There is a CD that belongs with this book.
Ask at the Circulation Desk.   PLEASE DO
NOT DESENSITIZE OR SENSITIZE CD.   THANK YOU.

The Garland Encyclopedia of World Music
Volume 8

Europe

Garland Reference Library of the Humanities, Volume 1169

THE GARLAND ENCYCLOPEDIA OF WORLD MUSIC

Advisory Editors
Bruno Nettl and Ruth M. Stone

Founding Editors
James Porter and Timothy Rice

The Garland Encyclopedia of World Music
Volume 8

Europe

Timothy Rice, James Porter,
and Chris Goertzen
Editors

GARLAND PUBLISHING, INC.
A member of the Taylor and Francis Group
New York and London
2000

The initial planning of The Garland Encyclopedia of World Music was assisted by a grant from the National Endowment for the Humanities.

Published by Garland Publishing, Inc.
A member of the Taylor & Francis Group
19 Union Square West
New York, New York 10003

Library of Congress Cataloging-in-Publication Data

The Garland encyclopedia of world music / [advisory editors, Bruno Nettl and Ruth M. Stone ; founding editors, James Porter and Timothy Rice].
        p.   cm.
    Includes bibliographical references, discographies, and indexes.
    Contents: v. 8. Europe / Timothy Rice, James Porter, and Chris Goertzen, editors
    ISBN 0-8240-6034-2 (alk. paper)
    1. Music—Encyclopedias.   2. Folk music—Encyclopedias.
3. Popular music—Encyclopedias.   I. Nettl, Bruno, 1930–   .
II. Stone, Ruth M.   III. Porter, James, 1937–   . IV. Rice, Timothy, 1945–
ML100.G16   1998
780'.9—dc21

                                           97-9671
                                             CIP
                                           MN

For Garland Publishing:

President: Colin Jones
Publisher: Ken Wright
Editor, Music: Soo Mee Kwon
Assistant Editor, Music: Gillian Rodger
Production Director: Laura-Ann Robb
Project Editor: Eleanor Castellano
Copy Editor: J. Wainwright Love
Proofreader: Laura Daly
Desktop publishing: Betty and Don Probert (Special Projects Group)
Index: Marilyn Bliss
Music typesetting: Hyunjung Choi
Maps: Indiana University Graphic Services
Cover design: Lawrence Wolfson Design, New York

Cover illustration: Local playing accordion, Golden Lane, Prague, Czech Republic. Photo by Anthony Cassidy. Used by permission of Tony Stone Images.

Printed on acid-free, 250-year-life paper
Manufactured in the United States of America

10 9 8 7 6 5 4 3 2 1

Contents

Part 3
Music Cultures of Europe   245

List of Audio Examples

The following examples are included on the accompanying audio compact disc packaged with this volume in the back of the book. Track numbers are also indicated on the pages listed below for easy reference to text discussions. Complete notes on each example can be found on pages 1077–1081.

List of Maps

About *The Garland Encyclopedia of World Music*

Scholars have created many kinds of encyclopedias devoted to preserving and transmitting knowledge about the world. The study of music has itself been the subject of numerous encyclopedias in many languages. Yet until now the term *music encyclopedia* has been synonymous with surveys of the history, theory, and performance practice of European-based traditions.

In July 1988, the editors of *The Garland Encyclopedia of World Music* gathered for a meeting to determine the nature and scope of a massive new undertaking. For this, the first encyclopedia devoted to the music of all the world's peoples, the editors decided against the traditional alphabetic approach to compartmentalizing knowledge from A to Z. Instead, they chose a geographic approach, with each volume devoted to a single region and coverage assigned to the world's experts on specific music cultures.

For several decades, ethnomusicologists (following the practice of previous generations of comparative musicologists) have been documenting the music of the world through fieldwork, recording, and analysis. Now, for the first time, they have created an encyclopedia that summarizes in one place the major findings that have resulted from the explosion in such documentation since the 1960s. The volumes in this series comprise contributions from all those specialists who have from the start defined the field of ethnomusicology: anthropologists, linguists, dance ethnologists, cultural historians, folklorists, literary scholars, and—of course—musicologists, composers, and performers. This multidisciplinary approach continues to enrich the field, and future generations of students and scholars will find *The Garland Encyclopedia of World Music* to be an invaluable resource that contributes to knowledge in all its varieties.

Each volume has a similar design and organization: three large sections that cover the major topics of a region from broad general issues to specific music practices. Each section consists of articles written by leading researchers, and extensive glossaries and indexes give the reader easy access to terms, names, and places of interest.

Part 1: an introduction to the region, its culture, and its music as well as a survey of previous music scholarship and research

Part 2: major issues and processes that link the musics of the region

Part 3: detailed accounts of individual music cultures

The editors of each volume have determined how this three-part structure is to be constructed and applied depending on the nature of their regions of interest. The concepts covered in Part 2 will therefore differ from volume to volume; likewise, the articles in Part 3 might be about the music of nations, ethnic groups, islands, or subregions. The picture of music presented in each volume is thus comprehensive yet remains focused on critical ideas and issues.

Complementing the texts of the encyclopedia's articles are numerous illustrations: photographs, drawings, maps, charts, song texts, and music examples. At the end of each volume is a useful set of study and research tools, including a glossary of terms, lists of audio and visual resources, and an extensive bibliography. An audio compact disc will be found inside the back cover of each volume, with sound examples that are linked (with a ⟨TRACK⟩ in the margin) to discussions in the text.

The Garland Encyclopedia of World Music represents the work of hundreds of specialists guided by a team of distinguished editors. With a sense of pride, Garland Publishing offers this new series to readers everywhere.

Preface

The music of Europe, especially so-called art or classical music, is probably the most extensively studied and documented of all the world's musical traditions. *The Garland Encyclopedia of World Music,* however, displaces European music from the center it often occupies in European-derived discourses on music and places it, not at the periphery, but in a constellation of world regions positioned without a center on the surface of a sphere. Though placing Europe in a global perspective represents a salutary move from an ethnomusicological point of view, it has created the problem of how to contain the vast knowledge of European music within a single volume.

In fact, of course, we cannot pretend to contain anything but the tiniest fraction of that knowledge here. Even in this volume, European classical music is decentered and treated as just one of many kinds of music available to ethnic groups and nations. Those interested in recovering the details of the history of European classical music—biographies of composers and performers, lists of compositions, analysis and history of styles—should look elsewhere.

European music history is usually told as if could be captured in a single, chronological trajectory, and we do here in a single article of perhaps ten thousand words—an incredibly short encapsulation. But such histories construct an imaginary story that underemphasizes or ignores the local histories and national experiences of this music in different places around the continent. These local histories, though abbreviated, are found in most of the articles on the music of individual countries.

An interest in and emphasis on folk and popular music and the position of music in European society and culture pervades this volume. Most of the articles in Parts 1 and 2 (with the exception of the historical section of Part 2) deal with comparative issues in the study of European traditional music. The articles on individual countries and cultures in Part 3 begin with folk music, often assumed (correctly or incorrectly) to have ancient roots that predate classical and popular traditions, which arise out of the history of the group and borrow from and influence folk tradition. Finally, modern musical life is presented as an amalgam of musical styles and values that mediate between poles of urban and rural, ancient and modern, supported and ignored, relevant and irrelevant.

HOW THIS VOLUME IS ORGANIZED

Like the other volumes in this encyclopedia, this volume is organized into three parts. Part 1 contains a broad overview of music on the continent, followed by a survey of the major trends in scholarship on traditional music.

Issues and processes

Part 2 focuses on major issues and topics of importance to the musical life of Europe. The first section deals with the history of music in Europe. Especially in the nineteenth and twentieth centuries, Europeans became absorbed with understanding themselves in historical terms, and the recovery of the history of so-called art music is at the center of the stories Europeans tell about themselves. This section begins with prehistory as understood by archaeology, briefly reviews ancient Greek music (the source of many ideas about music in European culture), continues with reflections on the role of notation and the idea of history in European music, and ends with a capsule summary of the history of art music.

The second section of Part 2 examines issues related primarily to traditional and popular music, studied from an ethnographic perspective. By surveying, for example, traditional and contemporary performance contexts across the continent, important parallels can be observed. The question of repertoire and genre is treated in complementary fashion from the outside, using scholars' classifications of song genres (such as ballad and epic), and from the inside, using the people's own words. General methods of musical transmission are examined, as are the links between music and ideology on one hand, and music and gender on the other. The variety of musical instruments in Europe has long inspired scholarly and public interest and is surveyed in two articles. Finally, popular music, until recently left out of many historical and ethnographic studies, is treated in four articles—one an overview, one on rock in Europe, one on "world music," and one on the music of recent immigrants to Europe, many from its colonial outposts.

Europe by region and country

Part 3 divides Europe into areas and within each area treats all the major countries and even a few important regions, such as (in France) Brittany and Corsica. No areal division for European music is well established, and the one used here may seem arbitrary and unusual to some. Two of the areas, United Kingdom and Ireland and the Balkans, are commonly used, though some might question the inclusion of Romania in the Balkans. The area known as Eastern Europe from 1944 to 1989 was a legacy of the Cold War and designated the communist countries of that region; however, many people in that part of the world think of themselves as Central Europeans, and Part 3 restores that older view. Furthermore, the Baltic states, once a part of the Soviet Union and thus Eastern Europe, are here placed in Northern Europe, with Finland and the Scandinavian countries, because of parallels in language, musical instruments, and a shared history that predates the Soviet era. Such divisions, however rationalized, inevitably illuminate some relationships while obscuring others.

Only in the last decade of the twentieth century did the last great European empire, the Soviet Union, fade from the map—though some might argue that the United Kingdom remains as a remnant of imperial ambitions. Part 3 gives the nation-states of Europe their due in most instances, though some readers may be struck by the exceptions. The United Kingdom appears in its parts, England, Scotland, and Wales, and Ireland is here united. The Low Countries include Belgium, the Netherlands, and Luxembourg. In separate articles, Sardinia, Corsica, Brittany, the Basque provinces, and North Caucasia peek out from under their national umbrellas. The Czech Republic and Slovakia have such a long shared history, compared to their recent separation, that one article seems efficient. The rump Yugoslavia is divided into its parts, Serbia and Montenegro, and the smallest principalities and city-states are omitted.

Using nations as the main organizing principle of Part 3 means that many ethnic minorities may have been overlooked. Some, such as the Jews and the Roma (Gypsies), are treated in the opening section of Part 3, on Transnational Minorities. Some minorities are mentioned within national articles, such as those on Finland, Hungary, and Russia. But in many national articles, the music of minorities is eclipsed by discussions of the majority's music—a hazard of this approach to the organization of the volume.

Each article in Part 3, with a few exceptions, proceeds along a common trajectory: a brief overview of demography, history, and geography; an overview of the style, function, and use of song genres; musical instruments, music history, popular music, revivalism, and the modern scene; and a survey of the history of scholarship. Many introductory overviews were silently supplied by the editors, and we take responsibility for any misinterpretations or errors that we may have introduced in them.

Research tools

Readers will find research aids throughout the volume. Maps of areas are found at the beginning of each section of Part 3. Where countries or ethnic groups are divided into ethnographic regions, additional, detailed maps are provided. For many of the place names, several spellings are acceptable. Every effort was made to use the most common spellings throughout the book, but some inconsistencies remain. Each article ends with an extensive bibliography and list of audiovisual resources, and highly selected guides to books, recordings, and films are given at the end of the volume. Numerous photographs, musical examples, and a compact disc of sound recordings illustrate the text, and a pronunciation guide to European languages follows the preface. A glossary and index aid access to material in the main text.

Musical examples

Perhaps more than some regions of the world [see, for example, the volume SOUTHEAST ASIA], European traditional music has a long history of representation in descriptive Western staff notation, and as a consequence many musical examples supplement this text. For those who read music, such examples can add telling detail to verbal descriptions of the basics of musical form, texture, rhythm and meter, scales and modes, and melodic shape. At the same time, they inadequately represent, or even fail to represent, important aspects of performance practice, such as untempered melodic intervals, timbres, nonmetrical rhythms, ornamentation, and the freedom and expressiveness of performance.

Many notated examples contain additional signs and other conventions that add to the descriptive possibilities of standard, prescriptive Western notation. For example, so-called key signatures are not intended in these transcriptions to indicate key per se, but indicate the relative pitches and intervals used; as a consequence, they may "break the rules" by including both sharps and flats and by placing the sharp or flat on the line or space of the actual melody note rather than in its conventional location. In some examples, the absence of time signatures and the use of dotted bar lines or half-lines illustrate the limits of Western metrical concepts. Other signs conventionally used in ethnomusicological transcriptions include the following:

↑ or ↓   pitches slightly higher or lower, respectively, than notated;

⌒ or ◡   durations slightly longer or shorter, respectively, than notated.

Glossary, index, and definitions

Because the encyclopedia is not organized alphabetically, an extensive glossary of virtually every native term for musical instruments, genre, or musical parts mentioned in the text is provided at the back of the volume. Names of individuals, organizations, and ethnic groups will be found in the index. Knowledge of basic musical terminology is assumed and so those terms are not defined. Some terminology associated with musical instruments and song genres is defined at the tops of pages in those articles.

Compact disc

To illustrate the text, the compact disc provides a selection of musical examples, which mainly come from fieldwork and were chosen to supplement material available on commercial recordings. A booklet of brief notes on the recordings is packaged with the CD on the back cover and printed on pages 1077–1081, preceding the index.

ACKNOWLEDGMENTS

A project of this magnitude requires dozens of minds and hands working at many levels. The coeditors' first debt is to the authors of the many long articles in this volume. They have borne with us during the periods of frustrating delay and frenetic activity that have characterized this project since its inception, in 1987. We thank them for their patience and helpful responses to our many queries. We deeply mourn the loss of one of our authors, JaFran Jones, a dear friend and colleague.

We must also thank the publisher, Garland Publishing, which originally approached us with the idea for this encyclopedia, and whose staff have helped us in many ways in the production of this volume. They include former Vice President Leo Balk, who expedited and advised the project in various phases; music and managing editor Soo Mee Kwon, whose gentle but firm planning and guidance brought the project to fruition; Eleanor Castellano, who coordinated the assembly of the volume; and Barbara Gerr, our perspicacious editor of music examples. J. W. Love proved extraordinarily adept at copyediting, spotting many a tricky inconsistency, odd misspelling, and questionable fact.

In addition to authors, many people contributed in small but critical ways, especially the translators of contributions submitted in languages other than English and the contributors of photographs and sound recordings. Marin Marian-Bălaşa of the Institute of Ethnography and Folklore in Bucharest Speranţa Rădulescu provided useful comments and material for the article on Romania. Most of these are acknowledged in the text, but special mention should be made of Maria Arko, who checked facts for the Slovenia article; Rita Karasiajus, who helped us with Lithuanian photographs; and those who contributed many photographs and/or sound recordings: Elsie Ivancich Dunin, Robert Garfias, Luisa Del Giudice, and Paula White. We are particularly grateful to Anna Chairetakis, who gave us permission to reproduce about twenty of Alan Lomax's photographs, and to Robert Godfried, who allowed us to use more than twenty images from his extraordinary collection of early-twentieth-century postcards. For picture research for the articles on Western art-music history, we used the Photographic Study Collection of the J. Paul Getty Museum in Los Angeles. Tracey Shuster, the manager, was particularly helpful in guiding neophytes to art history in searching the collection, and we thank the museum and the associated French and Co., which then supplied us with photographs of artworks to illustrate our texts. A UCLA graduate student, Patty Truchly, acted as our picture editor.

Generations of UCLA graduate students have acted as authors and research assistants for the volume. The authors are Valeriu Apan, Wanda Bryant, Roberto Catalano, Loren Chuse, Giuseppina Collicci, Paulette Gershen, Johanna Hoffman, and Elizabeth Miles. Brian Patrick Fox has been our chief assistant as the volume went to press, checking hundreds of facts, bibliographic and otherwise; he eventually compiled the pronunciation guide and the guides to recordings and films and videos. Pantelis Vassilakis helped master the compact disc. Other student helpers over the years have included Heidi Feldman, Meilu Ho, Laurel Isbister, Danielle Makler, Robert Reigle, Sonia Tamar Seeman, and Charles Sharp. We have undoubtedly left out a few, and to them we offer our sincerest apologies.

A major project such as this inevitably impacts the support staff and other professionals who work at the home institution. In our case, this includes Donna Armstrong, the chair's assistant in the Department of Ethnomusicology at UCLA, and the department's receptionist, Carol Pratt, both of whom helped with the enormous amount of mail that such a project entails. Louise Spear, the archivist in the Ethnomusicology Archive at UCLA, resolved many discographic queries, and Steven Fry, a music librarian at UCLA, made many valuable suggestions about sources for photographs and musical examples.

—TIMOTHY RICE

A Guide to Pronunciation
Brian Patrick Fox

This guide lists the approximate English pronunciation of the letters that appear in European languages.

GENERAL GUIDELINES

Unless otherwise noted, consonants and consonant clusters are pronounced roughly as their American equivalents. As in English, pronunciation of some letters varies with context, for example, *c* as in *coin* and *c* as in *cent,* and detailed guides for each language should be consulted.

Exceptions to American pronunciation and problematic consonants include:

r   usually rolled or trilled
j   usually pronounced like *y* in yes or the *h* in *hat*
w   usually pronounced like the *v* in *van*
x   usually pronounced like the *x* in *taxi* (exceptions noted below)
q   usually pronounced like the *k* in *kite*
c   like *ts* in *bits* (in Slavic and Baltic languages)

Commonly used diacritics include:

č   *ch* in *chin*
ć   *ch* in *chin*
dž   *j* in *judge*
ñ   *ni* in *onion*
š   *sh* in *shine*
ś   *sh* in *shine*
ž   *z* in *azure*

Some distinctions marked by diacritics, such as those between *č* and *ć* or *š* and *ś* in some Slavic languages, have no equivalents in English.

Vowels are generally pronounced as follows:

a   *a* in *father*
e   *e* in *bet*
i   *i* in *machine*
o   *o* in *open*
u   *u* in *rule*
æ   *a* in *cat*
y   *ü* in German *über* (in Albanian, Breton, Finnish, Scandinavian)

Diacritics added to vowels usually indicate a long form, and the unmarked vowel is correspondingly shortened.

INDIVIDUAL LANGUAGES
Transnational Ethnic Groups
Basque

dd	palatalized *d*; *dy* in *did you*
tt	palatalized *t*; *ty* in *next year*
tx	*ch* in *chin*
tz	*ts* in *bits*
x	*sh* in *ship*
z	*ss* in *miss*

Celtic languages (Welsh, Irish, Scottish Gaelic)

bh	*v* in *van*
ch	*ch* in Scottish *loch*; *h* in *help*
dd	*th* in *they*
dh	like French *r*; *y* in *yes*
fh	[silent]
gh	like French *r*; *y* in yes
ll	similar to *hl*
mh	*v* in *van*
s	*sh* in *ship*
sh	*h* in *hat*
th	*h* in *hat*
w	*u* in *June*
y	*o* in *for*

Scandinavia, Finland, and the Baltic States
Icelandic

ð	*th* in *the*
ll	*ttl* in *battle*
rl	*ttl* in *battle*
rn	like *tn* or *n*
z	*s* in *sell*
Þ	*th* in *thick*

Norwegian

qu	*kv*

Finnish

z	*s* or *ts* in *bits*

Latvian

ǵ	*gy*
ie	*ia* in *Philadelphia*
ķ	*ky*
ļ	*ly*
ņ	*ni* in *onion*

Lithuanian

ch	*k* in *kite*
ž	*j* in *job*

Western Europe
Dutch

g	*ch* in Scottish *loch*

French

ç	*c* in *cedar*
ch	*sh* in *ship*
j	*s* in *pleasure*

Breton

ch	*ch* in Scottish *loch* or *j* in Spanish *jota*

Portuguese

ç	*c* in *cedar*
h	[silent]
j	*s* in *pleasure*
nh	*ni* in *onion*
x	*sh* in *ship*, *ks* in *books*, *z* in *zone*

Spanish

c	in Spain, *th* in *thick*; elsewhere, *c* in *cent*
v	between *b* in *boy* and *v* in *van*
′	accent changes stress, not pronunciation

Italian

z	*ts* in *bits*

Maltese

c	*ch* in *chin*
g	*j* in *job*
gh	[mostly silent; lengthens vowel]
q	glottal stop
x	*sh* in *ship*
z	*z* in *zone*; *ts* in bits

Central Europe
German

v	*f* in *fight*
z	*ts* in *bits*

Polish

ch	*ch* in Scottish *loch* or *j* in Spanish *jota*
cz	*ch* in *chin*
dz	*ds* in *beds*

dż	*j* in *job*
ł	*w* in *will*
ń	*ni* in *onion*
rz	*s* in *pleasure*
sz	*sh* in *ship*
sczc	*shch* in *fresh cheese*
ś	between *s* in *sell* and *sh* in *ship*

Czech and Slovak

ch	*ch* in Scottish *loch* or *j* in Spanish *jota*
cz	*ts* in *bits*
gy	*j* in *job*
ŋ	*ni* in *onion*
ř	*rzh* in *Dvořák*
sz	*s* in *sell*
ý	*ie* in *field*

Hungarian

c	*ts* in *bits*
cs	*ch* in *chin*
dzs	*j* in *job*
gy	*dy* in *did you*; *d* in *adulation*
ly	*y* in *yes*
ny	*ni* in *onion*
s	*sh* in *ship*
sz	*s* in *sell* (not *s* in *rose*)
ty	*ty* in *Katya*
zs	*s* in *pleasure*

Double consonants are pronounced long

Eastern Europe
Russian

kh	*ch* in Scottish *loch*, or *j* in Spanish *jota*, or *kh* in *khan*
y	*wi* in *will*
'	palatalizes previous consonant: e.g., *ty* in *next year*

Belarusan

ch	*ch* in Scottish *loch*, or *j* in Spanish *jota*, or *kh* in *khan*
ł	*w* in *will*
ŭ	*i* in *big*

Ukrainian

ch	*ch* in Scottish *loch* or *j* in Spanish *jota*
z	*s* in *sell*
'	palatalizes previous consonant: e.g., *dy* in *did you*

Georgian

kh	*ch* in Scottish *loch*, or *j* in Spanish *jota*, or *kh* in *khan*

The Balkans
Romanian

ă	*a* in *sofa*
j	*s* in *pleasure*
ş	*sh* in *ship*
ţ	*ts* in *bits*

Bulgarian, Serbo-Croatian, Slovene, Macedonian

đ	*j* in *job*
ǵ	*gu* in *angular*
h	*ch* in Scottish *loch*, or *j* in Spanish *jota*, or *kh* in *khan*
ḱ	*cu* in *cure*
ŭ	*u* in *but*

Albanian

ă	*a* in *sofa*
c	*ts* in *bits*
ç	*ch* in *chin*
dh	*th* in *they*
ğ	[silent]
gj	*j* in *job*
l	*lli* in *million*
ll	*ll* in *wall*
q	*ch* in *chin* or the *ky* sound in *cute*
rr	rolled *r*
r	weak *r*
th	*th* in *thick*
x	*dz* in *adze*
xh	*dj* in *adjective*

Greek

g	rolled *g*
h	*ch* in Scottish *loch* or *j* in Spanish *jota*

List of Contributors

Valeriu Apan
Los Angeles, California, U.S.A.

Stephen Blum
City University of New York
New York, New York, U.S.A.

Philip V. Bohlman
University of Chicago
Chicago, Illinois, U.S.A.

Wim Bosmans
Muziekinstrumentenmuseum
Brussels, Belgium

Wanda Bryant
Sherman Oaks, California, U.S.A.

Salwa El-Shawan Castelo-Branco
Universidade Nova de Lisboa
Lisbon, Portugal

Roberto Catalano
Highland, California, U.S.A.

Anne Caufriez
European Society for Ethnomusicology
Brussels, Belgium

Loren Chuse
Berkeley, California, U.S.A.

Giuseppina Colicci
Pontecorvo, Italy

Jane K. Cowan
University of Sussex
Brighton, England

Ewa Dahlig
Institute of Arts, Polish Academy of Sciences
Warsaw, Poland

Silvia Delorenzi-Schenkel
Fonoteca Nazionale Svizzera
Biasca, Switzerland

Oskár Elschek
Institute of Musicology
Bratislava, Slovakia

Mark Forry
Santa Cruz, California, U.S.A.

Judit Frigyesi
Bar-Ilan University
Ramat-Gan, Israel

Vic Gammon
University of Leeds
Leeds, England

Paulette Gershen
Van Nuys, California, U.S.A.

Panicos Giorgoudes
University of Cyprus
Nicosia, Cyprus

Chris Goertzen
Earlham College
Richmond, Indiana, U.S.A.

Johanna Hoffman
Zurich, Switzerland

Pandora Hopkins
Brooklyn College of the City University of New York
Brooklyn, New York, U.S.A.

L. JaFran Jones (deceased)
University of Toledo
Toledo, Ohio, U.S.A.

Richard Jones-Bamman
Eastern Connecticut State University
Wilimantic, Connecticut, U.S.A.

Joseph Jordania
Northcote, Australia

Phyllis Kinney
Dyfed, Wales

Erik Kjellberg
Uppsala Universitet
Uppsala, Sweden

Ellen Koskoff
The University of Rochester's Eastman School of Music
Rochester, New York, U.S.A.

Lois Kuter
Jenkintown, Pennsylvania, U.S.A.

Wolfgang Laade
Music of Man Archive
Wädenswil, Switzerland

Denis Laborde
Centre National de Recherche Scientifique
Paris, France

Barbara Rose Lange
University of Houston
Houston, Texas, U.S.A.

Edward Larkey
University of Maryland, Baltimore County
Baltimore, Maryland, U.S.A.

Timo Leisiö
University of Tampere
Tampere, Finland

Jan Ling
Göteborgs Universitet
Göteborg, Sweden

Bernard Lortat-Jacob
Centre National de Recherche Scientifique
Paris, France

Krister Malm
Stockholm, Sweden

Elizabeth J. Miles
Los Angeles, California, U.S.A.

Zinaida Mozheiko
Institute of Musicology
Minsk, Belarus

Valdis Muktupāvels
University of Latvia
Riga, Latvia

Bruno Nettl
University of Illinois
Urbana, Illinois, U.S.A.

Svend Nielsen
Dansk Folkminde samling
Copenhagen, Denmark

William Noll
Center for the Study of Oral History and Culture
Kyïv, Ukraine

Edward J. P. O'Connor
Pinnacle, North Carolina, U.S.A.

Mira Omerzel-Terlep
Ljubljana, Slovenia

Ankica Petrović
Otok Hvar, Croatia

James Porter
University of Aberdeen
Aberdeen, Scotland

Timothy Rice
University of California at Los Angeles
Los Angeles, California, U.S.A.

Owe Ronström
Högskolan pa Gotland
Visby, Sweden

Wilhelm Schepping
Universität zu Köln
Köln, Germany

Albrecht Schneider
Universität Hamburg
Hamburg, Germany

David Schulenberg
University of South Dakota
Vermillion, South Dakota, U.S.A.

Tilman Seebass
Institut für Musikwissenschaft
Innsbruck, Austria

Hugh Shields
Trinity College
Dublin, Ireland

Carol Silverman
University of Oregon
Eugene, Oregon, U.S.A.

Marcello Sorce Keller
Pregassona, Switzerland

Jane Sugarman
State University of New York at Stony Brook
Stony Brook, New York, U.S.A.

Maria Paula Survilla
Wartburg College
Waverly, Iowa, U.S.A.

Johannes Tall
Flint, Michigan, U.S.A.

Magda Ferl Želinská
Hollywood, California, U.S.A.

Izaly Zemtsovsky
Berkeley, California, U.S.A.

Part 1
Europe as a Musical Area

The music of Europe arose and flourishes within four distinct, but interconnected, social and cultural spheres. The aristocratic and educated elite patronizes classical music. Folk music sprang from the life and work of rural peasants. Religious institutions have fostered special genres for their liturgies and community celebrations. Cities—where all classes rub shoulders, and commercial goods and intellectual ideas are traded internationally—are the wellsprings of popular music.

Each of these European music worlds possesses a characteristic sound, recognizable across the continent and reflecting the social and cultural milieu in which it is created and practiced. Musicians from each sphere, despite their differences, have long borrowed musical ideas from their counterparts in other spheres. And the music within each sphere, despite the similarities, exhibits significant variation among communities—differences that depend on language, nationality, and local history.

In the past, European traditional music was typically played by a single musician, who played a melody and sometimes provided his own accompaniment. Usually traditional musicians play one instrument, such as a bagpipe or a zither, on which they play a melody and drone accompaniment. In this photo, a musician plays two instruments. He plays a melody on a three-holed duct flute and strikes a zither with a stick to provide a rhythmic, dronelike accompaniment. Yebra de Basa, Aragón, Spain, 1952. Photo courtesy of the Alan Lomax Collection, New York.

The Music of Europe: Unity and Diversity

Timothy Rice

The Shared Culture of Music in Europe
Musical Similarities in Village Music
Distinctions in Music Style and Culture

MAP 1 Europe (*opposite page*)

Europe, though classified as one of the world's seven continents, is geographically a peninsula on the western end of the vast Eurasian landmass (map). Thus, its definition has always been cultural, rather than physical. Defying unity, however, the people of Europe have divided themselves by ethnicity, class, religion, language, and dialect. Each community has its own music and often believes this music to be a distinctive, even unique, representation of its identity. In 1999, Europe was divided into forty-two countries. This fine geopolitical mosaic contained even finer subdivisions by ethnic and linguistic groups. Despite the daunting political problems created by ethnic, linguistic, and religious differences, many factors can be cited in arguing for the cultural—and musical—unity of Europe.

The music of Europe has typically been understood as falling into three large categories: folk, classical, and popular. Created by intellectuals, these categories began as markers of social class as much as musical style. The concept of folk music, credited to the German writer Johann Gottfried von Herder (1778–1779), stood for the music of rural peasants, who intellectuals believed bore the soul of a nation. An important, even defining, feature was its supposed transmission in oral tradition (Karpeles 1955). Classical music, also known as art music, emerged as a category in the nineteenth century to label the work of a few supposed geniuses. Passed on in written form, it has come to be associated with urban, educated elites. The term *popular music* has been used to identify the music of the urban working and middle classes. In the twentieth century, it is transmitted primarily via electronic media—records, audiocassettes, compact discs, and radio and television broadcasts. These distinctions, invented in Europe by Europeans, work better for European music than they do in most other parts of the world. But even here, they cannot contain the shifts in musical style, practice, and meaning created by musicians with the passage of time (Frey and Siniveer 1987; Ling 1997).

The invention of the term *folk music* coincided with the beginnings of the industrial revolution in Europe. By the early nineteenth century peasants were moving in large numbers from the countryside into cities and towns to find work in factories and shops and form a new working class (figure 1). They brought their songs and music with them, invented new texts to suit new occupations, and adopted urban

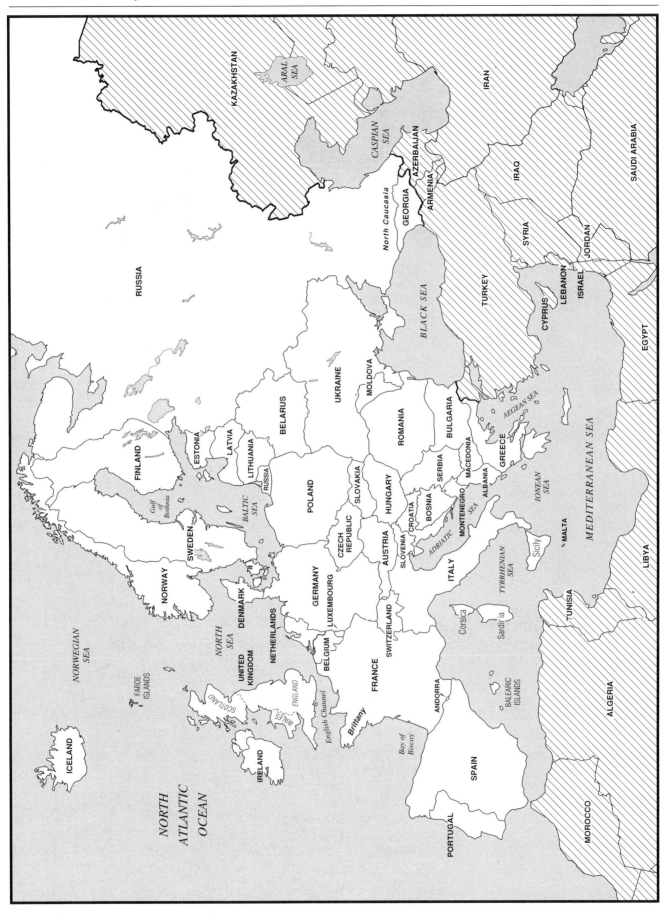

FIGURE 1 Urban working people, many of whom had come from rural villages, formed into bands that in their sizes and structures mirrored workplaces. The brass band was, and in some places still is, the most important type of town music, but this English concertina band, using instruments popular in the countryside, is an exception. Early-twentieth-century postcard. Courtesy of the Robert Godfried Collection, New York.

musical styles. Since the medieval period, trained musicians in churches and courts had incorporated the tunes of their country cousins, often with the goal of making their music more accessible and popular. In the nineteenth century, this practice became a crucial element of nationalism, as so-called classical composers utilized folk melodies to create national styles of art music. The music popular with the new urban classes of the nineteenth century used the instruments and harmonies of classical music, sometimes applied to tunes and dance styles originating in the villages. In the twentieth century these categories continue to mobilize great aesthetic and ideological differences, while musicians take advantage of the possibilities for fruitful interchange among them. Also, some scholars have begun substituting the label *traditional music* for the label *folk music,* which has become tainted by its association with the virulent nationalism that plagued Europe for most of the century.

Though classical music is the most prestigious and best studied of these three categories of European music, this volume of the *Garland Encyclopedia of World Music* places folk music at the center of its story throughout Parts 1, 2, and 3. It presents popular and classical music primarily in relation to traditional music and as social, more than aesthetic, practices. The remainder of this article reflects this point of view and examines traditional music cross-culturally and comparatively.

THE SHARED CULTURE OF MUSIC IN EUROPE

What factors contribute to the cultural and musical unity of Europe? First, ecologically most of the European continent lies in a temperate climatic zone. The length of growing and dormant seasons and the kinds of crops that can be grown vary significantly from south to north, but the continent has long been unified by similar patterns of summer agricultural work and winter rest. Common seasonal patterns have given rise to similar kinds of songs and dances for agricultural rituals and similar cycles of outdoor and indoor work and recreation (figure 2). Nearly every article devoted to a particular country in Part 3 opens with a review of the songs of the agricultural or calendrical cycle of songs. Though their musical forms differ, their functions are identical. In most of Europe, these functions have been lost, but the songs are remembered, especially in eastern and southern Europe, and are still sung at social gatherings and folk festivals. Because of their limited melodic ranges and short forms, many scholars regard them as belonging to the oldest layer of the European song repertoire. It is a tribute to the tenacity of tradition that they are still being sung at the end of the twentieth century, when urbanization, mechanization of labor, and scientific agricultural techniques have virtually eliminated the need to sing them for

their original functions: to assure fertility and lighten the burden of heavy manual labor.

A second factor unifying Europe has been the almost universal adoption of Christianity. Though many rituals and songs in Europe retain pre-Christian, pagan elements, such as worship of the sun and the moon, most of Europe was converted to Christianity by A.D. 1000. (The Lithuanians were the last to convert, in the 1300s.) Christian values and forms of worship have defined many aspects of life, including musical life, for Europeans ever since. The Christian calendar of holidays—Christmas, Lent, Easter, and others—overlays, but often retains, pagan fertility rituals. Christmas caroling during house-to-house visits is still known in many parts of Europe. The forty days of Lent were traditionally a period when most forms of traditional singing and dancing were prohibited, and other forms, such as song games, were substituted. Different national traditions share secular melodies derived from shared Christian liturgical music. The music to accompany the liturgy varies according to Christianity's main branches: Orthodoxy in the east; Roman Catholicism in the center, south, and west; and Protestantism in the north. Within a given branch, however, many aspects of musical style and musical life deriving from religious practice are shared across national and language boundaries. For example, Lutheran hymn tunes, some retained from Roman Catholic practice, are sung by Protestants throughout Europe.

Other shared features of European cultural life derive from a shared history that includes widespread literacy, interconnected imperial and princely courts, the rise of an urban bourgeoisie from the sixteenth to the twentieth centuries, and urbanization, industrialization, and the spread of the nation-state as the primary unit of political organization in the nineteenth and twentieth centuries. Though not all parts of

In Europe in the twentieth century, state interventions on behalf of folk music under all forms of government—democratic, fascist, and communist—led to widespread disillusionment, particularly among youth, with this kind of music.

Europe shared in this history in equal measure or at the same time, these processes have shaped a common European heritage. The invention of movable type and book printing in the 1400s enabled the spread of literacy and education, which, combined with musical notation and musical literacy, have defined musical life for the educated classes of Europe since the Renaissance. Literacy, coupled with a network of imperial and princely courts related by marriage and descent, created a shared European culture with many common features. Intellectual and musical ideas—and princesses and musicians—traveled with relative ease throughout most parts of Europe. Music from one country recorded in a shared notation was transported to other countries, so that within a few years, or in some cases months, the newest developments in Italy, for example, became part of the musical life of England, Germany, and Poland. Many of the country articles in Part 3 list the foreign musicians who established the earliest musical academies or orchestras and the emigrant musicians who gained fame abroad. Thus, classical music forms an important part of Europe's shared cultural landscape. In the twentieth century, mass media joined the book and the written score to aid the spread of musical culture, and shared forms of popular music knitted the disparate cultures of Europe even more tightly together.

Urban folklore

Finally, the industrial revolution and the urbanization it spawned have created similar patterns in the decline and revival of folk music all over Europe. These processes began in England in the eighteenth century, spread through most of Europe in the nineteenth century, and reached the remotest areas of eastern and southern Europe in the twentieth century. As agricultural efficiency and the population increased in the nineteenth and twentieth centuries, many people left their villages to seek their fortunes in the cities. The story of village music in Europe is in some respects a story of decline everywhere, though at different times and at different rates in different places. In Bulgaria, for example, the traditional wedding celebration was reduced in the late twentieth century from a weeklong affair with elaborate ritual singing by participants to a day or a day and a half with hired professional musicians. In Finland, a typical wedding once lasted a day with hired musicians, but at the end of the century it had been shortened to a few hours, with a disc jockey or without any music.

Counterbalancing this decline of village musical life all over Europe has been the rise of new forms of urban folklore. New urban genres include occupational songs of the working classes that developed in the nineteenth century [see, for example, DENMARK]. In Finland political parties in the nineteenth century each had their own brass bands to accompany the singing of songs advancing their points of view. In Russia a new urban middle class populated the outskirts of cities in a transitional suburban zone between the city and its surrounding villages; in this zone, all manner of popular songs, including improvised ditties (*chastushki*) and an important genre of soldiers' songs, took root. While most of these developments retain only local importance, some urban popular genres have gained international recognition. For example, new forms of couple dancing from Central Europe (mazurka, polka, schottische, waltz) and their tunes spread throughout most of Europe in the nineteenth century. In the 1920s, Greeks from Turkey were repatriated in a forced population exchange. In Athens and the port of Piraeus, they formed a new urban underclass, whose music, *rebetika* 'rebels' music', became internationally popular in the 1960s—as did the Portuguese urban genre, *fado*. The flamenco music of urban Gypsies in Spain has enjoyed similar international renown over an even longer period.

Throughout Europe, a less organic but still common response to the decline of village life and music has been the widespread support of efforts to preserve village folklore. In the nineteenth century, scholars, nationalists, and antiquarians initiated these efforts by collecting song texts (and more rarely, notated music) and publishing them in articles and books. In the twentieth century, preservationists' efforts took the form of grassroots "folk revivals," mainly in Western Europe, and state-supported performance troupes of professionals or amateurs, mainly in communist Central and Eastern Europe and the Balkans. These efforts at preservation and modernization of village traditions usually occur in urban settings and among educated youth and are sometimes disparagingly called folklorism, or even fakelore (Baumann 1976; Dorson 1976); however, they have undeniably altered and reshaped the way music originally produced in rural areas is heard, understood, and appreciated by modern audiences throughout Europe and the world.

In some cases, the motivation for these preservation efforts has been a romantic nostalgia for supposedly lost ways of life by urbanites otherwise anxious to reject most other aspects of village life, such as its drudgery, illiteracy, and poverty. But even more importantly, these rural traditions are associated nearly everywhere in Europe with the nation itself, precisely because they are local and not international. In the nineteenth century nationalists in Europe constructed an association between rural, village music and the people ("the folk") and soul of the nation. In the United States, the term *folk music* tends to retain the relatively innocent associations of the first meaning, that is, as rural, village, "old-time" music. In Europe in the twentieth century, however, state interventions on behalf of folk music under all forms of government—democratic, fascist, and communist—have led to widespread disillusionment, particularly among youth, with this kind of music in many countries. The term *folk* has been tainted by these political and ideological associations, and some scholars have substituted other, possibly more neutral, terms to describe what they are interested in: *traditional, village,* or *rural music,* for example. In this volume, the decision about how to label this music has been left up to each author. The people in villages, by the way, have their own, usually more functional, terms for their local musical practice [see LOCAL KNOWLEDGE OF MUSICAL GENRES AND ROLES]. At the most general level, they might call it our music, or more specifically, women's songs, wedding music, laments, shepherd's tunes, and so forth [for a discussion of the construction of the concept of Basque music as a result of nationalistic ideas, see BASQUE MUSIC].

MUSICAL SIMILARITIES IN VILLAGE MUSIC

Where traditional music is still vibrant, villagers often say that their music is unique, that the music of even the neighboring village is different. Similarly, many nations have striven in the last two centuries to define their rural music as a unique signifier of the nation in sharp contrast to the music of neighboring countries. Given these local views and national ideologies, which stress difference, can any common tendencies be found in the forms of European traditional music? There are a few.

Performance Practice

Performance contexts are remarkably similar across Europe. In the past, calendar rituals, based on the agricultural cycle of work and Christian religious holidays, provided important contexts for song and dance [see TRADITIONAL PERFORMANCE CONTEXTS]. The musically marked parts of the life cycle included wedding celebrations and lamenting the recently deceased. As traditional village culture waned, most calendric rituals and lamenting have tended to disappear, leaving the wedding as the most important traditional life-cycle ritual. Of course, informal social gatherings with song and dance as the main event continue nearly everywhere in the home, village square, and tavern (figure 3). In the second half of the twentieth century, concerts and festivals of rural music became common throughout Europe [see CONTEMPORARY PERFORMANCE CONTEXTS].

Village music is everywhere passed on in oral tradition, though there are frequent reports of musicians' and singers' using notebooks to help them remember tunes and song texts. There is no traditional notation system, and subtle variations from performance to performance are the rule. Descriptive speech about music is limited, though scholars have been able to collect local terminologies that constitute a kind of native musical theory of a given tradition [see LOCAL KNOWLEDGE OF MUSICAL GENRES AND ROLES].

Most European traditional cultures maintain a fundamental division between vocal and instrumental music. The common form of vocal music in all of Europe is the strophic song, in which the lyrics are sung to a repeated melodic structure. A narrative song genre, the ballad, has proved especially fruitful for the study of pan-European musical trends. Common ballad melodies have been found in neighboring countries, and, perhaps surprisingly, certain ballad themes—such as the star-crossed lovers in the English ballad known as "Barbara Allen"—have been documented in traditions as far removed as Scotland and Bulgaria (Buchan 1972; Entwhistle 1939; Vargyas 1983).

Instrumental music in Europe seems to have its roots in the practice of shepherds: flutes and bagpipes to pass the time; horns for signaling; and bells to identify animals. Instrumental music is also used nearly everywhere for dance music. The most common form consists of relatively short, repeated pairs of melodies (AA'BB'),

FIGURE 3   In Georgia, schoolchildren informally sing, accompanied by a plucked lute (*panduri*). Photo by Stuart Gelzer, 1995.

but in some traditions it has been extended with succeeding pairs of lines (CC′DD′ and so on) and improvisations. Musical instruments are important indicators of shared culture. The plucked zithers of Northern Europe and the double-reed oboes of southern Europe unify territories of great linguistic and cultural diversity. And modern manufactured instruments, especially the accordion and the violin, give the sound of European traditional music a similar timbre nearly everywhere (Deutsch and Heide 1975; Elschek 1969).

In the past, the most widespread performance style for song and instrumental music was probably the solo. The second most common practice for songs was unison or octave singing by a pair or group of singers. Unison performances by traditional instrumentalists, as in the violin section of a symphony orchestra, for example, was almost unknown until the early twentieth century. In Russia, Vasily Andreev experimented with orchestras of folk instruments, and this practice eventually spread throughout the Soviet Union and communist Central and Eastern Europe and the Balkans later in the century. About the same time, Swedish fiddlers formed societies that brought dozens of fiddlers together for festivals and competitions. In the 1960s, the famous Irish group The Chieftains used a pair of violins and occasionally a pair of tin whistles.

Other performance practices are widespread but not universal. Antiphonal singing by two soloists or groups is quite common, as is responsorial singing—solo call and choral response. Drone-based accompaniment in instrumental music is found virtually everywhere, but singing with drone accompaniment is common only in parts of Eastern and southeastern Europe (Deutsch 1981). The instrumental drone is often provided by a single instrument designed specifically to produce a melody plus drone, as with bagpipes, double-piped flutes, and bowed and plucked stringed instruments.

By the late twentieth century, village music everywhere in Europe had been influenced by urban music, with its chordal accompaniments primarily using triads build on the tonic (I), the subdominant (IV), and the dominant (V). Soloists and choruses are today typically accompanied by instrumentalists who play these chords, and instrumentalists form bands that double the melody in unison or play it in parallel thirds. Whatever drones might have existed in older practice are typically replaced by other instruments playing chords and a bass line.

Melody and rhythm

Generalizations about melodic and rhythmic structures can be made (Danckert 1970 [1939]; Karpeles 1956; Wiora 1957). In many regions of Europe, a presumably ancient layer of narrow-range (a fourth to a sixth) tunes that move diatonically by half steps and whole steps are still performed or were notated in the nineteenth century. More recent tunes extend the diatonic tendency over a wider range, to an octave or more. Pentatonic tunes, using five pitches within an octave, have a scattered distribution; not especially typical in Europe, they are important markers of regional or national identity where they occur [see HUNGARY].

Traditionally there were two treatments of rhythm: metrical, as in dance-music; and nonmetrical, as in table songs, by which guests were entertained while seated. Nonmetrical genres include Irish slow airs, the Russian *protiazhnaia pesnia* 'long-drawn-out song', the Romanian *doina,* and instrumental music such as the Greek *miroloyia* 'lament'. During the nineteenth century, whatever variety may have existed in European metrical constructions was reduced in most parts of Europe to duple and triple meters, influenced by emphasis on regular chordal harmonic rhythms, the spread of certain couple dances (especially the waltz, in 3/4 time, and the polka, in 2/4 time) and march rhythms (in 2/4 time), and other developments. A small num-

Many historical and geographical reasons contribute to the variety of European music, and many ideological factors, especially nationalism, lead Europeans to emphasize their differences and thus the variety in their musical styles and practices, rather than their similarities.

ber of songs in irregular or added meters have been collected in Northern Europe, suggesting a once common European practice, but only a few traditions in parts of Central and southeastern Europe consistently employ irregular, mixed, or additive meters (2 + 3, 2 + 2 + 3, and so on).

DISTINCTIONS IN MUSIC STYLE AND CULTURE

Refracted through a kind of comparative wide-angle lens that takes in the whole continent, Europe appears remarkably unified musically, whether we consider urban popular and classical music, village music, or religious music; however, Europeans on the ground, who hear music in the surrounding villages or in neighboring countries, are much more inclined to talk about differences among their musical practices and the uniqueness of their local style than to regard these practices and styles as contributing to a European, or even a national, manner of musical performance. In fact, many historical and geographical reasons contribute to the variety of European music, and many ideological factors, especially nationalism, lead Europeans to emphasize their differences and thus the variety in their musical styles and practices, rather than their similarities.

Geography and nationality

The European continent is broken up by peninsulas, islands, rivers, and mountain ranges—geographical features that tend to separate one group of people from another and have led over long periods of time to the development of metaphorical islands of local styles, some that transcend nationality. In southeastern Europe, for example, southern Albanians, Epirote Greeks, and western Macedonians share a presumably ancient three-part polyphonic singing style and pentatonic scale. Even in France, one of the oldest unified nations in Europe, regional languages and musical styles persist despite a long history of centralized education and industrialization.

In the nineteenth and early twentieth centuries, politicians created nation-states by unifying city-states and small principalities, as in Germany and Italy in the nineteenth century, or by dividing up the expired Austro-Hungarian, Ottoman, and Russian or Soviet empires. Partly because history has intervened to disperse and intermingle many ethnicities, the geographical distribution of ethnic groups and the boundaries of nations have never been as coterminous as national politicians have hoped or claimed. The result in the twentieth century has been a continuous series of wars between nations and within nations for national or ethnic rights and freedoms. In a more peaceful but nonetheless aggressive manner, musicians under the sway of nationalist politics have consciously used music as an important signifier of national and ethnic identity in these disputes. In a recent, tragic instance, Bosnian music, once a cosmopolitan mix, has, since the 1991 war among Serbians, Croatians, and Muslims, differentiated itself as each ethnicity emphasizes musical elements with connections to Serbia, Croatia, or the Middle East.

Religious differences

The image of Europe as a primarily Christian continent masks musically significant distinctions within Christianity and ignores the presence of other religions, especially Judaism and Islam. In Roman Catholic countries, the activities of religious brotherhoods provide important contexts for musical performance, especially in ritual processions. In Corsica and Sardinia, such brotherhoods preserve traditional styles of polyphonic sacred music. Protestants in some countries of Northern Europe perform religious hymns outside the liturgy for secular entertainment. Orthodox Christians believe the gravestone is a window on the other world, reachable through lamenting—a factor that has preserved lamenting into the present.

Europeans have repeatedly tried to purge the continent of Jews and Muslims: expelling Jews and Moors from Spain in 1492, pushing Ottoman Turks from the Balkans in the nineteenth century, engineering the Jewish Holocaust of the 1940s, and contriving the "ethnic cleansing" of Bosnia in the 1990s. However, Judaism and Islam have left their mark on European musical life and continue to inspire adherents. Jewish wedding musicians (*klezmorim*) played for their non-Jewish neighbors, especially in Poland, Ukraine, and Romania, and their tunes have become part of national repertoires in those countries. With the assimilation of Jewish populations in the urban cultures of many countries of Central and Eastern Europe and the Balkans, Jewish musicians became and remain among the most esteemed performers of European classical music. Since the 1980s or before, neotraditional and popular musicians in many parts of southern Europe—from the Balkans to southern Italy to Spain—have been reinvigorating their music with Middle Eastern elements. And in an ironic turnabout, a significant number of young Germans in the 1990s perform and listen to Jewish klezmer music as one way to deal with the legacy of the Holocaust.

Muslims still living in the Balkan Peninsula include Turkish minorities in Bulgaria, Cyprus, Greece, and Macedonia; minorities of Slavic-language-speaking adherents to Islam in Bosnia and Bulgaria; and the majority of Albanians. There are also Muslim groups in southern Russia, for example, Bashkirs, Chechens, Kalmyks, and Tatars (figure 4). Since the 1960s, many Muslims have immigrated to Western Europe—as "guest workers" in Germany (mainly Turks) and as the result of colonial collapse in France (mainly sub-Saharan and North Africans) and Great Britain (Arabs and Pakistanis). Besides a shared religious music and associated ritual occasions, such

FIGURE 4 An ensemble of Muslim Tatar musicians from Russia. Early-twentieth-century postcard. Courtesy of the Robert Godfried Collection, New York.

as Ramadan, many of these groups perform secular music with evident links to the Middle East—links that include stringed instruments such as short- and long-necked plucked lutes and melodic modes using augmented seconds and microtonal intervals.

Islamic rule in southern Spain from the ninth to the fifteenth centuries, and in the Balkans from the fourteenth to the early twentieth centuries, left its mark on the musical practices of Christians in Europe. Perhaps most importantly, the guitar and the violin, so important in contemporary European music, probably have their origins in Middle Eastern long-necked plucked lutes and bowed, pear-shaped fiddles, respectively. Early Christian religious music—some of whose melodies continue to resonate in modern religious and secular music—and some forms of Eastern Orthodox chant share features with Islamic and Jewish chanting. In Spain, flamenco retains elements of Arab music, especially in vocal style, ornamentation, and improvisatory practice. Many modes, meters, tunes, and ornaments of Balkan urbanized traditional music have Turkish analogs. The musical impact of late-twentieth-century Muslim immigrants from Asia and North Africa is perhaps too recent to judge, but Muslims in Paris and London have already become leading figures in the production of new forms of popular music known as world music or worldbeat music [see IMMIGRANT MUSIC IN EUROPE, WORLD MUSIC IN EUROPE].

Minorities

Europe is currently divided into forty-two sovereign countries, most so-called nation-states. (A few—Andorra, Liechtenstein, Luxembourg, Monaco, San Marino, and the Vatican—are tiny principalities and city-states, and one, the United Kingdom, contains three nations: England, Scotland, and Wales.) A nation-state consists of a large group of people supposedly homogeneous in language, history, and culture. This group, called a nation or nationality, is theoretically conceived as coterminous with the territory of the state or country. In fact, such states have never been able to contain all the nationalities of Europe, nor do many nation-states consist of a single nation, nor does a nation-state contain all members of its nationality. (Nationality in Europe in some respects resembles the American concept of ethnicity.) This inconsistency between the theory of nation-states—nationalism—and the on-the-ground reality of where people live has created conflicts between and within states: the Flemings and Walloons of Belgium, divided by language; Italy, split between northern and southern cultures; separatist movements of Basques, Bretons, and Corsicans in France and Basques, Galicians, and Catalans in Spain; east and west Germans (Ossies and Wessies), at odds after reunification; fighting among Roman Catholics, Eastern Orthodox, and Muslims in the former Yugoslavia and between Albanians and Serbs in Kosovo Province, Serbia; a buffer zone between Turks and Greeks in Cyprus; and a host of groups seeking political autonomy in Russia and Georgia.

Whether in conflict or living peacefully, each minority has its own music, which it uses to articulate and express its distinctness from the majority in the nation-state. Such national minorities include the Saami in Norway, Sweden, Finland, and Russia; the Basques, Bretons, and Corsicans in France; the Sardinians in Italy; the Turks in Bulgaria; and many other cases. Such variety extends the musical differences implicit in the division of Europe into nation-states and confounds nationalistic attempts to bring all of a country's music under a unified cultural umbrella. Minorities and nationalities who live in different nation-states often have different music. For example, though scholars located some common features of the music of the Jews and the Roma (Gypsies), Europe's largest transnational minorities, Jewish and Rom music varies according to contact with majority cultures (figure 5). Albanian music took on subtly different forms after World War II because of different national policies toward it in Albania and the former Yugoslavia. Many more cases could be cited.

FIGURE 5 In Macedonia, Rom (Gypsy) musicians play modern instruments at weddings for all ethnic groups. Photo by Carol Silverman, mid-1980s.

Thus, minority music adds to the sense of variety and difference in Europe's traditional music.

Urban-rural and class differences

At the local level, the social divisions among classes and the music associated with each constitutes an important source of difference in European musical life. Perhaps the most important division exists between rural and urban forms of musical performance. Urban societies contain a class division between an educated elite that patronizes classical music and a working class that has spawned various forms of urban popular music. Each country's musical life is notably varied, and most of the articles in Part 3 describe that complexity.

The urban-rural and class divisions of Europe play themselves out differently in different countries of Europe—a historical process that contributes to the variety of musical styles in Europe. Great Britain and Ireland and most of Northern, Western, and Central Europe, for example, underwent industrialization and urbanization in the nineteenth century, much earlier than countries in Eastern Europe and the Balkans. In areas with the longest histories of industrialization and urbanization, traditional village music is declining or being influenced by urban popular or classical music. Germany provides perhaps the clearest case of an almost completely lost rural-music tradition, to the point that scholars there have had to recast their notions of folk music to include urban and modern forms of music to find an object of study. By contrast, some industrialized countries (such as Ireland, Norway, and Switzerland) or somewhat isolated regions of industrialized countries (such as Brittany in France) preserve flourishing traditions of what might be called neofolk or neotraditional music, often transplanted into urban environments through processes of revival, folklorization, and nationalism. In parts of southeastern Europe, the decline of rural music as a result of industrialization and urbanization began only after World War II; there, however, the deleterious effects of these processes on village music were mitigated by government support of "people's music." As a consequence, many traditional practices uninfluenced by urban music, such as drone-based polyphonic singing and bagpiping, remain current. At the same time, many rural practices in southeast-

The use of manufactured acoustic and electronic instruments, jazzy chordal accompaniments, and newly composed tunes and songs signify tradition and modernity for villagers and urbanites wishing to assert their connection to both realities.

ern Europe, such as elaborate wedding music, have survived during the last fifty years by modernizing in line with developments in urban music. In Bulgaria and Serbia, the use of manufactured acoustic and electronic instruments, jazzy chordal accompaniments, and newly composed tunes and songs signify tradition and modernity for villagers and urbanites wishing to assert their connection to both realities.

Musical-style differences

At the level of musical style, each country, region, and village often seems anxious to assert its uniqueness, partly the result of nationalistic ideologies, but also of real experiences, such as the inability to dance to music from a neighboring village or valley. Examples of such uniqueness abound. The traditional, three- and four-part vocal polyphony of Georgia and the North Caucasus is known nowhere else in Europe, or indeed the world. Significant regional variations occur in traditional Bulgarian and Albanian part singing. Though ornamented singing and playing is typical throughout Europe, each region seems to have a unique style of ornamentation that identifies it. The singing of lengthy heroic epics, once possibly widespread in Europe, is still found in only a small area of the central Balkans (Lord 1960). Elaborate yodeling is limited to Europe's central alpine region. A rhythmic device known colloquially as the Scotch snap (a sixteenth note followed by a dotted eighth), though hardly unknown in other music, is so pervasive in Scottish music that it is taken as a sign of Scottish musical culture. Instances such as these, multiplied thousands of times, create the impression of enormous variety and differentiation, rather than similarity, in European traditional musical culture.

The articles in Part 2 of this volume explore some of the continentwide processes that have affected European music. The articles in Part 3 describe the music of each country—and of its minority groups and regions. Reading several country articles in close succession reveals striking similarities in the social and historical processes affecting music across the continent, just as it reveals the extraordinary variety of the results of these processes.

BIBLIOGRAPHY

Baumann, Max Peter. 1976. *Musikfolklor und Musikfolklorismus.* Winterthur: Amadeus-Verlag.

Buchan, David. 1972. *The Ballad and the Folk.* London: Routledge and Kegan Paul.

Danckert, Werner. 1970 [1939]. *Das europäische Volkslied.* 2d ed. Bonn: H. Bouvier.

Deutsch, Walter, ed. 1981. *Der Bordun in der europäische Volksmusik.* Vienna: A. Schendl.

Deutsch, Walter, and Gerlinde Heide, eds. 1975. *Die Geige in der europäischen Volksmusik.* Vienna: A. Schendl.

Dorson, Richard Mercer. 1976. *Folklore and Fakelore: Essays toward a Discipline of Folk Studies.* Cambridge: Harvard University Press.

Elschek, Oskár. 1969. "Typoligische Arbeitsverfahren bei Volksmusikinstrumenten." *Studia Instrumentorum Musicae Popularis* 1:23–40.

Entwhistle, William J. 1939. *European Balladry.* Oxford: Clarendon Press.

Frey, Jürgen, and Kaarel Siniveer. 1987. *Eine Geschichte der Folkmusik.* Reinbek bei Hamburg: Rowohlt.

Herder, Johann Gottfried von. 1778–1779. *Volkslieder.* 2 vols. Leipzig: Weygand.

Karpeles, Maud. 1955. "Definition of Folk Music." *Journal of the International Council on Traditional Music* 7:6–7.

———. 1956. *Folk Songs of Europe.* London: Novello.

Ling, Jan. 1997. *A History of European Folk Music.* Rochester, N.Y.: University of Rochester Press.

Lord, Albert B. 1960. *The Singer of Tales.* Cambridge: Harvard University Press.

Vargyas, Lajos. 1983. *Hungarian Ballads and the European Ballad Tradition.* 2 vols. Translated by Imre Gombos. Budapest: Akadémiai Kiadó.

Wiora, Walter. 1957. *Europäische Volksmusik und abendländische Tonkunst.* Kassel: J. P. Hinnenthal.

The Collection and Study of Traditional European Music

James Porter

Background to Early Collecting in Europe
The First Collections of Traditional Music
The Revolution of the Phonograph
The Organization of Research after World War II
The Influence of Anthropology and Folklore
Recent Developments

The integrated and systematic study of Europe's traditional music began only in the nineteenth century, though antiquarians had been collecting specimens of regional forms well before then.

BACKGROUND TO EARLY COLLECTING IN EUROPE

The first collections of popular songs as such appeared in the later seventeenth century, as the country dance and traditional forms of song and dance started to catch on in urban fashion. The songs were connected to domestic life, occupations, and love relationships at all social levels, or grew out of a need to express hardship, such as poverty or war, and were sometimes satirical and sometimes celebratory. Though not confined to one particular class, they had their basis among ordinary people and were often attached to saints' days, the seasons, and red-letter days in the life cycle: births, weddings, and funerals. They were sung in homes, village taverns, and fairs, or in city streets, in the last case sometimes by ordinary people, sometimes by semiprofessional balladeers singing from a bench (German *Bänkelsänger*, Italian *cantimbanchi*). Through unwritten canons of popular taste, the community, urban or rural, determined whether a song or dance was to be retained in the traditional repertoire.

Gradually, during the Enlightenment and into the nineteenth century, songs and dances came to have a more overtly regional and ideological role as nations, in the wake of the French Revolution, began to chafe under the imperial constraints of Austria or Russia. While the country population in most of Europe was fairly homogeneous, the cities were melting pots that attracted immigrants from other parts of Europe and beyond. But cities had already exerted their influence by the late seventeenth century, inculcating and disseminating notions of urban sophistication and rural backwardness. Unsurprisingly, therefore, the first song collections reflected a sense among urban intellectuals that "ancient" forms of expression could be rescued from rural peasants or people without formal education. These two groups, the peasants and the uneducated, were seen as manifestations of "timelessness"—one reason why they played an important role in such "out-of-time" events as carnival in Roman Catholic countries. The divided, post-Reformation world of Catholic, Orthodox, and Protestant Europe, which had considerable influence on folk song, was further complicated by the presence of Jews, Gypsies, and multifarious ethnic groups and religions.

By 1600, the demographic picture of Europe was complex, increasingly as voyages of discovery brought back exotic items that included musical forms. The French essayist Montaigne (1533–1592), for example, was especially fascinated by an account of Brazilian Indians. At the same time, street literature began to be a significant presence in the cities of Europe, as the popular press issued broadside sheets and chapbooks, which contained news of the day and were in fact an early form of tabloid newspaper. They also contained songs, sometimes with tunes, or indications of the tunes to which verses were to be sung. Thus they were one of the earliest means of collecting, printing, and disseminating popular songs. As literacy grew, so did their influence, though oral tradition played an equally important role in the transmission of popular forms. Figures from high culture paid attention to popular culture: Rabelais (ca. 1483–ca. 1553), the famous French satirist, drew on chapbook literature; the German composer Handel (1685–1759), visiting Italy in 1709, heard bagpipers from Abruzzi in Rome and imitated their music in his celebrated oratorio *Messiah* (1741).

THE FIRST COLLECTIONS OF TRADITIONAL MUSIC

The earliest collections of folklore and folk song in Europe were also inspired, in part, by philosophers such as Montaigne or essayists such as Joseph Addison (1672–1719). Montaigne, having traveled in Italy, remarked on the ability of illiterate peasants there to improvise verses, sometimes from hearing others reading or reciting the great Renaissance poets Ariosto or Tasso. Addison confirmed this ability from the example of ordinary Venetian singers, who would readily answer a first singer's verses derived from these poets. When the upper and middle classes in Europe realized that popular music, song, and dance were full of invention and interest and were to be imitated or adopted, the collection of such forms began in earnest. In Switzerland, with its centrality in Europe and prominence on trade routes, the cowherd's song known as *ranz des vaches* or *Kühreihen* appears early in the record (1545). Also in Central Europe, Georg Forster's *Frische teutsche Liedlein* (1539–1556) contains many traditional folk songs.

John Playford had begun to print collections of country dances in England in his *English Dancing Master* (1651), and more British and Irish popular songs and melodies appeared in Thomas D'Urfey's *Pills to Purge Melancholy* (1699–1700), the Neal brothers' collection of Irish tunes (1724), and William Thomson's *Orpheus Caledonius* (1725). In France, urban songs appeared in compilations such as Ballard's *La clef des chansonniers* (1717). Allan Ramsay's Scottish pastoral *The Gentle Shepherd* (1725) included traditional songs and later became a ballad opera following the astounding success of John Gay's *The Beggar's Opera* (1728). The fashion for ballad opera and "Scotch tunes" in Britain was a reaction against the wholesale importation of Italian musicians and styles, but helped to stimulate interest in older materials. The impact of James Macpherson's *Fragments of Ancient Poetry* (1760), which suggested the presence of ancient epics in the Scottish Highlands, and Thomas Percy's *Reliques of Ancient English Poetry* (1765), with its old ballads, was felt throughout the nineteenth century.

The person who began to draw theoretical attention to European musical traditions at this point was Johann Gottfried von Herder (1744–1803), who early in his career got to know Latvian folk songs in Riga. He believed that the soul of a people could be detected in its songs, and coined the term *Volkslied* 'folk song' in the early 1770s with his best-known collection, *Volkslieder* (1778–1779). This in turn influenced collections such as Achim von Arnim's *Des Knaben Wunderhorn* ('The Youth's

Magic Horn') (1806–1808). By this time, antiquarian interest in folk song had burgeoned. In Scotland, James Johnson, with the assistance of Robert Burns, published *The Scots Musical Museum* (6 vols., 1787–1803), L'vov and Prach issued their compilation of Russian folk songs (1790), and the material for Kirsha Danilov's collection of Russian epic songs was being put together in the 1780s, mostly in southwestern Siberia (2d ed., with melodies 1818). "National" collections of songs began to proliferate: in Sweden (Geijer and Afzelius 1814–1817), Austria (Tschischka and Schottky 1819), Germany (Erk and Irmer 1838–1841), Bohemia (Erben 1842–1843), and elsewhere.

Herder's interest in language, meantime, had launched the field of comparative philology and established affinities among the languages of Europe that derived from Sanskrit. At the same time, comparative folklore drew attention to similarities of theme and style in European tales and songs, while students of religion noted a common pattern of social organization in early European communities (ruler-priests, warriors, farmers). With this expansion of disciplines, collecting of music and songs in the field grew apace, marking an important retreat from idealistic, armchair collecting and appraisal of the material. Massive ethnographic collections were undertaken by scholars such as Oskar Kolberg in Poland (1961 [1857–1890]), Evald Tang Kristensen in Denmark (1868–1891), and the Czech painter and writer Ludvik Kuba, who assembled a vast collection of Slavic music (1884–1988). These compilations had political overtones: Kolberg's work, for example, was undertaken while Poland was still partitioned (1795–1914); Kuba's collecting was encouraged by President Thomas Masaryk after 1918, when Czechoslovakia became a republic.

THE REVOLUTION OF THE PHONOGRAPH

What happened next, however, was to revolutionize the study of music, song, and speech. The phonograph was invented independently by Thomas Alva Edison in the United States and Charles Cros in France (1877), and this invention led inevitably to the desire to capture manifestations of oral tradition with greater fidelity. Pioneers in recording music in Europe were Béla Vikár in Hungary (1896), Evgeniya Lineva in Russia (from 1897), Humbert Pernot in Greece (1898–1899), Hjalmar Thuren in the Faroes (1902), Karol Medvecky in Slovakia (1902), Zoltán Kodály (1905) and Béla Bartók (1906) in Hungary, Percy Grainger in England (1906), Otakar Zich in Bohemia (1909), and Matija Murko in Bosnia-Hercegovina (1912–1913). At this time, the phonogram archives in Vienna (1899) and Berlin (1900) were founded to house phonograph recordings, and the Berlin archive became especially important for the study of traditional music worldwide. Later national archives were established in Rome (Discoteca di Stato, 1928), London (the BBC Gramophone Library, 1931; British Institute of Recorded Sound, 1948), Paris (Phonothèque Nationale, 1938), and Geneva (International Archives of Traditional Music, 1944). The director of the Berlin phonogram archive until 1933, Erich M. von Hornbostel, published Bartók's important Romanian collection from Maramureş (1923).

Bartók, indeed, is central to this period in the collecting and editing of folk music in Central Europe and the Balkans. He produced editions of Hungarian (1924), Romanian (1913, 1923, 1935), Slovakian (1959–1970), and Yugoslavian (1951, 1954) musical traditions in addition to studies he made in North Africa and Asia Minor, and was the major force in comparative field-based studies (1934). No other scholar accomplished as much as he in this period, an incredible feat when one considers his brilliant achievement as a composer. His systematic analysis of each tradition goes beyond simple identification of scale or meter, and takes structural scrutiny and classification to extraordinary lengths. The influence of his methods, formed in the climate of positivistic science, has not always been beneficial: academies of science, especially in Eastern Europe, have tended to stress classification and structure to the point where many of the essential features of music making, such as affective communication or intonation, were minimized or lost. It could be argued that Bartók's best analyses of folk music are found in his arrangements, which synthesize many performative elements of folk music. The Romanian scholar Constantin Brăiloiu (1893–1958) extended Bartók's methods to specific genres (1984). Meantime, the climate of Stalinism in Russia and Ukraine created difficulties for field researchers such as Klyment Kvitka (1880–1953), whose contributions to comparative research, especially in the Slavic area, are noteworthy. Of the same generation, Vasil Stoin (1880–1938) collected more than nine thousand melodies in Bulgaria, and Adolf Chybiński (1880–1952), a notable historian of Polish music, carried out ethnomusicological studies of the Tatra Mountain people.

In Central Europe, the Austrian scholar Josef Pommer (1845–1918) founded the journal *Das deutsche Volkslied* (1899), which later became influential in the study of German-language folk-song types, such as the alpine yodel. The German scholar John Meier (1864–1953) founded the German Folk Song Archive in Freiburg in 1914 with the object of analyzing folk song, more particularly ballads, in important compilations, such as *Deutsche Volkslieder mit ihren Melodien* (1935–1982), but he also subscribed to the so-called reception theory with his concept of folk song's origins as *Kunstlieder im Volksmund* 'art song in the peoples' mouths', which in turn was grounded in the folklorist Hans Naumann's view of folklore as sunken culture (i.e., originating in the upper classes) and tended to minimize folk creativity. Reception theory was adopted in France by Patrice Coirault (1875–1959) in opposition to the ideas of Julien Tiersot (1857–1936) and others, who tended to follow Herder's original idea of collective creation by ordinary people.

Like Bartók in Central Europe and the Balkans, an inspired Cecil J. Sharp gathered a fair number of traditional songs in western England and the Appalachian Mountains of the United States. Bartók had felt at first that rural folk song represented the pure stream of Hungarian tradition, but he later came to see the creative contribution of urban and Gypsy music. Sharp, however, always saw folk song as essentially rural (1907). He conceived of it as consisting in a tripartite process of continuity, variation, and selection, factors resulting from stability over time, the input of singers, and the critical role of the community in retaining or rejecting individual items. His concept tended to idealize folk song, and indeed the ideological component in his thinking was wedded to a desire to imbue schoolchildren in England with a taste for folk song and inspire a national school of composers. The latter objective bore fruit in the work of Ralph Vaughan Williams, Gustav Holst, and others. But in transcribing and publishing the texts and tunes of folk songs, Sharp was less meticulous than Bartók and Grainger. He rejected the use of the phonograph because he felt it disturbed the singers. Though his energy dominated the Folk-Song Society in Britain from its founding (in 1898) and his disciple Maud Karpeles (1885–1976) carried his influence into a wider arena, his definition of folk song, adopted by the International Folk Music Council in 1954, was quietly abandoned by 1981, when this organization renamed itself the International Council for Traditional Music.

THE ORGANIZATION OF RESEARCH AFTER WORLD WAR II

The founding of the International Folk Music Council (London, 1947) was an attempt to coordinate the interests of researchers, most of whom then worked in Europe. In this development, Maud Karpeles was central, being honorary secretary from 1947 to 1965. The council's first president, Vaughan Williams, was succeeded by Jaap Kunst and Zoltán Kodály. All were involved with regional musical traditions in Europe (though Kunst carried out research on Dutch folk music, he was also not-

The methods for studying traditional music in Europe are still underdeveloped because the rise of ethnomusicology, strongly influenced by North American anthropology, posited the need for musical ethnographies of single cultures before comparative conclusions could be drawn.

ed for his research in Javanese music). The term *folk* was expunged from the title in 1981 because it was associated with romantic views of music production and was inappropriate for societies outside Europe. In Western and Central Europe, the trend to purge terms such as *folklore, folk music,* and *folk song* and substitute terms such as *traditional, popular,* and *vernacular* went hand in hand with a renaming of the discipline—which had been variously called music ethnology and music ethnography—as ethnomusicology (the earlier German term, *Musikethnologie,* has since begun to conform with the English-language term). The council produced a journal (*Journal of the International Folk Music Council*) that gave way to a yearbook (*Yearbook of the International Folk Music Council*), whose name changed again in 1981 (*Yearbook for Traditional Music*) and expanded its scope into diverse fields, such as history, iconography, and dance.

The methods for studying traditional music in Europe are still underdeveloped because the rise of ethnomusicology, strongly influenced by North American anthropology, posited the need for musical ethnographies of single cultures before comparative conclusions could be drawn. Curt Sachs (1881–1959) opened up the field of musical prehistory, which became a fertile field for students of musical archaeology (1936). Another Central European scholar, Werner Danckert (1900–1970), categorized musical idioms on the basis of language groups using methods of the Austrian historicist culture-circle school (1970 [1939], 1966). Later, Walter Wiora drew up a synoptic table of European folk melodies that he believed were genetically related over time (1952). Hungarian scholars eagerly pursued historical and comparative studies: Bartók's essay on the music of Hungary and that of its neighbors (1934) led the way. Bence Szabolcsi (1950) attempted a history of melody, like the German scholar Marius Schneider (1934, 1935, 1968), reaching beyond Europe to Asia to explain the presence in Europe of *maqam*-like structures and pentatonic scales. Another Hungarian, János Maróthy (1966), drew on Gyorgy Lukács's Marxist philosophy to analyze the history of European folk song.

The development of cross-cultural or comparative studies of melody was taken further by Mieczyslaw Kolinski, an assistant to Hornbostel at the Berlin Phonogramm-Archiv. Kolinski used European and other tunes to work out a system of melodic shapes by "tint affinity," derived from the circle of fifths (1965). In his study of the most common English-language folk song, "Barbara Allen," he used Croatian, French, Hungarian, Polish, and Slovakian songs (1968–1969). His study of seven Canadian versions of "Malbrough s'en va-t-en guerre" analyzed musical contour, rhythmic and metric structure, and pulse (1979). Similarly, George List used a well-known melodic formula ("Ah! vous dirai-je, maman") to raise issues of diffusion or polygenesis in the distribution of tune structures (1979).

By contrast, Alan Lomax, working in North America under the influence of behavioral anthropology, employed factors of singing style rather than structure or history to identify patterns in Europe as a whole. He posited an Old European, a

Northwestern (or Modern European), and an Old High Culture (or Eurasian) set of singing styles, the first tied to Central and Eastern Europe, the last to the Mediterranean (1974). His hypothesis holds that each culture has a dominant style, determined by such factors as means of subsistence, organization of the sexes, and social structure. The "old European" style he considers typical of societies where the agricultural cycle, country dance, and music making are linked; this zone stretches from Eastern Europe through southern Germany, northern Italy, and Spain to north-eastern France and Wales, employing a style that integrates music and text closely, is often polyphonic, and "reflects the communal, complementary character of the region." The "modern European" style Lomax finds typical of Northern Europe, where shepherds, woodsmen, and isolated farmers evolved the solo narrative song performed in an impersonal manner. The "Eurasian" style is found mainly in the Mediterranean, where "a complex system of irrigation is supported by specialized pas-toralism, centralized political systems, and a multilayered social stratification." These aspects are mirrored in ornate texts and long, through-composed, nonstrophic melodies ornamented by elaborate techniques of vocal production. Lomax's bold hypotheses are often based on uneven samples from each country or region (1976). Lomax also undertook important collecting in Europe, especially Britain, Ireland, and Italy. With Diego Carpitella, he produced a brilliant series of recordings of Italian folk music (figure 1).

The work of the study groups of the International Folk Music Council has advanced ethnographic and comparative methods in the study of European tradition-al music. The Group on Musical Instruments (founded in 1962) has produced vol-umes of proceedings of its annual meetings from 1969 (*Studia Instrumentorum Musicae Popularis*), and these cover such topics as typology, playing techniques, improvisation, performers' roles, children's instruments, and so on (figure 2). The group has sponsored a handbook series of regional instruments, including those of Hungary (Sárosi 1967), Czechoslovakia (Elschek 1983; Kunz 1974), Switzerland (Bachmann-Geiser 1981), and Slovenia (Kumer 1986). Independent surveys of instruments were contributed by Anoyanakis for Greece (1979), Atanassov for Bulgaria (1983), Veiga de Oliveira for Portugal (1966), and Vertkov for the U.S.S.R.

FIGURE 1 Alan Lomax kneels to adjust his recording equipment in Italy in the early 1950s—the decade when, in many parts of southern and Eastern Europe, the first extensive field recordings facilitated by small, portable, battery-operated tape recorders, were done. Photo courtesy of the Alan Lomax Collection, New York.

FIGURE 2   The Corsican collector Félix Quilici (1909–1980) records a threshing song (*trib-biera*), sung by farmers as they drive oxen around the threshing floor. Photo courtesy of the Collection Félix Quilici, Paris.

(1975 [1963]). Monographs on specific instruments have also appeared: e.g., on the Swedish keyed fiddle (Ling 1967), the Sardinian *launeddas* (Weis Bentzon 1969), the hurdy-gurdy (Bröcker 1973), and the balalaika (Ronström 1976). These studies examine past scholarship, historical sources, social use, symbolism, repertory, tunings, and so on. They complement broader organological writings such as Werner Bachmann's on the origins of bowing (1966) and more general surveys, such as that of Anthony Baines on European bagpipes (1960) and Harrison and Rimmer's overview of European folk instruments (1964). Symposia have addressed the use of the fiddle and the drone in European music (Deutsch 1975, 1981).

The International Musicological Society occasionally included panels on European traditional music in its conferences from the early 1960s, when ethnomusicologists brought growing influence to bear: panels dealt with such themes as the contribution of ethnomusicology to historical musicology, criteria for acculturation, oral and written traditions in the Mediterranean (1964), the problem of historicity in European folk song, traditional forms of epic singing, and sociology in music (1972); ethnomusicologists' influence in this organization reached its zenith when they participated in multiple sessions at the 1977 IMS Conference in Berkeley, California. The International Folk Music Council Conference at Regensburg (1975) included a panel on the current state of research into orally transmitted music. Bruno Nettl made the point at that time that scholars were becoming less interested in transcription, not only because of the arrival of automatic melody writers, such as that dubbed Mona at the University of Uppsala, Sweden, but because anthropological influence was turning scholars more toward questions of meaning and value in Western music (Nettl 1975).

The aim of the ICTM Study Groups was mainly to solve problems of documentation and classification—an issue taken up also by the Group on Analysis and Systematization of Folksong Melodies and the Group on Historical Sources of Folk Music. The urge to classify came from Bartók and Kodály, and was implemented by scholars such as Pál Járdányi (1961) within the framework of a national collection that grouped music into genres (*Corpus Musicae Popularis Hungaricae,* 1959–1987). Another early ICTM study group with a partial focus on Europe was that on ethnochoreology, in which members proposed a "European" approach to the holistic analysis of traditional dance (Giurghescu and Torp 1991). The first study groups of the 1960s were gradually joined, in the 1980s and 1990s, by those on Music Archaeology, Computer Aided Research, Iconography, Music and Gender, Maqam, Music of the Arab World, and Anthropology of Music in the Mediterranean (Elschek 1991; Magrini 1993; Michel 1991; Suppan 1991).

Genre studies

Genre studies have included pan-European forms, such as epic, ballad, lullaby, and lament. Research on epic songs and singing in the modern era began with Russian scholars of the later nineteenth century in their study of *byliny*–or *stariny,* as the people called them (Sokolov 1971). Research on these continued through the Soviet period (Dobrovol'sky and Korryzalov 1981). Meanwhile, South Slavic epic song was analyzed from the viewpoint of Homeric studies and in the context of creation and performance (Lord 1960), but also from folkloristic and musicological standpoints (Bartók 1942; Erdely 1995). Margaret Beissinger has scrutinized the text and music of Romanian epics (1988, 1991). Epic and ballad normally remain distinct genres, but in some areas, as in the former Yugoslavia, they overlap (Boskovic-Stulli 1991). The musical tradition of ballads has been compiled for Britain and North America by Bronson (1959–1972), for Denmark by Knudsen et al. (1976), for Germany by Suppan and Stief (1976), and for Judeo-Hispanic ballads by Katz (1982). Elsa Mahler studied laments in Russia (1935), as did Brǎiloiu in Romania (1938). Hungarian and Bulgarian scholars (Katsarova 1969; Rajezcky 1964, 1967) followed suit, and further work has occurred in Greece (Alexiou 1974; Auerbach 1989 [1987]), Ireland (O Madagáin 1978), and Italy (De Martino 1958). Like laments, lullabies exhibit features of structure and content in common with ballads, vendors' cries, dance tunes, and other genres (Greni 1960; O Madagáin 1989; Sanga 1979:41; Shields 1993:113).

THE INFLUENCE OF ANTHROPOLOGY AND FOLKLORE

In these developments, which tended to replace an emphasis on the analysis of musical structure with a more anthropological approach to musical performance and style, Central and Eastern European scholars preferred to develop more musicological techniques, such as use of a melograph for registering melodies with greater precision (as in Bratislava). Devices of this kind had also been developed in several centers of musicology: Los Angeles, Uppsala (Sweden), and Israel. But even in Eastern Europe, a diversity of concepts prevailed for classificatory purposes: melodic structure formed the basis for Hungarian researchers, while in Moravia, Poland, and Slovakia metrorhythmic features were preferred. The Ukrainian scholar Volodymyr Hoshovsky evolved a system to compare regional styles—a system that would, he believed, lead to an international catalogue of melodic types (1977). Feodosy Rubtsov looked for common intonational patterns in Slavic folk songs (1962); Nikolaj Kaufman sought common Slavic elements in Bulgarian and East Slavic music (1968); Anna Czekanowska analyzed narrow-range melodies in the Slavic countries using a taxonomic system (*dendrite*) developed in Wroclaw, Poland (1972, 1977) (figure 3).

Studies of individual singers or musicians are now complemented by detailed studies that view such performers as part of a process of "endofolklorization," cultivating their art as a response to tourism or a crisis of personal or regional identity.

FIGURE 3 Nikolaj Kaufman, Bulgaria's most prolific folk-song collector and musical folklorist in the period after World War II. In addition to his published collections and monographic studies, he was an avid folk-song arranger for state-sponsored folk choruses. Photo by Maria Kaufman 1990. Courtesy of Claire Levy.

Scholars in Soviet Russia also produced important genre studies, as of calendrical songs (Mozheiko 1985; Zemtsovsky 1975).

Current research on European traditional music is balanced between qualitative and quantitative patterns. Research on the latter in particular, now usually computer-driven, tends to investigate entire genres, though computers have also been used to analyze vocal timbre. Cybernetics and information theory have been harnessed (Hoshovsky 1965; Stockmann 1972), as have semiotics (Giurghescu 1973; Hoshovsky 1981) and linguistic methods of analysis (Sundberg and Lindblom 1976). An emergent "systematic" orientation in scholarship links up with the sociology of music on the one hand, and biological, perceptual, and acoustical studies on the other (Kaden 1984; Karbusicky 1979; A. Schneider 1993). A strong influence from hermeneutic philosophy and reflexive anthropology has placed much emphasis on eliciting musical "meaning" for performers and fieldworkers (Rice 1994). The spectrum of "folk" and "popular," with their mutual influence, continues to preoccupy some researchers, as does the formation and performance of political or religious songs with their strongly directed functions. Leydi and Rossi, for example, have looked at nonliturgical religious songs in Italy (1965). In this development, the sociology of music with its emphasis on urban-influenced styles has contributed useful perspectives (Kaden 1984; Karbusicky 1975), including the attempted redefinition of "folk song" as "group song" (Klusen 1969). The primary, face-to-face nature of the sung communication has been contrasted with artificial, staged versions of choral singing and yodeling, especially in Switzerland (Baumann 1976).

Large-scale comparative studies are now offset by field research into social groupings, urban and rural, following the pioneering studies of villages by Brăiloiu (1960, but effected in 1929–1932), Bringemeier (1931), Járdányi (1943), Klusen (1971 [1941]), and Vargyas (1941). Immigrant groups from Europe and beyond, e.g., the Roma, have become the focus of attention. Scattered studies of individual singers or musicians in an earlier phase (e.g., Henssen 1951; Katsarova 1952; Kvitka 1917; Tantsyura 1965) are now complemented by detailed studies that may view such performers as part of a process of "endofolklorization," cultivating their art as a response to tourism or a crisis of personal or regional identity (Lortat-Jacob 1983). Recent research has ranged from historical studies of the seventeenth-century Irish harper Carolan (O'Sullivan 1960) and the nineteenth-century Danish singer Selma Nielsen (Schiørring 1956) to studies of latter-day traditional singers, such as Maren Ole in Denmark (Nielsen 1973) and Jeannie Robertson in Lowland Scotland (Porter and Gower 1995). Instrumentalists have also been the focus of special studies (e.g., Stockmann 1981).

Field research has begun to include discussion of fieldworkers' roles and motives, and how researchers affect the subjects under study (Koning 1980) (figure 4). As a result, factors of gender, power, ideology, and metaphoric explanation mark a new phase in uncovering basic conceptions of music and how these might be considered

FIGURE 4 In Carpino, Puglia, Italy, in August 1954, shepherds listen to a playback of their songs. Interactions between collectors or field researchers and their local respondents, implicitly registered in this photo, have only recently become the subject of scholarly discussion. Photo courtesy of the Alan Lomax Collection, New York.

personal, regional, national, or even European; until more detailed information is available, however, cross-cultural methods are limited to broad features, such as history, content and style, structure, and texture (Ling 1997). The quality of evidence is obviously important here: who provided it, when, and where, and for whom? The mediation, interpretation, and representation of empirical data has become an essential question in the description and analysis of contemporary European ethnomusicology.

RECENT DEVELOPMENTS

The historical basis of research in European traditional music has always been present. "History of music" was a principal focus for scholars at the Budapest conference of the International Folk Music Council in 1964. The question of origins was integral to earlier studies, and even to a panel at the IMS Conference in Ljubljana in 1967, but became less so after 1970, when attention began to move toward chronology and musical archaeology (Hickmann and Hughes 1988). Apart from scholars such as Wiora, who continued to attempt a synthesis of historical and ethnomusicology, ahistorical approaches became the norm in the 1960s. Walter Graf in Vienna, for example, dealt with problems of musical perception, acoustics, and psychology (1980).

Aesthetics too began to engage researchers: in Finland, Armas Väisänen (1890–1969) had explored the topic in relation to instruments as early as 1938, and Hristo Vakarelski had discussed it in relation to Bulgarian singers (1957). Others began to take up the question of indigenous concepts of music, and this general approach was continued by Jan Ling in Sweden (1967), Radmila Petrović in Serbia (1971), Koraljka Kos in Yugoslavia (1972), Jan Stęszewski in Poland (1972), Ginette Dunn in England (1980), and Timothy Rice in Bulgaria (1980). In the 1970s and 1980s, emphasis on context and performance led to a group of studies that continued this trend: Hopkins, for instance, discussed the symbolic meanings of the Hardanger fiddle in Norway (1986), while Nielsen in Iceland (1982), Pekkilä and others in Finland (1983), and Porter in Scotland (1976, 1988) aimed at uncovering "emic" explanations of musical communication, meaning, and value and concepts of aesthetics, composition, and classification. These studies, in contrast to the comparative and historical research in vogue before 1960, disclose a burgeoning interest in the cognitive aspects of traditional music, its genesis and influence.

Attention has also been paid to composers and their relationship with traditional music. Composers, of course, have not only borrowed or transformed traditional elements; their compositions have sometimes entered the stream of popular musical consciousness. Wiora's study (1957) covers some of this ground. Other examples are Brăiloiu's study of Debussy's pentatonic structures (1958), studies by Geck (1970) and Vetterl (1968) on Janáček, that by Klusen on Mahler (1963), and continuing work on such prominent figures as Bartók, Stravinsky, and Vaughan Williams. Luciano Berio and Vinko Globokar are noted for their arrangements of folk music, and Solomon Volkov (1981) described the folkloristic wave of Soviet composers active in the late 1970s.

Work in the 1980s addressed topics such as the control and management of music production in complex societies (Henry 1989; Lortat-Jacob 1984), myth and ideology in Northern Europe (Donner 1985), class and identity in relation to music (Krader 1986; Manuel 1989), dance behavior (Garfias 1984; Giurghescu 1986), the acoustical analysis of herding calls in Sweden and Switzerland (Bolle-Zemp 1985; Johnson 1984), folk-hymn singing (Suojanen 1984), revival and innovation (Ledang 1986; Ling 1986), and music and trance (Rouget 1980). Urbanization of musical styles and interest in the iconographic aspects of traditional music likewise became the focus for research. It is widely accepted that "traditional music" covers an astonishing range of styles that vary within and among regions and countries.

The emphasis in current research on European traditional music, therefore, is on ethnographic reality and the interpenetration of concepts between performers and fieldworkers. The context for these exchanges, however, is often fraught with pressures—from market capitalism, issues of ideology and identity, and ethnic conflict. Awareness of past horrors, such as those experienced by European Jews or Roma during World War II, or recently in the former Yugoslavia, have drawn attention to the role of music as a symbol of ethnic identity and resistance to oppression (Flam 1992; Holý and Nečas 1993). Sensitive fieldwork forms part of this newer research mode, especially since ethical concerns continually confront researchers. The use of positivistic methods, whereby scholars distance themselves from musicians and objectify data through a process of descriptive analysis, is no longer possible or acceptable. Instead, a new awareness of the rich store of knowledge held by "traditional" and "revival" musicians has led ethnomusicologists to reach a more intersubjective understanding of their creative concepts.

BIBLIOGRAPHY

Alexiou, Margaret. 1974. *The Ritual Lament in Greek Tradition.* London: Cambridge University Press.

Anoyanakis, Fivos. 1979. *Greek Folk Musical Instruments.* Athens: National Bank of Greece.

Atanassov, Vergilij. 1983. *Die bulgarischen Volksinstrumente: Eine Systematik in Wort, Bild, und Ton.* Munich: E. Katzbichler.

Auerbach, Susan. 1989 [1987]. "From Singing to Lamenting: Women's Musical Role in a Greek Village." In *Women and Music in Cross-Cultural Perspective,* ed. Ellen Koskoff, 25–43. Urbana: University of Illinois Press.

Bachmann, Werner. 1966. *Die Anfänge des Streichinstrumentenspiels.* Leipzig: Breitkopf und Härtel. Translated by Norma Deane under the title *The Origins of Bowing.* London: Oxford University Press. 1969.

Bachmann-Geiser, Brigitte. 1981. *Die Volksmusikinstrumente der Schweiz.* Leipzig: VEB Deutscher Verlag für Musik.

Baines, Anthony. 1960. *Bagpipes.* Oxford: Oxford University Press.

Bartók, Béla. 1913. *Cântece poporale românești din comitatul Bihor* (Romanian folk songs from the Bihor region). Bucharest: Academia Română Librăriile Socec & Comp. și C. Sfetea.

———. 1923. *Volksmusik der Rumänen von Maramureș.* Munich: Drei Masken Verlag.

———. 1924. *A magyar népdal* (The Hungarian folk song). Albany: State University of New York Press.

———. 1934. *Népzenénk és a szomszéd népek népzenéje* (The folk music of the Magyars and neighboring peoples). Budapest: Somló Béla.

———. 1935. *Melodien der rumänischen Colinde.* Vienna: Universal Edition.

———. 1942. "Parry Collection of Yugoslav Folk Music." *New York Times* (28 June).

———. 1954. *Serbo-Croatian Heroic Songs.* Edited by Albert B. Lord. Cambridge: Harvard University Press.

———. 1959–1970. *Slovenské ľudové piesne* (Slovakian folk songs). 2 vols. New York: Universal Edition.

Bartók, Béla, and Albert B. Lord. 1951. *Serbo-Croatian Folk Songs.* New York: Columbia University Press.

Baumann, Max Peter. 1976. *Musikfolklore und Musikfolklorismus: Eine ethnomusikologische Untersuchung zum Funktionswandel des Jodels.* Winterhur: Amadeus-Verlag and Bernhard Pauler.

Beissinger, Margaret Hiebert. 1988. "Text and Music in Romanian Oral Epic." *Oral Tradition* 3:294–314.

———. 1991. *The Art of the Lautar: The Epic Tradition of Romania.* New York: Garland.

Bentzon, Andreas F. W. 1969. *The Launeddas: A Sardinian Folk Musical Instrument.* Copenhagen: Akademisk forlag.

Bolle-Zemp, Sylvie. 1985. "Lyoba: Appel au bétails et identité en Haute-Gruyère (Suisse)." *Yearbook for Traditional Music* 17:167–178.

Bosković-Stulli, Maja. 1991. "Balladic Forms of the Bugarstica and Epic Songs." *Oral Tradition* 6:225–238.

Brăiloiu, Constantin. 1938. "Bocete din Oaş" (Laments in Oaş). *Grai şi Suflet* 7:1–90.

———. 1958. "Pentatony in Debussy's Music." In *Studia Memoriae Béla Bartók Sacra,* 377–417. Budapest: Akadémiai Kiadó.

———. 1960. *Vie Musicale d'un village: Recherches sur le répertoire de Draguş (Roumanie), 1929–1932.* Paris: Institut Universitaire Roumain Charles 1er.

———. 1984. *Problems of Ethnomusicology.* Edited by A. L. Lloyd. Cambridge: University of Cambridge Press.

Bringemeier, Martha. 1931. *Gemeinschaft und Volkslied: Ein Beitrag zur Dorfkultur des Münsterlandes.* Münster: Aschendorff.

Bröcker, Marianne. 1973. *Die Drehleier: Ihr Bau und ihr Geschichte.* Düsseldorf: Gesellschaft zur Forderung der Systematischen Musikwissenschaft.

Bronson, Bertrand Harris. 1959–1972. *The Traditional Tunes of the Child Ballads.* 4 vols. Princeton, N.J.: Princeton University Press.

Czekanowska, Anna. 1972. *Ludowe melodie wąskiego zakresu w krajach słowiańskich* (Narrow-range folk melodies in Slavic countries). Warsaw: Polskie Wydawnictowo muzyczne.

———. 1977. "On the Theory and Definition of Melodic Type." *Yearbook of the International Folk Music Council* 8:108–116.

Danckert, Werner. 1970 [1939]. *Das europäische Volkslied.* 2d ed. Bonn: H. Bouvier.

———. 1966. *Das Volkslied im Abendland* (Folk song in the West). Berne and Munich: B. Hahnefeld.

De Martino, Ernesto. 1958. *Morte e pianto rituale nel mondo antico.* Turin: P. Boringhieri.

Deutsch, Walter, ed. 1975. *Die Geige in der europäischen Volksmusik.* Vienna: A. Schendl.

———, ed. 1981. *Die Bordun in der Europäischen Volksmusik.* Vienna: A. Schendl.

Deutsche Volksliedarchiv. 1935–1982. *Deutsche Volkslieden mit ihren Melodien.* Berlin: de Gruyter.

Dobrovol'sky, B. M., and V. V. Korryzalov. 1981. *Byliny: Russkii Muzykal'ny Epos.* Moscow: Sovietskii Kompozitor.

Donner, Philip, ed. 1985. *Idols and Myths in Music.* Musiikin Suunta, 7. Helsinki: Kirjastopalvelu.

Dunn, Ginette. 1980. *The Fellowship of Song: Popular Singing Traditions in East Suffolk.* London: Croom Helm.

Elschek, Oskár. 1983. *Die Volksmusikinstrumente der Tschechoslowakei.* Vol. 2. Leipzig: Deutscher Verlag.

———. 1991. "Publications, Studies and Activities of the ICTM Study Group on Analysis and Systematization of Folk Music." *Yearbook for Traditional Music* 23:181–189.

Erben, K. J. 1842. *Prostonárodni české pisně a řikadla* (National Czech songs and proverbs). Prague: Evropsky literarni klub.

Erdely, Stephen. 1995. *Music of Southslavic Epics from the Bihac Region of Bosnia.* New York: Garland.

Erk, Ludwig, and Wilhelm Irmer. 1838–1841. *Die deutschen Volkslieder mit ihren Singweisen.* Leipzig: B. Hermann.

Flam, Gila. 1992. *Singing for Survival: Songs of the Lodz Ghetto, 1940–1945.* Urbana and Chicago: University of Illinois Press.

Garfias, Robert. 1984. "Dance Among the Urban Gypsies of Romania." *Yearbook of the International Folk Music Council* 16:84–96.

Geck, Adelheid. 1970. "Das Volksliedmaterial Leoš Janáčeks." Ph.D. dissertation, University of Berlin.

Geijer, E. G., and A. A. Afzelius. 1814–1817. *Svenska folkvisor.* Stockholm: Z. Haggstrom.

Giurghescu, Anca. 1973. "La danse comme objet sémiotique." *Yearbook of the International Folk Music Council* 5:175–178.

———, ed. 1977. *First All-Union Seminar on Machine Aspects of Algorithmic Formalized Analysis of Musical Texts.* Yerevan: Publishing House of the University of Yerevan.

———. 1986. "Power and Charm: Interaction of Adolescent Men and Women in Traditional Settings of Transylvania." *Yearbook for Traditional Music* 18:37–46.

Giurghescu, Anca, and Lizbet Torp. 1991. "Theory and Methods in Dance Research: A European Approach to the Holistic Study of Dance." *Yearbook of the International Folk Music Council* 23:1–10.

Graf, Walter. 1980. *Vergleichende Musikwissenschaft: Ausgewählte Aufsätze.* Edited by Franz Födermayr. Vienna: Fohrenau.

Greni, Liv. 1960. "Bånsuller i Setesdal" (Lullabies in Setesdal). *Norveg* 7:13.

Harrison, Frank L., and Joan Rimmer. 1964. *European Musical Instruments.* London: Norton.

Henry, Edward O. 1989. "Institutions for the Promotion of Indigenous Music: The Case for Ireland's Comhaltas Ceoltoiri." *Ethnomusicology* 33:67–95.

Henssen, Gottfried. 1951. *Überlieferung und Persönlichkeit: Lieder und Erzählungen des Egbert Gerrits.* Münster: Archiv für Volkskunde Schriften.

Hickmann, Ellen, and David W. Hughes. 1988. *The Archaeology of Early Music Cultures.* Bonn: Verlag für Systematische Musikwissenschaft.

Holý, Dušan, and C. Nečas, 1993. *Žalujici písen: O osudu Romu v nacistických koncentracních táborech* (Lamenting song: The fate of Rom in Nazi concentration camps). Strážnice: Spisy Univerzity J. E. Purkyně v Brně.

Hopkins, Pandora. 1986. *Aural Thinking in Norway: Performance and Communication with the Hardingfele.* New York: Human Sciences Press.

Hoshovsky, Volodymyr. 1965. "The Experiment of Systematizing and Cataloguing Folk Tunes following the Principles of Musical Dialectology and Cybernetics." *Studia Musicologica* 7:273–286.

———. 1981. "Ukrainische Wechselgesänge der Ostkarpaten als semiotisches System." *Stratigraphische Probleme der Volksmusik in den Karpaten und auf dem Balkan,* ed. Alica Elscheková, 133–140. Bratislava: Veda.

Járdányi, Pál. 1943. *A kide magyarság világi zenéje* (Secular music of the Hungarian village of Kide). Kolosvár: no publisher.

———. 1961. *Magyar népdaltípusok* (Hungarian folk-song types). Budapest: Editio Musica.

Johnson, Anna. 1984. "Voice Physiology and Ethnomusicology: Physiological and Acoustical Studies of the Swedish Herding Song." *Yearbook for Traditional Music* 16:42–66.

Kaden, Christian. 1984. *Muziksoziologie.* Wilhelmshaven: Heinrichshofen.

Karbusicky, Vladimir. 1975. "Soziologische Aspekte der Volksliedforschung." *Handbuch des Volksliedes,* ed. R. W. Brednich, L. Röhrich, and Wolfgang Suppan, 45–88. Munich: W. Fink.

———. 1979. *Systematische Musikwissenschaft.* Munich: W. Fink.

Katsarova, Raina. 1952. "Tri pokolenija narodni pevici" (Three generations of folk singers). *Izvestiia na Instituta za Muzika* 1:43–91.

———. 1969. "Oplakvane na pokojnitsi" (Funeral laments). *Izvestia na Instituta za Muzyka* 13:177–190. Summary in French.

Katz, Israel J. 1982. *La música de los romances judeo-españoles.* Madrid: Seminario Menéndez Pidal.

Kaufman, Nikolaj. 1968. *Nyakoi obshti cherti mezhdu narodnata pesen na bulgarite i iztochnite slavyani* (Some common features of Bulgarian and East Slavic folk song). Sofia: Bulgarskata akademia na naukite.

Klusen, Ernst. 1963. "Gustav Mahler und das Volkslied seiner Heimat." *Journal of the International Folk Music Council* 15:29–37.

———. 1969. *Volkslied: Fund und Erfindung.* Cologne: Musikverlag.

———. 1971 [1941]. *Volksmusik in einem niederrheinischen Dorf: Studien zum Liedschatz der Gemeinde Hinsbeck.* Rev. ed. Bad Godesberg: Voggenreiter.

Knudsen, Thorkild, Svend Nielsen, and Nils Schiørring, eds. 1976. *Danmarks gamle folkeviser.* Melodier, vol. 11. Copenhagen: Akademisk forlag.

Kolberg, Oskar. 1961 [1857–1890]. *Piesni ludu polskiego* (Songs of the Polish people). Cracow: Polskie Wydawnictwo Muzyczne.

Kolinski, Mieczyslaw. 1965. "The Structure of Melodic Movement: A New Method of Analysis." *Studies in Ethnomusicology* 2:95–120.

———. 1968–1969. "'Barbara Allen': Tonal Versus Melodic Structure." *Ethnomusicology* 12(2):208–218, 13(1):1–73.

———. 1979. "*Malbrough s'en va-t-en guerre*: Seven Versions of a French Folksong." *Yearbook of the International Folk Music Council* 10:1–32.

Koning, Jos. 1980. "The Fieldworker as Performer: Fieldwork Objectives and Social Roles in County Clare, Ireland." *Ethnomusicology* 24:417–429.

Kos, Koraljka. 1972. "New Dimensions in Folk Music: A Contribution to the Study of Musical Tastes in Contemporary Yugoslav Society." *International Review of Aesthetics and the Sociology of Music* 3:61–75.

Krader, Barbara. 1986. "Slavic Folk Music: Forms of Singing and Self-Identity." *Ethnomusicology* 31:9–17.

Kristensen, Evald Tang. 1868–1891. *Jydske Folkeminder* (Folklore from Jutland). Copenhagen: C. G. Iversens Boghandel.

Kuba, Ludvík. 1884–1988. *Slovanstvo ve svých zpěvech* (The Slavic world in song). Nákladem Vydavatelovým: Komissi v Hoblíka v Pardubícich.

Kumer, Zmaga. 1986. *Die Volksmusikinstrumente in Slovenien.* Ljubljana: Slovenska akademija znanosti in umenosti.

Kunz, Ludvik. 1974. *Die Volksmusikinstrumente der Tschechoslowakei.* Vol. 1. Leipzig: Deutscher Verlag für Musik.

Kvitka, Klyment. 1917. *Narodni melodii z hološu Lesi Ukrainky* (Folk songs from the voice of Lesja Ukrainka). Kiev: Slovo.

Ledang, Ola Kai. 1986. "Revival and Innovation: The Case of the Norwegian Seljefløyte." *Yearbook for Traditional Music* 18:145–156.

Leydi, Roberto, and Annabella Rossi. 1965. *Osservazioni sul canti religiosi no liturgici.* Milan: Vedette Records.

Ling, Jan. 1967. *Nyckelharpan.* Stockholm: Norstedt.

———. 1986. "Folk Music Revival in Sweden: The Lille Edet Fiddle Club." *Yearbook for Traditional Music* 18:1–8.

———. 1991. *Nyckelharpan.* Stockholm: Sven fonogram.

———. 1997. *A History of European Folk Music.* Rochester, New York: University of Rochester Press.

List, George. 1979. "The Distribution of a Melodic Formula: Diffusion or Polygenesis?" *Yearbook of the International Folk Music Council* 10:33–52.

Lomax, Alan. 1974. "Singing." *Encyclopaedia Britannica,* 15th ed., 16:789. Chicago: Encyclopaedia Britannica.

———. 1976. *Cantometrics: A Method of Musical Anthropology.* Berkeley: University of California Extension Media Center.

Lord, Albert B. 1960. *The Singer of Tales.* Cambridge: Harvard University Press.

Lortat-Jacob, Bernard. 1983. "Theory and 'Bricolage': Attilio Cannargiu's Temperament." *Yearbook for Traditional Music* 14:45–54.

———. 1984. "Music and Complex Societies: Control and Management of Musical Production." *Yearbook for Traditional Music* 16:19–33.

L'vov, Nikolai, and Ivan Prach. 1790. *Sobraniie narodnikh russkikh pesen s ikh golosami* (Collection of Russian folk songs with their melodies). St. Petersburg: A. S. Suvorin.

Magrini, Tullia, ed. 1993. *Antropologia della musica e culture Mediterranee.* Bologna: Il Mulino.

Mahler, Elsa. 1935. *Die russische Totenklage.* Leipzig: O. Harrassowitz.

Manuel, Peter. 1989. "Andalusian, Gypsy, and Class Identity in the Contemporary Flamenco Complex." *Ethnomusicology* 33:47–65.

Maróthy, János. 1966. *Zéne es polgar—zéne es proletar* (Music and the bourgeois—music and the proletariat). Budapest: Akademiai Kiado.

Michel, Andreas. 1991. "Publications and Activities of the ICTM Study Group on Musical Instruments." *Yearbook for Traditional Music* 23:172–181.

Mozheyko, Zinaida. 1985. *Kalendarno-pessennaia kultura Belorussii: opyt sistemnotypologicheskogo issledovaniia* (Calendar-song culture in Belarus: Attempt at a systematic-typological study). Minsk: Nauka i tekhnika.

Nettl, Bruno. 1975. "The State of Research in Ethnomusicology and Recent Developments." *Current Musicology* 20:67–78.

Nielsen, Svend. 1973. "Om Maren Ole og hendes sange." *Folk og Kultur,* 87–112. Symposiumommidt-og Nordskaninavisk Kultur, Universitet i Trondheim, Norges Larerhogskole. Copenhagen: Akademisk forlag.

Nielsen, Svend. 1982. *Stability in Improvisation: A Repertoire of Icelandic Epic Songs (Rímur).* Translated by Kale Mahaffy. Copenhagen: Forlaget Kragen.

Ó Madagáin, Breandán. 1978. *Gnéithe den Chaointeoireacht* (The nature of lamenting). An Chéad Chlo: An Clóchomhar Tta.

———. 1989. "Gaelic Lullaby: A Charm to Protect the Baby?" *Scottish Studies* 29:29–38.

O'Sullivan, Donal. 1960. *Carolan: The Life and Times of an Irish Harper.* London: Routledge and Kegan Paul.

Pekkilä, Erkki, ed. 1983. *Suomen Antropologi* (Finnish anthropology). Vol. 4. Helsinki: Suomen Antropologinen Seura.

Petrović, Radmila. 1974. "Some Aspects of Formal Expression in Serbian Folk Songs." *Yearbook of the International Folk Music Council* 2:63–76.

Porter, James. 1976. "Jeannie Robertson's 'My Son David'": A Conceptual Performance Model." *Journal of American Folklore* 84:5–26.

———. 1988. "Context, Epistemics, and Value: A Conceptual Performance Model Reconsidered." *Selected Reports in Ethnomusicology* 7:69–97.

Porter, James, and Herschel Gower. 1995. *Jeannie Robertson: Emergent Singer, Transformative Voice.* Knoxville: University of Tennessee Press.

Rajezcky, Benjamin. 1964. "Zur Ambitusfrage der Klagelieder." *Studia Musicologica* 6:375–380.

———. 1967. "Ost und West in den hungarischen Klageliedern." *Festschrift für Walter Wiora,* ed. Ludwig Finscher and Christoph-Hellmut Mahling, 628–632. Kassel: Bärenreiter.

Rice, Timothy. 1980. "Aspects of Bulgarian Musical Thought." *Yearbook of the International Folk Music Council* 12:43–66.

———. 1994. *May It Fill Your Soul: Experiencing Bulgarian Music.* Chicago: University of Chicago Press.

Ronström, Owe. 1976. *Balalaijkan: Ein instrumentstudie.* Stockholm: no publisher.

Rouget, Gilbert. 1980. *Music and Trance: A Theory of the Relations between Music and Possession.* Chicago and London: University of Chicago Press.

Rubtsov, Feodosy. 1962. *Intonnacionoye siazi o pesennom tvorchestve slavianskikh narodov* (Intonational connections in the song art of the Slavic people). Leningrad: Sovetskii Kompozitor.

Sachs, Curt. 1936. "Towards a Prehistory of Occidental Music." *Proceedings of the American Musicological Society* 1937:91–112.

Sanga, Glauco. 1979. *La communicazione orale e scritta: Il linguaggio del canto popolare.* Brescia: Giunti/Marzocco.

Sárosi, Bálint. 1967. *Die Volksmusikinstrumente Ungarns.* Leipzig: Deutscher Verlag für Musik.

Schiørring, Nils. 1956. *Selma Nielsens Viser: Et repertoire af folkelige sange fra det 19 århundredes slutning.* Copenhagen: Munksgaard.

Schneider, Albrecht. 1993. "Systematische Musikwissenchaft: Traditionen, Ansätze, Aufgaben." *Systematische Musikwissenschaft: Tagungsbericht Moravany* 1(2):145–180.

Schneider, Marius. 1934, 1935, 1968. *Geschichte der Mehrstimmigkeit.* 3 vols. Tutzing: H. Schneider.

Sharp, Cecil J. 1907. *English Folk-Song: Some Conclusions.* London: Simpkins and Novello.

Shields, Hugh. 1993. *Narrative Singing in Ireland.* Dublin: Irish Academic Press.

Sokolov, Yuri M. 1971. *Russian Folklore.* Detroit: Folklore Associates.

Stęszewski, Jan. 1972. "Sachen, Bewusstsein und Benennungen in ethnomusicologischen Untersuchungen." *Jahrbuch für Volksliedforschung* 17:131–142.

Stockmann, Erich. 1972. "The Diffusion of Musical Instruments as a Process of Inter-Ethnic

Communication." *Yearbook of the International Folk Music Council* 3:128–137.

———, ed. 1981. *Studia Instrumentorum Musicae Popularis.* Vol. 7. Stockholm: Musikhistorike museet.

Sundberg, Johan, and Bjoern Lindblom. 1976. "Generative Theories in Language and Music Description." *Cognition* 4:99–122.

Suojanen, Päivikki. 1984. *Finnish Folk Hymn Singing: Study in Music Anthropology.* Tampere: University of Tampere Institute for Folk Tradition.

Suppan, Wolfgang. 1991. "Publications and Activities of the ICTM Study Group on Historical Sources of Folk Music." *Yearbook for Traditional Music* 23:189–194.

Suppan, Wolfgang, and Wiegand Stief. 1976. *Melodietypen des deutschen Volksgesanges.* Tutzing: H. Schneider.

Szabolcsi, Bence. 1950. *A melodia törtenete.* Budapest: Corvina. Translated by Cynthia Jolly and Sára Karig under the title *A History of Melody.* New York: St. Martin's Press, 1965.

Tantsyura, Hnat. 1965. *Pisni Yavdokhy Zuyikhy.* Kiev: Ukrainian Soviet Academy of Sciences.

Tschischka, Franz, and Julius Max Schottky. 1819. *Österreichische Volkslieder mit ihren Singweisen.* Leipzig: Deutsche Verlagsaktiengesellschaft.

Vakarelski, Hristo. 1957. "Belezhki po musikalnata teorija i estetika na naroda" (Notes on folk-musical theory and aesthetics). *Izvestiia na Instituta za Muzika* 4:123–151.

Vargyas, Lajos. 1941. *Aj falu zenei élete* (The musical life of the village of Aj). Budapest: Akadémiai Kiadó.

Veiga de Oliveira, Ernesto. 1966. *Instrumentos musicais populares portugueses.* Lisbon: Fundação Calouste Gulbenkian.

Vertkov, Konstantin, et al. 1975 [1963]. *Atlas of Musical Instruments of the Peoples Inhabiting the USSR.* Moscow: Muzyka.

Vetterl, Karel. 1968. "Janáček's Creative Relationship to Folk Music." *Colloquium Leoš Janáček et Musica Europaea,* 235–242. Brno: Janackova spolecnost, sekce ceske hudebni spolecnosti.

Volkov, Solomon. 1981. "The New 'Folkloristic' Wave in Contemporary Soviet Music as a Sociological Phenomenon." *International Musicological Society Congress Report, 1977,* 49–52. Berkeley: University of California Press.

Weis Bentzon, Andreas Fridolin. 1969. *The Launeddas, a Sardinian Folk-Music Instrument.* Copenhagen: Akademisk forlag.

Wiora, Walter. 1952. *Europäische Volksgesang: Gemeinsame Formen in charakteristische Abwandlungen.* Cologne: Arno Volk Verlag. Translated by Robert Kolben under the title *European Folk Song: Common Forms in Characteristic Modifications.* New York: Leeds Music, 1967.

———. 1957. *Europäische Volksmusik und abendländische Tonkunst.* Kassel: Bärenreiter.

Zemtsovsky, Izaly I. 1975. *Melodika kalendarnikh pesen* (Melodies of calendrical songs). Leningrad: Muzyka.

Part 2
Issues and Processes in European Music

European music can be understood from historical and ethnographic perspectives. Classical and religious music, because of their links to literacy and their use of musical notation, have an especially rich and well-documented history. Folk and popular music, preserved primarily in aural tradition (and recently in electronic media), have been best studied by musical ethnographers and collectors, who observe, interview, and record their contemporaries.

No matter whether folk or classical, popular or religious, singing is at the heart of most musical traditions in Europe. Often the way people sing and what they sing is a function of gender. Here a woman from La Mula, Ibiza, Spain, sings while accompanying herself on a drum. Photo courtesy of the Alan Lomax Collection, New York.

History of Music

The history of European classical and religious music can be traced in a nearly continuous line from around A.D. 800 to the present. Ancient Greek music has been influential less for its sound, which is almost impossible to reconstruct, than for giving Europeans the very name *music,* the idea of musical notation, basic concepts of music theory and terminology, and beliefs about the nature and meaning of music. Archaeology has uncovered potential links between the prehistoric past and modern folk instruments and practices. Musical notation has been crucial to the development and preservation of music history, and Europeans' seeming preference for older forms over newer ones deserves critical examination.

No instrument better symbolizes the history of European music and the links between classical, folk, and popular music than the violin. Developed from folk and medieval models of bowed fiddles and perfected by Italian master craftsmen in the 1600s for classical musicians, it was soon adopted by village musicians and tended to displace traditional, homemade instruments. For a small fee, this street violinist serenades strollers under the Via Rizzoli's arcade in Bologna, Italy. He plays tunes from the Italian classical repertory and of folk songs and dances. Photo by D. A. Sonneborn, 1988.

Archaeology of Music in Europe
Albrecht Schneider

Types of Sources and Their Interpretation
Culture Areas, Periods, Chronology
Classification, Typology, Development, Continuity
Other Research Directions

Archaeology investigates the material remains of musical instruments as primary sources for knowledge of the musical past, including the possible origins and early stages of musical development. This palaeo-organology, useful to ethnomusicology and music history (Scothern 1989), concentrates on the morphological description of recovered artifacts and makes inferences about the ergonomics of body position and motion in relation to instruments. Music archaeology, sometimes called archaeomusicology, starts from the description, conservation, and analysis of material objects interpreted as musical instruments, but seeks to place these objects or their remains into social, cultural, and presumably musical contexts—an approach called *Vorgeschichtsmusikanthropologie* 'prehistoric anthropology of music' (Lund 1980). Because of obvious historical implications, music archaeology has also been defined as *Traditionsforschung* 'research into tradition', an extension of music history using the archaeological record (Hickmann 1985). Music archaeology investigates the beginnings and early developments of musical behavior from biohistorical and anthropological perspectives, and it uses various types of source evidence (including excavated objects, iconographic and literary evidence, ethnographic data, and folklore) and methods (including experiments, fieldwork, laboratory research, hypothetical reconstruction of instruments, and trial of their musical capabilities) (Hickmann and Hughes 1988; Lund 1986).

In addition to the description and analysis of unearthed instruments and their sound properties, music archaeology makes inferences about prehistoric music and even composite soundscapes. This approach, which has already led to a number of illuminating recordings, is based upon, but goes beyond, archaeological evidence, which preserves no sounds, let alone actual music (Bibikov 1981; Lund 1974). Tunings, playing techniques, and pieces of music played on such instruments or replicas are hypothetical. Since historical reconstructions and archaeological interpretations are to some extent conjectural, history and archaeology use hypotheses and models to provide explanations, rather than simple descriptions, of factual evidence. In terms of method, historical narratives and archaeological interpretations of cultural systems and their change and evolution are constructs based on observations and other facts and the application of criteria of coherence, plausibility, and probability

(Schneider 1984, 1986). As a problem-oriented rather than an object-oriented discipline, music archaeology's research strategy combines different sources either to construct a theoretical model supported by factual evidence (Lawergren 1988), or to establish a kind of archaeological and historical narrative that reconstructs certain periods and developments in early music cultures (Vogel 1973, 1978).

Given the hypothetical nature of historical reconstruction, the use of models, analogy, and conjecture seems as legitimate as the experiments that have been successfully employed in archaeology and archaeomusicology (Coles 1973; Harrison 1978). Experiments test hypotheses and gain additional data for observation and measurement. Tonometric measurements have been applied to numerous excavated musical instruments to elucidate their acoustical and musical properties. Sophisticated instruments, such as the bronze horns of Ireland and Scandinavia (the latter called lurs), have been subjected to extensive laboratory investigation (Gottlieb 1986; Holmes 1979, 1986). The manufacturing process and the technology employed are now fairly well known, and the results can be used in the reconstruction of broken specimens and the fashioning of replicas.

Though it is customary in modern archaeology to distinguish between object-oriented and problem-oriented approaches, theoretical and anthropological issues are relevant to both kinds of research. In music archaeology, the special problem of musical origins calls for an interdisciplinary strategy and the combination of various types of sources (Geist 1970). Some have suggested that music played an important role in anthropogenesis, and thus is a genuine part of human nature from the beginning (Blacking 1976; Edström 1981; Wallin 1991). The roots of musical behavior and dance can be traced back even to nonhuman primates. They hypothesize that humans could sing before they invented articulate speech, and that the australopithecines developed the ability to sing in conjunction with signaling (Livingstone 1973). Thus, the most elementary music may have originated several hundred thousand years ago.

Somewhat different from these studies are surveys of excavated objects and their description and evaluation as musical instruments. In these studies, music archaeology is one of the historical disciplines. The objective of the field is to enlarge the scope and depth of music history by incorporating prehistoric periods before written records became available as source material. After an initial overview (Seewald 1934), comparable surveys followed covering specific areas of Europe, such as Scandinavia, the Netherlands, Austria, Poland and other parts of Eastern Europe, portions of Germany, and Spain. Some research is devoted to single classes of instruments, such as aerophones, idiophones, or membranophones, with listings of finds and sites, distribution, and chronological ordering, while other publications cover the material of a specific period, such as the Hallstatt culture of the eastern alpine region. Between 1975 and 1984, research groups in England, France, and Sweden specializing in music archaeology (*archéologie sonore*) were established (Homo-Lechner 1986; Lawson 1983; Reimers 1979). In Sweden alone, more than a thousand prehistoric musical instruments had been documented by 1978. As soon as such catalogues of inventoried data from various European countries become available, the basis for comparative and integrative studies will be much improved.

Since no music from the remote past has been preserved in sound or notation, the invoking of so-called ethnographic parallels—that is, analogies between existing and prehistoric music—is possibly inevitable. Such comparisons appear often in writings on the origins and early stages of music by older scholars, who believed that what they called the primitive music (a descriptive term related to evolutionary concepts) of contemporary ethnic groups retains basic features from the music and dance of prehistoric times (Sachs 1962; Wiora 1961). Parallels have been drawn between the music of the Kalahari Bushmen and that of hunter societies of the European Upper Palaeolithic (ca. 15,000–10,000 B.C.). Such analogies serve as heuristic devices to illustrate the uses and functions of music in its cultural setting, but the actual structure of Palaeolithic music remains a matter of speculation.

TYPES OF SOURCES AND THEIR INTERPRETATION

Music archaeology deals with seven types of source: objects that have been excavated or secured in different ways; iconographic material, including wall paintings in caves, rock engravings, depictions on pottery, coins, and metal vessels; linguistic sources, including terminology of music and musical instruments; written records, including clay tablets, classical Greek and Latin sources, and early historical documents; folklore and myth, including legends relating to the "singing bone" and the invention of certain instruments; evidence provided by physical anthropology and bioacoustics; and ethnographic data of use in drawing parallels or, alternatively, as explanatory or illustrative devices.

The number and quality of available sources varies considerably with time depth and geographical area. Evidence from musical instruments of the Palaeolithic and Mesolithic periods is scarce—a circumstance attributable to the fact that bone, wood, and other natural materials disintegrate over millennia. Chance largely determines the sampling of objects available for study. Fifty-nine complete or fragmented lurs of the Scandinavian Bronze Age III–IV (ca. 1300–650 B.C.) have been found (Lund 1986). In Ireland, a total of 122 items, many just fragments relating to bronze horns of the late Bronze Age, were once known (Coles 1963). Such samples allow comparisons, mapping of distributions, detection of common features, and typological ordering on the basis of morphological and technological traits; moreover, the study of finds and their context and of iconographic evidence offers clues on use, function, and the cultural background of music. Iconographic sources contain depictions of musical behavior such as singing, playing instruments, dancing, the formation of ensembles, and so on, including several hundred images relating to music on Greek pottery (Paquette 1984). Most instruments of the classical period are well documented, including their playing technique and cultural context. Further evidence can be derived from the study of the classics and other written sources and linguistic inquiry into the musical terminology of Indo-European and other languages (Gavazzi 1976; Nieminen 1963; Schneider 1985).

Problems often arise in evaluating sources. The rock carvings in Bohuslän, Sweden, or in Val Camonica, Italy, appear on first impression to be musical instruments, and yet they definitely are not. Literary sources occasionally mention the names of instruments—the biblical *nebel* (*nevel*) occurs in texts over a period of some seven hundred years—but no specimen exists. Names can also denote a variety of instruments; the term *zampogna* (*zanfoña, zumpogna*) may refer to a bagpipe, a hurdy-gurdy, or a mouth harp. As different as these instruments appear morphologically, they all produce a drone and a melodic line. Even excavated objects are not always easy to identify as musical instruments. In the 1980s, scholars debated whether the Palaeolithic flute existed; Christine Brade (1982) doubted that Upper Palaeolithic bones that exhibit one or more piercings (usually interpreted as finger holes and a blowhole) were made and used as flutes. Others challenged Brade's skepticism, pointing out that artifacts not initially made as musical instruments could be used as such, and in fact have been throughout history. Thus, objects suited for use as musical instruments can at least be considered potential sources in music archaeology.

So-called clay drums provide a good example of the problem. A large sample of Neolithic pottery is believed to represent clay drums, though no drumhead from these supposed membranophones survives (Maier 1960; Seewald 1934). Most specimens, including some sixty excavated from late Neolithic sites in Saxony and northern Germany, have similar hourglass or goblet shapes (Fischer 1951; Mildenberger 1952). Knobs or plugs, with or without holes, around the upper rim could have served to fasten a drumhead. Interpreting the pottery as drums is thus conjectural and rests on an analogy with actual drums of similar shape from North Africa, the Middle East, and the Balkans. Even conical clay objects have been defined as drums drawing on ethnographic parallels with African double-headed drums. Field experiments may provide a more conclusive method for testing the clay-drum hypothesis; one such experiment demonstrated that pottery of this kind could indeed have carried a drumhead and produced sounds for musical purposes (Lindahl 1986). Thus, experiments and ethnographic analogies support the hypothesis that pottery found in Neolithic sites of Central and Northern Europe were used as clay drums.

Though some scholars link the origins of music to anthropogenesis and the acquisition of language, material evidence for humans playing musical instruments is fairly late if we consider only artifacts that can be identified beyond doubt as instruments. Scholars have sought the beginnings of instrumental music in the Upper Palaeolithic, when groups of hunter-gatherers in large parts of Eurasia established fairly well-developed culture patterns. Hunting is depicted in a large number of rock paintings or so-called Palaeolithic cave art dating from ca. 35,000 B.C. to ca. 9,000 B.C. With the emergence of *Homo sapiens,* the advanced manufacture of tools, and the creation of artworks, a stage of evolution was reached in which signs of musical activity might be expected. Indeed, bone objects from the Aurignacian strata (ca. 35,000–18,000 B.C.) have long been interpreted as simple phalange whistles or as bone flutes with finger holes.

Other artifacts, such as the fine specimens of bone flutes from Pas de Miroir (Dordogne, France) and Ullö, Hungary, are most likely from a later period, and Brade (1975) has cast doubt on the existence of the Palaeolithic and Neolithic flute, with the possible exception of the well-known fragment from the Aurignacian site of Isturitz, which, because of its overall shape and the three holes, could well have been part of a bone flute, though definitive evaluation is difficult. Brade's (1982) critical account of the evidence thus far available has led to the conclusion that the existence of Palaeolithic and Neolithic flutes remains unproven. Even if some of the objects could and might have been used as flutes, the details of sound production are still unclear since no block-and-duct, the mechanism that creates the whistle, has been excavated. Putative reconstructions, such as that of a flute from Istállöskö, Hungary (Horusitzky 1955), rest on an assumption that the bone object was a cross flute rather than on the factual evidence that finds of the same age and area might provide.

Some objects, such as the lower jaw of a cave bear with three small holes pierced into the mandibular channel from the site of Potocka Zijalka, Slovenia, are almost certainly not musical instruments. The interpretation of mammoth bones excavated at Mezin, Ukraine, as part of a late Palaeolithic osteophone (bone idiophone) is also speculative. Though mammoth bones were commonly used in hunter culture for building houses and other purposes, to prove that the large bones had been worked to produce a musical instrument is not easy; it is possible, however, to produce sounds from such bone objects, as a recording demonstrates (Bibikov 1981), and they might have served as musical instruments. One scholar has hypothesized that all Palaeolithic musical instruments were closely related to hunting implements or were the by-products of hunting, and the Mezin osteophone might be viewed as such (Lawergren 1988).

A musical instrument related to hunting has been detected in the hands of the so-called sorcerer painted in the cave of Les Trois-Frères (Ariège, France) and dated to

Music archaeologists posit the Cyclades Islands and Crete as possible sites for the emergence of double aerophones and the harp family, both documented in ancient Asian and Egyptian sources.

ca. 13,000–11,000 B.C. The figure, dressed in animal skins, holds close to his mouth an object believed to be a flute or a musical bow. Since he is apparently dancing among wild animals, one may hypothesize, based on ethnographic parallels, that a hunting implement, the bow, was used as a musical instrument, singing and clapping may have accompanied the dancing, and the music may have been intended to have magical effects on the animals.

CULTURE AREAS, PERIODS, CHRONOLOGY

In prehistoric archaeology, cultures are customarily defined by artifact types (for example, the boat-ax culture of Sweden) or by leading sites (for example, Unetice, Bohemia). The type-site approach serves also to delimit larger culture areas and pre-historic periods (for example, Hallstatt and La Tène). The chief periodic framework for large parts of Europe covers the Palaeolithic, Mesolithic, and Neolithic, followed by the Copper, Bronze, and Iron ages, which were in turn succeeded by the Roman Empire and the period of migration (*Völkerwanderungszeit*) beginning in A.D. 375, and then the Middle Ages.

In most of Western and Central Europe, the Franconian Empire marked the transition to the Middle Ages, while, for example, the Iron Age in Scandinavia is defined to include the Viking period and thus ends only in A.D. 1050, the year of Christianization; the Middle Ages here cover the years 1050–1530. Every major period can be subdivided into smaller units with regard to space, time, and culture traits; some prehistoric cultures (e.g., Bandkeramik) cover large areas, and it is possible to detect regional "styles" in artifacts and culture contacts, including exchange, trade, and influence. Grouping palaeo-organological material with respect to archaeological culture areas and periods is likely to result in an uneven distribution because of several factors, only one of which is chance.

If Brade's criticism of the existence of Palaeolithic and Neolithic flutes is valid, the remaining material evidence before the late Neolithic and Copper Age is quite scarce and would be reduced to phalange whistles, idiophones such as scrapers and rattles, the Mezin osteophone, and free aerophones of the bull-roarer type, mainly from find complexes of hunter societies (Sidorov 1987). A rock painting from north-west Bulgaria, which appears to show a group of males and females, some of them dancing, one male apparently beating a drum and another handling a supposed musical bow, probably belongs to the Neolithic (Jantarski 1977). As with other iconographic sources, interpretation and dating are only tentative.

A find from a hunter-fisher society of the late third millennium (Mariupol, Ukraine) has been interpreted as a bone panpipe (Häusler 1960), with another late Neolithic specimen from the Kitoj culture (Baikal region, Russia). Evidence of panpipes in Central Europe is available only from the later Bronze Age onward, with finds from Poland (Przeczyce, Montelius V) and Germany (Klein-Kühnau, La Tène III), and representations on situlae dated to the sixth and fifth centuries B.C. from sites in northern Yugoslavia, Italy, and Austria (Megaw 1968). The panpipe from the famous site at Alesia, southeast France, with seven tubes carved into a solid oak block, is a refined type and probably even later, perhaps third century (Reinach 1906–1907).

It was suggested in the 1980s that some Neolithic pottery of the Iberian Peninsula might have carried skins as drumheads, while clay vessels could have served as aids to singing or as simple aerophones (Fernández de la Cuesta 1983). A flute with three holes found in a dolmen near Poitiers, France, belongs to Brade's (1975) doubtful-objects category of prehistoric flute. Instruments made of clay comprise rattles, objects believed to be bells, and, from considerably later, vessel flutes and horns. Vessel flutes made of flint have been found in Denmark and ascribed to the late Neolithic period (Lund 1972, 1974).

The picture becomes more complex in the third millennium B.C. because of culture contact between East and West in the Aegean culture area. Music archaeologists posit the Cyclades Islands and Crete as possible sites for the emergence of double aerophones and the harp family, both documented in ancient Asian and Egyptian sources. The Phrygians of Asia Minor are said, in classical sources, to have introduced important instruments, such as the *aulos* (a double aerophone), the *syrinx* (a panpipe), and the *kithara* (a lyre), with musical elements and customs, into what later became Greek music (Thiemer 1979). Probably the foundations of Greek music, and thus European tonal concepts, are related to the musical and sociocultural traditions of the East Mediterranean and Asia Minor, and can be traced well into the second millennium B.C. Given the processes of culture contact and diffusion around the Mediterranean basin, delimiting European music from Asian and North African music at that stage in music history is difficult or impossible. Source material for the distribution of double aerophones (presumably with reeds) is available from the Cyclades, Asia Minor, Crete, the Greek mainland, Sardinia, Etrurian sites, and the Roman Empire, where in the first century *tibiae pares* 'paired pipes' were taken as far north as the border settlement of Noviomagus, now Nijmegen, Netherlands (Rimmer 1976).

This importation of instruments into Europe from the East does not diminish the manufacturing achievement of the Scandinavian lurs and Irish bronze horns (Holmes 1979, 1986). Instruments of both groups have been praised for the outstanding craftsmanship required to master the technology of lost-wax casting (*cire perdue*). Unique as these instruments appear compared to the somewhat meager palaeoarchaeological record of the preceding periods, they seem to fit well into the culture of the northern Bronze Age, where lurs can be assigned to ca. 1300–600 B.C. and the Irish bronze horns to 750 B.C. and later (Coles 1963; Lund 1986). As to origins, uses, and functions, both groups have tentatively been conceived of as imitations of either wooden or animal horns, and have been linked largely to cultic and ceremonial functions for which there are indications, at least as far as the lurs are concerned, in rock art of the Bohuslän region of Sweden (Broholm et al. 1949; Nordbladh 1986).

The musical potential and actual music played on such instruments in the Bronze Age have been a matter of experiment and speculation. The Irish side-blown horns normally yield only one note, and the end-blown horns two to four, but one of the lurs from Brudevaelte, Denmark, can produce ten or more notes of the harmonic series, plus glissandi (O'Callaghan 1983). Even if Bronze Age people did not explore the full range of tones, accessible only with modern playing techniques, a relatively unskilled player could produce several harmonics. Lurs were tuned precisely in pairs, and, according to iconographic evidence, two and three players played simultaneously, perhaps implying harmony. Heterophonic playing, drone accompaniment, and other techniques are conceivable, but it seems unlikely that several lurs, such as the specimen from Brudevaelte, were skillfully crafted and tuned only to produce melodic lines in strict unison.

Other horns emerged in the first millennium B.C.: the Celtic *carnyx* of the La Tène period and the Etruscan and Roman *lituus*. The *carnyx* has been defined as an animal-headed trumpet (Piggott 1959) and a war trumpet popular throughout the Celtic world—which, if mapped from archaeological and literary sources, stretches from the shores of the Black Sea to the Iberian Peninsula and beyond to Britain and Ireland (Megaw 1968). Basically, it was a J-shaped metal aerophone with a rather lengthy, practically cylindrical tube joined by a curved conical horn plus the animal head, and a mouthpiece of uncertain shape. The instrument is depicted several times in widely scattered areas, the best-known source being the famous Gundestrup cauldron (first century B.C.), found in a Jutland bog but probably imported.

The Illyrians, who inhabited the Dalmatian area from Greece and Albania up to the foothills of the eastern Alps and from the coast as far inland as the Morava River (Coles and Harding 1979), may have introduced the lyre into the Celtic Eastern Hallstatt culture area, where there is some iconographical evidence from ca. 650 into the fourth century B.C. So-called Indo-European traces of the lyre have been identified on an engraving that shows a fifteen-stringed instrument on a funeral stela found close to Zaragoza, Spain and dated to the late Bronze Age (eighth century B.C.) (Álvarez 1985). Studies dealing with Celtic and Illyrian issues illustrate the problem of defining culture areas and of tracing the origin and diffusion of instruments assigned to specific ethnic groups. The lurs, for example, which have always been considered part of the Nordic Bronze Age, might also be viewed as separate traces of the unique activities of a very specialized group with a specialized place in the surrounding society (Moberg 1986). On the basis of historical and archaeological sources and ethnographic parallels, it has been suggested that the early history of music in the Near East, Asia Minor, and Greece is tied to small, probably clanlike groups of highly specialized professionals who mastered music, metalwork, and animal husbandry (Vogel 1973, 1978).

Future research will have to elaborate and test hypotheses concerning the context and social background of musical performance and thus go beyond palaeo-organological issues, such as identification, periodization, and the chronology of instruments. The difficulty of these tasks increases when, for instance, the survey and chronology of Celtic instruments suffers from huge gaps in the sequence of sources; tangible evidence is late and scarce, though a reasonable number of references to instruments and musical performance survive in ancient literary and iconographic sources (Harrison 1976). Also, long-extinct groups, such as the Picts in northeastern Scotland, left some traces of their musical instruments, though their history and ethnic character are debatable (Porter 1983).

CLASSIFICATION, TYPOLOGY, DEVELOPMENT, CONTINUITY

Paleo-organologists classify find material using the Hornbostel-Sachs system (1961 [1914]). While classification organizes a multitude of objects according to established criteria (for example, the primary vibrating material), music archaeologists who seek historical or genetic relationships among instruments employ a typological approach based on notions of relationship, similarity, constancy, and development of morphological features (Picken 1975; Schneider 1984, 1986). Similarity of formal features in the shape, size, construction, and ornamentation of lurs, for example, have been interpreted as evidence for the constancy of type. The relative sameness of type is then assumed to indicate historical continuity, especially if changes in certain features are slight and show no major break or gap. By contrast, decreasing similarity is interpreted as development if features are improved—for example, the number of strings in harplike chordophones judged from iconographic evidence. Such typological considerations of Scandinavian bronze lurs and Irish horns has led these instruments to be regarded as animal-horn instruments remade in metal (Coles 1963). Because the bronze instruments are advanced technologically, they probably presuppose the existence of extinct ancestral types, though scant persuasive evidence of animal or wooden ancestral types exists, perhaps because of the disintegration of organic material. Indeed, the opposite process, a translation from metal into wood, has been claimed for the Swiss alphorn's supposed descent from the Celtic *carnyx* (Zagiba 1967). The genetic links here are the mouthpiece, presumably once made of lead in the *carnyx* and the alphorn, and the comparable shape.

Though the heuristic usefulness of typological sequences appears incontestable, any hypotheses concerning the development of ancient instruments would require stratigraphic evidence or datable sources for confirmation. The bronze instruments may have had animal-horn or wooden predecessors, but the extant animal horns, such as the so-called *barva-lur* from Sweden and the more developed cow horn with finger holes from Konsterud, Denmark (Oldeberg 1950), are dated later and have been assigned to the Iron Age in northwest Europe (Raistrick et al. 1952).

The occurrence of more-developed types does not preclude the continued use of less-developed instruments. Bone flutes were in use in parts of Europe virtually up to the present, especially in pastoral communities (Atanassov 1977). Thus, one may assume for these instruments a typological continuity given a sequence of datable sources. Music played on such instruments has been recorded in Slovakia from rag pickers, who employed bone flutes with only two finger holes plus thumbhole to produce signals, songs, and instrumental pieces (Elschek 1983). Wooden trumpets and animal horns are still used in pastoral societies of alpine regions from Sweden to the Pyrenees and the Balkans (Elschek 1991; Emsheimer 1969). On the basis of historical and ethnographic evidence, scholars have suggested that the European pastoral complex, observed well into the twentieth century, did much to maintain older organological traditions and musical performances related to specific functions, such as signaling over a distance, defending herds against wild animals, and a belief in magic. Thus, the typological continuity of instruments is matched by a sociocultural configuration that appears to have retained archaic elements for a long time (Moberg 1971; Oldeberg 1950).

Contemporary traditional instruments such as the *vallehorn,* a wooden lur from central Sweden, and the Dutch *midwinterhoorn,* used in the context of seasonal customs, have been related to the lur-*carnyx-lituus* set of traditions (van Lennep 1959). They might be considered relics or survivals of extinct musical practice that may have existed for long periods without major change. Other survivals might include primitive folk instruments like willow flutes, bark trumpets, and simple clarinets made from ready-to-hand organic material, including leaves, stalks, and bark (Brockpähler 1971; Naselli 1951). According to classical sources, later historical sources, and ethnographic records, such instruments belong to a pastoral and agricultural environment, though by the late twentieth century they are mainly children's instruments (Emsheimer 1985). Though children's instruments may appear simple in comparison with more developed adult instruments, they provide an idea of how instruments originated and are valuable analogies for historical and prehistoric processes.

OTHER RESEARCH DIRECTIONS

This survey of research results, find materials, and methodological issues ignores potential sources such as folklore and myth and controversial issues, such as the development of plucked and bowed chordophones (Bruce-Mitford 1974), the intro-

In advocating an interdisciplinary approach, music archaeologists insist upon an anthropological perspective to complement and realize their historical and organological objectives, especially those regarding musical origins and the functions of music in early social and cultural configurations.

duction of the bow into Europe (Bachmann 1966), and the early history of reed instruments and bagpipes (Baines 1960; Becker 1966; Guizzi and Leydi 1985). Studies relating to medieval chordophones, such as the rote, the rebec, and the Welsh crowd (*crwth*), have mainly been undertaken by music historians, art historians, and philologists, and mark a transition to related fields of research. In advocating an interdisciplinary approach, music archaeologists insist upon an anthropological perspective to complement and realize their historical and organological objectives, especially those regarding musical origins and the functions of music in early social and cultural configurations.

BIBLIOGRAPHY

Álvarez, Rosario. 1985. "Presunto origen de la lira grabada en uno estela funeraria (ca. S. VIII a.C.) encontrada en Luna (Zaragoza)." *Revista de Musicologia* 8:207–228.

Atanassov, Vergillii. 1977. "Die historische Entwicklung der Hirteninstrumente in Bulgarien." *Studia Instrumentorum Musicae Populares* 5:81–83.

Bachmann, Werner. 1966. *Die Anfänge des Streichinstrumenspiels.* 2d ed. Leipzig: Breitkopf & Härtel.

Baines, Anthony. 1960. *Bagpipes.* Oxford: University Press.

Bajer, Bathja. 1968. "The Biblical Nebel." *Yuval* 1:89–131.

Bartha, Denes. 1934. *Die avarische Doppelschalmei von Janoshida.* Archaeologia Hungarica, 14. Budapest.

Becker, Heinz. 1966. *Zur Entwicklungsgeschichte der antiken und mittelalterlichen Rohrblattinstrumente.* Hamburg: Sikorski.

Bezic, Jerko, et al., eds. 1975. *Tradicijska narodna glazbela Jugoslavije.* Zagreb: Skolska Kniga.

Bibikov, Sergei Nikolaevich. 1981. *Drevneischii musikal'nii kompleks iz kostei Mamonta.* Kiev: Naukova Dumka.

Blacking, John. 1976. "Dance, Conceptual Thought and Production in the Archaeological Record." In *Problems in Economic and Social Archaeology,* ed. Gale de Giberne Sieveking, Ian Longworth, and K. E. Wilson, 3–13. London: Duckworth.

Brade, Christine. 1975. *Die mittelalterlichen Kerspaltflöten Mittel- und Nord-Europas.* Neumünster: Wachholtz.

———. 1982. "The Prehistoric Flute—Did It Exist?" *Galpin Society Journal* 35:138–146.

Brockpähler, Renate. 1971. "Rinden-Instrumente in Westfalen." *Jahrbuch für Volksliedforschung* 16:135–163.

Broholm, Hans Christian, W. P. Larsen, and G. Skjerne. 1949. *The Lurs of the Bronze Age.* Copenhagen: Gyldendalske Boghandel.

———. 1965. *Lurfundene fra Bronzealderen: En arkaeologisk studie.* Copenhagen: Nordisk Forlag.

Bruce-Mitford, Rupert Leo Scott. 1974. "The Sutton Hoo Lyre, Beowulf, and the Origins of the Frame Harp." In *Aspects of Anglo-Saxon Archaeology: Sutton Hoo and Other Discoveries,* ed. Rupert Bruce-Mitford, 188–197. London: Gollancz.

———. 1988. "Musical Instruments from Medieval Dublin: A Preliminary Survey." In *Early Music Cultures,* ed. Ellen Hickmann and David Hughes, 145–162. Bonn: Verlag für systematische Musikwissenschaft.

Coles, John. 1963. "Irish Bronze Horns and Their Relations with Northern Europe." *Proceedings of the Prehistoric Society* 19:326–356.

———. 1973. *Archaeology by Experiment.* London: Hutchinson.

Coles, John, and A. F. Harding. 1979. *The Bronze Age in Europe: An Introduction to the Prehistory of Europe ca. 2000–700 B.C.* London: Methuen.

Cosma, Voirel. 1966. "Archäologische musikalische Funde in Rumänien." *Beiträge zur Musikwissenschaft* 8:3–14.

Edström, Karl O. 1981. *The Roots of Music*. Musikvetenskapliga Institutionen vid Göteborgs Universitet stencilerade Skrifter, 8301. Göteborg: Tre Boecker.

Eibner, A. 1980. "Musikleben in der Hallstattzeit: Betrachtungen zur 'Mousiké' anhand der bildlichen Darstellungen." *Mitteilungen der österreichischen Arbeitsgemeinschaft für Ur- und Frühgeschichte* 30:121–148.

Elschek, Oskár. 1970. "Mensch—Musik—Instrument: Funktionelle Schichtung der Primärformen." In *Musik als Gestalt und Erlebnis: Festschrift für Walter Graf*, ed. Erich Schenck, 41–56. Wien: Böhlau.

———. 1983. *Die Slowakischen Volksmusikinstrumente*. Die Volksmusikinstrumente der Tschechoslowakei, 2. Leipzig: Deutscher Verlag für Musik.

———. 1991. *Slovenske l'udove pistaly*. Bratislava: Vydatel'stvo Slovenskei Akademie Vied.

Emsheimer, Ernst. 1969. "Zur Typologie der Schwedischen Holztrompeten." *Studia Instrumentorum Musicae Popularis* 1:87–97.

———. 1985. "Knallbüchse und Weidenpfeife—zwei traditionelle Kinderklanggeräte." *Studia Instrumentorum Musicae Popularis* 8:52–60.

Fages, G. 1983. "La flûte en os d'oiseau de la grotte sépulchrale de Veyreau (Aveyron) et inventaire des flûtes préhistoriques d'Europe." *Mémoires de la Société préhistorique française* 16: 95–103.

Fernández de la Cuesta, Ismael. 1983. *Historia de la musica española 1: desde los origines hasta el ars nova*. Madrid: Alianza música.

Fischer, Ulrich. 1951. "Zu den mitteldeutschen Trommeln." *Archaeologia geographica* 2:98–105.

Fleischhauer, Guenter. 1964. *Etrurien und Rom*. Leipzig: Deutscher Verlag für Musik.

Gavazzi, Milovan. 1976. "Die Namen der altslavischen Musikinstrumente." In *Die Volksmusik Sudosteuropas*, ed. Walter Wünsch, 34–49. Munich: Trofenik.

Geist, Bohumil. 1970. *Puvod hudby*. Prague-Bratislava: Editio Supraphon.

Gottlieb, Birthe. 1986. "X-Ray Analysis of a Lur Fragment." In *Second Conference of the ICTM Study Group on Music Archaeology*, ed. Cajsa Lund, 2:187–195. Stockholm: Kungl. Musikaliska akademien.

Guizzi, Febo, and Roberto Leydi. 1985. *Le Zampogne in Italia*. Milan: Ricordi.

Harrison, Frank. 1976. "Towards a Chronology of Celtic Folk Instruments." *Studia Instrumentorum Musicae Popularis* 4:98–101.

Harrison, R. 1978. "A Pierced Reindeer Phalanx from Banwell Bone Cave and Some Experimental Work on Phalangeal Whistles." *Proceedings of the University of Bristol Speleological Society* 15:7–22.

Häusler, Alexander. 1960. "Neue Funde steinzeitlicher Musikinstrumente in Osteuropa." *Wissenschaftliche Zeitschrift der Martin-Luther-Universität Halle-Wittenberg, Gesellschafts- und sprachwissenschaftliche Reihe* 9:321–331.

Hickmann, Ellen, and David Hughes, eds. 1988. *The Archaeology of Early Music Cultures*. Bonn: Verlag für Systematische Musikwissenschaft.

Hickmann, Hans. 1985. "Musikarchäologie als Traditionsforschung." *Acta Musicologica* 52:1–13.

Holmes, Peter. 1979. "The Manufacturing Technology of the Irish Bronze Age Horns." In *The Origins of Metallurgy in Atlantic Europe*, ed. Michael Ryan, 165–188. Dublin: Stationery Office.

———. 1986. "The Scandinavian Bronze Lurs." In *Second Conference of the ICTM Study Group on Music Archaeology*, ed. Cajsa Lund, 2:51–125. Stockholm: Kungl. Musikaliska akademien.

Homo-Lechner, Catherine. 1986. "L'Archéologie sonore en France: premiers résultats." In *Second Conference of the ICTM Study Group on Music Archaeology*, ed. Cajsa Lund, 1:157–161. Stockholm: Kungl. Musikaliska akademien.

Hornbostel, Erich Moritz von, and Curt Sachs. 1961 [1914]. "Classification of Musical Instruments: Translated from the Original German by Anthony Baines and Klaus P. Wachsmann." *The Galpin Society Journal* 14:3–29.

Horusitzky, Z. 1955. "Eine Knochenflöte aus der Höhle von Istállöskö." *Acta Archaeologica Academiae Scientiarum Hungaricae* 5:133–145.

Jantarski, Georgi. 1977. "Musikinstrumente auf einer steinzeitlichen Höhlenmalerei Bulgariens." *Musikforschung* 30:465–467.

Jazdzewski, Konrad. 1966. "O Zagadnienu Polskich Instrumentow Strunowych z Wczesnego Srendniowiecza." *Prace i Materialy Muzeum Archaeologicznego i Ethnograficznego w Lodzi* 12:7–35.

Lawergren, Bo. 1988. "The Origin of Musical Instruments and Sounds." *Anthropos* 83:31–45.

Lawson, Graeme, ed. 1983. *Current Research in European Archaeomusicology*. Music-Archaeological Research Project, Report 6. Cambridge, England.

Lennep, Henriette van. 1959. "De Midwinterhoorn: een oud Nederlands instrument." In *Honderd Eeuwen Nederland*, ed. Julianus Bogaers et al., 292–296. The Hague: Mouton.

Leroi-Gourhan, Andre. 1971. *Préhistoire de l'art occidental*. Paris: Éditions d'art Lucien Mazenod.

Lies, Hans. 1954. "Eine Tontrommel der älteren Megalithkultur von Gerwisch, Kreis Burg bei Magdeburg." *Jahresschrift für mitteldeutsche Vorgeschichte* 38:34–39.

Lindahl, Anders. 1986. "Simulated Manufacture of Prehistoric Ceramic Drums." In *Second Conference of the ICTM Study Group on Music Archaeology*, ed. Cajsa Lund, 1:29–39. Stockholm: Kungl. Musikaliska akademien.

Livingstone, Frank B. 1973. "Did Australopithecines Sing?" *Current Anthropology* 14:25–29.

Lund, Cajsa. 1974. *The Sound of Archeology*. Stockholm: Musikmuseet.

Lund, Cajsa. 1980. "Methoden und Probleme der nordischen Musikarchäologie." *Acta Musicologica* 52:1–13.

———. 1981. "The Archaeomusicology of Scandinavia." *World Archaeology* 12 (3):246–265.

———. ed. 1986. *Second Conference of the ICTM Study Group on Music Archaeology*, Stockholm, 1984. Vol. 1 *(General Studies)*, 2 (*The Bronze Lurs*). Stockholm: Royal Swedish Academy of Music.

Macak, Ivan. 1968. "Bemerkungen zu der Frage des Ursprungs der Streichbogen-Instrumente des Typus Rebeka in den Karpaten und auf dem Balkan." In *RAD XV-og Kongresa Saveza Udruzenja Folklorista Jugoslavije 1968 (Sarajevo)*, 341–345.

Maier, Rudolf Albert. 1960. "Zu den neolithischen Tontrommeln Mitteleuropas." *Germania* 38:424–426.

Malinowski, Tadeusz. 1981. "Archaeology and Musical Instruments in Poland." *World Archaeology* 12(3):266–272.

Megaw, Vincent. 1960–1961. "Penny Whistles and Prehistory." *Antiquity* 34:6–13; 35:55–57.

———. 1968. "Problems and Non-Problems in Palaeo-Organology: A Musical Miscellany." In *Studies in Ancient Europe: Essays Presented to Stuart Piggott*, ed. J. M. Coles and D. D. A. Simpson, 333–358. Leicester: Leicester University Press.

Meyer, Werner. 1977. "Von Maultrommeln, Flöten und Knochenschwirren: Ein Beitrag der Mittelalter-Archäologie zur Geschichte volkstümlicher Musikinstrumente der Schweiz." *Studia Instrumentorum Musicae Popularis* 5:33–38. Stockholm: Musikhistoriska museet.

Mildenberger, Gerhard. 1952. "Die neolithischen Tontrommeln." *Jahresschrift für mitteldeutsche Vorgeschichte* 36:30–41.

Moberg, Carl Allan. 1971. *Studien zur schwedischen Volksmusik*. Uppsala: Almqvist & Wiksell.

———. 1986. "'Lurs'—South-West Baltic Bronze Horns—and Sound Tools: Find Contexts." In *Second Conference of the ICTM Study Group on Music Archaeology*, ed. Cajsa Lund, 2:145–150. Stockholm: Kungl. Musikaliska akademien.

Moeck, Hermann. 1954. "Die skandinavischen Kernspaltflöten in Vorzeit und Tradition der Folklore." *Svensk Tidskrift for Musikforskning* 26:56–83.

———. 1967. *Typen europäischer Blockflöten in Vorzeit, Geschichte, und Uberlieferung*. Celle: Moeck.

Naselli, Carmellina. 1951. "Strumenti da suono e strumenti da musica del popolo siciliano." *Archivio storico per la Sicilia orientale* 4:251–280.

Nieminen, Eino. 1963. "Finnisch Kantele und die damit verbundenen Namen baltischer Musikinstrumente." *Studia Fennica* 10(2):1–43.

Nordbladh, Jarl. 1986. "The Bronze-Age Lurs in the Light of Rock Art Research." In *Second Conference of the ICTM Study Group on Music Archaeology*, ed. Cajsa Lund, 2:133–144. Stockholm: Kungl. Musikaliska akademien.

O'Callaghan, Donal. 1983. "A Brudevaelte Lur Re-examined: The Evidence for Ritual Music in the Scandinavian Late Bronze Age." *Galpin Society Journal* 36:104–108.

Oldeberg, Andreas. 1947. "A Contribution to the History of the Scandinavian Bronze Age Lur in the Bronze and Iron Age." *Acta Archaeologica* (Copenhagen) 18:1–91.

———. 1950. "Vallhorn, Lerdepipor och lurar." *Värmland förr och nu* 48:21–67.

Os'kin, A. 1987. "K probleme interpretazii archeologitscheskogo muzykal'nogo instrumentariia." In *Narodniie muzykal'niie instrumenty i instrumental'naia muzyka*, ed. Evard Gippius, 1:148–156. Moscow: Izdatel'stvo Muzyka.

Paquette, Daniel. 1984. *L'instrument de musique dans la céramique de la Grèce antique*. Paris: De Boccard/CNRS.

Passemard, Emmanuel. 1923. "Une flûte aurignacienne d'Isturitz." *Association française par l'avancement des sciences: Compte rendu de la 46ᵉ session Montpellier 1922* (Paris), 474–476.

Picken, Laurence Ernest Rowland. 1975. *Folk Musical Instruments of Turkey*. London: Oxford University Press.

Piggott, Stuart. 1959. "The Carnyx in Early Iron Age Britain." *Antiquaries Journal* 39:19–32.

Porter, James. 1983. "Harps, Pipes, and Silent Stones: The Problem of Pictish Music." *Selected Reports in Ethnomusicology* 4:243–267.

Raistrick, A., et al. 1952. "The Malham Iron-Age Pipe." *Galpin Society Journal* 5:2838.

Reimers, Christian. 1979. "Riksinventeringen— ett instrument för musikarkeologin." *Svensk Tidskrift för Musikforskning* 61:65–70.

Reinach, Théodore. 1906–1907. "La 'Flûte de Pan' d'Alesia." In *Pro Alesia* 1:161–169.

Rimmer, Joan. 1976. "The Tibiae Pares of Mook." *Galpin Society Journal* 29:42–46.

———. 1981. "An Archaeo-Organological Survey of the Netherlands." *World Archaeology* 12(3):233–245.

Rydbeck, Monica. 1968. "Maultrommeln in Funden aus dem schwedischen Mittelalter." *Archaeologica Lundensis* 3:252–261.

Sachs, Curt. 1962. *The Wellsprings of Music*. The Hague: Nijhoff.

Salmen, Walter. 1970. "Urgeschichtliche und mittelalterliche Musikinstrumente aus Schleswig-Holstein." *Offa* 27:5–19.

Schneider, Albrecht. 1984. *Analogie und Rekonstruktion: Studien zur Methodologie der Musikgeschichtsschreibung und zur Frühgeschichte der Musik*. Vol. 1. Bonn: Verlag für Systematische Musikwissenschaft.

———. 1985. "Charivari: ostwestliche Beziehungen untersucht anhand brauchtumsmässiger Ausdrücke und Sachverhalte: Ein linguistischer Beitrag zur Frühgeschichte der Musik." In

Historische Volksmusikforschung, ed. A. Mauerhofer, 121–161. Graz: Akad. Verlagsanstalt.

———. 1986. "ΑΡΧΑΙΟΛΟΓΕΩ: Some Comments on Methods and Sources in Music Archaeology." In *Second Conference of the ICTM Study Group on Music Archaeology,* ed. Cajsa Lund, 1:195–224. Stockholm: Kungl. Musikaliska akademien.

Scothern, Paula. 1987. "A Re-Evaluation of the Pas de Miroir Flute." *Archaeologica musicalis* 1:2–4.

———. 1989. "Palaeo-Organology, Ethnomusicology, and the Historical Dimension." In *Ethnomusicology and the Historical Dimension: Papers presented at the European Seminar in Ethnomusicology (London 1986),* ed. M. L. Philipp, 19–24. Ludwigsburg: Philipp.

Seewald, Otto. 1934. *Beiträge zur Kenntnis der steinzeitlichen Musikinstrumente.* Vienna: Scholl.

———. 1960. "Die Lyrendarstellungen der Ostalpinen Hallstattkultur." In *Festschrift Alfred Orel,* ed. Hellmut Federhofer, 159–171. Wien: R. M. Rohrer.

Sevåg, Reidar. 1973. *Det Gjaller og det Laet: Frå skremme-og lokkereiskapar til folkelege blåseinstrument.* Oslo: Norske Samlaget.

Sidorov, V. 1987. "Manok—muzikal'noi instrument epochi neolita." In *Narodnoie muzikal'niie instrumenty,* ed. Evard Gippius, 1:157–162. Moscow: Izdatel'stvo Muzyka.

Stockmann, Doris. 1985. "Music and Dance Behavior in Anthropogenesis." *Yearbook for Traditional Music* 17:16–30.

Stumpf, Carl. 1911. *Die Anfänge der Musik.* Leipzig: J. A. Barth.

Thiemer, Hannelore. 1979. *Der Einfluss der Phryger auf die altgriechische Musik.* Bonn: Verlag für Systematische Musikwissenschaft.

Vellekoop, Gerrit. 1966. "Voorlopers van onze Blokfuiten." *Tijdschrift van de Vereniging voor Nederlandse Muziekgeschiedenis* 20:178–185.

Vogel, Martin. 1973. *Onos Lyras: Der Esel mit der Leier.* 2 vols. Bonn: Verlag für Systematische Musikwissenschaft.

———. 1978. *Chiron, der Kentaur mit der Kithara.* 2 vols. Bonn: Verlag für Systematische Musikwissenschaft.

Wallin, Nils Lennart. 1991. *Biomusicology: Neurophysiological, Neuropsychological, and Evolutionary Perspectives on the Origins and Purposes of Music.* Stuyvesant, N.Y.: Pendragon Press.

Wille, Gunther. 1967. *Musica Romana.* Amsterdam: Schippers.

Wiora, Walter. 1949. *Zur Frühgeschichte der Musik in den Alpenländern.* Basel: Schweizer Gesellschaft für Volkskunde.

———. 1961. "Musikgeschichte und Urgeschichte." *Svensk Tidskrift för Musikforskning* 43:375–396.

———. 1974. "Zur Vor- und Frühgeschichte der musikalischen Grundbegriffe." *Acta musicologica* 46:125–152.

Zagiba, Frantisek. 1967. "Von der keltischen Carnyx I zum Alphorn." In *Festschrift für Walter Wiora,* ed. Ludwig Finscher, 609–612. Kassel: Bärenreiter.

———. 1976. *Musikgeschichte Mitteleuropas.* Wien: Verband der wissenschaftl. Gesellschaften Osterreichs.

AUDIOVISUAL RESOURCES

Lund, Cajsa. 1984. *Fornordiska klanger: The Sounds of Prehistoric Scandinavia.* Svensk musikhistopriska på fonogram/Swedish Music Anthology, MS 101. Stockholm: EMI-His Master's Voice 1361031. LP disk.

Ancient Greek Music

Wanda Bryant

Music in Daily Life
Musical Style
Written Theories of Music

The music of the ancient Greeks has long tantalized music scholars and historians. It has been reconstructed from extant musical examples (around a thousand measures from forty fragments of pieces covering a span of seven centuries), paintings on pottery, and writings about music, musical life, and philosophy by ancient scholars, most notably Aristoxenus and Plato (fourth century B.C.), Ptolemy (second century A.D.), and Quintilian (late third or early fourth century). Plato and Aristotle placed great importance on musical education, ethics, and influences, and discussed which types of music and instruments were appropriate for given occasions. Fragments of music and theoretical writings have answered some questions, but have raised others and prompted speculation on many fronts. Researchers continue to delve into areas such as musical intervals, modes and modality, pitch accent, instruments, performance practices, and the relationships of Greek music to that of other cultures (Near Eastern, western Christian) and times (Byzantine, modern Greek).

MUSIC IN DAILY LIFE

Music, including work songs, ceremonial songs, and sung epics, played a significant role in most important occasions in ancient Greek life. Choruses of men, women, or children performed for religious rituals, at marriages, funerals, and celebrations of famous persons and athletic victories, and in dramatic and dithyrambic competitions in Athens. The choruses of the cult of Dionysus remained an important element in comic and tragic plays until the fourth century B.C. The singers were amateurs, but all had received musical training as an essential part of a general education.

Choruses were accompanied by professional musicians playing the *kithara*, a seven- or eight-stringed plucked lyre, or the *aulos* (pl. *auloi*), a conical double-reed aerophone, typically played in pairs by one player. Professional instrumentalists competed at festivals, in solo singing accompanied by a *kithara* or an *aulos*, and solo instrumental playing not based on poetic origins (*nomos kitharōdikos* or *nomos aulōdikos*). The *kithara*, a fairly large instrument, had a solidly built wooden sound box with a curved back and arms joined by a crossbar that held a tuning apparatus. Strings of equal length stretched from a holder on the lower part of the sound box over a bridge to

FIGURE I An Attic red-figure terra cotta cup (*kylix*), 22.4 centimeters in diameter, attributed to the Dokimasia painter of Athens, ca. 510 B.C., depicts a man playing *auloi,* thought by most scholars to consist of two double- or single-reed pipes. The long staff suggests the man may be a shepherd. The instrument's closest modern European analogs are the Sardinian *launeddas,* which consists of three single-reed pipes played by a single player, and paired single-reed pipes, often with horns attached to form a bell, from the Basque provinces and the Dalmatian coast. Photo courtesy of the J. Paul Getty Museum, Los Angeles.

the crossbar. The instrument rested against the player's body as he plucked the strings by the fingers of his left hand or with a plectrum held in his right hand.

The skill of the professional *aulete* was an important factor in the success of competing choruses. The *aulos* was made of reed, wood, bone, ivory, or metal, open at the lower end, and with differing numbers of finger holes. Early pipes had three to five holes; later, in the fifth and sixth centuries, that number increased to as many as fifteen, with holes unnecessary for a particular scale being covered by a metal ring. Typically played in pairs, *auloi* were held in position by a band wrapped around the player's head and cheeks as a support. With separate mouthpieces, the pipes could speak alone or together, but it is believed that they sounded separately, each creating a portion of a single scale. Because of its early association with satyrs, Plato suggested banning the *aulos* (figure 1).

Amateur musicians played other instruments, such as lyres and harps. The lyre, smaller and simpler than the *kithara,* had an oxhide-covered sound box, made from a tortoise shell or a similarly shaped wooden frame. The *barbitos* or *barbiton,* a larger version with longer strings, was used to accompany erotic songs. Harps, such as the *psalterion,* the *trigonon,* and the *magadis,* with differing numbers of unequal-lengthed strings, were commonly played by women though philosophers disapproved of harp-accompanied music. The *syrinx* 'panpipes' was constructed of equal-sized pipes bound together in a row and stopped at graduated intervals.

MUSICAL STYLE

The music itself was primarily homophonic, sung in unisons or octaves. The accompanying *kithara* or *aulos* sounded notes either consonant (intervals of the octave, fourth or fifth) or dissonant, but probably not comprising a countermelody. Lyrics appear to have been preeminent. In performance, the songs most likely presented a clean melodic line without grace notes or melismas to obscure the words. The ancient Greek language employed pitch accents, imbuing it with its own melody; composers tended to follow the speech contour, or at least to avoid conflict with it—a tendency illustrated clearly by Delphic hymns. At some point, pitch accent gave way to stress accent, as in Byzantine and modern Greek. Rhythms, identical to existing poetic meters, were based on patterns of long and short syllables in each line or set of lines. The basic unit of metric and rhythmic theory was the poetic foot, rather than the musical measure.

WRITTEN THEORIES OF MUSIC

Greek music theory is derived from Pythagoras's concept of the numerical nature of consonances. The numbers 1, 2, 3, and 4 held great significance for ancient philosophers, and ratios derived from them represented the musical consonances: 2/1 (octave), 3/2 (fifth), 4/3 (fourth), 3/1 (octave plus fifth), and 4/1 (double octave). The fifth plus the fourth equals the octave, expressed arithmetically as the product of ratios, $3/2 \times 4/3 = 2/1$; the fifth minus the fourth defines the whole tone, expressed arithmetically as the quotient of ratios, $3/2 \div 4/3 = 9/8$.

Pythagorean theory was further developed by Aristides Quintilian, Ptolemy, and Aristoxenus, whose *Elements of Harmony* is the oldest extant European treatise containing a significant discussion of music. Using Aristotelian method, Aristoxenus devised a theory of music based on a geometric conception of musical space, which he viewed as infinitely divisible, but with the smallest musical interval the quarter tone (*diesis*). The tetrachord—four notes with three intervals, spanning a perfect fourth—was the basic building block; Aristoxenus considered the fourth to be exactly two and a half tones.

"Fixed" or "standing" notes formed the outer boundaries of the tetrachord. The inner two "movable" notes determined the tetrachord's genus: diatonic, enharmonic, or chromatic. Aristoxenus considered the tetrachord a system, a succession of intervals. Larger systems were created by combining tetrachords, either conjunct (sharing a note) or disjunct (separated by a whole tone). The Greater Perfect System (GPS), the standard for Greek musical theory, comprised four tetrachords plus a note one whole tone below the lowest tetrachord. The Lesser Perfect System (LPS) comprised the lower octave of the GPS plus a conjunct tetrachord at the top. Ptolemy later combined the two systems into the Immutable System, using the LPS for modulation from one mode (*tonos,* pl. *tonoi*) to another.

Issues of mode and key still perplex Greek music scholars. Aristoxenus and later scholars discuss tunings (*harmoniai*) and give the ethnic names of modes: dorian, lydian, phrygian, and others. These names are ascribed by Plato and Aristotle to the *harmoniai,* which they felt varied tonally and with respect to the *ethos* (character) of the ethnic groups after which the modes were named. Quintilian presents six ancient *harmoniai,* of which only the lydian matches those presented by Ptolemy. The second-century writer Cleonides added thirteen modes one half-step apart. Scholars are uncertain whether the *tonoi* included a sense of tonic or fundamental pitch and whether each *tonos* corresponded to a unique *ethos.*

In general, the philosophical and mathematical theories of Plato and the Pythagoreans were influential in the development of Western music. The very word *music*—forms of which appear in most modern European languages—comes from the Greek word *mousikē.* Though some of Aristoxenus's and Quintilian's ideas were incorporated into the music theory of the Middle Ages (by way of Martianus Capella's *De nuptiis Mercurii et Philologiae,* ca. A.D. 425), Pythagoras's theories were the most significant musical theories in Europe until the fifteenth century.

BIBLIOGRAPHY

Barbera, André. 1984. "The Consonant Eleventh and the Expansion of the Musical Tetractys: A Study of Ancient Pythagoreanism." *Journal of Music Theory* 28:191–223.

Litchfield, Malcolm. 1988. "Aristoxenus and Empiricism: A Reevaluation Based on His Theories." *Journal of Music Theory* 32(1):51–73.

Mass, Martha, and Jane McIntosh Snyder. 1989. *Stringed Instruments of Ancient Greece.* New Haven and London: Yale University Press.

Mathiesen, Thomas J. 1974. *A Bibliography of Sources for the Study of Ancient Greek Music.* Hackensack: N.J.: Joseph Boonin.

———. 1975. "An Annotated Translation of Euclid's Division of a Monochord." *Journal of Music Theory* 19(3):236–258.

———. 1981. "New Fragments of Ancient Greek Music." *Acta Musicologica* 53:14–32.

———. 1983. "Aristides Quintilianus and the Harmonics of Manuel Bryennius: A Study of Byzantine Music Theory." *Journal of Music Theory* 27(1):31–47.

———. 1984. "Harmonia and Ethos in Ancient Greek Music." *Journal of Musicology* 3(3):264–286.

Palisca, Claude V., et al. 1984. "The Ancient Harmoniai, Tonoi, and Octave Species in Theory and Practice." *Journal of Musicology* 3(3):211–286.

Quintilianus, Aristides. 1983. *On Music (In Three Books).* Translated, with introduction, commentary, and annotations, by Thomas J. Mathiesen. New Haven and London: Yale University Press.

West, M. L. 1992. *Ancient Greek Music.* Oxford: Clarendon Press.

Winnington-Ingram, Reginald P. 1936. *Mode in Ancient Greek Music.* Cambridge: Cambridge University Press.

Notation and Transmission in European Music History
Tilman Seebass

Notation, Composition, and Performance
The Relation of Written Music and Orally Transmitted Music
Modes of Musical Reproduction and Performance Practice

The ancient Greeks—who considered music an art with a strong theoretical and philosophical base, a rational tonal system, and a mathematical and cosmological component—invented a quasi-alphabetic notation for writing down certain aspects of music. However, the potential of notation and its associated concepts, which later became the core of Western art music, was not realized by the Greeks themselves. Instead, during Roman times, the philosophical and theoretical basis of music seems to have lost its prominent place and musical notation almost disappeared.

The so-called great migration of peoples throughout Europe beginning in A.D. 375 and the collapse of the Mediterranean world created very different conditions, where there was neither a social nor an academic basis for a "music as music theory" of this kind. Consequently, until the high Middle Ages, occidental history of music as a practice (*cantus* 'song' and the various instrumental genres) and music as a theory (*ars musica*) remained separated. During this period, theory was a highly speculative academic endeavor, pursued and transmitted inside the walls of ecclesiastical institutions; whereas music itself was practiced as an oral art, comparable to that of other cultures. Then conditions began to change again, literacy spread, and ecclesiastical, aristocratic, and civic centers began to burgeon. A music notation was invented for practical purposes and quickly changed the concept of what constitutes a piece of music. Laws and mechanisms for musical transmission began to become distinctly different from those of other cultures, including those of Eastern Christians; the music of higher society, "art music" or simply "music," was more and more integrated into the system of literate tradition and merged with *ars musica*.

NOTATION, COMPOSITION, AND PERFORMANCE

Neumatic chant notation was invented around A.D. 800 as an aid to oral tradition and a means to promote for political reasons one version of that tradition. Then, in the eleventh century, it changed into a tool for composing new music and in particular polyphonic music. The old academic, theoretical discipline of *ars musica* quite possibly played a decisive role in this. Contrary to cultures where polyphony is conceived and practiced heterophonically, the clerical singers were engaging in a type of

In oral and semiliterate traditions, part of the complexity of music is the chemistry between musicians and audiences, whereas in the European written music the complexity resides in design and construction.

polyphony that had a strictly organized verticality, note against note (*punctus contra punctum*), with precisely controlled vertical progressions. For such movement, knowledge of the theory of harmony was necessary. Composing music and in the process controlling most parameters of every performance, imply, by nature, a loosening of the links between music (as a process of sound produced in time) on the one hand, and the reactions and feelings among musicians and between musicians and audience on the other. Since then, a tendency toward the "absolute" or the idea of *l'art pour l'art* can be felt in much European art music. Nevertheless, pure art-for-art's-sake compositions—such as certain *Ars Subtilior* 'Subtler Art' pieces of the fourteenth century [see HISTORY OF EUROPEAN ART MUSIC] and certain twentieth-century serial works—are rare, because composers cannot but be a part of the system that embeds music in society, and performers and audiences are still left with possibilities of influencing the music when, through performance, it comes into being.

From the eleventh century on, musical notation developed into modal, mensural, and finally "postmensural" forms, gradually entrusting more elements of music to script and therewith separating a visualized sound structure from the performance while preserving the former. Over several centuries, notation spread into all branches of "art music" (that is, the music of the upper classes), promoted and enjoyed by literate clerical, courtly, and civic circles. But the process was complex. As late as the fourteenth and fifteenth centuries, when vocal sacred and secular polyphony reached a level of sophistication never to be surpassed, the manuscripts still give us the separate parts of a piece, not a score, suggesting that strong links to oral and heterophonic musical traditions still existed and the notation was the record of a music that was not necessarily composed at a desk, but put together in performance. Similarly, there is the practice of that time of improvising one or more lines over the chant line notated in the liturgical book, the so-called *cantus super librum*. (Important work on the history of notation is contained in Apel 1961; Arlt 1973–1982; Karkoschka 1972; Levy 1987; Treitler 1984; and Wolf 1913–1919; and is reviewed in Bent et al. 1980.)

The idea of writing out a score in which all parts are lined up synchronically had existed already in an earlier phase of vocal polyphony—since the ninth-century treatise *Musica Enchiriadis*—but did not become the standard mode until the sixteenth century as a result of the impact of instrumental tablatures (notations for polyphonic music on solo instruments), originally invented with the purpose of making multipart vocal music available to keyboardists. (Important editions of facsimiles of medieval music include *Paléographie musicale* 1889–, by the monks of Solesmes; Coussemaker 1966 [1852]; Nadas and Ziino 1990; Roesner, Avril, and Regalado 1990; and Rokseth 1935–1939.)

In principle, letter notation for pitches, neumes, and tablature are not different from notations found in the eastern parts of Asia, but the character and function of modal, mensural, and modern notation are tied to a new process (and a new concept) of musical creation. Here, music may be initially conceived in the mind only, or in an impromptu at the keyboard or the lute. Then its basic shape is "composed" by a process of visualization through script. Finally, the details and whatever the notation enables the author to prescribe are written down. Some musicians were so fascinated by the possibilities of visualization that they invented a music only apparent to the eyes, for example, with black notes symbolizing mourning. The relationship between the conceiving mind of the composer and the written product becomes discursive (dialectical), with notation inviting new structural designs and musical structures inviting notational devices. One consequence is that the composed and final musical product becomes a neighbor of a work of literature or a painting, assuming a *Werkbegriff* 'musical product as a finite, conceptual entity' similar to the one used in the sister arts. Another consequence is that the creator of music is split into a composer and a performer, the two functions becoming more and more separate. In no other culture has the prescriptive comprehensiveness of notation reached such extremes in the course of a millennium (Hammerstein 1966; Seidel 1987; Wiora 1965).

From the sixteenth century on, the development and function of notation and the division of music into composition and performance are linked to the history of music printing (King 1964). Previously, music had been written down by the small, highly educated, initially clerical class of writers and scribes, but for the next three hundred years handwritten music and printed music existed side by side. Which of the two modes was chosen was not so much a matter of the size of the ensemble and the complexity of the parts, but depended on the size of the group who used the notation and the possibilities of repeated performance. Complex scores with many parts, such as operas and oratorios, often performed only once during carnival season (prior to Lent), were not printed, but music for small ensembles, for example, Arcangelo Corelli's trio sonatas, could spread in innumerable editions.

In the nineteenth century, the conditions for transmitting music changed again. With the disappearance of musical patronage and the growth of an educated middle class, composers depended almost completely on the print medium for the distribution of music; royalties became an important economic factor. Except for operas and other works with large instrumentation (where only the parts were printed, until there was enough demand for full scores), the printing of parts and the score became standard. Economically and socially not much less important were the publications of arrangements of music for educated amateur pianists and chamber-music ensembles in bourgeois households, and increasingly for popular consumption in the *kaffeehaus,* ballrooms, for town and military bands, and so on.

As the ultimate version of a composition became more and more the printed one, the process by which composers arrived at the final product increased in complexity: from the jotting down of ideas in a notebook, to preliminary sketches, the *particello* 'score with only the most important voices', the *Urschrift* 'first full score', the *Reinschrift* 'conductor's copy for the first performance', the *Druckvorlage* 'printer's copy', and the corrected proofs. What is written in the composer's own hand, the autograph, today receives attention as a psychological document, a collectible, and a potential source for the scholarly study of the compositional process. (Facsimiles of musical autographs and studies based on them can be found in Hilmar 1990; Lichtenhahn and Seebass 1976; Marshall 1972; and Winternitz 1965.)

There is a direct correlation between the steadily increasing complexity of the process involved in writing music down and the increasing size of musical compositions. Whereas in oral and semiliterate traditions, part of the complexity of music is the chemistry between musicians and audiences, in the European written music the complexity resides in design and construction. The principle of orchestral music, with more than one musician playing the same part exactly in the same way, is in most other cultures neither feasible nor seen as desirable. Contrapuntal polyphony and uniformity in ensemble playing are the opposites of heterophony. Large-scale, complex structures with a dynamic outlay, in particular the sonata principle (found in orchestral and operatic genres), are the result of the technique of composition by script. Other, originally oral forms, such as variation and rondo, increased in complexity and length to a degree that they too became unthinkable without notation. The last to disappear were considered licenses of the performers: extemporaneous musical additions to the more or less faithful realization of a score survived into the twentieth century and disappeared before World War II, only to reappear a few decades later as constitutive elements prescribed by composers.

Nowhere outside Europe is script so central for a large portion of music. Consequently, the music outside the realm of script that lives as an orally created art separates itself earlier and more definitely than in other cultures from musical forms linked to a written tradition. Orally created music becomes gradually until the mid-nineteenth century an affair of the popular realm and lower classes, while written music is increasingly identified with the cultural activity of the upper class.

In the last few hundred years, the amount of written music has reached such immense proportions that it has set in motion a certain type of musicology, which operates with a *Werkbegriff,* derived from the idea of music being composed in writing and executed from the score, a *res facta,* unique, immobile, and eternal. As a consequence, the term *monument* (*Denkmal,* pl. *Denkmäler*) for a musical score has become common among scholars. On a conceptual level, European music historiography is congruent to European musical composition: the scholar sides with the composer and the written evidence, not with the musician. Thus, inherently the transmission of European art music through notation invites the assumption that what was visualized was the music itself. Not surprisingly, in English the term *music* can relate to both the sound and the score.

As to the ranking of this Western art music in the musical universe, to this day the insider and the outsider seem to have difficulties agreeing. Walter Wiora saw in its unique dependence on script a claim for superiority over all the others (1965:130–132). In fact, he made Western music the true bearer of what he called the fourth age of music, which he supposed had spread over the entire earth—a rather apocalyptic vision indeed. Writing the introduction to the (untranslated) second edition of Wiora's book in 1988, Carl Dahlhaus patently admired this concept of ethnocentric universal history. A Sicilian bagpiper, on the other hand, seems to respect Western art music while distancing himself from it: he calls written art music *musica,* and uses individual, concrete terms for his own forms of musical performance (oral communication Nico Staiti, November 1991). To most Asian musicians, finally, Western art music must appear as an interesting aberration from true music, because it has come to disregard the primordial dependence of structure on performance, time, and occasion.

THE RELATION OF WRITTEN MUSIC AND ORALLY TRANSMITTED MUSIC

There are many indirect and a few direct indications that throughout European music history the culture of orally transmitted music interacted with the composed music of the literati (see in particular Leydi 1991 and Knepler 1982:217–226). The reason for this is not only that written music becomes aural during the performance (as oral music does), or because many aspects of the musical event never enter the score, but because in vocal sacred or secular music and instrumental music the musicians were a social group who had ties into both directions of the system of social strata. The borderlines were particularly blurred before 1500, that is, during the many centuries when most instrumental music, even for literate audiences, was not written down.

The social and professional status of the musicians was of a kind that often makes it hard, sometimes plainly impossible, to separate folk or popular music culture from that of the upper strata, since the musical repertoire of students, lower clerics, and migrating professional musicians was mediated into both directions. An additional aspect is that sociocultural differences must be seen in tandem with the locale (urban or rural) and the geographic region. Since research into these gray zones often must operate without primary sources, scholars have tended to shun them. As research on the impact of Austrian folk music on the Viennese classics shows, it is possible to project twentieth-century, primary evidence of folk music backward and trace its influence in art music. (The relationship between art and folk music has been examined by Salmen 1983; Stockmann 1983; Szabolcsi 1965; Taruskin 1980; Wiora 1957; and others.)

Perhaps the most fascinating "mixed" culture is Italy, where from the Middle Ages to present times oral and written traditions continuously interacted. Genres of written literature and notated music were adopted and developed by reciters of epics, *gondolieri,* puppeteers, and religious groups in sacred or devotional practice (Leydi 1991). Conversely, popular vocal and instrumental genres, including dances, made it often into the repertoire of respected instrumentalists working for the higher classes, or were picked up by composers. (Even in Italy, scholarly attention to this phenomenon is recent; see Leydi 1991; Magrini 1986; and Staiti, Guidobaldi, and Bernardoni 1987.)

Though under certain circumstances music traveled between different social strata—sacred and secular songs and dance seem to have been particularly adaptable—from the sixteenth century to the eighteenth, written music of the literate society separated itself as "art music" more and more from oral traditions of illiterate and lower-class society. The growing bourgeois middle class adopted in the late eighteenth century common aesthetic standards for their music, and it appears that composers were aware of it, at least judging from Joseph Haydn's claim that his music appealed to this common standard—that it was for the whole world.

In the late eighteenth century, at the moment when music of the popular traditions seemed almost completely to disappear from the horizon of the literati, this music was reintroduced as an important part of it by Johann Gottfried von Herder (1744–1803), who advocated the recognition of cultural otherness of other historical periods, different social strata, and different geographical settings. With his discovery of folklore as a marker of cultural identity and a field of scholarly inquiry came the discovery of oral tradition (Burke 1978). What Herder started as a concept developed on the writer's desk became an important issue a generation later during the years of nationalist revivals. While Central European art music was establishing itself from the British Isles to St. Petersburg in performance and musical education, ethnic music was becoming a political issue and was beginning to influence the national music scenes. "Flavoring" musical compositions with ethnic elements, composers produced music that could serve as a national identifier. Throughout Europe, composers and audiences became increasingly interested in folk music. This process culminated twice, first among Chopin, Smetana, Dvořák, and other Central Europeans who resorted to their folklore as a means to color the tonal, rhythmic, and formal language of the late Romantic and post-Romantic phase, and then among the generation active in the first decades of the twentieth century, when folklore was the treasure trove to replace the worn-out parameters of Central European tonal language by new, even exotic ones. Since research in folkloristic and exotic aspects of Western art music requires a double expertise, it is hard to get a grip on the problem. So far,

A step into the almost limitless availability of music was reached with the introduction and expansion of the audiovisual electronic media. Contemporary music and music of the educated masses began to grow apart, with more and more people taking refuge in a music of past times, music that had long lost its new or avant-garde character.

scholars have almost exclusively dealt with this issue from the recipient's point of view; for a study from the donors' perspective, one would need the collaboration of folklorists and ethnomusicologists.

MODES OF MUSICAL REPRODUCTION AND PERFORMANCE PRACTICE

The performing arts—music, dance, and drama—have in common that their essence and existence reside in actualization. They are "arts-in-the-making" (Sheets 1966:36). Though in this respect Europe is not categorically different from other cultures, the increasing reliance on a written tradition did change some conditions for reproduction—synchronically between classes and occasions, and diachronically through time.

Synchronic reproduction

Western music history presents a wealth of examples for transformations of musical substance from one performance to another during a given time period. The Middle Ages, with its many oral or mixed traditions, was a particularly rich period. Chants were recomposed with tropes and sequences, melodies were adapted to new texts, and new melodies were adapted to given texts. Monophonic music formed the basis of new, polyphonic music in motets and masses, and sung tunes were intabulated on keyboard instruments and for a variety of instrumental realizations of dance tunes. Many of these possibilities lived on in the following centuries, yet they were reduced in importance with the increased role of composed music. By the mid-twentieth century, composers, musicians, scholars, and the public had so much become used to the idea that the music was the same if the score was the same, that one almost assumed that the changes from one performance to another did not affect the substance. Klaus Wachsmann (1981) correctly observed that the importance of context for musical form was greatly reduced in Western composed music. Nevertheless, there were always situations in which the original musical performance and the reproduction could grow apart—for example, if the work was performed by a larger set of instruments (a song for voice and keyboard being orchestrated) or a smaller one (a dance for string ensemble being reduced to a piece for lute). Reductions were often extemporized on the basis of the original score. The distance between the "original" and the new product was greater if a work was transferred from the written tradition of the literate society to the oral tradition of popular or rural culture, or if a performance from the realm of folk music and folk dance entered the written tradition, or if a change of taste in society made changes in the music necessary, as with Mozart's operas during the nineteenth century. Though in the course of the nineteenth century notation continued to assume ever greater precision, the *Werkbegriff* remained problematic. The most obvious example is the role of piano arrangements. With the spread of the piano into nearly every household of bourgeois society, piano arrangements as a means for domestic reproduction and consumption of music of theater, concert, and church grew to yet new dimensions.

A step into the almost limitless availability of music was reached with the introduction and expansion of the audiovisual electronic media, but simultaneously, and not surprisingly, a predilection for what is easy to the ears was increasing. Contemporary music and music of the educated masses began to grow apart, with more and more people taking refuge in a music of past times, music that had long lost its new or avant-garde character.

Diachronic reproduction

Though between 800 and 1800 the share of written music within music culture in general increased, this change did not alter the length of time during which a particular genre or individual work remained fashionable and remembered by society. Despite notation, most operas between 1600 and 1750 were performed once or a few times only. Then, at the end of the eighteenth century and the beginning of the nineteenth, historicism provided the incentive for rediscovering and reperforming a music that had ceased to be contemporary. The famous example is the performance of Bach's *St. Matthew Passion* under the baton of Felix Mendelssohn in 1829. This performance did not attempt a reconstruction of the original conditions. Mendelssohn chose modern state-of-the-art orchestras and large choirs, and thus brought the music up to date to the taste of the public. From then onward, the same piano and the same modern symphonic orchestra that served contemporary original (primary) or arranged (secondary) performances were used for bringing to life music of earlier periods written for different instruments and assuming different conventions of execution. It was in the 1920s that more scholars began to look into the original conditions of a performance, simultaneously with the appearance of numerous groups of "early music performers." The aims of musicologists and musicians had a new point of convergence.

Not surprisingly, the "early music" movement was stimulated by interest in three instruments, which had disappeared altogether (as with the harpsichord and the viola da gamba) or had undergone drastic changes in the nineteenth century (as with the organ). The events of the 1930s and World War II stopped the development of such studies and performances. Because large orchestras and the piano continued to appropriate whatever of the editions of earlier music came on the market for their public and private performance, the study of performance practice had a slow start in the 1950s. That it picked up at all is believed to have been due to the efforts of the German firm Polydor's budgeting a portion of its income from sales of singles of popular music for its Archiv Productions. An early music project could probably not have survived these critical years without outside funding. Even today, when live performances of early music on period instruments (original instruments or instruments build after originals) have considerably increased, the income from concerts would rarely suffice to keep musicians and instrument makers economically afloat. The early-music activity owes much of its existence to the audio industry. Another socioaesthetic change connected to the early-music movement is that the group of amateurs actively performing "classical" music has entered a crisis. They cannot afford to learn several techniques of playing and buy the "correct" instruments for playing the music of other periods, and are left with the choice of leaving active playing of early music to the historizing professionals, or continuing to play with modern instruments with the pretension that historicism is not their concern.

The early-music movement provided the first opportunity for historians to work "in the field," to use a term from ethnology. Accordingly, the *Werkbegriff* of scholars has begun to change (as has the public's and the self-consciousness of musicians), and research in those matters that are not evident from the score, yet relevant for the performance, has gained importance. Almost all the adjacent fields of music history, in particular organology and iconography, have received a boost from this, and editorial practices have begun to shift. (Important studies on early-music performance practice include Brown and Sadie 1990; Eggebrecht 1967; Haskell 1988; Kenyon 1988; and Neumann 1978; and journals devoted to the topic include *Early Music* and the *Basler Jahrbuch für historische Aufführungspraxis.*)

What started with historical performances in the nineteenth century became another feature by which Western art music separated itself from the rest of the globe. It created a mode of musical performance in which the original context had completely or almost completely disappeared and had been replaced by the new context of an "experience in concert" with its own purpose of historistic entertainment and edification. Of course, in non-Western musical performances the historical dimension can also be present; an example such as puppet (*wayang*) performances in Java, Bali, and Malaysia comes easily to mind; but in *wayang,* the contextual system, including its metaphysical purpose, has remained intact, and history is only experienced in its actualized form. In the West, an early-music performance is a historizing reconstruction of what fundamentally differs from the present.

BIBLIOGRAPHY

Apel, Willi. 1961. *The Notation of Polyphonic Music, 900–1600.* 5th ed. Cambridge: Mediaeval Academy of America.

Arlt, Wulf, ed. 1973–1982. *Paläographie der Musik.* Vol. 1. Cologne: Volk–Verlag Gerig.

Bent, Ian D., David Hiley, Margaret Bent, and Geoffrey Chew. 1980. "Notation." In *The New Grove.* Edited by Stanley Sadie. London: Macmillan.

Brown, Howard Mayer, and Stanley Sadie, eds. 1990. *Performance Practice.* New York: Norton.

Burke, Peter. 1978. *Popular Culture in Early Modern Europe.* New York: New York University Press.

Coussemaker, Charles Edmond Henri de. 1966 [1852]. *Histoire de l'harmonie au moyen âge.* Hildesheim: Gg. Olms.

Eggebrecht, Hans Heinrich. 1967. *Die Orgelbewegung.* Stuttgart: Musikwissenschaftliche Verlagsgesellschaft.

Ferand, Ernest T. 1938. *Die Improvisation in der Musik.* Zurich: Rhein–Verlag.

———. 1961. *The Improvisation in Nine Centuries of Western Music: An Anthology.* Cologne: A. Volk Verlag.

Hammerstein, Reinhold. 1966. "Musik als Komposition und Interpretation." *Deutsche Vierteljahrschrift für Literatur und Geistesgeschichte* 40:1–23.

Haskell, Harry. 1988. *The Early Music Revival: A History.* London: Thames and Hudson.

Hilmar, Ernst, ed. 1990. *Internationales Symposium Musikautographe, 5.–8. Juni, 1989, Wien.* Tutzing: H. Schneider.

Karkoschka, Erhard. 1972. *Notation in New Music.* London: Universal.

Kenyon, Nicholas, ed. 1988. *Authenticity and Early Music: A Symposium.* Oxford and New York: Oxford University Press.

King, A. Hyatt. 1964. *Four Hundred Years of Music Printing.* London: British Museum.

———. 1979. *Four Hundred Years of Music Printing.* 3d ed. London: British Library.

Knepler, Georg. 1982. *Geschichte als Weg zum Musikverstandnis: Zur Theorie, Methode und Geschichte der Musikgeschichtsschreibung.* 2d ed. Leipzig: Reclam.

Levy, Kenneth. 1987. "On the Origin of Neumes." *Early Music History* 7:59–90.

Leydi, Roberto. 1991. *L'altra musica: etnomusicologia: come abbiamo incontrato e creduto di conoscere le musiche delle tradizioni popolari ed etniche.* Milan: Ricordi.

Lichtenhahn, E., and Tilman Seebass. 1976. *Musikhandschriften aus der Sammlung Paul Sacher.* Basel: F. Hoffmann-LaRoche.

Magrini, Tullia. 1986. "'Dolce lo mio drudo': la prospettiva etnomusicologica." *Rivista italiana di musicologia* 22:215–235.

Marshall, Robert Lewis. 1972. *The Compositional Process of J. S. Bach: A Study of the Autograph Scores of the Vocal Works.* Princeton: Princeton University Press.

Nadas, John, and Agostino Ziino. 1990. *The Lucca Codex.* Lucca: Libreria Musicale Italiana.

Neumann, Frederick. 1978. *Argumentation in Baroque and Post-Baroque Music.* Princeton: Princeton University Press.

———. 1983. *Ornamentation in Baroque and Post-Baroque Music.* Princeton: Princeton University Press.

Paléographie musicale. 1989. Abbaye Saint-Pierre de Solesmes, ed. Berne: Herbert Lang.

Roesner, Edward H., François Avril, and Nancy Freeman Regalado, eds. 1990. *Le Roman de Fauvel in the Edition of Mesire Chaillou de Pesstain.* New York: Broude Brothers.

Rokseth, Yvonne. 1935–1939. *Polyphonie du XIIIe siècle.* Paris: Éditions de l'Oiseau Lyre.

Salmen, Walter, ed. 1983. *The Social Status of Professional Musicians from the Middle Ages to the 19th Century.* New York: Pendragon Press.

Seidel, Wilhelm. 1987. *Werk und Werkbegriff in der Musikgeschichte.* Darmstadt: Wissenschaftliche Buchgesellschaft.

Sheets, Maxine. 1966. *Phenomenology of Dance.* Madison: University of Wisconsin Press.

———. 1980. *Phenomenology of Dance.* New York: Books for Libraries.

Staiti, N., N. Guidobaldi, and V. Bernardoni. 1987. "Le musiche 'pastorali' e le novene per il natale in Italia." *International Musicological Society* 3:573–626.

Stockmann, Doris. 1983. "Musica vulgaris bei Johannes de Grocheo." *Beiträge zur Musikwissenschaft* 25:3–56.

Szabolcsi, Bence. 1965. "Folk Music—Art Music—History of Music." *Journal of the International Folk Music Council* 17(2):171–179.

Taruskin, Richard. 1980. "Russian Folk Melodies in The Rite of Spring." *Journal of the American Musicological Society* 33:501–543.

Treitler, Leo. 1984. "Reading and Singing: on the Genesis of Occidental Music-Writing." *Early Music History* 4:135–208.

Wachsmann, Klaus. 1981. "Applying Ethnomusicological Methods to Western Art Music." *The World of Music* 23(2):74–87.

Winternitz, Emmanuel. 1965. *Musical Autographs from Monteverdi to Hindemith.* 2 vols. New York: Dover Publications.

Wiora, Walter. 1957. *Europaische Volksmusik und abendländische Tonkunst.* Kassel: J. P. Hinnenthal.

———. 1965. *The Four Ages of Music.* Translated by M. D. Herter Norton. New York: Norton.

———. 1966. *European Folk Song: Common Forms in Characteristic Modifications.* Translated by Robert Kilben. New York: Leeds Music.

Wolf, Johannes. 1913–1919. *Handbuch der Notationskunde.* 2 vols. Leipzig: Breitkopf & Härtel.

The Role of History in Contemporary European Art-Music Culture

Bruno Nettl

The European Concept of Music History
The Sociology of Contemporary Performance: Past Dominates Present
Comparative Perspectives on the Uniqueness of European Music History

For Europeans, the art or classical musical repertory consists largely of works composed long ago, identified by their time of origin, and discussed in their chronological relationship to each other. Recent works are measured by their relationship to and departure from past works. The music most revered is that of the eighteenth and nineteenth centuries. It is reasonable to suggest that Western art-music culture is particularly oriented to and conscious of its history (Dahlhaus 1977; Knepler 1982).

The people of many societies emphasize that their music is ancient, is in some sense a pure expression of the society, is distinct from the music of other societies, and in many cases is of superior quality. Nowhere, possibly, is the specialness of a culture's music stressed more than among musicians and their audiences in Europe; and within that context, nowhere more than in the domain of European classical or art music.

According to Judith Becker (1986), Western musicians regard their music as superior in three respects: it is based on natural principles, which moved it to its present form (or more properly, to its form in the 1800s, its highest state of achievement) through stages now represented by other musics of the world; it is more complex than other musics, and, indeed, is in a totally different class of complexity; and it has meaning in ways that other musics do not. Similarly, Joseph Kerman, in suggesting that scholarship in Western art music requires an approach different from that required by other musics, writes, "Western music is just too different" (1985:174). Music-appreciation teachers sometimes distinguish between Western and other musics by asserting that the Western is dynamic and the rest of the musical world is static. There is ample ground on which to criticize these statements, but our task here is to use them to show that Western culture regards itself as different from other cultures, not only in degree, but in kind, and that its attitude toward music history reflects this.

THE EUROPEAN CONCEPT OF MUSIC HISTORY

Most adherents of European art music, people with a considerable general and at least somewhat formal musical education, look at music as a set of concentric circles, roughly like this: their own art music is in the center, surrounded by a circle of folk and popular musics (variously distant from the center, depending on similarities of styles, instruments, and contexts), with non-Western musics at the perimeter, art musics such as South Asian and Indonesian closer than the musics of smaller societies such as American Indians and Australian Aborigines. Their view of history may focus on the center alone, or on certain sectors, or even on the whole array of circles.

World music: a conspectus of "our" European history?

In listening to the musics of the world and considering musics that may have once existed but are no longer extant, many thoughtful scholars and other members of Western society regard world history as a single event, a line of development in which all cultures move through similar stages, but at different speeds. The culmination is Western music—in one respect, the accomplishments of nineteenth- and twentieth-century art music, and in another, the technological accomplishments of the twentieth century in the "new music" of the art-music world and the sphere of popular music. However, ethnomusicologists and a few music historians have expressed uneasiness about this kind of big-bang approach to world-music history (Blum, Bohlman, and Neuman 1990; Dahlhaus 1977), but it continues to be a major strand of the Western view of the musical past.

Folk music: illuminating national origins

To most Westerners, folk music is the music of rural and uneducated classes; but more important, it represents the early stages of their national cultures, early in a chronological sense, but also in the sense that this is the music of the unspoiled past, a time of cultural purity. Yet folk music continues to exist in isolated areas, suggesting, as in the view of world music, the simultaneous existence of various periods (Bohlman 1988). The European approach to music history can be seen as a struggle between accepting Europe as a unit and viewing music as the expression of different nationalities (Bohlman 1992). Folk-song scholarship has shown that certain tunes, instruments, and texts have wide distributions through Europe; but more importantly, each European culture or ethnic group has its own repertory and style of folk music. In the nineteenth and twentieth centuries, folk music has had significant functions in nationalistic movements of all directions, including German nationalism culminating in the Nazi period, nineteenth-century Czech liberation movements, Hungarian attempts to separate from Austrian domination, and the struggle for Irish political independence.

The history of art music: reconciling opposites

The value of the old, the value of change

In the world of European art music, historical consciousness probably did not play a major role until the Renaissance, with its desire to return to ancient classical ideals. By the 1700s and 1800s, the concept of progress and composers' desires to stay ahead of audiences and competitors had become established. At that point, music, to be alive, had always to be (or claim to be) changing. But as methods of transmission became more fixed—first through exclusively aural processes, and then through handwritten notation with little standardization, on to higher degrees of agreement, to printing, and eventually to recording and synthesis—the possibility of holding on to the old while forging ahead increased (Meyer 1982; Taruskin 1988).

In the twentieth century, a major motivating force has been the desire to see music expand (Cameron 1982, 1984). A paradox has resulted: on the one hand, new works ought to be new in their acoustic contents (themes, sequences of harmonies or tone series, and so on), and must show composers as innovators in compositional conception, method, and technique; but on the other hand, the art-music-loving populace, and even some ever-innovating composers, regard the best music as having been created in the past, especially in the 1700s and 1800s.

National and universal

In each nation, special attention is paid to local products, local popular music ensembles, local folk musicians who, no longer rural in culture or musical training, bring folklike music to urban populations and art-music composers, however little known in other countries. But throughout Europe, people recognize mainstreams of art and popular musical culture. In art music, this center is a constellation of universally respected great composers of the 1700s and 1800s, most of them German or Austrian. In popular music throughout the twentieth century, the stylistic center has been North America, with African-American musics a major source.

The importance of origins

Though the national origins of composers and pieces are a smaller issue in music than in visual art, the origins of pieces are of great importance. "Origin" includes the question of how compositions came about—the identity of composers, what they had in mind, how they worked, how they brought the materials together; stylistic and thematic sources, and the particular forms these sources had. The emphasis on origins resulted in the concern for authenticity of performance practice. But in the first instance, the character of a piece of music is ascribed to the time of its composition. If asked why two pieces are different, musicians go first to the temporal context of composition. And thus, one of the most important components in musicians' thought about music history is the concept of periods, each of which is assumed to have had a stylistically integrated character. Each period can be characterized by a set of stylistic features, typical genres, and aesthetic and cultural ideals; and European cultures are seen to have participated, not equally to be sure, in all or most of them.

Great masters, great works

European lovers of art music know that music history tells of innumerable phalanxes of composers and an almost infinite number of works, but they focus on a small number of masters and masterworks. The list is usually headed by Bach, Mozart, and Beethoven, and perhaps also Schubert, Handel, and Haydn, but while there would seem to be general agreement among Europeans about the stature of these composers (all ethnically Germanic), each nation has its preferences: Polish music lovers quickly add Chopin; Czechs add Smetana and Dvořák; Italians add Verdi, Puccini, and Monteverdi. But everywhere music is primarily the works of the great masters, composers who stand out because they composed not just one or two, but many masterworks. Europeans seem to be united in their elevation of certain works to the status of universal masterwork: Bach's *St. Matthew Passion,* Handel's *Messiah,* Mozart's *Don Giovanni,* Beethoven's Ninth Symphony, perhaps Schubert's song cycle *Die schöne Müllerin,* Wagner's *Ring,* Verdi's *Aida,* Stravinsky's *Rite of Spring*—all of these being large, complex works.

Popular music: art-music history telescoped

The world of art music sees itself as oriented to the past, but with an imperative to innovate; the world of popular music is similar, but takes a shorter time span as its measure. There is the constantly changing character of styles and repertories and the basic assumption that songs remain in the repertory briefly, after having for a short time been hits. But in trade magazines, on radio and television, occur frequent references to older recordings, early stars, songs from some kind of a classic period—the

1940s big-band era, Elvis Presley, the Beatles, Aretha Franklin, Hank Williams. The concepts of a classic era and classics of the repertory play a role here as they do in the art-music world. The impetus of nostalgia plays an important role, partly because of advances in the technology of recording and reissuing, improvements in quality, and the lengthening history of the recording industry itself. Altogether, the popular-music world reflects, or is reflected by, the temporal perspectives of the classical-music culture.

THE SOCIOLOGY OF CONTEMPORARY PERFORMANCE: PAST DOMINATES PRESENT

The relative importance of the past over the present in contemporary musical life manifests itself in many ways, including choice of repertory, the relationship between traditional musical structures and traditional family structures, formal dress codes at concerts, and even the temporal organization of music lessons.

Repertory

The concentration on music composed between 1730 and 1920 in the art music of European and European-derived societies is a recent development, dating perhaps to the end of World War I. At that point, according to Christopher Small, the repertory was "frozen" (1987:11–13). In the nineteenth century, European concerts consisted much more of recent and contemporary works. The change in attitude around 1920 results from several factors. Concerts, especially of large ensembles such as symphony orchestras, have become rituals in which a model of society—hierarchical, dominated by the middle and upper classes—to which most members of European society nevertheless do not subscribe is celebrated. Stylistic innovations in virtually each work began to outdistance the ability of audiences to absorb change, and a new and, to many people, incomprehensible set of musical languages was established. Composers' desires to produce great art for all time, rather than music for their contemporaries, introduced a split between composers and listeners. The development of technology and occupational specialization, and the idea that members of certain professions—scientists, physicians, engineers, social scientists—should properly use metalanguages unintelligible to the general public, encouraged composers to do the same with their music. The European art-music world came to be a society that idealized technological and social change, and expected composers to innovate radically, but remained tied to the enjoyment of music composed long ago, performed as much as possible as it would have been under its composers' direction.

Social structure in the music

The most significant and popular styles of Western art music have parts that fit together somewhat along the lines of Western societies. Most of the art music composed roughly between 1730 and 1920 consists of something accompanied by something else. The right hand of the piano and harpsichord is accompanied by the left, a violin is accompanied by a piano, first violins in the small orchestra are accompanied by other strings, and all the strings are accompanied by the winds in the large symphony orchestra. In opera, the solo singers are accompanied by the entire orchestra, within which, in turn, are all of the hierarchical elements of symphony orchestras generally; and on stage, solo with vocal accompaniment at various levels also exists. A piano concerto, the paradigmatic type of concerto, has the hierarchical elements of the piano, all of them as a unit, accompanied by an orchestra.

Interesting exceptions are musical genres in which all voices are thought to be equal and potential contrasts in timbre and sometimes tempo are deemphasized: fugues and their relatives, and string quartets. Fugues are particularly associated with

The conductor is a general, who, like real generals, stays on the sidelines and takes no risks, has supreme power, and communicates with the officers (first-chair players) by shaking hands with them after a performance. Playing in uniform (tuxedos or tails for orchestras, military-derived uniforms for bands) cements the association.

religion and otherwise with the concept of the serious, and they often appear as statements of climax or finality, as in the "Amen" of Handel's *Messiah,* the last movement of Mozart's *Jupiter* Symphony, the original fourth movement of Beethoven's String Quartet op. 130, and the end of Brahms's Variations on a Theme by Handel.

The ideal of European musical culture remains the ensemble, typically consisting of four parts or voices. Established in the seventeenth century, the soprano-alto-tenor-bass structure remains dominant in music theory, in the choral world, and in much instrumental ensemble music outside the framework of experimental art music. The relationship of this structure to an ideal European family structure suggests in some measure why it has retained its significance, and helps explain the dominance of eighteenth-century music in contemporary musical life. (For an attempt to show social structure reflected in harmony, see Norton 1984; and for related material, see McClary 1991 and Meyer 1967.)

The relationship among the musicians in an ensemble is a paramount criterion of success, and the degree to which an ensemble can maintain its unity of personnel makes a difference. Most members of an audience—especially those using radio or records—do not know and cannot find out the names of members of quartets or trios, and hardly anyone can name a member of an orchestra. It is the ensembles that are the primary units of thought.

The typical Western art-music ensemble is often identified with units (nation, state, city governments) that play a role in politics, and its internal social structure is related to political and military structures. According to Small (1977), it is also a replication of industrial structures. Indeed, an orchestra seems like a factory for producing a performance of music. There is the sharp distinction between conductor and players, as between management and labor (figure 1). The conductor gets credit and criticism for the quality of performances, and his name graces marquees and record covers. The orchestra is arranged in hierarchies, including concertmaster (whose leadership is symbolized by a separate entrance at a concert), section heads, and designations of string players by desk and of wind players by difficulty of the parts they play ("first," "second," and so on). Elements of class distinction derive from musical structure: melody-playing instruments such as first violins and woodwinds have the highest status; those playing bass—cellos, double basses—are next, and those inhabiting the inner acoustical territory (violas, second violins, trombones) are lowest.

We can also see the conductor as a general, who, like real generals, stays on the sidelines and takes no risks (does not play—"You never heard a baton play a wrong note" is a standard orchestra musicians' joke), has supreme power, and communicates with the officers (first-chair players) by shaking hands with them after a performance. Wind bands, especially marching bands—which more than orchestras are associated with towns or institutions, and are thus metaphorically armies that threaten and defend—have all these traits to a greater degree, as their physical movements are also

FIGURE 1   A symphony conductor rehearses the brass section of the orchestra, enacting a relationship that mimics that between management and labor. Photo courtesy of the Het Brabants Orchest, Eindhoven, Netherlands; Marc Soustrot, director. Photo by Cockie Donkers.

prescribed. The concept of playing in uniform (tuxedos or tails for orchestras, military-derived uniforms for bands) cements the association.

Concerts and other rituals

The principal ritual of the contemporary art-music world is the concert. The typical symphony orchestra concert is antihistorical in that it consists of works from various periods of history, various countries, and several possible social contexts. A concert might consist of an overture to a Mozart opera, a concerto by Grieg, and a symphony by Brahms, with an excerpt from a cantata by Bach as an encore. Materials from many sources are combined in a standardized ritual, in which introductory behavior (applause, tuning up, appearance of the concertmaster, who prepares the orchestra for the entry of the conductor, intermission, and closing behavior) are highly predictable. Printed programs and program notes, and a structure that gives places of honor to large works by famous composers or great masters, are essentially the same throughout Europe, whatever economic or political system dominates. Similar principles underlie piano recitals, chamber concerts, and other such events.

The audience of symphony orchestras and operas, at least in its subconscious, seems to wish to return to the eighteenth century, when patronage, lavish or parsimonious, would be provided by courts, churches, aristocrats, and the wealthy, and by associating with such persons and their establishments, the common people might be able to see and hear performances. Most patronage in the twentieth century is provided by national or local governments and industries; nevertheless, entering a concert hall often gives one a feeling that one is entering the predemocratic past. It is expressed most obviously in musicians' dress, costume, or uniform. White tie ("tails") is really nineteenth-century dress. It recalls suits worn by high-ranking servants, representing musicianship before it became a middle-class profession.

The taxonomy of musics is also made clear in performers' costumes. We see black tie (tuxedos) for the standard, 1710–1920 art music; Renaissance costumes for earlier music; turtleneck and non-uniform dress for the later twentieth century; non-Western dress for non-Western music, even if the musicians would wear Western dress otherwise; cowboy outfits for American country music when it is played in Europe; idiosyncratic dress in which no two members of an ensemble dress alike for rock; ethnic or rural dress ("folk costumes") for concerts of folk or folk-derived music; and military dress for large marching and even concertizing bands.

Secondary rituals

If we view the concert as the principal ritual of European art music, a ritual that embodies attitudes toward music and symbolizes important principles of social structure and culture as a whole, secondary rituals include practice sessions, rehearsals, and lessons. Individual students, teachers, conductors, and institutions vary enormously in the patterns of these events (more than in the patterning of concerts and recitals), and there is a dearth of concrete data, but there nevertheless appear to be some regularities. Most important, these patterns are derived from the pattern of concerts.

A typical orchestral rehearsal maintains the hierarchies and discipline of an orchestral concert, including respect for the conductor and first-chair players; indeed, direction from the top down is more important. Tuning up, the conductor's entry, intermission, and ordinarily the order of pieces duplicate those of the concert. One ordinarily rehearses for a particular concert.

Accomplished musicians and advanced students, who may practice many hours each day, develop idiosyncratic techniques of practicing. But most teachers impose a set of techniques and an order of events for the hour or so that other students devote to practicing. Frequently, it is a ritual that reflects the Western view of music history. A typical serious and moderately advanced piano student with a demanding teacher may practice, in order: scales; exercises derived from scales; an etude, such as those by Heller or Czerny; a work by J. S. Bach; a work by Robert Schumann; and a work by Béla Bartók. Three principles are followed. The student begins and ends with the least "musical," following the idea that the highest achievements are in the middle of the timeline; as in a concert, the *pièce de résistance* is in the middle. Like a concert, a practice session moves chronologically, the scales at the beginning a symbol of the beginnings of music. Similarly, one moves from melody to functional harmony to dissonance. One moves, as well, from musically (not technically) easy to musically difficult.

Lessons often follow the same pattern, but they may include elements of the orchestral rehearsal. Teachers sometimes conduct their students as they play, or hum along, or even perform in unison with them. They tend also to follow a typical order of events, presumably that which they expect to be followed in practicing. But in certain ways, a lesson is a small concert by the student, given for the teacher. You show what you have accomplished, and after each piece you receive applause, sometimes literally clapping, but more likely words of approval or encouragement. At the end of the lesson, a teacher may offer brief evaluative statements. Even the week before a lesson has a structure—technical, but perhaps more emotional, as the student works up to the climax of the week. The last practice session may be a dress rehearsal, full of excitement and anxiety.

Rehearsals, lessons, and practice sessions are minor versions of the concert ritual; and so are other events in the art-music world, such as auditions. There are material reasons for this, but in many societies, many rituals are microcosmic variations of a central one. European art-music culture has a sense of the way in which musical events should be ordered and the principles they should exhibit. Of these, the European view of history as a progression from easy to difficult, from introductory to great to decadent, from melody to harmony to dissonance, from warm-up to grand to light, is a major component.

COMPARATIVE PERSPECTIVES ON THE UNIQUENESS OF EUROPEAN MUSIC HISTORY

The European music intelligentsia used to assert that Western music was different from all others on account of its tendency constantly to change while the rest of the musical world was static. This characterization fits into an earlier attitude about the history of world music. Tribal music was seen to be the music of the Stone Age, and shows us what the beginnings of music may have been. Even a culturally neutral student would probably agree that guesses about the earliest human music may be best informed by the traits held in common by tribal peoples long or always isolated from each other. But the quasi-evolutionist view holds, further, that all non-Western musics have stopped developing, can thus be found at various stages of evolution, and by definition have become unchanging.

Looking at musical change in the world from a Western perspective provides concentration on musical style, and on composition, rather than other elements of music, such as repertory, performance practice, and social context. A Plains Indian, whose culture may have provided for rapid composing of new songs and discarding of older ones without great change in musical style, may consider Western music, in which concerts with the same pieces could be given in 1910 and 1970, as quite static. A folk culture in which communal recreation provides for many successive renditions of the same songs could consider the virtually identical performances of a nineteenth-century piece by twentieth-century pianists as evidence of the unchanging nature of Western art music.

The history of Western music features eras when musicians staked out claims for innovation: the Ars Nova, around the beginning of the 1300s; the beginning of the Baroque, about 1600; and the introduction of atonal techniques, shortly after 1900.

It is unfortunate that we can discuss the balance between change and nonchange only in the abstract, but the concrete information that we have about the history of European music and musicians' attitude toward it is not available in anywhere nearly the same quantity for other societies. We must travel in a theoretical and imaginary realm. But when all is said and done, and all ethnocentric biases are eliminated in favor of an evenhanded, culturally neutral analysis, it may still turn out that European musical culture is characterized, in comparison to most others, by rapid changeability.

But it is change that comes at intervals and alternates with conservative periods emphasizing the static; and it results from an attitude that is ambivalent, at least in the twentieth century. In the abstract, musicians and music lovers in European culture admire the experimental and scorn composers who write in older styles, reaching back to the ideals of the nineteenth century. But while they want composers to write things that are new, in content and style, they want to understand newer works in terms applicable to older music. And they cannot conceive that the composers of their own twentieth century or of the future will ever be able to compete with the grandeur of the past, of the period of Bach, Mozart, and Beethoven.

BIBLIOGRAPHY

Abraham, Gerald. 1974. *The Tradition of Western Music.* Berkeley: University of California Press.

Allen, Warren D. 1962. *Philosophies of Music History: A Study of General Histories of Music 1600–1960.* New York: Dover.

Ambros, August Wilhelm. 1862. *Geschichte der Musik.* Breslau: Leuckart.

Ames, David, and Anthony King. 1971. *Glossary of Hausa Music and Its Social Context.* Evanston: Northwestern University Press.

Attali, Jacques. 1985. *Noise: The Political Economy of Music.* Translated by Brian Massumi. Minneapolis: University of Minnesota Press.

Baumann, Max Peter. 1989. "The Musical Performing Group: Musical Norms, Tradition, and Identity." *The World of Music* 31(2):80–110.

Becker, Howard. 1982. *Art Worlds.* Berkeley: University of California Press.

Becker, Judith. 1986. "Is Western Art Music Superior?" *Musical Quarterly* 72(3):341–359.

Béhague, Gerard, ed. 1984. *Performance Practice: Ethnomusicological Perspectives.* Westport, Conn.: Greenwood Press.

Blacking, John. 1973. *How Musical Is Man?* Seattle: University of Washington Press.

———. 1987. *A Commonsense View of All Music: Reflections on Percy Grainger's Contribution to Ethnomusicology and Music Education.* Cambridge: Cambridge University Press.

Blaukopf, Kurt. 1972. "Musical Institution in a Changing World." *International Review of Music Aesthetics & Sociology* 1(1):35–54.

———. 1982. *Musik im Wandel der Gesellschaft.* Munich: R. Piper.

Blum, Stephen. 1975. "Towards a Social History of Ethnomusicological Technique." *Ethnomusicology* 19(2):207–232.

Blum, Stephen, Philip V. Bohlman, and Daniel M. Neuman, eds. 1990. *Ethnomusicology and Modern Music History.* Urbana: University of Illinois Press.

Bohlman, Philip V. 1988. *The Study of Folk Music in the Modern World.* Bloomington: Indiana University Press.

———. 1992. "Europe." In *Excursions in World Music,* ed. Bruno Nettl, Charles Capwell, Philip V. Bohlman, Isabel K. F. Wong, and Thomas Turino, 196–231. Englewood Cliffs, N.J.: Prentice Hall.

Bourdieu, Pierre. 1984. *Distinctions: A Social Critique of the Judgment of Taste.* Cambridge: Harvard University Press.

Brook, Barry S., Edward O. Downes, and Sherman Van Solkema, eds. 1972. *Perspectives in Musicology.* New York: Norton.

Caesar, Wendy. 1975. "'Asking a Mouse Who His Favourite Cat Is': Musicians' Stories about Conductors." *Western Folklore* 34(2):83–116.

Cameron, Catherine. 1982. "Dialectics in the Arts: Composer Ideology and Culture Change." Ph.D. dissertation, University of Illinois at Urbana-Champaign.

———. 1984. "Fighting with Words: American Composers' Commentary on their Work." *Comparative Study of Society and History* 27(3):430–460.

Canetti, Elias. 1962 [1960]. *Crowds and Power.* Translated from the German by Carol Stewart. New York: Viking Press.

Dahlhaus, Carl. 1977. *Grundlagen der Musikgeschichte.* Cologne: Hans Gerig.

———. 1989. *The Idea of Absolute Music.* Translated by Roger Lustig. Chicago: University of Chicago Press.

Feld, Steven. 1982. *Sound and Sentiment.* Philadelphia: University of Pennsylvania Press.

———. 1984. "Sound Structure as Social Structure." *Ethnomusicology* 28(3):383–410.

Finnegan, Ruth. 1988. *The Hidden Musicians.* Cambridge: Cambridge University Press.

Grout, Donald Jay. 1960. *A History of Western Music.* New York: Norton.

Harrison, Frank L. 1973. *Time, Place, and Music.* Amsterdam: F. Knuf.

Isherwood, Robert. 1978. "Popular Entertainment in Eighteenth-Century Paris." *International Review of Music Aesthetics & Sociology* 9(2):295–310.

Jones, Micheal Owen. 1971. "The Concept of Aesthetic in the Traditional Arts." *Western Folklore* 30(2):77–104.

Kaemmer, John. 1989. "Between the Event and the Tradition: A New Look at Music in Socio-Cultural Systems." *Ethnomusicology* 24(1):61–74.

Kavolis, V. 1968. *Artistic Expression: A Sociological Analysis.* Cornell University Press.

Keil, Charles, and Angeliki. 1966. "Musical Meaning: A Preliminary Report." *Ethnomusicology* 10:153–173.

Kerman, Joseph. 1985. *Contemplating Music: Challenges to Musicology.* Cambridge: Harvard University Press.

———. 1980. "How We Got into Analysis and How to Get out." *Critical Inquiry* 7(2):311–331.

Kingsbury, Henry. 1988. *Music, Talent, and Performance: A Conservatory Cultural System.* Philadelphia: Temple University Press.

———. 1991. "Sociological Factors in Musicological Poetics." *Ethnomusicology* 35:195–220.

Knepler, Georg. 1982. *Geschichte als Weg zum Musikverständnis.* 2d ed. Leipzig: Reclam.

Leppert, Richard. 1988. *Music and Image.* Cambridge: Cambridge University Press.

Levine, Lawrence W. 1988. *Highbrow/Lowbrow: The Emergence of Cultural Hierarchy in America.* Cambridge: Harvard University Press.

Lissa, Zofia. 1970. "Prolegomena to the Theory of Musical Tradition." *International Review of Music Aesthetics & Sociology* 1(1):35–54.

———. 1973. "Historical Awareness of Music and Its Role in Present-Day Culture." *International Review of Music Aesthetics & Sociology* 4(1):17–34.

Lomax, Alan, and others. 1968. *Folk Song Style and Culture.* Washington: American Association for the Advancement of Science.

McClary, Susan. 1991. *Feminine Endings: Music, Gender, and Sexuality.* Minneapolis: University of Minnesota Press.

McClary, Susan, and Richard Leppert, eds. 1987. *Music and Society: The Politics of Composition, Performance, and Reception.* Minneapolis: University of Minnesota Press.

Malm, William P. 1985. "On the Nature and Function of Symbolism in Western and Oriental Music." *Philosophy East and West* 19(3):235–246.

Manuel, Peter. 1988. *Popular Musics of the Non-Western World.* New York: Oxford University Press.

Martorella, Rosanne. 1975. "The Structure of Market and Market Style." *International Review of Music Aesthetics & Sociology* 6(2):241–254.

Mendoza de Arce, Daniel. 1981. "On Some of the Sociocultural Factors Affecting the General Characteristics of the Western Musical Styles during the Low Middle Ages." *International Review of Music Aesthetics & Sociology* 12(1):51–63.

Meyer, Leonard B. 1967. *Music, the Arts, and Ideas: Patterns and Predictions in Twentieth-Century Culture.* Chicago: University of Chicago Press.

———. 1982. "Innovation, Choice, and the History of Music." *Critical Inquiry* 9(3):517–544.

Nettl, Bruno. 1963. "A Technique of Ethnomusicology Applied to Western Culture." *Ethnomusicology* 7:221–224.

———. 1983. *The Study of Ethnomusicology.* Urbana: University of Illinois Press.

———. 1985. *The Western Impact on World Music.* New York: Schirmer Books.

———. 1989. "Mozart and the Ethnomusicological Study of Western Culture." *Yearbook for Traditional Music* 21:1–16.

Norton, Richard. 1984. *Tonality in Western Culture.* College Station: Pennsylvania State University Press.

Porter, James. 1984. "Work of Art, Art as Work, and the Arts of Working." *Western Folklore* 43(3):172–210.

———. 1993. "Verdi's *Attila*: An Ethnomusicological Analysis." In *Attila: The Man and His Image*, ed. Franz H. Bäuml and Marianna D. Birnbaum. Budapest: Corvina.

Powers, Harold S. 1979. "Classical Music, Culture Roots, and Colonial Rule: An Indic Musicologist Looks at the Muslim World." *Asian Music* 12(1):86–128.

Qureshi, Regula. 1987. "Music, Sound, and Social Contextual Input: A Performance Model for Musical Analysis." *Ethnomusicology* 31(1):56–86.

Rahn, Jay. 1983. *A Theory for All Music: Problems and Solutions in the Analysis of Non-Western Forms.* Toronto: University of Toronto Press.

Roseman, Marina. 1984. "The Social Structuring of Sound: The Temiar of Peninsular Malaysia." *Ethnomusicology* 28(3):411–445.

Sachs, Curt. 1948. *Our Musical Heritage.* New York: Prentice-Hall.

Schneider, Albrecht. 1984. *Analogie und Rekonstruktion: Studien zur Methodologie der*

Musikgeschichtsschreibung und zur Frühgeschichte der Musik. Vol. 1. Bonn: Verlag für systematische Musikwissenschaft.

Seeger, Charles. 1957. "Music and Class Structure in the United States." *American Quarterly* 9(3):281–294.

———. 1977. *Studies in Musicology, 1935–1975.* Berkeley: University of California Press.

Shepherd, John. 1976. "Serious Music: An A-Social Phenomenon?" *Contact* 14:3–1.

———. 1979. "Music & Social Control: An Essay on the Sociology of Musical Knowledge." *Catalyst* 13:1–54.

Small, Christopher. 1977. *Music, Society, Education.* London: John Calder.

———. 1987. "Performance as Ritual: Sketch for an Enquiry into the Nature of a Symphony Concert." In *Lost in Music: Culture, Style, and the Musical Event,* ed. Avron Levine White, 6–23. London: Routledge & Kegan Paul.

Spitzer, John. 1987. "Musical Attribution and Critical Judgment: The Rise and Fall of the Sinfonia Concertante for Winds, K. 297b." *Journal of Musicology* 5:319–355.

Stiperic, Erino. 1987. "The Social and Historical Status of Music and Musicians in Croatia in the Early Baroque Period." *International Review of Music Aesthetics & Sociology* 18(1):3–17.

Subotnik, Rose Rosengard. 1977. "The Cultural Message of Musical Semiology: Some Thoughts on Music, Language, and Criticism since the Enlightenment." *Critical Inquiry* 4(4):741–768.

———. 1979. "Tonality, Autonomy, and Competence in Post-Classical Music." *Critical Inquiry* 6(1):153–163.

Sudnow, David. 1978. *Ways of the Hand: The Organization of Improvised Conduct.* New York: Bantam.

Supicic, Ivo. 1982. "Music and Ceremony: Another Aspect." *International Review of Music Aesthetics & Sociology* 13(1):21–38.

Taruskin, Richard. 1988. "The Pastness of the Present." In *Authenticity and Early Music,* ed. Nicholas Kenyon, 137–207. London: Oxford University Press.

Tick, Judith. 1973. "Musician and Mécène: Some Observations on Patronage in Late 18th-Century France." *International Review of Music Aesthetics & Sociology* 4(2):245–256.

Virdan, Phil. 1977. "Some Observations on the Social Stratification of 20thC Music." In *Whose Music,* ed. John Shepherd, 155–166. London: Latimer.

Weber, William. 1977. "Mass Culture and the Reshaping of European Musical Taste, 1770–1870." *International Review of Music Aesthetics & Sociology* 8(1):5–22.

Wiora, Walter. 1965. *The Four Ages of Music.* New York: Norton.

———. 1983. *Das musikalische Kunstwerk.* Tutzing: Hans Schneider.

Wörner, Karl Heinrich. 1973. *History of Music: A Book for Study and Reference.* New York: Free Press.

Zolberg, Vera. 1980. "Displayed Act & Performed Music: Selective Innovation and the Structure of Artistic Media." *Sociological Quarterly* 21:219–231.

History of European Art Music
David Schulenberg

Medieval Music
Music in the Renaissance
Baroque Music
Classical and Romantic Music
Twentieth-Century Developments

The expression *European art music* is often applied to the music of the modern Western European concert-music tradition and its historical predecessors. Parallel terms include *Western music* and *classical music*. Some would restrict use of the term *art* to music composed only after the emergence in the nineteenth century of philosophies that understood music and other arts as objects valued for their own sakes, without respect for their real or perceived social or economic functions; however, evidence for an aesthetic appreciation of music can be found at earlier stages of Western music history, and it is arguable that certain fundamental functions of elite Western musics have remained constant since the Middle Ages.

This tradition is distinguished above all by its notation, which has permitted the preservation of music from as far back as the 800s. Diverse styles and genres have been preserved and remain in use. Particularly characteristic has been the use of polyphony, typical of European art music since the later Middle Ages. In addition, musicians in this tradition have typically been aware of foreign and past traditions transmitted orally and in writing, through notation and literary (historical and theoretical) works.

Technical features common to most Western art music include elaborate, hierarchically organized rhythmic and tonal structures and, since the tenth or eleventh century, systems of polyphony organized with equal complexity and regularity. These features have made possible the development of various musical forms, examples of which range in duration from half a minute to several hours. The early use of notation encouraged the development of a literate music culture and a dependence on fixed, unchanging musical texts; nevertheless, the performing traditions of most art-music repertories have included a substantial improvisatory element. Only in the 1800s, with the advent of precisely notated music for large ensembles, did the improvisatory tradition weaken. It was revived in certain genres in the twentieth century.

Though an elite tradition, Western art music cannot be uniquely associated with any particular economic or social class. Even within a given demographic group— whether the aristocracy of fifteenth-century France or the haute bourgeoisie of nine-teenth-century Germany and Austria—those practicing and patronizing art music have usually constituted a small minority of the population. The production of art music has tended to be concentrated in a few politically and economically important geographic centers. Hence, the history of Western art music is generally understood as consisting of innovations made within a limited number of cultural centers and spreading to geographically peripheral regions. France was of central importance during the Middle Ages (roughly 800–1450), followed by northern Italy in the Renaissance (1450–1600) and Baroque (1450–1700) and German-speaking Europe through the early twentieth century. In recent decades, musicians of the Americas, Asia, and Africa have joined those of Europe in playing important roles in the tradition.

Until the 1800s, the most frequent use of art music was probably in religious rituals. Religious institutions, particularly those of the Roman Catholic Church, have been prime patrons and users of art music. Through much of the history of the tradition, genres have been clearly distinguished as sacred or secular, though this distinction has not always held true for musical styles and techniques. Since the late 1700s, it has been customary to regard certain genres as distinctly religious in affect or mood, but this custom was not always true in earlier periods, when the same music might be employed for sacred and secular purposes.

MEDIEVAL MUSIC

The Western art-music tradition can be traced back to the Carolingian period (ninth century), when the earliest surviving Western musical notation was created and a corpus of theoretical writings took shape, chiefly in certain monasteries in what is now France. Important elements of the tradition derive from ancient Greece. These include the concept of the gamut or scale and the mathematical determination of available pitches, the ideas of mode and modal ethos (the relationship of affect to pitch structure), and notation. The organ, an instrument central to the Western tradition, is an ancient Greek invention, and most other instruments have ancient Greek analogs. Ancient Greek music remains imperfectly understood, despite the survival of notated fragments. That there was any continuity between the tradition represented by these fragments and later Western music is doubtful; nevertheless, a digest of ancient Greek writings on music prepared by the Roman writer Boethius (ca. 480–524) formed the basis of medieval musical thought. The convergence of this intellectual tradition with local musical practices can be considered the origin of Western art music. Local practices included those of the churches of early medieval Rome and pre-Carolingian France.

The establishment of a distinctive Western European tradition stems from the attempt by the emperor Charlemagne (742–814) to impose a uniform system of religious rituals throughout his realm, which included much of present-day France, Germany, and northern Italy. As in earlier Jewish and Christian worship, these rituals included chanted (sung) readings from the Bible and other fixed texts. Charlemagne intended the musical components of these rituals to follow the practice of Rome; actual practice, however, appears to have mixed Roman and northern traditions, and local variants had already been documented by the time of the earliest surviving notated sources, about a century later. Whether Carolingian chant was first transmitted orally or in writing remains controversial. Subsequent church musicians shared the concept of a fixed, historically authorized musical tradition and repertory conventionally, though wrongly, attributed to Pope Gregory the Great (reigned 590–604).

Gregorian chant

Gregorian chant is a repertory of several thousand melodies bearing Latin texts. Most of the melodies are intended for use in specified services on particular days of the church year. The repertory includes solo and choral items, each divided into various categories. Distinct to each category of chant is the degree of musical complexity, which may range from syllabic recitation on a single pitch to florid melismatic singing.

The concept of liturgical specificity for each musical item—each chant belongs to a genre defined by its liturgical function and is intended for a given day and service—has its origin in earlier practices at Rome and elsewhere. A few chant melodies have tentatively been traced to Eastern (Jewish and Byzantine) sources. The earliest Western notation gives only a rough outline of the pitch structure of each melody, and even the fully developed chant notations of the eleventh century and later leave rhythm, timbre, and other musical parameters largely indeterminate while sometimes including signs for ornaments and other elements whose nature remains uncertain.

The late Middle Ages saw a huge expansion of the melodic repertory of religious chant. Entirely new genres of chant, such as the sequence, were created, and perhaps thousands of new melodies (with new Latin texts) were compiled or composed. Composers responsible for the earlier chant repertory are mostly anonymous, but later additions to the repertory are often ascribed to individuals, among them the abbot Notker Balbulus (ca. 840–912), associated with the early sequence, and the abbess Hildegard of Bingen (1098–1179), one of the few women credited with significant compositions before 1600. In addition to such authors' liturgical or paraliturgical compositions, there is a substantial medieval repertory of Latin-texted songs, apparently composed by students or clerics for recreation or devotion.

The central Gregorian repertory was shared in principle by the members of each religious community, for whom its performance probably remained the most widespread musical activity through the Middle Ages. Teaching the rudiments of music was therefore an important element in medieval education, and a select few in certain institutions must have served as specialists in singing and teaching chant. With the development of notation, their activities would have included the composition and writing down of new chants alongside the copying of traditional ones (figure 1).

Music had been codified in late antiquity as a liberal art, constituting part of the quadrivium, alongside arithmetic, geometry, and astronomy, and as such it became the basis of many medieval treatises. At first designed as pragmatic guides to liturgical performance, these developed into a body of theoretical writings, whose tradition extends through the Renaissance to the present. Written for use at certain religious institutions and in the universities that emerged from them in the late Middle Ages, this literature provides, with notated music, our principal source for musical practice during the late Middle Ages and the Renaissance.

Medieval polyphony

An element of religious music first documented from the 800s or early 900s was polyphony, the intentional singing of distinct pitches simultaneously. Emphasized in modern music-history textbooks because of its later significance, polyphony was rare before the 1500s. Reserved for special sacred and secular occasions, it was largely restricted to soloists until the 1500s or later. It probably began as a form of improvised embellishment to the solo portions of certain chants. Treatises from around 900 describe several kinds of polyphonic singing, and repertories of written polyphony survive from the late tenth century on. The earliest examples are preserved, as with chant, in a highly indeterminate form of notation. More precisely decipherable are substantial twelfth-century repertories associated with southern France (Aquitaine) and the cathedral of Notre Dame in Paris. The latter was the source of a large collec-

FIGURE 1 *Coronation of the Virgin* (dated about 1420), by Gentile da Fabriano (Italy, ca. 1370–1427). In tempera and gold leaf on a wooden panel (87.5 × 64 centimeters), it depicts the use of musical notation for the singing of Gregorian chant. Photo courtesy of The J. Paul Getty Museum, Los Angeles.

tion of notated polyphony that remained in circulation through the 1200s, attributed by a later writer to two musicians: Leonin, who flourished in the late twelfth century, and Perotin, whose career possibly continued into the next century.

Early polyphony, called organum, consists of one or more newly composed melodic lines sung against an older chant. The combining of one line with another constitutes the technique known as counterpoint, which became fundamental to most later Western polyphony. By the late twelfth century, two types of counterpoint are evident, often used in alternation within a single musical item: note-against-note counterpoint, in which all voices move in approximately the same rhythmic style; and a more florid type, in which each note of the underlying chant is sustained while one or more added voices move in a more elaborate, sometimes highly embellished manner. Today, the latter is sometimes described as "free" organum, and *clausula, discantus,* and *conductus* are among the names for compositions of the former type. The earliest notated organa are for two voices, but later examples, including those associated with Perotin, are for three or occasionally four voices.

In such polyphony, the separate melodic lines repeatedly formed perfect consonances, defined in contemporary treatises as unisons, fourths, fifths, and octaves. Dissonant intervals may occur, but rarely at metrically stressed points. This type of structure favored regular metrical rhythm, and by 1200 or so, the notation of polyphony was including a durational element dependent on the use of regular meter. Unambiguous rhythmic notation was necessary for insuring that performers would properly coordinate the polyphonic lines, composed according to contrapuntal rules formulated by contemporary theorists, who described not only the conventions governing the use of consonance and dissonance, but also the increasingly precise forms of rhythmic notation.

Organum was employed, at first, only on particularly solemn liturgical occasions, and its practitioners must have been specially trained, hence present only at unusually wealthy or powerful institutions. During the later Middle Ages, polyphony and other forms of art music spread from monastic centers and became associated with the courts and private chapels of certain secular rulers.

An especially important late-medieval polyphonic genre, the motet, developed in thirteenth-century France. During the next two centuries, it spread to England, Italy, and elsewhere. Like certain early types of sequence, it originally involved the addition of new words to an existing melody; in this case, however, the melody had been composed as counterpoint to a preexisting chant. As a result, a motet usually contains at least two simultaneously sung texts, and other voices, each with its own text, could be added, not necessarily at the same time or by the same musician.

The earliest such compositions are often short, and the music of some can be identified with that of older *clausulae* or *conductus.* Later motets are longer; the last works in this tradition, dating from the early 1400s, employ isorhythm, a complex, highly structured type of rhythmic organization. They embody a shift in rhythmic theory and notation that took place around 1320, resulting in the so-called *ars nova* 'new art'—a term derived from the titles of two fourteenth-century treatises and now associated with French polyphony of the fourteenth century, especially motets and secular songs.

Unlike most earlier polyphony, many isorhythmic motets are attributed to individual composers and were composed for specific occasions. Guillaume Dufay's *Nuper rosarum flores* was composed for and presumably performed during the consecration of the cathedral of Florence, in 1436. In many motets, the presence of vernacular texts with secular, even erotic, subjects points to their use outside of religious ritual, though most retain an underlying chant melody. The attraction of this music must have been limited to a minority consisting primarily of highly educated clerics.

After 1500 the development of methods for printing music from movable type eased the dissemination of uniform musical texts and promoted a musical culture based on printed texts, paralleling the earlier development of a comparable literary culture.

The simultaneously sung texts would not have been intelligible to listeners, as the words often contain arcane literary and theological allusions.

Secular medieval monophony and polyphony

The earliest preserved secular songs with texts in a vernacular language began around 1100 in the form of poetry composed and perhaps sung by French nobles. The southern representatives of this tradition are known as troubadours, and their activity ended by about 1300. The northern representatives are called trouvères, and their tradition extends to the end of the Middle Ages, when it was taken over by nonaristocratic professionals, such as Guillaume de Machaut (ca. 1300–1377), the leading French poet and leading French musician of his time.

The musical component of the earliest vernacular medieval songs was monophonic. The poetry evolved into distinct, highly regulated formal designs, the so-called *formes fixes,* reflected in the musical forms. As with chant, the melodies were at first transmitted orally, producing substantial variants among versions of the same song. The performance traditions of this repertory are unclear; rhythm is often imprecisely notated, as in early chant, and it is uncertain whether instruments accompanied these or any other medieval songs. Literary evidence suggests that much of the repertory would have been sung—perhaps by professional court entertainers (*jongleurs*), rather than by the composers—at social gatherings, such as banquets.

The traditions of courtly song and learned polyphony merged in the late thirteenth and fourteenth centuries, above all in the works of Machaut, who composed motets with French and Latin texts and monophonic and polyphonic songs in *formes fixes* (figure 2). Related genres of secular polyphonic song are preserved from late medieval England, Germany, and especially Italy, where the blind organist Francesco Landini (ca. 1325–1397) was an important composer of polyphonic songs. Machaut, though a cleric, worked for the kings of France and Bohemia; whereas Landini and

FIGURE 2 The opening (the first text line) of Guillaume de Machaut's polyphonic setting of a ballade, one of the *formes fixes* popular in the courts of the thirteenth and fourteenth centuries. A ballade is an eight-line poetic form that employs the same rhymes in each stanza: ababccbR, in which R is a refrain. The musical form is AAB. To the monophonic song (*cantus*) with French text, the composer added a higher-pitched *triplum* and a lower-pitched tenor and sometimes contratenor, parts played by musical instruments. As indicated here, the notations were not in score form; rather, each part was notated separately. Transnotation by Timothy Rice from a photocopy of manuscript A.M.5.24, in the Biblioteca Estense, Modena, Italy. Courtesy of the UCLA Music Library.

other Italians worked for rulers of the emerging north Italian city-states, but compositions of both must have been intended for sophisticated aristocratic audiences. French and Italian polyphonic songs from the following two generations included increasingly complex types of rhythmic and melodic embellishment, leading to a style sometimes called the *ars subtilior* 'subtler art'.

Improvisation versus composition

An important development of the late Middle Ages was the emergence of the modern view of art music as a repertory of notationally fixed compositions attributed to distinct individuals. During the same period or slightly later, the distinction between improvisation and composition became increasingly clear, probably as growing numbers of performers came to depend on musical notation. Improvisation remained vitally important; traditions of improvised polyphony, sometimes in several parts, continued through the 1500s in sacred and secular settings. These traditions included practices fundamental to Western music: the singing of psalms and hymns, liturgical keyboard (organ) playing, instrumental dance music, and the sung recitation of poetry. In addition, the improvisatory elaboration and embellishment of existing polyphonic compositions would continue to be an important element of performance for singers and instrumentalists through the early 1800s.

Nevertheless, from the late Middle Ages on, the art-music performers' role was increasingly that of interpreting, ornamenting, or otherwise recreating notated compositions. Accordingly, composers came to occupy a central place in the tradition, and after 1500 or so they were routinely distinguished from other musicians, though they were not necessarily more highly valued. From this condition derives the customary modern view of art-music performance as the performance of notated musical compositions or works and a corresponding view of music history as primarily a history of compositional style and technique.

MUSIC IN THE RENAISSANCE

Guillaume Dufay (ca. 1400–1474) is usually regarded as one of the first major composers of the Renaissance. Application of the latter term to art-music history, though now customary, is problematical, since the period saw no "rebirth" of ancient Greek and Roman musical learning comparable to that witnessed in other disciplines, but significant changes in the techniques of musical composition and the social functions of art music are discernible during the 1400s and 1500s. Sociologically the most important development was the expansion in the number of environments in which art music was cultivated and, correspondingly, in the number of patrons and practitioners. Both latter groups increasingly included the bourgeoisie, especially in cities of northern Italy, northern France, and the Netherlands.

Particularly indicative of this trend shortly after 1500 was the development of methods for printing music from movable type. Though the transmission of music in manuscript remained important through the 1700s, printed music became an important industry. It eased the dissemination of uniform musical texts and promoted a musical culture based on printed texts, paralleling the earlier development of a comparable literary culture.

Despite the explosive growth of the Italian cities in wealth and power during the early Renaissance, the first few generations of Renaissance composers came primarily from northern France and the Netherlands. These composers included Dufay and his younger contemporaries Johannes Ockeghem (ca. 1425–1497) and Josquin des Prez (ca. 1440–1521). Dufay and Josquin spent important parts of their careers in Italy, as did sixteenth-century northern composers such as Orlando di Lasso (Rolande de

FIGURE 3   A nineteenth-century painting by Gustave-Clarence-Rodolphe Boulanger (1824–1888) portrays Giovanni Pierluigi da Palestrina at the organ, accompanying singers of his polyphonic music. Interest in history and the history of music was a hallmark of the nineteenth century, and fanciful paintings such as this reflect that interest. Photo courtesy of French and Company.

Lassus, ca. 1532–1594). Italian composers came into their own in the 1500s, when they emerged as the dominant group; the most influential, at least in sacred music, was Giovanni Pierluigi da Palestrina (ca. 1525–1594), who worked in Rome (figure 3).

By the late 1500s, polyphonic singing had become the norm at major services in most Western European churches and at musical entertainments at court or for private patrons. Singing was usually accompanied by instruments, such as the organ and other keyboard instruments, the lute, and various wind and stringed instruments, which often played in groups or consorts. Musical literacy was no longer confined to a narrow group of clerics, but had become a social requirement for members of the aristocracy and the bourgeoisie. Contemporary writings indicate the widespread practice of amateurs' after-dinner singing and playing of polyphonic music, presupposing the ability to sight-read complex musical compositions.

Perhaps the critical historical event of the sixteenth century was the Protestant Reformation, which, beginning in 1517, led to the splitting of Western Christianity into Protestant denominations in much of Northern Europe and the Roman Catholic Church in much of the south. The northern regions experienced the suppression of Roman Catholic services, including their music, and the substitution of new rites. In Germany, Martin Luther (1483–1546) and his followers created chorales, liturgical songs with vernacular texts in mostly syllabic settings. These served much as Gregorian chant in the Roman Catholic Church and became in turn the basis of various forms of polyphony.

The Roman Catholic response to the Protestant Reformation, known as the Counter-Reformation, resulted in a preference during the late 1500s for sacred music that featured the direct, comprehensible presentation of texts, as opposed to the elaborate technical feats of earlier medieval and Renaissance polyphony. This development reflected a trend evident in secular vocal music of the period. Under the influence of ancient Greek views on the expressive power of music, Renaissance humanist writers developed a concept now known as musical rhetoric. In this view, polyphonic vocal music was valued insofar as it uniquely and ingeniously reflected the syntax and the meaning of its verbal text. A musical setting and its performance were seen as parallels to the composition and public presentation of a poem or an oration, employing all the arts of verbal rhetoric.

In addition to producing new genres of vocal music, the Renaissance saw the first substantial repertories of instrumental composition, including works for solo instruments (chiefly organ and lute) and consorts (ensembles) of winds and strings. This development presupposed that instrumentalists, previously relegated to playing improvised dance music and the like, had acquired musical literacy and other training in the practice of art music. Amateurs and professionals cultivated certain instruments, notably the lute and the viola da gamba. Organists became a distinct class of professional musicians, often employed for secular purposes and as composers and players of other keyboard instruments, such as the harpsichord. Other professional instrumentalists organized themselves into guilds, raising their social status and becoming members of permanent church and court ensembles. During the same period, the manufacture of musical instruments developed into an important industry. Only from about 1500 and after do instruments survive in significant numbers, and their performance practices can be reconstructed with some precision. Most instruments in general use today can be traced to sixteenth-century antecedents.

Renaissance genres

Despite the influence of the Counter-Reformation, much music from the Renaissance and the following, Baroque period reflects an interest among professional musicians and their patrons in sophisticated techniques of composing and performing. An important development of the early Renaissance was the polyphonic Mass cycle, a musical setting of specified portions of the Latin liturgy, united by the use of a particular compositional device. Cyclic masses by Dufay, Josquin, Lasso, Palestrina, and others are most often unified by the reworking, in each movement, of music from the same melody or polyphonic composition. Though some such works, like much medieval polyphony, were based on Gregorian chant, others had secular sources. Several composers based masses on the same popular tune or composition, showing an interest in competitive emulation.

The Renaissance motet is a second major category of sacred vocal music. Cultivated by all the above-named composers, it differs from the medieval motet in usually employing a single text and sharing many compositional techniques with the cyclic Mass. Both Mass and motet exemplify the most important Renaissance contrapuntal innovation, tending toward equality and homogeneity of the vocal parts, which typically number from three to six. (Medieval counterpoint stratified the voices into distinct rhythmic and melodic types.) Renaissance polyphony was increasingly structured around sonorous harmonies of three pitches (triads) that form two imperfect consonances. Renaissance composers made wide use of imitation, whereby a melodic idea introduced by one voice is sung in turn by the others. Perfected by Josquin, imitation was employed in countless ways by subsequent composers. It served as a fundamental element of compositional technique and a major focus of interest for performers and listeners through the eighteenth century.

Though placing high value on such compositional craft, sixteenth-century commentators increasingly favored the rhetorical presentation of sacred texts; the motets of Josquin and Lasso were particularly praised in this regard. Additionally, the 1500s saw the rise of various genres of secular song whose primary function was the highly rhetorical setting of vernacular poetry. The most important genre of secular polyphony was probably the Italian madrigal, which emerged in the 1520s; there were also distinct types of French, German, and Spanish polyphonic songs. The Flemish com-

The term *baroque* in its literal sense ('lavish, highly ornamented') is particularly appropriate for productions that employed poets to write sung verses, costume designers to produce fanciful garments inspired by Greek and Roman antiquity, and artists and engineers to design theaters, sets, lighting, and special effects.

poser Adrian Willaert (1490–1562), working in Venice, applied to madrigals the contrapuntal techniques of masses and motets. Later composers, beginning with Willaert's student Cipriano de Rore (1516–1565), increasingly focused on means of representing the sense of specific words through distinctive harmonic and melodic ideas. This practice, known as text painting or word painting, remained central to vocal composition through the Baroque. Most such works are in principle purely vocal. In practice, instruments were increasingly substituted for one or more of the vocal parts. By 1600, William Byrd (1543–1623) and other English composers were writing polyphonic songs that included specific instrumental parts; songs for voice and lute were also composed by John Dowland (1562–1626) in England and on the continent. Byrd and Dowland were important composers of solo music for their own instruments—keyboard and lute, respectively.

Dance music for instrumental ensemble, though occasionally written down during the late Middle Ages, first became an important category of composition in the 1500s. The steps and patterns of the dances are known from various sources, but detailed choreographies are extremely rare before the 1700s; by then, the repertory of dances had changed drastically.

BAROQUE MUSIC

The period from about 1600 to 1750 is usually termed the Baroque, though the music-historical use of this term, like the term *Renaissance,* is sometimes questioned. The 1600s saw the continued use of many Renaissance genres, but these underwent sometimes radical changes in performance and composition. In the early Baroque, the Mass, the motet, and the madrigal tended away from the Renaissance emphasis on elaborate counterpoint toward simplified musical textures, sometimes employing but a single voice with instrumental accompaniment. The solo virtuoso singer or instrumentalist is the most characteristic element of Baroque music; many genres were invented or transformed to accommodate this trend. Impetus for this development came in part from popular fascination with public performance by virtuosos and in part from the continuing emphasis on musical rhetoric; solo singing came to be viewed as particularly effective for the vivid or expressive presentation of a verbal text.

Another fundamental development of Baroque music is the compositional integration of instruments with voices. From 1600 on, nearly every vocal composition included specified instrumental parts, and the ability to write idiomatically for the major instruments became a basic skill demanded of all composers, rather than a preoccupation of specialists. Particularly characteristic of Baroque ensemble music is the presence of a partially improvised part played by one or several instrumentalists, reading from a specially notated part known as the *basso continuo.* Members of the continuo group can include keyboard, plucked stringed instruments, low bowed strings, and winds.

Despite these changes, some Baroque musicians retained a sense of connection with the past, continuing to cultivate genres and in some cases perform compositions dating from the 1500s; hence, while espousing the most up-to-date musical developments, major figures, such as the Italian Claudio Monteverdi (1567–1643) and the Germans Heinrich Schütz (1585–1672) and Johann Sebastian Bach (1685–1750), also composed deliberately archaic works exemplifying practices of the past. Among these works are motets and masses that imitate sixteenth-century style.

The term *baroque* in its literal sense ('lavish, highly ornamented') is particularly appropriate for productions that, though documented from before the 1500s, were especially cultivated after 1600. Particularly at major courts and religious institutions, special occasions—festive masses, dynastic marriages, and other celebrations—might be marked by elaborate ceremonial or theatrical productions involving large numbers of musicians. Such events employed poets to write sung verses, costume designers to produce fanciful garments inspired by Greek and Roman antiquity, and artists and engineers to design theaters, sets, lighting, and special effects.

Though at first limited to occasional productions—in particular, musical interludes (*intermedi*) inserted into plays—these multimedia events were institutionalized around 1600 in the new genres of opera and oratorio. Particularly influential was Monteverdi's opera *L'Orfeo* (Orpheus, 1607). By the 1640s, permanent opera theaters offering regular performances existed in Venice. By the early 1700s, other major cities had followed suit. Some opera theaters, including those in Venice, Hamburg, and London, were privately owned commercial ventures; those in Paris, Vienna, and other monarchical seats were under governmental control and patronage.

Operas and related forms were often designed to display their sponsors' wealth and power. This purpose was particularly evident in France, where under King Louis XIV the composer Jean-Baptiste Lully (1632–1687) composed and produced operas and ballets for the court. Lully's works embodied a French manner distinct in compositional style and performance practice from the Italian. For subsequent generations, the French and Italian styles represented opposed versions of Baroque style; composers in Germany and other outlying regions selected from or combined the two. Particularly notable in the so-called Lullian style was the influence of dance rhythms (derived from the French court ballet) and the preference for precisely articulated vocal and instrumental performance over soloistic virtuosity.

Elsewhere, the advent of opera and related vocal genres paralleled a rise of virtuoso solo singers of secular music. Solo singers had emerged as an important professional category at late-sixteenth-century Italian courts. Among virtuoso performers were women, who appeared for the first time as professional musicians. Women—notably the Venetian Barbara Strozzi (1619–after 1677) and the Parisian Elizabeth Jacquet de La Guerre (1665–1729)—also figure in the Baroque for the first time as significant composers of polyphonic music. Outstanding among professional singers were *castrati,* men castrated at an early age to permit the retention of their high-pitched voices. Probably derived from Eastern practices, the custom spread during the 1600s from Italian sacred music to Italian opera. Except in France, where the practice never took hold, by the late 1600s and throughout the 1700s the exploits of ancient mythical gods and historical heroes—the usual subjects of opera—were most often represented by the virtuoso singing of high male voices. Women occasionally substituted for *castrati,* as they usually do in modern revivals of this music.

Baroque genres

Many Baroque genres were designed to serve as vehicles for virtuoso solo perfor-

From the 1500s to about 1800 choir schools and other church-related institutions continued to serve as principal sources of musical training. But by about 1800, the forerunners of the modern music school or conservatory had appeared in several Italian cities.

FIGURE 4 The opening measures of Arcangelo Corelli's Sonata op. 5, no. 1. Composed by the performer for his own use, the notation contains only a skeleton of what the performers would have played. To some of the quarter notes and half notes, the violinist would have added many grace notes, trills, turns, and more elaborate melodic figures, and the player of the keyboard (*cembalo*) would have added chords and rhythmic fills to the notated part played by the violoncello.

mance. Particularly important were the instrumental sonata and concerto and the vocal recitative and aria. The sonata, conceived in Italy around 1600 as an instrumental interlude during Roman Catholic devotional services, had spread throughout Western Europe by 1700. It became the principal instrumental genre, important for professional display and amateur music making by middle- and upper-class performers.

Sonatas called for one, two, or more instruments, plus continuo. At first chiefly for violins, sonatas were being written for most other instruments by the early eighteenth century. Many sonatas, such as those of the violinists Biagio Marini (ca. 1597–1665) and Arcangelo Corelli (1653–1713) in Italy, Heinrich Biber (1644–1704) in Germany, and Jean-Marie Leclair (1697–1764) in France, were composed by performers who presumably intended them for their own use in church or at court (figure 4). Sonatas for larger numbers of instruments evolved around 1700 into the concerto, which, by the 1720s, was most often a composition in which passages for a large group of instruments alternate with those for a virtuoso soloist, as in the works of the Venetian violinist Antonio Vivaldi (1678–1741).

Virtuosos of keyboard and plucked stringed instruments, including organ, harpsichord, lute, and harp, similarly composed works in various genres for their own soloistic display and teaching their students. Particularly in France, Germany, and the Netherlands, municipalities lavished considerable expenditures and craft on organs in major churches. The Renaissance tradition of performing and composing for these and other keyboard instruments continued in the Baroque, when player-composers such as the Italian Girolamo Frescobaldi (1583–1643) and the Germans Johann Jacob Froberger (1616–1667), Dietrich Buxtehude (ca. 1637–1707), and J. S. Bach created a substantial repertory of compositions, including toccatas and other virtuoso pieces in free form; in addition, fugues and other contrapuntal types, also composed for instrumental and vocal ensembles, continued the tradition of Renaissance imitative counterpoint.

Baroque vocal genres emphasized solo expressivity and virtuosity. Recitative, a form of dramatic musical declamation of poetry, probably derived from earlier improvisatory practices. It has played an important role in vocal music from about 1600 to the present, and is the major element in much early-Baroque vocal music, including the operas of Monteverdi and Lully; by 1700, however, it had been eclipsed by the aria as the principal vocal form, probably because the aria constituted a more effective vehicle for display by virtuoso singers. Late-Baroque operas and oratorios, such as those of the German composer George Frideric Handel (1685–1759), consist chiefly of elaborate arias linked by brief recitatives; the same is true of many of J. S. Bach's sacred vocal works, called cantatas. Though Handel's audiences in London theaters were probably more aristocratic than the bourgeois church congregations in Bach's Leipzig, both kinds of listener shared a view of musical rhetoric that upheld the aria as a supreme musical and poetic form, equivalent to a classical oration or dramatic monologue.

Middle- and upper-class amateurs in the Baroque imitated professional performance. Collections and arrangements of operatic arias were frequently copied in manuscript and published—implying use in homes. The sonata and other instrumental genres were also cultivated. Dance and dance-music constitute a further important area of activity. The same dances that received professional choreographies in the ballets of Lully and other French composers were studied by amateurs throughout Northern Europe, and dance-music became the basis of numerous suites, collections of pieces for solo keyboard, lute, and instrumental ensemble.

Renaissance and Baroque music education and theory

Music education and theory from the 1500s to about 1800 reflected the changes described above. Rudimentary training in musical notation, singing, and dance became a common element in upper- and, increasingly, middle-class education for men and women. For professionals, choir schools and other church-related institutions continued to serve as principal sources of musical training. By about 1800, the forerunners of the modern music school or conservatory had appeared in several Italian cities. Throughout the period, writings on music were published in increasing numbers, ranging from elementary instructional manuals to learned encyclopedic treatises encompassing all aspects of musical theory and practice.

An important technical development during this period was tonality, a system of tonal organization which, in its specifically Western form (known as common-practice tonality), replaced Renaissance modality in art music during 1600s. It was the principal structuring feature of Western art music from about 1650 to 1900, and it remains that of most Western popular music. It has made possible an increasingly varied array of elaborate, highly integrated musical forms, extending in duration to several hours.

CLASSICAL AND ROMANTIC MUSIC

The Baroque is usually viewed as having led in the mid-1700s to a so-called *galant* style, from which emerged many genres typical of the following period. Prominent composers included J. S. Bach's sons Carl Philipp Emanuel (1714–1788), important for his sonatas for solo keyboard instruments, and Johann Christian (1735–1787), who composed operas and symphonies. Both men's works influenced the three composers whom historians view as the chief representatives of the subsequent, Classical

Classical and Romantic music can be viewed as a single tradition, an important precondition of which was the emergence of professional public concerts, which encouraged the development of symphony orchestras.

style: Franz Josef Haydn (1732–1809), Wolfgang Amadeus Mozart (1756–1791), and Ludwig van Beethoven (1770–1827), all of whom worked primarily in Vienna.

The Classical style is regarded in turn as giving way to the Romantic, a period that lasted to about 1900; to some degree, however, the distinction between Classical and Romantic music rests more on convention than on a considered examination of music history in its broader cultural context. The Classical in music corresponds chronologically with Romantic styles in literature and the visual arts. The late works of Haydn and Mozart were regarded by some contemporaries as Romantic, and composers viewed today as late Romantics lived when other arts are judged to have moved to post-Romantic styles. Since the mid-1800s, the repertory of most symphony orchestras and other professional performers has been comprised primarily of Classical and Romantic music (with certain works of J. S. Bach and Handel); the three Viennese composers are "classical" only because their works were frequently studied by nineteenth-century musicians as models of form and style. Alongside the music of certain Romantic composers, these works have continued to constitute a canon, shared by professional musicians as part of a common educational curriculum.

Hence, Classical and Romantic music can be viewed as a single tradition that emerged out of the earlier 1700s. An important precondition was the emergence of professional public concerts, which encouraged the development of certain genres during the late 1700s, particularly the symphony and other types of orchestral music. The orchestra itself—a large instrumental body at first comprised chiefly of violins and other stringed instruments, joined from the 1700s onward by increasing numbers of wind and percussion instruments—had developed in close connection with late-Baroque opera. The symphony, the chief orchestral genre of the late eighteenth and nineteenth centuries, originated as the overture (opening instrumental movement) of eighteenth-century Italian opera. Removed from this context, it played a central role in many eighteenth-century concerts. During the 1700s, the concerto also developed into an orchestral concert genre, distinct from the symphony in its inclusion of a virtuoso soloist or multiple soloists.

At first, public concerts were given ad hoc, but already in Paris by 1725 a regular series, the Concert Spirituel, had been instituted. By the early 1800s, comparable series, in which vocal and instrumental works were performed, were regular events in other major European cities, often associated with permanently constituted orchestras and public societies (usually led by wealthy nonmusicians) that provided financial support. Simultaneously, the musical direction of most orchestras shifted from the principal violinist or other player to a conductor. During the 1800s, conductors took over what had been individual players' interpretive responsibilities. Thus was established the tradition whereby the public views conductors as the chief members of their ensembles.

In most countries, especially Italy, opera retained its earlier importance. Church music in the 1800s underwent a decline—a trend that continues. The role of art music in many churches has been diminished or entirely eliminated, and many leading musicians, including composers, have had little or no involvement with sacred music. A strong tradition of art-music performance by church organists and choirs survives, especially in select institutions in major European cities.

The same conditions that led to the rise of public concerts in the Classical and Romantic periods were probably responsible for the widespread founding of societies for the amateur performance of instrumental and vocal music, especially music for chorus. Among the most influential of these have been the Berlin Singakademie and the Gesellschaft der Musikfreunde in Vienna. Often under professional direction, such societies instigated significant numbers of compositions in the nineteenth century, especially oratorios and other choral works; a number of societies, in addition, founded and have continued to support public music libraries. More elite forms of amateur musical performance, descending from a tradition of upper-class salons and academies that dated back to the 1600s, continued. In such settings, prominent professional composers and performers often participated alongside wealthy amateurs in performing music, new and old. Both types of participatory music making declined in the twentieth century, particularly with regard to new compositions, interest in which tended to be limited to specialists.

The expansion of professional and amateur performance in the 1700s and 1800s paralleled the growth of industry and trade involving printed music. Aided by developments in engraving and printing technology, transport, and commercial distribution, publishers could issue music in increasingly large quantities and at reduced expense. By the mid-1800s, most Western art music was routinely published shortly after composition; this was true even of such works as the piano sonatas of Beethoven and the enormous musical scores of opera, which required performers to have professional-quality skill and training. Vast numbers of titles were issued for less sophisticated users. Among these was a growing repertory of songs and instrumental pieces, especially marches and dances, which occupied a gray area between art and popular music, leading to commercial popular music of the twentieth century.

Another development was that of increasingly large performance spaces. Concert halls and opera theaters were designed to accommodate growing audiences and expanding orchestral and choral ensembles, whose members by the early 1800s could number into the hundreds (figure 5). Accordingly, the 1800s saw significant changes in performing techniques and the construction of instruments; modern instruments

FIGURE 5 The arrangement of players for the Philharmonic Orchestra in England in 1846 differs significantly from most contemporary orchestral layouts. Instead of being confined to sections on the left or right of the conductor, as today, each string group—violins, violas, celli, and double basses—is spread across the entire stage. The principal violinist and bassist are in the center, rather than to the left and right, respectively, as today. After Adam von Ahn Carse, *The Orchestra from Beethoven to Berlioz* (New York: Broude Brothers, 1949).

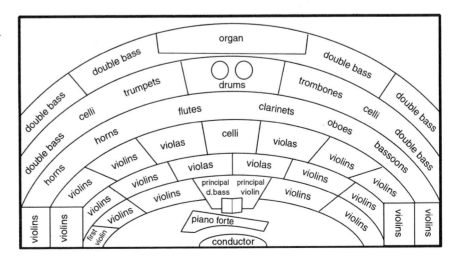

Composers from Beethoven onward wrote programmatic works depicting visual images, dramatic events, even autobiographical narratives. With the rise of European nationalism in the late 1800s, ethnic and patriotic matter, sometimes expressed through borrowings from folk songs, became an important topic for such music.

and techniques remain in many essential respects those of the late 1800s. Noteworthy by 1800 was the replacement of the harpsichord by the piano as the chief stringed keyboard instrument.

The 1800s also saw the transmission of the Western art-music tradition to Eastern Europe and the Americas. In many regions, musical activity was explicitly modeled on that of the central German, French, and Italian traditions, typically including the establishment of symphony orchestras and musical societies. An important role was played by newly founded national conservatories and opera theaters and similar institutions, as had existed in France and other Western European countries since the 1700s.

Classical and Romantic genres

By the late 1700s, firm distinctions had emerged between public, orchestral genres such as the symphony and the concerto, and genres such as the solo piano sonata and the string quartet (for two violins, viola, and cello), initially intended for use by amateurs or in semipublic performances in private houses or chambers—hence their designation as chamber music. Vocal music of the period shows corresponding distinctions between operatic and choral works for the stage or concert hall and more intimate songs for solo voice and piano; instrumental chamber works nevertheless tended to employ the styles and structures of orchestral genres, and by 1850 chamber music was commonly performed professionally in public recitals and concerts. Instrumental works in the larger chamber and orchestral genres usually have three or four distinct movements, each employing one of several common structural patterns. Particularly important among the latter is sonata-allegro form, developed by Viennese Classical composers and in various versions continuing in use (figure 6).

The sonata-allegro and other formal structures helped make possible the emergence of autonomous genres of instrumental music which, since the late 1700s, have been accorded status equal to that of vocal music in the European art-music tradition. Paradoxically, the recognition of such "absolute" music—instrumental music that is, in principle, nonrepresentational—was a product of Romantic thinking that encouraged a representational view of other types of instrumental music. Composers from Beethoven onward wrote programmatic works depicting visual images, dramatic events, even autobiographical narratives. With the rise of European nationalism in the late 1800s, ethnic and patriotic matter, sometimes expressed through borrowings from folk songs, became an important topic for such music. Both absolute and programmatic traditions claimed descent from Beethoven, who, though employing Classical structures in most works, evinced Romantic expressive aspirations and undertook such innovations as the introduction of solo voices and chorus in the final movement of his Ninth Symphony (1824).

Many later nineteenth-century composers resisted the impulse toward writing

FIGURE 6   The opening measures of Ludwig van Beethoven's Symphony No. 5 in C Minor, op. 67 (1807). The first of four distinct movements that typified the Classical and Romantic symphonic form, it unfolds in sonata-allegro form and is notable for its thorough and consistent development of the opening four-note motif.

explicitly programmatic music, at least in their symphonies and other larger instrumental works. Among them were the German and Austrian composers Franz Schubert (1797–1828), Felix Mendelssohn (1809–1847), Robert Schumann (1810–1856), Anton Bruckner (1824–1896), and Johannes Brahms (1833–1897). Schumann composed many shorter piano pieces with programmatic titles, and all composed numerous lieder, chamber settings of German poetry (most by contemporary Romantic poets) for voice and piano.

Among the proponents of a more programmatic approach to instrumental music were the French composer Hector Berlioz (1803–1869), whose Fantastic Symphony was premiered just three years after Beethoven's death, and the Hungarian-born virtuoso pianist Franz Liszt (1811–1886), who, like Berlioz, was a skilled conductor and symphonist. This tradition continued into the late- or post-Romantic period in the so-called tone poems of Richard Strauss (1864–1949) and the symphonies of Gustav Mahler (1860–1911), which incorporate vocal parts and other departures from the Classical tradition of instrumental music.

Closely associated with the programmatic tradition were the music-dramas of Richard Wagner (1813–1883), operas of unprecedented length and complexity whose texts, by Wagner himself, drew on Germanic myths and legends. Wagner's technical innovations in harmony and orchestration proved influential well into the twentieth century, though his aesthetics and politics (which included an unabashed racism) were controversial. Also notable among his accomplishments was the foundation of an opera theater at Bayreuth specially designed for the performance of his operas. Annual festivals, held there regularly since 1876, together with an older tradition of choral-music festivals, have served as models for what has become the widespread practice of devoting weeklong or monthlong festivals to public performances of a given kind of music.

The history of twentieth-century art music is bifurcated between the globalization of a static, homogeneous performance tradition and an innovative, diversified compositional practice, whose products are little known and rarely performed.

The genres of the Western European nineteenth-century tradition were enthusiastically taken up elsewhere. Distinctive developments occurred in Central and Eastern Europe, as in the operas and symphonic and chamber works of the Czech composers Bedřich Smetana (1824–1884) and Antonín Dvořák (1841–1904). A comparable development is represented by the Russians Modest Petrovich Mussorgsky (1839–1881), Peter Ilyich Tchaikovsky (1840–1893), and Nikolai Andreievich Rimsky-Korsakov (1844–1908).

The Classical and Romantic periods saw the continuation of the traditions of Italian opera and, to a lesser degree, Roman Catholic church music, as in the operas of Mozart and the masses of Haydn, Schubert, and Bruckner. The operas of the Italians Gioacchino Rossini (1792–1868) and Giuseppe Verdi (1813–1901) represent a form of musical Romanticism independent of more northern ones. Throughout nineteenth-century opera, the late-Baroque ideal of a stylized drama articulated into distinct recitatives and arias gradually gave way to an ostensibly more naturalistic form comprised of a nearly unbroken stream of musical invention, as in the late works of Verdi and Wagner.

TWENTIETH-CENTURY DEVELOPMENTS

The late nineteenth and twentieth centuries saw an unprecedented dissociation of performance from composition. The performance of eighteenth- and nineteenth-century European classics became a global tradition, and new approaches to writing art music proliferated, but few recent compositions have entered the repertory of major performing institutions, and the performance of new music has become a specialists' domain. Hence, the history of twentieth-century art music is bifurcated between the globalization of a static, homogeneous performance tradition and an innovative, diversified compositional practice, whose products are little known and rarely performed.

The years around 1900 are often said to have seen the dissolution of the common-practice tradition of the previous two centuries, yet many composers have continued to work in styles and idioms close to those of the nineteenth century. Some, such as the Italian opera composer Giacomo Puccini (1858–1924) and the Russian pianist-composer Sergei Rachmaninoff (1873–1943), achieved considerable popular success by adhering to late-nineteenth-century idioms. Others, such as the Russian composer Dmitri Shostakovich (1906–1975), were compositionally limited by externally imposed political compulsion. Still others, such as the British composer Benjamin Britten (1913–1976), chose to work in seemingly conservative idioms while remaining open to the use of nonconventional techniques.

Others have more purposefully sought new, sometimes radically innovative compositional techniques. A group centered around the Austrian Arnold Schoenberg (1874–1951) developed what is known as atonal style in the years immediately

FIGURE 7   In the nineteenth and twentieth centuries, the piano, played especially by young women, was an enormously popular instrument for home entertainment. The French composer Claude Debussy was a notable exponent of a new style known as impressionism, which featured novel approaches to timbre and harmony in music, and novel approaches to painting, as rendered here by Pierre-Auguste Renoir (1841–1919) in his *Two Girls at the Piano*. Photo courtesy of French and Company.

before World War I. This innovation led to the so-called twelve-tone (dodecaphonic) technique, which influenced academic composers in the United States, where Schoenberg took up residence after 1933. Paradoxically, many atonal and twelve-tone works fall into Classical genres, such as the string quartet, and employ Classical forms, especially the sonata-allegro. Serialism, a further development of Schoenberg's method, emerged in the 1950s in the works of French composer Pierre Boulez (b. 1925) and others. Not serial, but equally inspired by the modernist ethos of the mid-twentieth century, with its emphasis on strict constructionism, are works by the American composer Elliott Carter (b. 1908).

A less radical confrontation of innovation with tradition can be traced back to the French composer Claude Debussy (1862–1918), whose so-called impressionist works for solo piano and for orchestra emphasized novel approaches to harmony and timbre (figure 7). The early works of Igor Stravinsky (1882–1971) are an offshoot of this current, though they continue the Russian tradition of Stravinsky's teacher, Rimsky-Korsakov; in some late works, Stravinsky took up Schoenberg's twelve-tone technique.

During the 1920s and 1930s, Stravinsky and many other composers, particularly in France and the United States, adopted a Neoclassic style, which borrowed traits from older music, chiefly of the eighteenth and nineteenth centuries. Neoclassicism was part of a larger trend, toward music that imitates, quotes, or transforms, often with ironic effect, the music of past centuries, current popular music, and non-Western traditions. At the beginning of the century, such borrowings played an important role in the music of the American Charles Ives (1874–1954), and they occur in the otherwise disparate works of such contemporary composers as the Italian Luciano Berio (b. 1925) and the Russian Alfred Schnittke (1934–1998). Neoclassicism and transformed borrowing (from folk music) are also evident in works by the Hungarian composer and folklorist Béla Bartók (1881–1945), noted particularly for his six string quartets.

More extreme breaks with convention have occurred in so-called experimental music, which rejects not only past techniques and styles, but the entire ethos of the nineteenth-century concert-music tradition. Inspired by dadaism and related movements in the visual and literary arts, musicians such as the Americans Edgard Varèse (1883–1965) and John Cage (1912–1992) employed once exotic percussion instruments and sounds previously regarded as nonmusical; Cage's works have even incorporated ambient noises from the environment in which a work is performed. Cage and others have reintroduced elements of improvisation into musical composition and have employed methods of composition or performance involving the production of random (aleatoric) sounds. Electronically processed or synthesized sounds have been increasingly employed by certain composers since 1950.

The most important twentieth-century development in art-music performance has been the dissemination of commercial recordings. To a high degree, these have replaced live performance, and they have reinforced the trend toward the repetition of acknowledged masterworks, often in an increasingly homogeneous style of performing. Recordings have also permitted the dissemination of newly composed works that would otherwise have gone largely unheard.

A second major development has been the revival of music composed before the establishment of the canonic Classical and Romantic repertory. This development has been accompanied by the reconstruction of practices and instruments originally employed in the performance of older music; previously, older works were usually performed according to traditions conventional at the time of performance.

The revival of early music was encouraged by the inclusion of music history alongside art history and other humanistic disciplines in twentieth-century higher

The most important twentieth-century development in art-music performance has been the dissemination of commercial recordings. To a high degree, these have replaced live performance and permitted the dissemination of newly composed works that would otherwise have gone largely unheard.

education and scholarship. Though music history has been a concern of European writers since Greek antiquity, historical research founded on the systematic study of musical documents, including notated scores, began only in the 1700s. Nineteenth-century scholars, chiefly in Germany, borrowing techniques developed in the study of literary texts, prepared collected editions of works by composers of the past and placed particular emphasis on music seen as historically ancestral to the symphonic and operatic repertories, such as that of Handel, J. S. Bach, Mozart, and Beethoven.

Particularly since the 1950s, musical scholarship has expanded enormously in the range of its subjects. Scholarly editions have been published for music extending from medieval chant to mid-twentieth-century composers. Critical and theoretical methodologies range from technical analyses to feminist critiques and other approaches inspired by twentieth-century literary criticism. Recent decades have seen a shift in focus from individual composers and works to performance practices and works in their cultural and social contexts.

BIBLIOGRAPHY

A bibliography cannot begin to capture the breadth and depth of research on the history of European art music. The literature includes published primary sources, multi-volume encyclopedias, textbook surveys that list composers and trace the development of styles, composers' biographies, and monographs on selected topics, such as genres, institutions, periods, and places. Approaches and methods vary significantly and include studying composers' autographs as evidence of the creative process and analyzing instruments (organology), artwork (iconography), literature, and philosophy for evidence of performance practice and the relation among music, society, and culture. Each European country has its own academic journals and popular periodicals, too numerous to list here, devoted to music.

For a general orientation, English-language readers may turn to the following works, which include an annotated bibliography, a multivolume encyclopedia, the major American journal devoted to music history, four extensive series of publications, and a canonical music-history textbook.

Annotated bibliography

Duckles, Vincent, and Ida Reed. 1997. *Music Reference and Research Materials: An Annotated Bibliography.* 5th ed. New York: Schirmer.

Encyclopedia

The New Grove Dictionary of Music and Musicians. 1980. 20 vols. Edited by Stanley Sadie. London: Macmillan.

Journal

Journal of the American Musicological Society. 1948–.

Series

Garland Composer Resource Manuals. 1981–. New York: Garland.

Music Research and Information Guides. 1984–. New York: Garland. These contain annotated bibliographies of individual genres and composers of art music.

Music and Society. 1994–. Englewood Cliffs, N.J.: Prentice Hall. Published in the United Kingdom as Man and Music.

The Norton Introduction to Music History. 1978–. New York: Norton.

Textbook

Grout, Donald Jay, and Claude V. Palisca. 1988. *A History of Western Music.* 4th ed. New York: Norton.

Understanding Musical Performance and Ideas about Music

European folk and popular music participates in a world of cultural, social, political, and economic forces. Its musical instruments are products of local ecologies and the international economy. When and where music is performed—its contexts—respond to the divisions of social life, work and seasonal cycles, and beliefs about the power of music to enhance the celebration of major events in a person's and a community's life. How and why music is transmitted from generation to generation—and who learns it—depend on culturally shared ideas about gender, genre, and the meaning of music. Centuries-old forms of orally transmitted rural music continue to be performed and valued in Europe's modern, literate, and largely urban societies because musicians continually refresh them and societies give them aesthetic, economic, ideological, political, and practical value.

In Europe, folk and popular music is sung and played on many ritual and social occasions and in concerts. Whether vocal or instrumental, one of its most pervasive and important uses is to accompany dancing, which can take many forms. Here, a Hungarian couple from Kalotaszeg in the Transylvanian region of Romania dances to the accompaniment of a bass fiddle, part of a now-traditional string band. Photo by Paula A. White, 1994.

Ways of Transmitting Music
Pandora Hopkins

Recomposition: Creativity and Presentation
Cue-Systems
Transmission in Context

European musicians have used a variety of methods to transmit their traditions from person to person and generation to generation. Understanding these methods requires looking beyond established models of transmission (aural or written) and modes of music ownership (composed, interpreted, improvised, performed). Three factors continue to transform these models: the accumulation of information about contemporary music systems, the development of electronic media entailing combinations of transmission types, and a dramatic surge in the commercial importance of music products.

In Europe, special significance has been accorded the system of visual symbols we call music notation. Most formally educated Europeans consider graphic music notation to be a literal translation of sound structures and thus fundamental to the dissemination of those structures; indeed, notation is sometimes called music, as in "Who brought the music?" But in Europe, as elsewhere, many musical traditions continue to be transmitted aurally, entirely or in part, and this despite the fact that forms of notation have existed for at least six thousand years. The ancient Indian *Samaveda,* a treatise of the fourth millennium B.C., contains a description of the earliest known notational system, and notation is believed to have existed in China by 2000 B.C.

The development of music writing in Europe came much later. The ancient Greeks, whose influence over medieval European thinking was profound, used two notational systems, though extant fragments of notation shed some doubt on a clear distinction between the two: according to ancient Greek theorists, one system was devised for vocal music; the other, for instrumental pieces. The European system of notation with which we are most familiar is rooted almost entirely in a completely different source: linguistic accents that eventually evolved into neumatic symbols. They were useful to choir directors, who relayed their instructions to choristers largely through a system of aural and gestural symbols, a method common worldwide. But in Europe, musical notation gradually changed from a pragmatic aid in the Middle Ages to a touchstone for professionalism in the first half of the twentieth century.

All communicative structures reflect the genres they were designed to represent, and Western musical notation is no exception. The special problem with notation is that it has what linguists call an unmarked status, to convey supposedly universal properties of music in the abstract. The original edition of Harvard University Press's musical dictionary (Apel 1940) reflected this presumption in defining "any fully developed notational system" as one that "must be so designed as to clearly indicate the two main properties of a music sound: its pitch and its duration." In considering such a system "fully developed," the writer of the definition was apparently unaware of influences from Asian, African, and European traditions that were dramatically influencing European composers. Major Asian influence began during the last quarter of the nineteenth century (Chou 1971). African influence, better known because of commercial exploitation by record companies, dates largely from the beginning of the twentieth century, and the use of local musical resources was intertwined with the nineteenth-century growth of nationalism. A fundamental change in outlook, largely traceable to these influences, was the perception of timbre as a structural element. Formal recognition of this transformation began as early as 1938 when timbre was incorporated into Carl Seashore's talent-assessment tests (1967 [1938]). The inadequacy of staff notation to represent the new parameters of contemporary music led some composers to construct an original system of graphic representation for each new composition—a practice that negates the idea that staff notation is an unmarked system. Recent technology, especially in the form of digital synthesizers, has responded to the new directions already taken by avant-garde composers, and "banks of sounds" are now available on CDs for electronic composers; the Institut de Recherche et Coordination Acoustique/Musique (IRCAM) devoted a seminar to the subject of timbre in 1994 (Barrière et al., 1994); and a notational system for tone quality has been proposed (Slawson 1985).

What precisely is the relationship between symbols on paper and the sounds they represent? Clearly comparison is fundamental to this relationship; deciphering musical notation depends on a comparison of what is already known with what is pictured on paper (Hopkins 1966). In a similar vein, the 1986 edition of *The New Harvard Dictionary of Music* challenges the perceived distinction between written and aural transmission by pointing out that deciphering of graphic symbols depends on nonwritten knowledge; this observation quietly dispels the premise of a fundamental opposition between literate cultures (that is, those using music notation) and those that communicate aurally. We may fruitfully compare the 1940 definition of notation with one published in *The New Grove Dictionary of Music and Musicians:* "The concept of notation may be regarded as including formalized systems of signaling between musicians and systems of memorizing and teaching music with spoken syllables, words, or phrases" (Bent 1980:334; for a similarly broadened concept of notation, see Cole 1974).

The newly inclusive conception of European notation has necessarily caused a reassessment of previously accepted views on the process of music dissemination; it no longer seems so easy to make a clear distinction among composition, improvisation, and performance, nor even to decide with certainty when a piece began to be (or stopped being) created. A pool of resources and knowledge of their appropriate and inappropriate usage antedates the commonsense beginning of a "piece" of music (Tarasti 1983:193; see also Hopkins 1976 and Lévi-Strauss 1964). We need only think of J. S. Bach's reworkings of compositions completed by Vivaldi to realize that our contemporary assumptions about the origins of pieces of music do not hold for all times and places, even in Europe. Thus more generally applicable is the model devised by Leo Treitler to describe European medieval music. Treitler found that the concept had to accommodate "the idea that Generation and Dissemination can be a single category. . . . The transmission of music, then, may be understood as a process of its repeated and successive re-creation" (Treitler 1977:210; see also Finnegan 1992:112). Clearly, the designation of music authorship seems far less certain than formerly; yet the question of who has authority over compositions has become a matter of legal and economic concern. At the same time that European art music has ceased to seem unique by dint of its scores, aural artifacts drawn from all over the world have become commercially lucrative [see WORLD MUSIC IN EUROPE].

To account for all the ways music is transmitted in Europe requires a broadened concept of notation, with some new terminology. Most evident is the need for a rubric under which to classify the signal-systems used in musical communication: aural, tactile, gestural, and visual (notation); the term *cue-system*, introduced here, expresses this concept. To avoid confusion, the term *notation* has been reserved for systems of written symbols. The terms *recomposition* and *recompose* cover the seamless interaction of creativity and presentation.

RECOMPOSITION: CREATIVITY AND PRESENTATION

Musicians make choices with one of two underlying objectives in mind: to perpetuate a heritage or to develop a cultural legacy into something new, deemed better or more advanced. The first mission dominates most of the nonelite European traditions; it is well known to Europeans as the *classic* ideal. The second, a teleological perspective, derives from the definition of music as a branch of science and mathematics, disciplines expected to progress by the accumulation of knowledge.

Music as science: progress by accumulation

> Boethius and Cassiodorus are generally credited with transmitting the ancient Greek perception of music as a science. During the Middle Ages the seven liberal arts were divided into two categories, and music was taught as one of the *quadrivium* (along with Arithmetic, Geometry, and Astronomy), not as a member of the *trivium* (which included Grammar, Rhetoric, and Logic). As an eminent scholar has pointed out, the conception of music as a branch of mathematics is "a view that has never been and probably never will be altogether discarded since there is much truth in it." (Reese 1940:118)

The European classification of music as a science had its roots in Greek philosophy, though received in Central Europe through the preferences, translations, and interpretations of scholars from farther east. Twelfth- and thirteenth-century European theorists credit such Arabic philosophers as Al-Fārābī, Avicenna, and Averroes with casting off the Boethian threefold division of *musica mundana, musica humana,* and *musica theoretica.* Aristotle and Al-Fārābī (called The Second Teacher, the first being Aristotle) had a background in the physical sciences; therefore, it is not surprising that they advocated an empirical approach to the study of music and had little interest in the Pythagorean mysteries of *musica mundana.* Aristotle emphasized the inclusion of musical instrument training in a gentleman's education; however, he cautioned that practical instruction should be limited to five years—enough to criticize the performance of others, he pointed out, but not enough to become a professional musician (Aristotle 1932:1341a). Al-Fārābī, in the introduction to his *Kitābu l-Mūsīqī al Kabīr* (The great book on music), wrote that his work was unusual precisely because it devoted a portion—by far the largest—to practical music, while most other authors had limited themselves to the theoretical side (Al-Fārābī 1930:7). He considered the study of music performance an application of scientific method: "Aristotle proceeded thus in his natural history for all that pertains to animals and plants"; however, like Aristotle, he valued performance essentially as a means to the higher glory of theoretical understanding (1930:7; see Bacon 1962 [1928]:63 and

Cserba 1935). European music theory continues to reflect the teleological perspective, and the search for musical principles based on immutable scientific laws has long been a recurrent theme. Thus, the European composer Paul Hindemith, like Pythagoras, tried to construct systems of music theory on the basis of physical laws. The perception of music as a power that can directly induce specific emotions in auditors has been common throughout the world, including such contemporary ideas as "good-music" radio stations and religious leaders who try to censor certain styles as bad influences on the young. Such views are often closely associated with the physical basis of music.

Classical: transcending temporal contexts

The classic impulse to extend a heritage beyond its original context is found in elite and nonelite, religious and secular, aural and literate cultures in all parts of the world; it has always existed in certain European traditions. Especially obvious in formal liturgical rites, it has played a consistently important role in the local traditions of identity-conscious, nonelite ethnicities; however, when the term *classic* came into the world of mainstream European art music (at the end of the nineteenth century), it contradicted the long-held teleological perspective of music as science, the emphasis always on the new and the up-to-date: neither Bach nor Beethoven had considered the music of previous generations to be in viable currency, and Mendelssohn's celebrated rediscovery of Bach reflected a radically new interest in the past. In the latter half of the nineteenth century, the novel term was first applied to music by opponents of the latest—that is, the most modern—style of music (Blume 1970:8; see also Bukofzer 1947 and Hopkins 1986).

The dichotomy dilemma

In the European literate world, the *classic* concept became inexorably identified with musical notation; seen as a means of preserving composers' "authentic" works, the written document in music began to assume an authoritative, rather than only a prescriptive or speculative, status. The field of musicology was formed to provide authoritative editions known as *Urtexte* 'original texts'. This concept led to a separation of the performer and composer so complete that the former has been sarcastically called "the assimilation of the ideal interpreter as the perfect robot," and the latter, "the mythical divinity the composer has become" (Chailley 1967:7). Composers such as Arthur Honegger yearned for the time when "the performance of their works be entirely assured, in the near future, by mechanical agents, this mechanization marking the end of the interpreter's role" (Pincherle 1958:146). Even in the most influential institutions of Western culture, the desire to produce a comprehensive notational medium and the belief that it could be done were short-lived, perhaps only lasting, in its extreme form, three or four decades—a time one musicologist has tagged "the age of the god Paper" (Chailley 1967:7). Two and a half centuries earlier, improvisation was an expected ingredient of most styles of central European church and state music. J. S. Bach was severely criticized for including so much in his notation that should have been left to the interpreter's imagination (David and Mendel 1945:238). By 1900, European virtuosi were ceasing to take the interpretive liberties theretofore expected of them, liberties including the composition of original cadenzas; a complete turnaround, however, has occurred during the twentieth century, whose story contains ironic twists: first, in musical performance; then, in research about music; and finally, in composition.

The performer

By 1900, the myth of the supremacy of the printed page produced for European mainstream music such a curiously static interpretation of the notated score that its

Composers of notated "art" music in the nineteenth century manifested a desire to stretch beyond conventional boundaries. Interest in diverse musical resources was inspired, in some cases, by ethnographers' discoveries and, in other cases, by a newly awakened nationalistic interest in rural, nonelite musics in their own backyards.

fundamentally prescriptive function was obscured, and the authority of the composer loomed immense. The performer gradually became invisible as an artistic agent; however, interest in musical styles of the past, with the conviction that the one authentic interpretation of a work could indeed be uncovered, eventually led to research in the history of European performance practice. A player's correct usage of ornamentation, improvisation, and rhythmic and other conventions must be part of an authoritative performance to carry out the composer's intentions. Thus, the composer's authority led, ironically, to the performer's authority as the performer emerged into scholarly view directly from an increased textual emphasis.

The music researcher

During the eighteenth and nineteenth centuries, researchers in the new fields of folklore, anthropology, and comparative musicology adopted and adapted methods and terminology from the sciences; fieldwork methods were applied to study the aural traditions of cultures without literate documentation. As early as 1773, Johann Herder called the songs of "unpolished peoples" a natural archives and compared them to "natural history which describes plants and animals" (Feldman and Richardson 1972:22, 80). More than a century later, Benjamin Gilman reflected the prevailing anthropological view when he termed a collection of phonograph cylinders "specimens comparable in fidelity and reproduction and for convenience of study to casts or photographs of sculpture or painting" (Hood 1963:228). The "dichotomy dilemma" became exacerbated by the independent development of different research methods for the two bodies of musical material: ethnographic approaches of the social sciences for the music of "others," and the development of authorized texts for the elite musics of Europe.

The new fieldwork methods for research in aural traditions stimulated scholars from a variety of disciplines. Searching for the answer to a time-honored problem of classical scholarship, the genesis of the Homeric poems, Milman Parry and Albert B. Lord adopted ethnographic methods to study contemporary Yugoslav epics (Lord 1960). They described a process of composition in performance and emphasized constant variability combined with recurrent patterns they called formulas. Their "oral-formulaic theory" became highly influential in promoting a new concept of aural tradition in general, one that emphasized composition in performance and a state of constant flux. It lent scientific credibility to the perception of a fundamental difference between the two bodies of music (aural or folk and literate or art), emphasized by the recent static redefinition of "art" performance. In supplanting the old national or romantic notion of aural performers as passive transmitters of culture, the definition of oral poets as constantly and continuously creative produced an opposition with players who used scores—now considered to encapsulate the creative impulse. Within several decades, European perceptions of literate and nonliterate transmission had experienced a complete reversal: from change to nonchange in the literate world; from nonchange to change in the nonliterate one. Only the sense of a dichotomy persisted.

The composer

Another group of people who became interested in fieldwork methods for collecting music were composers of notated "art" music. In the nineteenth century, they manifested a desire to stretch beyond conventional boundaries; interest in diverse musical resources was inspired, in some cases, by ethnographers' discoveries and, in other cases, by a newly awakened nationalistic interest in rural, nonelite musics in their own backyards. One of the most eminent musicians to make use of the latter resources was Béla Bartók, whose lifespan (1881–1945) coincided with the period of almost unlimited respect for notation and the musical score, and it is important to recognize the significance of his change of outlook. Early in life, he questioned the creativity of the traditional musicians he had encountered in his recording trips: "Whether peasants are individually capable of inventing quite new tunes is open to debate," he wrote in 1931. This belief was tied to his viewpoint on aural transmission; he articulated his conviction that a completely representative system of notation could be devised if only enough symbols were created (Bartók 1931:2). His ultimate effort to produce such a notation system manifested itself in his transcriptions of Serbo-Croatian women's songs collected by Parry and Lord (Bartók and Lord 1954) (figure 1). In the introduction to this work, Bartók reversed his earlier opinion on notation: "The only really true notations are the soundtrack of the recording itself." As for the question of folk creativity in aural tradition, he again contradicted his original opinion: "The difference is not one of contrast, but one of degree. We must realize that even a performance of the same work of art music by the same performer will never occur twice in absolutely the same way" (Bartók and Lord 1954). In fact, years earlier, the psychologist Carl Seashore had conducted experiments that demonstrated this flexibility in performance from notation. After analyzing recordings made by well-known opera singers (such as Lawrence Tibbett), Seashore concluded:

> The conventional musical score—the composer's documentation of the tonal sequences which he feels will express beauty, emotion, and meaning —is for the singer only a schematic reference about which he weaves, through continuous variations in pitch, a nicely integrated melodic unity. In a very real sense, a singer never sings on pitch. (1967 [1938]:25–26)

FIGURE 1   The beginning of *Aj, polećela,* a Serbo-Croatian song transcribed by Béla Bartók, who tried to include every nuance in his notational symbols. In the introduction to this volume, however, Bartók reversed his earlier opinion concerning the possibility of creating a nearly perfect system of notation. After Bartók and Lord 1954:158.

Seashore found similar results in the playing of famous instrumentalists; he reported that such concert violinists as Fritz Kreisler and Yehudi Menuhin deviated "over 60% of the time from the tempered scale notes with deviations .05 tone or greater and over 31% of the time with deviations .1 tone or greater. . . .[Rhythmically,] the violinists deviated over 80% of the time from exact note values. Half the deviations were more than .15 sec" (1967 [1938]:202). Thus, notation provides only a rough approximation for components that seem as factual and standardized as pitch frequencies and rhythmic ratios.

Authority

The concept of music ownership is of recent vintage in Europe, even in the established traditions of church and state. Until about 1800, people gave little consideration to who had, or should have had, authority over a piece of music, a style, or its development. The impulse to develop a rank of classics—music products with clear beginnings and ends—naturally made individual rights seem more important than formerly. With the proliferation of a variety of aural and written artifacts created from so many different perspectives, the situation has become vastly more complicated by international regulations imposed by giants of the music industry (Frith 1992).

How does this global music industry affect the transmission of European music? The "cultural gray-out" once envisioned by Alan Lomax has still not taken place. Even rock has led to increased local creativity by youthful bands and individual styles in numerous countries (for Norwegian *trønderrock,* also called *dialektrock,* see Ledang 1985; for rock bands in an English town, see Finnegan 1989; see also Frith 1983, FAROE ISLANDS, and NORWAY). The multinational music industry has actually helped bring into the limelight hitherto obscured or forgotten traditions: one example is the international wave of enthusiasm for unadulterated Gregorian chant, initiated in 1994 by the unexpected popularity of *Chant,* a compact disc of religious pieces performed by the Benedictine monks of the Abbey of Santa Domingo de Silos (Angel CD 55138). Other examples include the catapulting to international attention of the indigenous music of the Saami people, especially their joiks—presented traditionally and adapted to all manner of jazz and rock styles [see NORWAY; SAAMI MUSIC]. But trial by mass market has victimized traditions that could not compete on those terms. The fundamental issue of who has control over music itself appears more and more difficult to answer. Krister Malm and Roger Wallis conclude their work on the music industry with a warning that we may be headed in one of two directions: complete standardization, on the one hand, or greater and greater diversity, on the other: "Whichever way it goes, technology will play an important role. But technology alone will not decide the outcome. People and governments will do that" (Wallis and Malm 1984:324).

Sociological theories, as valuable as they are, tend to ignore the individual human element in music as they have in language; by themselves, they cannot explain—or predict—the course of musical transmission within a culture. Unexpected shifts in this process can only be adequately understood by taking into account the control over change and permanence exercised by highly trained musicians. Much as speakers of language manipulate linguistic codes, players and singers negotiate rules of appropriateness known to cultural insiders (Hopkins 1986). This procedure takes place in aural and literate cultures:

> The technological determinism model is in any case often a misleading guide in the study of orality and literacy because of its focus on the medium. This focus draws attention away from the way people in practice use technologies, make choices and select from (or ignore or even oppose) what is available to them. (Finnegan 1988:160–161)

Today, the mainstream European composer's score, demystified from its timeless (classic) function, is once again perceived as a guide for performance, and in avant-garde styles seldom takes a conventional form. Sometimes (as in most electronic music) there is no score at all; sometimes areas are left for improvisation; and sometimes the score is of the once-only variety. As Roland Barthes put it, postserial music "has radically altered the role of the 'interpreter'," who often joins with the composer to coauthor the score, instead of merely "giving it 'expression'" (1977:163).

CUE-SYSTEMS

Most cue-systems are performance oriented, that is, they are intended for a prescriptive purpose. Tablatures, notations, solmization syllables, and gestural signs are widespread, all fundamentally methods for communicating to or among performers; however, there are other common, though less obvious, reasons for using systems of this kind. Not only do signs and symbols make ensemble performance possible, they also serve to regulate the individual contributions of players or singers. Cues may serve an exclusionary purpose, to control or even prevent communication. They may offer cross-modal comparison, and they sometimes provide theoretical information. Occasionally, they are used as an integral part of the performance itself, and at times have evolved into new genres.

The way cue-systems actually function in society frequently belies the practical reasons for which they were devised. Even the clues most closely related to performance serve to mark off inner circles of players, not only from the general public, but also from theorists and even other musicians. Part of the illusion sought from skilled performance lies in the mysterious ways members of a musical ensemble respond to secret signaling devices, whether the organization is an Italian village opera, a Faroese ballad-dancing group, or an Albanian instrumental ensemble accompanying traditional dancing. Signals may control participation within the ensemble itself. In the symphony orchestra, for example, different kinds of cues (scores, part books, gestures, and so on) reveal varying amounts and kinds of information according to the function of the user, whether that of soloist, section head, or rank-and-file player.

Perhaps the most ambitious use of cue-systems to affect widespread change was developed during the Protestant Reformation, as part of the mission to encourage congregational participation in church services. Singing seemed a natural way to effect this end, and the printing press was newly available. Therefore, the printing of special psalm books became a high priority with most Protestant denominations; however, the concept of a single, standard, proper way to worship—as to style of music and particular version—often overshadowed the essentially liberating purpose, and religious authorities actually went on the offensive, sometimes aided by royal decrees, against native improvisatory traditions. Chorale books were published and forced on unwilling parishioners, and singing schools were created to teach note reading. For those who had not yet learned to read notes, new aural cue-systems were developed to force musically illiterate parishioners into uniformity, the most common being the practice of "lining out." An ordinance of the Westminster Assembly (1644) read: "For the present, where many of the congregation cannot read, it is convenient that the minister, or some other fit person appointed by him and the other officers, do read the psalm, line by line, before the singing thereof" (Chase 1966:31). According to the English music historian Charles Burney, "singing by rule" was an unmusical expedient that resulted in psalms being "drawled out and bawled with . . . unmusical and unmeaning vehemence" (1935 [1789]:60; see also 1935 [1789]:38–59). In most Northern and Central European countries, parishioners responded against expectations; they tended to use the official psalm texts as springboards for a new version of their own improvisatory singing. In Scotland, popular

"Mannered notation" of fourteenth-century France
and Italy has been called pathological, and its period
a time when "musical notation far exceeds its natural
limitations as a servant to music, but rather becomes
its master, a goal in itself."

Within this croffe here may you find,
Foure parts in two be fure of this:
But firft feeke out to know my mind,
Or els this Cannon you may miffe.

FIGURE 2   Esoteric notation: a puzzle canon by
Thomas Morley (1597). Courtesy of the New
York Public Library for the Performing Arts.

psalmodic improvisation lasted almost to the present, the original tunes so highly
elaborated that they became unrecognizable without specialized research; lining out
(also called precentoring) led to another new tradition, a conventionalized melismatic
cantillation, which strays far from the original psalm tunes (Collinson 1966:261).

Sometimes, the expressed intention of a cue-system is not to facilitate, regulate,
synchronize, or achieve bonding, but actually to delimit accessability—to obfuscate,
embellish, or mystify. Thus the sixteenth- and seventeenth-century English organist
Thomas Morley observed that the French, though "generally accounted great masters, seldom or never would prick [notate] their lessons as they played them, much
less reveal anything in the thorough understanding of the instrument" (quoted in
Cole 1974). "Mannered notation" of fourteenth-century France and Italy has been
called pathological, and its period a time when "musical notation far exceeds its natural limitations as a servant to music, but rather becomes its master, a goal in itself
and an arena for intellectual sophistries" (Apel 1942:403). Puzzle canons were a
source of amusement in various times and places (figure 2).

A well-kept secret was the Scottish vocable system known as *canntaireachd,* the
method long used for the aural teaching of the classical piping tradition
(*piobaireachd*); it was unknown to competition judges in early-nineteenth-century
Scotland; when John Campbell, one of the competing pipers, showed them his
father's written-down versions, "The volume proved completely unintelligible to
them, and it occurred to none of them that it could be a musical notation," and even
today, "the editors of the Piobaireachd Society publications confess that their use of
canntaireachd has been 'a matter of some anxiety' as they admittedly have not yet got
sufficient information on many points" (Collinson 1975:190, 192). The avant-garde
composer Cornelius Cardew clearly expressed his desire to limit use of his music
through "once-only" notation; in a preface to his *Four Works,* he wrote:

> Pieces need camouflage to protect them from hostile forces in the early days of
> their life. One kind of protection is provided by the novelty and uniqueness of the
> notation; few musicians will take the trouble to decipher and learn the notations
> unless they have a positive interest in performing the works. (Cole 1974:148)

Cues sometimes transcend their original purpose altogether and function independently as an integral part of the musical communication process, occasionally
evolving into new and separate genres. European notational traditions are rife with
calligraphic examples that beg to be hung on walls—and indeed are often so exhibited: for example, European medieval manuscripts and "once-only" scores are clearly
visual interpretations of the sound structure (figure 3). Vocables originally designed
to convey theoretical information (rhythmic or melodic) may be used in performance, often imitating the playing of musical instruments.

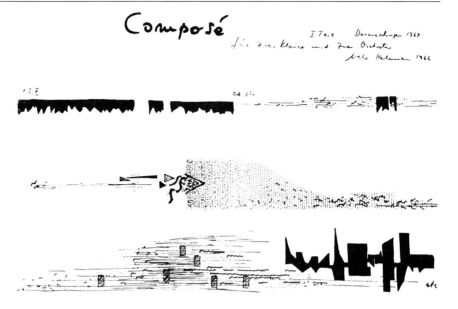

Tactile cue-systems

The tactile sensation has played, and doubtless always will play, a major role in music
communication, whether in Greek whispered duets or in awe-inspiring church organ
music at full blast: it is implied in the marketing tactics of the company that advertises an electronic instrument as one that "feels like a piano." In a book on the
Bulgarian bagpipe (*gajda*) tradition, Tim Rice recognized the importance of the tactile component in musical perception, another dimension in the complexity of musical transmission. Learning to play the *gajda*,

> I had made a distinction between accent and mordent and melody note, but now
> I realized that they should be integrated into a single concept located in a mental
> and physical image of how the hand worked to produce a complex of sounds. . . .
> This transformation in understanding unified at least four concepts into one, and
> simplified enormously the mental process of playing. . . . My new understanding
> added the hand motions necessary to produce the sounds: physical behavior
> became part of the conceptual source generating musical ideas. (Rice 1994:83)

Even the pitch system of a tradition may be discovered to emanate from finger patterns on adjacent strings, as may be attested by a peculiar scale, constructed of disjunct octave-overreaching tetrachords and found in the music of the Norwegian
Hardanger violin and the solo violin sonata of J. S. Bach (Hopkins 1986:162).
Various stratagems have been developed to train students to feel, rather than look at,
their instruments, be the instruments steel pans or pianos. Even a special device has
hit the market for this purpose: called a no-peek, it was designed to be placed on a
violin so as to shield a young student's eyes from the fingerboard.

Braille notation developed for blind musicians presents an organized system of
tactile messages; in a method similar to the one used for words, it indicates specific
pitches and rhythms by different configurations of embossed dots. To keep the symbols as brief and compact as possible, the system uses abbreviations and other strategies for triggering the player's memory. Pianists learn their music one hand at a time,
"reading" with one hand while performing with the other (Cole 1974:43). The
impressive number of blind musicians in many of the world's traditions speaks to the
importance of the tactile component of music, probably honed to the ultimate by
them (figure 4).

FIGURE 4   The tactile element: one of the many
traditions that attracted blind musicians was the
epic song tradition of the Ukrainian *kobzari*,
who accompanied themselves on their national
instrument, the *bandura*. Drawing, ca. 1910.

FIGURE 5   An artist's rendering of Egyptian cheironomy as represented on a relief decorating a fifth-dynasty tomb (ca. 2700 B.C.). Drawing by Barbara Perrin.

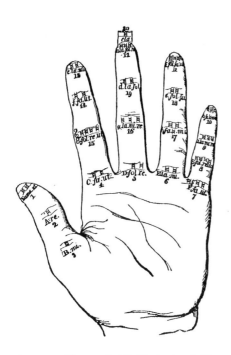

FIGURE 6   The so-called Guidonian hand. After Hawkins 1776:Vol. 1, 233. Courtesy of the New York Public Library for the Performing Arts.

Visual cue-systems

Gestures

The intimate association of music with physical movement includes instrumentalists' activated muscles, vocalists' dramatizations, conductors' gesticulations, dancers' interpretations, and auditors' physical responses, including clapping and stamping, but few people may be aware of the extent to which bodily motions serve as cues to carry out the recomposition process of music. Though gestures are conveyed visually, they sometimes have a tactile component and virtually always evoke a kinesthetic response in viewers. The term *cheironomy* implies more than hand motion. In general, hand and finger gestures are important in most kinds of music directing. In a historically restricted sense, cheironomic instructional practices may be found today, especially in sacred vocal tradition.

Cheironomy is a gesturing practice that has been intimately associated with notational and aural symbols for several thousand years. The term refers to a system of signaling in which a conductor directs a group of musicians with a variety of hand and finger motions and, in some traditions, motions of other parts of the body, frequently the head. The expression comes from the Greek word *cheír* 'hand', and has been applied to all similar systems, including the musical direction carved on walls of Egyptian temples and tombs from the fourth dynasty (2723–2563 B.C.) (figure 5); it was also used in the ancient cultures of Mesopotamia, India, China, Israel, and Byzantium, and is still thriving. The bulk of our direct knowledge about cheironomy, however, concerns its function within liturgical cantillation systems, where it manifests similar features among what has been termed a chain of cantillation styles from Muslim, Shinto, and Vedic religions, the diverse regional varieties of Buddhism, ancient and modern forms of Jewish chant, and the different national types related to the Eastern (Byzantine) and Western (Roman) branches of Christianity (Gerson-Kiwi 1961:66).

Cheironomy is an excellent example of cross-modality between cue-systems, as when, in the religious traditions, hand gestures were intimately allied with written neumes and liturgical accents. Most scholars feel that cheironomic gestural patterns influenced the shapes of neumes, and it is clear that accents and neumes were methods primarily intended to communicate traditionally important details of vocal inflection (Sendrey 1969:569). Of prime significance is the fact that all three systems—gestures, accents, neumes—have continued to coexist in several traditions, including the Jewish, Byzantine, and Egyptian-Coptic (Fétis 1895; Fleischer 1895; Gerson-Kiwi 1961, 1980; Hemsi 1930; Idelsohn 1944 [1929]; Reese 1940; Sendrey 1969; Werner 1959).

The use of the hand as a gestural-visual-tactile mnemonic device is widespread, having manifested itself in China, Japan, India, and Europe. During the eleventh century, the so-called Guidonian hand (attributed to Guido of Arezzo, though never actually mentioned by him) became enormously influential in Europe, sometimes even accorded mystical powers. According to medieval theoretical documents, this pedagogical tool was simply a sketch of a left hand, portions of which were inscribed with the solmisation syllables of the hexachord (figure 6). Though we have no direct evidence that the Guidonian hand was associated with gestures and visual symbolism, it seems likely, considering long-established practices elsewhere in the world. Hand signals are still important in numerous musical traditions, including the Kodály system (figure 7).

Choral directing today exhibits more of the characteristics of cheironomy than does orchestral conducting. Choral directors usually use both hands—in preference to a stick (baton)—and tend to concentrate on conveying aspects of the melody and

FIGURE 7   A contemporary example of hand signals for music transmission: the Kodály system.

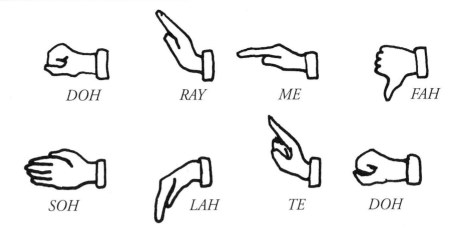

DOH   RAY   ME   FAH

SOH   LAH   TE   DOH

its interpretation (the expressive nuances of timbre and dynamics), with little emphasis on the symphonic director's cyclic beating of time (figure 8).

Some musical traditions require the constant presence of evenly spaced, unaccented pulses, sounded or not, a practical reference point for performers. It is especially suitable for part music characterized by highly complicated cross-rhythms; the players take care of all the technical and interpretive aspects of their individual parts. The least intrusive of all such systems must be the *tactus* of medieval Europe, a silent waving of the conductor's arm in a downward, upward alternation. This technique has reappeared occasionally in avant-garde European music, an expedient used especially in chamber works of noncyclic rhythmic structure. An outgrowth of this principle is manifested in the Greek composer Iannis Xenakis's *Strategie,* music governed by the evenly spaced blinking of colored lights dangling down from a frame.

In complete contrast to the unobtrusive pulse referent, there exists a kind of conducting in which the leader "plays" the musicians as instruments. The bell choir is probably the best known such institution: each participant operates one bell (sometimes two) and must wait for the director's signal to play. Similarly, the art of ringing bells allots a single note to each participant, usually with the director a participant.

Interplayer signaling within an instrumental ensemble is usually accomplished unobtrusively—a practical expedient to create an illusion of effortless discipline in a complex institution; players coordinate their parts through a prearranged system of cues, whether they are playing in a string quartet, a Ukrainian *bandura* chorus, a Russian balalaika orchestra, or a Greek dance ensemble.

In symphonic music, intrasection signals complement those of the orchestral director, who silently describes the cyclic beat structure through conventionalized patterns with one arm while expressing interpretive matters with the other, aided by facial expressions and other body movements; the conductor's signals, however, are seldom spontaneous, and their prime function is to remind the musicians of what they have learned during rehearsals. For this reason, the highly visible, baton-wielding conductor probably has more than simply a pragmatic function. The conductor's stick was controversial for nearly two hundred years in Europe. The typical seventeenth- and eighteenth-century European orchestra was under the dual direction of the keyboardist and the first violinist, whose contortions of heads, shoulders, and other body parts signaled the instrumentalists gathered around them; however, the conductor-controlled ensemble was already present in France in the second half of the seventeenth century, with Jean-Baptiste Lully and his small band of violinists. In London, performers greatly resisted the use of the baton. Handel continued to conduct from the keyboard, even while directing hundreds of oratorio performers in London, sometimes using wires to connect harpsichord and organ keyboards—a

FIGURE 8   A symphony conductor uses a baton to beat time and his free hand to signal expression. Marc Soustrot, chief conductor of Het Brabants Orchest, Eindoven, Netherlands. Photo courtesy of the orchestra.

The distribution of musical symbols on a page is determined by cultural metaphors, especially those governing passage through time. The direction of eye movement required to read the sequence of symbols equates closely with linguistic usage.

practice that was also used with more than five hundred participants in the Handel Commemoration concert of 1784: "Foreigners, particularly the French, must be much astonished at so numerous a band moving in such exact measure, without the assistance of a *Coryphaeus* to beat the time, either with a roll of paper, or a noisy baton, or truncheon" (Nettel 1948:89). English musicians held out against the baton until well into the nineteenth century, but the visiting Louis Spohr claimed success in 1820: "Quite alarmed at such novel procedure some of the Directors would have protested against it; but when I besought them to grant me at least one trial, they became pacified. The triumph of the baton, as a time-giver, was decisive" (Nettel 1948:119). Nevertheless, conductorless orchestras have continued to operate successfully, from the 1913 Philharmonic Society of London to the 1999 Orpheus Chamber Orchestra of New York.

Notation

The intimate relationship between music and graphic representation seems more difficult to understand than its association with the tactile and aural senses, both of which naturally come into play whenever music is performed; however, when one considers that gestures communicate kinetic energy through their affiliation with the sense of sight, it is possibly not surprising that one frequently finds high esteem expressed through elaborate ornamentation of musical artifacts (musical instruments, manuscripts, and prints), graphs and charts are often used for the transmission of theoretical concepts, and illustrations themselves, in several cultures, communicate the essence of ethical powers. In Europe, "emblematic" books sometimes included bits of musical notation among their verbal or pictorial formulaic "figures."

Scholars who have attempted to analyze the synesthetic equivalencies of sound and sight have emphasized their conventional basis. In reference to cross-modal comparisons, E. H. Gombrich stressed the importance of focusing "not on likeness of elements but on structural relationships within a scale or matrix" (1956:370). There is little doubt that the time-honored association of music with formal and structural patterning has contributed to the credibility of translating musical sounds into graphic terms—and perhaps shielded from view the less prosaic side of sign communication: "At a certain point the iconic representation, however stylized it may be, appears to be more true than the real experience, and people begin to look at things through the glasses of iconic convention" (Eco 1979:205).

This is the viewpoint that moved Lévi-Strauss to use musical forms as an intellectual framework for his monumental study of mythology (1964, 1967, 1968, 1971). He considered music's *capacité anagrammatique* a reflection of human thought patterning, a manifestation of which he found in the notated score (Hopkins 1977).

Music representation uses three main types of signs. Pictographs represent in graphic terms the perceived outline of the music structure (or other aspect of music);

they resemble what they signify—a kind of visual onomatopoeia. Ideographic nota-tion, in contrast, consists of conventionalized symbols representing complete musical ideas. Uniphonic notation consists of what one theorist called "units of dissection and another 'one-sound, one-sign'" (Cole 1974). These concepts are not opposition-al; all refer to ways people have described musical sounds through graphic designs.

Pictographs

The distribution of musical symbols on a page is determined by cultural metaphors, especially those governing duration (passage through time). The direction of eye movement required to read the sequence of symbols equates closely with linguistic usage. Thus, the characters of European, Javanese, Balinese, and Tibetan systems fol-low horizontal paths in left-to-right order. Chinese, Korean, and most instrumental Japanese signs are arranged in vertical columns that must be read from right to left; however, Japanese neumatic notations (*karifu* and *meyasu*), also in vertical columns, are read in left-to-right order. Many notations make use of the two dimensions offered on a flat surface to represent two dimensions of the music structure. Implicit in staff notation, for example, is the metaphoric equivalence of pitch with height: that is, a musical tone of few cycles per second is said to be low and is pictured toward the bottom of the staff. In tablatures for stringed instruments, however, the second dimension typically represents the fingerboard, and actual frequencies become unimportant. In instruments that use nonstandard tunings (*scordature*), they change their meaning according to the particular tuning being employed.

Musical notations make use of diagrams and pictures: grills, geometric figures, dots, wavy lines, and so on. Not all of them are (as is sometimes stated) group signs, for staccato dots, accent marks, and others are included in this category. The picto-graphic component is important in most systems. Many people who do not read music have been able to follow the direction of notes on the staff through sharing the pitch and time metaphors noted above. At least one popular textbook for an intro-ductory European music history course has exploited this social convention through the use of two-dimensional diagrams that communicate information about music structure without depending on previous study of music notation. Not only music structures, but also performance directions, have been transmitted iconically. Tablatures, for example, present a schematic diagram of part of a musical instrument (fingerboard, strings, frets, finger holes, keys), making use of letters or numbers to indicate discrete pitches in a scalar system. The generic terms *uniphon* and *uniphonic* are used here to denote this kind of system (figures 9 and 10).

All notations, simply through depicting passage through time, are pictographic in the most basic sense. Sometimes there is a further division of the original timeline into metrical units, marked off by vertical or horizontal lines, dots, circles, and so on. In a few cases, the relationship between timeline and time subdivisions is deliberately made proportional; more commonly, however, the pictographic element exists in conjunction with other types of signs (figure 11).

Ideographs

Pictographic signs are not (as is often assumed) universally comprehensible, but depend upon the cultural metaphors that influence visual perception itself. More immediately apparent, however, is the conventional nature of ideographic symbols. Compare a trill as it appears pictorially in European notation (figure 12*a*), with its ideographic representation (12*b*). Ideographs have been used to express most aspects of musical communication. In early European mensural notation, ligatures (an out-growth of the neumes) were group signs that conveyed matters of pitch and rhythm (that is, proportional relationships of the notes) according to rather elaborate rules.

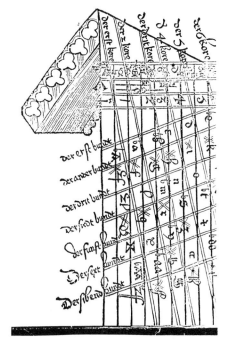

FIGURE 9   Pictographic notation: a sixteenth-century diagram showing a lute fingerboard for tablature instruction. After Lucinius 1536:52. Courtesy of the New York Public Library for the Performing Arts.

FIGURE 10 Lute piece from first book of lute intabulations printed by Ottaviano Petrucci (Venice 1507). Apel 1994:63.

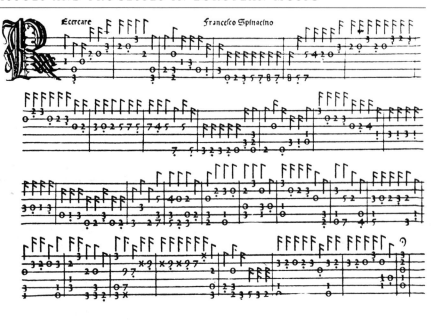

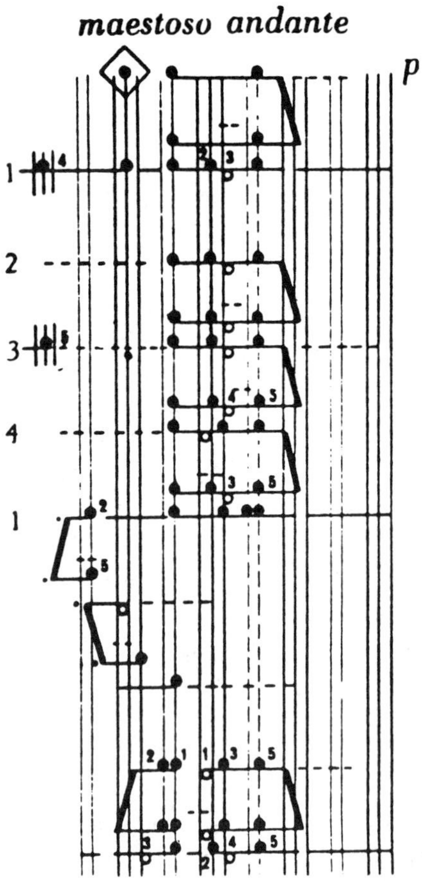

maestoso andante

FIGURE 11 An example of Klavierskribo, "Esperanto for keyboard notation," the mathematically proportional notational system invented and proposed by a Dutch electrical engineer. After Read 1987:76. Reproduced with permission of Greenwood Publishing Group, Inc., Westport, Conn.

In fourteenth-century Franconian notation, as in the ballade "*S'amours ne fait*" by Machaut (Apel 1940:350), there is no attempt to picture the descant and tenor as similar in length; even the "open" and "closed" endings of the phrase are obscured by this notation (figure 13).

The ideographic presentation of chords has long been common in Europe, from the *basso continuo* of Baroque tradition to contemporary lead sheets.

Uniphonic signs

Evidence for the use of systems of signs to name discrete pitches appears early in recorded history in documents from ancient Greece, India, and China. Scalar systems, in Europe as elsewhere, have displayed remarkable diversity, and their theoretical arrangement into scales and modes has usually followed (as it derived from) existing practice. One exception may be found in twelve-tone (serial) music, a system that derived its fundamental compositional material from the equal-tempered scale. Both familiar ways of naming and ordering such signs (as representing fixed or relative pitches) are found in ancient China. Today, the name of a tone can refer to the first scalar step or a specific pitch. Even the latter case shows variation: despite the establishment of an international pitch standard in 1939, discrepancies still exist from one instrument to another, and from one symphony orchestra to another.

A sharp distinction has often been drawn between alphabetical and syllabic (or other) methods of naming uniphonic systems. This differentiation appears to have little or no musical significance; whether or not the letters, numbers, or syllables have had a previous connotation is unimportant compared to the role they play in the musical structure.

Aural cue-systems

Memory feats performed by musicians in traditions seem to operate without any cues whatsoever. In the words of the Irish piper Tomás Ó Canainn:

A performance of traditional music is a thing of the moment—a few short minutes filled with music that is the result of many hours of practice, years of listening and perhaps generations of involvement in the tradition. In the past such a performance left no permanent record save in the mind of the listener. Does this mean

a   〰

b   *tr*

FIGURE 12   *a*, Pictographic and *b*, ideographic symbols contrasted.

that it is gone forever, without trace? In the traditional music context such a thing is unthinkable. (Cowdery 1990:4)

Vocalization undoubtedly manifests the most direct—and probably the most pervasive—method for the transmission of musical ideas. In many parts of the world, instrumentalists and singers learn music through vocal imitation; commonly, the methods that develop from this practice manifest elements of the particular musical structure and theoretical principles from which it was derived. Like other cue-systems, they may be used to help provide a framework for variation and change. Sometimes, these systems develop into genres of their own. Percussive sounds can be, and are, used to transmit rhythmic elements. Wherever the rhythmic component of music has been highly developed, there are likely to be aural methods for rhythmic instruction, and these have played an active and integral part in the musical fabric of several traditions.

Aural transmission often has a visual component. Instrumentalists learning through aural transmission usually fix their eyes on their teachers' hands, and the finger patterns they see form an important part of the process of memorization. Similarly, vocal students watch their instructors' mouths. A most interesting manifestation of this interrelationship has been suggested by Leo Treitler in reference to European liturgical neumes. He has postulated that neume contour identified which one of two types of vocal production was indicated for two general classes of sound: vocales (sounds like /a/) and semivocales (sounds like /n/). The sounds of

> vocales and semivocales can be made continuous—hence they are called nowadays "continuants." They, and only they, are the sounds that can be sung, and it is to them the neumes refer. From the beginning, it seems, neume systems provided for each neumatic character (virga, clivis, pes, etc.) a form to be written for singing semivocales, and one for singing vocales. The differentiation reflects the different shape of the mouth in singing the two sorts of sounds: wide open in singing vocales, closing down after singing the vocale sound in semivocales. . . . The liquescent neume in effect was a warning to the singer not to go on singing a wide-open sound. (Treitler 1992:18)

Thus, Treitler draws our attention to probable oral-aural-visual interaction in neumatic communication, a system also associated with cheironomy.

The practice of singing music without words is frequent, in performance and for instruction. Both of these functions are relevant to the subject at hand, because voca-

FIGURE 13
Ideographic notation: ligatures in Franconian notation in a passage from the fourteenth-century ballade "*S'amours ne fait*": *a*, discant; *b*, tenor; *c*, transcription into modern notation by Willi Apel. After Apel 1942.

In Scotland and Norway, even when certain instruments were clearly associated with male performers, mothers often taught their sons at least their first steps in learning them through vocal imitation. Both traditions exhibit instances of celebrated performers having been exclusively taught by their mothers in this way.

bles are used in transmitting music signals from teacher to student, from musician to musician, and as a technique preparatory to instrumental sight-reading. Sometimes even the instructional form of vocables becomes part of the performance. The common description of vocables as "meaningless" or "nonsense" syllables is misleading for a kind of singing that functions similarly to instrumental music, a phonemic structure within its musical context. Vocables are the aural side of uniphonic symbols, but they sometimes appear in written form as a kind of notation.

Untexted melismatic passages that decorated plainchant were central to medieval Roman Catholic church music. The *Alleluia* (from Hebrew *hallelujah* 'praise Yahweh'), originally a joyous exclamation grafted onto chant passages, eventually became a musical form of its own; its four vowels (continuants) made it an ideal vehicle for *vocalise*. Indeed, vocalizations have played an important role in a variety of European vocal traditions since, particularly as technical exercises and for virtuoso display. Limited strictly to an instructional function, two different systems of sol-fa syllables have long coexisted in Europe. In *solmization*, the sol-fa syllables represent interval relationships within the tonal scheme; the focal pitch of the series (*do*) can be placed at any pitch level, and thus it is considered a movable-*do* system. An influential reawakening of interest in solmization in nineteenth-century England was due mainly to the efforts of the English choir-director Sarah Glover (1786–1867). Long before her time, Guidonian solmization had developed an unsavory reputation as "pedantique gibberish," and Burney believed it would take great "meditation" to correct the system. Glover, in her own published method, took care to cite Burney and explain how her adaptation of sol-fa syllables had remedied its defects. Under the name *tonic sol-fa,* the method became enormously popular, especially in England, where it so remains. In contrast, the continental European system of solfège (Italian *solfeggio*) is a fixed-*do* system, in which vocables signify absolute pitches (that is, *sol* always designates G). It is sometimes called the Wilhem method, after Guillaume Louis Bocquillon Wilhem (1781–1842) but actually has been used, in one form or another, since the sixteenth century or before. In France, it continues to be a fixture in public-school education, and professional symphonic instrumentalists practice it before attempting to sight-read complicated orchestral parts on their instruments.

Canntaireachd, the Scottish vocable system for learning *piobaireachd* (the classical Highland bagpipe tradition), calls for technically skilled singers to reproduce intricate ornamentation. Figure 14 gives an example of *canntaireachd* in the *Nether Lord* system: first, the basic nine-step bagpipe scale, and then samples of traditional ornaments. The highly stylized ornaments are brought into prominence through percussive vocal sounds. The embellishing figures impart phrase articulations for music otherwise characterized by an uninterrupted flow of sound droning beneath the melody (Collinson 1975:161).

Ballads in Scotland and Norway often include vocal imitation of the national instruments (bagpipes and Hardanger violin, respectively), often as refrains. In

FIGURE 14   Aural signals: *canntaireachd,* the Scottish system of vocables for learning *piobaireachd,* the classical art of Highland piping. After Collinson 1966:162.

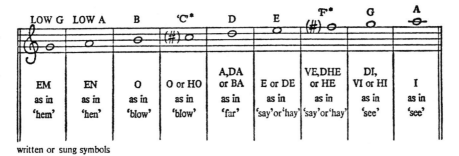

LOW G	LOW A	B	'C*'	D	E	F* (#)	G	A
EM as in 'hem'	EN as in 'hen'	O as in 'blow'	O or HO as in 'blow'	A,DA or BA as in 'far'	E or DE as in 'say' or 'hay'	VE,DHE or HE as in 'say' or 'hay'	DI, VI or HI as in 'see'	I as in 'see'

written or sung symbols

hin - barc   ho - bare   hio - bare

The *leumluath*.

hin - darid   ho - darid   hio - darid   etc.

The *taorluath* .

hin - bandre   ho - bandre   hio - bandre   etc.

The *crunluath,* or 'crowning movement,' of the *piobaireachd.*

Scotland, the practice is called mouth music; in Norway, *tralling (tulling, lolling, sulling)*; and in each country, the technique has led to a new genre, vocal renditions of entire pieces by singers who become renowned for executing the highly elaborate ornamentation involved. When these instruments were still clearly associated with male performers, mothers (in their function as original transmitters of culture) often taught their sons at least their first steps in learning them through vocal imitation. Both traditions exhibit instances of celebrated performers having been exclusively taught by their mothers in this way.

Like *canntaireachd, tralling* conveys more than melodic aspects of the music. It is particularly effective in reproducing the complicated rhythmic subtleties characteristic of the dance forms in their regional interpretations, and is commonly used in the

pa– ra– did– dle   pa– ra– did– dle

FIGURE 15   Contemporary drum mnemonics: "paradiddle, paradiddle."

transmission of Hardanger violin pieces from fiddler to fiddler. The following illustration gives a comparison of three dance rhythms (from Bjørndal and Alver 1966:117):

Halling: *Sut-tam sudluttam*
               sam-suttam-duttam-dei
               suttam-duttam-dudliodei

Gangar: *Samtamtam, susamtam*
               sutamtam—deia.

Springar: *Sam-tam-da ditam*
               ditt-um-dadli-dittum
               didl-i-dal-dittum
               samtamtam-du-di-dudl-i-du

The vocalization of percussive sounds is a common expedient in musical performance instruction. Players of wind instruments practice the technique of tonguing (articulations achieved by momentarily interrupting the windstream by the tongue) by repeating combinations of the letters *t* and *k;* for single tongueing, the player practices: *t—t . . . ;* for double tongueing: *t—k . . . ;* for triple tongueing: *t—k—t . . . ;* and for flutter tongueing *(flatterzunge): d—r—r—r.*

The rudiments of drumming are learned through practicing the rhythms of onomatopoeic words; for example, "stroke rolls" include the *paradiddle* (figure 15). As early as 1596, the French dancing master Thoinot Arbeau (Jehan Tabourot) published drum mnemonics (figure 16).

TRANSMISSION IN CONTEXT

Hugo Cole's observation that "all notations are indeterminate in so far as they fail to give a complete specification" (Cole 1974:137) may be extended to cue-systems in general. Cole makes it clear that he means "purposely" indeterminate, an important point in considering the discrepancies between music signs of all kinds and their realization in performance. Indeed, it is that unspecified area that is central to compre-

FIGURE 16   Sixteenth-century French drum mnemonics. The sketch shows a soldier following the aural signals of the drummer, whose function it is to lead the military outfit. After Arbeau 1588:35.

Colin tan plon   colin tan plon

hension of the tradition itself. Is it ignored because it is not relevant to the tradition in question or because it is too obvious to need specification? Or is it not present because its development is left in the performer's hands? The ability to decipher musical cues (whether cheironomic gestures, vocables, or graphic signs) depends on possessing knowledge of this kind, part of the pool of intellectual resources that is available to the knowledgeable musician of any culture.

The impulse to a broader perspective of music transmission may be understood in the larger context of a general abandonment of a belief in cultural progress. The search for a single truth in music no longer seems tenable (Bent 1980; Cole 1974; Finnegan 1988, 1992; Harvey 1990; Randel 1986; Tarasti 1983; Treitler 1977, 1992).

BIBLIOGRAPHY

Adorno, Theodor, and Max Horkheimer, 1977 [1944]. *Dialectic of Enlightenment*. Translated by John Cumming. New York: Herder & Herder.

Al-Fārābī. 1930. *Kitābu l-Mūsīqī al-Kabīr* (The great book on music). In *La musique arab*, ed. Rodolphe d'Erlanger, 1 (entire) and 2:1–101. Paris: P. Geuthner.

Apel, Willi. 1940. *The Harvard Dictionary of Music*. Cambridge: Harvard University Press.

———. 1942. *The Notation of Polyphonic Music, 900–1600*. Cambridge: Harvard University Press.

Arbeau, Thoinot. 1588. *Orchésographie*. Langres: Jeban de Preyz. Modern ed., trans. by Mary Stewart Evans. New York: Dover, 1967.

Aristotle. 1932. *Metaphysics I–IX*. Translated by Hugh Tredennick. London: William Heinemann.

Babitz, Sol. 1952. "A Problem of Rhythm in Baroque Music." *The Musical Quarterly* 38(5):533–565.

Bacon, Roger. 1962 [1928]. *Opus Majus*. Translated by R. B. Burke. Philadelphia: Russell and Russell.

Barrière, Jean-Baptiste, et al. 1994. *Harmonique: musique, recherche, théorie*. Paris: IRCAM.

Barthes, Roland. 1977. *Image—Music—Text*. Selected and translated by Stephen Heath. New York: Hill and Wang.

Bartók, Béla. 1931. *Hungarian Folk Music*. London: Oxford University Press.

Bartók, Béla, and Albert Lord. 1954. *Serbo-Croatian Heroic Songs*. Cambridge: Harvard University Press.

Béhague, Gerard. 1984. *Performance Practice: An Ethnomusicological Perspective*. Westport, Conn.: Greenwood Press.

Ben-Amos, Dan. 1982. *Folklore in Context*. New Delhi: South Asia Publications.

Bent, Ian. 1980. "Notation I and II." *The New Grove Dictionary of Music and Musicians*. Edited by Stanley Sadie. London: Macmillan.

Berliner, Paul. 1994. *Thinking in Jazz: The Infinite Art of Improvisation*. Chicago: Chicago University Press.

Bjørgum, Hallvard. 1987. "Dobbelsiger for Norsk Folkemusikk og Bygdedans" in *Spelemannsbladet Journal* 4:14.

Bjørndal, Arne, and B. Alver. 1966. *Og fela ho let*. Oslo: Universitetsforlaget.

Blume, Friedrich. 1970. *Classic and Romantic Music*. Translated by M. D. Herter Norton. New York: Norton.

Boretz, Benjamin. 1989. "The Logic of What?" *Journal of Music Theory* 33(1):107–116.

Bouissac, Paul. 1986. "Iconicity: Essays on the Nature of Culture." In *Festschrift for Thomas A. Sebeok on His 65th Birthday*, ed. Paul Bouissac et al. Tübingen: Stauffenburg Verlag.

Bourdieu, Pierre. 1977. *Outline of a Theory of Practice*. Cambridge University Press.

Bukofzer, Manfred. 1947. *Music in the Baroque Era*. New York: Norton.

Burney, Charles. 1935 [1789]. *A General History of Music*. Vol. 2. Edited by Frank Mercer. New York: Dover Publications.

Chailley, Jacques. 1967. *La Musique et le Signe*. Lausanne: Les Éditions Rencontre.

Chase, Gilbert. 1966. *America's Music*. 2d, rev. ed. New York: Macmillan.

Chou, Wen-Chung. 1971. "Asian Concepts and Twentieth-Century Western Composers." *The Musical Quarterly* 57(2):211–229.

Clifford, James. 1988. *The Predicament of Culture*. Cambridge: Harvard University Press.

Cohen, Anne, and Norm Cohen. 1973. "Tune Evolution as an Indicator of Traditional Musical Norms." *Journal of American Folklore* 36:44–52.

Cole, Hugo. 1974. *Sounds and Signs: Aspects of Musical Notation*. New York: Oxford University Press.

Collinson, Francis. 1966. *The Traditional and National Music of Scotland*. London: Routledge and Kegan Paul.

———. 1975. *The Bagpipe: The History of a Musical Instrument*. London: Routledge and Kegan Paul.

Connor, Steven. 1989. *Postmodernist Culture*. Oxford: Blackwell.

Cowdery, James. 1990. *The Melodic Traditions of Ireland*. Kent, Ohio: Kent State University Press.

Crane, Gregory. 1991. "Composing Culture: The Authority of an Electronic Text." *Current Anthropology* 32(3):293–311.

Cserba, Simon M., ed. 1935. *Tractatus de Musica* by Hieronymus de Moravia. Freiburger Studien zur Musikwissenschaft, 2. Resensburg: Friedrich Pustet.

David, Hans, and Arthur Mendel, eds. 1945. *The Bach Reader*. New York: Norton.

Dolmetsch, Arnold. 1916. *The Interpretation of Music From the XVIIth–XVIIIth Centuries*. London: Oxford University Press.

Eco, Umberto. 1979 [1976]. *A Theory of Semiotics*. Bloomington: University of Indiana Press.

———. 1986. *Art and Beauty in the Middle Ages*. New Haven: Yale University Press.

Escobar, Arturo, et al. 1994. "The Anthropology of Cyberculture." *Current Anthropology* 35(3):211–231.

Feld, Steven. 1995. "From Schizophonia to Schismogenesis: The Discourses and Practices of World Music and World Beat." In *The Traffic in Culture*, ed. George Marcus and Fred Myers, 96–127. Berkeley: University of California Press.

Feldman, Burton, and Robert Richardson, eds. 1972. *The Rise of Modern Mythology*. Bloomington: Indiana University Press.

Fétis, François. 1895. *Histoire générale de la musique*. 5 vols. Paris: Firmin Didot Frères.

Finnegan, Ruth. 1988. *Orality and Literacy*. Oxford: Blackwell.

———. 1989. *The Hidden Musicians: Music-Making in a Small Town*. Cambridge: Cambridge University Press.

———. 1992. *Oral Traditions and the Verbal Arts: A Guide to Research Practices*. London: Routledge.

Fleischer, Oskar. 1895. *Neumen-Studien.* 2 vols. Leipzig: Friedrich Fleisher.

Frith, Simon. 1983. *Sound Effects: Youth, Leisure and the Politics of Rock.* London: Constable.

————.1992. "The Industrialization of Popular Music." *Popular Music and Communication,* ed. James Lull, 49–74. 2d ed. Newbury Park: Sage.

————, ed. 1995. *Music and Copyright.* Edinburgh: Edinburgh University Press.

Gerson-Kiwi, Edith. 1961. "Religious Chant—A Pan-Asiatic Concept of Music." *Journal of the International Music Council* 13:64–67.

————. 1980. *Migrations and Mutations in Music East and West.* Tel-Aviv: Tel-Aviv University.

Gombrich, Otto. 1956. *Art and Illusion.* Princeton: Princeton University Press.

Gourlay, Kenneth A. 1978. "Towards a Reassessment of the Ethnomusicologist's Role in Research." *Ethnomusicology* 22(1):1–35.

Griffith, Paul. 1972. "Interview with Morton Feldman." *The Musical Times* (August), 758–759.

Gumperz, John J., and Del Hymes. 1972. *Directions in Sociolinguistics.* New York: Holt, Rinehart and Winston.

Harvey, David. 1990. *The Condition of Modernity: An Enquiry into the Origins of Cultural Change.* Oxford: Blackwell.

Hawkins, John. 1776. *A General History of the Science and Practice of Music.* 5 vols. London: T. Payne.

Heiniö, Mikko. 1989. "Post-Modernism—An Approach to Contemporary Finnish Music." In *Musiikki: Proceedings from the Nordic Musicological Congress in Turku/Åbo,* ed. Ilkka Oramo, 130–141. Turku/Åbo: Musicological Society of Finland.

Hemsi, Alberto. 1930. *La Musique de la Torah.* 2d ed. Alexandria, Egypt: Édition orientale de musique.

Herndon, Marcia, and W. Brynyate. 1976. *Form in Performance: Hard-Core Ethnography.* Proceedings of a symposium on the ethnography of performance held at the University of Texas. Austin: University of Texas Press.

Herndon, Marcia, and Norma McLeod. 1980. *The Ethnography of Musical Performance.* Norwood, Penn.: Norwood Editions.

Hirschhorn, Larry. 1984. *Beyond Mechanization: Work and Technology in a Post-Industrial Age.* Cambridge: M.I.T. Press.

Hood, Mantle. 1963. "Music the Unknown." In *Musicology,* ed. Claude V. Palisca, Frank L. Harrison, and Mantle Hood. Englewood Cliffs, N.J.: Prentice-Hall.

Hopkins, Pandora. 1966. "The Purposes of Transcription." *Ethnomusicology* 10(3):310–317.

————.1976. "Individual Choice the Control of Musical Change." *Journal of American Folklore* 89(354):449–462.

————. 1977. "The Homology of Music and Myth: Views of Levi-Strauss on Musical Structure." *Ethnomusicology* 21(2):247–261.

————. 1986. *Aural Thinking in Norway: Performance and Communication with the Hardingfele.* New York: Human Sciences Press.

————. 1989. "Nordic Musicology in International Perspective." In *Musiikki: Proceedings from the Nordic Musicological Congress in Turku/Åbo,* ed. Ilkka Oramo, 1–15. Turku/Åbo: Musicological Society of Finland.

Hymes, Dell. 1974. *Foundations in Sociolinguistics: An Ethnographic Approach.* Philadelphia: University of Pennsylvania Press.

Idelsohn, Abraham. 1944 [1929]. *Jewish Music in Its Historical Tradition.* New York: Holt.

Kubler, George. 1962. *The Shape of Time.* New Haven: Yale University Press.

Langer, Susanne K. 1951. *Philosophy in a New Key.* 2d ed. Cambridge: Harvard University Press.

Lévi-Strauss, Claude. 1964. *Mythologiques: Le cru et le cuit.* Paris: Plon.

————. 1967. *Mythologiques: Du miel aux cendres.* Paris: Plon.

————. 1968. *Mythologiques: L'origine des manières de table.* Paris: Plon.

————. 1971. *Mythologiques: L'homme nu.* Paris: Plon.

Longhurst, Brian. 1995. *Popular Music and Society.* Oxford: Blackwell.

Lord, Albert B. 1960. *The Singer of Tales.* Cambridge: Harvard University Press.

Lucinius, Ottomaro. 1536. *Musurgia.* Argentino: Ionnem Scottum.

Mathews, Max, and John Pierce, eds. 1989. *Current Directions in Computer Music Research.* Cambridge: M.I.T. Press.

Meyer, Leonard B. 1994 [1967]. *Music, the Arts, and Ideas: Patterns and Predictions in Twentieth-Century Culture.* 2d ed.

Nettel, Reginald. 1948. *The Orchestra in England: A Social History.* London: Jonathan Cape.

Pincherle, Marc. 1956. *Corelli: His Life and His Work.* Translated by Hubert Russell. New York: Norton.

————. 1958. "On the Rights of the Interpreter in the Performance of 17th- and 18th-Century Music." *Musical Quarterly* 44(2):145–166.

Randel, Don, ed. 1986. "Transmission." In *The New Harvard Dictionary of Music,* 866.

Read, Gardner. 1987. *Source Book of Proposed Music Notation Reforms.* New York: Greenwood Press.

Reese, Gustave. 1940. *Music in the Middle Ages.* New York: Norton.

Rice, Timothy. 1994. *May It Fill Your Soul: Experiencing Bulgarian Music.* Chicago: University of Chicago Press.

Saetveit, Joseph G., with Carl Seashore. 1940. *Seashore Measures of Musical Talents.* New York: Psychological Corporation.

Schenk, Erich. 1959. *Mozart and His Times.* New York: Knopf.

Schottstaedt, William. 1989. "A Computer Music Language." In *Current Directions in Computer Music Research,* ed. Max Mathews and John Pierce, 215–224. Cambridge: M.I.T. Press.

Seashore, Carl, 1967 [1938]. *Psychology of Music.* New York: Dover.

Seeger, Charles. 1971. "Prescriptive and Descriptive Music Writing." In *Readings in Ethnomusicology,* ed. David P. McAllester, 24–34. New York: Johnson Reprint Corporation.

Segall, Marshall, et al. 1990. *Human Behavior in Global Perspective.* New York: Pergamon Press.

Seidman, Steven, ed. 1994. *The Postmodern Turn.* Cambridge: Cambridge University Press.

Sendrey, Alfred. 1969. *Music in Ancient Israel.* New York: Philosophical Library.

Slawson, Wayne. 1985. *Sound Color.* Berkeley: University of California Press.

Steenberghen, Fernand van. 1955. *Aristotle in the West: The Origins of Latin Aristotelianism.* Translated and revised by Leonard Johnston. Louvain: E. Nauwela.

Strauss, Neil. 1997. "Whether or Not It Deserves It, the Music Industry Is Getting Its Own Press." *The New York Times* (17 Feb.), 47.

Strunk, Oliver. 1950. *Source Readings in Music History.* New York: Norton.

Tarasti, Eero. 1983. "Reflections on the Logic of Music Discourse." *Suomen Antropologi* 4(83):242–245.

Treitler, Leo. 1977. "Transmission and the Study of Music History." In *Report of the Twelfth Congress: International Musicological Society,* 202–211. Kassel: Bärenreiter.

————. 1992. "The 'Unwritten' and 'Written' Transmission of Medieval Chant and the Start-Up of Musical Notation." *Journal of Musicology* 10(2):131–191.

Turner, Victor. 1987. *The Anthropology of Performance.* New York: PAJ Publications.

Vansina, Jan. 1985. *Oral Tradition as History.* Madison: University of Wisconsin Press.

Wachsmann, Klaus. 1980. "Folk Music." In *The*

New Grove. Edited by Stanley Sadie. London: Macmillan.

———. 1982. "The Changeability of Musical Experience." *Ethnomusicology* 26(2):197–215.

AUDIOVISUAL RESOURCES

Fernández de la Cuesta, Ismael. 1994. *Chant.* Angel CD 55138. Compact disc.

Wallis, Roger, and Krister Malm. 1984. *Big Sounds from Small Peoples: The Music Industry in Small Countries.* London: Constable.

Werner, Eric. 1959. *The Sacred Bridge.* London: D. Dobson.

Local Knowledge of Musical Genres and Roles
Stephen Blum

The Names for Genres and Roles
The Ethics and Aesthetics of Reciprocity
Older and Newer Roles and Genres

FIGURE 1 In Bulgaria, two women sing in a close, two-voiced polyphony similar to Bosnian *ganga.* By sitting so close together as to touch shoulders, they can hear one another well and project their sound as if from one voice. Photo by Martha Forsyth, 1985.

Singers, dancers, and instrumentalists have reasons for doing what they do. Anyone who learns how to sing, dance, or play an instrument observes and participates in various events, and as experienced singers, dancers, and instrumentalists show the less experienced how to make the right moves, they may say something about why performers need to act in just this way in that particular setting. Verbal behavior is not necessarily external to musical performance: names, maxims, and evaluations convey information that helps performers do what is expected. Music-related statements that have been transmitted and collected in oral tradition are equally helpful to scholars and others who wish to understand the ethics and aesthetics of a musical practice. Common subjects of discourse about music include names for actors, actions, and situations; when and where to sing or not to sing; criteria for excellence in performance; the natural and supernatural worlds that are linked by singing or lamenting; who should lead and who should follow; when to compete and when to cooperate; and what sorts of local or national identities are negotiated through musical performance.

THE NAMES FOR GENRES AND ROLES

Our ability to call individuals, groups, objects, and actions by what we believe to be their correct names is indispensable to our collective existence. The names by which Europeans have identified performance genres and performers' roles have rich associations; performers often talk about what they are doing in terms of specific genres or roles, without generalizing about "music" or "performance." In Hercegovina and southern Bosnia, singers have said that the genre *ganga* "provokes the most pleasant feeling" and performers must blend their voices to "sound like one voice" (Petrović 1977:101). The ethics and aesthetics of *ganga* are articulated in such statements, with or without implicit comparisons to other arts and activities (figure 1).

Actors and actions

In many cases, words for actions are closely linked to words for the actors and the objects of their actions. Drawing on conversations with villagers, Tim Rice (1980a:45–47) lists five Bulgarian "verbal categories" that are "distinct behavioral or functional categories." Each is expressed by a transitive verb, "linked uniquely with specific cognate subjects and objects":

svirach sviri svirnya, a "tuner" "tunes" a tune
pevitsa pee pesen, a singer sings a song
tûguvashtiat tûguva tûga, a lamenter laments a lament
tûpanzhiya tupa tûpan, a drummer drums a drum
igrach igrae igra, a dancer dances a dance

"Tuning" (playing a chordophone or an aerophone), singing, lamenting, drumming, and dancing are different activities, each with its own area of meaning. Some (e.g., singing and lamenting) verge on being mutually exclusive, but others (e.g., drumming and dancing) usually happen at the same time. The five areas of skill do not constitute a larger whole, "music," and it would be impossible for a "master musician" to demonstrate full competence in all five areas—not least because drummers and instrumentalists are almost always men, but lamenters and most singers are women.

Situations

Names for many European traditional musical activities refer to the participants and the circumstances in which the activity normally takes place—the location, the time of year, the type of occasion. The name of one genre can call to mind a whole bundle of features, centering on the performer's situation and actions appropriate to it. In several regions of Poland, for example, local names for a genre of "open-air" song describe the landscape in which the singer's voice resounds: *leśna* 'of the forest' in Kurpie, *polne* 'of the fields' in Sandomierz, *lasowe* 'of the forest' in Zywieckie, *polanowe* 'of the mountain pasture land' (equivalent to French *alpage* 'alpine pasture') in the Beskidy Mountains, and *wierzchowe* 'of the peaks' in the Tatra highlands (figure 2). Though specific singing styles vary according to regional norms, each genre lets singers use their voices in ways that would be inappropriate in other genres. "Open-air" songs are often sung at a slower tempo than other genres, with more elaborate connections between the sung syllables, and for this reason the term *ciągnione* 'drawn out' may be used in place of *wierzchowe* (Stęszewski 1972). Such traits can be strong enough to remain intact when the songs are transferred to a different environment (i.e., sung indoors or at a wedding), but melodies commonly undergo stylistic changes as they pass from one set of circumstances to another. In Lubelskie, the melody used by a raftsman in singing the genre *flisak* might become a *podruznick*

FIGURE 2   In the Tatra highlands of southern Poland, a string band of three fiddles and a bass performs outdoors. Here, singing is often in a loud, outdoor style, even when performed indoors. Early-twentieth-century postcard. Courtesy of the Robert Godfried Collection, New York.

when played by instrumentalists to accompany a wedding procession, and the same melody could be called a *powiślak* 'over (or along) the Vistula' when sung by a group of women in the bride's home (Noll 1986:513).

In many cultures of southeastern Europe, genres appropriate to men's performance "at the table" (Greek *epí trapézios*, Bulgarian *na trapeza*) are distinguished from those sung "on the road" and/or those used for dancing. Singing for a group gathered around a table requires a man to display his vocal skills, and his listeners are in a strong position to exercise their aesthetic judgment. For the Serbs of Vojvodina, a distinction between table songs (*astalske pesme*) and street songs (*sokačke pesme*) may remain meaningful, even when songs of both genres are performed in cafes, rather than homes.

Obligations

Participants' identities are defined by immediate circumstances in such genres as lullabies, games, herding calls, laments for the dead, and bridal laments and other parts of marriage rituals. People, especially women, are often expected to be able to assume these identities as the occasion arises, and the learning process begins at an early age. For a young woman in some north Russian villages, not knowing how to lament would be as shameful as not knowing how to milk a cow (Mazo 1994:24). One also learns what not to do: when and where not to display some of the skills one may have acquired. In Epirus, northwesternmost Greece, women carry the primary responsibilities for mourning the dead—responsibilities that increase as they age: numerous occasions call for lamenting, but mature women are left with few opportunities to sing unless they are willing to incur blame (Auerbach 1987).

Situations in which people cannot easily evade a social obligation to perform are highly conducive to the reproduction of inherited musical practices. Bernard Lortat-Jacob (1984) suggests that the term *traditional* music is most applicable when people live together in relationships of "compulsory interdependence" and are constrained to meet their responsibilities to family members, neighbors, and ancestors. Other types of social relations may arise in circumstances of face-to-face contact or "interaction with others who are physically co-present" (Giddens 1984:64). To understand a musical practice is to understand the respects in which a musician's actions are "compulsory" or "voluntary," obligatory or optional—but in making this distinction, we should not forget that people often desire to meet others' expectations.

Willingness to carry out musical actions appropriate to one's standing in a community may not require any discussion of "tradition." Once an older way of life is recognized as such, people are more likely to speak about and reflect on the practices that have become "traditional" and somewhat more "optional" than before. Where no appeal to "tradition" is needed, the most useful terms of discourse are those that identify types of action and allow for evaluating performances.

Systems

Numerous genres may be understood as sets or systems of relationships used in performance—systems that define each participant's role in an ensemble. An early (1778) account of one such system is Henrik Gabriel Porthan's description of Finnish *runonlaulu,* the singing of old poems by a leader (*laulaja, päämies*) and a supporting singer (*puoltaja, säistäjä*), "surrounded by a circle of listeners who stand there attentively":

> [T]the singing is alternately shared in such a way that after the main singer has brought a verse to about the third syllable from the end, or to the last measure, the supporting singer comes in with his voice—for by estimating from the sense itself and from the meter one can easily finish off the rest of the measure—and

thus they both produce it. After that the supporting singer repeats the verse alone in a slightly varied tone as if he would give his unqualified approval. Meanwhile, the main singer remains silent until the supporting singer again reaches the final measure, which both utter in unison. . . .

The interval vouchsafed him while the supporting singer is repeating a previous verse the main singer, performing (*canens*) extemporaneously, uses to think up and compose (*concinnandum*) the coming verse. . . .

The *modus* that the main singer employs is always one and the same, with scarcely any variation. . . . The singers sit side by side or facing one another, close enough to bring in contact their right hands and also their knees . . . on which they prop their clasped hands. While singing, they move their bodies gently as if wanting to touch heads, and they assume a reflective and serious expression. (Porthan 1867 [1778]:362–365).

This description shows precisely what each singer does at specific points—something we now expect an ethnomusicological description to do. The system that obliges a second singer to enter on a final syllable of the first singer's line and repeat the same line, with the first singer joining in to end the repetition before proceeding with the next line, was used in other Finno-Ugric peoples' genres, such as the Estonian "swing song" (Ross 1989).

The components of a system are often named according to the qualities or actions that characterize each component in relation to the others. Several systems of vocal performance in the Baltic area and the Balkans use somewhat similar terms for the roles of "principal" and "supporting" singers; Marcu (1967) and Brambats (1983) have suggested that all these systems may have developed from a common source. The first singer may be said to "tell" or "cry"; the supporting singer, to "cut," "fold," "turn," or "trail"; and the other persons present, to "fill," "pull," or "drag" as they produce a drone.

Region	*Role*	*Action*
Latvia (west, central)	first soloist:	
	teiceja	*teikt* 'tells, says'
	sauceja	*saukt* 'calls, cries'
	second soloist:	
	locitaja	*locit* 'folds, bends'
	others: *vilcejas*	*vilkt* 'pull'
Greece (Epirus)	first soloist:	
	partis	["takes" melody]
	second soloist:	
	ghyristis	*ghyrizei* 'turns'
	tsakizei 'breaks, folds'	
	klostis	*klothei* 'spins'
	others: *issocrates*	[hold *ison*, drone]
Bulgaria	first voice:	*otivat po napred* 'goes in front'
	parvi glas	*izvikva* 'cries out'
		trese 'shakes'
		diga 'rises'
	second voice:	*otivat po nazad* 'goes behind'
	vtori glas	*vlachi* 'trails'
		slaga 'lies'
		trese 'shakes'
		krivo buchi 'bellows crookedly'
	[third voice]:	*pravo buchat* 'bellow straight'
	others:	*vlachat* 'trail'
Albania (Labs)	second soloist:	*ia kthen* 'turns it'
	others:	*ia mbush* 'fill it'

Performers often address themselves to both the living and the dead—and sometimes to a tree, a rock, or "Mother Earth." On many occasions, but particularly at weddings and funerals, performers can act as mediators, preparing the living to assume new roles or instructing the recently deceased as they find their way to the world of the dead.

The systems that come into play in solo vocal genres are sometimes learned as movement patterns: the singer remembers how it feels to articulate one type of vowel followed by another type of vowel, and reproduces this pattern time and again. In six swinging songs (*canti all'altalena*) of Basilicata, southern Italy, the vowels /a/ and /i/ serve as a system in two respects. First, they are sung as a pair in sequences from /i/ to /a/ and /a/ to /i/ more frequently than any other pair. Second, /a/ is preferred as the final vowel in 68 percent of the lines, but the first vowel in only 28 percent of them (Adamo 1984).

In genres performed by ensembles with fixed instrumentation, each instrumentalist assumes a specific role or set of roles within the overall system. In *fado,* which is performed in the Portuguese cities of Lisbon and Coimbra, one to four guitarists accompany a vocal soloist. One player of the *guitarra Portuguesa* contributes melodies that complement the singer's. A second player of this instrument, if present, adds melodies to mesh with those of the first. The most indispensable instrument, the *viola* (a guitar with six courses), provides the necessary harmonic and rhythmic support for the singer and the *guitarista*(s). The bass line may be played on the *viola baixo,* a larger *viola.* All players draw on a fund of conventional patterns, perhaps adding new ideas that fit the particular type of *fado* they are performing.

Sequences

Musical genres exist to be orchestrated: to be combined in appropriate sequences during one type of performance; to be distributed throughout the agricultural cycle and men's and women's life cycles; and to be differentiated in ways that can distinguish a descent group, a locality, a region, a class, or a means of livelihood. Each of these considerations (or a combination of them) comes to the fore in the name of one or another genre, and the processes of combination, distribution, and differentiation are often the subject of ethical and aesthetic judgments. The judgments are based on rules or norms and practices of interpreting, bending, and violating the rules.

Among the most common ways to orchestrate the genres of performance, particularly in southeastern Europe, is to associate specific genres with men's and women's life cycles. A celebration may be designed as an arrangement of the genres appropriate to people of different ages. Rice (1980b), for example, describes three phases in the dancing at a Macedonian *sobor,* with Rom (Gypsy) musicians playing different types of music for dancing by older men and women, middle-aged working men, and men and women in their late teens and early twenties. Each type had its distinctive meters, dance steps, and associations with regional or national norms. The musicians interacted most vigorously with the middle-aged wage-earning men, who gave them their fees and tips. For younger dancers, they provided music that more closely approached the national (pan-Yugoslavian and pan-Macedonian) norms of government-sponsored folkloric ensembles. The musicians had developed a "system" for matching genres with dancers.

THE ETHICS AND AESTHETICS OF RECIPROCITY

Why are a musician's actions so important as to be "compulsory" in some circumstances? The Romanian scholar Constantin Brăiloiu formulated one of the best answers to this question: because they amount to a "defense of life" (1984 [1946]:119). Of course, the actions may enhance life as much as they defend it—in which case they may seem to be more optional than obligatory. Yet in peasant communities, practices of mutual assistance (*clacă* in Romanian) might require a man who received help from his neighbors to provide music for dancing and food and drink; the pleasure that comes from dancing is often considered a necessary enhancement of life.

Copresence

The issue of physical copresence is a complicated one for students of musical performance, since performers often address themselves to both the living and the dead—and sometimes to a tree, a rock, or "Mother Earth." On many occasions, but particularly at weddings and funerals, performers can act as mediators, preparing the living to assume new roles or instructing the recently deceased as they find their way to the world of the dead. Specific musical genres are endowed with the power to bring about heightened relationships of copresence among ancestors, kinfolk, neighbors, animals, trees, and other features of the landscape or other inanimate objects. An outstanding instance is the joik (*juoi'gat*) of the Saami, to whom outsiders have applied the disparaging term *Lapps:* the most extensive joiks use narrative and singing to relate the singer's life history. Singers, "more often than not separated from each other by their kind of work, try to realize their 'social ties' by yoiking [*sic*] about the native environment: the mountains, lakes, herding places, animals, or even the mosquito girl who helps to drive the flocks faster, and about family members, neighbours and friends who may be far away or dead (for whom one is able to search by yoiking [*sic*] their personal tunes)" (D. Stockmann 1994:10). The most extensive joiks invoke presences of every kind, but others are more restricted in content.

The power to achieve copresence depends on performers' and listeners' skills of memory and abilities to enact what they know to exist. For Macedonian peasants in Debarca, copresence is made possible by the faculty of *ækil* (from Turkish *akıl*, Arabic *'aql* 'discernment'), through which any listener may grasp a piece of music as a whole, apprehending it as fully as does the performer (Marshall 1982:167–169). Joiking alone, a Saami woman may reach a state of deep emotion as her performance evokes the presences of deceased relatives. In all musical manifestations of copresence— which is almost to say in all music—more than one person participates in the motions that generate sounds; those present in performers' and listeners' memories can exert a powerful influence.

Excellence

The quality of some "solo" performances may be evaluated by the extent to which listeners join in. During the winter vigils (*kvöldvaka* 'evening watch') that were once held in Iceland, a performer [*kvæðamaður*] of *rímur*, ballads of up to one hundred stanzas, was most successful when his listeners "repeated almost every word" of the chanting (*kvæði*) according to the *kvæðamaður* Þórður Guðbjartsson (b. 1891). Performers normally recited "as clearly and slowly as they did so that people might be able to memorize the verses," and listeners participated in "drawing out" (*draga seiminn*) the last tone in each stanza; but the *kvæðamaður* might fail to elicit even the customary drawing out. If his listeners "repeated almost every word," he had managed to fully engage their attention and activate their memories of previous performances of the same ballad. Single stanzas or epigrams (*lausavísur* 'loose stanzas') that may have been improvised on a particular occasion are detached from their ballads, remembered, and quoted at appropriate moments in conversation (Nielsen 1982).

Memory comes into play when performers make the right moves at the right pace and moment. We can imagine a continuum extending from genres that most men or women perform at some time in their lives to those that demand a high degree of specialization—genres like narrative poetry, instrumental dance music, and, in some circumstances, improvised laments. Whether or not they receive money for their services, the best specialists have mastered the techniques of a "necessary improvisation that defines excellence" (Bourdieu 1977 [1972]:8). Specialists are often recognized for their sense of tact, their ability to find the performance gestures that "fit" or "work" at a given moment.

One such role is that of the *meraklis* (pl. *meraklides*) in the ritual celebrations known as *glendia* (sing. *glendi*) in Olymbos, a village on Karpathos, a Greek island. The *meraklis* has learned through experience how to animate the celebration, helping everyone present achieve a state of *kefi,* "a heightened form of experience—far more transported and serious than the carefree and festive mood that the term connotes in other parts of Greece" (Caraveli 1985:263). The primary form of communication during the celebration is the singing of rhyming or assonant couplets (*mantinadhes,* sing. *mantinadha*) to the accompaniment of *laouto, lyra,* and perhaps *tsambouna* 'bagpipe'. Whether improvised or quoted from memory, a *mantinadha* should "serve as a fitting response to something said before" or "make an apt allusion to past events." *Meraklides* play a crucial role in controlling who sings what, to whom, for how long, and when; to elicit appropriate contributions that will reconcile personal and communal interests according to the intricate rules of the *glendi,* they must be keenly sensitive to individual participants' concerns and emotional states. When the timing and delivery are right, a couplet or sequence of couplets is more likely to be remembered and reproduced at subsequent gatherings, acquiring new levels of meaning.

At Albanian men's gatherings (*muabet, mexhelis*), the role of the head elder (*kryeplak*) or leader (*kryetar*) is somewhat analogous to that of the *meraklides,* as is the overall dynamic and primary purpose of the event: "the coordinated attainment of elation" (Sugarman 1988:30). In comparison to the *glendi,* the seating arrangements and the order in which participants sing are perhaps more strictly regulated according to age: the *kryeplak* sings first, followed by other elders, men whose first children have not yet married, and unmarried youths. Flexibility occurs in the order of singing at a *muabet,* but the course of events in a *glendi* seems much more flexible; as the celebration proceeds, women sometimes sing *mantinadhes.* Ideally, several *meraklides* (rather than a single *kryeplak*) are present, and performance skills and age figure in the seating arrangements. Narrative songs (*syrmatika*) are performed before the exchange of *mantinadhes,* and "they are also interspersed throughout as means of restoring tranquility" after a long sequence of *mantinadhes* (Caraveli 1985:268). Here again, the Albanian ordering of genres is stricter: it moves from drawn-out songs (*këngë të shtruara*) to full-voice songs (*këngë të lartër*) to shorter and more strictly metric songs in quicker tempi, often followed by rhymed couplets (*bete*) in triple meter. Like *mantinadha, bete* may be improvised or quoted. The Albanian idiom differs from the solo singing of *mantinadhes* to instrumental accompaniment, yet for both performances, a successful gathering requires intensive interchange among voices at appropriate moments. Both types of event depend on hosts and guests proficient at improvisation.

"We may be Christian[,] but the *glendi* is our religion" (Caraveli 1985:267). "We live for *muabet,*" and "*muabet* is a necessity of life" (Sugarman 1988:8). Such statements proclaim a unity of ethics and aesthetics in performance. Genres are at once conditions and consequences of compulsory interdependence. Asked whether rich people lament, a peasant woman of Basilicata replied, "Yes, the rich lament, but not as we *pacchiani* [clods] do. We who are *villani* [rustics], *contadini* [peasants] lament more" (De Martino 1958:77). One who does not lament as we do is not one of us.

It is often assumed that a performer's actions should produce a sequence of sounds that fits or "harmonizes" with the immediately preceding sequence. In Maramureş, Romania, the couplets (*strigături*) shouted by men and women at weddings are judged according to how well they go together (*a să văji*); comparing the couplets in a sequence involves assessing "a complex correspondence (semantic, metaphoric, and symbolic) between a concrete situation . . . and the exigencies of a Law" (Karnoouh 1983, quoted in Kligman 1988:14). Similarly, in a Cretan mountain village, the effectiveness of the *mantinadhes* in a sequence is judged, not only by their "connectedness" (*sinekhia*), but more importantly, by the degree to which they "fit" (*teriazoun*) with one another and the immediate situation of the performance (Herzfeld 1985:140).

Stratification

In what circumstances must people demonstrate (or refrain from demonstrating) their command of a given genre? Different answers to this question are made as explicit or left as implicit in performers' actions and in many performers' responses to questions posed by ethnographers. A study of genres for calling cattle and other animals in Haute-Gruyère, Switzerland, shows that usage of the genres and of their names is constrained by "professional stratification" among the herdsmen. The boy (*bouèbo*) to whom the humblest tasks are assigned is said to chase (*acuy*) the cattle as he herds them toward the stable, whereas the *armailli,* who exercises the greatest authority, will *ayóbe* the animals: "*ayóber* is more melodious than *acuy;* it is an invitation, while *acuy* is an obligation," as one *armailli* explained (Bolle-Zemp 1985:175). In autumn during the annual descent (*rindja*) from the alpine pastures (a migration that has become a tourist event while retaining its main function), only the *armailli* performs the *lyóba por la rindja* 'calling-song for the descent'. A similar sequence of sounds performed by a lesser herdsman during the *rindja* is termed a *tchira* 'cry' or even a "simple cry," rather than a *lyóba,* and on this occasion, lesser herdsmen may adjust their habitual mode of calling so as not to compete with the *armailli.* The varieties of *lyóba,* combining attributes of song (*tsan,* from French *chant*) and cries, serve as representations of the alpine pasturage, the world of herdsmen and poor peasants (*petits paysans*), as opposed to the valleys, where the more prosperous peasants (*gros paysans*) live. Given the importance of cattle in this world, the *lyóba* is addressed to them almost exclusively; a call to a different animal or the *bouèbo* is a *tchira* (except that a few herdsmen use the term *lyóba* for calls to pigs).

The *lyóba* is an excellent example of a performance genre that allows for, indeed requires, enactment of the singer's identity—in relation not only to the cows, but to other herdsmen, residents of the alpine pastures and valleys, tourists witnessing the *rindja,* and even ethnographers. Yet almost any other genre would serve the same purpose equally well. Most Scandinavian herders have been women, and their music also functions for intercommunication among human beings and animals. As in Haute-Gruyère, some Scandinavian musical structures have become more elaborate than their immediate use requires, though they are not constrained by professional stratification and do not represent a way of life to tourists (Johnson 1984:44).

Over many centuries, European herders have developed vocal and instrumental resources that can serve several functions at once, among them the need to ward off evil spirits and beasts that might attack the herd while remaining in contact with one's own animals and other herders (Johnson 1984:43–44). Drawing on these

The Balkan peasant does not sing, as some specialists want us to believe, to make work bearable, but as a sign that his inner world is in order. Many Europeans share this understanding of music.

resources, a herder can improvise and "orchestrate" an appropriate response to the changing conditions encountered in each day's work.

Competition and solidarity

The enactment of identity through performance inevitably involves factors that augment and reduce some of the "distances" and differences between a performer and others. Caraveli's account of the singing of *mantinadhes* during the *glendia* of Olymbos stresses the reconciliation of personal and communal interests. For men in a Cretan mountain village, the improvisation of *mantinadhes* is normally a far more competitive activity, in line with such other tests of manhood as dancing, playing cards, rustling animals, and stealing brides (Herzfeld 1985:139), all of which involve "a poetics of social interaction" that makes possible the creation of meaning (*simasia*) (Herzfeld 1985:11, 18). Whatever the differences between this village and Olymbos, "the successful performance of selfhood depends upon an ability to identify the self with larger categories of identity" (Herzfeld 1985:10). Pride in being a shepherd, rather than a farmer, can be displayed in singing. The village "may be rather unusual among present-day rural Greek communities" in the extent to which social excellence (*filotimo*) requires a constant struggle for advantage over other men (Herzfeld 1985:289).

In much of Europe, responsibility for performing the genres deemed essential to the "defense of life" and the reproduction of the community falls disproportionately on women. The need for such genres as lullabies is so evident that it seems not to inspire much reflection or discussion. Women have much to say about their roles as lamenters, however, as is clear in studies of lamenting in southern Italy (De Martino 1958), Hungary (Kodály 1960 [1937]:76–81), Karelia (Tolbert 1990), northern Russia (Mazo 1994), Romania (Brăiloiu 1981 [1932], Kligman 1988), Macedonia (Sachs 1975), Crete (Caraveli 1986; Caraveli-Chaves 1980), and mainland Greece (Auerbach 1987). Among the most wide-ranging genres in content, laments link personal and domestic concerns to those of the community and allow for "fictive communication between the living and the dead" (Kligman 1988:154). In Europe, they are a subject of ethical and aesthetic reflection.

Local identities

That the qualities of individual lamenters and performances are so often discussed in detail helps us understand the process by which skills exercised on behalf of family and community can be developed in highly specialized ways, sometimes leading to the widespread recognition of outstanding performers. More often than not, however, the criteria by which performers and performances are evaluated emphasize a community's preference for certain sound qualities and ways of combining sounds. Women in the north Russian village of Tot'ma are unmoved and "wouldn't even think of crying" as they listen to laments from a nearby village: "We lament with a

FIGURE 3   From Telemark, Norway, Eivind Mo plays the *hardingfele,* a modified form of the violin with elaborate carving, inlay, and four sympathetic strings. It is played for listening, processing, and dancing, and in the last case the rhythms can be complex enough to make dancing to playing from other regions difficult. Photo by David Golber, 1990.

very thin [high-register], very poor (*bednen'kii*) voice—not like them. We lament and cry together. They just sing as though not lamenting at all" (Mazo 1994:25).

Singing, lamenting, instrumental music, and dancing are so important to many communities that people regard their local practices as unique, differentiated in numerous respects from those of neighboring communities. The differences may make an appropriate response impossible, whether by crying or by dancing. A Norwegian woman remarked: "I shall never be able to dance to the playing of my husband; for he was born and brought up in Hallingdal, while I was brought up on Telemark music" (Hopkins 1986:187). The woman *did* in fact dance in public to her husband's playing—but, for her, and presumably for others, this was different from dancing to the music of Telemark (figure 3). Similarly, local differences in Barbagia, Sardinia, are significant but not utterly insurmountable: "important enough to shed doubts on the execution of certain steps, but too fine to affect the basic cohesion of the collective dance" (Lortat-Jacob 1981:189). Musicians unpaid in their home villages may, as paid performers elsewhere, adjust their playing to meet dancers' demands, and dancers may or may not find fault with their efforts to meet these demands.

The fundamental significance of singing and some instrumental music to "the defense of life" is aptly summarized in Boris Kremenliev's remark: "The Balkan peasant . . . does not sing as some specialists want us to believe, to make work bearable, but as a sign that his inner world is in order" (1975:119). Many Europeans share this understanding of music. In some Portuguese districts, the ordering of one's inner world entails *encomendaçao das almas* 'recommending the souls' in ritual music (Dias and Dias 1953; Pina-Cabral 1986:229).

OLDER AND NEWER ROLES AND GENRES

Musical performance enables communities to dramatize differences between older and new ways of living. In some situations, performers who specialize in older genres are cherished for their knowledge and wisdom, but their activities have been deplored, and at times prohibited, by advocates of newer belief systems. Local distinctions between older and newer roles and genres shed light on a community's cultural life and relations with the outside world. Performers have done much to facilitate coexistence and symbiosis between opposing belief systems, and all nationalist movements have made use of performance genres that could be adapted to meet their needs.

Specialists

Certain repertoires and modes of performance are recognized as "older" than others and associated with certain types of performers. The Russian *starinshchik* was a specialist in the performance of *stariny* or *starinki,* 'old tales', known to scholars since the 1830s as *bylini* (Sokolov 1950 [1941]:291). A singer may open a performance by stressing the antiquity of the genre: "I will tell you, brother, but I won't tell a tale, I won't sing a song, but I'll sing you an ancient verse, a Kievan *bylina*" (Zemtsovsky 1980:392).

"Older" genres are often characterized by specific types of interaction among the performers, hence by musical demands that differ from those of newer genres. In Basque country, *kanta zaharak* 'old songs' are distinct from other genres because they require two voices; the *soñu zaharak* 'old melodies' notated in the early nineteenth century by Juan Ignacio de Iztueta are dance tunes with a variable number of bars to each phrase, in contrast to the eight-line, thirty-two-bar structure of the *zortziko* (De Barandiaran 2:242, 244).

In Wallachia, southern Oltenia, and elsewhere in Romania, professional musicians (*lăutari*) perform *cîntece bătrîneşti* 'old-time songs' at wedding banquets and on other occasions. Europeans identify dance genres, explicitly or implicitly, as "older" or "newer." The *starosvetská* 'old-world dance' of southeastern Moravia is done with "a calmer tempo and greater variety of dance figurations" than the more popular *sedlácká* 'peasant dance', and the *starodávny* 'old-time dance' of eastern Moravia uses some of the same figures as the *starosvetská* (Vetterl 1980:130). People of central and eastern Poland use many localized terms for "peasant style," but dance music in the "new style" is invariably *oberek* (Noll 1986:501–512).

Outsiders

The significance attached to older and newer genres is an issue where villagers' interests are intricately linked with those of outsiders, including scholars. Such links may involve relationships of mutual incomprehension, hostility and distrust, or collaboration and pursuit of common interests. Having identified an "old style" of Hungarian peasant music, Béla Bartók (1881–1945) had difficulty conveying his understanding of this style to the singers: "When we ask about old tunes, they serve up 'Ezt a kerek erdot járom én' or some other banalities of this kind, since these songs, in vogue during their youth, are 'very old' in their opinion" (Suchoff 1976:17). By the late 1960s and 1970s, researchers had learned to pay closer attention to the categories invoked by musicians. People of Gabela, a village in Hercegovina, distinguished between ancient (*starinske*) and present-day (*sadasnje*) songs (*pjesme*); the prestige of radio, television, and films was attached to the latter, but the former were more often sung (Christensen 1977:32).

The most important factors in marking specific idioms as ancient or archaic have been efforts by representatives of church and state to suppress or radically transform the rural practices that they regarded as pagan, backward, or irrational. Beginning in the sixteenth century, missionaries attempted to abolish all singing among the Saami by imposing severe penalties, and they succeeded in destroying most drums used by shamans. Representatives of church and state have often functioned as agents of the long process that Max Weber called disenchantment [*Entzauberung*] of the world, and as a result of their efforts, more and more Europeans lost the ability to communicate with spirits and ancestors through singing, lamenting, dancing, or producing sounds from drums or horns. Attempts to suppress singing because of its associations with magic and superstition have a longer history than efforts to suppress whole languages, since "repressive attitudes toward the languages and dialects of subject peoples seem to be distinctive only of European political policy in comparatively recent times" (Sapir 1933:167).

Coexistence and symbiosis

In the opening section of his *Skáldskaparmál* ('Poetic Diction'), the great Icelandic writer Snorri Sturluson (1179–1241) urged young poets not "to remove from poetry ancient kennings which the great poets of old permitted themselves to enjoy," even if, as Christians, they "must not believe in pagan gods" (1964 [1954]:10). Whether or not cultural practices of longstanding might prove compatible with one or another variety of Christianity has been debated by many writers and speakers, in Iceland and elsewhere. The first Icelandic psalmbook (1589) opened with a polemic against "undesirable poems of giants and heroes . . . loved by the peasantry of this land . . . to the delight of Satan and his spawn." The famous decree issued in 1648 by Tsar Alexis, "On the Righting of Morals and the Abolition of Superstitions," took particular aim at Russian popular entertainers (*skomorokhi*), who by 1700 were no longer widely active.

Compromises—like Snorri's proposal to retain "ancient kennings" while abjuring belief in pagan gods—have been represented by outside observers with such terms as the Russian *dvoverie* 'dual faith', a concept that "did not originate in an understanding of the beliefs of Russian peasants as they existed in actual practice," but helped theologians, ethnographers, and others articulate their sense of conflict between paganism and Christianity (Mazo 1991). A singer, however, may not perceive any such duality in her beliefs as she performs a *dukhovnyi stikh* 'spiritual verse' in which the Flying Serpent kidnaps the mother and horse of Saint Theodore Tyron (Mazo 1995:track 11).

By the late 1700s, as small groups of intellectuals in many parts of Europe began to record "popular antiquities" and "superstitions" (Burke 1978:3–22), there was considerable evidence of coexistence and symbiosis between "learned" and "popular" religion. At its sharpest, the conflict between the two involved disparities between so-called animist religion, with its emphasis on "equitable exchanges with nature, the dead, and fellow humans," and the values of religious reformers and protocapitalists (Schneider 1990:27). Peasants have sometimes responded to the intrusions of learned religion and the state by insisting on the failure of all attempts to "civilize" them: in the "almost proverbial phrase" attributed to peasants of Basilicata by the writer Carlo Levi (1947 [1945]), "Christ stopped short of here, at Eboli." Cretan villagers boasted to Herzfeld (1985:33) that "the law doesn't reach here." As communities take pride in self-consciously retaining supposedly archaic cultural practices, the practices are transformed for this reason.

Nationalism

Nationalist movements produced a new arsenal of techniques for distinguishing supposedly indigenous and therefore authentic cultural practices. These techniques served to isolate repertoires and practices labeled as foreign or regional, rather than national. The key issue is the creation—or radical transformation—of a "public sphere."

To transform a local dance genre into an emblem of national identity, activists needed to identify features that could be standardized and made to fit the environments in which the dance would be taught and performed. The dependence of nationalist movements on literacy ensured that the music of each national genre would be notated and that the notations would be heavily used in teaching. Writing, together with speech informed by the speaker's readings, was the primary medium for arguments about the correct forms and meanings of national genres. Much energy has been consumed by efforts to discourage or ban any borrowing of elements that do not belong to the presumed national heritage. For all the emphasis on unique identities, the formats adopted by nationalists are remarkably similar [see MUSIC AND IDEOLOGY].

Institutional networks through which national songs and dances might be diffused to villages were created in many parts of Europe. In eastern Ukraine around 1930, these include "houses of folk art" where village choirs rehearsed and performed; most choir directors followed written guidelines and a list of approved repertoire (Noll 1994). In Catalonia, no less than three hundred fifty societies were active in 1985 (three hundred of them outside Barcelona), teaching and propagating the national dance, the *sardana* (Brandes 1990:27). Use of a standardized instrumental ensemble—in this case, twelve instruments, played by eleven musicians—is one respect in which the *sardana* resembles other national genres.

Nationalist institutions inevitably alter musicians' working conditions with respect to such matters as who will have access to what resources, and who will be invited (or required) to produce performances, publications, and recordings that meet certain specifications and standards. These policies, incentives, and pressures

Representatives of church and state have often functioned as agents of the long process that Max Weber called disenchantment of the world, and as a result of their efforts, more and more Europeans lost the ability to communicate with spirits and ancestors through singing, lamenting, dancing, or producing sounds from drums or horns.

generate such strong constraints that all concerned may easily forget about the constraints that operate in situations that are local or transnational, rather than national. The real constraints exerted by national institutions produce illusions about what people who live in a given nation actually do in their daily lives. The public sphere never takes in all of the social relationships that motivate musical performance.

BIBLIOGRAPHY

Adamo, Giorgio. 1984. "Towards a Grammar of Musical Performance: A Study of a Vocal Style." In *Musical Grammars and Computer Analysis:* Atti del Convegno, Modena 4–6 ottobre 1982, ed. Marco Baroni and Luisa Callegari, 245–254. Florence: Olschki.

Auerbach, Susan. 1987. "From Singing to Lamenting: Women's Musical Role in a Greek Village." In *Women and Music in Cross-Cultural Perspective*, ed. Ellen Koskoff, 25–43. Westport, Conn.: Greenwood Press.

Barandiaran, Gaizka de. 1980. "Basque Music." *The New Grove*, ed. Stanley Sadie. London: Macmillan.

Bolle-Zemp, Sylvie. 1985. "Lyoba: Appels au bétail et identité en Haute-Gruyère (Suisse)." *Yearbook for Traditional Music* 17:167–197.

Bourdieu, Pierre. 1977 [1972]. *Outline of a Theory of Practice*. Translated by Richard Nice. Cambridge Studies in Social Anthropology, 16. Cambridge: Cambridge University Press.

Brăiloiu, Constantin. 1981 [1932]. "Despre bocetul de la Drăguş (Jud. Făgăraş)." In *Opere*, ed. Emilia Comişel, 5:115–194. Bucharest: Editura Muzical.

———. 1984 [1946]. "On a Romanian Ballad." In *Problems of Ethnomusicology*, ed. and trans. A. L. Lloyd. 113–119. Cambridge: Cambridge University Press.

Brambats, Karl. 1983. "The Vocal Drone in the Baltic Countries: Problems of Chronology and Provenance." *Journal of Baltic Studies* 14(1):24–34.

Brandes, Stanley. 1990. "The Sardana: Catalan Dance and Catalan National Identity." *Journal of American Folklore* 103:24–41.

Burke, Peter. 1978. *Popular Culture in Early Modern Europe*. New York: Harper & Row.

Caraveli, Anna. 1985. "The Symbolic Village: Community Born in Performance." *Journal of American Folklore* 98:259–286.

———. 1986. "The Bitter Wounding: The Lament as Social Protest in Rural Greece." In *Gender and Power in Rural Greece,* ed. Jill Dubisch, 169–194. Princeton: Princeton University Press.

Caraveli-Chaves, Anna. 1980. "Bridge Between Worlds: The Greek Women's Lament as Communicative Event." *Journal of American Folklore* 93:113–128.

Castelo-Branco, Salwa El-Shawan. 1994. "The Dialogue between Voices and Guitars in Fado Performance." In *Fado: Voices and Shadows*, 125–140. Lisbon: Museu Nacional de Etnologia.

Christensen, Dieter. 1977. "Kategorien mehrstimmiger Lieder des Dorfes Gabela, Herzegovina." *Die Musikforschung* 30:30–42.

De Barandiaran, Gaizka. 1980. "Basque Music." *The New Grove,* ed. Stanley Sadie. London: Macmillan.

De Martino, Ernesto. 1958. *Morte e pianto rituale*. Turin: Boringhieri.

Dias, Jorge, and Margot Dias. 1953. *A encomendaáao das almas*. Oporto: Impresa Portuguesa.

Giddens, Anthony. 1984. *The Constitution of Society: Outline of the Theory of Structuration*. Berkeley and Los Angeles: University of California Press.

Herzfeld, Michael. 1985. *The Poetics of Manhood: Contest and Identity in a Cretan Mountain Village*. Princeton: Princeton University Press.

Hopkins, Pandora. 1986. *Aural Thinking in Norway: Performance and Communication with the Hardingfele*. New York: Human Sciences Press.

Johnson, Anna. 1984. "Voice Physiology and Ethnomusicology: Physiological and Acoustical Studies of the Swedish Herding Song." *Yearbook for Traditional Music* 16:42–66.

Karnoouh, C. 1983. *Le rite et le discours: introduction à la lecture de la versification populaire.* Ghent: Communication and Cognition.

Kligman, Gail. 1988. *The Wedding of the Dead: Ritual, Poetics, and Popular Culture in Transylvania.* Berkeley and Los Angeles: University of California Press.

Kodály, Zoltán. 1960 [1937]. *Folk Music of Hungary.* Translated by Ronald Tempest and Cynthia Jolly. London: Barrie & Rockliff.

Kremenliev, Boris. 1975. "Social and Cultural Changes in Balkan Music." *Western Folklore* 34:117–136.

Levi, Carlo. 1947 [1945]. *Christ Stopped at Eboli.* Trans. by Frances Frenaye. New York: Farrar, Straus.

Lortat-Jacob, Bernard. 1981. "Community Music and the Rise of Professionalism: A Sardinian Example." *Ethnomusicology* 25:185–197.

———. 1984. "Music and Complex Societies: Control and Management of Musical Production." *Yearbook for Traditional Music* 16:17–33.

Marcu, George. 1967. "Un sistem identic de execuţie polifonică a cîntecelor populare, întîlnit la unele popoare din Peninsula Balcanică." *Revista de etnografie şi folclor* 13:545–554.

Marshall, Christopher. 1982. "Towards a Comparative Aesthetics of Music." In *Cross-Cultural Perspectives on Music,* ed. Robert Falck and Timothy Rice, 162–173. Toronto: University of Toronto Press.

Martí Pérez, Josep. 1994. "The Sardana as a Socio-Cultural Phenomenon in Contemporary Catalonia." *Yearbook for Traditional Music* 26:39–46.

Mazo, Margarita. 1991. "'We Don't Summon Spring in the Summer': Traditional Music and Beliefs of the Contemporary Russian Village." In *Christianity and the Arts in Russia,* ed. W. C. Brumfield and M. M. Velimirovic, 73–94. Cambridge: Cambridge University Press.

———. 1994. "Wedding Laments in North Russian Villages." In *Music-Cultures in Contact: Convergences and Collisions,* ed. Margaret J. Kartomi and Stephen Blum, 21–39. Australian Studies in the History, Philosophy, and Social Studies of Music, 2. Sydney: Currency Press.

———. 1995. Notes to compact disc, *Old Believers: Songs of the Nekrasov Cossacks.* Smithsonian Folkways SF CD 40462.

Nielsen, Svend. 1982. *Stability in Musical Improvisation: A Repertoire of Icelandic Epic Songs (Rímur).* Acta Ethnomusicologica Danica, 3. Copenhagen: Kragen.

Noll, William H. 1986. "Peasant Music Ensembles in Poland: A Culture History." Ph.D. dissertation, University of Washington.

———. 1991. "Economics of Music Patronage among Polish and Ukrainian Peasants to 1939." *Ethnomusicology* 35:349–379.

———. 1994. "Cultural Contact through Music Institutions in Ukrainian Lands, 1920–1948." In *Music-Cultures in Contact: Convergences and Collisions,* ed. Margaret J. Kartomi and Stephen Blum, 204–219. Australian Studies in the History, Philosophy, and Social Studies of Music, 2. Sydney: Currency Press.

Petrović, Ankica. 1977. "*Ganga,* a Form of Traditional Rural Singing in Yugoslavia." Ph.D. dissertation, Queen's University of Belfast.

Pina-Cabral, João de. 1986. *Sons of Adam, Daughters of Eve: The Peasant Worldview of the Alto Minho.* Oxford: Clarendon Press.

Porthan, Henrik Gabriel. 1867 [1778]. "Dissertation de poësia fennica," repr. in *Opera Selecta.* Helsinki: Finska Litteratur-Sällskapats Tryckeri, 3:303–381. Partial Eng. trans in *The Kalevala,* by Elias Lönnrot. Translated by Francis Peabody Magoun, Jr., 380–382. Cambridge, Mass.: Harvard University Press.

Rice, Timothy F. 1980a. "Aspects of Bulgarian Musical Thought." *Yearbook of the International Folk Music Council* 12:43–66.

———. 1980b. "A Macedonian *Sobor:* Anatomy of a Celebration." *Journal of American Folklore* 93:113–128.

Ross, Jaan. 1989. "A Study of Timing in an Estonian Runic Song." *Journal of the Acoustical Society of America* 86:1671–1677.

Sachs, Nahoma. 1975. "Music and Meaning: Musical Symbolism in a Macedonian Village." Ph.D. dissertation, Indiana University.

Sapir, Edward. 1933. "Language." In *Enyclopaedia of the Social Sciences,* ed. Edwin R. A. Seligman, 9:155–169. New York: Macmillan.

Schneider, Jane. 1990. "Spirits and the Spirit of Capitalism." In *Religious Orthodoxy and Popular Faith in European Society,* ed. Ellen Badone, 24–54. Princeton: Princeton University Press.

Sokolov, Yuri M. 1950 [1941]. *Russian Folklore.* Translated by Catharine Ruth Smith. New York: Macmillan.

Stęszewski, Jan. 1972. "Sachen, Bewusstein, und Benemungen in ethnomikologischen Untersungen." *Jahrbuch für Volksliedforschung* 17:131–170.

Stockmann, Doris. 1994. "Investigation and Documentation of Traditional Musical Styles Today: Traditional Sami Yoiking in Scandinavia." In *Music-Cultures in Contact: Convergences and Collisions,* ed. Margaret J. Kartomi and Stephen Blum, 1–12. Australian Studies in the History, Philosophy, and Social Studies of Music, 2. Sydney: Currency Press.

Sturluson, Snorri. 1964 [1954]. *The Prose Edda of Snorri Sturluson: Tales from Norse Mythology.* Translated by Jean I. Young. Cambridge: Bowes & Bowes.

Suchoff, Benjamin, ed. 1976. *Béla Bartók Essays.* New York: St. Martin's Press.

Sugarman, Jane C. 1988. "Making *Muabet:* The Social Basis of Singing among Prespa Albanian Men." *Selected Reports in Ethnomusicology* 7:1–42.

Todorov, Todor. 1987. "Old Forms of Professionalism in Bulgarian Folk Music." *International Folklore Review* 5:39–42.

Tolbert, Elizabeth. 1990. "Women Cry with Words: Symbolization of Affect in the Karelian Lament." *Yearbook for Traditional Music* 22:80–105.

Vetterl, Karel. 1980. "Czechoslovakia, II. Folk Music, 1. Bohemia and Moravia." In *The New Grove,* ed. Stanley Sadie. London: Macmillan.

Zemtsovsky, Izaly. 1978 [1974]. "Folk Music." In *Great Soviet Encyclopedia,* 3d ed., ed. A. M. Prokhorov, 17:58–59. New York: Macmillan.

———. 1980. "Union of Soviet Socialist Republics, IX. Russian SFSR, 2. Russian Folk Music." In *The New Grove,* ed. Stanley Sadie. London: Macmillan.

Zguta, Russell. 1978. *Russian Minstrels: A History of the Skomorokhi.* Oxford: Clarendon Press.

Song Genres
James Porter

Nonstrophic Song Forms
Strophic Song Forms

Europe has a wide variety of song genres in oral tradition. These genres and their structures are often difficult to separate from the singing styles and contexts that give rise to them. Some genres, such as shepherds' or cowherds' cries, are intimately connected to work or occupation; others, such as laments or weddings, are intimately connected to life-cycle events. Many surviving genres have their origins in the later Middle Ages; others stem from the modern period, especially the 1700s, with the growth of cities. Depending on how the cultural borders of Europe are conceived, some genres from Saami, Uralic, or Mediterranean cultures contrast strikingly with the conventional picture of predominantly strophic melodies across the continent. Song genres can be grouped in complementary ways: by content, form, function, situation, or performance style.

A broadly comprehensive grouping of songs by form distinguishes strophic and nonstrophic types. A more detailed structural division, used especially in Eastern Europe, is by the length of melodic sections, in turn determined by the number of syllables: isometric melodies have sections of the same length; heterometric melodies, of different lengths. Strophic and nonstrophic types have evolved in regional variations over many centuries since their original appearance, and they have subsequently been modified in local contexts.

Groupings of songs by content and situation can be arranged within the strophic-nonstrophic scheme, though the following are not exclusive categories: life-cycle and calendrical songs (e.g., wedding and harvest songs); songs of work or occupation (e.g., mining songs, shanties, outlaws' songs); songs of domestic provenance (e.g., ballads, lyric songs); and songs for public occasions (e.g., political and religious songs). Songs involving a special technique or form (e.g., falsetto cries, chants, yodels, epigrams, polyphony) can be enclosed within the above grouping on grounds of their purely musical features. Another broad subdivision that is sometimes made—into narrative and lyric—is best regarded as a spectrum reflecting verbal-semantic, rather than musical-semantic, content.

NONSTROPHIC SONG FORMS

Nonstrophic song forms are often rhetorical, involving communication over distance

ballad Narrative song in oral tradition but also transmitted in printed form with the spread of literacy

epic songs Long narrative songs, usually with text and music composed in a string of single lines and phrases

lyric songs Nonnarrative songs, often expressing emotions or describing the ritual action they accompany

nonstrophic songs Songs in which text and music are performed without the formal conventions of strophic songs

stichic songs Songs that repeat in performance a single musical phrase corresponding to the single line of verse

strophic songs Songs in which the same music, usually two to four phrases with or without a refrain, is repeated for each new stanza (strophe) of text

FIGURE 1 Ostjak song based on leaps of a fourth and a fifth. After Väisänen 1937:241, #153.

or with a different spiritual world: songs of the Vogul, Ostjak, and Saami peoples express a ritualized relationship with the natural world of animals; a woman's song after a bear hunt moves through a range of a sixth, with prominent leaps of a fifth. Ostjak songs commemorate a parallel relationship with this world in their leaping fourths and fifths (figure 1). Karl Tirén (1942) includes calls to shepherd dogs and reindeer. Open tritonic or tetratonic structures form the basis for most shepherding calls in pastoral areas of Europe, such as the Alps, the Norwegian highlands, and the Carpathian chain. Sometimes the vocal tendency to follow the natural overtone series shows up in a sharpened fourth or a variable third degree (Andersson 1922–1938; Pommer 1942).

Shepherd calls often involve virtuosic stretches of the voice: to a high F, E-flat, and D above the treble-clef staff (Johnsson 1984; Kotek and Zoder 1950). Others take the form of a dialogue song between herders (Hoshovsky 1981; Trébucq 1912). Before the arrival of twentieth-century technology, French plowmen signaled to their oxen in the recitative known as *briolage*, mentioned by the writer George Sand about 1850 (Davenson 1944). The Swiss Alpine blessing (*Betruf*) was a call to prayer that, across the range of a fifth, has acquired the status of a national ideology (Bolle-Zemp 1992). The melismatic Swiss cattle calls (*Kühreihen*) were notated as early as 1545 (Tobler 1890), and similar forms are found in pastoral contexts from Sweden to the Caucasus, with types such as the Romanian *hora lunga* and its spun-out, repeated notes (figure 2).

Solo yodels in pastoral societies are frequently cast in free form and develop the range between head and chest voice, sometimes in a range of up to two octaves (Pommer 1942). Multipart yodels, however, tend to construct regular groupings of four, eight, or sixteen measures. Laments for the dead embody a significant group of open forms. Often narrow in range, they can encompass an octave, usually descending in an affective curve that is well documented in, for example, the Irish *caoine* (Ó Madagáin 1978), Hungary (Kiss and Rajeczky 1966), and Italy (De Martino 1958).

FIGURE 2 A
Romanian *hora lun-
ga*. After Bartók
1923:16, #23b.

Epic songs and singing

Stichic songs, composed in an open form, line by line, rather than in the rounded, closed form of the four-lined strophic song, are no longer plentiful in Europe. Stichic composition was a feature of epic songs, from Homer's *Iliad* and *Odyssey* to the French *Chanson de Roland*, the German *Niebelungenlied*, the Icelandic heroic songs, the Spanish epics of *El Cid*, the Russian *byliny* (sing. *bylina*), and the Ukrainian *dumy,* though epics had regional markings and were by no means uniform in theme or musical style. In modern times, stichic technique is chiefly known through the study of Yugoslav, and to some extent Greek, epic or heroic songs (Bartók and Lord 1951; Notopoulos 1959). The stichic principle in Yugoslavia, with its ten-syllable line (*deseterac*), allows the singer's free embellishment of the story and its episodes, and songs of two thousand to four thousand or five thousand lines are not unusual. Some complete transcriptions of recorded performances have been made (e.g., Erdely 1994).

Epic singing has also been studied in Russia, in regard to *byliny* (or *stariny*, as the singers called them). About twenty-five hundred records of these (with about 120 topics) exist, dating from the seventeenth century, though most are from the late nineteenth century, when scholars published important collections. The first manuscript collection with melodies was made in the mid-1700s (by Kirsha Danilov); sound recordings were made at the end of the 1800s. Once widespread in the 1500s and 1600s, *byliny* have a diverse historical content: most surviving examples are from the Kiev or Vladimir cycle and tell of heroes such as Il'ya Muromets. As an active form, the *bylina* gradually gave way to historical songs after the 1700s. Brought to Russia by itinerant musicians in the late Middle Ages, *byliny* survived best in northern Russia, where peasants were less oppressed by serfdom; there too the style was mainly one of solo singing. Choral singing of *byliny* was common in parts of the north and among the Don and Terek Cossacks of southern Russia.

The melodies of *byliny* rework tunes popularly known by singer and audience, but distinctively compressed. This convention of form distinguishes the *bylina* from other songs with similar melodies: "I won't sing a song, but I'll sing you an ancient verse, a Kievan *bylina*," one singer said (Astakhova 1938–1951). Good *bylina* singers always had a "special talent" for this form, immersed themselves in their content, and made creative changes in the text. The *bylina* had several types of tune, a "tranquil, even stately" one and a "swift, gay" one (Sokolov 1971). The collector P. N. Rybnikov described the singing of the sixty-five-year-old singer T. G. Ryabinin from the Lake Onega region: "The tune of the *byliny* was very monotonous, the voice of Ryabinin . . . was not very loud, but his wonderful ability as a storyteller gave a special meaning to every verse" (Sokolov 1971:313).

In the Soviet period, when song themes were severely modified and *noviny* (new songs celebrating Soviet life) became the order of the day, women singers of *byliny* enjoyed fame: A. M. Krukova from the White Sea area had a repertory that included more than two-thirds of all Russian epic subjects, and an indigent peasant woman from the River Pinega, M. D. Krivopolenova, was brought to Moscow at seventy-two years of age to astonish audiences with her art. The latter would become excited just before singing, but when she began her beloved *byliny* before an audience of thousands, she felt free. At certain points in her "cheerful" *byliny*, she would represent specific episodes with gestures. But in serious *byliny*, quite another mood overtook her: for instance, she would weep as she sang "How Prince Roman Lost His Wife" (Sokolov 1971).

The epic singer in Greece and Yugoslavia, in contrast, was invariably male, and sang heroic songs for a male audience. This was especially true with the Muslim singers of Bosnia, whose repertoire frequently consisted of thirty songs, one for each night of Ramadan (holy month of fasting), when men of a community would gather in the coffeehouse from dusk to listen to epic singing. The repertoire in the former Yugoslavia consisted of songs about late medieval heroes, such as Marko Kraljević, or after World War II, partisans fighting Nazi invaders. The singer would accompany his singing on a one-stringed bowed lute (*gusle*), taking care to engage his audience in the plot of the song. In Greece, the main heroic cycle concerns the late medieval figure Digenis Akritas, and in Crete, especially, the singer accompanies his fifteen-syllable lines on the bowed *lyra*. The melodic line in both traditions is almost always narrow, within the range of a fifth or sixth, and the singer plays ornamental interludes at pauses in his singing.

The American scholars Milman Parry and Albert Lord visited Bosnia in the 1930s to understand the technique of composing epic songs, especially Homer. The result was a collection of more than two thousand recorded songs, the best of which have been published in the series *Serbo-Croatian Heroic Songs* (Parry, Lord, and Bynum 1953–). The different versions were conveyed to these scholars in three ways: through singing, reciting, and dictating. The absence of errors in the last medium led Parry and Lord to believe that the *Iliad* and *Odyssey* texts as they survive today were dictated. The melodic formulas, however, have changed less in performance for Romanian epic singers; these, like the story and the verbal formulas (at least into recent times), are "remembered" rather than "memorized," that is, as models they are followed closely, but not slavishly (Beissinger 1991).

Since the field studies of Parry and Lord, the situation has changed. Singers, now believing that written or published variants are more authentic than orally transmitted versions, tend to read and memorize those that are transcribed in archives and libraries. The coming of general literacy to Yugoslavia after World War II and the

FIGURE 3 The first seven ten-syllable lines of a 2,682-line Serbo-Croatian epic ballad in stichic form, sung by Mujo Velić in 1935. Recorded by Milman Parry. Note the subtle pitch, melodic, and ornamental variation from line to line. After Erdely 1995:55.

state's desire to eradicate illiteracy were contributing factors. Thus, singers like Avdo Međedović, who could recompose an epic of four thousand lines that he had just heard into a longer version through his mastery of traditional verbal formulas (which the singer manipulates at will in oral tradition) are no longer found. Epic singing has not died out completely, but it has undergone profound changes in structure, transmission, and context (figure 3).

STROPHIC SONG FORMS

Strophic songs by far outnumber nonstrophic and stichic forms. Structurally, songs are found in long single lines and two-line strophes, such as in Faroese ballads or Lithuanian *dainas*. Strophes also result from the free repetition of three long lines, as in some calendric songs (e.g., Romanian *colinde*) and game, harvest, and wedding songs. Three-line melodies proper often have a close tie to religious or life-cycle events, such as the sacred song at weddings in Tesin, Silesia, at the turn of the twentieth century (Bartoš and Janáček 1901).

Four-line melodies form the largest class for several reasons. The danced forms of the late Middle Ages came to have a strong influence on song forms. Epic songs, closely associated with feudal society, gave way to the ballad with its more domestic concerns of an expanding bourgeoisie. Since the ballad was originally danced in parts of Europe (e.g., Denmark) and still is (the Faroes), the stanza structure, sometimes with separated or interlaced refrains, became a standard form. At the same time, the preference for a rounded four-line tune, usually with one note per syllable, is paralleled in the Gregorian antiphon and the Protestant chorale, especially in north-central Europe, though in Eastern Europe ornamental types can be found, such as the song of parting that Bartók recorded in Hungary (Bartók 1981 [1925] and the recitative-style melody noted from Eastern European Jews (Idelsohn 1914–1932).

Albanians term the emotional lament "the lament by tears" and the more formal lament "the lament by voice." This conceptual division was observed in Ireland: the keen beside the body was distinct from the poetic lament composed later.

Lyric songs

This category covers many song types used for different purposes and occasions. Their generally nonnarrative content sets them apart from ballads and epics, and they may be embedded in rituals of the life-cycle or annual calendar. Wedding songs are especially important since the wedding alters the social structure of the community. Laments for the dead are often thought to be a separate genre because of contextual and stylistic features; but in Eastern Europe, laments were performed in the wedding to express the bride's fear of the perils ahead when she leaves her home. Before the 1917 revolution in Russia, professional weepers or criers—usually poor women, widows, or orphans—were specially invited to realize these fears in singing. Funeral laments, likewise, had parallels in the laments sung for departing soldiers or recruits. In modern times, Finnish Karelian singers have shown mastery of the older lament style. Albanians term the emotional lament "the lament by tears" and the more formal lament "the lament by voice." This conceptual division was observed in Ireland: the keen beside the body was distinct from the poetic lament composed later.

Plowing, seedtime, and harvest provided the frame for many songs associated with seasonal activity. The symbols of fertility (seed, rake, threshing machine) entered songs of amorous and bawdy content. In France, plowing was accompanied by ritual *briolées,* farmer's cries urging on his team of horses, and plowmen may have felt the need to use protective magic in this formula. Harvest songs, however, suggest fertility. While reaping, female ballad singers (as in Portugal and Spain) sing ballads that include references to women's impregnation and pregnancy.

Seasonal songs such as carols sometimes incorporated older beliefs, like the English wassail at Christmastide (figure 4). But carols were once well known throughout the church year, at Easter as well as Christmas. The form of the medieval carol was related to continental forms such as the *rondeau, virelai,* and *ballade,* and to the Italian *laude spirituale.* The English carol is linked to the French *carole,* a dance song that was popular and courtly. From the 1300s, the carol seems to have become a festive song, as with boar's-head carols, in which the ceremonial carrying in of the head precedes ritual feasting; another type, like the *carole,* was associated with

FIGURE 4 A Romanian New Year's carol (*colinde*), a strophic, lyric song with verses of three lines set to three phrases of music in ABA form. After Bartók 1975:142, #86a.

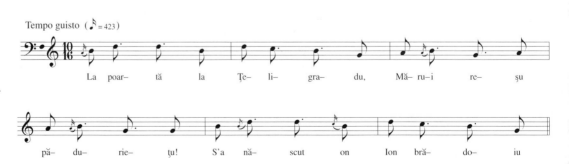

amorous games (e.g., "The Holly and the Ivy"). Religious carol texts may have been written by minor clerics who adapted their texts to popular melodies.

The carol in its older open, or processional, form is preserved in the May Day celebration of the hobby horse at Padstow, Cornwall. As the man inside an elaborately decorated hobby horse proceeds through the town, accompanied by a troupe who sing a "Morning Song" and a "Day Song," he and his companions stand still during the singing of stanzas and advance when the change to the burden (refrain) is made. The Padstow dance and song appear to be survivals of the medieval round dance and open procession, as the first lines of the chorus make clear ("With the merry ring, adieu the merry spring").

Wedding songs, especially in Eastern Europe, are deeply embedded in ritual, even when they are drawn from a source external to the wedding. Divorced from the ceremony, many lyric songs that emerge during a peasant wedding would lose their symbolic frame of meaning. Particular songs mark the stages of a wedding, and come to be associated closely with that function, even when sung on different occasions. Wedding laments are now extremely rare, even in Eastern Europe, most obviously because of the increase in literacy and the transformation of social and especially rural life. Laments for the dead, however, continue to be found in scattered regions of the Mediterranean and the Balkans.

Love songs form the largest body of lyrical songs. Numerous as they are, they encompass a variety of experience and theme: from tragic to humorous situations, from satire and derision to praise and ecstasy, from the joys of physical love to the bitterness of betrayal. Almost every collection in Europe has a preponderance of such songs, though they have been less studied, on the whole, than narrative types. As with the ballad, because the form is usually concise and flexible, lyric songs often merge with lullabies, wedding songs, and other types or genres. Many songs express a close or symbolic relationship with nature: with seasons (sun, moon, stars, wind, rain, snow), natural features (e.g., rocks, mountains, rivers, forests), birds (e.g., falcon, lark, nightingale, partridge, peacock, eagle, swan), animals (e.g., lion, bear, horse, wolf, fox, deer, fish), trees (e.g., oak, ash, holly, ivy, birch), plants (e.g., lily, rose, violet, rue, thyme, rosemary), and so on. But the symbols are not always interpreted in the same way. For instance, the swan in Russia symbolizes a bride; in Celtic countries, a supernatural creature.

Work songs split into two well-defined groups: those about a particular occupation (e.g., miners', soldiers', robbers' songs) and those accompanying actual labor (e.g., fulling cloth, milking cows, rowing, hauling barges). The latter type has given way to the former as modern technology has assumed tasks formerly accomplished by hand. Scottish Highland *waulking* songs to accompany the shrinking of tweed had ritual aspects: no song could be repeated during the process, and the texts came from many quarters, including heroic lays and other work songs. Other such songs (e.g., milking songs) have apotropaic elements, meant to protect animals from supernatural forces. Of occupational songs that cover a wide range of types, miners' songs are among the oldest collected (the German *Bergreihen*, 1531).

Lyric songs may stand on their own or be drawn into ritual occasions, such as weddings. These changes of context may result in alteration of the musical style, as in the cadential formula. The lyric song in Russia ranges from simple forms to elaborate, polyphonic long-drawn-out (*protiazhniie*) songs that evolved in the 1300s through 1600s. This part-singing was based on syllable count per line, not stress pattern. Such songs always encompass a single melodic unit, normally a fourth or fifth, which the singers develop into an intricate polyphonic web. These were recorded on the phonograph by Evgeniya Lineva and later published in a novel notation, with descriptions of the singers and contexts (English version, 1905–1912).

Polyphonic types of song in Europe range from the highly developed Russian forms to the heterophonic singing of Gaelic psalms in the Hebrides. Scholars have focused special attention on a belt of polyphonic singing that stretches from Sardinia through Italy and Sicily to the Caucasus. The character of rural polyphony in the central Mediterranean area has given rise to speculation that these types may have preceded, or at least paralleled, the development of European polyphony in the Middle Ages as it was first written down, in the *Musica Enchiriadis* (about A.D. 900). Especially noteworthy is the florid six-part polyphony of male singing around the port of Genoa (*trallalero*), the *vatoccu* 'bell clapper' style of central Italy that has links to medieval discant, and the nasal polyphony of Sardinian shepherds with its animal-like sounds and droning accompaniment. Two-part singing in the Balkans, with its typically clashing seconds, also seems to be a rural development distinct from Byzantine church practice.

Some song forms occur in a context of public competition among singers, such as the contests still known in the Basque country, Portugal, and Corsica. Other regional styles ask for command of a particular formal type: Portuguese *fado*, Spanish *cante jondo*, the Russian *chastushka*, or the Norwegian *stev*. Portuguese *fado,* resembling the song duels of Minho and the Azores, migrated from the countryside to city cafes in developing its somber themes, couched in musical arrangements showing strong Latin American influence. *Cante jondo*'s development is complex, but traditional performance demands a high degree of skill in singing, dancing, and guitar playing from members of the performing group (*cuadro*). The *chastushka* is an instrumental-vocal genre in short, single-stanza couplets, usually with four lines and accompanied by accordion or balalaika. It can be performed solo, as a duet, or by a chorus. The *stev* (or *nystev*, 'new *stev*', originating about 1800) has four lines of nearly identical couplets and archaic melodies. *Stev* are performed in a parlando-rubato style with scope for variation, but have an asymmetrical rhythmic mode with a basic unit of one short beat followed by a longer one.

The musical features of lyric songs vary from region to region, context to context, and singer to singer. It is therefore difficult to reduce this mass of material to any single, unified, or convincing arrangement that covers the continent. Scholars have usually dealt with lyric songs within a study of a community's repertoire as a whole, or as falling within a particular context or occasion (e.g., wedding songs). The range of such songs across the subcontinent in music, text, context, and performance is astounding and is frequently dependent on local taste.

The ballad

The ballad as a song form came to dominate from about 1350, spreading from France and the Low Countries to the rest of Western Europe. Though analogous proto-narrative songs may have been already present in many areas, the ballad emerged as the preferred form of the middle and lower classes in the period 1300 to 1500. The most condensed and cohesive are British and Danish ballads, often related in topic. Formulas as important structural elements are present in ballad and epic, but these aid ballads in being concise and reductive, whereas epics are expansive. Some ballads are historical in content; others deal with the supernatural, or with tragic situations of rivalry in love. In French, German, and Italian traditions, the lyric element tends to dominate over the ballad narrative. Spain has a large body of ballads (*romances*), quasi-historical like the cycle surrounding El Cid, the eleventh-century warrior whose exploits against the Moors gave rise to songs. Few Spanish *romances*, however, show cross-cultural affinities in content; the form too does not adopt the stanza pattern and is usually cast in hexameter couplets with a caesura in the middle of each line.

FIGURE 5 A Scottish four-phrase strophic ballad, "Lord Donald," sung by Jeannie Robertson of Aberdeen. Collected by Hamish Henderson. Transcribed by James Porter. Two strophes are shown here to illustrate melodic variation from strophe to strophe; the second strophe begins at "St. 2." After Bronson 1976:50, #43.2.

1. "Whaur hae ye been all the day,
    Lord Donald, my son?
    Whaur hae ye been all the day,
    My jolly young man?"

2. "Awa coortin, mither—
    Mak my bed soon,
    For I am seik at the hairt,
    An I fain wud lie doon."

In content and style, Hungarian ballads owe a great deal to French and Walloon influence, while in the Balkans, ballads in Slovenia are closest to central European ballad traditions. Ukrainian ballads frequently draw on a common Slavic epic tradition with its decasyllabic line and nonstanzaic patterns of versification. The British ballad, influenced by French and Scandinavian types in subject matter, alternates four-stress and three-stress lines. Ballads have interacted with other genres: apart from ties to epic tradition in Spain and Eastern Europe, ballads have been found as lullabies, laments, or children's games, and parodies of well-known ballads are known in modern times.

The popular ballad melody has influenced the formation of the stanza structure, the tune's points of emphasis in a four-lined type being the cadence at the end of the second and fourth lines (figure 5). The normal rhyme occurs at the same junctures. The most popular melodic pattern in the British ballads, and those North American ballads that derive from them, is the nonrecurrent ABCD (and ABCDE), which avoids the repetition of other common forms (e.g., ABAB). The pattern ABAC is the next most frequent, phrase A being separated from its identical self by the more prominent melody lines B and C. The refrains and commonplaces reveal the powerful influence of melody (and dance) on the poetics and overall strophic form. If traditional ballads were at one time, like epics, recreated anew in performance, modern singers now "memorize" rather than "remember" their ballads, since ballads are comparatively short.

Ballad singers, especially women, have been studied since the late 1700s. The middle-class Scottish singer Anna Brown provided Sir Walter Scott with ballads for his collection (1802–1803), as did the working-class Agnes Lyle for William Motherwell about the same time (1827), and post–World War II folk-music-revival singers have come increasingly under scrutiny for their views on ballads and singing.

The most remarkable aspect of ballad performance is the objective stance of the singer, who, though emotionally involved in the events of the ballad plot, avoids injecting subjective opinion. It is rare that a singer overtly expresses emotion while singing traditional ballads, since he or she normally allows the events to speak for themselves.

FIGURE 6   Two Flemish ballad singers hawk printed song sheets at a market, accompanied by two accordionists. Photo courtesy of Wim Bosmans.

Ballad singers who have been studied in other parts of Europe include Jeannie Robertson in Scotland (Porter and Gower 1995), Egbert Gerrits in Germany (Henssen 1951), Meen van Eycken in Belgium (Top 1981), Franciska Jemec, Veriska Gáspár, and Matjaz Kostric from Slovenia (Kumer 1981), and Javdoxa Zujixa in West Ukraine (Tancjura 1965). Descriptions of these attitudes to ballads reveal how the form captivated ordinary people for its insights into human behavior. Studies of ballad content, however, gradually dominated ballad studies in the nineteenth century, when great compilations of texts appeared: those of Svend Grundtvig (1966–1976) in Denmark (twelve volumes beginning in 1853), Francis J. Child for English and Scottish ballad texts (1882–1898), and Geijer and Afzelius in Sweden (1880). The inclusion of ballad tunes for these and other collections—for example, Bronson (1959–1972)—happened only as the influence of historicist and positivist studies waned. In the late twentieth century, interest in ballad singers has been renewed, and attention to context, performance, reception, and feedback is a scholarly norm (figure 6).

The contexts of ballad singing have been variable—from humble cottage to drawing room, from marketplace to concert hall, from tavern to local festival. In rural Portugal, the harvest is a special time for singing ballads (*romanceiros*) in a collective setting. In Slovenia, an unusual ballad-singing context was during a wake, beside the corpse, when laments and religious songs would also be sung. Traditional ballad singing is still vigorous in pockets of Europe, but the folk revival after World War II again sparked interest in these songs. New ballads, more often than not political or satirical in thrust, have added to the repertoire, and the revival concert or folk club now provide newer situations for ballad performance.

The most remarkable aspect of ballad performance is the objective stance of the singer, who, though emotionally involved in the events of the ballad plot, avoids injecting subjective opinion. This stance is central to the ballad aesthetic. It is rare that a singer overtly expresses emotion while singing traditional ballads, since he or she normally allows the events to speak for themselves. In recent times, however, singers have been known to interject spoken elements between stanzas to continue a part of the tale they may have forgotten. In later ballad traditions, especially from 1700 to 1850, the broadsheets (broadsides) and chapbooks (pocket books) sold at fairs and in the city streets throughout Europe recycled older ballads and added new ones. Ballads with a more subjective cast and explicit moral are found in great quantities in the 1800s, and political ballads, known since the eighteenth century, have again flourished in the twentieth.

BIBLIOGRAPHY

Andersen, Flemming G. 1991. "Technique, Text, and Context: Formulaic Narrative Mode and the Question of Genre." In *The Ballad and Oral Literature*, ed. Joseph Harris, 18–39. Cambridge: Harvard University Press.

Andersson, Nils. 1922–1938. *Svenska låtar*. Stockholm: P. A. Norstedt and soner.

Astakhova, A. M., ed. 1938–1951. *Bylini severa*. Moscow and Leningrad: Gos. izdatelstvo Karelo-finskoi.

Bartók, Béla. 1923. *Volksmusik der Rumänen von Maramures*. Munich: Drei Masken Verlag.

———. 1975. *Rumanian Folk Music*. Vol. 4. ed. Benjamin Suchoff. The Hague: Martinus Nijhoff.

———. 1981 [1925]. *The Hungarian Folk Song*. Edited by Benjamin Suchoff. Translated by M. D. Calvocoressi. Albany: State University of New York Press.

Bartók, Béla, and Albert Bates Lord. 1951. *Serbo-Croatian Folk Songs*. New York: Columbia University Press.

Bartoš, František, and Leoš Janáček. 1901. *Národní pisně moravské v nově nasbírané*. Prague: Nakladen české akademie.

Beissinger, Margaret H. 1991. *The Art of the Lautar: The Epic Tradition of Romania*. New York: Garland Publishing.

Bolle-Zemp, Sylvie. 1992. *Le réenchantement de la montagne: aspects du folklore musical en Haute-Gruyère*. Geneva: Gerog Editeur. Basel: Société Suisse des traditions populaires.

Bronson, Bertrand H. 1959–1972. *The Traditional Tunes of the Child Ballads*. Princeton, N.J.: Princeton University Press.

———. 1976. *The Singing Tradition of Child's Popular Ballads*. Princeton, N.J.: Princeton University Press.

Buchan, David. 1972. *The Ballad and the Folk*. London: Routledge & Kegan Paul.

Burke, Peter. 1978. *Popular Culture in Early Modern Europe*. New York: Harper.

Catalán, Diego ed. 1988. *Pan-Hispanic Ballad Catalogue: General Theory*. Madrid: Seminario Menéndez-Pidal.

Child, Francis James, ed. 1882–1898. *The English and Scottish Popular Ballads*. 5 vols. Boston: Houghton Mifflin.

Danckert, Werner. 1939 [1970]. *Das europäische Volkslied*. Bonn: H. Bouvier.

———. 1966. *Das Volkslied im Abendland*. Munich: Francke.

———. 1976–1978. *Symbol, Metapher, Allegorie im Lied der Völker*. Bonn-Bad Godesberg: Verlag für systematische Musikwissenschaft.

Davenson, Henri. 1944. *Le livre des chansons*. Neuchatel: Editions de la Baconnière.

De Martino, Ernesto. 1958. *Morte e pianto rituale nel mondo antico; dal lamento pagano al pianto di Maria*. Torino: Edizione Scientifiche Einaudi.

Emsheimer, Ernst. 1964. "Some Thoughts on European Folk Polyphony." *Journal of the International Folk Music Council* 16:43–53.

Entwistle, William. 1951 [1939]. *European Balladry*. Oxford: Clarendon Press.

Erdely, Stephen. 1994. *The Music of Four Serbo-Croatian Heroic Songs: A Study*. New York: Garland Publishing.

———. 1995. *Music of Southslavic Epics from the Bihać Region of Bosnia*. New York: Garland.

Finnegan, Ruth. 1986. "The Relation between Composition and Performance: Three Alternative Modes." In *The Oral and the Literate in Music*, ed. Yoshihiko Tokumaru and Osamu Yamaguti, 73–87. Tokyo: Academia Music.

Foley, John Miles. 1988. *The Theory of Oral Composition*. Bloomington: Indiana University Press.

Geijer, Erik Gustaf, and Arvid August Afzelius. 1880. *Svenska folkvisor*. Uppsala: Bokverks Forlag.

Greene, Richard, ed. 1962. *A Selection of English Carols*. Oxford: Clarendon Press.

Grundtvig, Svend. 1861. *Nels Ebbesen, dansk folkevise fra 14 die aarhundrede, efter kilderne*. Copenhagen: Gryldenal.

———. 1966–1976. *Danmarks gamle folkeviser*. Copenhagen: Akademisk forlag.

Heilfurth, Gerhard. 1954. *Das Bergmannslied:Wesen, Leben, Funktion*. Kassel: Bärenreiter-Verlag.

Henssen, Gottfried. 1951. *Überlieferung und Persönlichkeit: Lieder und Erzählungen des Egbert Gerrits*. Aschendorff: Archiv für volkskunde Schrifften.

Hoshowskyj, Volodymyr. 1981. "Ukrainische Wechselgesänge der Ostkarpaten als semiotische System." In *Stratigraphische Probleme der Volksmusik in den Karpaten und auf dem Balkan*, ed. Alica Elscheková, 133–140. Bratislava: Veda.

Idelsohn, A. Z. 1914–1932. *Hebräische-orientalischer Melodienschatz*. Leipzig: Breitkopf und Härtel.

Johnson, Anna. 1984. "Voice Physiology and Ethnomusicology: Physiological and Acoustical Studies of the Swedish Herding Song." *Yearbook for Traditional Music* 16:42–66.

Kiss, Lajos, and Benjamin Rajeczky, eds. 1966. *Siratók* (Laments). Budapest: Hungarian Academy of Sciences.

Klymasz, Robert B., and James Porter. 1974. "Traditional Ukrainian Balladry in Canada." *Western Folklore* 33:89–132.

Kotek, J., and R. Zoder. 1950. *Im Heimgarten: Ein österreichisches Volksliederbuch*. Vienna: Österreicheischen Bundesverlag.

Kumer, Zmaga. 1981. "Singers' Repertories as the Consequence of Their Biographies." *Lore and Language* 3(4–5):49–54.

Lineva, Evgeniia Eduardovna Paporits. 1893. *Russian Folksongs as Sung by the People and Peasant Wedding Ceremonies Customary in Northern and Central Russia*. Chicago: C. F. Summey.

———. 1905–1912. *The Peasant Songs of Great Russia as They Are in the Folk's Harmonization*. 2 vols. St. Petersburg: Imperial Academy of Science.

Ling, Jan. 1989. *Europas musikhistoria: Folkmusiken 1730–1980*. Göteborg: Akademiförlaget.

Lord, Albert Bates. 1960. *The Singer of Tales*. Cambridge: Harvard University Press.

Mazo, Margarita. 1990. "Stravinsky's *Les Noces* and Russian Village Wedding Ritual." *Journal of the American Musicological Society* 43:99–142.

Motherwell, William, ed. 1827 [1819]. *Minstrelsy: Ancient and Modern*. Glasgow: J. Wylie.

Nenola-Kallio, Aili. 1982. *Studies in Ingrian Laments*. Helsinki: Folklore Fellows.

Notopoulos, James A. 1959. *Modern Greek Heroic Oral Poetry*. Notes, "Modern Greek Heroic Oral Poetry and Its Relevance to Homer." Folkways Records FE4468. LP disk.

Ó Madagáin, Breandán. 1978. *Gnéithe den chaointeoireacht* (Symposium on keening). Dublin: An Clóchomhar Tta.

Parry, Milman, Albert B. Lord, and David E. Bynum eds. 1953– . *Serbo-Croatian Heroic Songs*. Cambridge: Harvard University Press.

Pommer, Josef. 1942. *444 Jodler und Juechzer aus Steiermark und der steirischen-österreichischen Grenzgebiete*. Vienna: Buchhandler Vertrieb durch Adolf Robitschek.

Porter, James. 1977. "Prolegomena to a Comparative Study of European Folk Music." *Ethnomusicology* 21(3):435–451.

Porter, James, and Herschel Gower. 1995. *Jeannie Robertson: Emergent Singer, Transformative Voice*. Knoxville: University of Tennessee Press.

Propp, Vladimir. 1976. *Fol'klor i deistvitel'nost': lzbrannye stat'i*. Moskva: Nauka.

Rajković, Zorica ed. 1988. *Ballads and Other Genres*. Zagreb: Zavod na istrazivanje folklora.

Sachs, Curt. 1962. *The Wellsprings of Music*. Edited by Jaap Kunst. The Hague: Martinus Nijhoff.

Schneider, Marius. 1954. *Singende Steine: Rhythmus-Studien an drei katalanischen Kreuzgangen romanischen Stils*. Kassel: Bareintes-Verlag.

———. 1969 [1934–1935]. *Geschichte der Mehrstimmigkeit*. Tutzing: H. Schneider.

Scott, Walter, Sir. 1802–1803. *Minstrelsy of the Scottish Border*. 2 vols. Paris: Baudry's European Library.

———. 1968 [1802–1803]. *Minstrelsy of the Scottish Border*. Edited by T. F. Henderson. 2 vols. Detroit: Singing Tree Press.

Shepard, Leslie. 1978 [1962]. *The Broadside Ballad: The Development of the Street Ballad from Traditional Song to Popular Newspaper*. London: Herbert Jenkins.

Sokolov, Y. M. 1971. *Russian Folklore*. Translated by Catherine Ruth Smith. Detroit: Folklore Associates.

Szabolcsi, Bence. 1965. *A History of Melody*. London: Barrie & Rockliff.

Tancjura, Hnat. 1965. *Pisni Javdoxy Zujixy*. Kyjiv: Soviet Ukrainian Academy of Sciences.

Tirén, Karl. 1942. *Die lappische Volksmusik*. Stockholm: H. Geber.

Tobler, Alfred. 1890. *Kühreihen oder Kühreigen, Jodler und Jodellied in Appenzell*. Leipzig, Zurich: Gebruder Hug.

Top, Stefaan. 1981. "Studien zum Repertoire einer 88jährigen flämischen Volksliedsängerin: Zielsetzung, Problematik und europäischen Ergebnisse." In *11. Arbeitstagung über Probleme der europäischen Volksballade*, ed. Rolf Wilhelm Brednich, 179–186. Ioannina, Greece: Faculty of Arts, University of Ioannina.

Trébucq, S. 1912. *La chanson populaire et la vie rurale des Pyrénées à la Vendée*. 2 vols. Bordeaux: Feret et fils.

Väisänen, Armas Otto. 1937. *Wogulische und ost-jakische Melodien*. Helsinki: Suomalais-ugrilainen seura.

Vargyas, Lajos. 1983. *Hungarian Ballads and the European Ballad Tradition*. 2 vols. Budapest: Akadémiai Kiadó.

Voigt, Vilmos. 1991. "Not a Simple Pan-Slavic Genre (Bride's Lament in Hungarian Folklore)." In *Finnish-Hungarian Symposium on Music & Folklore Research 15.–21.11.1987,* ed. Antti Koiranen, 96–103. Tampere: Tempereen Yliopisto.

Wiora, Walter. 1952. *Europäischer Volksgesang: Gemeinsame Formen in charakteristischen Abwandlungen*. Cologne: Arno Volk.

Traditional Performance Contexts
Timothy Rice

Calendar Customs
Songs for Seasonal Work and Recreation
Pastoral Music
Nonagricultural Work
Nonseasonal Recreation
Life-Cycle Rituals or Rites of Passage
Music and Song in Life Stages
Music in Institutional Society

Europe possesses a wide variety of musical styles, but those styles are or were performed in remarkably similar traditional performance contexts across the continent. If the stylistic differences are created by various ethnicities in a complex geography of mountains, plains, river valleys, and access to or isolation from oceans and seas, the similarities in performance contexts are due to a shared temperate climate suitable to agriculture, a shared Christian religious practice with common holidays, and a shared human condition with its inexorable arc of birth, childhood, marriage, aging, and death. In Europe, the agricultural work of plowing, planting, hoeing, harvesting, and resting follows the seasons of the year. Pagan rituals to ensure the fertility of land and animals during the passing seasons were long ago syncretized with Christian annual holidays (including Christmas, the forty-day fast of Lent, Easter, and saints' days) to produce a vital cycle of similar calendar rituals across the length and breadth of Europe. The life cycle, aided by religious beliefs and social practices, produces its own transitional moments, each marked by rites of passage, also called life-cycle rituals, particularly birth, marriage, and death. Stages in life have characteristic songs and dances, especially before marriage, when lullabies, children's games, and courtship songs are common.

Calendar and life-cycle rituals once provided some of the most important contexts for music, dance, and song, and at the same time provided rest from work and relief from the drudgery of everyday life. But traditional musical life was supported on a daily, weekly, or monthly basis by more regularly recurring events, such as informal social gatherings of family, friends, and fellow workers, usually in evenings after work, and by weekly religious observances.

CALENDAR CUSTOMS

Across Europe, the most characteristic features of many calendar customs are house-to-house "luck visits," called caroling in English. Groups of people, often youths, go from house to house singing special songs, or playing music unique to that time of year, blessing the house and those in it with wishes for good luck and fertility, and in return receiving food, drink, and token amounts of money. Caroling at Christmas is only the most durable of a set of such rituals that recurred annually from December

Whether an Irish *céili,* a Scottish *waulking* (wool shrinking), a Breton *fest noz,* a French *viellée,* an Icelandic *kvöldvaka,* or a Bulgarian *sedyanka,* evening gatherings in the home, often around the kitchen table, constituted the main forms of recreation in European villages before television.

FIGURE 1 May dancing around a maypole in Wales, 1994. Courtesy of the Museum of Welsh Life.

until harvest in the fall. In Wales, a "gray-mare" holiday marked the winter solstice with luck visits and wassailing, the transition from winter to spring was celebrated on 2 February with another luck visit, and there were carols for Shrove Tuesday (the day before Ash Wednesday) and May Day (figure 1). In the Balkans, there were luck visits at Christmas or New Year's (*koleda, colinde*), before Lent (day of the *kuker*), and on the Saturday before Palm Sunday (*lazarovden*). Celebrating the end of the harvest is not so widespread or so well marked as these efforts to ensure its fertility—efforts that have waned as the agriculture-devoted population in Europe has decreased and belief in the power of fertilizer and scientific agricultural practices has increased.

Situated within a religious calendar, the pagan origins of luck visits as fertility rituals are usually obvious in ritual actions and song texts. English wassailing songs wish animals well ("Here is to Dobbin and to his right eye"). In Switzerland, the Basque country, and parts of the Balkans, Carnival, a celebration before Lent, is celebrated by masked characters dressed in animal skins with bells tied to their waists. In Bulgaria, the *kukeri* jump up and down to jingle their bells (shake their balls) and toss their phallic-pointed hats on the ground at each house, ritually seeding it. These carnival characters, called *chläuse* in Switzerland, are conceptual ancestors of Santa Claus [see SWITZERLAND, figure 1]. In many parts of Europe, the procession from house to house has evolved into massive public parades of costumed marchers and masked characters to the accompaniment of bands and noisemakers. Some instruments are brought out and played during certain seasons of the year. In Central Europe, cog-ratchet rattles sound on Good Friday, and friction drums, with their sexual mimicry, are a favorite at Carnival [see SPAIN, figure 1, p. 590].

Often luck visits were the province of marginalized social groups, particularly children and youths, sometimes segregated by sex. In the Balkans, New Year's, Christmas, and Carnival luck visits are typically performed by boys, but *lazarovden* and the rain-begging luck visits that occur during summer droughts are performed by girls. In some cases, other marginal groups, such as Rom in the Balkans and handicapped and jobless adults in the Low Countries, caroled to receive charity in exchange for songs and blessings.

Easter and summertime saints' days provided pretexts for Sunday fairs and occasions for dancing and musical performance, the latter sometimes provided by professional musicians. Across Europe, the summer solstice is marked by dancing around bonfires, especially in the Scandinavian countries, where the seemingly unending midsummer's night is especially dramatic.

Many calendar customs, especially carnival with its masquerades, have a dramatic and narrative character, and with enactments of religious stories provided the main forms of folk theater before the rise of the urban theatrical tradition. Theater per se is not an especially widespread context for making music in the European tradition. Exceptions include the English Soul-Caking Play, the Italian *Maggio,* the pastoral and passion plays in Roman Catholic areas of Central and southern Europe, and the

Jewish Purim play (Yiddish *Purimspil*), which recounts the narrative of persecution and freedom from the Book of Esther. As Europe urbanized, the theater, rather than the calendar custom, became an important institution for displaying the important issues of life, and some theater used music prominently, including Yiddish theater, German *liederspiele* 'song plays', and Serbian *komad s pevanjem* 'dramatic play with singing'.

SONGS FOR SEASONAL WORK AND RECREATION

Each season brought characteristic forms of work, and that work was accompanied by singing. Men sang special plowing songs. Hoers and harvesters, often women, sang to relieve the boredom and exhaustion of physically demanding work. Though singing accompanies fieldwork in most of Europe, transverse flutes and snare drums accompany fieldwork in French-speaking areas of Switzerland. European fieldwork songs are not strongly metrical and therefore do not function to encourage coordinated movements; rather, they tend to be nonmetrical and unlinked to the rhythm of work. Their main function was psychological; they described the work and in the process lightened it, and they could be sung during the work and in rest periods. In winter, life moved into the home, where women gathered to sing as they spun thread, knitted, or embroidered, or people socialized, drank, sang, and danced. Whether an Irish *céili,* a Scottish *waulking* (wool shrinking), a Breton *fest noz*, a French *viellée,* an Icelandic *kvöldvaka,* or a Bulgarian *sedyanka*, these evening gatherings in the home, often around the kitchen table, constituted the main forms of recreation in European villages before television (figure 2). Some song genres took their name from the main feature of the venue, as in Greek "table songs." In addition to the metrical dance tunes that might be played, sitting around a table provides a context for enjoying richly ornamented, nonmetrical instrumental "listening tunes" in Norway, "slow airs" in Ireland, "laments" in Greece, and "slow songs" in Bulgaria.

FIGURE 2 An Italian family gathering with singing, guitar playing, food, and drink in Terracina, Lazio. Photo by Luisa Del Giudice, 1986.

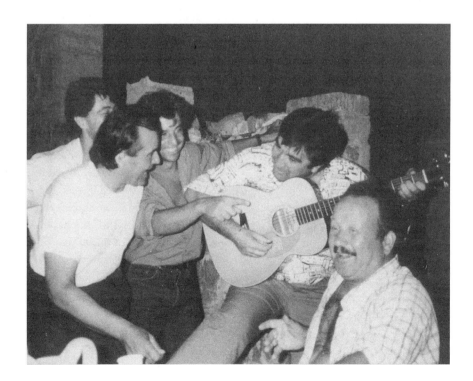

PASTORAL MUSIC

Farming was once the most widespread traditional occupation in Europe, and the husbandry of animal herds was an important part of that life. In mountainous regions of nonarable land, large flocks of sheep and goats provided the primary source of life, and the rhythms and sounds of work in shepherding communities differed significantly from those of farming communities. To provide adequate pasture for their animals, herdsmen and women moved their flocks from summer highlands to winter lowlands in a two-season transhumant cycle. The boredom of long days watching animals eat was relieved by playing musical instruments. The endless hours provided talented musicians with an opportunity outside courtly patronage to develop virtuosic techniques on their instruments. Across Europe, shepherds and shepherdesses played, and still play, similar instruments (flutes, horns, bagpipes) in a remarkable variety of specific types [see TRADITIONAL MUSICAL INSTRUMENTS]. In the French Pyrenees, pig-gelders and goatherds played panpipes. Music on the bagpipe and the flute was meant for personal amusement, and according to some shepherds the amusement of the sheep, while horns were and are used for signaling over great distances. In Switzerland, songs accompanied different herding activities (milking, feeding, blessing), and people believed they could entrance and control animals with music, cattle calls, and yodeling. In Norway, shepherdesses developed elaborate, highly ornamented techniques for their horn signaling, which differed for each type of animal. In Albania, girls in pairs watch flocks and amuse themselves by singing and simultaneously tapping a finger against their larynx to produce a vibrating sound. Shepherds tie bells around the necks of their animals, often carefully selecting the pitches they sound. In the Balkans, each species of animal wears a distinct type of bell, the types differing from each other in material and shape.

NONAGRICULTURAL WORK

Romantic ideas place folk song and folk music primarily in rural, farming communities; however, many traditional genres have emerged in towns since the Middle Ages, and since at least the 1800s in most of Europe, nonagricultural occupational groups have generated distinctive song and music traditions. In Denmark and the Low Countries, each trade had its repertoire: millers, weavers, wool workers, lacemakers, bargemen, miners, soldiers, builders, and children's nurses. Most of these songs tended to be about the work and the problems of the occupation, rather than accompaniments to work. Exceptions included sea chanteys sung by Atlantic sailors while hoisting sails (probably influenced by African slaves in the West Indies), and Sicilian fishermen's songs, sung while pulling nets [see ITALY, figure 1, p. 606]. In Italy, Spain, and the Mediterranean islands, mule-drivers moved goods down the road with special nonstrophic songs that combined melody with whoops and calls. As trucks replaced animal-drawn carts, this repertoire declined; but in Sicily, truck drivers congregate at rest stops instead of stables to continue a tradition of song dueling that originated among animal drivers (figure 3).

Urban environments and the interaction between urban and rural communities generated its own set of occupations: merchants, itinerant hawkers, and vagrant musicians. As more people moved from subsistence farming into a monied economy, music making became an occupation for respectable town-settled professionals and vagrants, beggars, travellers, and itinerant music teachers. At one time, each product's seller had his or her identifying songlike call or cry. Ballad singers, some with printed broadsides containing the words and even the tunes of their songs, traveled from market to market selling their songs. In Northern Europe, certain instruments, like the hurdy-gurdy and the pipe and tabor, were identified with vagrant street musicians; in the Balkans, nomadic Rom with bears on chains played the tambourine or

FIGURE 3 A cart driver sings in Bagheria, Sicily, July 1954. Courtesy of the Alan Lomax Collection, New York.

bowed lute as they beg for money in return for their blessings. Physical handicaps and joblessness often induced men to take up roles as vagrant musicians. Blindness in particular was the mark of professional minstrels, such as Italian *cantastorie* 'song-storytellers' and Ukrainian *lirnyky*. In Ireland, traveling schoolmasters who could teach singing, Latin, and Greek made their living tutoring at so-called hedge schools.

NONSEASONAL RECREATION

As wealth increased and more varied indoor work not directly tied to the seasons became the norm, people could afford and support entertainment outside homes. Taverns and pubs became gathering places, especially for men, including specially designated singing pubs in England, the pub session where instrumentalists gather to make music in Ireland, Greek tavernas with their urban *rebetika* 'rebel music', and Serbian cafés where male youths (*bećarci*) gather to sing and carouse. Certain ensemble formations came to characterize these places, such as the Hungarian Rom orchestra and the Bavarian bar-music ensemble.

Private amusement, relaxation, and passing the time during work and at odd moments of the day provide important contexts for musical performance throughout Europe. Housewives and farmers often sing whatever songs come to mind as they work alone. Certain small instruments, like mouth harps, duct flutes, and harmonicas, are ideal for carrying in the pocket, to be pulled out in spare moments. In Iceland, which had few traditional instruments, people recited and sang rhymed verses (*lausavísur*) while shepherding, traveling, and fishing.

Encounters between friends and acquaintances provided contexts for exchanging improvised or traditional verses. In Sardinia, improvised sung witticisms often punctuated gambling, discussions, conflicts, and jokes. In Iceland, people insert rhymed verses into conversations, arguments, and challenges. The Saami (Lapps) use joiks as a form of greeting and insert them into conversations. In Greece, cleverly improvised couplets help gatherings of friends achieve heightened enjoyment (*kefi*).

LIFE-CYCLE RITUALS OR RITES OF PASSAGE

In the Christian cultures of Europe, marriage is the only universally celebrated rite of passage marked by elaborate music. Customs associated with birth usually include no music, and the formalized lamenting that occurs at death and burials, though it bears many features of music and song, belongs to a separate category of activity distinguished by labels such as keening in Ireland, wailing, lament, and dirge. In some Roman Catholic countries, adolescents' confirmation in the church is marked by special parties, and in the second half of the twentieth century, the sending off of young conscripts to the military has become an increasingly important pretext for celebrations with music. The *bar mitzvah* in Jewish culture and the circumcision in Muslim cultures mark the beginning of male adolescence with elaborate celebrations, including music (figure 4).

The wedding in traditionally patriarchal, patrilocal European societies was not simply the union of two people, but the union of two families in a new relationship and the transfer of the bride from her natal to her affinal family. So important a rite of passage required elaborate preparation, execution, and confirmation, often over long periods of time. It began with engagement parties months before the marriage, lasted through a week of festivities and rituals at the time of the wedding, and continued for months with ritual visits between the bride and bridegroom's families, often including such rituals as the French *charivari*, teasing noisemaking outside the couples' house during the wedding night. Musical performance tended to take two forms. In-home singing by close friends and relatives of the bride and groom accom-

Adolescence is the time par excellence for singing, dancing, and making courtship-linked music. Young people use these forms to express their attractiveness and their attractions to others in formalized, socially sanctioned ways.

FIGURE 4   Albanian women at a circumcision ceremony (*sunet*) in Prizren, Kosovo, Serbia. Photo by Elsie Ivancich Dunin, 1967.

FIGURE 5   A Macedonian bride leads the dance, accompanied by professional Gypsy musicians on an accordion and a vase-shaped drum (*tarabuka*). Photo by Jane Sugarman, 1980.

panied such ritual actions as toasts, the exchange of gifts, the bride's veiling, the groom's shaving, the presentation of the bride to the groom's family, the bride's farewell to her parents, and processions to the church. Instrumental music, often made by professional or semiprofessional instrumentalists, accompanied processions and celebratory feasting and dancing (figure 5). As the pace of life increased with urbanization and industrial work in the twentieth century, the time devoted to weddings has decreased, but music continues to play an important role in the celebration. In Bulgaria during the 1980s, lavish, ostentatious weddings spawned major new developments in traditional musical styles, though the wedding now lasts a weekend instead of a week. In Finland, the once traditional weekend wedding has shrunk to an afternoon party sponsored by the couple themselves, rather than by their families.

The grief unleashed by death continues to be expressed in songlike laments in many parts of Eastern and southern Europe, while they are rarely performed in Northern and Western Europe. A nearly universal descending melodic shape, mixed with stylized forms of weeping, seems to provide an icon of waves of pain subsiding into emotional exhaustion. Laments occur as the body is prepared for burial, during the funeral, and at the grave for days and months after the burial. Though usually performed by close female relatives of the deceased, laments may be performed by male and female professional lamenters. In parts of Albania and Greece, lamenting is performed by groups of women, sometimes polyphonically. In Corsica, the lament is an honored poetic genre, and people remember and use the best laments in other contexts, including ridiculing candidates during elections. In some communities, the playing of a tambourine signals a death.

MUSIC AND SONG IN LIFE STAGES

Infancy, childhood, and adolescence are times to sing, play, dance, and be sung to. Most cultures use lullabies or recited rhymes to comfort children—and perhaps the mother. Children's games share common features: versions of the English game "London Bridge Is Falling Down" are played as far away as Bulgaria. In parts of north-central Europe, children constantly renew and invent new narrow-range game songs, constituting in some cases the only part of traditional culture where new forms are created, rather than merely preserved. Adolescence is the time par excellence for singing, dancing, and making courtship-linked music. Young people use these forms to express their attractiveness and their attractions to others in formalized, socially sanctioned ways. Those ways vary across the continent—from Italian and Spanish boys' serenades from the street to the balcony of their beloved across rigidly enforced spaces that separate the sexes, to dialogue-courtship songs sung as Welsh lovers lay in the same bed separated only by a board, a practice resembling bundling in the United States. In some Muslim communities in the Balkans, the alluring quality of singing and dancing required women to stop those activities in public after marriage. In the Low Countries, moving house, normally an unmarked stage of life, occasions singing parties. In many traditional communities, the death of a close relative required those in mourning to cease singing and dancing for a year or more. In Albania and Greece, older women may abandon the modest dance and singing styles demanded of girls and younger women in favor of the more rambunctious, overtly expressive styles of men. Since women are charged with primary responsibility for mourning, as they age and endure more and more deaths in the family, many wear black constantly and stop singing altogether at some point in their lives.

MUSIC IN INSTITUTIONAL SOCIETY

The rituals of peasant society focus on human and agricultural reproduction, but at least since the Middle Ages these activities existed at the bottom of a social scale whose higher reaches had created their own institutions dedicated to other goals: control, taxation, expansion, defense, education, and spiritual guidance. The first patrons of music outside villages were the courts of the nobility and Christian churches. Both institutions borrowed styles and musicians from the surrounding countryside to perform and in some cases create elaborate new styles that benefited from the money these institutions could lavish upon them.

The weekly, and in some cases daily, services of organized religions have for centuries provided important contexts for musical performance, sometimes led by trained musicians, like the Jewish cantor or Christian organist and choirmaster, often joined by amateur singers from the congregation. Though the liturgical repertoire differs significantly in form and function from secular folk songs, the differences have not prevented important interrelationships from developing. Traditional melodies have been borrowed for use in the church, perhaps most notably by Martin Luther during the Protestant Reformation, and religious tunes and styles have influenced secular styles. In Sardinia, Corsica, and parts of the Balkans, striking similarities between secular and sacred polyphony occur. In Roman Catholic countries, the singing of religious songs outside the church is common, while in Protestant Northern Europe, the singing of psalm tunes in highly elaborate call-and-response versions—a process called lining-out in English—was once a popular form of home entertainment in devout families (figure 6).

Medieval nobility provided the first secular patronage of musicians, who

FIGURE 6 Musicians from the Azores (Atlantic islands belonging to Portugal), dressed for a religious festival. Postcard from the early 1900s. Courtesy of the Robert Godfried Collection, New York.

undoubtedly brought melodies from the countryside to the court. The melodies and texts of French trouvères and troubadours and German minnesingers and meistersingers have been preserved in manuscripts. Only the texts of Welsh and Irish bards and Norwegian and Icelandic skalds are known today; their music, never written down, is lost, though some texts describe performers' improvisatory skill on the harp and other instruments. Such courts also transformed the shepherds' horn into the horns of battle, notably the Northern European lur, which existed in wooden and bronze forms [see ARCHAEOLOGY OF MUSIC IN EUROPE].

As governmental and economic institutions increased in complexity and power, the contexts for making music multiplied. By the 1800s, court trumpeters had evolved into full-fledged military brass bands, which in towns throughout Europe spawned municipal bands that played at civic parades and religious and wedding processions, fairs, markets, and jubilees. In Germany, town musicians formed guilds. In Malta and Portugal, communities compete for prestige in band competitions. In Macedonia and Serbia, bandsmen trained in the military brought their instruments home to form small wedding bands. Schools and schoolyards became important places for the performance of folk songs, song games, and dances to songs, sometimes brought there for recreation at recess by the children themselves, sometimes taught to them in class by their teachers. As Europe industrialized, factories, mines, and labor unions spawned their own bands and choirs to achieve solidarity and reinforce their social views. In nineteenth-century Finland, each political party had its own band and choir that performed songs at political rallies extolling its distinctive political philosophy in a distinctive musical style. In the Trentino area of northern Italy and the Basque country, choral societies formed for the pleasure of singing, their four-part harmonies significantly altering older singing practices. In at least one well-known instance, jail became a context for making music when Greek urban hood-lums and political prisoners commented on their condition and society's ills in songs accompanied on tiny homemade instruments in a style known as *rebetika* 'rebel music'. Finally, the European penchant for competition led as early as the late 1700s to competitive festivals such as the *eisteddfod* in Wales, a process intensified after World War II [see CONTEMPORARY PERFORMANCE CONTEXTS].

Throughout the 1800s and up to World War II, industrialization, urbanization, and education gradually changed the worldview and lifeways of Europe's people. A decreasing percentage of the population devoted themselves to agriculture, and as a consequence traditional contexts for making music, especially calendar rituals and agricultural work songs, disappeared, though at different rates in Western and Eastern Europe. World War II seems to have been a watershed for the practice of tra-ditional music in Europe. After that war, socialist governments in Eastern Europe accelerated the rate of industrialization, and transformed music and other aspects of culture into matters for cultural and ideological control. Western Europe rebuilt itself rapidly, in the process creating unprecedented urban prosperity. The new technolo-gies of television, long-playing records, and cassette recorders created new modes of self-entertainment in homes and taverns and on the street. Modernization in all its forms has conspired to eliminate or reduce in importance many traditional contexts for making music. Simultaneously, governments, commercial media companies, aca-demics, and private citizens have organized efforts to preserve the musical traditions they fear they are losing. In these efforts, organizations and individuals have created new contexts, with their own dynamic effects on the practice of music.

BIBLIOGRAPHY

Alexiou, Margaret. 1974. *The Ritual Lament in Greek Tradition*. Cambridge: Cambridge University Press.

Courtney, Margaret Ann. 1890. *Cornish Feasts and Folklore*. Penzance: Beare and Son.

Dadak-Kozicka, Katarzyna. 1990. *Levels of Formal Organization of Spring Carols from Northeast Poland*. Bern: Lang.

Danforth, Loring. 1989. *Firewalking and Religious Healing: The Anastinaria of Greece and the American Firewalking Movement*. Princeton: Princeton University Press.

Duthaler, Georg. 1985. *Trommeln und Pfeifen in Basel*. Basel: Merian.

Falassi, Alessandro. 1987. *Time Out of Time: Essays on the Festival*. Albuquerque: University of New Mexico Press.

Glassie, Henry. 1982. *Passing the Time in Ballymenone: Culture and History of an Ulster Community*. Philadelphia: University of Pennsylvania Press.

Ivanova, Radost. 1987. *Traditional Bulgarian Wedding*. Sofia: Svyat Publishers.

Kligman, Gail. 1981. *Caluş: Symbolic Transformation in Romanian Ritual*. Chicago: University of Illinois Press.

———. 1988. *The Wedding of the Dead: Ritual, Poetics, and Popular Culture in Transylvania*. Berkeley: University of California Press.

Kück, Eduard. 1911. *Feste und Spiel des Deutschen Landvolks: Herausgegeben von E. Kück und Heinrich Sohnrey*. Berlin: Deutsche Landbuchhandlung.

Paxton, Frederick S. 1990. *Christianizing Death: The Creation of a Ritual Process in Early Medieval Europe*. Ithaca, N.Y.: Cornell University Press.

Pol'skii, Il'ia. 1977. "Christmas-Carol Cycles in the Ukraine and in Belorussia and Their

Increasing Ties with the New Socialist Rituals."
Ph.D. dissertation, Leningraskii Institut Teatra,
Muzyki i Kinematograf II. In Russian.

Sikkarulidze, Ksenia. 1979. *Rituals and Songs of Weather in Georgian Poetic Folklore*. The Hague: Mouton.

Willetts, R. F. 1962. *Cretan Cults and Festivals*. New York: Barnes & Noble.

Zemaitiene, Ursule. 1953. *Wedding Customs of Suvalkieciai*. Cleveland: Lietuviu Tautosakos Lobyvias.

Contemporary Performance Contexts

Owe Ronström
Krister Malm

Live Performances
Mediated Performances

In Europe since the 1950s, significant changes—including festivalization, orientation toward public performance, professionalization, internationalization, institutionalization, and mediazation—have taken place in performance contexts for traditional music. Many of these changes began during the 1800s, but since World War II they have accelerated, leading typically to a shift from local, amateur, private, and nonstaged contexts to regional or national, professional, public, and staged contexts.

LIVE PERFORMANCES

With the entry of folk music into performance situations typical of classical and popular music, situations such as festivals, clubs, concerts, and musical conservatories, traditional musicians have come to adopt many of the performance practices expected at these contexts. As a result, new forms of traditional music, influenced by symphonic music, chamber music, jazz, rock, and different kinds of popular dance music, have developed. New performance contexts have affected every aspect of performance practice: temporal, spatial, social, aesthetic, and cognitive.

Festivals of traditional music

Organized all over Europe, festivals provide one of the most important new contexts for traditional music. Festivals orient musicians toward public performances, fixed arrangements, and objectified traditions—traits that shift aesthetic experience from the musical activity to the product of the activity. The festivalization of a musical tradition often leads to the development of a codified tradition and a set of institutions for socially controlling musicians and their playing styles.

Klapa singing in the former Yugoslavia changed in 1967, when the first *klapa* festival was arranged in Omiš, with the goal of attracting young people and tourists. *Klapa* 'club, group of friends' refers to songs and a singing style in four parts performed by men in urban areas along the Dalmatia coast. In the prefestival style, four to five men would gather in a small cafe, arranging themselves around a table, facing inward, leaning forward, singing quietly with simple harmonies and improvising the parts. In the postfestival style, five to eight members, men or women, arrange themselves in a line or a half circle and focus their performance outward to an audience. Their singing is louder; the songs, musical arrangement, and manner of performance

Since the 1960s, folk-music artists have won
international fame and toured the world, performing
at the same kinds of sports arenas and concert halls
as famous rock and jazz groups.

are rehearsed; and complex compositions and harmonies have been introduced.
Rehearsals for public performance have become especially important, and it is likely
that rehearsals constitute the greatest part of traditional musical activity.

Public staged performances of traditional music have led to the professionalization of musicians and the internationalization of styles. Since the 1960s, folk-music
artists have won international fame and toured the world, performing at the same
kinds of sports arenas and concert halls as famous rock and jazz groups, including the
Romanian panpipe virtuoso Gheorghe Zamfir, the Spanish guitarist Paco de Lucía,
and the Bulgarian singers Trio Bulgarka.

Such professionalization also occurs at the national level, where folk artists have
become famous by touring and performing on television, radio, and recordings. In
the former communist countries of Eastern Europe such artists had official titles and
permanent employment; professional folk musicians are also well known in most
Western European countries.

Traditional music was once closely related to the agricultural calendar of work
and leisure [see TRADITIONAL PERFORMANCE CONTEXTS], but today it is related more
to industrial and educational calendars. Public performance often occurs only during
summer months when festivals abound; the rest of the year is devoted to training,
rehearsing, and occasionally performing.

Folklore ensembles in festival contexts

From June to September, national folk-music and dance festivals and competitions
are arranged all over Europe, where concepts of tradition and authenticity are
enforced (Dubinskas 1981; Sremac 1978). Musicians perform as soloists, in small
groups or larger folk-dance groups or folklore ensembles. Each musician or group is
given five to ten minutes to perform authentic, representative songs and dances from
its home region. Large festivals are held regularly in such Eastern European towns as
Gjirokastër (Albania), Koprivshtitsa (Bulgaria), and Zagreb (Croatia), but there are
equivalents in most Western European countries (figure 1). In Norway, fiddlers' competitions, *kappleikar,* started in 1888 and have become important manifestations of
Norwegian national cultural heritage. The four-day *landskappleik* of 1990, in
Norfjordeid, presented more than fifteen hundred fiddlers to a jury of specialists and
an audience of twenty thousand spectators (figure 2). In Sweden, the famous painter
Anders Zorn organized the first fiddlers' contest in 1906. These fiddlers' gatherings
(*spelmansstämmor*) became social events, with emphasis on informal, spontaneous
playing rather than rehearsed, formal, competitively staged performances. Today,
they attract thousands of musicians and listeners from all over Sweden. Such gatherings have led to a preference for group playing, improvisation, the development of
various techniques of accompaniment, and a standardized repertoire of *allspelslåtar,*
tunes that everyone is supposed to know.

FIGURE 1   At the festival Pirin Pee ('Pirin Sings'), young Muslim women from the Bansko district of Pirin, Bulgaria, recreate the rainmaking ritual (*peperuda*). Photo by Jane Sugarman, 1980.

National festivals in the late nineteenth and early twentieth centuries mainly intended to represent the "folk" of a country to its own inhabitants. According to the prevailing Romantic ideology, the "folk" meant "peasants," as opposed to the upper classes or urban workers. After World War II, new festivals and ensembles were created to represent a "folk" now taken to mean peasants and workers, that is, the whole population of a country, and the intended audiences became people of other countries—a major step in the internationalization of folk music and dance. Similar forms of presentation soon became common to many groups, making it possible to compare groups from different countries, and competition became an important feature of international folklore festivals such as the International Eisteddfod in Wales.

The Second World Youth Festival, held in Prague in 1947, was particularly important for these developments. First prize went to the Soviet-Russian group led by the famous choreographer Igor Moiseyev; second prize, to the amateur ensemble Joža Vlahović, consisting of young students from Zagreb, led by the choreographer Zvonimir Ljevaković. As a result of success in this competition, the members of Joža

FIGURE 2   The Lom Juniorlag, the children's fiddle club of Lom, Norway, competes in the *landskappleik* ('National Fiddle Contest'). The fiddlers play tunes proper to Lom on the regular fiddle native to their home. The photo montage behind the fiddlers celebrates the logging heritage of Trysil, site of the contest. To be nationalistic in Norway is to conserve one's local heritage. Photo by Chris Goertzen, 1989.

FIGURE 3   The Croatian folk ensemble Varažden performs at a Yugoslav folk festival in Croatia. Photo by Owe Ronström, 1987.

Vlahović gained employment as professional artists in the new Croatian state folklore ensemble (later named Lado), one of the first in the Balkans (figure 3).

The first professional folklore ensembles were created in the Soviet Union between the world wars. After World War II, state folklore ensembles were created in all the socialist countries (Kosacheva 1990). These ensembles created large new orchestras of traditional instruments modeled on symphony orchestras, and the sound and the texture of traditional music changed dramatically.

The professional state folklore ensembles became a major vehicle for national and state propaganda on an international level, and these ensembles have had a profound impact on images of, and ideas about, Eastern European culture. By setting new, higher standards for good technique for musicians and dancers, the ensembles became important models for amateur and professional folklore ensembles in many countries. Official Yugoslav statistics show that, in 1975, folk-dance and music ensembles were the most popular organized cultural activities (Dedić 1981).

In Western Europe, there are few professional folklore ensembles of the Eastern European type. Nevertheless, the ideological ideas and aesthetic values behind the formation of such groups have influenced the development of new contexts for folk music in Western Europe. After World War II, the orchestra of Gunnar Hahn played arrangements of Swedish folk melodies on Swedish radio for many years. In Sweden, fiddlers' ensembles (*spelmanslag*) are counterparts to folklore ensembles of Eastern Europe. The first, formed in 1947, consisted of violins playing improvised second and third parts to traditional melodies. They performed at local dance events, concerts, and shows, where they acted as representatives of their community or region in front of visiting officials and tourists. Later, accordions, guitars, and double basses were introduced. With them, written arrangements and the sound and texture of the music changed in a fashion resembling that of Eastern European folklore ensembles.

Folk groups, folk clubs, and folk festivals

In Western Europe, new contexts arose from the wave of folk-music interest in most European countries in the late 1960s and early 1970s. This was the era of folk groups, typically consisting of four or five musicians and singers, in many cases combining instruments that had never before been played together; for example, Irish groups combined bagpipes, fiddle, banjo, bouzouki, harp, guitar, flutes, and other instruments. These groups directed their efforts mainly toward staged performances for listening audiences, either in smaller venues, such as folk clubs, or at local or regional festivals. In the early 1980s in Milton Keynes, a city in England with about two hundred thousand inhabitants, a dozen groups of this kind performed regularly at the five or six local folk-music clubs. These groups comprised a small minority of well-educated urban professionals, including teachers, bankers, chemists, and accountants. Some of them "lived for folk" and spent almost every evening of the week at folk clubs. They were connected to a countrywide network of folk musicians and folk clubs, through festivals, periodicals, and small booklets (Finnegan 1989). The folk-music world of Milton Keynes is not exceptional. The number of folk groups in many parts of Europe is large, and the folk clubs and folk festivals created by and for these groups are among the most important public-performance contexts for folk music.

In some countries, like the United Kingdom, the folk festival has become an institution with ever-growing popularity. The 1989 *Folkweave Festival Guide* listed more than a hundred events in England and Scotland.

Many new folk groups in Europe are dedicated primarily to dance music. Young people in Budapest, for example, cultivated folk dance to live performance beginning in the early 1970s, in the so-called *tánchás* (dance-house) movement [see HUNGARY]. A survey of the musicians connected to this movement from 1984 listed ninety-one groups, all of them consisting of three to six members, mostly male, age twenty to thirty-five years old, playing older traditional dance melodies on the folk instruments of Hungary and Transylvania (violins, bagpipes, hurdy-gurdies, flutes), all of which they learned through records, cassettes, videos, informal courses, and occasionally by serving as apprentices to famous village musicians (Ronström 1990).

Many young folk musicians and dancers directed their efforts against older forms of staged folk music and dance, especially forms cultivated by the large professional state folklore ensembles. For the young generation in Budapest, old, supposedly authentic, unarranged folklore became a symbol of a national culture unaffected by socialist and Stalinist ideology and cultural policy. Dance houses, modeled on the Hungarian *tánchás,* were created in Romania, Czechoslovakia, East and West Germany, and Sweden (figure 4).

FIGURE 4   A dancing house (*danshus*) in Stockholm, Sweden, modeled after a Hungarian dance house (*tánchás*). Photo by Owe Ronström, mid-1980s.

At the Falun Folk Music Festival in Sweden, "national representation," "tradition," and "authenticity" are no longer important concepts. Musicians emphasize modernity, diversity, and variety and use words such as *hybrid, creole, bastard, mixed,* and *syncretic* to describe their music in a strongly positive sense.

Folklore und Mitmachen is the German label for part of this movement and the name of a bulletin published by Folkklub Hamburg. Its calendar for November, 1988, listed sixty-two festivals and dance events in Germany and the Netherlands, many of them lasting from three days to a week. Significantly, the German clubs and groups connected to the folk-revival movement use the English term *folk* instead of the German *volk,* used by older folklore ensembles and *trachten-gruppen* 'folk-costume groups'.

Closely related to these groups and the subcultures that form around them are new folk-music ensembles—including Leegajus in Tallin, Estonia, and the Dmitri Pokrovsky ensemble in Moscow—that consist of young, well-educated urbanites aiming to restore old and disappearing musical styles by studying with older people in villages and performing their music in cities. As a result of these students' interest, villagers have been stimulated to remember songs and value them more highly (Krader 1990). The ethnographic concert, another expression of interest in so-called authentic folklore, is in the former Soviet Union and Eastern Europe connected to the ongoing dissolution of the socialist system. For urban audiences in such concerts, villagers perform their own traditional songs and dances, often by invitation of an ethnologist or ethnomusicologist. These concerts have been instrumental in the reformulation of national and cultural identity, creating new contexts and ascribing new social roles for older types of traditional music and dance, and creating new contexts and roles for ethnologists and ethnomusicologists, for example, the appointment of the ethnologist Bertalan Andrasfalvy as Hungarian cultural minister in the cabinet of 1989.

New types of festivals

Several new types of festivals have emerged since the 1970s. One type specializes in a particular musical style or instrument, for example, the bagpipe festival in Järna, Sweden, which contributed to the revival of the bagpipe in Sweden (Ronström 1989). Another type involves contemporary folk music, world music, and fusions and mixtures of styles from around the world, for example the Derde Werde Festival (Third World Festival), held in 1989 in Tilburg, Netherlands, and the Falun Folk Music Festival, held annually since 1985 in Falun, Sweden. In the latter case, the festival committee consists of many folk musicians, for whom "national representation," "tradition," and "authenticity" are no longer important concepts. These musicians emphasize modernity, diversity, and variety. Performers at these festivals use words such as *hybrid, creole, bastard, mixed,* and *syncretic* to describe their music in a strongly positive sense (figure 5).

Educational institutions

All over Europe, folk musicians have penetrated the educational system, either as teachers or as visiting artists. For pedagogical and therapeutic purposes, folk music is also presented at hospitals and prisons.

FIGURE 5   At a festival in Järna, Sweden, in the mid-1980s, the Swedish folk group Orientexpressen performs with Hungarian flutist Joszef Kozak (*left*). Courtesy of Owe Ronström (*third from left*).

Probably the first formal education on folk-music instruments was set up in the former Soviet Union, where, soon after the 1917 Revolution, it was possible to study balalaika, *domra,* and accordion at Russian conservatories. Following the Soviet model, folk-music schools were begun in many Eastern European countries; in Bulgaria for example, two folk-music high schools and a post-secondary conservatory devoted to folk-music pedagogy prepared students to become professional folk artists employed by state folklore ensembles or as directors of amateur ensembles. Today, indigenous folk music and instruments are taught at secondary schools in many countries, including the Sibelius Academy in Helsinki and conservatories in Oslo and Stockholm, and folk musicians have benefited from increased social status and new career possibilities.

MEDIATED PERFORMANCES

Perhaps the most significant development for the dissemination and popularization of all kinds of music in the twentieth century has been the various forms of mass media, including radio and television broadcasting and records, cassettes, and CDs.

Radio and television broadcasting

Until the 1980s, the European tradition of broadcasting normally followed a public-service model with a limited number of commercial radio channels. Though folk music was aired on and off during the 1920s and 1930s, it was broadcast more systematically only in the final years of the 1940s and the beginning of the 1950s. Special producers of folk-music programs were employed at many broadcasting companies, and program slots were set aside for documentary programs on folk music in Eastern and Western Europe. Academically trained folk-music experts played an important role in these broadcasts, partly to dissociate folk music from its nationalist connotations before and during World War II. Three factors contributed to the increased attention to folk music: the upsurge of nationalism caused by World War II; a sense of responsibility for folk-music traditions on the part of some media decision makers; and new magnetic recording technology. At the beginning of the 1950s, radio stations were the only institutions in Europe where tape-recording equipment was available. Many collectors quickly realized the value of this technology in documenting folk music, and collaborated with the radio stations in organizing field-recording trips, which provided material for radio programs and the foundation of folk-music archives.

Active folk-music producers at European radio stations formed a Radio Committee within the International Folk Music Council (now the International

Council for Traditional Music) in 1952 to collect information on recorded folk-music collections and cooperate with broadcasting corporations and institutions specializing in folk music in the recording, preservation, and dissemination of authentic folk music, with special reference to the presentation of broadcast programs and the international exchange of programs and recordings (Slocombe 1956). From 1954, the committee began to produce radio programs that were broadcast all over Europe, the first two of these being "Folk Music Associated with the Summer Solstice" and "Songs and Instrumental Music of Shepherds and Herdsmen." The practical cooperation among members of the IFMC Radio Committee resulted in a pan-European relationship that remained constant between folk music and radio stations into the 1980s.

Programs on folk music fall into several categories. Educational programs, often a lecture where a specialist presents field recordings with comments (Sárosi 1986), were directed to an intellectual or a popular audience. In 1953–1954, the BBC Light Programme broadcast, for six months, an extensive series of programs of folk music collected by the BBC in Great Britain and Ireland during 1952 and 1953. In the 1980s, Swedish Educational Broadcasting devised a series of programs that systematically taught folk songs from different regions of the country; the songs were also published in booklets, one for each region, and the programs were made available on audiocassettes. Broadcasts from folk-music festivals and other live music events constitute a second program type. Studio broadcasts where folk musicians and dancers were brought in for live or recorded broadcasts were often conceptualized as entertainment, and the folk music that was performed tended to be in a more contemporary style, with accordion, guitar, and added harmonies. Broadcasts of folk music arranged for choirs, string orchestras, and folk-music ensembles made up of professional musicians attempting to recreate folk-performance styles often involved ensembles employed by the broadcasting corporations.

Tape technology made the recording of folk events possible, even in quite remote villages, but performing in front of a microphone was a completely new context for most folk musicians. Though many collectors and radio producers aimed at some kind of authenticity in their recordings, they often directed the musicians not to stamp their feet or not to play loudly. The music was usually recorded outside its original context to avoid intrusive noise from dancers and other participants.

The studio environment was even more alien to many folk performers, and many were unable to adapt to it (figure 6). Others tailored their performance to the situation by adding virtuosic elements to the music or increasing the tempo of dance tunes.

Educators often found it hard to interest urban radio audiences in field recordings and resorted to arrangements. To play the arrangements, many stations employed semiprofessional folk musicians, including some with conservatory training, and formed folk-music ensembles to play for weekly and even daily broadcasts. The Swedish Broadcasting Corporation used the same ensemble, the Gunnar Hahn Folk Dance Orchestra, throughout the 1950s and most of the 1960s, while in Eastern Europe village musicians formed new radio ensembles under the direction of classically trained composers. Many of these professional folk-music ensembles, in their efforts to recreate traditional music, created new performance styles, closer to European art-music styles. The transferring of the folk repertory to radio ensembles also meant the transformation of the repertory.

Folk-music performances on radio were mainly designed by folk-music experts with academic training. Some had rather puritanical attitudes toward folk traditions, striving for authentic presentations and the preservation of old traditions. As media gatekeepers, they often tried to exclude newer trends from the medium. This situa-

FIGURE 6 The Hungarian cimbalom player Kalman Balogh records in a studio in Stockholm, Sweden. Photo by Owe Ronström, mid-1980s.

tion disappeared in some countries with the breakthrough of television in the 1960s. Documentary films on folk-music traditions were made for television, and folk music was brought into entertainment programs; in most European countries, however, folk music and dance have not been a significant part of television programming, except in the former Soviet Union and some Eastern European countries, where music and dance of professional and semiprofessional ensembles were prominent features of television programs. In the 1980s, a consortium of television stations started an annual folk-music festival with performers from different countries, to be broadcast over the television networks of participating stations. In 1989 and 1990, the producers demanded that all participating groups perform "in playback" (lip-syncing and playing to a recorded sound track)—a far-reaching transformation and festivalization of performance practice, caused by television's demand for a flawless production.

Records and cassettes

Radio stations were the chief folk-music collectors and the first to issue folk music on records as a spin-off from their collecting and programming. Some of these records became commercial hits, for example, the record with a team of fiddlers playing a traditional tune, "Gärdebylåten," issued by the Swedish Broadcasting Corporation in 1949.

Record companies, state-owned and independent, followed the documentary line of radio stations and began to release series of records based mainly on archive collections. These series systematically covered different styles and repertories, and in many cases contained extensive written commentaries. This development occurred in Eastern and Western Europe, and, with the exception of folk-music styles resembling that of popular music (released on purely commercial records), was the main channel for releasing folk music on records until the 1970s. Records of radio-broadcasted folk-music ensembles were issued in some countries.

Since few folk-music recordings were made especially for the record medium before 1970, the medium hardly affected folk performance; however, folk music was picked up in popular music. Some European jazz musicians used folk tunes as raw material for their improvisations, for example, the Swedes Lars Gullin and Jan Johansson and the Croatians Davor Kajfeš and Boško Petrović. During the 1960s, records issued by U.S. record companies spread to Western Europe the North American style of folksinging.

Cheaper recording technology and audiocassettes created a boom in folk-music releases in the 1970s. The more official issues of the 1960s and radio and television tended to neglect the folk music of ethnic minorities, and in the 1970s these came to the fore on records and cassette tapes. In Brittany during the 1970s and 1980s, a great deal of Breton folk music was issued on records and cassettes (Kuter 1990), and small record companies in Wales in the 1970s began to issue Welsh folk music (Wallis and Malm 1983).

In the 1970s, a new wave of interest in folk music spread among urban youths in Europe. Many new groups were formed outside media and other institutions—a process that has continued into the 1990s. These groups, experimenting with the revival and renewal of older styles, started to play in folk-music clubs and pubs. Their music was, and still is, recorded and released on records and cassettes, sometimes by record companies, sometimes by the groups themselves. Some records and cassettes are marketed through regular distribution channels; others are sold only by the groups at their performances. Since many groups have toured throughout Europe, these recordings have contributed to the international network among these groups, and to an international collection of styles. During the 1980s, recordings with

In live performances, new combinations of traditional instruments and electronic devices are used in performance of traditional repertoires. Some European folk-music festivals have come to resemble rock festivals, with huge towers of loudspeakers.

younger performers have gradually replaced the archived recordings in the radio broadcasts of many Western European countries.

A constant exchange and interdependence between the live folk-music scene and mediated folk music is evident. Live music performances are broadcast and released on records, and many younger performers have learned much of their repertory from documentary records, radio broadcasts, and cassette tapes. The music of deceased folk musicians recorded around 1950 was revived in the 1970s by young performers seeking their roots. These performers are also influenced by the constantly increasing flow of mediated music from all parts of Europe and the world.

In the 1990s, the rise of the iron curtain did not much influence the folk-music scene, since many formal and informal contacts between young performers had occurred through the 1970s and 1980s; however, the flow of mediated music from beyond Europe and access to low-cost media technology have influenced young folk-music performers. In live performances, new combinations of traditional instruments and electronic devices are used in performance of traditional repertoires. Elements from folk and popular music from different countries are mixed into local or regional styles. Some European folk-music festivals have come to resemble rock festivals, with huge towers of loudspeakers.

In recorded music, there has been a shift from cassettes to compact discs and from live music recorded in festivals and clubs to music recorded and edited in studios. Hence, traditional music as issued on recordings is increasingly becoming conditioned by the possibilities of shaping the sound and remixing offered by studio technology, and is thus gradually becoming separated from music heard in live scenes; however, most young performers remain skilled in traditional styles.

BIBLIOGRAPHY

Dedić, Milutin. 1981. "Cultural-Artistic Amateurism." *Yugoslav Survey* 22(2):121–140.

Dubinskas, Frank A. 1981. "Ritual on Stage: Folkloric Performance as Symbolic Action." In *Folklore and Oral Communication,* 93–106. Zagreb: Zavod za istraživanje folklora Instituta za filologiju i folkloristiku.

Finnegan, Ruth. 1989. *The Hidden Musicians: Music Making in an English Town.* Cambridge: Cambridge University Press.

Folklore und Mitmachen: Folkzeitschrift. 1988. Hamburg: Folkklub.

Kaeppler, Adrienne L., ed. 1988. *Come Mek Me Hol' You Hand: The Impact of Tourism on Traditional Music.* Kingston: Jamaica Memory Bank.

Kosacheva, Rimma. 1990. "Traditional Music in the Context of the Social-Political Development in the USSR." *Yearbook for Traditional Music* 22:17–19.

Krader, Barbara. 1990. "Recent Achievments in Soviet Ethnomusicology with Remarks on Russian Terminology." *Yearbook for Traditional Music* 22:1–16.

Kuter, Lois. 1990. "A Musical Renaissance in Brittany." *Resound* 9(4):1–5.

Magrini, Tullia. 1990. "Recorded Documentation of Italian Traditional Music (1955–90)." *Yearbook for Traditional Music* 22:172–184.

Razzi, Giulio. 1950. "Folk Music and Italian Broadcasting." *Journal of the International Folk Music Council* 2:47–48.

Ronström, Owe. 1989. "Making Use of History: The Revival of the Bagpipe in Sweden in the 1980s." *Yearbook for Traditional Music* 21:95–108.

———. 1990. "Danhusrörelsen i Ungern." In *Musik och Kultur,* ed. Owe Ronström. Lund: Studentlitteratur.

Sárosi, Bálint. 1986. *Folk Music: The Hungarian Music Idiom.* Budapest: Corvina.

Slocombe, Marie. 1955. "British Broadcasting Corporation, London." *Journal of the International Folk Music Council* 7:60–62.

———. 1956. "Report of the Radio Commission." *Journal of the International Folk Music Council* 8:51–52.

Sremac, Stjepan. 1978. "Smotre folklora u Hrvatskoj nekad i danas." *Narodna umjetnost* 15:97–116.

Stojanović, Josip. 1959. "Some Methods Applied to Broadcasting Folk Music at the Yugoslav Broadcasting Stations: Genuine Musical Folklore and Reconstructions." *Journal of the International Folk Music Council* 11:79–81.

Wallis, Roger, and Krister Malm. 1983. "Sain Cymru: The Role of the Welsh Record Industry in the Development of a Welsh-Language Pop/Rock/Folk Scene." *Popular Music* 3:107–120.

———. 1984. *Big Sounds from Small Peoples: The Music Industry in Small Countries.* London: Constable.

Wilkins, Jim. 1989. *1989 Folkweave Festival Guide.* London: author.

Dance in Europe
Timothy Rice

Theatrical Dance
Traditional and Social Dance

In Europe, dance, like music, has been classified into three main types, which index the social strata that created each type. So-called traditional dance, once and sometimes still called folk dance, originated among rural villagers. Artisanal and working classes continued it in the eighteenth and nineteenth centuries; intellectuals labeled and collected it in the nineteenth and early twentieth centuries; students and governments arranged and revived it in the late twentieth century. So-called theatrical dance began in the aristocratic courts of the fifteenth through the eighteenth centuries; it became professionalized as theatrical art and entertainment for urban elites in the nineteenth century. *Social dance* and *ballroom dance* are terms used mainly to describe courtly or urban nontheatrical, participant dancing from the seventeenth to the nineteenth century—dances that, in the twentieth century, were enjoyed by all strata of society in many parts of Europe.

THEATRICAL DANCE

Of these three main types, theatrical dance, like classical music, has the best-studied history, which includes genres, lionized dancers and choreographers, and important institutions (dance companies). Theatrical dancing was known in ancient Greece, and it may have played a role in early Christian religious practice, but its modern history began during the Renaissance in fifteenth- and sixteenth-century Italian courts, where presentations of social dances, taught by dancing masters, were called *balletti*. The noble carriage of the courtiers who performed them undoubtedly is the source for the strikingly erect postures of classical ballet. Monarchs and aristocrats hosted lavish spectacles to commemorate births, weddings, and events of state. These entertainments—known as *intermedi* in Italy, *ballets de cour* in France, and masques in England—used elaborate scenery, costumes, music, poetry, and dance to present pastoral, heroic, allegorical, and mythological themes.

In the seventeenth and eighteenth centuries, ballet flourished in France with the patronage of King Louis XIV, an avid dancer. The first professional female dancers took to the stage in 1681. Ballet played an important role in the new Baroque musical genre, opera, notably operas of Jean-Baptiste Lully (1632–1687) and Jean-Philippe Rameau (1683–1764). At the end of the seventeenth century, a new genre, *opéra-ballet,* told its stories in a series of dances, called *entrées,* unified by subject, and during the eighteenth century verbal texts were eliminated from ballets.

In 1827, Marie Taglioni (1804–1884) revolutionized ballet technique by dancing on her toes with astonishing agility—a technique designed to portray the lightness of the nymphs and fairies then in vogue at the Paris Opéra. The first classics of the ballet repertory, still performed, emerged in this period and included *La Sylphide* (1832), *Giselle* (1841), *Coppélia* (1870), and *Sylvia* (1876). In the late nineteenth century, two other cities rivaled Paris: Copenhagen, where August Bournonville (1805–1879) created a distinctive style for the Royal Danish Ballet, and St. Petersburg, where Marius Petipa (1819–1910) defined the structure of the *pas de deux* and elaborated the role of the *corps de ballet.* His productions included *Sleeping Beauty* (1890), *The Nutcracker* (1892), and *Swan Lake* (1895), all with music by Peter Ilyich Tchaikovsky (1840–1893).

In 1909, Sergei Diaghilev (1872–1929) formed the Ballets Russes, which emphasized the unity of the arts in ballet. He hired leading artists, such as Pablo Picasso, to design his productions and commissioned the outstanding composers of the day, notably Igor Stravinsky *(Petrushka, Le sacre du printemps),* Claude Debussy, Darius Milhaud, and Maurice Ravel. After the Soviet revolution in 1917, the choreographers (George Balanchine, Michel Fokine) and stars (Vaclav Nijinsky, Anna Pavlova) of Russian ballet dispersed to take Russian technical standards to ballet companies around the globe. The Soviet Union continued the Russian tradition, producing such stars as Rudolf Nureyev and Mikhail Baryshnikov, who eventually emigrated.

Modern dance emerged in the early twentieth century as a search for more flexible physical forms in response to the formality of ballet. Though Europeans participated in these experiments, the leaders (Isadora Duncan, Martha Graham, Ruth St. Denis, and Ted Shawn) came from the United States. In the 1980s, Pina Bausch emerged from Germany as a major choreographer. Also, music halls, cabarets, musical comedies, and televised variety shows provided venues for what might be called popular theatrical dance, linked to popular music.

TRADITIONAL AND SOCIAL DANCE

Traditional village and urban social dancing are so linked in Western, Northern, and Central Europe that a distinction between village and urban is difficult to maintain. In parts of southern and eastern Europe, by contrast, traditional village dances differ significantly in form and function from urban social dances. In urban areas throughout the continent, European forms of social dancing can be distinguished from forms of social dancing imported from the United States, and in the second half of the twentieth century, theatrical dance influenced the staged versions of traditional dance, blurring the distinctions further.

Traditional dance in Europe has had four basic functions: ritual, ceremonial, social-participatory, and presentational-competitive (Reynolds 1998). These functions seem to bear some relation to dance form.

Ritual dances

Ritual dances are believed to have a magical effect on nature or the human body and psyche and are usually linked to the agricultural or Christian calendar. Men perform some healing rituals, such as *căluş* in Romania (Kligman 1981), and agricultural fertility rituals, such as the masked carnival dances of Switzerland and Bulgaria. In Bulgaria, women and girls perform ritual dances as part of rain-begging rituals (*peperuda*) and spring fertility rituals (*lazarovden*). Because of elaborate costuming (such as heavy bells and dresses of leaves) and handheld props (such as flowers and sticks), the

FIGURE 1   In Romania, dancers for the spring healing ritual (*căluş*) carry sticks and swords as they dance in a circle without holding hands. Photo by Gail Kligman, 1976.

dancers often make similar steps but without touching—in lines, circles, or pairs (figure 1). In these cases, men dance to the accompaniment of instrumental music made by men, and women dance to women's—often their own—singing. During the rituals, often at the end, participants may join hands and perform a chain dance. Whatever the form, the dances are usually simple, involving just a few steps in place, but they can be demanding and virtuosic, as with Romanian *căluşari*. Such dances are still found mainly in eastern and southeastern Europe, but most scholars assume that they were once known throughout Europe. Dancing around bonfires during mid-summer's-eve festivities in much of Northern Europe may be a vestige of this function.

Ceremonial dances

Ceremonial dances dignify important moments in life-cycle rituals, rites of passage, and festive, secular events. Such moments include weddings, house-raising parties, military recruitment (such as the Hungarian dance *verbunkos*), meetings of crafts-men's guilds and political parties, and national holidays. Though ceremonial dances admit of a wide variety of forms, typical might be solo and pair dancing, the latter without touching. Soloists dance during ceremonial occasions when one participant honors another by dancing, as when the sponsor of the wedding dances for the bride and groom in Macedonia; or when an individual such as a military recruiter displays his dancing prowess to impress recruits; or when an individual is singled out for attention or honor, as at a guild festivity. Paired dancing without touching occurs to express the social divisions that ceremonies often exist to express, mediate, or remember. For example, at a Macedonian Rom (Gypsy) wedding, female relatives of the bride and groom dance opposite one another to express symbolically the transferral of the bride from one household to the other (figure 2). In much of southern Europe, men perform sword dances in opposed pairs (or lines and circles) to celebrate histori-cal battles against the Turks and Moors. Because the social group (family, in-laws, guild, political party) at a ceremony focuses its attention on the dancing of one, two, or a few individuals, these dances are often quite elaborate, with fast turns, masculine leg lifts, acrobatic flips, intricate steps, and graceful or dramatic arm motions—ges-tures whose character usually depends on whether a woman or man makes them. These paired ceremonial forms, which structurally relate to a form of social dance in

FIGURE 2   In Macedonia, Roma (Gypsies) trans-fer the bride from her natal family to that of the groom in a ceremonial dance that pairs a female relative of the bride (*left*) with a female relative of the groom. Photo by Elsie Ivancich Dunin, 1970.

FIGURE 3   In southern Spain, which the Moors
occupied for hundreds of years, a couple dances
without touching. Monteagudo, Murcia,
December 1952. Courtesy of the Alan Lomax
Collection, New York.

FIGURE 3   In southern Spain, which the Moors occupied for hundreds of years, a couple dances without touching. Monteagudo, Murcia, December 1952. Courtesy of the Alan Lomax Collection, New York.

which the pair does not touch, are typical of southern, Roman Catholic Europe (Portugal, Spain, Italy, Croatia), where Islamic influence may have been felt in ideas about gender segregation (figure 3).

Ceremonies can require all members of a social group to dance or process together at certain moments to express their solidarity. These dances usually replicate common forms of social or participant dancing. Other physical and ceremonial activities accompanied by music, including walking in processions and marching in parades, might join ceremonial dance in a common, though unnamed, category. The ceremonial dances once associated with life-cycle rituals such as weddings are performed only in a few isolated regions of Europe (social dancing of course remains important at weddings), but continue to exist, often in revived forms, as part of civic and national holidays and other newly invented traditions throughout Europe.

Intimate life-cycle ceremonial dances were sometimes accompanied by the dancers' singing, but the more festive, public occasions often attracted the services of specialized or even professional musicians, who played music that was as showy as the dances.

Social or participant dances

Social or participant dances are danced, in principle, by all present whenever people gather socially. Unlike ritual and ceremonial dances, they are not limited to a particular ceremony, occasion, or time of year, though they may be important parts of such events. Social events with dancing might consist of a few people in someone's home, fifty to a hundred in a specially designated dance hall, or hundreds in a village square. Social dancing appears to function as recreation at one level, but it also contains powerful expressions of gender, age, and ethnic identity.

Social dancing is almost always about gendered forms of behavior and relations between the sexes. In the Balkans, for example, when boys learn or are taught dances, they are enjoined and shown how to act like men, actions that include bold physical gestures. Girls are taught to restrain their motions (and emotions) in and through dance and to act demurely, even in moments of intense enjoyment. Dances also display and put into ritualized practice culturally shared ideas about the relations between the sexes. In areas still under Islamic influence, men and women may not touch each other in the dance. As traditional rules of this type relaxed, mixed lines and couple dancing became possible. In couple dances, men usually lead or direct

Social dances give visible form to gender, age, and ethnic differences and allow those differences to be expressed with pride and joy.

FIGURE 4   In Bulgaria, a chain of hand-holding dancers moves in a circular form at a village celebration. Standing in the center to face the dancers, musicians play, *left to right:* a drum (*tŭpan*), a bagpipe (*gajda*), a wooden flute (*kaval*), and an accordion. Photo by Mark Levy, 1980.

FIGURE 5   In Crete, Greece, the leader of a chain dance executes elaborate leaps at the head of the line. Photo by Cornelia Herzfeld, mid-1970s.

women—a way of dancing that reinforces ideas about the subordination of women in everyday life. For youth, social dancing has a courtship function, and even after marriage it remains a way for people to display their physical attractiveness and grace to others in sensual, but culturally appropriate ways. Social dance styles also give visible form to age and ethnic differences, and allow those differences to be expressed with pride and joy.

Chain dances

The oldest forms of social dancing in Europe are probably the so-called chain dances, in which an indeterminate number of dancers hold hands (or shoulders or belts). Dances of this type were recorded in prehistoric cave paintings in Sweden (Oetke 1982), and fifteenth- and sixteenth-century paintings from Central Europe record peasant chain dancing. With nineteenth-century ethnographic accounts of such dances in northern areas, this evidence suggests that chain dances were once widespread throughout the continent. By the nineteenth century, they had disappeared from most of Central, Northern, and Western Europe. At the end of the twentieth century, they were still common only in the Balkans and parts of Eastern Europe, but pockets of such dances exist in the Faroe Islands, Iceland, Brittany, and elsewhere.

The most common chain dances consist of closed or open circles that move counterclockwise, though a few move clockwise (figure 4). In open circles, the leader of the line may have a marked ceremonial role, such as the bride or sponsor of a wedding, or a marked dance role as a caller of steps or an improviser of elaborate variations, as for example in Greek dancing (figure 5). Leaders of such dances can form the chain into other shapes, such as lines (usually short), or even opposing lines, spirals, and serpentines, or they can lead the head of the chain through its length at some point. These shapes lead to alternate names for this type of dancing: circle dances, line dances, serpentine dances, and so forth.

Chains of dancers are often organized internally by social principles, such as gender, age, kinship, and friendship. Women may dance side by side in one part of the chain and men in the other. Within one gender group, young men may dance in one subgroup and older men in another. For some wedding dances in the Balkans, dancers arrange themselves according to the closeness of their relationship to the bride or groom. In Greece, a chain may consist only of a *parea* 'group of friends', who have requested and paid the musicians for the dance.

Though the variations in step patterns seem virtually unlimited, one simple, six-step (six-beat) structure is found throughout Europe. It consists of two traveling steps, followed by a step and pause-touch-swing in place, and then a step and pause-touch-swing in the opposite direction. The underlying structures may be simple, but the leader or others within the chain may elaborate the pattern with fancy footwork and improvised variations. In a spectacular version from Georgia, a chain of dancers stands on the shoulders of a another chain to form a so-called two-story dance.

Chain dances were once commonly performed to the dancers' own singing. The most famous extant example is ballad dancing in the Faroe Islands. In the Balkans, where chain dances are still the rule, once-common sung dances died out after World War II, except in folkloric performances, and dances are now accompanied exclusively by instrumental music. The music is typically organized in a series of four-measure (eight-beat), repeated phrases—a process that sets up a polymeter with the typical three-measure (six-beat) dance phrase. While the dance pattern repeats with subtle variation, the musicians string together melody after melody, precomposed or improvised, only repeating when they run out of ideas.

Couple dances

Much younger in Europe than chain dances are couple dances, which became the rage in Central and Northern Europe and the British Isles in the 1600s and possibly earlier. In these dances, each partner in the couple uses both hands to hold the other's hands, waist, or shoulders. By the 1800s, when folklorists began collecting traditional village dances, couple dances had completely replaced chain dances in most of Central and Northern Europe, where dances in villages, towns, and courts had all been done in this form. By contrast, in parts of the Balkans and Eastern Europe, couple dances have never entered village social life, nor have they been especially important in urban social life, where chain dances remain popular. Instrumental music is typical of couple dances. Singing of any kind is rare, though in some areas, dancers shout couplets, as, for example, the *strigături* couplets in Romania.

Couple dances are organized in two basic ways, of which the first to become widely popular in Europe was the so-called longways set—two opposed straight lines, usually women in one and men in the other, paired as couples. Participants dance a series of figures consisting of place changes, figure eights, advances and withdrawals, and circles around or processions up and down the set. Generically labeled set or figure dances, they first became widely popular among all classes in seventeenth-century England, where they were called country dances and were documented by John Playford (1957 [1651]). In the eighteenth century, their popularity spread to France, where they were called *contredanses*. In the nineteenth century, the favorite form became a square with four couples, called a quadrille or cotillion. A typical dance consisted of five eight- or sixteen-measure figures, and music was composed to fit the dance form exactly. Common dance rhythms included reels, in 2/4 time, and jigs, in 6/8.

The second way of performing swept across Europe in the nineteenth century. In these dances, individual couples perform a short (often just four-beat) repeated pattern of steps. They move at will around the dance floor or form a circle of couples and follow the circle around the floor. They may for a while break apart completely, hold by only one hand, and execute turns and elaborate arm movements. Usually the man leads and directs his partner around the floor and in the execution of the turns and other movements. The first pan-European dance in this form, the waltz (in 3/4 time), probably originated in German-speaking areas of Central Europe around 1780 and spread to other parts of Europe in the first two decades of the nineteenth century. By mid-century, the polka (in 2/4 time) had conquered Europe, followed a few decades later by the schottische (in 2/4 time) and the mazurka (in 3/4 time). Local variations abound, especially in Scandinavia. In Central Europe, a special type, called *zwiefachen* 'two-timers' in Bavaria and *matenik* 'muddle' in Czech, alternates duple and triple meter in various combinations.

Presentational and competitive dances

Presentational and competitive dancing displays individual dance skills. It involves a separation of performers from an audience in a manner not associated with the other kinds of dance and probably developed in importance as the specialization of labor proliferated in European society. It may have its origins in certain kinds of ceremonial dances, where the participants stop to watch a socially important actor in the ceremony perform his role through solo dance or two protagonists in a ritualized drama pantomime a sword fight. Also, excellent social dancers can occasionally cause others to pause and observe them. Scottish and Irish step dancing, perhaps once a form of social dancing, have become highly virtuosic competitive dances. Specialized presentation dances—for example, the Norwegian *halling,* the Austrian-German *Schuhplattler,* and the Scottish solo dance over crossed swords—often involve demanding technique and physical strength and are danced typically by men.

In the twentieth century, dance presentations and competitions became especially important means for the preservation of traditional forms of dance. All forms of ritual, ceremonial, and social dancing are now presented on stage at venues such as festivals (often with competitions) and tourist destinations by amateur and professional folk dance troupes [see CONTEMPORARY PERFORMANCE CONTEXTS]. Sometimes the dances are presented in something like their original forms. More typically, professional choreographers break up the pairs, couples, circles, semicircles, spirals, serpentines, lines, opposed lines, and squares into a rapidly changing kaleidoscope of patterns meant to entertain a passive audience increasingly alienated from traditional dance forms. In these presentations and competitions, traditional and theatrical dance effectively become indistinguishable.

BIBLIOGRAPHY

Alford, Violet. 1937. *Pyrenean Festivals, Calendar Customs, Music and Magic, Drama and Dance.* London: Chatto and Windus.

———. 1962. *Sword Dance and Drama.* London: Merlin.

Arbeau, Thoinot. 1967 [1589]. *Orchesography.* Translated by Mary Stewart Evans. New York: Dover.

Backman, Eugène Louis. 1977. *Religious Dances* in the Christian Church and in Popular Medicine. Translated by E. Classen. Westport, Conn.: Greenwood Press.

Böhme, Franz M. 1886. *Geschichte des Tanzes in Deutschland.* 2 vols. Leipzig: Breitkopf und Härtel.

Breathnach, Breandán. 1977. *Folk Music and Dances of Ireland.* Dublin: Mercier.

Bröcker, Marianne, ed. 1992. *Tanz und*

Tanzmusik in Überlieferung und Gegenwart. Bamberg: Deutsche Gesellschaft für Volkskunde.

Chandler, Keith. 1993. *"Ribbons, Bells, and Squeaking Fiddles": The Social History of Morris Dancing in the English South Midlands, 1660-1900.* Enfield Lock, Middlesex: Hisarlik.

Corrsin, Stephen D. 1996. *Sword Dancing: A History.* Enfield Lock, Middlesex: Hisarlik.

Cowan, Jane. 1990. *Dance and the Body Politic in Northern Greece.* Princeton: Princeton University Press.

Daniels, Marilyn. 1981. *The Dance in Christianity.* New York: Paulist Press.

Davies, J. G. 1984. *Liturgical Dance: An Historical, Theological, and Practical Handbook.* London: SCM Press.

Dunin, Elsie Ivancich. 1984. *Dance Occasions and Festive Dress in Yugoslavia.* Los Angeles: UCLA Museum of Cultural History.

Emmerson, George S. 1967. *Scotland through Her Country Dances.* London: Johnson.

Flett, J. F., and T. M. Flett. 1985. *Traditional Dancing in Scotland.* London: Routledge and Kegan Paul.

García Matos, Manuel 1971. *Danzas populares de España: Andalucía.* Madrid: Sección Femenina de Movimiento Nacional.

Gasnault, François. 1986. *Guingettes et lorettes: bals publics et danse social à Paris entre 1830 et 1870.* Paris: Aubier.

Guilcher, Jean-Michel. 1969. *La contredanse et les renouvellements de la danse française.* Paris: Mouton.

Hilton, Wendy. 1981. *Dance of Court and Theater: The French Noble Style, 1690–1725.* Princeton, N.J.: Princeton Book Company.

Hoerburger, Felix. 1956. *Die Zwiefachen: Gestaltung und Umgestaltung der Tanzmelodien im nördlichen Altbayern.* Berlin: Akademie-Verlag.

———. 1961. *Volkstanzkunde.* 2 vols. Kassel: Bärenreiter.

———. 1994. *Valle popullare: Tanz und Tanzmusik der Albaner in Kosovo und Makedonien.* New York: Peter Lang.

Hudson, Richard. 1986. *The Allemande, the Balletto, and the Tanz.* Cambridge: Cambridge University Press.

Ilieva, Anna. 1977. *Bulgarian Dance Folklore.* Translated by Thomas Roncevic. Pittsburgh: Dutifa-Tamburitza Press.

Katsarova-Kukudova, Raina, and Kiril Djenev. 1976. *Bulgarian Folk Dances.* Translated by Nevena Geliazhkova and Marguerite Alexieva. Cambridge, Mass.: Slavica Publishers.

Kirstein, Lincoln. 1935. *Dance: A Short History of Classical Theatrical Dancing.* New York: Putnam.

———. 1984. *Four Centuries of Ballet.* New York: Dover.

Kligman, Gail. 1981. *Caluş: Symbolic Transformation in Romanian Ritual.* Chicago: University of Chicago Press.

Lawler, Lillian B. 1978. *The Dance in Ancient Greece.* Middletown, Conn.: Wesleyan University Press.

Lonsdale, Steven H. 1993. *Dance and Ritual Play in Greek Religion.* Baltimore: Johns Hopkins University Press.

Louis, Maurice L. A. 1963. *Le folklore et la danse.* Paris: Maisonneuve et Larose.

Oetke, Herbert. 1982. *Der Deutsche Volkstanz.* 2 vols. Wilhelmshaven: Heinrichschofen's Verlag.

Playford, John. 1957 [1651]. *English Dancing Master, 1651.* Edited by Margaret Dean-Smith. London: Schott.

Reynolds, William C. 1998. "European Traditional Dance." In *International Encyclopedia of Dance,* edited by Selma Cohen et al., 536–561. New York: Oxford University Press.

Salvén, Erik. 1949. *Dances of Sweden.* Translated by Veronica Wright. New York: Chanticleer.

Sharp, Cecil. 1978. *The Sword-Dances of Northern England.* 3 vols. Wakefield: EP Publishing.

———, and A. P. Oppé. 1924. *The Dance: An Historical Survey of Dancing in Europe.* London: Halton and Truscott Smith.

Torp, Lisbet. 1990. *Chain and Round Dance Patterns: A Method for Structural Analysis and Its Application to European Material.* 3 vols. Copenhagen: University of Copenhagen, Museum Tusculanum Press.

Williams, W. S. Gwynn. 1933. *Welsh National Music and Dance.* London: J. Curwen.

Wolfram, Richard. 1951. *Die Volkstänze in Österreich und Verwandte Tänze in Europa.* Salzburg: O. Müller.

Zoder, Raimund. 1950. *Volkslied, Volkstanz, und Volksbrauch in Österreich.* Vienna: L. Doblinger.

Traditional Musical Instruments
Oskár Elschek

Distinguishing European folk musical instruments from those used in art music or even from those outside Europe is difficult because such instruments often have common origins and histories. Some of the most archaic instruments still in use, though changed in form from the oldest versions, include bells, clappers, horns, trumpets, and drums, which originally functioned as signaling instruments for religious rituals and the work of miners, soldiers, and shepherds.

Children's instruments, such as a simple bark flute made in springtime, often display archaic roots and common features all over Europe. A somewhat later historical stage is represented by European folk- and art-music instruments that derive from West Asian and North African types imported during contact with the Arab, Byzantine, and Ottoman empires. Stringed and wind instruments from the Balkans preserve evidence of this borrowing. The territory of the former Yugoslavia alone contains a plucked zither (*kanun*) and a shawm (*zurla*) in Macedonia; a santurlike hammered dulcimer in the Vojvodina region; fretted, long-necked plucked lutes (*tambura* and *saz*) in Bosnia, Croatia, and Serbia; and the bowed *lira* and *gusle* in the central Dinaric Mountains.

In the twentieth century, with growing interest in world music and a revival of European folk music, instruments from Africa and the Americas, such as xylophones, drums, rattles, and banjos, entered European folk and popular music—a process that is creating a new global music culture.

The differentiation and complexity of European instruments and instrumental music increased in the late Middle Ages, when migratory musicians, such as minstrels and troubadours, expanded and spread secular musical practice. In the 1500s, instrumental music for military bands and dances or dance suites gained prominence. Instrumental music gained importance as new instrumental ensembles incorporated newly developed instruments, such as bagpipes, recorders, shawms, and violins from the 1600s to the 1800s, and accordions, clarinets, and keyed brass instruments in the 1800s. These instruments and ensembles played increasingly numerous dance types, which spread widely throughout Europe in folk- and art-music circles: jig (gigue), sarabande, courante, allemande, hornpipe, reel, polonaise, mazurka, minuet, polka, ländler, contredanse, schottische, and waltz.

Instruments closely connected with art music had a more dynamic and rapid development, caused by changes in the style, structure, and character of European art music. But the history of folk- and art-music instruments in Europe is permanently intertwined. Bagpipes and hurdy-gurdies, for example, have passed back and forth among street singers, rural shepherds, and aristocratic courtiers. Folk-music instruments are defined not by their morphology, but by their function and social use, closely connected with the lifestyles, rituals, ceremonies, and entertainments of peasants and shepherds.

COMMON EUROPEAN INSTRUMENT TYPES

Europe's musical instruments embody features and types that form part of a worldwide pattern of distribution, for example, duct flutes made from bone, clay, or wood. Within Europe, many common types of instruments are widely distributed, but with a great deal of diversity in the details of their structures, materials, shapes, and sizes.

Among the most important European idiophones, bells are used in all shepherd cultures (Alps, Balkans, Carpathians, Pyrenees, Scandinavia), often without huge differences, but with great typological variation. Traditional Slovakian bells come in ninety-one types, forms, and sizes (Elschek 1983). Other widespread idiophones include wooden clappers, rattles made from clay, wooden ratchet or cog rattles with one or more wooden tongues, and mouth harps (figures 1 and 2).

Common membranophones include small, simple drums with one or two membranes used as military and signaling instruments, scraped and friction drums, frame drums, and kazoolike instruments used by children and hunters.

Widespread European chordophones include the violin, plucked and struck zithers, and plucked, fretted lutes in a variety of forms (balalaika, bouzouki, guitar, mandolin, *tambura*).

The most widespread European aerophone is the bagpipe. Other common aerophones include ducted shepherd's flutes with five or six finger holes, large natural trumpets (shepherd's typical signaling instrument), natural horns made from bark, horn, or wood, and single- and double-tube idioglot clarinets.

CONCEPTS AND FUNCTIONS

Differing and changing functions for instruments and concepts about instruments and instrumental music are probably the most important factors driving technological, morphological, and acoustic diversity. The same instrumental type may be found in many cultures, but with quite different playing techniques, functions, and repertory.

Changing musical concepts induce change in the construction and technology of instruments. New tonal material, scales, technical demands, tone colors, and differences in structures are much more developed in instruments of a complex technical and technological construction. The bagpipe, for example, involves combinations of conical and cylindrical wooden tubes of various lengths and numbers, single and double reeds, mouth and bellows blowing, and skin bags from different animals, left uncut or sewn into a variety of shapes.

More or less autonomous development in different regions and countries has led to musically and structurally important differences between the Irish *uilleann* pipes, the Scottish Highland bagpipe, the French *musette,* the Italian *zampogna,* the Croatian *diple,* and the Bulgarian *gajda* (figure 3). Even one culture can manifest remarkable diversity, such as the *zampogna* and *surdulina* in central and southern Italy, Istria on the Adriatic coast, and Sicily (Leydi and Guizzi 1985).

INSTRUMENTS BY REGION

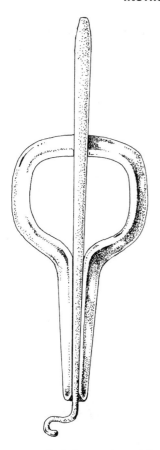

FIGURE 1   An Italian metal mouth harp. Drawing by Dan Beltran.

FIGURE 2   Michele Cabiddu, a shepherd from Villanova Strisaili, Sardinia, plays a mouth harp: he strikes the tongue of the instrument, whose vibrations make a drone, and creates melodies by changing the size of his oral cavity to resonate different overtones. Photo by Sabina Magliocco, 1992.

Different histories and similar living conditions have created six main regions for musical instruments in Europe. These regions are not isolated from one another, but are connected through the exchange of instruments and instrumental music.

Northwestern Europe

In Great Britain, Ireland, and the islands north of the mainland, the most widespread instruments are bagpipes, duct flutes, fiddles, harps, and free-reed bellows instruments such as concertinas.

Northern Europe

The most widespread instruments are bowed fiddles, zithers, and a wide range of shepherd's trumpets and horns, dating back to the old Scandinavian lurs. Small, plucked zithers include the *langeleik* (Norway), the *kantele* (Finland), the *kannel* (Estonia), the *kanklės* (Lithuania), and the *kokles* (Latvia). Bowed fiddles include the violin, but also local variants like the *nyckelharpa,* a Swedish keyed, bowed fiddle, and the *hardingfele,* a Norwegian fiddle with sympathetic strings and inlaid soundboard.

Western Europe

In France, Germany, Switzerland, the Netherlands, and Belgium, the most important instruments were bagpipes; hurdy-gurdies and the street barrel organs that developed from them; the violin; hammered dulcimers; free-reed, bellows instruments, such as the bandoneon, the concertina, and accordions; and tower-bell sets (carillons). Ensembles of bowed stringed instruments were typical, augmented by an accordion and brasses.

Southern Europe

The isolation of Europe's southern peninsulas—Iberian, Apennine, Balkan—has contributed to greater heterogeneity of instruments than elsewhere in Europe, though bagpipes are prominent in all three. For centuries, the Balkans had close ties with the Middle East, which exported long-necked plucked lutes, pear-shaped bowed lutes, and the double-reed shawm (*zurna*). Italy continued some older Roman traditions of flutes and reeds. From North Africa and the Arab world, Italy and Spain borrowed such instruments as the Sardinian *launeddas,* castanets, and the tambourine. Arab influence manifested itself in a varied group of short-necked plucked lutes, including the guitar, the mandolin, and the *vihuela.*

Eastern Europe

Contact with Asia enriched old Slavic and Byzantine instrumental traditions. Virtually every instrumental type is represented, including horns, trumpets, and simple bagpipes; fretted zithers and bowed or plucked lutes; and rattles, scraped and rubbed idiophones, cog rattles, and bells.

Central Europe

Austria, Slovakia, the Czech Republic, Poland, and Hungary have had contact across the Carpathian Mountains to the Balkans; across the Alps to Italy and France; and over vast plains to Western Europe and the Baltic countries. As a result of historical contact, Central Europe shares many common types of idiophones, aerophones, and chordophones with those regions. A shared dance-music repertory (including the minuet, the polka, and the waltz) have tended to unify instrumental styles in this region played by ensembles of bowed strings or brass instruments. Solo playing is preserved in aerophones shared with Eastern Europe.

FIGURE 3   In Sicily, a man plays an Italian bag-pipe (*zampogna* 'symphony') with two melody pipes and two drone pipes. Postcard postmarked 1916. Courtesy of the Robert Godfried Collection, New York.

UNIQUE INSTRUMENT TYPES

Most European instruments are distributed over a wide area of the continent, but some, closely bound to one culture, carry a representative, ethnic, or symbolic musical meaning. Basques in Spain, for example, play the *alboka,* a double-tube, single-reed hornpipe, symmetrically finished with two richly carved horns, one of them used as a cap for the reeds.

Basques also use an idiophone (*txalaparta*), consisting of one or more wooden planks beaten by the players to create different rhythmic patterns. Their characteristic ensemble consists of a single player playing in the left hand the *txistu* (a long, slim flute with three finger holes) while the right hand beats a drum (*tamboril*) [see BASQUE MUSIC].

Another unique European aerophone is the 2-meter-long Slovak duct flute (*fujara*) with three finger holes, supplemented by a shorter blowing tube. The sound has an extraordinary character, caused by a clearly perceivable overtone structure that reaches the tenth to the twelfth harmonic.

Definitions and Examples of Instrument Types (the definitions are quoted from Hornbostel and Sachs 1961)

Idiophones: "The substance of the intrument itself, owing to its solidity and elasticity, yields the sounds, without requiring stretched membranes or strings." Includes clappers, cymbals, gongs, bells, rattles, scrapers, and the mouth harp.

Membranophones: "The sound is excited by tightly stretched membranes." Commonly called drums, the main types are defined by the shape of the body: kettle, cylindrical, barrel-shaped, hour-glass-shaped, goblet-shaped, and frame.

Chordophones: "One or more strings are stretched between fixed points." Commonly called string instruments, the main types are zithers, lutes, lyres, and harps.

Aerophones: "The air itself is the vibrator in the primary sense." Commonly called wind instruments, the main types are reeds, flutes, and trumpets (and horns).

RESEARCH ON MUSICAL INSTRUMENTS

Since the 1950s, many approaches to the study of musical instruments in Europe have been taken. A Romanian study places them in ethnocultural context (Alexandru 1956); the historical development of instruments of the Sorbs (a Slavic people in Germany) has been reconstructed (Raupp 1963); systematic analysis and classification characterizes work on Bulgarian and Slovak instruments (Atanasov 1977; Leng 1967); and geographic distribution and description has been used for Finnish and Yugoslav instruments (Bezić et al. 1975; Leisiö 1983). Folk-music instruments have been included in large ethnographic cartography projects to clarify functional and cultural connections. For the Slovak ethnographic atlas, twenty-five instruments were investigated using questionnaires in 250 villages (Kovačevičová 1990). Morphological, technological, sociological, and functional processes and ensemble combinations were summarized in a set of more than twenty synthetic maps, which greatly improved understanding of these folk-instrument traditions. These studies, dissimilar in concept and approach, express contrasting views of European folk-music instruments.

A series of handbooks, *Handbuch der europäischen Volksmusikinstrumente,* tried to unify such views, systematize and compare single traditions as autonomous cultural units in a framework of countries and ethnic areas, and provide statistics for folk instruments in use (Emsheimer and Stockmann 1960). Individual studies in the series yielded fifty-three types of folk-music instruments in Hungary (Sárosi 1967); eighty-eight in Bohemia and Moravia (Kunz 1974); sixty-nine in Switzerland (Bachmann-Geiser 1981); and 171 in Slovakia (Elschek 1983), expanded to 203 in a later study (Elschek 1991).

BIBLIOGRAPHY

Acht, Rob J. M. van. 1983. *Volksmuziek en volksinstrumenten in Europa.* The Hague: Haags Gementemuseum.

Alexandru, Tiberiu. 1956. *Instrumentele muzicale ale popolurui Romin.* Bucharest: Editura de stat pentru literatur i art.

Anoyanakis, Fivos. 1979. *Greek Folk Musical Instruments.* Athens: National Bank of Greece.

Atanasov, Vergillij. 1977. *Sistematika na blgarskite narodni muzikalni instrumenti.* Sofia: Izdatelstvo blgarskata akademija naukite.

Bachmann-Geiser, Brigitte. 1981. *Die Volksmusikinstrumente der Schweiz.* Leipzig: Deutscher Verlag für Musik.

Baines, Anthony. 1973 [1960]. *Bagpipes.* Revised ed. Oxford: Oxford University Press.

Becker, Heinz. 1966. *Zur Entwicklungsgeschichte der antiken und mittelalterlichen Rohrblattinstrumente.* Hamburg: Musikverlag H. Sikorski.

Beregovskij, Moshe. 1987. *Jevrejskaja narodnaja instrumentalnaja muzyka.* Moscow: Sovjetskij Kompozitor.

Bezić, Jerko, et al., eds. 1975. *Traditional Folk Music Instruments of Jugoslavia.* Zagreb: Kolska Knjiga.

Bose, Fritz. 1975. "Arabische Elemente in der südspanischen Volksmusik." Bässler-Archiv 23(1):231–238.

Bröcker, Marianne. 1973. *Die Drehleier: Ihr Bau und ihre Geschichte.* 2 vols. Düsseldorf: Verlag für Systematische Musikwissenschaft.

Buchner, Alexander. 1957. *Musical Automats.* Prague: Artia.

Camp, John. 1974. *Bell Ringing, Chimes, Carillons, Handbells: The World of the Bell and the Ringer.* Newton Abbot, New York: David & Charles.

Campbell, Richard G. 1968. *Zur Typologie der Schalenhalslaute.* Baden-Baden: Verlag Heitz.

Donostia, José Antonio de. 1947. "Instrumentos de música popular española." *Anuario Musical* 2:105–150.

———. 1952. "Instrumentos populares del pueblo vasco." *Anuario Musical* 7:3–49.

Dunkel, Maria. 1987. *Bandonion und Konzertina. Ein Beitrag zur Darstellung des Instrumententyps.* Munich and Salzburg: E. Katzbichler.

Elschek, Oskar. 1969. "Hudobnovedecká Systematika a Etnoorganológia: Musikwissenschaftliche Systematik und Ethnoorganologie." *Musicologica Slovaca* 1:5–41.

———. 1970. "Mensch–Musik–Instrument: Funktionelle Schichtung der Primärformen." In *Musik als Gestalt und Erlebnis,* ed. Erich Schenk, 41–56. Vienna: H. B. Böhlau.

———. 1976. "Historische Quellentypen der Instrumentenkunde und die ihnen angemessenen quellenkritischen Methoden." *Studia Instrumentorum Musicae Popularis* 4:10–30.

———. 1983. *Die slowakischen Volksmusikinstrumente.* Die Volksmusikinstrumente der Tschechoslowakei, 2. Leipzig: VEB Deutscher Verlag für Musik.

———. 1991. *Slovenské ľudové píšťaly a dälše aerofóny* (Slovak folk flutes and other aerophones). Bratislava: Veda Slovenská Akadémia Vied.

Emsheimer, Ernst, and Erich Stockmann. 1960. "Vorbemerkungen zu einem Handbuch der europäischen Volskmusikinstrumente." *Acta Musicologica* 32:47–50.

Geiringer, Karl. 1978. *Instruments in the History of Western Music.* London: Allen & Unwin.

Gippius, V., ed. 1987. *Narodnye muzykanye instrumenty i instrumentanaja muzyka.* 2 vols. Moscow: Sovetskij Kompozitor.

Hoerburger, Felix. 1966. *Musica vulgaris: Lebensgesetze der instrumentalen Volksmusik.* Erlangen: Universitätsbund.

———. 1986. *Volksmusikforschung: Aufsätze and Vorträge 1953–1984 über Volkstanz and instrumentale Volksmusik.* Laaber: Laaber-Verlag.

Hornbostel, Erich. M. von, and Curt Sachs. 1961 [1914]. "Classification of Musical Instruments." *Galpin Society Journal* 14:3–29.

Kartomi, Margaret J. 1990. *On Concepts and Classifications of Musical Instruments.* Chicago and London: University of Chicago Press.

Kovačevičová, Soňa, ed. 1990. *Etnograficky atlas Slovenska.* Bratislava: Veda Slovenská Akadémia Vied.

Kunz, Ludwig. 1974. *Die Volksmusikinstrumente der Tschechoslowakei.* Leipzig: VEB Deutscher Verlag für Musik.

Leisiö, Timo. 1983. *Suomen ja Karjalan vanhakantaiset torvija pillisoittimet.* Kaustinen: Kansanmusiikki-Instituutin Julkaisuja.

Leng, Ladislav. 1967. *Slovenske ľudove hudobne nastroje.* Bratislava: Vydavateľstvo Slovenskej Akadémia Vied.

Leydi, Roberto, and Febo Guizzi. 1985. *Le zampogne in Italia.* Milan: Ricordi.

Ling, Jan. 1989. *Europas musikhistoria: Folkmusiken 1730–1980.* Göteborg: Akademi Förlaget.

Ling, Jan, et al. 1991. *The Nyckelharpa: Present and Past.* Stockholm: Svea Fonogram.

Midgley, Ruth, ed. 1976. *Musical Instruments of the World.* London: Paddington Press.

Moeck, Hermann. 1967. *Typen europäischer Blockflöten in Vorzeit, Geschichte and Volksüberlieferung.* Celle: Moeck Verlag.

Müller, Mette. 1972. *From Bone Pipe and Cattle Horn to Fiddle and Psaltery.* Stockholm: Musikhistoriska Museum.

———. 1974. *Keramik med Musik.* Stockholm: Musikhistoriska Museum.

Nixdorff, Heide. 1974. *Tönender Ton: Tongefässflöten and Tonpfeifen aus Europa.* Berlin: Museum für Völkerkunde.

Otterbach, Friedmann. 1980. *Die Geschichte der europäischen Tanzmusik.* Wilhelmshaven: Heinrichshofen.

Perkuhn, Eva Ruth. 1976. *Die Theorien zum arabischen Einfluss auf die europäische Musik des Mittelalters.* Walldorf-Hessen: Verlag für Orientkunde.

Plate, Regina. 1992. *Kulturgeschichte der Maultrommel.* Bonn: Verlag für systematische Musikwissenschaft.

Podnos, Theodor H. 1974. *Bagpipe and Tuning.* Detroit: Information Coordinators.

Praetorius, Michael. 1958 [1619]. *Syntagma Musicum: De Organographia.* Vol. 2. Facsimile. Kassel: Bärenreiter.

Raupp, Jan. 1963. *Sorbische Volksmusikanten und Musikinstrumente.* Bautzen: VEB Domowina-Verlag.

Rice, William Gorham. 1977 [1925]. *Carillon Music and Singing Towers of the Old World and the New.* New York: Dodd, Mead.

Rimmer, Joan. 1977 [1969]. *The Irish Harp.* 2d ed. Cork: The Mercier Press.

Sachs, Curt. 1929. *Geist und Werden der Musikinstrumente.* Berlin: J. Bard.

Sárosi, Bálint. 1967. *Die Volksmusikinstrumente Ungarns.* Leipzig: Deutscher Verlag für Musik.

Staššiková-Štukovska, Danica K. 1981. "Problematike stredoeurópskych aerofónov v 7.–13. stor." *Slovenska Archeologica* 29(2):392–420.

Stockmann, Erich. 1961. "Zum Terminus 'Volksmusikinstrument'." *Forschung in Fortschritt* 35:337–340.

————. 1965. "Toward a History of European Folk Music Instruments." *Studia Musicologica* 7(1–4):155–164.

————. 1966. "Volksmusikinstrumente und Arbeit." *Deutsches Jahrbuch für Volkskunde* 10:245–259.

————. 1974. "Das Instrument als Gegenstand anthropologischer und historischer Forschung." *Report of the 11th Congress of the International Musicological Society Copenhagen* 1:131–135.

Stradner, Gerhard. 1983. *Spielpraxis und Instrumentarium um 1500: Dargestellt an Sebastian Virdung's "Musica getutscht" (Basel 1511)*. Vienna: Vienna University.

Suppan, Wolfgang. 1976 [1973]. *Lexikon des Blasmusikwesens*. 2nd ed. Freiburg: Schulz Verlag.

Vertkov, Konstantin Aleksandrovich, et al., eds. 1963. *Atlas narodnych instrumentov narodov SSSR*. Moscow: Gosudarstvennoje Muzykalnoje Izdatelstvo.

Winternitz, Emmanuel. 1967. *Musical Instruments and Their Symbolism in Western Art*. London: Faber and Faber.

Organology and Traditional Musical Instruments in Museums

Anne Caufriez

The First Public Collections
Organology: The Science of Collections
Collections Today: Their Management and Goals
Principal European Collections

The traditional musical instruments of Europe, whether they originated in the countryside or were inherited from the city, are included in collections exhibited in museums. Some rural instruments are still actively played, but others have become silent. Their decline in the life of the countryside has conferred on them the value of nostalgia; however, they appeared late in museum display cases. They were long relegated to the periphery of the material arts as ornaments, serving to illustrate a historical epoch or a civilization, or to complete a gallery of paintings or sculptures.

To accord instruments an autonomous exposition space is an idea that appeared only around 1900 and for several reasons was developed much later. Interest in rural instruments was initially overshadowed by the discovery of so-called exotic instruments. Rustic instruments appeared to come from a minor musical culture, compared to the culture imposed by the cities; however, the first expositions of musical instruments originating from all of the countries of the world, such as those displayed in the Universal Exposition of Paris (1890), awakened an interest in the rural European heritage. Music historians, folklorists, and lovers of peasant customs met and shared their experiences, but the large collections of rural instruments appeared only forty or fifty years later (Marcel-Dubois 1958:33, 38).

Instruments of the countryside were little by little extracted from their social context and conserved, inanimate and mute, in public institutions or by individual collectors. It would be necessary to wait for the folk revival of the 1960s for these instruments to sound anew, this time in the city. It was to the old rural masters that the musicians of this revival would go, becoming students of this or that regional instrument. Today, some folk traditions, now in decline, are revived at festivals by the occasional appearances of village musicians who orient themselves more and more toward reconstituting the repertoires of their region or country (figure 1). Some traditional instruments of Europe are taught in conservatories of music and primary schools, or through specialized instruction (figure 2).

THE FIRST PUBLIC COLLECTIONS

Collections of instruments open to the public were established around 1850 in Austria and Germany, and the concept spread to other countries, but systematically

Though outlines of instrumental taxonomy were proposed as early as classical antiquity, the first great classifications of instruments appeared with the creation of the first museums and sound-recording archives.

FIGURE 1   A Bulgarian orchestra of traditional folk instruments at a communist-era regional festival sanctioned at the national level, as evidenced by the portrait of the country's leader in the background. By reconstituting for the modern stage a regional or national repertoire, such orchestras function as living museums. This orchestra comes from southwestern Pirin, as seen, *far right,* in the large number of long-necked plucked lutes (*tamburi*), the instrument emblematic of Pirin. Other instruments are, *left to right:* a drum (*tarabuka*), four wooden flutes (*kavali*), a bagpipe (*gajda*), and a bowed fiddle (*gŭdulka*). Photo by Mark Levy, 1985.

collecting traditional musical instruments in their original homelands was not well under way before 1945. The first collections of musical instruments were housed in museums of art, history, or ethnology, museums of popular arts and traditions or folklore, private museums, and finally in their own, much rarer, museums of musical instruments.

Because of political reasons or lack of space, certain museums opened their doors much later than when their collections were established. For instance, the collections of Barcelona's Museu de la Música did not find a permanent space until 1981, though they had been established in 1921. No representative historical model for the origins of European collections exists. But the Musée Instrumental of Brussels serves as one example. It is the first museum of musical instruments created in Europe and the first institution to have proposed a scientific classification of musical instruments. It was founded as part of a collection of classical musical instruments and assorted traditional instruments from China, India, Indonesia, and Japan. It began with the collection of François-Joseph Fétis (1784–1871), director of the Conservatoire Royal de Musique of Brussels. Packed away upon Fétis's death, in 1878, these instruments served as the nucleus of a museum. In 1886, the collection was expanded when curator Victor-Charles Mahillon (1841–1924) received from the Raja of Tagore a collection of north Indian musical instruments. Because of a lack of personnel, Mahillon kept the Musée Instrumental open only two hours per week. The Fétis collection did not include traditional European instruments, but Mahillon rapidly acquired European examples: Italian instruments, such as ocarinas; some flutes, a bagpipe, and a *vièle* from Dalmatia; a Norwegian Hardanger fiddle (figure 3); a hurdy-gurdy from France; a guitar from Portugal; a balalaika from Russia; and a *tambour* from French

FIGURE 2   Teaching Swedish folk fiddle at a festival in Falun. Photo by Owe Ronström, 1990.

FIGURE 3   A Norwegian *hardingfele* (Hardanger fiddle), with a characteristic inlaid neck and floral drawings on its body. Four bowed strings run over the neck, and four strings that vibrate in sympathy with the bowed strings run under the neck. Photo by Dave Golber.

Béarn. The European part of this collection was initially modest, as priority was accorded to other continents' traditional instruments, whose number never ceased growing.

The first tries to preserve musical instruments began as a byproduct of the collecting of songs and popular poetry in Europe. This collecting, particularly of literature, began early in the 1800s under the impulse of Romanticism—in 1819 for Austria, in 1833 for Hungary, and in 1852 for France, where such activity was not fully under way until around 1900, with regional folklorists such as Bourgault-Ducoudray and Tiersot. In the 1700s, Bishop Percy at first revised the popular songs he heard, but later more carefully gathered and notated them. Toward the end of the 1800s, the collecting of popular songs was supported by the creation of an essential technology, that of the gramophone (invented independently by Frenchman Charles Cros and American Thomas A. Edison in 1877), though the recording of European rural music began to take hold only in the decade 1920–1930, with Béla Bartók's work.

Early archives of phonograph records, assembled just before 1900, awakened the idea of collecting instruments in their original contexts and preserving them in situ. Recordings formed the basis of a new scientific movement, which, as early as 1914, inspired Erich M. von Hornbostel and Curt Sachs to propose a universal classification of musical instruments.

ORGANOLOGY: THE SCIENCE OF COLLECTIONS

The birth of collections and their installation in fixed places, where they were presented to the public, created the need to catalog instruments. The objective of these collections, beyond the didactic and the concrete, quickly touched the more abstract domain of organology. Though outlines of instrumental taxonomy were proposed as early as classical antiquity, the first great classifications of instruments appeared with the creation of the first museums and sound-recording archives. It is the transition of the instrument as a producer of sound to that of an inanimate object placed in public view that prompted the first tentative scientific classifications of musical instruments. Michael Praetorius (1986), one of the first to propose systematizing European musical instruments in 1618, based his classificatory logic on the nature of musical instruments from many continents.

In acoustics and construction, rural European instruments do not differ fundamentally from instruments of European art music or of instruments of other continents. This is why the classifications of Mahillon and Hornbostel and Sachs have endured, though modified and refined. In the late twentieth century, the study of instruments in their cultural contexts disrupted organology. The discipline currently reveals two main tendencies: the sonic approach and the cultural approach. The latter proposes gathering complementary data: the historical and social dimension of the instrument and its geographic distribution on one hand, and the practical dimension of the instrument (its playing technique, scales, and repertories) on the other.

Rural musical instruments thus find a place in the various major traditional classifications:

- The classification of Mahillon (1893 [1880]), founded on the criteria of morphological and functional acoustic order. This divides instruments into four categories: autophone, membrane, wind, and stringed instruments. Autophone instruments have a solid body. This system is especially effective for the winds (Mahillon's specialty as an instrument maker), but it remains less applicable to strings.

- The classification of Hornbostel and Sachs (1914), follows the same principles but brings to bear supplementary acoustical precision and new subdivisions. They renamed Mahillon's categories idiophones, membranophones, aerophones, and chordophones.

- The binary approach by Schaeffner (1936), which divides instruments into those with vibrating bodies (solid bodies susceptible or not to tension, flexible solid bodies) and those with vibrating air (ambient air, cavity, so-called wind instruments). Even if all the instruments could be divided into these two categories, this classification loses efficiency in the enumeration of materials used for the construction of the instruments and in descriptive considerations.

Beyond the systematization of instruments developed by these pioneers, other classifications have been proposed. Indeed, there are more than five hundred different organological classifications.

Fifty years would pass before an organology specific to traditional European instruments appeared. Though this system did not challenge the preceding classifications (based on the instrument as a producer of sound), it passed from the domain of macrotaxonomy (which characterizes the preceding systems) to that of microtaxonomy, following the new current of non-European organology. Erich Stockmann and Ernst Emsheimer, Germans who in 1962 created the first Study Group on European instruments under the auspices of the International Folk Music Council, did not find a classification more adequate than that of Hornbostel and Sachs's international system; however, they criticized the fact that this system did not take into account the environment in which each instrument is played (Emsheimer and Stockmann 1967–1986). Their research has the merit of being broadly based, taking into account archaeological artifacts, pieces collected in the field, literary and iconographical sources, and sound archives (Kartomi 1990:198).

Though limited to a single type of instrument (flutes), the classification of the Slovak researchers Oskár Elschek and his wife, Alica Elscheková, represents a refinement of the preceding classifications. These researchers emphasize the incompleteness of the earlier systematic method, which they view as a top-down taxonomy, taking into account certain instrumental traits. Their typological method, in contrast, operates in the opposite direction: the detailed intimate observations of each instrument lead to the definition of groups. The authors treat the morphological, technological, acoustical, and design data of the instruments. Their publications include graphic schemes and symbols that illustrate the types of embouchures and positions of lips and fingers, reported in synoptic tables. Their classification of any musical instrument is determined by the collection of its variants.

Finally, Timo Leisiö devised a taxonomy as an investigative tool for retracing the history of Finno-Karelian musical regions. The evolution of the terminology of instruments over time permits him to determine the cultural connections between the Finns and the Germans and to expound a theory on the evolution of Finno-Karelian music over five millennia. Here, organology enters the cultural dimension of musical instruments. Leisiö describes the instrumental classification adopted by the Finno-Karelians themselves and tries to elucidate certain aspects of it. He believes the two categories of aerophones found among them were distinguished by material criteria and harmonic possibilities. This classification, essentially historical, is reinforced by a group of archaeologically, folklorically, linguistically, musically, and sociologically complementary data.

Beyond these studies, European organology seems to have undergone little development. The symbolic and social dimension of an instrument, its inclusion in local systems of representation, and the description and typology of its repertories are themes rarely explored in European organology—and too often treated anecdotally (Yacoub 1986). In instrumental practice, few studies reveal evidence of the specific performance techniques unique to particular villages. There are practically no studies of the construction techniques of instruments across microregions of Europe, or of living instrument makers. In short, organology of traditional Europe has preferred laboratory research over ethnological field work.

COLLECTIONS TODAY: THEIR MANAGEMENT AND GOALS

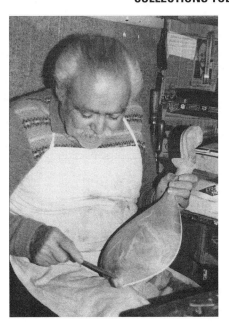

FIGURE 4   In a workshop on Crete, a traditional maker of the Greek bowed lute (*lyra*) carves a detail on an instrument. Traditional makers usually follow intuitive rules of thumb, rather than the exact measurements employed by modern makers of facsimiles. Photo by Cornelia Herzfeld, mid-1980s.

Museography, the museum-based method of classification, has evolved considerably, as museums have been modernizing to suit growing and diverse publics. Museums of the past century, which catered to elite visitors and their informed relation with the collections, has been transformed into a leisure-oriented art gallery, accessible to the general public—children, students, professional groups, families, tourists, and visitors, who browse daily, rather than studying intensively.

To respond to the pedagogical needs of this public, a form of direct commentary was inaugurated: the use of lectures and guided visits. Space for specialists and researchers is protected by the appearance of galleries and study collections. These collections resolved the problem of access to exposition-room showcases, which are sometimes crowded, or access to instruments in storage, which can be difficult. For many years, there has been a new type of visitor: musical instrument makers who come to examine and measure the instruments in reserved rooms so they can construct facsimiles of ancient instruments (figure 4). Finally, traditional European musical instruments have become particularly popular objects for temporary exhibitions, which feature certain instruments of a collection, brought out from storage or borrowed from foreign museums. Such exhibitions are served by new types of exhibition catalogs, which range from simple booklets to utilitarian tools and those that are luxuriously illustrated works of art. Their variety matches the diversity of the publics whom these catalogs address.

The development of museology has highlighted the importance of musical instruments as collectible objects. To display their traditional instruments, museums have gradually abandoned older methods of displaying classical musical instruments, as by dividing them by type and era (figure 5). Instead, the social and cultural dimen-

Some exhibitions try to foreground the social functions of musical instruments across many regions by choosing, for example, the theme of the bell in different villages of France, where the bell fills a role that is at once religious, therapeutic, symbolic, and parareligious.

FIGURE 5   A display in the Museum of Music, Tallinn, Estonia, organizes musical instruments by type. *From left:* two panels of bagpipes, two panels of bowed lyres, and a panel of bowed lyres and zithers. In the foreground, a box displays a diatonic button accordion. Photo by Johannes Tall.

sions of traditional instruments are becoming progressively more respected, and the division of traditional European instruments by geographic region is beginning to be abandoned, in favor of themes common to many regions. Little by little, museums are embracing the idea of a uniquely European "musical civilization," in which instruments are presented in all their diverse forms and local variations.

Organological arrangements

Most museums still display their collections of instruments according to the typological division adopted by major organological classifications from before World War II (idiophones, membranophones, aerophones, chordophones) and sometimes impose a chronology on this system. Though this kind of presentation does not consider the sociocultural context in which instruments appear, it permits the comparison of various traditions and puts into relief the varied means of construction.

Barcelona's Museu de la Música and Copenhagen's Musikhistorisk Museum og Carl Claudius are examples where instruments of Western art music and traditional European music are exhibited in the same rooms. The Museu de la Música, following Hornbostel and Sachs's classification, divides each category into secondary groups. It offers a linear vision of musical instruments without a hierarchy of musical genres. Among the stringed instruments stand, side by side in the same room or the same gallery of display cases, a classic zither from the Italian renaissance, a banjo made in Spain, and a balalaika from Russia. Though all epochs and musical cultures are typologically mixed together, a geographic distinction is made between the European instruments and those of other continents.

The Musikhistorisk Museum og Carl Claudius, which has a good collection of traditional Scandinavian instruments, adopts many systems of presentation at the same time: typological divisions (grouping classical and traditional instruments), geographical divisions (separating European instruments from those of other continents), and sociological divisions. Finally, there is a presentation of the construction of an instrument: a traditional Danish mandolin is displayed in all stages of its production, accompanied by photographs. This museum has chosen a flexible, varied mode of presenting its instruments.

Geographical arrangements

Another way of classifying instruments is by geographical area. This is illustrated by Lisbon's Museu Etnografico, which devotes a small part of its collection to musical instruments. It offers a panorama of instruments used in Portuguese-speaking countries. The display is presented in the form of a voyage around the world: one leaves the western coast of Africa (with Guinea, the Cape Verde Islands, Angola, and São Tomé) to go to the eastern coast (Mozambique), passing by the Azores, Madeira, Latin America (Brazil), and Hawai'i, and ending in Portugal. For continental Portugal, the instruments are organized according to their region of origin.

Sociological arrangements

Some museums present musical instruments according to their social context. Examples of this policy are the Musée Instrumentale of Brussels and the Musée des Arts et Traditions Populaires of Paris. In 1980, the latter, which presents the traditions and the technologies of each region of France, opened an exhibition of 450 musical instruments from throughout France. This exhibition tried to foreground the social functions of musical instruments across many regions by choosing, for example, the theme of the bell in different villages of France, where the bell fills a role that is at once religious, therapeutic, symbolic, and parareligious, as in penitents' processions. The exhibit showed that tinkling and pealing do not have the same meaning. It also presented the zither across its social functions and the geographic courses of instruments that traveled from one social milieu to another.

PRINCIPAL EUROPEAN COLLECTIONS

The following is a selected list of the principal European institutions maintaining collections of traditional European musical instruments. The collections listed may be important for their quantity of traditional European instruments, or they may have few traditional European instruments in comparison to their collection of traditional instruments originating on other continents. The numbers of instruments are approximate.

AUSTRIA

Vienna. Österreichisches Museum für Volkskunde, Laudongasse 15–19, A–1080 Vienna VIII. Five hundred instruments of Austria and Central Europe.

BELGIUM

Anvers. Volkskundemuseum, Gildekamersstraat 2–6, B–2000 Anvers. Three hundred instruments of Flanders.

Brussels. Musées Instrumental de Bruxelles (Musées Royaux d'Art et d'Histoire de Bruxelles), Petit Sablon 17, B–1000 Brussels. One thousand instruments of many European countries.

FINLAND

Helsinki. National Museum of Finland, Exotica, Mannerhelmintie 34, box 913, SF–001101 Helsinki. About 450 Finnish and Finno-Hungarian instruments and other European instruments.

Kaustinen. Kansanmusiikki Instituutti (Folk Music Institute), SF–69600 Kaustinen. Three hundred Finnish instruments.

FRANCE

Paris. Musée des Arts et Traditions Populaires, Département de la musique, Phonothèque, ave. du Mahatma Gandhi, 6, F–75116 Paris. Thirteen hundred instruments of regions of France.

Paris. Musée de l'Homme, Département d'Ethnomusicologie, Palais de Chaillot, Place du Trocadéro 17, F–75116 Paris. Nine hundred instruments of most European countries.

GERMANY

Berlin. Museum für Völkerkunde (Abteilung Musikethnologie), Arnimalee 23–27, D–1000 Berlin 33. Two hundred instruments of many European countries.

Göttingen. Georg-August-Universität, Göttingen (Musikinstrumenten Sammlung des Musikwissenschaftlichen Seminars), Kurze Geismarstrasse 1, D–3400 Göttingen. Six hundred instruments of many European countries, including Greece and Yugoslavia.

Markneukirchen. Musikinstrumenten-Museum, Bienengarten 2, D–0–9659 Markneukirchen. Two thousand instruments of many European countries.

Munich. Münchner Stadtmuseum (Musikinstrumentenmuseum), St. Jakobsplatz 1, D–8000 Munich 2. One thousand instruments of many European countries.

Nuremberg. Germanisches Nationalmuseum, Box 9580 Kornmarkt, D-8500 Nuremberg 11. Three hundred instruments of many European countries.

NORWAY

Trondheim. Ringve Museum, Pb. 3064 Lade, N–7002 Trondheim. About 650 European instruments.

POLAND

Poznań. Muzeum Instrumentów Muzycznych, Stary Rynek 45, PL–61 772 Poznań. About 275 Polish instruments.

Szydtowiec. Muzeum Ludowych Instrumentow Muzycznych (Museum of Folk Musical Instruments) ul. Sowinskiego, 2, PL–26500 Szydtowiec. About 1,340 Polish instruments.

Warsaw. Panstwowe Muzeum Etnograficzne (State Ethnographical Museum), ul. Kredytowa, 1, PL–00056 Warsaw. Four hundred Polish instruments.

PORTUGAL

Estoril. Museu da Música Regional Portuguesa, Casa Verdades de Faria, Av. de Saboia, 1146B, 2765 Estoril. Two hundred Portuguese instruments.

SLOVAKIA

Bratislava. Slovenské Narodné Muzeum, Music Department, Vajanskeho nábr., 2, CS–814 36 Bratislava. One thousand Slovakian instruments.

SPAIN

Barcelona. Museu de la Música, Avenida Diagonal, 373, 080008 Barcelona. Three hundred Spanish instruments.

Valladolid. Centro Etnográfico de Documentación Joaquim Díaz, Diputación de Valladolid, 47071 Valladolid. Five hundred instruments of Castile and León.

UNITED KINGDOM

Edinburgh. National Museums of Scotland–Royal Museum of Scotland, Chambers Street, Edinburgh EH2 1JD. Six hundred English, Irish, Scottish, and European bagpipes.

London. British Museum, Museum of Mankind, Burlington Gardens, 6, London W1X 2EX. European musical instruments.

London. Horniman Museum & Library, London Road, Forest Hill, London S.E.23 3PQ. Five hundred European musical instruments.

—TRANSLATED BY STEPHANIE P. SCHLAGEL

BIBLIOGRAPHY

Becker, Heinz. 1972. "Historische und systematische Aspekte der Instrumentenkunde." *Studia Instrumentorum Musicae Popularis* 2:184–196.

————. 1976. "Das Volksmusikinstrument in der Rezeption des Musikhistorikers." *Studia Instrumentorum Musicae Popularis* 4:30–38.

Bessaraboff, Nicholas. 1941. *Ancient European Musical Instruments.* Cambridge: Harvard University Press.

Brown, Howard Mayer, and Joan Lascelle. 1972. *Musical Iconography: A Manual for Cataloguing Subjects in Western Art before 1800.* Cambridge: Harvard University Press.

Buchner, Alexandre. 1969. *Les instruments de musique populaire.* Paris: Gründ.

Caufriez, Anne. 1988. *L'instrument de musique traditionnnel ibérique.* Brussels: Musée Instrumental de Bruxelles.

Drèger, Hans Heinz. 1947. *Prinzip einer Systematik der Musikinstrumente.* Kassel and Basel: Bärenreiter.

Elschek, Oskár. 1969. *System of Graphical and Symbolic Signs for the Typology of Aerophones.* Bratislava: Vydatelstvo Slovenskej Académie Vied.

————. 1969. "Typologische Arbeitsverfahren

bei Volksmusikinstrumenten." *Studia Instrumentorum Musicae Popularis* 1:23–40.

Elschek, Oskár, and Erich Stockmann. 1969. "Zur Typologie der Volksmusikinstrumente." *Studia Instrumentorum Musicae Popularis* 1:11–22.

Elscheková, Alica. 1975. "Systematisierung, Klassifikation, und Katalogisierung von Volksliedweisen." *Handbuch des Volkslieds,* ed. Rolf Wilhelm Brednich, Lutz Rohrich, and Wolfgang Suppan, 2:549–582. Munich: Fink.

Emsheimer, Ernst, and Erich Stockmann, eds. 1967–1986. *Handbuch der europäischen Volksmusikinstrumente.* Series 1, parts 1–5. Leipzig: VEB Deutscher Verlag für Musik. Llubljana: Slovenska akademija znanostie in umetnosti, Institut za slovensko narodopisje.

———. 1969–1985. "Studia Instrumentorum Musicae Popularis." *Studia Instrumentorum Musicae Popularis* 1–8. Stockholm: Musikhistoriska Museet.

Galpin, Francis. 1965 [1910]. *Old English Instruments of Music: Their History and Character.* London: Shenval.

———. 1937. *A Textbook of European Musical Instruments: Their Origin, History, and Character.* London: Williams and Nowgate.

Hickmann, Ellen. 1971. *Musica Instrumentalis: Studien zur Klassifikation des Musikinstrumentarium im Mittelalter.* Baden-Baden: Valentin Koerner.

Hornbostel, Erich M. von, and Curt Sachs. 1914. "Systematik der Musikinstrumente: Ein Versuch." *Zeitschrift für Ethnologie* 45. Translated by Anthony Baines and Klaus Wachsmann, under the title "A Classification of Musical Instruments." *Galpin Society Journal* 14 (1961):3–29.

Kartomi, Margaret J. 1990. *On Concepts and Classifications of Musical Instruments.* Chicago, London: University of Chicago Press.

Ledang, Ola Kai. 1972. "On the Acoustics and the Systematic Classification of the Jew's-Harp." *Yearbook of the International Folk Music Council* 4:94–103.

Leisiö, Timo. 1977. "The Taxonomy and Historical Interpretation of the Finnish Pastoral Aerophones." *Studia Instrumentorum Musicae Popularis* 5:45–50.

Lyskoff, René T. A., and Jim Matson. 1985. "A New Approach to the Classification of Sound-Producing Instruments." *Ethnomusicology* 29:213–236.

Mahillon, Victor-Charles. 1893 [1880]. *Catalogue descriptif et analytique du Musée Instrumental du Conservatoire Royal de musique de Bruxelles.* Paris: Gand.

Marcel-Dubois, Claudie. 1958. "L'ethnomusicologie." In *Précis de musicologie,* ed. Jacques Chailley, 53–62. Paris: Presses Universitaires de France.

———. 1980. *L'instrument de musique populaire (usage et symboles).* Paris: La Réunion des Musées Nationaux.

Montandon, Georges. 1919. "La généalogie des instruments de musique et les cycles de civilisation: étude suivie du catalogue des instruments de musique du Musée Ethnographique de Genève." *Archives Suisses d'Anthropologie Générale* 3:1–120.

Müller, Mette. 1972. *From Bone Pipe and Cattle Horn to Fiddle and Psaltery: Folk Music Instruments from Denmark, Finland, Iceland, Norway and Sweden.* Copenhagen: Musikhistorisk Museum.

Norlind, Tobias. 1932. "Musikinstrumentensystematik." *Svensk Tidskrift für Musikforskning* 14:95–123.

Praetorius, Michael. 1986. *Syntagma Musica II: De Organographie, Parts I and II.* trans. and ed. David Z. Crookes. Oxford: Clarendon Press.

Ramey, Michael. 1974. "A Classification of Musical Instruments for Comparative Study." Ph.D. dissertation, University of California, Los Angeles.

Reinecke, Hans-Peter. 1974. "Einige Bermerkungen zur methodologischen Basis instrumentaler Forschung." *Studia Instrumentorum Musicae Popularis* 3:176–179.

Sachs, Curt. 1940. *The History of Musical Instruments.* New York: Norton.

Sadie, Stanley, ed. 1984. *The New Grove Dictionary of Musical Instruments.* London: Macmillan.

Sárosi, Bálint. 1967. *Die Volksmusikinstrumente Ungarns: Handbuch der europäischen Volksmusikinstrumente.* Vol. 1. Leipzig: VEB Deutscher Verlag für Musik.

Schaeffner, André. 1932. "D'une nouvelle classification méthodique des instruments de musique." *Revue Musicale* 30:215–231.

———. 1936. *Origine des instruments de musique.* Paris: Payot.

Stockmann, Erich. 1964. "Die europäischen Volksmusikinstrumente: Möglichkeiten und Probleme ihrer Darstellung in eine Handbuch." *Deutsches Jahrbuch für Volkskunde* 10:238–253.

Veiga de Oliveira, Ernesto. 1966. *Instrumentos musicais populares portugueses.* Lisbon: Fundação Calouste Gulbenkian.

Yacoub, Gabriel. 1986. *Les instruments de musique populaire et leurs anecdotes.* Paris: MA Éditions.

Music and Ideology
James Porter

Nationalism
Social Class

Music making, like all artistic activity, is never value free. Even the most abstract piece of music is brought into being in a human context by a creator who has been enculturated in a specific society. That person derives values first from upbringing and exposure to the social norms of the society, and second from a more general worldview. The myth of the autonomous work of art, the symphony, opera, or string quartet that is somehow fashioned into a masterpiece out of thin air by an other-worldly composer divorced from economic or political realities, has long been exploded. The Romantic idea of such autonomy was driven by a belief in heaven-sent conditions attending artistic creation by a spiritually inspired composer. That notion, tantamount to an ideology, was widespread in eighteenth- and nineteenth-century Europe but began to change in the twentieth century with the crisis brought on by modernist experimentation in concert music, as in other arts.

Ideology is a set of beliefs that suffuses the worldview of individual makers and consumers of music, whether composers of concert music, traditional singers, instrumentalists, audiences, or those who study them. Communities, ethnic groups, and nation-states also form around ideologies in which music plays a central role. Inasmuch as ideology is closely bound up with worldview, it is linked to collective and individual identities. It extends into, and determines, conceptions of history, tradition, social structure, political organization, and cultural life. It is normally associated with secular beliefs, but religious or cultic notions may carry over into it and fuse with it. Ideology itself is a fairly modern concept, having entered usage with the French Revolutionary philosopher Destutt de Tracy (1970 [1801]), who wished to use ameliorative "ideas" as the basis of social and educational improvement. In Hegelian and Marxist philosophy, however, Friedrich Engels began to refer to ideology pejoratively as false consciousness. Ideology, in this view, is a set of beliefs by which people deceive themselves.

NATIONALISM

In the twentieth century, ideological concerns revolved around three major principles or types of secular organization: fascism, nationalism, and socialism (or communism). Of these, nationalism remains powerful, especially when wedded to concepts

FIGURE 1   *"Das Horst Wessel-Lied,"* a popular Nazi "fatherland and soldier song," composed by Hermann Blume for a German folk-song competition.

of ethnic identity. In Finland, for example, scholars have been at pains to expose nationalistic elements in their traditional life and worldview. With the demise of fascist states after World War II (after Franco's death in Spain) and the Soviet Union and its satellites after 1989, newer ideals include regionalism, feminism, and ethnic or cultural identity. Fascism and communism, however, gave rise to many kinds of artistic and musical expression, often in ways that closely resemble one another (figure 1). Nazi songs and Communist Party songs often used the same means to achieve the goal of ideological euphoria. These songs usually embodied semantic themes of positive value as regards the party and its dissemination of songs (Karbusicky and Pletka 1973). Musically, the songs adopt a hymnlike or marchlike character, derived from Protestant chorales or student songs, with easily remembered, concise melodies that are strongly diatonic and stay within the range of an octave. Based on folk or folklike melodies, the tunes were meant to drive home the import of the texts at affective levels.

Such songs are overtly propagandistic. But political songs as a broad category have played a central role in Europe and have often arisen from working-class experience (Steinitz 1954, 1962). Miners' songs, for example, such as the Bergreihen collection of 1531, have been known and collected in Germany since the sixteenth century. (Some with music are those of 1551 and 1602.) That certain laboring occupations would give rise to political songs is unsurprising, given the conditions of employment before the rise of trade unions in the late 1800s. But the growth of invented traditions in the same period (about 1870–1914) is also instructive: these include Bastille Day, the Olympic Games, and the labor holiday May Day (figure 2).

Many national ideologies spring from a sense of being overtaken by the modern world and such forces as commercialism, tourism, technology, imperialism, or simply a cultural majority. This was true for the Welsh, who, as a minority Celtic people, have been sidelined by English imperial designs since the 1200s. Edward Jones (1752–1824), harpist to George IV, helped turn Welsh culture from a decaying, unself-conscious state into a self-conscious, revivalist mode. The *eisteddfod* 'session', an occasion for musical competition, was reconceived during the 1700s, and by 1819 Edward Williams (1747–1826), a stonemason from Glamorgan, who, using the pseudonym Iolo Morganwg, inserted into the competition the druidic and bardic elements that it still preserves [see WALES]. In such ways, minority cultures, when threatened with extinction, have often responded by reinventing their imagined past. The term *Celtic music* is now used by some to project a sense of musical unity among peoples speaking a Celtic language when commonalities are hard to detect because of long separation. In any case, the Celtic peoples of the Late Iron Age were by no means a homogeneous people [see CELTIC MUSIC].

In Ireland and Scotland, languages and oral traditions similar to those in Wales were associated with political resistance to English conquest from the post-Norman period (after 1200). In the 1700s, the oral traditions and customs associated with them had to be recast for a world that was intent on modernizing. Caught between allegiance to an antiquated, paternalistic social system (the clan) and the need to adapt to a world of enlightenment and progress, James Macpherson recreated heroic songs and tales he had heard as a boy in the Scottish Highlands in his Ossianic *Fragments of Ancient Poetry* (1760), which influenced Goethe, Herder, Thomas Jefferson, Napoleon, and others. In producing free English versions of oral traditions, Macpherson echoed the procedures of late medieval Celtic writers such as Geoffrey of Monmouth (d. 1155), who, for his Norman patrons, reinvented early British history and a heroic, expansionist ideology around King Arthur. Macpherson caught the flavor of an oral tradition that was often rife with poetic invention and the antithesis of eighteenth-century "cultivated" taste.

Majority cultures, even those caught up in imperial and colonial expansion, such as Britain in the 1800s, have also needed to express their ideologies through musical means. The English musical renaissance, the architect of which was Hubert Parry (1848–1918), was accompanied by a growing enthusiasm for patriotic hymns: more choral settings of the national anthem ("God Save the King") appeared in the years 1890–1910 than any period before or since. The freshly ritualized coronations of Edward VII (1902) and George V (1911) had works specially commissioned from Parry, Edward Elgar, Arthur Sullivan, and others. Even in the mid-twentieth century, Gustav Holst, William Walton, and Ralph Vaughan Williams wrote music on command for the coronations of George VI (1937) and Elizabeth II (1953).

Beyond extending to the context of musical creation, ideology can influence the essential structures of music. It is no accident that profound changes occurred in the classical forms of Haydn, Mozart, and Beethoven at the time that "ideology" entered the world of ideas. The necessity of composing easily remembered tunes that might become popular was constantly inculcated in Mozart by his father. That popularity, in turn, would translate into hard cash for a composer abandoning a corrupt world of aristocratic and church patronage and seeking the patronage of the increasingly influential bourgeoisie. The patterned structures of the late classical symphony, in creating

FIGURE 3 In the nineteenth century, opera became an important vehicle for the expression of nationalist aspirations, a tendency that continues to the present. A scene from the world premiere of Aulis Sallinen's nationalist opera, *Kullervo,* based on the Kalevala, the national epic of Finland. Performed by the Finnish National Opera in association with the Los Angeles Music Center Opera, 25 February 1992. Photo by Ohringer/Millared. Courtesy of Los Angeles Opera.

a sense of symmetry and balance, are deceptive, for though they create an ideal world, their melodic clashes, contrapuntal inversions, and shifting harmonies embody a longing for a new musical and social order. Beethoven rejected the false ideology of Napoleon to embrace an ideology of universal brotherhood in his Ninth Symphony. The ideological element intensified with Frédéric Chopin (1810–1849) and his identification with Polish claims to freedom from Hapsburg and Russian imperialism. Race emerged with nationalism as powerful artistic modifiers in the operas of Richard Wagner (1813–1883), especially the Ring cycle (1869–1876) and *Die Meistersinger von Nürnberg* (1868). Giuseppe Verdi (1813– 1901) was a symbol of aspiring nationhood to Italians, not only because of the royal acronym of his name (*Vittore Emmanuele Re d'Italia* 'Victor Emanuel, King of Italy'), but through operas such as *Nabucco* (1842), which drew a pointed parallel with captive Israel in biblical times. Even in the late twentieth century, opera reflected nationalist ideals (figure 3).

The social orders that came into being in Europe around 1900 distorted history for ideological ends. The rise of fascism in Italy (1922–1945) was an outgrowth of nationalism. Its leader, Benito Mussolini (1883–1945), contributed an article on fascism to the *Enciclopedia italiana* (1932), and songs were created to further the fascist cause. Likewise, in Hitler's Germany, songs were adapted from older sources, either genuine folk songs or folklike productions of the 1800s. These creations transformed the older sources (where they existed) and their generally stoic or neutral ideology into positive-sounding texts with marchlike tunes in major tonality.

Similarly, the ideology of Soviet songs stressed positive goals and aspirations through musical means. Because the older, rural traditions had expressed a fateful irony or stoicism, the Soviets insisted that new songs should be created around and by the urban proletariat, who would form the avant-garde of the socialist movement. Folk songs were no longer to reflect the conditions of the peasant class: they were to show the way toward a politically empowered future. In 1964, the Soviet folklorist L. Zemljanova argued that the only genuine folk songs were those that revealed the plight of the working masses under capitalism, and the only admirable folk-song scholars were those whose collections or writings sympathized with the people. "Bourgeois folklorists" did not fall into this group. At about the same time, the

The disdain in which many professional critics hold traditional or folk music itself reflects an ideology of power relations in society. "Serious music" is for the higher social classes and intellectuals; the masses can be content with the "simple" music that makes them into docile consumers.

Hungarian János Maróthy attacked the German musicologist Walter Wiora for his "bourgeois" views on European folk song; these views included a second existence (*zweites Dasein*) for folk song in inauthentic or adapted settings.

SOCIAL CLASS

Cecil Sharp, likewise, has been roundly criticized for the middle-class selectivity he brought to his view of English folk song. In collecting and publishing folk songs, Sharp had two goals in mind: laying the basis for a national English school of composition, and providing schoolchildren with genuine, rather than "national," songs. In the first goal, he succeeded to some extent, as the achievements of Holst and Vaughan Williams indicate. In education, the results are harder to estimate because pedagogical fashions change. Sharp was a Fabian socialist, believing in gradualism and the ameliorating effect of rural folk song, which he recorded from lower-class artisans in Somerset. By contrast, a later English scholar, A. L. Lloyd, was a convinced Marxist who championed industrial folk song. Sharp's ideology was built around songs of the rural artisan, but Lloyd idealized mine workers and ploughmen for their creative use of folk songs.

The ideology of social class can permeate beliefs about popular creativity. Béla Bartók, convinced that Eastern European peasant song could be as perfect as the grandest pieces of musical art, nevertheless doubted that peasants were capable of inventing new tunes. He recognized clearly the ability to vary and recreate songs current in their community and appreciated the talent that gifted performers could bring to the art of variation. But he may well have underestimated peasants' capacities for original musical thinking. Intent on gathering as much as he could before these village cultures disappeared, he may have failed to distinguish between creative singers, who substantially alter or recompose songs, and workaday ones. Bartók's ideology of folk creation survives in Eastern Europe. Many scholars believe that every folk song has been collected, and only variants can now be found. This "devolutionary" view of creativity—that is, folk songs are perpetually in decline—stems from an ideology of class structure and progress that obtained earlier in the twentieth century.

With the rise of urban popular music, the ideology of production and consumption has shown the need for careful analysis. At the same time, the crisis of classical or concert music has created a gulf between the selling of musical commodities (cassettes, CDs) and the need to support musical organizations (symphony orchestras, opera companies) whose repertoire is confined to works of the 1700s and 1800s and whose performing conditions are costly. The polemics of a musical critic such as T. W. Adorno (1998), against, for instance, "pleasurable" music and the "culture industry," have only served to isolate from popular appeal "difficult" European composers, such as Pierre Boulez and Karlheinz Stockhausen, who still believe in "modern music." With culture brokers' realization that many societies value tradition more than modernity, the "ideology of the new" (as it has been called) has come increasingly under scrutiny.

The disdain in which many professional critics hold traditional or folk music—which, after all, commands a considerable audience throughout the world, and is not limited to consumer products—itself reflects an ideology of power relations in society. "Serious music" is for the higher social classes and intellectuals; the masses can be content with the "simple" music that makes them into docile consumers. Modernist ideologies now seem dated and unrealistic, saddled by a nineteenth-century historicist belief in progress. Traditional music, on the other hand, has shown an ability to renew itself, simply because it is based on participatory practice and the constantly evolving ideology of those who practice and perpetuate it. The ideals of European regionalism, feminism, or ethnic identity as they appear in folk and popular songs or in scholarly analyses appear more realizable because these ideals are keyed to European society as it is: multicultural, pluralistic, and conflict ridden, as ethnic groups strive for empowerment and capital and labor struggle over economic means, the distribution of wealth, and artistic and musical activity.

BIBLIOGRAPHY

Adorno, Theodor W. 1998. *Essays on Modern Music.* Trans. Rodney Livingstone. London: Verso.

Boyes, Georgina. 1994. *The Imagined Village.* Manchester: Manchester University Press.

Burke, Peter. 1978. *Popular Culture in Early Modern Europe.* New York: Harper.

Danckert, Werner. 1939 [1970]. *Das europäische Volkslied.* Bonn: H. Bouvier.

De Martino, Ernesto. 1961. *La terra del rimorso: contributo a una storia religiosa del Sud.* Milan: Il Saggiatore.

Destutt de Tracy, Antoine Louis Claude. 1970 [1801]. *Elemens* [sic] *d'idéologie.* Paris: J. Vrin.

Donner, Philip, ed. 1985. *Idols and Myths in Music.* Musiikin Suunta, 1. Helsinki: Finnish Society for Ethnomusicology.

Elsner, Jürgen, and Giwi Ordshonikidse, eds. 1977. *Sozialistische Musikkultur: Traditionen, Probleme, Perspektiven.* Berlin: Verlag Neue Musik.

Gammon, Vic. 1986. "A. L. Lloyd and History: A Reconsideration of Aspects of 'Folk Song in England' and Some of His Other Writings." In *Singer, Song and Scholar,* ed. Ian Russell, 147–164. Sheffield: Sheffield Academic Press.

Hobsbawm, Eric, and Terence Ranger, eds. 1983. *The Invention of Tradition.* Cambridge: Cambridge University Press.

Kamenetsky, Christa. 1972. "Folklore as a Political Tool in Nazi Germany." *Journal of American Folklore* 85:221–235.

Karbusicky, Vladimir, and V. Pletka. 1958. *Dělnické písně* (Workers' songs). Prague: Státní nakladatelství krásné literatury, hudby a umění.

———. 1973. *Ideologie im Lied: Lied in der Ideologie.* Cologne: Hans Gerig.

Klusen, Ernst. 1969. *Volkslied: Fund und Erfindung.* Cologne: Hans Gerig.

Koskoff, Ellen, ed. 1989. *Women and Music in Cross-Cultural Perspective.* Urbana: University of Illinois Press.

Kurkela, Vesa. 1983. "Varkaus: Worker's Music in a Finnish Industrial Town." *Suomen Antropologi* 4:218–223.

———. 1991. "Idealistic 'Folksiness' in the Folk Music of Finnish Popular Movements." In *Finnish-Hungarian Symposium on Music & Folklore Research, 15.–21.11.1987,* ed. Antti Koiranen, 50–53. Tampere: Kansanperinteen Laitos.

Leydi, Roberto, ed. 1972. *Trasformazioni socioeconomiche e cultura tradizionale in Lombardia.* Milan: Assessorato alla Cultura, Informazione e Partecipazione della Regione Lombardia (series "Quaderni di documentazione regionale"), 5–6.

Lloyd, A. L. 1952. *Come All Ye Bold Miners: Ballads and Songs of the Coalfields.* London: Lawrence and Wishart.

———. 1967. *Folk Song in England.* London: Lawrence and Wishart.

Lombardi-Satriani, Luigi. 1974. "Folklore as Culture of Contestation." *Journal of the Folklore Institute* 11:99–121.

Maróthy, János. 1974. *Music and the Bourgeois, Music and the Proletarian.* Budapest: Akadémiai Kiadó.

Oinas, Felix J., ed. 1978. *Folklore, Nationalism, and Politics.* Columbus, Ohio: Slavica Publishers.

Pekkilä, Erkki. 1991. "Folk Music, Tourism and Authenticity." In *Finnish-Hungarian Symposium on Music & Folklore Research 15.–21.11.1987,* ed. Antti Koiranen, 74–78. Tampere: Kansanoeriteen Laitos.

Rosen, Charles. 1971. *The Classical Style.* New York: Viking.

Sharp, Cecil J. 1907. *English Folk-Song: Some Conclusions.* London: Simpkin, Novello.

Simeone, William E. 1978. "Fascists and

Folklorists in Italy." *Journal of American Folklore* 91:543–557.

Steinitz, Wolfgang. 1954. *Deutsche Volkslieder demokratischen Charakters aus sechs Jahrhunderten.* Vol 1. Berlin: Akademie-Verlag.

———. 1962. *Deutsche Volkslieder demokratischen Charakters aus sechs Jahrhunderten.* Vol. 2. Berlin: Akademie-Verlag.

———. 1965. *Arbeiterlied und Volkslied.* Berlin: Akademie-Verlag.

Stockmann, Erich, and Hermann Strobach, eds. 1967. *Sowjetische Volkslied- und Volksmusikforschung: Ausgewählte Studien.* Berlin: Akademie-Verlag.

Stokes, Martin, ed. 1994. *Ethnicity, Identity and Music: The Musical Construction of Place.* Providence: Berg.

Strobach, Hermann. 1964. *Bauernklagen: Untersuchungen zum sozialkritischen deutschen Lied.* Berlin: Berlin: Akademie-Verlag.

Wiora, Walter. 1959. "Der Untergang des Volksliedes und sein zweites Dasein." *Musikalische Zeitfragen* 7:9–25.

Zemljanova, L. M. 1964. "The Struggle between the Reactionary and the Progressive Forces in Contemporary American Folkloristics." *Journal of the Folklore Institute* 1:130–144.

Gender and Music
Ellen Koskoff

The use of gender as an analytic category has been a recent development in the study of traditional and classical European musics. Early scholars and collectors frequently noted differences in men's and women's repertoires, performance styles, and contexts, but until the 1980s, little attention had been paid to the role that gender plays in structuring, maintaining, or subverting the gender-based division of musical and social roles.

GENDER AS A CATEGORY OF ANALYSIS

Gender is a socially constructed category (i.e., man or woman), derived predominantly from one's biological sex (i.e., male or female), and continuously negotiated within a given cultural template or framework. All societies recognize biological and social differences between men and women, and these commonly serve as the primary basis for a general division of labor in economic, political, expressive, and other domains. While biological categories are fairly static (few people are born with a combination of male and female sexual traits), gender categories are often dynamic, with boundaries between men's and women's attributes or behaviors constantly in flux, so that so-called masculinity or femininity can appear variously in both sexes. Further, specific notions of masculinity and femininity change over time and across cultures, so that any examination of gender relations and their effect upon music making must be contextualized for such an examination to have meaning.

Anthropologists and others have coined the term *gender ideology* to denote a conceptual and valuative framework that underlies appropriate behaviors for men and women. Gender ideologies can be, and often are, codified within religious, legal, or moral institutions and provide seemingly natural justifications for various gender arrangements. A given society's *gender style* can be understood in terms of the value and subsequent power given to and maintained by one gender over another. Gender styles can range theoretically from near-equal autonomy and value for men and women (complementarity) to a lack of equality in autonomy and value (gender stratification). European historical and contemporary societies have shown a diversity of gender styles, with a corresponding variety in men's and women's musical roles and practices.

Music making can be based on gender alone, possibly the oldest arrangement, where women and men are physically separated from each other while making music, essentially creating two separate, self-contained music cultures.

SCHOLARSHIP AND THEORETICAL ISSUES

Until the 1980s, most scholarship on music, especially within the Western art tradition, focused solely on men's activities, presenting a male-centered view of music making and history. Thus, locating women's musical activities and placing men's and women's music making within a broader context of gender relations has been a new scholarly phenomenon.

Scholarship on gender and music in Europe can be divided into four distinct, yet overlapping categories, showing a variety of disciplinary approaches. The earliest scholarship produced ethnographies and collections of folk materials that showed a strict division of musical labor between men and women, based on men's and women's differing social, economic, and political roles within the largely agrarian culture of eighteenth- and nineteenth-century Europe. In such collections, differences in repertoires, uses of musical instruments, contexts, and performing styles have been consistently noted, but not necessarily contextualized. The second category of scholarship, developing largely from the political struggles of the early women's movement (about 1960 to 1970) and continuing to the present, has produced studies of European classical and nonclassical musics that focus solely upon women's music making to balance the prevailing male-centered historical and contemporary descriptions. Category three, studies informed by Marxist and Lévi-Straussian-derived feminist theory, developed largely within anthropology and sociology since the 1970s, have placed women's and men's music making within a broader cultural context of prevailing gender and power ideologies. These works have stressed a holistic approach, where music making is integrated into other prevailing belief systems and practices.

The fourth, most recent form of scholarship has produced works influenced by postmodern literary and cultural criticism, where gender and music issues are interpreted through a variety of frames, such as social class, psychological theory, and sexual orientation. This scholarship owes much to the literary criticism of Jacques Derrida and Michel Foucault and the psychological theories of Sigmund Freud, Jacques Lacan, and others. Of special importance to postmodern music scholarship has been the notion of *différance,* a view suggesting that meaning is situated in language or text (Derrida 1976) and that deconstructing the politics of texts of all kinds, including pieces of so-called absolute music, with supposedly no reference to extra-musical cultural domains, can expose power relations between selves and others. Though some critics have characterized the postmodern view as Western- and text-centric, largely ahistorical, and undertheorized from the viewpoint of human agency, much recent work in music scholarship has been heavily influenced by postmodern criticism.

In this literature, certain broad theoretical questions concerning the nature of gender differences and their relationship to European historical and contemporary musical practices have emerged. First, how does the context of music making frame the gender distribution of musical roles? How is gender-based music making related to the overall pattern of social, cultural, and economic gender differentiation, and how does such music making maintain or subvert underlying belief systems and validating social institutions? What is the relationship between class and gender, and how does this intersection divide musical roles between men and women? And, finally, how have recent changes in the political, economic, and social lives of Europeans changed the gender-based division of musical roles?

Three forms of gendered music making can be identified, and though each may have been initially associated with a given historical period in European history, all three persist to the present day. First, music making can be based on gender alone, possibly the oldest arrangement, where women and men are physically separated from each other while making music, essentially creating two separate, self-contained music cultures. Here, men and women perform different genres, but both engage in all musical activities primarily for same-gender audiences. Second, gendered music making can be based on musical activity, where men and women perform together in mixed groups, often for mixed audiences, but divide up the musical activities along gender lines, with women most often singing and dancing and men most often playing musical instruments. Third, music making can show a breakdown of gender divisions, usually found in prosperous times, such as the late twentieth century, with musical activities more or less shared by men and women. All three forms of gendered music making can, and often do, appear within the same community at the same time.

PERFORMING IN SINGLE-GENDER GROUPS

It is within the agrarian context that the first form of gendered music making, that which creates two separate and distinct social and expressive spheres for men and women, is most prominent. Before 1800, about 90 percent of the European population was dependent upon an agrarian economy, and even today much of Europe remains a rural culture, regulated by the passing of the seasons and the stages of life. This form of economy, passed down from feudal times, with its heavy reliance upon sheer strength and hard physical labor, often required many people to work the land. Families were traditionally large, with one man having as many as eight or ten living children and, because of a high mortality rate during childbirth, possibly two or three wives within his lifetime.

Men and women commonly worked the fields, tended livestock, and prepared small gardens for family use, but women alone were responsible for rearing children, doing many domestic chores, healing the sick, and often preparing bodies for burial. Men's responsibilities traditionally took the form of more overarching community duties, such as governing, recounting historical tales, and defending families, communities, and the ruling elite that owned the lands they farmed; however, while it may be tempting to see women's domains as private and men's as public, what is more likely is that men and women performed various musics publicly and privately, yet maintained forms of segregation, or separation from each other. For gendered music making, this gender-based division of labor, validated by centuries of religious, social, and political influence, created contexts that have perpetuated and validated these roles to the present day.

Women's music

In most European societies, women have had clearly defined responsibilities to sing for calendric and life-cycle rituals, including burial laments and wedding songs, as well as their own repertoire of ballads, courtship songs, healing and work songs, instrumental music, and dances.

Calendric and life-cycle rituals

The yearly seasonal calendar, overlaid through the centuries by Jewish, Muslim, and predominantly Christian festivals and holy days, and the individual calendar of one's life cycle, provided the richest contexts for gender-based music making. Traditional beliefs link the Christian calendar to the cycle of four seasons: the autumn harvest and wedding time, around Michaelmas (29 September); Michaelmas to Christmas, when foodstuffs are prepared for winter; Christmas to Easter, when indoor activities prevail; and Easter to September, the major planting and growing season, and the season for courting (Anderson and Zinsser 1988). Each season and occasion, such as a wedding or a death, has its corresponding musical genres, styles, and performing contexts, in which women and men, each occupied with different activities, create their own musical cultures (figure 1).

The most prominent gender divisions in calendrical music performance seem to be found in eastern and southern Europe, where women are largely responsible for songs celebrating the calendrical festivals. Separate repertoires exist for men and women, for example in Albania, where women exclusively perform an important genre of lyric song, to celebrate the harvest, usually accompanying themselves on large frame drums, and during the Christmas season, girls wander through villages singing carols. In Romania, the harvest ritual includes the *drăgaica,* performed by girls, and in Serbia, women perform lyric love songs and ballads to celebrate the harvest. Romanian Gypsy girls perform a summer rainmaking ceremonial genre, *paparuda,* in which peasants deck them with greenery and sprinkle them with water.

In Northern and Central Europe, throughout Finland, Sweden, Norway, and as far south as the Czech and Slovak republics, women and girls were traditionally responsible for herding cattle and maintaining summer pastures during the growing season, and certain musical genres developed in these contexts, including songs, interspersed with yodels, calls, shouts, and signals. In Sweden, women often accompanied themselves on bark horns, instruments usually played by men and boys elsewhere in Europe. Butter-making songs and songs for communication across mountain ranges—songs often characterized by heavy improvisation and ornamentation—were developed in these communities.

FIGURE 1   In Macedonia in May, women wearing and holding bouquets of green leaves sing ritual songs for St. George's Day. Photo by Jane Sugarman, 1981.

FIGURE 2   In Albania, Muslim women accompany their singing with frame drums and a violin. Early-twentieth-century postcard. Courtesy of the Robert Godfried Collection, New York.

Ballads

Ballads were commonly performed communally or alone by women throughout agrarian Europe, and indeed, some of the earliest collections of traditional music were based on the repertoires of female ballad singers in Scotland, England, Ukraine, Sweden, and Germany. Ballads were usually performed without accompaniment, and texts, such as those found in Portugal, Bosnia, Bulgaria, among the Rom in Albania, and Sephardic Jews in Spain, often focused on love, fulfilled and unrequited. Occasionally, women would accompany themselves on a small frame drum, especially among Muslim populations in rural Albania and other parts of southern Europe (figures 2 and 3). In Scotland and England, women were the chief carriers of the ballad tradition, and texts show a close relationship of ballads with domestic life. Some song texts from the Low Countries tell of women's feelings about "bitter relations with lovers, husbands, fathers, and their longings for lost sons and lovers" [see LOW COUNTRIES].

FIGURE 3   In northern Spain, women sing and play drum and tambourines. Porea-Llanes, Asturias, November 1952. Courtesy of the Alan Lomax Collection, New York.

Until the twentieth century, women were rarely known as instrumentalists, and in many parts of rural Europe, especially in cultures influenced by Muslim and Jewish beliefs, women played musical instruments only at all-female gatherings.

Burial laments

The burial lament, especially in northern and southern Europe, was, and remains traditionally, a female performing genre. Seen as having the primary responsibility for birth and death, women often became well known as professional and semiprofessional lamenters in Finland, Georgia, Greece, Italy, Albania, and Ireland, where they performed keening (*caoineadh na marbh*). In Corsica, lament formulas were often borrowed and adapted as lullabies, another exclusively woman's genre. In Romania and other parts of the Balkans and southern Europe, two genres of burial laments were common: *cîntece ceremoniale* 'ceremonial songs' performed by groups of professional women not related to the deceased, often using set pieces performed in a unison, antiphonal style, with melodies moving slowly in narrow ranges; and *bocete,* laments constructed from improvised narratives sung by female relations or friends. Begun at the moment of death and continuing until burial, this form of solo singing was often interspersed with stylized and real weeping [see ROMANIA].

Courtship and wedding songs

Courtship and weddings also provided contexts for women's music making. At harvesttime, for example, girls might sit and sing songs about their boyfriends or spurned lovers, and in spring in Spain and elsewhere, girls frequently sang to the Virgin Mary to initiate the courtship season. In most of Europe, but especially in Eastern Europe, weddings were one of the most important ritual contexts for making music. Often lasting six months or more, preparations for the wedding and the ceremony itself provided contexts for constant music.

One of the most important genres was, and continues to be, the wedding lament, often performed by the bride's relatives and friends. Much like the burial lament, these songs marked the passage from girlhood to adulthood and often contained texts filled with stories about women's hardships in married life. Other songs accompanied the braiding of the bride's hair and the ritual of the henna dye. In Ukraine, wedding music was perhaps a woman's most important ritual genre. Women vocalists had significant amounts of power in the villages, often gaining high social status if they performed the hundreds of ritual texts well [see UKRAINE]. Among Romanian Gypsies, as in Ukraine, the wedding, often a three- or four-day event, was the most important ritual context for female singers.

Healing and work songs

Women were also responsible, especially before modern times, for assisting in childbirth and healing, and many became adept shamans and ritual-healing specialists, especially in Northern Europe, Russia, Finland, and Iceland. In winter, when most work took place indoors, women were the organizers and main performers in working bees, where various songs associated with women's work, such as cooking, lulling, and dandling, developed. In Ukraine, for example, the working bee (*dosvitky*) brought unmarried girls ten and older together to sew, embroider, make hemp rope, and sing and dance for hours; and in Scotland, wool-shrinking (*waulking*) songs are still performed exclusively by women.

Dance and instrumental musics

Dancing was also an important aspect of ritual and everyday life for women in rural Europe, and many separate dance genres, such as the chain and round dance, developed with song genres within the contexts of work, courtship, and marriage. Generally, dancing highlighted differences between men's and women's socialized roles and became in effect displays of appropriate gender behavior. Throughout Europe, women's dance steps were smaller, more regularly metered, and less athletic than men's, with none of the leaping or virtuosic displays so common among men's dance genres. In Italy, the tarantella, a fast 6/8 dance, was performed exclusively by women as a therapy for psychological problems. A soloist, often dancing into a trance, would simulate the movements of a person bitten by the tarantula spider until her symptoms passed.

Until the twentieth century, women were rarely known as instrumentalists, and in many parts of rural Europe, especially in cultures influenced by Muslim and Jewish beliefs, women played musical instruments only at all-female gatherings. Where women did play instruments, these instruments became associated with them almost exclusively, and would not be played by men. For example, the Ossetians of Georgia still consider the accordion a woman's instrument, one that is given to her by her groom at her wedding and buried with her. In Italy, women traditionally played only the concertina and the harp; in Norway, only the *langeleik,* a slim, oblong plucked zither. Women were sometimes known as fiddlers in parts of Norway, and had the responsibility of teaching fiddling to their children through the use of sung mnemonics. In cultures influenced by Arabic or Turkish music (in countries such as Spain, Portugal, and Albania), women perform on frame drums with jingles; and in Serbia, on drums and castanets.

The increasing importance of Christianity in Europe during the Middle Ages (about 800 to 1450), provided women with new roles and contexts for musical composition and performance outside the traditional structure of marriage and family. The Roman Catholic church welcomed women into its religious institutions, and during the ninth to the thirteenth centuries, great abbeys arose throughout Europe, where women, like men, could devote themselves to prayer and study (Anderson and Zinsser 1988). Young women, largely from the rural and village surroundings, flocked to the cloistered life as an alternative to a life of hard and constant labor; within the church, however, women and men developed parallel spheres for social and religious activities, mirroring those of agrarian life.

The Roman Catholic Church also became the context for the development of Western art music. Composed and performed by men and women living within monasteries and convents of medieval Europe, this music eventually became the foundation of Western ritual, classical, and popular musics. During the Middle Ages, especially in Italy, Germany, and France, women were active as church musicians, performing necessary musical duties, including composing, singing, performing musical instruments to accompany singing, and, occasionally, dancing. For example, the most influential musician of her day, the abbess and mystic Hildegard von Bingen (1098–1179) of the convent of Rupertsburg, was a prolific composer, poet, and worldly politician.

Men's music

In many traditional cultures, men had a more limited musical role in ritual life than did women. They were, however, the main performers of instrumental dance music and of historical songs.

FIGURE 4   A Romanian Rom (Gypsy) violinist. In many parts of the Balkans, men often sing historical ballads and epics while accompanying themselves on traditional fiddles or violins. Photo by Wayne Kraft, 1995.

Historical songs

Most standard music scholarship has focused exclusively on men's music making, taking it for the norm in all European societies. Therefore it would be redundant here to restate the many important contributions that men have made to European music throughout history; however, certain widespread trends can be seen if we look at European men's musical activities in relation to those of women.

Men participate in many of the same forms of music making as women in agrarian life, sometimes even performing healing songs and burial laments (or in Italy, parodies of burial laments), but the most important men's genre within agrarian and village contexts is the epic, or historical narrative song. Historical songs, especially in Greece and throughout the Balkans, reflect the concerns and histories of European men as fighters and defenders of their families and communities, and of their work as providers. Such songs retell the stories of heroic exploits, clashes between Muslim and Christian warriors, and honor and shame (figure 4).

Historical songs were traditionally performed in small coffeehouses or taverns for an exclusively male audience. Even today in Muslim Albania, Greece, and Bosnia, men will gather, especially during Ramadan, to listen to epic performances recounting tales of medieval or present-day heroes. In Malta, a historical song genre, *ghana,* is performed in public exclusively by men. Women will perform it, but privately, and will teach their sons to sing it, transmitting traditions they are barred from performing [see MALTA]. In Albania, *virgjineshe,* women sworn not to marry, play male roles in life: biologically female but socially male, they dress as men, become heads of households, and sometimes perform songs in male narrative genres.

Historical songs are usually composed on fixed texts, using formulaic melodic and rhythmic patterns, and are performed by solo singers, who frequently accompany themselves on the *gusle,* the *tambura,* or related chordophones. Men use a predominantly flamboyant style, heavily accented and ornamented.

Instrumental and dance musics

Throughout Europe, men (rarely women) have traditionally performed musical instruments to accompany singing or dancing, or as part of instrumental ensembles. Many written accounts tell of men performing instruments at public celebrations, such as those associated with the seasonal cycles of planting and harvesting, and for summer herding, weddings, and working bees. Among herders in Denmark, Croatia, and Bulgaria, and among the Vlachs (as, for example, with the *rikalo,* a bark trumpet), the birch leaf and other aerophones are played exclusively by men, even today.

Men's dances, as public displays of gender, developed in Europe alongside men's vocal and instrumental genres. Characterized by bold leaps, virtuosic movements, and a certain militaristic style, many men's dances simulated actual disputes or warlike behavior. Sword dances became highly developed in Scotland, Ireland, and Spain, where the fiesta, a context for dance performance, substituted as a ritual replacement for feuds. During fiestas, highly competitive male performances of pole dances (*coplas*) involved mock combat [see SPAIN]. In Romania, the *călușari,* a group dance performed by men, displayed intricate, virtuoso steps that enhanced the dancers' status, and in Portugal, the fandango, a dance for two men, was essentially a choreographed duel.

PERFORMING IN MIXED GROUPS

With the development of a monarch-based economy and the rise of a merchant class, contexts for making music began to change significantly in Europe. From the thirteenth through the eighteenth centuries, as many people began to leave rural culture for the towns and cities, gender began to recede somewhat in importance, or perhaps to change in significance as a defining social category. In court life, with the development of court-based musical traditions, men's and women's musical roles began to change; and with the growth of the cities and the rise of a middle class that could support musical activities, the beginnings of professionalism in music provided new opportunities for male and female musicians.

The court and the city

As feudal times waned and much of Europe became divided among powerful monarchies, a ruling class that required entertainment in the form of poetry, music, and dance developed. Noblemen and male serfs who worked the land would customarily farm for a few months and then depart for war, leaving their wives and daughters to control their holdings. Thus, medieval Europe was a time of relative power and autonomy for women, many of whom owned land, raised armies, and occasionally fought alongside their male counterparts. In Northern and Western Europe, especially in France, women might even have assumed power, as did Eleanor of Aquitaine, who in 1132 became the ruler of an enormous and powerful duchy.

Around 1100, especially in Northern and Western Europe, male and occasionally female musicians began to take up secular musical performance as a way of life. Two classes of musician-composers developed: the traveling musician (troubadour) and the musician attached more or less permanently to a court (courtier). A few of these musicians were women, known in France as *jongleresses,* who traveled throughout the countryside performing for harvest gatherings and the aristocratic elite's amusement. Courtesans, female musicians who attached themselves to the great courts of Europe, became well known, especially as singers and dancers. The first courtesans were probably Jewish and Arabic slaves and harem women brought to Spain and France during the Moorish occupation of Spain.

At court, as in the agrarian and church contexts of the same period, women were predominantly singers; men, instrumentalists. Three things had changed, though, reflecting new ideas about men's and women's roles and responsibilities to each other and their communities: the introduction of mixed-gender performing ensembles; mixed-gender audiences; and the essential nature of musicians, seen now as more or less professionals.

The court, alongside the church, was the primary context for the development of classical music. In addition to the works of secular vocal and instrumental musics by male composers, notably Monteverdi, Bach, and Haydn, women, such as the renowned singers at the sixteenth-century court of Ferrara in northern Italy, and composers and singers, such as Francesca Caccini (1587–ca. 1640), Barbara Strozzi (1619–ca. 1644), and Elizabeth Claude Jacquet de la Guerre (ca. 1666–1729), and many others, contributed to the rise of secular musics in the sixteenth, seventeenth, and eighteenth centuries. Even outside the major art-musical centers of eighteenth-century Europe—in Russia, for example—most courts employed a Rom (Gypsy) chorus, comprised of female singers and male instrumentalists. Among the eighteenth-century Hungarian Gypsies, Panna Czinka became the first professional female violinist, under the patronage of a wealthy landowner, who gave her a house, land, and a red uniform every three years [see ROM (GYPSY) MUSIC].

As cities developed and prospered, European society saw the rise of a merchant middle class and the development of professional guild musicians and new musical genres created especially for this class, such as the opera, where women excelled as singers, and various domestic musics, such as keyboard works and accompanied songs. Materials for keyboard, vocal, and symphonic works were often borrowed and adapted from the older traditional peasant, or Turkish-derived musics, and newly set for new contexts, such as the parlor and the salon, where women were leading per-

Sweeping social and political changes occurred in the late twentieth century, but ingrained gender and music ideologies that link men with solo, public, instrumental, and modern performance, and women with domestic, singer-dancer or choral performance, and older musical forms, persist.

formers (usually until they married) and patrons (after marriage). In much of Northern and Western Europe, women often played the lute, and later the clavichord, harpsichord, piano, and cittern as an accompaniment to singing. Some women, such as the eighteenth-century Scottish ballad composer Mrs. Anna Brown and the nineteenth-century pianist and composer Clara Schumann (1819–1896) and Swedish fiddler Elisabeth Olofsdotter, became well-known professionals.

MODERN CONTEXTS

The twentieth century saw a partial breakdown of older gender roles and gender-based musical activity. With a change from a largely agrarian to a capitalist economy, the growth of major European cities, and relative prosperity, women and men began to take on more equal musical roles. Older gender ideologies persist, but more opportunities than ever before enable men and women to share musical activities of all kinds.

Three forms of gender rearrangement have taken place within twentieth-century European musical culture. First, musical roles have been redistributed, with women now participating in some formerly all-male performance contexts, and vice versa. Second, gender-based professionalism finds women and men participating in all kinds of musical activities, but men taking on a professional, or semiprofessional role more often, as in classical music ensembles and at public ceremonies like weddings. Third, women and men participate more or less equally in all types of musical activity, but perform using appropriate gender-based singing, dancing, or playing style, with women generally performing in a more relaxed, less flamboyant style than men.

The redistribution of musical roles is the most common form of change in modern times. Among Gypsies in Romania, female violinists were beginning to become known in Bucharest in the early 1920s and today are common as instrumentalists in urban musical settings. In Georgia and the Northern Caucasus men now play the accordion, traditionally considered a woman's instrument, and women have begun to sing in men's choirs. In Wales, women have begun to form all-female choirs and now predominate as harpists, while in Bulgaria, men and women now sing laments. Even within the traditionally male-dominated art-music culture, women have begun to make their mark as composers, performers, and teachers.

From the 1960s on, especially in England and Scotland, women such as Jeannie Robertson, Jane Turriff, and Lizzie Higgins became prominent professional ballad singers and revivalists. In Finland, women's folk and popular ensembles now play folk-rock and arrangements of folk materials in urban, professional contexts, and in Germany, women can now be found playing in the formerly all-male Turkish janissary bands, if not quite yet in the Berlin Philharmonic. Even Turkish-derived musical cultures, still structured along strict gender lines, have become more integrated. In Macedonia, Rom (Gypsy) *čalgija* ensembles, performing vocal and instrumental music based on *makam*, now regularly employ male and female professionals; and the

FIGURE 5   For tourists in a restaurant in Prague, Czech Republic, a young woman plays the bagpipe, traditionally an instrument played only by men. This new possibility for women marks a rearrangement of traditional patterns of gendered music making in Europe. Photo by Phyllis Berggreen, 1998.

čoček, a Turkish-derived solo dance, traditionally performed by and for women in private settings, is now often danced in public for mixed audiences.

One impetus for a breakdown of gender segregation in musical activity was the origin of the state-supported choral and instrumental ensembles found most predominantly in the Balkans and Eastern Europe during the second half of the twentieth century. Throughout the Balkans, for example, notions of modernization, professionalism, and Westernization led to a mixing of men and women's ensembles and performances of private women's songs for public audiences. The Bulgarian National Ensemble of Folk Songs and Dances, under the direction of Filip Kutev, and other state-supported folk and popular music ensembles, have frequently performed throughout Europe and the United States since the 1950s. Though women predominated as singers in state-supported ensembles, men usually acted as conductors and instrumentalists. In Russia, the *bylina,* once an all-male epic genre, is now occasionally performed by a woman, and in Ukraine, the all-male tradition of playing the *trembitary,* a long, cylindrical wooden trumpet, is being passed to women. Even the bagpipe, with its phallic symbolism and traditional association with male herders and the military, is being played occasionally by women in Brittany, Bulgaria, the Czech Republic, and Scotland (figure 5); however, certain instruments, including the *zurla* and the *tapan,* are still played exclusively by adult men.

BROAD PATTERNS OF GENDERED MUSIC MAKING

Some broad patterns of gendered music making today can be discerned if we examine Europe as a unified musical culture. Sweeping social and political changes occurred in the late twentieth century, but ingrained gender and music ideologies that link men with solo, public, instrumental, and modern performance, and women with domestic, singer-dancer or choral performance, and older musical forms, persist. This pattern seems especially true of ritual music making, where gender segregation is still the norm, and of classical music activities, where men still predominate. Newer forms, however, such as popular, jazz, and national musics, are breaking down these gender barriers, for women and men, as late-twentieth-century Europe underwent rapid change.

BIBLIOGRAPHY

Alexiou, Margaret. 1974. *The Ritual Lament in Greek Tradition.* Cambridge: Cambridge University Press.

Anderson, Bonnie S., and Judith P. Zinsser. 1988. *A History of Their Own: Women in Europe from Prehistory to the Present.* 2 vols. New York: Harper & Row.

Auerbach, Susan. 1987. "From Singing to Lamenting: Women's Musical Role in a Greek Village." In *Women and Music in Cross-Cultural Perspective,* ed. Ellen Koskoff, 25–44. Westport, Conn.: Greenwood Press.

Bartók, Béla, and Albert B. Lord. 1961. *Serbo-Croatian Folk Songs.* New York: Columbia University Press.

———. 1978. *Yugoslav Folk Music.* Edited by Benjamin Suchoff. Albany: State University of New York Press.

Baud-Bovy, Samuel. 1983. *Essai sur la chanson populaire Grècque.* Nafplion: Foundation Ethnographique du Péloponnèse.

Bohlmann, Philip V., and Katherine Bergeron, eds. 1992. *Disciplining Music: Musicology and Its Canons.* Chicago: University of Chicago Press.

Bowers, Jane, and Judith Tick, eds. 1986. *Women Making Music: The Western Art Tradition, 1150–1950.* Urbana: University of Illinois Press.

Bridenthal, Renate, Claudia Koontz, and Susan Stuard, eds. 1987. *Becoming Visible: Women in European History.* 2d ed. Boston: Houghton Mifflin.

Briscoe, James. 1987. *Historical Anthology of Music by Women.* Bloomington: Indiana University Press.

Caraveli-Chaves, Anna. 1980. "Bridge between Worlds: The Greek Women's Lament as Communicative Event." *Journal of American Folklore* 93(368):129–157.

Citron, Marcia J. 1993. *Gender and the Musical Canon.* Cambridge: Cambridge University Press.

Clement, Catherine. 1988. *Opera, or the Undoing of Women.* Translated by Betsy Wing. Minneapolis: University of Minnesota Press.

College Music Society. 1988. *Women's Studies/Women's Status.* Report 5. Boulder, Colo.: College Music Society.

Cook, Susan C., and Judy S. Tsou, eds. 1994. *Cecilia Reclaimed: Feminist Perspectives on Gender and Music.* Urbana: University of Illinois Press.

Czekanowska, Anna. 1990. "Towards a Concert of Slavonic Women's Repertoire." In *Music, Gender, and Culture,* ed. Marcia Herndon and Susanne Ziegler, 57–70. Wilhelmshaven: Florian Noetzel.

Derrida, Jacques. 1976. *Of Grammatology.* Gayatri Chakravorty, trans. Baltimore: Johns Hopkins University Press.

Drinker, Sophie. 1948. *Music and Women: the Story of Women in Their Relation to Music.* New York: Coward-McCann.

Foucault, Michel. 1978. *A History of Sexuality.* Translated by Robert Hurly. New York: Pantheon Books.

Garfias, Robert. 1981. "Survivals of Turkish Characteristics in Romanian Musica Lautareasca." *Yearbook for Traditional Music* 13:97–107.

Hajdú, Peter. 1978. "The Nenets Shaman Song and Its Text." In *Shamanism in Siberia,* ed. Peter Hajdú, 355–372. Budapest: Académiai Kiadó.

Herndon, Marcia, and Susanne Ziegler, eds. 1990. *Music, Gender, and Culture.* Wilhelmshaven: Florian Noetzel.

———. 1991. *Women in Music and Music Research.* Special issue. *The World of Music: Journal of the International Institute for Traditional Music* 33.

Hixon, Donald L. 1975. *Women in Music: A Bio-Bibliography.* Metuchen, N.J.: Scarecrow Press.

Hoch-Smith, Judith, and Anita Spring, eds. 1978. *Women in Ritual and Symbolic Roles.* New York: Plenum Press.

Johnson, Anna. 1990. "The Sprite in the Water and the Siren of the Woods: On Swedish Folk Music and Gender." In *Music, Gender, and Culture,* ed. Marcia Herndon and Susanne Ziegler, 27–40. Wilhelmshaven: Florian Noetzel.

Koskoff, Ellen, ed. 1989. *Women and Music in Cross-Cultural Perspective.* 2nd ed. Urbana: University of Illinois Press.

Kramer, Lawrence, ed. 1990. *Music as Cultural Practice.* Berkeley: University of California Press.

Laade, Wolfgang. 1962. *Die Struktur der Korsischen Lanto-Melodik.* Strasbourg: P. H. Heitz.

Leonardo, Micaela di, ed. 1991. *Gender at the Crossroads of Knowledge: Feminist Anthropology in the Postmodern Era.* Berkeley: University of California Press.

Le Page, Jane Weiner. 1980. *Women Composers, Conductors, and Musicians of the Twentieth Century.* 3 vols. Metuchen, N.J.: Scarecrow Press.

Lloyd, A. L. 1967. *Folk Song in England.* New York: International Publishers.

Lord, Albert Bates. 1960. *The Singer of Tales.* Cambridge: Harvard University Press.

———. 1991. *Epic Singers and Oral Tradition.* Ithaca: Cornell University Press.

McClary, Susan. 1991. *Feminine Endings: Music, Gender, and Sexuality.* Minneapolis: University of Minnesota Press.

Macormack, Carol, and Marilyn Strathern, eds. 1986. *Nature, Culture, and Gender.* Cambridge: Cambridge University Press.

Marshall, Kimberly, ed. 1993. *Rediscovering the Muses: Women's Musical Traditions.* Boston: Northeastern University Press.

Masson, Georgina. 1975. *Courtesans of the Italian Renaissance.* London: Secker & Warburg.

Neuls-Bates, Carol, ed. 1982. *Women in Music: An Anthology of Source Readings from the Middle Ages to the Present.* New York: Harper and Row.

Parry, Milman, and Albert Bates Lord. 1954. *Serbocroatian Heroic Songs.* Cambridge: Harvard University Press.

Pendle, Karin, ed. 1991. *Women and Music: A History.* Bloomington: Indiana University Press.

Petrović, Ankica. 1977. "*Ganga:* A Form of Traditional Rural Singing in Yugoslavia." Ph.D. dissertation, Queen's University of Belfast.

Porter, James, and Hershel Gower. 1995. *Jeannie Robertson: Emergent Singer, Transformative Voice.* Knoxville: University of Tennessee Press.

Reich, Nancy. 1985. *Clara Schumann: The Artist and the Woman.* Ithaca: Cornell University Press.

Reiter, Rayna Rapp, ed. 1975. *Toward an Anthropology of Women.* New York: Monthly Review Press.

Rice, Timothy. 1980. "A Macedonian *Sobor:* Anatomy of a Celebration." *Journal of American Folklore* 93:113–128.

———. 1994. *May It Fill Your Soul: Experiencing Bulgarian Music.* Chicago: University of Chicago Press.

Rieger, Eva. 1981. *Frau, Musik und Männerherrschaft.* Frankfurt: Verlag Ulstein.

Rosaldo, Michelle, and Louise Lamphere, eds. 1974. *Women, Culture, and Society.* Stanford: Stanford University Press.

Rouget, Gilbert. 1985. *Music and Trance: A Theory of the Relations Between Music and Possession.* Translated by Brunhilde Biebuyck. Chicago: University of Chicago Press.

Sarkissian, Margaret. 1992. "Gender and Music." In *Ethnomusicology: An Introduction,* ed. Helen Myers, 337–348. New York: Norton.

Sárosi, Bálint. 1978. *Gypsy Music.* Translated by Fred Macnicol. Budapest: Corvina Press.

Senelick, Laurence, ed. 1992. *Gender in Performance: The Presentation of Difference in the Performing Arts.* Hanover and London: University Press of New England.

Seremetakis, C. Nadia. 1991. *The Last Word: Women, Death, and Divination in Inner Mani.* Chicago: University of Chicago Press.

Sharp, Cecil. 1965. *English Folk Song: Some Conclusions.* 4th ed. London: Heinemann.

Shepherd, John. 1987. "Music and Male Hegemony." In *Music and Society: The Politics of Composition, Performance, and Reception,* ed. Richard Leppert and Susan McClary, 151–172. Cambridge: Cambridge University Press.

Solie, Ruth A., ed. 1993. *Musicology and Difference: Gender and Sexuality in Music Scholarship.* Berkeley: University of California Press.

Sugarman, Jane. 1997. *Engendering Song: Singing and Subjectivity at Prespa Albanian Weddings.* Chicago: University of Chicago Press.

Tolbert, Elizabeth. 1990. "Magico-Religious Power and Gender in the Karelian Lament." In *Music, Gender, and Culture,* ed. Marcia Herndon and Susanne Ziegler, 41–56. Wilhelmshaven: Florian Noetzel.

Wood, Elizabeth. 1980. "Women in Music." *Signs: Journal of Women in Culture and Society* 6(2):283–297.

Zaimont, Judith Lang, et al., eds. 1983. *The Musical Woman: An International Perspective.* Westport: Greenwood Press.

Popular Music in Europe
Marcello Sorce Keller

Local Popular-Music Traditions
Patterns of Contact
Popular-Music Scholarship
Pan-European Trends

For many conservatory-trained musicians and musicologists, two kinds of music exist: *classical music,* produced by geniuses, eccentric and isolated personalities, frequently misunderstood by their contemporaries; and *folk music,* mysteriously produced by illiterate people in areas protected from urban civilization. Missing from this picture is the largest amount of music that most people across the world listen to: a kaleidoscopic cluster of genres and styles, produced and disseminated by the mass media. Only in the 1980s did a few researchers (including Birrer 1985; Cutler 1985; and Middleton 1981) begin defining the concept.

The term *popular music* to describe this mass-mediated music is often borrowed by languages other than English to cover Anglo-American imports and locally produced music modeled on them. Most European languages have developed native terms to designate locally produced songs in vernacular styles*: musica leggera* in Italy, *chanson* in France, *schlager* in Germany*, zabavna muzika* in the former Yugoslavia, *iskelmä* in Finland, and so on. Popular music includes all the truly international styles or repertoires recognized under the general labels of bluegrass, country, disco, jazz, funk, new wave, rock (with its subcategories from rockabilly to punk, from death metal to jazz-rock fusion), and so on; all international styles still carrying an ethnic-geographic identification of origin such as Jamaican reggae; and local genres such as *rebetik*a and bouzouki music in Greece, *arabesk* in Turkey, *fado* in Portugal, flamenco-style rumba, *nueva canción andaluza* and *rumba catalán* in Spain, and Neapolitan rock in Italy.

Popular music is predominantly vocal, with instrumental accompaniment. This emphasis contrasts with the Western art-music ideal of absolute music, in which purely instrumental compositions are the most prestigious. Equally important in popular music is that the singer, rather than the composer, enjoys higher status. In art music, however famous the virtuoso performer, the public always feels the need to know the composer's name, but in popular music, awareness of the composer is secondary, and for a good reason: the popular composer never produces such an accurately notated original as to suggest that the performer should feel bound to a literal or faithful performance of the original. The performer or performers always adapt the song to the circumstances, to the musical means available, and try to give a distinctively personal rendition of it. The performer may be the author of the song, but more often the author is actually more than one person. A song is often composed by two or three people plus a lyricist, with the intervention of an arranger and a sound engineer: in popular music, the compositional process has stages that continue to accumulate as long as a given song remains in circulation.

Early examples of popular-music compositions in the nineteenth century include the success of Viennese lighter music by Joseph Lanner (1801–1843) and Johann Strauss senior (1804–1849) and Parisian lighter music by Jacques Offenbach (1819–1880). A more dramatic turning point occurred when European drawing-room music encountered the music of American blacks. This is not to minimize the popularity of nineteenth-century opera in Europe and the United States, and of songs that in harmony and melodic profile betray operatic influences, albeit adapted for nonprofessional singers, as in America, songs by Henry Russell (1812–1901), John Hill Hewitt (1801–1890), and Stephen Collins Foster (1826–1864), and in Italy and England, *romanze* by Francesco Paolo Tosti (1846–1916).

LOCAL POPULAR-MUSIC TRADITIONS

Pop music is far from being an international product echoing Anglo-American models. Though the mass media generate a sameness wherever they reach, radio stations serving local audiences standardize style only in a limited sense. A layer of imported Anglo-American popular music may be found almost everywhere, but its share of airtime varies widely. It dominates most in countries, such as Norway, that until the 1960s did not have a native popular-music tradition, but whose radio stations replayed international hits sung in local translations. Its pervasiveness does not interfere with the development of local repertoires. It may help local styles retain essential meanings, and even favor their development, as if it offered a reference point by which their otherness could be gauged. In Europe, most European-made popular musics circulate primarily within the borders of their countries of origin, or even in smaller confines. In Italy and France, much local popular music still seems linked with the national art-music traditions, but in the popular music of Hungary and Poland, one senses the connection with the orally transmitted music of the land.

Even a cursory sample of radiobroadcasting reveals the variety of genres targeted to the same audience: a cluster of repertoires revealing an approximation of the average musical taste across a given nation. The emerging picture shows the influence that some local repertoires exert on each other, which repertoires are shared by different regions as a common property to be recontextualized according to local needs, which repertoires coexist in the same region, and which local products travel, and how much.

A bird's-eye view of European pop music shows one point clearly: effective as the mass media may be in triggering all sorts of change, numerous genres exist—and newer ones are being born almost every year—that show apparent vernacular traits. That has been true of *fado* styles in Portugal and, in Spain, of flamenco-style rumba, the *nueva canción andaluza,* the *rumbita catalán,* and other genres. What is fascinating about these repertoires is that they are at once contemporary, hybridized, and uniquely local (Ordovás 1986).

Rebetika and other national and vernacular genres

Some European popular repertoires are more localized than others. Especially in southern Europe, Western music merges with non-Western vernacular styles (Manuel 1988). The repertoires resulting from this synthesis remain local because it is often only one culture or subculture that finds the result fully satisfactory, though people of different origins may find in them something to their liking. In time, a minority style

FIGURE 1   Playing in Toronto, Canada, a Greek nightclub band combines elements of urban popular music (*rebetika*) with regional folk music [see GREECE]. The Greek émigré population considers this kind of music a symbol of national and sometimes regional identity. *Left to right:* Tassos Marinos (bouzouki), Yannis Antos (singer and keyboardist), Leigh Cline (electric guitar), Nikos Kaltsas (clarinet). Except for Cline, a Canadian, the musicians live and work in Greece, but travel abroad occasionally to perform for emigrant communities. Photo by Bev Cline, 1978.

of that sort may become more widely accepted and recognized as an identity symbol by a larger group, even a nation.

Hybrid repertoires—as for genres as diverse as *rebetika* in Greece and the forms of *volksmusik* in Swiss or Italian dialects—cater to audiences often considerably smaller than a nation. An Anglo-American strain is frequently one element of even the most local mix, for example, in the music of *schwyzerörgeli quartetten* 'Swiss button-accordion quartets'.

The case of *rebetika*, perhaps the most distinctive popular genre of Greece, is telling. It is an urban popular music that arose, mainly in Athens and Piraeus, during the first decades of the twentieth century. Its uniqueness derives from specific sources nourishing it: Greek folk music (*dhimotika*) and Gypsy music, then Near Eastern and Turkish influences, especially evident in the use of improvised sections resembling the *taksim* of Turkish music, and additive meters. Some early recordings of *rebetika* are almost completely modal, with extensive improvised passages. More recently, *rebetika* have incorporated Western harmonies, major and minor scales, and added to the traditional bouzouki an electric bass, a piano, a Western drum set, and other non-Greek instruments. Even so, no one could question the Greek connotations of the genre, least of all the Central European uninitiated listener, who would instantly recognize its exoticism. Though in Greece the degree of acceptability of *rebetika* varies from one social milieu to another, most Greeks consider this music a symbol of national identity, especially when they are away from their homeland (figure 1).

PATTERNS OF CONTACT

Minorities unrepresented in traditional songs of their nation or imported Western styles often develop new vernacular genres (Manuel 1988). Hybrid genres also grow in subcultures that, possibly because of their marginality, identify less strongly with the core values of their society and are more likely to accept influences that in other circles would subvert social or regional identity

Local repertoires

A repertoire resulting from musical hybridization does not pave the way for the appreciation of source repertoires, nor does it have a better chance of enjoying wide appeal. When people create a style by borrowing and mixing diverse elements, outsiders to their group may dislike their music precisely because they recognize something familiar in it, that is, because the new genre seems a grotesque imitation of music they loved. The more composite a repertoire is, the more it can be perceived as local, distinct, and typically theirs by those who are primarily exposed to it, though outsiders may easily notice linkages with other repertoires.

One such repertoire is that of Italian *liscio,* songs accompanied almost exclusively with tonic and dominant chords, made especially for rural dance, popular across the plains of northern Italy (the so-called *bassa padana* of Emilia Romagna). A genre living within confined geographical and social boundaries, it parallels American country music and the *volksmusik* and *volkstümliche lieder* heard across Switzerland, Bavaria, and Austria.

In localized vernacular repertoires, cultural barriers can be permeable. The Sud Sound System, an Italian pop group from southern Italy, meshes Jamaican ragamuffin and the local tradition of the *tarantolati* of the Salento area, the musical ritual once employed as a therapy for people bitten by the *taranta* spider. The group's texts are in the local vernacular. Probably for that reason, its music enjoys local circulation. But singing that vernacular restricts their popularity to that area, since the words are hardly comprehensible to nonlocal listeners. Musically, the use of the style typical of the therapeutic rituals of Salento is just as localized, but the group's instrumentation and arrangements usually rely on mainstream Italian popular music. With clichés derived from Jamaican popular styles, language and folk-musical elements cater to local taste and people's desire to hear "their own" music. At the same time, identification with Italy at large remains possible, and the presence of exotic elements gives a feeling of modernity and innovation where the sense of insularity—of isolation from the main centers of the nation—is strong. The music of the Sud Sound System characterizes not the area at large, but the younger audience of one small area; it is an intersection of musical elements that makes sense of components that could not coexist anywhere else.

Though mass media are believed to be most effective in promoting total uniformity, some cultural barriers remain effective. Cultures still succeed in excluding each other, even when modern communications could easily allow much more integration. For example, no one seems to be doing much listening to foreign radio stations, though such listening has never been forbidden, at least in Western Europe. Any objection that foreign songs are sung to a foreign language does not hold. After all, teenagers worldwide listen to English-language songs. One may wonder why they are unwilling to listen to music sung in yet other languages, even when such music stylistically resembles the music they habitually like. Clearly the products of some cultures are acceptable in new contexts, and others are not. Mere accessibility is not the issue.

Western Europe

In each European country (in fact, any country), the musical landscape spans a continuum including local, folk-music-related styles (*rebetika* in Greece and Neapolitan rock in Italy are good examples), foreign music locally produced by immigrant communities (like *bhangra,* an electrified version of Punjabi folk music popular among Punjabi immigrants in Britain), locally produced rock and pop in the mainstream Western idiom (for instance the Swedish, but English-singing, rock group ABBA during the 1970s, or nowadays the equally English-singing but Italian female singer Spagna), and outright musical imports (Michael Jackson, Madonna, and others). But what is more interesting is the presence or absence of musical interchange. It is intriguing to observe, not only the types of popular music one can hear in a given country, but also the types one does *not* get to hear.

One might assume that a song making the charts in France might easily cross

Italians are exposed almost solely to mainstream Anglo-American pop and Italian vernacular genres. Italy seems to have erected impenetrable barriers excluding the popular music of all other countries.

borders into Spain and Italy. But few songs become popular all across southern Europe, or even across the Romance-language area (from Portugal to Spain, France, Italy, and eventually Romania), where similar languages are spoken. Few Italian songs travel to Spain and Portugal. Even fewer travel in the reverse direction. Exceptionally, some French songs are translated and forcefully marketed abroad. At any rate, any Italian teenager would be hard put to mention offhand the title of a Spanish or French song making the charts currently in its country of origin.

Italians are exposed almost solely to mainstream international pop (read: Anglo-American) and Italian vernacular genres. Little comes from France, Spain, and Portugal, but nothing comes from Yugoslavia, Greece, Turkey, and the Middle East, except perhaps in the 1990s in Sicily. Italy is extreme in this respect: it seems to have erected impenetrable barriers excluding the popular music of all other countries (European or not), with the sole exception of Anglo-American imports, and a narrow sample of American musics at that. One may well hear an Italian song broadcast from Radio Zagreb, but one almost never hears a Croatian or a Greek song on Italian radio. Such renowned performers as Sheller in France, Nena Venetsanou and Manos Hadjidakis in Greece, and Rex Gildo and Manuela in Germany have never found any audience in Italy. Rock star Herbert Grönemeyer can easily gather ten thousand of his fans in Germany but could walk the streets of Madrid or Rome without being noticed. Considering that Spanish and Italian are closely related, it is remarkable that musicians such as Tijeritas, Queco, Serrat, and Paco Ibáñez are effectively stopped at the border.

The case of France parallels that of Italy. Though the French people receive some music from Muslim Africa, that music seems mainly targeted toward Muslim immigrant communities. Pop music from sub-Saharan Africa has a wider appeal. That is surprising, since the French have a national song tradition which, from Juliette Greco to Sheller, is so monochromatically Western that it constantly recycles old-fashioned harmonies of the eighteenth century. Nevertheless, something so quintessentially Western coexists with musics from faraway non-Western countries. Through colonialism, the French have gotten used to exotic sounds.

Spain enjoys a horizon enriched by the music it receives from Latin America. Also, some of its flamenco repertories circulate across the African Maghreb.

Each country in Europe has its peculiarities. The close cultural links among francophone Belgium, francophone Switzerland, and France favor more intense musical exchanges across this language area. Similar is the case of Holland and Flemish-speaking Belgium. Particularly significant is also the interchange between Iceland, Norway, Sweden, and to a degree Finland. However, exchanges *among* these supranational areas remain minimal. The opposite phenomenon is the exchange of singers whom one might term export products. For example, during the 1960s in Central Europe and Northern Europe, singers Vico Torriani and Robertino—perceived to be typically Italian—enjoyed considerable success in German-speaking lands and Scandinavia but remained unknown in Italy. Similar is the case of the American rock singer Rocky Roberts, whose popularity around 1970 was confined to Italy.

Eastern Europe

A different picture comes from the countries of Eastern Europe after the fall of the communist regimes. The Iron Curtain kept Western popular music from being openly commercialized. Except in the former Yugoslavia, where the barrier was relatively permeable (more in Slovenia and Croatia than in Serbia or Macedonia), the population could hear Western music only in roundabout ways. In the formerly socialist countries, the profession of popular musician was a "state job," just like that of classical musician. Training was institutionalized, and the level of musical literacy among popular musicians was quite high. A form of popular music absent in Western Europe, institutionalized folk music, at various levels involved many people. Though some forms of influence coming from Western musical styles arrived through underground channels (even secret jazz groups existed), one cannot talk of direct or pervasive forms of contact. The situation has dramatically changed. The collapse of cultural censorship and commercial barriers has allowed Western popular music to flood the ex-communist countries.

Pan-European pop

A thin layer of pan-European pop, songs produced in one European country and circulated in others, nonetheless exists. This is a limited phenomenon, intriguing because it is hard to figure out why some products enjoy some international circulation and apparently similar products do not. Typical examples are Italian artists such as Zucchero, Gianna Nannini, and Paolo Conte. Their popularity in parts of Western Europe can be accounted for, in part, by aggressive marketing. It may also be a sign that the European public is willing to listen to music sung in a foreign language other than English. Until 1970, the only method of marketing popular songs abroad was to issue recordings with lyrics translated into the language of the target area. This practice persists; instances of international, multilingual stars are the Italian Milva and the German Ute Lemper.

Some linguistic areas (including the German- and French-speaking areas) cross national boundaries, and in some European nations (including Switzerland, Belgium, Spain, and Finland) more than one language is spoken. English is commonly a second language in Holland, Norway, and Sweden. Of these countries, Switzerland is perhaps the most singular case: its German-speaking radio station (DRS 1) broadcasts massive doses of popularized *volksmusik,* with a remarkable variety of German, Italian, and French popular songs, understandably since those are the three major languages of the Swiss Confederation. Virtually absent is popular music in any other European language. Italophone and francophone radio stations broadcast almost solely music sung in the language of their areas.

In Europe as elsewhere, a repertoire of old and old-fashioned songs that still maintain an appeal and circulate in new arrangements, preferably instrumental, continue to exist. This repertoire, called evergreens in Europe, is heterogeneous. It includes songs performed by the Beatles and Frank Sinatra and European songs that over the years have reached an international audience, such as "*Volare*" by Modugno, "*Quando quando*" by Tony Renis, a few bestsellers by Edith Piaf, Yves Montand, Charles Aznavour, songs made popular by the sound tracks of famous movies, and others. In America such evergreens are the basis for easy-listening arrangements, broadcast by specialized radio stations, but in Europe such stations do not exist. Instrumental arrangements of evergreens make only occasional appearances on the airwaves, a little more, perhaps, in the United Kingdom and the German-speaking countries (the bands of Hazy Osterwald, Helmuth Zacharias and James Last are a part of the memories of any German who is now middle-aged) than in the Latin countries, which prefer vocal music more. Intertwined with the evergreen phenomenon is that of the revival of songs of decades past. Quite often such revivals produce additions to the evergreens, songs that had not entered the circle of the "everlasting" during their first life cycle, but do so once they are revamped.

Another phenomenon is that of Henryk Mikolai Górecki, a Polish art-music composer, whose Third Symphony became a hit among fans of R.E.M., U2, and other popular bands. In less than a year (1992–1993) Górecki went from obscurity to international fame. The Nonesuch release of his Third Symphony sold more than two hundred thousand copies worldwide; two thirds of those sales were in the United Kingdom, where the piece became a pop-culture phenomenon. Nourished by intensive airplay on Britain's new Classic FM radio network, it achieved unparalleled success, topping the classical charts (the first time a work by a living composer has done so) and reaching sixth on the pop charts, ahead of new records by Madonna, Annie Lennox, and Cher. Portentous as this event was, it is much too early to infer whether it might be a signal that the divide between popular and serious music may some day be bridged.

World music

World music is a recent and intriguing phenomenon. The more correct term would probably be *world pop music*; some call it worldbeat. It is East-West-North-South fusion music, essentially non-European-influenced jazz or pop. Prominent influences on it come from Africa, a source of basic elements of blues, jazz, and pop.

American culture was crucial in starting musical hybridizations on a grand scale leading to what is known today as world music (the African-American tradition living side by side with the Latin American), but Europe is playing a significant role. If the larger American cities are becoming more multicultural, European cities are catching up with considerable speed as the nations of Europe begin to receive waves of immigration from Africa and the ex-socialist countries of Eastern Europe. Paris, Frankfurt, Amsterdam, and Rome already offer most of the world musics. Cities such as Frankfurt and Paris have become centers of production for non-Western music conceived to be circulated not only among the immigrant population, but also in the country of origin. Some Turkish music produced in Frankfurt is later commercialized in Turkey, and *rai* music by Cheb Khaled, who lives in Paris, is smuggled into Algeria. In such fertile multicultural territories, mixed bands, made up of European and non-European musicians, are growing in number. They are creating an audience keen on East-West-North-South fusion music, an audience willing to listen to virtually anything from the Oriental Pop of Ofra Haza to the klezmer Yiddish music of Mony Ovadia to the Turkish rock of the German group Dissidenten (figure 2).

POPULAR-MUSIC SCHOLARSHIP

Most contributions to the study of European-American popular music have appeared in English or German (Brackett 1995; Frith 1981; Middleton 1990; Taylor 1985). A few scholarly journals, such as *American Music* and *Popular Music and Society,* focus on this music, while others, such as the German music-education journal *Musik und Bildung,* occasionally publish articles on the topic. These contributions tend to be historical or analytical.

A wider literature on the topic than in musicological journals appears in monographs marketed mostly to nonmusicological audiences. Much of this literature is devoted to texts, biographies of singers (less frequently composers and arrangers), and

FIGURE 2   Members of the Swedish fusion group Yeni Sesler (New Sounds) pose for a publicity photo during a studio recording. Photo by Tayfun Tuncelli, early 1990s. Courtesy of Owe Ronström.

the social relevance of particular repertoires, groups, or styles (literarily defined) and their political connotations and sociological import. Rather large is the literature on the popular-music business. Many discographies are available.

Music-industry periodicals and fan-oriented magazines may not be scholarly, but are often quite informative. The oldest one is *Billboard,* founded in the United States in 1894. Its best-selling record charts, introduced in an elementary form in the 1940s, have proved especially useful and valuable indicators of popular music trends. Others include *Rolling Stone* (rock), *Rhythm Music* (worldbeat), and *Down Beat* (jazz) in the United States; *New Musical Express* and *Record Retailer and Music Industry News* in England; *Musikmarkt* in Germany; and *Musica e dischi* in Italy. In other major languages, most contributions focus on national repertoires.

Popular and rock music of Anglo-American descent proliferated even in the socialist countries. Their history has only begun to be written. They had to contend with a censorship that, from country to country, from time to time, was more or less strict. Today the situation is changing. Popular music is gaining increasing acceptance as a legitimate field for scholarly work.

PAN-EUROPEAN TRENDS

The overall picture of popular music in Europe is stunningly complex. At one end of the spectrum, Anglo-American mainstream pop is everywhere. At the other end of it, one encounters vernacular genres, largely unknown outside their country of origin, and often unappreciated by most listeners within those borders.

Pop music across Europe is far from being a homogeneous hash of internationalized Anglo-American elements. National or vernacular traditions are flourishing and show no signs of being overwhelmed by foreign inroads; their variety reveals a complex pattern of cultural contacts, signaling conditions that allow musical styles to relate to other styles. The terms of the relationships may vary greatly: different musical styles may sometimes merge but sometimes ignore each other and live side by side, or one of them may succeed in dominating the territory, quashing any competition.

The complexity of this situation partly reflects the fact that communication across various types and levels of borders is sometimes allowed and sometimes

The collision between our awareness of being citizens of the world and a matrix of local cultures that repeatedly reassert their individuality illustrates how cultures and individuals vacillate between aspirations of modernity and reassurances of tradition.

denied. Supernational, national, or vernacular traditions reveal, in their diversity, the fruits of complex patterns of cultural contact in certain places, balanced by almost total isolation elsewhere. These places seldom coincide with language areas or national borders. Across Europe, different social groups of the same time and place share some repertoires and do not share others. The diffusion of music is no simple matter of spatial distribution, but a matter of cultural exchanges regulated by social filters.

Such patterns illustrate the encounter—indeed, the collision—between our awareness of being citizens of the world with a matrix of local cultures that repeatedly reassert their individuality in the larger society, defending with obstinacy their right to be heard. The extent to which they hybridize with other cultures illustrates how cultures and individuals vacillate between bewilderment and a sense of belonging— between aspirations of modernity and reassurances of tradition.

BIBLIOGRAPHY

Adorno, Theodor W. 1976 [1962]. *Introduction to the Sociology of Music.* Translated by E. B. Ashton. New York: Seabury Press.

Benjamin, Walter. 1963. *Das Kunstwerk im Zeitalter seiner technischen Reproduzierbarkeit.* Frankfurt: Suhrkamp.

Birrer, Frans A. J. 1985. "Definitions and Research Orientation: Do We Need a Definition of Popular Music?" *Popular Music Perspectives* 2:99–105.

Brackett, David. 1995. *Interpreting Popular Music.* Cambridge: Cambridge University Press.

Bright, Terry. 1985. "Soviet Crusade Against Pop." *Popular Music* 5:121–148.

Butterworth, Katherine, and Sara Schneider. 1975. *Rebetika: Songs from the Old Greek Underworld.* Athens: Kolomboi.

Carrera, Alessandro. 1980. *Musica e pubblico giovanile: L'evoluzione del gusto musicale dagli anni sessanta ad oggi.* Milan: Feltinelli.

Cutler, Chris. 1985. "What Is Popular Music?" *Popular Music Perspectives* 2:3–12.

Del Grosso Destreri, Luigi. 1972. *Europäisches Hit-Panorama: Erfolgsschlager in vier europäischen Ländern—Aussagen, Inhalte, Analyse.* Musik und Gesellschaft, 12. Karlsruhe: G. Braun.

Fabbri, Franco. 1989 [1985]. "The System of the Canzone in Italy Today." In *World Music, Politics and Social Change,* ed. Simon Frith, 122–142. Manchester: Manchester University Press.

Flender, Reinhard, and Hermann Rauhe. 1989. *Popmusik: Geschichte, Funktion, Wirkung und Ästhetik.* Darmstadt: Wissenschaftliche Buchgesellschaft.

Frith, Simon. 1978. *Sociology of Rock.* London: Constable.

———. 1981. *Sound Effects: Youth, Leisure, and the Politics of Rock 'n' Roll.* New York: Pantheon.

———, ed. 1989. *World Music, Politics and Social Change: Papers from the International Association for the Study of Popular Music.* Manchester: Manchester University Press.

Gammond, Peter. 1991. *The Oxford Companion to Popular Music.* Oxford: Oxford University Press.

Gans, Herbert. 1974. *Popular Culture and High Culture: An Analysis and Evaluation of Taste.* New York: Basic Books.

Goertzen, Chris. 1988. "Popular Music Transfer and Transformation: The Case of American Country Music in Vienna." *Ethnomusicology* 32(1):1–22.

Gronow, Pekka. 1969. "International Trends in Popular Music." *Ethnomusicology* 13(2):313–316.

———. 1973. "Popular Music in Finland." *Ethnomusicology* 17(1):52–71.

———. 1983. "The Record Industry: Growth of a Mass Medium." *Popular Music* 3:53–76.

Günther, Ehnert. 1979. *Rock in Deutschland.* Hamburg: Taurus Press.

Hartwich-Wiechell, Doerte. 1974. *Pop-Musik: Analysen und Interpretationen.* Cologne: Volk.

Helt, Richard C., and Ulrich Mahrius. 1979. "The West-German Country Music Fan." *Popular Music and Society* 6:324–330.

Kneif, Tibor. 1978. *Sachlexikon Rockmusik.* Hamburg: Rowoholt.

———. 1979. *Einführung in die Rockmusik.* Wilhelmshaven: Heinrichshofen Verlag.

Kos, Koraljika. 1972. "New Dimensions in Folk Music: A Contribution to the Study of Musical Tastes in Contemporary Yugoslav Society." *International Review of the Aesthetics and Sociology of Music* 3(1):61–73.

Laade, Wolfgang. 1975. "Von Country & Western zum Hard Rock." *Musik und Bildung* 6:322–329.

Larkey, Edward. 1992. "Austropop: Popular Music and National Identity in Austria." *Popular Music* 12(2):151–185.

Larkin, Colin, ed. 1992. *The Guinness Encyclopedia of Popular Music.* 4 vols. London: Guinness Publishing.

Lartigot, Jean-Claude, and Eric Sprogis. 1975. *Libérer la musique.* Paris: Éditions Universitaires.

Malm, Krister. 1982. "Phonograms and cultural policy in Sweden." In *The Phonogram in Cultural Communication,* ed. Kurt Blaukopf, 43–73. Vienna and New York: Springer-Verlag.

Manuel, Peter. 1988. *Popular Musics of the Non-Western World.* New York: Oxford University Press.

Middleton, Richard. 1981. "Editor's Introduction to Volume 1." *Popular Music* 1:3–7.

———. 1985. "Popular Music, Class Conflict, and the Music-Historical Field." *Popular Music Perspectives* 2:24–26.

———. 1990. *Studying Popular Music.* Milton Keynes: Open University Press.

Mignon, Patrick, and Antoine Hennion, eds. 1991. *Rock: De l'histoire au mythe.* Paris: Economica.

Numminen, Mauri A. 1974. "An Inside View of Pop Music in Finland." In *New Patterns of Musical Behavior of the Young Generation in Industrialized Societies,* ed. Irmgard Bontinck, 60–65. Vienna: Universal Edition.

Ordovás, Jesús. 1986. *Historia de la música pop española.* Madrid: Alianza Editorial.

Pond, Irina. 1987. "Soviet Rock Lyrics: Their Content and Poetics." *Popular Music and Society* 11:75–92.

Rauke, Hermann. 1975. "Popularität in der Musik." *Musik und Gesellschaft* 13(14):1–61.

Rauth, Robert. 1982. "Back in the USSR—Rock and Roll in the Soviet Union." *Popular Music and Society* 8:3–12.

Ryback, Timothy W. 1990. *Rock Around the Bloc: A History of Rock Music in Eastern Europe and the Soviet Union, 1954–1988.* New York: Oxford University Press.

Salmoni, Fabrizio. 1980. "Country Music in Italy: A Matter of Controversy." *John Edwards Memorial Foundation Quarterly* 16:175–180.

Sandner, Wolfgang, ed. 1979. *Rock Musik (Aspekte zur Geschichte, Ästhetik, Produktion).* Mainz: Schott's Söhne.

Schroder, Horst. 1968. "Aspekte der deutschen 'Folk Song' Bewegung." *Kontakte* 6:194–214.

Stoelting, Elke. 1975. *Deutsche Schlager und Anglische Popmusik in Deutschland.* Bonn: Bouvier Verlag.

Taylor, Paul. 1985. *Popular Music since 1955: A Critical Guide to the Literature.* London and New York: Mansell.

Troitsky, Artemy. 1987. *Back in the USSR: The True Story of Rock in Russia.* Boston and London: Faber.

Vulliamy, Graham, and Ed Lee, eds. 1980. *Pop Music in Schools.* Cambridge: Cambridge University Press.

———. 1982. *Pop, Rock and Ethnic Music in School.* Cambridge: Cambridge University Press.

Wallis, Roger, and Krister Malm. 1984. *Big Sounds from Small Peoples: The Music Industry in Small Countries.* New York: Pendragon Press.

Rock Music in Europe
Wanda Bryant

Rock in Western Europe
Rock in Eastern Europe

Rock music in Europe has mostly mirrored its development in the United States. It has been the voice of rebellion, accompanying social and political change. The use of politicized rock as opposition and the social impact of rock in Western Europe closely resembles its use in the United States; however, in former communist countries, especially during the dissolution of the Soviet Union, rock played perhaps a more significant political role.

Evolutionary similarities occurred throughout Europe. These included imitation of Anglo-American styles in the 1950s and early 1960s, the importance of the Beatles, the rise of original music making and the incorporation of local languages and indigenous musical elements in the 1970s, the rise of punk in the late 1970s, the onslaught of heavy metal in the 1980s, and the proliferation of rhythm and blues (R&B), rap, dance-club music, and alternative rock in the 1990s.

ROCK IN WESTERN EUROPE

Musicians in Western Europe have been playing rock almost as long as American musicians. England, Ireland, and Germany especially have been strongholds of rock since its inception, and remain so today.

Britain and Ireland

In the 1950s, garage bands, often consisting of unemployed young men, covered American hits, imitating the sounds and styles of R&B and rockabilly artists like Chuck Berry, Little Richard, Elvis Presley, and Buddy Holly. In the 1960s, British musicians began to create and export original rock music in two styles: one, strongly blues-oriented, was represented by artists like the Rolling Stones, the Who, the Kinks, the Yardbirds, the Animals, Cream, and preeminent guitarists Eric Clapton, Jimmy Page, and Jeff Beck; the other, more pop-oriented and called the beat or Mersey beat, was represented by the Beatles and other artists, including the Searchers, Gerry and the Pacemakers, Billy J. Kramer, the Hollies, the Dave Clark Five, and Herman's Hermits. As rock in Europe developed, English and Irish musicians routinely toured the United States, invigorating the genre and making important musical and sociopolitical contributions.

Near the end of the 1960s, the musical language of rock was expanded and enriched by artists exploring jazz, folk, country, classical, and other musical genres. The blending of rock with classical music brought about "art rock" or "classical rock," which utilized classical forms (e.g., the song cycle, the concerto, the symphony, and opera) and partnerships with classical ensembles to create extended works in rock style. British groups—most notably King Crimson, the Moody Blues, Deep Purple, Procol Harum, Pink Floyd, Jethro Tull, and the Who (with their rock opera, *Tommy*)—led the way.

In the 1970s, the phenomenon known as punk, a raw, angry sound with heavy, repeated chords, spread among a limited crowd in New York and then more widely in Europe. The social conditions to which the punk movement responded in Britain were especially dire and fostered groups like the Sex Pistols, who, with the release of "Anarchy in the UK," established themselves as the vanguard of this movement. Their "God Save the Queen" openly accused the monarchy of being a fascist regime, relentlessly attacked social problems, and made rock "dangerous" again. Another major punk group, the Clash, confronted issues of racism and unemployment, taking up the cause of working-class Britons.

In Britain, the organization Rock Against Racism (RAR, begun in 1976) used punk rock to inspire a political movement. It used explicitly socialist tactics to mobilize the nation's youth. Inspired by Eric Clapton's infamous remark that he wanted to keep Britain white, RAR drew on punk style and rhetoric as the medium for its political statement. RAR-sponsored festivals teamed punk artists like the Clash and Elvis Costello with black reggae artists like Aswad and Steel Pulse. Interracial bands, like The Specials, Madness, and English Beat, popularized ska, an upbeat Jamaican-styled dance-music. RAR's organizers felt that the value of their music lay in its performers' expressive authority: just as soul and R&B expressed the values of working-class African-American audiences, reggae stood for working-class Afro-Caribbeans and punk for working-class whites.

Blues-based rock in the 1970s began to fragment, in one case evolving into heavy metal, an exaggeration of mainstream hard rock. Led Zeppelin, an early prototype, used a pounding duple subdivision of the beat, distorted guitar riffs, extended guitar solos, and screaming vocals. Other heavy metal groups, like Black Sabbath and Ozzy Osbourne, were fascinated with the occult and the macabre. Glitter rock (glam rock) combined heavy metal with bizarre theatrical makeup and costumes; elaborate lights, sets, and staging; and the musicians' assumption of strange onstage personas. The foremost proponent of this style was David Bowie in his Ziggy Stardust character; his influence on other British performers, such as Boy George and Elton John, and Americans Alice Cooper and KISS, is apparent. New wave rock offered a pop-oriented offshoot of punk, represented by The Police, Billy Idol, the Cure, and the Pretenders. Another side of mainstream rock, less outrageous and less deafening, produced numerous successful artists, most notably Elton John (with the look of glitter but the softer sound of pop-based rock) and Fleetwood Mac, which began as a blues-based band, but as a result of personnel changes in the early 1970s softened its sound.

In the 1980s, rock saw a proliferation of heavy metal bands (e.g., Iron Maiden, Judas Priest, and Whitesnake), the rise of pop metal, increased synthesizer use (electro-pop), politicized music, and benefit concerts. Pop metal groups like Def Leppard, by incorporating various tempos, shorter and rapid-fire guitar solos, lighter bass lines, and vocal harmonies, presented a less offensive, smoother version of heavy metal. Electro-pop groups like Duran Duran, Depeche Mode, and Spandau Ballet featured upbeat, pop-style dance-tunes played on synthesizers, sequencers, and drum machines producing disco beats. Several Irish artists, including U2, Van Morrison, and Sinéad O'Connor, became international stars, bringing 1960s-like political sentiments back into rock. Similarly, international concern for humanitarian causes sparked numerous benefit rock concerts, of which one of the earliest was Live Aid, in 1985: organized by Bob Geldof, of the Irish band The Boomtown Rats, it was simulcast from London, Philadelphia, Moscow, and other cities via nine satellites to an audience of 1.6 billion viewers (Garofalo 1997:378), and it raised $40 million for relief of famine-stricken Ethiopia.

Germany and Austria

The early rock scene in Austria and Germany consisted primarily of German-language covers recorded in West Germany. Most rock in German-speaking countries was produced by the German-dominated *schlager* 'pop-music' industry. Much of the actual recording took place in Austria, where costs were lower (Larkey 1993:97). Austrian rock remained a peripheral genre until the mid-1960s; members of the youth subculture known as *halbstarke* were the initial consumers of rock. As with similar groups, including Russia's *stilyagi* (Troitsky 1987:15), Britain's mods and rockers, and 1970s punk rockers, *halbstarke*—leather-jacketed, ducktailed "hoodlums," who got into trouble hanging around street corners listening to loud music on transistor radios—used music, media, clothing, and language as a means of separating themselves from contemporary social values and norms. They were less radical in Austria, partly from the lack of important urban centers and a media blackout concerning concertgoers' "deviant" behavior in Germany and elsewhere. In addition, the rebelliousness of the English lyrics was usually lost in translation. The prominence of the Beatles and other British groups in the 1960s, however, led to wider acceptance of four Anglo-American traditions still found in Austria: the Anglo-based folk-song tradition, the "beat" tradition (Beatles), the rock tradition (dance-based, Rolling Stones style), and the soul and blues traditions. Not until the 1970s did any digression from these traditions—the development of a transcultural Austropop tradition—occur [see AUSTRIA] (figure 1).

Punk in Austria differed from the better-known versions in England and Germany. As elsewhere, Austrian punk was the music of a minority, but it had more symbolic value as an element of participation in an international youth-culture movement. It was soon co-opted by the music industry, made accessible to broader audiences, and stripped of its initial rebelliousness. Like beat and rock in the 1960s and heavy metal in the 1980s, punk and new wave underwent various changes, eventually merging with the mainstream pop and *schlager* traditions.

Scandinavia and Finland

In Scandinavia, rock followed Anglo-American models until the late 1960s, when a strong, well-organized grassroots youth-music movement, featuring domestic rock with realist or progressive lyrics, arose. In Sweden, domestic rock artists and bands like Pugh Rogefelt, Peps, Blå Tåget, Nynningen, and Nationalteatern found outlets through record companies and rock clubs; Kontaktnäten (Contact Network, an organization of music clubs), formed in 1974, still exists. This movement culminated in the 1980s with punk and groups like KSMB, Ebba Grön, and Attentat. Scandinavian rock has persisted and expanded, with internationally known artists like the Swedish groups ABBA, Roxette, and Yngwie Malmsteen, and the Icelandic singer Björk. The infrastructure of rock clubs, recording companies, and rock festivals has also expanded, with more than a hundred thousand rock performers out of a population of 8.5 million in 1995. Rock and other styles of pop are the most common leisure interest in Sweden, and Swedish teens are avid music buyers and listeners (Fornäs, Lindberg, and Sernhede 1995:x).

FIGURE 1   Since the 1980s, Willi Resetarits, an Austrian who sang with the political folk group Schmetterlinge (Butterflies) throughout the 1970s, has performed as Ostbahn-Kurti, a fictitious working-class rock hero. Photo by Edward Larkey, 1991.

Early rock musicians in Finland translated the lyrics of American and European hits into Finnish. American rock and associated media, like the U.S. film *Blackboard Jungle* (1955), with its hit song by Bill Haley and the Comets, were the ideal; there was even a competition to find the Finnish Elvis. In the 1960s, folk-rock bands and beat groups covered British hits in Finnish. Bands making original music, including the progressive blues bands Wigwam and Tasavallan Presidentti (The President of the Republic), both of which had English vocalists, had limited success outside Finland. In the late 1960s, Finnish rock voiced its own note of rebellion: "Finland was too cold a country for the Hippie [*sic*] movement and flower power, so their place was taken by political opposition" (Juntunen 1980:2).

In the 1970s in Finland, domestically produced rock—fast, loud, and basic—featured Finnish lyrics with realistic images of everyday life. Rockers wrote original songs with social or political messages criticizing society, often about the high rate of unemployment and the number of Finns forced to seek work in Sweden. The year 1977 saw the rise of punk groups, for whom "playing with gusto was the most important thing" (Juntunen 1980:5). Artists like Hanoi Rocks (the most successful Finnish rock band), Eppu Normaali, Hannu "Tuomari" Nurmio, and Hassinen Kone (Hassinen's Machine) flourished, singing lyrics that voiced melancholic Finnish views.

Contemporary Finnish rock exhibits influences of soul and R&B, Afro-Caribbean rhythms, thrash metal, Finnish melodies, rockabilly, jazz rock, and early classic rock. Newcomers like Melrose, Hearthill, Boycott, Gringo Locos, and Honey B & the T-Bones (with a female singer, a rarity in Finland) sing primarily in English. ELMU, a society for live music founded in 1970s, continues to establish rock clubs, publish books and magazines, and sponsor a radio station. A thriving rock press and dozens of radio stations, apart from the government channel, concentrate on rock. Twenty or more rock festivals are crammed into Finland's brief summer.

ROCK IN EASTERN EUROPE

To young people in communist Eastern Europe, America seemed a distant Utopia, and American rock, by presenting a mythical version of 1950s and 1960s U.S. society, offered an escape from the harsh realities of daily life. "Unquestionably the single most pervasive form of mass culture in the Soviet bloc" (Ryback 1990:5), rock transformed communist society and altered the policies and structures of Soviet-bloc governments. Officials in the 1950s and 1960s tried to suppress rock, arguing that it was not in accordance with the goals of a socialist society, because of the bourgeois influence it implied and the challenge it delivered to ideological goals and sexual taboos.

Antirock sentiments among communist party officials ran deep, evoking strong reactions to "the inalienably democratic character of the grassroots cultural movement of young people" (Wicke 1992:82). Rock groups were oppressed or banned throughout communist Central and Eastern Europe and the U.S.S.R. Vicious attacks on rock appeared in the Czech party weekly, and Bulgarian rockers were condemned as "apostles of the hostile ideology" for imitating American styles and trying to live and think as Americans (Ryback 1990:5). But once the communist authorities accepted that rock would not go away, they tried to get it to work for them. Romanian officials pressured rock groups to perform patriotic social and political themes. Hungarian cultural commissars tried to get rock musicians to make socialism attractive to youth. In the U.S.S.R., the Ministry of Culture regulated rock groups, allowing only rock that extolled socialism. In the German Democratic Republic (GDR) and Yugoslavia, socialist youth organizations organized and supervised rock concerts.

Though initially repressed, rock became a medium of resistance more or less

Rock musicians created and disseminated their ideas in underground or grassroots movements, and eventually contributed to the erosion of totalitarian regimes throughout Eastern Europe.

impossible to control. It allowed people to express themselves using only guitars, drum sets, and amplifiers (sometimes just simple radios). Rock culture within a modern socialist industrial context differed from that of the West in that it emerged and operated in the absence of a market system for its production and distribution; capital had no influence over the dynamics of cultural production. Rock musicians created and disseminated their ideas via rock in underground or grassroots movements, well outside the control or influence of the state or commercial markets. And because music can shape patterns of behavior, rock eventually contributed to the erosion of totalitarian regimes throughout Eastern Europe.

The Soviet Union

The Soviet Union had an official antirock policy in place from the 1950s. Rock was on a list of subversive dangers, condemned as a form of spiritual poison, and blamed for myriad social ills, from juvenile delinquency and alcoholism to vandalism and sexual assaults. The government attempted to eradicate rock through denunciations, ordinances, and police action. The police crashed concerts, forcibly shaved long-haired attendees' heads, and imprisoned rock musicians for offenses ranging from public disturbance to political subversion and tax evasion. But though public demonstrations (like concerts) could be dealt with, the Soviet government could not control the private acts of rebellion by youth at home listening to Radio Luxembourg, Radio Free Europe, and bootleg cassettes. Western rock culture disproved Marxist-Leninist assumptions about the state's ability to control its citizens.

The Beatles broke through the Iron Curtain in 1964 and were the biggest influence on rock in the socialist bloc. The Soviet government in Moscow even considered hiring them for a concert. Early Russian rock artists emulated the Beatles, imitating the original recordings as closely as possible. Gradually, Russian musicians developed their own style, with later influences coming from rock bands T. Rex, Led Zeppelin, and Deep Purple, and guitarists Johnny Winter and Jimi Hendrix. The sound was Western rock, but, following the indigenous traditions of Russian guitar-accompanied poetry, the lyrical content was considered more important (Cushman 1995:42–43; Troitsky 1987:39–40).

Punk and new wave were not so popular in the U.S.S.R. as elsewhere in Central and Eastern Europe. They were not considered prestigious—meaning they were without complex musical arrangements, technical virtuosity, and poetic lyrics (Troitsky 1987:49). The punk style of playing—loud, fast, and dirty—was incompatible with Russian style. In addition, the image of punks as Nazis was unwelcome. When punk did arrive, in 1980–1981, its rough lyrics brought a new street aesthetic and realistic lyrics, including singing about sex, previously taboo.

During the 1970s and 1980s, the Soviet state tried to co-opt the rock tradition and invent its own tradition of state-sponsored rock. It offered musicians financial and material support in exchange for not writing songs with antigovernmental or

FIGURE 2   From the former Soviet Union, the Belarusan rock band Ulis performs in concert in Minsk for a taping of the television program "Rock Island." *Left to right:* Viačaslaŭ Koryjan, Siarhiej Kniš, Aleh Tumašaŭ, Siarhiej Kraŭčanka. Photo by Maria Paula Survilla, 1993.

other rebellious lyrics. Government-sponsored institutes, like the Leningrad Rock Club, enabled public performance of independent rock, but also eased surveillance of the rock scene. Some rock musicians found themselves used by political reformers "to illustrate the authenticity of *glasnost* ['openness']" (Cushman 1995:xii). With *glasnost* came a loosening of prohibitions against rock, a more positive press, and rock radio programming. Politicians hoped that art rock (like Emerson, Lake, and Palmer's *Pictures at an Exhibition* and the rock opera *Jesus Christ Superstar*) could prepare young people to appreciate classical works (Troitsky 1987:33). By 1989, rock musicians in urban centers were allowed to perform without significant official interference (figure 2).

Communist Central and Southeastern Europe

In a study of rock in the German Democratic Republic, Peter Wicke noted that rock musicians helped set in motion the events that "led to the destruction of the Berlin Wall and the disappearance of the GDR" (1992:81). The Central Committee of the Communist Party reversed its policy against rock in 1972, renaming it youth dance-music and bringing it under state-imposed discipline, but they were losing the battle against its spread. Political Engagement Through Music became the rockers' slogan. The state's estimation of the political effectiveness of the lyrics and the subversive potential of the genre led to prohibitions against performance of rock songs with unapproved lyrics—prohibitions that led many popular musicians to leave the GDR; those remaining had to rely on the state for support and be more conservative in their political orientation.

In 1983, annual Rock for Peace festivals began throughout the GDR, some symbolically held at the House of Parliament and attended by street youth and party officials side by side. The musicians turned these festivals to their own purposes, realizing that their popularity gave them remarkable political power. The group Pankow challenged authorities at a 1987 festival, attacking the hypocrisy of the state's "peace policy." The state newspaper harshly attacked them, but their popularity soared. The 1987 release of the album *Battalion d'Amour* by the group Silly did not have state authorities' approval. Lyrics became more aggressive and openly oppositional on subjects covering a wide range of social issues, from the destruction of the environment to the dissolution of meaningful public discourse. Between September and October 1989, fifteen hundred rock musicians and disc jockeys signed a declaration demanding public dialogue about the state of affairs in the GDR and recognition of democratically constituted groups of citizens. This declaration sparked violent confrontations with police at rock concerts. Feeling pressure from hundreds of thousands of protestors nationwide, the communist state crumbled, on 9 November 1989.

Bulgaria

In Bulgaria, domestic rock failed to supplant the popularity of Western classical music. Communist Party opposition to rock was strong, and concert facilities, technical expertise, and equipment were limited. Western rock was directly available only to elite urban consumers, who had access to Western concerts, discos, magazines, stereos, and recordings through travel, family connections, and possession of hard currency. The rest of the population, living in villages and rural areas, heard rock only through radiobroadcasts and duplicated tapes, brought into the country by the elite. In the 1960s and 1970s, politicians frequently called for a ban on Western rock and certain Western artists, like David Bowie, but state propaganda had little impact on the popularity of rock among Bulgarian youth.

Rock thrived among Bulgarian youth but was barely assimilated beyond performers' copying the sound and imitating the outward appearance. The favored styles and artists were neither the musical virtuosos or those with complex lyrics, nor those who focused on Western issues; the most popular were British groups, including the Beatles, the Rolling Stones, Queen, Deep Purple, and Duran Duran. In the 1990s, Madonna, Michael Jackson, and the artist formerly known as Prince became favorites. Punk culture arrived in the early 1980s, but did not develop into a genuine movement. Though punk and new wave had some impact, the most successful bands were those who compromised with governmental authorities.

In the mid-1980s, some Bulgarian rock bands began to address issues like the environment, AIDS, drugs, conflicts with parents, lack of effective national political independence, and limited career expectations. Two bands, the Shturtsi and FSB, have dominated Bulgarian rock since the 1970s. The Shturtsi, a heavy-metal band, have a reputation for songs with insidious meanings, like "Wedding Day," a rock lament for the loss of freedom (Ashley 1994:145). This band has had numerous conflicts with the state. By contrast, FSB is primarily an instrumental group, and it has been awarded greater freedom, especially in recording. In the late 1980s, the Communist Party paper called for cultural liberalization, including uncensored performances of all types of rock. Recent trends include incorporation of Bulgarian folk music into rock, popularized among many rockers by the Bulgarian State Radio and Television Female Vocal Choir's 1987 recording *Le mystère des voix bulgares* and supported by Western musicians like George Harrison, Linda Ronstadt, and Kate Bush, whose album *The Sensual World* (1989) included backup vocals by the well-known folk singers Trio Bulgarka. The political revolution of 1989–1990 and the disappearance of censorship invigorated the synthesis of Western rock and Bulgarian traditional music. A new climate of tolerance has given rise to numerous outrageous and controversial new groups, including heavy-metal, thrash-metal, and rap bands.

Poland and Hungary

Of all the Soviet-influenced communist states, Poland and Hungary afforded rock musicians the most freedom. In the early 1980s, Hungary saw a loosening of centralized political control over production and consumption of rock, enabling innovative and influential new styles—punk, new wave, avant-garde rock, and independent musical performance—to create their own subcultural space, eventually helping undermine the social order. Hungarian punks, well-informed about British and American prototypes, reworked the Western European punk ideology, adopting the dress and hairstyles of Western punk but adding their own particular views and experiences. Despite relaxed governmental controls, most rock musicians faced some degree of censorship. To get around these restraints, they gave their lyrics multiple layers of meaning, extensively deployed double entendres, and used allusiveness as a poetic and political strategy to avoid confrontation with gatekeepers of radio, TV, and record companies. Punk lyrics were politically outspoken and anarchistic; their music provided a medium through which the subculture of homeless and jobless young men could articulate their frustration with the realities of their own existence.

The Hungarian avant-garde or new-wave art-punk movement was a subtler, more individualistic form of artistic expression, rooted in the middle class. Art-punk musicians adopted the term *rockandroll* to differentiate their music from the rock-and-roll dance-music style of the 1950s, give it a broader meaning (with elitist connotations of authenticity and relevance), and highlight their preoccupation with sex and drugs. Taking provocative names, such as Albert Einstein Committee (an allusion to the Central Committee of the Hungarian Communist Party) and URH (a reference to a police patrol of the same acronym), art punk created an alternative social space by mocking and challenging the "real" world. New-wave bands also encountered censorship: of the seven or eight most prominent bands, only two received official opportunities to issue albums, and those albums contained material at least three years old. A grassroots movement of new-wave enthusiasts developed through an extensive noncommercial system, which circulated duplicated tapes and videos through barter.

Despite more liberal governmental attitudes, Polish rock was not at all free: the government tolerated no intrusion into politics. Rock burst on the scene in 1957, with singer Boguslaw Wyrobek and his band Rhythm and Blues. Audiences soon became so frenzied at R&B concerts that the group was banned. Renamed big beat, to avoid any open connection with the subversive rock and roll, rock was originally sung in English, but performers soon saw political expediency in singing in Polish. The scarcity of Polish-language rock songs prompted the trend toward Polish folk-rock. In the 1960s, influence from the Beatles and blues rock, after a tour by The Animals in 1965, was most prominent.

Punk was not especially popular in Poland, but it did have a small, devoted following. Only during the 1980s, the years of martial law, did it acquire the hard, openly political edge seen in other socialist countries. The repression instilled in Polish society by martial law ignored rock, viewed as an innocent relief valve for adolescent frustration, and allowed it easy access to airwaves, recording studios, and concert venues. The punk scene grew to include festivals with twenty thousand participants. The band SS-20, named after Soviet nuclear missiles, brought antimilitary rock to the younger generation; other groups took aim at the Roman Catholic Church and Polish society in general. The band Perfect, openly antigovernment and pro-Solidarity movement, was banned from performing in 1983. It staged a comeback in 1987 in Warsaw and Gdánsk with its most controversial songs, but its leader, Zbiggy Holdys, sent a letter to the government denying any political intent and became an embarrassment to the radical movement.

Rock in the postcommunist era

Today, rock is heard blaring from stereos and in sports stadium concerts throughout Europe. Governments now sponsor rock bands, recordings, rock radio, and TV programming. Since the end of the 1980s, though, the role of rock in Central and Eastern Europe has been ambivalent. Some groups play in honor of socialist causes;

Many musicians in postcommunist European countries find themselves in the paradoxical position of having escaped overt political constraints on their freedom of expression only to find that they are subject to economic constraints for which their pasts have not prepared them.

others maintain a rebellious posture. Before reunification, East and West Berlin staged battling rock concerts. After the fall of the Berlin Wall (1989), a new rock movement began to emerge in eastern Germany. Power From The East Side is the new slogan. Former East German rock bands are performing again, with a renewed sense of freedom but no loss of the social conscience that aided in the unification of Germany. Many musicians in Central and Eastern Europe continue to defy authorities and sing "dangerous" songs, but many political-protest groups seem to have lost their energy.

Postcommunist European countries are faced with deregulation of musical life. State broadcasting and recording entities have lost their monopolies, and concerts and festivals have been deregulated, raising the question of who will step in to fill the financial gaps. Fluctuating economic policies play a major role in producing music. In the move toward a market economy, many musicians find themselves in the paradoxical position of having escaped overt political constraints on their freedom of expression only to find that they are subject to economic constraints for which their pasts have not prepared them. Other issues facing contemporary European musicians include music as identity, especially the roles of rock and traditional folk music in contemporary musical life, and a broader worldview of a global or transnational musical culture that incorporates a sensitivity toward local characteristics while forming new musical fusions.

BIBLIOGRAPHY

Ashley, Stephen. 1994. "The Bulgarian Rock Scene under Communism (1962–1990)." In *Rocking the State: Rock Music and Politics in Eastern Europe and Russia,* ed. Sabrina Petra Ramet, 141–163. Boulder, Colo.: Westview Press.

Bradley, Dick. 1992. *Understanding Rock 'n' Roll: Popular Music in Britain 1955–1964.* Buckingham and Philadelphia: Open University Press.

Chambers, Iain. 1985. *Urban Rhythms: Pop Music and Popular Culture.* London: Macmillan.

Cushman, Thomas. 1995. *Notes from Underground: Rock Music Counterculture in Russia.* Albany: State University of New York Press.

Fornäs, Johan, Ulf Lindberg, and Ove Sernhede. 1995. *In Garageland: Rock Youth and Modernity.* Translated by Jan Teeland. London and New York: Routledge.

Frith, Simon. 1981. *Sound Effects: Youth, Leisure and the Politics of Rock 'n' Roll.* New York: Pantheon.

Garofalo, Reebee, ed. 1992. *Rockin' the Boat: Mass Music and Mass Movements.* Boston: South End Press.

———. 1997. *Rockin' Out: Popular Music in the USA.* Boston: Allyn and Bacon.

Juntunen, Juho. 1980. *Rock: Is There Any in Finland?* Text translated by Susan Sinisalo. Lyrics translated by Herbert Lomas. Helsinki: Interprint Oy.

Kurkela, Vesa. 1993. "Deregulation of Popular Music in the European Post-Communist Countries: Business, Identity and Cultural Collage." *The World of Music* 35(3):80–105.

Larkey, Edward. 1993. *Pungent Sounds: Constructing Identity with Popular Music in Austria.* New York: Peter Lang Publishing.

Prendergast, Mark J. 1987. *Isle of Noises: Rock and Roll's Roots in Ireland.* New York: St. Martin's Press.

Przedpelsak, Beata. 1997. "Poland's Sweet Noise Aims to Rock Out with 'Ghetto'." *Billboard* (12 April), 49–50.

Ramet, Sabrina Petra, ed. 1994. *Rocking the State: Rock Music and Politics in Eastern Europe and Russia.* Boulder, Colo.: Westview Press.

Ryback, Timothy W. 1990. *Rock Around the Bloc: A History of Rock Music in Eastern Europe and the Soviet Union, 1954–1988.* New York: Oxford University Press.

Savage, Jon. 1992. *England's Dreaming: Anarchy, Sex Pistols, Punk Rock, and Beyond.* New York: St. Martin's Press.

Stuessy, Joe. 1994. *Rock and Roll: Its History and Stylistic Development.* 2nd ed. Englewood Cliffs, N.J.: Prentice Hall.

Szemere, Anna. 1985. "Pop Music in Hungary." *Communication Research* 12(3):401–411.

Troitsky, Artemy. 1987. *Back in the USSR: The True Story of Rock in Russia.* Boston and London: Faber and Faber.

Wicke, Peter. 1992. "'The Times They Are A-Changin': Rock Music and Political Change in East Germany." In *Rockin' the Boat: Mass Music and Mass Movements,* ed. Reebee Garofalo, 81–92. Boston: South End Press.

World Music in Europe

Timothy Rice

The World-Music Culture
World Music in Historical Perspective

The popular-music marketplace—recording companies, distributors, retailers, broad-casters, critics, and consumers—has variously labeled the market sector that contains neotraditional forms of rural music. In the 1980s, older labels, such as *ethnic, folk,* and *international,* gave way to newer ones, such as *worldbeat, ethnopop,* and *world-fusion* (Taylor 1997). This terminological change signaled changes in production, reception, and aesthetics. First, the older terms covered styles conceived as authentic and traditional, even when arranged and neotraditional, but the newer terms acknowledged the value of hybridity and the fusion of traditional music with popu-lar, African-American-influenced, beat-driven music. Second, the older terms empha-sized the national, local, or ethnic character of the music and implicitly its limited marketability, but the newer ones treated this new music as a worldwide phenome-non with broad appeal. The postcolonial, global, mass-mediated market of the last decades of the twentieth century had spread beyond Europe and North America to embrace Asia, Africa, Latin America, and the Pacific—that is, the world. No matter where the traditions originate, however, Europe has played a central role in their pro-duction and distribution [see IMMIGRANT MUSIC IN EUROPE].

THE WORLD-MUSIC CULTURE

Apparently believing that the plethora of old and new terms for this kind of popular, neotraditional music hurt efforts to market it, twenty-five representatives of indepen-dent labels met in Britain in the summer of 1987 and agreed to substitute the term *world music* for these old and new terms. Some record companies in the United States followed suit, and in 1990 *Billboard* magazine introduced a world-music chart (Taylor 1997). By 1987, the term *world music* was in use by some ethnomusicologists to describe their object of study, all the world's music, not just its neotraditional, mass-mediated, popular forms. Independently of developments in the music busi-ness, these scholars had used the term *world music* to replace the term *non-Western music,* to name a graduate program at Wesleyan University, and to entitle this ency-clopedia, then in its planning stages.

Musically, most recordings in this category combine traditional melodies, rhythms, vocal timbres, ornamentation, and instruments with classical and pop-music harmonies and rock beats and instruments (electric guitar and bass, drum set, synthesizer). The cultural patterns spawning the production and reception of this kind of music include the postcolonial movement of people from former colonies in African and Asia to Europe, an increasingly global economy for electronic media (radio, television, recordings), and a so-called postmodern aesthetic sensibility that rejects modernist distinctions between low and high culture and embraces borrowing of past and distant materials to create meaningful new work.

In Europe, other cultural themes are also being worked out in this music. One is identity: young people, especially, seem to turn to these fusions of traditional and modern elements to express ethnic, regional, or local identities and sentiments in opposition to rabid nationalism, European unity, and global capitalism. Other modern conditions and ideologies feeding these new forms of expression in Europe include the breakup of communist Eastern Europe, green politics, and feminism. By combining or fusing traditional and modern elements rather than choosing between them, they use the making of music to create a symbolic image or icon of how they understand themselves and experience their world: simultaneously global and local, of the past and the present, traditional and modern, national and international.

In Europe in the 1990s, the products—that is, the recordings—on the world-music market, fell into four categories: the Afropop and indiepop of postcolonial immigrants to the former imperial capitals of Paris and London (for example, Angélique Kidjo and Sheila Chandra, respectively); classical music picked up, somewhat surprisingly, by the popular music market (for example, recordings of Gregorian chant by the Benedictine monks of Santo Domingo de Silos); the productions of popular musicians such as Peter Gabriel, who sample "world" sounds or collaborate with "world" musicians; and the fusions of musicians representing nations, regions, or ethnicities and seeking to modernize their traditions.

The samplers and appropriators

Perhaps the musicians best known for their appropriation of traditional music into their own popular music are the British rocker Peter Gabriel and the American singer-songwriter Paul Simon. Peter Gabriel, in his albums *Us* and *Passion,* includes an eclectic sampling of European traditional music from England, France, Ireland, and Russia, and music from the Middle East and Africa. Gabriel seems to want to create an imaginary world that mirrors his understanding of the modern condition as no longer rooted in a particular place, but rooted in a "no-man's land." Though such efforts have found a receptive audience among like-minded youth seeking sonic novelty in Europe, America, and elsewhere, these and similar recordings can appear to represent an exploitation of the powerless by the powerful. Because the original styles are overwhelmed by the creations of the rock stars who produce them, and because the producers copyright and profit from the recordings, many critics view this tendency in world music as economic and legal colonialism. Mitigating these criticisms, Gabriel has established a recording company, Real World Records, and a music festival, WOMAD (World of Music, Arts and Dance), with numerous venues around the world to showcase the music and musicians he admires and borrows from (Taylor 1997).

Other commercially successful efforts include the German rock band Dissenten, who borrow elements from Arabic and Indian music, and the French duo Deep Forest (Eric Mouquet and Michel Sánchez), who in 1995 won a Grammy for *Bohème,* which featured pop-synthesizer mixes and samples of Eastern European traditional music (Zemp 1996). An Italian compact-disc production entitled *From Bulgaria with Love* combined Bulgarian choral folk music with hip-hop and techno beats. Beyond the issue of economic and artistic exploitation, the Bulgarian recording raises other ethical questions, since the production seems to mock the music it appropriates (Buchanan 1996). A group from England, 3 Mustaphas 3, eschewed sampling and learned to play some of the instruments, rhythms, and tunes of European traditional music, but they sometimes appear to parody these traditions in their dress, stage names, and some arrangements.

Not all these efforts come from Western Europe, now that Russia, with its own imperial legacy, has entered the global marketplace. In 1996 the Russian jazz composer Mikhail Alperin tried his hand at combining a Bulgarian choir called Angelite with multiphonic throat-singing by a Tuvan (Central Asian) group called Huun Huur Tu and adding Russian folk music and jazz into a mix fueled by romantic, speculative notions of a historical connection between Tuvans and Bulgars.

Local music becomes world music

Local musicians have usually created their fusions of traditional with popular or classical music as a response to local conditions rather than the world-music market. Being picked up by that market has been secondary to their original goals, though it has been economically beneficial to them. Only recently have some local traditional musicians begun to develop a world-music sensibility for the popular-music market. For example, The Chieftains, Ireland's most famous traditional music group, used Chinese musical elements on *In China,* and they collaborated with popular singers such as Mick Jagger, Van Morrison, and Sinéad O'Connor on *The Long Black Veil.*

Generally European traditional music with a world-music appeal has been governed by a classical-music or a pop-rock-jazz sensibility, both with the intent to reach a local audience. In the former camp, The Chieftains and the Bulgarian choirs have been the most popular. In both cases, traditional musical forms, instruments, and vocal timbres were made the centerpiece, but arranged in ways that reflected the influence of classical music. The Chieftains operate like a small chamber ensemble, combining individual tunes into extended suites and adding classical harmonies and counterpoint. The Bulgarian folk choirs use massed singers, as in the classical tradition, to sing in full-throated, powerful polyphony written by trained composers. In different ways, both groups project a sonic image at once traditional and modern, authentically rural and suspiciously urbane. In 1995, the Norwegian Hardanger fiddler Annbjørg Lien, working with the Swedish arranger Roger Tallroth, combined the traditional, intricate, double-stopped fiddle technique of that instrument with guitar, mandolin, and organ to create a restrained fusion almost classical in its effect.

Pop-traditional fusions have also been effective. Perhaps the most successful have involved pop-flamenco fusions, especially the Gipsy [*sic*] Kings from Andalucía and the Spanish guitarist Paco de Lucía, who helped spawn *nuevo flamenco,* many of whose artists have enjoyed enormous local popularity without breaking onto the world music charts. Ireland has provided numerous models for such fusions. In the 1950s and 1960s, groups like the Clancy brothers, Finbar and Eddie Furey, and Clannad combined traditional music with guitar accompaniment. Andy Irvine employed Bulgarian asymmetric meters and collaborated with the Hungarian singer Márta Sebestyén (figure 1). The Pogues combine rock and traditional music, and accordionist Sharon Shannon employs a potpourri of jazz and country accompanimental styles and continental polka and Finnish fiddle tunes. In Scotland, groups like The Battlefield Band have created a trad-rock fusion. The emergence of Celtic music as a marketing subcategory within the world-music category has improved the commercial prospects of many Celtic musicians—for example, Talitha MacKenzie, an American singer now resident in Scotland, and Milladoiro, a group from Galicia. The Bulgarian Rom (Gypsy) clarinetist Ivo Papazov, enormously important in a

FIGURE 1 The Hungarian singer Márta Sebestyén and the Hungarian string band Muzsikás in concert in Canada. The world-music market has facilitated her popularity outside Hungary, where she has worked with like-minded musicians from other traditions. Photo by Paula A. White, 1998.

politically sensitive tradition of wedding music in Bulgaria, has enjoyed modest recognition on the world-music market. In Finland, the vocal group Värttinä has combined the results of archival and field research into Finno-Ugric forms with their own compositions, a rock-influenced backup band, and modern clothes and stage behaviors to create a dynamic presentation with international appeal, even as it constructs notions of Finnish identity.

WORLD MUSIC IN HISTORICAL PERSPECTIVE

Though scholars have constructed the well-known categories of folk, popular, and classical music to describe broad patterns of musical performance, adventuresome musicians and their audiences, searching for new musical ideas, have persistently ignored these patterns. The musical categories may once have registered broad social categories: folk music for rural peasants, popular music for an urban middle class, and classical music for aristocracies and educated urban elites. The class boundaries may once have been fairly rigid, but the musical categories have always been permeable, and musicians from a given category have throughout history borrowed musical styles, instruments, and ideas from other categories.

Though world music is a new marketing category in the music business, the impulse to make and embrace cross-category and international fusions is at least three centuries old in Europe. By the 1990s, modernity and capitalism—the conditions usually cited for the emergence of world music—had spread around the globe. But these conditions existed first in Europe. If world music is understood as a musical process of fusion and hybridity, then this process has been going on for centuries in Europe, and world music is only its most recent manifestation. Even before the modern era, international or at least broadly European music arose first with Christian chant in the medieval period and later with the internationalization of secular music styles in the Renaissance [see HISTORY OF EUROPEAN ART MUSIC].

Modern patterns of musical exchange between categories began in the 1700s. Classical musicians in the Baroque and Classical periods borrowed folk tunes and drone techniques to reference rural, peasant music, and rural musicians began to substitute the professionally crafted violin and clarinet for homemade fiddles and bagpipes. In Northern and Western Europe, courtly figure dances and their music entered rural practice. In the 1800s, these processes continued as urban intellectuals romanticized and nationalized the countryside (and its inhabitants and music) as

New forms of rural music, originally conceived to preserve endangered styles of music and enable the expression of distinct regional, national, or local identities, entered the mass-media, global market for popular music, where audiences all over Europe and the world could consume, appropriate, and interpret them for their own purposes.

symbols of nation-states. Composers in every corner of Europe created national musical styles by incorporating rural tunes into an otherwise international style of harmony, form, and orchestral and choral timbres. More manufactured instruments found their way into village music, especially brass-band instruments and the accordion, as did classical harmony, added to formerly monophonic or drone-based rural traditions. The massive urbanization and industrialization of the 1800s also saw the rise of urban working and middle classes, for whom musicians created new kinds of music, generically labeled popular music. New genres in this style included music-hall songs and dance music for the waltz and polka, new couple dances that all classes enjoyed.

The twentieth century featured three new developments in these centuries-old patterns, developments that made world music possible in the 1990s. First, the dissemination of all categories of music was aided by the invention of electronic media: the phonograph record, radio, television, audiocassettes, and compact discs. For the spread of music, the physical distance between rural and urban spaces and between widely separated countries became immaterial. Face-to-face contact between musicians and their audiences was no longer required, and anyone with access to a radio or phonograph record had the opportunity to hear all types of music: urban and rural, folk and classical, popular and esoteric, national and international. Second, American popular music, with its seemingly unending series of African-American-derived stylistic innovations (ragtime, jazz, swing, blues, rock, and rap) and its new rhythms or beats, crossed the Atlantic to take European popular music by storm. Third, in the second half of the century, rural depopulation and the spread of popular and elite culture via the media and education seriously threatened traditional patterns of village life and music. Urban and rural musicians responded to this threat with efforts at resuscitation—a practice often called revivalism or folklorism.

During the so-called folk-music revival of the 1960s and 1970s in Western Europe, young people seeking their roots turned to older singers and musicians and researched folk-song collectors' archives. Some performed in traditional, solo, unaccompanied styles. Others, hoping to make old traditions appeal to a younger, urban, educated audience, added acoustic guitar accompaniments, sang in parallel thirds, and created their own songs with new texts in the style of folk songs (figure 2). In the countries of communist Eastern Europe, the state managed the preservation of folklore. As a symbol of the state and its ideology, these efforts took on grandiose forms, with large choruses and orchestras. These trends, widespread in Europe at the time, created many of the groups eventually picked up by the market for world music in the 1980s and 1990s. These new forms of rural music, originally conceived to preserve endangered styles of music and enable the expression of distinct regional, national, or local identities, entered the mass-media, global market for popular music, where audiences all over Europe and the world could consume, appropriate, and interpret them for their own purposes.

FIGURE 2   The Swedish band Orientexpressen in 1978. They and many similar bands in Northern Europe were borrowing Balkan music a decade before the concept "world music" had given this tendency a name. Photo courtesy of Owe Ronström.

BIBLIOGRAPHY

Broughton, Simon, et al., eds. 1994. *World Music: The Rough Guide.* London: Rough Guides.

Buchanan, Donna. 1996. "Dispelling the Mystery: The Commodification of Women and Musical Tradition in *Le Mystère des Voix Bulgares.*" *Balkanistica* 9(2):193–210.

Burnett, Robert. 1996. *The Global Jukebox: The International Music Industry.* London: Routledge.

Erlmann, Veit. 1996. "The Aesthetics of the Global Imagination: Reflections on World Music in the 1990s." *Public Culture* 8:467–487.

Feld, Steven. 1995. "From Schizophonia to Schismogenesis: The Discourses and Practices of World Music and World Beat." In *The Traffic in Culture: Refiguring Art and Anthropology,* ed. George E. Marcus and Fred R. Myers, 96–126. Berkeley: University of California Press.

Frith, Simon, ed. 1989. *World Music, Politics, and Social Change.* Manchester: Manchester University Press.

Garofalo, Reebee. 1993. "Whose World, What Beat: The Transnational Music Industry, Identity, and Cultural Imperialism." *World of Music* 35:16–32.

Goodwin, Andrew, and Joe Gore. 1990. "World Beat and the Cultural Imperialism Debate." *Socialist Review* 20:63–80.

Guilbault, Jocelyne. 1993. "On Redefining the 'Local' Through World Music." *World of Music* 32:33–47.

Jowers, Peter. 1993. "Beating New Tracks: WOMAD and the British World Music Movement." In *The Last Post: Music After Modernism,* ed. Simon Miller, 52–87. Manchester: Manchester University Press.

Lipsitz, George. 1994. *Dangerous Crossroads: Popular Music, Postmodernism, and the Poetics of Place.* New York: Verso.

Robinson, Deanna Campbell, Elizabeth B. Buck, and Marlene Cuthbert. 1991. *Music at the Margins: Popular Music and Global Cultural Diversity.* Newbury Park, Calif.: Sage Publications.

Spencer, Peter. 1992. *World Beat: A Listener's Guide to Contemporary World Music on CD.* Pennington, N.J.: A Cappella Books.

Taylor, Timothy. 1997. *Global Pop: World Music, World Markets.* New York: Routledge.

Zemp, Hugo. 1996. "The/An Ethnomusicologist and the Record Business." *Yearbook for Traditional Music* 28:36–56.

AUDIOVISUAL RESOURCES

3 Mustaphas 3. 1989. *Heart of Uncle.* Ace Records CDORB 043. Compact disc.

Battlefield Band, The. 1993. *Quiet Days.* Temple COMD-2050. Compact disc.

Benedictine Monks of Santo Domingo de Silos, The. 1993. *Chant.* Angel CDC 7243 5 55138 2 3. Compact disc.

Bulgarian Voices—Angelite and Huun Huur Tu. 1996. *Fly, Fly My Sadness.* Shanachie 64071. Compact disc.

Chandra, Sheila. 1995. *Nada Brahma.* Caroline CAROL 1780-2. Compact disc.

Chieftains, The. 1991. *Chieftains 1.* Shanachie CD-79021. Compact disc.

———. 1989. *In China.* Shanachie CD-79050. Compact disc.

———. 1995. *The Long Black Veil.* BMG 09026–62702–2. Compact disc.

De Lucía, Paco. 1992. *Zyryab.* Verve.

Deep Forest. 1995. *Bohème.* Epic BK 67115. Compact disc.

Dissidenten. 1993. *The Jungle Book.* Worldly Dance Music 7202–2. Compact disc.

Le Mystère des Voix Bulgares. 1987. Electra/Nonesuch 79165–2. Compact disc.

———. 1992. *From Bulgaria with Love.* Mesa R2 79049. Compact disc.

Gabriel, Peter. 1989. *Passion: Music for "The Last Temptation of Christ."* Geffen Records M5G 24206. Compact disc.

———. 1992. *Us.* Real World GEFD 24473. Compact disc.

Gipsy Kings. 1992. *Gipsy Kings Live.* Electra/Musician 61390-2.

Irvine, Andy. 1994. *East Wind.* Tara 3027. Compact disc.

Kidjo, Angélique. 1996. *Fifa.* Mango 162-531 039–2. Compact disc.

Latcho Drom: Bande Originale du Film. 1993. Caroline CAROL 1776–2. Compact disc.

Lien, Annbjørg. 1995. *Felefeber: Norwegian Fiddle Fantasia.* Shanachie 64060. Compact disc.

MacKenzie, Talitha. 1994. *Solas.* Shanachie 79084. Compact disc.

Milladoiro. 1991. *Castellum Honesti.* Green Linnet Records GLCD 3055. Compact disc.

Papazov, Ivo. *Balkanology.* 1991. Hannibal HDCD 1363. Compact disc.

Sebestyén, Márta. 1997. *The Best of Márta Sebestyén.* Hannibal HNCD 1412. Compact disc.

Shannon, Sharon. 1995. *Out The Gap.* Green Linnet Records GLCD 3099. Compact disc.

Värttinä. 1995. *Aitara.* Xenophile Records XENO 4026. Compact disc.

Immigrant Music in Europe
Elizabeth J. Miles

Understanding Immigrant Music in Europe
Colonialism before World War II
Colonialism after World War II
From the 1980s to the Present

The legacy of colonialism and booming post-World-War-II industrial economies have attracted large and diverse immigrant populations to Europe, especially the metropolitan centers of Berlin, London, and Paris. Immigrants to Europe, mostly arrived since 1945, have produced musical practices that reflect the intersection of home cultural values, immigrant experiences, and interaction with eclectic cultural environments.

Little scholarly research has addressed immigrant music in Europe. Ethnomusicologists have focused on the traditional musics of discrete immigrant communities as windows to cultures left behind. But as immigrant populations integrate to varying degrees, forming identifiable but heterogeneous urban cultures, their musics have been transformed by the dialogue between multiple cultures, mass communication, and the struggle for immigrant identity. European cities since the 1960s have become symbols and cultural manifestations of globalism, and the musics of their immigrants reflect complex cultural, commercial, political, and social networks.

UNDERSTANDING IMMIGRANT MUSIC IN EUROPE

Understanding immigrant music in Europe involves making at least five kinds of distinctions. The first is between ethnic and national origins. In England, large populations have come from South Asia (India, Pakistan, Bangladesh), Africa (Nigeria, Ghana, Uganda), and the Caribbean (Jamaica, Trinidad). France hosts emigrants from Algeria, Cameroon, Congo, the Gambia, Guadeloupe, Guinea, Ivory Coast, Mali, Martinique, Morocco, Senegal, and Zaire. Many Indonesians now reside in Holland, and scattered immigrant groups live in many other European cities, such as Turks and Yugoslavs in both Berlin and Stockholm. While musical interaction between immigrant groups and host cultures has been relatively limited in England, communities in France have shared many musical styles and contexts.

A second distinction is between temporary and permanent musical presence. Immigrant musical life encompasses musicians who come to Europe to perform, record, or visit immigrant communities there, and permanent immigrants who bring music to their new environment as part of their cultural heritage. Since temporary visitors often decide to stay, and prosperous long-term residents often maintain dual

West African griots, such as pop star Mory Kanté,
perform with rock-style bands composed of
musicians from many countries, making
sophisticated multitrack recordings for
international record labels and conducting
world concert tours.

residences in Europe and their home countries, this distinction is flexible and interactive. In England, for instance, resident African musicians used to perform mostly in jazz and Caribbean bands, while touring bands from Nigeria and Ghana were generally favored for performances of *jùjú* and highlife. Since the 1970s, however, immigrant musicians from diverse African cultures have formed pan-African bands that fuse various musical styles, thus sharing African immigrant music culture with visiting musicians from abroad. The exchange of recordings between home and immigrant communities opens further avenues of communication, and recorded music flows from immigrant to home cultures, often as much as in the opposite direction.

A third distinction is between professional and nonprofessional musicians. Many non- or semiprofessional African musicians migrate to Paris in the hope of professional employment as musicians; by contrast, Khalifa Muslim musicians from Pakistan lost their professional status when they immigrated to England.

A fourth distinction involves music directed primarily inside or outside the community. Much immigrant music is performed for the immediate immigrant community, but an increasing proportion is directed toward a larger audience. Jamaican reggae in England began as a strong symbol of West Indian minority pride, but its subcultural message caused it to be adopted by white British punk rockers as an expression of rebellion and marketed to international white rock audiences by white-owned record companies. Popular *bhangra* dance music of Punjabis in England experienced a brief wave of popularity with white audiences, but ultimately the localized nature of its performance and the traditional Punjabi identity of its musicians and audiences have maintained it as an insider's music. Conversely, many African musicians in Paris consciously direct their recording and touring equally toward their home countries, Europe, the United States, and Japan.

A final and increasingly complex distinction among immigrant musicians is between traditional culture bearers and musicians who seek to interact with the musical styles and technology that they encounter in Europe. Many immigrant musicians occupy shifting positions along the traditional-acculturated axis, deploying new influences and tools to diverse ends. Many West African griots (traditional musicians by inheritance) follow their patrons, when the latter immigrate to Paris, to play traditional music in traditional contexts for celebrations and ceremonies. Temporary visitors without work permits, these musicians supplement their income with itinerant work in Parisian restaurants, where they perform for mixed audiences, perhaps using amplification and drums, singing in French, and performing with musicians from other ethnic groups. Other West African griots, such as pop star Mory Kanté, perform with rock-style bands composed of musicians from many countries, making sophisticated multitrack recordings for international record labels and conducting world concert tours. In Britain, Indian ghazal and *bhangra* musicians have adopted instruments from Western popular music, but ghazal singers reject the sampled disco sounds of dance-floor *bhangra*.

COLONIALISM BEFORE WORLD WAR II

The colonizers' cultural relationships with the colonized have had a long-term impact on the nature of immigrant music in Europe. The French actively encouraged colonized peoples to consider themselves part of French culture, while encouraging and taking an interest in native cultural expression. The result was a musical inclination toward internationalism among musicians in Africa and those who traveled to France to perform. In Algeria, for instance, Bedouin tribes migrating to the western coastal capital of Oran in the 1940s brought an earthy music celebrating personal freedom and sexuality, accompanied by flutes and a goblet-shaped drum (*darbouka*). In the international climate of Oran, musicians incorporated the influences of European music, Spanish flamenco, and Moroccan *gnawa* to form a style known as *rai*. Rebellious against the strictures of Islamic fundamentalism, *rai* became popular for weddings, parties, and nightclub performances.

The French conducted extensive musical research and recording in the African colonies, culminating in ambitious field excursions by the Musée de l'Homme during the 1950s and 1960s. These excursions established a precedent for the exploration of African music by French commercial record companies in recent decades.

In contrast to French colonial practice, the British sharply demarcated between ruler and subject, overlooking most native cultural forms as they imposed European-style education. Many British subjects took up the instruments and styles of military bands, producing an array of hybrids, such as Ghanaian highlife, designed to please or mimic the white rulers. Subjects also found ingenious ways around British cultural constrictions, such as the development of Trinidadian steelbands, which played on discarded oil drums when the playing of African drums was forbidden.

Some of the first evidence of immigrant music in Europe is historical mentions of West Indian sailors' shanties, performed in ports in the early 1800s. In the latter half of the 1800s, African and Asian populations grew in London's East End, and a series of government-sponsored "Foreigners' Fêtes" celebrated their arts and cultures, including folk music; however, pre–World War II immigrant populations in Europe were small, and the primary outside influence on European music came from touring African Americans: minstrels, spiritual singers, and then jazz musicians. American jazz was enormously popular in Europe, and many jazz musicians visited or immigrated to Paris, where there were an active performance circuit and enthusiastic audiences. In 1935, the popularity of touring American jazz bands in Britain instigated a Musicians' Union ban on performance by musicians from abroad. In the vacuum thus created, pan-Caribbean immigrant bands formed to play popular music, including jazz and rumba, for white audiences, providing the main source of live jazz performance until the ban was lifted in 1956.

COLONIALISM AFTER WORLD WAR II

The two decades following World War II brought the demobilization of soldiers from the European colonies, then colonial independence. Both events contributed to unprecedented waves of immigrants who sought expanded work and educational opportunities in the former mother countries. Many settled in metropolitan centers, in cohesive immigrant quarters connected in differing degrees to the surrounding community. Parallel to this movement was a global wave of urbanization. As people migrated to cities worldwide, urban music cultures everywhere experienced increasing contact and diversification. The cities of former European colonies produced a new generation of musicians, looking outward to the recording and media technology that could expand their musical worlds. Recorded musical exchanges between home countries and immigrant communities became increasingly bidirectional. The confluence of urban diversity, European cultural curiosity, and the affluence and resources of the industrialized world created a new internationalized cultural milieu, in which musical practices in former colonies and Europe underwent transformation and adaptation.

France

After independence, Martinique, Guadeloupe, and all the former French colonies except Guinea and Mauritania remained tied to the French franc. Free currency exchange enabled free musical exchange, as musicians could easily travel to Paris to record and return home to distribute their records. Some of the earliest active participants were performers of Congolese rumba, a popular, upbeat, electric, guitar-driven dance style blending Central African and Cuban rumba styles. Eventually called *soukous,* the style became the first African popular music to be appreciated throughout the continent, and recordings by artists such as Tabu Ley, Doctor Nico, and Franco were in high demand. Producers such as Ibrahima Sylla of Senegal made low-technology recordings in francophone Africa, distributing them throughout the continent via a vast but disorganized cassette market. Many club or party bands in the former French colonies favored a repertoire of *variété,* which mixed local and international styles with Western popular instrumentation.

African musicians in France became increasingly specialized and professionalized, using French recording technology and marketing methods to share their music with Europeans and Africans. The Zairian *soukous* band Tabu Ley appeared on French television in 1971, sparking national interest in this genre. In the same year Manu Dibango, a Cameroonian immigrant in Paris, sold more than three million copies of his recording "Soul Makossa." The free international flow of musicians and recordings spurred dissemination of African musics in Africa and Europe.

In Algeria, urbanization and independence brought *rai* into contact with electric guitars, trumpets, synthesizers, drum sets, and recording technology. Soon the music of young male (*cheb*) and young female (*chaba*) singers became the emblem of rebellious postcolonial Algerian youth, and cassette sales flourished (figure 1).

FIGURE 1   At a festival in Los Angeles, Chaba Fedela (*left*) and Cheb Sahraoui (*right*) perform Algerian *rai* music. Photo by Elizabeth J. Miles, 1991.

Concurrently, young Algerians were emigrating to Marseilles and Paris in large numbers, fleeing poverty and political repression. To young Algerian immigrants, ignored and discriminated against in France, *rai* was a true exile's music, celebrating freedom, rebellion against established values, and the daily pleasures of sensual life. Live performance and cassette recordings of *rai* were popular in both French cities.

Britain

Immigrants in Britain experienced far less interaction with their home and new host cultures than their counterparts in France. As a result, most immigrant music of the period was strongly insider identified. During the 1950s, Britain actively encouraged immigration from its colonies to bolster a labor force reduced by the war. Immigrants settled in London and its suburbs and the cities of the West Midlands. Most lived in densely populated quarters divided along ethnic lines, with inadequate housing, health care, employment, and law enforcement. More than half the immigrants shared a socioeconomic identity with working-class whites but played little part in British cultural life.

West Indians were already established as popular musicians, and increased immigration expanded the population enough to create a cohesive West Indian musical audience. The most popular style was Trinidadian calypso, a topical-song genre typically sung at carnival. An active West Indian nightclub scene developed in Soho, and a flurry of British calypso recordings, many spearheaded by journalist Denis Preston, provided wide dissemination of calypso to immigrants in England and Trinidadians back home.

The international spirit fostered by postwar immigration led to the 1951 Festival of Britain, a celebration of multicultural arts. The first festival featured a Trinidadian steelband concert by the Trinidad All Steel Percussion Orchestra. Their instruments were steel drums ("pans"), whose surfaces had been heated and beaten into multiple raised areas, each tuned to a set pitch. The ensemble impressed British audiences with its bright melodic and rhythmic sound and diverse repertoire, including calypsos, marches, opera excerpts, and orchestral music. The number of West Indian immigrants playing in steelbands in Britain increased steadily through the decade, despite a shortage of qualified pan makers and inhospitable places, such as abandoned warehouses and factories, for their manufacture. As community groups formed to play for festivals and carnival, the repertoire incorporated more European concert music, and pitch precision tempered to the chromatic scale became an increasingly important aspect of performance. In 1959, the first West Indian Mardi Gras was held at London's Paddington Town Hall. The festival continues as the Notting Hill Carnival, the most important annual celebration of immigrant culture in and around London.

During the early 1960s, a long-term dialectic began between immigrant West Indian music and white working-class youth subcultures. British West Indians were listening to ska, a Jamaican frenetic dance music performed by a small rock-style band, disseminated in England by underground distribution of recordings from Jamaica. Ska's pace and sophistication appealed to young white mods (trend seekers), who adopted it as their music. In the late 1960s, ska in Jamaica gave way to the more relaxed rock steady, which was dropped by the mods but taken up by a quite different white youth subculture, the skinheads. This embrace by rebellious youth further alienated West Indian music from mainstream culture, and BBC Radio, which played black music in the form of American soul, eschewed ska and rock steady.

As the religion of Rastafarianism permeated Jamaican music during the 1970s to form the new genre of reggae, West Indian immigrant culture in Britain underwent a transformation toward self-definition and cultural pride. The heavy "dub" sound of

Though the Dutch avidly listened to rock and roll, by 1956, Indonesian bands such as the Bellboys, the Room Rockers, the Hap Cats, and the Hot Jumpers were the accepted proponents of rock and roll in Holland.

reggae music, alien to white pop aesthetics, became symbolic of the black identity of West Indian immigrants. Reggae sound systems (mobile discos) circulated through West Indian communities. Despite the great popularity of reggae with immigrants, mainstream culture continued to ignore Jamaican music until white rock star Eric Clapton recorded a cover of reggae musician Bob Marley's song "I Shot the Sheriff." This mainstream musical endorsement brought acknowledgment and appreciation of Jamaican music, and soon a new British record label, Island Records, was marketing reggae on a grand scale to white rock audiences in Europe and the United States. English reggae bands, such as Steel Pulse and Aswad, supplemented the flow of reggae records from Jamaica.

Notwithstanding reggae's newfound broad appeal, the heavier, politically indignant dub styles still attracted British white punk rockers, and during the late 1970s an uneasy alliance grew through reggae between the punks and the West Indian community. This resulted in the playing and circulation of reggae in the punk community, a fusion "punk dub" style, and a series of Rock Against Racism concerts, featuring punk and reggae performers. This was perhaps the first instance of widespread musical collaboration, rather than co-option, between immigrant and white musicians in Britain.

Unlike the threatening sounds of ska, rock steady, and reggae, the sounds of steelbands were embraced by English educators as a benign, communal musical form, unburdened with Western theory and notation, appealing to a multiracial student body. While steelbands in Trinidad were increasingly becoming professionalized, with corporate sponsorship and intense interband rivalry, steelband music in England was incorporated into the school curriculum, resulting in youth festivals and competitions that involved students who had various ethnic identities.

Though West Indian immigration to Britain stabilized in the 1960s, political events intensified the flow of South Asian immigrants: the partition of India and Pakistan, then Bangladesh; the independence of Kenya in 1963, and subsequent Kenyanization, which encouraged ninety thousand South Asian residents of Kenya to choose British citizenship; and Idi Amin's expulsion of South Asians from Uganda in 1972. The resulting broadly designated South Asian community in England included Hindus, Muslims, and Sikhs from Bangladesh, India, and Pakistan, many via residency in Kenya and Uganda. More than half the South Asian immigrants were Punjabis from western India, and it was their *bhangra* that became the first musical South Asian presence in Britain. A traditional Punjabi rural and urban folk music played to celebrate the new year and the harvest season, *bhangra* features double-sided *dhol* and *dholki* drums playing rhythmic, exuberant music. In the 1960s, Punjabis in Britain began to form amateur *bhangra* bands, which performed traditional repertoires and styles at weddings, parties, and other celebrations. Though *bhangra* was a vital part of South Asian life, few other British residents encountered the genre during this period.

Germany

Since the formation of the European Economic Community (EEC) in the 1960s, millions of people have migrated from the overpopulated and indigent regions of the Mediterranean Basin to richer Northern European countries. The Treaty of Rome (1960) provided the opportunity for millions of Arabs from the Maghreb to migrate to France and Belgium, large communities of Turks to settle in Belgium, Germany, and Sweden, and numerous Yugoslavs, Portuguese, Greeks, and Spaniards to seek greater opportunity and prosperity in the North.

A bilateral agreement between Turkey and Germany, signed in 1961, led to the migration of more than a million guest workers (*gastarbeiter*) to the poorer areas of German cities. The term, still favored today in Turkish and German communities, is indicative of their perceived impermanent status in German society. Many *gastarbeiter* have no rights of self-determination, and legislation of the early 1990s sought to undermine their legal status and encourage their repatriation.

Despite these adversities, strong Turkish musical communities developed in many German cities. Financial necessity forced many professional musicians from Turkey to give up their professional status upon arrival in their new home; they perform exclusively for small private and semiprivate gatherings of Turkish migrants. Others chose to integrate their musical identities and widen their appeal to non-Turkish audiences, often through the financial support of German government agencies, by adopting Western tonality and European instrumentation.

Far from being a homogeneous group, Turkish migrants in Germany have adopted conformist and nonconformist attitudes toward cultural integration. Intercultural performances by Turkish Alevi (a religious sect) musicians are included in many German socialist events, and some Turkish youth have been perceived as a degenerate, fringe element that denigrates all aspects of Turkish music in favor of Western popular genres or the rebellious sounds of *arabesk* disco. Since the 1980s, a renaissance of interest in more traditional Turkish musical genres and a genuine desire to create a unified musical identity for *gastarbeiter* culture have been found in these migrant communities.

The Netherlands

Another nexus for immigrants' musical performance during the postwar period was Holland, where newly independent Indonesian immigrants became the first musicians in Europe to perform American rock and roll. Many Indonesian immigrants to Holland exercised little choice in their migration decision or subsequent living arrangements. They were comprised primarily of Indos, people of mixed Asian and European origin who bore Dutch names and found it uncomfortable to remain in politically charged, postindependence Indonesia, and of Moluccans from the Dutch East Indies who had been recruited into the Dutch army, then forcibly repatriated to Holland to avoid complicating the Indonesian-Moluccan war. Indos lived in subsidized housing, apart from mainstream Dutch society, and Moluccans stayed in temporary camps. Thus isolated, musicians from both groups filled their time listening to rock and roll on the radio and forming family-based bands to perform in imitation of the style.

Though the Dutch avidly listened to rock and roll, white Dutch musicians did not perform the genre. Indo and Moluccan bands jumped into the breach, playing in pubs with guitars, homemade basses and amplifiers, and the occasional but optional microphone. By 1956, Indonesian bands such as the Bellboys, the Room Rockers, the Hap Cats, and the Hot Jumpers were the accepted proponents of rock and roll in Holland. Viewed as a rebellious dance-hall style by media and the music industry,

Indonesian rock was little documented or recorded, but young mixed audiences supported an active live-performance scene centered in The Hague.

An invitational performance in Germany by one of these bands, the Tielman Brothers, sparked a German craze for Indonesian rock, fed by fascination with the immigrants' exotic style and the large American military audience. Many Dutch bands toured Germany or relocated there, creating a reputation for wild behavior and earning large performance fees.

With the success and popularity of the immigrant bands, white Dutch musicians began to perform rock and roll. By the mid-1960s, Indonesian rock had been eclipsed by Nederbeat, white Dutch rock in the style of the Beatles. Indonesian dominance of Dutch rock receded, but revival movements persist in Holland and Germany. A 1981 revival concert festival in The Hague retrospectively applied the term *Indorock* to the genre and period. The Indonesian-Dutch alliance with rock and roll is currently evidenced in the work of American rock guitarist Eddie Van Halen, a Dutchman of Indo origins, who emigrated to the United States as a child.

FROM THE 1980S TO THE PRESENT

In the 1980s, immigrant music in Europe was transformed by increasing contact among immigrant cultures, growing global awareness in industrialized countries that resulted in curiosity toward the world's musics, and the intercession of high-technology recording facilities and the music industry. Though music continued to be an emblem of ethnic identity, it began to serve several layers of audience: immigrants in the immediate community; white Europeans in the immediate community; Americans and Japanese, purchasing records through developing international distribution networks; home communities attracted to the stylistic and technological transformation of local music culture; and diasporic immigrant communities, buying records produced in Europe, but representing the music of home.

France

The 1981 election of socialist President François Mitterrand generated a politically sanctioned celebration of cultural diversity in France. With more than four million immigrants, about 30 percent of whom had come from West and North Africa, France began to promote immigrant music as an alternative to imported American and British rock and a symbol of French cultural vitality. Minister of Culture Jack Lang supported African musicians by helping them legally and financially and providing governmental support for world music concerts and recordings. These concerts included Africa Fête, an annual concert of African popular music, organized since 1978 by Paris-based manager and promoter Mamadou Konté, an émigré from Mali.

Africa Fête, featuring performers from many African music cultures, served as a symbol of a new spirit of pan-Africanism. Many recordings mixed the stylistic influences of Antillean *zouk,* Zairian *soukous,* Cameroonian *makossa,* and the popular West African style termed Mande Sound by some ethnomusicologists. In 1984, musicians from four African countries (Salif Keita from Mali, Mory Kanté from Guinea, Souzy Kasseya from Zaire, and Touré Kunda from Senegal) collaborated on a recording to benefit Ethiopia. Algerian *rai* singer Khaled's album *Kutché* featured sub-Saharan African drumming and showed influences of African American funk, hip-hop, and house music. Cross-cultural immigrant musical collaborations reflected contemporary ideas of multiculturalism and linked disparate identity struggles through a shared expression of difference. Many musicians in Paris rejected the

FIGURE 2   At a festival in Los Angeles, the West African *kora* player Mory Kanté sings. To his right, the neck of the *kora,* a harp-lute, sticks up above the monitor. Photo by Elizabeth Miles, 1991.

immigrant paradigm of insular communities to forge a popular-music movement that expressed a conglomerate postcolonial identity.

The international record industry was reluctant to support this movement, but French enterprises provided musical outlets. The record companies Celluloid and Pathé-Marconi contracted with producer Ibrahima Sylla to record African artists for distribution to European markets. The establishment of FM radio frequencies in France led three stations—Radio Nova, Tropic, and Oui—to feature eclectic international programming. In addition to countless small cassette stores selling immigrant music, large retailers, such as Fnac and the Virgin Megastore, began selling immigrants' recordings.

A series of hit world-music albums and songs signaled the music's growing audience. Kassav, a *zouk* band from the Antilles, sold enough copies of its album *Zouk La Se Sel Medikaman Nou Ni* to qualify for the record industry's gold designation in 1983. Reggae singer Alpha Blondy from the Ivory Coast followed suit in 1987 with his song "Jerusalem." In that year, international record labels began showing interest in popular music from around the world; record executives officially declared worldbeat a marketing category, and many companies began to record worldbeat artists for their own or subsidiary labels, marketing in Europe, Japan, and the United States.

The British record company Barclay was among the first that succeeded in this endeavor; in 1988, "*Ye Ke Ye Ke,*" by *kora* player Mory Kanté, became the top-selling record in France and Germany (figure 2). Meanwhile, some immigrant music began to unhinge itself from its home base. Algerian *rai* singer Cheb Kader, who had immigrated to Paris at an early age, had top-ten records in Germany and Switzerland, television coverage in France, and international concert tours, but remained relatively unknown in Algeria.

Britain

In England, interest in world music among whites ran high, but the focus was on imported artists. An organization in Wiltshire, World of Music, Arts and Dance (WOMAD), supported by British rock musician Peter Gabriel, sponsored the first of an ongoing series of world-music festivals in 1981, featuring musicians from around

Though the highly synthesized, sampled sounds of *bhangra* appear modern and rebellious, the traditionally based song texts and strictly observed cultural and behavioral codes of *bhangra* performances serve to reinforce young immigrants' ties to their parents' culture.

the world, but without reference to immigrants in Britain. London's GlobeStyle Records, founded in 1985 by two white world-music aficionados, pioneered the recording of musicians from around the world, then packaging and marketing the product worldwide as popular music; but again, the exotic and unknown were favored. Many British record companies contracted with immigrant artists living in Paris but ignored the music of locally resident African, Caribbean, and South Asian immigrants.

Within the South Asian musical community, the availability of recording technology and eclectic musical influences spawned genres that have attracted international attention. *Filmi,* the music of Hindu films, is popular in Britain with many young South Asian immigrants, whose parents forbid them to attend Western-style nightclubs. *Filmi* functions as a proprietary popular music outside the Western realm, from which young South Asians are excluded by whites and their own parents. As British bands have formed to perform film music live, the original songs have been transformed by the influence of Western pop. The recreation of *filmi* in live performance in Britain has created a new musical form, liberated from its original context.

Another movement among young South Asian immigrant musicians blends classical Indian music with Western instruments and contexts. In the mid-1980s, the British record company Triple Earth asked a young second-generation Indian singer, Najma Akhtar, to record an album of Urdu ghazals, adding a saxophone to the violin and tabla accompaniment. The resulting new-ghazal album *Qareeb,* released in 1988, was popular with British South Asians and held enough international appeal to be released in the United States by Shanachie Records. With a degree in engineering and little training in classical Indian music, Akhtar experiments with the classical tradition instead of the more popularized Asian styles. Singer Sheila Chandra performs in a similar vein. Her album title, *Weaving My Ancestors' Voices,* involves a conscious recreation and transformation of preimmigrant identity. Akhtar and Chandra have achieved fame within the South Asian community and abroad.

The most popular musical style among young South Asian immigrants remains Punjabi *bhangra,* which has absorbed diverse stylistic influences since the 1980s to form new designations, such as *bhangra* beat, rock *bhangra,* and house *bhangra.* From the London suburb of Southall to towns throughout southeast England and the Midlands, *bhangra* bands play in expected nightclub settings and daytimers, afternoon performances for teenagers whose parents forbid nighttime socializing. Attendees skip classes and change from school uniforms to traditional Punjabi clothing. Though truantism and the highly synthesized, sampled sounds of *bhangra* appear modern and rebellious, the traditionally based song texts and strictly observed cultural and behavioral codes of *bhangra* performances serve to reinforce young immigrants' ties to their parents' culture, allowing them to experience the environment of young, urban England in a self-defined manner.

Successful *bhangra* bands, including Alaap, Golden Star, Heera, and Holle Holle, have made many recordings for the British record company Multitone and the Gramophone Company of India—recordings that appeal to South Asian immigrants of diverse ethnic and religious backgrounds. In 1987, a brief *bhangra* craze brought the style to mainstream attention through a media-brokered fascination with its exotic roots; however, major international record companies have overlooked the style, and it remains essentially a community-based phenomenon, a dynamic compromise between South Asian heritage and European environment.

Immigrant music is currently recorded in Europe by record labels including Barclay, Earthworks, GlobeStyle, Island, Real World, Stern's, Triple Earth, and World Circuit in England; Blue Silver, BUDA Musique, Celluloid/Mélodie, Pathé Marconi, and Sonodisc in France; Crammed Discs in Belgium; and Elektra, Mango, Nonesuch, Rounder, Rykodisc, and Shanachie in the United States. Record stores and nightclubs featuring world music thrive in Paris, London, Amsterdam, Stockholm, Berlin, Lisbon, and Milan. The WOMAD and Africa Fête festivals now tour the world, playing major cities in Europe, Canada, and the United States. The European Forum of Worldwide Music Festivals in Helsinki, Finland, tracks large-scale world-music festivals annually.

BIBLIOGRAPHY

Anhegger, Robert. 1981. "Lieder über Gastarbeiter, Lieder von Gastarbeitern." *Ästhetik und Kommunikation* 44:83–90.

Arnston Harris, Laura. 1990. "Jatigui: Tata Bambo Kouyate." *Ethnomusicology* 34(3):516–520.

Banerji, Sabita. 1988. "Ghazals to Bhangra in Great Britain." *Popular Music* 7(2):207–213.

Barlow, Sean, and Ned Sublette, eds. 1993. *Afropop Worldwide Listener's Guide.* Washington, D.C.: World Music Productions.

Baumann, Gerd. 1990. "The Re-Invention of *Bhangra*: Social Change and Aesthetic Shifts in a Punjabi Music in Britain." *The World of Music* 32(2):81–98.

Baumann, Max Peter. 1979. *Musikalische Streiflichter einer Grosstadt.* Berlin: Fachrichtung vergleichenden Musikwissenschaft des FB 14 der Freie Universität Berlin.

———. 1985. *Musik der Turken in Deutschland.* Berlin: Fachrichtung vergleichenden Musikwissenschaft des FB 14 der Freie Universität Berlin.

Collins, John. 1985. *African Pop Roots.* London: W. Foulsham.

Coplan, David. 1982. "The Urbanisation of African Music: Some Theoretical Observations." *Popular Music* 2:113–130.

Ewens, Graeme. 1992. *Africa A Ye! A Celebration of African Music.* New York: Da Capo Press.

Fairley, Jan. 1989. "Analysing Performance: Narrative and Ideology in Concerts by Karaxû!" *Popular Music* 8(1):1–30.

Farrell, Gerry. 1988. "Reflecting Surfaces: Indian Music in Popular Music and Jazz." *Popular Music* 7(2):189–205.

Feld, Steven. "Notes on World Beat." *Public Culture Bulletin* 1(1):31–37.

Fletcher, Peter. 1988. "Teaching Music in a British School Environment: Leicestershire's Indian Music Project." *ISME Yearbook* 15:117–121.

Frith, Simon. 1989. *World Music, Politics, and Social Change.* Manchester: Manchester University Press.

Ghazal and Beat. Southall, Middlesex: Derbar Publishers.

Graham, Ronnie. 1988. *The Da Capo Guide to Contemporary African Music.* New York: Da Capo Press.

Hanly, Francis, and Tim May, eds. 1989. *Rhythms of the World.* London: BBC Books.

Hebdige, Dick. 1979. *Subculture: The Meaning of Style.* London: Methuen.

———. 1987. *Cut 'n' Mix: Culture, Identity and Caribbean Music.* London: Comedia/Methuen.

Horn, David, and Philip Tagg. 1982. *Popular Music Perspectives: Papers from the First International Conference on Popular Music Research, Amsterdam, June 1981.* Gothenburg and Exeter: International Association for the Study of Popular Music.

Horn, Pierre L., ed. 1991. *Handbook of French Popular Culture.* New York: Greenwood Press.

Kebede, Ashenafi. 1991. "Aster Aweke." *Ethnomusicology* 35(1):157–160.

Knight, Roderick C. 1989. "The Mande Sound: African Popular Music on Records." *Ethnomusicology* 33(2):371–376.

———. 1991. "Music Out of Africa: Mande Jaliya in Paris." *The World of Music* 33(1):52–69.

Lee, Hélène. 1988. *Rockers d'Afrique: Alpha Blondy, Mory Kanté, Salif Keita, Touré Kunda et les autres.* Paris: Éditions Albin Michel.

Manuel, Peter. 1988. *Popular Musics of the Non-Western World.* New York: Oxford University Press.

Meintjes, Louise. 1990. "Paul Simon's Graceland, South Africa, and the Mediation of Musical Meaning." *Ethnomusicology* 34(1):37–73.

Mermoud, Laurence. 1988. "Mamadou M'a Dit." *Emois, Mensual Européen* 12:45–47.

Mutsaers, Lutgard. 1990. "Indorock: An Early Eurorock Style." *Popular Music* 9(3):307–320.

Nettl, Bruno. 1985. *The Western Impact on World Music.* New York: Schirmer Books.

O'Connell, John Morgan. 1991. "A Turkish Alevi Musician in Berlin: An Artist's Individual View and the Assumptions of a General Musical Tradition." M.A. thesis, University of California, Los Angeles.

Oliver, Paul. 1988. "Introduction: Aspects of the South Asia/West Crossover." *Popular Music* 7(2):119–122.

———, ed. 1990. *Black Music in Britain: Essays on the Afro-Asian Contribution to Popular Music.* Popular Music in Britain Series. Milton Keynes and Philadelphia: Open University Press.

Reck, David C. 1985. "Beatles Orientalis: Influences from Asia in a Popular Song Form." *Asian Music* 16(1):83–150.

Reinhard, Ursula. 1987. "Turkische Musik: Ihre Interpreten in West-Berlin und in der Heimat." *Jahrbuch für Volksliedforschung* 32:81–92.

Roberts, John Storm. 1972. *Black Music of Two Worlds.* New York: Praeger.

Robinson, Deanna Campbell, Elizabeth B. Buck, and Marlene Cuthbert. 1991. *Music at the Margins.* Newbury Park: Sage Publications.

Ronstrom, Owe. 1991. "*Folklor:* Staged Folk Music and Folk Dance Performances of Yugoslavs in Stockholm." *Yearbook for Traditional Music* 23:69–77.

Shepherd, John. 1988. "Africa in the World of Popular Music." *Popular Music* 7(1):101–103.

Slobin, Mark. 1993. *Subcultural Sounds: Micromusics of the West.* Hanover: Wesleyan University Press.

Snowden, Don. 1992. "Najma: Luminous Lady of the Love Poems." *The Beat* 11(2):36–39.

Stapleton, Chris, and Chris May. 1987. *African All-Stars: The Pop Music of a Continent.* London: Quartet.

Stern's World Music Review: Tradewind. London: Stern's African Music Center.

Stewart, Gary. 1993. "The Music of Sierra Leone: Maringa Roots, Rokoto Shoots." *The Beat* 12(1):45–47.

Tarte, Bob. 1988. "GlobeStyle: The Record Company That Shook the World." *Reggae and African Beat* 7(1):26–30.

Tillman, June B. 1988. "Some Reflections on the Collection and Use of Intercultural Material for British Education." *ISME Yearbook* 15:141–147.

Wallis, Roger, and Krister Malm. 1984. *Big Sounds from Small Peoples: The Music Industry in Small Countries.* New York: Pendragon Press.

Waterman, Christopher Alan. 1990. *Jùjú: A Social History and Ethnography of an African Popular Music.* Chicago: University of Chicago Press.

Wentz, Brooke. "Salif Keita and the Coup d'État." *The Beat* 10(5):38–45.

AUDIOVISUAL RESOURCES

Adé, King Sunny. 1984. *Aura.* Produced by Martin Meissonnier. Island Records 7567-90177. Compact disc.

Alaap. 1984. *Teri Chunni De Sitare.* Arishma Records. LP disk.

Aweke, Aster. 1989. *Aster Aweke.* Produced by Iain Scott and Bunt Stafford. Triple Earth 107. LP disk.

Chandra, Sheila. 1992. *Weaving My Ancestors' Voices.* Real World/Virgin 1704-62322. Compact disc.

Dibango, Manu. 1980. *Gone Clear.* Mango/Island Records 16253-9539. LP disk.

Fadela, Chaba. 1988. *You Are Mine.* Produced by Rachid Baba-Ahmed. Mango/Island Records 9827. LP disk.

Kader, Cheb. 1990. *From Oran to Paris.* 1990. Shanachie Records 64029. Compact disc.

Kanté, Mory. 1990. *Touma.* Mango/Island Records 16253-9903. Compact disc.

Kassav. 1992. *Tékit Easy.* One World Records/Sony Music France COL 472873. Compact disc.

Keita, Salif. 1987. *Soro.* Produced by Ibrahima Sylla. Mango/Island Records 9808. LP disk.

Khaled, Cheb, and Safy Boutella. 1989. *Kutchè.* Produced by Martin Meissonnier. Capitol/Intuition 7-90934. Compact disc.

Kouyate, Tata Bambo. 1989. *Jatigui.* Produced by Baba Cissoko Foutanga. Notes by Lucy Duran. GlobeStyle ORB042. Compact disc.

Lema, Ray, and Professor Stefanov. N.d. *Ray Lema and Professor Stefanov.* Buda Records. LP disk.

Najma. 1989. *Qareeb.* Produced by Iain Scott and Bunt Stafford-Clark. Shanachie Records 64009. Compact disc.

N'Dour, Youssou. 1988. *Immigrés.* Earthworks/Virgin 7567-91020. LP disk.

Our Boys Steel Orchestra. 1991. *Pan Progress.* Mango/Island Records 162 539 610–2, 162 539 916–4. Compact disc, cassette.

Steel Pulse. 1978. *Handsworth Revolution.*
Mango/Island Records 16253-9502. LP disk.

Tabu Ley Signeur Rochereau and Afrisa
International Orchestra. 1989. *Babeti Soukous.*
Real World/Virgin 259-943-222. LP disk.

Part 3
Music Cultures of Europe

Only in the twentieth century was the political map of Europe divided consistently into nation-states. This recent pattern and current political reality provide the basis for the organization of this part of the encyclopedia. For most of history, parts of Europe were divided into hundreds of tiny principalities and city-states, while other parts were united into huge, multiethnic empires. This much longer history undercuts a simplistic view of European music as divided into many national musics.

To take this complicated history into account, the articles in Part 3 should be read at many different levels. Some musical styles may have a national character and be expressive of national identity. Others maintain local, regional, or minority identities. Reflecting long histories of shared cultural experience within far-flung empires, the same or similar musical styles, customs, and instruments are common to ethnically distinct neighbors. And some aspects of musical life—strophic songs, the structure of instrumental dance tunes, calendar and life-cycle customs, and professional art music—link many far-flung traditions in a pan-European web.

Bowed lute (*lijerica*) player from Osojnik, Croatia, near Dubrovnik. Photo by Elsie Ivancich Dunin, 1973.

Transnational Ethnic Groups

The European political landscape consists of many small nation-states that tend to be viewed as ethnically homogeneous. In fact, few are, or ever were. They contain minority groups from neighboring countries, as Swedes in Finland and Turks in Greece; a mix of ethnicities, as in Russia or Bosnia-Hercegovina; minorities lacking their own state, as the Basques of Spain and France; and pan-European minorities, including Jews and Gypsies (Roma). For transnational ethnic minorities, music is a marker of ethnic and cultural difference. It expresses a distinctive cultural identity, which becomes highly meaningful when that identity is suppressed, censored, or persecuted by the mainstream. For certain minorities, including the Saami of the Arctic, the Basques of the Iberian Peninsula, and the Celtic peoples of northwestern Europe, singing songs gives new life to ancient languages in danger of being lost and affords a sense of identity distinct from that of the nation-state in which they find themselves.

A Basque street musician plays a bagpipe.
Ergoven, Basque Provinces of Spain, 1952.
Photo courtesy of the Alan Lomax Collection,
New York.

Jewish Music in Europe
Philip V. Bohlman

Contexts for Music
Music Systems
Song Texts
Conceptions of Music
Instrumental Music
Social Groups and Music
History of Music
History of Scholarship

Jewish music in Europe comprises cultural and historical phenomena that stretch across national and linguistic borders, and even beyond the continental boundaries. European Jews were not an isolated religious or linguistic group. Jewish music is found in different domains of European music history and culture, not simply in Jewish communities or the musical practices of Judaism.

Jews have never lived in large numbers in Europe. The first European Jewish communities formed in the wake of the destruction of the Second Temple by the Romans (70 C.E.), when Jews were forced into diaspora and settled in Mediterranean Europe. During the first centuries of the Common Era, Jews accompanied Roman expansion into Central and Western Europe, settling in areas of administrative and financial importance to the Roman Empire. Despite this dispersion and the small numbers of Jews, contact among the communities was common, particularly as Jews established centers of learning, for example, at Worms, an imperial seat of power on the Rhine River, which students from elsewhere in Europe frequently visited. The dispersion of Jewish communities responded further to large-scale European events. During the Black Death, the great series of plagues during the 1300s, Jews were severely persecuted, and many were forced to migrate from Central Europe to Eastern Europe. At the final expulsion of North African Muslims from the Iberian Peninsula at the end of the 1400s, Jews were expelled from the peninsula. These European events and the centuries-long presence of Jews in Europe have left indelible marks on contemporary Jewry, for example, in the designation of the two largest groups of Jews as Ashkenazic (German) and Sephardic (Spanish).

Greater Jewish integration into all aspects of European culture began with the Renaissance and the Age of Discovery, the so-called early modern era of European history, when regional differences among European Jewish communities intensified. The centers of Sephardism shifted from the Iberian Peninsula and southern France to the Balkans, the British Isles, the Netherlands, North Africa, and the Middle East. Eastern Ashkenazic communities flourished, and the cultural area identified with the Yiddish language grew in size and importance in Poland, Russia, the Baltic States, Ukraine, and the northern part of southeastern Europe. The geography of Jewish Europe had largely established itself by the 1700s, when the Enlightenment affected the cultures of Europe, including its Jewish communities. The *haskalah* ('learning, rationalism', the European Jewish Enlightenment) in Central and Eastern Europe and the explosive growth of Hasidism in Eastern Europe were responses to the Enlightenment, the *haskalah* leading to modernization of European Jewish culture and Hasidism to a protection of conservative values through new forms of mysticism.

The Jewish polity in Europe was never the product of nationalism and the political structures of statehood. Instead, it anchored itself in religion, understood as a spiritual, aesthetic, linguistic, political, and institutional framework. Music, concepts of music, and systems of music arose as part of Judaism and the complex interactions inherent in Jewish polity. Jewish music exists within a historical dynamic that is pan-European, rather than simply local. Non-Jewish repertories, styles, and contexts influenced Jewish music, which bears witness historically to influences from elsewhere.

Any account of Jewish music in Europe must recognize that Jews were active as musicians outside Jewish society. Indeed, music, particularly specialized performance, often served as a cultural domain in non-Jewish society where Jews were able to excel. In the Mediterranean world of antiquity, Jews were noted as specialists in non-Jewish cultures, but they increasingly became musical specialists in Europe during the modern era. Modern European music history reflects this encounter between non-Jewish society and a society that provided a model for internal "otherness" during a period when Europe was encountering external "otherness" as the result of colonial expansion. These patterns of otherness determine categories of music and musical life. Nationalism and the invention of various forms of folk music came to characterize European music in general during the 1800s, and Jewish music responded to the historical necessity of developing a music that expressed a distinctive cultural identity.

Like European musical thought in general, Jewish musical thought is motivated by historicism—the need to understand the present in relationship to the past, and to recover aspects of the past for the present. Religious music has explicit and implicit connections to the past, the music of ancient Israel, if not the Temple, and these are manifest in the recitation of biblical texts, sung prayers, the music of the synagogue, and festival music at other historical moments. The essential historical question is not whether these connections can be proved or not, rather just how they produce systems of music and influence musical life. At every historical moment, this historicism heightens the debates about Jewish music and its role in Jewish life. In the course of European Jewish history, it resulted in constant reexamination of the relation between Jewish music as a cultural metaphor and the musical culture of the external culture, and it undergirded the need to regard the Israel of the past and present as a source for music and ideas about music.

European Jewish history effectively ended with the Holocaust and the pan-European Jewish community's near-total annihilation, from which, excepting a few large Jewish communities (as in London), Jewish life in Europe has not recovered. European Jewish music has taken its place in a larger, contemporary process, in which the past is vital to an understanding of what Jewish music is and has been. Without the Jewish presence in European music, modern Jewish musical thought would be inconceivable

CONTEXTS FOR MUSIC

Many contexts for European Jewish music are religious and belong to the ritualized activities of the family and the community. Music accompanies holidays and rites of passage, with many genres fixed in the liturgy or customs associated with these and others spawned by the forms of celebration that surrounded them. Religious contexts include specific religious texts, liturgical and paraliturgical, that have become the basis for musical performance, but oral traditions are no less present, permitting variation and the influence of local musical traditions. Thus, at one level, the religious contexts for Jewish music serve to unify European traditions, and at another level, they make it possible for local variation to enter the musical life of individual communities.

Seasonal rituals

Seasonal rituals rely on narrative texts with specific historical references, and the music of these rituals often serves as a means of recounting these narratives and situating them in specific performance contexts. Hanukkah, a holiday falling in late November or December, celebrates the struggle of Judas Maccabaeus against the forces of hellenization in ancient Israel during the year 164 B.C.E. Children's songs and games refer directly to the symbols of this struggle, for example, the miracle of Temple lamps burning for eight days.

Many seasonal rituals rely on narratives that describe the confrontation between Jews and non-Jewish culture, the most persistent historical theme. Passover recounts Jews' encounter with ancient Egypt and their exodus, and this narrative is performed from the text of the Haggadah, a written narrative that contains many musical genres, sung by different members of the family, ranging from the youngest child to the head of the household. Seasonal rituals generate specific musical genres appropriate to their narrative, for example the laments that are most characteristic of the mourning of the destruction of the Temple (Tishah-b'Av) in July or August.

Seasonal rituals centered in the synagogue, for example, the High Holidays of Rosh Hashanah (New Year) and Yom Kippur (Atonement Day), require musical specialists for those ritual aspects that take place in the community. The High Holidays, despite their solemnity, are the single occasion in which all forms of Judaism tolerate instrumental music in the synagogue, namely the blowing of the shofar (figure 1). Certain genres of liturgical music—notably the Kol Nidre of Yom Kippur, which became a vehicle for cantorial virtuosity in the 1800s and a source for art-music settings in the nineteenth and twentieth centuries, for example, that by Arnold Schoenberg (1874–1951)—have been elevated because of their association with these holidays.

Life-cycle rituals

Secular and religious music takes place during life-cycle rituals and other rites of passage, including several of the most widespread folk-song genres, like lullabies and love songs. Whether or not these were traditionally designated folk songs in indigenous thinking about music, Jewish folk-music scholars and editors identified them as typical of the folk culture of the European community.

Weddings have long served as a life-cycle ritual in which several forms of Jewish music making converge. During the ritual, music is bound to religious texts and ritual performance. Framing the wedding in Ashkenazic rituals were several forms of secular and semireligious music, provided by instrumental musicians hired for the wedding procession, a dance after the wedding, and other secular celebrations. These musicians undergirded the transitional stages in the wedding ceremony—the preparation of the liminal moment during which the wedding was performed and the retransition of the married couple into the secular life of the Jewish community.

The genres that these life-cycle rituals embodied juxtaposed the secular and the sacred through performance, in effect multiplying the possibility for many forms of music making to coexist in a society whose polity was fundamentally religious.

FIGURE 1   A man blows a shofar at a service in the 1970s. Photo courtesy of YIVO Institute for Jewish Research, New York.

Narratives and dramas

Several genres of European Jewish music lend themselves to performance in narrative and dramatic contexts. Certain festivals are celebrated using narratives, from biblical texts or special texts traditionally performed during the holidays. The narrative of the exodus of the Jews from ancient Egypt is the best example of a text, the Haggadah, connected to a specific holiday, Passover, and performed using song and sung prayer. Purim is the holiday with the most widespread dramatic traditions, namely the performance of a Purim play (Yiddish *purimspil*) that recounts the narrative of persecution and freedom as told in the Book of Esther. Purim plays employ music to create a larger narrative fabric or accompany certain scenes or texts within the drama. These musical sections of Purim plays often spawn genres of song that then exist outside the drama itself, for example, the *stanzl*, based on Purim texts and found in the rural areas of the former Hapsburg Empire, where this narrative genre is widespread in non-Jewish communities.

Yiddish theater, the best-known dramatic form that developed within Jewish Europe, existed in many forms, some of which incorporated music that was more popular, others undergoing processes of classicization that eventually produced more extensive musical dramas. Yiddish theater in the immigrant setting of the United States influenced many other areas of musical activity, in Jewish and non-Jewish cultures. This was also true in Europe, with the exception that the impact of Yiddish theater and its music largely did not spill over into non-Jewish society.

Dance

Only recently have scholars begun to study the genres of dance in European Jewish society. Dance first appears in iconographic sources as stylized movement accompanying ritual or rites of passage, such as the processions that accompany weddings. Dance followed the wedding itself, and its importance is evident in the numerous accounts of instrumental musicians, such as klezmer bands, which garnered a large part of their livelihood playing for wedding dances. Community dances also accompanied certain holidays, particularly Purim. The Hasidim have traditionally used dance as a means of celebration, often as a part of events in which some form of trance enhances the believer's relationship to God.

Dance has a similar function when used to celebrate the autumn religious holiday, Simchas Torah (Hebrew *śimḥath tōrāh* 'rejoicing of the Torah'), in which processions and ecstatic dances are common. Research by Walter Salmen has revealed that secular dance in European Jewish communities may have played a central social role. Salmen located the presence of many large dance halls in the medieval Jewish cities of Central Europe, many of them near the center of the city. Salmen has further discovered that a large percentage of dance schools in fin-de-siècle Vienna had Jewish proprietors, suggesting that social dance served as one means of facilitating Jewish entrance into bourgeois society. Further studies of the relation between music and dance in European Jewish society may prove to be one of the most fruitful areas for future research.

Entertainments and concerts

Early designations of European Jewish musical professionals—as *badhanim, letzim,* and *klezmorim,* for example—suggest that music often functioned as entertainment. Settings for entertainment ranged from rituals and holidays to the salons and theaters of modern Jewish Europe. Weddings provided a setting at which the *badhan,* a combination of trickster, acrobat, and jester, entertained while mediating certain aspects of the performance of the ritual. *Letzim* and *klezmorim* also performed at weddings and other festivities, though their role as entertainers was more clearly defined by their specialty, as instrumentalists. During the nineteenth and twentieth centuries,

During the nineteenth and twentieth centuries, certain genres of entertainment, such as cabaret in cities like Berlin, Munich, Vienna, and Warsaw, would be unthinkable without the contributions of Jewish musicians.

Jewish musicians were increasingly active as entertainers in Eastern and Central Europe, and certain genres of entertainment, such as cabaret in cities like Berlin, Munich, Vienna, and Warsaw, would be unthinkable without the contributions of Jewish musicians and the traditions of Jewish secular entertainment that Jewish broadside and theater publications document.

As performers and audiences, Jews supported concert life of all kinds in Europe. Between World War I and the rise of Nazism in the 1930s, many concerts outside the Jewish community effectively shifted back to the Jewish community. Particularly in Central Europe, Jewish communities began to form their own orchestras, large and small chamber ensembles, and choruses, whose repertories ranged from folk songs to liturgical compositions. New concert halls were built, and music education, formal and informal, responded to this transformation of the concert setting, for which Jewish composers, like Ernest Bloch, Mario Castelnuovo-Tedesco, and Darius Milhaud, created new works, secular and sacred. The concert thus entered a period when it was traditionalized, responding perhaps to the Jewish community's modernization and emancipation during the previous century. Even in the most secular musical genres, the encounter of European Jews with non-Jewish society had not undermined the centrality of the community and its traditions.

MUSIC SYSTEMS

In most European Jewish music, especially religious music, melody functions as a means of clarifying the text and enhancing its meaning. Ideally, music must never obscure the text or acquire greater importance than the text. The performance of psalmody, for example, relies on responsorial and antiphonal forms, which, through the repetition of formulas or the use of repetition, assist congregations in performance.

The musical systems characterizing secular music, particularly genres of folk music, retain a close association with words and the text in a vernacular language, for example, Yiddish, Ladino, or their dialects, rather than those abstracted from religious texts. Logocentric, these melodic principles allow melody to sound non-Jewish—to reflect the influences from outside religious musical systems.

The intimate relation between text and melody further influences rhythms immanent in language. The organization of musical rhythm depends in large part on the forms and structures that express language. In religious and secular repertories, an efficacious rhythmic system clarifies and enhances the text. The recitation or cantillation of biblical texts and prayers depends entirely on textual rhythm. Many rhythmic forms, therefore, are syllabic. These do not exclude the possibility of melismas or extended melodies, which break free from strict adherence to textual rhythm; nor do they prevent the development of musical forms (for example, response and antiphony in psalmody), in which abstract form influences the regularization of rhythmic patterns. Genres did develop in which rhythmic formulas allowed the expansive exten-

FIGURE 2   Two common Ashkenazic modes (*shtayger*): *a*, "*Ahava rabbah*"; *b*, "*Adonai malakh.*"

sion of melody, particularly Sephardic melodic forms, in part because of their importance in Arabic and Iberian musical systems. The Ashkenazic *nusah,* a localized style of sung prayer, also developed as expansive, developmental melody, based on flexible rhythmic and melodic units, which retain a distinctive relation to the texts and assist in the efficacious performance of these texts.

Scholars have long maintained that one of the most distinctive markers of Jewish music, in comparison with non-Jewish music from neighboring musical cultures, is a modal system that unifies religious genres and influences secular genres. The distinguishing characteristic of this system is its reliance on tetrachords, rather than on octaves. It is difficult to prove just how extensively European repertories remained anchored in this tetrachordal modal system; only Sephardic melodies collected in Mediterranean communities retained a great deal from this system, and it is at best vestigial in Ashkenazic melody. The modal system of Ashkenazic music was codified as an aspect of liturgical styles and genres. Called *shtayger* (Yiddish 'something that climbs'), the modes have distinctive names, usually taken from the texts with which they are most frequently associated. The two most common modes in recent centuries have been the *ahavah rabbah* and the *adonai malakh,* examples that reflect a larger musical context in which Jewish melody is distinctive (figure 2). Certain distinctive *shtayger* traits also characterize secular Ashkenazic melody, at least in the attempts to stylize these, as in the augmented second in folk and popular melodies during the nineteenth and twentieth centuries. The destruction of the Ashkenazic community in Europe makes it impossible to determine if, in fact, the *shtayger* formed a system that underlay the entire Ashkenazic musical culture.

European Jewish music also permits the differences that develop with specific regions and communities and subsumes them under the concept *minhag,* which might best be glossed 'local tradition'. *Minhag* is an early concept of musical system, appearing during the Talmudic period of the first millennium. Early commentary on *minhag* apparently resulted from the practical necessity of providing rabbis and *hazzanim* (Hebrew 'those serving' the community; in modern times, the *hazzan* is the cantor, whose duties are largely musical) with guides for the transmission of local practice, in essence providing guidelines for channeling oral tradition. *Minhag* is historically important as a concept of musical system because of the different ways it permitted local communities to respond to non-Jewish musical influences. Whether a conservative or permissive response to these influences, it prescribed limitations on the musical system that were grounded in tradition, in the religious polity, but were inclusive and practical.

The Sephardic and Ashkenazic communities have historically maintained two distinctive musical cultures, with a variety of smaller musical systems developing within these. The *haskalah,* or eighteenth-century Enlightenment, of Ashkenazic Jews, for example, produced folk songs called *haskalah* songs, which reveal various types of response—positive and negative—to the transformation of Ashkenazic culture. In Sephardic areas of Europe, the most characteristic religious genre has been the hymn (*piyyut,* pl. *piyyutim,* a nonliturgical sacred song, but etymologically related to the Indo-European root for 'poetry' and 'poet'). *Hazzanim,* the professional singers in the community, created new *piyyutim* using the beginning and ending sections of preexisting melodies, and then improvising in the middle. *Piyyutim* remained anchored in traditional practice (such as liturgical metric structures) while incorporating influences from Arabic melodic style and Spanish poetry—a dualism typical of many European Jewish musical systems.

The most distinctive Sephardic secular genre to survive into the modern era has been the *romancero,* a narrative ballad form that accompanied Sephardic communities as they dispersed from the Iberian Peninsula. The subject matter of Sephardic *romanceros* often resembles that of Spanish and Portuguese narratives, but the forms and internal structures have changed less than those found in Spain and Portugal. *Romanceros* have thus served as a means of preservation, not just of Ladino (the language of Sephardic Jews), but of musical practices that lend Sephardic communities their identity.

SONG TEXTS

Song texts function in complex ways to specify the ways in which music expresses specific Jewish identities or mediates between Jewish and non-Jewish society. Strictly speaking, the Jewish identity of recited or musically performed biblical texts is unassailable because of the specific nature of the text. It is more difficult to lay claim to an unassailable identity in texts for which variants are possible, even when these take the form of Hebrew texts. The composition of contrafacta that use Hebrew texts, nevertheless, has long proved one of the commonest ways of creating a new piece of Jewish music. During the period of a return to a more easily identifiable Jewish structure in the European community (in the decades before World War II), the translation of non-Hebrew texts in works by non-Jews (like Handel's oratorios) served at least as a temporary gesture of using musical texts as a means of mediating identity.

So central is this question of song text that one of the most distinctive forms of European Jewish folk songs is intentionally textless. The *niggun* is a genre that first appeared as an expressive form sung by adherents to the movement known as Hasidism (from Hebrew *ḥāsīdh* 'pious') in Poland and the Ukraine during the 1700s. Hasidism was a spiritual movement in which disciples expressed ecstatic pietism through devotion to a charismatic rabbi and forms of worship that established a more direct communication with God. Words were regarded as a hindrance to forming such communication because they drew attention to themselves. Such attitudes toward song texts, however, were a natural extension and variation of Jewish musical aesthetics, in which melody should not draw attention only to itself.

TRACK 1

Niggunim employed easily sung vocables as texts and borrowed melodies from various sources, including existing folk songs (figure 3). Many *niggunim* became popular, passing into oral tradition and becoming the basis for texted variants and folk dances. How extensively *niggunim* contributed to the formation of folk-dance genres is difficult to prove, but dance was often an aspect of performance, not least because dance enhances the potential for an ecstatic experience. Particularly during the half century before the Holocaust, the *niggun* became popular beyond the Hasidic movement, a symbol of a secular Jewish identity in other parts of Europe. Some *niggunim* served as the basis for new versions of the hora, particularly as it traveled with early Zionists from the Balkans to Palestine. Few Ashkenazic folk-song anthologies lacked sections devoted to *niggunim,* and *niggun* melodies found their way into theatrical and classical compositions, where their ability to mediate identity without specific texts assumed new forms.

Text may enter the music history of a community as an unchanging element that permits different melodic ideas to influence the community, even those that clearly

FIGURE 3   A Hasidic textless folk song (*niggun*). After Jacobsen and Jospe 1988 [1935]:40 and Frankl and Frankl 1981:196.

come from an external musical system. The genre known as *pizmon* often takes pre-existing texts, particularly those for important holidays, and allows variant musical settings. The text in "*Shofet kol ha-aretz*" ('Judge of all the earth'), a *pizmon,* is often performed as part of the Yom Kippur service, though it was originally a poem by the medieval poet Salomon ibn Gabirol. Despite its sacred position in the music of the High Holidays, it has a complex history of change in many European Jewish communities, and many of its variants bear witness to contact with non-Jewish traditions. The example of it in figure 4 was sung by an Israeli who had immigrated from Germany, but its melodic structures suggest that it is a variant of a tune known to the Italian composer Benedetto Marcello (1686–1739). In *Estro poetico armonico,* his musical settings of the first fifty psalms, he used as cantus firmi eleven synagogal melodies, from the Ashkenazic and Sephardic traditions of Italy. His setting itself, however, may be indebted to another melodic tradition, namely that of German Protestant chorales. Howsoever direct or indirect these possible connections, the melodic history that proceeded the Israeli performance in figure 4 is surely complex and extensive. Amid the variability of this history, however, the song text itself

FIGURE 4   "*Shofet kol ha-aretz,*" a *pizmon* often performed as part of the Yom Kippur service, as sung by Hillel Baum from Shaveh-Zion, Israel. Phonothèque, Israel National and University Library, Jerusalem Y-3402. Transcription by Philip V. Bohlman.

The exclusion of women's voices from the Orthodox synagogue concerns the nature of the voice: the female voice draws attention to itself because of its beauty or, in some traditions, because of its seductiveness and thus distracts worshipers from the meaning of religious texts.

FIGURE 5   "*Las quejas de Jimena*" ('Jimena's Complaint'), a *romancero* from the *El Cid* epic cycle, as sung by a Moroccan immigrant living in Jerusalem in 1978. After Armistead and Silverman 1986:76–77.

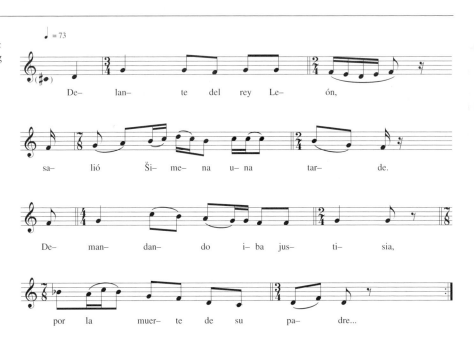

remains the same, anchoring oral tradition through the use of the Hebrew language and the religious symbolism associated with it.

The stories that song texts recount undergird the stability of oral tradition and maintain repertories over centuries, even during diaspora and migration. Whether retelling ancient history in Israel or reframing the traditions of the non-Jewish societies in Europe in which Jews lived, the narratives are extremely important agents of history and historicism, linking Jewish communities to numerous events of their own past. Many narrative song texts are therefore inseparable from a specific historical moment, an ethnic community for which this moment has powerful symbolism, a form of ritualized performance, and a genre or repertory of song within the larger oral tradition. For example, "*Las quejas de Jimena*" ('Jimena's Complaint'), a *romancero* from the *El Cid* epic cycle of Spain, entered Sephardic Jews' oral tradition during their centuries of residence in the Iberian Peninsula or contact with the Andalusian culture, and its story is central to the confrontation between the Cid and North African Moors. The version in figure 5 was sung in 1978 by an immigrant from Morocco living in Jerusalem, and it therefore serves as a musical documentation of the Sephardic Jews since their expulsion from Spain, in 1492 (Armistead et al. 1979).

Just as song texts encouraged the musical representation of the past, they became emblems of the confrontation of European Jews with the contemporary world, particularly around 1800 and in the early decades of the twentieth century. Yiddish song texts from Eastern Europe came to symbolize traditional Jewish culture for Central Europeans concerned about the deterioration of their connections to that culture. Collections of Jewish folk songs grappled with the Yiddish texts, presenting them as a form of classicized folk-song traditions for Central European Jews, most of whom had no previous knowledge of Yiddish, particularly the Eastern European dialects of the songs. These collections, published by distinguished Jewish presses (such as Schocken Verlag), often had a pedagogical intent, with transliterations and special accents placed in the text so they were more easily learned in the modern Jewish community of Berlin or Frankfurt. As Jewish communities expanded in the large cities of Central and East-Central Europe around 1900, new song texts emerged in the repertories of favorite theater or cabaret singers and were published inexpensively as broadsides. Often parodies in which High German and Yiddish texts are woven together in the same song, they exaggerated but demonstrated the difficulties that traditional Jews from Eastern Europe, perhaps from the eastern territories of the Hapsburg Empire, had in their confrontation with life in Vienna or Berlin.

CONCEPTIONS OF MUSIC

Jewish conceptions of music privilege the human voice. Vocal music provides an ideal vehicle for praise, prayer, cantillation of biblical texts, and interpreting a range of other religious texts. This fundamental conception of music regards the voice as important because it has a physical connection to language, and it clarifies and interprets the meaning of religious texts. A central body of learning, the religious law (*halakhah*), addresses aesthetic questions about the voice, identifying certain controversies over what constitutes traditional religious music, such as the appropriateness of musical instruments. The exclusion of women's voices from the Orthodox synagogue concerns the nature of the voice: the female voice draws attention to itself because of its beauty or, in some traditions, because of its seductiveness. This proscription carries an implicit aesthetic message—that the text and its meaning take precedence over the beauty of singing for its own sake.

Concerns arising from the relation between language and music also determine differences between sacred and secular practices, music of the community and music that originates outside the community, and gender roles, and among various types of Jewish musical professionals. Hebrew, the language of religious tradition, provides a basis for sacred practices, and the importance of literacy among men privileges musical repertories that employ Hebrew and musicians able to perform these. This tendency does not exclude other repertories from religious performance, but requires that they be connected to religious practice by other means. For example, setting preexisting melodies to Hebrew texts theoretically provides a way of drawing musics from outside Jewish society into a strictly religious context, and Ashkenazic and Sephardic *piyyutim* have been composed on this basis.

The contrast between a Jewish identity and "otherness" expresses itself in many conceptions of Jewish music. Clearly, "otherness" assumes its simplest form when language comes from a non-Jewish tradition. Folk songs in Yiddish and Ladino express a Jewish identity, and it was precisely this identity that traditionalizing movements, such as Hasidism in the 1700s and, in a different way, Zionism in the twentieth century, intended to capture.

Instrumental music does not rely exclusively on the community's traditional religious language. It obtains its instruments by borrowing from "other" communities, thus transforming instruments themselves into symbols of otherness. Instrumentalists, particularly popular, and dance musicians are professionals who can make their livelihood only from playing in variously different contexts, Jewish and non-Jewish. Though such forms of musical otherness were sometimes shunned, they sometimes engendered important processes of musical change in European Jewish communities. Jewish instrumentalists in the Central European region of most intensive rural Jewish settlement, Burgenland in eastern Austria and western Hungary, functioned as conduits for the encounter between the Jewish communities of this region and their multiethnic neighbors. These musicians became one factor among several that allowed for an ongoing encounter with otherness, inside and outside the community, and empowered it to function creatively in the history and aesthetics of Jewish culture in Burgenland.

In Jewish society, music often serves as an arena of vehement ideological debate. The central ideological questions result from the difficulty of locating Jewish identity in music—in other words, of determining whether music is or is not Jewish. At one ideological extreme, most arguments hold that Jewish music must have a Jewish religious function; at the other extreme, social concerns determine the basic criteria, usually taking some form of the claim that Jewish music involves music making by Jews. Between these extremes, ideological positions are staked out according to the role of language (Hebrew, Yiddish, Ladino), venue (a religious institution), and function (holidays, rites of passage, and so on). These positions extend into the aesthetics of music, as into considerations of typically Jewish modes, melodic patterns, rhythmic structures, and harmonic possibilities. Some ideological positions claim that the question of identity is not important, that it is a limitation on the creativity of Jewish musicians, and that Jewish music would thrive if musicians had more aesthetic freedom to interact with other musics.

These debates have been so important they have sometimes been crippling, and have sometimes enabled certain genres and styles to flourish in new ways. As Jewish folk-song specialists in Central Europe and Eastern Europe debated the identity of Jewish folk song during the late nineteenth and early twentieth centuries, they succeeded in producing a wealth of new anthologies, effecting a revival of interest in Jewish folk songs among diverse social groups. This revival was possible only with an invention of Jewish folk song (that is, the setting of new texts and the creation of new social contexts), but this invention contributed considerably to ideological debates concerning Jewish identity in other types of music. Ideological differences arising from coexisting Sephardic and Ashkenazic synagogal traditions in Amsterdam meant that both communities vigorously cultivated their own musics, resulting in a richer Jewish musical life overall. Ideological concerns also provided a means of protecting tradition, maintaining it in the midst of a vastly larger society. Conceptions of Jewish music in Europe were never without ideological inflection, never without debate about whether music was or was not Jewish, but this situation, in turn, intensified the presence of music in European Jewish society as a complex symbol of identity.

INSTRUMENTAL MUSIC

The centrality of language in Jewish music influences the concepts and practices of instrumental music. Many of the most virulent debates concerning synagogal practices during the 1800s, for example, arose from interest in placing an organ in the synagogue. Instruments sometimes acquired the aura of outsider status, that is, as a means of distancing a certain genre of music or type of musician from tradition. But outsider status could also transform musical instruments into a conduit of encounter with music outside the Jewish community, thus providing the musician with a means of specializing and excelling in several domains.

Debates about music and the frequent proscriptions against them contrast with the evidence about instrumental music that biblical texts provide and archaeological evidence from ancient Israel reveals. The instruments of ancient Israel were numerous, including instruments borrowed from other cultures and those found only in traditional settings. Already in the fourth chapter of Genesis, the mythical inventor of instrumental music, Jubal (Hebrew Yuval), is mentioned, historically grounding instrumental music in ritual; etymologically, the name Jubal relates to *yovel* 'ram's horn', and to 'jubilee', the occasion when the ram's horn is blown with ritual functions.

Instruments were apparently an important part of ritual and musical activity in the Temple, and they probably accompanied the performance of some biblical texts; with the destruction of the Temple and the diaspora, however, prohibitions against musical instruments begin to appear. Many justifications for banning instruments did not differ in substance from those in early Christianity or in Islam; the prohibitions, however, differ in kind, first because they refer historically to a particular moment in the history of Judaism, the destruction of the Temple, and second because they have persisted in various forms until the present, despite challenges to them.

The one instrument whose presence in sacred Jewish music has been unassailable has been the shofar, the ram's horn, blown as a signal instrument during the rituals of Rosh Hashanah and Yom Kippur. Explanations of the permissibility of the shofar range from recognition of its early appearance in biblical mythology (the 'Akedah', or Sacrifice of Isaac) to the nature of its ritualistic repertory. It serves as a reminder of the Temple period at solemn, reflective moments of the Jewish calendar, while never competing with liturgy and language. Though this repertory might appear circumscribed (and even insignificant from a musical perspective), it has had considerable importance in European Jewish musical life. The shofar has an extraordinary iconographic presence throughout European Jewish historiography, visually symbolizing religious music making in Jewish communities. Some communities even have a specialist who plays the shofar, the *ba'al tokeah* ('master of blowing', 'person in charge of signaling'; *tako'ah* is the biblical word for trumpet, and *tokeah* describes, among other things, the blowing of a trumpetlike instrument, in particular the shofar). The roles of the one instrument whose presence is always allowed further emblematize some of the central issues that surround the presence of musical instruments in European Jewish society, particularly the significance of musical specialists and the constant renegotiation of even the most basic conceptions of music over time.

Despite the proscriptions against instrumental music that appear in Talmudic writings and in medieval philosophical treatises, musical instruments did not disappear from Jewish society, and Jews excelled as instrumentalists. Accounts of the occupations in which Jews were active in the late Middle Ages and Renaissance reveal that numerous men made their livelihood from instrumental performance. Walter Salmen has succeeded in locating areas (as in the Hunsrück region, southwest of Mainz), where Jews were instrumentalists to such an extraordinary degree that one can properly speak of communities of instrumentalists. The specific identification of these specialists (*letzim, klezmorim, badhanim*) and the appearance of such designations in Jewish and non-Jewish sources is conclusive evidence of the role Jews played as instrumentalists in European society—a role that lasted until the Holocaust and emerged again at the end of the twentieth century as one of the most vigorous forms of European Jewish musical historicism.

Klezmorim and other instrumental specialists functioned in several distinctive capacities. Within the Jewish community, they were essential to the performance of music at rituals and rites of passage. At weddings, they performed for the religious wedding procession and the secular wedding dance. In Central and Eastern Europe, the bass violin was essential to the wedding klezmer, and performers found they had to strap it around their shoulders using a belt of some kind, giving the instrument a portability necessary for the wedding procession and lending its form and repertory a

Jewish instrumental repertories derive a large measure of their creativity from an ability to borrow and assimilate from other music cultures and to create a music that has primarily Jewish functions.

FIGURE 6   *Klezmorim* in 1912. Photo courtesy of YIVO Institute for Jewish Research, New York.

distinct Jewishness. *Klezmorim* also played as specialists outside the Jewish community, where they needed a repertory appropriate to sacred and secular non-Jewish settings (figure 6).

There is no single set of European Jewish musical instruments. Distinctiveness accrues to instrumental music in European Jewish society because of the flexible functions and uses that instruments acquire, such as the portable bass violin of the klezmer. More often, its effects are evident in distinctive instrumental combinations and repertories. Most characteristic is an inclusiveness that was also characteristic of instrumental music in ancient Israel, when periods of prolonged contact with other cultures led to an enrichment of the Jewish instrumentarium. Jewish instrumental repertories therefore derive a large measure of their creativity from an ability to borrow and assimilate from other music cultures and to create a music that has primarily Jewish functions.

The negotiation of Jewish instrumentalists between Jewish and non-Jewish societies in Europe was not limited to religious, folk, and dance repertories, but became one of the most distinctive aspects of the rise of bourgeois Jewish society in Europe after the *haskalah*. During the 1800s in the European cities to which Jews moved in increasingly greater numbers, Jewish homes were often the most important literary and artistic salons, offering central venues for chamber music. Jews came to excel as chamber musicians, forming important ensembles and establishing the Jewish community as a center for secular music making. In several European centers, chamber orchestras formed first within the Jewish community. Instrumental music provided one of the few paths open for a more extensive integration of Jews in the Soviet Union, and it is hardly surprising that Soviet Jews excelled on the concert stages of that nation and internationally during most of the twentieth century.

SOCIAL GROUPS AND MUSIC

As in most cultures, Jewish music differs significantly by gender, age, class, ethnicity, and whether it is performed in rural or urban settings.

Gender

One of the most striking social markers in European Jewish music is the presence of distinctions of gender. The widespread presence of repertories and social contexts differentiated according to gender predates the formation of Jewish communities in Europe and is clearly evident in accounts of Jewish musical life in ancient Israel. Men and women played different musical roles in the synagogue and the Temple, and many instruments had specific associations with male or female performers. Further distinctions result from the customary division of social labor and learning, thus forming women's repertories as part of the folkways of the home, and men's repertories generally in relation to community life outside the home. Surviving evidence about medieval European Jewish music refers almost entirely to men, partly the result of sources about literate genres performed in religious institutions. Women's genres, being more often strictly oral, restricted to the home, and performed with specific customs, fail to enter the accounts of Jewish music making until recent centuries.

The central venue in which gender differences are apparent is the synagogue, where traditionally men and women are separated, not just by the spaces they occupy but by their participation in the service—men are active participants, women are not—and in the strictest adherence to tradition, remain separated so their voices will not be heard. This means that women traditionally do not participate in congregational prayer and recitation; nor in the 1800s, while musical activity in the synagogue was diversifying, did they sing in choruses or serve as professional musicians, such as cantors. In contrast, the first collections and anthologies of Jewish folk songs concentrated on women's songs. Classificatory systems relied further on this apparent predominance and created categories and genres based on the contribution of women to the folkways in the home and the life cycle of the family; lullabies, love songs, and even soldiers' songs, therefore, seem to derive from women's perspective, though this perspective is often also that of the folk-song collector or editor. The role of women in Jewish music became a controversial issue during the modernization of Jewish communities following the *haskalah,* particularly as communities entered into extended debate about the appropriateness of mixed choruses or the integration of women into public prayer. During the same period, women expanded the role of music in the home. They often transformed the wealthier homes of urban centers into public salons, in which intellectuals met and musicians performed. By 1900, issues of gender were central to the modernization of European Jewish musical life.

Age

Children too have distinctive repertories and musical practices, many associated with the celebration of holidays. Among the most famous children's songs are those sung during Hanukkah, the festival of lights, when the activities of the holiday, such as playing with a top (*dredl*) are accompanied by singing. Other holiday celebrations require that children sing special songs, often as a part of larger musical cycles, for example, when the youngest child of a family sings "*Chad gadya*" ('One Kid') during the Passover seder. Other holidays lend themselves particularly well to children's performance, for example, Purim, when children enact the narrative of the Book of Esther.

An abundance of European Jewish folk songs concerns children, usually performed by the mother, though children probably also sing their own versions of specific songs. Distinctions of gender also mark some children's songs as a result of traditional social roles: boys learn songs as part of their studies in school, and girls acquire songs as part of their duties at home. During the various stages of the European folk-music revival in the nineteenth and twentieth centuries, Jewish youth movements formed, and, as in the case of the Zionist Blau-Weiss youth group, developed special repertories of folk songs and published these in important collections.

Class

Before the 1700s, distinctions of class were far less significant in Jewish society than in non-Jewish. Jews overwhelmingly lived in egalitarian traditional communities, and they were legally prevented from acquiring land and from owning other forms of property that would have led to widespread social stratification. Musical life too was relatively egalitarian, with repertories and social contexts for music in which all community members, at least theoretically, participated.

Social class became a factor in European Jewish musical life during the nineteenth and early twentieth centuries as laws restricting Jewish financial activities relaxed, and as many Jewish communities sought to modernize themselves. Jewish communities in various parts of Europe changed at varying paces during this period, some rapidly, others not at all, thus making the process of modernization a factor in the formation of social distinctions, which also took the form of ethnic differences.

The confrontation between Eastern and Central European Ashkenazic cultures became a factor of Jewish identity in Berlin, Prague, Vienna, and other cities of the Central European monarchies, as in the cultural life of shtetls along the borders between these monarchies and their Eastern European counterparts. This ethnic confrontation became especially important during the folk-music revival of the late nineteenth and twentieth centuries.

Rural settings

Because of the need to negotiate its relation to non-Jewish society, the Jewish community of Europe relied on an adaptability to rural and urban settings. The rural community could depend on a somewhat less problematic relation with the surrounding culture, and could rely on the stability of traditional culture—that is, however, if the population was large enough to permit a full Jewish polity. The shtetl of Eastern Europe was the most complex form of the rural community, though it had many historical antecedents in other parts of the continent. The urban community, in contrast, benefited from the financial and intellectual exchange of the city. It is possible to view European Jewish history as a dynamic tension between rural and urban cultures. Music reflected this tension, indirectly and directly. One indirect manifestation is evident in the centripetal pull of tradition and the centrifugal force of modernization that coexisted in many repertories; the rural community anchored tradition, whereas the urban community was constantly exposed to external influences and change. Folk-song repertories also contained genres that embodied some aspects of this tension, for example, songs decrying the working conditions of industrial centers in Eastern Europe during the nineteenth and twentieth centuries.

Ethnicity

The musical evidence for interaction among ethnic communities was most often evident at the cultural borders, where different communities came in contact with each other; the Ashkenazic and Sephardic sacred repertories of Amsterdam, for example, have remained distinct since the first settlement of Sephardic Jews in the Netherlands, in the 1500s. Ethnic differences are endemic to Jewish polity, for example, in the designation of an ethnic community as a *kehillah,* which implicitly recognizes differences between Italian Sephardic traditions and Bosnian Sephardic traditions; *kehillah* can therefore refer to different forms of culture and music culture, ranging from the local polity embodied by a synagogue and its members to ethnic characteristics at a regional level. As attempts to discover and cultivate a more expansive Jewish identity and musical aesthetic began in the late 1800s (in Central Europe, as the result of a growing interest in more traditional forms of ethnic identity, in Eastern Europe as a component of Zionism), musicians created repertories that deliberately juxtaposed ethnic differences. Central European anthologizers incorporated into their books increasingly numerous Yiddish songs, while Zionist aestheticians turned to the diverse repertories of southeastern Europe and Palestine for influences. Ethnic juxtapositions include melodies, musical styles, texts, and instrumental forms.

Urban settings

During the period of modernization known as *haskalah,* members of one social group in Jewish society enjoyed increasing access to the music of other social groups: women participated more often in the music of the synagogue. Publication of some genres of music, like the new compositions of liturgical music for the synagogue or Jewish broadsides in fin-de-siècle urban centers, meant greater distribution of Jewish music throughout and beyond the community. Modernization opened up new opportunities for Jews from all social groups to participate in musical activities in other Jewish communities and in non-Jewish communities, and the mobility of Jewish musicians increased during the nineteenth and twentieth centuries. The different sectors of European musical life, in fact, provided one of the greatest possibilities for social mobility for Jews in all parts of Europe. The complex social structure of music making in European Jewish society, and the added impetus of the modernization of that social structure, made it possible for Jews to contribute far more extensively to European musical life on the eve of the Holocaust than in all previous centuries of Jewish culture in Europe.

HISTORY OF MUSIC

History provides the most significant context for the music of Jewish Europe at the end of the twentieth century. On the destruction of most Jewish communities during the Holocaust and the relocation of the primary centers of Jewish culture outside Europe, primarily in Israel and the United States, history becomes for Jewish music and musicians a way of signifying the past, of resituating it in contemporary Europe, and of giving voice to its meanings in the present. Because of the recontextualization afforded by music, European Jewish culture has come to exert its presence in many new ways. For European Jewish communities themselves, music has a powerful symbolic presence, because of the ways it reminds European Jews of the past and the ways it emblematizes the uniqueness of European Jewry within the non-Jewish cultural environment.

Jewish folk and popular music, which has enjoyed a revival since the early 1970s, has embraced ever more genres during the ensuing decades, and it shows no sign of abating. This revival exhibited a decidedly pan-European character, particularly in its reliance on and dissemination of Yiddish repertories, or its spawning of a standard form of klezmer music, which, though in some ways artificial and exaggerated, attracted considerable interest throughout the continent. Jewish religious and art music also found new interest. In general, individual communities sought to reinvigorate specific religious repertories, for example, in the anthologizing of *hazzanut* traditions and compositions in Amsterdam, and in the revitalization of compositions of Salomon Sulzer in the central synagogue of Vienna. Motivating all these attempts to recover Jewish music was a pervasive belief that music empowered European Jews

Motivating these attempts to recover Jewish music was a pervasive belief that music empowered European Jews with a means of understanding their past and living in a cultural context that was Jewish and European.

with a means of understanding their past and living in a cultural context that was Jewish and European.

The earliest records of the concepts of Jewish music were not treatises about music theory, but tracts on philosophy or ethical questions. Much of the earliest evidence of Jewish musical life in the Middle Ages comes from non-Jewish sources, which describe the activities of Jewish instrumentalists or include observations about Jewish rituals and the music making that accompanied them. The humanism that began with the Renaissance stimulated an interest in Jewish religious music because of its potential relation to Christian religious music and its position in the past and the body of texts that both shared. These sources make it possible to reinterpret the interaction between Jewish musicians and composers and the institutions of non-Jewish society, for example, the Renaissance composer, Salomone Rossi, active in the court of Mantua, Italy, in the early 1600s. This humanistic interest in Jewish music was a quintessential component of modern European musical historiography, particularly during the 1600s and 1700s.

Jewish community records also document the history of Jewish music in Europe. Such records contain references to musical specialization in the religious musical life of the community, notably the differentiation of professional and semiprofessional roles of prayer leaders and *hazzanim*. Community records often became the venue for debates about music in the life of European Jews, for example, about the permissibility of music sung in part by women or choral music in the synagogue. Though many records of this kind were destroyed during World War II, a remarkable number survived and became available for research for the first time as a result of the political changes in Eastern Europe that began in 1989 and 1990. Because of the individual character of the discussions and concerns that each community included in its records, study of these documents suggests the possibility of a new direction in European Jewish music historiography—the investigation of individual music histories, and the ways they contribute to a larger Jewish music history for the entire continent.

Another fruitful area for the study of European Jewish music history is the influence of Jewish music and musicians on other musics. Jewish music has often shaped style in European art music. Particularly at the beginning of the twentieth century, composers such as Ernest Bloch and Arnold Schoenberg, in radically different ways, sought to use Jewish music as a font for stylistic elements in their compositions. Such endeavors came to have great importance in Israel, especially between 1930 and 1960, the period when immigrant composers from Europe tried to form a national style. The influences of Jewish musicians were particularly important to European jazz and popular music during the decades before World War II. Jewish musicians and entertainers made decisive contributions to the European cabaret, many of which, particularly those in large Central European cities, may have had a largely Jewish clientele; in general, however, the systematic historical study of Jewish influence on European popular music remains an open field, one that might well lead to widespread reevaluation of how ethnic, religious, and cultural differences relied on popular music for a voice in European society.

The history of European Jewry and of its music is inseparable from the tragedy of the Holocaust and the destruction of the communities that constituted European Jewry. Jewish culture in Europe, though inestimably diminished by the destruction of the Holocaust, survives. Its contemporary presence—in the growth of urban communities in Paris or London, the resettlement of Russian Jews in Germany, and the problems and challenges of persistent anti-Semitism and the rejection of otherness—means that it continues to exert its presence as a voice for the expression of the past and present histories of Europe.

HISTORY OF SCHOLARSHIP

Scholarship on Jewish music falls under two general categories. The first comprises a long intellectual history, in which Jewish music existed within a larger historical context, functioning as a source from which Christian and European cultures developed. The second concerns itself largely with questions of Jewish identity in music, as a larger unifying concept and a product of many differences among diverse Jewish communities.

It is hardly surprising that most scholars writing under the first category have been non-Jews, and in contrast, the scholars of the second tradition have been almost exclusively Jewish. The importance of this distinction is a matter not just of perspective, but primarily of ideology. The two traditions weight their central questions according to different ideological criteria, the first locating the significance of Jewish music in its relation to non-Jewish history and music, and the second claiming Jewish music as an essential domain for understanding the uniqueness of Jewish identity.

The learned writings of medieval European Jews, though grounded in religious and philosophical thought, often consider music. As in much Arabic-Islamic and Christian writing in the Middle Ages, music rarely appears as an isolated topic; it is considered because of its ethical and scientific associations. Medieval Jewish writers most concerned with ethical problems in music, for example, Maimonides (1135–1204) argued for music making and conceptions of music that sustained a fundamental dichotomy of music as sacred or profane, which appears already in biblical writings; Maimonides attacked any possible influences from non-Jewish musics, for example, the *muwashshah* of Muslim Andalucía. Other writers concentrated more on scientific questions, placing music in the medieval quadrivium, thus freeing it from a dependence on biblical connections. Central questions of identity in music—whether and when it is Jewish—therefore began to take a place in European thinking about music in the Middle Ages.

The first systematic study of music in ancient Israel and biblical sources appears in initial attempts to survey what was understood to be the position of music in the entire course of human history. Employing titles often claiming to be "universal histories of music," the tomes produced by such historiography reflect a particularly European stance, which would have been impossible without the colonialism that accompanied European expansion, especially in the 1600s and 1700s, when the genres of modern musical scholarship arose. Major works from this period, like Athanasius Kircher's *Musurgia Universalis* (1650) and Charles Burney's *A General History of Music from the Earliest Ages to the Present Period* (1789), accorded biblical music fairly extensive treatment. Other studies, usually written by musical scholars concerned with religious genres, tried to draw parallels between Jewish and Christian chant, again accounting for these by relying on their putatively common historical origins. By the 1800s, the combination of comparative and historical treatments had shifted scholarship into areas recognized today as ethnomusicological, especially as new information about other music cultures of the Middle East—Jewish, Christian, Muslim—loosened Jewish music from its moorings in an ancient period, and documented its diversity in a contemporary period. The most remarkable examples of resituating Jewish music into contemporary cultural contexts are found in multivolume music histories of the mid- and late nineteenth century, for example, François Joseph Fétis's *Histoire générale de la musique depuis les temps anciens à nos jours* (1869–1876) and August Wilhelm Ambros's *Geschichte der Musik* (1862–1878). It is because of this scholarship and the presence of nascent ethnomusicological approaches in it that Jewish music appeared in much European comparative musicology during the twentieth century, as in the works of Curt Sachs (*The Rise of Music in the Ancient World,* 1943), who employed broadly historical and comparative methods to deal with more universal concepts of music.

Questions of the uniqueness of Jewish identity in music have a more recent historiography, first taking their place in European scholarship in the 1800s. The issues of Jewish identity that arose in the 1800s resulted in part from the modernization of European Jewish society and in part from motivations evident in other domains of European thought, like romanticism and nationalism. Thus, the need to identify and document Jewish folk songs or the oral traditions of synagogal melody reflected similar undertakings in other European traditions of musical scholarship. The most scientific collections were those of Eastern Europe, particularly those of S. M. Ginsburg and P. S. Marek, which served as models for other collections throughout Jewish Europe, and as the most important source for Yiddish folk songs in European anthologies during the first half of the twentieth century. The collection and study of Sephardic secular music focused almost entirely on the *romancero,* with Ramón Menéndez Pidal's studies from around 1900 serving as models for a flourishing tradition of scholarship. Several scholarly practices influenced these endeavors, ranging from the systematic folkloristic methods of Max Grunwald to the discipline called Jewish science (*Wissenschaft des Judentums* 'scholarly study of Judaism'), which flourished in Berlin's liberal and Reformed Jewish sectors, fostering new directions also in Jewish musical scholarship, as in Emil Breslauer's study of sacred music in oral tradition (1898).

European Jewish musical scholarship developed rapidly during the early twentieth century as the result of increasing access to the institutions of European musical scholarship. The settlement of Palestine stimulated a new historicism and dramatically expanded the field for comparative research. These institutional and historiographic changes motivated scholars such as Abraham Zvi Idelsohn to travel to Palestine and to collect the music of the communities of Jews living near Jerusalem. Idelsohn's compendium of music from the Jewish ethnic communities, *Hebräisch-orientalischer Melodienschatz* (1914–1932), combines methodologies from German folk-song research and comparative musicology. Scholars including Robert Lachmann, Edith Gerson-Kiwi, and Hanoch Avenary, who immigrated to Palestine in the 1930s, combined Idelsohn's techniques with methods developed from German musicology and ethnomusicology, laying the groundwork for the programs of ethnomusicological research that would develop in Israel after independence (1948).

The scholarship devoted to European Jewish music after World War II has taken place on an international scale, with scholars and research projects located throughout the world. In the decades immediately after the Holocaust, the music and folklore of survivors were the subjects of many collecting projects, but many of the largest collections, among them the YIVO Institute in New York and the Phonothèque in the Jewish National and University Library in Jerusalem, have many holdings that remain to be studied. Israeli scholars have made especially important contributions to ethnomusicology, developing new approaches to the comparative study of Jewish musics and musical life. The problem of studying European Jewish music in Europe has persisted because of the destruction of human and material resources during the Holocaust and because many academic and scientific institutions have resisted accepting responsibility for studying the Jewish past of Europe. Research in Eastern Europe, for example, was often hampered before the dissolution of communist governments through latent and officially sanctioned anti-Semitism.

Ethnomusicologists employing historical approaches have begun to change this situation. The works of Gila Flam and Mark Slobin have incorporated, rather than avoided, the ideological and political dilemmas faced by Jewish musicians during the first part of the century, with Flam concentrating on the music of the Holocaust and Slobin on Jewish ethnomusicology and music in the Soviet Union. Philip V. Bohlman and Walter Salmen have studied Central European Jewish music, in particular the presence of secular music making in Jewish society. Sephardic traditions have received considerable interest, in philological studies by Samuel G. Armistead and Joseph H. Silverman, folkloristic studies by Isaac Jack Lévy, and ethnomusicological studies by Israel J. Katz and Edwin Seroussi. Other scholars, including Avenary, Eric Werner, and Lionel Wohlberger, have continued to locate religious music at the center of their studies, extending to it a comparative and analytical approach. Because of the destruction and dispersion of European Jewry, it has been more difficult to sustain in-depth sociological studies of European Jewish music since World War II, but intensive study of surviving communities and those that have begun growing again may prove to be a fruitful area for ethnomusicological research in the twenty-first century. The most noticeable trend in European Jewish musical scholarship at the end of the twentieth century has been the return to the continent itself by scholars incorporating fieldwork and ethnography into their historical studies, suggesting that future musical scholarship of all kinds will increasingly be guided by ethnomusicological concerns and methods.

BIBLIOGRAPHY

Adler, Israel. 1966. *La pratique musicale savante dans quelques communautés juives en Europe aux XVIe et XVIIIe siècles.* Paris: Mouton.

———. 1974. *Musical Life and Traditions of the Portuguese Jewish Community of Amsterdam in the XVIIIth Century.* Yuval Monograph Series, 1. Jerusalem: Magnes Press of the Hebrew University.

———. 1975. *Hebrew Writings Concerning Music: In Manuscripts and Printed Books from Geonic Times up to 1800.* Munich: G. Henle.

Adler, Israel, and Judith Cohen. 1976. *A. Z. Idelsohn Archives at the Jewish National and University Library—Catalogue.* Yuval Monograph Series, 4. Jerusalem: Magnes Press of the Hebrew University.

Armistead, Samuel G. 1971. *Folk Literature of the Sephardic Jews: The Judeo-Spanish Ballad Chapbooks of Yacob Abraham Yoná.* Berkeley and Los Angeles: University of California Press.

———. 1979. *Tres calas en el romancero sefardí (Rodas, Jerusalén, Estados Unidos).* Madrid: Castalia.

———, with the collaboration of Biljana Sljivic-

Simsic. 1971. *Judeo-Spanish Ballads from Bosnia.* Philadelphia: University of Pennsylvania Press.

———, with musical transcriptions and studies by Israel J. Katz. 1986. "Epic Ballads." In *Judeo-Spanish Ballads from Oral Tradition*, Vol. 2, Part 1. Berkeley and Los Angeles: University of California Press.

Armistead, Samuel G., Israel J. Katz, and Joseph H. Silverman. 1979. "Judeo-Spanish Folk Poetry from Morocco (The Boas-Nahón Collection)." *Yearbook of the International Folk Music Council* 11:59–75.

Armistead, Samuel G., and Joseph H. Silverman. 1986. *Judeo-Spanish Ballads from Oral Tradition.* Folk Literature of the Sephardic Jews, 2. Berkeley and Los Angeles: University of California Press.

Attias, Moshe. 1961. *Romancero judeo-español: Romanzas y cantes populares en judeo-español.* 2nd ed. Jerusalem: Ben-Zvi Institute.

———. 1972. *Cancionero judeo-español: Canciones populares en judeo-español.* Jerusalem: Centro de Estudios sobre el Judaísmos de Salónica.

Avenary, Hanoch. 1968. "The Cantorial Fantasia of the 18th and 19th Centuries." *Yuval* 1:67–85.

———. 1974. "Der Einfluss der jüdischen Mystik auf den Synagogen-Gesang." *Kairos* 26(1):79–87.

———. 1976. *Melodies of the Pentateuch in the Ashkenazic Tradition.* Tel Aviv: Tel Aviv University Press.

———. 1985. *Kantor Salomon Sulzer und seine Zeit: Eine Dokumentation.* Sigmaringen: Jan Thorbecke Verlag.

Baer, Abraham, ed. 1953. *Ba'al Tefiloh, oder der praktische Vorbeter.* New York: Hebrew Union College, Jewish Institute of Religion Sacred Music Press.

Bénichou, Paul. 1968. *Romancero judeo-español de Marruecos.* Madrid: Castalia.

Benmayor, Rina. 1979. *Romances judeo-españoles de Oriente.* Madrid: Catedra-Seminario Menéndez Pidal.

Berliner, Abraham. 1937 [1900]. *Aus dem Leben der Juden Deutschlands im Mittelalter.* Berlin: Schocken Verlag.

Bezalel, Itzhak, ed. 1984. *Ha-masoret ha-musikah shel yehudeh sfarad ve-mizrah* (The Musical traditions of Sephardic and Eastern Jews). *Pe'amim* 19, special edition.

Birnbaum, Eduard. 1893. *Jüdische Musiker am Hofe zu Mantua.* Vienna: M. Waizner.

Bloemendal, Hans, comp. 1990. *Amsterdams Chazzanoet: Synagogale muziek van de Ashkenazische Gemeente.* 2 vols. Buren: Uitgeverij Frits Knuf.

Bohlman, Philip V. 1989a. *"The Land Where Two Streams Flow": Music in the German-Jewish Community of Israel.* Urbana: University of Illinois Press.

———. 1989b. "Die Volksmusik und die Verstädterung der deutsch-jüdischen Gemeinde in den Jahrzehnten vor dem Zweiten Weltkrieg." *Jahrbuch für Volksliedforschung* 34:25–40.

———. 1992. *The World Centre for Jewish Music in Palestine, 1936–1940: Jewish Musical Life on the Eve of World War II.* Oxford: Oxford University Press.

———. 1995. "Musik als Widerstand—am Beispiel jüdischer Musik in Deutschland 1933–1940." *Jahrbuch für Volksliedforschung* 40: 49–74.

Braun, Joachim. 1978. *Jews and Jewish Elements in Soviet Music.* Tel Aviv: Israel Music Publications.

———. 1988. "Mosche Beregovski: Zum Schicksal eines sowjetischen Ethnomusikologen." *Jahrbuch für Volksliedforschung* 33:70–80.

Braun, Joachim, Vladimir Karbusicky, and Heidi Tamar Hoffmann, eds. 1995. *Verfemte Musik: Komponisten in den Diktaturen unseres Jahrhunderts.* Frankfurt am Main: Peter Lang.

Breslauer, Emil. 1898. *Sind originale Synagogen- und Volks-Melodien bei den Juden geschichtlich nachweisbar?* Leipzig: Breitkopf & Härtel.

Brod, Max. 1976 [1951]. *Die Musik Israels,* rev. and expanded by Yehuda Walter Cohen. Kassel: Bärenreiter.

Cahan, Yehudeh-Leib. 1952. *Shtudies vegn Yiddisher Folks-Shaffung* (Studies in Yiddish folklore). New York: YIVO.

———. 1957. *Yiddishe Folkslider mit Melodies* (Yiddish folk songs with melodies). Edited by Michael Weinreich. New York: YIVO.

Cohen, Judith R. 1982. "Judeo-Spanish Traditional Songs in Montreal and Toronto." *Canadian Folk Music Journal* 10:40–47.

Crews, Cynthia M. 1979. "Textos judeo-españoles de Salónica y Sarajevo con comentarios lingüísticos y glosario." *Estudios Sefardíes* 2:91–249.

Eliasberg, Ahron, ed. 1913. *Die jüdische Gemeinschaft.* Berlin: Jüdischer Verlag.

Eliasberg, Alexander, ed. 1918. *Ostjüdische Volkslieder.* Munich: Georg Müller.

Flam, Gila. 1992. *Singing for Survival: Songs of the Lodz Ghetto, 1940–1945.* Urbana: University of Illinois Press.

Frankl, Hai, and Topsy Frankl. 1981. *Jiddische Lieder: Texte und Noten mit Begleit-Akkorden.* Frankfurt am Main: Fischer.

Freund, Florian, Franz Ruttner, and Hans Safrian, eds. *Ess firt kejn weg zurik . . . : Geschichte und Lieder des Ghettos von Wilna 1941–1943.* Vienna: Picus Verlag.

Gerson-Kiwi, Edith. 1958. "Jüdische Volksmusik." In *Die Musik in der Geschichte und Gegenwart,* ed. Friedrich Blume. Vol. 7, cols. 261–280. Kassel: Bärenreiter.

Gerson-Kiwi, Edith, and Amnon Shiloah. 1981. "Musicology in Israel, 1960–1980." *Acta Musicologica* 53(2):200–216.

Geshuri, Meir Shimon. 1955. *Ha-nigun ve-ha-richud be-hassidut.* Vol. 2. Tel Aviv: Hotsaat Netsah.

Gil, Rodolfo. 1911. *Romancero judeo-español.* Madrid: Imprenta Alemana.

Ginsburg, S. M., and P. S. Marek. 1901. *Evreiskie noradnye pesni v Rossii.* St. Petersburg: Voskhod.

Glaser, Karl, ed. 1918 [1914]. *Blau-Weiß Liederbuch.* 2nd ed. Berlin: Jüdischer Verlag.

Gradenwitz, Peter, ed. 1988. *Die schönsten jiddische Liebeslieder.* Wiesbaden: Fourier.

Grunwald, Max. 1924–1925. *Mattersdorf.* Single edition of *Jahrbuch für jüdische Volkskunde,* 402–563.

Heiske, Wilhelm. 1964. "Deutsche Volkslieder in jiddischem Sprachgewand." *Jahrbuch für Volksliedforschung* 9:31–44.

Hemsi, Alberto. 1932–1973. *Coplas sefardíes.* 10 vols. Alexandria: Édition Orientale de Musique.

Heskes, Irene. 1994. *Passport to Jewish Music: Its History, Traditions, and Culture.* Contributions to the Study of Music and Dance, 33. Westport, Conn.: Greenwood Press.

Hirshberg, Jehoash. 1982. "Heinrich Schalit and Paul Ben-Haim in Munich." *Yuval* 4:131–149.

Holzapfel, Otto, and Philip V. Bohlman. Forthcoming. *Folk Songs of the German- and Yiddish-Speaking Jews.* Madison, Wis.: A-R Editions.

Idelsohn, A. Z. 1914–1932. *Hebräisch-orientalischer Melodienschatz.* 10 vols. Berlin: Benjamin Harz.

———. 1939. "The Mogen-Ovos-Mode: Study in Folklore." *Hebrew Union College Annual* 14:559–574.

———. 1967 [1929]. *Jewish Music in Its Historical Development.* New York: Schocken.

Jacobsen, Joseph, and Erwin Jospe, eds. 1935. *Hawa Naschira! (Auf! Lasst uns singen!): Liederbuch für Unterricht, Bund und Haus.* Leipzig and Hamburg: Anton J. Benjamin.

———. 1988 [1935]. *Das Buch der jüdischen Lieder.* Augsburg: Ölbaum Verlag.

Jaldati, Lin, and Eberhard Rebling. 1985. *Es brennt Brüder, es brennt: Jiddische Lieder.* Berlin: Rütten und Loening.

Janda, Elsbeth, and Max M. Sprecher. 1962. *Lieder aus dem Ghetto: Fünfzig Lieder jiddisch und deutsch mit Noten.* Munich: Ehrenwirth.

Kaludova, Stamatka. 1970. "Sur la poésie et la musique des juifs de la Péninsule Balkanique, du XVe au XXe siècle." *Études balcaniques* 6(2):98–123.

Kaminski, Nathan, ed. 1935. *Jüdisches Liederbuch—"Makkabi."* Berlin: Jüdischer Verlag.

Karas, Joža. 1985. *Music in Terezín, 1941–1945.* New York: Beaufort.

Katz, Israel J. 1971, 1975. *Judeo-Spanish Traditional Ballads from Jerusalem: An Ethnomusicological Study.* 2 vols. Brooklyn: Institute of Mediaeval Music.

Laks, Szymon. 1989. *Music of Another World.* Translated by Chester A. Kisiel. Evanston, Ill.: Northwestern University Press.

Landsmann, Salcia. 1985. "Die Volkslieder der Juden." *Jahrbuch für Volksliedforschung* 26:93–98.

Larrea Palacín, Arcadio. 1954. *Canciones rituales hispano-judías: celebraciones familiares de tránsito y ciclo festivo anual.* Madrid: Instituto de Estudios Africanos.

Leitner, Franz. 1906. *Der gottesdienstliche Volksgesang im jüdischen und christlichen Altertum.* Freiburg im Breisgau: Herder.

Lévy, Isaac. 1959–1973. *Chants judéo-espagnols.* 4 vols. London: Fédération Séphardite Mondiale.

———. 1964–1980. *Antología de liturgia judeo-espanola.* 10 vols. Jerusalem: División de Cultura del Ministerio de Educación y Cultura.

Loewe, Heinrich, ed. 1894. *Lieder-Buch für jüdische Vereine.* Berlin: Hugo Schildberger.

Migdal, Ulrike, ed. 1986. *Und die Musik spielt dazu: Chansons und Satiren aus dem KZ Theresienstadt.* Munich: Piper Verlag.

Milner, Chanah, and Paul Storm. 1974. *Sefardische liederen en balladen: Romanzas.* The Hague: Alberson.

Mitteilungen zur jüdischen Volkskunde. Later changed to *Jahrbuch für jüdische Volkskunde.* 1892–1932. Hamburg and Vienna.

Musica Hebraica 1–2 (1938). Jerusalem.

Nadel, Arno, ed. 1923. *Jüdische Liebeslieder.* Berlin and Vienna: Verlag Benjamin Harz.

Nettl, Paul. 1923. *Alte jüdische Spielleute in Prag.* Prague: Josef Flesch.

Pollack, Herman. 1971. *Jewish Folkways in Germanic Lands (1648–1806): Studies in Aspects of Daily Life.* Cambridge: MIT Press.

Projektgruppe Musik und Nationalsozialismus, ed. 1988. *Zündende Lieder—Verbrannte Musik: Folgen des Nationalsozialismus für Hamburger Musiker und Musikerinnen.* Hamburg: VSA-Verlag.

Ringer, Alexander L. 1990. *Arnold Schoenberg: The Composer as Jew.* Oxford: Oxford University Press.

Romero, Elena. 1979. *El teatro de los sefardíes orientales.* 3 vols. Madrid: Instituto "Arias Montano."

Rosenfeld, Morris. 1902?. *Lieder des Ghetto.* 6th ed. Berlin: Hermann Seemann.

Rubin, Ruth. 1964. *A Treasury of Jewish Folksong.* 2nd ed. New York: Schocken.

———. 1979. *Voices of a People: The Story of Yiddish Folksong.* Philadelphia: Jewish Publication Society of America.

Salmen, Walter. 1990. "Das Bild vom Klezmer in Liedern und Erzählungen." In *Festgabe für Lutz Röhrich zu seiner Emeritierung,* ed. Leander Petzoldt and Stefaan Top, 201–212. Frankfurt am Main: Peter Lang.

———. 1991. "*. . . denn die Fidel macht das fest*": *Jüdische Musikanten und Tänzer vom 13. bis 20. Jahrhundert.* Innsbruck: Edition Helbling.

Schleifer, Elihu, ed. 1983. *Anthology of Hasidic Music: Chemjo Vinaver.* Jerusalem: Magnes Press of the Hebrew University.

Schönberg, Jakob. 1926. *Die traditionellen Gesänge des israelitischen Gottesdienstes in Deutschland.* Nürnberg: Erich Spandel.

———. 1938. *Shireh Eretz Yisrael* (Songs of Eretz Yisrael). Berlin: Schocken.

Shiloah, Amnon. 1977. *Music Subjects in the Zohar: Texts and Indices.* Yuval Monograph Series, 5. Jerusalem: Magnes Press of the Hebrew University.

———. 1992. *Jewish Musical Traditions.* Detroit: Wayne State University Press.

Slobin, Mark, ed. and trans. 1982a. *Old Jewish Folk Music: The Collections and Writings of Moshe Beregovski.* Philadelphia: University of Pennsylvania Press.

———. 1982b. *Tenement Songs: The Popular Music of the Jewish Immigrants.* Urbana: University of Illinois Press.

———. 1989. *Chosen Voices: The Story of the American Cantorate.* Urbana: University of Illinois Press.

Steinschneider, M. 1903. *Purim und Parodie.* Frankfurt am Main.

Strauss, Ludwig, ed. 1935. *Jüdische Volkslieder.* Berlin: Schocken Verlag.

Stutschewsky, Joachim. 1959. *Ha-klezmorim: Toldotehem, orekhchaimhem ve-yetzirotehem* (The *klezmorim*: their history, life, and compositions). Jerusalem: Mosad Byalik.

Weisser, Albert. 1983 [1954]. *The Modern Renaissance of Jewish Music.* Music Reprint Series. New York: Da Capo Press.

Werner, Eric. 1976. *A Voice Still Heard. . . . The Sacred Songs of the Ashkenazic Jews.* University Park: Pennsylvania State University Press.

Zirker, Max, ed. 1905. *Vereinsliederbuch für Jung-Juda.* Berlin: Jüdischer Turnverein "Bar Kochba."

AUDIOVISUAL RESOURCES

Almonds and Raisins: A History of Yiddish Cinema. 1988. Teaneck, N.J.: Ergo Media. LP disk.

Beth Hatfutsoth Museum of the Jewish Diaspora. 1989. *The Danzig Tradition.* Jewish Musical Heritage BTR 8901. Compact disc.

———. 1990. *The Koenigsberg Tradition: The High Holidays.* Jewish Musical Heritage BTR 8601. Compact disc.

Cantorial Festival in Moscow, 1990. 1991. Miami: American Society for the Advancement of Cantorial Arts/Gila and Haim Wiener Foundation. Compact disc.

Cantorial Festival 1900: Zum 100. Todestag von Salomon Sulzer. 1991. Miami: American Society for the Advancement of Cantorial Arts/Gila and Haim Wiener Foundation 5750. Compact disc.

Dem Khazn's Zindl (The cantor's son). 1937. Teaneck, N.J.: Ergo Media 767. Video.

Der Purimshpiler (The Purim actor). 1937. Teaneck, N.J.: Ergo Media 715. Video.

The Dybbuk (Der Dibuk). 1937. Teaneck, N.J.: Ergo Media. Video.

Gojim. 1992. *Ess firt kejn weg . . . : Jiddische Lieder aus dem Ghetto in Wilna 1941–1943.* Extraplatte EX 139 CD. Compact disc.

Great Cantors of the Golden Age. 1990. Waltham, Mass.: National Centre for Jewish Film. Video.

Jewish Music Research Centre. 1976. *Hassidic Tunes for Dancing and Rejoicing.* Anthology of Musical Traditions in Israel. The Hebrew University of Jerusalem, RCA YJRL 1-029. LP disk.

———. 1979. *Synagogal Art Music XIIth–XVIIIth Centuries: Religious Poems, Cantatas and Choral Works.* Anthology of Musical Traditions in Israel. The Hebrew University of Jerusalem, AMTI 7901 Stereo. LP disk.

———. 1991. *Synagogal Music in the Baroque.* Anthology of Musical Traditions in Israel. The Hebrew University of Jerusalem, AMTI CD 9101. LP disk.

Jüdisches Worms: Musik aus der Raschi-Synagoge der "Heiligen Gemeinde Worms." N.d. Rheinelektra B-0761. LP disk.

Kirshenblatt-Gimblett, Barbara, et al. 1986. *Folksongs in the East European Jewish Tradition from the Repertoire of Miriam Nirenberg: Selections from the Max and Frieda Weinstein Archive of YIVO Sound Recordings.* New York: YIVO/Global Village Music C 117. LP disk.

Klezmer Music 1910–1942. 1981. Folkways FSS 34021. LP disk.

Klezmorim. 1977. *East-Side Wedding.* Arhoolie 3006. LP disk.

Lang, Marcel Moshe. 1985. *Synagogale und jüdische Musik.* Boba-Records 185. LP disk.

Legendary Voices: Cantors of Yesteryear. 1991. Teaneck, N.J.: Ergo Media. Video.

Mamele. 1938. Teaneck, N.J.: Ergo Media. Video.

Müther, Katharina. 1989. *Es ist Zeit, dass der Stein sich zu blühen bequemt: Jiddische Lieder II.* Calren Records KAT 1013601. LP disk.

Remember the Children: Songs for and by Children of the Holocaust. 1991. Washington, D.C.: United States Holocaust Memorial Museum, HMC 1901. Compact disc.

Rubin, Ruth. 1958. *Jewish Life: "The Old Country."* New York: Folkways 03801. LP disk.

———. 1992. *A Life in Song: A Portrait of Ruth Rubin.* Teaneck, N.J.: Ergo Media. Video.

Schwadron, Abraham A., ed. 1982. *Chad Gadya* (One kid). Folkways FR 8920. LP disk.

Schwartz, Martin, coll. 1983. *Greek-Oriental*

Smyrniac-Rebetic Songs and Dances (The Golden Years: 1927–1937). El Cerrito, Calif.: Folklyric Records. LP disk.

———. 1991. *Yikhes: Frühe Klezmer-Aufnahmen von 1907–1939.* Munich: Trikont US-0179. Compact disc.

Shalom—Songs of Polish Jews. 1988. Warsaw: ITI Video. Video.

Shiloah, Amnon. 1971. *Jewish Music.* Philips 6586 001. Unesco Collection: Musical Sources: Religious Psalmody, IV–1 (European, North African, and Middle Eastern). LP disk.

———. 1978a. *Greek-Jewish Musical Traditions.* Ethnic Folkways Records FE 4205. LP disk.

———. 1978b. *"Morasha": Traditional Jewish Musical Heritage.* Ethnic Folkways Records FE 4203. LP disk.

Song of the Sephardi: The Songs and Traditions of the Spanish Jews. n.d. Los Angeles: Zohar Productions. LP disk.

Tarras, Dave. N.d. *Dave Tarras Plays Again.* Colonial ST-LP-718. LP disk.

———. 1979. *Dave Tarras: Master of the Jewish Clarinet.* Balkan Arts US-1002. LP disk.

Voices from Sepharad. 1991. Waltham, Mass.: National Center for Jewish Film. Video.

Wandering Stars. 1987. London: London Museum of Jewish Life. Compact disc.

Yankl der Schmid (The singing blacksmith). 1938. Teaneck, N.J.: Ergo Media. Video.

Yidn mitn Fidl (The Jew with a fiddle). 1936. Teaneck, N.J.: Ergo Media. Video.

Rom (Gypsy) Music
Carol Silverman

Central Europe
The Balkans
Eastern Europe
Western and Northern Europe

That Roma are often musicians is a commonplace; yet the nature of Rom music has received little scholarly attention. Misunderstandings of it vary from the position that Roma merely borrow and have no music of their own (Bhattacharya 1965; Starkie 1933) to the position that all Hungarian music is Rom music (Liszt 1859). Roma have been hailed as the most authentic preservers of peasant music (Vekerdi 1976) and assailed as its corrupters and distorters (Bartók 1976 [1931]). The historical situation, however, is much more complex: for more than five hundred years, Roma in Eastern Europe have been professional musicians, playing for non-Rom peasants for remuneration in taverns and at weddings, baptisms, circumcisions, fairs, village dances, and other events. This professional niche, primarily for male instrumentalists, requires Roma to know and creatively interact with local repertoires. A nomadic lifestyle, often enforced upon Roma through harassment and prejudice, gave them opportunities to enlarge their repertoires and become multimusical and multilingual.

In addition to nomadic Roma, numerous sedentary Roma in major European cities professionally play urban folk, classical, and/or popular music. In Hungary, Russia, and Spain, certain forms of Rom music became national music, veritable emblems of the country. The music that professional Rom musicians play for their own people may or may not differ from the music they play for others. Many Roma are not professional musicians, but have their own music. All these groups have migrated within Europe, to varying degrees.

The label *Rom* (plural *Roma*), rather than the more common English label, *Gypsy,* is used here because of its political connotations. The term *Gypsy,* with cognates including *Gitan* (French), *Gitano* (Spanish), *Yiftos* (Greek), and *Gjuptsi* (Macedonian), is usually an outsider's term, with strongly negative connotations, which derive from the false belief that these people's ancestors came from Egypt. Another label, including *Tsigan* (found in Slavic languages) and *Zigeuner* (German), comes from the Greek *Atsingani,* the name of a heretical Christian sect active in the Byzantine Empire during the twelfth and thirteenth centuries. Roma distinguish themselves by names describing region, occupation, religion, and dialect. *Roma* has become a unifying term in the 1990s, as political consciousness is mobilized through unions, political parties, conferences, and congresses. In all these forums, music has played an important role in symbolizing Rom creativity and affirming Rom contributions to European culture.

Neither one worldwide nor one pan-European Rom music exists, despite an emerging awareness of ethnic unity. A Finnish Rom song may have more in common with an ethnic Finnish song than with a Greek Rom song, reflecting five centuries of coterritorial musical traffic. In contrast, some stylistic and performance elements, such as the propensity to improvise, are perhaps common to many European Rom musics (Kovalcsik 1987). In Eastern Europe, we hear and read of Rom virtuosic performances that move people to tears, of seemingly endless variations in Rom melodies, and of Rom readiness to adopt new influences, especially commercial popular music (Pettan 1992b; Vidić 1990b). Proverbs attest that "a wedding without a Gypsy isn't worth anything" (Bulgarian) and "Give a Hungarian a glass of water and a Gypsy fiddler, and he will become completely drunk" (Hungarian). Despite the prominence of Gypsy music in Eastern Europe, however, national governments there, though they preserved folk music during the communist era, marginalized and ignored most Rom music.

Linguistic evidence shows that Rom ancestors migrated from northwestern India in the eleventh century. Seeking the universal and unique in Rom music, some scholars have claimed to have found musical links with present-day Indian peoples, like the Gadolia Lothars (Bhattacharya 1965; *Latcho Drom* 1993; Manush 1987; Mercier 1993), but this work is highly speculative. Romani, the Rom language, is descended from Sanskrit and closely related to Hindi. By A.D. 1500, Roma were established throughout Europe, where some settled and others remained nomadic. Roma have indispensably supplied diverse services: music, entertainment, fortune-telling, metalworking, horse dealing, woodworking, sieve and comb making, basketry, and seasonal agricultural work. Many of these trades required nomadism. From economic necessity, musicians often had skills in several trades.

In Europe, curiosity about Roma quickly gave way to hatred and discrimination, which continue today virtually everywhere. From the fourteenth to the nineteenth centuries in the Romanian principalities of Wallachia and Moldavia, Roma were slaves owned by noblemen, monasteries, and the state; they were sold, bartered, and flogged, and even their marriages were regulated. As slaves, Roma provided skills in panning for and preparing gold, training bears, carving wood, blacksmithing, and making music. Slavery was abolished in 1864, but exploitation continues.

Roma were viewed as intruders, probably because of their dark skin, association with invading Muslims, and foreign ways. Despite their small numbers (often less than one percent of the total population), they inspired fear and mistrust and were expelled from virtually every European territory. Bounties were paid for their capture, dead or alive. Repressive measures included confiscation of property and children, forced labor, imprisonment, whipping, branding, and other forms of physical mutilation. Assimilation was tried in the Austro-Hungarian Empire during the reigns of Maria Theresa (1740–1780) and her eldest son, Joseph (1780–1790), who outlawed Romani and Rom music, dress, and nomadism and banned traditional Rom occupations. Similar legislation was in force in Spain from 1499 to 1800 and in Eastern European communist countries after World War II. In Europe in the 1930s, persecution escalated with the Nazis' rise to power. Roma faced a campaign of extermination only now being investigated: more than six hundred thousand—one-fifth to one-fourth of all Roma—were murdered.

In the 1990s, harassment and violence toward the 10 million Roma of Europe have increased, as have marginalization and poverty. The largest minority group in Europe, Roma have the lowest standard of living in every country. In Eastern Europe, political and human rights activism among Roma has increased, particularly since the

1989 revolutions and the subsequent rise in scapegoating of Roma and violence against them in the form of mob attacks, skinhead targeting, and police brutality. On a more positive note, since 1989, European Rom music festivals—some international, some annual—have been held in Austria, Bulgaria, the Czech Republic, France, Hungary, Poland, Macedonia, and Switzerland. Such cultural displays play an important role in the politicization of the Roma. Public attention to Rom music was heightened in and after 1993, when the film *Latcho Drom,* a musically staged documentary of the Rom journey from India to Spain, was released. A glossier extravaganza is André Heller's German festival *Magneten,* which features internationally known Rom musical groups.

The remainder of this article describes Rom music and its relationships to the music of the coterritorial peoples. It concentrates on countries for which the most documentation is available. The division of Rom music into regions differs slightly from the division used in the rest of Part 3. For flamenco music in Spain, see SPAIN, and for Travellers' music in the British Isles, see TRAVELLERS' MUSIC.

CENTRAL EUROPE

Hungary

There are three major groups of Roma in Hungary: 300,000 Romungre, who are urban and sedentary and speak Hungarian; 100,000 Vlach Roma, who were nomadic until the early twentieth century and speak Romani; and 35,000 Boyash, who speak a dialect of Romanian. These groups neither intersocialize nor intermarry, and their musics differ markedly: Romungre music is professional and instrumental; Vlach Rom music is vocal and nonprofessional; research on Boyash music began with Katalin Kovalcsik's analysis of melody and texts and two new songbooks and cassettes for elementary school students (1994, 1996).

Romungre are so famous in Europe for their professional string bands that many people mistakenly believe that this is the only type of Rom music. In the nineteenth century, they captured Western classical composers' attention, toured the best European concert halls, and became the representatives of Hungarian national music (figure 1). Franz Liszt in 1859 claimed they were the source and creators of all worthy Hungarian music. Bálint Sárosi (1978 [1970]) provided an excellent historical

FIGURE 1 A Hungarian Rom string orchestra of the early twentieth century. Their nineteenth-century costumes and their music were taken by many as symbols of Hungarian national identity—an interpretation criticized by Béla Bartók and others. The hammered dulcimer (cimbalom), resting on its side in the center, was an important instrument, literally at the center of these orchestras. Postcard courtesy of the Robert Godfried Collection, New York.

overview of Romungre music. In the eighteenth century, Panna Czinka became the first well-known Rom violinist and bandleader, one of the few women to enter this profession. In her band, one violin played melody, and the other (the *kontras*) played harmonic accompaniment in a repeated rhythmic pattern; the other instruments were a double bass and a cimbalom—a combination still popular. Ensembles like Czinka's, drawn from members of one family, were (and are) common, and players acquired their skills informally at home. Czinka's band had the patronage of a landowner who provided a house, land, and a red uniform every three years.

In the late 1700s, the *verbunkos,* a recruiting dance, became the characteristic Romungre genre. *Verbunkos* tunes, usually derived from folk songs, are distinguished by rich ornamentation, also a feature of European classical music, being partly improvised even in written works. Traditional song lines are elaborated with scalar patterns including augmented seconds between the third and fourth and between the sixth and seventh degrees of the scale. Augmented seconds are less evident in twentieth-century versions, in which major and minor scales are more common. The *verbunkos* scale has been termed the Gypsy scale—a gross generalization of a localized practice. The most famous Rom *verbunkos* composer, János Bihari, was a violinist and bandleader who played at royal military events and toured every important city in Central Europe. Roma were often sent by their patrons to music schools or private teachers (usually Germans and Czechs) to learn classical harmony, orchestration, arranging, and notation (Spur 1947–1949). It is ironic that the incorporation of these "foreign" elements forged a style that became the national symbol of Hungary in the nineteenth century.

From the mid nineteenth century to the early twentieth, Roma helped disseminate a new genre, the Hungarian popular art song (*nóta*). Songs of this genre were always harmonized, by piano on the printed page or Rom stringed ensembles in performance. Texts reflected lyrical love themes. *Nóta* can be divided into two groups: the slow, rhythmically free *hallgató* and the 2/4 czardas (*csárdás*). Rom bands applied the *verbunkos* formulas to art songs, creating overnight hits, and the public clamored for their repeated performance. Though most art-song composers were not Rom, one famous Rom composer, Pista Dankó, wrote more than four hundred songs. During this era, the populace accorded virtuosic Rom performers great respect. Aristocrats learned from them, made music with them, and even gave them their daughters in marriage. Composers such as Debussy and Liszt praised their talent. *Verbunkos* themes appear as early as 1766 in works of Haydn, and later in works of Schubert, Brahms, Tchaikovsky, and most notably Franz Liszt (Baumann 1996; Bellman 1993). Liszt's 1859 book created a controversy by claiming that what everyone was calling Gypsy music was in fact created by Roma, not Hungarians: Hungarians were merely patrons for the Rom genius. Critics, including Bartók, have countered that Gypsy music is not created by Roma; rather, it is popular Hungarian art music played by Roma. This controversy has many levels, which continue to the present day. Liszt erringly dismissed the rich Hungarian rural peasant repertoire (collected a half century later), romanticized about Eastern survivals of Roma, and defended Roma as creative interpreters of urban songs. The opposite camp reproached Roma for inhibiting the development of Hungarian creativity in music. Roma are neither bereft of music of their own nor merely cultural sponges. Because of their professional niche, Hungarian Roma creatively molded the popular repertoire and interacted dynamically with Hungarian folk music. The music became Rom just as much as it was Hungarian music and played by Hungarian Roma as their own.

The popularity of Romungre music remains strong. In the 1930s, a school for gifted Rom children was created, and by the 1960s, Romungre professional musicians numbered about eight thousand (Sárosi 1978 [1970]:10). The modern reper-

Rom ensembles' style of performance is so standardized that any good musician can sit in with any band, yet it is so individualized that bandleaders can easily distinguish among performers.

toire of urban bands includes popular art songs, folk songs, *verbunkos* and czardas music, selections from operas and operettas, international dance music (such as polkas and waltzes), international folk songs, and jazz. Ensembles string short tunes together, starting with the slowest and ending with the fastest. Their style of performance is so standardized that any good musician can sit in with any band, yet it is so individualized that bandleaders can easily distinguish among performers. What has been called the essential ants'-nest bustle in the music is achieved by heterophony, that is, two or more instruments simultaneously playing the melody with variant ornamentation. In the 1980s, Pentecostalism spread widely among Roma of Western, then Eastern Europe, with music and a cassette industry playing a significant role in prayer (Lange 1993, 1996).

Rural Hungarian Rom musicians tend to be poorer and less assimilated than urban Rom musicians, and supplement music with other trades. Since the eighteenth century, they have been indispensable for providing music at weddings, funerals, inns, fairs, and markets. Until the twentieth century, they were nomadic: only in the larger towns were they able to stay long without a nobleman's patronage (Sárosi 1978 [1970]:16–17). Except for instrumentation, their repertoire has little in common with the urban repertoire. Rural professional music was virtually unstudied before the early twentieth century, when Bartók and Kodály made pioneering collections of peasant music. Since the 1950s, the Folk Music Research Group of the Hungarian Academy of Sciences and the Folk Music Department of the Budapest Ethnographic Museum have made numerous recordings.

Rom string bands have gradually taken over the peasants' bagpipe repertoire, including the drone (tonic and fifth) accompaniments. A typical rural Rom band includes a violin, a second violin or a viola, a cimbalom, a cello, and a bass. The cimbalom is less common in rural bands, perhaps because its arpeggios suit the more Westernized harmonic structures of urban music (figure 2). Among the Hungarian Székelys of the Csík area of Transylvania, a violin supplies melodies, rhythmically accompanied by a *gardon,* a cello struck with a stick. Before the era of mass communication, "Gypsy musicians . . . were the musical fashion creators in the Hungarian villages. . . . Being professionals, . . . they were . . . expected to know things beyond what was required by the traditions of the village. . . . While bringing foreign trends, . . . they were . . . the first to 'Magyarize', or assimilate them" (Sárosi 1978 [1970]:234–235). They were often a musical link between gentry and peasant, between city and village, and among neighboring regions.

Vlach Rom music received virtually no scholarly attention until the 1940s, when the Csenki brothers, inspired by Bartók's and Kodály's work among peasants, collected thousands of folk songs. It was not until the 1940s that collections were published—first the Csenkis' (1943), then the work of André Hajdú (1962, 1964), Rudolf Víg (1974; *Gypsy Folk Songs of Hungary,* 1976), and Kovalcsik (1985 to the present). Vlach Rom music is primarily nonprofessional and vocal, and is performed

FIGURE 2 A rural Rom string band from the village of Szászcsávás, Transylvania (Romania). Such bands typically lack the cimbalom, characteristic of urban Rom bands. Photo by Paula A. White, 1998.

by men and women. Hungarians rarely perform or listen to Vlach Rom music. Songs are divided into two categories, slow and dance. Slow songs (*loki djili*) have a descending structure (according to Kovalcsik an influence from Hungarian folk music), a range of more than an octave, major or minor tonality, and four-line melodies. They are performed parlando-rubato with interpolated exclamations, such as *hej*, *de*, and *jaj*. Unlike Romungre music, but like Hungarian folk songs, Vlach Rom songs do not have elaborate ornamentation. The melody of a song is highly variable; the singer has in mind an ideal tune, which may take a different shape from verse to verse (Kovalcsik 1986:197). Vlach Roma compose songs from a limited stock of melodic formulas (Wilkinson 1990). The performance style of slow songs is interactive: the soloist greets the people and asks for permission to sing, and the people verbally give it. Facial expressions, comments, and gestures are made, and people may interrupt. At the end, the performer expresses good wishes. Occasions for singing include in-group Rom events, such as weddings, baptisms, departures for military service, funerals, *mulatshago*s (drinking and singing celebrations), and daily life. Texts, usually in Romani but occasionally in Hungarian, are improvised and deal with the pain of life, poverty, imprisonment, and love, and make formalized statements about what it is to be a Rom (Stewart 1989, 1997). Through song, Rom men experience a sense of brotherhood, in contrast to daily conflicts (Stewart 1989). Rom singers still perform Hungarian ballads, which have died out in non-Rom contexts. Though these songs have been preserved during decades of industrialization and collectivism, texts, melodies, and performance contexts have undergone changes in the direction of the Romani *loki djili* (Vekerdi 1976; Víg 1974).

Vlach Roma do not usually play instruments but dance to duple-meter songs (*khelimaski djili*), sung with sounds imitating instruments. Vocables are rolled (sung rhythmically) and backed up with oral double bassing, short, exclaimed syncopated vocables, sung on upbeats. Singers make the bassing blowing into their hands or buzzing their lips. They and sometimes the audience snap fingers, clap, drum on water cans, and tap spoons, creating a dense rhythmic texture. Vlach Rom music is thus distinguished from Hungarian music by melodic and textual improvisation, prolonged endings of slow songs, dance-songs with rolled vocables, and the absence of instrumental music.

As part of the urban revival of rural music in the 1970s, Rom youth formed bands such as Ando Drom, Fracilor, Kalyi Jag, and Romafolk and began performing for non-Roma. The most famous of the bands, Kalyi Jag, performs mainly Vlach Rom music with concert harmonizations and arrangements. The 1981 National Gathering of Rom Groups, the 1990 Ethnic Folk Music Gala, and the publication of Balazs's 1995 book have contributed to the popularization of Vlach Rom music. Vlach Rom music is taught to Hungarians and foreigners at dance workshops and camps (Kovalcsik 1987).

Czech Republic and Slovakia

Three groups of Roma live in Slovakia: Romungre, ethnically identical to the Romungre of Hungary, with whom they share professional string-band music; Slovak Roma, rarely professional musicians, who sing Hungarian and Slovak popular songs with Romani words and Slovak folk songs in slower tempi (Kovalcsik 1985:27, 1990:178); and Vlach Roma, who form one musical system with the Vlach Roma of Hungary. Some performers pronounce improvised introductory poetry before singing—an old style of performance. Old melodies are repeatedly set to new texts, especially treating the problems of modern life. New texts are also composed to rock and popular melodies by urban Rom ensembles such as Točkolotoč. Two song collections (Davidová and Žižka 1991; Hübschmannová 1980–1981) are important resources. A musical genre that deserves more attention is Holocaust songs, which scholars rarely collect (Holý and Nečas 1993; Nečas and Holý 1991), but are significant historical documents. In 1992, Romathan, a Rom theatrical ensemble including musicians, was formed in Kosice, Slovakia. The Czech Rom singer Věra Bílá and her group, Kale, which performs songs in Romani and popular-folk fusions reminiscent of the Gipsy Kings, have become well known in recent years.

Poland

In comparison with the Roma of Hungary, the Roma of Poland have had a smaller role in professional folk music, except in the Carpathian Mountains. In the fifteenth and sixteenth centuries, Roma were professional musicians at Polish royal courts, where they played bagpipes, violins, and zithers, but with the partition of Poland (at the end of the eighteenth century), discrimination increased, travel declined, and patronage ended. At the end of the nineteenth century, the immigration of Kalderash and Lovari Roma introduced new musical styles into Poland. Rom groups from Central Europe often share the same songs but interpret them differently (Kovalcsik 1990). Before World War II, improvised sung poetry was a major genre.

After World War II, the lowland Roma were forced to settle. They had a rich in-group Romani musical tradition, which declined because they began performing songs as a source of income in towns. The highland Roma play professionally in string bands and sing in Romani for in-group events. The texts of their songs center on poverty, marginalization, and loneliness. In structure and conciseness, the songs resemble non-Rom Polish highland folk songs. Many express the Rom experience in Nazi concentration camps and are modeled on songs of prison life and other laments (Karsai 1991). Most Rom songs tend not to depict specific historic periods and events and, rather, speak of eternal themes, such as love and poverty, but Holocaust songs often include the names of concentration camps. In recent years, they are sung less and less, performed only by the older generation:

> I shall never get out of here now,
> I shall never see my brothers and sisters!
> They brought us through the gateway
> And let us out through the chimneys. (Ficowski 1991:109)

Polish Rom music began to be popularized to wider audiences in the 1960s. Michaj Burano, a young Lovari, became a star by singing Romani songs with non-Rom Polish groups, and vocalist Sylwester Masio-Kwiek became popular. The professional music and dance ensemble Terno (with singer Randia) was formed by recruiting among the lowland Roma.

Romania

From the fourteenth to the nineteenth centuries, Romanian Rom musician-slaves brought high prices. Many affluent landowners maintained bands (Lloyd 1963–1964:18), and musician-slaves generated profits for their owners by playing in their taverns, inns, and mills (Sárosi 1978 [1970]:40). In the 1860s, when the slaves were freed, peasants began to hire Rom musicians, and in the early 1900s small Rom string bands began replacing peasants' bagpipes and flutes. Also at that time, Roma settled in large cities, where they performed *cîntece de mahala* 'songs of the neighborhood'.

Romanians use the word *lăutar* to denote a professional musician. *Musica lăutărească* refers to the urban Rom music of southern Romania. In the 1960s, about 95 percent (Lloyd 1963–1964:15) or, more realistically, 80 percent (Rădulescu 1984) of *lăutari* were Roma, and the percentage varies greatly by area; in Maramureş, and other northern areas, about half the professional musicians are Roma, but south of the Carpathians, almost all professional musicians are Roma (Ciobanu 1969). A few female violinists, such as Catinica in Bucharest in the 1920s, have been professional musicians, but the overwhelming majority are males (Starkie 1933:354). In Oltenia, women sing and play the guitar and other instruments until marriage, but only if their immediate family has no male heir.

Rural *lăutari* play local folk music at village events, but urban *lăutari* play an eclectic repertoire of light classical works, popular music, and arrangements of local folk music in restaurants and ensembles. Urban Rom music has influenced rural Rom music (Garfias 1981).

The Romanian Rom ensemble (*taraf*) consists of a melody instrument, an accompanying instrument (which varies regionally), and a double bass (Rădulescu 1984). In 1900 in Moldavia and Muntenia, a *taraf* consisted of a violin, a *cobza* (a plucked short-necked lute), and a bass. After World War I, the *cobza* was replaced by the *ţambal* 'portable cimbalom', and more recently by the accordion and the electric organ (figure 3). Today, the electric organ is widespread, but the older instruments are still used for processions. The *cobza* almost disappeared in the twentieth century but was revived by government-sponsored folk ensembles. The *nai* 'panpipes' was the melody instrument in some *tarafs*, but it had almost disappeared by 1900. The 1960s saw a revival of interest in the *nai* because of governmental sponsorship and the efforts of the Luca family, whose members have been makers and players for generations. Some *nai* players adopt the name Luca, even if they are not in the family. The *nai* player Fanica Luca refused to reveal his secrets, even to his son, until he was on his deathbed. Today, the *nai* is played mainly by Romanians and is found in large ensembles; it is not popular in villages.

Dance music, constructed of repeated motifs, is the most important part of the *taraf* repertoire: musicians string together melodies of contrasting mode and tonality to produce dances of varying lengths. According to Anca Giurchescu (personal communication), Roma have a distinct dance style (*hora tsigăneasca* or *hora lăutarescă*), characterized by improvisation, abrupt changes in direction, bent torso, upward arm swings, high energy stamps, and syncopation. When doing couple dances, Roma do not touch: each person does small, syncopated, crossing and stamping steps while clapping hands and snapping his or her fingers.

FIGURE 3 A Rom musician plays a small *ţambal,* a hammered dulcimer that can be slung from a strap and carried through the village. Photo by Gail Kligman, 1976.

Many Romanian studies of music ignore the Roma's role in performing and composing epics, while hailing epics as national treasures—a hypocrisy also prevalent in Bulgarian, Greek, and other European scholarship on Rom music.

Though much of *musica lutarească* is based on Western European major and minor scales, Turkish influence can be inferred from history, musical structure, and terminology (Garfias 1981). Rom musicians absorbed Turkish music during the eighteenth century, when Greeks from the Fanar quarter of Constantinople ruled Romania. The *manea,* a dance and musical form unique to urban Romanian Rom, showed strong Turkish influence. Its rhythm, *čiftečeli* (in 4/4 time, the pattern of an eighth note, a quarter, an eighth, and two quarters), is also found in the southern Balkans and the Middle East, and the dance is a female solo improvisation with demure torso movements. The *manea* may originally have been an improvised vocal form having the ornamented quality of Turkish and Greek popular song. *Manea*s of the famous singer Romica Puceanu are imitated throughout urban Romania.

Rom vocal traditions consist largely of ritual songs, epics, improvised lyric songs (*doina*s), and fixed-meter songs. Rom ritual songs include *paparuda,* in which, to encourage summer rain, peasants sprinkle water onto young Rom girls dressed in greenery. The *paparuda* is also found in Bulgaria and Yugoslavia, with the same history: in the last few decades, Rom girls, by assuming the peasant girls' roles, have kept the ritual alive, probably because it enables them to collect foodstuffs and coins.

Before the twentieth century, *lăutari* performed epics throughout Romania, but today, epic singers perform only in the southern provinces. Accompanied by a *taraf,* each typically plays a violin and never performs an epic the same way twice, displaying originality in using textual and melodic formulas.

The most important ritual context for singing is the wedding, during which music heralds every important moment. The head *lăutar* often acts as master of ceremonies. For generations, some traditional *lăutar* families have derived their livelihood from music. They might devote several hours a day to instruction, based on imitation, leading to mastery of one or a few instruments. Mastery means that a *lăutar* can hear a new song, and after one hearing, perform his own version of it—that is, compose while performing (Beissinger 1991).

Paradoxically, *lăutari* occupy a venerated position in music, yet are socially spurned and mistreated by peasants (figure 4). Many Romanian studies of music ignore the Roma's role in performing and composing epics, while hailing epics as national treasures—a hypocrisy also prevalent in Bulgarian, Greek, and other European scholarship on Rom music.

In Bucharest in 1949, the socialist government created the Barbu Lăutaru State Folk Orchestra, initiating widespread formation of conductor-led large folk orchestras of *lăutari.* Roma played and continue to play dominant roles in these ensembles. In the late 1970s, the Romanian government's policy of homogenization became more oppressive and began targeting Rom culture. Some Roma were removed from ensembles, where they made up 90 percent of professional musicians. The Rom ethnicity of musicians was frequently covered up, and Roma were not allowed to perform in-group music, such as songs in Romani for television and radio.

FIGURE 4 Two Rom violinists from Romania play at a village event. Photo by Gail Kligman, 1976.

After the 1989 revolution, life has worsened for Romania's approximately 2.5 million Roma. They can now organize their own cultural and political organizations, but they suffer numerous attacks on their possessions, their homes, and their persons. Some Rom bands' repertoires are eclectic; southern Balkan Rom music influences, such as the *čiftečeli* rhythm, can be heard in the newly popular genre *muzica orientala*. Some Rom women have become vocalists with instrumental groups.

THE BALKANS

Croatia, Bosnia, and Yugoslavia

The former Yugoslavian territories were home to more than 1 million Roma, divided into many different groups. Roma had a virtual monopoly on some musical forms and were largely absent from others (such as Istrian, Dalmatian, and Slovenian music and bagpipe, flute, and epic traditions), in which they could not earn a steady income. The earliest evidence of Rom music is found in the fifteenth-century archives of Dubrovnik (Gojković 1986:190). In 1828, the most prominent musician at the court of Serbian Prince Miloś Obrenović was a Rom *zurna* (keyless oboe) player. During the Ottoman period, Roma facilitated the spread of musical styles. Rom musicians in Vojvodina primarily played violin and bagpipes until the 1930s, when they became heavily involved in *tamburica* (orchestra of long-necked, plucked lutes), formed on the model of Hungarian Rom string bands (figure 5). Rural Rom musicians developed new performative techniques, which have become standard. The trend-setting Radio Beograd orchestra, formed in the 1930s, recruited the best Rom *tamburaši* (*tamburica* players) from the cafés and promoted musical literacy (Forry 1990). Roma continue to play important roles in professional *tamburica* music, but since the 1960s, their repertoires have been affected by the popularity of newly composed folk music (*novokomponovana narodna muzika*), influenced by popular urban styles.

In the interplay of Turkish-influenced style, marketing, and Rom identity, Roma have played a vital role in facilitating interaction among distinct musical genres: village folk music, urban folk music, popular music, and *novokompanovana narodna muzika*. Serbian Rom singer Šaban Bajramović popularized the song "*Dželem, Dželem*" ('I walked and walked'), composed at the 1971 World Romani Congress by Jarko Jovanović; it became the Rom anthem (Marushiakova and Popov 1994–1995). Perhaps because of its theme of wandering, or because of its style—a combination of

FIGURE 5 An early-twentieth-century Rom orchestra from Serbia plays long-necked plucked lutes (*tamburica*s). Postcard courtesy of the Robert Godfried Collection, New York.

Serbisch-ungarische Original-Zigeunertruppe „Balkan"
(Dir.: J. Kocsis)

Turkish-influenced vocal improvisation, unpretentious emotionalism, and urban salon accompaniment typical of old city songs (Rasmussen 1991)—it now exists in many variants throughout Europe.

In south Serbia, the brass-band tradition, which arose in the 1940s, is shared by Roma and Serbs. Rom bands are professional and play a Turkish-influenced repertoire. Government-sponsored festivals, such as those at Leskovac and Guča, have given wider visibility to this tradition and introduced a sense of hierarchy through the awarding of prizes.

Professional male Rom bear trainers have been found in all Balkan countries since the sixteenth century, teaching their bears to perform to tambourine and voice accompaniment. In nineteenth-century Lithuania, an Academy for Bear Training was founded (Ficowski 1991:94–95). In southeastern Europe, bears still entertain peasants at fairs and in courtyards; according to the Bulgarian proverb, "A festival without a bear trainer is a waste of time."

Macedonia

Roma have a virtual monopoly of southern Balkan professional ensembles consisting of one or two *zurla*s (Macedonian *surla,* Bulgarian *zurna,* Greek *pipiza*), a double-reed conical-bore instrument, plus one or two *tapani* (Bulgarian *tŭpan,* Greek *davul*), double-headed cylindrical drums (figure 6). Some ethnomusicologists, citing evidence from a fourteenth-century fresco in Ohrid, believe the Roma brought the *zurla* and the *tapan* to the Balkans before the Ottoman Turks' arrival. Currently, *zurla* and *tapan* ensembles play at large public events, as in the former Yugoslav Republic of Macedonia, the Macedonian province of Greece, and the Bulgarian region of Pirin. Among Muslim Skopje Roma, *zurla* and *tapan* music is essential for ritual moments, such as the application of henna to the bride's hair, hands, and feet, the act of male circumcision, and the slaughter of a lamb on St. George's Day. *Zurla* and *tapan* ensembles vitally coexist with amplified modern bands because of their ritual function, their role in playing traditional dance music, and their symbolic association with Rom identity (Silverman 1996b). In the 1960s in Macedonia, *zurla* and *tapan* players were even hired by radio and government-sponsored ensembles.

Zurla and *tapan* playing is reserved for men and transmitted along kin lines. In

FIGURE 6 In Pirin, Bulgaria, the player of a Rom *zurla* 'double-reed, conical-bore aerophone' faces the leader of the dance line as he plays requested tunes. The player of the *tŭpan* 'bass drum' is at right. Photo by Carol Silverman, 1984.

the villages around Galičnik, western Macedonia, most *zurla* players are from a single Rom family [see MACEDONIA, figure 7]. Training takes place on the job, from elder to younger, and repertoire and technique are learned by listening and watching. Typically, one *zurla* has the melody while the other drones. Occasionally, both *zurla*s play in heterophonic unison, in octaves or, more recently, in parallel thirds, and the lead *zurla* player does free rhythmic improvisations (*mane,* from Greek *amanedhes*) and metric improvisations. These devices alternate for varying lengths of times. Size of repertoire and technical virtuosity distinguish good *zurla* players. Ornamentation consists of rapid and even finger trills, mordents, and grace notes (Rice 1982). Master *tapan* players improvise rhythmically and texturally, using the sounds of two drumheads to create complex polyrhythmic interactions between the *zurla* player and the *tapan* player (Arbatsky 1953).

Roma were the majority of performers in urban professional *čalgija* ensembles, which flourished until World War II playing Ottoman-derived vocal and instrumental music in a heterophonic style based on the *makam* system, emphasizing innovation and improvisation. Each ensemble originally consisted of a violin, an *ud* 'plucked, short-necked, fretless lute', a *kanun* 'plucked zither', a *dajre* 'a frame drum with jingles', and a voice, but grew to feature a *džumbuš* 'long-necked plucked lute with a skin face', a clarinet, a *truba* 'trumpet', an accordion, and a *tarabuka* 'goblet-shaped drum'. Families of sedentary Roma have played *čalgija* for generations. Though the tradition is predominantly male, female professionals, usually relatives of male musicians, played for female guests in segregated Muslim events, and their

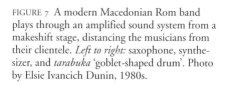

ensemble consisted of a violin, a *dajre,* and sometimes an *ud,* and the women accompanied their own singing. Women and young male Roma were hired to perform solo dancing in coffeehouses and at weddings. Currently, women are among the best singers, and Rom dance is almost exclusively female.

The *čalgija* repertoire included light Turkish classical pieces, rural folk music, and urban popular songs in the languages of the Ottoman city; it flourished in contexts such as coffeehouses, weddings, and other life-cycle celebrations, fairs, and saint's-day celebrations. Profound changes in the 1960s, such as the migration of rural populations into urban centers, the spread of Western harmony and instruments, and the introduction of amplification, affected the style and texture of *čalgija* (figure 7). Its tradition continues with electrified bands consisting of a clarinet and/or a sax-

FIGURE 7 A modern Macedonian Rom band plays through an amplified sound system from a makeshift stage, distancing the musicians from their clientele. *Left to right:* saxophone, synthesizer, and *tarabuka* 'goblet-shaped drum'. Photo by Elsie Ivancich Dunin, 1980s.

Esma Redžepova, born in Skopje, was the first
popularizer of songs in Romani among non-Roma,
via concerts and recordings. In 1976, she and her
husband, Stevo Teodosievski, were crowned "King
and Queen of Romani Music" at the World Romani
Congress in India.

ophone, an accordion and/or a synthesizer, a guitar and/or a *džumbuš,* an electric
bass, and a drum set and/or a *tarabuka,* plus a vocalist (Seeman 1990a, 1990b).

An important part of the repertoire is *čoček* in 2/4 (3–3–2), 7/16 (3–2–2), or
9/16 (2–2–2–3), marked by *mane,* an improvised free-rhythmic exploration of the
makam, using stock motifs and figures, played over a metric ostinato. The dance
čoček is solo and improvised, and utilizes torso and hand movements. Until the
1970s, it was danced by men and women, but separately. Women danced in homes
to the accompaniment of a female *dajre* player and women's singing; to dance for
men was considered crude (Dunin 1971, 1973, 1997). By the 1980s, women were
dancing *čoček* in public, and sexual segregation in dance was less pronounced
(Silverman 1996b).

Nonprofessional singing at ritual events occurs at weddings and for calendrical
holidays such as Vasilica (14 January), the most important winter holiday, and St.
George's Day (6 May), the most important spring holiday. Ritual songs are usually
unaccompanied and sung by women, and deal with themes of good luck and prosperity (Petrovski 1993).

The Rom singer most recognized by Roma and non-Roma alike is Esma
Redžepova, born in Skopje (figure 8). As part of the Stevo Teodosievski Ensemble
(which included Rom clarinetist Medo Čun and Slavic Macedonians like Stevo), she
was the first popularizer of songs in Romani among non-Roma, via concerts and
recordings. In the late 1950s, her trademark song, "*Čhaje Šukarija,*" took Yugoslavia
by storm—heard via concerts, records, radio, and television. She toured the world,
singing in packed halls and stadiums. Her renditions were fiery, emotional, and dramatic to the point of acting and dancing the text. In 1976, she and her husband,
Stevo Teodosievski, were crowned "King and Queen of Romani Music" at the World
Romani Congress in India. Their home, in Belgrade, was a training ground for
young, talented Roma. In 1993, she and Stevo founded a museum in Skopje to
archive their musical materials.

Macedonian Roma are particularly fond of Turkish music. Since the 1970s, their
repertoire has included Indian-inspired melodies and songs, reflecting their growing
historical awareness and rising ethnic consciousness.

Bulgaria

Currently home to about nine hundred thousand Roma (half Muslim, half Eastern
Orthodox), Bulgaria has a musical history of Rom professionalism since the fourteenth century. Instrumental music is transmitted in the male line with informal on-
the-job instruction. The most typical Bulgarian Rom instrumental genre, *kjuček,* can
be found in two metric patterns: *Turski kjuček* (in duple meter) and *Ciganski kjuček*
(in 9/8). Both sexes sing, but dancing is a female specialty. Unlike the situation in
Macedonia, Croatia, and Serbia, Bulgarian Roma play traditional village instruments
such as the *gŭdulka* 'bowed lute', the *gajda* 'bagpipe', the *kaval* 'end-blown flute', and

FIGURE 8 Esma Redžepova, perhaps the most
famous of all Rom singers, in performance.
Photo by Paula A. White, 1998.

the *tambura* 'plucked long-necked lute', in addition to Western European instruments. For example, Roma bear and monkey trainers in Bulgaria play a vertically held three-stringed pear-shaped bowed lute (*gŭdulka,* in Macedonia *kemene*). Many make their own instruments. In addition to playing dance music, to which the animal performs, they play and sing improvised historical ballads or humorous songs, sometimes providing social commentary (Silverman 1986:55). The Bulgarian socialist government strictly regulated animal trainers' travel and earnings, but since 1989, it has eased restrictions, and animal trainers now work in parks and playgrounds of major cities (figure 9). Rom *gajda* players were and are well respected throughout Thrace and Strandža.

In 1949, the theater ensemble Roma was founded, and folklorist Jašar Malikov became its orchestra director. In 1958 he started the first radio show featuring Rom music. He composed many songs, among them the first songs in Romani to be released by the state phonograph record company. One such song, "*Lele Devla,*" contains familiar themes of despair; it was arranged by Anželo Malikov, Jašar's son (also a composer) and performed by Katja Safedimova and Ani Garova on BHM 3423:

Lele Devla, so kergjan?	Oh God, what have you done?
Nasvalipe man dinjan.	You made me sick.
Mandar terni so mangjan?	What did you want of me so young?
Mo ternipe so liljan?	Why did you take my youth?
De, de mande, de mande	Give, give me, give me
Kerke draba te pijav, te pijav, te pijav.	Bitter medicine to drink, to drink, to drink.
Oke romel, ka merav, ka merav.	Behold Roma, I will die, I will die.

These recordings are distinguished by their Turkish influence, such as repeated descending phrases, fluid improvisations, and heterophonic textures.

The most important genre of Rom-shaped contemporary Bulgarian music is wedding music, which developed along new lines in the 1970s, when amplification was introduced into village settings. In wedding bands, Roma often play with Bulgarian Turks and/or Bulgarians. What defines wedding music is a combination of instrumentation, repertoire, and style. Wedding music is also performed at baptisms, house-warmings, soldier-send-off celebrations, and other major ritual events in village and urban contexts. Instrumentation typically consists of a clarinet, a saxophone, an accordion, an electric bass guitar, and a trap-drum set. Less often one finds a violin or traditional village instruments. The repertoire consists mainly of songs and village dances with a Thracian emphasis. It also includes, especially at Rom events, *kjučeks*, whose tunes are composed by wedding musicians, inspired by folk and popular music from Serbia, Macedonia, Greece, and Turkey, film scores from the West, cartoon music, Middle Eastern music, Indian film music, and other sources. The emphasis is on originality and cleverness. Above all else, the ability to improvise is valued. The style of wedding singers emphasizes wide vibrato and extensive ornamentation. The unquestioned guru of wedding music is Ivo Papazov, a Turkish Roma, who founded the band Trakija in 1974. For two decades, he was the highest-paid wedding musician in the country, being in such demand that people waited for months to engage him. Now he prefers to play concerts and international events.

From the early 1970s until the 1989 revolution, all music specifically identified as Rom or in the Romani language was prohibited from media and public performance as part of the government's program to suppress minority ethnic identities. This prohibition included the playing and dancing of *kjučeks*. The *zurna* and the *tŭpan* were excluded from government-sponsored folk music schools (Silverman 1989). As part of the (anti-Turkish, anti-Muslim) Bulgarization campaign of the 1980s, *zurna* playing was prohibited in private and public settings. It survived, however, in unofficial contexts. Fines were levied, and licenses to perform were revoked, when violations occurred (Buchanan 1996). Rom musical forms thrived anyway—in private settings and through cassette distribution. Since the 1989 revolution, Rom music has been revitalized and rehabilitated. Many new groups, such as Džipsi Aver, have formed, and annual Festivals of Rom Music and Song have been held since June 1993. Compact discs with Rom music are being released by fledgling private companies, and experimentation with hybrid styles, such as rap, is developing (Silverman 1996a).

Greece

By about A.D. 1400, numerous Roma inhabited the Adriatic coast. Throughout Ottoman times, Roma had an active musical life at the Turkish court in Ioanina, Epirus. At the end of the eighteenth century, Murat IV (known as Ali Pasha), and later his sons, recruited court musicians and singers from the Rom ghetto, located close to the palace, and from Athens (Brandl 1996). The court music of Ioanina included songs praising the pasha. Their texts are evidence that Roma imported the distich or strophic verse into this area. The melodies for the songs are similar to those of urban music of Constantinople (Baud-Bovy 1983:67–72).

In 1870, A. G. Paspati's linguistic study of Roma in the Ottoman Empire included more than four hundred song texts, about half collected from Christian sedentary Roma of Istanbul and half from Muslim nomadic Roma of Rumelia, the Ottoman province encompassing southern Bulgaria, Albania, Montenegro, southern Serbia, Macedonia, Thrace, and mainland Greece. A selection of Paspati's texts has been reprinted (Sampson 1947–1948).

Until World War II, virtually all professional Greek musicians, especially instrumentalists, of the Greek mainland were Roma. Many still are. The Halkias family of Epirus, for example, has had professional musicians in its male line for more than 150 years. *Yiftos,* a Greek word for Roma, is synonymous with 'musician'. As in Macedonia, Roma do not generally play the village and shepherding instruments of the mainland, but play clarinet, violin, *lauto* 'plucked lute', *santouri* 'struck zither' (introduced from Turkey in the last century), *darabuka* 'hand drum', *zurna,* and *dauli,* and sing professionally. The *outi,* a plucked, short-necked, fretless lute, though not a major mainland instrument, can be found in Thrace and parts of Macedonia in urban-influenced bands. The clarinet, the principal melodic instrument of the mainland, was introduced to Greece in the first half of the nineteenth century but did not take over until the 1920s. It spread from northern Greece to southern Greece along two main routes established by the first generation of Muslim Rom players (Mazaraki 1984 [1959]). The clarinet replaced the *zurna* and the *gaida* in much of the mainland, but in Macedonia, *zurna* playing continues. Roma are not professional musicians in the Greek islands.

Music is transmitted orally through apprenticeship with a master performer; students gradually learn melodic ornamentation, the foundation of Greek music. In a recorded comparison of two versions of the same Thessaly table song sung by a Greek villager and an Epirot Roma, the Rom version was more richly ornamented (Baud-Bovy 1983:67–72). With a few exceptions, Roma seem not to have been active in the urban genres of *rebetika* 'rebels music' and music of the Greek population in the Anatolian city of Smyrna [see GREECE]. In the early *cafe amans* (clubs where the Ottoman genre *amanedhes* were sung), wandering street players, many of them Roma, would play for a short time and move on; they appear not to have been part of the regular *koumpania*s 'bands'. Rom (and Jewish) female dancers performed in these clubs (Baud-Bovy 1983:67–73).

In the 1950 and1960s, numerous Roma—including Kostas Hadzis, Manolis Angelopoulos, and Anestis Athanasiou (known as *O Yiftos*)—achieved fame in popular bouzouki circles singing in Greek. In the 1990s, recordings such as *Yorgos Mangas, Tsigánika Traghúdhia,* and *Songs of Greece's Gypsies* were released with songs in Romani, providing a glimpse into the in-group musical repertoire of Roma in Greece—a topic severely neglected by researchers.

Albania

Albanian Roma live in the nation of Albania, in western Macedonia and Kosova (Serbian, Kosovo) province of Yugoslavia. In 1938, the British traveler and amateur ethnographer Margaret Hasluck published a comprehensive article that includes material on Albanian Rom music and ritual song texts. Sedentary Roma, the chief musicians of Albania, play at celebrations in sexually segregated family groups. Common ensembles consist of *zurna*s and *davul*s or a combination of a clarinet, a violin, and a frame drum (*def*). In the north, the *lauto* is played, and around Dibra (Debar, in western Macedonia), the plucked long-necked lute (*çiteli*) is common. Female Rom sometimes perform "action songs," in which, for example, they enact a story of unrequited love. In the cities, Rom women are sometimes professional dancers at Albanian weddings and cafes. In the early 1920s, such vast sums of money were spent on tips for dancing women that the Albanian government forbade Roma to dance in places of public entertainment. In 1934, the rule was relaxed, but café owners still had to pay a tax on entertainment, as during Ottoman times (Hasluck 1938).

The music of Kosova Roma can be divided into four groups, of which the first and the fourth are most widespread (Pettan 1992a). The first is the *zurla* and *tapan* group (see above), which accompanies men's dance cycles, horse races, and traditional wrestling. The audience for this group is mainly rural, and the professional relationship between a celebrating family and a *zurla* player's family may last for generations. The second is the frame drum (*dajre def*) ensemble, usually consisting of two female players and singers, one of whom may dance. The audience is rural women. The third group consists of Western brass band instruments, used mainly to accompany singing. The audience is primarily Serbs and Croatians. In the early 1990s only one

Russian audiences, especially writers and poets, were fascinated by Rom music. Pushkin's and Tolstoy's writings about Roma sparked curiosity, interest, and a degree of respect. Among the educated classes, almost every family had an album of piano transcriptions of Rom romances, which the nobility often performed.

Rom brass band existed in Kosova, but many others exist in southern Serbia and are hired to play in Kosova, sometimes at funerals. Unlike the other ensembles, brass bands play at funerals. The fourth group, called *čalgija* during the early twentieth century, consisted of a violin, a clarinet, a *tarabuka*, and a *def*, and sometimes an *ud,* a *džumbuš,* and a plucked zither (*kanun*), and resembled Macedonian *čalgija* ensembles in its instrumentation and use of heterophony. It went through profound changes following World War II: the accordion was introduced, facilitating the performance of Serbian popular harmonically based music. In the 1970s , the saxophone began to replace the clarinet, the drum set (*džez*) began to replace the *tarabuka* and the *def,* the electronic keyboard and synthesizer began to replace the accordion, and the bass was introduced, all becoming electrically amplified; processions, however, used the older instruments. Currently, older and newer groupings exist simultaneously and musicians often play different instruments in them.

The principal Rom musical genre in Kosova is *talava,* vocal dance music with a lively, strong, usually duple rhythm, improvised lyrics (often about the host family), melodic vocal improvisation on the word *aman,* and instrumental improvisation (*taksim*). Usually sung in Albanian, rarely in Romani, it originated with women's songs accompanied by a tambourine (*def*). Men and women perform it with amplified bands (Pettan 1992a).

In Kosova, Roma interact with all local ethnic groups. In the 1980s, the main sources of new tunes were Indian film music, Turkish popular music (*arabesk*), Bosnian and Serbian newly composed folk music, and Bulgarian Rom music. Roma have tried to avoid the conflict between Serbs and Albanians in Kosova by refusing to play music perceived as nationalist, but they have been unwittingly pulled into the conflict (Pettan 1996b).

EASTERN EUROPE

Russia

Sedentary Russian Rom musicians had the patronage of the aristocracy in the late eighteenth century, when Count Orloff brought Rom singers to St. Petersburg. They were much in demand and could often be heard at soirees offered by members of Catherine the Great's circle of nobility. Stesha, the singer known as the nightingale, was the object of Napoleon's admiration. She performed in Moscow with a male violinist, a male guitarist, and two female singers. Russian audiences, especially writers and poets, were fascinated by Rom music. Pushkin's and Tolstoy's writings about Roma, which emphasized their free spirit, sparked curiosity, interest, and a degree of respect toward Roma. Prominent princes, soldiers, merchants, and counts fell in love with Rom women (especially singers), married them, and showed them off proudly (Rom-Lebedev 1990). Among the educated classes, almost every family had an album of piano transcriptions of Rom romances, which the nobility often performed (Bobri 1961:20).

Women had the main role as singers and dancers, with males playing guitar, sometimes singing, and often leading the choruses. In choirs, women also played guitar. The characteristic seven-stringed Russian guitar was developed in the nineteenth century: it had a detachable neck; its sound was softer, deeper, and more velvety than other guitars (Bobri 1961). Performances included improvisation and rapid arpeggios; the repertoire, transmitted orally, consisted of Russian romances and folk songs, sung in Russian and Romani, with Western triadic harmony in an emotional, dramatic style. Choruses were often organized by families—a tendency that encouraged stability and preserved morality and family honor. The Poliakov chorus played in the best restaurants and toured villages, fairs, and concert halls. Famous soloists from the turn of the century supposedly received diamonds from their admirers. In addition to urban choruses, rural Roma cultivated music among multiple trades, sang at fairs and markets, and had an active in-group musical culture. Little is known of their music, but they learned the urban romances. Conversely, the chorus Roma learned some songs and dances from the "camp" Roma, but urban audiences did not receive these items well (Rom-Lebedev 1990).

A few ethnographic collections of nomadic Rom songs were published during the Soviet period, often with transcriptions such as those by Druts and Gessler in 1985 and 1988. Demeter and Demeter's 1981 collection consists of material collected from R. S. Demeter's father (born in Hungary in 1879), who told stories and sang in Hungarian, Russian, Romanian, Serbian, Polish, and Romani. Rural singing was not professional or accompanied, except for clapping or boot slapping, and often had vowel exclamations inserted into the Romani text to fill up the rhythm. Song genres include laments, songs of everyday life, wedding songs, dance songs, and joking songs.

In Moscow in 1931, the communist government formed the Teatr Romen to "preserve a national culture" and "aid the assimilation, sedentarization and education of nomadic peoples" (Lemon 1991:360). Romani literary activity then included the publication of hundreds of books in Romani, written in the Cyrillic alphabet. Performers were actors, musicians, singers, and dancers, auditioned from the nomadic camps and the sedentary communities.

Western musical notation, acting techniques, and ballet were taught at the theater, as was general literacy. Some performers worked in choruses in the evening, though such work was strictly prohibited. The repertoire included historical and dramatic plays, including foreign classics, and many plays showcased music. New pieces were commissioned and classics were altered, especially to fit the stereotype Russians had of Roma and the requirements of socialist realism. Until 1936, performances were in Romani; with Stalin's Russification programs, Russian replaced Romani. By 1947, the Teatr consisted of one hundred performers. The Soviet label Melodiya released many recordings, and several feature films highlighted the theater. The songs are typically in major and minor with a wide range and in 2/4 or free rhythm, and have chordal accompaniment. The vocal style emphasizes glissando and vibrato to express emotion. For Roma today, music remains a part of family gatherings, as shown in the video *T'an Bakhtale! Roma (Gypsies) in Russia*. Teatr Romen connects Roma from all over Russia and includes several generations of the same families, who comprise a Rom elite in Moscow. No longer an instrument of Soviet propaganda, Teatr Romen is viewed by some Roma as the caretaker of Rom culture (Lemon 1991). Since 1980, there have been many spin-off groups, such as the Trio Romen, the Kolpakov Trio, Loyko, and Djang, plus groups in the Russian Rom diaspora in Western Europe.

WESTERN AND NORTHERN EUROPE

France

The current French Rom musical scene is dominated by Manouch jazz, a style of playing that crystallized in the 1920s with the popularity of guitarist Django Reinhardt (1910–1953). Django's father led a family orchestra (violin, piano, guitar, and contrabass) that played popular music professionally for dances and in restaurants. The family was extremely poor, and Django, who was practically illiterate and never learned to read music, did not acquire his own instrument, a banjo-guitar, until he was twelve, when he began working professionally in dance halls. Badly burned in a fire in 1928, he lost the use of two fingers of his left hand. After two years of therapy, he devised a unique fingering system to overcome his handicap. In 1934, he and violinist Stephane Grappelli founded the ensemble later known as Quintette du Hot Club de France, which recorded many albums. Reinhardt became an international celebrity and inspired numerous imitators. In 1946, he played in England and Switzerland and toured the United States as a soloist with Duke Ellington's band, playing amplified guitar for the first time. Called the genius of the guitar and blessed with an exceptional ear, he had a melodic and harmonic inventiveness that revamped the role of the guitar in jazz groups. His repertoire included blues, swing, waltzes, and rhythm and blues.

Despite his fame, Django remained a member of the Manouch community, a Rom subgroup. Some critics have condemned him for the Rom quality of his playing (usually labeled romantic), but others credit him with successfully blending Rom elements and jazz. The journal *Études Tsiganes* has published many discographies of Rom jazz (Antonietto 1988). It periodically compiles discographies on Rom music elsewhere in Europe, sells selected recordings, and runs a Rom music archive. Django's sons Lousson and Babik are also fine guitarists, and many other Rom—including Bireli Langrene, Boulou Ferre, and Elio Ferre—have followed in his style in Belgium, France, Germany, and the Netherlands. The Rosenberg Trio, consisting of Stochelo Rosenberg and his cousins, is popular in the Netherlands. Indeed, Manouch jazz has developed a following throughout Western Europe, and festivals of Rom jazz have been held regularly in France.

In nonprofessional music, André Hajdú (1962, 1964) has published on the Kalderash Roma of Paris, especially their slow songs sung during traditional celebrations. In 1976, the French television series "*Tsiganes Sans Frontières*" covered many Rom musical styles; the sound track was released in two phonograph recordings. Another context for French Rom music, the Pentecostal church, has attracted a large following since the late 1980s and now disseminates cassettes throughout the Rom Pentecostal community.

Germany

Contemporary German Rom music encompasses a large array of styles and repertoires, in part because Germany's policy of liberal asylum, in effect until 1993, attracted Roma from other countries. In Germany, Macedonian, Turkish, Russian, Polish, Romanian, Hungarian, Spanish, and French Rom music is played for ingroup events and professionally for others. A Rom jazz scene and a political song movement flourishes (Weiss 1984). Django Reinhardt's successors, especially his second cousin, violinist Schnuckenack Reinhardt, have a large following. Reinhardt's band plays jazz standards and a few traditional songs of the Sinti, a group of German Roma, but it has recorded with urban Hungarian Rom musicians (*Music of the German Gypsies*). Indeed, nineteenth-century German Roma played mostly urban

Hungarian music. Other famous Sinti jazz musicians are Hansche Weiss, guitar, and Titi Winterstein, violin.

"*Lass Maro Tschatschepen*" ('We Finally Want Justice'), first performed in 1978 by the Hansche Weiss Quintett, inspired a political-song movement that crystallized with the formation of Duo Z, consisting of Rudko Kawczynski from Poland and Tornado Rosenberg from Hamburg. *Z,* short for *Zigeuner* 'Gypsy', is the symbol the Nazis forced the Roma to wear. The duo met in 1979 at a demonstration in front of Bergen-Belsen, the concentration camp where Sinti were demanding reparations for the Holocaust and an end to discrimination. Their goal is to use music to teach non-Roma about Rom history and human rights, and to foster communication between the Sinti and other Roma. Duo Z participated in the 1980 hunger strike in Dachau and the 1981 World Romani Congress in Göttingen, and they organized the 1980 Hamburg Rom festival. In 1980, they founded the Rom and Sinti Union of Hamburg. Kawczynski remains active in many Rom human rights movements. Duo Z sang mostly in German. It inspired a Rom political-song movement that in many Wesern European countries gained adherents, including Biermann in Hamburg, Hans Calderash in Sweden, and Hortto Kaalo in Finland. Kaalo's signature piece, "Why Do They Close the Doors on Us," refers to laws that prohibited the Rom from dining in restaurants in Finland.

Austria

Austria has four Rom groups: the Burgenland Roma, who came from Croatia and Hungary in the 1500s; the Sinti, who came from Bohemia and southern Germany in the 1800s and after World War I; the Lovara, who came from Hungary and Slovakia in the 1800s; and the Yugoslav Roma, who came after 1960 as guest workers. Ursula Hemetek, of the Institut für Volksmusikforschung, has documented the music of all these groups. The compact disc *Romamusik 1: Amare Gila—Unsere Leider* presents the repertoire of a Lovara singer at the center of the Austrian Rom musical scene. Hemetek has collected Holocaust songs and has worked with Mozes Heinschink to document Heinschink's collection of music of Macedonian Roma living in Vienna (Hemetek and Heinschink 1992).

Finland

Finnish Rom music is known through the collections of the Folklore Archives of the Finnish Literary Society, which holds more than one thousand hours of Rom music and has released a two-album collection. *Finnish Gypsies Sing* includes unaccompanied songs in Romani and Finnish, especially lyrical love songs, whose content and melody resemble Finnish folk songs. Other categories include songs from broadside sheets, prison songs, boasting songs (sung by men in conflict situations), and songs commemorating specific persons. The oldest melodic layer consists of songs in a minor scale—natural when ascending, but with the second degree lowered a semitone when descending. This scalar structure is common in Indian, Middle Eastern, and Balkan music, but unknown in Finnish folk music. Also different from Finnish folk music is the use of vibrato, trills, glissandos, and rhythmic variations, the most striking of which is the lengthening of the final note, the mark of a "good" singer. Around 1900, Rom music began to be heavily influenced by Finnish folk music and popular Russian romances and waltzes. In addition to in-group nonprofessional singers, some male Roma have become professional musicians and are among the country's top vocalists. Roma also have a significant role in composing and performing tangos. In the early 1980s, Rom writer Veijo Baltzar organized a Rom theater.

BIBLIOGRAPHY

Antonietto, Alain. 1988. "Discographie du Jazz Tsigane." *Études Tsiganes* 1:36–41.

Arbatsky, Yuri. 1953. *Beating the Tupan in the Central Balkans.* Chicago: Newberry Library.

Balazs, Gusztav. 1995. *A Nagyescedi Olah Cigányok Tánchagyományá.* Budapest: Magyar Néprajzi Társaság.

Bartók, Béla. 1976 [1931]. "Gypsy Music or Hungarian Music?" In *Béla Bartók Essays,* ed. Benjamin Suchoff, 206–223. New York: St. Martin's.

Baud-Bovy, Samuel. 1983. *Essai sur la chanson populaire grèque.* Nafplion: Fondation Ethnographique du Péloponnèse.

Baumann, Max Peter. 1996. "The Reflection of the Roma in European Art Music." *The World of Music* 38(1):95–138.

Beissinger, Margaret. 1988. "Text and Music in Romanian Oral Epic." *Oral Tradition* 3(3):292–314.

———. 1991. *The Art of the Lăutar: The Epic Tradition of Romania.* New York: Garland Publishing.

Bellman, Johnathan. 1993. *The Style Hongrois in the Music of Western Europe.* Boston: Northeastern University Press.

Bhattacharya, Deben. 1965. *The Gypsies.* London: Record Books.

Bobri, B. 1961. "Gypsies and Gypsy Choruses of Old Russia." *Journal of the Gypsy Lore Society,* series 3, 40:112–120.

Brandl, Rudolf. 1996. "The *Yiftoi* and the Music of Greece: Role and Function." *The World of Music* 38(1):7–32.

Buchanan, Donna. 1996. "Wedding Music, Political Transition, and National Consciousness in Bulgaria." In *Retuning Culture: Musical Changes in Central and Eastern Europe,* ed. Mark Slobin, 200–230. Durham, N.C.: Duke University Press.

Buckley, Ann. 1994. "Professional Musicians, Dancing and Patronage: Continuity and Change in a Transylvanian Community." *The World of Music* 36(3):31–48.

Ciobanu, Gheorghe. 1969. *Lăutari din Clejani: Repertoriu şi stil de interpretare.* Bucharest: Editura Muzicală.

Csenki, Imre, and Sándor Csenki. 1943. *Népdalgyüjtés a Magyarországi Cigányok Között.* Budapest: Kodály-emlékkönyv.

Davidová, Eva, and Jan Žižka. 1991. *Folk Music of the Sedentary Gypsies of Czechoslovakia.* Budapest: Institute for Musicology of the Hungarian Academy of Sciences.

Delaunay, Charles. 1961. *Django Reinhardt.* New York: Da Capo Press.

Demeter, R. S., and P. S. Demeter. 1981. *Obraztsy Fol'klora Cigan Kelderari.* Moscow: Eastern Literatures Press.

Druts, Efim, and Aleksei Gessler. 1985. *Skazi i pesni Rozhdennie v Doroge.* Moscow: Nauka.

———. 1988. *Narodnie pesni Ruskikh Cigan.* Moscow: Sovetskii Kompozitor.

Dunin, Elsie Ivancich. 1971. "Gypsy Wedding: Dance and Customs." *Makedonski Folklor* 4(7–8):317–326.

———. 1973. "Čoček as a Ritual Dance Among Gypsy Women." *Makedonski Folklor* 6(12)193–197.

———. 1977. "The Newest Changes in Rom Dance (Serbia and Macedonia)." *Journal of the Association of Graduate Dance Ethnologists, University of California, Los Angeles* 1(Spring):12–17.

———. 1985. "Dance Change in the Context of the Gypsy St. George's Day, Skopje, Yugoslavia, 1967–1977." In *Papers from the Fourth and Fifth Annual Meetings, Gypsy Lore Society, North American Chapter,* 110–120. New York: North American Chapter, Gypsy Lore Society.

———. 1997. *Gypsy St. George's Day, Coming of Summer: Romski Gjurgjovden, Romano Gjurgjovdani—Erdelezi, Skopje Macedonia 1967–1997.* Skopje: Združenie na Ljuboteli na Romska Foklorna Umetnost Romano Ilo.

Fennesz-Juhasz, Christiane. 1996. "Me ka džav ko gurbeti. . . . Klage- und Abschiedslieder Mazedonischer Roma-Migranten." In *Echo der Vielfalt, Echoes of Diversity: Traditional Music of Ethnic Groups,* ed. Ursula Hemetek and Emil Lubej, 255–270. Vienna: Böhlau.

Ficowski, Jerzy. 1991. *The Gypsies in Poland.* Warsaw: Interpress.

Forry, Mark. 1990. "The Mediation of 'Tradition' and 'Culture' in the Tamburica Music of Vojvodina (Yugoslavia)." Ph.D. dissertation, University of California, Los Angeles.

Garfias, Robert. 1981. "Survivals of Turkish Characteristics of Romanian Musica Lautareasca." *Yearbook for Traditional Music* 13:97–107.

———. 1984. "Dance Among the Urban Gypsies of Romania." *Yearbook for Traditional Music* 16:84–96.

Giannakopoulos, Takis. 1981. *Oi Yifti kai to Dimoyko Mas Tragoudi.* Athens: Thoukididis.

———. 1982. *Tsinganika Laika Tragoudia kai Balantes.* Athens: n.p.

Gojković, Adriana. 1986. "Music of Yugoslav Gipsies." *Traditional Music of Ethnic Groups—Minorities: Proceedings of the Meeting of Ethnomusicologists on the Occasion of the European Year of Music 1985* 7:187–194.

Hajdú, André. 1962. "Le Folklore Tsigane." *Études Tsiganes* 8(1–2):1–33.

———. 1964. "La Loki Djili des Tsiganes Kelderash." *Arts et Traditions Populaires* 12:139–176.

Hasluck, Margaret. 1938. "The Gypsies of Albania." *Journal of the Gypsy Lore Society,* series 3, 17:20–30.

Heinschink, Mozes, and Christiane Juhasz. 1992. "Koti džal o mulo. . . . Lieder österreichischer Sinti." *Jahrbuch des Österreich* 41:63–88.

Hemetek, Ursula. 1994. "Musik im Leben der Roma." In *Roma: Das Unbekannte Volk: Schicksal und Kultur,* ed. Ursula Hemetek and Mozes Heinschink, 150–170. Vienna: Böhlag Verlag.

———, et al. 1992. *Romane Ğila: Lieder und Tänze der Roma in Österreich.* With cassette IDI-TON 23. Vienna: Österreichischen Dialektautoren und Institut für Volksmusikforschung an der Hochschule für Musik und darstellende Kunst.

Hemetek, Ursula, and Mozes Heinschink, eds. 1992. "Lieder im Leid: Zu KZ-Liedern der Roma in Österreich." *Dokumentations-archiv des Österreichischen Widerstandes Jahrbuch* 76–94.

———. 1996. "Roma: Einen österreichische Volksgruppe: Die Rolle der traditionellen Musik im Prozess der Identitätsfindung." In *Echo der Vielfalt, Echoes of Diversity: Traditional Music of Ethnic Groups,* ed. Ursula Hemetek and Emil Lubej, 271–284. Vienna: Böhlau.

Holý, Dušan, and Ctibor Nečas. 1993. *O Sudo Romii v Nacistickýcch Koncentračnicch Táborech.* Strážnici: Vydal Ústav Lidové Kultuy.

Hübschmannová, Milena. 1980–1981. "Romane Gila." *Lacio Drom* 16(3–4):2–9; 16(6):2–4; 17(1):2–5.

Hunt, Yvonne. 1990. "The Dance of the Tzamála of Flámbouro, Serres." In *Proceedings of the Third International Conference on Traditional Dance,* 144–147. Larissa, Greece: International Organization of Folk Arts.

———. 1995. "Ta Kechékia—A Greek Gypsy Carnival Event." In *Dance and Ritual: Proceedings of the 18th Symposium of the ICTM Study Group on Ethnochoreography,* 97–103. Warsaw: Institute of Art, Polish Academy of Sciences.

Karsai, László. 1991. "Hungarian Gypsy Songs About the Holocaust." *Cahiers de Littérature Orale* 30:37–44.

Konstas, K. S. 1960. "I Zygia sti Dytiki Roumeli." *Laografia* 19:325–369.

Kovalcsik, Katalin. 1985. *Vlach Gypsy Folk Songs in Slovakia.* Budapest: Institute for Music of the Hungarian Academy of Sciences.

———. 1986. "The Place of Gipsies' Tradition in the Folk Music of Eastern Europe." *Traditional Music of Ethnic Groups—Minorities: Proceedings of the Meeting of Ethnomusicologists on the Occasion of the European Year of Music 1985* 7:176–182.

———. 1987. "Popular Dance Music Elements in the Folk Music of Gypsies in Hungary." *Popular Music* 6(1):45–66.

———. 1990. "On the Historical Music Layers of the Gypsies of Hungary." *100 Years of Gypsy Studies,* ed. Matt Salo, 177–192. Cheverly, Md.: The Gypsy Lore Society.

———. 1991. "Chansons tsiganes lentes sur l'experience personnelle." *Cahiers de Littérature Orale* 30:45–64.

———. 1992. *Ernö Király Collection of Gypsy Folk Music from Voivodina.* Budapest: Institute for

Musicology of the Hungarian Academy of Sciences.

———. 1994. *Florilyé Dă Primavárá I and II: Tavaszi Virágok, Beás Cigány Iskolai Énekeskönyv*. With cassettes GK1 and GK2. Pécs: Gandhi Középiskola.

———. 1996. "Roma or Boyash Identity? The Music of the 'Ard' elan' Boyashes in Hungary." *The World of Music* 38(1):77–94.

Kovalcsik, Katalin, and Endre Tálos. 1991. "The Little Maple Tree: A Transylvanian Gypsy Folk Tale with Songs." *Journal of the Gypsy Lore Society*, series 5, 1(2):103–125.

Lange, Barbara Rose. 1993. "Holy Brotherhood: The Negotiation of Musical Style in a Gypsy and Magyar Pentecostal Church." Ph.D. dissertation, University of Washington.

———. 1996. "Gender, Politics, and Musical Performers in the Isten Gyulekezet." *Journal of American Folklore* 109(431):60–76.

———. 1997a. "Hungarian Rom (Gypsy) Political Activism and the Development of *Folklór* Ensemble Music." *The World of Music* 39(3):5–30.

———. 1997b. "What Was That Conquering Magic . . .": The Power of Discontinuity in Hungarian Gypsy *Nóta*." *Ethnomusicology* 41(3):517–537.

Lemon, Alaina. 1991. "Roma (Gypsies) in the Soviet Union and the Moscow Teatr 'Romen'." *Nationalities Papers* 19(3):359–372.

———. 1996. "Hot Blood and Black Pearls: Socialism, Society and Authenticity at the Moscow Teatr Romen." *Theatre Journal* 48:479–494.

Liszt. Franz. 1859. *Des Bohémiens et de leur musique en Hongrie*. Paris: Bourdillat.

Lloyd, A. L. 1963–1964. "The Music of Rumanian Gypsies." *Proceedings of the Royal Musical Society*. 90th session, 15–26.

Manush, Leksa. 1987. "The Problem of the Folk Music of the Gypsies (Sources of Gypsy Music in Europe)." *Soviet Anthropology and Archaeology* 25(3):17–34.

Marre, Jeremy, and Hannah Charlton. 1985. "The Romany Trail." In *Beats of the Heart: Popular Music of the World*, 167–197. New York: Pantheon.

Marushiakova, Elena, and Veselin Popov. 1994–1995. *Studii Romani*. 2 vols. Sofia: Club '90 Publishers.

Mazaraki, Despoinas B. 1984 [1959]. *To Laiko Klarino Stin Ellada*. Athens: Kedras.

Mercier, Denis. 1993. *Latcho Drom: Un Film de Tony Gatlif*. Paris: K. G. Productions.

Nećas, Ctibor, and Dušan Holý. 1991. "À Auschwitz il y a une grande prison: Ausviate hi Kher Baro." *Cahiers de Littérature Orale* 30:15–35.

Pejcheva, Lozanka. 1993. "Nabludeniya vŭrhu zurnadzhiskata traditsiya v yugozapadna Bulgaria." *Bŭlgarski Folklor* 19(2):48–58.

———. 1994. "V Bŭlgaria—mezhdu Kalkuta I Viena: Muzikata na bulgarskite Romi s gidove Hasan Cinciri i Kiril Lambov." *Bŭlgarski Folklor* 20(2):83–91.

Pejcheva, Lozanka, Ventsislav Dimov, and Svetla Krŭsteva. 1997. *Romska Muzika: Priturka kŭm uchebnitsite po muzika za 5-8 klas*. Sofia: Papagal OOD.

Petrovski, Trajan. 1993. *Kalendarski Običai kaj Romite vo Skopje i Okolina*. Skopje, Macedonia: Feniks.

Pettan, Svanibor. 1992a. "Gypsy Music in Kosovo: Interaction and Creativity." Ph.D. dissertation, University of Maryland, Baltimore.

———. 1992b. "'Lambada in Kosovo: A Case Study in Gypsy Creativity." *Journal of the Gypsy Lore Society*, series 5, 2(2):117–130.

———. 1996a. "Female to Male—Male to Female: *Third Gender* in the Musical Life of the Gypsies in Kosovo." *Narodna Umjetnost* 33(2):311–324.

———. 1996b. "Gypsies, Music and Politics in the Balkans: A Case Study from Kosovo." *The World of Music* 38(1):33–61.

———. 1996c. "Selling Music: Rom Musicians and the Music Market in Kosovo." In *Echo der Vielfalt, Echoes of Diversity: Traditional Music of Ethnic Groups*, ed. Ursula Hemetek and Emil Lubej, 233–245. Vienna: Böhlau.

Rădulescu, Speranța. 1984. *Taraful și acompaniamentul armonic în muzica de joc*. Bucharest: Editura Muzicală.

Rasmussen, Ljerka Vidić. 1991. "Gypsy Music in Yugoslavia: Inside the Popular Culture Tradition." *Journal of the Gypsy Lore Society*, series 5, 1(2):127–139.

———. 1996. "Orientalism, Rom Gypsy, and the Culture at Intersection." In *Echo der Vielfalt, Echoes of Diversity: Traditional Music of Ethnic Groups*, ed. Ursula Hemetek and Emil Lubej, 247–253. Vienna: Böhlau.

Rice, Timothy. 1982. "The Surla and Tapan Tradition in Yugoslav Macedonia." *Galpin Society Journal* 35:122–137.

Rom-Lebedev, Ivan. 1990. *Ot Tsyganskogo Hora k Teatru Romen*. Moscow: Isskustvo.

Sampson, John. 1947–1948. "Folk-Songs of the Tchinghianés Extracted from the Études of Dr. A. G. Paspati." *Journal of the Gypsy Lore Society*, series 3, 26(1–2):53–73; 26(3–4):156–159; 27(1–2):47–65.

Sárosi, Bálint. 1978 [1970]. *Gypsy Music*. Translated by Fred Macnicol. Budapest: Corvina.

Seeman, Sonia Tamar. 1990a. "Music in the Service of Prestation: The Case of the Rom of Skopje." M.A. thesis, University of Washington.

———. 1990b. "Continuity and Transformation in the Macedonian Genre of *Čalgija*: Past Perfect and Present Imperfective." M.A. thesis, University of Washington.

Silverman, Carol. 1986. "Bulgarian Gypsies: Adaptation in a Socialist Context." *Nomadic Peoples* 21–22:51–61.

———. 1989. "Reconstructing Folklore: Media and Cultural Policy in Eastern Europe." *Communication* 11(2):141–160.

———. 1996a. "Music Marginality: The Roma (Gypsies) of Bulgaria and Macedonia." In *Retuning Culture: Musical Changes in Central and Eastern Europe*, ed. Mark Slobin, 231–253. Durham, N.C.: Duke University Press.

———. 1996b. "Music and Power: Gender and Performance Among Roma (Gypsies) of Skopje, Macedonia." *The World of Music* 38(1):63–76.

Sinclair, A. T. 1907. "Gypsy and Oriental Music." *Journal of American Folklore* 20(76):16–32.

Spur, Endre. 1947–1949. "Jozsi the Second: The Problem of a Gypsy Musician's Career." *Journal of the Gypsy Lore Society*, series 3, 25(3–4):134–145; 27(3–4):117–132; 28(3–4):97–115.

Stanley, Denise, et al. 1986. *The Romano Drom Songbook*. Brentwood, U.K.: Romanestan Publications.

Starkie, Walter. 1933. *Raggle-Taggle: Adventures with a Fiddle in Hungary and Romania*. London: John Murray.

Stewart, Michael. 1987. "Brothers in Song: The Persistence of Gypsy Identity and Community in Socialist Hungary." Ph.D. dissertation, University of London.

———. 1989. "'True Speech': Song and the Moral Order of a Hungarian Vlach Community." *Man* 24(1):79–102.

———. 1997. *The Time of the Gypsies*. Boulder, Colo.: Westview Press.

Strom, Yale. 1993. *Uncertain Roads: Searching for the Gypsies*. New York: Four Winds Press.

Vekerdi, Jozsef. 1967. "Gypsy Folk Songs." *Acta Orientalia Academiae Scientiarum Hungaricae* 20(3):339–352.

———. 1976. "The Gypsy's Role in the Preservation of Non-Gypsy Folklore." *Journal of the Gypsy Lore Society*, series 4, 1(2):79–86.

Vidić, Ljerka. 1990a. "Musical Practice of Nomadic Rom in Bosnia." M.A. thesis, Wesleyan University.

———. 1990b. "Musical Practice of Nomadic Rom in Bosnia." In *100 Years of Gypsy Studies*, ed. Matt Salo, 203–213. Cheverly, Md.: The Gypsy Lore Society.

Víg, Rudolf. 1974. "Gypsy Folk Songs from the Béla Bartók and Zoltán Kodály Collections." *Studia Musicologica Academiae Scientiarum Hungaricae* 16:89–131.

Vukanović, Tatomir. 1959. "Gypsy Bear Leaders in the Balkan Peninsula." *Journal of the Gypsy Lore Society*, series 3, 38:106–127.

———. 1962. "Musical Culture among the Gypsies of Yugoslavia." *Journal of the Gypsy Lore Society*, series 3, 41:41–61.

Weiss, Norbert. 1984. *Besprechungen in der Gegenüberstellung*. Duisburg: Masstäbe.

Wilkinson, Irén Kertész. 1990. "Lokes Phen! An Investigation into the Musical Tempo Feeling of a Hungarian Gypsy Community Based on Their Own Evaluation." In *100 Years of Gypsy Studies,* ed. Matt Salo, 193–201. Cheverly, Md.: The Gypsy Lore Sociey.

———. 1992. "Genuine and Adopted Songs in the Vlach Gypsy Repertoire: A Controversy Re-Examined." *British Journal of Ethnomusicology* 1:111–136.

———. 1994. "Diversity in Unity: A Study of Individual Creativity through the Performance of Songs among the Vlach Gypsies of South-Eastern Hungary." Ph.D. dissertation, Goldsmiths College, London.

———. 1996a. "Differences among One's Own and Similarities with the Other: The Dual Role of Adopted Songs and Texts among Hungarian Vlach Gypsies." In *Echo der Vielfalt, Echoes of Diversity: Traditional Music of Ethnic Groups,* ed. Ursula Hemetek and Emil Lubej, 225–231. Vienna: Böhlau.

———. 1997. "Song Performance: A Model for Social Interaction among Vlach Gypsies in South-Eastern Hungary." In *Romani Culture and Gypsy Identity,* ed. Thomas Acton and Gary Mundy, 97–126. Hertfordshire, England: University of Hertfordshire Press.

Williams, Partick. 1991. *Django.* Montpelier, France: Éditions du Limon.

AUDIOVISUAL RESOURCES

Amari Luma: Rom 2001, Mongo Stojka. 1994. Sing Sang Records (Austria) SSR 4023. Compact disc.

Ando Drom: Chants Tsiganes de Hongrie. 1992. Planett WM 334 242 041. Compact disc.

Ando Drom: Gypsy Life on the Road. 1995. North Pacific Music (Portland, Oregon) NPM LD 004. Compact disc.

Artists of the Gipsy Theatre "Romen." N.d. Moscow: Melodiya C 01261. LP disk.

Balkanology: Ivo Papasov and His Orchestra. 1991. Commentary by Carol Silverman. Ryko HNCD 1363. Compact disc.

Blow Besir Blow: Jova Stojilkovic "Besir" and His Brass Orkestar. 1995. Commentary by Kim Burton. GlobeStyle CD ORBD 038. Compact disc.

Bratsch: Gypsy Music from the Heart of Europe. 1993. World Network 55832. Compact disc.

Bratsch: Transport en Commun. N.d. GRI 19021–2. Compact disc.

Ciganski Tabor: Hasan Cinciri. 1994. Sofia: Lazarov Records. Cassette.

Djang: Gypsy Song Ensemble. 1988. Commentary by V. Demeter. Moscow: Melodiya C60 26865 004. LP disk.

Django Rheinhardt: Le Quintette du Hot Club de France. 1996. RCR 40009. Compact disc.

Django Rheinhardt. N.d. Everest: Archive of Folk Music FS 212. LP disk.

Duo Z, Ganz Anders: Deutsche Zigeunerlieder. N.d. Plane LP 88 257. Compact disc.

Epirotika with Periclis Halkias. 1981. Commentary by Sotirios Chianis. Folkways FSS 34024–5. 2 LP disks.

Esma (Esma Redžepova-Teodosievska). 1998. Skopje: Dom na humanosta i Muzej na Muzikata "Esma i Stevo Teodosievski." 2 compact discs.

Famille Lela de Përmet (Albania). 1992. Label Bleu/Harmonia Mundi LBLC 2503/HM83. Compact disc.

Finnish Gypsies Sing. Commentary by Jalkanen Pekka. Love Records 2 LXLP-508–9. LP disk.

Florilyé Da Primavárá: Tavaszi Virágok, Beas Cigány Iskolai Énekeskönyv. 1994. Recordings and commentary by Katalin Kovalcsik. Pecs: Gandhi Középiskola GK1. 2 cassettes.

Folk Music of Rumania. 1963. Commentary by Tiberiu Alexandru and A. L. Lloyd. Columbia World Library of Folk and Primitive Music, 18. LP disk.

Folk Songs of Hungarian Gypsies. 1984. Recordings by Rudolf Víg. Commentary by Katalin Kovalcsik. Hungaroton SLPX 18082. LP disk.

Fragile Traditions: The Art of Pericles Halkias, an Epirot Greek Musician in America. 1989. Ethnic Folk Arts Center A8901. LP disk.

Gipsy Music of Macedonia and Neighbouring Countries: Zurle—tapan/davul—zurna/daouli—zournas. 1996. Notes by Wolf Dietrich. Topic TSCD 914. Compact disc.

Gypsy Folk Songs from Hungary. 1976. Recordings and commentary by Rudolf Víg. Hungaroton SLPX 18028–29. LP disk.

Gypsy Holiday. 1991. Jovica Nikolić Orchestra. Intersound CDM 4010. Compact disc.

Gypsy Songs: Angelo Malikov. 1992. Commentary by Manol Todorov. Sofia: Gega GD 128. Compact disc.

Hungary and Romania: Descendants of the Itinerant Gypsies, Melodies of Sorrow and Joy. 1997. Commentary by Kazuyuki Tanimoto. Multicultural Media MCM 3010. Compact disc.

Ibro Lolov: Gypsy Music from Bulgaria. 1998. Arc Music 1476. Compact disc.

Kalyi Jag: Cigányszerelem: Gipsy Love. 1998. Kalyi CDK 001. Compact disc and CD-ROM.

Kalyi Jag: Gypsy Folk Songs from Hungary. 1987. Hungaroton MK 18132. Cassette.

Kalyi Jag: Karingszo Me Phirav: Gypsy Folk Songs from Hungary. 1990. Notes by Katalin Kovalcsik. Hungaroton HCD 18199. Cassette.

Kalyi Jag: Lungoj O Drom Angla Mande: Gipsy Folk Songs from Hungary. 1994. Notes by Katalin Kovalcsik. Hungaroton HCD 18179. Compact disc.

Kalyi Jag: O Sono/The Dream/Az Alom: Gipsy Folk Songs from Hungary. 1995. Hungaroton HCD 18211. Compact disc.

King Ferus: Ferus Mustafov, Macedonian Wedding Soul Cooking. 1995. Globestyle CD ORBD 089. Compact disc.

Kočani: A Gypsy Brass Band. 1994. Long Distance 592324. Compact disc.

Kolpakov Trio: Rodava Tut. 1995. Zurich: Opre OPCD 001. Compact disc.

La Grande Voix Tzigane d'aujourd'hui: The Greatest Living Gypsy Voice: Nicolae Gutsa, Romania. 1996. France: Auvidis Silex Y 225058. Compact disc.

Laila Dimitrievitch: Chants du Peuple Rom. N.d. Le Chant du Monde LDX 74527. LP disk.

Langzaam Janken: De Trompet in Servie. 1988. Rob Boonzajer Flaes, Carel Kuyl, and Maarten Rens. Netherlands. Video.

Latcho Drom. 1993. Tony Gatlif. Shadow Distribution, Waterville, Maine. 16mm film and video. Also Caroline 1776-2. Compact disc.

Laver Bariu, Songs from the City of Roses. 1995. Notes by Kim Burton. GlobeStyle CDORBD 091. Compact disc.

Le Taraf de Cléjanie: Musique des Tsiganes de Valachie. 1988. OCORA c 559036. Compact disc.

Loyko: Road of the Gypsies. 1994. World Network, 26 (Russia). Compact disc.

Muharem: Ciganska Duša. N.d. Muharem Serbezovksi. TCD 016. Compact disc.

Mulatok, Mert Jó Kedvem Van: Cigánydalok (Gipsy Songs). 1989. Qualiton HCD 10240. Compact disc.

Music of the German Gypsies. 1975. Commentary by Siefried Maeker. Musical Heritage Society, MHS 1058. LP disk.

Musique Populaire Hongroise de la Transylvanie: Sandor "Neti" Fodor. 1989. Hungaroton/Harmonica Mundi HCD 18122. Compact disc.

Nomad's Land: Gypsies on the Move. 1994. Playsound PS 65134. Compact disc.

Pericles Halkias Family Orchestra. 1984. Balkan Arts US 1003. LP disk.

Pilem, Pilem: Pera Petrovic, Rromano Centar. 1995. Zurich: Opre OPCD 002. Compact disc.

Pouro Sinto: Musiques des Tziganes de France (Manouches). 1992. Planett WM 242 034. Compact disc.

Pŭrvi Romski Festival '93 Stara Zagora. 1993. Payner. Cassette.

Road of the Gypsies. 1997. Commentary by Alain Weber. Frankfurt: Network CD 24756. 2 compact discs.

Romafolk: Kövecselik az Utakat (Hungary). N.d. Horváth Aladár. Cassette.

Romamusik 1: Amare Gíla—Unsere Lieder. 1994.

The Music of Ružo Nikolić-Lakatos. Recordings and commentary by Ursula Hemetek. Tondokumente zur Volksmusik in Österreich, 4. Institut für Volksmusikforschung RST 91571–2. Compact discs.

Romane Ǵila: Lieder und Tänze der Roma in Österreich. 1992. Recordings and commentary by Ursula Hemetek et al. Österreichischen Dialekautoren und Institut für Volksmusikforschung IDI-TON 23, Ex 138MC. Cassette.

Romani Ǵil'a: Anthology of Gypsy Songs. 1973. Recordings and commentary by Eva Davidová and Jaromir Gélnar. Prague: Supraphon 0171389. LP disk.

Romany Trail, Part Two: Gypsy Music into Europe. 1992 [1981]. Jeremy Marre. Shanachie 1211. Video.

Rromno Dives, Ćhaj Zibede, Musique Rromani d'Albanie. 1996. ALCD 172, M7 853. Compact disc.

Songs of a Macedonian Gypsy. 1994. Featuring Esma Redžepova and Usnija Jašarova. Monitor MCD 71496. Compact disc.

Songs of Greece's Gypsies. 1996. FM records 322. Compact disc.

T'an Bakhtale! Roma (Gypsies) in Russia. 1995. Produced and directed by Alaina Lemon and Midori Nakamura. Documentary Education Resources. 75 minutes. Video.

Taraf: Romanian Gypsy Music. 1996. Notes by Speranţa Rădulescu. Music of the World CDT 137. Compact disc.

Taraf de Haïdouks: Dumbala Dumba. 1998. Cramworld CRAW CDS 21. Compact disc.

Taraf de Haïdouks: Honourable Brigands, Magic Horses and Evil Eye. 1996. CRAW CDS 13.

Taraf de Haïdouks: Musique des Tziganes de Roumanie. 1991. CRAW CDS 2. Compact disc.

Traditional Gypsy Music from the Balkans: Zoltan and His Gypsy Ensemble. 1997? Legacy 434. Compact disc.

Tsiganes sans Frontières. 1976. Commentary by Claude Vernick. Barclay 930006–7. LP disk.

Tsigánika Traghúdhia: Me Tom Yiórgho Vasilíu. N.d. GSF CYS 190. Cassette.

Tzigane! Songs and Dances of the Balkan Gypsies. N.d. Monitor MFS 747. LP disk.

Tziganes Paris/Berlin/Budapest 1910–1935. 1993. Frémeaux and Associates FA 006. 2 compact discs.

Věra Bílá and Kale: Rom Pop. 1995. Recorded in Prague. Montrouge: Last Call Records 7422510. Compact disc.

Yiorgos Mangas. 1985. GlobeStyle/Media CDORB 021. Compact disc.

Yuri Yunakov Ensemble: Balada, Bulgarian Wedding Music. 1999. Notes by Lauren Brody. Traditional Crossroads CD 4291. Compact disc.

Yuri Yunakov Ensemble: New Colors in Bulgarian Wedding Music. 1997. Notes by Carol Silverman. Traditional Crossroads CD 4283. Compact disc.

Zournades Ke Doulia Christos Gevgelis. N.d. General Grammmophone GMG 4003. Compact disc.

Travellers' Music
James Porter

The Music of Irish Travellers
The Music of Scottish Travellers

Travellers are nomadic or seminomadic groups in Ireland and Scotland; similar groups live in Scandinavia. For their metalworking skills, they were formerly known as tinkers, cognate with names for Rom such as *zingaro* and *tsigane*. But because *tinker* has pejorative connotations, they prefer the term *traveller* (compare the Rom rejection of the word *Gypsy*). Their lifestyle has made oral tradition important to them in transmitting songs long thought to be extinct in the country they traverse.

Travellers' origins are obscure. They possibly originated in a metalworking caste from ancient times: a Celtic tinsmithing group is recorded in the city of Perth in the twelfth century. It is possible that they found a great deal in common with Rom who arrived in Scotland in 1505 and may have merged to some extent with them, though the two groups now regard themselves as distinct and separate. Interactions may well have occurred from the 1500s, so that by the 1700s the term *tinker* was synonymous with *Gypsy* or *Egyptian*. The metalworking skills and nomadic life may have been sufficiently common factors to promote intermarriage. Further, their ways of speaking (in Scotland, Beurla-reagad, that is, *Beurlacheard* 'language of the cairds' for Highland Travellers, cant for Lowland Travellers) were developed as a protective device. A small amount of Romany is interspersed with disguised terms, and songs sometimes contain cant words (Court 1985; Gentleman and Swift 1971; G. Gmelch 1977; S. Gmelch 1986; Rehfisch 1975).

The song and tune repertoires of Irish and Scottish Travellers have received the most attention from scholars in recent times. Regional manifestations of the folk-music revival have played a valuable role in rehabilitating Travellers in the eyes of a settled population that formerly despised them as predators.

THE MUSIC OF IRISH TRAVELLERS

Travellers in Ireland have been especially noted for singing old ballads. A general picture of their style is available from the LP disk *Songs of the Irish Travellers* (Munnelly 1983). A trait of Traveller singing noted by Hugh Shields (1993) is to repeat the second half of a four-line strophe; in other words, quatrains may be sung with a repeat of their second half with its verbal text. Individual Traveller singers have not been

FIGURE 1 "The Well Below the Valley," a Child ballad sung by John Reilly, a settled Traveller from Boyle, County Roscommon, Ireland. Recorded by Tom Munnelly and D. K. & E. Wilgus. After Bronson 1976:83–85. This transcription shows how the melody was improvised and changed over three verses.

studied as much as in Scotland, but their ability to preserve older styles, and in many cases freer styles of singing, makes their lives and contexts worthy of study.

One such singer, John "Jacko" Reilly, a settled Traveller, born about 1926 in Ballaghaderreen, County Roscommon, and living alone in Boyle (also in Roscommon), was recorded in 1967 (Munnelly 1972). He sang thirty-six ballads, including the first orally recorded version of "The Well Below the Valley" ("The Maid and the Palmer," Child 21), and others: "What Put the Blood?" ("Edward," Child 13) and two versions of "The Dark-Eyed Gipsy." John had learned all his songs from parents and immediate friends of his family. His singing style, now of a type quite rare, improvised the basic melody line from stanza to stanza (figure 1).

Another singer, Michael "Mikeen" McCarthy, a Traveller born about 1932 at Cahirciveen, County Kerry, and brought up in Ireland, was living in 1975 in London (Carroll 1986). His parents followed the traditional trades of tinsmithing, horse dealing, hawking, and chimney sweeping, spending eight months on the road and renting a house for the winter. His mother was a *ullagoner,* a woman called on to keen or lament at funerals. As a young man, McCarthy worked selling ballad song sheets. He described how, in the 1950s, he would slip his father's songs to printers in small Munster towns for printing. Mikeen had a strong visual sense: interviewed about "Betsy of Ballentown Brae" (Laws P28) and "Early in the Month of Spring" (Laws K12), he imagined what the characters looked like, what they wore, where they lived, and their surroundings, as if watching a film or television. In the folk clubs of London, he would select a member of the audience as a focal point, and totally engrossed in the song, sing to that person.

THE MUSIC OF SCOTTISH TRAVELLERS

Low in the social scale, Scottish Lowland Travellers and their music were excluded from the picture of traditional music and song until after World War II, when Hamish Henderson and other scholars bivouacked with them in the seasonal berrying fields of Perthshire and opened the door to a rich repertoire of songs, fiddle and pipe music, and other Traveller arts, including storytelling. From the 1950s, Traveller singers have participated in the folk-music revival: Lizzie Higgins; Jeannie Robertson; Belle, Cathie, Davie, Lucy, and Sheila Stewart; Jane Turriff; Betsy Whyte; and Duncan Williamson. Their singing style could be intense and forceful (Jeannie Robertson, Sheila Stewart), gentle and ironic (Belle Stewart, Lucy Stewart, Betsy Whyte), or rhapsodic (Jane Turriff, Davie Stewart, Duncan Williamson). Their repertoire, like that of Irish Travellers, reveals relationships to songs and ballads such as "Son David" (Child 13) and "Thomas Rymer" (Child 37), derived from lived experience. Close to nature and living rough at least part of the time, imbued to vendettas and internecine quarrels, they incorporate in their singing an elemental quality that sometimes emerges as a nasal whine, but can be powerfully assertive (Munro 1996:139).

MacColl and Seeger's (1977) survey collection of songs, made between 1960 and 1975, draws from English Rom and Travellers from central and northeast Scotland. The latter group, who contributed seventy songs, includes eleven singers, most of them born around 1900. Differences in style and attitude between the Scottish Travellers and English Rom are apparent: while the most common singing style among both groups was an open-throated, direct delivery, the Scots Travellers' texts were more coherent and structurally sound; the singers were more articulate and had a fuller vocabulary.

Each of the Traveller singers had distinct preferences in types of song, tunes, and meters. Charlotte Higgins (1893–1971) of Blairgowrie, Perthshire, central Scotland, contributed sixteen songs, of which one was a song in cant, three were Child ballads, five Laws (broadside) ballads, and the others lyric songs; John MacDonald gave five Child ballads, six Laws ballads, and several bothy (housing for seasonal farm workers) songs, derived from his experience as hawker and farm servant. The Scottish Traveller songs recorded in this collection as a whole are in triple meter and major mode by a ratio of two to one, and the same ratio obtains for the combined number of tunes in the plagal or mixed ranges over the authentic range. The most common textual forms are AABB and ABCB, and the most common tune forms, in order of frequency, are ABCD (twenty), ABAC (seventeen), ABBA (thirteen), and ABCA (nine). Hexatonic tunes amount to about one-third of the sample; five tunes end on a note other than the tonic.

More detailed studies of Scottish Lowland Travellers have been made. MacColl and Seeger published their account of the Stewart family of Blairgowrie after several years of work with them (1986). This study deals with social background and other expressive forms such as folktales, but songs occupy fully one-half of the book. Some seventy-one songs from the family include twelve Child Ballads, nine Laws ballads, lyric songs of great variety, and an overlooked repertoire, that of Traveller children's songs and rhymes, some of which were sung by children, others by adults to amuse or instruct infants. Yet another aspect is the creative inventing of songs (mak'-ye-ups), often parodic or satirical, within the family as a kind of humorous competition. In its orientation, this study takes up the relationships within a Traveller family, and includes liberal quotations from the performers. Searching questions of Belle Stewart's learning and style of composition, in which parody and satire take prominent places, are explored in another study (Porter 1985).

A different family study discusses a tripartite relationship in which the daughter of a Traveller, Jane Stewart, had married a non-Traveller, Cameron Turriff (Porter 1978). Jane's mother, Tina Stewart, was a Traveller of the old school, with a repertoire of songs embedded in the traditional Traveller life. Jane herself, disabled as a young woman and widowed after an early marriage, was always eager to make up songs and try them out on friends. Cameron, her second husband, sang mostly bothy songs from the northeast farmlands, and their repertoires give some indication of the points at which northeast farming life and Traveller life intersect and diverge. Jane's repertoire lies about halfway between that of her mother and that of Cameron, with an admixture of traditional ballads and her own, freshly composed songs. Her style is rhapsodic as she accompanies herself on the harmonium or accordion (figure 2).

The alteration of style as a factor affecting the emergence of Travellers as leading singers in the folk-music revival of the 1950s and 1960s in Scotland is addressed in another study (Porter 1976, 1988). In this case the singing style of Jeannie Robertson was affected as she became accustomed to larger arenas and the demands of the media. Her singing of the ballad "Son David" (Child 13) slowed in delivery but shortened in text as she adjusted to new contexts and elevated this particular song in her repertoire to special status because outsiders, especially scholars and fieldworkers, perceived it as a rarity. The spacious halls for concertizing and Jeannie's own perception of herself and the songs as representing a central incident in her life (the death of her young son) also contributed to the lament-like character of the song as she finally recorded it. Her life and repertoire have been the subject of a recent study (Porter and Gower 1995).

An additional study of Traveller singing style deals with strophic variation, especially in narrative songs or ballads (Williamson 1985). Taking up MacColl's point that if singers could not remember the correct melody they would substitute another tune, one with the same meter, mode, and general feeling (MacColl and Seeger 1977:22), the study concludes that some Traveller singers construct their songs, or the strophes within these songs, phrase by phrase, with each recreated phrase affecting the further process of recreating as the singer's mind interacts with the immediate stages of construction. Singers do not sing just anything that comes into their head when they cannot produce "the correct form" of the tune; they sing something that has a meter and mood fitting for the proper tune and is comparable to it. Thus, melodic variation in Traveller singing has a freer quality than that of singers in the settled population, who are influenced by bookish notions of a "correct" tune and text. This may be a key aspect of Traveller singing as a whole, and to that extent it reflects, as well, a less fettered mode of living.

FIGURE 2   Jane Stewart Turiff, a Traveller singer from Fetterangus, Aberdeenshire. Photo by James Porter, 1972.

BIBLIOGRAPHY

Bronson, Bertrand H. 1976. *The Singing Tradition of Child's Popular Ballads.* Princeton: Princeton University Press.

Carroll, Jim. 1986. "Michael McCarthy, Singer and Ballad Seller." In *Singer, Song and Scholar,* ed. Ian Russell, 19–29. Sheffield: Sheffield Academic Press.

Court, Artelia, ed. 1985. *Puck of the Droms: The Lives and Literature of the Irish Tinkers.* Berkeley: University of California Press.

Gentleman, Hugh, and Susan Swift. 1971. *Scotland's Travelling People: Problems and Solutions.* Edinburgh: Her Majesty's Government Stationery Office.

Gmelch, George. 1977. *The Irish Tinkers: The Urbanization of an Itinerant People.* Menlo Park, Calif.: Cummings Publishing.

Gmelch, Sharon. 1986. *Nan: The Life of an Irish Travelling Woman.* New York: Norton.

Goldstein, Kenneth S. 1992. *Alias MacAlias: Writings on Songs, Folk and Literature.* Edinburgh: Polygon.

MacColl, Ewan, and Peggy Seeger. 1977. *Travellers' Songs from England and Scotland.* Knoxville: University of Tennessee Press.

———. 1986. *Till Domsday in the Afternoon. The Folklore of a Family of Scots Travellers, the Stewarts of Blairgowie.* Manchester, Manchester University Press.

McCarthy, William B. 1995. "Sheila Stewart's 'Twa Brothers' (Child 49)." In *Ballads and Boundaries: Narrative Singing in an Intercultural Context,* ed. James Porter, 218–221. Los Angeles: Department of Ethnomusicology and Systematic Musicology, University of California at Los Angeles.

Munnelly, Tom. 1972. "The Man and His Music . . . John Reilly." *Ceol* 4 (1):2–8.

Munro, Ailie. 1970. "Lizzie Higgins and the Oral Transmission of Ten Child Ballads." *Scottish Studies* 14:155–188.

———. 1996. *The Folk Music Revival in Scotland.* Rev. ed. Aberdeen: Scottish Cultural Press.

Niles, John D. 1995. The Role of the Strong Tradition-Bearer in the Making of an Oral Culture. In *Ballads and Boundaries: Narrative Singing in an Intercultural Context,* ed. James Porter, 231–240. Los Angeles: Department of Ethnomusicology and Systematic Musicology, University of California at Los Angeles.

Porter, James. 1976. "Jeannie Robertson's 'My Son David': A Conceptual Performance Model." *Journal of American Folklore* 89:7–26.

———. 1978. "The Turriff Family of Fetterangus: Society, Learning, Creation and Re-Creation of Traditional Song." *Folk Life* 16:5–26.

———. 1985. "Parody and Satire as Mediators of Change in the Traditional Songs of Belle Stewart." In *Narrative Folksong: New Directions,* ed. Carol L. Edwards and Kathleen E. B. Manley, 305–338. Boulder, Colo.: Westview Press.

———. 1988. "Context, Epistemics, and Value: A Conceptual Performance Model Reconsidered." *Selected Reports in Ethnomusicology* 7:69–97.

Porter, James, and Herschel Gower. 1995. *Jeannie Robertson: Emergent Singer, Transformative Voice.* Knoxville: University of Tennessee Press.

Rehfisch, Farnham. 1975. *Gypsies, Tinkers and Other Travellers.* New York: Academic Press.

Robertson, Stanley. 1990. *Exodus to Alford.* Inverness: Balnain Press.

Russell, Ian, ed. 1986. *Singer, Song and Scholar.* Sheffield: Sheffield Academic Press.

Shields, Hugh. 1993. *Narrative Singing in Ireland: Lays, Ballads, Come-All-Yes and Other Songs.* Dublin: Irish Academic Press.

Smith, Stephanie D. L. 1975. "A Study of Lizzie Higgins as a Transitional Figure in the Development of Oral Tradition in the North-East of Scotland." M.Litt. thesis, University of Edinburgh.

Whyte, Betsy. 1986. *Yellow on the Broom.* 2nd ed. London: Futura.

———. 1991. *Red Rowans and Wild Honey: In the Open, a Bitter-Sweet Life.* Edinburgh: Polygon.

Williamson, Linda J. 1985. "Narrative Singing Among the Scots Travellers: A Study of Strophic Variation in Ballad Performance." Ph.D. dissertation, University of Edinburgh.

AUDIOVISUAL RESOURCES

Goldstein, Kenneth S. 1954. *Jeannie Robertson: Songs of a Scots Tinker Lady.* Riverside RLP 12–633. LP disk.

———. 1961. *Lucy Stewart: Traditional Singer from Aberdeenshire.* Folkways FG 3519. LP disk.

Hall, Peter. 1969. *Lizzie Higgins: Princess of the Thistle.* Topic 12T185. LP disk.

———. 1975. *Lizzie Higgins: Up an' awa wi' the Laverock.* Topic 12TS260.

Henderson, Hamish. 1959. *Jeannie Robertson, the Great Scots Traditional Ballad Singer.* Topic 12T96. LP disk.

———. 1978. *Davie Stewart.* Topic 12T293. LP disk.

Henderson, Hamish, and Ailie Munro, eds. 1992 [1975, 1979]. *The Muckle Sangs.* Scottish Tradition, 5. Greentrax CDTRAX 9005. Compact disc.

Kennedy, Peter, ed. 1975. *What a Voice.* Lismor LIFL 7004. LP disk.

———. 1982. *Irish Tinker Singers.* Folktracks FSA 60.166–8. 3 LP disks.

MacDougall, Carl. 1968. *The Travelling Stewarts.* Topic. 12T179. LP disk.

Munelly, Tom. 1983. *Songs of the Irish Travellers.* European Ethnic Oral Traditions. LP disk.

Neat, Timothy, and Hamish Henderson. 1977. *The Summer Walkers.* Dundee: Duncan Jordanstone College of Art. Film.

Reilly, John. 1978. *The Bonny Green Tree.* Topic 12T359. LP disk.

Saami Music

Richard Jones-Bamman

Musical Meaning and Structure
Cultural Meaning
The Saami Drum
Modern Contexts
History of Study

The Saami (formerly Lapps or Laplanders) are the indigenous people of northern-most Europe. Currently they are spread across four nations: Norway (with a Saami population of about thirty-five thousand), Sweden (eighteen thousand), Finland (four thousand to five thousand), and Russia (two thousand on the Kola Peninsula).

The more familiar name, *Lapp,* derives historically from *lappalainen,* a Finnish word for the Saami people, but this has been abandoned in recent years in favor of *Saami* (or *Sámi*), taken from *Sábmelas,* the native term. Consequently, Lapland is now called Saamiland (Sápmi), and the language (formerly Lappish) is called Saami.

The only indigenous Saami musical genre is a style of vocalizing known as joik (pronounced "yoik"), from the Saami verb *joigat* 'to produce musical sound' and an anglicization of the Swedish *jojk.* Traditionally this is performed solo and without any accompaniment, but since the late 1960s it has also been presented with instrumental ensembles, from simple acoustic guitars to rock-and-roll bands (figure 1).

Whether performed unaccompanied or with instruments, the sound of joiking is unmistakable. Among knowledgeable audiences, its performance constitutes an important element of Saami identity. Though this effect is particularly evident in contemporary performances, it is largely explained within a broader historical frame, for the joik and its practitioners have often been subjects of official opposition and derision from dominant Scandinavian cultures. Joiking, and even listening to joiks, have long been a means of demarcating ethnicity.

MUSICAL MEANING AND STRUCTURE

It is difficult to discuss the joik in general musical terms without taking into account several of its distinct regional dialects, which differ from one another considerably in fine points of structure and emphasis on specific elements. The Eastern Saami, in northeastern Finland and on the Kola Peninsula, have not been sufficiently studied, but some traits are common enough to all regional styles of joiking to develop an overview.

One of the most distinctive qualities of the joik is the frequent use of vocables instead of, or mixed in with, lexically meaningful words. These vocables are quite often monosyllabic, featuring long final vowels: *no, na*; *lo, la, lai*; *vo, yo* (for a joik

Words in a joik are frequently cryptic, hinting at the subject, rather than addressing it directly. People who listen to the performance derive extra meaning or pleasure from deciphering the clues.

FIGURE 1   Joik singer Ingor Ántte Áitu Gaup performs on stage in Stockholm with the popular-music group Bolon X. Photo by Richard Jones-Bamman, 1992.

that uses these exclusively, see figure 2). These syllables are not considered meaningful in a conventional sense, nor are they necessarily repeated from one performance of a joik to the next. Some communities may even support a tendency to replace existing words with vocables, a specific joik becoming less text-oriented over time, without any perceived degradation of the overall meaning. This is not to imply that the function of these vocables is merely the substitution of words, for they are considered an essential element of the structure of joiks: their presence contributes to the overall sound of the genre, clearly marking the performance as a Saami expression.

In this light, words as meaning-bearing devices are effectively subordinate to melody and rhythm. Words that do exist in a particular joik are therefore frequently cryptic, hinting at the subject, rather than addressing it directly. In most cases, their presence is crucial only to the extent that people listening to the performance derive extra meaning or pleasure from deciphering the clues, presented within an already complete musical vehicle, at least in the Saami conception of the genre; as with vocables, however, the inclusion of text in a joik is subject to regional and personal interpretation, in composition and performative enactment.

Another trait of the genre is the flexibility of its form, including an emphasis on improvisation. In particular, when an individual joiks unaccompanied, he or she does not conceive the desired result with the same precision that many other systems of music demand. The resulting subtle shadings of pitch, for example, do not constitute mistakes in most instances, nor do they necessarily connote meaning in any concrete sense. Instead, they indicate a broader predilection for improvisation, an attribute of

FIGURE 2   A South
Saami joik about a
mountain, performed
in 1992 by Lars-Jonas
Johansson. Its text con-
sists entirely of voca-
bles. The range is lim-
ited to a perfect fifth.
Transcription by
Richard Jones-
Bamman.

performance that complicates attempts to discuss the genre in terms of codified structure. To demonstrate this, figure 3 presents three repetitions of the same joik as performed; despite pointed differences in choice of pitches and overall rhythmic scheme from one phrase to the next, the joiker considers each to be a complete statement. Melodic and rhythmic figures agree in numerous places, yet what unites these realizations (or other similar examples) is not easily reducible to single components, though such may surface through analysis. Rather, it resides in a *Gestalt* to which the performer refers but does not feel compelled constantly to reiterate; the ideal is not to repeat the form verbatim, but to joik around it.

Regional dialects

Numerous dialects of joik correspond roughly to dialectal distinctions in the Saami language. It is expedient to divide these subgenres into two gross categories (North and South Saami), representative of a basic cultural bifurcation that includes language and handcrafts in its purview. Generalizations resulting from this division should be interpreted with caution, for in many examples of joiking, performers routinely cross or combine these styles.

The North Saami joik (or *luohti,* as it is called in this dialect) is the more predominant style (as is its linguistic analogue), found throughout most of northern Norway, Sweden, and Finland. It is characterized melodically by a wide range (often exceeding an octave), disjunct melodic motion (occasionally involving leaps of as much as a major tenth), and a general triadic orientation (figure 3).

Rhythmically, North Saami joiks can be equally complicated, with much use of complex meters (nine beats divided 2–3–2–2, or ten beats divided 2–3–3–2) and variable metric units (9–10–9–10–10–10). Just as typically, however, each repetition of a complete joik phrase may have its own rhythmic organization, as in figure 3. Alternatively, a North Saami performer may prefer a simple duple or triple meter for a particular joik.

The South Saami variant (*orvuolle*) is currently found in just a few locations in the central parts of Norway and Sweden. This is hardly surprising, for this population of Saami have been subjected to a much longer period of continuous contact

FIGURE 3   A North
Saami personal joik,
performed in 1992 by
Ingor Ántte Áitu
Gaup. It has a wide
range of an octave
plus a fourth with dis-
junct melodic motion.
The example contains
three variant repeti-
tions of the same joik.
Transcription by
Richard Jones-
Bamman.

FIGURE 4   Noted Lule Saami performer Lars Pirak, who is equally known for his paintings of Saami subjects and his skills in traditional handicrafts. Photo by Richard Jones-Bamman, 1992.

with neighboring Scandinavians, and have suffered a subsequent decline in language and other cultural expressions; despite the genre's moribund state, however, notable general differences in joiks from this region remain, when compared with those found in the north.

Melodically, South Saami joiks exhibit a narrower range (rarely exceeding a major sixth, more commonly a perfect fifth), with more conjunct motion and many so-called gliding notes, which often make discrete pitches hard to identify. Rhythmically, these joiks are less complex, with basic duple and triple meter organization predominating. Performers in the South Saami region have a tendency to use more vocables than those in the north.

Features of performance

Joiking typically involves much use of the throat and nasopharynx, contributing to what may be described as a harsh or nasal vocal timbre; these qualities are accentuated if the joiker does so loudly, as often happens (figure 4). Another notable trait is the relationship between breath control and phrasing. Unlike vocal genres that emphasize the coordination of breathing with musical and textual phrases, joiking has no such parameters. The individual performing a joik usually proceeds until running out of breath, pauses momentarily to inhale, and continues from where he ceased; within this aesthetic, it is acceptable to stop altogether, whether or not an entire exposition of the joik has been completed.

A third general feature common to many joik performances is a steady rise in the basic pitch, such that any given example of joiking is likely to end at a noticeably higher point than where it began. This can be quite subtle, with the shift taking place across several repetitions, or it can be strikingly abrupt (Arnberg et al. 1969).

A final consideration is the use of mimesis or gesture to reinforce a joik. An individual will occasionally interject the specific traits of an animal or a person into a joik, imitating his or her calls or in some way using the body to suggest the figure in question; however, the efficacy of a performance in no way depends on the use of such devices, a joik being conceived as a unified structure of meaning consisting essentially of melody, rhythm, and text (if present), and mimicry is an adjunct to these elements.

CULTURAL MEANING

According to the Saami author Johan Turi (1931), joiking is a way of remembering people, animals, places, or events. Yet a person who joiks does not simply invoke these memories through performance, musing over them as one might expect, but is in effect transforming them into a tangible and interpretable configuration. Underlying all performances is an understanding that a given joik is an accurate description of its subject. This is conceived as a one-to-one relationship, with the joik directly recreating that which it is describing. Thus, by making a memory audible, the joiker is conceptually communing with the subject, at least for the duration of the joik. In such a manner, family and friends (not to mention animals and places) are perceived to remain viable for individuals, as long as they joik them into existence whenever feeling inspired to do so.

The great preponderance of joiks, regardless of the region where they are found, are personal joiks, created to describe another individual, never oneself, most often in a positive light. Performers approach this process differently, but the goal is to encapsulate the desired subject, by concentrating on a physical attribute (strength, a way of walking, a notable facial feature), a personality trait (friendly, sad), or often a combination of these. These descriptions, in turn, are created using the same building blocks discussed above: melody, rhythmic figures, to a lesser extent text, and perhaps even cogent gestures. Figure 3, for example, is a woman's personal joik.

As Johan Turi noted, however, humans are not the only suitable subjects for this art. Because of the prominence of reindeer in Saami culture, this animal is often joiked, in an abstract sense (joiking a generic reindeer calf), or from a personal perspective (joiking a favorite draft animal, or even one's herd). Other animals frequently found in joik repertoires are birds (ptarmigan, wood grouse) and mammalian predators (wolves, wolverines, lynxes), which as fellow participants in the life cycle of reindeer are recognized for their roles. Like several other arctic and subarctic peoples, the Saami have long celebrated a particular relationship with bears, which they feared and respected, as exemplified in joiks (Manker 1972). Joiks describing places or events are conceived in the same manner as those portraying animate objects, drawing on attributes or specific facts that can be captured in performance. Figure 2, for example, is a joik describing a mountain in southern Saamiland.

Social function

Another important aspect of this genre, which builds upon its descriptive abilities, is the means by which the joik has traditionally been used to construct a sense of community among those who perform and listen to it. When a person is joiked by another for the first time, this performance constitutes a process of incorporation for the listener, similar to receiving a name. Furthermore, this relationship is conceived to be strengthened each time the personal joik is repeated, even if the subject is not physically present. By contrast, individuals do not joik themselves, for to do so would negate the validity of the incorporative experience.

This relationship is not limited to the duality comprising performer and subject, for it can easily be extended within a community. Those who hear a person joiked, if sufficiently knowledgeable, are equally engaged by this process, their own roles as interpreters constituting another important element of the joik milieu (Jernsletten 1978). It is within the interpretive collective that an individual achieves full recognition—develops a concrete Saami identity—and the personal joik makes this transformation possible. For the moment of performance at least, the subject, the performer, and the audience conflate into a single conception of community, made explicit by joiking.

Not every Saami person has a personal joik, particularly in contemporary Saami culture, since joiking has declined in many regions of Saamiland. The promulgation of the genre through staged performances, recordings, and the broadcast media has led some Saami to question whether the new performer-audience roles dictated by these phenomena have any place in the intimate relationships once expressed within the joik milieu (Gaski 1991). To a great extent, these challenges to the traditional conception of the function of the joik reveal changes within Saami culture as a whole, which has increasingly expanded its sphere of concern from the local community out toward the establishment of a pan-Saami corporate identity (Svensson 1976).

Learning and transmission

Under ideal conditions, people learn to joik in the same type of community that the joik milieu represents, wherein joiking is heard frequently as part of the Saami soundscape. Performance in this environment is not restricted in any way, by age or by gender; however, there are no formal means of teaching the genre to others. Until the late twentieth century, the Saami had an oral-aural culture, with few examples of written literature but ample evidence of literary skills, manifest in myriad stories, sagas, and joiks (Fjellström 1985). Learning to joik has thus been primarily depen-

Many Saami have resorted to joiking while alone to relieve the solitude or calm their animals if engaged in herding. When a solitary individual joiks another person in this context, the joiker is no longer alone.

dent on a process of repetition and trial; unlike the stories and sagas, however, joiking has not successfully transferred to a written form. Dependent on improvisation, it has proven difficult to capture on the musical staff. Consequently, those learning to joik must rely greatly on nonwritten sources.

Whereas these sources used to consist of a person's immediate friends and family, increasingly these have been replaced by recordings. These developments have had some negative effects on regional dialects, but the new resources have proven highly beneficial as teaching materials, providing inspiration and models of performance. In a parallel development, joik workshops have been held throughout Saamiland, typically sponsored by local Saami organizations. The latter have been effective in reviving interest in the genre where it has been more or less dormant for several generations.

Contexts for joik performance

Before the implantation of Christianity throughout Saamiland (in the 1600s and 1700s), the joik was an integral element in shamanic ritual, being used by the shaman (*noaidi*) to self-induce a state of trance, often with drumming. The shaman had several different roles within the community, all of them predicated on his ability to commune with beings and deities in other realms of existence. Most Saami shamans, according to historical sources, were male. In some instances the shaman was called upon to heal the grievously ill; in others, to rid a community of predators or control the influence of spiritual beings. Another service he provided was to ensure the success of hunts and predict the community's future. In each of these instances, he relied on joiks specific to the task. Once his journey was under way, other members of the community often joiked as a reminder of the task at hand, or to provide a sonic beacon to aid in the return to the human realm; most historical sources cite this as a role for women (Edström 1978).

Because of the migratory cycle followed by many Saami communities, the larger collectives that typically comprised several families periodically split up—meaning that a shaman was not always present in each of the smaller groups. When this was the case, the head of each household (usually male) took over some shamanic functions, including joiking to aid in healing; some of these joiks were learned from the shaman, to be used in his absence. In addition, most families kept a drum that they consulted to divine the future before making important decisions; these were not used for soul travel, however, that task remaining the shaman's responsibility (Bäckman 1978).

Though these rituals and therapies captured the attention of outside reporters almost to the exclusion of other uses of joik, the genre simultaneously fulfilled more mundane functions, some of which remain important in contemporary Saami life. Saami culture has no traditional concept of entertainment (or of dance or theater), but joiking has often served in this role informally.

Many Saami have resorted to joiking while alone to relieve the solitude or calm their animals if engaged in herding (Kjellström et al. 1988). What makes the genre effective in such situations is the perceived relationship between the joiking person and the subject of the joik: when a solitary individual joiks another person in this context, the joiker is no longer alone. Joiking can also serve as a form of greeting, as when individuals joik each other upon meeting; occasionally it is inserted into conversation among friends.

These examples show that joiking is impromptu in any but a ritual context. To joik is to respond to stimuli, externally or internally generated, in a specifically Saami fashion. It has no rules governing its exposition, except as applied from outside the culture. Yet even where such proscriptions have been most harshly enforced, as in some religious communities in Scandinavia, joiking has not disappeared—it has simply become a practice reserved for private, or even secretive, performance.

THE SAAMI DRUM

The drum used by the shaman, and to a lesser extent by families, came in two basic types, again conforming to the north-south division of the culture. The South Saami instrument (*gievrie*) was an ovoid-shaped frame drum, constructed by bending and securing a thin strip of wood, over which a single membrane of reindeer skin was stretched. To facilitate playing and reinforce the frame, a cross-member (or two, forming an X) was attached, spanning the diameter of the rim. To the resulting handle, the shaman would often attach bits of his personal spiritual regalia, including strips of sinew, coins, and other pieces of metal (Kjellström and Rydving 1988).

The North Saami version (*gobdas*) was a basin drum, carved like a shallow bowl in an oval shape, from a single piece of wood. Like its southern counterpart, it had a membrane of reindeer skin stretched across its top surface. Its back was typically pierced by a pair of ovals situated parallel to each other, creating a convenient handle; often the entire back was ornately carved, or incised with geometric shapes.

Both types of drum featured elaborate paintings done directly on the playing surface of the skin. The most common display had a central design representing the sun (usually rhomboid shaped), around which were grouped stylized designs depicting animals, people, and geometric shapes. These paintings are thought to portray the Saami cosmological system, emphasizing the sun as progenitor and arranging spiritual and mundane beings concentrically in some order of importance.

The method of playing the drum was identical, regardless of its shape or where it was found. The shaman (or head of the household) would hold the instrument parallel to the ground, striking it with a T-shaped hammer made of reindeer antler. If the drum was used for divination, a small pointer was placed on the membrane; the individual lightly struck the surface, causing this piece to jump, and subsequently interpreted its movement and the painted figures where the pointer came to rest.

Little is known of how a journeying shaman coordinated his joiking and drumming, but from historical and ethnographic accounts of other arctic cultures, scholars assume that the Saami conceived of joiking and drumming as separate but mutually reinforcing activities, rather than a vocal part with accompaniment. All records agree that only the shaman performed in this section of the ritual, drumming and joiking simultaneously (Edström 1978).

MODERN CONTEXTS

In the late 1960s, the Saami joik was heard for the first time on a commercial recording made by Nils-Aslak Valkeapää, a young Saami man from Finland. Rather than

FIGURE 5   A young woman joiks on stage during the Saami Grand Prix, an annual music competition in Kautokeino, Norway. Photo by Richard Jones-Bamman, 1995.

present the genre in its traditional format, Valkeapää combined his joiks with acoustic guitar and string bass, plus ambient noises—such as sounds associated with herding reindeer—added to suggest a Saami environment.

While this approach provoked controversy within Saami culture, by and large it proved successful among audiences throughout Saamiland. Within a few years, other young Saami were actively involved in what has been dubbed the joik renaissance, not only experimenting with the genre, but in some instances actually stimulating a revival of joik in its more traditional contexts.

As part of this development, a Saami music industry emerged, making it possible to record and distribute albums and cassettes specifically targeted for a burgeoning Saami audience without relying on similar systems within the dominant Scandinavian cultures. In response to listeners' demand, Saami radio stations in Norway, Sweden, and Finland began broadcasting joiks regularly, playing material from recent recordings and occasionally featuring live performances. As a result of this activity and the pervasive quality of the broadcast media, the joik was arguably more audible in Saamiland by the end of the 1970s than it had been for generations.

Such developments rarely occur in a cultural vacuum, and the speed with which this renaissance blossomed and the quantity of material it produced—more than thirty records and cassettes in twenty years—suggest that this was essentially a movement whose time had come. For centuries, traditional joiks had been the focus of contempt and derision from many people outside Saami culture. As Christianity gained a foothold in Saami communities, effectively casting out the shamans, the clergy's concern in many areas shifted to the joik, a genre closely associated with the deposed spiritual leaders. If anything, this situation was exacerbated when local churches came under the control of converted Saami, who recognized the need to supplant the existing worldview and its expressions before new religious ideology and dogma could be successfully introduced (Outakoski 1991).

As the most easily recognizable physical manifestation of the pre-Christian era (other than the shaman himself), most drums in Saamiland were gathered up by missionaries. Some of these instruments ended up in museums, but most were burned in public ceremonies to demonstrate the power of the new religion.

For joiking to assume a public role once more, a context that momentarily severed the genre from these negative cultural moorings had to develop, and this is precisely what the new performers of the late 1960s and early 1970s accomplished. By surrounding otherwise traditional joiks with the trappings of popular music, the joik became an acceptable practice again in all but the most stalwart Christian Saami communities. The ensuing experimentation has produced ways of using joiks in new and challenging contexts, but the most significant testimony to the continued importance of the genre in Saami culture lies in the reemergence of the traditional joik as a familiar sound heard once again throughout Saamiland (figure 5).

HISTORY OF STUDY

While the study of joik as a discrete musical expression is a development of the twentieth century, the genre has been the subject of speculation and interest since the beginning of the 1600s or before, as documented in accounts by travelers, clergy, and governmental officials. The cause for notoriety, judging from the sources themselves, was the relationship between joiking and Saami ritual behavior, most often brought into focus for outsiders in the guise of shamans, who used joiks with drumming to go into a trance, and it was in this context that the genre was most often reported, frequently with hyperbole.

Whether cited primarily for its use in rituals or judged on its musical merits, joiking was a topic in many accounts of those who visited Saamiland into the early 1900s. Unfortunately for current scholarship, most of these resources are tainted by the prejudices of their authors, most of whom found the genre primitive at best. Nevertheless, a few important examples of early scholarship deserve mention.

Among the most important and influential of these is Johannes Schefferus' *Lapponia,* published in Latin in Sweden in 1673 and subsequently translated into English and German (1674 and 1675, respectively). While Schefferus devoted considerable attention to the joik as it appeared in shamanic ritual (entirely drawn from secondhand and thirdhand accounts), he included a pair of joik texts (without melodies), dictated to him by a young Saami man, Olof Sirma, studying for the priesthood. Because of Sirma's poetics in his joiks, these two examples demonstrated, for the first time to a broad audience, the potential the genre had as a means of expressing personal emotions. Sirma's texts proved so popular that they circulated around the Western world (in translated form as "Winter Song" and "Spring Song") for nearly two centuries as examples of so-called folk poetry, usually without explanation of their origins (Kjellström et al. 1988). Johann Gottfried von Herder included them in his *Stimmen der Völker in Liedern* (1778–1779), and even Henry Wadsworth Longfellow paid homage to them in his poem "My Lost Youth."

The writings of Jacob Fellman (1795–1875) and Anders Fjellner (1795–1876), another unusual but significant contribution to joik literature, challenged preconceptions about the genre. Fellman and Fjellner, a Saami himself, were priests in Saamiland. Both men collected, edited, and published examples of joik texts (Fellman 1912; Fjellner in Donner 1876), which, for the length and complexity of their narrative style and their treatment of mythological subjects, scholars subsequently labeled epic or epiclike (Gaski 1987). In neither case, however, did the collector-editors transcribe the melodies for these poems, leaving their audiences with little conception of their appropriate melodic structure and how these joiks were contextually performed.

It was not until the early 1900s that folklorists, ethnologists, and musicologists took a more active interest in joik and produced the first works to present the genre in its complete musical format. The Finnish researcher Armas Launis (1908) drew upon two years of fieldwork and more than eight hundred collected melodies and variants to produce the first critical musical analysis of the genre. He was followed by a Swede, Karl Tirén, who captured an unprecedented number of joiks on a cylinder-recording machine and transcribed most of them. His landmark book (1942), based on his collection, was characterized by his interest in categorizing joiks by type and his comparison of the basic structure of the genre with the concept of leitmotif.

Later work on the subject has diverged little from the paradigms established by Launis and Tirén. Much emphasis has been given to musical analysis of fairly large field collections (Grundström and Väisänen 1958; Lüderwaldt 1976). Notable exceptions to this trend include Karl-Olaf Edström's reporting on the joik as an object of study (1978), Ola Graff's work with a single individual and his repertoire (1985), and a book by Rolf Kjellström, Gunnar Ternhag, and Håkan Rydving for a more general audience (1988). All works to date have been concerned with Saami performances of the joik in its most traditional contexts and do not address the more modern manifestations of the genre.

The drum, associated with joiking in shamanic rituals, has also been the object of study. The most thorough work on it was produced by Ernst Manker (1938, 1950), who primarily worked among specimens of Saami drums housed in the Nordic Museum in Stockholm. A monograph by Kjellström and Rydving (1988) distills material contained in Manker's books. Also noteworthy is Juha Pentikäinen's article (1987).

BIBLIOGRAPHY

Arnberg, Matts, Håkan Unsgaard, and Israel Ruong. 1969. *Jojk/Yoik.* Stockholm: Sveriges Radio.

Bäckman, Louise. 1978. "Types of Shaman: Comparative Perspectives." In *Studies in Lapp Shamanism,* ed. Louise Bäckman and Åke Hultkrantz. Stockholm: Almqvist & Wiksell.

Donner, Otto. 1876. "Lappalaisia Lauluja." *Suomi* 2(11).

Edström, Karl-Olaf. 1978. *Den samiska Musikkulturen.* Göteborg, Sweden: Musikvetenskapliga Institutionen.

Fellman, Jacob. 1912. *Lapska sånger I: Isak Fellman.* Handlingar och uppsatser angående finska lappmarken och lapparne, 3. Helsinki.

Fjellström, Phebe. 1985. *Samernas samhälle.* Stockholm: P. A. Norstedt & Söners.

Gaski, Harald. 1987. *Med ord skal tyvene fordrives.* Karasjok, Norway: Davvi Media O. S.

———. 1991. "Og ønskeplata er: En joik med Kjell Karlsens orkester—Om joiken i mediesamfunnet." In *Joikens frie lyder nar engre enn mange ord,* ed. Ola Graff, 97–108. Tromsø, Norway: University of Tromsø.

Graff, Ola. 1985. "Joik som musikalisk språk: Litt om nordsamisk joik ut fra Per Hœtta som tradisjonsformidler." M.A. thesis, University of Oslo.

Grundström, Harald, and A. O. Väisänen. 1958. *Lapska sånger I: Jonas Eriksson Steggos sånger.* Landsmåls—Och Folkminnesarkivet i Uppsala, C-2. Uppsala: A. B. Lundquistska Bokhandeln.

Jernsletten, Nils. 1978. "Joik og kommunikasjon." *By og Bygd* 26:109–122.

Jones-Bamman, Richard Wiren. 1993. "As Long as We Continue to Joik, We'll Remember Who We Are: Negotiating Identity and the Performance of Culture: The Saami Joik." Ph.D.

dissertation, University of Washington.

Kjellström, Rolf, and Håkan Rydving. 1988. *Den samiska trumman.* Stockholm: Nordic Museum.

Kjellström, Rolf, Gunnar Ternhag, and Håkan Rydving. 1988. *Om jojk.* Hedemora, Sweden: Gidlunds Bokförlag.

Launis, Armas. 1908. *Lappische Jouigos-Melodien.* Helsinki: MFSOu.

Lüderwaldt, Andreas. 1976. *Joiken aus Norwegen.* Bremen: Übersee-Museum.

Manker, Ernst. 1938. *Die lappische Zaubertrommel.* Vol. 1. Acta Lapponica, 1. Stockholm: Nordic Museum.

———. 1950. *Die lappische Zaubertrommel.* Vol. 2. Acta Lapponica, 6. Stockholm: Nordic Museum.

———. 1972. *The Bear Feast.* Luleå, Sweden: Norrbotten Museum.

Outakoski, Nilla. 1991. *Lars Levi Laestadiuksen Saarnojen Maahiskuva.* Oulu, Finland: Oulun Historiaseuran julkaisuja.

Pentikäinen, Juha. 1987. "The Saami Shamanic Drum in Rome." In *Saami Religion,* ed. Tore Ahlbäck, 139–156. Stockholm: Scripta Instituti Donneriani Aboensis.

Schefferus, Johannes. 1956 [1673]. *Lappland.* Translated by Henrik Sundin. Acta Lapponica, 8. Stockholm: Nordic Museum.

Svensson, Tom G. 1976. *Ethnicity and Mobilization in Sami Politics.* Stockholm: Department of Social Anthropology, University of Stockholm.

Tirén, Karl. 1942. *Die lappische Volksmusik.* Acta Lapponica, 3. Stockholm: Nordic Museum.

Turi, Johan. 1931. *Turi's Book of Lappland.* New York: Harper.

AUDIOVISUAL RESOURCES

Boine, Marie. 1993. *Goaskinviellja Rnebror.* Lean MBCD 62. Compact disc.

Christensen, Dieter, and Wolfgang Laade. 1992 (1956). *Lappish Joik Songs from Northern Norway.* Smithsonian Folkways Records 04007 (P 1007). Compact disc.

Fernández, M. M. Jocelyne. 1984. *Chants et Poésies des Sames Laponie.* Orstom Selaf CETO 806. LP disk.

Koch, Erland von. 1977. *Lappland-Metamorphoser; Impulsi; Echi; Ritmi.* Swedish Society Discofil SLT 33259. LP disk.

Lapsk Folkmusik: Jojkning/Lappish Folkmusic: Yoiking. 195?. Sveriges Radios Forlag RELP 1029. LP disk.

Nordland, Berit. 1992. *Muittut.* Lasis CD-1. Compact disc.

Persen, Mari Boine. 1990. *Gula Gula.* Virgin 91631–4. Compact disc.

Samisk Musik: Forvandling. 1988. Caprice CAP 1351. Compact disc.

Basque Music
Denis Laborde

Musical Structures and Styles
Musical Instruments
Musical Contexts, Politics, and Identity
History of Musical Scholarship

Basque territory lies in southern France and northwestern Spain along the Bay of Biscay and the western foothills of the Pyrenees (map 2). The origin of the Basque people, who number about two hundred fifty thousand in France and two and a half million in Spain, is obscure. Their language, Euskara, is not Indo-European, but derives from that of the Vascones and Aquitani of Roman times, groups whose successors resisted in turn Visigoths, Franks, Normans, and Moors. Historically important Basques include Saint Ignatius of Loyola (1491–1556), founder of the Jesuit Order, and Saint Francis Xavier (1506–1552), Jesuit missionary to India and Japan. Maurice Ravel (1875–1937) is the most famous Basque composer.

Basque national aspirations, language, and customs began to be recorded in the 1800s. During the Spanish Civil War (1936–1937), the bombing and burning of Guérnica, a symbol of the Basque nation, inspired Picasso's famous painting. Many Basques emigrated to the Americas after World War II, and a Basque national government operates in Paris and New York.

MUSICAL STRUCTURES AND STYLES

Diverse musical practices constitute Basque music—a concept that emerged in the 1800s, when the modern structure of Europe began to be formed by its large nation-states, and Basque (or Euskadian) society came into existence, giving meaning to the phrase. Music, with language, customs, and the special character of the Basque house (*etxe*), took its place as an identifying characteristic of this human group, one of the oldest on the European continent. The editorial selections made by musicologists and the limitations of musical transcription created a new reality for Basque music, based on its written form. Musical analysis became the means of defining Basque music by the criteria of melodic scale, rhythm, and formal structure.

Most collected melodies were tonal, the majority in a major key, but about twenty-five percent were modal. The use of modes was rare, but there were still grounds to assume that Basques were familiar with modal scales. Most melodies were transcribed in regular meters until J. A. Arana Martija (1985) suggested that combinations of measures—for example, 6/8 + 3/4 or 5/8 + 2/4—would yield a more accurate approach. When instrumental melodies from Soule were transcribed, no meter

MAP 2   The Basque Provinces. Basque
names are on top; Spanish and French
names are in parentheses.

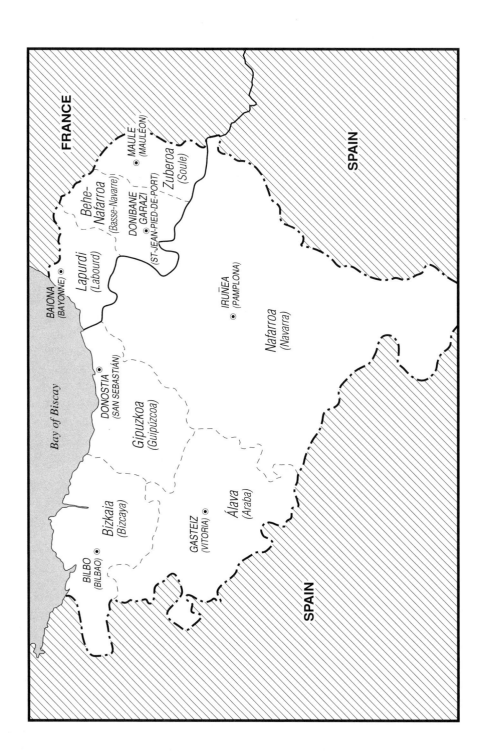

was indicated, and so the complexity of this tradition's rhythmic structures remains an unsolved problem. The most popular dance-song type, *zortziko* 'made of eights', whose name refers to the eight steps of the dances it accompanies, presents similar problems. Its meter consists of two different asymmetric patterns—a duple one (2 + 3)/8 and a triple one (2 + 3 + 3)/8—whose combination creates an even more complex asymmetric meter. Jean Bergara, the famous Basque flutist of Saint Pée, said, "I don't know why, but I feel we are born with this rhythm." The rhythm has become symbolic of Basque identity, and the national anthem, José María Iparraguirre's "*Guernikako Arbola*" ('The Tree of Guérnica') is a *zortziko* (figure 1).

Song strophes have a three-part structure, ABA, often stretched to AABA (figure 2). The stanza-and-chorus format, common in France and Spain, is rare in Basque country. The syllabic style, in which each syllable of the lyrics corresponds to just one note of the melody, allows many borrowings: the same words can be sung to different melodies and timbres, and the same melody can be put to different words.

Versifiers (*bertsulari*) take pride in their ability to improvise new verses (*bertsu*) for an existing tune. They improvise in informal social occasions and hotly contested organized competitions. They use four-verse structures, depending on whether the stanzas consist of four couplets (as in the *zortziko*) or five couplets (as in the *hamar-reko*) and on whether the couplets contain thirteen or eighteen syllables. The former, divided into seven- and six-syllable hemistichs, are called *ttiki* 'small' lines; the latter, divided into ten- and eight-syllable hemistichs, are called *haundi* 'big' lines.

Another common form, *bederatzi puntuko,* consists of nine couplets or lines, all with the same rhyme, of varying numbers of syllables: 13 (7 + 6), 12 (7 + 5), 13 (7 + 6), 13 (7 + 6), 6, 6, 6, 6, and 12 (7 + 5). *Bertsulari* love to improvise on such formally complex structures—an art requiring great skill (figure 3). Subtle mnemonic devices in this art demand a good memory.

The role of musical improviser is becoming increasingly professionalized, and schools have been founded for the best improvisers to teach their techniques. The themes they improvise on are quite varied. Some take the form of a dialogue: "You

FIGURE 1
"*Guernikako Arbola*" ('The Tree of Guérnica'), the Basque national anthem, in *zortziko* rhythm and with piano accompaniment. Music and text composed by José María Iparraguirre in 1853.

FIGURE 2   Two strophic songs: *a*, in ABA form, as performed by D. Ignacio Pérez Arregui at Ezkioga in 1912; *b*, in AABA form, as performed by Juana Lekuberri at Zugarramurdi in 1944.

two were born in the same village. You make a great pair. You, you work for the ETA [the nationalist organization], and you for the police. Today you take your friend to prison. Dialogue between two friends." Other social themes are imaginable: "Your son comes to ask for pocket money. You know he's going to buy drugs. Dialogue between a father and son." Sometimes, a satirical slant is required: "You went to the village festival. Returning, you were drunk. Instead of sleeping in your bed, you got into your mother-in-law's bed. Dialogue between a son-in-law and mother-in-law." When the *bertsulari* improvises alone, the theme is more literary: "You are an ancient mariner. Your life has been spent on the sea. Today you're confined to your room, and through the open window you hear the sea."

At the finals of the 1982 championship, the jury demanded that each finalist improvise a *bertsu* about his adversary. The *bertsu* of Xabier Amuriza about Jon Lopategui (see figure 3) has a monorhyme on *stea*.

> Hauxe da orain sortu diguten nastea,
> bata lengoa eta ni ez gastea,
> nai zuten hemen lagun hauek ikustea.
> Neure auzoa haiz ta ez egon tristea:
> herri bat askea,
> baitaemaztea,
> lagunen eskea,
> hori nik ustea
> ez diat sentiko hik irabaztea. [*Berris*]

FIGURE 3   A *bertsu* performed by Xabier Amuriza at Donostia in 1982. Transcription by Denis Laborde.

Here then is the imbroglio they've invented,
between an old guy and me, who's not so young,
and in which, my friend, you're going to assist.
You're my partner, and must not be sad:
a free country,
a woman,
a family,
and as for me, I would not want
at all for you to win this competition. [*Repeat*]

Amuriza improvised this *bertsu* on a tune transmitted for a long time in Basque country—the tune on which, in 1799, Fernando Amezketara (1764–1823) had com-

In 1936 use of the Basque language was outlawed, as was any demonstration of Basque culture. But Basque music became synonymous with resistance. For twenty-four years, despite the official cultural blackout, versifiers continued improvising in secret and in isolated villages.

posed the famous song "*Urrestilgo semea.*" Amuriza sang in a clear, powerful voice in a high, tenor register, but never in a head voice. *Bertsulari* must sing in a throat voice and a declamatory manner, so the words can be understood. The syllabic character of the singing is indispensable for this purpose.

MUSICAL INSTRUMENTS

FIGURE 4 Mixel Etchecopar plays a duct flute (*txirula*) and a struck zither (*ttunttun*). Courtesy of the Institut Culturel Basque, Mstaritz, France.

Most traditional Basque instruments are wind instruments. One of the most important, the *txistu,* is a three-holed duct flute, usually in the key of F, made of ebony, boxwood, or plastic, encircled by metal bands, with a metal mouthpiece. Flutists (*txistulari*) usually accompany dances solo, playing the *txistu* in their left hand while with a stick striking a snare drum (*danbolin*) suspended from their elbow. Groups of flutists may form bands. They also play in small groups of *txistu, silbote* (a side-blown wooden flute), and *atabal* (a drum larger than the *danbolin*). In Soule, the combination of *txirula,* a small, shrill wooden flute in the key of C, and *ttunttun,* a carved hollow wooden body across which six strings are stretched and struck with a wooden stick, is considered an ancestor of the modern *txistu*-drum duo (figure 4).

In addition to a single musician playing two instruments, duets of two musicians are also common. Since the 1980s, the *trikitixa,* a duet consisting of a diatonic accordion, a Basque drum, and singing, has been extremely popular. The musicians play for parades and chain dances, including *jotas,* fandangos, and *arinarins,* which everyone in Basque country knows. Another duet, from Alaba in Nafarroa, consists of a drum with a *gaita,* a double-reed instrument of Arab origin with eight finger holes; the variant in Soule is called *txanbela.* A third duet, played in Bizkaia, combines a frame drum (*pandero*) with *alboka,* two pipes each with a single reed and a horn at both ends, one acting as a bell, the other as a mouthpiece. Finally, the *txalaparta* is a percussion instrument made of two wooden boards about one and a half meters long and struck by two musicians with wooden sticks (figure 5).

As with versifiers, playing traditional instruments is becoming a profession, and these instruments are gradually beginning to be taught in conservatories in France and Spain. Their use is governed mainly by federations that organize annual contests, which declare one musician a champion and stimulate musical interest among other Basques. *Trikitilari gazteen txapelketa* 'young *trikitixa* players', for example, brings together *trikitixa* players, and hundreds of children come to hear each other sing at *haur kantu txapelketa* 'the songs of children'. The popularity of these events is partly a function of their providing a context for a party or celebration.

MUSICAL CONTEXTS, POLITICS, AND IDENTITY

Traditional musicians are in great demand for carnivals, masquerades, *pastorales souletines* 'popular theater of Soule', and village celebrations. Joaldunak, the symbolic

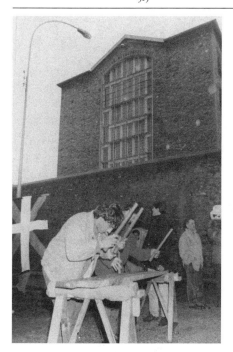

FIGURE 5   In front of Fresnes Prison, Paris, where Basque political prisoners are detained, two musicians play a resonant board (*txalaparta*). Copyright 1990 Enbata, Bayonne, France.

characters at the carnivals of Ituren and Zubieta (Nafarroa), dress in sheepskins from which hang bells that ring as they walk; they are today part of many cultural events that fill the streets. All the traditional instruments are present during Basque independence celebrations, which take place annually during October in Bilbao, attracting almost two hundred thousand participants, and for parades on behalf of the Basque language and the schools that teach it.

Numerous folkloric groups and many bands enliven local festivities. The Basque choral movement, one of the most active in Europe, takes the form of the *oxote,* eight unaccompanied male voices. In Gipuzkoa and Bizkaia, several vocal-harmony groups work with instrumentalists. In Soule, an entire village (different each year) presents a *pastorale,* a play accompanied by songs and dances. Supposedly descended from medieval mystery plays, they have been documented in performance since the 1500s. Every summer, more than five thousand people swarm into Soule's narrow valleys to participate in open-air, three-hour-long performances.

The versifiers' traditional improvisational art became popular in 1935, when Manuel de Lekuona published *Aozko Literature,* the first work devoted to the versifier's art, and Jose "Aitzol" Ariztimuño organized the first versifying championship. The contest was intended to be an annual one, but on 17 October 1936, Aitzol was shot by Francisco Franco's soldiers in Hernani (Gipuzkoa). Use of the Basque language was outlawed, as was any demonstration of Basque culture. But Basque music became synonymous with resistance: the Basque choral group Eresoinka sang throughout the world, and the dance group Dindirri performed throughout Basque lands, flouting the silence imposed on them. Singer Xabier Lete also defied Franco's censorship. For twenty-four years, despite the official cultural blackout, versifiers continued improvising in secret and in isolated villages. In 1960, a third championship occurred, organized just months after the birth in Bilbao in 1959 of Euskadi Ta Askatasuna (ETA, 'Basque Nation and Freedom'), a secret, armed group that fought the Spanish dictatorship for Basque independence. Versifiers reappeared in public as Basques, reclaimed their identity, and versifying championships took place in 1962, 1965, and 1967.

In 1968, armed conflict between the Spanish Civil Guard and ETA resulted in further repressing and silencing versifiers, who could not organize championships until 1980. Since then, championships have occurred every four years. The finals in Anoeta (Gipuzkoa), widely broadcast and publicized by the media, provide the twelve thousand spectators with a symbolic satisfaction that relieves their feelings of frustration (figure 6). The competitions reinforce the traditionally vital role of versifiers in the call to reclaim Basque identity. Versifiers regularly pay homage to Basque political prisoners—numbering about seven hundred—incarcerated in French and Spanish prisons. The *gaita* was heard in the Baigorri Valley at the burial of a member of Iparretarrak (the armed independence movement operating within France), and the *txalaparta* performs at the funerals of ETA militants.

The recording industry allows traditional singers like Peio Serbielle and Bena Achiary, and groups like Oskorri, to reach a wider audience, but it also puts out hard rock, trash, funk, and reggae-style music by Basque bands like Negu Gorriak and Hertzainak, who practice what might be called an art of citation. Negu Gorriak's "Bertso Hop" borrows a famous *bertsu* improvised during a championship. Some *trikitixa* duets make use of a synthesizer.

Traditional music in this sense is not a reservoir of musical styles from times past. The frequent reuse of old forms in new guises feeds a Basque music that is not simply a collection of structural properties that have the academic stamp of authenticity. Instead, in varying situations, at particular times and places, and within shifting contexts, musicians perform music for listeners who recognize it as Basque music.

TRACK 5

FIGURE 6 Before a crowd of twelve thousand spectators at the final of the 1993 championship, the vocal improvisers (*bertsulari*) Andoni Egana and Xabier Euskitze extemporize a poetic duel. The other men on stage are contestants waiting to perform. Photo by Denis Laborde.

In this way, Basque music is being made on the spot, within a partnership between listeners and performers, whose shared knowledge creates a common culture.

HISTORY OF MUSICAL SCHOLARSHIP

The earliest evidence of musical practice in this mountainous area is a 22,000-year-old, three-holed, bird-bone flute discovered in the city of Izturitz in northern Basque country (Labourd), a possible ancestor of the *txirula* and *txistu.* To the south, in Atxeta near Gernika (Bizkaia), a small horn dating from the Azilian era (8,000 B.C.) has been found (Barandiaran 1973). Latin songbooks demonstrate a tradition of Basque religious song during the Middle Ages. Bernat Dechepare's *Linguae Vasconum Primitiae* (1980 [1545]) suggests a centuries-old practice of singing poetry. The performances of the famous *txistulari,* Domingo Likona, in the late 1500s are documented, and dances, though popular, were prohibited from being performed in church by the Bishop of Pamplona (Nafarroa) in 1531.

During the 1800s, a variety of different traditions began to be called Basque when threatened by the consolidation of nation-states. Certain widespread practices were named, identified, distinguished, and highlighted as markers of identity, designed for staged performance. Campaigns arose to save the newly identified traditions, and Basque music was born paradoxically when it became part of a recognized cultural legacy, not just a standard part of everyday social practice. In 1826, Juan Ignacio de Iztueta published *Euscaldun Anciña Anciñaco,* a collection he intended as a monument that later generations should receive and preserve as their ancestors' cultural legacy. Subsequent published collections often omitted musical notation, but in 1870, Jean-Dominique-Julien Sallaberry published his *Chants Populaires du Pays Basque,* a record of words and music, with harmonies to certain songs adjusted to fit educated tastes. José Manterola published the three volumes of his *Cancionero Vasco* (1877–1880). Between 1833 and 1898, the Bayonne-based publisher Lasserre printed four successive editions of Dr. A. Goyeneche's *Euskaldun Kantaria,* and in 1894, *Euscaldun Anciña Anciñaco* was reprinted in Bordeaux.

Even before the birth of the Basque Language Academy (Euskaltzaindia) in

Bilbao (1918), the four southern Basque provinces organized a contest in 1912 to promote collections of Basque popular songs. Two eminent musicologists, Don Resurrección Maria de Azkue Aberasturi and Father J. G. de Zulaika Arregi de Donostia, participated and subsequently published, respectively, *Música popular vasca: su existencia,* with 1,810 songs for voice and instruments, and *Gure Abendaren Ereserkiak,* containing 523 songs. These two collections inspired a dynamic period of collecting, publishing, and composing that ultimately defined Basque music.

BIBLIOGRAPHY

Arana Martija, Jose Antonio. 1985. *Musica vasca.* 2nd ed. Bilbao: Caja de Ahorros Vizcaina.

Aulestia, Gorka. 1995. *Improvisational Poetry from the Basque Country.* Reno: University of Nevada Press.

Azkue Aberasturi, Resurrección Maria de. 1919. *Música popular vasca: su existencia.* Bilbao: J. J. Rachelt.

———. 1968 [1923]. *Cancionero popular vasco,* 2nd ed. Bilbao: Biblioteca de la Gran Enciclopedia Vasca.

Barandiaran, José Miguel de. 1973. *Eusko-Folklore.* Vol. 2. Bilbao: Editorial La Gran Enciclopedia Vasca.

Dechepare, Bernat. 1980 [1545]. *Linguae Vasconum Primitiae.* Bilbao: Real Academia de la Lengua Vasca: Editiones Mensajero.

Donostia, José G. de Zulaika Arregi de. 1994. *Obras completas.* 9 vols. Donostia: Eusko Ikaskuntza.

Fagoaga, Isidore de. 1944. *La musique représentative basque.* Bayonne: La Presse.

Gascue, Francisco. 1913. *Origen de la música popular vascongada.* Paris: H. Champion.

Guilcher, Jean-Michel. 1984. *La tradition de danse en Béarn et Pays Basque français.* Paris: Éditions de la Maison des Sciences de l'Homme.

Laborde, Denis. 1996. *Tout un monde de musiques.* Paris: L'Harmattan.

Landart, Daniel. 1988. *L'improvisation chantée en Pays Basque.* Bayonne: Centre Culturel du Pays Basque.

López Aguirre, Elena. 1996. *Del txistu a la telecaster: crónica del rock vasco.* Vitoria and Gasteiz: Edition Aianai.

Madina, Francisco de. 1960. *Orreaga: Basque Suite.* New York: E. F. Kalmus.

Manterola, José. 1877–1880. *Cancionero vasco.* 9 vols. San Sebastian: J. Oses.

Sagaseta, Miguel Angel. 1977. *Danzas de Valcarlos (Navarra).* Pamplona: Disputación Foral de Navarra, Institución Príncipe de Viana, Consejo Superior de Investigaciones Científicas.

Sallaberry, Jean-Dominique-Julien. 1992 [1870]. *Chants populaires du Pays Basque.* Nîmes: Lacour.

AUDIOVISUAL RESOURCES

Achiary, Benat. 1988. *Pays Basques Arranoa.* Ocora C 559045. LP disk.

Adixkideak. N.d. *Urte.* Agorila AG CD 185. Compact disc.

Basque Music of Today. 1997. Auvidis/Silex Y 225 069. 2 compact discs.

Coro Easo. N.d. *Abesbatza.* Elkar KD 282/283. 2 compact discs.

Kepa, Zabaleta, and Imanol. 1990. *Triki up.* Elkar KD 241. Compact disc.

Laboa, Mikel. N.d. *Euskal kanta berria.* Elkar KD HG 210. Compact disc.

Lagun Arteak. 1993. *Chants du Pays Basque.* Arion ARN 64223. LP disk.

Leidor de Tolosa, Pottoroak de Bayonne. N.d. *Polyphonies basques.* Sony GRI 19045 2. Compact disc.

Lertxundi, Benito. N.d. *Hundikora kuttunak.* Elkar KD 394/395. 2 compact discs.

Lizarrako Gaiteroak. N.d. Iruñea CD IZ 224/289KD. Compact disc.

Lomax, Alan. 1969. *The Spanish Basques.* Westminster W9812. LP disk.

Martikorena, Erramun. N.d. *Herrian.* Agorila AG CD 155. Compact disc.

Maurizia, Leon eta Basilio. N.d. *Alboka eta trikitixa.* Elkar KD-165. Compact disc.

Mystère des chœur basques. N.d. Agorila and Sony Music Entertainment VER 487402 2. Compact disc.

Negu Gorriak. N.d. Oihuka 0-190 CD. Compact disc.

Onatibia, Juan. 1991. *Euzkadi: Songs and Dances of the Basque.* Smithsonian Folkways FW 6830. LP disk.

Orfeon Donostiarra. N.d. *Donostiko kantu zarak.* RCA CD 35730 (K2). 2 compact discs.

Oskorri. 1984. *Musik aus dem Baskenland.* Folkfreak FF 40.4014. LP disk.

Oskorri and the Pub Ibiltaria. Elkarlanean KD 487/488, KD 469/470. 2 compact discs.

Peio Serbielle. N.d. *Euskadi kanta lur.* Déclic 8429542, Virgin. Compact disc.

Tapia eta Leturia 1998. Triki Elkarlanean KD 498/499. Compact disc.

Trikitixa! An Introduction. Erde Records RDCD 003. Compact disc.

Xaramela. N.d. Mixed choir. Covadia 1650101-2. Compact disc.

Celtic Music
Lois Kuter

Applying *Celtic* to Music
Contemporary Developments

The term *Celtic* refers to Bronze Age civilizations that expanded their territorial hold throughout Europe until the early years of Christianity. Archaeologists have identified two periods of these civilizations: Hallstatt (800–450 B.C.) and La Tène (450–55 B.C.). By the second and first centuries B.C., Celts had occupied Europe from the British Isles to Ukraine and Turkey, including northern Italy, France, and Spain. From then, historians, archaeologists, and linguists have documented their movements, not as conquerors, but as peoples retreating from the onslaught of expanding, colonizing groups: Romans, Angles, Saxons, and Vikings (Delaney 1986).

Celtic also denotes cultural traits that persist from earlier ages, specifically the Celtic family of Indo-European languages with its branches: Goidelic (Irish and Scottish Gaelic, Manx) and Brythonic (Welsh, Breton, Cornish). These languages survive in Ireland, Scotland, Wales, and Brittany. Cornish and Manx have been revived and put into use by scholars and militants in Cornwall and the Isle of Man, respectively, and Wales has about five hundred thousand speakers of Welsh, about 25 percent of the population. Brittany has at least 250,000 native speakers and possibly another six hundred thousand familiar with the language (TMO Ouest 1991). Few monolingual speakers of Gaelic live in Ireland and Scotland. Each country has about a hundred thousand mostly bilingual speakers who use Gaelic as their first language. Census figures should be interpreted with caution, since "knowledge" of the language varies even within a single household.

The Celtic languages are minority languages everywhere they survive—the victims of suppression by English and French authorities, who for centuries have stifled the development of education and media in Celtic languages. This situation is changing—in Ireland, politically independent since 1921, and during the 1980s and 1990s in Wales and Scotland, countries experiencing an upsurge of interest in Welsh and Gaelic, respectively, even by nonnative speakers. Celtic studies have almost exclusively focused on ancient or medieval language and literature or history, with some attention to art, archaeology, and law. Scholars examine modern Celtic languages, too, but have trouble identifying which elements speakers of non-Celtic languages in Celtic countries have inherited from their Celtic ancestors.

No scholar has established a set of sonic traits that can qualify or disqualify music as Celtic. *Celtic* is just a convenient way to bundle the musical traditions of different Celtic countries whose differences often seem more striking than the commonalities.

APPLYING *CELTIC* TO MUSIC

Though the definition of Celtic languages results from criteria that allow linguists to trace the historical evolution of these languages and identify Celtic elements in other languages, scholars have never fully clarified their application of the adjective *Celtic* to music. Suggesting the establishment of Celtic music studies as part of the wider field, Mícheál Ó Súilleabháin (1986) has pointed out the difficulty of even gathering scholars to identify a "common Celtic cultural thread" running from the past to modern nonverbal expressions like music and dance. René Abjean (1975) has emphasized that there is not one Celtic music, but several.

Attempting a beginning to the study of these musics, Frank Harrison proposed the following working definition: "those musical practices in Celtic or partly Celtic regions which have or had some characteristics differentiated to recognizable extents from those in contemporary non-Celtic societies" (1986:252). Yet the difficulty of showing separation or overlap of musical styles between Celtic-speaking and English-speaking communities, has received scant attention and is limited to a few studies (Purser 1992; Shields 1971; and others). The incorporation of "foreign" elements into specific traditions has been little studied (Rimmer 1984–1985).

No scholar has established a set of sonic traits that can qualify or disqualify music as Celtic. This adjective, however, is applied to music—mostly music unique to, or typical of, each of those countries called Celtic—because the Celtic languages remain part of a cultural heritage transmitted from ancient times. When used in relation to music, *Celtic* has a geographical sense, indicating places where recognizably different musical styles exist—music not shared by non-Celtic neighbors and often unique to just one country, or even one small region within it. *Celtic* is a convenient way to bundle the musical traditions of different Celtic countries. Recordings listed in the Green Linnet record catalog with titles such as *Celtic Music, The Next Generation, Masters of the Celtic Accordion, The Celts Rise Again,* and *The Celtic Fiddle Collection* are samplers, featuring musicians from Ireland and Scotland, and in one instance, Brittany. Similarly, music festivals billed as Celtic present diverse styles of music from two or more of the Celtic countries, plus Galicia and Asturias in Spain. Though Galicia and Asturias do not have the linguistic link Celtic scholars demand, there are common elements of ancient history and traces of a common heritage in oral tradition.

Those studying music and dance in the Celtic countries have not broached the subject of commonalties. Instead, scholars have concentrated on documenting individual styles found primarily among Celtic-speaking populations—usually music transmitted through oral transmission and assumed to be old in origin. The task of sorting out what is Irish or Welsh, for instance, is formidable. Celtic peoples on their islands and peninsulas have centuries of experience in sea travel—experience that makes it difficult to trace the history of song texts, dances, musical instruments, rhythms, and melodies. Looking at Celtic music in general and Breton music in particular, Alan Stivell, a noted musician and student of Celtic languages and history, has said that in music, trying to determine what is typically Celtic and specifically Breton means forgetting what is most important: Breton people's ability to incorporate and transform exterior influences (1979:56).

Recognizing that a propensity toward borrowing and change may be an important defining characteristic of Celtic culture, scholars who track the diversity found in just one of these countries would require years of study to achieve their goal. For good reason, they have avoided defining what might be Celtic in the music of Celtic countries: "Celtic musics, by whatever definition in whatever places, have never existed in total isolation, and looking for a 'pure' musical Celticity is an unrealistic pursuit" (Harrison 1986:263). To illustrate the difficulty of isolating Celtic elements from more widely found practices, Harrison has offered many examples of musical instruments—from bells, horns, and lyres in early depictions, to later literary descriptions that use ambiguous terminology. The reliability of such descriptions, and of musical transcriptions in later centuries, does not improve with the imposition of outsiders' concepts on a different musical tradition. Edward Bunting's (1796) transcriptions of "ancient Irish music" that he took down at the Belfast Harp Festival of 1792 are a case in point; their undoubted value as documents of the past is colored by the drawing-room taste of the period.

The problem of isolating Celtic elements of musical practice is not easier for those examining early Celtic culture. The difficulty of analyzing scant archaeological evidence is summarized by Megaw (1991), who has described fragments of musical instruments and early depictions of music making and dancing on coins and metalwork of the Hallstatt and La Tène civilizations. Only in the early centuries A.D., when the northward expansion of the Roman Empire introduced and reintroduced Mediterranean instruments, does evidence of musical artifacts among Celtic peoples increase in quantity.

CONTEMPORARY DEVELOPMENTS

Musicians and audiences have experienced renewed interest in Celtic musics, but few scholars study these styles, and few have taken a comparative look at musical traditions in Celtic countries. The differences often seem more striking than the commonalities (Shields 1985). The Breton piper Polig Montjarret, who for fifty years has studied the vocal and instrumental traditions of western Brittany, suggests that the unique qualities of Breton music might lie in European medieval music. Citing Seán Ó Riada's (1982) conviction that Irish music is not European, Montjarret (1984) questions the wisdom of considering Breton music Celtic, and proposes that the many differences between Breton music and that of Ireland and Scotland stem from a long separation, which has tapped different roots: European versus oriental.

Alan Stivell, as a performer of Celtic harp, bagpipes, and song, has examined different traditions in the Celtic countries. He admits he has found a certain common "feeling" in learning to perform different styles from those countries, but neither he nor music scholars have succeeded in defining this feeling clearly, nor has anyone defined the sense of swing that is common to, but not identical in, various Celtic traditions. Stivell has identified tendencies found more often in Celtic music than anywhere else, including a sense of cyclic, rather than unidirectional, melodic construction—for example, a tendency to use pentatonic scales, or a rhythmic swing due to shifts between binary and tertiary rhythms. He is hesitant to define traits or collate musical common denominators shared by all Celtic countries. Musicians can feel some common tendencies in learning to perform different styles, but no one has identified specific structural, melodic, or rhythmic elements that can be isolated as

Celtic. Scotland and Ireland, however, share common elements because of an originally contiguous culture, and this tendency is evident in some musical structures (Bruford 1972–1973).

The Celtic aspect of the 1970s phenomenon called Celtic rock by Nuala O'Connor (1991:122–124) is the conscious attention musicians give to ancient Celtic myths and legends, plus their use of Celtic languages in song. O'Connor cites the Irish band Horslips, who reinterpreted early Irish legends to an electric rock beat. This trend has also occurred in Brittany, where Alan Stivell has experimented with a rock band as a medium suitable for reinterpreting ancient Celtic themes and traditional songs in Breton. The Scottish rock band Runrig has gathered a sizable audience for its songs, often with a bitter edge, referring to historical experience in the Hebrides (Morton 1991). Though musicians—including the Scot Robin Williamson, the Welsh Dafydd Iwan, and the Canadian Loreena McKennitt—are drawing, or have drawn, from ancient Celtic mythology for rock, folk, or classical arrangements or compositions, this mythology has been a criterion for the application of the term *Celtic* to music.

We may ask if it is the sound, or the reference to earlier civilizations, that should be examined in applying that term to music. What have the ancient Celts transmitted to those living in Celtic countries today? Is it a manner of thinking about music or music making—for instance, an association of music with uninhibited feasting and drinking, or an exalted emotional state, rather than the structure of the music itself (Ó Madagáin 1993)?

It is hard to separate out the many constructions placed on the term *Celtic,* but two views are broadly perceptible: for scholars, it refers mainly to linguistic and historical questions and only secondarily to cultural ones; its popular sense, however, reverses this order of priorities, attaching to music and art unsubtle aspects of nineteenth-century medievalism and twentieth-century New Age colorations in an idealized Arthurian vision of a golden age, originally projected by late medieval writers such as Geoffrey of Monmouth.

Current musical manifestations of Celtic ethnicities may be overwhelming the linguistic because of the difficulty of learning the languages (Chapman 1994). Comparative research on Celtic musical traditions, and their relationship to language skills, is scanty. But cross-cultural investigation of regional styles and their historical evolution, including the Celtic diaspora (Campbell 1990; Creighton and MacLeod 1964; MacDonell 1982; Williams 1980) and contemporary performances at individual and pan-Celtic music festivals—such as the Fête Interceltique, held every August at Lorient, Brittany—may begin to clarify these issues.

BIBLIOGRAPHY

Abjean, René. 1975. *La musique bretonne.* Chateaulin: Éditions JOS Le Doaré.

Bruford, Alan. 1972–1973. "The Sea-Divided Gaels." *Irish Folk Music Studies* 1:3–27.

Bunting, Edward. 1796. *A General Collection of the Ancient Music of Ireland.* London: Clementi & Co.

Campbell, John L. 1990. *Songs Remembered in Exile.* Aberdeen: Aberdeen University Press.

Chapman, Malcolm. 1994. "Thoughts on Celtic Music." In *Ethnicity, Identity and Music: The Musical Construction of Place,* ed. Martin Stokes, 29–44. Oxford and Providence: Berg.

Creighton, Helen, and Calum MacLeod. 1964. *Gaelic Songs in Nova Scotia.* Ottawa: Department of the Secretary of State. National Museum of Canada, bulletin 198.

Delaney, Frank. 1986. *The Celts.* London: Hodder & Stoughton.

Harrison, Frank. 1976. "Towards a Chronology of Celtic Folk Instruments." *Studia instrumentorum musicae popularis* 4:98–101.

———. 1986. "Celtic Musics: Characteristics and Chronology." In *History and Culture of the Celts/Geschichte und Kultur der Kelten,* ed. Karl Horst Schmidt, 252–263. Heidelberg: Carl Winter-Universitäts Verlag.

Herman, Janet. 1994. "British Folk-Rock; Celtic Rock." *Journal of American Folklore* 107:419–423.

MacDonell, Margaret. 1982. *The Emigrant Experience: Songs of Highland Emigrants in North America.* Toronto: University of Toronto Press.

Megaw, J. V. S. 1991. "Music Archaeology and the Ancient Celts." In *The Celts,* ed. S. Moscati et al., 643–648. London: Thames and Hudson.

Monjarret, Polig. 1984. *Toniou Breizh-Izel/Folk Music of Western Brittany.* Rennes: Éditions B.A.S.

Morton, Tom. 1991. *Going Home: The Runrig Story.* Edinburgh and London: Mainstream Publishing.

O'Connor, Nuala. 1991. *Bringing It All Back Home.* London: British Broadcasting Corporation and Radio Telefís Eireann.

Ó Madagáin, Breandán. 1993. "Song for Emotional Release in the Gaelic Tradition." In *Music and the Church,* ed. Gerard Gillen and Harry White, 254–275. Irish Musical Studies, 2. Dublin: Irish Academic Press.

Ó Riada, Seán. 1982. *Our Musical Heritage.* Mountrath, Ireland: Fundúireacht an Riadaigh/Dolman Press.

Ó Súilleabháin, Mícheál. 1986. "Celtic Music Studies." *Celtic Studies Newsletter* 4 (November):13–16.

Purser, John. 1992. *Scotland's Music: A History of the Traditional and Classical Music of Scotland from Earliest Times to the Present Day.* Edinburgh and London: Mainstream Publishing.

Rimmer, Joan. 1984–1985. "Foreign Elements in Irish 18th Century Dance Music." *Historical Dance* 2(4):28–35.

Shields, Hugh. 1971. "Singing Traditions of a Bilingual Parish in Northwest Ireland." *Yearbook of the International Folk Music Council* 3:109–119.

————, ed. 1985. *Scéalamhráin Cheilteacha* (Narrative songs in the Celtic languages). Baile Atha Cliath: An Clóchomhar Tta.

————. 1994. *Narrative Singing in Ireland.* Dublin: Irish Academic Press.

Stivell, Alan, with Jacques Erwan and Marc Legras. 1979. *Racines interdites/Gwriziad difennet.* Paris: J. C. Lattes.

TMO Ouest. 1991. *La pratique du Breton—les principaux résultats.* Rennes: TMO Ouest, Jean de Legge et Associés.

Williams, W. H. A. 1980. "Irish Traditional Music in the United States." In *America and Ireland, 1776–1976: The American Identity and the Irish Connection,* ed. David Noel Doyle and Owen Dudley Edwards, 279–293. Westport, Conn.: Greenwood Press.

AUDIOVISUAL RESOURCES

The Celtic Heartbeat Collection. 1995. Celtic Heartbeat 82732. Compact disc.

Celtic Thunder. 1982. *The Light of Other Days.* Green Linnet GLCD-1086. Compact disc.

The Celts Rise Again. 1990. Green Linnet. GLCD-104. Compact disc.

Chieftains. 1998. *Celtic Wedding.* RCA Victor 63120.

DeDanann. N.d. *DeDanann.* Celtic Collections, K-Tel International 6266. Compact disc.

Fureys. N.d. *The Fureys.* Celtic Collections, K-Tel International 6265. Compact disc.

Horslips. 1996. *Horslips.* Celtic Collections, K-Tel International 6270. Compact disc.

Reid, Sandra, and Randy Crafton. 1995. *Songs of the Six Celtic Nations: Hal-An-Tow.* Lyrichord LYRCD 7425. Compact disc.

Stivell, Alan. 1989. *Journée à la Maison.* Rounder Records 3062. Compact disc.

————. 1995. *Symphonie Celtique.* Dreyfus DRYCD-36196. Compact disc.

The Twentieth-Anniversary Collection. 1996. Ivers, Eileen [Irish-American fiddler], Wolfstone [Scottish contemporary folk ensemble], Milladoiro [Galician ensemble], and others. Green Linnet GLCD-106. Compact disc.

United Kingdom and Ireland

The United Kingdom and Ireland are musically linked mainly by songs in the English language, though other languages are also used. No matter whether from England, Scotland, Wales, or Ireland, many songs also have similar features, including a four-line form, most often AABA; the use of similar diatonic modes; and a relatively relaxed, unpretentious manner of singing. Today, instrumental dance-music, often performed without dancers, seems more important in England, Ireland, and Scotland than in Wales. The tunes possess similar structures (AABB) and meters (2/4, 6/8)—and the fiddle and bagpipes, though constructed differently, are everywhere the most popular instruments.

Songs and instrumental music are mainly performed in informal settings among friends at home or the local pub, though a few calendar customs, especially Christmas caroling, include singing. Competitive festivals are another important context for performing and preserving traditional music. A folk revival, begun in the 1950s and 1960s, has helped invigorate once rural musical traditions threatened by urbanization and industrialization.

MAP 3   United Kingdom and Ireland

England

Vic Gammon

Singing Style and Song Types
Dance-Music and Instruments
Contexts for Music and Song
Transmission and Education
Musicians and Creativity
Conceptions of Music
Social Groups and Music
History of Scholarship

England is the largest of the four countries that constitute the United Kingdom and displays dramatic contrasts of population and topography. Geographically it divides into a lowland south and east, an area of crop production and mixed farming, and the upland north and west, where sheep farming predominates. London, the old administrative and business center, and industrial cities such as Manchester and Birmingham have been transformed since World War II by multiethnic immigration, mainly from countries of the old British Empire. The country has long been ethnically mixed, with invasions and settlements by Celts, Romans, Saxons, Vikings, and Normans before A.D. 1100 and Welsh, Scots, Irish, Huguenot French, and Eastern European Jews in more recent centuries.

The present population of England is 47 million, living in an area of 130,000 square kilometers. In the eighteenth and nineteenth centuries, England was at the forefront of the Industrial Revolution, a fact that brought benefits and disadvantages and marked the landscape permanently. Many areas now demonstrate contrasts between the declining old "heavy" industries (the manufacturing of metals and cloth, shipbuilding, and mining) and the developing newer manufacturing, service, and financial industries. In a country once described as the workshop of the world, only about 20 percent of the population are engaged in manufacturing. England was also a leader in developing the study of popular customs. The term *folklore,* derived from the German *Volkskunde,* was introduced into scholarship by the antiquarian W. J. Thoms in 1846. The cognate terms *folk song* and *folk music* followed, and growing interest in musical idioms led to the founding of the Folk-Song Society in 1898.

SINGING STYLE AND SONG TYPES

The solo-singing style of English traditional singers is declamatory. Melody is a vehicle for words, and telling the story is most singers' prime consideration. Singing tends to be unemotional or stoical, in the sense that dramatic elements in the narrative are not stressed. English traditional singing is an art of understatement, but the singer's involvement with the song is total. Vocal production is full, open-throated, and sometimes nasal in quality, though there is considerable variety in vocal techniques used. The English collector Cecil J. Sharp contended (1907) that the quality of the

FIGURE I In the first two decades of the twentieth century, Cecil Sharp recorded many singers, including Louie Hooper, shown here, whom he recorded in 1903, 1904, and 1906. Photo courtesy of the Vaughan Williams Memorial Library, Cecil Sharp House, London.

voice of the average singer is "thin and poor" because singers were old. This is true of some recorded singers, but not of all. Others, from Joseph Taylor (recorded in 1908) to later, post–World War II singers of above middle age, such as Harry Cox, George Spicer, Bob and Ron Copper, and Phoebe Smith, have been superb vocalists in the traditional style (figure 1).

Most recorded English song has been performed unaccompanied—a fact that has profoundly influenced singing style. Singers are free to vary the pace of delivery, to engage in metrical irregularity, and to vary the melodic line. They are also free to decorate the musical line, though the degree to which they do varies from singer to singer and region to region and decoration is hardly ever as pronounced as in the *sean-nós* style of the west of Ireland. Traditional songs are built on rounded structures such as four-line stanzas, with repeats that contain some element of variation. Sometimes variation is used to accommodate different syllabic line lengths and textual variations, but more usually it appears to result from singers' fancy and musicality.

English traditional song is not "pure melody" uninfluenced by harmony. Church and military bands played in harmony in the eighteenth and nineteenth centuries, and were widely heard and sung to. Traditional singing in harmony has been recorded extensively, notably in the performances of the Copper family of Rottingdean, Sussex, whose style has been explained as deriving from eighteenth-century glee singing, a form of amateur music making in three or more unaccompanied parts. Many traditional tunes have implicit harmony and are built on triadic structures (figure 2). Even tunes that are not in the major mode often seem to make use of triadic structures within their particular modality. Many dorian, mixolydian, and aeolian tunes appear to base themselves around the tonic chord and the triad based on the minor seventh degree of the scale, with some use of the subdominant (figure 3).

It is clear from early collectors' encounters with traditional music that much of it did not follow the conventions of the major-minor system of Western theory and practice (Kidson and Neal 1915). In the first volume of the *Journal of the Folk-Song Society* (1899), this difference was explained as "modal survival." Collectors were greatly taken with "modal" tunes and published a greater proportion of these than they notated in the field. In an influential book, *English Folk-Song: Some Conclusions* (1907), Sharp characterized English tunes as being cast in the dorian, phrygian, mixolydian, aeolian, and ionian (major) modes, and occasionally in the minor, accepting thereby a modal theory of English folk song that he used to classify melodies, though he clearly understood that some materials were variable. One year later, in 1908, Percy Grainger put forward a radically different explanation of the modality of English traditional song. For Grainger, there was but "one single loosely-knit modal folk-song scale" with certain unstable points, notably the 3rd, the 6th, and the 7th. Having made phonograph recordings, Grainger carefully transcribed entire songs, criticizing the "typical verse" practice of Sharp's method of transcription. Both explanations fit the evidence as recorded. The theories of Sharp and Grainger may not, however, be incompatible. Sharp's modalism works well enough as a classificatory scheme. Grainger's unstable scale appears to work at a deeper structural level

FIGURE 2 A tune for the ballad "Lord Randal," sung by Mrs. Eliza Hutchings of Langport, Somerset, for Cecil Sharp in 1904. The tune outlines one octave of the major mode and emphasizes the notes of the G-major triad (g–b–d). Its four-line form is AABC. After Bronson 1959–1972:1:198.

FIGURE 3 A tune for the ballad called "A Wager, A Wager," sung by Mrs. Powell near Weobley, Herefordshire, for Ralph Vaughan Williams in 1910. The four-line tune in the dorian mode has an ABCD structure (after Bronson 1959–1972: vol. 1, p. 344).

and can explain how tunes change mode in the process of transmission. It can also deal with tunes that vary particular intervals and with singers who employ flexible intonation. The American scholar Bertrand Bronson (1902–1986), while neither affirming nor denying a possible evolutionary development from pentatonic to heptatonic modes, sought to understand melodic variation "through the chinks of the hexatonic and pentatonic systems," the points of difference between one mode and another, and the points that are absent in the pentatonic system. As Bronson demonstrates in his *Traditional Tunes of the Child Ballads* (1959–1972), it is possible to find the same essential tune cast in different modes.

Songs performed by traditional singers can be notated in common time, 4/4, 3/4, and 6/8 being the most frequent, with 5/4 also represented. Nine-eight and 7/4 are not unknown, and some songs display a marked irregularity in rhythm. Songs are normally set in four-line stanzas in common or ballad meter (4.3.4.3 as four-line alternating stresses) or long meter (8.8.8.8), with or without repeats or choruses, but a great variety of other metrical forms are found, some with interpolated chorus lines. Two- and eight-line forms are also encountered, and nineteenth-century songwriting, some of which was absorbed into the tradition, took delight in more elaborate forms.

Melodic patterns are quite varied. Some tunes use internal repetition, sequence, and phrase transposition, while others draw their coherence from an overall structure that does not use such devices. Thus, ABCD is a common musical verse form for a song in ballad meter, but so too is ABBA for songs in long meter, and a wealth of other forms are found, including AABA, AABCD, ABB, ABACDEDF, ABCBC, and many more (see figures 2 and 3). The survival of a popular kind of church music known as west gallery (ca. 1750–1850) in oral tradition means that some elaborate fuguing tunes with highly melismatic melodies held a firm place in popular memory. Many examples of this type of material survive in the vigorous carol-singing traditions of South Yorkshire.

The actual repertory of English songs is made up of many layers. Versions of "The Miller and His Lass" can be traced back to the later Middle Ages, and "The Frog and the Mouse" and "The Three Ravens" are songs that were current in the Tudor period and survive into the present. Others were originated and sustained in tradition by the broadside press, which issued masses of cheap song sheets between about 1500 and 1900. Numerous songs by broadside poets passed into oral tradition and were reshaped by it. Some of these were later collected and reissued in their reshaped form. Thus, broadside ballads, stage songs, music-hall songs, and popular songs from different periods contributed to the layering of the English traditional repertory.

It has been common since the time of the early collectors to group songs according to their subject matter and textual style. In *The English and Scottish Popular Ballads* (1882–1898), the American ballad scholar and anthologist Francis J. Child

FIGURE 4   A procession of morris dancers led by a concertina player, from Winster in Derbyshire, around 1908. Photo courtesy of the Vaughan Williams Memorial Library, Cecil Sharp House, London.

published and annotated texts longer than normal, mostly older narrative pieces with the characteristic features of oral transmission. Though Child included a few tunes, Bronson compiled the tunes extant for many of these ballads in *The Traditional Tunes of the Child Ballads* (1959–1972), printing additional texts.

Songs that were lyric and subjective, rather than narrative in tone, were less attractive, aesthetically, to the early collectors. For Sharp, the words of most traditional songs were vastly inferior to the tunes. He believed they had been corrupted by the broadside press—which, because melodies were rarely printed, was a fate the tunes escaped. Sharp's notions of the quality of folk poetry derived mainly from Child, who despised broadside texts. But modern scholarship has established beyond doubt that the broadside press was a vital influence on traditional singers' repertories.

Interest in the words of traditional songs in England dates from the publication of Alfred Williams's *Folk-Songs of the Upper Thames* (1923). As editor of the collection, Williams wanted "to describe how the people spent their days and nights, in what employments, recreations and amusements. In a word, I wished to show how they lived." Williams argued that such a goal was impossible without dealing with folk songs, and that nothing less than a representative collection would suffice. The first collector from a working-class background, Williams wanted to gain an understanding of the social context in which the songs were performed. This desire in turn led more recent researchers toward a study of English social history.

The world of traditional song is largely the world of preindustrial and protoindustrial England, a land of fields, towns, cottages, alehouses, sailors, agricultural workers, and so on. Yet when scholars consider the narrative or lyric content of the songs, they face substantial problems in interpreting class attitudes, crime, sexual relations, and other themes, quite apart from the problem of differentiated repertories, used by different social groups on various occasions. Songs tell a great deal about the mentality, attitudes, and assumptions of the people for whom singing was important. Yet the meaning of these songs is not always obvious, since meaning is relative to precise contexts and individuals. Clearly the same song sung in an eighteenth-century cottage, an Edwardian drawing room, or a 1960s folk club has the potential for generating quite distinct meanings.

DANCE-MUSIC AND INSTRUMENTS

Like song texts and tunes, the English dance-tune repertory stems from various historical periods. Some seventeenth-century tunes have been played continuously since then, but much of the repertory seems to be eighteenth and early nineteenth century in origin. In the nineteenth century, traditional musicians began to assimilate new dance forms from the continent (like the polka and the waltz), and instrumentalists have readily incorporated twentieth-century dance tunes, provided these are adaptable to rhythmic and melodic conventions.

Just as printed broadsides have been an important influence on traditional singers' repertories, so the interaction among print, manuscript, and oral-aural traditions has been a feature of instrumental music. English traditional dance-music, however, has been collected and studied much less than traditional song. Dance tunes are typically more regular in shape than tunes not meant for dancing. A form of AABB (in which each letter represents an eight-bar strain) is the most common, though AABA and AABBCC crop up. An exception to this regularity is the music for Cotswold morris dancing, a central and south Midlands tradition, wherein the music often follows the dance closely. The pattern of sections can be complex, and many dances contain "caper" sections, which require the instrumentalist to play at a slower tempo, or at half speed (with note values doubled), while the dancers perform high leaps (figure 4).

Dance-music in England is used in three important situations: for mixed social dancing (country dancing), for single-sex display (ceremonial dancing), and socially without dancing.

The time signatures and tune types of English dance music are hornpipes in 4/4, jigs in 6/8, polkas in 2/4, and waltzes in 3/4. The hornpipe, often used to accompany different types of step or clog dancing, is played either straight (with equal eighth-note values) or dotted (with the eighth note followed by a sixteenth). In both cases, the tune typically ends with three stressed quarter notes. A few triple-time hornpipes, common in eighteenth-century printed collections, survive in 3/2 or 6/4, or in a hemiola mixture of both. Jig tunes in 9/8 occasionally appear. Marches in duple or triple time abound but often shade into other categories. The reel, the characteristic dance form of Ireland, cast in 4/4 time with eight equal eighth-note pulses to the bar, is hardly present in English music outside Northumbria.

English dance tunes are overwhelmingly major in tonality, though a few striking tunes make use of other modes. The repertory includes recognizably Scottish or Irish tunes, but the performance of English dance music differs strongly from that of Scotland and Ireland. English music has a contrasting rhythmic feel, is usually slower in tempo, and uses anacrusis, syncopation, Scotch snap, and other devices. Each section of the music, usually four or eight bars, is clearly marked. When played by more than one instrumentalist, the tune is heterophonic, rather than unison. Bass parts were traditionally added to dance tunes by the use of a cello, bassoon, or serpent (an undulating, wooden, lip-vibrated aerophone, with six finger holes), and other parts may have been added to dance tunes during the period that west-gallery church bands flourished. Some musicians' manuscript tune books contain harmony parts for dance tunes.

English fiddle playing distinctively places a great deal of emphasis on rhythmic thrust. The fiddle, however, seems to have suffered a relative decline in the nineteenth century, with the introduction of free-reed instruments, notably the melodeon (button accordion), the Anglo-German concertina (the "anglo"), and the mouth organ, each of whose reeds produces different pitches, depending on the direction of air over the reed. How much these instruments contributed to the development of traditional style and how much they fitted with what already existed, are matters for conjecture: the particular jaggedness of sound produced by the push-and-pull bellows action (allowing no overlapping of notes) appears entirely appropriate for English traditional music. In the twentieth century, the widespread adoption of the piano accordion and the English concertina, instruments that produce the same notes whichever direction the bellows is played, has been seen by many as diluting and enfeebling the traditional style.

Fipple flutes are represented by various kinds of six-holed pipes. Early examples are made of wood, but in the nineteenth century, instruments such as the tin whistle or penny whistle were widely produced commercially. A related instrument is the three-holed pipe played with one hand only, leaving the other free to beat a small drum, called a tabor; the combination was called whittle and dub (whistle and drum). A primitive one-man band, used since the Middle Ages, it was a common

FIGURE 5 Pauline Cato, Official Piper to the mayor of Gateshead, playing the Northumbrian smallpipes in 1996. The bag of the smallpipes is supplied with air from a bellows held under the arm. Modern instruments have added keys to the chanter and multiple dronepipes that can be opened or closed, additions that enable playing in a number of keys. Photo by Danny Cato.

TRACK 6

accompaniment for morris dancing. A parallel example of melody and percussion combined, at times, in one musician is the tambourine, sometimes played with the mouth organ. Other percussion has come into play at various times: military drums, spoons, bones, or beer glasses. Some traditional bands incorporated twentieth-century drum kits into their combinations.

The bagpipe survives in one part of England only as the bellows-blown Northumbrian smallpipes (figure 5). Evidence shows that the dance music of Northumbria differs markedly in style from that of the rest of England. It appears to have more in common with Irish music, and especially with Scottish music. Yet it is also to some extent unique. The Northumbrian pipes emerged as central to a nineteenth-century regional revival, which tried self-consciously to develop a distinctive regional identity, and the smallpipes served as a convenient icon. In no other part of England does the instrumental contest, developed after World War II, have such an important influence, since it not only serves as a mechanism for improving standards but also develops a normative competition style.

A flourishing Northumbrian Pipers' Society encourages practice of the instrument, and highly skilled players live in many parts of the country. Some Northumbrian tunes have a typical bitonal or double-tonic structure, based on the alternation of tonic major and supertonic minor chords. Another distinctive aspect of the repertory is the performance of tunes with variations. These are not simply embellishments of the tune ad libitum, but thoroughly worked-out sets of variations, often of increasing difficulty, calculated to demonstrate the piper's skill. This practice goes back at least to the sixteenth century, when playing divisions on a known melody was common among elite composers and popular musicians. Hornpipes, jigs, polkas, and notably reels form the mainstay of the repertory, and some triple-time hornpipes survive in Northumbria. The tune books published by the pipers' society confirm the distinctiveness of Northumbrian tunes and strong Scottish influence on the repertory.

Traditional musicians play the instruments they can get their hands on or make, and other instruments used by traditional instrumentalists include the hammer dulcimer, the clarinet, the piano, and after the success of black-face minstrelsy in the nineteenth century, the banjo. The historical record shows that such instruments as the hurdy-gurdy and the English guitar, a small cittern, were once used by street musicians.

CONTEXTS FOR MUSIC AND SONG

Singing regularly formed, and still forms, part of social events and calendar customs such as hunt suppers, harvest homes (completion of summer harvest), friendly society feasts, and so on. At Padstow, Cornwall, the "'Oss" (hobbyhorse) dances to a song accompanied by melodeons and drums. Some traditional plays, such as the Soul-Caking Play at Antrobus, Cheshire, have songs integral to them. Other carol-singing and wassailing customs combine house visiting with the performance of specific songs. More often, people sang for simple enjoyment at home or in the pub. Some alehouses gained a reputation as singing pubs. Occasionally, a degree of formality affected pub singing, with one person acting as a chairman or master of ceremonies, but more often singing occurred informally.

Dance-music in England is used in three important situations: for mixed social dancing (country dancing), for single-sex display (ceremonial dancing), and socially without dancing. These contexts can intermingle. Music-only sessions might include solo step dancing, and social dancing might follow dancing for display. Dance-music might be performed in different social spaces. Display dances by their nature were public, being enacted in streets and gardens normally at special times of the year.

Social dances took place at servants' halls, in dancing booths at fairs, in barns, on village greens, and in pubs and houses. In the twentieth century, the development of community and village halls, and of schools with large halls, provided for the continuation of country dancing. The performance of dance-music, like singing, took place in public and private spaces, most commonly at home or in the pub.

The post–World War II folk revival gave rise to informal folk clubs, which usually met in rooms over pubs. At their height, in the 1960s, they numbered in the thousands. Though they still exist in most areas, their numbers have declined considerably since then. The music performed at these venues varied widely in type and quality, but the pubs provided a public platform for traditional performers. Festivals are the most prominent legacy of the later revival: to those with an interest in traditional music, those at Sidmouth, Whitby, and Sutton Bonnington offer both a meeting place and a chance to hear traditional styles.

TRANSMISSION AND EDUCATION

The image of the traditional singer given by the early collectors tended to be that of a naive bearer of ancient survivals, unaware of the significance of what he or she knew, uncorrupted by modernism and commercialism. But the traditional singer or instrumentalist is an individual belonging to his or her age, not an ahistorical fantasy. Traditional performers are self-conscious about their art. They have tended to be artisan tradespeople or working-class people, though examples exist from other social groups. Henry Burstow, shoemaker-singer-bellringer, one of the most important singers encountered by early collectors, produced an illuminating book of reminiscences toward the end of his life. Having read some of the major intellectual works of his day, including those of Darwin and Lyle, and having thought through his own religious views, he had become a convinced atheist. Bob Copper helped sustain his family's unique singing tradition through the interwar period, when interest in traditional singing was at a low ebb, and became an important collector in the 1950s, when interest revived. Having collected blues records from the United States since the 1930s, he became a successful broadcaster and author of books about his experiences and country life.

The Copper family, like many other traditional singers, kept manuscript books of song texts. Other singers, such as Harry Cox, collected broadsides. A significant number of village instrumentalists wrote out their tunes in manuscript books. Professional or semiprofessional street musicians and ballad sellers were common in England well into the late nineteenth century. Traditional music in England is communicated via oral-aural tradition, with its characteristics of fluidity and constant change. But the tendency for decay and recreation was constantly modified by the influence of print and manuscript. Print and manuscript, though subject to these processes of change and decay, likely had a tendency to stabilize songs and to replant into active use pieces that might have become extinct without this intervention.

Sharp was particularly successful at convincing educationalists of the value of traditional songs and dances, thereby securing for them a place in the curriculum of state schools. Despite changes in fashion and emphasis, they tentatively retain that place. That these highly arranged pieces bore only superficial resemblance to their traditional originals did not worry Sharp; in fact, the process of mediation was seen to be the aim of the endeavor, for Sharp, Vaughan Williams, and their contemporaries believed they could effect a sort of cultural revolution by disseminating modified and conventionalized folk music.

This attitude was most evident in the modern collectors' work of composition and arranging. Vaughan Williams is the most significant of these, since his direct and indirect use of folk tunes is a vital aspect of his creative output. From a long list,

Grainger, George Butterworth, and E. J. Moeran also spring to mind. The musical language of another important composer, Gustav Holst, was deeply affected by folk music, though he was not directly involved in the process of collecting. Frederick Delius came under the spell of African-American folk music in one phase of his creative life, and his orchestral rhapsody *Brigg Fair* (1907) was inspired partly by the song of that name that Grainger had in 1905 noted from Joseph Taylor of Saxby-All-Saints, Lincolnshire, and partly by Grainger's own choral setting of it.

This folk-music-based movement in classical composition lost its impetus in the interwar years, and younger composers began to feel the effects of folk music on composition as a constraint, rather than something enabling. The study of folk music in conservatories and colleges of music did not take hold. With a waning of interest in the style and methods of the English nationalist composers, it could be safely relegated to a minor aspect of background study, where it has remained. England has no university program devoted to the study of its own traditional music, and the existence of the English Folk Dance and Song Society, a voluntary organization run by amateurs, has served as a convenient excuse for not establishing a properly funded, institutional resource.

MUSICIANS AND CREATIVITY

Many traditional performers were content to create within the conventions that the tradition allowed. The famous example of peasant poets, such as Stephen Duck and John Clare, coming to adopt the conventions of learned literature should not blind us to the fact that many songwriters were happy to remain within traditional bounds. Sometimes we know the name of a local songwriter. Recent studies of such popular songwriters as Robert Anderson, an early-nineteenth-century songsmith from Cumbria, inspired by Robert Burns, have done much to illumine our understanding, even if many questions on their goals and methods remain unanswered.

Local satirical ballads—a genre that collectors tended to ignore—have a long history and are sometimes cited in the church-court records of the sixteenth and seventeenth centuries. They are songs composed to make fun of or slander unpopular members of the community. Sometimes they were a means for the powerless to attack their social superiors. The local satirical ballad remains a largely unstudied form, yet it was obviously created within its community of origin. The growth of interest in popular church music since 1980 has shown that in the west-gallery period (ca. 1750–1860), many local people composed pieces in the style. These composers were often of humble origin, their names unknown, even when some of their pieces maintain a vigorous life.

A significant number of traditional dance tunes are locally composed, though the distinction between composition, adaptation, adoption, and recreation is often difficult to make. The Sussex concertina player Scan Tester seems to have made tunes from common elements put together in the act of playing, and this is probably true of musicians from many other parts of England. In Northumbria, where musical literacy has long been associated with piping, composers have left compositions and elaborate sets of variations, which test pipers' artistic and technical skills. These tunes have come down in both written and printed forms.

Performance is also a locus of creativity. The formal variation of Northumbrian music is often mirrored by the much less formal use of elaboration and variation in traditional performances. The transcription of tunes that Grainger pioneered demonstrated the creative role of the singer in performance. Variation within repetition is the general rule in English traditional music, songs, and dance tunes. The heterophonic style of group performance in dance tunes adds variation within the context of simultaneous performance.

Many traditional singers adjusted their repertories to what they perceived to be prevailing notions of folk song. Some felt unease about whether items in their repertory fitted prevailing notions, introducing a song with the words "I don't know if it's a folk song or not, but I'm going to sing it anyway."

Creativity is affected by context, to which traditional performers are highly sensitive. In a session I observed many years ago, George Spicer, a singer from Sussex responded to changes in the mood of the session over a period of about three hours, both in his choice of material and manner of performance. Recordings of Spicer made in his home and in a pub demonstrate his performing the same song differently: at home, his performance is relaxed, not especially animated, and in a relatively low key; in front of a pub audience, his performance is lively, more directed, and in a higher key. The role of the audience, in fact, can be a decisive factor in creativity. Intervention such as the singing and harmonizing of a chorus may result in a communication that the performer alone could not achieve, and may be unique to that particular context and performance. This, in turn, may affect and modify future performances of the piece. The study of the pragmatics of performance is in an undeveloped state, but some recent work has shown it to be a promising area for future research.

CONCEPTIONS OF MUSIC

Popular aesthetic notions are usually demonstrated through practices that reveal underlying attitudes and values, such as the inclusion or exclusion of stylistic elements, items of repertory, and so on. Occasionally a popular aesthetic can be glimpsed in the testimony of performers, or in aesthetic views that, through conflict, cause attitudes to be articulated. I have sometimes heard traditional performers criticize others for aspects of style. I heard an excellent singer from Norfolk, Walter Pardon, express distaste at the way another singer gesticulated during a song. To Pardon, songs should be performed as he himself performed them: in the sustained, stoical idiom of much traditional singing, which sets the tone for a song and maintains it to the end, without emphasizing or dramatizing moments in the narrative.

Some traditional performers, defying the vagaries of fashion and popular taste on a wider plane, have kept their musical traditions alive. The Copper family, discovered by the first folk-music revival with songs that appear in the first volume of the *Journal of the Folk-Song Society,* maintained their custom of singing traditional songs in harmony, out of the gaze of the public, until their reemergence on radio and in public performances after World War II. The revival of the postwar period led to the discovery of a great number of traditional singers and instrumentalists. In performing and perpetuating their music in the face of public disinterest, such performers were making a statement about the value of traditional music to them.

Style of performance is one medium through which a popular aesthetic is articulated. Earlier collectors (with the exception of Grainger) were more interested in appropriating the pieces they discovered for uses other than in the way the pieces were performed. Lack of understanding tended to characterize the encounter between middle-class people and traditional singers and instrumentalists. The nineteenth-century reformers of popular church music, who thought it an awful noise, were not joined in this view by its performers. Many nineteenth-century descriptions of traditional music making were dismissive and negative. Around 1900, the documented encounters between collectors (with their newly invented notions of what constituted folk song) and their informants (who had no such term in their vocabulary, and held no such concept) speak volumes. Traditional singers often simply could not understand why the collector wanted only some items and not others.

Many traditional singers who found a new audience and platform in the second folk-music revival adjusted their repertories to what they perceived to be prevailing notions of folk song. Some felt unease about whether items in their repertory fitted prevailing notions. I remember the singer George Spicer introducing a song with the words "I don't know if it's a folk song or not, but I'm going to sing it anyway." Clearly, performers did not usually hold such views, though once articulated, such elements of discourse tend to crop up frequently in the most unlikely settings, sometimes even in traditional performers' mouths.

In a wider perspective, the popular notion and evaluation of folk music has had its supporters and detractors over time and has been subject to fashion. In the 1960s, the folk-music boom caused many people to embrace the idea of a music that was often presented in anodyne and distorted ways, without any sense of the reality of traditional music making or its generative context. In the 1970s and 1980s, with the decline of the revival, popular affection gave way to a general rejection of the idea that folk music had any value. This view, however, seems to be yielding to a less dismissive approach. But it is also true that one now encounters a broader range of opinions about the value of English folk music than formerly.

SOCIAL GROUPS AND MUSIC

Several historians have persuasively argued the thesis of a widely shared traditional culture, fragmented by the withdrawal of elite and middle classes in eighteenth- and nineteenth-century England. A view of this kind admits, however, of many exceptions. Analysis has been clouded by unconscious adoption of the Germanic notion of *das Volk,* variously identified as "the people," "the peasantry," rural dwellers generally, the uneducated or, in its more polite version, the unlettered. In another version of this assumption, traditional music and song are seen as the cultural inheritance of ordinary people or the working class. Research in the 1990s painted a more complex, if incomplete, picture.

Important points emerge from an analysis of performers' social origins. Scholars' perception of traditional music as the possession of the lower strata of society may partly arise from the early collectors' preoccupation with this social class. Many of the informants in England from whom songs were collected were laborers, but they were also farmers, shopkeepers, and publicans, even occasionally clergymen. Study of church bands before the 1850s reveals that these were dominated by artisanal tradesmen.

Different patterns emerge in different parts of the country. In the highly capitalistic agricultural areas of East Anglia, where the process of proletarianizing the work force developed furthest, traditional performers have almost exclusively been drawn from the rural working class. Elsewhere, such as in Sussex and the West Country (Cornwall, Devon, Somerset), significant performers have been members of lower-middle-class, agricultural, or artisanal segments of society. There have even been examples of the gentry maintaining an active participation in traditional music, especially where this is identified with paternalistic values and "Old England." Against this we have to set the invisibility of much traditional culture to the late Victorian and Edwardian middle and upper classes.

The role of women in traditional music is significant. Formerly barred from many activities and confined to a largely domestic sphere, women have nevertheless been important traditional performers, especially in singing: Mrs. Verrall, Louie Hooper (figure 1), and Mrs. Overd in the first revival, and later, "Queen" Carolyne Hughes, Mary Ann Haynes, and Phoebe Smith. Their repertories were often extensive and of high quality. In instrumental and dance-music performance, however, women were normally absent. West-gallery bands sometimes included women, but as singers, not instrumentalists. Women had a role in social dance, but even here the structure of dances often says a lot about the subordination of women's roles. With changing social norms in the late twentieth century, women have begun to take a larger part in traditional music and dance. Women in single-sex groups (school, college, sports, military), like their male counterparts, possess an oral culture that exhibits characteristic features. They also transmit traditional culture in different forms to children, especially younger children. Children themselves retain an extensive oral culture of the street and playground. The work of Peter and Iona Opie (1959), which has built upon that of such pioneers as Lady Alice Gomme (1984 [1898]), has documented the richness of this youth culture.

The major motivation for performing traditional music is, and probably always was, pleasure. Nevertheless, income, in cash or kind, could be had from different types of performance. The occasional income that dance teams could generate, for example, was considerable. Busking for money and playing or singing for drinks in pubs are well documented. Even the relationship between collector and informant sometimes led to financial exchange and the creation of a quasi-client relationship. When one considers that performers' wages were low, such income was significant.

Gypsies (most politely known as Travellers in England, as elsewhere) maintained a distinctive lifestyle, specialized in performing for money. Itinerant and separated from the settled population, they were alternatively and simultaneously scorned and romanticized. Traveller music has, however, been an integral part of the English repertory for centuries and has retained idiosyncratic features. Their repertory largely overlaps with that of settled English country singers, though it sometimes contains pieces that employ a Romany vocabulary. Traveller singing style is often nasal, and singers delight in an elongated delivery, which makes use of slurs and ornaments [see ROM (GYPSY) MUSIC; TRAVELLERS' MUSIC].

The movement of population from Ireland and Scotland has left discernible traces on the repertories of English singers and instrumentalists. But migratory patterns are complex, and it is difficult to tell in which direction a piece has moved: common songs and tunes crop up over many parts of Britain and Ireland. In terms of texts, the dissemination of ballad sheets was evidently important in this process. Some aspects of English singing style may have been influenced by Irish music, but there is no substantial proof that the process was not the reverse, or that the influence was not mutual. Tunes exist in common in the repertories of each country, though instrumentalists from England south of Yorkshire do not traditionally include reels, the most characteristic dance-tune form of Scotland and Ireland.

Immigrant groups—French Huguenots, Italians, Jews, Poles, Ukrainians, Hungarians, and later Chinese, Indians, Pakistanis, and West Indians—have brought traditional and popular forms of music with them. Few of them have had any direct influence on traditional English forms of music making, with the possible exception of German bands and Italian street musicians, common in nineteenth-century England, whose descendants were still found playing on London streets until the late twentieth century. It is possible that the rather "European" style of English traditional instrumental music owes something to this influence. It is possible to hear Irish music in almost any large English city, and the traditions and history of such Irish music are now receiving researchers' attention.

HISTORY OF SCHOLARSHIP

The scholarly collection and study of traditional music in England began in the 1880s. Earlier, in mid-century, antiquarian collectors such as John Broadwood, James Dixon, and Robert Bell had produced collections of songs, some complete with melodies and accompaniments, and the library research of William Chappell in England and Child in the United States had resulted in the publication of popular material taken from printed and manuscript sources. But it was a flurry of publication around 1889–1893, notably by Lucy Broadwood, Frank Kidson, and the Reverend Sabine Baring-Gould, that marked the beginning of the first folk revival.

In 1898, the creation of the Folk-Song Society provided an institutional focus for fieldwork. The development of folklore as a popular field of study, too, had made the collection of cultural items an acceptable pursuit for educated members of Victorian society, even though this meant the temporary crossing of social barriers. Interest in the music of peoples falling under British imperial rule also contributed to the study of music current among "uneducated" English people.

A particular intellectual climate favored the emergence of the folk-song movement. Constitutive of this were the somewhat mystical ideas of "the folk" derived from the German folk-song theorist J. G. Herder (1744–1803) and the growth of "Englishness" (a romantic nationalism that valued the spirit of the nation and sought out those things that expressed it), and on the continent the development of national schools of composition gave rise to self-questioning as to why the English had no such material and added to feelings of inferiority about English music compared with the products of the continent. In this context, the discovery of English traditional music became an urgent and deeply satisfying task. The goal was twofold: to lay the basis for a national school of composition, and to give folk song back to the people as the basis of a cultural and social renaissance.

The entry of collectors from around 1903 initiated a decade of notable achievement by Sharp, Vaughan Williams, Grainger, and others. In 1907, after four years' work in the field, Sharp produced his *English Folk-Song: Some Conclusions,* the first systematic analysis of English traditional song (figure 6). This book was to influence theory and method in folk song, in England and beyond, until the late twentieth century. Sharp was a passionate, energetic, driven man. He created ardent disciples on the one hand, and enemies and detractors on the other. Some who admired his work as collector did not rate highly his ability as musician and arranger. Yet for all his failings, he had a strong influence on the English educational system and shaped the understanding of what "folk song" was for later generations. His amanuensis and inheritor, Maud Karpeles, ensured that his doctrine had a wide and prolonged airing. His ideas are still widely accepted, especially by those with little interest in the field.

Sharp proposed a neo-Darwinian model of the process of folk song, with three stages: *continuity,* the passing on of a tradition in a way that links the past and the present; *variation,* the conscious or unconscious alteration of sung material; and *selection,* the adoption or rejection of songs according to communal taste. An evolutionary model, while powerful, it may also be capable of explaining creative processes beyond the genre of folk song. If so, it cannot be used to mark out folk music as a unique area of human creativity. Sharp's definition of folk song was ultimately exclusive: it was "the song which has been created by the common people," used "in contradistinction to the song, popular or otherwise, which has been created by the educated," even if the latter was also popularly performed by the same people who gave collectors the former.

Nevertheless, Sharp was willing to accept as "authentic folk song" material of "educated" origin that had been transmuted by the evolutionary process. His definition means, though, that to distinguish the authentic from the inauthentic, the col-

FIGURE 6   Cecil Sharp collecting from Edwin Clay of Brailes, Warwickshire, in 1910. Few early collectors used the newly available but cumbersome phonographs, and instead transcribed tunes by ear in the field. Photo courtesy of the Vaughan Williams Memorial Library, Cecil Sharp House, London.

The prestige of traditional music in England varied greatly in the twentieth century. Generally, its status was low, despite particular moments of prominence. From the viewpoint of high art, it seemed a convenient quarry, a source of useful and even unique material, but not of much value in its own right.

lector has to make aesthetic judgments from the moment of contact. Since Sharp (and Child before him) posed the problem in this way, questions of authenticity have bedeviled research. Further, his approach ignored the aesthetics of traditional performers. It disregarded actual practice, preferring an idealized version of the traditional repertory. Some traditional performers found it difficult to understand exactly what collectors working within Sharp's definition wanted.

The emphasis of the first revival was on song. Some collectors developed an interest in dance and, occasionally, its music, but this music was little studied because Sharp showed an overwhelming preference for the display and ceremonial dances (morris, sword, and processional dances, normally performed by men only) as opposed to social dances for both sexes. Thus, the pioneers little considered the richness of the tradition of instrumental music, played for its own sake or to accompany social dancing. Disappointed with the social dances he found, Sharp turned to the interpretation of published dances from the seventeenth and eighteenth centuries to stimulate the folk-dance revival.

The death of many revival pioneers during or after World War I severely impacted the movement. Little collecting was done in the interwar years, compared with the halcyon period 1903–1914. The weakness of the movement was epitomized in 1932 when the Folk-Song Society was, in effect, swallowed up by the English Folk-Dance Society, the main aim of which was to popularize traditional dancing, not to study folk music. In the years after World War II, a new spirit emerged. Of crucial importance were the BBC radio series entitled "As I Roved Out" (from 1955) and, later, the *Folk Songs of Britain,* a series of commercial recordings. From the work of collectors like Peter Kennedy and the singer-collector Bob Copper, it became evident that, though traditional music making in England had declined in significance over the years, it was not dead. The involvement of the American collector Alan Lomax was of particular importance. In bringing together A. L. Lloyd and Ewan MacColl, Lomax laid the foundation for the second revival. Lloyd and MacColl were politically left-wing performers and self-educated intellectuals, who had a powerful effect on younger performers seeking an alternative (from pop music) on which to base their musical practice. This development was fed by the contribution of American scholars, notably Bronson, D. K. Wilgus, Samuel P. Bayard, and G. Malcolm Laws, whose work in the main continued the tradition of Chappell and Child, but was also of a high analytical order.

The apex of this period from a scholarly point of view was the publication of Lloyd's *Folk Song in England* (1967), a heroic attempt to understand English folk song musically, socially, and historically. The book drew on three significant intellectual traditions: Sharpian folk-song scholarship; international folklore scholarship, especially from Eastern Europe and the work of Bartók and Brăiloiu; and radical and Marxist historical writing. Lloyd tried to comprehend folk song as a historical process, one that was not divorced from the experiential world, not relegated to some mythical past, nor the product of a mythicized folk, but as the product of men and women engaged in real social relations, experiencing a range of human emotions. Lloyd was criticized by the political right for his Marxism, but none of his critics produced a work so persuasive, so elegant, in such command of its material.

None of the younger generation has yet produced a work to compare in stature with that of Lloyd. We can see, however, in the diverse and sometimes conflicting work of Georgina Boyes, Vic Gammon, Reg Hall, Dave Harker, Alun Howkins, Michael Pickering, and Ian Russell (and in the collections made by John Howson, "Doc" Rowe, Keith Summers, and Mike Yates) the formation of a more robust view of the English vernacular music tradition. These scholars prefer the term *traditional music* (used earlier by Lucy Broadwood and Frank Kidson), implying music from any source subject to the processes of popular tradition, to *folk music,* which they see as too restrictive and laden with previous ideologies to be of analytical value. In the 1980s and 1990s, the term *vernacular music,* which suggests a social use of the music, had some currency. It can be helpful in the context of discussing Western classical music, where *traditional* refers to music of a tonal (rather than atonal) character. But *folk music* continues to be used, as in the title of the leading English journal in the field (*Folk Music Journal,* begun in 1965).

The prestige of traditional music in England varied greatly in the twentieth century. Generally, its status was low, despite particular moments of prominence. From the viewpoint of high art, it seemed a convenient quarry, a source of useful and even unique material, but not of much value in its own right. As fashions in art music changed, so folk music was relegated to a footnote, something that plays a necessary role in the evolutionary scheme, but is unimportant. In the 1960s, the influence of folk music on popular music was considerable, but journalists of the 1970s delighted in labeling traditional music as boring, ear-hole music. Traditional music appears to be rising again in esteem, since it can be considered a homegrown example of world music. The folk-music revival, however, a vital force in the 1960s, is largely a spent force, its adherents aging and often inward looking, though the best performers can still pack venues and turn in thrilling performances.

Traditional culture is held in low esteem in England because many English symbols of nationhood are associated with imperialism, rather than with national identity or, in particular, resistance to a foreign, invading power. In any case, English identity cannot be separated from class identity. Even the romantic nationalism of composers such as Vaughan Williams, a continuing and potent force in some quarters, was merely an expression of Englishness, an appropriation of traditional music from its social and contextual reality. Yet English traditional music remains a dynamic resource. The cultural history of the past two centuries suggests that people feel a periodic need to return, appraise, and reuse material that helps them create or recreate their identity; traditional music has this potential.

BIBLIOGRAPHY

Armstrong, Frankie, and Brian Pearson. 1979. "Some Reflections on the English Folk Revival." *History Workshop Journal* 7:95–100.

Bird, John. 1976. *Percy Grainger.* London: Faber.

Boyes, Georgina. 1993. *The Imagined Village.* Manchester: Manchester University Press.

Broadwood, Lucy. 1906. "On the Collecting of English Folk Songs." *Journal of the Royal Musical Association* 31:89–110.

Bronson, Bertrand H. 1959–1972. *The*

Traditional Tunes of the Child Ballads. 4 vols. Princeton: Princeton University Press.

Cannon, R. D. 1972. "English Bagpipe Music." *Folk Music Journal* 2(3):176–219.

Chandler, Keith. 1993. *"Ribbons, Bells, and Squeaking Fiddles": The Social History of Morris Dancing in the English South Midlands, 1660–1900.* Enfield Lock: Hisarlik Press.

Chappell, William. 1965. *Popular Music of the Olden Time.* New York: Dover.

Child, Francis James. 1882–1898. *The English and Scottish Popular Ballads.* 5 vols. Boston: Houghton Mifflin.

Clissold, Ivor, Frank Purslow, and John R. Baldwin. 1969. "Alfred Williams . . . A Symposium." *Folk Music Journal* 1(5):315–349.

Copper, Bob. 1971. *A Song for Every Season.* London: Heinemann.

Davies, Gwilym. 1992. "Percy Grainger's Folk Music Research in Gloucestershire, Worcestershire and Warwickshire." *Folk Music Journal* 6(3):339–358.

Dawney, Michael. 1976. "George Butterworth's Folk Music Manuscripts." *Folk Music Journal* 3(2):99–113.

Dean-Smith, Margaret. 1954. *A Guide to English Folk Song Collections 1822–1952.* Liverpool: University Press of Liverpool.

Dickinson, Bickford H. C. 1970. *Sabine Baring Gould: Squarson, Writer & Folklorist.* Newton Abbot: Batsford.

Dunn, Ginette. 1980. *The Fellowship of Song.* London: Croom Helm.

D'Urfey, Thomas. 1959 [1719–1720]. *Pills to Purge Melancholy.* New York: Folklore Library Publishers.

Elbourne, Roger. 1980. *Music and Tradition in Early Industrial Lancashire.* Woodbridge: Brewer.

Fox Strangways, A. H. 1933. *Cecil Sharp.* London: Oxford University Press.

Gammon, Vic. 1980. "Folk Song Collecting in Sussex and Surrey, 1843–1914." *History Workshop Journal* 10:61–89.

———. 1981. "'Babylonian Performances': The Rise and Suppression of Popular Church Music in England, 1660–1870." In *Popular Culture and Class Conflict,* ed. Eileen Yeo and Stephen Yeo, 62–88. Brighton: Harvester Press.

———. 1982. "Song, Sex and Society in England, 1600–1850." *Folk Music Journal* 4(3):208–245.

———. 1988. "Singing and Popular Funeral Practices in the Eighteenth and Nineteenth Centuries." *Folk Music Journal* 5(4):412–447.

Gerould, Gordon Hall. 1957. *The Ballad of Tradition.* New York: Galaxy Books.

Gomme, Lady Alice Bertha. 1984 [1898]. *The Traditional Games of England, Ireland, and Scotland.* London: Thames & Hudson.

Grainger, Percy. 1908. "Collecting with the Phonograph." *Journal of the Folk-Song Society* 12:147–169.

Hall, Reg. 1990. "*I Never Played to Many Posh Dances. . . .*": Scan Tester, Sussex Musician, 1887–1972. Rochford: Musical Traditions.

Harker, Dave. 1972. "Cecil Sharp in Somerset— Some Conclusions." *Folk Music Journal* 2(3):220–240.

———. 1980. *One for the Money: Politics and Popular Song.* London: Hutchinson.

———. 1985a. *Fakesong: The Manufacture of British "Folksong" 1700 to the Present Day.* Milton Keynes: Open University Press.

———, ed. 1985b. *Songs from the Manuscript Collection of John Bell.* Durham: The Surtees Society.

Howes, Frank. 1969. *The Folk Music of Britain— and Beyond.* London: Methuen.

Howkins, Alun, and Ian C. Dyck. 1987. "'The Time's Alteration': Popular Ballads, Rural Radicalism and William Cobbett." *History Workshop Journal* 23:20–38.

Karpeles, Maud. 1987 [1973]. *An Introduction to English Folk Song.* London: Oxford University Press.

Kennedy, Peter. 1975. *The Folksongs of Britain and Ireland.* London: Cassell.

Kidson, Frank, and Mary Neal. 1915. *English Folk-Song and Dance.* Cambridge: Cambridge University Press.

Laing, Dave, Karl Dallas, Robin Denselow, and Robert Shelton. 1975. *The Electric Muse.* London: Methuen.

Lloyd, A. L. 1967. *Folk Song in England.* London: Lawrence & Wishart.

Opie, Peter, and Iona Opie. 1959. *The Lore & Language of Schoolchildren.* Oxford: Clarendon Press.

Pickering. Michael. 1982. *Village Song and Culture.* London: Croom Helm.

———. 1990. "Recent Folk Music Scholarship in England: A Critique." *Folk Music Journal* 6(1):37–64.

Purcell, William. 1957. *Onward Christian Soldier: A Life of Sabine Baring Gould.* London: Longman.

Purslow, Frank. 1967. "The George Gardiner Folk Song Collection." *Folk Music Journal* 1(3):129–157.

———. 1968. "The Hammond Brothers' Folk Song Collection." *Folk Music Journal* 1(4):236–266.

Russell, Ian. 1970. "A Survey of Christmas Singing in South Yorkshire." *Lore and Language* 1(3):1–15.

———, ed. 1986. *Singer, Song and Scholar.* Sheffield: Sheffield Academic Press.

Sharp, Cecil J. 1907. *English Folk-Song: Some Conclusions.* London: Novello, Simpkin.

Shepard, Leslie. 1962. *The Broadside Ballad.* Hatboro, Penn.: Legacy Books.

Turner, Christopher. 1997. *The Gallery Tradition: Aspects of Georgean [sic] Psalmody.* Ketton: SG Publishing.

Van Der Merwe, Peter. 1992 [1989]. *Origins of the Popular Style.* Oxford: Oxford University Press.

Vaughan Williams, Ralph. 1934. *National Music.* London: Oxford University Press.

Vaughan Williams, Ursula. 1964. *RVW.* London: Oxford University Press.

Williams, Alfred. 1923. *Folk-Songs of the Upper Thames.* London: Duckworth.

Williams, Iolo. 1935. *English Folk-Song and Dance.* London: Longman.

Yates, Michael. 1975. "English Gypsy Songs." *Folk Music Journal* 3(1):63–80.

———. 1982. "Percy Grainger and the Impact of the Phonograph." *Folk Music Journal* 4(3):265–275.

AUDIOVISUAL RESOURCES

The Brave Ploughboy: Songs and Stories in a Sussex Pub. 1975. Xtra XTRS 1150. LP disk.

Callaghan, Barry. 1979. *Billy Bennington—Norfolk Dulcimer Player.* Sheffield: Garland Films/EFDSS. 16mm film.

Cann, Bob, and Mark Bazeley. 1988. *Five Generations: The Music and Songs of a Dartmoor Family.* Veteran Tapes VT110. Cassette.

Coe, Pete. 1990. *Catch Me If You Can: Songs From Cornish Travellers.* Veteran Tapes VT119. Cassette.

Cohen, John. 1983. *The Ballad and the Source.* Vaughan Williams Memorial Library. 16mm film.

Copper, Bob, and Ron Copper. 1963. *Bob and Ron Copper.* EFDSS LP 1002. LP disk.

Cox, Cyril D. 1989. *Sword Dancers (and a Tup!).* The Cyril D. Cox Folk Collection, 5. Simril Video. Video.

The Folk Songs of Britain. 1968–1969. Field recordings, originally published on the Caedmon label. Topic 12T157–161, 194–198. 10 LP disks.

Hall, Reg, and Mervyn Plunkett. 1976. *English Country Music.* Topic 12T296. LP disk.

Hinchliffe, Frank. 1977. *In Sheffield Park: Traditional Songs from South Yorkshire.* Topic 12TS308. LP disk.

Hugill, Stan. 1993. *Sailing Days: Shanties and Sea Songs of the Mersey Shanty Man.* Veteran Tapes VT127. Cassette.

Kennedy, Peter. 1955. *The Barleymow.* VWML. 16mm film.

Kennedy, Peter, Alan Simpson, and S. Coles. 1954. *Walk in St. George.* VWML. 16mm film.

Kimber, William. 1974. *The Art of William Kimber.* Topic 12T249. LP disk.

Larner, Sam. 1974. *A Garland for Sam.* Topic 12T244. LP disk.

The Leaves of Life: Songs, Stories, Tunes and a Play from Eight English Counties. 1989. Field recordings of Fred Hamer. Vaughan Williams Memorial Library Audio Cassette VWML 003. Cassette.

The Ling Family: Singing Traditions of a Suffolk Family. 1977. Topic 12TS292. LP disk.

Many a Good Horseman: Traditional Music Making from Mid Suffolk. 1986. Produced by John Howson. Vintage Tapes 005. Cassette.

Maynard, George. 1976. *Ye Subjects of England: Traditional Songs from Sussex.* Topic 12T286. LP disk.

Morrissey, Tommy, and Charlie Pitman. 1992. *Pass Around the Grog: The Songs of Two Cornishmen.* Veteran Tapes VT122. Cassette.

Noble, Will. 1992. *In That Beautiful Dale: South West Yorkshire Songs from Will Noble.* Veteran Tapes VT124. Cassette.

Pardon, Walter. 1975. *A Proper Sort.* Leader LED 2063. LP disk.

Pass the Jug Round: Songs of Cumberland from Archive Recordings. N.d. Produced and engineered by Bernard Whitty. Reynard Records RR–002. LP disk.

Pigg, Billy. 1971. *Billy Pigg the Border Minstrel.* Leader LEA 4006. LP disk.

Rowe, Doc. 1988. *"Rouse, Rouse": Traditional Christmas Carols from Padstow in Cornwall.* Veteran Tapes VT117. Cassette.

Russell, Ian. 1988. *Arise Rejoice and Sing: Village Carols from the Blue Ball Inn, Worrall.* Village Carols VC002. Cassette.

Russell, Ian, and Barry Callaghan. 1971–1972. *The Derby Tup.* Sheffield: Garland Films. 16mm film.

Shergold, Francis, and Bampton Traditional Morris Dancers. 1988. *Greeney Up: Songs Dances and Reminiscences (Oxfordshire).* Veteran Tapes VT111. Cassette.

Smith, Phoebe. 1970. *Once I Had a True Love.* Topic 12T193. LP disk.

Spicer, George. 1974. *Blackberry Fold.* Topic 12T235. LP disk.

Tester, Scan. 1990. *Scan Tester 1887–1972: "I Never Played to Many Posh Dances.* Topic 2–12T455/6. 2 LP disks.

Unto Brigg Fair: Joseph Taylor and Other Traditional Lincolnshire Singers Recorded in 1908 by Percy Grainger. 1972. Leader LEA 4050. LP disk.

Yates, Mike. 1975a. *Songs of the Open Road: Gypsies, Travellers & Country Singers.* Topic 12T253. LP disk.

———. 1975b. *When Sheep Shearing's Done: Countryside Songs from Southern England.* Topic 12T254. LP disk.

———. 1976. *Green Grow the Laurels: Country Singers from the South.* Topic 12TS285. LP disk.

———. 1987. *Ripest Apples: Traditional Singing in Sussex.* Veteran Tapes VT107. Cassette.

Wales
Phyllis Kinney

Wales (Cymru in the Welsh language) occupies a mountainous peninsula along the central west coast of Great Britain. Its nearly three million people live in an area of 20,768 square kilometers. The greatest portion of Wales has always been given over to agriculture, but the southeastern valleys were heavily industrialized from the late eighteenth century to the 1980s. Today, tourism employs far more people than heavy industry.

About 25 percent of the population speak English and Welsh, part of the Brythonic or British (as opposed to Gaelic) subdivision of the Celtic language family. With English, the Welsh language, the most flourishing of the Celtic languages, is an official language of Wales, promoted since 1970 through bilingual education and regular broadcasts on television and radio.

Musically, Wales is most famous for its traditional harp playing (which formerly accompanied the singing of courtly bards) and choral singing and its annual competitive music festivals, The Royal National Eisteddfod and the International Music Eisteddfod.

MUSICAL GENRES AND CONTEXTS

The oldest songs in Welsh traditions are probably those associated with calendric customs. Around the winter solstice, farm work was suspended so people could indulge in seasonal festivities, including a horse ceremony (Mari Lwyd 'Gray Mare'), in which a party outside sang to gain admittance and defenders inside answered in song. At least sixteen examples of the song have been noted. The example with the most variants features considerable repetition—which suggests its suitability as a vehicle for improvisation.

Other customs popular around the winter solstice were the wren hunt and New Year's luck visits, with wassailing. Though the wren hunt had died out in Wales by the early 1900s, several songs connected with it survived, one type praising the wren as king, and the other being a question-and-answer song, sung in processions. Until the early decades of the twentieth century, New Year's was considered more important than Christmas in Wales. It was an occasion for luck visiting, which included songs asking for *calennig* 'money, food, wassail' and wishing luck to the family in return.

Also associated with the winter solstice, but in the Christian tradition, are *plygain* carols (see below). In the 1600s and 1700s, they were sung to complex, extended tunes, including non-Welsh melodies with words in *cynghanedd,* a verbal embroidery including alliteration and internal rhyme. In the nineteenth century under the influence of hymns, carols became simpler in text and tune.

The change from winter to spring also had its festivals, beginning on Candlemas (2 February), celebrated in Wales as Gŵyl Fair y Canhwyllau. Here too a musical contest between outdoor wassailers and indoor responders was an important element, this time in the form of musical tests—of memory or the ability to sing long sections on a single breath (according to some references, while dancing) or say tongue-twisting words faster than anyone else. Though the festival has not survived, many of its songs give tantalizing glimpses of their role to accompany dressing in animal costumes and masks.

Shrove Tuesday, the prelude to Lent, was celebrated by children, who went from door to door chanting a song asking for pancakes or the ingredients to make them. Later, in the spring, came May carols, sung outdoors during early May mornings, with words, usually serious and Christian in tone, celebrating the coming of spring. An older and more boisterous element in May celebrations came with May dancing (*dawnsio ha*), which included Cadi, a man dressed in women's clothes wielding a broom, accompanied by dancers with blackened faces. The dancers' song mentions leaping and, like some of the musical tests, carries suggestions of animal guising.

Love songs form the largest category of Welsh folk song. In addition to the usual types—eulogies to a sweetheart, laments for disappointed love, night-visit songs, *chansons d'aventure*—there are some less common traits. One of these is the device of sending a bird as a messenger of love—a concept called *llatai* in classical Welsh poetry, but also popular among folk poets. The chosen messenger is usually a blackbird, but one enthusiastic suitor sent a nightingale, a lark, and some little mountain birds. Two bird-messenger songs contain Welsh and English lines in alternation.

Dialogue songs of courtship are popular. In print, some were bowdlerized to suit the moral taste of the period. At least two found in manuscript mention courting in bed (*caru yn y gwely*), a practice similar to bundling in New England, but those references were excised when the songs appeared in print. Similarly, no songs using sexual metaphors were printed in songbooks before 1974, though the words to some were to be found on ballad sheets and in manuscripts. They are usually on the theme of mowing the hay, but one is based on the collier's work and tools.

After love songs, broadside ballads are among the most popular forms of traditional song in Wales. They are of two main types: seventeenth- and eighteenth-century ballads on many of the same melodies as the *plygain* carols, with words in *cynghanedd,* and simpler tunes, often of four equal phrases, with words in folk meters. The older type is as much a vehicle for poetic display as a means of storytelling; simpler nineteenth-century ballads, often sung to English, Irish, or American tunes, deal with topics as diverse as murder, deportation to Australia, and most aspects of love, including parental interference. Versions of only two Child ballads—"Lord Randal" and "Our Goodman"—have been collected from Welsh oral tradition; both are of a type well known in Europe, rather than of purely British origin.

Texts frequently reference the natural world. The fox is the subject of several ballads, in dialogues and descriptions of fox hunts. Domesticated animals tend to appear in humorous guises, but a ballad of two stallions has a thread of bitterness running through it. Birds, in addition to being messengers of love, take part in serious or humorous conversations with humans, and the blackbird acts as a counselor in a dialogue with a prospective suitor. The holly is praised as the finest tree in the wood; flowers and herbs play a conventional role, with red roses standing for love, white lilies for purity, and thyme for virginity. Perhaps the most important aspect of the natural world is the sense of place, strong among Welsh people and found in songs praising a favorite spot or enumerating places on a journey. The latter element is especially prominent in sailors' farewell ballads, which note familiar landmarks on the way out to the open sea.

The oldest known category of Welsh work songs is undoubtedly the oxen songs, mentioned in the 1100s and still used in plowing until about 1900. The singer was the plowboy (*geilwad*), whose job was to walk backward facing the oxen and sing to keep the oxen calm. The songs were usually in the form of quatrains on any subject, serious or satirical, but the distinguishing mark was a call to the oxen at the end of each verse. Some twenty-one of these songs survive, including several different tunes. Other examples of work songs include one sung by the smithy while striking the anvil and an industrial song with a refrain. The only Welsh-language sea shanty so far found was used as a capstan or rope shanty.

Most Welsh occupational songs refer to or describe some aspect of work, rather than accompany it. These include miners' songs, a dialogue between a gull and a fisherman, and songs describing begging, milling, plowing, shearing sheep, and tinkering.

Foreign influences on Welsh folk song were mostly English, and to a lesser extent Irish. Nineteenth-century American minstrel shows gave rise to Welsh songs on tunes such as "Oh Susanna" and "Just Before the Battle, Mother," and these have entered the Welsh repertoire. The latter tune was used with Christmas words by a male trio in a rural *plygain* carol service as recently as January 1990.

STRUCTURES OF SONGS

The first scientific analysis of Welsh tonal structures (Crossley-Holland 1968), based on a sample of four hundred tunes, found that about two-thirds of Welsh tunes are in diatonic five-, six-, and seven-tone patterns. Four-note scales are rare, and pentatonic scales are uncharacteristic of Welsh folk songs. Most are in some form of major or minor scale, but a few are in the mixolydian and phrygian modes. The melodic range varies from a fifth to a thirteenth, with more than half in a range of eight or nine tones. Wide-range melodies are more frequently found in ballad and carol tunes, but rarely in older kinds of song. The balance of mode appears to be closer to that of England than of Ireland or Scotland. The tonic is more often placed low than centrally, and tonic and final are identical, apart from eight circular tunes whose final is usually the dominant.

Some wide-range tunes derive from non-Welsh sources. The Welsh ballads and carols mentioned above include variants of the seventeenth-century English ballads "See the Building" (*'Gwel yr Adeilad'*) and "Let Mary Live Long" (*'Hir Oes i Fair'*), both with a range of ten tones. An Irish tune, "St. Patrick's Day," gave birth to almost two dozen Welsh variants in a ten- to twelve-tone compass. A study of Welsh narrow-range tunes (Kinney 1986) found sixty pentachordal songs; this category is extremely rare in English folk songs, and some narrow-range songs may have begun as descants to the harp. Examples of singing with the strings published in 1885 show the singer chanting a descant, sometimes following the harp melody and sometimes in harmony, frequently in a range of five or six tones, with considerable doubling of notes. Most pentachordal tunes are unornamented. Perhaps the tradition of declaiming poetry influenced the vocal range and the ornamentation; many of these tunes were sung to words in traditional Welsh poetic meters, popular in rural contests among singers.

FIGURE 1 *"Y Fenyw Fain"* ('The Slender Girl'), a secular song, whose opening phrase, repeating the fifth degree of the scale, shows the influence of religious declamations.

Tra– fei– les i dre Llun– den, do, Ac he– fyd dre– fydd mawr, do, Ac

he– fyd Sbaen a Scot–land, do, Ac he– fyd Sbaen a Scot–land, do. I chil– io am fen– yw fain.

I traveled to London town, yes, and also great towns, yes, and also Spain and Scotland, yes, to search for a slender girl.

Poetic declamation reached new heights with the *hwyl,* a declamatory technique used by Welsh preachers in the 1800s and early 1900s to heighten religious fervor. Further declamatory influence may be found in songs that open with the voice chanting on the fifth degree of the scale (figure 1). About thirty Welsh folk songs have been noted with openings that are to some degree declamatory, usually on the fifth, but one song opens by chanting the first three phrases on the tonic, mediant, and dominant, respectively.

Declamation in the Welsh folk tradition is still to be heard in *canu'r pwnc* 'singing the text'. As now practiced in southwest Wales, the tradition is connected with reciting biblical scriptures at catechismal festivals, which became prevalent in the early 1800s. The style of sung recitation may, however, be much older. In a typical example, a passage from the Bible is announced, and the precentor sounds the note. One group enters immediately on the same note, a second part comes in at a fifth above, and the two parts chant together at that interval. The rhythm of the chant is even, the tone firm and rather staccato, the diction clear. Phrasing is according to punctuation: the reciting tone dips slightly on each strong accent; but at cadences on commas or periods in the text, the dip may reach as much as a fourth. These cadences are snapped sharply, in a sixteenth-and-dotted-eighth rhythm. The alternation of voices adds variety, as children chant in unison, then women in unison, then men, and then the entire congregation once more in two parts.

The Welsh language, whose words tend to be polysyllabic, puts a strong accent almost invariably on the penultimate syllable, and so well over a quarter of Welsh folk songs finish with a so-called feminine cadence, reaching the tonic after the first beat of the last measure. Songs in trochaic meters, where all cadences are feminine, are not uncommon. Some of these are simple quatrains; others may be couplets or quatrains with interlaced refrains. Some refrains, originally instrumental, received nonsense syllables later. That was the case with *"Triban Gwyr Morganwg"* ('The Glamorgan Men's *Triban*'), sung in the 1700s with instrumental interludes, called symphonies. In 1844, it appeared in print as *"Triban Morganwg,"* much shortened and with two of the symphonies incorporated in the vocal part to the syllables *"ffal lal la."* About a century later, it surfaced again, with *"ffal lal la"* replaced by *"bwmba didl dei."*

Ornamentation consists predominantly of passing tones or slurs, long melismas are extremely rare, and about 40 percent of Welsh tunes have no ornamentation. In contrast, less than 18 percent of Welsh folk songs are highly ornamented; most are older ballads and carols, including variants of English and Irish tunes. Songs may have been more highly decorated in the past, especially perhaps in south Wales. The proportion of ornaments including graces, trills, turns, and melismas in *Ancient National Airs of Gwent and Morganwg* (Huws 1988) is high: only one song out of the forty-three is unornamented, and three-quarters of the songs are heavily embellished

The origins of the harp (*telyn*), symbolically the most important Welsh musical instrument, are obscure. Whatever its ancestry, the harp in Wales quickly achieved a dominant position, undoubtedly due to the close connection between harp music and poetry.

FIGURE 2   *"Pan own y gwanwyn,"* a highly embellished Welsh melody, collected in *Ancient National Airs of Gwent and Morganwg*. After Huws 1988.

Pan own y gwan– wyn   ar u– chel–fryn Yn   gwyl–io'r de–   faid

gy– da'r ŵyn,   Clywn lais   fy nghar– iad   bêr ei chan– iad Yn

sein– io'n llaw–   en   yn y llwyn;   Oedd gwawr llaw– e–   nydd

ar ei deu–   rudd,   O mor hardd   ei   lliw a'i llun,   A

min–nau'n syll– u   ac   ym–hyf–ry– du Gan   har–dded hwyl   fy   an– nwyl fun.

(figure 2). One informant mentioned "slurring and quavering," and Welsh hymn singers were admonished for "overloading each note with three or four and sometimes half a dozen grace notes" (*Y Cerddor Cymreig* 1873:37). Nevertheless, the ornamentation found in *Ancient National Airs of Gwent and Morganwg*—with its double appoggiaturas and cadential trills—probably owes more to the art music of the period than to the folk tradition.

The most characteristic rhythmic element in Welsh song is the snap. Snapping feminine endings gives syncopation; if the cadence is snapped at a slow tempo, it has the effect of an appoggiatura. Another means of adding rhythmic variety is to sing verses of different meters to the same tune—a custom that probably evolved out of competitive singing of verses to the harp. Occasionally, rhythmic contrast is provided in the course of a song by changing between duple and triple meter. This effect is particularly noticeable in some carols, but traditional Welsh verses are not uncommonly followed by a refrain in a contrasting rhythmic pattern.

About two-thirds of Welsh folk tunes consist of four equal phrases, the most popular patterns being AABA and ABCD. Almost half the AABA examples in the *Journal of the Welsh Folk-Song Society* printed before World War I include wide-ranging variants of Anglo-Irish tunes. The ABCD tunes, largely medium-range, show considerably more differentiation in type, including ballads and farewells, May carols, and solo-and-chorus items. Songs in the older categories tend to have phrases of irregular length, as do seventeenth- and eighteenth-century ballads and carols. These items are mostly long, often consisting of seven or more phrases, due to the repetition of each section to accommodate the extended poetic stanza. The style of singing may also contribute to phrasal irregularity: *plygain* carol singers, for example, tend to extend and hold upbeats and cadences, whereas verses sung to the harp may be regularized by the harpist.

MUSICAL INSTRUMENTS

The origins of the harp (*telyn*), symbolically the most important Welsh musical instrument, are obscure. Though there are numerous medieval references to it, no native instrument survives from before about 1700. Whatever its ancestry, the harp in Wales quickly achieved a dominant position, which it has retained. Undoubtedly the close connection between harp music and poetry—a connection that never completely disappeared—ensured the survival of the instrument. Literary references suggest that the medieval and Renaissance harp was small, with about thirty strings; later, single-string Welsh harps became increasingly larger. The silver model of a harp awarded at the 1523 Caerwys competition appears to show a single-stringed Renaissance harp.

The Italian chromatic harp (the triple harp), introduced into England by the mid-1600s, became so popular in Wales that it was known as the Welsh harp until the 1800s, when the pedal harp largely displaced it (for this and other Welsh instruments, see figure 3). The triple harp, held in Wales on the performer's left shoulder, had a range of about five octaves, with about ninety-five strings set in three rows: diatonic, the outer rows were tuned in unison; chromatic notes were played on the inner row. This instrument was well suited to brilliant solo displays, as talented Welsh Gypsy performers demonstrated in the 1800s.

FIGURE 3 "The Musical Instruments of the Welsh." Portrayal by Edward Jones, "the king's bard," in Jones 1825 [1784]. Courtesy of the National Museum of Welsh Life, Cardiff.

FIGURE 4 Gypsy fiddlers. Photo by David H. Smith. Courtesy of the National Museum of Welsh Life, Cardiff.

Efforts to preserve the triple harp as the national instrument failed, and its use declined. The last traditionally trained triple harpist, Nansi Richards, died in 1979, but some of her pupils had learned to master the instrument, and some still play it. The pedal harp survives and flourishes as a popular instrument in Wales.

The crowd (*crwth*) developed from the Celtic lyre, which accompanied bardic declamation as early as the first century B.C. Rectangular in shape, it had from three to six strings, probably of horsehair, stopped by the fingers of the left hand. Flat, the bridge, which enabled the performer to produce chords, had one leg lengthened to go through a sound hole and act as a sound post. Some time after the tenth century, the bow was adopted and two drone strings were added, to be plucked with the left hand while the melody was played on the other strings. The crowd accompanied the voice in the declamation of poetry, played variations on melodies, and accompanied dancing, as a solo instrument or in combination with others, especially the harp. The status of harp and crowd was officially acknowledged in medieval and Renaissance Welsh courts, but "in the houses of the gentry" the crowd's popularity later declined; by the 1700s it had been displaced by the fiddle, which for a while borrowed the crowd's name. The fiddle never attained the status of the harp, but the two instruments were often heard together; a carol of 1759 calls for "Two men and two boys with harp and fiddle."

Throughout the 1800s, fiddlers were indispensable at fairs, weddings, wakes, feasts, and dances. During the 1800s and early 1900s, the Welsh fiddling tradition became increasingly confined to Gypsy players (figure 4).

The third main type of traditional instrument in medieval and Renaissance Wales included pipes (*pibau*) of various kinds. The status of the pipes was lower than that of the harp and the crowd, because it was not acknowledged in the music making of the bardic order. The *pibgorn* was a single-reed hornpipe with cow-horn bells and wood or bone barrels, pierced by seven finger holes. Once popular in Wales, it fell into disuse, like the crowd, in the 1700s. Bagpipes (*pibau cod*) were depicted in an early seventeenth-century manuscript, which, in addition to crude drawings of a harp and a three-string crowd, shows two sets of pipes: one is a single-chanter bagpipe; the other has a double chanter. Though the *pibgorn* died out, the bagpipe continued to play an important part in rural "horseback weddings" into the early 1800s.

According to Edward Jones (1825 [1784]), the Welsh in earlier times had a drum called a *tabwrdd* and a semicircular bugle horn known as the *corn buellin.*

Several folk instruments enjoying periods of popularity after the medieval period included the *cornicyll,* a concealed-reed instrument like the *pibgorn,* with a mouthpiece that screwed on and off. The mouth harp (*bibaw, sturmant*), made of wood or metal, was held between the teeth and struck with a finger; it remained popular in Wales until the early 1900s, when it was superseded by the harmonica, which, like the *sturmant* and the concertina, was popular in taverns and among farmhands in the stable loft (*llofft-stabal,* which gave its name to the informal entertainment of farmhands quartered there).

THE BARDIC TRADITION

The history of Wales as a territorial unit with a distinct language stems from the 500s, when the population, which had settled in that part of Britain about 300 B.C., separated from their fellow Celts because of Anglo-Saxon invasions. For the next thousand years, the Welsh musical tradition other than the liturgical music of the Christian Church was almost entirely oral, and our knowledge of the place of music in early Wales is based on historical and literary sources. Sixth-century references indicate that high-status bards declaimed the king's praises in a style different from that of singing in church, and that declamation was accompanied on the crowd.

In the late 1100s, an ecclesiastic, Giraldus Cambrensis, noted that the Welsh had three kinds of musical instruments: harp, crowd, and pipes. About 1300, Wales lost its independence, through conquest by the English crown. The patronage of the native royal courts fell away, and their place was taken by the Welsh gentry, who continued to dispense patronage to bards and musicians. Among the twenty-four accomplishments expected of a Welsh noble were poetry, singing to an instrument, and playing the harp.

The end of the fifteenth century saw a Welsh dynasty, the Tudors, ruling England, and Welsh gentlemen flocked to London for status and profit. Many became so Anglicized that poets and musicians who depended on them lost their patronage. By 1523, the formal bardic system was in disarray; an *eisteddfod* (pl. *eisteddfodau,* a competitive meeting of bards and musicians) was held in that year to try to bring order into the system, and another followed in 1567.

Shortly afterward, harper-bard Robert ap Huw compiled a manuscript in an attempt to record elements of the bardic tradition in its dying years. Though one page is dated 1613, part of it may have been written by a harper honored in the 1567 *eisteddfod.* Present-day opinion seems to accept that the music was intended for the harp, rather than the crowd. It was written in tablature, substituting the first seven letters of the alphabet for notes on a stave. The music was homophonic, based on a highly systematized treatment of two chords, *tyniad* and *cyweirdant,* which in various combinations made up twenty-four patterns, called measures; the measure (*cainc*) was the smallest complete musical unit out of which longer pieces were made. The notes of the chords were not struck together, but could be varied in order and length, and seventeen types of ornament gave further variety. The manuscript cites five different scales and states that others can be developed from those, probably entailing altered tunings. Because scholars do not agree as to how these scales were tuned, we cannot be sure how the music sounded.

Though Robert ap Huw does not mention singing or declaiming, musical treatises and literature of the period show that the relationship between music and words was exceptionally close. Many acknowledged poets played the harp, and they may well have declaimed their poetry to pieces in this manuscript, for the treatises say these are the pieces singers should know. Sixteenth-century poems indicate that declaiming or singing to a stringed instrument was popular with ordinary people, who substituted their own verses and shorter forms of classical poetry for formal bardic declamation.

THE TRADITION OF PSALMS AND HYMNS

After 1588, when the Bible was translated into Welsh, there was a call for metrical psalms in the vernacular, and in 1621 the first book of psalms with music appeared in Wales. The religious turbulence of the 1600s saw the birth of the simple, folklike *halsingod* of south Wales, some of which were sung on psalm tunes, and the north Wales *plygain* carols set to longer and more complex tunes from Wales, England, and France. The *plygain* service, still to be heard in north Wales and undergoing something of a revival, began when state Protestantism was establishing itself, and probably took the place of the midnight Christmas Mass.

After the Reformation, singing carols became part of the Welsh Christmas service. Poets who wrote carols for the seventeenth- and eighteenth-century *plygain* adapted the intricate alliterative poetic devices of bardic poetry to the meters dictated by the tunes, thus continuing the relationship between music and poetry characteristic of Welsh culture. During the Puritan period and after, when the Christmas carol had almost died out in England, the Welsh carol flourished. This survival was due partly to doctrines embedded in carols, which celebrated the nativity with moral

Poetic competition in song, a feature of the ancient bardic tradition, lived on as a popular entertainment in the 1800s. The harp struck up a tune to start the contest. The feat was twofold: always to enter the tune at the place that would let the singer finish with the harp; and never to repeat a verse.

advice and exhortation, and partly to the social function of the *plygain* in isolated rural areas. The carols are sung, not by the congregation, but by single voices or small groups, one of the commonest being a male trio with the melody in the middle voice (figure 5). The singing is usually unaccompanied, but a 1696 book of carol words directs some carols to be "sung with strings," and the harp is known to have been used.

Hymns, which unlike carols were meant for congregational singing, began to replace metrical psalms in the 1700s, especially after the Methodist revival of 1736. Religious revivals of the 1800s were reflected musically in the flood of hymns that for a time permeated every aspect of Welsh musical culture, and tended to straitjacket some of the old modal tunes into major or minor. Older harmonies, melismas, and fuguing entries gave way to smoother melodies with choralelike harmonies. This change was due largely to two men: John Roberts (known as Ieuan Gwyllt), who collected and arranged the hymns into a standardized volume, and John Curwen, who devised Tonic Sol-fa, a notational system based on a movable *doh,* making publication cheap and music reading easy for the masses. These developments enabled the Cymanfa Ganu, a Welsh hymn-singing festival, to become a medium of musical religious expression throughout the land. They are still held, though in Wales the old enthusiasm has become decorous, and in Welsh communities abroad, the language of the hymns is now sometimes English.

SINGING TO THE HARP IN THE 1700s AND 1800s

Even after the demise of the bardic tradition, the harp continued to be indispensable in secular singing into the modern period. Eighteenth-century manuscripts give examples of this style of singing, called in Welsh *canu gyda'r tannau* 'singing with the strings' or *canu penillion* 'singing verses', where instrumental symphonies are an integral part of the presentation, appearing at the beginning and between verses, or as interpolations in the stanzas of verse. In a performance, the harp began alone; after a few bars, the singer entered with a verse, probably improvising the vocal part to suit the harmonies of the harp and fitting the chosen verse to the length of the tune, with occasional instrumental interludes between verses; the voice and the harp then finished together.

Poetic competition in song, a feature of the ancient bardic tradition, lived on as a popular entertainment with folk verses instead of classical odes. A traveler in 1781 described the custom: the evening began with dancing; later, the harp struck up a tune to start the contest. The feat was twofold: always to enter the tune at the place that would let the singer finish with the harp; and never to repeat a verse—a condition demanding a prodigious memory, or the ability to improvise verses.

The 1700s, with strong antiquarian interests, saw the earliest appearance in print of Welsh music for the harp. The first important publication for the harp was the 1742 collection of twenty-four untitled tunes, *Antient* [sic] *British Music,* compiled in

FIGURE 5 The *plygain* carol "*Ffarwel Ned Puw.*" The singing opens with solos in the treble and tenor voices, followed by a repeated section in three-part harmony, as sung by the brothers known as Parti Fronheulog at a Montgomeryshire Congregational Chapel in 1967.

This is the best morning of all which has made known to the world the birth of the blessed Jesus to bring us out of ignorance. Our great King and Brother appeared in human form. How wonderful to see the Son of God on the fair breast of the Virgin.

This is a wonder that will never cease. May God inspire us to sing joyfully.

A carol which tells a story and nothing else is not enough; the believer needs the experience of the divine Christ.

FIGURE 6   A contest at an 1824 *eisteddfod*, with singers gathered around the harp. Drawing, artist unknown. Courtesy of the Museum of Welsh Life, Cardiff.

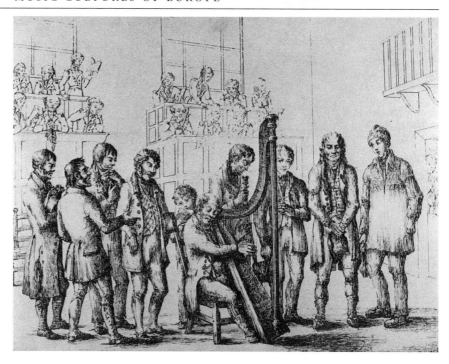

London by Blind John Parry (master of the triple harp) and Evan Williams. In 1781, John Parry published *British Harmony*, a collection of forty-two tunes, many with variations, in simple, tuneful arrangements, without words. Three years later, Edward Jones brought out *Musical and Poetical Relicks of the Welsh Bards*, followed in 1794 by an extended version with 103 tunes arranged in late Baroque and early Classical styles.

During the 1700s, Welsh lifestyles changed. The population grew substantially, and by the end of the century it was largely literate. Industrial development drew people from the sparsely populated uplands, and many customs associated with rural Wales were dying out. The competitive element of the traditional singing had played an essential role in many old customs—nuptial celebrations, Candlemas rituals, and luck visits at the time of the winter solstice. After about 1800, the competitive element began to be transferred more and more to the *eisteddfod*. A drawing of a contest at an 1824 *eisteddfod* shows singers standing around a harp (figure 6). The judges and the harper chose a tune, the singers drew lots to learn who would start, and the harper played the tune through once. On the second playing, the first singer entered the tune with a verse of any meter, at a place that would enable singer and harp to finish together. Then the harper began the tune again, and the second singer entered with another verse in the same meter as the previous contestant's verse. The competition continued until the process eliminated those who had forgotten their words, or had chosen a verse of the wrong meter, or had failed to finish with the harp, and only one was left.

The institution of the *eisteddfod* provided the context for the appearance of the first printed books of Welsh folk songs with Welsh words. The 1837 Abergavenny *eisteddfod* offered a prize for the best collection of "airs, with the words, as sung by the peasantry of Wales" (Huws 1988). The collection of the winner, Maria Jane Williams, a gentlewoman from a family known for its patronage of Welsh bards, formed the nucleus for a book of forty-three songs with accompaniments for harp or pianoforte, *Ancient National Airs of Gwent and Morganwg* (Huws 1988), published in 1844 and dedicated to Queen Victoria.

The growth of industry in the 1800s, particularly in south Wales, concentrated much of the population in towns and cities. The flood of incomers to the industrial areas eventually resulted in a decline in the numbers of Welsh speakers. Street ballads, concerts, music halls, male choirs, and the piano in the parlor took the place of traditional singing to the harp, which increasingly retreated to the upland farming areas of the north. Even there, the harp's traditional status was under threat because of religious revivals that periodically swept the country. Religious enthusiasts condemned its connection with singing and dancing at fairs and taverns, raising the maypole, and the *gŵyl mabsant* (a boisterous patron-saint festival); after a spiritual experience, one harper buried his harp in peat, and one who joined the Methodists threw his harp under the bed, where it fell to pieces. Traditional dancing never recovered, and most Welsh folk dancing today is a reconstruction of old dances, though clog dancing and stepping continued in taverns and stable lofts.

THE REVIVAL OF TRADITION

Increasing educational opportunities in the 1800s boosted professional music-making. Welsh artists of international stature still tended to be either singers or harpists, and composers wrote mostly music for the voice, but this began to change as the end of the 1800s saw the establishment of University Colleges in Wales with departments of music. Between 1900 and 1910, other cultural institutions followed, including the National Library of Wales and the National Museum of Wales, with its later offshoot, the Welsh Folk Museum. From the standpoint of traditional music, however, the most important development was the founding of the Welsh Folk-Song Society, in 1908.

A handful of enthusiasts, including a lecturer in botany, a farmer, a few college students, the English wife of a Welsh member of Parliament, and some classically trained sopranos were the pioneers who collected, arranged, and published songs that would otherwise have been lost. The giant among them was the botanist John Lloyd Williams (1854–1945), who collected more than the rest put together, exhorted others, edited the *Journal of the Welsh Folk-Song Society* from the first issue (1909) until his death, lectured indefatigably, promoted the use of folk songs in schools and in the *eisteddfod,* and established sound analytical principles for Welsh songs (figure 7).

With few exceptions, traditional Welsh tunes or styles of performance have had little or no influence on Welsh composers. Wales has never produced a composer-collector like England's Ralph Vaughan Williams, and the general reaction of classically trained musicians has been apathetic at best. In part, this may be due to sociological factors. The industrial developments that concentrated the population into towns and cities large enough to support concert halls, choirs, and orchestras dealt a mortal blow to the Welsh language in those areas; by about 1950, two-thirds of the population did not speak Welsh or have familiarity with native musical traditions. Young Welsh-speaking musicians were cut off from their traditional roots: until about 1950, Wales supported no musical academies resembling those in England; and until the early 1980s, students training in the music departments of the University of Wales had no access to a course in Welsh traditional music.

Specialist societies formed by amateur enthusiasts, though largely ignored by professional musicians, began to flourish and contribute to the preservation or revival of various aspects of traditional music. Of these, undoubtedly the most important was the establishment (1934) of a society to promote and regulate the tradition of singing to the harp. It was called the Cerdd Dant Society—after a medieval term, *cerdd dant* 'the craft of the string'. Among its aims were the reconsideration and reform of the rules of performance, particularly in competitions such as the National Eisteddfod, held every year in August, and the Cerdd Dant Festival each November. With the arrival of written settings, singing with the harp has been extended beyond

FIGURE 7   Dr. J. Lloyd Williams (1854–1945), probably the most important figure in the history of the Welsh Folk-Song Society. Courtesy of the Museum of Welsh Life, Cardiff.

Traditional musical styles from England and Ireland have been influential, and American country music has long been popular in Wales, giving birth in the 1950s to skiffle bands, which included guitar, banjo, mouth organ, concertina, and washboard.

solo singers to small groups, and even to choirs. The audiences at the *eisteddfod* competitions and the festival are large, knowledgeable, and enthusiastic.

The harp gradually regained its former status. The Welsh Harp Society was formed in 1961, and peripatetic harp teachers popularized the instrument in schools. Increasing affluence has enabled young people, even in mountainous rural districts, to rent or buy harps, and there is no shortage of performers, particularly in connection with *cerdd dant,* though now women predominate.

Folk dancing began to revive and prosper after 1949, when the Welsh Folk Dance Society was started. Numerous people, Welsh-speakers and not, having formed and joined organizations throughout Wales, hold weekend schools to teach traditional dances, compete in various *eisteddfodau,* and dance in festivals abroad.

In all these activities, The National Eisteddfod plays a significant part by providing a focus for performers. It is held for an entire week at the beginning of August in a different place each year, moving alternately between North Wales and South Wales. It aims to include all aspects of culture in Wales, classical and traditional. In a country of about five hundred thousand Welsh speakers, it attracts between fifteen thousand and twenty-five thousand visitors each day to the arts-and-crafts exhibition, the literary pavilion for the poetry competitions, the music studio for the competitions and instrumental performances, and the main pavilion for competitions in the traditional arts of dancing, folksinging, *cerdd dant,* recitation, and classical singing and playing. The Welsh League of Youth promotes Welsh-language activities for young people up to the age of twenty-five, inside and outside schools, and holds its *eisteddfod* annually at the end of May.

Little has been written about the traditional music of the population who do not speak Welsh, and few of their songs have been published. Phil Tanner (1862–1950), a fine Welsh singer who was not Welsh-speaking, favored English songs, such as "The Parson and the Clerk" and "Barbara Allen" (figure 8). A collection of miners' songs from south Wales is mostly in English, though several of the tunes are Welsh. The contemporary folk scene has given rise to Ar Log, Plethyn, Aberjaber, Carreg Lafar, and other new groups, Welsh-speaking and not, which interpret traditional Welsh music in different ways.

The strongest influence in this tradition has been from Ireland. Though some groups have featured such traditionally Welsh instruments as the harp, the bagpipe, the fiddle, and even the crowd, imported folk instruments—*bodhrán* (an Irish frame drum played with a stick), pennywhistle, guitar, bouzouki, mandolin—are even more popular.

Folk clubs abound, a bilingual magazine, *Taplas,* appears every other month, and Sain, an enterprising recording company, puts out everything from mainstream Welsh traditional music to rock-based folk bands and contemporary songs of protest.

Since the early 1980s, S4C, one of the main television channels in Wales, has devoted about thirty hours each week to Welsh-language programs, which include

FIGURE 8   Phil Tanner (1862–1950), a farm laborer and well-known singer from Gower. Courtesy of the Museum of Welsh Life, Cardiff.

broadcasts from The National Eisteddfod, the Welsh League of Youth Eisteddfod, the Cerdd Dant Festival, entertainment by folk-rock groups, and occasionally feature programs with folkloric content.

CHANGE AND ADAPTATION

Since the end of World War II, Wales has seen considerable changes in the purpose, style, and function of its traditional music. Increasing affluence, tourism, and mass media have played an important role in these changes. Affluence has enabled performers to travel to any part of the country by car, carrying large, unwieldy instruments, like harps, and it has increased the number of people who can afford to buy harps, adding substantially to interest in the art of *cerdd dant*. Tourism, radio, television, and record companies have provided new sites for performance and wider audiences, calling for a higher degree of professionalism.

Traditional musical styles from England and Ireland have been influential, and American country music has long been popular in Wales, giving birth in the 1950s to skiffle bands, which included guitar, banjo, mouth organ, concertina, and washboard. Guitars as accompanying instruments began to supersede pianos and harps, except in *cerdd dant*. Irish influence is dominant among the proliferating instrumental groups, and in most cases instruments from other cultures have replaced or augmented the harp and fiddle.

English influence, which has historically been the most pervasive, seems to be less important in Wales today than styles of performance from Ireland and to a lesser extent Brittany. In the 1970s, there was almost no crossover in Wales between English-speaking and Welsh-speaking folk groups, particularly in south Wales. This has begun to change, and in English-speaking areas of Wales it is not uncommon for folk-club guests to sing English songs, followed by local groups singing Welsh songs in English or setting the words of Anglo-Welsh poets to Welsh tunes; however, most Welsh groups that concentrate on singing English material tend to gravitate toward England and do not become part of the Welsh scene. The Pan-Celtic influence, however, in part because it is instrumental and stylistic, rather than linguistic, appeals across a broad spectrum [see CELTIC MUSIC].

Changes are most marked in instrumental music. One of the most important figures in this development is the triple harpist, Robin Huw Bowen (b. 1957), a Welsh-speaker who combines the functions of professional performer, scholar, and music publisher, expanding the instrumental repertoire through his publications of dance tunes transcribed from manuscripts (figure 9). In addition to providing fresh music for the folk-dance revival, this material has stimulated groups of players to meet without dancers from time to time for purely instrumental sessions. The growth of this tradition is reflected in the revival of the *twmpath* (the tump or mound where musicians traditionally stood to play for dancing), which has given its name to a kind of country dancing with callers. The *twmpath*, once replaced by discos, has begun to be popular again for family and communal celebrations, such as weddings, birthday parties, anniversaries, and Parent-Teachers Association evenings. It appeals to all ages, classes, and language groups.

An important development in this area was the establishment, in 1996, of the Society for the Traditional Instruments of Wales, "to safeguard the instrumental tradition in Wales and reinstate it to its rightful place in Welsh life" (*Society Newsletter* 1). Prominent among the members are triple harpist Robin Huw Bowen, Stephen Rees, formerly fiddler in the folk group Ar Log, who lectures in music at the University of Wales at Bangor, and Robert Evans, harp and crowd maker who specializes in early Welsh music. The society, which hopes to awaken interest in crowd, *pib-*

FIGURE 9   Robin Huw Bowen (b. 1957), Welsh triple harpist. Courtesy of the Museum of Welsh Life, Cardiff.

gorn, harp, and fiddle, organizes throughout Wales workshops for traditional music making and teaching and performing sessions at various locations.

Welsh groups have also been active in various styles of popular music, including hard rock, funk, and reggae, where there is some overlap with traditional material. It is not unusual for releases by Welsh-language bands to contain occasional rock settings of traditional songs, and some singers move easily between the two styles. Because few of these bands are full-time professionals, they do not tour extensively outside the British Isles and Brittany, and most groups break up after a few years. Jazz has had only a minor effect on Welsh styles of performance; there are some jazz groups and a major festival, but almost no crossover into Welsh pop or traditional music.

Wales has only two cities of any size, Cardiff and Swansea. Folk clubs and festivals in these places provide an opportunity to hear international groups, many of which also perform in smaller centers and theaters outside the cities. The Welsh folk-club scene, though active, is not economically strong enough to support full-time professional Welsh groups: most musicians, having other jobs, are not free to tour; they perform only at night and on weekends. Apart from club and community activities, much of the work is seasonal, depending on festivals, museum displays, and tourism. Most folk clubs are situated in South Wales, but there are outlets for Welsh-language groups in *eisteddfodau,* festivals, and traditional Welsh entertainment for tourists. *Eisteddfodau* continue to promote competitions for unaccompanied performances of traditional song. Folk festivals, sometimes promoted and in part financed by tourism, have widened the horizons of performers and audiences, increased the repertoire, and encouraged a higher professional standard. These effects have spilled over into some of the folk clubs, where traditional performance is being elevated to the level of concert music—and the audience goes to listen, rather than to participate.

From the 1960s, much Welsh singing has focused on the struggle to save the Welsh language. The leader of this movement is Dafydd Iwan, who, as a student in the late 1960s, started singing the songs of Bob Dylan and Woody Guthrie to his own guitar accompaniment. Fitting traditional Welsh words to the tunes, or translating American folk songs into Welsh, finally led him to write his own words and music, and he is now the most prolific song composer in Wales. His songs, usually written for a social, political, or linguistic purpose, are widely known and sung throughout Welsh-speaking Wales. He is one of the founders of the Sain Record Company, which produces an immense amount of recorded music.

TRACK 7

Possibly the only area of Welsh traditional music that has received no influence from the international folk scene is *cerdd dant.* Though that art developed considerably after the 1940s, its strongest influence is probably from classical music, via Welsh university music students, who have used classical techniques in their settings of the words, particularly those for choirs. Its performance standards are extremely high. Though around 1900 the most proficient performers tended to be men (singing alone with the harp), now choral competitions are the highlight of *cerdd dant* festivals—and these are almost invariably won by women's choirs.

BIBLIOGRAPHY

Barrington, Daines. 1770. "Some Account of Two Musical Instruments Used in Wales." *Archaeologia* 3:30–34.

Blake, Lois. 1975. "The General Characteristics of Welsh Folk Dance." *Dawns* 1974–1975:19–26.

Bullock-Davies, Constance. 1973. "Welsh Minstrels at the Courts of Edward I and Edward

II." *Transactions of the Honourable Society of Cymmrodorion* 1972–1973:104–122.

Cawte, E. C. 1978. "The Mari Lwyd in South Wales." In *Ritual Animal Disguise,* 94–109. Cambridge: D. S. Brewer

Conran, Tony. 1986. *Welsh Verse.* Bridgend: Poetry Wales Press.

Cooper, Barry. 1996. "The Welsh Folk-Song Melodies Set by Beethoven: A Preliminary Investigation." *Welsh Music History* 1: 5–22.

Crossley-Holland, Peter. 1942. "Secular Homophonic Music in Wales in the Middle Ages." *Music and Letters* 23(2):135–162.

————, ed. 1948. *Music in Wales.* London: Hinrichsen Edition.

————. 1968. "The Tonal Limits of Welsh Folk-Song." *Journal of the Welsh Folk Song Society* 5(2):46–73.

Daniell, Alfred. 1910. "Remarks on the Tonality of Some Welsh Melodies." *Journal of the Welsh Folk-Song Society* 1(2):51–59.

————. 1911. "Some Remarks on Certain Vocal Traditions in Wales." *Transactions of the Honourable Society of Cymmrodorion* 1909–1910:4–59.

Dart, Thurston. 1968. "Robert ap Huw's Manuscript of Welsh Harp Music (c. 1613)." *Galpin Society Journal* 22:52–65.

Davies, Malcolm Sior. 1972. "The Pibgorn." *Welsh Music* 4(1):5–10.

de Lloyd, David. 1931. *Forty Welsh Traditional Tunes.* London: Oxford University Press.

Edwards, Hywel Teifi. 1990. *The Eisteddfod.* Cardiff: University of Wales Press.

Edwards, Owain T. 1972. "Music in Wales." In *Anatomy of Wales,* ed. R. Brinley Jones, 207–226. Peterson-super-Ely: Gwerin Publications.

Ellis, Osian. 1991. *The Story of the Harp in Wales.* Cardiff: University of Wales Press.

Evans, Meredydd. 1985. "Deuair Fyrion ac Alawon" (The *deuair fyrion* meter and its tunes). *Canu Gwerin* 8:16–31.

————. 1980–1981. "Y Canu Gwasael yn Llawysgrif Richard Morris o Gerddi" (The wassail songs in the Richard Morris manuscript). *Llên Cymru* 13(3–4):207–235.

————. 1990. "Canu Jim Cro: Caneuon Americanaidd yng Nghymru" (American minstrel songs in Wales). Annual lecture of the Welsh Folk-Song Society.

————. 1996. "Contest Singing." *Welsh Music History* 1:84–91.

Evans, Meredydd, and Kinney, Phyllis. 1981. "Hanes a Datblygiad Canu Gyda'r Tannau" (The history and development of *canu gyda'r tannau*). In *Gŵyr Wrth Gerdd,* 72–91. Welshpool: Cyngor Gwasanaethau Gwirfoddol Clwyd.

Evans, T. C. [Cadrawd, pseud.]. 1991. "Ploughing with Oxen in Glamorgan." *Canu Gwerin* 14:30–39.

Huws, Daniel. 1983. "Dr. J. Lloyd Williams and Traditional Music." *Canu Gwerin* 6:40–46.

————. 1985–1986. "Melus-Seiniau Cymru" (The *Melus-Seiniau* manuscript of Ifor Ceri). *Canu Gwerin* 8:32–50, 9:47–57.

Huws, Daniel, ed. 1988. *Ancient National Airs of Gwent and Morganwg Collected and Arranged by Maria Jane Williams.* London: The Welsh Folk-Song Society.

Jarman, Alfred Owen Hughes, and Gwilym Rees Hughes, eds. 1976, 1979. *A Guide to Welsh Literature.* 2 vols. Swansea: Christopher Davies.

"John Lloyd Williams (1854–1945)." 1995. *Canu Gwerin* 18:3–8.

Jones, Edward. 1825 [1784]. *Musical and Poetical Relicks of the Welsh Bards.* 4th ed. London: R. Rees.

Jones, John [Idris Vychan, pseud.]. 1885. *Hanes ac Henafiath Canu Gyda'r Tannau. An Essay on Penillion Singing.* London: The Honourable Society of Cymmrodorion.

Jones, John Gwynfor. 1981–1983. "Cerdd a Bonedd yng Nghymru" (Music and the gentry in Wales). *Welsh Music* 6(9):22–33, 7(1):25–40, 7(3):3–47.

Jones, Lewis D. 1911. "Hunting the Wren." *Journal of the Welsh Folk-Song Society* 1(3):99–113.

Kennedy, Peter, ed. 1975. *The Folksongs of Britain and Ireland.* London: Cassell & Company.

Kinney, Phyllis. 1979. "The Tunes of 'Yr Hen Benillion.'" *Canu Gwerin* 2:30–45.

————. 1984. "Vocal and Instrumental Interaction in Earlier 'Canu Penillion.'" *Canu Gwerin* 7:28–38.

————. 1986. "Narrow Compass Tunes in Welsh Folk-Song." *Canu Gwerin* 9:12–29.

————. 1988–1989. "The Tunes of the Welsh Christmas Carols." *Canu Gwerin* 11:28–57, 12:5–29.

————. 1994. "Contraboncin, Pigransi" (Country bumpkin, Peg a Ramsey). *Canu Gwerin* 17:18–27.

————. 1996. "An Irish/Welsh Tune Family." *Welsh Music History* 1:114–121.

Kinney, Phyllis, and Meredydd Evans, eds. 1981. *Caneuon Gwerin i Blant* (Folk songs for children). Llandysul: The Welsh Folk-Song Society.

————, eds. 1984, 1987. *Canu'r Cymry* (Welsh folk songs). 2 vols. Arfon: The Welsh Folk-Song Society.

————, eds. 1986. "Canu'r Ychen" (Oxen songs). *Transactions of the Honourable Society of Cymmrodorion,* pp. 99–113.

————, eds. 1993. *Hen Alawon (Carolau a Cherddi) Casgliad John Owen, Dwyran* (Old melodies [carols and songs] collected by John Owen of Dwyran). Cymdeithas: Alawon Gwerin Cymru.

Ley, Rachel. 1996. "Lady Llanover and the Triple Harp." *Welsh Music History* 1:136–143.

Mabsant. 1991. *Casgliad o hoff ganeuon gwerin Cymru: A Collection of Popular Welsh Folk Songs.* Talybont: Y Lolfa.

Morgan, Prys. 1981. *An Eighteenth Century Renaissance.* Llandybie: Christopher Davies.

Owen, Trefor. 1959. *Welsh Folk Customs.* Cardiff: National Museum of Wales, Welsh Folk Musuem.

Parry, John. 1761. *A Collection of Welsh, English and Scotch Airs.* London: John Johnson.

————. 1781. *British Harmony.* London.

Parry, John [Bardd Alaw, pseud.], ed. 1839, 1848. *The Welsh Harper.* 2 vols. London: D'Almaine.

Parry, John, and Evan Williams. 1742. *Antient British Music.* London.

Parry, Thomas. 1955. *A History of Welsh Literature.* Translated by Idris H. Bell. Oxford: Clarendon Press.

Peate, Iowerth C. 1972. "Music and Dance." In *Tradition and Folk Life: A Welsh View,* 86–102. London: Faber & Faber.

Rees, A. J. Heward. 1997. "Henry Brinley Richards (1817–1885): A Nineteenth-Century Propagandist for Welsh Music." *Welsh Music History* 2:173–192.

Richards, Brinley. 1873. *Songs of Wales.* London, New York: Boosey & Hawkes.

Rimmer, Joan. 1965–1966. "The Morphology of the Triple Harp." *Galpin Society Journal* 18:90–103, 19:61–64.

————. 1982. "Telynores Maldwyn: Nansi Richards (1888–1979)." *Welsh Music* 6(10):18–32.

————. 1987. "Edward Jones's Musical and Poetical Relicks of the Welsh Bards, 1784: A Re-Assessment." *Canu Gwerin* 10:26–42.

Roberts, Enid P. 1966. "Marwnadau Telynorion" (Elegies in memory of harpers). *Denbighshire Historical Society Transactions* 15:80–117.

Roberts, Richard. 1829. *Cambrian Harmony.* Dublin and Caernarfon: author.

Rosser, Ann. 1981. *Telyn a Thelynor: Hanes y Delyn yng Nghymru 1700–1900* (Harp and harper: The story of the harper in Wales 1700–1900). Cardiff: National Museum of Wales, Welsh Folk Museum.

Saer, D. Roy. 1969. "The Christmas Carol-Singing Tradition in the Tanad Valley." *Folk Life* 7:14–42.

————. 1974. *Caneuon Llafar Gwlad* (Songs from oral tradition). Cardiff: National Museum of Wales, Welsh Folk Museum.

————. 1974, 1994. *Caneuon Llafar Gwlad: Songs from Oral Tradition.* 2 vols. Cardiff: Welsh Folk Museum, National Museum of Wales.

————. 1977. "An Account of May-Dancing in Holywell." *Dawns* 1976–1977:3–10.

————. 1982. "Llen Gwerin a Defod a Chan" (Folklore and ritual and song). *Canu Gwerin* 5:19–32.

————. 1982–1983. "Y Bibgod yng Nghymru: Rhai Cyfeiriadau Diweddar" (The bagpipe in Wales: Some recent references). *Welsh Music* 7(2):31–38.

————, ed. 1983a. *Famous Fiddlers by the Reverend W. Meredith Morris.* Cardiff: National Museum of Wales, Welsh Folk Museum.

————. 1983b. "Tôn 'Hen Ddarbi' a'i Theulu" (The tune 'Old Darby' and its family). *Canu Gwerin* 1:17–26

————. 1983–1984. "A Midnight *Plygain* at Llanymawddwy Church." *Folk Life* 22:99–106.

————. 1984. "Traditional Dance in Wales During the Eighteenth Century." *Dawns* 1983–1984:5–24.

————. 1985. "Carol y Cymro ac Anthem y

Sais" (God save the king: The Welsh carol and the English anthem). *Welsh Music* 7(9–10):6–17.

Schuurmans, Theo, and D. Roy Saer. 1987. "The Bagpipe." *Taplas* 21:12–15.

Shorland, Jonathan. 1986. "The Pibgorn." *Taplas* 17:15.

Thomas, Ceinwen H. 1974. "Inaugural Address of the Easter Course [The *nantgarw* dances]." *Dawns* 1973–1974:10–22.

Thomas, Gwyn. 1967. *The Caerwys Eisteddfodau.* Cardiff: University of Wales Press.

Thomas, Wyn. 1982. *Traditional Music in Wales: A Bibliography.* Cardiff: National Museum of Wales Welsh Folk Museum.

———, ed. 1987. *Musica: The Robert ap Huw Manuscript.* Facsimile edition. Godstone, Surrey: Gregg International.

———. 1996a. *A Bibliography: Traditional Music in Wales.* Denbigh: Gwasg Gee.

———. 1996b. "John Roberts: 'Telynor Cymru' 1816–1894." *Welsh Music History* 1:173–179.

Vaughan-Jones, Geraint. 1987. *Hen Garolau Plygain* (Old *plygain* carols). Talybont: Y Lolfa.

———. 1990. *Mwy o Garolau Plygain* (More *plygain* carols). Talybont: Y Lolfa.

Wallis, Roger, and Krister Malm. 1983. "Sain Cymru: The Role of the Welsh Phonographic Industry in the Development of a Welsh Language Pop/Rock/Folk Scene." *Popular Music: Producers and Markets* 3:77–105.

Weller, Philip. 1997. "Gerald of Wales's View of Music." *Welsh Music History* 2:1–32.

Williams, Gwyn A. 1985. *When Was Wales?* Harmondsworth, England: Penguin Books.

Williams, J. Lloyd. 1908. "Welsh National Melodies and Folk-Song." *Transactions of the Honourable Society of Cymmrodorion,* 1907–1908:1–46.

———. 1991. "Yr Hwyl Gymreig" (The Welsh *hwyl*). *Canu Gwerin* 14:15–29.

———. 1995. "The History of the Welsh Folk-Song Society." *Canu Gwerin* 18:9–26.

Williams, W. S. Gwynn. 1927. *Old Welsh Folk-Songs.* Llangollen: Gwynn Publishing.

———. 1932. *Welsh National Music and Dance.* London: J. Curwen & Sons.

AUDIOVISUAL RESOURCES

Aber-dau-jaber. 1988. Sain C610N/1410M. Cassette, LP disk.

Ar Lan y Môr (Beside the shore). 1976. Sain C561/1061D. Cassette, LP disk.

Ar Log. 1988. *Ar Log V.* Sain C668N. Cassette.

———. 1991. *O IV i V* (From iv to v). Sain SCD9068. Compact disc.

Bennett Elinor. 1985. *Y Delyn Gymreig* (The Welsh harp). Sain C931/1331D. Cassette, LP disk.

———. 1991. *Telynau a Chân* (Folksongs and harps). Sain C441/SCD4041. Cassette, compact disc.

Bowen, Robert Huw. 1988. *Cyfarch y Delyn* (The harp's greeting). Sain C660. Cassette.

———. 1991. *Cyfarch y Delyn* (Saluting the harp). Sain C474/SCD4074. Cassette, compact disc.

Calennig. 1990. *Dŵr Glan* (Clear water). Sain C425N/SCD4025. Cassette, Compact disc.

———. 1994. *Trade Winds.* Sain C2091N/SCD2091. Cassette, compact disc.

Cân Cymru 2: The Song of Wales 2. 1981. Sain C811G. Cassette.

Caneuon Gwerin i Blant (Folk songs for children). 1984. Sain C909N. Cassette.

Caneuon Llofft Stabal (Stable-loft songs). 1980. Sain C764N. Cassette.

Caneuon y Siroedd (Songs from the old Welsh counties). 1984. Sain C891/1291D. Cassette, LP disk.

Carolau Plygain (Christmas carols). 1977. Cain 700N. Cassette.

Carolau Plygain (*Plygain* carols). 1966. Welsh commentary. St. Fagans, Cardiff: Welsh Folk Museum. 16mm, black-and-white.

Casgliad Gwerin Newydd: New Folk Compilation. 1997. Sain C2146/SCD2146. Cassette, compact disc.

Casglu Caneuon Gwerin yn Llyn (Collecting folksongs in the Llyn Peninsula). 1964. Welsh commentary. St. Fagans, Cardiff: Welsh Folk Museum. 16mm, black-and-white.

Clwt y Ddawns. 1975, 1978, 1982. Sain C535/1035D, C595/1098D, C867/1267D. 3 cassettes and 3 LP disks.

Clychau'r Gôg (Bluebells). 1991. Sain C467. Cassette.

Côr Godre'r Aran. 1981. *Côr Godre'r Aran* (Godre'r Aran male choir). Sain C783/1183D. Cassette, LP disk.

Côr Gwerin y Gader. 1982. *Melys Seiniau* (Sweet sounds). Sain C847/1247D. Cassette, LP disk.

Côr Merched y Garth. 1988. Sain C621. Cassette.

Davies, Aled Lloyd. 1978. *Hen Win* (Old wine). Sain C717/1117D. Cassette, LP disk.

Davies, Walter Haydn, and Ifor Owen. 1980. *Mining Ballads and Pieces.* Private recording. Cassette.

Dolmetsch, Mable. 1937. *Excerpts from the Penllyn Manuscript.* The Early Welsh Music Society, DR1–DR3. 3 78-RPM disks.

Ebillion, Bob Delyn a'r. 1990. *Sgwarnogod Bach Bob* (Bob's little hares). [Sain] Crai C005A. Cassette.

Ebillion, Bob Delyn a'r. 1993. *Gedon.* Sain CF52E. Video.

Ellis, Osian. 1969. *17th and 18th Century Harp Music.* Decca (L'Oiseau Lyre) SOL 309. LP disk.

———. 1990. *Clymau Cytgerdd: Diversions.* Sain C438/SCD4038. Cassette, compact disc.

Endaf Emlyn. 1974. *Salem.* Sain 1012M. LP disk.

Evans, Meredydd. 1954. *Welsh Folk Songs.* Folkways Records FP835. LP disk.

———. 1962. *Traditional Welsh Songs.* Tradition Everest TR 2078-A. LP disk.

———. 1977. *Merêd.* Sain C576/1076D. Cassette, LP disk.

The Fruitful Year. 1951. Brunner Lloyd Co.: Central Film Library, London. 16mm and 35mm, black-and-white; English commentary.

Gorau Gwerin (The best of Welsh folk music). 1984, 1986. Sain C878G/1278H, C933G/1333H. 2 cassettes, 2 LP disks.

Gorau Gwerin (The best of Welsh folk music). 1992. Sain SCD2006. Compact disc.

Gŵyl Gerdd Dant y Bala a'r Bylch (The Bala *cerdd dant* festival). 1983. Sain C884. Cassette.

Iwan, Dafydd. 1979. *Bod yn Rhydd* (Being free). Sain C558/1250M. Cassette, LP disk.

———. 1990. *Bod yn Rhydd/Gwinllan a Roddwyd.* Sain SCD 8085. Compact disc.

Iwan, Dafydd, et al. 1990. *Dafydd Iwan yng Nghorwen.* Sain CF80C. Video.

James, Siân. 1992. *Cysgodion Karma* (The shadows of karma). Sain C437N/SCD4037. Cassette, compact disc.

Jenkins, Tomi. 1991. *Folk Songs of Swansea and Gower.* Sain C483. Cassette.

Llanelli Male Choir. 1991. *Goreuon Côr Meibion Llanelli.* Sain SCD7034. Compact disc.

Mabsant. 1983. *A Trip to Glamorgan.* Folktrax 60–054. Cassette.

———. 1990. *Tôn Gron* (Round). Fflach C075G. Compact disc.

Mari Lwyd/The Mari (The Mari Lwyd wassailing ceremony). 1966. Welsh commentary. St. Fagans, Cardiff: Welsh Folk Museum. 16mm, black-and-white.

Meibion Menlli. 1981. *Tân Glyndwr* (Glyndwr's fire). Sain C524/1024D. Cassette, LP disk.

Miner's Pittances. 1975. Folktrax FTX 60–055. Cassette.

Mynediad am Ddim. 1978. *Torth o Fara* (A loaf of bread). Sain C737N/1137M. Cassette, LP disk.

———. 1993. *Dyma Mynediad am Ddim.* Sain CF49C. Video.

Penceirddiaid Cymru. 1997. *Penceirddiaid Cymru.* Sain C2130/SCD2130. Cassette, compact disc.

Phil Tanner. 1967–1968. English Folk Dance and Song Society: Folk Classics Series, LP1005. LP disk.

Plethyn. 1979. *Blas y Pridd* (The taste of earth). Sain C745N. Cassette.

———. 1984. *Caneuon Gwerin i Blant* (Folksongs for children). Sain 1309/C909N. Cassette, LP disk.

———. 1991. *Blas y Pridd/Golau Tan Gwmwl.* Sain SCD6045. Compact disc.

Plygain. 1977. St. Fagans, Cardiff: Welsh Folk Museum. Color; English commentary. Video.

Richards, Nansi. 1973. *The Art of Nansi Richards.* Qualiton Squad 115, Sain Cambrian DCRC 331. LP disk.

———. 1975. *Harps and Hornpipes: Music and Memories of Welsh Gipsies* [sic]. Folktrax FTX-053-C60. Cassette.

———. 1980. *Nansi Richards: The Bells of Aberdovey.* Folktrax FTX 60– 351. Cassette.

Roberts, Bob. 1976. *Bob Roberts Tai'r Felin 1.* Sain C558G/1058H. Cassette, LP disk.

Roberts, Bob, and John Thomas. 1976. *Bob Roberts a John Thomas.* Sain C568G/1068H. Cassette, LP disk.

Saer, D. Roy. 1977. *Carolau Plygain* (*Plygain* carols). Sain C700N/1100M. Cassette, LP disk.

———. 1980. *Caneuon Llofft Stabal* (Stable-loft songs). Sain C764N/1164M. Cassette, LP disk.

Saith Rhyfeddod (Seven wonders). 1977. Sain C700N. Cassette.

Step y Glocsen (Clog dancing). 1960. St. Fagans, Cardiff: Welsh Folk Museum. 16mm, black-and-white.

Tanner, Phil. N.d. *Phil Tanner.* English Folk Dance and Song Society, Folk Classics Series LP 1005. LP disk.

———. 1975. *Phil Tanner: Folksinger of the Gower Peninsula.* Folktrax FTX 60–057. Cassette.

Telyn Cymru (The harp of Wales). 1976, 1977, 1978, 1979, 1982. Sain C523/1023D, C580/1080D, C736/1136D, 1160D, C849/1249D. 4 cassettes, 5 LP disks.

Telyn Teilo Choir. 1994. *Goreuon Côr Telyn Teilo* (The best of the Telyn Teilo Choir). Sain SCD2093. Compact disc.

Thomas, John, and Elizabeth Thomas. 1975. *Old Welsh Ballads and Penillion.* Folktrax FTX 60–051. Cassette.

Tomi Jenkins. 1991. Sain C483. Compact disc.

Traditional Welsh Music. 1981. Adlonni Audio Tapes AH2. Cassette.

Trelawnyd. 1981. *Folk Songs of Wales.* Sain C802/1202D. Cassette, LP disk.

Welsh and English Songs from Pembrokeshire. 1975. Folktrax FTX 60–052. Cassette.

Williams, Sioned. 1981. *Harp Music by John Parry.* Meridian E45002. LP disk.

Wood, Hywel. 1962–1963. *Hywel Wood yn Ffair y Bala* (Hywel Wood at Bala Fair). St. Fagans, Cardiff: Welsh Folk Museum. 16mm, black-and-white; silent.

Y Delyn (The Welsh harp). 1968. Welsh commentary. St. Fagans, Cardiff: Welsh Folk Museum. 16mm, black-and-white.

Y Delyn Deir-rhes (The queen of harps). 1970. Welsh commentary. St. Fagans, Cardiff: Welsh Folk Museum. 16mm, black-and-white.

Y Fari Lwyd/The Mari (The Mari Lwyd wassailing ceremony). 1961. St. Fagans, Cardiff: Welsh Folk Museum. 16mm, black-and-white; Welsh commentary.

Scotland

James Porter

Song and Instrumental Music
History of Music
Performers and Contexts
The Folk-Music Revival
History of Collection and Research

With a population of 5 million that has remained stable for a century, Scotland occupies the northern part of Great Britain and lies on the North Atlantic sea route between Ireland and Scandinavia. Historically, this position has affected its patterns of settlement and culture, though influences from the continent and even the Mediterranean are evident. Scotland's stormy past reflects invasions by Celts, Romans, Vikings, Normans, English, and others before and after the beginning of the Christian era. These invasions set up regions (in a land of almost 80,000 square kilometers) and religious affiliations critical to Scotland's cultural and political diversity: the Highland and Lowland division; northeast (conservative, Scandinavian-derived) and southwest (progressive, Celtic-inflected); Roman Catholic in the southern and Presbyterian in the northern Hebrides. Apart from the industrial belt between the cities of Glasgow and Edinburgh, Scotland has large tracts of mountainous terrain (north and west) and agricultural land (east and southwest), as well as hundreds of offshore islands.

In addition to English, Scotland maintains two languages, Gaelic and Scots. Gaelic has receded since the 1700s, but is still spoken in the Hebridean islands and pockets of the western mainland. Scots, in many regional dialects, is the vernacular language of the Lowlands. Both languages have given rise to musical genres that interact and overlap in melody and theme.

SONG AND INSTRUMENTAL MUSIC

Two distinct musical regions can be distinguished: the Highlands and Hebridean Islands, and the Lowlands and Northern Isles.

Highlands and Hebridean Islands vocal music

Gaelic-speakers perpetuate musical genres attached to the life cycle and the pastoral, clan-based society before 1700. Lullabies and laments, which often drew on related melodic material because of their social function and shared features in their refrains, can be related to two of three ancient divisions of Celtic music: those for sorrow (lament) and sleep (lullaby); that for laughter (dance-music) was the third. As with many Gaelic songs, the refrain precedes the verses. A lament such as "*Grigor*

FIGURE 1 Women sing while waulking (shrinking) tweed in the Hebrides Islands. Photo by W. Kissling, 1934. Courtesy of School of Scottish Studies, The University of Edinburgh.

Criodhal" ('Beloved Gregor'), which dates from 1570, refers to the execution of Gregor of Glenstrae by his father-in-law, Duncan Campbell of Glenlyon, who thought him unworthy to marry his daughter. The song, possibly composed by Gregor's widow, uses the lullaby formula *Ba ba mo leanabh* "Ba, ba, my child." Verbal and melodic formulas may stem from earlier times in suggesting magical or protective power; charms were recorded in the Hebrides during the twentieth century. The presence of history, in songs of clan warfare, and the overtones of natural magic in Gaelic songs have kept them alive despite the predicted demise of the language.

Hebridean labor songs accompanied milking, churning, dandling infants, rowing, and other activities integral to a pastoral society. Of special note are songs for waulking (shrinking) the tweed, a process performed by women until the introduction of technology in the twentieth century. Because tweed was important to the economy, care was taken in its manufacture, which involved spinning and carding the sheep's wool, soaking the cloth in urine, and shrinking the cloth by pounding it by hand while passing it clockwise around a table for an extended time (figure 1).

The repertoire of waulking songs, which involves a call-and-response pattern, is enormous and drew its themes and melodies from diverse sources. Repetition of any song was considered bad luck, but the chorus is sung after every line to prolong the song, and repetition within text and melody is evident. "*Am Bron Binn*" ('The Sweet Sorrow') is also sung as a lay (*laoidh* or *duan* 'narrative song', figure 2). It tells of a beautiful woman who beheads King Arthur:

> The King of Scotland saw in a dream
> The woman of fairest hue under the sun.
> He would rather be beloved of her
> Than to converse with a man like himself.
> Fios-falaich spoke to Fiann:
> "I shall go seek her for you
> I and my servant, and my dog
> The three of us, to seek the woman."

FIGURE 2 The narrative song (lay) *Am Bron Binn* ('The Sweet Sorrow'), as sung by Mrs. Kate MacCormick of Benbecula. Recorded by J. L. Campbell. Transcribed by Francis Collinson. After Collinson 1966:47.

'S chunnaic Righ Al–(a)ba   'na shuain   'N aon– a bhean bu ghil– e snuagh fo'n ghréin,

'S gum b'fheàrr leis tuit–eam dha cion, Na còmhr–adh fir mar bha(a) fhéin. Labh–air Fios Fal–aich gu fi–al,

Théid mis– e' ga h–iarr–aidh dhut, Mi fhìn 's mo ghill– e 's mo chù Na còmhr–adh fir mar bha a fhéin.

Unusually, the verse in this rendition comes first.

The themes of the lay deal with legendary heroic figures: Fionn, Fraoch, Ossian, and their adventures. The first lay to be written down, "*Laoidh Mhanus*" (by the Rev. Patrick MacDonald in 1784), was recorded as late as 1968 in the Hebrides with similarities in text and tune. The "Lay of Fraoch" illustrates the declamatory style of some singers (figure 3). The Gaelic text of stanza 1 shows the style.

Medieval bards employed meters based on the number of syllables per line (syllabic meters), but later came to use the stressed meters more common in Western Europe. Traditionally the province of male bards, lays have been recorded from women and men in the twentieth century.

Bards used music to praise or satirize the chieftain or his family. Some musicians were itinerant in Scotland and Ireland: Ruairidh Dall Morrison (ca. 1656–ca. 1714), who had studied *clàrsach* 'harp' in Ireland, returned to work for the chieftain of Clan MacLeod at Dunvegan Castle in Skye. With the dispersal of the clans after the Battle of Culloden (1746), bards, harpers, and pipers lost their patrons. Many bards sailed with their clanspeople to the New World, where they coined heartfelt elegies praising their homeland (MacDonell 1982). What evolved in their place, after harsh anti-Gaelic laws and the emigration of the Highland Clearances, were local bards, singers, and composers. Such a local bard in recent times was Calum Ruadh Nicholson (1902–1978) of Skye, who composed satires and laments that were recorded in the 1960s.

Psalm singing in the strictly Protestant areas of the northern Hebrides and mainland developed a unique character. Congregations still sing only the Psalms of David in Gaelic (no hymns or organ are permitted) in an elaborate, long-drawn-out style guided by a precentor who lines out the psalm—that is, he sings each line of text before the congregation responds by repeating the line [see WAYS OF TRANSMITTING MUSIC]. In home worship, the singing is more ornamental, at times like the decora-

FIGURE 3 The "Lay of Fraoch" employs a declamatory style characteristic of the genre. Recorded by P. McCaughery and Fred Kent, 1965. Transcription by James Porter.

Laigh éa–   slain– te throm,   throm   Air nigh–ean Maigh– re nan còrn fi– al:

Sin   'nuair chuir i fios air fra– och   'S dh'fhios– raich a' laoch gu dé 'mi– ann.

A sore, sore sickness fell upon the daughter of Maighre of the bounteous goblets;
That was when she sent for Fraoch, and the warrior asked what was her wish.

FIGURE 4 A Gaelic song about fairies, as sung by Flora MacNeil. After Purser 1992:30.

A phiu– thrag 's a phiu– thar,   Hù   rù;   A ghaoil, a phiu– thar,   Hù   rù,   Nach tru– agh leat fhéin,   Hó ha– la leó,   A nochd   mo chu–mha   Hù   rù.

tions of *piobaireachd,* and builds its devotional character from a heterophonic texture set by a lead singer. These styles have analogs in Denmark and Norway, but nowhere else is the performance so intense; the syllabic tunes of the sixteenth-century Reformers are now severely devotional melodies that match the people's piety.

The current impetus in Gaelic secular folk song stems from a few older singers, such as William Matheson of North Uist and Flora MacNeil of the mostly Roman Catholic island of Barra. MacNeil's repertoire includes a song that echoes Highland belief in the preternatural: a girl carried off by fairies to a nearby hill tells her sister how she may be rescued (figure 4). A younger generation of singers has come to prominence through competing in the National Mod, an annual gathering of Gaelic speakers held since 1892. Local Mods, too, offer a context for gifted instrumentalists and singers to renew the tradition. These competitions have been geared to the expectations of outside adjudicators, whose authority has been open to question. But younger singers, such as Anne Lorne Gillies, Mairi MacInnes, Karen Matheson, and Christine Primrose, recreate local traditions with songs tied to specific landscapes or historical events, communicating their art through television programs, commercial recordings, and videotapes.

Highlands and Hebridean Islands instrumental music

Pipers were also part of the clan retinue, and whole families (MacCrimmons, MacArthurs) evolved traditions of teaching and composition, e.g., by the use of mnemonic syllables, which influence pipers today. The Highland bagpipe chanter has a nine-note scale of g′–a′–b′–c♯″–d″–e″–f♯″–g″–a″ and the instrument has two tenor drones on a and one bass drone on A (figure 5). A major form that emerged in the 1600s was *piobaireachd* (English pibroch, "piping"), which may have evolved from clan-gathering tunes or laments. *Piobaireachd* (or better, *ceòl mór* 'great music') is a theme-and-variation form that can test a piper's mastery, especially in the cumulative effect of proliferating grace notes as the variations advance until the music returns to the theme or ground (*urlar*) at its conclusion. The singing of pibroch vocables (*canntaireachd*) was often linked to *port-a-beul* 'mouth music', for dancing when no instrument was available, especially after the harsh laws imposed by the British government on the Highlands after the battle of Culloden. Realizing the powerful effect of massed bagpipers, the government enlisted pipers as part of its army, and still does. The dispersal of Scottish pipers over the British Empire spread the assertive sound of the instrument into countries that had bagpipes of their own, from continental Europe to India, displacing or dominating indigenous instruments through sheer volume of sound.

Bagpipe music includes song, march, and dance tunes (*ceòl beag* 'little music'), a suite of which forms the basis of modern piping competitions (figure 6). Bagpipe and clan associations flourish throughout the Anglophone world, an index of the massive emigration of the 1700s and 1800s: the World Pipe Band Championship competition has been won by a Canadian band. Contemporary pipers of recognized skill who also compose tunes include John D. Burgess, John MacFadyen, Robert Wallace, Allan MacDonald, and Murray Henderson (from New Zealand). Alex Duthart intro-

FIGURE 5 Calum Johnston plays the bagpipes at his home, Eoligarry, Barra. A blowpipe fills the bag with air, which then passes over a double reed in the chanter and single reeds in the three dronepipes. Photo by Peter Cooke, 1972. Courtesy of School of Scottish Studies, The University of Edinburgh.

The lyrics of songs of rural life often refer to plowing, seedtime, and harvest, metaphors for physical love. Later nineteenth-century songwriters often sanitized such songs for middle-class taste.

FIGURE 6 The slow air "Maiden of Morven," as played with characteristic ornamentation on the bagpipes. After MacLellan 1988:35.

duced Swiss styles into Scottish drumming, and virtuoso side-drum performance is part of the pipe-band repertoire (Boag 1975).

The *clàrsach* (harp), obsolescent in Scotland and Ireland by about 1800, was revived at the first Mod in 1892. It was further boosted by the Clàrsach Society in 1931. The number of skilled players today includes Patsy Seddon and Mary McMaster of the group Sileas. Some harpists play the older wire-strung harp as well as the later version with gut strings. The fiddle, which had begun to displace the bagpipe in the more domesticated taste of the middle classes after 1700, took over much of the piping repertoire and added more dance tunes. Niel Gow, the most famous Highland fiddler, composed tunes that imitate the bagpipe scale and the characteristic double-tonic device: figuration repeated a whole tone below or above. A pupil of Niel Gow, James McIntosh, taught the grandfather of Hector MacAndrew, one of the skilled twentieth-century fiddlers in the Northeast.

The folk revival has led to the formation of pop groups who draw from Gaelic tradition: Na h-Oganaich and Runrig, in particular, mix their song tradition with rock music. Runrig, with members from Skye and other Hebridean islands, are steeped in Hebridean tradition but adapt their compositions in rock arrangements [see CELTIC MUSIC]. One song, "*Tir an airm*" ('Land of the Army'), protests against militarism and the British government's exploitation of the Hebrides and its people.

The band's video, *City of Lights,* which contains Gaelic- and English-language songs, won a major prize at the 1991 Celtic Film and Television Festival.

Lowland and Northern Isles songs

The Lowland tradition is noted for ballads and lyric songs. The ballad focuses on a single incident and weds the plot and stanzaic form to a concise, rounded tune. Ballads arose in the late Middle Ages as the favored genre of a merchant class, but the genre itself is heterogeneous. Narrative content tends to the familial and domestic: many types work out, often tragically, a triangular love relationship; other topics are battles and historical events. Ancient tales appear in ballads recovered in modern times: that of "King Orfeo," collected in the Shetland Isles in 1880 and 1947, tells the classical legend of Orpheus as he plays the "notes of joy" and the "notes of noy" (unhappiness), a contrast that recalls the ancient Celtic division of music into types for laughter, sorrow, and sleep.

The Scots language emerged in the 1100s. Ballads with otherworld themes, such as that of "Thomas the Rhymer," "Tam Lin," "The Great Silkie of Sule Skerry," and "The Wife of Usher's Well," reflect older beliefs. Historical or legendary events also appear in ballad form. The date of their composition remains uncertain, and "history" is dramatic rather than factual, as in "The Battle of Otterburn," an affray between the English Percys and the Scottish Douglasses in 1388, and "Harlaw," a battle between Donald, Lord of the Isles, and the Earl of Mar over disputed territory in 1411. Ahistorical ballads—"Edward," "The Broomfield Hill," "Sweet William's Ghost," and others—treat familial relationships in a stoic, nonjudgmental vein. Later types, with more recognizable historical figures, e.g., "Andrew Lammie" and "The Laird o' Drum," are still sung in the Northeast. The industrial lowlands also produced ballads: "The Blantyre Explosion" and "The Starlaw Disaster" commemorate twentieth-century mining tragedies (Henderson 1992).

The lyrics of songs of rural life often refer to plowing, seedtime, and harvest, metaphors for physical love. "The Shearin's No' for You" tells of a young woman whose pregnancy prevents her bending to shear the wheat. Later nineteenth-century songwriters often sanitized such songs for middle-class taste; for example, "The Shearin'" became the genteel "Kelvingrove." Ploughmen in the reign of Queen Victoria (1819–1901) evolved the bothy song, especially in northeast Scotland, where the bothy was housing for seasonal farm laborers. Though celebrating the all-male farmhand life, these songs cast a wry look at social mores, criticizing thankless toil and poor wages.

Ballads and songs are transmitted orally and by print. Hawkers sold chapbooks and broadsheets widely in the 1700s and 1800s, recirculating songs to rural and urban populations and adding topical items. Songwriters penned political ballads at the time of Union with England (1707) and continued with Jacobite, anti-Hanoverian songs in the 1800s. In the twentieth century, Ewan MacColl, Norman Buchan, Andy Hunter, and others renewed a tradition of protest or satirical songs: Hamish Henderson's "Freedom Come-All-Ye" and "Free Mandela" were composed during the Cold War and the nuclear weapons race. Political songs are largely pro-freedom, antiroyalist, and anti-Westminster, as the movement for national independence has grown since World War II.

Lowland and Northern Isles instrumental music

The fiddle has been the instrument most favored since the 1700s. In the twentieth century, the bandleader Jimmy Shand developed a combination of fiddles, accordion, piano, and drum set playing in strict tempo. Regional tradition is strong in the northeast and especially in the Shetland Isles, where almost every house has a fiddle hanging on the wall. The whaling tradition of the 1800s led to the composition of many Shetland tunes: ships from southern ports would take a fiddler on board as they steamed north to the whaling grounds. The Shetland style is energetic and flowing; brilliant exponents (e.g., Tom Anderson, Aly Bain) have won it admirers within the Revival (Cooke 1986).

The *clàrsach* (harp) has Highland and Lowland adherents: exponents include Alison Kinnaird, Marie-Louise Napier, Rhona Mackay, Judith Peacock, Wendy Stewart, and Savourna Stevenson. The bagpipe, like the harp, has not been exclusively Highland since the eighteenth century, when the British Government formed Scottish regiments for its colonial wars. Thus the Highland bagpipe has been cultivated by players who are neither Highland nor even Scottish. It has been used in Revival groups (e.g., the Battlefield Band) and classical music (e.g., Peter Maxwell Davies' *An Orkney Wedding*). The Lowland bagpipe, in construction bellows-blown but with a chanter and three drones, died out in the early 1800s but has been revived by skilled players, such as Gordon Mooney and Hamish Moore. An array of instruments besides the harp, bagpipe, and fiddle was traditionally used in popular contexts: the mouth harp (trump) and hornpipe (stock and horn) were later joined or displaced by the accordion and, in the Revival period, by guitar, saxophone, bouzouki, and world-music instruments.

HISTORY OF MUSIC

Early history shows Scotland to have a shared musical culture with Ireland. The oldest fragment (ca. eighth century B.C.) is that of a bronze side-blown horn that resembles Irish types. These, like the end-blown horns buried with them, were probably played by circular breathing and may have had a ritual significance. Rock gongs have also been identified as a means, perhaps, for creating pitched rhythms that held preternatural significance. Horns were also used at a later date for gathering kinfolk. From the historical period a bronze Celtic war trumpet, the carnyx, was found in the Northeast and is contemporary with the Roman occupation (first century A.D.).

Christianity brought with it the *cruit*, a small, triangular handheld harp or lyre which accompanied missionaries from Ireland. The larger triangular harp, developed later, is shown on the Pictish symbol stones that stand along the Northeastern coast. The Picts, whose origins are obscure and who later merged with Celts of Irish origin, left a number of these standing stones, many depicting a musician who is probably King David. The triangular frame harp as we know it was developed in the border area between Pict, Celt, and Northumbrian culture since both harp and lyre are carved on an eighth-century cross from northeast England. Special types of singing were developed by Celtic monks, and early Celtic chant is contained in the thirteenth-century *Inchcolm Antiphoner*. The sequence, a genre prominent mainly on the continent from 850 to 1150, probably originated in Celtic text and music (Crocker 1977). Another medieval link to Europe is the famous mid-thirteenth-century *St. Andrews Music Book*, compiled at St. Andrews and removed to Wolfenbüttel, Germany, in 1553. It contains, in addition to music of the French school of Leonin and Perotin, important native pieces (conductus, tropes, motets) written for the Cathedral of St. Andrews, the primary ecclesiastical center in Scotland in the late Middle Ages (Hiley 1980).

The Renaissance brought brilliant composers, such as Robert Douglas and especially Robert Carver (ca. 1485–ca. 1568), who was aware of Flemish masters such as Guillaume Dufay. Polyphonic settings of the Mass (e.g., *Missa L'Homme Armé*) and motets (e.g., the nineteen-part *O Bone Jesu*) show Carver experimenting with novel harmonies and textures (Darvas 1975). Much of his output is extant in the *Carvor Choirbook* (ca. 1500–ca. 1560), with pieces written in his own hand (Woods 1984).

After 1560, the Reformers urged a plain, syllabic style of singing in church, though ornamental singing by Lowland congregations survived into the 1700s (Bremner 1765). A significant figure in this stressful Reformation period is Robert Johnson (ca. 1500–ca. 1560), a priest who fled to England and wrote homophonic anthems in English instead of polyphonic settings in Latin: his anthem "Defyled is my name" has traditionally been linked with Anne Boleyn (d. 1536). More dutiful composers of Reformed church music included Andro Blackhall, Andrew Kemp, and David Peebles; Thomas Wood's *Partbooks* (1562–ca. 1592) contain revealing vocal styles from this period.

The Lowland instrumental tradition developed in the 1600s around the cittern, lute, lyra-viol, spinet, or virginals, for the last of which William Kinloch wrote his brilliant piece "The Battle of Pavie" (ca. 1610). Kinloch used extended variation structure in his galliards and other keyboard compositions (Elliott 1958, 1967). That instruments were widely cultivated by affluent or noble families is evident from the number of manuscripts compiled between 1680 and 1740 (Johnson 1972). In the 1700s, the fiddle, harpsichord (or fortepiano), and German flute (introduced in 1725) emerged as the preferred instruments of the monied classes.

In the Highlands, a group of bards emerged that reflected the looming crisis for their society: Mary MacLeod (ca. 1615–ca. 1706) praised the music of harp, pipe, and fiddle; Iain Luim MacDonald (1625–?) composed a famous elegy on the Battle of Inverlochy (1645); Sileas MacDonald (ca. 1660–ca. 1730) probably played *clàrsach* to accompany her "Lament for Blind Lachlan"; Ruairidh Dall Morrison (ca. 1656–ca. 1714) composed the well-known "Lament for the Lost Harp Key." Rob Donn Mackay, Alexander MacDonald, and Duncan Ban Macintyre were other outstanding poets. In the 1750s, Duncan Ban composed a splendid song of more than five hundred lines, "*Moladh Ben Dorain*" (in praise of a mountain), intended to be sung like a *piobaireachd,* with theme and variations.

Composition in the Lowlands blossomed after the Union (1707). James Oswald, Robert Bremner, and William McGibbon, talented writers of the "Scotch tunes" that came into vogue in London and elsewhere, were also publishers. Social dancing had returned to fashion, and demand for hornpipes, jigs, reels, and strathspeys gave musicians Nathaniel Gow, William Marshall, and Donald Dow opportunities to write jaunty, sixteen-bar tunes that are still performed. Violin makers such as Matthew Hardie began a long line of these up to the present. The Earl of Kelly, born in 1732, studied composition in Mannheim, Germany, and produced symphonies, string quartets, and trio sonatas; the Scots piano builder John Broadwood (also b. 1732) took his family enterprise to London in 1761.

The flute, violin, and harpsichord (or piano) were used by Beethoven, Haydn, and others in mostly inept arrangements of Scottish tunes for the publisher George Thomson. These composers, clearly puzzled by the modality of the tunes and effects derived from bagpipe technique (such as the double tonic or a freely pentatonic structure), could not understand why some tunes did not end on the "tonic" or home key. Yet by 1800, the fame of Scottish minstrelsy had spread to Europe, first through James Macpherson's *Ossian* poems (1760), then through the works of Robert Burns (1759–1796) and Sir Walter Scott (1771–1832). An astonishing array of composers, from Bizet, Brahms, and Donizetti to Rossini, Schubert, and Schumann wrote works based on, or inspired by, Scottish or Ossianic themes (Fiske 1983).

Popular songs in the vernacular form a huge subclass. Burns collected more than two hundred of them for James Johnson's *The Scots Musical Museum* (1787–1803). Many reworked by Burns closely resemble genuine folk songs. Though Stephen

After the disintegration of the clan system, Queen Victoria and the British establishment embraced Highland life and customs with their patronage. The art of piping was transmitted often within the context of the British Army.

Clarke arranged the tunes, Burns was also a useful musician (Bronson 1969:307). His songs "My Luve Is Like a Red, Red Rose," "Ae Fond Kiss," and "Ay Waukin O" are fine examples of refurbishing old tunes (or new ones, as by James Oswald) with words. In identifying with popular tradition, Burns occupies a central role, not simply in the preservation, but also in the recomposition of vernacular song.

At the popular level, women were the chief carriers of ballads and songs—hardly surprising, given the economic realities of male outdoor work and the link between ballads and domestic life. Later in the 1700s, women from the upper classes—including Mrs. Grant of Carron, Joanna Baillie, Lady Wardlaw, and Lady Nairne—wrote songs. The context, however, moved from the fields into the drawing room, and sentimental pastiche tended to take the place of real experience. At the same time, popular chapbooks recycled material of a more political cast: the ballad "Jamie Raeburn" (ca. 1820), about the deportation of a Glasgow man widely believed innocent, sold a hundred thousand copies.

Burns influenced most vernacular songwriting in the nineteenth century, just as Mendelssohn did for middle-class musical taste. The pianoforte, moreover, began to dominate the arrangements of such songs. John Thomson (1805–1841), Finlay Dun (1795–1853), and others worked in the extended forms of Romanticism; Mendelssohn met Thomson and admired one of his trios. Later, Alexander Mackenzie (1847–1935) and Hamish MacCunn (1868–1916) contributed orchestral and chamber works. Mackenzie had personal contact with continental musicians of his time: Liszt, Sarasate, Hans von Bulow, Paderewski, and Grieg (a descendant of the Scottish family of Greig; see Gavin Greig, below).

MacCunn's opera *Jeannie Deans* (1894), based on Scott's novel *The Heart of Midlothian,* was successful in London and Edinburgh. William Wallace (1860–1940), Learmont Drysdale (1866–1909), and John MacEwen (1868–1948) also drew on national themes. In contrast, James Scott Skinner (1843–1927) was a traditional fiddler who combined classical technique with vernacular idiom for his airs, reels, and strathspeys. Marjory Kennedy-Fraser (1857–1930) adapted Highland songs she collected for concert performance, not entirely with success.

After the disintegration of the clan system, Queen Victoria and the British establishment embraced Highland life and customs with their patronage. The last of the great hereditary pipers, Donal Ruadh MacCrimmon, had died in 1825, but the art was transmitted through pupils, often within the context of the British Army. Angus MacKay, the queen's official piper, was succeeded by William Ross, and both published collections of pipe music. In 1778, the Highland Society of London instituted annual pibroch competitions that continue today, but a shortage of pipers able to master pibroch led to the founding of the Piobaireachd Society (1902).

In the twentieth century, composers had to struggle against public indifference. Francis George Scott (1880–1958) is noted for his settings of Hugh MacDiarmid's poetry. Erik Chisholm (1904–1965), who authored a violin concerto and two piano concertos as well as operas, was a formidable organizer: the first in the world to mount a complete performance of Berlioz's opera *The Trojans* (in Glasgow, 1935), he organized more than two hundred first performances, many of them by the composers, including Béla Bartók and Paul Hindemith. The conductor of the BBC Scottish Orchestra from 1945, Ian Whyte (1901–1960), was one of the few composers to pair the bagpipes with the symphony orchestra in his ballet *Donald of the Burthens* (1951). Cedric Thorpe Davie (1913–1983) wrote music for films (e.g., Disney's *Rob Roy*) and the theater.

Robin Orr (b. 1909), mainly a composer of songs and operas, helped found Scottish Opera and assumed the chair at the University of Glasgow (founded 1929). Donald Francis Tovey (1875–1940), Reid Professor at Edinburgh, forged an international reputation as a music analyst. Iain Hamilton (b. 1922), Thea Musgrave (b. 1928), and Thomas Wilson (b. 1928) have made their names in opera and symphonic composition. Musgrave and Wilson have used Scottish subjects for their operas *Mary, Queen of Scots* (1977) and *Confessions of a Justified Sinner* (1976), respectively. Ronald Stevenson (b. 1928) has composed vocal and piano music on Scottish themes.

Of younger composers who draw on native material, Edward McGuire (b. 1948) has included the bagpipes in an orchestral context, namely his symphonic piece *Calgacus,* named for the resister of Roman invasion. John Geddes (b. 1941) has used the psalm tune "Stornoway" as a basis for his solo cello piece *Callanish IV,* and William Sweeney (b. 1950), who shows the influence of jazz, also draws on Gaelic psalm singing for his *Salm an Fhearainn* (Psalm of the Land), the first use of Gaelic in a classical work. James Macmillan's symphonic work *The Trial of Isobel Goudie,* which reflects on seventeenth-century witch-hunts, was a commission from the London Promenade Concert season.

In popular music, American influence seeped into Scotland in the 1920s and 1930s with singers such as Jimmie Rodgers. By the 1950s, hillbilly and rhythm and blues styles were popular. The Glasgow singer Lonnie Donegan and his skiffle group reached the Top Ten in Britain and the United States with "Rock Island Line" (1956). Glasgow acted as a ready conduit for transatlantic styles, and Scottish beat groups in the 1960s, such as Lulu and the Luvvers and Alex Harvey's Big Soul Band, became international successes. The Sensational Alex Harvey Band of the 1970s mixed mime, vaudeville, hard rock, Jacques Brel songs, and vernacular speech in their live performances.

At the same time, the Incredible String Band and Jethro Tull attempted to blend native and exoteric musical styles—a tack taken up lately by Talitha MacKenzie in mixing Gaelic mouth music with African idioms. In the 1970s, other successful rock bands emerged: the Average White Band, the Bay City Rollers, Nazareth, and Frankie Miller. Punk soon entered from London with Scottish bands such as the Skids, the Scars, the Jolt, Johnny and the Self Abusers, and Simple Minds, who reached No. 1 in the United States with "Don't You Forget About Me" (1984). Glasgow was again the center for bands: the Big Dish, the Blue Nile, Deacon Blue, Horse, Hue and Cry, Love and Money, Texas, and Wet Wet Wet. Though these have been supported by organizations (the Music in Scotland Trust, Scottish Record Industry, Scottish Enterprise), there are no major Scottish labels or Scottish-based distributors.

PERFORMERS AND CONTEXTS

Ballads and songs were the economic stock in trade of the broadside and chapbook vendors from 1600 to 1850. The antiquarians of eighteenth-century Scotland developed an interest in how singers such as the long-lived Charles Leslie (1677–1782) came by their "curious" or "ancient" songs. One such singer, Mrs. Anna Brown (1747–1810), learned her ballads from the singing of her mother, an aunt, and an old nurse. The aunt, who had learned the ballads from women in the Braemar district (west of Aberdeen), was her chief source. Mrs. Brown was no peasant, but an educated, middle-class woman for whom supernatural or romantic ballads had a special appeal. She compiled a manuscript of her songs, and Sir Walter Scott mentions her in the preface to his *Minstrelsy.* The fifteen tunes for her ballads, however, are inexpertly taken down, though that for "Clark Colven" (Child 42) reiterates a haunting tetrachordal structure D–G–A–D as its basis (Bronson 1976:365).

Agnes Lyle (b. ca. 1775) of Kilbarchan in Ayrshire (southwest Scotland), a weaver's daughter, was born into a radical community that suffered from brutal English suppression in 1820, when three weavers who had protested a decline in wages were hanged. Her songs were taken down by William Motherwell, a young lawyer who sympathized with her lot (McCarthy 1990). Motherwell remarked on her sometimes bitter choice of subjects and emotional singing; she wept on one occasion while singing "Sheath and Knife" (Child 16), a ballad about incest.

An even greater contrast is afforded by singers of "concert music." The famous castrato Giusto Ferdinando Tenducci (ca. 1735–1790) was praised for his performance, in Edinburgh and London, of "Scotch" songs arranged for him by his friend Johann Christian Bach (1735–1782). George Thomson the publisher and William Tytler the antiquarian, who heard him sing, remarked on the touching effect of his "Gilderoy," "Lochaber no more," "The Braes of Bellenden," and "Roslin Castle." The contexts for these performances and arrangements transformed the songs into refined products for a refined audience; J. C. Bach was, after all, the music teacher of the royal family at the time.

Scottish singers appeared on the operatic stage: John Sinclair (1791–1857) came to the notice of Rossini, who wrote a part in *Semiramide* for him. John Wilson (1800–1849) sang on the London stage, but in 1838 went to the United States, where he began a series of "Scottish entertainments" that were rapturously received. David Kennedy (1825–1886), father of Marjory Kennedy-Fraser, made concert tours of the United States, Canada, Australia, and New Zealand as a tenor specializing in older Scottish songs. Jessie McLachlan (1866–1916) sang Gaelic songs at the Highland Society of London and gave a command performance for Queen Victoria at Balmoral in 1892. By far the best-known stage singer was Mary Garden (1874–1967), born in Aberdeen and taken to the United States as a child. She studied singing in Chicago and Paris, and was chosen by Debussy to create Mélisande in his opera *Pelléas et Mélisande* (1902).

With the Revival, traditional singers came back into prominence, many of them from the ranks of the Travellers. Studies have been made of Jeannie Robertson (Porter and Gower 1995), the Stewart family (MacColl and Seeger 1986), Jane Turriff, and Duncan Williamson [see TRAVELLERS' MUSIC]. Studies of Highland singers are rare, but Calum Ruadh Nicholson has demonstrated his compositional method on a commercial disc (Knudsen 1969), and Thomas A. McKean's study of another Skye songmaker, Iain MacNeacail, has underlined the importance of local bards in the Hebrides (1997).

THE FOLK-MUSIC REVIVAL

Public awareness of vernacular music making in the later 1800s was assisted by a revival that emerged just before World War I and again after World War II. Marjory Kennedy-Fraser had latched onto the Celtic revival begun in the wake of James MacPherson's Ossian poems (1760), and the Edinburgh Reel and Strathspey Society was formed in 1881 with a reawakening of interest in old dances. Concert halls and ballrooms had replaced taverns and theaters in the early 1800s as the middle class demanded spacious, comfortable arenas. Societies founded by Gaels living in exile (Edinburgh, Glasgow, London) put on concerts and *ceilidh* 'evening entertainments'. Choirs were formed and taught to use harmony; traditional singers were trained in voice production. The National Mod (1892) set up competitions, the music and adjudication of performance often being by outsiders to the singing tradition.

The Folklore Institute of Scotland began to record Gaelic songs in 1947. John Lorne Campbell and Margaret Fay Shaw gathered traditions in South Uist and Barra, and Alan Lomax recorded material later published on the Columbia World Library label. Broadcasting of traditional songs in Gaelic took a new and influential turn with singers such as Alasdair Fraser (Wester Ross), Flora MacNeil, and Calum Johnston (Barra). These singers were occasionally at odds with their communities, who preferred to sing popular songs of the day, but attitudes changed. In turn, An Comunn Gaidhealach, the Gaelic Society responsible for organizing the National Mod, began to accept a more authentic style of singing. The School of Scottish Studies at Edinburgh University, founded in 1951, created an archive that houses an extensive collection of Gaelic and Lowland music.

An Comunn later allowed folk-group contests at the Mod: groups such as Na h-Oganaich, the Lochies, and Sound of Mull thus added to the repertoire of Gaelic song. Some bands, such as Capercaillie, are noted for uncompromising arrangements of traditional Gaelic material. The taste among most young Gaels, nevertheless, is for pop music such as that evolved by Runrig, or for Gaelic country and western and other hybrid forms. In social terms, the folk-club circuit of the 1970s has given way to the rock-music arenas of the 1980s and 1990s, with media coverage and the proliferation of musical tapes, CDs, and books.

In the Lowlands, field collecting had been undertaken since the early 1800s: Motherwell, Robert Jamieson, and George Kinloch all published ballad collections. In the Northeast, Gavin Greig and the Rev. James B. Duncan amassed, before World War I, the most extensive collection of songs in the Anglophone world: 3,050 song texts and 3,100 tunes. The contributors were ordinary people, though the class consciousness of the day prevented Traveller songs from being included. In Scotland between the wars, an American, James Madison Carpenter, collected many songs that remain unpublished.

After World War II, the Revival took on a more overtly political cast. Hamish Henderson was a key figure in the People's Festival Ceilidhs of 1951–1953, which he organized for the Edinburgh Labour Party as a counter to the elitist Edinburgh International Festival (1947). With Alan Lomax, Francis Collinson, and Calum MacLean, Henderson made many field recordings. Peter Kennedy's BBC radio program *As I Roved Out* (1955) broadcast twelve programs that included songs from Galloway (southwest), Skye, and Barra. In 1957, Henderson and Lomax aired eight programs entitled *A Ballad Hunter Looks at Britain*, and in 1960 a series of six programs on collectors, *As They Roved Out*. Ewan MacColl's series, *The Radio Ballads*, contained significant material from Scotland.

A backdrop for songwriting was young nationalists' removal of the Stone of Destiny from Westminster Abbey in 1950. Songbooks with antigovernment and antinuclear songs appeared, and folk clubs proliferated. Activist songwriters such as Thurso Berwick and Matt McGinn exploited the British government's neglect of Scottish affairs. Glasgow schoolteachers, including Morris Blythman (Allan Glen's School) and Norman Buchan (Rutherglen Academy), started folk-song clubs at the classroom level. An influential popular journal, *Chapbook* (1964–1969), grew out of the Aberdeen Folk Club newsletter. In 1965, the founding of the Traditional Music and Song Association of Scotland paved the way for folk festivals that still flourish.

George Thomson commissioned famous composers to arrange songs for his *Select Collection of Original Scotish* [*sic*] *Airs* (1793–1841). But Haydn, Beethoven, and others failed to understand the modality of the tunes, even when they found them attractive, and cast them in continental harmonies.

A powerful incentive to the Revival were traditional performers who emerged from their communities, many of them seminomadic Travellers: Jeannie Robertson, the Stewarts, Jane Turriff, Lizzie Higgins, and Duncan Williamson. Farm workers, shepherds, and journeymen from the northeast and Borders were also prominent: Jimmy MacBeath, Willie Mathieson, John Strachan, Willie Scott, as well as Aberdeen's Norman Kennedy (who sings in both Gaelic and Scots) and outstanding women singers, e.g., Jean Redpath and Isabel Sutherland.

Younger singers and songwriters, including Eric Bogle, Dick Gaughan, and Andy Hunter, have exploited a taste for parody and satire. Since the 1980s, local and source singers—shipyard, mine, and factory workers, as well as rural dwellers—have emerged (Douglas 1992). In the 1970s, instrumental music advanced prominently, especially the fiddle and concertina in groups like The Gaugers (Aberdeen) and The Clutha (Glasgow). Following the success of the Irish band The Chieftains, groups like Silly Wizard, Ossian, and The Battlefield Band produced impressive albums. In the world of "electric folk," Five Hand Reel, J.S.D., and The Tannahill Weavers are notable (Cowan 1980; Henderson 1992; MacLeod 1996; Munro 1996 [1984]).

HISTORY OF COLLECTION AND RESEARCH

Scotland has one of the longest European traditions of studying its native music. At first, collectors such as Allan Ramsay (1686–1758) printed songs to meet a genteel eighteenth-century taste. Then, musicians latched onto the craze for "Scots tunes" as the country dance took hold in Edinburgh, Glasgow, and London. Though tunes of Scottish provenance appear in works by the Playfords, such as *Apollo's Banquet* (1690) and *Original Scotch Tunes* (1700), the first to publish Scots song texts with their tunes was William Thomson in his *Orpheus Caledonius* (1725, 1733). In response, Ramsay sought a tune book for his best-selling *Tea-Table Miscellany* (1724), and Alexander Stuart obliged with his *Musick* (ca. 1726). Adam Craig (1730) and Alexander Munro (1732) brought out their compilations of instrumental tunes, the latter collection published in Paris. The fifteen volumes of *The Caledonian Pocket Companion* (ca. 1742–1760), by James Oswald (1711–1769), was a landmark publication. William McGibbon (ca. 1690–1756) and Robert Bremner (ca. 1713–1789) added to a growing list of collections embodying the rediscovery and performance of traditional tunes.

An Italian musician resident in Edinburgh, Francesco Barsanti, was so taken with native airs that he published his own collection (1742). Other Italians in Edinburgh, Domenico Corri (1783) and Pietro Urbani (1792–1804), drew the ire of Scottish critics who thought the "graces" in their settings of Scots songs improper to the character of the tunes. Thereafter, George Thomson commissioned more famous composers to arrange songs for his *Select Collection of Original Scotish* [*sic*] *Airs* (1793–1841). But Haydn, Beethoven, and others failed to understand the modality of the tunes, even when they found them attractive, and cast them in continental harmonies. Old dance tunes fared better: Bremner's collection (1757–1761) was followed by those of Neil Stewart (1761–1765), Alexander McGlashan (1778), Joshua Campbell, Angus Cumming, and Robert Ross (all 1780), James Aird (1782), Niel Gow (1784–1800), and Nathaniel Gow (1797) in fairly authentic versions.

A primary compilation, *A Collection of Highland Vocal Airs,* was published by the Rev. Patrick MacDonald in 1784. The lack of qualified collectors for Highland music is evident in the light of the effort put into James Johnson's *The Scots Musical Museum* (1787–1803) by Burns and others; William Stenhouse (1839) and David Laing (1853) added historical annotations to the *Museum.* Song scholarship had changed direction with David Herd, whose *Ancient and Modern Scottish Songs* (1769, 1776) is trustworthy. The English critic Joseph Ritson contributed a useful account in his *Scottish Songs* (1794), as did Alexander Campbell in *Albyn's Anthology* (1816–1818), which contains Highland and Lowland tunes. In a similar vein of historical research, William Dauney's *Ancient Scotish* [sic] *Melodies* (1838) studies early music, especially the Skene manuscript (1615–1635), transcribed from lute tablature by G. F. Graham. A similar work of learned cast, Sir John Graham Dalyell's *Musical Memoirs of Scotland* (1849), is a painstaking study of older musical instruments.

After that of Patrick MacDonald, a second important Highland publication is Simon Fraser's *Airs and Melodies Peculiar to the Scottish Highlands* (1816), said to have been gathered in the period 1715–1745, the time of the Jacobite uprisings. Joseph MacDonald's (1803), Angus MacKay's (1838), and William Ross's (1869) collections are indispensable for the study of bagpipe music. Donald Campbell's *Treatise* (1862) contains tunes in basic settings, while Charles Stewart's *Killin Collection of Gaelic Songs* (1884) is a valuable contribution. The Glen family of Edinburgh issued useful collections of bagpipe music by the end of the century.

R. A. Smith's *Scotish* [sic] *Minstrel* (1820–1824) raised the quality of Lowland song publications. Its popularity led Finlay Dun and John Thomson to issue their *Vocal Melodies of Scotland* (1836–1838), which restored the tunes to their unembellished state; Dun also published a collection of Gaelic song, *Orain na'h Albain* (1848). The standard nineteenth-century collection of Lowland songs with historical notes (1848–1849) was collated by G. F. Graham and later revised by J. Muir Wood (1884). In the northeast, Dean William Christie compiled his *Traditional Ballad Airs* (1876–1881). Robert Ford's *Vagabond Songs of Scotland* (1899–1901) from the same area is important, as is David Balfour's *Ancient Orkney Melodies* (1885), which brought tunes from the remoter northern isles to public notice. John Ord's *Bothy Songs and Ballads* (1990 [1930]) records an important genre with roots in the farm life of the 1800s.

By 1900, scholars had introduced a new scrupulousness into their work: Lucy Broadwood (1858–1929) collected in the Highlands, and Anne Gilchrist (1863–1954) contributed to the study of Gaelic scale structure. Frances Tolmie's collection of songs from Skye (1911) is accurate and important, notably for the study of women's songs, and offers a contrast to the adaptations of Kennedy-Fraser, in which, despite skillful arrangements, the vital character of the songs is lost (Bassin 1977). Kennedy-Fraser's account of her life and work, however, is not without interest (1987 [1929]).

John Lorne Campbell and Margaret Fay Shaw largely redress the distortions wrought by Kennedy-Fraser. With Francis Collinson, Campbell analyzes waulking songs in historical and structural detail (1969–1981). As well as an account of Gaelic songs in Nova Scotia (1990), Campbell's study of Highland Jacobite songs (1933) provides a corrective to Hogg's *Relics of Jacobite Poetry* (1819–1821). Shaw produced an exemplary study of the folklore and songs of South Uist (1955). Archibald Campbell's *Kilberry Book of Ceòl Mor* (1953), and Roderick Ross's *Binneas is Boreraig*

(1959) are noted pibroch collections. Of several studies, A. J. Haddow's (1982) is possibly the best analysis of its subject to date; the accounts by Seamus MacNeill (1976 [1968]) and Roderick D. Cannon (1988) are also useful. William Matheson's portrait of the eighteenth-century harper Ruairidh Dall Morrison (1970) and Colm O'Baoill's similar study of the bard Sileas MacDonald of Keppoch (1972) are valuable for their inclusion of music. Alistair Campsie's highly critical *The MacCrimmon Legend* (1980) clears away myths about the famous piping family, as does William Donaldson's *The Jacobite Song* (1988) for "seditious songs" in a similar period.

In studies of song, J. C. Dick's *Notes on the Songs of Robert Burns* (1962 [1903]) updates the work of Stenhouse, Laing, and C. K. Sharpe. Claude M. Simpson's *The British Broadside Ballad and Its Music* (1966) discusses tune histories in detail. Bertrand H. Bronson's compilation of ballad tunes (1959–1972) is a major monument of tune scholarship. But histories of Scottish music are rare: H. G. Farmer's (1970 [1947]) improves upon David Baptie's (1894). John Purser's *Scottish Music* (1992), a synthesis of scholarship on all types of Scottish music, grew out of a BBC Radio series of talks. Accounts of the Revival are in Cowan (1980), Henderson (1992), and Munro (1996 [1984]). Collinson's landmark survey (1966) is based on field collecting, as is MacColl and Seeger's Traveller songs (1977). The most extensive harvest of Anglophone songs anywhere had a proportion edited by Alexander Keith (Greig and Keith 1925), but the entire collection is currently appearing in eight volumes as *The Greig-Duncan Folk Song Collection* (1981–).

BIBLIOGRAPHY

Collections (chronological)

Forbes, John. 1662, 1666, 1682. *Cantus, Songs and Fancies*. Aberdeen.

Playford, Henry. 1690. *The Banquet of Musick: Or, A Collection of the Newest and Best Songs Sung at Court*. London: E. Jones.

Playford, John. 1690. *Apollo's Banquet*. London: E. Jones.

Playford, Henry. 1700. *A Collection of Original Scotch Tunes*. London.

Thomson, William. 1725, 1733. *Orpheus Caledonius*. London.

Stuart, Alexander. Ca. 1726. *Musick for the Tea-Table Miscellany*. Edinburgh.

Craig, Adam. 1730. *A Collection of the Choicest Scots Tunes*. Edinburgh.

Munro, Alexander. 1732. *A Collection of the Best Scots Tunes*. Paris.

Barsanti, Francesco. 1742. *A Collection of Old Scots Tunes*. Edinburgh.

McGibbon, William. 1742, 1746, 1755. *A Collection of Scots Tunes*. Edinburgh.

Oswald, James. ca. 1742–1760. *The Caledonian Pocket Companion*. London.

Bremner, Robert. 1757–1761. *A Collection of Scots Reels and Country Dances*. Edinburgh.

———. 1765. *A Collection of Scots Reels*. London.

Stewart, Neil. 1761. *A Collection of the Newest and Best Reels or Country Dances*. Edinburgh.

McGlashan, Alexander. 1778. *A Collection of Strathspey Reels*. Edinburgh

Campbell, Joshua. 1780. *A Collection of the Newest and Best Reels and Minuets*. Glasgow.

Cumming, Angus. 1780. *A Collection of Strathspey, or Old Highland Reels*. Edinburgh.

Ross, Robert. 1780. *A Choice Collection of Scots Reels*. Edinburgh.

Marshall, William. 1781. *A Collection of Strathspey Reels*. Edinburgh.

Aird, James. 1782. *A Selection of Scottish, English, Irish, and Foreign Airs*. 6 vols. Edinburgh.

Corri, Domenico. 1783. *A New and Complete Collection of the Most Favorite Scots Songs*. Edinburgh.

Gow, Niel. 1784–1800. *A Collection of Strathspey Reels*. 4 vols. Edinburgh.

MacDonald, Patrick. 1784. *A Collection of Highland Vocal Airs*. Edinburgh.

Johnson, James. 1787–1803. *The Scots Musical Museum*. Edinburgh.

Urbani, Pietro. 1792–1804. *A Selection of Scots Songs*. Edinburgh.

Thomson, George. 1793–1841. *A Select Collection of Original Scottish Airs for the Voice*. Edinburgh.

Ritson, Joseph. 1794. *Scottish Songs*. London.

Gow, Nathaniel. 1797. *A Collection of Strathspey Reels*. Edinburgh.

MacDonald, Joseph. 1927 [1803]. *A Compleat Theory of the Scots Highland Bagpipe*. Glasgow: Alexander MacDonald.

Campbell, Alexander. 1816–1818. *Albyn's Anthology*. Edinburgh.

Fraser, Simon. 1816. *Airs and Melodies Peculiar to the Highlands of Scotland and the Isles.* Edinburgh.

Hogg, James. 1819–1821. *The Jacobite Relics of Scotland.* Edinburgh.

Smith, R. A. 1820–1824. *The Scotish [sic] Minstrel.* Edinburgh: R. Purdie.

MacDonald, Donald. 1974 [ca. 1822]. *A Collection of the Ancient Martial Music of Caledonia.* Wakefield: EP Publishing.

Dun, Finlay, and John Thomson. 1836–1838. *Vocal Melodies of Scotland.* Edinburgh: Paterson.

MacKay, Angus. 1838. *A Collection of Ancient Piobaireachd or Highland Pipe Music.* Edinburgh.

Stenhouse, William. 1839. *Illustrations of the Lyric Poetry and Music of Scotland.* Edinburgh.

———. 1848. *Orain na'h Albain.*

Graham, George Farquhar. 1848–1849. *The Songs of Scotland.* Edinburgh: Wood and Co.

Laing, David, ed. 1853. *Illustrations of the Lyric Poetry and Music of Scotland.* Edinburgh.

Christie, Dean William. 1876–1881. *Traditional Ballad Airs.* 2 vols. Edinburgh: Edmonston and Douglas.

Stewart, Charles. 1884. *Killin Collection of Gaelic Songs.* Edinburgh: Maclachlan and Stewart.

Wood, J. Muir. 1884. *The Popular Songs and Melodies of Scotland.* Edinburgh.

Balfour, David. 1885. *Ancient Orkney Melodies.* Edinburgh.

Thomason, General. 1975 [1893]. *Ceòl Mor.* Wakefield: EP Publishing.

MacDonald, Keith Norman. 1895. *The Gesto Collection of Highland Music.* Leipzig.

Ford, Robert. 1899–1901. *Vagabond Songs of Scotland.* Paisley: A. Gardner.

Glen, David. [last of 17 parts ca. 1902–1907]. *David Glen's Collection.* Edinburgh: Glen.

Kennedy-Fraser, Marjory. 1909, 1917, 1923. *Songs of the Hebrides.* 3 vols. London.

Tolmie, Frances. 1911. "Notes and Reminiscences: One Hundred and Five Songs of Occupation from the Western Isles of Scotland." *Journal of the Folk-Song Society* 4(16):143–276.

Greig, Gavin, and Alexander Keith. 1925. *Last Leaves of Traditional Ballads and Ballad Airs.* Aberdeen: The Buchan Club.

Ord, John. 1990 [1930]. *Bothy Songs and Ballads.* Edinburgh: John Donald.

Campbell, Archibald. 1953. *Kilberry Book of Ceòl Mor.* Glasgow: J. Smith.

Ross, Roderick. 1959. *Binneas is Boreraig.* Edinburgh: Macdonald Publishers.

MacColl, Ewan, and Peggy Seeger. 1977. *Travellers' Songs from England and Scotland.* Knoxville: University of Tennessee Press.

Hardie, Alistair. 1981. *The Caledonian Companion.* Edinburgh: EMI Music Publishing.

Shuldham-Shaw, Patrick, and Emily B. Lyle, eds. 1981, 1983, 1987, 1989–. *The Greig-Duncan Folk Song Collection.* Aberdeen: Aberdeen University Press (vols. 1–4). Edinburgh: The Mercat Press (vols. 5–7).

Mooney, Gordon. 1982. *A Collection of the Choicest Scots Tunes.* Edinburgh: Lowland Pipers Society.

Wallace, Robert. 1986. *The Glasgow Collection of Bagpipe Music.* Glasgow: Scottish Music Publishing.

MacDonald, Allan. 1991. *The Moidart Collection.* Edinburgh: School of Scottish Studies.

Studies (alphabetical)

Alburger, Mary Anne. 1983. *Scottish Fiddlers and Their Music.* London: Gollancz.

Armstrong, R. B. 1904. *The Highland Harp.* Edinburgh.

Baptie, David. 1894. *Musical Scotland.* Paisley: J. and R. Parlane.

Bassin, Ethel. 1977. *The Old Songs of Skye.* London: Routledge and Kegan Paul.

Boag, William. 1975. *The Tenor Drum, Drums on Parade: The Rise of the Scottish Style of Side Drumming, Pipers in the Scottish Regiments.* N.p.: Military Historical Society.

Bronson, Bertrand H. 1959–1972. *The Traditional Tunes of the Child Ballads.* 4 vols. Princeton, N.J.: Princeton University Press.

———. 1969. *The Ballad as Song.* Berkeley: University of California Press.

———. 1976. *The Singing Tradition of Child's Popular Ballads.* Princeton, N.J.: Princeton University Press.

Bruford, Alan. 1986. "The Singing of Fenian and Similar Lays in Scotland." In *Ballad Research,* ed. Hugh Shields, 55–70. Dublin: Folk Song Society of Ireland.

Campbell, Donald. 1862. *A Treatise on the Language, Poetry and Music of the Highland Clans.* Edinburgh: Collie.

Campbell, John Lorne. 1933. *Highland Songs of the Forty-Five.* Edinburgh: John Grant.

———. 1990. *Songs Remembered in Exile.* Aberdeen: Aberdeen University Press.

Campbell, John Lorne, and Francis Collinson. 1969, 1977, 1981. *Hebridean Folksongs.* 3 vols. Oxford: Clarendon Press.

Campsie, Alistair. 1980. *The MacCrimmon Legend: The Madness of Angus Mackay.* Edinburgh: Canongate.

Cannon, Roderick D. 1980. *A Bibliography of Bagpipe Music.* Edinburgh: John Donald.

———. 1988. *The Highland Bagpipe and Its Music.* Edinburgh: John Donald.

Collinson, Francis. 1966. *The Traditional and National Music of Scotland.* London: Routledge and Kegan Paul.

Cooke, Peter. 1986. *The Fiddle Tradition of the Shetland Isles.* Cambridge: Cambridge University Press.

Cowan, Edward J., ed. 1980. *The People's Past.* Edinburgh: EU Publications Board.

Crocker, Richard. 1977. *The Early Medieval Sequence.* Berkeley: University of California Press.

Dalyell, J. G. 1849. *Musical Memoirs of Scotland.* Edinburgh and London: no publisher.

Darvas, Garbor. 1975. *L'Homme Armé.* Budapest: Editio Musica.

Dauney, William. 1838. *Ancient Scotish [sic] Melodies.* Edinburgh: Bannatyne Club.

Dick, J. C. 1962 [1903]. *Notes on the Songs of Robert Burns.* Hatboro: Folklore Associates.

Donaldson, William. 1988. *The Jacobite Song.* Aberdeen: Aberdeen University Press.

Douglas, Sheila, ed. 1992. *The Sang's the Thing.* Edinburgh: Polygon.

Elliott, Kenneth. 1958, 1967. *Early Scottish Keyboard Music.* London: Stainer & Bell.

Elliott, Kenneth, and Helena Mennie Shire, eds. 1957, 1964, 1975. *Music of Scotland 1500–1700.* Musica Britannica, 15. London: Stainer & Bell.

Emmerson, George S. 1971. *Rantin' Pipe and Tremblin' String.* London: Dent.

Everist, Mark. 1990. "From Paris to St. Andrews: The Origins of W$_1$." *Journal of the American Musicological Society* 43:1–42.

Farmer, Henry George. 1970 [1947]. *A History of Music in Scotland.* New York: Da Capo Press.

Fiske, Roger. 1983. *Scotland in Music.* Cambridge: Cambridge University Press.

Gillies, Anne Lorne. 1990. *Song of Myself.* Edinburgh: Mainstream.

Glen, John. 1900. *Early Scottish Melodies.* Edinburgh: J. & R. Glen.

Haddow, Alexander John. 1982. *The History and Structure of Ceòl Mor.* Privately printed.

Henderson, Hamish. 1992. *Alias MacAlias: Writing on Songs, Folk and Literature.* Edinburgh: Polygon.

Hiley, David. 1980. "Sources, MS IV, 1: Organum and Discant." In *The New Grove Dictionary of Music and Musicians,* ed. Stanley Sadie, 17:653. London: Macmillan.

Johnson, David. 1972. *Music and Society in Lowland Scotland in the Eighteenth Century.* London: Oxford University Press.

———. 1997 [1984]. *Scottish Fiddle Music in the 18th Century.* Edinburgh: Mercat Press.

Kennedy-Fraser, Marjory. 1987 [1929]. *A Life of Song.* Corte Madera: Arno Communications.

Kinnaird, Alison. 1992. *The Tree of Strings: Crann nan teud: A History of the Harp in Scotland.* Edinburgh: Kinmor Music.

MacColl, Ewan, and Peggy Seeger. 1986. *Till Doomsday in the Afternoon: The Folklore of a Family of Scots Travellers, the Stewarts of Blairgowrie.* Manchester: Manchester University Press.

MacDonell, Margaret. 1982. *The Emigrant Experience: Songs of Highland Emigrants in North America.* Toronto: University of Toronto Press.

McKean, Thomas A. 1997. *Hebridean Song-Maker: Iain MacNeacail of the Isle of Skye.* Edinburgh: Polygon.

MacLellan, John A. 1988. *Music for the Highland Bagpipe.* Edinburgh: self-published.

MacLeod, Morag. 1996. "Folk Revival in Gaelic Song." In *The Democratic Muse: Folk Music Revival in Scotland,* ed. Ailie Munro, 124–137. Aberdeen: Scottish Cultural Press.

MacNeill, Seamus. 1976 [1968]. *Piobaireachd.* Glasgow: BBC Publications.

Matheson, William. 1970. *An Clarsair Dall* (The blind harper). Edinburgh: Scottish Gaelic Texts Society.

Morton, Tom. 1991. *Going Home: The Runrig Story.* Edinburgh: Mainstream Publishing.

Munro, Ailie. 1996 [1984]. *The Democratic Muse: Folk Music Revival in Scotland.* Rev. ed. Aberdeen: Scottish Cultural Press.

O'Baoill, Colm. 1972. *Bardachd Shilis na Ceapaich* (Songs of Sileas MacDonald of Keppoch). Edinburgh: Scottish Gaelic Texts Society.

Patrick, Millar. 1949. *Four Centuries of Scottish Psalmody.* London: Oxford University Press.

Porter, James, and Herschel Gower. 1995. *Jeannie Robertson: Emergent Singer, Transformative Voice.* Knoxville: University of Tennessee Press.

Purser, John. 1992. *Scotland's Music.* Edinburgh: Mainstream Publishing.

Robertson, Stanley. 1990. *Exodus to Alford.* Inverness: Balnain Press.

Ross, G. F. 1926. *Some Piobaireachd Studies.* Glasgow: Peter Henderson.

Sampson, Claude M. 1966. *The British Broadside Ballad and Its Music.* Piscataway, N.J.: Rutgers University Press.

Shaw, Margaret Fay. 1986 [1955]. *Folklore and Folksongs of South Uist.* 3rd ed. Aberdeen: Aberdeen University Press.

Shire, Helena Mennie. 1969. *Song, Dance, and Poetry of the Court of Scotland under King James VI.* Cambridge: Cambridge University Press.

Ward, John M. 1967. "Apropos the British Ballad and Its Music." *Journal of the American Musicological Society* 20:28–86.

Woods, Isobel. 1984. "The Carvor Choirbook." Ph.D. diss., Princeton University.

AUDIOVISUAL RESOURCES

Bothy Ballads: Music from the North-East. 1993. Scottish Tradition, 1. Greentrax CDTRAX 9001. Compact disc.

Calum & Annie Johnston: Songs, Stories & Piping from Barra. 1995. Scottish Tradition, 13. Greentrax CTRAX 9013. Cassette.

Calum Ruadh, Bard of Skye. 1994. Scottish Tradition, 7. Greentrax CTRAX 9007. Cassette.

Capercaille. 1989. *Sidewaulk.* Green Linnet 1094. Compact disc.

———. 1993. *Secret People.* Green Linnet 3104. Compact disc.

The Fiddler and His Art. 1993. Scottish Tradition, 9. Greentrax CDTRAX 9009. Compact disc.

Gaelic Psalms from Lewis. 1994. Scottish Tradition, 6. Greentrax CDTRAX 9006. Compact disc.

Gillies, Anne Lorne. 1991. *Songs of the Gael.* Lochshore LOCLP 1014. LP disk.

James Campbell of Kintail, Gaelic Songs. 1994. Scottish Tradition, 8. Greentrax CTRAX 9008. Cassette.

Knudsen, Thorkild. 1969. *Calum Ruadh, Bard of Skye.* Scottish Tradition, 7. Tangent TN6M 128. LP disk.

McCusker, John. 1995. *John McCusker.* Temple Records COMD 2059. Compact disc.

McLachan, Iain. 1997. *A Island Heritage: Traditional Music of the Western Isles.* Springthyme Records. SPRCD 1022. Compact disc.

Miller, Jo. N.d. [1998]. *Mary Macqueen's Ballads.* Scottish Texts Society. Cassette tape.

The Muckle Sangs: Classic Scots Ballads. 1992. Scottish Tradition, 5. Greentrax CDTRAX 9005. Compact disc.

Music from the Western Isles. 1992. Scottish Tradition, 2. Greentrax CDTRAX 9002. Compact disc.

Musique Celtique. N.d. Ocora 45. LP disk.

New Recordings from the North East Folklore Archive. 1994. Northeast Tradition 1. Banff & Buchan District Council. Cassette.

Notes of Noy, Notes of Joy: Early Scottish Music for Lute, Clàrsach and Voice. 1994. The Rowallan Consort. Temple Records COMD 2058. Compact disc.

Pibroch: George Moss. 1995. Scottish Tradition, 15. Greentrax CTRAX 9015. Cassette.

Pibroch: Pipe-Major Robert Brown. 1995. Scottish Tradition, 11. Greentrax CTRAX 9011. Cassette.

Pibroch: Pipe-Major Robert Nicol. 1995. Scottish Tradition, 12. Greentrax CTRAX 9012. Cassette.

Shetland Fiddle Music. 1993. Scottish Tradition, 4. Greentrax CDTRAX 9004. Compact disc.

Turriff, Jane. 1996. *Singin is Ma Life.* Springthyme Records SPRCD 1038. Compact disc.

Waulking Songs from Barra. 1993. Scottish Tradition, 3. Greentrax CDTRAX 9003. Compact disc.

William Matheson, Gaelic Bards and Minstrels. 1993. Scottish Tradition, 16. Greentrax CTRAX 9016D. 2 cassettes.

Ireland

Hugh Shields
Paulette Gershen

The Republic of Ireland occupies about 85 percent of Ireland's 84,431 square kilometers and is predominantly Roman Catholic, while the remainder is covered by Northern Ireland, a primarily Protestant part of the United Kingdom. More than 40 percent of the island's five million inhabitants live in rural areas, where agriculture formed the economic base until industry began to expand, in the mid-1950s. Irish Gaelic, with English as the major language, is spoken by less than 20 percent of the population (including much fewer native Irish-speakers), mainly in the western and southwestern parts of the republic.

Ireland was already famous as a center of learning since the early Middle Ages, when Irish missionaries traveled to the continent to teach Christianity and to found monasteries. Major Irish authors have included Samuel Beckett, James Joyce, Sean O'Casey, George Bernard Shaw, Jonathan Swift, and William Butler Yeats. Two Irish classical musicians—the pianist John Field (1782–1837), composer of nocturnes that influenced Frédéric Chopin, and the tenor John McCormack (1884–1945)—achieved international recognition.

TRADITIONAL GENRES OF SONG AND STYLES OF SINGING

Irish traditional musical and poetic forms have much in common with those of Britain. Pentatonic forms common in Scotland recur in Ulster, and heptatonic modes are distributed in Ireland in much the same proportions as in England: more than half of the stock of tunes are major, and less than half are mixolydian, dorian, or aeolian, in that order of frequency. Irish songs are a thorough cultural mix; their texts, musical or verbal, are often recognizably of British origin, and Irish music uses the dance forms of England, Scotland, and the Continent.

Old Gaelic genres

Certain old Gaelic genres, though no longer performed, were in use until recently. The death lament (*caoineadh na marbh,* anglicized as "keening"), a custom cited by Giraldus Cambrensis as early as the 1180s, involved both singing and spoken lament: melody mixed with speech heightened by emotion, in relatively free form (Partridge 1983). The term *caoineadh* seems to have been applied specially to the laudatory and

FIGURE 1 "*Caoineadh Airt Uí Laoghaire*" ('Lament for Art Ó Laoghaire'), a late-eighteenth-century death lament, sung by Máire Uí Chonaill, of Ballyvourney, County Cork. The widow is reacting to an assertion that she went to bed on the night of her husband's wake. Many features of this example are considered typical of the genre. The scale, which ranges over an octave, is missing the fourth degree, and the melodic phrases generally have a descending shape. De Noraidh 1965:28.

descriptive verse lament, sung by one or more women (less by men), and *gol* 'weeping' was the textually unfixed, partly sung, partly sobbing expression of grief. Written documents usually record a single musical phrase without the fourth heptatonic degree, descending through an octave by way of preferred cadences on the sixth and major third. The descending melody has served in many songs of lament that are not strictly keens, and recurs in most examples of a rare category, the so-called plow whistles (Joyce 1909; Petrie 1978 [1855]; Stanford 1902–1905). Apparently the phrase could be drawn out to accommodate monorhyme lines of varying length and number. In Gaelic, rhyme is assonantal. A striking traditional embodiment of the genre is the late-eighteenth-century "*Caoineadh Airt Uí Laoghaire*" ('Lament for Art Ó Laoghaire') (figure 1).

Another old genre, the Fenian or Ossianic heroic lay (*laoi Fiannaíochta*), is better preserved than the keen, in plentiful verbal texts of a vernacular manuscript tradition that supported singing and in scanty, badly notated versions of their tunes (Shields 1993). This tradition inspired James MacPherson's "Ossian" (1760s), which he claimed to have translated from old Scottish Gaelic manuscripts. The Irish versions contrast with better-preserved Scottish ones, which are faster in tempo and are often sung by women, while most Irish singers of heroic songs, such as the lays of Fionn mac Cumhaill, with their narratives of hunts, invasions, extravagant battles, and otherworldly enemies, have been men. Lays continued to be sung until the mid-twentieth century, to music that most observers have called chant: parlando melodies with irregular stresses and quatrain form often musically well defined though at times replaced by rhapsodic grouping of varying numbers of lines or obscured by alteration of the pattern of phrases or cadences.

Lyric and narrative songs and "lilting"

The lays were more formally defined than the later Irish- and English-language lyric and narrative songs, but quatrain form was practiced, early and late, in both languages, and after the Middle Ages verses of eight or four long lines have been common in musical forms AABA, AA^2BA^2, and so on, especially in Irish. ABBA form, borrowed more than two centuries ago from the British broadside ballad (figure 2), has been much commoner in English, though increasingly used in songs in Irish. An old and now probably extinct feature of quatrain form more noticeable in English is the repetition of the words and music of the last two lines of every verse. The couplet rhyme and symmetrical musical repetition of English songs serve plain expression, while Irish uses the often more extended AABA form for "difficult" expression (a term not usually depreciative in Irish), covering form and content and exemplified in lexical diversity and complicated rhyme. Despite such contrasts, cultural interaction has caused the introduction of features of each language and its song forms into the other.

The length of phrases helps make melody the most interesting musical feature of Irish song. An open cadence is usually followed by a closed one, and a low register by

FIGURE 2 "Ann Jane Thornton," a narrative song, sung in English by Robert Butcher, of Magilligan, County Derry. From the broadside ballad tradition, songs such as this, in quatrain (four-line) form, in this case ABBA, had come to Ireland by the eighteenth century. Shields 1964:42.

a high one. Airs, the conventional label for vocal melodies, may encompass a wide range, such as an eleventh or a twelfth—a trait sufficiently Irish for a melody of uncertain traditional status, the "Londonderry Air," which runs to a fourteenth in its published form, to have become a world-renowned representative of the flowery, well developed, usually major, Gaelic tunes in AABA form.

The old, so-called Child ballads [see ENGLAND; SCOTLAND] were popular in Ireland, though the genre was no longer productive, even in the 1600s, when it arrived. These ballads have short, four-phrase melodies (usually *abcd*), corresponding to the twice-as-long A and B phrases of the later, less oral ballads. A few old ballads with refrains entered Ireland, but the characteristic refrains of some British and many continental ballads left little mark on Irish practice. Since refrains are associated with choral singing and dancing, the long Irish history of solo singing and the lack of evidence that songs ever served to accompany dancing could explain the rarity of ballads with refrains.

Lilt (*portaireacht*), the singing of instrumental dance tunes to nonlexical syllables, is the only vocal music for dancing, but little used for that purpose today (figure 3). Occasional verses of words may surface among the syllables of lilt, but they usually belong, not to songs, but to a repertoire of verses serving on occasions when they may amuse the company.

Performance styles and practices

Singers usually modify strict meter by means of pauses or lengthening, not only at cadences, but at climaxes within lines. The degrees of rubato vary with the singer, the language, and the region. The slower and more rubato the song, the greater the opportunity for melodic ornamentation, used plentifully and traditionally in the Gaeltachts (native Irish-speaking areas) of Munster and Connaught, but not Donegal. This style, for which *sean-nós* 'old manner' is a recent label, is strongest in Connemara, where ornamentation embellishes notes, filling melodic intervals, and the extent of rubato contrasts in lingering and hurrying passages (CD track 9). Such performance may be most effectively transcribed in measures determined by poetic meter. Connemara *sean-nós* singing has influenced many young singers from all over Ireland and elsewhere, though its songs in Irish and their metrical verses recur in the other Gaeltachts, and the melodies are found throughout Ireland. Both parlando-

FIGURE 3 "All the Ways to Go," a jig in AABB form, lilted after being played on the melodeon. Jigs are dances in 6/8 time. Performed by Packy Boner, of Arranmore Island, County Donegal. Shields 1984:10.

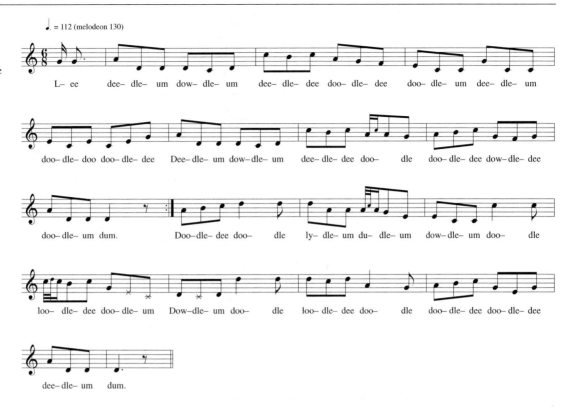

rubato rhythm and melismatic style recur with less intensity in the English singing of Ireland (Ó Muirithe 1982).

The underlying structure of singing is basically syllabic. Melodic ornamentation has its verbal counterpart in the nonlexical syllables that singers intercalate freely in the words of songs. These syllables also are clearly intended as ornament. A musical ornament not much favored by younger singers is the bleating quality in held notes, broken up by reiterated glottal stops, a kind of glottal vibrato. Big, sonorous voices are not favored, though a certain degree of pitch vibrato, far from the classical model, is at times audible. Traditional style is more inclined to diminish sonority in varied ways, as by emphasizing the voiceless sounds in the verbal text. Though the rhythm is relaxed, a certain tenseness often leads to sharpening of pitch as the song progresses, so that it may end a third or a fourth higher than it began. Songs may also end in speech, for it is old tradition to descend into speech in the concluding line, phrase, or word.

Traditional songs (and instrumental music) are transmitted and performed orally: performers do not countenance singing or playing from written music. "Help" in the performance of song may be supplied vocally by a second singer, and singing in duet is commoner than first appears; but it remains a monophonic variant on solo practice. The islanders of Tory, off northwest Donegal, favor duet or even loose choral singing more than singers elsewhere. In Gaeltachts, cohesion between the singer and the audience is achieved when those sitting close by take the singer's hand and "wind" it to and fro during the song.

Irish music found more than temporary quarters in America, the chief destination of Irish emigrants since the late 1700s. Irish music has flourished there, and the exchange of players, more often than singers, between the homeland and what used to be called the New Island (*An tOileán Úr*) became common in the second half of the twentieth century. Songs of parting—from a locality, a family, or a loved one—are among the most enduring in both languages.

Dance-music is played fast, with ornamentation, and today's technically skilled young players often take tempos as fast as possible. Most players prefer reels, and some play nothing else.

INSTRUMENTAL MUSIC

The instrumental repertory, traditionally played solo, but since the mid-twentieth century also in groups, consists mainly of dance music. Though often played without dancing, it has experienced a renewal of its earlier function as a result of the revival of set dancing since the 1970s. As a vernacular adaptation of the socially superior quadrilles, set dancing replaced older kinds of native dancing during the 1800s. It drew largely on native musical material to nourish a limited range of dance forms adopted from abroad: the jig, in 6/8 meter (with the slip jig in 9/8, and the slide in 12/8); the reel, in 4/4 or 2/2; the hornpipe, in 4/4; the polka, in 2/4; and the march, in 2/4 or 6/8. Dance-music is played fast, with ornamentation, and today's technically skilled young players often take tempos as fast as possible.

Most players prefer reels, and some play nothing else (figure 4). Dance tunes consist typically of two sections, traditionally called the tune (*fonn*) and the turn (*casadh*), each consisting of two four-measure phrases. The sections are usually repeated to make an AABB form. A few tunes with more than two sections may vary the order of their repetition (for example, ABCBAB). A performance conventionally consists of a series of two or more tunes in the same meter, even when not played for dancing, but items in different meters that are variants of one tune may be perceived as such and played successively. "The Blackbird," a Jacobite song, serves in hornpipe meter for a (solo) step dance, and its variants may function successively as music for listening. The same may apply to old native marches in 2/4 that have been remade as jigs in 6/8. Despite the fanciful or suggestive titles of many tunes, instrumental music rarely has any meaning other than musical, though two old descriptive pieces—"The Fox Hunt" (Moylan 1981) and "Allisdrum's March" (*Mairseáil Alasdruim*) (Breathnach 1968–1969)—are still played: the latter was noted in 1750 as "a wild rhapsody," said to commemorate a battle and treacherous killing in 1647.

Some instrumentalists also play "slow airs" taken from songs and played exclusively for listening. The basic meter is that of the song in question, which brings in 3/4 meter, not otherwise represented in the instrumental repertoire, but the 3/4 or other song meter is played intentionally rubato. Some players successfully introduce considerable variation into their airs, and the flexible rhythm and melodic ornamentation resemble the Connemara *sean-nós* style.

Musicians usually provide interest by making rhythmic and melodic variations in successive repetitions and ornamenting notes somewhat as in the more ornate styles of singing, by adding single grace notes one or more degrees above the melody note, inserting trills and rolls (groups of three descending grace notes, the second of which is equal in pitch to the main note), and articulating ("cutting") successive main notes of identical pitch. On low notes, pipers have "cranning," a more elaborate ornament of this kind. These features enhance solo playing and the heterophonic group playing associated with a solo tradition.

FIGURE 4   "Jenny, Tie Your Bonnet," a reel in AABB form, played on *uilleann* pipes by Willy Clancy, of Miltown Malbay, County Clare. Reels are dances in 4/4 time. These bagpipes are bellows-blown; in addition to a chanter (melody pipe) and drones, they have a set of two or more pipes with keys, called regulators, which, depending on the player's skill and inclination, can be pressed down by the player's wrist to create rhythmic accompaniments or harmonic effects. The drone pipes sound D, d, and d'. Transcription by Hugh Shields from *The Pipering of Willie Clancy* 1980: track B9.

The reel "Corny is coming" follows without a pause.

MUSICAL INSTRUMENTS

The range of instruments played traditionally today is small—principally fiddle, wooden, side-blown flute, tin whistle (a six-hole whistle flute), pipes (by which is meant bellows-blown bagpipes, while the term *bagpipes* is being more and more reserved for mouth-blown "warpipes" of the Scots type), concertina, and diatonic accordion. All these but the last two, if we take into account their respective precursors, have a long, even millennial, history. The contexts of their use are almost wholly recreational and without ritual significance.

Medieval instruments include the harp (*cláirseach* or *cruit*) often mentioned in early literature, though *cruit,* the older term, was used for other instruments before the harp was introduced, and so may leave doubt as to the instrument it describes. The earliest extant harp, from the late Middle Ages, is named after Brian Boru, killed in 1014. It shows the solidity of construction that permitted the use of brass wire strings, which the player plucked with long fingernails—a technique still used by Dennis Hempson, the oldest harper at the Belfast festival of 1792 (Carolan 1984; Rimmer 1969). From the 1800s, "Irish" harps were made on the old model and strung with gut. Since the 1960s, a few makers have reconstructed the medieval harp more scrupulously, so that its tone—much more sonorous than that of modern harps—may be heard again. The *tiompán,* Old Irish *timpan,* was not a drum, as the Latin *tympanum* would suggest, but a plucked or bowed chordophone. Like the harp, it is often mentioned in literature, but it fell from use before the harp. No surviving specimens of it or the fiddle (*fidil*), also mentioned in a medieval text, have been discovered (Buckley 1978). A variety of medieval terms occur for aerophones, and the oldest surviving Irish instruments are bronze trumpets, evidently used in hunting or war. The terms *feadán, cuisle,* and *píopaí* suggest, respectively, 'whistle', 'pipe(s)' or 'flute(s)', and 'bagpipes', but firmer facts cannot be elicited from the contexts. Among the artifacts excavated from Viking Dublin are some twelfth-century bone whistles [see ARCHAEOLOGY OF MUSIC IN EUROPE].

At the end of the Middle Ages, the harp and the bagpipes stand out as characteristic national instruments: the former proper to performances in polite society, the latter mouth-blown and associated with war and other occasions of celebration or mourning, but these warpipes, as convention now calls them (Donnelly 1981–1984), fairly soon declined and disappeared, probably because they lacked large enough public performative contexts in the 1600s. By the mid-1700s, the warpipes were replaced by bellows-blown "union" pipes (later *uilleann* pipes), with a range of about two octaves, a softer tone (suitable for indoor use), and the potential for further evolution.

The use of bellows for the pipes was a continental innovation, but the *uilleann* pipes developed new features, and are thus distinguished as the only traditional Irish instrument now in use which is of native elaboration. Like warpipes, they now have three drones tuned in octaves. To these were added a set of three pipes ("regulators"), each with a few metal keys depressed by the player's wrist to create limited harmonic accompaniment. Treatment of this facility is individualistic, sometimes seeking rhythmic more than harmonic effect. The style of playing may be legato with open fingering, or staccato with closed ("tight") fingering. Because their construction and maintenance are complex, *uilleann* pipes have tended to focus much of the discussion of traditional playing through the opportunely founded society, *Na Píobairí Uilleann* (Irish Pipers' Society). During the twentieth century, playing of the instrument declined to such an extent that its extinction seemed imminent, but revival since the 1970s has been impressive, and societies of players now exist, not only in Ireland, but in Britain, Europe, America, and Australia.

In 1674, a visitor reported "in every field a fiddle" at the Sunday dancing (Breathnach 1971). Whether the Irish were playing a prototype of the modern fiddle he does not say, but this certainly became the case in the course of the 1700s. The violin (always called fiddle by traditional musicians) enjoyed a boom in Dublin music publishing then, and music for it was composed, or borrowed from popular tradition. The instrument is not played in the classical manner. It is held lower and at a different angle, and the upper end of the bow is used most of the time. Northern style prefers a single stroke to a note, and tends to be nonlegato (Feldman and O'Doherty 1979). Fiddling was somewhat better sustained than piping until the late-twentieth-century revival; some distinctiveness of style by region survived, notably in Kerry, Sligo, and Donegal. The fiddling of Michael Coleman, a Sligo emigrant to the United States, is the best example of the influence of discs made in America in the 1920s and 1930s by Irish players living there. Coleman's influence is still felt in the style and repertory of fiddling in Ireland.

Whistles, or end-blown duct flutes, have been long in use, but the first firm evidence of a modern tradition of flute playing is from the 1700s, when published music often recommends itself for the "German" flute, that is, the keyed concert flute, which Irish traditional players have used since then, and continue to use in its

FIGURE 5 Sean Ryan, a tin whistle (duct flute with six finger holes) player from Tipperary. Most popular models of this instrument are made of metal, but other materials, such as plastic (as here), are also used. Photo by Paulette Gershen, 1992.

modern, fully keyed or its older, single-keyed form. As with the open and tight styles of piping, the flute and the whistle are played in legato and nonlegato styles. The flute remains strong, especially in the counties of Sligo, Leitrim, Roscommon, Galway (Connaught), Clare (Munster), and Fermanagh (Ulster). In outdoor demonstrations and parades of the Orange Order and at competitions, a keyless fife, not much used today, has served in Ulster to accompany large, two-headed "Lambeg" drums. More widely played is the tin whistle, formerly the penny whistle, which serves as a learning instrument, but also has its skilled exponents, including Mary Bergin and the late Micho Russell, who play in contrasting styles (figure 5).

The melodeon ("box"), concertina, and mouth organ ("French fiddle"), free-reed instruments that produce different pitches on a given key or hole, depending on whether air is pushed or pulled through the reeds, have been in traditional use since at least the late 1800s (CD track 10). Since then, the melodeon has been largely replaced by the diatonic accordion, and traditional music is also played on the piano accordion. All these free-reed instruments except the piano accordion are treated as monophonic instruments, and their harmonic provisions are used for drone effects or chords lightly imitative of those of pipes and fiddle. Instrumental traditions, mainly of fiddling, have been impressively adapted to the accordion and concertina by good local, and younger, musicians, like Noel Hill and Tony McMahon (Ward 1976).

Other instruments figure more marginally in the tradition: reports of earlier use of an ivy leaf (vibrating against the upper lip like a reed) are not supported by recordings, any more than those of the mouth harp. More regrettable is the lack of illustration of whistling without the aid of a pipe, for Henry Hudson's mid-nineteenth-century notation entitled "boy whistling for divartion [diversion]" illustrates a formerly common practice. Irish traditional music has little use for percussion, other than the player's foot in the case of instrumental music, but the *bodhrán* was a domestic utensil formerly used in some southwestern counties as a single-headed frame drum played with a short stick, and the revival has caused it to proliferate as an accompaniment to melody. Percussion is similarly provided by spoons and bones. The hammered dulcimer has few exponents. The imported tenor banjo, the mandolin, and the Irish bouzouki flourish in the revival environment, and warpipes, in their Scottish form, have recolonized Ireland through adoption of the Scottish tradition of pipe bands.

EDUCATION AND TRANSMISSION

Uncolonized by Rome, Ireland received Christianity in the fifth century—and with it, an international tradition of written scholarship in Latin. But early Irish literature of pagan inspiration, mainly extant in manuscripts only from the twelfth century, shows evidence of an older, learned, oral tradition. Respect for learning is a persistent feature of the later popular tradition, manifested as respect for old lore (*seanchas*).

Writing intervened early in the environment of traditional music, though it was a socially deprived environment, in which formal education came for a time from "hedge schools," run by poor traveling masters, some of whom could dispense Latin or Greek besides "rehearsing"—the learning of lessons by "reading aloud or humming together." Remnants of a profession of scribes, who continued to copy, among other things, the words of the lays of Fionn mac Cumhaill in versions some centuries old, lingered into the late 1800s.

The early popular tradition of Gaelic leaves a scarce musical and poetic record. English was used and taught in schools from the 1600s, and cheap printed matter, including song texts, was published to suit all tastes; the Gaelic tradition, however, stayed aloof. During this period, Gaelic culture was not immune from outside influ-

There is no modern evidence of extended improvisation in performance, though remnants of the *caoineadh* and a few spinning songs suggest that improvisation was former practice in those genres.

ence, but it exerted little influence outside its own community, and it was perceived by most English-speakers as linguistically and culturally remote.

The steady acquisition of English by native Irish speakers is seen in macaronic songs, chiefly of the nineteenth century. These alternate lines or verses of Irish and English, nonrepetitively or with the English translating the Irish. Some of these songs, with others wholly in Irish, appear on ballad sheets, whose chief function was probably to confer status on the language—a foreshadowing of the Gaelic revival movement, which began in the 1890s. Their conventions of spelling indicated what kind of literacy was expected, for they were those of English, not Irish (Shields 1990). Thus, while traditional songs in English were plentiful on the sheets, those in Irish were rare and belated in their appearance. Songs in Irish, apart from the handwritten lays, continued to be transmitted almost wholly by oral means.

In both languages, orality comes first. The notion of a "ballet" is familiar: a printed broadside or its later equivalents in writing, print, or photocopy. But singing or playing from *music* in company is unheard of, unless in church. One singer, whose father picked up songs "as quick as you would sing them, and tunes," describes the older man's incredulity in the 1930s at the news that a visiting pianist at a parish event had to play from music (Byrne 1989:39). Many traditional players today do learn from music, many reading imperfectly, some not at all; teachers of instruments vary in their use or avoidance of notation, which may take some simplified alphabetic or numerical form. Singers continue to learn the air by heart, though they might use a "ballet" of the words. Such aids to learning can be observed, but the processes of learning, retention, and recall cannot; performers find them difficult to talk about, and no useful study of them has been undertaken.

Schools have made little impression on the broad public perception of traditional music, and the music departments of universities are mainly concerned with classical studies: Irish music, as traditional music is usually called in the absence of a strong native classical tradition, has tended to appeal more to departments of Irish. Organizations providing opportunities for learning instruments are Comhaltas Ceoltóirí Éireann (Association of Irish Musicians), founded in 1951, and Na Píobairí Uilleann (Irish Pipers' Society). Radio and television have intermittent input into popular education; they review new publications and report numerous urban and rural events, held chiefly in summer, for example, the Willie Clancy Summer School, a major annual gathering of traditional musicians in the town of Miltown Malbay, County Clare. Such activities, organized mainly by local amateurs, provide Irish traditional music with its most effective educational contexts.

MUSIC AND CREATIVITY

Around 1840, the collector Edward Bunting declared that "the last airs having any Irish character" were those of the late-eighteenth-century piper Jackson (d. 1798). On hearing this, Bunting's junior, Henry Hudson, set about composing and publishing some airs of his own, which in due course the master seems to have admired as "genuine Irish" (or so Hudson says in manuscript notes dated 1 October 1841 and February 1844). The fraud is typical of its epoch, but it did not test the product on the proper public. For traditional musicians of the present day, the most successful new music is unattributable on grounds of style, perhaps like "The Mist-Covered Mountain," a jig commonly ascribed to the late Junior Crehan, a well-known County Clare fiddler. Songsmiths usually stay even closer to tradition by setting new texts to minimally adapted existing airs. Sheets and chapbooks often emphasized this practice by stating that a song is sung "to the air of" an older or more widely known one.

Variation provides the clearest indication of creativity. Traditional performers ignore detailed variation, as when an Ulster singer praised his father's singing by saying, "He neither put till nor took from." Deliberate and involuntary variations are not easily distinguished, but it is clear that players cultivate varied ornaments and alter the melodic line intentionally. In doing so, they produce idiomatic variants, but it is rare to hear rhythmic and chromatic effects as eccentric as those of the late Tommy Potts' fiddling. Idiomatic variation, easy to notice in successive repetitions within a rendition, is a rich source of invention, whether preserved from the past or in the concurrent versions that exist orally today. A particularly revealing case of this last kind is in the verbal texts of lyric songs in Irish. As a rule, these have no sequential narrative, but refer implicitly to narrative circumstances, or to a fact or a body of facts—*an t-údar* 'authority, authentication'—that the song may recall or celebrate (Shields 1993). To a degree uncommon in West European traditions, verses may be sung or omitted, or may suffer changes of order, or be supplemented by verses usually found in a different song or invented by the singer.

The modern notion of creativity is not prominent in the older tradition. The actual writing of song words has long been familiar in both languages, in English notably since the surge of patriotic songs with known or conjectured authors that began around 1798 and influenced oral tradition. Later, "folk songs" were made by Yeats and some of his precursors and successors. Cló Iar-Chonnachta publishes, in print and on cassette, Irish-language songs: songs that Raidió na Gaeltachta broadcasts; songs mainly from the Connemara Gaeltacht, including an assortment of old lyrics, new lyrics, in more or less traditional style, and pop songs.

The revival of dance music has had great success, prompting the composition of half-traditional, half-classical narrative suites: Shaun Davey's "The Brendan Voyage" (ca. 1980) and Charlie Lennon's "An Island Wedding" (1992). Probably most players compose on their instrument, and most singers make songs orally "to the lie of a good tune" (Ó Baoill 1959).

There is no modern evidence of extended improvisation in performance, though remnants of the *caoineadh* and a few spinning songs suggest that improvisation was former practice in those genres (Stanford 1902–1905, nos. 1172–1175, 1366–1368, 1473–1475). Róise Rua (Red-Haired Rose), a noted Donegal Gaelic singer recorded in the 1950s, tells of an Arranmore Island girl who, to get knitting wool distributed early and get home, by land and sea, before nightfall, extemporized verses praising the mainland shopkeepers (Ua Cnáimhsí 1988).

CONCEPTIONS OF MUSIC

The traditional community regards instrumental music and song as serious matters, though their present function is essentially recreational. Performance, especially of songs, entails absorption in the communicative act, and singing may be demanding: "That's a heavy old song" is a singer's frequent comment. Sometimes a tune is attributed to fairies, from whom the player is said to have learned or stolen it, the second case often leading to some sort of retribution.

Such motifs or beliefs, including the three-part classification of music commonplace in early Irish literature, should not be underestimated or overinterpreted. One text describes music as the birth of three sons (Goltraige, Gentraige, Suantraige) of a water goddess. Etymologically they relate, respectively, to sorrow, mirth, and sleep, and they have often been cited in modern traditional music, though their significance as a medieval or modern taxonomic ordering cannot be assumed. More interesting is their emphasis on potency. Used as narrative motifs, they signify the power of different kinds of music to induce sleep or inspire grief or joy. Another motif, which brutally confirms the power of music, is the magic lyre on the wall of a palace, which kills several men before coming to Dagda, the good god. These images are remote from modern traditional life, but we find parallels in such common situations as courtship, when a western suitor makes an Irish-language song that induces a girl to marry him (Ó Tiománaidhe 1906:47–48). In early literature, words and music have power, and the effect of words enhances the poet's status, especially in satire. The idea of the coercive power of medieval Irish poets appears in Yeats's play *The King's Threshold* (1904).

Songs seem to differ collectively from instrumental music in being more often classed as old, whether the term refers to age or takes affective value (an "oul' come-all-ye"). *Old* or *Irish* (a vaguer term) traditional music has had national appeal. Extreme republicans may find a message simply in its idiom, and some northern Protestants react by distancing themselves from what they hear as republican music. Both mistake the whole tradition for just "party" (sectarian) songs. Party songs there are, and with other political and patriotic songs they begin to appear, in English, around the 1790s, but the only thoroughly patriotic genre—in Irish—was probably the medieval *laoi Fiannaíochta.*

CONTEXTS FOR MUSIC

Of music with special cyclical or occupational associations, only a few remnants have been noted: the death lament, choral practices, domestic spinning songs, plow whistles, Gaelic lullabies, and religious songs (*amhráin bheannaithe* or *dánta*) at Easter. A few seasonal ceremonies with music are in limited use: mumming at Christmas in Ulster and Leinster, celebration of the days of Christmas, "wren boys" begging on St. Stephen's day, 26 December (MacDonogh 1983), and "Biddy boys" on St. Bridget's day, 1 February in Munster. The political celebrations of the Protestant Orange Order in Ulster (12 July) were conceived some two centuries ago, when varied outdoor activity was common. Fairs and other occasions gave ballad singers good opportunity to hawk their wares (Murphy 1979).

Despite public diversity, it was domestic practice, largely lacking any apparent formal organization, that dominated performance in the past. Irish has a surprising number of terms for domestic evening entertainment and visiting; the most widely known, *céilí,* underwent a change of meaning in the 1920s and 1930s, when it was applied to the simplified traditional dances held in halls with a "*céilí* band" (McCann 1983). The traditional fireside *céilí* is not extinct, though singing and playing has moved more into pubs and clubs, where one usually finds only singing or, much oftener, playing (Carson 1986).

Instruments are in good supply today. Radio, television, and the recording industry, when they intervene in traditional music, often present good players and wide variety, potential models and a source of repertory. They unavoidably process the product in varying degrees, and combine with other agencies to serve new audiences best described collectively as a tourist public. Concert halls represent an inter-

FIGURE 6 Singing and playing in informal gatherings in a home, a pub, or a club are often considered the most enjoyable and original contexts for performing and listening to Irish traditional music. Without the formality and distance between performers and audiences, such sessions feature intimate gatherings of family and friends, many of whom are expert singers and musicians. In this gathering, of *sean-nós* 'old-style' singers in 1998, Caitlín Ní Dhomhnaill of Ranafast, County Donegal, sings for other singers, who listen intently. Photo courtesy of Lillis Ó Laoire.

mediate state, but old-style programs held in the National Concert Hall (Dublin) have been cool affairs, ruled by refined acoustics. Perhaps the most useful function of concerts is to bring together the participants in an ensuing musical session (figure 6).

SOCIAL GROUPS

In the 1500s, the serious decline of monolingual Gaelic society began, and poets of courtly formation began to adapt themselves to humbler conditions of life. Music, then still undocumented, tended to follow this evolution. By the 1600s, most Roman Catholic Irish-speakers were landless peasants, while the Protestant religion and the English were associated with the socially ascendant. Some popular songs in Irish, like the love song "*Eibhlín a Rún*" ('Eileen My Treasure'), leave a record in the concerts and spectacles of English-speaking Dublin society of the 1700s—though urban polite society looked to London and Europe for its music. Despite historical inequalities, class consciousness is not particularly divisive in Ireland; some of the wealthy and the academically endowed practiced traditional music from at least the time of piper Jackson (fl. 1770s–1798) (Breathnach 1976). Much of the traditional music of Ulster was taken there by Protestant settlers, mainly from Scotland. Irish migrant workers (*spailpíní,* later "tattie-howkers") and Travellers ("tinkers") have been important disseminators of song and music, in Ireland and between Ireland and Britain. With the democratization of education in the twentieth century, the cultivation of traditional music has passed partly into the hands of teachers and other graduates or academically trained people for whom music is usually an amateur interest, though good exponents may be of recent rural ancestry and "bring the music with them."

English- and Scots-speaking women have sung lyric songs in general; Irish-speaking women singers have also flourished in specifically female genres (*caoineadh* 'lament', *amhráin bheannaithe* or *dánta* 'religious songs', and lullabies), not sung now, or little sung. Since the revival, women instrumentalists have been more common. Previously they played socially acceptable instruments: traditionally the concertina and on concert platforms or in broadcast performances, the harp. Young children seem to maintain the play-song tradition—a tradition more of the English lan-

At sessions the boundary between performers and the audience is subtle and shifting; moreover, the socializing within the session can be as important as the music itself.

guage than of the Irish. Most children have scarce opportunities for learning adult music traditionally and every incentive to find more commercially viable musical interests.

—HUGH SHIELDS

THE REVIVAL OF IRISH MUSIC

Music and dance were highly valued social practices in rural Ireland during the nineteenth and early twentieth centuries, when traditional instrumental music was usually played to accompany dancing. Contexts included crossroads dances, at which professional or semiprofessional itinerant musicians, usually a piper or fiddler, played outdoors for local residents, who danced and socialized, and the *céilí*, where friends and neighbors gathered to drink, sing, dance, tell stories, and play music for one another (Glassie 1982). Singing was traditionally unaccompanied, but instrumental music, though often solo, was played in unison by informal, impermanent groups of two or three musicians.

Traditional dancing and the rural *céilí* suffered a serious decline during the economic downturn of the 1930s. The Dance Hall Act of 1935 banned crossroads dancing, many dance halls closed, and the lack of employment at home led many rural musicians, with their neighbors, to leave the countryside to find work in Dublin, London, and the United States. The loss of traditional contexts for dancing led to a decline in the playing of traditional music throughout the country. During the 1940s and 1950s, the Pipers' Club in Dublin became a gathering place for many dispossessed rural musicians, including the fiddlers John Kelly and Tommy Potts, the pipers Leo Rowsome and Tommy Reck, and the whistle player Seán Potts.

Though the dance-music tradition declined in rural Ireland, it was reinterpreted as the *céilí* band in urban contexts among Irish emigrant communities of Britain and America. Influenced by popular dance bands of the 1920s to 1950s and consisting of multiple fiddles, flutes, accordions, piano, and drum set, *céilí* bands presented dance tunes in a danceable style in which rhythm, harmony, and collective playing eliminated much of the ornamental subtlety of traditional solo playing. Initially a creation of the nationalist organization Conradh na Gaeilge (The Gaelic League) in the late 1800s, the *céilí* band was an early example of collective playing in Irish music, and by the 1950s it had become extremely popular, throughout Ireland and in emigrant communities.

In the 1950s, an aesthetic reaction against *céilí* bands by intellectuals and the influence of commercialized American folk music, followed by an unprecedented increase in economic prosperity in rural Ireland in the 1960s, combined to form the basis for a so-called revival of Irish traditional music along four paths: an increase in recording and broadcasting traditional music, the development of sponsored competitions and group instrumental playing, a so-called ballad boom, and the innovations of the composer Seán Ó Riada (Hamilton 1998).

In 1947, Radio Éireann, which since its inception (1926) had broadcast traditional singers and musicians from its Dublin studios, set up a mobile broadcast unit and began recording in rural areas of Ireland. Recorded for the unit by collectors including famed *uilleann* piper Séamus Ennis, Proinsias Ó Conluain, and Ciarán Mac Mathúna, the programs increased public awareness of the richness of Irish traditional music, and a generation of older rural singers and musicians became known to, and admired by, the Irish public.

In 1951, members of the Pipers' Club formed the musicians' organization Comhaltas Ceoltóirí Éireann. They organized competitive local, regional, and national festivals each year, culminating in the Fleadh Cheoil na hÉireann (Festival of Music of Ireland). The competitions spurred interest among young people, who, in increasing numbers, began learning to play traditional musical instruments, especially the *uilleann* pipes, the tin whistle, the concert flute, the fiddle, the concertina, and the button accordion. Looking for opportunities to play informally, experienced and beginning musicians began to gather in so-called pub sessions; in the process, they created a new tradition of collective playing. Combining music and socializing, sessions usually occur once a week on a specified night in a selected pub or in someone's home, though in some towns, they occur every night in every pub. At sessions, the boundary between performers and audience is subtle and shifting, and the socializing within the session can be as important as the music itself. The repertoire is almost exclusively dance music (predominantly reels), but dancing, except in certain rural districts (including parts of County Clare), was largely absent from instrumental sessions until the 1970s, when an active revival of set dancing fostered dancing as part of the social atmosphere of the evening.

A third influence on the Irish revival came from the folk revival in the United States. The Clancy Brothers and Tommy Makem, emigrants from Ireland and aspiring actors in New York in the 1950s, began playing Irish songs in the folk-club scene in Greenwich Village, accompanying themselves on guitars and banjo and singing in unison, on the model of American groups like the Weavers. Their popularity and commercial success inspired similar groups in Ireland (the Dubliners and the Wolfe Tones) and Scotland (the Corries), and an active scene in pubs and folk clubs in Ireland and Great Britain, called ballad singing. In this context, the word *ballad* refers not to the narrative songs favored by scholars, but to what folk revivalists might have generically called a folk song.

Seán Ó Riada (1931–1971)—a classically trained composer, who served as music director at Radio Éireann and later at Dublin's renowned Abbey Theatre and was affiliated with Gael-Linn, an organization that encouraged the use of the Irish language and became one of Ireland's main record companies—developed a fourth element of the Irish folk revival. In 1960, for Bryan MacMahon's folk play *The Song of the Anvil* at the Abbey Theatre, he organized traditional musicians into a group that became known as Ceoltóirí Chualann (Musicians of Cualann, a region of Dublin). Through his selection of instruments and his arrangements, he effectively invented a new tradition, a fusion of his training in classical music, his ideas about Irish music, particularly the harp tradition as exemplified by Turlough Ó Carolan (1670–1738), and the tunes and styles of living musicians. His choice of instruments included *uilleann* pipes, two fiddles, a flute, a whistle, a button accordion, a concertina, a harpsichord (which he played), and a *bodhrán,* a goatskin frame drum associated with the Wren Boys ritual on St. Stephen's Day. He carefully orchestrated alternating solos and instrument combinations, and added countermelodies and chords in a way that highlighted the ornamental style of individual musicians and contrasted sharply with the *céilí*-band style. He revived Carolan's music, no longer in the oral tradition, but which had been recently compiled, edited, and published by Donal

FIGURE 7   A poster advertises a concert in
August 1973, following the release of Planxty's
first (and seminal) album. *Clockwise from top
left:* Christy Moore, Andy Irvine, Donal Lunny,
Liam Ó Floinn. Photo by Paulette Gershen.

O'Sullivan (1983 [1958]). His group became extremely popular with the urban middle class and the artistic scene in Dublin. They recorded several influential albums for
Gael-Linn. Affiliated musicians, under the leadership of the piper Paddy Moloney,
became The Chieftains, who recorded their first album (1963) for the newly founded
Claddagh Records, and went on to become world-famous as performers of Irish
music and a model for other touring bands, who perform at pubs, folk festivals, folk
clubs, and formal concerts.

In the 1970s, some famed and widely imitated bands, inspired by two seminal
groups (the Johnstons and Sweeney's Men) and led by innovative musicians (including Paul Brady, Christy Moore, Andy Irvine, and Donal Lunny), fused the traditional
instruments of bands like The Chieftains with guitar-based ballad singing and influences from rock and jazz to produce arrangements with complex instrumental
accompaniments and virtuosic, hard-driving instrumentals—a tradition set by
Planxty, The Bothy Band, De Danann, and Clannad, and continued into the 1980s
and 1990s by Altan and many others (figure 7).

From the 1970s to the 1990s, the revival flourished in the hands of scores of
young instrumentalists and singers who emerged from the competitive festival
(*fleadh*) and sessions to make influential recordings, which in turn fed the revival. For
some of these musicians, the boundaries between traditional music and rock were
permeable. The rock band Horslips incorporated traditional material in the 1970s,
and in the 1980s Moore and Lunny formed Moving Hearts, a band that fused traditional and rock music and combined saxophone and *uilleann* pipes. In the 1990s,
The Chieftains recorded with Mick Jagger, Tom Jones, Van Morrison, Sinéad
O'Connor, and Ricky Skaggs. In the late 1980s and 1990s, several Irish bands and
singers became prominent in international popular music. These included the
Cranberries, the Hothouse Flowers, the Pogues, Sinéad O'Connor, and U2. They
sometimes credit Irish traditional music and its associated cultural experience as a
source of inspiration, even when traditional elements are not obviously present in
their music.

—PAULETTE GERSHEN

HISTORY OF SCHOLARSHIP

In an enthusiastic page on the Irish harping seen and heard in the 1180s, the Welsh-Norman visitor Giraldus Cambrensis looks like the first in a line of commentators on Irish music, but he lacked successors, and the Irish themselves long refrained from objective study of it. Medieval records include sung or chanted poems, but omit their music. The oldest extant manuscript collection of traditional Irish tunes seems to date only from the 1780s. By then, many native tunes had survived in publications aimed at leisured music readers. Sixteenth-century English music collections contain some titles that suggest Irish origin, but the tunes themselves are less encouraging. The Irishness of even the most likely of them, "Callino custure me" ('I am a young girl from beside the River Suir [?]') is uncertain. The English-speakers of eighteenth-century Dublin leave us more familiar tunes in ballad operas or printed in collections or on sheets with "symphonies" for keyboard or guitar. John and William Neal (1986 [1724]) give mainly harp tunes. The Irish harp has had a long history, and in the 1780s it became an object of attempted revival (Walker 1818). It was associated with poetry of the legendary Irish bard Ossian, whose European celebrity stimulated the publishing of songs and lays in Irish and writings about them. Harp festivals, notably one at Belfast in 1792, were held. Harp societies, founded to teach blind children the instrument, were sustained for a time, but were finally abandoned (McClelland 1975). By the mid-1800s, the harp-playing tradition admired by Giraldus had disappeared.

Edward Bunting, transcriber of music at the 1792 festival, wrote down some remnants of harp music. He was the first of a line of major nineteenth-century collectors of music, including William Forde, Henry Hudson, George Petrie, J. E. Pigot, James Goodman, and P. W. Joyce. Francis O'Neill's collections were made in Chicago during the early twentieth century from emigrants and personal recall; his volumes (especially 1965 [1907]) have long been used by traditional players who can read music.

Nineteenth-century collectors, knowing little Irish and not caring for the songs in English that came their way, satisfied their patriotic sentiments by collecting Irish melodies. They often preserved songs as airs without words—a famous example is the "Londonderry Air." Linguistic scholars of Irish recorded songs as words without airs—a traditional practice, linked to Gaelic fascination with words. In 1936, the strength of the verbal tradition in folklore prompted the founding of the Irish Folklore Commission, now the Department of Irish Folklore at University College Dublin. The commission's chief aim was to collect spoken texts, primarily in Irish, but in the 1940s it had a notable collector of Gaelic songs in Séamus Ennis, and for the department since the 1970s, Tom Munnelly has recorded on tape a substantial collection of songs mainly in English. In 1987, the Irish Traditional Music Archive, an active and independent organization directed by Nicholas Carolan, was founded in Dublin.

In the twentieth century, a certain number of unpublished music collections—Goodman 1998, vol. 1 (of two to date); Henry 1990 [1923–1939], a newspaper series; Joyce 1909; Petrie's by Stanford, 1902–1905—were edited. Bunting's three volumes (1796, 1809, 1840) have been substantially reedited. Numerous smaller collections have appeared, and some of them represent the music better than their predecessors could do: collections of songs in English (Morton 1970, 1973; Munnelly 1994; Shields 1981), songs in Irish (Costello 1990 [1919]); De Noraidh 1965, 1994–; Freeman 1920–1922), and instrumental music (Breathnach 1963, 1976, 1985; Mitchell 1976; Mitchell and Small 1986; O'Leary 1994). Many sound recordings have been issued, as have numerous editions in book form, complemented by sound recordings.

Breandán Breathnach, founder of the journal *Ceol* (1963–1986), was closely involved with *uilleann* pipers and in 1968 was the prime mover of the pipers' society, Na Píobairí Uilleann. In 1971, he and others founded the Folk Music Society of Ireland.

FIGURE 8   Breandán Breathnach, one of Ireland's leading folk-music scholars. Photo by Paulette Gershen, 1978.

The *Journal of the Irish Folk Song Society* began publishing in the early twentieth century (1905–1939). By mid-century, one of the society's members, Donal O'Sullivan, was almost the only scholar writing on traditional Irish music. He placed more emphasis on historical context than on music—a method suited to his edition of the harper Carolan (O'Sullivan 1983 [1958]). In contrast, Breandán Breathnach, founder of the journal *Ceol* (1963–1986), was closely involved with *uilleann* pipers and in 1968 was the prime mover of the pipers' society, Na Píobairí Uilleann. In 1971, he and others founded the Folk Music Society of Ireland (figure 8). The two organizations have published the newsletters *An Píobaire* (which continues at present) and *Ceol Tíre,* both mainly in English, with notes of interest to researchers. The Folk Music Society publishes an occasional journal, *Irish Folk Music Studies,* and both societies have produced books, pamphlets, and tapes. Other journals with articles of scholarly musical interest include *Ceol na hÉireann, Béaloideas, Dal gCais,* and *Ulster Folklife.*

Irish traditional music is not well covered in higher institutions in Ireland. At Queen's University, Belfast, John Blacking (1928–1990) initiated a center for ethnomusicology, mainly concerned with non-European research. University College Cork focuses on Irish music in a tradition influenced by the late Seán Ó Riada. In 1994, Mícheál Ó Súilleabháin founded the Irish World Music Centre at the University of Limerick. At University College Dublin, Thérèse Smith's research interests are African-American and Irish traditional music. Research on traditional Irish music is also conducted by Ann Buckley on historical organology, Nicholas Carolan on discography and early sources, Sean Donnelly on history of instruments, Breandán Ó Madagáin on music in Gaelic society, Paul McGettrick on music technology, Colette Moloney on Bunting's manuscripts, Colm Ó Baoill on music and Irish language, Tom Munnelly on songs (especially ballads) in English, and Hugh Shields on singing and narrative song. The Limerick-born emigrant folklorist Mick Moloney writes on Irish music in America. Non-Irish scholars who have contributed to the study of Irish music are Joan Rimmer on historical organology, Albrecht Schneider on musical evolution, James Cowdery on melody, G.-D. Zimmermann on songs in history, Jos Koning on dance-music, and Lawrence McCullough on style. For references to sources, there are a discography (Carolan 1987), a bibliography of songs (Shields 1985), and an annotated bibliography dealing with Ireland in the context of the British Isles (Porter 1989).

—HUGH SHIELDS

BIBLIOGRAPHY

Acton, Charles. 1978. *Irish Music and Musicians.* Dublin: Eason and Sons.

Bodley, Seóirse. 1973. "Technique and Structure in 'Sean-Nós' Singing." *Irish Folk Music Studies* 1:44–53.

Bradshaw, Harry. 1991. *Michael Coleman: 1891–1945.* Dublin: Viva Voce. Booklet with 2 cassettes.

Brady, Eilis. 1975. *All in! All in! A Selection of Dublin Children's Traditional Street Games with Rhymes and Music.* Dublin: Comhairle Bhéaloideas Éireann.

Breathnach, Breandán, ed. 1963, 1976, 1985. *Ceol Rince na hÉireann.* 3 vols. Dublin: An Gúm.

———. 1968–1969. "Mairseáil Alasdruim." *Ceol* 3(2):38–42; 3(3):79–85; see also 2(3) [1966?] 71, 75–76.

———. 1971. *Folk Music and Dances of Ireland.* Dublin: Talbot Press.

———. 1976. "Piper Jackson." *Irish Folk Music Studies* 2:41–57.

———. 1983. *Dancing in Ireland.* Miltown Malbay: Dal gCais.

———. 1989. *Ceol agus Rince na hÉireann.* Dublin: An Gúm. Translation and revision of Breathnach 1971 in Irish, with added references.

Buckley, Ann. 1978. "What Was the Tiompán?" *Jahrbuch für musikalische Volks- und Völkerkunde* 9:53–88.

———. 1990. "Musical Instruments in Ireland from the Ninth to the Fourteenth Centuries." In *Musicology in Ireland,* ed. Gerard Gillen and Harry White, 13–57. Irish Musical Studies, 1. Dublin: Irish Academic Press.

Bunting, Edward, ed. 1796, 1809, 1840. The three collections reedited from the original manuscripts. Corresponding to 1796 and 1809: Donal O'Sullivan, "The Bunting Collection of Irish Folk Music and Songs," *Journal of the Irish Folk Song Society* 22–39, 6 parts, 1927–1939. Corresponding to 1840: Donal O'Sullivan and Mícheál Ó Súilleabháin, *Bunting's Ancient Music of Ireland* (Cork: Cork University Press, 1983).

Byrne, Packie Manus. 1989. *Recollections of a Donegal Man.* Edited by Stephen Jones. Lampeter: Roger Millington.

Carolan, Nicholas. 1984. "Two Irish Harps in Co. Dublin." *Ceol* 7(1–2):40–45.

———. 1987. *A Short Discography of Irish Folk Music.* Dublin: Folk Music Society of Ireland.

———. 1997. *A Harvest Saved: Francis O'Neill and Irish Music in Chicago.* Cork: Ossian Publications.

Carson, Ciarán. 1986. *Irish Traditional Music.* Belfast: Appletree Press.

———. 1996. *Last Night's Fun: A Book about Irish Traditional Music.* London: Jonathan Cape.

Ceol na hÉireann. 1993–. Dublin: Na Píobairí Uilleann.

Costello, Eileen, ed. 1990 [1919]. *Amhráin Mhuighe Seola: Traditional Folk Songs from Galway and Mayo.* County Galway: Cló Iar-Chonnachta, Indreabhán.

Cowdery, James. 1990. *The Melodic Tradition of Ireland.* Kent, Ohio: Kent State University Press.

De Noraidh, Liam, ed. 1965. *Ceol ón Mumhan.* Dublin: An Clóchomhar.

———. 1994. *A Collection of Songs and Airs Made in East Munster.* Edited by Dáithí Ó hÓgáin. Binneas thar Meon, 1. Dublin: Comhairle Bhéaloideas Éireann.

Donnelly, Seán. 1981–1984. "The Warpipes in Ireland." *Ceol* 5(1):19–24, 5(2):55–59, 6(1):19–23, 6(2):54–58.

Fairbairn, Hazel. 1994. "Changing Contexts for Traditional Dance Music in Ireland: The Rise of Group Performance Practice." *Folk Music Journal* 6(5):566–599.

Feldman, Allen, and Eamonn O'Doherty, eds. 1979. *The Northern Fiddler.* Belfast: Blackstaff Press.

Freeman, A. M., ed. 1920–1922. "Irish Folk Songs from Ballyvourney [County Cork]." *Journal of the Folk Song Society* 6(23–25):vii–xxviii, 95–342.

Glassie, Henry. 1982. *Passing the Time.* Dublin: O'Brien Press.

Goan, Cathal, Hugh Shields, Douglas Sealy, et al. 1985. *Scéalamhráin Cheilteacha.* Dublin: An Clóchomhar.

Goodman, James, collector. 1998. *Tunes of the Munster Pipers.* Vol. 1. Edited by Hugh Shields. Dublin: Irish Traditional Music Archive.

Gronow, Pekka. 1979. *The Columbia 33000-f Irish Series.* Los Angeles: John Edwards Memorial Foundation, University of California at Los Angeles.

Hamilton, Samuel Colin. 1990. *The Irish Flute Player's Handbook.* Cork: Breac Publications.

———. 1998. "The Role of Commercial Recordings in the Development and Survival of Irish Traditional Music, 1899–1993." Ph.D. diss. University College, Cork.

Harris, Bernard, and Grattan Freyer. 1981. *Integrating Tradition: The Achievement of Seán Ó Riada.* Terrybaun, Bofeenaun, Ballina: Irish Humanities Centre & Keohanes.

Harrison, Frank. 1976. "Towards a Chronology of Celtic Folk Instruments." *Studia Instrumentorum Musicae Popularis* 4:98–101.

———. 1988. *Irish Traditional Music: Fossil or Resource?* Ó Riada Memorial Lecture 3. Cork: University College.

Henebry, Richard. 1928. *A Handbook of Irish Music.* Cork: Cork University Press.

[Henry, Sam, ed.]. 1990. *Sam Henry's Songs of the People.* Edited by Gale Huntington and Lani Herrmann, with John Moulden. Athens and London: University of Georgia Press.

Jackson, W[alker]. 1790. *Jackson's Celebrated Irish Tunes.* Dublin: John Lee.

Joyce, Patrick Weston, ed. 1909. *Old Irish Folk Music and Songs.* Dublin: University Press.

Koning, Jos. 1979. "'That Old Plaintive Touch': On the Relation Between Tonality in Irish Traditional Dance-Music and the Left Hand Technique of Fiddlers in East Co. Clare, Ireland." *Studia Instrumentorum Musicae Popularis* 6:80–84.

———. 1980. "The Fieldworker as Performer: Fieldwork Objectives and Social Roles in County Clare, Ireland." *Ethnomusicology* 24:417–429.

Lynch, Larry. 1989. *Set Dances of Ireland: Tradition & Evolution.* San Francisco and Miltown Malbay, County Clare: Séadna Books.

McCann, May. 1983. "Belfast Ceilidhes: The Heyday." *Ulster Folklife* 29:55–69.

McClelland, Aiken. 1975. "The Irish Harp Society." *Ulster Folklife* 21:15–24.

McCullough, Lawrence E. 1977. "Style in Traditional Irish Music." *Ethnomusicology* 21:85–97.

MacDonogh, Steve. 1983. *Green and Gold: The Wren Boys of Dingle.* Dingle, County Kerry: Brandon Books.

Mac Lochlainn, Alf. 1967. "Broadside Ballads in Irish." *Éigse* 12(2):115–122.

McNamee, Peter, ed. 1991. *Traditional Music: Whose Music?* Belfast: Institute of Irish Studies.

Macpherson, James. 1760. *Fragments of Ancient Poetry, Collected in the Highlands of Scotland, and Translated from the Galic [sic] or Erse Language.*

Meek, Bill. 1987. *Paddy Moloney and the Chieftains.* London: Gill and Macmillan.

Mitchell, Pat, ed. 1976. *The Dance Music of Willie Clancy.* Dublin and Cork: Mercier.

———, and Jackie Small, eds. 1986. *The Piping of Patsy Touhey.* Dublin: Na Píobairí Uilleann.

Morton, Robin, ed. 1970. *Folk Songs Sung in Ulster.* Cork: Mercier.

———. ed. 1973. *Come Day, Go Day, God Send Sunday: The Songs and Life Story . . . of John Maguire.* London: Routledge and Kegan Paul.

Moylan, Terry, ed. 1981. *Ceol an Phíobaire.* Dublin: Na Píobairí Uilleann.

Munnelly, Tom. 1975. "The Singing Traditions of Irish Travellers." *Folk Music Journal* 3(1):3–30.

———. 1980–1981. "Songs of the Sea: A General Description with Special Reference to Recent Oral Literature in Ireland." *Béaloideas* 48–49:30–58.

———. 1986. "Narrative Songs in West Clare." In *Ballad Research: The Stranger in Ballad Narrative and Other Topics,* ed. Hugh Shields, 35–48. Dublin: Folk Music Society of Ireland.

———. ed. 1994. *The Mount Callan Garland: Songs of Tom Lenihan, Co. Clare.* Dublin: Comhairle Bhéaloideas Éireann. Book with 2 cassettes.

Murphy, Maura. 1979. "The Balladsinger and the Role of the Seditious Ballad in 19th-Century Ireland: Dublin Castle's View." *Ulster Folklife* 25:79–102.

Neal, John, and William Neal, eds. 1986 [1724]. *A Collection of the Most Celebrated Irish Tunes.* Facsimile edition. Edited by Nicholas Carolan. Dublin: Folk Music Society of Ireland.

[Ó Baoill] Ó Baoighill, Seán, ed. 1944. *Cnuasacht de Cheoltaí Uladh.* [Newry:] Comhaltas Uladh.

[Ó Baoill] O'Boyle, Sean. 1959. "The Sources of Ulster Folk Song." *Ulster Folklife* 5:48–53.

———. ed. 1976. *The Irish Song Tradition.* Dublin: Gilbert Dalton.

———. 1980. *Ogham: The Poet's Secret.* Dublin: Gilbert Dalton.

Ó Canainn, Tomás. 1978. *Traditional Music in Ireland.* London: Routledge and Kegan Paul.

O'Connor, Nuala. 1991. *Bringing It All Back Home: The Influence of Irish Music.* London: BBC Books.

O'Leary, Johnny. 1994. *Johnny O'Leary of Sliabh Luachra: Dance Music from the Cork-Kerry Border.* Edited by Terry Moylan. Dublin: Lilliput Press.

Ó Lochlainn, Colm. 1967. *Songwriters of Ireland in the English Tongue.* Dublin: Three Candles Press.

Ó Madagáin, Breandán. 1985. "Functions of Irish Song in the Nineteenth Century." *Béaloideas* 53:130–216.

———. 1993. "Song for Emotional Release in the Gaelic Tradition." In *Music and the Church,* ed. Gerard Gillen and Harry White, 254–275. Irish Musical Studies, 2. Dublin: Irish Academic Press.

Ó Muirithe, Diarmuid, ed. 1980. *An tAmhrán Macarónach* (The macaronic song). Dublin: An Clóchomhar.

———, ed. 1982. *The Wexford Carols.* Dublin: Dolmen.

O'Neill, Francis, ed. 1963 [1903]. *O'Neill's Music of Ireland: 1850 Melodies.* New York: Dan Collins.

———, ed. 1965 [1907]. *The Dance Music of Ireland: 1001 Gems.* Dublin: Walton.

———. 1973 [1910]. *Irish Folk Music: A Fascinating Hobby,* with introduction by Barry O'Neill. Darby, Pennsylvania: Norwood Editions.

———. 1973 [1913]. *Irish Minstrels and Musicians.* Introduction by Barry O'Neill. Darby, Pa.: Norwood Editions.

Ó Riada, Seán. 1982. *Our Musical Heritage.* Edited by Tomás Kinsella and Tomás Ó Canainn. Mountrath: Fundúireacht an Riadaigh and Dolmen Press.

Ó Súilleabháin, Mícheál. 1990. "The Creative Process in Irish Traditional Dance Music." In *Musicology in Ireland,* ed. Gerard Gillen and Harry White, 117–130. Irish Musical Studies, 1. Dublin: Irish Academic Press.

O'Sullivan, Donal, ed. 1981 [1960]. *Songs of the Irish.* Cork: Mercier.

———, ed. 1983 [1958]. *Carolan: The Life, Times and Music of an Irish Harper.* 2 vols. Louth, Lincolnshire: Celtic Music.

Ó Tiománaidhe, Mícheál, ed. 1906. *Abhráin Ghaedhilge an Iarthair.* Vol. 1. Dublin: Gill.

Partridge (Bourke), Angela. 1983. *Caoineadh na dTrí Muire: Téama na Páise i bhFilíocht Bhéil na Gaeilge* (The lament of the three Marys: An Easter theme of oral poetry in Irish). Dublin: An Clóchomhar.

Partridge (Bourke), Angela, and Hugh Shields, eds. 1981. "Amhráin Bheannaithe as Co. na Gaillimhe agus as Tír Chonaill." *Irish Folk Music Studies* 3:18–44.

Petrie, George, ed. 1978 [1855, 1882]. *Ancient Music of Ireland.* 2 vols. reprinted in 1. Kansas City, Mo.: Gregg International.

Porter, James. 1989. *The Traditional Music of Britain and Ireland: A Select Bibliography and Research Guide.* New York and London: Garland.

Ranson, Joseph, ed. 1975 [1948]. *Songs of the Wexford Coast.* Darby, Pa.: Norwood Editions.

Rimmer, Joan. 1969. *The Irish Harp.* Cork: Mercier Press.

Schneider, Albrecht. 1981. "Orale Tradition, Musikgeschichte und Folklorismus in Irland: Das Kontinuitätsproblem und die historische Volksmusikforschung." *Historische Volksmusikforschung,* 117–157. Graz: Akademischer Druck.

Shields, Hugh, ed. 1964. "Some Bonny Female Sailors." *Ulster Folklife* 10:35–45.

———. 1971a. "Singing Traditions in a Bilingual Parish in N.-W. Ireland [Glencolumbkille]." *Yearbook of the International Folk Music Council* 3:109–119.

———. 1971b, 1972a. "Some 'Songs and Ballads in use in the Province of Ulster . . . 1845'." *Ulster Folklife* 17:3–24, 18:34–65.

———. 1972b. "Old British Ballads in Ireland." *Folklife* 10:68–103.

———. 1973. "Supplementary Syllables in Anglo-Irish Folk Singing." *Yearbook of the International Folk Music Council* 5:62–71.

———, ed. 1981. *Shamrock, Rose and Thistle: Folk Singing in North Derry.* Belfast: Blackstaff Press.

———. 1982. "Literacy and the Ballad Genre in Ireland." In *Proceedings of the 12th International Folk Ballad Conference (Alden Biesen, 22–26 July 1981),* ed. Stefaan Top, 151–165. Brussels: Centrum voor Vlaamse Volkscultuur.

———. 1984. "Singing in Arranmore, 1977." *Ceol* 7(1–2):3–12.

———. 1985. *A Short Bibliography of Irish Folk Song.* Dublin: Folk Music Society of Ireland.

———. 1990. "Printed Aids to Folk Singing, 1700–1900." In *The Origins of Popular Literacy in Ireland,* ed. Mary Daly and David Dickson, 139–152. Dublin: Trinity College Dublin and University College Dublin.

———. 1991. "Popular Modes of Narration and the Popular Ballad." In *The Ballad and Oral Literature,* ed. Joseph Harris, 40–59. Cambridge: Harvard University Press.

———. 1993. *Narrative Singing in Ireland: Lays, Ballads, Come-All-Yes and Other Songs.* Dublin: Irish Academic Press.

Stanford, C. V., ed. 1902–1905. *The Complete Petrie Collection of Irish Music.* 3 vols. London: Boosey & Co.

Taylor, Barry. 1984. "The Irish Ceili Band—A Break With Tradition?" *Dal gCais* 7:67–74.

Tunney, Paddy. 1979. *The Stone Fiddle: My Way to Traditional Song.* Dublin: Gilbert Dalton.

Ua Cnáimhsí, Pádraig. 1988. *Róise Rua.* Dublin: Sairséal and Ó Marcaigh.

Walker, Joseph Cooper. 1818. *Historical Memoirs of the Irish Bards.* 2nd ed. 2 vols. Dublin: J. Christie.

Ward, Allan. 1976. "Music from Sliabh Luachra." *Traditional music* 5:1–31.

White, Harry. 1984. "The Need for a Sociology of Irish Folk Music: A Review of Writings on 'Traditional' Music in Ireland, with some Responses and Proposals." *International Review of the Aesthetics and Sociology of Music* 15(1):3–13.

Zimmermann, G.-D. 1967. *Songs of Irish Rebellion.* Dublin: Allen Figgis.

———. 1981. "What Is an Irish Ballad?" *Irish Folk Music Studies* 3:5–17.

AUDIOVISUAL RESOURCES

Altan. 1995. *The First Ten Years of Altan.* Green Linnet Records GLCD 1153. Compact disc.

Barry, Margaret. 1976. *Ireland's Own Margaret Barry.* Outlet SOLP 1029. LP disk.

Bergin, Mary. 1979. *Feadóga Stáin [Tin Whistles].* Gael-Linn CEF 071. LP disk.

Bothy Band. 1975. *The Bothy Band 1975.* Mulligan LUN 002. LP disk.

Brady, Paul. 1978. *Welcome Here Kind Stranger.* Mulligan LUN024. Cassette.

Breathnach, Breandán, ed. 1971. *Folk Music and Dances of Ireland.* Mercier MCT 344. Cassette.

Burke, Joe. 1974. *Traditional Music of Ireland.* Shaskeen OS 361. LP disk.

Burke, Kevin. 1978. *If the Cap Fits.* Mulligan LUN 021. Compact disc.

Butcher, Eddie. 1976. *Shamrock, Rose and Thistle.* Leader LED 2070. LP disk.

Byrne, Packie Manus. 1975. *Songs of a Donegal Man.* Topic 12TS 257. LP disk.

Canny, Paddy, and P. J. Hayes. 1960. *All-Ireland Champions.* DU-LP 1003. LP disk.

Casey, Bobby. 1979. *Taking Flight.* Dublin: Mulligan LUN 018. LP disk.

Chieftains, The. 1963. *Chieftains.* Ceirníní Cladaigh CC2. LP disk.

Children's Songs. 1974. *Green Peas and Barley O!* Arts Council of Northern Ireland LPS 3018. LP disk.

Cinnamond, Robert. 1975. *You Rambling Boys of Pleasure.* Topic 12T 269. LP disk.

Clancy Brothers and Tommy Makem. 1963. *In Person at Carnegie Hall.* CBS BPG 62020. Cassette.

Clancy, Willie. 1967. *Willie Clancy, the Minstrel from Clare.* Topic 12T175. LP disk.

Clannad. 1974. *Clannad 2.* Gael-Linn CEF 041. LP disk.

Coleman, Michael. 1976. *The Legacy of Michael Coleman.* Shanachie 33002. LP disk.

Corcoran, Sean, ed. 1986. *Here Is a Health.* Arts Council of Northern Ireland. Cassette with booklet.

Cowell, Sidney Robertson, ed. 1957. *Songs of Aran.* Folkways FM 4002. LP disk.

Cronin, Elizabeth. 1981. *Cucanandy.* Folktracks FSP60–160. Cassette.

De Danann. 1981. *Star-Spangled Molly.* Shanachie 79018. LP disk.

Doherty, John. 1979. *John Doherty*. Gael-Linn CEF 072–073. 2 LP disks.

De hÓra, Seán. 1977. *Seán de hÓra*. Gael-Linn CEF 063. LP disk.

Donegal Fiddlers. 1987. *The Brass Fiddle*. Ceirníní Cladaigh CC 44. LP disk.

Ennis, Seamus. 1976. *Forty Years of Irish Piping*. Free Reed FRR 001-002. 2 LP disks.

Hanna, Geordie. 1978. *Geordie Hanna sings*. Eagrán MD 0002. LP disk.

Harte, Frank. 1967. *Dublin Street Songs*. Topic 12T 172. LP disk.

Heaney, Joe [Seosamh Ó hÉanaí]. 1963. *Irish Traditional Songs in Gaelic and English*. Topic 12T 91. LP disk.

Hill, Noel, and Tony McMahon. 1985. *I gCnoc na Graí*. Gael-Linn CEF 114. LP disk.

Holmes, Joe, and Len Graham. 1976. *Chaste Muses, Bards and Sages*. Free Reed FRR 007. LP disk.

Johnstons, The. 1968. *The Johnstons*. Transatlantic TRA 169. LP disk.

Keane, Sarah, and Rita Keane. 1968. *Once I Loved*. Ceirníní Cladaigh CC4. LP disk.

Keenan, Paddy. 1983. *Port an Phíobaire*. Gael-Linn CEF 099. LP disk.

Kilfenora Ceili Band. 1960. *The Kilfenora Ceili Band*. DU-LP 1004. LP disk.

Lee, Ian, ed. N.d. *Amhráin ar an Sean-Nós*. RTE CD 185. Compact disc.

Lenihan, Tom. 1978. *Paddy's Panacea*. Topic 12TS 363. LP disk.

Lomax, Alan, et al., eds. 1961–1968. *Folk Songs of Britain: 1–10*. Caedmon (reissued Topic) TC 1142–1146, 1162–1164, 1224–1225. 10 LP disks.

McCafferty, Joe. 1984. *Ceolta agus Seanchas Thír Chonaill*. European Ethnic. Cassette.

McConnell, Cathal. 1978. *On Lough Erne's Shore*. Topic 12TS377. LP disk.

[M]ac Donncha, Seán. 1971. *An Aill Bháin*. Ceirníní Cladaigh CC9. LP disk.

[Mac Grianna] Mhic Grianna, Róise. 1994. *Róise na nAmhrán: Songs of a Donegal Woman*. RTE, CD 178. Compact disc.

Maguire, John. 1973. *Come Day, Go Day, God Send Sunday*. Leader LEE 4062. LP disk.

Makem, Sarah. 1968. *Sarah Makem, Ulster Ballad Singer*. Topic 12T 182. LP disk.

Mitchell, Kevin. 1977. *Free and Easy*. Topic 12TS 314. LP disk.

Molloy, Matt. 1976. *Matt Molloy*. Mulligan LUN 004 LP disk.

Moore, Christy. 1972. *Prosperous*. Tara 1001. Cassette.

Morton, Robin, ed. 1971–1972. *Folk Songs Sung in Ulster*. Mercier Irl. 11–12. 2 LP disks.

Moving Hearts. 1981. *Moving Hearts*. WEA (Ireland) IR 58387. LP disk.

Munnelly, Tom, ed. 1983. *Songs of the Irish Travellers*. European Ethnic. Cassette.

Munnelly, Tom, and Hugh Shields, eds. 1985. *Early Ballads in Ireland, 1968–85*. Dublin: European Ethnic. Cassette.

Ní Dhonnchadha, Máire Áine. 1970. *Deora Aille*. Ceirníní Cladaigh CC6. LP disk.

Ní Ghuairim, Sorcha. 1957. *Traditional Irish Songs*. Folkways FW6861. LP disk.

Ó Flatharta, Vail. 1987. *Bláth na nAirní*. Ceirníní Cladaigh CC 45. LP disk.

O'Keefe, Pádraig, Denis Murphy, and Julia Clifford. 1977. *Kerry Fiddles*. Topic 12T 309. LP disk.

O'Leary, Johnny. 1989. *Johnny O'Leary: An Calmfhear: The Trooper*. Gael-Linn CEF CD 132. Compact disc.

Ó Riada, Seán, with Ceoltóirí Chualann. 1962. *Reacaireacht an Riadaigh*. Gael-Linn CEF 010. LP disk.

The Pipering of Willie Clancy. 1980. Ceirníní Cladaigh CC 32. LP disk.

Planxty. 1973. *Planxty*. Polydor 2383186. LP disk.

Potts, Tommy. 1972. *The Liffey Banks*. Ceirníní Cladaigh CC 13. LP disk.

Reilly, John. 1978. *The Bonny Green Tree*. Topic 12T 359. LP disk.

Rowsome, Leo. 1961. *Rí na bPíobairí*. Ceirníní Cladaigh CC1. LP disk.

Russell, Micho. 1976. *Traditional Country Music of Co. Clare*. Free Reed 004. LP disk.

Scéalamhráin Cheilteacha. 1985. *Narrative Songs in Irish, Scottish Gaelic, Welsh, Manx and Breton*. Dublin: European Ethnic. Cassette.

Shields, Hugh, ed. 1972. *Folk Ballads of Derry and Donegal*. Leader LEA 4055. LP disk.

———, ed. 1983. *Shamrock Rose and Thistle, 2–3*. European Ethnic. 2 cassettes.

Sweeney's Men. 1968. *Sweeney's Men*. London: Transatlantic TRA 170. LP disk.

Tóibín, Nioclás. 1977. *Nioclás Tóibín*. Gael-Linn CEF 062. LP disk.

Touhey, Patsy. 1986. *The Piping of Patsy Touhey*. Na Píobairí Uilleann NPU 001. Cassette.

Tubridy, Michael. 1979. *The Eagle's Whistle*. Ceirníní Cladaigh CC 27. LP disk.

Tunney, Paddy. 1978 [1963]. *The Man of Songs*. Folk Legacy FSE 7. Reissued as *Lough Erne Shore*. Sruthán/Mulligan LUNA 334. LP disk.

Various artists. 1992. *Music at Matt Molloy's*. RealWorld CD RW 26. Compact disc.

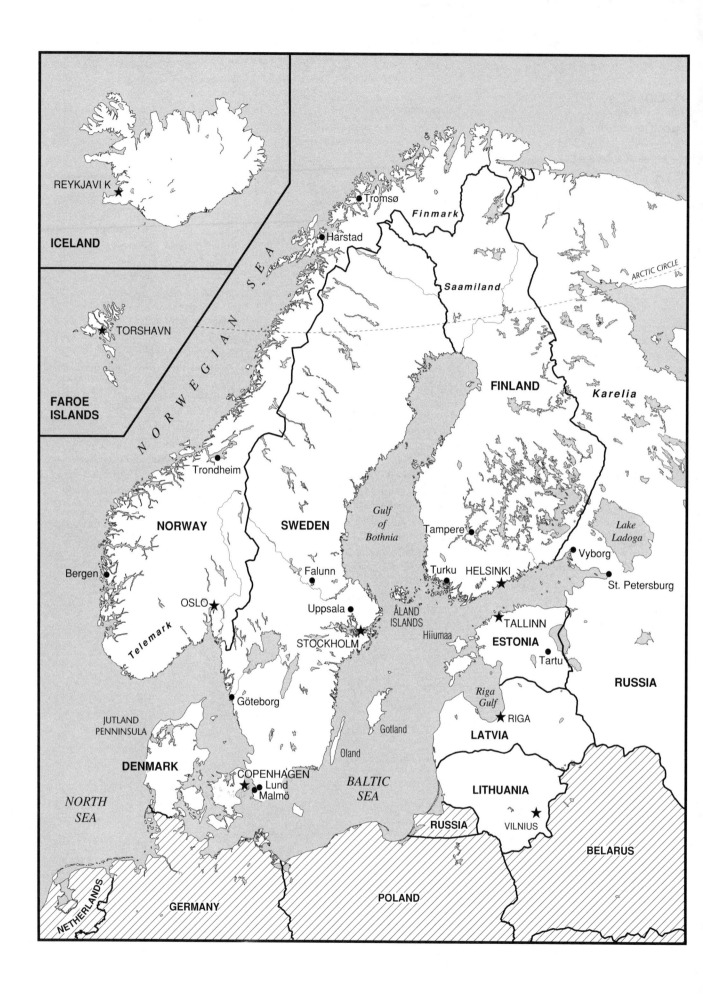

Northern Europe: Scandinavia, Finland, and the Baltic States

The people of Northern Europe speak languages in three families: Scandinavian, Baltic (Latvian and Lithuanian), and the non-Indo-European, Finno-Ugric languages (Finnish, Estonian, and Saami). Many countries of the region share the historical experience of Swedish or Russian rule. Except for Roman Catholic Lithuania, Protestant denominations are the norm, and as a consequence devotional singing has been a popular form of entertainment in many areas.

Epic poems and long historical ballads are still sung in Iceland and the Faroe Islands, and have been written down in Finland. Most singing is monophonic, but traditional forms of polyphony persist in Iceland and certain regions of each Baltic country. The most characteristic instrument of the region, the plucked or bowed zither, is found in nearly every country. The long midsummer's eve is probably the most important calendar custom here. Many countries have contributed important composers and performers to the history of classical music. In the twentieth century, jazz became particularly popular in parts of Scandinavia and Finland, while festivals of choral music became important manifestations of national aspirations in the Baltic states.

MAP 4   Northern Europe: Scandinavia, Finland, and the Baltic states

Iceland
Pandora Hopkins

Vocal Genres
History of Textual Forms
Musical Instruments
"New Music"
Trends in Traditional and Popular Music

Europe's second-largest island at 103,000 square kilometers, Iceland lies in the North Sea, 240 kilometers southeast of Greenland, 800 kilometers northwest of Scotland. Geologically a new body of land, it seethes with geothermal activity, concentrating the population—sparse, at about 260,000—along the coast. In the 1990s, 90 percent of the population lived in cities and towns, and fishing and fish processing were the major industries.

Iceland was originally settled within a short span (A.D. 870–930), largely by immigrants from western Scandinavia. Some of these refugees came by way of Ireland and nearby islands, where they were joined by Celtic individuals as spouses, servants, and slaves, the degree and nature of whose influence has become a matter of interest to historians.

The government of Iceland, established in 930 at Thingvellir, near Reykjavík, the Icelandic capital, was ruled by a legal code whose statutes were recited annually at the Althing, the oldest still-functioning representative assembly in the world. The first Icelandic written documents were the code of laws that had been recited at the Althing, and these manuscripts were illuminated with the care reserved for Bibles in continental Europe.

Of the Scandinavian countries, Iceland has attracted the most interest among foreign historians, linguists, and social scientists—an interest dominated by a romantic-antiquarian perspective. Musicologists have viewed Icelandic culture as static, dominated by a sense of history and mythology. In fact, Icelandic musical traditions are a vital communicative force, on national and international levels; the persistence of certain aspects of Icelandic culture has been remarkable, but it is due to active, not passive, causes.

VOCAL GENRES

Rímur

Rímur 'rhymes' (sing. *ríma*) are lengthy epic poems that used to be chanted informally when Icelandic family members gathered in the evening—an occasion called *kvöldvaka* 'evening awakening', which, for almost six centuries, was an enormously popular means of cultural expression. Though it no longer serves a function in con-

FIGURE 1 A *ríma* melody performed in the songlike, diatonic style preferred by some twentieth-century performers. Recorded and transcribed by Pandora Hopkins from a performance by Halldor Einarsson taped en route to Iceland on the freighter *Dettifoss*, 1965. Translation by Hallberg Hallmundsson.

1. Lík– a– frón og lags– menn tveir,
3. Fram– ar gnæf– a fjöll– in há;

ljós– ið dags nær fá að skoð– a,
firð– a þreyt– ir leið– in hál– a

kveð– ja hjón og því– næst þeir
allt að kveld– i er þeir sjá

það– an und– ir fjöll– in troð– a.
á– kaf–leg– a mik– inn skál– a.

Stanza 1.
Líkafrón and his two companions,
as they see dawn break,
take leave of the couple and then
walk from there toward the mountains.

Stanza 3.
Ahead, the high mountains tower;
the slippery way tires the men
until the evening, when they see
an enormously big hall.

temporary life, *rímnakveðskapur,* the art of composing *rímur,* continues within the structure of clubs, organizations more relevant to the urban milieu.

A strophic form, that of *rímur* combines a highly esoteric versification technique with a short, reiterated melody, traditionally intoned in a performance style between singing and speaking. The melody of a *ríma* may be of the simplest litany type, using as few as two pitches; other styles, however, manifest developmental subtleties and sometimes vie with the text in rhythmic intricacy. A more songlike, diatonic style is preferred by twentieth-century performers (figure 1). In Breiðafjörður, western Iceland, embellishments characterize the musical style: figures *2a* and *2b* are different interpretations of the same melody, yet the performers, Ingibjörg Sumarliðadóttir and Karl Guðmundsson, learned their art from the same person, Ingibjörg's father (Steingrímsson 1975). Despite transformations that obscure the melody, the outlining of the tritone F–B is evident in both examples. This interval is a prominent melodic feature of the genre, and of Icelandic music in general.

From the inception of the tradition, plentiful written documentation exists for *rímnakveðskapur,* including manuscripts and descriptions of performances. This unusual degree of documentation for an oral tradition is made possible by the fact that singers of *rímur* have never considered oral and literate means of transmission to be mutually exclusive; the tradition has always used both forms of communication (Ólafsson 1975). At the turn of the twentieth century, when Bjarni Þorsteinsson was gathering material for his collection of traditional music from literate and oral sources, the singers themselves provided numerous transcriptions (Þorsteinsson 1906–1909).

Rímur functioned in various contexts, including sheepherding, fishing, and traveling, and they were a source of livelihood for itinerant performers. Characteristic of the tradition was the evening awakening (*kvöldvaka*), when a family gathered to hear legendary lore or history, read or recited by a chanter (*kvæðamaður*), who might be a family member, a neighbor, or an itinerant musician, renowned for special abilities.

The characteristic metrical shift at the beginning of each chapter (*ríma*) and the metrical manipulations within each chapter are a musical and textual device to sustain interest throughout a long narrative. A single *rímnaflokkur*—an entire cycle or a series of chapters—could consist of thousands of stanzas, using hundreds of metrical variations. The performance of a cycle of *rímur* includes the lengthening of the final note of each strophe; final tones are made prominent by an idiosyncratic ornament (*dilla* or *dillandi*), executed with vibrato (figure 2b). The characteristic timbre of the chanting has an intensity that heightens excitement as the recitation proceeds—an

TRACK 11

FIGURE 2 Variants of the same *ríma,* performed in an embellished style typical of Breiðafjörður: *a,* from a performance by Ingibjörg Sumarliðadóttir (translation by Jóhann Sölvason); *b,* from a performance by Karl Guðmundsson (translation by Hallberg Hallmundsson). Transcriptions by Hreinn Steingrímsson.

a

Nú kemst ekk– i nótt– in lengr' en neðst í da– li– nn með– an bless– uð
sum– ar sól– in sveig– ir fyr– ir norð– ur pól– inn.

Now the night cannot reach farther than the bottom of the valley
while the blessed summer sun passes by the North Pole.

b

Allt– af má ég aug– um svon– a á þig mæn– a– ná– er (e) væng̈j– u– m
vo– na mi– nn– a vax– ið haf til stran– da þi– nn– a.

I must ever gaze at you this way,
now the wingspan of my hopes
has (been) extended to your shores.

effect often enhanced by the abrupt raising in pitch of the last note of each stanza by a semitone. In traditional performances of *kvöldvaka,* the audience customarily joins in on the last note—a practice called *taka undir* 'to take under'.

The word *kveða* (*kveðir, kvað, kveðið*), embedded in the term *rímnakveðskapur,* can mean 'compose, write poetry, tell, pronounce, narrate, chant, intone'. No matter what the melodic style of *rímur,* the vocal timbre used by the chanter is an intense, guttural sound, and the performance is accomplished in a slow, dirgelike tempo. Records show that *rímur* were once associated with dancing (Samsonarson 1964), and perhaps dances influenced the metrical form of *rímur* (Einarsson 1957). Melodies of *rímur,* called *bragir* and *stemmur,* may come from a body of existing tunes, or they may be newly created; a chanter who selects an existing melody may adapt it to various metrical configurations.

Intimately related to the tradition is the performance of quatrains (*lausavísur*), normally improvised on the spot, spoken or chanted as part of a conversation, an argument, or a challenge (Nielsen 1982). Involving complex rules of versification, a metrical challenge (*að kveðast á*) may still be offered by one person to another. Such intricacies as palindromic rhymes can be used to deliver coded messages in *sléttubönd,* an elaborate verse form. *Lausavísur* may also consist of separate strophes, detached in performance from cycles of *rímur.* Whatever the function, the chanter has always been adept at elaborate word manipulation. *Lausavísur* are often recited with only speech melody, but they may also be *kveðnar* in the manner characteristic of *rímur.*

Tvísöngur

Iceland's other major indigenous vocal tradition is *tvísöngur* 'two-singing'. Usually thought of as a form, *tvísöngur* is more accurately described as a technique used to

FIGURE 3 *Tvísöngur*
'two-singing' in par-
allel fifths. In the
first phrase, the voic-
es cross after the first
two measures; in the
second, the top
voice leaps a tritone
and in stepwise
motion outlines a
high-pitched arch.
After a transcription
sent to Bjarni
þorsteinsson by
Benedict Jónsson
about 1900
(þorsteinsson
1906–1909:212; see
also Helgason
1980:114–115).

The light comes long and slender, long and slender, long and slender.
The light comes long and slender, flames glittering on stalks of cotton grass.

enhance the performance of sacred and secular vocal melodies, including those of *rímur.* This technique involves, in its simplest form, the accompanying of one voice by another in parallel fifths; the melody is accompanied by an extemporized second part, which begins a fifth below the melody and crosses it to conclude a fifth above (figure 3). This procedure, formerly called taking it up, reflected a soloist's skill; the melody could be sung by multiple voices (Helgason 1980). More elaborate versions of *tvísöngur,* with doublings at the octave for other vocal parts, and a great variety of freer forms, were performed in sacred and secular settings.

The *tvísöngur* has been applied in Iceland to a wide range of monophonic pieces, from flippant courting songs and the melodies of traditional *rímur* to Gregorian chants and psalm tunes. Figure 3 illustrates the oldest type. In the last phrase, the second voice crosses the melody; it begins the final ascent with the melodic leap of a tritone, and continues by outlining another tritone, obliterating any feeling of tonal center. In a slightly less rigid form of *tvísöngur* (figure 4), sections in unison alternate with sections of parallel fifths. Modest embellishments in the second voice provide a trace of heterophonic dialogue. Figures 3 and 4 show applications of *tvísöngur* technique to the tunes of *rímur.*

Musicologists have studied the long-standing existence of *tvísöngur* because of its possible bearing on the development of organum, a kind of parallel singing [see HISTORY OF EUROPEAN ART MUSIC]. In medieval Europe, written documentation was largely in the hands of ecclesiastical scribes, so scholars have had difficulty making authoritative generalizations about secular use of the technique.

Ballad singing

Icelandic balladry is metrically related to danced *rímur* and other dances dating from as early as the 1200s. Little is known, however, about individual ballads until the

FIGURE 4 *Tvísöngur*
'two-singing' that
opens in unison
before moving into
parallel fifths.
Performed by Páll
Stefánsson and Gísli
Ólafsson, 1960.
Transcription by
Pandora Hopkins.
Translation by
Jóhann Sölvason.

For seventeen straight years, I have fallen asleep—an overnight guest.
So far my strength has not given up, always renewed by expressing myself in poetry.

Words, written or spoken, have had an almost
totemic significance in Iceland from runic days.
Icelanders are proud that their schoolchildren can
read the language of twelfth- and thirteenth-century
chronicles with less trouble than English speakers
experience with sixteenth-century English.

1600s. Unlike ballads in the rest of Europe, ballads were never central to local culture. Perhaps there was a sociological reason, since Icelanders never experienced a
period of chivalry. In addition, the typical balladic structure may have seemed simplistic to Icelanders, who were accustomed to complicated alliterative verse (Hallberg
1962).

Little is known, but there is much speculation, about another type of dance
song, the *vikivakalag,* a strophic song with refrain, performed responsorially by
dancers (1500s to 1700s); it was named after its refrain (*vikivaka kvæði*).

Religious singing

The first Icelandic printing of musical notation occurred in 1589, nearly six decades
after the beginning of the Reformation in Denmark (1530); melodies were included
in the *Psalma Bok,* compiled by Bishop Guðbrandur Þorlaksson. The volume contained a diatribe against *rímur,* which the bishop called undesirable poems of giants
and heroes and wicked and evil recitation. In 1594, he issued his Gradual (*Grallari*),
containing Latin chants and Lutheran chorales. For more than two centuries, it functioned as a linchpin of Icelandic religious vocal tradition, and its influence is still felt.
It went through nineteen editions. A method of instruction, included from its sixth
edition on, became the established Icelandic text for analyzing European tonal harmony; however, Danish imperial decrees aimed at enforcing standardization did not
succeed in supplanting indigenous Icelandic culture, musical or verbal. Bishop
Guðbrandur, a prolific publisher of religious material for more than fifty years, eventually tried to use the "immoral" idiom against itself, but his publications of religious
rímur in 1612—the first published *rímur*—had no chance of success against the
time-honored themes of classical antiquity.

Religious authorities also inveighed against the style of religious singing in the
service. Even as late as the 1800s, the leading singers would not confine themselves to
the notes as printed, but insisted on continuing the practice of applying ornaments
and improvisation until the hymn tunes seemed utterly unrecognizable. Singing the
notes was called singing the new way. Despite the ecclesiastical insistence on "correct"
musical worship, the people viewed hymn singing as an integral part of their own
domain, and continued informally, at least through the 1800s, to sing hymns in traditionally melismatic styles.

HISTORY OF TEXTUAL FORMS

Words, written or spoken, have had an almost totemic significance in Iceland from
runic days. Since the early 1800s, protective legislation has prevented linguistic
change; Icelanders are proud that their schoolchildren can read the language of
twelfth- and thirteenth-century chronicles with less trouble than English speakers
experience with sixteenth-century English.

The original Scandinavian and Celtic immigrants to Iceland brought with them their runic alphabets and a body of traditional lore, including fiction and history, plus the skills of the professional oral historian. The elite tradition of official Norwegian court poets followed the emigrants to Iceland, and by the year 1000, the Icelandic skalds had established a monopoly: Norway had become completely dependent upon Icelandic poet-musicians, imported to carry on the elaborately complex, highly stylized, and politically influential oral art of the court poet (*hirðskáld*).

The texts of most of these are oral chronicles of Icelandic family sagas and events of the tenth and eleventh centuries, though none was committed to writing until after 1200. Many scholarly discussions have probed the historical accuracy, as opposed to the literary creativity, of these documents, which testify to an exceptional and primarily Icelandic tradition of performance.

From these sources, we learn much about the esteem in which Icelanders held the poetic art: rhyming and harping were among the essential accomplishments (*íþróttir*) of a well-educated gentleman. The skalds' profession was by no means an anonymous one: the names of some two hundred fifty skalds from before the 1300s have come down to us. One of the most renowned was Egill Skallagrímsson, whose biography is contained in *Egil's Saga*. A skald could save his head by improvising an inspired set of verses for a hostile potentate; so important was the skald's function that warriors could be kept on hold, delaying their fight until a skald-king took the opportunity to revise and make metrically more elaborate his prebattle verses. The preservation of these records in written form was due principally to the efforts of the remarkable author, compiler, and statesman Snorri Sturluson (1179–1241). In the preface to *Heimskringla,* his monumental history of the Norse kings, he articulated the reasons for including "old songs and ballads" as legitimate sources of information.

A major source for skaldic verse and the narrative style of Eddic poetry is the so-called *Prose Edda*. In this work, Snorri's purpose was to perpetuate a tradition that had come under the fire of religious zealots by providing a textbook, a codification of the rules for composing skaldic poetry, and he used Eddic verse for illustrative material. The other principal compilation of Eddic material is now known as the *Poetic Edda,* our main source for information about the Æsir religion. Though Eddic verse is various in content, uncomplicated in style, and possibly reflective of an informal narrative function, it shares an alliterative construction with skaldic verse.

In Eddic and other ancient sources, references to the use of music for supernatural purposes are frequent, including abundant references to male and female chanters being accorded special powers. In defining the concept of speech (*mál*), Snorri includes what are more generally considered forms of musical performance: as parallel speech terms, he lists song (*söngur*), incantation (*galdur*), and recitation (*kveðandi*) alongside talk or tale (*tala*), story or history (*saga*), and quarrel (*senna*) (Sturluson 1975).

Many have believed that indigenous Icelandic traditions were created and perpetuated because of Iceland's isolation from the rest of the world. In fact, the skaldic tradition often received ideas from all peoples of the Nordic world and beyond. Active communication between Iceland and other parts of Europe during the Commonwealth Era (900s to 1300s) was not limited to the skalds and their retinues, however, but formed part of a more general picture. We know that, almost as a matter of course during this period, for example, Icelandic youth were sent abroad to study.

MUSICAL INSTRUMENTS

Two instruments, both bowed zithers, are unique to Iceland, though they share features with other northern European bowed lyres.

The *fiðla* (figure 5) has two or more horsehair strings (later, metal or gut), which

FIGURE 5   Sigurður Rúnar Jónsson plays a two-stringed, fretless, bowed zither (*fiðla*), which he has constructed. He stops the strings with the fingernails of his left hand underneath the strings. Photo by Egill Sigurðsson with the help of Njáll Sigurðsson, 1998.

run the full length of a slightly trapezoidal sound chamber. It is placed on a table top, or laid across the knees of the player, who holds the bow like a pencil. The *fiðla* uses neither fingerboard nor bridge, resulting in the production of a constant drone from simultaneously sounding strings. All strings but one are drones. The melody string is stopped from below, palm up. The technique employed on this instrument is similar to that used on the medieval bowed lyres typical of northern Europe and found in such extant examples as the Swedish-Estonian *talharpa* and the Finnish *jouhikantele*. The *fiðla,* which had almost disappeared from active use by the early 1800s, was revived in the twentieth century, based on an eyewitness account from 1905 (Jóhannsdóttir 1972, 1975).

The other traditional instrument, the *langspil* (figure 6), is also a bowed zither, usually with two to six strings (originally horsehair, later gut or wire) strung over a narrow, rectangular, box-shaped sound chamber, which has a sound hole at the lower end, where it flares out slightly. The fingers of the player's left hand press the melody string down onto frets, the drone strings are tuned in unison or to the fifth above the melody string, and the player holds the bow like a pencil. There is no bridge, and the bow actuates all strings simultaneously, producing a constant, thick-textured sound, typical of northern European bowed instruments of different categories: lute, lyre, and zither. In 1855, an *Instruction Manual for Playing the Langspil and for Learning Psalm Melodies from the Notation* was published to instruct people, through the use of the *langspil,* to sing any psalm tune "correctly" and "from the given notation"— another example of utilizing an indigenous tradition to promote the international idiom, and of identifying musical notation with the correct rendering of spiritual music (Sæmundsen 1855).

"NEW MUSIC"

Mainstream European musical instruments were imported by wealthier people since at least the 1700s, but their adoption by serious musicians as part of Icelandic music began to develop only during the late 1800s. The cathedral in Reykjavík installed its first pipe organ in 1840; under the direction of Pétur Guðjohnsen, the cathedral became the center for the promotion of "new music"—four-part harmony, the tonal idiom of mainstream Europe, and staff notation.

The pianist and composer Sveinbjörn Sveinbjörnsson (1847–1927) became the first internationally known virtuoso from Iceland; after having receiving a conservatory education in Germany, he spent most of his professional life in Scotland.

Symbolic of the new focus was the choice of music for the celebration of the thousandth anniversary of the Icelandic parliament, in 1930: an orchestra and a chorus were assembled to perform the *Alþing Festival Cantata* by Páll Ísólfsson (1893–1974), organist of the cathedral in Reykjavík. The conservatory of music and the Iceland State Broadcasting Service were founded in that same year, with Ísólfsson as the principal and musical director, respectively. Shortly thereafter came the establishment of the Icelandic Composers' Society and the Performing Rights Society. The Iceland Symphony Orchestra was founded in 1950, with four to six Icelandic works included in each orchestral season. One of the prime influences on contemporary Icelandic composition, Thorkell Sigurbjörnsson (b. 1938), has used electronic facilities in Holland and the United States; in 1960, his piece *Leikar No. 3* was included in the first Icelandic concert of electronic music.

A central figure in establishing the credibility of the national idiom was the musicologist-composer Hallgrímur Helgason (b. 1914), who studied composition with Paul Hindemith and wrote a dissertation on Icelandic traditional music. In constructing a national idiom for symphonic forms, he drew on concepts from Icelandic music, and his musical analysis of the Icelandic epic-song tradition is a landmark

FIGURE 6   Sigurður Rúnar Jónsson plays a three-stringed, bowed zither (*langspil*), which he has constructed. It has a fret board for the melody string, played with the thumb. Two strings, tuned in a perfect fifth, provide a drone. Photo by Egill Sigurðsson with the help of Njáll Sigurðsson, 1998.

publication (Helgason 1980). Jón Nordal (b. 1926), perhaps the most cosmopolitan and widely known of all Icelandic composers, grew up with Icelandic and mainstream European culture: his father, the well-known literary scholar Sigurður Nordal, served as Iceland's ambassador to Denmark. Attracted to Anton Webern's music, the young Nordal was part of a post–World War II group of young avant-garde composers who reacted strongly against the nationalism of earlier composers. He eventually became the director of the Reykjavík Conservatory of Music.

TRENDS IN TRADITIONAL AND POPULAR MUSIC

In 1929 and 1930, two institutions devoted to *rímur* were founded: in Reykjavík, Kvæðamannafélagið Íðunn (Íðunn Chanters' Society, named for Íðunn, a Norse goddess), and in Hafnarfjördur, Kvædamannafélag Hafnarfjardar (Hafnarfjardar Chanters' Society). Their purpose was to provide the opportunity to collect, perform, and create new *rímur* and *tvísöngur,* and in 1930 they established an annual field trip to further their goals. Since then, on the northern coast, another similar organization, Kvædamannafélag Siglufjardar, has been formed. With the newly flourishing economy, the *kvöldvaka* had come to an abrupt end, and the *rímur*-devoted organizations conceived their role more in terms of cultural preservation than of development; there was much concern about the demise of a way of life, of which the *kvöldvaka* was the most obvious cultural manifestation.

A trio of traditional musicians—Njáll Sigurðsson, Bára Grímsdóttir, and Sigurður Rúnar Jónsson—have recently found themselves in demand for performances and lecture-demonstrations of Icelandic vocal and instrumental traditions, especially in Europe. Jónsson is one of the few Icelandic musicians to play the *langspil* and the *fiðla,* which he demonstrates on these programs(see figures 5 and 6). Since the 1950s, Anna Thorhallsdóttir has introduced audiences to the *langspil,* with which she accompanies her singing of hymns and other traditional material.

The folk-rock group Íslandica, with Gísli Helgason (recorder) and Herdís Hallvarðsdóttir (bass and vocalist), has gradually become more interested in exploring and presenting authentic Icelandic idioms. In 1987, the Sugarcubes, best known for its female vocalist, Björk Guðmundsdóttir, became the first commercial band to win an international award, when the British magazine *Melody Maker* chose the Sugarcubes' song "Birthday" as the single of the week. Since then, Björk has become an international celebrity on her own. Other bands—Mezzoforte, the Reptiles, Ham, and Bless—are experimenting with fusion, rock, and other styles of popular music.

Traditional modes of expression have continued to persevere informally without the *kvöldvaka.* The chanting of *rímur* had always served multiple objectives: education, entertainment, protest, and competition—precisely the same purposes it continues to serve. A few *kvæðamenn* 'chanter-men' and *kvædakonur* 'chanter-women' reside in rural areas: in Akureyri in 1990, Jóhann Björn Jónsson (b. 1900), who still sang the traditional repertory, was periodically continuing to send tape recordings of *lausavísur* to his grandson in Reykjavík. In the cities, founding members of *rímur*-devoted organizations tend to be persons brought up in rural traditions, and they participate in weekly walking clubs for the creation of *lausavísur* in new urban settings.

Traditional idioms have continued to comment on contemporary issues. After World War II, a *sléttubönd* by Sigurður Norland was circulated to protest the founding of the American military base in Iceland. Some Icelanders still meet one another with a metrical-verse challenge; a few years ago, a Reykjavík university student (now a published poet) showed dissatisfaction with his university education by circulating a *sléttubönd* on the subject. When Sveinn Jónsson, a member of the Reykjavík *rímur*-devoted organization and a senior executive of a refrigerator company, represented his

Sveinbjörn Beinteinsson, a farmer known for his skill at versification and a self-proclaimed priest of Ásatrú, the ancient Nordic religion, used chants to curse the symbols of the military-industrial complex that has engulfed Iceland ever since its location became geopolitically strategic.

firm at a pan-Nordic environmental conference in Norway, he distributed to delegates a set of newly composed verses in the style of *rímur* (*lausavísur*) on the dangers of damage to the ozone layer.

Kvæðamannafélagið Íðunn, now with about 150 members, has always had a core of skilled musicians and versifiers. The organization undertakes field collecting and serves as a running documentary of the tradition itself. A member of the ministry of education, Njáll Sigurðsson, has recently edited grammar-school textbooks that, with traditional tunes from other countries, include simple examples of Icelandic melodies that typically have uneven beat structures. A detailed method for instruction in metrical versification, appropriate for older students and adults, has also been published (Aðalsteinsson 1990). Sveinbjörn Beinteinsson, a farmer known for his skill at versification, became the leader of a group of protesters against war, nuclear weapons, environmental devastation, and NATO's presence in Iceland. Calling himself a priest of Ásatrú, the ancient Nordic religion, he used chants to curse the symbols of the military-industrial complex that has engulfed Iceland ever since its location became geopolitically strategic.

Perhaps the most important shot in the arm to indigenous Icelandic culture happened in 1971, when the manuscript collection named after its original, eighteenth-century collector, Árni Magnússon, began to be returned to Iceland from the University of Copenhagen; the institute created for it by the University of Iceland sponsors publications and fieldwork and maintains a staff of specialist-scholars who conduct research.

BIBLIOGRAPHY

Aðalsteinsson, Ragnar. 1990. *Bögubókin.* Reykjavík: Fanafold.

Aksdal, Bjørn. 1982. *Med Piber og Basuner, Skalmeye og Fiol.* Trondheim: Universitetsforlaget.

Andersson, Otto. 1930. *The Bowed-Harp: A Study in the History of Early Musical Instruments.* London: Oxford University Press.

————. 1970. "The Bowed Harp of Trondheim Cathedral and Related Instruments East and West." *Galpin Society Journal* 23:4–34.

Auden, Wystan Hugh, and Louis MacNeice. 1969 [1937]. *Letters from Iceland.* Revised edition. New York: Random House.

Bergendal, Goran. 1981. *Musiken pa Island: om Isolering och Internationalism.* Stockholm: Konserthusstiftelse.

————. 1992. *New Music in Iceland.* Reykjavík: I.M.I.C.

Byock, Jesse. 1982. *Feud in the Icelandic Saga.* Berkeley: University of California Press.

Chase, Gilbert. 1966. *America's Music.* Revised edition. New York: Macmillan.

Chadwick, Hector Munro, with N. Chadwick. 1932–1949. *The Growth of Literature.* 3 vols. Cambridge: Cambridge University Press.

Coles, John. 1882. *Summer Travelling in Iceland.* London: John Murray.

Craigie, William. 1934. *Sýnisbók Íslenzkra Rímna.* 3 vols. Specimens of the Icelandic Metrical Romances. London and New York: Thomas Nelson & Sons.

Dasent, George Webbe. 1964. *Icelandic Sagas.* 3 vols. London: Kraus Reprints.

Davíðsson, Ólafur. 1888–1892. *Íslenzkar gátur, skemtanir, vikivakar og þulur.* 4 vols. in 2. Reykjavík: Hið islenska bókmenntafélag.

Einarsson, Stefán. 1957. *A History of Icelandic Literature.* Baltimore: Johns Hopkins Press.

———. 1986. *Studies in Germanic Philology.* Hamburg: H. Buske.

Eiríksson, Hallfreður Orn. 1975. "On Icelandic Rímur: An Orientation." *Tidskrift för Nordisk Folkminnesforskning* 31:139–150.

Eiríksson, Hallfreðou Orn, and Helga Johanssdóttir. 1974. *Recordings of Icelandic Folklore.* Reykjavík: Stofnun Arna Magnussonar a Islandi.

Faulkes, Anthony, ed. 1987. *Snorri Sturluson: Edda.* London: Dent.

Hallberg, Peter. 1962. *Old Icelandic Poetry.* Lincoln: University of Nebraska Press.

Hammerich, Angel. 1899. "Studien über isländische Musik." *Sammelbände der internationalen Musikgesellschaft* 1:341–362.

———. 1920. *Dansk Musikhistorie.* Copenhagen: Gad.

Hastrup, Kirsten. 1985. *Culture and History in Medieval Iceland: An Anthropological Analysis of Structure and Change.* Oxford: Clarendon Press.

Helgason, Hallgrimur. 1977. *Tónmenntir.* 2 vols. Reykjavík: Bókáutgáfa Menningarsjóðs og Þjóðvinafélagsins.

———. 1980. *Das Heldenlied auf Island: seine Vorgeschichte, Struktur Vortragsform: ein Beitrag zur älteren Musikgeschichte.* Graz, Austria: Akademische Druck und Verlagsanstalt.

Hollander, Lee. 1968. *The Skalds.* Ann Arbor: University of Michigan.

Jóhannsdóttir, Helga. 1972. "The Fidla of Iceland." In *From Bone Pipe and Cattle Horn to Fiddle and Psaltery,* ed. M. Muller, 27–31. Copenhagen: Musikhistorisk Museum.

———. 1975. "Fiðla," "Ísland: Folkmusik," and "Langspil." In *Sohlmans Musiklexikon* 2:561, 3:612–613, 4:256–257. Stockholm: Sohlmans Forlag.

Liestøl, Knut. 1930. *The Origin of the Icelandic Family Sagas.* Oslo: H. Aschehoug.

Mackenzie, George. 1841. *Travels in Iceland.* Revised edition. Edinburgh: William & Robert Chambers.

Marchand, James. 1975. "The Old Icelandic Allegory of the Church Modes." *Musical Quarterly* 61:553–559.

Marcuse, Sibyl. 1975. *A Survey of Musical Instruments.* New York and London: Harper & Row.

Nielsen, Svend. 1982. *Stability in Improvisation: A Repertoire of Icelandic Epic Songs (Rímur).* Translated by Kate Mahaffy. Copenhagen: Forlaget Kragen.

Nordal. Sigurður. 1931. "Introduction." In *Codex Wormianus.* Facsimile edition. Copenhagen: Levin and Munksgaard.

———. 1960. *Bibliography of Old Norse-Icelandic Studies.* Copenhagen: Munksgaard.

———. 1990. *Icelandic Culture.* Ithaca, N.Y.: Cornell University Library.

Norland, Sigurður. 1965. *Nokkur kvæði og vísur.* Reykjavík: Norland.

Ólafsson, Eggert. 1975. *Travels in Iceland Performed 1752–1757 by Order of his Danish Majesty.* Revised English edition. Reykjavík: Bókáutgáfan Örn og Örlygur.

Ottósson, R. A. 1980. "Iceland: Folk Music." *The New Grove,* ed. Stanley Sadie. London: Macmillan.

Pálsson, Gisli, and E. Durrenberger, eds. 1989. *Anthropology of Iceland.* Iowa City: University of Iowa Press.

Pfeiffer, Ida. 1852. *Visit to Iceland.* London: Ingram, Cooke.

Raschella, Fabrizio, ed. *The So-Called Second Grammatical Treatise: An Orthographic Pattern of Late Thirteenth-Century Icelandic.* Florence, Italy: F. Le Monnier.

Ryscamp, Charles. 1982. *Icelandic Sagas, Eddas, and Art.* New York: Pierpont Morgan Library.

Sachs, Curt. 1930. *Handbuch der Musikinstrumentenkunde.* Leipzig: Breitkopf und Härtel.

Sæmundsen, Ari. 1855. *Leiðarvísir til að spila á langspil og til ad læra Salmalog eptir notum.* Akureyri: H. Helgasyni.

Salus, Peter H., ed. 1968. *Völuspá: The Song of the Sybil.* Translated by Paul B. Taylor and W. H. Auden. Iowa City: University of Iowa Press.

Samsonarson, Jón, ed. 1964. *Kvæði og dansleikir.* 2 vols. Reykjavík: Almenna Bókafélagið.

Sigurðsson, Njáll. 1989. "Um rímur, kvedska-parlist og kvædalog." *Kvædamannafélagid Íðunn* 60:13–18.

Sigurjónsson, Jón Hrolfur. 1994. "Electro-Acoustic and Computer Music in Iceland." *Nordic Sounds* 2:10–14.

Steingrímsson, Hreinn. 1975. "Problemer i forbindelse med klassifisering av rimur-melodier." *Svensk tidskrift för musikforskning* 57(2):11–14.

Sturluson, Snorri. 1975. *Edda Snorra Sturlusonar.* Edited by Arni Bjornsson. Reykjavík: Íðunn.

Turville-Petre, Edward. 1976. *Scaldic Poetry.* Oxford: Clarendon Press.

Þorolfsson, Bjorn Karl. 1934. *Rímur fyrir 1600.* Reykjavík: Hið íslenzka bókmenntafélag.

Þorsteinsson, Bjarni. 1906–1909. *Íslenzk Þjóðlög.* Copenhagen: S. L. Møller.

AUDIOVISUAL RESOURCES

Eiriksdottir, Karolina. N.d. *Portrait.* ITM 7–01. LP disk.

———, et al. 1985. *Íslensk Fiðlutonlist* (Violin music from Iceland). ITM 5–02. LP disk.

Grímsson, Lárus Halldór, and Þorsteinn Hauksson. 1985. *Íslensk raftónlist/Electronic Music From Iceland.* ITM 5–04. LP disk.

Helgason, Gisli. 1985. *Ástarjátning.* Þor 005. LP disk.

Helgason, Hallgrimur. N.d. *Rondo Islandia.* (4'). ICE-MIC. 78-RPM disk.

———.1936. *Sonata No. 1.* Musica Islandica, 3. (18'). ICE-MIC. 78-RPM disk.

———.1939. *Sonata No. 2.* ICE-MIC. 78-RPM disk.

Hjálmarsdóttir, Margrét. 1980. *þetta er gamall þjóðarsiður.* SG-136. LP disk.

Islandica. 1990. *Rammislensk.* Icelandair FIM-MUND 001. LP disk.

Islenzkur Kvædamannafelg Hafnarfjardar. N.d. SG–147. LP disk.

Kvæðamannafélagið Íðunn. 1979. *100 íslensk kvæðalög.* Iðunn SG-122. LP disk.

Nordal, Jón. 1991. *Portrait.* ITM 7–04. LP disk.

———, et al. 1989. *Four Icelandic Orchestral Works.* ITM 6–02. LP disk.

Reykjavík Rímur Society. 1979. *100 Islensk Kvadalog.* Íðunn SG–122. LP disk.

Sigurbjörnsson, Hroðmar I., et al. 1990. *What Have They Done to Gudny's Clarinet?* ITM 6–03. LP disk.

The Hamrahlid Choir and þorgerdur Ingolfsdóttir. N.d. *Islenzk pjodlog* (Icelandic folk songs). TM 8–05. LP disk.

Thorhallsdóttir, Anna. 197?. *Folk Songs of Iceland.* Lyrichord LLST 7335. LP disk.

Norway

Pandora Hopkins

From shortly before 1400 to shortly after 1900, Norway was ruled by non-Norwegian powers: first by Denmark, then by Sweden. During this time, Norway did without a nobility, a military, and a court culture, thus occupying a special position outside the European mainstream. The end of Danish rule (1819) inspired a nationalist movement to construct a written Norwegian from diverse dialects, and the resultant language, *nynorsk* 'New Norsk', now enjoys equal status with older written Norwegian, *bokmal* 'Dano-Norsk', a form of Danish—reflecting a situation described as two nations within one (Smith 1962:23). The indigenous Hardanger violin tradition, also characterized by dialectal diversity, was heralded as the national music of Norway. Since regaining independence as a constitutional monarchy (in 1905), Norway has continued to develop strong regional and local affiliations on one hand, and a nationalist mission on the other.

Norway occupies a 1,756-kilometer-long, narrow strip of land along the western coastline of the Scandinavian Peninsula. Fjords indent the (often mountainous) coast to create natural harbors, and 75 percent of the population of 4.3 million lives within 16 kilometers of the sea. Lengthy mountain chains divide the southern sector of the country into western and eastern regions, and distinguish the northern, arctic half from the broadened-out base in the southern highlands. Though these topographical features have inspired strong feelings of local identity, the ever-present waterways have provided exceptional opportunities for contact among valley communities and even with far-off countries. Thus, cultural diversity has more to do with conscious choice than physical necessity (Blom 1986).

About forty thousand Saami (formerly called Lapps) live in Finnmark, Norway's northernmost province [see SAAMI MUSIC]. The Saami received their own parliament in 1989. Norway has three official languages: the two derivatives of Old Norse mentioned above, and Saami. Internationally, Norway's most widely known musician was Edvard Grieg (1843–1907), whose originality, especially in harmony, has only recently been fully appreciated. Just as famous, not only within the closely knit confines of the indigenous musical tradition but throughout Norway, are two nineteenth-century Hardanger violinist-composers from Telemark: Torgeir Augundson

> The principal Norwegian indigenous vocal genres are *sæter* songs, including songs that accompanied the making of food, such as the butter-making song, ornamented and individualistic animal calls, such as goat calls, cow calls, and hog calls; and elaborated shouts and hollers, which communicated from person to person across long distances.

(1801–1872), called Myllarguten (The Miller's Boy), and Håvard Gibøen (1809–1873). Both established styles of playing that remain influential.

VOCAL GENRES

The principal Norwegian indigenous vocal genres are *sæter* songs, including songs to accompany work on mountain farms and shouting songs, designed to communicate from one mountaintop to another; ballads, strophic narrative songs called *viser, folkeviser,* and *balladar; stev* tunes, single-strophe melodies sung to a special kind of traditional poetry; religious songs; a song competition (*stevleik*) between two persons; and the singing of fiddle pieces (*slåttestev*).

Sæter songs

In Norwegian mountain communities during the most fruitful season of the year, women were in charge of the *sæter,* a summer farm for highland pasturing. Special traditions grew up around farm activity: songs that accompanied the making of food, such as the butter-making song (*smørbon*); ornamented and individualistic animal calls, such as goat calls (*geitlokkar*), cow calls (*kulokkar*), and hog calls (*sauelokkar*); and elaborated shouts and hollers (*laling, huving*), which communicated from person to person across long distances. *Kulokkar,* generically animal calls, were highly idiosyncratic: yodeling, shouting, and singing were applied to an ornamented melodic line with microtonal inflections, often in a style between speaking and singing (figure 1). Variation in performance indicates that the genre offered scope for individual creativity within a traditional form (Sevåg 1980).

FIGURE 1   A cow call (*kulokk*) with ornamented melody. A yodel-like refrain follows three texted phrases. Original pitch is a minor third lower. Sung by Hanne Kjersti Buen in Bø, Telemark, 1972. Recording and transcription by Pandora Hopkins.

Kom Su– mar– lauv, kom Sa–   le, kom Bran– de– rygg og Sva– le.   Kom

Lur– (re)–ve, kom Lar–   ve og Li–   ti–   blom.   Rek– kje og Snek– kje,

Skau– te   og Rau– te. Et– te kje– me Sin– fak– se   Sju– li– brand. Plu– lo, lu– lo– lo,

lu– lo lu–   lo lu– lo lu– lo   lo.   Lu– lu– lu–   lo.

Come, Sumarlauv! Come Sale! Come Branderygg and Svale! Come Lurve! Come, Larve and Little-Blossom! Rekkje and Snekkje, Skaute and Raute! After comes Sinfakse Sjulibrand.

Ballads

Ballads have been the primary means of transmitting historical narratives and legendary lore in Norway. They have been categorized according to subject matter: heroic songs (*kjempevisene*); knightly songs (*riddarvisene*), influenced by European romances; ancient, indigenous songs about the supernatural (*trollvisene*); sacred songs (*heilagvisene*), both Christian and pre-Christian; and animal songs (*dyrevisene*), humorous, often with a moral function. The heroic songs, still current in tradition-rich regions, stylistically resemble other epic-song traditions of northern Europe. In strophic form, each stanza is usually followed (occasionally preceded) by a refrain. The original practice of dancing to the ballads, long in disuse in Norway, was revived early in the twentieth century on the basis of fieldwork in the Faroe Islands, whose people maintain an unbroken tradition [see FAROE ISLANDS]. Ballads are sung in a rhythm freely governed by speech accents in a vibratoless throat tone, a style of singing called *kveding,* which lets the singer control a high degree of ornamentation—a characteristic of much ballad performance in Norway.

The most famous sacred ballad, *Draumkvædet,* a medieval visionary poem, combines popular Christian (pre-Reformation) beliefs with mystic elements from earlier Norse religion. It tells of Olav Åsteson, who during a supernatural sleep from Christmas Eve to Epiphany receives a vision of heaven, hell, and doomsday. Four melodies are successively used in its fifty-two stanzas, each melody believed to be relevant to a particular portion of the story. In oral tradition, the melodic material is felt to be as old as the text.

Stev tunes

Older ballads, including *Draumkvædet* and most *kjempevisene,* use the old *stev* (*gamlestev*) structure for each stanza:

```
/ u / u / u / u
/ u / u / u
/ u / u / u / u
/ u / u / u
```

This is a four-line stanza of trochaic tetrameter alternating with trochaic trimeter, with lines usually rhyming ABCB, though rhymes and meters are not standardized. The old *stev,* now virtually extinct, was a single stanza of popular poetry, a form that had its roots in the medieval period. It began to be supplanted during the nineteenth century by the new *stev* (*nystev*), which, though also containing four lines, differs in metrical construction and textual character. The text of the *stev,* old and new, has been the basis for vocal and instrumental improvisation. Singers have tended to regard the *stev* as a way of singing, a basis for personal interpretation of text and melody, in contradistinction to songs that exist in songbooks or notated psalms (Myklebust 1982).

The new *stev* (*nystev*), though also containing four lines, differs in metrical construction. Each of its lines contains four stressed syllables, and end rhyme links the first two and the last two lines. *Nystev* singing, with its uneven-beat patterning (sometimes reinforced with foot stamping), is sometimes associated with fiddle music; a *nystev* may have a ribald text, which frequently communicates an in-group joke or mockery. Fiddlers are usually adamant that the *nystev* grows out of the fiddle pieces, not the other way around (figure 2).

Religious songs

In the Reformed Church, the first Danish-Norwegian chorale book did not appear until 1764, but evidence that handwritten examples were in use from as early as 1600

FIGURE 2 "Anne sit heime å tullar fe båne" (Anne sits at home singing [*tulling*] to her baby), a fragment of a vocal *nystev*, highly ornamented in the manner of instrumental music (after Buen et al. 1978:85).

Sov mi sø— te sul— le gjæ— va— re hell gul— le!

Bli lik snil— le pa— pa din, han er ful— la gut— en sin: og

han låg au i tul— le! Tral—la— la— lei, tra— la— lei,

tral— la— la— la lei— a.

Eveningtime brings shadows,
Mama embraces her baby,
Nothing dreadful can happen
To frighten her young one,
While Mama is rocking the cradle.

exists. Royal decrees from Copenhagen authorizing particular chorale books sought to impose on the most isolated Norwegian parishioners the prevalent musical style, the new liturgy, and the vernacular texts, at first in German, and later in Danish. Thus, Denmark posed a serious threat to psalmodic improvisation, an integral part of popular religious observance at home and in church. The last Danish-Norwegian chorale book, issued in 1801, saw the triumph of regularized, isometric chorales. However, instead of letting the existence of authorized texts destroy their creative performance tradition, performers used the printed chorale melodies as springboards for extemporizations that were melismatic, often modal, and rarely foursquare in rhythm. In informal devotionals at home, parishioners successfully resisted the imposition of central authority, perpetuating different styles of singing hymns, and improvising on the originals to create new material. Ludvig Mathias Lindeman (1812–1887), one of the earliest to collect directly from singers, published editions of religious and secular songs, including more than a thousand melodies. In 1848–1849, he transcribed almost a hundred hymns from the singing of A. E. Vang of Valdres, with melismatic elaborations of the melodies published in one of the official Danish-Norwegian psalters, Thomas Kingo's authorized Gradual of 1699 (Gaukstad 1973) [see DENMARK].

MUSICAL INSTRUMENTS AND INSTRUMENTAL MUSIC

The most important instruments in use today are chordophones, but aerophones are still used in pastoral settings.

The *langeleik*

A slim, oblong, plucked zither, the *langeleik* normally has eight steel strings, all but one drones. In performance, it lies on a table. The melody string runs over frets and is stroked by a plectrum held in the right hand. Between these strokes, the drones are plucked, being stopped by three left-hand fingers. The earliest evidence of the *langeleik* is a painting dated 1560. In early instruments, the distances between frets imply the use of a unique scale. Within a fairly constant frame of perfect fifth and octave, the smaller intervals vary, but they are all larger than a tempered half step and smaller than a tempered whole step—a system termed anhemitonic heptatonicism (Sevåg 1974).

The instrument has always been most closely associated with women, but it has attracted unconventional men, like Johannes Viken (1844–1936), who, when his hands became too large for the fiddle, learned from his mother, Ragnhild Viken (1810–ca.1895). Both were professional musicians and earned money to support their families by playing at markets, hotels, and special events. A renowned player was Berit Pynten (1812–1900). A great deal of information has come down to us about individual performers from well before 1800. As early as the late seventeenth century, we find documented evidence of the popularity of the *langeleik:* Sunday-evening concerts were regularly given by performers with a following from the community, such as Sissel Luth and Kirsti of Norbø (Landstad quoted in Ledang 1979:20; Ledang 1974a; Myklebust 1982). Valdres continues to support an unbroken tradition of *langeleik* playing.

The *langeleik* was played on *sæter* and in rural districts (*bygdene,* sing. *bygd*). Pieces for listening (*lydarslåttar*) were played in early evenings, when *sæter* women did their weaving and embroidering; in late evenings, the *langeleik* accompanied social dancing.

Bowed strings

During the 1600s, members of the violin family began to be played in Norway (Aksdal 1982), and the violin gradually took over the functions of the *langeleik,* which faded from view except in Valdres, where both instruments flourish. A second kind of violin also emerged, and two kinds of playing became associated with physically different violins; culturally, they divided up the country between them. The internationally known variety, called flat violin (*flatfele*) or usual or ordinary violin (*vanleg fele*), flourished in the northern, central, and eastern regions. The other variety, unique to Norway, was the Hardanger violin (*hardingfele* 'Harding violin'), which held sway in the west and the south-central inner-mountain valleys.

The hardingfele

The *hardingfele,* an elaborately ornamented violin with four or five sympathetic strings running beneath the fingerboard, has remained virtually unchanged for three centuries. It must have been in existence by 1700 (Aksdal 1982; Alver and Bjørndal 1966; Blom 1985; Sevåg, Blom, and Nyhus 1971), and to about 1850, it was not professionally built, as the flat violin usually was. It survived a period of intense religious persecution and increased in influence during the twentieth century—the same period that saw the disappearance of the pastoral-seafaring complex, to which it had belonged. The body of the *hardingfele* resembles the shape and size of a Baroque violin—smaller than the contemporary violin, with a more rounded body and a shorter neck. In addition to its most prominent feature, the sympathetic strings, it has a flatter bridge and fingerboard; elongated f-holes are so deeply cut into the belly that a protruding upper edge is formed; and its peg box, surmounted by a carved animal's head, is resplendent with gilt and reminiscent of the figureheads on Viking prows. The body is typically ornamented with mother-of-pearl inlay outlining traditional symbolic patterns on the fingerboard and elsewhere, while intricate *fela-rosa* 'rose painting for fiddles', drawn freehand with pen and India ink, adorns the edges (figure 3).

The *hardingfele* produces an unwavering background of upper-partial resonance created by the sympathetic strings (figure 4). Other factors contribute to a thick tex-

Traditional music for the *hardingfele* uses at least twenty different tunings, which are important for the communication of extramusical connotations— for example, Light Blue, a tuning to be used at dawn, and Troll Tuning, used only between midnight and dawn.

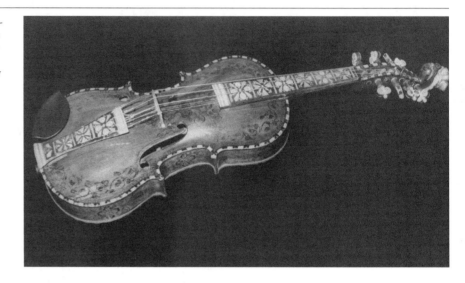

FIGURE 3   A *hardingfele* 'Harding violin', elaborately decorated with inlaid mother-of-pearl on the fingerboard and elsewhere, India-ink drawings of flowers (*fela-rosa*), and a gilded animal head reminiscent of the figurehead on the prow of a Viking ship. Photo by Betty Dunn, 1976.

FIGURE 4   Detail of a *hardingfele,* showing the four sympathetic strings beneath the four bowed strings, the *fela-rosa,* and the inlay. Photo by Betty Dunn, 1976.

ture, especially a seamless bowing technique applied to double and triple stopping, facilitated by a flatter bridge and alternate tunings (*scordatura*), which augment the number of open strings available for sympathetic resonance. The *hardingfele* produces its own melody and accompaniment and is primarily a solo instrument.

Aurally transmitted, traditional music for the *hardingfele* uses at least twenty different tunings. The instrument is normally pitched a whole tone to a tone and a half higher than standard A=440 cps. A Hardanger fiddle piece is called a *slått* (pl. *slåttar*; from *slå* 'to beat, to strike'). The tuning bound to any *slått* is important to its internal structure and the communication of extramusical connotations—for example, Light Blue, a tuning to be used at dawn, and Troll Tuning, used only between midnight and dawn. Though players no longer follow these rules strictly, they form part of the associations conveyed to knowledgeable listeners.

Slått music is not strictly tonal, but is usually constructed from disjunct tetrachords, often resulting in a scale not bounded by the octave, but including chromatic pitches. The musical structure can manifest an intricate melodic device that has been called inherent rhythms, single-line polyphony, and compound melodic line (Hopkins 1986). Players have a special predilection for the tritone (a characteristic of music in other Nordic lands and the *seljefløyte,* a flute without finger holes, which relies on the overtone series to produce melodies). *Slått* variations involve chains of motives, each slightly varied from its predecessor—a procedure that has been called metamorphosis technique (Kydland 1983). The overall structure of a *slått* is hierarchical. When a *slått* is played for listening (not dancing), it is usually performed twice, each presentation called a realization (*fremføring*). Each realization is likely to divide into two or more rounds (*omganger*); each round consists of about ten to fourteen phrases (*vendingar,* sing. *ei vending;* also *vek*); it is within the *vending* that the metamorphic chain of motivic variants occurs, more or less according to the basic dance form, the regional tradition, and the individual style (Alver and Bjørndal 1966; Hopkins 1986; Kvifte 1981).

Rhythm is extremely complex; counterrhythms are heard against a firm backdrop of a repeating beat cycle; in a structure resembling that of the Indian tala system, competing voices come together at periodic rest points. Three further devices obscure the overall structure: elision between sections, bowing across the beat, and a general practice of what Baroque theorists called rhythmic alteration, the unequal performance of subdivisions of the beat. It is customary for player (*spelemann*) and audience to stamp their feet to the basic cyclical pattern throughout a performance. Sometimes the fundamental pattern is asymmetrical—that is, it consists of uneven beats.

Music for dancing and listening

Like the *langeleik,* the *hardingfele* has always served two functions, listening and dancing. It traditionally accompanies *bygdedansar,* the indigenous dances of Norway, which fall into two general categories according to their rhythmic makeup and type of step. Three dances in 2/4 or 6/8 meter—*gangar, rull,* and *halling* (*lausdans*)—are characterized by a slow and heavy, but flexible, gait. One dance—*springar*—is in triple meter, characterized by light, almost running steps or uneven, limping ones. The *halling* (*lausdans*) is an acrobatic solo dance, and the other three are couple dances (Blom 1981).

Fiddler and dancers closely coordinate their actions in all these dances, the fiddler surrounded by the dancing couples. These dances are highly esoteric and difficult to perform; like *bygde* music, they are for trained specialists, not the general public. Recent research concerns the question of whether the dancer and the fiddler perceive the music identically (Bakka, Seland, Vårdal, and Egeland 1990; Kvifte 1983).

In earlier times, at marketplaces, local courts of law, and informal gatherings, *slåttar* were played for listening. During the 1800s, fiddlers made names for themselves in formal concerts, and some even undertook concert tours to the United States. Figure 5 is the Telemark *springar* "*Rakstejenta*" as performed by its composer, Johannes Dahle. He makes no attempt to reproduce the Telemark *springar* dance rhythm, which consists of three uneven beats.

The most famous *hardingfele* player, Myllarguten, preferred to play music for listening (Berge and Fjalestad 1972). The styles of listening pieces differ according to time and place: some are program music, some are fantasias in tempo rubato, and others could be danced but are not. Figure 6 is a fantasia type taken from a performance by Finn Vabø, who played it to illustrate music understood only by connoisseurs (Hopkins 1986).

TRACK 12

One of the earliest known *hardingfele* players was Ola Hildan (1755–1826) from Oda, Hardanger; he was said to have spread the tradition to Telemark and places farther west. Jorn Hilme (1778–1854) was a founder of the Valdres tradition; Knut Lurås (1782–1843), an itinerant rose painter and *spelemann,* was an early disseminator of the tradition. As mentioned above, Håvard Gibøen and Torgeir Augundson (Myllarguten) have become household names in Norway. Neri Neset (1838–1883) introduced the *hardingfele* to Setesdal, and Ola Mosafinn (1858–1912) is considered the western counterpart of Augundson; with Sjur Helgeland (1828–1924), he founded the western Voss tradition. In Telemark, Knut Dahle (1834–1921) and his grandsons Johannes (1890–1980) and Gunnar (b. 1902) drew from Gibøen and Augundson to fuel a tradition that has been characterized by the coexistence of old and new: Gunnar has tended to treat the traditional repertory with more latitude,

FIGURE 5
"*Rakstejenta,*" a Telemark *springar,* composed and performed for listening by Johannes Dahle of Tinn, Telemark, in 1967. Recording and transcription by Pandora Hopkins.

but Johannes has contributed many new compositions to it (figure 7). (Of 434 pieces recorded by Johannes for the Norwegian State Broadcasting Company, sixty are his own works.) The principal inheritor of this Telemark tradition is Ola Øyaland (b. 1922, from Tinn); but in Bø (also Telemark), the celebrated Hauk (b. 1933) and Knut (b. 1948) Buen have developed the repertory in another way.

The European violin (flatfele 'flat fiddle')

The internationally known violin, in Norway called *flatfele* 'flat fiddle' and *vanleg fele* 'customary fiddle', appeared earlier than the *hardingfele.* The thick-textured sound produced by the *hardingfele,* however, had long been characteristic of bowed instruments in Nordic lands, where stringed instruments were designed to have drone strings and permit the simultaneous bowing of several strings. Early music for the European violin, when it was first being imported into Norway, exhibited elements of this style: drones and *scordatura* tunings were common, and sometimes players even flattened the bridges of their instruments. The emergence of the *hardingfele* may

FIGURE 6
*"Myllarguten's Siste
Slått,"* by Finn Vabø
of Bergen, performed
in 1965 to illustrate
music for listening.
Recording and tran-
scription by Pandora
Hopkins.

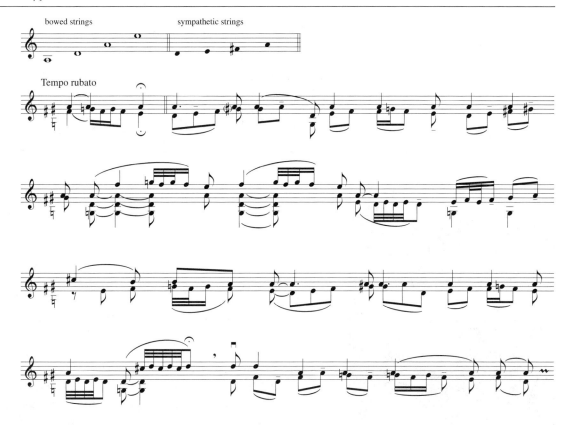

be seen as the result of a gradual adaptation of the Baroque violin body to accommodate a preexistent musical sound—a feature that has characterized the idiosyncratic
musical traditions of north, central, and eastern Norway, through the development of
diverse individual styles. Once the *hardingfele* had taken hold, the European violin
began to be used more specifically to play the treble part in ensembles that accompanied the mazurkas, polkas, *reinlanders,* waltzes, and other pan-European dances that
swept into Norway during the 1800s, known today as the old dances (*gammaldansane*).

The *flatfele* has never been associated with virtuosity to the extent that the *hardingfele* has, though names of performers admired within the bounds of their immediate localities have come down to us. An exception, Jakup Lom (also known as Fel-
Jakup and Loms-Jakup) (1821–1876) from Gudbrandsdalen, widely influenced the
tradition.

The earliest-named fiddler from Røros was Ellev Ellevsen Vintervold (1775–
1855), father of Ellev Ellevsen Holm (1812–1890), whose farm became a meeting
place for fiddlers in the area. *Flatfele* player Per Mathiasen Bolstad (1833–1910), first
in an important family line in Nordfjord, taught Jens Maurseth (1863–1927), member of another influential dynasty. Margrete Maurset was a fiddler and the teacher of
her son, Magne Maurset, who later learned *slåttar* from an itinerant musician,
Blinde-Rasmus (Blind Rasmus), who taught Samuline Seljeset (1804–1872), another
woman professional.

Setesdal was European violin territory until well into the nineteenth century,
when Neri Neset (1838–1883) introduced the *hardingfele* from farther east and
began a wholesale conversion to that instrument among violinists. Around 1900, one
of the great *flatfele* players of Nordfjord, Ivar Kjellstad (1868–1914), following a
trend promoting the *hardingfele* as the national instrument of Norway, switched to
the *hardingfele*. Those who sought to establish a national identity showcased the one
uniquely Norwegian musical instrument. Also, the *hardingfele* had always served for

FIGURE 7 Johannes Dahle (1890–1980), an
important composer of new compositions in the
Telemark *hardingfele* tradition. Photo by
Pandora Hopkins, 1972.

Men and women used mnemonic syllables as a kind of mouth music for singing fiddle pieces—a practice called *tralling*. Women, in their pedagogical role, often used *tralling* to teach their children the first steps of fiddle playing, and *tralling* became an art in itself.

FIGURE 8   Knut Buen (b. 1948) from Bø, an important figure in the Telemark *hardingfele* tradition, tours from time to time in America. Photo by Laila Amdahl, 1981.

listening, which became more important in rural areas. In the wake of pietistic religious fervor in the late 1800s, many *hardingfele* were burned or smashed, and dancing suffered even more. It was more acceptable to give concerts in areas where dancing was prohibited, and top *hardingfele* players easily set up concert tours, especially in America (figure 8). Thus, the switch from *flatfele* to *hardingfele* may in some cases have been a practical expedient.

The greatest threat to the *hardingfele* was another solo instrument, the accordion. Shortly before 1900, an accordion (*trekkspil*) could be purchased in Norway for only two kronor (then the cost of about half a barrel of potatoes), and it soon became wildly popular in cities and the countryside. Acclaimed as a virtuoso instrument, it imposed the equal-tempered tuning system wherever it went, and soon became associated with *gammaldansane* flooding the country. In ensemble with the *flatfele* and the string bass, it blended well. In some parts of the country (Hardanger, Setesdal, Sogn), it and the *hardingfele* continue to coexist (Aksdal 1986; Faukstad 1978).

Aerophones

The Norwegian version of the alpine horn, a 1.5-meter-long, bark-bound, split-tubed, unkeyed, conical, wooden trumpet (*lur*), was tied to *sæter* culture. Performance on it went beyond signaling. *Sæter* women produced upper partials to allow the playing of fiddle pieces and other melodies—an impressive feat on an open-tubed instrument. Sometimes they both made and played their instruments, using alder bark to blow through as they herded the goats. Improvisation in making instruments too was common; different-sized lurs with single or double reeds were tried, and in one case someone experimented with a crooked form (Sevåg 1973).

Herdsmen needed easily portable instruments. The buck horn (*bukkehorn*) existed from the earliest recorded time to the present, with and without finger holes, and its signals were more functional than artistic. Just as portable was the mouth harp (*mundharp*).

The willow flute (*seljefløyte*), an overblown bark flute without finger holes, sometimes as much as 60 centimeters long, was easily made with a knife during the spring months. By opening and closing the end of the tube with a finger, the player produced a scale formed by the interlocking overtone series of closed and open tubes. In modern times, it has become a symbol of bucolic life.

With violins, violas da gamba, and lutes, continental aerophones began to be imported into Norway during the sixteenth and seventeenth centuries. North German traders unloaded their instruments in Bergen, but some instruments found their way to the principal marketplaces: Kongsberg (East Norway) and Lærdal (West Norway), and thence to more remote areas. In this way, musicians employed by cities and churches or recruited for the military bands of the Danish civil service acquired bassoons, clarinets, French horns, oboes, shawms, transverse flutes of bone or wood, trombones, trumpets, and vertical flutes (recorders).

GENDER AND MUSIC

As in other sea or mountain cultures, women were often closely associated with agricultural work and men with the sea—and in some parts of Norway, herding or logging, also activities practiced away from home. Until the mid-twentieth century, transhumance—the summer nomadism that was an integral part of highland farming—resulted in separate gender milieux, each with its own traditions. Women were in charge of the *sæter,* a summer farm for highland pasturing, and vocal traditions were important in bringing up the next generation, largely a feminine responsibility, on and off the *sæter.* Lullabies (*bånsuller*) had a melodic simplicity and a regular rhythm meant to lull the baby, a kind of work song often called *voggevise* 'rocking song'. A second type of lullaby transmitted cultural attitudes; for it, the parent might transform almost any existing song (Buen, Garnås, and Myhren 1978; Greni 1960).

Men and women used mnemonic syllables as a kind of mouth music for singing fiddle pieces—a practice called *tralling, tulling, lulling,* or *sulling.* In the absence of a fiddler, a singer would *trall* the fiddle piece to accompany dancing; *tralling* continues for the transmission of tunes from fiddler to fiddler. Women, in their pedagogical role, often used *tralling* to teach their children the first steps of fiddle playing, and *tralling* became an art in itself. The singing of Kari Dalen from Valdres was so admired that one of her favorite fiddle pieces came to be called by her name, and Sissel from Hallingdal was such a clever *slått* singer that her singing was almost like listening to the fiddle.

The Hardanger violin developed as a male tradition, its symbolism associated with the sea, woodworking, and horsemanship (figure 9); the players were often itinerants who built reputations by playing at weddings, fairs, and other events. During the twentieth century, it became more and more common for women to play the Hardanger violin. One of the pioneers was Kristiane Lund (1889–1976). Toward the end of the century, about the same number of girls as boys were studying the instrument, and feminine Class-A *spelemenn* were no longer unusual. One of the most renowned of these, Annbjørg Lien, tours with her rock band. In contrast, the European violin drew women players at an early date, at least from the late eighteenth century, and some played professionally and taught the instrument. Margrete

FIGURE 9   Finn Vabø teaches his son, Øivind, who also became an outstanding *hardingfele* player. This once mainly male tradition has changed, and now as many women as men play the instrument. Photo by Pandora Hopkins, 1980.

Maurset, who had played at weddings from the time "when she was so little they had to sit her up on a table," was the first teacher of her son, the renowned Magne Maurset (1824–1916) of Njordfjord (Myklebust 1982). In the twentieth century, the Hallingdal fiddler Odd Bakkarud learned from his mother, who played only at home. Hauk Buen, the great Telemark player, learned from his mother's *tralling*; his sister, the equally accomplished singer Agnes Buen Garnås, remembered a children's piece that their mother would *trall* and their father play the *hardingfele* (Buen, Garnås, and Myhren 1978:855).

While the Hardanger violin was almost exclusively the domain of men, the *langeleik* was almost always played by women, some of whom became celebrated as concert performers within their local communities. Like the *hardingfele,* the *langeleik* functioned as an instrument for accompanying dancing and one to be listened to by an admiring audience; players performed different pieces for dancing and listening. Women earned their livings playing it at markets and dances in the winter; on the summer farm (*sæter*), they played in the evening while others wove or plied another handicraft after a day of work in the fields.

In urban as in rural areas, a dichotomy of gender was evident; at home, instruments were associated with women in their function as teachers and transmitters of culture. The lute was a drawing-room instrument, and of the woman who presided there from the 1500s to the mid-1600s. It was superseded by the clavichord (*klavikordet*) in the last half of the 1600s, the harpsichord (*cembalo*) around 1700, and the piano (*hammerklaver*) around 1800. The cittern, considered primarily an amateur's instrument, was associated with self-accompanied women's singing.

The children of the Norwegian urban middle class traveled to Germany and Denmark, and less often, to other European countries. Agathe Ursula Backer (1847–1907), a shipowner's daughter, studied with some of the most famous musicians of the era, including Hans von Bülow in Florence and Franz Liszt in Weimar. Though the eighteen-year-old Backer did not become a concert performer, George Bernard Shaw thought her one of the greatest pianists in Europe. She is remembered for having composed short piano pieces and songs.

ARCHAEOLOGY AND THE EARLY HISTORY OF MUSIC

With the exception of bronze trumpets, dated from about 1100 to about 500 B.C., Norway's music history began during the Viking Age, from the 800s to the 1000s.

The lur

The earliest evidence of musical practice in the area of present-day Norway consists of archaeological specimens. Several dozen bronze curved trumpets have been dated about 1100–500 B.C. [see ARCHAEOLOGY OF MUSIC IN EUROPE]. The first of these was excavated in Denmark in 1797, when the ambiguous name *lurer* (sing. *lur*) was applied to them. Since then, four more examples have been discovered in Norway. The lur was a 1.5-to-2.5-meter-long, conical bronze tube with a built-in cup mouthpiece and a circular plate projected perpendicularly to the tube, where one would expect to find the flaring out of a bell. Highly ornamented, this plate may have had religious significance.

From excavated ships and more conventional archaeological sites of the Viking Age (800s–1000s), various idiophones have been found in ancient Norway, many associated with the so-called horse culture. One, the *rangle,* is a special kind of rattle: large and small iron rings were loosely interconnected, to each other and a main ring, so as to jingle freely. In Vestfold, Oppland, and Valdres, more than 150 specimens have been found. Archaeologists believe these rattles were attached to horses and wagons (or sleighs), but they may have served more than a purely practical function (Sevåg 1973).

Animal horns (with and without finger holes), duct flutes made of bark or bone, and long wooden horns similar to the alphorn are known to have existed in Norway from well before Viking days. Also called *lurer,* they were straight, conical-bore, wooden tubes 1.4 to 1.7 meters long, some much longer. One variety was made of hollowed-out wood; the other, of a wooden tube split lengthwise and bound spirally with birch bark. The lur mentioned in ancient Nordic literature (*lúður* in Old Norse) was associated with ceremonial and military functions, but no depiction of it exists.

The *harpa*

Old Norse manuscripts suggest that playing the *harpa* and creating poetry were accomplishments an educated young gentleman was expected to develop. The Norwegian king Harold Sigurdarson (*harðráði*) (1015–1056) is said to have boasted, "Of art-skills, eight have I"; with shooting, boating, swimming, brewing beer, horseback riding, and skiing, he includes "riming" and harping "with my hands" (Hollander 1968 [1945]). Harold was exceptional in being both king and poet (*skáld*). Skalds were upper-class poet-chanters, who occupied politically powerful, semiofficial posts as court poets, esteemed advisors to kings, and keepers of history. The early ones were all Norwegian, but the art tended to migrate to Iceland during its settlement (870–930). By the eleventh century, Icelanders had a monopoly on the tradition in Norway: the words were composed by Icelanders, but the reported events had occurred in many northern places, since these poets were also itinerant within Nordic high society. They do not seem to have used instrumental accompaniment; as far as can be determined, instrumental playing and chanting poetry were separate activities.

In literary sources, the most frequently mentioned instrument is the *harpa,* named as early as the tenth-century Eddic poem *Völuspá.* Harp playing was a tradition of itinerant musicians and gentlemen. The instrument is never described in writing; however, it was clearly a generic term for a stringed instrument, sometimes bowed, sometimes plucked. Iconographic sources depict the hero Gunnar in the snake pit, charming snakes with his *harpa*; from these representations, the word usually seems to have denoted a lyre, rarely a harp. One of the few extant medieval instruments is a seven-stringed lyre from Numedal; and a thirteenth-century stone carving in Trondheim Cathedral depicts a musician playing a bowed lyre, prevalent in Scandinavia during the Middle Ages. Available sources show that the bowed lyre outlasted the plucked instrument in the Nordic area, and indeed is still found in Finland (*jouhikantele*) and the Swedish settlements of Estonia (*talharpa*) (Andersson 1970). It was probably the instrument that ancient Nordic writings called a *fiðla*—a term that occurs from the beginning of the 1100s (Andersson 1970).

Early part-singing

After the establishment of the Nidaros bishopric (1152–1153), cathedral schools were set up in Bergen, Christiania, Nidaros, and Stavangar. No evidence of polyphony in Norwegian churches exists, but in a description of part singing in England and Wales, the twelfth-century author Giraldus Cambrensis wrote that he believed the natives had learned polyphonic singing from Danes and Norwegians (Reese 1940). We have no way of knowing precisely what kind of part singing was meant—whether it proceeded in fourths, fifths, and octaves, as in Icelandic *tvísöngur*; or whether it utilized the parallel-third style found in a hymn to St. Magnus from the Orkney Islands

The first Norwegian musician to achieve international fame was the swashbuckling violinist Ole Bull (1810–1889), whose admirers and detractors alike noted his improvisatory abilities and a technical skill that included double, triple, and even quadruple stopping.

and included in a thirteenth-century manuscript. For centuries, Iceland and the Orkneys were within the Norwegian sphere of influence.

MUSIC AND IDENTITY IN THE NINETEENTH CENTURY

The end of Danish rule and the beginning of the association with Sweden (1814) brought with it a new interest in Norwegian cultural identity. The first Norwegian musician to achieve international fame was the swashbuckling violinist Ole Bull (1810–1889), whose admirers and detractors alike noted his improvisatory abilities and a technical skill that included double, triple, and even quadruple stopping, facilitated by the use of a flatter-than-usual bridge in a style reminiscent of the older styles to which that instrument was traditional.

In his early years, Ole Bull studied with European-trained teachers during the winter in Bergen, but he never received conservatory training. The extent to which he was taught by *flatfele* players in Valestrand, where his family spent their summer vacations, is probably underestimated (Bjørndal 1940). His critics complained that he rarely applied his technical ability to mainstream European music, that he improvised too much, and that he used incorrect voice leading when he committed his music to paper. He was a popular success in most European countries and consistently played to overflow crowds in major cities of the United States, which he toured several times. He traveled to Havana, where, delighting his audience, he improvised on Cuban melodies.

In 1848, Bull's friends and colleagues pressured him to interrupt his tours, come home, and contribute to the movement for national identity. He purchased the Bergen theater as a national performance space and held public auditions to attract aspiring musicians, dancers, and actors from rural districts. He invited the great *hardingfele* virtuoso Myllarguten to give a recital on 15 January 1849. Though the people of the rural southern highlands revered Myllarguten as a genius, urbanites were as unprepared for this exotic music from their own backyard as for the new dialect-based language that had suddenly arisen, and the result was a cultural collision (*kulturkollisjon*) (Ledang 1980).

The barrier between urban-written and rural-aural traditions was surmounted by the appearance of printed folk-song collections. The availability of published, simplified transcriptions with piano accompaniments, or four-part choral arrangements, provided easy access and lent a sense of legitimacy, through the presence of a printed document, to material about which native composers had little knowledge. Ludvig Lindeman, a pioneer collector of indigenous music, was extraordinary among his peers in not having had a continental European conservatory education. A product of the same informal mode of instruction as the rural ballad singer or fiddle player, he received musical training from his father (Grinde 1991). In his *Norske Fjeldmelodier* (Norwegian mountain melodies) and *Ældre og nyere Norske Fjeldmelodier* (Old and new Norwegian mountain melodies), he provided piano accompaniments for the songs and otherwise adapted the melodies to the taste and expectations of the day. Commissioned to put together a new psalter, he refused to include traditional material, despite his interest in the indigenous music. The contradictions within Lindeman himself represented conflicts within most urban musicians at this time, and his revisions of traditional material began to take on a life of their own.

Halfdan Kjerulf, at first an opponent of the movement for Norwegian cultural identity, later published two collections of what he called folk dances and folk ballads with piano accompaniments, influenced by Lindeman's treatment of folk songs. The building blocks of Norwegian music—augmented fourth, parallel fifths and octaves, pedal points, asymmetrical rhythms, and other features—formed the basis for a style of music that developed an important existence but bore faint resemblance to indigenous Norwegian idioms (Anker 1983 [1943]; Gurvin 1940).

In this context, the originality of Edvard Grieg and misunderstandings concerning the national character of his music may be understood. Grieg grew up in Bergen, a cosmopolitan city; as a young student at the Leipzig Conservatory (1858–1862), he interested himself in avant-garde theories of harmony (Benestad and Schjelderup-Ebbe 1988). He has been underrated for his role in loosening the bounds of tonality; in his harmony, he anticipated the work of Debussy and Ravel. His music and its assumed connection with "the folk" received international acclaim when there was great interest in "exotic" national idioms; but later, with fluctuations of international taste, his music was belittled for much the same reason. Recently, Grieg has been newly respected for his original contributions to modernist composition.

Within regions of *bygde* culture, the classical ideal has long been highly regarded. Improvisations and compositions of acknowledged masters of the tradition are carefully remembered and perpetuated, coexisting with each other and new works. In the late 1880s, Hardanger violinist Knut Dahle (1834–1921), concerned about the effect of religious revivalism on the traditional music in his township (Tinn, in Telemark), wrote to Grieg to ask him to transcribe this heritage, most of it handed down from previous generations, some pieces composed by himself. Grieg sent violinist-composer Johan Halvorsen to meet Dahle in Oslo; Halvorsen and Grieg, when he received the Halvorsen transcriptions, expressed admiration for a body of music that had been unfamiliar to them. Despite warnings that it would be "sinful" to arrange this music for keyboard, Grieg published an edition for piano (opus 72 of his *Lyric Pieces*), and Halvorsen published his transcriptions as violin pieces (both published by Peters Publishing Company). Because of the generally accepted view that folk music was not individually composed and was therefore available to be "raised . . . to an artistic level" (as Grieg said in his introduction), it was not thought necessary to name Knut Dahle or the Tinn tradition in these publications. Transcriptive inaccuracies stem, not from Halvorsen and Grieg's lack of musicianship, but from their unfamiliarity with the tradition; preparing for recording these pieces, the pianist Einar Steen-Nøkleberg found it a "revelation" to inject the correct rhythmic and other traits as he had learned them from Knut Buen. Contrary to Knut Dahle's expectations, the Tinn repertory had survived in aural tradition, not in notation (Anker 1983 [1943]; Hopkins 1986).

NATIONALISM AND MUSIC IN THE TWENTIETH CENTURY

The next generation did not develop Grieg's harmonic leads, but followed the inheritance of German Romanticism beyond the time when audiences were receptive to the style. Christian Sinding (1856–1941), who spent half of his life in Germany, is the most famous of these composers. Exceptions were Pauline Hall (1890–1969), who, breaking with tradition, studied in Paris and made original use of the impressionist idiom; and Fartein Valen (1887–1952), whose individual development of the twelve-tone style drew increasing attention in the 1990s.

Between 1925 and 1950, composers who grew up with *bygde* musical traditions tried to construct an indigenous musical culture that would be internationally comprehensible. Probably the two most original composers of this group were Geirr Tveitt (1908–1981) and Eivind Groven (1901–1977). Tveitt, skilled in the traditions of his native Hardanger, sought to combine a theoretical structure built on the peculiar modality of this music with experimental idioms, especially those relating to new ways of manipulating musical timbre. Eivind Groven composed new *slåttar* for the *hardingfele,* on which he was a skilled player, and symphonic works that drew on features such as the Telemark *springar* rhythm, the metamorphosis variation technique for melodic development, and the nonequal-tempered pitch systems of the *bygde* traditions; he invented an electronic organ capable of playing the nontempered pitches of indigenous scales.

Groven, appointed director of folk music for the Norwegian Broadcasting Company, made effective use of radio to bring aural traditions directly into homes. His program, "The Folk Music Half Hour," which aired for the first time in 1931, was a new experience for urban listeners, many of whom wrote angry letters to the station, complaining about out-of-tune pitches, singers not properly accompanied by the piano, and so on. "The Folk Music Half Hour" soon began to function as a weekly ritual for rural and urban Norwegians and became a major influence in promoting the importance of indigenous music to new generations of urbanites, who remember having been expected to listen respectfully as a cultural duty. In the late 1990s, two decades after Groven's death, the cultural significance of the program has not diminished, judging by the storm of protest at the news of its intended removal from prime-time scheduling.

The new school of nationalist composers bore the brunt of the reaction against romanticism, and an even stronger reaction against nationalism after World War II. Influenced by the acoustically based theory of Hindemith (then living in the United States), young Scandinavian musicians formed the Monday Group (*Mandagsgruppen*) in Stockholm on Monday, 5 May 1945, the day the German occupation of Norway and Denmark ended [see SWEDEN]. They declared themselves opposed to the "old national-romantic" and vowed to seek "absolute objectivity" (Wallner 1968). Norwegian members of the group included Olav Gurvin, who became the first Norwegian professor of musicology (1956), with an interest in the use of technology in musical analysis, and the jazz performer Gunnar Sonstevold (b. 1912), who in original compositions united his experience with jazz and his knowledge of atonal techniques.

INSTITUTIONS FOR MUSIC

After World War I, *bygde* musicians felt the need for a formal organization that would provide a meeting place for practice, instruction, and music swapping; a structure for competitions, concerts, and festivals; and an institution that would support their cause. The formalization of these activities led to a state-sponsored nationwide network of fiddlers' groups, Landslaget for Spelemenn (National Fiddlers' Association), founded in 1923, an organization that grew to include more than 125 affiliated groups. Though founded only to develop *hardingfele* playing and *bygde* dancing, this organization opened its doors to the *flatfele* in 1946, and in the 1970s to competitive *kveðing,* the singing style associated with the performance of the traditional vocal repertory, especially *stevs* and old ballads. Since 1972, offerings have expanded to include the accordion, the buck horn, the guitar, the harp, the recorder (*tussefløyte*), and ensemble groups of all kinds.

By the early 1980s, the National Fiddlers' Association was geared more toward the production of mass festivals than to maintaining the hierarchical network of competitions (local, regional, national) that had been designed to hone the abilities of *bygde* dancers and players. This change aroused protest, and in 1986 the sponsorship of a national festival for *gammaldans* touched off a major controversy. The result was the founding of a new organization, Norsk Folkemusikk og Danselag (Norwegian Folk Music and Dance Society), based on the old principles.

In 1919, in both Bergen and Oslo, symphony orchestra societies were reorganized on a permanent basis. After 1945, official cultural policy was to grant fixed appropriations to such institutions as the Norwegian Opera Company, founded in 1959. The Bergen Festival became a permanent annual event in 1953, and new concert halls were established in Oslo (1970), Bergen (1978), and Stavangar (1980). The Norwegian chapter of the International Society for Contemporary Music gained visibility through its sponsorship of the ISCM International Festival in 1953. The Norwegian Jazz Federation was founded in the same year, and the club Metropol Jazz Centre became internationally prominent in the 1960s, as did the annual jazz festival in Molde.

The twentieth century saw an increase in educational institutions of all kinds, not only local music schools and organized courses for traditional music, but also institutions of higher learning, research institutes, archival collections, and scholarly societies. Norway gained its first major conservatory of music in 1973, when the government-sponsored Norwegian State Academy of Music was founded, in Oslo. Musicology departments were added to the University of Oslo in 1956 and the University of Trondheim in 1961 (presently headed by Ola Kai Ledang). Since 1989, students have been able to major in folk dance scholarship at the University of Trondheim, using the facilities of Rådet for Folkemusikk og Folkedans, a program developed by Egil Bakka, the first professor of dance in Norway, and Bjørn Aksdal, organologist and curator of the musical instrument collection at the Ringve Museum. Students can study at the University of Oslo through the Norsk Folkemusikksamling (Norwegian Folk Music Archive), directed by Reidar Sevåg. Other important archives with recording programs are at Norwegian Radio, under the leadership of Sven Nyhus, and Trondheim University.

Norway's first musicological society (Samfund for Musikkgranskning) issued an annual periodical, *Norsk Musikkgranskning,* from 1937 to 1961. The Norsk Musikkforskerlag (Norwegian Association for Musicological Research), founded in 1964, publishes *Studia Musicologica Norvegica.* Ole Bull Akademiet, a center for research and instruction in traditional music, was established in Voss (1977). Its program was created and developed by Sigbjørn Osa (1910–1990), a *hardingfele* player and popular promoter of the tradition through radio, TV, and personal appearances. Music majors at some teachers' colleges and conservatories are required to take a prescribed number of credits at this academy.

In the twentieth century, musicologists tended to come from the ranks of musicians; most of the more than two thousand *slåttar* in the monumental seven-volume series of *hardingfele* transcriptions, *Norsk Folkemusikk,* were drawn from the repertoires of the editors, several of whom were collectors and transcribers (Gurvin et al. 1958–1967; Sevåg et al. 1971, 1981).

Technology has made it possible to bring the organization of music research into remote localities. The Buen Kulturverkstad in Tuddal, Telemark, publishes and markets phonograms (LPs and CDs), books, and artifacts. Several phonograms consist of performances by the Buen family, especially the master fiddlers Hauk and Knut Buen and the great traditional singer Agnes Buen Garnås; they represent the fifth generation of musicians in their family, and all three receive government stipends for their

From the late 1960s through the 1970s, northern youths began to experiment with combining their traditional styles with almost every available idiom—from rock to symphonic—to form various kinds of ethno-jazz, jazz-rock, and new music groups.

contribution to Norwegian culture. The compositions of Knut Buen range from traditional to experimental idioms. The organization also houses a small folk-life museum, the setting for an annual festival of traditional music with demonstrations by musicians and artisans.

SAAMI MUSIC IN NORWAY

According to the first authoritative written source on the Saami (Scheffer 1963 [1674]), the Saami lived a nomadic life supported by egalitarian socioeconomic communities called *siidas* and a religion that revolved around a spiritual leader (*naid*). Fundamental to their society and their mode of worship was the joik 'to sing in the Saami way', that is, with a distinctive tone quality achieved by a constricted throat, a slightly open mouth, and frequent *glissandi*. The texts—about people, animals, and the scenery—often expressed intensely personal thoughts about the individual qualities of a particular person.

As colonists and missionaries arrived during the 1600s and 1700s, the Saami suffered industrial exploitation and intense religious persecution. Their religion was destroyed, and their special ceremonial drums, *runebommene*, were burned. The joik tradition, despite being declared illegal, was never annihilated. After World War II, the Saami gradually succeeded in changing official attitudes and governmental policies toward their culture, and through a series of adaptations to new social requirements, the joik has prospered.

Until the 1960s, Saami music was unfamiliar to most Norwegians. Probably the first authoritative information on Saami music available to the general public was an NRK documentary made on location in Tromsø. In 1974 in Kautokeino (a city that still had an ordinance banning the singing of joiks), the Joint Nordic Saami Institute was established for the study of Saami culture. From the late 1960s through the 1970s, northern youths began to experiment with combining their traditional styles with almost every available idiom—from rock to symphonic—to form various kinds of ethno-jazz, jazz-rock, and new music groups.

This direction continues, as conservatory-trained composers, including Folk Stromholm and John Person (both b. 1941), employ joiks in avant-garde styles. The latter's neoexpressionist and postserial style and prizewinning pieces with titles like *CSV* ("Dare to show that you are Saami") display almost militant assertions of Saami culture (Grinde 1991). In 1981, Nils-Aslak Valkeapää, the most influential Saami artist, composed a prologue for the nearly twenty-year-old music festival at Harstad (about 250 kilometers north of the Arctic Circle) as part of a new policy of incorporating local culture into the already established festival. In 1991, Valkeapää, an equally skilled musician, poet, and artist, composed a multimedia work for the festival. The Saami Musicians Association (Sapmi Musihkariid Searvi) was founded in 1983. In 1990, the internationally known Norwegian saxophonist Jan Garbarek collaborated with Saami singers Mari Boine Persen and Ingor Ántte Áitu Gaup on a recording, *I Took Up the Runes*.

The composers who have made a permanent place in Norwegian culture for Saami music are all insiders to the tradition, a style of music strikingly dissimilar to other musical systems of the Scandinavian area. Almost every musical style available in Norway since the 1970s has been combined with joik singing, which does not assimilate to, but coexists virtually unchanged with, the other traditions to which it is joined [see SAAMI MUSIC].

MUSIC AND CULTURAL POLICY

The Norwegian government's new cultural policy of the 1970s extended the boundaries of the welfare state to include artists, and definitions of "culture" and "art" came under close political scrutiny (Klausen 1977). From 1975 to 1985, the new policy underwent a decentralized phase, when the concept of culture grew to include informal manifestations. The government instituted a policy of distribution from the state-sponsored theater, opera, and concert groups out to regional localities, and the NRK Television Orchestra became an especially important means of cultural distribution. In 1981, a governmental white paper on culture announced an expansion of the government arts-subsidy program, through which most top-ranking artists, including *hardingfele* fiddlers, receive lifetime stipends. Since 1985, policy has shifted to a localized infrastructure so dialectal differences could be maintained, not just to support indigenous regional traditions, but also to promote local styles of rock (called *dialekt-rock*), jazz, and other community-based idioms (figure 10).

FIGURE 10 This bust of Hardanger fiddler Johannes Dahle, displayed in the foyer of the Tinn public school during his lifetime, reflects the unusual esteem in which Dahle was held by the local inhabitants and the strong support for local traditions, especially by farmers, taxi drivers, and teachers. Photo by Pandora Hopkins, 1972.

The Norsk Musikk-Kongress was held in Sundvollen (1986), and a conference on community control of culture was held in Sogn og Fjordane (1987). These meetings led to a proposal by the Norwegian Song and Music Council, an umbrella organization for more than twenty music institutions (including symphony orchestras, church-music groups, jazz groups, and the National Fiddlers' Association) to recommend a course of governmental action to benefit its member organizations; the result, the report "Charting the Musical Life of Norway," gives music a political-economic function and stresses the need to support local traditions for international interaction.

The main sponsor of ULTIMA, a Norwegian contemporary-music festival founded in 1990, is the multinational oil company Fina Exploration Norway. Attracting a nonspecialist audience, ULTIMA has twice collaborated with more esoteric festivals, World Music Days (1990) and Nordic Music Days (1992).

POPULAR MUSIC

Norwegian interest in rock goes back to the late 1950s, when Bill Haley's "Rock Around the Clock" was imported with the film *The Blackboard Jungle* (Bakken 1983). At the Kalvoya Festival (1972), the jazz singer-composer Åge Aleksandersen coined the term *Trønderrock* to describe the style of his group, Prudence, whose members had decided to dispense with English-language texts in favor of their own dialect, *Trøndersk,* and to experiment by incorporating local musical traits. *Trønderrock* became popular all over the country, followed by an explosive growth of amateur rock groups, each using the linguistic and musical dialects of its locality—a new wave of styles dubbed *dialekt-rock* by Aleksandersen (Ledang 1980).

In the 1980s, Norwegians became interested in combining traditional music with other idioms. In 1989, a young *hardingfele* player, Annbjørg Lien (b. 1971), issued a recording (*Annbjørg*) of her rock and new-music ensemble; it contains classics of the *slått* repertory, backed by synthesizer with wind and rhythm instruments. Once acclaimed as a child prodigy and featured in a TV special, "Miller-Girl," Lien has worked her way up to Class A in national *hardingfele* competitions.

The flood of U.S. recordings that became available in the early part of the twentieth century inspired an interest in jazz. Two international jazz festivals, established in Molde and Kongsberg during the 1960s, remain permanent institutions. Norway has several internationally known jazz composers and virtuosi, including Jan Garbarek, the guitarist Terje Rypdal (both b. 1947), and Rolf Walin (b. 1957). Now the spotlight is turned on unconventional combinations of instrumental or vocal idioms, sometimes called new music, ethno-jazz, or world beat.

Norwegian styles of jazz and *bygde* music seem to have an affinity, perhaps because the performers share highly developed improvisatory skills, a special interest in complexity and the esoteric, and the ability to play in different styles. Knut Buen's composition *Valssorm-visa* sets the traditional-style epic singing of Agnes Buen Garnås against the background of *hardingfele* (Buen), synthesizer and saxophone; together they produce a tone painting of the Seljord Worm (*Valssorm*), a Norwegian version of the Loch Ness monster. On the same cassette is an equally original composition, *"På gamle tufter,"* a traditional solo *slått* with an innovative development of modal interplay (*På gamle tufter* 1985).

The first LP to feature the *langeleik* was issued the following year (1986); one of the finest *langeleik* performers, Elisabeth Kværne, plays traditional pieces while an unobtrusive accompaniment is provided by a small ensemble of lute, recorder, clarinet, and *hardingfele*. In Setesdal, electric bassist Arild Andersen's original compositions include the voice of the traditional singer Kirsten Bråten Berg, works that have been recorded and performed at the Voss Jazz Festival, once again without any confluence of styles. In l989, Jan Garbarek collaborated with Agnes Buen on a compact disc (Solberg 1989).

International has replaced *national* as the buzzword of Norwegian music. An argument for governmental subsidy extols the commercial utility of music as an international language; the *gammaldans* is being promoted for its accessibility across national borders, while advocates of the *hardingfele* justify special support for their tradition because its distinctiveness makes it a contribution to world culture. The increasingly articulate voices of what were once called folk and popular musicians and a postmodernist point of view have ended the supremacy of conservatory-trained musicians and their music. The single value system typical of modernism has given way to multiple value systems, and cultural pluralism expresses both the actuality of the musical scene in Norway and intellectual theories about it.

BIBLIOGRAPHY

Aksdal, Bjørn. 1982. *Med piber og basuner, skalmeye og fiol.* Trondheim: Universitetsforlaget.

———. 1986. "Samspillformer innen folkemusikken—et historisk perspektiv." *Spelemannsbladet* 45(6):14–17.

Alver, Brynjulf, and Arne Bjørndal. 1966. *Og fela ho lét.* Oslo: Universitetsforlaget.

Alver, Brynijulf, and Ingrid Gjertsen. 1985. *Arne Bjørndals hundrears-minne: Seminar i Bergen 3.-5. mars 1982.* Bergen: Forlaget folkekultur.

Andersson, Otto. 1930. *The Bowed-Harp: A Study in the History of Early Musical Instruments.* Translated by Kathleen Schlesinger. London: Oxford University Press.

———. 1970. "The Bowed Harp of Trondheim Cathedral and Related Instruments East and West." *Galpin Society Journal* 23:4–34.

Anker, Øyvind. 1983 [1943]. "Knut Dale—Edv. Grieg—Johan Halvorsen." In *Som gofa spølå,* ed. Knut Buen, 71–95. Tuddal: Rupesekken forlag, 1983. Partial English translation in *Aural Thinking in Norway: Performance and Communication with the Hardingfele,* by Pandora Hopkins, 247–251. New York: Human Sciences Press, 1986.

Anmarkrud, Björn. 1975. "De Ulike Felestille i Hardingfeletradisjonene." Ph.D. dissertation, University of Oslo.

Arneberg, Halfdan. 1949. *Norsk Folkekunst: Kvinnearbeid.* Oslo: Universitetsforlaget.

Bach, Dagfinu. 1989. *Misikklivet i Norge: Hovudrapport frå prosjektet "Kartlegging av musikklivet i Norge."* Sogndal: Kommunenes Sentralforbund med Kultur-og vitskapsdepartementet som bidragsytar.

Bachmann, Werner. 1969. *The Origins of Bowing and the Development of Bowed Instruments up to the Thirteenth Century.* Translated by N. Deane. London: Oxford University Press.

Bakka, Egil. 1978. *Norske dansetradisjonar.* Oslo: Det Norske samlaget.

———. 1982. *Springar, Gangar, Rull og Pols.* Trondheim: Rådet for folkemusikk og folkedans.

Bakka, Egil, Brit Seland, Dag Vårdal, and Ånon

Egeland. 1990. *Dansetradisjonar frå Vest-Agder.* Trondheim: Vest-Agder Ungdomslag and Rådet for folkemusikk og folkedans.

Bakken, Willy. 1983. *Norge i rock, beat og blues.* Oslo: E. Sandberg.

Balchen, Bernt. 1987. "'Meiningslaus splitting' herr formann?" *Spelemannsbladet* 4:13.

Benestad, Finn, and Dag Schjelderup-Ebbe. 1988. *Edvard Grieg: The Man and the Artist.* Translated by William Halverson and Leland Sateren. Lincoln: University of Nebraska Press.

Berge, Rikard, and Olav Fjalestad. 1972. *Myllarguten/Gibøen.* Oslo: Noregs Boklag.

Bjørgum, Hallvard. 1986. "Norsk Folkemusikk og Danselag." *Spelemannsbladet* 3:6.

———. 1987. "Dobbelsiger for Norsk Folkemusikk and Bygdedans." *Spelemannsbladet* 4:14.

Bjørndal, Arne. 1940. *Ole Bull og norske folkemusikk.* Bergen: Forlaget Folkekutt.

Blom, Jan-Petter. 1981. "Dansen i hardingfelemusikken." Norsk Folkemusikk, 7. Oslo: Universitetsforlaget.

———. 1985. "Hvor gammel er fela?" *Arne Bjørndals hundreårs-minne,* ed. Brynjulf Alver and Ingrid Gjertsen, 191–208. Bergen: Forlaget Folkekultur.

———. 1986. "Foreword." In *Aural Thinking in Norway: Performance and Communication with the Hardingfele,* by Pandora Hopkins, 11–13. New York: Human Sciences Press, 1986.

Blom, Jan-Petter, and Tellef Kvifte. 1986. "On the Problem of Inferential Ambivalence in Musical Meter." *Ethnomusicology* 30:491–517.

Bø, Olav. 1957. *Stev.* Norske folkedikting 5. Oslo: Det Norske Samlaget.

Brincker, Jens. 1982. "Three Modern Nordic Composers." *Nordic Sounds* 1:22–26.

Buen, Hanne, Agnes Buen Garnås, and Dagne Groven Myhren. 1978. *Ei Vise vil eg kveda: Songar på folkemunn i Telemark.* Oslo: Tiden Norsk Forlag.

Buen, Knut. 1983. *Som gofa spølå.* Tuddal: Rupesekken forlag.

Bull, Edvard, et al. 1929. *Det norske folkliv og historie gjennom tidene 8.* Oslo: H. Aschehoug.

Burney, Charles. 1957 [1776]. *A General History of Music.* New York: Dover.

Dahm, Cecilie. 1987. *Kvinner Komponerer: Ni portretter av norske kvinnelige komponister i tiden 1840–1930.* Oslo: Solum Forlag.

Durrenberger, E. Paul, and Gisli Palsson, eds. 1989. *The Anthropology of Iceland.* Iowa City: University of Iowa Press.

Edstrom, Karl-Olaf. 1989. "Avspeglar den stilistiska skillnaden inom jojken samernas forhistoria?" *Musiikki* 1(4):294–312.

Einung, H. H. 1942. *Tinn Soga.* 2 vols. Rjukan: Eigi Forlag.

Ekgren, Jacqueline. 1983. "Musical Tradition in the Repertoire of Folk Singer ('Kvedar') Aslak Brekke: 'Stev' and 'Viser'." *Studia Musicologica Norvegica* 9:43–72.

Engeset, Bergljot. 1985. "Kvinner skal lytle og danse!" *Spelemannsbladet* 6:6–7.

———. 1986a. "Hornindalsområdet med Landsrekord." *Spelemannsbladet* 1:4–5.

———. 1986b. "Musikk fra mor til son." *Spelemannsbladet* 2:6–8.

Faukstad, Jon. 1978. *Ein-raderen i norsk folkemusikk.* Oslo: Universitetsforlaget.

Fischer, Gerhard. 1965. *Domkirken i Trondheim.* 2 vols. Oslo: Land og Kirke.

Fjalestad, Olav, ed. 1971. *Eivind Groven: Heiderskrift til 70-årsdagen.* Oslo: Noregs Boklag.

Fritzner, Johan, Carl Unger, and Sophus Bugge. 1886–1896. *Ordbog over det gamle norske sprog.* Kristiania: Den Norske Forlagsforening.

Garnås, Agnes. 1980. "Kvedarskogen har runne pa ny i 70-åra." *Årbok for Telemark* 1980:115–137.

Gaukstad, Øystein. 1973. *Toner fra Valdres.* Valdres: Valdres Bygdeboksforlag.

Goertzen, Chris. 1997. *Fiddling for Norway: Revival and Identity.* Chicago: University of Chicago Press.

Greni, Liv. 1960. "Bånsuler i Setesdal." *Norveg* 7:13–28.

Grinde, Nils. 1991. *A History of Norwegian Music.* Translated by William Halversen and Leland Sateren. Lincoln: University of Nebraska Press.

Groven, Eivind. 1969. "Equal Temperament and Pure Tuning." Unpublished manuscript.

————. 1971. "Musikkstudiar–ikkje utgjevne for." In *Eivind Groven: Heiderskrift til 70-årsdagen,* ed. Olav Fjalestad, 93–119. Oslo: Noregs Boklag.

————. 1972. "Myllar-Spel og Håvard-Spel." In *Myllarguten/Gibøen,* ed. Rikard Berge and Olav Fjalestad, 233–238. Oslo: Universitetsforlaget.

Gurvin, Olav. 1940. "Norske serdrag i musikken." *Norsk Musikkgranskming Årbok* 50.

Gurvin, Olav, A. Bjørndal, Eivind Groven, and Trulls Ørpen, eds. 1958–1967. *Norsk folkemusikk.* 5 vols. Oslo: Universitetsforlaget.

Heiniö, Mikko. 1989. "Post-Modernism—An Approach to Contemporary Finnish Music." *Musiikki* 1(4):130–139.

Hollander, Lee. 1968 [1945]. *The Skalds: A Selection of Their Poems.* Ann Arbor: University of Michigan Press.

Hopkins, Pandora. 1986. *Aural Thinking in Norway: Performance and Communication with the Hardingfele.* New York: Human Sciences Press.

————. 1989. "Nordic Musicology in International Perspective." In *Musiikki: Proceedings from the Nordic Musicological Congress in Turku/Åbo 1988,* 1–15.

Huldt-Nystrøm, Hampus. 1959. "Scandinavian Music Till the Baroque Period." In *Scandinavia Past and Present I: From the Viking Age to Absolute Monarchy,* ed. Jørgen Bukdahl et al., 591–601. Copenhagen: Edvard Henriksen.

Klausen, Arne Martin. 1977. *Kunstsosiologi.* Oslo: Gyldendal Norsk Forlag.

————, ed. 1984. *Den norske væremaaten.* Oslo: J. W. Cappelens Forlag.

Kortsen, Bjarne. 1965. *Fartein Valen: Life and Music.* 3 vols. Oslo: Johan Grundt Tanum.

————. 1975. *Norwegian Music and Musicians.* Bergen: Author.

Kvifte, Tellef. 1981. "On Variability, Ambiguity and Formal Structure in the Harding Fiddle Music." *Studia instrumentorum musicae popularis* 7:102–107.

————. 1983. "Om flertydighet i opplevelse av metrum." *Studia musicologica norvegica* 9:27–42.

————. 1990. "Jan Garbarek: Jazz, Ethnic Romanticism, World Music or Personal Expression?" *Nordic Sounds* 4:8.

Kydland, Anne. 1983. "Eivind Grovens I. Symfoni: en studie i hans metamorfose-teknikk." Ph.D. dissertation, Oslo University.

Ledang, Ola Kai. 1974a. "Instrument—Player—Music on the Norwegian *Langleik.*" *Studia Instrumentorum Musicæ Popularis* 3:107–118.

————. 1974b. "Folkemusikk i smeltedigelen: Frå Hardanger til Trøndelag." *Forskningens lys* 1:311–327.

————. 1979. *Norsk Folkemusikk.* Oslo: H. Aschehoug.

————. 1980. "Trønderrock–Folkemusikk eller kva? Om Age Aleksandersen og musikken hans." *Studia Musicologica Norvegica* 6:59–79.

————. 1981. "Africanst Musikki dag it Global Kraftsentrum." *Forsknings Nytt* 6:18–23.

————. 1989. "Norwegian Musicology—Stagnation or Development?" *Musiikki* 1(4):56–73.

Ledang, Ola Kai. 1980. "Trønderrock—folkemusikk eller kva?" *Studia Musicologica Wovegica* 6:59–79.

Lindeman, Ludvig Mathias. 1853–1867. *Ældre og Nyere norske fjeldmelodier.* Christiania: C. Warmuths Musikkforlag.

Lodgaard, S. H. Hveem, and K. Skjelsbaek, eds. 1984. *Vår plass i verden.* Oslo: Gylddal Norsk forlag.

Mace, Thomas. 1958, 1966 [1676]. *Musick's Monument.* 2 vols. Facsimile of 2nd edition. Paris: Editions du centre national de la recherche scientifique.

Mersenne, Marin. 1957 [1636]. *Harmonie universelle.* Translated by Roger E. Chapman. The Hague: Nijhoff.

Myhren, Magne. 1985. "Opplæring i hardingfele-spel. Serleg tilhova i 1950 åra." In *Arne Bjørndals*

Hundre ars-minne: Seminar i Bergen 3.–5. Mars 1982, 103–116. Bergen: Forlaget Folkekultur.

Myklebust, Rolf. 1982. *Femti år med folkemusikk.* Oslo: Det Norske Samlaget.

Nyhus, Sven, 1973. *Pols i Rørostraktom.* Oslo: Universitetsforlaget.

Reese, Gustave. 1940. *Music in the Middle Ages.* New York: Norton.

Sachs, Curt. 1920. *Handbuch der Musikinstrumentenkunde.* Leipzig: Breitkopf & Hartel.

Scheffer, Johannes. 1963 [1674]. *Lapponia: HameenlinnaL Lapin tatkimussearan.* Minneapolis, Minn.: A. A. Kariat.

Sevåg, Reidar. 1972. "The Harding Fiddle." In *From Bone Pipe and Cattle Horn to Fiddle and Psaltery,* ed. M. Muller, 18–24. Copenhagen: Musikhistorisk Museum.

————. 1973. *Det Gjallar og det Læt: Fra skremme-og lokkereiskapar til folkelege blaseinstrument.* Oslo: Det norske samlaget.

————. 1974. "Neutral Tones and the Problem of Mode in Norwegian Folk Music." *Studia Instrumentorum Musicæ Popularis* 3:207–213.

————. 1979. "Die Hardingfele: Instrument—Spieltechnik—Musik." *Studia instrumentorum musicæ popularis* 6:71–79.

————. 1980. "Norway ii: Folk Music." *The New Grove Dictionary of Music and Musicians.* Edited by Stanley Sadie. London: Macmillan.

Sevåg, Reidar, Jan-Petter Blom, and Sven Nyhus. 1971, 1981. *Norsk Folkemusikk.* Vols. 6 and 7. Oslo: Universitetsforlaget.

Smith, Leslie Francis. 1962. *Modern Norwegian Historiography.* Trondheim: Universitetsforlaget.

Solberg, Leif. 1989. "Sterke musikere = Sterk musikk = Rosensfole!" *Spelemannsbladet* 9:20.

Tiren, Karl. 1942. *Die Lappische Volksmusik.* Acta Lapponica, 3. Stockholm: H. Geber.

Wallner, Bo 1968. *40 En Klippbok om Mandagsgruppen och det svenska musiklivet.* Stockholm: Institutet for rikskonserter.

AUDIOVISUAL RESOURCES

Alexandersen, Hilman, et al. 1994. *Hjartsespel Hilman Alexandersen spelar ag fortel.* Norway: Buen Kulturverkstad BKCD 7. Compact disc.

Bjørgen, Amund, and Bjørn Odde. 1993. *Slåttemusik frå Lom.* Heil CD 804. Compact disc.

Boine, Mari. 1993. *Geaskinviellja Ørnebror mo italíy* (Eagle brother). Lean MBCD 62. Compact disc.

Brăiloiu, Constantin. 1958. *Norvegiens.* Unesco Conseil Internationale de la Musique A1 108/109. LP disk.

Bratland, Sondre. 1994. *Gjest i verda.* Kirkelig Kulturverskkted. FXCD 135. Compact disc.

Buen, Hauk, and Knut Buen. 1992. *Myllargutens Minne.* Buen Kulturverkstad BKCD 2. Compact disc.

Bukkene Bruse. 1993. *Bukkene Bruse.* Oslo, Norway: Grappa GRCD 4053. Compact disc.

Courlander, Edward, ed. 1954. *Songs and Dances of Norway.* Smithsonian Folkways FW 04008. LP disk.

Dahle, Andris. 1993. *Gofalåtten.* Heilo HCD 7090. Compact disc.

Dahle, Johannes, and Knut Dahle. 1993. *Griegslåttane.* Musikkhuset Forlag. M-H 2642 CD. The original classical Telemark pieces,

arranged for piano by Grieg and published as peasant dances, op. 72. Compact disc.

Danko, Rick. 1993. *Danko/Fjeld/Andersen.* Rykodisc RCD 10270. Compact disc.

Faukstadt, Jon, and Per Sæmund Bjørkum. 1994. *Slåtter frå Torger Olstads notebok.* Bergen Digital Studios. BCDC 7018. Compact disc.

Fjøllmanntonar: Folkemusikk frå Vinje, Rauland og Møsstrand. 1993. Heilo HCD 7083. Compact disc.

Folk Music From Norway. 1993. Heilo HCD 7078. Compact disc.

Folk Music of Norway. 1977. Topic 12TS351. LP disk.

Highlights—Landskappleiken '94. 1994. National Contest for Traditional Music. Heilo HCD 7103. Compact disc.

Indre Sunnfjord Spelemannslag. 1984. Heilo HO 7030. LP disk.

Jan Garbarek Group. *Twelve Moons.* 1993. ECM 519 500–2. 2 compact discs.

Joner, Pelle. 1992. *Norwegian Folk Songs Sung With Guitar by Pelle Joner.* Smithsonian Folkways FW 08725. Compact disc.

Kalenda, Maya. 1989. *Norske middelalderballader.* Kirkelig Kulturverksted FYCD 82. Compact disc.

Laade, Wolfgang, ed. 1992. *Lappish Joik Songs from Northern Norway.* Smithsonian Folkways FW 04007. Compact disc.

Norwegian Information Service. 1994. *Buskerudtonat med Tradisjonar* (Traditional folk music from Norway). Vol. 2. Buskerud Folkemusikklag BFCD 9102. Compact disc.

Nyhus, Sven. 1989. *Traditional Norwegian Fiddle Music.* Shanachie SH- 21003. Compact disc.

Paulsen, Ståle. 1993. *Slåtter frå Helgeland.* Heilo HCD 7082. Compact disc.

Porsanger, Sverre. 1993. *Lavlu Lavlla.* Idut ICD 932. Compact disc.

Saami Music and Change. 1988. Ole Edstrom Caprice 1351. LP disk.

Sdorbye, Lief. 1986. *Songs and Stories from Norway.* Golden Bough LSC 101. LP disk.

Tiriltunga. 1992. *Det Tungvint fri.* CD Plant KHGCD 02. Compact disc.

Valkeapää, Nils-Aslak. 1994. *Dálveleaikkat—Wintergames.* Guovdageaidnu DATCD 17. Compact disc.

Sweden

Jan Ling
Erik Kjellberg
Owe Ronström

Regional Styles of Traditional Music	**Dance**
Musical Types and Structures	**Music Education and Transmission**
Conceptions of Music	**History of Music**
Age, Class, Gender	**Popular Music and Jazz**
Musical Instruments	**History of Research**

Geographically the fourth largest country in Europe, Sweden has about 8.5 million inhabitants, most of them clustered densely in a small part of an area of 449,750 square kilometers. The center and north of the country are heavily forested, with numerous lakes. The south supports an agrarian society, though 85 percent of the population lives in urban areas. The three major metropolitan areas—Stockholm (the capital), Göteborg, and Malmö—more than doubled in population between 1910 and 1970.

Evangelical Lutheranism, the state church, claims 90 percent of the population. Sweden's ethnic, linguistic, and religious homogeneity is modified by seventeen thousand indigenous Saami and a post–World War II immigration from Finland, the Baltic countries, Italy, the Balkans, Iran, Turkey, and Latin America—immigration that accounts for about one-eighth of the population. Sweden's most famous artists include the filmmaker Ingmar Bergman and several renowned singers: Jenny Lind (1820–1887), Christine Nilsson (1843–1921), Jussi Björling (1911–1960), Birgit Nilsson (b. 1918), and Anne Sofie von Otter (b. 1955).

REGIONAL STYLES OF TRADITIONAL MUSIC

A common way to describe stylistic differences within Sweden is to speak of "musical dialects," as if musical styles were direct counterparts to linguistic dialects. At local levels, an abundance of dialects has been identified—in Dalecarlia, for example, one for each village. These dialects combine to form larger dialectal districts, which in turn combine to form twenty-four regions (sing. *landskap*) corresponding closely to the twenty-four administrative counties (*län*).

Another common way to divide Sweden, especially among folk musicians, is based on the character and distribution of instrumental tunes for the *polska*, a dance in 3/4 time, known in Sweden from the late 1500s and most popular before the early twentieth century. The dance has two parts: walking and turning. Free-form and improvisatory, it has many types and variants. It was the fiddlers' favorite genre. Tens of thousands of its tunes have been preserved, many of them primarily intended for listening, rather than dancing; the tunes also exist in many types, forms, and variants.

Until around 1650, parts of southern Sweden (Skåne, Blekinge, Småland,

Halland) belonged to Denmark, and proximity to Danish and German culture is clearly recognizable in local music there. An important part of the repertoire shows influences from the music of the upper classes of the 1600s and 1700s, but older styles are present. The south of Sweden, the east coast, and the islands of the Baltic sea (Gotland and Öland) reflect the economic boom in the 1700s, which, to even the remotest villages, brought new instruments, dances, musical forms, and styles. In Ångermanland, Hälsingland, and Gotland, violin music dominated dance-music in a style known as folk baroque. In southern and eastern Sweden, major modes are common, especially in tunes of modern origin. There are many *åttondelspolskor* (*polska* in eighth-note rhythms), though the predominant type is *sextondelspolskor* (in sixteenth-note rhythms).

In central and western Sweden, many old-style tunes in minor modes survive. From Lake Mälaren northward, except for the eastern coast, *åttondelspolskor* are common; in western Sweden, triplet *polskas* (*triolpolskor*) proliferate. The folk-music styles of western Sweden have traits similar to those of eastern Norway, and in many respects the territory of the Scandic Mountains forms a homogeneous culture area. Farther south, along the western coast, are many traces of contact with inhabitants of Britain.

Folk music in the far north reflects different waves of colonization in the seventeenth, eighteenth and nineteenth centuries. Along the coast and east-flowing rivers are old and new styles, but farther north and west, in more recently colonized areas, popular idioms of the late 1800s predominate. Influences from Finnish folk music are perceptible in more populous areas along the border with Finland. The music of the Saami, scattered over vast expanses of northern Sweden, has left few marks on the music of the Saami's neighbors.

MUSICAL TYPES AND STRUCTURES

The oldest layer of music in Sweden, probably of medieval origin, consists of songs, ballads, herding music, and dance music—genres that share such traits as modal scales, narrow ranges, and short, repeated melodic formulas, heard in herding calls, lyrical songs, and melodies for flute, bagpipe, and violin.

In musical practice, the tones 1, 4, 5, and 8 of this scale are stable. The other degrees vary from one performance to another, within one rendition of a tune, or even within a given melodic phrase. Most collections and studies bear few signs of this musical practice, since the first generation of collectors and scholars often "corrected" the alterations on the grounds that they were mistakes or the result of poor intonation.

Ballads, many originating in the medieval period and once widespread throughout Sweden, have parallels throughout Scandinavia, Britain, and other European countries. Collected since the 1600s and praised by intellectuals as the most important folk-song genre, ballads mostly went out of oral currency in the 1700s. Broadside ballads (*skillingtryck*) and lyrical songs, which took over their function in the 1700s and 1800s, were preserved through a dialectical interplay between the oral versions and written or printed texts.

A second historical layer consists of dance music and songs of the 1700s, often deriving from popular dance-music in Baroque style; the tunes have many formal and structural traits in common with the *galant* style: theme-development-theme form, sequential chains of sixteenth notes, a wide range (often over two octaves), and arpeggios or broken chords (figure 1).

A third historical layer consists of music for the galop, the polka, the schottische, the waltz, and other dances, all introduced in the 1800s with newer instruments and ensembles: button accordions, mouth harps, and brass bands. This layer exhibits sim-

FIGURE 1 A typical eighteenth-century dance tune, characterized by sixteenth notes in melodic sequences, arpeggiation, and a range of more than two octaves.

ple diatonic, stepwise melodies built on major or minor scales, with implicit harmonic progressions mainly in sixteenth-note rhythms (figure 2).

Other popular genres are drinking songs and erotic songs. Thousands of the former type still live in everyday practice, and many are known by almost every Swede. New versions, often of a burlesque character, are continually composed. A large number of erotic songs are still sung by teenagers. As with drinking songs, new variants are constantly appearing, often set to popular melodies. Most drinking and erotic songs have been and still are orally transmitted without the support of printed texts. Dance songs also exist with lyrical, comic, or burlesque texts. Many have "meaningless" words that function more to serve easier recall of the tune. A specific way of singing—diddling (*trallning*), where the voice imitates the fiddle by means of onomatopoeic syllables, like *tidadi* and *dili-diliadi*—has developed in Dalecarlia and elsewhere.

Swedish folk songs are usually sung monophonically and in a fairly straightforward, unemotional manner: in a low or medium register and a slow tempo, with low volume and few ornaments; many folk songs have a solemn character, and have actually been sung as hymns; a few melismatic idioms, however, exist, as does singing at a high pitch, for example, cattle calls (*kulning*). Songs accompanying work, festivities, or dancing are sung in a more lively and rhythmic fashion.

CONCEPTIONS OF MUSIC

In Sweden, the term *folkmusik* usually denotes orally transmitted music of the rural classes in old peasant society. *Populärmusik* normally denotes modern music, created first and foremost for a city audience. As a result of the interchange between these two concepts, there emerged an urban folklore, which, around 1920, was embodied in *gammeldans* 'old-time dance-music'. Since about the 1970s, the term *folklig musik* 'folkloric music' has served as an umbrella term for folk music, *gammeldans,* and

FIGURE 2 A typical nineteenth-century dance tune, with mostly diatonic stepwise melodic movement.

some other forms of popular music. In the 1990s, the terms *ethnic music* and *world music* were introduced, most often for modernized forms of non-Swedish folk and popular music.

Swedish folk music is a composite of many heterogeneous styles and genres, accumulated for centuries. These traditions, genres, forms, and styles seem homogeneous in comparison to today's musical diversity. Their homogeneity is, however, a result of powerful processes of ideological filtering—processes that have seriously reduced the heterogeneity of rural musical traditions.

The homogenizing of Swedish folk music began in the late 1700s with the introduction of national-romantic ideas from German and French intellectuals—ideals such as the notion of a folk in regard to a specifically Swedish cultural tradition. Another important period was 1880–1930, when numerous musical transcriptions were collected and published—for example, *Svenska låtar* (Andersson 1974 [1922–1940]), with about eight thousand vocal and instrumental tunes from most of Sweden. The publication of this and other large collections gave rise to a standard repertoire that subsequently became the national Swedish folk-music tradition. A third important period was the 1970s and 1980s, the years of the folk-music revival, when many young musicians began searching for historically authentic styles of local or regional origin. Many of these styles, which had become more or less extinct, became available again through collections and recordings of original musicians. The search for roots led to an increasing diversity of folk music in Sweden, though the homogenization and nationalization of folk music continued, and was even reinforced. During this period, Swedish folk music was strongly influenced by jazz, classical music, and English and American pop and folk.

In constructing the Swedish national folk-music tradition, collectors and researchers often had rather narrow preconceptions of what an original, authentic, national, folk music should sound like. In articles published from the early 1800s to the present, the most common approach to folk music has been a combination of two different perspectives, the historical and the geographical. The historical perspective is often a paradoxical combination of evolutionary and devolutionary ideas: on the one hand, folk music constantly develops from simple to complex, from primitive to cultivated; on the other, it is constantly corrupted and distorted, vanishing gradually as a result of modernization and urbanization. From the geographical perspective, Sweden is treated either as a single homogeneous unit, or as consisting of several enclosed units. In the latter 1800s, the *landskap,* a medieval administrative unit, was reintroduced as a symbolic, imagined community. It has become firmly established in folk taxonomy as the main organizing unit of folk traditions.

The historical-geographical perspective was seriously challenged about 1950 by the introduction of structural-functionalist ideas, which underlined the forms, the functions, and the social origins of folk music. A representative of this perspective is the musicologist Jan Ling, whose views have been influential on the Swedish folk scene since the mid-1960s.

In the 1970s and 1980s, young folk-music revivalists began to apply class perspectives to folk music. This resulted in a peculiar alliance between two idealized concepts, that of the romantic "folk" and the socialist "people." Most recently, there has also been a growing interest in folk music and gender. Age, another potentially fruitful criterion, has been almost totally neglected, except for the musical traditions of children.

AGE, CLASS, GENDER

As in many other countries in Europe, men have been more closely connected to instrumental music and women to vocal music. But men also sing lyrical songs, com-

Olof Jonsson From lived in Hälsingland, in the early 1800s. For every wedding, he composed two new tunes (according to his own notes, he played at 416 weddings). His brilliance earned him the reputation of having learned from Nacken, a mythical figure living in streams and waterfalls.

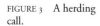 FIGURE 3   A herding call.

Kos— si jän— ten mi— na sa ja å, kom nu mi— na kor.

Kol— le—kos— san mi— na mi— na ko—

n, ko— n kos— san, ko— n å

Ro— sa, Li— sa, Snäl— la, From— ma, Lin— da, Stäl— la, kom nu mi— na

kor. Kos— si jän— ten mi— na, kol— li kos— sen mi— na.

ic songs, drinking songs, work songs, and rhymes. Women also play instruments: female fiddlers were not uncommon in northern Sweden.

A large repertoire of songs and instrumental tunes relates to intensive cattle-breeding methods traditionally employed in the north. Breeding cattle was considered solely a female task, and thus only women worked as shepherds, except in Skåne. Female shepherds engaged in singing, shouting, and playing on horns and birch-bark lurs in different situations [see NORWAY].

Besides the music used at work, music was performed for its own aesthetic qualities. Herding calls (*lockrop*) developed complex aesthetic structures. High-pitched, based on a few structural tones richly elaborated with improvised melismatic figures, they are sung with a tense larynx. This kind of vocal technique is used outside its original context, in staged folk-music performances, jazz, and art music, often as an audible symbol of "old rural Sweden" (figure 3).

Typical gender differences in Swedish folk music are seen in the lives of Florsen Burs and Elisabeth Olofsdotter, a married couple who, as indigent peasants, lived in Gotland in the mid-1800s. Both were active musically, and a large part of their repertoires was collected and published by their son, himself a famous fiddler. Florsen Burs became the most famous fiddler of his time. Many of his tunes, especially those his son wished to preserve, are elegant, sometimes even virtuosic dance tunes of the kind that became fashionable among peasants in Gotland in the early 1800s.

Though the husband's repertoire was intended for use in public, the wife's musical activity—in regard to her repertoire of lyrical songs, love songs, lullabies, and ditties—was restricted to the domestic sphere. Stylistically, her repertoire belonged to

FIGURE 4   The most
common lullaby tune,
based on a penta-
chordal scale.

FIGURE 4   The most common lullaby tune, based on a pentachordal scale.

the oldest layer of Swedish folk music. In this case, as in the traditional musical culture of Sweden up to recent times, the male, instrumental, public, and modern are closely connected, as are the female, vocal, domestic, and old.

The most common type of lullaby, recorded in thousands of variants, is based on a simple five-tone formulaic melody, which parallels a tune found in a twelfth-century French manuscript (figure 4). These motives and others remain common among children, with more recent genres, such as clapping games, which have spread especially among eight- to ten-year-old girls since the mid-1970s or later.

Scrutiny reveals that Swedish folk music is a mixture from diverse sources, a result of a constant process of interchange between high and low, new and old, rural and urban, local and foreign. Nevertheless, important differences that existed among rural classes have often been overlooked. These can be illustrated by a comparison of two fiddlers and their repertoires.

The first fiddler, Olof Jonsson From, known as From Olle, lived in Järvsö Parish, in Hälsingland, in the early 1800s. As the most renowned fiddler of his day, he was hired to play at weddings of better-off peasants all over Hälsingland. For every wedding, he composed two new tunes (according to his own notes, he played at 416 weddings). His brilliance earned him the reputation of having learned from Nacken, a mythical figure living in streams and waterfalls. From Olle's compositions, most of which have been preserved in local traditions, bear marks of his technique: they bristle with arpeggios and leaps and closely relate to the popular dance-music of the upper classes.

In the same period, in Bergsjö (not far from Järvsö, Hälsingland), lived Hultkläppen, another renowned fiddler, who made a living walking from village to village and playing for food. An odd character, with long hair, dressed in old-fashioned, worn-out clothes, and wearing birch-bark shoes, he was known to play wildly and loudly. Many of his tunes have been preserved in local traditions. In contrast to From Olle's tunes, they recall older stylistic layers: often modal, with a narrow range and repeated formulaic motives.

These two fiddlers represent the opposite ends of an aesthetic continuum—from high to low, from modern to old—from which today's notion of Swedish folk music is derived.

MUSICAL INSTRUMENTS

Archaeological finds of flutes, lurs, and other instruments are evidence of musical activity from prehistoric times [see ARCHAEOLOGY OF MUSIC IN EUROPE]. Lurs—made of bronze, modeled on cattle horns, and lavishly decorated—date back to about 1500 B.C. Prestigious for various reasons, they were probably played in pairs and used in ritual situations as symbols of fertility and power (Lund 1974).

In the Middle Ages, Swedish musical culture was based on instruments found in other parts of Europe: the *hummel* (a plucked dulcimer), the *mungiga* (a mouth harp), the *spelpipa* (a duct flute), the *säckpipa* (a bagpipe), the *vevlira* (a hurdy-gurdy), the *nyckelharpa* (a keyed fiddle), and the fiddle. These are still played as folk instruments. In the 1400s, church mural paintings depicted instruments and musicians for symbolic purposes. Heaven and hell, fundamental sources of medieval inspiration,

FIGURE 5   Two violinists and a keyed-fiddle (*nyckelharpa*) player. Postcard, postmarked 1919. Courtesy of the Robert Godfried Collection, New York.

were associated with different types of instruments and contexts: the music of heaven is played by angels on lutes as a symbol of purity, but the bagpipe is played by animals or itinerants as a symbol of luxury and other sins. In the 1800s, many of these symbols were still alive in folk tradition. To European instruments, Sweden contributed several prototypes, including the keyed fiddle, the Swedish lute, the Swedish clavichord (in use well into the 1800s), and the Swedish organ—all the result of a strong domestic instrument-building tradition that began to flourish in the 1700s.

The violin was brought to Sweden no later than the 1640s by French musicians hired to perform at the court of Queen Christina; in the 1700s, it conquered the rural population, among whom it soon became the most popular instrument (figure 5). Musicians continued to play the same type of tunes as before, but they also learned styles related to virtuoso late Baroque music and pre-Classical violin music. Some musicians learned to play from musical notation.

The keyed fiddle was once played only in a small zone northeast of Stockholm, but after a vigorous revival in the 1970s and 1980s, it is played all over Sweden. The bagpipe enjoyed a similar revival in the 1980s. Though there are traces of at least three different types of bagpipes in Sweden from medieval times, it was probably never commonly played. A peculiar type—with a small stitched bag, one chanter, and a short drone—was played in villages in western Dalecarlia until the 1940s. This type, which provided the model for the revival, is now known as the Swedish bagpipe (figure 6).

An important but often overlooked instrument is the *psalmodikon,* a bowed monochord, invented in Denmark and popularized in Sweden by the priest Johannes Dillner in the 1840s to support psalm singing at home. In the mid-1800s, the clarinet became popular through the influence of military bands. Trumpets were played at royal and noble Swedish courts from the 1500s well into the 1700s, and trombones were used in church and school music beginning in the 1600s. From 1850, Ahlberg & Ohlsson was a well-known manufacturer of brass instruments. The Swedish cornet (flügelhorn in E♭ or B♭) was in use by versatile Swedish civilian bands, organized especially in industrial communities and based on a liberal-national-Christian ideology. These bands remained active in the early twentieth century. For

FIGURE 6   A bagpipe and a musical saw played during a festival (*spelmansstämma*) in Bingsjö, Dalarna. Photo by Owe Ronström, 1979.

entertainment and dancing, they had an extensive repertory, from arrangements of light classics and marches to popular songs and dances. From the 1700s to modern times, brass instruments and reeds were in use by military bands, the chief suppliers of professionally educated brass musicians, who also played in other musical settings, including symphony, opera, and theater orchestras. Military bands were organized according to international standards, but in educational, sociological, and musical importance, they were gradually replaced by big bands, which came out of the dance and jazz movement of the 1920s and 1930s.

By the late 1800s, the accordion had become popular, especially among urban working-class people. Because it became a symbol of progress, modernity, and industrialization, it was furiously opposed by spokesmen for supposedly authentic or original folk culture, most of whom belonged to the urban bourgeoisie and promoted the violin as the symbol of Sweden's folk heritage. In their view, the violin and its music were positive, because the instrument was handmade, precious, noble, cultivated, and Swedish, whereas the accordion was negative, because it was factory-made, cheap, simple, uncultivated, and foreign. Among many educated persons, these attitudes still prevail; among others, however, the fiddle and the accordion soon became an inseparable pair. The *gammeldans* 'old-time dance-music', a popular synthesis of old and new, is typically performed by bands consisting of accordions, fiddle, guitar, string bass, and drums.

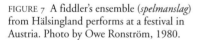 Folk music in Sweden was traditionally performed solo, or by two musicians playing in unison or octaves. In the late 1800s, specialized accompaniments became based on simple harmonic progressions or the improvisation of a second voice, using octaves, thirds, and sixths. In the mid-twentieth century, the latter way of accompanying spread, and is now the norm all over Sweden.

A popular ensemble that developed in the first half of the twentieth century under the influence of military brass bands and middle-class dance music is the fiddler's ensemble (*spelmanslag*). Early ensembles consisted of five to fifty fiddlers. Modern ones still consist mainly of fiddlers, but many include accordions, flutes, guitars, string basses, and drums. The ensembles perform folk music or *gammeldans,* each according to its own musical functions and ideologies (figure 7).

FIGURE 7 A fiddler's ensemble (*spelmanslag*) from Hälsingland performs at a festival in Austria. Photo by Owe Ronström, 1980.

Swedish folk music is played on older instruments (violins, keyed fiddles, bagpipes, and duct flutes), but many modern kinds are being introduced, including synthesizers, electric guitars, saxophones, and drum sets, often in combination with instruments from abroad.

Swedish folk music of the twentieth century consists of older styles and idioms consciously revived and reinterpreted for aesthetics or politics, plus newer forms and styles typified by enlarged forms, more and longer phrases, wider ranges, and more complex harmonic structures. Stylistic expansion is coupled to an expansion of instruments: Swedish folk music is played on older instruments (violins, keyed fiddles, bagpipes, and duct flutes), but many modern kinds are being introduced, including synthesizers, electric guitars, saxophones, and drum sets, often in combination with instruments from abroad, such as the *berimbau* (Brazilian musical bow), congas, and the *darbuka* (a Near Eastern vase-shaped drum). In turn, this expansion has furthered a search for new folk-music functions: on stage as chamber music, and in dance halls as popular dance music.

DANCE

Line dances have been widespread, at least since the Middle Ages. Many are still widely danced at midsummer and Christmas (figure 8). The *polska* has been the most popular dance from the 1600s to the present. The great variation in *polska* dancing can be explained by its popularity and the renaming and assimilating of older dances into the *polska* type.

During the 1700s, numerous contra dances (*kadrilj, anglas, cottiljon*) entered the repertoire, especially in southern and eastern Sweden. Free-form, these dances were danced by one or two couples at a time, or by many people, arranged in lines, circles,

FIGURE 8   A folk-dance ensemble performs a line dance at a summer festival in Gotland. Photo by Owe Ronström, 1981.

and squares. In contrast, the dances that became popular in the nineteenth century (mazurka, polka, schottische, and waltz) were danced by many couples following one another in a large circle.

Around 1900, to meet the needs of these new dance forms, the people of almost every village built large, outdoor pavilions, where the old *polska* became replaced by its modernized version, the regulated, nonimprovised *hambo,* and the fiddlers were replaced by accordionists as the main instrumentalists.

Fashionable North American dances—the one-step, the two-step, the foxtrot, the shimmy, the Charleston, and others—were introduced in the 1910s and 1920s. Dance establishments, from lavishly decorated dance palaces in Stockholm and Göteborg to humbler dance spots, were formed in most cities in Sweden. Outdoor amusement parks (*folkparker*), built around 1900 for the benefit of working-class entertainment, became important venues for dance music of the modern and old types. Local variations of ballroom dances—for example, the two-step (*jumpa*)—emerged. During summer seasons (May to September) until the late 1950s, *folkparker* were the most important arenas for popular music and live jazz of all types, including bebop. In the 1960s, *jazz balett* emerged as an artistic free ballet accompanied by live jazz, but the term served as a catchword for a loosely gymnastic movement for young people and adults, accompanied by jazz or jazz-derived recordings. Since the 1970s, practically all educational and other official gymnastic group exercise—reflecting an ideology that dates back to the early 1800s, with Pehr-Henrik Ling as a pioneer—has most often been accompanied by loudspeakers blasting contemporary, preferably stridently rhythmic, rock and pop music.

Immigration to Sweden has brought a wide variety of dances, performed at local communities and festivals. In the 1990s, "oriental" and samba festivals, with hundreds of participants, are not uncommon. For ethnic dancing, education, and other goals, an important arena for ethnic musicians of diverse nationalities is Falun Music Festival, held every summer.

MUSIC EDUCATION AND TRANSMISSION

Music in Sweden was formerly transmitted by ear, except among a small group of professional musicians, and later by middle-class urban people who had access to musical education. In the Middle Ages, written music was familiar in churches and cloisters, and cantors, organists, and other professional musicians gave music instruction at schools and in courts; but up to the 1800s, the ability to read music was not widespread. During the 1500s and 1600s, immigrant professional musicians cultivated European art music at the court in Stockholm and wherever nobles introduced cultural manners from the continent, while the hymns of the Protestant church fashioned a new idiom of folksinging.

The Swedish Royal Academy of Music was founded in Stockholm in 1771, during the reign of King Gustav III; musical education now had a defined structure. In the 1800s, higher education in music was channeled into a conservatory with methods following German practice. Music education in the twentieth century was furthered through the founding of symphony orchestras (as in Göteborg) and other musical activities; today, Sweden has six conservatories of music. Music education on a wider level, aiming at professional and amateur musical performance, began in the 1930s; today, it functions through music schools operated by municipalities all over the country, reaching about five hundred thousand pupils.

HISTORY OF MUSIC

Some extant liturgical books used in Swedish religious institutions from the 1300s to 1400s and containing music notation give evidence for polyphonic singing at the cathedral of Uppsala in 1298. King Gustav Vasa (reigned 1523–1560) eliminated papal control of Christianity in Sweden and introduced the Protestant faith. The Reformation resulted in many handwritten hymnbooks that reflected local traditions; in 1697, the first official collection of hymns was published.

In 1620, King Gustav II Adolf (reigned 1611–1632) reestablished the royal court ensemble and a royal trumpet corps, mainly with German musicians. During the reign of Queen Christina (1644–1654), French and Italian musicians performed ballet, church, and stage music at court, and large sums were spent on entertainment and propaganda demonstrations.

In the late seventeenth century, Gustav Düben (1628–1690), son of a German immigrant musician and court-ensemble leader (*hovkapellmästare*), assembled a huge collection of manuscripts and prints from different parts of Europe; Dietrich Buxtehude and many of his contemporaries in Germany, Italy, Poland, and France are represented in this collection. Among works connected with the Swedish court are a large collection of dance suites in the French style. The first song collection with Swedish text was *Odae Sveticae* (1674) by Samuel Columbus (text) and Gustav Düben (music).

From 1720 to 1809, the middle class became an important force besides the royal court and the nobility, and the cultivation of music all over Sweden was concentrated among urban parish houses, manor houses, and musical societies. In 1731, the composer Johan Helmich Roman (1694–1753) arranged the first public concert in Sweden. Roman, who had studied abroad, is regarded as the first important Swedish composer. He composed many notable instrumental and vocal works, for example, his Swedish Mass (*Svenska mässan*). King Gustav III (reigned 1772–1791), a highly influential patron of the arts, established a national Swedish opera in 1773 and participated in producing operas; he collaborated on the libretto of Johann Gottlieb Naumann's *Gustav Vasa* (1786), which mixes German art-musical and folklike melodies.

The German lied and the French chanson were cultivated by musical amateurs in the 1700s, and a Swedish counterpart was created by the singing poet Carl Michael Bellman (1740–1795). In poems sung mostly to borrowed melodies, Bellman's collections, *Fredmans Epistlar* (1790) and *Fredmans Sånger* (1791), depict the artistic bohemian life of Stockholm.

The first important Swedish music printer was the composer Olof Åhlström (1756–1835), who from 1789 to 1834 published and distributed all over Sweden the periodical *Musikaliskt Tidsfördrif,* which included popular instrumental pieces and songs.

Several large choral societies were founded in Sweden in the early 1800s, when choral and solo vocal music dominated the local production and reception of music. August Söderman (1832–1876) was popular for his choral and stage music. A special milieu was created at the universities of Uppsala and Lund, where students cultivated a tradition of singing with a patriotic orientation. Solid compositional training was available only abroad. Franz Berwald (1796–1868), a highly talented composer from an immigrant German music family, was little acknowledged during his lifetime, but his symphonies and string quartets reveal a composer of stature, and he was important in professionalizing Swedish instrumental music.

Shortly before 1900, several gifted composers made their debut. Hugo Alfvén (1872–1960), Wilhelm Peterson-Berger (1867–1942), and Wilhelm Stenhammar (1871–1927) cultivated instrumental and vocal genres. Influenced by late romantic German music and Scandinavian composers such as Edvard Grieg, Jean Sibelius, and Carl Nielsen, these composers infused a distinctive, personal flavor into their work.

In art music from 1920 to 1945, trends still centered around ideas of national romanticism or classical-romantic ideals, but innovations from Vienna and Paris were assimilated by Hilding Rosenberg (1892–1985), Gösta Nystroem (1890–1966), and others. In the 1930s and 1940s, Lars-Erik Larsson (1908–1986) and others moved toward neoclassical ideals.

After World War II, the prestige of avant-garde European art music led a new generation of Swedish composers away from older romantic or national-romantic forms and attitudes. Some composers, performers, and musicologists founded the Monday Group (*Måndagsgruppen*), influenced by Hindemith, Bartók, Stravinsky, and later Schoenberg and Webern.

The best-known composers of the 1950s and 1960s were Ingvar Lidholm (b. 1921) and Karl-Birger Blomdahl (1916–1968), the latter known for his "space opera" *Aniara* (1959). Jan W. Morthenson (b. 1940), inspired by the German music critic T. W. Adorno, formulated cultural and social criticism as author and composer, with articles and the book *Nonfigurative Music* (1966) and compositions such as *Antifonia I–III* (1963–1970) and *Alla marcia* (1973), the latter illustrating social violence and relationships between human beings and machines.

In the 1960s, many composers operated outside mainstream avant-garde movements. Allan Petterson (1911–1980) expressed bitterness in a style reminiscent of Mahler and Bruckner. Åke Hermanson (b. 1923), inspired by the dramatic nature and climate of the Swedish west coast, created orchestral and chamber work in a highly personal style. The Electronic Music Studio (EMS, founded 1964) and other electronic studios in Sweden have eased the production of compositions by numerous poet-musicians. Daniel Börtz (b. 1943) and Sven-David Sundström (b. 1942) are among the leading composers of their generation, with a large and varied output of vocal and instrumental works. A young generation of composers born since World War II—including Karin Rehnqvist (b. 1957), a female composer close to the avant-garde of the folk-music revival—combine various styles and topics.

POPULAR MUSIC AND JAZZ

In the twentieth century, light popular music, largely produced and distributed in the new media of radio, gramophone, and (from the 1930s) movies, reached virtually everyone in the country, bringing fame to numerous popular-song composers and performers. The composer and performer Evert Taube (1890–1976) still appeals to a large public in Sweden. His delivery had a quality that enhanced the spirit of texts depicting distant, exotic countries or the poetic moments of Swedish life. The trumpeter Gösta Törner (1912–1982) and others set high standards for American dance music and jazz in Sweden.

Until the 1950s, the bulk of Swedish popular music consisted of songs in Swedish with melodies composed by Swedes. In the 1960s, an influx of popular music from the United States and Britain resulted in a fascination with British-American music and English-language texts that propagated novel lifestyles. Composers and singers like Gösta "Snoddas" Nordgren (1926–1981) and Thore Skogman (b. 1931) led a reaction against this by promoting an ideology of nostalgia for the countryside. In more intellectual and elaborate ways, others adapted new musical idioms to the Swedish musical heritage. Among them, Povel Ramel (b. 1922) became a central figure in the artistic organization that produced the revues, films, and recordings that played a dominant role in Swedish popular music well into the 1960s.

After World War II, new impulses in jazz followed visits to Sweden by Dizzy Gillespie, Charlie Parker, and Stan Getz. Swedish musicians emulated these performers' styles, and for a while Swedish jazz was widely known in the United States, mainly through outstanding recordings. Clarinetists Åke "Stan" Hasselgård (1922–1948)

In the folk-music revival, young people searching for identity rejected modish classical and popular music and began playing old instruments and practicing older vocal styles. Soon, a synthesis had emerged from the interaction between folk and popular music.

and Putte Wickman (b. 1924), trumpeter Rolf Ericson (1922–1997), saxophonists Arne Domnérus (b. 1924) and Bernt Rosengren (b. 1937), trombonists Åke Persson (1932–1975) and Eje Thelin (1938–1990), pianists Reinhold Svensson (1919–1968), Bengt Hallberg (b. 1931), and others formed the basis for the Swedish modern jazz tradition. A special coloration was introduced by baritone saxophonist and composer Lars Gullin (1928–1976), who fused cool jazz with Nordic folk music and the national romantic idiom, as in "Danny's Dream" (1954). In the 1963 album *Jazz på svenska* (Jazz in Swedish), jazz pianist Jan Johansson (1931–1968), a versatile and adventurous composer-arranger, brought folk music to the attention of a wider public. He interpreted folk melodies with an improvisational touch—a trait the public considered innovative yet comprehensible.

In its avant-garde phase, jazz began to lose its earlier appeal, and young people turned to rock, soul, and pop, dominated by performers like Elvis Presley, Ray Charles, Aretha Franklin, Bob Dylan, the Beatles and others. Among Swedish artists from this era may be mentioned singers Owe Törnquist (b. 1929), Siw Malmkvist (b. 1936), Cornelis Vreeswijk (1937–1987), and Jerry Williams (pseudonym of Erik Fernström, b. 1942). In the 1960s, several Swedish pop bands, including the Hep Stars and Made in Sweden, flourished.

Around 1970, the explosion of rock, interest in the music of minorities and folks from various corners of the world, and the revival of Swedish folk music and music of the workers' movement were strongly formative factors. There was criticism of commercial music, perhaps represented by the world-famous band ABBA, founded in 1972, and the hegemony of the avant-garde in serious music. Ideologically, popular music was dominated by left-wing groups, like the band Hoola Bandoola, and large demonstrations, like the 1977 *Vi äro tusenden* (We Are Thousands).

In the folk-music revival, young people searching for identity rejected modish classical and popular music and began playing old instruments and practicing older vocal styles. Soon, a synthesis had emerged from the interaction between folk and popular music. Groups such as Sevda, Egba, Rena Rama, and Opposite Corner sought the integration of folk music from around the world with jazz and improvisational techniques. In the late 1980s, pop artist Benny Andersson (b. 1946) was making music with fiddlers in the area of Orsa in Dalarna, an important folk-music center in Sweden.

During the 1980s, several young professional musicians turned to forms of folk music and jazz as their most direct way to communicate their musical thoughts and feelings. These included the keyed fiddler Åsa Jinder (b. 1963), the singer Lena Willemark (b. 1960), jazz pianists Per-Henrik Wallin (b. 1963) and Lars Jansson (b. 1951), and the jazz tenor sax player Joakim Milder (b. 1941).

Ethnically rather homogeneous, Sweden has an indigenous population of Saami in the north (Lappland) and, since World War II, a growing number of immigrants from Finland and the Baltics and from southern Europe and Turkey. Saami songs (*juoigos*) reference various subjects, and singing (*juoi'gat*) is used to master an inhospitable environment. Pitch variation, glissandi, and a gradual pitch rise characterize Saami singing, which varies locally: in southern Saami, singers employ a limited set of pitches and numerous glissandos; in northern Saami, they sing heptatonic modes, including the major scale [see SAAMI].

The music of immigrants from the Balkans and Turkey is just beginning to be studied. Academic studies consist of ethnographic reports on activities of groups and individuals, plus musical analysis of performative styles, many of which have changed only minimally in Swedish contexts (Hammarlund 1993; Lundberg 1994; Ronström 1992).

HISTORY OF RESEARCH

By the 1700s, dissertations in the philosophy of music and acoustics were being published at the University of Uppsala. The first music historian, Abraham Abrahmson Hülphers (1734–1798), wrote a general history of music, including a history of ecclesiastical music and organ music in Sweden. Carl M. Envallsson (1756–1806) published the first Swedish musical dictionary (1802).

An antiquarian movement in the 1800s inspired intellectuals and music amateurs to notate songs and instrumental pieces from peasant farmers throughout Sweden. The first important song collection was that of Erik Gustaf Geijer (1783–1847) and Arvid A. Afzelius (1785–1871), *Svenska folkvisor från forntiden* (1814–1817). In the same decade, Afzelius and O. Åhlström published an instrumental collection, *Traditioner af Svenska Folkdansar* (1814–1815). Intended for drawing-room performers, these collections were adapted to art-music norms, arranged for solo voice and piano. Studies of the time include Johann Christian Friedrich Haeffner's "Anmärkningar öfver den gamla nordiska sången" (1818). Later in the 1800s, collections closer in style to folk songs and traditional instrumental performances were assembled; large compilations of instrumental folk music were created by August Fredin. At the beginning of the twentieth century, more were assembled by Nils and Olof Andersson in *Svenska låtar* (N. Andersson 1974 [1922–1940]).

A musicological tradition was created at the University of Uppsala, where J. A. Josephson defended a thesis on musical aesthetics in 1844. The music critics Karl Valentin (1853–1918), Adolf Lindgren (1846–1905), and others were the first Swedish musicologists in a modern sense. In the first decade of the 1900s, musicology as a university discipline was established by Tobias Norlind (1879–1947). His main task was to create a Swedish national music history, but he also laid the foundation of Swedish research in ethnomusicology. His interest in biology and other sciences and his emphasis on the importance of primary sources were the main points of departure for his scholarly output. The most important of his doctoral students, Carl-Allan Moberg (1896–1978), studied Gregorian chant, but also published important studies on Swedish music history and folk music; with the music theorist Sven E. Svensson and the music historian Stig Walin (b. 1907), Moberg founded the so-called Uppsala School.

In the 1930s, three eminent German-Jewish scholars emigrated to Sweden: Richard Engländer (1889–1966), Ernst Emsheimer (1904–1989), and Hans Eppstein (b. 1911). Engländer conducted research into Swedish music history of the 1700s; Emsheimer intensified the ethnomusicological tradition in Sweden; and Eppstein, besides researching J. S. Bach's chamber music and the music of the German romantic era, worked as editor in the series *Monumenta Musicae Svecicae.*

The first Swedish chair in musicology was established in 1947 at the University of Uppsala, with Carl-Allan Moberg the first professor. Of Moberg's pupils, Martin Tegen (b. 1919) studied nineteenth-century art and popular music, Ingmar

Bengtsson (1920–1989) studied stylistic analysis and systematic musicology, and Bo Wallner (b. 1923) studied twentieth-century musical aesthetics and avant-garde music. In the 1960s and 1970s, the next generation developed new topics: Jan Ling (b. 1934) studied the sociology of music and ethnomusicology, Johan Sundberg (b. 1936) studied musical acoustics, Alf Gabrielsson (b. 1936) studied musical psychology, and Erik Kjellberg (b. 1939) studied the social history of music and jazz.

The 1980s introduced research into contemporary popular music into Sweden by Philip Tagg (b. 1944) and others; Owe Ronström and others study the folk revival and the music of immigrant communities.

Institutes for documentation, research, and publication include the Svenskt Visarkiv (Center for Swedish Folk Song, Folk Music, and Jazz Research), the Musikmuseet (Music Museum), the Svenskt Musikhistoriskt Arkiv (Swedish Music History Archive), the Arkivet för Ljud och Bild (Swedish National Archive of Recorded Sound and Moving Images), and the Kungliga Musikaliska Akademien (Royal Swedish Academy of Music), all in Stockholm.

BIBLIOGRAPHY

Afzelius, Arvid A., and O. Åhlström. 1972 [1814–1815]. *Traditioner af Svenska Folkdansar* (Traditions of Swedish folk dances). Stockholm: Bok och bild.

Andersson, Nilss. 1895–1916. *Skånska melodier* (Tunes from Skåne). Stockholm: Norstedt.

————. 1974 [1922–1940]. *Svenska låtar* (Swedish tunes). Stockholm: Gidlunds förlag.

Andersson, Otto, ed. 1934. *Musik och musikinstrument.* Nordisk Kultur, 25. Stockholm, Oslo, and Copenhagen: Bonnier.

Arnberg, Mats. 1962. *Den medeltida balladen: én orientering och kommentar till Sveriges radios inspelningar* (The medieval ballad: an introduction and commentary to Swedish radio recordings). English summary. Stockholm: Sveriges Radio.

Arvidsson, Alf. 1991. *Sågarnas sång: folkligt musicerande i sågverkssamhället Holmsund 1850–1980* (Song of the sawmills: popular musical performance in the sawmill community of Holmsund, 1850–1980). English summary. Umeå: Acta Universitatis Umensis.

Arwidsson, Adolf Ivar. 1834–1842. *Svenska fornsånger* (Early Swedish songs). Stockholm: Norstedt and Söner.

Barkefors, Laila. 1995. *Gallret ocg stärnan: Allan Petterssons väg genom Barfotasånger till Symfoni* (The grating and the start: Allan Pettersson's path from *barfotasånger* to symphony). English summary. Göteborg: Musikvetenskapliga avdelningen, Musikhögskolan.

Barth Magnus, Ingebørg, and Birgit Kjellström. 1993. *Musikmotiv i svensk kyrkokonst: Uppland fram till 1625* (Musical motifs in Swedish church art: Uppland up to 1625). In Swedish and English. Stockholm: Svenska RIdIM-kommittén.

Bengtsson, Ingmar. 1974. "On Notation of Time, Signature and Rhythm in Swedish Polskas." *Studia Instrumentorum Musicae Popularis* 3:22–31.

Brolinson, Per-Erik, and H. Larsen. 1984. *När*

rocken slog i Sverige: Svensk rockhistoria 1955–1965. Stockholm: Sweden Music.

Connor, Herbert. 1977. *Från Midsommarvaka till Aniara.* Svensk musik, 2. Stockholm: Bonniers.

Davidsson, Åke. 1980 [1948]. *Bibliografi över svensk musiklitteratur 1800–1945.* Stockholm: Almqvist & Wiksell.

Dicander, Jorgen. 1975. *Folkliga koraler från Dalarna* (Folk hymns from Dalarna]. Falun: Dalarnas Museum.

Dybeck, Richard. 1974 [1846]. *Svenska vallvisor och hornlåtar* (Swedish herding songs and horn tunes). Stockholm: J. L. Brudins.

Edström, Karl-Olof (Olle). 1978. *Den samiska musikkulturen.* Göteborg: Musikvetenskapliga Institutionen.

————. 1989. *Schlager i Sverige 1910–1940.* Göteborg: Musikvetenskap, Göteborgs Universitet.

————. 1996. *Göteborgs riks musikliv: en översikt mellan världskrigen* (The rich musical life of Göteborg: a survey of the interwar period [1919–1939]). Göteborg: Musikvetenskapliga avdelningen, Musikhögskolan.

Emsheimer, Ernst. 1969. "Zur Typologie der schwedischen Holztrompeten." *Studia Instrumentorum Musicae Popularis* 1:87–97.

————. 1977. "Schwedische Schellenmagie." *Studia Instrumentorum Musicae Popularis* 5:10–19.

Engländer, Richard. 1959. "Die Gustavianische Oper." *Archiv für Musikwissenschaft* 16:314–327.

Envallsson, Carl Magnus. 1802. *Svenskt musikaliskt lexikon.* Stockholm: C. F. Marquard.

Fredin, August. 1909–1933. *Gotlandstoner* (Melodies from Gotland). Stockholm: P. A. Norstedt.

Geijer, Erik Gustaf, and Arvid A. Afzelius. 1957–1860 [1814–1817]. *Svenska folkvisor från forntiden* (Swedish folk songs from early times). Stockholm: Bokverks Forlag.

Göransson, Harald. 1992. *Koralpsalmboken 1697: studier i svensk koralhistoria* (The 1697 hymnal: Studies in Swedish choral history). English summary. Uppsala: Gidlunds.

————. 1997. *Koral och andlig visa i Sverige* (Choral and sacred song in Sweden). German summary. Stockholm: Norstedts.

Grusnick, Bruno. 1964, 1966. "Die Dübensammlung: Ein Versuch Ihrer Chronologischen Ordnung." *Svensk tidskrift för musikforskning* 46:27–82, 48:63–186.

Gustavian Opera: Swedish Opera, Dance, and Theatre 1771–1809. 1991. Stockholm: Kungliga musikaliska akademien.

Hammarlund, Anders. 1993. *Yeni Sesler—Nya Stämmor: En väg till Musiken i det turksika Sverige.* Studier i Musikvetenskap, 1. Stockholm: Stockholm Universitet.

Hedwall, Lennart. 1996. *Svensk musikhistoria: en handbok* (Swedish music history: A textbook). Stockholm: Edition Reimers.

Jacobsson, Stig, ed. 1986. *Svenska tonsättare: Diskografi* (Swedish composers: a discography). Stockholm: Svenska Rikskonserter.

————. 1993. *Swedish Composers of the Twentieth Century.* Stockholm: Swedish Music Information Center.

Jersild, Margareta. 1975. *Skillingtryck: studie i svensk folklig vissång före 1800* (Broadsides: Studies on Swedish popular ballads before 1800). English summary. Stockholm: Svenskt Visarkiv.

Johnson, Anna. 1984. "Voice Physiology and Ethnomusicology." *Yearbook for Traditional Music* 16:42–66.

Jonsson, Bengt R., et al. 1978. *The Types of Scandinavian Medieval Ballad.* Stockholm: Svenskt Visarkiv.

Jonsson, Leif. 1990. *Ljusets riddarvakt: 1800-alets studentsång utövad som offentlig samhällskonst* (Guardians of enlightenment: Nineteenth-century student songs as a form of public art). German summary. Uppsala: Studia Musicologica Upsaliensia.

Jonsson, Leif, et al. 1992–1995. *Musiken i Sverige* (Music in Sweden). 4 vols. Stockholm: T. Fischer & Co.

Karlsson, Henrik. 1980. *Musikspelet: Det svenska musiksamhället av idag.* Göteborg: Göteborgs Universitet, Musikhögskolan.

Kjellberg, Erik. 1979. *Kungliga musiker i Sverige: studier kring deras organisation, verksamheter och status ca 1620–ca 1720* (Royal musicians in Sweden: Studies of their organization, activities, and status from about 1620 to about 1720). English summary. Uppsala: Institutionen för musikvetenskap.

———. 1985. *Svensk jazzhistoria: En översikt.* Stockholm: Norstedts.

———. 1993a. *Grieg and Sweden.* Studia Musicologica Norwegica, 19. Oslo and Stockholm: Scandinavian University Press.

———. 1993b. "'Old Folklore in Swedish Modern': Zum Thema Volksmusik und Jazz in Schweden." In *Jazz in Europa,* ed. Wolfgang Knauer, 221–231. Darmstädter Beiträge zur Jazzforschung, 3. Darmstadt.

———. 1994. "Frankreich und Schweden: Ein Beitrag zur Geschichte der musikalischen Migration im 17. Jahrhundert." In *Europa in Scandinavia: Kulturelle und sozziale Dialoge in der frühen Neuzeit,* ed. Robert Bohn. Frankfurt: Peter Lang.

Kjellberg, Eric, and Jan Ling. 1991. *Klingande Sverige: Musikens vägar genom historien* (Resounding Sweden: Along the paths of music through history). Göteborg: Akademiförlaget.

Kjellström, Birgit. 1977. "Zur schwedischen Spilopipa." *Studia Instrumentorum Musicae Populares* 5:39–44.

———, et al. 1985. *Folkmusikvågen: The Folk Music Vogue.* Stockholm: Rikskonserter.

Larsson, Gunnar. 1979. "Die estnisch-schwedische Streichleier, ihre Spieltechnik und ihr Repertoire." *Studia Instrumentorum Musicae Populares* 6:87–92.

Leffler, Karl Peter. 1982 [1899–1900]. *Folkmusik från norra Södermanland.* Nyköping: Sodermanlands Museum.

———. 1899. *Om nyckelharpospelet på Skansen* (Keyed-fiddle playing in Skansen). Stockholm: Nordiska Museet.

———. 1921–1924. *Folkmusiken i Norrland.* Härnösand: Föreningen för norrländsk hembygdsforskning.

Ling, Jan. 1964. *Svensk folkmusik: bondens musik i helg och söcken* (Swedish folk music: Peasant music for holidays and weekdays). Stockholm: Prisma.

———. 1967. *Nyckelharpan: studier i ett folkligt musikinstrument.* Stockholm: Norstedts.

———. 1981. "Spieler von Volksmusikinstrumenten in der Industriegesellschaft Schwedens." *Studia Instrumentorum Musicae Popularis* 7:53–57.

Ling, Jan, et al. 1980. *Folkmusikboken.* Stockholm: Prisma.

———, eds. 1983. *Vi äro musikanter alltifrån Skaraborg: Studier i västgötsk musikhistoria.* Falköping: Gummeson.

Lund, Cajsa. 1974. *The Sound of Archaeology.* Stockholm: Musikmuseet.

Lundberg, Dan. 1994. *Persikoträdgårdarnas musik: En studie av modal improvisation i turkisk folk- och populärmusik baserad på improvisationer av Ziya Aytekin.* Studier i Musikvetenskap, 3. Stockholm: Stockholm Universitet.

Lundberg, Dan, and Gunnar Ternhag. N.d. *Folkmusik i Sverige* (Folk music in Sweden). Hedemora: Gidlunds.

Moberg, Carl-Allan. 1955. "Om vallåtar: en studie i de svenska fäbodarnas musikaliska organisation" (On herding calls: A study of the musical organization of the Swedish summer pasture). *Svensk tidskrift för musikforskning* 37:7–9.

———. 1959. "Om vallåtar II: musikaliska strukturproblem." *Svensk tidskrift för musikforskning* 41:10–57.

———. 1971a [1942]. *Från kyrkooch hovmusik till offentlig Konsert: Studier i stormaldstidens Svenska musikhistoria.* Uppsala: Acta Universitatis Upsalienses.

———. 1971b. *Studien zur schwedischen Volksmusik.* Uppsala: Uppsala Universitet.

Monumenta Musicae Svecicae. 1958–. 10+ vols. Stockholm: Svenska Samfundet för musikforskning.

Musik i Norden (Music in the Nordic countries). 1997. Stockholm: Kungliga musikaliska akademien.

Nordlander, Johan. 1971 [1886]. *Svenska barnvisor och barnrim* (Swedish children's songs and children's rhymes). Stockholm: Bok och bild.

Öhrström, Eva. 1987. *Borgerliga kvinnors musicerande i 1800-talets Sverige* (Bourgeois female musicians in nineteenth-century Sweden). English summary. Göteborg: Musikvetenskapliga institutionen.

Ramsten, Märta, ed. 1982. *Einar Övergaards folkmusiksamling.* Stockholm: Almqvist & Wiksell.

———. 1992. *Återklang: Svensk folkmusik i förändring, 1950–1980* (Reverberations: Swedish folk music in a state of change, 1950–1980). English summary. Svenskt visarkivs handlingar, 4. Göteborg: Musikvetenskapliga institutionen.

Ronström, Owe. 1992. *Att gestalta ett ursprung: en musiketnologisk studie av dansande och musicerande bland jugoslaver i Stockholm.* Stockholm: Institutet för Folklivsforsning.

Ronström, Owe, and Gunnar Ternhag. 1974. *Texter om svensk folkmusik från Haeffner till Ling* (Texts on Swedish folk music from Haeffner to Ling). Stockholm: Kungliga musikaliska akademien.

Rosenberg, A. G. 1969 [1876–1882]. *420 svenska danspolskor.* Göteborg: Nordisk folkmusik.

Säve, Per Arvid. 1949–1955. *Gotländska visor* (Folk songs from Gotland). Uppsala: Gustav Adolfs Akademien.

Ternhag, Gunnar. 1992. *Hjort Anders Olsson—spelman, artist* (Hjort Anders Olsson—player artist). English summary. Hedemora: Gidlunds.

Tillhagen, Carl Herman, and N. Dencker. 1949–1959. *Svenska folklekar och danser* (Swedish folk games and dances). Stockholm: Bokverk.

Tillman, Joakim. 1995. *Ingvar Lidholm och tolvtonstekniken: analytiska och historiska perspektiv på Ingvar Lidholms musik från 1950-talet* (Ingvar Lidholm and twelve-tone technique: Analytical and historical perspectives on Ingvar Lidholm's music during the 1950s). English summary. Stockholm: Musikvetenskapliga institutionen.

Tirén, Karl. 1942. *Die Lappische Volksmusik.* Acta Lapponica, 3. Stockholm: Nordiska museet/Hugo Gebers förlag.

Walin, Stig Alfred Ferdinand. 1952. *Die schwedische Hummel.* Stockholm: Nordiska Museet.

Wallner, Bo. 1965. "Scandinavian Music after the Second World War." *Musical Quarterly* 51:111–143.

AUDIOVISUAL RESOURCES

Arnberg, Mats. 196?. *Svensk Folkmusik.* Sveriges Radio RAEP 1–22. 22 LP disks.

Babs, Alice. 1974. *Om Sommaren Sköna.* Swedish Society Discofil, SLT 33231. LP disk.

Folkmusik i Förvandling (Folk music in transition). 1982. Caprice CAP 1168. LP disk.

Folkmusik i Sverige. 1973–1988. Compilations of recordings released between 1969 and 1982.

Caprice CAP 1092–1351 (irregular numeration). 28 LP disks.

Folkmusik Vagean (The folk-music vogue). 1985. Caprice CAP 11309. LP disk.

Gammal Svensk Folkmusik från 78-varvare. 1987. Schilling Records SR001–002. 2 LP disks.

Hans, Pers, Kalle Almlof, and Björn Stabi. 1991. *Three Swedish Fiddlers.* Shanachie Records 21002. Compact disc.

Johansson, Jan. 1963. *Jazz på svenska* (Jazz in Swedish). LP disk.

Music in Sweden. 1977–1982. Caprice CAP 1121, 1123, 1131, 1140–1141, 1163–1164, 1168, 1183. 9 LP disks.

Songs and Music of Varmland. 1976. EMI Svenska 4E 256–35326 Columbia. LP disk.

Stabi, Björn, and Ole Hjorth. 1970. *Folk Fiddling*

from Sweden: Traditional Fiddling Tunes from Dalarna. Nonesuch, H 72033. LP disk.

Suède-Norvège: Musiques des Vallées Scandinaves. 1993. Ocora C 560008. LP disk.

Svart, Kaffe. 1993. *Musique traditionnelle vivante de Suède.* Planett 242054. Compact disc.

Svensk jazz. 1996. Six 30-minute television pro-grams on the history of jazz in Sweden, from about 1920 to about 1995. Sveriges Utbildningsradio AB, S-113 95.

Svensk Jazzhistoria. 1979. Caprice CAP 22037–22041. 5 compact discs.

Taube, Sven-Bertil. 1991. *Swedish Folk Songs and Ballads Sung by Sven-Bertil Taube.* Smithsonian Folkways 06844. Compact disc.

The Swedish Fiddlers Music from the Gathering of the Fiddlers at Delsbo. 1978. Folkways Records FW 8471. LP disk.

Vasen. 1993. *Essence Musique Suédoise.* Auvidis Ethnic B 6787. Compact disc.

Denmark

Svend Nielsen

Denmark, a constitutional monarchy of some five million people, occupies 43,069 square kilometers on the Jutland Peninsula (north of Germany) and six islands in the strait between the peninsula and Sweden. The economy, traditionally based on agriculture, shipping, and fishing, expanded after World War II to include manufacturing and services, including a furniture industry famous for its designs and craftsmanship. Lutheranism is the established religion.

Denmark's most famous intellectuals include the fairy-tale and travel writer Hans Christian Andersen (1805–1875), the existentialist philosopher Søren Kierkegaard (1813–1855), the composer Carl Nielsen (1865–1931), and the writer Isak Dinesen (1885–1962), whose autobiographical *Out of Africa* (1937) became a popular film in 1989.

TRADITIONAL SONG GENRES

Until 1958, genre analysis of Danish folk song was based on the form and content of texts. Scholars considered the main genre to be ballads—narrative, strophic songs with end rhymes, with or without a chorus and a middle refrain. Nonstrophic or monostrophic song types could be grouped on the basis of content as jingles, lullabies, street cries, and dance rhymes. Finally, singing games, which could be strophic or nonstrophic, often had texts referring to the particular dance or game.

Of primary interest to scholars, ballads became subject to another level of classification, which has three historical divisions. The first category, medieval ballads, consisted of two- or four-line stanzas with a special end-rhyme formation (*aa*, or *abcb*) and a chorus and possibly a middle refrain. According to their content, they were grouped into folk ballads (concerning persons of rank or encounters with the supernatural), and jesting ballads (concerning ordinary people, often involving successful transgressions of religious norms and taboos); jesting ballads have been considered parodies of folk ballads. Folk ballads have been extensively published (Grundtvig et al. 1853–1976); the jesting ballads, only selectively (Kristensen 1901).

The second ballad category includes echoing songs (*Efterklangsviser*), known from written sources as far back as the 1500s. Similar to medieval ballads in text and

The transmission of Danish traditional songs in the last 150 years has essentially taken place through broadsides, prints that in the 1800s were sold in great numbers by balladmongers who appeared at markets or went from farm to farm.

FIGURE 1   The cover and back page of a typical late-nineteenth-century broadside: "The fallen woman. A serious song about her life and the reason why." It contains words but no musical notation.

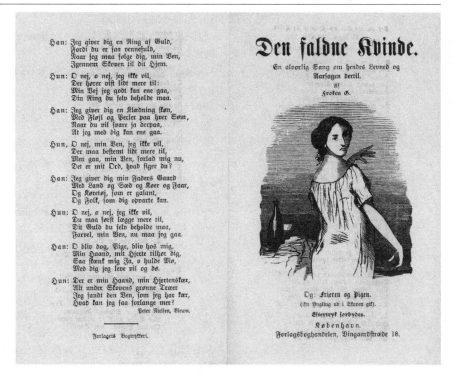

content, they have a different metrical structure. They can be grouped by content as spiritual, secular (lyrical, lyrical-epic, and epic), and historical ballads (Piø 1985).

A third major ballad category comprises ballads from the 1700s to the present, sorted into subcategories according to content—murder ballads, ballads of misfortune, and love, war, and sailors' songs.

Parallel to the ballad genre is the popular singing of hymns having authorized texts, hymns whose original tunes have been transformed (Knudsen and Nørgaard 1963).

After 1958, when the center of scholarly interest shifted toward individuals and various groups of people with ballads in their repertory, folk songs were primarily differentiated by affinities with groups and functions in society. Ballads sustained work—carding, milking, spinning, hauling an anchor, hoisting a sail, or working with a pile driver. Singing could sustain a motoric process in conjunction with dance music, lullabies, and rhythmic rhymes. Communication was effected by love songs, street cries, and shepherds' calls, and group identity was emphasized through manorhouse and shack ballads and revival and drinking songs. In some cases, the function is reflected not in musical and textual structures (for example, ballads sung by sailors when hoisting a mainsail), but in the situation in which it is performed.

The transmission of Danish traditional songs in the last 150 years has essentially taken place through broadsides (figure 1), prints that in the 1800s were sold in great

FIGURE 2 The children's song *"Save save brænde,"* set to a hexachordal melodic formula. Transcription by Svend Nielsen.

numbers by balladmongers who appeared at markets or went from farm to farm (Piø 1974). The tunes were often from already known ballads; if they were not, they were sung on the spot by the balladeer so people could learn them. The broadside served as a model that spread all over the country, causing later texts and tunes to display set forms and a certain standardization.

MUSICAL STRUCTURE OF SONGS AND INSTRUMENTAL MUSIC

When adults sing lullabies and ride-a-cock-horse rhymes to children, and when children play their own singing games and bantering cries, they freely link formulas related to hexachordal melodies commonly found across Western Europe (figure 2).

Most tunes for folk ballads, many jesting ballads, and a few nineteenth-century ballads belong to an early musical stratum that predates seven-tone modes. Individual tunes are structured as combinations of short melodic phrases, usually the length of a line in a diatonic scale with the range of a fourth, a fifth, or a sixth; a few pentatonic tunes also exist. Typical forms have two identical halves followed by a refrain—ABABC in four-line stanzas, AAB in two-line stanzas. Many seem to depend on one melodic model, with a limited number of perhaps ten to twenty such models (figure 3).

Ballad tunes and texts from the 1500s and 1600s were borrowed from Germany. The tunes usually have a more modal and metrical character than those discussed above, and are linked to particular texts. The ballad in figure 4 tells of a knight who wishes to bring a maiden out of a convent.

During the 1700s and 1800s, numerous tunes marked by major-minor tonality appeared, often with an extended range. The influence of triadic harmony is evident in them, and their forms are more symmetrical than earlier tunes. Presumably, there was a close connection between instrumental dance tunes and the ballad tunes of the time. During the 1800s, the major mode became predominant in ballad tunes. Two new musical forms account for about half the tunes: the ABCD form, with an overall arch shape; and the AABA form, with phrase B at a higher pitch than phrase A. The latter form is found in fiddlers' tunes and nineteenth-century love ballads (figure 5).

Fiddle music can be divided into two historical strata. Old melodies, related to

FIGURE 3 The medieval ballad *"Dronning Dagmar ligger i Ribe,"* with a melody having the range of a fifth. The form is ABABA, and the last line of the text is a refrain. Transcription by Svend Nielsen.

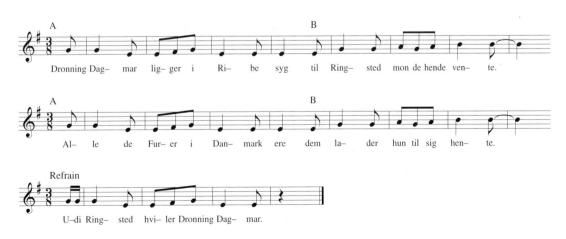

FIGURE 4 The sixteenth-century ballad tune "*En pige gik op på højeste bjerg,*" in G major, with a range of more than an octave and having AAB form. Transcription by Svend Nielsen.

dances like the minuet and the *polska,* first appeared in music books before 1800 and are still performed in a few areas, such as Fanø and Lësø. In these tunes, the feeling of an underlying beat is stronger than that of a particular meter. The melody consists of one- or two-measure melodic and rhythmic motifs, repeated or transposed; phrases may include five, six, seven, eight, and nine bars (figure 6). Newer melodies, the major part of the instrumental repertoire, are far more symmetrical and stereotypical, each phrase consisting of eight bars, normally repeated, and each melody, firmly based on major triads, evoking a tonic, a dominant, and a subdominant (figure 7).

FOLK INSTRUMENTS

Around 1700, the *fedel,* a stringed instrument of the violin type, and the drum appeared as the most important instruments in peasant music. The bagpipe, the hurdy-gurdy, and the mouth harp were undoubtedly used in this period, but their geographical distributions are uncertain. In later times, wandering musicians from southern Europe occasionally played the bagpipe in Denmark.

From the 1700s, the violin became village musicians' predominant instrument, with the clarinet, the flute and, more rarely, the string bass. Military instruments, used by discharged soldiers, were primarily the French horn, the oboe (shawm), and the bassoon. In the 1730s, an ensemble of two violins and a bass was reported to be playing in pubs near Copenhagen.

From the early 1800s, Danish musical instruments were to a large extent professionally made—and possibly in some cases, factory made. Trumpets, cornets, and trombones were played outdoors, but toward the end of the century, they went inside and joined ballroom orchestras, which sometimes included six persons or more.

In the late 1800s, accordions appeared. By about 1900, they were competing

FIGURE 5 The nineteenth-century ballad tune "*I et vinhus vil jeg sige,*" in F major and having characteristic AA'BA form. Transcription by Svend Nielsen.

FIGURE 6 An old-style dance tune. The first phrase (A) consists primarily of a one-measure motif; the second phrase (B), slightly more varied, but still based on this motif for three of its six measures, is in a higher pitch range. Transcription by Svend Nielsen.

with violins as the predominant dance instruments. Though in the twentieth century musicians have come to use larger and more advanced accordions, many accordion players' styles are still closely related to that of the two-row accordion. With the arrival of American dances in the 1920s and 1930s, the piano and drums found their way into dance bands.

In the nineteenth century and at the beginning of the twentieth, the guitar seems to have been the predominant instrument among street musicians (figure 8). Sellers of fake medicines used the barker's stick (*rumsterstang*), and primitive, home-made versions were used at bricklayers' shack parties. In the early twentieth century, vagrants and street singers used the saw blade and spoons as instruments.

Homemade instruments were fashioned in the nineteenth and early twentieth centuries. Clarinet-shawms are known in several forms made of pine, split and hollowed out, and bound or wedged together. A cow horn, possibly with one or more finger holes, was used as a bugle to call together the people of a village. The rumble pot (*rumlepotte*), a friction drum made from a pot sealed with the skin of a pig's bladder and having a goose quill or a piece of reed attached to the middle, was used particularly in connection with New Year celebrations in Jutland and on Fuen Island.

The bull roarer (*svingbruse*) consists of a hollow tile, or a small oblong wooden plate with a hole, tied to the end of a string that can be swung in circles to produce a whirring sound. Whirring may also be produced by a different type of bull roarer (*hvësegasse*): a button or a round piece of cardboard set in rotation by rhythmically tightening or slackening an unlaid string noose threaded through two holes in the middle of the plate or button and held in outstretched hands.

FIGURE 7 A new-style dance tune, with two repeated eight-measure phrases in AABB form. The melody prominently outlines tonic (G–B–D) and dominant (D–F♯–A) triads. Transcription by Svend Nielsen.

Few instrumentalists earned their living solely by playing. They were usually artisans, blacksmiths, bricklayers, carpenters, smallholders, or farmhands, with music an important sideline. In addition to being hired for dances, weddings, and seasonal celebrations, instrumentalists were hired to mark the pace and rhythm of work.

FIGURE 8   Street musicians in Copenhagen. *From left:* a singer holding a tray to collect money, a guitarist, and an accordionist. Photo by Svend Nielsen, 1983.

All these instruments were made by grownups, but children and shepherd boys constructed various other instruments. The music produced by these instruments is often limited to a single tone, and in many cases they may be regarded as toys, where the main entertainment is the manufacture of the instrument, rather than its playing. Boys played on a leaf from a beech tree or a grass blade, which they stretched between their thumbs while slightly cupping their hands and blowing toward the edge of the leaf. They could change the pitch by varying the tension. They made temporary shawms from the stem of a dandelion pressed together at one end so that it is split, forming a double reed. Finger holes poked in the stem enable the player to produce several unstable pitches.

The bark lur consists of an idioglot reed (*skrëme*), inserted into a funnel made from a spiral coil of willow bark, held together at the end by a thorn or a thin twig sewn through the bark. More durable shepherd's instruments include duct flutes, with or without finger holes. Another type of flute, made on a large scale by grownups, was the clay pipe, a vessel flute, often fashioned in the shape of an animal and sold at markets. It had two varieties: the squeaky-bum horse (*piv-i-røv-hest*) and the clay cuckoo (*lergøg*).

MUSIC OF OCCUPATIONAL, SOCIAL, AND RELIGIOUS GROUPS

Danish musical dialects differ somewhat by region, but balladic and instrumental repertoires can be distinguished by social groups, marked by occupation, religion, political affiliation, age, and sex, and three main groups of professional, traditional musicians—instrumentalists (fiddlers), who mainly play at dances in the country, street singers, and tavern musicians in towns.

Many of the most famous street singers and tavern and circus musicians come from a distinct social group—vagrants (*de rejsende*), who consist of families who have traveled around in house wagons since the early 1800s and make their living as circus people and street singers, selling homemade wares and repairing kitchen utensils.

Instrumentalists

Between 1650 and 1800, the state gave professional borough instrumentalists a monopoly on providing music for private and public celebrations in towns and the countryside, but court cases show that in that period, tradesmen made a living, at least in part, from playing at dances and parties celebrating annual events: Shrovetide, Easter, Whitsunday, Midsummer Day, harvest festivals, and Christmas. Most often, their instrument appears to have been the violin, but some used other instruments. In the decades immediately after 1800, the borough musicians' monopoly was gradually revoked, and since then, the trade has been open to anyone. Few instrumentalists earned their living solely by playing. They were usually artisans, blacksmiths, bricklayers, carpenters, smallholders, or farmhands, with music an important sideline. In addition to being hired for dances, weddings, and seasonal celebrations, instrumentalists were hired to mark the pace and rhythm of work, for example, the threshing of rape and long straw.

Self-taught, many instrumentalists play by ear, having memorized their music. Others have received instruction in childhood, or have been apprenticed to an experienced instrumentalist who taught them dance tunes and how to read music. After a while, an instrumentalist would take his apprentice with him to gain experience in playing at dances. As a rule, only one musician played at a dance, and the instruments most often used were the violin and the accordion. Nineteenth-century dance ensembles included combinations of one or two violins, a clarinet or a flute, a trumpet, and a string bass. From the late 1800s, the accordion gained a foothold as an instrument for accompanying dancing; in the twentieth century, the piano and drums have also come into use.

Fiddlers play a variety of couple dances (fox-trot, *gammel vals* 'old-fashioned waltz,' galop, mazurka, polka, schottische, tango, waltz) and figure dances (*schottische anglaise,* minuet, and *polska*). Most instrumental dance tunes are played all over the country, but some—such as the figure dances in Thy and Sønderho and the *fannike* on Fanø—are specific to a certain area. Musicians in isolated areas, like Fanø and Lësø, play in a melodic style that differs notably from the common one (Grüner-Nielsen 1976).

Street musicians

Street musicians set up in the streets or backyards and sang or played for money; unlike professional or semiprofessional instrumentalists, they had no other occupation. Many came from vagrant families, but outside these circles, some families have been street musicians for generations. Formal musical instruction was rare, but children learned to help at an early age, and thus acquired the trade. During the Great Depression of the 1930s, street musicians were temporarily joined by a large number of tavern and restaurant musicians, forced out of their preferred field of work.

Being a street musician was problematic. Singing and playing in public places was not allowed unless one had a special permit from the local police. Since permits were difficult to obtain and were valid in a particular town for only a short period, musicians often played without a permit, risking fines and the confiscation of their earnings.

The major part of street singers' repertoire was simply the music that was most popular. Before 1900, it consisted of broadside ballads and theatrical songs, and later it would include hits or dance music made popular by films or the radio. Apart from those examples, however, a few songs and tunes became associated with street singers; these included certain hits, broadsheet ballads about the dregs of society, prison ballads, and ballads about street singer's circumstances. The presentation, rather than the repertoire, is characteristic of street singing and street music: a fairly free and rather personal style allowed a rubato and melodic ornamentation with grace notes and glissandi. Street musicians might perform on their own, singing and playing at the same time, in pairs, or in larger ensembles.

In the 1800s, street musicians relied on the same group of instruments professionals used, but especially the guitar. In the twentieth century, the instruments were primarily the accordion, the banjo, the guitar, the saw blade, and spoons.

Tavern musicians

Tavern musicians often belonged to vagrant families, and many street musicians were from time to time employed in taverns and beer gardens. Some, when they married and settled into a home, became tavern musicians. The tavern style resembles that of vagrants and street musicians, but its repertoire reflects the audience's demand to hear the most popular contemporary tunes.

Farmers' songs

Ignoring professional musicians and occupational groups, early collectors viewed farmers and smallholders' musical traditions as manifestations of Danish folksinging as a whole. Well into the twentieth century, this group by far constituted the majority of the population. For the celebration of festivals such as New Year, Twelfth Night, Shrovetide, Easter, Whitsunday, and Midsummer Day, villages had processions that used special songs. Some tunes are related to ballad tunes, but many are more recent.

Singing accompanied women's work (carding, milking, spinning), but the work is reflected less in the words or the tunes than in the style of singing, in which the rhythmical stress was evened out so the song could be sung independently of the rhythms of the work. Playing with little children, women also sang nursery rhymes and lullabies, especially ride-a-cock-horse rhymes, often spoken, but also sung to special tunes; lullabies also had special tunes.

In rural areas, an important context for singing was twilighting—when young people sat in the dark, or did indoor work before lamps were lit, closely watched by a farmer and his wife. In the summer, they sat in roadside ditches, went for walks in groups, and met in farmhands' rooms, where the songs had a touch of eroticism.

Migrant workers' songs

Until the 1950s, when agriculture became mechanized, large estates and manor houses depended on manor-house navvies, vagrant day laborers, who went from farm to farm in search of work. When they gathered in the servants' hall after work, singing was common entertainment, as it was when they left in a group for the local village hall to dance and enjoy their leisure.

Some navvy and manor-house ballads, sung to tunes similar to jesting ballads, concern the navvies' circumstances (like wretched food and miserable rooms); some defame the master and mistress, the farm bailiff, and the cook. Navvies also sang jesting ballads in the servants' halls—an important factor in the continuation of this genre. They sang many newer songs and tunes, and their mobility ensured a large and diverse repertoire.

Builders' songs

Builders passed the time singing, and they had a repertoire of songs related to their work, with songs also known by tavern musicians and street singers. When it rained, for instance, builders could not work, but were obliged to stay on site until past noon to see if the weather would improve. Waiting in the workmen's shack, they accompanied their singing with a shack organ (*skur-orgel*, a barker's stick, made from building materials), teaspoons in empty beer bottles, wooden shoes stamped on floorboards, and hands and elbows alternately banged on a table.

Sailors' and fishermen's songs

During the era of sailing ships, sailors sang work songs, often English shanties in leader-chorus style, but also Danish and other Scandinavian shanties with tunes related to ballad melodies. The words were often heroic, but from time to time singers improvised satirical verses about onboard situations and individuals. The leader customarily sang the verse, and the others sang the middle refrain and chorus.

The character of the songs differed according to the nature of the work. For heavy hauls (like hoisting the mainsail), songs with short middle refrains and choruses were used, and the men hauled only on stressed syllables. For pulling the rope around the capstan, many kinds of songs could be used, with or without a chorus. In port and on watch below, narrative ballads (love songs) and ballads about the conditions on ships were sung. The tunes of these ballads derive from more recent musical styles.

TRACK 14

Sailors' and fishermen's song traditions are closely connected. Fishermen usually sent their sons away as sailors before allowing them to join the fishing trade at home; thus, sailors' musical traditions have become part of the fishermen's repertoire. Fishermen sang work songs while hauling boats in, and cried work cries while hammering fishing stakes down. They also sang while not at work, as when storms kept boats in port, or when a whole family was mending the nets, or when fishermen went visiting in winter.

Religious songs

Some religious movements have distinct musical forms. As late as the 1960s, Jutlanders employed a hymn-singing style that had been fairly common until the mid-1800s. Using *kingotoner,* tunes in a hymnbook compiled by Bishop Thomas Kingo (1634–1703), they sang in a slow tempo, with inserted passing tones and ornamentation [see SCOTLAND].

The Home Mission, an evangelical branch of the Church of Denmark, strongly opposes public dancing, and as a result has retained the tradition of letting groups of engaged couples play singing games when they gather, after meetings or at private parties. Young people in the Home Mission used old traditional singing games, but they also invented new ones, often with words and tunes from official, patriotic songs. Religious circles created a large stock of edifying, revivalist ballads, sung at meetings and in the home. Many tunes and texts were taken from similar Swedish and English songs.

Children's songs

In the late twentieth century, children have the most animated traditional musical culture in Denmark, a tradition still capable of renewing itself by producing new forms of words and tunes (E. K. Nielsen 1986; S. Nielsen 1980a, 1980b). Children perform bantering cries and songs when playing and competing; boys also direct songs at adults, teachers, and bus drivers. Girls have a repertoire of swing songs and a

In the mid-1960s—when the international folk-music revival reached Denmark—American, Irish, and English music prevailed, inspiring young musicians to incorporate foreign musical elements into their music.

unique way of singing them; when they sit together in a quiet corner, they sing long, narrative children's ballads.

In the 1960s, singing games were still the most conspicuous musical activity among girls, who had a large, active repertoire of old and new songs. Since the mid-1970s, however, these games have almost disappeared, and only a few types can still be observed. Since 1970, a genre of songs with clapping has appeared, and new material is produced all the time. The clapping songs are part of an apparently new international tradition of play, and the inspiration from abroad is evident. Other children's songs are taken from the adult world and its media, rephrased according to the children's liking and needs.

ART MUSIC AND FOLK MUSIC

Danish composers have made little use of indigenous folk music, and they have done so in two well-defined periods. During the romantic period (from the late 1820s to the 1850s), composers such as Friedrich Kuhlau (1786–1832), Johann P. E. Hartmann (1805–1900), Niels W. Gade (1817–1890), and the lesser-known Johann Frølich (1806–1860) drew on folk material. Kuhlau's incidental music to the play *Elverhøj* (The Elf's Hill, 1828) uses ballad tunes from Nyerup and Rasmussen's folk-ballad edition of 1821. Hartmann's opera *Liden Kirsten* (Little Christina, 1846) evokes the atmosphere of the medieval ballads. Gade's overture *Efterklange af Ossian* (Echoes of Ossian, 1840) echoed James Macpherson's Celtic epic's impact on European intellectuals, and Frøhlich used popular ballads and folk tunes in his ballet scores, including *Erik Menveds barndom* (Erik Menved's Childhood, 1843), based on a historical novel by B. S. Ingemann.

Denmark's greatest modern composer, Carl Nielsen (1865–1931), was profoundly affected by his rural upbringing on Funen, and though he developed a style of composition based more on classical than romantic principles, he early in his career wrote songs related to the Danish tradition of classical lieder. In the spring of 1914, he composed around fifty hymn tunes, and at the suggestion of his friend Thomas Laub, they collaborated on a reform of Danish secular song, simplifying the songs and purifying them of their romantic and liederlike qualities to make them accessible. After World War I, he became involved in popular-music education. His work with high schools resulted in the publication of *Folkehøjskolens melodibog* (1922) and considerably influenced a later generation.

The 1920s and 1930s saw some mining of folk tunes by composers such as Poul Hamburger (1901–1972) and Oluf Ring (1884–1946), but it was the Australian composer Percy Grainger who made the most ambitious use of Danish folk melodies (figure 9). Drawing from fieldwork that he and Evald Tang Kristensen had undertaken, he composed pieces for piano (including "Jutish Melody," 1927), chamber music, and the "Suite on Danish Folk Songs," arranged for different instrumental combinations over the period 1922–1950. In the 1990s, jazz pianist and composer Ole Koch

FIGURE 9 Evald Tang Kristensen, *left,* and Percy Grainger, *center,* record the singer Jens Kristian Jensen on a wax-cylinder phonograph, 1925. Photo by H. P. Hansen, Herning Museum.

Hansen (b. 1945) has made arrangements of Danish folk music, his primary source being Berggreen (1869).

THE FOLK REVIVAL

In 1901, students and university graduates, taking their inspiration from Sweden, founded the Association for the Promotion of Folk Dance; local associations soon appeared all over the country. Its object was to preserve Danish folk dances and keep them alive in the manner in which they had been danced over the period from 1750 to 1850. To achieve this objective, members collected, taught, and performed dances. On the basis of an extensive and concentrated collection of descriptions of dances, members selected, choreographed, and published dances from particular regions, to be used at rehearsals and public performances. As a result of their methods and ideology, which included special regional costumes, some dances and tunes, all in fixed forms, came to be regarded as authorized versions. In 1929, the associations, many belonging to gymnastic clubs, joined to form the Danish Folk-Dancers; in 1946, the associations' musicians formed a subsidiary organization, Danish Folk-Dancers' Association of Fiddlers. In the 1990s, fifteen thousand to twenty thousand persons belonged to these associations.

In the mid-1960s—when the international folk-music revival reached Denmark—American, Irish, and English music prevailed, inspiring young musicians to incorporate foreign musical elements into their music. The interest in using Danish musical material then declined, except within leftist youth groups opposed to Denmark's joining the Common Market. At the beginning of the 1970s, in Hoager, Thorkild Knudsen founded the Folk-Music House, which started a movement that met the need for a physical and social setting for folk-musical activities. Folk-Music Houses were particularly interested in preserving ballad dancing. In them, young people who have no folk-musical tradition meet the older bearers of folk music, learn from them, and continue the tradition. They can also learn to play an instrument and dance, and in some localities they collected folk music.

In theory, instrumental and vocal folk music are of interest, but in practice, vocal music has receded into the background. Activities of the Folk-Music Houses ended in the early 1980s, but some associations still continue. Because of the attention the houses gave to fiddlers' music, young professional and semiprofessional musicians of the 1970s and 1980s began to use Danish folk music as a starting point for their music. Some of them combined folk music with jazz, rock, and music from Latin America; others worked with historical instruments and music from the 1700s.

TRADITIONAL MUSIC TODAY

In Denmark today, many types of traditional music are still in use, but they lead mostly an unobtrusive, sometimes hidden life, in the form of personal repertoires, used for private amusement without an audience, or in the form of family repertoires, used within a small circle of individuals. A single type still widely practiced is the song for a particular occasion, where the singer writes the words to a commonly known tune or has the song made by someone who specializes in the production of occasional songs.

The entire structure of occupational life underwent enormous changes in the twentieth century, especially after World War II. These changes have caused some occupational groups with musical traditions to disappear—sailors on sailing ships in the 1920s and 1930s, and manor-house navvies in the 1940s. Some occupational groups survive, but their occasions for singing have disappeared: cow-milking singing ceased with the arrival of milking machines, and twilight singing faded with the introduction of electricity and higher standards of living.

Changes in social convention have had musical consequences. Spontaneous visits with friends and family have more or less stopped, and when they do take place, television has replaced singing and conversation as the focus of social intercourse. Similarly, grownups' singing and reciting rhymes and ballads to children has to a large extent been replaced by cassettes, television, and videotapes. No new musical situations arise in modern occupational groups, work, or forms of social intercourse. This situation presumably reflects changes in attitude toward the use of traditions—changes fostered by influences from art and commercial music, where self-made music is replaced by consumers who buy musical products.

During the last 150 years, traditional musical culture in Denmark has increasingly renounced the possibility of transforming words and tunes according to its immediate needs, and has perceived ballads and instrumental tunes to be fixed and sacrosanct. An exception is children's music, where one may still find that not only new words and tunes, but also entirely new song forms, are being developed, as in the case of songs with clapping. However, one can also envisage problems in this group: in the late 1960s, children adhered to their own musical culture until the age of fourteen or fifteen, but now they drop it at the age of eleven or twelve, in favor of a predominantly commercial youth culture.

In the long view, a fixed musical tradition may signal the end of folk song, because if people do not secure an infusion of new texts and tunes by composing them themselves or adopting them from others, or if they refrain from transforming already existing lyrics and tunes, the musical repertoire gradually becomes antiquated, and representing a society and issues that existed perhaps a hundred years ago, it fails to reflect present concerns, except in general terms; however, folk music in Denmark, proving tenacious, has survived scholarly death warrants, and despite everything, it may yet endure.

Since 1970, new developments have taken place: street singers have partly been replaced by musicians who perform in pedestrian areas. These buskers are mostly young people (often students from America, Britain, and Latin America) on a tour of Europe, staying for a time and earning money by playing music from their home countries; young dancers too follow in their footsteps, mostly with a repertoire taken from commercial music. Since the 1960s, new populations—primarily from the former Yugoslavia, Turkey, and Pakistan—have brought their own music with them. The immediate question is whether they will influence the musical culture of Denmark in the long run.

COLLECTION AND RESEARCH

Before the nineteenth century, knowledge of folk music in Denmark is confined to archaeological finds of instruments, especially lurs [see ARCHAEOLOGY OF MUSIC IN EUROPE], pictorial renderings (such as medieval murals in village churches), and written sources. In all these cases, problems of interpretation are great, and existing accounts show traces of having been written by outsiders with different cultural backgrounds—and consequently negative attitudes toward what they are depicting.

Vocal music

In 1809, the historian Rasmus Nyerup initiated the actual collecting of Danish folk music, the focus of which was medieval ballads. The result was about 250 tunes, most of which were published in the five-volume work he and two other scholars edited (Abrahamson, Nyerup, and Rahbek 1812–1814). A far more comprehensive collection was organized from 1840 to 1877 by the folklorist and philologist Svend Grundtvig, assisted by the organist Andreas Peter Berggreen, who supervised the musical aspects. They brought ballad texts and tunes together with general folkloric material: fairy tales, legends, popular beliefs, customs, riddles, and proverbs. Though Grundtvig's interest was still directed mainly at medieval ballads, a strong attraction to lyrical love ballads makes itself felt; however, the collection was clearly historical in orientation, and more recent ballads were of little interest. Berggreen (1869) published a fairly large selection of the eleven hundred tunes they collected, the emphasis being almost exclusively on the origin and tonality of the tunes.

In 1868, the schoolmaster Evald Tang Kristensen, from West Jutland, began his own collection of folklore, which he continued until his death, in 1929. At first he restricted work to his local area, but later he traveled through Jutland on state grants, and others would send him tunes they had collected. From 1883, he administered a national association of people collecting folkloric materials for him. His collection, like Grundtvig's, comprises all folkloric genres. Some of the ballad tunes he found in the moors of West Jutland apparently belong to a musical style older than those previously found, and he gives much more information about the ballads than other collectors (Kristensen 1871, 1876, 1891, 1901).

The Danish Folklore Archives was established in 1904, with Hakon Grüner-Nielsen in charge of collecting music. He conducted fieldwork, organized collecting by using persons from all over the country, and began publishing the tunes for Grundtvig's compilation. In his depiction of the inhabitants on Læsø, he was the first to describe the role of music in a local community and demonstrate examples of musical situations and the functions of music (1924). About 1900, the cantor Hans Johansen, of the town of Rønne, on Bornholm Island, collected songs and dance tunes from the island; from 1908 to 1911, he published some of the songs. In 1940, the composer Vagn Holmboe (1988) collected and studied Danish street cries, which he grouped into half cries, and static, dynamic, or ecstatic recitations.

The use of the phonograph in Danish collecting began in 1907, with Grüner-Nielsen as the leading figure. In 1922, 1925, and 1927, the Australian composer

Analyzing Danish folk tunes, Thorkild Knudsen introduced the concepts of type and model—*type* referring to closely related melodic variants, often linked to the same kind of lyric, and *model* being the tonal or melodic idea that forms the basis for melodic variants grouped by type.

Percy Grainger (1882–1961), with Evald Tang Kristensen, recorded eighty waltzes, and by 1952, 311 separate waltz tunes had been recorded (see figure 9).

In the 1940s, collecting ebbed. It resumed in 1958, when a younger generation, equipped with magnetic tape recorders and headed by Thorkild Knudsen of the Danish Folklore Archives, began to conduct research. Analyzing Danish folk tunes, Knudsen introduced the concepts of type and model—*type* referring to closely related melodic variants, often linked to the same kind of lyric, and *model* being the tonal or melodic idea that forms the basis for melodic variants grouped by type; variants within the model need not have the same lyrics (1961a, 1961b).

With Knudsen and others, folk-musical research moved in the direction of studying individual singers or musicians, special groups, and society at large. Nils Schiørring (1956) published the repertoire of the traditional singer Selma Nielsen, and other singers have been studied (Clausen 1975 [1958]; Knudsen 1961a, 1961b; Koudal 1985; S. Nielsen 1973, 1980b). Interest moved in the direction of ethnology, to the people who made the music and the environments in which recordings were made; the new concept of an urban folk song, for example, among ragpickers and children, became a subject of interest. From the early 1960s, broadcasts on radio were a means of collecting, and through them emphasis was directed back to the rural environment and older genres, such as medieval ballads. Between 1960 and 1968, songs in the collections of the 1800s, with some recently collected songs, were published (Knudsen and Schiørring 1960–1968). In 1975, Svend Nielsen (1977, 1980), who had been collecting since 1963, began documenting the songs in groups other than that of country folk: builders, day laborers, fishermen, religious groups, sailors, and children. He has also written on the use of satirical songs (1979) and singers' views of their songs (1974).

Geographically defined studies have been presented in Åge Skjelborg's book on singing and music on the island of Anholt (1975), and in Kirsten Sass Bak, Elsemarie Dam-Jensen, and Birgit Lauritsen's book (1983) on singing in southern Jutland.

From 1979, scholars began using videotape for collecting musical material: they have recorded a large number of dancing and singing games and ballad singing in various contexts. In the 1980s, parallel to collecting with tape recorders, Jens Henrik Koudal studied archives and discovered valuable sources illustrating folk music before 1800 (Koudal 1982, 1983–1984, 1985). From 1958 to 1990, about twenty-seven hundred tapes (thirteen hundred hours' playing time) were filled with perhaps twenty thousand recordings of music, and about 250 videotapes were made (Koudal 1989).

Besides the Danish Folklore Archives, the Sanghistorisk Arkiv (Historical Song Archives) in Arhus has organized a large collection of popular songs, mainly in southern Jutland (Clausen 1962, 1975 [1958]). Thorkild Knudsen, who has been working at the Folk-Music House in Hogager since 1971, has organized his own collecting methods, especially for fiddle music, and in the 1970s and 1980s other local Folk-Music Houses recorded folk-musical materials.

Instrumental music

Collecting in the 1800s rarely dealt with instrumental music: only about a hundred tunes were written down by the collectors in the same way as ballad tunes. This was possibly because a great deal of music existed in written form in musicians' manuscripts, and their versions were regarded as more original than those that collectors could write down. Toward the end of the century, however, Evald Tang Kristensen began collecting these manuscripts, and collecting continued in the twentieth century, organized by the Danish Folklore Archives, the Danish Folk-Dancers' Association of Fiddlers, and private individuals acting individually, particularly Christian Olsen and Sven Jørgensen (Olsen 1923–1928). Today, the collections, kept at the Danish Folklore Archives, total about twelve hundred manuscripts containing about eighty thousand tunes. The manuscripts were written between about 1750 and 1950, the greater part being from about 1850 to about 1900, nearly all of them music for the violin.

Between 1909 and 1916, Grüner Nielsen recorded about a hundred dance tunes with a phonograph, primarily tunes from Sønderho on Fanø (Grüner-Nielsen 1976), but then such collecting ceased for about forty years. Only in 1958, with the arrival of tape recorders, did the actual recording of instrumental music resume, at first in interview situations. After the introduction of videotape, dance situations became the subject of interest. From 1979 to 1990, about fifty hours of dance music and a large number of explanatory conversations with musicians were recorded on video.

BIBLIOGRAPHY

Abrahamsen, Erik. 1923. *Éléments romans et allemands dans le chant grégorien et la chanson populaire.* Copenhagen: P. Haase & Fils.

Abrahamson, Werner Hans Frederik, Rasmus Nyerup, and K. M. Rahbek. 1812–1814. *Udvalgte Danske viser fra Middelalderen.* 5 vols. Copenhagen: J. F. Schultz

Bak, Kirsten Sass. 1988. "Folkemusik og musikvidenskab—Fra Laub til folkemusikdebatten." In *Otte ekkoer af musikforskning i Arhus,* 21–61. Århus:

Bak, Kirsten Sass, Elsemarie Dam-Jensen, and Birgit Lauritsen. 1983. *Æ har høør . . . Sønderjyder synger.* Aabenraa: Institut for Grænseregionsforskning.

Berggreen, Andreas Peter. 1869. *Danske Folke-Sange og Melodier.* 3d ed. Copenhagen: C. A. Reitzel.

Bødker, Knud. 1978. *Hej spil op! Jyske spillemænd og melodier.* Rønde: Si-Mi Tryk, Ökdbenhavnë.

Clausen, Karl. 1962. "Tille Davidsen og hendes viser." *Sønderjysk Maanedsskrift* 1–8.

———. 1975 [1958]. *Dansk Folkesang gennem 150 år.* Copenhagen: Tingluti.

Dal, Erik. 1956. *Nordisk folkeviseforskning siden 1800.* Universitets-jubilæets danske samfund, 376. Copenhagen: J. H. Schultz.

Danske Folkedanseres Spillemandskreds: 358+358 danske Folkedanselodier. 1963, 1984. 2 vols.

Enevig, Anders. 1963. *Prinser og vagabonder.* Copenhagen: Forlaget Fremad.

———. 1964. *Klunsere og kræmmere.* Copenhagen: Forlaget Fremad.

Grundtvig, Svend, et al., eds. 1853–1976. *Danmarks gamle Folkeviser.* 12 vols. Copenhagen: Samfundet til den Danske Literaturs Fremme.

Grüner-Nielsen, Hakon Harald. 1917. *Vore ældste Folkedanse, Langdans og Polskdans.* Copenhagen: Det Schønbergske Forlag.

———. 1920. *Folkelig vals.* Copenhagen: Det Schønbergske Forlag.

———. 1924. *Læsøfolk i gamle dage.* Danmarks Folkeminder, 29. Copenhagen: Det Schønbergske Forlag.

———. 1947. "Din skaal og min Skaal; En undersøgelse vedrørende de danske folkelige sunge Skaalevers og deres Historie." *Kulturminder* : 51–118.

———. 1949. "Degnesang ('Kingotoner') i Herning-egnen i 1860'erne." In *Festskrift til Museumsforstander H. P. Hansen,* ed. Peter Skautrup, 239–249. Copenhagen: Rosenkilde og Bagger.

Holmboe, Vagn. 1988. *Danish Street Cries: A Study of Their Musical Structure, and a Complete Edition of Tunes with Words Collected Before 1960.* Acta Ethnomusicologica Danica, 5. Copenhagen: Forlaget Kragen.

Johansen, Hans. 1911. *Viser i bornholmsk Mundart.* Rønne: Colberg.

Knudsen, Thorkild. 1958. "Structures prémodales et pseudo-grégoriennes dans les mélodies des ballades danoises." *Journal of the International Folk Music Council* 10:1–14.

———. 1961a. "Ingeborg Munchs viser." *Folkeminder* 7:89–104.

———. 1961b. "Model, type og variant." *Dansk Musiktedsskrift* 3:79–92. Reprinted in 1961 as "Modell, Type und Variante," *Wissenschaftliche Zeitschrift der Ernst-Moritz-Arnd-Universität Greifswald* 10:77–89.

———. 1967. On the Nature of Ballad Tunes. Copenhagen:

———, and Nils Schiørring. 1960–1968. *Folkevisen i Danmark: Efteroptegnelser i Dansk Folkemindesamling*, no. 1-8. Copenhagen: Musikhøjskolens Forlag.

Koudal, Jens Henrik. 1982. "Rasmus Nyerups visearbejde og folkeviseindsamlingen 1809–21." *Musik og Forskning* 8:5–79.

———. 1983–1984. "Evald Tang Kristensen som folkevisesamler og udgiverbelyst ud fra Jens Mikkelsen og Niels Albrektsen i Kølvrå 1874." *Musik og Forskning* 9:68–141.

———. 1984. *To sangere fra den jyske hede: Efter optegnelser i Dansk Folkemindesamling af Evald Tang Kristensen 1874*. Copenhagen: Forlaget Folkeminder.

———. 1985. "En frontsoldat i kampen om folkeviserne: Om Frederik Snedorff Birch 1805–69." *Sumlen: årsbok för vis—och folkmusikforskning*:69–95.

———. 1987. *Rasmus Storms nodebog: En fynsk tjenestekarls dansemelodier o. 1760*. Copenhagen: Forlaget Kragen.

———. 1989. *Sang og musik på Dansk Folkemindesamling: En indføring*. Copenhagen: Forlaget Folkeminder.

Kristensen, Evald Tang, ed. 1871, 1876, 1891. *Jyske Folkeminder*. Vols. 1, 2, and 11. Viborg and Copenhagen: Gyldendal.

———, ed. 1901. *Et hundrede gamle danske skjëmteviser efter nutidssang*. Arhus: J. Zeuner.

Nielsen, Erik Kaas. 1986. *Jeg vil synge en sang: Børns viser og sange før og nu*. Copenhagen: Fremad.

Nielsen, Svend. 1973. "Maren Ole og hendes sange." *Folk og Kultur*:87–112.

———. 1974. *Den gode vise, den sande vise*. Copenhagen: Dansk Folkemindesamling.

———. 1978. *Glimt af dansk folkemusik: Tekster, melodier & kommentarer*. Copenhagen: Kragen.

———. 1979. *Når visen får brod: Om nidviser, smædeviser, drilleviser og protestsange: Et våben for de svage i samfundet*. Århus.

———. 1980a. *Flyv lille påfugl: Tekster, melodier og kommentarer til traditionel sang blandt børn*. Copenhagen: Kragen.

———. 1980b. "Selma Nielsens remser." *Musik og Forskning* 6:142–151.

———. 1983. "Spillemand på fonograf." *Folk og Kultur*:20–37.

———. 1985. *Go'morgen Karl Baj! Sang blandt prinser og klunsere på Nørrebro i København, optaget i 1958 af Anders Enevig*. Copenhagen: Kragen.

Olsen, Christian. 1923–1928. *Gamle Danse fra Nordvestsjælland*. 3 vols. Torpelund pr Eskebjerg.

Piø, Iørn. 1974. "Julius Strandbergs skillingsvise-produktion 1861–1903." *Folk og Kultur*:17–49.

———. 1985. *Nye veje til folkevisen; Studier i Danmarks gamle Folkeviser*. Copenhagen: Gyldendal.

Schiørring, Nils. 1950. *Det 16. og 17. århundredes verdslige danske visesang*. 2 vols. Copenhagen: Thaning & Appel.

———. 1956. *Selma Nielsens viser: Et repertoire af folkelige sange fra det 19 århundredes slutning*. Copenhagen: Munksgaard.

Skjelborg, Åge. 1975. *Folk og musik på Anholt*. Ry: Laboratorium for Folkloristik Samfundsforskning.

Thyregod, S. Tværmose. 1907. *Børnenes leg, gamle danske sanglege*. Copenhagen and Christiania.

———, ed. 1931. *Danmarks Sanglege*. Copenhagen: Det Schønbergske Forlag.

Tonn-Petersen, Anette. 1985. "Spillemandens rolle: Om spillemanden og festtraditionerne i 1800-tallet." *Folk og Kultur*:84–136.

Urup, Henning. 1976. "Dansk spille-mandsmusiks forudsætninger, kilder og særlige karakertræk." *Musik og Forskning* 2:31–47.

AUDIOVISUAL RESOURCES

Christensen, Anders, Svend Nielsen, and Sven E. Ottosen. 1989. *Gammeldans på Snedsted Kro*. Kragen DFS 4. LP disk.

Jensen, Ole, and Stig Larsen. 1989. *Viggo Gade i Albertslund*. Albertslund AFMH MC1. LP disk.

Knudsen, Thorkild, and Anelise Nørgaard. 1963. *Dansk Folkemusik: Ballader 1–2, Himmerland 1–2 og Kingotoner 1*. RCA DFS 451–454. 4 LP disks.

Nielsen, Svend. 1977. *Glimt af dansk Folkemusik*. Kragen DFS 1. LP disk.

———. 1979. *Når visen får brod*. Kragen DFS 101. LP disk.

———. 1980. *Flyv lille påfugl; Traditionel sang blandt børn*. Kragen DFS 2. LP disk.

———. 1985. *Go'morgen Karl Baj! Sang blandt prinser og klunsere på Nørrebro iKøbenhavn: Optaget i 1958 af Anders Enevig*. Kragen DFS 3. LP disk.

———. 1988. *Her'er sild! Danske gaderåb optaget i perioden 1935–88*. Kragen DFS103. LP disk.

Nyberg, Bo. 1989. *Polskan i Norden: Traditionsindspilninger från Sverige, Norge, Danmark og Finland.* Svea fonogram SVMC 2. LP disk.

Skjelborg, Åge. 1975? *Folk og musik på Anholt.* SLA FSLD 1. LP disk.

Ternhag. Gunnar, ed. 1983. *Prillarhorn och knaverparpa: Folkliga musikinstrument i Norden.* Caprice CAP 1146. LP disk.

Faroe Islands
Pandora Hopkins

Indigenous Musical Traditions
International Traditions
Institutions for Culture and Music

Part of the Atlantic Ridge, the Faroe Islands are a small archipelago of eighteen volcanic islands (seventeen inhabited) that rise precipitously out of the North Sea about halfway between Iceland and Scotland, 305 kilometers northwest of the Shetland Isles. Only about 6 percent of their 1397 square kilometers is arable.

Most of the forty-eight thousand inhabitants support themselves by fishing, and a few by catching birds or shepherding. They ascribe a particular significance to whaling, which they explain, not only in practical terms, but also as a cultural focus, without which they would lose their ballad-dancing tradition and therefore their place in history.

In the eleventh century, the Faroes became part of the Norraena Empire, ruled by Norway until it was forced to yield to the Danish crown in 1380. In 1846, V. U. Hammershaimb published an orthography for Faroese, which in 1948 received legal status as the official language of the islands. In 1948, the Faroe Islands were accorded political self-determination in some regards, especially those dealing with culture and communication, but not others, including formal education.

INDIGENOUS MUSICAL TRADITIONS

The esteem that the Faroese have always bestowed upon their ballad dancing—a collaboration of music, poetry, dance, and drama—accounts for its continuing viability. The dance, technically known as a chain dance (*ketudansur*), is sometimes called a ring dance or, archaically, a long dance. Most commonly today, people call it the Faroese dance. The Faroese never seem to have had indigenous musical instruments, and those that were imported did not attract any measure of enthusiasm until the beginning of the twentieth century, when accordions and violins began to be plentiful. At that time, the ballad dance not only continued to exist, but actually increased in importance. In the 1880s and 1890s, Ólavsøka (King Olav's Week) was celebrated by two different dances: the Faroese, danced by most people, and international dances, performed by the elite, including daughters of Danish officials and Faroese university students home from Denmark for the holidays. By 1902, according to contemporary sources, the governor himself was proud to participate in a ballad dance held in the parliament building.

Faroese musical traditions fall into four musically related vocal types. *Kvæði* (sing. and pl.), lengthy Faroese heroic ballads dramatized by performers in a line dance, have been perpetuated through oral transmission from medieval times. *Kempurvísur*, performed similarly, are Danish heroic ballads that have coexisted with *kvæði* since the 1600s, have fewer stanzas, are livelier in tempo, and have been transmitted in published song collections; they are usually called simply *vísur* (sing. *vísa*). *Tættir* (sing. *táttur*), also chain-danced, are satirical ballads that deal with topical events, often ridiculing famous personalities; they continue to be composed. Kingo tunes are Danish hymns named for items in Bishop Kingo's gradual [see DENMARK]; the people used them as the basis for extensive improvisation in informal worship services at home.

Kvæði

As in the Icelandic *rímur* [see ICELAND], a short, reiterated, usually preexisting melody functions as a vehicle for the singing of a lengthy epiclike ballad; a typical *kvæðir* contains more than a hundred stanzas, and one has six hundred, organized in nine chapters. Dramatized, danced, and sung, these narratives deal with medieval topics, including the Sjúrðarkvæði with Germanic mythology (legends about Sigurd the Dragonslayer) and the Rolantskvæði with the exploits of the ninth-century Frankish king Charlemagne (Karlamagnus), his uncle, Pepin, and Pepin's daughter, Óluva (figure 1). The Óluva sagas, as the last have come to be known, are especially associated with celebrations at carnival (Shrovetide).

A second body of texts deals with legends that derive from the ancient Icelandic sagas. One of the prime saga heroes was Nornagest, whose name means "guest of the Norns" (Nordic mythological fates), and his accomplishments, among those required of a gentleman, included harp playing and poetic ability.

The Faroes never had a court, and therefore did not require the services of formal oral historians, so the mode of transmission was in nonprofessional, home-oriented performance. Few Faroese epics deal with Faroese topics; an exception, the

FIGURE 1 The Óluva ballad treats a popular *kvæði* subject: King Pepin's daughter, Charlemagne's sister. After Thuren and Nielsen 1923:93 (#13d). Translation by Pandora Hopkins.

Pipin, king of Frankenland,
has a wife, has he.
Olua, that's the name of her daughter
stately and proud is she.
Refrain
Oh, tread we hard on the floor, save we not our shoes!
God, advise us what our toast will be next Yule.

Sigmundarkvæði, contains a verse from the Færeyinga saga, an account of the original settlement of the islands.

Most Faroese *kvæði* were composed in the late Middle Ages, but some may date from later. In the old days, *kvæði* were not always danced; they were sometimes narrated in informal home gatherings to while away winter nights. At such times, a soloist sang, or probably more often chanted, the epic; refrains characteristic of danced performances were truncated or omitted. Still important to the culture, the chain dance is performed on Sundays, at weddings, during St. Olaf's week, and on other holidays and special occasions, especially during the "dancing period" from Christmas to Lent.

Ballad dancing is an expressive outlet for all ages, and both sexes participate in it. Dancing is "one of the few activities in which all Faroese—and only Faroese—may participate fully; foreigners may learn the steps but are unlikely to learn the words, let alone become leaders (*skiparar*). The dancing thus distinguishes the popular culture from the official management of Faroese affairs, as represented by the sheriff and his appointees" (Wylie and Margolin 1981:117).

The basic dance pattern, repeated as often as necessary, consists of six steps, occasionally interrupted by a high jump on an individual dancer's part. The lead singer-dancer directs the rest, whose interlocked hands are held at hip level and rocked back and forth. The Faroese take pains to express the meaning of the words and evoke the appropriate mood through kinetic motion portraying and imitating the action of the narrative and through the music, whose interpretation includes such devices as extreme variation in timbre and tempo. The dancers weave in and out of crowded rooms, forming new lines as additional participants present themselves, maintaining close physical proximity to their neighbors in the line of dancers and to new lines, as they wend their way through the narrow rooms.

The repeated six beats of the fundamental dance pattern contradict the rhythms of the melodies, which follow the metrical design of the text. Each stanza consists of two or four lines: in the first case, the couplet has two lines of four stresses each; in the second case, the quatrain contains four lines with alternating beat patterns, 4–3–4–3. The refrain, which varies in length from two to thirty stresses, may be an abbreviated cadential formula or an independent melody, itself made up of formulaic patterns (Luihn 1980:91). The stanza is chanted to recitativelike motives; sometimes existing tunes are borrowed from Celtic or Nordic traditions.

Musical and textual variations used to be the province of the leader, who, chanting or singing the body of the text, was given the expressive license to vary as he or she saw fit; the refrain, however, always sung in chorus, did not change. This distinction is seldom maintained today, when performances usually have all performers singing the entire song throughout. The responsorial effect, however, is still maintained through the ringing out of the leader's voice at the beginning of each stanza. Individual creativity is in the realm of dramatic action, each dancer interpreting the text in his or her own way through a wide variety of facial expressions and bodily gestures.

Kempurvísur

Literally meaning 'giant songs', these Danish (and some Norwegian) ballad texts date from the Middle Ages, when chain dancing to the responsorial performance of narrative songs was characteristic of most northern peoples. *Kempurvísur* quickly became part of the Faroese repertory, and are still performed in precisely the same manner. Many of these texts are found in Anders Sorenson Vedel's collection of Danish ballads (the earliest such anthology, published in 1591), but today they are danced only in the Faroes. Despite Danish-language texts and a clear Danish provenance, they are not a medieval Danish tradition but a second Faroese genre. Numerous differences set the two ballad types apart: the *vísur* are much shorter, and their music is more melodic and does not have a recitativelike quality. As to the dancing, the *vísur* have more dance steps, and strong and weak beats are usually stepped (Luihn 1980:471). The Faroese-Danish ballads have long been partly propagated by printed songbooks, unlike the *kvæði,* which were always transmitted aurally.

Tættir

Satirical lampoons, *tættir* date from the 1600s and are still alive in some localities. The songs are performed in the same danced, responsorial fashion as *kvæði* and *kempurvísur.* They deal with topical subjects, usually ridiculing individuals' absurdities or transgressions, thus serving a punitive function. It used to be the custom to force the victim to take part in the dance, a strong dancer holding fast to his or her hands in the chain until the lampoon was accomplished.

This genre has long served for political satire, and some contemporary scholars see its function transferred to electronic media. Radio singers perform the satirical verses to tunes of European-international pop styles. This function may also be found in newspaper cartoons and special cartoon books published for Ólavsøka, the national holiday (Galvin 1989).

Kingosang

In the Faroes, the imposition of a prescribed body of religious songs, and the attempt to enforce an inflexible standard through the use of a printed text, had the opposite effect, and the Faroese turned the authorized Kingo tunes to their own advantage. Informal family devotionals developed an extensive and creative form of improvisation, using the notes of the hymns in the officially recognized published edition only as a springboard for an elaboration that grew from verse to verse. The new style involved transforming the old free-flowing melodies to simple tunes in duple meter, as the new emphasis on congregational participation in singing had brought with it the concept of uniformity in performance and correctness according to the printed page.

INTERNATIONAL TRADITIONS

Faroese culture has been an agent and a recipient of international influence. Most European orchestral instruments were known on the islands long before the Faroese showed an interest in them. The philologist Jan Christian Svabo (1746–1824), a prime mover in the preservation of Faroese language and ballads, was considered a violinist of the first rank. Napoleon Nolsøe, member of an esteemed musical family, became the first organist in Tórshavn, in 1831. The Danish immigrant Georg Caspar Hansen (1844–1924), a baker, played and taught all the major symphonic instruments, developed choral and instrumental groups, and inaugurated a brass-band tradition that achieved popularity.

Composition in a pan-European style is of more recent date: Joen (Jogvan) Waagstein (1879–1949) and others composed strophic songs in the tonal idiom; Pauli i Sandágerði (b. 1955) has written orchestral music and pieces for piano and other instruments; Sunleif Rasmussen (b. 1969), the first Faroese to study composition at the Royal Danish Academy of Music in Copenhagen, believes the traditional milieu of his formative years was a rich foundation for modernist composition. The Faroese Jazzband Triumf, founded early in the 1920s (about 1923), performed consistently until 1976, and then on a sporadic basis. The most participatory contemporary musical genre is the volunteer choir. There are twenty to thirty choirs in the Faroes, some dating back to the early decades of the twentieth century.

Throughout the last two centuries, most players of symphonic instruments were

The Danish composer and pianist Kristian Blak (b. 1947) went to the Faroes when he was twenty-five years old and is now a major influence in local musical life. He is responsible for the development of the Tórshavn Jazzclub; Players of Hoydølum, a folk-music organization; the record company TUTL; and the pan-Nordic performance group Yggdrasil.

FIGURE 2 Kristian Blak (b. 1947) composes and arranges in a variety of styles, including jazz, rock, folk, and classical. Photo courtesy of Kristian Blak.

immigrants who brought their instruments and skills with them from Central European countries and continued to ply their trade in the islands. A present-day example is the Danish composer and pianist Kristian Blak (b. 1947). Trained at the Music Department of Aarhus University in Denmark, he went to the Faroes when he was twenty-five years old and is now a major influence in local musical life (figure 2). He is responsible for the development of formal institutions, including the Havnar Jazzfelag (Tórshavn Jazzclub), Spælimenninir í Hoydølum (Players of Hoydølum, a folk-music organization), the record company TUTL (which produces three series: jazz and rock, folk, and classical), and the pan-Nordic performance group Yggdrasil. Most of his recordings, including the music for two ballets, have been made by Yggdrasil. In 1989, he collaborated with Faroese and Icelandic artists for the production of *Harra Pætur og Elinborg,* his interpretation of an ancient Faroese ballad about stalwart young women who force a wayward lover back to his homeland and his betrothed.

The movement for pan-Nordic cooperation is symbolized in Tórshavn by the presence of the Nordic Cultural Centre, the setting for the premiere performances of Blak's ballets. Immigrant artists make up part of a semiprofessional symphony orchestra, the Føroya Symphony Orchestra, founded by a Danish violinist (Kanny Sambleben) and a Norwegian clarinetist (Magne Synnevåg). Pioneer rock bands in the 1960s, such as The Faroe Boys, were purposely imitative in style; an independent tradition that includes Faroese lyrics has begun to develop. Small groups have been formed to play in a wide variety of idioms, from funk to rock and jazz to new music. Plúmm, which has tried all of them, is perhaps the most famous; its guitarist, Lejvar Thomsen, is highly regarded as a jazz composer. Other contemporary Faroese rock bands include Devon and Frændur.

INSTITUTIONS FOR CULTURE AND MUSIC

Though higher education in most fields usually takes place outside the islands, the study of Faroese language and literature (of increasing interest to Faroese nationals and outside scholars) may best be accomplished in the islands. For education and research, the Fróðskaparsetur Føroya (Faroese Academy of Higher Learning) was founded in Tórshavn in 1965 and later accorded official status as a university. The Føroya Fróðskaparfelag (Faroese Scientific Society), founded in 1952 to provide cooperation in all fields of learning, has published books on Faroese culture. Its official organ, the yearly periodical *Fróðskaparrit,* is published in Faroese with English translations.

Local book publishing began with the bookseller H. N. Jacobsen in 1870, and the twentieth century has seen the development of publishing companies, including Fróðskaparfelag, which concentrates on the arts and publishes the country's leading literary journal, *Vardin.* Faroese radio communication began with the founding of Útvarp Føroya in 1957. In 1978, when private, local TV companies began to transmit foreign programs, the Faroe Islands became one of the last countries in Europe to acquire television. Sjónvarp Føroya (the public Faroese television station) began transmitting in 1984; it still operates on a limited basis, broadcasting only certain hours on select days of the week.

BIBLIOGRAPHY

Andreassen, Eyðn. 1986. *Úv Søgn og Søgu.* Tórshavn: Føroya Skúlabókagrunnur.

———. 1991. "Strofeformev, rytme og metrum i balladediktningen." *Fróðkaparrit* 26:33–51.

———. 1995. "Folkelig kultur på massemedias daasovðen." In *Nostalgi og sensasjoners: Folklorisk perspektiv på mediekulturen,* 223–245.

———, et al. 1995. *Alfagurt ljóðav min tunga.* Tórhavn: Føroya Skúlabókagrunnur.

Blak, Kristian, with Erhard Jacobsen. 1992. "Jazz í Føroyum." *Jazz Tídindí* 2:14–16.

Conroy, Patricia. 1978. "Snioluv Kvaði: The Growth of a Ballad Cycle." *Fróðskaparrit* 26:33–53.

———. 1979. "Ballad Composition in Faroese Heroic Tradition: The Case of Hernilds *Kvæði.*" *Fróðskaparrit* 27:73–101.

Debes, Lucas. 1676. *Færoiæ et Færoa reserata: that Is, A Description of the Islands and Inhabitants of Færoe.* Translated by J. Sterpin. London: W. Isles.

Dhurhuus, Napoleon, Christian Matras, et al., eds. 1951–1972. *Foroya Kvæði: Corpus carminum Færoensium.* 6 vols. Copenhagen: Einar Munksgaard [vols. 1–3]; Akademisk Forlag [vols. 4–6]; and Universitets-Jubilaeets Danske Samfund [all vols.].

Fjeldsøe, Michael. 1993–1994. "En nordisk naturlyriker: Et trait af komponisten Sunleif Rasmussen." *Dansk Musik Tidsskrift* 7:234–239.

Galvin, Seán. 1989. *The Many Faces of Satiric Ballads in the Faroe Islands: Identity Formation, National Pride and Charter for Everyday Life.* Bloomington: Indiana University Press.

Grinde, Nils. 1991. *A History of Norwegian Music.* 3d ed. Translated by William Halversen and Leland Sateren. Lincoln: University of Nebraska Press.

Hammershaimb, Venceslaus Ulricus, ed. 1891a. *Færöiske Kvæder.* Copenhagen: Det Nordiske Literatur-Samfund.

———. 1891b. *Færøsk Anthologi.* 2 vols. Copenhagen: S. L. Møller (Møller and Thomsen). Facsmile edition, 1969. Tórshavn: Hammershaimbsgrunnarin.

Haugen, Einar. 1981. "Foreword." In *The Ring of Dancers: Images of Faroese Culture,* by Jonathan Wylie and David Margolin, xiii–xx. Philadelphia: University of Pennsylvania Press.

Henriksen, Jeffrei. 1992. *Kvæða- og vísuskrá.* Tórshavn: Føroya Skúlabókagrunnur.

Joensen, Joan Pauli. 1980. *Faroisk folkkultur: en oversikt.* Lund: Liber Laromedal.

Johannesen, Marius. 1978 [1966–1974]. *Tættir.*

Vols. 1–3. Tórshavn: Tingakrossur. 1, *Nólsoyar Páll,* 1966. 2, *Hoyberatáttur, Brókartáttur, Lorvókspáll, Ananiasartáttur,* 1969. 3, *Simunartáttur and other tættir.*

———. 1978 [1974]. *Tættir.* Vols 4–6. Tórshavn: Grønalið.

Jóhansen, Johannes. 1971. "A Paleobotanical Study Indicating a Pre-Viking Settlement in Tjørnuvík, Faroe Islands." *Fróðskaparrit* 19:147–157.

Johnston, George, ed. and trans. 1975. *The Faroe Islanders' Saga.* Ottawa: Oberon.

Ketting, Knud. 1989. "Kristian Blak." *Nordic Sounds* (March), 6–7.

Knudsen, Thorkild. 1968. *Ornamental Hymn-Psalm Singing in Denmark, the Faroe Islands and the Hebrides.* DFS Information, 68/2. Copenhagen: Danish Folklore Archives.

———. 1980. "Faeroes." In *The New Grove,* ed. Stanley Sadie. London: Macmillan.

Lindholm, Steen. 1990. "Music in the Faroes." *Musical Denmark* 43(2):2–7.

Louis-Jensen, Jonna. 1992. "Om Ólif og Landrés, vers og prosa samt kuìnder og poefer." In *Eyvindarbok: Festskrift til Eyvind Fjeld Halvorsen,* ed. Finn Hødnebø et al., 217–230. Oslo

Luihn, Astrid. 1980. *Føroyskur dansur: Studier i sangdanstradisjonen på Færøyene.* Trondheim: Prådet for folkemusikk og folkedans.

Metcalfe, Frederick. 1861. *The Oxonian in Iceland.* London: Longman & Roberts.

Nolsøe, Mortan. 1977. "The Faroese Dance: The Poetry." *Faroe Isles Review* 2(2):29–33.

———. 1985. "The Heroic Ballad in Faroese Tradition." In *The Heroic Process: Form, Function and Fantasy in Folk Epic,* 395–412. Proceedings of the International Folk Epic Conference, University College, Dublin.

O'Neil, Wayne. 1970. "The Oral-Formulaic Structure of the Faroese *Kvæði.*" *Fróðdskaparrit* 18:59–68.

Schiørring, Nils. 1980. "Denmark, II, Folk Music, parts 1–4." In *The New Grove,* ed. Stanley Sadie. London: Macmillan.

Steenstrup, Johannes. 1968 [1914]. *The Medieval Popular Ballad.* Translated by Edward Cox. Seattle and London: University of Washington Press.

Thuren, Hjalmar. 1908. *Folkesangen paa Færøerne.* Copenhagen: A. F. Höst & Sons forlag.

Thuren, Hjalmar, and H. Gruner Nielsen. 1923. *Færöske melodier til danske kæmpeviser.* Copenhagen: I kommission hos J. H. Schultz Forlag.

West, John F. 1972. *Faroe: The Emergence of a Nation*. London and New York: C. Hurst & Paul S. Eriksson.

Wylie, Jonathan, and David Margolin. 1981. *The Ring of Dancers: Images of Faroese Culture*. Philadelphia: University of Pennsylvania Press.

———. 1987. *The Faroe Islands: Interpretation of History*. Lexington, Ky.: University Press of Kentucky.

AUDIOVISUAL RESOURCES

Blak, Kristian. 1984. *Yggdrasil: Concerto Grosso*. SHD 7. LP disk.

———. 1988. *Antiphonale*. HJF 20. LP disk.

Blak, Kristian, and Sunleif Rasmussen. 1991. *Avaringar*. FKT 4. Compact disc.

———, et al. 1993. *Boreas*. FKT 6. Compact disc.

Laumann, Holger, and Plúmm. 1991. *Allar Ættir*. HJF 25. Compact disc.

Spælimenninir. 1984. *Rekavidur*. SHD 7. LP disk.

Finland

Timo Leisiö

Traditional Singing and Genres of Song
Musical Instruments
Music Education and Transmission
Conceptions of Music
History of Music
Contemporary Musical Life
Ethnic Minorities
History of Scholarship

Finland (*Suomi* in Finnish) is a republic of five million people, of whom more than three hundred thousand are Swedes and other minorities. Finnish, one of the few non–Indo European languages in Europe, belongs to the Finnic branch of the Uralic language family, which includes Hungarian and Samoyed, a Siberian tongue. Other Baltic Finnic groups include Karelians, Veps, Votyans, Ingrians, Estonians, and Livonians; ethnic relatives also include the Saami of Saamiland, and the Mordvins and Maris of Russia's Volga basin.

A province of Sweden from 1150 to 1809, and of Russia from 1809 to 1917, Finland first became an independent country in 1917. Finland can be divided into three basic cultural zones: the west, influenced by Western Europe; the east, influenced by Eastern Europe and Russians via Karelia, an area in Finland and Russia; and the north, a zone of mixed Saami, Finno-Karelian, and Scandinavian elements. Older cultural elements survive mainly in the east, in the north, and in Russian Karelia; modern influence has entered primarily through the southern ports: Turku, Viipuri, and Helsinki.

TRADITIONAL SINGING AND GENRES OF SONG

The oldest Finnish genres of song are the lament (*itku* 'cry, weep') and the song (*runo* or *laulu*). The underlying structure of both genres is a tetrachordal or pentachordal scale (C–D–E–F–G) with an unstable third degree, sung minor, major, and neutral, sometimes in the same song. (The *kantele,* the Finnish zither, is also tuned to a pentachordal scale.) The *runo* scale is sometimes expanded by the addition of a fourth below the tonic and a neutral sixth, a major seventh, and an octave above it. The song and lament are sung syllabically.

The Karelian *itku* has no fixed textual meter. The singer starts on a high note and descends slowly to the tonic—a gesture repeated several times in improvised, heterometric lines (figure 1). Containing mythic elements, laments convey symbolic expressions outside normal language. Women lamented departures in life and at death, especially when, as in Russia, the bride bade her home farewell and left for the bridegroom's house. Lamenting was a socially regulated way to express sorrow for

In the 1520s, when Sweden became a Protestant country, the Finns received from Germany new kinds of modal, and later tonal, songs with rhymed texts organized into stanzas. Many of the melodies, used as psalm tunes by the church, were borrowed from the popular love songs and ballads of the 1400s to 1600s.

FIGURE 1   Excerpt from a Karelian lament (*itku*), consisting of a series of descending phrases of various lengths.

weeks or months after death and a protection against destructive supernatural powers. Traditionally, the Karelian lament was restricted to women. All other genres were sung, and many instruments were played, by men and women, though semiprofessional wedding musicians were exclusively male. Children's songs included lullabies and chain songs with texts in Kalevala meter; many are still performed, but usually sung by adults.

Strictly metric, the *runo* is the genre in which the text of the Finno-Karelian epic, Kalevala, was sung. Kalevala songs were used in all social occasions, from feasts and rituals to work and amusement. The textual meter consists of four trochaic feet: the first foot may have two, three, or four syllables, and the others have two syllables; hence, each line is composed of eight, nine, or ten syllables and melodic notes. The musical form was iterative: the singer repeated one isometric line (AAAA), or he would repeat two isometric lines that differed from each other (ABABAB). Since the 1700s, the basic unit of structure has become a four-line stanza (ABCB). In Finland, the musical meter used to be 5/4 or 5/8 and 2/4 (figure 2), but mixed meters were also usual, especially in Karelia. *Runo* texts in both genres employed alliteration, but not rhyme. Because the main stress in Finnish is always on the first syllable, upbeats

FIGURE 2 Three
Kalevala melodies:
a, East Finnish
tetrachordal melody;
b, East Finnish pen-
tachordal pastoral
song; *c,* West
Finnish cradle song,
with an octave range
in A minor. After
*Suomen Kansan
Sävelniä,* vol. 4.

are virtually nonexistent, and a stressed syllable tends to have a higher pitch than an unstressed one. Song texts in Kalevala meter have four feet per line:

Is-ki ker-ran, is-ki toi-sen.   He struck it once, he struck it twice.

Kalevala song texts include mythic, magical, and shamanic themes, sea adventures from the Viking age (ca. A.D. 800–1000), Christian legends, ballads, and dance-songs.

In the 1520s, when Sweden became a Protestant country, the Finns received from Germany new kinds of modal, and later tonal, songs with rhymed texts organized into stanzas. Many of the melodies, used as psalm tunes by the church, were borrowed from the popular love songs and ballads of the 1400s to 1600s. These new melodic principles, rhyme, and the structural principles of runos evolved into a new Finnish genre, *rekilaulu* (round-dance song), in which melodies are modal, major, or mixed. The musical meter is usually 2/4 or 4/4, the last two syllables sung with a double duration (figure 3). Many genres originated in instrumental dance rhythms: the *polska,* for example, spawned corresponding *polska* songs with characteristic verse meter. *Reki* meter has seven feet per line, with a variable number of unstressed syllables per foot. The lines below share a structure of 4 + 3 feet and an assonantal end rhyme, here italicized:

Kak-si mark-kaa mull on ra-haa, | puo-let sii-tä on *vel-kaa.* |
En-kös tyt-tö mam-mal-le-si, | vä-vy-po-jaks *kel-paa?*

I've got two dollars in my pocket, | half of it indebted.
Ain't I quite a guy, my darling, | to be a son-in-law to your mom?

FIGURE 3 West
Finnish love song in
rekilaulu style.

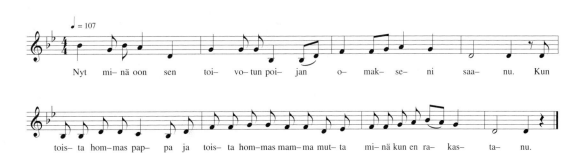

Rekilaulu, whether lyric or epic, recount historical tales of people and events. Since the metric structure of *rekilaulu* was used to improvise texts, and since any text of *rekilaulu* could be applied to any melody in mazurka rhythm, mazurka songs became popular around 1900. This poetic structure is still evident in popular music; for example, the text for a punk-rock melody from the early 1980s, "*Meidän stadi*" ('Our City'), by Ralf Örn, uses the *rekilaulu* seven-foot structure with upbeats, characteristic of newer forms.

The Finno-Karelian style of singing is characterized by a relaxed voice in mid-register. The tempo is rather slow. The melody is not embellished, except in the singing of members of a Lutheran folk movement, the revivalists (*heränneet*), who decorate their performance of psalms. Singing used to be solo or in collective unison until the 1800s, when mixed four-part choirs became popular.

MUSICAL INSTRUMENTS

Musical instruments were played mostly by men, although women working as shepherds played wind instruments such as animal horns. Women avoided acting as dance musicians, mainly because part of the salary was often paid as alcohol; in the late twentieth century, however, women play every instrument. Finland had no folk ensembles before the 1800s, when clarinet, violin, and later brass ensembles became popular. In the 1940s, a newer ensemble—two violins, plucked double bass, and school organ—developed in the western village of Kaustinen. Since the late 1960s, it has become the model for many players of old fiddle tunes (figure 4).

More than three hundred older, local dialectal names for musical instruments persist. Some, like *soittu* 'a sounding one', belong to the indigenous vocabulary; others are of Proto-Germanic, German, Scandinavian, or East Slavic origin. Only three instruments, however, are widespread among Finns and Karelians: *torvi,* a natural trumpet, made of cow horn (or ox horn), or birch bark (or alder bark); *pilli,* a reed pipe or simple clarinet; and a duct flute made of willow wood. These were used for signaling, or for summoning people, and for the magical control of animals.

FIGURE 4   The group JPP from Kaustinen. *From left:* Timo Alakotila, Janne Virkkala, Matti Mäkelä, Tommi Pyykönen, Mauno Järvelä, Arto Järvelä. Photo by Aki Paavola, 1995. Courtesy of the Archive of the Kaustinen Folk Music Institute.

FIGURE 5   A musician plays a nine-stringed *kantele* in 1917. Photographer unknown. Courtesy of the National Museum of Finland.

A fourth common instrument might have been the zither known as *kantele,* but its practice ceased in western Finland after the 1600s (figure 5). Used to accompany singing, and possibly for magical purposes, it disappeared in the west when Finns there learned social dances accompanied by violin (*viulu*), the main musical instrument to appear before the accordion. Another stringed instrument, a bowed lyre (*jouhikko*), was mainly East Finnish and South Karelian, though it may have had a western origin. Most *kantele* and *jouhikko* transcriptions are Karelian dance tunes, and in the twentieth century Finland and Karelia have experienced a significant *kantele* revival.

Some instruments have symbolic associations. The *torvi* implies the meaning "a simple-minded and awkward fellow," and the harp (*harppu*) implies the meaning "an older female with a sharp tongue." Some had predictable Christian associations: the *kantele* and harp, for instance, were heavenly instruments. In the early 1800s, the *kantele* was chosen as the symbol of Finnish culture. Many religious movements accepted neither the dance nor the fiddle, and even the accordion was called "the Devil's lungs."

At the end of the 1800s, powerful social, political, and cultural mass movements, such as socialism and secular enlightenment, arose. Each of these movements expressed itself musically by means of brass bands, which became a symbol of the new ideas, just as new kinds of personal freedom were expressed by drum sets in the 1930s, saxophones in the 1950s, and electric guitars since the 1960s. Since the 1940s, educated urbanites in the south of Finland began to look down on the popular accordion as a symbol of romanticized folk music, and lovers of art music have long abhorred it. In contrast, these classes tend to view the piano, the organ, and the violin as symbols of civilization, toward which Finnish backwoodsmen might develop with the help of enlightened projects.

MUSIC EDUCATION AND TRANSMISSION

Though most people of Finland could read and write since the mid-1700s, musical transmission among them was aural. The publication of broadside ballads with nota-

Playing instruments was mainly aural magic, not music. The louder the noise, the better the player. Farmers and cattle breeders would blow sounds to ensure the fertility of the crop, attract a good-luck snake, produce winds or storms, and ensure the safety of cattle.

tion began in 1622, but only in the early 1800s did publishing song collections with notation become profitable. People learned texts and melodies, and the techniques to improvise them, by imitation. The *itku*, the *runo*, and the *rekilaulu* had clear and easy rules for spontaneous and endless invention. In the late twentieth century, however, few people had the skill to improvise melodies and texts in traditional genres; such skill had passed into the domain of rock music.

Because of negative religious attitudes toward instrumental music, especially in western Finland, parents declined to pass on their skills to their children. Children had to listen to them in secret, or learn from someone outside the family. To remember dance melodies in the absence of notation, musicians invented an often bawdy text for the beginning of a tune. Some highly talented fiddlers in the early 1900s were reluctant to transmit their skills to youngsters since they earned their living as wandering musicians. It was not until the revival of old dance music after 1968 that people had systematic training in folk music. Since the early 1970s, training was arranged by many newly organized associations, such as the Finnish Fiddlers' Club (*Suomen pelimanniyhdistys*) and Central Organization for Folk Music (*Kansanmusiikin keskusliitto*). In summers, the Ala-Könni Academy in Turku, with the Folk Music Institute, offers special classes on folk and older popular music, including instruction in improvising, playing instruments, and dancing.

CONCEPTIONS OF MUSIC

Finnish has no native term for music. People began to use the term *musiikki* in the early twentieth century after learning it at school. Because the main function of sonic activities was practical communication, the product, whether *musikki* or song, was not so important as the process of singing or playing. The situation is reversed at present; music is chiefly regarded as someone's output and is protected by a complex system of copyrights.

Finns created musical sound mostly for practical and perhaps magical purposes: playing an instrument attracted male birds to a fowler; singing lulled a child to sleep or lent a common rhythm to a working group. The original meaning of *laulaa* 'to sing' was 'to enchant', and the enchanting was carried out with spoken or sung magical formulas in Kalevala meter. Every song (*laulu*) could be called *runo,* a loanword from Proto-Germans, who knew it as *rúnó* 'secrecy' (it may also be cognate with Old Norse *rún*) more than two thousand years ago. Since the age of the words *runo* and *laulu* is similar, the meaning of the Bronze Age Proto-Finnic *laulaa* may have been 'to enchant someone (with a help of secret formulas in Kalevala meter).' The lament (*itku*) is always sung, but it is never 'singing', rather 'crying'. It was also termed *virsi,* which refers to a Lutheran psalm in modern Finnish.

People enjoyed a beautiful voice, but singers were not respected if they did not have knowledge of magical powers. The more words a singer knew, the greater the respect he or she would command; a person with above-average knowledge was called *tietäjä* 'knower, soothsayer'. Contests were arranged to see who could sing the longest, and the music was less important then the text.

Playing instruments was mainly aural magic, not music. The louder the noise (or the longer the bark trumpet), the better the player. Instrumental magic was especially important to farmers and cattle breeders; they would blow ("speak out") sounds to ensure the fertility of the crop, sound a free double reed (wild-chervil pipe) to attract a good-luck snake, play small bark flutes to produce winds or storms, and rattle all manner of idiophones to ensure the safety of cattle.

The *kantele* is an exception to this notion of musical instrument as magical noisemaker. According to myths sung in Kalevala meter, it was invented by the hero Väinämöinen, by making it from wood or fish bones lying on the seabed. When he invented *kantele* music, it sounded so beautiful and emotional that all living things in the sky, forest, and water came to listen to his playing with tears in their eyes; thus the *kantele* was sometimes called *ilo* 'joy'. This myth expresses a musical aesthetic completely different from the one the Balto-Finnic nations knew at the time of its adoption, presumably from the Black Sea area, in the first millennium B.C. The concept of composer, moreover, was unknown in Finno-Karelian folk culture, since nothing was more natural than to create music by improvisation. The music (*soitto* 'improvisation') was played without end, and players did not dampen their strings after plucking, but let them ring.

Since the 1600s, new musical instruments, social dances, and songs with composed texts divided into stanzas and with heptatonic melodies were adopted. The largest collections of musical instruments are in the Sibelius Museum (Turku), the Department of Folk Tradition in Tampere University, the National Museum (Helsinki), and the Finnish Museum of Folk Music Instruments (Kaustinen). Ethnographic data (manuscripts, photos, tape recordings and videos) are mostly in the Department of Folk Culture, Finnish Literature Society, and the Finland-Swedish Archive of Folk Culture (Helsinki).

HISTORY OF MUSIC

Because Finland's soil has lost most of its calcium, it preserves virtually no cultural traces from before the late Middle Ages. A sonorous stone in Karelia may be prehistoric; five-thousand-year-old rock paintings, however, lack depiction of musical instruments. Some nine-thousand-year-old bones may have been used as side-blown flutes [see ARCHAEOLOGY OF MUSIC IN EUROPE]. The earliest unambiguous duct flute made of bone comes from Ahvenanmaa in southwestern Finland and belongs to the West European, bone-flute belt of about A.D. 1000. A side-blown flute with two finger holes, dating from the early 1500s, and a tiny pocket fiddle perhaps used by a seventeenth-century dancing master, have been found in Turku.

Since Swedish was the official language for centuries, scant written documents in Finnish exist before the 1800s. Roman Catholicism was introduced to the Turku area by a Swedish crusade of 1155, and priests composed texts sung in Kalevala meter. Somewhat earlier, the Karelians had become Greek Orthodox; they sang their ritual music in Russian, though some traits of Karelian laments (like repetitions of the final) were adopted. The first compositions in a Western style date from the 1100s. Some form part of *Piae Cantiones* (Devotional Songs), a medieval collection of male students' songs in Turku; it was printed in mensural notation in 1582. Sixteenth-century Swedish documents chronicle music in the castle of Turku (Swedish Åbo) and the beginnings of Lutheran liturgical singing, but they do not record the music of forest-dwelling Finns, or that of Orthodox Karelians.

Lutheranism came to Finland in the 1500s and had a profound effect on tradition. Lutherans banned Kalevala singing as the main source of pagan culture. As people abandoned this tradition, they adopted new ones from western Finland, such as dancing to the accompaniment of violins, new rhyming stanzaic structures for texts, and a new tonal system.

Until the late 1600s, formal education was limited to about 5 percent of the Finnish population. During the 1600s, mostly uneducated Lutheran cantors taught people Lutheran psalms—a process that created melodic variants in each congregation. The first psalm book with musical notation was published in 1702, but denominational agreement on the melodies was not reached until the late 1800s. The number of schools increased during and after the 1600s, when primary schools were founded in every parish; the teaching of psalms remained the principal subject of education until the late 1800s. The best schooling system existed in the army, which fought almost continuously for two centuries until the 1740s, especially against the Russians. The peaceful era that began in 1743 saw the founding of a musical ensemble at the Academy in Turku, where several public concerts were offered in 1774, the first given in Finland. The educational system was reorganized in the late 1800s, and the first conservatory and symphony orchestra were founded in Helsinki in 1882. Today, Finland has some music high schools and more than 130 music colleges (*musiikkiopisto*).

Erik Tulindberg (1761–1814), who composed six string quartets in the style of Haydn and Mozart, is regarded as the first Finnish composer. The German violist and composer Fredrik Pacius (1809–1891), who came to Helsinki in the early 1830s, brought with him a South German folk song that became the national anthem of Finland in 1848. Another German, Filip von Schantz (1834–1865), was the first in Finland to write an orchestral overture, which he named *Kullervo* after a tragic character in the old *runo*. In 1890, Richard Faltin (d. 1918) composed the first large vocal composition based on the Kalevala; he arranged many Finnish folk songs. Karl Collan, a Finn (d. 1871) and Pacius's son-in-law, pioneered as a collector and arranger of East Finnish folk melodies in a style suitable to the upper classes.

Jean Sibelius (1865–1957), a Finnish Swede who is the founder of the Finnish national romantic style, is the greatest native composer of modern times. Influenced by Karelian and Ingrian songs and the Kalevala, he did not use *runo* melodies as such, but preferred elements of their modal style, especially the dorian mode. Finns immediately identified his personal style as Finnish, and his seven symphonies, violin concerto, symphonic poems such as *Tapiola* (Mythic Forest), and songs are widely admired in Finland as the first truly native compositions. Inspired by modern French music, Uuno Klami wrote music based on national elements, such as *Kalevala Suite* (1932), *Lemminkäinen* (1934), and *Fantaisie Tschérémisse* (1931) based on Mari melodies.

Industrialization began in the 1860s, and mass movements initiated cultural, political, and social changes that tended to homogenize Finnish life. In the east and north, the violin, adopted in the 1800s, replaced the bowed lyre, and the eastern Finnish Kalevala tradition started to decline. During the 1800s, when the upper classes sought political and national independence, they developed contradictory attitudes toward rural, traditional music. On the one hand, they used Karelian *runo* as a symbolic weapon to unite Finns against the Russian government and against Swedes in Finland; on the other hand, these classes viewed rural music and culture as hopelessly backward, and consciously used the educational system to enculturate the younger generation in the values of urban culture.

At the end of the 1700s, new organizations promoting socialism, temperance, folk and youth enlightenment, and voluntary fire brigades were founded. To attract members, they formed musical ensembles and composed songs based on European art-music models. The musical style was the same for each group; only the texts dif-

fered to reflect the ideology. These songs acted as symbols for collective ideology, and
thereby introduced this style of music to rural folks, who, from the 1880s, sang them
in mixed choirs and played them in horn septets. Even the smallest villages had horn
septets, one for a right-wing organization, another for a socialist one (figure 6).
Modernized folk music and, since the 1920s, popular music were viewed by many in
the upper classes as a threat to national unity and these ideologies. Little has changed
in this area of culture since the 1930s.

In rural and urban areas since the late 1800s, thousands of choirs, horn orchestras, and classical-music ensembles were founded. Jazz (*jatsi*) and the tango became
popular in the mid-1920s. In Helsinki, Turku, and Vyborg, youths played jazz (ragtime, foxtrots) in bands modeled on German groups and a Finnish-American group
that visited Helsinki in 1926. In 1925, young workers founded a band, Dallappé,
that made recordings and traveled around the country into the 1930s. Dallappé
spread their own version of jazz, mixing elements of American foxtrot, polkalike
dances, *rekilaulu,* and Russian romances. This style is now known as *humppa*;
because one of its major instruments was the accordion, it is also called accordion
jazz (figure 7). The Finnish tango employs slow, intimate movements, without the
elaborate poses of the Argentinian original. *Humppa* involves lively movements taken
over from the charleston, the polka, and the two-step. About 1900, many mass
movements, even in small villages, financed themselves by arranging *iltamat,* public
entertainment concluding with a one-hour dance; because of television, this tradition
ceased in the late 1950s.

Until the end of the 1800s, the official language in Finland was Swedish, and the
social distinction between Finnish-speaking peasants (so-called forest folk) and
Swedish-speaking upper classes (priests, nobles, bourgeoisie) was explicit and deep.
Each group had its own musical traditions. The Finns despised the nobility and their
culture. As a result of centuries-old mistrust, though the social system has changed
radically during the past hundred years, many rural and working-class people still
view art music as a nonsensical, upper-class tradition. No longer a class-based activi-

Wedding customs used to consist of two or three days of celebration, led by a fiddler, as a symbol of a family's prosperity. The only ceremonial music today is a church-organ wedding march and a waltz danced by the couple to open the celebration.

FIGURE 7   The jazz band Humina ('Ramble') from a village in southwest Finland, 1930s. Photographer unknown.

ty, concert music still functions as a symbol of social and economic power, of influential religious and scientific institutions, and of the state. The only musical genre that competes for prestige with art music is traditional folk music, conceived as Finnish in character.

By the early 1900s, a clear distinction between rural and urban traditions had emerged. Everything old was labeled birch-bark culture and consciously exchanged for new, European, and American innovations. In Russian Karelia, however, older elements are still culturally active. Finns who wish to learn about rural traditions must go to Karelia, or to archives. The main urban-rural differences center around repertoire and venue. In the countryside, dancers represent all generations, dance in outdoor pavilions, gather at bars with a jukebox in the local gas station, and continue to enjoy older fiddle music, the accordion, and dances (*humppa,* polka, schottische, tango, waltz).

After World War II, the main trends have included an intensified contact with the United States, the coming of rock, and the strengthening of music education and public support for research into music and the arts. Rock sung in Finnish began to sound like punk rock since the late 1970s and is covered by a number of journals: *Soundi* (Sound), *Blues News, Ratbeat, Rumba,* and *Suosikki* (Fave). Since the early 1970s, radio programs and ethnic records have led to the appearance of world-music bands, and opera experienced a boom starting in the late 1970s.

CONTEMPORARY MUSICAL LIFE

Finland is divided into 461 communes, most with two thousand to eight thousand

FIGURE 8   The folk group Tallari with harmonium (*left*), *kantele,* bowed lyres, idioglot clarinets, and bark trumpets. Courtesy of the Archive of the Kaustinen Folk Music Institute, 1988.

FIGURE 8   The folk group Tallari with harmonium (*left*), *kantele,* bowed lyres, idioglot clarinets, and bark trumpets. Courtesy of the Archive of the Kaustinen Folk Music Institute, 1988.

inhabitants and a church choir, two or more mixed or male choirs, a dance or rock band, a folk-music group, and at least one ensemble or orchestra playing classical music. Amateur singers, musicians, and dancers number more than a hundred thousand. One professional folk-music ensemble, Tallari, performs practically all the Finno-Karelian genres of folk music (figure 8). A few professional orchestras for symphonic, theatrical, and operatic music work in Helsinki, Turku, and Tampere. Most classical performers—singers including Karita Mattila, Tom Krause, Tero Hannula, and Martti Talvela (d. 1990), and conductors including Leif Seferstam, Jukka Pekka Saraste, Esa-Pekka Salonen, and Okko Kamu—work abroad. Jazz is no longer as popular in Finland as it once was, but a few musicians, like Heikki Sarmanto, are highly skilled. Performers of *humppa,* tango, and rock, like Juice Leskinen, are popular with fans.

In the 1990s, music represented a variety of worldviews, stamped with extramusical associations: concert music stood for political, social, and artistic authority; African-American styles, for personal freedom of youth; Latin American music, for the right to bodily communication; jazz, for intelligence; Russian romance- or march-based popular music, for left-wing steadfastness; old-fashioned fiddle music, for the right of different value systems to coexist; and new folk music, for so-called green values.

May Day—a springtime festival for workers, university, and polytechnic students—is an open-air occasion when political parties demonstrate their power through public speeches and the symbolic music of horn orchestras and collective singing. On Midsummer Eve (*juhannus,* 21 June), when the sun does not set, rural people gather in lakeshore dance pavilions. The month before Christmas, Little Christmas, is a season of feasting, drinking, and dancing.

Wedding customs used to consist of two or three days of celebration, led by a fiddler, as a symbol of a family's prosperity. Now, a young couple typically organizes its own half-day party. The only ceremonial music today is a church-organ wedding march and a waltz danced by the couple to open the celebration.

In the 1990s, tango and *humppa* were still the favorite dances of those who do not like rock, and dance is one of the most popular forms of entertainment, in spite of having once been regarded as a sinful activity by many religious movements.

Restaurants, athletic clubs, and associations, to finance their other functions, organize dances. Restaurants offer afternoon dances for pensioners, ladies'-choice dances, and evening dances. Music may be played on tape, as in discos, or by Finnish or foreign bands. An older type of dance band, consisting of accordion, bass guitar, drum set, and perhaps a synthesizer, plays *humppa,* tango, waltz, and Latin American music.

In June, July, and August, more than three thousand summer festivals, most organized around music, take place. The most important are held in Tampere, Mäntsälä, and the small village of Kaustinen in northwestern Finland, the last a nine-day affair. Festivals for popular and accordion music take place in Ikaalinen and Hyvinkää; other festivals feature classical music, jazz, rock, world music, *humppa,* tango, and dance, including folk dance in Haapavesi. Because Finns frequently travel abroad, some Mediterranean idioms, such as Greek dances, have become popular. Tourism in Finland itself, however, has had no discernible effect on the content or practice of music.

Until the mid-1980s, Finland had only one radio company, Finnish Broadcasting Company, a noncommercial service, which began in 1926 and is still the nation's largest. Now there are fifty-four local radio companies, including, in Tampere, University Radio, whose broadcasts consist mainly of music. The leading Finnish record company, Fazer Musiikki, produces many labels and acts as an agent for Polygram. Smaller companies specializing in folk music include the Folk Music Institute and Olarin Musiikki Oy.

Interest in folk music intensified after 1968, when instruction in it, led by Heikki Laitinen, a researcher, composer, and singer, began at the Sibelius Academy. All kinds of musical instruments are now combined, and musical elements from different parts of the world have been joined with Finno-Karelian elements to produce a neofolk music that is distinctly national in character. In the 1990s, the group Värttinä became popular at home and abroad. Consisting of four young female singers accompanied by a folk-rock band that adds *kantele,* violin, and accordion to the usual guitar, bass, and drums, Värttinä make their own arrangements of songs they collected in Russian Karelia and among other Finnic groups in Russia. They also compose songs based on these styles and on Finnish archival collections. They sing forcefully in the open-throated style associated with East European and Balkan singing, employ traditional and neotraditional drone-based polyphony, revel in the asymmetric meters of traditional styles, and dress and behave on stage like a contemporary pop group.

ETHNIC MINORITIES

About three hundred thousand Karelians, who speak a language close to Finnish, emigrated from Soviet Karelia to Finland after World War II. They have assimilated into Finnish culture, with the exception of their Eastern Orthodox liturgical music. In Finland's Karelia region, elements of older folk music, such as singing in Kalevala style and playing *kantele,* is kept alive as a folkloristic phenomenon.

About twenty-five hundred Saami people live in Finland's far north, in close contact with nature; their music belongs to an arctic, circumpolar zone that includes the musics of Siberian and native American peoples. They divide into three groups. The eastern Skolts number about five hundred, and their main genre, *lev'dd,* consists of epic songs about animals, nature, and past events. Songs are complex, varied rhythmically, improvised on a three-to-eight-note scale, often recitative in character, some with unequal line lengths. The texts are difficult to understand, since the order of syllables in a word may be changed, and special filling syllables may be added to a word. Traditional songs are almost extinct among the central Inari Saami, but they

FIGURE 9 Saami joik singer Wimme Saari performs with banjo and bass clarinet at the 1997 Rudolstadt Festival. Photo by Tapio Korus.

remain a vital part of culture among the reindeer-breeding Fjeld Saamis, who live in the west, near Norway. Their singing is termed joiking (*juoigan*). Unlike *lev'dd,* it is mostly pentatonic and without much improvisation, and the musical form consists usually of two or four short, repeated lines. The text has only a few words of everyday language, and most words are short expressions like *nun-nu-go* or *lol-lo,* whose meaning is kept secret from outsiders. Everyone has a personal joik, performed by his companions, usually not by the owner. A rich variety of joiks describe elements of nature such as animals, mountains, and rivers. The most famous Finnish joiker, Nils-Aslak Valkeapää, known as Aillohas, also an honored painter and poet, has expanded joiking by combining it with African-American elements and using various musical instruments with it (figure 9).

The Swedes in Finland form a large minority (about 310,000). Their ancestors migrated to the south and west coast of Finland in the 1200s, and to the Åland Islands (Ahvenanmaa) even earlier. Their music differs little from music in Sweden, but it differs from Finnish music in at least three ways: Swedes love triple meter, while Finns prefer duple meter; upbeats are typical among Swedes, but rare among Finns (a difference attributable to linguistic features); and Swedish folk ensembles were traditionally groups of violins without bass instruments or chordal accompaniment, while Finns have long used accordions and bass instruments in harmony. Finns adopted the first two elements since the 1920s and 1930s under the influence of an enormously popular musician, Georg Malmsten, a Finnish Swede, who sang waltz-like melodies in Swedish and Finnish. The Swedes have been active and influential in Finnish art and popular music on all levels.

Gypsy immigration from Sweden into Finland started in the late 1500s, and from Russia during the 1800s. These Gypsies did not play musical instruments, but had a repertoire of songs they sang to Finns for money. The oldest Gypsy songs resemble Finnish *rekilaulu* in structure but are sung with a sentimental vibrato, rather free use of rhythm, and in a phrygian hexachord (D–E♭–F–G–A–B♭). Though only sixty-five hundred Gypsies live in Finland, they are musically talented and have had a strong influence on Finnish popular music.

Jews began to immigrate to Finland from Russia at the end of the 1700s; currently, they number about 1,400 and preserve religious music and some Russian tunes sung in Yiddish; the Jewish Choir in Helsinki has contributed to their ethnic identity.

Russians settled in the Helsinki area about the time of the Russian Revolution in 1917, and today they number about five thousand. Russian styles had an appreciable effect on Finnish popular music. The Russian minority, while assimilating to Finnish culture, has kept its traditions alive through liturgical music and an active balalaika orchestra.

Since the late 1800s, about a thousand Mescher-Tatars have immigrated to southern Finland. They have special traditions, some connected to Islam, and some to Turkic traditions south of Kazan, Russia, where they still have cultural contacts. Though the old traditions of melismatic *ozyn köj* 'long tone', syllabic *kyska köj* 'short tone', short and spontaneously created *takmak,* and dance-songs are nearly forgotten, Soviet-Tatar elements such as their accordion-playing style are preserved in their popular music.

HISTORY OF SCHOLARSHIP

Turku Academy, founded in 1640, produced a few studies dealing with music. Literature from the 1500s to the 1800s contains sporadic data on the uses, magical functions, and texts of ancient *runo.* In 1766–1778, H. G. Porthan, a history professor, published the first academic study on Finnish folk song in his *De Poesi Fennica*

Emerging romantic nationalism of the 1800s created an interest in folk music among the ruling classes. The collecting and studying of Karelian *runo* functioned mostly to unite Finns into a nation and to provide them with a history in the absence of a written one.

(On Finnish Poetic Creation). Emerging romantic nationalism of the 1800s created an interest in folk music among the ruling classes. The collecting and studying of Karelian *runo* functioned mostly to unite Finns into a nation and to provide them with a history in the absence of a written one. In 1831, Carl Gottlund published the first study on folk music with notation (for *kantele* and horn).

Though melodies continued to be collected, the main interest was still in texts, written down mostly in Karelia and Ingria. In 1840, Elias Lönnrot published notations for forty-three Finnish and Karelian songs in *Kanteletar* (Lady Kantele), an anthology of lyric *runo*. Lönnrot, who undertook field collecting in Finland and Estonia, collated folk songs and in the process compiled the Kalevala, which appeared in 1835 and in a new, expanded edition in 1849. Nineteenth-century collectors wrote down only those melodies that satisfied art-music aesthetics and values, so only a fraction of the tradition is known—a state of affairs that continued into the 1960s and later. The notations of A. A. Borenius-Lähteenkorva, however, who wrote down more than a thousand melodies from the 1870s, are fairly reliable.

The academic study of folklore arrived with the Krohn family from Germany. Julius Krohn and his son Kaarle generated a comparative method, the so-called Finnish method, for studying the origin and distribution of song texts. Ilmari Krohn, Kaarle's brother, was the first to complete a Ph.D. dissertation on folk music (at Helsinki University, 1899), after studying Finnish Lutheran folk psalms; he also tried to solve the problem of classifying melodies. Objective research on upper-class musical traditions began in the 1890s.

In the early 1900s, Ilmari Krohn, an adjunct professor at Helsinki University between 1918 and 1935, coined a Finnish vocabulary of musical terms in his books on the theory of concert music. The first regular professor was Armas Otto Väisänen (1956–1961), the most prominent Finnish folk-music researcher of the century. In 1926, the Department of Musicology in Swedish-speaking Åbo Akademi, Turku, was established, with Otto Andersson as professor until 1946. The Finnish Society of Musicology (founded in 1916) has published the journal *Musiikki* since 1971.

Folk music was first collected mainly in eastern Finland, Karelia, Saamiland (Lappland), and among the Samoyeds and Finno-Ugric peoples living in Russia. The linguists Heikki Paasonen, working among the Mordvins in 1898, and K. F. Karjalainen, working among the Khantys (Ostyaks) in 1900, made the first phonograph recordings of music in Finland. Early objects of research were Balto-Finnic *runo* singing, melodies of the Khantys and Mansis near the Ob River, folk-musical instruments, Saami *lev'dd* and joik, Karelian *joik* and lament, fiddle music, and old notation books. Researchers showed little interest in West Finnish music (fiddle music, old books containing notation) until the 1940s, when Erkki Ala-Könni started intensive fieldwork in West Finland.

Ala-Könni (1956) was the first to use the word "ethnomusicology" in Finland, but it was not until the late 1960s that the concepts and methods of ethnomusicology were brought to Finland from the United States by Pekka Gronow, the first scholar to study popular music and the recording industry. Ethnomusicology started in Helsinki University in 1972 under the leadership of Philip Donner; thereafter, research was enlarged to embrace questions of musical worldview (through cognitive anthropology), the social, political, religious and national functions of music in large mass movements, and the music of continents such as Africa and Asia. New ideas were also adopted from semiotics and cognitive psychology. Pekka Jalkanen was the first to write a dissertation on the history of African-American musical appropriations in Finland. Few foreign scholars have treated Finnish music, with the exception of the Karelian lament (Tolbert 1990) and the *kantele* (Rahkonen 1989).

At present, the Department of Folk Tradition (founded 1974) at the University of Tampere has a leading role in ethnomusicology under professor Timo Leisiö; research extends to all musics and sociomusical phenomena through a theoretical pluralism. Special areas of research are popular music, the folk music of arctic and subarctic peoples (including Russians), the anthropology of dance, and organology. Research is also conducted in other universities, the Sibelius Academy, and five independent music-research institutes: the Folk Music Institute, the Folk Music Institute of Swedes in Finland, the World Music Institute, the Institute of Popular Music, and the Institute of Accordion Music. The Finnish Society for Ethnomusicology has published a journal, *Musiikin Suunta,* since 1979 and a bulletin since 1988.

BIBLIOGRAPHY

Aho, Kalevi. 1992. *After Sibelius: Finnish Music Past and Present.* Helsinki: Finnish Music Information Center.

Ala-Könni, Erkki. 1956. "Die Polska-Tänze in Finnland: Eine ethno-musikologische Untersuchung." Ph.D dissertation, Suomen muinaismuistoyhdistys.

———. 1969. "Kansanmusiikin keruun ja tutkimuksen vaiheita" (History of folk-music collection and research). *Kalevalaseuran vuosikiria* 49:267–271.

Andersson, Otto. 1964, 1969. *Studier i Musik och Folklore.* 2 vols. Åbo: Svenska Litteratursälleskapet i Finland.

Burchenal, Elizabeth, ed. 1915. *Folk-Dances from Finland: Containing Sixty-Five Dances.* New York: Schirmer.

De Gorog, Lisa S. 1989. *From Sibelius to Sallinen: Finnish Nationalism and the Music of Finland.* New York: Greenwood Press.

Donner, Philip. 1983. "The Frame of Reference of Music: Two Realities." *Suomen Antropologi* 4:184–197.

———, ed. 1986. *Aaneton pauhu! Hahmotelmia 70-luvan poliittisesta laululiikkeesta* (Sketches of the political-song movement in the 1970s). Helsinki: Tyovaenmusiikki-instituutti.

Granholm, Åke. 1974. *Finnish Jazz: History, Musicians, Discography.* Helsinki: Foundation for the Promotion of Finnish Music, Finnish Music Information Center.

Gronow, Pekka. 1963. "Popular Music in Finland: A Preliminary Survey." *Ethnomusicology* 17:52–71.

Helisto, Paavo. 1973. *Finnish Folk Music.* Helsinki: Foundation for the Promotion of Finnish Music, Finnish Music Information Center.

Juntunen, Juho. 1990. *Finnish rock? Then it must B. Goode!* Helsinki: Finnish Music Information Center.

Kaipainen, Marja. 1985. "Where Is the Source of Song?" *Form: Function* 2:18–19.

Knuuttila, Seppo. 1985. "The Last Rune Singer." *Musiikin Suunta* 1:59–65.

Koiranen, Antti, ed. 1991. *Finnish-Hungarian Symposium on Music and Folklore, 1987: Tampere, Finland.* Tampere: Tampereen yliopiston, kansanperinteen.

Kolehmainen, Ilkka. 1989. "Do Not Dance to the Screeching, Insidious Accordions; Burn Them: The Accordion in Finnish Folk Music." *Finnish Music Quarterly* 1989(2):29–31.

———. 1990. "The Kalevalaic Musical Variation Technique in Karelia." *Congressus Septimus Internationalis Fenno-Ugristarum 4,* ed. Elek Bartha et al. Debrecen, Hungary.

Komulainen, Orvokki. 1965. *Old Finnish Folk Dances.* Helsinki: Suomalaisen Kansantanssin Ystavat.

Konttinen, Matti. 1982. *Finnish Jazz.* Helsinki: Foundation for the Promotion of Finnish Music, Finnish Music Information Center.

Korhonen, Teppo. 1983. "On the Metamorphosis of the Ob-Ugrian Arched Harp." *Suomen Antropologi* 4:224–233.

Krohn, Ilmari. 1899. *Über die Art und Entstehung der geistlichen Volksmelodien in Finnland.* Helsinki: Druckerei der Finnischen Litteratur-Gesellschaft.

Kurkela, Vesa. 1983. "Varkaus: Workers' Music in a Finnish Industrial Town." *Suomen Antropologi* 4:218–223.

———. 1985. "Interest in Folklore and Its Myths in the Finnish Workers' Movement." *Musiikin Suunta* 7:34–44.

———. 1991. "Idealistic Folksiness in the Folk Music of Finnish Popular Movements." In *Finnish-Hungarian Symposium on Music and Folklore Research, 1987,* ed. Antti Koiranen, 50–53. Tampere: Department of Folk Tradition, University of Tampere.

———. 1992. "Long-term Fusions and Lost Traditions: Towards a Historiography of Finnish Popular Music." *Popular Music Perspectives* 3:25–31.

———. 1993. "Deregulation of Popular Music in the European Post-Communist Countries: Business, Identity and Cultural Collage." *The World of Music* 35(3):80–106.

Laitinen, Heikki. 1985. "Rune-Singing, the Musical Vernacular." *Finnish Music Quarterly* 1985(1–2):36–41.

Latvala, Raimo. 1985. *Rapapallit ja Lakuttimet* (Ancient Finnish musical instruments). Helsinki: Kansanmusiikki-instituutti.

Launis, Armas. 1908. *Lappische Juoigos-Melodien.* Suomalmis-ugrilaisen seuran toimituksia, 26. Helsinki: Druckerei der Finnischen Litteraturgesellschaft.

———. 1910. *Über Art, Entstehung und Verbreitung der estnisch-finnischen Runenmelodien.*

Helsinki: Druckerei der Finnischen Literatur-Gesellschaft.

———. 1930. *Karjalan runosavelmat* (Ancient songs from Karelia). Suomen kansan savelmia, 4. Helsinki: Suomalaisen Kirjallisuuden Seura.

Leisiö, Timo. 1977. "The Taxonomy and Historical Interpretation of the Finnish Pastoral Aerophone." *Studia Instrumentorum Musicae Popularis* 5:45–50.

———. 1983. "Surface and Deep Structure in Music: An Expedition into Finnish Musical Culture." *Suomen Anthropologi* 4:198–208.

———. 1985. "Turu Luru, Turu Luru! Myth and Reality in a Finnish Folk Tale." *Musiikin Suunta* 1:6–14.

Louhivuori, Jukka. 1990. "Computer Aided Analysis of Finnish Spiritual Folk Melodies." In *Probleme der Volksmusikforschung,* ed. Hartmut Braun. Bern: Peter Lang.

———. 1992. "The Symbiosis of Church and Folk Music." *Finnish Musical Quarterly* (2):27–30.

Makinen, Timo. 1985. *Musica Fennica: An Outline of Music in Finland.* Helsinki: Helsingissa Kustannusosakeyhtio Otava.

Marvia, Einari, ed. 1987. *Song of Finland.* Porvoo: WSOY.

Moisala, Pirkko, ed. 1994. "Ethnomusicology in Finland." *Ethnomusicology* 38:399–422.

Pekkilä, Erkki. 1983. "'Musiikki' and 'Kappalevalikoima': Aspects of the Ethno-Theory of a Finnish Folk Musician." *Suomen Anthropologi* 4:209–217.

———. 1986. "Ideal Patterns in the Finnish Juoksuvalssi: A Paradigmatic Segment Analysis." In *The Oral and the Literate in Music,* ed. Yoshihiko Tokumaru and Osamu Yamaguti, 206–220. Tokyo: Academia Music LTD.

———. 1987. "A History of Finnish Ethnomusicology." In *Kalevala et traditions orales du monde,* ed. M. M. Jocelyn Fernandez. Paris: CNRS.

———. 1991. "Folk Music, Tourism, and Authenticity." In *Finnish-Hungarian Symposium on Music and Folklore Research,* ed. Antti Koiranen, 74–78. Tampere: Department of Folk Tradition, University of Tampere.

Pentikäinen, Juha. 1978. *Oral Repertoire and World View: An Anthropological Study of Marina Takalo's Life History.* Helsinki: Suomalainen Tiedeakatemia.

Rahkonen, Carl. 1989. "The Kantele Traditions of Finland." Ph.D. dissertation, Indiana University.

Saha, Hannu. 1987. "De nouveaux enjeux pour la musique Kalevaléenne." In *Kalevala et Traditions Orales du Monde,* ed. M. M. Jocelyne Fernandez-Vest. Paris: CNRS.

———. 1984. "Kantele—New Life for Finland's National Instrument." *Finnish Music Quarterly* 1:20–29.

———. 1990. "Problems of the Survival of Traditional Playing Styles in Modern Finland." In *Congressus Septimus Internationalis Fenno-Ugristarum 4,* ed. Elek Bartha et al. Debrecen, Hungary.

———. 1993. "The Revival of Finnish Folk Music." *Finnish Features.* Helsinki: Ministry for Foreign Affairs.

Saunio, Ilpo, et al. 1978. *Edesta aattehen: Suomalaisia tyovaenlauluja 1890–1938* (Finnish Workers' Songs 1890–1938). Helsinki: Tammi.

Suojanen, Päivikki. 1984. *Finnish Folk Hymn Singing: Study in Music Anthropology.* Tampere: Institute for Folk Tradition, University of Tampere.

Suomen Kansan Sävelmiä (Finnish folk tunes). 1893–1933. 5 vols. Helsinki: Suomalaisen Kirjallisuuden Seura.

Tolbert, Elizabeth. 1990. "Women Cry with Words: Symbolization of Affect in the Karelian Lament." *Yearbook for Traditional Music* 22:80–105.

Väisänen, A. O. 1917. "Suomen kansan savel-main kerays" (A collection of Finnish folk music). *Suomi: Kirjoituksia isanmaallisista aineista* 76(2):I–XI, 1–139.

———. 1928. *Kantele—ja jouhikkosavelmia* (Music for the *kantele* and the *jouhikko*). Jyvaskylassa: Jyvaskylan Kirjapainossa.

———. 1937. "Wogulische und Ostjakische Melodien." In *Phonographisch Aufgenommen von Artturi Kannisto und K. F. Karjalainen.* Edited by A. O. Väisänen. Suomalais-ugrilaisen Seuran toimituksia, 73. Helsinki: Suomalaisugrilainen seura.

———. 1939. *Untersuchung über die Ob-ugrischen Melodien.* Suomala ugrilaisen Seuran toimituksia, 80. Helsinki: Suomalaisen Kirjallisuuden Seuran Kirjapainon Oy.

———. 1949. "Kalevalan savelma" (The music of the Kalevala). *Kalevalaseuran vuosikirja* 29:401–438.

Vierimaa, Irma. 1985. "Music in the Struggle Between Good and Evil: Mythical Motifs in Finnish Medieval Frescoes." *Musiikin Suunta* 1:21–31.

Virtanen, L. 1968. *Kalevalainen laulutapa Karjalassa* (The Kalevala song tradition in Karelia). Helsinki: Suomalaisen Kirjallisuuden Seura.

AUDIOVISUAL RESOURCES

Aarnion Sisarukset. 1993. *Hameen polkka: Finnish Folk Music from the 1930s.* Kansanmusiikki-instituutti KICD 28. Compact disc.

Archbishop Paul of Karelia and All Finland. 1976? *Orthodox Church Music from Finland.* IKON Records IKO 4F. LP disk.

Bhattacharya, Deben. 196-?. *The Kantele Music of Finland.* Philips 427 035 NE. LP disk.

———. 1967. *Music from the Far North.* Argo ZFB 43. LP disk.

Finnish Jazz '88. 1988. Finnish Jazz Federation FJLP 902. LP disk.

JPP. 1992. *Devil's Polska.* Linnet Records CSIF 4012. Compact disc.

Jylha, Konsta. 1993. *Finnish Folk Music.* Finlandia 566072/566082. Compact disc.

Kaale Dzambena Suomen mustalaiset laulavat (Finnish Gypsies sing). 1993. Global Music Center GMCD 9302. Compact disc.

Kalaniemi, Maria. 1994. *Maria Kalaniemi.* Green Linnet Records GLCD 4013. Compact disc.

Lahti, Heikki. 1989. *Traditional Finnish Mandolin.* Mandocrucian's Digest MD 001. Compact disc.

Niekku 3. 1989. *Niekku 3.* Olarin Musiikki OMCD 27. Compact disc.

Ottopasuuna. 1993. *Ottopasuuna.* Green Linnet Records GLCD 4005. Compact disc.

Pokela, Martti. 1990. *Kantele.* Finlandia FACD 018. Compact disc.

Rikka, Sirrka and Kantele. 1959. *Finland Through Song and Dance.* Bruno BR 50025. LP disk.

Stark, John. 1992. *Tunes and Songs of Finland.* Folkways Records 06856. Compact disc.

Tulikari, Eino. 1993. *Eino Tulikari, kantele.* Kansanmusiikki-instituutti KICD1. Compact disc.

Tulikulkku. 1993. Kansanmusiiki-instituutti KICD 30. Compact disc.

Värttinä. 1994. *Aitara.* Green Linnet Records 4026. Compact disc.

Estonia
Johannes Tall

Vocal Folk Music
Instrumental Folk Music
Art Music
History of Scholarship

Estonia (*Eesti Vabariik* in Estonian) is a republic of 1.5 million people with an area of about 50,000 square kilometers. Bordered on land by Russia and Latvia, Estonia has coastal borders on the Gulf of Finland and the Baltic Sea. Estonians speak a Finno-Ugric language and use a Latin script. About 45 percent of Estonians are Evangelical Lutherans. Other denominations include Methodist, Baptist, Russian Orthodox, and Roman Catholic. Boasting a literacy rate of 100 percent for citizens over fifteen years of age, Estonia's ethnic groups include Estonians, Swedes, Russians, Ukrainians, Belarusans, and Finns. The presence of ethnic Estonians in this territory dates back to about 3000 B.C. German invaders forcibly Christianized the population in the thirteenth century, and since then Estonians have almost continually lived under foreign rule, including rule by Sweden (in the seventeenth century), Russia (1710–1918), the Soviet Union (1940–1941 and 1944–1991), and Germany (1941–1944). In August of 1991, Estonia declared independence from the Soviet Union, and in June of the following year adopted the country's current constitution.

VOCAL FOLK MUSIC

In Estonia, folksingers were primarily women, and instrumental music was almost exclusively a man's domain. Most folk songs deal with subjects that more appropriately belonged to women: love and intrigue, domestic life, and household activities such as spinning and weaving. Heroic songs of an epic character are rare. Even in them, romantic feelings seem to dominate, as in "*Venna Sõjalugu*" ('Brother's War Tale'), where the sister, more concerned for her brother's safe return than his heroic deeds, gives the following advice:

> Oh my darling brother,
> When you go to waging war,
> Do not rush to the front of the battle,
> Close to the standard-bearer!
> The first ones are sacrificed,
> The last ones are slaughtered,
> The ones in the middle will return.

The most popular, almost legendary Estonian folk instrument is the *kannel,* a zither resembling the Finnish *kantele,* first mentioned in the Finnish national epic, the Kalevala. The Finns and Estonians consider this their national instrument, as do other Finno-Ugric peoples living at or near the Baltic Sea.

FIGURE 1
"Kadrilaul," a runic folk song (*regivärss*) for the fall season. The melody has the range of a fourth and a changing meter. The text uses nature metaphors to encourage members of the household to get out of bed and light a fire to warm the house. Tampere 1956–1965.

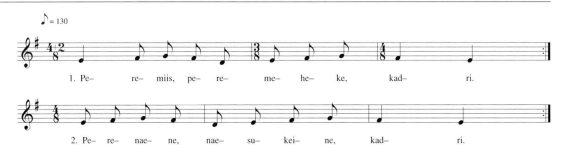

Melodies in Estonian folk songs can be divided into two distinct styles, reflecting contrasting historical periods. The older types have narrow-range recitativelike melodies, with each syllable usually corresponding to one melodic pitch and melodic movement being mostly diatonic and stepwise. If leaps occur, they are narrow (a third, seldom a fourth), while chromaticism is absent (figure 1). These are called "runic" melodies (*regivärss*). The term *runo* refers to Finnish-Estonian folklore types, "runic verse" or "runic melody," whose phrases basically have four disyllabic feet. In performing these songs, the main emphasis was on the words, which abundantly use alliteration, assonance, and parallelism, and lack stanzaic arrangement and rhyme. In the older type of folk songs, even the choice of melody for a given text is optional. The primary consideration seems to have been whether the melodic style and poetic meter fit together. These songs are associated primarily with work, rituals, children's games, and charms and incantations.

In the nineteenth century, a new, rhyming folk-song form (*vemmalvärss*) superseded the runic song, though the old tradition is still perpetuated in isolated areas, including southeastern Estonia and islands such as Kihnu, in the Baltic Sea. The newer form primarily includes lyric songs for nonceremonial situations and narrative songs. The style of these songs is newer, the melody is more developed, the melodic range is wider, and the modes are about equally divided between major and minor. The minor-mode melodies commonly use the scale in its natural form, with the lowered leading tone. For these newer melodies, an easy step was the use of functional harmony in nineteenth-century style. The newer folk melodies also exhibit more rhythmic variety (figure 2). The most important deviation from the archaic melodies is in musical construction: the melodic structure depends more on musical than poetic considerations. The influence of art music of Central Europe and Scandinavia is clearly evident. The texts of these songs, influenced by the poetry that became prevalent in the nineteenth century, use strophic structures and end rhymes.

Estonia has few religious folk songs, perhaps partly reflecting lack of interest on the part of collectors. A style of devotional song closely related to the Lutheran chorale has a melodic structure clearly identifiable as AABA (figure 3).

The oldest Estonian folk songs are mostly monophonic. Polyphony occurs in Setu, the southeast region. Though some observers have heard Russian influence in

FIGURE 2 *"Kus on, kus on kurva kodu,"* a nineteenth-century folk song in the minor mode and 3/4 time. The text reflects sadness. Aavik 1965.

this style, Setu polyphony differs from the neighboring Russian style in having less independent voice leading (figure 4). In Setu songs, the lower voice, the main melody, is carried by the lead singer and the chorus (or secondary voice) enters with the upper part, rather restricted in its melodic range (a second or third)—and in a few songs, the upper voice remains on one pitch (Rüütel 1988).

INSTRUMENTAL FOLK MUSIC

The most popular, almost legendary Estonian folk instrument is the *kannel,* a zither resembling the Finnish *kantele,* first mentioned in the Finnish national epic, the Kalevala (figure 5). The Finns and Estonians consider this their national instrument, as do other Finno-Ugric peoples living at or near the Baltic Sea: Karelians call it *kandeleh;* Livonians, *kandla;* Votians, *kannöl;* and so on. The early five-stringed *kannel* served for playing the ancient runic *regivärss* on its open strings. As the melodic range of accompanied tunes increased, strings were added. Developments in construction were matched by changes in playing techniques. Older instruments, with limited range, were played by plucking open strings singly, producing melodies. As more strings were added (as many as twenty to thirty, tuned diatonically), new playing techniques, such as stopping certain strings with left-hand fingers while strumming with the right hand, producing chords and sometimes chords plus melody, were invented. During the nineteenth century, three bass strings were added, tuned to the tonic, dominant, and subdominant, to the existing melody strings. The melody strings were plucked with the bass to produce harmony.

A further development was the placement of groups of higher strings adjacent to bass strings to produce tonic, dominant, and subdominant chords, making it much easier to play the melody and a chordal accompaniment. Modern folksingers use this type of *kannel,* which has never had one standard shape or size. Regional differences exist, and even in one locality various shapes and sizes occur, as do many different playing techniques (figure 6).

Another popular string instrument was the *hiiukannel* or *rootsikannel,* a bowed instrument with three or four strings. One or two of the strings were used for playing melodies, and the others sounded drones. The name implies that the instrument was particularly popular in Hiiumaa, the second largest island of Estonia in the Baltic Sea, and also that it came from Sweden and was used by Swedish people in Estonia in the eighteenth and nineteenth centuries. Its music had a narrow range, and since it

FIGURE 3 *"Mu süda ärka üles,"* a religious folk song that praises the Creator in AABA form. Aavik 1965.

FIGURE 4 *"Nakeks köne köi poisi vöi,"* a Setu polyphonic song. A soloist begins, and the other singers add thirds, fifths, and an occasional triad. Transcription by Johannes Tall.

1. Na– keks kõ– ne kõ– i poi– si või lo– lõks– ko– zõ– mai– e võ– ie

laul– ge ko– zõ va poi– si või lau– lo– ge ko– ze– ge laul

2. I– ne na– kõks kooh nu vai i– lo– jal– le– ta– ma võ– ie

i– ne kas ko– zõ koo– na ka– vai i– lo vai kas ko– zõ kooh

FIGURE 5 Igor Tönurist, of the folk-music ensemble Leegajus (from Tallinn), plays a zither (*kannel*) made in or near Leningrad in 1920. Photo by E. Kärmas.

served primarily for weddings and other festive occasions, the style was derived from popular folk dances. It was displaced by the violin in the nineteenth century. Folk-music enthusiasts made modern copies in the late twentieth century.

Of wind instruments, one of the oldest and most popular is a reed instrument, the bagpipe (*torupill*). One pipe sounds the melody, and the others drone on the tonic and dominant (figure 7). Each pipe has a single reed. The melodic range of the *torupill* is limited to an octave of the diatonic major scale. According to old documents and chronicles, the *torupill* was popular as early as the fourteenth century. An outdoor instrument, it had many practical functions, such as accompanying wedding processions and providing entertainment at harvesttime (to encourage people to work faster) and village dances and festivities.

Other homemade wind instruments include trumpets, such as the *sokusarv* (a buck horn, often with finger holes) and the *karjapasun* (a herding trumpet, made of wood). Pipes, with or without a reed, include the *roopill* (a reed pipe). Cut into the upper end of the reed, an opening creates a vibrating tongue, similar to a clarinet reed. The pipe has four to six finger holes, capable of playing simple melodies in a narrow range, embellished with grace notes. On the *pajupill* or *vilepill* (a willow flute), a popular instrument, the tone production resembles that of a recorder or a whistle; however, the player modifies the pitch by sliding a piece of wood up and down the tube.

Musical repertory for these instruments depended on the limitations of the instruments and players' skill. The development of new playing techniques influenced improvements gradually made to the instruments themselves. This in turn eased the formation of instrumental ensembles, some as early as the end of the eighteenth century, though they became common only during the nineteenth century. In the early twentieth century, harmonicas and button accordions became popular. To these were added such instruments as violins, string basses, and even a piano, when available.

ART MUSIC

Centuries of foreign rule delayed the development of art music in Estonia. In 1561, northern Estonia came under Swedish rule while Poland occupied the south, which in 1629 also came under Swedish rule. This began a lengthy period of peace, and the

FIGURE 6 Estonian zithers (*kannel*) in various shapes and sizes, with varying numbers of strings. Drawings by Dan Beltran.

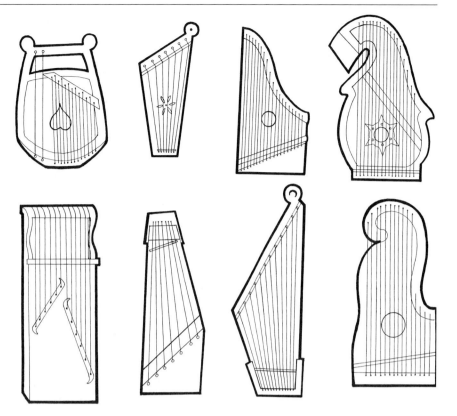

Swedish government took steps toward social, economic, and educational improvements. In 1694, the Protestant church was established as it was in Sweden, and churches became practical centers for learning. Schools too were established, among them the university in Tartu, founded in 1632 by King Gustav II Adolf.

Choral singing

The beginning of a choral-music tradition in Estonia grew directly out of the musical interest and activities of the Moravian Brethren, who at the end of the eighteenth and in the nineteenth century came to the Baltic area, where they found employment as music teachers in the houses of wealthy landowners, most of whom were Baltic Germans. Their expertise in music reached the common folk, and as early as the 1820s, the Moravians established a private school in Röngu, in southern Tartumaa.

The main purpose of Moravian music instruction was to raise the quality of singing in church. Thanks to their inspiration and leadership, Estonians' first efforts at choral singing reached back into the thirties and forties of the nineteenth century. The leaders of these groups were amateurs, mostly schoolteachers with some musical training. These choirs sang mainly German melodies set to Estonian texts. They were attached to churches, and their primary task was to provide music in services. For this reason, the clergy supported the development of these choirs and tried to secure suitable music for them. Gradually, however, the interests of these choirs broadened to include in their repertory secular songs.

Choral singing gained new and wider impetus from the initiative of Johann Voldemar Jannsen (1819–1890), an editor, publisher, and influential social leader, who organized and led the first Estonian Song Festival, held in 1869 in Tartu. Such festivals became an important aspect of musical life and boosted national pride. By the year of independence (1918), seven festivals had been held. The beginning of original Estonian art-music composition followed: the first composers were Aleksander Saebelmann-Kunileid (1845–1875), and Aleksander Edward Thomson

FIGURE 7   A man plays an Estonian bagpipe (*torupill*). Photographer and date unknown. Photo courtesy of Johannes Tall.

National song festivals became a national tradition and have continued once every five years, except during the war years. At the one held in 1994 in Tallinn, thirty-four thousand singers participated, and the audience was estimated at half a million.

(1845–1917). Jannsen wrote some songs, and in 1862 published a collection of one hundred twenty songs, which he called Estonian songs, though they were actually translations from German, or original Estonian verses by Jannsen set to German tunes.

In the first National Song Festival, forty male choirs from around the country participated, with a total of about eight hundred singers. Though this festival emphasized German songs, it included two works by an Estonian composer, Sabelmann-Kunielid: *"Sind Surmani"* ('I will hold you dear until I die') and *"Mu Isamaa on Minu Arm"* ('My Gracious Fatherland'). A melody by the Finnish composer Fredrik Pacius (1809–1891) served for Jannsen's text, *"Mu Isamaa mu Õnn ja Rõõm"* ('My Fatherland, My Fortune and Joy'), which later became the Estonian national anthem. This festival helped inspire the creation of a national art music, particularly in choral composition. Many first-generation composers came from families of amateur choir directors and singers, or from families of schoolteachers and church organists. During this period of national awakening, three song festivals took place: the first in Tartu (1869), the second also in Tartu (1879), and the third in Tallinn (1880).

The idea for the fourth song festival (1891) came from the Estonian Literary Society. For the first three festivals, the general directors had been Baltic Germans, but for the fourth one, the artist and professor Johann Köler (1826–1899) was chosen. He was the first Estonian artist to gain international recognition, and his choice added popularity to the undertaking. More than twenty-five hundred singers and instrumentalists went to Tartu, and the number of listeners increased proportionally. In this festival, mixed choirs participated for the first time. The artistic standard was higher, in that the program included works by such composers as Haydn, Mozart, and Beethoven. More works by Estonian composers were performed, and folk-song settings were included for the first time. These changes indicated the diminishing cultural and political influence of the Baltic-German elite.

These festivals became a national tradition and have continued once every five years, except during the war years. At the one held in 1994 in Tallinn, thirty-four thousand singers participated, and the audience was estimated at half a million (figure 8).

Instrumental music

The Moravian Brethren also initiated Estonian instrumental art music. Instruments accompanied congregational singing in church. At first, any available instruments were used, mainly wind instruments. As early as 1818, an orchestra in Tartu consisted of fourteen to fifteen players; about 1825, strings joined the ensemble. Instrumental ensembles soon spread throughout the country. Capable schoolteachers provided instruction on various instruments, and by the 1860s, some ensembles, such as the instrumental choir Vaagvere Pillikoor, under the direction of David Otto Virkhaus (1837–1912), had gained a wide reputation for their quality.

FIGURE 8 The choir of thirty-four thousand singers at the Song Festival in Tallinn. Photo by Johannes Tall, 1994.

By 1871, Estonia had more than one hundred amateur instrumental ensembles. Their value lay in their contribution to the development of cultural awareness and interest among the people, because their efforts represented a national expression, which laid an important foundation for the artistic developments that occurred during the years of independence, 1918–1940.

The first Estonian musicians with conservatory training, Johannes Kappel (1855–1907), Miina Härma (1864–1941), and Konstantin Türnpu (1865–1927), were graduates of the Imperial Conservatory of Music in St. Petersburg. All of them contributed to the development of Estonian music, but because of economic conditions, they could not devote themselves to full-time musical activities in Estonia, but had to seek employment abroad.

The beginning of the twentieth century brought changes in Estonian musical life. These reflected economic improvements and an increase in the number of idealistic and nationalistic musicians with professional training and education. The first professional Estonian orchestras date from the early part of the century and are closely connected with two theaters: Vanemuise in Tartu and Estonia in Tallinn. The primary focus for both was stage presentation, but each also presented symphonic music. In 1919, the Conservatory of Music in Tallinn was established. The first graduates of that institution provided a new and younger generation of professional musicians, trained in independent Estonia, who became active in musical life as performers, composers, and teachers. Of the first instructors at the conservatory, 53 percent were Estonians and 47 percent were from other nations, mainly Germany and Russia. In addition to the conservatory in Tallinn, other music schools of higher learning were established in Tartu, Valga, and elsewhere. All of these contributed to a high standard of professional music in Estonia, and they have graduated outstanding musicians, some with international reputations.

Several of the next generation's musicians received their training at the Imperial Conservatory in St. Petersburg with internationally recognized professors, such as Homilius, Rimsky-Korsakov, Liadov, and others. These students included Rudolf Tobias (1873–1918), Artur Kapp (1878–1952), Mihkel Lüdig (1880–1958), Mart Saar (1882–1952), Peeter Süda (1883–1920), and Juhan Aavik (1884–1982). Most were strongly influenced by Russian music, particularly that of Rimsky-Korsakov. However, Mart Saar made a complete break with that style, finding inspiration in

Estonian folk song. Cyrillus Kreek (1889–1962), another composer who dedicated his creative life to working with folk materials, systematically collected folk tunes— the first Estonian to do this with the help of a phonograph. He composed many polyphonic settings of folk tunes. Heino Eller (1887–1970), basically an instrumental composer, laid the foundation for Estonian symphonic music. In addition to his work as composer and teacher, several of his best students have proven themselves masters of the symphonic style, including Eduard Tubin (1905–1982) and Arvo Pärt (b. 1935).

During the years of Soviet occupation in Estonia, performing musicians and composers were forced to work under severe state-imposed restrictions. Soviet ideology and doctrine suppressed individual creativity in favor of building up and supporting communist ideology. Estonian artists, musicians, and composers, working under strict rules, sought to reconcile the limits of their consciences with the dictates of the state. Estonian folk song provided an obvious source of inspiration. The younger generation of composers has been particularly interested in runic folk songs, as can be heard clearly in the works of two composers: Veljo Tormis (b. 1930), primarily in vocal music, and Anti Marguste (b. 1931), in instrumental music.

Since 1991, freedom of expression, artistic and otherwise, has been restored in Estonia. There is no shortage of creative talent, and many talented performers and composers have had excellent education and training. With the reestablishment of communication with Western Europe, Estonian music has found a place in concert halls abroad.

HISTORY OF SCHOLARSHIP

The earliest written record of an Estonian folk-song text, now in the archives of the city of Pärnu, dates from 1680. Early specimens are rare, and they do not represent any organized effort of collecting. More systematic collecting started in the second half of the nineteenth century, as a sign of the national awakening among Estonians. The earliest systematic collectors were Jakob Hurt (1839–1907) and Oskar Kallas (1868–1946), the first to study Estonian folk songs in a scholarly manner. The most important researchers since World War II have been Herbert Tampere and Ingrid Rüütel.

BIBLIOGRAPHY

Aavik, Johannes, et al. 1961. *Aspects of Estonian Culture*. London: Boreas Publishing.

Aavik, Juhan. 1965. *Eesti Muusika Ajalugu* (The history of Estonian music). Rootsis: Esti Lauljaskond.

Andersson, Otto. 1930. *The Bowed-Harp*. London: William Reeves Bookseller.

Hirvesoo, Avo, ed. 1990. *Eesti Muusika Biograafiline Leksikon* (Biographical lexicon of Estonian music). Tallinn: Valgus.

Jürisson, Johannes, et al. 1968. *Eesti Muusika* (Estonian music). Tallinn: Eesti Raamat.

Põldmäe, Rudolf. 1969. *Esimene Eesti Laulupidu* (First Estonian song festival). Tallinn: Eesti Raamat.

———. 1976. *Kaks Laulupidu* (Two song festivals). Tallinn: Eesti Raamat.

Rüütel, Ingrid. 1988. *Setu Rahvalaulu Kihistused ja Ethnokultuuriline* (Setu folk songs in ethnocultural perspective). Tallinn: Taust.

Tall, Johannes. 1985. *Estonian Song Festivals and Nationalism in Music toward the End of the Nineteenth Century*. Stockholm: Acta Universitatis.

Tampere, Herbert. 1956–1965. *Eesti Rahvalaulud Viisidega* (Estonian folk songs with melodies). Kirjastus: Eesti Riiklik.

———. 1975. *Eesti Rahvapillid ja Rahvatantsud* (Estonian folk instruments and folk dances). Tallinn: Eesti Raamat.

AUDIOVISUAL RESOURCES

Eesti rahvalaulude ja pillilugude (Estonian folk songs and instrumental tunes). 1970, 1974. 2 vols. Melodiia 33D-25519–28; 33D-032783–86, 032797–800, 033283–84. Five 10-inch LP disks and five 12-inch LP disks.

Estonia in Song and Dance. 1958. Around the World Series. Bruno BR 50018. LP disk.

Estonian Songs and Dances. 1961. Monitor MF317. LP disk.

Narodnaia muzyka Estonskoi SSR (The folk music of Estonian S.S.R.). 1986. Melodiia GUST 5289-80. LP disk.

Songs from Estonia. 1979. Request Records SRLP 8236. LP disk.

Latvia
Valdis Muktupāvels

Vocal Music
Seasonal and Life-Cycle Songs
Musical Instruments and Instrumental Music
History of Music
History of Scholarship

The Republic of Latvia rests on the eastern shore of the Baltic Sea, neighboring Estonia, Lithuania, Russia, and Belarus. The original inhabitants were Balt tribes—Indo-European speaking Curonians, Semigallians, Latgalians, and Selonians, and Finno-Ugric Livs. Latvia's 65,791 square kilometers house a population of more than 2.5 million, of whom almost a million live in its capital, Riga.

Ethnographically, Latvia subdivides into four regions: Kurzeme (Courland) in the west, Zemgale (Semigallia) in the center and south, Vidzeme (Liefland) in the center and north, and Latgale in the east. After the German crusaders' conquest in the 1200, Latvia and Estonia were ruled, under the name of Livonia, by the Livonian Order, a military brotherhood of the Roman Catholic Church. Livonia was dissolved in 1561. The Russian conquest came in the 1700s. Latvia achieved political independence in 1918, was occupied by the Soviet Union in 1940, and regained its independence in 1991.

Latvian traditional culture has remained conservative. The Latvian language has changed little over millennia, and with Lithuanian is regarded as an old Indo-European language. Before World War II most Latvians (64 percent) were Lutherans, and a prominent minority (26 percent), basically in Latgale and the Suiti region of Kurzeme, was Roman Catholic.

VOCAL MUSIC

Musical practices in the Lutheran and Roman Catholic parts of Latvia are much the same, yet major differences in musical style and repertoire exist between Latgale and the rest of the country. On the whole, traditional singing is better preserved in Latgale and southwestern Kurzeme. Recent lyrical and other popular styles are common in most of Vidzeme and Kurzeme, particularly in the central, northern part and along the Riga Gulf.

Singing in rural Latvia is mostly women's domain. Communal singing is characteristic for calendar and family celebrations and joint field labor.

Old Latvian had no umbrella term for *music*. Two terms, *dziedāt* and *gavilēt*, describe vocal music. *Dziedāt* 'to sing' stands for most musical vocal forms. *Gavilēt*

FIGURE 1 *"Godu balss,"* a funeral tune from the Suiti region, sung in vocal drone style. Transcription by Emilis Melngailis.

'to cheer, to exult, to shout, to howl' refers to a loud, outdoor, solo song, including characteristic cheering or howling formulas. *Gavilēšana* (the nominative form of *gavilēt*) was practiced mostly by shepherds, plowmen, and fishermen at, for instance, climaxes of calendric festivities.

Songs in folk tradition are often known by their textual incipit. In other cases, titles refer to a specific refrain or after an event, when the melodic formula *balss* is applied; thus, the term *godu balss* 'tune of life-cycle (usually wedding) rituals and communal feasts' is known in many parts of Latvia. Other such titles used in Latgale include *talku balss* 'tune of joint fieldworks' and *rudzu balss* 'rye-field tune'.

The *daina,* the basic form of a Latvian folk-song text, is a short self-contained quatrain of two nonrhyming couplets. About 95 percent of these texts are in octosyllabic trochaic meter; the rest, in dactylic. This uniformity contrasts with a great variety of meters, from simple or compound duple to complex asymmetrical and mixed (5/8, 5/4, 7/8, 6/4=2/4+4/4, 7/4, and others). Though each quatrain is short, the singing can go on for hours. *Daina* are mostly lyrical in sentiment. They only rarely tell stories, but comment on performed rituals, express feelings, or condense folk wisdom into epigrams.

Recited songs (*teicamās dziesmas*) are a part of traditional events and celebrations, such as weddings, lullabies, field labor, and breeding cattle. The melodic formulas composing a recited song are varied according to the textual prosody. The "spoken" character of these songs is reinforced by their narrow tonal ranges (rarely exceeding a fifth), the lack of melodic ornamentation, and their syllabic structure. Performance, often by a group during a celebration, can be responsorial.

In some areas, above all in the Suiti region, vocal drones accompany this style of singing. The performers are elderly women. A soloist (*teicēja* 'the one who says, recites') performs half of the four-line stanza, which is then repeated by one or several *locītājas* 'those who twist, inflect, vary', while a vocal drone is performed by *vilcējas* 'those who drawl, pull (a tone)'. Soloist and countersinger sometimes overlap at the ends of phrases. The drone on /e/ is in unison with the last tones of the soloist, then rises a tone to join the countersinger. Simultaneously, the drone changes from /e/ to /o/ (figure 1). Other varieties of vocal drone are known throughout Latvia.

In contrast, "sung" songs (*dziedamās, dziesmas*) are less connected with traditional festivities. These songs are performed mostly solo. Two- or three-part singing, resembling that of western Lithuanian homophony, is typical of southwestern Kurzeme. Singing in thirds with the melody in the upper voice can be heard all over Latgale—a style influenced by liturgical singing. These songs, with ranges often exceeding an octave, are basically as important as their texts. Their lyrical character can be reinforced through refinements, such as ornamentation, short vocalizations, and refrains.

SEASONAL AND LIFE-CYCLE SONGS

As the result of changing social and economic conditions in the late 1800s, traditional contexts for singing disappeared from urbanized areas. In most rural districts, the traditional calendar was still observed, and singing was still meant to assure the efficacy of seasonal rituals. At Easter morning, girls greeted spring and the "jumping sun" with singing. On Easter Monday, young people walked from house to house, collecting eggs and singing good wishes. On still evenings from then until Whitsunday, girls practiced the custom known as *rotāšana*. They gathered on hillsides, from where their singing could be heard afar. The term *rotāšana* refers to the refrain (*rotā*), which followed each textual line. Spring songs with vocal drone but without refrain were sung in western Kurzeme. Spring-singing traditions differed in Latgale: every evening in May until Whitsunday, women and girls gathered by a roadside crucifix, where they sang psalms and religious folk songs.

One of the most complex vocal genres, *līgotnes,* is connected with *Jāņi*, the midsummer solstice celebration, which joins features of solar, phallic, and fertility rites. Singing of *līgotnes* can start a fortnight before and can continue a week after the solstice, with a climax on the evening and the subsequent night of the celebration. A refrain (*līgo*) follows each textual line. A soloist sings the first line, others join with the refrain, and all sing a quatrain. Midsummer songs with the refrain *rūtō* are specific to eastern Latgale (figure 2).

Singing accompanied some autumn activities. Grinding grain, formerly a woman's job, was accompanied by grinding songs with their characteristic mythological motifs, narrow tonal ranges and some tones held at the ends of phrases. Another

FIGURE 2   Singing at *Jāņi*, the midsummer solstice celebration. Photo by Laimonis Skride, 1983.

The central musical event at the wedding and the associated feast was *apdziedāšanās,* antiphonal, humorous, competitive singing, involving two opposite teams of singers (boys and girls, relatives of bride and bridegroom, hosts and guests); each group sang in turn, teasing or making fun of the other, with texts largely improvised.

situation requiring singing was *vakarēšana,* joint needlework and handicrafts in autumn and winter evenings.

Masked processions started on St. Martin's day (locally 10 November) in Lutheran territory and on Christmas in Roman Catholic areas. Noisy crowds of carolers walked from house to house, requesting gifts, making jokes, and often dragging a log to be burnt. These Christmas songs, melodically similar to *līgotnes,* have narrow ranges and regionally specific refrains. *Budeļi,* masked revelers in Kurzeme and western Zemgale, employed simple responsorial singing: a monotonously recited couplet was repeated one fourth lower. Throughout Latvia, the revelers were called Gypsies (*čigāni*). Their songs have long refrains, sung once or even twice after each couplet—a structure meant to evoke the image of Gypsies (Roma).

Latvians observed major life-cycle events with church services, but informal, elaborate surrounding events overwhelmed the religious center. After a christening in a church, singing was part of a feast in a house. In southwestern Kurzeme, this was followed by *dīdīšana,* ritual swinging and rocking of the baby by all participants of the celebration, accompanied by special songs, expressing good wishes for the baby's future. Rural weddings started in the bride's house, where a farewell party occurred. The bride's girlfriends would sing songs that in Latgale and eastern Vidzeme resembled some funeral songs.

Following marriage ceremonies, singing and dancing added to the joyful noise of the celebration. The central musical event at the wedding and the associated feast was *apdziedāšanās,* antiphonal, humorous, competitive singing, involving two opposite teams of singers (boys and girls, relatives of bride and bridegroom, hosts and guests); each group sang in turn, teasing or making fun of the other, with texts largely improvised. A melodic formula (*godu balss* 'family celebration tune' or *kāzu balss* 'wedding tune') was employed. Since the 1970s, when the traditional terminology was partly lost, people have called this tune a melody with which one sings all song texts. In most cases, this is a recited-style tune.

In Latgale, semiprofessional women singers were invited to wedding parties. Apart from singing at the doorway and the table, they performed *apdziedāšana,* witty, humorous, sometimes licentious quatrains, offered to the new couple and in turn to every guest. The last song for this event came at about midnight, when the bride's crown was taken off and the woman's headdress was put on.

Funeral singing has a strong relationship to Christian ceremony. Psalms and parts of the liturgy were sung in the house, on the way to the cemetery, and by the grave. The funeral was anticipated by a wake (*vāķēšana*), around 1900 still observed throughout the country, but nowadays only in Latgale. So recently as the early 1900s, some communities in western Kurzeme practiced a special activity, *vāķu rotaļas* 'games performed beside the corpse the night before funeral'. Traits of such games are recited-style melodies, often restricted to two or three pitches.

Men and women sing at the table during feasts, in pubs, and on other social occasions. Courting and wedding motifs are the most common, but certain mythological, orphan, recruiting, soldiers', humorous, sailors', or drinking songs are also important. When youths gathered on certain occasions, a popular pastime was *iet rotaļās* 'to play games, usually circle dances with singing'. This singing focused on courting and marriage, frequently invoking the symbolism of animals or plants.

MUSICAL INSTRUMENTS AND INSTRUMENTAL MUSIC

In connection with herding, *svilpes* 'bark or clay whistles', *stabules* 'wooden flutes with six or seven finger holes or reeds', *ragi* 'horns, hornpipes', and *taures* 'wooden and birch-bark trumpets with mouthpiece or a single reed' were made and played. These instruments were recreational and functional; players say they have used their trumpets to collect the herd in the morning and signal the return in the evening. They used hornpipes to calm the herd or to direct its movement.

Music for Latvian flutes is purely instrumental, rather than instrumental versions of vocal music. In some cases, short tetratonic or pentatonic motifs are repeated with variations. Bark whistles, about 50 to 70 centimeters long and without finger holes, were used as overtone instruments; playing techniques involved overblowing combined with stopping and opening the end hole with a finger.

Horns with metal mouthpieces and bronze or silver fittings and trumpets were used for signaling, particularly to announce weddings and important moments of wedding rituals. Goat horns, usually with three finger holes, were played during *mēslu talka* 'spreading manure on the fields' or within matchmaking ceremonies. Because of its role announcing the initiation of sexual relations, the goat horn has obtained a kind of phallic symbolism in folklore texts. There are a few melodies of two goat horns playing antiphonally, but its music normally consists of solo variations within a range of a tetrachord.

Making and playing instruments, except shepherds' instruments, was basically men's business, but a group of rattle-sticks—*trīdeksnis,* a wooden stick with hanging bells and jingles; *eglīte,* a fir-tree top decorated with colored feathers and hanging bells and jingles; *puškaitis,* a wooden stick heavily decorated with colored feathers, strips of cloth, and bells—are played mostly by women. They were formerly used to accompany singing of *godu balss* in wedding or winter-solstice rituals: women marked the rhythm by hitting the table with the sticks.

The most characteristic and significant instrument in Latvian traditional music is the *kokles,* a board zither with five to twelve strings. It is related to similar instruments in lands east and north of the Baltic Sea: the Lithuanian *kanklės,* the Estonian *kannel,* the northwestern Russian *gusli,* the Karelian *kandeleh,* and the Finnish *kantele.* Instruments were carved from a single wooden plank, to which an ornamented soundboard was added. Strings were made of steel, bronze, or possibly natural fibers, and tuned with wooden pegs. An instrumental drone was characteristic in the case of five-to-nine-stringed instruments: the longest string, tuned a fourth below the tonic, was often plucked or touched during play; therefore it was named *dziedātāja* 'the singer'. The tuning was a diatonic scale, so for the seven-stringed *kokles* it would be a_1–g_1–f_1–e_1–d_1–c_1–g. When played, the instrument is placed on a table or the player's knees. A special damping technique is used: some strings are damped with the left-hand fingers; when the strings are plucked with the right hand, only undamped strings produce tones, while the left-hand fingers pick up some offbeat notes.

Though the repertoire of the *kokles* is mostly dance tunes and in a few cases song melodies, the instrument was not used for dance accompaniment and was only seldom used for song accompaniment. The heavenly aura and fine, deeply touching tone quality have made the *kokles* a symbol of national music for Latvians, but by

FIGURE 3   Jānis Poriķis, the last surviving *kokles* player. Photo by Vaira Strautniece, 1982.

1900, the instrument's playing traditions had diminished, and five-to-twelve-stringed instruments remained in use only in some places in Kurzeme, particularly in the Suiti region and Latgale (figure 3). Simultaneously, hybrid forms, influenced by zithers, developed, usually with seventeen to fifty strings.

Historical sources bear witness to the special role of bagpipes in peasants' life from the 1500s through the 1800s: they were often the only instruments played at weddings, and were used in other ceremonies and for dancing. Latvian bagpipes have a chanter with four to seven finger holes and one or two drones, each with a single reed. The bag is made of a sheep or dog skin or seal stomach, and bellows could be attached. One can distinguish between two kinds of bagpipe tunes: *uzsaukums* 'call' or 'air' (slow-tempo variations) and *dancis* 'dance'. The oldest evidence of an ensemble with bagpipes is an engraving in Münster's *Cosmography* (1598, the engraving possibly made in 1549): it shows devils and witches dancing and three musicians playing—a kind of lute, hurdy-gurdy, and bagpipes.

The violin probably arrived between 1650 and 1700. Gradually replacing the old instruments, especially bagpipes, and partly adopting their repertoires, the violin became the most popular folk-music instrument in and after the 1800s. Solo violin playing was the most characteristic musical texture, and not by chance does the basic meaning of the Latvian term *spēlmanis* 'player' (but mostly 'violin player, fiddler') point toward the Swedish *spelman,* traditionally glossed 'solo violinist'.

After about 1850, rural violinists played in ensemble with other instruments: zither, accordion, mandolin, guitar, hammer dulcimer, double bass, and percussion. Frequently the ensemble consisted of one or two violins, zither, and drums, or of violin, zither, and accordion. The dominance of the accordion increased after about 1950, and this is now the main dance-music instrument.

A favorite dance for four couples was *četrpāru dancis.* The third of four or more sections was usually *sudmaliņas* 'mill', which could be a separate dance. Walking was the most characteristic action of several other dances, among which the *diždancis,* a solemn couple dance, performed at the beginning of a wedding feast, is the most important. *Krusta dancis,* dancing and jumping over crossed poles or swords, enabled solo dancers to demonstrate their skill or compete with others.

HISTORY OF MUSIC

Much Latvian popular music in oral tradition originated in printed sources. The first collections of *ziņģes,* Latvian popular songs of the 1700s and 1800s—*Jaunās ziņģes* ('The new *ziņģes*', 1774) and *Ziņģu lustes* ('The joy of singing *ziņģes*', 1783)—were published by the Lutheran priest Gothard Friedrich Stender (1714–1796). Intended to replace Latvian peasants' traditional repertoire with translations of popular German songs and thus "to enlighten peasants in a more gentle sentimental mood," *Ziņģu lustes* remained the most popular secular song collection until the mid-1800s. It influenced the spread of the new musical style, which resembled that of broadside ballads (*Flugblattlieder* 'flying sheets'). Only texts with references to well-known German melodies of that time—lyrical songs and *Singspiel* music—were published, but later publications added advice on how to improvise one's own melody. By 1900, the popularity of the *ziņģes* style had declined. In cities and towns, the style gave way to romances, student songs, theater music, and other genres, but pub dancing and vocal and instrumental music-making dominated rural musical life.

After the mid-1800s, when serfdom was abolished, Latvian social life burgeoned. Singing societies emerged all over the country, and sought a repertoire that would reflect an emerging feeling of unity and nationalism. Four-part harmonizations of Latvian folk songs served this purpose well, so more and more composers drew on folklore materials.

Jānis Cimze (1814–1881) was the first important arranger, though his *Dziesmu rota* ('Garland of Songs') was reminiscent of Protestant chorales. The choral works of Andrejs Jurjāns (1856–1922) finally created and defined the so-called national style of professional music, which Emilis Melngailis (1874–1954) developed and perfected.

The first Latvian Song Festival, held in 1873, became a political event of the first rank. It symbolized the reawakening and unity of the new nation. Later festivals, by concentrating on national aspirations and involving thousands of participants, won the status of central national musical events.

After World War II, Latvian musical culture was heavily influenced by Soviet ideology, which advocated the disappearance of national aspirations. Yet a formal aspect of national musical culture was planned as the "improvement" of "folk music" (a mixture of traditional and popular music, viewed through the prism of art music) to reach amateur and professional levels. Choral singing fit well in this scheme as amateur art, as it could involve the masses, and its "folkishness" could be ensured by including arrangements of traditional music in its repertoire. The Song Festival, an important symbol in the definition of national culture, was reinterpreted in terms of Soviet ideology and successfully accommodated into the new regime's musical life. This festival became huge: its thirty thousand to one hundred thousand participants constituted up to 4 percent of the population. Yet a certain charm was added by the sincere greeting and summoning of conductors, and an informal collective identity and nationalism were cultivated.

Between the world wars, urban and rural music flowered in professional and popular forms. Though traditional music had lost its significance in much of the country, it continued to flourish in remote districts, especially in Latgale and western Kurzeme. At the same time, though a national style in Latvian art music had been established, attempts to practice "more Latvian" music were undertaken, as, for instance, within the neopagan movement *dievturīc,* whose members (*dievturi*) developed a special choral style, which they named the Latvian style. Avoiding chromaticisms, frequent use of drones, antiphonal singing, and special treatment of soloists or groups of soloists are characteristics of this style. Members if the *dievturi* community tried to "improve" old, forgotten instruments, especially the *kokles,* increasing the number of strings and changing the construction to make it possible for people to play it in different tonalities. The Soviet occupation of 1940 and the following war curtailed this movement.

The "modernizations" of traditional instruments continued after the war. Following the Soviet model, *kokles* ensembles and other folk-song and folk-dance ensembles were established in numerous "culture houses," "Pioneer houses," music schools, and conservatories. Though the activities of such groups fit into the regime's model of culture, they achieved broad acceptance, and even today are generally recognized as an expression of national music and national dance.

A significant formal "folklore" movement arrived later in Latvia than in other Baltic countries—that is, in the 1970s. However, the seeds of the movement were sown much earlier. The earliest performances with "ethnographic singing" occurred during the first Latvian ethnographic exhibition, in 1896. In the 1920s and 1930s, singers and musicians from Alsunga and other Kurzeme regions performed in Riga. The folklore movement skipped over the new, institutionalized strata of folklore to concentrate on the oldest traditional music. New folklore ensembles that emerged early in the 1980s tried to practice authentic local styles.

Deliberate attempts were made to revive older instruments, such as the five-to-twelve-stringed *kokles,* bagpipes, zithers, pipes, reeds, and so on. These were then played in calendar festivities, folklore festivals, and other contexts. Folklorists now

The renewed ethnic music traditions in the 1980s was allied to the national resistance movement, opposing Soviet totalitarianism and russification. However, such music did not become a generally accepted national symbol, and in the 1990s its sphere narrowed.

FIGURE 4 In Riga during a street procession at the folklore festival Baltica '88, old national flags are publicly displayed for the first time under Soviet rule. Photo by Pēteris Korsaks, 1988.

arranged dance parties, singing, instrument playing, dancing workshops, clubs, and other events, cultivating the view that all could participate in such activities. These enthusiasts tried to renew repertoires and traditional rituals and other contexts.

Cultivating the renewed ethnic music traditions in the 1980s was allied to the national resistance movement, opposing Soviet totalitarianism and russification. The most striking expression of this movement was the folklore festival Baltica '88, during which a symbol of prewar Latvia—the national flag—was flown (figure 4). However, such music did not become a generally accepted national symbol, and in the 1990s its sphere narrowed.

HISTORY OF SCHOLARSHIP

Extensive systematic collection of Latvian folk songs and instrumental melodies started in the 1870s. Andrejs Jurjāns's still important six-volume *Latvju tautas mūzikas materiāli* ('Materials of Latvian folk music', 1894–1926) contains more than eleven hundred items, with descriptions of customs and traditional contexts and field observations. Similarly, Krišjānis Barons's six-volume collection of Latvian folk-song texts, *Latvju dainas* (Latvian *dainas*, 1895–1914), remains fundamental.

In 1925, soon after the establishment of the independent Latvian State, the Latvian Folklore Repository (Latviešu Folkloras Krātuve) was founded. It organized the collection of folklore materials, basically folk-song texts, beliefs, riddles, and similar verbal lore. Folk music was not counted among these priorities, though 155 wax cylinders and a number of discs were recorded in and after 1926.

Another important collector and publisher of Latvian folk music was Emilis Melngailis, whose most active period of collecting was the 1920s and 1930s. By 1941, he had collected about forty-five hundred tunes. From 1951 to 1953, three large volumes of his—*Latviešu mūzikas folkloras materiāli* (Materials of Latvian Musical Folklore), containing thousands of items, were published.

After World War II, the Latvian Folklore Repository was gradually transformed into the Department of Folklore of the Institute of Language and Literature within the Academy of Sciences of the Latvian Soviet Socialist Republic. It instigated systematic folklore-collection field work. In the 1940s and 1950s, special support was aimed at the collection of something that did not exist: so-called Soviet folklore, "folk songs" about Stalin and Lenin, communism, revolution, one's happy life under communism, and so on. But between May 1945 and 1990, about fourteen thousand newly transcribed musical items were archived, and the number of transcriptions exceeded thirty thousand.

From the early 1950s until 1977, the foremost authority on Latvian folk-music scholarship was Jēkabs Vītoliņš. The series *Latviešu tautas mūzika* (Latvian folk music) was compiled under his guidance. Through 1997, five volumes were published, and the sixth was in press.

The number of institutions dealing with folk music has recently increased. The collection of folk-music audio recordings at the Music Department of Latvian Radio was developed by the ethnomusicologist and music editor Gita Lancere. The archives of folk-music recordings of the Latvian Academy of Music, founded in 1990, was led until 1993 by Mārtiņš Boiko. The Center for Ethnic Studies of the University of Latvia, founded in 1992 by Māra Mellēna, Valdis Muktupāvels, and Ernests Spīčs, developed an approach toward traditional culture in modern education, integrating music, choreography, narrative genres, ceremonies, ornaments, and symbols. An independent Folk Music Center, led by Māris Jansons, concentrates on collecting and disseminating audio and video recordings. The Baltic Institute of Folklore, founded in 1994, aims to coordinate and promote folklore studies and research in all three Baltic States—Latvia, Lithuania, and Estonia.

BIBLIOGRAPHY

Apanavičius, Romualdas. 1992. *Baltu etnoinstrumentologija* (Baltic ethno-organology). Kaunas: Kauno lietuviu tautinés kultūros centras.

Apkalns, Longins. 1959. "Die lettische Volksmusik aus der Sicht der kulturhistorischen Gegebenheiten des baltischen Raumes." *Anthropos* 54:765–795.

———. 1984. "Folk Music." In *Latvia*, ed. Vito Vitauts Sīmanis, 87. St. Charles: The Book Latvia.

Bielenstein, August. 1918. *Die Holzbauten und Holzgeräte der Letten.* Vol. 2. Petrograd: N.p.

Boiko, Martin. 1994. "Latvian Ethnomusicology: Past and Present." *Yearbook for Traditional Music,* 47–65.

Brambats, Karl. 1969. "Die lettische Volkspoesie in musikwissenschaftlicher Sicht, I: Musikinstrumente im Spiegel des lettischen Volksliedes." *Musik des Ostens* 5:25–48.

———. 1982. "Ein frühes Zeugnis livländischen Singens" *Musik des Ostens* 8:9–29.

———. 1983. "The Vocal Drone in the Baltic Countries: Problems of Chronology and Provenance." *Journal of Baltic Studies* 14(1):24–34.

Braun, Joachim. 1971. "Die Anfänge des Musikinstrumentenspiels in Lettland." *Musik des Ostens* 6:88–125.

Braun, Joachim, and Karl Brambats. 1985. *Rakstu izlase par latviešu mūziku: Bibliogrāfija: Selected Writings on Latvian Music: A Bibliography.* Münster: Verlag Latvija.

Jaremko, Christina. 1980. "The Baltic Folk Zithers: An Ethnological and Structural Analysis." M.A. thesis, University of California at Los Angeles.

———. 1984. "Traditional Musical Instruments." In *Latvia,* ed. Vito Vitauts Sīmanis, 89. St. Charles: The Book Latvia.

Jurjāns, Andrejs. 1894–1926. *Latvju tautas mūzikas materiāli* (Materials of Latvian folk music). 6 vols. Riga: N.p.

Klotiņš, Arnolds, and Valdis Muktupāvels. 1989. "Traditional Musical Instruments and the Semantics of Their Functions in Latvian Folk Songs." In *Linguistics and Poetics of Latvian Folk Songs,* ed. Vaira Vīķis-Freibergs, 186–217. Kingston and Montreal: McGill-Queen's University Press.

Melngailis, Emilis. 1951–1953. *Latviešu mūzikas folkloras materiāli* (Materials of Latvian musical folklore). 3 vols. Riga: Latvijas Valsts izdevniecība.

Muktupāvels, Valdis. 1987. *Tautas mūzikas instrumenti Latvijas PSR teritorijā* (Folk-musical instruments in the territory of the Latvian S.S.R.). Riga: E. Melngaiļa Republikas tautas mākslas un kultūras izglītības darba zinātniski metodiskais centrs.

Münster, Solomon. 1598. *Cosmography: Das ist, beschreibung aller Länder.* Basel: N.p.

Priedīte, Īrisa. 1983. *Ko spēlēja sendienās* (What they played in the days of yore). Riga: Zvaigzne.

———. 1988. *Tautas mūzikas instrumenti* (Folk-musical instruments). German summary. Riga: Avots.

———. 1993. *Cītaras un meistari: Katalogs* (Zithers and their makers: A catalog [German summary]). Riga: Latvijas Etnogrāfiskais brīvd-abas muzejs.

Reynolds, Stephen. 1983. "The Baltic Psaltery and Musical Instruments of Gods and Devils."

Journal of Baltic Studies 14(1):5–23.

Rinks, Johanna, and Jānis Ošs. 1934–1936. *Latvju tautas dejas* (Latvian folk dances). 4 vols. Riga: Valters un Rapa.

Silņa, Elza. 1939. *Latviešu deja* (Latvian Dance [German summary]). Riga: Latviešu folkloras krātuve.

Sūna, Harijs. 1966. *Latviešu rotaļas un rotaļdejas* Latvian folk dances accompanied by singing). Riga: Zinātne.

Vīķis-Freibergs, Vaira, ed. 1989a. *Linguistics and Poetics of Latvian Folk Songs.* Kingston and Montreal: McGill-Queen's University Press.

———. 1989b. "Oral Tradition as Cultural History in the Lyrical World of the Latvian Daina." In *Linguistics and Poetics of Latvian Folk Songs,* ed. Vaira Vīķis-Freibergs, 3–13. Kingston and Montreal: McGill-Queen's University Press.

Vītoliņš, Jēkabs. 1958. *Darba dziesmas* (Work songs). Riga: Latvijas Valsts izdevniecība.

———. 1967. "Die lettischen Hirtenlieder." *Deutsches Jahrbuch für Volkskunde* 13:213–222.

———. 1968. *Kāzu dziesmas* (Wedding songs). Riga: Zinātne.

———. 1971. *Bērnu dziesmu cikls: Bēru dziesmas* (Children's-song cycle: Funeral songs). Riga: Zinātne.

———. 1973. *Gadskārtu ieražu dziesmas* (Seasonal ritual songs). Riga: Zinātne.

———. 1986. *Precību dziesmas* (Matchmaking songs). Riga: Zinātne.

AUDIOVISUAL RESOURCES

Kapusts, Andris. 1994. *Balsis no Latvijas* (Voices from Latvia). Auss RS 001. Cassette, compact disc.

Klotiņš, Arnolds, and Vilis Bendorfs. 1986. *Latvijas PSR muzikālā folklora* (Musical folklore of Latvian S.S.R.). Melodija M30 46913 005. LP disk.

Lancere, Gita. 1994. *Voix des Pays Baltes: chants traditionnels de l'Lettonie, Lituanie, Estonie: documents d'archives.* INEDIT, Maison des Cultures du Monde W 260055. Compact disc.

Muktupāvels, Valdis. 1993. *Zelta Kokles* (Golden kokles). Micrec. Cassette.

———. 1995. *Lettonie: Musiques des rites solaires: Ensemble RASA.* INEDIT, Maison des Cultures du Monde W 260062. Compact disc.

Musical Art of the Peoples of the USSR: Estonian/Latvian Instrumental Music. 1985. Melodija C90 23253-23254/Le Chant du Monde LDX 74006. LP disk.

Reizniece, Ilga. 1993. *Ilģi: Bāremu dziesmes.* Cassette, compact disc.

———. 1996. *Ilģi: Riti.* Cassette, compact disc.

Seasonal Songs of Latvia: Beyond the River. 1998. Hemisphere 7243 49334120. Compact disc.

Lithuania
Chris Goertzen

Vocal Music
Musical Instruments
History, Ideology, and Contemporary Developments

The southernmost and largest of the Baltic states (65,201 square kilometers), Lithuania shares borders with Latvia in the north, Belarus in the east, and Poland in the southwest. Its 100 kilometers of Baltic coastline afford it a moderate climate for such a northern location. Though it has extensive forested areas and wetlands, about half its territory is splendid farmland. About 80 percent of the population (of just under four million) are ethnic Lithuanians, with 9 percent ethnic Russians (most of whom recently voted for independence from Russia) and small populations of Poles, Belarusans, Ukrainians, and Jews. A majority are Roman Catholic. The Lithuanian language is in the Baltic branch of Indo-European languages.

Lithuania became a grand duchy in 1236 and officially became Christian in 1386—the last country in Europe to do so. It was absorbed by Poland in the early 1500s, and then gradually taken over by Russia. When the Russian empire collapsed, during World War I, Lithuania achieved independence, though not stability. Its reannexation by the U.S.S.R. during World War II was accompanied by horrific repression, including the exiling of more than three hundred fifty thousand Lithuanians to Siberia. When the Soviet empire weakened, Lithuania was the first republic to declare independence, in 1990. Independence was achieved by 1991, and the time since has been filled with attempts to stabilize the economy and define the nation—a task to which music and dance have contributed enormously.

VOCAL MUSIC

Lithuania harbors a remarkable legacy of vocal repertoires. Because the economy remained largely agricultural until after World War II, thousands of work and calendric songs, with historical ballads and political songs from earlier in the century, remained in use in oral tradition to that time. Then industrialization (the enemy of functional song) and repressive recolonization by the Soviet Union inspired Lithuanians to seek nonconfrontational ways to remind themselves of earlier, better times. What better way to do this than through song? When the formal folk revival moved into high gear, in the late 1960s, plenty of tradition bearers who had nurtured their repertoires carefully were still alive, allowing this revival to be rich.

The most general characteristics of prewar Lithuanian traditional song texts are

Szen–dien ger– sim, bu– stą– kel– sim, Ry– toj' szwen– tą isz–mie– go– sim. (isz–mie– gos'.)

FIGURE 1   Untitled song about drinking and flirting, first published in Bartsch 1886:184. The text, translated from Lithuanian, reads: "Today, we will drink heartily. Tomorrow, Sunday, we will sleep." In the remaining stanzas, three young, lusty soldiers ride through a field and a meadow to a riverbank, then up a mountain to ancient trees and a cool spring, where three maidens are washing clothes. The soldiers offer beer to the girls, who show them only wreaths, symbolizing innocence.

that they are more often lyrical than narrative, and are not extremely dramatic, and that nature and associated imagery loom large, as do mythological and metaphorical references. Since women were the primary bearers of tradition, most song lyrics reflect a female perspective. Plenty of songs are calendric, linked to festivals (Christmas, Easter, Shrove Tuesday, the summer solstice) or many events in the agricultural year. Wedding songs are varied and important. The lyrics, neither extremely light nor excessively serious, make up a body of engaging but calm verse, usually set strophically, occasionally linked with a variety of dances (Balys 1935).

Just as most texts are straightforward, albeit with a rich vocabulary of nature-infused symbolism (Balys 1961; Sruoga 1932), modal practice tends not to surprise. The vast majority of melodies are firmly in a major key. A significant minority are in the aeolian mode; more recently, some of these have been transformed into the melodic minor mode, perhaps under the influence of younger melodies, which arrived with instruments such as the accordion. Other modes, notably mixolydian and rarely lydian, appear, though the most common deviation from fully fleshed major are melodies that fit within the major mode but use fewer pitches in a narrower range. Folk melodies have fueled a nationalist school of art-music composition, which, though little known outside the country, has produced a substantial body of learned and vigorous works. Lithuanian composers have participated in many widely known twentieth-century compositional styles, but nationalism remains the most important trend (Nakas 1974, 1975; Tauragis 1971; Venclauskas 1990).

Text setting in Lithuanian folk songs is mostly syllabic, with the addition of a few short passing notes. Meter can be flexible, though not extremely complicated. Most tunes are in simple duple or simple triple meter, with a fair number combining duple and triple sections or measures (figure 1). Phrasing tends toward being balanced, but with later phrases often extended by a measure or two. Just as "extra" measures add weight to the ends of phrases, some songs repeat their last line or two. Overall forms are rounded: AABA, ABAC, and so on.

Perhaps the most striking type of Lithuanian traditional vocal music is the *sutartinė*, a family of polyphonic song types (coupled with dances) originally from the southeast, from the northern portion of the province of Aukštaitija. Texts, which tend to be short and simple, concern work, though parts of many are nonsense syllables. These songs are in clear-cut duple meter, often containing much syncopation. The vast majority are in two to four vocal or sometimes instrumental parts. The nature of the polyphony varies: some seem just a step away from heterophony, but more are canonic or in loosely imitative counterpoint. Melodic motion is generally minimal, with many repeated pitches and very shallow melodic curves. What is most remarkable about the genre is that quite a few examples feature series of dissonant seconds, and may even move in parallel seconds (figure 2). Since this feature makes the genre quite distinctive, it has become a favorite of revival ensembles throughout the country and in immigrant communities.

Tradition in Lithuanian song has never flagged, though performance venues have changed with how work has been performed and new events have spawned new genres of song. For instance, the most recent exile—the mass deportations to Siberia

FIGURE 2   The *sutartinė* "Obelyt, gražuolyt" for instruments, first published in Baltrėnienė and Apanavičius 1991:41. Note the shallow melodic contour and the dissonance produced by parallel motion in seconds.

♩ = 84

combined with escapes to the West—produced its own body of songs, with texts such as, "In spring all the birds fly home, / But we, will we ever return?" (Kelmickaitė 1998:73). New performance venues overlap with the older ones. There is less singing while at work, since agriculture and industry involve less physical labor and less rhythmic motion than before. Family gatherings and such convivial and significant occasions as weddings continue to be graced with song, and new venues have appeared in the choral concerts and other revival settings discussed below.

MUSICAL INSTRUMENTS

Lithuania is rich in indigenous and imported musical instruments. The best-known stringed instrument is the *kanklės,* a native plucked zither in a family of zithers found in each neighboring country. It has four to a dozen or more strings, stretched over a flat, trapezoidal body, the longest (and thus lowest-sounding) strings along the longer side of the body. The soundboard is fashioned from spruce, and the rest of the instrument of native hardwoods, such as dogwood, aspen, and oak. It is usually tuned to a pentachordal scale—most often the first five members of the natural minor scale (for instance, d–e–f–g–a). It has been used to accompany song (often in religious ceremonies) and to play alone. Though the instrument has looked much the same for centuries (several sizes have regularly been in use), it has moved up and down the social ladder—relative refinement of construction and physical ornamentation corresponds roughly to number of strings and upper-class use (Baltrėnienė and Apanavičius 1991:33–37). Though moribund earlier in the twentieth century, it became arguably more popular than before in the recent folk revival, much as have the American lap dulcimer and the Swedish keyed fiddle. Today, most *kanklės* are elegantly crafted, have many strings, and are often played in ensembles of about ten instruments.

Other plucked stringed instruments found in Lithuania include variously sized hammered dulcimers, much like the Hungarian cimbalom, and the psaltery. Bowed strings include the rare *manikarka* (a one-stringed cello, used in the church), and the rarer *boselis,* with an air- and pea-filled bladder as a bridge. A violin with a skin face has largely been replaced by the modern violin, which had become the only bowed stringed instrument in frequent use in prerevival oral tradition.

Žilevičius (1935, 1957) describes Lithuanian folk wind instruments in detail. The simplest are pipes, and among these the most primitive is the *skudutis* (plural *skudučiai*), individual panpipes used in ensembles of three to seven (the first five tuned to, for example, d–e–f–g–a, the others, if present, within a semitone above the a). In performance, two to five players produce simultaneous seconds in instrumental versions of the *sutartinė.* These days, larger groups of pipes are played by larger groups of performers, each of whom takes up to three pipes (Baltrėnienė and Apanavičius 1991:83). The *vamzdis* is a wooden flute with a few finger holes. The most visually arresting instruments in this group are clay ocarinas shaped like and named for barnyard animals.

Reed instruments include the *birbynė,* which has a single reed and sounds rather like a clarinet, and the formerly popular *labanorų dūda,* a bagpipe held under the arm, with blow pipe, melody pipe, and drone pipe.

A wooden trumpet, the *ragas,* is made from complementary hollowed-out pieces of ash. It is treated much like the *skudutis*—that is, each instrument plays one note, and ensembles consist of variously sized trumpets, which together can play a scale. Relatives of the *ragas* include a larger wooden trumpet (100 to 250 centimeters long), the *trimitis,* which produces a natural scale through overblowing, and the *ožragis,* a goat horn with four or five finger holes. This and various fipple flutes are pastoral instruments, played alone or in pairs.

Nearly nine hundred ensembles were formed between 1980 and 1989, some of them village groups that drew directly on local tradition—so-called ethnographic ensembles—and some "folklore" ensembles that adapted or recreated traditions.

Accordions, which became popular during the twentieth century, are often played in village ensembles with bowed stringed instruments and clarinet types.

Percussion instruments include tambourines, drums made from hollowed-out tree trunks, wooden bells in many sizes and shapes (some played by groups of people, one player per bell, others suspended from racks in sets played by an individual), ratchets, and the use of simple boards and body parts to create rhythms.

Brass-band instruments join the accordion and violin as welcomed imports, played in ensembles whose instrumentation is often much the same as elsewhere in Europe. The most remarkable aspect of instrumental practice in Lithuania is the long-standing preference for ensembles of considerable size, of even the simplest instruments. Folk revivals throughout Europe have featured more and larger ensembles than had been found in oral tradition, but in Lithuania, the spirit of cooperation and habit of playing in ensembles constitute an unusually valid basis for such revival practices.

HISTORY, IDEOLOGY, AND CONTEMPORARY DEVELOPMENTS

That the Baltic countries have seldom been independent in modern times invests nationalism in each with special urgency, and has inspired the use of song as national symbol for centuries. The national-romantic use of folk song behind Johann Gottfried Herder's *Volkslieder* (first published in 1778–1779) resonated in Lithuania. Herder's collections contained eight Lithuanian folk-song texts, perhaps in part because there was a large expatriate population of Lithuanians in German-speaking territory; however, a nationalist movement took hold in Lithuania proper somewhat later than in the neighboring Baltic states. Lithuania was more rural, and serfdom was abolished there only in 1861, decades later than in Latvia and Estonia. Also, the 1863 Polish revolt against Russia, which included Lithuanian nobles (who spoke Polish), was savagely repressed. The first large self-consciously patriotic Lithuanian choral concerts were held in Lithuanian communities of East Prussia in the 1890s. Such concerts were not allowed in Russian-controlled Lithuania.

The first song festival in Lithuania came relatively late, in 1924, yet it featured seventy-six choirs with three thousand members. The early festivals followed German practice, that is, relatively genteel performance of arrangements of songs with three- or four-part harmony. Performance practice was civilized rather than accurate: the words were what mattered. Indeed, most published collections of Lithuanian song have been of texts only. Melodies came second, and offered good raw material for a vigorous national school of art composition. Actual folk-harmonic practices, harsh and loud vocal timbres, and rhythmic aspects, were neglected.

The time between the world wars gave the Baltic States a brief but precious respite from Russian rule. Subsequent Soviet domination was stunningly brutal, and, as time passed, quite thorough. The idea of the song festival appealed to the new

FIGURE 3   Massed line dancers at the "Day of Dance" at the 1998 World Song Festival in Vilnius. Photo by ELTA.

oppressors as an ideological tool, though continuing with these festivals remained a valuable emotional outlet for thousands of Lithuanians. Government subsidies increased the number, size, and quality of choirs. These groups spent enormous amounts of time and effort with pieces such as a cantata about Stalin, but the sheer act of group singing, plus the rare occasion to do Lithuanian songs with flexible meanings (e.g., about the glory of collectives, but ones made up of Lithuanians), became a form of "hidden national resistance" (Šmidchens 1996:107–109).

As time passed and the Soviet grip relaxed incrementally, massive choral spectacle was supplemented by small-scale local folklorism, emphasizing musical and poetic forms that antedated rural urbanization and agricultural collectivization. The Soviet model, embodied in the performances of the professional state folk ensemble of the Lithuanian S.S.R., Lietuva, was slick and European, with harmonizations and vocal style that were attractive but by no stretch of the imagination traditional. At the same time, groups of students at Vilnius University sang folk songs together, and a fair number became amateur ethnographers. Since Lithuania had been the least industrialized of the Baltic states, still retaining substantial rural areas after World War II, many of these students still had strong ties to village culture. Their fieldwork in specific villages—much of it long-term and participatory—yielded an interesting collage of ethnographies, beginning in the late 1960s. The Ramuva movement, named for sacred pagan groves, had a general interest in the authentic ethnic culture of Lithuania and a special focus on music. About fifteen hundred students and professors took part in movement-sponsored fieldwork between 1968 and 1998. These collectors formed student societies and lively small ensembles, many of which survived Soviet crackdowns in 1971 and 1983, eventually achieving a measure of uneasy tolerance. Nearly nine hundred ensembles were formed between 1980 and 1989, some of them village groups that drew directly on local tradition—so-called ethnographic ensembles—and some "folklore" ensembles that adapted or recreated traditions (Kelmickaitė 1998:75).

The ethnography-based folk movement moved steadily in the direction of mass tradition, both drawing on and opposing Soviet-sponsored activities. The young movement regularly sought to create participatory, inclusive singing communities, charting a path contrasting vividly with that of groups like Lietuva, with its trained specialists. Following a few regional festivals, 1976 witnessed the first of what would become a series of annual festivals in Vilnius. It had many debts to the Soviet festival model, but experiments in size and setting of festivals' constituent events produced a durable balance of large and small concerts. An international festival, Baltica, rotated among the Baltic countries beginning in 1987, but was most successful in Lithuania: the first of these festivals, held in Vilnius, lasted five event-crowded days. The Soviet overseers were in a quandary: "To ensure massive public participation in the festival, the folklore ensembles were allowed into portions of the official program. It was these ensembles, and their songs and dances continuing through the nights," that ensured the festival's success and impressed visitors (Šmidchens 1996:146). In time, older people contributed partisan and exile songs, formerly sung in private. These songs spread quickly, uniting people and acting as weapons of resistance (Kelmickaitė 1998:75).

A projected return of Baltica to Vilnius in 1990 was stifled, but not entirely squelched, by a Soviet blockade. Finally, in September of 1991, thousands of Lithuanians gathered on the Song Festival grounds in Vilnius to celebrate independence, with folk ensembles participating from all the Baltic states. Just as the Soviet model of slick "folk" performances for passive audiences had been incrementally overwhelmed by a festival model based on public participation, power had changed hands with less violence than anyone would have expected. The demonstrations of solidarity in the song festivals had done much to convince the Soviets that they had to let go of Lithuania and soon the other Baltic States, justifying a frequently heard slogan, *The Singing Revolution.*

Just as folk ensembles played a major role in Lithuania's achieving national independence, they continued to be central in encouraging and defining national culture (figure 3). Both stages of musical nationalism were vigorously supported, in Lithuania proper and abroad. Streams of immigration at various periods created Lithuanian communities supporting many music and dance ensembles, for instance in the United States and Canada (Braun 1983; Liubinienė and Kelly 1997). Back home, groups such as the Vilnius University Ensemble are large, extremely active, and fascinatingly complex in how they draw on older folk culture. Carefully restricted use of musical notation, something of a calendric rotation of repertoire, and emphasizing groups over stars within them all express some allegiance to older folk practice, even as a new folk practice is defined. Some ensembles draw on families of performers, but create new families too, as many marriages occur between members who had not known one another before joining the groups. Many of the top scholars of Lithuanian folk music work with revival ensembles.

BIBLIOGRAPHY

Ambrazevičius, Rytis, comp. 1994. *Lithuanian Roots: An Overview of Lithuanian Traditional Culture.* Vilnius: Lithuanian Folk Culture Center.

Baltrėnienė, Marija, and Romualdas Apanavičius. 1991. *Lietuviu liaudies muzikos instrumentai* (Lithuanian folk-musical instruments). Vilnius: Vilnius Mintis.

Balys, Jonas. 1935. "Lithuanian Folk Dances." *Journal of the English Folk Dance and Song Society* 2:139–142.

———. 1958. *Lithuanian Folksongs in America: Narrative Songs and Ballads.* Boston: Lithuanian Encyclopedia Publishers.

———. 1961. "The Lithuanian Daina." *Lituanus* 7(1):21–23.

Bartsch, Christian, ed. 1886. *Dainu Balsai:*

Melodieen litauischer Volkslieder. Heidelberg: Carl Winters Universitäts-Buchhandlung.

Braun, Joachim. 1983. "One or Two Baltic Musics?" *Journal of Baltic Studies* 14(1):67–75.

Katzenelenbogen, Uriah. 1935. *The Daina: An Anthology of Lithuanian and Latvian Folk-Songs.* Chicago: Lithuanian News Publishing.

Kelmickaitė, Zita. 1998. "The Tenacity of Tradition." *Smithsonian Folklife Festival 1998.* Washington, D.C.: Smithsonian Institution.

Landsbergis, Algirdas, and Clark Mills. 1964. *The Green Linden: Selected Lithuanian Folksongs.* New York: Voyages Press.

Liubinienė, Vilmantė, and Mary E. Kelly. 1997. "Some Aspects of Lithuanian Folklore and the United States." *Lituanus* 43(2):56–75.

Nakas, Vytas. 1974. "The Music of Lithuania: A Historical Sketch." *Lituanus* 20(4):55–61.

———. 1975. "Gražina: The First Lithuanian National Opera." *Lituanus* 21(1):45–62.

Šmidchens, Guntis. 1996. "A Baltic Music: The Folklore Movement in Lithuania, Latvia, and Estonia, 1968–1991." Ph.D. dissertation, Indiana University.

Sruoga, Balys. 1932. "Lithuanian Folk Songs (Dainos)." Translated by E. J. Harrison. *Folk-Lore* 43(3):301–324.

Tauragis, Adeodatas. 1971. *Lithuanian Music Past and Present.* Translated by M. Ginsburgas and N. Kameneckate. Vilnius: Gintaras.

Venclauskas, Loreta. 1990. "Modern Twentieth-Century Lithuanian Music." *Lituanus* 36(3):72–81.

Žilevicius, Juozas. 1935. "Native Lithuanian Musical Instruments." *Musical Quarterly* 21(1):99–106.

———. 1957. "Native Musical Instruments." *Lituanus* 1(10):12–15.

AUDIOVISUAL RESOURCES

Beliajus, V. F. 195?. *Lithuanian Songs and Dances.* Monitor MF 305. LP disk.

Lietuva Musical Group. 1969. *Lietuva lietuviu liaudies muzikos instrumentai ansamblyje* (Lithuanian folk-instrumental music ensembles). Riga: Melodija 33D-252 73–80. Four LP disks.

Lituanie, le pays des chansons. 1997. Ocora C 600005. Compact disc.

Western Europe

The countries of Western Europe are predominantly Roman Catholic, a religion whose calendar of holidays, processions, and pilgrimages provides many occasions for making music. The languages of the region belong primarily to the Romance family of languages. Rhyming couplets form the basis for an important genre of song dueling in Portugal, Spain, and the Mediterranean islands (Corsica, Sardinia, Sicily, and Malta). Narrative ballads are more prevalent north of the Mediterranean. Singing is mainly monophonic, but polyphonic styles exist in Sardinia, Corsica, and certain parts of Italy.

Tambourines and shawms, as well as a high-pitched, tense vocal production, are probably remnants of Arabic influence. The guitar is perhaps the instrument most associated with southwestern Europe, but diatonic accordions and violins are also found throughout the region. Municipal brass bands form an important part of musical life and play arrangements of popular pieces from the classical tradition.

MAP 5   Western Europe

Low Countries
Wim Bosmans

Vocal Music and Song Types
Context and Performance
Instrumental Music
Musical Instruments
Sources and the Results of Their Study

The Low Countries, so called because large parts lie below or just above sea level and on the deltas of major river systems such as the Rhine, include Belgium, the Netherlands, Luxembourg, and French Flanders. Tucked on about 74,000 square kilometers between France, Germany, and the North Sea, these countries have long been among Europe's leading centers of finance, commerce, sea trade, and industry.

The Netherlands' fifteen million people speak Dutch, though in the northern province of Friesland, Frisian (the Germanic language most closely resembling English) is an official language. Belgium, with about ten million people, has three official languages: the Flemings of northern Belgium, known as Flanders, speak Dutch; the people in French Flanders also speak Dutch dialects; the Walloons are French-speakers from southern Belgium, known as Wallonia; and German is spoken in eastern Belgium.

The music of this last area and of Luxembourg will not be discussed here, since little research has been conducted on these regions. The Low Countries are not separated from Germany and France by major natural borders, so they have always been open to political, cultural, and musical influence from abroad. Only the Dutch-French language boundary in Belgium constitutes an ethnic frontier in some respects.

Since the Middle Ages, the Low Countries have been among the most urbanized areas of Europe. From the 1400s to about 1600, scholars, painters, and musicians—the last including Guillaume Dufay, Gilles Binchois, Johannes Ockeghem, Josquin des Pres, and others—played a leading role in the Renaissance. Amsterdam's Concertgebouw Orchestra has long been one of the world's leading orchestras. Urban, middle-class musical practice borrowed from and influenced folk culture. Since urbanites often have an ambiguous attitude toward folk culture, simultaneously desiring to preserve it while distancing themselves from it, and since traditional musicians and singers have adopted manufactured instruments and classical-music tonal systems, it is often hard to draw a line between middle-class and lower-class, urban and rural, musical culture.

VOCAL MUSIC AND SONG TYPES

The traditional repertoire of songs in the Low Countries can be divided roughly into

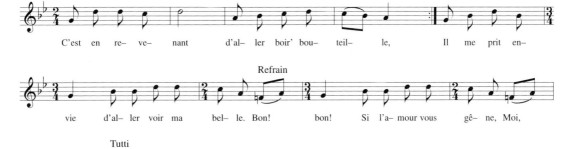

FIGURE 1 *Crâmignon* chain-dance song from Liège. After Terry and Chaumont 1889:48–49.

2. Il me prit envie d'aller voir ma belle.
   Je vis trois rivaux assis auprès d'elle.
   Refrain: Bon! bon!
        Si l'amour vous gêne,
         Moi, non!

3. Je vis trois rivaux assis auprès d'elle.
   Et quand ils m'ont vu, s' sont retirés d'elle.
        Bon, etc.

4. Et quand ils m'ont vu s' sont retirés d'elle.
   Restez, mes rivaux, assis auprès d'elle.
        Bon, etc.

5. Restez, mes rivaux, assis auprès d'elle;
   Vous n'aurez jamais ce que j'ai eu d'elle.

6. Vous n'aurez jamais ce que j'ai eu d'elle,
   J'ai eu de son coeur la fleur la plus belle.
        Bon, etc.

7. J'ai eu de son coeur la fleur la plus belle
   C'est en revenant d'aller boir' bouteille.
   Refrain: Bon! bon!
   Si l'amour vous gêne,
        Moi, non!

two groups, according to whether they originated first in oral tradition or in written form. Songs in oral tradition are generally cheerful. Dance-songs and game songs are sung by a group. As a rule, they are in binary measure and strict tempo. Particularly in Flanders, they are often sung in dialect. Each verse contains only one or two "new" elements or lines; the rest of the verse consists of repetitions of those lines and ever-returning fixed lines (refrains), among which are nonlexical syllables, such as *van falderadiere, van falderada* and *tradérira, luron, lurette.* Since these songs are constructed with mnemonic devices of this kind, they are hardly ever written down. Songs of this group are known in countless variants, but with different text and tune lengths (figure 1).

The second group includes songs whose lyrics were originally written down in manuscripts or broadsides. Their content relates positive and negative experiences, and they are usually sung solo. They can be in ternary measure, and the serious songs

FIGURE 2 Broadside ballad "*Genoveva van Brabant.*" Sung by Arthur De Winter (b. 1896), at Aaigem, West-Vlaanderen Province, Belgium. Collected and transcribed by Hubert Boone.

are often performed in *parlando rubato* (figure 2). As a rule, the text is in a kind of standard French or Dutch. The verses contain four to eight or more lines, of which the last one or two are in some instances repeated. They were also transmitted orally, but this process usually resulted in a qualitative deterioration of the lyrics.

In the Low Countries, folksinging is essentially monodic. Accompanying harmony is only rarely provided by a musical instrument. Spontaneous two-part singing has been recorded sporadically, but this seems to be a nineteenth-century phenomenon. The melodic outline of traditional songs is usually undulating and fluent, with a marked preference for small intervals up to a fourth. Tunes, too, are essentially syllabic; melismas only occur exceptionally, and practically never exceed two notes to a syllable.

Among the most archaic vocal forms are the calls of herdsmen and hawkers, who often use nonfixed intervals. Only the Walloon herdsmen's calls have been studied: their nucleus is a (mostly major) third, which can be divided into two tones and completed with an additional whole tone, or more recently a semitone, at the bottom or top of the scale. Also archaic are bichordal or trichordal chains of short motives sung by children. A study of Flemish children's repertoires reveals that the most representative tritonic scale is A–C–D, with C the central degree (Gelber 1972). Children also make great use of scales of four, five or six tones, the most frequent scales being G–A–B–C–D(–E–G) and (G–)C–D–E(–G). Such scales may have been transmitted since premedieval times.

Tunes of more than four phrases are exceptional, and melodies often consist of only two phrases. One quarter of extant Dutch ballads have the form AB, the other most common forms being AAB, AABB, and ABC. Until about 1900, songs built on the varied repetition of a single phrase were collected from laceworkers in West-Vlaanderen Province. Most melodies range between an octave and an octave and a fourth, and have a major heptatonic scale. About a third of the folk songs from the adult repertoire collected in Flanders in the 1800s and the early 1900s were in various modal scales; the rest are in major or minor keys.

FIGURE 3 Ornamented singing from Volendam.
After Veurman 1968:236.

Few melodies modulate. Two-thirds of Dutch ballads have a plagal scale, and half the plagal tunes in a major scale start with the dominant followed by the tonic. The final note is usually the tonic, and sometimes the third degree. A lot of Dutch ballad tunes in a major scale are built around broken triads, predominantly I–III–V and less often II–V–VI.

Singers in the Low Countries show a marked preference for binary meters. Most songs are entirely isometric; however, tunes with heterometric features are not uncommon, the most frequent combinations in Dutch ballad tunes being 3/4 + 4/4, 6/8 + 9/8 and 2/4 + 3/4. The presence of heterometer can be structural or incidental, because of the singer's adapting the measure to the text, or pausing at the end of a phrase. Most melodies start with an upbeat, and syncopation is extremely rare.

The style of singing is sober, without grace notes, except in Volendam (Noord-Holland Province), where singers like to embellish their singing with turns on long notes, trills, and less frequently mordants on short notes. The generic local term for these notes is *trararetje* (figure 3). More common is the use of glissando; there is little variety in dynamics.

The marked decline of traditional singing was caused by the mechanization of agriculture, industrialization, the radio, the increasing ease of transportation, and the advent of electric lighting, by means of which twilight—the best time for singing in the family circle—was removed.

CONTEXT AND PERFORMANCE

Until the early 1900s, singing played an important part in everyday life, at work and leisure. Part of the repertoire is linked with important moments in human lives, such as conscription, marriage, or moving one's residence; hardly any songs, however, are connected with birth and death. Another important group consists of seasonal songs—luck-visit songs during carnival and Holy Week, on May Day, Midsummer, and Martinmas, and in the period from Christmas to Epiphany. Until about 1900, many luck-visit singers were handicapped or jobless adults, though they are now children and teenagers who go singing from door to door, and are given money or food, mostly biscuits, sweets, and fruits. Singers in nineteenth-century singing pubs (*cafés chantants*) were also paid.

So-called market singers sang and sold broadsides from the 1500s until about 1900, and in Flanders even until about 1950. They were a familiar sight anywhere people gathered, as for instance at markets and outside a Roman Catholic church after Mass. Usually the singer would stand on a raised platform; with a stick or fiddlestick he would point at the main scenes of his song, depicted on a piece of cloth. Broadside singers accompanied themselves on the fiddle, and later on the accordion. Their repertoire dealt chiefly with love stories, and even more with sensational news (crimes, wars, disasters), with the odd religious song for variety. In the 1800s, the content of this repertoire was quite varied: bawdy and pathetic songs appeared side by side with antimilitarist topics. One of the last Flemish broadside singers, Hubert Geens (b. 1917), had a high opinion of his profession and its artistry, which he contrasted with that of ordinary street singers, who begged from door to door as they sang (Top 1985a) [see SONG GENRES, figure 6, p. 136].

Dance-songs are now only to be found on the playgrounds of elementary schools, though until about 1900 they were performed by adolescents and adults. Instances of once popular sung round dances are *'t patertje* (a kissing dance from the Dutch-language area), sung dances round the maypole or under the *rozenhoed* (hat of roses, Dutch-language area), the *zevensprong* or *danse des sept sauts* 'seven-step dance', and dancing around bonfires during autumn and Lent, and at Midsummer and Easter. A repertoire of songs was linked with the *alion* ceremony in the Borinage area (Hainaut Province), held on a Sunday in Lent, which included a big fire. A rich variety of songs also accompanied the *crâmignon,* an open-air chain dance, performed until about 1960 in Liège, and still known in a few villages between Liège and Maastricht (Dutch province of Limburg), though now mostly accompanied by just a brass band. *Crâmignon* songs consist of distichs or quatrains, the second half of which constitutes the beginning of the next verse. A related chain dance is the *vlöggelen* of Ootmarsum (Overijssel Province), performed by more than a thousand men on Easter Sunday and Monday, and accompanied by religious Easter songs.

Most songs collected since the mid-1800s are not older than the 1700s. However, the origin of some songs still known can be traced back as far as the 1500s.

Some ballads even have medieval roots. Already in the 1800s, collectors were worried about the marked decline of traditional singing, and this decline was accelerated in the twentieth century by a combination of factors, the most important being the gradual loss of function. According to the Dutch fieldworker Ate Doornbosch, this was caused mainly by the mechanization of agriculture, industrialization, and the radio, and the growing influence of business on entertainment, the increasing ease of transportation by which the isolation of the islands and remote villages was overcome, and the advent of electric lighting, by means of which twilight—the best time for singing in the family circle—was removed. Doornbosch's (1986) field study of the ballad "*Heer Halewijn*" (or "*Jan Alberts*") documents the decline of a ballad tradition in Flanders and Friesland.

INSTRUMENTAL MUSIC

Before the 1700s, folk musicians played by ear, and the nature of their repertoire can be derived only from iconographical sources and financial accounts. In the 1400s and 1500s, the repertoire included morris and sword dances, performed for public festivities. The oldest mention of sword dancing in Europe is found in the Bruges town accounts of 1388–1389. It has survived only in two Belgian villages: as the unaccompanied *danse des pèlerins* 'pilgrims' dance' in Marbisoux (Brabant Province), and as the *trawantel* or *traweitel* (uncertain meaning) in Westerlo (Antwerp Province), where it is accompanied on a side drum only. Sixteenth- and seventeenth-century paintings chiefly show round dances, long dances, and pair dances.

Though folk musicians did not leave written music, many traditional tunes found their way into collections printed for middle-class amateurs. For instance, the brawls (*branles*) published by Tielman Susato in Antwerp (1543–1551) and by Pierre Phalèse in Leuven (1571) and Antwerp (1583) are unmistakably rooted in the Western European popular tradition. A wealth of traditional music is also found in the *Oude en Nieuwe Hollantse Boerenlieties en Contredansen* 'Old and New Dutch Peasant Songs and Country Dances', published in Amsterdam by Estienne Roger and Pierre Mortier (1700–1716). This is the largest collection of tunes ever published in the Low Countries. It contains more than a thousand folk-song melodies, marches, and dances known in Holland at that time, many of them of foreign (mainly French and English) origin. The oldest tunes date back to the late 1500s. About 1900, Theophiel Peeters collected a dozen, probably medieval, modal dance tunes from older folk musicians in Antwerp Province.

From all these sources and the instruments used, it appears that until around 1700 there was no notable distinction between instrumental and vocal music in the Low Countries; tunes were often sung and played. The scarcity of bands points to the fact that, contrary to middle-class music, folk music of the region was essentially monodic, drones being the common form of accompaniment. The fiddle-and-bass combination was introduced about 1600, but it is unclear whether the bass was used to play a drone, or whether it already had a harmonic function.

Eighteenth-century tunes are found in manuscripts and printed collections made by fiddlers, dancing masters, and carillon players, whose varied forms suggest they were often adopted from aural tradition.

Around the mid-1700s, popular music became predominantly tonal. It was still largely diatonic, but gradually moved away from vocal music. The drone accompaniment gave way to harmony—a fact that may explain the decline of the bagpipe. Some sources give an idea of the ensemble playing that was undoubtedly also adopted by country bands. The second part is mostly isorhythmic, a third or a sixth below the first voice. The bass is often limited to triadic roots, with transitional notes sometimes intervening. Occasionally, the bass part is more melodically elaborated.

Most mid-eighteenth-century sources chiefly contain marches in 2/2 time and minuets in 3/4 time. The tunes usually have an AABB structure, both units consisting of an even number of usually eight to sixteen bars, with eight-bar units predominating. Unit B is often longer than unit A. In some villages in Brabant Province, the minuet survived until about 1900. In the second half of the 1700s, the minuet gave way to the contradance (Dutch *contredans, conterdans*; French *contredanse*) in 2/2, 2/4, or 6/8 time. The "English" longways (French *colonne, [contredanse] anglaise*) and the "French" square dances (French *contredanse française, quadrille*) became immensely popular, and dance masters published important collections of country dances. All these collections contain description of the figures. The tunes were now often extended to three or even four units, each consisting of usually eight and sometimes sixteen bars, and modulation to closely related keys was no longer exceptional.

Some nineteenth-century fiddlers left manuscript collections of tunes that are among the most accessible sources for the study of popular dances and marches in this period. These manuscripts also contain numerous tunes and dances of French, German, and British origin; apparently, the minuet was still lingering on at that time. Much more popular were all kinds of country dances, such as the *anglois* 'English' in Friesland and the *passe-pied* (or *pas-py*), the *allemande* 'German', and the *amoureuse* 'love dance' in Luxembourg Province. The term *matelotte* 'sailor's dance' introduced in the second half of the 1700s, was deformed to *madlot* in Friesland (in 6/8 time), and to *maclotte* in the provinces of Liège and Luxembourg (in 2/4 or 6/8 time).

Frisian manuscripts contain a sizeable number of tunes with the title *schotz* or *schots*. Melodically, these tunes are mostly un-Scottish, but rhythmically they often appear to be related to Scottish strathspey reels or jigs, hornpipes, and marches. In the second half of the 1800s, the *Skotse trije* 'Scottish three' became the "national" dance of Friesland. Originally danced by three dancers, by about 1900 it had become a widespread square dance. Other "Scottish" square dances popular at that time, and later, include the *Skotse fjoar* (from the island of Terschelling) and the *boerenschots* (from the West-Friesland area, Noord-Holland Province). The *schots* is not to be confounded with the schottische (Dutch *schottisch,* French *scottish*), a pair dance imported from Germany in the mid-1800s.

Shortly after 1815, the first waltzes (Dutch *wals,* French *valse*), akin to the Alpine ländler [see SWITZERLAND], appeared in the north of the Netherlands and the south of Belgium. The polka was introduced in 1844, and it immediately conquered even the remotest villages. Other couple dances imported around that time include the galop, the mazurka, the *redowa,* and the schottische. The quadrille (Dutch *kadril,* French *quadrille*) was introduced in the mid-1800s. A descendant of country dances, it usually consisted of four to five figures, with different tunes in 2/4 or 6/8 time.

The instrumental tradition reached its greatest complexity in the second half of the 1800s. The handwritten scores of Belgian wind bands and mixed bands give a first and a second part, offbeat chords, and a bass. Bands whose players were literate mostly played couple dances with the structure AABBACCAABBA, each unit consisting of eight or sixteen bars. Sections B and C (called *trio*) modulate to different related (mostly) major keys, usually to the dominant and subdominant, respectively.

Literate and illiterate musicians, however, continued to play older and simpler forms of instrumental music and dance until well into the 1900s. Old rounds, country dances, quadrilles, and pair dances were best preserved in the Twente area (Overijssel Province), the Achterhoek area (Gelderland Province), on the island of Terschelling, in the West-Friesland area (Noord-Holland Province), in Antwerp Province, in the central part of Brabant Province, and in the Ardennes (Liège and Luxembourg provinces). Some communities carried on the local tradition into the

1990s. In the 1920s and 1930s, the repertoire of dances was extended with dances of American origin, such as the foxtrot, the quickstep, and the tango.

MUSICAL INSTRUMENTS

Though a large variety of instruments can be documented historically, many had disappeared from everyday practice by 1900, or are now played only in one or a few locales.

Noisemakers

A whole series of instruments are solely meant to produce an indefinite, nonmusical, and nonrhythmical sound: buzzers, whirled friction drums, whizzing discs, popguns, hammer clappers, cog rattles, oboes made of a rolled-up strip of bark, hooters, earthenware whistles, "spring" whistles made of a twig, and humming tops. In a few Belgian villages, hammer clappers and cog rattles—formerly also instruments announcing lepers and night watchmen—are still used in Holy Week by youths collecting eggs from door to door.

The custom of making noise (Dutch *scharminkelen, de bef jagen*; French *charivari*) on all kinds of instruments and utensils around the house of a villager who has misbehaved is now extinct.

Idiophones

Another group of instruments can be classified as noisemakers and rhythm instruments: shaken rattles, clappers, whips, and bells, which form part of the costume worn by the *gille,* the typical carnival character in Binche (Hainaut Province) and the surrounding villages; the *gille* wears one bell on his chest and a belt of bells around his waist.

The *hanske knap* is a clapper in the form of a wolf's or bear's head, made of a clog. This instrument accompanies luck-visit singing on Plow Monday in a few villages north of Antwerp (figure 4). A related instrument is the *knaptand,* a wild animal-like mask in the pageant (*ommegang*) of Dendermonde (West-Vlaanderen Province). Other concussion idiophones include spoons, plaque clappers, and the

FIGURE 4 Clog clappers (*hanske knap*), played in 1987 at Zandvliet, Antwerpen Province, Belgium. Photo by Marc Wouters, © W & F.

Conical tin whistles in C or D were played for amusement, mainly by young people; they were also popular with cowherds. Around 1900, this type of flute was quite often part of informal dance bands in Belgium, usually with an accordion and one or two rhythm instruments, and often with a fiddle and a cello.

FIGURE 5 Friction drums (*rommelpot*) played in 1950–1955 at Kessenich, Limburg Province, Belgium. Photographer unknown.

sticks or swords used in sword dances, such as the *trawantel* in Westerlo (Antwerp Province) and the pilgrims' dance (*danse des pèlerins*) in Marbisoux (Brabant Province).

A pseudo-bass—formerly used in informal village bands—consists of a long stick normally provided with two to four metal strings that run over a tin box or small drum as resonator and are scraped with a toothed stick. It is nearly always mounted with several additional noisemakers, such as bells, cymbals, and a sistrum.

The mouth harp (Dutch *mondtrom, mondharp, tromp(e)*; French *guimbarde, gawe*) is first mentioned at the end of the 1300s, but extant examples may be older. Archaeological research has yielded hundreds of examples from the 1400s to the 1600s, some of which may be of foreign origin, since they closely resemble examples excavated elsewhere in Western Europe. The mouth harp was played by boys and young men for their own pleasure, and in public by the Brussels virtuoso Joseph Mattau (1788–1867). Between roughly 1850 and 1900, it was in decline, but in Belgium it was sporadically played until about 1930. The most interesting specimen, a richly decorated sixteenth-century example from Oudenaarde (West-Vlaanderen Province), is housed in the Museum of Musical Instruments, Brussels.

Membranophones

The friction drum (*rommelpot*, also called *foekepot, goebe, koenkelpot*, and other terms), consists of a pot over whose lip a membrane—usually part of a pig's bladder—has been stretched (figure 5). A stick is moved up and down through a central hole in the membrane, or, more commonly, tied into the membrane and rubbed with moistened fingers. The *rommelpot* usually accompanies luck-visit singing at Shrovetide or between Christmas and Epiphany—a tradition still alive in some villages (see figure 5).

Since its introduction at the end of the 1400s, the side drum has been one of the most important open-air instruments. From the 1700s on, it was also combined with other wind instruments than the fife. A high standard of drumming is achieved by the carnival drummers of Binche and surrounding villages (Hainaut Province), whose rhythms display a fascinating asymmetry.

Aerophones

Horns

Horns are undoubtedly from premedieval times. The most revealing type, the *midwinterhoorn*, is played in the Twente area (eastern Overijssel Province) during Advent. It is made from a long stem of willow, ash, or birch, about 15 centimeters thick and 100 to 120 long. It is usually played with its bell above a well. Originally it was probably meant to inject new life into nature.

Flutes

Since the Middle Ages, the Low Countries have used a rich variety of duct flutes. Archaeological research has yielded dozens of bone duct flutes, most of which were excavated in the area of mounds (*terpengebied*) along the coast of Friesland and Groningen (Netherlands). The oldest examples cannot be dated before A.D. 1100 (Brade 1975) [see ARCHAEOLOGY OF MUSIC IN EUROPE].

The use of bone flutes seems to have died out in the 1700s. These flutes were often made from a goat's or sheep's shinbone or upper arm bone, and less frequently from a swan's ulna or other bird bone. Most examples have two to four finger holes and sometimes one thumb hole; a few specimens have six finger holes and one thumb hole. Not a single block has been preserved, and in some cases the duct may have been formed with the tongue or the lower lip.

In Belgium, a few traces of a pastoral horn-flute tradition have been found; the known examples are all made from cow horn. The duct could be formed by means of a wooden block, but the last traditional player, Henri Crasson (from Waimes, Liège Province), used his lower lip. His horn (*cwène*) has four finger holes and one thumb hole, and is played with the left hand only, to produce the hexachordal scale C–D–E–F–G–A.

Noteworthy are the enormously varied birdcalls, mostly whistles, some of which are still used illegally in Belgium by aged bird catchers. Six-hole lathe-turned duct flutes, however, were among the most popular traditional instruments of the Low Countries until the early 1900s, particularly in Belgium, where the last traditional players were recorded in the 1970s.

After the mid-1800s, these flutes were superseded by factory-made metal and plastic instruments imported from France, Germany, and England. The cheapest and consequently most widespread type was the conical tin whistle in C or D. The style of playing is characterized by a nonlegato to staccato delivery, with brisk tonguing and an economy of ornamentation. Simple or double grace notes mostly decorate the first note of the bar. Triplets replacing one note occur in nineteenth-century dance music (mazurkas, polkas, schottisches, waltzes). Six-hole duct flutes were played for amusement, mainly by young people; they were also popular with cowherds. Around 1900, this type of flute was quite often part of informal dance bands in Belgium, usually with an accordion and one or two rhythm instruments, and often with a fiddle and a cello.

The ocarina, an earthenware flute, was introduced from France into Belgium in 1876 and shortly afterward in the Netherlands; some examples of homemade instruments are known. The ocarina has the same repertoire and style of playing as the six-hole duct flute. Ocarina playing was mainly an individual pastime, but around 1900 Belgium supported several ocarina bands, playing different sizes of the instrument, from bass (with seven finger holes) to sopranino (with eight finger holes and two thumb holes). The popularity of the instrument was rather short-lived; the last good players were all born around 1900.

Pipe and tabor

The tabor pipe, a duct flute with two finger holes plus thumb hole, was portrayed for the first time about 1275–1300. It flourished later, however, from about 1450 to about 1650, and the Low Countries (the west Netherlands in particular) have preserved more tabor pipes older than 1650 than the rest of Europe. The pipe and tabor (side drum), an instrumental combination played by one person, was commonly used by professional entertainers, wandering musicians, buffoons, and jugglers, usually to accompany dances.

Until about 1540, written and iconographical sources document the use of the pipe and tabor in upper-class or middle-class circles. It is then depicted solo or in ensembles with stringed instruments (harp and lute) or other wind instruments (bombarde, cornet, shawm, trumpet). Around 1550, the pipe and tabor seems to have fallen to a more lowly status: from then on, it is shown only in the popular environment of country weddings, fairs, and the like, where it often plays with a fiddle, a bagpipe, or a hurdy-gurdy. Apparently the pipe and tabor tradition died out in the second half of the 1600s, and no tabor from the Low Countries has been preserved. Iconographical sources show a cylindrical shell, about 20 to 35 centimeters in diameter and from 10 to 35 centimeters deep.

Fife and drum

The combination of fife (a side-blown flute: Dutch *fijfer, fijfel, pijper[s]fluit*; French *fifre, sife*) and side drum was introduced in the Low Countries at the end of the 1400s, probably by or under the influence of the Swiss mercenaries. In the 1500s and 1600s, the instruments portrayed are nearly as long as the present orchestral flute. In Flanders, the keyless fife was gradually ousted by the orchestral piccolo during the 1800s.

In Wallonia, and more particularly in the area between the rivers Sambre and Meuse (Hainaut and Namur provinces), traditional keyless fifes are still being made, and the tradition is still alive there. The players, in post-Napoleonic uniforms, form part of a military escort for religious processions, and their repertoire consists of dozens of marches and signals (figure 6). The tradition is also kept up in a few towns of West-Vlaanderen Province, where as a rule the fife and drum are accompanied by a dancing buffoon. In Flanders, fifers hired by guilds of archers or other societies were often supposed to play their signature tune only.

Between Sambre and Meuse, the style of playing is characterized by a sparse use of slurring and ornamentation, with the exception of trills, which often replace long notes. In the West-Vlaanderen Province, fife playing, on the contrary, is more slurred and ornamented, mainly with single and double grace notes on downbeats. Typical of Flanders and Wallonia are slurred triplets. In the early 1900s, Theophiel Peeters collected examples of modal dance music played on the fife, but most are in major keys. Nearly all music for fifes is in 2/4 or 6/8 time (figure 7).

Bagpipe

The oldest written references to the bagpipe (Dutch *moezel(zak), doedelzak, pijpzak*;

FIGURE 6   A fife and drum band plays at Thuin, Hainaut Province, Belguim. Photo by J. Heylemans, 1986.

French *muchosa, muchafou, pipsac*) in the Low Countries date from 1275–1300. Some pictures from the period 1450–1550 show a small, primitive, droneless type, with a bag made from a bladder, and a slightly conical one-piece chanter. In the 1300s and 1400s, the most widespread type had a large, sewn bag, a conical one-piece chanter, and one cylindrical, two-jointed drone, lathe-turned and held in stocks.

Around 1500, a second, tenor, drone, added to a common stock, played an octave or a fourth below the bass drone. There is only one extant example of this type (in the Kunsthistorisches Museum, Vienna), but it is probably of German origin. In the 1700s and 1800s, Hainaut Province favored a type with a parallel arrangement of chanter and small drone in the same stock, while the bass drone rested against the shoulder. The three surviving examples of this type are all in the Museum of Musical Instruments, Brussels.

The bagpipe was played chiefly by shepherds in processions and at fairs and weddings. It was sometimes accompanied by other instruments, such as the pipe and tabor, the hurdy-gurdy, and the fiddle. It was already declining in the 1700s, when it was ousted by the fiddle and bass combination. In some areas, the tradition lingered on until about 1900; the last players were chiefly beggars (in Antwerp and Brabant provinces) and shepherds (in the north of Hainaut Province). Apparently none of these last players was recorded; consequently, little is known about their repertoire and style of playing. The tunes remembered by older informants have a range of an octave, and they are mostly in the authentic A mode or the plagal C mode. Vibrato was much used in slow tunes.

Factory-made aerophones

In the early 1800s, the manufacture of wind instruments underwent a revolution. From then on, brasses and woodwinds were made on an industrial scale, a result of the rising popularity of wind bands. In the second half of the 1800s, one or more wind bands were founded in almost every village. This form of organized ensemble playing naturally demanded a knowledge of musical notation, and numerous books of music, written by literate musicians in the late 1800s or the early 1900s, have been preserved. The best musicians of the village wind bands formed small dance bands, which often consisted of a clarinet, a cornet, a trombone, and a tuba. There could

The accordion became a truly popular instrument around 1880, with the import of cheap, industrially made German models and the start of mass production in Belgium. In no time, the accordion dethroned the fiddle as the main folk instrument for all musical occasions except religious ceremonies.

FIGURE 7   Fife tune, played by Hendrik Bruyneel of Mater, West-Vlaanderen Province, Belgium. Collected in 1953 by Hendrik Daems. Transcribed by Wim Bosmans (1998:115).

also be a second clarinet, a flute, one or two flügelhorns, and a bombardon (a bass saxhorn or a bass tuba). In Belgium, the saxophone—despite its invention (about 1840) by a Belgian, Adolphe Sax—was adopted by rural musicians in Belgium only from the 1920s on. Until the 1930s, wind bands were the most common type of band for large village dance halls.

Mouth organ

The mouth organ (harmonica) was one of the most popular instruments of amateur musicians in the Low Countries between 1900 and 1950. Nearly all models sold in the Low Countries were of the Hohner brand, made in Trossingen, Germany.

Accordion

The accordion (Dutch *accordeon, (har)monika, trekzak, trekorgel, open-en-toe, tienbasser, trekbuul, troet*; French *accordéon, harmonica*) was first made in Belgium just after 1840 by François Verhasselt (1813–1853). His double-action accordions are closely related to the Parisian models of that time, with two rows of melody keys. They also have two bass keys, sounding a bass note and its chord. These accordions are fine pieces of workmanship, decorated with precious materials.

Shortly after 1870, Vital Scheerlinck and the Italian Jean Solari established workshops in Brussels. They produced double-action accordions with two or three rows of melody keys. They provided the bass side with six to ten spoon-shaped keys, and sometimes a few additional buttons.

The first workshop outside Brussels was set up around 1880 by Felix Callewaert of Zwevezele (West-Vlaanderen Province). After its transfer to Lichtervelde in 1890, this workshop quickly became the Belgian market leader. In its heyday, between 1900 and 1925, it produced up to seventy models, some entirely made in Belgium, others assembled with mainly German parts. A bestseller was the double-action model with two melody rows and ten bass keys, of which five keys sound bass notes and the other five their chords (figure 8). The success of the Callewaert accordions inspired other Flemish craftsmen to start their own workshops.

In Wallonia, the first accordions were made in 1884 by Jean-Joseph Vassart of Auvelais (Namur Province), whose instruments closely resemble the models made by Solari and Scheerlinck. Vassart was possibly the first to make only single-action accordions. Both sides have three rows of keys; the bass keys sound only one note each—which means the player has to form the chords himself.

Besides the above-mentioned single- and double-action accordions, the Belgian makers from the period 1890–1935 produced an amazing variety of hybrid models with a single-action melody keyboard and a double-action bass keyboard, or vice versa.

In Belgium, the production of double-action and hybrid accordions ceased around 1940. Locally made accordions had lost the competitive struggle against cheaper Italian imports. In the Netherlands, however, where accordion making had been virtually nonexistent, the Flemish double-action model with ten spoon-shaped bass keys was still made until well into the 1980s by Cees Eekels in Vught (Noord-Brabant Province).

The foot bass, a bass accordion (Dutch *voetbas*; French *basse aux pieds*), was invented in 1894 by Joseph Alexandry. It consists of a large bellows, on top of which is a sound box with one row of nine to twelve buttons, depressed with both feet. The foot bass was especially popular in Namur Province and neighboring areas between 1900 and 1945.

The accordion became a truly popular instrument around 1880, with the import of cheap, industrially made German models and the start of mass production in Belgium. In no time, the accordion dethroned the fiddle as the main folk instrument for all musical occasions except religious ceremonies. The accordionists often played alone, though some performers accompanied themselves on a drum set or a bass accordion, played with both feet. Frequently, the accordion also constituted the heart of dance bands. Clubs of amateur accordionists, which constitute an important social phenomenon, are still flourishing in Belgium. A few older musicians, all born before 1914, have kept playing double-action accordions until the present day, especially in Flanders (figure 8).

Chordophones

The bowed pseudo-bass (Dutch *blazeveer, huibe*; French *criniki, ramoncelle*) is functionally related to the friction drum. It consists of a lath or a bow and usually one or two gut or fiber strings running over a bladder as resonator.

FIGURE 8 Fons De Groen (b. 1897) plays a double-action accordion in Wolvertem, Vlaams-Brabant Province, Belguim. Photo by Wim Bosmans, 1979.

Fiddle

The violin is first shown in popular contexts after about 1550; some fiddles made by rural musicians show archaic (Baroque) features. In the twentieth century, a classically inspired and a more archaic style of playing have been recorded. The latter survived until the 1970s, though only in the Walloon provinces of Liège and Luxembourg. The archaic style is characterized by nonlegato playing (single-stroke style), the use of drone strings, the absence of vibrato, economy of ornamentation, and some glissando. The fiddle can be used to play a second part or a rhythmic, generally offbeat accompaniment consisting of two notes, usually a third or a sixth, sometimes a fourth apart.

The fiddle was by far the most popular instrument for dancing in the 1700s and 1800s, until it was superseded by the accordion. Quite often it was accompanied by a bass or a cello; this duo survived in the provinces of Brabant and Antwerp until about 1920. Until about 1900, dance bands in the West-Friesland area (Noord-Holland Province) usually consisted of two fiddles and a bass. The fiddle was often combined with brasses or woodwinds.

In Flanders, burlesque imitations of the fiddle were popular until about 1900. The most widespread was the clog fiddle, the sound box of which is made from a clog [see SWEDEN]. There are basically two types: neckless instruments, on which only open strings are bowed, and instruments provided with a neck, played more or less like an ordinary fiddle. Clog fiddles were mainly used by luck-visit singers in the period between Christmas Eve and Epiphany and during carnival.

Hurdy-gurdy

The hurdy-gurdy (Dutch *(draai)lier*; French *vielle (à roue), tiesse di tch'vå, chiphonie*) was first mentioned in the 1200s. Its oldest pictorial representations date from the mid-1400s, when the instrument was already well established. Among the hurdy-gurdies preserved in museums and private collections, twelve specimens may have been made in the Low Countries, all dating from 1500 to 1800. They can be divided into two groups: valuable, sophisticated instruments, undoubtedly played by well-to-do amateurs; and truly popular, rather rudimentary, examples. Both kinds have a flat back in common. The French, lute-shaped type seems to have been exceptional, though the forms of the sound boxes show a great deal of variation. Some iconographical documents depict a pear-shaped sound box, obviously often made of a hollowed-out log; most eighteenth-century examples, however, are guitar-shaped.

The hurdy-gurdy usually has one or two melody strings and two to four drone strings; a single row of ten to fourteen keys produces a diatonic scale: some examples have a second row of keys for a full chromatic scale. From about 1500, the hurdy-gurdy is usually shown in the hands of humble, wandering minstrels, many of them blind beggars, who played for villagers as they danced and feasted. The hurdy-gurdy was sometimes depicted in more socially elevated company.

The tradition of playing hurdy-gurdies was alive until well into the 1800s; in Belgium, the last players were seen around 1920. Not a single example of their repertoire has ever been recorded.

Dulcimer

The hammered dulcimer

The trapezoidal hammered dulcimer (Dutch *hakkebord*; French *tympanon*), with seventeen to twenty-three triple and quadruple courses of metal strings, was first depicted between 1420 and 1435. The name *santoer*, mentioned in sources from about 1350 till the 1500s, probably also referred to it. The instrument may have been imported to Western Europe in the 1100s by Flemish crusaders returning from the Near East.

Only a few hammered dulcimers made in the southern Low Countries in the 1600s or 1700s have been preserved. Nearly all iconographical documents show female, upper- or middle-class players. There are, however, a few indications that the hammered dulcimer was also played by wandering street musicians until the mid-1800s.

The plucked dulcimer

The history of the plucked dulcimer (Dutch *hommel, noordse balk, vlier, (e)pinet, blokviool*; French *épinette*) starts with a Dutch instrument dated 1608 (Gemeentemuseum, The Hague), probably the oldest extant example in Europe. The instrument is usually placed on a table, and is occasionally also held across the lap or knees. In twentieth-century Belgium, the plucked dulcimer was exclusively played with a piece of cane or hardwood for fretting and a plectrum for plucking. Formerly in Noord-Holland and Friesland, the instruments with one or two melody strings were probably also played with a bow.

The plucked dulcimer was popular chiefly among farmers, craftsmen, barge men, miners, and factory workers, and also among soldiers at the Belgian front during World War I; it was the only instrument often played by women. Occasionally it accompanied religious music. In Belgium in the early 1900s, a single plucked dulcimer often supplied the music for informal dances in pubs, or at family and neighborhood gatherings. Sometimes it was also played in bands, often with an accordion and one or more other stringed or woodwind instruments.

Though the plucked dulcimer was virtually extinct in the Netherlands by around 1900, its popularity in Belgium peaked after World War I. In the late 1930s, the instrument went out of fashion; but especially in West-Vlaanderen and the south of Antwerp Province, some musicians, all born before 1920, continued to play regularly.

Other chordophones

Musicians in the Low Countries also played other plucked stringed instruments—lutes and citterns in the Middle Ages and Renaissance, the guitar from the 1800s, the mandolin in the twentieth century, and the banjo mainly in the 1920s and 1930s. Under the influence of Anglo-American pop, the electric guitar became one of the most popular instruments after World War II.

SOURCES AND THE RESULTS OF THEIR STUDY

The first important source for Dutch song in the Middle Ages is the Gruuthuse Songbook, a manuscript made in the last quarter of the 1300s. This collection contains 147 songs, some of which may also have been sung by common people. The first Walloon collection, of only nine songs, dates from the early 1400s, and was probably written by Noël de Fleurus and his son Jehan, lawyers in Namur.

The first printed collections of the texts and melodies of Dutch sacred songs date from the mid-1500s: *Een devoot ende profitelyck boecxken* and the *Souter Liedekens* (Antwerp, 1539 and 1540, respectively). Both these sources supply the tunes to many of the 221 texts in *Een Schoon Liedekens-Boeck,* the so-called Antwerp Songbook (1544), the most important sixteenth-century collection of secular songs of the Low Countries. According to these sources, the tunes were predominantly hexatonic and modal until the mid-1500s. More than half of them are in the D mode or the A mode, followed in popularity by the C mode (the later major scale)

The revival of native traditional instruments was started in 1968 by Hubert Boone's band, De Vlier. At first, the revival caught on chiefly among university students and visual artists as a reaction against the alienating and leveling effect of the international commercial music business; it has often had strong links with regional and ecological movements.

and the G mode. Some tunes testify to the strength of the link between popular and ecclesiastical singing.

Until the mid-1500s, collections of songs mostly contain melodies of which no foreign versions are known. From about 1600, however, indigenous tunes are gradually superseded by imports: Adriaan Valerius's *Nederlandtsche Gedenck-clanck* (1626), a collection of religious and political songs against the Spanish invaders, mainly contains tunes of French, Italian, or English origin. The French influence was especially strong in Belgium in the 1700s and 1800s, when many melodies from vaudeville, *opéra-comique,* and tune collections (such as *La Clé du Caveau*) were eagerly adopted. According to written sources, the transition from modal to tonal music took place in the 1600s, but modal music held its ground among the people until the mid-1800s; even in the twentieth century it did not completely die out.

Nineteenth-century collectors were mainly interested in songs they considered old and beautiful, or at least remarkable. A more scientific approach, also taking into account aesthetically less satisfactory songs, broke through only in the second half of the twentieth century. Folk-song research began in earnest in the mid-1800s, at first from written sources (Hoffmann von Fallersleben 1833, 1856; Willems 1989 [1848]); Edmond de Coussemaker (1976 [1856]) was the first to collect songs from oral tradition in French Flanders, followed by other regionally based field collections (Blyau and Tasseel 1962; Bols 1992 [1897], 1939, 1949; Lambrechts 1995 [1936–1937]; Lootens and Feys 1990 [1879]; Peeters 1998 [1952]). Gerrit Kalff (1972 [1884]) and Florimond Van Duyse (1896, 1902) were the first to study texts and tunes of folk songs in the Dutch language; Van Duyse compiled the results of nineteenth-century research in *Het oude Nederlandsche lied* (1903–1908), a masterly, standard work.

In the Netherlands, Jaap Kunst (1951) undertook the first serious fieldwork in 1910 on the island of Terschelling. In the 1930s, Pol Heyns (1942) of Flemish radio made the first field recordings, and Will Scheepers (1963) followed suit in the Netherlands around 1950. Many Flemish and Dutch twentieth-century fieldworkers followed with important work (Bartelink 1967; Franken 1978; Gelber 1982–1983; Hessel 1980; Van der Molen 1970; Veurman 1968; Veurman and Bax 1944).

The most prolific fieldworker is Ate Doornbosch, until 1986 head of the Dutch Folk Song Archives at the P. J. Meertens Institute, Amsterdam. For his popular radio program "Onder de groene linde," which began in 1957, he managed to record some ten thousand songs, mainly among country people in the south and the east of the Netherlands, and in the islands. Since 1975, the Folklore Seminar of Leuven University, under the guidance of Stefaan Top (1985b), has specialized in research on Flemish folk-song texts. Building on the work of De Cock and Teirlinck (1902–1908), Top has also written on Flemish children's songs (1986a, 1986b).

Like the Netherlands, Wallonia showed little interest in its folk songs in the 1800s. Bailleux and Dejardin published a first collection of songs from greater Liège in 1844, but then there was a gap of nearly half a century, until an important collection of *crâmignon* songs and other traditional songs from Liège (Terry and Chaumont 1889) was published. Later collectors concentrated on specific regions and genres (Doutrepont 1909; Gilson 1894; Jouret 1889; Lebierre 1966; Libiez and Pinon 1939–1972; Maes, Vaisière, and Pinon 1965; Senny and Pinon 1961–1962; Simon and Denée 1937). The eminent specialist in Walloon folk-song texts, Roger Pinon, has edited much of this material for the Belgian Commission Royale de Folklore. The most important overall study on Flemish and Walloon traditional songs to date is by Paul Collaer (1974).

Nineteenth- and twentieth-century research on dance, dance music, and instruments can be traced to studies of Flemish processional music in the 1860s (Vander Straeten 1969 [1867–1888]; Wytsman 1868), followed in the first decade of the twentieth century with the first collection of dance tunes (Peeters 1952). In Flanders, systematic research on folk dancing has been undertaken only since the foundation of the Vlaams Dansarchief, in 1964. In the Netherlands, Jaap Kunst's pioneering work in Terschelling was followed by others in the interwar years (Sanson-Catz and De Koe 1930–1935; Van der Ven and Van der Ven-Ten Bensel 1942). The first articles on Walloon folk dancing appeared in the folklore magazine *Wallonia* in the last decade of the 1800s. The most important collections and studies were, however, published from the 1960s on (for example, Thisse-Derouette 1960). Musical instruments were the least documented aspect of traditional music until Hubert Boone started his research in the late 1960s. Since then, the study of traditional instruments in the Low Countries has been coordinated by the Museum of Musical Instruments in Brussels.

Revivals

Since around 1900, many traditional songs from the above-mentioned collections have been propagated in a cultivated form through schools, youth movements, and choral societies. Folk dancing was revived after World War I by youth movements of all kinds, mainly with educational goals, as a means to counter the growing popularity of the supposedly degenerate, newly imported couple dances of American origin.

Since the early 1900s, folk dances have also been cultivated and demonstrated by folklore groups, including the guilds of archers in Brabant and Antwerp provinces, some of which draw their repertoire from local tradition. In the mid-1960s, the Antwerp singer Wannes Van de Velde was the first of his generation to resume the traditional style of singing. Since the late 1970s, folk-dance nights (French *bal folk,* Dutch *volksbal*) have stimulated spontaneous dancing, mainly in Belgium.

The revival of native traditional instruments was started in 1968 by Hubert Boone's band, De Vlier. In Wallonia and the Netherlands, the revival of indigenous folk music began in 1973, largely under the influence of Flemish bands such as De Vlier and 't Kliekske, the quartet of folk instrument maker Herman Dewit. At first, the revival caught on chiefly among university students and visual artists as a reaction against the alienating and leveling effect of the international commercial music business; it has often had strong links with regional and ecological movements.

In contrast with older performers and organizations, revivalistic ensembles have not limited themselves to the preservation of tradition in its most recent form, as it was collected among surviving, mostly older musicians. Revivalistic bands also go back in time by drawing from older, written sources, and by reconstructing and playing virtually extinct instruments.

An important tendency within the revival aims at making traditional music relevant by means of arrangements, techniques, instruments, and instrumental combinations formerly unknown to tradition. Many of the new bands are strongly influenced by foreign—and **more particularly** Irish, British, and central French—revival music.

FIGURE 9 Het Brabants Volksorkest, led by Hubert Boone. Photo by Marc Masschelein, 1998.

The internationally most famous traditional-style band is Hubert Boone's Het Brabants Volksorkest (figure 9).

Since the 1970s, the number of musicians, bands, recordings, workshops, instrument makers, organizations, and publications has grown. Though traditional music is locally a marginal genre, it seems to have found a lasting place in the contemporary music scene of the Low Countries.

BIBLIOGRAPHY

Achtel, zalig oord! Volksleven en danstradities uit Achtel. 1997. Schoten: Instituut voor Vlaamse Volkskunst.

Aelbrouck, Jean-Philippe Van. 1986. *Les contredanses du journal musical liégeois "L'Echo" (1758–1773).* Brussels: Commission Royale Belge de Folklore.

B[alleux] and D[ejardin]. 1844. *Choix de chansons et poésies wallonnes (Pays de Liège).* Liège: F. Oudard.

Bartelink, G. J. M. 1967. "Twents volksleven." *Neerlands Volksleven* 17(3):1–152.

Blyau, Albert, and Marcellus Tasseel. 1962. *Iepersch oud-liedboek.* Brussels: Koninklijke Belgische Commissie voor Volkskunde.

Bols, Jan. 1992 [1897]. *Honderd oude Vlaamsche liederen.* Antwerp: K. C. Peeters-Instituut voor Volkskunde.

———. 1939. *Godsdienstige kalenderliederen.* Brussels: Schott.

———. 1949. *Wereldlijke volksliederen.* 2 vols. Brussels: Schott.

Boone, Hubert. 1976a. *De hommel in de Lage Landen.* Brussels: Instrumentenmuseum and Musicological Research Association.

———. 1976b. "Beknopte bijdrage tot de geschiedenis van het hakkebord in de Lage Landen." *Volkskunde* 77:203–216.

———. 1983. *De doedelzak.* Brussels: Renaissance du Livre.

———. 1986. *De mondtrom.* Brussels: Renaissanee du Livre.

———. 1990. *Het accordeon en de voetbas in België.* Leuven: Peeters.

———. 1991. "Gestreken en geschraapte pseudo-bassen in Vlaanderen en Wallonië." In *Liber Amicorum prof. dr. Jozef Van Haver,* 35–46. Brussels: Koninklijke Belgische Commissie voor Volkskunde.

Boone, Hubert, and Wim Bosmans. 1995. *Volksinstrumenten in Vlaanderen en Wallonië,* Leuven: Peeters.

Bosmans, Wim. 1991. *Eenhandsfluit en Trom in de Lage Landen: The Pipe and Tabor in the Low Countries.* Peer: Alamire.

———. 1994. "De volksliedtraditie in Woluwe." In *Volkscultuur in Brabant,* ed. Fernand Vanhemelrijck, 143–180. Brussels: Centrum voor Brabantse geschiedenis.

———. 1996. "La *Cwène* d'Henri Crasson, ménétrier de Gueuzaine." In *Studium et Museum:*

Mélanges Édouard Remouchamps, 1:9–22. Liège: Éditions du Musée de la Vie Wallonne.

———. 1998. *Fijfer en Trom in het Vlaamse Land: The Fife and Drum in Flanders.* Peer: Alamine.

Brade, Christine. 1975. *Die mittelalterlichen Kernspaltflöten Mittel- und Nordeuropas.* Neumünster: K. Wachholtz.

Büshing, Johann Gustav, and Friedrich Heinrich Von der Hagen. 1807. *Sammlung deutscher Volkslieder.* Berlin: F. Braunes.

Closson, Ernest. 1913. *Notes sur la chanson populaire en Belgique.* Brussels: Schott.

Collaer, Paul. 1974. *La musique populaire traditionnelle en Belgique.* Brussels: Académie Royale de Belgique.

Dansen en volksleven uit Duffel. 1992. Schoten: Instituut voor Vlaamse Volkskunst.

Dansen uit de Vlaamse gewesten. 1967–1991. 12 vols. Schoten: Vlaams Dansarchief.

De Bra, André, and Nora Vande Voorde-Hendriks. 1987. *Gentse kontradansen.* Antwerp: Vlaamse Volkskunstbeweging.

De Cock, Alfons, and Isidoor Teirlinck. 1902–1908. *Kinderspel & kinderlust in Zuid-Nederland.* 8 vols. Ghent: A. Siffer.

De Coussemaker, Edmond. 1976 [1856]. *Chants populaires des Flamands de France.* Kemmel/Steenvoorde: Werkgroep Malegijs.

De Gruijtters, Johannes. 1971 [1746]. *Beiaardboek.* Amsterdam: Broekmans & Van Poppel.

De Hen, Ferdinand J. 1972. "Folk Instruments of Belgium." *Galpin Society Journal* 25:87–132.

———. 1973. "Folk Instruments of Belgium." *Galpin Society Journal* 26:86–129.

De Vuyst, Julien. 1967a. *Het Nederlandse volkslied: Bibliographie: 1800–1965.* Brussels: Belgische Commissie voor Bibliografie.

———. 1967b. *Het sterrelied in het gebied van Dender en Schelde.* Ghent: Koninklijke Bond der Oostvlaamse Volkskundigen.

Despringre, André-Marie. 1993. *Fête en Flandre: rites et chants populaires du Westhoek français, 1975–1981.* Paris: Institut d'Ethnologie, Musée de l'Homme.

Dewit, Herman, Hugo Heughebaert, and Jozef Robijns, eds. 1983. *Op harpen en snaren: Volksmuziek, Volksdansen, Volksinstrumenten in Vlaanderen.* Antwerp: De Nederlanden.

Doornbosch, Ate, et al. 1987–1991. *Onder de*

groene linde: Verhalende liederen uit de mondelinge overlevering. 3 vols. Amsterdam: Uniepers.

———. 1986. "Twentieth Century 'Halewijn' Recordings in the Netherlands: A Matter of Survival and Persistence." In *Ballad Research: Dublin 1985,* ed. Hugh Shields, 187–197. Dublin: Folk Music Society of Ireland.

Doren, Lode Van. 1964. *Kinder-volksliedjes uit de Vlaamse gewesten.* Brussels: Ministerie van Nationale Opvoeding en Cultuur, Koninklijke Belgische Commissie voor Volkskunde.

Doutrepont, Auguste. 1909. *Les noëls wallons.* Liège: Société liègeoise de Littérature Wallonne.

Duyse, Florimond Van. 1896. *Het eenstemmig Fransch en Nederlandsch wereldlijk lied.* Ghent: J. Vuylsteke.

———. 1902. *De melodie van het Nederlandsche lied en hare rhythmische vormen.* The Hague: Martinus Nijhoff.

———. 1965 [1903–1908]. *Het oude Nederlandsche lied.* 3 vols. Hilversum: Frits A. M. Knuf.

Foulon, Pierre-Jean. 1991. "Tambours et fifres d'Entre-Sambre-et-Meuse." In *Liber Amicorum prof. dr. Jozef Van Haver,* 107–121. Brussels: Koninklijke Belgische Commissie voor Volkskunde.

Franken, Harrie. 1978. *Liederen en dansen uit de Kempen.* Hapert: Brabants Heem.

Gelber, Lucy. 1972. *De melopee van de Vlaamse kinderzang.* Ghent: Rijksuniversiteit Gent, Seminarie en laboratorium voor psychologische en experimentele pedagogiek, Interuniversitair centrum voor jeugdproblematiek.

———. 1982–1983. *Encyclopedie van het levende Vlaamse Volkslied.* 2 vols. Sint-Martens-Latem: Aurelia.

Ghesquiere, Remi. 1905. *Kinderspelen uit Vlaamsch België.* Ghent: A. Siffer.

Gilson, P. 1894. *Chants populaires du pays Borain.* Brussels.

Heeroma, K., and C. W. H. Lindenburg. 1966. *Liederen en gedichten uit het Gruuthuse-handschrift.* Leiden: E. J. Brill.

Hessel, Roger. 1980. *Het volkslied in West-Vlaanderen.* Bruges: R. Hessel.

Heyns, Pol. 1942. *Volksliederen.* Antwerp: De Nederlandsche Boekhandel.

Hiel, Laura. 1931. *Kinderspelen en liedjes uit het land van Dendermonde.* Ghent: Bond van Oost-Vlaamsche folkloristen.

Hoffmann von Fallersleben, August Heinrich. 1833. *Holländische Volkslieder.* Breslau: Grass, Barth.

———. 1856. *Niederländische Volkslieder.* Hannover: C. Rumpler.

Huybens, Gilbert, and Eugeen Schreurs, eds. 1995. *T'Haegelant: Vier 18de-eeuwse muziekboekjes uit Diest: Quatre recueils de musique du XVIIIᵉ siècle de Diest.* Peer: Alamire.

———. 1996. *Speelmansboek uit Maastricht.* Peer: Alamire.

Huyghe, Jan. 1982. "The Flemish Broadside-Singer Achille Coppenolle (1885–1954)." In *12de Internationale Volksballadentagung (Alden Biesen 22–26 Juli, 1981),* ed. Stefaan Top and E. Tielemans, 45–53. Brussels: Centrum voor Vlaamse volkscultuur.

Jans, Everhard. 1995. *Het midwinterhoornblazen.* Enschede: Van de Berg.

Jansen, Rolf. 1984. *We hebben gezongen en niks gehad: Muzikanten en liederen uit Midden-Brabant.* Tilburg and Breda: Gianotten.

Jouret, Leon. 1889. *Chansons du pays d'Ath.* Brussels: Schott.

Kalff, Gerrit. 1972 [1884]. *Het lied in de middeleeuwen.* Arnhem: Gysbers & Van Loon.

Koning, Jos. 1983. *De folkbeweging in Nederland: Analyse van een hedendaagse muziek-subcultuur.* Ph.D. dissertation, Universiteit van Amsterdam.

Kunst, Jaap. 1951. *Terschellinger Volksleven.* The Hague: H. P. Leopold.

Lambrechts, Lambrecht. 1995 [1936–1937]. *Limburgsche Liederen.* Antwerp: K. C. Peeters-Instituut voor Volkskunde.

Lebierre, Olivier. 1966. *Lyre mâmediène.* Brussels: Schott.

Lempereur, Françoise. 1982. "Le Folklore Musical." In *La Musique en Wallonie et à Bruxelles,* ed. R. Wangermee & P. Mercier, 2:303–328. Brussels: Renaissance du Livre.

Libiez, Albert, and Roger Pinon, eds. 1939–1972. *Chansons populaires de l'ancien Hainaut.* 12 vols. Brussels: Schott.

Lootens, Adolphe, and J. M. Feys. 1990 [1879]. *Chants Populaires Flamands.* Antwerp: K. C. Peeters-Instituut voor Volkskunde.

Maes, Léon, Maurice Vaisière, and Roger Pinon, eds. 1965. *Chansons populaires de la Flandre Wallonne.* 2 vols. Brussels: Commission Royale Belge de Folklore.

Moises, Luce. 1986. *La vielle à roue.* Brussels: Renaissance du Livre.

Molen, S. J. Van der. 1970. *De Friese tjalk.* The Hague: Kruseman.

Montellier, Erneste. 1939. *14 chansons du XVe siècle extraites des archives namuroises.* Brussels: Commission de la vieille Chanson populaire.

Peeters, Theophiel. 1998 [1952]. *Oudkempische volksliederen en dansen.* Antwerp: K. C. Peeters Instituut Voor Volkskunde.

Phalèse, Pierre. 1962a [1583]. *Antwerpener Tanzbuch.* 2 vols. Wilhelmshaven: Heinrichshofen's Verlag.

———. 1962b [1571]. *Löwener Tanzbuch.* 2 vols. Wilhelmshaven: Heinrichshofen's Verlag.

Pinon, Roger. 1963. "Contribution à l'étude du folklore poético-musical des pâtres en Wallonie." *Enquêtes du Musée de la Vie wallonne* 10:19–63. Liège: Musée de la Vie Wallonne.

———. 1968. "L'étude du folklore musical en Wallonie." *Jahrbuch für musikalische Volks- und Völkerkunde* 4:25–58.

———. 1972. *Contribution au folklore poético-musical de la ville de Charleroi.* Yearbook 18 (1966). Commission royale belge de Folklore.

———. 1996. *Ainsi chantait le pays de l'Ourthe: Chants, cris et formulettes de l'Ardenne wallonne, région de La Roche—Houffalize.* Rixensart: Amélie Mélo.

Prick van Wely, Max. 1949. *Het bloeitijdperk van het Nederlandse volkslied.* Heemstede: De Toorts.

Recueil de Contredanses avec Premier Violon et la Basse Continue dont les figures sont de Monsieur Trappeniers. 1987 [ca. 1775–1779]. 3 vols. Brussels: Commission Royale Belge de Folklore.

Rimmer, Joan. 1978. *Two Dance Collections from Friesland.* Grins: Frysk Ynstitut oan de Ryksuniversiteit.

Rombouts, Luc, and Gilbert Huybens, eds. 1990. *Het liedeken van de Lovenaers: Een 18de-eeuws Leuvens beiaardhandschrift.* Leuven: Universitaire Pers.

Roger, Estienne, and Pierre Mortier. 1700–1716. *Oude en Nieuwe Hollantse Boerenlieties en Contredansen.* Amsterdam:

Sanson-Catz, Anna Henriette, and A. De Koe. 1930–1935. *Oude Nederlandsche volksdansen.* 2 vols. Amsterdam: Stichting de Jeugd.

Seelen, Antoon. 1981. *Het volkslied in Nederland: Heden en verleden van een ideaaltype.* Nijmegen: N.p.

Senny, Edouard, and Roger Pinon, eds. 1961–1962. *Chansons populaires de l'Ardenne Septentrionale (Lorcé et Filot).* 2 vols. Brussels: Schott.

Sepieter, Jean-Paul. 1981. *De muziek van het Vlaamse volk.* Dunkirk: Westhoek-Editions.

Simon, Léon, and Maguerite Denée. 1937. *Chansons populaires condruziennes.* Gand: Volksdrukkerij and Commission de la Vieille Chanson Populaire.

Terry, Léonard, and Léopold Chaumont. 1889. *Recueil d'airs de crâmignons et de chansons populaires à Liège.* Liège: H. Vaillant-Carmanne.

Thisse-Derouette, Rose. 1960. *Le recueil de danses manuscrit d'un ménétrier ardennais.* Arlon: Fasbender.

———. 1962–1978. *Danses populaires de Wallonie.* 10 vols. Brussels: Commission Royale Belge de Folklore.

Top, Stefaan. 1985a. "The Flemish Broadside-Singer Hubert Geens and the Second World War." In *The Ballad Today: History, Performance and Revival,* ed. Georgina Boyes, 23–35. Doncaster: January Books.

———. 1985b. *Komt vrienden, luistert naar mijn lied: Aspecten van de marktzanger in Vlaanderen (1750–1950).* Tielt: Lannoo.

———. 1986a. "Strangers in Flemish Children's Songs." In *Ballad Research: Dublin 1985,* ed. Hugh Shields, 85–101. Dublin: Folk Music Society of Ireland.

———. 1986b. "Death in the Present-Day Flemish Children's Song." In *Tod und Jenseits im europäischen Volkslied,* ed. Walter Puchner, 111–130. Ioannina: Société Hellenique de Laographie.

Valerius, Adriaan. 1942 [1626]. *Nederlandtsche Gedenck-clanck.* Amsterdam: N. V. Wereldbibliotheek.

Vander Straeten, Edmond. 1969 [1867–1888]. *La musique aux Pays-Bas avant le XIXᵉ siècle.* 8 vols. New York: Dover Publications.

Vandereuse, J., and Roger Pinon. 1958–1959. "Quelques danses curieuses de Wallonie." *Commission Royale Belge de Folklore Yearbook* 12:184–267.

Veldhuyzen, Marie, ed. 1972. *Oude en Nieuwe Hollantse Boerenlieties en Contredansen.* Amsterdam: Frits Knuf.

Ven, Dirk Jan Van der, and Elise Van der Ven-Ten Bensel. 1942. *De volksdans in Nederland.* Naarden: A. Rutgers.

Vermeersch, Bart. 1982. "The Flemish Broadside Singer Alberic Cattebeke (1894–1975)." In *12de Internationale Volksballadentagung (Alden Biesen 22–26 Juli, 1981),* ed. Stefaan Top and E. Tielemans, 29–38. Brussels: Centrum voor Vlaamse Volkscultuur.

Verstraete, Eugeen. 1985. *Zwaarddansen in Vlaanderen.* Sint-Niklaas: Stadsbestuur.

Veurman, B. W. E. 1968. *Volendam, leven en lied.* Arnhem: Gijsbers & Van Loon.

Veurman, B., and Dirk Bax. 1944. *Liederen en dansen uit West-Friesland.* The Hague: Nijhoff.

Voskuil, J. J. 1981. "Het tijdelijke met het eeuwige verwisseld, of: op de klank van de midwinterhoorn de eeuwigheid in." *Volkskundig Bulletin* 7:1–50.

Willems, Jan Frans. 1989 [1848]. *Oude Vlaemsche Liederen.* Antwerp: K. C. Peeters–Instituut voor Volkskunde.

Wirth, H. F. 1911. *Der Untergang des Niederländischen Volksliedes.* The Hague: Nijhoff.

Wytsman, Klemens. 1868. *Anciens airs et chansons populaires de Termonde.* Termonde: E. Ducaju.

AUDIOVISUAL RESOURCES

Les authentiques airs de Gilles de Binche. 1989. Folklore Records 1507. Compact disc.

Belgique: Ballades, danses et chansons de Flandre et de Wallonie. 1994. Ocora 580061. Compact disc.

Belgique: Le Carnaval de Binche/Belgium: The Carnival of Binche. N.d. Buda Records 82516-2. Compact disc.

Boone, Hubert. 1997. *Musique Populaire de la Belgique: Volksmuziek uit België: Folk Music from Belgium.* Auvidis Ethnic B 6844. 2 compact discs.

Boone, Hubert and Egide Vissenaekens. 1970. *Etnische Instrumentale Muziek uit de Brabantse Gewesten.* Alpha AL 5005. LP disk.Brabants Volksorkest. 1996. *Crispijn.* Auvidis B 6827. Compact disc.

Daems, Hendrik. 1967. *Etnische Muziek in België.* BRT DL 111 427. LP disk.

Despringre, André-Marie. 1982. *Volksmuziek uit Frans Vlaanderen: Vie Musicale Populaire en Flandre Française.* Alpha 5030. LP disk.

Doornbosch, Ate. 1996. *Pays-Bas: Chansons oubliées: The Netherlands: Songs Adrift.* Ocora C600003. Compact disc.

Doornbosch, Ate, and Marleen van Winkoop-Deurvorst. 1980. *Van een heer die in een wijnhuis zat . . . en 15 andere mondeling overgeleverde liederen.* P. J. Meertens-Instituut and Nederlandse Omroep Stichting 6814 230. LP disk.

Flagel, Claude. 1991. *Airs de fête en Wallonie: Chansons et musiques traditionnelles.* Fonti Musicali FMD 188. Compact disc.

———. 1994. *Tambours et fifres d'Entre-Sambre-et-Meuse.* Fonti Musicali FMD 198. Compact disc.

Flagel, Claude, and Françoise Lempereur. 1974–1981. *Anthologie du folklore wallon.* CACEF FM 33 003/04/05/06/09/10. 7 LP disks.

Gilles de Binche: Les airs du "Mardi Gras." 1991. Ariola Express 290 837. Compact disc.

Jouster Boerebrulloft: Farmer's Wedding in Joure. 1994. Pan Records 2004. Compact disc.

Scheepers, Will. 1963. *Folksongs and Dances of the Netherlands.* Ethnic Folkways Library FE 4036. LP disk.

Tromp, Frans. 1983. *Piet de Jong en Willem de Hek: Harmonikamuziek van Terschelling.* Cadans 15042. LP disk.

France
Hugh Shields

Songs and Singing
Performance
Instruments and Instrumental Music
Contexts for Music and Dance
Urban Popular Music and Folk-Music Revival
Transmission, Performance, and Conceptions of Music
History of Scholarship

France, a country of some fifty-six million people living in an area of 547,000 square kilometers, was, from the 1700s to the mid-1900s, one of the most influential cultural centers in Europe and the world. With 37 percent of its land arable and extremely fertile, its economy provided the basis for a rural, traditional music. Since World War II, however, the pace of industrialization has increased to the point where only 7 percent of the population engage in agricultural work.

Most of the population is a long-term European one, but the end of French colonialism has seen the immigration of peoples from West and North Africa. The main traditional religion is Roman Catholicism. Extensive education has led to the dominance of standard French on the whole national territory, but there remain dialects (*patois*), other Romance languages (Provençal, Catalan, and Corsican [see Corsica]), the non-Romance Breton [see Brittany], Basque [see Basque Music], Flemish language, and the German dialects of Alsace and Lorraine—all still used, chiefly in rural areas and revival contexts.

SONGS AND SINGING

Most French traditional music is monophonic, with simple, short tunes, elaborated in strophic form or as dance tunes, usually of isometric phrases, repeated (in whole or part) without much use of new melodic material, but the dominance of strophic forms was less complete in the past. Genres or items existed that we may call stichic (repeating in performance a single musical phrase corresponding to a single line of verse) or rhapsodic (tending with some degree of improvisation to use motifs of variable length, rather than measured phrases). The *chansons de geste* (long heroic songs) of the twelfth century and earlier appear to have belonged to the first category (Chailley 1948; Gennrich 1923). Detailed comment is speculative, for only one line of melody remains, and that from a thirteenth-century parody of the genre (figure 1);

FIGURE 1 A thirteenth-century parody of a *chanson de geste,* the only surviving musical fragment of long heroic epics in France. Adam de la Halle: *Jeu de Robin et Marion.*

"Au– di– gier," dist Raim– ber– ge, "bou– se vous di."

Using a team of oxen, a plowman sang to his animals—and to an unknown number of nearby humans, for these airs carried well. This music is characterized by phrases of varying length; general rubato; parlando passages; nonlexical vocables; verbal exhortation (some spoken) to the animals; perhaps a final whoop rising about an octave.

FIGURE 2 Excerpt from a plowing song sung to animals by the plowman, who combines meaningful text ("Go," "Let's walk," "Let's go") with vocables. In a free, spoken rhythm (*rubato parlando*), it employs various effects, including partially spoken passages, indistinct tones, and tremolo. Transcription by Hugh Shields. Le Père Berger, La Châtre, Berry, on *Anthologie de la musique traditionelle* 3, B 12.

yet its musical naïveté is plausible, suggesting the strong verbal orientation of epic style.

Some rural cries and work songs of interest here are of the second category, and they take advantage of an outdoor situation; most versions are from the Massif Central. Using a team of oxen, a plowman sang to his animals—and to an unknown number of nearby humans, for these airs carried well (figure 2). This music is characterized by phrases of varying length; general rubato; parlando passages; held notes on a high pitch, possibly sharpening; stepwise movement with descents to lower pitch; nonlexical vocables; verbal exhortation (some spoken) to the animals; perhaps a final whoop rising about an octave. Similar in style was the singing by shepherds, or perhaps more often shepherdesses, in a genre (*huchage* 'calling') known in the thirteenth century to Adam de le Halle, used in his play *Robin et Marion* and quoted again by a sixteenth-century writer (Davenson 1944:445). Rather than work songs, these were dialogues with distant companions over elevated terrain (Canteloube 1951:2:130, 267–269, 3:298–299). They could include songs in strict rhythm, consisting of part-improvised teasing matches. Cries also served for herding flocks and in towns for selling goods and services.

The term *strophic* is used here to describe songs with a recurrent musical structure corresponding to a verse (*couplet*) or a verse with its refrain. Strophic songs have great formal variety, and only the main features can be outlined. The *chanson de danse* or *chanson en laisse* is well known from the Middle Ages onward. It consists of one or sometimes more series of discursive isosyllabic lines of six to sixteen syllables. As in the *chanson de geste*, a series of lines (*laisse*) is defined by its monorhyme asso-

FIGURE 3 *"Le petit moine"* ('The Little Monk'), a song built on the repetition of short phrases. Transcription by Hugh Shields.

nance at line endings, but the lyric *laisse* differs from the heroic in that the recurrent refrain, combining with it, breaks it into regular strophes of one or two, occasionally three, lines. The *chansons de danse* originated as dance-songs, and some have continued to function, or have been revived, as an accompaniment to dancing unsupported by instruments. Verse and refrain need not agree in their verbal discourse; the refrain may intervene within and outside the verse; and it may contribute new (possibly preexisting) rhythmic or even melodic material. Rather than disunity, a sort of dialogue is thus established, reflecting the formerly more common solo-choral execution. The tune, embracing both parts, impresses unity on the whole by musical repetition or similitude. Dance-songs make up a large part of the category of mainly recreative song, which may include religious ballads (*cantiques*).

The other strophic songs—of strophes formed not simply by subdividing a *laisse,* but by combining lines in a repeating verse structure—often have no refrain, or, if they have, give it less importance than it has in dance-songs. Among their forms, the commonest are verses of four and of three lines or—probably a later development of these—of eight or six short lines. Songs in these forms are usually isosyllabic, but variety arises from the popular songs of literate character, or their imitations, which have entered and remain in oral tradition. Two other features, both traditional, have bearing on strophic form. Some *enumerative songs*—a popular category in France—are recapitulative, augmenting the strophe progressively. Litanylike, the words newly intercalated repeat musical matter taken mainly from the tune as used in the first verse, which thus stretches out in lingering fashion. Or *new words* are set to dance tunes, usually instrumental, forming single, loose verses, which may accompany dancing but do not become songs merely by being strung together.

Other songs make similar use of simple repetition, especially if phrases are short (figure 3). When refrains of songs add or intercalate heterometric musical elements, these are usually more distinguished in rhythm than in melody, so that the phrases of the verse do not lose prominence. Some strophic tunes consist of a single repeated phrase (Canteloube 1951:1:313), but in a larger minority of others, little or no repetition of phrases occurs in the strophe, the pattern ABCD, for example, existing in a variety of songs.

Aside from some "rhapsodic" pastoral songs, the common meters of French music are those of Western Europe: 2/4, 4/4, 3/4, 3/2, 3/8, 6/8, 9/8, sometimes 5/8, grouped in two-bar or three-bar units or multiples of these. Uneven rhythms arise from variations in the length of the units, especially from short sections of different meter—features that introduce contrasts into otherwise regular development. Most frequent are mixtures of duple and triple time: 3/4 occurring in 2/4, or 9/8 in 6/8. These effects are often associated with the presence of a refrain, but not exclusively, and they evidently have an ornamental quality, desired for its own sake. They belong

TRACK 18

mostly to an abundant repertory of fast tunes, in which other departures from strict meter are unlikely to go further than lengthening or shortening at the ends of phrases. In slow tunes, a certain amount of rubato is more general, but long-drawn-out effects belong chiefly to some plowing songs or other work songs, which do not admit of measured analysis.

Much French music has a narrow melodic compass; it is common to find hexachordal tunes or ones that develop almost wholly within a range of a fifth, including children's game songs, lullabies (*berceuses*), plowing songs (*briolage,* figure 2), some street cries, and what we know of medieval epics (figure 1). Widest are some flowery tunes not associated with any specific social function, probably not of great age, but characteristic of sentimental songs on love themes: tunes extending to a tenth or an eleventh. Intermediate tunes, the majority, range from a sixth to an octave.

Melodic idiom can be plainly discerned as collectively diatonic. Scales coincide at times with the ecclesiastic modal tradition, but at others they differ from it by the absence or the variation of certain tones. Variation and absence are particularly common in the case of the seventh. When all seven tones are used, one may identify, in order of frequency, tunes in the ionian, aeolian, dorian, and rarely mixolydian or phrygian modes, while pentatonic tunes are very rare. In a country productive of much medieval plainchant, religious song has naturally influenced the popular musical tradition as a source of melodic and idiomatic borrowings.

PERFORMANCE

Centuries of classical polyphony have made little impression on the monophonic popular tradition and its realization mainly as solo performance. From the activity of the single ballad seller to the traditionally high cost of instruments, the soloist has also been confirmed by social, even commercial, factors. The monophonic solo tradition has been dominant, but not exclusive. Some ballad sellers and other singers have had instrumental accompaniment, usually fiddle, and the development of instrument making (*facture, lutherie*) reflects increased affluence today in a public interested in collective performance. Singing to a fiddle recalls the *vièle* accompaniment that the medieval minstrel (*jongleur*) gave his heroic chant, and the ancient and modern practices have no doubt been largely heterophonic. Heterophonic also in varying degrees is the responsorial singing of dance-songs (*chansons à repouner* in the west), and of chanties (*chansons de bord:* see Colleu 1991; Hayet 1971 [1934]), ceremonial choral performances such as the "*Bacchu-Ber*" at Pont-de-Cervières in Dauphiné (Alford 1940; Canteloube 1951:2:50), collective bagpipe playing (Chassaing 1982:111), general instrumental duets, and the technique of singing called *tuilage* (two voices alternate and slightly overlap) mainly in Breton, but noticed also in French. Other practices involve explicit harmonic features, including practices of some antiquity.

Two-part polyphony, striking in its dissonances, is an insular tradition that Corsica shares with Sardinia [see CORSICA; SARDINIA]. In Corsica, *paghjelle* are polyphonic religious songs of wholly secular tradition (*Musique corse de tradition orale* 1982); on the mainland, polyphonic practices exist in parts of the south. In the southeast (Haut-Dauphiné), semipopular songs in the eighteenth-century pastoral tradition have been provided with suitably mellow harmonic sections. This practice resembles the formerly widespread traditions of Christmas carols (*noëls*), often composed by church organists. In the southwest, an older tradition of two-part singing has its focus in the Basque country [see BASQUE MUSIC], but is found in neighboring Romance-speaking Béarn (figure 4).

This tradition, whether or not proper to Basque culture, puts nicely into relief the solidly monophonic tradition of most of Romance-speaking France. This was further emphasized for me in Limousin by Henri Rouland, a Romance bilingual singer,

FIGURE 4 Two-part singing from Béarn of the song "*M'a pres per fantesia*" ('A Fancy Took Me'). Transcription by Hugh Shields from *Les traditions populaires en France* 4, A 3.

who once produced extempore organum through inability to adjust his pitch to his Parisian grandson's accordion. The effect might be described as a two-part equivalent of heterophony; while contributing a lower part, of pitch at times uncertain, the singer seems to have perceived the whole as strictly monophonic.

INSTRUMENTS AND INSTRUMENTAL MUSIC

Accompaniment to melody on solo instruments is limited to the use of drones (*bourdons*) on violin, hurdy-gurdy, and bagpipes. In Auvergne and Limousin, drones declined in the later 1800s, partly because of collective performance, in which they seemed superfluous (Chassaing 1982), but playing in the twentieth century has seen a revival of their use; solo bagpipe playing, however, continued in Auvergne to produce an effective drone by *picotage,* alternating a low note with a melody (figure 5).

A single player's drumming to a flute gives a kind of drone, or an actual drone of fixed pitch in the case of the string drum (*ttunttun*) of the southwest [see BASQUE MUSIC]. With the increasing availability of instruments and skill at reading music, playing in parts became more common in the twentieth century; certain regions have traditions of popular, literate bands of music: oboes, clarinets, and so on in Roussillon; brass in many places, notably Alsace. With these, we approach the playing in parts characteristic of classical music, or *musique savante* 'learned music', as the French often call it; vocal music, however, shows less tendency in that direction.

At first glance, the range of French folk instruments contained in the Musée des Arts et Traditions Populaires (Paris) seems to reflect great variety of practice, but the limits of many of these instruments are geographically or historically narrow, and it would be of interest to know how many of those that are chiefly percussive, or tonally or acoustically primitive, would be considered musical in traditional terms. In a different way, the modern revival also implies abundance, but abundance that an anonymous copywriter no doubt justly attributed to *la boulimie instrumentale*

FIGURE 5 "*Bourrée de Salers,*" a piece for bagpipe, with intermittent drone on G. Transcription by Hugh Shields.

Known in French as vielle—or *vielle à roue* 'with wheel'—the hurdy-gurdy is firmly considered proper to Auvergne and Brittany, but chiefly the former, whose cheeses and salamis use an icon of it on their wrappings.

ambiante 'the current hunger for instrumental novelty' (*Trad'Magazine* no. 10:52). Evidence of traditional practice in recent generations gives a different picture, one in which only a small range of instruments was habitually used in every locality, each of them playable solo, or at times in small ensembles, whose music remains essentially monophonic.

Certain paramusical agents of human elaboration contribute to the soundscape of France. Most obvious are bells. The churches of seventeenth-century Beauvais (in Picardy) had 135 great bells and a few dozen little ones, muted in time of epidemic out of consideration for the sick. Notably in northern France, church bells remain a feature of urban life. On a smaller scale, cowbells (*clarines*) and sheep bells (*tintenelles, grelots,* in varying sizes) color the rural scene in the south. Various instruments requiring little skill, now usually treated as toys, have formerly had special applications: examples are the panpipes used in the Pyrenees by pig gelders and goatherds, friction drums in Flanders and elsewhere, and rattles and bird whistles generally. To some a ritual function may attach, as when the *réveillez* 'night-visiting boys collecting eggs and other gifts for Easter' replace bells by rattles during days leading up to Easter. This image of spiritual disorder is paralleled elsewhere in an image of social disorder: mock bands of "music" formerly directed at unevenly matched couples in the *charivaris* 'satiric ceremonies at unequal marriages' of carnival (see below).

Of instruments producing more elaborate music, the violin was the most widely used until relegated to second place by the accordion. The two continue in extensive use. Both are historical borrowings, one classical, the other conceived in a society of increasing factory production (accordions have been manufactured at Tulle, Corrèze, since 1919). This environment is perhaps what renders the accordion readily adaptable from traditional styles to urban *chansonnier* styles or innovating folk styles of today; the violin, however, had its traditional precursors from early times in France, and seems popularly to be associated with conservative tradition: the *crin-crin* 'fiddle' suitable for balls and weddings.

Neither instrument has any particular geographic association. While the accordion is popular, the view of it as typically French seems more a foreign than a native one, based not so much on national as on urban practice, and on the music of *cabarets* and *chansonniers*. The popularity of the chromatic accordion is evoked by a Norman dance-hall manager, who said he played the instrument because "it was greatly liked" (Redhon, Piraud, and Le Vraux 1984:67), but the diatonic accordion is probably more common in traditional performance, and revival has once more accentuated its suitability to traditional monophony.

The two older instruments that do have geographic associations—bagpipe and hurdy-gurdy—owe these, no doubt, to the trend that has caused them to disappear from many places where they were formerly played and are often being revived (figure 6). Bagpipes are commonplace and widespread in medieval French iconogra-

FIGURE 6 A hurdy-gurdy player (*vielleux*) on the sidewalk, probably seeking donations. Early-twentieth-century postcard, courtesy of the Robert Godfried Collection, New York.

phy—so user-friendly that, in a fresco of the crypt of Bayeux cathedral, even an angel plays them. A hurdy-gurdy (organistrum, French *chifonie*) was also known from the twelfth century. From the 1600s, the bagpipe and the hurdy-gurdy had success in polite society, with effects that influenced popular practice. The musette-type (bellows-blown) bagpipe was developed and later was partly adopted for popular use; the hurdy-gurdy was given its characteristic form and was borrowed or gained strength as a popular instrument. Known in French as vielle—or *vielle à roue* 'with wheel', to distinguish it from the medieval fiddle-type vielle or *vièle*—the hurdy-gurdy is firmly considered proper to Auvergne and Brittany, but chiefly the former, whose cheeses and salamis use an icon of it on their wrappings. The same two provinces are also known for their native bagpipes: the Breton *biniou* [see BRITTANY] and the Auvergnat (bellows-blown) *cabreta* (or Limousine *chabreta*).

Among other instruments used traditionally, the *épinette des Vosges*, a native plucked dulcimer, is the only notable chordophone, though revived only after near extinction. A traditional example of its playing (from 1972) may be heard on *Anthologie de la musique traditionnelle française* 1975. The rest are chiefly aerophones that may conveniently participate in ensembles: clarinet, oboe, trumpet in groups of two to four or more. Older are end-blown flutes, some of which may be played with a drum by a single performer—a practice already noted as southwestern in the sixteenth century (Arbeau 1967 [1589]:47; Arma 1951). Three-holed flutes are played thus in Provence (*galoubet* with *tambourin,* a snare drum about 70 centimeters deep) and in the Basque country and adjacent Gascony (*chirula* with *ttunttun*). The drum in these areas is usually strung to produce rhythmic drones. Functionally dissimilar from all these is the harmonica, formerly appreciated for its mouth music (*musique à bouche*) and easy transportation.

In support of today's traditional players, a flourishing small industry has sprung up, providing instruments of traditional design. The Agence des Musiques Traditionnelles d'Auvergne issued a folder presenting the work of a selection of makers, and the International Assembly of Instrument Makers and Master Players takes place at Saint-Chartier (Berry) every year in July.

CONTEXTS FOR MUSIC AND DANCE

Contexts for music, and especially singing, have been greatly formalized by French tradition. Opportunities for ceremony and song are often defined narrowly: the departure of a batch of conscripts to the army, the making of reed or boxwood flutes at summer pastures (*en estive*) (*L'Aubrac: Etude ethnologique, linguistique, agronomique, et économique d'un établissement humain* 2:148). Such a narrow definition is especially characteristic of work songs (*chansons de métier, chansons de travail*), a plentiful category in France, the least documented of which are probably sea chanties (*chansons de bord*). The formalized contexts characteristic of traditional life are today greatly diminished; yet they were once familiar enough to attract to themselves songs not originally proper to them: flowing 3/4 ballads accompanying hand reaping, and songs on miscellaneous religious subjects sung by the *réveillez*. Among seasonal customs, the *réveillez* are probably the best preserved. They have provided material for various cassettes of songs from Auvergne (*Ardes-sur-Couze* 1986), and are the subject of a revival feature on cassette (*Compagnie chez Bousca*); they have begun to include girls in their number; and they have prompted a magazine appeal (*Musique bretonne* no. 107, Dec. 1990) aiming to discover how extensively the custom is maintained.

As for the life cycle, no rituals pertaining to it have been so important as those of marriage, or have inspired so many contextually defined songs: songs to visit the fiancée, sung by young men; songs of mock abduction; marches to walk to or from the civil and religious ceremonies (played on bagpipe and fiddle, later bagpipe and accordion); songs and loose, sometimes bawdy, verses warning the bride of her duties and prospects; other songs to sing at and after the banquet; others while visiting the bedded couple; others that tell what the bed says; and so on. Small wonder that a chatty old countrywoman in Corrèze asked me with a puzzled look why the young don't want to get married nowadays!

Among wedding songs, those that suit the banquet have the best chance of survival, for meals are a traditional focus of conviviality. The custom of singing after them is a well-rooted one: a fact at times evident from paramusical touches, such as the recurrent choral tinkling of knives against glasses (*drin, drin*) or a balancing act with a knife and plate, performed by a cook while singing a song during the meal, as illustrated on the disk *Musiques de France* (Marcel-Dubois and Andral 1969). Singing after meals, at least on special occasions, is likely now practiced more than singing at evening gatherings not associated with meals (*veillées*), whose demise, under the influence of television and other media, it has become French fashion to deplore. The *veillée* was undoubtedly the major context for recreative singing. Like other contexts, it often attracted suitable musical items, such as the march on the bagpipe, played to help the visitors walk home (Bergheaud 1980?). Modern sessions, workshops, and such events naturally take account of the traditional contexts of *veillées* and after-dinner entertainment; weekend functions usually end with a Sunday lunch and informal music.

Much of the energy of the folk-music revival goes into organized spectacle, ranging from local concerts and competitions to the more expensive offerings of broadcasting. The distancing effect of the electronic media is perceived and variously reacted to, often with recognition that "we are no longer living in old-style village communities," sometimes with apparent satisfaction that "today's musicians are putting on a show" (*Musiques traditionnelles: musiques professionnelles?* 1987:17). Sound recording provides good traditional performances on compact discs and cassettes, with emphasis on singing more than playing.

The perception of media as distancing is not generally extended from the electronic to merely written media. Much of the effort of cultural organizations goes toward documentary publicity in the expectation that books, editions, and articles will indeed be read and used by musicians and their public. For traditional music, such documentary support would form a cultural context whose effect, if any, will not be apparent for some time. From what we know of the past, literate influences have not weighed heavily on the qualities of popular musical or poetic style that are broadly attributable to an oral environment, but some genres of religious inspiration are an exception, being more deeply marked by learning and their popular didactic intention: especially the traditional practice of *noëls*. For bibliography of Christmas carols, see Van Gennep 1938:805–812; of Catalan *goigs,* Courcelles 1984; of Protestant psalms, Cheyronnaud and Hameline 1979a:247–250; of some hymns (*cantiques*) and *complaintes* drawing on hagiography for narrative matter, like the story of St. Genevieve of Brabant, probably for centuries the most famous composition of its kind, Davenson 1944:547–549 and *French Popular Imagery* 1974:42–43.

Music and dancing

French traditions of dancing emerged from medieval ring dances and chain dances: *carole* and *tresche,* later *branle*—closed in the *ronde,* open as in the *farandole* (Torp 1986; for the *farandole,* see Alford 1932). Arbeau gives plenty of evidence of brawls (*branles*) as popular court dances in his own day. They began to yield first to the contredanse, a figure dance that apparently was borrowed from the English country dance in the late 1600s, and in due course yielded to quadrilles; branles, however, are reported as popular even in the early 1900s. *Rondes* are usually sung and danced by the dancers, and their persistence in tradition has obviously sustained the link of singing with dancing: not only the practice of dancing to the vocal accompaniment of a nondancer, but also the responsorial style to which the refrains of songs still named *chansons de danse* correspond, whether the songs are sung to dancing or not. Some respectable responses from a large (seated) audience are audible on the tape *Chants traditionnels de Haute-Bretagne* (Bouthillier et al. 1991).

All the chordophones and aerophones popular in tradition seem to have accompanied dancing. In Orléanais, Ephraïm Grenadou danced to the fiddle (Grenadou and Prévost 1966:55); in Paris, at *bals musette,* the Auvergnat Antonin Bouscatel played his native musette, the *cabreta,* soon to be replaced in that tradition by the accordion and its *style musette*; in Dauphiné, the mouth organ (*musique à bouche*) could suffice for a rigaudon, though the violin was preferable (Guilcher 1984b:30–32). Locally available instruments naturally prevailed, and since the players' natural function was to provide the needful (*faire danser*), their repertories include more dance-music than song tunes.

Instrumental music for dance-tunes and marches is usually limited to two short phrases. The phrases are often repeated (*aabb*), with little variation unless in phrase *b* an open cadence is followed by a closing one.

URBAN POPULAR MUSIC AND FOLK-MUSIC REVIVAL

Public taste in France has put considerable emphasis on the separation of courtly or learned from popular art and literature, and on their respective users, and the modern survival of folk music in rural society, its emergence as an object of scrutiny, and many of its themes and applications, all suggest that its users have been coterminous with a supposedly peasant class. In French, the corresponding term lacks the depreciative quality of the English term *peasant*: many *paysans* have enjoyed not only stable, but prosperous, conditions of life, but traditional music has generally been collected from the less prosperous peasantry or villagers in similar circumstances (in France, a village may have two to three thousand inhabitants). With the advanced development of literacy and the arts, the negative effect of urban spread on traditional music may have begun quite early, but the poet Gérard de Nerval wrote down a varied folk-song repertory close to Paris in the 1840s, and more recently, Auvergnat migrants have exerted musical influence in Paris.

A little by luck, Tiersot (1931:68–108) found that Nerval had sung for his Parisian artistic friends some of the versions of songs he had collected in Valois, and that they were still remembered in Paris—with their tunes, which Nerval had not noted—in a kind of secondary oral tradition toward the end of the 1800s. In a different situation, I recorded in 1986 some ballads learned decades earlier from fellow pupils—who may have learned them from printed sources—by Nicole Marzac, a former boarding pupil at a girls' college in the west of France. Thus, chance may reveal how music may reach a larger public than we are usually able to identify: in these cases, a more educated public or one of town as well as country. Today, the urban reception of traditional music in new conditions of revival is much more evident, and perhaps more active. Provincial loyalty causes modern revival in France to focus strongly on the habitats in which the music was discovered, but its presence is also felt in towns and cities, in conservative and in adapted rendition, while the abundance of musical workshops, festivals, and such events, organized locally throughout the country (and announced regularly in *Trad'Magazine*), stimulates a specialized tourism, particularly in summer, with a native, youthful, and largely urban clientele, more homogeneous in their motivation than in their social background.

During the 1970s and 1980s, funding from the Ministry of Culture and Communications allowed active groups to set up regional cultural centers, some of them devoted largely to traditional music, or giving it prominence in their activities, emphasizing in varying degrees the traditional (or *ethnographique*) and the revival or acculturative aspects.

The popular urban music that relies more heavily on literacy and professionalism also has, however, like the music called traditional, a long tradition. Relevant to that tradition, the French term *vaudeville* (sometimes *voix-de-ville*) is at least as old as the sixteenth century. From being understood as "a song with an easy tune sung by the common people," it had by the eighteenth century acquired additional meanings: satiric, topical, catchy, "runs through the town" (Coirault 1942:181). At that time, vaudevilles seemed hardly different from *pont-neufs,* a term arising from association with a place of sale—the Pont-Neuf in Paris—and evidently adding to the meanings just mentioned only a suggestion of the object sold (printed words) and its commerce. The early eighteenth century saw the rise of urban musical and convivial fraternities of middle- and lower-class members, poets and artists among them. Most famous were the Caveau (1729 to about 1857, with intermissions) and its politically objectionable associate Pierre-Jean Béranger, who wrote of a younger poet after his early death that "his songs would live on sung by the sons of those now singing them" (1833:143). Possibly they did, but as the music of popular urban inspiration became a bigger and better-organized business, personal communication in performance diminished, and exponents figured more as public property in a rapidly renewed and eventually international hit parade (now a French term, like many similar ones); the general flavor is given in the pictorial survey of French pop song by Saka and Brosseau (1983), yet despite such trends (everywhere manifest), there subsists an old, peculiarly French tradition of "literary" popular song, in which the performers (*chansonniers*) are often also poets and musicians. Though its conditions of subsistence make it an increasingly esoteric art, it from time to time produces artists who, like Georges Brassens and Jacques Brel (born in Belgium), are acclaimed through the media by the public.

Much as the theater, urban popular music has long been open to women vocalists, less to women instrumentalists. Traditional society, for its part, has been familiar with women singers in a small range of social functions, such as herding and nursing, and more generally on the domestic scene, where older women, if confronted by a stranger, tend to emphasize their domestic role by performing tasks while singing: kindling the fire, preparing food, and so on. Outside familiar environments with known audiences, women have sung less, and it is doubtful whether they have commonly played instruments at all, unless perhaps ones perceived as less demanding, such as the *épinette des Vosges*. The revival of traditional music, in assimilating it to spectacle, gives young women the greater scope generally available in popular urban performing art. Male instrumentalists, it is true, continue to outnumber them. The only girl member of the Grande Bande of bagpipers thought she would be "a bit jealous" if another girl joined (*Trad'Magazine* 1989(6):12–13, 1990(10):10–13), and though the Grande Bande has a kind of counterpart in Roulez Fillettes (1992(20):10–12), this group of five young women is better known for singing than for playing.

TRANSMISSION, PERFORMANCE, AND CONCEPTIONS OF MUSIC

Transmission

Given the early and varied uses of literacy in France, one would expect strong influence of literate traditions on the learning and transmission of mainly oral music. Many singers made and kept notebooks of verbal texts of songs, and singing received support from the popular press, in the form of broadsides (*feuilles volantes*), small chapbook collections of words (*livrets de colportage*), and later more substantial songbooks. Pictures provided song sellers with an accessory found elsewhere in continental Europe: in strip-cartoon form, they displayed the action of a narrative and with a cane pointed while singing to the scene appropriate to the verse (for illustration of this practice, see frontispieces of Davenson 1944 and *French Popular Imagery* 1974). The French popular press seems to have used fewer traditional songs than the English and to have been more inclined to digest and renovate them in the light of contemporary fashion, but these tendencies are hardly needed to explain the absence of songs in traditional style—though local poetry is by no means absent—from the broadsides used in a study of working-class culture in the northern industrial town of Roubaix down to the early 1900s (Marty 1982).

Since playing is more open to observation and analysis than singing, it is unremarkable that players have resorted more than singers to the use of musical notation. Music writing developed in the medieval period in France, but it would be difficult to put a date on its adoption by traditional musicians. Some Provençal *tambourinaires* (pipe and tabor players) seem to have had manuscript tune books from the nineteenth century (Tennevin and Texier 1951:14); a Norman fiddle tutor of the early twentieth century (Redhon et al. 1984:27) contains notations of recent dances and a smaller number of older ones. Until the recent revival, music notations must have been used only by a small proportion of practicing musicians.

Important developments arising from the revival movement, now in progress, are changing the picture just drawn. During the 1970s and 1980s, funding from the Ministry of Culture and Communications and other sources responded to local initiatives, allowing active groups to set up regional cultural centers, some of them devoted largely to traditional music, or giving it prominence in their activities, emphasizing in varying degrees the traditional (or *ethnographique*) and the revival or acculturative aspects. Names and addresses of the chief organizations serving such interests and founded since 1970 are Conservatoire Occitan (CO), 1 rue Jacques-Darré, 31024 Toulouse (Languedoc, Pyrénées); Dastum, 16 rue de Penhoët, 35000 Rennes (Brittany, including French-speaking Upper Brittany); UPCP, Maison des Ruralies, Vouillé, 79230 Prahecq (Poitou, Vendée, Charentes); Agence des Musiques Traditionnelles d'Auvergne (AMTA), place Eugène-Rouher, 63200 Riom (Auvergne, Limousin); Centre Régional de Musiques et Danses Traditionnelles (Ris-Orangis), rue Johnstone-Reckitt, 91130 Ris-Orangis (Paris region).

The revival has had an educative effect. Festivals and workshops, mainly in summer, complement a winter season of singing, instrumental classes, and dancing classes. New in the case of singing, the effects of teaching will be mainly for the next generation to judge. Much will depend on the use of an expected increase in music literacy. On an academic level, the Ministry of Culture instituted in 1986 a certificate of aptitude for teachers of traditional music in music schools and conservatories. Rather less unusual in the French intellectual climate, but innovative in traditional music, is the cultural centers' publishing effort, which includes books, disks, and tapes, and seeks a clientele among new readers of and about music. These developments postdate the Paris student revolt in 1968 and belong to the context of educational reforms in the ensuing period.

Performance and creativity

Creativity in French traditional music must be looked for mainly in performance and in the processes of variation. Most music is anonymous for reasons that are familiar in Western popular traditions. If a name attached to a song is not that of a performer, it will be the name of the author of the words (actual or supposed), and the tune will almost always be a borrowed one. *Timbre* is the French word for the borrowed tune or its title, and *contrafact,* a term for similar borrowing in medieval music, can already be applied from the twelfth century to one genre of courtly poetry, the troubadour satiric song (*sirventes*). Borrowing music is the usual practice of the modern maker of local songs, the only traditional genre that still gives evidence of having makers. Music, in fact, has been and remains an ancillary art: instruments are ancillary to dance and song, and melody is ancillary to words.

Nor have French traditions encouraged the folk-musical virtuoso. The old tradition of song selling, for its part, will be "a good trade"—in the words of a songbook of 1861—"when hens have teeth" (Bibl. nat. Res. mus. Vm 298, LII). Now and then, a performer-composer leaves a memory and perhaps some semitraditional texts lacking tunes; however, if a player expresses deeply felt admiration for a master, like the *cabretaire* Jean Bergheaud (1980?) for his teacher Bouscatel, it is usually for his playing, rather than for compositions attributed to him.

Good performers cannot fail to inspire admiration in their community, and admiration may confer on them, given the circumstances, at least semiprofessional status. Those who received payment for their music would mainly have been persons famed for their singing or playing at balls and weddings.

Conceptions of music

We might expect the French, with their "strong taste for verbal expression" (Coirault 1942:196, translated) to have views on their traditional music well formulated in writing, but since about 1600, probably no European nation has so completely divorced its literate art from the deeds and utterances of common tradition. It is not that writers have been uniformly ignorant of popular art, unmoved by traditional music: there is plentiful historical information to the contrary (Bénichou 1970; Laforte 1973; Tiersot 1931). It is rather that the major themes of French literature, typically not national ones, have not tended to find inspiration in popular native sources; nor has such influence often been explicit in classical, or "learned," music, though, from Adam de le Halle in the thirteenth century onward, recurrent interest in traditional music has been shown by some composers through pastiches: madrigal settings by Guillaume Dufay and others, dance tunes in Jean-Philippe Rameau and Georges Bizet, popular airs or snatches evoked in larger works by Vincent d'Indy and Arthur Honegger. However, national idiom has probably been remarked on as much in the classical as in the traditional music of France, and a comparison of the two would be useful. Even today, French intellectual and artistic interest in popular traditional art tends strongly to seek satisfaction outside the national frontiers.

To obtain a genuinely popular perspective on traditional music, one should perhaps try to elicit it from indirect expression: for example, from the narrative motifs referring to music that often occur in French traditional songs. Instruments provide images of merrymaking and socializing in these, sometimes with erotic touches. A boy makes a whistle and it tells him to woo the neighbor's daughter; a girl grieves at her elder sister's wedding while rejoicing that next year it will be her turn ("Fiddle and pipes will play for me," Canteloube 1951:3:326; Shields 1974). Singing motifs are more common and usually erotic. A girl's singing attracts a man, whom she evades; a man's singing entices a girl and leads to her dishonor or death ("*La Fille aux chansons*"). If these motifs hint that music is a kind of enchantment, they only barely envisage the irrational; even the natural image of the ancient and ubiquitous nightin-gale is a simple reflection of the erotic, at times an antithesis of the moral, in ordinary human relations.

The uses of music emphasize the traditional importance of music to the ordered cohesion of community and family. France has an abundance and variety of songs with practical applications. Such exceptional events as averted incest, infanticide, murder, and rape provide admonitory topics of song familiar in Western tradition; marriage, however, is an expected rite, celebrated by a profusion of custom in which music takes the lead. The fiddle and pipes that led wedding parties to church have become accordion and pipes at a wedding photographed in 1966 (*L'Aubrac: Etude ethnologique, linguistique, agronomique, et économique d'un établissement humain* 3(1): facing 118). Mobilized today, the party may have to make do with car horns. Thus, a practice can survive, if less musically, but modern custom will hardly see a revival of the *charivari,* an occasional ceremony of moral censure, in which crowds gathered to express distaste at untoward matrimonial behavior: a widower or a former nun who marries, a husband with a domineering wife, and such. The custom in the southwest is described by Jean-Michel Guilcher (1984a:453–489); it had its songs and cacopho-nies (Canteloube 1951:2:304), and it could appropriate songs. A nineteenth-century document describes how the ballad "*Corbleu, Marion!*" (compare the Scots "Our Goodman") formed the centerpiece of scenes of conjugal dispute acted during carni-val at Istres, Bouches-du-Rhône (Bibl. nat. n. a. 3340, fols. 80^r–91^r).

About the same time, instrumental music was becoming a cultural support for provincial communities of migrants moving from country to town—an encourage-ment to endogamy and eventual repatriation. Auvergnats in Paris have been especial-ly noted for their high profile in traditional music and their social cohesiveness and organization.

But modern urban life is less and less conducive to the persistence of provincial subcultures, and since 1944 a high level of rural depopulation in France has turned many more provincials into undifferentiated town dwellers. The traditional-music revival has partly been a response to the loss of ancestral links, but whereas tradition is often silent on questions that seem to call for exposition or evaluation, revival talks. Thus, the present revival is ready to distinguish categories of music: *de collectage* 'field' (recordings), *résidus* 'remnants, survivals', *ethnographique* 'traditional', *métissée* 'acculturated, half-caste'. *Musique* itself is no longer just a collective singular, but countable (*ces musiques)* and countless (each country, district, person, and member of a conference has his, her, or its own). From before such descriptive luxuriance date less articulate ideologies: song the servant of minority languages, or song part of an ensemble that wears music as a badge, the audible in *son-et-lumière.* From the inter-war years, these attitudes endured until reacted against in the 1970s by the talking revival. Folk music, say the *écolos,* goes with ecology. We have helped bring about the deauthentification of traditional music, says Gilles Remignard (*Musiques tradition-nelles: musiques professionelles?* 16). The peoples of France are not minorities, but nationalities, each getting sensuous pleasure (*une jouissance)* from its *musique folk* (Pécout 1978:135, 181). Traditional music has no ideologies, its purpose was to live it up, *faire la fête* (Redhon et al., 1984:85). Indeed, its character and usage make the recreative function evident, yet its intricate relations with domestic, communal and social life at many points also signify a serious cultural evaluation that goes beyond the casual or voguish quality of the comments just cited.

HISTORY OF SCHOLARSHIP

The history of studies of folk song and folklore has a kind of beginning in the inven-tion of two terms: German *volkslied* (1780s) and English *folk-lore* (1846). It was with

Soon after the appearance of long-playing disks, non-Western music began to be published in this format, notably by the Musée de l'Homme, OCORA, and Boîte à Musique. Thus, ethnomusicologists briskly took advantage of the French public's liking for novelty and strangeness.

a certain hesitation that French drew on these models, adopting *le folklore* by the 1870s, and from it deriving the adjective *folklorique* not later than 1884. Many authors preferred *populaire,* possibly guided by instinct, for by the 1960s *folklorique* had enlarged its reference to include 'facilely picturesque, unserious' and in this sense took the familiar form *folklo.* By then, to describe the sciences, scholars were gladly embracing, in preference, the learned terms previously reserved for non-Western civilizations: *ethnographie* (1819), *ethnologie* (later 1800s), *ethnomusicologie* (1954), so that the problem of describing the immaterial artifacts was left more or less intact.

Artistic, and mainly literary, interest in traditional song activated modern research. The most noteworthy literary event in this respect was the appearance, in the 1760s, of James Macpherson's writings based on Ossianic poetry, in their day an attractive, if fraudulent, recreation of old heroic lays taken from Scottish Gaelic [see IRELAND; SCOTLAND]. Macpherson's work inspired in France a desire to find native specimens of comparable traditional poetry, but it was only much later that similar enthusiasm was generated by something nearer home. Also of dubious authenticity, this was La Villemarqué's collection of Breton songs *Barzaz Breiz* 1963 [(1839]), mainly genuine, but silently interspersed with poetry composed in Breton and translated into French by the editor himself [see BRITTANY] (Laurent 1989). Their writings produced controversy, but they worked their effect. Already under Napoleon, by 1805, had been founded the Celtic Academy (Académie celtique), which in its questionnaire of 1807 showed substantial interest in music (Belmont 1975:63–91; Cheyronnaud 1986:73). The Académie aimed to seek and preserve traces not simply of Breton traditions, but of the substratum of Gaulish culture believed to exist from antiquity in the greater part of France. The underlying conception of popular arts as a relic of the remote past was carried to some lengths here, and may have soon been found embarrassing, for in 1814 the Académie was replaced by a more prosaically named Société des Antiquaires de France.

In the 1850s, researchers made another attempt to elicit a national record of traditional art: songs only this time, and the initiative came from a government minister, Hippolyte Fortoul. Now usually called the *enquête Fortoul,* this project comprised a central, mainly academic committee and a network of provincial informants, whose job was to collect popular poetry, with or without its music. A printed booklet of instructions (Ampère 1853) included specimens of traditional song of wide dissemination. Sources could be local, mainly peasant singers themselves, but could also be in libraries, for items already collected might exist in manuscript, or even in print. This obvious dilution of emphasis on orality gave room for misunderstanding, but at the period in question, a great measure of success was hardly to be expected. The resulting collection, preserved in six large volumes in the National Library, contains more verbal than musical texts, and is uneven in value. It was never published even moderately complete, though after 1876 some of its contents appeared (see especially Rolland 1883–1890).

The emphasis on song so far noticed is not surprising in the Romantic age. Julien Tiersot (1931) usefully documented the interest in traditional French song that postrevolutionary literary writers often expressed in their works. Early studies of Western traditional music took a more literary than musical orientation, and in France linguistic and dialectal diversity no doubt encouraged concentration on verbal texts. Emphasis on the study of song, once established, persisted through generations to the considerable exclusion of the study of instruments and their music.

Down to the beginning of World War I (1914), song collections appeared plentifully, some general and many regional, with or without music, variable in their documentation and the quality of their texts: a mixed tradition of what was not yet generally called ethnography. The merits and shortcomings of this tradition are sketched from a folklorist's point of view in Arnold Van Gennep's critical bibliography (1938), to which Patrice Coirault (1942:406–422) links a more musically oriented sequel.

Down to 1914, only one substantial work (Tiersot 1889) treated French traditional music even partly from a musicological point of view. Tiersot also acted as musical editor of the only strict collection of (narrative) French ballads (Doncieux 1904) to appear before Laforte and Jutras 1997. In the interwar years, a new figure emerged, the folk-song scholar Coirault, more a musical folklorist than a musicologist. His publications (1927–1932, 1942, 1953–1963) were presented as an organized whole, dealing with oral tradition and the relationship of folk song to printed sources and the works of written literature. Preoccupations with high and low literature are developed in the introduction to Henri Davenson's comprehensive anthology of song (1944).

In 1938, the state made new provision for archives and museums. The founding of the Musée de l'Homme (1878) was reaffirmed (1938), responding to increasing French interest in the study of non-Western peoples including their music, particularly that of the overseas territories making up what would be called from 1946 the *Union française*. At the same time were founded a national ethnographic museum for France itself (Musée National des Arts et Traditions Populaires, 1937) and a general sound archive (Phonothèque Nationale, 1938), now part of the National Library. These institutions continue to include traditional music among their responsibilities.

After World War II, articles—and more rarely, books—continued to present songs newly collected, usually with their music, but often sparsely documented. Claudie Marcel-Dubois and Maguy P. Andral (1954), though dealing with Lower (Breton-speaking) Brittany, included a few songs sung there in French, in some cases making full notations of the repetitions of melodies, but it was soon to become evident that detail in performance was best obtained from published sound recordings. Soon after the appearance of long-playing disks, non-Western music began to be published in this format, notably by the Musée de l'Homme, OCORA, and Boîte à Musique. Thus, ethnomusicologists briskly took advantage of the French public's liking for novelty and strangeness. From the 1960s, French ethnomusicology was to be reckoned with as a serious discipline, and it already had produced a manual (Daniélou 1959). French researchers on foreign music became numerous, and foreign ones were attracted to Paris and settled there. The French contribution to the European Seminar in Ethnomusicology has been considerable since its inception (1981–1982), including a national follow-up colloquium after a European seminar in Paris on musical improvisation, and publication of work presented at both events (Lortat-Jacob 1987). By the 1980s, the common interests of ethnomusicology and what people were calling less and less musical folklore were widely appreciated.

Neither radio nor the record industry was quick to give space to native traditional music. For a generation, these media had been dominated in that field by regional folklore groups, and the first commercial disks of older traditions actually came out in the U.S.; these included *Folk Music of France* (Arma 1951) and *France,* the fourth disk in the Columbia World Library of Folk and Primitive Music (Marcel-Dubois 1954). The Musée des Arts et Traditions Populaires issued one small disk, *Musiques de France* (Marcel-Dubois and Andral 1969), but it was only as the 1970s advanced that recordings of performances of native music caught up with those of foreign music. Native-music studies thus continued to rely chiefly on publication in print. In 1971, *Ethnologie française,* a new journal (replacing *Arts et Traditions populaires* and, like it, including French music in its scope), implied in its title a closer approach to methods already used for non-Western cultures. From the early 1970s also dates the massive collaborative study of the ethnography of Aubrac, a region in Auvergne, including sections on its music.

Traditional disciplines have continued to contribute to the subject: the medievalist Jacques Chailley (1964) on popular and classical polyphony; Paul Bénichou (1970) on the history of literary views of folk song. In 1983, the medieval literary scholar Paul Zumthor produced the first general book in French on oral poetry, and from 1969 to 1984, Jean-Michel Guilcher ranged over widely separate provinces in an investigative study of the near-contemporary and historical traditions of dance.

The folk-music revival, already familiar in English-speaking countries, began to make an impression in France only in the later 1970s (significantly named *le revival*), and some of its eventual consequences began to be felt. Record production boomed, including the LPs called *ethnographiques,* from field tapes of old traditions. A few that may stand for many are *French Folksongs from Corrèze* (Shields 1974), *Anthologie de chants et musiques populaires du Haut-Poitou* (Valière et al. 1977), *Collectage de musiques et chansons traditionnelles en Basse-Normandie* (Redhon et al. 1980), *Musique corse de tradition orale* (1982), Chant du Monde's series *Anthologie de la musique traditionnelle française* and OCORA's (1975–1980), series *Les Traditions populaires en France* (1980–1982). Audiocassettes followed, their usefulness for small-scale publishing of regional traditions being quickly recognized. The Auvergne cassette series *Musique du canton* (*Ardes-sur-Couze* 1986) is the most abundant, and is so far the most narrowly localized of these records. Often they are the work of cultural centers that have set up sound archives of their regions, rapidly enlarging the amount of music available for consultation.

Recent research in print is also more plentiful, reflecting in part the movement of revival. Some of it comes from abroad: the Swiss scholar Wolfgang Laade's work goes back to the 1950s, and the Canadian scholar Conrad Laforte's monumental *Catalogue* (1976, 1977–1987) is an excellent bibliography and classification of French traditional song everywhere, but young native writers are active also. Among them are Jean-Noël Pelen and Daniel Travier (1974) on song in the Cévennes, Jean-François Chassaing (1982, 1987) on instruments, and Jacques Cheyronnaud (1986) on collecting and archiving. The first two of these began as academic dissertations.

The successive magazines of the revival for their part provide useful kinds of documentation, notably on instrumental practice and through interviews with musicians, not to mention current activities. These publications include *Escargot folk,* in the 1970s; *Modal: La Revue des musiques traditionnelles,* 1982–1986; *Tradition vivante,* 1984–1987; and *Trad'Magazine,* 1988–.

BIBLIOGRAPHY

Alford, Violet. 1932. "The Farandole." *Journal of the English Folk Dance and Song Society* 1(1):18–33.

———. 1940. "The Baccubert." *Journal of the English Folk Dance and Song Society* 4(1):8–14.

Ampère, Jean-Jacques. 1853. *Instructions relatives aux poésies populaires de la France.* Paris: Imprimerie impériale.

Arbaud, Damase, ed. 1862–1864. *Chants populaires de la Provence.* 2 vols. Aix-en-Provence: Makaire.

Arbeau, Thoinot [Jean Tabourot]. 1967 [1589]. *Orchésography.* Translated by Mary Stewart Evans. New York: Dover.

Arnaudin, Félix, ed. 1970 [1912]. *Chants populaires de la Grande-Lande et des régions voisines: Musique, patois et traduction française.* Paris: Champion.

Arts et Traditions populaires. 1953–1970. 18 vols. Paris: Maisonneuve et Larose.

L'Aubrac: Étude ethnologique, linguistique, agronomique, et économique d'un établissement humain. 1971–1975. Paris: Centre National de Recherche Scientifique.

Barbillat, Emile, and Laurian Touraine, eds. 1930–1931. *Chansons populaires dans le Bas-Berry.* 5 vols. Paris: E. Rey.

Baucomont, Jean, et al., eds. 1961. *Les Comptines de langue française recueillies et commentées.* Paris: Seghers.

Beauquier, Charles, ed. 1894. *Chansons populaires recueillies en Franche-Comté.* Paris: Leroux.

Belmont, Nicole. 1975. "L'Académie celtique et George Sand: Les débuts des recherches folkloriques en France." *Romantisme* 9:29–38.

Bénichou, Paul. 1970. *Nerval et la chanson folklorique.* Paris: J. Corti.

Béranger, Pierre-Jean. 1833. *Chansons nouvelles et dernières.* Paris: Pérotin.

Bladé, Jean-François, ed. 1967 [1881–1882]. *Poésies populaires de la Gascogne: Texte gascon et traduction française.* 3 vols. Paris: Maisonneuve et Larose.

Bujeaud, Jérôme, ed. 1895 [1866]. *Chants et Chansons populaires des provinces de l'Ouest.* 2d, enlarged edition. 2 vols. Niort: L. Clouzot.

Canteloube, Joseph, ed. 1951. *Anthologie des chants populaires français.* 4 vols. Paris: Durand.

Capelle, Paul, ed. 1872 [1811]. *La Clé du caveau.* 4th ed. Paris: A. Cotelle.

Chailley, Jacques. 1948. "Études musicales sur la chanson de geste et ses origines." *Revue de musicologie* 27:1–27.

———. 1964. "Comment entendre la musique populaire?" *Journal of the International Folk Music Council* 16:47–49.

Les Chansons de France. 1907–1913. 7 vols., nos. 1–28.

Chassaing, Jean-François. 1982. *La Tradition de cornemuse en Basse-Auvergne et Sud-Bourbonnais.* N.p.: Ipomée.

———. 1987. *La Vielle et les luthiers de Jenzat.* Combronde: Aux Amoureux de science.

Cheyronnaud, Jacques. 1986. *Mémoires ou Recueils: Jalons pour une histoire des collectes musicales en terrain français.* N.p.: Office départemental d'action culturelle de l'Hérault.

Cheyronnaud, Jacques, and Jean-Yves Hameline. 1979a. "L'Hymnodie d'usage dans les églises protestantes." In *Religions et Traditions populaires,* ed. Jean Cuisenier et al., 247–250. Paris: Réunion des Musées Nationaux.

———. 1979b. "L'Hymnodie religieuse d'usage dans l'église catholique." In *Religions et Traditions populaires,* ed. Jean Cuisenier et al., 239–247. Paris: Réunion des Musées Nationaux.

Coirault, Patrice. 1927–1932. *Recherches sur notre ancienne chanson populaire traditionnelle.* 5 parts. Paris: various publishers.

———. 1942. *Notre Chanson folklorique: Étude d'information générale.* Paris: A. Picard.

———. 1953–1963. *La Formation de nos chansons folkloriques.* 4 vols. Paris: Éditions Scarabée.

Collection Phonothèque nationale (Paris). 1952. Archives de la musique enregistrée, C/1. Paris: Unesco.

Colleu, Michel. 1991. "The Songs of the French Sailors." *Musical Traditions* 9:18–30.

Courcelles, Dominique de. 1984. "Les Goigs en Catalogne." *Ethnologie française* 14:281–294.

Coussemaker, Edmond de, ed. 1856. *Chants populaires des Flamands de France.* Ghent: Gyselynck.

Cuisenier, Jean, Claudie Marcel-Dubois, and Maguy P. Andral. 1980. *L'Instrument de musique populaire: Usages et symboles.* Paris: Ministère de la Culture.

Daniélou, Alain. 1959. *Traité de musicologie comparée.* Paris: Hermann.

Davenson, Henri [Henri-Irénée Marrou], ed. 1944. *Le Livre des chansons.* Neuchâtel: Éditions La Baconnière.

Decitre, Monique. 1960. *Dansez la France: Danses des provinces françaises.* 2 vols. Saint-Etienne: Éditions Dumas.

Decombe, Lucien, ed. 1884. *Chansons populaires recueillies dans le département d'Ille-et-Vilaine.* Rennes: H. Caillière.

Delarue, Georges. 1973. "Chansons folkloriques de la Renaissance: Libres propos à partir d'une publication récente." *Monde alpin* 1:51–66.

———, ed. 1977. *Chansons populaires du Nivernais et du Morvan recueillies par Achille Millien, airs notés par J.-G. Penavaire.* Grenoble: Centre Alpin et Rhodanien d'Ethnologie.

D'Indy, Vincent, ed. 1900. *Chansons populaires du Vivarais.* Paris: Durand.

Doncieux, Georges, ed. 1904. *Le Romancéro populaire de la France.* Paris: E. Bouillon.

Duchemin. 1768–1792. "Chansons, Vaudevilles et Ariettes choisies." Bibl. nat., mus. rés. Vm. Coirault 270.

Dumersan, and Noël Ségur, eds. 1846. *Chansons nationales et populaires de France.* 2 vols. Paris: G. de Gonet.

Ethnologie française. 1971–, 1–. Paris: Armand Colin. Proceedings of a seminar on the ethnomusicology of France. vol. 3.

French Popular Imagery: Five Centuries of Prints. 1974. London: Arts Council of Great Britain.

Gastoué, Amédée. 1924. *Le Cantique populaire en France: ses sources, son histoire.* Lyon: Janin.

Gaultier Garguille [Hugues Guéru]. 1658 [1631]. *Les Chansons de Gaultier Garguille.* New edition. Bibl. nat., mus. rés. Vm. Coirault 174. London.

Gennrich, Friedrich. 1923. *Der musikalische Vortrag der altfranzösischen Chansons de geste.* Halle: M. Niemeyer.

Gérold, Théodore, ed. 1921. *Le Manuscrit de Bayeux: Texte et musique d'un recueil de chansons du quinzième siècle.* Strasbourg: Publications de la Faculté des Lettres.

Goubert, Pierre. 1968. *Cent Mille Provinciaux au dix-septième siècle: Beauvais et le Beauvaisis de 1600 à 1730.* Paris: Flammarion.

Grenadou, Ephraïm, and Alain Prévost. 1966. *Grenadou, paysan français.* Paris: Éditions du seuil.

Guilcher, Jean-Michel. 1969. *La Contredanse et les renouvellements de la danse française.* Paris and The Hague.

———. 1984a. *La Tradition de danse en Béarn et Pays basque français.* Paris: Maison des Sciences de l'Homme.

———. 1984b. "Le Domaine du rigodon: une province originale de la danse." *Monde alpin* 12:7–72.

Hayet, Armand, ed. 1971 [1934]. *Dictons, tirades et chansons des anciens de la voile.* Paris: Denoël.

Kennedy, Peter, ed. 1975. *Folksongs of Britain and Ireland.* London: Cassell.

Laforte, Conrad. 1973. *La Chanson folklorique et les écrivains au dix-neuvième siècle (en France et au Québec).* Montreal: Hurtubise.

———. 1976. *Poétiques de la chanson traditionnelle française.* Quebec: Presses Université Laval.

———. 1977–1987. *Le Catalogue de la chanson folklorique française.* 6 vols. Quebec: Presses Université Laval.

Laforte, Conrad, and Monique Jutras, eds. 1997. *Vision d'une société par les chansons de tradition orale à caractèrr épique et tragique.* Sainte-Foy, Que.: Université Laval.

Lambert, Louis, ed. 1908–1912. Songs mainly in Occitanian and from Languedoc, variously titled, in *Revue des langues romanes:* 51(1908):111–142, 448–478, 512–544, work songs, street cries; 53(1910):5–25, same; 54(1911):5–36, "pastoral" songs; 55(1912):5–59, same.

Laurent, Donatien. 1989. *Aux sources du Barzaz-Breiz: La mémoire d'un peuple.* Douarnenez: Ar Men.

La Villemarqué, Hersart de, ed. 1963 [1839]. *Barzaz-Breiz: Chants populaires de la Bretagne.* Paris: Perrin.

Lortat-Jacob, Bernard, ed. 1987. *L'Improvisation dans les musiques de tradition orale.* Paris: SELAF.

Marcel-Dubois, Claudie. 1961. "Principes essentiels de l'enquête ethnomusicologique: Quelques applications françaises." *Journal of the International Folk Music Council* 13:13–18.

Marcel-Dubois, Claudie, and Maguy P. Andral, eds. 1954. "Musique populaire vocale de l'île de Batz." *Arts et Traditions populaires* 2:193–250.

Marty, Laurent. 1982. *Chanter pour survivre: Culture ouvrière, travail et techniques dans le textile, Roubaix 1850–1914*. N.p.: Fédé Léo Lagrange.

Massin. 1978. *Les Cris de la ville: Commerces ambulants et petits métiers de la rue*. Paris: Albin Michel.

Mélusine: Recueil de mythologie, littérature populaire, traditions et usages. 1878–1887. Paris.

Modal: La Revue des musiques traditionnelles. 1982–1986, nos. 2–11. Lyon and other places. Successor to *Plein Jeu: Cahiers d'écomusique* 1, n.d. [1981].

Le Monde alpin et rhodanien. 1973–, 1–. Grenoble.

Montel, Achille, and Louis Lambert, eds. 1975 [1880]. *Chants populaires du Languedoc*. Marseille: Lafitte.

Musiques d'en France: Guide des musiques et danses traditionnelles. [1984.] N.p.: Centre National de l'Action Musicale.

Musiques traditionnelles: musiques professionnelles? Actes du Colloque international MIDEM, 27–28 January 1987. Paris: CENAM.

Paris, Bibliothèque nationale. MSS nouv. acq. fr. 3338–43.

Paris, Gaston, ed. 1875. *Chansons du quinzième siècle*. Paris: Société des Anciens Textes Français.

Pécout, Roland. 1978. *La Musique folk des peuples de France*. Paris: Stock.

Pelen, Jean-Noël, and Daniel Travier, eds. 1974. *Le Temps cévenol*, 3(1). N.p.: Sédilan.

Pinck, Louis, ed. 1926–1933. *Verklingende Weisen: Lothringer Volkslieder*. 3 vols. Metz: Lothringer Verlag.

Pirkin [François Célor], ed. 1904. *Chansons populaires et Bourrées recueillies en Limousin*. Brive: Roche.

Poueigh, Jean, ed. 1926. *Chansons populaires des Pyrénées françaises: Traditions, mœurs, usages*. Paris: Champion.

Puymaigre, Comte de, ed. 1881 [1865]. *Chants populaires recueillis dans le Pays messin*. 2d ed. 2 vols. Paris: Champion.

Ratel, Jeanne, ed. 1978. *Bessans chante: Noëls, chants sacrés, chansons profanes*. 73230 Saint-Alban Leysse: N.p.

Redhon, François, Anne Piraud, and Denis Le Vraux. 1984. *Musiques traditionnelles en Mayenne, 1789–1984*. [Laval]: Éditions de l'Oribus.

Revue des traditions populaires. 1886–1919, 1–34. Paris.

Revue des langues romanes. 1870–, 1–. Montpellier: Université Paul-Valéry.

Rolland, Eugène, ed. 1883–1890. *Recueil de chansons populaires*. 3 vols. Paris: Maisonneuve et Larose.

Saka, Pierre, and J.-M. Brosseau. 1983. *La Chanson française*. Paris: F. Nathan.

Servettaz, Claudius, ed. 1963 [1910]. *Vieilles chansons savoyardes*. Annecy and Paris: E. Leroux.

Shields, Hugh. 1986. "A quand une édition critique de la chanson narrative française?" In *Ballad Research: The Stranger in Ballad Narrative and other Topics*, ed. Hugh Shields, 241–250. Dublin: Folk Music Society of Ireland.

———. 1989. "Chanson de toile et ballade populaire: Problématique d'une comparaison." In *Ballades et Chansons folkloriques*, ed. Conrad Laforte, 319–331. Quebec: CELAT, Université Laval.

———. 1991. "Popular Modes of Narration and the Popular Ballad." In *The Ballad and Oral Literature*, ed. Joseph Harris, 40–59. Cambridge: Harvard University Press.

Simonsen, Michèle. 1987. "French Traditional Ballads." In *UNIFOL Årsberetning 1986*, 17–56. Copenhagen: Institut for folkemindevidenskab.

Tennevin, Nicolette, and Marie Texier. 1951. *Provence and Alsace*. Dances of France, 2. London: M. Parrish.

Tiersot, Julien. 1889. *Histoire de la chanson populaire en France*. Paris: Plon.

———, ed. 1903. *Chansons populaires recueillies dans les Alpes françaises (Savoie et Dauphiné)*. Grenoble: Falgue et Perrin.

———. 1931. *La Chanson populaire et les écrivains romantiques*. Paris: Plon.

Torp, Lisbet. 1986. "European Chain and Round Dances." *Dance Studies* 10:13–48.

Trad' Magazine. 1988, Nov.–, 1–. 62350 Robecq.

Tradition vivante. 1984–1987, nos. 1–14. Lorient, France.

Tran Van Khê. 1963. "Sur la présentation de documents authentiques de la musique traditionnelle populaire et savante à la radio." *International Folk Music Council Bulletin* 24(Oct.):25–30.

Van Gennep, Arnold. 1938. *Manuel de folklore français contemporain*. 4 vols. Paris: A. Picard.

Vargyas, Lajos. 1967. *Researches into the Medieval History of Folk Ballad*. Budapest: Akademiai Kiadó.

Verrier, Paul. 1931–1932. *Le Vers français: Formes primitives, développement, diffusion*. 3 vols. Paris: H. Didier.

Weckerlin, Jean-Baptiste, ed. 1883. *Chansons populaires de l'Alsace, avec airs notés*. 2 vols. Paris: Maisonneuve.

Zumthor, Paul. 1983. *Introduction à la poésie orale*. Paris: Éditions du seuil.

AUDIOVISUAL RESOURCES

Anthologie de la musique traditionnelle française. 1975–1980. Paris: Chant du Monde. 1, *Musique traditionnelle des pays de France* (1975), ed. J. F. Dutertre et al., LDX 74516. 2, *Violoneux et Chanteurs traditionnels en Auvergne: Cantal* (1977), ed. Alain Ribardière, LDX 74635. 3, *Musique traditionnelle du Berry* (1977), LDX 74653. 4, *Violoneux et Chanteurs traditionnels du Dauphiné* (1978?), LDX 74687. 5, *Chants traditionnels des marins pêcheurs de Fécamp (Haute-Normandie)* (1979), ed. Michel Colleu, LDX 74704. 6, *Musique traditionnelle du Haut-Poitou* (1980), ed. Alain Ribardière, LDX 74726. 6 LP disks.

Ardes-sur-Couze. 1986. Musique du canton, 1. Cassette.

Arma, Paul, ed. 1951. *Folk Music of France*. Folkways FE 4414. LP disk.

[Bergheaud]. 1980? *Musique d'Auvergne: Jean Bergheaud*. 29290 Milizac: Discovale WM 56. Cabreta. LP disk.

Bouthillier, Robert, et al., eds. 1990. *Chansons traditionnelles du pays de Fougères: Mélanie Houëdry*. Rennes: Dastum DAS-111. Cassette.

———. 1991. *Chants traditionnels de Haute-Bretagne*. Rennes: Dastum DAS-117. Cassette.

Compagnie chez Bousca: Chants de quête de la période de Pâques. 1989. Paris: Ocora 4559085. Cassette.

Dubreuil, José, et al., ed. 1990. *Cantal: Musiques traditionnelles*. Riom, France: AMTA/ADMD 001. 2 cassettes.

Guillot, Yves, et al., eds. 1983? *Les Sarthois chantent, dansent et racontent*. 61350 Passais-la-Conception: Pluriel PL 3342. 2 LP disks.

Kennedy, Peter, ed. 1975a. *Au bord d'une fontaine: Folksongs from Guernsey and Sark*. Folktracks FSB 011. Cassette.

———. 1975b. *Au logis de mon père: Folksongs from Jersey and Alderney*. Folktracks FSB 012. Cassette.

Marcel-Dubois, Claudie, ed. 1954. *France*. Columbia World Library of Folk and Primitive Music, 4. Columbia SL 207. LP disk.

Marcel-Dubois, Claudie, and M.-M. Andral, eds. 1969. *Musiques de France*. Paris: Musée national des Arts et Traditions Populaires ATP 69.1. 7-inch LP disk.

Musique corse de tradition orale (mission Félix Quilici, 1961–63). 1982. Paris: Phonothèque nationale APN 82.1-3. 3 LP disks.

Pays de Saulieu. 1977. Chanteurs et Musiciens de villages en Morvan, 2. Autun: Lai Pouèlée VDES 022. LP disk.

Redhon, François, et al., eds. 1980. *Collectage de musiques et chansons traditionnelles en Basse-Normandie*. 61350 Passais-la-Conception: Pluriel CCEN 101. 4 LP disks.

Shields, Hugh, ed. 1974. *French Folksongs from Corrèze: Chants corréziens*. Topic 12T 246. LP disk.

Sonneurs de vielle traditionnels en Bretagne. [1980s]. Douarnenez: Le Chasse-Marée CM 004. 2 LP disks.

Les traditions populaires en France. 1980–1982. Paris: OCORA. 1, *Louise Reichert* (1980), 558 520; 3, *Vendée: Le Marais,* Pierre Burgaud (1982),

ed. John Wright and Catherine Perrier, 558 605; 4, *Béarn: Veillées en Vallée d'Ossau: Pierre Arrius-Mesplé* (1982), 558 604. 3 LP disks.

Valière, Michel, ed. 1977? *Albert Guillet: Accordéon diatonique en Poitou.* 86160 Gençay: UPCP La Marchoise LM 001. Cassette.

———, et al., eds. 1977. *Anthologie de chants et musiques populaires du Haut-Poitou.* 86160 Gençay: UPCOOP 008. LP disk.

Violoneux corréziens. [1978]. N.p. [Lyon?]: *Musiciens Routiniers.* MR 4001. LP disk.

Brittany
Lois Kuter

Dance and Genres of Song
Musical Instruments
History of Music
Institutions for Music and Dance
New Contexts for Traditional Music

Brittany comprises 34,200 square kilometers in the westernmost parts of France on the Atlantic littoral, including the department of Loire-Atlantique, administratively cut off from Brittany by the French government in 1941, to the continued protests of Bretons. According to the 1990 census, Brittany has a population of 3.8 million.

Archaeological evidence traces a local human presence as far back as Palaeolithic times. Between 4,000 and 1,500 B.C., pre-Celtic peoples built megalithic monuments, and though little is known about these peoples, they have left a rich archaeological record, such as the standing stones of Carnac. The first Celts to settle in Brittany were from the La Tène culture, between 500 and 300 B.C. Romans called the Celtic nations in Western Europe Gauls, and Julius Caesar identified five Celtic nations in Brittany (called Armorica) in 58 B.C., when he conquered it. Celts from Britain, primarily from Wales, Devon, and Cornwall, settled in Brittany between A.D. 100 and 600. They shared a language that would later develop into Welsh, Breton, and Cornish.

Brittany is subdivided in several parts, each with a different cultural or administrative significance. At the highest level, Upper Brittany (French *Haute-Bretagne,* Breton *Breizh-Uhel*) forms the eastern part, where standard French and a French-based dialect, Gallo, predominate. Lower Brittany (French *Basse-Bretagne,* Breton *Breizh-Izel*) forms the western part, where Breton, closely related to Welsh as part of the Brythonic subgroup of Celtic languages, is spoken daily by more than 250,000, but perhaps as many as six hundred thousand have some knowledge of it. At the next level, however, the government-defined, administrative *départements* of Brittany (Finistère, Morbihan, Côtes d'Armor, Ille-et-Vilaine, and Loire-Atlantique) often crosscut cultural borders. At a third level, the Roman Catholic dioceses in western Brittany (Leon, Treger, Kernev, Gwened), established between A.D. 600 and 900, correspond to the major dialects of the Breton language. Eastern Brittany has five dioceses: Dol, Penthièvre, Nantes, Rennes, and Saint Malo. At the lowest level, Brittany is divided into "countries" (French *pays,* Breton *broiou,* sing. *bro*), to which the Breton sense of cultural identity is strongly linked, each marked by distinctive music, song, dance, costume, and architecture, and subtleties of language and economy. Since the borders between these cultural features may not coincide exactly, the borders of *pays* are indefinite, though they can be approximated on a map.

DANCE AND GENRES OF SONG

Traditional Breton music is perpetuated through oral transmission, supported by books and recordings from institutions that organize workshops and classes. Traditional styles continue to be performed because they are a part of people's social life, integrated into everyday activities and performed at special events, such as concerts, contests, dances, and festivals. In the practice and transmission of what Bretons define as traditional Breton music, friendship and socializing are critical to the relation between teachers and learners (Moëlo 1989).

Traditional Breton singing is unaccompanied. Dance-songs are sung in unison, and most ballad singing is performed solo. In contrast to some other areas of Western Europe, responsorial singing is common in French and Breton, especially for dancing. *Kan ha diskan,* a distinctive type of such singing, is found in the Breton-speaking areas of western Brittany. It is most often sung by two people: a singer (*kaner*) begins each phrase, and a countersinger (*diskaner*) repeats it. The singers overlap as they sing the last few syllables of each other's phrases.

Bretons distinguish four genres of song. The *gwerz* (French *complainte*) includes ballads or narrative songs in Breton, recounting historical, legendary, or dramatic events. The *son* (French *chanson*) includes lighter topics, such as love, drinking, and counting songs. The *kantig* (French *cantique*) are religious hymns. The *kan da gorell* (French *chanson à danser*) 'songs for dancing' draw texts from ballads and lighter songs, set to varying melodies.

The modernization of maritime industries means that sailors and fishermen no longer perform the work songs and tunes for diversion used on board the large sailing ships of the late 1800s and early 1900s, but songs relating to Brittany's maritime heritage remain part of the oral tradition, relating maritime history, shipwrecks, piracy, and the hard life of fishermen and sailors separated from loved ones.

Dance tunes are named by type, often including a reference to the *pays* without any other title (Guilcher 1995 [1963]). Three distinct types are found in Brittany. The oldest are performed in a three-part suite, commonly danced in lines or circles, and include such dances as the *an dro,* the *dans plinn,* the gavotte, the *hanter dro,* and the *laridé* (or *ridée*). The second, more recent type includes the *bals,* the *jabadao,* and the *pach-pi,* figure dances influenced by British dances of the 1600s or French contredanses of the 1700s. The third type includes couple dances, such as the mazurka, the polka, and the schottische, introduced to Brittany in the 1800s and 1900s and locally transformed.

MUSICAL INSTRUMENTS

Aerophones (reeds)

The instruments most strongly symbolic of Brittany and its cultural revival and autonomy—the *biniou koz* 'old bagpipe' or *biniou bihan* 'little bagpipe' and the *bombarde* 'shawm'—are played together by two performers, the *sonerion* (Breton) or *sonneurs de couple* (French) (figure 1). The *biniou koz* is a mouth-blown *biniou* with one drone. Pitched an octave above the Scottish Highland bagpipe, its usage and key (G♯, A, B, or C) varies from area to area, and research is under way to document fully its history and function. The *bombarde* has a range of two octaves with its lower range pitched an octave below that of the *biniou*.

Two other forms of bagpipes are played in Brittany. Scottish bagpipes (*biniou bras,* French *cornemuse*) were introduced in the late 1800s but did not become popular until the late 1930s, when they began to replace the *biniou koz* in duets with the

86 · MŒURS ET TYPES BRETONS. — Les Biniou. — LL.

FIGURE 1   For dancing, two men play a *biniou* 'bagpipe' and a *bombarde* 'double-reed shawm'. The barrels they sit on function as a raised stage and are seen in many pictures. Early-twentieth-century postcard courtesy of the Robert Godfried Collection, New York.

bombarde. In the 1950s, a tradition of Breton bagpipe bands (*bagad*, pl. *bagadou*) with drum corps, similar to those of Scottish bands, developed, but with the addition of *bombardes*. The *veuze*, a single-drone bagpipe, is found in southeastern Brittany and in the northern part of the Vendée (Pays de la Loire). Played alone or with accordion or fiddle, it is perhaps the oldest *biniou* in Brittany and has changed little since the Middle Ages. Its tone is similar to that of the *gaita* of Galicia, Spain, and the *cabrette* of Limousin and Auvergne, in France. It disappeared from Brittany for several dozen years before musicians began to research it and locate older instruments. A real revival began in the 1970s, mainly because of the efforts of the organization Sonneurs de Veuze, which reconstructed instruments. In the 1990s, about eighty musicians played the instrument.

With a strong tradition in southwest Brittany, the *biniou* and *bombarde* pair is found today throughout Brittany, where at least four hundred pairs of musicians perform. Paired playing has been documented as far back as the 1700s, and some scholars think this use dates at least back to the 1500s in Brittany. Until the mid-twentieth century a drum was often found to form a trio.

The *treujenn gaol* 'cabbage stump' is a clarinet with four or five keys, often made of boxwood. More common are clarinets with thirteen keys, made of boxwood or ebony. The manufacture of these in Brittany dates to the 1800s, and their use is concentrated in central-western Brittany. Modern clarinets with twenty-four keys are also played, though traditional performers tend to stay within one octave. Clarinets are often paired to perform in a style like those of the *biniou-bombarde* duo and responsorial singing for dancing. The organization Paotred an Dreujenn Gaol (Clarinet Men) has been active in promoting research into, and documentation and performance of, this instrument.

The diatonic accordion, and later the chromatic accordion, gained in popularity from around 1900, especially in eastern Brittany and in coastal areas, where maritime traditions remained strong. It often supplanted the *biniou* but has developed a tradition of its own. Though it imported a repertoire to replace local styles, Breton musicians have adapted it to uniquely Breton tastes.

Chordophones

The fiddle (*violon*), first noted in Brittany in the 1600s, has been cultivated mainly in eastern Brittany. Most fiddlers were artisans—wood workers and furniture makers—who made their own instrument. The height of its popularity was around 1900, when it led wedding processions and dances. After World War I, it gradually gave way to the accordion. Only about forty traditional fiddlers could be found in the 1970s, but the collection of their tunes and knowledge has maintained the fiddle's currency. Irish fiddling has been a source of inspiration for younger Bretons.

The hurdy-gurdy (*vielle à roue*) was developed in France in the 1700s. Eastern Brittany, with the French regions of Bourbonnais, Berry, and Auvergne, are active areas for the instrument. As with other traditional Breton instruments, its use declined between the World Wars as the accordion gained ground. A revival in Brittany by the Cercles Celtiques (Celtic Circles) of Rennes, St. Malo, Penthievre, St. Brieuc, and Dinan began in the 1950s; the circles specialize in perpetuating local Breton dance, music, and costumes. The hurdy-gurdy remains in the oral-aural tradition of northeastern Brittany, where it accompanies dancing and weddings and appears in local festivals.

The small Celtic harp (*telenn*) had a golden era in the Middle Ages, and a great deal of musical exchange during that period is recorded among the harpers of Brittany, Wales, Ireland and Scotland. Economic, social, political, and cultural changes led to its decline, and harps disappeared from Brittany by about 1800. A local rebirth of the Celtic harp can be dated to the 1950s, when Jord Cochevelou (father of Alan Stivell, the most famous Breton harper) began reconstructing ancient models. By the early 1970s, the popularity of the Celtic harp had grown, and today hundreds of Bretons are playing it at annual competitions and festivals, solo and in groups.

HISTORY OF MUSIC

Since little was recorded in writing in early Breton society, the origins of Breton music are difficult to trace. Until about 1800, information about music is found only in references to popular traditions in the poetry and texts of royal courts and the Roman Catholic Church.

Early texts refer to a bardic tradition that Bretons in Britain shared with the Welsh, the Irish, and the Scots. What information we have about bardic traditions, song, poetry, and musical instruments sheds light on an elite whose practices may have been quite distinct from those of the rest of the population. Songs with medieval Arthurian themes stemming from common Celtic sources are still found in Breton tradition.

Chansons de geste, dating from the eleventh and twelfth centuries in Brittany, include elements characteristic of traditional song: fantasy, a drawn-out development of the drama, short phrases with concise ideas, and considerable repetition. The lay, however, reached its full development in the 1100s to 1300s, and is most famous from the compositions of Marie de France, who claimed it was of ancient Breton origin. The earliest written song texts, from religious plays, date from the 1300s, with some melodies borrowed from secular traditions.

Early references to popular music are scarce but appear in religious writings that condemn the supposedly corrupting influence of singing and dancing. An injunction against pagan traditions, such as dancing around a fire on St. John's Eve, dates to the 600s, when St. Eloi instructed his followers to refrain from such activity. Despite repeated admonitions by religious authorities, this tradition has survived. The earliest references to the instrumental music of the *biniou,* the *bombarde,* and drums are also found in religious writings from the 1600s, and in visual depictions of diabolical animals—such as goats, pigs, and monkeys—playing these instruments.

Beginning in the 1600s with religious songs, the oral song tradition was supplemented by written texts in the form of broadsides (*feuilles volantes* 'flying sheets'). Identifiable authors, who signed these broadsides and came from all walks of life, would print as many as fifteen hundred copies and try to sell them at fairs after performing them. Subjects included the events of the day (crimes, accidents, politics), moral or instructive messages on family life, love, and conscription into the army (Ollivier 1942). Satirical and humorous songs had a central place in this repertoire, as did religious topics, and the genre survived into the 1960s.

Documentation of the oral song tradition began in the 1800s. The most widely known collection, *Barzaz-Breiz* (Villemarqué 1963 [1867]), provided evidence that Brittany had a rich cultural heritage, and lent prestige to the Breton language. It was often bitterly attacked by other Breton scholars for supposed liberties taken with the texts, especially those glorifying Brittany's independence from France. While Villemarqué never adequately defended his work, a detailed study by Donatien Laurent (1989) has shown that he did not invent the texts, as some of his accusers claimed. He had a good knowledge of Breton and gathered the texts with care, even if he revised them for publication to suit nineteenth-century tastes. Between 1869 and 1890, François-Marie Luzel (1821–1895), another influential collector, published more than four hundred lyrics from the Tregor region of northern Brittany. In contrast to the literary retouching of Villemarqué and other collectors, Luzel's texts

Though contests have often been an excuse to convene musicians and dancers, they have been taken seriously, and are especially effective in adding prestige to the performance of traditional music. Contests for the paired *biniou* and *bombarde* have a long history, dating from 1881.

were closely representative of his singers' renditions. The composers and musicologists L. A. Bourgault-Ducoudray (1840–1910) and Maurice Duhamel (1884–1940) included musical transcriptions and analyses in their collections.

Recordings of Breton music date from 1900, when an otherwise unknown Dr. Azoulay recorded on wax cylinders performances of "peoples of the world" at the Exposition Universelle de Paris. In Brittany in 1900, François Vallée recorded Marc'harid Fulup, a renowned singer and the primary informant for Luzel's collections in the 1870s and 1880s. The Austrian Rudolf von Trebitsch made recordings in 1908, as did the Musée des Arts et Traditions Populaires (Paris) in 1939, but neither collection has been released. The collecting of singing and musical traditions was dampened by World War I, in which many young Bretons—about 240,000 from a population of 3.2 million—died. This marked a period of rural exodus and an increasing influence of governmental and educational institutions that promoted a standardized culture from Paris.

INSTITUTIONS FOR MUSIC AND DANCE

While many Bretons continued the oral tradition, others consciously developed institutions to teach and preserve music and dance. The first Cercle Celtique was founded in Paris in 1929 to help Breton emigrants maintain their cultural identity in an alien environment. The fastest growth of this institution came in the early 1950s, in Breton emigrant communities and small towns throughout Brittany itself. In the circles, young Bretons began to learn about native traditions that had not been transmitted to them within their families because their parents had been taught that being Breton held one back from economic progress.

About 150 Celtic Circles (120 in Brittany, thirty in Breton emigrant communities) form part of two major cultural federations, Kendalc'h 'Continuation' and Wa'r Leur 'On the Floor'; both organize classes, contests, and festivals, set standards for the quality of performance, and support their members' travel throughout Europe. The circles study and master the differences among the traditional dances of Brittany, but also choreograph new dances based on Breton traditions. Many aspects of culture are learned in the circles, but their work is most famous for the performance of traditional dances in costumes particular to the part of Brittany where the circle is based. The costumes themselves are now rarely worn outside of weddings and annual religious festivals (*pardons*).

Parallel to the Celtic Circles was the growth of a new ensemble, the *bagad*, a *biniou* band modeled after Scottish bands, though these include *bombardes* and Scottish-style bagpipes and drums. Often accompanying a performance by a Celtic Circle, these may be officially linked with a particular circle to form a larger troupe. Typically, a *bagad* has eight Scottish bagpipes, eight *bombardes*, four snare drums, two tenor drums, and one bass drum. Members wear uniforms, often a simplified version of older traditional dress, incorporating perhaps an embroidered vest, but not a traditional hat or trousers. Though the *bagad* has always been a popular part of festival parades, these ensembles also perform Breton dance music, arranging tunes from the traditional repertoire of singers or the paired playing of the *biniou* and the *bombarde*. As their technique has improved, *bagadou* have developed innovative arrangements and composed new music. Annual contests for different levels of competence showcase orchestrations these ensembles have developed.

More of the sixty or so *bagadou* in Brittany are part of the federation Bodadeg ar Sonerion (Association of Bagpipers), founded in 1942. This federation publishes a magazine (*Ar Soner*), and organizes classes and contests for pipers and *bombarde* players.

Another important institution, Dastum, a center for documenting Breton culture, has contributed to the development of Breton musical traditions. After grassroots beginnings (1972), it has expanded its collection of tapes and texts, and now functions as an archive for photographs and documents, with over thirty thousand recordings, thirty thousand pages of manuscripts and lyrics, twenty thousand old postcards and photographs, and more than fifty-five thousand press clippings, all catalogued and indexed by computer. Dastum also publishes a magazine (*Musique bretonne*), books, and well-documented recordings. Collectors for Dastum are volunteers, often musicians. Local collectors are the basis of Dastum's activity, and they are effective because of the closeness of their ties to local communities; they are not outsiders, but participants in a living tradition.

Smaller organizations, run by volunteers, create new contexts for music by developing local and Brittanywide festivals and competitions and teach in schools to foster Breton music culture. In the late 1980s, the curricula of state-administered schools and conservatories began incorporating classes in traditional Breton music. The French Ministry of Culture has set up means for educators to become certified to teach traditional Breton music.

NEW CONTEXTS FOR TRADITIONAL MUSIC

Several kinds of event currently provide musicians with incomes. A prominent context is the *fest noz* 'night festival', originally a gathering of family and neighbors after communal work, when songs and dances were performed. *Fest noz* of the 1950s began in small villages and first included contests to encourage singers and dancers. Microphones were introduced as the event grew larger, separating singers from dancers, but the style of singing was not greatly affected.

Contests, usually embedded in a larger festival, have become a powerful medium for encouraging Breton music. Cutting across all styles of music, these involve championships for all Brittany, or for just a small area. Though contests have often been an excuse to convene musicians and dancers, they have been taken seriously, and are especially effective in adding prestige to the performance of traditional music. Contests for the paired *biniou* and *bombarde* have a long history, dating from 1881.

Festivals have become important occasions. Dozens of established ones—like the Fêtes de Cornouaille and the Interceltic Festival at Lorient—gather four thousand or more performers and two hundred thousand spectators over a week's duration, or, in annual village festivals, perhaps a few hundred participants for a weekend. Festivals promote vocal styles (like Kan ar Bobl, Bogue d'Or, Breizh a Gan), specific instruments (Rencontre International de la Clarinette Populaire, Fête du Violon, Fête de la Veuze), dance (Concours de la Ronde de Loudéac, Festival Fanch-Plinn, Festival de la Danse Bretonne et de la Saint Loup), a specific region or Breton culture as a whole (Fête de Rigodailles, Assemblé de la Boueze, Carrefour de la Gallesie, Tombés de la Nuit, Festival des Ajoncs d'Or, Fête des Filets Bleu, Tregor en Fête), or maritime culture (Fête du Chant Marin, Fête Internationale de la Voile).

Social gatherings in small towns, at a bar or a café, also serve as a context for performance of various Breton musical idioms. Modeled after pub sessions of Ireland, the café is a new context, not so widespread in Brittany. In most cases, musicians are hired to perform at a café, and their performance leads to less formal music making.

Magazines produced by Breton cultural organizations are a critical resource for knowledge of Breton music. The following, published four to six times a year, focus primarily on Breton music. The publishing organization is in parentheses: *Ar Soner* (Bodadeg ar Sonerion); *Breizh,* replaced in 1988 by *Keleier Kendalc'h* (Kendalc'h); *Evit Koroll* (Federation Celtique de la Danse); *Kazel ha Kazel,* replaced in 1989 by *Keleier War'l Leur* (War'l Leur); *Musique bretonne* (Dastum); *Telennourien Vreizh—Le journal de la harpe* (Telennourien Vreizh).

The availability of cassette recorders encouraged performers to become collectors in the 1960s and 1970s. These and compact-disc recordings provide inspiration for younger singers and instrumentalists. Commercial recordings have not only allowed greater access to repertoires, but have given new prestige to traditional performers. The 1960s and 1970s saw the growth of ensembles of younger musicians, who used a variety of acoustic and electric instruments. Young Bretons who had grown up in urban settings began to study rural traditions, while those in small rural communities took a new interest in the older styles around them. Many younger musicians mastered both traditional and contemporary popular styles, just as their parents had temporarily put aside *biniou* and fiddles to play in jazz bands in the 1930s. In the 1990s, performers switched styles to adapt to different audiences and contexts, and new technologies supported the continuation of the oral tradition, rather than replaced it.

BIBLIOGRAPHY

Badone, Ellen. 1987. "Ethnicity, Folklore, and Local Identity in Rural Brittany." *Journal of American Folklore* 100:161–190.

Becker, Roland, and Laure Le Gurun. 1994. *La Musique bretonne.* Spezet: Coop Breizh.

Dastum. 1999. *Guide de la musique bretonne.* 3d, augmented edition. Rennes: Dastum.

Defrance, Yves. 1996. *Sonnoux et sonerien.* Musiques traditionnelles de Bretagne, 1. Morlaix: Skol Vreizh.

Giraudon, Daniel. 1985. *Chansons populaires de Basse-Bretagne sur feuilles volantes.* Morlaix: Skol Vreizh, nos. 2–3.

Guilcher, Jean-Michel. 1995 [1963]. *La tradition populaire de danse en Basse-Bretagne.* Chasse-Marée: Ar Men.

Kuter, Lois. 1981. "Music and Identity in Brittany, France." In *Discourse in Ethnomusicology II: A Tribute to Alan P. Merriam,* 15–41. Bloomington, Ind.: Ethnomusicology Publications Group.

———. 1985. "Labelling People: Who Are the Bretons?" *Anthropological Quarterly* 58:13–29.

Laurent, Donatien. 1989. *Aux sources du Barzaz-Breiz: la mémoire d'un peuple.* Douarnenez: Ar Men.

Luzel, François Marie. 1971 [1869–1890]. *Chants et chansons populaires de la Basse-Bretagne, Gwerziou, Soniou.* 4 vols. Paris: Maisonneuve et Larose.

Malrieu, Patrick. 1983. *Histoire de la chanson populaire bretonne.* Rennes: Dastum and Skol.

Moëlo, Serge. 1989. *Guide de la musique bretonne 1990.* Rennes: Direction Régionale des Affaires Culturelles, Direction Régionale de la Jeunesse et des Sports, Sonerion ha Kanerien Vreizh, and Dastum.

Montjarret, Polig. 1984. *Toniou Breizh-Izel/Folk Music of West Brittany.* Rennes: Bodadeg ar Sonerion.

Musique bretonne—histoire des sonneurs de tradition. 1997. Douarnenez: Le Chasse Marée/Ar Men.

Ollivier, Joseph. 1942. *Catalogue bibliographique de la chanson populaire sur feuilles volantes.* Quimper: Le Goaziou.

Villemarqué, Vicomte Hersart de la. 1963 [1867]. *Barzaz-Breiz: chants populaires de la Bretagne.* Paris: Librairie Perrin.

AUDIOVISUAL RESOURCES

Accordéons diatoniques en Bretagne. 1990. Keltia Musique KMCD 08. Compact disc.

Au coeur de la musique bretonne. 1997. Escalibur CD 874. Compact disc.

Barzaz Breizh—c'hoazh hag adarre. 1990. FR3 Bretagne/Le Lagon Bleu LBCD 03. Compact disc. LBK 03. Cassette

Becker, Roland. 1993. *Musiques traditionnelles en Bretagne Morbihannaise.* Arfolk CD 423. Compact disc.

Clarinettes et anciennes danses populaires de Tregor. 1991. Chanteurs et musiciens de Bretagne, 5. Dastum Bro Dreger/Dastum DAS 1115. Cassette.

Fest deiz, fest noz: Printemps de Châteauneuf. 1997. Printemps de Châteauneuf/Coop Breizh CD 113. Compact disc.

Gouel 20 vloaz Dastum: Tradition vivante de Bretagne. 1993. Dastum DAS 119. Compact disc.

Musiques de Bretagne/The Sounds of Brittany. 1991. Keltia Musique KMCD 19. Compact disc.

Quand les Bretons passent à table. 1994. Dastum DAS 121. Compact disc.

Sonneurs d'accordéon en Bretagne. 1994. Anthologie des chants et musiques de Bretagne, 7. Ar Men/La Boueze SCM 034. Compact disc.

Sonneurs de clarinette en Bretagne/Sonerien treujenn-gaol. 1992. Anthologie des chants et musiques de Bretagne, 3. Le Chasse-Marée/Ar Men SCM 026. Compact disc.

Sonneurs traditionnels de Bretagne. 1994. Anthologie des chants et musiques de Bretagne, 7. Ar Men/La Boueze SCM 034. Compact disc.

Sonneurs de vielle traditionnels en Bretagne. 1993. Anthologie des chants et musiques de Bretagne, 3. Dastum/Le Chasse-Marée SCM 027. Compact disc.

Sonneurs de veuze en Bretagne et marais breton vendéen. 1993. Anthologie des chants et musiques de Bretagne, 4. Le Chasse-Marée/Ar Men SCM 026. Compact disc.

Sonneurs de violon traditionnels en Bretagne. 1993. Anthologie des chants et musiques de Bretagne, 5. Le Chasse-Marée/Ar Men SCM 031. Compact disc.

Tradition chantée de Bretagne: Aux sources du Barzaz Breiz. 1989. Ar Men and Dastum SCM 013. Compact disc.

Voix de Bretagne. 1992. Le Quartz/France 3. Keltia Musique RSCD 205. Compact disc.

War an Hent. 1995. Gwerz Pladenn GWP 010. Compact disc.

Zantzinger, Gei, Lois Kuter, and Michael Bailey. 1997. *Of Pipers and Wrens.* Constant Spring Productions.

Corsica
Wolfgang Laade

Traditional Musical Genres and Performance Practices
Musical Instruments
History of Music and Scholarship

Corsica, at 8,680 square kilometers the smallest and northernmost of the three major islands in the Tyrrhenian Sea, is mountainous and wooded in the center, with an alluvial plain on the east coast. Libyans, Iberians, and Ligurians formed the earliest populations, and Phoenicians, Etruscans, and Greeks had colonies at various times in the coastal areas. In the third century B.C., the island became part of the Roman Empire; later, Goths, Vandals, Byzantines, Lombards, and Saracens followed. From the eleventh to the eighteenth centuries, the island belonged in succession to the Italian cities of Pisa and Genoa. It became a French possession in 1768, just in time to make Napoleon Bonaparte, born in 1769 in Ajaccio (Corsica's largest city), a French citizen. The Corsican language, like Sardinian and Sicilian, is not an Italian dialect, but grew directly out of Latin.

Throughout Corsican history, foreign influences chiefly affected the coastal areas. The local people retreated to the mountains, where they continued to lead a migratory, semipastoral life. Poverty and unending political unrest induced many Corsican men to seek their fortune in the French army and colonial service. A massive emigration to France began between the world wars, and traditional culture was finally disrupted after World War II by increasing socioeconomic changes. The population, of about 240,000, supports itself by raising goats and sheep, growing wheat, olives, citrus fruits, and grapes, and making cheese and wine. A movement for independence has been active since the 1970s.

TRADITIONAL MUSICAL GENRES AND PERFORMANCE PRACTICES

In Corsica, singing and the oral poetry it supports are far more important than instrumental music, and many distinct song genres can be identified, though the free use of existing tunes across genres leads to a certain amount of overlap. The traditional repertoire consists of laments (*lamenti,* especially for the dead), lullabies, work songs performed when driving animals, responsorial song duels and improvised songs to violin accompaniment, polyphonic songs (*paghjelle*), Italian-style songs, and children's songs. After World War II, the original contexts for these songs declined in importance.

The *lamentu* (pl. *lamenti*; also *voceru, ballata, compitu*) is by far the most impor-

FIGURE 1 *Lamentu* on a Minor Scale. Transcription by Wolfgang Laade.

tant and richest category of traditional song. Women composed and sang *lamenti,* and men borrowed their tunes for their own songs of sorrow. The lamenter sings slowly and syllabically, dwelling on the semifinals and finals of each line, in a relaxed voice in the middle register, with melodies built on a minor pentachord (figure 1). Some individual tunes exist in this repertoire, but singers chiefly use a few melodic models, which appear in endless and varied metamorphosis (Laade 1962). The tunes have also been used for other genres of song.

Some writers have distinguished between the normal *lamentu,* sung for a natural death, and the *voceru* (*buceru, bucerata*) sung for a violent death, but the people do not make this distinction. The term *ballata* (*abbaddata* in the south) may denote a dance once performed around the corpse. The ordinary *lamentu* recalls the dead person's good qualities, but in the case of a violent death, angry verses ask male relatives to carry out a vendetta, their inescapable duty. *Lamentu* tunes also serve for songs of farewell, love, and departing recruits. The last farewells for recruits were composed during the French-Algerian conflict of the 1950s. *Lamenti* on the death of an animal, sincere or satirical, serve to ridicule people, especially during elections. *Lamenti di banditi* tell "autobiographical" tales of famous bandits—men who, under the compulsion of the vendetta, left home to live in the *macchia,* the impenetrable forest, to fulfill their revenge. The tune of any *lamentu* can serve for a bandit's lament, but this category has a special tune with many variants, which in turn have been used for other subjects.

Corsican women, always dressed in black, sang lullabies (sing. *ninna-nanna*) in a lamentlike mood and style, probably because incessant wars, the vendetta, and emigration left them with *lamentu* texts and tunes in mind, even when nursing a baby. Tender lyrics describe the beauty of a girl or the strength of a boy, wishing them luck and wealth. Scholars regard the lyrics of the *lamentu* and the *ninna-nanna* as the finest traditional poetry composed on the island. Many outstanding laments and lullabies have survived and become well-known folk songs.

Two kinds of work song, connected with animal driving, belonged to the male repertoire. Driving a pair of oxen pulling a heavy stone roller (*tribbiu*) over wheat spread on a stone platform, farmers formerly sang a threshing song (*tribbiera*) in free meter with a strained voice (figure 2). Each stanza describes the labor and the animals before moving into a drawn-out descending melisma and downward glissando and ending with calls, like *hooka hokijoooh,* urging the animals to move on without tiring (figure 3). The form is AA', or slightly extended, A(a + a) B(b + b), and the vocal line covers a fifth, the first phrase rising from the third to the fifth and descending to the tonic, the second descending from the fourth to the tonic. The mule driver (*mulatteru*) sang songs with a similarly drawn-out, call-like quality as he transported goods

FIGURE 2 Farmers threshing wheat with *tribbiu* and singing. After Galletti 1863.

from the towns to the villages. The advent of trucks and automobiles led to the disappearance of this genre. Until the early 1950s, street vendors selling fish, seafood, cheese, or bread and cakes performed various melodic calls in Bastia, the main northern city.

Corsicans loved to improvise songs in ordinary family gatherings and at fairs, and men and women competed in this art. An existing tune was often the basis for composing a new text, set in a standard three-line model, which literati called tercet form and the people called making *puesia*. Any subject could be the theme of a *puesia:* reminiscences of friends or mountain walks, greetings to relatives, congratulations on a wedding or a birthday, patriotic themes, love, satire, or respectful praise—often in the form of a letter, sometimes written from overseas. There were three main styles of performance. The poetic contest known as call and response (*chiam' e rispondi*) often developed spontaneously between two or more participants after a meal or in competitions at fairs. Each singer responded in alternation to his or her rival's improvised text; in the rare *tercets proverbes,* a traditional proverb had to be answered with another suitable one. For *u contrastu,* two lovers or a married couple improvised a poetic dialogue. A *currente* (from *corre* 'to run') was an improvised poem accompanied by a violin, normally played by the singer; the term may refer to the accompaniment, which consists of a two-part drone on open strings during the singing, and fast melodic runs between verses. The musical style of the violin accompaniment no doubt derives from that of the bagpipes. A *currente* sung at a wedding, with good wishes to the newlyweds, was called a serenade for the couple (*sirinata a i sposi*).

FIGURE 3 *Tribbiera* (threshing song). Transcription by Wolfgang Laade.

Vì– a, vì– a, vì– a, vì– a! Vin– ti sol– di fà u– na li– ra.

U– na li– ra fà un fran– cu. Ve–ne trib– bia chi– sò stan– cu.

In the 1700s and 1800s, many foreign travelers characterized the Corsicans as a race of poets. Almost everyone could improvise poetry, and many illiterate people could recite long poems. In the 1950s, many could still improvise common tercets, and some improvisers were famous all over the island. Alisandru Ambrosi (Lisandru di Rustinu, 1798–1842), the first illiterate village poet whose verses survive, composed a satirical poem that cost him his life (Laade 1981:1:157–158).

The tercet form contains three musical phrases set to three sixteen-syllable poetic lines with end rhyme. Each poetic line and musical phrase is constructed of two half phrases and two eight-syllable poetic lines, as in the following stanza from a *chiam' e rispondi* (after Marcel-Dubois 1955):

> I svegliati la mio musa, e pro dati di curaju!
> Sta sera ai vole a canta per a fiera di lu Pratu,
> Un locu cusi famosu, chi da tutti acclamatu.

> Waken, oh my muse, and do your best for me!
> This evening I must sing at the fair of Pratu,
> A famous place, and praised by all.

The three melodic lines are most frequently organized as ABB, less often as AAA or AAB. A few songs have the two-part form AB or AABB. The A phrase is usually subdivided a + a, and the B phrase can be b + b or b + b′. Laments of the bandits have a twelve-syllable pattern, from which another group of variants derives.

Nineteenth-century travelers often mentioned *paghjella,* Corsican polyphony sung on social occasions. Since *lamenti* have lost their original contexts, there remains little more typically Corsican than *paghjelle,* and so they play a central role in young Corsicans' revival of traditional music. Three male soloists normally sing in three parts in a style reminiscent of twelfth- and thirteenth-century medieval polyphony; other males may join the bass or the final cadence (figure 4). The highest voice is called *secunda* (there is no *prima*); the middle voice, *terza*; and the lowest, *bassa*. The *secunda* sings the main tune solo, in major or minor pentachords. The *bassa,* moving in a way that implies tonal harmony, joins the *secunda,* and both proceed together, ending the first half verse on the subdominant. The *terza* joins for the second half verse. The two phrases of a *paghjella* can accommodate only one full sixteen-syllable line, so, since a poetic stanza contains three sixteen-syllable lines, the *paghjella* must be sung three times to accommodate one stanza. The term *paghjella* (from *paghja* 'pair') seems to refer to the pair of half verses, which together make one line of the poem and a sung strophe.

The singers normally stand close together, concentrating on the lines sung by their neighbors. To hear their own voice more clearly, they cup their right hand

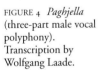

FIGURE 4 *Paghjella* (three-part male vocal polyphony). Transcription by Wolfgang Laade.

Terza

Secunda

Bassa

Many songs for elections were satirical, witty, malicious, and crude. For these songs, the poets often used a tune printed with the song the soldiers of Pasquale Paoli, Corsica's liberator from Genoese rule, are said to have sung in their last fight against the French, at Ponte Nuovo, on 8 May 1769.

FIGURE 5 Three singers of *paghjella* with hands cupped around their ears to hear their own voice better. Photo by Wolfgang Laade.

around their right ear, eyes often closed, neck and forehead muscles tense, the torso moving to and fro with the musical accents (figure 5). To make the sound pleasing and create a clear and transparent polyphony, they sing with contrasting timbres: the *terza* harsh and metallic; the *secunda* high and strained, but less harsh than the *terza*; and the *bassa* more relaxed, in medium register, with a darker timbre than the others. When the singers change vocal roles, as they sometimes do, they change their vocal timbre to suit the part. There are clear standards for good *paghjella* singing: a good ear, for example, or listening to the voices of one's partners. The melismas (*ricucetti*) must be sung precisely; they guide the voices to the semifinal and final cadences, thus playing an important part in organizing the strophes. Corsicans could clearly explain why a *secunda,* a *terza,* or a *bassa* was well intoned, whether a voice was too hard and inflexible, and whether the entries of the voices were imprecise or the ornaments blurred. Before the revival, *paghjelle* were sung only in the mountains of northern Corsica, with the exception of Cape Corse. In the 1950s, the best singers could be found in the province of Castagniccia, in Orezza, and in the Casinca. Because of the proximity of multipart singing in Sardinia, the lack of polyvocal singing in the south is surprising [see SARDINIA].

Italian song types preserved in Corsica include *madrigali, sirinati,* barcaroles, *brindisi,* and dance songs. *Madrigali,* a form cultivated in northern Italy during the 1300s, are sung in three parts with the leading voice (*secunda*) in the middle. Each madrigal has its own tune, but only a few have been recorded, and those only from one family in Orezza, where this tradition appears to have been strongest. Serenades (*sirinati*) and barcaroles (songs modeled on Venetian gondolier songs) comprise a single genre. Some serenades are purely Corsican: locally composed and sung to *lamentu* or *puesia* tunes. The Italian tunes, introduced chiefly in the 1700s, differ from these in every respect: they are major, rather than minor, and in a brisk 6/8 meter. Songs of this type became very popular, including "*Tre surelle*," "*U pescator' dell'onda*," and "*O Frederi*," all Corsican adaptations of "*La pesca dell'anello*," known throughout Italy and the Italian Swiss region of Ticino. Songs of Italian or French origin are always sung in a relaxed voice, and many village and urban singers sing Italian and modern Corsican songs in an operatic *bel canto* voice.

Dances of Italian origin and their corresponding songs found their way into Corsican towns and then spread to rural areas. Bastia and Calvi were influenced largely by northern and central Italy, but Ajaccio displays Neapolitan character and style. Period dances of Italian origin include the *cerca*, the *conca*, the *monferina*, the saltarello, and the tarantella, all known in the mid-1800s [see ITALY]. Since about 1800, dances such as *la tarascona* and *la marsigliana*, both of Provençal origin, were adopted from France. By 1900, these had given way to the contredanse, the *marcia*, the mazurka, the quadrille (*quadriglia*), the schottische (*sciotiscia*), and the waltz (*valsu*).

By the 1950s, it was difficult to observe indigenous Corsican children's songs. Early in the twentieth century, French *rondes enfantines* and patriotic chants learned at school had replaced the traditional repertoire, which had largely consisted of *filastrocche* (from *filare* 'to spin', or from *filia* 'row, line') whose name refers to rows of verses, often with nonlexical words, linked together like a chain. These were not sung, but recited, in fast tempo on two neighboring notes. Children's games such as *torra, cascola, ingermatura,* and *scallamanu* were accompanied by verses.

Songs for communal and cantonal elections continued after World War II, but by the seventies had ceased to exist. Elections were accompanied by exuberant behavior, including singing solo verses with a choral refrain. Poets, hoping that the new leader would bring change, composed long songs describing the grievances of the village. Many songs for elections were satirical, witty, malicious, and crude. For these songs, the poets often used a tune printed with the song the soldiers of Pasquale Paoli, Corsica's liberator from Genoese rule, are said to have sung in their last fight against the French, at Ponte Nuovo, on 8 May 1769.

MUSICAL INSTRUMENTS

Three kinds of Corsican musical instruments can be distinguished: pastoral flutes and reeds; noisemaking idiophones and membranophones; and more refined instruments, like the bagpipe and the *cetera* 'cittern', both introduced from Italy and used for dance music and to accompany singing. Most of these had fallen out of use between the mid-1800s and the mid-1900s, replaced by the violin, the guitar, and the accordion, but some have been rediscovered by the folk-music revival.

Signaling instruments

Signaling instruments include the conch-shell trumpet (*cornu, cornu marinu, culombu*), associated at times with the struggle for independence; a simple idioglot clarinet (*tromba*), whose thick mouthpiece was fastened to a conical funnel made of chestnut bark, and whose sound called the herd together; and the hornpipe (*zampogna*), a small tube with an idioglot single reed attached to a cow or goat horn.

The bagpipes (*caramusa*), introduced from Italy in the 1700s, consisted of a goatskin bag with a blowpipe, a single-reed chanter, and one or two drone pipes. The *cialambella* or *cialamella* (in the south, *cialambedda, cialamedda*) is a single-reed instrument with a slightly conical wooden body and bell and six finger holes. Shepherd's flutes were traditionally duct flutes: the *pirula* or *fischju* was a long, narrow, reed flute with three to six finger holes, usually cut for immediate use. The cow or goat horn is actually a duct flute (called *pivana*) with six finger holes and a wooden plug at the wide end to create a duct.

A metal mouth harp (*riebula, riberbula, rivergula*), made by local blacksmiths, was especially popular in the 1700s, and continued to be used to the mid-twentieth century. Despite the picture of a Corsican shepherd playing panpipes (*cornamusa*) in Abbé Jean-Ange Galletti's *Histoire illustré de la Corse* (1863), the existence of panpipes on the island has never been substantiated.

Noisemakers

Drums and idiophones served mainly as noisemakers during Holy Week and to create rhythms for marching in a procession or dancing, with or without songs or instrumental tunes. The drum of the poor was the *cassella* (also *paghjolu, nacchere*), a kitchen kettle with a piece of cow skin tied over it. During the Good Friday procession in Erbalunga, on Cape Corse, this instrument gave the beat for marching. Another type of *cassella* was made from a kettle, but without the skin.

Written sources mention that a small kettle was placed upside-down inside a larger one and beaten with two sticks, accompanying the saltarello and the *charivari,* when the community drew attention, with noisemaking outside the newlyweds' house, to the wedding of a former widow or widower—a custom that died out after World War II.

A large frame drum, some 40 centimeters in diameter, also called a *cassella,* was played with a pair of sticks and accompanied certain dances, notably the *tarasco* (*tarascona*). It formerly announced deaths, usually in the middle of the night.

The friction drum (*pignatu*) was a bellied clay pot with a cat skin tied over its opening and a stick, about 30 centimeters long, inserted in the center. Its sound, a deep rumbling, produced by rubbing the stick with a moistened rag, was used as a drone accompaniment to the music of guitars and mandolins in Corte as late as the 1930s.

A triangle (*u timpanu*), usually fashioned by the local blacksmith, was a popular pairing with the bagpipe or violin, later the accordion or guitar.

As in other Roman Catholic countries, bells were silent from the Mass of Maundy Thursday to the first Mass of Easter, but processions included the noise of simple whistles and reeds and wooden instruments: clappers, castanets, rattles, and scrapers of all kinds: *traccule* (small wooden slabs, played like castanets), *taccule* (a wooden board with beaters), *martellu* (a wooden hammer, fixed in a forked handle), *ragana* (a mechanized wooden rasp, having various local names).

Refined instruments

The cittern (*cetera*), the most important stringed instrument, was imported from Italy in the late 1600s. A favorite instrument in Corsica until the mid-1800s, it was still played until World War II to accompany songs and dances. Recent research has discovered nine instruments kept by families on the island. Basically a pear-shaped lute with a flat-bottomed, wooden sound box and a wide, fretted neck, the *cetera* has eight pairs of wire strings, plucked with the fingers or a plectrum (*penna*). The recently discovered instruments are nineteenth century in origin, with chromatic frets; only one still retains an older, diatonic system. A newly found manuscript with *cetera* tablature for twenty-six dance pieces includes a *cerca*, a *gagliarda*, a *minuetto*, and a saltarello. Young musicians are currently reconstructing and reviving performance on the instrument, which the violin (*viulinu*) and the guitar (*guitarra*) eclipsed in the late 1800s and early 1900s, only in turn to be eclipsed by the accordion (figure 6).

FIGURE 6 A revival musician playing the *cetera*. Photographer and date unknown.

HISTORY OF MUSIC AND SCHOLARSHIP

In the 1600s, remarks about Corsican poetry and music began sporadically to appear in the literature. The 1700s saw a renewed period of Italian influence: Italian, the official language, continued to dominate in educated families well past the mid-1800s. Knowledge of the great poetic works of the Renaissance reached even illiterate shepherds in the mountains, some of whom, according to early travelers, could recite whole *canti* of Dante, Petrarch, Ariosto, and Tasso, and whose own poetry absorbed elements from these sources. The *cetera* and the violin became popular, the latter rivaling bagpipes as the instrument for weddings and dances. Both accompanied the serenades, barcaroles, and Italian dances that had newly been imported, and the violin's accompanying the *currente* was a transference from the bagpipe's function and style.

In the mid-1700s, when French troops occupied and then annexed the island, soldiers (chiefly from the south of France) introduced French military and drinking songs, which possibly became the model for Corsican songs of elections. Dances from southern France, the *tarascona* and *marsigliana,* were probably variants of the Provençal *farandole.* But by the mid-1800s, the bagpipe and the *cetera* had become rare and were played only sporadically, even in remote villages.

In the late 1800s, however, the influence of the Provençal *félibres,* poets and intellectuals dedicated to the revival of their own regional dialects and the advancement of their literary value, spread to other regions of France, and Corsican literati began to form associations and publish periodicals with articles on Corsican folklore and poetry, short stories, and comedies in Corsican. They also began to compose songs in folk styles—nostalgic songs about the island, its natural beauty, and their personal memories. They composed hundreds of songs between 1870 and the mid-twentieth century. A few such songs have become popular, even standard. Some songwriters composed text and tune; others adapted words to an existing tune, even an opera tune of the day.

In the middle of the twentieth century, professional musicians began to compose neofolkloric songs heard on radio and records, in Corsican bars and cabarets in Paris and Marseilles, and in tourist spots on the island. The dominant instrument accompanying these songs was the guitar. The texts, rarely in Corsican, were cast in French for general consumption.

In the seventies, younger Corsican musicians combined scholarship and performance in a revival movement aimed at resurrecting styles of singing and musical instruments that were in decline or had disappeared. They produced a book on Corsican musical instruments (*Voce di u Cumune* 1980) that covers an area not previously studied; they apply their research in villages to the revival of older practices. Traditional polyphonic singing is again practiced; *paghjelle* especially have become a symbol of Corsican identity. Devoted revivalists play the violin once again in a traditional style, and have reconstructed and play the *cetera,* the *cialambella,* and the *pirula.* Besides recreating the most popular traditional forms, these performers have created a new Corsican music, casting traditional elements into contemporary forms.

Written studies of Corsican music

Authors writing in Italian compiled the first collections of Corsican folk song with Italian texts and no music notation (Tommaseo 1841; Viale 1984 [1855]). Antoine Laurent Apollinaire Fée (1985 [1850]) produced the first collection of the texts of Corsican folk songs. At the end of the 1800s, two collectors (Marcaggi 1898; Ortoli 1887) supplemented Fée's texts, but without additional tunes, and two musicians from Bastia (Clementi and Graziani 1890) published an important collection of songs popular in their city at that time. Austin de Croze (1911), after three years of

In 1948, Félix Quilici (1909–1980), a violist in the French National Orchestra and an enthusiastic collector of Corsican music, documented traditional songs for the Phonothèque Nationale and the Musée des Arts et Traditions Populaires (Paris). In Paris, he created his own folklore group, A Cirnea.

military service in Corsica, published more songs, texts, and tunes in a simple and convincing notation; he provided the first, though brief and somewhat speculative, discussion of Corsican poetic talent, the music of traditional songs, their origins, and cross-cultural connections. Xavier Tomasi (1932), father of the Corsican-French composer Henri Tomasi, published a substantial collection of traditional songs with piano accompaniment, and Edith Southwell-Colucci (1933) published the results of fieldwork, in a completely new collection of folk-song texts without tunes. In 1951, the Corsican portion of Joseph Canteloube's monumental anthology of French folk songs followed.

In 1948, Félix Quilici (1909–1980), a violist in the French National Orchestra and an enthusiastic collector of Corsican music, began to make regular recording trips to his home island, where he documented traditional songs for the Phonothèque Nationale and the Musée des Arts et Traditions Populaires (Paris) [see THE COLLECTION AND STUDY OF TRADITIONAL EUROPEAN MUSIC, figure 2, p. 22]. In Paris, he created his own folklore group, A Cirnea. Wolfgang Laade's fieldwork followed, in 1955, 1956, 1958, and 1973, and Markus Römer in the 1970s documented Corsican church-singing traditions; their work resulted in the first comprehensive studies of Corsican traditional music (Laade 1962, 1981, 1987; Römer 1983). Laade transcribed and analyzed 284 Corsican folk songs, which he discussed in their ethnographic and historical setting and in the wider Mediterranean context. Combining the experience and methods of a music historian and an ethnomusicologist, Römer studied the traditions of the polyvocal Latin liturgical songs and Corsican *laudi*, handed down within Roman Catholic lay brotherhoods in rural areas. The source of local oral traditions lay in Franciscan musical manuscripts of the 1600s and 1700s, held in Corsican archives.

BIBLIOGRAPHY

Canteloube, Joseph. 1951. *Anthologie des chants populaires français*. Vol. 1. Paris: Durand.

Casanova, Petru. N.d. *Apellamanu: Ghjochi nustrali e usanze festie*. Nice: SEF.

Clementi, Antoine Nicolas, and Dominique Graziani. 1890. *La lyre corse*. Marseille: La Lyre Corse.

Collectivité Territoriale de la Corse, ed. 1993. *Cinq instruments de musique traditionnels corses*. Ajaccio: Collectivité Territoriale de la Corse.

Croze, Austin de. 1911. *La chanson populaire de l'île de Corse*. Paris: H. Champion.

DeZerbi, Ghjermana, and François Diani. 1983 [1981]. *Cantu Nustrale*. Ajaccio: C.R.D.P.

———. 1992. *Cantu Corsu: Contours d'une expression populaire: Raccolta di e cronache di Kyrn*. Ajaccio: Cyrnos et Méditerranée.

DeZerbi, Ghjermana, and Mighele Raffaelli. 1993. *Antulugia di u cantu nustrale*. Ajaccio: La Marge.

Fée, Antoine Laurent Apollinaire. 1985 [1850]. *Voceri, chanson populaire de l'île de Corse*. Paris: Benelli.

Firruloni, Guy, and Collectivité de la Corse, eds. 1993. *Canta u Populu Corsu*. Levie: Albiana.

Galletti, Jean Ange. 1863. *Histoire illustrée de la Corse*. Paris: Pillet fils.

Giacomo-Marcellesi, Mathée. 1989. *Contra*

Salvatica: Contes et légendes de corse du sud suivis des chansons de Jean-André Culioli. Aix-en-Provence: Edisud.

Knudsen, Anne. 1994. "Corps silencieux et âmes chantantes: Chants mortuaires corses." *Travaux du Centre d'Études Corses* 2:59–72.

Laade, Wolfgang. 1962. *Die Struktur der korsischen Lamento-Melodik.* Baden-Baden: Koerner.

———. 1981, 1987. *Das korsische Volkslied: Ethnographie und Geschichte, Gattungen und Stil.* 3 vols. Wiesbaden: Steiner.

Le chant traditionnel. 1992. LETTERA (A): Revue Gratuite d'Informations Culturelles de A Stampata, 5. Bastia: N.p.

Marcaggi, Jean-Baptiste. 1898. *Chants de la mort et de la vendetta de la Corse.* Paris: Perrin.

———. 1926. *Lamenti, voceri, chansons populaires de la Corse.* Ajaccio: J. Rombaldi.

Ortoli, Frédéric. 1887. *Les voceri de l'île de Corse.* Paris: E. Leroux.

———. 1992 [1887]. *Les voceri de l'île de Corse.* New printing, with a supplement containing *lamenti* collected by Roccu Multedu. Edited by Marie-Jean Vinciguerra. Petricaghju: Cismonte e Pumonti.

Pasquali, Iviu. 1993. *Pulifunie—eri, oghje, dumani/Poliphonies—hier, aujourd'hui, demain.* Petricaghju: Cismonte e Pumonti.

Pérès, Marcel, ed. 1996. *Le chant religieux corse: État—comparaisons— perspectives.* Actes du colloque de Corte, 1990. Les Cahiers du Centre Européen pour la Recherche et l'Interprétation des Musiques Médiévales (Foundation Royaumont). N.p.

Quilici, Félix. 1971a. "Chants sacrés traditionnels en Corse." In *Encyclopédie des Musiques Sacrées,* 3:584–588. Paris: Labergerie.

———. 1971b. "La recherche et l'étude scientifique de la musique corse traditionnelle." In *Mélanges d'études corses offerts à Paul Arrighi,* 2:201–210. Aix-en-Provence: N.p.

Römer, Markus. 1983. *Schriftliche und mündliche Traditionen geistlicher Gesänge auf Korsika.* Wiesbaden: F. Steiner.

———. 1992. *Elementi stilistici e storici del canto polivocale in Corsica.* Culture Musicale, 1–2. Rome: N.p.

———. 1996. "Korsika." *Musik in Geschichte und Gegenwart.* 2d ed. Kassel: Bärenreiter.

Southwell-Colucci, Edith. 1933. *Canti popolari corsi.* Leghorn: Giusti.

Tomasi, Xavier. 1932. *Les Chansons de Cyrnos.* Marseille: F. Detaille.

Tommaseo, Nicolo. 1841. *Canto popolari toscani, corsi, illirici, e greci,* 2d ed. Bologna: A. Forni.

Viale, Salvatore. 1984 [1855]. *Canti popolari corsi,* 2d ed. Bologna: A. Forni.

Voce di u Cumune. 1980. *État des recherches sur les instruments traditionnels en Corse.* Calinzana: L'Accademia di Vagabondi.

Voci di u Cumune, ed. 1986. *État de recherches sur le chjama e rispondi.* Pigna: E Voce di u Cumune with the Centre National des Lettres and the Accademia di Vagabondi, Scola Corsa.

———. 1992. *Polyphonies vocales et orgue.* Contributions aux recherches sur le chant corse, 1. N.p.: Musée des Arts et Traditions Populaires.

Zerbi, Ghjermana de. 1992?. *Ghjermana de Zerbi, François Diani presentent cantu corsu.* Ajaccio: Éditions Cyrnos et Mediterranée.

AUDIOVISUAL RESOURCES

Caramusa. 1990. *Canti e musica tradiziunali di l'isula di Corsica.* Ricordu CDR 062. Compact disc.

Cloarec, Jacques, and Jacques Chailley. 1989 [1977]. *Religious Music of Oral Tradition from Rusiu.* Unesco Collection Musical Sources: European Polyphony: Sources of European Polyphony, 13–1. Auvidis D 8012. LP disk.

Laade, Wolfgang. 1990. *Corsica: Traditional Songs and Music.* Jecklin Disco JD650-2. Compact disc.

Marcel-Dubois, Claudie. 1955. *French Folk Songs.* Columbia World Library of Folk and Primitive Music, 4. Columbia Masterworks SL 207. LP disk.

Micaelli, Jacky. 1996. *Corsica Sacra: Chants corses sacrés/Sacred Songs of Corsica.* Compact disc.

Pasquali, Yves. 1992. *Madricale, Polyphonies corses.* Consul CM 88–19. Compact disc.

Pérès, Marcel. 1994. *Chant corse: Manuscrits franciscains (xvii-xviii siècles).* Ensemble Organum, directed by Marcel Pérès. Harmonia Mundi 901495. Compact disc.

Poletti, Jean-Paul. 1996. *Polyphonies corses/Corsican Polyphony.* Le choeur d'hommes de Sartène. Compact disc.

Quilici, Félix. 1975. *Messa corsa in Rusiu.* Disques Adès 10.007. LP disk.

———. 1981. *Musique corse de tradition orale.* Archives Sonores de la Phonothèque Nationale. Bibliothèque Nationale APN81–83. 3 LP disks.

Raffaelli, Michel. 1989. *Canti corsi in tradizioni.* Fonti Musicali fmd-158. Compact disc.

Tavagna. 1993. *A cappella: Chants polyphoniques corses profanes et sacrés.* Compact disc.

Portugal
Salwa El-Shawan Castelo-Branco

Twentieth-century Portuguese Culture
Performance Contexts and Song Genres
Formally Structured Performance Groups
Song Style
Dances
Instruments and Instrumental Ensembles
Music in Urban Settings
Popular Music since 1974
Documentation and Research

Portugal occupies a rectangular area of approximately 89,000 square kilometers at the southwestern edge of Europe, sharing the Iberian Peninsula with Spain. The Atlantic archipelagos of Madeira and Azores have been part of Portugal since their discovery and occupation, in the 1400s. Mainland Portugal is characterized by notable contrasts between the "Atlantic north" and the "Mediterranean south," and between the coast and the interior. Administratively, Portugal is divided into districts, each with a capital city.

Portugal emerged as a country in 1128, when the first Portuguese king, Afonso Henriques (ruled 1128–1185), seceded from the kingdom of Castile; he later expanded his reign to the Muslim-dominated south. Afonso III (ruled 1246–1279) established the boundaries that continental Portugal has had since.

Portuguese history was marked by maritime exploration and overseas colonization. During the 1400s and 1500s, the Portuguese were the first Europeans to conquer territories in Africa, Asia, and South America. To these lands, they carried Christianity and their language and culture, and they brought back trading goods, slaves, new crops, and cultural influences.

The Portuguese monarchy ended with the first parliamentary republic (1910–1926). A military coup in 1926 led to António de Oliveira Salazar's dictatorship, which advocated a nationalistic ideology based on traditional values. The revolution of 25 April 1974 established democracy and ended colonial rule. Portugal joined the European Community in 1985, embarking on a program of modernization and economic development.

The population, of 9,371,448 (1991 census), is concentrated in the coastal areas—in Lisbon, the capital, and Oporto, the largest northern city. Large Portuguese emigrant communities exist in the Americas, France, and South Africa. Metropolitan Lisbon contains immigrant communities from the former colonies: Cape Verdians, Angolans, Mozambicans, Brazilians, Goanese, and Timorese.

TWENTIETH-CENTURY PORTUGUESE CULTURE

The musical traditions of Portugal are highly diverse. Some styles and instruments, including ballads, guitars, and vocal polyphony, partake of pan-European and pan-

FIGURE 1   Maria Amélia Fonseca from the village of Monsanto, district of Castelo-Branco, accompanies her singing on the *adufe.* Photo by João Tuna, 1997.

Hispanic traditions. Other styles and instruments were molded through Portugal's encounters with non-European peoples (Castelo-Branco 1997a). The *adufe* (a square frame drum, adapted from the North African *duff,* figure 1), modal structures with neutral intervals, and *fado* (which originated in nineteenth-century Lisbon from a synthesis of Portuguese and Brazilian vocal genres and dances) are examples.

Until the 1950s, a few isolated rural areas preserved musical practices and styles documented around 1900; however, rural Portugal has undergone profound changes. The mechanization of agriculture at mid-century removed manual agricultural work as a context for making music. Emigration since the mid-1800s and migration to urban areas since the 1950s depopulated many areas, weakening traditions there. But migrant communities in urban areas have vigorously maintained their traditions, and through participation and sponsorship returned emigrants have contributed to the continuity of ritual practices, such as religious festivities (*festas*) and pilgrimages (*romarias*), and Portuguese communities abroad maintain traditional music through the activities of formally structured groups.

Cultural policy during Salazar's rule promoted the regime's ideology through national and local institutions and controlled artistic activities. Within the domain of traditional expressive behavior, an ideologically charged concept of *folclore* was central. A model for a folklore group (*rancho folclórico*), a formally organized music and dance-revival group, crystallized (Castelo-Branco 1991, 1992a, 1997b) (figure 2). Until the 1980s, researchers regarded *ranchos* as undesirable distortions of traditional practices, and condemned their political ties with Salazar's dictatorship.

Numerous *ranchos,* formed between the 1930s and 1950s, were affiliated with the Fundação Nacional para a Alegria no Trabalho (FNAT, National Foundation for Joy at Work), a national organization inspired by the German fascist Kraft durch Freude (Valente 1995:10). Another government agency, Sociedade de Propaganda Nacional (SPN), organized the landmark competition of A Aldeia mais Portuguesa (The Most Portuguese Village), in which villages competed for a prize in recognition of their preserving local architecture, costumes, music, and dance. To qualify, competing villages had to have a *rancho folclórico.* Many *ranchos* were formed for this event. By 1957, sixty-one were affiliated with FNAT (Ramos do Ó 1993:218).

FIGURE 2   The Rancho Folclórico das Lavradeiras de Mosteiró, São Miguel de Matos, plays at the Harvest Fair (Feira da Colheita) of Arouca, district of Aveiro. Photo by Salwa El-Shawan Castelo-Branco, 1995.

Since 1974, these groupings have multiplied, but their association with Salazar's regime has gradually dissipated. Many are affiliated with the Portuguese Federation of Folklore, a private association, which regulates their activities and functions as a "seal of quality," encouraging *ranchos* to participate in hundreds of folklore festivals held in Portugal every year.

The establishment of radio (1935) and television (1957) had a major impact on rural life. Radio brought urban music, such as *fado,* to the remotest villages. Television brought urban images and sounds to every home, and altered the patterns of domestic sociability, replacing conversation and singing. The growth of tourism during the 1960s and 1970s, especially along the southern and northwestern coasts and in Madeira, has affected musical life by inspiring the adaptation of traditional genres for performances staged for tourists. Finally, Portugal's entry into the European Economic Community, while contributing to overall development, has affected its agriculture, driving rural populations from their land.

PERFORMANCE CONTEXTS AND SONG GENRES

In rural Portugal, singing, instrumental performance, and dance accompanied agricultural and domestic work, marked life-cycle events, entertained families and communities, and has been a basic ingredient in sacred and secular rituals.

Before mechanization, agricultural labor was often accompanied by singing, by workers or hired musicians. Work songs are predominantly strophic, including songs accompanying plowing, threshing, harvesting, and olive gathering.

Ballads (*romances*) have been collected throughout Portugal. They are usually sung or recited by women without instrumental accompaniment. Their texts feature historical, religious, and social themes. Most ballads are strophic. The same text can be sung to multiple melodies, and the same melody can be used for multiple texts.

Throughout the district of Beja (southern Alentejo), agricultural workers of either sex formerly sang unaccompanied polyphonic songs (*modas*) while working. These songs now thrive in contexts such as taverns, and in performances by formally TRACK 19 structured choral groups (figure 3). A *moda* consists of rhymed verses sung polyphonically in strophic form. Between the 1930s and the 1970s, nearly two dozen formally structured men's choral groups were formed in the district of Beja. Since 25 April

FIGURE 3 The Grupo Coral da Caixa Social e Cultural da Câmara Municipal de Beja plays during a parade of Alentejan choral groups in Lisbon. Photo by Salwa El-Shawan Castelo-Branco, 1997.

1974, 179 such groups have arisen in Alentejo and among Alentejano migrants to the Lisbon metropolitan area.

Monophonic or homophonic strophic songs marking life-cycle events—including lullabies, courting songs, wedding songs, and mourning songs—have been collected throughout rural Portugal. Today, most of this repertoire is no longer active outside of *ranchos folclóricos*.

Religious rituals continue to provide vigorous contexts for making music. These contexts include occasions in the official religious calendar and festivities and pilgrimages honoring the Virgin Mary and other saints. Each ritual event has repertoires that vary regionally, for instance, songs for the Christmas season, January songs (sung by children and adults at villagers' doorsteps, wishing happy holidays and requesting donations of food), "kings' songs" (sung at doorsteps on the eve of Epiphany, 6 January), carnival songs, Lent songs, and Easter songs.

Religious festivities and pilgrimages are complex community events lasting from one to several days. Though these vary in their scope and ritual detail, a basic pattern can be established for the main day of festivities, especially for northern and central Portugal (Lameiro 1997):

1. *Alvorada:* A civil wind band or bagpipe-and-drum ensemble announces the beginning of the festivities by performing marches or other compositions throughout the village or town streets.
2. *Arruada, peditório, recolha de andores:* The band performs marches throughout the village, stopping in front of houses whose occupants donate money and goods (such as cakes and wine, mounted on decorated handbarrows) to be sold to benefit the festivities and the parish.
3. *Missa:* A sung Mass in church is the only liturgical event required for the festivities. In some churches, the choir and some members of the band sing the proper and the ordinary and whatever other musical material may occur in the service, while other members of the band provide instrumental accompaniment.
4. *Procissão:* The high point of the festivities, the procession combines sacred and secular symbols. Departing from and returning to the church, it moves solemnly through the village's main streets to the rhythm of marches performed by the band. Typically, the procession includes statues of the Virgin Mary and/or another celebrated saint carried on handbarrows, a cross, a banner representing the parish saint, one or more priests, the festivities' organizers, donations carried on decorated handbarrows, one or more bands, villagers, and visitors.
5. *Arraial,* a secular celebration beginning immediately after the procession and ending in the late evening. It includes the sale of donations, performances by several groups (such as civil wind bands, folklore groups, popular singers, and ensembles), and a dance for local youths.

FORMALLY STRUCTURED PERFORMANCE GROUPS

Today, traditional music and dance is enacted primarily by close to three thousand formally structured groups in religious and secular rituals (Castelo-Branco and Lima 1998). These are legally constituted named groups that have a fixed membership and artistic and administrative directors, rehearse, and perform regularly.

Nonprofessional civil wind bands, which emerged in the mid-1800s, modeled after military bands, are the most enduring and vital musical institutions in Portugal. Today, more than seven hundred bands are indispensable in local religious and secular festivities (figure 4). Occasionally, they perform in church services, weddings, and

Creativity with words is particularly valued in "improvised" song duels, usually between two or more singers with instrumental accompaniment.

FIGURE 4 The civil wind band Sociedade Artística Musical dos Pousos plays during the *peditório* of the feast of Our Lady of the Rosary (Festa da Nossa Senhora do Rosário). Alqueidão da Serra, district of Leiria. Photo by Salwa el-Shawan Castelo-Branco, 1995.

funerals. Their repertoire includes marches, religious music, arrangements of traditional, popular, and classical music, and original compositions by band conductors.

Some bands are affiliated with cultural and social institutions. Others are independent organizations, which run a music school for children, training them to become instrumentalists. In many areas, band-music schools are the only training institutions locally available; their uniqueness and effectiveness have earned them government and private support.

Ranchos folclóricos abound throughout Portugal: today, there are more than two thousand *ranchos,* plus hundreds more among Portuguese emigrant communities abroad. In many areas of Portugal, *ranchos* have been the main repositories for traditional music and dance. They are part of a wide-ranging effort for the revival and preservation of tradition, which characterized some sectors of Portuguese musical life in the twentieth century. They play in local festivities and hundreds of annual folklore festivals. The nonprofessional instrumentalists, singers, and dancers constituting *ranchos* perform staged revivals of the traditions of their region or specific locale. Performances by *ranchos folclóricos* range from those adhering closely to local traditions to those presenting new interpretations or products.

The two or three to ten instrumentalists in a given *rancho* often include an accordion. In fact, accordionists are the only paid musicians in the ensemble. The other instruments differ from one area to another and include different kinds of traditional guitars and percussion. The vocal section usually includes one or two soloists and a chorus of up to ten men and women. *Ranchos* usually have from five to ten pairs of dancers. Each *rancho* often has an artistic director, who usually collects the repertoire, adapts it for staged performances, and transmits it to *rancho* members. Regionally emblematic costumes and dances are highlighted.

Another type of formal ensemble includes polyphonic choral groups, which in southern Alentejo and among Alentejano migrants in the Lisbon metropolitan area have fifteen to thirty men. They perform in costumes that represent social classes and professional groups in their area earlier in the twentieth century. Typical venues include religious and national holidays, festivities, and their own competitions, which feature up to thirty ensembles. These groups have contributed to the preservation of a vast repertoire of *modas,* and to the maintenance and solidification of Alentejano identity.

SONG STYLE

Vocal music, with or without instrumental accompaniment, is predominant in Portugal. Most vocal music is precomposed, but authorship is seldom known. (Some texts are attributed to local oral poets.) Throughout the country and in most genres, different texts are set to the same melodies. Since the 1970s, creativity in some genres has been practically limited to texts. Creativity with words is particularly valued in "improvised" vocal genres, known as *desgarradas, cantares ao desafio,* and *despiques.* These are song duels, usually between two or more singers with instrumental accompaniment. The words are improvised to a fixed melodic and harmonic pattern.

Metered strophic songs, with or without a refrain, predominate, and the quatrain provides the most common poetic structure for songs usually designated by the generic terms *cantiga* 'song' and *moda* 'fashion'. In much vocal music, a musical phrase is usually set to one, two, or four lines of text. Singing is predominantly syllabic. Melismatic singing occurs primarily in the solo parts of the polyphonic modas in Beja, and in solo songs in the east-central districts.

Lyric songs with homophonic instrumental accompaniment are common in much of the country. Triadic vocal polyphony in two, three, and four voices occurs in the northwestern districts of Viana do Castelo, Braga, and Aveiro, in the eastern and central districts of Viseu and Castelo-Branco, and in the southern district of Beja. Except for Beja, where multipart singing is primarily a men's practice, vocal polyphony is performed by women.

In much of the country, tonality is organized within the major and minor modes, and harmonic accompaniment centers on the alternation of tonic and dominant chords. Church modes and other modal structures that do not correspond to so-called European common practice occur in areas that have preserved archaic practices, especially the districts of Castelo-Branco and Beja. Melodic ranges usually do not exceed a fifth or sixth beyond an octave. Duple and triple meters are most common in vocal music, including dance-songs.

Song texts deal with all aspects of rural life, past and present: agricultural work, nature, the local village or town, life-cycle events, love, emigration, religious themes, and historical and political events.

DANCES

Dances—some local, some widespread—range from medieval sword dances to adaptations of eighteenth- and nineteenth-century Central European salon dances. Dances are distinguished by their choreography, meter, and musical repertoire, and are usually performed to strophic dance-songs; duple or triple meter predominate.

Three widespread dances, each with local variants, are the *vira,* the *chula,* and the *malhão.* The *vira,* one of the oldest Portuguese couple dances, occurs throughout the north and center, but it is especially popular in the northwest. It is in 6/8 meter. *Chula,* known throughout northwestern Portugal, is a couple circle dance in duple meter, traditionally accompanied by an improvised song duel. In the absence of contenders for the song duel, the *chula* is danced to a solo song with a fixed text, or to an instrumental accompaniment. The *malhão,* a circle dance of the western coast from the north down to central Portugal, especially the districts of Oporto and Aveiro, is in duple meter.

The fandango, a dance of Spanish origin, once widespread, is today mainly found in the district of Santarém. It can be danced by a mixed couple, two men, or two women; however, it has been popularized by *ranchos folclóricos* as a choreographic duel between two men, who use rapid footwork while their upper torso remains practically motionless. Its instrumental accompaniment, in 6/8, consists of a single, much-repeated phrase. A second local dance, the *corridinho,* is a virtuosic couple dance, practically limited to the southern district of Faro. Characterized by duple meter, fast tempo, and rapid dance turns, the *corridinho* has been used as a tourist attraction by *ranchos folclóricos.*

INSTRUMENTS AND INSTRUMENTAL ENSEMBLES

Diatonic and chromatic accordions are dominant in *ranchos folclóricos.* Guitars of various sizes and types accompany vocal music and dance in many rural and urban traditions. The bagpipe, accompanied by a bass drum and a snare drum, has been central in religious festivities in the northeast and the coastal area from the north to the center. In the east-central area, square frame drums accompany song and dance, transverse flutes are played by shepherds, and a sharply waisted guitar is used to accompany singing. Fewer instruments are used in the south.

Portuguese idiophones include castanets, a wood scraper (*reque reque*), a triangle (*ferrinhos,* common in *ranchos folclóricos*), a large clay pot (*cântaro com abano*), which the player holds below his left arm while hitting the opening with a straw or leather fan), and the *cana* (a cane tube about 60 centimeters long, cut vertically through the middle, creating two parts, which the player strikes together).

Of membranophones, a snare drum (*caixa*), with two skins and one or two sympathetic strings, is struck on the upper skin with two wooden drumsticks. It is played in ensemble with a bass drum (*bombo*). Other drums include two kinds of frame drums. The *adufe* is square, with two skins and interior metal jingles. Each side of the frame is about 45 centimeters long. This instrument is played exclusively by women, who hold it with the thumbs of both hands and the index finger of the left hand, leaving the remaining fingers free for playing the instrument. The *pandeiro,* a round frame drum about 20 centimeters in diameter, with a single skin and metal jingles, is found mainly in the district of Evora, near the Spanish border. The *pandeireta,* a smaller *pandeiro,* is popular throughout the country as an accompaniment to informal singing and dancing and in string ensembles known as *tuna.* The northwestern friction drum (*sarronca*) is a clay pot with a narrow opening, covered with a skin that vibrates through the movement of a friction stick.

Chordophones constitute the richest, most varied category of Portuguese musical instruments. Guitars (called *violas*) usually having five double or three double and two triple courses of metal strings, exist in many local variants, known by different names, including *amarantina, braguesa,* and *toeira.* The term *viola* also denotes the "Spanish guitar," with six metal strings. The *cavaquinho,* a small guitar with four courses of strings, is widespread in the northwest and Madeira, where it is called *braguinha* (figure 5). Easy to transport and play, it was widely diffused by Portuguese settlers and emigrants—for instance, to Hawai'i (where it is called *'ukelele*), Brazil,

FIGURE 5 A *cavaquinho* player of the Rancho Folclórico de Viana do Castelo. Photo by Elise Ralston, 1988.

and Indonesia (where it is called *kroncong*). The *guitarra,* also designated *guitarra Portuguesa* 'Portuguese guitar', has a pear-shaped sound board and six double courses of metal strings. It is a local adaptation of the "English guitar," introduced to Portugal in the second half of the 1700s through the British colony in Oporto. Once used in the salons of Oporto's bourgeoisie, it diffused to Lisbon and Coimbra, in both locations eventually adapted to accompany *fado.*

Of aerophones, the bagpipe (*gaita-de-foles*), documented in Portugal since the 1300s, has been used on ceremonial occasions on the northwestern coast down to Coimbra and throughout the northeast. Also in the northeast, an end-blown flute is accompanied by the *tamboril,* a small cylindrical drum. A transverse cane flute with six holes, a shepherd's instrument, is found in the east-central area.

Ranchos folclóricos, the most widespread ensembles for the performance of revivalist traditional music and dance, usually include one or several accordions, stringed and percussion instruments, a chorus, and one or more solo vocalists. *Tunas,* ensembles primarily formed by families of stringed instruments (including different sizes of mandolin, *viola,* and *viola baixo* 'bass guitar'), are found mainly in the north. Smaller ensembles, such as a bagpipe with bass drum and snare drum, are also found.

MUSIC IN URBAN SETTINGS

In urban settings, particular musical genres developed, rural traditions were revived and reinvented by migrants, musical traditions from the former Portuguese colonies were transplanted, and new styles were created.

Fado emerged in poor neighborhoods of Lisbon between 1825 and 1850 as a synthesis of song-and-dance genres already popular in Lisbon and newly imported genres, such as the *lundum,* a Brazilian dance and vocal genre of African origin, brought from Brazil when the Portuguese court returned to Lisbon after a stay in Rio de Janeiro (1808–1822); the *modinha,* a genre of salon "art song," which developed in Portugal and Brazil from the mid-1700s to the mid-1800s; the fandango, a Portuguese dance of Spanish origin; the *fado,* a Brazilian dance still found in rural areas in the state of Rio de Janeiro; and the *fofa,* a dance found in Brazil and Portugal. Extremely involved, the subsequent history of *fado* passed through Lisbon's slums and salons, Portuguese vaudeville, the recording industry, and radio. During Salazar's dictatorship, *fado* was promoted as Portugal's "national song." Its texts were censored, its performers were required to obtain a license to practice their profession, and touristic restaurants (*casas típicas*) were instituted for its performance. Much of this period coincided with the careers of some of its most brilliant and celebrated figures: *fado* singers Amália Rodrigues (b. 1920) and Alfredo Marceneiro (1891–1992) and *fado* composers and guitarists Armandinho (Salgado Armando Freire, 1891–1846) and Martinho d'Assunção (1914–1992).

Today, *fado* can be heard in tourist restaurants, concerts in large auditoriums, neighborhood associations, taverns, and local restaurants, and through radio, television, and phonograms. *Fado* performances involve a solo vocalist, instrumental accompanists, and audiences in a communicative process using verbal, musical, facial, and bodily expression. The vocalist (*fadista*) is the dominant figure. The first *guitarrista* (the *guitarra* is pear-shaped), regarded as a second soloist, provides a melodic counterpoint and harmonic support to the main melody. When included, a second *guitarrista* furnishes a second melodic counterpoint and harmonic support. The *viola* is mandatory, and provides a harmonic and rhythmic grounding, allowing the *fadista* and the *guitarristas* to improvise. A *viola baixo* is occasionally used to provide bass progressions in a regular rhythm.

Fado practitioners classify their repertoire into *fado castiço* 'authentic *fado*' (relatively old) and *fado canção* 'song *fado*'. Within the former, a distinction is made

After 1850, a distinct *fado* tradition developed within the university community of Coimbra, Portugal's central city. Essentially a male tradition, it is a synthesis of Italian *bel canto,* traditional music brought by students from various parts of the country, and Lisbon's *fado.*

between three anonymous *fados* presumed to be the oldest, basic *fados* (*corrido, menor,* and *mouraria*) and nearly one hundred *fados* attributed to nineteenth- and twentieth-century composers. *Fados castiços* have fixed rhythmic and harmonic schemes (usually I–V–I) and accompanimental patterns, but their melodies can be improvised or precomposed. The *fado canção* has a poetic and musical structure that alternates stanzas and refrains, more complex harmonic structures than those of the *fado castiço,* fixed melodies, and a flexible accompanimental pattern developed within the basic harmonic scheme. *Fado* texts feature early *fado* performance contexts, such as houses of prostitution, Lisbon's old neighborhoods, *fado*-connected personages, specific events, feelings, the mother figure, and political struggle.

After 1850, a distinct *fado* tradition developed within the university community of Coimbra, Portugal's central city. Essentially a male tradition, it is a synthesis of Italian *bel canto,* traditional music brought by students from various parts of the country, and Lisbon's *fado.*

POPULAR MUSIC SINCE 1974

Musical expression, central to the opposition to Salazar's dictatorship, contributed to the political processes that culminated in the revolution of 1974 and the consolidation of revolutionary ideals. During the three decades preceding the revolution, the *canção de intervenção* 'song of intervention' became an important vehicle for political protest. The songs of one of its main protagonists, the poet-composer-singer José Afonso (1929–1987), were set to politically engaged poetic texts and integrated elements from the *fado* of Coimbra, Portuguese rural traditions, African music, and French popular song. His song "*Grândola Vila Morena*"—broadcast on radio on the eve of the revolution as a signal for insurgent troops to advance—became an emblem of the revolution.

For about a decade after the revolution, a movement for the revival of traditional music emerged among university students and young professionals. Inspired by the revolution, some groups were involved in political and social action in rural areas, where they collected traditional music with the purpose of salvaging disappearing practices by reproducing them on stage for urban audiences. More than a dozen groups that formed between the mid-1970s and mid-1980s typically performed traditional songs and tunes (reproducing rural repertoires) and recreations of those.

The 1980s and 1990s were marked by the search for a new musical discourse for urban popular music, the commodification and industrialization of musical production, and a sizable increase in the production and consumption of phonograms. The recording industry, essentially controlled by multinational companies (BMG, EMI, Polygram, Sony, Warner) and more than two dozen independent local producers, has played a central role in shaping and disseminating urban popular music.

Increasingly various styles of urban music are produced and consumed in Portugal. Local pop and rock styles developed during the 1980s and 1990s, jazz performances by Portuguese and foreign artists increased considerably, and a local style of rap and varieties of African music thrive in Lisbon. Two broad tendencies can be observed in productions of popular music: a musical style that vindicates its Portugueseness through its connection to traditional music or *fado* and a musical discourse created by Portuguese musicians and integrated within the major developments of commercial popular music.

DOCUMENTATION AND RESEARCH

Interest in collecting and studying rural musical traditions goes back to the late 1800s, inspired by Portuguese literary romanticism and philological and ethnological research. Musical transcriptions, sound recordings, and verbal descriptions of rural traditions were presented with the aim of salvaging and disseminating them through documentation and revival. For some composers, the collected corpus represented an important source for creating a nationalist art music (Castelo-Branco and Toscano 1988:158–162).

The first musical transcriptions of rural traditions were published by Neves e Melo in 1872. Three landmark volumes of harmonized transcriptions of rural and urban songs followed (Neves and Campos 1893, 1895, 1898). From the 1920s to the 1970s, the quantity and quality of documentation and research increased, focusing on regional repertoires (e.g., Marvão 1955; Sampaio 1986 [1940]). A few publications focus on musical genres, instruments and their distribution (Lima 1962; Oliveira 1982). A handful of researchers endeavored to survey musical traditions throughout continental Portugal (Gallop 1933a, 1933b, 1936, 1960; Graça 1974; Leça 1922, 1942).

Beginning with the 1940s, sound recording became the main form of documentation. In 1940, the composer Armando Leça was sponsored by the radio (Emissora Nacional) to carry out the first recorded survey of rural traditions. From the late 1950s to the early 1980s, the Corsican researcher Michel Giacometti documented rural traditions in mainland Portugal. This endeavor resulted in the publication of a multiple-volume recorded anthology (1998) initially published between 1959 and 1970, a volume of musical transcriptions by Giacometti and Fernando Lopes Graça (1981), and the television series "*Povo que Canta*" ('Singing Folk', 1972–1973), documenting musical performance in various areas of the country. The composer-pedagogue Artur Santos published a recorded anthology of Azorian musical traditions (1956a, 1956b, 1963, 1965).

Between the 1920s and the 1970s, researchers tried to analyze music systematically. Musical transcriptions no longer constituted the focus of publications, but illustrated verbal descriptions of musical style. Researchers made a clear distinction between transcription as a form of documentation and harmonization of traditional melodies for choral performance.

In the 1980s, a new phase of research began. Ethnomusicology as an academic discipline was introduced with the founding of the musicology department at the Universidade Nova de Lisboa (UNL). Since the mid-1980s, students and graduates of the UNL have carried out research in Portugal and Portuguese-influenced countries abroad, focusing on rural-urban migration, ethnicity, cultural policy, revival, identity in postcolonial settings, popular music, the recording industry, and other issues. An Institute for Ethnomusicology was founded in 1995 within UNL to provide a framework for ethnomusicological research and establish a sound archive.

BIBLIOGRAPHY

Brito, Joaquim Pais de. 1983. "O Fado: Um Canto na Cidade." *Ethnologia* 1:149–184.

———, ed. 1994. *Fado: Voices and Shadows.* Translated by James Ormiston. Lisbon: Museum of Ethnology.

Carvalho, Pinto de. 1982 [1903]. *História do Fado.* Lisbon: Dom Quixote.

Carvalho, Ruben. 1994. *As Músicas do Fado.* Lisbon: Campo das Letras.

Castelo-Branco, Salwa El-Shawan. 1991. "Culture Policy and Traditional Music in Portugal since 1974." In *Music in the Dialogue of Culture: Traditional Music and Cultural Policy,* ed. Max Peter Baumann, 95–107. Wilhelmshaven: Florian Noetzel.

———. 1992a. "Safeguarding Traditional Music in Contemporary Portugal." In *World Music, Musics of the World: Aspects of Documentation, Mass Media and Acculturation,* ed. Max Peter Baumann, 177–190. Wilhelmshaven: Florian Noetzel.

———. 1992b. "Some Aspects of the 'Cante' Tradition of Cuba: A Town in Southern Alentejo, Portugal." In *Livro de Homenagem a Macário Santiago Kastner,* ed. Rui Vieira Nery, Manuel Morais, and Fernanda Cidrais, 547–561. Lisbon: Fundação Calouste Gulbenkian.

———. 1994. "The Dialogue between Voices and Guitars in *Fado* Performance Practice." In *Fado: Voices and Shadows,* ed. Joaquim Pais de Brito, 125–141. Lisbon: Museum of Ethnology.

———, ed. 1997a. *Portugal and the World: The Encounter of Cultures in Music.* Lisbon: Dom Quixote.

———. 1997b. *Voix du Portugal.* Paris and Arles: Cité de la Musique and Actes Sud. Book with compact disc.

Castelo-Branco, Salwa El-Shawan, and Maria João Lima. 1998. "'Práticas musicais locais: alguns indicadores preliminares." *Obs 4 Publicação Periódica do Observatório das Actividades culturas* 10–13.

Castelo-Branco, Salwa El-Shawan, and Maria Manuela Toscano. 1988."'In Search of a Lost World': An Overview of Documentation and Research on the Traditional Music of Portugal." *Yearbook for Traditional Music* 20:158–192.

Freitas, Frederico. 1969. "Fado." In *Enciclopédia Luso-Brasileira de Cultura.* Lisbon: Verbo.

Gallop, Rodney 1933a. "The Folk Music of Portugal 1." *Music and Letters* 14(3):222–231.

———. 1933b. "The Folk Music of Portugal 2." *Music and Letters* 14(4):343–355.

———. 1936. *Portugal: A Book of Folk-Ways.* Cambridge: University Press.

———. 1960. *Cantares do povo Portugués.* Lisbon: Instituto de Alta Cultura.

Giacometti, Michel, and Fernando Lopes Graça. 1981. *Cancioneiro Popular Português.* Lisbon: Círculo de Leitores.

Graça, Fernando Lopes. 1974. *A Canção Popular Portuguesa,* 2d ed. Lisbon: Publicações Europa América.

Lameiro, Paulo. 1997. "Práticas musicais nas festas religiosas do concelho de Leiria: O lugar privilegiado das Bandas Filarmónicas." *Actas dos 2$^{\underline{o}}$s Cursos Internacionais de Verão de Cascais (17a22 Julho),* 1–14. Cascais: Câmara Municipal.

Leça, Armando. 1922. *Da Música Portuguesa.* Lisboa: Lumen.

———. 1942. *Música Popular Portuguesa.* Porto: Editorial Domingos Barreira.

Lima, Fernando de Castro Pires de. 1962. *Chula: Verdadeira Canção Nacional.* Lisbon: Fundação Nacional para Alegria no Trabalho-Gabinete de Etnografia.

Martins, Firmino. 1928. *Folklore do Concelho de Vinhais.* Vol. 1. Coimbra: Imprensa da Universidade.

———. 1938. *Folklore do Concelho de Vinhais.* Vol. 2. Lisbon: Imprensa Nacional.

Marvão, António. 1955. *Cancioneiro Alentejano: Corais Majestosos, Coreográficos e Religiosos do Baixo Alentejo.* Braga: Tipografia da Editorial Franciscana.

Mourinho, António. 1984. *Cancioneiro Tradicional e Danças Populares Mirandesas.* Bragança: Escola Tipográfica.

Neves, César das, and Gualdino Campos. 1893, 1895, 1898. *Cancioneiro de Músicas Populares.* 3 vols. Porto Tipografia Ocidental (vol. 1) and Impresa Editorial (vols. 2 and 3).

Neves e Melo, Adelino António. 1872. *Músicas e Cantigas Populares Colligidas da Tradição.* Lisbon: Imprensa Nacional.

Ó, Jorge Ramos do. 1993. "O dispositivo cultural nos anos da política do Espirito (1933–1949): Ideologia, Instituições, Agentes e Práticas." M.A. thesis, Universidade Nova de Lisboa.

Oliveira, Ernesto Veiga de. 1982. *Instrumentos Musicais Populares Portugueses,* 2d ed. Lisbon: Fundação Calouste Gulbenkian.

Ribeiro, Mário Sampayo. 1936. *As 'Guitarras de Alcácer' e a Guitarra Portuguesa'.* Lisbon: Separata do Arquivo Histórico de Portugal.

Sampaio, Gonçalo. 1986 [1940]. *Cancioneiro Minhoto,* 3d ed. Braga: Grupo Folclórico Dr. Gonçalo Sampaio.

Tinhorão, José Ramos. 1994. *Fado: Dança do Brasil Cantar de Lisboa—O Fim de Um Mito.* Lisbon: Caminho da Música.

Travassos, Elizabete. 1987. "O Fado." In *M. E. P. Marchiari,* ed. Quisamã, 166–180. Rio de Janeiro: Fundação Nacional Pró-Memória.

Valente, José Carlos. 1995. "A FNAT: das Origens a 1941: Estado Novo e Alegria no Trabalho." *História* 6:4–17.

AUDIOVISUAL RESOURCES

Alfredo Marceneiro: A Casa da Mariquinhas. 1996 [1960]. EMI—Valentim de Carvalho 72438 52856 22. Compact disc.

Amália Rodrigues: Abbey Road. 1992 [1952]. EMI—Valentim de Carvalho 07777 81195 24. Compact disc.

Biografia do Fado. 1994. An anthology of *fado* recordings since 1927. EMI—Valentim de Carvalho 7243831965 2 4. 2 compact discs.

Brigada Vitor Jara: 15 Anos de Recriação da Música Tradicional Portuguesa. 1992. Caravela CV-9202. Compact disc.

Fado de Coimbra (1926–1930). 1992. Arquivos do Fado, 2. Interstate HTCD 15 and Tradisom TRAD005. Compact disc.

O Folclore musical nas ilhas dos Açores: Antologia sonora—ilha de São Miguel. 1956a. Recordings collected by Artur Santos. Instituto cultural de Ponta Delgada F100.000.21–F100.030. 10 78-RPM disks.

O Folclore musical nas ilhas dos Açores: Antologia sonora—ilha Terceira. 1956b. Recordings collected by Artur Santos. Junta geral do distrito autónomo de Angra doi Heroísmo F100.000 H–F100.019. 18 78-RPM disks.

O Folclore musical nas ilhas dos Açores: Antologia sonora—ilha de Santa Maria. 1963. Recordings collected by Artur Santos. Instituto cultural de Ponta Delgada ASF034–045. 12 45-RPM disks.

O Folclore musical nas ilhas dos Açores: Antologia sonora—ilha de São Miguel. 1965. Recordings collected by Artur Santos. Instituto cultural de Ponta Delgada ASF046–052. 7 45-RPM disks.

José Afonso: Cantigas do Maio. 1996 [1971]. Movieplay JA 80004. Compact disc.

Musical Traditions of Portugal. 1994. Recordings by Max Peter Baumann and Tiago de Oliveira Pinto. Notes by Salwa El-Shawan Castelo-Branco. Smithsonian Folkways SF40435. Compact disc.

Music from the Edge of Europe. 1997. EMI—Hemisphere 7243859270 27. Compact disc.

Portugal Today: Rui Veloso, Trovante, Madredeus, Sétima Legião, António Pinho Vargas, etc. 1991. EMI—Valentim de Carvalho 797836 2. Compact disc.

Portugal: Trás-os-Montes: Chants du Ble et Cornemuses de Berger. N.d. Recordings and notes by Anne Caufriez. Ocora 558547. Compact disc.

Portuguese Folk Music: Minho, Trás-os-Montes, Beiras, Alentejo, Algarve. 1998 [1959–1970]. Recordings compiled by Michel Giacometti. Notes by Fernando Lopes Graça. Portulgalsom/Strauss SP4198–SP4202. 5 compact discs.

Songs and Dances of Portugal. 1994. Recordings by Michel Giacometti. Notes by Fernando Lopes Graça and Michel Giacometti. Strauss SP 4031. Compact disc.

Tempos de Coimbra: Oito Décadas no Canto e na Guitarra. 1992. Commentary by António Brojo and António Portugal. EMI 0777 79960729. 3 compact discs.

Spain
Elizabeth J. Miles
Loren Chuse

Singing Styles and Vocal Genres
Musical Instruments and Instrumental Music
Regionalism
Music and the Roman Catholic Church
Social Groups and Music
Flamenco
Contemporary Developments
History of Art Music in Spain
History of Spanish Scholarship

With four spoken languages, several dialects, and seventeen culturally and politically distinct regions, Spain is a historically diverse nation. Its thirty-nine million inhabitants live in a 505,000-square-kilometer peninsula whose geography has isolated its people from the rest of Europe and served as a gateway between Europe and North Africa.

Once inhabited by Iberian tribes, Spain hosted Celtic, Phoenician, Hebrew, Greek, and Carthaginian cultures before a six-century occupation by the Romans (second century B.C. to the fifth century of the common era), followed by three hundred years of Visigothic rule. The invasion by Moors from North Africa (711–1492) led to the creation of the Arab kingdom of Al-Andalus, which ruled most of the Iberian peninsula and left an enduring and distinctive imprint on Spanish culture. The Christian reconquest from the Moors led to the reactionary religious zealotry that fueled the Inquisition (1478), the expulsion of the Jews (1492), and the forced Christian conversion of the indigenous peoples of the newly conquered Americas.

The weight of traditionalism slowed Spain's democratization after World War II, when the rest of Europe underwent rapid political and social change. Reflecting isolation and adherence to tradition, Spain has been little touched by the wave of globalism that has swept other parts of Western Europe since the 1960s. Without the influx of immigrants from former colonies—immigrants who arrived in France, England, Germany, and the Netherlands—and with the inhospitable atmosphere of a bloody civil war (1936–1939) and Francisco Franco's repressive regime (1939–1975), Spain's ethnographics remained relatively stable over the latter half of the twentieth century. Spain approved its first constitution in 1978, setting the stage for reintegration into the modern European mainstream after nearly a century of isolation. About three-quarters of the population now live in cities, the largest of which are Madrid, Barcelona, Valencia, and Seville, but a stubborn tradition is embodied in the persistent, though diminished, practice of traditional music in *pueblos,* the rural towns that many urban dwellers cite as home, even after generations in the city.

Personal connections to *pueblos* reinforce regional identity in Spain, while the many mountain ranges that divide the country provide topological boundaries to its regions. Certain regions are famous for a typical musical form—Aragón for the *jota,*

Castile for *seguidillas*, Andalucía for the fandango. Yet these forms have spread to local traditions throughout Spain.

Fiesta: Spanish folk music and its contexts

The word *fiesta* depicts the synergy between the sacred and the secular, the solemn and the celebratory, common to Spanish culture. *Fiesta* means 'feast, holy day, party, celebration', and encompasses occasions ranging from religious processions to disco dancing. Traditional occasions for music-filled fiestas follow an annual cycle of religious and secular events, many of which suggest roots in ancient pagan rites (Crivillé i Bargalló 1988), plus such life-cycle occasions as courtship and weddings.

Spanish music involves variation on central themes, including the observation of annual and life-cycle events (sacred and secular); the prevalence of monophonic vocal song (solo or small-group), which might be accompanied by a small instrumental ensemble; song forms that juxtapose text and musical phrases to achieve deeply nuanced musicopoetic meaning; dialogic or call-and-response singing; portamento at the ends of vocal phrases; high-trilling vocal cries (*relinchidos*) to frame musical events; and melodic and rhythmic systems that can be roughly grouped into European (diatonic, metric, syllabic, symmetrical), Arabic (modal, melismatic, unmetered, asymmetrical), and admixtures of the two.

The instruments most commonly deployed in traditional music include an extended family of guitars, a flute-and-drum duo, shawms, bagpipes, and other winds with rural associations.

SINGING STYLES AND VOCAL GENRES

The principal Spanish song genres are associated with the annual ritual calendar.

The Christmas cycle

The Christmas cycle includes carols and serenades, narrative songs and ballads, and number songs. The Christmas carol (*villancico*) serves as an expressive emblem of the conceptual complexity of fiesta. Texts, even as they narrate the birth of Christ, can be amorous, picaresque, or satirical, and their historical roots may go back to pre-Christian solstice celebrations. Christmas carols—at once sacred and secular, devotional and festive—are sung throughout Spain, accompanied by guitars, frame drums, friction drums, triangles, and brass mortars (figure 1).

The *romance* 'ballad', the national Spanish poetic form, has roots in the epic narrative tradition, palace minstrel song, and fifteenth-century vernacular song. Its texts concern love, vengeance, history, legend, myth, crime, the supernatural, burlesque, and the Bible. They are still sung in rural areas throughout Spain, especially from Christmas to Lent. They are performed by a soloist or an unaccompanied unison choir, or are accompanied in an Arabic style by a *rabel* fiddle (figure 2) or a violin in heterophonic imitation of the vocal line or with an ensemble of hurdy-gurdy (*zanfona*), guitar, and *vihuela* (a type of guitar).

Music for carnival and Lent

The carnival and Lent cycle encompasses songs of childhood (lullabies and play songs), lovers' serenades, and songs for Lent and Holy Week. *Cuñeros*, cradle songs or lullabies, are often called by names such as *arroró* and *arrolo,* which refer to the repeated syllables used to lull the baby to sleep. *Cuñeros* are often in an unmetered, melismatic style bearing evidence of eastern influence and antiquity. *Infantiles* are children's play songs, usually simple in meter and mode, with symmetric structure and syllabic settings. The celebration of carnival thrives in Spain under many names,

FIGURE 1 Two women play friction drums (*xim-bombas*). Lagartera, Castille, 1952. Courtesy of the Alan Lomax Collection, New York.

FIGURE 1 Two women play friction drums (*xim-bombas*). Lagartera, Castille, 1952. Courtesy of the Alan Lomax Collection, New York.

with local traditions of musical masquerades and burlesques. Carnival songs are noisily accompanied by bull roarers and cowbells.

Rondas 'round songs' comprise the largest, best loved, and least regionally varied part of the repertoire of collective songs. Their name refers to the tradition of rounding, in which young male musicians serenade the general public or, more likely, young women at the windows of their homes. Rounding can serve for the performance of Christmas songs (*aguinaldos*), *cantares de ayuda* for the gathering of alms, and *auroras* to call people to the rosary. The *ronda* form, usually of solo-chorus alternations of an octosyllabic quatrain, is most typical of traditional Spanish song (Crivillé i Bargalló 1988:150). *Ronda* groups, though apparently casually formed, can be quite competitive between or within *pueblos*, and serve to mark the territory of each group of young men.

FIGURE 2 As a woman watches, a man plays a bowed fiddle (*rabel*). Lagartera, Castille, 1952. Courtesy of the Alan Lomax Collection, New York.

Lent and Holy Week were traditionally times of musical prohibition, in which only songs specifically prescribed for various observances could be performed. These included *rondas* performed by young women to collect contributions toward the celebration of Maundy Thursday.

Music for spring and summer

The May cycle features prayer songs, marches, and songs celebrating spring. Musical processions and ceremonies involve boughs and crosses adorned with flowers. May is also the time for *rogativas*, prayer songs to local patron saints, asking for the crop's protection from drought and disease.

The summer cycle includes announcements, work songs, and songs for St. John the Baptist. The town crier (*pregonero*) was a familiar figure in *pueblos* until recently, announcing the hours, weather, and news with songs that ranged from simple recitative to highly developed melodies.

Work songs divide into three groups. The first is for food-gathering tasks, such as hunting, fishing, threshing, and picking olives. Many of these songs demonstrate Mediterranean influence in *maqam*-like scales, supple meter, melisma, and descending melodies. The second group is for jobs such as milling, mining coal, and shearing sheep. These songs are often dialogues between two singers or a soloist and a chorus, utilizing repeated phrases with variations, wide tonal ranges, and rhythms keyed to the task. The third group is for domestic chores, such as cooking, cleaning, washing, and keeping taverns. Its repertoire shares musical traits with the second group.

Music for autumn

The autumn cycle includes wedding songs and a constellation of religious songs for pilgrimages, rosaries, saints, and various fiestas. The importance of weddings in Spanish culture is evidenced by the complexity of musical customs surrounding them, many with idiosyncratic regional variations. The festivities might begin on the eve of the ceremony with songs announcing the wedding and perhaps inviting the guests. The day typically begins with dawn songs, sung by young men in honor of the couple and their parents, and sometimes melodically complex and melismatic. The wedding banquet is followed by traditional regional dances. Most wedding songs are in the form of *rondas*.

The religious songs of the autumn cycle include *ramos*, songs for processionals bearing boughs (as in the May celebrations) and narrating the lives of saints, the Virgin Mary, and Christ; *romerías*, sacred and secular songs to accompany pilgrimages to local shrines; *exvotos*, songs of thanks for miracle cures, providential intercessions, and such; *ánimas*, gory descriptions of the sufferings of souls in purgatory, often sung in rounding style and followed by prayers for the dead; and *gozos* or *goigs*, a semipopular medieval genre that recounts the Virgin Mary's seven joys as catalogued by popular medieval culture.

Poetic song forms

Spanish song forms break down into the metric style brought from elsewhere in Europe by eleventh- to thirteenth-century troubadours, and usually containing verses and refrains with a degree of textual improvisation and instrumental interludes; and the free, unmetered songs of the Arabic tradition, which survive mostly in lullabies, work songs, and the Andalusian *cante jondo*.

Among the metric types, the *copla* 'couplet' is used broadly to denote lyrics or poetry in general and specifically to describe a common song form employing quatrains of octosyllabic lines with consonant or assonant rhymes in the even-numbered verses. The stanza can be followed by an *estribillo* 'refrain'. The octosyllabic quatrain

Relinchidos 'onomatopoeic shouts' could be viewed as relief from textual formality, or a typically Spanish juxtaposition of emotional exclamation with pious or solemn expression.

FIGURE 3   In triple meter and a major scale, a *seguidilla* alternates five- and seven-syllable lines. After Crivillé i Bargalló 1988:219.

of *coplas* provides the poetic scheme for many lyric songs (*rondas, villancicos,* and others), most ballads (*romances*), and the *jota,* a widely known dance.

Another prevalent metric-song form is the *cuarteta* or *copla de seguidilla* (*seguidilla* quatrain or couplet). The *seguidilla* is a dance form that shapes vocal and instrumental songs throughout the country, demonstrating characteristic Spanish fluidity between dance and song genres. Quatrains of *coplas de seguidilla* alternate lines of seven and five syllables with rhymes linking the even-numbered lines, and are often followed by an *estribillo volante,* a tercet with lines of five, six, and five syllables. This form, known in Spain as early as the eleventh century, is widely dispersed (figure 3).

Given the formality of Spanish poetic structures and the refinement of lyric verses, the prevalence of *relinchidos* 'onomatopoeic shouts' might seem incongruous, but they are found everywhere. *Relinchidos* could be viewed as relief from textual formality, or a typically Spanish juxtaposition of emotional exclamation with pious or solemn expression.

FIGURE 4 The *maqam*-like scale of Andalucía, with chromatic alterations of the second and third scalar degrees. After Crivillé i Bargalló 1988:312.

Melodic and rhythmic systems

In Spanish song, with few exceptions, monody prevails. Many traditional songs employ descending, terraced melodies built on an E mode, with chromaticisms that probably originate with Arabic modes (figure 4). The raised third degree of this mode reflects the influence of the Arabic *maqam* "Hijaz Kar" or the Persian *dastgah* "Tchahargah." The forces of diatonicism, seeking to avoid the resulting augmented second, eventually added the option of a natural third degree, so a raised and a natural tone can appear within a single song.

The Andalusian scale underlies melodies throughout the Iberian peninsula, but especially in Andalucía, Extremadura, Castile, and León. Such songs often conclude with four descending triads in parallel thirds—a distinctively Spanish cadential pattern. Other common modalities include the major mode, the minor mode, and alternations between the two within a song.

The solo vocal repertoire includes melismatic, asymmetric songs in Mediterranean-influenced free rhythm: work songs, lullabies, improvisations, and flamenco's *cante jondo* (see below). Most of the remaining repertoire is metric, in duple and triple meters. Spanish rhythms are often flavored with hemiola (*sesquiáltera*), which may involve alternation between 3/4 and 6/8 times or the insertion of a 3/2 bar in a 3/4 melody, creating polyrhythm against the accompaniment. Another rhythmic trait is *aksak*, the "limping" asymmetrical rhythms common to Turkish and Eastern European music (Preciado 1984–1985). Usually five-beat measures grouped into three and two beats, *aksak* meters are found in the *seguidillas* and *peteneras* of flamenco, *charradas* of Salamanca, *corridos* of León, and widespread *ruedas* (circle dances).

MUSICAL INSTRUMENTS AND INSTRUMENTAL MUSIC

Much traditional instrumental music in Spain is monophonic. Though Spain is well known for the guitar, the Spanish instrumental tradition relies upon flutes, shawms, and bagpipes, with rhythm provided by many types of frame drum, and a festive textural layer added by metallic idiophones including bells and triangles, particularly favored for religious occasions.

In the twentieth century, traditional instrumental ensembles have been harder hit by mass-mediated music and external influences than vocal genres, as demands for musical performance have been met by jazz and then pop and rock bands. But certain ensembles have proved resilient and enduring, foremost among them the flute-and-drum duo played by a single musician. Such flutes are typically wooden with finger holes; accompanying is a drum whose generic name is *tambor*.

Similar to the flute-and-drum duo is that of the shawm or bagpipe with drum. The shawm is particularly popular in central Spain; the bagpipe, in northern Spain. Made of a goatskin bag, a breath tube, drone tubes, and one melody tube, the bagpipe is most frequently called *gaita*. The stridency of the shawm and bagpipe suit this ensemble for outdoor performances.

Another widespread and important instrumental ensemble is the *rondalla*, the guitar-based band that accompanies *rondas*. Typically composed of variously sized guitars and optional rhythmic accompaniment by a *pandereta*, castanets, triangles, and a large earthen jug, the *rondalla* has functions that extend far beyond the *ronda* to accompany various dances.

The Catalonian *cobla* is a departure from the spare instrumental prototype of Spain. Born in the 1300s of indigenous instruments, including a flute and drum

FIGURE 5 Men play a guitar and a *bandurria.* Monteagudo, Murcia, December 1952. Courtesy of the Alan Lomax Collection, New York.

played by one performer, and first and second soprano and tenor oboes, *coblas* in the 1880s began to incorporate European concert instruments including trumpet, trombone, flügelhorn, and double bass. In addition to instrumental performances, the *cobla* accompanies the *sardana,* a vital urban-rural circle dance, serving as an emblem of Catalonian identity.

Less distinctive than the *cobla* but idiomatically similar is the *banda de música,* a municipal wind-band tradition that extends throughout Spain. Performing repertoires mixing traditional and popular pieces, bands stage inter-*pueblo* competitions and serve as symbols of civic pride.

Beyond the components of these ensembles, many instruments—particularly idiophones, such as church bells, cowbells, and jingle bells (*cascabeles*)—make traditional Spanish music. Important among the simple and old idiophones used in Spanish folk music are castanets (*castañuelas* 'chestnuts'), paired concave wooden clappers.

The violin has insinuated itself into traditional and popular repertoires, often supplementing traditional ensembles to accompany Spanish dances and those of Continental origin, such as the contra dance, the gavotte, the mazurka, the minuet, and the polka. Of historical interest but little current usage is the *rabel,* a relative of the Arabic *rabab,* once common throughout Spain (see figure 2). The five-stringed hurdy-gurdy (*zanfona*) is considered characteristic of Galicia; its two drone strings identify the instrument with the region.

The prominence of the guitar in Spanish music is well known. Today, there is an extensive complex of guitars, from the large and low-pitched *guitarrón* to several small and high ones, including the *requinto,* the *timple,* the *vihuela,* the *guitarillo,* the *tiple,* the *triplo,* and the *tiplillo* (figure 5). In central and southern Spain, the guitar often accompanies solo singing, as in flamenco; elsewhere, it is often played in an ensemble, such as the *rondalla.*

A uniquely Spanish instrument is the *alboka* of Basque country—a double clarinet that plays two simultaneous notes in unison or fifths. The player employs circular breathing to create a continuous tone.

Many Spanish instruments bear evidence of Muslim influence. These include lutes, rebecs, psalteries, transverse flutes, shawm, trumpets, frame drums, tambourines, and castanets. Instrumental names that begin with the vowel /a/ derive from Arabic. These include *adufe* 'tambourine', *ajabeba* 'transverse flute', *alboka,* *añafil* 'long, straight trumpet', and *sonajas de azófar* 'metal castanets'.

Dance forms

Spain's dances include the *jota,* the "mother dance" of the culture, with many variants; the *seguidillas*; and the fandango. All three are couple dances in quick triple time, encapsulating essential traits of Spanish music: dialoguing or solo-chorus vocal performance, small-group instrumental accompaniment, and evocative, poetic texts [see DANCE IN EUROPE, figure 3, p. 163].

The *jota* has an instrumental introduction (*variaciones*), followed by octosyllabic quatrains of *copla*s interspersed with refrains (*estribillos*) and instrumental interludes. The harmonies alternate between tonic and dominant chords. A complicating factor is that the four-line textual verse extends over a period of seven musical phrases, with the fourth, fifth, sixth, and seventh tending to group into two longer phrases, interrupted by held cadential notes—a pattern that, coupled with repetition of the fourth line of text, marks the dramatic high point of the verse. The resulting musical-textual structure is generally (Crivillé i Bargalló 1988:211):

Musical phrases:	A	B	A	C	D	C	E
Textual phrases:	A	B	A	C	D	D	B

FIGURE 6 Music for the *jota*, the "mother dance" of Spanish culture: the musical sections are ABACDCE; the textual sections, BABCD-DA. After Crivillé i Bargalló 1988:210–211.

The cumulative effect of this musical-textual layering and repetition is of a nonlinear system that continues to loop back upon itself; surprise is heightened by the tendency to begin vocal phrases on the second beat of the measure, working against an emphatic downbeat in the accompaniment. An example of a *jota* verse (figure 6) inverts—to BAB—the usual textual order of the first three lines.

Seguidillas have long been linked with La Mancha, though no written evidence confirms their origin there. Their form is similar to that of the *jota*.

The fandango, most closely associated with Andalucía, is widely dispersed, with regional variations. It features sensual movements, laughter, and cries; these attributes combine with harmonic complexities to make it stylistically more expressive than the *jota*. The music begins with instrumental passages, followed by one or more chords to mark the beginning of the *coplas*. A stanza of five octosyllabic lines is sung over six musical phrases, with a complex harmonic progression.

REGIONALISM

Spanish musical scholarship has historically been intensely regional. The most useful regional designations are broad; once the analyst perceives the huge variety of regional names and variants of any given genre, instrument, or practice, lists of designations can provide little insight into Spanish traditional music as a whole.

Folk musics in the north of Spain tend to share similarities with European folk-song style by utilizing mostly major and some minor keys, syllabic settings, and symmetric phrases. Northern dances accent masculine power in war and courtship contexts; circle dances are more popular there than elsewhere. Galicia and Basque Country use their own languages and have unique instrumental traditions [see BASQUE MUSIC].

Catalonia, in the northeast, serves as a transitional area between Spain and

The ambiguous status of flamenco musicians reflects societal distrust of the *gitanos* and international admiration for their music. The development of flamenco—from the rural song of Andalucía to what is arguably the most urbanized, professionalized form of traditional Spanish music—symbolizes the urbanization of Spanish culture.

France. Eastern Spain, including Aragón, the Levante, and the Balearic Islands, favors formal and elegant performance, as embodied in the music and dance of the *jota*. In central and eastern Spain, areas of Castile-León and Extremadura preserve much of the heart of the traditional repertoire: *alboradas, romances, rondas, seguidillas,* and *villancicos.* Andalusian and Murcian music is livelier and more rhythmically complex than that of the rest of Spain; *cante jondo* introduces an aesthetic of introspection unknown elsewhere. The Andalusian scale prevails in Andalucía and Murcia, and asymmetric phrasing and free meter delineate southern from northern style.

MUSIC AND THE ROMAN CATHOLIC CHURCH

For religious observations and ceremonies, the Spanish church embraced and adapted many musical practices with probable pagan roots, as in the fertility-based songs of the May cycle. An array of secular songs and dances has gained religious associations strictly through their performance on sacred occasions. Many Spanish secular folk songs freely mix praise of the Virgin Mary with lyrics of earthly love and secular celebration, again demonstrating the fluidity of meaning in fiestas.

Dance has been associated with Roman Catholic worship since pilgrims performed circle dances at shrines such as Santiago de Compostela and Nuestra Señora de Montserrat; ritual dancing was an integral aspect of Mass in cathedrals during medieval times. In the 1600s, the clergy prohibited dancing during the Mass. Nevertheless, a host of dances, performed before or after Mass and processionals, remain closely associated with religious occasions.

SOCIAL GROUPS AND MUSIC

Much traditional musical practice is the domain of young men, the usual performers of courtship *rondas.* Older, less popular songs, such as work songs and some ballads, are of necessity now in the domain of older musicians. Women traditionally sing; as instrumentalists, they usually play drums and castanets.

Judeo-Spanish music, a vital force in Spanish culture before the expulsion of the Jews, survives outside Spain in the Ladino musical styles practiced in Greece, Libya, Morocco, and Tunisia. Since the expulsion of the Jews, the only significant social minority in Spain has been the Gypsies (*gitanos*). The ambiguous status of flamenco musicians reflects societal distrust of the *gitanos* and international admiration for their music. The development of flamenco—from the rural song of Andalucía to what is arguably the most urbanized, professionalized form of traditional Spanish music—symbolizes the urbanization of Spanish culture.

—Elizabeth J. Miles

FLAMENCO

Flamenco, the music and dance traditionally associated with the Gypsies (*gitanos*) of southern Spain, unites song (*cante*), guitar (*toque*), and dance (*baile*) in an emotional,

FIGURE 7   In a café in Moron de la Frontera,
Diego del Castor (guitar) accompanies singers
Joselero (left) and Antonini Del Puerto. Photo
by Robert Garfias, 1968.

deeply expressive art form. [Known as Rom elsewhere in Europe, Gypsies receive broader attention in the article ROM (GYPSY) MUSIC.] Flamenco music is the fusion of *gitano* musical traits and stylings with traditional and popular forms of Spanish music. Initially a *gitano* expression, it soon came to be practiced by non-*gitanos* (*payos*). Historically, its most important aspect is the *cante,* originally performed unaccompanied, with rhythmic accompaniment from a stick (*palo seco*) or sometimes claps (*palmas*). Later, in the era of the singing cafés (*cafés cantantes*), guitar accompaniment became a feature of the style (figure 7).

As the origins of the *cante* are obscure, many scholars prefer to sort its forms (*palos*) into three groups: *cante jondo* 'deep song', *cante intermedio* 'intermediate song' (also known as *cante flamenco*), and *cante chico* 'light song'. *Cante jondo,* considered the oldest and most serious group, includes the important *palos siguiriyas* and *soleá,* both based on a complex, twelve-beat rhythmic structure (*compás*). *Cante intermedio* is a hybrid, created from the fusion of *cante jondo* and forms from Spanish folk and popular music styles, in particular the fandango, originally a dance of Arabic origin. The rhythmic structure of the *cante chico* is not so complex as that of the *jondo,* with the exception of the festive *bulerías,* also based on a twelve-beat structure. Primarily rooted in Andalusian folklore, it has assimilated Latin American musical traits.

TRACK 20

History of flamenco

The earliest accounts of flamenco, dating from the early nineteenth century, document parties in *gitano* homes and jam sessions (*juergas*), in taverns, bars, and brothels. The jam sessions were patronized by members of the wealthy, *señorito* class of Andalusian landed gentry, who sought entertainment among the lower rungs of the social ladder. *Cafés cantantes,* which appeared about 1840 in Madrid and Seville, offered flamenco artists regular contracts with fixed salaries and gave flamenco a reenergized, creative thrust. Purists have decried this period as the beginning of commercialization in flamenco, but it is now acknowledged as having been tremendously important in the artistic development of flamenco, particularly in the creation of new forms of *cante,* the addition of the guitar as an accompanimental instrument, and the growing importance of the dance.

After the *café cantante* era, flamenco was taken to the theatrical stage in the period known as flamenco opera (*operismo*). This period, which lasted through the

1920s, transformed more "authentic" styles of flamenco into the commercialized forms that held sway until the renaissance of older, more serious styles in the 1950s and 1960s. With sentimental songs (called *cuplé flamenco*), borrowings from Spanish zarzuela and popular South American song, use of sensational and melismatic vocal tricks, theatrical affectations, and florid lyrics, *operismo* came under attack by intellectuals led by the composer Manuel de Falla and the poet Federico García Lorca, who together organized the *Concurso de cante jondo* in Granada in 1922 in an attempt to restore flamenco to respect as an art form. To counteract the consequences of commercialization, Falla, García Lorca, and their followers went to the opposite extreme and developed a romanticized, mythic, spiritual interpretation of flamenco as the "soul of Andalucía," in which they developed the concept of transcendent emotion (*duende*) as the inspiration of flamenco. Under Francisco Franco's dictatorship, this artistic development was quashed by a recommercialized flamenco, whose superficial gaiety was encouraged by state cultural policies.

In the early 1950s, a renaissance of serious, "pure" flamenco began, brought about partly by the influence of Spanish dance companies, whose touring resulted in the interest of international scholars and aficionados. In Jerez de la Frontera in 1958, the Cáthedra de Flamenco (Institute of Flamenco Studies) was created. Nightclubs (*tablaos*) that offered performances of more "artistic" flamenco, were opened in Barcelona, Madrid, and Seville. The 1960s saw the beginnings of small flamenco clubs (*peñas*), regional flamenco festivals throughout Andalucía, and the many contests (*concursos*) of *cante* and *toque*, in which important new flamenco artists got their first recognition. Thus, in little more than a century, flamenco has moved from the intimate setting of the *juerga* to *cafés cantantes*, contemporary professional *tablaos*, festival circuits, and concert stages.

Traits of the genre

The guitar was introduced during the *café cantante* era, solely for accompaniment. The characteristic playing style—strumming (*rasgueado*), alternating with plucked melodic phrases (*falsetas*)—is an integral part of the ensemble of singer, dancer, and guitarist. The guitar style was soon expanded through the introduction of complex arpeggios, the four-finger tremolo, and more difficult left-hand work. The intense period of creativity and renovation that flamenco has enjoyed since the late 1960s is largely due to the work of young, innovative guitarists, whose incorporation of classical and jazz guitar techniques and Latin American rhythms and genres has influenced all aspects of flamenco, including the sung and danced elements.

In traditional flamenco contexts, onlookers played important roles. Their participation in the *jaleo*, a series of encouraging and admiring shouts from the audience, added an essential element to the ambiance. An audience of aficionados participates with claps (*palmas*) and finger snaps (*pitos*). Flamenco *palmas* are rhythmic patterns based on the rhythmic structures of the *cante*. Members of the flamenco *cuadro* (dancers, singers, and guitarist) and skilled aficionados perform complex counter-rhythms in the *compás*, complementing the guitar's rhythms and the dancers' footwork (*zapateo*). The influence of the audience in the *jaleo* is less evident in concert and festival contexts, but it prevails in more intimate settings where flamenco is performed (figure 8).

The texts of *cante flamenco* consist of "couplets" (*coplas*), three- to five-line stanzas. Most flamenco lyrics are sung in the Andalusian dialect of Spanish. Flamenco singers rely on traditional lyrics, which they enhance with variations. Some *coplas* are anonymous, but many were composed by famous poets, including Manuel Machado, Manuel Balmaseda, and García Lorca. The use of sophisticated flamenco lyrics has become common, largely reflecting the influence of García Lorca.

FIGURE 8 In a cave in Albaicín, a woman dances, accompanied by a guitarist and clapping. Photo by Robert Garfias, 1968.

Themes of *cante jondo* communicate personal suffering in personal vignettes with directness, simplicity, and lyricism, and evoke a deep sense of fatalism and nihilism. Death is a principal theme, as are the conflicts between hope and despair, love and the pains of love, guilt and atonement, and evil and divine protection. Verses of the *cante chico* tend to express humor and sarcasm, but they too reveal an underlying tragic or ironic sense. Since Franco's demise, some *coplas* have addressed overtly political themes.

Nuevo Flamenco

Nuevo Flamenco is the term given since the 1960s to fusions of flamenco with idioms as varied as Western popular music, blues, and Latin American, Arabic, and African music. The brilliant guitarist Paco de Lucía, a pioneer of this genre, created fusions of jazz and Latin American rhythms in the early 1970s and had a tremendous influence on contemporary flamenco artists. Working with popular gitano singer Camarón, he made arrangements that, by featuring bass, percussion, flute, and synthesizer, forged new paths in flamenco, and raised Camarón to superstar status in Spain with hits like "Soy Gitano" and "Caminando." At the same time, popular duo Lole y Manuel were drawing a new, younger audience to flamenco with their fusions of flamenco and newly composed poetry and expanded instrumental forms. Their 1975 recording "*Nuevo Día*" ('New Day'), released just after Franco's death, heralded a new era of idealism and freedom. They also fused flamenco with Arab music to create *flamenco arabe*.

In the mid-1980s, the group Ketama and the duo Pata Negra continued these trends, adding salsa and blues, respectively, to the mix. Composed of younger singers and guitarists from well-known flamenco lineages, these groups and their successors have moved flamenco into the realm of commercial music. In the 1990s, Barbería del Sur continues the Latin trend, Navajita Plátea mixes flamenco with rhythm and blues, and Tomasito (known as Niño Robot) has created an innovative rap-flamenco fusion. Some singers, like Niña Pastori from Cádiz (with her 1996 release "*Tu me camelas*"), have had hit records that feature a mix of flamenco with pop styles.

Contemporary forms of flamenco fusion coexist with the older forms seen in festival and *tablao* contexts. The old and the new flamenco are commercial, internation-

The old and the new flamenco are commercial, internationally successful musical styles, whose Andalusian *gitano* roots continue to be expressed in creative ways in social and musical contexts that address the present while acknowledging the past.

ally successful musical styles, whose Andalusian *gitano* roots continue to be expressed in creative ways in social and musical contexts that address the present while acknowledging the past.

—LOREN CHUSE

CONTEMPORARY DEVELOPMENTS

Television is enormously popular in Spanish homes. The channels are state-run, and programming favors dubbed American shows and Spanish soap operas. Radio plays pop music from Spain and the rest of Europe. Dance clubs playing current hit records from Europe and the United States are important social centers for a broad spectrum of urban youth.

Spain's popular-music exports span a spectrum from the Gregorian chant of the Benedictine monks of Santo Domingo, whose dance-floor mixes returned plainsong to popular and classical music charts throughout the Western world, to flamenco-based pop artists and ensembles, such as Ketama and Malou, which employ a rock-oriented style of performance.

The contemporary conception of *folklorismo* in Spain results in the conscious re-creation of folk performances for goals from the commercial to the social to the personal; but Spain's conservative nature seems to have lessened the critical gap between creative and re-creative performance, and the country's contested cultural history appears to lend a generous degree of continuity to the inexorable process of change.

HISTORY OF ART MUSIC IN SPAIN

Spain's documented music history is quite ancient. Cave paintings of dance from Lérida, Castellón, and Albaceta date to the Palaeolithic Age. The Basque *txistu* is believed to descend from bone flutes found in the caves of Isturitz; documents as early as the 700s mention its prehistoric origins. Greeks and Latins in pre-Roman Iberia wrote of war and burial dances and songs, circle dances, and festive dances accompanied by flute and cornet.

In 711, the Moors' arrival made a strong impression on Spanish culture. Arabic musical treatises were translated into Latin and disseminated throughout Spain, and Muslim musicians performed in Christian courts. Spain served as the gateway for the Arabic lute to the rest of Europe. The courts were important forces in the sponsorship and study of music. That of Alfonso X (1221–1284) engaged the services of Castilian, Galician, Hebrew, Muslim, and Provençal minstrels.

Polyphony arrived in Spain during the Middle Ages. One of the first instances was at the cathedral at Santiago de Compostela, the shrine that symbolized the Christian struggle against the Moors and became the destination of pilgrimages from all over Europe. The twelfth-century Codex Calixtinus contains the cathedral's chant repertory for feast days, including twenty pieces in a new two-voiced polyphonic style tracing to France and Aquitania. The codex documents that pilgrims played citterns, lyres, kettledrums, flutes, flageolets, trumpets, harps, and violins at the shrine.

Cancioneros—literary anthologies of poetic texts, with or without music—began to be published in the 1200s. These anthologies provide a rich, if highly mediated, documentary of Spanish music through the centuries.

The Renaissance brought a clear distinction between the *romance* 'ballad' and the *villancico,* which then denoted all lyric art songs, sacred and secular. Literary references to *seguidillas,* beginning in the mid-1400s, document the differentiation of rural and urban forms by 1500. *Vihuela* tablatures were first published in the mid-1500s, adding instrumental music to the written tradition.

Important developments of the 1600s included the zarzuela, a court-based musical play with sung choruses and *coplas* alternating with spoken lines. The *tonadilla escénica,* a short comic opera of the late 1700s, used folk and popular melodies and temporarily displaced the zarzuela, which, however, returned to popularity with a revival in the 1800s spearheaded by Francisco Asenjo Barbieri (1823–1894), who, in the Romantic spirit of nationalism, added folk melodies and popular dances.

Zarzuelas provided an early compositional forum for Manuel de Falla (1876–1946), one of Spain's first internationally famous composers. Other important art-music composers of the time included the pianists Enrique Granados (1867–1916), famous for his *Goyescas* for piano, and Isaac Albéniz (1860–1909), known for the *Suite Iberia* for piano. The 1800s also brought the first folk *cancioneros,* transcriptions of song collection undertaken in the same nationalistic vein driving folk collections throughout Europe (see below).

Twentieth-century art music has followed international trends. Few composers working in progressive contemporary forms have achieved international fame, but composer Joaquín Rodrigo and pianist Alicia de Larrocha are well known for mingling classicism with Hispanicism.

HISTORY OF SPANISH SCHOLARSHIP

Scholarship in traditional Spanish music has often focused on individual, localized traditions at the expense of a broad overview of Spanish music culture. Folk-song collecting in Spain began early with the work of Francisco de Salinas (1513–1590), whose text collections were eventually published with the intent to prove Spanish music superior to the Italian styles currently in fashion at the courts. Further text collecting followed in the 1800s, but it was not until the 1870s that the first musical transcriptions were published—transcriptions of Basque songs.

The twentieth century brought extensive, though spotty, fieldwork. Collections and recordings continued to target regional differences and focus on the interplay between folk and art musics. Many regional folk and popular *cancioneros* were compiled and published during the first three decades of the century.

The first important recording effort, yielding 281 field recordings, was spearheaded in the 1930s by the German-American composer Kurt Schindler, whose extensive transcriptions and analyses, covering more than one thousand songs arranged by province, were published posthumously (1941).

The Civil War and World War II interrupted research, but work resumed in 1943, when Higinio de Anglés founded the Instituto Español de Musicología in Barcelona. Manuel García Matos collaborated with Unesco and the Spanish record company Hispavox to release an annotated, regionally organized anthology of Spanish folk music in 1959; it was rereleased in the United States in 1972. Important archival collections are housed at the Instituto Español de Musicología in Barcelona and Madrid, the Centro de Historia del Folklore y de la Danza at the Real Escuela

Superior de Arte Dramático y Danza in Madrid, and the Biblioteca del Orfeo Catalá in Barcelona.

Most studies of folk *cancioneros,* collections, and recordings have sought to define regional or generic styles, trace the roots of extant folk melodies, or detect folk elements in nineteenth- and twentieth-century art music, especially the zarzuela (Katz 1974). The resulting body of literature is rich in monographs but poor in comprehensive overviews and synthetic approaches. Josep Crivillé i Bargalló filled that void with a book on Spanish folk music (1988).

—ELIZABETH J. MILES

BIBLIOGRAPHY

Álvarez, Caballero. 1988. *Gitanos, payos y flamencos en los orígenes del flamenco.* Madrid: Editorial Cinterco.

———. 1994. *El Cante flamenco.* Madrid: Editorial Alianza.

Anglés, Higinio, ed. 1943. *La música de las Cantigas de Santa María del Rey Alfonso el Sabio.* Barcelona: Biblioteca Central.

Arana Martija, Jos Antonio. 1985. *Basque Music.* Bilbao: Basque Government.

Blas Vega, José, and Manuel Rios Ruiz. 1988. *Diccionario-enciclopedia ilustreado del flamenco.* 2 vols. Madrid: Editorial Cinterco.

Carrera, Adolf. 1910–1916. *Cançons populars catalanes.* Barcelona: Tipografía "L'Avenc."

Chase, Gilbert. 1959. *The Music of Spain.* 2d, rev. ed. New York: Dover Publications.

Crivillé i Bargalló, Josep. 1988. *Historia de la música española.* 2d ed. El folklore musical, 7. Madrid: Alianza Editorial.

Diaz Viana, Luis. 1985 *Canciones populares de la Guerra Civil.* Madrid: Taurus Editions.

Echevarría, F. 1912. *Cantos y bailes populares de Valencia.* Valencia.

Etzion, Judith, and Susana Weich-Shahak. 1988a. "The Music of the Judeo-Spanish Romancero: Stylistic Features." *Anuario Musical* 43:221–255.

———. 1988b. The Spanish and the Sephardic Romances: Musical Links." *Ethnomusicology* 32:1–37.

Farmer, Henry George. 1929. *History of Arabian Music to the Thirteenth Century.* London: Luzac.

García Gomez, Génesis. 1993. *Cante flamenco, cante minero.* Barcelona: Editorial Anthropos.

García Matos, Manuel. 1958. *Spanish Folk Music and Dance.* Translated by Clover de Pertínez. Madrid: Inter-Ministerial Organizing Committee for the Spanish Pavillion.

———, comp. 1982. *Cancionero popular de la provincia de Cáceres.* Critical edition by Josep Crivillé i Bargalló. Lírica popular de la Alta Extremadura, 2. Barcelona: Consejo Superior de Investigaciones Científicas.

García Matos, Manuel, and Rodríguez Mata, comps. 1951–1960. *Cancionero popular de la provincia de Madrid.* 3 vols. Critical edition by José Romeo Figueras, Marius Schneider, and Juan

Tomás Parés. Madrid: Consejo Superior de Investigaciones Científicas.

Gil García, Bonifacio. 1931–1956. *Cancionero popular de Extremadura.* 2 vols. Valls and Bajadoz: E. Castells.

———, comp. 1987. *Cancionero popular de La Rioja.* Edited by José Romeo Figueras et al. Barcelona: Consejo Superior de Investigaciones Científicas.

González Climent Anselmo. 1989. *Flamencología.* 2d ed. Córdoba: Publicaciones del Ayuntamiento de Córdoba.

Grande, Félix. 1992. *García Lorca y el flamenco.* Madrid: Mondadori.

Inzenga, José. 1888. *Cantos y bailes de España.* 3 vols. Madrid: Romero.

Katz, Israel J. 1972. *Judeo-Spanish Traditional Ballads from Jerusalem: An Ethnomusicological Study.* 2 vols. Preface by Samuel G. Armistead and Joseph H. Silverman. New York: Institute of Mediaeval Music.

———. 1974. "The Traditional Folk Music of Spain: Explorations and Perspectives." *Yearbook of the International Folk Music Council* 6:64–85.

Labajo Valdez, Joaquina. 1988. *Pianos, voces y panderetas: Apuntes para una historia social de la música en España.* Madrid: Ediciones Endymion.

Larrea Palacín, Arcadio de. 1957. *La música hispano-árabe.* Madrid: Ateneo.

———. 1968. "Aspectos de la música popular española." In *El folklore español,* ed. J. M. Gómez-Tabanera, 297–318. Madrid: Instituto Español de Antropología Aplicada.

Leblon, Bernard. 1991. *El Cante flamenco: entre las músicas gitanas y las tradiciones andaluzas.* Madrid: Editorial Cinterco.

Liu, Benjamin M., and James T. Monroe. 1989. *Ten Hispano-Arabic Strophic Songs in the Modern Oral Tradition: Music and Texts.* University of California Publications in Modern Philology, 5. Berkeley: University of California Press.

Livermore, Ann. 1972. *A Short History of Spanish Music.* New York: Vienna House.

Manuel, Peter. 1986. "Evolution and Structure in Flamenco Harmony." *Current Musicology* 33(1):47–64.

———. 1988. "Andalusian, Gypsy and Class Identity in the Contemporary Flamenco Complex." *Ethnomusicology* 42:46–57.

Mitchell, Timothy. 1988. *Violence and Piety in Spanish Folklore*. Philadelphia: University of Pennsylvania Press.

———. 1990. *Passional Culture*. Philadelphia: University of Pennsylvania Press.

———. 1994. *Flamenco Deep Song*. New Haven, London: Yale University Press.

Ortiz Nuevo, José Luis. 1985. *Pensamiento político en el cante flamenco*. Seville: Biblioteca de la Cultura Andaluza.

Pedrell, Felipe. 1919–1922. *Cancionero musical popular español*. 4 vols. Barcelona: Boileau.

Pohren, Don. 1992a. *The Art of Flamenco*. 3d ed. Seville: Society of Spanish Studies.

———. 1992b. *Paco de Lucía and Family: The Master Plan*. Madrid: Society of Spanish Studies.

Preciado, Dionisio. 1969. *Folklore español: música, danza, y ballet*. Madrid: Studium Ediciones.

———. 1984–1985. "Veteranía de algunos ritmos 'aksak' en la música antigua española." *Anuario Musical* 39-40:239–247.

Pujol, Francisco, et al. 1926–1929. *Obra del cançoner popular de Catalunya: materials*. Barcelona: Imprenta Elzeviriana.

———. 1946. "Clasificación de las canciones populares." *Anuario Musical* 1:19–29.

Ribera y Tarragó, Julián. 1970 [1922]. *Music in Ancient Arabia and Spain*. English translation of

La Música de las Cántigas: estudio sobre su origen y naturaleza, vol. 3. New York: Da Capo Press.

Schindler, Kurt. 1941. *Folk Music and Poetry of Spain and Portugal*. Edited by Federico de Onis. New York: Hispanic Institute.

Schneider, Marius. 1946. "A propósito del influjo árabe: ensayo de etnografía musical de la España medieval." *Anuario Musical* 1:31–141.

Seguí, Salvador. 1980. *Cancionero musical de la provincia de Valencia*. Valencia: Institución Alfonso el Magnánimo.

Seroussi, Edwin. 1990. "La música arábigo-andaluza en las *baqqashot* judeo-marroquíen: estudio histórico y musical." *Anuario Musical* 45:297–315.

Steingress, Gerhard. 1991. *Sociología del cante flamenco*. Jerez: Centro Andaluz de Flamenco.

Stevenson, Robert M. 1964 [1960]. *Spanish Music in the Age of Columbus*. The Hague: Martinus Nijhoff.

Subira, José. 1953. *Historia de la música española e hispánoamericana*. Barcelona, Madrid: Salvat Editores.

Washabaugh, William. 1995. "Ironies in the History of Flamenco." *Theory, Culture, and Society* 12:133–155.

———. 1996. *Flamenco: Passion, Politics and Popular Culture*. Oxford and Washington, D.C.: Berg.

AUDIOVISUAL RESOURCES

Innumerable discs issued by individual artists are not listed here.

El Ángel. 1992. Documentaries produced by Richard Pachon for Spanish Television RTVE. Six videos.

Anthology of Spanish Folklore Music. 1972. Recordings by Roberto Pla. Notes by Manuel García Matos. Everest 3286/4. Reissue of volume 1 of *Antología del folklore musical de España*, Hispavox 10-356/7/8/9, 1959. LP disk.

El Cante Flamenco: Antología Histórica. 1991. Directed by José Blas Vega. Philips and Polygram Ibérica. Compact disc.

Duende. 1994. Ellipsis Arts ELLI CD 3353. 3 compact discs.

Early Cante Flamenco: Classic Recordings from the 1930s. 1990. Compiled by John Parth. Arhoolie CD 326. Compact disc.

Flamenco: Great Figures. 1992. Compiled by Mario Bois. Harmonia Mundi Le Chant du Monde LDX 274 944 CM 234. Compact disc.

Music of Spain. 1951. Notes by Emilio de Torre. Folkways 4411. LP disk.

Nuevas Generaciones. 1992. Documentary on the new flamenco. Produced by Catalán Productions, Barcelona. Video.

Sequentia. 1992. *Sons of Thunder: Music for St. James the Apostle from the Codex Calixtinus*. Vox Iberica, 1. Notes by Richard Crocker and Benjamin Bagby. Deutsche Harmonia Mundi 77199. Compact disc.

Songs and Dances of Spain. N.d. Recordings and notes by Alan Lomax. Westminster 12001–12005, 12018–12023. 9 LP disks.

Spanish Folk Music. N.d. Recordings by Alan Lomax and Jeanette Bell. Notes by Eduardo Martínez Torner and Alan Lomax. Columbia World Library of Folk and Primitive Music, 14. Columbia KL-216. LP disk.

Waverly Consort. 1995. *Traveler: Pilgrim Songs from the "Llibre Vermell" of Montserrat, Seven "cantigas de amor" from the Martin Codex, Traditional Judeo-Spanish Ballads*. Notes by Israel J. Katz. Angel 55559. Compact disc.

Italy

Marcello Sorce Keller
Roberto Catalano
Giuseppina Colicci

Contexts and Genres of Traditional Song and Music
Musical Style, Performance Practice, and Aesthetics
Musical Instruments
Songs of Ethnic Minorities
Popular Music
History of Musical Scholarship

Italy's 56 million people have evolved traditions that share common elements with continental Europe and the Mediterranean. Consequently, some scholars have suggested that, while northern Italy is musically the south of Europe, southern Italy belongs to the north of Africa. The musical tradition of the Piedmont (in the north), for example, may relate more closely to the traditions of France, Spain, the British Isles, German-speaking countries, and Scandinavia than to those of Calabria or Sicily.

Along the peninsula, the transition from European to Mediterranean musical idioms occurs gradually, but on the basis of structure, manner of performance, and textual elements, Italy has four main regions of musical style: the Mediterranean (or south) and Sicily; the central region; the north; and Sardinia [see SARDINIA]. The clearest division in musical, linguistic, and social styles is between north and south, bounded by the Apennines chain that links La Spezia and Pesaro (map 6). Heavy migration from south to north after 1945 further complicated the social landscape.

Musical styles and practices vary from those reminiscent of Austrian folk music to others resembling Arabic melismatic singing. Linguistic isolates, clearly related to traditions outside Italy, add to the variety: Albanian (in Calabria, Basilicata, and Sicily), Greek (in Apulia and Sicily), German (in Alto Adige, Trentino, and Veneto), Provençal (in Piedmont), and Catalan (in Sardinia). In these musical areas, little in the way of syncretism or acculturation has occurred. The Italian peninsula is thus a mosaic of local traditions, confined at times within a region, town, or family. From this point of view, there is no "Italian folk music." Rarely shared at the national level, folk song in Italy never became a national symbol. Instead, during the second half of the nineteenth and part of the twentieth century, opera and so-called Neapolitan popular song served such purposes.

Art music bonded Italy's 310,000 square kilometers into a cultural unit. In the 1800s, for instance, the middle class from Piedmont to Sicily enjoyed opera, and composers such as Donizetti were equally popular in Milan and Naples. At the rural level, however, where music circulates orally for the most part, Italy was by no means unified, and still is not. Sensing this diversity in region and class, the Austrian politician Metternich (1773–1859) remarked that Italy was not a nation but a geographic expression.

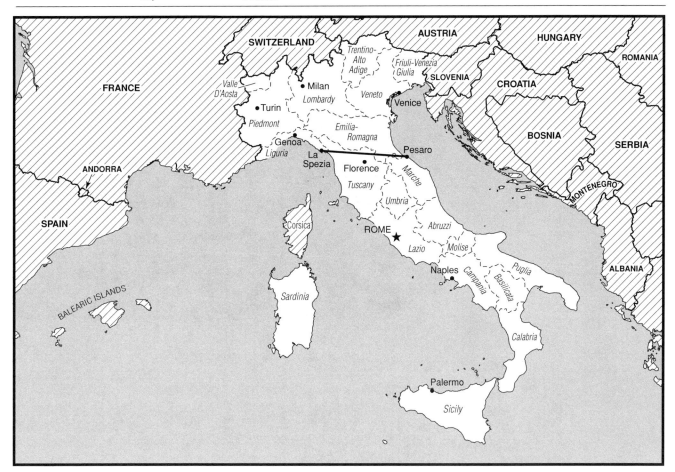

MAP 6   Italy

CONTEXTS AND GENRES OF TRADITIONAL SONG AND MUSIC

Singing in Italy has many uses, occasions, and associations: life-cycle ritual songs (baptism, wedding, burial), calendric carols (Christmas, spring, carnival), occupational songs (shepherds', soldiers', vendors', fishermen's), recreational songs (including dance songs), family songs (lullabies, children's songs), cattle calls, and so on (figure 1).

Genres of song

Two important types of Italian folk song are ballads (often called *canti epico-lirici*) and lyric songs (*canti lirico-monostrofici*). Ballads are found mostly in the north, where older dialects favored the spread of balladry from France. Lyric songs are more common south of the Apennines, where pre-Latin languages (Latino-Faliscan, Osco-Umbrian, Sabellian) were widespread. Scholars around 1900 constructed this theory of linguistic substrata by focusing solely on the narrative content of songs and bypassing their musical component. Though research has not shown exactly why such correlation between linguistic background and song types exists, it has demonstrated that the north-south dichotomy holds true, not only in the literary content of songs, but in musical style, including the type of vocal production, the mode of performance, and the compositional process.

Ballads

Ballads in Italy share narrative themes with those of the Anglo-American canon

FIGURE 1   Tuna fishermen sing while working, August 1954. Vibo Valentia Marina, Calabria. Photo by Alan Lomax. Courtesy of the Alan Lomax Collection, New York.

established by Francis James Child [see ENGLAND; IRELAND; SCOTLAND]. Found in oral tradition and on broadsides (*fogli volanti*), several Italian ballads have exact correspondences in the English repertoire, among them Child 4, "Lady Isabel and the Elf Knight" (*L'eroina*); Child 12, "Lord Randal" (*L'avvelenato*); Child 43, "The Broomfield Hill" (*La bevanda sonnifera*); and Child 73, "Lord Thomas and Fair Eleanor" (*Danze e funerali*). Literature devoted to the topic of such correspondences includes Francello (1946) and Regnoni-Macera (1964).

Narrative themes are sometimes close to those of the Child ballads, but Italian melodic types differ considerably from those of the Anglo-American tradition, where tunes frequently have modal features, often with flatted thirds or sevenths. In Italy, melodies for ballads usually have a clearly tonal character, at times resembling those of French-speaking territories. The resemblance is not coincidental. Evidence strengthens the thesis, formulated by Costantino Nigra, that most Italian ballads came to northern Italy from francophone territories (Sorce Keller 1989).

From Piedmont eastward across Lombardy and Veneto to Trentino and Friuli, one often encounters fanfarelike tunes that display a distinct French flavor. Piedmont, where local dialects still maintain a strong French coloration, may have functioned as a bridge between France and the eastern Italian areas north of the Apennines. In the 1800s, the cultural ties between northern Italy and France were strengthened in the wake of the Napoleonic wars. Themes in folklore and folk songs, such as that of France as the land where young people go "never to return" (a reference to the military draft), demonstrate these ties.

Lyric songs

Italian lyric songs exist in a bewildering variety (*stornelli, strambotti, rispetti, stranotti, canti alla boara, canti a vatoccu, canti alla stesa, canti alla longa, canti a pera, villotte*), mostly in southern Italy and in the northeast; a frequent term for such songs in Sicily is *canzune*. Some (like *maitinade* and *polesane*) are *canzoni a ballo,* songs originally intended for dancing [see GREECE]. Lyric songs function as lullabies, work songs, and serenades. They are also, to some degree, improvised. In performing, the singer draws on a repertoire of traditional versification and verbal formulas. Sometimes the singer will use ready-made stanzas that, with some variation, can be adapted to almost any

theme. The text is coupled to a small number of melodic types, embellished and molded to the circumstance.

A lyric song can comprise a single stanza or, more often, several stanzas in which each unit expresses a complete thought. Whereas a single stanza from a narrative song would suffer from lack of context or completeness, a monostrophic *canto lirico* usually expresses a self-contained idea. Lyric songs have been much less studied from the musical point of view than ballads. Tullia Magrini and Giuseppe Bellosi (1982) found that, though much was known about song texts, the internal organization of a text owes much more to the music than was formerly supposed.

Diffusion may also have affected the central and southern *canti lirico-monostrofici*. Some philologists believe that lyric songs may have originated in Provençe, since generic names such as *stornello* comes from the Provençal *estorn* 'to challenge', and *strambotto* comes from the Provençal *estribar* 'to lash'. The *canti a vatoccu* 'songs in the manner of a bell clapper' resemble singing styles typical of the Balkan area, where the flattened, narrow intervals between pitches are said to "ring like a bell" [see BULGARIA] (figures 2, 3).

Funeral laments, still practiced in the southernmost reaches of the peninsula, remind us that in antiquity Italy was part of the Greek world (De Martino 1958), and Greek remained the everyday language long after the Roman conquest. Lyric-song versification in southern Italy resembles a form of textual fragmentation used in the Greek islands of the eastern Mediterranean (Magrini 1985, 1986a).

Other genres

In comparison to ballads and lyric songs, other song types are rare. Epic songs of the kind widespread across the Balkan area and eastern Europe are found in Italy only to a limited degree. The most famous case is that of the *maggio* (May) celebration, typical of Tuscany and Emilia. It features epic-dramatic themes, adapted for singing and acting, delivered before a popular audience. Religious songs have been studied less than other types. Among them, *laude*, strophic songs in Latin or the vernacular, are perhaps most famous. In medieval times, they constituted an important repertoire of monodic, nonliturgical songs, and some survive in oral tradition.

A limited repertoire of nonstrophic songs still exists. Professional female wailers in southern Italy commonly sing dirges that have analogies elsewhere in Europe; men, however, sing only satirical or parodic dirges at carnival. Some cattle calls survive, as do, in the alpine area, a smaller number of yodels, to which native scholars have given little attention.

Poetic forms in Italian traditional music have been well studied in terms of versification, rhyme, stanzaic pattern, and narrative content. Few scholars have tried to understand how poetic versification (the *sistema metrico,* to use Diego Carpitella's phrase) and musical accents or beats (the *sistema ritmico*) interact. In northern Italy, most lines are seven, eight, or (least frequently) nine syllables long. The *maitinade* of the north, most typical of Trento Province, were composed of quatrains or six-line stanzas of eleven-syllable lines. Sung by a young man below the window of his beloved, often supported by accordion interludes, they seem to have dropped out of use after World War II. In central Italy, the hendecasyllabic line, with occasional missing or added syllables, is dominant in rhyming distichs and *ottava rima*, a strophe of eight lines (*abababcc* or *abababab*). A literary device in Italy until the 1500s, it

FIGURE 3   A couple sings a *canto a vatoccu.* Marche, December 1954. Courtesy of the Alan Lomax Collection, New York.

The tarantella, a vivacious dance in 6/8, derives its name from the tarantula and from the dance-therapy ritual that took place when the tarantula had supposedly bitten someone.

became a popular form of folk composition and a means of improvising lyric-song genres in central Italy (Tuscany, Umbria, Lazio).

Seasonal rituals and theatrical forms

Students of Italian literature are familiar with carnival (*carnevale*) through the so-called *canti carnascialeschi* 'carnival songs' of renaissance Florence, which originated in Tuscany and spread to other areas. A cluster of heterogeneous genres—*testamenti, canzoni a ballo,* lyric songs—these were composed by literate artists (Lorenzo dei Medici, Giulio Cesare Croce) who imitated traditional performances. In twentieth-century Italy, the most famous carnival celebration was the *carnevale di Bagolino,* from the village of that name in Brescia. During this celebration, complex scenic action takes place while an instrumental ensemble (three or four violins, one or two guitars, one mandolin, and a double bass) provide dance music.

An age-old mid-Lenten ceremony, *Sega la vecchia* 'the sawing of the witch' (the embodiment of Lent) or, in Umbria, *La condanna della vecchiaccia,* 'the condemnation of the crone' ushers in spring. Lent is conceived as an evil spirit dwelling in an oak, tried for killing carnival, and sentenced to death, and the tree is sawn in two. Preceded by a procession of choral singers, brass bands, and people in sixteenth-century costumes, the action divides into four parts: trial, sentence, testament, and final chorus.

The most famous seasonal celebrations are *maggi,* widespread across central Italy (mainly Romagna, Tuscany, and Umbria). These songs, whose origins go back to *rappresentazioni* of the 1400s and 1500s, have lost much of their ritual function. The socialist celebration of May Day, a modern refunctionalization, recalls the ancient custom. The *maggio* includes rituals such as the offering of branches, flowers, and eggs, choosing a May queen, planting a tree and dancing around it, serenading combined with the collection of alms, and the staging of a drama with music and singing. This drama, the *maggio drammatico,* consists of scenes performed by peasant actors who sing songs with interludes on violin or accordion. The subject matter is the life of a saint or a historical hero, the latter often derived from poetry by Ariosto, Dante, or Tasso and sometimes from classical poetry (Virgil, Ovid) or chronicles of current events. Love songs are *maggi a serenata.*

Canti di questua 'begging songs' are performed in winter (the winter solstice, Saint Martin, New Year's Eve, Epiphany, Saint Anthony the Abbot), spring (*tratto marzo, scacciamarzo,* and so forth), Holy Week (*Passione*), and the *maggio* celebration (*cantamaggio*). The *canto della passione,* a begging song widespread in central Italy, is performed the week before Easter. Often noted in collections as the *orologio della passione,* 'clock of the passion', because the text follows, hour by hour, the trial, crucifixion, death, and resurrection of Jesus, these songs contrast the devotional tone required by the subject and the occasion with the saltarello, a dance that evokes joy and hope for the resurrection of Christ. A diatonic accordion (*organetto*) player and

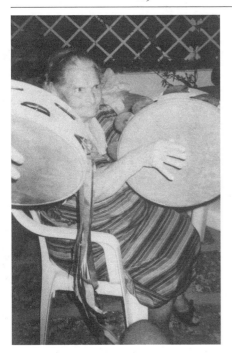

FIGURE 4 Nonna Spella Catamo, more than ninety years old and once a frequent musician for the *tarantate* 'women "bitten" by the spider' in the *tarantismo* ritual in the Salento (Apulia, southern Italy), plays a frame drum (*tamburello*). Photo by Luisa Del Giudice, 1996.

two singers, who accompany themselves on a hammered dulcimer (*cembalo*) and tambourines (*tamburini)*, alternate stanzas. In parts of the Marche, an ensemble of accordion and violins involves up to ten people. From house to house, the singers wish good health and receive food and wine in return.

Dances

The tarantella, a vivacious dance in 6/8, derives its name from that of the tarantula, the large, supposedly poisonous spider found in central and southern Italy, and from the dance-therapy ritual that took place when the tarantula had supposedly bitten someone. Though the spider's poison did not cause hysterical or psychotic behavior, the patient or her relatives—it was most often women who were spider-poisoned (*tarantate*)—blamed it on the spider, rather than on social or psychological reasons, which they preferred not to acknowledge. After the "poisoning," townspeople and a few musicians with a fiddle, guitar, accordion, and frame drum (*tamburello*), produced excited and incessant music from which the tarantella supposedly originated (figure 4). The patient danced to the music until she went into a trance, collapsed on the floor, and recuperated. The ritual is called *tarantismo* in the area of Apulia, where it occurred until the late 1950s. A similar ritual in Sardinia was *argismo* (from *argia* 'spider').

The *monferrina*, a dance accompanied by instrumental and vocal music, was once popular in the valleys of Fassa and Rendena in northeastern Italy and Monferrato (Piedmont) in the northwest, where it may have originated. Partners circled around the couple who danced the best. The *monferrina* enjoyed a short life in art music: the pianist and composer Muzio Clementi (1752–1832) and others published *monferrine* for the piano.

The *tammuriata* (from *tammorra* or *tammurro* 'tambourine') of Campania is danced by man-woman, man-man, and woman-woman couples to syllabic *strambotti*, 'lyric songs', whose scale with an augmented fourth resembles the lydian mode. A tambourine accompanies the singing with a reiterated rhythmic formula that constantly undergoes microvariations, often joined by castanets, friction drum, mouth harp, and other noisemakers.

Many types of saltarello formerly existed all across central Italy. Still frequently encountered with variant names such as *saltarella, savatarelle, ballarella,* and *stuzzichetto,* they belong to a large group of courting dances. Contrary to its name (*saltarello* implies quick jumping), the dance can be gentle and slow, not strenuous and acrobatic, though it is so in the Marche. The *organetto* in central Italy and a type of friction drum in the central-southern area usually accompany the dancing (figure 5).

Dances may have accompanied ballads, though evidence is scant. Documents from Trentino suggest that ballads were accompanied instrumentally and danced to the beat of the saltarello and the *monferrina* until about 1900.

MUSICAL STYLE, PERFORMANCE PRACTICE, AND AESTHETICS

Tonal and rhythmic organization

The oral repertoires of Italy may be conceived as a tonal continuum. At one end, and by far the most conspicuous, are melodies that function according to the principles of classical functional harmony; at the other is music whose tonal material is organized into a variety of modal scales. Tonal melodies have a clear tonal center (or tonic), a dominant, and a leading tone (which seldom moves forcefully to the tonic). Neither vocal nor instrumental music in oral tradition follows the tempered scale, except in

FIGURE 5   A young man dances a sword dance (*danza dei coltelli* 'dance of the knives', though hand gestures have replaced swords or knives), accompanied by a diatonic accordion (*organetto*) and a frame drum (*tamburello*). Torrepaduli, the Salento, Apulia, southern Italy. Photo by Luisa Del Giudice, 1996.

the case of instruments with mechanically fixed sound production: the accordion and its humble relative the *organetto* (small diatonic accordion), which has gradually replaced bagpipes in many area.

Most of the nontempered diatonic scales in Italian folk music resemble the major scale. In modal tunes, there is always a tonal center of sorts, though functional notes such as the leading tone or the subdominant may be absent. Occasionally, "exotic" features occur, such as a lydian scale, often limited to the pentachordal series D♭–E♭–F–G–A♭ in the Neapolitan area or, in Sicily, modal formulas reminiscent of the tetrachord of Middle Eastern classical music. In the alpine area, the tritone serves, though rarely, as a melodic and a harmonic interval. Anhemitonic pentatonic scales occur infrequently, as among the Albanians of Calabria.

The Italian tradition contains metric music in strict time or *parlando rubato* 'robbed speaking' (with speechlike, variable beat) and nonmetric music. In the north, divisive meters predominate; in central and southern Italy, additive meters and other complex forms occur. Binary organization is almost as common as ternary, except in the alpine area, where ternary meter is more common. Frequent shifts between binary and ternary are a trait of alpine style in Austria, France, and Switzerland.

The organization of performances

Italian performances include virtually all possible combinations of vocal, instrumental, and vocal-instrumental interaction. The range of vocal practices covers monophonic singing, drone-based polyphony, various kinds of heterophony, and choral polyphony. Antiphonal and responsorial performances are typical, especially in religious, quasi-liturgical songs, occasionally sung in Latin; perhaps the most famous responsorial performances are the tuna-fishing songs of Sicily, sung in unison or octaves.

Most practices, forms, and genres are localized. Choral singing belongs mainly to the alpine area and the north, where a variable number of singers sing two, three, or four parts (CD track 21). The accompanying part sings below the leading part or, less commonly, above it. This type of polyphony, structured in thirds or sixths, is widespread from the southern German territories to the valley of the river Po, and into Slovenia, Dalmatia, and northern Croatia (figure 6). In playfulness and intricacy of texture, the richest polyphonic forms include the *tiir*, from the town of Premana in Lombardy; the *trallalero,* in the area around Genoa, in which five vocal parts imitate various instruments; and the *bei* in Tuscany. These styles are neither song forms nor song types, but polyphonic procedures applied to different kinds of songs.

Northern polyphony reaches somewhat farther south into the Apennines of Abruzzi and the Marche, where we find more archaic forms like the *canto a vatoccu,* known also in Tuscany as *canto a dispetto* 'song of the despised'. Distributed along the eastern Adriatic litoral, these songs feature a clash between the two parts, producing an interval of a second reminiscent of Bulgarian two-part singing [see BULGARIA]. The phenomenon of voices proceeding in parallel seconds is extremely rare, and scholars consider this style, which probably originated with medieval discant, archaic—one of the oldest forms of polyphony in Europe.

FIGURE 6   "*Sul castel che 'l mira ben,*" an alpine song from the Trentino area, sung in parallel diatonic thirds and a major mode. Transcription by Renato Morelli.

South of Naples, solo singing is predominant. Polyphony is seldom choral (in which participants join in and try to blend), but instead is unison singing that borders on heterophony, or two or three parts carried by single voices.

Textures cut across genres. Ballads, for instance, are performed solo or in chorus depending on the area and on the availability of singers; in the alpine area, choral performance is the most common. According to Roberto Leydi (1977), the polyphonic singing of ballads is gradually replacing solo performances. Lyric songs like *cantu a vatoccu,* traditionally sung by two or three people at the most, are now sometimes performed chorally. The coexistence of different ways of performing the same repertoire can be interpreted as evidence of a transition in the making. A few exceptions resist choral performance: *stornelli,* for instance, are solo songs in which an extemporized, formulaic construction of the text makes the collaboration of two or more people impossible.

Vocal production differs sharply between the north and the south. In the north, especially the alpine area, choral singing of ballads is syllabic, the words are clearly intelligible, the tempo is strict, and the melody is unaffected by the content of the text; voices are full and relaxed, come from the chest, and aim at blending. Southward from the Apennines, choral singing gradually disappears, the tempo becomes *rubato,* the meter shifts from divisive to additive, and a nonblending, strained vocal production predominates. In Sicily, where the relationship of the Italian south to eastern and southern Mediterranean cultures goes back to antiquity, a nasal timbre and florid, embellished melodies resemble those of Arabic styles (figure 7). From about A.D. 800 to 1000, Sicily was ruled by Arabs. From 1816 to 1860, like most of southern Italy, it was under Spanish Bourbon rule, from which it received indirect Muslim influence because of former Arab hegemony on the Iberian peninsula.

Song performance is also a gendered practice, which varies from genre to genre. Lullabies and dirges are sung only by women, and solo lyric songs are sung only by men. Polyphonic lyric songs such as the *canti a vatoccu* are usually sung by women, and song collectors have found women more ready than men to sing ballads. Though choral performance may once have been a male domain, women join in spontaneous performances, even when they give the impression that they feel uncomfortable within the ensemble. The rarity of mixed singing groups is another sign of the exceptional and uncommon collaboration of women with men in the social life of music.

Performers and audiences

Broadsides used to be performed by itinerant professional bards (*cantastorie*), who often took up singing as a consequence of a handicap (blindness, paralysis) that made them unfit for other work. They perform almost solely in Sicily and accompany themselves with the *chitarra battente* 'beaten guitar' (a guitar played with a plectrum), illustrating their narrative with painted pictures that portray the often tragic or gruesome main events. The fantastic exploits of Ariosto's Orlando, for example, are still perpetuated by Sicilian puppeteers and followed by enthusiastic audiences.

Broadside ballads circulating in southern Italy and Sicily belong to the repertoire of the *cantastorie.* The most widely known ballad, *"Baronessa di Carini,"* occurs all across the Italian south; Salomone Marino (1847–1916), a Sicilian and one of the first folklorists in Italy, found thirty-nine variants.

While *cantastorie,* like *poeti a braccio,* perform for a nonspecialist public, choral singing tends to merge performers and audience, most commonly in the alpine area. The atmosphere of the singing event encourages active participation, and men and women, as they sit at table with a bottle of wine, join the performance.

Traditional aesthetics

Traditional music in Italy is as yet uninfluenced by any Romantic or post-Romantic

A folk-music revival in Italy, occurring in the late 1970s, showed similar traits to that of the United States in the 1950s and 1960s. Since the political left viewed folk music as a cultural product of unprivileged classes, folk music was the natural vehicle of protest against free-market capitalism.

FIGURE 7   A florid song (*canzuna*) from Palermo, Sicily. Its melismatic style and ornamentation suggest Arab influence. After Leydi 1973:186–188.

aesthetic ideas about the creative process, the individual character of art, or its enduring value in time. Whereas performers of popular music often verbalize about their musical practices with the same terminology and conceptual apparatus as those of art music, the aesthetic domain in orally transmitted music is hardly verbalized at all. North of the Apennines and in the Alps, where choral singing is pervasive, the voice is produced at mid chest, with relaxed open throat and no vibrato; melodies are accordingly simple and unembellished, and the texture oscillates between homophony and heterophony. According to Alan Lomax (1955–1956, 1968), this kind of singing is an indicator of sociability and interaction among social groups, and is typical of continental Europe. In this area, a "good singer" knows an extensive repertoire, but does not necessarily have an outstanding voice. People believe that an especially good, but personal and idiosyncratic, voice might be detrimental to the cohesion of their ensembles. For collective singing, they prefer singers who remember a great many songs and whose voices can blend effectively with those of the others—though they ignore this criterion when women join men in spontaneous singing.

The aesthetics of singing in Mediterranean Italy differs from that of the north. In the Neapolitan area, vibrato is common in traditional and popular song. Solo singing allows voices to develop personal traits and idiosyncrasies. Voices are throat- and head-centered, rather than chest-centered, and in the far south, they incline toward nasality.

The ideology of music

A folk-music revival in Italy, occurring in the late 1970s, showed similar traits to that of the United States in the 1950s and 1960s. Record companies took an interest in folk music as soon as they discovered its value as a commodity, and recordings played an important role in the revival, as did periodicals like *Il nuovo canzoniere italiano* and *Il cantastorie,* the Italian equivalents of *Sing Out* and *Caravan.* Several collectors—including Roberto Leydi, Sergio Liberovici, and Michele L. Straniero—were notably active in that context. Professional folksingers—including Maria Carta, Il Duo di Piadena, Otello Profazio, and La Nuova Compagnia di Canto Popolare—became almost as popular as their American counterparts. They did not, however, gain an international reputation, and their influence in Italy was limited partly by the revival's politics. Since the political left viewed folk music as a cultural product of unprivileged classes (termed *classi subalterne* by the social philosopher Antonio Gramsci), folk music was the natural vehicle of protest against free-market capitalism. As a by-product of the revival, commercial labels such as Dischi del Sole, Divergo, and Vedette-Albatros Records released field recordings, which reintroduced material into the oral tradition and reinforced the oral circulation of some melodic types.

Professional alpine choirs played only a minor part in the revival, but the sale of their recordings benefited from the wider interest in folk or folk-inspired music it generated. The historical origin of these choirs is obscure: numerous male choirs exist across the alpine area, and their highest concentration is in northeastern Trentino, Alto Adige. While some of their practices and tunes derive directly from folk tradition, their repertoire depends on mass media for its circulation. Alpine choral singers, however, do not usually identify with the political left, especially in Trentino, a strongly Roman Catholic area. As with the revival, the choirs fashion folk songs into a popular product that depends for its circulation largely on the mass media: neither the folk-song revival nor this type of choral practice would have been conceivable without the existence of radio, television, and records.

Electronic media have created "mediamorphosis," a feedback or reintroduction mechanism, by which, from the media, the carriers of oral tradition relearn music they already know. The reintroduced version often becomes the only rendition, or the correct one. Carefully studied only in Trentino by alpine choirs, the process results in a decreasing amount of melodic variation, a contraction or shrinkage of the textual narrative, a rigidity of tempo, and the strong association of a given tune with a particular text.

Outside Trentino and the alpine area, the repertoire of alpine choirs is unfamiliar to the general public, but most Italians have heard some performances and recognize the alpine sound. The music appeals primarily to older people who served in World War II in northern Italy and heard the alpine music circulating there among Italian troops. To their generation, many of these songs ring with patriotic overtones. With Neapolitan songs, they are the closest thing to a musical symbol of national identity.

MUSICAL INSTRUMENTS

Instrumental performances accompany dance, song, and ritual. The celebration of the *maggio* includes a choral or instrumental introduction, plus a recitative with choral or instrumental interludes. For lyric songs, as in the *maitinade* of Trentino, instrumental interludes were also once customary. In the south, particularly in the Neapolitan area, the dance *tammuriata* takes its name from the *tamburello* 'little drum' that performs a rhythmic formula with microvariations. Celebrants of the winter solstice in Predazzo (Trento Province) and many other villages of the alpine area ring cowbells as they gather around a huge fire in the middle of a square or clearing.

Though the use of most instruments remains confined to their local areas, some manufactured instruments enjoy nationwide use. The diatonic button accordion (*organetto*) has largely replaced many types of bagpipe (figure 8). It typically plays the saltarello. Performers develop a virtuosic technique that they test in public competitions. Though the *organetto* still circulates widely in the central areas of the Marche

FIGURE 8   A musician plays a diatonic accordion (*organetto*). Monte San Angelo, Puglia, August 1954. Courtesy of the Alan Lomax Collection, New York.

(Lazio, Abruzzi, and Umbria), it has been replaced by the chromatic accordion in the north. Standard brass or woodwind instruments are usually played by those trained to perform in municipal brass bands. These musicians do not usually engage in spontaneous performances, but play at gatherings promoted by revival groups, whose ensembles commonly include violin, accordion, clarinet, and small drums with bells, and provide music for dancing in traditional costume. Violins are still employed in many areas, but no repertory specific to them exists. In areas such as the Italian part of southern Tyrol, they were used until World War I (1914), though not quite as extensively as in Austria, in an ensemble consisting of two fiddles (a *Vorgeige* or a *Primgeige,* and a *Sekundgeige*), a bass (*Bassgeige*), and sometimes a harp or dulcimer (*Hackbrett*).

Many traditional instruments continue to be made without noticeable differences from local models of the 1890s. The profound socioeconomic transformation of the country since then has not caused substantial organological changes, except in the substitution of materials.

Chordophones

Many stringed instruments are found only locally. The harp exists in Viggiano, in southern Basilicata; iconographic sources point to its former use in Lazio, Abruzzi, and Calabria. The hurdy-gurdy (*ghironda*) is confined to small areas in Piedmont, Lombardy, and Emilia. Variations of the *lira* of Calabria (a bowed, three-stringed fiddle, played on the knee) are played elsewhere in the eastern Mediterranean, especially in Crete and the Balkans. Other chordophones include zithers in the German-speaking Alto Adige and the one-stringed, bowed fiddle (*torototela*) in the northeast.

In the north, the guitar has the standard six-stringed form, but in central and southern Italy, the *chitarra battente,* has four or five courses of steel strings, tuned to suit rhythmic strumming in basically tonic-and-dominant patterns. The body is deep, with a highly arched back, rounded edges, and a slight waist; the belly bends to form a slope just below the bridge. Older instruments have double courses of strings, but later instruments normally have three strings to a course. The middle course may be an unfingered short string, attached to a peg near the bottom of the neck. Traditionally, the *chitarra battente* accompanies singing and dancing and is not a solo instrument (figure 9).

From historical records, like Marin Mersenne's *Harmonie Universelle* (1963 [1636–1637]) and iconographic sources, it appears that the *cannacione,* a countrified version of the medieval lute (*colascione*) used between 1750 and 1800, was the only stringed instrument deriving from Turkish, Arabic, and Greek long-necked lutes. It was popular around Venice, whose trade promoted continuous contact with the Middle East between about 1400 and about 1700.

Idiophones and membranophones

Idiophones include crotals, *triccheballacche* (the rattle of Naples, with three or five mallets inserted in a wooden frame, so the center one is fixed and the outer ones are free to strike against it), bells of various kinds, castanets, and *raganelle* (cog rattles). The mouth harp (*scacciapensieri* 'care-chaser') occurs only in the extreme north of the alpine area and in the deep south of Sicily (where it takes the name of *marranzanu*) [see TRADITIONAL MUSICAL INSTRUMENTS, figures 1, 2, p. 170]. Elsewhere it is known as *ribeba* 'rebab', *trunfa* 'trump', or *tromba degli zingari* 'trumpet of the Gypsies'. Church bells in Italy are played in complex and melodious rounds.

Membranophones comprise various types of tambourines (*tamburini, tamburello*) and *putipù* (friction drum).

It is hard to imagine the extent to which opera was a popular form of entertainment during the 1800s, and how widely it was disseminated through actual productions, transcriptions for brass bands and many other ensembles, itinerant groups of various sorts, and carillons and mechanical musical devices.

FIGURE 9 Shepherds sing and play *chitarra battente*. Carpino, Puglia, August 1954. The singer with his hand to his ear, presumably to hear himself better, adopts a pose typical of many Mediterranean cultures. Courtesy of the Alan Lomax Collection, New York.

FIGURE 10 Accompanying carolers, a bagpiper plays a *zampogna a chiave*. Caggiano, Campania, January 1955. Courtesy of the Alan Lomax Archive.

Aerophones

Aerophones include a variety of flutes: the *firlinfeu* 'pan flute', single and double duct flutes, transverse duct flutes, open transverse flutes, and globular flutes. The double flute exists in Campania, Calabria, and Sicily (Carpitella 1975). While some flutes—such as an end-blown duct flute, made from chestnut bark in northern Italy—have disappeared, others have emerged to take their place: in 1867 Giuseppe Donati of Budrio invented the ocarina, an earthenware, globular flute.

Reed aerophones include single- and double-reed pipes (*ciaramella* and *piffero*, respectively), which can be played in sets of two or three, plus two distinct types of bagpipes. In the north, where bagpipes are now virtually extinct, they had one chanter and one or two drones, each coming out from its own stock. Similar to bagpipes in continental Western Europe, the *piva* in Lombardy had a double-reed, conical chanter with seven finger holes, sometimes with a rear thumb hole, and two single-reed, tunable drones.

The central and southern Italian bagpipe (*zampogna*) features two chanters (the player's hands divided between them) and one or more drones, all mounted in a single frontal stock attached to the skin of the bag (figure 10). Its association with Christmas has preserved its use but limited its repertoire to a single carol ("*Tu scendi dalle stelle* 'You came down from the stars'") and a few other pieces based on traditional dance tunes and songs.

SONGS OF ETHNIC MINORITIES

In north and south, some linguistic minorities still maintain their original language. The major groups are Albanians (Calabria, Basilicata, Sicily), Slavs (Molise, Carnia), Germans (Alto Adige, Trentino, Veneto), Ladins or Rhaetoromanisch speakers (Trentino), Occitans (Piedmont), and Catalans (northwestern Sardinia). No specific studies have been undertaken to ascertain how song repertoires in the native vernacular survive in these enclaves, but when they do, such repertoires are very small. In two areas of Trentino, the local languages are spoken, but songs in them have disappeared. In Ladin- and German-speaking Val di Fassa (northern Trentino), where eight thousand people thrive on tourism, most songs are in Italian. A few are in German, but none is in Ladin, a language still spoken and enjoying a revival. The isolation of the village of Luserna has not saved its musical repertoire in Cimbrian, a Germanic language still spoken there: its six hundred inhabitants sing in Italian or German.

Songs in vernacular languages do not necessarily disappear under the pressure of major languages, and many linguistic enclaves have managed to preserve at least a small repertoire. In Valle dei Mocheni (Trentino), songs in Mocheno-German exist side by side with songs in Italian and German. The three coexisting languages are associated with three different musical styles, the most archaic of which appears to correspond to the native vernacular. In other Germanic enclaves of northern Italy (such as Vicenza and Verona), songs in the local vernacular also survive. In the far south, songs in Greek and Albanian have been documented; they constitute a case of marginal survival, since in some instances the singers no longer understood the original significance of the words.

POPULAR MUSIC

In the late Middle Ages and Renaissance, art music imitated traditional models. Some sixteenth-century madrigals and frottola melodies bear a strong resemblance to those still sung in oral tradition by poet-singers who improvise lyric songs (Laki 1990). In the 1800s, the amount of art music patterned after traditional melodic types was small, whereas tunes belonging to the literate tradition were accepted and transformed in the oral environment: in Italy, where the phrase *art music* normally refers to opera, arias are heard in the villages.

Popular music in the 1800s

It is hard to imagine the extent to which opera was a popular form of entertainment during the 1800s, and how widely it was disseminated through actual productions, transcriptions for brass bands and many other ensembles, itinerant groups of various sorts, and carillons and mechanical musical devices. Small villages that never had an operatic season saw the occasional production of works which had been successful in the large operatic centers. Such provincial productions helped reduce the distance that normally exists between urban music and rural music.

In Italy, brass bands were an important link between art and folk music. Though Italy is the land of bel canto, a country where people sing rather than play musical instruments, brass bands have been extremely popular since before the 1890s, and most villages have a civic band (*banda comunale*). Bands traditionally performed an operatic repertoire: a cornet substituted for the female voices, and a trombone or a fluegelhorn for the male singers. Wagner's operas were first heard in Rome through the band transcriptions of Alessandro Vessella. Most Italian popular music, at least until World War II, was a by-product of opera, rather than an adaptation of folk material.

Operatic tunes were also disseminated by itinerant ensembles, such as *Viggianesi* (from the town of Viggiano, in southern Basilicata), which traveled across Italy, Europe, and Turkey during the 1800s. The ensemble consisted of a diatonic harp, a viol or violin, and at times a transverse flute or clarinet. A boy played the triangle and solicited alms (Leydi 1988).

Because earlier Italian scholars presumed extensive contact between the oral and literate traditions, they believed that folk songs had not survived in great numbers into the twentieth century; research since 1945 has proven that idea false. The "operatic atmosphere" was thought to have reached into the most remote corners of the countryside. In Ticino, the Italian-speaking canton of Switzerland, even liturgical texts are occasionally sung to operatic airs (Bianchi 1984). At times, Italian traditional music shows the effect of contact with opera and with the popular-song tradition, a subsidiary stream of opera in the 1800s. Tunes from famous and obscure works—including those of Mercadante, Meyerbeer, Donizetti, and Verdi—occasionally filtered into the oral tradition (Sorce Keller 1990). In some instances, the tunes diverge little from the original. Nonnarrative drinking songs in the north have a melodramatic effect, and the melodic contour, delivered with an emphatic and rhetorical operatic vocal quality, recalls Verdi's "*Deh, libiam nei lieti calici*" and Mascagni's "*Viva il vino spumeggiante.*"

Neapolitan song, whose origins go back to at least the 1100s, has been nourished by oral and literate traditions. Usually sung in a soft voice, with an intimate and sentimental sound quality, it is known to non-Italians through the renditions of tenors such as Caruso, Di Stefano, Pavarotti, and Domingo. By musically setting texts in the Neapolitan vernacular, numerous composers—including Orlando di Lasso, Leonardo Vinci, Alessandro Scarlatti, G. B. Pergolesi, and Giovanni Paisiello—contributed to the art and popular traditions of Naples. Many nineteenth-century composers—including Gaetano Donizetti (1797–1848) and Francesco Paolo Tosti (1846–1916), the latter perhaps the most popular of such composers—wrote Neapolitan songs that became internationally famous.

Two features identify the Neapolitan style. First, songs have two sections (narrative verse and repeated refrain), often in contrasting relative or parallel major and minor keys. Second, they use simple harmonies, with occasional Neapolitan sixths or diminished-seventh chords that, in nineteenth-century operas, evoked trite dramatic effects. Some Neapolitan songs are in an intentionally folklike style, which, despite the efforts of their authors, bears little resemblance to the actual sound of folk music anywhere in the peninsula. Examples are Tosti's *Canti popolari abbruzzesi* for vocal duet and the popular *Reginella campagnola* by Eldo Di Lazzaro (b. 1902). The tradition maintained its identity until the early 1950s, after which it fragmented into a variety of substreams and hybrids, among them "Neapolitan rock."

Popular music in the early twentieth century

Between 1918 and 1939, some influences from American jazz began to be felt in Italian popular song, though jazz itself was then virtually unknown in Italy. From 1922, when Mussolini assumed power, to the end of World War II, Italy was nearly closed off from external influence. Fascist policy favored *autarchia* (protectionism, in economic and cultural life), emphasized extreme nationalism, and idealized purity in language, music, and race. Between 1920 and 1925, when Stravinsky's *Les Noces,* Varèse's *Intégrales,* and Berg's *Wozzek* received their premieres, Italy produced provincial pieces such as *I cavalieri di Ekebu* by Riccardo Zandonai (1883–1944), *Belfagor* by Ottorino Respighi (1879–1936), and *Gli amanti sposi* by Ermanno Wolf-Ferrari (1876–1948).

Art and popular music escaped censorship to some degree, and the orally transmitted repertoires were virtually unknown at the time, except to a handful of folk-lorists. Popular musicians and arrangers traveled and met colleagues from other European countries and the Americas, and heard new musical idioms. For popular bands (a novelty in Italy at the time), Pippo Barzizza (b. 1902) published a manual of orchestration that contained tricks of the trade and clichés he had learned in his travels.

The effectiveness of the recording industry as a channel for disseminating music from overseas is hard to evaluate. Songs from abroad were occasionally reissued on 78-RPM disks, and though the public did not buy many of them, musicians had access to them. Alberto Rabagliati (1908–1974), for instance, spent four years in Hollywood, and returned home with a swinging quality in his voice—a quality that became his trademark. With Ernesto Lecuona (1896–1972), he worked in Paris, where he heard American and Latin American music. Gorni Kramer (b. 1913), Lelio Luttazzi (b. 1920), and other composers listened to the Voice of America, though Fascist and Nazi authorities prohibited it. Through these broadcasts, composers kept abreast of trends that affected the tunes they wrote for variety shows and the musical theater.

Three imported features contributed to Italian popular songs of the 1930s. First, melodic and harmonic elements borrowed from early jazz or blues were inserted into a context in which they do not seem to belong. Second, composers used occasional, more complex harmonies, like major chords with an added sixth, dominant-seventh chords with an added ninth, and dominant-seventh chords that do not resolve. Third, they employed the rhythms of Latin American ballroom dances like the beguine, the rumba, and the tango. Neapolitan songs enjoyed great popularity in Latin America, and during this period Italian composers began to write in a Latin American idiom. The Brazilian *modinha* and other genres share features such as the verse-and-refrain form, with its contrast of major and minor; and the *habanera* accompaniment (in 2/4 time with dotted eighth, sixteenth, and two eighths) was common in the Neapolitan repertoire. The syncopation of Latin American music is foreign to Italian style, but whenever Latin American music and jazz weave themselves into the fabric of Italian songs, the former merges naturally into the texture, and the latter stands out as foreign.

—Marcello Sorce Keller

Popular music in the second half of the twentieth century

In the 1950s and 1960s technological innovations, such as television, the juke box, and 45-RPM records, and an efflorescence of song festivals—the first and most famous is Festival di Sanremo—contributed to the discovery of new singers and the composition of new *canzone italiana* 'Italian song'. Influenced by rock and roll and rhythm and blues, a new generation of singers (*urlatori* 'shouters') added a more strident vocal quality and theatrical movements to the Italian popular style. The most famous singers of the period were Tony Dallara, Mina, and Domenico Modugno, whose "*Nel Blu Di Pinto Di Blu,*" also known as "*Volare,*" became a worldwide hit. Under the spell of the Beatles and the Rolling Stones, the soft-rock groups (*complessi*) Equipe 84, Dik Dik, Nomadi, and Giganti enjoyed considerable success.

New singers emerged in the late 1950s and early 1960s—the *cantautori* 'singer-songwriters' who combined the talents of singer, storyteller, and poet. Songs by Gino Paoli, Gianni Meccia, and Umberto Bindi were perceived as astonishingly innovative. Lucio Battisti, the representative of this movement in the late 1960s, combined a raucous vocal quality, slightly out-of-tune singing, fresh melodies, and the surreal lyrics of Mogol into memorable songs. In the 1970s, Francesco De Gregori, the most important *cantautor,* and the rock group Premiata Forneria Marconi used a new,

In the 1970s, Francesco De Gregori, the most important *cantautor,* and the rock group Premiata Forneria Marconi used a new, harsh musical style to express their concern with changing mores and the political and social unrest of the period, which included the terrorism of the Red Brigades, student riots, and the shooting of magistrates.

harsh musical style to express their concern with changing mores and the political and social unrest of the period, which included the terrorism of the Red Brigades, student riots, and the shooting of magistrates.

The 1980s introduced a variety of styles, some continuing to comment on the sociopolitical confusion, others turning to a more pensive, introverted mood: hard-rockers like Vasco Rossi; punk-rockers like Donatella Rettore; romantic balladeers like Eros Ramazzotti; folk-fusion revivalists like Teresa De Sio; intellectuals like Fiorella Mannoia; the funk orientation of Zucchero; and Pino Daniele's fusion of traditional Neapolitan song with rock, jazz, and blues. Daniele mixed Neapolitan and black musical styles and lyrics with English and Neapolitan dialect to create a parallelism between the conditions of African-Americans in the United States and those of the poor and alienated peoples of southern Italy.

In the 1990s a host of young artists, led by Jovanotti, appropriated rap and hip-hop to create pungent texts adapted to their interpersonal and sociopolitical concerns.

Various forms of popular and classical music, Italian and non-Italian, played on thousands of radio stations twenty-four hours a day, absorb the attention of most Italians. Though the consumption of music via electronic media has tended to drown out the face-to-face music making of rural traditions, religious life continues to provide important contexts for traditional singing and instrumental music. Interest in world beat is causing a revitalization of older instruments and their associated techniques.

—ROBERTO CATALANO and GIUSEPPINA COLICCI

HISTORY OF MUSICAL SCHOLARSHIP

Scholarly interest in Italian traditional music began around 1850 and developed as a by-product of scholarship dealing with what was termed, in the early years of philological ethnography, *letteratura* or *poesia popolare.* Such investigation, represented in the work of Niccolo Tommaseo (1973 [1841]), Alessandro D'Ancona (1878), and Costantino Nigra (1974 [1888]), was aimed not at studying the nature of oral tradition, but at revealing whatever sense of national identity lay in traditional peninsular repertoires.

After 1860, when Italy became a unified nation, politicians needed, as Massimo d'Azeglio said, "to *invent* the Italian people." To achieve this aim, the educational system taught the cultural history, language, and literature behind local dialects and customs. The literary content of folk songs, rather than the music, provided common ground for comparison. Only a handful of the major works dealing with oral poetry from about 1850 to about 1900 contain musical annotations or transcriptions (Busk 1977 [1887]; Nigra 1974 [1888]; Pitré 1891). Important contributions from this period appeared in two folklore journals: *Rivista Italiana delle Tradizioni Popolari* (founded in 1894) and *Lares* (founded in 1912 and running to 1943, when it interrupted publication because of World War II; it resumed publication in 1949). The emphasis on folk poetry over music, especially among those trained in folklore (*tradizioni popolari*), dominated scholarship until the early 1960s (Barbi 1939; Bronzini 1956; Santoli 1940). This emphasis continues to parallel ethnomusicological studies that began in the 1960s.

The earliest important studies of music were Mario Giulio Fara's work (1913, 1914) on the *launeddas,* a Sardinian clarinet; Alberto Favara's substantial collection of Sicilian music, published posthumously (1957), and Francesco Balilla Pratella's (1941) research on the music of Emilia Romagna. These scholars worked in isolation from developments in comparative musicology in Austria, Germany, and Hungary (Gizzarelli 1938).

Despite Italy's colonialist adventures in Ethiopia (1935–1941), researchers had little serious interest in African music (see, however, Barblan 1941), possibly because such episodes were short and came too late to leave deep traces on the mainland. An expedition to Uganda in the 1930s, organized by the Discoteca di Stato and sponsored by the Rockefeller Foundation, was disappointing, since the wax cylinders it produced did not survive long enough to be examined.

At the end of World War II, Italy still did not possess sound recordings of its traditional music; a few exceptions were made by Gavino Gabriel, Cesare Caravaglios, and Giorgio Nataletti between 1920 and 1930. On the initiative of Nataletti and Guido Razzi, the Centro Nazionale Studi di Musica Popolare (CNSMP) was established in Rome in 1948 (Centro Nazionale Studi di Musica Popolare 1963; Nataletti 1950) with the support of Italian Radio and Television (Radiotelevisione Italiana 1977) and the Accademia Nazionale di Santa Cecilia, where in 1940 Nataletti began to teach a course on Italian folk music. The CNSMP, concerned almost exclusively with the collection and preservation of oral repertoires in the Italian peninsula, sponsored several collecting trips, mainly to central and southern Italy. With Nataletti, Luigi Colacicchi, Ernesto de Martino, Alberto M. Cirese, Diego Carpitella, and others, it made large numbers of recordings (figure 11). Carpitella and Alan Lomax surveyed the entire peninsula in 1954 (Lomax 1955–1956; Lomax and Carpitella 1957a, 1957b). In 1956, the old Museo di etnografia italiana (founded in 1906)

FIGURE 11   Italian folk-song collector Diego Carpitella (1924–1990), with a peasant. Mammola, Calabria, July 1954. Courtesy of the Alan Lomax Collection, New York.

changed its name to Museo nazionale di arti e tradizioni popolari and began, under the coordination of Annabella Rossi, a collection of phonograph recordings. In 1962, also in Rome, the Discoteca di Stato, acting on a proposal by Anna Barone and Diego Carpitella, opened the Archivio etnico-linguistico-musicale, the largest and most accessible archive of its kind in the country.

In the 1950s, scholars worked intensively in central and southern Italy on the assumption, later proven wrong, that the industrialized north was no longer a reservoir of folklore. Prominent figures included Leo Levi, Ottavio Tiby (who continued the work of Favara in Sicily, with the collaboration of Marius Schneider, Paul Collaer, Claudie Marcel-Dubois, and Maguy Andral), Antonio Sanna, Pietro Sassu, Antonino Uccello, and Tullio Seppilli (Collaer 1980). Extensive research in northern Italy in the early 1960s under the impetus of the "folk-music revival" focused attention on rural and urban traditions (Leydi 1972). This revival created widespread interest in local traditions and inspired serious scholarship. Roberto Leydi was the driving force behind many expeditions, which became the training ground for his associates, many of whom later undertook field work on their own in Lombardy, Piedmont, and other areas.

Between 1973 and 1976, the Museo nazionale sponsored ethnomusicological investigation by Roberto de Simone in Campania, the area around Naples, where some believed orally transmitted repertoires no longer existed since Neapolitan popular song had been so thoroughly disseminated there (De Simone 1979).

From 1945 until about 1970, researchers devoted most of their efforts to documentary recordings. It was a productive period: the collected material created a detailed sound picture of Italian traditional music from the Alps to the Mediterranean islands. Between 1970 and 1980, the first two Italian professorships in ethnomusicology were established, with chairs held by Diego Carpitella at the University of Rome and Roberto Leydi at the University of Bologna. Stimulated by their work, younger scholars undertook research, mainly in their area of residence. These included Glauco Sanga, Italo Sordi, and Bruno Pianta (Lombardy); Marcello Conati and Tullia Magrini (Emilia Romagna); Amerigo Vigliermo (Piedmont); Edward Neill (Liguria); Sandro Biagiola (Molise and Campania); Roberta Tucci and Luigi Cinque (Calabria and Basilicata); and Leonardo Sole and Pietro Sassu (Sardinia). Their efforts documented the oral repertoires of the peninsula, and their recordings are readily available on commercial records and cassettes (on labels including Dischi del Sole, Vedette-Albatros, and Divergo).

By the 1990s, the folk-music collecting of the postwar years had not been matched by ethnomusicological studies of the material. The urge to record as many items as possible had come from scholars' fear that oral traditions were dying under the impact of social and economic changes (Leydi 1980). Now that local traditions have been documented in recordings made over a fifty-year period, a younger generation of scholars is more interested in developing theoretical studies of organology, oral transmission, the compositional process, performance practice, and musical change.

Slight attention has been devoted to the music of Italian immigrants in the United States (Bianco 1973; Chairetakis 1986a, 1986b, 1986c; Ramirez 1941; Sorce Keller 1986b) and Australia (Barwick 1987). In the 1980s, several Italian scholars began research on non-Italian and non-Western traditions (*Etnomusicologia italiana fuori casa* 1988). A few non-Italian scholars have dealt with the traditional music of Italy: Andreas Weis Bentzon, Bernard Lortat-Jacob, and Emil H. Lubej were attracted by the "exotic" sounds of Sardinia, an island whose music can be considered only marginally Italian [see SARDINIA].

The historical details of research in Italian traditional music are available from several sources (Balilla Pratella 1941; Carpitella 1960, 1973, 1974; Magrini 1982; Simeone 1978). A useful bibliography (Carriuolo 1974) can be supplemented by more recent contributions (Biagiola, Giuriati, and Macedonio 1983). Tucci (1982) provides an excellent listing of commercially available recordings, and the Associazione Italiana Museo Vivo (1973) publishes an inventory of sound sources. Leydi's 1973 collection of transcriptions with annotations contains an initial overview of the musical styles of the peninsula.

—MARCELLO SORCE KELLER

BIBLIOGRAPHY

Associazione Italiana Museo Vivo. 1973. *Inventario delle fonti sonore della musica di tradizione orale italiana*. Rome: Istituto Accademico.

Baldazzi, Gianfranco. 1989. *La Canzone Italiana del Novecento: da Piedigrotta al Festival di Sanremo, dal Caffè-Concerto all'Opera Rock, una Storia della Società Italiana Attraverso le sue Canzoni Più Belle e i Loro Grandi Interpreti, da Enrico Caruso a Eros Ramazotti*. Rome: Newton Compton.

Balilla Pratella, Francesco. 1941. *Le arti e le tradizioni popolari in Italia. Primo documentario per la storia dell'etnofonia in Italia*. Udine: Edizioni Idea.

Barbi, Michele. 1939. *Poesia popolare italiana: Studi e proposte*. Florence: Sansoni.

Barblan, Guglielmo. 1941. *Musiche e strumenti dell'Africa orientale italiana*. Naples: Edizioni della triennale d'oltremare.

Barwick, Linda. 1987. "Italian Traditional Music in Adelaide." *Australian Folklore* 1:44–66.

Biagiola, Sandro, Giovanni Giuriati, and Mauro Macedonio. 1983. "Primo contributo ad una bibliografia etnomusicologica italiana con esempi musicali." *Culture musicali* 3:121–180.

Bianco, Carla. 1973. *The Two Rosetos*. Bloomington: Indiana University Press.

Biella, Valter. 1985. *Ricerca sulla piva nel bergamasco*. Bologna: Dipartimento di Musica e Spettacolo, Università degli Studi di Bologna.

Borgna, Gianni. 1985. *Storia Della Canzone Italiana*. Rome: Laterza.

Bronzini, G. B. 1956. *La canzone epico-lirica nell'Italia centro-meridionale*. Rome: Signorelli.

Busk, R. Harriette. 1977 [1887]. *The Folk-Songs of Italy*. Musical examples by Giuseppe Pitré. New York: Arno.

Carpitella, Diego. 1960. "Rassegna bibliografica degli studi di etnomusicologia in Italia dal 1945 ad oggi." *Acta Musicologica* 23:77–113.

———. 1961. "Folk Music (Italian)." In *Grove's Dictionary of Music and Musicians: Supplementary Volume to the Fifth Edition*, ed. Eric Blom. London: Macmillan

———. 1973. "L'etnomusicologia in Italia." *Analecta musicologica* 12:23–38.

———. 1974. "Ethnomusicology in Italy." *Journal of the Folklore Institute* 11:82–98.

———. 1975. "Der Diaulos des Celestino." *Musikforschung* 18:422–428.

Carriuolo, R. Eugene. 1974. "Materials for the Study of Italian Folk Music." Ph.D. dissertation, Wesleyan University.

Centro Nazionale Studi di Musica Popolare. 1963. *Catalogo delle registrazioni 1948–1962*. Rome: Accademia Nazionale Santa Cecilia, RAI Radiotelevisione Italiana.

Cleopatra, Franco, and Mario Sarica. 1985. *Ricerche sul doppio flauto in Italia*. Università degli Studi di Bologna, Dipartimento di Musica e Spettacolo.

Collaer, Paul. 1980. *Musique traditionelle sicilienne*. Tervuren: Fonds Paul Collaer.

D'Ancona, Alessandro. 1878. *La poesia popolare italiana*. Leghorn: Giusti.

De Martino, Ernesto. 1958. *Morte e pianto rituale*. Turin: Boringhieri.

———. 1961. *La terra del rimorso*. Milan: Il Saggiatore.

De Simone, Roberto. 1979. *Canti e tradizioni popolari in Campania*. Rome: Lato Side Editori.

Etnomusicologia italiana fuori casa. 1988. *Culture musicali* 10–11 (1986–1987). Special issue. Florence: Usher.

Fara, Mario Giulio. 1913, 1914. "Su uno strumento musicale sardo." *Rivista musicale italiana* 20:763–791, 21:13–51.

Favara, Alberto. 1957. *Corpus di musiche popolari siciliane*. Edited by Ottavio Tiby. Palermo: Accademia di Scienze Lettere e Arti.

Ferand, Ernest T. 1939. "The Howling in Seconds of the Lombards." *Musical Quarterly* 25:313–324.

Fontana, Sesto. 1964. *Il maggio*. Florence: Leo S. Olschki.

Francello, Elvira. 1946. "The Maid Freed from the Gallows." *New York Folklore Quarterly* 2:139–140.

Germi, Linda. 1977. "Sugli strumenti musicali popolari in Italia." *Nuova Rivista Musicale Italiana* 11:58–76.

Giannattasio, Francesco. 1979. *L'organetto*. Rome: Bulzoni Editore.

Giuriati, Giovanni, ed. 1985. *Forme e comportamenti della musica folklorica italiana*. Milan: Unicopli.

Gizzarelli, E. Francis. 1938. "An Historical Survey of Italian Folk Song and a Critical Estimate of Modern Research." Ph.D. dissertation, Cornell University.

Guizzi, Febo. 1983. "Per la conoscenza, lo studio e la conservazione degli strumenti della musica popolare." *Culture musicali* 2:9–30.

Guizzi, Febo, and Roberto Leydi. 1983. "Alcune schede su strumenti popolari italiani." *Culture musicali* 2:100–306.

———. 1985. *Le zampogne in Italia.* Milan: Ricordi.

Hirdt, Willi. 1979. *Italienischer Baenkelsang.* Frankfurt am Main: Vittorio Klostermann.

Laki, Peter. 1990. "Arie da cantar ottave." Paper presented at the fifty-sixth annual meeting of the American Musicological Society, Oakland, California.

Lavena, Vincenza. 1986. *La zampogna nella Calabria settentrionale.* Università degli Studi di Bologna, Dipartimento di Musica e Spettacolo.

Leydi, Roberto. 1967. "Venti anni di ricerche sulla musica popolare in Italia." *Nuova Rivista Musicale Italiana* 1:785–788.

———, ed. 1972. *Il folk music revival.* Palermo: Flaccovio.

———. 1973. *I canti popolari italiani.* Milan: Mondadori.

———. 1977. "Appunti per lo studio della ballata popolare in Piemonte." *Ricerche musichali* 1:82–118.

———. 1980. "Italy, Folk Music." *The New Grove Dictionary of Music and Musicians.* Edited by Stanley Sadie. London: Macmillan.

———. 1988. "Diffusione e volgarizzazione." In *Storia dell'opera italiana,* ed. Lorenzo Bianconi e Giorgio Pestelli, 6:303–392. Turin: EDT Musica.

Lomax, Alan. 1955–1956. "Nuova ipotesi sul canto folcloristico italiano nel quadro della musica popolare mondiale." *Nuovi argomenti* 17–18:109–135.

———. 1968. *Folk Song Style and Culture.* Washington, D.C.: American Association for the Advancement of Science.

Magrini, Tullia. 1982. "Etnomusicologia." In *Vent'anni di musicologia in Italia,* ed. F. A. Gallo et al. *Acta Musicologica* 54(1–2):80–83.

———. 1985. *Forme della musica vocale e strumentale a Creta.* Milan: Ricordi.

———. 1986a. "Dolce lo mio Drudo." *Rivista Italiana di Musicologia* 21(2):215–235.

———. 1986b. *Canti d'amore e di sdegno.* Milan: Franco Angeli.

———. 1992. *Il maggio drammatico: una tradizione di teatro in musica.* Bologna: Analisi.

Magrini, Tullia, and Giuseppe Bellosi. 1982. *Vi do la buona sera: Studi sul canto popolare in Romagna: Il rapportor lirico.* Bologna: Editrice Clueb.

Mersenne, Marin. 1963 [1636–1637]. *Harmonie Universelle, contenant la théorie et la pratique de la musique.* Paris: Centre National de la Recherche Scientifique.

Nataletti, Giorgio. 1950. "Report." *Journal of the International Folk Music Council* 2:61–62.

Nigra, Costantino. 1974 [1888]. *Canti popolari del Piemonte.* Turin: Einaudi.

Pitré, Giuseppe. 1891. *Canti popolari siciliani.* Palermo: Carlo Clausen.

Radiotelevisione Italiana. 1977. *Documenti Sonori: Catalogo informativo delle registrazioni musicali originali.* Turin: Edizioni ERI Radiotelevisione Italiana.

Ramirez, Manuel D. 1941. "Italian Folklore from Tampa, Florida." *Southern Folklore Quarterly* 5:101–106.

Regnoni-Macera, Clara. 1964. "The Song of May." *Western Folklore* 23:23–26.

Santoli, Vittorio. 1940. *I canti popolari italiani. Ricerche e questioni.* Florence: Sansoni.

Simeone, William E. 1978. "Fascists and Folklorists in Italy." *Journal of American Folklore* 91:543–557.

Sorce Keller, Marcello. 1984. "Folk Music in Trentino: Oral Transmission and the Use of Vernacular Languages." *Ethnomusicology* 28:75–89.

———. 1986a. "Life of a Traditional Ballad in Oral Tradition and Choral Practice." *Ethnomusicology* 30:449–469.

———. 1986b. "European-American Music: Italian." *The New Grove Dictionary of American Music.* Edited by H. Wiley Hitchcock and Stanley Sadie. New York: Macmillan.

———. 1988. "Segmental Procedures in the Transmission of Folk Songs in Trentino." *Sonus* 8:37–45.

———. 1989. "Costantino Nigra and Ballad Scholarship: New Considerations Concerning the Relationship Between Northern-Italian and French Folk Ballads." Paper presented at the thirtieth conference of the International Council on Traditional Music, Schladming, Austria.

———. 1990. "'Gesunkenes Kulturgut' and Neapolitan Songs: Verdi, Donizetti, and the Folk and Popular Tradition." *Atti del XIV Congresso della Società Internazionale di Musicologia* (Turin) 3:401–405.

Staiti, Nico. 1988. "La formula di discanto di *Ruggiero.*" *Culture musicali* 12–14:47–79.

Tommaseo, Niccolo. 1973 [1841]. *Canti popolari toscani, corsi, illirici e greci.* Bologna: Forni.

Tucci, Roberta. 1982. "Discografia del folklore musicale italiano in microsolco (1955–1980)." *Culture musicali* 1:125–148.

Tucci, Roberta, and Antonello Ricci. 1985. "The Chitarra Battente in Calabria." *Galpin Society Journal* 38:78–105.

Weis Bentzon, Andreas Fridolin. 1969. *The Launeddas, A Sardinian Folk Instrument.* 2 vols. Acta Ethnomusicologica Danica, 1. Copenhagen: Akademsk Forlag.

AUDIOVISUAL RESOURCES

Biagiola, Sandro. 1979. *Calabria 2: venditori ambulanti*. Cetra SU 5002. LP disk.

Bianchi, Pietro. 1984. *Canti liturgici popolari nel Ticino*. Serie discografica 1. Berne: Societa Svizzera per le Tradizioni Popolari FM 84022. LP disk.

Carlio, Ludovico, Gino Carlio, Andrea Polo, and Santino Scotto. 1972. *Il trallalero genovese*. Vedette-Albatros VPA 8164. LP disk.

Carpitella, Diego, Pietro Sassu, and Leonardo Sole. 1973. *Musica Sarda*. Vedette-Albatros VPA 8150, 8151, 8152. 3 LP disks.

Chairetakis, Anna L. 1986a. *Chesta e la voci ca canuscite: Southern Italian Mountain Music*. Recorded in the Niagara Frontier Region. Global Village Music 675. LP disk.

———. 1986b. *La Baronessa di Carini: Sicilian Traditional Song and Music*. Recorded in the Niagara Frontier Region. Global Village Music 676–677. LP disk.

———. 1986c. *Cantate con noi: Choral and Popular Songs from Northern and South-Central Italy*. Recorded in the Niagara Frontier Region. Global Village Music 678. LP disk.

Guggino, Elsa. 1974. *Canti del lavoro*. Vedette-Albatros VPA 8206. LP disk. Reissued as *Work Songs, vol. 1 (Folk Music and Songs of Sicily)*, Lyrichord LLST 7333. LP disk.

La Brigata Petrolana. 1973. *Canti popolari dell'umbria: il vatoccu e altri canti tradizionali*. Vedette-Albatros VPA 8145. LP disk.

Leydi, Roberto. 1969a. *Italia vol. 1: i balli, gli strumenti, i canti religiosi*. Vedette-Albatros VPA 8082. LP disk.

———. 1969b. *Italia vol 2: la canzone narrativa, lo spettacolo popolare*. Vedette-Albatros VPA 8088. LP disk.

Leydi, Roberto, and Bruno Pianta. 1972. *La zampogna in italia e le launeddas*. Vedette-Albatros VPA 8149. LP disk.

Lomax, Alan, and Diego Carpitella. 1957a. *The Folk Music of Northern Italy. The Folk Music of Central Italy*. The Columbia World Library of Folk and Primitive Music, 15. Columbia KL 5173. LP disk.

———. 1957b. *The Folk Music of Southern Italy and the Islands*. The Columbia World Library of Folk and Primitive Music, 16. Columbia KL 5174. LP disk.

———. 1958. *Music and Song of Italy*. Tradition Records TLP 1030. LP disk.

Lomax, Alan, Diego Carpitella, and Carla Bianco. 1972a. *Italian Folk Music, vol. 1: Piedmont, Emelia, Lombardy*. Ethnic Folkways FE 4261. LP disk.

Lomax, Alan, Diego Carpitella, Carla Bianco, and Anna Lomax. 1972b. *Italian Folk Music, vol. 2: Naples, Campania*. Ethnic Folkways FE 4265. LP disk.

McNeish, James. 1965. *Sicily in Music and Song*. Argo ZFB 71. LP disk.

Pagliaro, Antonino, and Diego Carpitella. 1973. *Documenti dell'archivio etnico linguistico-musicale della Discoteca di Stato*. Presidenza del Consiglio dei Ministrei Ufficio della Proprieta Letterarra, Artistica, e Scientifica 2G3K P 19321–22, 19323–24, 19329–30. 3 LP disks.

Tucci, Roberta, and Carol Crivelli. 1979. *Calabria 1: strumenti*. Cetra SU 5001. LP disk.

Sardinia

Bernard Lortat-Jacob

Musical Styles and Instruments
Musical Aesthetics
History of Music and Scholarship

Sardinia, a 24,000-square-kilometer island off the west coast of the Italian peninsula, is culturally distinct from Italy. Some call it almost a continent. They point to the persistence of Sardinian (a non-Italian, neo-Latin language) at the expense of Italian and the current presence of a traditional Sardinian way of life, still going on despite technological upheavals. Sardinia's economy and culture, based mainly on sheepherding and secondarily on farming and raising cattle, solicits summer tourism, above all on the coasts. Moving toward a European standard of living, the 1.6 million Sardinians have sought neither a nostalgic "revival" nor cultural autonomy; rather, they affirm their identity through traditional culture, especially in the center of the island, where people practice music intensively in a largely communal society.

Sardinian music suffuses daily life, whether men singing in bars or families making music at *spuntini,* weekend picnics for large groups of people. Discussions, entertainment, and jokes involve music: male polyphony, dance music on a triple clarinet (*launeddas*) or a small diatonic accordion (*sonettu*), sung poetry, and musical games. Music is an integral part of religious celebrations, summer saints' days, and other village parties, notably the one organized under the auspices of the ex-Communist Party and known under the name of parties of unity. These parties always feature a *launeddas* or a *sonettu,* which require virtuosic performance; each village has a unique style, realized by a group of either professional or peasant musicians.

The cultural vitality evident in village styles has protected Sardinia from folklorization; however, since probably the 1970s, nearly every village has had its *gruppo folk*. Supported by the local village administration or a regional organization, these groups include some of the best local instrumentalists, singers, and dancers. Young people join these groups because they are invited to attend not only local festivals, but those in Italy and abroad. They solicit older people informally for their knowledge of songs and costumes.

Sardinian cities, especially Sassari in the north and Cagliari in the south, are cut off from rural traditions, and urban dwellers consume Italian and international pop music. Piero Marras and a few other popular artists sing in Sardinian, and some young musicians—-notably Angelo Branduardi and the groups Cordas a Cannas and Tazenda—-have tried to work elements of traditional music into their compositions.

MUSICAL STYLES AND INSTRUMENTS

Musical styles in Sardinia correspond approximately to three administrative provinces: Sassari (north), Nuoro (central), and Cagliari (south); a fourth province, Oristano (in the west), attained the status of a province after administrative reform in the late 1970s. The mountainous center, which the Romans named Barbagia (after the Latin *barbaria* 'foreign country'), is home to secular vocal polyphony, known as *a tenore*, and the *sonettu*, used exclusively for dance music. In the north, religious polyphony sung by brotherhoods (groups of men who serve the Roman Catholic Church) and *canto a chiterra* 'guitar-accompanied song' are characteristic. The south has the *launeddas* and the large chromatic accordion (*fisarmonica*). The most common dance, *ballu*, plays an important role everywhere, except in some villages in Sassari, notably Anglona. Local variations confound these generalizations: the drum-and-flute combination, for example, occurs in the village of Gavoi in Barbagia; and rare instruments like the *serragia*, a bowed, one-stringed, stick zither with a pig-bladder resonator, serves as an instrument for carnival. Giovanni Dore (1976) described sixty Sardinian instruments, including an idioglot clarinet, wood and iron idiophones, different types of drums, mouth harps, and flutes, most of them unevenly distributed on the island.

Secular polyphony

Polyphonic singing *a tenore*, a common practice among amateurs (shepherds above all), occurs in Barbagia and eastern Sardinia (Baronia). Polyphony *a tenore* consists of a soloist, who sings the text while the others sing syllabic formulas in triadic harmony (figure 1). Standing or sitting close to one another, they place their hands against their ears—a common gesture in all the Mediterranean area, allowing singers better to hear their own voices (figure 2). The vocal technique of the two high-pitched voices (*boghe* 'voice' and *mesa boghe* 'high voice') has the tense, nasal quality of Mediterranean singing. The lowest-pitched voices (*contra* and *basu*) produce a forced, slightly nasal sound, whose audible overtones mix with the fundamentals of the other voices to produce a characteristic harmonic thickness. The traditional style differs from that of some modern choirs, which perform in a new fashion, doubling or tripling the voices and including harmonies not found in the original style.

TRACK-22   The *a tenore* repertory includes many genres with traditional texts: *boghe'e notte* or *a sa seria* (songs in slow tempo based on "serious" themes), *mutu* or *mutettu* (a poetic form, usually about love), *goso* (religious hymns), *anninnia* (cradle songs), and various dance songs. In addition, the three-person chorus, *su concordu*, can provide a simple accompaniment to poets' sung jousts (*gara poetica*).

Religious polyphony

Orally transmitted religious polyphony is nowadays concentrated in the northern Sassari Province (centered in the villages of the northwestern Castelsardo area) and around Oristani, particularly the villages of Santulussurgiu and Cuglieri. Brotherhoods (*confraternite*), each acting as a *schola cantorum* of the oral tradition (Carpitella et al. 1973), preserve and teach songs at rehearsals in their chapel. They perform them in church and during processions for funerals (at Castelsardo) and feasts of the Roman Catholic calendar. Like the *a tenore*, religious polyphony consists of four voices (rarely five, as in Aggius in Sassari Province) in triadic harmonies. But these voices have a different timbre, and the harmonic system permits unprepared modulations. From bass to treble, the four parts are *bassu*, *contra* (often a fifth above the bass), *bogi* 'voice' (usually an octave above the bass), and *falzittu* (a third above the *bogi*), which, despite the name, is not sung in falsetto. The polyphony exploits

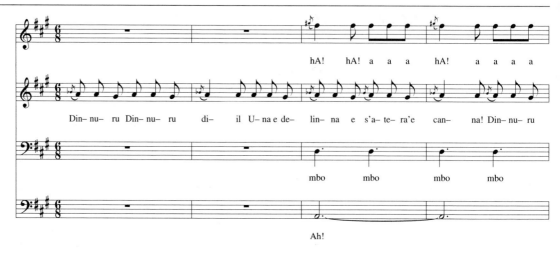

FIGURE 1 A song
a tenore. After
Fara 1940:157.

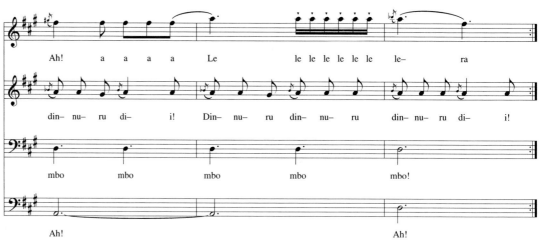

modulations, ornaments, and ritardandi. The texts are religious verses, such as *Miserere* (Psalm 51, or 50 in the Roman Catholic Bible) and *Stabat Mater* (a medieval poem with numerous polyphonic settings), which develop over long, slow, semimeasured phrases.

FIGURE 2 Three of the four men who sing traditional four-part polyphony (*a tenore*). Two hold their hands to their ears. This gesture allows them to hear their own voice better and is common in cultures around the Mediterranean. Photo by Bernard Lortat-Jacob.

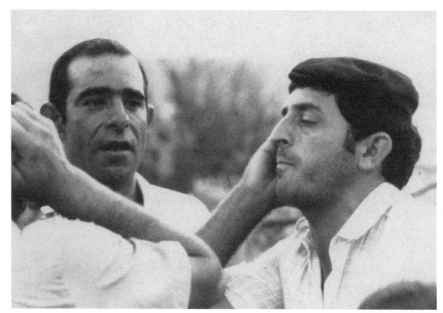

FIGURE 3 Excerpt from "*Canarinu avventuradu*" ('Adventurous Canary'), a guitar-accompanied song in D. After a picked introduction and a strummed transition, the first singer enters. Roman numerals denote chords, strummed rhythmically as notated. Transcription by Bernard Lortat-Jacob.

Guitar-accompanied song

The genre known as guitar-accompanied song (*canto a chiterra*) may have originated in the north around Logudoro and Anglona, perhaps through Spanish influence, but is common throughout the island. The accompaniment originally consisted of two chords, but since the 1960s has used additional chords. The singer leads the musical interaction by inviting the guitarist to follow and harmonize an improvised, melismatic melody.

The *canto a chiterra* is performed by amateurs in bars, at *spuntini*, and, more formally, on festival stages by professional singers and guitarists. The competition (*gara*) between singers—usually men, but women can compete—lasts about three hours and consists of many different poetic and melodic structures. Each song is named after either the place where it originated (*Nuorese* 'from Nuori'; *Tempiesina* 'from Tempio') or its melodic and harmonic features (*canto in re* 'song in D'; *mi e la* '[song in] E and A').

Figure 3 is an excerpt from a guitar-accompanied song in D (*canto in re*), recorded in a bar in Irgoli, Nuoro, in 1979. A song in D always uses paired couplets of eight-syllable lines, rhyming *abab*. Other genres use couplets of eleven-syllable lines (Cirese 1977, 1988). In a typical performance, one singer sings two lines twice, another sings two more twice, a third sings two more twice, and so on, making a slowly unfolding chain of couplets:

Of Sardinia's musical instruments, the triple clarinet (*launeddas*) is perhaps most important to Sardinians, because it serves as a symbol of local culture.

FIGURE 4   Giovanni Mele, from Cabras, Oristano Province, plays a *launeddas*. Weis Bentzon 1969.

Singer 1.	Canarinu avventuradu	Adventurous canary
	De s'ermosa Flora mia	of my beautiful Flora
Singer 2.	Bella e'sa serenada	How beautiful is your serenade
	Fisarmonica e chiterra	to the accordion and guitar
Singer 3.	Rosa, naschida in levante	Rose, born in the Levant
	In d'una istaione bella	during the beautiful season

Each singer tries to surpass his rival or rivals with surprising and original melodic microvariations. In guitar-accompanied songs, most of the texts have a written source (as of published poems). In *a tenore* songs, the texts mostly come out of oral tradition, and it is not uncommon that the singers themselves are the authors.

Launeddas

Of Sardinia's musical instruments, the triple clarinet (*launeddas*) is perhaps most important to Sardinians, because it serves as a symbol of local culture (figure 4). One drone (*tumbu*) and two melody pipes (*mankosedda* and *mankosa*), each with a single reed, are constructed out of cane and uniquely tuned. The player inhales through the nose while squeezing air from his cheeks—a process called circular breathing. A few professional musicians, each with his own repertory, perform in villages in the south; the most highly valued musicians have a large repertory. The *launeddas* accompanies processions and sometimes singing, but its chief role is to accompany dance, traditionally performed in the village square. To play dance music for long periods, musicians develop themes and improvise variations.

A *launeddas* composition (*sonata*) realizes thematic formulas partly corresponding to the figures of the dance. Some pieces contain more than thirty memorized formulas. Called *nodas* or *pikkiadas* (terms that first appear in Oneto 1841), they have been transmitted from one generation to another and, insofar as the music of *launeddas* benefits from formalized learning, from master to pupil. The music is not always improvised, but each musician may insert personal, but thematically related, variations (*passeggius*).

Dance-music

A developed tradition of sung dances, performed polyphonically or with guitar accompaniment, exists in the center and south of the island. The two main types of dancing, *ballu* and *danza*, include two basic choreographic steps: a slide (often called *a passu* or *a passu seriu*) and a jump (*trincada* or *brincada*). In manner of performance, tempo, and melodic formulas, both genres (also accompanied by *sonettu*, *fisarmonica*, or *launeddas*) differ from place to place. The *ballu*, called *ballu tundu* when it is danced in a circle, is a chain dance, with arms joined one over the other in an

FIGURE 5   A *ballu* accompanied by a *sonettu* (Oliena, Nuoro Province). Photo by Bernard Lortat-Jacob.

FIGURE 6   The basic rhythm of the *danza*. Transcription by Bernard Lortat-Jacob.

interwoven pattern (figure 5). It features the rhythmic pattern of two eighth notes followed by two quarter notes. The accented first and third beats correspond to steps. The *danza*, a couple dance of some virtuosity, takes many forms rhythmically related to the dance. The *passu torrau* is based on a six-note rhythmic pattern (figure 6).

MUSICAL AESTHETICS

Sardinian genres and local styles resist a simple musical analysis. The Sardinian ethnomusicologist Pietro Sassu reduced the musical scales to a simple trichord covering a major third, found in women's genres, such as funeral laments (largely obsolete), lullabies, and *duru-duru* (infant-dandling songs). The more modern repertoire, and especially dance music, first added a major third above and later a minor third below this nucleus. In every song, the importance of the major third is evident, but pentachordal structure is always affirmed with conjunct melodic movement.

Sardinian music is a microsystem in which "musical sounds correspond to some extremely limited choices" (Carpitella et al. 1973:9): a few rhythmic figures with displaced accents, algorhythmic transformations of small amounts of poetic and musical material, changes in the vocal coloration of identical harmonic patterns, plays with assonance in women's monophonic songs, and small modifications of melodic cells and phrases in dance music for *launeddas* or accordion. Regulated by an economy of means and unity at the smallest level of detail, Sardinian music continues to evolve, without academic influence.

HISTORY OF MUSIC AND SCHOLARSHIP

The first evidence of music in Sardinia comes from its bronze age (fifteenth to sixth centuries B.C.) in the form of small bronze statues (*bronzetti*). One, dated from the eighth or seventh century B.C. and stored in the Cagliari Museum, represents a nude musician with an erect penis, playing a double or triple flute or clarinet, the ancestor of the *launeddas*. Phoenicians, Arabs, Latins (from Rome, Pisa, and Genoa), and, from the 1300s to the 1700s, Spaniards from Aragon successively occupied Sardinia, militarily or administratively. In 1861, the Kingdom of Italy annexed it, and it became an autonomous region in 1948. Sardinia's musical history rests largely on oral tradition, and therefore little is known of it.

Matteo Madau (1792), a priest, provides the first references to four-part folk polyphony and musical instruments. Travelers' accounts in the late 1700s and early 1800s (notably La Marmora 1826) include descriptions of funeral music and ceremonies, with information on the location of *launeddas.* Nicolò Oneto's *Memoria sopra le cose musicali di Sardegna* (1841) commented on the *launeddas* and its typology; the *cetera,* a type of lute no longer in use; four-part polyphony in Campidano; the harmonic and melodic system; and instrumentalists' techniques of melodic variation. Auguste Bouiller (1916), Gavino Gabriel (1923), and Giulio Fara (1940) made the first precise musical notations of Sardinian songs accompanied by guitar, and Fara transcribed a polyphonic, polyrhythmic dance-song (*a tenore*), including ornamentation (figure 1). Clara Gallini (1967) described *argia,* the spider-poisoning ritual [see ITALY], the Danish scholar Andreas Weis Bentzon (1969) published an excellent monograph on the *launeddas,* and Diego Carpitella, Pietro Sassu, and Leonardo Sole (1973) compiled and annotated a three-record album of Sardinian music.

—TRANSLATED BY JOHN MORGAN O'CONNELL

BIBLIOGRAPHY

Bouiller, Auguste. 1916. *Canti popolari della Sardegna.* Bologna: Multigrafica Editrice.

Caria, Clemente. 1981. *Canto sacro-popolare in Sardegna.* Oristano: Edizione S'alvure.

Carpitella, Diego. 1961. "Folk Music (Italian)." *Grove's Dictionary of Music and Musicians: Supplementary Volume to the Fifth Edition,* ed. Eric Blom. London: Macmillan.

———. 1973. *Musica e tradizione orale.* Palermo: Flaccorio.

Catalano, Roberto. 1995. "Sonu de Canna: The Revitalization of Sas Enas, a Sardinian Cane Clarinet." M.A. thesis, University of California at Los Angeles.

Cirese, Alberto Mario. 1977. *Struttura e origine morfologica dei mutettus sardi e alcune questioni terminologiche in materia di poesia popolare sarda: mutu, muttetu, battorina, taja.* Cagliari: Edizione 3T.

———. 1988. *Ragioni metriche.* Palermo: Sellerio.

Dore, Giovanni. 1976. *Gli instrumenti della musica popolare della Sardegna.* Cagliari: Edizione 3T.

Fara, Giulio. 1913. "Su uno strumento musicale sardo." *Rivista musicale italiana* 20:763–791.

———. 1940. *L'anima della Sardegna: La musica tradizionale.* Udine: Istituto delle edizioni accademiche.

Gabriel, Gavino. 1923. *Canti di Sardegna.* Milan: G. Ricordi.

———. 1936. "Musica: Sardegna." *Enciclopedia italiana* 30:861–865.

Gallini, Clara. 1967. *I rituali dell'argia.* Padua: CEDAM.

La Marmora, Alberto. 1826. *Voyage en Sardaigne de 1819 à 1825.* Paris: Delaforest.

Lortat-Jacob, Bernard. 1981. "Community Music and the Rise of Professionalism, a Sardinian Example." *Ethnomusicology* 24(2):185–197.

———. 1982. "Improvisation et modèle: le chant à guitare sarde." *L'Homme* 24(1):65–89. With disc enclosed.

———. 1990. "Pouvoir la chanter, savoir en parler: chants de la Passion en Sardaigne." *Cahiers de musiques traditionnelles* 3:5–22.

———. 1993. "En accord, polyphonies de Sardaigne: quatre voix qui n'en font qu'une." *Cahiers de musiques traditionnelles* 6:69–86.

———. 1994. *Sardinian Chronicles.* Chicago: University of Chicago Press.

———. 1996. *Canti di Passione, Castelsardo, Sardegna.* Lucca: Libreria Musicala italiana. Translated into French under the title *Chants de Passion.* Paris: Éditions du cerf, 1998.

Madau, Matteo. 1792. *Dissertazioni storiche apologetiche critiche della sarda antichità.* Cagliari: Nella Reale Stamperia.

Oneto, Nicolò. 1841. *Memoria sopre le cose musicali di Sardegna.* Cagliari: n.p.

Weis Bentzon, Andreas-Fridolin. 1969. *The Launeddas, A Sardinian Folk Instrument.* 2 vols. Acta Ethnomusicologica Danica, 1. Copenhagen: Akademisk Forlag.

AUDIOVISUAL RESOURCES

Carpitella, Diego, Pietro Sassu, and Leonardo Sole. 1973. *Musica Sarda* (Music of Sardinia). Albatros VPA 8150, 8151, 8152. 3 LP disks, 49-page booklet.

Giannattasio, Francesco, and Bernard Lortat-Jacob. 1982. *Sardegna 1, Organetto.* Collection "I Suoni." Cetra SU 5007. LP disk, 24-page booklet.

Lortat-Jacob, Bernard. 1981. *Polyphonies de Sardaigne.* Collection CNRS/Musée de l'Homme. Le Chant du Monde LDX 74760. LP disk. Reissued (1991) as LDX 274760. Compact disc.

———. 1984. *Sardaigne, Launeddas.* Collection Ocora. Radio-France 558611. LP disk.

———. 1992. *Sardaigne, Polyphonies de la Semaine Sainte.* CNRS/Musée de l'Homme, Le Chant du Monde LDX CD 274936. Compact disc.

Lortat-Jacob, Bernard, and Georges Luneau. 1990. *Musica Sarda.* Paris: Tara Production et la Sept. 70 min., color. Video.

Malta

L. JaFran Jones

Traditional Genres of Song
Contexts for Musical Performance
Musical Instruments
Gender and Music
Dance
Western Art Music

Malta, an insular republic, occupies a strategic midpoint of the Mediterranean Sea between Sicily and North Africa. It has three inhabited islands: Malta, Gozo (Ghawdex), and Comino (Kemmuna), with a total area of 320 square kilometers, about the size of the city of Munich. Malta has a large, deep, sheltered harbor, the key to its importance throughout Mediterranean history, and the magnet that has attracted foreign domination.

Of a population numbering about 350,000, slightly over half is concentrated in the capital, Valleta, and in the conurbation around Grand Harbor. Smaller and rural, Gozo and Comino have about twenty-five thousand inhabitants. Many Maltese live and work abroad, chiefly in Australia, the United States, Canada, and Britain. From a wholly client economy under foreign domination, autonomous Malta has the task of forging economic independence. Efforts in this direction have enjoyed mixed success but have reverberated with changes throughout the sociocultural fabric, creating a nation in transition.

The Maltese people have led a shadowy existence, obscured by the strategic importance of their islands and the succession of powerful nations that have dominated them. Scarcely noticed by outsiders, their culture has survived, though under-appreciated and only marginally acknowledged, even by many Maltese.

Archaeology dates human habitation of the islands from 4000 B.C., but no archaeological evidence of music has been reported. Malta first appeared in history as Melita, a *municipium* of the Roman Empire, under the administration of Sicily. For modern Maltese, the most important event of the Roman era was St. Paul's legendary shipwreck on Melita, from which local people date their Christianity. By 870, Malta was absorbed into the empire of Islam, expanding from Arabia and Africa. It was reconquered in 1090 by Christian Normans. Arab-African and Islamic hegemony, though temporary, gave Malta a unique language and has provided a pretext for wistful assertions about the supposed origins of Maltese music.

The period of nominal rule from Aragón (1283–1530) established Spanish roots for Maltese music. The islands' destiny took a major turn in 1530, when Charles V bestowed on them the religious military order of the Knights of St. John of Jerusalem, Hospitaler. The knights' rule, marginally longer than that of the North

Africans, indelibly marked the islands. The demography underwent significant transformations during these centuries, through decimation by pirates and plagues, repopulation (chiefly from Sicily), and the influx of Muslim slaves. Poorly documented, these changes make it difficult to determine what relation modern Maltese may have to their medieval ancestors.

At the Great Siege of 1565, the Maltese and their masters repelled a formidable Ottoman army, but success was otherwise rare in encounters with Turks and pirates. Frequent raids on defenseless Maltese villages brought tragedy to many families. These disasters bore fruit, however, in the minds of local bards, giving Malta a poignant corpus of ballads, some of which are still sung. The knights left Malta ingloriously after defeat in 1798 by Napoleon's army, which in turn promptly bowed to British occupation. Malta became independent in 1964, and the British military departed in 1979.

The most striking feature of Maltese culture is its language, a variety of North African Arabic with several apparently eastern Arabic features and many Italian and English loanwords. The Arabic component is more prominent in the language of poets and singers than in that of the educated—leading in part to a subtle stigma attached to folk song. Without diminishing the authenticity of local Roman Catholicism, the Maltese worship an Arabic-named God (Alla) and observe an Arabic-named Lent (Randan). Virtually all customs that invite folklorists' attention—including secular song sessions held in bars on Sunday mornings—have a religious pretext. Current Maltese culture, however, is leaving the religious domain increasingly behind: there is no dearth of exposure to mainstream media and trends in Europe and beyond, and the people have little will to oppose these in defense of traditional culture.

TRADITIONAL GENRES OF SONG

Traditional Maltese music is predominantly vocal, with a limited melodic repertoire and strong emphasis on textual content. Singers typically improvise their words without preparation, but traditional texts have some use, as in the case of ballads. In keeping with the preference for improvisation, there is little tradition of choral singing. Strictly solo performance is also uncommon.

The normal context for singing is an antiphonal dialogue between two or more singers, with or without guitar accompaniment. Public singing is chiefly the domain of men, though in principle women are not excluded.

Ghana

Ghana 'song' serves the Maltese as a generic name for their traditional music; it is restricted to forms that are perceived as authentically Maltese. Other varieties of traditional music considered imported or imitative of foreign models, however remote their naturalization and however integral their function in folklife, receive other names. The clear affiliation of *ghana* with the Arabic *ghinā'* 'song' need not support any assumptions about the origins of the genre. *Ghana* has unique musical features, but fits comfortably within the European music system.

Though generally acknowledged as quintessential Maltese music, *ghana* does not enjoy the unreserved affection of all Maltese. Attitudes toward it may coincide with long-standing class divisions in Maltese society and may provide a gauge to Maltese problems of ethnic identity. Only less well-off, less educated, working people appreciate the genre wholeheartedly. Affluent, educated, professional Maltese tend to treat it condescendingly or with contempt, using tags like *gharbi* 'Arab' to express their distaste. In liberal intellectual circles, it is fashionable to accord *ghana* respect but not to admit genuinely liking it.

FIGURE 1   The
underlying *spirtu
pront* melody, which
varies widely with
each repetition.
Transcription by
L. JaFran Jones.

Repartee singing: spirtu pront

The most robust and accessible sort of Maltese singing is described as *ghana ta' spirtu pront* 'quick-witted song'. This is a cluster of similar types of improvised witty repartee (*botta u risposta*), dialogue singing between two or more individuals, which uses rhymed quatrains and a single underlying melody. In performance, an even number of singers in alternating pairs takes turns through several rounds, improvising four-line stanzas rhyming *abcb* in response to their respective partners. Two or three accompanying guitars play stanza-length, partly improvised interludes between singers. A set ends with an eight-line cadence (*gadenza*), a stanza set to a modified, extended form of the melody, usually without a guitar interlude. There is normally a guitar prelude and postlude.

Repartee singing probably realizes a single underlying melody (figure 1). That a single melody is involved has not been proven through musical analysis, but it appears to reflect the perceptions of Maltese and foreign hearers. The origin of the melody is unidentified, but echoes of it abound in southern Italy. Other musical and nonmusical details prove more fruitful for those prone to seek the exotic: vocal timbre, melisma, certain gestures, and the language suggest possible Middle Eastern or North African origins.

In principle, singers improvise the melody and the text in each stanza. In practice, the range of melodic variability is narrow. Each singer has a signature version of the core melody, by which aficionados may easily recognize him. He does not reproduce it identically each time (as only an unimaginative rote singer would), but his improvisational departures are limited, cued perhaps by rhetorical intentions or audience response. Most singers (and guitarists) prefer the key of A major. Melisma is minimal, except in the second line and the virtuosity of a few singers. Microtonal intervals occur but can hardly be considered systematic. Delivery is typically loud, in the higher reaches of a singer's register, but not falsetto, and with conscious aim at the comprehensibility of the words over musical considerations.

Words are clearly at the heart of *spirtu pront,* composed in metered, rhymed verse at the moment of singing. It is the witty repartee, the clever rhyme, the delicate double entendre, the well-poised metaphor, the two-edged compliment, the playful innuendo, the graceful parry, with virtuosic adherence to canons of etiquette, rhetoric, and poetic form, that singers strive to cultivate, earning connoisseurs' approval. A singer must be attentive to his listeners' musical expectations, but it is proverbial that a sweet voice is no substitute for quick-witted verse.

Spirtu pront uses the eight-syllable quatrains that pervade *ghana* and are common in folk poetry throughout the Mediterranean [see CORSICA]. The intended meter is trochaic, corresponding to the melody's rhythm, which calls for stanzas of 8–7–8–7 syllables. In practice, the singer-poet appears to aim at four stressed syllables per line, with at least one weak syllable between stresses. Metrical circumspection ranks below wit, originality, and rhyme, possibly also below musical pitch, and singers take considerable license. A singer must meet more exacting expectations for rhyme, a touchstone of his craft; indeed, the art is also called rhyming (*taqbil*). Lines two and four of each stanza must rhyme according to accepted canons, which involve more than phonetic rules. Singers must avoid facile, conventional rhymes and seek those that give their verses an unexpected, wily twist. They must stay with the established subject and respond promptly to their interlocutors. Errors are not overlooked, and repetition is shunned. Singers are not necessarily illiterate. Their tradition is oral, however, and their techniques of composing or improvising are independent of literacy. Few singers and guitarists have had formal training in music, or can read musical notation.

Antiquated songs: bormliza

Bormliza (of Bormla, a town) is a loose term for types of improvised and partly improvised *ghana* that share certain vocal features and the fact that they have fallen into disuse. Older people still occasionally sing *bormliza,* but the genre is no longer appreciated or programmed at events that feature *ghana.* Assertions of its antiquity, or millennial descent from North African occupation, rely chiefly on presumption or prejudice. *Bormliza* could be a relic of a formerly more prevalent song style; or it could reflect influence from other regions of the Mediterranean and be a recent fashion, initiated, as some informants believe, by a singer from Bormla "years ago," and now out of vogue.

Though dated, *bormliza* merits attention, since it blossomed in *ghana* milieux, yet displays a facet of Maltese music not obviously discernible in other genres. The voice is forced and tense, but not nasal. Melodic lines are long, with abundant melismas and falling contours. Unusual melodic intervals that occur in melismas have not been evaluated sufficiently to resolve questions of possibly non-Western modal substrata.

Textual units, improvised or not, are short: one or two lines, usually similar to eight-syllable *ghana* lines. Contrary to the syllabic clarity of the delivery of *spirtu pront,* words are stretched and distorted across long ornamental passages, virtually incomprehensible to any but the initiated. This feature is most often cited, with the genre's supposed difficulty, as reason for the lack of interest in keeping *bormliza* alive.

Ballads: fatt

The oldest documented traditional Maltese song is the ballad (*fatt* 'fact, true story') "*Il-Gharusa ta' Mosta*" ('The Bride of Mosta'), traceable to events in the 1500s and still sung. *Ghana tall-fatt* stands out as the leading nonimprovised form of *ghana.* Its melody ranks with those of *spirtu pront* and il-Maltija, the national dance, as a signature tune of Maltese music. The ballad tradition, as yet sparsely studied, is a chronicle of Maltese history from the people's viewpoint. Literacy and the mass media are usurping its practical function, transforming it from a productive medium into a museum piece.

Traditionally every serious, significant event called for the composition of a ballad: natural disasters, accidents, wars, notorious crimes, and eminent personal tragedies were its domain. The ruthless raids of Barbary pirates on defenseless Maltese villages provided fertile material for the oldest and best remembered examples. A ballad is expected to be solemn, poignant, detailed, and scrupulously factual.

A repertoire of several major- and minor-mode melodies is claimed for the genre, but only one melody (figure 2), always minor, counts as the archetype. Standard variations exist for lighter ballads, and as with *spirtu pront,* each singer has his own version, which does not stray far from the basic melody and remains constant from stanza to stanza. Many Maltese guitar pieces, whatever their title, are elaborations of this melody, which can be heard in southern Italy, where it may have originated. Particularly apt for ballads, it has been appropriated by non-Maltese artists, including Fairouz, a popular Lebanese singer.

In the 1960s and 1970s, *ghana* gained a broader audience and were exceptionally lively. Song sessions were frequent and animated, piqued rivalries between factions of singers emerged, and aficionados (*dilettanti*) abounded. Leading singers and guitarists enjoyed a brief windfall of popularity and modest profit, with a taste of stardom for a few.

FIGURE 2   A minor-mode melody for the ballad form, *fatt*. Transcription by L. JaFran Jones.

A ballad requires a different setting and a differently disposed audience from those of *spirtu pront*. It is sung by one man, without chorus or respondent, but with guitar accompaniment as in *spirtu pront,* including interludes between stanzas. Delivery is in the singer's normal register, syllabic, without marked melisma, but with attention to textual intelligibility.

Other genres

Genres outside *ghana* include lullabies, children's songs, festive songs, work songs and marine songs, laments and keens, and religious songs and hymns. Scant research is available on these subjects, with virtually no reliable musical data; it is not known how much of this repertoire remains alive. A substantial part has succumbed to mass-media pressure, as witnessed in Christmas songs, most of which are simply translations from famous European and American versions, including those referencing weather that never occurs in Malta. Folkloric troupes perform song-and-dance routines labeled traditional. Given the paucity of data, their claim to authenticity is implausible. Likely adaptations of foreign material in local garb, they may utilize melodies gleaned from folk-flavored works of Maltese composers.

The Maltese mingle music with most religious and solemn observances; they have hymns and special songs for festive processions and sacramental ceremonies. The extent and provenance of this repertoire have not been assessed. Guitars may be used in church, and folk Masses are not uncommon in some parishes. *Ghana* is excluded. The national anthem, "*Lil din l-Art Helwa,*" uses verses by Dun Karm Psaila, Malta's first great poet, with music by Robert Samut, M.D., with no apparent connection to folk song.

The *kanzunetta* 'popular song' and the *makkjetta* 'comic sketch' (sometimes employing spoken segments) bridge folk and pop. Light vignettes, these are products of *ghana* singers at play. They enjoy a wide audience and account for the stardom some singers achieved during the 1960s and 1970s. They typically adapt *ghana* melodies and exploit other conventions of the genre but are not dignified with the title of *ghana,* though they are frequently composed and performed by leading singers of *spirtu pront*. *Ghana* remains a serious, cerebral art, however jocular and unbuttoned it may wax.

CONTEXTS FOR MUSICAL PERFORMANCE

In the 1960s and 1970s, independence and an accelerated expansion of tourism brought a surge of national consciousness, which lavished attention on local folk arts, even reviving musical genres and instruments that had lapsed into disuse. During this period, *ghana* gained a broader audience and were exceptionally lively. Song sessions were frequent and animated, piqued rivalries between factions of singers emerged, and aficionados (*dilettanti*) abounded. Leading singers and guitarists enjoyed a brief windfall of popularity and modest profit, with a taste of stardom for a few. One singer (*ghannej*) had a hit that reached the top of the local charts, and several others cashed in with similar recordings. By the 1980s, the wave of euphoria had run its course, a less optimistic calm had settled over many areas of Maltese life (including the popular arts), and *ghana* had retreated to the shadows. In the late 1990s, however, *spirtu pront* was alive, if less ostentatiously than in its halcyon days.

The standard venue for singing is bars. There are regular weekly sessions, typically on Sunday mornings, always in the same bars and with regular groups of friends, including singers, guitarists, aficionados, and learners. The spirit is social, recreational, amicable, with ample consideration for novices anxious to learn and old-timers wanting to keep in form or savor past glories. Somewhat more serious sessions are organized ad hoc on weeknights.

Gatherings in bars usually consist of one or two one-hour sets by established singers and guitarists, with considerable practicing before and after by less-experienced aspirants. Tape recorders are required. The *spirtu pront* set, called a 'tape' (*zigarella*), is staged to just fill one side of a 120-minute cassette. Often the "official" singers and guitarists leave fairly early, and the rest continue drinking and chatting into the night. As drink flows, impromptu singing discussions may develop, in which practically everyone participates, with animation and aplomb.

Xandir Malta, national radio, programs a half hour of sanitized *spirtu pront* each week on its AM station. Recording for Xandir is currently the only paying gig available to *ghana* artists, but they earn only enough for a few days' cigarettes. Some traditional festivals include formal contests in *spirtu pront*. The most prestigious is l-Imnarja (29 June, commemorating saints Peter and Paul), held in the Buskett Gardens in connection with an agricultural fair.

MUSICAL INSTRUMENTS

The guitar is the pervasive instrument of Maltese folk music and the traditional province of men. In the twentieth century, it became virtually inseparable from *ghana*. Early accounts mention other instruments used with *ghana*, such as mandolin, accordion, and tambourine; but the guitar alone remains. Guitar without song (*kitarra biss*) is not uncommon, but would seem anomalous in a context that did not include singing. Some consider it a recent, and still dubious, innovation.

The standard ensemble, for accompaniment or *kitarra biss*, consists of three guitarists, but two may suffice: one always plays the lead (*prejjem*), and the others provide chords. The basic tuning (*lah*), used for backup, is E–A–D–G–B–E. For melodic excursions, the *prim* tunes to *sol*, G♯–B–E–A–C♯–E. The other accompanist uses standard *lah*, or, if he has the skill, the special *doh* tuning, E–F♯–B–E–G♯–C♯, with more melodic figures. Many guitarists have difficulty tuning their instruments. Older traditionalists disapprove of the pick (*pinna*). During song, all three play their respective conventional chords. At the beginning and end of a set, and between stanzas, the *prim* provides melodic improvisations.

Kitarra biss may be performed as a separate piece between *zigarelli,* or after official singing has concluded. Standard guitars suffice throughout, but the special Maltese guitar is preferred for *prejjem.* It has a normal-length fingerboard with a slightly smaller body—shorter, shallower, more slender. This shape yields a timbre that makes the *prejjem* stand out and suggests peculiarities of Maltese vocal style. It also creates a captive market, at home and in emigrant communities, for Maltese guitar makers.

Bands

Bands, the concept of which reached Malta by the mid-1700s, ostensibly evoke the most general enthusiasm and command the most abundant funds. With the Roman Church as patron, they assumed a leading role in processions, *festas,* fireworks, and fairs. They also became a focus of rivalries between villages and between parishes within a village, in a curious mix of religion, politics, and music, sometimes erupting in open conflict.

In principle, every local parish has a band, loyally funded by parishioners and defended against rivals. Besides processions on saints' days and high holidays, they hold concerts and always attract an enthusiastic crowd. Many maintain clubhouses with bars, recreational facilities, youth programs, and auditoriums. Some foster folkloric troupes and musical training. The two principal bands on Gozo each have a theater capable of staging larger operatic productions than are possible in Valletta. Bands, which receive ample coverage by Xandir, also make commercial recordings that enjoy brisk sales among local and emigrant dilettantes and tourists.

The bands' repertoire, the work of Maltese composers, employs European conventions difficult to distinguish from foreign counterparts, except for occasional echoes of *ghana* melody. New compositions are expected for each year's *festa,* providing a modicum of income for amateur composers. Wealthy bands retain their own composers; others commission works. The music is seldom published.

Bagpipes and other instruments

Bands and guitars effectively exhaust the catalog of the instrumental music of Malta today. Other instruments and ensembles remain fossils of bygone customs, susceptible only to artificial resuscitation for folkloric festivals and touristic entertainment. Of these, the Maltese bagpipe (*zaqq* 'belly') has received the most scholarly attention. Rhythm instruments always accompany it, usually tambourine (*tanbur*) and friction drum (*zavzava*). Wind instruments used in outdoor music are a shepherd's reed pipe (*flejguta*) and a fife (*fifra*), the latter together with a bass drum (*katuba*) for public announcements (*bandu*). A whistle (*betbut*) and a mouth harp (*bijambò*) provide private amusement.

Small ensembles, using combinations of violin, contrabass (*bordi*), mandolin, guitar, shawm (*kurnetta*), accordion, and *orgni* (variously harmonica, concertina, portable harmonium, hurdy-gurdy) with tambourine, cymbals, bells, or castanets (*taqtuqa*), are formed for ambulatory street music, or are hired for weddings, parties, and picnics (figure 3). For amusement and dancing, a *terrimaxka*—an elaborate barrel organ on wheels, with clockwork dancing figures, often accompanied by a monkey—could appear on Sundays and feasts. Normally imported, it brought the latest foreign popular tunes to Malta in the 1800s and early 1900s.

GENDER AND MUSIC

Many people, women and men, can sing *spirtu pront* and other varieties of *ghana,* and do so informally for their own enjoyment. Few, however, profess the title *ghannej* and exhibit their skills publicly. A leading singer estimated in 1991 that the

FIGURE 3 An ensemble of three violins and a contrabass (*bordi*), from Gozo. Postcard from the early 1900s. Courtesy of the Robert Godfried Collection, New York.

islands have roughly forty acknowledged singers, all men, of whom about twelve are in demand and rank from good to excellent. There were still female singers in the 1970s; their disappearance results, not from prohibition, but from a multitude of changes in Maltese society, responsible for the reduced number of male singers.

Women's music has received only passing notice in Malta. Traditional roles for Maltese women parallel those of other southern European cultures: general restriction to the domestic sphere, which serves as the stage for women's music. Their minimal representation in public *ghana* is consistent with this. Because women's music is more private, it is more difficult to investigate, but certain manifestations of it, infrequently witnessed today, have become legendary in recollections: washing at public wells, threshing and winnowing grain, pressing grapes, repairing roofs, having fun at picnics and *festas*. In these contexts, women, among themselves or with family, bandy *ghana* with the same acumen and delectation as men.

Domestic employees of wealthy families are known for animated singing conversations with neighbors' servants, sometimes causing contretemps between households. To avoid singing openly, women may conduct *ghana* dialogues by proxy, devising their repartees and sending a child out to sing them. Boys who later become singers gain initial experience with the art in this way. Women frequently transmit musical traditions they themselves are barred from performing.

DANCE

Il-Maltija, billed as Malta's national dance, is not a folk dance like the polka and the square dance, but conscious folklore, performed by a trained troupe on special occasions. It apparently began in the 1700s as a contredanse for high society in courtly settings. As the fashion faded and customs changed, it was eventually elevated to the status of folklore. It is seen today at carnival and folklore festivals and in tourist hotels. Of chief importance is its principal theme (figure 4), which functions, alongside those of *ghana*, as a hallmark of Maltese music. Its origin may be sought among European contredanses; it occurs in "*Joyeux Paris*," by Émile Waldteufel (1837–1915).

With the fading of traditional customs, new ethnic self-consciousness, and expansion of tourism, a folkloristic industry has emerged in Malta. In the years following independence, Malta experienced a revival of folklore, and enterprising Maltese mastered the idiom and launched folklore products. The *zaqq* was resurrect-

In the years following independence, Malta experienced a revival of folklore, and enterprising Maltese mastered the idiom and launched folklore products. The *zaqq* was resurrected, il-Maltija choreographed, costumes designed, customs devised, folk songs composed, and enthusiastic young people trained to perform for uncritical audiences.

FIGURE 4 The tune for il-Maltija, the national dance, is in a major mode. Transcription by L. JaFran Jones.

ed, il-Maltija choreographed, costumes designed, customs devised, folk songs composed, and enthusiastic young people trained to perform for uncritical audiences.

Much was assimilated from the revival of folklore during the same period in Europe and the Anglophone world. *Ghana* artists rode the wave too, with their *kanzunetta* and *makkjetta,* hits of the 1970s, and some enduring music emerged, though in the idiom of 1960s folk with Maltese overlay. The vogue has apparently subsided, but its products have acquired the aura of a bygone age—a curious popular repertoire, not authentic, yet endowed with nostalgia and romance, a sort of postmodern ersatz folklore.

WESTERN ART MUSIC

Malta's foreign rulers and the Roman Catholic Church have always fostered the European music of their class in Malta and have extended to Maltese the opportunity for exposure, training, and participation in it. Through most of history the church encompassed all music, sacred and profane. Multinational, the knights secularized the musical climate and facilitated openings for Maltese. The Manoel Theater, inaugurated in 1732 and still in use, intensified musical activity and opportunity. Europe began to take note of Maltese composers, who concentrated their talents on opera and sacred music in the Italian style of the day.

Giuseppe Balzano (1616–1700) and Pietro Grixti (1696–1738) blazed trails, followed by Mikelangelo Vella (1715–1792) and his distinguished pupils, Francesco Azzopardi (1748–1809) and Nicolò Isouard (1775–1818). The latter is revered as Malta's greatest early composer, the first to enjoy renown beyond Italy. Contact with Britain in the 1800s brought diversity to Maltese music, an era dominated by two musical dynasties, the Nani and Bugeja families. It ended in 1890, with establishment of a musical lyceum.

Carmelo Pace (1906–1993) is the senior composer of the twentieth century. Charles Camilleri (b. 1931), his pupil, a talented and productive musician, enjoys the most success abroad. Both weave Maltese musical motifs into their works, Pace in his Fantasia and Camilleri in his Malta suite and Maltese dances. Both diligently foster younger talents. Joseph Vella is prominent as composer, educator, conductor, and researcher, and has unearthed and performed many valuable manuscripts from the archives of Mdina Cathedral. The younger generation includes composers Dion

Buhagiar, John Galea, and Pawlu Grech. Malta boasts several singers of international repute, two significant orchestras, and opera companies in Valletta and Gozo.

BIBLIOGRAPHY

Azzopardi, Giovanni. 1988. *La cappella musicale della cathedrale di Malta e i suoi rapporti con la Sicilia.* Musica sacra in Sicilia tra rinascimento e barocco, 5. Palermo: Flaccovio.

Boissevain, Jeremy. 1965. *Saints and Fireworks: Religion and Politics in Rural Malta.* London School of Economics Monographs in Social Anthropology, 30. London: Athlone Press.

Bruni, Franco. 1993. *Musica sacra a Malta: Le cappelle della Cattedrale di S. Paolo e della Concattedrale di S. Giovanni Battista nel XIX secolo.* Marsa, Malta: Publishers Enterprises Group.

Cassar-Pullicino, Joseph. 1976. *Studies in Maltese Folklore.* Msida, Malta: University of Malta Press.

Cassar-Pullicino, Joseph, and Micheline Galley. 1981. *Femmes de Malte dans les chants traditionnels.* Paris: Éditions du CNRS.

Herndon, Marcia. 1971. "Singing and Politics: Maltese Folk Music and Musicians." Ph.D. dissertation, Tulane University.

———. 1987. "Toward Evaluating Musical Change Through Musical Potential." *Ethnomusicology* 31(3):455–468.

Herndon, Marcia, and Norma McLeod, eds. 1979. *Music as Culture.* Darby, Penn.: Norwood Editions.

Ilg, Bertha, and Hans Stumme. 1909. *Maltesische Volkslieder im Urtext mit deutscher Übersetzung.* Leipzig: J. C. Hinrichs'sche Buchhandlung.

McLeod, Norma, and Marcia Herndon. 1975. "The Bormliza: Maltese Folk Song Style and Women." *Journal of American Folklore* 88:81–100.

———. 1980. "The Interrelationship of Style and Occasion in the Maltese *Spirtu Pront.*" In *The Ethnography of Musical Performance,* ed. Norma McLeod and Marcia Herndon, 147–166. Norwood, Penn.: Norwood Editions.

Partridge, J. K., and Frank Jeal. 1977. "The Maltese Żaqq." *The Galpin Society Journal* 30:112–144.

AUDIOVISUAL RESOURCES

Baldachino, Frans, and Karmenu Bonnici. 1992. *Malte, ballades et joutes chantées.* Maison des cultures du monde W 260040. Compact disc.

Bonavia, George. 1993. *Folk Songs and Music from Malta.* Smithsonian Folkways Records 04047. Compact disc.

Il-banda Immexxija. 196-? *Marci Maltin.* Center RCLP 1009. LP disk.

Pace, Tony, et al. 1974. *Il-Maltija and Other Folk Tunes from Malta.* Circle MRB LP1. LP disk.

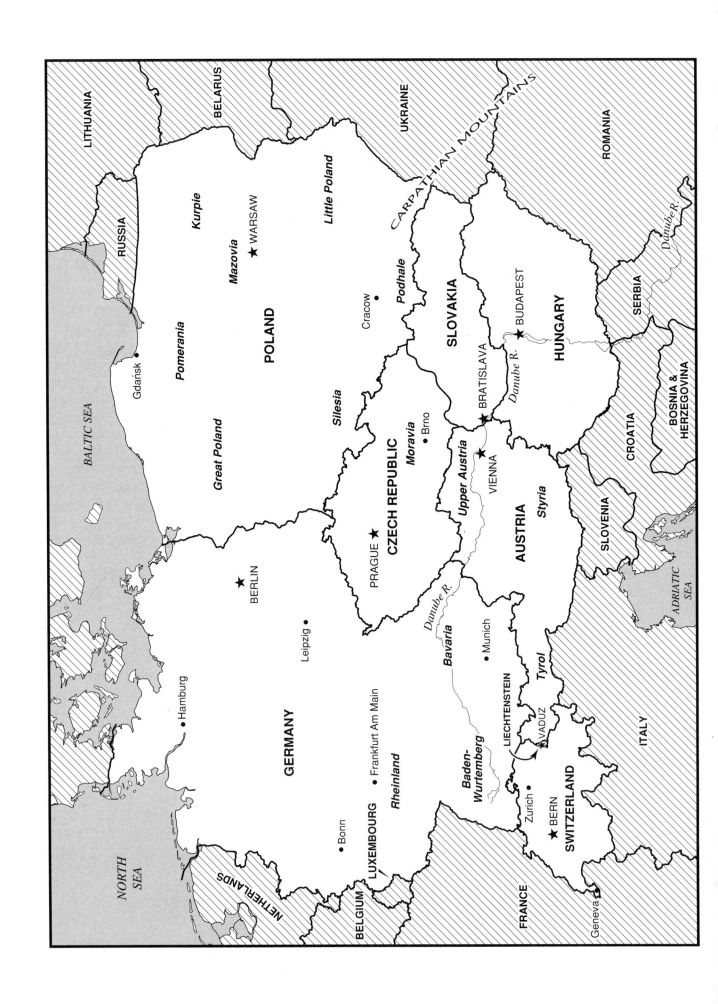

Central Europe

Central Europe borders on all the other major geographical regions of continental Europe. The music of German-speaking countries (Germany, Austria, and parts of Switzerland) has some archaic features—such as the prominence of horns and trumpets and vocal cattle calls—with parallels in northern Europe. In the Slavic-speaking countries (Poland, the Czech Republic, and Slovakia), the ritual occasions for singing resemble ones in eastern and southeastern Europe, as do those of the Hungarians, who speak a non-Indo-European, Finno-Ugric language. As centers of literacy since the Middle Ages, the musical traditions of this region have perhaps the longest and richest recorded histories of folk and art music in all of Europe. The link among them is illustrated by the popularity of string bands and brass ensembles at all levels of society. The association of music with ideology and politics in this region has been particularly striking, whether the form of government was fascist in the 1930s and 1940s, communist from the late 1940s to 1990, or democratic.

MAP 7   Central Europe

Germany

Wilhelm Schepping

One of the largest countries in Europe at 356,735 square kilometers, Germany was for much of its history a geographical term for an area of smaller states and principalities. Politically unified from 1871 to 1945, Germany led two world wars in the first half of the twentieth century. From 1945 to 1990, it was divided into the communist German Democratic Republic and the democratic German Federal Republic. Highly urbanized, its population of eighty million is about 45 percent Protestant (mainly in the north) and about 37 percent Roman Catholic (mainly in the south, in Rhineland and Bavaria).

Bordering on nine countries, Germany has produced an influential musical culture with such composers as Heinrich Schütz, George Frideric Handel, members of the Bach family, Christoph Willibald Gluck, Carl Maria von Weber, Ludwig van Beethoven, Robert Schumann, Felix Mendelssohn-Bartholdy, Johannes Brahms, Richard Wagner, Richard Strauss, Paul Hindemith, Karlheinz Stockhausen, Hans Werner Henze, Kurt Weill, and others. Important German poet-dramatists were Johann Wolfgang von Goethe (1749–1832), Friedrich Schiller (1759–1805), Joseph von Eichendorff (1788–1857), Eduard Möricke (1804–1875), Gerhart Hauptmann (1862–1946), Bertolt Brecht (1898–1956), and others, whose writings, especially Goethe's *Faust,* have inspired countless musical settings.

GERMAN CONCEPTS OF FOLK MUSIC

Given the complexity and richness of the documentation of Germany's history, the urbanization and literacy of its society, and the role of its intellectuals in defining concepts of "folk" and applying them to song, dance, and instrumental music, German ethnomusicologists have recently rethought their object of study.

Traditional criteria

The notion of folk song (*Volkslied*) put forward by the poet, philosopher, and Protestant preacher Johann Gottfried von Herder (1744–1809) as "the living voice of the people, indeed humanity" (188? [1773]) has been fertile for German cultural and intellectual history. Folk culture, preserved in publications on folk music and in archival manuscript and print collections of songs, ballads, dances, and folk music, has influenced the arts and even political life, where it has served for the development of regional and national identities.

After 1945, Ernst Klusen, founder of the Lower Rhine Folk-Song Archive (1938) and the Institute for Musical Folklore in Neuss (1964; since 1985, at Cologne University), and other scholars recognized that Herder's concept was in many respects more invention than discovery, more fiction than reality. They reacted against the interpretation of folk song as "the song of the lower classes," or, in socialist parlance, the song of the "working class" (Strobach 1980). They noted that folksinging runs "straight through the social pyramid" (Klusen 1969) and "folk" must be understood purely as "many people" or "the population" (Braun 1985). Others criticized object-oriented definitions of folk songs by demonstrating that earlier criteria binding them to oral transmission, general circulation among the people, ever-changing textual and melodic formation, unknown authorship, aesthetic-moral qualities, and multigenerational traditions have never corresponded to what people really sang (Schepping 1994).

Early on, popular songs were orally transmitted through singing, but since the Middle Ages also through manuscripts and handwritten songbooks. The theory of the purely mnemonic retention of songs has been gradually revealed as a scientific fiction, and the notion of solely oral transmission abandoned (Röhrich 1992). The invention of the printing press (in the fifteenth century) accelerated the writing of folkloric traditions and the simultaneous oral transmission of printed matter. Song-pamphlets, whose texts were sung to well-known melodies, and books of songs became increasingly important for the transmission of songs (Brednich 1974). Since the general spread of electronic media, songs have mostly been transmitted electronically, in an indirectly oral fashion. Phonographs, tape recorders, or CD players have become the companion of each generation (Schepping 1991a), enabling pop fans and others to sing along with German and international pop, rock, and folk groups the songs they have learned in English, German, and even dialects, from tapes and compact discs.

Popularity is likewise a trait of folk song. But many songs, even in our media age, live in social, local, or regional contexts too limited to be ascribed to broad distribution and general popularity, demanded by the traditional conception of folk song (Böhme 1970 [1895]). This recognition fueled Klusen's attempt to substitute the term "group song" for Herder's "folk song" (Klusen 1967), but "popularity," in the sense of "applicability to everybody's singing," is indeed a determining factor of folk song.

Variability is also a typical feature of folk song, dance, and instrumental music, because the practitioners, who determine all aspects of the text, melody, rhythm, harmony, and arrangement, are partially bound by regional or stylistic conventions, beyond which they freely and creatively adapt all sorts of music to their purposes, a process observable, for example, in the differences between performed and printed versions of the same music; however, many singers remain so tied to every subtle rhythmic or intonational finesse of the traditional, written, or recorded versions (illustrated through playback) that variants possibly remain the exception.

Anonymity has been a defining feature of folk song since Herder's time, but it was vigorously disputed in Germany early in the twentieth century. Proponents of so-called production theory, led by the Austrian scholar Josef Pommer, believed with Herder that the authorship of folk song was collective, emanating from the "creative folk spirit or soul." Another camp formed around "reception theory," which viewed the "folk" as an uncultured lower class, which did not create, but simply adapted cultural material from the upper class. John Meier, the principal advocate of this theory (1971 [1906]), later modified his thesis to credit the people with creatively appropriating these "art songs" (Meier 1940); Ernst Meier (1977 [1855]), however, had already found empirical evidence that people customize their songs by adapting them to their purposes and tastes. In this way, the community participates in the creation of folk songs and instrumental music in a manner unattainable by any individual.

Attempts to restrict "folk songs" through the application of normative, subjective values, like worthiness or moral qualities, remain questionable. Compressing these songs into aesthetic and ethical precepts has led collectors and editors, contrary to Herder's postulate, but not to his own practice, to revise, falsify, and recompose texts and melodies (Wiora 1953).

Antiquity or longevity as a criterion for folk songs, folk dances, and folk instrumental pieces has long been disputed. Herder's disciple F. D. Gräter (1968 [1794]) felt that a "folk song" must be "transferred for centuries from mouth to mouth." The prevailing opinion today is that, in addition to traditional songs, contemporary folk songs, dances, and instrumental pieces are appropriate objects of research and collection. Otherwise, one would be forced to share Wiora's (1959) erroneous belief in the "downfall of folk song" and the "decline" of folk music and dance, without acknowledging the continued ability of folk culture to transform the repertoire and its performance.

In identifying folk song, conservative musical folklorists focused on the object, but the folk-music field is defined today through criteria relating to the subject: the function of music in social life; the interaction of singers, dancers, and players; and how practitioners handle musical and textual materials.

Function and performance

Viewed functionally, folk music is not primarily music for performance, but rather is utilitarian music (Besseler 1925). It originates from concrete individual or communal needs; one applies the music like a tool appropriate to the situation. Individuals use music in singing, to express sadness, joy, fear, gratitude, or love, or simply entertain a child or help it sleep. Even singing along with electronic media (according to statistics, practiced by about 70 percent of the German populace), can serve this function. Group practice includes singing in church, with family members or members of a club, during carnival, soccer matches, and demonstrations, at work, pop concerts, and play, and while hiking and dancing. Purely functional instrumental music can accompany dancing, hiking, marching, and training in gymnastics and fitness; it is played in the streets of towns and cities. This, too, counts as folk music, and it is included in the field of musical folklore.

Viewed in terms of action, folk music lives not as a performance by a few musicians for many (as in concert halls), but in collective performance with a high degree of participation and interaction by all present (Klusen 1975). Most of the audience are also performers: they sing, hum, sway, dance, or clap together. Most participants are only nominally interested in the origin and type of musical material. It is insignificant to them whether it is "art" or "folk" music, or derives from a subculture; whether it is composed for instruments or voices; whether it is traditional or contemporary, of "inferior" or "superior" quality, already popular or freshly written, from an unknown or celebrated hand, or is transmitted orally or from printed or electronic media; and whether the text suits the situation or function at hand. The determining factor is whether the music or the dance provides the opportunity for performers and audience to participate in the immediate situation.

The function and intensity of interaction in performance influence music-related behavior (Baumann 1976)—that is, how the performers handle the text and music, which are treated with complete freedom and disregard for any rights to an original version or the intention of an author. Instead, through parody, retexting, recomposition, and musical modification, practitioners adapt the musical material to their conditions, situations, instruments, and abilities. Despite their dependence on existing models or conventions, these alterations deeply mark songs, dances, and instrumental pieces, and can be empirically ascertained and analyzed.

Hundreds of versions of the same ballad documented in *Deutsche Volkslieder mit ihren Melodien* (Deutsches Volksliedarchiv 1935–) impressively demonstrate this practice. The same can be said for the variants of songs, dances, and instrumental pieces in German archives. These collections and editions confirm that every recorded folk song, dance, or instrumental piece preserves only one of its potential forms, alongside countless other previous and subsequent mutations. Even widely disseminated editions of music and dance cannot check the further development and change of their content.

Education and folk-music research, from Herder to the present, have defined our knowledge: the decisive features defining folk music, German or otherwise, are neither the instrument, nor the means of transmission, nor the music itself. Every instrument, regardless of how it is learned—saxophone, piano, electric piano, synthesizer, harmonium, Hammond and electric organs, and the orchestral instruments—is a potential folk instrument. Likewise, nearly every kind of music is potentially folk music. Three criteria define folk music in this modern sense. First, it occurs in the context of a social situation or need more than in a performance, and maintains functional, rather than performative, qualities. Second, it initiates a high degree of communication and interaction, with substantial participation, action, and reaction by the performers. Third, it becomes the productive, creative property of its practitioners, more or less unfettered by any media, and largely independent of its historical origin, notation, and source.

If one redefines the field and subjects of musical folklore by these criteria, the complete range of functional songs, dances, and instrumental pieces must be included in it: every vocal and instrumental practice that corresponds to these criteria must become a subject of ethnomusicological research. The music must be analyzed independently of its categorization as "art" or "popular" music, its social provenance, or the musical education or abilities of its practitioners, and three areas of research need to be considered: the musical material, its nature, and origin; music making, including practices, performances, instruments, motivation, function, and effects; and the practitioners themselves, and their recipients or consumers.

Social situations and events with this kind of functional folk-musical action and interaction can almost always be found. These include diverse regional, music-related customs at festivities of carnival and Shrovetide (Fastnacht), whose music and dance are quantitatively the largest, and have spread independently through almost all German regions; certain children's activities, like candlelight processions on Saint Martin's Day in the Rhineland; domestic and institutional festivals, and spontaneous plays and dances; and traditional yearly festivals of sacred and secular customs, whose folkloric qualities are paradoxically endangered and advanced through commercial support and touristic exploitation. In the lower and central Rhineland, these last run from the song-intensive activities of May or Whitweek, with its "Queen" and "Boy game," to the song-, dance-, and music-filled Oktoberfest and harvest feast days; from singing at Advent, Christmas, and Epiphany to school parties, which have increasingly become more musically inventive; the often boisterous student semester-end or graduation celebrations; the anniversary, company, and inauguration parties; parish, street, bridge, quarter, and city festivals (Reimers 1995); and strikes and demonstrations (Schepping 1992). These are all events in which functional instrumental music, with functional singing and dancing, has gained increasing significance and quality, but even musical customs whose traditional functions have

In battle, calls were blown on animal horns, such as the oliphant. According to the song of Roland (1100s), Charlemagne's loyal paladin Roland, before his death during an attack by Basques in 778 in the Spanish Pyrenees, blew on this horn until it broke.

remained nearly unchanged exhibit tendencies toward modernization and updating, including an effortless integration of folklore, jazz, pop, rap, rock, and techno.

Regionally differentiated, Germany's population and location engendered a diverse musical culture, long influenced by neighboring musical communities, and never achieved or aspired to a countrywide or uniform musical identity. Blanket statements, therefore, about the tonality, rhythm, melody, forms, and structures of traditional German folk music cannot easily be made, and many contemporary forms can best be explained by a review of German folk music from the Middle Ages to the present.

THE MIDDLE AGES

Knowledge about music in Germany in the first millennium is sketchy at best. Only indirect records of early German music exist before the first documented song, an Old High German song text of the Freisinger Petruslied (ninth century). Unfortunately, the melody, written in neumatic notation without a staff, cannot be deciphered, but musical traits in notations of the 1100s and other indirect sources allow conclusions about that epoch, despite the superimposition of Gregorian and Mediterranean musical styles.

Medieval German song

A range of musical parameters already existed. The tonal ambit included the three-tone formula preserved today in children's songs (figure 1). Pentatonic tendencies and hexachordal structures can be found at this time; these were eventually expanded to include the full heptatonic scale through the addition of the seventh scalar degree, flattened or as a leading tone. This type was found mainly among church-modal scales, which eventually began to approach the minor and major tonalities.

Melodically, early German song was marked by its closeness to Gregorian chant. Most early German spiritual folk songs were derived from textual parodies of Gregorian melodies (primarily sequences), or syllabic settings (tropes) of previously melismatic melodies. Even dance melodies were modeled on forms borrowed from the structure of sequences. The exclamatory intervals found in Kyrie tropes, in extra-liturgical battle, pilgrim, procession, and crusade songs, and in recitative songs (*Sprechgesänge*) on repeated tones, may all have roots in the late Middle Ages. Secular songs in Gregorian modes, with rich melismatic material, the flowery ornaments of Nuremberg's famous Meistersinger Hans Sachs (1494–1576), and metrically unfettered melodies, closely parallel Gregorian chorales.

FIGURE 1   The children's song *"Backe, backe Kuchen,"* based on a three-tone formula.

Bak– ke, bak– ke Ku– chen, der Bäk– ker hat ge– ru– fen

FIGURE 2 The famous
Christmas carol
"*Joseph lieber Josef
mein,*" based on a tri-
adic melody.

Music correction to be
made by Hyunjung.

The dance-songs and rounds of the Middle Ages, typified through bar form
(mostly AABA), had a different tonal and melodic orientation: pentatonic or triadic
melodies. The rhythms of these melodies closely follow the meter of the verse. The
same tendency can be seen in folkloric Christmas carols, particularly cradle songs
(*Wiegenlieder,* for the custom of "rocking to sleep the Christ-child") in 6/8 or 3/4
meter with triadic melodies (figure 2). But triadic melodies too were particularly
characteristic of the alpine yodel, a nearly textless singing, which even today influences the melodies of Bavaria's secular and religious music. The people of the region
of the Harz Mountains also cultivated the yodel [see SWITZERLAND].

Medieval documentation reports the existence of unaccompanied singing for
dancing, drinking, magic, and cult singing, particularly at funerals and weddings.
Christian music in the Middle Ages included pilgrims' songs and crusaders' songs,
and the songs and religious dances of the fourteenth-century flagellants, which flared
up intermittently in Germany, especially in times of plague. Such information
demonstrates the existence of a widespread vernacular song culture associated with
folk religion (Hübner 1931; Runge 1900). Canonic singing manifested itself astonishingly early, at the genesis of polyphony. The significant manuscript collections of
songs of the late Middle Ages—Jenaer, ca. 1350; Lochamer, ca. 1452–1460;
Kolmarer, ca. 1460; Schedelsches, 1461–1467; Rostocker, ca. 1475; Glogauer, before
1488—contain songs originating in the repertoire of folk songs, fashioned into art-
ful, mixed vocal and instrumental pieces.

Medieval instruments and instrumental music

In the Middle Ages, the leading instruments for accompaniment to singing were the
hand harp (*Minnesängerharfe*) and the vielle (*Fidel*), whether bowed or strummed.
The great verse epics, like the Nibelung and Hildebrand songs, were probably performed with these instruments. The psaltery (dulcimer) and hurdy-gurdy later augmented them.

Instrumental music was also played for worship, dance, and certain routines of
work, and in battle. Lurs, prehistoric paired large S-form bronze trumpets found in
northern Germany and Scandinavia, were blown at religious ceremonies and were
capable of playing signals [see ARCHAEOLOGY OF MUSIC IN EUROPE]. In battle, calls
were blown on animal horns, such as the oliphant. According to the song of Roland
(1100s), Charlemagne's loyal paladin Roland, before his death during an attack by
Basques in 778 in the Spanish Pyrenees, blew on this horn until it broke.

Instrumental music accompanied daily activities in the countryside.
Iconographic evidence implies that bells, drums, horns, and flutes were used to herd
animals with signals (D. Stockmann 1992). In the Middle Ages, instrumental music
was played most often as an accompaniment for dancing, and it was sounded at
parades, folk plays, markets, and celebrations. Important folk instruments included
bagpipes, the hurdy-gurdy, the hornpipe, the trumpet, the animal horn, the mouth
harp, the duct flute, the zither, the shawm, the friction drum, and later the alphorn
(figure 3).

In cities, these performances came under the control of musician's guilds

FIGURE 3   The zither entered German folk music in the Middle Ages and continues to be popular in the German-speaking areas of Central Europe. Die lustigen Tölzer, a music, song, and dance group, accompanied by a variety of zithers and double-necked guitars that mimic the capability of zithers to provide melody and chordal accompaniment. Early-twentieth-century postcard, courtesy of the Robert Godfried Collection, New York.

(*Stadtmusikanten*). In town and country, traveling musicians, often itinerant clerics and students, disseminated instrumental and vocal music. This is illustrated, for example, by *Carmina Burana,* a thirteenth-century musical manuscript from the Benediktbeuren monastery, in Bavaria. It has more than three hundred pieces that demonstrate the internationality and formal diversity of music of its time.

FROM THE 1400s THROUGH THE 1700s
Song style

In the 1400s, the major mode became increasingly popular, especially in dance music. This status was officially recognized by the Swiss theorist Glareanus (educated in Cologne, later professor in Freiburg) in 1547. To the existing eight modes, he added two major modes, dubbed *ionicus* 'ionian', and two minor modes, dubbed *aeolus* 'aeolian', and thus created a system of twelve modes, which collectively he called *dodekachordon.* Johannes Kepler gave them their modern names in 1619, calling the first *genus durum* 'hard kind' (German *dur,* English *major*) and the second *genus molle* 'soft kind' (German *moll,* English *minor*). These terms had been prepared in the Middle Ages with the hexachord system, which distinguished between *b durum* (*hexachordum durum,* with a major third between the first and third tones) and *b molle* (*hexachordum molle,* with a minor third). The empirical basis of these theoretical observations was displayed in German folk music of the Renaissance, whose major-minor dualism slowly yielded to the sovereignty of the major mode. All forms of singing and dancing, sacred and secular, followed this inclination.

In the 1500s and 1600s, the sacred songs of the Reformation and Counter-Reformation revived the old modes, dominated by the aeolian and dorian scales. This regregorianization, begun in the Middle Ages with the practice of writing German songs to Gregorian melodies, was promoted in the Reformation by Martin Luther. Modality also lived on in secular song. Even the somewhat antiquated melismata were reborn for expressive purposes. In this period, sacred and secular singing became more and more bound to metrical organization in measures. Now and then, syncopation or metrical change relieved metrical rigidity (figure 4).

Melodic modernization began in the late 1600s with more motivic unity, symmetrical phrasal periods, systematic shifts in modulation, phrasal repetitions (sometimes still based on the bar form of the Middle Ages), and conscious expressive use of major-minor polarity. During the 1700s and 1800s, these changes in sacred and sec-

FIGURE 4 The secular song "*Es ist ein Schnitter*," probably from the 1500s or 1600s, exhibiting a modal character and metrical change, rather than the metrical rigidity that came to characterize music in later periods.

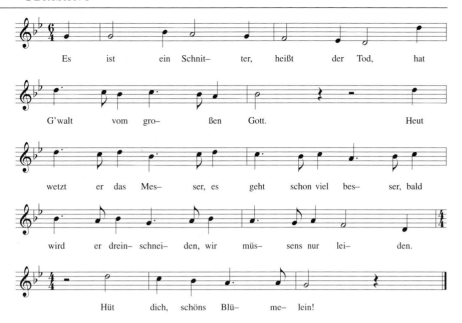

ular folk song were harmonically supported within the limits of the tonic-subdominant-dominant cadential progression. German *Liederschulen* (song schools in Berlin, Leipzig, and Swabia) greatly influenced this development, as did the folkloric *Liederspiele,* a musical theater related to the singspiel, with spoken parts alternating with folkloric song, composed by J. F. Reichardt, Felix Mendelssohn, and others. The character and content of the text were often melodically reinforced.

Instrumental music

Urban musical culture, organized into guilds during the Renaissance, provided accompaniment to religious, vocational, and urban activities. On flutes, hammered dulcimers, shawms, crumhorns, trombones, and eventually trumpets and timpani (especially at tournaments) and stringed instruments, professional town musicians (*Stadtpfeifer*) performed music for religious and communal feasts, church services and festivals, receptions and jubilees, weddings and funerals, city-council meetings and market days. They also sounded daily hours from city towers, day and night, and at Christmas and New Year's. Their repertoire included not only signals and chorales, but also dances and songs. Enjoying regular employment, they were constantly under pressure from competing traveling musicians (*Spielleute*), organized into regional brotherhoods, the so-called piper's kingdoms. Military music, too, was a branch of folk music.

Instrumental folk music and folk song attracted art musicians at this time, and thus became an important secondary source for ethnomusicologists later. Suites of instrumental variations of songs and dances, and of arrangements of polyphonic songs, were based on dances or folk and community songs recorded in manuscript songbooks. New compositions were published, for instance in Georg Forster's *Frische teutsche Liedlein* (1539–1556), Hans Leo Hassler's *Neue deutsche Gesänge* (1596), and J. H. Schein's *Venuskränzlein* (1609), *Waldliederlein* (1621–1628), and *Studentenschmaus* (1626); market and street cries, for example, were artfully treated in *Der Kölner Markt,* by Nikolaus Zangius (1603).

The practitioners of this vocal and instrumental culture included not only town musicians, cantors, and other professionals, but also school choirs, student *collegia musica,* and educated, noble amateurs or bourgeois dilettantes from the world of business and trade. The parts varied among vocal, mixed vocal-instrumental, and

The content of Johann Christoph Weigel's series of prints, *Musicalisches Theatrum* (1720) overcomes the allegorical posture of its frontispiece: Apollo, representing courtly instruments, strides victoriously over the prostrate Dionysius, whose folk instruments (panpipes, dulcimer, timbrel, tambourine, triangle) lie strewn on the ground around him.

completely instrumental performance on instruments such as lute, organ, harpsichord, viola da gamba, and recorder. Improvisation figured prominently in performance, and performances took place in churches, schools, castles, city offices, dance halls, and coffeehouses.

In the Baroque era, folk music and dance were often integrated into music for court celebrations and dedication cantatas (Bach's *Bauernkantate* and *Kaffeekantate*; Telemann's *Singende und klingende Geographie*). Religious and folk-song melodies appeared in motets, cantatas, passions, oratorios, chorale preludes, and variations, and in programmatic works like battle pieces (*batta[g]lia*), biblical sonatas (Kuhnau), and *kirchfahrten* (Biber's *Pauern-Kirchfahrt*). Dance tunes and worldly songs and melodies, including coachmen's and hunting calls, were artfully incorporated into capricci (Bach's *Auf die Abreise*), overtures (Telemann's *Ouverture des Nations anciens et modernes*), sonatas, suites (Telemann's *La Poutaine*), and variations (Bach's *Goldberg Variations*).

Early Baroque composers imitated folk instruments as a special effect. The double bass, when prepared with paper under the strings, could mimic the snare drum, the violin played in the higher positions recalls a fife (*Schwegel*) or a shawm, and droning double stops invoke the sound of a hurdy-gurdy or a bagpipe. The humorous effects of these imitations on the connoisseur were sometimes achieved at the cost of mocking the despised folk instrument. That folk instruments were considered inferior was vividly described in two copiously illustrated German organological publications: Sebastian Virdung's *Musica getutscht und aussgezogen* (1970 [1511]) and Michael Praetorius's *Syntagma musicum* (1958 [1619]). Both publications included folk instruments only "to make them known to science—not to practice," and qualified them as stupid and useless (Virdung) or as peasant instruments (Praetorius).

The content of Johann Christoph Weigel's series of prints, *Musicalisches Theatrum* (1961 [1720]), overcomes the allegorical posture of its frontispiece: Apollo, representing courtly instruments, strides victoriously over the prostrate Dionysius, whose folk instruments (panpipes, dulcimer, timbrel, tambourine, triangle) lie strewn on the ground around him. Though part I of Weigel's book depicts the common classical musical instruments in use at the time, part II, aptly titled *Des Musicalischen Theatri Lustiges Nachspiel* 'The Musical Theater's Humorous Epilogue', accurately portrays twenty-three typical German folk instruments in performance: barrel organ, carried under the left arm and played with the right hand; hammered dulcimer, played with two spoon-shaped mallets; *Rindentrompete* made from a bark scroll; wooden alphorn; shawm and its little version, the *Dudey*, with reed cap; two forms of bagpipe, with bellows ("the Polish goat") or mouth blown; small transverse flute, similar to the piccolo; fife, a thin end-blown flute played with one hand; mouth harp; tenor drum; a "guitar," still in cittern form and with a bass cittern in the picture; the five-stringed hurdy-gurdy, tenderly played by a feminine hand like the hammered dulcimer and barrel organ. The last instrument was still counted among

FIGURE 5   Wooden alphorns and bark-scroll trumpets were depicted as early as the 1720s. Though horns came to be important accouterments of the aristocratic hunt and later the symphony orchestra, they began as signaling instruments, used especially by shepherds, such as this little boy, with his small trumpet draped around his neck. Künzig 1958: plate 15. Courtesy of the Johannes Künzig-Institute für ost Deutsche Volkskunde, Freiburg.

art instruments in the Middle Ages because of its polyphonic abilities; here it has "sunk" to the folk level. Two other folk instruments are presented in part I of the *Musicalisches Theatrum:* two different types of kit (dancing master's fiddle, a Renaissance holdover) hang next to the court violist; and finally, spied through the open window of the court horn player can be seen his rural counterpart, the hunter with his horn, sounding hunting calls (figure 5).

Weigel's comprehensive survey of German folk instruments omitted but a few: the trumpetlike bullhorn; the traditional bull roarer or thunderstick (*Schwirrholz*); the popular Bavarian musical spoons; a variety of alpine zithers (see figure 3), from *Raffele* to scratch zither and later the emerging Salzburg-Mittenwald zither; the stick zither; the eerily beautiful Good Friday cog rattles; and the Rhenish-Flemish friction drum, indispensable at carnival.

THE 1800S AND 1900S

Songs

The major mode proliferated in secular and sacred song in the 1700s and especially the 1800s. In the music of the Roman Catholic Church, modal melody was consciously suppressed, especially in the attempt to substitute German sung Masses (*Liedmessen*) for the music of the Latin Ordinary. Works by Joseph Haydn and the polyphonic version of Franz Schubert's *Deutsche Messe* ("Heilig, heilig, heilig") became widely known.

During the 1800s, melody evolved under harmonic influence but retained its periodic formal structure. Modulation became almost the rule, often with chromatic development, intervallic leaps, or suspensions of the fourth, sixth, and seventh scale degrees, and harmonically determined chordal melodies. This melodic type established itself speedily in song, folk music, and dance (especially the waltz). Patriotic songs, songs of the homeland or the Rhine, wine songs, students' songs, and church songs were disseminated through civic male choirs (mostly called *Liedertafel*), worker or factory choirs, and schools. This sort of melody still influences carnival songs and popular and commercial folk music. Such uniformity is resisted, at least rhythmically, in a Bavarian musical form that non-Bavarians can savor only with difficulty: the *Zwiefache,* a lively dance-song, which shifts abruptly between 2/4 and 3/4 time (figure 6).

In the early twentieth century, the German youth movement, initiated in 1896 by the creation of outdoor clubs (*Wandervogel*), quickly tired of such songs and dances, and began a countermovement by establishing its own repertoire. Hans Breuer's *Der Zupfgeigenhansl* (1908), the most famous songbook of the day, has been reprinted more than any other. It stimulated the composition of new songs, for two reasons: first, through the revival of old German songs (in part a consequence of

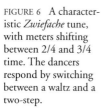

FIGURE 6 A characteristic *Zwiefache* tune, with meters shifting between 2/4 and 3/4 time. The dancers respond by switching between a waltz and a two-step.

Herder's original folk-song movement), and through the assimilation of little-known national and regional folkloric or "wander" songs, chiefly taken from Erk-Böhme's *Deutscher Liederhort* (1893–1894) and Kretzschmer-Zuccalmaglio's *Deutsche Volkslieder mit ihren Originalweisen* (1840); second, through songs from neighboring countries, partially compiled from the travels of the *Wandervogel*. The movement's new songs were composed partly from historicized melodic, tonal, and formal models from the 1500s to the 1700s, and partly from new melodic types and songs with traits from Slavic, Balkan, and Scandinavian folk songs or marches. Some of this repertoire has achieved recent popularity in concerts and recordings by the German hit-song star Heino.

Musical instruments

The melodies of several of Weigel's folk instruments filled the air of European cities well into the twentieth century. The hurdy-gurdy, for instance, accompanied the dramatic songs of street singers with music and with painted pictures. Schubert's socially critical song "The Hurdy-Gurdy Man" from his song cycle *Die Winterreise,* realistically depicts in the piano part the three-stringed model, which has two drone strings and one mechanically stopped string. Today, the hurdy-gurdy has appeared on the streets again—a nostalgic reference to earlier times.

Several folk instruments have made a comeback in the German alpine region. The hammered dulcimer has been integrated into Bavarian *Stubenmusi* (parlor music) ensemble: folkloric chamber-music groups consisting of combinations of zither, harp, double bass, guitar, fiddle, clarinet, accordion or mouth harp, which perform in concert or as accompaniment to dancing. The alphorn is often played in duos, trios, or quartets. The mouth harp, esteemed in the Middle Ages, but reduced to an instrument for beggars and revelers at carnival, has been reinstated as an art instrument, even among the ranks of rock musicians.

The revival of these historical instruments began with the rediscovery of the lute and the recorder by the youth movement of the 1920s, and accelerated in the 1960s by folk musicians and their interest in early music. Instruments like the zither (*Scheitholz*), the Appalachian dulcimer, the psaltery, the cittern, the fiddle, the hurdy-gurdy, the tambourine, musical spoons, the tenor drum, the shawm, and bagpipes took their place next to those of foreign origin: the banjo, the bouzouki, the guitar, the *güiro* (a gourd scraper), rumba rattles and castanets, and bongos and congas (figure 7). Through this array of instruments, with their associated styles and musics, German folklore has undergone a stylistic internationalization whose authenticity is self-evident in concerts, festivals, media productions, and folk competitions.

Marching bands and wind bands

In enthusiasm for the Middle Ages, German youth groups in the 1920s rediscovered the mercenary's drum (*Landsknechttrommel*). After 1933, the tenor drum was revived in less sympathetic hands. The Music Corps of the Hitler Youth appropriated this instrument for their purposes, a tradition continued today by neo-Nazis; however, the marching bands of the annual, interregional, and nonmartial civil-militia "celebrations" (*Schützenfest*) employ the same drum as a rhythmic basis for their parades.

These parades are frequently accompanied by drum corps composed of transverse pipes and marching drums; both instruments have belonged to typical German military and march music ensembles since the late Middle Ages. Today, brass marching bands, successors of the eighteenth-century military wind bands with Turkish Janissary music, make up the most important component of these parades. Brass instruments and clarinets dominate these groups but are nearly always supplemented by saxophones. In addition, young women now take part in these groups.

FIGURE 7   A revival group plays folk music on violins, a guitar, and a bowed zither. Instruments shown on the wall behind them include another zither, a tambourine, a mouth harp, and duct flutes. Photo by H. Röttgers, Aachen, 1983.

A similar type of band participates in parades and processions. For example, the traditional songs of the St. Martin's Day children's procession by lantern light (*Fackelzüge*), especially popular in the Rhineland, are sometimes accompanied by wind bands, but without the usual cymbals. Similar ensembles participate in festivities, concerts, and assemblies, especially in Bavaria and Swabia, again during carnival and in South Germany's Shrove Tuesday (*Fastnacht*), functioning as a tourist attraction, and in *Volksmusik* productions by the broadcasting media. Naturally, these activities have been commercialized and professionalized in a way that, to an increasing degree, undermines their "real-folk-music" status.

Groups composed of trombones (*Posaunenchöre*), often augmented with trumpets and flügelhorns, perform in Protestant church festivities and services, and at Christmas and New Year's, and even play from the towers of some Roman Catholic churches. Revived on Baroque models, these groups became popular before and after World Wars I and II, but they have now somewhat waned.

Wind, drum, and fanfare groups mostly train their musicians themselves. Newer recruits are never in financial need, in part because players can earn an attractive supplemental income. Despite the vast difference between this musical style and modern pop music, the younger generation often participate because the musicians frequently regroup, sometimes with other instruments, to play jazz, pop, and rock numbers for dancing and entertainment.

The accordion

Song-and-dance accompaniment in modern Germany are the domain of a relatively young, originally German, but now internationalized arrival: the accordion (vernacular German *Ziehharmonika*). The incipient form of this instrument, the *Mundäoline*, was invented in Berlin by F. Buschmann in 1821. With the addition of the folded bellows, it was renamed *Handäoline* in 1822, and a later evolution was called the concertina. Bass keys and a renaming as accordion were Viennese contributions, whereas the Buschmann invention came to be called the *deutsche Harmonika*. A variant form of the instrument, known the world over, bears the name of its builder, H. Band of Krefeld, namely the bandoneon.

The musical dimensions of today's instrument have been extended through a

After the Russian Revolution of 1917, emerging German workers' songs were greatly influenced by the Russian and Bolshevik heritage. They were spread during the period of the Weimar Republic (1919–1933) by communist agitators and by wind bands and musical parades of the Red Front-Line Society.

highly developed system of buttons, keyboard, and register keys. Dilettantes and folk musicians were quick to recognize the accordion's potential as "the poor man's orchestra," an easily transported instrument, which could play chords at the push of a button. Whether in solo playing or in accompanying songs or dances, it is the ideal partner for a one-man band. Consequently, at festivities and dances, in pubs, and at markets, numerous German traveling musicians of the nineteenth and twentieth centuries earned their living playing it with the harp, stringed, and wind instruments (Piechura 1995; Sell 1988). It has found a place in modern classical music too. The mouth harmonica, playable by children and adults, has a similar history and function, though a much smaller range. Both instruments can be found in large groups of even orchestral dimensions and constitute an alternative to the usual wind bands in popular entertainment and folkloric concerts [see THE MUSIC OF EUROPE, figure 1, p. 4].

The mandolin

Comparable in function to these two is an older European folk instrument, the mandolin, which, especially in the Baroque era, was used in art music too, as in Vivaldi's concertos. Like the harmonica, it is mostly played solo, especially for accompanying songs; between the world wars and after 1945, however, German mandolins were built in various sizes, supplemented by other plucked instruments, and frequently grouped into mandolin orchestras. Though the repertoire of the mandolin orchestras encompasses popular music not unlike that of the harmonica bands, idiomatically adapted symphonic literature can be heard on the concert stage.

The guitar

The guitar was always an art and a folk instrument. In the folk music of Europe and the Americas, it has played a leading role, and in Bavaria it has shared this position with the cittern and the dulcimer. Because of the instrument's popularity in jazz, beat, rock, and folk, nearly every music school in Germany, public or private, offers guitar courses (fewer offer *Harmonika* courses). And plectrum-instrument ensembles, which often include guitar and perform primarily folk music, have increasingly freed themselves from a folk image by adding to their repertoires adaptations of classical pieces or fully modern works.

The guitar nevertheless remains a folk instrument in Germany, partly because of its popularity in the 1800s. Nearly every pub in the alpine regions had an instrument at hand, and many people played it. The enthusiasm of the German youth movement for singing around 1900 is unimaginable without the guitar. Dangling on a neck strap, the instrument was the constant companion on outings, hikes, and camping trips. Though the number of youth groups has declined, the guitar's role in accompanying songs has prevailed. This result can be attributed to the prominence of the guitar in jazz, beat, and rock. The guitar accompanies songs in kindergartens and schools, and likewise the new Christian songs of Protestant and Roman Catholic services for youth. The amplified electric guitar and electric bass have expanded the campfire sounds of the past to the enormous sing-along, dance-along, interactive audiences at pop and rock concerts in sports arenas and stadiums.

Folk-music pedagogy

Folk-music instruction occurs in music schools and academic institutions, and nowadays has become an academic discipline, often in courses offered by public colleges (*Volkshochschulen*), schools, and youth centers. In Bavaria and Baden-Württemberg, where folk music is particularly popular, musical instruction has become increasingly organized by qualified personnel at musical seminars and courses. Like jazz, pop, and rock, folk music is frequently offered in the institutional curriculum. Not only special folk-music schools (like the Munich school for Bavarian music) but also conservatories and universities offer instruction in folk-music performance.

In 1925, Fritz Jöde, an important pedagogue of the youth-music movement, launched study programs for folk and youth music at the Berlin Academy for Church and School Music (Akademie für Kirchen- und Schulmusik). This initiative was revived in the former German Democratic Republic, where folk music became a discipline in many musical institutions. Likewise in the 1960s, West Germany instituted seminars for folk and youth music, like those instituted by the ethnomusicologist Hans Mersmann at the Cologne Conservatory of Music. Even competitions today are important for the performance of folk music and the spread of folk instruments. Thus performance, composition, and ensemble skills are elevated, while audiences profit from exposure to a new array of players, styles, and music.

MUSIC AND IDEOLOGY

During the later 1800s, the proletarian song (workers' song, combat song) of the communist movement gradually influenced singing. At first, these songs were modeled on the "Marseillaise" (1772) and songs of the Paris Commune, like the "Internationale" (German text: "*Wacht auf, Verbannte dieser Erde*"; original French text by Eugène Pottier, 1871; music by Pierre Degeyter, 1888), called the hymn of the world proletariat.

The early twentieth century

After the Russian Revolution of 1917, emerging German workers' songs were greatly influenced by the Russian and Bolshevik heritage ("*Brüder, zur Sonne, zur Freiheit*," original Russian text by Leonid P. Radin, 1897; German text by Hermann Scherchen). Song texts by Bertolt Brecht and Erich Weinert, set to music by Hanns Eisler and Paul Dessau, led the field in the late 1920s ("*Solidaritätslied*"; "*Vorwärts, und nie vergessen*"; "*Einheitsfrontlied*"). These songs have a marchlike character, an upbeat nature, dotted rhythms, triadic melodies, signal motives, and modulatory multisectional forms, often marked by the alternation of a minor-mode strophe and a major-mode refrain ("In Paris, in Copenhagen, Zurich, Prague"). They were spread during the period of the Weimar Republic (1919–1933) by communist agitators and by wind bands and musical parades of the Roter Frontkämpferbund (Red Front-Line Society). Even more effective were the "brass shawm bands" (Hinze 1994), whose instruments, developed from the automobile horn (*Martinshorn*), produced penetrating tones by means of vibrating metal tongues.

In comparison, little impression was left for about twenty years on folk singing by the mighty jazz wave that swamped Europe in the 1920s. Only commercial dance music was clearly influenced by jazz, cabaret, film music, and avant-garde opera, just a few of whose popular hits found their way into the common repertoire ("*Mackie*

Messer" from Brecht and Kurt Weill's *Threepenny Opera*; "*Jonny's Triumphlied*" and the blues "*Leb wohl, mein Schatz*" from Ernst Krenek's *Jonny spielt auf*). Compact and syncopated, with melodies brimming with rests, and harmonies fresh and jazz-related, their style of singing brought to popular music revolutionary innovations, which could be fully realized in Germany only after Hitler's demise.

The Nazi period

After 1933, the Nazis abruptly ended the free development of music and youth song, and of socialist and communist singing. Hitler liquidated all political parties and their organizations, and banned nearly all youth groups, their songs, and songbooks. In their place, he offered Nazi-movement songs, circulated by schools, Nazi youth organizations (all adolescents were forced into membership), military, government-controlled organizations, radio, recordings, and films. This repertoire encompassed not only retexted songs of the communists and socialists, but also older and modern military and marching songs, enlarged with traditional, politically neutral folk-song material, the latter tolerated thanks to a patriotic German folk ideology (*Blut und Boden* 'blood and soil'). Also, folk songs, dances, and instrumental music were pressed into service to shape the new "national-socialist person."

In November 1933, Germany's musical life fell under the control of the newly established Reichsmusikkammer (State Music Office). Directly supervised by "propagandaminister" Joseph Goebbels, this body tried to suppress all foreign or non-Aryan influences by regulating the work permits necessary for publicly practicing professional and amateur musicians. The purpose of this effort was to stanch the supposed subversion of the "moral strength of the people"—and beyond this, beginning five years later, after the terrible pogroms of "Crystal Night," by deportations and mass executions to destroy a flourishing old Jewish (especially Yiddish) German folk-music culture, with its fascinating folk songs and a vital—today by young German musicians partly renewed—klezmer music.

After the United States entered the war, the campaign against jazz and swing heightened, except for their peculiar function as an approved part of "Germany Calling," the daily propaganda broadcast to enemy military forces. The prohibition of "hot jazz," syncopated rhythms, lengthy drum solos, and the saxophone, with popular American dances like the foxtrot, the charleston, and the Lambeth Walk, hardly reduced the swing fever of the 1930s, which had swept through Germany and the rest of Europe. The Reichsmusik-Prüfstelle (State Music Commission) supervised all popular- and nonpopular-music pieces proposed for print, recording, or broadcast. The regime also tried, with little success, to develop traditional elements into new "social dances" and a "new German dance music" and to introduce them to the people. Some dance bands defended themselves from these attacks by camouflaging outlawed jazz standards with false German names and titles: "A Tisket, a Tasket" became "Old German Children's Song" ("*Laterne, Laterne*"); the "St. Louis Blues" became "*Lied vom blauen Ludwig*" ('Song of the Blue Ludwig'); "Tiger Rag" became "*Wo ist der Papa?*" ('Where's Daddy?') (Fackler 1994).

Newer Nazi songs, like "*Die Fahne hoch*" (the hymn of Hitler's combat group "SA"), "*Vorwärts schmettern die hellen Fanfaren*" (the hymn of the Hitler-Jugend, the Nazi youth organization), and the soldier's song "*Erika,*" became ever more rigid and strict in rhythm, beat, tonality, and structure. Marchlike rhythms dominated, and the major mode expelled the supposedly non-Aryan minor mode. Hard, accented meters, short phrases, stiff dotted rhythms, triadic horn-signal melodies, ostinato motives, and the refrain form permeated this music [see MUSIC AND IDEOLOGY, figure 1, p. 185]. Paradoxically, these traits sometimes appeared in the work and protest songs of Hitler's opponents (Karbusicky 1973).

Banned and persecuted with other nonfascist organizations, the churches (the Roman Catholic Church and the Protestant "Confessing Church"), youth groups, communists, and socialists fought back. Underground singing by these groups in concentration camps (Probst-Effah 1989), prisons, churches, and secret meetings became an effective means of political resistance or protest (Schepping 1993a). For those in the underground, these songs at times served as a code or a means of identification and became a medium for sometimes obvious, sometimes concealed, political or religious opposition, and in songs traditional and newly composed (Schepping 1995). The rebellious texts of the Roman Catholic churchman Georg Thurmair, often set to melodies by Adolf Lohmann in church or minor modes, became popular, and were even issued in an ecclesiastical recording series between 1934 and 1939. In forbidden Russian Cossack songs and parodies, the so-called *Edelweisspiraten* 'edelweiss pirates' opposed Hitler most conspicuously, operating out of bombed-out cities along the Rhine and the Ruhr, specifically Cologne and Wuppertal (Buscher 1988).

By confiscating songbooks, sheet music, and instruments, by searching houses, by interrogating, torturing, and imprisoning individuals, by setting up special concentration camps for young political convicts and penal battalions, and by expelling students from schools and universities, the Nazis tried to suppress the activities of these groups and others. Swing-Jugend (Swing Youth), a provocative opposition movement active in the cities and towns of occupied Europe, was an informal group of youthful enthusiasts of jazz and dance. Groups of young people mimed the clothing, hair, and lifestyles of their American contemporaries, opposing thereby the uniformed Nazi society and its conformist state youth groups (Fackler 1994). Nazi authorities mercilessly persecuted this movement.

After World War II

After the demise of the Third Reich, West German youth organizations regrouped and reclaimed songs forbidden during the dictatorship and those of earlier times. Schools endeavored to create a new repertoire, based on experiments in the 1930s with tonality, rhythm, harmony and irregular phrases and freed from traditional constraints. Several of these songs—Karl Marx's "*Jeden Morgen geht die Sonne auf*" ('Every Morning the Sun Rises'), G. Wolters' "*Freunde, lasst uns fröhlich loben*" ('Friends, Let's Gaily Praise'), W. Gneist's "*Es tagt der Sonne Morgenstrahl*" ('The Sun's Morning Rays Dawn'), and H. Lau's "*Singt ein Vogel*" ('A Bird Sings')—became popular and were published in school songbooks and elsewhere. In response to the Nazi regime's adulteration of German folk songs, foreign folkloric items found their way into German youth singing and songbooks.

Postwar contact with the flood of African-American spirituals, blues, and jazz that swept through popular music radically changed the tone of German singing. Blues and jazz harmonies, and above all, jazz rhythms and phrasing, influenced popular singing, dancing, and instrumental music. The high proportion of this music in the media first conquered the musical practices of the younger generation, then of their parents, and even children's singing and dancing (Segler 1990–1992). Finally, these developments overflowed into young people's new religious music, in which the unusual harmonies and syncopations at first overwhelmed congregations' musical abilities (Bubmann 1990; Malessa 1980; Schepping 1993b; Zenetti 1966). Later, melodic and rhythmic re-Europization softened these effects.

Folk music took a different course in the communist German Democratic Republic (DDR), founded in 1949. The state supervised all cultural activities, including "folk art," which had to make a contribution to the education and creation of the socialist individual (Meyer 1994). The martial, optimistic march style dominated in communist battle songs and socialist collective songs of the Freie Deutsche

Folk-song research and collection in Germany began with Herder's wish to set down the songs of the people, "exactly as they are, in their original language, with sufficient commentary, but unchanged, without ridicule and in no way edited or improved; if at all possible with their melodies and all that belongs to the life of the people."

Jugend (Free German Youth), the Communist Party, unions, "industrial battle groups," and the National People's Army.

In the mid-1960s, hootenannies (folk singers' meetings for public entertainment) broadened the style and content of state-regulated singing; however, folk music, which included not only folk song and dance, but also jazz, beat, rock, and the music of discotheques, remained under state control and organization. The authorities limited undesirable influences by requiring permits for professional and amateur musicians and controlling the conditions for education, scholarships, and competitions. Besides the regulation of the Oktoberklub (earlier, Hootenanny-Club), the Singebewegung (Song Movement), with its workshops, festivals, competitions, and public folk-music meetings, was subject to approval from the state censor, and music was accepted or rejected according to its geopolitical origin. In 1963, the erection of the Berlin Wall and the prohibition on travel completed a series of disciplinary and isolationist actions. Dissenters like the Canadian folksinger Perry Friedman, a DDR resident since 1959, were forbidden to perform, publish, or broadcast, and in 1976 the politically critical songwriter Wolf Biermann was driven into exile.

Protectionist methods did not prevail: already in 1970, at the yearly meeting of the Festival of Political Song, contact between international participants from "kindred countries" and leftist Western folk groups had introduced inevitable political criticism. Finally, Western radio and television broke down all frontiers. In the mid-1980s, the restrictions had to be loosened, and music functioned increasingly as a political outlet, unifying artists and their audience. Texts carried hidden political messages that the public could easily decipher. Singing was incorporated into a growing oppositional movement, in part prepared by prayers for peace and singing in churches, which played a far-reaching part in the fall of the DDR in 1989 (Kirchenwitz 1993).

HISTORY OF SCHOLARSHIP

Folk-song research and collection in Germany began with Herder's wish to set down the songs of the people, "exactly as they are, in their original language, with sufficient commentary, but unchanged, without ridicule and in no way edited or improved; if at all possible with their melodies and all that belongs to the life of the people" (188? [1777]). Herder's formulation outlined goals that are still important: the authentic documentation of texts and melodies, with accompanying description of the cultural context from which they develop. Additionally, Herder stimulated research into folk culture as a whole—an investigation that folk-song scholars led and that eventually evolved into the science of ethnology. For many years, research on folk songs dominated the discipline of ethnomusicology—until, at the turn of the twentieth century, scholars also began studying dance and instrumental music.

Herder's new term, *Volkslied,* formulated in 1771 on the analogy of the English term *popular song* and the French *chanson populaire,* first appeared in print in 1773. Its precise definition and content have been the subject of debate ever since (Heimann 1982; Klusen 1969; Linder-Beroud 1989; Meier 1971 [1906]; Pulikowski 1933; Schepping 1994; Wiora 1962 [1950]); Herder's impetus, however, released a wave of enthusiasm for folk song and a frenzy of collecting that carried over into dance and instrumental music. Song collectors in the initial aesthetic-prescientific stage (Linder-Beroud 1989) limited themselves to assembling, editing, and often revising song texts. This held, not only for Herder's own editions (1778, 1779) of German songs and European songs in German translation, but also for the earliest and most famous anthology after Herder, *Des Knaben Wunderhorn: Alte deutsche Lieder* (1806–1808). These three volumes, edited by the prominent German Romantic poets Achim von Arnim and Clemens Brentano, contained more than seven hundred song texts (without melodies), including sacred and profane songs, children's songs, love songs, and ballads. The texts of this collection soon found new musical settings in symphonies, orchestral songs, and other works by Gustav Mahler, and in choral and solo songs by Brahms, Schumann, and Richard Strauss. A great number of melodies belonging to these texts have been rediscovered (E. Stockmann 1958).

The multivolume anthologies of German folk song by F. K. von Erlach (1834–1837), Ludwig Uhland (1968 [1844–1866]), and F. W. von Ditfurth (1871, 1872a, 1872b, 1874a, 1874b, 1874c, 1875a, 1875b, 1876) were also composed purely of song texts. During this phase of research, authors and editors rarely followed Herder's approach. One who did was the young Goethe, who, in 1771, while collecting songs "from the throats of the oldest grandmothers" in Alsace, notated melodies and song texts; though these melodies were lost, they have been reconstructed (Müller-Blattau 1955; Pinck 1935 [1932]).

The largest and most important early editions of song texts and melodies (Erk 1856, expanded into Erk and Böhme 1963 [1893–1894]; Erk and Irmer 1838–1845) belong to the prescientific phase on account of their methods of collecting, processing, and editing. Böhme's collections of 1877 and 1893 extended the aesthetic and historical definition of folk song to folklike song (*volksthümliches Lied*) by including oral evidence from folk culture, with texts and melodies. Böhme was the first to incorporate traditional and social dance into folk-music research in a significant publication and was the first researcher to make children's songs and games accessible.

Among the anthologies published in rapid succession in the 1800s were comprehensive collections that established songs as a significant mirror of historical events, though songs in part were themselves prey to nationalistic inclinations. Much earlier, parallel to *Des Knaben Wunderhorn,* anthologies with songs from the German countryside appeared, often with texts in regional dialects. These publications were the result of Germany's regional distinctions, with their differences in dialect, religion, culture, and (until the 1800s) political life. Folk-music research was marked from the beginning by the same regional divisions. It began with the Deutsches Volksliedarchiv (German Folk-Song Archive) in Freiburg-i-Breisgau, founded in 1914 by John Meier (figure 8), which has remained a leading institute for folk-song research in Germany. Later, other regional archives opened with individual emphases and aims, each active in collecting, researching, and publishing.

In the early 1900s, some regional anthologies attempted a more authentic reproduction of folk melodies. A more accurate record of rhythm and meter was demonstrated by Heeger and Wüst in a 1909 song collection from Rheinpfalz. A comparable recording of melodic accuracy can be found in a 1911 collection by Georg Amft from the duchy of Glatz, which impressively documents, through variants, the free

FIGURE 8   John Meier, founder in 1914 of the German Folk-Song Archive, Seemann 1954.

formation of text and melody in live performance. The most significant and exhaustive rural-song collection before World War II deepened this approach to folk songs from Alsace-Lorraine (Pinck 1926–1939, 1962).

When the phonograph became available, research captured the nuances of text and melody in performance. In German-speaking countries, wax cylinders were used early by Josef Pommer in 1908, Georg Schünemann (1923), and Kurt Huber, who recorded old Bavarian songs in 1925 (Huber and Kiem 1930, 1936, 1937) and traditional Bosnian songs and musical folklore from Sarajevo in 1937. After 1939, the newly developed AEG tape recorder was used by workers from the State Institute for German Music Research in Berlin to document musical folklore until 1943, including thousands of examples of sacred and secular, monophonic and polyphonic songs, and dances and instrumental music from the so-called reimmigrants forced back into Germany by Hitler's racist policies: ethnic Germans from Russia, Romania, the Tirol, and forced laborers from Ukraine.

These recordings illustrate how folk-music research in the Third Reich was dependent on Nazi political goals. The Nazis made every effort to press folk-music research and publications into the service of the state. Research into the musical culture of ethnic Germans outside Germany was misused for the hegemonic and racist politics of the Third Reich. Huge efforts were made to Germanize and mythologize the complete early folk heritage, and to de-Christianize religious folk customs and songs, or at least suppress them through new repertoires (Lang 1941). The *Lieder der Bewegung* 'songs of the [Nazi] movement', called new folk songs, were propagated and encouraged. Ethnomusicologists were coerced into working within political-ideological frameworks, which even the opponents of the regime found difficult to shun. For at least a decade, folk-musical research was debilitated and compromised.

Trends after World War II

After World War II, ethnomusicology struggled to cleanse itself of Nazi ideology. Regaining objectivity, scholars tried to embrace the new approaches influenced in particular by sociology (Klusen 1974–1975). Folk-music editions returned to production soon after the end of World War II. Publications of songs of the Middle Ages and the Renaissance, customary songs (*Brauchtumslieder*), broadside ballads, politically critical songs, and erotic songs appeared, as did reprints of important historical collections and facsimiles. Several anthologies by East German researchers, though politically tendentious, proved particularly significant. These editions dealt with sung material that earlier collectors and editors had almost completely overlooked—the satirical and protest songs of the lower classes, including workers, peasants, craftsmen, soldiers, revolutionaries, and prisoners. The most important publication (Steinitz 1954–1962) greatly influenced youth singing in both German states. Even socialist publications, including somewhat one-sided editions and recordings of workers' songs, peasants' laments, songs from the fascist concentration camps, and the series Das Lied im Kampf geboren ('Song Born in Struggle') of 1957–1967 from the Worker's Song Commission of the GDR Academy of Arts, and anthologies on Berlin's *Gassenhauer* 'popular street songs' (Richter 1969), filled real gaps in research on West German folk songs.

Editions of songs adapted to modern technologies appeared with printed melodies and texts, with recorded examples. In Freiburg, the Künzig Institute for East German Folklore, founded in 1951, led the field in quality and quantity of song, dance, and musical matter collected from residents of German extraction in East European countries (figure 9). By phonetically notating texts and original pronunciations in the LP series *Quellen deutscher Volkskunde* (Künzig, Werner, and Habenicht 1967–), it created a model edition of vocal folk music.

FIGURE 9 A string band from a German community living in Eastern Europe. The band, which uses three homemade fiddles and a bass that the player can play while the instrument hangs from a strap around his neck, is based on a model typical of the Carpathian Mountain region, stretching from Romania through Slovakia to Poland. Künzig 1958: plate 2.

Contrary to the popularly held opinion that folk music is in decline, modern German society shows a marked increase in the number and kinds of primarily functional musical occasions, including collective singing, music making, and impromptu dancing by audiences in the thousands at sporting events, civic carnivals and festivals, and folk, pop, and rock concerts. German ethnomusicologists are devoting themselves increasingly, and with less prejudice, to this field of action and interaction.

BIBLIOGRAPHY

Amft, Georg. 1911. *Volkslieder der Grafschaft Glatz.* Habelschwerdt: J. Wolf.

Arnim, Achim von, and Clemens Brentano. 1806–1808. *Des Knaben Wunderhorn.* 3 vols. Heidelberg: Mohr und Winter.

Bachmann, Fritz. 1972. *Rezeptionskundliche Untersuchungen zur Tanzmusik in der Deutschen Demokratischen Republik.* Leipzig: VEB Deutscher Verlag für Musik.

Baumann, Max Peter. 1976. *Musikfolklore und Musikfolklorismus: eine ethnologische Untersuchung zum Funktionswandel des Jodelns.* Winterthur: Amadeus-Verlag.

Besseler, Heinrich. 1925. "Grundfragen des musikalischen Hörens." *Jahrbuch Peters* 32:35–52.

Böhme, Franz Magnus. 1966 [1877]. *Altdeutsches Liederbuch.* Hildesheim: Olms.

———. 1967a [1897]. *Deutsches Kinderlied und Kinderspiel.* Wiesbaden: Breitkopf und Härtel.

———. 1967b [1886]. *Geschichte des Tanzes in Deutschland.* Hildesheim: Olms.

———. 1970 [1895]. *Volksthümliche Lieder der Deutschen.* Hildesheim: Olms.

Boletta, W. L. 1967. "The Role of Music in Medieval German Drama: Easter Plays and Passion Plays." Ph.D. dissertation, Vanderbilt University.

Braun, Hartmut. 1985. *Einführung in die musikalische Volkskunde.* Darmstadt: Wissenschaftliche Buchgesellschaft.

Brednich, Rolf Wilhelm. 1974. *Die Liedpublizistik im Flugblatt des 15–17 Jahrhunderts.* 2 vols. Baden-Baden.

———. 1979. *Erotische Lieder aus 500 Jahren.* Frankfurt: Fischer.

———, Lutz Röhrich, and Wolfgang Suppan. 1973, 1975. *Handbuch des Volksliedes.* 2 vols. Munich: Wilhelm Fink.

Breuer, Hans. 1908. *Der Zupfgeigenhansl.* Leipzig: Hofmeister.

Bringemeier, Martha. 1931. *Gemeinschaft und Volkslied: Ein Beitrag zur Dorfkultur des Münsterlandes.* Münster: Aschendorff.

Bröcker, Marianne, ed., 1992. *Tanz und Tanzmusik in Überlieferung und Gegenwart.* Bamberg: Universitätsbibliothek Bamberg.

Bubmann, Peter. 1990. *Sound zwischen Himmel und Erde: Populäre christliche Musik.* Stuttgart: Quell-Verlag.

Buscher, Paulus. 1988. *Das Stigma "Edelweiss-Pirat."* Koblenz: Siegfried Bublies.

Danckert, Werner. 1966. *Das Volkslied im Abendland.* Bern and Munich: Francke.

Deutsch, Ernst, and Wilhelm Schepping. 1988. *Musik im Brauch der Gegenwart.* Vienna: A. Schendl.

Deutsche Volkstänze. 1926–1963. 57 vols. Kassel: Bärenreiter.

Deutsches Volksliedarchiv. 1924–1972. *Landschaftliche Volkslieder mit ihren Weisen.* Kassel, London, New York: Bärenreiter.

———. 1928–. *Jahrbuch für Volksliedforschung.* 4 vols. to date.

———. 1935–. *Deutsche Volkslieder mit ihren*

Melodien. 10 vols. to date. Berlin and Leipzig: Walter de Gruyter (vols. 1–4). Freiburg: DVA.

———. 1986. *Studien zur Volksliedforschung.* Bern, Frankfurt, New York, and Paris: Peter Lang.

Ditfurth, Franz-Wilhelm von. 1871, 1872a, 1877. *Die historischen Volkslieder.* 3 vols. Berlin, Heilbronn: Franz Lipperheide.

———. 1872b. *Deutsche Volks- und Gesellschaftslieder des 17. und 18. Jahrhundert.* Nördlingen: C. H. Beck.

———. 1874a. *Balladen: 16.–18. Jahrhundert.* Stuttgart: G. J. Göschen.

———. 1874b. *Balladen und Liebeslieder: 16. Jahrhundert.* Stuttgart: G. J. Göschen.

———. 1874c. *52 ungedruckte Balladen des 16., 17. und 18. Jahrhunderts aus fliegenden Blättern, handschriftlichen Quellen und mündlichen Über-lieferungen.* Stuttgart: G. J. Göschen

———. 1875a. *Einhundertundzehn Volks- und Gesellschaftslieder des 16., 17. und 18. Jahrhunderts mit und ohne Singweisen nach fliegenden Blättern, handschriftlichen Quellen und dem Volksmunde.* Stuttgart: G. J. Göschen.

———. 1875b. *Volks- und Gesellschaftslieder: 16. Jahrhundert.* Stuttgart: G. J. Göschen.

———. 1876. *Lieder des 16. und 17. Jahrhunderts mit ihren zweistimmigen Singweisen.* Stuttgart: G. J. Göschen.

Döring, Alois. 1988. *Glockenbeiern im Rheinland.* Cologne: Rheinland-Verlag

Eberwein, Michl. 1980. *Das Eberwein-Liederbuch: Eine Zwiefachen- und Liedersammlung vom Eberwein-Vater.* Munich, Vienna, Zürich: BLV-Verlag.

Ehrenwerth, Manfrid. 1992. *Teufelsgeige und ländliche Musikkapellen in Westfalen.* Münster: Coppenrath.

Eichstedt, Astrid, and Bernd Polster. 1985. *Wie die Wilden: Tänze auf der Höhe ihrer Zeit.* Berlin: Rotbuch-Verlag.

Eisenburg, Beni. 1977. *Volkstanz in Bayern.* Munich: Preissler.

Erk, Ludwig. 1856. *Deutscher Liederhort.* Berlin: Enslin.

Erk, Ludwig, and Wilhelm Irmer, eds. 1838–1845. *Die deutschen Volkslieder mit ihren Singweisen.* 13 vols. Berlin and Potsdam: Ludwig Voggenreiter.

Erk, Ludwig, and Franz Magnus Böhme. 1963 [1893–1894]. *Deutscher Liederhort: Auswahl der vorzüglicheren Deutschen Volkslieder nach Wort und Weise aus der Vorzeit und Gegenwart, gesammelt und erläutert von Ludwig Erk.* Wiesbaden: Held.

Erlach, Friedrich Karl von. 1834–1837. *Die Volkslieder der Deutschen.* 5 vols. Mannheim: Heinrich Hoff.

Fackler, Guido. 1994. "Zwischen (musikalischem) Widerstand und Propaganda-Jazz im 'Dritten Reich'." In *Musikalische Volkskultur und die politis-*

che Macht, ed. Günther Noll, 437–484. Essen: Die Blaue Eule.

Frey, Jürgen, and Karel Siniveer. 1987. *Eine Geschichte der Folkmusik.* Reinbek: Rowohlt.

Gansberg, Ingeborg. 1986. *Volksliedsammlungen und historischer Kontext: Kontinuität über zwei Jahrhunderte?* Frankfurt, Bern, New York, Paris: Peter Lang.

Gennrich, Friedrich, ed. 1960 [1951]. *Troubadours, Trouvères, Minne- und Meistergesang.* Cologne: Arno-Volk-Verlag.

Goldschmidt, Änne. 1967. *Handbuch des deutschen Volktanzes: Systematische Darstellung der gebräuchlichsten deutschen Volktänze.* Berlin: Henschelverlag Kunst und Gesellschaft.

Gräter, Friedrich David. 1968 [1794]. "Ueber die teutschen Volkslieder und ihre Musik." In *Gräters Beitrag zur Volksliedforschung,* ed. Hermann Bausinger. *Jahrbuch Wuerttembergisch-Franken* 52:201–226.

Habenicht, Gottfried. 1996. *Leid im Lied: Südost- und ostdeutsche Lagerlieder und Lieder von Flucht, Vertreibung und Verschleppung.* Freiburg: Johannes Künzig–Institut für Ostdeutsche Volkskunde.

Heeger, Georg, and Wilhelm Wüst. 1963 [1909]. *Volkslieder aus der Rheinpfalz.* 2 vols. Edited by Joseph Müller-Blattau. Mainz: Schott.

Heimann, Walter. 1982. *Musikalische Interaktion.* Cologne: Gerig.

Heising, Elvira, and Sigrid Römer. 1994. *Der Tanz im "Künstlerischen Volksschaffen" der DDR: Amateurbühnentanz—Volkstanz zum Mitmachen.* Tanzhistorische Studien, 8. Informationen zum Tanz, 21. Remscheid: Deutscher Bundesverband Tanz.

Herder, Johann Gottfried. 188? [1773]. "Aus deutscher Art und Kunst I: Auszug aus einem Briefwechsel über Ossian und die Lieder alter Völker." In *Stimmen der Völker in Liedern,* 9–48. Halle: Otto Hendel.

———. 188? [1777]. "Ähnlichkeit der mittlern englischen und deutschen Dichtkunst: Aus dem deutschen Museum." In *Stimmen der Völker in Liedern,* 49–60. Halle: Otto Hendel.

———. 1778. *Volkslieder I.* Leipzig: Weygand.

———. 1779. *Volkslieder II.* Leipzig: Weygand.

Hinze, Werner. 1994. "Instrumentalmusik im politischen Kampf der zwanziger Jahre am Beispiel der Schalmei." In *Musikalische Volkskultur und die politische Macht,* ed. Günther Noll, 301–329. Essen: Die Blaue Eule.

Hoerburger, Felix. 1956. *Die Zwiefachen: Gestaltung und Umgestaltungen der Tanzmelodien im nördlichen Altbayern.* Berlin: Akademie-Verlag.

———. 1961, 1964. *Volkstanzkunde.* 2 vols. Kassel: Bärenreiter.

———. 1966. *Musica vulgaris: Lebensgesetze der instrumentalen Volksmusik.* Erlangen: Universitätsbund Erlangen-Nürnberg

Holzapfel, Otto, ed. 1993. *Das Deutsche Volsliedarchiv Freiburg im Breisgau.* Bern, Frankfurt, New York, Paris: Peter Lang.

———. 1996. *Lexikon folkloristischer Begriffe und Theorien (Volksliedforschung).* Bern, Berlin, Frankfurt, New York, Paris, and Vienna: Peter Lang.

Huber, Kurt, and Paul Kiem 1930, 1937. *Oberbayrische Volkslieder mit Bildern und Weisen.* Munich: Knorr und Hirth.

———. 1936. *Altbairisches Liederbuch.* Mainz: Schott.

Hübner, Arthur. 1931. *Die deutschen Geisslerlieder: Studien zum Volkslied des Mittelalters.* Berlin: Walter de Gruyter.

Jöde, Fritz. 1923. *Ringel, Rangel, Rosen: 150 Singspiele und 100 Abzählreime, nach mündlicher Überlieferung gesammelt.* Berlin: Teubner.

Karbusicky, Vladimir. 1973. *Ideologie im Lied, Lied in der Ideologie.* Köln: Gerig.

Kirchenwitz, Lutz. 1993. *Folk, Chanson und Liedermacher in der DDR: Chronisten, Kritiker, Kaisergeburtstagssänger.* Berlin: Dietz.

Klusen, Ernst, ed. 1963 [1875]. *Hans zurmühlen, Des Dülkener Fiedlers Liederbuch.* Viersen and Krefeld: Verein Linker Niederrhein.

———. 1967. "Das Gruppenlied als Gegenstand." *Jahrbuch für Volksliedforschung* 12:21–41.

———. 1969. *Volkslied: Fund und Erfindung.* Cologne: Gerig.

———. 1974–1975. *Zur Situation des Singens in der Bundesrepublik Deutschland.* 2 vols. Cologne: Gerig.

———. 1975. "Zwischen Symphonie und Hit: Folklore?" In *Musikpädagogik heute,* ed. Heinz Antholz und Willi Gundlach, 79–91. Düsseldorf: Schwann.

———. 1986. "The Group Song as Object." In *German Volkskunde,* ed. James R. Dow and Hannjost Lixfeld, 184–202. Bloomington: Indiana University Press.

Korth, Michael. 1979. *Carmina burana: Lateinisch–Deutsch: Gesamtausgabe der mittelalter-lichen Melodien mit den dazugehörigen Texten.* Munich: Heimeran.

Krafeld, Franz Joseph. 1985. *Wir tanzen nicht nach eurer Pfeife: Zur Sozialgeschichte von Volkstanz und Volkstanzpflege in Deutschland.* Lilienthal and Bremen: Eres Edition.

Künzig, Johannes. 1958. *Ehe sie verklingen . . . Alte Deutsche Volksweisen vom Böhmerwald bis zur Wolga.* Freiburg: Verlag Herder.

Künzig, Johannes, and Waltraud Werner. 1975. *Volksballaden und Erzähllieder: Ein Repertorium unserer Tonaufnahmen.* Freiburg: Volkskunde-Tonarchiv des Instituts für ostdeutsche Volkskunde Freiburg.

Künzig, Johannes, Waltraud Werner-Künzig, and

Gottfried Habenicht, eds. 1977. *Legendenlieder: Ein Repertorium unserer Tonaufnahmen.* Freiburg: Volkskunde-Tonarchiv des Instituts für ostdeutsche Volkskunde Freiburg.

Lang, Ilse, ed. 1941. *Lieder zur Weihnachtszeit.* Wolfenbüttel, Berlin: Kallmeyer.

Linder-Beroud, Waltraud. 1989. *Von der Mündlichkeit zur Schriftlichkeit?* Frankfurt, Bern, New York, Paris: Peter Lang.

Linker, Robert White. 1962. *Music of the Minnesinger and Early Meistersinger: A Bibliography.* Chapel Hill: University of North Carolina.

Maerker, Bruno. 1941. "Gregorianischer Gesang und deutsches Volkslied." *Jahrbuch für Volksliedforschung* 7:71–127.

Malessa, Andreas. 1980. *Der neue Sound: Christliche Popmusik—Geschichte und Geschichten.* Wuppertal: Brockhaus.

Meier, Ernst. 1977 [1855]. *Schwäbische Volkslieder mit ausgewählten Melodien.* Kirchheim/Teck: Verlag Jürgen Schweier.

Meier, John. 1971 [1906]. *Kunstlieder im Volksmunde.* Hildesheim: Verlag Olms.

———. 1940. "Volksliedsammlung und Volksliedforschung in Deutschland." *Deutsche Kultur im Leben der Völker* 15:190–210.

Meyer, Thomas. 1994. "Musiker zwischen Repression und Förderung—-Bemerkungen zum kulturpolitischen System der DDR." In *Musikalische Volkskultur und die politische Macht,* ed. Günther Noll, 43–55. Essen: Die Blaue Eule.

Moser, Hugo, and Joseph Müller-Blattau. 1968. *Deutsche Lieder des Mittelalters von Walther v. d. Vogelweide bis zum Lochamer Liederbuch.* Stuttgart: Klett.

———. 1977. *Die Volksliedsammlung des jungen Goethe.* Kassel: Bärenreiter.

Noll, Günther, ed. 1992. *Musikalische Volkskunde—heute.* Cologne: Cologne University.

———, ed. 1994. *Musikalische Volkskultur und die politische Macht.* Essen: Die Blaue Eule.

Noll, Günther, and Wilhelm Schepping, eds. 1992. *Musikalische Volkskultur in der Stadt der Gegenwart.* Hanover: Metzler.

———. 1995. *30 Jahre Institut für Musikalische Volkskunde 1964–1994.* Cologne: Cologne University.

Oetke, Herbert. 1951, 1951, 1952. *Volkstänze unserer Heimat.* 3 vols. Berlin: Neues Leben.

———. 1982. *Der deutsche Volkstanz.* 2 vols. Wilhelmshaven: Heinrichshofens' Verlag.

Petermann, Kurt. 1982. *Wechselbeziehungen zwischen Volks- und Gesellschaftstanz.* Berlin: Deutscher Bundesverband Tanz.

Piechura, Sabine. 1995. "Beruf: Wandermusiker: Lokaltradition und Biographie in Interviews mit ehemaligen Wandermusikern und -musikerinnen

aus dem eichsfeldischen Hundeshagen." In *Musikalische Volkskultur als soziale Chance,* ed. Günther Noll and Helga Stein, 319–340. Essen: Die Blaue Eule.

Pinck, Louis. 1926–1939, 1962. *Verklingende Weisen.* 5 vols. Kassel and Metz: Bärenreiter.

———, ed. 1935 [1932]. *Volkslieder von Goethe im Elsass gesammelt.* Saarbrücken: Saarbrücker Druckerei und Verlag.

Pommer, Josef. 1912. "Meine Definition des Begriffes 'Volkslied'." *Das deutsche Volkslied* 14:99–100.

Praetorius, Michael. 1958 [1619]. *Syntagma Musicum,* vol. 2: *De Organographia.* Kassel: Bärenreiter.

Probst-Effah, Gisela. 1989. "Das Lied im NS-Widerstand: Ein Beitrag zur Rolle der Musik in den nationalsozialistischen Konzentrationslagern." In *Musikpädagogische Forschung,* ed. Christa Nauck-Börner, 79–89. Laaber: Laaber Verlag.

———. 1995. *Lieder gegen "das Dunkel in den Köpfen": Untersuchungen zur Folkbewegung in der Bundesrepublik Deutschland.* Essen: Die Blaue Eule.

Pulikowski, Julian von. 1933. *Geschichte des Begriffes "Volkslied" im musikalischen Schrifttum.* Heidelberg: Carl Winters Universitäts-Buchhandlung.

Reimers, Astrid. 1995. *Laienmusizieren in Köln.* Cologne: Bachem.

Richter, Lukas. 1969. *Der berliner Gassenhauer.* Leipzig: Deutscher Verlag für musik.

Röhrich, Lutz. 1992. "Volkstümliche Lieder zwischen Mündlichkeit und Schriftlichkeit." In *Musikalische Volkskunde—heute,* ed. Günther Noll, 131–177. Cologne: Universität zu Köln.

Rölleke, Heinz, ed. 1979. *Des Knaben Wunderhorn: alte deutsche Lieder gesammelt von Achim von Arnim und Clemens Brentano.* Stuttgart: Kohlhammer. Studienausgabe in neun Bänden, mit Lesarten und Erläuterungen.

———, ed. 1975. *Stimmen der Völker in Liedern: Volkslieder.* 2 vols. Stuttgart: Reclam.

———. 1993. *Das Volksliederbuch.* Cologne: Kiepenheuer & Witsch.

Roth, Klaus. 1977. *Ehebruchschwänke in Liedform: Eine Untersuchung zur deutsch- und englischsprachigen Schwankballade.* Munich: Wilhelm Fink.

Runge, Paul. 1900. *Die Lieder und Melodien der Geissler des Jahres 1349 nach der Aufzeichnung Hugos von Reutlingen.* Leipzig: Breitkopf & Härtel.

Salmen, Walter. 1951. *Das Lochamer Liederbuch: Eine musikgeschichtliche Studie.* Leipzig: Breitkopf & Härtel.

———. 1983. *Der Spielmann im Mittelalter.* Innsbruck: Edition Helbling.

———. 1991a. "Singen—ein Grundbedürfnis

des Menschen?" In *Singen in Bayern: Alte und neue Singformen "überlieferter" Lieder,* ed. Bayerischer Landesverein für Heimatpflege, 9–22. Munich: Bayerischer Landesverein für Heimatpflege.

———. 1991b. "Zur Situation des Dialektliedes heute: Belege aus dem Niederrheinraum." *Jahrbuch für Volksliedforschung* 36:29–47.

———. 1992. "Probleme gegenwartsorientierter Forschung und Dokumentation in der Musikalischen Volkskunde." In *Musikalische Volkskunde—heute,* ed. Günther Noll, 35–58. Cologne: Cologne University.

———. 1993a. "Menschen seid wachsam." *Widerständisches Liedgut der Jugend in der NS-Zeit.* Munich: Museumspädagogisches Zentrum.

———. 1993b. "Zwischen Popularität und 'Opus-Musik': Das Neue Geistliche Lied im rheinischen Raum." In *Musikalische Volkskultur im Rheinland: Aktuelle Forschungsbeiträge,* ed. Günther Noll, 9–49. Kassel: Merseburger.

———. 1994. "*Lied- und Musikforschung.*" In *Grundriss der Volkskunde: Einführung in die Forschungsfelder der Europäischen Ethnologie,* ed. Rolf Wilhelm Brednich, 467–492. Berlin: Dietrich Reimer.

———. 1995. "Annotation und Konnotation im oppositionellen Liedgut der NS-Zeit." In *Kunst und Widerstand,* ed. Hildegard Vieregg and Hinrich Siefken, 171–210. Munich: Iudicium Verlag.

Schünemann, Georg. 1923. *Das Lied der deutschen Kolonisten in Russland.* Munich: Drei Masken Verlag.

Seemann, Erich. 1954. *John Meier: Sein Leben, Forschen, und Wirken.* Freiburg-im-Breisgau: Hans Ferdinand Schultz Verlag.

Segler, Helmut. 1990–1992. *Tänze der Kinder in Europa: Mit einer Analyse des sozialen Kontextes von Günther Batel.* 2 vols. Celle: Moeck.

Sell, Manfred, ed. 1988. *Musikantenleben: Zur Volkskunde und Sozialgeschichte ländlich lebender Musikanten im ausgehenden 19. Jahrhundert.* Schriften des Freilichtmuseums am Kiekeberg. Ehestorf: Freilichtmuseum am Kiekeberg.

Steinitz, Wolfgang. 1954–1962. *Deutsche Volkslieder demokratischen Charakters aus fünf Jahrhunderten.* 2 vols. Berlin: Akademie-Verlag.

Stief, Wiegand. 1976–1984. *Melodietypen des deutschen Volksgesanges.* 4 vols. Graz: Akademische Druck- und Verlagsanstalt.

Stockmann, Doris, ed. 1992. *Volks- und Popularmusik in Europa.* Laaber: Laaber Verlag.

Stockmann, Erich, ed. 1958. *"Des Knaben Wunderhorn" in den Weisen seiner Zeit.* Berlin: Akademie-Verlag.

Strobach, Hermann. 1980. *Deutsches Volkslied in Geschichte und Gegenwart.* Berlin: Akademie-Verlag.

Suppan, Wolfgang. 1978. *Volkslied: Seine Sammlung und Erforschung.* Stuttgart: Vandenhoek.

———. 1983. *Blasmusik in Baden: Geschichte und Gegenwart einer traditionsreichen Blasmusiklandschaft.* Freiburg: Fritz Schulz.

Thiel, Helga. 1970. *Die deutschen Volktänze in Böhmen, Mähren und Schlesien.* Marburg: Elwert Verlag.

Uhland, Ludwig. 1968 [1844–1866]. *Alte hoch- und niederdeutsche Volkslieder.* Hildesheim: Olms.

Virdung, Sebastian. 1970 [1511]. *Musica getutscht und aussgezogen.* Kassel: Bärenreiter.

Vogt, Margrit. 1986. *Alte niederdeutsche Volkstänze.* Münster: F. Coppenrath.

Weigel, Johann Christoph. 1961 [1720].

Musicalisches Theatrum. Facsimile edition, ed. A. Berner. Kassel, Basel, London, New York: Bärenreiter.

Wiora, Walter. 1949a. "Alpenländische Liedweisen der Frühzeit und des Mittelalters im Lichte vergleichender Forschung." In *Festschrift J. Meier,* 169–198. Lahr: Schauenberg.

———. 1949b. *Zur Frühgeschichte der Musik in den Alpenländern.* Basel: Schweizerische Gesellschaft für Volkskunde— Verlagsbuchhandlung G. Krebs.

———. 1962 [1950]. "Das echte Volkslied." Heidelberg: Müller-Thiergarten.

———. 1953. *Die rheinisch-bergischen Melodien bei Zuccalmaglio und Brahms.* Bad Godesberg: Voggenreiter.

———. 1959. "Der Untergang des Volkslieds

und sein zweites Dasein." In *Volkslied heute,* ed. Walter Wiora, 9–25. Kassel and Basel: Bärenreiter.

Wolf, Jürgen B., and Eric Kross. 1987. *Bibliographie der Literatur zum deutschen Volkslied: Mit Standortangaben an den wichtigsten Archiven und Bibliotheken der DDR.* Leipzig: Zentralhaus-Publikation.

Zachmeier, Edwin, ed. 1991 [1911]. *Tafelmeiers Tanzmusik.* Munich: L. Stimme.

Zenetti, Lothar. 1966. *Heisse [W]Eisen: Jazz, Spirituals, Beatsongs und Schlager in der Kirche.* Munich: J. Pfeiffer.

Zurmühlen, Hans, ed. 1875. *Des Dülkener Fiedlers Liederbuch.* Viersen: Verein Linker Niederrhein.

AUDIOVISUAL RESOURCES

10 Jahre neue Lieder in der Kirche: Eine Dokumentation. 1972. Schwann Verlag Düsseldorf DP F 60.557–61. 5 LP disks.

50 Jahre Schlager 1900–1950. n.d. Marcato 63651–5. Ariola 63656. 6 LP disks.

Allmein Gedanken, die ich hab: Volkslieder aus 4 Jahrhunderten in Sätzen von Ernst Klusen. N.d. Aulos Viersen Aul 53586. LP disk.

Augsburger Vokal-Ensemble. 1984. *Bet' und arbeit! Ruft die Welt: Arbeiterlieder des 19. Jahrhunderts in Bayern.* Leitung: Christian Ridil. CLG 30 809. LP disk.

Bairische Volksmusik. 1982. Teldec Telefunken-Decca 6.28609. LP disk.

Bartmann, Manfred. 1991. *Das Beiern der Glocken in der Grafschaft Bentheim, Denekamp (NL) und Ostfriesland.* Philipp Verlag und Bauer Studios GmbH, Ludwigsburg. 080491–2. Cassette.

Baumann, Max Peter. 1984. *Volksmusik in Franken: Eine ethnomusikologische Dokumentation.* Oberfränkische Verlagsanstalt und Druckerei GmbH Hof. Dynasound 51/0584. 2 LP disks.

Brandl, Rudolf M., Marianne Bröcker, und Annette Erler, ed. 1989. *Dokumentation des Musiklebens in Niedersachsen: Lüneburg und Umgebung.* Göttingen: Edition RE. Cassette.

Busch, Ernst. N.d. *Legenden, Lieder und Balladen von 1914–1934.* Text: Bertolt Brecht. Eterna 8 10 017. LP disk.

Dokumente regionaler Musikkultur. 1994–. Edition Volksmusik-archiv des Bezirks Oberbayern. Bruckmühl. CD series.

Ehe sie verklingen. . . . Alte deutsche Volksweisen vom Böhmerwald bis zur Wolga. 1958. Freiburg: Herder. LP disk.

Frankl, Hai, and Topsy Frankl. 1981. *Wacht Oif! Jiddische Arbeiter- und Widerstandslieder.* FolkFreak/Ebergötzen FF 2002. LP disk.

Fürsten in Lumpen und Loden: "Zollfrei": Lieder der Jugendbewegung: Bündische Jugend seit der Jahrhundertwende. 1990. Vive le Gues Verlag GmbH, Dirk Hespers and Mönchengladbach DHGD 06. LP disk.

Gebirtig, Mordechaj, Manfred Lemm, and Ensemble. 1985. *Gehat hob ich a Hejm: Jiddische Lieder des Volkssängers und Arbeiterdichters, Pläne.* Verlag EK 17 10 52. LP disk.

Hein & Oss. 1966. *Soldatenlieder.* CBS S 62 909. LP disk.

———. 1982. *Lieder vom Hambacher Fest.* Büchergilde Gutenberg 20 606/0. LP disk.

Hellkuhl, Antoinette, ed. 1989. *Traditionelle Volkslieder aus dem Ruhrgebiet, 1.* Verlag Peter Pomp, 89 355–043. LP disk.

Jacobus, Hans. 1973. *100 Jahre Deutsches Arbeiterlied. Eine Dokumentation.* Eterna 8 10 015–016. 2 LP disks.

Kreuzfidel im Alpenland: Original alpenländische Volksmusik. N.d. Saphir 25 702–2 SB. LP disk.

Küchen-Lieder. N.d. Europa E 301. LP disk.

Künzig, Johannes, Waltraud Werner, and Gottfried Habenicht, eds. 1967–. *Quellen deutscher Volkskunde.* Freiburg: Volkskunde-Tonarchiv des Instituts für ostdeutsche Volkskunde Freiburg. Veröffentlichungen aus dem Volkskunde-Tonarchiv Freiburg. 13 LP disks to date.

Kuwest, Georg. N.d. *Der Leierkastenmann.* Ariola 202 140–241. LP disk.

Lammel, Inge. 1971. *Vorwärts und nicht vergessen: Musik der Arbeiterbewegung in Dokumentaufnahmen.* 8 10 052. LP disk. Berlin: Verlag VEB Deutscheplatten.

Lied-Wort-Dokument im deutschen antifaschistischen Widerstand 1933–1945. N.d. Eterna Stereo 8 15 097–098. 2 LP disks.

"Liederbücher" I. 1964–1979. Polydor 2630 110. 2 LP disks.

"Liederbücher" II. 1966–1981. Polydor 2679 082. 2 LP disks.

Martinslieder. 1977. Freiburg: Christopherus Verlag SCGLV 75 967. LP disk.

Met Trööte un Trumme: Lieder und Märsche aus dem Rheinland mit dem Kölner Kinderchor. N.d. Fidula FON 3032. LP disk.

Müller-Blattau, Wendelin. 1968–1969. *Goldene Lieder des Mittelalters.* MPS Records GmbH 0188.043. LP disk.

———. 1983. *Der Schwartenhals: Schöne alte Landsknechtslieder.* Thorofon FTH 262. LP disk.

Piechura, Sabine. 1993. *Mit Musik gegangen.* N.p. Video.

Pinck, Louis, and Fritz Neumeyer. 1975. *Lothringer Lieder & Balladen: Aus 'Verklingende Weisen.'* Harmonia Mundi 29 21531-8. 2 LP disks.

Sachsenhausenkomitee West-Berlin. N.d. . . . *denn in uns zieht die Hoffnung mit Lieder, gesungen im Konzentrationslager Sachsenhausen.* Sachsenhausenkomitee West-Berlin, c/o VVN and Verband der Antifaschisten. Cassette.

Schnitzfolgen, Suppinger. N.d. *"No en Sotta": Schwäbische Lieder & Tänze.* Tonstudio F. Mauermann, Ostfildern 1 (Ruit), MAS 130. LP disk.

Segler, Helmut, und Doris C. Kleindienst-Andrée. 1982. *Tänze der Kinder aus dem südlichen Niedersachsen.* Göttingen: Institut für den Wissenschaftlichen Film C1468.

Sie krieh'n uns nit kaputt. Mainzer Karneval in Tondokumenten. 1976. Helau 00 176. LP disk.

So leben wir, so leben wir . . . 500 Jahre deutsche Militärmusik. 1977. Teldec Telefunken-Decca Schallplatten GmbH DX 6.30111. 3 LP disks.

Speelemann, Speele. N.d. *De Goldmüehle: Niederdeutsche Volkslieder.* Autogram Records ALLP-216. LP disk.

Stockmann, Erich. 1985. *Folk's Tanz Haus.* VEB Deutsche Schallplatten Berlin DDR Sstereo 845289. LP disk.

Studio der frühen Musik. 1972. *Oswald von Wolkenstein.* EMI 29 653-3 Stereo LP disk.

Tibbe, Monika, and Manfred Bronson. 1981. *Folk, Folklore, Volkslied.* J. B. Metzler 30185. 2 LP disks.

Tränenlieder aus der Küche. N.d. Europa E 373. LP disk.

Ulrich, Manfred. 1984. *Deutsche Volkslieder: 1, Soldaten—Demokraten.* Autogram Records ALLP–909. LP disk.

Unvergängliche Volksmusik: Lieder und Weisen aus Bayern, dem Bayerischen Wald, dem Salzburger Land und Tirol. N.d. Polydor Stereo 2630 121. 3 LP disks.

Völker, hört die Signale: Internationale Arbeiterkampflieder. N.d. VEB Deutsche Schallplatten Berlin DDR, Eterna 8 15 061. LP disk.

Wiora, Walter, and Gottfried Wolters, eds. 1961–1962. *Deutsche Volkslieder: Eine Dokumentation des Deutschen Musikrates. I, Alte Lieder aus mündlicher Überlieferung; II, Liedsätze aus älterer und neuerer Zeit.* Wolfenbüttel und Zürich: Verlag Mösler DP 008 701–4. 4 LP disks.

Austria

Chris Goertzen
Edward Larkey

Art Music
Folk Music
Popular Music

Austria, a land-locked nation of 83,849 square kilometers, is bordered on the west by Switzerland, the northwest by Germany, the northeast by the Czech Republic, the east by Hungary, the southeast by Croatia, and the southwest by Italy. Nearly all its 7.5 million citizens speak German (often in dialect); just over half are urbanites, and 90 percent are Roman Catholic. Physically and ideologically, the country centers on the valleys of the Danube River and its tributaries, valleys home to modern, productive agriculture. About 40 percent of the country is forested and mountainous. A common aphorism has it that Austria is not large, but tall. Its current borders date from the end of World War I. Before then, its capital, Vienna, was the seat of the Austro-Hungarian Empire. Prosperous and highly industrialized, modern Austria is a federal republic offering many welfare services.

More than a little of the psychological and cultural flavor of Austria responds to its history, that is, that it once was much more powerful. Two trends in musical taste illustrate this: the affection for a grander past, shown through widespread respect for art and folk music; and an unusual tolerance for musical variety within today's national borders. In the early twentieth century, the varieties of music heard on the streets and in the cafes of Vienna reflected the processes of empire: the capital was a powerful economic and cultural magnet. Today, though most of the many non-Austrian cultures that had been under the imperial umbrella are politically independent, the magnet still attracts, and the flow of culture to Vienna remains strong.

ART MUSIC

Most countries find national glory more in the past than the present, but Austrians have more than the average factual basis for such feelings, and thus an unusual predilection for respecting and liking music associated with the national (imperial) past. Many citizens, when asked to specify the most Austrian music, immediately recite a list of composers of art music, awarding special honor to Mozart, Schubert, and the Strauss family [see HISTORY OF EUROPEAN ART MUSIC]. The reasons behind the widespread respect for and knowledge of art music in Austria are straightforward. Much of this music is wonderful. Its aesthetic weight and grace suggest that the land that nurtured it must be culturally powerful. Cultural strength is harder to gauge than political influence: the waning of Austria as a world power may be balanced by its continued importance in art. At the same time, this music evokes eras when Austria played a more prominent international role.

FOLK MUSIC

The split between what some believe to be a glorious past and a crass present is nowhere more strongly—and willfully—limned than in attitudes toward the folk's musical tastes. The bygone folk were rural dwellers, whose agriculture-based lives gave rise to the functional—and, not incidentally, lovely—music today considered real *Volksmusik,* a set of repertoires with no more than a tenuous hold on oral tradition today, but dear to academics, the cultural elite, and some tourists. The most direct living sociological parallel to the Austrian folk of the past are blue-collar workers—truck drivers, domestics, owners of small stores—who tune their radios to one or another station featuring folksy music (*Volkstümlichemusik*), an array of regional styles bearing some relation to older folk music, but played by brass- or accordion-based ensembles and rendered relentlessly cheerful—the sort of music to which one might swing a stein of beer (figure 1). This branch of pop music, which in function and status roughly parallels country music in the United States and old-time dance music (*Gammaldansmusik*) in Scandinavia, enjoys a large market share.

"Authentic" Austrian folk music is remarkably unified, though practitioners and scholars subdivide it into distinct regional repertoires. The common ground between these repertoires is largely in musical sound, especially mode, melody, meter, and rhythm, in addition to typical song topics, while how instrumental ensembles are constituted and vocal dialects are specific to regions. The yodel (*Jodler, Dudler*)—a family of song types that permeates alpine regions, within and near Austria—aptly illustrates connections and divergences in Austrian folk music. A typical yodel from the Tyrolian Alps (which spill into Italy) has a title and a text invoking its home through employing local dialect: *O du schiane, süasse Nåchtigåll* 'Oh you pretty, sweet nightingale' would be spelled *O du schöne, süsse Nachtigall* in formal German (figure 2). The theme, however, does not surprise. Light, cheerful, nonnarrative texts invoking the out-of-doors are ubiquitous.

No country in Europe has folk music more thoroughly wedded to the diatonic major mode and the fleshing out of harmony than Austria. A few songs are in some

TRACK 23

FIGURE 1   A Central European brass band performing in a town square, 1969. Such bands, found in the alpine regions of Austria, Germany, and Switzerland, are associated with beer drinking and other activities. Photo by Timothy Rice.

form of diatonic minor (for example, the Wienerlied in Deutsch 1984:38). In the yodel of figure 1, as in most yodels, harmonies are simple: in the first two measures, we hear a tonic chord, then, in the third measure, the dominant (including the seventh, as is common), which immediately resolves back to the tonic; the fifth measure goes to the subdominant, which will again return through the dominant seventh (ornamented by an appoggiatura in the third beat of the seventh measure) to the tonic. Few songs are more adventurous—and few less so. Such three-chord schemes dictate a body of melodies many of which are strikingly disjunct. Frequent leaps of thirds, sixths, and even sevenths and tritone outline chords, and are easy to hear and to perform precisely because they do that.

This melody relaxes easily into triple meter, recalling a ländler (the most common family of folk dances), just as many folk melodies can easily be classified as nineteenth-century social dances in meter, rhythm, and tempo. In addition to ländler, songs that sound like waltzes (also in triple time), several types of polkas and marches (both in forthright duple meter, but the latter at a slower tempo) can be found in much of the country. Many melodies feature dotted rhythms, but few include much syncopation. Most readers in Europe and the United States will find these melodies simple—a judgment based partly on fact, but reflecting widespread musical experience: centuries of mutual influence between art and folk music in Austria have produced folk repertoires that seem to ape the basic and most accessible features of the eighteenth- and nineteenth-century art music most often heard in European and American concert halls.

Regional styles

The most prominent scholar of Austrian folk music, Walter Deutsch, has described regional subdivisions in Austrian folk music in several publications (1980, 1984, and others), summarized here.

The Tyrol, which has nurtured folk music with unusual persistence, adds Christmas and Easter carols, historical ballads, and songs about hunting to a repertoire of yodels. It is difficult to distinguish between older yodeling styles and several recent waves of commercial yodels. Harps and a form of xylophone are still played.

Verlag Frz.Huber, Mooskirchen. Aufnahme F. Pirnat, Photogr., Graz, Kaiser-Josef-Platz 3.

Mooskirchner Altsteirer Musik

Steira san ma, Steira bleib' ma, so lang' uns's Herz thuat schlog'n,
Und so leb' ma und so bleib' ma, bis dass' uns aussi trog'n.

String ensembles survive in some areas, though the most common dance ensemble, dating from after World War II, features a chromatic hammered dulcimer, a zither, a guitar, a harp, and a bass.

The Salzkammergut, a region of mountains cradling chains of lakes, joins the province of Salzburg with Styria and parts of Upper Austria. Its most typical forms of vocal music respond to this geography. There are three- and four-part homophonic yodels, other multipart mountain pasture songs, and the *Almschroa,* a solo dairy-maid's yodel. The most typical dance ensemble includes a pair of violins, a string bass, and a button accordion, which may also be played alone. Salzburg is home to a unique repertoire of songs for the Christmas season. Upper Austria (bordering on Germany and the Czech Republic) features numerous musical traditions of considerable antiquity. In addition to its own yodels, it is home to a contrasting form, the four-line song (*Vierzeiler*), and gives special attention to an elaborately performed and rhythmically complex form of the Ländler. Styria's most characteristic dance is named for the province: the *Stierische* is a multipart sectional Ländler—the increased rhythmic density of successive sections adds considerable excitement—and the form of button accordion that often plays that genre. The local hammered dulcimer (*Steirisch*) is often played with that accordion and a bass, or, in a formerly more widely distributed ensemble, with fiddles and a bass (figure 3). Yodels are common.

In the Vorarlberg, in the far west, older traditional music has largely given way to new forms. For instance, older dance ensembles focusing on clarinets and flügelhorns have in many places been replaced by groups featuring accordions, zithers, and guitars.

Vienna, the capital, is far to the east. In earlier centuries, its location placed it nearer the center of the empire. It is home to performances of folk music from throughout the country, its own harmonically and chromatically enriched form of the waltz, and the artistic and nostalgically texted *Wienerlied.* Musical variety obtains in the geographically varied surrounding province of Lower Austria. Especially notable are the hymns of the wine country north and east of Vienna. In these hymns,

Austrian popular music has accommodated the internationally produced popular musics from outside its borders and produced specific critical responses to them, responses like new folk and Austropop, which combine musical elements and sounds of the international industry, Austrian dialect lyrics, and alpine folklore.

lines for a pair of leaders alternate with lines for the congregation, still in two parts, but with each now doubled at the octave. Much Austrian folk music follows the yodel in belonging to the alpine stylistic category, but this hymn, like many Austrian religious folk songs, ballads, and soldiers' songs, fits into more general Germanic melodic style. Last, at weddings in the wine country, people dance the ländler and polkas to ensembles led by clarinets or fluegelhorns and including a button accordion and a bass flügelhorn.

Just as Tyrol and its music are not entirely within the national boundaries of Austria (Tyrolian styles extend into Italy), two Austrian provinces include substantial ethnic minorities and their music. Burgenland, bordering on Hungary, nurtures quite a few typical (and some atypical) Austrian traditions, such as ballads, alongside the *tamburica* bands of the substantial Croatian minority (the term *tamburica* encompasses related and variously sized long-necked fretted lutes) and some Hungarian traditions. Last, in Carinthia, bordering on Croatia, home to the *Kärntnerlied,* a special Austrian love song, performed by choruses in four-part harmony. The Slovenian minority cultivates polyphonic songs sounding much like the *Kärntnerlied.*

POPULAR MUSIC

From 1945 until the mid-1980s, popular music in Austria was distinguished from German and Anglo-American models by specific responses, rooted in Austrian social, cultural, political, and economic realities. These responses—including hits (*Schlager,* originally referring to commercially successful twentieth-century operetta- and folk-music-derived popular dance-music), jazz, rock and roll, disco, and new wave—did not always result in musical or lyric distinctiveness. Since no appreciable ethnomusicological research on popular music (with the possible exception of certain types of folk music and a study on music among foreign youths in Vienna) is available, its role in society is difficult to determine precisely. Austrian popular music has accommodated the internationally produced popular musics from outside its borders (in Germany and the United States) and produced specific critical responses to them, responses like new folk and Austropop, which combine musical elements and sounds of the international industry, Austrian dialect lyrics, and alpine folklore, the last two to mark Austrian contributions.

In 1952, actor-cabaretist Helmut Qualtinger and songwriter Gerhard Bronner teamed up to produce musical parodies of youth culture, including one of the earliest postwar Austrian popular songs, the boogie-woogie song "*Der g'schupfte Ferdl*" ('Clever Ferdinand', with an ironic usage of the adjective *clever*), about a small-time Viennese hoodlum, who, with his girlfriend, returns week after week to the same dance club to get beat up by other small-time hoodlums. In 1956, Bronner and Qualtinger continued with the "Bundesbahn Blues," an ironic song about the stations of the federal railway system, mixing English and Viennese-German, allegedly

FIGURE 4   Heli Deinboek, a regular performer in the Viennese blues scene, sings and plays electric guitar in concert. Photo by Edward Larkey, 1991.

about the time Louis Armstrong failed to get off his train at the right station for a performance, and the song "*Der Marlon Brando mit seiner Maschin*" ('Marlon Brando with His Motorcycle', referring to the movie *The Wild One,* in which Brando starred). In 1959, their song "*Der Papa wird's schon richten*" ('Father Will Take Care of Things') parodied the cover-up of a fatal automobile accident by the son of the president of the Austrian National Council. Qualtinger, Georg Kreisler, and other cabaretists exposed the superficiality of conservative Austrian postwar social "normality" as a thin veneer, concealing unreconstructed and unrepentant Nazi fellow travelers.

Anglo-American culture transmitted into the country by the mass media, live performances, and phonograph recordings transplanted the blues, rock and roll, heavy metal, and country music. Because of their continuous reception, cultivation, and development in Austria, these styles have become Austrianized. This metamorphosis occurred especially in the Vienna blues scene, with a small but dedicated sector of acoustic-blues aficionados, represented above all by Al Cook, who started his career as an Elvis Presley clone and proselytizes to retain the "purity" and "authenticity" of acoustic blues. Dutch expatriate Hans Theesink can also be included among them, as can city-blues rocker Heli Deinboek, who started out as a student singer-songwriter allied with the political folk-music and critical songwriters of the late 1960s and early 1970s. Some of Deinboek's songs are narratives about the seedier sides of Viennese life; others are ironic or comic plays on words seen in his job as an advertising copywriter (figure 4).

Volkstümlichemusik

Commercialized folk music seems to denote a quintessential Austrian identity, despite its roots in the brass-band march music and folklore of Slavko Avsenik's Original Oberkrainer Band, from Slovenia, south of the Austrian state of Carinthia. This music received its first big boost through the commercial success of the Kern Buam band in 1962. The style has also proliferated in Germany, with Heino its primary representative (*Blau blüht der Enzian*), but Austrian groups like the Original Fidelen Mölltaler and the duo of Klaus und Ferdl have persisted in popularity. Since the mid-1980s, the South Tyrolian Kastelruther Spatzen has become one of the leading groups in the *volkstümlich* market—a popularity fueled in part by the growth in the number of TV shows catering to this genre in all German-speaking countries. To promote the music and its ensembles, the public-service broadcasters of the German-speaking countries sponsor a major competition, the Grand Prix of *volkstümlich* music. *Volkmusik* purists and rock music adherents consider the genre to be a kitsch-laden money-maker for the commercial recording industry, without appreciable authenticity in the general population; however, the genre is the largest sector of the recording industry in Austria, a sector dominated by Koch Records.

The "Austrian" element of popular Austrian music denotes not merely the usage of Austrian dialects in the lyrics, but also the specific nostalgic or ironic usages of *Schlager, volkstümlich,* and other domestic music traditions. Alpine folklore and folk music from the Austrian territories and including Italian South Tyrol, considered inherently Austrian by many of its amateur and professional practitioners in Austria, are closely intertwined with nostalgic aspects of Austrian identities, rooted in rural, unspoiled nature as a refuge from the stress of urban life—images and ideologies cultivated by the German-dominated tourist industry and embodied and propagated by TV shows, like "*Musikantenstadl*" ('Musician's Barn'), one of the most popular in the German-speaking countries, broadcast several times a year, usually from a different German-speaking location in Europe (it was once broadcast from Canada) and featuring different groups playing *volkstümlich* music from all over. The tourist-industry-driven *volkstümlich* scene has been parodied by rock and pop musicians, who embark on musical critiques of the industry's tendency to simplistically label the *volkstümlich* type of music a genuine and authentic Austrian music. In the late 1970s, Wilfried Scheutz took a leading role in these parodies, with a mixed rock and *volkstümlich* rendition of the "*Kufstein-Lied*" ('Kufstein Song'). The Erste Allgemeine Verunsicherung ('First General Insecurity', a play on the name of the insurance company Erste Allgemeine Versicherung) has intermittently released songs containing parodic critiques of that type of music, songs such as Hans Alber's parody "*Auf der Reeperbahn nachts um halb eins*" ('On the Reeperbahn at 12:30 A.M.'), a film song referring to Hamburg's red-light district), and "*Alpen Rap*" ('Alpine Rap'), about a greedy New York music producer who visits the Austrian Alps to seek the latest trends in folkloric peasants' yodel music.

By far the most serious cultural critique of *volkstümlich* music has been the New Folk Music (Seiler 1995). Several Austrian musicians and bands have cultivated a mixture of Anglo-American "folk" with German-Austrian alpine *Volkmusik,* combining these with elements of jazz, *Schrammel* (a nineteenth-century Viennese restaurant genre popularized by the brothers Hans and Josel Schrammel, using a contrabass-guitar or an accordion, a clarinet, two violins, and one or two voices), rock, blues, punk, and hip-hop. Attwenger, for instance, a duo from Upper Austria, has fused punk and hip-hop (played with an electrically amplified accordion and drum-computer) with an archaic-sounding *Volkmusik* to achieve a unique musical profile that implicitly practices an active critique of *volkstümlich* music. Hubert Achleitner, an Upper Austrian musician who lived in Canada in the early 1980s, performed in Austria in the late 1980s and early 1990s, calling himself Hubert von Goisern (his hometown in Upper Austria) and cultivating a rock-influenced *Volkmusik,* combining old folk-dance tunes with syncopated and blues-influenced music, played on folk instruments like the Upper Austrian button accordion. The Styrian-based band Broadlahn incorporates jazz elements into its reworked *Volkmusik,* producing a soft but powerfully melodic music that caters to an enthusiastic but small group of followers.

One of the most commercially successful bands to fuse the *volkstümlich* tradition with rock has been a group originally calling itself Zillertaler Schürzenjäger (Zillertal Apron-Chasers), a name derived from the *volk* and *volkstümlich* practice of identifying music according to its alleged local roots (in the Ziller River Valley in Tyrol). With three core members, who played electronically amplified *volkstümlich* music containing elements of *Schlager* music, the band built up a reputation of attracting diverse social groups to its concerts. After issuing commercially successful records, adding two more musicians, and spending years on tour, the band changed its identity by replacing a guitarist who opposed the change, dropping the designation *Zillertal,* and incorporating rock and *Schlager* with hardly any musical references to its *volkstümlich* origins.

Austropop

The term *Austropop* was in the 1960s applied to dialect-sung pop music mixing influences from the student folk movement, underground rock and blues music, and elements of *Schlager*. Arik Brauer, André Heller, and other artists were at the forefront in the usage of Austrian dialect lyrics with chanson-style songs, much like the style of Reinhard Mey in Germany. One of the first of the Austropop lineage was actress Marianne Mendt's song "*Wia a Glockn*" ('Like a Church Bell'), which Eva-Maria Kaiser produced for a 1970 *Schlager* competition sponsored by the Austrian Broadcasting Service (ÖRF). The quintessential Austropop song, however, was "*Da Hofa*" ('The Outcast'), composed and performed by Wolfgang Ambros. Its lyrics, written by Josef Prokopetz, told about an outcast lynched by upstanding citizens merely for being different. It achieved popularity because it implicitly criticized society, no longer dominated by Nazis, but still intolerant of nonconformity. Prokopetz wrote most of Ambros' early lyrics, which employed black humor, solidarity with social underdogs, irony, and satire, using blues-based structures and Austrian dialectal words.

In 1974, a vocal duo calling itself Waterloo + Robinson recorded "Hollywood," a song composed by Christian Kolonovits, until then the keyboardist for the folk group Milestones. A sentimental song with English lyrics, it bemoaned the death of the old Hollywood heroes and proclaimed in its refrain "Good old Hollywood is dying. / Good old Hollywood is dead." Because its lyrics were in English, it was apparently not perceived as a drippy, crooner's tune (*Schnulze*)—which would have meant exclusion from ÖRF playlists. Many background singers and instrumentalists in the recording session came from the student folk and music scenes and included members of the Milestones and Schmetterlinge (Butterflies), the left-wing political folk-rock band that in the Eurovision song contest in 1977 represented Austria with "*Bum, Bum Bumerang*" ('Boom, Boom, Boomerang'), a satirical parody of recording-industry commercialism and greed. Formed in 1969, Schmetterlinge worked with poet Heinz R. Unger and after 1976 became famous in the German-speaking political folk circuit for producing, with financial advances from the Eurovision, *Proletenpassion* ('Passion of the Proletariat'), a three-hour studio production singing the history of working-class suffering at the hands of the bourgeoisie. After the mid-1990s, Danzer, Ambros, and Rainhard Fendrich recorded songs together as the band Austria 3.

In the late 1970s, Ambros, after success with several records, including "Long Live the Central Cemetery," an LP whose title song celebrated the centennial of Vienna's Central Cemetery by inviting all the dead people buried there to a party to which no living person was allowed, released *Wie im Schlaf* ('Like Sleeping'), a collection of Bob Dylan songs with Viennese lyrics. In a period marked by heavy drug usage and depressing lyrics of personal hopelessness, Ambros produced a solo album, *Weiss wie Schnee* ('White as Snow'), after he had separated from his partner, Josey Prokopetz. Ambros produced musicals and a long series of highly popular LP recordings with his band Nr. 1 des Wienerwalds (*Nummer Eins des Wienerwalds* 'Number One of the Vienna Forest'). Until well into the 1980s, Ambros was Austria's most successful popular music star throughout German-speaking lands.

At the end of the 1970s, a second generation of Austropop emerged in productions by Stefanie Werger, Fendrich, the Erste Allgemeine Verunsicherung (EAV, based in Graz), and Opus. Werger and her backup band sang about personal and individual conflicts and topics connected with femininity and relationships. Fendrich's songs satirically or ironically focused on daily banalities, like the bodybuilding craze and summer romances. Early EAV productions satirized trendiness among intellectuals and students and latent and not-so-latent fascist tendencies in Austrian society. EAV gradually became more formulaic and superficial in treating socially relevant topics, like Austrian tourists, greed, and provincialism. One of its most commercially successful and linguistically inventive albums, the 1985 LP disk *Geld oder Leben* ('Your Money or Your Life'), had three number-one successes: "*Banküberfall*" ('Bank Robbery'), "*Heisse Nächste in Palermo*" ('Hot Nights in Palermo', an ironic song poking fun at the Italian Mafia), and "*Der Märchenprinz*" ('Fairy Prince', satirizing the behavior of city slickers who drive out to rural discotheques to pick up already attached country bumpkins and on the way home get stopped by the police for an alcohol test, which they fail). EAV combines a cutting-edge-engineered dance-music sound crafted by Peter J. Müller with a uniquely inventive, ironic usage of slang and dialect to attain one of the broadest audiences ever achieved in Austria.

German tourists in Austrian vacation resorts form an important audience for Austrian performers. These vacationers return home with recordings and pleasant memories of holiday experiences and buy recordings or attend performances of these groups in Germany.

Throughout the 1970s, Willi Resetarits sang with Schmetterlinge. As that project stagnated and the market for left-wing political rock faded, he turned to author Günter Brödl's fictitious working-class rock hero Ostbahn-Kurti to produce "Ostbahn-Kurti und die Chefpartie" (*Ostbahn* 'eastern railway', *Kurti* 'Kurt', *Chefpartie* 'good old boys'), a project portraying escapades in Vienna's working-class neighborhoods, where Resetarits grew up. The concept of the rock novel or soap opera can be applied to the group, now called Dr. Kurt Ostbahn [see ROCK MUSIC IN EUROPE, figure 1, p. 216]. The music, taken primarily from U.S. rock tunes, is redone with Viennese-Austrian dialect lyrics, and each LP or CD features a unique concept or experience.

Another Graz-based band in the Austropop tradition is STS (Schiffkowitz, Timischl, Steinbäcker), whose folk-rock music style is closely related to that of Neil Young, the Mamas and Papas, and Bob Dylan. Their first big success was "Fürstenfeld," an ironic country-style tune, which proclaimed "I want to go home to Fürstenfeld" and complained about the lack of roots when traveling throughout the world.

Austria as a German *Schlager* province

The postwar *Schlager* industry in Austria was dominated by German-based record companies, reestablished in the mid-1950s in Vienna as Columbia, EMI, and Polydor, joining the Austrian Amadeo Schallplatten (later bought by Polydor). These offices were not production facilities, but served to promote sales of U.S., British, and German vocalists, combos, and orchestras. Polydor concentrated on *Schlager* tunes, and EMI, through its London subsidiary, became an importer of rock and roll recordings. In the 1950s and early 1960s, Polydor producer Gerhard Mendelson assembled Austrian and German musicians and vocalists in Vienna to record songs popular in the United States and remade as German versions. He continued to do so until the Austrian finance ministry decided that Polydor was not an Austrian operation but an export, and would need to pay higher taxes. Mendelson closed down the operation and moved to Germany.

The so-called Weisswurst ('White Sausage') Line in southern Germany (primarily Bavaria), a cultural and ethnic boundary for Bavarian-German speakers, represents the northernmost border for Austrian popular music artists singing with dialect lyrics. Most Austrian dialects derive from Bavaria. In the westernmost Austrian state, Vorarlberg, people speak Alemannic dialects shared with Swiss-Germans and Swabians in southern Germany. German tourists in Austrian vacation resorts form an important audience for Austrian performers. These vacationers return home with recordings and pleasant memories of holiday experiences—in summer mountain and hiking activities or winter ski trips—and buy recordings or attend performances of these groups in Germany. Most highly successful Austropop performers schedule up to two-thirds of their performances in Germany, hiring German agents to plan their schedules and gain them sufficient airplay and other types of media exposure, like interviews on private radio and TV stations.

Austrian *Schlager* vocalists played a prominent role in the German *Schlager* industry, particularly in the 1960s. One of the earliest, popular in the late 1950s and early sixties, was Freddy Quinn (born Franz Eugen Helmuth Manfred Nidl-Petz), whose first success, the 1956 song "*Heimweh*" ('Homesickness'), sold more than 2 million recordings. Recounting feelings of loneliness, farewell, and longing for a home, his songs are the quintessential embodiment of *Schnulze.* By 1966, his record sales had totaled 17 million, and he had starred in numerous films. Peter Neumayer, an Austrian singer who used the stage name Peter Alexander, had a German producer, Kurt Feltz. In addition to appearing in more than forty films by the early 1970s, he proved to be an extremely popular television entertainer, with some of the highest ratings in German television entertainment. In 1966, Udo Jürgens (born Udo Jürgen Bockelmann), who grew up in Carinthia, won the Eurovision song contest for Austria with the song "*Merci, Cheri*" ('Thanks, Cheri'), and went on numerous European and international tours arranged by a German manager, Hans Beierlein. Jürgens composed many of his own tunes, wrote his own lyrics, and did the arrangements for his productions. In the 1970s, by infusing his lyrics with French chanson-derived social criticism, he led innovations in *Schlager,* making the genre reflect concrete realities.

In the mid-1960s, the Beatles' success and popularity meant that *Schlager* in Austria, as in Germany, was on the defensive; however, the situation was not so drastic as in Germany, where 1964 was the key year of transition (Herrwerth 1995:70). As in Germany and other countries, teenagers flocked to concerts featuring the Beatles, the Rolling Stones, and other British groups. Many started to sing or play the guitar or drums. The most prominent German beat groups, like the Rattles and the Lords, went to England to perform, but Austrian bands, including the Mimes, the Thunderbirds, Johnny and the Shamrocks, and the Guitarmen, achieved local prominence in Austria or Germany while touring with British or American groups. The Beatles' popularity meant that bands with *Schlager,* or at least a pre-Beatles background—bands like the Bambis, popular in the 1950s and early 1960s as a mixed German-Austrian group specializing in renditions of the newest *Schlager*-oriented hit-parade songs—were suddenly obsolete or relegated to *Schnulzen.* The Beatles filmed *A Hard Day's Night* partly in Salzburg and created a huge impact on local youths and businesses. Falco, who in 1988 died in an automobile accident in the Dominican Republic, and Opus were two of the more prominent Austrian popular music figures to achieve international prominence outside the German-speaking world.

BIBLIOGRAPHY

Bailer, Noraldine, et al. 1994. *Zwischen zwei Kulturen: Kulturelle Verhaltensweisen von jugendlichen Migranten in Wien, unter besonderer Berücksichtigung der Musik.* Vienna: Hochschule für Musik und darstellende Kunst.

Beck, Lukas, and Christian Seiler. 1993. *Ostbahn-Kurti und die Chefpartie.* Vienna: Edition Tau.

Bloemke, Rüdiger. 1996. *Roll Over Beethoven: Wie der Rock'n'Roll nach Deutschland kam.* St. Andrä-Wördern: Hannibal.

Brödl, Günter, ed. 1982. *Die guten Kräfte: Neue Rockmusik aus Österreich.* St. Andrä-Wördern: Hannibal.

Bronner, Gerhard. 1995. *Die goldene Zeit des Wiener Cabarets—Anekdoten, Texte, Erinnerungen.* St. Andrä-Wördern: Hannibal.

Chmelar, Dieter. 1995. *Rainhard Fendrich—Texte, Bilder, Geschichten.* Vienna: Fechter Verlag.

Deutsch, Walter. 1980. "Austria, II: Folk Music." In *The New Grove Dictionary of Music and Musicians.* Edited by Stanley Sadie. London: Macmillan.

———. 1984. "Volksmusiklandschaft Österreich." In *Volksmusik in Österreich,* ed. Walter Deutsch, Harald Dreo, Gerlinde Haid, and Karl

Horak, 9–44. Vienna: Österreichischer Bundesverlag.

Deutsch, Walter, Gerlinde Haid, and Herbert Zeman. 1993. *Das Volksleid in Österreich: Ein gattungsgeschichtliches Handbuch.* Vienna: Holzhauser.

———. 1995. *Lieder des Weihnachts Festkreises: Steirmark.* Vienna: Böhlau.

Fielhauer, Helmut, ed. 1962. *Volkskunde und Volkskultur.* Vienna: Schendl.

Finkentey, Matthias. 1994. *Handbuch für Musiker und Komponisten.* Vienna: Buchkultur Verlagsges.

Fuchs, Harry. 1996. "Austropop: Entstehungsgeschichte: Rahmenbedingungen und Kommunikationswissenschaftliche Relevanz einer nationalen populären Kultur." Diplomarbeit, Institut für Publizistik und Kommunikationswissenschaft, Universität Vienna.

Goertzen, Chris. 1988. "Popular Music Transfer and Transformation: The Case of American Country Music in Vienna." *Ethnomusicology* 32(1):1–21.

Gröbchen, Walter. ed. 1995. *Heimspiel: Eine Chronik des Austropop.* St. Andrä-Wördern: Hannibal.

Gugitz, Gustav. 1954. *Lieder der Strasse: die Bänkelsänger im josephinischen Wien.* Vienna: Brüder Hollinek.

Gürmen, Lilá, and Alexander Leitner. 1995. *Austropop.* Vienna: Verlag des ÖGB.

Herrwerth, Thommi. 1995. *Itsy Bitsy Teenie Weenie: Die deutschen Hits der Sixties.* Marburg: Jonas Verlag.

Hodina, Karl, ed. 1991. *O du lieber Augustin: Die schönsten Wienerlieder.* Vienna: J&V Edition Wien Verlagsgesellschaft.

Horak, Karl. 1985. *Instrumentale Volksmusik aus Tirol.* Innsbruck: Author.

———. 1988. *Musikalische Volkskultur in Burgenland: Ein Rückblick auf 60 Jahre Volksmusikforschung.* Eisenstadt: Bezirks Oberbayern.

———. 1989. *Ältere Zeugnisse zur Volksmusik des steirischen Ennsbereiches.* [Trautenfels]: Verein Schloss Trautenfels.

Humann, Klaus, and Carl-Ludwig Reichert, eds. 1981. *Eurorock.* Reinbeck bei Hamburg: Rowohlt Taschenbuchverlag.

Ilka, Peter. 1983. *Tanzbeschiebungern, Tanzforschung.* Vienna: Österreichischer Bundesverlag.

Institut für Publizistik und Kommunikationswissenschaft der Universität Salzburg. 1993. *Massenmedien in Österreich.* Medienbericht 4. Vienna: Buchkultur Verlagsgesellschaft.

Janig, Herbert, et al., eds. 1988. *Schöner Vogel Jugend: Analysen zur Lebenssituation Jugendlicher.* Linz: Universitätsverlag Rudolf Trauner.

Juhasz, Christiane. 1995. *Kritische Liedermacher und Politrock in Österreich.* Vienna: Peter Lang Publishing.

Jürgens, Udo. 1994. *Unterm Smoking Gänsehaut.* Munich: C. Bertelsmann.

Kehlmann, Michael, and Georg Biron. 1995. *Der Qualtinger: Ein Porträt.* St. Andrä-Wördern: Hannibal.

Klier, Karl M. 1950. *Das Neujahrssingen im Burgenland.* Eisenstadt: n.p.

———. 1956. *Das totenwacht-Singer in Burgenland.* Eisenstadt: n.p.

Koller, Josef. 1931. *Das Wiener Volkssängertum in alter und neuer Zeit.* Vienna: Gerlach and Wiedling.

Kolneder, Walter. 1981. *Die vokale Mehrstimmigkeit in der Volksmusik der österreichischen Alpenländer.* Winterthur, Switzerland: Amadeus.

Lach, Robert. 1923. *Eine Tiroler Liederhandschrift aus dem 18. Jahrhundert.* Vienna: Hölder-Pichler-Tempsky.

Larkey, Edward. 1993. *Pungent Sounds: Constructing Identity with Popular Music in Austria.* Austrian Culture, 9. New York: Peter Lang.

Leopold, Peter, ed. 1988. *Erste Allgemeine Verunsicherung—Kann denn Schwachsinn Sünde sein?* Vienna: Überreuter.

Maurer, Philipp. 1987. *Danke, man lebt: Kritische Lieder aus Wien 1968–1983.* Vienna: Österreichischer Bundesverlag.

Mitchell, Tony. 1996. *Popular Music and Local Identity.* London, New York: Leicester University Press.

Moissl, Rudolf Alexander. 1943. *Die Schrammel-Dynastie.* St. Pölten: St. Pöltners Zeitungsverlag.

Moser, Johannes. 1988. *Der "Volksliedmacher" Wolfgang Ambros: Eine Untersuchung über Möglichkeiten zur Erweiterung des Volksliedbegriffes.* Bonn: Holos.

Neckheim, Hans, and Josef Pommer. 1891. *222 Echte Kärntnerlieder.* Vienna: Verlag des Deutschen Volksgesang-Vereines.

Pauswek, Peter, and Gerald Teufel. 1995. *Ganz Privat: Österreichische Popstarts, wie sie niemand kennt.* Vienna: List & Partner Verlagsgesellschaft.

Seiler, Christian, ed. 1995. *Schräg dahoam—Neue Volksmusik und ihre Zukunft.* St. Andrä-Wördern: Hannibal.

Seminar für Volksmusikforschung. 1972. *Volkslied, Volksmusik, Volkstanz: Kärnten und seine Nachbarn.* Klagenfurt: Verlag des Landesmuseums für Kärnten.

Staribacher, Wolfgang. 1994. *Untenoben.* Alpinkatzen: author.

Suppan, Wolfgang. 1981. *Das grosse steirische Blasmusikbuch.* Vienna: Molden.

———. 1984. *Volksmusik im Bezirk Liezen.* Trautenfels: Verein Schloss Trautenfels.

VÖM. 1996. *Österreichischer Musikatlas.* Vienna: Vereinigte Österreichische Musikförderer.

Wagnleitner, Reinbold. 1994. *Coca-Colonization and the Cold War: The Cultural Mission of the United States in Austria after the Second World War.* Translated by Diana M. Wolf. Chapel Hill and London: University of North Carolina Press.

Wittmann, Wolfgang. *1984 Österreichisches Hit-Lexikon 1956–1984.* Graz: DBV Verlag.

Zink, Wolfgang. 1989. *Austro-Rock-Lexikon: 20 Jahre Austro-Rock von A–Z.* Neufeld: Author.

Zoder, Raimund. 1950. *Volkslied, Volkstanz, Volksbrauch in Österreich.* Vienna: L. Doblinger.

Switzerland

Johanna Hoffman
Silvia Delorenzi-Schenkel

Early and Traditional Musical Contexts
Musical Instruments
Musical Areas
Education in Traditional Music
Mutual Influence of Art and Folk
Late-Twentieth-Century Developments and Trends

Switzerland was founded in 1291 as a confederation of the three *waldstätte* (today called cantons) Uri, Schwyz, and Unterwalden. In the following centuries, more cantons joined, until 1848, when the Swiss Confederation was established by the federal constitution, with twenty-five cantons. In 1978, the confederation accepted the French-speaking part of the canton Bern as the new, autonomous canton Jura. Switzerland comprises four distinct cultural and linguistic areas: Swiss-German, French, Italian, and Romansh, the last a collection of Rhaeto-Romanic dialects, spoken in canton Graubünden and adjacent parts of Italy. Though the country has fewer than seven million inhabitants within 41,288 square kilometers and almost two-thirds of that area consists of sparsely inhabited mountains, distinct regions and many cantons or smaller areas have distinct musical traditions. Despite attempts to use folk music to forge a sense of national identity, many Swiss traditions are specific to certain isolated valleys or cities in which local history has forged strong feelings of communal identity. Until the early 1970s, differentiations of gender were important factors, since most public traditions were maintained by males.

Identification of the alpine region as "the psychological center of Swiss cultural identity" (Weiss 1946:19) often conflicts with the cultural and social diversity of the national population. The exodus of rural people to the cities has been so great that today, less than 4 percent of the people practice or are in direct contact with the musical styles they claim as their own.

EARLY AND TRADITIONAL MUSICAL CONTEXTS

Artifacts found in Neolithic sites point to the use of musical instruments in the geographical area of Switzerland, where archaeologists have unearthed bark trumpets, bull roarers, flutes (of wood, bark, and bone), ratchets, and snail-shell shakers. Some of these artifacts have turned up near megalithic constructions and on sites formerly used for astronomic calculations—facts that point to the ritual use of musical instruments.

The rural economy of Switzerland gave rise to a repertoire of songs associated with agriculture, herding cattle, calendrical events, and life-cycle stages. Shepherds of the alpine regions preserved a large part of this repertoire, including songs accompanying milking, feeding animals, and blessing cattle. People believed they could entrance and control various animals with vocal music. This repertoire, maintained in isolated areas until about 1900, has been preserved in part. Its elementary forms include signal calls, yells, recitatives, a three-tone yodel, and melodic vocalizing.

Melismatic, nonmetrical calls (*löckler*) were performed solo, frequently accompanied by the bells of moving cattle. Group performances now occur in small closed circles, one man yodeling melodies and the others holding a drone. These calls often contain the word *loba,* which in different parts of the country appears as *lobela, liauba,* or *liôba*—a term that, some commentators have speculated, refers to an ancient cattle deity, whose cult may have been commonly observed by cattle-tending peoples in this area of Europe.

Another archaic genre, the cattle call (*kuhreigen* or *kuhreihen*), was formerly used in cow-naming ceremonies and music for dancing. Consisting of two or three melodic formulas sung in alternate slow and fast tempos over the range of a fifth, calls would end with a descending third. When their texts contain the word *loba,* they (like *löckler*) are melismatic and in free rhythm; however, longer texts are syllabic and move in strict meter.

Documentation of cattle calls printed in 1826 contains evidence of alteration to suit an urban, rather than a peasant, audience (Wiora 1949). With harmonizations supplied by the composer F. F. Huber (1791–1863), and often sung by classically trained singers, some calls resemble classical lieder in their musical style, and their texts contain insertions of political ideology concerning international neutrality, homeland, and family descent.

Contemporary performance of early styles

Though archaic vocal styles have been widely replaced by newer ones, Switzerland's musical past maintains a presence, despite changed contexts. Musical traditions connected to calendrical events have been retained in cities and villages. Ancient beliefs in the power of so-called noisemaking instruments are at the core of many such events.

All kinds of bells are involved in most Swiss festivals occurring during midwinter (November through January). In many places, St. Nicholas Day (6 December), Christmas Eve, and New Year's Eve are marked by processions of men or boys, who around their waist or in their hands have a clapper bell (*chlause* in Kaltbrunn, St. Gallen; *nachttrichjer* in Fiesch, Valais; *kalusschellen* in canton Glarus; *silvesterchlausen* in Wald, Zurich; *achetringele* in Laupen, Bern; *nünichlingler* in Ziefen, Baselland) or various types and sizes of jingle bells on a harness (*chlausjage* in Hallwil, Aargau; *silvesterklüuse* in Oberschau, St. Gallen). In other places, the bell-ringing groups walk with groups of drummers or a brass band and with whip crackers (*trychlen* and *übersitz* in Meiringen, Bern; *klausjagen* in Küssnacht am Rhein, Schwyz; *haaggeri* in Richterswil, Zurich).

In Urnäsch, Appenzell Ausserrhoden, on 31 December and 13 January (New Year's Eve in the Julian calendar) groups of men disguised as *silvesterchläuse* move from one farmyard to another and wish farmers a happy New Year, singing a polyphonic natural yodel (*zäuerli*). They accompany themselves with cow bells and large pellet balls, worn on their bodies. They form in two groups (*schuppel*), the beautiful and the ugly. The beautiful *chläuse* are four masculine figures and two feminine figures. The masculine figures wear on their chests and backs a cowbell (*sänntumsschölle*), each pair having a different size and tone. The feminine figures usually wear thirteen pellet bells (*rolli*). The *rollichläuse* make their bells sound by hopping and moving around with tripping steps, while the *schellenchläuse* sound their bells by swaying their upper torsos (figure 1).

FIGURE I *Silvesterchläuse* from the so-called beautiful group with bells, Urnäsch, Appenzell. The four masculine characters wear on their chests and backs one large cowbell; the female characters, played by men, wear a skirt, a vertical headdress, and usually thirteen smaller pellet bells. Photo by Amelia Magro.

Till around 1900 in many places in canton Aargau, threshing in rhythmic patterns was a well-known custom on New Year's Eve. Nowadays, this *silväschtertrösche,* by three to six persons, survives only in Hallwil.

In Wil, St. Gallen, a procession of children with homemade lanterns accompanied by drumming and carol singing, is associated with the inspection of lanterns, which each household was formerly required to have for emergency lighting.

Another event—with an origin that predates the fourteenth century and has its roots in guild-based and military traditions—is the griffin pageant, which takes place in the second half of January in Basel. Drumming accompanies three mythical figures: a griffin (*vogel gryff*), a wild man (*wild ma*), and a lion (*leu*), which dance on a raft drifting down the Rhine and on the bridge that connects Grossbasel with Kleinbasel. This pageant commemorates and reinforces the local identity of Kleinbasel. Similar to the figures of the griffin pageant, in Steinen, canton Schwyz, the dance of the *nüssler,* traditional maskers wearing pellet bells on their costumes, is accompanied by drums. Both events are forerunners for the Swiss carnival traditions that begin in some places in January and end everywhere in the week after Ash Wednesday.

In Solothurn on the Thursday before Ash Wednesday, the beginning of carnival is marked by the *chesslete.* Around 4:00 A.M., people walk through the streets, dressed in white nightshirts and nightcaps, in a parade accompanied with cowbells, pellet bells, rattles, clappers, and other homemade noisemakers.

A distinctive carnival music originating in Stans, canton Nidwalden, is the *guggemusig,* played by costumed marching bands on various (formerly homemade) brass instruments and noisemakers. In Lucerne, earlier carnival traditions changed after World War II, when two carnival associations and two guilds began working together and organizing three days of masked balls and merrymaking in the streets of the city. In the 1950s, the first *guggenmusige* were founded, and today the city of Lucerne has more than sixty such bands, some of which travel around Switzerland and participate in carnival parades in various places in central Switzerland, Ticino, and north and northeast Switzerland. Fasnacht, the largest organized carnival in the country, takes place in Basel during the week after Ash Wednesday. Large fife-and-drum bands (*cliquen*) parade the streets in masks and costumes (figure 2). Small ensembles travel from bar to bar singing *schnitzelbänke,* derisive songs, critiquing political and social events of the past year; the ensembles accompany themselves on guitars, accordions, or street organs.

The end of winter is often marked by the revival of archaic traditions, coordinated with Christian holidays. During carnival in Lötschental, a remote valley in canton Valais, occurs a festival (*roitschäggäta*), in which masked men, the *tschäggätä* 'dappled ones', representing demons and evil spirits, walk the streets, howling songs and accompanying themselves with large cowbells. In Engadin and other Rhaeto-Romanic valleys of Graubünden on 1 March, during the *chalandamarz* celebration, winter is chased away by groups of boys ringing cowbells, cracking whips, and singing songs that praise the coming spring.

In Zurich during the festival of Sechseläuten in April, at 6:00 P.M., the *böög,* a "snowman" made of cotton wool and stuffed with explosives, symbolizing wintertime, is burned on a huge stake. This tradition, which originated in fourteenth-century trade guilds, is accompanied by the ringing of church bells and the *sechseläuten* march, while the riders of the guilds gallop on horses around the burning *böög.*

MUSICAL INSTRUMENTS

Idiophones

Idiophones, found in Switzerland in great variety, have retained much of their archaic significance. Tuned clapper bells made of copper or sheet iron are hung on the necks of cattle, and their pitches allow shepherds to locate the individual animals. Cowbells with an almost rectangular opening (*trychle, gunggele*) are still made in Muotatal. These bells have been employed since the early sixteenth century for the lead cow in a herd. Bigger bells are used when the cattle are taken in festive processions to and from the alpine summer pastures. In Appenzell, the three largest bells are removed from the cows in the last and steepest part of the climb, and are carried by two men. When they reach the alpine hut, they sing a few *zäuerli* while ringing the bells (*schellenschötte* 'bell shaking') in a regular rhythm. Cowbells and pellet bells of different sizes provide accompanying noises during various calendrical festivals and at skiing competitions.

Most festivals and calendric events, whether Christian or not, are marked by the extensive ringing of church bells, blessed and named according to traditions believed to reach back to the eleventh century. In remote areas, church bells still signal a person's death, different rhythms identifying the deceased individual.

In Valais, cast bells hanging in churches or towers as early as 1414 have been played as musical instruments since around 1800—a practice inspired by Flemish mechanical bell ringing. The bells are played by ropes tied to the player's hands and feet—which gives him control over the rhythmic and dynamic variations of his performance. Several strokes—*à la volée* 'flying', *tinter* 'to ring softly', *sonner* 'to ring', *bourdonner* 'to buzz'—are recognized, and the tradition is passed on from father to son. Some current traditions go back to the mid-1800s. The repertoire includes popular songs, religious songs, rhythmic ringing, and melodic ringing. A similar tradition exists in Ticino, though there the bells, activated by mechanical means, play arpeggiated improvised patterns.

Ratchets—wooden noisemakers, swung on the end of a stick, or turned with a handle, and called by various local names (including *raffle, rüffle,* and *rärri*)—are found near megalithic sites, conceptually related to bells, and used in various con-

FIGURE 2   During Fasnacht in Basel, maskers play fifes and a drum. Photo by Peter Armbruster.

The art of making flutes is depicted in oral traditions as having been taught to shepherd boys by Alpbütz, a diabolical bogeyman. A presumably phallic invocation of saints ('Oh Saint Lawrence, make it so that my flute doesn't fail me') accompanies the manufacture of flutes in Aargau and other areas.

texts. Like bells, they serve as noisemakers in various parades and church contexts, especially in central Switzerland and Graubünden. During Holy Week, especially in Roman Catholic areas, ratchets played in great numbers replace bell ringing and are even used inside churches.

Coin rolling (*talerschwingen*) was probably invented in Appenzell around 1900. A five-franc piece is rolled around the inside of an earthenware bowl, held on the palm of one hand and slowly rotated. The sound produced by this coin blends well with the local yodeling (*zäuerli*).

Membranophones

The most important and widely used drums in Switzerland are military drums. Drummers of the Swiss army are trained by an instructor, and the Schweizerischer Tambourenverband (Swiss Drummers' Association), founded in 1906, regularly organizes competitions with drumming on a high level. Since Swiss military drummers are allowed to take their instruments home and keep them, the military drum has become a popular folk-music instrument. In peacetime since the sixteenth century, drums and fifes have accompanied dancing. Drum bands take part in many calendrical and carnival-related events. The Basel drum, recognizable by its height and black-and-white hoop decoration (the Swiss military drum has a red-and-white decoration), is played for the griffin pageant and during carnival. In Valais, fifes and drums accompany the year's first work in the vineyards; and in Graubünden and Appenzell Ausserrhoden, they accompany the open-air parliaments (*landsgemeinde*). In Altdorf, Uri, more than one hundred bass drums are played in the morning parade on Mardi Gras.

Chordophones

The use of chordophones in Swiss traditional music was first documented in 1447, when the nightly playing of trapezoidal hammered dulcimers (*hackbretter*) provoked a riot in Zurich. The *Luzerner Chronik* (1509) documented the use of other chordophones as solo instruments: the violin, the dulcimer, and the long-necked cittern (*halszither*). Today, the violin, the acoustic double bass, and the guitar are the most widely used chordophones.

The tradition of constructing and playing the *hackbrett,* once a popular instrument in Switzerland, survives only in Appenzell and the Goms Valley, Upper Valais. In Appenzell, the *hackbrett* is played in so-called Appenzell string music (two violins, cello, double bass, dulcimer); since the early twentieth century, it has been customary in Valais to play the dulcimer four-handed. In the second half of the nineteenth century, two types of board zither were locally introduced: the *schwyzer zither* and the *glarner zither,* both named after the canton where they remain in use. In earlier times, the zither was played for small dance events, with a violin and a double bass. Now it is an instrument played mainly by women for self-entertainment.

Long-necked citterns are still made and played in Toggenburg, St. Gallen, and Kriens, Lucerne. The *toggenburger halszither* has a flat body, shaped like half a pear, and it is performed as an accompanimental instrument. The *krienser halszither* resembles a guitar, and it is played with other citterns or in ensembles with guitars, lutes, and mandolins.

Mainly in southern Switzerland, mandolins are played as solo instruments and in small ensembles and orchestras with guitars.

Aerophones

Years ago, whips were used in handling animals. Today, two types of whip are popular as free aerophones in folk customs and whip-cracking (*chlepfe*) competitions. One type, formerly used by drivers of horse-drawn vehicles, has a supple grip and a lash about 1 meter long, with a knot at the end of the strap. The second type, the herdsman's whip, has a short grip with a heavy, strongly tapered cord, up to 5 meters long. Cracking the short whip involves an overhead action (*chrüzlistreich*), in which the whip is swung backward and flicked forward in the form of a crossed loop. The longer whip, swung only horizontally, produces a muffled sound similar to that of a bull roarer. Whip crackers (*geissler*) compete with each other, displaying control over rhythmic and dynamic variations.

The simplest type of Swiss aerophone is a ribbon reed—a leaf or a blade of grass—held between the thumbs and blown through to produce whistling sounds. Primarily a children's toy, it is used by hunters to attract game. Several may be played in duets, trios, or quartets.

Duct flutes and fifes

The art of making flutes is depicted in oral traditions as having been taught to shepherd boys by Alpbütz, a diabolical bogeyman. A presumably phallic invocation of saints (*O heilige Lorenz, mach ass mer d'Pfyfe nit verschränzt* 'Oh Saint Lawrence, make it so that my flute doesn't fail me') accompanies the manufacture of flutes in Aargau and other areas. During the 1500s, duct flutes were used in Appenzell to accompany dancing.

Fifes, originally military instruments, play a prominent role in much of the parade music heard in Lucerne, Basel, and Bern. The *schwyzerpfyf,* a side-blown flute, is a soldier's instrument; others, such as the *schwegepfyfli,* a piccololike side-blown flute, accompany dancing and singing. Since 1507, professional fifers have organized themselves into brotherhoods under the direction of regional "kings."

Alphorn

The alphorn, a wooden trumpet, is the most famous Swiss aerophone. Its distribution stretches from Appenzell to Valais, in rural and mountainous areas, with significant regional variations. Archaeological evidence in the form of bark trumpets indicates that its origins reach back to the Neolithic period. Old-style contemporary horns in the Bündner Oberland, Graubünden, and other relatively remote areas are handmade from wood (occasionally from metal pipes) and are about 2.5 meters long.

In Muotatal, two types of alphorn are found: the *grada büchel,* a straight, hollowed-out fir-tree trunk wrapped in birch bark, with a curved bell, is from 4 to 10 meters long; and the *büchel,* a smaller horn, whose coiled shape, first mentioned in 1820 in Grindelwald, seems to have been inspired by the modern trumpet. The *büchel* can be played at faster tempos and higher pitches than the *grada büchel.* Mouthpieces for all alphorns are of turned boxwood, crafted in various shapes and sizes, depending on the intended type of playing.

FIGURE 3   Anton Wicky and his son Andreas play alphorns (sg. *grada büchel*). A *büchel* lies on the tree trunk at left. Courtesy of Anton Wicky-Hediger.

Players once fabricated their own horns, but specialists in alphorn construction began to appear around 1900, and were then replaced by new technologies, such as mechanical carving and glueing. Currently, thirty factories in the Berner Oberland are producing alphorns (figure 3).

The instrument restricts players to the overtone series of open tubes. The intonation of the eleventh partial (F in a C scale), characteristically sharp, is commonly called alphorn-*fa*—a pitch frequently found in traditional vocal performance of so-called *naturjodel* 'natural yodel'.

Conrad Gessner contributed the first written detailed and illustrated mention of an alphorn, which he called a *lituus alpinus* in the *Zürcher Naturgelehrte* of 1555. A few years later, in 1563, a document attested to the hiring of a Swiss alphornist by the Duke of Orleans. Local names for the instrument include *touta* in Anniviers, *tiba* in Bündner Oberland, and *pichel* in Uri. Until about 1900, the alphorn was played as a solo instrument to pacify cattle and send signals. Today, it is much played by amateur musicians in alphorn duets, trios, quartets, and larger ensembles. In the early 1970s, the alphorn made its entry into concert halls with compositions by the Swiss composers Jean Daetwyler, Étienne Isoz, André Besançon, Albert Benz, and others; then it entered pop music, and more recently, it and the *büchel* have appeared in jazz. Nowadays, the alphorn is generally considered Switzerland's national instrument. During battle, cow, sheep, goat, and mountain-goat horns functioned as military instruments in signaling, but today, when they are used at all, they simply help summon cattle.

Brass ensembles

Brass ensembles are found in nearly every village or precinct. In 1987, 79,989 bands, organized in 1,991 sections, were registered in the Eidgenössische Musikverband (Federal Music Association). The biggest brass-band formation in the country is the Swiss Armeespiel, the collective of all military bands of the Swiss army.

Brass ensembles are an integral part of public activity. They perform at ecclesiastical festivities, public elections, and parades on national holidays. Modern brass ensembles came into existence in the early 1800s, when the German instrument makers Stölzel und Blühmel invented the valve system, allowing diatonic and chromatic scales to be played more easily than before.

Two types of ensemble are common: those with a *harmoniebesetzung* incorporate woodwinds and are usually found in larger localities; those with a *blechbesetzung* are composed of brass instruments with the addition of saxophones and occasionally other woodwinds, in the *fanfares mixtes* of the French-speaking area of Switzerland. In the 1950s, the band Musikgesellschaft Speicher from Appenzell introduced the English brass-band formation (brass instruments only, without trumpets) as a popular innovation. This formation is well established in Switzerland.

Harmonicas, accordions, clarinets, saxophones, and trumpets have gradually been introduced into the traditional dance-music repertoire and form its main contemporary instrumentation.

MUSICAL AREAS

Stereotypical notions of Switzerland as a mountainous region of alphorns, yodels, cowbells, and brass bands fail to do justice to the country's local musical practices, which differ significantly by language area, and even from canton to canton.

Swiss-German areas

The most popular contemporary Swiss-German instrumental ensemble is the *ländlerkappelle*. The term, coined in 1880 to replace the term *burämusig* 'farmer's music', also denotes the corresponding style of dancing and its accompanying music. The standard *ländlerkappelle* consists of a clarinet, accordions (often the diatonic *schwyzerörgeli*), and a double bass. When the ensemble plays for dancing, the clarinet may alternate with a saxophone, and in the 1990s, a trombone sometimes joined the ensemble. A good *ländlermusig* is played *lüpfig* 'lifting', meaning the music must induce the audience to get up and dance.

Since 1965, three distinct regional styles—the *bündnerstil*, from Graubünden; the *schwyzerstil*, from central Switzerland; and the *bernerstil*, from Bern—have been recognized. The *bündnerstil* is played by two clarinets in A, a *schwyzerörgeli* in A, and a double bass. Elsewhere in Switzerland, this style has enjoyed increasing popularity under the influence of bandleader Peter Zinsli, from Chur, Graubünden. The central Swiss style, played by a B-flat clarinet, a *schwyzerürgeli*, a piano, and a double bass, is distinguished by the accordionist's quick rhythmic play. The most prominent performer in this style was the clarinetist and *ländlermusig* composer Kasi Geisser (1899–1943), from Arth, Schwyz. In the *bernerstil*, a chromatic accordion is played, and the melody of the clarinet imitates the Bernese style of yodeling.

In Engadin, Graubünden, in the second half of the nineteenth century, the blind violinist and composer Franz Waser (1858–1895), from Tschlin, created a style of *ländlermusig* called, after his nickname, Fränzli music. The ensemble consisted of two violins, a clarinet, and a double bass, and a trumpet was added later on. In Engadin in the 1980s, Fränzli music was revived by five musicians, who named their band Ils Fränzlis da Tschlin.

Late-twentieth-century trends include experimentation, collaboration with Dixieland bands, classical string orchestras, and Latin American and Brazilian traditional music, the institution of national competitions, and the composition of international *ländler* hits.

The repertoire of *ländler* bands (*ländlerkappellen*) was always adapted to the fashions of the times. Since the 1700s, the bands have played in styles imported from Austria, England, France, Germany, Hungary, Poland, Scotland, and the United States. In genres such as the waltz, dancers added complicated mimetic figures to the

Many distinctive local styles have been replaced by standardized repertoires and practices since the first "festival of singers," in 1825. The main agents of change were choral societies, yodeling clubs, and ecclesiastical choirs, which trained singers and provided a new repertoire of written music.

steps and solo dancing, such as male footwork (*bödele*) in central Switzerland and competitive heelwork (*bääle, schlottere, solo-doppeliere*) in Appenzell. In the 1700s and 1800s, Northern and Central European dances were integrated into traditional dancing, performed in cycles of dances.

In central Switzerland, a common cycle (*räschtli*) consists of a schottische, a waltz, a polka, a mazurka, and a *ländler,* as called out by the dance master. After World War II, the tango, the foxtrot, and the one-step were introduced, especially in the more cosmopolitan areas of the country, while the alpine territory resisted these trends. Today, the most widespread dances include the polka (a slow 2/4), the schottische (a fast 2/4), the *ländler* (a fast 3/4), and the mazurka (a slow 3/4). The *galopp* and the *kreuzpolka* are regional variations.

The string band

In canton Appenzell and Toggenburg, St. Gallen, a *striichmusig* 'bowed music' is a band consisting of a violin, a dulcimer, a bowed double bass, and a chromatic accordion or a piano. In the *original appenzeller striichmusig* 'original Appenzell string band' are two violins, a cello, a dulcimer, and a bowed double bass. This type of ensemble can be traced back to the early nineteenth century. A violin and a dulcimer playing for a dance event was first mentioned in 1804, and dance music for string band was first printed in 1826. About 40 percent of the string-band repertoire consists of waltzes and all other musical styles played by the *ländlermusig.* A specialty of this ensemble is the instrumental *zäuerli,* the polyphonic natural yodel, transposed for stringed instruments. During breaks, the musicians may sing a *zäuerli* and accompany it with *talerschwinge.* Every string band has its own repertoire, transmitted in one family over several generations, as in the case of the Alder family, an *original appenzeller striichmusig* from Urnäsch, Appenzell Ausserrhoden, founded in 1884 (figure 4).

Yodeling

Yodeling can be heard in the Swiss-German language area from the north slope of the Alps into Appenzell and central Switzerland. The *jodel* is a vocal technique in which the singer alternates rapidly between chest voice and head voice.

In Muotatal, natural yodeling (*jüüz, jüüzli*) features a tense voice, falling glissandos, and zigzagging melodies (figure 5). The intonational margin is wide, the alphorn-*fa* is employed, and dynamic accentuation is strong. Polyphonic performances include a bass (alternately sounding tonic and dominant), a second voice, and a soloist, who improvises in a higher register. Sometimes the second voice sings above the leader—a technique called *überjüüza.*

In Appenzell, yodeling (*zäuerle,* Appenzell Ausserrhoden; *ruggusserle,* Appenzell Innerrhoden) involves a lower vocal range, relaxed vocal quality, slow tempo, free

rhythm, slides between notes, a gradually rising intonation, and the alphorn-*fa*. On the tonic and the dominant, the soloist (*vorzäurer*) is accompanied by drones (*gradhäbe* 'to keep it straight'), which may be sounded above or below the soloist's pitch. Yodels are structured in two or three parts, each of which is repeated (in form, AABB or AABBCC).

Yodeling in Appenzell, famous since the 1600s, involves a tense vocal style, fairly rapid yodeling with a pulsating quality, and soloists accompanied by drones sung in triads or larger chords. Many ornaments, such as grace notes and trills, are used. Accelerating yodels are called *schnelzer*. Songs involving the alphorn-*fa* (*chindli jodel*) function mainly as lullabies. Yodeling competitions, which include telling jokes and demonstrating intricate footwork, are held in Appenzell.

In other areas, yodeling is present but is not the main component of the local style. In the Lucerne region, people sing in a circle, accompanying the leader with a triadic drone on I, ii⁶, IV, V, and V⁷ chords. The rhythm is flexible, and the leader may introduce *rallentandos* and *accelerandos*. When used, yodeling is performed in slow tempo. In the region of Solothurn, singing was formerly accompanied by clapping hands, slapping thighs, or drumming on a table. Other movements—holding the hand or little finger to the ear, pressing the throat to manipulate vocal quality, and other techniques—were commonly associated with singing in many areas. Tight closed circles, in which singers held their heads close together, commonly occurred.

Many distinctive local styles have been replaced by standardized repertoires and practices since the first "festival of singers," in 1825. The main agents of change were

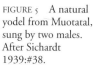

FIGURE 5   A natural yodel from Muotatal, sung by two males. After Sichardt 1939:#38.

choral societies, yodeling clubs, and ecclesiastical choirs, which trained singers and provided a new repertoire of written music. These institutions encouraged a sense of national pride but cast indigenous idioms into the background. Literate music education rapidly replaced the oral transmission of musical traditions, song structures were narrowed to strophic forms, Swiss-German dialect was sometimes replaced by standard German texts, and vocal style became standardized. Intonation conformed to tempered tuning, minor keys and modes were mostly replaced by major keys, descending melodic patterns fell into disuse, functional harmony and modulations were introduced, and yodels were incorporated as choruses into verse songs (*jodellied*).

In 1910, the 115 members of different regional choral societies formed the Swiss Yodeling Association (Eidgenössischer Jodlerverband), which by the 1990s had grown to more than twenty-five thousand participants, only 20 percent of whom were farmers. The association organizes periodic competitive festivals, where performers are rated by fight judges (*kampfrichter*). This organization and its composers—above all the cofounder, Oskar Friedrich Schmalz (1881–1960), and others, including Max Lienert (1903–1964), Alfred Leonz Gassmann (1876–1962), Hans Walter Schneller (1893–1982), Jean Clémençon (b. 1900), Jakob Ummel (1895–1992), Robert Fellmann (1885–1951), Paul Müller-Egger (1885–1979), and Adolf Stähli (b. 1925)—have permanently altered the repertory of folk songs and *jodellieder,* and even created new local styles.

The Romansh-speaking area

As in the German-speaking areas, the most popular contemporary Romansh instrumental ensemble and genre is the *ländlermusig.*

Religious songs formed a large part of the folk repertoire. As early as the mid-1500s, religious songs were published in songbooks such as *Philomela* (by Johannes Martinus ex Martinis) and *Consolaziun dell'olma devoziusa*; these became unique reference books for Rhaeto-Romanic folk music. Their texts, inspired by indigenous Romansh and German sources, were sung in German, Italian, Latin, and Romansh. Early themes included homesickness, the sadness of leaving, or archaic legends, as in "*Canzun da Sontga Margriata.*" These books were continuously updated throughout the 1700s and 1800s, and their repertoire was used not only in church, but in daily activities and events of calendrical cycles and individual lives.

For religious songs, a strong, high, metallic vocal quality was preferred, especially outdoors. Extremely high pitches were chosen for special occasions. This vocal timbre was first described in the 1700s, as "generally an ugly yelling and screaming," and in a newspaper concert critique (1990) as "similar to the sound of an Eastern European vocal ensemble." Formerly, young adults were trained for vocal performance in singing societies (*cantaduras* or *cantadurs*) that performed in large groups, usually in two to four parts a cappella—a practice alive today, during pilgrimages, processions, and wakes.

Introduction of the organ and its repertoire into churches during the 1800s reduced the use of traditional songbooks, forced *cantaduras* out of churches, and severely cut the Romansh folk-song repertoire, though some of the songs are still known. In 1904, to maintain the Romansh cultural heritage and republish Romansh religious folk and other ancient songs, the organization L'Uniun dals Grischs was established. Composers of the 1990s, including Duri Sialm and Gion Antoni Derungs, are readapting ancient folk songs, encouraging their increased performance.

The French-speaking area

Having been frequently suppressed, instrumental music in this area is not nearly so

FIGURE 6 A flutist and a drummer accompany work in the vineyards of Sierre, Valais. Photo by Albert Nyfeler, around 1930.

well defined as in the others. During Bern's occupation of Vaud (1536–1798), music and dance came under unprecedented pressures. The guidelines of the Calvinist Reformation strictly forbade instrumental music making, dancing, and masking, and imposed heavy sanctions on disobedient musicians. Music became a topic of considerable friction between the people of Vaud and the authorities, who never fully succeeded in repressing local musical performance. Reminders of the former ban on music and dance are the absence of carnival festivities in all French-speaking Protestant cantons and the lack of indigenous instrumental folk traditions—a situation many local people resent.

In Roman Catholic French-speaking areas, however, musical traditions have remained part of daily life. In the Val d'Anniviers, where side-blown flutes and snare drums accompany fieldwork, a winegrower's proverb says "No flutes, no work" (figure 6). In the Val d'Illiez, the group Champéry 1830 features an unusual instrumentation: clarinets, flügelhorn, trombone, accordion, harmonica, bass drum, jingling johnny (Turkish crescent), and triangle. As the band's name suggests, the oldest instruments in the ensemble date from the nineteenth century. The jingling johnny was introduced into Switzerland during the French invasion of 1788.

In other parts of the French-speaking area, the accordion has become the main instrument in the *orchestre champêtre,* a formation deriving from the *ländlerkappelle.* It is also played solo and in duets and big accordion orchestras. In the Jura region, the musette-tuned accordion (*accordéon jurassien*) has enjoyed a tradition dating back to 1944, when the accordionist Gilbert Schwab founded a duo with his star pupil André Nicolet. The new ambassadors of this accordion are today the young Chapuis sisters, Corinne and Fabienne.

A few songs—"*Ranz des Vaches,*" "*Coraula du Moléson,*" "*Comte de Gruyère,*" "*Chanson du Comte Vert*"—are still partly performed in dialect. In canton Fribourg, this tradition was preserved and developed by Joseph Bovet (1879–1951), a composer, conductor, teacher, organist, and priest from Sâles. His choral song "*Ranz des vaches fribourgeois,*" which emerged from the vocal tradition of the Gruyère region, enjoys the status of a quasi-national anthem among French-speaking Swiss. Most popular songs, however, can be traced to the French regions of Burgundy, Piedmont, Provence, and Languedoc and from Spanish Catalonia, from where they have been continuously imported by mercenary soldiers, merchants, and traveling musicians since the 1400s. Local individuals then reworked this repertoire to fit contemporary situations, creating distinctive regional traditions. The texts of many songs feature historical events or patriotic feelings, and many versions of the same song appear throughout French-speaking Switzerland.

The early repertoire included work songs for different trades: reapers sang *lityerse;* millers, *hymée* or *épiaulie;* weavers, *élive;* cattle tenders, *bucoliasme;* wool workers, *yule;* and children's nurses, *catabaucalise* or *nunnie.* Children's songs, military songs, pastoral songs, drinking songs, religious songs, and many types of songs for dancing were common. Texts often took the form of a *complainte,* which dealt with religious themes or became political satire, and consisted of a stereotypical introduction and strophes of six or eight verses (as in "*Complainte de Saint Nicolas,*" "*Trois Petits Enfants,*" and "*Vie des Saints*").

Pastoral songs (*pastourelles*) survived in Switzerland without being influenced by the poetry that transformed the parallel French tradition. Similarly, many old dance-song forms survive in French-speaking Switzerland. The *riondâ,* a dialect word for singing and dancing, designated dances such as the *coraula,* during which two choruses answered each other; the *voeyesi,* performed around fountains during field burnings (*les brandons*); and a communal dance (*la grande coquille de Gruyère*), which involved the whole population of the area of Gruyère. Songs to accompany such

The only places of active singing by old and young are churches and taverns, particularly open-air taverns (*grottos*). There is almost no distinction between liturgical and secular songs: secular melodies are sung to liturgical texts and vice versa.

dances were usually performed in 6/8 or 2/4 time, and made extensive use of the minor mode. Newer songs for dancing mostly accompany ring dances (*ronde*) in 3/4 time, make extensive use of the major mode, and involve onomatopoeic imitations of musical instruments (*turlututu, rantamplan, roupioupiou,* and others).

In French-speaking Switzerland, vocal music differs from Swiss-German styles in many ways. Some German melodies are performed to French texts, rhythms tend to be in 4/4 (rather than 3/4), and songs are usually performed in alternation by a soloist and a chorus, with melodies sung in unison.

Since most French-speaking cantons were incorporated into Switzerland much later than the German cantons (and under a variety of turbulent circumstances), many patriotic and political songs record historical events, such as the independence of the canton of Vaud (1798), the establishment of the République Lémanique (1798), the *Acte de Médiation* (1803), and the Federal Pact (1815). In Geneva, the "*Chant de L'Escalade*" commemorates the battle against the Duke of Savoy in 1602. In Neuchâtel, many songs about the confrontations between royalist and republican partisans reflect the canton's involvement in the Austro-German power struggle.

The Italian-speaking area

Switzerland's Italian-speaking regions consist of three valleys in canton Graubünden and the whole of canton Ticino. Culturally, these areas belong to the alpine arch (reaching from the French Alps to the Slavonic Alps), but have more in common with the adjoining regions of Italy (especially Lombardy and Piedmont) than with the rest of Switzerland.

In this area, the guitar and diatonic accordion (*fisarmonica a nümar* 'figure-accordion') have been the main accompanying instruments for folksinging, but the violin, the mandolin, the hurdy-gurdy (*viula di orbi* 'blind man's viola'), and the mechanical piano (*il verticale*) have also been popular. In the mid-1980s, a bagpipe (*piva*) similar to those found in northern Italy was revived. Ensembles include the *bandella* (clarinet and four brass instruments), with a repertoire of polkas, mazurkas, waltzes, and schottisches.

Far from representing remnants of archaic traditions, the culture of the small, remoter valleys in the Alps has been influenced by foreign cultural traits, adopted and integrated into local ones; polyvocal singing in thirds, disseminated chiefly by organized alpine choirs, is the dominant model throughout the alpine region (Leydi 1987). This holds true for Ticino only as regards songs written by local composers, often the directors of such choirs. In Ticino, the most famous composer of this genre, Vittorio Castelnuovo (b. 1915), has written more than a hundred songs, many of them in local dialect and with easygoing melodies of the sort noted by Leydi. They were written with the feeling of a native who loves his home, and this is the reason many of his songs have been labeled authentic Ticinese folk song.

There is some evidence of singing in the spinning mills and small factories of this area, but otherwise little spontaneous singing is known from Ticino (Lurati 1987). The only places of active singing by old and young are churches and taverns, particularly open-air taverns (*grottos*). An instructive link exists between the music sung in such locations and the kinds of songs and melodies used. There is almost no distinction between liturgical and secular songs: secular melodies are sung to liturgical texts and vice versa. The older, "narrative" tradition of ballads or epic-lyric songs is preserved only by a few elderly people. Many songs too have been disseminated by story singers (*cantastorie,* locally *torototéla*).

Since the 1970s, the people who remember these songs have become the most important sources for the local folk-revival movement. In Ticino, this revival was begun by the ethnomusicologist Pietro Bianchi, whose first studies were based on material collected since about 1900, particularly the collections of Hans in der Gand (1935, known as the Swiss Bartók) and his follower Arnold Geering (1949–1951). The first fruits of this research were a documentary long-playing disk (Bianchi 1984). Bianchi's later position as director of a program for folk and ethnic music allowed him to encourage others, including the folk-revival group Vox Blenii (Voice of the Blenio [Valley]), which since 1984 has reinterpreted traditional songs and organized a three-day folk festival every fall for singers from Switzerland and abroad. Vox Blenii has thus helped win the interest of local people in the musical traditions of Ticino and restore the cultural identity of the Ticinese people.

Like most of Switzerland, Ticino has an old brass-band tradition and even a famous native composer, Gian Battista Mantegazzi (1889–1958), some of whose compositions for brass band and military band (such as the "Bellinzona March," dedicated to the capital of Ticino) are known worldwide. The *bandella,* a reduced version of the *banda* (brass band), exists in Ticino, where it uses one or two clarinets, a trumpet, a tenor, and a baritone flügelhorn, a key trombone, and a bass tuba. Unlike the brass band, the *bandella* plays exclusively for public dances (figure 7).

In the late 1800s, the mandolin was introduced into the southern parts of Ticino, especially around Lake Lugano, and it gradually superseded the violin. Duos and trios with mandolin and guitar became the instruments preferred for accompa-

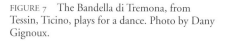

FIGURE 7   The Bandella di Tremona, from Tessin, Ticino, plays for a dance. Photo by Dany Gignoux.

nying local folk songs. In 1926, Aurora di Vacallo, the first group of mandolin players in Ticino, was founded. This ensemble is a real mandolin orchestra, with a repertoire that covers local folk tunes and classical compositions for orchestra by well-known Italian and contemporary Swiss composers.

As in other parts of the country, the accordion has replaced older instruments, like the shawm and the bagpipe, but folk-revival musicians have founded groups with a traditional flavor, such as groups with one violin, an accordion, and a double bass, or with a violin, a guitar, and an accordion. Some have accepted into their ensembles the recorder or brass instruments. Normally, one or more of the instrumentalists in these groups are also singers, and thus the repertoire contains folk-dance tunes and vocal types. As elsewhere in Switzerland and the whole alpine area, the most frequently played dance tunes of Ticino are waltzes, polkas, mazurkas, schottisches, and the *monfrina*, a dance in 6/8 time, originally from Monferrato, in the Italian province of Piedmont.

EDUCATION IN TRADITIONAL MUSIC

In some cantons, traditional Swiss folk songs are introduced in elementary and intermediate schools. Local-language songs are usually chosen at the elementary level; songs from other regions and in other languages are taught at the intermediate level. This policy depends on the educational program of the canton and the individual teacher. In the absence of music education in schools, the only way to learn folk music was in the family or in a children's choir or a brass band.

In some regions, certain genres have been transmitted for generations in the same family, for example, the Ribary family of clarinetists and the Alder family's typical Appenzell string ensemble. The children decide young whether they want to sing, or which instrument to play. Traditional structures, such as the yodel, are often transmitted within a family. Learning is normally through imitation. Scholastic training offers motivated children insight into musical genres—an evolution that has enriched traditional music through new interpretations or compositions in traditional style.

Some folk musicians have begun to give young people private lessons on traditional instruments. The 1988 bulletin of the Gesellschaft für die Volksmusik in der Schweiz (Society for Folk Music in Switzerland) lists twenty-four private music schools for the *schwyzerörgeli*. The Swiss dulcimer is taught by teachers in the cantons of Zurich, Bern, Valais, and East Switzerland, where the tradition of this instrument survives. A few other teachers offer instruction in alphorn, side-blown flute of Valais, or yodeling (Gesellschaft für die Volksmusik in der Schweiz 1988:32–34).

MUTUAL INFLUENCE OF ART AND FOLK

Since the foundation of the Société Helvétique de Musique in Lucerne (1808), the influence of art music on Swiss musical activities has grown. The promotion and performance of classical music pushed folk styles into the background of people's musical awareness, and classical music benefited from the influence of these styles. This interaction can be observed in events such as the Einsiedler Passion plays and the Fête des Vignerons at Vevey. The latter, a celebration of local winegrowers and cattle tenders, is based on the *festspiel,* a German form of folk theater. Held on a small scale in 1819, 1833, 1851, and 1865, it evolved in 1889 into a musical event uniting traditional musicians and dancers, choral associations, regional brass ensembles, and classical musicians under a single director, then composer Hugo de Senger. The Fête des Vignerons, which has taken place every twenty-five years, has been the springboard for many new popular songs, and has acted as a powerful agent for reconciling notions of art and folk.

Art-music composers in Switzerland, including Arthur Honegger, Frank Martin,

Gustave Doret, and Jean Daetwyler, have been affected by the distinctive musical idioms of folk music. On a broader cultural level, the collaboration of Igor Stravinsky, author Alphonse Ramuz, and graphic artist René Auberjenois resulted in the production of *L'Histoire du Soldat* (1918).

Many Swiss compositions for classical orchestra have tried to incorporate traditional instruments. These include Jean Daetwyler's Concerto for alphorn and orchestra and Montagnard Suite for flute, alphorn, and organ; Étienne Isoz's Concerto and Prayer for alphorn and orchestra; André Besançon's Rustic Sonata for alphorn and horn quartet; and Heinz Holliger's *Alb-Chehr* for dulcimer.

In the Romansh area especially, composers—under constant pressure from the German cultural majority—incorporate folk elements into their compositions. Several of these composers collect traditional songs in Rhaeto-Romanic dialects.

LATE-TWENTIETH-CENTURY DEVELOPMENTS AND TRENDS

Switzerland has experienced a steady immigration of peoples: Italians, Spaniards, and South Slavs, all seeking employment, and refugees from countries such as the Czech Republic, Portugal, Mali, Slovakia, Sri Lanka, Tibet, Turkey, Vietnam, and Zaïre. Since Swiss policy proscribes the creation of ghettos, the children of immigrants attend school with Swiss children and learn the local language; in turn, Swiss children come into contact with foreign cultures, directly and through radio and television. At the second and third level of elementary school and in high school, music-education programs recommend the introduction of international folk songs, often at individual teachers' discretion and knowledge.

Some cantons, including Saint Gall, Thurgau, and Zurich, offer a manual containing fifty-one folk songs, a few from Switzerland, but most from the rest of Europe and North America (Gohl, Juon, Messmer, and Willisegger 1976:34–65). The selection is based on the didactic value of the songs, rather than on cultural interaction through the music—which has become an issue for schoolteachers whose classes contain more than 50 percent non-Swiss pupils.

Pedagogical issues inspired the forum Schule für eine Welt (School for One World), which produced a catalog (1985) and teaching materials. In 1985, the Swiss Committee of UNICEF published a collection containing traditional and newly composed children's songs, with dances from twenty-five countries in the Americas, Africa, Europe, Asia, and Australia, with instructions on making simple musical instruments representing those countries. These songs, selected from items submitted for the International Contest for New Children's songs, are available on record and cassette (UNICEF, Schweizerisches Komitee 1982). In the 1980s and 1990s, young people's and adults' interest has grown in international folk music through courses in music and dance at the Ateliers d'ethnomusicologie in Geneva and the Völkerkundemuseum in Basel and Zurich.

The internationalization of Swiss education in music is balanced by the restrengthening of Swiss folk music. The immediacy of European union has produced a reaction in which individuals and associations insist on preserving Swiss folk music: older musical instruments (bagpipe, lute, hurdy-gurdy), some of which have not been played for more than a century, are restored or reconstructed, and a few schools teach folk instruments, including dulcimer, zither, and alphorn and various types of accordion.

The first step toward a more integrated program of teaching music in schools came in 1984 at a seminar for music teachers at the Musikschule Münsingen, Bern. Subsequently, Ulrich Mooser compiled a textbook on instrumental folk music (1988). In 1988, the founder and director of the Münsingen school, Werner Schmitt, was appointed director of the Bern conservatory, where he has introduced

Since 1967, when the Montreux Jazz Festival was
established, Switzerland has become a world-famous
center for urban popular music. Other renowned
Swiss festivals include the Rock Festival at Leysin,
the Tropical Music Festival in Winterthur, and the
Paleo Folk Music Festival in Nyon.

lessons on folk-music instruments for teachers and students. His efforts in promoting
folk music in schools were aimed toward the founding of a folk-music academy in
canton Bern by the year 2000. Meanwhile, new textbooks were written by the young
musician and composer Fabian Müller, on the use of the cello in folk music (1992)
and the dulcimer (1990), and by Arnold Alder, leading violionist of the Appenzell
string band Alder, on the violin in Appenzeller Streichmusik (1995).

Since 1967, when the Montreux Jazz Festival was established, Switzerland has
become a world-famous center for urban popular music. Founded by Claude Nobs,
this festival grew from a three-day event, originally dedicated to jazz, to a three-week
series of concerts, hosting international artists in the mediums of classical, contemporary, and modern jazz, blues, folk, pop, and rock. Other renowned Swiss festivals
include the Rock Festival at Leysin, the Tropical Music Festival in Winterthur, and
the Paleo Folk Music Festival in Nyon.

Beginning with the so-called Folk-Festival at the castle of Lenzburg in 1971, the
tradition of singer-songwriters—as of the blind traveling singer Alois Glutz, of the
early nineteenth century, and Gilles and Hans Roelli, of the first half of the twentieth—was revived by a new generation of *liedermacher, chansonniers,* and *cantautori*
from all parts of Switzerland, singing songs in their native languages and dialects and
accompanying themselves on the guitar. They influence the repertory of Swiss pop
singers and rock bands, which remain active regionally, and many promote strong
activist messages. Swiss-German and Romansh bands emphasize their linguistic and
cultural identity through their original compositions, whose texts stress environmental and political issues.

BIBLIOGRAPHY

Alder, Arnold. 1995. *Die Geige in der Appenzellemusik: Anleitung für den Gebrauch der Violine in der Appenzeller Streichmusik.* Zurich: Mülirad-Verlag.

Altwegg, Wilhelm. 1949. "Les Archives Suisses de la Chanson Populaire." *Journal of the International Folk Music Council* 1:8–11.

Ansermet, Ernest. 1970. "Ansermet parle d'Ansermet." *Journal de Genève* serie littéraire 1.

Bachmann-Geiser, Brigitte. 1981. "Die Volksmusikinstrumente der Schweiz." *Handbuch der europäischen Volksmusikinstrumente,* ed. Ernst Emsheimer and Erich Stockmann, 1(4). Zurich and Freiburg i. Br.: Atlantis Musikbuch-Verlag.

Baumann, Max Peter. 1976. *Musikfolklore und Musikfolklorismus.* Winterthur: Amadeus.

———. 1981. *Bibliographie zur ethnomusikologis-chen Literatur der Schweiz.* Winterthur: Amadeus.

Bendix, Regina. 1985. *Progress and nostalgia: Silvesterklausen in Urnäsch, Switzerland.* Berkeley: University of California Press.

Bolle-Zemp, Sylvie. 1992. *Le réenchentement de la montagne: Aspects du folklore musical en Haute-Gruyère.* Mémoires de la Société Suisse des Traditions Populaires, 74. Basel: Société Suisse des Traditions Populaires. Geneva: Georg Editeur.

Burdet, Jacques. 1958. *La danse populaire dans le pays de Vaud sous le régime Bernois.* Edited by Société Suisse des Traditions Populaires. Basel: Krebs.

Colzani, Alberto, ed. 1987. *Musica, dialetti e tradizioni popolari nell'arco alpino: Atti del Convegno di studi sul tema "Cultura popolare del-l'arco alpino", Montagnola, 29 giugno 1985.* Lugano: Ricerche musicali nella Svizzera italiana.

Dedual, Marietta, Jacques Guidon, and Theo

Candinas. 1985. *Romanisch Bünden.* Chur: Tierra Grischuna Buchverlag.

Deplazes, Gion. 1988. *Istorgia de la litteratura rumantscha per scola e pievel.* Vol. 2. Funtaunas, Chur: Lia rumantscha.

Eidgenössischer Jodelverband. 1976. *Alphorn Bläserschule.* Thun, Aargau: Schaer.

Eidgenössischer Musikverband. 1987. *125 Jahre Eidgenössischer Musikverband: Unsere Blasmusik in Geschichte und Gegenwart 1862–1987.* Lucerne: Keller & Co. and Eidgenössischer Musikverband.

Fricker, Robert. 1949. "The Vogel Gryff Pageant." *International Folk Music Journal* 1:7–8.

Gassman, Alfred Leon. 1906. *Volkslieder im Luzerner Wiggental und Hinterland.* Basel: Verlag der Schweizerischen Gesellschaft für Volkskunde.

———. 1961. *Was Unsere Väter Sangen.* Basel:

Verlag der Schweizerischen Gesellschaft für Volkskunde.

Gattlen, A. 1951. "Walliser Musikleben." *Schweizerische Musikzeitung* 91(5):196–199.

Gerstner-Hirzel. 1985. *Reime, Gebete, Lieder und Spiele aus Bosco Gurin*. Basel: Verlag der Schweizerischen Gesellschaft für Volkskunde.

Gesellschaft für die Volksmusik in der Schweiz. 1985. *Volksmusik in der Schweiz: Herkunft und Geschichte, instrumentale Musik, Volkstanz, Jodel, Volkslied, Chor- und Blasmusik, Liedermacher, Volksmusik und Brauchtum*. Zurich: Ringier.

———. 1988. *Informationsblatt Nr. 13/14.* Zurich: Gesellschaft für die Volksmusik in der Schweiz/Société pour la musique populaire en Suisse/Società per la musica popolare in Svizzera/Societad per la musica populara en Svizra.

Gohl, Willi, Andreas Juon, Fredy Messmer, and Hansruedi Willisegger, eds. 1976. *Musik auf der Oberstufe*. Amriswil: Gemeinschaftsverlag der Sekundarlehrerkonferenzen der Kantone St. Gallen, Thurgau und Zürich, Verlag Schweizer Singbuch Oberstufe.

Grolimund, Sigmund. 1910. *Volkslieder aus dem Kanton Solothurn*. Basel: Verlag der Schweizerische Gesellschaft für Volkskunde.

Hürlemann, Hans, and Amelia Magro. 1984. "Brummbass, Geige, Hackbrett: 100 Jahre Appenzeller Streichmusik Alder." *Appenzeller Brauchtum* 2. St. Gall: VGS Verlagsgemeinschaft St. Gallen.

Kleeb, Sales, Gustav Ineichen, and Bruno Leuthold, eds. 1990. *Albert Benz, ein Leben für die Blasmusik*. Zurich: Atlantis Musikbuch-Verlag.

Leuthold, Heinrich J. 1981. *Der Naturjodel in der Schweiz*. Altdorf: Robert Fellmann-Liederverlag.

Leydi, Roberto. 1987. "Musica e musiche della tradizione alpina." In *Musica, dialetti e tradizioni popolari nell'arco alpino: Atti del Convegno di studi sul tema "Cultura popolare dell'arco alpino," Montagnola, 29 giugno 1985*, ed. Alberto Colzani,

21–38. Lugano: Ricerche musicali nella Svizzera italiana, 1987.

Lurati, Ottavio. 1987. "Forme e modi della cultura orale nella Svizzera italiana con una raccolta di formalizzatii inediti." In *Musica, dialetti e tradizioni popolari nell'arco alpino: Atti del Convegno di studi sul tema "Cultura popolare dell'arco alpino," Montagnola, 29 giugno 1985,* ed. Alberto Colzani, 39–60. Lugano: Ricerche musicali nella Svizzera italiana, 1987.

Maissen, Alfons, and Werner Wehrli. 1945. *Die Lieder der Consolaziun dell'olma devoziusa*. Basel: Verlag der Schweizerischen Gesellschaft für Volkskunde.

Matthey, Jean-Louis, ed. 1983. *Ernest Ansermet 1883–1969: Catalogue de l'exposition Ernest Ansermet organizée à l'occasion du centenaire de la naissance du chef d'orchestre*. Lausanne: Bibliothèque cantonale et universitaire and Association Ernest Ansermet. Denges: Roth et Sauter.

Mooser, Ueli. 1988. *Die instrumentale Volksmusik: Grundlagen und Musizierpraxis der Ländlermusik: Formen—Modelle—Beispiele—Anregungen*. Edited by Gesellschaft für die Volksmusik in der Schweiz. Bern: Musikverlag Müller & Schade.

Müller, Fabian. 1990. *Neue Hackbrettschule: Lehrgang für chromatisches Mittelsteghackbrett*. Zurich: Mülirad-Verlag.

———. 1992. *Das Cello in unserer Volksmusik: Lehrgang für den Gebrauch des Cellos in unserer und anderer alpenländischer Volksmusik*. Zurich: Mülirad-Verlag.

Popular Customs and Festivals in Switzerland. N.d. Zurich: Swiss National Tourist Office.

Roberti, Arlette. 1990. "L'art choral en Suisse Romande." *Revue Musicale de Suisse Romande* 2(June):111–114.

Rossat, Arthur. 1917. *La chanson populaire dans la Suisse Romande*. Lausanne: Foetisch Frères.

Das Rote Büchlein zur 700-Jahrfeier. 1991. Bern: Büro der Delegierten, 700 Jahre Eidgenossenschaft.

Roth, Ernst. 1982. *Kasi Geisser: Leben und Schaffen des berühmten Schweizer Volksmusikanten*. Altdorf: Gamma & Cie.

———. 1987. *Lexikon der Schweizer Volksmusikanten*. Aarau: AT Verlag.

———. 1993. *Schwyzerörgeli: Eine Kulturgeschichte und Instrumentenkunde*. Aarau: AT Verlag.

———. 1994. *Nachtrag zum Lexikon der Schweizer Volksmusikanten*. Adliswil: Eigenverlag Ernst Roth.

Schmid, Camille. 1903. *Bellwald, Sach- und Sprechwandel seit 1890*. Basel: Krebs.

Schwaller, Robert. 1996. *Treicheln Schellen Glocken: Sonnailes et Cloches*. Schmitten: Glockenbuch/Livre de cloches Dr. R. Schwaller.

Sichardt, Wolfgang. 1939. "Der alpenländische Jodler und der Ursprung des Jodelns." *Schriften zur Volksliedkunde und völkerkundlichen Musikwissenschaft*, ed. Werner Danckert. Berlin: Bernhard Hahnefeld Verlag.

Sprecher, J. A. 1976 [1875]. *Kulturgeschichte der drei Bünde im 18. Jahrhundert*. Chur: Verlag Bischofberger.

Tobler, Alfred. 1903. *Das Volkslied im Appenzellerlande*. Zürich: Verlag der Schweizerischen Gesellschaft für Volkskunde.

Vernet, Marc. 1965. *Les Carillons du Valais*. Edited by Société Suisse des Traditions Populaires. Basel: Krebs.

Weber, Conrad. 1985. *Brauchtum in der Schweiz*. Zurich: Werner Classen.

Weiss, Richard. 1946. *Volkskunde der Schweiz*. Zurich: Eugen Rentsch.

Willi, Hansjürg. 1997. *Bündner Musikantenführer: Volksmusikanten proträtiert von Hansjürg Willi*. Schiers: AG Buchdruckerei Schiers.

Wiora, Walter. 1949. *Zur Frühgeschichte der Musik in den Alpenländern*. Basel: Krebs.

AUDIOVISUAL RESOURCES

Am alte Silveschter z'Umäsch: Zäuerli aus Appenzell Ausserrhoden. 1991. CSR Records CSR Schwing 91662. Compact disc.

Appenzell, Toggenburg, St. Galler Oberland. N.d. Anthologie authentischer Volksmusik aus den Schweizer Bergen/Anthologie de musique populaire originale des régions montagnardes suisses/Antologia di musica popolare originale delle regioni svizzere di montagne/Antologia da musica populara autentica dallas muntognas svizras, 7. Forum Alpinum 9007. LP disk.

Bachmann-Geiser, Brigitte. 1996. *Die Volksmusikinstrumente der Schweiz: Les instruments de musique traditionnels suisses: Traditional Swiss Musical Instruments*. Claves Records CD 50-9621. Compact disc.

Berner Oberland, Emmental. N.d. Anthologie

authentischer Volksmusik aus den Schweizer Bergen/Anthologie de musique populaire originale des régions montagnardes suisses/Antologia di musica popolare originale delle regioni svizzere di montagne/Antologia da musica populara autentica dallas muntognas svizras, 3. Forum Alpinum 9003. LP disk.

Bianchi, Pietro, ed. 1984. *Canti liturgici popolari nel Ticino*. Berne: Production Cooperativa Fata Morgana. Serie discografica 1, Schweizerische Gesellschaft für Volkskunde/Société svizzera per le tradizioni popolari FMM 84022. LP disk.

Brailoiu, Constantin. 1984 [1951–1958]. *Collection universelle de musique populaire enregistrée: World Collection of Recorded Folk Music*. Geneva: VDE-Gallo VDE 30–425 to 30–430. 6 LP disks.

———. 1986. *Musique populaire suisse: Schweizerische Volksmusic: Swiss Folk Music*. Geneva: VDE-Gallo VDE 30–477 to 30–478. 2 LP disks.

Cellier, Marcel. 1994. *Zäuerli: Polyphonies traditionnelles d'Appenzell: The Secular Swiss Yodeling*. Marcel Cellier Collection. Recorded in 1975 in Appenzell Ausserrhoden. Disques Cellier 750008. Compact disc.

Chante Jura. 1988. Series discografica, 5. Bern: Genossenschaft Fata Morgana 85736. LP disk.

Douce Romandie: Les plus belles mélodies et chansons de la Suisse Romande. 1992. Tell Records 7561 ATC. Compact disc.

Drey Dääg im Schuss: Querschnitt durch die Basler Fasnacht 1996. Basel: Grammohaus Lothar

Löffler, Schweizer Radio DRS BFCD 1996. Compact disc.

Extraits des Fêtes des Vignerons. N.d. Swiss Composers, 64–27. Communauté de travail pour la diffusion de la musique suisse CT 64–27. LP disk.

Fêtes des Vignerons, Lausanne '91. 1992. Migros Genossenschafts-Bund MGB 6113. Compact disc.

Fête des Vignerons: Mélodies populaires et chants célèbres de Suisse Romande. 1977. Tell Records 5182 TLP. LP disk.

Fête des Vignerons, Vevey 1955. 1987 [1955]. Souvenir album. Polygram Records Philips 832 318-2. Compact disc.

Fête des Vignerons, Vevey 1977. 1987. Polygram Records Philips 832 000-2, 832 0001-2. 2 compact discs.

Ils Fränzlis da Tschlin: Pariampampam. 1996. Zytglogge Vergag ZYT 3813. Compact disc.

Geisser, Kasi. 1996. *Historische Originalaufnahmen von 1928.* Vol. 1. Stein am Rhein: Phonographen Museum Phonodisc 0196. Compact disc.

————. 1997. *Historische Originalaufnahmen von 1928.* Vol. 2. Stein am Rhein: Phonographen Museum Phonodisc 0296. Compact disc.

Graubünden/Grischun. N.d. Anthologie authentischer Volksmusik aus den Schweizer Bergen/Anthologie de musique populaire originale des régions montagnardes suisses/Antologia di musica popolare originale delle regioni svizzere di montagne/Antologia da musica populara autentica dallas muntognas svizras, 61. Forum Alpinum 9006. LP disk.

Graubünden singt Canzuns e chants dils Retoromans. 1975. Canzuns Popularas 30–477. LP disk.

Gustave Doret: Fêtes des Vignerons de Vevey, 1905 & 1927: Les plus belles chansons. 1993. Disques Office RSR 65109–65111. 3 compact discs.

Jura, Gruyère, Alpes Vaudoises. N.d. Anthologie authentischer Volksmusik aus den Schweizer Bergen/Anthologie de musique populaire originale des régions montagnardes suisses/Antologia di musica popolare originale delle regioni svizzere di montagne/Antologia da musica populara autentica dallas muntognas svizras, 1. Forum Alpinum 9001. LP disk.

Jura, Valais, Berner Oberland, Emmental, Uri, Unterwalden, Ticino, Graubünden, Grischun, Appenzell, Toggenburg. N.d. Anthologie authentischer Volksmusik aus den Schweizer Bergen/Anthologie de musique populaire origi-

nale des régions montagnardes suisses/Antologia di musica popolare originale delle regioni svizzere di montagne/Antologia da musica populara autentica dallas muntognas svizras, 1–7. Forum Alpinum 9008. LP disk.

Juuzli: Jodel du Muotatal. 1979. Le Chant du Monde LDX 74716. LP disk.

Kantons-Märsche aus der ganzen Schweiz: Marches Cantonales de toute la Suisse: Marce cantonali di tutta la Svizzera. 1991. K-tel International 330006–2, 330007–2. Compact disc.

Music of the Swiss Alps. 1960. Capitol Records DT 10009. LP disk.

Naare uff's Schiff: Querschnitt durch die Basler Fasnacht 1995. Basel: Grammohaus Lothar Löffler, Schweizer Radio DRC BFCD 1995. Compact disc.

Numme Schutt und Gröll: Querschnitt durch die Basler Fasnacht 1992. Basel: Grammohaus Lothar Löffler, Schweizer Radio DRS BFCD 1992. Compact disc.

The Popular Folk Music of Switzerland. 1961. Vee-Jay Records 6407. LP disk.

Que serra: Querschnitt durch die Basler Fasnacht 1994. Basel: Grammohaus Lothar Löffler, Schweizer Radio DRS BFCD 1994. Compact disc.

Querschnitt durch die Basler Fasnacht 1986. Radio DRS Studio Basel Musik HUG HBL 120. LP disk.

Romandie: Chants et musique populaires: Chants, jodels, harmonicas, cor des Alpes et orchestre. 1992. Disques Office 65078. 3 compact discs.

S Theater goot wyter: Querschnitt durch die Basler Fasnacht 1993. Basel: Grammohaus Lothar Löffler, Schweizer Radio DRS BFCD 1993. Compact disc.

Schweizer Armeespiel. 1977. *Patriotische Schweizerlieder und -märsche: Chansons et marches patriotiques suisses: Canzoni e marce patriotiche svizzere: Patriotic Swiss Songs and Marches.* Musica Helvetica, 1. Swiss Broadcasting Corporation MH SE-1. LP disk.

————. 1981. *Schweizer Märsche.* CBS Schallplatten AG 84860. LP disk.

Schweizer Lieder aus allen Kantonen: Chansons suisses de tous les cantons: Canzoni svizzere di tutti i cantoni. N.d. K-tel International AG 330008–2, 330009–2. 2 compact discs.

Schweizer Volksmusik: Traditional Swiss Music: Tag der Schweizer Volksmusik IMF Luzern. N.d. Gümligen: DRS, Zytglogge 4532. 2 compact discs.

Schweizer Volksmusik im Jahreskreis: Les saisons et la musique populaire suisse: Le stagioni e la musica popolare svizzera: The Seasons and Swiss Traditional Music. 1991–1993. Zurich: SRG/SSR, Kornhaus Burgdorf, Gesellschaft für die Volksmusik in der Schweiz SMPS CD 001–004. 4 compact discs.

700 Joor yschtoo: Querschnitt durch die Basler Fasnacht 1991. Basel: Grammohaus Lothar Löffler, Schweizer Radio DRS BFCD 1991. Compact disc.

Switzerland: Suisse: Zäuerli: Yodel of Appenzell: Yodel d'Appenzell. 1980. Recordings by Hugo Zemp. Unesco Collection, Musics & Musicians of the World. Unesco D 8026, Auvidis. Compact disc.

Ticino: Genuine Folk Music from Southern Switzerland. 1989. Musica Helvetica, 2. Swiss Broadcasting Corporation MH CD 71.2. Compact disc.

Ticino, Grigioni italiano. N.d. Anthologie authentischer Volksmusik aus den Schweizer Bergen/Anthologie de musique populaire originale des régions montagnardes suisses/Antologia di musica popolare originale delle regioni svizzere di montagne/Antologia da musica populara autentica dallas muntognas svizras, 5. Forum Alpinum 9005. LP disk.

20 Jahre Guggenmusig Noggeler, Luzern: In Concert. 1991. Phonoplay-Tonstudio Luzern and Joe Käslin Phonoplay 7222. Compact disc.

2000 Johr [sic] *Mählsuppe: Ein Querschnitt von der Basler Fasnacht 1957.* The Gramophone Company His Master's Voice ZFLP 116. LP disk.

UNICEF, Schweizerisches Komitee, ed. 1982. *Sing mit uns! Die schönsten, neuen Kinderlieder aus 25 Ländern, entnommen dem Internationalen Kinderlieder-Wettbewerb der UNICEF: Bereichert durch alte Kinderlieder, Tänze und Instrumente zum Selberbasteln.* Zurich: Edition Melodie Pick 100–260/2. 2 LP disks. Pick 1260/2. 2 cassettes.

Unsere Märsche: Nos marches. 1982–1991. Tonstudio Amos, Theo Fuog 5525, 5530, 5540, 5550. 4 compact discs.

Valais/Wallis. N.d. Anthologie authentischer Volksmusik aus den Schweizer Bergen/Anthologie de musique populaire originale des régions montagnardes suisses/Antologia di musica popolare originale delle regioni svizzere di montagne/Antologia da musica populara autentica dallas muntognas svizras, 2. Forum Alpinum 9002. LP disk.

Der Volksliedsänger und -forscher Hans in der Gand. Serie discografica, 2. Bern: Genossenschaft Fata Morgana 84023. LP disk.

Poland

Ewa Dahlig

Singing Styles and Vocal Genres
Musical Instruments and Instrumental Music
Social Processes of Making Music
History of Music
Contemporary Developments
History of Scholarship

A large lowland region of thick forests and fertile soil, Poland is bounded in the south by the Carpathian Mountains and in the north by the Baltic Sea. Some 40 million people, of whom 98 percent are Poles, inhabit its 312,000 square kilometers. Ethnic minorities include Belorusans, Czechs, Germans, Lithuanians, Slovaks, Ukrainians, and small groups of Gypsies and Jews. Between Germany in the west and Ukraine, Lithuania, Belarus, and Russia in the east, Poland's territory has been a battlefield throughout history.

Five main Slavic tribes populated the area: Polans (the most important), Vistulans, Silesians, Mazovians, and Pomeranians. They were converted to Latin Christianity at the end of the tenth century with the help of Czech missionaries. The absence of centralized authority from 1138 to 1314 contributed to the regional diversity of modern Poland. From the 1400s to the 1600s, the Polish kingdom, in union with Lithuania, was a great power, extending far eastward from Poland's present border. In the late 1700s, the country was partitioned among the Great Powers (Austria, Prussia, and Russia), and its sovereignty was not restored until the end of World War I. The German invasion of 1939 interrupted this period of independence and led to unprecedented material and human losses, laboriously and painfully recovered during nearly fifty years of subjugation to communist rule, which ended in 1989 with the electoral victory of the labor movement, Solidarity. In the late 1990s, Poland espoused a liberal, market-oriented economy and was headed toward membership in the European Union. Its economy is based on industrial workers and small farmers, the latter the repositories of folk culture.

SINGING STYLES AND VOCAL GENRES

Poland's history and geography have combined to yield five major cultural and musical regions, three of which preserve the names of the Slavic tribes who settled there: Pomorze (Pomerania) in the north, Mazowsze (Mazovia) in the center and northeast, Małopolska (Little Poland) with the Carpathian area in the south and southeast, Wielkopolska (Great Poland) in the west, and Silesia in the southwest. Natural conditions in each region favor certain kinds of economy with implications for musical culture: hunting and fishing in the north, agriculture in the center, and sheep-farm-

Generally, singers sing in high registers, especially in Podhale in the Tatra Mountains, where men use strained voices on the fringe of screaming. The use of high, loud voices in Great Poland is sometimes explained as analogous to the sound of Polish bagpipes.

FIGURE 1   A wedding in Ojców in the 1800s. *Życie Polskie* 1914:167.

ing in the southern mountains. During the nineteenth-century partition of Poland, cultural differences among Austria, Prussia, and Russia divided Poland into a more progressive west and a more traditional east; in the west, for example, singing is far less lyrical and expressive than in the east.

Genres and contexts

Traditional musical practice is organized in two cycles: an annual cycle (New Year's caroling, Lent, Easter caroling, midsummer, harvesting, and Advent) and a life cycle (birth, childhood, wedding, marital life, death). The most important musical event, the wedding, has preserved the oldest strata of vocal repertoire (figure 1).

Among the oldest vocal forms are women's calls (*wiskanie*) in the southern mountain area. These calls have a free rhythmic structure and descending melody, in which only the first and last note have definite pitch. Ancient spring songs dedicated to the end of winter and the coming of summer, once prohibited by the Roman Catholic Church and preserved mostly in western and southern Poland, are limited today to the children's repertoire and consist of short recited formulae of three or four notes on repeated rhythmic patterns. Old ritual songs from eastern regions, especially wedding songs and laments, are often free recitations. Funeral laments, which vanished long ago, have been replaced by a religious repertoire sung by professional performers. This repertoire plays a special role in Pomerania, especially in the Cassubia subregion, where group singing in the house of the dead during so-called empty

FIGURE 2 A narrow-range wedding song from Lubelskie, eastern Poland. Transcription by Ludwik Bielawski.

Za stol Ka–sien–ku, za stol, za stol, Ka–sien–ku, za stol, ej, bo juz przy–sedl cas twoj

nights (*puste noce*) is customary. Solstice songs, which accompany dancing around fires, have strong sexual symbolism. Nearly forgotten, they are of two types: the eastern one refers to the pagan demon Kupała; the western one, to St. John the Baptist.

Folk-song structures

Polish folk songs may be differentiated into short forms (dance songs) and long forms (narrative songs). The inhabitants of the Kurpie region in northeastern Poland, the so-called foresters, have their own local classification of songs along these lines: *przytrampywane* 'songs with foot tapping', performed with dancelike movements, and *leśne* 'forest songs', slow, melismatic songs, sung in the open in woods and fields. The structure of vocal forms mostly depends on their function. In scales, rhythms, and content, ritual songs of the annual and life cycles have preserved the oldest musical features, including remnants of pentatonic and narrow-range scales (figure 2). Most Polish folk songs, however, are based on modal scales (figure 3).

Most Polish folk songs have a strophic structure, with melodies consisting of two four-bar phrases. The most popular type is the so-called *przyśpiewka* 'ditty', with a two-line text, often improvised, that refers to the situation or contains malicious remarks about participants in the events.

As a rule, Polish folk songs are syllabic, with occasional glissandi or melismas. Melismatic singing is typical of eastern regions and Kurpie. In northern areas (Kurpie, Mazuria, and Podlasie), an archaic performance manner, *apocope* 'whispering or omitting the last syllable of a song', was practiced. *Tempo rubato* is typical, especially of the central and southern part of Poland, where it combines with *mazurka* rhythms to create an oscillation between duple and triple time (figure 4). In most regions, folk songs are performed monophonically, though heterophonic singing may have been practiced in the past. Only in the Carpathian area is polyphonic singing found. There, one singer initiates a song, and after a few notes others join in; some take the main melody while the rest add a voice below (figure 5).

Performance style

Generally, singers sing in high registers, especially in Podhale in the Tatra Mountains, where men use strained voices on the fringe of screaming, while women sing quietly in low-pitched registers. In Kieleckie (in Little Poland), men and women sing in high tessituras. In the north, west, and east, registers are lower. The use of high, loud voices in Great Poland is sometimes explained as analogous to the sound of Polish bagpipes. In Mazovia, vocal timbres are more delicate.

In Kieleckie, songs often end with high-pitched shouts, and in Podhale, with women's calls. Vocal performances, especially those of Little Poland and the Carpathian area, are accompanied by spontaneous behavior like vivid gesturing, stomping, and shouting.

FIGURE 3 A long modal song (ballad) from Mazovia. After Kolberg 1979 [1961]:1:119.

Na Po– do– lu mo– dry ka– miń na Po– do– lu mo– dry ka– miń

Po– do– lan– ka sie– dzi na nim Po– do– lan– ka sie– dzi na nim.

FIGURE 4   An *oberek* from the Kielce region, Little Poland. Transcription by Ewa Dahlig.

MUSICAL INSTRUMENTS AND INSTRUMENTAL MUSIC

The oldest instruments found in the Polish area are drums, originating in the Neolithic period. In contemporary folk music, membranophones play an important role as rhythmic drones. The friction drum (*burczybas*), for example, was used in carnival masquerades in Pomerania. The frame drum with jingles (*grajcary, cykace*) is typical of ensembles in central and eastern regions, where it is played with a certain virtuosity. In the 1920s and 1930s, it was replaced in some areas by a large two-headed drum (*baraban*), sometimes with an added cymbal or triangle.

Idiophones are represented by clappers (*kołatki, terkotki*) used in annual church ceremonies, especially on Good Friday.

The simplest aerophones have signaling functions and vary in length from short clarinets (*bekace*) to long wooden trumpets and horns, known in Mazovia as *ligawka*, in Pomerania as *bazuna,* and in Silesia as *trembita*. In the Carpathian area, numerous flutes are used: end-blown, ductless shepherd's flutes without holes (*fujarka*); duct flutes with six to seven holes (*fulyrka*); and a duct flute with a double pipe (*piszczałka*). Reed pipes are represented by the bagpipe, the only wind instrument traditionally used in folk ensembles.

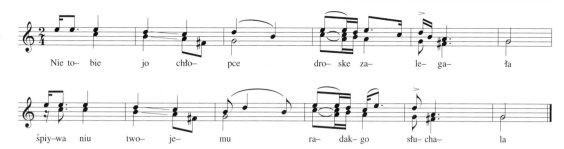

FIGURE 5 Carpathian polyphonic singing on a tune type called *nuta wierchowa*. After Sadownik 1971:275.

Nie to— bie   jo chło— pce   dro— ske za— le— ga— ła

śpiy—wa niu   two— je— mu   ra— dak— go słu— cha— la

Ensembles

Ensemble playing in Poland has been dominated by bowed stringed instruments. Traditionally, the most important melodic instrument was a fiddle (today a violin), popular all over the country. A musical band could be created by a fiddle with only one accompanying rhythmic (drum) or drone (bagpipe) or rhythmic-drone (bass) instrument (figure 6). The importance of the fiddle is mirrored in folktales, many of which relate a common belief in the supernatural power of this instrument and of its player.

The origin of bowing in Polish and other Slavic areas is obscure. Three archaeological findings (two examples of so-called *gęśle* from Opole from the eleventh century and one *gęśle* from Gdańsk from the thirteenth century), morphologically close to northern European bowed lyres preserved in Finland and Estonia, may have been bowed. Two major groups of bowed chordophones were formerly known in Poland. Instruments played in a vertical position—mentioned in the old Polish literature as belly fiddles and in all probability a folk version of Polish violins described by Martin Agricola in his *Musica instrumentalis deudsch* (1545)—had disappeared by 1900, their last trace the so-called *suka* 'bitch', whose only example was documented in 1888. Depictions show that the *suka* had a bridge resting on two long legs on the back of the resonance box, with no contact with the face. The proportions and dimensions of the resonance box, the presence of a fingerboard, and the form of the

FIGURE 6 A traditional music ensemble with fiddle, clarinet, pedal accordion, and frame drum, from the Kurpie region. Photo by Jacek Chodyna.

In Great Poland, the *maryna* combines the function of a chordophone with an idiophone. The player holds the bow motionless in his right hand, and his left hand rotates the instrument to bow it. At the same time, he strikes the leg of the *maryna* against the floor, causing jingles on its head to sound.

tailpiece show the influence of violins commonly used in folk traditions at that time. Historical analogs to *suka* may be found on a seventeenth-century woodcut and in well-preserved instruments from the 1500s, found in Plock (Central Poland) in archaeological excavations. This instrument has a bridge of two unequally long legs; the longer one passes to the bottom of the resonance box through the resonance-hole while the short one rests on the belly. Such a bridge was also found on the small fiddle (*mazanki*) from western Poland and the two-stringed bass from the Kalisz District (Great Poland).

Polish belly fiddles seem to belong to the same tradition as the Russian *gudok*. It seems probable that after being replaced by the violin, they took on the role of accompanying instruments, limited to the function of rhythmic drone, thus becoming predecessors of modern small bass instruments.

Three main groups of horizontally played fiddles have survived in folk practice: the *mazanki* (a small, figure-8-shaped fiddle from Wielkopolska, with a bridge having two unequal legs); the *złóbcoki* (a small, rebeclike fiddle of the Polish highlanders in the Tatra mountains); and the violin (*skrzypce*). The *mazanki* and *złóbcoki* basically disappeared around 1900, and their present comeback results from revivals of local traditions. The *mazanki* was played with a bagpipe (*kozioł*), often by shepherds. In the mid-1800s, it was replaced by factory-made violins retuned to the bagpipe (*kozioł*) by binding the neck and strings at one third of their length to form a capo (hence the name *skrzypce podwiązane* 'bound-up violin'). *Złóbcoki* was a solo instrument in the late 1800s. Quieter than the violin, it was taken up in the 1950s by some ensembles as a musical symbol of Podhale.

Traditionally, fiddlers finger the strings in first position. In newer types of ensembles with loud melodic instruments like accordion or saxophone, they use higher violin registers and higher positions to obtain more audibility. They play without vibrato, make extensive use of open strings, and do not use their little finger. They prefer nonlegato bowing techniques and reserve pizzicato for special effects only, as in certain game-dances, in which switching from bowing to pizzicato indicates a change of partners.

Bass chordophones, used exclusively as accompanying instruments, exist in many regional versions varying from small local forms (like the two-stringed bass of the Kalisz area in the west) to standard double bass. Some local variants are also found, for example, in Great Poland, the *maryna*, an instrument combining the function of a chordophone with an idiophone. The player holds the bow motionless in his right hand, and his left hand rotates the instrument to bow it. At the same time, he strikes the leg of the *maryna* against the floor, causing jingles on its head to sound. Another bowed chordophone, the hurdy-gurdy, was formerly known as an instrument of wandering beggars, usually of Ukrainian or Belorusan origin [see UKRAINE]. Struck chordophones include the dulcimer (*cymbały*) known at least from the 1600s and today existing in two local versions: a large one in the east and south (the area of

FIGURE 7   A bagpipe (*koza*) from Podhale. Photo by Jan Świderski, year unknown.

TRACK 25

Rzeszów), used mostly to play in ensembles as an accompanying instrument; and a smaller one in the east and north on the Lithuanian border, used as a solo melodic instrument.

In some regions, the bagpipe plays an important role as an ensemble instrument. In Wielkopolska (Western Poland) five types of bagpipe can be found: two regional types of *dudy* 'bagpipe', *kozioł biały* 'white he-goat', *czarny kozioł doślubny* 'black he-goat of the wedding' and *sierszeńki* 'tiny hornet', each unique in size, tuning, and function. The *kozioł* is ornamented with an imitation of the he-goat head. In the white version, the skin has white hair outside. Smaller, the black *kozioł*, with black hair outside, was played only at weddings, with *mazanki*. The *sierszeńki* (also called *siesieńki* and *pancharzyna*) is a learner's instrument, used by boys and made of one or two animal bladders with a melodic pipe. Other bagpipes are known in Podhale (*koza*), Żywiec (*dudy*), and Silesia in Beskid Śląski (*gajdy*). Bagpipes from Great Poland and Silesia are equipped with a bellows; and in the Carpathian area (Podhale and Żywiec), with a blowpipe. All Polish bagpipes have single reeds and one drone pipe, though until the late 1800s, forms with many drones were documented. In Żywiec, an ensemble of bagpipe and violin is popular, but in Podhale, the bagpipe is a solo instrument (figure 7).

In central and eastern Poland, bands consisting of a violin, a single-headed frame drum, and/or a bass were popular. In larger ensembles, the violin was doubled: the first player played the so-called *prym* (main melody) and the second one the *sekund,* a harmonic and rhythmic accompaniment. The frame drum was eventually replaced by large two-headed drums with triangle and/or cymbals. Since the 1930s, other instruments have been adapted to folk-band use. These include the clarinet, the trumpet, and, above all, various accordions, from the simplest concertinas to the piano accordion and an accordion with an air pump attached to the instrument by a long, thin tube (see figure 6). The bass, originally small and two- or three-stringed and used mostly as a rhythmic drone with no harmonic function, eventually became larger and four-stringed, and was used for playing harmonies; stopping strings is typical especially for Podhale. Nowadays, especially in large bands, the traditional homemade bass is often replaced by a double bass, which the player bows or plucks. In the sub-Carpathian area (Rzeszów), the dulcimer is used in ensembles.

In Podhale, string ensembles are typical. They consist of one *prymista* (a melody-playing fiddle), two or more *sekund,* and a bass [see LOCAL KNOWLEDGE OF MUSICAL GENRES AND ROLES, figure 2, p. 113]. Ensemble playing in Podhale is uniquely oriented toward chordal harmony (ornamented melody played against chords). The typical instrumental repertoire of the region consists of cycles of tunes starting with a moderate tempo but increasing in speed. A central musical notion of Podhale is the tune (*nuta* 'note'), a concept of a certain harmonic structure identified by its name and often referring to the name of the musician who invented it (figure 8).

There are many types of ensembles in Wielkopolska: two to three violins and bass; violin, two-stringed bass (typical of towns of the Kalisz area), and drum; bound-up violin and *dudy; kozioł,* violin, and clarinet; and violin, clarinet in C, and *maryna.*

Instrumental music

As a rule, Polish folk-instrumental music is dance music. The only exceptions are signals played on wooden trumpets and horns and shepherds' tunes. Most instrumental dance tunes derive from vocal melodies, though the words are often forgotten. Instrumental versions differ from vocal ones in musical form (often phrases or single bars are repeated many times) and rich ornamentation, which consists of formulas typical of a given instrument. Typical traditional dance tunes of vocal origin are built of two phrases (in Central Poland, they are called *kolano* 'knee'), each four bars long.

FIGURE 8   Jędrzej Bronisławski's *nuta ozwodna* from Podhale. Transcription by Ewa Dahlig.

The first phrase is repeated twice and the second ad libitum. The melody is opened and closed by a special fiddle formula, the function of which is to inform other members of the ensemble and dancers of the type and tempo of the dance.

Triple-meter dances create the image of Polishness in music. These dances are based on rhythms that refer to the movement pattern and reflect the specificity of the Polish language. Polish words formerly had an initial accent, but today they have the accent on the penultimate syllable. This linguistic history contributes to the constitution of mazurka rhythms with their typical measures of two sixteenth notes followed by two eighth notes. Such rhythms are typical of the family of dances known and dominant in Polish folk music from the Renaissance and Baroque period and consisting of dances performed in different tempos: *oberek* (the fastest), *mazurek* (mazurka), *kujawiak, chodzony* (a walking dance) and, finally, the slowest one, *polonez* (polonaise).

Like the mazurka-type dances, the most popular duple-meter dance, the *krakowiak,* has entered the canon of Polish national dances. Regional dance tunes, *wiwat* (in duple or triple time) are popular in Great Poland, and the Carpathian area has preserved distinct local dances, including a couple dance (*góralski* 'highlanders' dance') and a men's dance (*zbójnicki* 'robbers' dance').

SOCIAL PROCESSES OF MAKING MUSIC

Generally, Polish folk music is transmitted orally and is connected to family and social life. Singing is learned while people work in groups and attend musical events. The learning of instrumental play is more institutionalized and requires a master-pupil relationship. A multistage process, it includes learning to tune the instrument, practicing exercises in fingering, repeating melodies by ear, and learning basic musical notions necessary in making music. Musical theory is rather limited and oriented toward practice: it includes the minimum of knowledge indispensable to play, without much reflection or an elaborated terminology. Musicians highly appreciate the knowledge of musical notation, since it provides an additional source of repertoire beyond memory, though they commonly believe that playing from the score limits their improvisational skills. At a minimum, in singing and playing, performers are expected to reproduce melodies correctly. Singers are judged according to the quality of the voice and instrumentalists according to their ability to ornament the melody. Individual creation adds to the common treasure and remains mostly anonymous. The names of the most distinguished fiddlers may survive in the titles of dance tunes.

Traditional music in Poland never referred to politics, but was influenced by ideologies coming from the outside world. As early as the 1700s, and especially during the 1800s, traditional music played an important role in the growth of a national consciousness and identity. An example of this process was the conscious stylization of folk dances, in which the mazurka, the polonaise, and the *krakowiak* were incorporated into a canon of so-called national dances. Even if these developments did not benefit Polish peasants directly, they resulted in the first serious attempts by intellectuals to document and preserve peasant music in written form. In the 1920s and 1930s, folk culture underwent a major transformation under new economic conditions. New educational programs and amateur initiatives directed toward folk music were institutionalized. Many folk musicians born in that time attended schools, had contact with urban musicians, learned music notation, and were able to buy factory-made instruments.

After 1945, communist rule created new conditions for massive undertakings in folk music, to some extent following Soviet patterns. A large-scale documentation of folk traditions was undertaken, and folkloristic ensembles of professionals performing what some village musicians called "embellished" folk music were promoted. The official promotion of folk music, heard on radio and seen in concerts accompanying state ceremonies, resulted from the conviction that in a nation-state of workers and peasants, folk music of the once lowest and now leading social strata should serve as an official musical emblem. The reaction was the opposite, however, and many people rejected folk music, as either a symbol of difficult living conditions and poverty or a tool of official policy.

After 1989, when the country opened itself to Western Europe, the attitude toward folk music changed in accordance with Western ideas that forgotten and underestimated traditional values may enrich present-day culture. The ideology associated with this movement is based on terms like *music ecology* and *back to the roots,* rather than on political notions.

HISTORY OF MUSIC

Polish musical culture emerged between the twelfth and the fifteenth centuries on the basis of old Slavic and Western European culture, the latter including mostly imported Roman Catholic church music (tropes and sequences are said to have had a decisive influence on Polish modality) and secular elements, such as ballads and dance music. In the 1300s and 1400s, new institutional forms, like choirs and instrumental ensembles, emerged.

In the 1990s, as in many Western European countries decades earlier, a trend developed to merge folk elements into popular music. Such experiments helped young people find an identity in an age of transnational music and provided a source of inspiration for new music.

FIGURE 9   A mazurka in a nineteenth-century lithograph. *Życie Polskie* 1914:168.

In the Middle Ages, the Roman Catholic Church directed its activities against Slavic paganism, leading to the eradication of pre-Christian repertoires. Only in eastern areas, influenced by the Greek and Russian Orthodox churches, did old Slavic traits (musical scales, structure, and symbolism) survive, perhaps best in the wedding ritual. In the Middle Ages, folk songs penetrated religious repertoires, however, and religious songs, in turn, exist today as one of the most important folk genres. The mixture of religious content with folk melodies can be best heard in the repertoire of Christmas carols.

Polish art music, from its earliest days, has gained inspiration from folk music, and in the process has achieved a national flavor. In return, folk music adopted formal and stylistic features of art music, and even whole tunes.

Some sixteenth- and seventeenth-century tablatures include melodies now identified as folk tunes; at least their rhythmic structures show the influence of so-called mazurka rhythms. Not many Polish sources from then survive, but this repertoire migrated to many European countries under the names of *chorea polonica, polnischer Tanz, balletto polacco,* and *danse polonaise.*

In the late 1700s, a new wave of interest in folk music resulted in music quotations, especially in operas by Józef Elsner (1769–1854) and Karol Kurpiński (1785–1857). Dances of folk origin, like the polonaise, the mazurka, and the *krakowiak,* became national dances, were accepted by the upper social classes, and were reflected especially in the piano works of Prince Michał Kleofas Ogiński (1765–1833) and Maria Szymanowska (1789–1831) (figure 9). The work of Frédéric (Fryderyk) Chopin (1810–1849) is the best example of the synthesis of national elements rooted in folk music with the texture of the piano music of his time. In rhythms, tonality, and emotions, his music is unmistakably Polish, and especially close to the Mazovian tradition of *oberek* and *kujawiak.* Operas by Stanisław Moniuszko (1819–1872), based on Polish themes, were popular in Poland, though they never became internationally renowned.

In the twentieth century, Polish folk music found its admirer in Karol Szymanowski (1882–1937). Inspired by Skierkowski's folk-song collection from Kurpie (1928–1934), Szymanowski composed his six choral and twelve solo *Kurpie Songs* on this material. Folk music from Podhale became an invaluable source of inspiration for this composer and contributed to his concept of a Polish folkloristic style using new musical language. From then on, folk-music stylizations do not find much place in composers' works, and the impact of folk culture on contemporary art music is limited.

CONTEMPORARY DEVELOPMENTS

Contemporary folk culture is still changing. In the twentieth century, it changed much faster than before. The first half of the century witnessed a growth of large urban centers. The second half brought changes in social consciousness to varying degrees in different regions. In Great Poland, for example, an orientation toward Western Europe, local pride, and the awareness of local culture have helped to preserve regional cultural resources and adapt them to modern ways of cultural transmission. The situation in Silesia is similar, though difficult living conditions in this region formerly resulted in some disintegration of the deepest strata of the music repertoire. The situation in Little Poland, where no institutional support has developed, endangers the existence of local folk traditions. The Carpathian area, especially Podhale, has a strong musical idiom that forms the most important element of local identity and therefore is relatively resistant to change.

Modernizing processes have strongly influenced performance practice, destroying the organic unity of dance-music. Performers' reactions often lack spontaneity and sensitivity to the social functions of music, and the traditional lack of differentiation between performers and audience has been replaced by a clear distinction. Since many traditional contexts for transmission involving group performance have disappeared, "group memory," once a main source of the repertoire, does not function as before. Neutral thirds, flexible time units, and traditional vocal timbres are disappearing in favor of major-minor tonalities, regular rhythms, and so-called clear singing, with no melismas, glissandi, or apocope (whispering or dropping the last sound of the word). The decline of narrative songs reflects the deaths of women singers of the older generation, who did not teach their special knowledge to the next generation.

Despite these changes, obvious elements of traditional thinking still allow people from a peasant background to combine two time dimensions: modern everyday reality and old customs. In modern society, folk culture has lost many of its functions in favor of being a source of inspiration in other types of music, a factor in social identity, and a means of recreation. Since many traditional contexts for folk-musical practice have disintegrated, new contexts have had to be created, especially folk-music festivals. The most important ones are Festiwal Kapel i Śpiewaków Ludowych (Festival of Folk Ensembles and Singers) in Kazimierz and Festiwal Folkloru Ziem Górskich (Festival of Highland Folklore) in Zakopane.

In Poland, folk music never gained a significance comparable to that in other Slavic countries, and therefore its impact on contemporary art music is limited. Instead, pop music seems to be the music most hospitable to promoting traditional values. After decades of artificially supported life under socialism, Polish folk music was moribund. Meaningful only to old villagers, it was rejected by others, including young people, who did not find an identity in folk tradition. But in the 1990s, as in many Western European countries decades earlier, a trend developed to merge folk elements into popular music. Such experiments helped young people find an identity in an age of transnational music and provided a source of inspiration for new music.

Traditional and pop music elements have been combined in five different ways: folk tradition is followed completely, using folk instruments, repertoires, and performing styles, as by Kapela Domu Tańca (Dance House Ensemble); folk music is played by professionals in an artistically sophisticated form, as by Ensemble Polonais; folk music and pop music coexist as two overlapping clichés, as when the Trebunie-Tutki Family Band plays with the Jamaican reggae band Twinkle Brothers; traditional repertoire in pop music is used as an inspiration only, as by the Jorgi Quartett; and repertoire not originally from the folk tradition is folklorized, played in a traditional manner, as when the Ensemble Polonais experiments with playing Chopin's mazurkas in a folklike manner. Such experiments have changed the general attitude toward pure tradition, which in the 1990s was more respected than when it was promoted by the state.

HISTORY OF SCHOLARSHIP

FIGURE 10   Oskar Kolberg (1814–1890). Photo by A. Regulski, year unknown. Bielawski and Dadak-Kozicka 1995: cover.

Studies of Polish folklore occurred in three stages. From 1801 to 1857, collectors were interested mostly in folk-song texts. Melodies, if included, had piano accompaniment. Even Oskar Kolberg, the most distinguished Polish ethnographer of this stage, published *Pieśni ludu polskiego* (Songs of the Polish people, 1842) in such a form. From 1857, however, his volume under the same title but in a new style started a new chapter in the history of folk-song research. A survey of Polish folk songs, it concentrated on the music and text of folk repertoire and was followed by many regional monographs showing music in the context of folk customs, beliefs, rituals, tales, and everyday life. Kolberg was the first collector to complement his collection with precise documentation, comments, and references (figures 10, 11). This new work marks a second period in Polish folkloristic studies (1857–1890). In the third stage, 1890–1950, his work was followed, though not on such a large scale, by many folklorists: Jan Stanisław Bystroń, Józef Ligęza, and Stefan M. Stoiński in Silesia; Władysław Skierkowski in the northeastern part of Poland; and Stanisław Mierczyński in the Tatra Mountains.

In 1912 and 1913, musicology was established as a university discipline in Cracow and Lvov, and in 1913 the first phonograph recordings—of Bartek Obrochta, a renowned fiddler from Podhale—were made. Helena Windakiewiczowa (1897) wrote valuable studies on Polish folk-rhythmic structures and relationships between Chopin's music and Polish folk music. Adolf Chybiński (1961) wrote the first study of Polish folk-musical instruments, devoted to Podhale.

Systematic recordings of folk music started in the 1930s at the Phonographic Archive of the Poznań University, led by Łucjan Kamieński. In 1935, Julian Pulikowski created the Central Phonographic Archive in the National Library in Warsaw. Both collections were destroyed in World War II.

In the late 1940s, the Institute of Art in Warsaw organized a large-scale documentation of folk music in all the regions of Poland. Collectors, the most important of whom were Jadwiga and Marian Sobieski, did intensive field research in Pomerania, Olsztyn, Kielce, Cracow, Poznań, the Warsaw area, and Silesia. From 1949 to 1953, about sixty thousand tunes were recorded. Now stored in the Marian Sobieski Phonographic Archive of the Institute of Art, they have been followed by intensive recording from the 1970s to the present. Large collections of recorded music may be found in the Centre of Folk Culture of the Polish Radio in Warsaw.

In the 1960s and 1970s, old methodological trends—oriented mostly toward diachronic and regional studies—gave way to multidisciplinary research. Generally, Polish ethnomusicology combines methods typical of the humanities with those of empirical disciplines. Mathematical methods have been applied to the exploration of vocal repertoire (Czekanowska 1972), the modeling of *shashmaqam* structures (Żerańska-Kominek 1986), the classification of musical instruments (E. Dahlig 1991), and a "zonal" theory of time (Bielawski 1975). Other important recent studies include a monograph on Polish folk music (Czekanowska 1990) and specialized studies of rhythms (Bielawski 1970), the consciousness of Polish folk performers (P. Dahlig 1993), Carpathian musical instruments (Kopoczek 1984), the fiddle and fiddling (E. Dahlig 1991), the melodic form of Polish folk songs (Przerembski 1994), and folk dances (Dąbrowska 1980, Lange 1978).

BIBLIOGRAPHY

Bartkowski, Bolesław. 1987. *Polskie śpiewy religijne w Żywej tradycji: Style i formy* (Polish religious folk chants in the living tradition: Styles and forms). Cracow: Polskie Wydawnictwo Muzyczne.

Bielawski, Ludwik. 1970. *Rytmika polskiej pieśni*

ludowej (Rhythms of Polish folk songs). Cracow: Polskie Wydawnictwo Muzyczne.

———. 1975. *Strefowa teoria czasu i jej znaczenie dla antropologii muzycznej* (The zonal theory of time and its significance for the anthropology of

FIGURE 11   In the nineteenth century collectors mainly focused on song texts while artists rendered village scenes such as this harvest celebration. *Zycie Polskie* 1914.

music). Cracow: Polskie Wydawnictwo Muzyczne.

Bielawski, Ludwik, and Katarzyna Dadak-Kozicka, ed. 1995. *Oskar Kolberg: Prekursor antropologii kultury* (Oskar Kolberg, precursor of cultural anthropology). Warsaw: ISPAN.

Bobrowska, Jadwiga. 1981. *Pieśni ludowe regionu Żywieckiego* (Folk songs from the Żywiec area). Cracow: Polskie Wydawnictwo Muzyczne.

Chybiński, Adolf. 1961. *O polskiej muzyce ludowej* (On Polish folk music). Ludwik Bielawski ed.). Cracow: Polskie Wydawnictwo Muzyczne.

Czekanowska Anna. 1972. *Ludowe melodie wąskiego zakresu w krajach słowiańskich* (Narrow-range folk melodies in Slavic countries). Cracow: Polskie Wydawnictwo Muzyczne.

———. 1990. *Polish Folk Music: Slavonic Heritage—Polish Tradition—Contemporary Trends.* Cambridge: Cambridge University Press.

Dąbrowska, Grażyna. 1980. *Taniec ludowy na Mazowszu* (Folk dance in Mazovia). Cracow: Polskie Wydawnictwo Muzyczne.

Dahlig, Ewa. 1991. *Ludowa gra skrzypcowa w Kieleckiem* (Fiddling in the Kielce region). Cracow: Polskie Wydawnictwo Muzyczne.

Dahlig, Piotr. 1993. *Ludowa praktyka muzyczna* (Folk-musical practice). Warsaw: Wydawnictwo ISPAN.

Dygacz, Adolf. 1975. *Ludowe pieśni górnicze w Zagłębiu Dąbrowskim* (Miners' songs in Zagłębie Dąbrowskie). Katowice: Śląski Instytut Naukowy.

Kamiński, Włodzimierz. 1971. *Instrumenty muzyczne na ziemiach polskich* (Musical instruments in Poland). Cracow: Polskie Wydawnictwo Muzyczne.

Karłowicz, Jan. "Narzędzia muzyczne na wystawie muzycznej w Warszawie, na wiosnę. 1888." (Musical instruments in the Warsaw exhibition in 1888). *Wisła* 1888:431–435.

Kolberg, Oskar. 1979 [1961]. *Dzieła wszystkie* (Collected works). Vols. 1–57. Wrocław, Poznań, Warsaw, and Cracow: Polskie Wydawnictwo Muzyczne.

Kopoczek, Alojzy. 1984. *Instrumenty muzyczne Beskidu śląskiego i Żywieckiego: Aerofony proste i ich repertuar* (Musical instruments of the Beskid: Simple aerophones and their repertoire). Bielsko-Biała: Beskidzka Oficyna Wydawnicza.

Krzyżaniak, Barbara, Aleksander Pawlak, and Jarosław Lisakowski. 1975. *Kujawy.* Folk music, vol. 1. Texts, vol. 2. Cracow: Polskie Wydawnictwo Muzyczne.

Lange, Roderyk. 1978. *Tradycyjny taniec ludowy w Polsce i jego przeobrażenia w czasie i przestrzeni* (Traditional folk dance in Poland and its changes in time and space). London: Veritas Foundation Press.

Linette, Bogusław. 1981. *Obrzędowe pieśnie weselne w Rzeszowskiem* (Wedding songs in the Rzeszów area). Rzeszów: Krajowa Agencja Wydawnicza.

Mierczyński, Stanisław. 1930. *Muzyka Podhala.* Cracow: Polskie Wydawnictwo Muzyczne.

Moszyński, Kazimierz. 1968 [1939]. *Kultura ludowa Słowian* (Folk culture of the Slavs). Vol. 2. Warsaw: Książka i Wiedza.

Noll, William Henry. 1986. "Peasant Music Ensembles in Poland. A Culture History." Ph.D. dissertation, University of Washington, Seattle.

Pawlak, Aleksander. 1981. Folklor muzyczny

Kujaw (Folklore of Kujawy). Cracow: Polskie Wydawnictwo Muzyczne.

Przerembski, Zbigniew. 1994. *Style i formy melodyczne polskich pieśni ludowych* (Style and form of the Polish folk song). Warsaw: Wydawnictwo ISPAN.

Pietruszyńska (=Sobieska), Jadwiga. 1936. *Dudy Wielkopolskie* (Bagpipes of Great Poland). Poznań: Gebethner i Wolff.

Sadownik, Jan, ed. 1971. Pieśni Podhala (Folk songs from Podhale). Cracow: Polskie Wydawnictwo Muzyczne.

Skierkowski, Władysław. 1928–1934. Puszcza kurpiowska w pieśni (The Kurpie Forest in folk song). Vol. 1–3. Płock: Wydawnictwo Towarzystwa Naukowego Płockiego.

Sobiescy, Jadwiga, and Marian Sobieski. 1973. *Polska muzyka ludowa i jej problemy* (Polish folk music and questions about it). Edited by Ludwik Bielawski. Cracow: Polskie Wydawnictwo Muzyczne.

Stęszewska, Zofia. 1965. "Z zagadnień kształě towania się stylu narodowego w muzyce polskiej XVI do XVIII w" (On the formation of Polish national style in music from the sixteenth to eighteenth centuries). *Muzyka* 1965(3):3–33.

Stęszewski, Jan. 1972. "Sachen, Bewusstsein und Benennungen in ethnomusikologischen Untersuchungen." *Jahrbuch für Volksliedforschung* 17:131–170.

Windakiewiczowa, Helena. 1897. "Rytmika muzyki polskiej ludowej" (Rhythms of Polish folk music). *Wisła* 1897:716–737.

———. 1926. "Wzory polskiej muzyki ludowej w mazurkach Chopina" (Folk music patterns in Mazurkas by Chopin). *Rozprawy Wydziału Filologicznego PAU*, series 3, 16:3–50.

Żerańska-Kominek, Sławomira. 1986. *Symbole czasu i przestrzeni w muzyce Asji Centralnej* (Time and space symbols in the music of Central Asia). Cracow: Polskie Wydawnictwo Muzyczne.

Życie Polskie. 1914–. Warsaw: Księgarnia Altenberg, Seyharth, Wende.

AUDIOVISUAL RESOURCES

Baliszewska, Maria. 1995. *Pologne. Instruments populaires*. Radio France & Polish Radio. OCORA C 600 001. Compact disc.

Domański, Marian. 1982. *Maśniaki Ensemble from Zakopane (Podhale)*. Polskie Nagrania, Muza sx 1716-1717. LP disk.

Ensemble Polonais. 1995. *Muzyka nizin* (Music of the lowlands). Agencja Artystyczna MTJ CD 024. CD

———. 1996. *Oj chmielu*. Agencja Artystyczna MTJ CD 005. CD

Krywań. 1995. *Dwie tęsknoty '95* (Two melancholies '95). Ryszard Music CRM 005. Cassette.

Podhale śpiewa (Tunes of Tatra highlands). 1967. Polskie Nagrania xL 0337. LP disk.

Polish Folk Music. 1990. Edited by Joanna Kalinowska. *The Feliks Dzierżanowski Polish Folk Band: Krakowiaks and Polonaises*. Polskie Nagrania CK 062. *Podhale Tunes of Tatra Highlands*. Polskie Nagrania CK 1006. *Polish Song and Dance Ensemble "Mazowsze."* Polskie Nagrania CK068, CK083. *Polish Song and Dance Ensemble Śląsk*. Polskie Nagrania CK1003, CK1004. *Polish Ensemble Kurpianka*. Polskie Nagrania CK1005. *Polish Song and Dance Ensemble Wielkopolska*. Polskie Nagrania CK *290*. *The Sowa Family Band of Piątkowa Village*. Polskie Nagrania CK 512, CK 519. *The Stefan Maciejewski Clarinet Band. Polkas and Obereks*. Polskie Nagrania CK 054. *The Tadeusz Wesołowski Accordion Band*. Polskie Nagrania CK 086. 12 cassettes.

Polkas from Poland. N.d. Polskie Nagrania PNCD 023 ADD. Compact disc.

Sobieska, Jadwiga, ed. 1976. *Grajcie dudy, grajcie basy* (Play shawms, play basses). Part 1, Music from Mazovia and Great Poland, Polskie Nagrania, Muza sx 1125. Part 2, Music from Little Poland and Carpathian area, Polskie Nagrania, Muza sx1126. 2 LP disks.

———, ed. N.d. *Folk Music from the Rzeszów area*. Polskie Nagrania Muza sx 2348-2349. LP disk.

———, ed. N.d. *Grajcie dudy, grajcie basy* (Play shawms, play basses). Songs and Music from Poland. Polskie Nagrania PNCD 048. Compact disc.

Sources of Polish Folk Music. 1996–. *Maria Baliszewska and Anna Szotkowska: Mazowsze (Mazovia)*. Polish Radio PRCD 150. *Maria Baliszewska and Anna Szotkowska: Podhale (The Tatra foothills)*. Polish Radio PRCD 151. *Anna Szewczuk-Czech and Anna Szotkowska: Młopolska Północna (Northern Little Poland)*. Polish Radio PRCD 152. *Anna Szewczuk-Czech and Anna Szotkowska: Lubelskie (The Lublin area)*. Polish Radio PRCD 153. *Anna Szewczuk-Czech and Anna Szotkowska: Wielkopolska (Great Poland)*. Polish Radio PRCD 154. *Anna Szewczuk-Czech and Anna Szotkowska: Kurpie*. Polish Radio PRCD 155. 6 compact discs in series, with more in process.

Sowa Family Band. N.d. *Songs and Music from the Village of Piątkowa*. Polskie Nagrania PNCD 049. Compact disc.

Stęszewski, Jan, ed. N.d. *Podhale parts 1–3*. Veriton sxv-728, sxv-729, sxv-730. 3 LP disks.

———, ed. N.d. *Polish Ensemble Kurpianka from Kadzidło (Kurpie)*. Polskie Nagrania Muza sxl 0683. LP disk.

Szałaśna, Anna. N.d. *Rzeszów Folk Bands*. Polskie Nagrania Muza sx 0876. LP disk.

Szurmiak Bogucka, Aleksandra, ed. N.d. *Lachy Folk Ensemble from Nowy Sącz*. Polskie Nagrania Muza sx 1023. LP.

Tańce polskie: Śladami Oskara Kolberga (Polish Dances: Following Oskar Kolberg). N.d. Fundacja Kultury Wsi (Foundation of Folk Culture). 15 videotapes in series, with more in process.

Trebunia Family Band and Twinkle Brothers. 1995. *Comeback*. Polish Radio CRM 0002. Cassette.

Czech Republic and Slovakia

Magda Ferl Želinská

Edward J. P. O'Connor

Traditional Music

Modern Processes of Folk-Music Revival and Preservation

History of Music

Jazz and Popular and Underground Music

Music in the Postcommunist Period

History of Scholarship

From A.D. 450 to 550, the Czechs settled in the Central European region of Bohemia (Čechy), with its gently rolling fields interspersed with forests, lakes, and rivers. Bohemia, ruled by the Premysl family for about four hundred years (895–1306), later became a semi-independent kingdom within the Holy Roman Empire. It reached its cultural and political peak under Charles IV, the Holy Roman Emperor, who ruled from 1346 to 1378, the period when Prague became the empire's leading city.

Slovakia lies among Slavic peoples in the west, north, and east (Czechs, Poles, and Ruthenians, respectively) and Magyars (Hungarians) to the south. Whether under their ancient name, *Slovieni,* or its modern equivalents, *Slovaci* and *Slovaks,* the Slovak people identify themselves as "people of the word," based on the Slavic term *slovo* 'word'. By the fifth century, the Slavic tribes who were to become the Slovak nation were well established between the Carpathian Mountains and the Danube River.

Moravia, where certain Slavic tribes settled during the fifth century, lies between Bohemia and Slovakia. In the ninth century, these tribes united with other Slavic tribes to form the Great Moravian Empire, which Magyar invasions subsequently destroyed. In 1029, the Bohemian Kingdom formally incorporated Moravia as a separate territory, customarily ruled by a younger son of the Bohemian king.

Bohemia and Moravia became provinces of the Hapsburg Empire in 1526, when Ferdinand I, Holy Roman Emperor, was elected king of Bohemia. The throne of Bohemia became a hereditary possession of the Hapsburg archduchy of Austria, which from 1804 until 1914 was known as the Austro-Hungarian Empire. In October 1918, the first Czechoslovak Republic was formed as a result of the reorganization of the former Austro-Hungarian Empire. Industrialization and urbanization, already apparent in the nineteenth century, increased during the 1920s and 1930s. German expansion forced a temporary dissolution of the republic (1939–1945), and Bohemia and Moravia were formed into a protectorate of the German Reich. From 1945, Czechs, Moravians, Slovaks, and various minorities (a total of more than fourteen million) lived in Czechoslovakia, a state renamed the Czech and Slovak Federal Republic in 1989. On 1 January 1993, the federation dissolved into independent Czech and Slovak republics. In 1996, the Czech Republic (78,703 square kilometers) had an estimated population of 10,321,000; Slovakia (48,845 square kilometers), an estimated population of 5,374,000.

—MAGDA FERL ŽELINSKÁ

TRADITIONAL MUSIC

The Czech Republic and Slovakia have rich folk-music traditions, documented in more than a hundred thousand archived folk songs. The extent to which folk music remains a living tradition throughout both republics, however, is the subject of scholarly debate. In Bohemia, urbanization and industrialization have been blamed for the demise of the living tradition, with the daily performance of music and dance retained primarily in Chodsko, a small ethnographic district in the southwest. In general, the farther east through Moravia and Slovakia, the stronger is the living tradition; yet some occasions, including weddings, holidays, and festivals, require folk music and dance throughout Bohemia.

Historical, cultural, and geographic factors have resulted in substantial regional differences. Carpathian and alpine mountain ranges and valleys served to isolate certain peoples, resulting in the development of numerous musical dialects and the perpetuation of local traditions. Influences from surrounding peoples have also had their effects; for example, yodeling is found in Bohemia near the border with Bavaria, strummed zither bands occur in southern Slovakia near the Hungarian border, and the unique singing and dance style of the Goral (Highland) culture straddles the borders of northern Moravia, Slovakia, and Poland.

Commonalities

Despite regional differences, the folk music and dance of the Czech and Slovak republics share some common traits. Perhaps foremost is the relationship between music and dance. In several regions, as much as 80 percent of the music is intended to accompany dance. Often, the rhythm of the music is adapted to the length and pace of the dance steps. In the Bohemian *sousedská* (a moderate waltz), the second beat tends to be anticipated as the dancers rise on the balls of their feet; in the *danaj* (a duple-meter couple's turning dance) of southeast Moravia, a hesitation in the step on the last eighth note creates a lilting 5/8 pattern; and in the *verbunk* 'recruit's dance' of Moravia and Slovakia, a figure of short and long steps makes a duple rhythm in which no eighth notes in a measure are the same length, and different violinists play the rhythms nonidentically (Holý 1969). Some dance forms, including the *chorovod* 'line dances' (particularly for young women), turning dances for couples (who rotate in place), and couple's round dances, occur throughout both republics. Everywhere each stanza of a song commonly alternates with dancing. In both republics, dances are punctuated with whistles, squeals, shouts, foot stamps, and slapping of the thighs and heels.

A second commonality is the relationship between language and music. Though Czech (spoken in Moravia also) and Slovak are different languages, both share two elements that bear on music: stress always falls on the first syllable of a word, and vowels are long or short, as indicated in writing by diacritics (unmarked vowels are short, and vowels with an acute accent are long). Because of first-syllable stress, pickup notes rarely occur, and phrases sometimes end on an unstressed beat or an offbeat to match an unstressed final syllable. Each line of a strophic song may display a unique rhythm, as long and short vowels fall on different beats. Vowel lengths and stresses distinguish Czech and Slovak music from that of neighboring peoples.

A third commonality is that in all three regions, some portion of the repertoire involves mixed meters, which, though they do not make up a large share of the Czech repertoire, are associated with some prominent dances. Duple and triple meter may

FIGURE 1 "*Zelenyj kúsek*," a texted Czech dance from Chodsko, alternates sections in triple (3/8) and duple (2/4) meter. Two people sing the text in parallel thirds while two others sing the vocable *hó* on a drone at the interval of a fifth, imitating the bagpipe.

alternate or occur simultaneously in several combinations; for example, a complete waltz section may alternate with a complete polka section. In the dance *zelenyj kúsek,* triple and duple alternate in one-, two-, or four-measure sequences (figure 1). The *furiant* has a basic triple meter throughout (written 3/4 or 6/8), but melodic accents result in alternating duple and triple two-measure patterns (figure 2). The *furiant* dance figure includes two measures of duple hops followed by two measures of waltz steps. In eastern Moravia and Slovakia, songs not unusually have a duple rhythm in the accompaniment while the melody is written mainly in triplets, resulting in two against three. To capture some of the rhythmic flexibility of Moravian music, the collector Vladimír Úlehla (1888–1947) often wrote groups of notes in 3, 5, and 7 against a duple accompaniment with phrases starting on an offbeat. In the protracted parlando-rubato style prominent in Moravian and Slovak songs, some collectors have omitted metric signatures altogether.

FIGURE 2   The dance *furiant* is written in triple meter, but internal melodic accents, repeated words, and dancers' hops suggest duple meter that crosses the bar line.

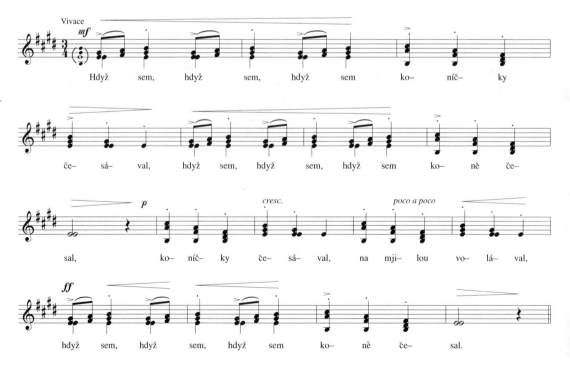

FIGURE 3 Slovakia, especially, is known for its tremendous variety of flutes. Perhaps the most impressive and unusual is the 2-meter-long *fujara,* a duct flute that emits an impressive series of overtones. Played by Anton Lupták from Veľký Krtíš, Slovakia. Photo by Marie-Barbara Le Gonidec, 1991.

Fourth, phrases may vary in length, more in some regions than in others. Though most Czech songs have balanced phrases, eight-bar phrases may be divided into 3 + 5 bars, or a combination of 4 + 4 + 6 bars or 6 + 6 + 7 + 7 bars may occur. A protracted parlando-rubato Moravian song may have phrases of 1 + 2 + 3 bars. Phrase length often is closely related to the syllabic structure of the text; for example, a Slovak song with a bimetric syllable structure of 8 + 8 + 7 + 7 may have two four-bar phrases followed by two three-bar phrases.

Fifth, text is an important aspect of songs and covers a wide range of subjects, particularly those related to life-cycle and calendar-cycle events, work, the military, nature, and love. Most dance-tunes have texts. Even a solitary shepherd alternates between singing and playing tunes on the flute or bagpipes (figure 3). Text setting is largely syllabic, with melismas used primarily for embellishment. Vocables are rare and tend to occur in refrains—*tra, la, la,* for example.

Sixth, traditional instrumental ensembles in both republics tend not to be large. Czech ensembles began when a violin and a clarinet joined a bagpipe (*dudy, gajdy*) in an ensemble known as *malá selcká muzika* 'small rustic band'. Later, an additional violin and clarinet and a string bass and a second bagpiper joined the ensemble to form the *velké muzika* 'large band'. In eastern Moravia and Slovakia, two types of small ensembles became prominent: the *slácikóvá muzika* (string band) of two to four stringed instruments and the *cimbalóvá muzika* (dulcimer band) generally consisting of two violins, one or two violas, one or two clarinets, string bass, and large hammered dulcimer (*cimbál*) (figure 4). During the communist period, the state and radio folk-instrument ensembles expanded to include eleven to twenty musicians. Throughout both republics, brass bands (*dechovka muzika*) developed a separate tradition, averaging fourteen to eighteen musicians each.

Seventh, vocal and instrumental musical styles bear a close relationship. Musicians comment on the similarity between vocal and instrumental timbres. Where the bagpipe is prominent, singers tend to imitate the bagpipe sound in their vocal timbre. Also, vocal range can be affected by instrumental pitch. String ensembles of eastern Moravia and northern Slovakia, for example, play in the key of D, forcing vocalists to sing in a high register. Czech bagpipes in E♭ do the same. Some singers even try to sing an octave above the bagpipe register, to be heard over its penetrating sound. Then there is the matter of key. Certain instruments play in a particular mode. The Slovak *koncovka* (flute without finger holes) plays in the lydian mode, and the large Slovak shepherd's flute with three holes (*fujara*) plays in the mixolydian. Singers perform in the same modes as instruments. Singers are praised for their ability to match instrumental styles, particularly in regard to the use of ornamentation, whether the grace notes and other embellishments of Czech bagpipers or the portamento and cadential formulas of eastern ensembles.

Eighth, improvisation is a common feature of folk music. Czech bagpipers are expected to develop their own variations on tunes and to change those variations with each performance. Variation techniques include the use of neighboring tones, passing and harmonic tones, grace notes, anticipations, turns, mordents and inverted mordents, trills, and rapid repetitions of a single tone. In protracted Moravian songs, elaborately embellished transitions occur from one phrase to the next on the parts of the first violinist, the clarinetist, and the *cimbál* player. Moravian dance-songs employ rhythmic variations. The same instruments in Slovak ensembles intricately ornament the melodies.

Ninth, polyphonic singing occurs to varying degrees throughout both republics. Collections show that polyphonic singing has not been common in most of Bohemia; however, in Chodsko, singing in parallel thirds and sixths has been popular. The lines of a duet may so intertwine that it is difficult to tell which has the

Polyphonic singing is more common in Moravia and Slovakia than in Bohemia. In one Slovak locale, it is considered a special talent for a singer to manipulate the pitch of the third of the chord by raising or lowering it slightly.

FIGURE 4   A dulcimer band typical of eastern Moravia and Slovakia consists of four clarinets, two violins, a hammered dulcimer (*cimbál*), and a bass. Early-twentieth-century postcard from the Robert Godfried Collection, New York.

melody. Three- and four-part singing occurs, with the lower lines imitating the bagpipe on a wordless drone (figure 1). Polyphonic singing is more common in Moravia and Slovakia than in Bohemia. Polyphonic Moravian singing is primarily in parallel thirds and sixths, usually in two parts, but sometimes in three. Slovak singers tend to start with a solo voice intoning the first phrase, or the group beginning on a unison pitch, proceeding in parallel thirds, and ending in unison; however, in some districts, at certain points in a song, singers may expand the texture to three or four tones in a chord. In one Slovak locale, it is considered a special talent for a singer to manipulate the pitch of the third of the chord by raising or lowering it slightly.

Tenth, many of the same musical genres are found throughout both republics, with some more prominent in certain districts than others. In some districts, a given genre may still be performed as part of daily life, but in others it may occur only in staged festivals. Seasonal activities begin with songs and dances for celebrating the death of winter, children's spring game songs in meadows, carnival, and Easter songs, and continue with songs for summer farm work, pasturing, herding, cutting timber, doing other work, St. John's day, fall harvest activities, winter spinning and plucking down, and Christmas caroling. Wedding songs accompany all ritual stages, from women's instructions to the bride, her farewell to her mother, the "capping" ceremony during the wedding service (when she joins the ranks of married women), to the transportation of the bed to the new residence. Lullabies, children's songs, and songs about love and nature are common in all districts.

Ethnographic districts

In the mid-nineteenth century, the song collector Karel J. Erben (1811–1870) identified ten ethnographic districts in Bohemia (1984–1990 [1842, 1862–1864, 1886–1888]). František Bartoš's (1837–1906) collection (1901) of Moravian songs shows five ethnographic districts with six, ten, four, seven, and eight subdistricts, respectively. More recently, Alica Elscheková and Oskár Elschek (1956) described four major districts in Slovakia with numerous subdistricts.

On the broadest level is the distinction between western and eastern styles. Moravia, between Bohemia and Slovakia, is the transitional region. The dividing line between styles is roughly the Morava River, which flows through the center of Moravia. In music and dance, Bohemia and western Moravia are oriented toward the Western European style, whose music tends to be based on instrumental forms (waltz, polka); song texts consist primarily of metered poetry with regular, balanced phrases; the harmonic-melodic system is rooted in the major-minor structure, with the major mode most prominent; and, historically, triple meter predominated, though it no longer does. Melodies tended to originate for the bagpipe, with several different sets of lyrics for any given tune. The prominence of the bagpipe style resulted in legato melodies of stepwise motion, broken chordal passages, or a combination of the two. Though there are many lyrical songs, such as love songs, much of the music is based on dance forms, such as the triple-meter *sousedská* (a couple's round dance), the duple-meter *obkročák* (a couple's turning dance), and the mixed-meter *zelenyj kúsek.*

In eastern Moravia and Slovakia, music tends to be based on vocal forms, in which stress falls on the most prominent words in the melody, rather than on the first beat of each measure. In nondance music, a parlando-rubato style with considerable rhythmic freedom is popular; the term *táhle,* meaning 'protracted' or 'drawn-out', is used by collectors to define this style. Uneven phrase lengths are common (5 + 5 + 4 + 5 measures, for example), as are the minor mode and duple meter. Dance forms have resulted in distinctive rhythmic practices, such as the uneven, offbeat-accented Moravian *sedlácká,* which increases from a slow to a rapid tempo, often in medleys of four tunes; women's circle dances of eastern Slovakia (e.g., *karicka*), with complex heel-stamping patterns; and variations of the czardas (*čardáš*), in which couples may compete with increasingly rapid, improvised steps.

Though these general traits are described in the literature, the actual practice has been much more complex. For example, whereas triple meter predominated in Bohemia in the nineteenth century, an examination of collections from the middle of that century shows a gradual decrease in the percentage of songs in triple meter from 80 percent near the western border to 50 percent near the Moravian border. Regional stylistic distinctions are defined by the extent to which melodies are stepwise or chordal, the application of passing tones, prominent rhythmic patterns, the types of embellishments used, and the ratio of monophonic songs to polyphonic songs.

Among the distinctive features of east Moravian music is melodic and harmonic coloration, to which two aspects, described by folk-music theorists as fiddler's functions, contribute (Trojan 1980). One, the use of fluctuating tones in the melody, derives from preharmonic practice, in which performers temporarily raised or lowered scalar tones, ranging from major-minor alternation to the adjustment of as many as four pitches in a scale. This practice also results in hybrid scales. The other aspect is the derivation of chord progressions from modes, particularly the lydian and the mixolydian. For example, in parallel motion from C major to D major, or the reverse, the F♯ in the D-major chord, derives from the raised fourth of the lydian mode. Similarly, in a movement of a G-major chord to F major, the F is the mixolydian lowered seventh. Lydian chords are formed from the step above the tonic, subdominant, and dominant chords; mixolydian chords, from the step below. These progressions can result in temporary shifts of the tonal center, with neutral chords (a chord that has one function in the temporary key and a different function in the primary key), secondary dominants, and dominants used to return to the original. Whether these shifts are defined as modulations is the subject of scholarly debate, though the shift to the lowered seventh is so common as to be called the Moravian modulation by folk-music collectors and theorists.

Subregional distinctions within Slovakia and eastern Moravia have resulted from three historical periods. The first period includes preharmonic, "old-style" songs, associated primarily with rituals to influence fate and control nature. Retained primarily in west and south Slovakia, they have a predominant range of a second or a third (the ambitus may be greater, but these intervals form the framework of the melody), with short, repeated rhythmic formulas. A predominant range of a fourth characterizes a large repertoire of farmers' fieldwork and harvest songs and songs for weddings and other rituals, widely dispersed in the country. Old-style shepherds' songs, sung in mountainous areas, have a predominant range of a fifth and employ improvisatory techniques.

The second period is characterized by nonharmonic songs, primarily in lydian, mixolydian, hypoionian, and dorian modes. Shepherds' and new ritual songs, performed in a rhapsodic style, have four-section melodies with symmetrical verses in duple meter. Robbers' songs, reflecting harsh economic conditions, grew out of the shepherds' songs and showed a wide range and five- and six-section melodies, often with bimetric structures; the second half of robbers' dance-songs are often a fifth lower than the first half. Songs of this period predominate in north, central, and eastern Slovakia.

The new-style period, stabilized before the nineteenth century, consists of three types of songs, all based on major-minor tonal principles: songs with old-style rhythms and open construction (ABCD, AABB), "new-Hungarian" style syncopated songs, and songs reflecting Western melodic and harmonic influences. The second and third types have closed forms (AABA, AA⁵BA), with transposition of phrases and extended bimetric structures. (The sign A^5 indicates that phrase A is repeated a fifth higher.) Common in the new-style period are lyrical, military, social, and epic songs. Ritual songs are essentially absent. New-style songs now predominate in the west and south.

MODERN PROCESSES OF FOLK-MUSIC REVIVAL AND PRESERVATION

From the nineteenth century on, intellectuals and others have taken special measures to preserve Czech and Slovak traditions.

Festivals

Festivals have been a major factor in the preservation and revival of folk music and dance traditions. They grew out of the life-cycle and calendar-cycle festivities of feudal times. On completing the fall harvest, peasants expected landowners to reward them with food, drink, and money, which they celebrated during harvest feasts with songs, dances, and rituals. Other festive occasions included religious observances, the death of winter, the awakening of spring, carnival, and weddings.

With industrialization and the decline of such traditional activities, the concept of special public performances of folk music and dances began to take hold in the late nineteenth century and spread during the 1920s and 1930s. A major impetus, the Ethnographic Czech-Slovak Exhibition in Prague in 1895, led to the formation of local exhibits, museums, and performances. Especially after World War II, annual festivals were established in numerous locations, of which some of the most important were Strakonice in Bohemia, Strážnice in Moravia, and Vychodná in Slovakia. In addition to the major festivals, annual regional, district, and local festivals now feature traditional folklore.

The Strážnice festival

The growth of the festivals, and issues that arose around them, may be illustrated by the example of the Strážnice festival (Tomeš 1974). It began in 1946 as Czechoslovakia in Dance and Song, a celebration of liberation after World War II. It was sponsored by the Institute of Folk Arts in the town of Strážnice and authorized by the Czecho-Slovak government as the first all-state ethnographic festival. Performers from eight districts participated in competitions of fiddlers, singers, dancers, and ensembles. They were judged on technical merit and stylistic purity. Before long, changes and issues emerged. Though organizers of the festival aimed to contribute to the survival of ethnographic traditions, the Regional National Committee tried to influence the foundation of new ensembles in villages and the formation of youth ensembles in cities and on collective farms. In 1949, the university ensemble Lúčnica, from Bratislava, introduced new technical standards that led to new criteria for evaluating ensembles at these festivals. In 1950, special programs for army and youth ensembles were added, as was, in 1951, an international evening and a children's folklore program.

After 1950, competitions for newly composed songs were held. Contrary to the original intent, programs began moving toward more theatrical formats, such as "The Collective Farm's Harvest." To balance this trend in 1953, organizers introduced the concept of "The Treasury" (*Klenotnice*), with the aim of supporting collectors, reviving village folk arts, and presenting the best amateur ensembles. The Treasury became a permanent part of the festival, taking on particular themes, such as "From the Beskedy Mountain Ridge."

By 1964, programs were divided into three categories: authentic folklore, featuring seasonal traditions and family customs; stylized programs with unified themes, such as "From My Homeland"; and foreign ensembles. Competitions were dropped, groups participated by invitation, and local programs began to be featured

Since the 1970s, the festival has continued to focus on authentic folklore and public entertainment (Jančář 1995). From the outset of the festival, the programs have been recorded, and a scientific-educational program, including ethnological symposia, has covered such topics as bagpipe music and miners' songs. Recordings have been issued from Strážnice and other festivals.

Folk music under socialism

On the election of a communist government in 1948, President Clement Gottwald spoke of the need for cultural renewal: "It is not only a matter of making existing culture accessible, our people also need a new culture of today, living today and contributing to today" (Šimek and Dewetter 1986). That philosophy led to a revival of interest in traditional folk music on the one hand, and to professionalization of practice on the other. According to Šimek and Dewetter, official policy—known as *the principle of popularization,* "serving the current and prospective needs of the masses"—fostered the growth of folk-music activity through a system of sponsorship. Before World War II, ensembles were essentially self-supporting: they depended on the dues from their members and profits from public performances. After 1948, under the Czech and Slovak ministries of culture, through regional, district, and local committees, cultural clubs, trade unions, institutes, and youth organizations, ensembles received financial support. By 1975, 3,955 folk bands had 41,373 members. At the thirtieth anniversary concert of the *cimbálová muzika* ensemble Olsava in eastern

In some locations, folk musicians still learn their performance techniques and repertoires traditionally. In mountain areas, children learn the game songs of pasturing and other seasonal activities by participating in them. Bagpipers listen to other pipers and develop their own variation techniques.

Moravia in 1981, officials mentioned that the community Uherský Brod had two youth ensembles and two adult ensembles, including Olsava, which frequently broadcast on radio, recorded, and toured internationally. One of the musicians pointed out that thirty years before, the community had had just one band, which played in a tavern.

Under *the principle of the scientific approach*, the Czech and Slovak academies of science sponsored folk-music research through the Institute of Folklore and Ethnography, in Prague and Brno, and the ethnomusicology division of the Institute of Musicology, in Bratislava. Both centers developed substantial archives. Publishing of folk-music studies, collections, and recordings was centralized in the state publishing houses, such as the State Publisher of Fine Literature, Music, and Art, in Prague; the houses of Supraphon and Panton, in the Czech Republic; and Opus and the Academy of Science, in Slovakia.

The state-run system had advantages and disadvantages. It focused attention on traditional practice, in which participation expanded. Systematic research, while not new to this era, was encouraged. Public awareness of folk music and dance expanded through festivals and other public venues, including radiobroadcasts and recordings. However, certain limitations resulted from official policy. Restricted editions of books and recordings—perhaps only four hundred to five hundred copies—made obtaining materials difficult. This policy was attributed to the concept of having a frequent turnover of materials in book and record stores. Research support in the institutes was subject to directors' whims. By 1988, the folk-music staff at the Institute of Folklore and Ethnography had been assigned to other areas, so that folk-music research in Bohemia ceased; at the same time, funds for ethnomusicology were severely cut back at the Institute for Musicology.

The movement toward professionalizing folk music and folk dance created a complex and controversial situation. In contrast to village traditions, ensembles with conservatory-trained performers gained a high level of technical proficiency, developed stylized arrangements of music and dance, and performed on radio, recorded, and toured nationally and internationally. The state ensembles became dedicated to the development of a new art form. For example, the state ensemble in Bratislava—the Slovak Folk Arts Collective (SLUK), founded in 1949—adopted the purpose professionally to develop and conventionalize tradition-based popular art and modify it for the stage, using contemporary artistic forms.

In general, only members of the radio and state ensembles were considered professional. Other musicians, no matter how proficient or how often they performed (some as many as a hundred concerts a year), were classified as amateurs because they also worked at other jobs.

Education

In some locations, folk musicians still learn their performance techniques and repertoires traditionally. In mountain areas, children learn the game songs of pasturing and other seasonal activities by participating in them. Bagpipers learn their art as apprentices to a master piper; they listen to other pipers and develop their own variation techniques.

Folk songs have long been in the elementary-school curriculum. Students who show talent in music and dance at an early age attend a public school of the arts, where folk music and dance are supplementarily covered. At the secondary level, students may attend a conservatory of music and dance, where they follow a five- to six-year curriculum of study on one or more folk instruments or dance, and they perform in ensembles. In higher education, they study at an academy of music and dramatic art, or they pursue such fields as ethnography and folklore at a university. Graduates of conservatories and academies usually perform in a professional state or radio ensemble.

In the mid-twentieth century and later, numerous musicians left their villages to study at conservatories in the classical field, then returned home to learn to play folk music "in the tradition." They not only learned the local repertoire but went to archives to draw additional materials from collections. Often their knowledge of performance styles allowed them to incorporate these pieces with appropriate inflections, but sometimes their recordings showed they were playing the notation exactly as written and did not reflect the traditional style. This result seems to occur particularly where a break in the tradition had lasted for several years.

Folk music and composers

Interest in folk music on the part of composers of the nineteenth-century nationalist revival, including Bedřich Smetana (1824–1884) and Antonín Dvořák (1841–1904), is well known. This interest widely infected the next generation. The Czech composer Jindřich Jindřich (1876–1967) was sufficiently active as a collector of folk music and other artifacts of his native Chodsko to establish a local museum. He published several volumes of collected songs and his settings of songs with piano accompaniment. The Moravian Leoš Janáček (1854–1928) was a devoted student of folk music and the relation of folk song to speech. The piano accompaniments in his setting of *Ukvalská lidová poezie v písních* ('Ukvald Folk Poetry in Song') are particularly sensitive to folk-instrumental style and such aspects as cadential embellishments. The Slovak composer Mikuláš Schneider-Trnavsky (1881–1958) published five volumes of folk-song settings (*Slovenské národné piesne*). The Czech Bohuslav Martinů (1890–1959) drew heavily on folk-musical elements for such works as his *Český tanec* ('Czech Dances'), *Písničky na jednu stránku* ('Songs on One Page'), and the choral work *Otvírání studánek* ('Opening the Wells'), depicting a folk spring ritual. In the mid-twentieth century, Slovak Ján Cikker (1911–1989) participated in a major collecting effort in Slovakia and later recorded his setting of five Slovak songs for soprano and orchestra (*Pat' ľudových piesní*).

During the period of socialist realism, starting in the 1950s, composers were encouraged to use folk music as a basis for their works, so that the masses could understand the music. Some song settings reflected traditional folk styles, but others had simple arpeggiated accompaniments that bore no relation to the character of folk ensembles. Some composers wrote accompaniments that enhance the text, rather than attempting to imitate the folk style. In Petr Eben's (b. 1929) *Písně z Těšínska* ('Songs from Těšín') (1952), the piano setting in the song "Rain" uses descending sixteenth notes to depict falling rain. For soprano, clarinet, viola, and piano, the Czech composer and ethnomusicologist Arnošt Košťál (b. 1920) wrote a work based on "*Vandrovali hudci*" ('Wandering Musicians'), a text traced to the fourteenth century or earlier and appearing in several collections. Only the first phrase of the composition is related to a collected tune. The remainder is a composition that features folk elements, including rhythmic freedom, three-measure phrases, and free textual declamation.

Finally, compositions deliberately celebrate the folk traditions. In 1973, organizers of the twenty-fifth anniversary of the Czechoslovak State Folk Ensemble of Songs and Dances engaged Václav Trojan (1907–1983) to compose music for a staged poem, "*Zlatá brána*" ('The Golden Gate'), based on Bohemian, Moravian, and Slovakian folk motifs and following the calendric cycle of events. Several composers became directors and principal arrangers for major ensembles.

—EDWARD J. P. O'CONNOR

HISTORY OF MUSIC

A new musical tradition, different from peasant music, began around A.D. 863, when the Byzantine missionaries Cyril and Methodius brought Christianity in the Slavonic tongue to the Great Moravian Empire. The Roman church resolutely opposed the Slavonic liturgy, which Pope Stephen V banned in 885. The finest conditions for liturgical singing were found in monasteries established in urban centers, particularly in Prague (Bohemia) and Brno and Olomouc (Moravia), and later in the countryside. The oldest monastery, Zobor, near Nitra in Slovakia, was founded in the late ninth century. The monasteries were centers for developing and disseminating church music. One of the most important activities of the monks was copying manuscripts, of which the oldest known is the *Codex nitriensis* (Nitra Codex) from the eleventh century.

Clergy of the Middle Ages vehemently discouraged secular music. The first social class to show an interest in secular music, composed and interpreted by professional musicians and singers called *jokulatori,* was the aristocracy. As early as about 1350, Slovakian cities, mainly Bardejov and Banská Stiavnica, began to employ professional musicians. German minnesingers and French trouvères, invited to the Prague court during the thirteenth and fourteenth centuries, brought fashionable secular songs. French influences of the *Ars Nova* flourished during the reign of Charles IV (1346–1378), and such composers as Magister Závis of Prague University (founded in 1348) and Jan from Jenstejn, Archbishop of Prague, contributed to the evolution of polyphonic compositions.

Religious folk songs became the basis for Hussite songs of the early fifteenth century. The Hussites, members of a Christian sect that followed the teachings of the Bohemian religious reformer Jan Hus (1372–1415), were chiefly interested in church reform rather than theological doctrine, and used religious songs as the primary instrument for disseminating their faith and developing music in the Czech language. These songs reflected public opinion on politics and religion. Their melodies inspired the chorales and hymns of the Czech Brethren hymnals and the Lutheran chorales of Germany.

The 1400s and 1500s

During the Hussite era, music was transferred from the hands of musically trained clergy to the amateur laity. Societies known as *literátska bratrstva* 'literary fraternities' and their choirs, the first founded in Prague in 1439, were the most prominent musical institutions in the post-Hussite era. Consisting mainly of educated middle-class townsmen and some tradesmen and local aristocrats, the choirs had eight to twenty men's and boys' voices, and sang monophonic and polyphonic music, often produced by local composers, including Jan Trajan Turnovský (1550–1595) and Krištof Harant of Polžice (1564–1621).

In Bohemia and Moravia, the desire to emulate European art music resulted in a music culture centering on the castles of the nobility. Instrumental music—especially that of horns, lute, trumpets, trombones, and organ—enjoyed immense popularity. With the beginning of Hapsburg rule in 1526, Prague's castle, Hradčany, became an influential music center. Holy Roman Emperor Ferdinand I (1503–1564) founded one of the largest European orchestras, the Prague-Viennese, which performed frequently in St. Vitus Cathedral.

"Wayside songs," found on single leaflets and in manuscripts and sung by traveling musicians, were important in this period. Their themes vary from religious and national to those of war and personal experience. "Wayside songs" not only served as entertainment but provided information and news.

In Slovakia, towns and cities gradually became centers of musical culture. Elsewhere in Europe during the Renaissance, the emperor's courts and nobility decided on musical direction, but Slovak urban merchants and tradesmen, as patrons of music, regularly sponsored modest, traditional performances. Town trumpeters, who formed guilds and trained their own apprentices, were prominent in daily musical life: they announced the time of the day, often using the style of polyphonic motets and church music, and they participated in church services, city functions, and public and private celebrations. Churches and schools were important institutions. Each was directed by a *kantor* 'schoolmaster', responsible for musical aspects of religious and public city life. In the sixteenth century, Slovakia had more than two hundred schools. Students received an excellent musical education, and were thus essential to urban musical activities. They formed an integral part of every community, singing in churches and performing for social occasions, including dances, weddings, baptisms, funerals, and numerous celebrations.

Baroque music

The most distinctive Czech composer of the early Baroque was an Italian-influenced school organist, Adam Michna from Otradovice (ca.1600–1676), who used indigenous elements in his music. He orchestrated the *Svatováclavská mše* (St. Wenceslas Mass) for six solo voices, six-part choir, and an orchestra that included trumpets. His work found its way into the folk repertoire, and to this day his carol "*Chtíc aby spal*" ('Wanting Him to Sleep') is still sung.

Among the most important Baroque documents in Slovakia, dance-music collections show clearly the relationship between folk and professional music and the overlapping of musical expression among various social milieus.

The classical period

Eighteenth-century classicism in Bohemia is connected to major European composers: Haydn, Gluck, Mozart, and Beethoven, whose contact with Czech musicians and the Czech aristocracy was especially fruitful. The premieres of Mozart's operas in Prague, the first being *Le Nozze di Figaro* (The Marriage of Figaro) in 1786, met with great success.

For a century after 1723, when Charles VI was crowned emperor and moved his court to Vienna, Prague became a provincial city. Few posts were available for musicians, who were forced to emigrate, especially to Vienna and Germany. Many emigrant musicians became well known: Johann Stamitz (1717–1757) and his two sons, Karel (1745–1801) and Antonín (1750–1789), for example, and František Xaver Richter (1709–1789), who contributed to the development of the pre-Classical symphony at Mannheim.

Several important musicians emigrated to Paris. In 1768, Josef Kohout

At the beginning of the twentieth century, Slovak music suffered from Hungarian oppression. The Slovak middle class was unable to appropriate decision making regarding music culture from the hands of the Hungarian and German bourgeoisie. Until the fall of the Austro-Hungarian Empire (1918), Slovak musicians remained amateurs.

(1738–1793) contributed to the *opéra comique* with his *Sophie, ou le mariage caché.* Antonín Rejcha (1770–1836), among whose students were Berlioz and Gounod, experimented with modern composition and is best known for his thirty-six fugues for piano (ca. 1803).

An important figure of early classicism in Slovakia was the organist and conductor Anton Zimmerman (1741–1781), many of whose compositions were published in Vienna and performed throughout Central Europe.

Nineteenth-century national music

At the beginning of the nineteenth century, composers engaged with the idea of "national" music sought mainly to use the Czech language as the basis of song and opera, though the notion of using folk songs in musical compositions also attracted them. A figure of note is the composer and bandmaster František Skroup (1801–1862), creator in 1834 of the future (1918) Czech national anthem, "*Kde domov muj*" ('Where Is My Home'). Bedřich Smetana, after his return from Sweden (in the early 1860s), channeled his energy and talent into developing Czech music. His melodic style, influenced by native Bohemian folk songs and dances, helped portray national life in such works as his comic opera, *Prodaná nevěsta* (The Bartered Bride, 1866) and his cycle of six symphonic poems, *Má vlast* (My Country, 1874–1879). Antonín Dvořák's reputation grew rapidly after he composed his *Slovanské tance* (Slavonic Dances, 1878). Near the end of his life, his *Rusalka* (1901), a fairy-tale opera, became synonymous with Czech culture. Leoš Janáček (1854–1928) was powerfully influenced by Moravian folk music. His mature style repeated brief melodic and rhythmic fragments (*napevky*) to create a musical mosaic. He received public recognition late in life with his opera *Její pastorkyňa,* known abroad as *Jenůfa* (Brno, 1904), after which his reputation rose, nationally and internationally.

The beginnings of romanticism in Slovakia can be traced to the 1820s, when the aristocracy championed Hungarian culture while urban patricians favored German culture, the latter direction falling in line with the official political stance of the Austrian court.

Modern composition

In the early years of the twentieth century, the quality of Czech musical life improved with the establishment of professional orchestras; the Czech Philharmonic, for example, became a catalyst for many new orchestral works. During this era many Czech singers, instrumentalists, and conductors—including virtuoso violinist Josef Suk (1874–1935) and the celebrated soprano Ema Destinnová (1878–1930), who sang with Enrico Caruso at the Metropolitan Opera—enjoyed international fame.

Vítezslav Novák's (1870–1949) personal style was shaped to some extent by Moravian and, later, Slovak folk music. His compositions, which made him famous outside his country, include the symphonies *V Tatrách* (In the Tatras, 1902) and *O věčne touze* (The Song of Eternal Desire). Otakar Zich's (1879–1934) compositions are predominantly vocal arrangements of folk songs, choruses, cantatas, operas, and a melodrama. Oskar Nedbal (1874–1930), though a Czech, headed the National Theater in Bratislava and contributed greatly to the musical life of Slovakia by staging Slovak operas, such as Viliam Figuš-Bystry's (1875–1937) *Detvan* in 1928.

The main contributors to the Czech interwar avant-garde were Bohuslav Martinů (1890–1959) and Alois Hába (1893–1973). Martinů, a figure of international merit and one of the most prolific composers of the twentieth century, used Czech folk music pervasively in his songs, cantatas, and symphonies, to shape his melodic and rhythmic invention. Eventually, to maintain his artistic freedom, he went into exile. Hába, composer, theorist, and teacher, originated the use of quarter and sixth tones in Western art music. His opera *Matka* (The Mother) is an example of his compositions employing quarter tones.

Emil František Burian (1904–1959), best known for his theater productions, was greatly influenced by folk music, as reflected in his folk play *Vojna* (The War), which incorporated fair songs, urban music, and national songs.

At the beginning of the twentieth century, Slovak music suffered from Hungarian oppression. The Slovak middle class was unable to appropriate decision making regarding music culture from the hands of the Hungarian and German bourgeoisie. Until the fall of the Austro-Hungarian Empire (1918), Slovak musicians remained amateurs.

The professionalization of Slovak music culture emerged after 1918, when until 1945 it was closely tied to the development of Czech music. In reality, many institutions in Slovakia, though called Slovak, such as *Slovenská filharmónia* (The Slovak Philharmonic) and *Slovenské narodné divadlo* (The Slovak National Theater) in Bratislava, primarily served Czech musicians and audiences. The first directors of the Slovak National Theater were Bedřich Jerábek, who opened the theater in 1920 with Smetana's opera *Hubička* (The Kiss), and Oskar Nedbal, who took over in 1923 and staged several Slovak operas.

In the 1930s, the most prominent musical direction was known as *moderna*. Its representative figures were Ján Cikker, Alexander Moyzes (1906–1984), and Eugeň Suchoň (b. 1908). To create Slovak national music, these composers utilized folk songs in their compositions. Moyzes, who was fairly progressive in employing folklore, used robbers' and mountain outlaws' motifs in his composition *Jánošíkovi chlapci* (Janosik's Rebels).

The communist period

Immediately after World War II, a new phase of musical life began in the Czechoslovak Socialist Republic. For the next forty years, the development of Czech, Moravian, and Slovak music was closely tied to political goals. Surviving music institutions were reorganized, and the socialist spirit prevailed. New symphony orchestras, chamber orchestras, and festivals were founded. After the film studios were nationalized, film orchestras, in addition to radio orchestras in Prague, Brno, Ostrava, and Pilsen, were founded.

After 1945 and into the mid-1950s, the government widely promoted folk cantatas and mass songs, many of which had questionable artistic value. The most championed composers of these genres were Miloslav Kabeláč (1908–1979), inspired by Czech folklore and non-European musical cultures; Jan Seidel (b. 1908), a folk-song enthusiast, who published several volumes of national songs, *Písně o rodné zemi* (Songs of the Homeland), and myriad mass songs; and Václav Dobiáš (1909–1978), a leader of the new, socialist postwar musical life, who composed *Buduj vlast—posíliš mír* (Build the Nation—You Will Strengthen Peace), songs with contemporary themes. In *The Joke*, the Bohemian novelist Milan Kundera refers to the difficulty folk music traditions face in an ideologically oriented nation-state, and says that folk musicians often mocked, in late-night private sessions after public concerts, the ideological cast to state-sponsored performances.

From 1945 through 1948, the development of Slovak music became a controversial issue. Government officials viewed folk expression as reflecting the ideology of the past ruling classes, and thus discouraged it. They advocated a new type of folklore, which they promoted to reflect the goals of the new society and a new international humanitarianism. In music, a fresh voice, that of the young composer and theoretician Oto Ferenczy (b. 1921), championed international trends, criticized the modernist movement for its ethnocentric Slovak tendencies, encouraged the fusion of Slovak national music with the world's music, and sought inspiration from the works of prominent twentieth-century composers, including Bartók, Stravinsky, and Hindemith.

In 1950, the creation of the first professional symphonic orchestra, *Slovenská filharmónia* (The Slovak Philharmonic), was important for the development of concert life in Bratislava and Slovak music culture in general. A Czech, the conductor Václav Talich, set high artistic standards for this orchestra, and its repertoire was predominantly Slovak.

JAZZ AND POPULAR AND UNDERGROUND MUSIC

After 1948, jazz was considered a bourgeois product and strongly discouraged. In the 1970s, jazz musicians, working without official approval, staged performances, published jazz bulletins, and supported multigenre underground music. The publication of the important journal *Rock 2000* (now known as *Art Forum*) began, and the music scene witnessed a synthesis of jazz and rock.

Because the government opposed jazz, dance-music, which had been based on jazz music since the 1920s, was profoundly affected. In response, folk music was substituted in a popular format (*lidovky*), introduced primarily by the Polatov Wind Band; however, only the older generation accepted this change. Reacting to public pressure, swing was restored during the early 1950s. A pioneering performing group was the dance orchestra of Karel Vlach, who, with Gustav Brom and his band, worked for Czechoslovak Radio.

In popular entertainment, perhaps the most important performer was Jiří Suchy, who sang for the theatrical company Divadlo na zabradli, and with entertainer Jiří Slitr started the famous Semafor Theater. Performances at the Semafor were known for criticizing the communist regime. Musicians often escaped censorship and consequently developed unofficial, nontraditional, avant-garde, underground music.

The late sixties ushered in a new symbiosis between popular folk singers (*písničkáři*) and rock musicians, resulting in *folkníci,* who dominated the musical scene of the 1970s and 1980s. In Prague, *folkníci* included Vladimír Merta, Petr Lutka, Dagmar Andrtová-Voňková, and Jaroslav Hutka. In the 1970s, the center of folk activities was a Prague organization, *Malostranska beseda*, under whose auspices jam sessions, performances, seminars, and publishing centers were organized. Supraphon, a national record company, released singles and long-playing records by many of these musicians, who fought the political system. Many were constantly at odds with the law—for which they were periodically prohibited from working. Their compositions were not published, and they were often interrogated by the police.

The only musicians to be imprisoned were members of the rock band Plastic People of the Universe. Established in 1969 and soon the most influential pop-music phenomenon of its time in Czechoslovakia, the band provided ideological leadership for the younger generation.

Between 1968 and 1989 musicians labored under systematic restrictions. Their attitudes ranged from refusing to collaborate to using the system for personal gain. The most important figure in Czech alternative rock of the 1970s and 1980s was Mikoláš Chadima, a performer-composer-ideologue, who postulated that rock is not only entertainment, but a unique multimedia art, which reflects individuals' feelings. A member of Rock and Jokes Extempore Band, led by folksinger Jaroslav Jeroným Neduha, Chadima composed music that incorporated elements of rock, jazz improvisation, and the experimental avant-garde—genres linked to political criticism. In 1979, this band's performances featured black humor and violence, in which musicians used jazz or rock structures with new-wave and punk elements.

The Composers' Union, an organization for the party elite, replete with extensive privileges, banned such talented professional artists as Jan Novák and Antonín Tučapský, who eventually went into exile. Václav Kučera, known for using instruments and lyrics from cultures unfamiliar to the Czechoslovak public, was also banned. His music is now extremely popular.

In Slovakia during the 1960s, neofolkloristic tendencies strengthened, as artists took their inspiration from jazz, popular, and non-European musics. One of the most active musicians in Slovak rock was Ján Baláž from Nitra, who cofounded the band Modus, which performed at home and abroad with a repertoire based on Western contemporary hits. The period of the mid-1970s to the mid-1980s represents the height of Slovak popular music. Leading the way were vocalists and composers Peter Nagy from Prešov, Marika Gombitová from Turany nad Ondavou, and Miroslav Zbírka from Bratislava.

—MAGDA FERL ŽELINSKÁ

MUSIC IN THE POSTCOMMUNIST PERIOD

After 1989, when communism fell, the musical infrastructure changed only slightly. Many people who had held high positions in the previous system continue to do so, perpetuating the same ideology and affecting the direction of today's music; however, the postrevolutionary political system permits more freedom in Czech society and fosters more opportunities for free artistic expression and the exchange of musical ideas with the rest of the world.

Most institutions associated with folk music now function like those in other democracies. Since the birth of an independent Slovak Republic in 1993, traditional folklore has been promoted there as a unifying factor for Slovaks and a merchandising tool for tourists. Support for and policy on folk music have decentralized. Organizations and institutions receive funds from their supporting agencies, but for new or special projects they must usually seek grants or raise funds in other ways, as by selling their goods and services. As a consequence, musicians increasingly seek international collaboration to meet the challenges of the newly open market system. Some critics have expressed concern that at least one major ensemble has altered its style to cater to tourists; however, many ensembles continue to tour internationally with their traditional repertoires, and the festivals remain active.

Teachers now have greater flexibility in selecting materials, and students have more curricular choices. Private and parochial schools have opened. Several new institutions of higher education have been founded, some with folk music in the curriculum and affiliated institutes that include folk-music research. The institutes of the academies of science in Prague and Bratislava have continued their research and expanded their publishing. The publishing houses have been privatized. Opus still issues folk-music books and records under its old name. Supraphon has divided into

Often the early collectors were teachers, ministers, and organists—persons with some schooling in music. Prominent among these collectors was František Sušil (1804–1868), who published more than 2,350 Moravian songs in 1832 and reissued them in 1859.

Supraphon Records for sound materials and Editio Supraphon for printed materials; affiliated with Bärenreiter, the latter has reissued hundreds of out-of-print items.

HISTORY OF SCHOLARSHIP

The collection of folk music has occurred systematically throughout the republics since at least the early nineteenth century, and it has been characterized by increasing sophistication. Some of the earliest collections began under governmental sponsorship. In Bohemia in 1822, Count František Antonín of Kolovrat Libsteinsky commissioned one of the first major collections of songs. The collectors often were not musically sophisticated, nor were publishers familiar with the material—leading later collectors to criticize the accuracy of the collections (Erben 1984–1990 [1842, 1862–1864, 1886–1888]). In 1819, a collecting effort for all of the Austro-Hungarian Empire, initiated under the Gesellschaft der Musikfreunde in Vienna, resulted in a collection of some 1,174 songs and instrumental pieces from Moravia and Silesia—items systematically studied and reissued by Karel Vetterl (1898–1979) and Olga Hrabalová (1994).

In 1834–1835, Jan Kollar (1793–1852) published two volumes, *Národnié zpiewanky cili pisne swetské Slowáku w Uhrách* (Folk songs or secular songs of Slovaks in Hungary). With its twenty-five hundred songs, this publication is an important folkloric collection of the early European romantic period; it played an influential role, not only for Slovak national revivalists, but also for Czechs, Croats, Serbs, and Russians.

Often the early collectors were teachers, ministers, and organists—persons with some schooling in music. Their collections tended to lack such indications as tempo markings and deviations in pitch. Prominent among these collectors was František Sušil (1804–1868), who published more than 2,350 Moravian songs in 1832 and reissued them in 1859. His collection remains a major source for scholars (Sušil 1951). Karel J. Erben was one of the first collectors to travel throughout Bohemia, systematically classified songs by district and type, and studied musical variants. The introduction to his collection reveals his perspective and methods.

Later, composers took an interest in systematically collecting and publishing folk songs in various locales. In addition to Jindřich, Karel Weis (1862–1944) collected in southern Bohemia in the 1920s and published fifteen volumes of songs with piano accompaniment (1928–1941). Leoš Janáček's studies of Moravian folk music at the turn of the century resulted in a scholarly work (1955) and many published settings of folk songs with close attention to traditional styles.

A major national collecting effort in Slovakia, beginning in the 1880s, led to the publication of the multivolume *Slovenské spevy* (Slovak Songs), containing two thousand songs. It was revised, enlarged, and reissued in the 1980s. The increasing sophistication of collecting is seen in a multiyear Slovak effort, in which the preface to the first edition notes that greater attention was given to such factors as the extent to which pitches deviate from major-minor intonation (Hudec and Poloczek, 1950–1964). Meanwhile, scholars were furthering the theory of folk music. Josef Kresánek's *Slovenska l'udová pieseň so stanoviska hudobného* (1951) laid the foundation for much subsequent research on Slovak folk music. The publications of Dušan Holý (1969) and Jan Trojan (1980) are other detailed theoretical expositions.

Since the mid-twentieth century, staffers at the institutes in Prague, Brno, Strážnice, and Bratislava have published numerous scientific articles for journals (e.g., *Český lid, Národopisné aktuality,* and *Musicologica Slovaca*) and have presented papers at national ethnomusicological conferences and elsewhere. They have produced books of local studies (Burlasová 1987), genre studies (Burlasová 1991), instruments (Elschek 1983, 1991), and educational materials (Elscheková 1995; Mázorová, Ondrejka, et al. 1991). In the 1990s, to assess the extent of preservation and change in folk-music practice, Slovak ethnomusicologists revisited villages where they had done field research twenty to thirty years earlier.

—MAGDA FERL ŽELINSKÁ, EDWARD J. P. O'CONNOR

BIBLIOGRAPHY

Bartoš, František. 1901. *Národní písně moravské* (Moravian folk songs). Revised ed. Brno.

Bonuš, František. 1996. *Lidové tance: Výbor lidových tanců z Čech, Moravy, a Slezska* (Folk dances: A collection of Czech, Moravian, and Silesian folk dances). Strážnice: Ústav lidové kultury Strážnice.

Burlas, Ladislav. 1957. *Alexander Moyzes.* Bratislava: Slovenské vydavatel'stvo krasnej literatury.

Burlasová, Soňa. 1987. *L'udová pieseň na Horehroní* (Folk song in Horehronie). Bratislava: Opus.

———. 1991. *Vojenské a regrútske piesne* (Soldiers' and recruits' songs). Bratislava: Veda, vydavatel'stvo Slovenskej akadémie vied.

Černy, Jaromir, Jan Kouba, Vladimír Lebl, Jitka Ludvová, Zdenka Pilková, Jiří Sehnal, and Petr Vit. 1983. *Hudba v českých dějinach* (Music in Czech history). Prague: Supraphon.

Demo, Ondrej, and Olga Hrabalová. 1961. *L'udová vokálna a inštrumentálna hudba v Púchovskej doline* (Vocal and instrumental folk music in the Púchov Valley). Bratislava.

Drenko, Jozef. 1986. "Panna Cinková (1711–1772) a l'udová hudba v Gemeri" (Panna Cinková (1711–1772) and folk music in Gemer). *Vlastivedné Štúdie Gemera* 4:174–210.

Dúžek, Stanislav, ed. 1993. "Teória slovenskej l'udovej piesne (Theory of Slovak folk song)." *Ethnomusicologicum* 1(1).

Elschek, Oskár. 1965. "Problems of Variation in Eighteenth-Century Slovak Folk Music Manuscripts." *Studia Musicologica* 7:47.

———. 1966. "Methodological Problems in Slovak Ethnomusicology." *Ethnomusicology* 10:191.

———. 1972. "Charakteristické znaky súčasnej slovenskej etnomuzikológie" (Characteristic fea-

tures of contemporary Slovak ethnomusicology). *Slovenský národopis* 20:253.

———. 1983. *Die slowakischen Volksmusikinstrumente.* Die Volksmusikinstrumente der Tschechoslowakei, 2. Handbuch der europäischen Volksmusikinstrumente, series l. Edited by Ernst Emsheimer and Erich Stockman. Leipzig: VEB Deutscher Verlag für Musik.

———, ed. 1985. *Slovenská l'udová nástrojová hudba a l'udové piesne* (Slovak folk-instrumental music and folk songs). Musicologica Slovaca, 10. Bratislava: Veda, vydavatel'stvo Slovenskej académie vied.

———, ed. 1989. *L'udové hudobné a tanečné zvykoslovie* (Folk music and folk dance customs). Musicologica Slovaca, 15. Bratislava: Veda, vydavatel'stvo Slovenskej akadémie vied.

———. 1991. *Slovenské l'udové píšťaly a d'alsie aereofóny* (Slovak folk flutes and other aerophones). Bratislava: Veda, vydavatel'stvo Slovenskej vied.

———, ed. 1996. *Dejiny slovenskej hudby najstarších čia po súčasnost'* (History of Slovak music from its beginning to the present). English summaries to chapter 8 ("Slovak Folk Musical Culture," "Slovak Folk Song," by Alica Elscheková) and chapter 9 ("Folk Music Instruments and Instrumental Music," by Oskár Elschek). Bratislava: Ústav hudobnej vedy SAVASCO.

Elscheková, Alica. 1960. "Stilgeschichten der slowakischen Volksmusik." *Deutsches Jahrbuch für Volkskunde* 6:353.

———. 1978. "Stilbegriff und Stilgeschichten in der slowakischen Volksmusik." *Studia Musicologica* 20:263–303.

———. 1989. "Svadba a svadobné piesne" (The wedding and wedding songs). In *L'udové hudobné a tanečné zvykoslovie* (Folk music and folk dance

customs), ed. Oskár Elschek, 72–122. Musicologica Slovaca, 15. Bratislava: Veda, vydavatel'stvo Slovenskej akadémie vied.

———. 1990. "Text—Melos—Funktionen in ihren Gattungszusammenhängen." In *Probleme der Volksmusikforschung,* ed. H. Braun, 202–230.

———. 1993–1994. "Volksliedforschung und Volksliedsammlung in der Slowakei." *Jahrbuch des Österreichischen Volksliedwerkes* 42–43:186–192.

———. 1994. "Regionale Volksmusikaktivitäten im städtischen Bereich der Slowakei." In *Ländliche Kulturformen—ein Phänomen in der Stadt,* ed. H. Schnur, 85–101. Graz: Weishaupt-Verlag.

———. 1995. *Slovenské l'udové spevy* (Slovak folk songs). Bratislava: Ústav hudobnej vedy Slovenskej akadémie vied, ASCO.

Elscheková, Alica, and Oskár Elschek. 1956. *O slovenskej l'udovej piesni a l'udovej hudbe* (Slovak folk songs and folk music). Martin: Vydavatel'stvo Osveta.

———. 1980, 1982. *Slovenské l'udové piesne a nástrojová hudba—Antológia* (Slovak folk songs and instrumental music—an anthology). 2 vols. Bratislava: Osvetový ústav.

———. 1996 [1962]. *Uvod do stúdia slovenskej l'udovej hudby* (Introduction to the study of Slovak folk music). Bratislava: Národné osvetové centrum.

Erben, Karel J. 1984–1990 [1842, 1862–1864, 1886–1888]. *Prostonárodní české písně a říkadla* (National Czech songs and proverbs). Prague: Panton.

Födermayr, Franz, and Walter Deutsch. 1995. "Die Spielweise slowakischer Primgeiger im Lichte akustisch-digitaler Signalverarbeitung." *Studia Instrumentorum Musicae Popularis* 11:103–112.

Garaj, Bernard. 1990. "Der Dudelsack in der

Dörflichen Tanzmusik in der Slowakei." In *Döflichen Tanzmusik im westpannonischen Raum*, ed. Walter Deutsch and Rudolf Pietsch, 209–230. Vienna: A Schendl.

———, ed. 1993. *Gajdoške piesne z Malej Lehoty, Veľkej Lehoty a Jedľových Kostolian* (Bagpipers' songs from Malá Lehota, Velká Lehota, and Jedľový Kostolian). Nitra: Západoslovenské folklórne združenie.

———. 1995a. *Gajdy a gajdosská tradícia na Slovensku* (Bagpipes and the bagpiper's tradition in Slovakia). Bratislava: Ústav hudobnej vedy Slovenskej akadémie vied, ASCO.

———. 1995b. "Zungenaerophone in der Slowakei." *Studia Instrumentorum Musicae Popularis* 11:132–138.

Gasparíková, Viera. 1980. *Interetnické vzťahy vo folklóre karpatskej oblasti* (Interethnic relationships in folklore of the Carpathian district). Bratislava: Veda, vydavateľstvo Slovenskej akadémie vied.

Gelnár, Jaromír, and Oldřich Sirovátka. 1957. *Slezské písně z Třinecka a Jablunkovska* (Silesian songs from Třinec and Jablunkov). Prague.

Helfert, Vladimír. 1946. *Czechoslovak Music.* Prague: Orbis.

Holas, Čenek. 1908–1910. *České národní písně a tance* (Czech folk songs and dances). Prague.

Holý, Dušan. 1969. *Probleme der Entwicklung und des Stils der Volksmusik.* Brno: Universita J. E. Purkyně.

Horák, Jiří, and Karel Plicka. 1946. *Naše lidová píseň* (Our folk song). Prague.

———. 1965. *Zbojnícke piesne slovenského ľudu* (Highwaymen's songs of the Slovak people). Bratislava: Slovenské vydavateľstvo krásnej literatúry.

Hudec, Konštantín, and František Poloczek. 1950–1964. *Slovenské ľudové piesne* (Slovak folk songs). Bratislava: Vydavateľstvo Slovenskej akadémie vied.

Janáček, Leoš. 1955. *O lidové písní a lidové hudbě* (On folk song and folk music). Edited by Jiří Vysloužil. Prague: Státní nakladatelství krásné literatury, hudby a umění.

Jančář, Josef. 1995. *Strážnická ohlédnutí* (Reminiscence of Strážnice). Strážnice: Ustav lidové kultury Strážnice.

Jindřich, Jindřich. 1926–1955. *Chodský zpěvník* (A Chodsko songbook). 8 vols. Domažlice: Nákladem vlastním v Domažlicích. Prague: Státní nakladatelství krásné literatury, hudby a umění.

Kovačicová, Olga. 1986. *Piesne z Brezovej* (Songs from Brezová). Bratislava: Opus.

Kováčová, Júlia. 1989. "Dievčenské spevy v jarnom zvykosloví na Slovensku" (Girls' songs in yearly customs in Slovakia). In *Ľudové hudobné a tanečné zvykoslovie* (Folk music and folk dance customs), ed. Oskár Elschek, 20–71. Musicologica Slovaca, 15. Bratislava: Veda, vydavateľstvo Slovenskej akadémie vied.

Krekovičová, Eva. 1989. *O živote folklóru v súčasnosti (Ľudová pieseň)* (On the life of contemporary folklore [folk song]). Bratislava: Národopisný ústav.

———. 1992. *Slovenské koledy* (Slovak carols). Bratislava: Práca.

Kresánek, Josef. 1951. *Slovenská ľudová pieseň so stanoviska hudobného* (Slovak folk song from the standpoint of the music). Bratislava: Slovenská akadémia vied a umení.

Leng, Ladislav. 1958. *Slovenský ľudový spev a ľudová hudba* (Slovak folk songs and folk music). Bratislava: Slovenské pedagogické nakladateľstvo.

———. 1961. *Slovenský hudobný folklór* (Slovak musical folklore). Bratislava: Slovenské pedagogické nakladateľstvo.

———. 1967. *Slovenské ľudové hudobné nástroje* (Slovak folk-musical instruments). Bratislava: Veda, vydavateľstvo Slovenskej akadémie vied.

———, ed. 1984 [1966–1973]. *Variačná technika predníkov v oblasti západného, stredného a východného Slovenska* (Variational technical preferences in the western, central, and eastern districts of Slovakia). Edited by Oskár Elschek. 2d ed. Bratislava: Osvetový ústav.

———. 1993 [1965]. *Slovenské hudobné nárečia* (Slovak folk laments). 2d ed. Bratislava: Osvetovy ústav.

Leščák, Milan and Oldřich Sirovátka. 1982. *Folklór a folkloristika* (Folklore and folklorism). Bratislava: Smena.

———, ed. 1985. *Folklór a festivaly* (Folklore and festivals). Bratislava: Osvetový ústav.

Lichard, Milan. 1934. "Príspevky k teórii slovenskej ľudovej piesne" (Contributions toward a theory of Slovak folk songs). *Sborník Matice slovenskej* 9–12:1–58.

Lubej, Emil H. 1995. "Akustische Analysen slowakischer Aerophone: Fujara und Píšťala." *Studia instrumentorum musicae popularis* 11:122–126.

Mačák, Ivan. 1969. "Typologie der slowakischen Sackpfeifen." In *Studia Instrumentorum Musicae Popularis* 1:113–127.

———. 1989. "Die Persönlichkeit der Hersteller der 'Fujara'." *Studia Instrumentorum Musicae Popularis* 9:47–59.

———. 1990. "Zur Entwicklung der Musikinstrumente im westpannonischen Raum aus der Sicht der geographischen Determination." In *Dörfliche Tanzmusik im westpannonischen Raum*, ed. Walter Deutsch and Rudolf Pietsch, 198–207. Vienna: A. Schendl.

Markl, Jaroslav. 1987. *Nejstarší sbírky ceskych lidovych písní* (The oldest collections of Czech folk songs). Prague: Editio Supraphon.

Markl, Jaroslav, and Vladimír Karbusický. 1962. *Česká dudácká hudba: partitury Ludvíka Kuby* (Czech bagpipe music: the scores of Ludvík Kuba). Prague.

———. 1963. "Bohemian Folk Music: Traditional and Contemporary Aspects." *Journal of the Folk Music Council* 15:25–29.

Martinková, Alena. 1985. *Češti skladatele současnosti* (Czech contemporary composers). Prague: Panton.

Matzner, Antonin, et al. 1990. *Encyklopedie jazzu a moderní populární hudby* (The encyclopedia of jazz and contemporary popular music). Prague: Editio Supraphon.

Mázorová, Mária, Kliment Ondrejka, et al. 1991. *Slovenské ľudové tance* (Slovak folk dances). Bratislava: Slovenské pedagogické nakladateľstvo.

Michalovič, Peter. 1995. "Die Streich-Hackbrett-Ensembles in der Slowakei." *Studia Instrumentorum Musicae Popularis* 11:139–142.

Mikušová, Lýdia, ed. 1995. *Cimbál: jeho zaciatky, vyvoj a súcasnost'* (The hammered dulcimer: Its beginning, development, and present). Bratislava: Asociácia cimbalistov Slovenska.

Móži, Alexander. 1989. *Slovenský hudobný folklór* (Slovak musical folklore). Bratislava: Vysoká škola múzických umení v Bratislave.

———. 1995. "Volkstümliche Streichermusik aus dem nödlichen Orava." *Studia Instrumentorum Musicae Popularis* 11:143–150.

Němeček, Jan. 1956. *Zpěvy 17. a 18. století* (Songs of the seventeenth and eighteenth centuries). Prague.

Newmarch, Rosa. 1942. *The Music of Czechoslovakia.* London: Oxford University Press.

Ondrejka, Kliment. 1969. *Systematika pohybu a jej aplikácia na odzemkové motívy* (Systematic movement and its application in *odzemek* motifs). Bratislava: Osvetový ústav.

Plicka, Karel. 1924. "O sbieraní ľudových piesní" (On the collection of folk songs). *Sborník matice slovenskej* 2:49.

Pohanka, Jaroslav. 1958. *Dějiny české hudby v příkladech* (The history of Czech music in examples). Prague.

Potúček, Juraj, ed. 1965–1973. *Hudobná folkloristika na Slovensku v rokoch 1853–1963* (Musical folklorism in Slovakia in the years 1853 to 1963). 6 vols. Bratislava: Ústav hudobnej vedy Slovenská akadémie vied.

Rittersberk, Jan. 1825. *České národní písně* (Czech folk songs). Prague.

Rusko, Milan, and Sachia Daržagin. 1995. "Basic Research on Acoustic Characteristics of Slovak Reed Aerophones." *Studia Instrumentorum Musicae Popularis* 11:127–131.

Rybarič, Richard. 1984. *Dejiny hudobnej kultury na Slovensku* (The history of musical culture in Slovakia). Vol. 1. Bratislava: Opus.

Šimek, Milan, and Jaroslav Dewetter. 1986. *Cultural Policy in Czechoslovakia.* 2d ed. Paris: Unesco.

Slovenska spevy (Slovak songs). 1973–1983 [1880–1926]. 6 vols. Bratislava: Opus.

Sojáková, Miriam. 1995. *Ľudová sláčková hudba z Čierneho Balogu.* (Folk string music from Čierny Balog). *Ethnomusicologicum* 2:37–75.

Sušil, František. 1951. *Moravské národní písně* (Moravian folk songs). 4th ed. Prague: Nakladatelství vyšehrad.

Švehlák, Svätozar, and Igor Kovačevič, eds. 1979. *Podpol'anie: tradície a súčasnosť* (Podpol'anie: Tradition and present). Bratislava: Obzor.

Sychra, Antonín. 1948. *Hudba a slovo v lidové písni* (Music and word in folk song). Prague.

Tomeš, Josef. 1974. "Mezinárodní folkloristický festival ve Strážnici" (International folklore festival in Strážnici). In *Živé píseň Strážnice* (The living song of Strážnice), 1–14. Prague: Supraphon.

Tóth, Stefan. 1959. "Pohybové skupiny slovenského l'udového tance" (Movement groups of Slovak folk dance). *Hudobnovedné štúdie* 3:43–118.

Trojan, Jan. 1980. *Moravská lidová píseň: Melodika/Harmonika* (Moravian folk song: Melody or harmony). Prague: Edition Supraphon.

Úlehla, Vladimír. 1949. *Žvá píšen* (Living song). Prague: Fr. Borový.

Václavek, Bedřich, and Robert Smetana. 1950. *O české písni lidové a zlidovělé* (On Czech folk song and popularized song). Prague.

Vetterl, Karel, and Olga Hrabalová. 1994. *Guberniální sbírka písní a instrumentální hudby z Moravy a Slezska z roku 1819* (The gubernatorial collection of vocal and instrumental music from Moravia and Silesia from the year 1819). Strážnice: Ustav lidové kultury Strážnice.

Vetterl, Karel, and Zdenka Jelínková, eds. 1960. *Lidové písně a tance z Valašškokloboucka* (Folk songs and dances from Valašské Klobouky). Prague: Nakladatelství československé akademie věd.

Weis, Karel. 1928–1941. *Český jih a Šumava v lidové písni* (South Bohemia and Šumava in folk song). 15 vols. Prague: Národohospodářský sbor jihočeský.

Zálešák, Cyril. 1976. *Prehl'ad slovenských l'udových tancov* (Survey of Slovak folk dances). Bratislava: Osvetovy ústav.

———. 1982. *Folklórne hnutie na Slovensku* (The folklore movement in Slovakia). Bratislava: Obzor.

Želinská, Magda Ferl. 1989. "Folklore and Government-Sponsored Festival: The Czechoslovak Case." *Folklore & Mythology Studies* 13:42–52. Los Angeles: University of California, Los Angeles.

Zeman, Martin. 1951. *Hořňácké tance* (Horňácko dances). Prague.

AUDIOVISUAL RESOURCES

Bláha, Zdeněk, ed. 1972. *Antologie Chodské lidové hudby* (Anthology of Chodsko folk music). Music of Chodsko, southwest Bohemia. Supraphon S 1 17 1391–92. 2 LP disks.

———.1978. *Lidové písně ze západních Čech* (Folk songs from west Bohemia). Supraphon S 1117 2445 G. LP disk.

Czechoslovakian Folk Songs. N.d. SLUK, Slovak State Folk Ensemble. Olympic Records 6132. LP disk.

Demo, Ondrej, ed. 1975. *Rozsutec, Rozsutec.* Music of Terchová, northwest Slovakia. Opus S 9117 1434. LP disk.

———. 1986. *Už si ty, Anička, naša: tradicná svadba z Vajnor* (You are all ready, our Annie: A traditional wedding from Vajnor). Opus S 9117 1834. LP disk.

Elschek, Oskár. ed. 1982 *Slovenská l'udová nástrojová hudba antológia/Slovak Instrumental Folk Music Anthology.* Opus S 9117 10210–23. 3 LP disks.

———. 1988. *Spevy slovenského l'udu* (Songs of the Slovak people). Opus S 9117 1699–700. 2 LP disks.

Folk Songs and Dances from Czechoslovakia. N.d. Professional ensembles. Monitor Records S MFS 465. LP disk.

Gelnár, Jaromír, ed. 1978. *Jasénka.* An ensemble from Valašsko, Moravia. Panton S 110747 G. LP disk.

———. 1979. *Od Opavy k Těšínu: hudební folklór Slezské oblasti* (From Opavsko to Tesínsko: Musical folklore of the Silesian district). Supraphon S 1117 2319 G. LP disk.

Holý, Dušan ed. 1981. *Samko Dudík.* A fiddler and ensemble from Myjava, west Slovakia. Opus M 9017 1128. LP disk.

Jakubíček, Jaroslav, ed. 1988. *Ej, Brode, Brodečku.* Songs from Uhersky Brod and Kopanice, east Moravia. Supraphon S 11 0059 1711 G. LP disk.

Jančář, Josef, ed. 1980. *Slávek Volavý: písně ze Stráýnicka* (Vítězslav Volavý: Songs from Strážnice). Supraphon S 1117 2829 G. LP disk.

———. 1979. *Zapomínaná krása: lidové písně z Brněnska, Hané a Jihlavska* (Faded beauty: Folk songs from Brněnsko, Haná, and Jihlavsko). Songs of central and west Moravia. Panton S 8117 0112 G. LP disk.

Móži, Alexander, ed. 1986. *Javorovie husličky a hodvábny sláčik* (Maple violins and silk strings). Datelinka Ensemble from Detva, central Slovakia. Opus S 9117 1735. LP disk.

Něcas, Jaromír, ed. 1978. *Hoš, Podluýí! Písně a tance od Břeclavi* (Hoš, Podluží! Songs and dances from Břeclav). Music of southeast Moravia. Supraphon S 1 17 2379 G. LP disk.

Plicka, Karel, Libuše Hynková, and Václav Holzknecht, eds. 1974. *Zlatá brána* (The golden gate). Supraphon S 1 17 1491–92 G. 2 LP disks.

Pokora, Miloš, ed. 1978. *Hořňácké pěsničky* (Horňácko songs). Music of the southeast Moravian highlands. Supraphon 1117 2447 G. LP disk.

Stika, Jaroslav, ed. 1986. *Zbojné písně moravské* (Moravian outlaws' songs). Supraphon S 1117 3923 G. LP disk.

Stračina, Svatozár, and Viliam Gruska, eds. *Liptov: panoráma l'udovaj piesňovej a hudobnej kultúry* (Liptov: Panorama of folk song and musical culture). Music of Slovakia. Opus S 9117 1211–14. 4 LP disks.

Stračina, Svatozár, and Igor Kovačovič, eds. 1986. *Podpol'anie: panoráma l'udovej hudobnej kultúry* (Podpol'anie: Panorama of folk-musical culture). Music of Slovakia. Opus S 9117 1541–44. 4 LP disks.

———. 1990. *Kysuce: panoráma l'udovej piesňovej a hudobnej kultúry* (Kysuce: Panorama of folk song and musical culture). Music of Slovakia. Opus. 4 LP disks.

Stračina, Svatozár, and Igor Medlen, eds. 1981. *Pohronie: panoráma l'udovej piesňovej a hudobnej kultúry* (Pohronie: Panorama of folk song and musical culture). Music of Slovakia. Opus S 9117 1121–24. 4 LP disks.

Szarka, Viktor, ed. 1978. *Malokarpatská kapela* (Small Carpathian brass band). Opus S 9114 0673. 2 LP disks.

———. 1981. *Večar je, večar je: l'udové piesne zo Šariša* (It's evening, it's evening: Folk songs from Šariš). Music of east Slovakia. Opus S 9117 0957. LP disk.

Hungary

Judit Frigyesi
Barbara Rose Lange

History of Folk Music
Contexts for Vocal Music and Aesthetic Concepts
Genre, Style, and Performance
Melodic Types
Instrumental Music
Hungarian Pop and Rock Music

Hungary (Magyarország), with a population of slightly more than ten million, occupies 93,030 square kilometers in the Carpathian Basin. Predominantly a plain known to the Romans as Pannonia, it is bisected from north to south by the Danube. Ninety percent of its population are Magyars, 4 percent are Gypsies, and smaller minorities include Croats, Germans, Jews, Serbs, and Slovaks. Hungarians are significant minorities in the neighboring countries of Slovakia, Romania (especially in Transylvania), Serbia (especially in Vojvodina), and Croatia.

The Magyars, originally a Finno-Ugric people, who speak one of the few non-Indo-European languages in Europe, took control of Pannonia in the tenth century and converted to Christianity under the rule of the country's first king, Saint Stephen (977–1038). During the Middle Ages and the Renaissance, until the Ottoman occupation, Hungary was an important power within feudal Europe. For part of the sixteenth and seventeenth centuries, Hungary fell under Ottoman suzerainty, and in the eighteenth century under Hapsburg rule. Since the Counter-Reformation, the majority of the population, including the high aristocracy, has been Roman Catholic. A smaller part, though Protestant (Calvinist, Lutheran, Evangelist), has included a politically and culturally important segment of the middle nobility. In 1867, a dual monarchy, Austria-Hungary, was declared. For a few months in 1918–1919, Hungary became a republic, then a constitutional monarchy with right-wing political leadership, until the communist takeover in 1949. Since 1989, Hungary has been a multiparty republic.

HISTORY OF FOLK MUSIC

During centuries-long migrations from Asia, the Magyars encountered many ethnic groups. For centuries after the conquest of the present Hungarian lands, the Magyars continued to interact with the ethnic groups that coexisted in the Carpathian Basin. Because of this history and dramatic changes in Hungary's political, economic, religious, and social life in the past millennium, Hungarian folk music is a repository of multiple cultural resources. Historical and linguistic evidence, notated monophonic art songs since the sixteenth century, and recorded oral traditions since about 1900 allow for the proposal of a possible history for the parts of the folk-music tradition that survived into the era of recording.

The oldest layer of peasant music consists of so-called old-style songs—fifth-shifting, pentatonic types, the "psalmody" style, and the "lament" style—and certain children's and ritual songs and funeral laments. These styles may have retained Finno-Ugric musical elements, or at least may derive from genres that existed before the Hungarian conquest. During the first centuries of the Hungarian kingdom (established shortly after the conquest, in 1000), Magyars came into contact with European melodic styles and Gregorian chants. In the countryside, chant singing was widespread up to the Reformation. Though no piece in the surviving repertoire can be considered representative of what may have been sung centuries ago, scholars consider these old styles to contain Finno-Ugric, Turkic, and medieval European folk and chant elements.

It is unclear how the century-and-a-half-long Ottoman domination (1526–1686) influenced Hungarian folk music. The presence of the Turkish aristocracy may have facilitated the spread of professional Gypsy musicians, though Gypsy ensembles were insignificant in Hungary before the nineteenth century (Sárosi 1970). This period, which coincided with the beginning of the Reformation, brought a new wave of Hungarian monophonic music and vernacular poetry, much of it preserved in manuscripts and print. Its most important genres were Hungarian-texted religious songs based on Gregorian chants; historic-epic songs; humanist, metric songs; and lyric songs, including those called flower songs (*virágének*). This textual classification does not mean musical categories: the same melody appeared with various texts.

This period is also characterized by the dissolution of aristocratic establishments, internal migrations of the lower and middle classes (peasants, soldiers, teachers, priests, merchants, wandering musicians), and an awakening of national consciousness—changes that contributed to the spread of these monophonic genres to large and varied segments of society, including the peasantry. Some pieces were likely based on the peasant repertoire or continued an earlier practice of epic singing. Numerous melody types of modern peasant music can be identified with notated melodies found in sixteenth- and seventeenth-century manuscripts (Szendrei, Dobszay, and Rajeczky 1979; Szabolcsi 1972).

The second half of the eighteenth century witnessed the development of the *verbunkos* 'recruiting dance', an instrumental dance-music style. It probably originated with the "Hungarian dances" found in manuscripts and printed collections from the Renaissance and Baroque eras and which had national connotations. The eighteenth-century *verbunkos* shared certain features with much European music of the period (periodic structure, tonic and dominant triads, melodic turns), but it had unique traits, including characteristic figures of dotted rhythms, triplets, descending note-pairs, cadential syncopations, and ornaments attached to long notes. The *verbunkos* appears to have been known to all strata of society and was soon recognized as "national music"; it is unclear, however, with which segment of society or in which geographical area it originated, and how much of a role the growing number of professional Gypsy musicians had in its evolution.

The popularity of the *verbunkos* reached its peak in the nineteenth century. Several modern dances derive from it, and its characteristic ornamentation and rhythmic and melodic figures are recognizable in virtually all forms of instrumental music among Hungarian peasants. It penetrated into Hungarian Romantic art music, influencing piano pieces, symphonies, and chamber music. It continued to influence late-nineteenth- and twentieth-century composers, including Bihari, Csermák, Lavotta, Rózsavölgyi, Mosonyi, Erkel, Liszt, Bartók, and Kodály. The nineteenth century also brought a new wave of song composition, which soon divided into two repertoires: one, known among the peasantry, is called, in scholarly writing, the new

FIGURE 1   A Hungarian Gypsy restaurant orchestra of the early twentieth century. The association with nationalism and military recruiting music (*verbunkos*) is mirrored in the stylized military costumes the musicians wear. Only the leader wears the white tie and tails of the symphony conductor and the upper-class social occasion. In addition to the four violins, viola, cello, and bass, the orchestra is augmented with a cimbalom (struck zither) and a clarinet. Early-twentieth-century postcard from the Robert Godfried Collection, New York.

style folk song (*új stílusú népdal*); the other, composed mainly by amateurs of the urban middle class, is today usually called art song (*műdal*), folklike art song (*népies műdal*), or Hungarian song (*magyar nóta*). Stylistic differences notwithstanding, the two branches were related to each other and to older folk and art music, and the social distinction was not absolute, for *magyar nóta* was known to the peasants, and some new-style songs circulated among all social classes.

Scholarly studies have proved that these melodies originated with songs of the middle class—songs composed mostly in the first half of the nineteenth century. Many circulated with revolutionary texts or as military music during the 1848–1849 War of Independence. Others were sung by soldiers for marching or entertainment. The meeting of people from various regions and social groups in the army and the need for music suitable for common singing eased the development and spread of the new style. Within decades, it became known throughout the country. Unlike old-style folk songs (typically performed solo in rubato rhythm), the new songs are mostly in metric rhythm and performed chorally.

The rise of the *verbunkos* and the creation of new song styles coincided with the development of instrumental string ensembles and the spread of professional Gypsy musicians (figure 1). Gypsies were employed first by the aristocracy and the lesser nobility, but because of the rising standard of living among the peasantry, more and more villages could afford to pay a professional ensemble. By the end of the nineteenth century, Gypsies were the primary professional musicians, even in smaller villages; in Hungarian usage, however, "Gypsy music" normally connotes not all the music Gypsies play, but the repertoire and style they play in taverns and restaurants.

In the nineteenth century, the main patrons of restaurant-Gypsy music were the impoverished middle nobility, the so-called gentry. The leading conservative politicians of the day promoted the image of the gentry as the embodiment of the "real Hungarian"—as opposed to workers, peasants, Jews, and members of the urban middle class. Consequently, Gypsy music, the gentry's music par excellence, came to be viewed as "the real Hungarian music." In the 1930s and 1940s, such a view became a tool in the hands of chauvinistic politicians to gain the population's sympathy for a racist ideology.

Reaction to this ideology played a major role in the government's policy after World War II. The dissemination of "pure" (that is, unaccompanied, vocal, and often old-style) folk song was fostered through state-supported publications, radio programs, folk festivals, and competitions. Peasant music was included in the music curriculum from elementary school through university, and students were required to memorize, sing, and analyze peasant songs. They were taught almost exclusively with written notation, and most members of the middle class never heard a peasant performance.

During this period, peasant and Gypsy music continued to be performed in their traditional contexts. Though out of favor, Gypsy music continued to be broadcast and played in restaurants; its audience in the main urban centers was shrinking, however, not so much because of lack of state support, but because the postwar generation preferred other kinds of popular music.

The situation of peasant music in Hungary today differs from one region to another. In more developed areas, many elements of the traditional way of life, including old rituals and songs, became extinct, the repertoire became more limited, and popular styles broadcast on radio became dominant. Certain instruments (e.g., bagpipe), performing styles (old style, ornamental singing), rituals (funeral lamenting, etc.), and genres (night-watchman songs) became rare or died out; nevertheless, genres and idioms thought to have disappeared by the 1970s can be still found in the less industrial areas, or wherever Hungarians are a minority. Musicians of the revival movement in the 1970s could study older instrumental styles (known from historical recordings) and learn dances directly from Gypsy or peasant musicians of the Hungarian minority in Transylvania.

The urban revival started at the end of the 1960s among university students in Budapest, who composed, taught, performed, and organized regular dance meetings, called dancehouses (*táncház*). New compositions, often to texts by modern Hungarian poets, were inspired by various styles, including those of old-style folk songs (e.g., psalmody style), modern popular music, and Balkan folk music.

Though regions of Hungarian folk music show differences in their political, economic, ethnic, social, and cultural development, the folk musics of all Hungarian regions share some basic features. Vocal music, whether solo or choral, is uniformly monophonic, typically strophic, and performed in either rubato or *giusto* rhythm, and it includes a wide variety of musical and textual substyles. Instrumental music manifests a distinction between solo-peasant-amateur style and ensemble-Gypsy-professional style. The virtuoso instrument is the violin, the core of the professional ensemble is the string family, most of the professional repertoire is dance-music, and most of the amateur-solo repertoire is based on vocal music.

CONTEXTS FOR VOCAL MUSIC AND AESTHETIC CONCEPTS

In the peasant society, singing is a form of personal and social expression, an inherent part of community life. Therefore the performers of vocal music are not professionals, though good voice and musical ability is recognized and, in certain functions, required. But even the best peasant singer is "untrained"—meaning that the art of singing is not transmitted in a guild, nor is it considered a profession. Though peasants may occasionally earn money by singing, they normally despise making a living as a performer. Unlike professional instrumentalists, who provide music for patrons, most singers in traditional contexts do not perform for an audience, but sing to themselves or act out their role in a ritualistic setting; in exceptional cases, the ritual may become an occasional performance, as in the Bethlehem play, whose performers rehearse and receive remuneration.

Vocal pieces may or may not be associated with ritual, and many songs occur in more than one context. Rituals are basically of two types: those of the life cycle and those of the yearly cycle. The most important life-cycle rituals are funerals and weddings, both of which last for several days, containing series of ceremonies accompanied by vocal and instrumental pieces. The yearly cycle, based on the Roman

The only Hungarian vocal genre that calls for extensive textual and melodic improvisation is the funeral lament. Lamenting is a moral obligation, a service to the deceased, carried out by the dead person's closest female relative(s).

Catholic calendar, emphasizes Christmas, Easter, Pentecost, and about two hundred other Christian holidays. Tradition has preserved fragments of religious and secular customs of the Middle Ages and the Renaissance and elements of paganism and shamanism—all of which are now merged into integral ceremonies associated with a Christian holiday. The Bethlehem play (at Christmas) and the fire-jumping ceremony (on 24 June, St. John the Baptist's Day) are in several parts, with dramatic action and a series of musical items. Smaller rituals may consist of only one song ("Saying," "Greeting"), performed by a small group going from house to house.

Most vocal pieces do not directly relate to ritual, but they are not entirely "free of context" either. Participants agree on which songs are appropriate for a given situation or mood, how they should be performed, and by whom. What is considered appropriate or beautiful depends on the genre of the song, the age, gender, and number of performers, the ritual or social context, and the occasion. For example, it is inappropriate for older women to sing songs in some areas, yet this restriction does not apply to all genres, and not at all to the funeral lament, which is not considered "song."

The most important song genres are children's songs, *párosító* 'pairing songs', dance-songs, bagpipe songs, beggars' songs, drinking songs, ballads (*ballada*), *keserves* 'bitter songs' (i.e., lamenting songs), shepherds' songs, and soldiers' songs (Dobszay 1984). Musical traits may or may not be relevant in defining a genre; in most cases, various elements—text, music, performance, and mood—are equally important. For example, in Transylvania and Moldavia, old-style songs, performed in a parlando-rubato manner and having sad texts that relate to love or prisoners' lives, are known as *keserves*. These songs do not always have a fixed form; combining existing poetic lines and stanzas with their own invention, singers improvise them to express their sorrows. For peasants, it is the sad mood, the free performing style, and the personal content that primarily define this genre (Kallós 1969).

GENRE, STYLE, AND PERFORMANCE

The only Hungarian vocal genre that calls for extensive textual and melodic improvisation is the funeral lament (*sirató*) (Dobszay 1983). Lamenting is a moral obligation, a service to the deceased, carried out by the dead person's closest female relative(s). The ritual and melody of lamenting seem to derive from pre-Christian practice and possibly relate to commemorative heroic epics. Lamenting is done beside the bier and during the funeral, but a lament may be sung apart from the ritual, even years after the funeral, as a token of remembrance. Texts are improvised on the spot for the occasion, making use of traditional textual patterns. The melody, performed parlando-rubato, is roughly an extended descending line, whose fragments are repeated, varied, and rearranged in performance. Laments fall into two melodic styles: the so-called diatonic style used to be performed all over the country, but the so-called pentatonic style is known only in Transylvania.

Children's music includes counting songs, games, dance-songs, rhymes, and greetings for various occasions of everyday life and holidays. It is usually metric, with each item composed of loosely related poetic-musical lines. Some words and phrases may have no apparent meaning, but they often turn out to be textual fragments referring to extinct customs, shamanistic rituals, and pagan beliefs.

The core of Hungarian vocal music consists of strophic songs, usually composed of four isosyllabic six-, seven-, eight-, eleven- and twelve-syllable lines; within this framework, however, songs show great melodic and rhythmic variety. Collected Hungarian peasant songs amount to several tens of thousands, not counting variant performances of the same song. The old-style songs alone number more than fifty-five thousand pieces, representing more than eighteen hundred melody types.

Songs are performed in either of two rhythmic styles: parlando-rubato and *giusto*. Theoretically, the term *parlando-rubato* refers to a manner of performance that follows the natural rhythm of the spoken text; such a definition, however, does not entirely hold true. Some performances follow the natural rhythm of the text more than others, but all have an underlying rhythmic pattern, repeated in all strophes. In all instances, the music reflects poetic rhythm, rather than the natural accentuation of phrases. In some performances, the syllables flow in a series of undifferentiated, even eighth notes; in others, the rhythm approximates metrical line-schemes. Asymmetrical rhythmic formations may recur and become fixed patterns within the performance; Bartók called this phenomenon frozen rubato.

In *giusto,* the rhythm is executed according to a metric framework, yet there is slight and subtle flexibility in the durational values. Like parlando-rubato, *giusto* is a generic term for various performing styles, of which some may emphasize metric accents, others may have a somewhat blurred metric structure, and again others may be nearly as flexible as parlando-rubato though with a feeling of regular pulsation.

Parlando-rubato performance is almost exclusively solo, and choral performance is typically *giusto*. Since a melodic type may be used with different texts, it can be performed in various rhythmic styles, having parlando and *giusto* versions. A metric song may become parlando-rubato when performed by one person; nevertheless, some melodic and textual types occur almost exclusively in one or the other style: for example, psalmody style and *keserves* are almost always parlando-rubato, but bagpipe songs are always *giusto.*

In general, Hungarian vocal melodies can be called syllabic, but ornamentation is often substantial, and older recordings suggest that ornaments may have been much longer and structurally more important before the twentieth century. In contemporary performances, ornamental notes are usually distinguished from the "main" melodic notes: they are usually shorter, often reduced in dynamics, and/or performed with a different vocal quality. Styles of ornamentation show considerable regional differences: for example, north Hungary has a unique tradition: in contrast with general practice, new-style songs are performed with ornaments (Paksa 1987).

MELODIC TYPES

Hungarian scholars conceive of peasant songs in terms of thousands of related melodic types (*tipus*), which form about ten type-groups (*tömb*), also called melody styles. Scholars distinguish the following types: fifth-shifting, pentatonic, and related types; major-mode, descending, octave-range types; psalmody style; lament style; Rákóczy songs and related types; bagpipe and swineherd songs and related types; old-style pentachordal and hexachordal types; new-style pentachordal and hexachordal types; wide-ambit, ascending types; and the new style proper. These type-groups are coherent to various degrees: for instance, the old- and new-style pentachordal and hexachordal type-groups form one supergroup, which contains only loosely related

FIGURE 2 The new-style folk song "*De Nekem is volt éde-sanyém . . . ,*" as performed in 1963 by Istváan Gömbér, age 65, of Felsővály (Gomor). Like many songs in this style, this one has a pentatonic scale, the second line repeats a fifth above the first, and each phrase has an arch shape. After *Anthology of Hungarian Folk Music II: The North* 1986:2:4.4.c.

melodic types, but the psalmody-, lament-, and new-style type-groups also form a supergroup, remarkably coherent in melody, rhythm, performing style, function, and text. The history of some type-groups can be well established; for others, however, there is merely structural similarity among pieces. Some styles are the product of the nineteenth century; in this sense, the distinction between new and old styles, a basic framework of Kodály's and Bartók's classifications, is still meaningful. The so-called new style proper continues to be the most popular: it contains about eight hundred melody types. Songs in this style are usually of a wide range, often with an arch shape (ascending-descending), and within the strophe, the last line is the recapitulation of the first. New-style songs are typically in *giusto* rhythm and performed chorally (figure 2).

The oldest surviving melodies are those of the psalmody and lament styles. Songs in the former style, known only in Transylvania, are tonally related to pentatonic laments: their performance is almost always a recitativelike parlando-rubato; their texts belong to so-called lamenting textual genres, such as ballads, *keserves*, prisoners' songs, beggars' songs, and soldiers' laments (and their related parody texts) (figure 3). Songs in the latter style appear to have originated with the diatonic lament, whose melodic motives and typical lines they share. Their melodies, found among seventeenth- and eighteenth-century notated monophonic art songs, are often related to heroic, epic, and religious texts in the art and folk traditions. Texts thus provide contextual links between psalmody- and lament-style songs and funeral laments: the essence of laments and epic poetry is commemoration (Szendrei, Dobszay, and Rajeczky 1979).

INSTRUMENTAL MUSIC

In Hungarian instrumental music, two categories can roughly be distinguished: solo-amateur-peasant and ensemble-professional-"gypsy" music (Sárosi 1981). In peasant society, solo instrumental music is a form of private entertainment; its use in rituals and social ceremonies, if it exists at all, is secondary to the use of vocal genres and professional instrumental music. Solo instrumentalists are not professionals, but peasants, who earn their living from agricultural labor. They are amateurs, have no formal training, and learn to play the instrument rather late in life, for their own enjoyment. They might be asked to play at lesser social occasions, and they normally

FIGURE 3 The ballad "*Anyám éde-sanyám . . . ,*" in psalmody style, the oldest surviving melodic style in Hungary, as performed in 1963 by Mrs. Jano Anna Demeter of Lécped (Moldavia). Like many songs in this style, it is performed in a recitativelike parlando-rubato and a pentatonic scale (with the addition of an ornamental E♭), with no internal repeats of melodic material. After *Hungarian Folk Music I* n.d.:1.1.

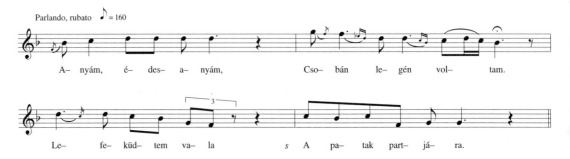

FIGURE 4 A Gypsy fiddler accompanies village singers from the Hungarian minority in Moldavia, Romania, in a style quite different from that of urban Gypsy music. Photo by Wayne Kraft, 1995.

do so, without expecting remuneration. They are rarely called to play at weddings, dancehouses, or important rituals.

Solo instrumental music is almost entirely based on the vocal repertoire. Typically, the peasants play what they can also sing, and in some performances the instrumental rendition hardly differs from the vocal model (figure 4). Nevertheless, the more skilled performers alter the songs considerably: they not only add ornaments but transform melodic lines and rhythms with great creativity. In fact, the virtuosity and imagination in the best of such performances differ in no essential way from what may be produced by the leading violinist of a professional ensemble.

To make musical sounds, peasants use signal instruments (bell, cow horn), professional implements (whip), and improvised devices, such as leaves and spoons. Traditionally, even the more developed solo instruments were homemade, though today factory-made substitutes are also used. These solo instruments include various flutes, the *tárogató* 'Hungarian clarinet', the cane pipe, the zither, the *tambura,* the harp, types of cimbalom, the ocarina, the mouth harp, and, for rhythmic accompaniment, friction drums and the *gardon* (see below). Among more modern, factory-made instruments, the most popular are the orchestral flute, the clarinet, and the accordion.

Unlike these instruments, two other solo instruments were associated with professionalism. In preceding centuries, the bagpipe (*duda*) was a professional instrument, and bagpipers were occasionally hired by aristocrats. The hurdy-gurdy (*tekerő*) has traditionally been a beggar's instrument, having a less prestigious "professional" role. In recent times, the duo of hurdy-gurdy and clarinet has been used to accompany dancing. Players of these instruments tended to be outsiders, or even outcasts, in relation to the society whose members paid them.

From the early nineteenth century, the bagpipe was gradually replaced by the modern peasant string ensemble. At the beginning of the twentieth century, bagpipers and the hurdy-gurdy-clarinet duo were still called to play at poorer weddings, or to perform for parts of the ceremony (Sárosi 1981). The genuinely amateur instruments survived the growing popularity of the string ensemble, but the bagpipe died out, precisely because it was a professional instrument and as such depended on its market. Today's professional folk ensemble is the outcome of almost two centuries of development. First a solo violin, then a violin duo was used. At the end of the nine-

The contexts for dancing are most importantly weddings, but there are regions with regular dance parties *táncház* 'dancehouses'. Dancing takes place sometimes two or three times a week; dancing at weddings may last for thirty hours.

FIGURE 5   In Gyimes, Mihály Mihók plays a violin accompanied by a *gardon,* a cello struck with a stick. Photo by Wayne Kraft, 1995.

teenth century, the violin duo was still sufficient at social occasions. When only two violins play together, both may play the melody, each with different ornamentation, together producing a heterophonic-sounding, dissonant, but expressive style—a performing practice that survives only in the so-called instrumental *keserves*. In what appears to be a more modern practice, the violins have different roles, and their parts are called accordingly: *príma* 'lead melody' and *kontra* 'rhythmic-harmonic support'. The players are thus the *prímás* and the *kontrás*.

The basis of today's string ensemble is *príma, kontra* (played by a violin and a viola or a three-stringed viola), and bass (cello or double bass). To these instruments, another violin or viola, a clarinet, a cimbalom, and occasionally an accordion may be added. Because of the popularity of the instrumental-ensemble repertoire and the outstanding Gypsy player Aladár Rácz, the modern Schunda cimbalom gained national recognition among classical instruments. Rácz taught cimbalom at the Academy of Music since the 1950s, and today the instrument is used prominently in contemporary compositions, such as those by György Kurtág.

The violin and *gardon* ensemble is known in only a few regions, particularly Gyimes, Transylvania (figure 5). Normally, a man plays the violin while a woman, often his wife, accompanies him on the *gardon.* The *gardon* has roughly the shape and size of a violoncello and serves as a percussion accompaniment; a factory-made cello or a homemade imitation of it can be used. The player beats the strings, located in one plane, with a wooden stick, and combines the beat with plucking, picking up the thinner, side string and letting it strike the fingerboard, thus producing extremely complex rhythms, often in asymmetrical meters (*aksak*).

TRACK 26

Unlike most other instrumental styles, string-ensemble music is flourishing in the villages and has served as the basis of the urban revival movement. Since only remnants of the once-virtuoso bagpipe repertoire were recorded, we will never know how closely the virtuosity of the violin resembled that of the bagpipe, which it replaced in the same function. Some structural traits—for instance, the alternation of strophes and interludes—appear to be similar.

Though the bagpipe was played by Hungarian peasants, stringed instruments have been played by peasants, Gypsies, Jews, and mixed ensembles. Professional string players today are usually Gypsies. It is impossible to determine whether there ever was a decisive difference between the performing style of peasant and Gypsy ensembles, but no such difference now exists.

In villages, string ensemble music is primarily for dancing. The contexts for dancing are most importantly weddings, but there are regions with regular dance parties (*táncház* 'dancehouses', referring to the location and the event). In Szék, each section of the village has its own dancehouse and musicians. Dancing takes place sometimes two or three times a week; dancing at weddings may last for thirty hours. The success of the dancehouse depends largely on the musicians, primarily on the *prímás.* Each individual has a favorite piece, and the *prímás* is supposed to know it and play it specifically to him or her. The musicians decide the final form of each dance, the dance cycle, and to some extent the entire event.

Most Hungarian dances are couple dances, but men's solo dances, women's (young girls') chain dances, and dueling war dances can still be found in some regions (Martin 1974, 1988). Hungarian dance-music is cyclic: three to six dances follow in series in a regionally typical traditional order. Dance cycles show great variety regionally, and there may be variant traditions even in one village.

The tempo and rhythmic outlines of individual pieces are defined primarily by the dance type, but this framework permits ample opportunity for improvisation. Hungarian dances are usually in duple meter. The most important distinction is between slow and fast dance types: they differ in rhythm, performing style, and accompaniment. In most dances, traces of old Hungarian dances and *verbunkos* music can be discovered. Typically, the "melody" is played by the *prímás* in a freely ornamented style; the *kontrás* and the bass play repetitive rhythms, almost always with major chords, regardless of the modality of the melody. Slow dances are often accompanied by *dűvő* rhythm, a regular rhythm with slurred, offbeat accentuation. Fast dances are almost always accompanied by even eighth-note chords. Outside Gyimes, asymmetrical (*aksak*) accompanying rhythms are uncommon, but rhythmic asymmetry is created by the clash of the stable accompaniment and the ornamental rubato melody of the *prímás*. The form of each dance of the cycle is open; structural elements may be repeated, lengthened, and added as needed. In general, the *prímás* improvises the form of the piece, combining alternating sections of symmetrically structured units.

Instrumental music should be understood not in terms of variants of complete pieces, but as the variation and combination of small structural elements, such as musical line, pair of measures, and pair of lines. The compositional method of combining small structural units into larger pieces differs from that of vocal songs, where invention occurs mostly within the preconceived framework of strophes. Instrumental music, both structural types and melodic elements, originated in and developed in connection with the Western instrumental dance tradition of the seventeenth and eighteenth centuries (Sárosi 1987, 1988a, 1988b).

In traditional contexts, instrumental genres are usually played for dancing, but certain pieces are intended for listening; for example, the *lassú* 'slow' of the Szék dance cycle is often requested at wedding tables. An exceptional genre is the instrumental *keserves,* an unusually rich, ornamented, virtuoso fantasia, usually based on a *keserves* song and played by one or two violins in slow tempo without rhythmic accompaniment. The instrumental *keserves* has a specific ritualistic function in the funeral ceremony of Gyimes.

Since the nineteenth century, Gypsy ensembles were the main entertainers in restaurants, where they created a repertoire and performing style usually defined as urban Gypsy music, but better called restaurant music (see figure 1). In villages, musicians are usually chosen by peasants and hired primarily for dancing. The lead violinist's virtuosity is appreciated but is less important than sensitivity to the dance and individual dancers' special needs. In contrast, urban Gypsy ensembles are hired by the restaurant management to provide background music and accompany the guests' singing, and only secondarily to lead dance events. The restaurant ensemble serves less a community event than individual patrons by playing patrons' favorite tunes; hence, much of its repertoire consists of instrumental renditions of popular tunes, ranging from *magyar nóta* and folk songs to modern popular songs. Even when playing for dancing, restaurant bands typically choose songs that customers can sing. The performing style differs from that of old-style village dances in its rhythm, fuller harmonic progression, and denser texture. When not bound by the rhythm of dancing, performers may indulge in extreme rubato, ornamentation, tempo changes, and virtuosic displays. Restaurant bands have created a characteristic instrumental genre: the slow, rubato fantasia, a type likely to have been the model for Liszt's Hungarian Rhapsodies. As attested by nineteenth- and twentieth-century literature, it came to be seen as the most representative genre of the Hungarian popular tradition.

—JUDIT FRIGYESI

HUNGARIAN POP AND ROCK MUSIC

In the twentieth century, Hungarian popular music followed Western styles; varying restrictions during forty years of socialist rule, however, gave the music political significance. In the 1930s, professional entertainers in Hungary's urban nightclubs and film stars like Pál Jávor and Katalin Karády popularized European dance-music with jazz elements and cabaret songs (*kuplés*). This music provided Hungarians with their first exposure to features of African-American style. The term *táncdalok* 'dance-songs' has remained a general designation for pop music. From 1948 to 1953, Stalinist cultural policymakers tried to promote mass song, a genre in which fanfare motives, major tonalities, and ascending melodic lines signified a grand future, and texts praised communist heroes and mobilization programs (Tokaji 1983). For a brief period, the repertoire of dance-music and jazz was confined within ideological lines, and privately owned music venues were closed. Dance-songs, accompanied by large orchestras, regained prominence by the early 1960s.

The British music of the 1960s inspired the genre known as beat, including original songs and covers of Western rock. This music was sung at a fast tempo and accompanied in straight 4/4 time by amplified guitars. The first identifiable youth culture in Hungary developed around beat. Amateurs played for their peers at culture houses and university clubs (Bácskai et al. 1969; Vitányi 1974). The founding members of the groups Illés, Metró, and Omega gained a prominence that they held through the early 1980s.

After 1970, the citizenry accepted and valued Hungarian rock, and the state guardedly supported it. The Young Communists' League provided performance venues ranging from camps to arena concerts. The state-run company Hungaroton issued many albums during this decade, but a few groups, such as Locomotiv GT and Omega, dominated the media and played to large audiences. Relying on the studio staffs of state radio and television, pop singers utilized a bel canto style and orchestral accompaniment. From 1975 to 1980, technically accomplished guitarists introduced jazz-rock and country styles. Numerous Hungarian rock musicians successfully toured Britain, Northern and Western Europe, and the United States, and musicians composed the first Hungarian blues and rock opera. Some groups experimented with folk-rock, a blend of East European folk music, jazz, and rock, but they were eclipsed by the *táncház* revival movement (Balázs 1983), and audiences felt a wave of nostalgia for 1930s film music (Hankiss 1987 [1984]).

In the 1980s, musicians experimented with punk and avant-garde styles. Punk audiences and musicians were primarily working-class; lyrics were openly rebellious, sometimes expressing fascist sentiments (Kürti 1991). The songs and stage demeanor of Feró Nagy and his group, Beatrice, provoked controversy. The avant-garde groups A. E. Bizottság, Európa Kiadó, and Kontroll Csoport utilized multiple media, found instruments (household objects used as instruments), prepared guitars (guitars with unusual tunings), and special vocal effects (Szemere 1992). They performed in small Budapest venues to audiences of their peers and distributed independent recordings. Surrealism was the dominant textual style, but groups led by Péter Müller, including URH and Európa Kiadó, directly criticized the government. The 1970s virtuoso style retained a broad audience, as evidenced by the success of the rock opera *Stephen the King,* composed by Illés founders Levente Szörényi and János Bródy and dramatizing the religious conversion of Hungary's first Christian ruler.

In the late 1980s, *lakodalmas* 'wedding' rock formed the basis for an independent cassette industry in Hungary (Lange 1996). Performers like the group 3 + 2 and Lagzi Lajcsi played *magyar nóta,* early-twentieth-century popular songs, and original music on electronic instruments—an indication that the musical tastes of ordinary people had changed little during the socialist period (Losonczi 1969).

Stylistic influences

Hungarian musicians have adopted elements from Western European and American pop styles. Hungarian popular music has comparatively little rhythmic complexity, electronic distortion, or variety of vocal effect. The chunky beat accompanying the czardas (*csárdás*) in *lakodalmas* rock resembles that of polkas in the United States. In Hungary, rock opera is considered a high, rather than a popular, art. One indigenous stylistic element permeates Hungarian popular song: parlando, the temporal patterns based on Hungarian speech rhythms, is found in folk song, rock opera, blues, pop, and *magyar nóta.* Lyrics of a sarcastic or ironic nature in punk, 1970s rock, and *lakodalmas* rock resemble the folk *gúnydals* 'mocking songs' of marketplaces. Since the 1970s, musicians from the intelligentsia have consciously incorporated folk instrumentation and melodic motives.

The politics of popular music

Hungarians have frequently used popular music as political criticism. *Magyar nóta* and *lakodalmas* rock were a locus of Hungarian identity. Believing that only folk music should be identified with the Hungarian national character, intellectuals objected to both genres (Bartók 1947 [1931]; Lange 1996; Losonczi 1968). In the 1940s and 1950s, Stalinist cultural policymakers emphasized rationalism by determining and encouraging, along ideological lines, the musical styles thought to be close to the people. Operetta, dance-music, and jazz, because they were used for recreation, threatened to undermine this rationalism; subsequently, Hungarian rock musicians satirized it with parodies of mass song. In the early 1970s, artists like Szörényi and Bródy, Gábor Presser, and Zsuzsa Koncz expressed dissatisfaction with Hungarian society, particularly the government's role in the 1968 invasion of Czechoslovakia. Sociologists and adherents of the 1970s revivals asserted that the importance of this music lay in its association with simple entertainment and its lack of edifying value.

After the early 1960s, cultural policymakers alternated between openness and repression. Allowing the broadcast of Western rock music—possibly meant to head off wholesale youth rebellion—strengthened the independence of beat musicians and audiences. Authorities had a three-phase policy—of banning, tolerating, or supporting music. Overt crackdowns and arrests were rare, except in the case of punk, but during the 1970s, songs by nearly every major group were censored or banned. The state could marginalize performers by limiting the broadcasts of their music, restricting their performances to small venues, and supporting rival groups with similar musical styles. This was the case with politically oriented music of the 1960s (*polbeat*), the avant-garde idiom, and other music.

Lyricists of the 1970s and 1980s expressed social criticism elliptically; the presence of many professional actors in rock groups during the 1980s enhanced the music's capacity to transmit double meanings. For example, the 1970s folk revival and rock operas on historical themes celebrated Hungarian national culture, symbolically objecting to Hungary's subject status in the Soviet bloc. Avant-garde and punk bands utilized the no-future ideology to protest the social, economic, and artistic

During the 1970s, songs by nearly every major popular-music group were censored or banned. In the 1990s, artists openly celebrating their histories of opposition reissued recordings and gave reunion concerts. Musicians realigned themselves politically, becoming spokespeople for parties across the political spectrum.

rigidities of 1980s Hungarian society. Musicians suffered an ethical paradox because of the state's media monopoly: they wanted to release records, but to do so, they had to capitulate to state censorship of texts and styles; as a result, musicians lost credibility. Much journalistic criticism subtly questioned the right of rock and pop to exist, but sociological analyses of popular music addressed important social and political issues (Bácskai et al. 1969; Losonczi 1969). In regional journals with limited circulation, dissident writers interviewed marginalized musicians and discussed the restrictions on musical performance. In the 1990s, artists openly celebrating their histories of opposition reissued recordings and gave reunion concerts. Musicians realigned themselves politically, becoming spokespeople for parties across the political spectrum.

—BARBARA ROSE LANGE

BIBLIOGRAPHY

This bibliography complements those published as part of the articles "Bartók, Béla," "Hungary," and "Kodály, Zoltán" in the *The New Grove Dictionary of Music and Musicians*, edited by Stanley Sadie (London: Macmillan, 1980). Works that appear there are not listed here, except for Bartók and Kodály 1951–1973.

Primary collections

Bartók, Béla, and Zoltán Kodály, general eds. 1951–1973. *Corpus Musicae Popularis Hungaricae (A Magyar Népzene Tara)* (The corpus of Hungarian popular music). Vol. 1, *Gyermekjatekok* (Children's games), edited by György Kerenyi, 1951. Vol. 2, *Jeles napok* (Calendar-custom tunes), edited by György Kerenyi, 1953. Vol. 3, *Lakodalom* (Wedding), edited by Lajos Kiss, 1955–1956. Vol. 4, *Parositok* (Matchmaking songs), edited by György Kerenyi, 1959. Vol. 5, *Siratok* (Laments), edited by Benjamin Rajeczky and Lajos Kiss, 1966. Vol. 6, *Népdaltipusok* (Folk-song types), edited by Pál Járdányi and Imre Olsvai, 1973. Budapest: Akademiai.

Falvy, Zoltán, general ed. 1988. *A magyar népdalok katalogusa stilusok szerint rendezve* (Catalog of Hungarian folk songs according to styles). Vol. 1. Introduction by László Dobszay and Janka Szendrei. Budapest: Magyar Tudomanyos Akademia.

Scholarly journals and yearbooks

Ethnographia. In Hungarian.

Magyar Zene (Hungarian music). In Hungarian.

Népzene es Zenetortenet (Folk music and music history). Budapest: Editio Musica. In Hungarian with English summaries.

Studia Musicologica. In English, German, French, and Russian.

Zenetudományi Dolgozatok (Studies in musicology). Budapest: A MTA Zenetudományi Intezete. In Hungarian with English summaries.

Collections, books, and articles

Bálint, Sándor. 1976. *Karacsony, husvet, punkosd: a nagyunnépek hazai es kozep-europai hagyomanyvilagabol* (Christmas, Easter, Pentecost: The great holy days in the Hungarian and the Central European tradition). Budapest: Szent Istvan tarsulat.

———. 1977. *Unnépi kalendarium: a Maria unnépek es jelesebb napok hazai es kozep-europai hagyomanyvilagabol* (Calendar of holy days: St. Mary's and other holy days in the Hungarian and Central European tradition). Budapest: Szent Istvan tarsulat.

Dobszay, László. 1978. "Der Begriff 'Typus' in der ungarischen Volksmusikforschung." *Studia Musicologica* 20:227–243.

———. 1983. *A siratóstilus dallamkore zenetortenetunkben es népzenenkben* (The melodic style of the lament in Hungarian folk and art music). Budapest: Akademiai.

———. 1984. *A magyar dal konyve* (The book of the Hungarian song). Budapest: Zeneműkiadó.

Frigyesi, Judit. 1998. *Béla Bartók and Turn-of-the-century Budapest*. Berkeley: University of California Press.

Halmos, Béla. 1980. "Adam Istvan széki prímás" (Istvan Adam, a lead violinist from Szék). *Zenetudományi Dolgozatok,* 85–114. Budapest: A MTA Zenetudományi Intezete.

———. 1981. "Kozjatekok egy széki vonosbanda tánczenejeben" (Interludes in the dance-music of a string band from Szék). In *Zenetudományi Dolgozatok,* 191–220. Budapest: A MTA Zenetudományi Intezete.

———. 1982. "Tizenket széki csárdás" (Twelve czardas from Szék). *Népzene es Zenetortenet* (Folk music and music history) 4:157–225.

Járdányi, Pál. 1962. "Die Ordnung der ungarischen Volkslieder." *Studia Musicologica* 2:3–32.

———. 1965. "Experiences and Results in Systematizing Hungarian Folksongs." *Studia Musicologica* 7:287–291.

Kallós, Zoltán. 1969. "A keservesekrol I–II" (About the *keserves* 1–2). *Muvelodes* 22(3):48–49, 22(4):37–41.

Lajtha, László. 1988. *Instrumental Music from Western Hungary: From the Repertoire of an Urban Gypsy Band.* Edited by Bálint Sárosi. Studies in Central and Eastern European Music, 3. Budapest: Akademiai.

Martin, György. 1974. *A magyar nép táncai* (Hungarian folk dances). Budapest: Corvina.

———. 1984. "Népi tánchagyomány es nemzeti tánctipusok Kelet-Kozep-Europában a XVI–XIX. században" (Folk-dance tradition and national-dance types in east-central Europe in the sixteenth to the nineteenth centuries). *Ethnographia* 95:353–361.

———. 1988. *Hungarian Folk Dances.* Budapest: Corvina.

Ortutay, Gyula. 1972. *Hungarian Folklore: Essays.* Budapest: Akademiai.

Paksa, Katalin. 1982. "Gyimesi tetraton-triton dalok diszitesi modja" (Ornamentation of four-tone and three-tone melodies from Gyimes). In *Népzene es Zenetortenet* (Folk music and music history) 4:110–156.

———. 1985. "Stilusjelensegek a magyar népdaldiszitesben" (Ornamentation styles in Hungarian folk song). In *Zenetudományi dolgozatok,* 157–166. Budapest: A MTA Zenetudományi Intezete.

———. 1987. "Népdaldiszites es népzenei dialektusok" (Regional dialects of folk-song ornamentation). In *Zenetudományi dolgozatok,* 151–170. Budapest: A MTA Zenetudományi Intezete.

Sagi, Maria. N.d. "Sebo Ferenc es Halmos Béla utja avagy a Sebo egyuttes" (The road of Ferenc Sebo and Béla Halmos, or the Sebo-ensemble). In *"Huzzad, huzzad muzsikasom . . .": a hangszeres népzene feltamadasa* ("Hooray, hooray, musicians . . .": The revival of instrumental folk music), ed. Jeno Szell, 14–22. Budapest: Muzsak.

Sárosi, Bálint. 1970. *Gypsy Music.* Budapest: Corvina.

———. 1981. "Professionelle und nichtprofessionelle Volkmusikanten in Ungarn." *Studia Instrumentorum Musicae Popularis* 7:10–16.

———. 1985. "An Instrumental Melody." *Yearbook for Traditional Music* 17:198–205.

———. 1986. *Folk Music: Hungarian Musical Idiom.* Budapest: Corvina.

———. 1987. "A hangszeres magyar népzene utempáros retege" (The pair of measures in Hungarian instrumental folk music). *Magyar Zene* 28(4):335–378.

———. 1988a. "A hangszeres magyar népi dallam: sorok" (Hungarian instrumental folk melody: Lines). *Magyar Zene* 29(1):28–42.

———. 1988b. "A hangszeres magyar népi dallam: sorpárok I" (Hungarian instrumental folk melody: Pairs of lines, 1). *Magyar Zene* 29(2):197–218.

Szabolcsi, Bence. 1972. *Vers es dallam: tanulmanyok a magyar irodalom korebol* (Poem and melody: Essays in Hungarian literature). Budapest: Akademiai.

Szell, Jeno, ed. N.d. *"Huzzad, huzzad muzsikasom . . .": a hangszeres népzene feltamadasa* (*"Huzzad, huzzad muzsikasom . . .":* The revival of instrumental folk music). Budapest: Muzsak.

Szendrei, Janka, László Dobszay, and Benjamin Rajeczky. 1979. *XVI–XVII századi dallamaink a népi emlekezetben* (Sixteenth- and seventeenth-century melodies in the folk tradition). 2 vols. Budapest: Akademiai.

Szomjas-Schiffert, György. 1972. *Hajnal vagyon szep piros . . . : enekes várvirrasztók es órakiáltók* (It is a beautiful, red dawn . . . : Songs of Hungarian night watchmen). Budapest: Magveto.

Ullmann, Peter. 1986. "Halottvirrasztas egy magyar erdelyi faluban" (Waking in a Hungarian village in Transylvania). In *"Mert ezt Isten hagyta . . .": tanulmanyok a nei vallasossag korebol* ("For God let it happen . . .": Essays in folk religion), ed. Gabor Tuskes, 481–495. Budapest: Magveto.

Vargyas, Lajos. 1983. *Hungarian Ballads and the European Ballad Tradition.* Translated by Imre Gombos. Budapest: Akademiai.

Viragvolgyi, Marta. 1981. "Egy magyar paraszt-prímás Széken" (A Hungarian peasant lead violinist from Szék). In *Zenetudományi Dolgozatok,* 221–233. Budapest: AMTA Zenetudományi Intezete.

Hungarian pop and rock music

Bácskai, Erika, Péter Makara, Róbert Manchin, László Váradi, and Iván Vitányi. 1969. *Beat.* Budapest: Zeneműkiadó.

Balázs, János. 1983. "Young People's Folk Music Movement in Hungary: Revival or Failure?" *International Society for Music Education Yearbook* 10:36–45.

Bartók, Béla. 1947 [1931]. "Gypsy Music or Hungarian Music?" *Musical Quarterly* 33(2):240–257.

Hadas, Miklós. 1983. "'Úgy dalalok, ahogy én akarok': A popzenei ipar működésének vázlata" ('I sing the way I want': A sketch of the workings of the pop-music industry). *Valóság* 26(9):71–78.

Hankiss, Ágnes. 1987 [1984]. "Karády Katalin—1979/1980." In *Kötéltánc* (Tightrope walk), 286–316. Budapest: Hankiss.

Hánkiss, Elemér. 1969. "Sorrentói narancsfák közt . . .': A magyar slágerszövegekről" (Among the orange trees of Sorrento . . .': On Hungarian popular song texts). In *Népdaltól az abszurd drámáig* (From folk song to absurd drama), 195–315. Budapest: Magvető.

Kürti, László. 1991. "Rocking the State: Youth and Rock Music Culture in Hungary, 1976–1990." *East European Politics and Societies* 5(3):483–513.

Lange, Barbara Rose. 1996. "*Lakodalmas* Rock and the Rejection of Popular Culture in Post-Socialist Hungary." In *Retuning Culture,* ed. Mark Slobin, 76–91. Durham: Duke University Press.

Lévai, Júlia, and Iván Vitányi. 1973. *Miből lesz a sláger?* (What's in a hit song?). Budapest: Zeneműkiadó.

———. 1982. "Egy elkallódott forradalom után" (After a wasted revolution). *Kultúra és Közösség* 1–2:202–214.

Losonczi, Ágnes. 1968. "Magyar nóta, népdal, dszessz—és a közönség" (*Magyar nóta,* folk song, jazz—and the audience). *Valóság* 11(5): 38–48.

———. 1969. *A zene életének szociológiája* (The sociology of musical life). Budapest: Zeneműkiadó.

Sebők, János. 1983–1984. *Magya-Rock.* 2 vols. Budapest: Zeneműkiadó.

Szemere, Anna. 1983. "Some Institutional Aspects of Pop and Rock Music in Hungary." *Popular Music* 3:120–142.

———. 1985a. "A jövő itt van és sose lesz vége: Tér- és időképzetek az Európa Kiadóegyüttes zene- és szövegvilágában" (The future is here and it will never end: Concepts of space and time in the musical and textual world of the Európa Kiadó Ensemble). *Magyar Zene* 1:70–74.

———. 1985b. "Pop Music in Hungary." *Communication Research* 12:401–414.

———. 1992. "The Politics of Marginality." In *Rockin' the Boat: Mass Music and Mass Movements,* ed. Reebee Garofalo, 93–114. Boston: South End Press.

Tardos, Péter. 1981. "Rock in Ungarn." In *Eurorock,* ed. Klaus Humann and Carl-Ludwig Reichert, 292–298. Hamburg: Rohwohlt EuroRock.

Tokaji, András. 1983. *Mozgalom és hivatal* (Movement and bureaucracy). Budapest: Zeneműkiadó.

Vitányi, Iván. 1974. "The Musical and Social Influence of Beat Music in Hungary." In *New Patterns of Musical Behaviour of the Young Generation in Industrial Societies,* ed. Irmgard Bontinck, 69–79. Vienna: Universal Edition.

AUDIOVISUAL RESOURCES

This discography contains commercial publications of field recordings only. Revival ensembles are published among others in the series Elo Népzene by Hungaroton. All Hungaroton publications listed below contain transcriptions and/or extensive notes.

Comprehensive collections

Anthology of Hungarian Folk Music I: Dance Music. 1985. Selected from the collection of the Musicological Institute of the Hungarian Academy of Sciences by György Martin, Istvan Nemeth, and Erno Pesovar. Hungaroton LPX 18112–16. 5 LP disks.

Anthology of Hungarian Folk Music II: The North. 1986. Selected from the collection of the Musicological Institute of the Hungarian Academy of Sciences by Lujza Tari and László Vikar. Hungaroton LPX 18124–28. 5 LP disks.

Hungarian Folk Music: I. N.d. From the collection of the Hungarian Academy of Sciences. Edited by Benjamin Rajeczky. In cooperation with Unesco. Hungaroton LPX 18001–04. 4 LP disks.

Hungarian Folk Music: II. N.d. From the collection of the Hungarian Academy of Sciences. Edited by Benjamin Rajeczky. In cooperation with Unesco. Hungaroton LPX 18050–53. 4 LP disks.

Hungarian Folk Music: III. 1982. From the collection of the Hungarian Academy of Sciences. Edited by Benjamin Rajeczky. In cooperation with Unesco. Hungaroton LPX 13050–53. 4 LP disks.

Hungarian Instrumental Folk Music. 1980. From the collection of the Hungarian Academy of Sciences. Edited by Bálint Sárosi. Hungaroton LPX 18045–47. 3 LP disks.

Reissued archival recordings

Hungarian Folk Music Collected by Béla Bartók: Phonograph Cylinders. 1981. Edited by Bálint Sárosi. Hungaroton LPX 18069. LP disk.

Hungarian Folk Music Collected by Zoltán Kodály: Phonograph Cylinders. 1983. Edited by Lujza Tari. Hungaroton LPX 19075–76. 2 LP disks.

Hungarian Folk Music: Gramophone Records with Béla Bartók's Transcription. 1981. Edited by László Somfai. Hungaroton LPX 18058–60. 3 LP disks.

Regional collections

"Este a Gyimesbe jartam": Csango Folk Music of Gyimes. 1987. Performed by János Zerkula (fiddle, voice) and Regina Fiko (*gardon*). Collected by Ferenc Sara. Hungaroton SLPX 18130. LP disk.

Gyimesi népzene. N.d. Performed by János Pulika, Mihaly Vandor, János Zerkula, and Regina Zerkula. Electrecord EPE 02686. LP disk.

Hungarian Folk Music of Bukovinian Szeklers. 1988. Collected and edited by Ferenc Sebo. Hungaroton SLPX 18131. LP disk.

Hungarian Folk Music of the Csangos of Moldavia. 1987. Collected and edited by Ferenc Sebo. Hungaroton SLPX 18096. LP disk.

Hungarian Folk Music from Gyimes. 1988. Performed by Mihaly Halmagyi (fiddle) and Gizella Adam (*gardon*). Edited by Andras Jánosi. Hungaroton SLPX 18145. LP disk.

Hungarian Folk Music from Rumania (Mezoseg): I, Bonchida, Valaszut; II, Buza; III, Ordongosfuzes; IV, Magyarszovat. 1985. Recorded by Zoltán Kallos and György Martin. From the collection of the Musicological Institute of the Hungarian Academy of Sciences. Edited by Béla Halmos. Hungaroton LPX 18107–9, 18111. 3 LP disks.

Hungarian Folk Music from Szék. 1985. Collected and transcribed by László Lajtha. Edited by Ferenc Sebo. Hungaroton LPX 18092–4. 3 LP disks.

Eastern Europe

For most of the last two hundred years, Eastern Europe would have been called the Russian Empire (1800s) or the Soviet Union (most of the 1900s). More than other regions of Europe, the musical cultures of Eastern Europe feature singing in general, and traditional polyphonic singing in particular, over instrumental music. The Slavic-speaking people of Russia, Ukraine, and Belarus share similar styles of two-voiced singing, some related to Slavic-language polyphonic singing in southeastern Europe. In North Caucasia and Georgia, where non-Indo-European languages are spoken, people sing in unique, rather complex, three- and four-voiced polyphonic styles.

During the Soviet period, folk-music practice came under nearly complete state sponsorship and control. The state's ideology fundamentally changed traditional soloistic and small-group practices by remolding them into large orchestras of folk instruments and choruses. Musical scholarship has been rather sophisticated in this region but, because of language barriers, little known outside of it.

MAP 8   Eastern Europe

Russia

Izaly Zemtsovsky

Historical Overview of Music
The Structures of Village Music
Musical Dialects and Genres
Musical Instruments and Instrumental Music
Music of Minorities
Urban Revivalism
History of Music
History of Scholarship

Though 80 percent of Russian territory is in Asia, the historical and cultural heart of Russia—between the Karelian peninsula in the west and the Ural Mountains in the east—is in Eastern Europe. The population grew from ten to twelve million people in the seventeenth century to 55 million in 1897, and was 147.7 million in 1996.

The European part of contemporary Russia is a multiethnic territory whose geographical position has brought ethnic Russians in constant contact with Finno-Ugric, Baltic, Turkic, and other ethnicities, with interethnic mixtures and assimilations of different historical depths. As a result, many place-names and river names are not Russian in origin. Physical features, elements of pre-Christian beliefs, and musical traditions have traces of these peoples. The area between the Volga and Oka rivers, where Slavic and Finnic tribes interacted as early as the ninth or tenth centuries, is considered the historical core of Russia. By the twelfth century, it had given rise to 224 cities, which attracted Russian immigrants from elsewhere.

The northern area, Pomorie ('along the sea'), consisted of the delta of the North Dvina, Onega, and Pechora rivers, and included many aboriginal peoples (Karels, Komi, Lopars, Nenets, and Veps.) This area was colonized by two streams of Russians, first from Novgorod and then from Rostov and Suzdal. A third area, the middle Volga, known as Povolzh'e ('along the Volga'), was formed in the sixteenth and seventeenth centuries, and was the only area that supported fishermen. The other two areas supported the cultivation of grain, whose various types figure prominently in folk-song texts.

HISTORICAL OVERVIEW OF MUSIC

It is impossible to generalize about the structures, performance styles, and texts of Russian folk songs because of the rich variety of forms and styles at local levels. Historically these styles never became integrated into a national style: in no one place did a population know all the genres of Russian folklore; cultural isolates in some areas have no known duplicates in others. Even the famed Russian epics (*byliny*) were known in just a few northern regions; their cultural importance arises from the efforts and attention of folklorists, journalists, painters, composers, and others, not because epics are widespread. These musical dialects were fixed in place by feudal subdivision up to national consolidation in the seventeenth century; until then, folklore had been known to all social strata in society, not just the peasantry.

The seventeenth century saw a massive buildup of new national institutions, like the army, the postal system, the church, and European-style theater at the tsar's court. In response to church reform, Old Believers maintained (and still maintain) older ways of performing religious music, and the army gave rise to new genres of recruiting songs and military-band music. At the same time, some aspects of traditional culture disappeared. Traditional musical instruments were ordered destroyed as the organ was being introduced, and Russian traditional minstrels were banned and forcibly removed to the north. In the next century, the building of St. Petersburg and the growth of suburbs around older cities represented the beginning of a division of society into classes and strata that left rural folklore behind. The population was split into several regional and social classes (for example, the Pomory, the Cossacks, and the Posads) that acted as mediators between the distinctive musical cultures of villages and cities. Changes in society and culture accelerated in the 1700s, and led to peasant rebellions in 1825 and the freeing of the serfs in 1861, the growth of a merchant class, intervillage travel for seasonal work, the growth of a city culture, and the emergence of self-consciousness among students, workers, and middle-class intellectuals.

As a result of the split between village and city culture, a romantic interest in folklore emerged in the 1760s, though until the collections by Mikhail Stakhovich (1850s) and Mily Balakirev (1957 [1866]), which presented village music in harmonized arrangements, manuscripts contained composed urban reflections on and imitations of village culture, preserved as chapbooks for voice and fortepiano, voice and guitar, guitar solo, and violin, and in a genre called *kant,* a three-part singing style with top voices in parallel thirds and an independent third voice. These efforts constitute an early form of what has been called folklorism, a process that would take many other forms in succeeding years. Contexts for these performances of village songs included homes, army camps, schools, markets (where singers sang songs from *lubok* 'chapbooks', which they sold), and concert tours by choirs and soloists. These venues and tours enabled these forms of urban folklore to become better known than rural folklore and came in some sense to be considered pan-Russian. The discovery of "authentic" Russian folklore began only in the early years of the twentieth century, with the gift of a phonograph from Thomas A. Edison to Russian scholar Evgeniya Lineva. That process continues.

THE STRUCTURES OF VILLAGE MUSIC

Russian scholars have theorized about Russian village music under three main categories: rhythmics, the underlying rhythmic structures, particularly in the relation of musical rhythm to poetic rhythm and versification; melodics, the basic modal and structural principles on which melodies are built; and polyphony, the way two or more melodic lines are combined.

Rhythmics

Traditional Russian songs employ three systems of versification—syllabic verses with caesuras (word boundaries or poetic cadences), segmented syllabic or tonic-accented verses (with a fixed number of main stresses but a variable number of syllables per line), and tonic nonsegmented verse (usually short musical-poetic lines, lacking subdivisions of syllables)—and three types of formal organization: a verse as a rhythmical period; a stanza as a combination of two or more rhythmic periods; and a so-called *tirade,* which consists of an unstable grouping of rhythmic periods.

Modern Russian ethnomusicology analyzes the rhythmic relationship between words and melodies, especially the rhythm of sung speech. It focuses on rhythmic thinking. Folksingers recognize only larger units, such as stanza, line, and half line; they do not conceptualize poetic feet and musical measures. The rhythmic coordination of melody and words depends on any of three types of versification. The first two have what is called a syllabic musical-rhythmic form. In the first type, the musical accent matches the verse accent; in the second type, the coordination of verse and melody occurs in larger blocks, where a fixed number of syllables is marked by a melodic caesura. A third type exists in the nonmetrical "drawn-out song" (*protiazhnaia pesnia*), in which a single syllable is lengthened and set to many melodic tones, sometimes making a melodic phrase. In such songs, people hear and remember not the rhythm of syllables, but a rhythm within a syllable. Songs with verses that combine syllables with tonic accents—a new phenomenon among Russian folk songs—reflect the influence of the literary poetic tradition and the harmonic structure of Western European music.

Melodics

Melodics refers not just to contours and scales, but to the formal regularities, types, and tendencies of melodies. These features are performed in a characteristically energetic style.

To describe Russian melodics, Russian scholars use three principles. The first is captured in the term *popevka,* borrowed from the analysis of church music and referring to typical melodic turns, motifs, and models. In many songs, these elements are repeated over and over to form a musical lexicon with its own grammar. Some scholars have even imagined a melodic dictionary of such models with the potential for semantic meaning.

The second principle, developed by Boris Asaf'ev, contains two laws relevant to "pure melody," without any chordal implications. The first law ("shifting") describes melodies consisting of a series of important tones, which create a "magnetic field" that attracts other notes. In one phrase, a given note may be the main note; in a succeeding phrase, it may depend on another (temporarily central) tone. The second law ("filling") involves the notion that melodic leaps are always immediately filled in with a melodic gesture that includes the passed-over tones.

The third principle, proposed by Izaly Zemtsovsky (1975), refers to a so-called intonational field, which contains mobile melodic elements. Within a given field of movement, all melodic versions and variants are conceived as equivalent and representative of an ideal unity.

The logic of melodic formal structures can be reduced to three basic types borrowed from the syntactic structure of sentences in ordinary language—simple, compound, and complex. Simple structures are found in ritual, seasonal, and wedding songs. Compound structures are found in *tirade.* Complex structures are found in lyric and "drawn-out songs." Dance songs have yet another structure, which lacks a melodic cadence that might signal the end of a melodic sentence, but instead creates a cumulative form similar to some children's folktales and rhymes.

Polyphony

The existence of Russian folk polyphony was doubted until 1879, when Yuly Melgunov published *Russian Songs . . . Recorded Directly from People's Voices.* In this collection, whose songs are arranged for piano and voice, Melgunov described some fundamentals of Russian folk polyphony, such as the dependence of all voices on one tune, the uses of unison to mark sections, the aesthetic value of the voices, and voice-leading principles different from classical European harmony. To describe polyphonic singing, he introduced the terms *zapev* to label the solo introduction to a choral song and *podgolosok* to denote subsidiary voices. In 1905–1912 Evgeniya Lineva published the first Russian edition of *The Peasant Songs of Great Russia as They Are in the Folk's*

Harmonization, transcribed with the aid of phonograph recordings, which documented the existence of such polyphony. Evgeny Gippius and Zinaida Evald (1937) pointed out that the functional differentiation of voices in north Russian choirs was reflected in folk terminology. In 1979, musicologists from Moscow used multichannel recordings to capture each voice separately, proving that Russian polyphony was not based simply on a main voice plus subsidiary voices; rather, that analysis of the recordings led to a much more sophisticated understanding of the variety of polyphonic styles.

Two types of singing ensembles exist. The first involves groups with "locked" membership: the same people sing together for years. The second type is open to all who know the tradition and would like to participate, but in practice such groups are limited to not more than about eighteen people. The second type is connected to collective activities, such as line dances, harvesting, and indoor working parties.

The latest fieldwork documents five main types of Russian polyphony. The first is monodic: the singing is almost in unison, sometimes described as a wide unison. The second is heterophonic and the most widespread, from the Smolensk district in the west to the White Sea in the north, with many local and structural versions; it includes parallel octaves in the Ural Mountains. These types can be distinguished by the performers' intentions: in the first, the intention is monophonic with a heterophonic result; in the second, the intention is polyphonic, and creates a heterophonic structure.

The third type, a drone sung to a text, is especially typical of the Bryansk district in the west and the Voronezh district in the south. At cadences, the drone disappears into a unison or an octave with the melody. It may be above or below the melody, or it may frame the melody from above and below. A particular subtype, from the Belgorod district, frames the melody within drone pitches a fifth apart. Along the Oka, people sing a so-called fake drone: no one voice sings the drone, but the illusion of a drone emerges from the combination of voices.

The fourth type, involving two functionally different voices, is the most widespread and characteristic. Songs of this type contrast in range, register, timbre, and melody. The leading voice is the lower one. It is sung by a chorus, sometime heterophonically, and is called the bass or thick (*tolsty*) voice, no matter whether sung by men or women. Among Cossacks in the south, the higher voice is sung by a solo singer (*golosnik, dishkant*), who sings an anhemitonic tune without text. In the north, the higher voice is sung by a chorus of singers on the same melody one octave higher than the bass voice. In central Russia, Russians and Finno-Ugric peoples, including the Mordvinians, the Udmurts, and the Komi-Permiaks, favor a type with a lower voice and improvised descant, the *podvodka* (Engovatova 1989).

The fifth type, three-part polyphony with functionally distinct voices, is found in central and southern Russia, around Belgorod, Voronezh, and Riazan and among the Don Cossacks and Mordvinians (figure 1). Most of these peoples perform a texted part called bass. The second voice, *golosnik,* is a sometimes textless upper drone. The third voice, called thin voice (*tonki golos*), is performed by two or more women in a tense voice in heterophony with the bass voice. Dmitri Pokrovsky (1980), using participant observation, discovered a fourth functional part among the Cossacks. It has fairly stable bass, a decorative and relatively independent discant (*dishkant*), an unnamed and previously unrecognized part that somehow coordinates the other parts, and a voice called *tenor,* in close contact with the third part.

In general, the more complicated the polyphonic structure, the fewer the singers involved. It has become clear that the complicated traditions require specialization, and certain master singers can create complex forms while leading performances.

In the Russian north in the 1920s, Gippius recorded duets and trios sung by

> In the north, the dominant genres are epic songs and laments; in the southwest, calendric songs, with characteristic yells (*gukania*); in eastern Vologda, laments; in the south, circle dances.

men with uniquely independent voices, but this style seems to have disappeared. Another kind of polyphony occurs when different songs are sung simultaneously at weddings, in spring-summer circles, during women's lamenting in a cemetery, or for other ritual events.

MUSICAL DIALECTS AND GENRES

Not accidentally, musical dialectology is the most important approach in Russian ethnomusicology. Recent research has revealed strictly limited, local, unique musical styles and genres. In fact, there is not a pan-Russian system of genres. Every region has its own system. Early nineteenth- and twentieth-century anthologies of songs tended to create the impression of a certain pan-Russian uniformity, but this impression was mistaken. The first important regional collection, Gippius and Evald's *Pesni Pinezh'ia* (1937), revealed the specificity of this regional style, including performance, scale, and melodic structure, polyphony; it represented a revolution in Russian ethnomusicology. So different was this style from stereotypical ideas about Russian folk songs that some critics did not trust the transcriptions.

Subsequent studies confirmed the reality of regional styles and dominant genres: in the north, the dominant genres are epic songs and laments; in the southwest, calendric songs, with characteristic yells (*gukania*); in eastern Vologda, laments; in the south, circle dances. Some regions have unique ritual genres, including certain Easter songs, carnival (Shrovetide) songs, and Christmas carols. To account for this variety, researchers classify genres in either of two systems, one based only on what exists in a local tradition and the other a constructed system that includes all possible types. The intersection and coordination of these systems gives the best idea of Russian folklore in all its historical and geographical variety.

Calendric songs

Calendric songs linked to the yearly cycle of agricultural work were once considered the most fundamental folk-song genres of Russian music culture, but these songs exist in European Russia only in the areas bordering other ethnic groups. Though described here in the present tense, most are no longer performed in their original contexts. The richest area for such songs is in western Russia, on the border with Belarus, historically linked to a tribe known as Krivichi, whose people lived around Briansk, Smolensk, Pskov, and Tver. The second area is the border with Ukraine, especially around Kursk and Belgorod. The third is the upper Volga area on the ethnic border with Mordvinians around Riazan, Vladimir, and Lower Novgorod. Wherever these songs exist, they constitute the core of the local song tradition. The only really widespread calendric song ritual is *koliada*, caroling at Vasil's Day (New Year's), and Christmas in the Orthodox Christian calendar.

Winter rituals, mainly New Year greetings during Svyatki, the complex period of holy days from 24 December to 6 January, include *koliada*, a general name for a wide variety of customs named primarily for the sung refrain, including *shchedrovki, ovsen-*

FIGURE 1   *"Okh, kalina s malinoiu,"* the "daughter-bird" ballad, a three-part polyphonic song. Recorded in Kotelino Village, Riazan region, in 1967 by Izaly Zemtsovsky. Transcription by Marina Petrashen and Yuri Boiko. Each voice is melodically and rhythmically independent, with phrase endings at the octave. After Zemtsovsky 1972:65.

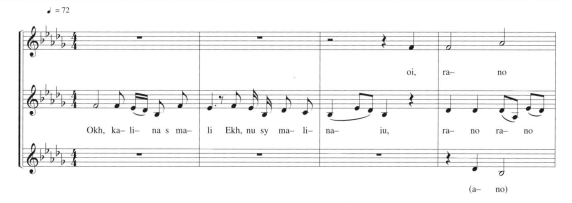

ki, and *vinogradia.* Other genres include *podbliudnye pesni* 'fortune-telling songs', with refrains such as *lado moe* and *slava* and Shrovetide (*maslenitsa*) songs at carnival, with texts about the passage from winter to spring (figure 2). This ritual occurs in the play *The Snow Maiden,* by Aleksandr Ostrovsky (1823–1886), which Nikolai Andreievich Rimsky-Korsakov (1844–1908) turned into an opera in 1881.

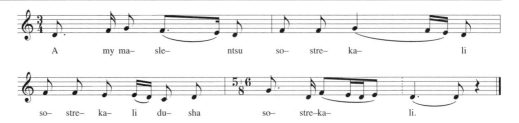

FIGURE 2   *"A my maslentsu sostrekali,"* a Shrovetide song (*maslenitsa*), with a range of a perfect fifth, its narrowness characteristic of songs in the calendric ritual. After Zemtsovsky 1967a:3.

The first songs of spring are sung in March at the Annunciation, when chanted invocations to spring birds substitute for songs proper, which custom forbids at that time of year. The next cycle consists of songs for St. George's Day (23 April), when cattle are led to summer pastures. Easter is marked by *volochebnye pesni* 'trudging songs', named for the singers' manner of walking from village to village on roads muddied by spring rains. Their festive melodies are unique in the calendric cycle. On the first Sunday after Easter in the Kostroma region near the Volga, carolers go to newlyweds' houses to sing newlywed songs (*viunishnye pesni*).

Summer rituals are celebrated mainly in Krivichi territory. The first ritual is *troitskie* (Whitsunday)—normally the fiftieth day after Easter, between the beginning of May and the middle of June. On 22 June, the summer-solstice songs, *kupalskie pesni,* are sung in western areas on Midsummer's Day (23 June), the eve of St. John's Day, as villagers holding a scarecrow (*kupala*) leap over a fire. The texts are ballads about the magical origin of plants, and melodies show links to many other agricultural ritual songs for spring and for the harvest and the melodies of refrains are even reminiscent of *koliada* songs. After St. Peter's Day (12 July), haymaking (*senokos* or *pokos*) begins, and fieldwork is accompanied by special songs. During the harvest, each village gathers to help one family, which in return for the work provides a big meal, at which collective-help songs (*tolochnye pesni*) are sung. Harvest songs and associated rituals differentiated the harvest into beginning, middle, and end. Though harvest songs do not belong to events in the calendric cycle itself, they demonstrate many musical links to other genres of calendric songs and help establish the musical unity of the entire yearly cycle.

The time around summer solstice is believed to be a time of magic. To drive away the evil spirits, the ritual cacophony called *borona* 'harrow', which may refer to the noise produced by harrowing machines, is produced by as many women simultaneously singing calendric songs from all the seasons of the year. Singing these songs together apparently increases their inherent power to affect nature, and helps demonstrate their conceptual unity as expressions of magical power in relation to the seasons and associated agricultural work. Events such as *borona* demonstrate that though the songs may be separated by season, they share a common function. Another confirmation of this unity is contained in New Year's fortune-telling songs (*podbliudnye pesni*), in which the scales and motifs of all calendric songs are found, a kind of musical prediction of the future (Zemtsovsky 1975:59).

Calendric rituals contain a unity of speech, heightened speech, song, movement, and dance. They are performed outdoors with loud, shouting voices and unusual vocal timbres, addressing nature, spirits, birds, and heaven. In tandem with this manner of performance, the scales are untempered and difficult to notate. One form of this dialogue with nature is *aukan'e* 'helloing', not a calendric song, but a lament, sung to birds in the forest by solo women (Lobanov 1997). A typical stanzaic structure of calendric songs repeats the text of the first phrase in the second phrase, but compresses it into a shorter time span with new music. The third phrase then contains a new line of text and new music.

Weddings

Nearly two-thirds of all songs collected during fieldwork are wedding songs, which continue to be performed and remain in the memories of women who have not performed them for many years. No two villages share the same music for wedding songs, even when they share the texts and the general order of rituals. A given village has five to twelve tune formulas, but a few villages have just one or two. The songs accompanying the main events of the wedding are sung forcefully, with each syllable stressed and accompanied by foot stomping, tapping on the table, and ecstatic shouting. Despite the musical variety, it is possible to generalize about the sequence of ritual events in weddings throughout European Russia, each event with characteristic musical and theatrical elements: the matchmaking and courtship, the engagement and wedding contract, the ritual clasping of hands, the bridal shower, the farewell to the bride's maidenly beauty and freedom and the braiding of the bride's hair before the groom arrives, the bride's ritual bath, the blessing of the bridal wreath, the greeting and sendoff of the wedding procession, the return from the church, the nuptial feast at the groom's home, and the feast on the following day at the bride's former home.

The main genres are lyric songs, farewell songs to the bride, songs praising the groom and other guests, teasing songs, taunting ditties (*draznilki*), *chastushki*, ritual-bread songs, processional songs, laments by or for the bride, and songs that describe each wedding event. These last songs, which resound during the entire sequence of events, are unique to weddings and, unlike the other nuptial genres, have no structural parallels in other genres. Songs detailing the protocol of the wedding and wedding lyric songs have musical features unique to the Russian song tradition and distinct from those of neighboring traditions.

Russian culture has developed two kinds of weddings: joyful weddings and funereal weddings. The former are typical of the west and south; the latter, of the north. Songs for the former are stylistically related to calendric songs; songs for the latter, to funeral laments. In the north, a verb for crying (*nevestitsia*) is a cognate of the word for bride (*nevesta*). Joyful weddings are conducted in the bride's and the groom's houses, in parallel ritual events. Funereal weddings are conducted in sequence in the two houses. Joyful weddings link Russian wedding rituals to those of other Slavic peoples. They feature "song wars" and other forms of ritual antagonism between the two families. Funereal weddings feature the bride lamenting while her girlfriends sing, or lamenting while others dance or vocally imitate instrumental music (figure 3). In some areas, the bride engages in ritual crying without text on vocables, such as *u-u, ha-ha,* and *oi-oi*. In some areas, the bride's girlfriends go into the field to "shout" a lament to the dawn on her behalf. In some areas, the bride laments by improvising texts as she addresses the guests at the wedding. If she is an orphan, she laments on her parents' grave, using a tune for funeral laments. Group lamenting at weddings has many features of songs but is understood as lamenting by the people. This tradition is known among other people of northeastern Europe, including Karelians, Komis, and Veps.

Laments and dirges

The Russian tradition has many kinds of laments (*prichitaniia, vopli*). The funeral lament proper provides the model for all others, which include laments at memorials observed at specified times after the funeral; wedding laments; recruiting laments in times of peace; laments for sending soldiers to war; widows' laments; and laments on bad times, such as fires, floods, crop failures, epidemic animal diseases, and forced separation from relatives. For the lamenter, lamenting (or keening) has a cathartic emotional function with respect to grief and sorrow, but the texts, addressed to the

The Russian tradition has many kinds of laments, including laments at memorials observed at specified times after the funeral; wedding laments; recruiting laments in times of peace; laments for sending soldiers to war; widows' laments; and laments on bad times, such as fires, floods, crop failures, epidemic animal diseases, and forced separation from relatives.

FIGURE 3 Excerpt from a bride's lament, sung while the bride's girlfriends are singing a polyphonic song. Recorded in Kotelino Village, Riazan region, in 1967 by Izaly Zemtsovsky. Transcription by Marina Petrashen. The bride's lamenting (uppermost staff) is not rhythmically coordinated with the girlfriends' song, and her indistinct pitches (notated with an *x*) and descending glissandos recall the sounds of weeping. After Zemtsovsky 1972:80.

FIGURE 4 A funeral lament (*prichitaniia*), performed in a style resembling epic or liturgical singing, with a wide melodic range and in free rhythm. After Zemtsovsky 1967a:61.

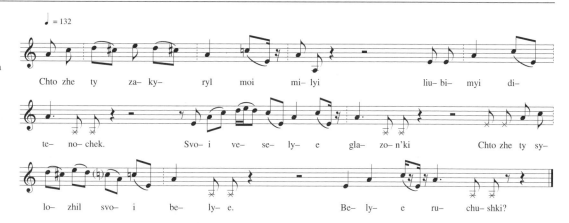

dead person, contain incantational formulas that suggest a magical power to raise the dead.

Performers improvise using formulaic structures or models. The core of this tradition is in the Russian north. One singer, Irina Fedosova (1831–1899), filled three volumes—a total of thirty thousand lines—with her funeral, wedding, and recruiting laments (Barsov 1872). In performance style, which often invokes crying, they are clearly distinguishable from all other genres; in structure, however, they are clearly linked to other song genres from the same village or region.

Russian lament melodies occur in four main types. The first, a cry or shout, contains melodic structures and a performance manner related to the structures and magical energy of calendric and work songs. The second type (*prichitaniia*, containing the root *chit-* 'to read') resembles epic and liturgical narrative singing (figure 4). Highly chaotic and emotional, lamenting at the grave follows strict musical and textual formulas, which lamenters (keeners) sometimes recite quietly at home in the manner of liturgical recitations. The third type is built on the same scales as certain lyric songs, a minor tetrachord or pentachord. The fourth type is stereotypical moaning on a descending, untempered, three-tone, minor-third formula, which Russian composers have used so often that it has become a symbol of Russian lamenting, but ethnographically it is not the most fundamental type of Russian lamenting.

Epic song (*bylina*)

To denote sung epics, scholars introduced the term *bylina* 'what it was', taken from the first line of the famous *Igor's Tale.* Folk terminology calls the genre *starina* 'old song'. It has about a hundred different plots. The average *bylina* is about a thousand lines long, and *bylini* vary from five hundred to two thousand lines. Some stories reflect Russian history from before the first medieval state, in the tenth century; others reflect more internationally known themes, such as the husband returning to remarry his wife (known from Homer's *Odyssey,* for example) and the father fighting with his unrecognized son; yet others reflect mythological and fairy-tale themes.

In Russian education and intellectual life, the *bylina* occupies the highest position in the hierarchy of traditional culture. Examples have been collected in a scholarly edition in English (Bailey and Ivanova 1998). The history of research in this genre can be divided into five periods.

The first saw the publication at the beginning of the nineteenth century of the first anthology of Russian epics, *Sbornik Kirshi Danilova.* Compiled not later than about 1750 from manuscripts left by a singer and collector named Kiril (Kirsha) Danilov, the collection was remarkable for folkloristics of the period, because it included not just authentic texts, but notated music (Danilov 1977).

The second period occurred in the 1860s and the early 1870s, when a living epic tradition was discovered in the Russian north. In the wake of this discovery, epic singers toured St. Petersburg, Moscow, and other major cities, and brought this tradition to broad public attention. Their songs were notated and almost immediately adapted in works by Modest Petrovich Mussorgsky (1839–1881), Rimsky-Korsakov, and Anton Arensky (1861–1906), whose Fantasy on Themes of Riabinin (the famous epic singer Trofim G. Riabinin, c. 1791–1885) for piano and orchestra became so popular that it stands today as a musical symbol of the genre, though the melody is known only along part of the shoreline of Lake Onega.

The third period occurs at the end of the nineteenth century and the beginning of the twentieth, when Aleksandr Grigor'ev made the first sound recordings in the field. Grigor'ev's collection contains 213 texts and 174 tunes from the previously unknown Archangelsk tradition. Julius Block (1858–1934), who introduced the Edison phonograph to Russia, made the first phonographic record of a *bylina*—from a performance by Ivan Riabinin, in St. Petersburg in January 1892. A bit later, about two hundred short so-called epic songs about epic heroes were recorded in the Russian south, among the Don Cossacks, and the first scholarly articles about the music of epics were published (Maslov 1911; Yanchuk 1919).

The fourth period includes the publication of the first scholarly anthology of Russian musical epics (Dobrovol'sky and Korguzalov 1981), the first collection of scholarly articles (Zemtsovsky 1989), and several dissertations. The fifth period saw new publications in the scholarly annual *Russkii Fol'klor* and an annual series of international conferences in memory of the American scholar Albert Bates Lord (1912–1991).

In the nineteenth century, epics were unknown to most Russian peasants, limited as the genre was to the north, but mass propaganda promoted the *bylina* as the true source of a pan-Russian tradition, even as late as the 1981 anthology cited above.

Some scholars have contended that epic songs were originally created by professional minstrels at princely courts, but the tradition has been collected from peasants, fishermen, net-makers, shoemakers, and tailors. Epics are an important genre among Old Believers, who sing them even during Lent, when other forms of singing are prohibited. Epic singers are held in high regard for their memory and skill, passed on within families known as epic dynasties; the most famous such dynasty is the Riabinin family. Most solo epic singers are male, but group singing can mix male and female singers, often from the same family. The last recordings of this tradition were made in the 1970s, but the themes, heroes, and selected texts continue to enjoy a second life in literature, schoolbooks, classical music, films, paintings, and other forms of popular culture.

The recordings of the last hundred years are exclusively vocal, but most scholars assume a distantly past tradition of epics accompanied by a *gusli* 'zither' and a *gudok* 'bowed lute'. Epics have three main performance styles: rhapsodic singing, alternating with recitation that uniquely combines fast speech with hints of exact pitch; ensemble performance without real polyphony, but more melodic than the first type; and group polyphonic singing in song style (figure 5). Each epic text does not have its own tune; rather, tunes belong to the performer, who may have one or two tunes to which he sings all the epic texts he knows. The structure of stanzas is flexible and can change, for example, to a simpler structure as the singer tires. During a performance, the pitch often rises.

Epic tunes are structured around short melodic motifs (*popevki*), which can be made to accommodate three main types of stanzaic structure: twelve to fourteen syllables per line, with three main accents; eight to eleven syllables, with two main accents; and irregular stanzas, set to regular musical phrases of twenty rhythmic beats,

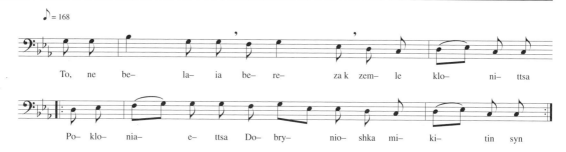

FIGURE 5 Excerpt from an epic song (*bylina*) about the epic hero Dobrynia of the Onega region, performed by an ensemble with distinct pitches but without polyphony. After Astakhova 1951: no. 3.

To, ne be— la— ia be— re— za k zem— le klo— ni— ttsa

Po— klo— nia— e— ttsa Do— bry— nio— shka mi— ki— tin syn

with three held notes to mark a three-syllable cadence in each line. Each line of text is set to a single melodic phrase. One important exception, the so-called *tirade* from the Lake Onega region, creates stanzas of varying lengths by following an opening emphatic melodic line with variable numbers of repeated melodic lines.

Lyric songs

Lyric songs, perhaps more than other genres, belong to all strata of society: from villages to suburbs to cities; peasants, seasonal and factory workers, servants, students, soldiers, prisoners, homeless people, and even thieves; and ethnic minorities, such as Gypsies. Performed at occasions not limited by function, place, or time, they include different musical styles and belong to different historical stages of Russian musical consciousness. The most archaic surviving style is limited to a range of four or five diatonic tones, and is most typical of the western Russian tradition.

From scalar, rhythmic, and structural points of view, the most elaborated forms of peasant lyric songs are the so-called long-drawn-out songs (*protiazhnye pesni* 'protracted songs'), known practically everywhere in Russia and featuring extended melodic motifs (*popevki*) on selected syllables, effectively creating two rhythms: one based on the duration of syllables and one the result of intrasyllabic melodic rhythms (Zemtsovsky 1967a). Long-drawn-out songs evolved simultaneously with Russian liturgical music during the fourteenth to seventeenth centuries, when the Russian nation formed. The same singers (*raspevshchiki*) probably participated in both developments. Both genres became symbols of national culture and points of national pride. The favored locale is outdoors, where lyric songs are performed with an open, loud sound (*na vole* 'with freedom, without walls'); in contrast, lyric songs that have come to villages from cities are typically performed in houses at social gatherings (*posidelki*).

Lyric songs can be performed by a soloist, a chorus of people gathered to socialize or work together, or a trio of professional singers; this last tradition, which flourished until the 1930s, no longer survives (figure 6). Scholars distinguish two performance styles: a strict style and a free style, with virtuoso embellishments and expressivity. Lyric songs, more than other genres, have a one-to-one linkage between text and melody, and variants of a single song are recognizable; however, when given texts pass from one social stratum to another or from one genre to another, they move beyond melodic variants to new versions or entirely different tunes.

Lyric songs circulated between villages and cities in both directions, though typically not directly. They passed through a buffer zone, a suburban area (*sloboda, posad*), which represented a third type of culture in Russian tradition. Populated by former soldiers and a literate middle class who had broken their connection with the peasantry but had not attained many trappings of city culture, this cultural stratum, though neglected by scholars, has been enormously influential on village and city cultures. Its dominant genres are soldiers' songs, so-called "cruel romances" or "sufferings" (*stradaniia*), sentimental drawing-room songs (some in waltz rhythm), and songs with texts from eighteenth- and nineteenth-century literary sources (*knizhnye*

Zhanna Bichevskaya has retuned her guitar to enable herself to play it like an American banjo, and with it she creates arrangements of Russian village and city songs that resemble American country music—a musical, nontextual symbol of ideological opposition to official Soviet culture.

FIGURE 6 "*Za rechen'koi bylo za Nevagoiu*," a lyric song performed by a male duet in an expressive style involving free rhythm and virtuoso embellishments. After Gippius 1979: no. 1.

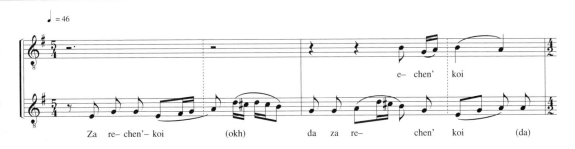

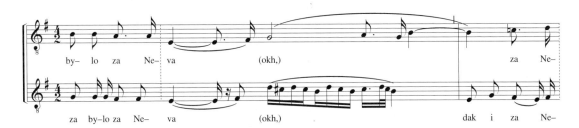

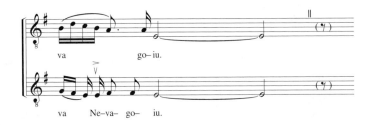

pesni), though their origin is unknown to the singers. Some songs entered the Russian tradition from street barrel-organs (*sharmanka*, from a French popular song, "*Charmante Catherine*"), which played an international repertory of popular songs (including Neapolitan songs, and even Argentinian tangos), which music boxes, musical clocks, and other mechanical devices spread further. Another important source for oral traditions were manuscript and published songbooks (*pesenniki*), which flourished during and after the reign of Catherine the Great (1762–1796). They included songs from the theater, outdoor parties (*gulyaniya*), courtly masquerades, and ballroom dances new to Russian society, including the polka, the quadrille, and the waltz. According to one count, eighteenth-century manuscript songbooks alone included some 450 different themes in 870 variants (Pozdneev 1996). Many published songbooks contain a separate section of Ukrainian songs—an indication of their popularity and influence in Russian cities. Other ethnic groups' songs were represented in multiethnic cities, including St. Petersburg, where a report of one outdoor party in 1825 listed among participants, in addition to Russians and Ukrainians, Finns, Germans, Tatars, Kalmyks, and Jews. Gradually the lyric-song legacy of St. Petersburg became part of the suburban culture of every Russian city.

The most popular instrument for accompanying city lyric songs after about 1800 was the seven-stringed guitar, modified from the six-stringed guitar by Antonin O. Sikhra (1773–1850). So popular was this guitar that it became a symbol of Russian city culture. Perhaps the most creative performance style involves taking printed lyrics and improvising a melody over standard chord progressions that came to define a new Russian harmony. This manner, still especially popular among student hikers and mountain climbers, has given birth to a new genre, after-ski songs, which, in the post-Stalinist period, were revived with new texts, having a strong political, even anti-Soviet, cast. The most popular performers—Bulat Okudzhava (1924–1997), Vladimir Vysotskii (1938–1980), and Aleksandr Galich (1918–1977)—had their songs circulated via samizdat (self-published) cassette tapes (*magnitizdat'*), and their songs were widely sung by young people to create a feeling of freedom from authoritarianism. The importance of these songs, also known as *avtorskie pesni* 'authored songs', was recognized by the publication of special indexes and bibliographies devoted to them in the 1980s, though Galich, exiled in France, remained absent from these reference works. In another variant of the guitar-song tradition, Zhanna Bichevskaya has retuned her guitar to enable herself to play it like an American banjo, and with it she creates arrangements of Russian village and city songs that resemble American country music—a musical, nontextual symbol of ideological opposition to official Soviet culture.

Other popular accompaniments and arrangements of lyric songs were performed on solo violin or solo piano. Despite Russian society's sharp division between rural and urban culture, the same songs could be heard in oral and written traditions, though in different styles: one version transformed into traditional village style, another provided with one or more of these urban arrangements. Urban lyric songs served a new class of people, a public with leisure time, a new concept in Russian society.

The new Russian harmony and polyphony was influenced by *kant,* a subgenre of *knizhnaia pesnia. Kant* had texts written by anonymous authors and well-known eighteenth-century poets. The melodies were transformed from hymn tunes and Polish and Ukrainian songs, one of whose features was the use of sequences and dominant-tonic cadences. Their most distinctive feature was performance in three-part polyphony. The two upper voices sang in parallel thirds while the lowest voice sang countermelodies outlining Western European harmonies new to Russia at the time (figure 7). This style provided Russians with one of their earliest experiences of Western European musical culture, and it became extremely popular among urban upper and middle classes. Though Asaf'ev (1957:5:285) believed "[t]his worst kind of homophony infected the suburbs and villages," the genre managed to "blend in language, themes, and music Russian medieval, European secular, and Russian folk elements" (Bailey 1983:123–124).

These new city songs accommodated new dance rhythms and march rhythms, which added a particularly clear-cut movement to *kant* melodies and harmonies. This style was taken up by soldiers' songs (*soldatskie pesni*), which added sharp accents, fanfarelike melodies, and special refrains. These songs have been a hallmark of Russian and Soviet military music for more than two centuries.

One feature of city culture consists of the performance of village music by urban immigrants, who gather once a week in corners (*piatachki* 'heel') of city parks to keep alive their musical culture and other aspects of village culture, such as matchmaking. In the process, they create dialogues and fusions among different local traditions.

FIGURE 7 *"Kak na matushke na Nevereke,"* a *kant,* a subgenre of published city songs, from a mid-eighteenth-century collection. Its use of parallel thirds over a bass part and Polish and Ukrainian melodies reveals one of the first experiences of Western European musical culture in Russia. After Zemtsovsky 1987:50.

Kak na ma- tush- ke na Ne- ve- re- ke, na Va- sil'- ev- skom slav- nom o- stro- ve.

Short ditties (*chastushki*)

Short ditties (*chastushki*) include many genres and forms, and represent a synthesis of sung ditties, instrumental accompaniment, and sometimes dancing. *Chastushki* burgeoned in the 1860s, when long-drawn-out songs and the *bylina* appeared to be waning; their popularity continues. The whole country, including people of all ages and social classes, became involved in their creation. Many ethnic groups adapted and improvised ditties in their own languages to Russian-style melodies. They are sung at any time, except during funerals. They contain themes drawn from all aspects of life—a fact reflected in collections with titles like "echo," "mirror," "village newspaper," "notebook of simple folk," "factory *chastushka*," and so on. Despite the freedom with which these collections were compiled, they were heavily censored; during the Stalinist period at the Institute of Russian Literature in the Academy of Sciences, for example, a three-person commission destroyed all critical and anti-Soviet texts; however, because of the popularity of the genre, the authorities adapted it to create written texts for propaganda, put it on the stage, and published many collections. In an electoral campaign in the 1990s to head the popular social movement Russia Is Our Home, the politician Viktor Chernomyrdin used one. The poetic texts juxtapose ideas almost meaninglessly to create humorous effects; also common are plays on words and neologisms. The first publication of music for *chastushki* (Lineva 1904) used graphic notation, rather than standard musical notation. The standard form, known everywhere in Russia, consists of four lines (8 + 7 + 8 + 7 syllables each); the second and fourth lines rhyme. An instrument, usually a balalaika (a three-stringed, long-necked, finger-strummed lute with a triangular body) or accordion, provides a rhythmic and harmonic ostinato using the harmonic formula IV(II)–I–V–I (figure 8). The syllables are sung in a rapid patter on fixed pitches that outline the harmonic formula. Each variant is named for a word in the first line of all the texts sung to that variant; for example, *russkogo* 'of Russians'; *semenovna* 'daughter of Simeon'; *tsyganochka* 'beautiful Gypsy girl'; *iablochko* 'beautiful apple'; and many others. In addition to the standard form, local variants abound. In *spasovskaia*, named for a locality where this tune is sung, words in the second line repeat in the fourth and consequently vary and extend the harmonic formula V–I–IV–I–V–I–IV$^6_4$–I. Many singers know only one local tune, to which they sing many songs. In the Volga and Voronezh regions, the subgenre *chastushka* called *stradaniia* 'sufferings' contains two rhyming lines about the problems of a girl in love. In western Russia (the Pskov district), the *chastushka* called *pod draku* 'at a fight' is sung as men engage in fisticuffs. *Chastushki* can be performed solo, in chorus, by soloists and a chorus with an accordion, and with dancing and without. In the absence of instruments, singers accompany a soloist by performing instrumental tunes vocally (*pod iazyk* 'under the tongue'). Sometimes a social event is created around improvised antiphonal dialogues or song dueling using *chastushki*. Competition can also occur between a singer and an accordionist, who improvises textural and melodic variants. The event ends with a *chastushka* dedicated to the accordionist, showing his importance. An indicator of the instrument's importance is its use as the title of some collections of *chastushka* texts, for example, *Talyanka* 'Italian accordion'.

FIGURE 8 *"Uzh kak Meleksa ne gorod,"* a four-line *chatushka,* performed with a *spasovskia* tune to balalaika accompaniment. Recorded in the Leningrad district by Lidiya Kershner. Transcription by Lidiya Kershner. After Kotikova 1961:86.

Dances and singing for traditional dances

Russian culture has two types of dances: individual, solo dances (*pliasky*), accompanied by instrumental ostinato dance tunes (*naigryt'* 'dance until you drop'); and collective circle and figure dances (sing. *khorovod, tanok,* pl. *krugi* 'circles'), accompanied by the dancers' singing and/or, in the late twentieth century, instrumental music. In some places, a *khorovod* is performed exclusively by girls, and elsewhere girls are the main performers, sometimes paired with bachelors. There are three main types of *khorovod.* One is the dance game (*igrovoi khorovod*) with pantomiming soloists inside a circle of singers. Another is the dancing *khorovod* (*pliasovoi khorovod*), with solo dancers inside a circle of dancers who step lightly in place; sometimes the dance rhythms and the song rhythms create polyrhythmic effects. The third is the walking *khorovod* (*khodovoi khorovod* or *khodiachii* or *zmeika* 'snake'), in which all participants walk in a circle or in a serpentine movement down a street. Often the dancers move asynchronically with the song rhythm, and the verb used to describe the movement is typically 'to walk', rather than 'to dance'. To accompany dancing, the relationship between dance rhythms and music rhythms is more precise. One accordionist remarked, "I listen to the dancers' feet." *Khorovod*s were danced outdoors in spring and summer; during the winter, indoors and outdoors on icebound rivers and lakes. Often the texts are humorous, but they also contain themes from the calendric-ritual cycle or ballads. In addition to its entertainment value, *khorovod*s were believed to influence magically the harvest of flax and hemp. Dances can occur during rituals

In the west (Briansk) and south (Kursk and Belgorod), women still play *khorovod*s (dance tunes) on archaic panpipes (*kugikly, kuvikly*), interlocking their blown pitches with vocal pitches. Each woman plays two unbound pipes.

and celebrations (such as weddings) or as independent events, when they constitute an entire domain of traditional culture, on a par with weddings.

MUSICAL INSTRUMENTS AND INSTRUMENTAL MUSIC

FIGURE 9 A man plays a zither (*gusli*). Photo by Ulrich Morgenstern, 1995.

Russian instrumental music underwent two historical crises, in which authorities tried to annihilate important parts of the tradition. In the seventeenth century, Tsar Aleksei Mikhailovich, the father of Peter the Great, became vehemently Orthodox and destroyed the stringed instruments of secular minstrels (*skomorokhi*), including the *gudok* 'bowed fiddle' and the *gusli* 'plucked zither', neither of which fully recovered from this tragedy (figure 9). In the 1920s and 1930s, Stalinist authorities collected and burned villagers' homemade violins and other stringed instruments, which they considered symbols of bourgeois culture; instead, they promoted military band instruments as the ideal of a new society.

Except for minstrels, the best performers of instrumental music were traditionally shepherds and wedding musicians. Shepherds played mainly aerophones. A duct flute (*dudka, sopel, pizhatka*) had five or six finger holes. Single reeds were placed in one or two pipes with a horn bell (*zhaleika, pishchik*). One pipe might have three holes, the other pipe, six. A shepherd could play two contrapuntal melodies. In the morning, pipers played the tune "The sun rises; the shepherd goes crazy"; in the evening, they played the tune "The sun sets; the shepherd enjoys himself." A wooden trumpet (*rozhok*) of various sizes had five finger holes and one thumb hole. Shepherds remembered their signals with verbal mnemonics, which suggested the melody and rhythm; some (like *telenka* 'calf') were addressed to their animals: others called to other shepherds, always with the name *Kirila*. In the Vladimir and Yaroslavl districts, the *rozhok* tradition called for ensembles of up to 120 players; since good players imitated vocal polyphony, they were said to sing with their horns, and each ensemble was called a chorus of horns. The first sound recordings of *rozhok* were made by Evgeniya Lineva before 1917.

In the west (Briansk) and south (Kursk and Belgorod), women still play *khorovod*s on archaic panpipes (*kugikly, kuvikly*), interlocking their blown pitches with vocal pitches. Each woman plays two unbound pipes.

The most popular Russian traditional instrument is the balalaika, a three-stringed strummed lute with a triangular sound box. Played solo, or since the 1930s in ensembles, it accompanies songs, *chastushki,* and dances. The most popular tuning of its strings are a major triad (*gitarnyi*); two unison strings and one up a fourth (*balalaechnyi*); and a minor triad (in the north) or a major second and a minor third (in the south), both called *medornyi* or *minornyi*.

The oldest Russian bowed stringed instrument was a three-stringed pear-shaped fiddle (*gudok*), made from one piece of wood; its successor, a violin (*skripka* 'to squeak') homemade from glued pieces of wood, also had three strings. The center of this tradition was west Russia, where this violin was exclusively a wedding instru-

TRACK 27

FIGURE 10 A man sings and accompanies himself on a button accordion (*garmon'*). Photo by Ulrich Morgenstern, 1995.

ment, traditionally played seated, in a manner peasants call *po-skomorosh'i* 'like a minstrel'. Today, most violinists play four-stringed manufactured instruments, and when they play standing, they call it modern. Since the 1920s, a violin has been played with an accordion for weddings.

The diatonic button accordion (*garmon', garmoshka, garmonika*) was widespread in Russia by the 1840s, and from the 1860s to 1880s it was the most popular Russian folk instrument. Its main center of production was the Tula region, south of Moscow. It had one row of buttons, which produced one set of pitches when the bellows was pushed and another set when the bellows was pulled. Later developments included the ability to produce the same pitch when pushing or pulling and the addition of several chromatic tones (figure 10). The developed instrument, the so-called *khromka* 'chromatic', remains popular. In many places, the *garmonika* replaced the *zhaleika* and the balalaika. Many European dance tunes were introduced to Russia via the accordion and then passed on from Russian to minority groups. A feature of Russian harmony as realized on the accordion is the substitution of a minor chord on the second degree for subdominant and dominant chords: in harmonizing a descending tetrachord (F–E–D–C) in accompanying a *chastushki,* IV–I–V–I becomes ii–I–ii–I. A fully chromatic button accordion (*bayan*), introduced in the early twentieth century, became extremely popular. Its earliest versions had chords preset on the buttons of the left, while the right hand played the melody. Later versions had individual notes in the left hand.

MUSIC OF MINORITIES

Russian history is inextricably linked to the history of Russia's Eurasian minorities. Traces of historical links survive in linguistic dialects and toponymies, ornaments on clothes and utensils, peasant beliefs and superstitions, folklore, and the oldest genres of music in oral tradition. Russian history and culture can hardly be understood without acknowledging the influence of its minorities. In the Soviet period, however, opportunities for these so-called brotherly peoples to become members of a united Soviet family were rather limited, and they were considered outsiders. Such attitudes did not reflect the variety of nations in the country.

Three main groups of minorities can be distinguished: Finnish-speaking minorities in the north and northwest; the Jews; and a host of groups living along the Volga and between the Volga and the Ural Mountains. Other groups include Germans and the Kalmyks, who live in the southeast part of European Russia. The Kalmyks' language belongs to the Mongolian language family, and their monumental Dzhángar epic and protracted lyrical songs (*ut dun*) have parallels in the Mongolian long song (*urtyn dun*) (Shivlianova 1990).

Finnish-speaking minorities in the north and northwest

Finnish-speaking minorities, such as Saami, Nenets, Karels, Veps, and others, live in a region called Ingermanlandia and another called Setu, near Pskov, inhabited by Estonian-speakers, of the Orthodox religion (Slezkine 1994). These minorities' impact on Russian peasant folklore and the influence of Russian traditional music on their cultures are well known. Russian ethnomusicologists have demonstrated Russian epic musical borrowings from Vep laments and the preservation of ancient Russian musical style in the Vep wedding repertory.

Jews

The Jews entered Russia as a mass population with the first two divisions of Poland (1772, 1793), though Jews in Eastern Europe have been neighbors of Slavic and other peoples for more than a millennium. Traces of other peoples' influence can be detected in Yiddish songs and instrumental tunes, and Jewish influence can be heard in the music of other nations (Goldin 1989). Restricted to the western pale for most of the nineteenth century, some Jews were able as students to migrate to cities, where they created their own cultural institutions, including the Society for Jewish Folk Music, which, operating from 1908 to the beginning of the 1920s, supported composers, performers, and ethnomusicologists, most of them students of Nikolai Rimsky-Korsakov. Despite many difficulties, Zusman Kiselgof (1878–1939) and Moshe Beregovsky (1892–1961) documented the Jewish folk-music tradition, and in 1994 the first musical anthology of Jewish folk songs in Yiddish (Zemtsovsky 1994) was published in Russia.

The Volga-Ural historic-ethnographic region

The areas near the Volga and Kama rivers and from the Volga to the Ural Mountains, known collectively as the Volga-Ural historic-ethnographic region, has been the meeting place of Finno-Ugric, Turkic, and Slavic populations for many centuries. Mutual influence in music and culture has occurred, despite religious differences among Christians, Muslims, and pagans. (One group, the Udmurts, professes all three religions.) The minorities belong to two main language families: the Turkic branch of Altaic languages (Tatars, Bashkirs, and Chuvash) and the Finnish branch of Finno-Ugric languages (Mari-Cheremis, Mordvinian-Erzia, Mordvinian-Moksha, Udmurt-Votyak, Komi-Zyriane, and Komi-Permiaki). László Vikár, a Hungarian ethnomusicologist, has pointed out (1989) that the music of these groups can only be understood in reference to other groups. Many of these groups are segmented into unique local traditions or dialectal subgroups, differing greatly from one another. For instance, the Mordvinians split into two main groups with different languages (Erzia and Moksha); the Mari, into three (the Eastern in Bashkiria, the Forest, and the Mountain, the last also known as the Hill and Meadow Maris); the Chuvash, into three (the upstream Vir'yal, the downstream Anatri, and the Anat Enchi, a geographically distinct "middle-low" dialect); and the Tatars, into numerous subgroups, including the Volga Kazans, the Mishars, the Kriashen "Christians," and others in Crimea, Kasimov, and Astrakhan. In the 1990s, several microethnic groups, like the Tatarized Mordvinian-Karatai and the enigmatic Bessermian tribe of northern Udmurtland, have been investigated by local ethnomusicologists.

Some of the music of these minorities has become internationally known through recordings: the Bashkirs' throat singing (*uzliau*), similar to the Mongolian and Tuvinian *khöömei;* the protracted and ornamented tunes of the Bashkirian *kurai,* a rim-blown flute made of a plant stem with five holes for fingering and a diatonic scale; the Tatars' long-drawn-out lyric songs (*ozyn-kyi*); and the Mordvinians' multi-part choral songs. However, little-known and recently discovered local musical traits and microdialects abound; for instance, Chuvash polyphony and brides' laments are known only among the Anatri subgroup, whereas the drum as a wedding instrument is in use only among the Vir'yal subgroup. The southern Udmurt, who live near Turkic groups, perhaps for that reason sing collectively in unison or heterophony, whereas, the northern Udmurt, which have had contact with Russians, have different kinds of polyphony. In some Udmurt villages, all calendric songs used to be performed on the basis of one melody, a tune-formula. The northern Udmurt have so-called personal songs resembling those of indigenous Siberian and Far Eastern peoples. The performance of Mordvinian epic songs by two singers resembles the ancient tradition of Karelian-Finnish epic runes [see FINLAND]. The Udmurts used a local wedding tune (*siuan*) as the musical symbol of crucial moments of the existence of any being, human or nonhuman.

The situation for these minority groups is gradually changing. National schools are beginning to open anew, and significant publications on these peoples' history, language, and culture, including musical folklore and archaeology, have recently appeared. The most significant are new collections of transcriptions of minorities' music of the oral tradition in many volumes that supplement three well-known volumes edited by László Vikár and Gabor Bereczki (1971, 1979, 1989). Numerous new recordings document the most archaic styles of pagan rites and vanishing forms of musical performance in traditional villages undergoing rapid transformation. The hundreds of ethnomusicological publications in Russian and national languages are contributing to the understanding of their identity.

The most characteristic musical feature of the Volga-Ural minorities is pentatonicism (Brazhnik et al. 1995). This is the most homogeneous zone of pentatonicism in Eastern Europe, and even Russian songs proper from this area incorporate the same modal structure (Pal'chikov 1888). In addition to anhemitonic forms of pentatonicism, the Chuvash and the Mari have hemitonic forms. All have two types of pentatonicism: type "d" (d–e–g–a–b) and type "e" (e–g–a–b–d^1). None has type "b" (b–d^1–e^1–g^1–a^1). Type "g" (g–a–b–d^1–e^1) is known among the Tatars and the Mari and unknown to the Chuvash.

Musics in this multiethnic territory have some common rhythmic features, for instance, the iambic combination of short-and-long components in a rhythmic cell as basic building material. Many of them, especially the Chuvash, have a stable system of quantitative rhythm, independent of, and apparently much older than, Arab and Persian metrical systems. Mikhail Kondrat'ev (1990) points out that present-day Chuvash quantitative rhythm has a musical, not a poetical or syncretic, musical-poetical nature. He describes more than a hundred fifty types of rhythmic patterns in Chuvash vocal music and a structure of rhythmic feet and cells in folk songs of Chuvash neighbors, the Mari, Volga Tatar, Bashkir, and Udmurt peoples. Quantitative rhythms resembling those of the Chuvash are found in archaic layers of the song heritage of other Eurasian peoples, including Russian, Hungarian, and Estonian peasant songs. Quantitative rhythmic patterns (clichés) have been demonstrated in the vocal music of the Tatar Kriashen people of the Middle Volga area (Almeeva 1986).

The third important feature of this region is part-singing, of which the Mordvinian three-part choral tradition includes two types. Its choirs have a melody, a drone, and an additional solo voice above the main voices (*podvodka*); some remark-

At the beginning of the twentieth century, staged interpretations of Russian folklore were one of three main trends that profoundly affected Russian musical life. The other two were cheaply printed and widely sold songbooks and gramophone records.

able examples are included in Piatnitsky (1914; numbers 3, 4, 8, and 9). This type of polyphony unites Mordvinian and Russian styles, whereas the ancient heterophonic and diaphonic styles of Mordvinian music reflect the Setu legacy in western Russia. Though it was once believed that Finno-Ugrian peoples (the Volga-Ural peoples in particular) did not sing polyphonically, this belief turned out to be wrong. Musics of the Mordvinian and Komi cultures are completely polyphonic, and some dialects of all other Volga-Ural peoples have one or another of these types of part-singing.

Unusual genres constitute a fourth aspect of the musical life of Volga-Ural minorities. The Komi-Zyriane, for example, perform collective polyphonic wedding song-laments. This genre unites Komi-Zyriane music with north Russian musical dialects and shows the Zyrian substratum of eastern Vologda wedding lamentation. Other unique genres of traditional music include the guests' songs (*gostevye*) in Udmurt, Mari, Chuvash, and Tatar-Kriashen folklore. A guest ritual alternates solo and collective songs and recitatives, and forms a kind of folk opera (Almeeva 1986).

A fifth aspect of musical culture is the use of musical instruments. Especially typical are wing-shaped or helmet-shaped zithers. Called *gusli* by Russians and Tatars, they include the Mari *kyuslë* (a twenty- or twenty-two-stringed box zither), the Mordvinian *kaiga*, the Chuvash *guslya* and *kyoslë*, the Komi *brungan*, the Udmurt *krez'* (the same word also means 'song' and 'melody'), the Karelian *kantele*, and so on. In the past, it was mainly an instrument of pagan priests. At Tatar weddings, two types of instruments—a violin among the Muslims and a *gusli* among the Kriashen—were played; but today, the accordion (*garmoshka*) prevails in both communities. The Mordvinian traditional violin had three strings, but today, Mordvinians prefer to take off the lower string of factory-made violins and play just on three strings. Another important traditional instrument was the bagpipe (Russian *volynka*, Mari *shuvyr*, Chuvash *shapar* or *sarnai*, the Mordvinian *skamóra, fam, válonka,* or *puzyr'* 'bladder', the Udmurt *byz*, and so on). A men's instrument, it was often used for weddings. Flutes, including the Komi panpipe (*pöliannez* or *pölian'ias*) and the Bashkir and Tatar *kurai*, with its rich repertoire of programmatic instrumental tone poems, were also important. During the Soviet era, the accordion and the Russian balalaika replaced many indigenous instruments (Beregovsky 1987; Boyarkin 1995; Chistalev 1980, 1984; Saha and Lindblad, 1994; Shurov 1995; Turovsky 1997a).

URBAN REVIVALISM

Urbanization, industrialization, and other modernizing forces of the twentieth century inevitably had a deleterious effect on folklore. Five major tendencies to keep folklore alive and meaningful can be identified: folklore on the stage; folklore at festivals and holidays, including so-called new rituals associated with collective farms and urban weddings; folklore in education and scholarship; folklore in professional music; and folklore in mass media and entertainment, including TV, radio, films, CDs, cassettes, advertisements, restaurants, cafes, and public transportation.

FIGURE 11   A balalaika orchestra of the early twentieth century. To form an orchestra along the lines of a symphony orchestra, the original folk instrument was constructed in many sizes, from soprano to bass, and the musicians played under a conductor's direction. Postcard postmarked 1908. Courtesy of the Robert Godfried Collection, New York.

Folklore in professional music

In professional music, the Russian version of nineteenth-century European Romantic nationalism is well known in the work of composers such as the Russian five (see below). One of the earliest exponents of folk music was a pan-Slavic enthusiast, Dmitri Agrenev-Slaviansky (1834–1908), who in the 1860s traveled to all the Slavic countries of Europe and returned to perform folk songs from all these traditions on concert stages with splendid but fake medieval and folk costumes and orchestral accompaniment.

Though this attempt at urban revivalism was largely forgotten, Vasily Andreev (1861–1918) from St. Petersburg, inspired by these performances but with Russian nationalism in mind, took Russian instrumental music in a new direction. Believing that Russian instrumental folk traditions were declining, he sought to return this tradition to the people. He began by collecting folk instruments in markets and villages, but soon realized that they were ineffective when presented on stage, so he tried to improve them by recreating them along the lines of a symphony orchestra. In addition to having more than one play at a time, he had each instrument rebuilt in sizes from soprano to bass, and wrote new music for the resulting orchestra, which he called the Great Russian Orchestra of Folk Instruments, a name that distinguished it from other eastern Slavic traditions (figure 11). Well-received by the prerevolutionary intelligentsia, these orchestras became the hallmark of Soviet-period staged folklore and were later adopted by all Soviet republics. From the 1920s, musical schools and colleges were established to teach these instruments and the new orchestral style. Eventually, these orchestras performed European classical music.

At the beginning of the twentieth century, staged interpretations of Russian folklore were one of three main trends that profoundly affected Russian musical life. The other two were cheaply printed and widely sold songbooks and gramophone records.

Staged performances

Staged concerts of Russian, Ukrainian, and Gypsy choirs, balalaika orchestras, solo and duo accordionists, instrumental and vocal combos (balalaika and mandolin, singer and accordionist), and dancers who acted out the content of folk songs were enormously popular in Moscow, St. Petersburg, and Kiev, and toured provincial cities. In 1913, Andreev's orchestra celebrated its twenty-fifth anniversary, to great acclaim. In his honor in 1921, this orchestra was renamed The State Great Russian Orchestra Named after Andreev.

The most popular genre of stage music, especially with prominent members of the Russian intelligentsia, were Gypsy romances, performed by soloists and choirs in restaurants on the outskirts of Moscow and St. Petersburg. The choirs, always composed of Gypsies, sang in Russian and Romani in a characteristic Gypsy style [see ROM (GYPSY) MUSIC]. Except for a few famous singers, such as the legendary Stesha (1787–1822) from the Gypsy choir of Ilya Sokolov (1777–1848) and Varvara Panina (1872–1911), the soloists were usually non-Gypsies, attracted to the genre by its popularity and the possibility of making good money. The biggest star, an Armenian from Tbilisi who moved his audience to tears with his singing, took the stage name Sasha Davydov (1850–1911). Nataliya Tamara (d. 1934), a Russian peasant, became an extremely popular and wealthy "Gypsy" singer. Another peasant, Anastasiya Vial'tseva (1871–1913), pioneered a genre of petit bourgeois salon romances, combining traits of Gypsy and arranged folk songs; she brought a unique business acumen to her concerts and tours and died one of the wealthiest women in Russia. Nadezhda Plevitskaya (1884–1940) added a folk character to Gypsy romances, and after 1914 added Russian peasant songs to her repertoire. Paradoxically this most popular of Russian singers emigrated in 1920. During her American tours, she was accompanied on piano by Sergei Rachmaninoff. Imprisoned by the Nazis, she died in Paris in 1940.

Though less popular than Gypsy music, unarranged, but staged, traditional music had its well-known exponents, including Mitrofan Pyatnitsky (1864–1927), Olga Kovaleva (1881–1962), and Piotr Yarkov (1875–1945). Perhaps the first influential Russian singer-songwriter (*poiushchii poet* 'singing poet'), Aleksandr Vertinsky (1889–1957), created a new genre for the stage by combining intimately declaimed melodies with an extremely elaborate plasticity of gesture and the whiteface of a Russian Pierrot, a famous French mimed, comic character. He emigrated in 1919. His songs, despite being banned, became symbols of freedom and individualism to many Soviet admirers. Stalin allowed him to return and sing his songs from 1943 until his death.

Songbooks (pesenniki)

The third trend began about 1900, when inexpensive songbooks containing popular folk songs from the stage repertoire, many with texts only, flooded markets in Moscow, St. Petersburg, and Kiev. Each of about ten publishers produced about twenty thousand copies per year; this publishing peaked in 1911, when 180 new books were published. Most of the songs were so-called cruel romances about unhappy love affairs, suicides, and murders. A subcategory of these books included songs of thieves, convicts, and hobos. About a dozen were produced by a Swede, Wilhelm N. Garteveld (1862–1928). These books helped spread newly composed folk songs, creating the first folk songs known throughout Russia and not limited to a particular region. Even today, Russian ethnomusicologists find these songs the best preserved and easiest to collect in Russian villages.

Hundreds of thousands of individual songs were published as sheet music; in Moscow, the Iambor Company systematically published in pocket-size editions music of virtually every kind: popular, folk, student, Gypsy, music-hall, and even favorite classical songs, marches, and dances, including waltzes and the two-step. Russian folk songs in popular arrangements and with singers' photographs were also published by Semyon Iambor between 1907 and 1914.

The gramophone

The fourth trend at the beginning of the century was the boom in the production and sales of the gramophone, a machine that, like the songbooks, helped join city culture with villages culture. From 1900 to 1907, half a million gramophones were sold in Russia. By 1915, Gramophone and Pathé, English and French companies, respectively, were selling up to twenty million phonograph records (*plastinky*) of Russian stage performers annually, in addition to sales from their international catalog. Other gramophone companies included Sirena Record, Stella Record, Orpheon, Lirophone, Ekstraphone, and Zonophone Record.

Listening to recordings on the gramophone became a part of everyday social life, not just among urban elites, but in provincial areas. During World War I, so-called gramophone concerts became popular, especially on ships and in hospitals. On the street, in parallel with phonograph recordings, barrel organs played cylinders of the stage repertory.

Jazz

In 1922, Leonid Utesov (1895–1982), a Jew originally named Weissbein, migrated from Odessa to Leningrad, where in 1929 he founded the group Tea-Jazz (with the word *Tea* shortened from *teatr* 'theater'). Utesov became the leading jazz singer in the Soviet Union and retained his popularity during the 1940s and 1950s, when jazz was essentially banned. Like Vertinsky, he almost declaimed his songs, though not his own songs, but stage and thieves' songs. Unlike Vertinsky's voice, his voice was not refined, intimate, and expressive of individual feeling, but hoarse and soft, musically penetrating, and expressing of collective feelings. The style of music (jazz) and the songs' contents (lives of convicts and similar outcasts) expressed the idea of freedom for a repressed people. He and his cheerfulness reminded people of their humanity.

Mainstream revivalism and folklorism

Looking at the early years of the twentieth century from the perspective of the end of the century, we see that six main streams of music making and styles of presentation have continued from the prerevolutionary period through the communist era to the present.

First, big choruses, like Agrenev-Slaviansky's Cappella, and folk-instrument orchestras, like Andreev's, both of which performed folk and composed music, became state choruses and orchestras such as The Red Army Ensemble of Songs and Dances, founded in 1928 and now named after its founder and director, Aleksandr Aleksandrov (1883–1946); the State Academic Russian Choir, named after Aleksandr Sveshnikov (1890–1980); and since 1937 the State Ensemble of Folk Dance, under the direction of Igor Moiseyev (b. 1906). Such ensembles continue to perform and tour with the pretension that their performances are less politicized and closer to the folk tradition than they were under Soviet regimentation.

Second, smaller regional choruses, like those of Pyatnitsky and Yarkov, became state folk choruses and models for other regional folklore groups, such as those from the northern Russian, Voronezh, Ural, and Don regions. These groups concentrated on arrangements of local folk traditions; in many of them, skillful village singers would start singing in a traditional, polyphonic manner before the large chorus entered. Today, no such traditional singers are living, and younger performers are unable to compromise between traditional and staged styles.

Third, universally popular prerevolutionary solo singers, such as Nadezhda Plevitskaya and Olga Kovaleva, had counterparts during the Soviet period in the art of other Russian folk-style soloists, like Lidiya Ruslanova, Lyudmila Zykina, and countless graduates of the Musical Academy Named after the Gnesin Family, which had a unique department devoted to folksinging, a department established by Nina Meshko (b. 1917) and now directed by Lyudmila Shamina (b. 1936).

Fourth, the so-called Silver Age of Russian poetry (between 1898 and the 1920s), which included Aleksandr Blok (1880–1921) and Osip Mandel'shtam (1891–1938), had its parallel in the staged-singing tradition of Aleksandr Vertinsky,

In Russian villages, two styles coexist: a communal style that everyone can perform and that has become the basis for the repertoire of state choruses, large and small; and a more personal, virtuosic (masterful) style of a few adept and talented individuals.

who spawned the tradition of guitar songs (*avtorskie pesni* 'authors' songs'), which before perestroika were published only by the underground *magnitizdat'* and samizdat press. Called Russian bards (*bardy*), the most famous were Aleksandr Galich and Bulat Okudzhava, who acknowledged Vertinsky as the father of authors' songs. It remains a flourishing genre of Russian popular poetry and music.

Fifth, Leonid Utesov's coarser approach to singing and his humorous, democratic approach to already composed songs endeared him to his public and gave birth to a tradition in which songs intended for the masses seemed to speak from person to person, from soul to soul. The best exponent of this tradition was another Jew, the singer Mark Bernes (1911–1969). Utesov's approach has found its way into Russian rock, performed by Boris Grebenshchikov and his group, Aquarium; Aleksandr Bashlachev (1960–1988); Tatyana Kabanova; and others.

The sixth stream of twentieth-century musical life consists of professional composers and performers in the European art tradition (see below).

Other revival trends

The foregoing streams do not carry all aspects of Russian musical life: important eddies deserve scrutiny. In the 1930s and 1940s, the singer Irma Yaunzem (1897–1975) collected and performed folk songs of Soviet minorities. In 1960, with the first so-called ethnographic concert, villagers performed on stage in Moscow. This tradition continues: in St. Petersburg in 1996, such concerts included Old Believers from Oregon; in 1998, the festival St. Petersburg Musical Spring included native Americans from northern California.

Third, from the 1970s to the 1990s, an ensemble led by Dmitri Pokrovsky (1944–1996) started a folklore group in which ethnomusicologists became singers by conducting fieldwork and learning directly from traditional singers. Their goal was not merely to imitate traditional singing but to improvise according to traditional principles. Pokrovsky's approach inspired numerous followers, such as the St. Petersburg Studio, directed by Aleksandr Romodin, and a Don Cossack group, led by Tatyana Rudichenko. The names of other groups incorporated words—like *circle, folk, holiday,* and *talk*—that suggested the groups aimed for a sense of participation and interrelationship between themselves and their audiences, rather than a formal concert presentation. In Russian villages, two styles coexist: a communal style that everyone can perform and that has become the basis for the repertoire of state choruses, large and small; and a more personal, virtuosic (masterful) style of a few adept and talented individuals. Pokrovsky's and other ensembles set their sights on the latter part of village traditions, and their performances had a liveliness and freshness lacking in the older state groups, which aimed for a representation of collective unity.

A fourth eddy consists of teenagers' public musical life on streets and in markets, entryways to buildings, and empty fields on urban outskirts. These spaces are laboratories for new Russian guitar songs and pop and rock. Performers have developed new experimental genres. In performances they call mimic-jazz-rock-theater, groups act out the words of the song. In the genre called picture drawers (*kartinniki*), performers draw pictures suggested by songs and throw the pictures into the audience. During the 1980s, the group Working Afternoon became a professional cooperative of street musicians, and obtained a permit to work on the street. Kino, the rock group of Viktor Tsoi (1962–1990), was one of the most popular with Russian youth from 1980 to 1990.

Russian versus Western models

The history of Russian music in the twentieth century can be interpreted as flowing from nineteenth-century debates between advocates of vernacular Russian traditions (*slavianofily* 'Slavophiles', 'Russophiles') and advocates of a Western cultural model (*zapadniki* 'Westernizers'). During Stalin's era, the composer Isaak Dunayevsky's (1900–1955) popular songs in march and waltz rhythms with Western-like melodies and harmonies contrasted with Vladimir Zaharov's (1901–1956) new Russian folk songs for the Pyatnitsky chorus. Each style had its favorite singer: Leonid Utesov for Western-like music; Lidiya Ruslanova and Maria Mordasova for popular Russian music (songs and *chastushki*). In between was the singer Irma Yaunzem, who sang the songs of different nations. During the Khrushchev era, Mikhail Tariverdiev (b. 1931) composed popular songs in a Western-oriented style, while Vasily Solovev-Sedoi (1907–1979) composed Russian-style songs, including "*Podmoskovnye vechera*" ('Moscow suburb nights'). Edita Piekha was the most popular Western-style singer; Valentina Tolkunova and others were the most popular Russian-style singers. Underground bards fell into one camp or the other. During the Brezhnev era, Alla Pugacheva, a Western-oriented singer, and Lyudmila Zykina, a Russian folk-style singer, enjoyed enormous popularity. Zhanna Bichevskaya is an intermediate stylist. Today, American-style pop, rock, and rap—all performed in Russian—compete for popularity with Nadezhda Babkina and her group, Russian Song. A philosophical and ideological difference is manifested in the continued coexistence of distinct musical styles.

HISTORY OF MUSIC

The history of Russian professional art music involves deep interrelationships with folk and church music.

Church music to the eighteenth century

In Russia, the word for Christian and peasant is nearly the same, and any sense of opposition between folk and church music is more imaginary than real. Sacred and secular music coexisted in the same person, who could sing in both contexts. Even melodic structure, in which one textual syllable corresponds to a musical phrase, is known to both traditions and bears nearly the same name: *rospev* for religious chants and *raspev* for long-drawn-out secular songs. From common roots, folk and religious musics have been marked by mutual influence, and both have affected and been affected by the history of professional art music.

Unlike folk music, church music has a history preserved in numerous manuscripts, of which the earliest, in a neumatic notation called *kriuk* 'hook', have not been deciphered. The first indisputably readable manuscripts come from the seventeenth century, though Russian scholars, especially Maksim Brazhnikov (1904–1973) and his students, claim they can read much older notations. Notations of *znamenny rospev* 'chanting by signs' may be the closest we can come to an understanding of how long-drawn-out songs sounded when they were new. Until the seventeenth century, Russian chant was monophonic, but in performance it was probably full of heterophonic variation. It was based on a system of eight melodic modes (*glas* 'voice'), each of which had a unique scale and set of melodic motifs (*popevki*).

Polyphonic compositions, begun in the seventeenth century with influence from the Ukrainian and Polish Catholic churches, eventually replaced monophonic chants, except among Old Believers, one-third of the population. In the new style, the *cantus firmus* of many compositions was based on folk material. A new genre of polyphonic music—*kant*—emerged and united church and folk music. Its texture features a freely moving music bass and two parts above it, moving in parallel thirds.

The emergence of art music

For most of the eighteenth century, professional composers devoted themselves to compositions for the church. The most important figure, Dmitry Bortnyansky (1751–1825), was a serf who trained in Italy. He was the first director of the famous Russian Court Singing Cappella (*Pridvornaia Pevcheskaia Kapella*). In the late eighteenth century, he wrote one of the first Russian operas, as did such composers as Vasily Pashkevich (1742–1797), founder of the opera genre in Russia, Mikhail Matinsky (1750–c. 1820s), also a freed serf, and Evstigney Fomin (1761–1800), who used folk tunes in his operas and composed comic operas, including *The Americans* (1788). In the early nineteenth century, Aleksei Verstovsky (1799–1862), trained by the Irishman John Field (1782–1837) and other foreign teachers living in Russia, composed many popular operas using Russian folk melodies; his most popular was *Askold's Tomb* (1835).

The acknowledged father of the Russian national school of music was Mikhail Glinka (1804–1857), who briefly studied piano with John Field. He studied in Italy and Germany, where he systematized his knowledge of composition. His most important operas were *A Life for the Tsar* (1836) and *Ruslan and Lyudmila* (1842). He was the first important Russian composer of instrumental music. His overture *Kamarinskaia* (1848), based on two folk melodies, is a cornerstone of the Russian symphonic tradition. According to Tchaikovsky's well-known dictum, that tradition is "contained in *Kamarinskaia,* just as the whole oak is contained in the acorn." Glinka created many new songs and romances that helped set the Russian melodic style. Early operatic and symphonic performances were sponsored by wealthy private individuals, including those at the imperial court. In youth, Glinka, for example, had an instrumental "chapel" of serfs to perform his music.

The St. Petersburg Philharmonic Society, the oldest surviving public Russian musical organization, began in 1802, but it was not until the 1860s that publicly organized performances flourished and musical training was established—first in St. Petersburg and later in Moscow. These changes in musical life paralleled larger social changes, such as the emancipation of the serfs (1861) and its consequences. To organize and sponsor concerts and Russian musical activities, the Russian Musical Society, eventually with branches in most major cities, was formed in 1859 (St. Petersburg) and 1860 (Moscow). The first conservatories were established by Jewish brothers: Anton Rubinstein (1829–1894), composer and pianist, in St. Petersburg (1862), and Nikolai Rubinstein (1835–1881), conductor and pianist, in Moscow (1866). The St. Petersburg Society of Chamber Music was founded in 1872, and other groups followed in later years. The Russian-French musical journal *Muzykal'nyi Svet/Le Monde Musical* was published in St. Petersburg (1847–1878), and in 1872–1877, the first musical newspaper, *Muzykal'nyi Listok* (Musical Leaflet) was founded in St. Petersburg, with the help of composer, ethnomusicologist, and critic Aleksandr Famintsyn (1841–1896). The first musical-theatrical newspaper, *Nuvellist,* was published from 1878 to 1902.

The flowering of Russian art music

During the second half of the nineteenth century, five composers—Mily Balakirev

(1836–1910), Alexander Borodin (1833–1887), César Cui (1835–1918), Modest Mussorgsky, and Rimsky-Korsakov—united under the banner "New Russian School." In Russia, they subsequently came to be called The Mighty Handful; in the West, The Russian Five. Three of them were outstanding, and their work continues to be performed, in Russia and abroad: Borodin, Mussorgsky, and Rimsky-Korsakov. Borodin established a new kind of "epic symphony," with a musical narrative free of intrinsic dramatic conflicts. His most famous works are the opera *Prince Igor* and the second symphony, *Bogatyr* 'Epic Hero'. Mussorgsky, who wrote mainly operas (the most famous is *Boris Godunov*) and romances, was adept at creating melodies that mimicked Russian speech. Rimsky-Korsakov, a composer of fifteen operas filled with folk motifs, absorbed Western compositional principles more completely than his colleagues and became the first great Russian teacher of composition. He wrote important books on orchestration and harmony, both of which have been translated into English. Many of his students at the St. Petersburg Conservatory were from Russian minorities; his most famous student was Igor Stravinsky (1882–1971).

The most popular Russian composer, Peter Ilyich Tchaikovsky (1840–1893), studied with Anton Rubinstein at the St. Petersburg Conservatory. Tchaikovsky, whose popularity in music might be compared to Dostoevsky's in literature, was oriented, like Dostoevsky, toward the human psyche and the depths of the soul. He was the first to compose in all the established genres of Western music: ballets, operas, symphonies, instrumental concertos, symphonic overtures, chamber music, piano music, songs, and romances. He created a new kind of melody, cantilena-narration, which seems to speak without words. Like Rimsky-Korsakov and Balakirev, Tchaikovsky published collections of folk songs. His most important musical heir, who established a unique style, was the pianist and composer Sergei Rachmaninoff (1873–1943), who left Russia in 1917.

Russian music in the twentieth century

The Russian avant-garde emerged in 1900 with the performance of Aleksandr Scriabin's (1872–1915) First Symphony. Scriabin was the first Russian composer to break away from the folk-song tradition and create an idiosyncratic approach to melody and harmony. Another avant-garde figure, Igor Stravinsky, in his Russian period (before World War I), was inspired by folk ideas and musical elements evocative of the pre-Christian era. In the early 1920s he shared in the ideas of the "Eurasianists" Piotr Suvchinsky, Nikolai Trubetskoi, and others (Taruskin 1996).

Among many Russian Soviet composers, two—Sergei Prokofiev (1891–1953) and Dmitri Shostakovich (1906–1975)—have already joined the canon of great Western composers. Both graduated from the St. Petersburg conservatory as composers and pianists, and both published arrangements of Russian folk songs. Working in all contemporary genres, they composed masterly operas, symphonies, ballets, and chamber works, in which they created musical idioms of their own. Prokofiev, temporarily a student of Rimsky-Korsakov, started, like Stravinsky, with exuberant images of wild, pagan Russia inexorably moving toward revolution (*Ala and Lolly: A Scythian Suite for Orchestra,* 1914). However, in his mature orchestral music he followed the line of Borodin's epic symphonism. In general, his music is marked by wide dynamics and sunny energy, and reflects Russian vigor, health, and humor. Shostakovich, being younger, from the beginning of his career had to work under Soviet rule. Following Dostoevsky's line of modern Russian culture and Mahler's line in music, he was never limited by images of individual horror, but portrayed the social catastrophe of the Soviet people. He was called the musical conscience of his period. His Fifth Symphony (1937) is known as the Hamlet Symphony. His Seventh Symphony (1942) has become a monument to World War II. Though Russian, he

In the mid-1960s, as part of a "new folkloric wave" in Soviet music, a "new Russian wave" began. Many young composers, without an official directive, turned to folk music as the means of a new concept, *narodnost'* 'nationality, peopleness, national identity', and a new musical language.

wrote deep Jewish music as a symbol of the suffering of all human souls. During his lifetime, many of his works were the subject of sharp discussion and state suppression. His opera *Lady Macbeth of the Mtsensk District* was banned from 1936 to 1961. Despite these challenges, he continued to travel a uniquely thorny path.

Shostakovich, when he was allowed to be a teacher, had many excellent students, among whom was Georgy Sviridov (1915–1998), a composer of mainly vocal music, predominantly of Russian folk and sometimes liturgical character. He has become a spiritual and stylistic leader of Russian nationalist ideology in music. He understands and employs Russian music in all its historical and stylistic variety: musical styles equally of villages and suburbs, countries and cities, and factories and churches. He understands Russian people in all their richness. He prefers not to quote folklore, but to create music of his own to generalize and poeticize the national character.

In the mid-1960s, as part of a "new folkloric wave" in Soviet music, a "new Russian wave" began. Many young composers, without an official directive, turned to folk music as the means of a new concept, *narodnost'* 'nationality, peopleness, national identity', and a new musical language. This wave resulted from the so-called ideological thaw and an avalanche of ethnomusicological discoveries of traditional music in remote villages. Composers hoped to portray their own people realistically. For some, like Valery Gavrilin (1939–1999), Sviridov was an ideal and an authority. But two contrasting trends emerged: the state sponsored the folklore-oriented one, but the experimental one, which followed the Western avant-garde, became the new underground and included Alfred Schnittke (1934–1998), Edison Denisov (1929–1997), Sofia Gubaidulina (b. 1931), and others, of whom one, Galina Ustvolskaya (b. 1919), an extremely avant-garde and religious student of Shostakovich, became known to the musical world only after 1985. For years, she could write only for private consumption. As the *New York Times* pointed out, "[A]n imposing figure in twentieth-century musical history has stepped out of the mist" (28 May 1995:23).

Alongside these trends (folkloric and avant-garde), a third current included neither classic nor modernist composers, but writers of beautiful and extremely popular song-romances, including Mikhail Tariverdiev, Igor Egikov (b. 1936), Aleksei Rybnikov (b. 1945), and others.

HISTORY OF SCHOLARSHIP

Russian musicology and ethnomusicology (the latter called in Russia musical ethnography and musical folkloristics) are marked by several outstanding achievements.

Nineteenth-century trends

Numerous publications have come out since the beginning of the nineteenth century, but the first thinkers who spoke as specialists were Vladimir Odoevsky (1803–1869), a romantic writer and musical folklorist, whose legacy is still known only partially, and Aleksandr Serov (1820–1871), a well-known composer and critic, and the author of the first brochure on Russian folk song as a subject of scholarly study. The nineteenth century saw other important figures: the bellicose ideologue of the Five, Vladimir Stasov (1824–1906); the music critics Hermann Laroche (1845–1904), the first critic who had a theoretical conservatory education; Nikolai Kashkin (1839–1920); Nikolai Findeizen (1868–1928), author of *Sketches for the History of Music in Russia* (1928); Joel Engel (1868–1927), an indefatigable Russian critic and Jewish composer; Ivan Lipaev (1865–1942); and Vyacheslav Karatygin (1875–1925). All participated in the movement to create a Russian musical school in contrast with Western ways. Other specialists included the outstanding ethnomusicologist and composer Piotr Sokalsky (1832–1887), author of a fundamental and unsurpassed study (1888), and the discoverer of Russian folk polyphony, Yuly Melgunov (1846–1892). Later outstanding musical folklorists were Aleksandr Maslov (1876–1914), Evgeniya Lineva (1853–1919), Aleksandr Listopadov (1873–1949), and Aleksandr Kastalsky (1856–1926), composer of church and other choral music.

The first modern periodical, the *Russian Musical Gazette*, published by Nikolai Findeizen in St. Petersburg between 1894 and 1918, devoted articles to musical ethnography and liturgical singing. Other magazines included *Muzyka i Penie* (Music and Singing, St. Petersburg, 1895–1902), *Gramophone and Phonograph* (St. Petersburg, 1902), and the popular weekly *Music* (Moscow, 1910–1916). Between the revolutions of 1905 and 1917, about forty musical journals and newspapers were founded in Russia.

Theory in the early twentieth century

In musical theory, the most important book is *Counterpoint in the Strict Style* (1906) by the composer Sergei Taneev (1856–1915), teacher of another great theoretician and scholar, Boleslav Yavorsky (1877–1942). Yavorsky and Boris Asaf'ev (1884–1949) were the first Russian theorists to create a system applying to all music. Their legacy is the cornerstone of Russian musicology. Most musicological concepts and terms used by Russian scholars today were created by Yavorsky and partly picked up and developed by Asaf'ev and others. These include *intonatsiia* 'intonation' (as a structural and semantic notion); *vnutrenniaia slukhovaia nastroika* 'inner auditory tuning'; *slukhovoe tiagotenie* 'auditory gravitation', concepts of mode, modal rhythm, musical thought, and so on. The most important is the concept of *intonatsiia,* the primary formal and expressive cell (McQuere 1983; Zemtsovsky 1997). Both Yavorsky and Asaf'ev studied written and oral traditional music, because, according to them, art music follows the same principles as folk music.

In the prerevolutionary period, Yavorsky worked for the musical-ethnographic commission of Moscow University. Just after the 1917 revolution, Asaf'ev taught, for the first time in Russia, Russian musical folklore and musical ethnography as a discipline at the Russian Institute for the History of the Arts, St. Petersburg. Among his pupils were Zinaida Evald (1894–1941) and Evgeny Gippius (1903–1985), founders of Russian ethnomusicology and the Russian phonogram archive in St. Petersburg. Though Asaf'ev never wrote a book about folklore, his references to music of the oral tradition (as he called it) were so numerous and so conceptually important, they filled a book published posthumously on the basis of his published and unpublished writings (Asaf'ev 1987). Among his most important concepts were *intonatsiia* 'intonation', by which he meant musical thought and music's basic communicative element; "oral vocabulary of intonations"; "common intonations of the era"; "symphonism"; "melodiousness"; *tonnost'* 'toneness'; and *pesennost'* 'songness'. He viewed every ethnic or social intonational (musical) system as a function of social or mass consciousness, and saw such systems, taken together, as a means of communication between human beings.

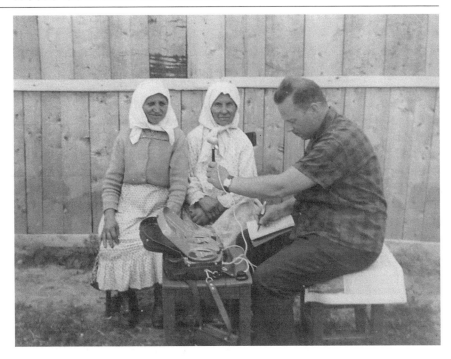

Soviet ethnomusicology

Russian ethnomusicology since 1917 is too complex and contradictory for easy generalizations, though, as in musical life, two contrasting main streams and a third eddy
can be identified. The main trend belongs to the St. Petersburg school, Asaf'ev and
his students: Evald, Gippius, Michael Druskin (1905–1991), Semyon Ginzburg
(1901–1978), Roman Gruber (1895–1962), Lidiya Kershner (1905–1968),
Christopher Kushnarev (1890–1960), Sofya Maggid (1892–1954), and Pavel Vulfius
(1908–1977). Later followers of this tradition included Tatyana Bershadskaya (b.
1921), Boris Dobrovolsky (1914–1976), Aleksandr Gorkovenko (1939–1972),
Viktor Lapin (b. 1941), Igor Matsievsky (b. 1941), Feodosy Rubtsov (1904–1986),
and Izaly Zemtsovsky (b. 1936). Most of them worked or are still working at the
Russian Institute for the History of the Arts (figure 12). Their sources included
Asaf'ev and other main figures of prerevolutionary scholarship, starting with Serov.
Already in 1869 Serov had imagined a research program for "one common enormous
science of 'humanology'"—anthropology in a general sense, including the science of
folk-music art (that is, folk songs), a field that would be closely related to physiology,
ethnography, history, and philology, "chiefly, in the unwritten, traditional monuments, since the musical embryos in each nation precede its written language"
(Vulfius 1979:127). The realization of this program began with so-called complex
artists' expeditions to the Russian north, initiated by Asaf'ev in the 1920s. On the
basis of those expeditions, the phonogram archive was founded, in 1927, and the
first important ethnomusicological book was published, in 1937 (Korguzalov and
Troitskaya 1993). This school does not confine itself to the music of oral tradition,
but studies such problems as "folklore and the composer," "music and ethnogenesis,"
and so on. It does not limit itself to the traditions of Russian scholarship, but keeps
in touch with scholarly trends around the world. It does not restrict itself to one ethnic tradition, but studies the music of all Russian minorities—and, indeed, the
world's music. It argues that, while folklore can be strictly local, folkloristics and ethnomusicology cannot be.

A second main trend is connected with two scholars: Klyment Kvitka
(1880–1953) after the 1930s, when he moved from Ukraine to Moscow; and
Gippius after World War II, when he moved from St. Petersburg to Moscow. They

sought to be critical of all published material and pay special attention to performers and their knowledge of traditions under study. Since the 1940s, they taught at the Moscow Conservatory. Their most significant period was the 1970s and 1980s, when Borislava Efimenkova (1933–1996) and other ethnomusicologists at the Musical-Pedagogical Institute Named after the Gnesins became Gippius's students. As a result, their school has two particular features: first, their fieldwork is purposefully directed to particular Russian localities and traditions, with no generalizations beyond the local material; second, their notations and analyses focus on the structural and compositional coordination between words and music, with an emphasis on rhythmic structure, rather than melody—a discipline that might be called philological ethnomusicology.

A third eddy, which might be called empirical ethnomusicology, includes people who collect material without generalizing or reflecting much on methodologies—for example, the collections of Natalya Kotikova (1909–1981) and a recent, important collection by Elena Razumovskaya (1998).

The post-Soviet period

The post-Soviet period of Russian ethnomusicology is marked by an extension of fieldwork into the archaic layers of Russian traditional (mainly peasant) culture, their local (dialectal) investigation, and the study of formerly banned genres—for example, spiritual verses with religious content. Whereas, in the oral traditions of modern life, Russian folkloristics has begun to concern itself with modern genres and sexual and political issues, Russian academic ethnomusicologists remain more attracted to the history and dialectology of ethnic music and to the oldest systems of musical performance and the traditional bearers of these systems. This research is being published in *Russkii Fol'klor* (St. Petersburg), *Musical Academy,* and, since 1994, *Zhivaia Starina* ('Living Antiquity', Moscow). Grants from abroad have enabled the publication of new collections and monographs. A new textbook, *Ethnosolfège on the Data of Russian Village Traditional Song,* was published in 1996 by Mikhail Lobanov.

BIBLIOGRAPHY

Alekseeva, Galina. 1983. *Drevnerusskoe pevcheskoe iskusstvo: muzykal'naia organizatsiia znamennogo rospeva* (Ancient Russian liturgical art: The musical structure of chanting by signs). Vladivostok: Izdatel'stvo Dalnevostochnogo universiteta.

Almeeva, Naila. 1986. "Pesennaia kul'tura tatar-kriashen: zhanrovaia sistema i mnogogolosie" (The song art of the Tatar-Kriashen: Generic system and polyphony). Ph.D. dissertation, Russian Institute for the History of the Arts.

———, ed. 1989. *Traditsionnaia muzyka narodov Povolzh'ia i Priural'ia: voprosy teorii i istorii* (Traditional music of the peoples of the Volga and the Urals: Problems of theory and history). Kazan: Academy of Sciences.

———. 1990. "Traditsiia gostevogo obshcheniia u tatar-kriashen" (The tradition of guest relationships of the Tatar-Kriashen). In *Zrelishchno-igrovye formy narodnoi kul'tury* (Spectacle-game forms of folk culture), ed. Larisa Ivleva, 180–191. Leningrad: Ministry of Culture.

Arom, Simha, and Christian Meyer, eds. 1993. *Les Polyphonies populaires russes.* Edited by Anne-Helene Trottier. Paris: Éditions Creaphis (with accompanying compact disc).

Asaf'ev, Boris. 1952–1957. *Izbrannye trudy* (Selected works). 5 vols. Moscow: Akademia Nauk S.S.S.R.

———. 1953. *Russian Music from the Beginning of the Nineteenth Century.* Translated by Alfred J. Swan. Ann Arbor: J. W. Edwards, for the American Council of Learned Societies.

———. 1982. *A Book about Stravinsky.* Translated by Richard F. French. Introduction by Robert Craft. Russian Music Studies, 5. Ann Arbor: UMI Research Press.

———. 1987. *O narodnoi muzyke* (On folk music). Reconstructed and edited by Izaly Zemtsovsky and Alma Kunanbaeva. Leningrad: Muzyka.

Astakhova, Anna. 1951. *Byliny Severa* (The Bylinas of the North). Vol. 2. Moscow-Leningrad: Akademiya Nauk S.S.S.R.

Bachinskaya, Nina, comp. 1962. *Narodnye pesni v tvorchestve russkikh kompozitorov* (Folk songs in Russian composers' creations). Moscow: Muzgiz.

Bailey, James. 1993. *Three Russian Lyric Folk-Song Meters.* Columbus, Ohio: Slavica Publishers.

Bailey, James, and Tatyana Ivanova. 1998. *An Anthology of Russian Folk Epics.* New York: M. E. Sharpe.

Balakirev, Mily. 1957 [1866]. *Russkie narodnie pesni: dlia odnogo golosa s soprovozhdeniem fortepiano: redaktsiia, predislovie, issledovanie i primechaniia E. V. Gippiusa* (Russian folk songs: For solo voice with piano accompaniment: Edition, introduction, research, and commentary by Evgeny Gippius). Moscow: Muzgiz.

Balashov, Dmitry, Yury Marchenko, and Nina Kalmykova. 1985. *Russkaia svad'ba* (The Russian wedding). Moscow: Sovremennik.

Banin, Aleksandr. 1997. *Russkaia instrumental'naia muzyka fol'klornoi traditsii* (Russian instrumental music of the folkloric tradition). Moscow: Gosudarstvennii respublikanskii tsentr russkogo fol'klora.

Barsov, Elpidifor V. 1872. *Prichitaniia severnogo kraia* (Laments of the northern region). Vol. 1. Moscow: Tipografiia "Sovremennye izvestiia."

Batser, David, and Boleslav Rabinovich, eds. 1981, 1984. *Russkaia narodnaia muzyka: notograf-ficheskii ukazatel, 1776–1973* (Russian folk music: Index, 1776–1973). 2 vols. Moscow: Sovetskii kompozitor.

Beliaev, Viktor. 1990. *Viktor Mikhailovich Beliaev: 1888–1968: Izbrannoe* (Viktor Mikhailovich Beliaev: 1888–1968: Selected works). Compiled by Aleks Beliaev. Edited by Irina Travina. Moscow: Sovetskii kompozitor.

Beregovsky, Moshe. 1982. *Old Jewish Folk Music: The Collections and Writings.* Edited by Mark Slobin. Philadelphia: University of Pennsylvania Press.

———. 1987. *Evreiskaia narodnaia instrumental'naia musyka* (Jewish folk-instrumental music). Edited by Max Goldin. Moscow: Sovetskii kompozitor.

Bogdanova, Anna. 1995. *Muzyka i vlast': poststalinskii period* (Music and authority: The post-Stalin period). Moscow: Nasledie.

Boiarkin, Nikolai. 1981, 1984, 1988. *Pamiatniki mordovskogo narodnogo muzykal'nogo iskusstva* (Monuments of the Mordvinian folk-musical art). 3 vols. Saransk: Academy of Sciences.

———. 1983. *Mordovskoe narodnoe muzykal'noe iskusstvo* (The Mordvinian folk-musical art). Saransk: Knizhnoe isdatel'stvo.

———. 1995. "Fenomen traditsionnogo instrumental'nogo mnogogolosiia: na materiale mordovskoi muzyki" (The phenomenon of traditional instrumental polyphony: On the basis of Mordvinian music). Doctor's dissertation, Russian Institute for the History of the Arts.

Boikova, Elena, and Tatyana Vladykina. 1992. *Pesni iuzhnykh udmurtov* (Songs of the south Urdmurts). Vol. 1. Izhevsk: Academy of Sciences.

Brazhnik, Larisa, Naila Almeeva, Aleksandr Makligin, and Shamil Monasipov, eds. 1995. *Pentatonika v kontekste mirovoi muzykal'noi kul'tury* (Pentatonicism in the context of world-musical culture). Kazan: State Conservatory and the Academy of Sciences.

Brazhnikov, Maksim. 1972. *Drevnerusskaia teoriia muzyki: po rukopisnym materialam XV–XVIII vv.* (Ancient Russian theory of music: On manuscript material of the fifteenth to eighteenth centuries). Moscow: Muzyka.

Brill, Nicholas. 1980. *History of Russian Church Music: 988–1917.* Bloomington: Indiana University Press.

Brown, Malcolm, ed. 1984. *Russian and Soviet Music: Essays for Boris Schwarz.* Russian Music Studies, 11. Ann Arbor: UMI Research Press.

Campbell, Stuart, ed. and trans. 1994. *Russians on Russian Music, 1830–1880: An Anthology.* Cambridge and New York: Cambridge University Press.

Cherednichenko, Tatyana. 1994. *Tipologiia sovetskoi massovoi kul'tury: mezhdu "Brezhnevym" i "Pugachevoi"* (The typology of Soviet mass culture: Between Brezhnev and Pugacheva). Moscow: RIK "Kul'tura."

Chistalev, Prometei. 1980. *Die Musikinstrumente der permischen Völker.* Syktyvkar: Academy of Sciences.

———. 1984. *Komi narodnye muzykal'nye instrumenty* (Komi folk-musical instruments). Syktyvkar: Knizhnoe isdatel'stvo.

Cui, Cesar. 1993 [1896]. *Russkii romans* (The Russian romance). Translated by James Walker. Classical Essays on the Development of the Russian Art Song, and Twenty-Seven Outstanding Russian Romances of the Eighteenth and Nineteenth Centuries. Nerstrand, Minn.: James Walker.

Cushman, Thomas. 1995. *Notes from the Underground: Rock Music Counterculture in Russia.* Albany: State University of New York Press.

Danilov, Kirsha. 1977. *Drevnie rossiiskie stikhotvoreniia* (Ancient Russian verses). 2d ed. Edited by Alexandra Evgeneva and Boris Putilov. Moscow and Leningrad: Nauka.

Dobrovol'sky, Boris, and Vsevolod Korguzalov. 1981. *Byliny: Russkii muzykal'nyi epos* (Byliny: Russian musical epics). Moscow: Sovetskii kompozitor.

Dobrovol'sky, Boris, and Aleksei Soimonov. 1956. *Russkie narodnie pesni o krest'ianskikh voinakh i vosstaniiakh* (Russian folk songs about peasant wars and revolts). Moscow: Akademia Nauk SSSR.

Dolskaya, Olga, ed. 1995. *Vasily Titov and the Russian Baroque: Selected Choral Works.* Monuments of Russian Sacred Music, series 13, vol. 1. Madison, Conn.: Musica Russica.

———, ed. 1996. *Spiritual Songs in Seventeenth-Century Russia: Edition of the MS 1938 from Muzejnoe Sobranie of the State Historical Muzeum in Moscow (GIM).* Bausteine zur slavischen Philologie und Kulturgeschichte, series B, new series, vol. 4. Cologne: Bohlau.

Efimenkova, Borislava. 1980. *Severnorusskaia prichet* (North Russian laments). Moscow: Sovetskii kompozitor.

———. 1993. *Ritmika russkikh narodnykh pesen* (The rhythm of Russian folk songs). Moscow: Institut kultury imeni Gnesinykh, Rossiiskaia Akademia Muzyki.

Engovatova, Margarita. 1989. "Dvukhgolosie s podvodkoi v kul'ture russkoi liricheskoi pesni" (Two-part singing with *podvodka* in the culture of Russian lyric songs). In *Pesennoe mnogogolosie narodov Rossii* (Song polyphony of the peoples of Russia), 23–27. Moscow-Voronezh: Union of Composers.

Famintsyn, Aleksandr. 1995 [1889]. *Skomorokhi na Rusi* (The Russian minstrels). St. Petersburg: Aleteiia.

Feigin, Leo, ed. 1985. *Russian Jazz: New Identity.* London and New York: Quartet Books.

Findeizen, Nikolai. In press. [1928–1929]. *Ocherki po istorii muzyki v Rossii s drevneishikh vremen do kontsa XVIII veka* (Sketches of the history of music in Russia from the most ancient times until the end of the eighteenth century). 2 vols. Moscow and Leningrad: Muzgiz. English translation by S. W. Pring. Edited, with addenda and comments, by Milos Velimirovic and Claudia Jensen.

———. 1993 [1904]. *Russkaia khudozhestvennaia pesnia* (The Russian art song). Translated by James Walker. Classical Essays on the Development of the Russian Art Song, and Twenty-Seven Outstanding Russian Romances of the Eighteenth and Nineteenth Century. Nerstrand, Minn.: James Walker.

Geldern, James von, and Richard Stites, eds. 1995. *Mass Culture in Soviet Russia: Tales, Poems, Songs, Movies, Plays, and Folklore, 1917–1953.* Bloomington: Indiana University Press.

Gerasimowa-Persidskaya, Nina, ed. 1993. *Altrussische Musik: Einführung in ihre Geschichte und Probleme.* Grazer musikwissenschaftliche Arbeiten, 10. Graz: Akademische Druk- u. Verlagsanstalt.

———. 1994. *Russkaia muzyka XVII veka: vstrecha dvukh epokh* (Seventeenth-century Russian music: The conjunction of two epochs). Moscow: Muzyka.

Gippius, Evgeny. 1936. "Intonatsionnye elementy russkoi chastushki" (The intonational elements of Russian short ditties). *Sovetskii Fol'klor* 4–5:97–142.

———. 1979. *Dvadtsat' russkikh narodnykh pesen v rannkh zvukozaposiakh: 1897–1935* [Twenty Russian folk songs in the early phonorecords: 1897–1935]. Moscow: Sovetskii Kompozitor.

Gippius, Evgeny, and Zinaida Evald, eds. 1937. *Pesni Pinezh'ia: materialy fonogram-arkhiva* (The Pinega songs: The Phonogram-Archive's material). Vol. 2. Moscow: Gosudarstvennoe Muzykal'noe Izdatel'stvo.

———. 1989. *Udmurtskie narodnye pesni* (Udmurt folk songs). Izhevsk: Academy of Sciences.

Goldin, Max. 1989. *On Musical Connections between Jews and the Neighboring Peoples of Eastern and Western Europe.* Translated and edited by Robert Rothstein. Amherst: University of Massachusetts at Amherst.

Granovsky, Bernard. 1998. *Pesni pevtsov-samorodkov Ivana Fomina i Ivana Molchanova v sobranii V. F. Odoevskogo* (Songs of the born singers Ivan Fomin and Ivan Molchanov in the collection of Vladimir Odoevsky). Moscow: Gosudarstvennyi Fol'klornyi Tsentr "Russkaia pesnia."

Grigor'eva, Inga. 1995. *Muzykal'naia kul'tura ingermanlandskikh finnov vtoroi poloviny 19 i 20 stoletii* (Musical culture of the Ingermanland Finns of the second half of the nineteenth and twentieth centuries). St. Petersburg: Bukva.

Imkhanitsky, Mikhail. 1987. *U istokov russkoi narodnoi orkestrovoi kul'tury* (The origins of the Russian folk-instrument-orchestra tradition). Moscow: Muzyka.

Keldysh, Yury. 1965. *Russkaia muzyka XVIII veka* (Russian music of the eighteenth century). Moscow: Nauka.

Kondrat'ev, Mikhail. 1990. *O ritme chuvashskoi narodnoi pesni: k probleme kvantitativnosti v narodnoi muzyke* (On the rhythm of Chuvash folk song: Toward the problem of quantitativeness in folk music). Moscow: Sovetskii kompozitor.

Konen, Valentina. 1994. *Tretii plast: novye massovye zhanry v muzyke XX veka* (The third layer: New mass genres in the music of the twentieth century). Moscow: Muzyka.

Korguzalov, Vsevold, and Elena Troitskaya. 1993. "The Phonogram Archive of the Institute of Russian Literature (Pushkin House) of the Russian Academy of Sciences, St. Petersburg." *The World of Music* 35(1):115–120.

Kotikova, Natalia, comp. 1961. *Russkie chastushki, stradaniia, pripevki* (Russian short ditties, "sufferings," and *pripevki*). Leningrad: Muzgiz.

———. 1966. *Narodnye pesni Pskovskoi oblasti* (Folk songs of the Pskov district). Moscow: Muzyka.

Krasnopolskaya, Tamara, comp. 1987. *Pesni Zaonezh'ia v zapisiakh 1880–1980 godov* (Songs of the Onega region in recordings from 1880 to 1980). Leningrad: Sovetskii kompozitor.

Kremlev, Yuly, 1954–1960. *Russkaia mysl' o muzyke* (Russian thought on music). 3 vols. Moscow: Muzyka.

Lapin, Viktor. 1995. *Russkii muzykal'nyi fol'klor i istoria: k fenomenologii muzykal'nykh traditsii: ocherki i etiudy* (Russian musical folklore and history: Toward a phenomenology of musical traditions: Sketches and studies). Moscow: Russkaia Pesnia.

Lineva, Evgeniya, ed. 1905–1912. *The Peasant Songs of Great Russia as They Are in the Folk's Harmonization*. St. Petersburg: Imperial Academy of Science. London: D. Nutt.

Lobanov, Mikhail, ed. 1996a. *Ekspeditsionnye otkrytiia poslednikh let: Narodnaia muzyka v zapisiakh 1970–1990-kh godov* (Fieldwork discoveries of the latest summer: Folk music in recordings of the 1970s to the 1990s). St. Petersburg: Institut istorii iskusstv.

———. 1996b. *Etnosol'fedzhio na materiale traditsionnoi pesni russkoi derevni: uchebnoe posobie dlia starshikh klassov detskikh muzykal'nykh shkol i srednikh spetsial'nykh uchebnykh zavedenii* (Ethnosolfège on the data of Russian village traditional song: For musical schools and colleges). St. Petersburg: Severnyi Olen'.

———. 1997. *Lesnye klichi: vokalnye melodii-signaly na severo-zapade Rossii* (Forest calls: Vocal melody-signals in northwest Russia). St. Petersburg: Izdatel'stvo S.-Peterburgskogo Universiteta.

———, et al., ed. 1998. *Nizhegorodskaia svad'ba: Pushkinskiie mesta— Nizhegorodskoie povolzh'e— Vetluzhskii krai: obriady, pesni, prichitaniia, prigovory* (The Nizhnii Novgorod Wedding: Pushkin places—Nizhnii Novgorod Povolzh'e—Vetluga District: Rites, songs, laments, sayings). St. Petersburg: Kultinformpress.

Lopatin, Nikolai, and Vasily Prokunin. 1956 [1889]. *Russkie narodnye liricheskie pesni: opyt sistematicheskogo svoda liricheskikh pesen* (Russian folk lyric songs: The experience of the systematic *svod* of lyric songs). Moscow: Muzgiz.

Lvov, Nikolai, and Ivan Prach. 1987 [1790]. *Sobranie russkikh narodnykh pesen s ikh golosami* (A collection of Russian folk songs with their tunes).

Edited by Malcolm Brown. Introduction and appendices by Margarita Mazo. Classics of Russian Musical Folklore in Facsimile, Russian Music Studies, 13. Ann Arbor: UMI Research Press.

Maslov, Aleksandr. 1911. "Byliny, ikh proiskhozhdenie, ritmicheskii i melodicheskii sklad" (*Byliny,* their genesis, rhythmic and melodic structure). In *Trudy Muzykal'no-Etnograficheskoi Kommissii,* 2:299–329. Moscow: University Publishers.

Matsievsky, Igor, ed. 1987–1988. *Narodnye muzykal'nye instrumenty i instrumental'naia muzyka* (Folk-musical instruments and instrumental music). 2 vols. Edited by Evgeny Gippius. Moscow: Sovetskii kompozitor.

McQuere, Gordon, ed. 1983. *Russian Theoretical Thought in Music.* Russian Music Studies, 10. Ann Arbor: UMI Research Press.

Melgunov, Yuly. 1879, 1885. *Russkiie piesni: dlia fortepiano v 2 ruki neposredstvenno s golosov naroda zapisannye i s ob'iasneniiami izdannye* (Russian songs: For two-handed piano recorded directly from people's voices and published with comments). Part 1: Moscow: Tipografia E. Lissner i IU. Roman. Part 2: St. Petersburg: V. Bessel'.

Mischakoff, Anne. 1983. *Khandoshkin and the Beginning of Russian String Music.* Russian Music Studies, 9. Ann Arbor: UMI Research Press.

Morgenstern, Ulrich. 1995. *Volksmusikinstrumente und instrumentale Volksmusik in Russland.* Studia Slavica Musicologica, 2. Berlin: E. Kuhn.

Morris, Jeremy. 1994. *The Russian Piano Concerto.* Bloomington: Indiana University Press.

Nestev, Izrail. 1974. *Zvezdy russkoi estrady: Panina, Vyal'tseva, Plevitskaya: ocherki o russkikh estradnykh pevitsakh nachala XX v.* (Stars of the Russian stage: Panina, Vyal'tseva, Plevitskaya: Sketches of Russian concert singers at the start of the twentieth century). 2d, supplementary ed. Moscow: Sovetskii kompozitor.

The New Grove Russian Masters. 1986. 2 vols. Glinka, Mikhail, 1804–1857; Borodin, Aleksandr, 1833–1887; Balakirev, Milii, 1837–1910; Mussorgsky, Modest, 1839–1881; Tchaikovsky, Peter, 1840–1893; Rimsky-Korsakov, Nikolay, 1844–1908; Scriabin, Aleksandr, 1872–1915; Rachmaninoff, Sergei, 1873–1943; Prokofiev, Sergei, 1891–1953; Shostakovich, Dmitrii, 1906–1975. New York: Norton.

Noebel, David. 1974. *The Marxist Minstrels: A Handbook on Communist Subversion of Music.* Tulsa: American Christian College Press.

Novikov, Anatoly, 1936–1937. *Russkie narodnye pesni* (Russian folk songs). 3 vols. Moscow: Gosudarstvennoe voennoe Izdatel'stvo narodnogo komissariata oborony SSSR.

Olkhovsky, Yury. 1983. *Vladimir Stasov and Russian National Culture.* Ann Arbor: Michigan University Press.

Pal'chikov, Nikolai. 1888. *Krest'ianskie pesni zapisannye v sele Nikolaevka Menzelinskogo uezda,*

Ufimskoi gubernii (Peasant songs recorded in Nikolaevka Village, Menzelinsk District, Ufa Region). St. Petersburg: A. E. Pal'chikov's Publishers.

Piatnitsky, Mitrofan. 1914. *Kontserty M. E. Piatnitskogo s krest'ianami* (The concerts of Mitrofan Piatnitsky with the peasants). Moscow: Robert Kents.

Pokrovsky, Dimitri. 1980. "Fol'klor i muzykal'noe vospriiatie" (Folklore and musical perception). In *Vospriiatie muzyki* (The perception of music), ed. Vladimir Maksimov, 244–256. Moscow: Muzyka.

Polyakova, Lyudmila. 1961. *La musique soviétique.* Moscow: Éditions en Langues Étrangères.

Porfireva, Anna, ed. 1996, 1998. *Muzykalnyi Peterburg: entsiklopedicheskii slovar'* (Musical St. Petersburg: An encyclopedic dictionary). Vol. 1. St. Petersburg: Kompozitor.

Porter, James, ed. 1997. *Folklore and Traditional Music in the Former Soviet Union and Eastern Europe.* Los Angeles: Department of Ethnomusicology, University of California, Los Angeles.

Pozdneev, Aleksandr. 1996. *Rukopisnye pesenniki XVII–XVIII vv.: iz istorii pesennoi sillabicheskoi poezii* (Songbook manuscripts of the seventeenth and eighteenth centuries: From the history of sung syllabic poetry). Moscow: Nauka.

Razumovskaya, Elena, ed. 1998. *Traditsionnaia muzyka russkogo Poozer'a: po materialam ekspeditsii 1971–1992 godov* (Traditional music of Russian Poozer'ye: In fieldwork material from 1971 to 1992). Supplement in 3 cassettes. St. Petersburg: Kompozitor.

Rubtsov, Feodosy. 1973. *Stati po muzykal'nomu fol'kloru* (Articles on musical folklore). Leningrad: Sovetskii kompozitor.

Rudneva, Anna. 1975. *Kurskie tanki i karagody* (Russian circle dances of Kursk). Moscow: Sovetskii kompozitor.

Rudneva, Anna, Vyacheslav Shchurov, and Svetlana Pushkina. 1979. *Russkie narodnye pesni v mnogomikrofonnoi zapisi* (Russian folk songs in multimicrophone recording). Moscow: Sovetskii kompozitor.

———. 1994. *Russkoe narodnoe muzykal'noe tvorchestvo: ocherki po teorii fol'klora* (Russian folk-musical creation: Sketches on the theory of folklore). Edited by Natalia Giliarova and Larisa Kostiukovets. Moscow: Kompozitor.

Rüütel, Ingrid, ed. 1977. *Muzykal'noe nasledie finno-ugorskikh narodov* (The musical legacy of the Finno-Ugric peoples). Tallinn: Eesti raamat.

———. 1980. *Finno-ugorskii muzykal'nyi fol'klor i vzaimosviazi s sosednimi kul'turami* (Finno-Ugric musical folklore and interconnections with neighboring cultures). Tallinn: Eesti raamat.

———. 1986. *Muzyka v svadebnom obriade finno-ugrov i sosednikh narodov* (Music in the wedding rite of the Finno-Ugric and neighboring peoples). Tallinn: Eesti raamat.

Sabaneev, Leonid. 1967. *Modern Russian Composers.* Freeport, N.Y.: Books for Libraries Press.

Saidasheva, Zemfira, ed. 1984. *Muzykal'nyi fol'klor i tvorchestvo kompozitorov Povolzh'ia* (Musical folklore and the Volga composers' art). Moscow: Musical-Pedagogical Institute Named after the Gnesins.

Schwarz, Boris. 1983. *Music and Musical Life in Soviet Russia: Enlarged Ed., 1917–1981.* Bloomington: Indiana University Press.

Serov, Aleksandr. 1955 [1869–1871]. "Das russische Volkslied als Gegenstand der Wissenschaft." In *Aufsätze zur Musikgeschichte,* by Alexander Serow [*sic*], 119–154. German edition edited by Nathan Notowicz. Translated by Felix Loesch. Berlin: Aufbau-Verlag.

Shamina, Lyudmila. 1997. *Shkola russkogo narodnogo peniia* (The school of Russian folksinging). Moscow: Russkaia pesnia.

Shchurov, Vyacheslav. 1987. *Iuzhnorusskaia pesennaia traditsiia* (The South-Russian song tradition). Moscow: Sovetskii kompozitor.

Shivlianova, Viktoriia. 1990. *Muzyka "Dzhangara": Sbornik epicheskikh napevov* (Dzhángar music: A collection of epic tunes). Elista: Kalmyk Book Publishers.

Sitsky, Larry. 1994. *Music of the Repressed Russian Avant-Garde, 1900–1929.* Contributions to the Study of Music and Dance, 31. Westport, Conn.: Greenwood Press.

Slezkine, Yuri. 1994. *Arctic Mirrors: Russians and the Small Peoples of the North.* Ithaca, N.Y.: Cornell University Press.

Smith, Gerald. 1984. *Songs to Seven Strings: Russian Guitar Poetry and Soviet "Mass" Song.* Bloomington: Indiana University Press.

Sokalsky, Piotr. 1888. *Russkaia narodnaia muzyka Velikorusskaia i Malorusskaia v ee stroenii melodicheskom i ritmicheskom i otlichiia ee ot osnov sovremennoi garmonicheskoi muzyki* (Great Russian and Little Russian folk music in its melodic and rhythmic structure and its distinction from the fundamentals of modern harmonic music). Kharkov: Tipografiia Adolfa Darre.

Sokhor, Arnold. 1959. *Russkaia sovetskaia pesnia* (Russian soviet song). Leningrad: Sovetskii kompozitor.

Starr, S. Frederic. 1994. *Red and Hot: The Fate of Jazz in the Soviet Union, 1917–1991.* New York: Limelight Editions.

Stasov, Vladimir. 1980. *Selected Essays on Music.* Translated by Florence Jonas. Introduced by Gerald Abraham. New York: Da Capo Press.

Stockmann, Erich, and Hermann Strobach, eds. 1967. *Sowjetische Volkslied- und Volksmusikforschung.* Ausgewählte Studien in Zusammenarbeit mit Kirill Cistov und Eugen Hippius [*sic*]. Berlin: Akademie-Verlag.

Stupel, Aleksandr. 1980. *Russkaia mysl' o muzyke: 1895–1917* (Russian thought on music: 1895–1917). Leningrad: Muzyka.

Swan, Alfred. 1973. *Russian Music and Its Sources in Chant and Folk-Song.* London: J. Baker. New York: Norton.

Taneev, Sergei. 1909. *Podvizhnoi kontrapunkt strogogo pis'ma* [Mobile counterpoint in the strict style]. Leipzig: M. P. Beliaev.

———. 1994. *Die Lehre vom Kanon. Herausgegeben, aus dem Russischen ubersetzt und mit einem Vorwort sowie erganzenden Anmerkungen versehen von Andreas Wehrmeyer.* Berlin: E. Kuhn.

Taruskin, Richard. 1996. *Stravinsky and the Russian Traditions: A Biography of the Works through Mavra.* Berkeley: University of California Press. 2 vols.

———. 1997a. *Defining Russia Musically: Historical and Hermeneutical Essays.* Princeton, N.J.: Princeton University Press.

———. 1997b [1993]. *Mussorgsky: Eight Essays and an Epilogue.* Berkeley: University of California Press.

Tosin, Sergeu. 1998. *Kolokola i zvony v Rossii* [Bells and ringing in Russia]. Novosibirsk: Novonikolaevsk.

Tsukkerman, Viktor. 1957. *"Kamarinskaia" Glinki i ee traditsii v russkoi muzyke* (Glinka's *Kamarinskaia* and its traditions in Russian music). Moscow: Muzgiz.

Tull, James. 1977. "B. V. Asafev's Musical Form as a Process: Translation and Commentary in 3 Vols." Ph.D. dissertation, Ohio State Univerity.

Uspensky, Nikolay. 1971. *Obraztsy drevnerusskogo pevcheskogo iskusstva: muzykal'nyi material s istoriko-teoreticheskimi kommentariiami i illiustratsiiami* (Examples of ancient Russian liturgical art: musical material with historic-theoretical commentaries and illustrations). 2d, supplementary ed. Leningrad: Muzyka.

Vertkov, Konstantin. 1975. *Russkie narodnye muzykal'nye instrumenty* (Russian folk-musical instruments). Leningrad: Muzyka.

Vertkov, Konstantin, Georgy Blagodatov, and Elsa Iazovitskaia. 1975. *Atlas muzykal'nykh instrumentov narodov SSSR* (Atlas of the musical instruments of peoples of the U.S.S.R.). 2d ed. Moscow: Muzyka.

Vikár, László, and Gabor Bereczki. 1971. *Cheremis Folksongs.* Budapest: Académia Kiadó.

———. 1979. *Chuvash Folksongs.* Budapest: Académia Kiadó.

———. 1989. *Votyak Folksongs.* Budapest: Académia Kiadó.

Vinogradov, Viktor, ed. 1988. *Russkie pesennitsy nashikh dnei* (Russian folksingers of today). Narodnye pevtsy i muzykanty (Folksingers and instrumentalists), 11. Moscow: Sovetskii kompozitor.

Vulfius, Pavel. 1979. *Russkaia mysl' o muzykal'nom fol'klor: materialy i dokumenty* (Russian thought on musical folklore). Moscow: Muzyka.

Vysotsky, Vladimir. 1990. *Hamlet with a Guitar.* Compiled by Yuri Andreyev and Iosif

Boguslavsky. Translated by Sergei Roy. Moscow: Progress.

Warner, Elizabeth, and Evgeny Kustovskii. 1990. *Russian Traditional Folk Song.* Hull, England: Hull University Press.

Yanchuk, Nikolay. 1919. "O muzyke bylin v sviazi s istoriei ikh izucheniia" (On the music of *byliny* in connection with the history of their study). In *Russkaia ustnaia slovesnost'* (Russian oral literature), 2:527–570. Moscow: Sabashnikovykh.

Yoffe, Elkhonon. 1986. *Tchaikovsky in America: The Composer's Visit in 1891.* New York: Oxford University Press.

Zemtsovsky, Izaly. 1967a. *Russkaia protiazhnaia pesnia* (The Russian long-drawn-out song). Leningrad: Muzyka.

———. 1967b. *Toropetskie pesni: pesni rodiny M. Musorgskogo* (Songs of Toropets: Songs from M. Mussorgsky's homeland). Leningrad: Muzyka.

———. 1972. *Obraztsy narodogo mnogogolosiia* [Examples of (Russian) folk (song) polyphony]. Leningrad: Sovetskii kompozitor.

———. 1973. *Problemy muzykal'nogo fol'klora narodov SSSR* (Problems of musical folklore of the peoples of the U.S.S.R.). Moscow: Muzyka.

———. 1975. *Melodika kalendarnykh pesen* (The melodics of calendric songs). Leningrad: Muzyka.

———. 1978. *Fol'klor i kompozitor* (Folklore and the composer). Leningrad: Sovetskii kompozitor.

———, comp. and ed. 1982. *Narodnaia muzyka SSSR i sovremennost'* (Folk music and current lifestyles in the U.S.S.R.). Leningrad: Muzyka.

———. 1987. *Po sledam vesnianki iz fortepiannogo kontserta Petra Chaikovskogo: istoricheskaia morfologiia narodnoi pesni* (On the trail of the "Vesnianka" melody in Tchaikovsky's Piano Concerto: The historical morphology of the folk song). Leningrad: Muzyka.

———, comp. and ed. 1989. *Muzyka eposa* (Music of the epic). Yoshkar-Ola: Union of Composers.

———, comp. and ed. 1991. *Narodnaia muzyka SSSR: opyt diskografii* (Folk music of the U.S.S.R.: A discography). Moscow: Ministry of Culture.

———. 1994. *Jewish Folk Songs: An Anthology.* Compiled by Max Goldin. Commentary by Max Goldin and Izaly Zemtsovsky. Yiddish texts edited by Larisa Pecherskaya. St. Petersburg: Kompozitor.

———, comp. and ed. 1995. *Russkaia narodnaia pesnia: neizvestnye stranitsy muzykal'noi istorii* (The Russian folk song: The unknown pages of musical history). St. Petersburg: Institute for History of the Arts.

———. 1997. "An Attempt at a Synthetic Paradigm." *Ethnomusicology* 41(2):185–205.

AUDIOVISUAL RESOURCES

This discography lists only compact discs; for LP disks, see Zemtsovsky 1991.

Agafonnikov, Igor, artistic director. 1992. *Slavonic Farewell: The Alexandrov Choir Today.* Recorded in 1992 in Moscow. Album 1. LAD. MK 427064. Compact disc.

Asplund, Anneli, ed. 1995. *The Kalevala Heritage: Archive Recordings of Ancient Finnish, Karelian, and Inger Songs.* ODE 849–2. Compact disc.

Babkina, Nadezhda, director. 1995. *Shumel kamysh* (A reed makes a noise). Ensemble Russkaia Pesnia. Records Bekar (Sweden) SZCD 0299. Compact disc.

Boone, Hubert, and Elena Drozhzhina, eds. 1996. *Songs of the Volga: Traditional Music from Chuvashia and Mordovia.* Auvidis Ethnic B 6835. Compact disc.

Devyatov, Vladimir. 1993. *Russian Songs and Romances.* Russkie Napevy (Russian Tunes) Ensemble. Melodiya MEL CD 20 00686. Compact disc.

Dorokhova, Ekaterina. 1993. *Songs of the Earth: Narodnyi Prazdnik* (Folk holiday). Moscow Folk Ensemble. Russian Compact Disc RCD 17001. Compact disc.

Dorokhova, Ekaterina, and Tamara Pavlova, producers. 1994. *Songs of the Peoples of Russia: Regions of Briansk, Tula, Arkhangelsk, Sverdlovsk, and Others.* Le Chant du Monde CDM CMT 274978. Compact disc.

Georgevskaya, Marusya. 1992. *A Treasury of Russian Gypsy Songs.* Marusya Georgevskaya, vocals, and Sergei Krotkoff, guitar. Music of the World. Monitor International MCD 71565. Compact disc.

Horowitz, Joshua, ed. and performer. 1997. *Budowitz: Mother Tongue: Music of the 19th Century Klezmorim on Original Instruments.* Koch Schwann 3–1261–2 H1. Compact disc.

Howe, Jovan, comp. 1996. *Sinjie Lipjagi: Village of Blue Linden Trees.* Ethnic Series: South Russian Wedding. Recorded by Irina Raspopova and Jovan Howe in 1993. PAN and Paradox Records 2039CD. Compact disc.

Kuzma, Marika, director and producer. 1995. *Icons of Slavic Music: 17th to 20th Century Sacred Music from Ukraine and Russia.* Chamber Chorus of the University of California. Compact disc.

Lapin, Viktor. 1991. *Russian Northern Wedding: An Ancient Traditional Wedding Performance with Dialogues and Songs.* Recorded by Viktor Lapin in 1989. Melodiya Records SUCD 11–00325. Compact disc.

Lyadov, Anatoly. 1997. *Russian Folksongs: Three Symphonic Sketches: Baba-Yaga, Kikimora, The Enchanted Lake.* Arranged and composed by Anatoly Lyadov (1855–1914). Recorded in 1991 and 1996 in Moscow. Tradition and Fantasy of the Russian People. Harmonia Mundi HM 90. Russkii Sezon RUS 288 144. Compact disc.

Mazo, Margarita, comp. 1995. *Old Believers: Songs of the Nekrasov Cossacks.* Compiled and annotated by Margarita Mazo, with the assistance of Olga Velichkina. Smithsonian Folkways CD 40462. Compact disc.

Pokrovsky, Dmitri, director. N.d. *The Wild Field.* The Dmitry Pokrovsky Ensemble. Womad Production. RealWorld 91736–2. Compact disc.

Romodin, Aleksandr, director. N.d. *Igrai, dudka! Spiel, dudelsack! Play, Pipe!* Studio St. Petersburg. Notes in German by Ulrich Morgenstern. LuboMusik LBC 1001. LC 7154. Compact disc.

Saha, Hannu, and Kurt Lindblad, eds. 1994. *Teppo Repo, Shepherd's Musician: Herdsman's Music from Ingria.* Kaustinen, Finland: The Folk Music Institute KICD 7. Compact disc.

Sapoznick, Henry, ed. 1980. *Klezmer Music: Recordings from the YIVO Archives 1910–1942.* Global Village CD 104. Compact disc.

———. 1992. *Dave Tarras: Yiddish-American Klezmer Music 1925–1956.* Yazoo 7001. Compact disc.

Sapoznick, Henry, and Dick Spottswood, eds. 1993. *Klezmer Pioneers: European and American Recordings 1905–1952.* Rounder CD 1089. Compact disc.

Schwartz, Martin, ed. 1997. *Klezmer Music: Early Yiddish Instrumental Music: The First Recordings: 1908–1927.* Arhoolie Folklyric CD 7034. Compact disc.

Sedletsky, Georgii. 1993. *Russkie napevy* (Russian tunes). Recorded in 1993. Ensemble Korogod. Produced by Georgii Sedlesky. Anima Vox CDAV 91 7001 2, R-54001. Compact disc.

Shchurov, Viacheslav. 1991a. *Sigray, Vanya* (Play, Vanya). Folk instrumental music and its vocal counterpart in southern, western and central Russia. Recorded in 1968 and 1989. Ethnic Series. Produced by Vyacheslav Shchurov. PAN 2002CD. Compact disc.

———. 1991b. *Tam Letal Pavlin* (A peacock once went flying). Songs from Belgorod and the Oskol River (Belgorod Prioskolye). Recorded in 1967–1969 and 1982–1987. Produced by Vyacheslav Shchurov. Ethnic Series. PAN 2001CD. Compact disc.

———. 1997. *Solovka* (A little nightingale). The Moscow Folk Song Ensemble, directed by Vyacheslav Shchurov. Recorded in 1978–1985 and 1995. Choral Series. PAN 7008CD. Compact disc.

Sholokhova, Lydmila, ed. 1997. *Treasury of Jewish Culture in Ukraine: Reproduced from Phono Cylinders Recorded in 1912–1945.* Vol. 1. Vernadsky National Library of Ukraine. Institute for Information Recording. Compact disc.

Shurov, Vyacheslav, ed. 1995. *Chilik: Songs and Melodies of the Nagaybaks.* PAN Records 7003 CD. Compact disc.

Sysoeva, Galina, ed. 1997a. *Proleteli vse nashi goda* (The years have flown by). Sung by Folklore ensembles of Ilovka Village, Podserednee Belgorod, and of Pchelnikovka Village, Voronezh. Recorded in 1997. Voronezh: The Black Box Studio DDD 97340. Compact disc.

———, art director. 1997b. *V slavnom gorode Voronezhe* (In the glorious city of Voronezh). Sung by the Folklore Ensemble "Volya" of the Voronezh State Institute of the Arts. Recorded in 1997. Voronezh: The Black Box Studio. Produced by Tony Korologos. Fast Forward Recording DDD 97339. Compact disc.

Turovsky, Henrich, artistic director. 1997a. *The Karelian Folk Music Ensemble: Ingrian Folk Instruments.* Gadfly Records 501. Compact disc.

———. 1997b. *The Karelian Folk Music Ensemble: Ingian Folk Songs.* Gadfly Records 504. Compact disc.

Utesov, Leonid. 1995. *Vse pesni iz repertuara L. O. Utesova* (All the songs in the repertory of L. O. Utesov). Produced by Sergei Zhiltsov. Restoration by AnimaVox. Kominform-Tsentr KIC-R 00011–12–13–14. 4 compact discs.

Vikár, László, ed. 1995. *Music of the Tatar People.* Topic Records TSCD 912.

Vikár, László, and Gabor Bereczki, eds. 1996. *Finno-Ugrian and Turkic Melodies in the Volka-Kama Area. Selection from the Collection of László Vikár and Gabor Berecski, 1958–1979.* HCD 18229.

Vysotsky, Vladimir, author-performer. 1987. *Vladimir Vysotsky.* With 72-page booklet. New York: Apollon Foundation. 7 LP disks.

Zina. 1993. *Sing, Gypsy! Zina Pavlova Sings Russian-Gypsy Songs and the Balalaika of Sasha Polinoff with the Russian-Gypsy Ensemble of Kostya Poliansky.* Music of the World. Monitor International MCD 71475. Compact disc.

Belarus

Zinaida Mozheiko
Maria Paula Survilla

The Rural Song Tradition
Instrumental Folk Music
History of Music
Urban Music
History of Scholarship

Modern-day Belarus lies at the eastern threshold of Europe. Its area, 207,599 square kilometers, is bordered by Russia to the east, Lithuania to the northwest, Latvia to the north, Ukraine to the south, and Poland to the west. Of the 10,400,000 inhabitants, 1.8 million live in the capital, Miensk. Major urban centers comprise 67 percent of the population; the remainder live in rural areas, villages, and small towns.

The ethnic foundation of Belarus is defined by the ancient settlements of the eastern Slavic tribes: Kryvichans, Drehavichans, and Radzimichans. As part of the Grand Duchy of Litva (with Samogitia), Belarus experienced a golden era between the fifteenth and the seventeenth centuries, when scholarship, the arts, and religious freedom flourished, with Belarusan the official language. This period is best reflected in the art and writing of Frančišak Skaryna (1490–1552), the first Eastern European printer, who remains a prominent and celebrated symbol in Belarusan history. In 1569, Belarus entered a commonwealth with the Kingdom of Poland to strengthen its stand against Russia. With the final partition of this commonwealth in 1795, Belarus was colonized as a province of Russia. The eighteenth century saw cultural and religious persecution in Belarus, including the prohibition of the Belarusan language. By the mid-nineteenth century, despite Russian censorship, Belarusan literature and history were inspiring new generations. The early twentieth century is marked by the Naša Niva period, which produced two of Belarus's most important writers, Janka Kupala and Jacub Kolas. The first declaration of independence in modern times took place on 25 March 1918, but was overturned by the Bolsheviks in 1919 with the creation of the Byelorussian Soviet Socialist Republic (B.S.S.R.). Under the Soviets, Belarus experienced censorship and the devaluing of its culture which persisted only among the intelligentsia and in grass-roots communities. State sovereignty was declared on 27 July 1990, followed by a declaration of independence on 25 August 1991.

THE RURAL SONG TRADITION

The song tradition of Belarus can be divided into music reflecting three main historical periods. The oldest songs are found in seasonal and family-ritual cycles. A second

FIGURE 1 A girl dressed as a mermaid (*rusalka*) for the calendrical celebration of the beginning of summer. Damamierka, southeastern Belarus, July 1993. Photo courtesy of Maria Paula Survilla.

set of material—nonritual songs—developed between 1400 and 1700. A third set developed as an urban style in the nineteenth century.

The calendric song cycle

As elsewhere in Europe, village singing in Belarus was once governed by seasonal song cycles. During the twentieth century, as agricultural practices changed, the songs linked to those practices became symbols of the seasons and seasonal work, supported by memory, tradition, and performance practices linked to ritual repertoires and customs. The winter song cycle includes carols (*kaladki*) and *ščadroŭki*, songs originally sung during the celebration of the winter solstice, which later were sung at Christmas. The spring song cycle consists of *Maśleničnyja pieśni*, performed the day after Ash Wednesday, mainly on swings; *zaklikańnie viasny*, invoking the spring season; *vałačobnyja pieśni*, performed by singers wandering in groups from village to village originally announcing spring, later Easter, St. George's Day (*Jurjeŭskija*), and Trinity (*Troickija*), including the so-called bush (*kust*) songs, for which on Pentecost (*Zialonyja śviatki* or *Siomucha*), a girl clothed in greenery is taken around the village; and *rusalnyja pieśni* 'water-nymph songs' (figure 1). The summer cycle includes *kupalskija pieśni*, songs celebrating the summer solstice (*Kupalle*), harvesting songs (*žniŭnyja pieśni*), and end-of-harvest songs (*dažynačnyja pieśni*).

FIGURE 2   Women from Jelck, Paleśśie, sing harvest songs for the taping of the Belarusan television program "Viacorki," July 1993. Photo courtesy of Maria Paula Survilla.

Autumn songs include *jaravyja pieśni,* sung during the harvest of the spring sowing; *lnovyja,* sung during the flax harvest; and *vasieńnija pieśni* 'general autumn songs' (figure 2).

The agricultural calendric tradition also includes spring and summer round dances (*karahody*). In the southern Belarusan tradition, playful winter songs are associated with the main character of the caroling masquerades, the goat; in the northern Belarusan tradition, with the comic game Tereshka's marriage (*žanićba Ciareśki*), in which a symbolic mother and father, chosen from the older members of the community, pair young unmarried men and women and "marry" them. The women run from the men, who pursue them. The game includes various dances, especially the *biarozka,* the *byńk,* and polkas. Spring, summer, and autumn team songs (*tałočnyja pieśni*) are performed by groups gathered to help fellow farmers.

The agricultural calendar cycle also comprises ancient epic and lyrical songs that coincide with an appointed time, place, or symbolic circumstance. These include the so-called pre-Christmas songs (*Pilipaŭskija pieśni*), performed throughout Advent, when celebrations and weddings were banned by the church and women sang while spinning linen at night. Other agrarian calendrical songs include songs for haying (*sienakosnyja*), weeding (*prapołačnyja*), and pasture (*paśbišča*), and songs for meadow (*łuhovyja*), field (*palavyja*), and forest (*lesavyja*), sung respectively in meadows, fields, and forests.

The seasonal agricultural songs interweave themes of work with those of everyday life, pagan celebrations, historical themes in the carols, antifeudal themes in harvest songs, and ballad themes in summer-solstice songs. The imagery and poetic description contained in such texts communicate the mood of each calendrical moment. Spring songs evoke picturesque colors, but the autumn songs are melancholy and psychologically profound. The emotional intensity and refined poetic expression draw upon vivid and clear sketches of nature, for example, the endless fields and unrelenting scorching sun of the harvest songs. The agricultural song cycle ends with the autumn songs and begins the new year with carols.

Compared to nonritual lyrical songs, calendric songs are not simply sung, but rather arise in consciousness, as if spontaneously, at a certain time. The special significance of these songs, the solemnity of their performance, and their high social status

FIGURE 3   The singer Evdokim Markević, the duct flute (*dudka*) player Vasil' Sved, and the fiddler Mihail Skodun perform at a wedding in Paleśsie. Photo by Zinaida Mozheiko, 1986.

are emphasized in the poetic texts of the rituals, for example, in the "wandering" spring songs (*vałačobnyja pieśni*), when the singers address the head of the household: "But we, infrequent guests, / Can come only once a year."

Songs in the family-ritual cycle

The family-ritual cycle includes wedding songs, birth songs, and funeral laments. Lullabies may also be classified within this cycle.

Wedding songs (*viasielnyja pieśni*) accompany all stages of the wedding ritual: the engagement; the preparation of the round wedding bread (*karavaj* 'ritual bread'); the bridal fair (*dziavočnik, subornaja subota, "na viankach"*), when the girls gather the day before the wedding; the groom riding out to the bride; the unbraiding of the bride's hair; when an orphaned bride is given away; the bride's farewell to her parents' home; the weeping lament of the bride and sometimes of her mother; the ride to and from the wedding ceremony; the exchange of the wreath for the married woman's headdress at the groom's home; the division of the wedding bread; the eating of the feast; and the matchmakers' numerous tableside comic squabbles, in which some sing while others add exclamations to the musical texture.

The diversity of wedding songs can be narrowed to three emotional and conceptual frameworks: festive songs, including opening songs, with an appeal to the god of marriage, Kuzma-Demian, the praise of the bride and groom, and songs around the round wedding bread; lyrical dramatic songs, including the engagement, the bridal fair, the marriage of the orphan, the bride's farewell to her parents' home, and her lament; and comic songs, associated with the matchmakers' ritual laughing contests and the bride's and groom's wedding parties (figure 3).

Birth songs (*radzilnyja pieśni*) include ritual praises of the parents of the newborn and the midwife, and comic songs addressing the midwife and the godparents. Most songs of this cycle are table songs (*biasiednyja pieśni*).

Laments (*hałaśeńni*) in Belarus derive their name from the word *hałaśić* 'to voice one's grief'. They are improvisatory dramatic recitatives, performed for the death of a loved one. Besides funeral laments, Belarusan folklore includes marriage and social laments, for example, ones performed after a fire. There once existed army-recruitment laments, which are now completely forgotten. During disastrous periods, laments were revived in the form of collective wailing (*kalektyŭnaje hałaśeńnie*), which reappeared during World War II in the form of collective mourning for Soviet soldiers, partisans, and inhabitants of burned villages. After the Chernobyl catastrophe of 1986, a collective lament arose in southern and eastern Belarus for lost land and forests polluted by radioactivity.

The determining trait of the agricultural-calendar songs and the family-ritual cycle is their strict association with a season or circumstance. Originally governed by the corresponding ritual function, the songs are now performed according to seasonal associations and traditions. Established melodic formulas are condensed into multitexted melodies to suit the diverse poetic texts of a given genre. Each melody carries symbolic meaning, for example, of spring or the harvest. Village folksingers, the repositories of folklore tradition, understand these formulas as songs, and as referencing many aspects of life and belief.

Ritual song forms and singing styles

Calendric and family-ritual songs, based on ancient forms with a narrow melodic range and short strophic forms, draw expressive strength from the subtleties of each melodic detail and the dramaturgical significance of every aspect of musical expression: melody with rhythmic subtleties, ornamental detail, and timbre. The manner of performance, which has evolved into a stylistic school of vocal singing (*hałasnoha śpievu* 'open-air singing', or by folk definition *na voli* 'singing freely'), includes reso-

Clear, loud singing in the open air has its own aesthetic rules and criteria, such as the ability to "hold the voice for a while" (to sing long-drawn-out tones on a deep breath) and to "lift a song" (to sing it with a clear lead).

nant exclamations and a glissando completion of phrases or melodic strophes, particularly in spring songs. An important role is played by nontextual elements, including ritual noises: knocking, jingling, verbal shouting, and body movement, such as foot stomping in carols and wedding songs.

The melodies of these songs can be subdivided into two types. Songs of the first type are declamatory with a narrow or medium range (a third, often with a fourth and a fifth), and have defined rhythmic patterns depending on the syllabic structure of a verse. Lines with 5 + 5 syllables with a prolongation of the last syllables are typical of carols, but lines with 5 + 3 syllables with prolongations at the end of each phrase are typical of wedding songs. Melodies of this type are found mainly in festive "walkabout" songs (*abchodnyja pieśni*), sung while villagers make the rounds of their neighbors' homesteads (in winter caroling and in spring "wandering" songs), round dances (*karahody*), numerous wedding songs, and some birth, spring, and summer-solstice songs. Songs of the second type have a narrow range and harmonic structures similar to those of the first type, but seem more developed, thanks to the flexibility of the melodic line, with extended end-of-phrase drones (in southern Belarus, the fermata may last more than twenty beats), expressive melismas, and partly improvised rhythmic structures, which gracefully soften the distinct pulses of the syllabic structure. In addition to harvest songs (the most characteristic of this type), this type comprises most autumn songs and some spring- and summer-solstice songs and wedding songs. The lament genre includes tensely improvised recitations resembling natural weeping, as in funeral laments (*pachavalnyja hałašeńni*), and stable verse structures whose melodic-rhythmic form suggests a songlike character, as in wedding laments (*viasielnyja halašeńni*).

Except for ritual ceremonial songs, such as "wandering" songs and carols sung mainly by men, the calendric and family-ritual songs are typically monophonic and are performed by a group or solo, mainly by women. As a rule, group singing is heterophonic and especially elaborate in the south. There are two types of heterophonic song: dissonant two-part singing (figure 4) and multirhythmic monody, in which the

FIGURE 4 Two slightly varied verses of a narrow-range melody that features dissonant polyphony based on seconds, from southwestern Belarus. Transcription by Zinaida Mozheiko.

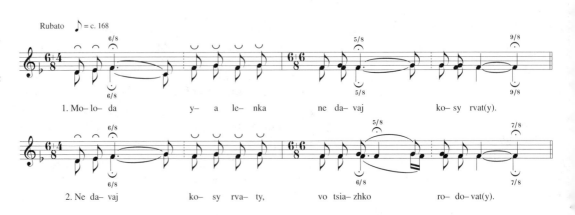

FIGURE 5 A Christmas carol (*kaladka*) from western Belarus, sung heterophonically. Transcription by Zinaida Mozheiko.

Oj, pod ga— i— kom, pod zia—lye— ne—n'kim ko—lia— do, pod zia—lye— nen'— kim, ko—lia— do!

divergence from unison arises from variations in the fundamental melody because of differences in ornamentation (figure 5). This variety of heterophonic singing is particularly characteristic of harvest songs.

Clear, loud singing in the open air has its own aesthetic rules and criteria, such as the ability to "hold the voice for a while" (to sing long-drawn-out tones on a deep breath) and to "lift a song" (to sing it with a clear lead). Prominent masters of singing are found mainly among shepherds, foresters, milkmaids, field hands, deliverymen, and river navigators and raftsmen.

Nonritual songs

Nonritual songs constitute the second historical layer of song creation. They were developed primarily in the fourteenth century and continued through the period of the Cossack peasant uprising (sixteenth to eighteenth centuries). In addition to nonritual lyrics on themes of love and daily life and ballads, this style is strongly represented by male sociolyrical epic poetry: Chumak songs (*čumackija pieśni*) (the Chumaks were peasants who traveled to Crimea for salt), barge-hauler songs (*burłackija pieśni*), Cossack songs, songs of military events and about leaders of peasant uprisings, and soldiers' songs, which continue the recruitment-song tradition. Nonritual songs differ from songs of the ancient style in their brilliant graphic individualization of the musical poetic image and the spontaneity of performance. In Belarusan folk terminology, they were sung *aby-kali* 'whenever suitable'. Songs of the peasant uprising are unique in their energy and intensity, and the love lyrics are characterized by a wealth of psychological nuances. They exist in many choral and solo variants. Particular melodic openings play an important role in this musical expression, and melodies are distinguished by melodic movement, the diversity of rhythmic structures, and the development of the song strophe.

Associated with male and female performances in this style is a developed multivoiced texture related to the polyphonic structure common throughout southern, central, and eastern Belarus. Two parts are clearly specified. The basic melody, performed by a chorus, is always sounded in a lower range. The high solo voice sings in counterpoint to the lower chorus. The singers recognize the artistic function of the voices in their own terminology. Singers performing the lower part are called *basy* 'the basses', and *basavać* means to sing the bass part. Those performing the high-pitched solo contrapuntal voice are called those who lead up (*padvodka*) or the little voices (*hałaśnik*), and are said to lift the song or lead it upward (*brać na padhałosak*).

An examination of ritual and nonritual song creation shows that Belarus can be divided into five regions: northern (including Viciebščyna-Paazieryje), eastern (Mahiloŭščyna), western (Horadzienščyna), southern (including Bieraściejščyna and Homielščyna-Paleśsie), and central (Mienščyna). Certain genres—e.g., "wandering" songs in the northern region, carols in the southern region, and game-play and round-dance songs in the eastern region—stylistic nuances, and melodic peculiarities predominate in certain regions. Most noticeable are differences between Paazieryje and Paleśsie. The songs of Paazieryje characteristically have straightforwardness and thematic conciseness, the predominance of solo singing, and the choral performance of one-voiced songs with an insignificant digression from the unison. The songs of

Paleśsie have a more extensive melodic character, extensive accented ornamentation, and a rich vocal timbre. Choral heterophony or monody with an upward-leading singer (*hałaśnik*) predominates and can be described as melodic painting.

Nineteenth-century urban-influenced songs

In the nineteenth century, a third historical style of Belarusan song developed from urban folklore. It includes farm-laborer and migrant-worker songs, labor and revolutionary songs, literary songs based on the words of professional poets and refrains (*častuški*), and rhymed poems of several lines on humorous themes. These songs bear the influence of peasant-uprising lyrics of the seventeenth and eighteenth centuries, Polish revolutionary anthems disseminated in the second half of the eighteenth century, and Russian and Ukrainian democratic social romances influenced by nineteenth-century revolutionary songs. Belarusan and eastern Slavic religious chants influenced several song genres, including festive ceremonial table-side comic and soldier songs and revolutionary anthems.

In the Soviet period, the development of the folk-song tradition saw the fusion of peasant oral folklore with the urban literary tradition—a process typical of the partisan songs of 1941–1944, a rich and specific layer of Belarusan contemporary folklore. Partisan folklore developed in three directions: heroic songs and anthems, lyrical songs, and satirical and comic refrains (*častuški*). Individual authorship of songs became an important aspect of musical folklore in partisan detachments and brigades. In the postwar era, such songs continued to be created by individuals, and were then refined and perfected in amateur rural ensembles (*kalektyvy*) approximating the models of the anonymous oral song tradition (figure 6).

INSTRUMENTAL FOLK MUSIC

The most widely disseminated and socially significant stringed instruments are a fiddle or violin (*skrypka*), a hammered dulcimer (*cymbaly*), the bass fiddle (*basetla*), the balalaika, and the mandolin; the hurdy-gurdy (*lira, rela, kobza*) is no longer widely used.

Aerophones include single- and double-pipe duct flutes and, since the beginnning of the twentieth century, the ocarina (*akaryna*), made of clay in an oval

FIGURE 7   Some Belarusan aerophones. *Top to bottom:* (*a*) horn (*berestiankka*), (*b*) horn (*mastušij rožok*), (*c*) duct flute (*dudka*), (*d*) reed pipe (*žalejka*), (*e*) reed pipe (*pištik*), (*f*) ocarina (*akaryna*), (*g*) reed horn (*dudka jazyčkovaia*). Photo by Zinaida Mozheiko.

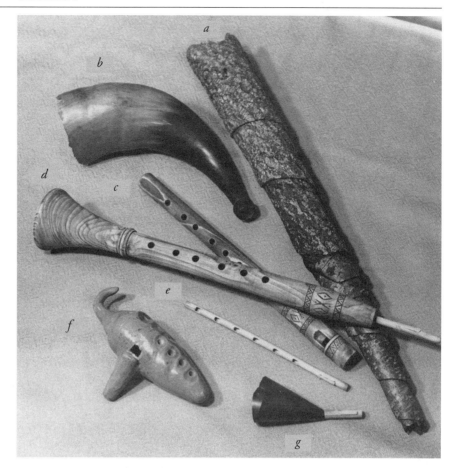

form, with eight to ten finger holes. Horns (*roh*) are 30 to 45 centimeters long and can be made of animal horn, wood, or metal. Shepherds' trumpets (*truba*), in various conical shapes, are made of coniferous woods wrapped in birch bark, or of hammered metal, and can range from 1.25 to 3 meters long. A large family of "reeds" (*žalejki, dudki, ražki, piščyki, čarotki*) are distinguished by their material (reeds, wood, straw, goose feathers) and finger holes (from none to twelve). The reed can be cut into the body of the instrument or tied on (figure 7). More elaborate reed instruments include the clarinet and, until the latter half of the twentieth century, bagpipes (*duda*), known in Belarus since the sixteenth century, and free reed instruments like the accordion (*harmonik*).

The most common drums were the tambourine (*buben z brazhotkami*), with jingles tied across the underside of a wooden or metallic frame, and the drum with cymbals (*baraban z talerkami*), a cylindrical double-headed drum of various sizes with a brass cymbal attached to the top of the frame. Idiophones commonly used for ensemble accompaniment are bronze, pitched and nonpitched clappered bells (*zvon*), two-clappered hand bells (*zvanočak*) of metal and wood, a triangle (*stalki*), rattles (*brazhotki*), jingle bells (*šarkuny*), spoons (*łyžki*), and other everyday objects.

Only a few of these instruments—mainly the accordion and tambourine and less so the violin, the *cymbaly,* and flutes—continue to function in the musical life of Belarusan villages. Researchers must search diligently for double-pipe flutes and reeds. Other instruments, such as the bagpipe and the hurdy-gurdy, exist only in instrumentalists' and singers' memories, though they are appearing again in the hands of noninstitutionally supported youth and rock ensembles as they explore their regional and cultural roots.

Improvisation is central in a genre of pieces depicting socially and naturally produced sounds. Popular among these is *ciałušačka,* which musically depicts how everyone laments the loss of the calf and rejoices when it is found.

FIGURE 8   The accordionist (*bayan*) Vitali Maroz and a tambourinist rest between performances by the Motal Musical Collective, August 1993. Photo courtesy of Maria Paula Survilla.

In villages, musical instruments are used for solo playing and in instrumental ensembles and vocal-instrumental combinations. Traditional folk instrumental ensembles are called *muzyki* 'musicians' (also *kapela, hurt-kampanija, skamarochi* 'minstrels', and *viasielnyja muzyki* 'wedding musicians'). The most common have two instruments: violin (or accordion) and drum (or dulcimer or bass fiddle) (figure 8). Ensembles known as "tripled music" in Belarusan and Ukrainian tradition include three instruments: a violin (or flute), a dulcimer (or accordion), and a tambourine. The most popular instrumental quartets include violin, dulcimer, accordion, and drums; or two violins, dulcimer, and tambourine. In the west, larger ensembles, called orchestras (*arkiestry*), include two violins, accordion, clarinet, drums, and rattles; or violin, two dulcimers, accordion, and drums.

Folk terminology assigns specific terms to the instrumental ensemble performers' functions. For example, in an ensemble of two violins and a tambourine, the first violinist "supports the top" of the folk melody, the second "supports the bass," and the tambourinist holds the rhythm.

The character of Belarusan instrumental music depends primarily on its social function. The oldest style, patterned on folk tunes formerly associated with signaling in hunters' and shepherds' everyday lives, consists of one or more tones from the natural overtone series. Dance and song folk tunes associated with the spring ("wandering") songs, winter rituals (game-play songs and dance tunes), and summer work songs are also characteristic of the old style. A later style consists of widely disseminated wedding marches, performed during dramatically important moments of the ritual. The melodic structure of instrumental music seems to have influenced some older song styles. For example, the intonation of the shepherds' trumpet may be detected in spring songs, of the violin in "wandering" songs, and of the hurdy-gurdy in old ballads and so-called spiritual verses.

Folk tunes performed by a skillful musician are distinguishable by an improvisational liberty that embellishes the melody ornamentally and rhythmically. Improvisational mastery can dominate instrumental folk tunes, acquiring the name *by oneself* (*sam pa sabie* 'free of restrictions'). Improvisation is also central in a genre of pieces depicting socially and naturally produced sounds. Popular among these is *ciałušačka*, which musically depicts how everyone laments the loss of the calf and rejoices when it is found, and includes sonic imitations, as in the songs "How the Wind Strolls the Fields" and "How the Grasses Stir and the Birds Caw."

Folk musicians understand the art of playing as *independent* (that is, by folk definition, they are natural musicians), or imitation of family tradition (they are *descendant* musicians), or imitations of local master musicians (those renowned among the community, who in effect create their own performance schools). For example, the polka is prevalent throughout Belarus in numerous musical and ethnographic variants, often in villages called by musicians' names: "Ivan's Polka," "Stepan's Polka," "Kyril's Polka." Several self-taught Belarusan musicians are manufacturers of instruments and possess the secret knowledge of the qualities of the raw materials from which the instruments are made.

On stage, where many folk-instrumental traditions have been transferred for performance by organized amateur village collectives, folk-instrumental and folk-song traditions do not always appear in their authentic forms, though they are still practiced in traditional ways in Belarusan villages.

HISTORY OF MUSIC

Authentic Belarusan musical folklore performed by amateurs or professionals has exerted a noticeable influence on Belarusan musical life. The first professional folk artists were minstrels (*skamarochi*), whose performances on Belarusan territory have been documented since the twelfth century. Elements of their art have been a part of two forms of popular folk theater since the sixteenth century: one with live actors, the other a puppet theater (*batlejka*), similar to the Ukrainian *vertep* (Nativity play) and the Polish *szopka* (Christmas puppet story).

With the expansion of artistic life and education in the sixteenth century, ecclesiastical singing and secular choruses and orchestras developed, and theater was added to some school curriculums. In the seventeenth and eighteenth centuries, theatrical troupes originated at the courts of prominent feudal lords. Plays written by local authors appeared on school stages and in court theaters, as did secular choruses and orchestras, and these works include elements adapted from peasant musical folklore.

In the nineteenth century, musical folklore penetrated more widely into urban amateur and professional groups, partly because of the expanding practice of fieldwork collection. During this century, folklore changed significantly, as it was made to meet the standards of urban musical life.

At present, in addition to original, authentic performance contexts, musical folk tradition is well known in Belarus in its secondary forms. Most modern performances are organized by cultural educational institutions and rural and urban amateur collectives. The most famous professional collectives based on folk tradition are the Hienadś Citovič State Academic Folk Choir of Belarus, the Zynovič State National Orchestra of Belarus, and the Šyrma State Academic Choir of Belarus.

As in many other European countries, the musical folklore of Belarus has played a crucial role in the establishment of a national school of composers. Nearly all Belarusan composers of all generations—including Mikoła Aładoŭ, Uładzimir Ałoŭnikaŭ, Jaŭhien Cikocki, Jaŭhień Hlebaŭ, Ivan Kuzniacoŭ, Ryhor Pukt, Juyij Siemianiaka, Dzimitry Smolski, and Ihar Òučanok—have appealed to folklore sources in some way. Each composer converts folklore material in accordance with his or her creative individuality and the genres produced (song, cantata, orchestral miniature, symphony, opera). A general tendency may be noticed progressing from the initial citation of folklore material (characteristic of the compositions of the prewar and initial postwar periods) to the more abstract comprehension of folk principles in musical expression (harmonies, polyrhythm, and so on). Belarusan musical folklore has been integrated most clearly in the works of Russian composers Modest Mussorgsky and Igor Stravinsky, independent of concrete quotations from folk melodies. The intonational structure of folk songs is so perceptible that some composers' songs—including "The Forest Song" of Uladzimir Ałoŭnikaŭ and the songs of Niescer Sakalo`ski—are easily folklorized and enter oral tradition.

—Zinaida Mozheiko

URBAN MUSIC

Since the mid-1980s, music in urban Belarus has reflected and often shaped the movement toward cultural and national assertion known as the Belarusan Renaissance (*Adradžeńnie*). Within this climate, performers, journalists, scholars, and audiences search for the parameters of Belarusan expression, including the popularization of the Belarusan language, while evaluating the impact of Soviet ideology on traditional folk repertoires. The music heard in live performance, on radio, and on television includes staged folk-derived performance, regional nonmediated vocal music, bardic songs, variety-show balladry, and rock music.

Staged folklore

The Soviet approach to folk practices was characterized by the collection and cataloguing of repertoires for ethnographic scholarship and the transposition of folk-music genres to the urban stage. The resulting management of traditional repertoires established a system of education and performance based on cultural institutes and folk ensembles (*kalektyvy*).

The Soviet process of mediating and standardizing folk practice upheld the political mandate of producing a contemporary musical mirror of a historically and ethnically united Soviet society. Accomplished stage ensembles were state supported, participated in international performance tours, and produced recordings through the state-owned Melodya label. Professional, urban-trained "culture workers" (*kultrabotniki*) managed local houses of culture (*dom kultury*) and directed regional performance groups. In some cases, repertoires were regulated or censored by such management. Repertoires most at risk were those with ritual functions that could be linked to regional, spiritual, and Belarusan-specific identity, such as the celebration of summer solstice and ritual community renewal.

The urban management of folklore has culminated in a genre of performance separate from grass-roots musical practice. For performances, many ensembles use musical-theater frameworks, including choreographed interaction between performers, dramatizations of scenarios described in the songs, and the suggestion of rural settings, including the *kirmaš* 'marketplace'. A more formal approach bypasses the suggestion of the original village context and offers a highly stylized interpretation of folk songs and dances. Staged performances can combine folk repertoire and traditional instrumentation with ballet-inspired choreography of traditional dances; harmonized, arpeggiated arrangements of folk tunes; a more nasal vocal projection for female voices (a trait borrowed from Russian vocal practice); and costumes that synthesize elements from Belarusan and Russian traditional dress. The regional and symbolic significance of Belarusan color, embroideries, and woven decorations are superseded in favor of large geometric shapes in colors that mask any regional or national connections.

In post-Soviet Belarus, institutions continue to produce ethnographers, specialists for the stage, and staff for cultural centers. Staged performance is an established genre and remains popular with urban audiences. The advent of the Belarusan Renaissance has generated two responses to such performance. Some observers reject staged folklore, and value instead what they consider nonmediated authentic folk practice. Others consider staged folklore an established performative Belarusan genre, which can be used to reeducate Belarusans about their cultural roots in the postcolonial climate.

The recent emphasis on Belarusan culture also relies on presenting regional performance groups through television and radio. Programming specifically focuses on nonmediated regional performance or, as with the program "Viacorki," of Belarus Television, highlights regional musicians in prepared village or studio settings. Several young urban ensembles, such as Uladzimir Biarbierau's Lićviny, independently research traditional repertoire and performance styles and consciously offer what they consider authentic performances of vocal and instrumental music. The debate between mediated and nonmediated Belarusan music continues and most often defines the nature of scholarship and performance practice.

Bardic traditions

The urban bard (*bard*) reflects the importance of poetic form, metaphor, and symbolism in Belarusan traditional and literary repertoire. Through poetry and live performances, bards such as Valžyna Ciareščanka, Aleś Kamocki, Liza Lambovič, Andrej Mielnikau, and Siaržuk Sokalau-Vojuš became public advocates of the Belarusan language in the time leading up to the Belarusan Renaissance. Performers combine social commentary, poetic expertise, and emotional delivery with varied singing ability, strophic melodies, and simple guitar accompaniments. Bards perform for many audiences, including the literary elite in Miensk's House of Literature and youth audiences at Belarusan rock festivals, or vie for awards against bards from other Slavic traditions in yearly competitions.

Popular music

Variety performance (*estradnaja muzyka* 'stage music'), a stylized genre highlighting a solo singer with an orchestral, big-band, or jazz-style accompaniment, requires showmanship, black-tie costumes, and skilled instrumental ensembles, such as musicians from the Miensk Philharmonic. Performers participate in the pan-Slavic music festival Słavianski Bazar, the national music festival Maładěčna, and other such events. Unlike Belarusan bardic and rock music, *estradnyja* are often sung in Russian.

Rock

Eastern European rock has most often been analyzed for its political commentary and the quality of its texts. Belarusan bands realize they have an impact on attitudes in the public sphere, but they are quick to emphasize that they are part of a larger musical process, with challenging lifestyle and inconsistent opportunities for success. These musicians want to be considered for their music and their messages, their creativity, and their artistic choices.

Belarusan rock borrows from local folk tradition, American and British popular

Belarusan rock is defined by overt or masked reference to current events, the use of folk sources, the choice of language, and a curiosity about musical trends outside Belarus.

music, and world music trends. Since the early 1980s, Belarusan rockers have also chosen to sing in Belarusan. Before the 1991 legislation that made Belarusan the only official language, Belarusan had suffered under the Russification policies of the Soviet regime. Initially, rock musicians' choice of language and negative image kept most groups from finding performance venues, producing studio recordings, and making a living as rock musicians. The evolution of signature styles and the distribution of cassettes and records encouraged an underground following, including media support from print journalists, radio, and television.

Bands depend on a loose patronage system—educational institutes, businessmen, and factory managers—to provide monthly stipends, rehearsal spaces, and equipment. Several bands have local managers, who organize performances and solicit recording opportunities. Without access to the Soviet-built Melodiia studios in Moscow and Riga, recordings are engineered after hours in the Belarus Radio studios, and video production is rare; nevertheless, bands keep releasing cassettes and records, and most recently compact discs, without the support of a national music industry.

Five bands dominate Belarusan rock. Krama (Shop) uses a blues-based, straight-ahead rock style (figure 9). They attracted the interest of British REX Records in 1993 and produced an English cover of their album *Addicted to Rock 'n Roll* (rereleased in English *Vodka on Ice*). Ulis (Ulysses) projects musical energy with inventive percussion, electric bass, guitar, male vocals, and lyrics by poet Feliks Akšencaŭ. Their concept album, *A LONGWHITECLOUDLAND* (Ulis 1991b), begins and ends with traditional songs performed by Taćciana Marchiel. Within these traditional bookends, the band explores, critiques, and celebrates life in Belarus. Mroja (Dream) changed their name to NRM (National Republic of Mroja) in 1995. Together since 1981, this all-male heavy-metal-style band sings compelling texts about the human condition, individualism, and current events, including the impact of the Chernobyl disaster on the Belarusan psyche. Novaje Nieba (New Sky) was formed in 1993, when then-bard Kacia Kamockaja joined forces with NRM lead Lavon Volski. They define their style as the most avant-garde among their peers. Over electronic keyboard, percussion, bass, and acoustic or electric guitar accompaniment, Kamockaja sings in a low alto that ranges from lyrical to aggressive in quality. Her texts, often philosophical, openly address contemporary Belarusan frustrations. For example, in *President Go Home* (Novaje Nieba 1995) she speaks directly to populist Belarusan president Lukashenko, suggesting that he return home to Russia. *Palac* (Palace) consciously reshapes folk repertoires and original compositions, combining traditional texts and melodies with synthesized tracks, saxophone, recorder, electric guitar, and male vocals. This self-described "folk-modern" style includes vocals sung with appropriated Palessie-derived female vocal projection, English-language rap interludes, and techno, hip-hop, reggae, and Afro-Cuban instrumentals.

Through overt or masked reference to current events, the use of folk sources, the choice of language, and a curiosity about musical trends outside Belarus, these bands

FIGURE 9   In Miensk in September 1993, the rock band Krama performs for the taping of the Belarusan television program "Rock Island." Photo courtesy of Maria Paula Survilla.

suggest a broad definition of Belarusan rock. Despite the variety of styles, these performers are conscious of the Belarusan stamp on their music as they explore their local resources and those of other musics to produce a unique contemporary Belarusan voice.

—MARIA PAULA SURVILLA

HISTORY OF SCHOLARSHIP

Ethnomusicological studies began with song collecting, which burgeoned in the second half of the nineteenth century, thanks to numerous Belarusan folklorists and ethnographers, including Mitrafan Doŭnar-Zapolski, Mikoła Jančuk, Mikoła Nikifaroŭski, Jeŭdakim Ramanaŭ, and Pavel Šejn. These and other folkorists' initial publications focused on song texts, occasionally supplemented with musical examples.

Belarusan ethnomusicology began as a scholarly activity focused on music with the work of the Belarusan, Ukrainian, and Russian Slavist Mikoła Jančuk, who in 1901 founded and was the director of the Musical Ethnographic Commission of the Society of Friends of Natural Science, Anthropology, and Ethnography at Moscow University. Polish ethnographers and folklorists, such as Oskar Kolberg, and Ukrainian ethnomusicological folklorists, such as F. Kolessa and K. Kvitka, also played an important early role in Belarusan studies.

The Russian Leningrad school led by Evgeny Gippius and Zinaida Evald furthered research strategies and determined the general movement and conceptual direction of Belarusan ethnomusicology. As students of Boris Asaf'ev, scholars considered folk music through the theory of intonation—where the music of oral tradition, as a form of culture similar to language, is the conveyor of logical, symbolic, national, and social meaning. From this viewpoint, folk music is a language of direct, live social intercourse.

The issues of systematization (especially of folk instruments), transcription, and acoustic measurement of melodies and folk tunes are related to those highlighted by various Western European schools. Gippius and Evald played significant roles in establishing these relations. They were acquainted with the founding work of the Berlin school of comparative musicology (led by Erich M. von Hornbostel and Curt Sachs) and the work of foreign scholars centered at the beginning of the twentieth century at the Berlin Phonogram Archives, founded by Karl Stumpf.

In 1927, Gippius established the Leningrad Phonogram Archive in the Institute of Art History (now located in the Institute of Russian Literature of the Russian Academy of Sciences, known as the Pushkin House), which remains the most prominent musical center for the study of the folklore of the Slavic, Finno-Ugric, and Turkic peoples of the former Soviet Union.

Musical ethnographic expeditions were conducted in Belarus in the 1930s by Gippius and Evald, with ethnographer Mikhail Hrynblat of the Belarusan Academy of Sciences. Since then, field work by Belarusan ethnomusicologists has been led by directors of the Citoviç State Academic Folk Choir of Belarus and director of the Šyrma State Choral Academic Capella, with theoretical work by professors Lidiia S. Mukharinskaia and Viktor I. Elatov.

Ethnomusicological work is currently conducted in three main centers: the Institute of Art Studies, Ethnography, and Folklore, of the Belarusan Academy of Sciences; the Belarusan State Conservatory; and the Union of Belarusan Composers. The basic directions of Belarusan scholars' ethnomusicological research include systematic typological, regional, structural-stylistic, and socioethnopsychological approaches, including the problems of visual anthropology. These studies, affected by the integrity of musical folklore, whose core can be considered the genetic foundation of the national musical language, are related to the ritual song of what has been called the Old Slavic historical style. The guiding principle of such research is based on the Leningrad school's intonational approach [see RUSSIA].

—ZINAIDA MOZHEIKO

BIBLIOGRAPHY

Asaf'ev, Boris. 1987. *O narodnoi muzyke* (On folk music). Leningrad: Muzyka.

Bandarchyk, Vasilii, et al. 1978. "Balady u dziukh knihakh" (Ballads in two volumes). In *Belaruskaia narodnaia tvorchasts* (Belarusan folk creations). Minsk: Navuka i tekhnika.

Bartashevich, Halina, and L. Salavei. 1979. "Vesnavyia pesni" (Spring songs). In *Belaruskaia narodnaia tvorchasts* (Belarusan folk creations). Minsk: Navuka i tekhnika.

Blagoveshchenskii, Igor. 1965. *Nekotoriye voprosy muzykal'nogo iskusstva: pedagogika, estetika, folklor* (Some issues of musical art: pedagogy, aesthetics, folklore). Minsk. Navuka i tekhnika.

Elatov, Viktor I. 1977. *Pesni vostochnykh Slovian* (Songs of the eastern Slavs). Minsk. Navuka i tekhnika.

Evald, Zinaida. 1979. *Pesni belorusskogo Polesia* (Songs of Belarusan Palessie). Moscow: Sovieskii kompozitor.

Fiadosik, Anatol, ed. 1990. *Viaselle: melodyi in Belaruskaia narodnaia tvorchasts* (Wedding: Melodies in Belarusan folk creations). Minsk: Navuka i tekhnika.

Gippius, Evgenii. 1980. *Obshcheteoreticheskii vzglad na problemu katalogizatsii norodnikh melodii: aktualnyie problemy sovremennoi fol'kloristiki: sbornik stat'ei i materiolov* (Sociotheoretical aspects of the problem of a catalogue of cataloguing folk melodies: Present problems of contemporary folkloristics: Compilation of articles and documents). Leningrad.

———. 1982. *Problemy arealnogo issledovania traditsionnoi russkoi pesni v oblastiakh ukrainskogo i belorusskogo pogranichia: traditsionoe narodnoe muzykal'noie isskusstvo i sovremennost': voprosy tipologii* (Problems in the study of traditional regional Russian songs along Ukrainian and Belarusan border regions: Traditional folk-musical art and the present: Issues of typology). Moscow: Sovietskii kompozitor.

Hilevich, Nil. 1959–1976. *Belaruskiia narodnyia pesni: zapis' Ryhora Shyrmy* (Belarusan folk songs: Recorded by Ryhor Shyrma). 4 vols. Minsk: Dziarzhaunaie vydavietstva BSSR.

———. 1974. *Pesni narodnykh sviat i abradau* (Songs of folk celebrations and rituals). Minsk: Vydavietstva imia Lenina.

———. 1975. *Antalohiia belaruskai narodnai pesni* (Anthology of Belarusan folk song). Edited and with an introduction by H. Tsitovich. Minsk: Belarus.

Hlushchanka, Heorhii, et al. 1971. *Historyia belaruskai savetskai muzyki* (History of Belarusan Soviet music). Minsk: Vyshejshaia shkola.

Hrynblat, Mikhail. 1968. *Belorusy: ocher-proiskhoshdzenia*. Minsk: Navuka i tekhnika.

———. 1972. *Belaruskaia etnahrafiia i falk-larystyka: bibliiahrafichny pakazalnik, 1945–1970* (Belarusan ethnography and folkloristics: A bibliographical guide, 1945–1970). Minsk: Navuka i tekhnika.

Kaladzinski, Mikhail, et al. 1983. "Narodny teatr" (Folk theater). In *Belaruskaia narodnaia tvorchasts* (Belarusan folk creations). Minsk: Navuka i tekhnika.

Lozka, Ales. 1993. *Belaruski narodny kaliandar* (The Belarusan folk calendar). Minsk: Polymia.

Martynienka, Vitaut, and Anatol Mialhui. 1989. *Praz rok-pryzmu: zbornik artykulau i interviu* (Through the prism of rock: A collection of articles and interviews). English introduction by Maria Paula Survilla. New York: Instytut Navuki i Mastatstva.

Mozheiko, Zinaida. 1971. *Pesennaia kul'tura belorusskogo Polesia* (Song culture of Belarusan Palessie). Minsk: Nauka i tekhnika.

———. 1981. *Pesni belorusskogo Paazer'ia* (Songs of Belarusan Poozer'ye). Minsk: Navuka i tekhnika.

———. 1983. *Pesni belorusskogo Polesia* (Songs of Belarusan Palessie). 2 vols. Moscow: Sovietskii kompozitor.

———. 1985. *Kalendarno-pesennaia kultura Belorussii: opyt sistemnotipologicheskogo issledovaniia* (Calendar-song culture of Belarus: A case of typological-systematic research). Minsk: Navuka i tekhnika.

Mukharinskaia, Lidiia S. 1968. *Belaruskaia narodnaia partizanskaia pesnia (1941–1945)* (Belarusan folk-partisan song (1941–1945)). Minsk.

———. 1977. *Belaruskaia narodnaia pesnia: istoricheskoie razvitie* (Belarusan folk song: a historical study). Minsk: Nauka i tekhnika.

Nazina, Inna. 1979. *Belorusskie narodnye muzykal'nye instrumenty: samozvuchnye, udarnye, dukhovye* (Belarusan folk-musical instruments: Idiophones, percussions, winds). Minsk: Navuka i tekhnika.

———. 1982. *Belorusskie narodnye muzykal'nye instrumenty: strunnie* (Belarusan folk-musical instruments: Strings). Minsk: Navuka i tekhnika.

———, et al. 1993. "Zhanits'ba Tsiareshki" (Tereshka's marriage). In *Belaruskaia narodnaia tvorchasts* (Belarusan folk creations). Minsk: Navuka i tekhnika.

Survilla, Maria Paula. 1994. "Rock Music in Belarus." In *Rocking the State,* ed. Sabrina Ramet, 219–242. Oxford: Westview Press.

Varfolomeeva, T. B. 1988. *Severobelorusskaia svadʹba: obriad, pesenno-melodichskie tipy* (North Belarusan wedding: Ritual, song-melodic types). Minsk: Navuka i tekhnika.

Zhynovich I. I. 1975. *Atlas: muzykalʹnye instrumenty narodau SSSR* (Atlas: Musical instruments of the peoples of the U.S.S.R.). 2d ed. Moscow.

AUDIOVISUAL RESOURCES

Folk music

Belaruskaia tradytsianalʹnaia instrumentalʹnaia muzyka (Belarusan traditional instrumental music). 1989. Notation, editing, and equalization by Inna Nazina. Minsk. Compact disc.

Marchenko, Yurii. 1983. *Kalendarnie pesni Belorusskogo Polesia* (Calendric songs of Belarusan Paleśsie). Melodya C20 19893 001. Compact disc.

Marchenko, Yurii, and L. Petrova. 1989. *Traditsionnie pesni Polesia* (Traditional songs of Paleśsie). Melodiia C20 28043 005. Compact disc.

Mozheiko, Zinaida, and Inna Nazina. 1988. *Musical Folklore of the Byelorussian Polessye.* Audivis-Unesco D 8005. Compact disc.

———, et al. 1990. *Bielaruskii muzykalʹni falʹklor* (Belarusan musical folklore). Melodiia M30 49231 009. Compact disc.

Popular music and rock

Krama. 1993. *Hei tam nalivai.* Minsk. Compact disc.

———. 1994. *Vodka on Ice.* REX Records. Compact disc.

Mroja (NRM). 1990. *28th Star.* Melodya C60 30401 001. Compact disc.

———. 1993. *Vybranie piesni 1989–1993.* Compact disc.

———. 1995. *Łałałała 1995.* Kovcheg 00295. Compact disc.

Novaje Nieba. 1994. *Son i tramvai.* Kovcheg. Compact disc.

———. 1995. *Go Home.* Novaje Nieba. Compact disc.

Palats. 1996. *Palace Folk-Modern Palac.* Vigma 0360. Compact disc.

Ulis. 1991a. *Čuwzanica.* Melodiia. Compact disc.

———. 1991b. *Kraina doŭhai biełai chmary.* Polskie Nagrania. Compact disc.

———. 1993. *Dances on the Roof '93.* Dainova. Compact disc.

———. 1996. *Blukannie.* Kovcheh 02096. Compact disc.

Ukraine
William Noll

Ukraine, the second largest country (603,700 square kilometers) in Europe after Russia, consists of forests in the north, steppes in the south and east, and mountains (the Carpathians) in the southwest (map 9). Until the 1970s, the northwest was a marshy area, which has since been drained. From roughly the late 1600s, much of central and eastern Ukraine was part of the Russian Empire and then the Soviet Union. Western Ukraine, known historically as Galicia (in Ukrainian, Halychyna), was part of Polish or Austrian states from the 1300s until 1939. At the time of the disintegration of the Soviet Union (in 1991), more than 96 percent of the Ukrainian population voted for independence. In the 1990s, much of the population of more than 52 million works in industry, mining, aeronautics, metals, service, and agriculture.

VILLAGE VOCAL MUSIC BEFORE COLLECTIVIZATION

In peasant Ukraine before collectivization (in the 1930s), most village musical life was formally organized around the Christian calendar of feasts and fasts, or longstanding institutions of civil society, such as weddings, funerals, seasonal or agricultural celebrations, and ritual and nonritual evening social gatherings of various kinds. Church choirs and the occasional military band in a market town were the only socially organized music practices not primarily local or regional in character.

The social organization of singing

Genres, repertories, and other performance practices were divided between women and men. Most ritual vocal music was performed by women and girls, though men also participated; most instrumental music was played by men and boys, though women also participated; and women and men or girls and boys shared numerous nonritual vocal genres and certain musical instruments more or less equally. Women and men and girls and boys performed some nonritual genres, such as lyrical ballads, love songs, and soldiers' songs, sung informally by anyone at any time.

Most ritual musical performances in villages were specific to certain contexts and people. Wedding ceremonies were acted out in a sequence of events over the course of three to seven days. Most wedding rituals required songs, some of which were real-

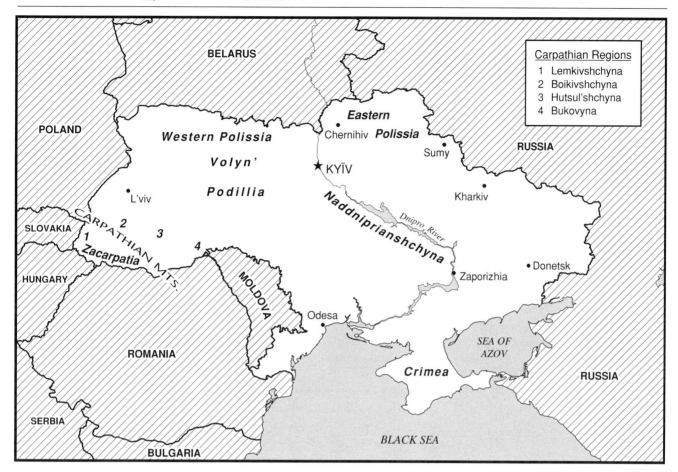

MAP 9   Ukraine

ized in groups, some rendered solo, still others a combination of group and solo singing. The singing lasted for hours, as hundreds of ritual texts were rendered, mainly by women acting in specific roles: the bride, the bridesmaids, an older woman acting as a sergeant-at-arms for the women, the bridegroom's sisters, the bride's mother, and the bridegroom's mother.

Women had to learn hundreds of ritual texts, numerous melodies, and the sequence of events that included ritual dances. Most men knew far fewer texts, for, with only a few exceptions (e.g., the *boiary* 'groomsmen'), men did not customarily have ritual wedding roles to fulfill. The music of the wedding sequence was part of a series of social obligations into which a woman was born. Not knowing these texts and melodies would have been a breach of custom. Ritual songs could be extremely long, with hundreds of strophes. Each village sometimes had only ten or twenty melodies to which the texts were sung. Some melodies, those with a range of a fourth or a fifth, were among the oldest elements of local music culture (figure 1).

Music practice reflected village social structure. Girls from one place (a *kutok* or "corner" of the village) and one generation shared a common aesthetic and musical knowledge. Large villages could have five or even ten "corners," and a small village might have two or three. In wedding and other ritual contexts, specific people sang specific songs. As girls entered young adulthood, their roles, ritual obligations, and music practices changed. As they aged into mature women, their roles and music practices changed again, but it was still among their musicosocial group, based on generation and "corners," that these practices were realized. Each stage in life required a different set of ritual songs for a given generation of a particular "corner."

Though ritual wedding music may have been known to all women, all women

FIGURE 1 A narrow-range wedding melody, "*Si pojdu ia ta do Dunaiu*," in a major mode with a range of a fifth above the tonal center. After Chubyns'kyi and Lysenko 1970 [1877]:90.

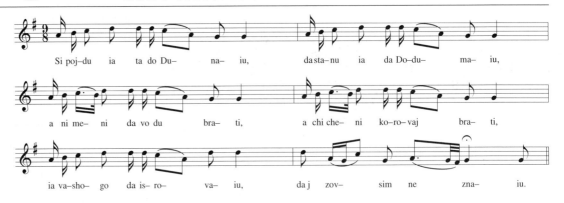

did not know it equally well. Some were leaders, to whom others looked when no one else could remember a line of text or which melody or ritual came next. The best local singers were expected to lead the ritual life of the village. Whenever possible, they were invited to weddings. Though not paid cash for their services, they were greatly admired for their skill and memory. In contrast to instrumental musicians, who had an ambiguous status bordering on the lowly, the best female singers' status was high, and they were respected individuals.

Women vocalists' artistry was still evident in the 1990s, when folkloric ensembles in Ukraine and most of Eastern Europe contained perhaps ten times more women than men; thus, this gender-specific role survived as a folkloric element. Village women's prominence as vocal musicians reinforced their social power. They controlled most aspects of village ritual and the social calendar—which in turn put them in a position to influence social activities and relationships.

Another context for singing dominated by women was *dosvitky*. Between late September and Lent, virtually all girls from the age of ten until they became engaged had for their primary social activity the participation in *dosvitky*, for which they gathered nearly every evening (and some days) to sew, weave, embroider, make hemp rope, sing, and dance. The girls usually sang while they worked at the home of a widow or childless adult woman, whom the girls paid in labor, food, and firewood. Boys sometimes came later in the evening. Sometimes they hired a music ensemble, and the dancing was intense and virtually without a break for hours at a time. The girls organized the *dosvitky* and decided who could attend. During the Christmas and New Year season, more control of the social calendar and the planning and paying for social activities was taken over by boys, but girls took over again until Lent, when *dosvitky* shut down until the next season began.

In the spring, girls sang *vesnianky* 'spring songs' in groups of two or more in open or cleared spaces in or near the village. In some regions, they sang as loudly as possible, so the sound would carry long distances and everyone could hear them. In many regions, certain musical games were played only on the day after Easter. In eastern Ukraine, one such game and its songs were called *perepelka,* and only girls of a given *kutok* played it together. In some western Ukrainian regions, all ages and both sexes participated in these games (known in some areas as *haïvky*), which could be boisterous.

Other ritual genres heard only once a year included *koliadky* 'Christmas carols'. In the summer, the night before Ivan Kupalo (July 7) included special songs, often on a single melody, repeated over and over by mostly young people gathered around a fire.

Singing styles

Vocal music among peasants in Ukraine varied by region and genre. A succinct regionalization of vocal practice is hard to formulate because practices overlapped from region to region in ways that defy easy description and classification. As a result, the ethnographic and musicological literature about Ukraine includes no detailed study of regionalism in vocal music.

A few generalizations are possible, however. In most regions vocal production is with an open throat, with higher registers resonated in the head, especially in women, giving the sound a slightly nasal quality. This nasality is more pronounced in eastern regions and Polissia, and less pronounced in lowland Halychyna. Differences in vocal practice between eastern and western Ukraine provide the most obvious basis for regional differentiation. In eastern regions (including Chernihivshchyna, Kharkivshchyna, Poltavshchyna, and Sumshchyna) and many central regions (Cherkashchyna, most of Kyïvshchyna, eastern Polissia) two- and three-part harmony is more prevalent than in western Ukraine.

In most of western Ukraine, monophony is common for certain genres, notably the narrow-range wedding melodies known in most of lowland western Ukraine as *ladkana;* however, in some locales certain of these melodies are sung in two voices. In village lexicons in most regions, the two or three voices had specific names. The upper-register voice that begins in measure four is said to draw or pull (*tiahnuty*) or to lead (*vyvodyty*), while the other voices sing bass (*tiamkyiut'* or in other regions *basuiut*).

Wedding ritual music and narrow-range spring songs do not fit into a neat modal pattern. Above the lowest pitch (which should not be confused with a tonic), the second degree is usually a major interval, the third may be major, minor, or missing, and the fourth and fifth are usually perfect. Other melodies are pentatonic or hexatonic. In the Carpathians, an augmented fourth is commonly heard. Lyrical songs, soldiers' songs, and several other genres are more predictably in major or minor scales, with other modal characteristics rare.

VILLAGE INSTRUMENTAL MUSIC AND MUSICIANS BEFORE COLLECTIVIZATION

In Ukraine, four types of instrumentalists existed before collectivization: part-time specialists, who played in regionally specific ensembles for weddings and various social events; specialists found only in certain regions; *kobzari* and *lirnyky,* blind peasant minstrels; and nonspecialists, who played for their own amusement or to accompany singing at informal social gatherings

Part-time specialists

Part-time music specialists performed instrumental music for weddings, *dosvitky,* baptismal parties, and other evening gatherings, and in some regions in village inns. They were farmers who relied for their livelihood primarily on agricultural labor and home industries. Instrumental music was a part-time service or craft, and professionals rarely lived in villages. Instrumental musicians were not different from the local blacksmith, wheelwright, or miller, all of whom farmed the land and organized most of their family labor around agricultural activities. Most musical instruments were handmade by local masters who supplemented their agricultural income by selling them to local specialists or minstrels.

With few exceptions, the instruments of village specialists in Ukraine resemble those of most of Eastern Europe. In the 1800s, the violin or fiddle (*skrypka*) was widely made by village craftsmen, usually on the model of the classical violin. The bass (*bas*), about the size and shape of a violoncello, seems to have had three strings in most areas, with variant tunings (1–5–8 or 1–4–8 or 1–4–m7) that enabled the performer to play two sets of rhythmic drones (figure 2). In the twentieth century, this instrument was often replaced by a contrabass.

In Ukraine, Poland, and Belarus, peasants played the trapezoidal hammered dul-

In virtually all regions, it was common in the 1980s and 1990s to find a mixture of electrified instruments (guitars and keyboards) and a standard percussion trap set used in combination with acoustic instruments from the village past.

FIGURE 2 A fiddle and a bass play an excerpt of a *kolomyka* from the Boikivshchyna region of the Carpathians. The bass part contains a rhythmic drone on two notes a fifth apart. After Khai 1989b:8.

cimer (*tsymbaly*). Not a typical Gypsy instrument as in Romania, Moldavia, and much of Hungary since the early 1800s or before, it was widely distributed among Jews, and can be regarded as the main Eastern European Jewish instrument until about 1900. In village practice among Christians and Jews, it was small, usually with triple, quadruple, or quintuple courses of strings, and was played in a range of about three and one-half octaves. At the time of collectivization, it was still common in western Boikivshchyna and Hutsul'shchyna, but rarer elsewhere (figure 3).

The single-headed frame drum (*bubon*) is characteristically played with a small wooden mallet. The double-headed field drum or side drum (*baraban*) has been known over all lowland Ukraine since at least the early twentieth century and in some regions perhaps from as early as the 1700s. Until the mid-twentieth century, most village drums were made by local masters, but since then they have often been replaced with small bass drums purchased in stores. Since World War I, the bass drum has often had an attached metal cymbal. Since the 1930s or so, but especially after World War II, local musicians sometimes called the drum-cymbal combination *dzhaz* 'jazz'.

Specialists on these instruments performed for weddings, *dosvitky*, and other evening gatherings, and in some regions in the village inn. They performed in regional ensembles that differed over time and space. The following ensembles were common between 1890 and 1920 in territories where Ukrainians lived.

1. In southeastern Poland (Peremyshchyna), a fiddle and a *bas*, with or without *tsymbaly* and sometimes with clarinet
2. In highland southeastern Poland and northern Slovakia (Lemkivshchyna), one or two fiddles and a *bas*
3. In lowland western Ukraine (Halychyna), one or two fiddles with a *bas*, or one or two fiddles and a *bubon* or *baraban*, with or without a *tsymbaly*
4. In the forests and swamps of northwestern Ukraine (western Polissia and parts of Volyn'), one or two fiddles and a *bubon*
5. In highland western Ukraine (Boikivshchyna and Hutsul'shchyna), a bagpipe and a fiddle, a fiddle (or two) and a *bas*, a fiddle and a *tsymbaly* (with or without a *bas*), or two fiddles, with or without a *bubon*

FIGURE 3   A band of violin, *tsymbaly* (trape-zoidal hammered zither), and drum (*baraban*) from the Hutsul region (Hutsul'shchyna) accompanies a circle dance. Courtesy of the Robert Godfried Collection, New York.

6. In central and eastern Ukraine (Chernihivshchyna, Kharkivshchyna, Kyïvshchyna, eastern Podillia, and Poltavshchyna,), a box fiddle and *bas* with or without *tsymbaly*, or one or two fiddles and a *bubon* or *baraban*

These ensembles had dozens of variations, including those with wind instruments, which were increasingly common from after World War I until the 1960s and 1970s, when the electrification of village ensembles began. The most common wind instruments included an E♭ or B♭ clarinet, a trumpet or a cornet, a saxophone (often in C), and occasionally a flute. From the 1920s, and in some locales perhaps a generation earlier, brass bands replaced local ensembles of mostly stringed instruments, especially in Volyn' and parts of Halychyna and western Polissia. These bands consisted of trumpets, two or three sizes of baritone horns, and a small tuba—in all, from five to ten players, who played part of the string-band repertory and added popular urban tunes of their day.

A free-reed, button accordion (*harmoniia*) entered peasant practice in Eastern Europe at the turn of the twentieth century and gained favor among villagers throughout the twentieth century. By the mid-twentieth century it was known in varieties widely dispersed throughout Europe, as was the piano accordion, a larger instrument. As ensemble instruments in Ukraine, accordions were at first used in groups that included a fiddle, *bubon* or *baraban,* and sometimes *tsymbaly,* but by the end of World War II the fiddle had declined in many regions, and the *tsymbaly* even more so. By the 1960s, the fiddle was still in decline, and the *tsymbaly* was nearly defunct in most lowland regions. In the 1990s, the most common village ensembles that were not electrified consisted of *harmoniia* or accordion or the Russian variant known as *baian,* with *bubon* or *baraban* and wind instruments. The fiddle remained in use in some locales, but was often played only by elderly musicians who were rarely requested to perform. In the 1990s, the most obvious regional exception to these changes was Hutsul'shchyna, where younger performers played fiddle and regional instruments. In virtually all regions, it was common in the 1980s and 1990s to find a mixture of electrified instruments (guitars and keyboards) and a standard percussion trap set used in combination with acoustic instruments from the village past.

In the early twentieth century, some researchers began referring to village instrumental music as trio ensembles (*troïsta muzyka*), but this term was never commonly used by villagers, who called the local instrumental ensemble *muzyka* (accent on *y*), a variant of *muzyka* (accent on *u*) 'music'.

Many village ensembles were composed primarily of blood relatives (father, son, brother, uncle, cousin), though in the early twentieth century there were instances of husband-wife ensembles, usually with an instrumentation of fiddle and a *bas,* with the wife usually playing *bas.* In Hutsul'shchyna between about 1930 and 1970 (and perhaps earlier), women *tsymbaly* players performed with their husbands and sons.

Such ensembles earned income by playing at social gatherings, especially weddings. In most regions, they were paid for their services at weddings in a combination of cash and foodstuffs. In some regions, payment included ceremonial towels and kerchiefs. Ensembles performed local and regional dances, such as *hutsul'ka* in Hutsul'shchyna, accompanied ritual songs heard only at weddings, and played more widely distributed fare such as the Ukrainian *kozak* and *metelytsia,* polkas, and waltzes. By the 1930s, most ensembles played the tango and the foxtrot. By the 1970s, and continuously since then, regional ensembles might include acoustic and electric instruments (guitar, bass, and others), their repertory a mixture of older local or regional genres, Soviet or Ukrainian "national music," and international tunes current on the radio. An expanding grid of possible performance practices became ever more a part of village music as participation in the network economies of nation, continent, and world worked themselves into rural people's daily lives.

At *dosvitky,* instrumental musicians were hired by boys and young unmarried men, who pooled their resources to pay the musicians small amounts of cash, food, or drink (Kolomyichenko 1918a). Depending upon the region, other paying performance contexts included Sunday evening gatherings at someone's home and performances at the village inn, where musicians were often paid in alcohol.

In most regions, there seems to have been a hierarchy in terms of the amount of money earned when performing in ensemble. Fiddle players earned the most, *tsymbaly* and wind instrumentalists next, and *bas* players and drummers the least. The social status of village instrumental specialists often tended to be rather low, as they were viewed as individuals who drank too much and were frequently away from home for long periods of time, especially during village weddings. They were sometimes viewed as undesirable because of their perceived contacts with Satan or connections with black magic (Khotkevych 1930).

Regional specialists

Certain music specialists were unique to a given region. The *trembitary* of Hutsul'shchyna performed on the *trembita,* a long cylindrical wooden trumpet, which ranged in length from abut 2 to 5 meters. In the nineteenth and early twentieth centuries, the *trembita* was used to signal danger, as from a bear or a fire, or the death of a villager, and as ceremonial music during funeral services, when a *trembitary* trio played over the grave of the deceased. *Trembitary* were paid for their services during funerals, but not normally for their role as signaling agents. Before collectivization, all *trembitary* were men, but since 1970, some elderly performers have taught their granddaughters to play the instrument; however, women did not perform during funerals. In northwestern Ukraine (Polissia and Volyn'), regional specialists played the *truba,* a 1- to 2-meter-long conical wooden horn, slightly curved at the end. These funerary practices in the Carpathians and Polissia are defunct in all but a few locales.

The curved conical wooden horn (*rih*) was most common in Hutsul'shchyna and neighboring Carpathian regions, where people walked in groups from house to house singing local Christmas carols (*koliadky*), accompanied by one or several of these horns, as instrumental interludes between carols or simultaneously with the

FIGURE 4 A blind traveling singer (*starets*) with his boy guide, date unknown. Photo courtesy of the Center for the Study of Oral History and Culture, Kyïv, Ukraine.

singing. When three or four were played simultaneously, especially with singing, the effect was a raucous and boisterous cacophony. This practice did not die out in Hutsul'shchyna in the Soviet period: in the 1990s, it became more common again.

The bagpipe (*duda*) was common over virtually all of Ukraine in the 1700s, but by the mid-1800s it apparently survived only in some regions of the Carpathians, especially Hutsul'shchyna, and perhaps in western Polissia and northern Volyn'. In Hutsul'shchyna, the instrument was known as *dudka*. A local instrumental ensemble for weddings and other ceremonies was *dudka* and fiddle. The bagpipe was commonly played by adult male shepherds in the highlands, to which sheep and cattle were taken in warm months. Some performers played in market squares and village bazaars where they earned small amounts of cash, supplementing their earnings derived from agriculture. In these contexts, they primarily performed regional melodies, including *hutsul'ka do spivu* 'hutsul'ka for singing' (most commonly heard as a vocal genre during weddings) and assorted dance melodies. Performances in market squares and bazaars were common until the 1950s. By 1990, this practice had all but died out.

Blind minstrels

Ukraine's blind peasant minstrels were named, after the instruments they played, *kobzari* 'kobza players' and *lirnyky* 'lira players'. They are probably the most researched historical group in Ukraine. An enormous ethnographic literature in Ukrainian, Russian, and Polish provides a clear picture of their life, music, performance practices, and social roles from the mid-1800s until their demise, between about 1930 and 1950. Historical (nonethnographic) literature from before this time is too unreliable and lacking in detail to provide more than a tentative and general account.

Most blind minstrels had families and homes. They were not vagabonds or beggars, as they are frequently—but incorrectly—portrayed. They are better thought of as traveling musicians who worked on the road for part of the year and spent the other part at home. They traveled through villages and small towns, stopping and performing near or in markets, fairs, monasteries, and village houses (figure 4). From singing and playing, they earned cash and foods. They took most of the money home and pooled it with other family income. An especially lucrative performance context was the festival for the village patron saint. Some minstrels had students, others did not. Some wandered far away, while others traveled only in villages not far from their homes. Most often they, like other blind villagers, worked making rope by twisting hemp. Only blind village males were commonly *kobzari* and *lirnyky*. They studied with a master performer (*pan otets*) for periods ranging from a few days to eight years, but averaging one or two years. Usually they lived with him, providing him with labor and giving him their earnings for the period of their apprenticeship.

Contrary to most of what was written about the blind minstrels during the Soviet period, the main part of their repertory was not the heroic epic genre of Cossack Ukraine known as *dumy*, but Christian songs known in most regions as *psal'my*. Few minstrels knew more than two or three *dumy*, but they generally knew twelve, twenty, or more *psal'my*. They routinely performed satirical songs and dances. Until collectivization, they were apparently most often requested to perform, and earned the most money from, *psal'my*, which could be strophic or recitativelike, and treated themes such as "The Last Judgment," "Jesus, my great love," and "Lazarus" (figure 5).

⟨♦⟩ TRACK 29

The texts of their other main genre, *dumy*, described historical battles and legends of Cossack tragedy, prowess, or daily life ("About the Lament of the Captives," "About Ivan Konovchenko," "About a Poor Widow and Her Three Sons"). Formal

Villagers admired blind peasant minstrels for their spirituality and stoicism in the face of adversity (blindness, a life on the road). In the ethnographic literature, many minstrels are depicted as describing themselves, or being described, as messengers of God.

FIGURE 5 The *psal'ma* "Khrystu na kresti" ('Christ on the Cross'), in strophic form, performed by *lira* and voice. After Demutskii 1903:5.

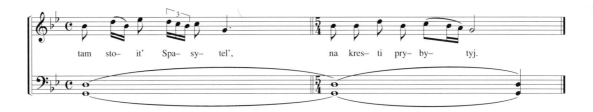

musical characteristics of *dumy* varied by performer, region, and probably time period. Most common was the recitative form (figure 6). Satirical songs and dances were virtually always simple melodies repeated over and over (figure 7). The minstrels' repertory, with its Christian themes and their blindness, lent them moral authority in the village. Villagers admired them for their spirituality and stoicism in the face of adversity (blindness, a life on the road). In the ethnographic literature, many minstrels are depicted as describing themselves, or being described, as messengers of God.

Villagers sometimes used the word *kobzar* to refer to all blind minstrels, both *kobzari* and *lirnyky*, no matter which instrument they played. In virtually all regions, blind minstrels and all other wandering blind street performers (and sometimes sim-

FIGURE 6 The *duma* "Pro sestru i brata," in recitative form, from the Poltava region, sung by Kobzar Opanas Bar'. After Kolessa 1969:187.

FIGURE 7 The
dance tune
"Metelitsia," played
on a *kobza*. After
Kolessa 1969:539.

FIGURE 7 The
dance tune
"Metelitsia," played
on a *kobza*. After
Kolessa 1969:539.

FIGURE 8 A blind minstrel (*lirnyk*) with a hurdy-gurdy (*lira*). Drawing courtesy of the Center for the Study of Oral History and Culture, Kyïv, Ukraine.

ple beggars) were collectively called *startsi* by villagers. The *lira* was the standard European hurdy-gurdy and did not vary greatly from the models known over much of Europe (figure 8). The *kobza* (called *bandura* by some researchers), a plucked bowl lute, has a complex history made confusing by contradictory or unreliable information in the historical ethnographic literature. In the late 1800s, the strings normally numbered from eight to about thirty, and were tuned to produce different scales, but especially those with a minor third, raised fourth, and minor seventh.

Because each *kobza* was handmade by a village craftsman, each was a unique instrument, with its own shape, measurements, sound, and to a certain extent, technique. *Kobzari* purchased their instruments from village masters. A given minstrel might own several instruments over the course of his lifetime, sometimes wearing one out, losing one, or having one stolen, or preferring the instrument of a particular master and purposely changing. A *kobza* could be from 5 to 20 centimeters thick, and the back could be more or less rounded, depending on the master. The body was often made from willow and the face from pine, though maple was sometimes used for more expensive instruments. The bass strings (*bunty*) usually numbered between four and six, with their tuning pegs on the neck. The short strings (*prystrunky*) numbered between six and about twenty-five. Their tuning pegs ran from back to front on the left side of the body of the instrument. Most strings were made of sheep gut in the 1800s, until copper and steel strings replaced these (KFUO 1882; Lysenko 1978). In the 1800s, most performers sounded the strings only in open position. The main exception to this may have been Ostap Veresai, who sometimes stopped the long strings with fingers of the left hand (Lysenko 1978). For virtually all other performers described in print, both hands were used to pluck open strings. *Kobza* and *lira* were usually played solo. In one style, a performer sang and played simultaneously. In another, a performer sang unaccompanied, sounding the instrument only during interludes between sections of the text.

The ethnographic literature is confused about the names that peasants used for the *kobza*. Peasants seldom distinguished between blind minstrels' instruments, and they sometimes used the word *kobza* to denote what is organologically a *lira* or a *kobza* (Kvitka 1928). In ethnographic literature from the 1800s, the minstrels themselves usually used the word *kobza* to refer to their plucked lute. The word *bandura* was often used by researchers and interviewers, but not usually by the performers; it is likely of literary origin, perhaps dating from the 1500s (Hrytsa 1979). It was apparently not used in villages in many regions until the 1920s or 1930s, but after then it became widely and commonly known. Mass production of the *bandura* began in the 1930s. Mass-produced instruments vary little from one manufacturer to another. They differ from the handmade village instruments of the past in shape, size, sound, playing technique, and repertory. The mass-produced *bandura* is normally larger and louder and customarily has sixty or more strings, tuned chromatically, fully or in part.

A separate and distinct group of performers, unresearched after collectivization, were *starchykhy* (women) and *startsi* (men), usually blind or crippled vocalists who wandered village roads and performed in regional markets and bazaars, next to churches and monasteries, or among village houses. Their repertory consisted of "begging recitations," the texts of which requested alms; songs about orphans; and several kinds of *psal'my*. Much of their repertoire overlapped that of *kobzari* and *lirnyky*. They generally had families and homes where they lived part of the year, journeying for days or weeks at a time to earn money from street performances.

Nonspecialized instruments and instrumentalists

Instrumentalists who occasionally played in nonritual settings, especially boys, performed for their own amusement on the *sopilka* 'end-blown flute', the *okarina* 'ocarina', the *drymba* 'mouth harp', and other instruments while pasturing cattle or other domesticated animals or gathering informally on a village street. In Hutsul'shchyna, the *drymba* was primarily a girls' instrument, on which girls played solo or accompanied each other when singing. In most other regions, it was played by girls and boys.

The flute (*sopilka*) has many regional and local names, sizes, and performance practices. Formerly a pastoral instrument played by boys for entertainment, it entered the practice of instrumental music specialists in the early twentieth century in Hutsul'shchyna, and later was frequently included in Soviet-period ensembles of *narodni muzychny instrumenty* 'folk-music instruments', though it was formerly a regionally specific, not a pan-Ukrainian, instrument.

Another regional instrument, a small wooden duct flute called *dudka* (not to be confused with the *dudka* of Hutsul'shchyna, a bagpipe), comes from Polissia. It is played by adult males to accompany nonritual songs sung by the player's wife or daughter or their friends, or solo when pasturing domesticated animals. It is about 50 centimeters long, with six holes in front. *Dviina fleita* 'double flute' has two pipes leading from one mouthpiece, each pipe with a separate fingering system.

In the late nineteenth and early twentieth centuries, the balalaika, a long-necked lute with triangular body, became widespread in eastern Ukrainian regions (where it was often known as *balabaika*) and some central Ukrainian regions [see RUSSIA]. Characteristically boys, more rarely girls, played it on the street in accompaniment to ribald songs, games, and dances.

Musical toys came in a wide variety and included whistles, end-blown flutes, and bells, spoons, and other idiophones.

VILLAGE MUSIC AFTER COLLECTIVIZATION

Village musical life in Ukraine and research about that music changed in profound ways in the 1930s, when the Soviet Union under Joseph Stalin instituted collectivization of land and industrial production, mass deportations and executions in villages, purges of the intelligentsia (including music researchers), proscriptive and prescriptive administrative controls over music performance in villages, and administrative control over music-research methods, aims, and content. These changes, which have continued to influence village musical practice and music research in Ukraine, can be described as part of a "modernization program," the "destruction of the peasantry," the "repression of Ukrainian culture," or the "repression of traditional culture," but however characterized, they represent an important turning point in village musical life and its research. Evaluation of current music practice cannot be reasonably undertaken without considering the institutional changes in music practice early in the Soviet period.

In rural Ukraine, many musical activities associated with this turning point took place in each village "club," a building or even a house in which Soviet cultural activities were organized. This building was often constructed on the spot where the village church (then recently destroyed by government agents) had stood, usually in the center of the village. In other cases, a house that had formerly been someone's home, usually of a family deported to Siberia or executed, was used. At the club, many social activities—including plays, reading circles, a choir, *komsomol* 'communist youth' meetings, and the like—were organized.

The clubs were also the primary performance context of a then recently invented Soviet music culture, one distributed widely to the village population, often including an instrumental ensemble. Such ensembles had little to do with village musical life before collectivization. Their repertory, instruments, and performance practices were derived from mass activities designed, controlled, and distributed through a network of governmental institutions, far removed from village practice and civil society. In most villages, the directors of music ensembles were not native to the area. They were professionals trained in the special urban institutions of Narkomos (Narodnii Komisariiat Osvity, People's Commissariat of Education) and sent to villages to teach this mass musical activity, sometimes using music notation, in other cases teaching by rote. Especially common were instrumental ensembles of plucked lutes, homogeneous groups of a mandolin, a guitar, a balalaika, or a *bandura*, or combinations of these (figure 9). Other ensembles consisted of so-called folk instruments (*narodni*

FIGURE 9   A *bandura* ensemble, around 1935. Photo courtesy of the Center for the Study of Oral History and Culture, Kyïv, Ukraine.

In vast competitions, participants in Soviet music culture gathered to perform on stage for an audience and a jury of party activists, who gave awards to performers who played in a highly virtuosic style. Village music practices, not normally a featured part of the program, seem to have been considered primitive and therefore undesirable.

instrumenty) with fiddles, end-blown flutes, a hammered dulcimer, drums of various kinds, and one or more of the plucked lutes mentioned above. They performed a mixed repertory, arranged or composed in styles consistent with state policy. Many of these ensembles became massive in size—"the bigger, the better," according to the prevailing ideology.

This repertory was controlled through "repertory lists" published in journals and provided to village music directors. Under threats of repression, state ensembles could not usually deviate far from these lists, which included stylized folk songs and dances, revolutionary marches, selections from the European classical music repertory, popular urban Soviet (mostly Russian) music, and arrangements accompanying hymns in praise of Lenin, Stalin, the Red Army, and war heroes and songs about tractors, collectivized agriculture, and the war against so-called class enemies. The state provided most of the components necessary for this music: the music institutions (village clubs), the social organization of the music (directors sent to villages to organize music activities, including music ensembles), the repertory (contained in the repertory lists), and special performance contexts. In villages, these contexts included gatherings sponsored or demanded by local party officials, Soviet holidays, and (somewhat later) elections. Some of these ensembles participated in vast competitions (*olimpiady* 'Olympics'), held periodically from 1931. Here, participants in Soviet music culture gathered locally, regionally, republic-wide, or even federally, to perform on stage for an audience and a jury of party activists, who gave awards to performers who played in a highly virtuosic style. Village music practices, not normally a featured part of the program, seem to have been considered primitive and therefore undesirable.

The virtuosic style of instrumental performance became the standard for participants in the state-funded music culture. In village clubs, small-town schools, and conservatories, this concept of instrumental performance dominated pedagogical fashions in the teaching of so-called folk instruments. Instruments were mass-produced in ways that altered their formerly diatonic capabilities, creating chromatic instruments that could perform the mostly urban music of the Soviet cultural elite. This process was euphemistically known as improving (*vdoskonalyty*) the musical instruments, or "creating new possibilities for performance," even as these changes virtually destroyed the *kobza, tsymbaly, bas, sopilka,* and other long-standing village practices.

This aesthetic was still widely held in the 1990s by numerous performers and pedagogues in all parts of the former Soviet Union, including Ukraine. In the 1980s and especially in the 1990s, as the ideological activities of the state were altered or focused less on villages, mass village ensembles lost part or most of their funding from the state. Interest among villagers in participating in them declined. By the mid-1990s, they did not exist in most villages.

After collectivization and the repression and regimentation of village civil society in the Stalinist period, research on *startsi* and their music practices virtually ceased. Performance was repressed by the police and party officials. By about 1960, performers were rarely seen. A few blind singers—unaccompanied, or self-accompanied on *harmoniia*—continued to perform in the northwest regions of Volyn' and Polissia in the 1990s. Their most typical performance context was a village market square or a regional bazaar. They frequently performed in neighboring villages on the Belarus side of the border, freely moving back and forth. They sang mostly in Russian, but with a lexicon drawn from Church Slavonic, Ukrainian, and Belarusan.

For music-derived income, blind minstrels had formerly relied on travel to distant villages. When the Soviet state forbade such travel and singing the Christian *psal'my* was increasingly difficult, blind minstrels' economic base was irretrievably altered. When working on the streets as musicians was no longer feasible, they disappeared. Some researchers have speculated that many were shot at a gathering of minstrels in 1934 (Khai 1989a), but no documentary evidence showing that such a gathering took place has emerged.

Not all instrumental music practices changed immediately with collectivization and the state's effort to alter music performance. In some regions, the instrumental practices of village wedding ensembles continued at least into the 1960s. In the mid-1990s, some instrumental ensembles not associated with state-funded or controlled collectives routinely performed at weddings a repertory that was at least in part regional or even local, as they had throughout the Soviet period. In some locales, these ensembles continued their grandparents' and great-grandparents' performance practices, mixing older local or regional genres, melodies, and dances with those of the 1950s, the 1960s, and the late twentieth century. This result particularly occurred in Hutsul'shchyna, Boikivshchyna, and parts of Bukovyna, as in various locales scattered throughout Ukraine.

In the 1990s, hundreds of folkloric vocal ensembles consisted mostly of elderly and middle-aged women. Such ensembles are a continuation of vocal ensembles from the Soviet period. They were first organized specially for public or stage presentations connected to state and party institutions and administration, and continued in the post-Soviet period only where an administrative organization from the past remained. To exist, such ensembles generally required organization from without. By the early 1990s, these ensembles probably numbered in the low hundreds—a decline from several thousands during the Soviet period. This need for outside organization does not indicate a practice closely associated with civil society, and most peasant music practices tied to civil society before collectivization did not survive in most locales into the late twentieth century. Much of what was left was a pale reflection of past practice, stylized in the context of Soviet and national institutional needs and requirements. Most villagers in the 1990s carried only a smattering of a regional music identity, and instead listened to or themselves played or sang music that was widely distributed through national institutions or commercial institutions of international media. With the dozens of exceptions just noted (and especially with the exception of Carpathian regions), the music identity and performance practices of most villagers had become similar to, or in some cases virtually indistinguishable from, those of urban dwellers. They were primarily passive consumers of a popular music culture or industry that included internationally distributed programs and locally produced styles and genres (mostly Russian and Ukrainian pop songs) of a commercial or patriotic nature. Many musical contexts and practices of peasant society were no longer observed by most rural dwellers.

URBAN COMPOSED MUSIC

In the 1800s, urban composers of art music in Ukraine, as in most other European lands, used musical materials that derived from the village, or that they believed derived from the village. Mykola Lysenko (1842–1912) was perhaps the most prominent Ukrainian composer of the late 1800s. Some of his compositions—for example, the operetta *Natalka Poltavka*—use what could be called folk-music elements. From the early twentieth century until the 1990s, most Ukrainian composers incorporated into their works material that supposedly represented rural practice. Among the most important of these composers were Nestor Nyzhankivs'kyi (1894–1940), Stanislav Liudkevych (1879–1979), Lev Revuts'kyi (1889–1977), Mykola Kolessa (b. 1904), and Myroslav Skoryk (b. 1938).

Their music was concert music, intended for an urban audience, not for villagers, most of whom did not hear it. Village music until World War II remained a mostly separate culture, or a group of regional cultures. These composers tried to draw on village culture, but they did not usually try to influence it directly.

HISTORY OF RESEARCH AND RECORDINGS

Research on the music of rural areas began in the early 1800s and was conducted by people of various backgrounds and training, including philologists, historians, ethnographers, folklorists, musicologists, and interested nonprofessionals. Much of it can be treated as oral history, mostly concerning peasantry, and to a lesser extent other village dwellers, such as rural gentry and Jewry. The ethnographic literature is written primarily in Ukrainian, Polish, and Russian. The Ukrainian population was overwhelmingly rural until the 1930s. Few studies regard the musical life of urban populations in Ukraine, other than sources on the history of the classical music of elite populations (largely standard European fare with significant local talents), and magazine articles on the popular-music industry.

The literature from the early 1800s is largely philological, formulated through period-specific strainers that compromise much of the data, such as the romantic quest for origins of distinct music practices and instruments. Between about 1860 and 1930, in any given year dozens of ethnographers were conducting field work in Ukraine. They covered hundreds of villages. Their publishing included articles, monographs, and encyclopedias. The result was an enormous ethnographic literature. Combined with ethnographies from other peasant lands of Eastern Europe, it amounts to thousands of articles and books detailing aspects of village life, including music—a literature that offers unique opportunities for comparative, cross-regional, and historical interpretations of field work.

Periodicals of uneven quality began appearing in the 1870s. By the 1890s, full-blown professionalism was evident in ethnographic publications in Ukraine, as in most of Eastern Europe. Most of these studies were not devoted exclusively to music, but the musicological information in them is bountiful, with detailed descriptions and interpretations of vocal and instrumental genres and ritual and nonritual performance contexts. Before the 1920s, only a few major studies were devoted specifically to music, usually with material gathered or organized regionally or by genre and consisting largely of hundreds of notated melodies with analyses of rhythm and scale and descriptions of performance contexts. These studies usually included information on the social organization of music, especially weddings and blind peasant minstrels. Filaret Kolessa's study of the music of the *kobzari* and *lirnyky*, the blind peasant-minstrels of Ukraine, is the most comprehensive (1969, from 1910 and 1913). Aside from complex analyses of musical scale, motive, and phrase endings, this work is incomparably valuable for its detailed music transcriptions, made from wax-cylinder recordings. A problem with many studies of the 1920s–30s is the failure to admit that it is a description of nineteenth-century performance practice, not an ethnographic document of current practice. These studies seldom refer to changes that had occurred in instrumental music in the early twentieth century.

The music of ethnic minorities (Armenians, Belarusans, Bulgarians, Czechs, Germans, Greeks, Gypsies, Jews, Poles, Russians, and others) in Ukraine was seldom systematically researched. Oskar Kolberg often briefly analyzed the music of Jews, Poles, and others in Ukrainian lands. In addition to hundreds of transcriptions of these groups' melodies, he frequently described practices and transcribed melodies that were apparently a confluence of Ukrainian and Jewish or Polish and Jewish (or Ukrainian-Jewish-Polish) musical concepts (see Kolberg 1964[1907]:56, example 662, "Jewish melody sung during the dressing of the bride," and 1964[1907]:57, example 2158, "Jewish *kozak*"). Moshe Beregovsky was one of the main researchers on Jewish musical life in Ukraine in the Soviet period. Some of his studies were translated into English by Mark Slobin (Beregovsky 1982).

The Ukrainian Academy of Sciences in the 1920s housed several research institutions, including the Music Cabinet under the administration of the Ethnographic Commission and the Cabinet of Primitive Culture under the administration of the Cultural-Historical Commission. In the 1930s, the NKVD (secret police) destroyed most of the field-work materials of the Cabinet of Primitive Culture, forcibly shut down periodicals, and sent many ethnomusicologists into exile or to labor camps or executed them (Kondrufor et al. 1992). One of the best known, Klyment Kvitka, was arrested in the early 1930s, spent an unknown amount of time in a labor camp, and was exiled to Moscow, forbidden to live or work again in Ukraine.

Competent ethnographic research did not resume in Ukraine until the late 1950s. Most sources on music research from the early 1930s to the mid-1950s are seriously flawed by the ideological constraints and prescriptions of the time and need to be approached with extreme caution. Many are excellent sources for gauging or understanding the degree of falsification to which a social science can be brought in the hands of committed activists. Field work undertaken in villages from about 1930 until about 1960, or even later, was often conducted to demonstrate a socialist content in contemporary music. From *komsomolists*, local party leaders, and other village party activists, researchers collected song texts about Lenin, Stalin, the Red Army, and tractors (Haidai 1939; Kharkiv 1932). In addition to being a highly selective view of music, these portrayals reflected some of the changes in the state-prescribed social organization of music and were part of the break with the past, the intellectual terrorism, and the territorial isolationism that characterized the Marxist-Leninist sociocultural program up to the 1980s.

By the late 1950s, many Ukrainian and other Soviet scholars were trying to publish the major or significant parts of the corpus of manuscripts held in archives and libraries, especially noncontroversial (and therefore publishable) genres of nonritual, nonreligious music practices, such as ballads and love, lyrical, and historical soldiers' songs. In the 1960s and 1970s, significant studies on regional music, village vocal harmony, and computer-assisted analyses of melodies were written. The main problem with the literature of this period was the omission of accounts of religious belief. Major village Ukrainian genres and practices—including important and pivotal moments in wedding sequences, funerary rituals, mourning laments, and blind itinerant singers' Christian psalms—were not studied.

In the 1980s and 1990s, as ideologically imposed constraints were relaxed, ethnographic research of great detail became the norm. Most of this work exists only in unpublished manuscripts, as dissertations. Much dissertation research on musical instruments was carried out in St. Petersburg under the guidance of Ihor Matsiievs'kyi (in Russian, Igor Matsievskii), whose dissertation (1970) was a forerunner of those of the 1980s. A weakness in research from the 1980s and 1990s is the

In the Stalinist period and after, field work in Ukraine was closely monitored by the security apparatus. From the late 1950s, field work was easier to conduct than in the 1930s, as the identification of unique regional or national genres and performance practices became more acceptable to state administrators.

paucity of musicosociological analysis. The blatant abuses of this topic under the influence of Marxism-Leninism perhaps led scholars to a suspicion of all analyses that focus on the relation of music and society. Thus, the social organization of musical life and the influence on, or significance for, music of political and economic institutions were not addressed systematically. In many cases, the problem was so deep that scholars even provided inadequate biographical information about their informants. There was virtually no mention of institutional influences, such as the proscriptions and prescriptions imposed by the state. Such research, as of 1999, was still not considered a serious topic by most scholars in the region. The lack of serious treatment of religious elements in village music continued and can be seen as a reflection of scholarly distortions from the Soviet past.

In the Stalinist period and after, field work in Ukraine was closely monitored by the security apparatus. From the late 1950s, field work was easier to conduct than in the 1930s, as the identification of unique regional or national genres and performance practices became more acceptable to state administrators. By the late 1980s, but especially in the 1990s, field work was difficult to conduct, not because of proscriptions of the state, but from a lack of funds. As the Soviet state began to wither away, funds for research were more difficult to obtain from such organs as the Academy of Science, a major source for funds to conduct field work since the 1920s. By the early 1990s, research funds from the Academy of Sciences had greatly decreased, and field work was carried out mostly by researchers from smaller institutions, such as the Tchaikovsky Music Academy (formerly Conservatory) in Kyïv, the Lysenko Music Institute (formerly Conservatory) in L'viv, and other music or ethnographic institutes and museums in Cherkasy, Kharkiv, Odesa, Rivno, Ternopil', and elsewhere.

Field and commercial recordings

The earliest sound recordings in Ukraine were made by Iosyf Rozdol's'kyi in 1900 in western Ukraine. By 1940, he had recorded at least twelve hundred wax cylinders, documenting a wide range of genres and styles, vocal and instrumental. Other scholars made and published transcriptions from these cylinders (Hnatiuk and Kolessa 1909; Liudkevych 1906, 1908). Wax-cylinder recordings were also made by Evgeniya Lineva, a Russian scholar, in 1903. In 1908, Filaret Kolessa, Opanas Slastion, and others, in an expedition to the Poltava region, recorded the music of the blind peasant minstrels, the *kobzari* and *lirnyky*. Some cylinders from these expeditions and recording sessions survive.

Field recordings were made in Ukraine throughout the Soviet period. From the late 1920s to World War II, Volodymyr Kharkiv and Moshe Beregovsky were among the most active recordists. Kharkiv's main contribution, of more than two hundred cylinders, was made in the Valkivs'kyi county of the Kharkiv region in eastern Ukraine in 1929. He recorded mostly *lirnyky*, but also other village street musicians.

From these, he and others transcribed dozens of *psal'my, dumy,* and dance melodies (Kharkiv 1929, 1930). Probably because of the religious content, this material was not published in the Soviet period, and is only now being comprehensively researched. Copies of many of these recordings, made in the early 1990s by the Library of Congress, are housed in the American Folklife Center, Washington, D.C. Beregovsky recorded hundreds of wax cylinders, from the music of village Jewry to urban operetta singers. These and other collections of Jewish music were locked up and sealed off by the KGB in the 1940s. They were reopened in the early 1990s, and scholars have begun to research their origins and history, using catalogs that describe their contents. As of 1995, they remained uncopied and thus unusable (Adler and Goisman 1995).

About fifteen hundred magnetic tapes, most recorded from 1950 to 1975, are housed at the Institute of Art, Folkloristics, and Ethnology (IMFE) of the National Academy of Sciences in Kyïv. These include high-fidelity recordings of widely various genres and performers, including blind minstrels. Students at the Lysenko Music Institute in L'viv have been recording in the field since the early 1970s, and at the Tchaikovsky Music Academy in Kyïv since the early 1980s. These institutions house hundreds of magnetic tapes. In addition, ethnographers and collecting enthusiasts hold dozens of private collections.

A wide variety of recorded music has been issued under numerous labels and is available on commercial formats, usually marketed as folk or traditional music. These recordings include highly stylized arrangements made by professional musicians trained specially in conservatories and music schools to render music in what they call a folk style—a phenomenon typical for several parts of the world. The recordings listed below, except Brăiloiu (1951–1958) and Khai (1997), fall into this format.

BIBLIOGRAPHY

Adler, Israël, and Mila Goisman. (1995). "À la recherche de chants perdus: La redécouverte des collections du 'Cabinet' de musique juive de Moisei I. Beregovski." In *Ndroje balendro: Musiques, terrains et disciplines,* ed. Vincent Dehoux et al., 247–267. Société d'Études Linguistiques et Anthropologiques de France, 27. Paris: Peeters.

Bazelevych, H. 1853. "Mestechko Aleksandrovka, Chernigovskoi gubernii sosnitskago uezda." *Etnograficheskii sbornik* 1:313–336.

Beauplan, Guillaume. 1990 [1650]. *Description d'Ukraine.* Kyïv: Naukova Dumka.

Beregovsky, Moshe. 1982. *Old Jewish Folk Music: The Collections and Writings of Moshe Beregovski.* Edited by Mark Slobin. Philadelphia: University of Pennsylvania Press.

Bezsonov, Peter A. 1861–1864. *Kaleki perekhozhie: Sbornik stikhov i izsledovannie.* 6 vols. Moscow: n.p.

Borzhkovskii, V. 1889. "Lirniki." *Kievskaia starina* 11:661–704.

Chubyns'kyi, Pavlo [in Russian, Pavel Chubinskii]. 1878. *Trudy etnografichesko-statisticheskoi ekspeditsii v zapadno-russkii krai.* St. Petersburg: Osudarstvennoe Geograficheskoe Obshchestvo.

Chubyns'kyi, Pavlo, and Mykola Lysenko. 1970

[1877]. "Vesillia v seli Boryspil' pereiaslavs'koho povitu poltavs'koï hubernii." In *Vesillia,* ed. O. A. Pravdiuk and M. M. Shubravs'ka, 1:81–146. Kyïv: Naukova Dumka.

Czekanowska, Anna. 1972. *Ludowe melodie wąskiego zakresu w krajach słowiańskich (przegląd dokumentacji źródłowych próba klasyfikacji metoda taksonomii wrocławskiej).* Cracow: Polskie Wydawnistwo Muzyczne.

Demutskii, P. 1903. *Lira i e motivy.* Kyïv: Leona Idzikovskago.

Domanitskii, V. 1904. "Kobzari i lirniki Kievskoi gubernii v 1903 godu." In *Pamiatnaia kniga na 1904,* ed. Nikolai Vasylenko, 4:1–65. Kyïv: Izdatelstvo Kievskogo Gubernskogo Komiteta.

Famintsyn, Aleksandr S. 1891. *Dombra i srodnye ei muzykal'nye instrumenty russkago naroda: Balalaika, kobza, bandura, torban, gitara.* St. Petersburg: n.p.

Harasymczuk, Roman. 1939. *Tańce huculskie.* Prace etnograficzne, 5, Wydawnictwo Towarzystwa Ludoznawczego we Lwowie. L'viv: Nakładem Towarzystwa Ludoznawczego.

Hnatiuk, Volodymyr. 1896. *Lirnyky.* Etnohrafichnyi Zbirnyk, 2:1–73. L'viv: Naukove Tovarystvo im. Shevchenka.

———. 1904. *Znadoby do halyts'ko-rus'koï demonolo'ogii.* Etnohgrafichnyi zbirnyk, 15. L'viv: Naukove Tovarystvo im. Shevchenka.

Hnatiuk, Volodymyr, and Filaret Kolessa. 1909. *Haïvky.* Materiialy do ukraïns'koï etnol'ogiï, 12. L'viv: Naukove Tovarystvo im. Shevchenka.

———, ed. 1919. *Ukraïns'ki vesil'ni obriady i zvychai.* Materiialy do ukraïns'koï etnol'ogii, 19–20. L'viv: Naukove Tovarystvo im. Shevchenka.

Holovatskii, Ia. O. 1878. *Narodnyia pesni halitskoi i uhorskoi rusi.* Part 3, section 2. Moscow: Izdanie Imperatorskogo Obshchestva Istorii et al.

Hoshovs'kyi, Volodymyr [in Russian, Vladimir Goshovskii]. 1968. *Ukrainskie pesni Zakarpat'ia.* Moscow: Sovetskii Kompozitor.

———. 1992. *Bio-bibliohrafichnyi pokazhchyk naukovykh prats'.* L'viv: L'vivs'ka Orhanizatsiia Spilka Kompozytoriv.

Hrinchenko, M. O. 1959 [written in or before 1940]. "Ukraïns'ka narodna instrumental'na muzyka." In *Vybrane,* ed. M. Hordiichuk, 55–103. Kyïv: Brazotvorche Mystetstvo.

Hrushevs'ka, Kateryna. 1927. *Ukraïns'ki narodni dumy.* Vol. 1. Kyïv: Derzhavne Vydavnytstvo Ukraïny.

Hrytsa, Sofia. 1979. *Melos ukraïns'koï narodnoï epiky.* Kyïv: Naukova Dumka.

Humeniuk, Andrei I. 1967. *Ukraïns'ki narodni muzychni instrumenty.* Kyïv: Naukova Dumka.

———. 1972. *Instrumental'na muzyka.* Kyïv: Naukova Dumka.

Iaremko, Bohdan. 1994. "Rol' vykonavstva u for-mubanni muzychnoï tradytsiï (na materiali ukraïns'koï sopilkovoï muzyky Prykarpattia)." Candidate's dissertation, Rosiiskii Institut Istorii Iskusstvovedeniia.

Iashchenko, Leopold. 1962. *Ukraïns'ke narodne bahotoholossia.* Kyïv: Muzychna Ukraïna.

KFUO [K. F. Ukhach-Okhorovych]. 1882. "Kobzar Ostap Veresai." *Kievskaia Starina* 7:259–282.

Khai, Mykhailo. 1989a. "Au, autentyka!" *Ukraïna* 5:17–18.

———. 1989b. "Narodnoe muzykal'noe ispol-nitel'stvo Boikovshchiny." Candidate's disserta-tion, LGITMiK.

———. 1993. "Lirnyts'ka tradytsiia iak fenomen ukraïns'koï dukhovnosti." *Rodovid* 6:37–43.

Kharkiv, Volodymyr. 1929. "Posterezhennia nad lirnykamy ta kobzariamy balkivs'koho raionu na kharkivshchyni." *IMFE* 6(2, part 23[2]).

———. 1930. "Dumy, psal'my (z melodiiamy)." *IMFE* 6(4, part 194).

———. 1932. "Muzychni pobut robitnykiv stal-inshchyny." *IMFE* (6–2, part 23[6]): 3–6.

Khotkevych, Hnat. 1930. *Muzychni instrumenty ukraïns'koho narodu.* Kharkiv: Derzhavne Vydavnytstvo Ukraïny.

Kolberg, Oskar. 1964–. *Dzieła wszystkie* 35, *Przemyskie* [first published in 1891]; 36, *Wołyń* [first published in 1907]; 52, *Białoruś-Polesie*; 54, *Ruś Karpacka*; 56:1, *Ruś Czerwona*; 57:2:2, *Ruś Czerwona.* Cracow: Polskie Wydawnistwo Muzyczne et al.

Kolessa, Filaret. 1909. *Haïvky.* Materiialy do ukraïns'koï etnol'ogiï, 12:1–100. L'viv: Naukove Tovarystvo im. Shevchenka.

———. 1929 [1910, 1913]. *Narodni pisni z halyts'koï lemkivshchyny.* Etnohrafichnyi Zbirnyk, 39–40. L'viv: Naukove Tovarystvo im. Shevchenka.

———. 1969 [1910, 1913]. *Melodiï ukraïns'kykh narodnykh dum.* Kyïv: Naukova Dumka.

Kolessa, Ivan. 1902. *Halyts'ko-rus'ki narodni pisni z mel'odiamy.* Etnohrafichnyi Zbirnyk, 11. L'viv: Naukove Tovarystvo im. Shevchenka.

Kolomyichenko, Fedir. 1918a. *Rizdviani obriady i zvychaï v Chernyhivshchyni (v seli Prokhorakh, Borzen. pov.).* Materiialy do ukraïns'koï etnol'ogiï, 18:142–154. L'viv: Naukove Tovarystvo im. Shevchenka.

———. 1918b. *Sil'ski zabavy v Chernyhivshchyni (vid Mariï Kolomyichenkovoï: Melodiï—V. M. Liashchenko).* Materiialy do ukraïns'koï etnol'ogiï, 18:123–141. L'viv: Naukove Tovarystvo im. Shevchenka.

———. 1919. *Vesillia v seli Prokhorakh, Borzens'koho povitu, Chernihivs'koï huberniï.* Materiialy do ukraïns'koï etnol'ogiï, 19–20:81–118. L'viv: Naukove Tovarystvo im. Shevchenka.

Kondrufor, IU. IU. et al. 1992. *Represovane*

kraieznavstvo (20–30–i roky).* Kyïv: Ridnyi Krai.

Kulish, Panteleimon O. 1856. *Zapiski o Iuzhnoi Rusi.* Vol 1. St. Petersburg: n.p

Kvitka, Klyment. 1924. *Profesional'ni narodni spivtsi i muzykanty na Ukraïni.* Kyïv: Zbirnyk Istorychno-Filolohichnoho Viddilu Ukraïns'koï Akademii Nauk.

———. 1928. "Do vyvchennia pobutu lirnykiv." *Pervisne hromadianstvo ta ioho perezhytky na Ukraïni* 2(3):115–129.

———. 1971. *K. V. Kvitka: Zbrannye trudy v dvukh tomakh.* Edited by Volodymyr Hoshovs'kyi [in Russian, Vladimir Goshovskii]. Moscow: Sovetskii Kompozitor.

———. 1985–1986. *Vybrani statti.* 2 vols. Edited by Anatolyi Ivanyts'kyi. Kyïv: Muzychna Ukraïna.

Kyrdan, Boris P. 1962. *Ukrainskie narodnye dumy (XV—nachalo XVII v.).* Moscow: Izdatel'stvo Akademii Nauk SSSR.

Kyrdan, Boris P., and A. Omel'chenko. 1980. *Narodni spivtsi-muzykanty na Ukraïni.* Kyïv: Muzychna Ukraïna.

Lavrov, F. 1940. "Kobzari v mynulomy i teper." *Narodna tvorchist'* 3:9–22.

Lineva, Evgenia. 1991. *Opyt zapisi ukrainskikh fonografom narodnykh pesen.* Kyïv: Muzychna Ukraïna. First published in *Trudy muzykal'no-etnograficheskoi komissii* (Moscow) 1, 1905.

Liudkevych, Stanislav. 1906. *Halyts'ko-rus'ki narodni mel'odiï zibrani na fonograf Iosyfom Rozdol's'kym.* Etnohrafichnyi Zbirnyk, 21. L'viv: Naukove Tovarystvo im. Shevchenka.

———. 1908. *Etnografichnyi zbirnyk.* 2 vols. L'viv: Naukove Tovarystvo im. Shevchenka.

Luhovs'kyi, Borys. 1926. "Chernihivs'ki startsi." *Pervisne hromadianstvo ta ioho perezhytky na Ukraïni* 3:131–177.

———. 1993 [fieldwork from 1926]. "Materiialy do iarmarkovoho repertuaru ta pobutu startsivstva v zakhidnii chernihivshchyni." *Rodovid* 6:83–120.

Lukaniuk, Bohdan. 1993. "Kul'turo-zhanrova kontseptsiia S. Liudkevycha: Do postanovky pytannia." In *Chetverta konferentsiia doslidnykiv narodnoï muzyky chervonorus'kykh ta sumizhnykh zemel',* ed. Bohdan Lukaniuk, 7–13. L'viv: Lysenko Music Institute.

Lysenko, Mykola. 1955 [1894]. *Narodni muzych-ni instrumenty na Ukraïni.* Kyïv: Mystetstvo. First published in *Zoria* 1 and 4–10.

———. 1978 [1874]. *Kharkterystyka muzychnykh osoblyvostei ukraïns'kykh dum i pisen' u vykonanni kobzaria Veresaia.* Kyïv: Muzychna Ukraïna. First published in *Sbornik Iugo-zapadnogo otdela russko-go geograficheskogo obshchestva* 1.

Lytvynovych-Bartosh, P. 1900. *Vesil'ni obriady i zvychaï u s. Zemliantsï, v Chernyhivshchynï.* Materiialy do ukraïns'koï etnol'ogiï, 3:70–173. L'viv: Naukove Tovarystvo im. Shevchenka.

Maslov, S. 1902. "Lirniki poltavskoi i chernigov-skoi gubernii." *Sbornik kharkovskogo istoriko-filo-logicheskogo obshchestva* 13:217–226.

———. 1903. "Lirniki orlovskoi gubernii, v svi-azi s istoricheskim ocherkom instrumenta 'mal-orossiiskoi liry'." *Etnograficheskoe obozrenie* 46:1–13.

Matsievskii, Igor [in Ukrainian, Ihor Matsiievs'kyi]. 1970. "Gutsul'skie skripichnye kompositsii." Candidate's dissertation, LGITMiK.

———. 1987. "Osnovnye problemy i aspekty isucheniia narodnykh muzykal'nykh instrumentov i instrumental'noi muzyki." In *Narodnye muzykal'nye instrumenty i instrumental'naia muzy-ka,* ed. Igor Matsievskii, 6–38. Moscow: Sovetskii Kompozitor.

Mierczyński, Stanisław. 1965. *Muzyka Huculszczyzny.* Cracow: Polskie Wydawnistwo Muzyczne.

Moszyński, Kazimierz. 1936. *Atlas kultury ludowej w Polsce.* Vol. 3. Cracow: Nakładem Polskiej Umiejętności.

Myshanych, Mykhailo. 1987. *Narodna vokal'na tvorchist' L'vivshchyny.* L'viv: author.

Myshanych, Stepan, and Sofia Hrytsa, eds. 1976. *Pisni Podillia.* Kyïv: Naukova Dumka.

Nezovybat'ko, O. 1976. *Ukraïns'ki tsymbaly.* Kyïv: Naukova Dumka.

Noll, William. 1991. "Economics of Music Patronage among Polish and Ukrainian Peasants to 1939." *Ethnomusicology* 35(3):349–379.

———. 1993. "Paralel'na kul'kura v Ukraïni u period stalinizmu." *Rodovid* 5:37–41.

———. 1994a. "Cultural Contact through Music Institutions in Ukrainian Lands, 1920–1948." In *Musical Cultures in Contact: Convergences and Collisions (Australian Studies in the History, Philosophy and Social Studies of Music),* ed. Margaret Kartomi and Stephen Blum, 2:204–219. Sydney: Currency Press.

———. 1994b. "The Social Role and Economic Status of Blind Peasant Minstrels in Ukraine." *Harvard Ukrainian Studies* 17(1–2):43–71.

———. 1997. "Selecting Partners: Questions of Personal Choice and Problems of History in Fieldwork and Its Interpretation." In *Shadows in the Field: New Perspectives for Fieldwork in Ethnomusicology,* ed. Gregory F. Barz and Timothy J. Cooley, 163–187. New York: Oxford University Press.

Nosov, Leonyd I. 1940. "Pershyi vsesoiuznyi ohli-ad vukonavtsiv na narodnykh instrumentakh." *Narodna tvorchist'* 1:51–60.

Oshurkevych, O. 1970. *Pisni z Volyni.* Kyïv: Muzychna Ukraïna.

Plosaikevych, L. and I. A. Senchyk. 1916. *Mel'odiï ukraïns'kykh narodnykh pisen' z Podillia i Kholmshchyny.* Materiialy do ukraïns'koï etnol'ogiï, 26. L'viv: Naukove Tovarystvo im. Shevchenka.

Polotai, M. 1940. "Mystetstvo kobzariv Radians'koï Ukraïny." *Radians'ka muzyka* 6:23–34.

Pravdiuk, Oleksandr A., and Mariia M.

Shubravs'ka, eds. 1970. *Vesillia*. 2 vols. Kyïv: Naukova Dumka.

Riptets'kyi, O. 1918. *Parubochi i divochi zvychaï v seli Andriiashivtsi Lokhvyts'koho povitu na Poltavshyni.* Materiialy do ukraïns'koï etnol'ogiï, 18:155–169. L'viv: Naukove Tovarystvo im. Shevchenka.

Saban, Larysa. 1989. "Synkhronnyi zapys narod-notantsiuval'noï tvorchosti." In *Aktual'ni pytannia metodyky fiksatsiï tvoriv narodnoï muzyky*, 37–40. Kyïv: Ministerstvo Kul'tury URSR.

———. 1995. "Dudky na Hutsul'shchyni." In *VI Konferentsiia doslidnykiv narodnoï muzyky Chervonorus'kykh ta Sumizhnykh zemel'*, ed. Bohdan Lukaniuk, 43–53. L'viv: Lysenko Music Institute.

Shchukhevych, V. 1904. *Hutsul'shchyna.* Materiialy do ukraïns'ko-rus'koï etnol'ogiï, 7, part 4. L'viv: Naukove Tovarystvo im. Shevchenka.

Shubravs'ka, Mariia M. 1982. *Vesil'ni pisni.* 2 vols. Kyïv: Naukova Dumka.

Slastion, Opanas. 1902. *Kobzar Mykhailo Kravchenko i ego dumy.* Kyïv: Imperatorskii Universitet sv. Vladimira.

———. 1908. "Melodiï ukraïns'kykh dum i ïkh zapysuvannia." *Ridnyi krai* 35:4–6, 38:5–7, 41:5–7, 43:4–7, 44:8–9.

———. 1909. "Zapysuvannia dum na fonohrafi." *Ridnyi krai* 22:8–9, 23:7–10, 24:6–8.

Speranskii, M. [in Ukrainian, M. Sperans'kyi] 1904. *Iuzhno-russkaia pesnia i sovremennye ee nositeli: Po povodu bandurista T. M. Parkhomenka.* Sbornik istoriko-filologicheskogo obshchestva pri institute Kn. Bezborodko v Nezhine, 5. Kyïv: I. I. Chokolov.

Tsertelev, Kniaz. 1827. "O narodnykh stykhotvoreniiakh (Pis'mo ko g-nu Maksimovichu)." *Vestnik Ievropy* 9:270–277.

Ukraïnka, Lesia. 1956. *Lysty, 1881–1913.* Vol. 5. Kyïv: Derzhavne Vydavnytstvo Khudozhn'oï Literatury.

Verkhovynets', Vasyl' M. 1970. "Vesillia v seli Shpychyntsi Skvurs'koho povity kyïvs'koï huberniï." In *Vesillia,* ed. O. A. Pravdiuk and M. M. Shubravs'ka, 1:220–280. Kyïv: Naukova Dumka. Manuscript from 1914.

Vodianyi, Volodymyr. 1993. "Narodna instrumental'na muzyka zakhidnoho Podillia: Problema evoliutsiï tradytsiinykh form muzykuvannia." Candidate's dissertation, Rosiiskii Institut Istoriï Iskusstvovedeniia.

AUDIOVISUAL RESOURCES

Brăiloiu, Constantin. 1951–1958. *Ukraïniens Roumanophones: Region du bong établie par Constantin Brăiloiu.* Unesco Conseil International de la Musique A1 59/58. LP disk.

Chants et danses d'Ukraine. 196?. Le Chant du Monde LD-S-4225. LP disk.

Khai, Mykhailo. 1997. *Isuse mii* and other titles. Kyïv: Ukrainian Experimental Folklore Laboratory. 18 unnumbered cassettes.

Konoplenko, Paul. 1961. *The Kobza: Songs and Tunes Played on the Kobza.* Folkways FW 8705. LP disk.

Music of the Ukraine. 1951. Ethnic Folkways Library FE 4443. LP disk.

Songs and Dances of the Ukraine. 1957–1958. Monitor MF 301 and MF 308. 2 LP disks.

Georgia
Joseph Jordania

Ethnographic Districts
Songs and Singing
Contexts for Musical Performance
Musical Instruments
Social Processes in Making Music
History of Music
Village Music in the Soviet Period
Popular Music: Jazz, Rock, Folk
History of Scholarship

Georgia (in Georgian, *Sakartvelo* 'Land of the Kartvels') is a mountainous country of 69,700 square kilometers, situated in the western Caucasus, south of the Caucasian Mountains and east of the Black Sea. About 5 million Georgians (Kartveli) live in Georgia and adjacent territories of Turkey and Azerbaijan. No sizable communities of Georgians live outside the Caucasus. Georgians speak the Georgian language (Kartuli), which has several dialects in different districts. In western and northwestern Georgia—districts known as Samegrelo and Svaneti, respectively—are languages of the Kartvelian family of languages: Megrelian (Megruli) and Svanetian (Svanuri), unconnected with any other language family and believed survivals from before Indo-European times. Georgia officially adopted Christianity in 337 and is one of the oldest Christian countries. Georgians are mostly Eastern Orthodox, with a small number of Roman Catholics. The population of Achara, southwestern Georgia, was Islamized during three centuries of Turkish dominance, starting in the sixteenth century. Despite religious differences, musical traditions are similar throughout Georgia.

Several ancient Georgian states existed in this territory: Kolchis (sixth to second century B.C.) along the Black Sea coast, where, according to ancient Greek mythology, the Argonauts arrived in search of the Golden Fleece; Iberia (fourth century B.C. to fourth century of the common era) in eastern Georgia; and Lazika (Egrisi) in western Georgia (second to sixth centuries). From the tenth to the twelfth centuries, all of Georgia was united as a kingdom under the eastern Georgian ethnic group Kartli, from whom the name *Sakartvelo* derives. The eleventh and twelfth centuries saw the climax of Georgian culture: the first major academies were founded, and architecture, poetry, and philosophy thrived. Beginning in the thirteenth century, Muslim countries threatened Georgia, whose king in 1783 responded by signing a contract of friendship with Russia. In 1801, Russia abrogated the contract, abolished the Georgian king's dynasty, and despite several rebellions incorporated Georgia into the Russian Empire. In 1918, after the Bolshevik revolution, Georgia became independent as the Republic of Georgia. In 1921, communist Russia reoccupied Georgia, which regained its independence in 1991 as the Republic of Georgia, with its capital Tbilisi. Post-Soviet ordeals—civil war and wars in Abkhazia and Ossetia—ravaged the Georgian economy and caused intensive migrations, within and outside the

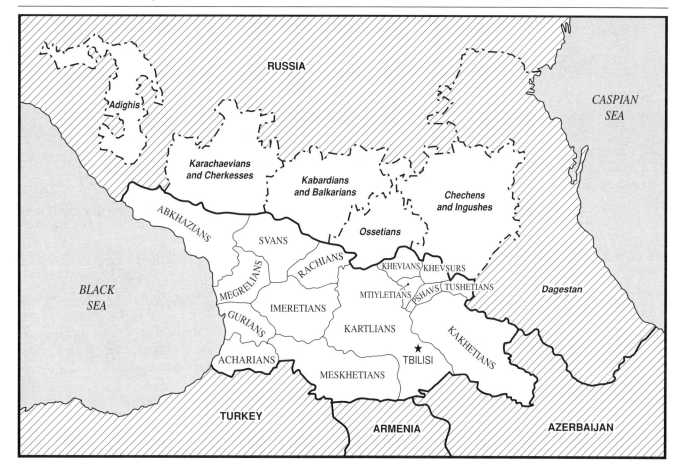

MAP 10   Georgia and North Caucasia.
Ethnographic regions are shown in Georgia, and
political regions are shown in North Caucasia.

country, mostly to Russia, European countries, and the United States of America.

Folk-musical traditions in Georgia are well preserved, especially in the mountainous areas. Overall, these traditions are actively negotiated in contemporary life. The study of Georgian music reveals the interaction of European and Asiatic musical traditions and the ongoing performance of archaic musical survivals, and affords an opportunity to examine the effect of media on contemporary musical life.

ETHNOGRAPHIC DISTRICTS

Georgian folk music is traditionally divided into fifteen ethnographic districts clustering in an eastern area (Khevians, Mtiyletians, Khevsurs, Pshavs, Tushetians, Kartlians, Kakhetians, Meskhetians) and a western area (Abkhazians, Svans, Rachians, Megrelians, Imeretians, Gurians, Acharians), but they can also be viewed as mountain districts (Abkhazians, Svans, Rachians, Khevians, Mtiyletians, Khevsurs, Pshavs, Tushetians) and valley districts (Megrelians, Imeretians, Gurians, Acharians, Kartlians, Kakhetians, Meskhetians) (map 10).

Kartli and Kakheti comprise the largest ethnographic traditions and share many musical features. Two- and three-part drone singing predominates. Examples of developed-drone style are found in Kakhetian table songs. In contrast, three hundred years of Ottoman rule considerably affected the Meshketi tradition, uniquely marked by an absence of part-singing. The last recordings of the polyphonic tradition were made in Meskheti in the 1960s.

Samegrelo is notable for its polyphonic songs and simpler two- and three-part drone songs. Imerety, in the center of west Georgia, specializes in three-part songs and urban songs. Guria is notable for extensive use of polyphony in three- and four-part songs. Achara divides its musical heritage into two subtraditions, valley and mountain: the valley music resembles Gurian music, but the mountain music favors two-part singing.

Because of historical links, Georgian practices have influenced Abkhazian folk music, notably in three-part singing, which in turn relates to Adighian music [see NORTH CAUCASIA: "Abkhazians"]. The geographic isolation of Svaneti, in the highest Caucasian mountain ranges, has contributed to the retention of archaic features, such as the absence of rhythmic poetry. Only three-part songs are found here. Racha, a mountain district, is marked by a prevalence of three-part songs with developed melodic lines.

Two- and three-part drone singing predominates in the east Georgian mountain districts of Khevi and Mtiuleti, some of whose songs share stylistic traits with those of Svaneti and Racha. Primitive solo and two-part songs comprise the musical traditions of the mountain districts of Khevsureti, Pshavi, and Tusheti, known for their developed poetic forms. The musical traditions of Tusheti, a pastoral territory, shows influence from the musical culture of Azerbaijan and Dagestan.

Two additional districts lie outside Georgia: Shavsheti in Turkey, with musical traditions closely resembling those of Acharia, and Saingilo in Azerbaijan, with music whose few known examples share musical features with the music of Kakheti.

SONGS AND SINGING

Part singing forms the basis of the Georgian musical system, which maintains no unison-singing tradition in choral performances. The rare occurrence of solo singing—for harvest songs and women's repertoires—reflects the particular natures of the contexts in which people sing the songs. *Orovela,* solo male songs connected with plowing, threshing, and winnowing, are found only in Kartli and Kakheti, and have parallels in Armenian, Azerbaijanian, and some Central Asian traditions. Women's solo songs are mostly lullabies and laments.

Part singing

More than sixty traditional terms describe the parts and their functions in three-part songs. Traditionally, the middle part (*tkma* 'to say') is considered the main part (*pirveli khma* 'first part'). Its performer (*mtkmeli* 'speaker') usually begins and leads the song.

The top voice (*modzakhili* 'follower') is considered the second voice (*meore khma*). It has several versions, including *tsvrili* 'thin' and *magali bani* 'high bass'. *Gamkivani* 'like the cock's sound' is known for its specific timbre. The most famous, *krimanchuli* 'distorted falsetto, distorted jaw', is a yodel, distributed in lowland areas of western Georgia (figure 1, top voice).

The lowest voice (*bani* 'bass') is the only part traditionally sung by a group. In highly developed polyphonic songs of the western Georgian lowland districts (Guria, Imereti, Samegrelo, Achara), all three voices are performed by soloists, and the bass is often the most melodically and rhythmically active part (figure 2). In four-part harvest songs (*naduri*) from Guria and Achara, a unique voice (*shemkhmobari* 'giving the voice') sounds a pedal drone between the high melodic voices (figure 3): also performed by a group of singers, it acts as a second bass voice.

Four Georgian polyphonic styles can be distinguished: drone (which may change its pitch several times during the song), ostinato, parallel, and free polyphony. These styles are often combined, as when a drone has an ostinato under a free polyphonic line (figure 3). Use of the pedal drone without words predominates in the eastern area (figure 4) but is rare in the western area, where free polyphony prevails

FIGURE 1 West Georgian three-part polyphony. The top voice (*krimanchuli*) uses yodeling, the middle voice (*tkma*) is considered the main part, and the lowest voice (*bani* 'bass') is the only part sung by a chorus, rather than a soloist. After Rosebashvili 1980:6.

FIGURE 2 Western Georgian three-part polyphony in which the bass part is most active and all three parts are sung by soloists. After an unpublished transcription by Edisher Garakanidze.

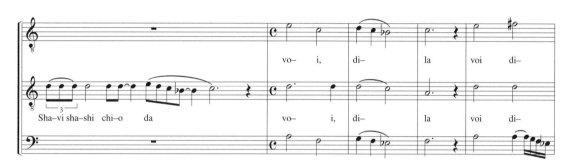

The guiding principle of Georgian aesthetics is the
avoidance of repetition. In music, it reveals itself
in the absence of unison singing, the lack of imitation and canonic forms, the primacy placed on
improvisation, and the avoidance of exact repetition
in vocal performance.

FIGURE 3 A western Georgian
four-part harvest song (*naduri*)
with two drones, one between
two melody voices.
Transcription by Joseph
Jordania.

(figures 1 and 2). Also found in western Georgia are an ostinato and a drone broken
up by recited words. Parallel polyphony is found in the western Georgian mountain
districts (figure 5).

Native aesthetics

The guiding principle of Georgian aesthetics is the avoidance of repetition. This
principle is evident in architecture and poetry. In music, it reveals itself in the absence
of unison singing, the lack of imitation and canonic forms, the primacy placed on
improvisation, and the avoidance of exact repetition in vocal performance.

Native articulations illustrate the connections among singing, the divine, and
nature. The eleventh-century philosopher Ioane Petritsi attributed three-part
polyphony to the Trinity, the Christian concept that the Father, the Son, and the
Holy Spirit attain unity as three persons in one godhead. Part-singing also represents
the sounds of nature and is said to resemble *aelebra,* the harmonious singing of a
flock of birds. Folk and classical poetry emphasizes the necessity of bass support. A
vocal performance without a bass is believed aesthetically inferior, as reflected in a
poetic phrase: "The song is adorned by the bass, the garden by the red apple."

The harmonic system is highly developed and unique. Polyphony in three- and
four-part songs results in chords that include dissonant intervals, such as seconds,
fourths, sevenths, and ninths. The purity of the perfect fifth has primary importance.
Harmonic functionality is based on second relations between the harmonic steps.
The scalar system is called unicentral because each scale has only one center. Each
tone is individual, and its function is not repeated by the same tone an octave higher
or lower. Complex tonal modulations serve as a foundation, especially in table songs

FIGURE 4 An eastern Georgian three-part polyphonic song with a moving, wordless drone supporting two melodic parts. After Rosebashvili 1980:33.

of eastern Georgia, also noted for unique cadences. Figure 4 shows the cadence that moves the tonal center a minor second below its initial tonality, from F to E.

Studies of eastern Georgian singing traditions are numerous, but those of western Georgia are few. Features of western Georgian polyphony illustrate important differences from the polyphony of Western Europe. These include the absence of repeated themes, the lack of imitation or canonic construction of the melodic lines, and the tendency for each voice to perform a uniquely distinctive melody. Polyphonic improvisations are governed by horizontal and vertical considerations. While improvising, each singer relies on a melodic axis or the central note and emphasizes consonant melodic intervals of thirds and fifths (figures 1 and 3). The vertical coordination of voices places the axes or central notes of different voices at dissonant harmonic intervals, for example, E–B♭–C–f–c in figure 3.

FIGURE 5 Three-part polyphony in roughly parallel motion, from the western Georgian mountains. One typical chord is built up of intervals of a fourth and a second (G–C–D). Transcription by Joseph Jordania.

Georgian scalar systems are nonoctave, unicentral scales. Ancient pentatonic and tetratonic scales survive in the mountain districts, mostly in eastern Georgia, and in some valley traditions. The most common pentatonic or tetratonic scale is A–c–(d)–e–g.

Diatonic scalar systems predominate, subdivided into those built on tetrachords and those built on pentachords. Table songs of eastern Georgia have scalar systems with tetrachordal and pentachordal elements. Tetrachordal scales without implications of pentachordal scalar elements are found only in monophonic harvest songs from eastern Georgia. Pure tetrachordal scales are not found in polyphonic songs. The pentachordal system has a much wider distribution, particularly in western Georgia.

Little research on the rhythmic systems of Georgian folk music has been done, though Georgian folk poetic meters have been studied thoroughly. In western Georgia, 2/4 and 4/4 meters predominate, but in eastern Georgia, 3/4 and 6/8 are highly popular. Among the Guria, the poetic text is subordinate to the musical rhythm. Gurian songs are usually independent of a text, Gurian singers frequently use the same text for different melodies, and the Gurian repertoire of untexted songs is large. The Khevsureti vocal tradition, from the eastern Georgian mountains, subordinates music to the poetic text. The Khevsuretian poetic tradition is highly developed, and good singers are known by their poetic talent.

Georgia has three main types of metric systems: changing meter, found occasionally among the Svans (of western Georgia) and groups of the eastern Georgian mountain districts; free meter, of solo harvest songs and table songs of the eastern Georgian valley districts; and fixed meter, mostly 4/4 in the western Georgian valley districts, and 4/4 and 6/8 in ritual songs and round-dance-songs of the eastern Georgian valley districts.

Performance practice

Universal participation is one of the most important features of Georgian folk-music performance. In western Georgia, only specialists engage in some types of singing (see figure 2), but elsewhere, in most performance contexts (such as working, riding,

FIGURE 6 A performance by Tetnuldi, a youth ensemble from Svaneti, with eight long-necked lutes (*panduris*) and one wooden cane flute (*salamuri*). Photo by Stuart Gelzer, 1995. Used by permission.

and drinking events), the chorus includes all the participants. The vocal quality is open and usually devoid of special vocal techniques.

Throughout Georgia, polyphony is performed by two lead soloists, who perform the top voices simultaneously or antiphonally, accompanied by a choral bass. Antiphonal performance by two choirs is ubiquitous. Antiphony includes two choirs, a choir and a trio of soloists, a choir and one soloist, two soloists (rarely found), and two soloists on the same drone. The last form is commonly found in the mountain districts of eastern Georgia.

The performance of vocal polyphony was always marked by a competitive spirit, in which each singer strives to present the best singing through improvisation. Competitions also occurred during ritual events. For a wedding, the singing groups of different villages met, and sessions that pitted the groom's and the bride's best friends against each other were important events. Competitiveness, an important element in traditional folk-music performance, has now been partially replaced by the institutionalization of competitions in festivals (figure 6).

The predominantly polyphonic nature of Georgian folk music requires an emphasis on collective creation, in which people place a primary value on improvisation. Connected to other singers, individuals follow a traditional structure, yet have great freedom in realizing melodic lines. In a sense, to perform is to compose, and the best singers never repeat themselves, creating a wide range of variations. This process creates difficulty in determining the origins of any given song, and Georgians regard folk-song composers as anonymous. Contemporary songs have known composers, but these are not regarded as folk songs, because the manner of their performance is set and they have been recorded, transcribed, and published.

The forms and structures of folk compositions are determined by social function. Lullabies have no fixed cadence, as the end is determined by the sleeping baby. The harvest song (*naduri*) has a dynamic structure comprising several sections, sung at progressively faster tempos and higher pitches, and moving from two- and three-part polyphony to four-part polyphony (figure 3). Such songs can last more than one hour. Eastern Georgian table songs are distinguished by their tonal modulations, free meter, melodic development, and melismas (figure 4). Many lyric songs are in couplets. Polyphonic funeral songs, such as the Gurian *zari,* have structures based on liturgical forms.

The rain-begging ritual, known as Lazaroba, is performed by girls and young women, who in a procession carry a female figure (called *guda, kuki,* or *gonja*) while singing the song "*Lazare.*" The ritual ends with the burial of the figure in a riverbank and a ritual feast.

A peculiarity of Georgian traditional music is the absence of developed epics. A group of epic songs, based on fragments of the Amirani epics, survives in Svaneti. These songs are performed in three-part harmony and are mostly accompanied by circle dances.

CONTEXTS FOR MUSICAL PERFORMANCE

As elsewhere in Europe, traditional singing was mainly occasioned by calendric and life-cycle rituals. Religious worship and social dancing provide the other main contexts.

Calendric rituals

The agricultural year begins in spring, when rituals center on death and resurrection. The main ritual complex, *kvelieri* (from *kveli* 'cheese', the last week of carnival), occurs during the week before Lent and involves several events. Masqueraders' performances (in rural areas, *berikaoba,* from the ancient Georgian word *ber* 'child'; in urban areas, *keenoba*) include a ritual plowing of water, a ritual lament for the plow, and a masqueraders' lament. Originally a pagan celebration, *kvelieri* became incorporated with Easter. In Svaneti, this event continues to be celebrated as *murkvamoba-kviriaoba,* a fertility ceremony, with elements of an ancient phallic cult.

In *chonaoba,* a ritual held on Palm Sunday (one week before Easter), maskers process through the village while singing a ritual song (*chona*). From listeners, they beg food and red eggs (a symbol of fertility), then hold a ritual feast.

The celebration of the Christian saint White George (Tetri Giorgi) on the fourteenth and fifteenth of August is the central summer ritual. It supplanted an archaic moon cult, which figured prominently in ancient Georgian beliefs and was connected to a bull-worshiping cult. The quarter moon is believed to symbolize the bull's horns. The celebratory climax occurs when the moon is full and a woman in trance foretells the future. The *dideba* 'glory', a women's circle dance, decorates the primary ritual music, performed antiphonally. Additional celebrations of St. George's Day occur on 23 April and 10 November. The existence of 363 Georgian churches dedicated to Saint George attests to this saint's popularity. In fact, St. George is the most popular and respected Christian saint in the country.

The mountain districts of eastern Georgia continue to celebrate Atengenoba, the biggest local celebration, originally connected with the Christian saint Atinogen and his ten students. Held from 16 to 29 July, it is celebrated with the sacrifice of sheep and the performance of circle dances. The rain-begging ritual, known as Lazaroba, Eliaoba, and Gonjaoba, is performed by girls and young women, who in a procession carry a female figure (called *guda, kuki,* or *gonja*) while singing the song "*Lazare.*" The ritual ends with the burial of the figure in a riverbank and a ritual feast.

Autumn is marked by harvest rituals. Celebrations are centered on the Christian saints George and Mary. Giorgoba, Saint George's Day, begins on 23 November and consists of ritual feasts and the performance of circle dances for several days. Mariamoba, the death of Saint Mary, was commemorated on 28 August. Its ritual theme centered on the concept of motherhood, and its enactment continued until the start of the nineteenth century.

Contrasting with the moon-based symbolism of summer rituals, the symbolism of winter rituals features the sun. Objects representing the shape of the sun—such as circular forms, fire circles, and gold coins—figure prominently. Folk mythology considered the sun female; the moon, male; therefore, winter celebrations are dedicated to a goddess. The ritual is best preserved in Svaneti, whose ritual song *riha* is connected to the Christmas celebration, also rich in ritual acts. The Christmas carol "*Alilo,*" found throughout Georgia, accompanies ritual processions in which food is gathered and homes are blessed, after which participants have a ritual feast.

Life-cycle rituals

In addition to calendric rituals, Georgian folk culture is rich in celebrations that mark an individual's life from birth to death.

The birth ritual, *dzeoba,* is marked by the obligatory performance of the song "*Mze shina*" ('The sun is inside'). A few days after a birth, a mother protects her infant by singing a ritual lullaby, *nana.* A rare instance of monophonic singing, it can be sung in polyphonic form by two or more persons. A two- and three-part curing song, known as *iavnana* in eastern Georgia and *batonebo* in western Georgia, is performed for whooping cough and the measles. The eastern version is sung by women, but the western version is performed by men. During the illness, the baby's room contains ritual decorations, and all people present try to create a calm atmosphere.

The next important celebration in an individual's life is the wedding (*kortsili*). The central event is the best man's songs, which begin in the bride's home and continue throughout the procession to, and arrival at, the groom's house. All wedding songs are polyphonic.

Funerals also rely on music. Each ethnographic district has its tradition of laments, which range from three-part polyphonic songs sung only by men to monophonic and polyphonic songs sung by women.

Religious music

Religious rituals are prominent in Georgian cultural life. Because Christianity is the official religion, religious music is a significant genre, with historical roots in Georgian professional music . Pagan rituals and their songs have survived in various places, particularly in the mountains, where Christian and pagan ritual elements are intertwined. Pre-Christian songs are best preserved in Svaneti. Songs such as *lile,* connected with the cult of the sun (figure 4), and *kviria,* connected to the fertility deity, are believed to be archaic. These and other ritual survivals can be attributed to the remoteness of the mountain areas, whose mode of life made establishing new religious traditions difficult and contributed significantly to the tenacity of pagan rituals. Pagan rites emphasize the relationship between humans and nature, important in the mountains. Though retaining their pagan practices, mountain dwellers vaunt Christianity as a means to solidify national and ethnic identity.

Ottoman rule in Achara, southwestern Georgia, led to the replacement of Christianity by Islam, whose restrictions, such as the prohibition of alcohol consumption, caused the loss of some traditional music genres, such as table songs. With the waning of state propaganda promoting atheism, a new generation of Acharians is

returning to Christianity (figure 7). Simultaneously from the late 1980s, the opening of the borders between Georgia and Turkey strengthened Islam.

Theater and dance

Georgian culture promoted rural and urban folk theater. The spring masquerade, *berikaoba*, ritually enacted the theme of death and resurrection. Its urban variant, *keenoba,* included elements of the historical battle with *kaeni* (or *khan*), the Muslim ruler. Singing, instrumental music, and dancing filled the day with long performances, in which many participated.

Found throughout Georgia is a wide variety of dance forms, of which the circle dance (*perkhuli*) is considered the most archaic. In Svaneti, vocal performance culminates in circle dances, some of which have ritual themes, such as hunting and fertility. Antiphonal performance of three-part polyphonic song accompanies Georgian circle dances. Men and women usually had different dances, but in western Georgia (particularly Svaneti) the tradition of mixed dancing survived. In some districts, one circle of dancers stands on the shoulders of another in a suite of dances whose successful performance, according to folk belief, ensures a bountiful harvest. Three-story circle dances occurred in Svaneti and Kartli. Noncircle or line dances (*perkhisa*) also could be one- and two-story. In Meskheti, two- or three-story line dances included the long dance-walk to another village to see relatives or friends and the return home. This tradition was alive as late as about 1900.

Among dances that use instrumental accompaniment are military dances and staged versions of folk dances. The *khorumi,* a military dance found among the Acharians and Gurians, is in 5/4 meter and uses instrumental accompaniment provided by a bagpipe (*chiboni*) and/or a drum (*doli*). The eastern Georgian mountain dance (*mtiuluri*) contained themes of battle and competition and now serves as the basis for modern folk dances accompanied by an accordion and a *doli*. Also by using instruments, staged versions of the women's dance *samaia* and the mixed couple dances *davluri* and *kartuli* depart from the traditional use of vocal accompaniment. Middle Eastern dance forms became popular in the 1700s and 1800s, with the migrations of craftsmen who settled in Tbilisi. Dances such as the *bagdaduri* and the *kintouri* were accompanied by Middle Eastern instruments, such as the *zurna* 'double-reed oboe', the *duduki* 'fipple flute', and the *doli*.

FIGURE 8 Members of the Tbilisi University ensemble Mtatsminda sing after dinner, accompanied by a *chonguri.* Photo by Stuart Gelzer, 1995. Used by permission.

Contemporary contexts

Today, because of changes in traditional life-styles and modernization, many life-cycle rituals are no longer practiced. Many work, riding, and ritual songs were transferred to the table, creating the impression that Georgian folk songs are mostly table songs (figure 8). In some localities (mostly urban ones), the tradition of singing is decreasing. For example, wedding celebrations now use amplified instrumental ensembles, rather than traditional table songs. Funeral rites have remained relatively stable, retaining specific local laments and the use of singer-specialists in western Georgia.

Staged folk-song performances have become a main form of traditional music in Georgia. The first modern concert of folk music took place in 1886 and was a great success. The format has changed little since then. New songs are brought to the stage every year, and folk material continues to be extracted from its ritual context for performance, often without the corresponding dances. Georgian professional and amateur choirs and dance ensembles continue to have a wide audience, within Georgia and abroad (figure 9). Performances of folk songs and dances have become important tourist attractions in Georgia.

Modern technological media have affected folk traditions: television and other media have led to the increased popularity of contemporary folk performers, the standardization of variant versions, the deemphasis of context, and rural performers' emulation of professional musicians. The younger generation's attitude toward folk music has been affected by viewing classical and popular music shows.

MUSICAL INSTRUMENTS

Georgian musical instruments reflect indigenous and foreign sources. Nonindigenous instruments are mostly from Middle Eastern cultures, identifiable as Arabian, Armenian, Azerbaijanian, Persian, and Turkish.

Idiophones and membranophones

A pair of copper plates found in archaeological excavations in central Georgia dates from the fourth century. No longer used, this instrument was known as *tsintsila* or *lini,* reflecting the Chinese *ling* 'small bell' and *ling dzo* 'gongs' (Javakhishvili 1990 [1938]). In Kartli, Kakheti, Tusheti, Racha, and Samegrelo, the *daphi* or *daira,* a frame drum with jingles, serves for performances in which a female dancer provides

The *chuniri*, a three-stringed bowed lute, has an important role in funeral rituals, in which it is believed able to bring home the soul of a deceased whose death occurred away from the house. In such cases, it is played where the death occurred until cockcrow, when it proceeds to the home of the deceased, playing music accompanied by the cock.

FIGURE 9   The Georgian choir Fazisi performs at a folk festival in Falun, Sweden. Photo by Owe Ronström, 1988.

her own musical accompaniment. Its names suggest external origins: *daphi* recalls Arabic *daf* and Hebrew *tof,* terms for squarish frame drums, and *daira* recalls Arabic *dā'ira* 'circular', a term for roundish frame drums (Sachs 1940). The *daphdaphi* or *doli,* a large double-headed drum, is played with an accordion to accompany dancing. The most popular percussion instrument, it is more often called *doli* (from Persian) than *daphdaphi*. The *diplipito* consists of two or occasionally three to five skin-covered clay pots, each sounding a unique pitch because of its size. Mostly struck with small sticks, the *diplipito* has parallels in the Armenian *nagara* and the Azerbaijani *gosha-nagara*. Its small version, known as *tablak,* is sometimes called *dumbul* in literary sources.

Chordophones

Plucked chordophones include long-necked lutes (*panduri, chonguri*) and harps (*ebani, knari, changi*). The *panduri,* a medium-sized fretted lute with three strings, tuned $g–a–c_1$, is one of the most popular instruments and accompanies dance and songs as in the context of folk-poetry competitions (*shairi*). It is found mostly in eastern Georgian mountain and valley districts. The *chonguri,* an unfretted medium-sized lute with four strings, tuned $f–a–c_1–e_1$ (or $f–a–c_1–f_1$), accompanies singing and dancing (figures 6, 8, 10, and 11). It is played primarily by Samegrelo and Guria women. The term *panduri* has been extant since the tenth century, but *chonguri* does not appear in literary sources until the eighteenth. In some areas of eastern Georgia, the term *chonguri* is applied to the *panduri*.

FIGURE 10   Riho, an ensemble from Svaneti, rehearses with a harp (*changi*) and a bowed lute (*chuniri*). Photo by Stuart Gelzer, 1995. Used by permission.

The *changi,* a harp (from Persian *chang*) found in Svaneti, provides accompaniment for three-part songs. The traditional *changi* has six strings and sometimes performs with the *chuniri,* a bowed lute.

Literary sources mention the *ebani* and the *knari,* harps that have fallen into disuse. There is no iconographical information about the *ebani,* though older historical writings often mention it. Javakhishvili (1990 [1938]) suggests an etymological connection between *ebani* and *bani,* the lowest voice of the polyphonic choir, and a possible historical connection to the "*tebuni*"—a nineteenth-century misspelling of Greek *tò buní,* designating the ancient Egyptian harp. The *knari* is cited in literary works of the early Middle Ages. The word may relate to the name of a South Indian stick zither, possibly reflecting the Hebrew King David's harp and the ancient Egyptian harp, both actually lyres (Sachs 1940). A clay figure from the fifth century B.C. shows a musician playing a stringed instrument apparently related to the *changi* and possibly the *ebani.*

The bowed chordophone (*chuniri*) is a three-stringed bowed lute tuned $a–c_1–d_1$, found in Svaneti; in Achara and Tusheti, it is called *chianuri.* It serves as a solo and accompanimental instrument, can perform three-part polyphony, and in Svaneti is sometimes joined by a *changi.* It has an important role in funeral rituals, in which it is believed able to bring home the soul of a deceased whose death occurred away from the house. In such cases, it is played where the death occurred until cockcrow, when it proceeds to the home of the deceased, playing music accompanied by the cock.

Aerophones

A wooden cane flute (*salamuri*) is found in eastern Georgia. An example made of bone has been unearthed in a young shepherd's grave from the fourteenth or fifteenth century B.C. Folk belief says the instrument originated as a gift from God, and it figures in the bull cult.

Of wooden aerophones (*stviri*), a Georgian variant of the panpipe is considered the oldest. It is widespread in western Georgia, where Gurians call it *soinari* 'the hollow' and *sastsrapo* 'urgent' and Samegrelians call it *larchemi* 'cane'. It consists of six cane tubes tied in a row, with the longest in the middle. Each tube takes its name from the corresponding part within the vocal polyphonic tradition. Two-part music

FIGURE 11 A Georgian bagpiper. Postcard from the early 1900s. Courtesy of the Robert Godfried Collection, New York.

is played on it. Samegrelians hold competitions in which, for a responsorial texture, performers divide a panpipe into two sets of three tubes. As with *chuniri,* rural people use panpipes to bring home the soul of a person who has died away from home, as by drowning. Megrelian shepherds played the *larchemi* to lure evil spirits into the instrument so as to not disturb the sheep. It and the *soinari* are believed to provide protection from reptiles and evil sources.

The bagpipe, played throughout Racha, Kartli, Pshavi, Achara, and Meshketi, has a melody pipe and a bass pipe, which sounds an ostinato on two or three pitches. It is known as *gudastviri* (*guda* 'bag', *stviri* 'pipe') in Racha, Kartli, and Pshavi, *chiboni* (or *chimoni*) in Achara, and *tulum* (Turkish, 'bag') in Meshketi. The *gudastviri* and *chiboni* accompany dancing and singing, for which the musician (*mestvire* '*stviri* performer') accompanies his own singing, emphasizing the poetry (figure 11). Such singing is an important tradition in Racha, where celebrations require the participation of numerous professional *mestvire,* who formerly sang a melodic ostinato in unison with the ostinato of the bass pipe.

Georgian metal aerophones include the *buki,* a large trumpet, popular at court in celebratory contexts and used by Samegrelians and Svanetians until about 1800. It also served in military contexts. The *zrokha kudi* 'cow's tail' was a small metal military instrument used in the Middle Ages, as mentioned in literary sources. It was frequently played with the metal percussion instrument *spilendz-churi* 'copper barrel', no longer extant. The *kvirostviri* 'loud-shouting *stviri*' was another metallic military instrument.

Urban instruments

From the 1600s to the 1800s, Tbilisi musical culture reflected the influence of a cosmopolitan mixture of Armenians, Azerbaijanis, Jews, Kurds, Persians, and others, to whom instrumental music was paramount. The instruments found in Georgian cities, mostly in Tbilisi, included various chordophones (for example, *saz, ud,* rebab, santur, *kanum, kemancha*) and aerophones (*duduk, zurna*). Only the *duduk,* the *zurna,* and the *doli* survive. In Tbilisi, urban ensembles consisting of two *duduk* and *daira,* or two *zurna* and *doli* remain popular, sometimes associated with the "old Tbilisi."

Georgian folk music has adopted two Western European instruments: the accordion (*garmon,* also *buzika,* from *muzika* 'music') and the guitar. Within the last two centuries, the former has been adopted in the musical culture of the mountainous areas of eastern Georgia. It fulfills an accompanimental role for solo and polyphonic songs and provides music for dancing. Use of the guitar to accompany urban songs dates from the nineteenth century. During the first half of the twentieth century, the Georgian guitar had seven strings and was known as the Russian guitar. It was particularly popular in Imereti: in Kutaisi, the center of Imereti, it was tuned d_1–b–g–d–C–G–D. From the 1960s, the popularity of the six-stringed version increased.

Ensembles

Traditional Georgian folk ensembles tended to consist of two instruments, such as a *panduri* and a *daira,* a *chonguri* and a *doli,* a *chiboni* and a *doli,* and a *changi* and a *chuniri.* The exceptions were the *mtskobri* military ensemble of Bukis, and the medieval court ensemble, which used mostly the metal aerophones *buki* and the membranophone *dumbuli.* Small ensembles of Middle Eastern musical instruments were known in Georgia, mostly in Tbilisi, as *sazandari.*

From the 1930s, the revival of folk instruments in line with Soviet ideology led to the creation of large orchestras of Georgian folk instruments, and traditional instruments were transformed into chromatic ones. Small ensembles of *salamuri, chonguri,* and *panduri* are popular with ensembles that play Georgian folk songs.

SOCIAL PROCESSES IN MAKING MUSIC

How music is transmitted, who performs it, and where it is performed profoundly affect its style.

Music education and transmission

Georgian musical transmission has been primarily aural. Learning occurred within family contexts and through participation in traditional celebrations, as during table rituals and traditional feasts (*supra*). Georgia is one of the world's oldest areas where wine was made, and Georgian traditional feasts are known for their complex structure of toasts, led by a toastmaster (*tamada*), and religious and folk songs. Families that produced good singers were locally well known. These included the Erkomaishvili in Guria, the Kavsadze and the Tarkhnishvili in Kakheti, and the Gvishiani in Svaneti. There was a marked tendency for intermarriage among musically talented families, especially in Guria.

The nineteenth century saw the penetration of liturgical music traditions into folk music, including the use of written neumes. In the 1960s, Artem Erkomaishvili, a performer unfamiliar with staff notation, used neumes to transcribe a liturgical song and transcribed folk songs in this manner as a memory aid.

During the Soviet period, institutional musical education for children was modeled on the European professional musical system of eighteenth- and nineteenth-century Europe. In many districts, traditional aural transmission survived. Most Georgian folksingers, including the members of state ensembles, do not read musical notation, so aural training remains the primary way of transmitting traditional music. The curriculum of musical colleges and conservatories consists of several courses of Georgian traditional music. A course in Georgian folk songs is offered for one year at musical colleges, and folksinging lessons last three years. Conservatories offer courses in folk-musical culture, history, Georgian folk harmony, and solfège. Ethnomusicologists are trained in the Department of Georgian Folk Music at Tbilisi State Conservatory.

Gender

Musical performances and repertoires are mostly segregated by sex, reflecting the Georgian aesthetic preference for hearing timbrally similar voices. Men perform most major vocal genres, except for women's lullabies and ritual songs. Women perform contemporary lyrical songs in Guria, Imereti, Samegrelo, and Tusheti. Solo and group singing in these districts is accompanied by instruments such as the *chonguri,* the *buzika,* and the guitar. Some ritual circle dances in the mountains of western Georgia (in Svaneti and Racha) are traditionally performed by mixed groups. Mixed choral singing also occurs within familial contexts.

Children's singing

Children's repertoires have been little studied. In general, children participate in making music during family celebrations. They retain their own game songs, which use simple melodies and texts, thought to reflect an archaic style. Most musical training occurs in childhood. Special schools of traditional singing were established in Guria in the 1980s, and today, there are several children's folk ensembles.

Urban music

Georgian musical culture has separate rural and urban traditions. Rural music, largely

The Greek historian Xenophon, traveling with Greek soldiers in 401 B.C., noted the use of marching songs by the Mossiniks, a southwestern Georgian tribe. He wrote that one person began singing, followed by the others, who marched in rhythm to the song, and that Georgians sang in a distinctive manner.

the product of peasant society, was rarely heard in courts, commercial areas, and urban centers; rather, musical instruments of Eastern origins, songs of foreign nationalities, and instrumental ensembles characterize urban areas.

Urban musical styles of eastern and western Georgia are distinct because of historical and geographical influences. Eastern Georgian urban music has been influenced by the traditions of neighboring peoples—Armenians, Azerbaijanis, Persians, and Turks. Tenth- and eleventh-century literary and iconographic sources provide evidence that non-Georgian musical instruments were introduced into eastern Georgian urban centers. Eastern melodies were particularly popular in nineteenth-century Tbilisi, which had a large nonindigenous population. Singing employed ornamentation and scales with augmented seconds, and was usually accompanied with Middle Eastern instruments. The ensemble of two *duduk* and *doli* or two *zurna* and *doli* was the most popular, and often the *doli* player accompanied his own singing. This style of music was mostly performed by ethnic minorities in Tbilisi. Some of these songs became popular among other Georgians, who used to sing them unaccompanied, turning one-part melodies into three-part versions. According to folk traditions, the original melody was performed by the middle part. The popularity of urban music has declined since about 1900, but the music is still performed.

Urban music of western Georgia dates to the nineteenth-century influence of European classical music, especially Italian opera and Russian romances. Kutaisi was its center, and its main stylistic features were the use of European harmonies, parallel thirds and sixths, three-part harmony, and a leading middle voice. Three-part songs are accompanied by a guitar or are performed unaccompanied. During the twentieth century, this tradition has become more popular than that of the eastern area, and serves as the stylistic basis for professional and western composers' contemporary popular genres. It strongly affected classical composers in the decade around 1900.

HISTORY OF MUSIC

Archaeological excavation has yielded the earliest instrument discovered in the Caucasus, a bone flute from the fourteenth or fifteenth centuries B.C. Found in a young boy's grave among the bones of domesticated animals, it is believed to show that the flute was then a shepherd's instrument. Findings from the Trialeti and Kazbegi excavations in east Georgia indicate that tribes in the second millennium B.C. performed circle dances and songs. Little is known about the musical traditions of the intervening periods.

The earliest written records on the musical activities of Georgian tribes are from foreign sources. Sargon II, King of Assyria and conqueror of Urartu in 714 B.C., described the bountiful gardens and fields of the Mana, people considered to be Georgian ancestors. He also described the joyful songs that accompanied work and the collective performance of harvest songs. The Greek historian Xenophon, traveling with Greek soldiers in 401 B.C., noted the use of marching songs by the Mossiniks, a southwestern Georgian tribe. He wrote that one person began singing, followed by the others, who marched in rhythm to the song, and that Georgians sang in a distinctive manner.

The development of Georgian orthography in the fifth century of the common era led to additional information on Georgian musical activity, especially from writings of the tenth to the twelfth centuries. Works from this era, known as the Golden Age of Georgia, devote attention to court and ecclesiastical music. Little is known about folk music during this time.

Church music

According to written evidence, medieval Georgian professional music had emerged by the seventh century and thrived from the eighth century to the twelfth. Several schools of professional composers (*khelovantmtavari* 'head of the arts') and translators of Greek liturgical texts worked in Georgian churches within and outside Georgia from the eighth century to the eleventh. The folk tradition of multipart singing influenced the initially monophonic melodies of the Eastern Orthodox church and made them polyphonic. Besides the polyphonic versions of Greek one-part liturgical melodies, many original Georgian church songs were composed by professional composers from the schools of Mikael Modrekili, Giorgi Khandzteli, Giorgi Merchule, Ioane Sabanisdze, Arsen the Katholikos, Ioane Zosime, and Ekvtime and Giorgi Mtatsmindeli.

Several manuscript collections of tenth- to twelfth-century church songs, written in neumatic notation, have survived. The neumes, placed above below poetic texts, were unique. The music they transcribe remains undeciphered.

After the political and cultural hardships of the thirteenth to eighteenth centuries, the severest ordeal for the Georgian church-singing tradition was the Russian Empire's abolition of the independent Georgian patriarchate (1811) and its suppression of Georgian singing in Georgian churches. In 1860, when the Council for the Resurrection of Georgian Church Song was created, several individuals still remembered the bulk of the repertoire. More than five thousand church songs were transcribed, and several major collections of eastern and western Georgian church songs were issued. After 1921, when the Soviet Union suppressed religious activity and banned the performance and study of church songs, the study of transcribed collections ceased. After the so-called milder period of the 1960s, minor collections of Georgian church songs appeared. But only after perestroika did Georgian musicologists return to the study of medieval Georgian church singing—a topic that has become a central field of Georgian musicology.

Art music

After 1850, European professional music penetrated Georgia. An opera house was opened in Tbilisi in 1851. In the 1890s, the first major compositions of European type—mostly operas—were created by Georgian composers, including Meliton Balanchivadze (1862–1933), composer of the first Georgian opera, *Malacious Tamar,* and father of American choreographer George Balanchine; Zakaria Paliashvili (1871–1933), composer of the operas *Abesalom and Etery, Daisi,* and *Latavra*; Dimitri Arakishvili (1873–1953), composer of the opera *The Legend of Shota Rustaveli*); and Viktor Dolidze (1890–1933), composer of the comic opera *Keto and Kote.* These operas used urban musical traditions and eastern Georgian traditional songs. Niko Sulkhanishvili (1871–1919), composer of classical unaccompanied vocal works, was an expert performer of Kakhetian songs.

The years of independence (1918–1921) were extremely fruitful for the development of Georgian musical culture: in 1919, the Tbilisi State Conservatory was founded, and the classical operas *Abesalom and Etery, The Legend of Shota Rustaveli,* and *Keto and Kote* debuted.

Soviet and post-Soviet period

Occupation of Georgia by the Red Army in February of 1921 stopped independent musical development. Politics penetrated the arts, always guarded by Soviet ideologists. The church-singing tradition was banned. Composers were obliged to create compositions dedicated to the "glorious" present and "brilliant" communist future of the peoples of the Soviet Union, and to the leaders of the Communist Party. Despite these constraints, some Georgian composers created internationally renowned musical compositions, employing folksinging traditions: Shalva Mshvelidze (1904–1984) used songs and scales from mountain areas of eastern Georgia, and Otar Taktakishvili (1924–1989) incorporated traditional songs from all districts of Georgia.

A new generation of Georgian composers appeared in the milder ideological period of the 1960s. They used contemporary compositional techniques of Western Europe. Gia Kancheli (b. 1935) is the most prominent representative of this generation of Georgian composers.

VILLAGE MUSIC IN THE SOVIET PERIOD

Forced collectivization in the 1930s destroyed many institutions of traditional village life. At the same time, traditional music and musicians gained the wide attention of the mass media. Soviet ideology tried to create the stereotype of happy people by encouraging performers to create new songs praising life in the U.S.S.R. and communist leaders. Many outstanding folk performers of this period had in their repertoires at least a couple of such songs to demonstrate their political loyalty. Such concessions allowed many outstanding performers, including Artem Erkomaishvili, Dzuku Lolua, Noko Khurtsia, and Sandro Kavsadze, to maintain and perform traditional music.

The Soviet government highly praised expert traditional singing, which became a profession. Well-known expert traditional singers formed ensembles and choirs and were often invited by authorities to set up ensembles outside their own districts. Teaching methods in those ensembles remained traditional—by rote without written notes.

From the end of the 1920s a series of big folk festivals was organized in Georgia. The special attention the Soviet government paid to traditional singing affected the natural development of traditional music and caused several major changes.

1. The number of performers in ensembles increased, as authorities in different districts competed with each other to display the biggest choir at the national folk festivals.
2. Numerous performers (sometimes more than a hundred) sang the three voices—a violation of traditional practice, where upper melodic lines were always performed by individuals. The new tradition of unison performance penetrated small ensembles.
3. Big ensembles had conductors, unknown in traditional groups.
4. The unison performance of all three voices inevitably required fixed versions of the songs, and traditional performers complained that free improvisation was lost.
5. Fixed versions of songs, performed by standard ensembles and broadcast by radio or TV usually turned into a standard variant for all ensembles, to the exclusion of different versions of the songs.

6. Following the Russian model, most traditional musical instruments were turned into chromatic ones, and new versions were created—for example, the *panduri*, in a variety of sizes from soprano to bass.

7. The establishment of large orchestras of Georgian folk instruments was unusual for Georgia, where traditional music was comprised primarily of unaccompanied vocal music. There had never been such large orchestras in rural Georgia, and so, by contrast, small ensembles became popular. A trio of *salamuri*, *chonguri*, and *panduri* in their original sizes and led by virtuoso *salamuri* player Omar Kelaptrishvili, became the standard for such ensembles in the 1970s and the 1980s.

POPULAR MUSIC: JAZZ, ROCK, FOLK

The Soviet government strictly controlled the development of popular music. During the Stalinist period, it banned the performing of American jazz, using mottos like "If you play jazz today, you'll betray the homeland tomorrow" and "There is only one step between the saxophone and the knife." As an alternative, Russian jazz was popularized by the Russian musician Leonid Utesov [see RUSSIA]. The jazz ensemble at the Georgian Polytechnic Institute was the first in Georgia. It mostly played compositions of contemporary Georgian composers and jazz versions of popular urban songs.

The milder ideological politics of the 1960s and the development of new audio technologies improved the situation. Rock ensembles, inspired by the local popularity of the Beatles, were formed in Tbilisi and other cities in the mid-1960s. Performances of Georgian rock ensembles did not occur on officially approved stages until the 1980s. The best representative of an official popular music in 1960s and 1970s was Orera. In its best compositions, Orera incorporated elements of contemporary lighter European pop music with Georgian urban and rural singing traditions, and was considered one of the best ensembles of the U.S.S.R. in the 1970s. In 1980, the first jazz festival in the Soviet Union was held, in Tbilisi.

During the milder ideological period, the tradition of Georgian church singing was partly revived by the influential ensemble Gordela. Later, ensembles of Georgian folk songs usually included several examples of church songs. One of Gordela's peculiarities was to separate songs from their traditionally accompanying dances. Singing with a more trained vocal quality and dynamic colors was another of Gordela's traits—features that became popular among ensembles that performed Georgian folk songs in the 1970s and 1980s. Hamlet Gonashvili, a member of the state ensemble Rustavi, was a brilliant performer of this type. Rustavi and other ensembles, including the Georgian State Ensemble of Folk Songs, Pazisi, and Georgian Voices, had enormous success during their international tours in many countries of Europe, Asia, America, and Australia. The ensembles Mtiebi and Mzetamze (the latter an all-female ensemble) try to bring to the stage the interaction of singing, dancing, and other traditional activities, especially processing, working, and lamenting. The ensemble Anchiskhati resurrects traditional church singing, mostly of western Georgian style.

During the post-Soviet period (after 1991), Georgia became a theater of fierce political and military clashes. During several wars, the economy was depressed. In the mid-1990s, a tendency toward stabilization appeared. The Georgian folksinging tradition had always been a hallmark of Georgian culture and national identity. In the 1980s and 1990s, the international popularity of Georgian polyphonic singing increased. Ensembles of Georgian traditional singing were established in several countries: Kartuli Ensemble and Kavkasia (United States of America), Marani (France), Darbazi (Canada), Cardiffian Georgian Choir (United Kingdom), and Golden Fleece (Australia).

During World War I, Robert Lach and Georg
Schünemann recorded songs from Georgian military
prisoners; these recordings are in the Berlin
Phonogramm-archiv.

HISTORY OF SCHOLARSHIP

The first studies of Georgian singing, written by amateurs, appeared in the 1860s,
followed in later decades by the first song collections (Kargareteli 1899, 1909). In the
1890s, Russian musicians interested in Georgian folk music recorded songs and
investigated the origins of Georgian singing style.

The greatest contributions to Georgian musical scholarship are the works of
Dimitri Arakishvili, who recorded songs from various districts, published them in
important collections, and contributed to the scientific investigation of central issues
in Georgian musical traditions.

In the first decades after 1900, the composer Zakaria Paliashvili recorded hundreds of folk songs and published one collection (1909); V. Steshenko-Kuftina published the first work on Georgian folk instruments (1936), which emphasized the
panpipe; and Ivane Javakhishvili's *The Basic Questions of the History of Georgian Music*
(1990 [1938]) presented information drawn from old Georgian, Greek, and
Armenian manuscripts.

Works by European musicologists appeared during the early twentieth century.
During World War I, Robert Lach and Georg Schünemann recorded songs from
Georgian military prisoners; these recordings are in the Berlin Phonogramm-archiv.
Siegfried Nadel (1933) drew comparisons between Georgian part-singing and
European medieval polyphony. Marius Schneider (1940) furthered this hypothesis
and suggested that Georgian part-singing had influenced European ecclesiastic
polyphony.

After World War II, Arakishvili published more studies. Among the most prominent postwar scholars were Grigol Chkhikvazde (1898–1985), who studied the history and dialectology of folksinging, and Shalva Aslanishvili (1896–1981), who studied
stylistic features of Georgian harmony.

The 1950s were marked by the appearance of a new generation of Georgian
ethnomusicologists. In addition to theoretical work, Mindia Jordania (modal
systems and terminological issues), Kakhi Rosebashvili (musical instruments
and church music), Vladimer Akhobadze (four-part singing tradition), and
Otar Chijavadze (ethnographic districts) published collections of Georgian folk
songs.

In the 1960s and 1970s, much research resulted from Georgian scholars connected with the Tbilisi Conservatory, which has specialized departments in Georgian
folk music, music theory, and music history. Among the areas covered are reconstruction of Meskhetian part-singing (Magradze 1987); emergence of the modal system
(Chokhonelidze 1988); song structures; harmony (Zhengti 1979); rhythmic systems;
origins of folk polyphony (Iashvili 1975); historical and comparative study of folk
polyphony (Joseph Jordania 1989b); musical instruments (Alavidze 1978); and song
collections (Kokeladze 1979, 1981, 1984, 1985, 1988). Nino Maisuradze, of the
Institute of History, Archaeology, and Ethnography, has examined (1989, 1990)

vocal traditions of eastern Georgia and historical aspects of folk music. Manana Shilakadze (1970) has focused on instruments and instrumental music.

Younger scholars have explored new topics, including musical dialects, funeral rites, women's singing, lullabies, the classification of polyphony, the comparative study of Georgian and Balkan music (Tsitsishvili 1990), and polyphonic instrumental music. Since the 1960s, conferences on various topics have been held, but economic hardship during the post-Soviet period stopped them, as it stopped intensive field work throughout Georgia.

European and American scholars carried out research on Georgian music after World War II. Among these were Ernst Emsheimer, who worked on folk polyphony; Paul Collaer, who explored connections among melodies found in the lullabies of Spain, Hungary, Bulgaria, and Georgia; and Erich Stockmann, who compared the polyphonic traditions of Albania and Georgia. Marius Schneider (1969) revived Nadel's hypothesis of Georgian influence on the development of European medieval polyphony. Ivette Grimaud in 1970 collected several hundred songs still unpublished. Susanne Ziegler, alone (1990) and with Andreas Traub (1990), has analyzed Georgian singing. Peter Gold (1972) collected songs from Georgians living in Turkey. Sylvie Bolle-Zemp (1994) collected Svanetian songs.

BIBLIOGRAPHY

Akhobadze, Vladimer. 1957. *Georgian (Svanetian) Folk Songs* (in Georgian). Tbilisi: Teknika da Shroma.

———. 1961. *Georgian (Acharian) Folk Songs* (in Georgian). Batumi: Sakhelgami.

Alavidze, Zurab. 1978. *Georgian and Distributed into Georgia Musical Instruments* (in Georgian). Tbilisi: Khelovneba.

Arakishvili, Dimitri. 1905. *Short Review of Development of Georgian (Kartlian and Kakhetian) Folk Songs* (in Russian). Moscow Comission of Music and Ethnography, 1. Moscow: K. Menshov.

———. 1908. *West Georgian Folk Songs* (in Russian). Moscow Comission of Music and Ethnography, 2. Moscow: K. Menshov.

———. 1916. *Georgian Folk Musical Heritage* (in Russian). Commission of Music and Ethnography, 5. Moscow: G. Lissner and D. Sobko.

———. 1925. *Georgian Music* (in Georgian). Kutaisi: Metsniereba Sakartveloshi.

———. 1940. *Review of Georgian Folk Musical Instruments* (in Georgian). Tbilisi: Teknika da Shroma.

———. 1948. Review of *East Georgian Folk Songs* (in Russian). Tbilisi: Gosizdat.

———. 1950a. *Rachian Folk Songs* (in Georgian). Tbilisi: Khelovneba.

———. 1950b. *Svanetian Folk Songs* (in Georgian). Tbilisi: Khelovneba.

———. 1954. *Scale System in West Georgian Folk Songs* (in Georgian). Tbilisi: Khelovneba.

Aslanishvili, Shalva. 1970 [1950]. *Harmony of the Karlian and Kakhetian Folk Choir Songs* (in Georgian). 2d ed. Tbilisi: Ganatleba. Published in 1978 in Russian. Moscow: Muzika.

———. 1954, 1956. *Essays on Georgian Music* (in Georgian). 2 vols. Tbilisi: Khelovneba.

Beliaev, Viktor. 1933. "The Folk Music of Georgia." *Musical Quarterly* 19:417–433.

Chijavadze, Otar. 1962, 1969. *Georgian Folk Songs (Kakhetian)* (in Georgian). 2 vols. Tbilisi: Ganatleba.

———. 1974. *Georgian Folk Songs (Megrelian)* (in Georgian). Tbilisi: Khelovneba.

Chijavadze, Otar, and Valerian Tsagareishvili. 1964. *Georgian Folk Songs* (in Russian). Moscow: Musica.

Chkhikvadze, Grigol. 1948. *Ancient Musical Culture of Georgian People* (in Georgian). Tbilisi: Muzfond.

———. 1961. *Georgian Folk Songs* (in Georgian and Russian). Tbilisi: Sabchota Sakartvelo.

———. 1964. "Main Types of Georgian Polyphonic Singing." Paper given at the 7th International Congress of Anthropological and Ethnological Sciences, August 1964. Moscow: Nauka.

Chokhonelidze, Evsevi. 1988. "Das Wesen der georgischen poliphonen Volksmusik." *Georgika* 11:63–66.

Collaer, Paul. 1954. "Notes concernant certains chants espagnols, hongrois, bulgares et géorgiens." *Annuario Musical* 9:153–160.

———. 1955. "Similitudes entre des chants espagnols, hongrois, bulgares et géorgiens (addendum)." *Annuario Musical* 10:109–110.

Conferences of the Coordinating Council of Georgian Folklore. 1958–1998. Abstracts (in Georgian).

Conferences of the Musical and Choreographical Society of Georgia. 1970–1991. Abstracts (in Georgian).

Dirr, Adolf. 1910. "Fünfundzwanzig georgische Volkslieder." *Anthropos* 5:483–512.

———. 1914. "Neunzehn swanische Lieder." *Anthropos* 9:597–621.

Donadze, Lado, Otar Chijavadze, and Grigol Chkhikvadze. 1990. *History of Georgian Music* (in Georgian). Edited by Gulbat Toradze. Tbilisi: Ganatleba.

Emsheimer, Ernst. 1950. "Schallaufnahmen georgischer Mehrstimmigkeit." *Kongressbericht, Gesellschaft für Musikforschung, Lüneburg,* 172–173.

———. 1967. "Georgian Folk Polyphony." *Journal of International Folk Music Council* 19:54–57.

———. 1979. "Georgische Volksmusik." *Die Musik in Geschichte und Gegenwart* 16 (suppl.):448–455.

Gochiashvili, Tamar, ed. 1995. *Georgian Chants* (in Georgian; English transcriptions and summary). Tbilisi: Georgian Patriarche Press.

Grimaud, Ivette. 1968. "Musique de tradition orale." *Bedi Kartlisa, revue de kartvelologie* 25:78–84.

———. 1977. "Musique vocale géorgienne (europe orientale)." *Bedi Kartlisa, revue de kartvelologie* 35:52–72.

Gvaramadze, Lili. 1987. *Georgian Folk Dances* (in Russian). Tbilisi: Khelovneba.

Gwacharia, Vazha. 1977. "Die Mehrstimmigkeit in der alten gruzinischen (georgischen) Muzik." *Musica Slavica: Beiträge zur Muzikgeschichte osteuropas,* 414–427. Wiesbaden: F. Steiner.

Iashvili, Mzia. 1977. *On the Problem of Georgian Polyphony* (in Georgian). Tbilisi: Khelovneba. Published in 1988 in Russian. Tbilisi: Khelovneba.

Javakhishvili, Ivane. 1990 [1938]. *The Basic Questions of the History of Georgian Music* (in Georgian). 2d ed. Tbilisi: Khelovneba.

Jordania, Joseph. 1980. "Gruusialaisten kansanlaulujen alkuperasesta polyfoniasta ja harmoniasta" (in Finnish). *Mussikki* 4:215–228. Helsinki.

———. 1984. "Georgian Folk-Singing: Its Sources, Emergence and Modern Development" (in Arabic, Chinese, English, French, and Spanish). *International Social Science Journal* 36(3):569–581. Paris, Unesco.

———. 1989a. "Folk Polyphony, Ethnogenesis, and Racegenesis" (in Bulgarian). *Muzikalni Xorizonti* 5:56–66.

———. 1989b. *Georgian Traditional Polyphony in the International Context of Polyphonic Cultures* (in Russian; English summary). Tbilisi: Tbilisi University Press.

Kargareteli, Ia. 1899. *Georgian Folk Songs in Notes* (in Georgian). Tbilisi: Literary Dissemination Society Press.

———. 1909. *Georgian Folk Songs* (in Georgian). Tbilisi: Literary Dissemination Society Press.

Kokeladze, Grigol. 1979. *Fifty Georgian Folk Songs* (in Georgian). Tbilisi: Muzfond.

———. 1981. *Thirty Georgian Folk Songs* (in Georgian). Tbilisi: Muzfond.

———. 1984. *One Hundred Georgian Folk Songs* (in Georgian). Tbilisi: Khelovneba.

———. 1985. *Georgian Folk Songs with Comments* (in Georgian and Russian). Tbilisi: Muzfond.

———. 1988. *Forty Georgian Folk Songs* (in Georgian). Tbilisi: Muzfond.

Korganov, B. D. 1898–1900. "Mestvirebi, die Troubadoure des Kaukasus." *Schriften der Internationalen Musikwissenschaftlichen Gesellschaft* 1:627-629.

———. 1904–1905. "La musique da Caucase." *Zeitschrift der Internationalen Musikgesellschaft* 6:24–29.

Lach, Robert. 1917. *Vorläufiger Bericht über die im Auftrage der Kaiserlichen Akademie der Wissenschaften erfolgte Aufnahme der Gesänge russischer Kriegsgefangener im August und September 1916.* Mitteilung der Phonogramm-Archiv-Kommission, Sitzungsbericht der Phil.-hist. Klasse der Akademie d. Wissenschft zu Wien, 183. Vienna: Phonogramm-Archiv-Kommission.

———. 1920. *Die Musik der turk-tatarischen, finnisch-ugrischen und Kaukasusvölker in ihrer entwicklungsgeschichtlichen und psychologischen Bedeutung für die Entstehung der musikalischen Formen.* Mitteilungen der Anthropologische Gesellschaft, 50. Vienna: Phonogramm-Archiv-Kommission.

———. 1927. *Kaukasische Volksgesänge, in Forschungen und Fortschritte.* Berlin.

———. 1928. *Georgische Gesänge.* Transcriptions and translations by Adolf Dirr. Gesänge russischer Kriegsgefangener, 3, part 1 (Kaukasusvölker), section 1. Mitteilung der Phonogramm-Archiv-Kommission, 55. Sitzungsbericht der Phil.-hist. Klasse der Akademie d. Wissenschaft zu Wien, 204. Vienna: Phonogramm-Archiv-Kommission.

———. 1931. *Mingrelische, abchasische, svanische und ossetische Gesänge.* Transcriptions and translations by Robert Bleichsteiner. Gesänge russischer Kriegsgefangener, 3 (Kaukasusvölker), part 2. Mitteilung der Phonogramm-Archiv-Kommission, 65. Sitzungsbericht der Phil.-hist. Klasse der Akademie d. Wissenschaft zu Wien, 205. Vienna: Phonogramm-Archiv-Kommission.

Lang, David M. 1970. "Popular and Courtly Elements in the Georgian Epic." *Revue de kartvelologie* 27:143–160.

Magradze, Valerian. 1987. *Georgian (Meskhetian) Folk Songs* (in Georgian). Tbilisi: Khelovneba.

Maisuradze, Nino. 1989. *Georgian Folk Music and Its Historical-Ethnographical Aspects* (in Georgian). Tbilisi: Metsniereba.

———. 1990. *The Oldest Stage of Development of Georgian Folk Music* (in Russian). Tbilisi: Metsniereba.

Mamaladze, Tamar. 1962. *Work Songs in Kakheti* (in Georgian). Tbilisi: Georgian Academy of Science Press.

———. 1970. *Georgian Urban Songs* (in Georgian and Russian). Tbilisi: Muzfond.

Musical Culture of Georgia (in Russian). 1957. Collection of articles. Tbilisi: Ganatleba.

Nadel, Siegfried. 1933. *Georgische Gesänge.* Leipzig: Verlag Otto Harrassowitz.

———. 1934. "Messungen an kaukasischen Grifflochpfeifen." *Anthropos* 29:469–475.

Paliashvili, Zakaria. 1909. *Georgian Folk Songs* (in Georgian and Russian). Tbilisi: Georgian Philharmony Society Press.

Problems of Folk Polyphony (in Russian; English summary). 1985, 1986, 1988. Abstracts of international conferences held in Tbilisi in 1984 and Borjomi in 1986 and 1988.

Rosebashvili, Kakhi. 1968. *Georgian Church Songs (Western Georgia)* (in Georgian). Tbilisi: Muzfond.

———. 1980. *Georgian Folk Songs* (in Georgian). Tbilisi: Muzfond.

Sachs, Curt. 1940. *The History of Musical Instruments.* New York: Norton.

Schneider, Marius. 1935. "Diskussionen zur übereuropäischen Mehrstimmigkeit." *Zeitschrift für Vergleichende Musikwissenschaft* 3(1–2):34–38.

———. 1940. "Kaukasische Parallelen zur mittelalterlichen Mehrstimmigkeit." *Acta Musicologica* 12:52–61.

———. 1969. *Geschichte der Mehrstimmigkeit.* 2nd, revised ed., part 3. Tutzing: Schneider.

Schunemann, Georg. 1920. "Über die Beziehungen der Vergleichenden Musikwissenschaft zur Musikgeschichte." *Archiv für Musikwissenschaft* 2:175–194.

Shilakadze, Manana. 1970. *Georgian Folk Instruments and Instrumental Music* (in Georgian). Tbilisi: Metsniereba.

Steshenko-Kuftina, V. 1936. *Ancient Instrumental Background of Georgian Music* (in Russian). Pan's Flute, 1. Tbilisi: Federacia.

Stockmann, Erich. 1957. Kaukasische und albanische Mehrstimmigkeit. *Bericht über den Internationalen Musikwissenschaftlichen Kongress, Hamburg 1956,* 229–231. Kassel: Bärenreiter.

Tsitsishvili, Nino. 1990. "Folklore Parallels between Georgians and South Slavs" (in Bulgarian; English summary). *Bulgarski Folklor* 16(4):20–29.

Zhenti, Ivane. *1979. Chrestomathy in Georgian Harmony* (in Georgian). Tbilisi: Ganatleba.

Ziegler, Susanne. 1990. "The Discovery of Georgian Polyphony—Varying Trends in a Century of Research." In *VII European Seminar in Ethnomusicology,* 509–516. Berlin:

Ziegler, Susanne, and Andreas Traub. 1990. "Mittelälterliche und kaukasische Mehrstimmigkeit: Neue Gedanken zu einem alten Thema." *Beiträge zur Musikwissenschaft* 3:214–227.

AUDIOVISUAL RESOURCES

Bolle-Zemp, Sylvie. 1994. *Géorgie: Polyphony of Svaneti.* CNRS and Musée de l'Homme. Compact disc.

Gold, Peter. 1972. *Georgian Folk Music from Turkey.* Recorded and noted by Peter Gold. LP disk.

North Caucasia
Joseph Jordania

Regional Musical Generalizations
Abkhazians
Adighis (Cherkesses and Kabardians)
Balkarians and Karachaevians
Ossetians
Chechens and Ingushes

About half the people living on the northern slopes of the Caucasus Mountains are indigenous Adighis, Balkarians, Chechens, Karachaevians, Ingushes, and Ossetians (see map 10, p. 827). The other half are Russians, since politically North Caucasia is in southern Russia. Three language families are found here. The Caucasian language family includes Abkhazian (in Georgia), Adighian, Chechen, Ingushian, and an array of Dagestanian languages. The Indo-European language family is represented by Ossetian. The Turkic language family is represented by Balkarian-Karachaevian. Writing systems are based on the Cyrillic alphabet, introduced mostly in the 1920s and 1930s. Despite linguistic diversity, North Caucasia, except for Ossetians, is united by Islam.

Several ethnocultural strata can be distinguished in the history of North Caucasia, a land of highlander hunters and agriculturists. The northern slopes of the Caucasian Mountains were populated by 6000 B.C. The indigenous Caucasian stratum is united by the identity of physical features of all the Caucasian groups and some shared elements of culture. The second known major immigration occurred in the first century of the common era, when the Alans, carriers of an Indo-Iranian language, spread their language to Ossetia and brought new cultural elements, including the Nart epic (see below). Turkish elements in North Caucasia were introduced during the seventeenth and eighteenth centuries, when a Turkic language spread among Balkarians and Karachaevians and the introduction of Islam in North Caucasia occurred. The Russian Empire incorporated the territory of North Caucasia during the eighteenth and nineteenth centuries, times marked by the struggle of Russian military forces with recalcitrant local highlanders—a struggle that continues in Chechnya. In 1944–1957, the Balkarians, the Karachaevians, the Chechens, and the Ingushes were banished to Central Asia. Despite political and economic dominance, however, the Russian language, Orthodox Christianity, and other major elements of Russian culture did not spread widely among local people.

North Caucasian culture remains firmly connected with traditional institutions. The society is patriarchal, and respect for elders is an important social value.

REGIONAL MUSICAL GENERALIZATIONS

For all the peoples of North Caucasia, folk music constitutes the most important part of musical culture. Local folk-musical traditions are united by several important features.

Vocal traditions predominate. Part-singing occurs everywhere, except in a couple of Adighian groups. The types of polyphony are similar: a drone or ostinato bass accompanies a melodic line. The drone does not remain on one pitch. In three-part singing, the leading melodic line is accompanied by two drones, an octave, fifth, or fourth apart. Melodic lines are performed by a solo singer, while the bass (drone or ostinato) is performed by a group. The society is not divided into performers and listeners, since everyone present at an event participates by singing. Scales are diatonic. Meter is often complex in traditional songs, but usually simple in contemporary songs. Texts of songs contain elaborate systems of meaningless words. Males perform most songs. Females perform lullabies, laments, lyrical songs (often with the accompaniment of an accordion), and some work songs.

Flutes and plucked and bowed chordophones proliferate in North Caucasia. Horns, double reeds, and bagpipes are less prominent. Many flutes and single-reed pipes are locally associated with shepherds. Rhythmic instruments consist of various types of idiophones. Most musical instruments are played by men. Women mostly play the Caucasian accordion.

The Nart epic is a central element of the traditional music of all the peoples of North Caucasia. The epic, which describes the adventures of *nart*s (epic heroes), is important for Ossetians, Balkarians, and Karachaevians, and less so for Chechens and Ingushes. Ossetians are considered the descendants (at least partially) of Alans, the Indo-Europeans thought to have brought this epic to North Caucasia. They retain the original performance style: solo singing with self-accompaniment on a chordophone. Other North Caucasians perform songs from this epic polyphonically, with the soloist's melody accompanied by a drone or an ostinato.

The proliferation of European forms of musical culture in North Caucasia mostly reflects the cultural politics of the Soviet Union from the 1920s to the 1940s. First, musical schools and colleges were opened, and religious activities were banned. State ensembles of folk songs and dances were established. In the 1930s in all the North Caucasian republics, new chromatic musical instruments of different sizes (piccolo, soprano, alto, tenor, bass, contrabass) were constructed, based on traditional wind and stringed instruments, and artificial orchestras of musical instruments were organized.

In the milder political climate of the 1960s, the first pop and rock ensembles were formed. The post-Soviet period has seen the reactivation of religious and nationalistic forces. Political and military clashes have arisen mostly from internal territorial conflicts (as between Ingushians and Ossetians) and struggles for independence (as between Chechnya and Russia).

ABKHAZIANS

Abkhazians (in Abkhazian, *Apsua*) live in the Abkhazian Autonomous Republic in the Republic of Georgia. The other North Caucasian peoples live within the Russian Federation. Autochthonous in the northwest fringe of Georgia, Abkhazians are thought to have coresided with Georgians in this territory since the fourth century B.C. In 1992, before the Abkhazian-Georgian war, Abkhazians constituted only 17 percent (about seventy thousand) of the population in Abkhazia. The remainder were Georgians (49 percent), Russians (17 percent), and Armenians (16 percent). The economy of Abkhazia was destroyed during the Georgian-Abkhazian war

FIGURE 1 Two-part Abkhazian choral polyphony with a melody and a wordless drone. After Akhobadze and Kortua 1957:233.

(1992–1994), when more than half the population, including two hundred thousand Georgians, had to leave Abkhazia. Political tensions remain high.

Abkhazian musical traditions are best preserved in Gudauta, where Abkhazians are in the majority. Elsewhere, as in Ochamchira, their musical tradition reflects Georgian influence. Classical European music is in a rudimentary state.

Song style

Abkhazian modes include the aeolian, mixolydian, dorian, phrygian and ionian. Two-part polyphony with a drone predominates (figure 1). Two types of three-part polyphony occur. In the North Caucasian type, the drone is divided into fourths, fifths, or octaves. In the Georgian type, two melodic voices (each called *akhkizkhuo*) are accompanied by a drone or an ostinato (*argizra*). Abkhazian cadences emphasize the harmony of a fourth.

Abkhazian musical performance emphasizes improvisation and the music over the text, since sometimes little text is used and nonsense syllables are employed. Oral transmission is the predominant mode of dissemination. The younger generation learns music in the context of family and community events, including wedding parties, group work, and funerals.

Singing and musical genres are segregated by gender, and men sing the bulk of the repertoire. Women perform mostly lullabies, work songs, and laments. Only recently have men and women begun singing together.

Musical instruments

The Abkhazian whistle flute (*acharpan*), made from the mountain grass from which it takes its name, is 700 to 800 millimeters long. Good performers often accompany themselves with a nasal vocal drone.

The two-stringed Abkhazian bowed lute (*apkhertsa*), which resembles the Svanetian *chuniri* (see below), occasionally has a lead role with a vocal chorus, for which it performs the melody while the voices provide the bass. The Abkhazian *apandur* and *achangur* are three- and four-stringed plucked lutes, respectively (see also Georgian *panduri* and *chonguri*). The Abkhazian *aijuma*, a fourteen-stringed harp, is no longer played. The Abkhazian *akhima* was a twenty-four-stringed zither but is also not played.

Membranophones are represented by the *adaul*, a double-headed drum. Idiophones include the rattles *akapkap* and *ainkjaga*. All these instruments are traditionally played by men. Women perform on an accordion, the *amirzakan*.

Performance genres and contexts

Traditional Abkhazian genres include healing songs (*atlarchopa*), heroic songs (*afirkhatsar-ashva*), hunting songs (*azhveipshaar-ashva, aerg*), harvest songs (*arashvara-ashva, aeag-ashva*), wedding songs (*atatsaagara-ashva*), funeral songs (*azar*), and nostalgic migrant songs (*mahadjiri-ashva*). Today, songs of most of these genres are no longer sung in traditional social contexts and are performed only during traditional feasts. Music is believed to have curative powers, as in the use of the "Song of the Wounded Man" to promote healing. "Saint Vitta's Illness," in which a young girl is made to dance, is attributed to the deity Atlarchopa, and performance of the *atlarchopa* song and circle dance around the afflicted person is believed to effect a cure. Hunting songs are performed to invoke good luck from the hunter's deity before the hunt and after the kill. The antiphonal performance of harvest songs occurs during the hoeing of corn and tobacco, with nonsense syllables as text.

Weddings last two to three days and accommodate several hundred guests. Wedding songs, *redada* or *uari-dada,* include those marking the appearance of the bride, wishes for good health, and humorous songs, and are performed exclusively by men. Men and women traditionally sit apart from each other at wedding parties.

Riding constitutes an important component of funerals. A ritual race honors the deceased, and funeral songs are performed by the participants in the race. Nonsense syllables serve as text. Migrant songs entered the repertoire after 1877, when a large portion of the population fled to Turkey to avoid Russian repression after the Abkhazian rebellion of 1866.

Many texts of so-called new songs were artificially created during the Soviet period. They celebrate Soviet life, Lenin, and the Communist Party. The texts are drawn from those of well-known poets, but researchers find the musical material less interesting than that of traditional repertoire. The collection of Akhobadze and Kortua (1957) contains many "new songs." Other areas of musical life, such as the intermixture of new and old traditions, children's and urban music, and the impact of media on musical performance, have yet to be investigated.

History of scholarship

Abkhazian musical material has been collected and published since the early nineteenth century; however, scholars have done little research and analysis, and the history of these musical traditions has received little attention. The first collection of Abkhazian music was attempted at the beginning of the twentieth century, yet the first transcriptions—of Georgian folk singer Dzuku Lolua—did not survive. Georgian ethnomusicologist and composer Dimitri Arakishvili published the earliest extant collection of Abkhazian folk songs (1916) and the first study of Abkhazian musical instruments (1940). K. Kovach and K. Dzidzaria contributed two works (1929, 1930). Georgian ethnomusicologist Vladimer Akhobadze and Abkhazian

Lullabies for the elderly constitute a unique Adhighian genre. Scholars believe these contain retentions of an ancient ritualized euthanasia, since the texts are imbued with grotesque elements.

FIGURE 2 Two-part Adighian polyphony with a wordless drone often a fifth below the melody. After *Folk Songs and Instrumental Tunes of Adighis* 1981:140.

composer I. Kortua (1957) published a collection of 168 songs, including vocal, instrumental, traditional, and contemporary works. More recent works include work on folk songs (Ashuba 1986), folk-musical instruments (Khashba 1967), harvest and ritual songs (Khashba 1977), and musical genres (Khashba 1983).

ADIGHIS (CHERKESSES AND KABARDIANS)

About 120,000 Adighis live in western North Caucasia. They are linguistically and ethnically related to Abkhazians, and their languages (Abkhazo-Adighian languages) are in the Caucasian language family. *Adighi* is the Russian name for ethnic groups including Abadzekhs, Beslenevs, Bzhedughis, Cherkesses (or Circassians), Kabardians, Mozdokian Kabardians, Shapsugs, and Temirgoians—all known in Europe as Circassians. Like the Abkhazians, they are autochthonous residents of the Caucasian mountains. In the Soviet Union, Adighis were politically mixed with Balkarians and Karachaevians. Kabardians are part of Kabardian-Balkarian Autonomous Republic, but other Adighis are united with Karachaevians in the Karachaevo-Adighian Autonomous Republic.

Song style

Adighian modes include the aeolian, mixolydian, dorian, phrygian, and ionian. Adighian temporal organization uses duple and triple meters simultaneously in two- and three-part polyphony. Two-part polyphony with a drone (or ostinato) predominates (figure 2). Kabardians use three-part polyphony in which a two-part drone is sustained at the fifth or the octave (figure 3). In Adighian polyphony, the bass (*ezhy* 'everybody') is performed by the group and has its own melody (*ueredjeiu* or *kikhezidzerem*). Circassians (Cherkesses) and Abadzekhs tend to sing in unison.

Adighian oral transmission is traditionally mediated by a *djeguako,* a semiprofessional composer, who submits his new material for older men's approval for conformity to tradition. The *djeguako,* who serves as community historian, was often present on the battlefield to record heroic actions. Nowadays, he is a poet-musician and humorist, indispensable for wedding celebrations, in which he acts as the cultural leader. Gender segregation in performance, typical of North Caucasia, is intensified by the tenets of Islam.

FIGURE 3 Three-part Kabardian polyphony with a melody and a wordless drone in octaves. After *Folk Songs and Instrumental Tunes of Adighis* 1981:132.

Musical instruments

The Adighian whistle flutes are the *camil* and *bzhami*. According to native beliefs, the *bzhami* had the power to find the bodies of drowned men through the performance of a ritual melody (*psikhere*) at a riverbank. The two-stringed *chishapshina*, a long-necked plucked lute, has an accompanying role in epic songs and two-part vocal polyphony. Adighis adopted the accordion (*pshine*) in the nineteenth century. Only women play it. The Adighian *pkhachich*, a rattle used for dance accompaniment, is sometimes replaced by clapping.

Performance genres and contexts

Adighian genres include healing songs, songs of acquittal, work songs, rain-begging songs, wedding and funeral songs, epic and historical songs, hunting songs, and songs for children and the elderly. Healing songs (*shiapshe yeredkher*), performed at the patient's bedside, are believed to cure illness and wounds, and even to draw out an arrow or a bullet. Songs of acquittal (*zerizaykheizh yeredkher*) try to persuade the community of the singer's innocence of a crime. Bekmurra Pachev, one of the first educated Adighian poets, began his career after twice using songs to clear his name.

The variety of work songs shows that singing accompanied many facets of Adighian life. Collective plowing had its own songs, with a special leader. Women were responsible for combing wool, a collective activity held at night and accompanied by specific songs. Magical songs, also performed before work, included wishes for prosperity (*hokh*). One genre existed to attract wild bees into hives built for them. A repertoire of hunting songs was dedicated to Pshimazitkhe, god of wild animals, and the existence of a secret hunter's language shows the former importance of this activity.

Rain and thunder deities figure in the vocal repertoire. Ritual songs dedicated to Khantseguashe or Ele (from Saint Elijah), goddess of rain, accompany a procession whose participants hold a representation of the deity while passing the villagers' houses, accumulating food. The procession culminates in a feast at the riverbank and ritual bathing. A circle dance (*shible ydj*), honoring the god of thunder, is accompanied by the song "*Ele tsopai*," and is performed where lightning has struck. Believing that God has descended to them, villagers celebrate lightning strikes with joy, even when a death has occurred. Funeral songs (*bzhe*), a women's genre, are performed for three days in the house of the deceased.

Historical songs were and are performed by the *djeguako*. Some lyrics were so well known that the audience could complete a given song. The Nart epic remains popular and is accompanied by a choral drone (*ezhy*), a chordophone (*chishapshina*), and a rattle (*pkhachich*).

The children's repertoire includes songs to make the child walk (*sabii zegakiye*) and the song of the first independent step (*leteuve yered*), an achievement still marked by a ritual song. Lullabies are believed to protect children. Songs dedicated to a firstborn are accompanied by a choral drone against calls and responses between a soloist and a choir. The elderly have an honored position. Gerontologists attribute their longevity to the important roles they play in traditional life. Lullabies for the elderly constitute a unique genre. Scholars believe these contain retentions of an ancient ritualized euthanasia, since the texts are imbued with grotesque elements.

Dance genres subdivide into two types. The circle dance (*udj*), a collective form, has many variants, employed in ritual processions during the gathering of food in the village. *Islamei* is a fast virtuoso solo dance. Couple and solo dances, such as *kafa,* are used for dance competitions and are more popular than the circle dance in contemporary society. Instrumental accompaniment, particularly by an accordion and a drum, has supplanted traditional songs for *kafa* dancing.

History of scholarship

The first literary record of Adighian music contained only texts and ethnographic descriptions and dates from the 1850s. Sultan Khan-Girei, a colonel in the Russian army, was a well-known author in this period. Russian composers Aleksandr Alijabiev, Mily Alekseevich Balakirev (1837–1910), and Aleksandr Sergeevich Taneev (1850–1918) transcribed musical examples, which they incorporated into their compositions. Kabardinian songs collected by Taneev in 1886 were first published in 1947. Materials collected by Arsenii Avraamov and T. Sheibler (1957) just before World War II were lost during the war, though the published versions survive. Russian musicians also collected and published songs from this area, such as Mikhail F. Gnesin's *Cherkesian Songs* (1937) and Alexander F. Grebniov's *Adighian (Cherkesian) Songs* (1941). *Folk Songs and Instrumental Tunes of Adighis* (1980, 1981, 1986), considered one of the best publications of traditional music in the Soviet Union, contains excellent analytical transcriptions.

BALKARIANS AND KARACHAEVIANS

Balkarians (about seventy thousand) and Karachaevians (about one hundred twenty thousand) have common historical, linguistic, and ethnic links and were once believed to have been Turkic immigrants. After about 1950, physical anthropologists came to the conclusion that Balkarians are in fact descendants of Caucasian tribes that adopted Islam and the Turkic language in the seventeenth and eighteenth centuries. Karachaevians are descendants of Balkarians who in the nineteenth century migrated from Balkaria to other Caucasian regions, their current homeland. The unevenness of the study of their music is the result of political hardships during the Soviet period. In 1944, the Soviet government exiled all Balkarians and Karachaevians to Central Asia, but in 1957 allowed them to return to their homeland.

Song style

Though practicing Islam and speaking a Turkic language, Balkarians and Karachaevians do not employ Middle Eastern modal concepts, such as *makam* and *mugam,* in traditional music. Though Taneev noted that Balkarians and Karachaevians used Eastern-influenced chromaticism, Balkarian and Karachaevian music features diatonic minor, phrygian, and dorian modes. Older genres, such as ritual and epic songs, use syncopation and the alternation of duple and triple rhythms. Free meter obtains in musical genres that emphasize textual roles, such as epic songs, whose melodic lines are in recitative style and follow the poetic meter.

Two- and three-part polyphony with a drone is widespread among Balkarians

FIGURE 4 Three-part Balkar and Karachaevi polyphony with a melody and a wordless drone in fifths. After Rakhaev 1988:8.

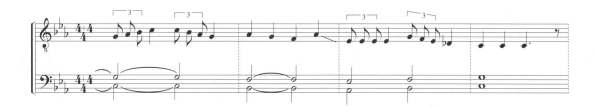

and Karachaevians (figure 4), who also use North Caucasian double-drone polyphony, sometimes adding a fourth to a fifth and an octave.

Balkar and Karachaevi songs are transmitted orally, and melodic improvisation is highly valued. As in other Caucasian groups, the melody is performed by an individual while the bass is being performed by a group. The term for melody, *zhir baschi* 'head of song', is Turkish, but the drone is identified by the Adighian word for bass (*ezhy* 'everybody'), because of the absence of a concept for polyphony in Turkic cultures. A large body of songs connected with the non-Muslim deity Teiri show the importance of this deity. Two forms of Teiri, kind and cruel, are described in a song that laments death due to lightning. A lament for a drowning mentions three Teiris: the mother of water, the water itself, and the earth. According to traditional beliefs, Teiri has greater importance than Allah.

Musical instruments

The Balkar and Karachaevi whistle flute (*sibizgi*) is popular among shepherds. The people play a double reed with flared bell (*sirijna*), a bowed lute (*zhil-kobuz*), a plucked lute (*kil-kobuz*), a harp (*kingir-kobuz*), and a rattle (*kars*). They use accordions, adopted in the nineteenth century, for accompanying dances. As in many other North Caucasian societies, all musical instruments but the accordion are played by men.

Performance genres and contexts

The epic constitutes the central body of songs performed polyphonically. In addition to the Nart epic, well known throughout North Caucasia, historical songs figure prominently. Many of them date from the eighteenth, nineteenth, and early twentieth centuries and through their documentation of events serve as oral histories. The song "Emina" describes the plagues of 1790–1800 and 1808–1814.

Balkarians and Karachaevians perform various agrarian songs, such as those that accompany the fall rituals Ozai and Tepina. Songs accompany a ritual procession, followed by gathering food, blessing the hosts, and consuming the ritual feast. Harvest songs accompany various tasks. Songs accompany preparing butter, threshing grain, and weaving cloth, the last performed by women. The first furrow, the beginning of sowing, and preparing the traditional feast have particular songs. Hunting follows songs about the deity Apsati, patron of wild animals and hunting. Apsati has counterparts among Abkhazians, Adighis, Ossetians, and Svanetians. Ritual songs mention pagan and Christian gods, including the god of thunder (Shiblu), the god of lightning (Elia), the god of the earth (Daucje), and the god of the wind (Geri-Geri).

Control of nature and fertility is believed to be affected by particular rituals,

As in all Caucasian polyphonic traditions, Ossetian society does not divide into performers and listeners, since all the participants in an event—mostly traditional feasts—join the bass part (*kirnin* or *fersag*).

such as the conjuration of the soul of a special stone, bathing a frog, and bathing a ritually masked person. Male participation in these rituals is unusual for the Caucasus. The collective fertility ritual known as Bairim is marked by special cult buildings, found in the Chegum gorge in Balkaria and decorated with depictions of male and female genitalia. A song to the pine-tree god Rauvazi illustrates the importance held by this deity until the twentieth century: *Allah seni djaningan bolsun, / Rauvazi meni djanimdan bolsun* 'Let Allah be with you, / And let Rauvazi be with me'.

The Caucasian practice of gender segregation in vocal performance is intensified by Islam. Lyrical songs, as of the genre *kjyy*, treat love as an illness and a sorrow, and the singer uses them to express her feelings. Weeping songs describe women's unfortunate fate. Antiphonal performance marks the singing of *kargish inar*, a song competition where improvisation is important. Lullabies (*beshik zhirla* 'cradle song'), based on formulaic ritual poetry, have themes concerning boys. In one of them, a giant tree in a boy's garden wants the boy to escape from the cradle. The epic tradition preserves evidence of matriarchy—a striking feature in reference to the role of women in Islam.

Children's songs have yet to be investigated. In addition to their own repertoire, children perform traditional adult songs, especially women's. The archaic ritual song "Ozai" has been recorded from a transformed version in children's performance.

Folk-dance genres, related to those of other North Caucasian and Georgian peoples, include circle and couple dances. The *tegerek-tepsey* and *gollu* are circle dances, and the *tjuz tepsey* is a couple dance. Overall, the dances of this area feature triplets, usually transcribed in 2/4 and 4/4 meters.

History of scholarship

There has been insufficient study of Balkarian and Karachaevian music, except of the epic tradition. Because their language is Turkic, musicologists have turned their attention to Turkish musical elements. For example, Taneev described the use of chromatic scales, though the modal system is diatonic. Other scholars made monophonic transcriptions of polyphonic songs by eliminating the drone.

The well-known Russian composers Balakirev and Taneev were the first collectors of Balkarian and Karachaevian music. Balakirev recorded eleven melodies, nine of which were Balkarian and Kabardinian, for use in his piano fantasy, *Islamei*. Taneev wrote an article (1886) that remains one of the most important studies of Balkarian and Karachaevian music. He also transcribed traditional music from this area. Material he recorded was republished in 1947, with many errors. The singer Ismail Urusbiev was the source for the musical materials transcribed by these Russian composers. Balkarian violinist Sulkhan-Bek Abaev, a student of Henryk Wieniawski, transcribed traditional folk music, but his recordings have been lost. A Hungarian scholar, Prele, collected and published Balkarian and Karachaevian songs. Exile stopped development of musicological studies between 1944 and 1957. Collections of Balkarian folk songs first appeared in an edition by O. Otarov and X. Kardanov (1962). It was followed by several minor collections. The first volume of the *Anthology of Balkarian and Karachaevian Folk Music*—a volume treating the Nart epic—awaits publication.

OSSETIANS

About three hundred thousand Ossetians (in Ossetian, *Iron*) live on both sides of the Caucasus Mountains in Russia and Georgia. Ossetians are believed to have descended from autochthonous Caucasians and Indo-European immigrants, the Alans, who spoke an Indo-Iranian language. The Ossetians' original homeland is in North Caucasia, but some Ossetians migrated to Georgia beginning in the sixteenth century and continuing in the seventeenth and eighteenth. In fact, Ossetian cultural elements are better preserved among those who migrated across the mountains than among those who stayed behind. Musically, Ossetian traditions have little in common with Indo-Iranian groups. Most Ossetians are Orthodox Christians, but some descend from people who converted to Islam in the seventeenth century. Religious differences are not reflected in their traditional music.

Song style

As in all Caucasian polyphonic traditions, society does not divide into performers and listeners, since all the participants in an event—mostly traditional feasts—join the bass part (*kirnin* or *fersag*). Male singing is predominant. Women perform only lullabies, some work songs, laments, and contemporary accordion-accompanied solo songs.

Aeolian, ionian, dorian, and mixolydian scales are widespread in older Ossetian music. Songs are metrically complex, and free rhythm, set by the recitative style of the leading voice, predominates, as does two-part polyphony with a drone or ostinato and a melody performed antiphonally by one or two people (figure 5).

Ossetians sing two types of three-part polyphony: in the North Caucasian type, the drone divides into fourths, fifths, or octaves; in the South Caucasian (or Georgian) type, the upper melodic voices move in parallel. Ossetian polyphony emphasizes harmonies of a fourth and a fifth, and cadences emphasize the fourth.

Musical instruments

Shepherds still play an ancient whistle flute (*uadindz*), mentioned in the Nart epic. From 500 to 700 millimeters long, it is sometimes made from a gun barrel. Shepherds also play the *stili,* a double clarinet 200 to 250 millimeters long. Its melody pipe has five holes and provides its own accompaniment with a single-hole drone pipe. The *fidiog,* made from the horn of a bull or wild goat, has four or five holes and a mouthpiece. No longer played, it was associated with hunting and had a signaling function. An instruments of lesser distribution is the *lalim uadindz,* a bagpipe with melody and drone pipes. Though rare today, it formerly had solo and accompanimental roles and was used for dance-music.

Kisin-fandir (or *khoiisar-fandir*), a two- or three-stringed bowed lute used to accompany epics, is the most popular Ossetian instrument. Since the 1950s, it has occasionally been replaced by the violin. In the 1930s, the creation of regional folk orchestras in the Soviet Union led to the creation of five sizes of *kisin-fandir:* soprano, alto, tenor, cello, and contrabass. This ensemble was not particularly popular. The Georgian plucked long-necked fretted lute (*panduri,* see below) has its parallel in the Ossetian *dala-fandir,* which originally had two or three strings but was developed into a chromatic version in six sizes (piccolo, soprano, alto, tenor, bass, contrabass)

FIGURE 5 Two-part Ossetian polyphony with changing meters and a movable drone. After Galaev 1964:44.

for use by the Ossetian State Ensemble in 1930s. The traditional instrument still serves for accompanying solo singing. The Ossetian harp (*duadastanon-fandir*) has ten to twelve diatonically tuned strings and was traditionally a men's instrument, believed to be a hero's instrument. According to the Nart epic, Nart Sirdon constructed it from his dead son's bones and sinews.

For Ossetians, the accordion (*iron-kandzal-fandir*) has become a women's instrument. Its popularity grew so that since the end of the nineteenth century the instrument became an obligatory wedding gift from the groom to the bride, and upon the woman's death her instrument was buried with her.

Ossetians use a wooden castanet (*kartsganag*) for dance accompaniment.

Performance genres and contexts

Heroic songs constitute the bulk of the Ossetian musical repertoire, as evidenced in Galaev's collection (1964), in which forty-two songs and instrumental pieces concern specific heroic figures. Still popular, these songs can be clearly dated from the event described. The hero's death is a necessary tragic component of the texts. Performance of heroic songs usually occur at traditional feasts, where they are performed polyphonically by all participants. In contrast, the epic song (*kadeg*) is performed by a soloist (*kadeganag*), who provides his own instrumental accompaniment. The best-known *kadeganag* was Bibo Dzugutov ('Blind Bibo') in the nineteenth century. Though solo performance of epic genres is typical across Asia, its Ossetian manifestation is unique for the Caucasus, where epic songs are ordinarily performed in polyphony.

During work or immediately after, people collectively performed harvest songs, which have lost their social context and are mostly performed during traditional feasts. Little is known about traditional wedding songs, with the exception of a large body of best-man's songs (*chindzembeltti zardjite* 'songs to accompany the bride').

Ritual dances were accompanied by polyphonic songs or instrumental music. The circle dance (*tsopai*), connected to the cult of thunder and lightning, was performed where lightning had killed someone. This dance has its parallels elsewhere in the Caucasus. The most popular dance, *simd,* has many variants, among which the *narton-simd* 'simd of Nart' had two sections and was accompanied by singing or instrumental playing. A version of it was performed during New Year celebrations. It was a two-story circle dance (one circle of dancers on the shoulders of another), performed around a fire. Couple dances include *khonga-kaft* or *kabardinka* and the *timbil-kaft* or *lezginka*. One virtuoso solo dance is known as *rog-kaft*. Traditionally dances were accompanied by polyphonic singing. Today, an accordion provides musical accompaniment for them.

Men's and women's repertoires have traditionally been segregated, but this division has broken down since the 1930s. In the past, women did not perform where men could hear them. The accordion was considered a women's instrument, but certain instruments, such as the *kisin-fandir,* were considered exclusively male. Most women's songs, such as the lullaby (*lolote*), were monophonic and connected to women's social life. A rare archaic example of women's polyphonic singing is demonstrated in the song *onai,* which accompanied the preparation of traditional clothing, such as felt and cloaks. Women also perform contemporary lyrical songs, accompanying themselves on an accordion.

Ossetian contemporary music consists of songs with known authors and little variation, performed solo with an accordion and other instruments.

History of scholarship

Composers greatly contributed to the recording of Ossetian folk songs in the late nineteenth century. Mikhail Mikhailovitch Ippolitov-Ivanov and Sergei Ivanovich Taneev transcribed material in 1883 and 1886. The work of Georgian composer and ethnomusicologist Dimitri Arakishvili was published at the beginning of the twentieth century. From 1900 to 1910, thirty-two discs of Ossetian songs were recorded by the Gramophone Company. In 1916, Robert Lach recorded and transcribed Ossetian songs performed by Ossetian and Georgian military prisoners (1917, 1931). Boris Galaev's *Ossetian Folk Songs* (1964) is considered the most important work on this music. An Ossetian composer and ethnomusicologist, Galaev presented a hundred songs and instrumental melodies, supplemented by texts and ethnographic analyses. In recent years, the study of Ossetian music has declined.

CHECHENS AND INGUSHES

About 1.2 million Chechens (in Chechen, *Nokhcha*) and two hundred thousand Ingushes (in Ingush, *Galgai*), carriers of languages of the Nakho-Dagestanian group of the Caucasian language family, live in North Caucasia, with Ossetians to the west, Dagestanians to the east, and Georgians to the south. Autochthonous residents of the Caucasus, Chechens became Muslims in the seventeenth and eighteenth centuries.

Because the creation of an alphabet for the Chechen languages occurred only in the 1920s, oral traditions still yield clues to Chechen history. The nineteenth and twentieth centuries held many tragedies for the Chechens and Ingushes. They were conquered by the Russian Empire during the nineteenth century. Three-quarters of

Matriarchal motifs, such as the evil forest-woman Almas and the giant cannibal-woman Gorbash, are prominent in local folklore, but men perform the bulk of the vocal repertoire. The women's repertoire consists of lullabies, which have polyphonic variants.

FIGURE 6   Two-part Chechen and Ingush polyphony with a melody and a drone. The sustained intervals between the melody and the drone include fourths, fifths, and minor sevenths, in addition to thirds and sixths. Transcription by Joseph Jordania.

the population was annihilated by a war waged by Russia from 1847 to 1860. From 1944 to 1957, the Soviet government exiled them to Central Asia. In 1992, the Checheno-Ingushian Autonomous Republic was divided into the Chechen and Ingushian republics, and the Chechens declared independence. The Chechen-Russian war, which started in 1992, is the extension of a series of battles for the independence of Chechnya, locally called the Republic of Ichkeria. As a consequence of this history, the traditional music of Chechens and Ingushess has received little study.

Song style

The dorian mode predominates among Chechens and Ingushes. One scale, also found in the Pshavi mountain district of eastern Georgia, uses the minor second, the minor third, and the major sixth. Older Chechens and Ingushes frequently alternate triple and duple meter.

The predominance of dissonance is noteworthy in two-part Chechen and Ingush polyphony (figure 6). In three-part polyphony, the middle voice carries the melody while the remaining voices sound a double drone at the fifth. Cadences often end on a dissonant three-tone chord, which comprises the tonic, fourth, and fifth (figure 7). The leading melodic line is performed by a soloist, who improvises the melody and text while accompanied by a choral drone or ostinato.

Traditional modes of performance are aurally transmitted within families, many of which, notably the Bisirkhoev family, are recognized for their outstanding performance of folk music. New songs (*kerla esharsh*), usually consisting of new text and traditional melodies, are composed and performed by individual singers (men and women) during traditional feasts. Men accompany themselves on stringed instruments, but women accompany themselves on an accordion (*komuk* or *kekhat-pondur*). Eastern and Western influences are evident in the combination of the augmented second and a waltzlike meter.

FIGURE 7 Three-part
Chechen and Ingush
polyphony, ending
on a dissonant three-
tone chord, F♯–B–C♯.
Transcription by
Joseph Jordania.

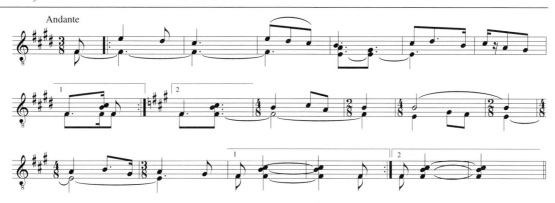

Matriarchal motifs, such as the evil forest-woman Almas and the giant cannibal-woman Gorbash, are prominent in local folklore, but men perform the bulk of the vocal repertoire. The women's repertoire consists of lullabies (Chechen *agadan iish,* Ingush *diadizha iish*), which have polyphonic variants. Solo songs known as *esharsh* are instrumentally accompanied but are usually transcribed solo. Singing has again begun to reflect the traditional practice of gender segregation, but women have sung in men's choirs since the 1920s.

Musical instruments

Chechen instrumental music includes pure instrumental music (*ladugiju iish* 'melodies for listening') and instrumental music accompanying dances, processions, and horse races (*khalkharan iish*).

The Chechen and Ingush shepherds' *dutra* 'whistle flute' is made from wood or a reed. The *shedag* 'double reed' has a straight pipe. The *tsuzam,* a children's instrument, is made from a goose feather or a stalk of grass. The *maa* 'horn' was once used during feasts and wedding celebrations.

The *adxoky-pondur,* a three-stringed bowed lute resembling the Georgian *chuniri* and bowed instruments of other North Caucasian peoples, is used as a solo and an accompanimental instrument. The *dechik-pondur,* a three-stringed long-necked plucked lute, is played by men, mostly for accompaniment.

Membranophones include a double-headed drum (*vota* or *gaval*) and a frame drum (*zhirga* or *tep*), both frequently played with a double-reed aerophone (*shedag*). The *gema* or *gemanash,* a rattle made from split wood, is played during traditional dances.

The Chechen and Ingush accordion (*komuk* or *kekhat-pondur*) became popular in the 1880s. The right-hand melody is accompanied by a melody in the left hand, rather than chords. Though the accordion has traditionally been a women's instrument, men have recently begun to play it. All other instruments are traditionally played by men.

Chechen and Ingush innovations in the 1930s included varied sizes of traditional instruments, which received chromatic capacity, and their inclusion in a large folk orchestra. Chechens and Ingushes have adopted the guitar and the Russian balalaika.

Performance genres and contexts

Musical genres include songs celebrating pagan gods, epic songs, hunting songs, humorous songs, songs for entertainment, dance-songs, and women's songs.

Wedding songs and songs in celebration of Miatsela, the main pagan deity, are numerous. The pantheon of deities includes Tutir, the protector of wolves, considered the totemic ancestor of Chechens and Ingushes; the goddess of fertility, Melererda (Ingush) and Tusholi (Chechen); the goddess of thunder and lightning,

Sela (Ingush) and Dardzin-Nana (Chechen); the goddess of the wind, Furki (Ingush); the mother of the water, Chacha; the protector of the forest, Tsu (Chechen); the god of the underground, Entr, Eter, or Dala (Chechen) and Dela (Ingush); the god of the sun, Dela-Molkh (Chechen); the mother of the moon, Chech-Kini (Chechen); and the god of sacrifices, Eshpor-Zhe (Ingush).

The epic genre, Nart-Orkhust (Nart of Evil Forces), is less extensive than that of the Ossetians, the Adighis, the Balkarians, and the Karachaevians. According to Chechen and Ingushian oral tradition, the original form of Nart epic came from Ossetia. Historical songs (*illi*), related to epic songs, are performed by a solo male performer known as *illancha,* who accompanies himself on the *dechik-pondur* or *adx-oky-pondur.* In this genre, text and music are only loosely connected, and melodies are mostly recitativelike.

Songs performed at celebrations are connected to cult activities and magical practices. Rituals intended to control weather included *musta guduchg* (Chechen) and *karshkuli* (Ingush), an event dedicated to the goddess of thunder and lightning, Sela, to invoke sunny weather. A procession involving a toy was held, food was begged from villagers, and finally a ritual feast was held. The hunting genre included a song concerning Nakhcho, ancestor of the Chechens, blinded by the goddess Elta when he tried to kill a white deer, a transformation of the goddess Elta.

Ethnographic evidence and literary sources show that Chechens and Ingushes had a large repertoire of work songs connected with agriculture and cattle herding, but little is known about current practices. Songs unconnected to ritual contexts include humorous songs (Chechen *zabarii iish,* Ingush *begii iish*) and table songs (*dottagialin iish*).

Dances include circle dances and dances for people of approximately the same age. Dance melodies are known as *khalkhar.* In pre-Christian times, men and women danced together with vocal accompaniment. Today, mostly instruments, such as the accordion, usually provide accompaniment.

Religious songs performed by men, transcribed from the 1920s and 1930s, include examples of funeral prayers (*nazm* and *zikr*).

The Chechen-Russian war of the 1990s resulted in the reactivation of traditional forms of singing and dancing, particularly circle dancing, and inspired the creation of new heroic songs about national heroes of this war.

History of scholarship

Ivan Dobrovolski published the first collection of Chechen music in 1818. More than one hundred years elapsed before additional collections of Chechen and Ingush music appeared. Georgian ethnomusicologist and composer Dimitri Arakishvili made the first arrangements of Chechen folk melodies, in 1913. In 1925, Russian composer A. Davidenko collected eighty melodies, of which thirty tunes were published the following year, with an additional thirty tunes arranged for piano. The exile of Chechens and Ingushes to Central Asia temporarily halted the collection of folk music in this area. Nikolai Rechmenski published four works in the 1950s and 1960s.

BIBLIOGRAPHY

Abkhazians

Akhobadze, Vladimer, and I. Kortua. 1957. *Abkhazian Songs.* Moscow: Gosudarstvennoe Muzikalnoe Izdatelstvo. In Russian.

Arakishvili, Dimitri. 1916. "Georgian Folk-Musical Culture." In *Moscow Ethnographical and Anthropological Commission,* 5. Moscow: G. Lissner and S. Sobko. In Russian.

———. 1940. *Review of Folk-Musical Instruments.* Tbilisi: Tenkia da Shroma. In Georgian.

Ashuba, Vadim. 1986. *Abkhazian Folk Songs.* Tbilisi: Muzfond. In Russian.

Khashba, Meri. 1967. *Abkhazian Folk-Musical Instruments.* Sukhumi: Alashara. In Russian.

———. 1977. *Abkhazians' Work and Ritual Songs.* Sukhumi: Alashara. In Russian.

———. 1983. *Genres of Abkhazian Folk Songs.* Sukhumi: Alashara. In Russian.

Kovach, Konstantin V., and K. Dzidzaria. 1929. *One Hundred One Abkhazian Folk Songs.* Moscow: Izdanie Narkomprosa Abkhazii. In Russian.

———. 1930. *The Songs of Kodorian Abkhazians.* Sukhumi: Izdanie Narkomprosa Abkhazii. In Russian.

Shamba, Ivane. 1986. *Abkhazian Folk Songs.* Tbilisi: Muzfond. In Russian.

Adighis (Cherkesses and Kabardians)

Folk Songs and Instrumental Tunes of Adighis. 1980, 1981, 1986.

Gnesin, Mikhail F. 1937. *Cherkesskie pesni* (Cherkesian songs). Moscow: Muzgiz.

Grebniov, Alexander F. 1941. *Adige oredkher* (Adighian songs). Moscow and Leningrad: Muzgiz.

Sheibler, T. 1957. "Musical Culture of Kabardino-Balkarian SSR." In *Musical Culture of Autonomous Republics of Russian SFR.* Moscow: Muzgiz. In Russian.

Balkarians and Karachaevians

Balkarian Folk Songs. 1969. Nalchik. In Balkarian.

Daurov, Aslan. 1974. *Musical Culture of Peoples of Karachaevo-Cherkesia.* Cherkessk. In Russian.

Karachaevian Folk Songs. 1969. Moscow. In Russian.

Karaeva, A. 1961. *The Folklore Heritage of Karachaevian-Balkarian People.* Cherkessk: Stavropolskoe Knizhnoe Izdatelstvo. In Russian.

Malkonduev, X. 1978. "Genre and Poetics of Balkarian-Karachaevian Lyric: Before the Revolution." Ph.D. dissertation, Moscow. In Russian.

Ortabaeva, P. 1977. *Karachaevo-Balkarian Folk Songs.* Cherkessk: Stavropolskoe Knizhnoe Izdatelstvo. In Russian.

Otarov, O., and X. Kardanov. 1962. *Balkarian Folk Songs.* Nalchik. In Balkarian.

Rakhaev, Anatoli. 1988. *Musical Epic of Balkarians.* Nalchik: Elbrus. In Russian.

Sheibler, T. 1957. "Musical Culture of Kabardino-Balkarian SSR." In *Musical Culture of Autonomous Republics of Russian SFR.* Moscow: Muzgiz. In Russian.

Taneev, Sergei. 1947 [1886]. "On the Music of Mountain Tatars." 2d ed. In *In Memory of Sergei Ivanovich Taneev,* ed. Vladimer Protopopov with comments by Victor Beliaev, 195–199. Moscow and Leningrad: Muzgiz. In Russian.

Urusbieva, Fatima. 1979. *Karachaevo-Balkarian Folklore.* Cherkessk: Stavropolskoe Knizhnoe Izdatelstvo. In Russian.

Urusov, Iskhak, ed. 1982. *Karachaevian Folk Songs.* Cherkessk: Stavropolskoe Knizhnoe Izdatelstvo. In Karachaevian.

Ossetians

Dolidze, Victor. 1960. "Ossetian Folk Music." In *Messenger of North-Ossetian Scientific Institution,* 173–179. Orjonilidze. In Russian.

Galaev, Boris. 1964. *Ossetian Folk Songs.* Moscow: Muzgiz. In Russian.

Khakhanov, Dudar. 1972. "Ossetian Folk Songs." Ph.D. dissertation, Erevan. In Russian.

Lach, Robert. 1917. "Vorläufiger Bericht über die im Auftrage der Kaiserlichen Akademie der Wissenschaften erfolgte Aufnahme der Gesänge russisher Kriegsgefangener im August und September 1916." *Mitteilung der Phonogramm-Archives-Komission Wien* 46:62–78.

———. 1931. *Gesänge russischer Kriegsgefangener, aufgenommen und herausgegeben von Robert Lach.* Abteilung mingrelische, abchasisches, svanische und ossetische Gesänge 3, 2. Vienna and Leipzig.

Ossetian Musical Folklore. 1948. Moscow and Leningrad: Muzgiz. In Russian.

Tskhurbaeva, Ksenia. 1959. *Some Features of Ossetian Folk Music.* Orjonikidze. In Russian.

Chechens and Ingushes

Arakishvili, Dimitri. 1913. "Songs of Caucasian Mountain Peoples, Kurds, Turks." In *Works of Musical-Ethnographical Commission,* 4. Moscow.

Beibulatov, T. 1926. *Collection of Lyrics and Songs.* Buinaksk. In Russian.

Bekbulatov, Umar, comp. 1976. *Folk Music of Chechens and Ingushes.* Moscow: Muzika. In Russian.

Checheno-Ingushian Musical Folklore. 1963, 1965. 2 vols. Grozni: Knigoizdat. In Russian (vol. 1) and Chechnian (vol. 2).

Davidenko, Aleksander. 1926. *Collection of Chechenian Melodies and Songs.* Moscow: Muzikalniy sektor Gosizdata. In Russian.

Mepurnov, G. 1936. *Checheno-Ingushian Songs.* Moscow: Muzgiz. In Russian.

Rechmenski, Nikolai. 1957. "Checheno-Ingushian ASSR." In *Musical Culture of Autonomous Republics of Russian SFR.* Moscow: Sovietskii Kompozitor. In Russian.

———. 1962. *Chechenian and Ingushian Folk Melodies and Songs.* Moscow: Muzika. In Russian.

———. 1965. *Musical Culture of Checheno-Ingushian ASSR.* Moscow: Muzika. In Russian.

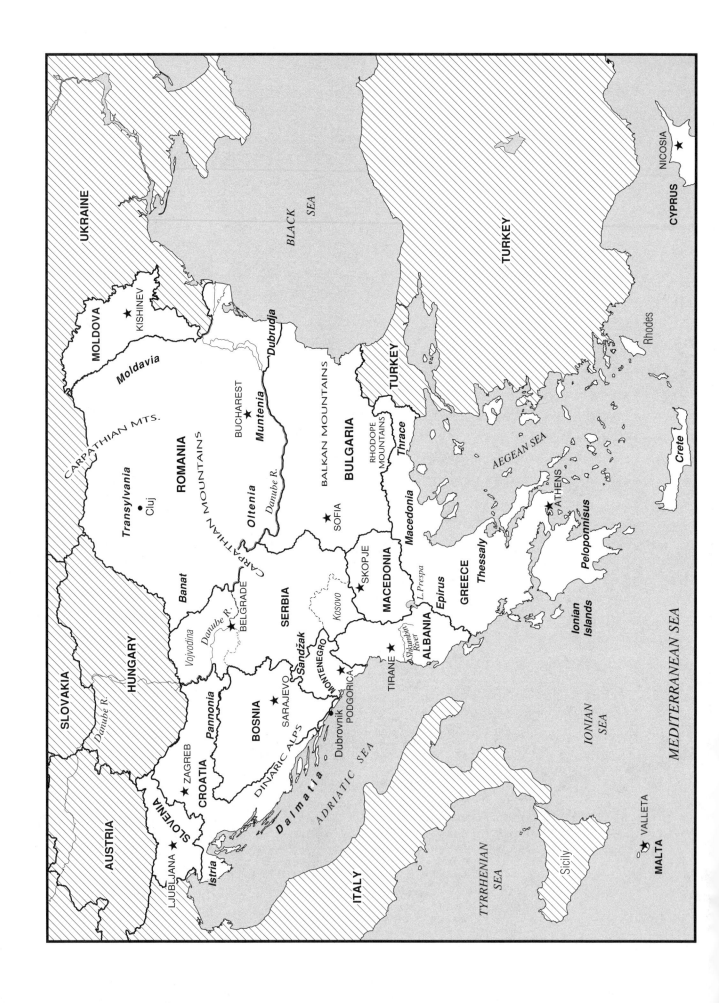

The Balkans

The Balkan Peninsula in southeastern Europe has given us the verb *balkanize* 'to break up into smaller and often hostile units'. The region is indeed home to an astonishing variety of ethnicities, languages, religions, regions, and musical styles. Despite this diversity, a number of common threads tie together the musical life of the region. Calendar and life-cycle rituals, especially weddings, are still vibrant occasions for musical performances. Narrow-range melodies, some sung in drone-based polyphonic styles, are sung in many rural areas. Traditional homemade instruments, especially flutes and bagpipes, figure prominently in musical life, often played in additive meters unusual in the rest of Europe.

A part of the Ottoman Empire for many centuries, the region features Middle Eastern instruments and performance genres, especially in towns. Gypsies (Roma) play an important role as professional musicians in all these cultures. Most of the region came under communist rule after World War II. These regimes supported staged, arranged, and choreographed versions of folklore as symbols of national identity and political ideology—a process that bolstered rural traditions threatened by industrialization and urbanization.

MAP 11   The Balkans

Romania
Valeriu Apan

Contexts for Music
Vocal Genres
Instrumental Music
Musical Instruments
Performance Practice
History of Music
History of Scholarship

Romania, with the Danube River to the south and the Black Sea to the east forming natural boundaries, has an area of nearly 238,000 square kilometers and a population of about 23 million. Romanians trace their ancestry and language to the Romans, though their ethnic origins include a mixture of peoples. Romanians form the majority of the population at 89 percent; other ethnic groups include Hungarians, Germans, Ukranians, Serbs, Croats, and Gypsies. About 75 percent of Romanian citizens belong to the Romanian Orthodox Church; the rest are Roman Catholics (Uniate) or Protestants, or have no religious affiliation. Widespread industrializaton and urbanization of a previously rural, agricultural economy and way of life began only after World War II.

Ancient Romania was inhabited by the Dacians, a northern branch of the Thracian tribes. The Roman conquest, of A.D. 105—106, gave way to Goth, Hun, Avar, Slav, Bulgar, and Hungarian invaders, from the fourth to the tenth centuries. The feudal principalities of Transylvania, Moldavia, and Wallachia (which included present-day Oltenia and Muntenia) emerged in the eleventh through the fifteenth centuries. In the first half of the sixteenth century, they became vassal states of the Ottoman Empire. The Austro-Hungarian Empire annexed Transylvania in 1699. Moldavia and Wallachia united under a single monarch in 1859, adopted the name *Romania* in 1862, and achieved independence from the Ottomans in 1878. With the defeat of the Austro-Hungarian Empire in 1918, Banat, Bucovina, and Transylvania united with Romania. The monarchy, established in 1881, was abolished in 1946, and a Romanian Peoples Republic was proclaimed, emphasizing industrialization, the formation of agricultural cooperatives, education, and culture. The communist era ended violently in December 1989.

Because of this history, Romanian traditional culture varies by region: Transylvania, Oltenia, Muntenia, Moldavia, Banat, Bucovina, Maramureş, Crişana, Banat, Hunedoara, Bihor, Năsăud, and Dobruja (map 12).

CONTEXTS FOR MUSIC

Most performances of Romanian folk music, song, and dance are directly tied to ritu-als and other traditional occasions: winter customs (Christmas and New Year), agrari-

MAP 12   Romania and Bulgaria ethnographic regions

an rites and feasts (planting and harvesting), and social and ritual events (weddings, burials, work parties). While some have historical roots in antiquity, many have lost their initial magical meanings and today are performed primarily for spectacle.

Calendric rituals

Since Roman times, the winter solstice has been celebrated with ritual songs, masked dancers, and ritual greetings. Caroling (*colinde*), the most important winter custom, begins on Christmas Eve or the day before, and lasts until Epiphany. Boys, girls, teens, and adults (*colindatori*), six to twelve in number, go from house to house, singing in unison (in some parts of Transylvania, antiphonally) or occasionally accompanied by instrumentalists. Their songs express hope for prosperity, good crops, health, and happiness; the hosts, in turn, treat the carolers with hospitality, gifts, food, and drinks. Sometimes the festivities conclude with dances involving hosts and singers.

The children's winter repertoire (*cîntece de stea* 'star songs') has texts inspired by biblical scriptures. The rhythms and melodies of these songs resemble Western European Christmas carols, but in some parts of Oltenia, texts incorporate the older *colinde* structures.

Children and youths engage in traditional greetings (*urările*) at Christmas and New Year. Sometimes humorous, these musical-poetical forms are spoken rhythmically or sung on simple melodies. One version, the *plugușorul* 'the little plow', is an ancient agrarian fertility rite in Bucovina, Moldavia, and Muntenia. On New Year's Day or New Year's Eve, children or young men go through the village carrying a colorfully decorated plough, sometimes pulled by oxen. Accompanied by a friction drum (*buhai*), a shepherd's flute, or other instruments playing nonmetrical melodies, they deliver long recitations depicting fieldwork. Jokes, shouts, the crack of whips, and bells punctuate the text and the instrumental tunes. Variants of this custom survive in Transylvania and Maramureş.

Masked dancing recalling Dionysian festivals occurs during winter feasts. Among the most remarkable are *capra* 'goat', found in Transylvania, Maramureş, Bucovina, Moldavia, and Muntenia; and *ursul* 'the bear' and *calul* or *caiuţi* 'hobby horses', found in north-central Moldavia and Bucovina. Some instrumental melodies are unique to these rituals, and musical instruments such as drums, bells, friction drums, cog rattles, alphorns, and horns add to the uproar with which the new year is greeted. During the communist era, festivals of masked dances were organized in Hunedoara, Maramureş, Bucovina, and Moldavia, and during the postcommunist era, they are still flourishing.

Spring and summer rituals

Spring and summer rituals relate to agriculture and sheepherding. In Muntenia, Oltenia, Banat, and Hunedoara, children perform *paparuda* 'rain-caller'. Dressed in greenery, they go from house to house singing a simple repeated melodic line and improvising steps and turns in asymmetrical rhythms. To ensure fertility, the householders sprinkle them with water. Another rain-begging ritual, *scaloian,* involves a mock funeral lament for a rag or clay doll, which after the singing is tossed into a river or a lake.

The beginning of the agricultural and pastoral seasons are often marked by feasts involving the entire community. In Maramureş, the first farmer to plough his fields is honored in a festive ceremony, *plugarul* 'the ploughman'. In Banat, Transylvania, and Maramureş, the taking of sheep to mountain pasturage is also ritually celebrated.

Harvest rituals include *drăgaica* in Muntenia, where on 24 June (St. John's Day) girls between eleven and fifteen years old perform a ritual song in asymmetrical meter, a circle dance (hora), or a suite of dances. In Transylvania, *cununa* 'the wreath' has survived as a significant traditional feast at the end of the harvest. It unfolds in several stages: the harvester's departure, making a wreath, carrying and watering the wreath, and a communal feast with dancing and music. A slow, ornamented, lyrical song accompanies the solemn procession. Some of the songs retain mythological elements, such as the dispute between the sun's sister and wind's sister over their brothers' qualities.

The *căluşul* 'little horse', a ritual dance performed at Whitsuntide (the fifth week after Easter) to create fecundity, or to heal or prevent illness, is practiced in Oltenia, Muntenia, and parts of Dobruja. The *căluşari*, a group of seven, nine, or eleven young men, dance intricate virtuosic figures in a circular promenade to the accompaniment of vigorous dance-music played on one or two violins and sometimes other instruments (figure 1).

Seasonal fieldwork intermingles with numerous social traditions involving song, music, and dance: work parties (*claca*), social evenings (*sezatoarea*), and village fairs.

Life-cycle rituals

In the human life cycle, marriage and death are marked by the most elaborate rituals and musical expressions.

Weddings

The wedding ritual includes actions, songs, dances, humor, symbolic gestures, orations, and *strigături* 'extemporized verses'. The most important moments in the wedding ritual, each accompanied by specific songs or instrumental tunes are *cununa* 'the

FIGURE 1 A line of dancers (*călușari*) for the
spring healing ritual (*căluș*), accompanied by
accordion. Photo by Gail Kligman, 1976.

FIGURE 1 A line of dancers (*călușari*) for the
spring healing ritual (*căluș*), accompanied by
accordion. Photo by Gail Kligman, 1976.

wreath', *steagul* 'the flag', *îmbrăcatul* 'the dressing of the bride', *iertările* 'the forgiveness', *cununia* 'the church ceremony', and *masa mare* 'the grand feast'. Wedding
music is vocal (dedicated to the bride, groom, mother-in-law, godfather, godmother,
dowry, fir tree, hen) and instrumental (dances, marches, music for the feast, dowry,
and processions). Traditional wedding melodies are performed by the guests accompanied by paid instrumentalists (Transylvania, Crișana, Maramureș, Bucovina) and
by professional folksingers and musicians (Muntenia, Oltenia, Banat, Moldavia, and
Dobruja).

Death

Romanian culture regards death as a passage from this world to another world, and
death rituals provide a transition that prevents the deceased from returning as a
ghost. Burial rituals are marked by numerous customs and special music, and end
with a religious ceremony and special feast. Their magnitude is a function of the family's relations and social status, the age of the deceased, and the cause of death. For
instance, an unexpected death or a teenager's death causes the entire community's
participation.

Burial rituals employ two main categories of music: *cîntece ceremoniale* 'ceremonial songs', found in northern Oltenia, Banat, and some areas of Transylvania; and
bocete 'laments', practiced everywhere. In both categories, the singers or lamenters
evoke the deceased's momentum toward transition, recall the deceased's life, and
express relatives' and acquaintances' grief. The ceremonial songs, sung by women not
closely related to the deceased but hired for this purpose, are performed in unison or
antiphonally with narrow-range, slow-moving melodies. Ceremonial songs include
"*Cîntecul Zorilor*" ('Dawn Song'), sung at sunrise as an announcement of the death;
"*Cîntecul Bradului*" ('Song of the Fir'), sung for those dying young and unmarried;
and songs accompanying each part of the ritual such as "*Al Drumului*" ('On the
Road') and "*Al Gropii*" ('At the Grave'). The laments are improvised narratives sung
by female relations or friends of the deceased. They begin at the moment of death,
continue through the burial, and reappear at commemorative dates after the burial
(figure 2). Their poetry combines elements from the deceased's life and the sentiments of those left to mourn. Three types can be distinguished: in Muntenia and
southern Moldavia, where the words are improvised without versification; in Oltenia
and some places in Banat, where the text is improvised in hexasyllabic lines; and in

FIGURE 2 Women lament at the gravestone of a
deceased relative. Photo by Gail Kligman, 1976.

Unique to Romania, the *doina* may be vocal or instrumental, and are performed by men and women, solo or with accompaniment. Their texts relate to themes of love, nature, longing, sorrow, and grief. Lullabies are sung to *doina* tunes.

FIGURE 3 A small ensemble (*taraf*) of Gypsy musicians: two violins, *ţambal,* bass, and accordion. Photo by Gail Kligman, 1976.

Transylvania, Banat, Bucovina, and northern Moldavia, where melodies and versified texts are preset and improvisation is limited to adapting the poetic formulas to the particular context. The solo singing (rarely in a group, as in Năsăud, northern Transylvania) is mingled with weeping usually at the cadence and may be accompanied by the shepherd's flute in Bucovina.

In some parts of Transylvania, *verşuri,* songs based on the literate tradition and used since the late eighteenth century, have been specifically composed for burial services. The *bucium* 'alphorn' is often used for burial services, especially when the deceased is a young person or a shepherd (northern Transylvania, Maramureş, Bucovina, and northern Moldavia). At certain points during the funeral, the musicians play melodies similar to laments or shepherd signals. Wakes (*priveghi*) involve humorous games and in some places (Vrancea, southern Moldavia) masked dancers. In Banat, the dance *jocul de pomana* 'alms dance' is performed for those who die young.

Dances

The repertoire of Romanian village dances varies regionally. Some villages in the southwest have forty to fifty dances differing in music and steps and performed for entertainment or ritual. They can be in a closed or open circle, a semicircle, a straight line, winding lines, or couples, are danced by the young and old of both sexes, and are always accompanied by music. Sung dances, where the dancers supply the music, used to be performed throughout the country, but in the late twentieth century they were found only in central Transylvania, danced by girls, and Bucovina, danced by older women.

The basic Romanian dances—hora, a circle dance; and *sîrba,* a line dance—are found, with variations, in most of the country. Each region has unique dances.

Polyrhythm, resulting from an overlapping of music, steps, shouted verses (*strigături*), calls (*comenzi*), interjections, cries, whistles, and clapping, is quite common. Some dance tunes have fixed forms comprised of two or three sections; others involve the varied repetition of one or a few motifs. Meters are binary or asymmetrical; triple meter is absent, except where it results from the blunting of asymmetrical meters, as in Moldavia. Instrumental accompaniment varies from a single musician (almost always men) to small bands using a variety of instruments: violin, *fluiere* 'duct flutes', *nai* 'panpipe', *taragot* (a wooden conical-bore, single-reed aerophone), cimbalom, accordion, guitar, and bass (figure 3). Many professional and amateur ensembles performing in Romania and abroad play transformed versions of dance music for stage presentations.

VOCAL GENRES

The most prominent vocal genres performed during rituals and social occasions are the *doina* 'improvised lyrical song' and the *cîntec* 'strophic song'.

FIGURE 4 A *doina* of love (*doina de dragoste*) from Muntenia, sung, after the opening descending melisma, in a spoken (parlando) rhythm. The curved lines over a note indicate a slight shortening of the duration as a way to capture the freedom in the rhythm. After Oprea and Agapie 1983:317.

Doina

Unique to Romania, the *doina* is found throughout the country under various names: "long song" (*hora lunga*), "song of the forest," and "song of sadness." *Doina* may be vocal or instrumental, and are performed by men and women, solo or with accompaniment. Their texts relate to themes of love, nature, longing, sorrow, and grief. Lullabies (*cîntece de leagăn*) are sung to *doina* tunes. The musical form is freely improvised, but the textual meter is octosyllabic, except when extended by *noduri* (glottal sounds) in Maramureş. Vocal sounds equivalent to the yodel (*hăulit*) are used in the Gorj zone of Oltenia. Three types of *doina* may be distinguished.

The first type, found in Maramureş, Năsăud, Bucovina, and northern Oltenia, has a narrow melodic range, and so most scholars presume it to be the oldest. The melodic line is typically diatonic major, with the fourth degree raised or natural. Singers begin with an introductory recitative on the fifth or fourth degree, which may be attacked directly or through a melodic passage from below. The introduction is succeeded by an improvisatory section developed around the fifth, fourth, third, and second degrees, involving repeated ornamental melodic variations. The concluding formula is usually a recitative on the tonic.

The second type is found in the previously mentioned zones and in some parts of Transylvania, Muntenia, and Moldavia. *Doina* of these types have a wider melodic range within a simple, less ornamented structure.

The third type, *de dragoste* 'of love', appears much newer, possibly of professional minstrel origins, and is found in the southern part of the country (Oltenia, Muntenia, Dobruja). *Lăutari* (professional musicians, many of them Gypsies) perform it during social occasions with romantic and sometimes erotic texts. Musicians and singers show off their expressive abilities in wide-ranging, highly ornamented, rubato melodies (figure 4).

Strophic songs

Strophic songs (*cîntece*), performed at social occasions, are used as ceremonial songs in wedding and funeral rituals, fertility rites, laments, epic songs, and lullabies. Songs have a regular strophic form with two to seven melodic lines and vary regionally in structure and style. Singers modify the basic structure with each repetition: they may repeat or omit a melodic line and vary the pitches and rhythms. Songs use major and minor modes and various approaches to rhythm. The poetry touches on a wide range of emotions and is organized as a succession of octosyllabic (or sometimes hexasyllabic) lines, with or without stanzaic organizational principles.

Song regions

In Hunedoara and Bihor, songs typically have three melodic lines with the cadence of the second line on the subtonic. Most scales are pentatonic or have a pentatonic substratum. Those from Bihor typically employ an augmented (lydian) fourth and are in free rhythm (rubato). Most songs from the Transylvanian plain have four-line forms with the second-line cadence on the third degree (occasionally the fifth). They have a narrow range and a pentatonic substratum. Additional syllables ("*şai, lai lai; trai, lai, lai*") extend the octosyllabic lines. Songs from Maramureş also have four-line melodic forms, usually AABB, with the second-line cadence on the tonic. In the last two lines, the verses may be replaced by a refrain of meaningless words ("*şapoi daina şi daina, şi iară daina daina*"). They have a limited musical range, and may be diatonic (G, A, D modes and D mode with a variable fourth) or pentatonic, with regular, repeated rhythms. Songs from Năsăud are long, extemporized, nonmetrical, richly ornamented forms with five, six, or seven lines. They require great vocal skill and possibly show the influence of instrumental music. Songs from Bucovina, like many from Moldavia, typically have a flat second at the final cadence and an occasional descending diminution of the fifth. In sub-Carpathian Muntenia and Oltenia, the older, indigenous songs are distinguished by their iambic rhythm, interwoven with trochaic or other rhythmic formulae. Songs from Banat have four melodic lines (AABC, ABBC) with the second-line cadence on the subtonic—a trait common to southern and southwestern Transylvania. Their modes are usually diatonic on G or D, with some pentatonic examples. Many songs from Banat include texted refrains in the last line or two. The final cadence usually occurs on the second, giving a semicadential impression.

Late-twentieth-century folk music adopted a style of dance songs that originated in Oltenia but became popular throughout the country because of professional singers' performing with instrumental accompaniment on radio, television, and recordings. Urban folk music generally has a heterogeneous character because of the mélange of people from different regions; however, in the suburbs of Bucharest, Gypsy musicians have developed a type of folk music preferred by audiences in Muntenia, with songs characterized by richly ornamented, chromatic melodies, showing strong Turkish influence and demanding great vocal skill. When they are performed instrumentally, they are described as 'listening' or 'table' songs. Under communist rule, the urban song repertoire also included an artificially created genre, revolutionary workers' songs. Inspired by the life and social issues of working-class people, these songs were based on folk tunes and served ideological purposes.

INSTRUMENTAL MUSIC

Romanian instrumental music perhaps has its origins as the pastime of shepherds, though song and dance accompaniments are its other important functions.

FIGURE 5 The first eight bars of a *sîrba* from Muntenia played by violin and *ţambal*. This melody would be repeated with slight variation followed by a contrasting eight-measure melody. After Suliţeanu 1976:n.p.

Shepherds' music

Shepherds' instruments include the *bucium* 'alphorn' and the *tilinca* (an end-blown flute, without a duct or holes for fingering), which produce notes based on overblowing the harmonic series. The richness of melodies depends on the player's skill. Shepherds also play widely various duct flutes (*fluier, caval*).

Many pieces refer to shepherds' work ("when the sheep are milked," "measuring the milk," "making cheese"). Some have melodies used with the movement of sheep ("when the sheep go to the mountains," "when the sheep run down the valley") and the grazing of flocks ("when the sheep graze on the slopes"). Some melodies are variants of *doina* tunes and have long phrases and wide ranges. Others consist of repeated melodic motifs. Shepherds play numerous signaling melodies on the alphorn to gather sheep to the fold and prepare them for the trip to summer pasturage or winter homes.

A particularly elaborate item in the shepherd's repertoire is an instrumental rendition of a tale about a shepherd losing his flock. Usually played on the *fluier,* it has many variants around the country. The piece portrays a shepherd's feelings while he searches for his flock in a series of episodes: a sad song, usually a *doina*; a lively melody, typically a dance tune; another sad song, the initial or another selection; and a lively melody. In some areas, the tale is amplified with episodes explained through recitation and illustrated by music.

Dance-music

Most dance melodies have fixed forms and binary and asymmetrical rhythms and are organized in a variety of modes. Western triple meter is not typical of Romanian dance. Duple and asymmetric meters are common. Most dance performances consist of two repeated phrases of four, eight, or sixteen measures. Each phrase is repeated and varied (figure 5).

Vocal-instrumental music

Romania's epic genre, *balade* 'ballads' (also called *cîntece bătrîneşti* 'old-time songs'), flourished in the feudal period between the sixteenth and nineteenth centuries. Most describe the conflicts, manners, and aspirations of that time, and though some are still performed in many parts of the country, they are gradually being replaced by other genres. In Bucovina and Transylvania, peasants sing epic texts to *doina*-type tunes or strophic-song melodies. In southern Moldavia, Dobruja, Muntenia, Oltenia, and Banat, professional musicians perform ballads with recitativelike melodies. The

Romanian musical instruments began as remarkably simple natural objects: a leaf, a blade of grass, a sliver of birch bark, the bony scale of a fish (or somewhat less naturally, a slip of plastic) placed between or in front of the lips and blown to produce a shrill, clear sound with wide melodic range.

communist period saw a revival of songs of this genre, performed by amateurs who sang at folk festivals and competitions.

In the past, peasant-bards sang ballads at different social occasions and accompanied themselves on the shepherd's flute, bagpipe, or other instrument. In the late twentieth century, professional musicians, accompanied on violin or a small ensemble of two violins, *cobza*, *ţambal* (cimbalom), and bass, sing them at weddings or other social gatherings at the guests' request. The musicians play a prelude, interludes, and a postlude and occasionally double the voice. The instrumental accompaniment consists of a continuous rhythmic figuration of the basic chords. The musicians conclude with a lively instrumental dance piece. The sung parts are interwoven with the instrumental solos and passages of spoken narrative. The performers may use mimicry and other dramatic effects to stress actions recounted in the text. The performance is free and improvisatory. The same ballad will be condensed or amplified according to the listeners' interest and the performers' disposition.

Amzulescu (1964) distinguishes ballads according to poetic content as "fantastic ballads" (with themes relating to nature), mythical narratives, magic, and fairies in the manner of fairy tales and legends; "ballads of bravery" (including "the cycle of the invaders," "the outlaws," and "the robbers"), which depict human relations and historical events; "pastoral ballads," concerned with nature and shepherds' lives; ballads about the feudal court; and "family ballads," which delve into personal relationships. A good singer may know around forty ballads or more.

MUSICAL INSTRUMENTS

Romanian musical instruments began as remarkably simple natural objects: a leaf, a blade of grass, a sliver of birch bark, the bony scale of a fish (or somewhat less naturally, a slip of plastic) placed between or in front of the lips and blown to produce a shrill, clear sound with wide melodic range.

Idiophones

Many children's instruments use naturally sonorous materials, such as wooden plates or swords clapped together, spurs, and whips. The *duruitoare,* a ratchet-type cog rattle whirled on a handle, is made by craftsmen and used for masked dances at New Year's and as a noisemaker to scare birds away. Other idiophones can vary their pitches, for instance, the mouth harp (*drîmba*) and bells (*clopote* and *zurgălăi*), cast in many sizes and used in New Year's ceremonies and weddings (decorating the nuptial banner) and hung around the necks of cattle and sheep as signal devices. The *toaca,* a wooden plank or metal plate struck with one or two wooden hammers, produces different percussive pitches depending on where it is hit. Monks and nuns use it in monasteries to announce Mass and other offices, and children play it during Lent in Oltenia, Banat, and Maramureş.

Membranophones

Membranophones are widespread and are used most often in rituals. They include the friction drum (*buhai*); various one-headed frame drums (*dairea, dara, vuvă*), about 25 centimeters in diameter (Oltenia and Muntenia), and *doba*, 80 centimeters in diameter (Moldavia); and double-headed drums (*tobe, dube*), with a diameter between 20 and 25 centimeters (Hunedoara, Banat, Bihor, and Arad). In some parts of the country, a snare drum (*darabana*) and a bass drum (*toba mare*), borrowed from military bands and jazz bands, and a cymbal are used alongside other instruments to accompany dancing.

Chordophones

Chordophones, especially important to professional musicians, include the *cobza* (a short-necked plucked lute), the *ţambal* 'cimbalom' (a trapezoidal hammered dulcimer), and the *vioara* 'violin'.

The *cobza,* a pear-shaped, bent-necked lute resembling the Middle Eastern *'ud,* is probably the oldest stringed instrument in Romania. Professional musicians use it to accompany melody instruments. It has eight to twelve gut or metal strings arranged in four courses of two or three strings each. Common tuning follows a pattern of fifths and fourths (d–a–d–g). Once widespread, it has largely been replaced by the guitar and the cimbalom.

The *ţambal* was first mentioned in Romania in 1546. Originally played in the castles of the nobility, it passed into the hands of professional, mainly Gypsy, folk musicians and was common in the nineteenth century. In Oltenia, Muntenia, and Moldavia, village Gypsy musicians play small, twenty- to twenty-five-course instruments suspended on a strap around their necks. City musicians play larger ones with four legs, thirty-five courses, and a pedal mute, perfected in Hungary by Jozsef V. Schunda in the late nineteenth century. These zithers are tuned in three ways: "Romanian" (chromatic succession), "Hungarian" (diatonic succession), and "transport" (chromatic-diatonic succession). The strings are struck with two mallets, wrapped in cloth or cotton to soften the sound. Various diatonic and chromatic passages and arpeggios can easily be produced, and the instrument is used as an accompaniment and a solo instrument. The accompanimental technique differs regionally. The *lăutari* of Muntenia, Oltenia, and Moldavia base their style on rhythmic-melodic formulas in which the rhythm prevails, but musicians from Banat and Transylvania use a harmonic accompaniment realized through arpeggios.

The violin (*vioara*), the mainstay of professional musicians since the 1700s, is found all over the country, sometimes modified, as in Vrancea, where up to eight sympathetic strings are added to the four that play the melody, and in Transylvania, where violins with flat bridges and three strings serve for accompaniment. Though the typical tuning in fifths has become standard, more than thirty *scordaturas* (tuning variations) ease the playing of certain fast dance melodies or the obtaining of special sound effects.

In the 1920s, a violin appeared with a metal horn in place of a sound box, with the bridge supported on a small membrane. Fiddles of this kind have been found in some parts of Transylvania, Banat, and Moldavia. Since the nineteenth century, *lăutari* have added a viola, a cello, or a double bass. Sometimes of rural manufacture, these accompanying instruments may have only two or three strings, which can be bowed, plucked, or struck with the wood of the bow. They are used as accompanying instruments in folk bands in Transylvania and Banat and folk orchestras in cities.

Aerophones

Aerophones were the mainstay of the rural, peasant tradition. The Carpathian

Mountains still echo with the powerful sound of the alphorn, an ancient pastoral instrument made of wood or (in northern Romania) metal, and played by men and women. Used during Roman times as a military instrument, it functioned primarily as a signaling instrument and in funeral processions. Five types of alphorns are differentiated by the shape of the tubing, the length (between 1.5 and 3 meters), and the materials used in manufacturing. All are blown in the manner of trumpets and can produce harmonics from the third to the sixteenth.

Flutes (*fluiere*) are the most common folk instruments, and researchers have identified seventeen types. Craftsmen throughout the country make them to sell at markets or fairs, or to artisans' stores. A few are described here.

The *fifa* (Oltenia) is the simplest Romanian flute. A notched hemlock tube about 20 centimeters long and closed at the lower end, it plays one pitch. Women play it while using a yodel-like technique in alternation with its note.

Another simple flute, the *tilinca,* is found in the northern part of the country. Made of wood, metal, or plastic, it is a tube from 50 to 80 centimeters long, open at both ends, with no holes for fingering. By alternately closing and opening the lower end of the tube with the forefinger while varying the blowing pressure, the player utilizes the interlocking harmonic series of closed and open pipes to produce elaborate *doina* and dance melodies. In Maramureş, a version made of willow bark has a duct.

The *caval,* common in the south and southeast of the country (Oltenia, Muntenia, Dobruja, and southern Moldavia), is a wooden duct flute from 60 to 95 centimeters long, with a cylindrical or slightly conical bore. It has five holes for fingering, plays a diatonic scale, and has a soft, velvety tone, well-suited to playing *doinas* and laments.

Most widespread of all wind instruments is the *fluier,* a variously sized six-holed duct flute, usually made of wood. A plug and a small opening cut in the tube form a duct that guides the breath over a beveled edge. The bore is slightly inversely conical (the lower aperture smaller than the duct end). Six finger holes, round or slightly elliptical and nearly equidistant in smaller instruments, are arranged in two groups of three in medium-sized and larger instruments. The scale is diatonic, with a range of almost three octaves. Chromatic tones can be obtained by half covering the holes or using cross fingerings. It is played solo and in orchestras.

The most famous of all Romanian flutes, the *nai* 'panpipe', has existed in Romania since ancient times, documented archaeologically and by the Roman poet Ovid, who saw it played by natives in the land of his exile, present-day Dobruja. More recent historical documentation, beginning in the sixteenth and seventeenth centuries, shows that after about 1750, professional musicians played it in ensembles (*tarafuri,* sing. *taraf*). The standard *nai* consists of a slightly concave row of twenty cane, bamboo, or wood pipes of different lengths and diameters, arranged according to size in the shape of a wing. Skilled craftsmen glue the pipes together and support them on a curved casing. To regulate the tuning, the pipes, open at the upper end and closed at the lower with poplar or cork plugs, are filled with beeswax. Sound is made by blowing across each pipe separately, enabling the musician to play a diatonic scale from b^1 to g^4 with f♯s. Chromatic pitches are produced by tilting the instrument. Since the 1960s, the lower register of the *nai* has been expanded by adding up to seven more pipes. The *nai* is employed in a great variety of musical genres, from free-form melodies to the most intricate dances. Professional musicians play it solo or in an orchestra, most frequently in Muntenia, Oltenia, Dobruja, Moldavia, and Bucovina.

The most important reed instrument, the *cimpoi* 'bagpipe', was once widespread and played at weddings. In the late twentieth century, other instruments have replaced it, and it is found mainly in the hands of elderly men in northern Oltenia,

Muntenia, Dobruja, Moldavia, western Transylvania, and Banat (figure 6). It is made of a large goatskin bag (*burduf*), equipped with two wooden pipes fitted with idioglot single cane or elder reeds and a blowpipe (*suflător*). The drone pipe (*bîzoi*) is usually made of three sections without holes for fingering, but the melody pipe (*carabă*) has five to eight holes. Six kinds of *cimpoi* have been identified, distinguished from one another by the chanter's form—cylindrical or conical, straight or curved, single or double. The scale of the instrument is usually diatonic, with a range of one octave. Dance melodies make up the bulk of the repertoire.

The *taragot,* a keyed, conical-bore instrument with clarinet mouthpiece and reed played in Banat and Transylvania, is an idealization of an older double-reed *zurna* instrument, invented at the end of the nineteenth century by Jozsef V. Schunda of Budapest. It is well-suited to *doina*, though it is played for fast dance melodies with astonishing virtuosity.

These folk instruments continue to be played, though the accordion, the clarinet, and the guitar (and, in cities, the electric guitar) are replacing the traditional accompanying instruments, *cobza* and small *ţambal*. Brass instruments, introduced in folk bands around the end of the nineteenth century, are still found in Moldavia and Banat. Many urban musicians now play electronic instruments.

In some parts of the country, especially at cultural events, folk festivals, and competitions, instruments from the same family play in groups—for example, flutes, bagpipes, alphorns, or panpipes. During the communist period, folk instruments were played together with Western instruments in bands (*tarafuri*) and large orchestras.

FIGURE 6 A peasant musician plays bagpipe (*cimpoi*) outside his home. Photo by Gail Kligman, 1976.

PERFORMANCE PRACTICE

Most Romanian folk music is performed monophonically, but polyphony and harmony occur in some vocal, instrumental, or vocal-instrumental group performances. These polyphonic and harmonic forms, which result from superimposed melodic lines or a drone or the use of chords, are typically rudimentary when played by villagers and more developed in professionals' practice.

In the vocal genres, antiphonal performance results in rudimentary forms of heterophony and polyphony, including funeral songs sung by two groups of women (in some parts of Banat, Transylvania, and Oltenia); laments sung by a woman leader and a group of women (Banat); songs sung by mixed groups of men and women during the nights of the death vigil (Moldavia); wedding ceremonial songs sung by men (Bihor) and mixed groups (Hunedoara-Transylvania); carols sung by men (south Transylvania); quatrains sung by girls during evening working parties (Bihor); and children's songs connected to different dance-games, found all over the country.

The use of a drone appears in funeral songs from Banat and a guttural vocal drone used in *fluier* and *caval* playing in Oltenia. Some instruments, including the *cimpoi* (comprising a melodic pipe and a drone pipe), play polyphonically. Violinists in Bihor and Alba-Transylvania utilize the open strings or double stopping to play polyphonically.

Heterophony occurs in instrumental and vocal-instrumental styles, especially in pieces in parlando rubato rhythm, like *doina*, strophic songs, ballads, and laments, because of the differences in technical possibilities of the voice and instruments and the numerous variants of the pieces known among players. Polyphonic forms with counter melodies accompanying the principal melodic line occur rarely and only in professional renditions.

In instrumental and vocal-instrumental performance, instrumental harmony as accompaniment appears in various forms and depends on the instruments used for

Turkish music was cultivated in the courts at Bucharest and Iaşi, with Dimitrie Cantemir (1673–1723) as its most famous exponent.

TRACK
30

accompaniment, the musical region, the genre, and the musicians' skill. For example, the *cobza,* the *chitara* (guitar), and the *zongora* (the guitar of Maramureş) play simple harmonic forms. *Cobza* players strum *ţiituri* 'rhythmic formulas', differentiated and named after dance type and musical form (fixed or free) and using bichords (fifths and fourths) and major and minor triads (tonic, dominant, and subdominant). Musicians also use *ţiituri* similar to those of the *sîrba* and the hora to accompany nonmetrical *doina,* songs proper, and ballads, an accompaniment style they call *mărunt* 'small' or *gonit* 'chased'. Musicians on other accompanying instruments (*ţambal,* guitar, accordion) derive their accompaniment technique from the *cobza's ţiituri.*

In Romanian and Hungarian music in parts of Transylvania, a second violin or viola (called *săcunda, braci,* and *contră*) and a cello or a double bass (called *gordună* and *broancă*) supply the rhythmic-harmonic accompaniment. The *braci* or *contră* has only three strings, tuned G–D–A, stretched on a flat bridge, which enables the player to maintain the same intensity on all strings while playing major, minor, and diminished chords. The *gorduna* usually has a tuning of g^1–d^2–g^2, and during the accompaniment plays the root of the chords played on the *braci.* In some parts of Arad, Hunedoara, Alba, and Banat, the strings are plucked or beaten with a stick or a bow while accompanying fast dances. In some parts of Banat and western Transylvania (Arad), two violins (each a *coantră*) or a second violin (*coantră*) and a viola (*braci*) serve for accompaniment.

The most complex harmonic forms in Romanian folk-musical accompaniments are played by the *ţambal,* which has a wide range and vast technical possibilities. The instrument plays triads (major, minor, diminished, augmented), major and minor triads with minor and major sevenths, and diminished chords with diminished sevenths, through arpeggios or by playing two pitches of the chord at the same time, in various melodic-rhythmic-harmonic figures. Most of the cimbalom's rhythmic formulas (*ţiituri*) were taken from the style of the *cobza,* enriched with fragments of the melodic line through grace notes, appoggiaturas, and diatonic and chromatic passages. Players from Muntenia, Oltenia, and Moldavia use melodic-rhythmic formulas (*ţiituri*) to emphasize the rhythm, while players from Banat and Transylvania use arpeggios and intervals to emphasize the harmony.

In the twentieth century, village bands throughout the country used the accordion (*acordeon*) to accompany melodies using basically the same *ţiituri* as the *chitara,* the *cobza,* and the *ţambal.* Some village bands also used a drum (*dobă*) to supply a rhythmic pedal.

Urban musicians, having adopted the traditional *ţiituri,* use a harmonic language strongly influenced by Western harmony. Concert bands and orchestras employ a more compact, complex, and richer harmonic style than is traditionally used for the *taraf*—a result of their formal training. Their style, heard in recordings and broadcasts, has influenced many village musicians around the country.

HISTORY OF MUSIC

Ceramics found in Moldavia and other relics of the late Neolithic Age (2800–1900 B.C.) show stylized human figures that suggest dance movement. As early as the seventh century B.C., the population of Dobruja enjoyed a flourishing cultural and musical life under Hellenic influence. The *Anabasis* by Xenophon (ca. 427–355 B.C.) and the notes made by the geographer Strabo (64 B.C. to A.D. 21) mention the Dacians' songs and dances, including genres such as the hymn, the lament, the ode, and a paean to Apollo.

The Roman conquest introduced the celebrations of the winter solstice (Calendae and Saturnalia) and the spring ritual Rosalia. The Romans contributed to the spread of trumpets and horns variously called *buccina, tibia,* and *cornua.*

Christianity, introduced to Romania in the second to fourth centuries, resulted in Latin musical forms. From the time of Justinian (sixth century), Eastern Orthodoxy and Byzantine music were adopted in many parts of the country. For nearly three centuries Latin and Greek were the languages of religious music, before the latter became dominant, in the ninth century. In the tenth century, ecclesiastical rituals began using Church Slavonic. Indigenous musical documents include the *Evangelic Lectionary* (tenth or eleventh century) in ekphonetic notation and manuscripts written in Greek from the thirteenth and fourteenth centuries, when Giobascus Vlachus (thirteenth century) and Filothei Cozianul (fourteenth century) composed Byzantine melodies on biblical texts. Byzantine and Gregorian chant developed simultaneously in the northern parts of Moldavia and Transylvania.

In the fifteenth and sixteenth centuries, the names of individual musicians such as military buglers, *buccina* players, trumpeters, and virtuoso guitarists and lutenists begin to appear. After 1400, the organ spread rapidly in Transylvania, as did virtuosi to play it, foremost among them Hieronymus Ostermayer (1500–1561) of Braşov. Other genres of the period included ballads and folk instrumental music, played by professional, often Gypsy, musicians. The invention of printing stimulated the publication of ritual books in the early 1500s.

In the 1600s, Western musical genres continued to develop, primarily in Transylvania. Composers Ioan Căianu (1629–1687) and Daniel Speer (1636–1707) incorporated Romanian folk-song and dance music into their work, and the church introduced texts in Romanian.

In the 1700s, Baroque instrumental polyphony stimulated the development of choral harmony at Blaj in Transylvania and Neamţ in Moldavia. The introduction into the Romanian language of psalm singing, by Filotei Sin Agai Jipei's *Psaltichia Româneasca* (The Romanian Psalm Reader's Handbook, 1713), when Turkish music was popular, resulted in the coexistence of two different musical styles: an old one with simple melodic lines in free rhythm, and a new one with richly ornamented Turkish chromatic inflections. Turkish music was cultivated in the courts at Bucharest and Iaşi, with Dimitrie Cantemir (1673–1723) as its most famous exponent. The eighteenth century saw increased cultural contact with Western Europe. A new type of instrumental ensemble, the collegium musicum, developed in Braşov, Sibiu, and Bucharest, as did vocal-instrumental ensembles in Oradea, Sibiu, Timişoara, and Bucharest. Michael Haydn, Karl Ditters von Dittersdorf, and Wenzel Pichel led professional ensembles in Oradea and Timişoara.

In the late eighteenth and early nineteenth centuries, a series of uprisings against Turkish and Austro-Hungarian authority—the Peasant's Revolt in Transylvania in 1784, and the uprising led by Tudor Vladimirescu in Wallachia in 1821—coincided with the development of national values in literature, theater, music, and journalism. In 1830, European fanfares replaced the Turkish *mehterhane*s (military bands), and between 1830 and 1854 Anton Pann issued a collection of nearly two hundred folk and secular songs. Folk music and musicians were especially popular during the nineteenth century, and a few folk musicians, including Barbu Lăutaru, Nicolae Picu, and Dumitrache Ochialbi, gained great fame. After independence (in 1878), nationalist composers wrote marches, drawing-room dances, potpourris, and overtures for military bands and symphony orchestras. Choral groups in the cities and towns such as Iaşi, Lugoj, Sibiu, and Braşov stimulated the creation of choral miniatures that drew on folk music, and numerous periodicals to educate the public in musical forms were launched.

Music education developed first in monasteries. During the Renaissance, Latin schools (*schola Latina*) formed in Braşov, Cotnari, Bistriţa, Alba-Iulia, and Putna. National artistic establishments arose in Bucharest (Philharmonic Society, 1833) and Iaşi (Philharmonic and Dramatic Conservatory, 1836). Musicians who could afford a more prestigious education attended music schools in various European cultural centers (Vienna, Rome, Paris, Berlin). The foundation of national theaters in Bucharest, Iaşi, and Craiova, and state conservatories in Iaşi (1860) and Bucharest (1864), and the founding of a permanent symphony orchestra (1866) and opera (1877) in Bucharest advanced the formation of a national school of music.

In the years just before World War I, Romanian composers showed increasing interest in traditional music and used psalm settings and folk genres, such as carols, ballads, and *doina*, exploring their nonclassical traits, including modality, free rhythm, and untempered intervals. The composer, violinist, and conductor Georges Enescu (1881–1955) is the best known of this generation. Professional and amateur musical activities flourished during this period, stimulated by numerous festivals and competitions and the newly emerging phonograph record.

The unification of the Romanian state (1918) stimulated the development of national art and culture during the interwar years, and composition based on folk sources was encouraged. Whether Western harmonizations and arrangements of traditional tunes or new melodies in folk style, both techniques resulted in original art music characterized by the modal structures, free rhythm, melismatic melodic lines, and polyrhythmic formulas of folk music. Many folk musicians—including the violinists Grisoraş Dinicu, Georges Boulanger (father of French composer and teacher Nadia Boulanger), and Nicolae Buica, the singer Maria Tanase, and the panpipe player Fanica Lucă—became famous during this period.

Musical Life in the Communist and Postcommunist Periods

The communist era (1946–1989) was characterized by increased state support for music, a continued high value placed on national sources for composition, and a centrally controlled ideology that molded and trained several generations of performers, composers, musicologists, folklorists, music critics, and teachers. Suites, rhapsodies, symphonic dances, ballets, and choral pieces—many inspired by folk-song melodies, Byzantine music, and folk-instrument sonorities—were especially popular. The desire to systematize the folkloric basis of composition led to the assertion of "Romanian modalism," which focused on homophonic melodic lines and monody or heterophony at the expense of counterpoint and narrowed the range of acceptable musical expression. Operas drew their texts from national epics, ballads, and other folk genres. In symphonic music, a younger generation of composers tried to synthesize modal and serial techniques and experimented with minimalism. In addition to art music, a number of musical groups created and performed new types of popular music, such as rock and jazz, for large followings. For most of these groups, folk music was the main source of inspiration. The panpipe player Gheorghe Zamfir became famous abroad with recordings of folk, popular, and classical music.

The installation of the people's republic brought adjustments to and restructuring of the existing educational system. Music education became an important part of general education from kindergarten through high school, and gifted students attended special music schools at the elementary through secondary levels in Bucharest, Cluj-Napoca, Iaşi, Timişoara, Craiova, and elsewhere.

"Cultural houses" and other organizations organized music groups for semiprofessionals and amateurs, including new groups involved with folklore. These institutions provided musical outlets for rural working-class people, and popularized folk music and dance within the country and abroad. During the communist period, as many as one hundred thousand amateur groups, professional chamber orchestras, military and civilian bands, choruses, jazz bands, pop and rock groups, and professional folk musicians existed throughout the country. A few groups specialized in the music of minorities—Hungarians, Germans, and Serbians.

Radio, television, and the state record company (Electrecord) had important roles in disseminating a great variety of music. During the communist period, directors at these agencies adjusted productions to fit the government's ethical, moral, and educational standards. The government organized numerous local and regional competitions, festivals, performances, symposiums, and conferences, encompassing art music, ballets, traditional music, folk customs, choral music, military music, and popular music. These activities brought together a large number of participants from throughout the country and abroad. Institutions such as the Union of Composers and Musicologists, the Institute of Ethnography and Folklore, and Electrecord, the national record company, organized these events to promote contemporary musical culture.

Between 1946 and the early 1960s, massive vocal genres with socialist-inspired texts (cantatas, oratorios, symphonic songs, and operettas) were the most favored, and only conservative works—based on popular or folk styles—were allowed. By the late 1960s, the conditions that fostered these styles were changing, and many composers, including Pascal Bentoiu, Cornel Ţăranu, Aurel Stroe, Anatol Vierus, and Stefan Niculescu, gained fame abroad with fully contemporary work.

During the 1970s and 1980s, important musical festivals were canceled, few internationally famous musicians visited Romania, and Romanian musicians defected to pursue their dream of a career abroad. One exception, the a cappella choir Madrigal, founded in 1963, enjoyed an international reputation. After 1989, cancellations and defections diminished, and since 1991, the International Week of New Music each May has provided an important venue for the hearing of new works by Romanian composers, international ensembles, and instrumentalists from abroad.

From 1976 to 1989, new emphasis was placed on a highly politicized National Festival of Political Education and Socialist Culture, called *Cîntarea României* 'Song of Romania', which included unending choral-music composition contests for songs that praised Nicolae Ceaucescu, the national and Communist Party leader. The festival fostered artistic expression at all levels of proficiency and professionalism, including performance of folk music. Peasant-singers and musicians were taught to memorize their self-introductions, which included their musical pedigree and the local origins of their repertoire and techniques. Folk-music specialists often advised these musicians and groups in ways that stimulated, encouraged, and promoted the oldest and most valuable traditional forms and repertoires. These festivals, which embodied official cultural policy in the work of scholars and peasants alike, seemed aimed at constructing an idealized image of village life. Folk-music performance became static and artificial, as if preserved in a museum (figure 7).

During the communist period, the government highly valued folk music and folk arts as symbols of national identity, partly because of the rurality of Romania's economy and the ideological definition of folk music as belonging to the "masses." In

During the last years of the communist regime, when the national TV channels broadcast only two hours per evening, the only cultural treat that continued to be offered was a weekly folk-music program. Such official support in fact alienated many people from traditional culture and folk music, which they came to hate more and more.

FIGURE 7 A choral group from a village near Sibiu, formed to perform at government-sponsored folk festivals, such as Song of Romania (*Cîntarea României*). Photographer unknown. Collection of Valeriu Apan.

the early years of communism, musicologists scoured the countryside for "songs of the new life"—songs that extolled the people's happiness and their love of communism, the party, and the leader. They searched in industrialized environments for working- or laboring-class songs, and in the 1950s and 1960s the journal *Revista de Folclor* abounded with articles on how sociopolitical changes were reflected in folk creativity. Though a few peasants have put new lyrics to old songs, it was left to trained, literate poets and composers to create the "songs of the new life," which were the basis for the socialist choral movement embodied in *Cîntarea României.*

During the last years of the communist regime, when the national TV channels broadcast only two hours per evening, the only cultural treat that continued to be offered was a weekly folk-music program. Such official support in fact alienated many people from traditional culture and folk music, which they came to hate more and more. During the same period, a dynamic, underground folk-music culture emerged in rural and urban areas, ignored by scholars, officials, and the state media. This music involved an amalgam of Serbian-influenced "Banat music," Turkish music (by way of Serbia), and some Gypsy-influenced music, performed at weddings and festivities and disseminated via privately recorded cassettes.

During the last ten years of the communist period, to fight off the influence of foreign popular music, Romanian broadcasters were required to devote more than 60 percent of their programs to Romanian material, and bars and discos were directed to devote 50 percent of their time to Romanian music. These policies helped prop up Romanian popular music and benefited many Romanian pop musicians.

During the communist period, ethnomusicology meant collecting, classifying, and publishing field collections. Larger issues, such as the interpretive purpose to which such collections could be turned, did not arise. From a few dozen in the 1950s, the number of ethnomusicologists at the Institute of Ethnography and Folklore shrank to seven. The journal *Revista de Folclor* shrank from six to three issues per year, and though communist ideology no longer guides editorial policy, nothing critical of communism can yet be published. Since 1989, the power of institutions such as the Union of Composers and Musicologists has decreased, and they have allowed their publishing house, Editura Muzicală, to die out, from a lack of funding. In 1994, a new yearbook, published in English and called *East European Meetings in Ethnomusicology,* was founded to open a worldwide dialogue on problems of traditional musical life in Eastern Europe.

HISTORY OF SCHOLARSHIP

Dimitrie Cantemir was the first scholar who attempted to provide a broad overview of Romanian cultural life. His *Descriptio Moldaviae* (1716) dealt with geographical, historical, ethnographic, and demographic aspects of Romanian customs, folk traditions, and music. F. J. Sulzer's *Geschichte des transalpinischen Daciens* (1781–1782) described rituals, dances, and vocal, instrumental music, with notated examples.

In the 1800s, town musicians notated, arranged, and printed numerous folksong collections of marginal documentary value. In the second half of the nineteenth century, Teodor T. Burada (1839–1923) studied folk customs, music, and instruments so thoroughly that he is considered the founder of Romanian musicology. He gathered the first collection of Romanian folk instruments and donated them to the Museum of Antiquities in Bucharest. Musical periodicals began publishing in the late nineteenth century, with the general review *Muzicul Român* (1861), followed by specialized journals devoted to folklore, Byzantinology, Gregorian chant, military fanfares, and musical instruments.

In 1908, the Romanian Academy began to issue a series of folk-music collections, such as that compiled by Béla Bartók in 1913 and several by Romanian scholars and even some musicians. Bartók's collection, comprising nearly thirty-five hundred tunes, was a model for transcription, analysis, and classification, although only a fraction of the songs was published during his lifetime. The collection was issued in 1967–1975, under the editorship of Benjamin Suchoff.

In 1927–1928, two archives that led to the application of more systematic research methods to Romanian folk music were founded. One was directed by George Breazul, a musicologist specializing in historiography of Romanian music, and the other was led by Constantin Brăiloiu, a musicologist and composer and a founder of the Society of Romanian Composers (1920). Brăiloiu emphasized fieldwork methodology, and outlined one of the first methods of musical folklore research in 1931. He considered folk music a social phenomenon to be observed and understood in its context; he focused on structural analysis and social, economic, functional, and aesthetic phenomena. His methodology, highly regarded by scholars abroad, was adopted and developed by many Romanian researchers and institutes. In 1949, the government amalgamated the two archives and founded the Institute of Folklore in Bucharest (renamed the Institute of Ethnology and Dialectology in 1974 and the Institute of Ethnography and Folklore "C. Brăiloiu" in 1990). The institute continued Brăiloiu's theoretical and methodological principles while fitting its research into a Marxist-Leninist ideology that ignored part of the actual musical life and restrained the research process. Many smaller cities and all the universities also established archives.

After 1950, folk-music studies published in *Revista de Folclor* (now *Revista de Etnografie și Folclor*) and those carried out by the Institute of Art History (founded in 1949) had a Marxist point of view, and many scholars of the older generation hesitated to express opinions that diverged from the state's philosophy. Songbooks—including regional collections and those representing ethnic minorities, such as Serbs and Hungarians—were compiled from the institute's archives. The most important folk-music scholars during this period were Tiberiu Alexandru, who published significant studies on musical instruments, and Emilia Comișel and Traian Mîrza, who studied musical structure, forms, and style. Constantin Costea and Vera Proca-Ciortea studied structure, movement techniques, and context in folk dance. Nearly twenty huge volumes of significant monographs and typologies, under the aegis of the "National Collection of Folklore," were dedicated to genres, repertories, and variants all over the country. Films were made by Alexandru Amzulescu (burial rites, 1969); Gottfried Habenicht (instrument-making and playing techniques, 1964); Anca Giurchescu (traditional customs, *călușari*, 1969); Mihai Pop (folk dances from Hunedoara, 1968); and Andrei Bucșan (folk dances from Sibiu, 1969). Ghizela Sulițeanu (1980) summarized the new methodological premises of Romanian ethnomusicology and the contribution of psychology to folk studies. Museum collections of folklore were established in Timișoara, Sibiu, Brașov, Iași, Cluj-Napoca, Constanța, Lugoj, Craiova, and Oradea.

In 1968–1969, nearly thirty short films of Romanian folk music and dance were published by Encyclopedia Cinematographica in Heidelberg, Germany. To date, research on Romania's ethnic groups (including Gypsies, Hungarians, Germans, Jews, and Serbians), with the exception of a few song collections, has not been published.

In historical musicology, Ioan D. Petrescu (1884–1970), writing before World War II, established comparative Byzantine musical paleography and the study of psalm transcriptions. Between 1960 and 1978, his most important successor, Gheorghe Ciobanu, worked on Byzantine sources, structure, and history. Vasile Tomescu, Octavian L. Cosma, and Viorel Cosma provided the most important general studies of the history of Romanian art music.

BIBLIOGRAPHY

Alexandru, Tiberiu. 1956. *Instrumentele Muzicale ale Poporului Roman* (Musical instruments of the Romanian people). Bucharest: Editura de Stat Pentru Literatură și Artă.

———. 1957. "The Tilinca, an Ancient Rumanian Folk Instrument." *Journal of the International Folk Music Council* 9:78–80.

———. 1971. "An Account of the Teaching Methods of Some Folk Instruments in Romania: The Panpipe." *Yearbook of the International Folk Music Council* 3:143–145.

———. 1978, 1980. *Folcloristică, Organologie, Muzicologie, Studii.* 2 vols. Bucharest: Editura Muzicală.

———. 1980. *Romanian Folk Music.* Bucharest: Musical Publishing House.

———. 1984. "Die Rumanische Panflote Monographische Skizze." *Tibia* 9:20–30.

Amzulescu, Alexandru I. 1964. *Balade Populare Românesti* (Romanian folk ballads). 3 vols. București: Editura Pentru Literatură și Artă.

———. 1974. *Cîntece Batrînești* (Old-time songs). Bucharest: Editura Minerva.

———. 1986. *Cîntecul Nostru Bătrînesc* (Our old-time song). Bucharest: Minerva.

Apan, Valeriu. 1994. "The Panpipe (*Nai*) in Contemporary Romanian Folk Music." Ph.D. dissertation, University of California, Los Angeles.

Bartók, Béla. 1956. *Insemnări Asupra Cîntec ului Popular* (Notes about folk song). Bucharest: Martinus Nijhoff.

———. 1967–1975. *Romanian Folk Music.* Edited by Benjamin Suchoff. The Hague: Mouton.

Berger, Wilhelm G. 1977. *Musica Simfonică Contemporană* (Contemporary symphonic music). Bucharest: Editura Muzicală.

Bîrlea, Ovidiu. 1981 and 1983. *Folclor Românesc-Momente și Sinteze* (Romanian folklore moments and synthesis). Bucharest: Editura Minerva.

Brăiloiu, Constantin. 1967, 1969, 1974, 1979, and 1981. *Opere* (Works). In Romanian and French. 5 vols. Edited by Emilia Comisel. Bucharest: Editura Muzicală.

———. 1984 [1931]. *Problems of Ethnomusicology.* London and New York: Cambridge University Press.

Brăncuși, Petre. 1978, 1980. *Muzica Românească și Marile ei Primeniri* (Romanian music and its great renewal). 2 vols. Bucharest: Editura Muzicală.

Brătulescu, Monica. 1981. *Colinda Românească* (The Romanian carol). Bucharest: Editura Minerva.

Breazul, George. 1966, 1970, 1974, 1977. *Pagini din Istoria Muzicii Românești* (Pages from the history of Romanian music). Bucharest: Editura Muzicală.

Brediceanu, Tiberiu. 1972. *Melodii Populare Românești din Banat* (Romanian folk melodies from Banat). Bucharest: Editura Muzicală a Uniumii Compozitorilor.

Bucșan, Andrei. 1971. *Specificul Dansului Popular Românesc* (The specific character of the Romanian folk dance) (French summary). Bucharest: Editura Academiei.

Burada, Teodor T. 1974, 1975. *Opere* (Works). 2 vols. Bucharest: Editura Muzicală.

———. 1978, 1980. *Opere: Folclor și Etnografie* (Works: folklore and ethnography). 2 vols. Bucharest: Editura Muzicală.

Cantemir, Dimitrie. 1958. *Descriptio Moldaviae* (Reprint). Bucharest: Editura Academiei.

Caraman, Petru. 1983. *Colindatul la Români, Slavi si la Alte Popoare* (Caroling among Romanians, Slavs and other people). Bucharest: Editura Minerva.

Carp, Paula, and Alexandru Amzulescu. 1964. *Cîntece și Jocuri din Muscel* (Songs and dances from Muscel). Bucharest: Editura Muzicală.

Cernea, Eugenia. 1977. *Melodii de Joc din Dobrogea* (Dance tunes from Dobruja) (French and English summary). Bucharest: Editura Muzicală.

Cernea, Eugenia, Monica Brătulescu, Vasile Nicolescu, and Nicolae Rădulescu. 1966. *Cîntece și Strigături Populare Noi* (New folk songs and *strigături*). Bucharest: Editura Muzicală.

Ciobanu, Gheorghe. 1969. *Lăutarii Din Clejani: Repertoriu și stil de Interpretare* (The *lăutari* of Clejani: Repertoire and performance style). Bucharest: Editura Muzicală.

———. 1974, 1979. *Studii de Etnomuzicologie si Byzantologie.* 2 vols. Bucharest: Editura Muzicală.

Ciobanu, Gheorghe, and Vasile Nicolescu. 1962. *200 Cîntece și Doine* (Two hundred songs and *doinas*). Bucharest: Editura Muzicală.

Cocișiu, Ilarion. 1960. *Cîntece Populare Românești* (Romanian folk songs). Bucharest: Editura Muzicală.

Comișel, Emilia. 1964. *Antologie Folclorică din ținutul Pădurenilor* (Folk-music anthology from Pădureni). Bucharest: Editura Muzicală.

———. 1967. *Folclor Muzical* (Musical folkore). Bucharest: Editura Didactică și Pedagogică.

———. 1982. *Folclorul Copiilor* (Children's folklore). Bucharest: Editura Muzicală.

———. 1986. *Studii de Ethnomusicologie* (Studies in ethnomusicology) (French summary). Bucharest: Editura Muzicală.

Cosma, Octavian Lazăr. 1973–1988. *Hronicul Muzicii Românești* (The chronicle of Romanian music). Bucharest: Editura Muzicală.

Cosma, Viorel. 1980. *Zweitausend Jahre Musik auf dem Boden Rumaniens.* Bucharest: Editura ion creangă.

———. 1982. *A Concise History of Romanian Music.* Bucharest: Editura științifică și Enciclopedică.

Costea, Constantin. 1961. *Jocuri Feciorești din Ardeal. Structura și Technica Mișcarii* (Men's dances from Transylvania: Structure and technique of the movements). Bucharest: Editura Muzicală.

Drăgoi, Sabin V. 1930. *303 Colinde cu Text și Melodie* (Three hundred three carols with texts and melodies). Craiova: Șcrisul Românesc.

Fira, G. H. 1916. *Cîntece și Hore* (Songs and dances). Bucharest: Editura Academiei.

Fochi, Adrian. 1985. *Cîntecul Epic Tradiţional Al Românilor: Încercare de Sinteză* (The traditional epic song of Romanians: A synthetic attempt) (English, French, and German summaries). Bucharest: Editura Minerva.

Friedwagner, Matthias. 1940. *Rumänische Volkslieder aus der Bukovina.* Wurzburg: Konrad Triltsch Verlag.

Georgescu, Corneliu Dan. 1968. *Melodii de Joc din Oltenia* (Dance music from Oltenia). Bucharest: Editura Muzicală.

———. 1984. *Jocul Popular Românesc: Tipologie Muzicala și Corpus De Melodii Instrumentale* (Romanian folk dance: Musical typology and corpus of instrumental melodies). Bucharest: Editura Muzicală.

Ghircoiașiu, Romeo. 1963. *Contribuţii la Istoria Muzicii Românești* (Contributions to Romanian music history). Bucharest: Editura Muzicală.

Giurchescu, Anca. 1974. "La Danse comme Object Sémiotique." *Yearbook of the International Folk Music Council* 5:175–178.

Habenicht, Gottfried. 1964. "Acompaniamentul Tarafurilor Năsăudene" (The accompaniment of *taraf*s from Năsaud). *Revista de Etnografie și Folclor* 9(2):159–174.

———. 1972. "Un Cimpoier Bănățean" (A bagpiper from Banat). *Revista de Etnografie și Folclor* 17(4):261–297.

———. 1973. "Cimpoiul Hunedorean" (The bagpipe of Hunedoara). *Revista de Etnografie și Folclor* 13(3):235–250.

Herţea, Iosif, and István Almási. 1970. *245 Melodii de Joc* (Two hundred forty-five dance tunes). Tîrgu Mureș: Comitetul Pentru Cultură și Artă.

Kiriac, Dumitru G. 1960. *Cîntece Populare Românești* (Romanian folk songs). Bucharest: Editura Muzicală.

Kligman, Gail. 1981. *Căluș: Symbolic Transformation in Romanian Ritual.* Chicago: University of Chicago Press.

——. 1988. *The Wedding of the Dead. Ritual, Poetics and Popular Culture in Transylvania.* Berkeley: University of California Press.

Laszlo, Francisc. 1976. *Béla Bartók și Muzica Românească* (Béla Bartók and Romanian music). Bucharest: Editura Muzicală.

Manolesco, Aurel. 1984. *Vechi Cîntece și Jocuri din Basarabia* (Old songs and dances from Bessarabia). Montreal: Patenteux.

Marcu, George. 1977. *Folclor Muzical Aromân* (Aromanian musical folklore) (English summary). Bucharest: Editura Muzicală.

Marin, Marian. 1991. *Chipul Geniului* (The image of genius). Bucharest: Editura Muzicală.

Medan, Virgil. 1968. *160 Melodii Populare instrumentale* (One hundred sixty folk-instrumental melodies). Cluj-Napocoa: Casa Județeană a Creației Populare.

——. 1980. *Folclorul Copiilor* (Children's Folklore). Cluj-Napoca: Casa Județeană a Creației Populare.

Meițoiu, Ioan. 1969. *Spectacolul Nunților: Monografie Folclorică* (The wedding spectacle: Folkloric monography). Bucharest: Casa Centrală a creației Populare.

Miller, Miamon. 1986. "Instrumental Music in Maramureș, Romania: The Zongora and Violin." M.A. thesis, University of California, Los Angeles.

Mîrza, Traian. 1966. "Cadențe Modale Finale in Cîntecul Popular Românesc." *Studii de Musicologie* 85–108.

——. 1972. "Ritmul Orchestic (Dans). Un Sistem Distinct Al Ritmicii Populare Românești." *Studii de Muzicologie* 8:231–262.

——. 1974. *Folclor Muzical din Bihor: Schiță Monografică* (Folk music from Bihor: Monograph sketch). Bucharest: Editura Muzicală.

——. 1979. "Ritmul Vocal Acomodat Pașilor din Marșul Ceremonios, un Tip Distinct al Ritmicii Populare Românesti." *Lucrări de Muzicologie* 10–11:245–259.

Nicola, Ion R., Ileana Szenic, and Traian Mîrza. 1963. *Curs de Folclor Muzical* (Course of musical folklore). Bucharest: Editura Muzicală.

Nicolescu, Vasile, and Constantin Prichici. 1963. *Cîntece și Jocuri Populare din Moldava* (Songs and folk dances from Moldavia). Bucharest: Editura Muzicală a Uniumii Compozitorilor.

Oprea, Gheorghe, and Larisa Agapie. 1983. *Folclor Muzical Românesc* (Romanian musical folklore). Bucharest: Editura Didactică și Pedagogică.

Pann, Anton. 1955. *Cîntece de Lume* (Secular songs). Bucharest: Institutul de Folclor.

Pennington, Anne E. 1985. *Music in Medieval Moldavia.* Bucharest: Editura Muzicală.

Petrescu, Ioan D. 1967. *Études de Paléographie Musicale Byzantine.* Bucharest: Editura Muzicală.

Pop, Mihai. 1976. *Obiceiuri Traditionale Românești* (Romanian traditional customs). Bucharest: Institutul de Cercetari Etnologice și Dialectologice.

Popa, Steluța. 1980. *Obiceiuri de Iarnă* (Winter customs). Bucharest: Editura Muzicală.

Popescu-Judetz, Eugenia. 1979. *Sixty Folk Dances of Romania.* Pittsburgh: Tamburitzans, Institute of Folk Arts, Duquesne University.

Popovici, Doru. 1970. *Muzica Românească Contemporană* (Contemporary Romanian music). Bucharest: Editura Albatros.

Proca-Ciortea, Vera. 1955. *Jocuri Populare Românesti* (Romanian folk dances). Bucharest: Editura de Stat Pentru Literatură și Artă.

Rădulescu, Speranța. 1984. *Taraful și Acompaniamentul Armonic in Muzica de Joc* (The *taraf* and harmonic accompaniment in dance music). Bucharest: Editura Muzicală.

——. 1985. "Ucenicia Lăutarului (The Apprenticeship of Lăutar)". *Revista de Etnografie si Folclor* 30(2):111–124.

——. 1988. "Ucenicia Lăutarului (The Apprenticeship of Lăutar)". *Cahiers de Musiques Traditionnelles* 87–99.

Schuursma, Ann. 1987. "Colinde Cu Dubă in Valea Mureșului, Southwestern Transylvania (Hunedoara Province, Romania)." 2 vols. Ph.D. dissertation, University of California, Los Angeles.

Suliteanu, Ghizela. 1976. *Muzica Dansurilor Populare din Muscel-Arges* (Dance tunes from Muscel-Arges-Muntenia). Bucharest: Editura Muzicală.

——. 1979. "Antiphonal Performance in Romanian Folk Music." *Yearbook of the International Folk Music Council* 2:40–58.

——. 1980. *Psihologia Folclorului Musical. Contributia Psihologiei la Studierea Limbajului Muzicii Populare* (The psychology of musical folklore: The contribution of psychology to studying the language of folk music). Bucharest: Editura Academiei.

——. 1986. *Cîntecul de Leagăn* (The lullaby) (English summary). Bucharest: Editura Muzicală.

Tomescu, Vasile. 1973. *Des origines au commencement du XXe siècle.* Histoire des relations musicales entre la France et la Roumanie, 1. Bucharest: Editura Muzicală.

——. 1978 and 1980. *Musica Daco-Romana.* 2 vols. Bucharest: Editura Muzicală.

Vancea, Zeno. 1968 and 1978. *Creatia Muzicală Românească* (Romanian musical creation). Bucharest: Editura Muzicală.

Viman, Alexandru. 1989. *Cu Cît Cînt Atîta Sînt*

(Folksingers of Maramureş). Baia-Mare: Centrul Judeţean de Îndrumare a Creaţiei Populare.

Zamfir, Gheorghe. 1975. *Traité du nai roumain, méthode de flûte de Pan.* Paris.

AUDIOVISUAL RESOURCES

Alexandru, Tiberiu. 1976. *Anthology of Romanian Folk Music.* 2nd ed. Electrecord, EPE 01220, EPE 01221, EPE 01222, EPE 01223, EPE 01224, EPE 01225. 6 LP disks.

Alexandru, Tiberiu, and Alexandru Amzulescu. 1963. *Cîntece Bătrîneşti* (Old-time songs). Electrecord EPD 1065-1066. LP disk, with notes in Romanian and French.

Alexandru, Tiberiu, and A. L. Lloyd. 1963. *Folk Music of Romania.* Columbia Records AKL 5799. LP disk.

Ballades et fêtes en Roumanie/Ballads and Festivals in Romania. 1985. Le Chant du Monde CM/801, LDX 74846/47. LP disk.

Comişel, Emilia, and Ovidiu Bîrlea. 1972. *Anthology of Romanian Folk Music—Carols.* Electrecord EPD 1257-1258. LP disk.

Les flûtes roumaines avec Gheorghe Zamfir. N.d. Documents inédits enrégistrés en Roumanie par Marcel Cellier. Arion 30T 073. LP disk.

Instrumentele Populare Romaneşti (Romanian folk instruments). N.d. Electrecord EPE 0431. LP disk.

Întilnire Cu Romania. N.d. Electrecord EPE 0890 (Oltenia); EPE 0891 (Maramureş); EPE 0932 (Caransebes, Banat); EPE 0963 (Bucovina); EPE 0997 (Bihor); EPE 01104 (Valea Someşului, Transylvania); EPE 01212 (Moldova). 7 LP disks.

Romania: Traditional Folk Music. N.d. Odeon-EMI Italiana- 3C 064-18120. LP disk.

Roumanie—polyphonie vocale des Aroumains/Romania—Vocal Polyphony of Arumanians. 1983. Le Chant du Monde LDX 74803. LP disk.

Taraful Tradiţional Romanesc (Traditional Romanian *taraf*s). Electrecord 02085, 02164, 02232, 02307, 02412, 02557 (Oltenia, Bucovina, Arad-Bihor, Cîmpia Dunarii, Cîmpia Transilvaniei, and Maramureş-Oaş, repectively). 6 LP disks.

Village Music from Romania: Oltenia-Moldavia-Transylvania. 1988. Collected by Constantin Brăiloiu and others in Romania in 1933–1943. Produced by International Archives of Folk Music, Geneva. VDE-Galloix-XI/CD 537–539. 3 compact discs, with notes in English and French.

Bulgaria
Timothy Rice

Though small, economically poor, and historically isolated, Bulgaria has produced a musical tradition that has won international respect for its traditional music and brilliant singers. In classical music, Bulgarian singers, including Nikolai Ghiaurov, Boris Christov, Raina Kabaivanska, and Ghena Dimitrova, have achieved fame in the world's finest opera houses. Women's, children's, and mixed choirs routinely win international choral competitions, such as the International Eistedfodd in Llangollen, Wales. Béla Bartók was only the most prominent of many outsiders to notice Bulgaria's vivid asymmetrical rhythms. In the 1960s, the colorful dancing, singing, and instrumental music of the National Ensemble for Folk Song and Dance, commonly known as the Filip Kutev Ensemble, made a vivid impression in Western Europe and North America, with its arrangements of folk songs sung with open-throated intensity by village singers trained to perform in three- and four-part harmony. In 1977, the Voyager space probe included among its collection of Earth's music a recording of a Bulgarian folk singer and two bagpipers from the Rhodope Mountains (Raim and Koenig 1970a:B1). In the late 1980s, Bulgarian folk-song arrangements, under the title *Le mystère des voix bulgares*, and the virtuosity of the folk clarinetist Ivo Papazov graced the worldbeat charts in Europe and North America. Such international recognition and success represent the tip of an iceberg of lively, rich, musical practice within a country of about nine million people and 110,994 square kilometers in southeastern Europe (see map 12, p. 869).

Bulgaria has absorbed various cultural influences over its history, each contributing to its music. Slavic settlers from the north displaced the Thraco-Illyrians in the 500s. In the 600s, the Bulgars, a tribe of warlike horsemen from Central Asia, assumed political control of the local Slav agriculturalists, but left few traces besides their name and the large states they established in the Middle Ages to battle the Byzantine Empire. Two Bulgarian Empires dominated large parts of the Balkans for much of the period from 800 to 1385, when the Ottoman Turks conquered the Bulgarian lands. Bulgarian culture was preserved mainly in oral village traditions until the 1800s, when a "national renaissance" began. Bulgaria reemerged politically as an independent principality in 1878 and an independent kingdom in 1908, under German and Austrian political and cultural influence. From 1944 to 1989—a period characterized by active state support of music and art and a move away from a primarily agriculture-based economy to an urban, industrialized one—Bulgaria was ruled by the Communist Party as one of the Soviet Union's most loyal allies. Since 1989, Bulgaria has become a multi-party democracy, and state support of the arts has declined.

MUSICAL STYLE

Regional variation confounds nearly every generalization about Bulgarian village musical style. Strophic songs, sung metrically or nonmetrically, provide the basis for vocal performance and instrumental music. Instrumental dance tunes often begin with song tunes before launching into instrumental variations, and nonmetrical instrumental tunes are usually improvisations based on nonmetrical song tunes.

Most metrical songs and tunes originally accompanied dancing and were sung antiphonally by two pairs of singers near the head of the dance line. Dance-songs typically consist of two phrases of four measures each, structured AA, AA′, or AB. Songs with pairs of three-, five-, and six-measure phrases are common, as are pairs of unequal-length phrases. Each phrase is typically set to an eight-syllable line of text, but six- and ten-syllable lines are also common. Sometimes refrains replace text, or are added at the end, unbalancing the symmetrical structure and requiring one or more measures of melodic material. The commonest meter is transcribed in 2/4 time. The melodic range is usually narrow, extending to a fifth above and a second below the tonic. Major, minor, and phrygian diatonic tetrachords are common, as are ones with augmented seconds. Some tunes include major and minor thirds or major and minor seconds. Various ornaments are typically applied to the basic tune.

Duple meter provides the metrical foundation for most songs and dances in Bulgaria, but the culture is justly famous for its so-called asymmetrical, additive, unequal-part, *aksak* (Turkish for 'limping') meters, which add variety to the music. These meters, performed at fast tempos, combine or add groups of two and three pulses to form meters of five, seven, nine, and eleven pulses, grouped into "beats" of unequal length. While no traditional music theory labels or distinguishes these meters (this analysis is the product of Western music theory, first applied to Bulgarian music by Dobri Hristov), dance names distinguish one meter from another, and certain names are now commonly associated with particular meters. The typical Bulgarian dance form, generically called *horo,* consists of an open or closed circle of dancers holding hands (figure 1).

In addition to metrical dance tunes, the Bulgarian repertoire of song and instrumental music consists of many nonmetrical songs typically sung while seated at wedding-banquet tables, at spinning bees, when guests gather in the home, or while resting from fieldwork. Formal principles of metrical songs include two phrases of similar length, modal variety, narrow range, and ornamentation. These songs allow for each of these features to be expanded in some way, for example, to three-phrase structures, slightly wider melodic ranges up to an octave and occasionally even more, correspondingly greater modal possibilities, and even richer ornamentation, especially on long-held notes (figure 2). Though song performances are constrained by the demands of the text, instrumentalists often use song tunes as the basis for extended improvisations.

MUSICAL INSTRUMENTS

Traditional instruments, once made primarily by the players (each using rules of thumb of his own invention), answered to few general rules or notions of absolute pitch, and varied significantly from region to region. During the socialist period, the professionalization of folk music, the creation of ensembles, and a growing sense of a

FIGURE 1 Women from the Pirin region of southwestern Bulgaria perform an open-circle dance to their own singing (*horo na pesen*). Photo by Timothy Rice, 1973.

FIGURE 1 Women from the Pirin region of southwestern Bulgaria perform an open-circle dance to their own singing (*horo na pesen*). Photo by Timothy Rice, 1973.

national style led to an increasing standardization. A small set of instruments, basic to the new folk orchestra (*narodni orkestri*) and constructed to an absolute pitch standard, strive to play a tempered scale and are widely distributed in the country (figure 3).

Traditionally, only men and boys played musical instruments. One of the first opportunities to learn to play was while herding cows, sheep, goats, and pigs in pastures outside villages. Boys' and shepherds' typical instrument were homemade flutes: the *duduk*, a short, end-blown whistle-flute with six finger holes; and the *svirka*, a short, end-blown, fippleless flute with six finger holes and perhaps a thumb hole. Also known was the *lokarina*, a clay, globular flute with eight finger holes and two thumb holes. All three flutes play diatonic melodies over a two-octave range.

The most advanced instrument in the flute category is the *kaval*, now standardized as a national instrument—a long, end-blown, rim-blown flute with seven finger holes and a thumb hole, made from three separate pieces of hardwood. Master craftsmen turn it on a lathe, adorn the joints with buffalo horn for added stability, and carve decorations on it. The bottom piece has four "devil's holes," which affect tuning and timbre. The finger holes are placed to produce a chromatic scale over three or more octaves, each register with a distinctive timbre. Many Bulgarians regard the *kaval*, with its wide range, honey (*meden*) tone, and rich ornamentation, to be the most expressive Bulgarian folk instrument. As many song texts say, "His *kaval* played and spoke."

The most widespread reed instrument is the bagpipe (*gajda*), a favorite instrument at outdoor celebrations, like weddings, fairs, and village dances because of its

FIGURE 2 A nonmetrical harvest song with extensive ornamentation from the region of Thrace. Sung by Todora Varimezova in 1978. Transcription by Timothy Rice.

FIGURE 3   On stage at the National Folklore Festival in Koprivshtitsa, a small group of musicians accompanies Yordanka Ilieva, a singer from Gabra in the Shop region. The five instruments that came to typify the Bulgarian folk orchestra are (*left to right*): *kaval* 'flute', *gajda* 'bagpipe', *kaval, gŭdulka* 'bowed lute', *tambura* 'long-necked lute', and *tŭpan* 'drum'. Photo by Jane Sugarman, 1976.

TRACK 31

loud sound. A common expression still is, "A wedding without a bagpipe can't happen." The bag consists of a whole goatskin. Wooden stocks, tied into the front-leg and neck holes, receive the melody pipe, drone pipe, and blow pipe. The melody pipe, with a single reed, has seven finger holes and a thumb hole and a range of a major ninth, and can play chromatically with cross-fingerings. In the southwestern region, the *zurna* (a double-reed, conical-bore oboe) is played by Rom musicians.

The main bowed-stringed instrument is the *gŭdulka,* a pear-shaped lute with three or four metal playing strings, played with a horsehair bow. The *gŭdulka* was used to accompany dancing and singing, in some cases with the musician playing and singing simultaneously. It was a favorite of blind beggars, and is still used by Rom beggars with trained bears or monkeys on chains (figure 4). The modern *gŭdulka* has about eight sympathetic strings lying underneath the playing strings and tuned to important notes in the scale, creating an instrument with an unusually loud, resonant, full-toned quality.

The traditional plucked string instrument is the long-necked lute (*tambura*). Undoubtedly a local descendant of the Turkish *saz*, it was originally popular where Turkish and Muslim influence was strongest and was used mainly to accompany male singing. The oldest forms were made from a hollowed-out, pear- and bowl-shaped piece of wood, covered with a wooden face with a few small holes for resonance. The instrument typically had four strings arranged in two double courses, tuned a fourth or a fifth apart. Using a plectrum, the player played the melody on one course and sounded a drone on the open string (figure 5). In folk orchestras formed in the 1950s, the *tambura* was transformed into an accompanying, chordal instrument of four double courses, tuned like the highest strings of the guitar: d–g–b–e. The body became flat-backed, and metal-and-plastic tuning machines replaced the wooden pegs. During solos, the players pluck out the melody monophonically on single strings.

The most common drum, *tŭpan* (barrel-shaped, double-headed drum), was the specialty of Rom (Gypsy) musicians. Slung over the left shoulder and struck with a

FIGURE 4   A Rom (Gypsy) bear trainer plays his *gŭdulka* as he leads his animal through a market in Sofia, the capital of Bulgaria. Photo by Martha Forsyth, 1992.

Recordings and broadcasts, controlled by state organizations, tended to keep traditional (*bitov*) ensembles distinct from those using Western instruments, but since the 1930s or before, some wedding bands routinely combined the two types of instruments.

FIGURE 5   Bulgarian Muslim (Pomak) women play the *tambura* on stage at a folk festival in the Rhodope Mountains. The backdrop—which combines an image of a woman in local head-dress with a drawing of Todor Zhivkov, the longtime head of the Bulgarian Communist Party—illustrates clearly the link between nationalism, politics, and folklore during the socialist period. Photo by Timothy Rice, 1969.

hefty stick on one head and a thin wand on the other, it was traditionally most popular in the southeastern and southwestern parts of the country, where it accompanied bagpipes and oboes at outdoor celebrations. During the socialist period, it became a fixture in folk orchestras. Two other drums, the vase-shaped, single-headed *darabuka* and the single-headed frame drum (*daire*), are played mainly by Turkish and Rom minorities.

In addition to these common musical instruments, there are a large variety of other sound makers, among them children's clay whistles in various shapes (pistols, vases, chickens), reed pipes made of grass, and idiophones such as tuned bronze bells tied to sheep, church bells, ankle bells on ritual costumes, wooden boards struck while circling the church, and scrapers on wagon axles (Atanasov 1983).

Village music began to change after 1878, as men served in the military and learned to play instruments in army brass bands. Small ensembles with clarinet, trumpet, trombone, baritone horns, and *tŭpan* with an added cymbal became popular at village and town weddings and fairs in many parts of the country, where they competed with and sometimes replaced traditional instruments (figure 6). Later, the accordion and violin were added to ensembles, whose instrumentation has never been standardized. In all areas of the country, accordion and clarinet became extremely popular, and many fine virtuosi developed to play them. In the western and northern parts of the country, accordions and clarinets often fit into brass bands; in the south and east by the 1960s, these instruments were often accompanied by violin, guitar, and string bass. In the 1970s, electric versions of all these instruments,

FIGURE 6   A Bulgarian village brass band plays in a small circle within a larger circle of dancers. This dance in the village square celebrated a marriage right after it was registered in the village council (*sŭvet*). Photo by Timothy Rice, 1973.

with saxophone and electric organ or synthesizer (*yonika*), were added. Recordings and broadcasts, controlled by state organizations, tended to keep traditional (*bitov*) ensembles distinct from those using Western instruments, but since the 1930s or before, some wedding bands routinely combined the two types of instruments.

REGIONAL STYLES

The preceding generalizations about musical styles and instruments are modified by regional variety resulting from combinations of mountainous terrain acting as a barrier to communication and centuries of restricted possibilities for travel. Musically, the country can be divided in different ways. Eastern regions use fewer asymmetric meters (typically only 5/16, 7/16, and 9/16), while people in the west, in addition to these meters, use longer, more complex meters. In the east, tempos are usually slower, and playing is more legato and highly ornamented than in the west, and most of the best contemporary ensemble musicians come from the east. No obvious geological boundaries distinguish east from west, but the Balkan Mountains divide Bulgaria into north and south, and some musical-style elements correspond to this division. Seemingly older styles of performance and types of instruments are preserved in the mountainous south, whereas the north, with its broad agricultural plains, has been subjected to modernizing and Westernizing influences for a longer period. In addition to these gross differences, Bulgarian scholars distinguish at least six main musical dialect regions, with some subregions and transitional zones.

In the southwest, the Pirin region, named after the dominant mountain range, is distinguished by a two-part singing style in which the second voice either holds a drone or performs a movable drone on two pitches. Meters common here (7=3 + 2 + 2, 8=3 + 2 + 3, and 3/8) are rare in other areas. Many Pirin songs, with their wide ranges and lyrical qualities, have become popular through recordings and broadcasts in towns and villages all over the country. Pirin has numerous Bulgarian Muslims (called Pomaks), who converted to Islam during the Ottoman period but speak Bulgarian. Perhaps as a consequence, instruments with close links to Turkey, especially *tambura*, *daire*, and the ensemble of one or two *zurna*s with *tŭpan,* are common here and rare elsewhere. Also known here is a pair of *kaval*s (*chift kavali*), each made

FIGURE 7   A song sung in two-part heterophony from a village near the town of Pazardzhik in 1973. The lower part sings the basic melody while the upper part sings a highly ornamented version of it, in the process creating the effect of harmonic seconds almost continuously. Transcription by Timothy Rice.

I- va-   ne   le

pro- vi- de-   lo sev- da   go- le-

in one piece and carried together in a case, played by two players in melody-and-drone duets.

In west-central Bulgaria, called the Shop region (after a label for the peasants around Sofia), another kind of two-part singing is characteristic. The second voice moves between the tonic and subtonic tones, which, combined with narrow-range melodies of a third or a fourth, creates a dissonant harmony of frequently sounding seconds. The singers find these harmonies pleasant, however, and try to make them "ring like bells." Also unique to this region is a type of historical ballad and associated solo monophonic recitative known as Krali Marko ballads, after a king of mythical proportions who fought against the Turks. Though Bulgarian scholars call them epics, they are usually a few hundred lines long, rather than the thousands of lines characteristic of the Bosnian and Montenegrin epics studied by Albert Lord in his *Singer of Tales*. The singing style, beginning with a highly ornamented, textless, melismatic descent from the fifth above the tonic, is unique to this region.

East of the Pirin and Shop regions, a transitional zone in the areas around the towns of Velingrad, Ihtiman, and Parardzhik separates these areas of two-part singing from the rest of Bulgaria, where only unison singing is found. In the western Rhodope Mountains and an area called the Sredna Gora (Middle Forest), two-part singing begins to take on a more heterophonic character, with a more active drone, an intermittent drone, or a conscious heterophony based on ornamented and unornamented versions of the melody (figure 7).

In the Rhodope Mountains of south-central Bulgaria, instrumental music and song are distinguished by an anhemitonic pentatonic scale stretching across an octave, rather than the diatonic pentachords typical of other areas. Also typical are the use of a low-pitched *kaba* (Turkish for 'large') *gajda* to the near exclusion of other instruments, though *chift kavali* and *tambura* are used by Pomaks (figure 8). Asymmetric meters are comparatively rare here, and, since the regional economy depends more on shepherding than on agriculture, the calendric cycle of music and song associated with fertility rituals is nearly absent.

Thrace, in the southeast, became the most important musical region during the socialist period, mainly because its virtuoso instrumentalists and singers joined ensembles all over the country, spreading its repertoire and performance style into the national media and many regional ensembles. Most of the best clarinet, accordion, bagpipe, and *kaval* players come from this region. Both the playing and the singing from Thrace are rich in ornamentation, with higher-pitched tones separating melody tones and a characteristic vibrato on held tones. In the southeast, the Strandzha

FIGURE 8   A player of the low-pitched bagpipe (*kaba gajda*) typical of the Rhodope Mountains. Photo by Timothy Rice, 1969.

Mountains form a subregion, distinguished by the frequent use of the phrygian (e–f–g–a–b) pentachord. Strandzha is the home of a dramatic fire-walking ritual called *nestinarstvo,* performed in two villages on 3 June, Saint Constantine and Saint Elena's Day, to the accompaniment of *gajda* and *tŭpan* and still performed occasionally for tourists.

Dobrudzha, the northeastern region, has passed between Bulgarian and Romanian control, and is currently split between the two countries. Since many of its residents are settlers from Thrace, Thracian musical features dominate its song style. Distinguishing Dobrudzhan characteristics include a small, three-stringed *gŭdulka,* played with a drone; preference for slightly higher-pitched bagpipes; and a unique set of slow-tempo dances with more arm and shoulder movements than usual.

In northern Bulgaria, a vast plain south of the Danube, brass bands have long been popular, and the whistle-flute (*duduk*) is the most important folk instrument, as it is in neighboring Romania (*fluier*) and Serbia (*frula*).

MOVEMENT AND DANCE

Bulgarian villagers distinguish at least four types of movement. *Igra* (game), the most general term, refers to all manner of games and dances and as a verb (*igrae*) means 'to dance'. More specifically, it refers to a set of children's musical games sung by girls to short texts to accompany various actions. The movements of carnival masqueraders (*kukeri*), who jump up and down to sound bells tied around their waists, are also called games (*kukerski igri*).

Horo is the generic name for line dances arranged commonly in an open circle with a leader, but indoors in a closed circle, and sometimes in straight or curving lines. The dancers normally hold hands, but sometimes hold the belts, or place their hands on the shoulders of the neighboring dancer, or even reach in front of their neighbor to take the hand of his or her neighbor, creating a woven effect called a "basket hold" in English. The line typically moves counterclockwise. Dance movements and patterns are concentrated in the legs, consisting mainly of steps and touches of the feet to the right, left, and front, plus other movements, such as hops, leg lifts, knee bends, leg circles, and leaps. The upper body occasionally bends forward, or the head turns in a prescribed manner. The hands come into play mainly in handholds as the arms swing to and fro or shake up and down in time to the music.

Dance movements are usually more varied and larger for men than women, and reflect and enact culturally appropriate behavior for each sex. The movements are organized into patterns typically lasting three measures—which contrasts with the typical four-measure phrases of the music. Though most of the dancers move in unison to a common pattern, men often improvise variants within the basic dance pattern. In the past, dancing to women's singing, especially for *pravo horo,* was common, two pairs of two singers leading the line and singing antiphonally. In the socialist period, instrumental accompaniment became the rule.

The *rŭchenitsa* ('hand' or 'handkerchief' dance) is a common dance, distinguished from *horo* by the fact that it is often not danced in a line with a set pattern, but is a solo dance with improvised steps and the possibility for hand-and-arm movements. *Rŭchenitsa* can be performed as a solo, in pairs, as a large group dance, and even as a led *horo,* and is typical of wedding processions and other parts of the wedding ritual (CD track 31).

Nonmetrical tunes songs performed *na pŭt* 'on the road' accompany movement from village to field and back, and ritual processions (figure 9). Songs performed *na trapeza* 'at the table' are sung by people sitting around a table, eating and drinking.

FIGURE 9 Three women from the village of Mala Tsŭrkva near Samokov sing on the road (*na pŭt*) on their way home from harvesting potatoes. Photo by Martha Forsyth, 1988.

Some songs depict happy unions between attractive couples, but most detail the trials and tribulations of life: interference from parents, infidelity and betrayal, untimely sickness, death, or even murder, unhappy family relations caused by marriage and remarriage, and suffering during the five hundred years "under Turkish slavery."

SONG TEXTS

Song texts are constructed of a series of lines (abcde . . .), each with the same number of syllables, but no additional verse structure, rhyme, or poetic rhythm. In a typical performance of a two-phrase song, the second line of text in a verse often becomes the first line of the next verse, yielding the performed structure ab bc cd de . . . The most common number of syllables per line is eight, but songs with lines of six, seven, and ten syllables are typical. The texts are constructed using the same formulaic principles detailed for Serbo-Croatian epic ballads in Albert Lord's *Singer of Tales*. Common formulas (cliché-like word clusters) recur in every song for bodily attributes (black eyes, white face, thin figure) and objects in the environment (cold water, white rock, well-fed horse). Though communal rather than solo singing and shorter-than-epic texts probably reduces the amount of variation, each performance varies according to the memory of the singers and the circumstances in which they sing. In many contemporary contexts, and especially on recordings, only a portion of the text is sung; listeners in principle know what happened or are content to guess.

The language used in song texts varies slightly according to regional dialects, but the contents of the songs are remarkably consistent across the country. They are usually told by a narrator in the third person and consist in large part of dialogue between a mother and her son or daughter, two lovers, a Turk and a Bulgarian, a mother-in-law and daughter-in-law, or a circle of friends. Some ritual songs and work songs simply describe the action they accompany (the bride goes to church with her family, the sun casts no shadow at noon, we are entering the host's home). Most are lyrical songs about human relationships or historical songs detailing the unhappiness caused by war or oppression. Rather than monologues pouring out inner feelings, the third-person, dialogic nature of the texts tends to leave feelings to be inferred or imputed empathetically, as situations are described or opinions stated rather matter-of-factly. One of the most common evocative techniques, usually at the beginning of a song, invokes an image from nature and then switches to a person, implicitly linking his or her feelings to something in nature: "the Vardar river flows with mud" signals the emotional turmoil of a bride at a wedding; "a thick fog fell" represents the feeling of the bride's parents as the groom's family arrives to take their daughter; "the sun shone in the meadow" turns out to be the joyful sighting of a beautiful girl. Some songs depict joking relations between lovers and happy unions between attractive couples (often he is a good musician, and she is a good singer or dancer), but most detail the trials and tribulations of life: interference from parents, infidelity and betrayal, untimely sickness, death, or even murder, unhappy family relations caused by marriage and remarriage, and suffering during the five hundred years "under Turkish slavery." Some songs preserve mythical elements, such as anthropomorphized sun and moon, snakes and dragons, or seductive fairies, and there is a cycle of songs about Krali Marko (King Marko), a mythical hero of superhuman dimensions and strength, who participated in the fourteenth-century war between Serbs and Turks.

So-called *hajduk* 'bandit' songs recall resistance to the Turks during the Ottoman period. In the twentieth century, folklorists collected new songs, possibly by stimulating their production, celebrating the efforts of early communists and Second World War partisans, and built on the model of earlier heroic and *hajduk* songs.

TRADITIONAL CONTEXTS FOR MUSIC

In every region and village of the country, musical life once moved to the larger rhythms of the seasons and their associated work. Many songs, instrumental tunes, and dances could be performed at any time or "whenever guests gathered together," but a substantial portion of the repertoire consisted of a lengthy music-and-song cycle performed over the course of a year, each piece performed only during the appropriate period or ritual. Not every ritual occurred in every region, but the most widespread ones are described here.

The most important winter ritual is *koleda*, a still-performed Christmas or New Year's caroling ritual, in which boys go from house to house singing songs and saying a blessing for the family's health, fertility, and happiness in the new year. The *koledari* (carolers) know twenty or more songs, each addressed to a specific class of person in the household: a landowner, his wife, an eligible bachelor, a young girl, a pregnant woman, a new baby. The songs often have refrains (*koledo le*), and many are in asymmetric meters.

In some areas, New Year's is celebrated with *laduvane,* a fortune-telling ritual for boys and girls, in which their rings are pulled from a container as they dance around it, and their fortunes—who will marry whom—are told. The songs use refrains like *oj lado lado*, and asymmetric meters are common.

The beginning of Lent was marked by house-to-house visits by carnival masqueraders, called *kukeri*, or *startsi* 'old men'. Dressed in costumes symbolizing male fertility (sheepskins with large bells tied to the waist and tall hats or fantastic masks), men go from house to house moving to the accompaniment of their own bells or sometimes bagpipes (figure 10). In each yard, they perform ritual plowing and sowing of seeds.

FIGURE 10   Carnival maskers (*kukeri*) dressed in animal skins covered with bells symbolize male fertility at a festival in Pernik in the Shop region. Photo by Donna Buchanan, 1988.

During the forty days of Lent, dancing proper was forbidden, and so musical games (*igri*), many with a kind of flirting character, were played, including songs sung by girls as boys pushed them in swings. *Na filek,* the most developed set of such singing games, existed in the Strandzha Mountains and included the game called bridge (*most*), which resembled the English game sung as "London Bridge Is Falling Down." The Saturday before Palm Sunday, called *lazarovden* (Lazar's Day), featured young girls caroling from house to house with a set of lyrical love songs and wearing, in the Shop region, elaborate headdresses. A special dance, often in 7/8 and performed by four girls arranged in a square pattern, was performed in each yard. In exchange for the girls' good wishes, performers received gifts symbolizing fertility, such as flour and eggs. Easter, called Velikden (Great Day), ended Lent and was celebrated with three days of dancing in the village square to a set of love songs reserved for the occasion.

The rain-begging ritual, *peperuda* 'butterfly', was performed as needed during spring and summer droughts. After covering a young girl (the butterfly) with greenery, a group of girls went from house to house singing a song asking God for rain. At each house, the female head of the household doused the girl with water from a pitcher, hoping a heavy rain would fall.

The heavy fieldwork of summer was relieved by frequent Sunday saint's day celebrations. People and musicians gathered to visit friends and relatives, show off musical and dance skills in the village square, and perhaps attend a wrestling match accompanied by music on *tŭpan* with bagpipes or oboes. The huge repertoire of instrumental dance music and summer dance-songs testifies to the importance of summer saint's days as a performance venue.

Fieldwork was accompanied by harvest or hoeing songs, sung nonmetrically by solo singers in antiphony while bent over at work, during rest periods, and on the way to and from the fields. The texts evoke the feelings at different times of the day: the sunrise, the growing heat, the need to rest at the hottest part of the day, and relief as the sun sets and the temperature drops. A few texts contain mythical themes, anthropomorphizing the relations between the sun, the moon, and stars.

In autumn, unmarried girls gathered at a neighbor's house for communal handwork, accompanied by singing. These gatherings, called *tlŭka* when the girls helped the hosts with some task (like shucking corn) and *sedyanka* 'sitting bee' when they worked on their own (spinning or doing embroidery), attracted bachelors, some with musical instruments, to an evening of flirting and dancing. *Sedyanka* songs treat historical and love themes and are often nonmetrical, with the largest ranges and most extended forms in the repertoire. The girls tease one another about boyfriends in short *pripevki*, dancelike songs, in which the names of boys and girls can be readily changed.

Finally, the wedding (*svatba*), normally classed as a life-cycle ritual, traditionally occurred during late autumn and winter, after the harvest, wine making, and food preservation had ensured the wherewithal to host a weeklong celebration. The wedding, in addition to the church ceremony and celebratore feasting, was a kind of folk drama, with all the emotions associated with transferring the bride from her home to her groom's family's home evoked in song and each ritual event accompanied by instrumental music, traditionally on bagpipes and now by a small band of Western or traditional instruments. The songs—sung by unmarried female relatives of the bride while braiding her hair and veiling her, as she bid's farewell to her mother on the way to the church—describe the bride's feelings, especially her fears, as she bids her youth, family, and friends goodby, and the joy of her new family as they accept her. The first stages of the wedding—the shaving of the groom, the procession of the groom's party to the bride's house, and the presentation of the veiled bride—are accompanied by nonmetrical instrumental tunes (*svirni*); then, after "taking" the bride, the youth of the wedding party dance a lively *rŭchenitsa* (line or solo dance in 7/16) during the procession to the church and later to the groom's house. Nonmetrical *sedyanka* songs with texts about engagements and marriages were sung at the wedding banquet.

Besides weddings, the only life-cycle rituals are those associated with births and deaths, and in Bulgaria these are rarely accompanied by music or song per se, but with genres possessing some musical characteristics, particularly the lament (*oplakvane*); lullabies take the form of sing-song recitations. Laments are performed by close female relatives of the deceased at the gate of the yard to announce the death, as the body is being prepared for burial, at the funeral, and at memorials for the deceased, held periodically after the funeral until grief subsides. In addition to assuaging grief, laments are signs of respect for the dead, and without them a burial would be considered shameful. The lamenter improvises a series of sentences and phrases with—unlike song—no recurring structure as she speaks to the deceased, complaining about the death and the grief it brings, and recalling happier times. She moves among whispering, reciting, and nonmetrical melody, interspersed with weeping, sighing, crying, and exhibiting a dynamic range unknown in song performance. The melodic sections vary from simple recitatives to melodies bearing some resemblance to local nonmetrical tunes for *sedyanka* or *trapeza*. In parts of Pirin, they are even performed with the characteristic drone.

Though Bulgarian women sing to their children, lullabies do not seem to exist as a named category. Children performed many of the most important ritual songs (*koleda*, *laduvane*, *peperuda*) and games (*na filek*), and young, unmarried girls were the most important singers at weddings.

CONTEMPORARY CONTEXTS AND PERFORMANCE PRACTICES

After 1944, the economic, social, and educational conditions in villages changed dramatically, ending many traditional practices and causing the decline of others. At the same time, the Communist Party and its propaganda organs, recognizing the value of the existing folk traditions and seeking to support them in new forms suitable for the new society it was creating, had an enormously rich store of village singers, musicians, and dancers and a huge repertoire of songs, dances, instrumental tunes, and ritual contexts to draw on. The government began creating new national institutions to replace the family, the village, and the local region as supporters of folk music. Among these were two (later nearly twenty) professional ensembles of folk song and dance, staffed originally by outstanding village musicians, singers, and dancers, and thousands of amateur town and village "collectives," organized by a central directorate of "artistic amateurs" to perform village traditions on stage, often under the supervision of personnel trained in music and choreography at schools established for that purpose (figures 3 and 5). The communists' desire to raise the people's cultural level led to the formation of at least seven professional symphony orchestras, five opera companies, many a cappella choirs, musical high schools (including two devoted to folk music), a post-secondary pedagogical institute for folk music, more than five hundred "children's musical schools," and other organizational structures (such as the Institute for Music at the Bulgarian Academy of Sciences), scientific and popular musical journals, and unions of composers and "musical activists."

With the mechanization of agricultural work, the discouragement of religious expression and "backward superstition," and a diminishing sense of personal involvement in the fruits of one's labors, the raison d'être and desire to perform agriculturally based rituals and music disappeared. Only the wedding remained an important context for music. In many cases, instrumental music, perhaps with a professional

Music for family celebrations—weddings, engagement parties, and sending sons off to the army—continued to flourish. Families poured enormous amounts of money into food, drink, and music for these events; musicians could make substantial livings in this market.

solo singer, replaced the extensive song repertoire performed by the female relatives of the bride and bridegroom. That traditional contexts and practices remain vivid in the Bulgarian consciousness is a function of living singers and musicians' memories and state efforts to keep them alive in village amateur performance ensembles, festivals, and competitions, and the choreographies of professional, "national" ensembles.

In the early 1950s, two professional ensembles were created: the National Ensemble of Folk Songs and Dances, under the direction of the composer Filip Kutev; and the Ensemble for Folk Songs, at Radio Sofia. Both held extensive auditions of village performers, collected their repertoires, harmonized their songs for three- and four-part a cappella female choirs, and arranged instrumental tunes and song accompaniments for a small orchestra of folk instruments: one or more bagpipes, two or more *kavals*, six or so *gŭdulkas*, two *tamburas*, *tŭpan*, cello, and bass. To their music and song arrangements, the Kutev ensemble added choreographies of village dances, weddings, and other customs.

To perform the new choral and orchestral arrangements effectively, musically illiterate villagers in professional ensembles were taught to read musical notation, and in the 1960s and 1970s high schools and post-secondary "higher institutes" were founded to teach repertoire, performance style, and the notational and conceptual skills necessary to arrange and choreograph folk music to the successors of the village musicians, youths who grew up in town and village environments less conducive to learning traditional music, song, and dance in all its richness.

The Kutev ensemble's harmonizations of traditional songs stimulated the formation of thousands of amateur choirs in villages, towns, and factories, and its choreographies influenced to varying degrees amateur village folk ensembles, whose repertoire and style of performance were organized by a central directorate of "artistic amateurism" within the Ministry of Education and Culture. As the larger ensembles in the main provincial towns improved in quality and mastered the complicated presentational style, many became professional, "national" ensembles, funded by the provincial government to tour and entertain villagers in the local province, around the country, and even abroad.

Somewhat independent of the state apparatus supporting folk-music presentation, music for family celebrations—weddings, engagement parties, and sending sons off to the army—continued to flourish. Families poured enormous amounts of money into food, drink, and music for these events; musicians, especially those playing Western instruments (like clarinet and accordion) not supported by folk music ensembles could make substantial livings in this market, and ensemble musicians supplemented their state income. Unlike the truncated, short, preservation-oriented performances presented on stage by the ensembles, these events lasted a day or more, demanded nearly continuous playing, and inspired innovation and technical display to attract clients. In this environment, technique became more virtuosic, and the repertoire grew in complexity through improvisation, some of it by musicians trained in music theory at the new schools for music. By the 1980s, the vibrant wedding music tradition had produced "stars"—the most famous of whom was the clarinetist Ivo Papazov—whose fame, technical brilliance, and improvisational skills seriously challenged the conservative aesthetics of the state-sponsored ensembles.

After 1944, the radio and its associated record company, Balkanton, monopolized the music industry, sponsoring and controlling frequent broadcasts and a large number of long-playing records. The performers were mainly members of professional ensembles drawn from all over the country, but especially from Thrace and Dobrudzha.

POPULAR MUSIC

Popular and urban music, as in most countries, remains one of the most heard but least studied aspects of Bulgarian musical life. The earliest sources for urban songs are chapbooks (*pesnopojki*) published outside Bulgaria during the mid-1800s. Important ones include the first, published in Budapest in 1842, with folk-song texts only; the first with neumatic musical notation, published in Istanbul in 1846; the first with "city songs," published in Bucharest in 1852, with texts by Bulgaria's first famous poet, Petko Slavejkov; and the first with Western musical notation, published in Moscow in 1854 (Kaufman 1968). Bulgarian scholars value most highly the patriotic and school songs written before and after the Liberation in 1878, many of them in waltz and march rhythms imported from Western Europe, Russia, and Ukraine, and written by some of Bulgaria's finest poets in rhyme. Less well studied is the character of love songs sung to the accompaniment of "salon orchestras" in bars, restaurants, and circuses before World War II, though some published versions show the influence of Turkish, Greek, Serbian, Jewish secular, and Bulgarian folk music.

Under the communists, Bulgarian popular music (*estradna muzika*), supervised and recorded at Radio Sofia and for Balkanton, resembled light European, especially Italian, popular music. Some Bulgarian jazz musicians, notably the pianist Milcho Leviev, who emigrated to the United States, developed considerable skills, but hard rock was heard primarily as performed by foreign bands. In the wake of *glasnost* in the 1980s, bands, musicians, and singers experimented with "folk-jazz" fusions and more complex mixes of avant-garde classical music with folk, jazz, rock, and Latin music.

MINORITY MUSIC

Since 1944, Bulgaria's attitudes and policies toward ethnic minorities (Turks, 9 percent; others, 6 percent) have vacillated between uncomfortable and hostile, and predictably little scholarly work has been devoted to them. Roma constitute the most important minority for folk music, providing many of Bulgaria's finest instrumentalists on traditional and Western instruments. Roma have their own traditions of songs sung in Romani, and dances such as the solo *kyuchek*. During the 1950s and 1960s, the largest ethnic groups, including Roma, Turks, Armenians, and Greeks, had their own amateur folk ensembles, and Balkanton recorded many of the best singers and musicians. A "Jewish Folk Choir" performed Jewish religious and Western classical music, and Jewish composers are active in folk, classical, and popular music. In the more repressive atmosphere of the 1970s and 1980s, these ensembles and recordings ceased, but after 1989, Balkanton began once again to record minority performers.

HISTORY OF MUSIC

Bulgarian scholars have scanned church documents and frescoes for traces of a musical history before 1978. The first act in the Slavicization of Byzantine religious ritual was its translation from Greek into the Slavonic language of the medieval period, and

Kliment of Ohrid is credited with having composed hymns with such texts by the beginning of the tenth century. Bulgarian scholars have uncovered evidence of local, Bulgarian variants on traditional Byzantine musical practice. Their attempts at decoding it are hampered, however, by the use of notations without enough information to reconstruct pitch and rhythm. In a thirteenth-century Bulgarian manuscript, the existence of neumes (notational signs) not found in standard Greek texts is taken as evidence of the possible existence of an independent Bulgarian musical practice. Decipherable evidence for such a "national" practice appeared in a new type of notation in seventeenth- and eighteenth-century manuscripts, preserved in Kiev, and identifying a so-called *bolgarski rospev* 'Bulgarian manner of singing'. Bulgarian scholars have been fascinated by the figure of Yoan Kukuzel, a reformer of Byzantine music and notation, who wrote a piece entitled "In Praise of Bulgarian Women" and may have been of Bulgarian descent. The monk Josif, educated at Mount Athos, established a school for singing in the Bulgarian language at the Rila Monastery in 1790, but the musical style was Byzantine. In the mid-1800s, as the Bulgarian church moved toward independence from the Greek Patriarchate (a Bulgarian Exarchate was established in 1872), more evidence of Bulgarian secular influence on church singing appeared. After 1878, Russian choirmasters assumed the directorship of many church choirs, and the Russian style of four-part, homophonic singing, in many cases arranged by a new group of trained Bulgarian composers, replaced the Greek style of monophonic or drone (*ison*) singing.

Only after 1878 did European classical music begin to take root in Bulgaria, first in the form of army brass bands taught and led by musicians from Prague. By 1889, twenty-four bands, called "musician's choirs," of thirty-five to forty players each, were active, and by the 1890s, the first Bulgarian composers were trained to write for them. By 1892, a Czech kapellmeister had formed a small symphony orchestra for the Royal Guards in Sofia, the capital, and by 1921, a national opera theater had been founded there. Despite these inroads, many Bulgarian scholars, intellectuals, and composers give pride of place to traditional music over classical music, at least partly as a symbol of national identity.

Early compositional work consisted primarily of arrangements of a potpourri or bouquet (*kitka*) of well-known folk and urban popular songs for bands or a cappella choirs. The first important Bulgarian composer, Emanuil Manolov (1860–1902), focused on school songs in march style, many still sung. Dobri Hristov (1875–1941), his most gifted successor and a notable folk-song scholar, championed a closer adherence to folk models and frequently used tunes in asymmetric meters for his choral and solo-song arrangements. In 1900, Manolov composed the first Bulgarian opera, for performance by his military band in the provincial town of Kazanlŭk. His and others' early efforts were superseded by the work of Georgi Atanasov the Maestro (1882–1931), who studied for three years at a conservatory in Italy and composed six operas, many based on folk themes and songs, some still in the repertoire. Compared to vocal music, instrumental music developed more slowly, though the opera orchestra, the symphony of the Royal Guards, directed by Georgi Atanasov, and military bands gave frequent concerts of European classics.

The interwar period saw an increased sophistication in musical life and compositions, though the role of bandmaster and music teacher continued to be the most important sources of income for professional musicians, many now trained in conservatories abroad. In 1933, the younger generation of composers were numerous enough to form an association called Contemporary Music (Sŭvremenna Muzika), but though some experimented with newer Viennese atonal models, most continued to argue for folk song as the basis for a Bulgarian musical style and composed in a late Romantic, Russian-influenced style. Though folk-song arrangements for unaccompanied choir continued to figure prominently in composers' output, increased mastery of European instrumental forms, which in Bulgarian contexts required a new balance between folk and personal elements, defines the work of the most important composers of the period, including Petko Stainov (1896–1977), Pancho Vladigerov (1899–1978), Veselin Stoyanov (1902–1969), Filip Kutev (1903–1982), Lyubomir Pipkov (1904–1974), and Marin Goleminov (b. 1908), all of whose symphonies, tone poems, and rhapsodies were based primarily on folk tunes or folklike themes of their own creation. In 1921, the expenses of the Bulgarian Opera Society were included in the national budget. In 1924, a National Academy of Music was founded, and by 1936, it was offering a four-year course. Its orchestra, founded in 1928 as the Academic Symphony Orchestra, became the Royal Military Symphony Orchestra in 1936 and the Sofia National Philharmonia in 1944.

The most important difference in Bulgarian musical life after 1944 was the extraordinary flowering of state support for music of all kinds: amateur and professional; folk, classical and popular; in Sofia and provincial towns and villages. Music was "nationalized," and its evolution and performance guided by an aesthetic ideology emanating from the highest levels of the Communist Party. Venelin Krŭstev, in *Bulgarian Music*, quotes Georgi Dimitrov, the first communist head of state, as hoping music and other arts would "help to raise the cultural level of our people, of our youth, as a mighty factor in the construction of a new socialist society in our country." He ordered composers "to express in new musical works both the heroic struggle of our people against fascism before 9 September 1944, and also its all-round development in the present." The new political climate unleashed a ten-year-long period of composition of new "mass songs" and symphonies with heroic themes based on Soviet models. The oratorio for chorus and orchestra emerged as a new and favored form; Filip Kutev, who, like many professional musicians before the war, worked for the military, composed the first, entitled *Ninth of September*, in 1946. By the mid-1950s, Bulgarian folk models, perhaps stimulated by the success of the new professional folk ensembles, reasserted themselves. Composers active in the 1930s continued to produce, and a younger generation of composers, including Parashkev Hadzhiev (1912–1992), Alexander Raichev (b. 1922), Ivan Spasov (1934–1996), and Krasimir Kyurkchijski (b. 1936), came to prominence, the last two experimenting with avant-garde techniques and moving in some of their compositions away from a complete dependence on folk tunes and style. Opera asserted itself as the public's most popular genre; composers wrote dozens of operas after 1955, and Bulgarian opera singers achieved international reputations. The success of Kutev's arrangements for his village singers and the formation of similar choirs throughout the country stimulated most composers to write for women's folk choirs—a variation on a tradition going back to the beginnings of Bulgaria's professional musical life, in the 1880s.

The communists' interest in music created an explosion of performance organizations and new economic opportunities for professional musicians, who were paid by the state to perform, conduct, compose, record, and teach. From one music academy, one opera theater, and one symphony in Sofia before the war, professional opera companies, symphony orchestras, and folk ensembles blossomed in nearly every major provincial town. A Higher Institute for Music Pedagogy, with a department of folk music, and specialized music high schools, including two for folk music in Kotel and Shiroka Lŭka, joined the conservatory in training the new generation of musicians. Hundreds of thousands of people participated in amateur folk and classical music ensembles, dance troupes, and choirs organized in every town and village and many civic organizations, from schools, youth groups, and universities, to unions, factories, ministries, and the military.

Since the demise of socialist totalitarianism in 1989, state support of classical

Since the demise of socialist totalitarianism in 1989, state support of classical and traditional music has dwindled, and many musicians in both traditions have sought to make a life for themselves outside Bulgaria.

and traditional music has dwindled, and many musicians in both traditions have sought to make a life for themselves outside Bulgaria.

HISTORY OF RESEARCH

The major focus of Bulgarian music research for more than a century beginning in the mid-1800s was the collection and publication of folk songs. The first major folk-song collections, published by Verkovich (1860) in Belgrade and the Miladinov brothers (1942 [1861]) in Zagreb, included only song texts. Continuous, systematic work began after 1878 with the publication of thousands of songs, many with melodies. The earliest transcribers distorted asymmetric meters into duple and triple meters, until Atanas Stoyanov, a teacher and amateur collector from Shumen, wrote the first transcriptions in 5/8 and 7/8 in 1886.

The leading figures in the first generation of scholars were Angel Bukoreshtliev (1870–1950), Dobri Hristov (1875–1941), and Vasil Stoin (1880–1939). Bukoreshtliev led the first fieldwork expedition to collect songs in a particular region. Dobri Hristov, the first important Bulgarian music theorist and a prominent composer, laid the foundation for all subsequent treatments of Bulgarian musical structure with the first systematic analysis of the "metrical basis" of Bulgarian music in 1913 and an analysis of more general structural issues in 1928. Stoin founded the Folk Music Section of the Ethnographic Museum in 1926, and organized song-collecting expeditions involving travel to particular regions with large teams of coworkers. Having no mechanical recording devices, he and his coworkers notated each song by ear on the spot with pencil and paper, and he eventually edited and published four massive collections (1928, 1931, 1934, 1939). After his death, his colleagues edited and published four more collections based on his work. Stoin wrote the first analysis of Bulgarian two-part singing, published in French in 1925.

Many in the second generation of Bulgarian scholars wrote doctoral dissertations in musicology at French, Austrian, and German universities. The most important in this group was Stoyan Dzhudzhev (1902–1998), who, at the Sorbonne in 1931, wrote his dissertation on rhythm and meter in Bulgarian music, inventing his own system of dance notation. In 1945, he published the first scholarly book on Bulgarian folk dance; later, he produced a four-volume *Theory of Bulgarian Folk Music* (1954, 1955, 1956, 1961). While he and most of his generation concentrated on describing the formal structure of Bulgarian music, Raina Katsarova (1901–1984), who worked with Erich von Hornbostel and Robert Lachmann in Berlin from 1925 to 1928 and had extensive foreign contacts, pioneered the study of music in context, writing extensively on music and dance, music in ritual, instrument making, and musicians' and singers' lives.

The third generation of Bulgarian musicologists, writing after 1944 under the influence of Russian folk-music scholarship and in a new ideological climate, continued collecting songs. With the help of tape recorders after 1955, they built an enormous archive of recorded materials, and published collections of folk songs from Pirin and the Rhodopes. They also began to write about more particular, special problems, including musical instruments (Ivan Kachulev, Manol Todorov, Vergilij Atanassov); musical dialects (Elena Stoin, Vasil Stoin's daughter); folk dance (Anna Ilieva); and music in contemporary life (Todor Todorov, Venelin Krŭstev). Nikolaj Kaufman, the most important figure in this generation, whose prodigious output spans a vast range of topics, has written books on "many-voiced singing," wedding songs, funeral laments, and the relations between Bulgarian and other Slavic groups' music, and has compiled song collections of workers, city songs (from Pirin and Rhodope), and Bulgarians living in Bessarabia, a region on the north coast of the Black Sea [see THE COLLECTION AND STUDY OF TRADITIONAL EUROPEAN MUSIC, figure 3, p. 24].

The youngest generation has begun to apply a wide range of methods borrowed from internationally known scholars and a wide range of disciplines, such as anthropology, structural linguistics, semiotics, psychology, folklore, and literary criticism, and is turning to an analysis of performers and performance, rather than musical structures (Svetla Zaharieva, Dimitrina Kaufman).

Bulgarian music has received the attention of non-Bulgarian scholars and enthusiasts. Henry Bernard published translations of Bulgarian folk songs in 1904. Boris Kremenliev, an expatriate Bulgarian composer, wrote articles and an introductory book (1952). Important recordings, many with helpful notes and song-text translations, have been produced. Barbara Krader has written an important survey of Bulgarian scholarship and biographies of Raina Katsarova and Vasil Stoin. Klaus and Juliana Roth have studied printed chapbooks and the gray area between oral and written tradition. Other topics receiving considerable attention include music in the Rhodopes (Levy, Rice, Sugarman), multipart singing (Markoff, Messner, Rice), and musical life under the communists (Buchanan, Rice, Silverman).

BIBLIOGRAPHY

Atanassov, Vergilij. 1979. "Die technischen Möglichkeiten der Sackpfeife in Bulgarien." *Studia instrumentorum musicae popularis* 6:126–129.

———. 1981. "Der Gadulkaspieler und die Multifunktonalität seines Instrumentes." *Studia instrumentorum musicae popularis* 7:120–126.

———. 1983. *Die bulgarischen Volksmusikinstrumente: Eine Systematik in Wort, Bild und Ton.* Munich: E. Katzbichler.

———. 1988. "Children's Folk Musical Instruments." *The World of Music* 29:188–213.

Bartók, Béla. 1976. "The So-called Bulgarian Rhythm." In *Essays*, ed. Benjamin Suchoff, 40–49. New York: St. Martin's Press.

Bernard, Henry. 1904. *The Shade of the Balkans.* London: D. Nutt.

Blom, Jan-Petter. 1978. "Principles of Rhythmic Structures in Balkan Folk Music." *Antropologiska Studier* 25–26:2–11.

Boone, Hubert. 1971. "De Volksinstrumente uit Balkan. I: Volksinstrumente uit Bulgarije." *The Brussels Museum of Musical Instruments* 1:79–92.

Bottger, Walter. 1966. "Bei einem bulgarischen Gaidar." *Mitteilungen aus dem Museum fur Völkerkunde zu Leipzig* 1(2):24–29.

Buchanan, Donna. 1991. "The Bulgarian Folk Orchestra: Cultural Performance, Symbol, and the Construction of National Identity in Socialist Bulgaria." Ph.D. dissertation, University of Texas at Austin.

———. 1995. "Metaphors of Power, Metaphors of Truth: The Politics of Music Professionalism in Bulgarian Folk Orchestras." *Ethnomusicology* 39(3):381–416.

———. 1996. "Wedding Musicians, Political Transition, and National Consciousness in Bulgaria." In *Retuning Culture: Musical Changes in Central and Eastern Europe*, ed. Mark Slobin, 200–230. Durham, N.C.: Duke University Press.

Bukoreshtliev, Angel. 1934. "Sredno-Rodopski pesni." *Sbornik za Narodni Umotvoreniya* 39:1–213.

Bukurestliev, Mihail, and Panaiot Madzharov. 1983. *Strandzhanski narodni pesni.* Sofia: Muzika.

Djoudjeff, Stoyan. 1931. *Rhythme et mesure dans la musique populaire bulgare.* Paris: Champion.

Dozon, Auguste. 1875. *Les chants populaire bulgares: rapport sur une mission littéraire en Macédoine.* Paris: Maisonneuve.

Dzhudzhev, Stoyan. 1945. *Bŭlgarska Narodna Horeografiya.* Sofia: Ministry of Public Instruction.

———. 1954–1961. *Teoriya na Bulgarskata narodna muzika.* 4 vols. Sofia: Bulgarian Academy of Sciences.

Hristov, Dobri. 1967 [1925]. "Metrichni I ritmichni osnovi na bŭlgarskata narodna muzika." In *Dobri Hristov: muzikalno-teoretichno i publitsistichesko nasledstvo,* ed. Venelin Krŭstev, 1:33–98. Sofia: Bulgarian Academy of Sciences.

———. 1970 [1928]. "Tehnicheskiya stroezh na bŭlgarskata narodna muzika." In *Dobri Hristov: muzikalno-teoretichesko i publitsistichesko nasledstvo,* ed. Venelin Krustev, 2:63–124. Sofia: Bulgarian Academy of Sciences.

Ilieva, Anna. 1976. "Bulgarian Dance Folklore." In *The Folk Arts of Bulgaria,* ed. Walter Kolar, 215–228. Pittsburgh: Tamburitzans Institute of Folk Arts, Duquesne University.

———. 1978. *Narodni tantsi ot Srednogorieto.* Sofia: Bulgarian Academy of Sciences.

———. 1983. "On Changes in the Style in the Bulgarian Dance Folklore." *Dance Studies* 7:57–72.

Istria, Dora d'. 1868. "La nationalité bulgare d'après les chants populaires." *Revue des deux mondes* 38(2d period):319–354.

Ivanova, Radost. 1987. *Traditional Bulgarian Wedding.* Sofia: Svyat Publishers.

Kachulev, Ivan. 1963. "Gadulkas in Bulgaria." *Galpin Society Journal* 16:95–107.

———. 1969. "Zweistimmige Volksmusikinstrumente in Bulgarien." *Studia instrumentorum musicae popularis* 1:142–158.

———. 1973. *Narodni pesni ot severoiztochna Bŭlgariya.* Vol. 2. Sofia: Bulgarian Academy of Sciences.

———. 1978. *Bulgarian Folk Music Instruments.* Pittsburgh: Tamburitza Press.

Katsarova, Raina. 1952. "Tri pokoleniya narodni pevitsi." *Izvestiya na Instituta za Muzika* 1:43–96.

———. 1959. *Narodni pesni ot zapadnite pokrainini.* Sofia: Bulgarian Academy of Sciences.

———. 1960. "L'ethnomusicologie en Bulgarie de 1945 à nos jours (1959)." *Acta Musicologica* 32:77–89.

———. 1962. *Narodni pesni ot severoiztochna Bŭlgariya.* Vol. 1. Sofia: Bulgarian Academy of Sciences.

———. 1964. "Phénomènes polyphoniques dans la musique populaire bulgare." *Studia Musicologica* 3:161–172.

———. 1965. "La classification des melodies populaires en Bulgarie." *Journal of the International Folk Music Council* 17:293–299.

———. 1981. "Narrative Melodien aus Graowo." In *Stratigraphische Probleme der Volksmusik in den Karpaten und auf dem Blakan,* ed. Alica Elschekova, 99–111. Bratislava: Veda.

———. 1982. "Bulgarian Funeral Laments." *International Folklore Review* 2:112–130.

Katsarova, Raina, and Kiril Djenev. 1976. *Bulgarian Folk Dances.* Cambridge, Mass.: Slavica.

Kaufman, Nikolai. 1959. *Pesni na bŭlgarskoto rabotnichesko dvizhenie 1891–1944.* Sofia: Bulgarian Academy of Sciences.

———. 1963. "Part-Singing in Bulgarian Folk Music." *Journal of the International Folk Music Council* 15:48–48.

———. 1966. "Die folkloristischen Traditionen und die Entwicklung des revolutionaren bulgarischen Arbeiterliedes." *Deutsches Jahrbuch für Volkskunde* 12:336–342.

———. 1968. *Bŭlgarskata mnogoglasna narodna pesen.* Sofia: Nauka i Izkustvo.

———. 1968. *Bŭlgarski Gradski Pesni.* Sofia: Bulgarian Academy of Sciences.

———. 1974. "Die instrumentale Volksmusik der Bulgarien aus Bassarabien und Taurien." *Studia instrumentorum musicae popularis* 3:87–94.

———. 1982. *Narodni pesni na bŭlgarite ot Ukrainska i Moldavska SSR.* Sofia: Bulgarian Academy of Sciences.

Kaufman, Nikolai, and Dimitrina Kaufman. 1988. *Pogrebalni i drugi oplakvaniya v Bŭlgariya.* Sofia: Bulgarian Academy of Sciences.

Kaufman, Nikolai, and Todor Todorov. 1967. *Narodni pesni ot yugozapadna Bŭlgariya.* Sofia: Bulgarian Academy of Sciences.

———. 1970. *Narodni pesni ot Rodopskiya krai.* Sofia: Bulgarian Academy of Sciences.

Kolar, Walter, ed. 1976. *The Folk Arts of Bulgaria.* Pittsburgh: Tamburitzans Institute of Folk Arts, Duquesne University.

Krader, Barbara. 1969. "Bulgarian Folk Music Research." *Ethnomusicology* 13:248–266.

———. 1980. "Vasil Stoin: Bulgarian Folk Song Collector." *Yearbook of the International Folk Music Council* 12:27–42.

———. 1981. "Raina D. Katsarova: A Birthday Appreciation and List of Publications." *Ethnomusicology* 25:287–294.

Kremenliev, Boris A. 1952. *Bulgarian-Macedonian Folk Music.* Berkeley: University of California Press.

———. 1956. "Some Social Aspects of Bulgarian Folksongs." *Journal of American Folklore* 69:310–319.

———. 1965. "Some Observations on Stress in Balkan Music." *Studies in Ethnomusicology* 2:75–94.

———. 1966. "Extension and Its Effect in Bulgarian Folk Song." *Selected Reports in Ethnomusicology* 1:1–27.

———. 1975. "Social and Cultural Changes in Balkan Music." *Western Folklore* 34:117–136.

———. 1976. "Bulgarian Folk Music: Some Recent Trends." In *Bulgaria Past and Present,* ed. Thomas Butler, 373–392. Columbus, Ohio: American Association for the Advancement of Slavic Studies.

———. 1976 [1978]. "Asymmetry as a Continuing and Defining Characteristic in Bulgarian Folk and Art Music." *Balkanistica* 3:74–90.

————. 1983. "*Mnogoglasie*: A Compositional Concept in Rural Bulgaria." *Selected Reports in Ethnomusicology* 4:181–203.

Krŭstev, Venelin. 1978. *Bulgarian Music*. Sofia: Sofia Press.

Lazarov, Stefan. 1975. "Die Bogomilen und die Musik." In *Beiträge zur Musikkultur des Balkans*, ed. Rudolf Flotzinger, 1:77–108. Graz: Akademische Druck- und Verlagsanstalt.

Levy, Mark. 1985. "The Bagpipe in the Rhodope Mountains of Bulgaria." Ph.D. dissertation, University of California at Los Angeles.

Lord, Albert B. 1976. "Studies in the Bulgarian Epic Tradition: Thematic Parallels." In *Bulgaria Past and Present*, ed. Thomas Butler, 349–358. Columbus, Ohio: American Association for the Advancement of Slavic Studies.

Markoff, Irene. 1975. "Two-Part Singing from the Razlog District of Southwestern Bulgaria." *Yearbook of the International Folk Music Council* 7:134–144.

Messner, Gerald Florian. 1980. *Die Schwebungsdiaphonie in Bistrica: Untersuchungen der mehrstimmigen Liedformen eines mittelwestbulgarischen Dorfes*. Tutzing: Schneider.

Miladinovi, Bratya. 1942 [1861]. *Bŭlgarski narodni pesni*. 3d edition. Sofia: Dŭrzhavna pechatnitsa.

Millien, Achille. 1894. *Ballades et chansons populaires tcheques et bulgares*. Paris: Lemerre.

Obreshkov, Christo. 1937. *Das bulgarische Volkslied*. Bern und Leipzig: P. Haupt.

Palikarova-Verdeil, Raina. 1953. *La musique byzantine chez les bulgares et les russes du IXe au XIVe siecle*. Boston: Byzantine Institute.

Pantaleoni, Hewitt. 1985. "Bulgarian Harmony that 'Rings like a Bell'." In *On the Nature of Music*, 139–163. Oneonta, N.Y.: Welkin Books.

Peitavi, P. S. 1905. "Les chansons populaires bulgares." *Le Mercure Musical* 1:354–363.

Pekkila, Erkki. 1985. "Culture, Non-Culture and Myth in Bulgarian Music-Folklorism." *Musiikin Suunta* 7:45–53.

Rice, Timothy. 1971. "Music of a Rhodope Village in Bulgaria." M.A. thesis, University of Washington.

————. 1977. "Polyphony in Bulgarian Folk Music." Ph.D. dissertation, University of Washington.

————. 1980. "Aspects of Bulgarian Musical Thought." *Yearbook of the International Folk Music Council* 12:43–67.

————. 1988. "Understanding Three-Part Singing in Bulgaria: The Interplay of Concept and Experience." *Selected Reports in Ethnomusicology* 7:43–57.

————. 1994. *May It Fill Your Soul: Experiencing Bulgarian Music*. Chicago: University of Chicago Press.

————. 1995. "The Dialectic of Music and Dance in Bulgaria." In *Dance, Music, Ritual:*

Proceedings of the 18th Symposium of the ICTM Study Group in Ethnochoreology, ed. Grazyna Dabrowska and Ludwik Bielawski, 217–228. Warsaw: Polish Academy of Sciences.

————. 1995. "Understanding and Producing the Variability of Oral Tradition: Learning from a Bulgarian Bagpiper." *Journal of American Folklore* 108(429):266–276.

————. 1996. "The Dialectic of Economics and Aesthetics in Bulgarian Music." In *Retuning Culture: Music and Change in Eastern Europe*, ed. Mark Slobin, 176–199. Durham, N.C.: Duke University Press.

Roth, Klaus, and Juliana Roth. 1983. "'Naj-nova pesnopojka s narodni pesni . . .': Populare Liederbücher und Liederheftchen in Bulgarien." *Jahrbuch für Volksliedforschung* 27–28:242–257.

————. 1985. "A Bulgarian Professional Singer and His Songs." In *Narrative Folk Song: New Directions: Essays in Appreciation of W. Edson Richmond*, ed. Carol Edwards and Kathleen Manley, 339–361. Boulder, Colo.: Westview Press.

Shehan, Patricia K. 1987. "Balkan Women as Preservers of Traditional Music and Culture." In *Women and Music in Cross-Cultural Perspective*, ed Ellen Koskoff, 45–53. New York: Greenwood Press.

Silverman, Carol. 1982. "Bulgarian Lore and American Folkloristics: The Case of Contemporary Bulgarian Folk Music." In *Culture and History of the Bulgarian People: Their Bulgarian and American Parallels*, ed. Walter Kolar, 65–78. Pittsburgh: Tamburitza Press.

————. 1983. "The Politics of Folklore in Bulgaria." *Anthropological Quarterly* 56:55–61.

————. 1986. "Bulgarian Gypsies: Adaptation in a Socialist Culture." *Nomadic Peoples* 21–22:51–62.

————. 1989. "Reconstructing Folklore: Media and Cultural Policy in Eastern Europe." *Communication* 11:141–160.

Spassov, Vassil. "Volksmusik, Volksmusikinstrumente und Tänze der Bulgaren." Ph.D. dissertation, University of Vienna.

Stainov, Petko et al. 1967. *Entsiklopediya na bŭlgarskata muzikalna kultura*. Sofia: Bulgarian Academy of Sciences.

Stoin, Elena. 1955. *Narodni partizanski pesni, 1923–1944*. Sofia: Bulgarian Academy of Sciences.

————. 1975. *Narodni pesni ot Samokov i Samokovsko*. Sofia: Bulgarian Academy of Sciences.

————. 1981. *Muzikalno-folklorni dialekti v Bŭlgariya*. Sofia: Muzika.

Stoin, Elena, and Ivan Kachulev. 1958. *Bŭlgarski sŭvremenni narodni pesni*. Sofia: Bulgarian Academy of Sciences.

Stoin, Vasil. 1925. "Hypothèse sur l'origine bulgare de la diaphonie." *La Bulgarie d'aujourd'hui* 8:3–44.

————. 1928. *Narodni pesni ot Timok do Vita.* Sofia: Ministry of Public Instruction.

————. 1931. *Narodni pesni ot sredna severna Bulgariya.* Sofia: Ministry of Public Instruction.

————. 1934. "Rodopski pesni." *Sbornik za narodni umotvoreniya* 39:1–313.

————. 1939. *Bŭlgarski narodni pesni ot iztochna i zapadna Trakiya.* Sofia: Institut de culture de Thrace.

Sugarman, Jane. 1985. "Singing in the Rhodope Region of Bulgaria: An Inquiry into the Determinants of Musical Practice." M.A. thesis, University of California at Los Angeles.

Todorov, Manol. 1972. "Instrumentalensembles in Bulgarien." *Studia instrumentorum musicae popularis* 2:152–157.

————. 1973. *Bŭlgarski narodni muzikalni instrumenti.* Sofia: Nauka i Izkustvo.

Todorov, Todor. 1978. *Sŭvremennost i narodna pesen.* Sofia: Muzika.

————. 1981. *Bŭlgarskata muzikalna folkloristika do 9.IX.1944.* Sofia: Bulgarian Academy of Sciences.

Traerup, Birthe. 1970. *East Macedonian Folk Songs: Contemporary Traditonal Material from Malesevo, Pijanec and the Razlog District.* Copenhagen: Akademisk Forlag.

Vakarelsi, Hristo. 1952. "Muzikata v rodnoto mi selo Momina Klisura." *Izvestiia na Instituta za Muzika* 1:167–203.

————. 1969. "Lieder, Musik, Tänze." In *Bulgarische Volkskunde,* 339–349, 364–371, 371–380. Berlin: De Gruyter.

Vakarelski, Hristo, and Anastas Primovski. 1956. "Muzikalno-folklorni proyavi v Plovdivskoto izlozhenie prez 1892 godina." *Izvestiia na Instituta za Muzika* 2–3:267–319.

Verkovich, Stefan. 1874. *Le Veda slave: chants populaires des Bulgares de Thrace et de Macédoine.* Belgrade: n.p.

————. 1966. *Narodni pesni na makedonskite Bulgari, Vol. 1: Zhenski pesni* (Folk Songs of the Macedonian Bulgarians, Vol. 1: Women's Songs). Sofia: Bŭlgarski Pisatel.

Zaharieva, Svetlana. 1987. *Svirachut vŭv folklorna kultura.* Sofia: Bulgarian Academy of Sciences.

AUDIOVISUAL RESOURCES

Balkanton, the Bulgarian national recording company, has produced many important LP records and CDs, but they are not well distributed abroad.

Bhattacharya, Deben. 1968. *Songs and Dances from Bulgaria.* Argo ZFB 47. LP disk.

Boyd, Joe. 1991. *Ivo Papazov and His Orchestra: Balkanology.* HNCD 1363. Compact disc.

Boyd, Joe, and Rumyana Tzintzarska. 1987. *Balkana: The Music of Bulgaria.* Hannibal HNCD 1335. Compact disc.

————. 1988. *The Trio Bulgarka: The Forest Is Crying (Lament for Indje Voivode).* Hannibal HNCD 1342. Compact disc.

————. 1989. *Ivo Papazov and His Bulgarian Wedding Band: Orpheus Ascending.* HNCD 1346.

Cellier, Marcel. 1987, 1988. *Le mystère des voix bulgares.* Vols. 1 and 2. Nonesuch 79165, 79201. 2 compact discs.

————. 1990. *Le mystère des voix bulgares.* Vol. 3. Polygram/Fortuna 846 626. Compact disc.

Forsyth, Martha. 1981, 1983. *Traditional Song in Southwestern Bulgaria.* Available from Martha Forsyth, 51 Davis Avenue, West Newton, MA 02165. Two 60-minute cassettes.

————. 1990. *Two Girls Started to Sing: Bulgarian Village Singing.* Rounder 1055. Compact disc.

Lloyd, A. L. 195–. *Bulgaria.* Columbia KL 5378. LP disk.

————. 1964. *Folk Music of Bulgaria.* Topic 12T 107. LP disk.

Music of Bulgaria. 1955. Nonesuch 72011. LP disk.

Raim, Ethel, and Martin Koenig. 1970a. *A Harvest, and Shepherd, a Bride: Village Music of Bulgaria.* Nonesuch 72034. LP disk.

————. 1970b. *In the Shadow of the Mountain: Songs and Dances of Pirin-Macedonia.* Nonesuch 72838. LP disk.

Slovenia

Mira Omerzel-Terlep

Contexts for Singing
Musical and Textual Traits of Folk Songs
Folk Musicians and Folk Ensembles
Musical Instruments
Slovene Folk Music in the Twentieth Century
Folk Styles in Classical Music
History of Research on Folk Music

Slovenia declared its independence from Yugoslavia in June 1991, becoming an independent state for the first time since the late 700s. For most of the intervening period, the Austrian Habsburg dynasty and the Austro-Hungarian Empire ruled Slovenia, which absorbed German, Austrian, and Hungarian influences. In 1918, it joined the Kingdom of Serbs, Croats, and Slovenes, renamed Yugoslavia in 1929. Nearly 2 million people, the predominantly Roman Catholic population live in a heavily forested alpine zone, of 20,251 square kilometers.

Slovene folk music has several regional traditions: Prekmurje and Porabje in the east; Styria in the northeast; Upper Carniola and Carinthia (on both sides of the border with Austria) in the north; Bela Krajina and Lower Carniola in the south; central Slovenia around Ljubljana; Notranjsko, Karst, and Brkini in the west; Istria and the littoral region on the coast; and Resia, Venetian Slovenia, Friuli, and the Kanal Valley on the Italian side of the western border.

CONTEXTS FOR SINGING

Singing formerly marked many events in the life cycle. Mothers usually sang ballads and narrative songs to their infants, rather than lullabies, which were rare. Riddles and songs accompanied children's games and dances, and youths sang serenades during courtship. Wedding songs accompanied the collecting of gifts for the newlyweds, musicians, and cooks, and the guests' return home. Laments (*naricanje*), sometimes sung by hired female lament singers, narrated the deceased's biography and praised his good deeds; they survived until World War II. Religious, narrative songs, "grief" songs, funeral and farewell songs, narrating the deceased's death, are still sung while people hold a vigil in the presence of the body of the deceased.

Songs are also sung during annual holidays. Carnival masqueraders' songs employ rhymed requests for gifts, wishes for fertile land, and dances for tall flax and large turnips. The custom survives, but without most of its ritual component. St. George's Day (Jurjevo) songs and customs used to be celebrated throughout Slovenia, but today the custom is alive only in Bela Krajina—as a tourist attraction. Midsummer Night (June 24) songs in Bela Krajina were sung by girls who, having visited the fields and vineyards, proceeded to the village singing in two antiphonal

Door-to-door caroling from Christmas until Epiphany (6 January) was sometimes accompanied by plays, with three carolers dressed as Magi. After the carolers sang the story of Epiphany in front of the house, they were invited inside and given food and money, gifts that often helped poor people survive the winter.

groups or pairs without pause, because any house where a pause occurred would be struck by bad luck. Before World War I, the girls were accompanied by a bagpiper; after World War II, by a double flute player. Door-to-door caroling (*koledovanje*), from Christmas until Epiphany (6 January), occurred, for example, in Carinthia, where the carolers (*koledniki*) sang in two groups, one group singing the main text and the other one responding with a refrain. The carols (*kolednice*) were sometimes accompanied by plays, with three carolers sometimes dressed as Magi. After the carolers sang the story of Epiphany in front of the house, they were invited inside and given food and money, gifts that often helped poor people survive the winter. The custom declined in the twentieth century, then was taken over by children. Wherever the custom survives, it is performed by folk musicians. Spanking songs (*tepežnice*), sung by children on 28 December, were supposed to bring fertility.

Other contexts for singing include songs at personal celebrations, such as name days and army recruitment parties, and during collective farm work, such as weeding, mowing, harvesting, shucking corn, spinning, and weaving.

Part of the folk-song tradition are the cries of peddlers from Prekmurje, who used to walk from house to house buying poultry, and the cries of potters and vendors of printed handbills, crafts, and vinegar. Prayers for rain and spells against diseases and injuries such as snakebite started dying out in the 1890s. They could be rhythmic texts or texted melodies.

MUSICAL AND TEXTUAL TRAITS OF FOLK SONGS

The oldest Slovene folk songs and instrumental music, especially children's, ritual, narrative songs from the Resia area employ just a few tones. Later songs—including old religious songs, Christmas carols, and many songs from Prekmurje and Porabje—employ pentatonic scales and heptatonic modes. Many of the scales cannot be described in standard musicological terms or in terms of a diatonic major or minor scale. The most remarkable, used in songs from Bela Krajina and Istria, is the so-called Istrian scale, which employs notes of unequal temperament. This scale has not yet been fully investigated [see CROATIA].

The rhythm of Slovene folk songs is characterized by frequent metrical changes (figure 1). A meter with five beats per measure (or alternating two and three beats per measure) is common in narrative and dance-songs and most characteristic of Resia, the most isolated region. The basic pattern is difficult to determine, as each measure is often unique. Rubato is characteristic of Slovene folk music in general, and particularly of narrative songs in which the text, being more important than the music, is recited on one note or to a repeated melodic phrase.

Slovene folk music does not employ variety in dynamics. In different regions, singers in the old style value quiet or loud singing in sharply different ways. For example, in Carinthia quiet singing is considered beautiful, but in Haloze and Resia extremely loud, guttural singing has the same value.

FIGURE 1 Four-part song with frequent metrical changes. After Kumer 1976:28c.

Slovenes employ one-, two-, three-, four-, and five-part singing. A single voice was mostly used for ritual and narrative songs and is still common in Prekmurje and Porabje. Two-part singing in parallel thirds or sixths is known throughout Slovene territory. The interval between the two voices is not always the same; it can be a fourth, a fifth, or a sixth instead of a third, and sometimes the voices even merge, as in Prekmurje. An older type of two-part singing utilizes a drone accompaniment to the melody, as in Resia. In Bela Krajina in some Midsummer Night songs and in Istria, two-part singing emphasizes the interval of a second, with some thirds and fourths and unison cadences (figure 2).

Three-part singing, most common in young men's singing in central Slovenia, has the leading voice in the middle (*naprej* 'forward'), the highest voice following a third higher (*čreiz* 'over'), and the lowest voice in the bass (*bas*). In four-part singing, three voices move above a bass (*na tretko*), with the third following in octaves or independently (see figure 1). In five-part singing, (*na štrtko,* four voices above the bass), a woman is often included in otherwise all-male singing. In all these types of polyphony, singers do not start singing simultaneously as in choral singing. Consecutively, they follow the lead singer, who has the same role as a conductor, is responsible for the intonation, and must know the words. Though the old types of singing have been preserved in some places, most types have been replaced by arranged four-part choral music.

FIGURE 2   Excerpt from a two-part song with harmony based on seconds, thirds, and fifths. Two groups sing antiphonally, overlapping for one beat. After Kumer 1976:238a.

The themes of Slovene folk songs deal with questions of life and death and the natural and supernatural worlds. They reveal old social, judicial, ethical, and even aesthetic norms. Slovenes have few heroic songs, perhaps because they were compelled to fight under the Hapsburg flag, rather than in their own national interest. Christianity furnished many Slovene folk songs with religious themes and personalities such as saints.

FOLK MUSICIANS AND FOLK ENSEMBLES

Performance on musical instruments formerly served as a source of money for low-income people, particularly in the winter. The best known instrumentalists were musicians from Trenta, Bovec, Kropa, and Idrija, and Gypsies who traveled throughout the Slovene territory with their instruments. Before World War I, groups from other parts of Europe visited Slovenia. These included groups from Bohemia, with harps and accordions; Slovakia, with bagpipes; Vlahs in Istria; Hungarians in Prekmurje; and in Bela Krajina, Croats and Uskoks, fifteenth- and sixteenth-century refugees from Turkish invasions to the east and south, most likely from Bosnia and Montenegro. These and other groups influenced musical taste and transmitted melodies and instruments in Slovene territory.

Besides playing an instrument, a folk musician had to be an entertainer, a joker, and a leader of rituals. Before World War II, only men took these roles, except that some zitherists were women, who mostly played at home (figure 3). The skills of playing and making folk instruments were handed down orally from one generation to the next.

Instrumental folk music accompanied all important events and customs. Certain instruments were typically used for specific events or rituals, for example, bells at death and on Easter morning and horns to turn away evil spirits at carnival and for St. George's Day.

MUSICAL INSTRUMENTS

Many kinds of Slovenian instruments can be distinguished, including traditional instruments, those from the Middle Ages, more recently borrowed instruments, European symphonic instruments, and the currently most popular instruments, the zither and the accordion.

FIGURE 3 Four blind women play the zither (*citre*) at home before World War II. Photographer unknown.

Traditional Instruments

Many Slovenian aerophones are successors of prehistoric, Indo-European instruments and are common to other Slavic groups: reed pipes (*trstenke*), bagpipes (*dude*), double reed-pipes (*diple*), horns (*rogovi*), clay whistles (*okarine* and *žvrgolci*), duct flutes (*žvegle* and *stranščice*), and leaf whistles (*pero*).

Panpipes (*trstene orglice*) are made of six to forty-seven reed tubes, tied together and graduated in length, so that the longest piece (producing the lowest note) is in the middle and the shortest ones are on both sides (figure 4). Caps made of beeswax and pitch are used for tuning, which differs from instrument to instrument. In this intonation, semitones are not of equal temperament. Before World War II, panpipes were used throughout Slovene territory, in some areas for dance-music. The last maker—in Haloze, northeastern Slovenia—died in 1998.

Bagpipes with melody pipes and two drone pipes were used until about 1900; historical data show that they were used as early as the thirteenth century in dance music and were known in various Slovene regions, but particularly in western Slovenia, with players from Istria and Italy. Another type of bagpipe (*diple z mehom* 'double pipe with bag')—with two melody pipes and no drone—was typical of Bela Krajina and used in dance music at Midsummer Night procession and weddings until World War I [see CROATIA].

Horns (*rogovi*) were made of cow, ox, or goat horns or of wood or bark. They were mostly used as a signaling instrument by shepherds and hunters, but also at certain customs, as on St. George's Day in Carinthia and by Christmas carolers and carnival masqueraders. Alphorns began disappearing in the 1600s and are not used by Slovenes today [see SWITZERLAND].

European instruments known since the Middle Ages

Children and shepherds throughout Slovene territory played simple end-blown flutes or pipes with one or more holes. In the littoral region, these instruments had four to six holes and were made of thick reed. The wooden transverse flute made of plum wood (*postranica, žvegla*) was known throughout entire alpine region, in Slovenia particularly in the north and east (Carinthia, Prekmurje, Styria). In Haloze (Styria), it came in nine different sizes, each a whole or half-tone apart and played in various

The *gudalo* is a clay pot covered with a pig's bladder, with a stroked reed or maize stalk or plucked piece of string inserted through the skin. Its sound was dark and muffled, believed appropriate for rituals intended to drive evil spirits away.

FIGURE 4   A panpipe (*trstene orglice*) player and transverse flute (*žvegla*) player from Haloze. Photo by Matija Terlep, 1982.

ensembles. The mid-sized variant, with shrill timbre and untempered tuning, was used in dance-music and for hunters' and shepherds' entertainment since the Middle Ages. Until World War II, it could be found in almost every house in Haloze, but it became obsolete after World War II.

The trapezoidal hammered dulcimer (*oprekelj, cimprekelj, pretl, brana, male cimbale*) was known throughout Slovene territory (hence its many different names), except in Bela Krajina. It was used by musicians who played from house to house and in ensembles with other instruments, as with two violins or a clarinet and a small bass (especially in Upper Carniola, the Zilja Valley, Carinthia). Various sound colors were achieved by the use of different materials on the hammers, including cork, wire, felt, and cotton, but the dulcimer's hundred strings were hard to tune and harder to keep in tune, and the dulcimer ceased to be used in ensembles with other instruments. The last expert Slovene player died in 1979.

The drum (*boben*) was folk more by use than origin. It accompanied public announcements of laws and bankruptcies and between 1850 and 1900 served in various ensembles, particularly in brass bands throughout Slovenia.

The *gudalo* (clay pot bass) is a clay pot covered with a pig's bladder, with a stroked reed or maize stalk or plucked piece of string inserted through the skin. Its sound was dark and muffled, believed appropriate for rituals intended to drive evil spirits away and as rhythmic accompaniment of Christmas carolers. After it had lost its ritual appeal, it became an instrument expressing joy, most often replacing a rhythmic instrument or a bass. In northeastern and eastern Slovenia, it still accompanies carnival processions and dances with syncopated rhythms.

People bought the mouth harp (*drumlica, drumelca, brnica*) at fairs, but it became obsolete after World War I. In Carinthia, it was used as a serenading instrument.

Slovene instruments borrowed from neighboring countries

The ocarina (*okarina*) was a popular instrument in the 1700s throughout Europe. Its predecessors were probably bird-shaped clay whistles with one or more holes. In Slovene territory, ocarinas used to be made by potters in Styria and Bela Krajina, but foreign-made ocarinas from Austria and Slovakia were also sold.

Long-necked plucked lutes (*tamburice*) were borrowed from Croatians and Serbians, who adopted them from Turks in the fourteenth or fifteenth century. The tradition of *tamburica* ensembles started between 1800 and 1850, during the Illyrian Movement, a nationalistic revival in Slovenia and Croatia [see CROATIA]. The *tamburica* became most popular in Bela Krajina, where it replaced the double flute and bagpipes. Between the world wars, the ensemble became known throughout Slovenia through *tamburica* societies, newspapers, and schools, which propagated ideas of South Slavic and pan-Slavic unity. The Slovene tuning of the instruments uses the so-called *Farkaš* tuning system: two double courses of strings tuned a fifth apart (d–g). Ensembles consist of first and second *bisernica,* playing the melody mostly in thirds; *brač,* improvising countermelodies and filling gaps between the melody instruments; *bugarija,* which plays chords in syncopated rhythms; and bass (*berda).*

The Hungarian pedal cimbalom (*velike cimbale*) was played mostly in Prekmurje and Porabje by Gypsies. The larger version was better suited to accompany bands (*bande* or *goslarije*) of two to four violins, one or two violas, one or two clarinets, a bass, and a cimbalom than the smaller, pedal-less version (*male cymbale*). Typical of the Gypsy style of playing was improvisation with melodic preludes and ornamentation. Until World War II, Gypsy, Prekmurje, and Hungarian bands competed for dominant position and market share in northeastern Slovenia. Since they played for varied rural and urban audiences, they developed extensive repertoires. They were named after their lead violinist (*primaš*) or their place of origin. One band, Beltinška Banda, is still active, but without a cimbalom player. In the twentieth century, wind instruments gained popularity in bands, which eventually became brass bands, and the cimbalom was replaced by the accordion.

TRACK -33

European classical music instruments

The cimbalom played in bands with instruments borrowed from classical music: violins, violas, bass, clarinet, and, after World War II, guitars.

The violin, only rarely made locally, was widely used in the 1700s and became the lead instrument of various ensembles in the 1800s. It has unusual features in Resia, where it is called *cítira*. The tuning is a third higher than usual, and only the top third of the bow, which has higher tension than normal, is used for playing. A seated player supports the instrument on his chest—the technique used by amateur Gypsy players in Prekmurje—and taps a foot on every beat. Players in Resia use two keys only, G and D major (sounding B and F♯). The two-part melody is first played in the basic key (G, called by players *na towstvo* 'at fat or low pitch'), then transposed to the dominant key (D, called *na tenko* 'at thin or high pitch'), and ends with an upward glissando (*cvik*), drawing on the open strings g and d (*cvak*).

In Resia, men play a small three-stringed bass (*b[r]unkula, ta-velika citira*), known in European music as a basset. Nowadays elsewhere in Slovenia, this instrument is replaced by a purchased cello or bass with a homemade bridge, strengthened to sustain higher string pressure. The horsehair on the bow is stretched by a piece of string, tightened to the frog, instead by a nut. This instrument accompanies violins on open strings. The player holds it under the neck, turning it to draw on desired strings by the bow in the right hand, which does not change position. This bass is considered an undemanding instrument, which can be played by anybody. The cello and the bass were also used instead of the three-stringed bass in other parts of Slovenia. In Istria, a two-stringed bass is still in use.

Other instruments used in Slovene folk bands were the viola, regularly used only in Prekmurje and Istrian bands, where it complemented the lead violin; the clarinet, which in the 1800s began to replace the violin in some ensembles, especially those with dulcimer, violin, and bass. In the nineteenth century, the trumpet, the tuba, and the French horn were introduced into ensembles. After World War II, the guitar was added.

The most popular instruments: zither and accordion

Two instruments can be said to monopolize Slovene folk music at the end of the twentieth century: the zither (*citre*) and the accordion (*harmonika*). The first mention of the zither in Slovene lands is from the 1600s, when a drone zither evolved from a simple medieval stringed instrument, called *Scheitholt* in German. The drone zither, which used to be made by folk musicians throughout Slovene lands, had one or two pairs of melody strings, usually tuned to the same pitch, and one, two, or more strings for accompaniment, harmonized in pure octaves and/or fifths. The player addressed the zither by pressing a piece of wood in his left hand against the frets, while plucking all the strings simultaneously with a quill or a plectrum in his right hand. The drone zither, manufactured as late as World War I, is still used in dance-music in Genterovci, a village in Prekmurje.

In the 1800s, when the zither became a popular instrument of urban salons, the limited range of the drone zither became inadequate and its tuning changed. The few accompanying strings were tuned to form triads, and eventually more strings were added to play the major and minor harmonies of melodies. To play thirds in alpine zones, players started using their left-hand fingers instead of a piece of wood. This innovation and the addition of multiple strings for accompaniment were the beginning of the "chord zither." Different types of zither developed, depending on sound coloring, pitch, and purpose. The golden age of the zither was the twentieth century. Carinthia, Styria, and Lower Carniola were famous for their zitherists, though they are rarely found in Bela Krajina and Istria. The zither is mostly played as a solo instrument for dancing and as accompaniment to singing (CD track 32).

The accordion, introduced to all Slovene regions but Resia between 1850 and 1900, became the major instrument for folk-dance music. There were several types: the diatonic with buttons (*frajtonarica*), the piano accordion (*klavirka*), and in western Slovenia the two-row diatonic (*plonarca*). They are homemade or imported from Austria or Germany.

Noisemakers and children's instruments

Simple or improvised instruments, mostly used for rhythmic accompaniment or entertainment, include clappers made of stalks or wood, rattles, lids, spoons, chains, scythes, saws, and numerous children's instruments and noisemakers.

People improvise violins by cutting one or more strings into maize stalks (*korizne goslice*), supporting the stalks with pieces of wood and rubbing two such stalks against each other. They turn these instruments into rattles by filling dry stalks with pebbles or seeds and into poppers by cutting the ends into flaps. Pot lids, wooden and metal spoons, and metal cans serve as rhythmic instruments. Nutshells can be made into simple castanets, into a top producing a wrenlike sound with a piece of thread across the shell and a piece of wood for scraping, or into a noisemaker making a rattling sound (*drdra*). A piece of wood or bone on a piece of string (*zingulca, brnkač*) produces a buzzing sound if spun above one's head.

Children's instruments include a rattle (*raglja*), used before Easter, when bells cannot be used; a paper-and-comb kazoo; whistles of thick reed stalks with a thin middle portion (*nunalca*), with thin paper on both ends that form vibrating membranes; whistles of willow, elderberry, reed, straw, or bark, with one or more holes and various tonal capacities; in Prekmurje and Lower Carniola, bird- or horse-shaped clay whistles (*žvrgolci*) with one to three holes, some using water and producing a warbling sound; in Bela Krajina, horns made of bark by shepherds in spring and used for St. George's procession; the mouth organ (*ustne orglic, ustne harmonike*), in the past most often purchased at fairs and given to children as a confirmation present.

Hurdy-gurdy

The hurdy-gurdy (*lajna*) was once common throughout Slovene territory, but the last player died at the beginning of the twentieth century. There were many types of hurdy-gurdy. One that originated in the Middle Ages was hung around the player's neck and played by pushing keys and turning a handle that caused a wheel to scrape the strings. Modern, automatic hurdy-gurdies hang around the players neck if small, and stand on legs (*lajerkosten*) if large. These instruments had melodies engraved in cylinders with nails or in discs with small holes and were used in inns for dance-music. They were made mostly in Austria, Germany, Bohemia, and Slovakia.

Bells

Ringing bells (*pritrkavanje z zvonovi*) at special, mostly festive occasions is done by striking the bells with the clapper or sometimes with a hammer in certain rhythmic patterns. The bells—at least three of them (large, medium, small)—are sounded consecutively. The clapper can be swung by hands or by rope tied to it. The rhythmic patterns differ from one place to another and are named by their provenience or other traits.

It is unclear when this custom started in Slovene lands. There is a mention that in the Gorica region on the day after All Saints' Day in the 1500s people rang bells to prevent misfortune and bad weather, but no reliable data survive from before 1800. Nowadays, special bell ringing is used in religious rituals, at deaths, and during or before weddings, as a warning. The custom is shared by other European nations, but the Slovene style is unique and has been systematically researched since the 1940s.

SLOVENE FOLK MUSIC IN THE TWENTIETH CENTURY

The process of losing distinctively Slovene musical elements began in the 1800s and accelerated after World War II, which interrupted the continuity of the Slovene musical heritage. Around industrial centers, the peasant majority's folk music was almost instantly lost, but some ancient forms of musical expression—panpipes, the music of Resia, Istrian music, and instruments made of natural materials—survive in daily life. Many forms of unique musical creativity, such as spontaneous improvisation, tempo rubato, and changing meters (especially five-beat meter), disappeared as a result of conforming to European and American styles after 1950. With the spread of radio and television (radio was already accessible in most Slovene villages before World War II), people's active and creative involvement in music was replaced by a

To Slovene immigrants, accordion-based folk-popular music is a symbol of Slovene identity. In fact, it is Europeanized and Americanized and represents, in some sense, the negation of the nation's identity.

FIGURE 5   A small band of button accordion (*frajtonarica*) and brass instruments during the 1940s. Photographer unknown.

passive one. The proliferation of the equal-tempered scale on instruments such as the accordion is affecting singers' intonation. Even in Resia and Istria, which retain the most archaic Slovene music, the erosion of naturally untempered scales has begun. Elsewhere in Slovenia, the old system can be detected only after careful observation.

Several musical trends have affected folk music adversely. In folk bands, button accordions (*frajtonarica*), imported into Slovene lands in the mid-1800s and then developed into a specifically Slovene variety, replaced older, mostly untempered instruments: hammered dulcimers, panpipes, flutes, hurdy-gurdies, bagpipes, and zithers. After becoming the most popular Slovene folk instruments of the early twentieth century, they were quickly replaced by the chromatic piano accordion, which has been an indispensable part of folk-popular bands (*narodno-zabavni ansambli*) since World War II (figure 5). The button accordion is on its way out, and the centuries-old melodies and musical styles that were popular before the world wars and shortly after World War II are rapidly disappearing. The introduction of wind instruments and brass bands, between 1850 and 1900, had a similar impact. Three- and five-part singing has mostly been replaced by four-part singing, promulgated by choral-singing groups that started in the cities.

Folk-popular music, which after World War II almost totally replaced folk music, grew into an extremely popular phenomenon. The public gave this music a mixed response: huge popularity on the one hand and great aversion on the other. For 2 million Slovenes, there are two hundred to three hundred folk-popular bands, which have become a trademark of Slovene music. To Slovene immigrants, they are a symbol of Slovene identity, and accordingly, other ethnic groups in the United States and Canada identify Slovenes with polkas and accordions. In fact, Slovene folk-popular music is Europeanized and Americanized, adapted for the simple musical taste of a passive mass audience. It represents, in some sense, the negation of the nation's identity.

Folk-dance groups throughout Slovenia keep alive folk dances, folk songs, and to some extent folk instruments. The earliest and best known group is the Academic Folklore Ensemble of France Marolt, from Ljubljana, founded in 1948. This group and others issue recordings of their music.

The political climate in Yugoslavia after World War II was not favorably disposed toward folk music. The first postwar presentation of more or less forgotten Slovene folk music and instruments was at a concert by ethnomusicologist Mira Omerzel-Terlep, flutist Matija Terlep, and singer Bogdana Herman in 1978. To the public, unfamiliar with its old folk music, this concert and others that followed came as a tremendous surprise. This trio, currently called Trutamora Slovenica, revitalized numerous folk songs from the archives of the Slovene Academy of Science and art and private field recordings by Omerzel-Terlep. (Trutamora is the pentagonal protective symbol traditionally painted on cradles to protect babies from nightmares.) Since 1978, other groups and individuals—including Istranova, Piščaci, Kras, Marko

Banda, Trinajsto Prase and Tolovaj Malaj, singer Ljuba Jenček, and the vocal group Katice—have been trying to revitalize traditional vocal-instrumental folk music. As concern with national identity rose in and after the years of the independence movement, interest in traditional folk music grew. The political climate in the newly independent Slovenia is much more favorably disposed toward folk tradition. In the mid-1990s, a combination of original folk and popular music gained popularity, particularly music by composer-performer Vlado Kreslin with the bands Beltinška Banda and Šukar.

FOLK STYLES IN CLASSICAL MUSIC

Classically trained Slovenian composers who used folk music in their symphonies, operas, and chamber works include Emil Adamič (1877–1936) in *Iz moje mladosti,* a suite for orchestra; Blaž Arnič (1901–1970) in the symphonies *Ples Čarovnic, Povodni Mož,* and *Divja Jaga;* Matija Bravničar (1897–1977) in the opera *Hlapec Jernej in Njegova Pravica* and the symphonies *Faronika* and *Hymnus Slavicus;* Marjan Kozina (1907–1966) in the symphonic poems *Davnina* and *Bela krajina;* Karel Pahor (1896–1974) in *Istrijanka* for wind instruments, *Tri Istrske Predigre* for orchestra and piano, and the six-part choral piece *Očenašphlapca Jerneja;* the neoromantic composer Risto Savin (1859–1948) in the operas *Lepa Vida* and *Matija Gubec;* and Rado Simoniti (1914–1981) with Istrian, Resian, and other South Slavic musical motifs in his choral compositions. Subtler influences of folk music can be found in Alojz Srebotnjak's (b. 1931) works *Kraška Suite* and *Slovenica* and Vilko Ukmar's (1905–1991) ballet *Lepa Vida.* Among the youngest composers using Classical techniques in his folk-music arrangements is Jani Golob (b. 1948), as in his *Štiri Slovenske Pesmi za Godala,* and Tomaš Svete (b. 1956), as in his *Komi bi Rože Trgala,* for soprano and string orchestra.

Avant-garde postwar composers have used folk-musical elements in their works: Marjan Lipovšek (1910–1996) in the symphony *Domovina: 30 Variacij na Ljudski Motiv,* and numerous solo vocal pieces entitled folk songs; Uroš Krek (b. 1922) in *Rapsodični Ples, Inventiones Ferales,* for a violin and bowed instruments, and *Pet Narodnih,* for voice and instruments; Pavle Merkù (b. 1927), a Slovene folk-music collector in the Trieste area, using this material in *Alo, sijaj, sijaj, sonce,* a rhapsody for bowed instruments, *Vojskin čas,* the opera *Kači Pastir* and numerous pieces for solo voice; Lojze Lebič (b. 1934), in *Korant* for orchestra; Vinko Globokar (b. 1934), in search of new instrumental sounds, often using old folk instruments, as in *Etude pour Folklore I–II* for orchestra; Pavel Šivic (b. 1908), in compositions for solo voice, choir, and orchestra, including *Medjimurska in kolo;* and Danilo Čvara (1902–1981), who reworked some older folk songs in choral compositions, including the folklore scherzo *Kako se Polžeku Mudi,* the folk-song variations *O Martinu Kebru,* the opera *Veronika Deseniška,* and symphonic works. Composers who used folk-musical and folk-song elements primarily in pieces for solo voice or choir are Jakob Jež (b. 1928), in the cantata *Brižinski Spomeniki* and many other choral compositions; Radovan Gobec (b. 1909), in numerous cantatas and choral adaptations of folk songs; and Jurij Gregorc (1916–1985).

HISTORY OF RESEARCH ON FOLK MUSIC

The first mention of a Slovene folk song and instruments, dating from the 1300s, is a passage of a song sung by Seifreid Helbling. In the 1700s appeared the first Slovene folk-song collectors, including Marko Pohlin, Valentin Vodnik, Žiga Zois, and Jože Rudež. The first organized collecting of Slovene folk songs was part of the program of collecting folk songs of all Hapsburg-ruled peoples, organized by the Society of

Friends of Music in Vienna. Questionnaires were sent out in 1819. The literary jour-nal *Kranjska Čbelica* (1830–1833, 1848) published numerous poetic folk-song re-creations, some of them by France Prešeren, considered the greatest Slovene poet. The collecting and recording of folk songs was unsystematic and usually failed to include music. The most prominent nineteenth-century collector, Karel Štrekelj, as a member of the Viennese committee for folk-song collection in the entire empire had access to collections made by various collectors. He edited a collection of 8,686 folk songs, published as *Slovenske Narode Pesmi* in sixteen volumes (1898–1923; the final volume was prepared by Jože Glonar and published after Štrekelj's death); it rarely adds musical notations to the texts. Between the world wars, folk songs were collect-ed by Stanko Vurnik, Davorin Beranič, France Cigan, Marko Bajuk, and others. The first phonograph recording of a Slovene folk song was made in 1913 by Jure Adlešič in Bela Krajina.

The Folklore Institute in Ljubljana was founded in 1934; after World War II, it was renamed the Institute for Musical Ethnography. Its phonographic archives began in 1955 with the acquisition of a tape recorder and the work of its first director, France Marolt, who collected folk music, instruments, and dances. At the present time, the institute, which became part of the Slovene Academy of Arts and Sciences in 1972, is commissioned to collect folk songs from the entire Slovene territory. The institute is currently preparing a ten-volume series, *Slovenske ljudske pesmi* ('Slovene Folk Songs'), intended to include every Slovene folk song ever collected, with music. Its first big volume (mythological and heroic songs) was published in 1971, the sec-ond one (ballads) in 1982, and the third one (narrative songs) in 1992. The authors of this project are Zmaga Kumer, who specializes in monographic publications of Slovene folk songs, theoretical works in ethnomusicology, and studies on folk instru-ments; Valens Vodušek, who specializes in Slovene folk-song rhythms, meters, and melodies; Mirko Ramovš, an ethnochoreographer; Julijan Strajnar, who writes on instrumental music and its transcription and on Resian folk music; and Marko Terseglav, Marjeika Golež, and Igor Cvetko, who work on folk-song texts and tran-scriptions. Today, the institute houses about forty-five thousand Slovene folk-music recordings.

Research on Slovene folk songs has been done at the Institute for Musical Ethnography and by individuals outside the institute. The department of folk music at the Slovene National Radio, founded in 1973, houses large archives of Slovene folk music and has published ten Slovene folk-song cassettes. The University of Ljubljana has no ethnomusicological program, but it offers a survey course within the field of musicology. Though numerous folk-song collections have been published, Slovene ethnomusicology lacks monographs presenting the musical character of individual Slovene regions and the essential general traits of Slovene folk music.

Published information on Slovene folk instruments and instrumental music is much more limited than published information on folk songs, since interest in folk music and instruments developed much later than interest in folk songs. Though nineteenth-century romantic folk-song collectors were not interested in music, two important sources of information on Slovene folk music and instruments—"Göth's Topography," a questionnaire from the Graz Archives in Austria, with information on Styria (eastern Slovenia) from 1811 to 1847, and a similar questionnaire for Carniola from 1838—survive from the nineteenth century. Systematic research on folk instruments began with the foundation of the Folklore Institute. Since then, general studies dealing with Slovene folk instruments by Zmaga Kumer and specific instruments or instruments of a specific region have been published. Extensive work in collecting and researching Slovene folk instruments and reproducing music played on those instruments in concerts and broadcasts has been done since the 1980s by

Mira Omerzel-Terlep and Matija Terlep, who maintain a collection of more than two hundred traditional Slovene musical instruments, and in Istria by Dario Marisičo Mira.

—Translated by Marta Pirnat-Greenberg

BIBLIOGRAPHY

Cvetko, Igor, et al. 1988. *Jest sem Vodovnik Jurij: O slovenskem ljudskem pevcu 1791–1858.* Ljubljana: Partizanska Knjiga.

———. 1991. "Otroška glasbila in zvočne igrače kot del glasbene (zvočne) tradicije otrok na Slovenskem." In *Med godci in glasbili/Among Folk Musicians and Instruments,* 51–90. Ljubljana: Etnografski Muzej, Znanstvenorazisko Valni Center, Inštitut za Slovensko Nardodpisje, Sekcija za Glasbeno Narodopisje.

———. 1992. *Slovenske ljudske pesmi.* Vol. 3. Ljubljana: Slovenska Matica.

Dravec, Josip. 1957. *Glasbena folklora Prekmurja.* Ljubljana: Slovenska Akademija Znanosti in Umetnosti.

———. 1981. *Glasbena folklora Prlekije.* Ljubljana: Slovenska Akademija Znanosti in Umetnosti.

Goljevšček, Alenka. 1982. *Mit in slovenska ljudska pesem.* Ljubljana: Slovenska Matica.

Hasl, Drago. 1977. "Haloška žvegla." *Traditiones* 4:89–114.

Hrovatin, Radoslav. 1964. "Bordunske citre v Sloveniji." *Rad kongresa saveza udruženja folklorista Jugoslavije* 7:301–307.

Košuta, Miran, et al. 1985. *Deklica podaj roko: Ljudske pesmi in noše Slovencev v Italiji.* Trieste: Založništvo Tržaškega Tiska.

Kumer, Zmaga. 1968. *Ljudska glasba med rešetarji in lončarji v Ribniški dolini.* Maribor: Obzorje.

———. 1972. *Slovenska ljudska glasbila in godci.* Maribor: Obzorje.

———. 1976. *Pesem slovenske dežele.* Maribor: Obzorje.

———. 1986a. *Ljudske pesmi Koroške.* 2 vols. Celovec: Drava.

———. 1986b. *Die Volksmusikinstrumente in Slowenien: Handbuch der europäischen Volksmusikinstrumenten.* Ljubljana: Slovanske Matica.

———. 1991. *Oj, ta vojaški boben! Slovenske Ljudske Pesmi: Vojaščini in Vojskovanju.* Celovec: Drava.

———. 1995. *Mi smo prišli nócoj k vam: Slovenske Kolednaške Pesmi.* Ljubljana: Kres.

———, et al. 1981. *Slovenske ljudske pesmi.* 2 vols. Ljubljana: Slovenska Matica.

Kuret, Primož. 1973. *Glasbeni inštrumenti na srednjeveških freskah na Slovenskem.* Ljubljana: Slovenska Matica.

Logar, Engelbert. 1988, 1990, 1991. *Vsaka vas ima svoj glas.* 3 vols. Celovec: Krščanska Kutturne Saveza.

———. 1993. *Slovenske ljudske pesmi iz Spodnje Podjune.* Celovec: Krščanska Kulturna Zveza v Celovcu, Katoliško Prosvetno Društvo 'Drava' v Žvabeku.

———. 1994. *Koroške ljudske pesmi iz Libelič na Koroškem.* Celovec: Krščanska Kulturna Zveza v Celovcu in Katoliško Prosvetno Društvo 'Drava' v Žvabeku.

Marolt, France. 1935, 1936, 1954. *Slovenske narodoslovne študije.* 4 vols. Ljubljana.

Marušič, Dario. 1992. *Predi, predi hčimoja: Ljudske pesmi slovenske Istre.* Koper: Lipa.

———. 1995. *Piskaj sona sopi-svjet istarskih glazbala: Universo degli strumenti musicali istriani.* Pula: Castropola.

Merkù, Pavle. 1976. *Ljudsko izročilo Slovencev v Italiji: La tradiozioni popolari degli Sloveni in Italia.* Trieste: Založništvo Tržaškega Tiska and Editorale Stampa Triestina.

Omerzel-Terlep, Mira. 1990. "Oprekelj na Slovenskem." *Traditiones* 19:177–210.

———. 1995. "Uglašeno in razglašeno v ljudski glasbi: kvantna fizika-izziv sodobni etnologiji in etnomusikologiji." In *Razvoj slovenske etnologije od štreklja in Murka do sodobnih etnoloških prizadevanj,* 109–117. Ljubljana: Slovensko Etnološko Društvo.

———. 1996. "Paleolitske koščene piščali, Pričetke slovenske, evropske in svetovne inštrumentalne glasbene zgodovine." *Etnolog* 62(6): 235–294. Ljubljana: Slovenski Etnografski Muzej.

———. 1997. "Tipologija koščenih žvižgavk, piščali in flavt ter domnevna paleolitska pihala Slovenije: Typology of Bone Whistles, Pipes and Flutes and Presumed Paleographic Wind Blowing Instruments of Slovenia" and "Moustérianska 'koščena pišč' in druge najdbe iz Divjih babi-Slovenija: Moustérian 'Bone Flute' and Other Finds from Divje Babe Cave Site—Slovenia." In *Opera instituti archaelogici Sloveniae,* ed. I. Turk, 2:199–218. Ljubljana.

Ramovš, Mirko. 1980. *Plesat me pelji.* Ljubljana: Cankarjeva Založba.

Ravnikar, Bruno. 1970. "Akustična študija drumeljce." *Muzikološki zbornik* 6:99–104.

———. 1972. "Analiza kurentovih zvoncev." *Traditiones* 1:55–60.

Starec, Roberto. 1990. *Strumenti e suonatori in Istria.* Udine: Pizzicato.

Strajnar, Julijan. 1972. "Ein slovenisches Instrumentalensambel in Resia." *Studia Instrumentorum Musicae Popularis* 2:158–162. Stockholm: ICTM, Musikhistoriska museet.

———. 1981. "Zur Frage der Personlichkeit des Voksmusikanten in Slowenien." In *Studia Instrumentorum Musicae Popularis* 7:37–

———. 1988. *Citira: La musica strumentale in Val Resia: Inštrumenatalna glasba v Reziji.* Udine: Pizzicato.

———. 1990. "Il canto delle campane." *Quaderni dell Archivio della cultura di base* 13:123–1129.

Štrekelj, Karel. 1898–1923. *Slovenske narodne pesmi.* 4 vols. Ljubljana: Slovenska Matica.

Šuštar, Marija, and France Marolí. 1958, 1968. *Slovenski ljudski plesi.* 3 vols. Ljubljana: Glasbeno Nardodopisni Institut.

Terseglav, Marko, and Julijen Strajnar. 1989. *Porabska pesmarica.* Budapest.

Videčnik, Aleksander. 1991. *Iz roda v rod. Domači godci v Gornji Savinjski dolini.* Nazarje: Mercator.

Vodušek, Valens, 1969. "Über den Ursprung eines Characteristischen slowenischen Volksliedrhythmus." *Alpes Orientales* 5:151–178.

AUDIOVISUAL RESOURCES

Istranova. 1982. *Istranova.* Ljubljana: RTV Ljubljana LD-0796. LP disk.

Jenče, Ljoba. 1992. *Ljudska pesem poje v meni: Slovene Folk Songs.* Sraka SCD 04. Compact disc with booklet.

Merku, Pavle. N.d. *Dolina Rezije.* Ljubljana: Helidon FLP-03-006. LP disk.

Omerzel-Terlep, Mira. 1991. *Des bleiche Mond: Bledi mesec: Alte instrumentale Volksmusik aus Slowenien.* Munich: Trikont US-0182. Compact disc.

Omerzel-Terlep, Mira, and Matija Terlep (with guests). 1980–1984. *Slovenska ljudska glasbila in goçi, serija TV dokumentarnih oddaj: I–Trstenke, II–Žvegla, III–Oprekelj, IV–Cimbalist Miško Baranja, V–Beltinška banda, VI–Razvoj citer, VII–Bordunske citre (Genterovci), VIII–Akordične citre, IX–Violinske citre (Jože Zajc).* Posnela TV Slovenija. LP disk.

Omerzel-Terlep, Mira, Matija Terlep, and Bogdena Herman. 1982, 1985. *Slovenske ljudske pesmi in glasbila.* Belgrade: RTV Beograd, LP 250065, 2510103. 2 LP disks.

Omerzel-Terlep, Mira, Matija Terlep, and Beti Jenko. *1987. Slovenske ljudske pesmi in glasbila.* Zvočnost Slovenskih Pokrajin, 3. Ljubljana: PS-29 LP/KA-3. LP disk.

Omerzel-Terlep, Mira, Matija Terlep, and Mojka Žagar. 1991. *Zvočnost slovenskih pokrajin.* Vol. 4. Ljubljana: Svetovni Slovenski Kongres in Terlap. Compact disc.

Omerzel-Terlep, Mira, et al. 1991. *Zvočnost slovenskih pokrajin: Sound Image of Slovene Regions.* Slovenske Ljudske Pesmi in Glasbila, 4. Ljubljana: Svetovni Slovenski Kongres in Terlep. Compact disc.

Strajnar, Julijan. 1979a. *Porabje.* Ljubljana: Helidon FLP 03-008. LP disk.

———. 1979b. *Slovenska glasba: Slovene Music—Porabje.* Ljubljana: Helidon FLP 03-013. LP disk with booklet.

———. 1983. *Koroška, Slovene Music, Carinthia.* Ljubljana: Helidon FLP 03-009/1–2. 2 LP disks.

———. 1985. *Pritrkavanje.* Ljubljana: Helidon LFP 03-013. LP disk.

———. 1992. *Rožmarin, Slovenske ljudske pesmi: Canti popolari: Slovene Folk Songs.* Udine zal Pizzicato C.o. 34, C.o. 35. 2 cassettes with booklet.

Strajnar, Julijan et al. 1996. *Junaške, zgodovinske, bajeslovne in pravljične pripovedne pesmi (iz arhiva Glasbenonarodopisnega inštituta).* Slovenske Ljudske Pesmi, 1. Ljubljana: ZRC SAZU. Compact disc.

Tolovaj, Mataj. 1996. *Kranjec, Marinoi-Peček, Jerneg-Ravnič, Roman-Marušič, Dario.* Compact disc.

Vidakovič, Jasna. 1995. *Authentic Traditional Music from the Archives of Radio Slovenia: Piano and Percussion.* Ljubljana: Radio Slovenija, RS 001. Compact disc.

Croatia
Mark Forry

Croatian Musical Culture
Urban, National, and Popular Music
Traditional Music in the Modern World
History of Scholarship

Croatia (in Croatian, *Hrvatska*) emerged in 1991 as an independent state for the first time since the Middle Ages. For most of the intervening period, it endured foreign domination, mostly by Austria and its allies, but in 1918, it joined Serbia and Slovenia to form the federated kingdom that became Yugoslavia in 1929. Croatia's and Slovenia's declarations of independence signaled the end of the postwar socialist Yugoslavia in a protracted war of succession. Within Yugoslavia, Croatia was a republic of about 56,500 square kilometers and a population of 4,551,000; however, disputed national boundaries and a massive forced population exchange with Serbians and Bosnian Muslims from the former Yugoslavia complicate the demographic data. The largest ethnic minority in Croatia before the war was Serbian, but most Serbians left during the war. Other ethnic minorities include Italians on the Istrian Peninsula, Hungarians and Slovaks in eastern Slavonia and Baranja, and numerous Bosnians in refugee camps.

CROATIAN MUSICAL CULTURE

Croatia's geographical diversity yields significant variety in musical and cultural styles; however, since many Croatian groups originate in the Dinaric Alps and share the Roman Catholic religion, a common cultural framework underlies musical practice throughout Croatia.

Social contexts for making music

Croatian traditional music is rooted in ways of life now abandoned or substantially altered, changing with the seasonal rhythms of land and sea and events in a person's life. There was a time and place for each piece of music.

Religious holidays—especially Lent, Easter, Assumption Day, and Christmas—included music and defined the annual ritual cycle, though seasonal festivities of pre-Christian origin often became syncretized with church celebrations. Round dances specific to Easter were held throughout Slavonia and northwestern Croatia. At carnival, the villages of the northern Adriatic coast resounded to the singing and antics of bell carriers (*zvončari*).

Collective rural work parties, such as gatherings of women to spin and sew (*pre-*

In parts of Croatia, people say that "without an accordion, there can be no partying!"

lo), stimulated music and dancing. During the late fall in Slavonia, communal hog-butchering parties (*kolinje, svinjokolje*) provided occasions for neighborhood singing, dancing, and merrymaking. Singing accompanied solitary work in genres such as traveling songs (*putničke pjesme*) and shepherds' songs (*čobanske pjesme*).

Calendric celebrations and work parties afforded opportunities for courtship as young people sang and danced together. *Kolo,* the word for dance, signifies a characteristic round dance and a village event, often held in front of the church after Sunday services, when young people sang and danced while their elders chaperoned them. Spontaneous dance parties (*igranke*) and serenades, for which groups of young men visited the households of prospective fiancées and sang beneath their windows, were other occasions for courting. The *samica,* a small long-necked lute, was played exclusively by young men while courting.

Marriage celebrations consisted of many events over several weeks, including several uninterrupted days of festivities, with ritual songs and celebratory instrumental music for dancing, often supplied by hired professionals. Singing marked other life-cycle events, including births, christenings, child care (*uspavanke* 'lullabies'), festivities for young men entering military service, and funerals.

Rural singing and dance styles

Singing by men and women still dominates rural musical expression. Though solo and unison singing are practiced in some genres and locales, polyphonic singing is widespread—in older, narrow-interval styles and newer, diatonic styles. Singers denote polyphonic vocal roles according to precedence and function. In Sinj, for example, in the genre *treskavice* (from *treskanje* 'shaking'), the initial singer "drives" (*goni*) the opening syllabic recitation and "sings *voj*" (*vojka* 'holds a long tone'), while the second voice "shakes" (*trese* 'performs a glottal ornament') (Bezić 1967–1968). In Slavonia, the first voice "leads" while the second "follows" (Dubinskas 1983).

Dances of South Slavic groups in Croatia are most frequently closed circles (*kolo*) of mixed genders, dancing in compact spatial formations. Small, rhythmic shaking movements, sometimes known as *šara* 'ornament, iridescence', characterize the gestures. Other groups have closed circle dances (*csárdás* among Hungarians and Slovaks), and all groups have couple dances. Fast duple dance meters predominate, often without correspondence between musical and dance phrases.

Rural instrumental music

Despite the predominance of singing in rural life, Croatia boasts many diverse rural instruments. Aerophones, once its most common instruments, were frequently played solo by young men and boys tending domestic animals, and these instruments retain their pastoral association. Some flutes and reeds have two pipes and play two-part pieces in styles corresponding closely to local two-part vocal styles.

Plucked chordophones, probably introduced into the Balkan Peninsula by

FIGURE 1   A *tamburica* trio. Postcard post-marked 1909. Courtesy of the Robert Godfried Collection, New York.

Ottoman armies, are widespread and were identified as *tambure* (sing. *tambura*) in Slavonia as early as 1762. The simplest *tambure* are usually played alone to accompany singing and dancing (notably in Lika and Slavonia), and are often called *samica* 'by itself' to distinguish them from ensemble instruments.

Tambure are most often encountered in ensembles known as *tamburaški orkestri* 'orchestras of *tambura* players' or *tamburica,* the diminutive of *tambura. Tamburica* apparently originated in Slavonia and Vojvodina, where they remain characteristic of instrumental style. Beginning in the late nineteenth century, these ensembles became popular in other parts of Croatia, facilitated by the expansion of labor markets and improved communication. Eventually, nationalist cultural institutions accounted for the establishment of *tamburica* in even the remotest places (figure 1).

Urban military bands, which provided popular middle-class entertainment in the nineteenth century, became increasingly common in villages in the early twentieth century. Known throughout Croatia, they are particularly popular on the Adriatic coast and in Medimurje, where distinctive brass-band styles have evolved.

The most popular modern instrument, the accordion, is played solo in accordion-led ensembles and groups, sharing a role with the violin, the *tamburica,* and other instruments. Most accordionists play piano or chromatic button accordions, but smaller, diatonic instruments are common in Istria and northwestern Croatia. In Lika, people say that "without an accordion, there can be no partying!"

Musical zones

The Dinaric Alps

Many Croatians view the Dinaric Alps as the wellspring of Croatian culture. When the lowlands were depopulated by war and the coasts harried by invaders, Dinaric communities retained their integrity.

Two musical styles dominate the Dinaric Alps: the narrow-interval style, sometimes called *seljačko* 'of the village'; and *na bas* 'on a bass' style, also known simply as *bas.* The narrow-interval style is manifested in locally distinct polyphonic forms, each with its own terminology and musical-textual traits. Around Sinj, a remarkable number of forms flourish; the best known is *ojkanje* 'singing with *oj*', which takes its name from the distinctive glottal melisma on the sound *oj* following a terse exposition of the text (figure 2).

The Dinaric Alps are the only places in Croatia where the tradition of epic singing, known among Croatian and Serbian populations, is maintained. Dinaric epic singers accompany themselves with a *gusle,* a one-string upright bowed lute, and are hence usually known now as *guslači* or *guslari.* They formerly sometimes accompanied themselves with a *tambura.* Epic texts are set in a ten-syllable poetic line (*deseterac*) with subject matter drawn largely from mythological topics and historical struggles with foreign invaders, usually Turks. Melodic phrases are formulaic, often like reciting tones, with initial and closing figures, though most *guslari* vary melodic lines according to inflections in the language and dramatic content. The instrumental part is a heterophonic variant of the vocal one, except for an instrumental introduction and interludes for the performer to rest his voice.

The *na bas* style originated in Slavonia (see below) and was introduced to the Dinaric Alps in the late nineteenth and early twentieth centuries by migrant workers returning home. Songs in *na bas* style are begun by a solo singer, whom one or more accompanying singers join. The upper voice leads and frequently moves within a range of a fifth or a sixth, ending on the second degree of the scale; the lower voice forms thirds with the upper but a fifth at cadences, yielding an implied harmonic movement of tonic to dominant. "*Pjevaj mi, pjevaj, sokole*" ('Sing to me, sing, fal-

FIGURE 2 *Ojkanje* 'singing with *oj*', a traditional style of polyphonic singing, from near Sinj. Transcription by Mark Forry.

con'), one of the best known among Dinaric Croatian and Serbian communities, is considered emblematic of Lika (figure 3).

Herders use flutes and reed instruments to entertain themselves while tending animals. The term *svirala* generically denotes wind instruments, but more commonly denotes duct flutes, also called *frula*. Double duct flutes (*dvojnice* or *dvojice* 'pair'), carved from a single piece of wood and drilled with three holes in one pipe and four in the other, are sold by the thousands to tourists on the Dalmatian coast. Similar double-reed pipes, called *diple* 'double pipe', are played with a wooden mouthpiece or as bagpipes, known as *diple s mijehom* 'double pipe with bag' and *mješnice*.

FIGURE 3 The well-known song "*Pjevaj mi, pjevaj, sokole*" ('Sing to me, sing, falcon'), as sung in *na bas* 'on-a-bass' style in Lika, Dinaric Alps. Transcription by Mark Forry.

FIGURE 4 Excerpt from "Gospin plač" ('The Madonna's Lament'), as sung in the Zastražišće, Hvar Island. After A. Petrović 1985:n.p.

The Dinaric *kolo* consists of powerful leaping movements over a large space in open or closed circles. Some of these dances have no instrumental accompaniment and are led by gestures of a dance leader (*kolovođa*). The only sounds heard are the dancers' footfalls and the bouncing coin jewelry of the women's costumes. According to legend, these so-called silent dances, such as the well-known *vrličko kolo* 'kolo from Vrlika', date from the Ottoman period, when public gatherings were proscribed and people danced silently to avoid detection by the authorities.

Dalmatia

Dalmatia proper includes the central Adriatic islands and a narrow coastal belt, though the term also refers to the entire Croatian coast south of Rijeka and all the islands. Common Mediterranean cultural forms abound in this zone, particularly Italian influences around Dubrovnik.

A diatonic, narrow-range, monophonic style dominates Dalmatian vocal music. Songs in the Dinaric narrow-interval style are rarely performed, except in the cycle *Gospin plač* 'The Madonna's Lament', performed during Holy Week by pilgrims to selected churches and shrines. The musical setting takes the form of an extended melismatic lament, sung in unison by two singers (*kantaduri*), with replies by one or two others (figure 4). The northern Dalmatian coast and Kvarner Gulf is the last remaining home of a liturgical and paraliturgical form dating from the tenth century: Glagolitic singing (*glagoljaška pjevanje*), in Croatianized Old Church Slavonic. Lay singers employ a musical style based on local secular practice (Bezić 1973).

In larger cities and towns, Italianate popular-musical forms have been widespread since the nineteenth century. The best-known of these forms, *klapa* 'gathering, club', is sung by four to eight men, who gather to sing and socialize. The *klapa* uses harmonic and melodic models derived from Italian sources (Bezić 1977). In the rhythms and inflections of local dialects, the texts reflect a young person's maritime labors and passions. In 1967, numerous Dalmatian singers and music directors sought to revitalize *klapa* singing by presenting fifteen *klape* at a festival in Omiš. The enthusiasm of the singers and the Dalmatian public has ensured the continuing success and growth of the festival, with virtuosic performances and new compositions in more complex harmonic and contrapuntal settings (figure 5).

TRACK 34

The Adriatic coast is home to various dance cycles, particularly in the south, where dancing is almost the only form of recreation (Ivančan 1973). The cycle known as *poskočica* 'leaping dance' and *lindo* (a nickname for the *lijerica* player accompanying the dancing) has become emblematic for all of Dalmatia. The *lijerica,* a three-stringed, pear-shaped bowed lute similar to the Cretan *lyra* [see GREECE], is used primarily to accompany dancing. A few couples execute turning and running figures about a central point occupied by a musician and a caller, who directs the dancers' movements by calling out dance steps, often embedded in humorous cou-

Singing in Slavonia was a privileged form of conversation, because in most social gatherings, singing took precedence over speech, and topics that could cause offense if spoken could be safely broached in song. At communal work parties, singing served to defuse tensions and motivate neighbors to continue working with each other.

FIGURE 5 The first stanza of "*Dobra večer uzorita*," a *klapa* song from Dalmatia in four-part harmony, as performed at the Fourth Festival of Dalmatian *Klapa* Singing, at Omiš in 1970. Arranged by Jakov Gotovac.

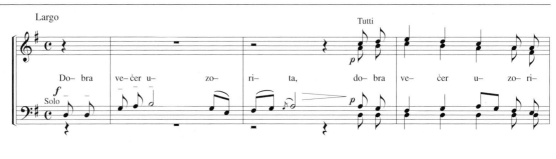

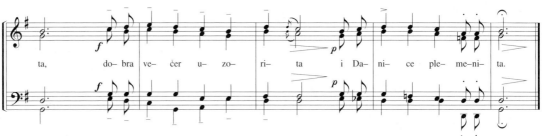

plets: "Give her wind [i.e., turn her fast enough to lift her skirts]: She's not your sister!"

Northern Adriatic zone: Istria and the Kvarner Gulf

The northern Adriatic coast constitutes a distinct cultural zone, including the Istrian Peninsula (Istria), the islands of the Kvarner Gulf (notably Krk, Cres, Lošinj, and Rab), and the coastline of the Kvarner Gulf from Rijeka to Senj. Italian cultural influences are noticeable, especially in dialects, and many people, mainly in Istria, are bilingual or trilingual—in Croatian, Slovenian, and Italian.

This zone is home to a distinctive vocal style with the so-called Istrian scale, consisting of alternating half and whole steps, which, particularly in older singers' and instrumentalists' renditions, are untempered. The songs are sung by pairs of singers (male, female, or mixed) in a characteristic two-part polyphony in minor thirds (or major sixths) with a cadence to a unison or an octave (figure 6). Singers distinguish the higher (*na tanko* 'thin') part from the lower (*na debelo* 'fat').

Reed aerophones are the most common musical instruments in this zone, and all are constructed of two tubes or played in pairs to render the polyphonic style based on the Istrian scale. On Krk, pairs of double-reed oboes (*sopile*) are the most common instrument; corresponding instruments in Istria are known as *roženice. Mišnice,* a pair of tubes drilled in a single piece of wood with single reeds for each tube and a wooden mouthpiece, has finger holes ordered to produce the Istrian scale. In Istria, the Italian minority uses an ensemble of double-chanter bagpipe (*pive*) and frame drum (*simbolo*).

Other ensembles include *gunci* or *gunjci* (also called *violine,* or simply *muzika*) and brass bands (*limena glazba*). Two- and three-row diatonic accordions (*harmonika, ramonika*), introduced in the late 1800s, quickly became the most prestigious instrument in Istria. Though often played solo, accordions appear in ensembles, sometimes with older, untempered instruments, such as *roženice.*

The dance style of the northern Adriatic zone has adapted many features of the Slovenian Alps, Italy, and Central Europe. The Italian influence is recorded in names of dances, such as *balun* (or *balon,* from Italian *balla*), and the term for dance leader, *kapobalo* 'head of the dance'. Most dances are turning couple dances, particularly in Istria; quadrilles and line dances are found on the Kvarner coast and islands.

Pannonia: Slavonia and Baranja

Pannonia includes the lowlands of the Danube, Sava, and lower Drava rivers, the plains and hills lying between them, and the territory of Slavonija and Baranja, with numerous communities of Šokci (old-stock settlers), who distinguish themselves from later-arriving Croatians. The musical styles of eastern Slavonia and Baranja closely resemble those of Serbian Vojvodina, which has its own Šokci communities in Bačka and Srem.

The dominant Pannonian vocal style, *na bas,* is thought to have originated in Pannonia and then spread, notably to Dinaric Bosnia and Croatia, and via Vojvodina to Serbia proper (figure 3). The songs are usually diatonic, but a few have scales with augmented seconds, suggesting Islamic influence.

Songs per se are more common now, but Slavonians formerly preferred *pismice* (also *pjesmice* 'small songs'), rhymed couplets in *deseterac,* set to the contextually most appropriate melody (*arija*). Villagers typically knew hundreds of fixed texts, but formulaic construction allowed singers to improvise texts to fit situations, for example, naming a particular person in a teasing verse. Singing in Slavonia was thus a privileged form of conversation, because in most social gatherings, singing took precedence over speech, and topics that could cause offense if spoken could be safely broached in song. At communal work parties, singing served to defuse tensions and motivate neighbors to continue working with each other (Dubinskas 1983: 256–257). Slavonians also sang or shouted *pismice* while dancing *kolo,* particularly in the dance *poskočice* 'small hops', whose form ranged from well-known stock couplets to extended topical conversation in verse: "Hey, all the maids love *tamburica* musicians, but neither maid nor wife loves the bassist."

With the exception of the single fipple flute (*frula*), played solo while the player

FIGURE 7   A Pannonian bagpiper plays a bellows-blown bagpipe (*duda*). Photo by Elsie Ivancich Dunin, 1970.

tended stock, most Slavonian instrumental music duplicates the tonal relations—diatonic and multivoiced—of the *na bas* vocal style. For example, the bagpipe (*duda*) has a double-bore chanter; one tube plays melodic figures while the other alternates between the tonic (the same note as the drone) and the dominant (similar to the accompanying voice in *na bas* singing). Bagpipes are inflated by an elbow bellows, allowing the piper to sing while playing (figure 7). Since the 1930s, chordophone ensembles—usually *tamburic*e or violin(s) with *tamburice*—have become the dominant instrumental medium. Renditions of amateur *tamburaši* are sometimes rudimentary, but many village musicians display virtuosity and sophistication, particularly in Slavonian *kolo* (*slavonsko kolo*), the most widespread and representative dance in the repertoire (figure 8).

Medimurje and upper Podravina

Medimurje (on the Mura River) and upper Podravina (the Drava River basin) comprise the riverine lowlands and surrounding hill country on the border between Croatia and Hungary and form a transition zone between South Slavic and Hungarian Pannonian cultures.

Many melodies in this zone conform to well-known Hungarian types classified by Bartók (1931) and others, especially Bartók's "new style" melodies: diatonic major or minor scales, four-part arch form, and dance rhythms. The form AA^5BA, where the first melody repeats a major fifth higher, is one of the most frequently encountered in Medimurje. The rhythm is reminiscent of the *csárdás,* a Hungarian dance, known by Medimurje Croatians. As in Pannonian Hungary, the melodies are sung monophonically without much ornamentation.

Tamburica, brasses, and accordions are the most popular instruments for accompanying village songs and dances, and instrumental music reflects Hungarian practice in the *esz-tam* rhythm, a Hungarian term used onomatopoeically to denote downbeat-offbeat rhythmic patterns. The dance repertoire also includes distinctively Croatian pieces known in other zones, pieces such as *drmeš* 'shaking dance' and *kolo.*

Northwestern Croatia

Northwestern Croatia, the transitional zone between Dinaric Croatia, the Pannonian lowlands, and alpine Slovenia, includes Hrvatsko Zagorje (the low mountains north

FIGURE 8   A Pannonian line dance (*kolo*), performed with a characteristic cross-hand hold. Photo by Elsie Ivancich Dunin, 1976.

of the capital Zagreb), the lowlands of Turopolje and upper Posavina, and the north-western highlands. Its musical style most closely resembles that of Central Europe: scales are diatonic and mostly tempered, most melodies end on the fundamental scalar tone, and polyphonic texture is usually in two or three parts.

For many years, ensembles known as *guci* or *gunci* 'fiddlers', consisting of one or more violins and a standard or adapted double bass (*bajs*), provided the preferred accompaniment to dancing and festive events. *Tamburica* instruments began to appear in the 1930s and in some places supplanted *guci* entirely; elsewhere, violins remained the lead instruments, but *tamburica* instruments and accordions were added to ensembles.

Dances of northwestern Croatia display many traits of the Alpine zone, including alpine Slovenia. They are mostly for couples, occasionally in groups of four, and especially where couples are arrayed in equal intervals about a circle, as in *sroteš* from Hrvatsko Zagorje and *drmeš* from Turopolje (*turopolski drmeš*); however, Pannonian traits, including compact, closed circles with energetic shaking gestures (as in the *drmeš*) are found here.

URBAN, NATIONAL, AND POPULAR MUSIC

During the nineteenth and early twentieth centuries, Croatian cities fell under external spheres of influence: Austria in the north and Italy on the Adriatic coast. Popular nineteenth-century classical and semiclassical forms, particularly opera and operetta, were fostered. Even after World War II, Viennese zither music was heard in Zagreb and Italian mandolin ensembles in Dalmatia. Nevertheless, in the nineteenth century, urban populations of Germanicized or Italianized Slavs discovered their own ethnicity.

Illyrians and the national revival

The proponents of the nineteenth-century national revival (*Hrvatski narodni preporod*) in Croatia called themselves Illyrians, after the ancient people who had inhabited parts of Croatia before the Slavs arrived. Like other Romantic nationalists, Illyrians were primarily intellectuals of a marginalized ethnicity. They believed that their political legitimacy was rooted in rural culture, manifested in language and to a lesser extent other rural expressive forms, including music. The Illyrians' promotion of village cultural symbols focused on wearing village costumes as a mark of national pride; the publication of oral literature, especially folk-song texts; the composition of folk-styled poetry, based on these publications; and the performance of village or quasi-village songs and dances, particularly at urban political events. These manipulations provided symbolic models for succeeding generations of nationalistically oriented folklorists.

Illyrian musicians' project—to establish a folk-music-based Croatian national style—was hampered by an inadequate acquaintance with the purported source of their inspiration. Though dedicated to romantic ideals and patriotic principles, few Illyrian composers had actual contacts with rural Croatian music; in fact, many were Germanized Slavs, for whom Croatian was a second language. It was not until Franjo Kuhač's (1834–1911) five volumes of South Slavic national songs, published in Zagreb from 1878 to 1881, that most Croatian urban musicians had a sense of the stylistic features and variety of native Croatian music. Among the Illyrian musicians publicized by Kuhač was Pajo Kolarić (1821–1876), composer and leader of the first known *tamburica*. The identification of *tamburica* music with the Illyrian Movement enabled its rapid spread through the urban centers where nationalist cultural organizations were active. In the succeeding generation, the operetta melodies of Ivo Tijardović (1895–1976) became widely popular in rural practice, and Emil Cossetto's

In the 1990s, contemporary popular musicians frequently exploited traditional motifs to lend national appeal to their work; for example, the hybrid style *techno-lindo* sets traditional Dalmatian dance music on electronic instruments.

(b. 1918) composition *Ladarke,* for chorus and *tamburica* orchestra, has become a standard in folklore ensembles.

The national revival also enabled the emergence of two cultural streams often seen as antithetical: commercial popular music (*zabavna muzika*) and organized performances of musical folklore.

The emergence of Croatian popular music

The nationalistic songs and marches favored by Illyrian patriots in the early years of the national revival represent the beginnings of Croatian popular music, often called *zabavna muzika* (recreational or entertainment music) by scholars and the popular media. Throughout the nineteenth and early twentieth centuries, solo songs of famous and obscure composers alike gained widespread popularity and a traditional status in urban repertoires. The popularity and nostalgic associations of these old-city songs *(starogradske pjesme)* have endured, and they have enjoyed a revival since the 1980s.

Between the world wars, two related genres became popular: *romanse,* rooted in the stylistic conventions of the earlier old city songs, and *šlageri* (hits, from German *schlager*), songs popularized in operettas and, after World War II, in films. Among the most successful composers in both genres was a native of Dubrovnik, Vlaho Paljetak (1893–1944), a popular chansonnier and for many years prompter at the Zagreb Opera. He composed his most popular songs in the styles of two Croatian dialects: those of the Zagreb hinterlands and Dalmatia. Local performers have accepted his most popular songs as original folklore, and his songs are widely imitated as models for so-called newly composed folk songs (*novokomponirane narodne pjesme*).

Since the 1980s, many popular singers, though oriented toward international popular music, have returned to traditional music. Vera Svoboda and Krunoslav "Kićo" Slabinac, for example, perform material from their native Slavonia, and their careers have been enhanced by the association of *tamburica* and national sentiments in their music. *Tamburaši* such as the ensemble Ex-Panonia have become national celebrities, and have spurred a renewed interest in *tamburica* music among younger musicians and listeners.

Rock, probably the most popular music among young Croatians, makes abundant use of traditional textual and musical material, but the hybrid result is still regarded as rock. A few pop groups incorporating local musical and textual themes into their work are perceived as representative of local musical culture and have gained a national following. The best known include Dubrovački Trubaduri (Dubrovnik Troubadours) and Novi Fosili (New Fossils), both active in the 1970s and 1980s, using Adriatic themes. In the 1990s, contemporary popular musicians frequently exploited traditional motifs to lend national appeal to their work; for example, the hybrid style *techno-lindo* sets traditional Dalmatian dance music on electronic instruments.

TRADITIONAL MUSIC IN THE MODERN WORLD

Contemporary musical occasions, rural and urban, are likely to include various musical compositions and styles: old-city songs; older rural songs and dances in staged adaptations; newly composed national songs (*novokomponirana narodna muzika*); contemporary South Slavic songs in pop or rock style (*zabavna muzika*); and popular international music, increasingly dominated by American rock.

Organized folklore

Village expressive culture was the putative object of Illyrian concerns, but village culture in itself received little attention until the late nineteenth century, when the scientific discipline of ethnography became established in Croatia. Antun Radić (1868–1919), editor of the first Croatian ethnographic journal, developed field-research guidelines that researchers used into the 1960s. His political activities with his brother Stjepan Radić (1871–1928) were oriented to a rural populism (still viable in Croatian politics) that celebrated village culture and sought rural political power through a program of education and consciousness-raising.

In 1904, they founded the Croatian Peasants' Party. In 1925, Stjepan Radić expanded the brothers' nationalist cultural program by founding Seljačka Sloga (Peasant Harmony) in 1925. Music and dance performances were at the center of Sloga's activity. Village choral societies, modeled on urban choral societies founded in the 1800s, performed arrangements of village music or artistic stylizations of rural vocal practice. Arrangements were distributed in the publications of Sloga and other rural cultural societies, and village singers were encouraged to sing from written music, though in practice, trained directors frequently taught them by rote.

After political changes in 1935, Sloga was reorganized, and performance practices in village chapters were reoriented to original (*izvorni*) material: songs and dances assumed to be ancient, native, and free from foreign influences. Folklore ensembles were formed to present village performers' dancing, singing, and playing instruments, all in "original" costumes. Performances took place at local and national festivals, of which the first, the Festival of Village Singing Choruses, was held in Zagreb in 1935. After this festival, a jury was formed to guarantee that materials presented at festivals were "authentic forms of folklore" and "truly of the folk"; the jury consisted of the presidents of the Croatian Peasants' Party and Peasant's Harmony, ethnologists from Zagreb University, and musicologists from the Music Academy. Its members visited performing groups in their villages and reprimanded villagers for infractions of their guidelines, including city-bought costumery, new dance steps, and the use of accordions. The structure of "original" organized folklore—juried performances at festivals—was reinstated after World War II and is still in use.

Presentation of folk music

Croatia has two forms of staged folklore, each based on the concepts of "spontaneous" (that is, traditional rural) and "adapted" contexts. In Yugoslavia after World War II, groups of both sorts were constituted as cultural artistic societies under the auspices of local and national cultural agencies, though each had its own organizations and they usually appeared at different festivals. The original (*izvorni*) folklore groups derive from the "spontaneous" performances of traditional village performers; hence their repertoire is exclusively local, and the performers are generally older. Amateur (*amaterski*) folklore groups are usually composed of urban young people who perform theatrically adapted music and dances from all over Croatia (previously Yugoslavia) that they learn from professional folklore performers and directors. These groups are closer in spirit to mid-nineteenth-century Illyrian ideals, whose adherents were mostly young urbanites unconnected to village life. The dance presentations most frequently derive from the choreographies of the noted Croatian dance ethnologists Zvonimir Ljevaković (1908–1981) and Ivan Ivančan (b. 1927), artistic directors and choreographers for the national professional ensemble, Lado. Named for a pagan Slavic deity, this ensemble has served as a model for amateur folklore ensembles since its inception, in 1949. In turn, Lado draws into its ranks the most talented performers from amateur ensembles.

The principal mass-media organization in Croatia is Radio-Televizija Zagreb. Pula, Osijek, Rijeka, Split, and other large towns have local stations. Before the war, folk music accounted for 10 percent of music broadcast on Radio Zagreb, as against 20 percent for "serious" and 70 percent for "popular." Folk music accounted for 80 percent of music shows broadcast on Televizija Zagreb. Since the 1980s, music-video production was adopted for folklore presentations, and broadcasts of these videos have boosted the careers of many contemporary folk artists. RTV Zagreb maintains two ensembles devoted to the performance of traditional music in adaptation: a *tamburica* orchestra and a mandolin sextet for Dalmatian old-city (*starogradski*) songs.

The principal recording institutions in Croatia are Croatia Records (formerly Jugoton) and Suzy Records. About 32 percent of their average production in 1990 was devoted to traditional music: 10 percent original village music and 22 percent folk music in some degree of adaptation. Both firms manufacture traditional music videotapes, which are popular with Croatian communities in Western Europe, the Americas, and Australia.

"Newly composed" Croatian folk music

There are four principal current trends in Croatian traditional music: traditional forms with little or no change; structural changes or changes in musical systems; acceptance of basically new phenomena and their adaptation; and newly composed folk music (Bezić 1988). Of these, newly composed folk music probably enjoys the broadest popularity. These items may include the commonly known *novokomponirana narodna muzika* 'newly composed folk music', though, because of its associations with Serbia, it is now rarely heard; new texts for long narrative songs, published in booklet form and frequently concerning the experiences of economic emigrants; new vocal and instrumental compositions by Slovenian artists and Croatian local compositions in this style; and local festival songs, composed with the express desire of popular acceptance in local musical practice.

Among the most successful of the latter are new *klapa* songs in Dalmatia; because new songs are required as audition criteria for the principal *klapa* festival at Omiš, many new songs are produced every year. Other festivals contributing new local material include those held in Krapina, Požega, and Split. The musical settings of these new songs often reflect those of commercial popular music, with contemporary studio orchestras and recording processes, but the songs are often perceived locally as appropriate to local musical culture.

HISTORY OF SCHOLARSHIP

Notations of Croatian music date from the sixteenth century, when the Dalmatian poet Petar Hektorović (1487–1572) published two melodies with an idyllic poem on the fisherman's life (1556). Organized ethnographic activity in Croatia began in the mid-nineteenth century, with the rise of the Illyrian Movement, which inspired the first field collections of folk songs. The seminal example is the work of Franjo Kuhač (1834–1911), whose five volumes of South Slavic melodies (1878–1881) have influenced generations of musicians and scholars. The Czech folklorist and musicologist Ludvik Kuba (1863–1956) made numerous expeditions between 1888 and 1912, resulting in several published collections of material from Dalmatia, Bosnia, and Hercegovina (1899, 1906–1909).

Scientific studies of folk music began immediately after World War I, when three scholars—Božidar Širola (1889–1956), Vinko Žganec (1890–1976), and Milovan Gavazzi (1895–1985?)—took primary responsibility for realizing the Radić brothers' cultural policies. Širola's musicological studies emphasized musical instruments (1922, 1932, 1937), but he also considered issues of classification. Žganec extended Širola's classification work by applying the Finnish musicologist Ilmari Krohn's comparative methodology to Croatian melodies. Gavazzi was primarily concerned with comparative ethnology within Croatia and with other South Slavs, and his work in this field is the basis for contemporary local stylistic classification (1939, 1942, 1956). The three were among the first to make audio recordings of traditional music (their recordings are preserved in the Phonogrammarchiv in Vienna), and their transcriptions have been the basis for most subsequent ethnomusicological investigations in Croatia. Their work in collection and classification has been continued by Jerko Bezić (b. 1929), one of the first Croatian ethnomusicologists to investigate the place of musical folklore in the modern world and ethnomusicologists' roles in its continued existence.

Younger scholars associated with the Folklore Institute include Grožđana Marošević, Krešimir Galin, Ruža Bonifačić, Naila Ceribašić, and Tvrtko Zebec; Gorana Doliner is associated with the Musicological Institute (attached to the Zagreb Music Academy), and Svanibor Pettan is associated with the Slovenian Music Academy. American scholars who have studied music and dance in Croatia include dance ethnologists Elsie Ivancich Dunin and Nadine Dougan, the late anthropologist Frank Dubinskas, the ethnomusicologist Mark Forry, and the folklorist Richard March.

The sisters Ljubica (1894–1974) and Danica (1898–1960) Janković, Serbian pioneers of dance ethnology, included studies of Croatian dances in their volume on dance in Yugoslavia (1952). Croatia's leading dance ethnologist since World War II, Ivan Ivančan (b. 1927), has completed detailed monographs on most Croatian zones, in addition to directions for staging folkloric dances. His younger colleague Stjepan Sremac researches contemporary dance events and the history of organized folklore presentations. Ivančan and Sremac are affiliated with the Folklore Institute in Zagreb and have been active with folklore-performing ensembles, particularly the ensemble Lado. Research on music and dance of the Croatian diaspora was conducted by composer and folklorist Tihomir Vujičić (1929–1975), who collected and arranged songs and instrumental pieces of South Slavs in Hungary; by Rudolf Pietsch, on the Gradišćani Croatian minority in Austrian Burgenland; and by Elsie Ivancich Dunin, Mark Forry, and Richard March, on Croatian communities in the Americas.

BIBLIOGRAPHY

Abbreviations:

INU   Institut za narodnu umjetnost (Institute for Folk Art) [later ZIF]

JAZU   Jugoslavenska akademija znanosti i umjetnosti (Yugoslav Academy of Sciences and Arts)

NU   *Narodna umjetnost: Godišnjak Instituta za etnologiju i folkloristiku* (Folk art: Yearbook of the Institute for Ethnology and Folkloristics)

ZIF   Zavod za istraživanje folklora (Institute for Folklore Research) [earlier INU]

ZNŽO   *Zbornik za narodni život i običaji* (Journal for Nnational Life and Customs)

Andreis, Josip. 1959. *Yugoslav Music.* Belgrade: Edition Yugoslavia.

———. 1982. *Music in Croatia.* 2d, enlarged edition. Zagreb: Institute of Musicology, Academy of Music.

Andrić, Josip. 1962. *Tamburaška glazba* (*Tamburica* music). Slavonska Požega: Matica Hrvatska.

Bartók, Béla. 1931. *Hungarian Folk Music.* London: Oxford University Press.

Bartók, Béla, and Albert B. Lord. 1978. *Yugoslav Folk Music.* Edited by Benjamin Suchoff. Foreword by George Herzog. Albany: State University of New York Press.

Bersa, Vladoje. 1944. *Zbirka narodnih popievaka (iz Dalmacije)* (A collection of folk songs [from Dalmatia]). Edited by Božidar Širola and Vladoje Dukat. Zagreb: Hrvatska akademija znanosti i umjetnosti.

Bezić, Jerko. 1967–1968. "Muzički folklor sinjske

krajine" (Musical folklore of the Sinj area). German summary. *NU* 5–6:175–275.

———. 1973. *Razvoj glagoljaškog pjevanja na zadarskom području* (The development of Glagolitic singing in the Zadar area). Zadar: Institut JAZU u Zadru.

———. 1976. "The Tonal Framework of Folk Music in Yugoslavia." In *The Folk Arts of Yugoslavia,* ed. Walter Kolar, 193–208. Pittsburgh: Tamburitzans Institute of Folk Arts, Duquesne University.

———. 1977. "Dalmatinska folklorna gradska pjesma kao predmet etnomuzikološkog istraživanja" (Dalmatian folkloric city songs as a subject of ethnomusicological research). *NU* 14:23–54.

———. 1988. "Contemporary Trends in the Folk Music of Yugoslavia." In *Contributions to the Study of Contemporary Folklore in Croatia,* ed. Zorica Rajković, 49–73. Special issue 9. Zagreb: ZIF.

Bonifačić, Ruža. 1991. "'Mi ćemo zakiantat glason od slavića': Koncepcije izvođača o tradicijsko pjevanju u Puntu na otoku Krku" ("We will sing with the voice of the nightingale": Conceptions of traditional singing held by performers on Krk Island). English summary. *NU* 28:49–86.

———. 1995. "Changing of Symbols: The Folk Instrument Tamburica as a Political and Cultural Phenomenon." *Collegium Antropologicum* 19(1).

Ceribašić, Naila. 1992. "Slavonska folklorna glazba kroz koncepcije smotri i istraživanja" (Slavonian traditional music through the concept of folklore festivals and research). English summary. *NU* 29:297–322.

———. 1995. "Gender Roles During the War: Representations in Croatian and Serbian Popular Music 1991–1992." *Collegium Antropologicum* 19(1).

Dobronić, Antun. 1915. "Ojkanje: Prilog za proučavanje geneze naše pučke popijevke" (Ojkanje: A contribution to research on the genesis of our popular melodies). *ZNŽO* 20(1).

Dubinskas, Frank Anthony. 1983. "Performing Slavonian Folklore: The Politics of Reminiscence and Recreating the Past." Ph.D. dissertation, Stanford University.

Forry, Mark. 1990. "The Mediation of 'Tradition' and 'Culture' in the Tamburica Music of Vojvodina (Yugoslavia) " Ph.D. dissertation, University of California, Los Angeles.

Gavazzi, Milovan. 1939. *Godina dana hrvatskih narodnih običaja* (The annual cycle of Croatian folk customs). 2 vols. Zagreb: Matica Hrvatska.

———. 1942. "Etnografijski sastav" (Ethnographic structure). In *Zemljopis Hrvatske* (Geography of Croatia), ed. Zvonimir Dugački. Zagreb: Matica Hrvatska.

———. 1956. "Die Kulturgeographische Gliederung Südosteuropas." *Südost-Forschungen* 15. Special issue.

Gojković, Andrijana. 1989. *Narodni muzički*

instrumenti (Folk-musical instruments). Belgrade: Vuk Karadžić.

Ivančan, Ivan. 1963. *Istarski narodni plesovi* (Istrian folk dances). English summary. Narodno stvaralaštvo Istre (Folk creation of Istra), 3. Zagreb: INU.

———. 1964. "Geografska podela narodnih plesova u Jugoslaviji" (Geographic distribution of folk dances in Yugoslavia). English summary. *NU* 3:17–38.

———. 1970. "Prilozi istraživanju socijalne uloge plesa u Hrvatskoj" (Contributions to the study of the social role of dances in Croatia). English summary. *NU* 7:97–106.

———. 1971. *Folklor i scena: priručnik za rukovodioce folklornih skupina* (Folklore and the stage: A manual for leaders of folklore groups). Zagreb: Prosvjetni sabor Hrvatske.

———. 1973. *Narodni plesovi Dalmacije, I: Od Konavala do Korčule* (Folk dances of Dalmatia, 1: From Konavle to Korčula). English summary. Posebna izdanja (special issue), 3. Zagreb: INU.

———. 1981. *Narodni plesovi i igre u Lici* (Folk dances and games in Lika). Zagreb: Prosvjetni sabor Hrvatske.

Janković, Ljubica C., and Danica C. Janković. 1952. *Narodni igre VII* (Folk dances 7). English summary. Belgrade: Prosveta.

Janković, Slavko. 1967–1974. *Šokačke pismice* (Šokci rhymed couplets). 3 vols. Vinkovci: Matica Hrvatska.

Karabaić, Nedeljko. 1956. *Muzički folklor hrvatskog primorja i Istre* (Musical folklore of the Croatian coast and Istra). Rijeka: Novi list.

Kljenek, Kresimir, and Josip Vlahović, eds. 1979. *Zbornik dalmatinskih klapskih pjesama (izvedenih na festivalima u Omišu od 1967 do 1976)* (Collection of Dalmatian *klapa* songs [performed at festivals in Omiš from 1967 to 1976]). Omiš: Festival dalmatinskih klapa Omiš.

Kobola, Alojz, ed. 1975. *Tradicijska narodna glazbala Jugoslavije* (Traditional folk music of Yugoslavia). Zagreb: Školska knjiga.

Kos, Koraljka. 1972. "Dimensions in Folk Music: A Contribution to the Study of Musical Tastes in Contemporary Yugoslav Society." *International Review of Aesthetics and the Sociology of Music* 3(1):61–73.

Kuba, Ludvik. 1899. "Narodna glazbena umjetnost u Dalmaciji" (Folk musical art in Dalmatia). *ZNŽO* 4:1–33,161–183.

———. 1906–1909. *Pjesme i napjevi iz Bosne i Hercegovine* (Songs and melodies from Bosnia and Hercegovina). Sarajevo: Glasnik Zemaljskog Muzeja za Bosnu i Hercegovinu.

Kuhač, Franjo Ksaver. 1877. "Prilog za povijest glasbe južnoslovenske: opis tanbure" (A contribution to the history of South Slavic music: A description of the *tambura*). *Rad JAZU* 39:5–103.

———. 1878–1881. *Južno-slovjenske narodne popievke* (South Slavic national songs). 4 vols. Zagreb: C. Albrecht.

———. 1893. *Ilirski glasbenici* (Illyrian musicians). Zagreb: Matica Hrvatska.

Lord, Albert B. 1960. *The Singer of Tales.* Cambridge: Harvard University Press.

March, Richard Anthony-Daniel. 1983. "The Tamburitza Tradition." Ph.D. dissertation, Indiana University.

Marošević, Grožđana. 1988. "Folk Music in Croatia in the Period from 1981 to 1985." In *Contributions to the Study of Contemporary Folklore in Croatia,* ed. Zorica Rajković, 75–98. Special Issue 9. Zagreb: ZIF.

———. 1992. "Culture as a Determinant of Folk-Singing Style, Group, and Solo Singing in the Karlovačko Pokuplje Region." *International Review of the Aesthetics and Sociology of Music* 23(2):207–221.

Milošević, Predrag. 1971. "Music Broadcast on Yugoslav Radio Stations in Figures and Percentages." *International Journal of Aesthetics and the Sociology of Music* 2(2):291–293.

Mladenović, Olivera. 1973. *Kolo u jušnih Slovena* (The *kolo* of the South Slavs). Belgrade: Etnografski institut, Srpska akademija nauka i umetnosti.

Njikoš, Julije. 1970. *Slavonijo zemljo plemenita: narodni običaji, pjesme, kola, i poskočice* (Oh, Slavonia, noble land: Folk customs, songs, dances, and dance couplets). Osijek: Matica Hrvatska.

Parry, Milman. 1953. *Serbocroatian Heroic Songs.* Collected by Milman Parry. Edited and translated by Albert Bates Lord. Cambridge: Harvard University Press. Belgrade: Serbian Academy of Sciences.

Pernić, Renato. 1985. *Narodne pjesme iz Istre* (Folk songs from Istria). Pula: Istarska naklada.

Petrović, Ankica. 1985. "Passion Chant from the Island of Hvar in Dalmatia: The Relations of Ritual and Music-Poetic Content." In *Musica Antiqua,* 3 [unpaginated]. Bydgoszcz, Poland: Filharmonia Pomorska Im. I. J. Paderewskiego.

Petrović, Radmila. 1968. "The Concept of Yugoslav Folk Music in the Twentieth Century." *Journal of the International Folk Music Council* 20:22–25.

———. 1976. "Folk Music in Yugoslavia." In *The Folk Arts in Yugoslavia,* 183–192. Pittsburgh: Tamburitzans Institute of Folk Arts, Duquesne University.

Radić, Antun. 1897. "Osnova za sabiranje i proučavanje građe o narodnom životu" (The foundation for collecting and studying material about national life). *ZNŽO* 2:1–88.

Rihtman, Cvjetko. 1976. "Yugoslav Folk Music Instruments." In *The Folk Arts in Yugoslavia,* 209–228. Pittsburgh: Tamburitzans Institute of Folk Arts, Duquesne University.

Rihtman-Augustin, Dunja. 1971. "Polozaj tradicionalne kulture u suvremenom društvu" (Status of traditional culture in contemporary society). *NU* 8:3–17.

———. 1978. "Traditional Culture, Folklore,

and Mass Culture in Contemporary Yugoslavia." In *Folklore in the Modern World,* ed. Richard M. Dorson, 163–172. The Hague and Paris: Mouton.

Širola, Božidar. 1933. "Kako se grade dangubice i druge tamburice" (How *dangubice* and other *tamburice* are constructed). *ZNŽO* 29(1):197–205.

———. 1937. *Sviraljke s udarnim jezičkom* (Wind instruments with beating reeds). Zagreb: JAZU.

———. 1940a. *Hrvatska narodna glazba* (Croatian folk music). Zagreb: Matica Hrvatska.

———. 1940b. "Smotre hrvatske seljačke kulture" (Festivals of Croatian village culture). *ZNŽO* 32(2):1–44.

Sremac, Stjepan. 1978. "Smotre folklora nekad i danas" (Folk festivals then and now). *NU* 15:97–116.

———. 1983. "O hrvatskom tancu, drmešu, čardašu i porijekla drmeša" (About the Croatian

tanac, drmeš, and czardas and the origin of the *drmeš*). *NU* 20:57–74.

Stepanov, Stjepan. 1966. "Muzički folklor Konavala" (Traditional music of Konavle). *Anali Historijskog instituta JAZU u Dubrovniku* 11–12:461– 549.

———. 1971. *Narodne pjesme iz Gorjana i Potnjana* (Folk songs from Gorjani and Potnjani). *ZNŽO* 44:283–421.

Stepanov, Stjepan, and Ivo Furić. 1966. *Narodne Pjesme i Kola iz Slavonije* (Folk songs and dances from Slavonia). Zagreb: Savez Muzičkih Društava i Organizacija SR Hrvatske.

Supek, Olga. 1988. "Ethnology in Croatia." *Etnološki pregled* 23–24:17–35.

Vujičić, Tihomir. 1978. *Muzičke tradicije južnih slovena u Madarskoj* (Musical traditions of South Slavs in Hungary). Budapest: Tankönyvkiadó (Preduzeće za izdavanje udžbenika).

Zebec, Tvrtko. 1991. "Prilog proučavanju drmeša

zagrebačkoga prigorja" (A contribution to the study of the *drmeč* of the Zagreb foothills). English summary. *NU* 28:143–158.

———. 1995. "The Dance Event as a Political Ritual: The *Kolo* Round Dance 'Slavonia at War'." *Collegium Antropologicum* 19(1):79–89.

Žganec, Vinko. 1950. *Narodne popijevke Hrvatskog Zagorja* (Folk songs from Hrvatsko Zagorje). Zagreb: JAZU.

———. 1958. "The Tonal and Modal Structure of Yugoslav Folk Music." *Journal of the International Folk Music Council* 110:18–21.

———. 1990–1992 [1924–1925]. *Hrvatske pučke popijevke iz Medimurja* (Croatian folk songs from Medimurje). 2 vols. Edited by Jerko Bezić and Grozdana Marošević. English summary. Zagreb: ZIF.

AUDIOVISUAL RESOURCES

Most sound and video recordings of Croatian traditional or national musics are available only in the former Yugoslav republics: recordings on the Croatia Records (formerly Jugoton) label are issued in Croatia; those on RTB (Radio-Televizija Beograd), in Serbia; and those on Suzy, in Slovenia. They are hard to find in Western Europe and North America, though Croatian and Serbian specialty shops may carry them. The following recordings are more readily available outside Croatia and Serbia.

Boulton, Laura. 1952. *Songs and Dances of Yugoslavia.* Folkways FW 6805. LP disk.

Boxell, Dennis. 197–. *Kad zaigra, pusta Slavonija* (When the Slavonian plains dance). Festival 7221B. LP disk.

Croatia—Traditional Music of Today/Croatie—Musiques Traditionnelles d'Aujourd'hui. 1997. Paris: Avudis-UNESCO-ICTM D 8276. Compact disc.

Croatie—Musiques d'autrefois. 1997. Paris: Ocora-Radio France, Ocora C 600006. Compact disc.

Dietrich, Wolf. 1973. *Folk Music of Yugoslavia.* Topic 12TS 224. LP disk.

Eredics, Gábor. 1992. *Chants et danses croates: Traditions musicales des peuples croates de Hongrie.* Quintana [Harmonia Mundi] QUI 903071. Compact disc.

Folk Dances of Yugoslavia: Dennis Boxell Presents "Jugoslavenski narodni plesovi." 198–? [1948]. Festival Records. 50 min. Videocassette.

Folk Music of Yugoslavia. 196–. Folkways FE4434. LP disk.

Gyurok, György. 1978. *Járd a kolót! Magyarországi Désláv Népzene—Igraj kolo—Dance the Kolo: Southern-Folk Music from Hungary.* Hungaroton SLPX 18036. LP disk.

Katsumasa, Takasago, and Yanko Trubic. 197–. *Yugoslav Folk Music.* Lyrichord LLST 7189. LP disk.

Kennedy, Peter, and Albert Lord. 195–. *Yugoslavia.* Columbia World Library of Folk and Primitive Music. Columbia K1217 4954. LP disk.

Koenig, Martin. 1971. *Village Music of Yugoslavia.* Nonesuch H72042. LP disk.

Laade, Wolfgang, and Dagmar Laade. 1975. *The Diaphonic Music of the Island of Krk, Yugoslavia.* Ethnic Folkways Library. Folkways FE 4060. LP disk.

Music of Yugoslavia: Dalmatia. 1960–1964. Monitor MF 349, 413. 2 LP disks.

Musiques de Yugoslavie. 1990? Musique du Monde. Buda 92490-2. Compact disc.

Roje, Ana. 196–. *Folk Songs and Dances of Yugoslavia.* Monitor MF 312. LP disk.

Romania, Yugoslavia, Bulgaria, Albania. 1988. JVC Video Anthology of World Music and Dance, 22. Europe, 3. Produced by Ichikawa Katsumori with the National Museum of Ethnology (Osaka) and Smithsonian Folkways Records. Notes in English, translated from Japanese. Distributed by Rounder Records. 59 min. Videocassette.

Songs and Dances of Dalmatia. 196–. Performed by the vocal ensemble Dalmacija and the Ljubca Stipišić Mandoline Ensemble. Music of Many Lands. Request Records SRLP 8132. LP disk.

Yugoslavia. 196–. Music of Many Lands. Request Records SRLP 8138. LP disk.

Serbia
Mark Forry

Serbia consists of three political and geographical zones, spread over 88,361 square kilometers: Serbia proper, with a Serbian majority; the ethnically diverse autonomous province of Vojvodina, a fertile plain to the north drained by the Danube, the Sava, and the Morava rivers; and Kosovo, a mountainous autonomous province to the south, with a majority Albanian population (map 11, p. 866).

The Serbs, who settled in the Balkans in the 600s, speak Serbo-Croatian (a Slavic language written in the Cyrillic alphabet) and profess the Serbian Orthodox faith. Their first kingdom, founded in 1168, effectively ended in defeat by the Ottoman Turks at the battle of Kosovo Polje (1389). In 1829, they gained, under Prince Miloš Obrenović (1780–1860), a measure of independence, which lasted until the end of World War II. In 1918, they joined the Kingdom of Serbs, Croats, and Slovenes, which in 1929 became Yugoslavia. From 1945 to 1991, Serbia formed one of six federal republics within Yugoslavia, a communist country, noted for its tolerance and encouragement of ethnic self-determination.

Since the breakup of Yugoslavia, in 1991, only Montenegro, with a Serbian Orthodox majority, remains with Serbia in the Yugoslav Federation [see MONTENEGRO]. Seventy percent of Serbia's 10 million people live in cities and towns, though before World War II, 70 percent lived in rural areas.

MUSICAL CONTEXTS AND GENRES

Singing accompanied activities of the rural agricultural calendar: ploughing in the spring, tending stock in the summer, mowing and harvesting in the fall, indoor women's work in the winter. These were not work songs in the sense of enforcing rhythmic unity for movement; songs accompanying such activities did not reinforce the rhythm of work, but functioned to maintain morale through humor or magical formulas for success.

Because tasks were divided into female and male spheres, the songs associated with these were sung only by men or women; songs of ploughing and mowing were sung only by men, while harvesting songs were sung almost exclusively by women. Activities that required the greatest number of participants have yielded the most songs; thus, the repertoires associated with harvest, tending sheep, and indoor working bees are the richest.

The annual ritual cycle included religious holidays from the calendar of the Serbian Orthodox Church and seasonal festivities of pre-Christian origin, often syncretized with church celebrations. Important ritual occasions were *koleda* (caroling at winter solstice), St. Lazarus' Day, St. George's Day, St. Jeremiah's Day, and *dodola* (rain begging in the summer). On St. Lazarus' Saturday, to mark the beginning of the agricultural work cycle, Lazarus' songs (*lazaričke pesme*) were sung by groups of young girls (*lazarice*). In addition to public holy days and celebrations, all Serbian Orthodox families celebrate *slava,* the patron saint's day of an individual, a family, or a village church, with songs to accompany ritual customs like the preparation of foods specific to the *slava,* and songs to entertain guests for pleasure and merriment.

The most important life-cycle celebration, the wedding, celebrates the newlyweds' change of status and publicly confirms the relationship between their families. Until the 1960s, the cycle of rituals before and after weddings could last up to a week; even now, when the industrial work week limits the duration of most nuptial celebrations to a weekend, elements of the older ritual survive. Some songs are linked to particular ritual moments, others to meals and general celebrations. The former category included songs sung at the bride's and bridegroom's house during the days before the wedding, and songs sung during the wedding to the bride and groom, the bride's mother, and especially the witness or godfather (*kum*). Songs for nuptial merrymaking comprise one of the largest parts of rural musical repertoire.

Other life-cycle events marked by singing included birth, first haircut (for boys), and festivities held when a young man departs for military service (*ispratnica*). Previously an informal family event, *ispratnica* has become a major folkloric tradition since the 1970s, almost equal in importance to the wedding. In some areas, laments (*tužbalica, zapevanje*) were sung for the dead. Occupying a border-area between song and speech, laments were usually sung by the wife and other female relatives of the deceased, in the home after the remains were prepared and at the graveyard. Laments were also sung at set intervals after deaths and at observances of All Souls' Day.

Singing occurred at informal gatherings of family and friends, and it was in such gatherings that epic singing, an important musical form, was practiced. Epics (*junačke pesme* 'heroic songs'), were sung mostly by men until about the 1980s. Serbian epic singing is first mentioned in a historical document of 1415, and some texts mention historical figures predating the Battle of Kosovo Polje.

Serbian epic songs are almost exclusively accompanied by a *gusle* (one-stringed bowed lute); for this reason, epic singers are often called *guslari* (in some areas, *guslači*). The *gusle* has a skin resonator and decorative carving, particularly on the head. Two-string *gusle* have been reported in southeastern Serbia, but they are quite rare and are apparently not used for epic singing. The frequency of horse imagery in the decoration and the component terminology and the use of horsehair for the string and the bow suggest the *gusle*'s origin with the Central Asian nomadic riders who invaded Europe from the 200s through the 800s. *Gusle* are generally made by the men who play them, though imitation instruments are sold as souvenirs (figure 1).

Epic singers improvise melodies in performance based on the content of the text, tones in the language (Serbo-Croatian has vocalic accents of pitch and duration), the ten-syllable poetic line (*deseterac*), and conventional melodic fragments. Depending on the occasion and the singer's skill, tales may be spun out in epic formulas similar to those found in the poetry of Homer (Lord 1960). Singers usually play on the *gusle* the same pitches they sing, but they may add embellishments on sustained vocal notes; singers usually provide instrumental introductions to epics and interject instrumental interludes to set off narrative sections and rest their voices (figure 2).

FIGURE 1 At Zonska Smotra Folklora, a regional folklore gathering in Sivac, Vojvodina, an epic ballad singer (*guslar*) from Vrbas sings and plays a *gusle,* a one-stringed bowed lute with a skin resonator and decorative carvings. Photo by Mark Forry, 1983.

FIGURE 2 The melody and accompaniment of the epic ballad "*Vino piju dva dobra junaka*" ('Two fine heroes drank wine'), as sung and played about 1980 by Dušan Dobričanin, of Rača, Kuršumlija, south Serbia. Transcription by Mark Forry.

Many village families boast at least one accomplished *guslar,* but professional *guslari* are played at public houses and fairs. These were often marginalized individuals: blind, physically handicapped, indigent, or members of low-status ethnic groups, like Muslims and Albanians. In the early 1900s, schools for the blind included instruction for *guslari,* and Vuk Karadžić, an informant for nineteenth-century folklorists and linguists, studied at such a school in Vojvodina.

CONCEPTS OF MUSICAL STRUCTURE

Most Serbian rural singers employ the concept of voice (*glas*) for the melodic aspect of their songs, and they identify the textual content simply as words (*reči*). *Glas,* known as *kajda* 'note' in some areas, may best be described as a melodic type with four attributes: social occasion, musical form, textual content, and ethnic or geographic designation. A song to accompany harvesting will be sung in harvest voice (*žetvarski glas*). A given singer will sing all harvest texts to a somewhat fixed melody, similar to the melodies used by other singers in the area for their harvest songs.

In addition to classification by social context, singers distinguish voices with respect to musical form: *kratki glas* 'short voice' denotes songs with syllabic textual settings, while songs in *dugački glas* 'long voice' include melismatic sections. Specification of a melodic type may be further refined by referring to textual features; for example, *glas na oj ubava* denotes a song with the refrain *o ubava* 'Oh, you pretty one'. Finally, singers can identify a *glas* as a melodic trait of a certain area, or even a certain village. By subtle variations in singing, rural Serbs can identify closer or more distant neighbors.

If sung by more than one person, songs are frequently in unison, but two-part singing of *na glas* is practiced by Serbs everywhere except in southwestern Serbia and Kosovo. The western style has melodic movement in the second voice, which sounds a second with the first voice, particularly at cadences (figure 3). The eastern style is common primarily in southeastern Serbia near the Macedonian and Bulgarian borders, where the interval of a second also predominates, but is formed as the lead voice moves against an accompanying vocal drone (figure 4). The manner of singing is intense, energetic, and full-voiced for men and women, who sing in separate groups. A solo singer begins and is joined by a group on the second part.

Serbian singers believe singing *na glas* is their oldest and most characteristic polyphonic form, but they identify another style as newer: *na bas* 'on a bass', also called *basiranje* 'bassing' or *na ariju* 'on a melody', now the most common vocal style among rural Serbs. In this style, the *bas* forms intervals in parallel thirds with the

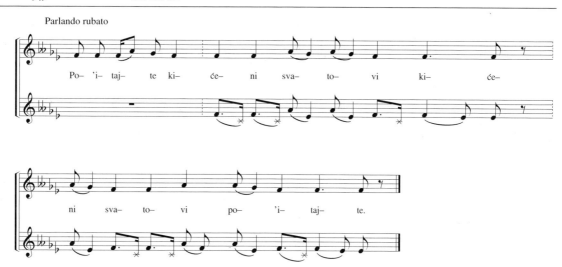

FIGURE 3   The wedding song "Po'itajte kićeni svatovi," as sung *na glas* in 1985 by women from Ribaševina, Užice, eastern Serbia, where the second voice moves and cadences are on a second. Transcription by Mark Forry.

melody, and forms a perfect fifth at the cadence (figure 5). Singing *na bas* probably began in Slavonia and Vojvodina, areas under Austrian control in the 1800s and hence with greater access to high culture. From there, it spread south into Serbia and Bosnia, reaching some isolated areas as late as the 1960s. It is increasingly common for men and women to sing *na bas* together, but many aspects of such singing have carried over into the performance of *na bas,* like the focused singing style and the solo-chorus structure.

RELIGIOUS SINGING

Since 1219, when St. Sava declared the independence of the Serbian church, the Hilandar Monastery on Mount Athos in Greece has been the source of Serbian liturgical practice. Its monks were familiar with Byzantine musical practices of other monasteries on Mount Athos (particularly Greek and Russian), but the Serbian monks who taught singing fostered and notated a distinctive style and carried it to Serbian communities abroad, where Hilandar manuscripts continue to be important in Serbian liturgical music practice.

In the mid-1800s, the composer Kornelije Stanković (1831–1865) notated and codified what had previously been the exclusively oral repertoire of the chant form known as Karlovo singing (*Karlovačko pojanje*). Using this form and other sources, he created the first polyphonic settings of Serbian chant. His work was disseminated through singing societies, and composers and arrangers based their work on his models. Even among contemporary village singers, many recognized singers of newer-style rural songs are skilled in liturgical chant.

INSTRUMENTAL MUSIC

During the twentieth century, most Serbs have moved away from a traditional rural economy toward a modern, cash-based market economy. This trend is manifest in

FIGURE 4   The grape-harvesting song "Pratila majka devojče u lojze" ('A mother sent a maiden to the vineyard'), as sung *na glas* in 1978 by women of Gornja Studena, Niš, southeastern Serbia, where a drone in the second voice is typical. The short vertical line is a glottal ornament. Transcription by Mark Forry.

While *gajde* (bagpipes) were indispensable for major events, *gajde* playing and making are declining in Serbia, the instrument having largely been supplanted by accordions and other ensembles.

FIGURE 5 The young rakes' song "*Sa planine vetar duva*," as sung *na bas* in 1978 by men of Korman, Kragujevac, central Serbia. Transcription by Mark Forry.

the popularity of factory-produced instruments, the production of indigenous instruments by specialized craftsmen, and a reduction in active rural instruments, as local variation gives way to standard instrumental practices. Nevertheless, specific regional styles have survived.

The most common rural Serbian instruments are duct flutes, most often known as *svirale* (sing. *svirala*). Based on the old Slavic root *vir-* 'breath', the term *svirala* is cognate with the verb *svirati* 'to play a musical instrument' and the noun *svirač* 'musician'. While *svirale* of various sizes and constructions have various names throughout Serbian lands, the *frula* (pl. *frule*) as currently made and played in Šumadija is the most famous. Its repertoire consists principally of songs, solo improvisations, dialogues among *frulaši* (*frula* players), and dance melodies. Today, *frule* are often used to add a so-called village scent in contemporary ensembles, and so are increasingly manufactured in standard keys with tempered intonation.

The most common multivoiced instruments are double fipple flutes (*dvojnice*). Cut and drilled from a single block of wood with two interior pipes, they usually have three holes for one pipe and four for the other, and are played to imitate the leading and accompanying roles of rural singing. The flutes may be constructed to produce *na glas* or *na bas* sonorities, though the range does not permit a final fifth on the cadence. As with *frule*, the repertoire for of *dvojnice* consists mainly of songs and dance melodies.

Serbian bagpipes, of various types, are usually called *gajde* (from the Old Gothic *gait* 'goat', as most *gajde* are made from goatskins). The reeds are idioglot (single-clarinet type); in addition to a drone pipe, there is a single or double chanter. The latter has two channels, drilled in a single piece of wood, one a melody pipe with a range of six to eight notes, the other an accompaniment pipe playing two notes, the tonic and a fourth below. The *gajde* is usually a solo instrument, though players sometimes perform with a drum (*tapan* in southern or eastern Serbia), or a violin (eastern Serbia).

Four types of bagpipes are found. In northeastern Serbia, Serbs and Vlahs (Romance-language-speaking pastoral nomads) play a small, two-voiced *gajde* similar to Bulgarian bagpipes; a notable feature in this style is a chirping, executed with the player's thumb, providing a rhythmic ostinato for accompanying dances (figure 6). The larger, two-voiced *gajde* of southern Serbia and Kosovo resembles Macedonian bagpipes and shares its more legato style of playing. The three-voiced *gajde* of south-

eastern Serbia (sometimes called *svrljiške gajde,* after the Svrljig area, where it is commonly found) also employs the chirping technique, but here it is performed on the accompanimental pipe to provide a one-note ostinato. The large, three-voice *gajde* of Vojvodina (often called *banatske gajde,* after the Banat area, where they were crafted) uses the accompanimental pipe, rhythmically and tonally. The Banat *gajde* are inflated with a small bellows strapped to the player's arm, which allows him to sing while he plays (figure 7). While *gajde* were indispensable for major events, *gajde* playing and making are declining in Serbia, the instrument having largely been supplanted by accordions and other ensembles.

Excepting *gusle,* stringed instruments are more recent additions to the Serbian rural instrumentarium. The violin, a popular rural instrument, is almost exclusively in the hands of Gypsy musicians, though many villages have a few Slav peasants (or Vlahs in eastern Serbia) who play it.

Some Serbian medieval frescoes depict lutes of various types, but these were probably court instruments, and like plucked lutes in use today, were probably of foreign origin. Nonetheless, *tambura* (long-necked plucked lute) ensembles (also known as *tamburica*) have come to be emblematic of traditional music in Vojvodina, where they are found among several ethnic groups, notably Croatians, Roma (Gypsies), Hungarians, and Serbs. Long-necked plucked lutes were brought into the Balkans in the years after the Turkish invasion of the 1300s. The first known orchestra was founded by Slavonian town dwellers in 1849 [see CROATIA].

FIGURE 7 A musician from Kovilj plays the large, three-voice, bellows-blown *gajde* of Vojvodina, using an accompanying pipe rhythmically and tonally. Photo by Mark Forry, 1985.

FIGURE 8   A Serbian brass band, featuring
flügelhorns and euphoniums, marches in a
folk-festival parade in Petrovac, northeastern
Serbia. Photo by Mark Forry, 1990.

Rural brass bands, popular in Čačak and Užice (western Serbia), Vranje and
Leskovac (southern Serbia), and Boljevac (eastern Serbia), have developed distinctively. Their origins are obscure, though they probably date from the period after World
War I. Known as *bleh-orkestri* or *bleh-muzika* (German *blechmusik* 'brass-band
music'), contemporary ensembles from these areas number five to ten players, usually
consisting of three flügelhorns, three or four euphoniums, one tuba, and one percus-
sionist playing a bass drum with a cymbal mounted on top (figure 8). In eastern
Serbia, such bands are found among the Vlah minority, though their ensembles usually include only a clarinet, a trumpet, and a drum. Brass-band repertoire is a diverse
mixture of rural songs and dance music, popular urban songs from the repertoire of
old city songs, military marches and Serbian patriotic songs, and novelty pieces. This
resembles other popular instrumental ensembles (such as accordion and *tamburica*
orchestras), except that Serbian patriotic music is held to be particularly appropriate.
Since 1970, brass bands have enjoyed a surge in popularity, doubtless aided by the
prominence of Zlatna Truba (Golden Horn), a festival in western Serbia. With the
sponsorship of a major Serbian periodical and coverage in the broadcast media, the
festival has grown from a small local event to an enormous national one, drawing
crowds of more than fifty thousand people to a remote rural area. Award-winning
ensembles from the festival appear on television and recordings, and thus become
famous throughout Serbia. The popularity of this festival and the media attention it
has received may account for brass-band music having become a musical emblem for
Serbia.

The most popular contemporary instrument among Serbs is the accordion.
Some of its forms were known to Austrian Serbs in Vojvodina and Slavonia before
1914, but only after World War II were accordions introduced massively into Serbia
proper. This influx may have resulted from Russian influence, especially through the
adoption of Soviet models of cultural organization. The rapid spread of accordions
throughout Serbia is probably explained by their versatility in playing new-style
melodies and their ability to play loudly for outdoor events (before amplification)
and replace several musicians in an ensemble, increasing each remaining musician's
pay.

The melodic style of contemporary accordion music can be traced to the instrumental idioms of *frula, gajde,* and violin ensembles. Conventional piano accordions and chromatic button accordions are equally popular, and each has distinctive capabilities; many ensembles have both instruments. Modern Serbian accordionists have attained high technical levels; virtuoso performances may be heard in the annual Prva Harmonika Srbije (First Accordion of Serbia), a competition in southern Serbia. In contemporary ensembles, accordions are frequently supplemented by electric guitars, electric bass, drums, and increasingly synthesizers.

RURAL DANCE STYLES

Within former Yugoslavia, Yugoslav dance ethnologists have identified six zones with distinctive choreological features, four partly in Serbia.

The Morava zone, including most of northern and central Serbia, comprises the lower basin of the Morava River. The dances of Vlahs in the east belong to this area. Most dances are open circles moving counterclockwise (*kolo*), in which men and women mix together. Many dances require intricate interweaving footwork (called *vez* 'embroidery' in Šumadija), and musical phrases synchronize with those of the dance.

The Dinaric zone comprises the area of the Dinaric Mountains, including parts of Croatia, Bosnia-Hercegovina, Montenegro, and Serbia. The Serbian parts include western and southwestern Serbia and northern Kosovo; Serbian settlements occur throughout Dinaric Croatia and Bosnia. One commonly encountered dance form is an open circle (*kolo*), often segregated by gender, accompanied only by the dancers' singing. The dances often cover a large area, in which they frequently make leaps.

The Vardar zone comprises the basin of the Vardar River, and thus is largely coterminous with the republic of Macedonia; however, recent research indicates that dance and instrumental forms of this zone may pertain to southern Serbia and Kosovo. Dances are mostly open circles (*oro*) with men and women dancing separately, or segregated in the same line of dancers. The men who lead the dance often make virtuosic gestures, including leaps and squats. Meters are frequently asymmetrical (7/8, 11/8, and so on), and dance phrases are frequently not synchronized with musical phrases.

The Pannonian zone includes Serbian Vojvodina and Croatian land north of the Sava River. Dances of the South Slavic groups in Vojvodina are most frequently closed circles (*kolo*) of mixed gender, dancing in compact spatial formation. Small rhythmic shakes, sometimes known as *šara* (ornament, iridescence), characterize the gestures of the dance. Other groups have closed circle dances (*csárdás* among Hungarians, *joc* among Romanians), and all groups have couple dances, though only South Slavs have dances for groups of two women and one man. Fast duple meters predominate, often without correspondence between musical phrases and dance phrases.

URBAN SOCIAL CONTEXTS AND MUSICAL STYLES

Until the late 1800s, Serbian society felt the pull of Turkish and Austrian poles of urban experience, both of which left their mark on Serbian music. Turkish influence receded as the Turkish border shifted southward; the areas of strongest Turkish influence remain southern Serbia and Kosovo. In the twentieth century, Central European musical practice gained ascendancy, and contemporary Serbian music draws on an increasingly international base.

Little is known of the musical life of Serbian cities under the Turkish regime, but the Serbian prince Miloš retained Turkish musicians at his court until 1831, when he retained Josif Šlezinger (1794–1870), charging him to make the musical life of his

After World War II state-sponsored cultural organizations sponsored festivals of traditional music and dance. The festivals are competitive, and winners at local festivals receive awards, proceed to higher levels, and appear on recordings and media broadcasts.

court in Kragujevac the equal of any other royal court in Europe. During his years at the Serbian royal court (1831–1840), Šlezinger founded and directed the first orchestras, European military bands, and choirs in Serbia, taught the musicians, and wrote original compositions and arrangements. He founded the first Serbian military band, Knjaževsko-Srpska Banda (Serbian Prince's Band) in 1831; in subsequent years, Czech bandmasters were active in Vojvodina and Serbia proper, and they continued to spread the form to the Balkans. Military music was a popular form of entertainment throughout the 1800s and well into the 1900s.

Šlezinger was one of the first composers of music for *komad s pevanjem* 'dramatic play with singing', a variant of the Central European *Singspiel*. As theatrical entertainment became increasingly popular with the Serbian middle class, particularly as a vehicle for national sentiments, *komad s pevanjem* became a leading Serbian musical form. The music was a mixture of original compositions, topical urban songs, and famous traditional songs. For many plays, the mixture of styles was so thorough that in later years it was unclear which traditional songs had predated the plays and which had been written for them. Composers for these plays include prominent Serbian musicians of the nineteenth and early twentieth centuries. Isidor Bajić (1878–1915) is particularly remembered for his compositions and arrangements.

While some songs from the plays later became identified with rural musical practice, many of them acquired an urban identification and became known to later generations as old, city songs (*starogradske pesme*). This repertoire of popular songs spread throughout Serbian middle-class society through singing-societies (*pevačka društva*). Modeled on nationalistic German organizations, the first Serbian singing societies were founded during the same period as Šlezinger's reforms. In addition to songs from the plays, the repertoire included political songs, the new four-part arrangements of liturgical music from Stanković and others, and selections from the international choral repertoire. Singing societies eventually reached all levels of Serbian society, and many are still active.

NEWLY COMPOSED FOLK MUSIC

Possibly the most popular form of music in Serbia is known among scholars as newly composed folk music (*novokomponovana narodna muzika*), hereafter NKNM, which most of its practitioners call *narodna muzika* 'folk music, national music'. Its features include musical allusions to rural musical practice; song texts mixing evocations of older, rural lifestyles with modern urban ones; instrumental settings combining rural instruments with modern, increasingly amplified ones; a commercial orientation emphasizing massive distribution through recordings and media; and a generally urban working-class audience, no more than a generation or two removed from rural life.

NKNM's rise probably dates from the confluence of three musical trends at the end of World War II: the string-orchestra arrangements of Serbian rural songs, like those of Vlastimir Pavlović-Carevac, who became the leader of the *narodna orchestra* at Radio Belgrade after 1945; the increasing popularity of the accordion, introduced through postwar Soviet influence; and the activities of composers such as Miodrag Todorović-Krnjevac (a famous accordionist), who began composing new songs on rural themes, in a musical style reminiscent of *na bas*. Early NKNM compositions were virtually indistinguishable from their models, central Serbian new-style rural melodies. Later melodies draw from Vlah arpeggiated melodies, southern Serbian melodies in Turkish-derived scales, international popular styles, and others.

Though NKNM features the accordion, most *narodnjaci* have relied on amplified instruments since the 1970s. Electric accordions, guitars, basses, and synthesizers predominate, while voices and instruments amplified through microphones are often heavily modulated with effects such as echo and reverb. The switch to amplified sound has significantly altered the relationship between audience and musician. Before amplification, musicians might be summoned from the bandstand to play at the tables of free-spending patrons, who themselves would often sing. Amplified ensembles are tied to their equipment, and often it is only the singer with a long microphone cord who can approach the tables.

NKNM artists and producers are making increasing use of the technologies and production values of contemporary popular music, but there has been little reciprocal interest in folk or national themes from Serbian popular musicians. Turbo folk of the 1990s, despite its name, is a more nationalistically oriented successor to NKNM. Notable exceptions are Smak (The End), a rock group active in the 1970s and early 1980s, which used rural musical themes; Rokeri s Moravu (Rockers from the Morava [River]), a comedy group, which combined parodies of NKNM with rock; and Đorđe Balašević, a singer-songwriter who uses musical and textual themes from his native Vojvodina. Contemporary urban and rural musical occasions feature various musical compositions and styles: old-city songs, older rural songs in contemporary instrumental settings, NKNM songs, patriotic songs, contemporary South Slavic songs in pop or rock style (*zabavna muzika*), and popular international music, mostly American.

TRADITIONAL MUSIC IN THE MODERN WORLD

In the years immediately after World War II, as villagers flocked to the cities, Yugoslavs became more acutely aware of the diversity of their rural cultures. Since the war was largely conducted in rural areas within the framework of rural society, traditional values were celebrated as the foundation for the success of the war effort. But since increasing contact with the outside world made villagers aware of their material poverty and limited social opportunities, traditional values came to be viewed as impediments to an improved quality of life.

This issue was addressed by state-sponsored cultural organizations, cooperating with academic institutions and the media, which sponsored festivals of traditional music and dance. Professional ethnologists helped identify stylistically representative regional performers, who went to regional festivals and later national and international festivals. The Sabor Narodnog Stvaralaštva (Gathering of National Creation) and BEMUS (Belgrade Music Festival) are among the most important Serbian festivals. Until the breakup of Yugoslavia, Serbian groups regularly participated in the Smotra Folkora (Folklore Gathering) in Zagreb and other Croatian festivals.

The festivals are competitive, and winners at local festivals receive awards, proceed to higher levels, and appear on recordings and media broadcasts. Certain winning characteristics are selected and reinforced by juries of professional ethnographers—a process with profound effects on traditional performers. Older genres and instruments are preferred, thus limiting innovation, and only a cross section of musical activity is deemed stageworthy, thus encouraging the abandonment of other material. So-called original ensembles (mostly older people performing local material) are distinguished from folklore ensembles (rural and urban youths, performing folklore from all parts of the country). This distinction has separated young people from the source of music and dances they perform, and assumes and encourages a rupture in cultural transmission.

Amateur performing groups are ubiquitous in Serbia; in addition to folk festivals, they perform at events ranging from political rallies to trade shows. Stylized images of rural expressive culture are thus widely available and serve in public communication to convey a sense of traditional continuity and idyllic rural life. As an organized activity for adolescents, young people pass through folklore performance organizations; some become members of professional ensembles or cultural institutions, but most retain a positive association of youth and folklore.

Perhaps because of the proximity of the national capital (Belgrade), the musical practice of north-central Serbia (particularly the Šumadija woodlands) has come to be emblematic of Serbian traditional music as a whole, despite the distinctive traditions of western, southern, and eastern Serbia. The singing known as *na bas* arrived here first, and the Šumadija vocal style and repertoire became the model for Serbian NKNM composers and singers. Likewise, the central Serbian round dance in six steps (*kolo u šest,* often called simply *kolo*) has effectively become the Serbian national dance among Serbs everywhere.

ETHNIC MINORITIES IN SERBIA PROPER

Vlachs and Roma are the most important musical minorities in Serbia proper.

Vlachs

Vlah (from Wallachia, southern Romania) is a term for nomadic pastoral groups that once roamed the Balkans; the Vlahs of eastern Serbia are a largely sedentary Slavic group who adopted a Romance language and cultural elements during their sojourn in Transylvania and the western Carpathians several hundred years ago. Vlah ritual music, especially for funerals and magic, has retained old Balkan cultural features. Among contemporary Vlah practices that have Carpathian counterparts is wordless singing; as in dialogue songs from the Oltenian region of Romania, Vlah girls sometimes omit words from love songs to hide their feelings from relatives.

To while away time spent tending animals, Vlahs played instruments, usually flutes. A larger *svirala,* known as *duduk,* was most common; these instruments are frequently played in eight-player ensembles, which sometimes include a cylindrical drum (*bubanj*). In ensemble playing, melodies usually sound in unison, though more modern arrangements, perhaps influenced by radio and television broadcasts, include homophonic accompanimental lines. In some areas, this ensemble has been replaced by brass bands.

Other Vlah traditional instruments include the *dudurejš,* a pair of stopped tubes, used by women for magical charms and ritual pieces; the *rikalo* (also known as *bušen*), a bark trumpet more than three meters long, played by men for St. George's Day festivities; and bagpipes (*gajde, karabe*).

Roma

One of the few remaining nomadic Rom professions is entertainment with animals, usually bears; its practitioners exhort the animals to "dance" by singing to the accompaniment of a frame drum or another percussive instrument. There was formerly a special bear-trainers' repertoire, but contemporary trainers usually sing NKNM songs. Violin ensembles (with bass and, increasingly, accordion) in Serbia are almost exclusively the province of Gypsy musicians. The ensemble came into Serbia proper from the north, but in north-central Serbia, it has developed a distinctive style, which bears little resemblance to that of Hungarian Gypsies.

Gypsy brass bands are found throughout Serbia. Their instrumentation is usually the same as that of Serbian ensembles, though southern bands often employ clarinets, a *tapan* (double-headed cylindrical drum), and a *tarabuka* (goblet drum). In non-Gypsy communities, Gypsy brass bands and NKNM ensembles have popularized *čoček* (Turkish *kücek* 'belly-dance hip movement'), a favorite dance among southern Serbian and Macedonian Gypsies. Younger Gypsy musicians are increasingly playing modern instruments and adopting the NKNM style, and like singer Šaban Bajramović and accordionist Bata Kanda, they are achieving popularity outside Gypsy communities.

AUTONOMOUS PROVINCE OF KOSOVO

Kosovo has a majority (77 percent) Albanian population, which, from internal migration and natural population growth since the 1300s, has been increasing steadily [see ALBANIAN MUSIC]. Other groups include Serbs (13 percent), Muslimani (Slavic Moslems), Turks (4 percent), and Gypsies (2 percent), and small communities of Montenegrins and Croats. This section refers to the cultural pluralism before the NATO intervention of 1999.

Serbs

Distinctive singing styles among Kosovo Serbs include the absence of polyphony and a type of singing focused on a copper pan (*tepsija*) turned on a low wooden table. The turning produces a rhythmic rumbling, from which those close to the singer experience a vibratolike effect.

Muslimani (Muslims)

The culture of the South Slavic Muslims of Kosovo remains little studied. The musical style of rural Muslimani divides sharply by gender, particularly in remote mountainous areas. Muslimani men's music, rural and urban, was open to Turkish influence, reflected in the adoption of a number of Turkish melodic modes (*makam*) and rhythmic modes (*usul*).

As in Bosnia, Muslimani vocal music is often accompanied by a Turkish *saz* (long-necked lute), whose frets have been adapted to local style. Muslimani women's music remained insular and rather conservative, retaining features of the older rural style common to other Slavic groups of the Dinaric highlands: narrow, nontempered intervals and a small melodic range. Women sing polyphonically, though part singing is uncommon among Kosovo Serbs.

Roma (Gypsies)

Kosovo Gypsies live in close social and economic cooperation with the other Kosovo ethnic groups. Gypsies' ability to synthesize new stylistic elements and repertory into their practice is especially true in Kosovo, with the diversity of its ethnic mix.

Based on Turkish practices like *taksim* (solo improvisation based on *makam*), supplemented with a dance-based rhythmic sensibility, Gypsy musicians perform songs and dances from all of Kosovo's ethnic groups and music popular with Gypsy audiences. The latter includes modern Indian film music, Turkish film music in the *arabesk* style, and international dance hits; the Brazilian-French version of the lambada was popular in the early 1990s.

Several types of Gypsy ensemble flourish in Kosovo, each corresponding to a given audience and musical style: shawm (*zurla*) and drum (*tapan*); brass bands; the

Vojvodina Serbs categorize music by where it usually takes place: home (*dom*), street or lane (*sokak*), and café (*kafana*). They further divide musical events into small and large occasions; small occasions were normally limited to singing, but large occasions added instrumental playing and dancing.

čalgija ensemble, of clarinet, accordion, violin, and frame drum (*def*); and ensembles of various electric instruments, saxophone, and drum set. Individual Gypsy musicians often play in more than one type of ensemble, and occasionally play with non-Gypsy ensembles.

AUTONOMOUS PROVINCE OF VOJVODINA

According to the 1981 census, Vojvodina was one of the most culturally diverse areas of Europe, home to Serbs (55 percent), Hungarians (19 percent), Croats (5 percent), Slovaks (3 percent), Romanians (2 percent), Ruthenians (1 percent), Gypsies (1 percent), and others. Before World War II, the population included significant minorities of Volksdeutsche (ethnic Germans) and Ashkenazic Jews. Since World War II, Dinaric Mountain Serbs have resettled areas previously inhabited by Germans, Jews, and other war refugees; similar demographic changes have followed the Yugoslav succession wars of the 1990s.

Serbian musical culture in Vojvodina

While Serbia proper languished under Ottoman rule, Serbs in Vojvodina gradually adopted Western European cultural features from their Austrian overlords and other neighboring peoples. Vojvodina Serbs categorize music not by *glas,* but by where it usually takes place: home (*dom*), street or lane (*sokak*), and café (*kafana*). They further divide musical events into small and large occasions; small occasions were normally limited to singing, but large occasions (Sunday gatherings, holidays, weddings) added instrumental playing and dancing.

Probably the largest group of songs in the village repertoire were street songs (*sokačke pesme*) sung by young people for street corners (*rogalj*), as their gatherings were called. One type, songs with a few melodic types but many texts (*bećarci* 'songs of the young rakes'), provided opportunities for verbal and musical improvisation. *Bećarac* could be sung in a *na bas* vocal setting, or accompanied by *gajde* or *tamburica* ensemble.

Much of the song repertoire sung in the cafés came from young people's street songs, but table songs (*astalske pesme*) are still known, particularly among *gajdaši* and *tamburaši* who entertain older men. Carousing *lumpovanje* (from German *lump* 'ragamuffin, ne'er-do-well') by prosperous young men in cafés, and its adjunct, *pratnja* 'being accompanied by instrumentalists', often costing enormous sums of money, are popular throughout Serbian lands.

The musical culture of Vojvodina's Bunjevci

Bunjevci, a Roman Catholic minority related to Croatians, inhabit the north of Bačka Province, on both sides of the Hungarian border. Their musical style and repertoire are distinct from those of neighboring Croatian Roman Catholic groups. Perhaps through the length of their historical association with Hungarians (many

FIGURE 9   At the regional festival Dan Berbe Grožđe (Day of the Grape Harvest), in Vršac, Vojvodina, a *tamburica* ensemble of the Bunjevci minority from Subotica performs on stage. Multilingual signs in Romanian, Ruthenian, Serbian, and Slovakian proclaim "Festival of Folkloric Traditions of Vojvodina." (Signs in Croatian and Hungarian are not shown.) Photo by Mark Forry, 1983.

Bunjevci are still bilingual), their rural vocal style tends to be monophonic, not in the prevalent *na bas* style of surrounding Serbs and Croats.

Preference and excellence in *tambura* playing most distinguishes Bunjevci (figure 9). Much earlier than other groups, Bunjevac *tamburica* reached the height of their development in the 1940s and 1950s; the virtuoso and composer Pero Tumbas-Hajo, who taught many musicians active at that time, remains influential. Though younger Bunjevci's interest in *tamburica* seems to be declining, distinctive Bunjevac melodies are still performed frequently; perhaps best known is their *momačko kolo,* a showy young men's dance.

Gypsy musical culture in Vojvodina

Though a few nomadic Gypsies still specialize in entertainment, most famous Gypsy musicians come from sedentary communities several generations old, the most celebrated at Deronje in central Bačka, whose musicians traveled throughout Yugoslavia and other European countries; a local legend says one of the most famous Balkan Gypsy songs, "Đelem đelem" ('I wander, I wander'), is from Deronje (figure 10).

Several Gypsy styles of performance in Vojvodina survive, each corresponding to an audience and a musical style: *tamburica*; Hungarian-style ensembles [see HUNGARY]; and itinerant Gypsies, who perform bear-trainers' songs and in violin ensembles and brass bands. Unlike Gypsy musicians of Kosovo, Gypsy musicians of Vojvodina rarely cross between styles.

FIGURE 10   The melody of "*Đelem đelem*" ('I wander, I wander'), one of the most famous Balkan Gypsy songs, as performed in 1997 by Esma Redžepova, from Skopje, Macedonia. Transcription by Mark Forry.

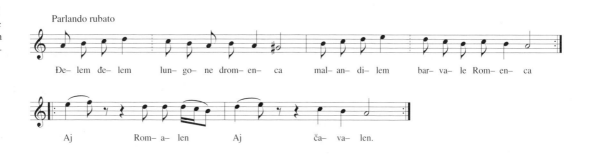

HISTORY OF SCHOLARSHIP

Vuk Stefanović Karadžić (1787–1864), generally credited as the impetus for reform of the Serbo-Croatian literary language and the development of a standardized orthography, believed that *narodna umotvorina* 'folk creation, folklore' could form the basis of an autochthonous South-Slavic civilization, and set out to collect, publish, and promote songs, proverbs, tales, and customs. His was the first scholarly work on Serbian epics, and it won the interest of Herder and other leading Romantic thinkers [see GERMANY]. Vuk's *Srpske narodne pesme* (*Serbian folk songs*, 1815) includes six melodies transcribed and arranged for the piano. Vuk's nationalism and the emerging Pan-Slavic movement inspired nineteenth-century composers to look to rural music as a source of musical inspiration: Kornelije Stanković was among the first to collect folk melodies from different regions, and collector-composers remain strongly represented in south Slavic ethnomusicology. Stevan Mokranjac (1856–1914), in addition to extensive work as a composer and conductor, may be considered the founder of Serbian ethnomusicology because his transcriptions, not published until 1966, show an attention to detail and ethnographic context that still renders them useful.

The most important Serbian ethnomusicologist after World War I was Miodrag Vasiljević (1903–1963). An active field worker and pedagogue, he collected more than fifteen hundred melodies in southern Serbia and Macedonia, insisting that rural melodies be a central part of the pedagogy of classical music. His students are the most influential Serbian scholars of their generation: Radmila Petrović has pioneered cognitive methodologies in Yugoslavia, Andrijana Gojković is famous for organological work, and Dragoslav Dević has authored numerous regional studies and theoretical papers on musical innovation.

Ethnomusicological studies in Kosovo were pioneered by Miodrag Vasiljević and continued by others (Sheholli, Vukanović, Pettan). The earliest studies in Vojvodina date from Vuk's time, but little further research was conducted until after World War II, when it was undertaken by contemporary researchers (Fracile, Mihalek, Vukosavljev, Forry).

The undisputed pioneers of dance ethnology were the sisters Ljubica (1894–1974) and Danica (1898–1960) Janković. They collected material all over Yugoslavia, with a special emphasis on Serbia and Macedonia. Their eight volumes of published work include field-methodology discussions, choreological descriptions in a system of their own invention, musical transcriptions, ethnographic notes, and photographs.

BIBLIOGRAPHY

Bartók, Béla, and Albert B. Lord. 1978. *Yugoslav Folk Music.* Edited by Benjamin Suchoff. Foreword by George Herzog. Albany: State University of New York Press.

Bezić, Jerko. 1976. "The Tonal Framework of Folk Music in Yugoslavia." In *The Folk Arts in Yugoslavia,* 193–208. Pittsburgh: Tamburitzans Institute of Folk Arts, Duquesne University.

———. 1981. "Stilovi folklorne glazbe u Jugoslaviji" (Styles of folk music in Yugoslavia). *Zvuk* 3:33–50.

Bingulac, Petar. 1968. "Uticaj radiodifuzije i gramofona na muzički folklor" (The influence of broadcasting and the record player on musical folklore). *Rad XIII-og kongresa Saveza folklorista Jugoslavije u Dojranu 1966 godine* (Proceedings of

the thirteenth congress of the Union of Folklorists of Yugoslavia in Dojran), 529–539.

Dević, Dragoslav. 1960. "Sakupljači narodnih melodija u Srbiji i njihove zbirke" (Collectors of folk melodies in Serbia and their collections). *Glasnik Etnografskog Muzeja* 22–23:99–122.

———. 1968. "Nove 'narodne' pesme—kompozicije 'Zlatne ploče'" (New 'folk' songs—compositions of 'Golden Record'). *Rad XIII-og kongresa Saveza folklorista Jugoslavije u Dojranu 1966 godine* (Proceedings of the thirteenth congress of the Union of Folklorists of Yugoslavia in Dojran in 1966), 191–214.

———. 1978. "Opšti pregled narodnih muzičkih instrumenata u Vojvodini, sa posebnim osvrtom na gajde u Srbiji" (General review of folk-musical

instruments in Vojvodina, with particular reference to the *gajde* in Serbia). *Rad XX-og kongresa Savez Folklorista Jugoslavije, Novi Sad* (Proceedings of the twentieth congress of the Union of Folklorists of Yugoslavia in Novi Sad), 173–190.

———. 1984a? *Narodna muzička tradicija: Srbija, instrumenti* (Traditional folk music: Serbia, instruments). Notes for an LP disk. Belgrade: Radio-televizija Beograd 2510030.

———. 1984b? *Narodna muzička tradicija: Srbija, instrumentalni ansambli* (Traditional folk music: Serbia, instrumental ensembles). Notes for an LP disk. Belgrade: Radio-televizija Beograd 2510049.

Đorđević, Vladimir R. 1931. *Srpske narodne melodije: Predratna Srbija* (Serbian folk songs:

Prewar Serbia). Skopje: Knjige Skopskog naučnog društva.

———. 1969. *Ogled srpske muzičke bibliografije do 1914* (Essay in Serbian musical bibliography until 1914). Belgrade: Nolit.

Đurić-Klajn, Stana. 1972 [1966]. *A survey of Serbian music through the ages.* Translated by Nada Čurčija-Prodanović. Belgrade: Savez kompozitora Srbije.

Forry, Mark. 1990. "The Mediation of 'Tradition' and 'Culture' in the *Tamburica* Music of Vojvodina (Yugoslavia)." Ph.D. dissertation, University of California, Los Angeles.

———. 1991. "'To the Café Every Night:' Tamburica Music and Café Life in Vojvodina." *Zbornik Matice Srpske za scenske umetnosti i muziku* 8–9:143–152.

Fracile, Nice. 1987. *Vokalni muzički folklor Srba i Rumuna u Vojvodini: Komparativna proučavanja* (Vocal musical folklore of Serbs and Romanians in Vojvodina: Comparative research). Novi Sad: Matica Srpska.

Gojković, Andrijana. 1983. "O muzici Roma" (On Gypsies' music). *Zvuk* 1:71–75.

———. 1989. *Narodni muzički instrumenti* (Folk-musical instruments). Belgrade: Vuk Karadžić.

Gojković, Andrijana, and Ivan Kirigin. 1962. "Tone Series of Serbian Pipes." *Ethnomusicology* 5:100–120.

Gvožđenović, Nada, ed. 1973. *Srpska muzika kroz vekova* (Serbian music through the ages). Belgrade: Savez Kompozitora Srbije.

Ilijin, Milica. 1978. "Orska tradicija naroda i narodnosti Vojvodine" (Popular Dances of the Peoples and Nationalities of Vojvodina). *Rad XX-og kongresa Savez Folklorista Jugoslavije, Novi Sad* (Proceedings of the twentieth congress of the Union of Folklorists of Yugoslavia in Novi Sad), 201–210.

Ivančan, Ivan. 1976. "Folk Dances in Various Regions of Yugoslavia." In *The Folk Arts in Yugoslavia,* 229–240. Pittsburgh: Tamburitzans Institute of Folk Arts, Duquesne University.

Janković, Ljubica C., and Danica C. Janković. 1949. *Narodne igre, I–VIII* (Folk dances, 1–8). Belgrade: Prosveta.

———. 1962. "Serbian Folk Dance Tradition in Prizren." *Ethnomusicology* 6(2):115–125.

Karadžić, Vuk Stefanović. 1965 [1814]. *Mala prostonarodnja slaveno-serbska pesnarica* (A small common man's Slavic-Serbian songbook). Belgrade: Prosveta.

Király, Ernö. 1962. *Madarske narodne pesme* (Hungarian folk songs). Novi Sad: Vojvodanski muzej.

Kolarevic, Emanuil. 1828. "Serbska narodna muzika" (Serbian folk music). *Letopis Matice srpske* 4(15):114–116.

Kos, Koraljka. 1972. "Dimensions in Folk Music: A Contribution to the Study of Musical Tastes in Contemporary Yugoslav Society." *International Review of Aesthetics and the Sociology of Music* 3(1):61–73.

Lord, Albert B. 1960. *The Singer of Tales.* Harvard Studies in Comparative Literature, 24. Cambridge: Harvard University Press.

Manojlović, Kosta. 1953. *Narodne melodije iz istočne Srbije* (Folk melodies from eastern Serbia). Belgrade: Prosveta.

Matović, Ana. 1978. "Melografski rad in Vojvodina" (A survey of melographic work in Vojvodina). *Rad XX-og kongresa Savez Folklorista Jugoslavije, Novi Sad* (Proceedings of the twentieth congress of the Union of Folklorists of Yugoslavia in Novi Sad), 191–200.

Međedović, Avdo. 1974. *The Wedding of Smailagić Meho.* Translated with introduction, notes, and commentary by Albert B. Lord. Translation of conversations concerning the singer's life and times by David E. Bynum. Publications of the Milman Parry Collection: Texts and Translations, Series, 1. Cambridge: Harvard University Press.

Milošević, Predrag. 1971. "Music Broadcast on Yugoslav Radio Stations in Figures and Percentages." *International Journal of Aesthetics and the Sociology of Music* 2(2):291–293.

Mladenović, Olivera. 1973. *Kolo u južnih Slovena* (The *kolo* dance of the South Slavs). Belgrade: Etnografski institut, Srpska akademija nauka i umetnosti.

Mokranjac, Stevan Stojanović. 1966. *Zapisi narodnih melodija* (Notations of folk melodies). Edited by Stana Đurić-Klajn. Belgrade: Naučno delo.

Nikolić, Rade. 1979. *Stih i zvuk: starogradske pesme na stihove naših pesenika* (Verse and sound: Old city songs in the verses of our poets). Knjaževac: IO Nota.

Parry, Milman, comp. 1953. *Serbocroatian Heroic Songs.* Edited and translated by Albert Bates Lord. Cambridge: Harvard University Press. Belgrade: Serbian Academy of Sciences.

Pejović, Roksanda. 1984. *Predstave muzičkih instrumenata u srednjovekovnoj Srbiji* (The representation of musical instruments in medieval Serbia). Belgrade: Srpska akademija nauka i umetnosti.

Pešić, Ljiljana. 1974. "Narodni muzički instrumenti na Kosovu i Metohiji" (Folk-musical instruments in Kosovo-Metohija). *Rad XIV-og kongresa Savez Folklorista Jugoslavije u Prizrenu* (Proceedings of the fourteenth congress of the Union of Folklorists of Yugoslavia, in Prizren), 87–99.

Petrović, Radmila. 1963. "Two Styles of Vocal Music in the Zlatibor Region of West Serbia." *Journal of the International Folk Music Council* 15:45–48.

———. 1968. "The Concept of Yugoslav Folk Music in the Twentieth Century." *Journal of the International Folk Music Council* 20:22–25.

———. 1970. "Some Aspects of Formal Expression in Serbian Folk Songs." *Yearbook of the International Folk Music Council* 63–70.

———. 1972. "Dvoglas u muzičkoj tradiciji Srbije" (Diaphony in the musical tradition of Serbia). *Rad XVII-og kongresa Savez Folklorista Jugoslavije—Poreč* (Proceedings of the seventeenth congress of the Union of Folklorists of Yugoslavia, in Poreč), 333–337.

———. 1974. "Folk Music of Eastern Yugoslavia: A Process of Acculturation." *International Review of the Aesthetics and Sociology of Music* 5(1):217–224.

———. 1976. "Folk Music in Yugoslavia." In *The Folk Arts in Yugoslavia,* 183–192. Pittsburgh: Tamburitzans Institute of Folk Arts, Duquesne University.

———. 1981. *Srpska narodna muzika* (Serbian folk music). Notes for an LP disk. Belgrade: Radio-televizija Beograd 2510057. Produced in cooperation with Srpska akademija nauka i umetnosti, Belgrade.

———. 1989. *Srpska narodna muzika: pesma kao izraz narodnog muzičkog mišljenja* (Serbian folk music: Song as an expression of musical thought). Belgrade: Srpska akademija nauka i imetnosti.

Pettan, Svanibor. 1992a. "Gypsy Music in Kosovo: Interaction and Creativity." Ph.D. dissertation, University of Maryland, Baltimore County.

———. 1992b. "'Lambada' in Kosovo: A Case Study in Gypsy Creativity." *Journal of the Gypsy Lore Society* 5(2):117–130.

Rihtman, Cvjetko. 1976. "Yugoslav Folk Music Instruments." In *The Folk Arts in Yugoslavia,* 209–228. Pittsburgh: Tamburitzans Institute of Folk Arts, Duquesne University.

Simić, Andrei. 1969. "Management of the Male Image in Yugoslavia." *Anthropological Quarterly* 42(2):89–101.

———. 1976. "Country 'n' Western Yugoslav Style: Contemporary Folk Music as a Mirror of Popular Culture." *Journal of Popular Culture* 10(1):156–166.

———. 1978–1979. "Commercial Folk Music in Yugoslavia: Idealization and Reality." *Journal of the Association of Graduate Dance Ethnology* 2:25–37.

Vasiljević, Miodrag. 1950. *Jugoslavenski muzicki folklor I: Narodne melodije koje se pevaju na Kosmetu* (Yugoslav musical folklore 1: Folk melodies sung in Kosmet). Belgrade: Prosveta.

———. 1952. "Les bases tonales de la musique populaire Serbe." *Journal of the International Folk Music Council* 4:19–23.

———. 1960. *Narodne Melodje Leskovačkog kraja* (Folk melodies from the Leskovac area). Belgrade: Naučno delo.

Vidić-Rasmussen, Ljerka. 1991. "Gypsy Music in Yugoslavia: Inside the Popular Culture Tradition." *Journal of the Gypsy Lore Society* 2:127–139.

Vlahović, Petar, ed. 1980. *Narodne pesme i igre u okolini Bujanovca* (Folk songs and dances in the Bujanovac area). Field material prepared by Olivera Vasić and Dimitrije Golemović. Summary in German. Belgrade: Etnografski Institut, Srpske akademije nauka i umetnosti.

Vujičić, Tihomir. 1978. *Muzičke tradicije južnih slovena u Mađarskoj* (Musical traditions of South Slavs in Hungary). Budapest: Tankönyvkiadó.

Vukanović, Tatomir P. 1956. "Pevanje narodnih pesama uz okretanje tepsije" (Singing folk songs while spinning a copper tray). *Glasnik Muzeja Kosova i Metohije* 1:117–163.

———. 1962. "Musical Culture Among the Gypsies in Yugoslavia." *Journal of the Gypsy Lore Society* 41(1–2):41–61.

Žganec, Vinko. 1958. "The Tonal and Modal Structure of Yugoslav Folk Music." *Journal of the International Folk Music Council* 110:18–21.

AUDIOVISUAL RESOURCES

Boulton, Laura. 1952. *Songs and Dances of Yugoslavia.* Folkways FW 6805. LP disk.

Dejanović, Jelena and Aleksandar, et al. 1970? *Pesme i igre iz Srbije—Songs and Dances of Serbia* [Vojvodina]. Request SRLP 8130. LP disk.

Golden Horns: Brass Band Music of Serbia. 1975. Olympic 6133. Reissue of RTB LP 1338. LP disk.

Gyurok, György. 1978. *Járd a kolót! Magyarországi Désláv Népzene—Igraj kolo—*

Dance the Kolo: Southern-Folk Music from Hungary. Hungaroton SLPX 18036. LP disk.

Liebman, Robert Henry. 1973. *Traditional Songs and Dances from the Soko Banja Area.* Balkan Heritage Series, 1. Festival Records: Selo Records LP-1. LP disk.

Musiques de Yugoslavie. 1990? Musique du Monde series. Buda 92490–2. Compact disc.

Roje, Ana. 1960? *Folk Songs and Dances of Yugoslavia.* Monitor MF 312. LP disk.

Vujicsics Ensemble. 1988. *Vujicsics: Serbian Music from Southern Hungary.* Hannibal HNBL 1310. LP disk.

Vuylsteke, Herman C. 1980. *Yougoslavie 1 (Serbie orientale): Les Bougies du Paradis.* Ocora 558548. LP disk.

———. 1991. *Serbie—Danses et melodies pastorales: Musiques traditionelles de la Serbie orientale.* Auvidis Ethnic B 6759. Compact disc.

Montenegro
Ankica Petrović

Rural Folk Music
Urban Folk Music
Folk-Musical Instruments
Religious Music
New Developments in Folk Music
Scholarship

Montenegro, the smallest republic of the former Yugoslavia, is a rocky, mountainous country of 13,812 square kilometers in the central Dinaric geographic and cultural region of the western Balkans. Since 1991 and 1992, when the six republics of the former Yugoslav federation split up, it remains one of two republics in present-day Yugoslavia. It has about six hundred thousand inhabitants, who still work primarily in agriculture, without a developed industrial base.

Most Montenegrins are Eastern Orthodox South Slavs who speak Serbo-Croatian and use the Cyrillic alphabet, as do the Serbs. Roman Catholic Croatians live in the Adriatic coastal region of Boka Kotorska Bay, and an Albanian minority of Muslims and Roman Catholics live in the eastern and southeastern regions of the republic. Other Montenegrins are Muslims, Serbo-Croatian-speaking ethnic Slavs, whose ancestors during the period of Ottoman Turkish governance (1514–1912) forged a synthesis of South Slavic and Islamic cultures, as did the Muslims of Bosnia and Hercegovina.

Montenegro's geographic, ethnic, and historical diversity can be classified into four basic musical regions: central and mountainous Montenegro, known as Old Montenegro and Hills; Sandžak, in the north and northeast, inhabited predominantly by Muslims of Slavic origin; the coastal region, which spreads from Boka Kotorska Bay south to the cities of Bar and Ulcinj; and the Plav-Gusinj and Malesia region, on the eastern border with Albania, populated only by Muslim and Roman Catholic Albanians.

RURAL FOLK MUSIC

The performance of rural folk music differs by region and ethnicity, though some common elements can be identified. Vocal forms predominate throughout the central regions of Montenegro, sharing stylistic elements with the folk songs of rural dwellers of nearby Dinaric Mountain territories in Bosnia and Hercegovina, Serbia, Croatia, and the nearby region where the Malisori, a subgroup of northern Albanian Gegs, live. These features include a narrow melodic range (of a diatonic trichord, tetrachord, or pentachord), using stepwise minor or major seconds, usually smaller than tempered intervals. Some older epic songs accompanied by the *gusle,* a bowed

Male vocalists accompany themselves with the *gusle* when performing heroic songs. In central Montenegro, the cultural importance of the *gusle* is shown by the presence of the instrument in every household. A person widely recognized as a good *gusle* player enjoys a high reputation in Montenegrin society.

one-stringed chordophone, base their melodic movement on a narrow-range chromatic tone row. Simple poetic-rhythmic forms are created on eight- or ten-syllable single lines or two-line couplets.

Montenegrin rural folk songs are usually slow. Only those that accompany dances (*poskočice*) may have faster tempos, also in 2/4 time. *Poskočice* are usually sung responsorially by a solo voice and group. Unlike the polyphony common to central regions of the Dinaric Alps, including music of the Malisori, monophonic texture dominates, but two-voiced singing with the characteristic interval of a major second occurs in shepherds' and wedding songs of the southwest region of Montenegro, on the border with Hercegovina, where the major second is treated as a consonance.

The older stratum of the rural folk-music tradition includes the male vocal genre *izvika* 'called out' or *izglasa* 'out loud', which employs a tense vocal technique, a sustained cadence that may include melismatic formulas, a narrow range, and narrowed, nontempered intervals approximating minor and major seconds. This genre resembles the eastern Hercegovina male wedding song (*svatovska pjesma*) and songs in the Turkish manner (*turčije*), and shares some features with the Malisori male music called *maje krahi* 'from the ear'. Shepherd songs (*čobanske pjesme*), usually lyrical, are performed by youngsters in the fields. Dance songs, rather than instrumental music, accompany *kolo* and *oro* dances, and constitute another genre.

In all ethnic and religious communities of rural Montenegro, wedding songs (*svadbene pjesme*) are the most persistent folk songs. They exist in various forms and accompany each phase of the wedding ceremony, including the gathering of the wedding guests in the bride's home, the arrival of the wedding party at the bride's home, the bride's farewell to her parents and her home, and the bringing of the bride to her new home and family. Other kinds of ritual songs—including Christmas carols (*koledarske pjesme*); St. Lazarus' Day songs (*lazaričke pjesme*); swinging songs, performed on St. George's Day (*culjke*); and rain-invocation songs (*prporuše*)—disappeared from folk-musical practice immediately after World War II.

The most characteristic Montenegrin vocal forms are narrative heroic songs (*junačke pjesme*), performed by men, and the lyrical lament (*tužbalica*), performed by women. Female lamenting, still passionately practiced by professional and nonprofessional mourners, is an everyday scene in rural and urban cemeteries. There is also a form of men's lamenting, in which single men or a male group announces a death over a large distance; Slavic Montenegrins call it *lelekanje,* referring to the repeated mourning exclamation *lele*. The Malisori call it *thirrje vaji* 'provocation of cry'. *Lelekanje* and *thirrje vaji* are closer to declamations than to songs or laments, yet they have pronounced rhythmic and melodic components, something like those of religious cantillations.

Musical patterns, subordinated to the poetic content of the texts, consist of a melorhythmic formula with a fixed tonal content and syllabic textual treatment. Singers express their individuality by following traditional rules for musical improvisation and variation. Male vocalists accompany themselves with the *gusle* when performing heroic songs. In central Montenegro, the cultural importance of the *gusle* is shown by the presence of the instrument in every household. A person widely recognized as a good *gusle* player (*guslar*) enjoys a high reputation in Montenegrin society. Epic songs, old and new, have been idealized as expressions of Montenegrin national pride. After World War II, the performance of epic songs extended beyond private gatherings in homes to concert stages, radio and TV programs, and festivals. The Montenegrin manner of singing epics and playing *gusle* became the most appreciated style among *guslari* elsewhere in the former Yugoslavia. In the 1990s, *guslarske junačke pjesme* served for expressing and strengthening Serbian nationalism, extended to Montenegro. The same genre of Albanian music and epic poetry, with different interpretations of history within the songs, did not receive the same recognition, and is beginning to disappear.

URBAN FOLK MUSIC

Because of ethnic and religious heterogeneity of the populations and the legacy of past cultural influences, various musical styles exist in urban areas. In Boka Kotorska Bay, most urban and suburban musical forms have Italian-influenced Mediterranean traits, but some older ritual forms such as wedding songs maintain ties with the musical practice of the interior continental region of Montenegro. Mediterranean influence is the most evident in the unaccompanied singing of *klapa*, songs in a two- and three-part choral style, typical of the Dalmatian coastal region [see CROATIA]. In settlements in Boka Kotorska Bay sometime around the 1880s, these songs came to be accompanied by *tamburica* orchestras [see CROATIA, SERBIA], formed by local or national cultural-artistic ensembles (*kulturno-umetnička društva*).

The urban areas of Sandžak, the region bordering Montenegro and Serbia, were subject to Ottoman Turkish rule until 1912, and therefore preserved Muslim urban traditions. As in Bosnia, lyrical songs incorporated Turkish musical elements, such as a wide tonal range, changing and asymmetrical (*aksak*) meters, distinctive melodic formulas, and augmented seconds. Unlike the Bosnian *sevdalinka* 'love song', however, urban lyrical folk songs from Sandžak do not use lengthy melismas (figure 1).

Urban folk songs from Podgorica (formerly Titograd) performed by the Muslim and Christian urban populations of central Montenegro represent a synthesis of Sandžak songs and coastal songs. Originally performed in unison or solo, in the 1930s they became accompanied by instrumental ensembles of accordion, clarinet, guitar and bass guitar, and were also arranged for singing in small groups.

TRACK 36   Albanians from the southeastern coast around Ulcinj perform an urban folk-song type that represents a fusion of Albanian, Mediterranean, Turkish, and Arabic elements. With wide-ranging melodies and asymmetrical meters, songs of this type are performed mainly by male groups singing in harmony and accompanied by accordion, guitar, and *darabuka*, a goblet-shaped drum. Traditional solo lyric and group weddings songs belong exclusively to the female repertory.

FOLK-MUSICAL INSTRUMENTS

The *gusle* is traditionally played by Slavic Montenegrins and Malisori, who call this instrument *lehut* and *gude*. Both groups claim it for their own traditions. Malisori also accompany their epic songs with a *tambura*, a long-necked lute with four strings (figure 2). Older people of Sandžak say that, as in Bosnia, the Turkish *saz* was formerly used to accompany lyric songs.

Montenegrin aerophones include the *diple* and the Albanian *zumare,* a single-reed double pipe with five or six finger holes in each pipe. A similar instrument, a goat-skin bagpipe also called *diple,* belonged to shepherds' older heritage in Bosnia,

FIGURE 1 An urban Muslim song from the Sandžak region. Each ten-syllable line of text is set to a short melody, which varies with each repetition. The meter changes with each measure, and the singing, though not melismatic, is highly ornamented. Transcription by Ankica Petrović.

FIGURE 1 An urban Muslim song from the Sandžak region. Each ten-syllable line of text is set to a short melody, which varies with each repetition. The meter changes with each measure, and the singing, though not melismatic, is highly ornamented. Transcription by Ankica Petrović.

Hercegovina, and Croatia. Until the 1950s, Montenegrin shepherds played the *duduk*, a rim-blown flute about 20 centimeters long, and the *dvojnice*, a duct flute with two pipes, each with three or four finger holes. Literary sources and folk songs mention a folk trumpet (*borije*) and a folk oboe (*zurne*), both of Ottoman origin and unused since about 1900. *Diple* or *zumare* and *duduk* served for the performance of shepherds' improvisations or, less commonly, the accompaniment of dances.

Some instruments of Turkish origin—*daulbas* 'double-headed drum', *zili* 'cymbals', and the *talambas* 'large kettle drum'—have fallen into disuse; however, to accompany Muslim and Albanian urban songs, the *darabuka* and the *def* (a frame drum, with or without jingles) are still used by ensembles with Western instruments, including accordion, guitar, violin, clarinet, bass guitar, and drum set.

RELIGIOUS MUSIC

Few European musical styles have taken root in Montenegro, except in Boka Kotorska Bay, which had political ties to Venice from 1420 to 1797. Roman Catholic liturgical singing, which in principle used Gregorian chant, deviated from the official model and incorporated local musical practices. The resulting style, named Glagolitic after the orthography used in Old Slavic texts of the Middle Ages, was in use in Boka Kotorska Bay until the late 1960s, when modern Croatian was introduced into Roman Catholic services. The Old Slavonic chant of Boka Kotorska parishes had common elements with the Glagolitic Mass of the Dalmatian coast, where people refused to sing in Latin and used Old Church Slavonic. This chant shared some features with local folk music and the liturgical chant of the Orthodox Church. Roman Catholic Albanians from eastern Montenegro, the Malisori, have retained the Latin liturgical tradition while incorporating some tonal relationships and melodic patterns borrowed from local rural music.

NEW DEVELOPMENTS IN FOLK MUSIC

During the twentieth century, because of the models provided by amateur folklore ensembles and Radio-Television Titograd, many folk songs, particularly urban ones, and dances have been transformed through new arrangements and choreographies. Some ritual and archaic musical forms have been lost because of modernization. *Gusle*-accompanied heroic songs are still performed, though with changes in musical and poetic content, performance contexts, the status of the *guslar*, and the presentation of the genre in electronic media. Since the 1950s, specialized *guslar* societies have organized public performances and festivals to support *guslari*, and radio and television programs have featured performances by *guslari*. The most successful *guslari* publish selections of texts from their most recent songs with contemporary themes and produce tapes and cassettes. Intensive communication between *guslari* with different local and personal styles has created hybrid forms. In performances of the newer songs, *guslari* rely more on written texts than spontaneous creation, the indispensable feature of earlier practice (Lord 1960). The newer heroic songs are shorter and more limited in poetic expression than the older songs.

Popular "newly composed folk songs," mainly from Serbia, have spread to Montenegro, but primarily for listening. Montenegrins have not created new songs in this style, probably because of the continuing predominance of the older genre of narratives.

FIGURE 2   Hamdija Šahinpašić accompanies with a *tambura* his singing of Sandžak urban songs. His repertoire is documented in Vasiljević 1967. Photo by Ankica Petrović.

SCHOLARSHIP

The study of folk music in Montenegro has not been undertaken in an organized fashion, as in the other republics of the former Yugoslavia, because of the lack of trained personnel and a specialized institution for its systematic study. Therefore, scholars from the other republics of the former Yugoslavia and from abroad, including the Czech folklorist Ludvik Kuba, the Croatian scholar Franjo Kuhač, and the Serbs Miloje Milojević, Miodrag Vasiljević, and Tihomir Đorđevic, have written most of the important studies on Montenegrin regional music.

BIBLIOGRAPHY

Bartók, Béla, and Albert Bates Lord 1951. *Serbo-Croatian Folk Songs*. New York: Columbia University Press.

Kuba, Ludvik. 1890a. *Album Černohorské—70 národnich pisni*. Prague: V. Praze Nakaldem Vlastnim.

———. 1890b. *Slovanstvo ve svých zpevech, VIII, Cernohorske*. Prague: V. Pardubieich.

Lord, Albert Bates. 1960. *The Singer of Tales*. Cambridge: Harvard University Press.

Munishi, Rexhep. 1987. *Kenget Malesorce Shqiptare*. Priština: Instituti Albanologik i Prishtines.

Petrović, Ankica. 1976. "Staroslavensko obredno pjevanje u Škaljarima u Boki Kotorskoj." *Zvuk* 1: 51–57.

———. 1986. "Narodni elementi u pjevanju latinske mise medju Malisorima u Tuzima (Crna Gora)." *Makedonski folklor* 19(37):201–211.

Vasiljević, Miodrag. 1965a. *Narodne melodije Crne Gore*. Belgrade: Naučno Delo.

———. 1965b. *Narodne melodije Crne Gore*. Belgrade: Naučno Delo.

———. 1967. *Jugoslavskie narodnie pesni iz Sandžaka, Zapisani ot narodnogo pevca Hamdii Šahinpašića*. Moscow: Izdatelstvo Muzika.

Vukičević, M. 1988. "Karakteristike diplarske svirke u staroj Crnoj Gori." *Zbornik radova XXXV Kongresa SUFJ (Rožaje, 1988)*, 370–377. Titograd: Savez udruženja folklorista Jugoslavije.

Wunsch, Walter. 1934. *Die Geigentechnik der südslawischen Guslaren*. Brno: R. M. Rohrer.

Bosnia-Hercegovina

Ankica Petrović

In the late 1990s, it is impossible to provide a well-documented presentation of the contemporary treatment of traditional music and the newest musical trends in Bosnia-Hercegovina. From April 1992 to November 1995, warfare destroyed the lives of hundreds of thousands of Bosnians. About 2 million Bosnians sought refuge outside the country's boundaries (according to a prewar census, 4,365,639 people live in Bosnia-Hercegovina). Territorial occupation by Serbians and Croatians, the expulsion of the Bosnian people, especially Muslims, from their ancestral homes, and the forceful division of the country along ethnic lines led to the violent destruction, exclusion, and denial of the cultures of "others." National and cultural pluralism in Bosnia-Hercegovina was destroyed to redefine people's identities and support new nationalistic politics. Because of the disruptions caused by the war, this article describes the musical traditions and processes in Bosnia-Hercegovina, with an area of 51,129 square kilometers, only until the early 1990s.

The population of Bosnia-Hercegovina consists of three main ethnic groups: Muslims, Serbs (Orthodox Christians), and Croats (Roman Catholics). The Muslims are Slavs whose ancestors converted to Islam at the beginning of the Ottoman period. From the government of Yugoslavia, they received official recognition as a distinct ethnic group in the 1960s on the basis of their cultural traditions and religion. Members of all three groups speak Serbo-Croatian. A small population of Sephardic Jews settled in Sarajevo in the 1500s. Until the beginning of World War II, their descendants preserved their distinct musical tradition, especially religious and secular singing in Hebrew and the Judeo-Spanish language, now known as Ladino.

FOLK MUSIC

The musical forms grouped under the name *narodna muzika* 'people's music' or 'folk music' have specific, pan-Balkan features. The shared traits result from common Balkan historical, social, and cultural processes. The rugged terrain of the Dinaric Alps has created natural boundaries to outside influences, and has contributed to a cultural conservatism that maintains unique older musical styles.

During the medieval period of the Bosnian kings (from the 900s to the 1400s) and Ottoman rule over Bosnia (1463–1878) and Hercegovina (1482–1878), *narod-*

na muzika was the predominant musical style. After 1878, with the beginning of Austro-Hungarian rule, Bosnia-Hercegovina began to follow Western European musical trends, and folk music was joined by other musical genres, especially classical and popular music; however, folk music remained the style preferred by every social class. *Narodna muzika* does not constitute a homogeneous style. It varies according to religious, ethnic, social, and class differences, can be found in archaic and changed forms, and has influenced more recent, popular music styles.

The main subdivision within *narodna muzika* is between rural and urban musical practices. Rural music constitutes the older musical layer. Urban music began during the Ottoman period, when much of the local urban population adopted elements of Turkish culture, including Islam. In the 1700s, when Christians began to settle the cities and take more significant positions in socioeconomic life, urban dwellers of all ethnicities voluntarily adopted Muslim secular musical elements and forms, though middle- and upper-class Muslims preserved and nurtured these forms most strongly.

RURAL SONGS AND SONG STYLES

The physical isolation of rural areas kept villages from adopting rapid social, cultural, or musical changes, and led them to preserve conservative attitudes toward newer musical trends and cultural changes. Vocal forms tied to rituals and daily life, which centers on animal husbandry, predominate where rituals survive in everyday life. These songs preserve remnants of archaic patriarchal rural society. Some ritual songs have been maintained outside their original performance contexts as memories of past traditions.

Wedding songs (*svatovske pjesme*) constitute the largest repertoire of ritual songs. Men and women perform these songs, but always separately. Women's wedding songs, usually performed by a group, accompany many different phases of the wedding ceremony with distinctive melodies and texts. Men's wedding songs consist of songs of salutation (*zdravice*). In eastern Hercegovina, they are performed as alternating solos, using the technique known as *potresanje* 'shaking' and *ojkanje* 'singing with an emphatic exclamatory section on the syllable *oj*', used also in performing table songs (*sofračke pjesme*), Turkish-style songs (*turčije*), and traveling (*putničke*) and caravan songs (*kiridžijske pjesme*), songs of merchants who traveled in caravans—a practice that had disappeared by the 1930s.

Other religious or pagan ritual songs included songs for masked ritual processions, such as *čarojičarske pjesme*, Bosnian Serbs mens' songs, performed throughout January, and wolf songs (*vučarske pjesme*), performed after hunting wolves in winter. Songs of Saint Lazarus (*Lazaričke pjesme*) were sung by groups of women or girls on St. Lazarus' Day, the Saturday before Palm Sunday. These songs fell out of practice in Bosnia-Hercegovina after World War II.

Other rural vocal genres include singing beside the cradle (*pjevanje uz bešiku*), laments (*tužbalice*), shepherds' songs (*čobanske pjesme*), and dance songs (*pjesme u kolu*), sung while dancing the *kolo,* a circle dance. Work songs include harvest songs (*želetačke pjesme*), wool-combing songs (*vlačiljske pjesme*), and grass-cutting songs (*kosačke pjesme*). The texts of these songs refer to the work context, but there is no relationship between the musical rhythm and the work movements, except for the dance-songs. Social situations elicit love songs and narrative women's songs of the ballad type, called long songs (*duge pjesme*). Men's epic songs are usually accompanied by the *gusle,* a one-stringed bowed fiddle, or the *tambura,* a small, long-necked lute. Older male or female singers sometimes sing comic or joking songs (*šaljive pjesme*), which could be lascivious. If performed by men, these songs were accompanied by a *gusle* and a two-stringed *tambura*, as were other men's narrative songs.

In addition to labeling songs by function, villagers recognize and differentiate certain stylistic traits, including polyphonic texture and the use of special ornamental tones, and they identify various regional and ethnic styles. They also distinguish between men's and women's styles in otherwise identical genres, for example, male (*muška*) and female (*ženska*) *ganga,* a song with new, often improvised, lyrics.

Rural melodies are based on diatonic or chromatic nontempered modes with a melodic range of a fourth or a fifth. Intervallic relations are unstable. Groups of two to five singers create a two-part (rarely three-part) polyphonic texture, in which the harmonic interval of a major second predominates. Most songs end on this interval, which singers experience as a consonance.

There are two kinds of rhythm: the rhythm of songs based on the flexible rhythm of the words (*uravan,* 'plain' singing) and those based on the stable rhythm of body movement (*podkorak* 'lined with the step'). Additive (*aksak,* Turkish for 'limping') rhythms are frequently used.

Villagers classify songs as short melodies (*kratki napjevi*) or long melodies (*dugi napjevi*), describing the relationship between text and melody. Short melodies subordinate the tune to the text, with many verses performed to one melodic pattern. Long melodies emphasize the tune over the text. In both styles, a single verse usually has eight (4 + 4 or 5 + 3) or ten (6 + 4 or 5 + 5) syllables. One musical strophe may embrace one or two lines, interpolate refrains and exclamations, and repeat verse lines and segments of lines. Singing in a loud, open-throated manner in a narrow range of the middle register is felt suitable for singing in open spaces. Certain ornamental notes are sung in a higher, falsetto register (figure 1). This style of polyphonic singing is also used for *ganga,* which use genre-specific ornaments called *sjecanje* 'cutting' or *jecanje* 'sobbing' (figure 2).

After 1920, a form of polyphonic singing called *na bas* 'on the bass', in which two voices sing in parallel thirds and cadence on a fifth, emerged. *Na bas* singing (also called *bećarac* 'bachelors' song') spread from Croatia to Bosnia-Hercegovina and western Serbia, in the process often supplanting older rural songs. Older versions of Bosnian *na bas* singing sometimes use seconds in alternation with thirds.

URBAN MUSIC

After the end of Ottoman rule (in 1878), musical forms nurtured in urban centers and smaller towns with elements adapted from Islamic culture spread throughout Bosnia-Hercegovina. In urban contexts, musical performances occurred indoors in intimate surroundings. Songs were performed by a solo singer—if a woman, unaccompanied; if a man, accompanied by the *saz,* a long-necked, plucked lute.

The texts of these songs can be categorized as narrative ballads, romances, and love songs. The earliest sources call them *turčije* 'Turkish-like songs', but since the late 1800s they have been known as *sevdalinke* 'love songs' (Turkish *sevda* 'passion'). Still among the most popular folk songs, they represent urban Muslim culture. Each employs a wide melodic range, based on *hidžaz makam,* a Turkish mode built on the tetrachord G–A♭–B–C (figure 3). Since the early twentieth century, the intervals have mostly been tempered. The player elaborates main melodic tones with melismas, expressing individual creativity. Repeating textual elements and interjecting exclamations (such as *aj!* and *aman!*) lengthen strophes. *Sevdalinke,* typically with a restrained emotional expressiveness, are performed quietly, especially by women, and have a more relaxed vocal production than rural songs.

Urban singing is monophonic. In *saz*-accompanied singing, musicians play the melody on the upper string, and the other strings provide rhythmic and drone accompaniment (figure 4). At the beginning of the twentieth century, the accordion began to add chordal accompaniment to *sevdalinke.* Eventually, two types of instru-

TRACK 37

FIGURE 1 The *ganga* "*Odkad seke, odkad seke, nismo zapjevale,*" in three parts. Except for the falsetto and the glottal "cries," the pitch material consists of four chromatic tones within the range of a minor third. The straight and sobbing voices are distinguished by their different styles of performance, not their pitches or rhythms. Transcription by Amy Wooley.

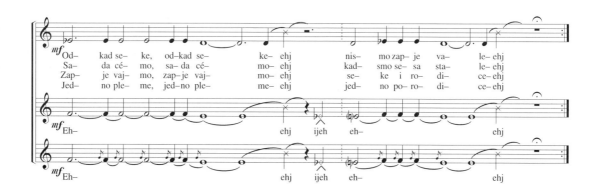

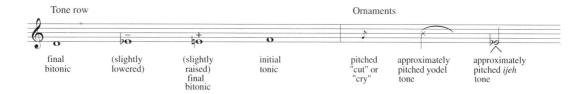

= slide between notes, occurring at end of first note's duration

= slide up to note

= approximately pitched falsetto yodel tone; slur over note indicates direction of tone

= pitched, falsetto, glottal prestrike grace note

1. How long we sisters haven't sung.
2. Now we'll do it because we've come together.
3. Let's sing, sisters and cousins.
4. One tribe, one family.

mental ensemble accompanied this genre. *Tamburica* ensembles, influenced by newer Croatian practice, consist of variously sized long-necked plucked lutes, designed to play chords in tempered tuning. Ensembles of European instruments including accordion, bass, guitar, clarinet, and violin also accompany *sevdalinke* in a manner linked more to Serbian traditions.

In urban Muslim music of the past, old heroic songs (*junačke pjesme*), narrative songs of epic character, retained structural elements found in similar rural forms. Singers performed without accompaniment or used the *pivačka tambura* 'singer's tambura', a long-necked two-stringed plucked instrument. In Bosnia-Hercegovina, as elsewhere in the Balkans, the broad diffusion of narrative epic (male) or lyric (female)

Membranophones and idiophones relate mainly to Muslim musical forms. Most of these membranophones and idiophones are played only by men. Urban Muslim and Sephardic Jewish women play tambourines and small cymbals to accompany rhythmic singing.

songs shows the depth of the tradition of composing texts with music. Accordingly, in addition to interpreting traditional songs, folksingers create new songs while maintaining structural patterns and aesthetic norms approved by people of their own social and cultural background. The authorship of text and music was a communal and an individual activity. At the end of the 1800s, however, a new concept of authorship, linked to the writing of poetic texts and music, emerged. In the twentieth century, this concept became a more accepted practice, particularly after 1960. One of the first recognized authors of urban written folk songs, Sahvet-beg Bašagić, composed new *sevdalinke* during the last part of the nineteenth century and the beginning of the twentieth. Most of his songs, and those of other authors, were accepted as real folk songs—and are retained as such, even today.

MUSICAL INSTRUMENTS

Urban and rural musical instruments are distinct in type and use. In rural environments, aerophones connected to herding cattle dominate: *jednojke* and *dvojnice* (single- and double-piped duct flutes), *diple* (single-reed pipe, with or without an air reservoir), and *rog* (animal horn, with single idioglot reed). Turkish military ensembles imported the *zurna* or *zurla*, a double-reed pipe, which the Muslim populations adopted for weddings and other celebrations. Professional and semiprofessional musicians—Rom (Gypsies) or Muslims from low social strata—play this instrument, usually in ensembles of two *zurnas* and a drum, *bubanj*.

The *gusle* was treated as the most traditional chordophone in Bosnia-Hercegovina. With one or, as in northwestern Bosnia, two strings, singers use this instrument to accompany narrative and heroic songs heterophonically. In southeastern Hercegovina, the *lirica*, a three-stringed bowed lute, accompanies *lindo*, a dance typical of southern Dalmatia [see CROATIA].

In rural areas of central and northern Bosnia, various long-necked plucked lutes, such as *tambura, šargija, karadjuzen,* and *bugarija,* predominate. The *tambura* has two to four double courses of strings, and the *šargija* has four to six. Urban populations prefer the *saz,* tuned in Bosnian *avaz,* a term meaning instrumental tuning and tune. Folk performers make their own *tambura* and *šargija,* but professional craftsmen build the urban *saz.*

The two-stringed *pivačka tambura* of northwestern Bosnia accompanies epic songs, and the four-course *tambura* and the *šargija* accompany ballads and lyric songs and dances. Urban Muslims use the *saz* to accompany singing and perform freemeter improvisations. At the beginning of the twentieth century, ensembles of smaller, factory-made *tambura* and ensembles of violin, clarinet, and accordion started to accompany urban songs. In the 1980s, an electric guitar and a synthesizer were added. Tunings of traditional urban instruments have been adjusted to the tempered system to ease ensemble performance with European instruments.

FIGURE 2   Three village women sing a *ganga.*
Photo by Ankica Petrović.

FIGURE 3 The first stanza of a *sevdalinke,* showing an octave range, a tetrachord (G–A♭–B–C), ABB′ form, and a melismatic style, sung by Selim Salihović. Transcription by Ankica Petrović.

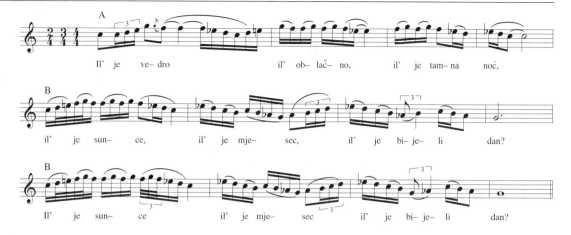

Membranophones and idiophones, less common instruments, relate mainly to Muslim musical forms. The former include double-headed drums (*bubnjevi*), a kettledrum (*talambas* or *dulbas*), and a single-headed frame drum with jingles (*def*). The latter include small cymbals (*čampareta*) and metal disks (*zili*), formerly imported by the Turkish military ensembles (*mehterhana*). Some Dervish rituals use *zili* and membranophones such as *kudum,* a small kettledrum, and *binbir halka,* a large tambourine, which takes its name from the fact that it supposedly has a circumference of a thousand and one finger widths in the interior part of the rim. Most of these membranophones and idiophones are played only by men. Urban Muslim and Sephardic Jewish women play *def* and *čampareta* to accompany rhythmic singing.

MUSLIM RELIGIOUS MUSIC

The most direct musical influences from the Islamic world were expressed in Islamic prayers, as they still are. Oral memorization served to teach religious chants in Arabic, a language foreign to Bosnian-Hercegovinan converts to Islam during the Ottoman period. The degree of Turkish influence varied. It was strongest in urban, administrative centers such as Sarajevo and Travnik. Educated religious authorities

FIGURE 4 Selim Salihović, an urban Muslim singer, sings a *sevdalinka,* accompanying himself on a *saz.* Photo by Ted Levin.

maintained the conservative Islamic belief that the interpretation of sacred Islamic texts constitutes the act of recitation, rather than singing; however, musical forms were fairly developed, and even with simple melodies, practicing laymen found this music meaningful and expressive. Sufi Muslim brotherhoods (Bektaši, Hamzevi, Kadiri, Mevlevi, and Naqšabandi) have a particularly developed treatment of music.

SEPHARDIC JEWISH MUSIC

FIGURE 5   Flory Jagoda, a well-known Sephardic singer originally from Sarajevo, accompanies herself on a guitar at a concert. Photo by Ankica Petrović.

Sephardic Jews, expelled from Spain in 1492, had arrived in Sarajevo by the middle of the 1500s. In the 1980s, Sephardic musical forms were no longer found in living tradition and could be reconstructed only from the memories of the oldest members of the community. Men performed religious songs in a style of singing called *bosanski mekam* 'Bosnian *maqam*' and *alaturka* 'in Turkish style'—like Muslim religious music, a synthesis of local Bosnian singing with Turkish musical practice. The religious tunes were sung in Hebrew. Lyric songs were sung in *djidjo,* the local name for Ladino. Some melodies of the Muslim paraliturgical practice, especially those of hymns (*ilahije*), were adopted into Sephardic religious musical practice.

At the beginning of the twentieth century, under the leadership of Sarajevo rabbi Avram Kapon (active from 1900 to 1920) and *hazzan* 'cantor' Isak Kalmi Altarac (active from 1930 to 1941), the Sarajevo Sephardic community modernized its liturgy and liturgical chants. Rabbi Kapon insisted that, during the service, the men of the congregation sing in unison, not individually, as they had been accustomed. He allowed female worshippers to sing the Saturday morning liturgical chants. Cantor Altarac, a Sarajevo native educated in Vienna, introduced the use of a boy's choir, and occasionally a girl's choir, or a choir composed of members of the vocal Sephardic group La Lira, active in Sarajevo from 1901 to 1941. It sang in the main Sephardic synagogue, Kal Grande, on the Sabbath and High Holidays. Altarac composed melodies and harmonizations that the choir sang in addition to traditional chants. He was known for his brilliant solos.

Jewish wedding songs, performed mainly by women, were retentions of Spanish ballads (*romances*) and other lyrical songs (figure 5). While retaining some aspects of the Spanish legacy, such as specific versification and the metrics of the poetic content in Ladino, Sephardim adopted stylistic features resembling those of local Bosnian Muslim practices, primarily *sevdalinke.* Common morphological traits appeared in a wide melodic range; congruence in modal concepts, though reduced in the twentieth century to the minor-major system; and emphasis on elaborate melismas and free rhythm.

Women performed dance songs on the *pandero,* a tambourine with jingles. Sephardic *romances* and religious songs disappeared from use during World War II, but some songs were revived by Sarajevo's student groups Ladino and Etno-Akademik (figure 6), formed in the mid 1980s and 1990s, respectively. They presented Sephardic songs in concerts and on Radio-Television Sarajevo.

NEW TRENDS IN FOLK MUSIC AND DANCE

At the end of the 1800s, ensembles devoted to performing folk songs and dances began to form. During the Communist period, these ensembles increased in number, under the name of cultural-artistic societies or KUDs (*kulturno-umjetnička društva*). They performed stylized folk songs and dances from all regions of Yugoslavia and emphasized virtuosic techniques not characteristic of the village traditions they supposedly represented.

After World War II, Radio-Televizija Sarajevo supported two full-time folk ensembles, a *tamburica* orchestra (*tamburaški orkestar*) and a folk orchestra (*narodni orkestar*), consisting of imported Western instruments. Well known in the country,

FIGURE 6   The student ensemble Etno-Akademik in the mountains outside Sarajevo. Photo by Ankica Petrović.

these ensembles collaborated with a large number of professional performers of folk songs and dances. Many Radio-Televizija Sarajevo's programs were reserved for arranged, stylized folk music from Bosnia-Hercegovina and other regions of Yugoslavia.

Since the 1960s, the development of newly composed folk songs (*novokomponovane narodne pjesme*) has become enormously popular in Serbia and Bosnia-Hercegovina. These songs appeal to the musical tastes of urban and suburban populations, and absorb musical elements from urban centers in the Balkans.

Traditional and arranged folk-music forms and the newly composed folk-song genre have received artistic recognition at numerous regional, republic, national (Yugoslav), and international music festivals. The record industry disseminates performances of these genres, with the exception of traditional folk-music forms, which are felt to lack commercial viability. Since 1990, the media have strongly supported religious folk music, such as Muslim paraliturgical religious hymns (*ilahije*) and odes (*kaside*).

Popularized folk-music forms have inspired popular and rock music, which began to develop during the 1970s in Sarajevo, the center of popular music in Yugoslavia. The rock group Bjelo Dugme (White Button) and its composer, Goran Bregović, were recognized as the most important figures. Bregović gained international acclaim as the composer of sound tracks with folk coloring for films by the renowned Sarajevo director Emir Kusturica.

For classical composers such as Vlado Milošević (1901–1988), Cvjetko Rihtman (1902–1990), Vojin Komadina (1933–1997), and Rada Nuić (b. 1942), the folk music of Bosnia-Hercegovina has served as an inspiration and as the dominant feature of compositional style. These composers have achieved national and international recognition for the originality of their treatment of musical folklore and the breadth of styles in which they have composed.

RESEARCH INSTITUTIONS AND ACTIVITIES

The first Bosnian-Hercegovinan ethnomusicological activities date from 1889, when the National Museum in Sarajevo engaged Ludvik Kuba, the Czech painter and folk-lorist, to collect and notate local folk songs. He collected more than a thousand tunes, mostly urban songs from Sarajevo.

Before 1947, the National Museum was the only institution in Bosnia-Hercegovina to sponsor the collection of musical works, including transcriptions, instruments, and information about musical practice. The museum has sporadically published articles on musical folklore in its journal, *Glasnik Zemaljskog Muzeja u Sarajevu* ('Report of the National Museum in Sarajevo'). In 1947, Cvjetko Rihtman formed the Institute for the Study of Folklore in Sarajevo. He directed its affairs until its close in 1957. In 1953, composer and ethnomusicologist Vlado Milošević formed the Banja Luka Center for Folk Songs, an institution that, with the Museum of the Bosnian Krajina, supported music research. Since the 1950s, ethnomusicological research projects have been organized by the Ethnographic Department of the National Museum in Sarajevo and through the Academy of Arts and Sciences. After the formation of the Music Academy in Sarajevo (in 1955), students have been trained in musical folklore in the Department of Musicology, which supports ethnomusicological study at the undergraduate and graduate levels.

BIBLIOGRAPHY

Bartók, Béla, and Albert B. Lord. 1951. *Serbo-Croatian Folk Songs*. New York: Columbia University Press.

Christensen, Dieter. 1977. "Kategorien mehrstimmiger Lieder des Dorfes Gabela, Herzegovina." *Essays for a Humanist, an Offering to Klaus Wachsmann*, 105–120. Spring Valley, N.Y.: Town House Press.

Dopudja, Jelena. 1971. "Narodne igre (plesovi) u području Jajca." In *Rad XV Kongresa SUFJ u Jajcu 1968*, 75–82. Sarajevo: SUFJ.

Gesemann, Gerhard, ed. 1925. *Erlengeski rukopis starih srpskohrvatskihnarodnih pjesama*. Belgrade: Srpska Kraljevska Akademija.

———, ed. 1926. *Studien zur südslawischen Volksepik*. Reichenberg: Verlag Gebrüder Stiepel.

———. 1937. "Prolegomena povodom gramofonskog snimanja bosanske narodne pjesme." *Prilozi proučavanju narodne poezije* 4:222–239.

Krader, Barbara. 1981. "A Bosnian Urban Love Song: The Sevdalinka." In *Report on the Twelfth Congress Berkeley 1977*, 29–35. London: Bärenreiter.

Kuba, Ludvik. 1906. "Pjesme i napjevi iz Bosne i Hercegovine." *Glasnik Zemaljskog Muzeja* 18:183, 355, 499.

———. 1907. "Pjesme i napjevi iz Bosne i Hercegovine." *Glasnik Zemaljskog Muzeja* 19:103, 244, 405, 629.

———. 1909. "Pjesme i napjevi iz Bosne i Hercegovine." *Glasnik Zemaljskog Muzeja* 21:303, 581.

———. 1910. "Pjesme i napjevi iz Bosne i Hercegovine." *Glasnik Zemaljskog Muzeja* 22:513.

Kuhač, Franjo. 1898. "Turski živalj u pučkoj glazbi Hrvata, Srba i Bugara." *Glasnik Zemaljskog Muzeja* 2(3):175–218.

Lord, Albert Bates. 1960. *The Singer of Tales*. Cambridge: Harvard University Press.

Marić, Branimir. 1933–1934. "Hercegovačke gange." *Hrvatski narodni kalendar* 105–108.

———. 1938. "Pentatonika u bosansko-hercegovačkoj pučkoj muzici." *Sveta Cecilija* 3–11.

———. 1940–1941. "Iz područja gange." *Hrvatski narodni kalendar* 41–47.

Milošević, Vlado. 1976 [1940]. "Seljačko pjevanje u Banjalučkoj Vrhovini." *Banjaluka* 22: 488–491.

———. 1954–1964. *Bosanske narodne pjesme*. 4 vols. Banja Luka: Narodni Muzej.

———. 1964. *Sevdalinke*. Banja Luka: Narodni Muzej.

———. 1984. *Ravna pjesma*. Banja Luka: Putevi.

Murko, Matija. 1913. *Bericht über phonographische Aufnahmen epischer, meist mohammedanischer Volkslieder im Nordwestlichen Bosnien im Sommer 1912*. Vienna: A. Holder.

———. 1915a. *Bericht über phonographische Aufnahmen epischer Volkslieder im mittleren Bosnien und in der Herzegowina im Sommer 1913*. Vienna: A. Holder.

———. 1915b. *Bericht über eine Reise zum Studium der Volksepik in Bosnien und Herzegowina im Jahre 1913*. Vienna: Kommission bei A. Holder.

———. 1929. *La poésie populaire épique en Yougoslavie au début du XXème siècle*. Paris: Ancienne Honore Champion.

Pennanen, Risto P. 1993–1994. "The God-Praising Drums in Sarajevo." *Asian Music* 25(1–2):1–7.

Petrović, Ankica. 1978. "Fenomen vokalnog stila u seoskoj muzičkoj praksi Bosne i Hercegovine." *Zvuk* 2:15–22.

———. 1982. "Sacred Sephardic Chants in Bosnia." *The World of Music* 24(3):35–51.

———. 1985. "Tradition and Compromise in the Musical Expression of the Sephardic Jews in Bosnia." In *Proceedings of the Meeting of Ethnomusicologists on the Occasion of the European Year of Music*, 166–178. Zagreb: Zavod za proučavanje folklora.

———. 1988. "Paradoxes of Muslim Music in Bosnia and Hercegovina." *Asian Music* 20:128–147.

———. 1990. "Correlation between the Musical Content of Sephardic Songs and Traditional Muslim Lyrics *Sevdalinka* in Bosnia." In *Proceedings of the Tenth World Congress of Jewish Studies, Division D, Vol. 2 (Art, Folklore, and Music)*, 165–171. Jerusalem: World Union of Jewish Studies.

———. 1991a. "The Musical Form *Ganga* as a Multi-Channeled Cultural Symbol in the Rural Society of Central Yugoslavia." In *Tradition and Its Future in Music: Report of the SIMS 1990, Tokio* [sic], 283–286. Osaka, Japan: Mita Press.

———. 1991b. "Les techniques du chant villageois dans les Alpes Dinariques (Yougoslavie)." *Cahiers de Musiques Traditionnelles* 4:103–115.

———. 1995. "Perceptions of Ganga." *The World of Music* 37(2):60–70.

Rihtman, Cvjetko. 1951. "Polifoni oblici u narodnoj muzici Bosne i Hercegovine." *Bilten instituta za proučavanje folklora u Sarajevu* 1:3–38.

———. 1966. "Formes polyphoniques dans la musique traditionelle Yougoslave." *Journal of the International Folk Music Council* 18:23–28.

———. 1967. "Orientalische Elemente in der traditionalen Musik Bosniens und der Herzegowina." In *Das Orientalische Elementam Balkan 2: Balkanologen-Tagung: Graz 1966*, 97–105. Grazer und Münchner Balkanologische Studien, 2. Munich.

———. 1974. *Zbornik napjeva narodnih pjesama Bosne i Hercegovine, Dječje pjesme*. Sarajevo: ANU-BIH, Gradja 19.

———. 1979. "Die gusle in Bosnien und der Herzegovina—Beziehungen zwischen Instrument, Spieltechnik und Music." *Studia Instrumentorum Musicae Popularis* 6:93–97.

———. 1981. "Die Spieler von Volksmusikinstrumenten in Bosnien und der Herzegowina." *Studia Instrumentorum Musicae Popularis* 7:40–42.

———. 1986. *Pjesme i napjevi iz Bosne i Hercegovine, 2: Svatovske Pjesme*. Sarajevo: Svjetlost.

Rihtman, Dunja. 1970. "Narodna muzička praksa listićkog područja." *Glasnik Zemaljskog muzeja Bosne i Hercegovine, Etnologija* 24–26:363–419.

———. 1982. "Narodna muzička tradicija Drežnice." *Glasnik Zemaljskog muzeja Bosne i Hercegovine, Etnologija* 37:137–164.

———. 1988–1989. "Muzička pratnja i zdravice u tradicionalnom obredu slave kod Srba u Bosni i Hercegovini." *Glasnik Zemaljskog muzeja Bosne i Hercegovine, Etnologija* 43–44:181–223.

Schmaus, Alfred. 1953. *Studije o Krajiškoj epici*. Zagreb: n.p.

Topić, Slavko. 1986. *Kirchenlieder der bosnischen Katholiken*. Regensburg: Gustav Bosse Verlag.

Vidić-Rasmussen, Ljerka. 1995. "From Source to Commodity: Newly-Composed Folk Music of Yugoslavia." *Popular Music* 14(2):241–256.

Weich-Shahak, Shoshana. 1990. "The Bosnian Judeo-Spanish Musical Repertoire in a Hundred Year Old Manuscript." *Jahrbuch für Musikalische Volks- und Volkerkunde* 14:97–122.

Wunsch, Walter. 1934. *Die Geigentechnik der südslawischen Guslaren*. Brno: R. M. Rohrer.

Macedonia

Timothy Rice

Rural Song Genres and Singing Styles
Village Musical Instruments and Instrumental Music
Dancing and Dance-Music
Urban Music
Folk Music during the Yugoslav Socialist Period
Music of National Minorities
Popular Music and Recent Developments
History of Scholarship

Macedonia, a land of deep valleys and rugged mountains in the south-central Balkans, asserted itself historically in the fourth century B.C., when King Philip II conquered Greece, and his son, Alexander the Great, created an empire stretching from western Asia to Egypt, Persia, and northwestern India. For centuries after the collapse of Alexander's empire (in the second century B.C.), Macedonia disappeared as a political entity, becoming a territory within the Roman and Byzantine empires, the Serbian and Bulgarian kingdoms, and eventually the Ottoman Empire. Settled by Slavs in the fifth century, its towns played host to the ethnic diversity of the Ottoman Empire from the late 1300s. These changes obliterated any historical relationship between ancient and modern Macedonia, but a symbolic relationship remains a matter of dispute in the region (compare Danforth 1995).

After the Balkan Wars of 1912–1913, the already-independent states of Bulgaria, Greece, and Serbia divided and absorbed what remained of European Turkey, denying the national aspirations of those who called themselves Macedonians at the end of the Ottoman period. In northern Greece, poor economic conditions and repressive cultural policies, especially toward the (Slavic) Macedonian language, led many Macedonians to emigrate in the interwar years to North America, Australia, and Bulgaria, and after World War II to Eastern European countries and as far away as Uzbekistan. Ethnic Macedonians were accorded political notice for the first time when, after World War II, the new Yugoslav government recognized Macedonia as a constituent republic within federal Yugoslavia, Macedonian as one of Yugoslavia's official languages, and the Macedonian Orthodox Church as an autocephalous body. Landlocked, the Macedonian republic, occupying 25,713 square kilometers, declared its independence in 1991, with Croatia and Slovenia, to become a multiparty republic struggling for international recognition and economic viability. Its population, of 2.2 million people, has been estimated as 67 percent ethnic Macedonians (Slavs), 23 percent Albanians [see ALBANIAN MUSIC], 4 percent Turks, 4 percent Rom [see ROM (GYPSY) MUSIC], and 2 percent Serbians, Bosnians, Vlachs, and others, but these percentages are disputed and may be unreliable. The flight of ethnic Albanian refugees from Kosovo in 1999 exacerbated tension between ethnic Macedonians and ethnic Albanians. Music is one of the most prominent markers of ethnic identity.

RURAL SONG GENRES AND SINGING STYLES

The 45 percent of ethnic Macedonians living in rural areas support a still dynamic traditional music culture despite extensive industrialization and urbanization and the nearly universal literacy achieved since the 1940s. Rituals of the pre-Christian agricultural and Christian calendar once supported a richly varied repertoire of songs, music, and dance: house-to-house caroling by boys at Christmas and New Year (*božik*) or young children before Easter (*lazarica*) and during droughts (*vajdudule*). Major holidays at Easter and St. George's Day (*ǵurǵovden*) in May and a succession of saint's day celebrations (*slava*s) at village churches continue to provide important occasions for dancing. The repertoire of nonmetrical plowing, hoeing, harvesting, and shepherding songs is still remembered by the oldest generation, but its practice has declined with mechanized farming and emigration by youths to cities and factories. Three-day-long weddings, each including a succession of dramatic ritual events marking taking of the bride by the bridegroom's family, once provided repeated opportunities for ritual singing, and continue to support celebratory music making and dancing. In the fall and winter, social gatherings of families and guests— and in the past, indoor working bees, where girls and women spun wool and embroidered cloth—provide additional contexts for singing, dancing, and homemade music. Many of the ritual songs describe the events they accompany and sketch the emotions people feel on such important occasions, but songs sung at social occasions treat more general themes important to the community: young lovers' courtship, betrothal, and feelings; tensions in extended, patriarchal family relationships; the history of subjugation under, and attempts at liberation from, the Ottoman Empire; and the necessity, given the relatively barren lands, for young men to search for work far from home, leaving family behind. In the 1800s, many men left their homes to find work in cities in other parts of the Ottoman Empire and as far away as North America. In the twentieth century, subsequent generations continued this pattern, emigrating to Australia and Germany—a process that has created an important genre of *pečalbarski pesni* 'songs of workers abroad', mourning their loss.

Men and women sing, solo or in gender-separated groups, using a throat-focused vocal production that produces a loud sound, thought suitable for outdoor singing. Listeners evaluate singers' performances with metaphors of birds and bells ("She sings like a nightingale" or, for two-voiced singing, "They sounded like bells") and characteristic humor ("She sings well, only her voice doesn't please me") (Bicevski 1986). Men's songs, sung mainly at social occasions in the home, taverns, weddings, and saints' days, deal with male experiences such as shepherding, fighting the Turks, adventures in the market, and their fiery attraction to girls. An important subcategory tells of a fruitless but honored uprising against the Turks on St. Elijah's Day in August 1903 (Ilinden), which has become a national holiday for Macedonians throughout the world. Girls and women once sang ritual, fieldwork, and working-bee songs that describe the ritual or work activity, register their feelings about it, and tell tales of their bitter relations with unwanted lovers, no-good husbands, strict fathers, and longing for lost sons and lovers.

Though men and women often sing in different contexts about different topics, their song structures and singing styles are rather similar. Men and women sing solo and in unison groups throughout the country; in addition, polyphonic singing occurs in three zones. Female singers in the east employ a two-part melody-and-drone style similar to eastern Serbian and southwestern Bulgarian styles (figure 1). Male and female singers in the northwest sing an accompanying part that moves in relation to the melody to emphasize the interval of a second. Macedonians from the areas around the town of Kostur (in Greek, Kastoria) near the Greek-Albanian border

FIGURE 1
Polyphonic drone
singing from
Pehčevo Village,
eastern Macedonia.
After Traerup
1970:#62.

sing in two- and three-part styles resembling southern Albanian singing [see
ALBANIAN MUSIC].

Song texts are based, not on rhymes or stanzaic structures, but on a series of
unrhymed lines, each with the same number of syllables, usually eight, but texts with
six- and ten-syllable lines are also common. A typical musical strophe consists of two
phrases, AA or AB, each phrase setting one line of text, but shorter and longer strophes exist, including ones with textual refrains. Villagers traditionally distinguish
between short, recitativelike songs (*gatački pesni*) and longer, more melodic ones
(*vozeni, glasoečki, or ikoečki pesni*). A typical monophonic village song covers the
range of a fourth or fifth above the tonic and a major second below it. Polyphonic,
ritual, and work songs often have a narrower range, but *soborski pesni* 'fair songs'—
well-known songs, probably reflecting contact with urban culture—range up to an
octave or ninth (Hadžimanov 1964). Printed song collections suggest that two-thirds
or more of song scales employ a minor third above the tonic, but all tetrachordal
modes exist, including songs with chromatic alternations of the second and third
degrees (Ziegler 1979). Urban-influenced *soborski pesni* use the augmented second
typical of the Turkish *hijaz* tetrachord more than do other categories of village song.
Song rhythms fall into two large categories: nearly 40 percent of songs are nonmetrical. These songs are particularly effective for recounting epic loves and battles. Most
metrical songs accompany dancing, but they are often sung by performers seated at
social events; often just their melodies are played by instrumentalists. The two most
common song meters are 2/4 and 7/8 (3 + 2 + 2), but many other asymmetric meters
exist [see BULGARIA].

As rural Macedonians have felt the effects of industrialization and the migration
of youth to the cities, singing, particularly the drone-based forms of polyphonic
singing during work and ritual occasions, has suffered, perhaps more than instrumental music and dance. In 1955, researchers found girls as young as ten years old
singing polyphonically (Bicevski 1986). During the socialist-led modernization campaigns that began around 1954, such singing and other village customs were regarded
as old-fashioned and backward, not progressive. Young people turned on the radio
and later television to find their cultural models. The ensembles and classical harmonies they heard accompanying singers with rather relaxed vocal production sounded little like unaccompanied monophonic or polyphonic village singing. In the
1980s, mainly middle-aged and older women sang in the old village styles, but young
people sang no songs or the urban *narodni pesni* 'folk songs' they learned at school or
from the radio.

VILLAGE MUSICAL INSTRUMENTS AND INSTRUMENTAL MUSIC

Village instrumental music, produced exclusively by men and boys, is based on song structures and a procedure unique to instrumental music, the "spinning out" of short melodic motifs. There are four main types: music played while herding animals; music for weddings, fairs, and social occasions, provided by the villagers themselves; music on similar occasions, played by professional Rom musicians; and accompaniment to singing, played on bowed and plucked stringed instruments. Parts of the soundscape on the margins of adult music making include children's noisemakers and simplified imitations of adult instruments; religious signals in the form of church bells and sonorous boards, the latter played during periods of mourning; bells hung from the necks of herd animals; and jingles and other noisemakers, attached to costumes, horses and mules, and wagons.

Shepherds used to while away the hours playing flutes, of which the most common was the *šupelka*, a short (240–350 millimeter) tube open at both ends, with six finger holes and no thumb hole, and played by blowing across the beveled rim at an oblique angle (figure 2). Shepherds also played the *duduk*, a six-holed duct flute similar to ones ubiquitous in Europe and beyond (possibly named for the tonguing technique) and the *dvojanka*, a double duct flute with a melody pipe and a drone pipe. The music consisted mainly of improvised fragments of song and dance tunes. Muslim Albanian shepherds played the *kaval*, a long (800-millimeter) bevel-edged, rim-blown flute with seven finger holes, a thumb hole, and four vent holes near the bottom. Elaborately decorated and played in pairs (*čift kavali*), one shepherd held a drone while the other played the melody. Found mostly in northern and western areas, *čift kavali* were played and are still manufactured mostly by Albanians [see ALBANIAN MUSIC].

Though villagers played flutes on social occasions for entertainment or to accompany dancing, the favored instrument they played for celebratory feasts and dancing at weddings and fairs is the bagpipe (*gajda*), consisting of a cylindrical chanter with an angled, hornlike projection at the bottom, a three-piece drone, a blowpipe, and a sheepskin bag. The wooden parts are typically made of boxwood, with joints and ends sheathed in horn. In eastern Macedonia, a rare variant of the instrument has an added high-pitched drone. Bagpipers, who often practice their technique while herding animals, accompany dances, play ritual tunes at key moments of weddings, and accompany singing, including their own (figure 3). Though typically a solo instrument, bagpipes are sometimes played in pairs.

The two other kinds of village instrumental music exist at the intersection of rural and urban life. For accompanying singing, particularly long, historical ballads, some villagers in eastern Macedonia played the *kemene*, a three-stringed, pear-shaped bowed lute. Elsewhere in Macedonia, particularly in towns, the same instrument, called *gusla,* was played by blind itinerant beggars (*guslari*), for whom singing and playing was a trade [see UKRAINE]. A few villagers learned to play the *tambura*, a long-necked, fretted plucked lute with two double courses of strings, which they probably first heard in urban markets played by Muslim townspeople, especially Turks. Both instruments played melody with drone accompaniments similar to those on bagpipes and *čift kavali.*

Another part of village musical life on public occasions continues to be that provided by outsiders to the village—Rom, who play loud, virtuosic music in an ensemble of two *zurla*s (double-reed, conical-bore oboes) and one or two *tapan*s (cylindrical, double-headed drums). Rom musicians, who usually live in or near towns, sell their musical services to villagers for weddings, saint's day celebrations, patriotic holidays, and, for Muslim communities, circumcisions and Bajram, the most important Islamic calendric feast. True professionals, they know the dance and ritual-tune reper-

FIGURE 2   A shepherd boy plays a *šupelka.* Photo by Blagoje Drnkov.

In one Greek Macedonian village, a "worker abroad" brought the first brass instruments to his village in the late 1800s after hearing a Salvation Army band in Toronto, Canada.

FIGURE 3   A bagpiper (*gajdar*) accompanies male singers at a village fair at a monastery near Bitda. Photo by Joan Friedberg, 1982.

toire specific to each ethnic community, including their own, and pass on their knowledge within extended families of specialists in *zurla* or *tapan* as part of an economic survival strategy (figure 4). A feature of Ottoman town culture they have introduced into village musical life is the *taksim,* a nonmetrical, virtuosic improvisation, played between sections of metrical melodies over a sustained drone and the beat of the drum during dancing [see ROM (GYPSY) MUSIC].

Of these types of village music making, traditional forms of self-entertainment at home or in the pasture are being replaced by other forms of entertainment, such as radio and television. The *zurla-tapan* ensemble and bagpipes are still common at saint's day celebrations. Bagpipes can still be heard at family social occasions, but the bagpipers and *zurla-tapan* ensembles must now compete, especially for wedding jobs, with ensembles of modern, manufactured instruments, typically consisting of clarinet, saxophone, accordion or electronic keyboard, and drum set, played by semiprofessional village musicians or professional Rom musicians.

The clarinet probably entered Macedonia during Ottoman times, and Western brass instruments became popular in the early twentieth century, particularly in the Greek part of Macedonia and the Bitola area. In one Greek Macedonian village, a "worker abroad" brought the first such instruments to his village in the late 1800s after hearing a Salvation Army band in Toronto, Canada. Brass bands (*duvački orkestri*), consisting of one or two trumpets, a clarinet, one or two valve trombones, a

tapan with attached cymbal, and a snare drum (*barabanče*), remain more typical of southwestern Macedonia than elsewhere. After 1912, young soldiers trained to play these instruments in military bands brought them home to play at village weddings. Those who took up the clarinet were often village bagpipers or Rom *zurla* players. Tale Ognenovski, a clarinet player at Radio Skopje after World War II, came from a Bitola-area family of *gajda* players (Seeman 1990), and in the early twentieth century a Rom *zurla* player named Lambro introduced the clarinet into Bitola urban-music ensembles called *čalgija* (Turkish 'music'), which had consisted mainly of stringed instruments (Aluševski 1980). In many urban and rural settings in the 1950s, an ensemble with a core of a clarinet, an accordion, and a drum set began to compete with and replace bagpipe, *zurla-tapan,* and *čalgija* ensembles for Macedonian weddings (figure 5).

FIGURE 5 At a village fair, Rom clarinet, accordion, and *tapan* players inspire the lead dancer's improvisation as the rest of the line of dancers wind behind them. The lead dancer has placed tips for the musicians in the drummer's mouth and under the bill of his cap. Photo by Timothy Rice, 1973.

DANCING AND DANCE-MUSIC

Dancing at social gatherings in the home, but especially outdoors at weddings and fairs and after church on Sundays, traditionally provided the principal entertainment and an important means for the display of gender and age roles in the village. Formally, a dance (*oro*) consists of an open circle of an unlimited number of dancers, who hold hands or place their hands on the shoulders of those next to them. The line of dancers moves to the right under the direction of a leader, who sometimes waves a handkerchief or beaded chain and occasionally improvises steps. The rest of the dancers in the line keep their bodies still and stiff from the hips up, while repeating patterns of steps, hops, and leg lifts, each dancer free to improvise slightly within the pattern. The most common dance, called *pravo* 'straight' or *lesno* 'easy' *oro* and performed in 2/4 and 7/8 time, has a pattern of steps that recurs every six beats, creating an overlapping relationship with typical four- and eight-beat dance-music phrases.

Each village typically has several social dances that both sexes dance and a few social dances for each sex alone. Some dances are well known throughout Macedonia; others are limited to a specific village or region. Children are not taught the dances, but learn them through trial and error by joining in the line with adults and older children who know the dances. Before World War II, dance lines were often segregated by age and gender, but since the war, men and women have often danced next to each other in the line. Though men and women perform the same steps, women typically dance with small, demure movements, and men may leap athletically and lift their legs proudly. Some dances, particularly those associated with weddings, are performed only by people of one sex or the other, for example, women's *nevestinsko oro* 'bride's dance' and men's *teško oro* 'heavy dance'. The latter is notable for its masculine leaping in a slow, meterless rhythm, which requires the drummer to follow the lead dancer's movements, rather than setting the beat for the dancers, while the *zurla* players play unmetered tunes.

In addition to dances in 2/4 and 7/8 (3 + 2 + 2) time, some dances are in longer asymmetric meters, similar to those found in Bulgaria. In the west and southwest, dances in 12/8 (3 + 2 + 2 + 3 + 2) time, variously known as *beranče, Ibraim Odža, krsteno,* and *pušteno oro*, are prominent, and are probably linked to Albanian tradition. The melody on the three-beat pulse can have four tones, creating a four-against-three pattern. On many musical beats, the dancers, rather than stepping, lift their legs, creating a light, graceful effect.

Though limited in number, the dance forms in a village supplies a seemingly inexhaustible resource for amusement and self-presentation at dance events lasting many hours, as each dance is repeated innumerably under the leadership of a different person, each of whom in turn directs the musicians, with a tip if they are paid professionals, to play a favorite tune, often a song tune. Each tune and the variety of tunes contribute significantly to the pleasure of the experience. The leader regulates the tempo of the dance; therefore, the same formal structure may be performed slow, medium, or fast. Depending on the leader, the context, and the sizes of tips, dances can last from five minutes to an hour or more, while the dancers talk to those around them, watch others in the dance line, vary their own movements in response to changing melodies and energy levels, and admire the leader's style and improvised variations.

URBAN MUSIC

Since the establishment of Radio Skopje (in 1943), urban music and musical values in various forms have been a prominent part of villagers' aural experience, inevitably influencing their musical taste. Villagers' migration into the cities has brought songs and dances to be incorporated into urban ensembles' arrangements, which have then been disseminated in urban and rural areas on radio.

In Macedonian cities, the older Ottoman and newer European styles, both with connections to classical music traditions, continue to influence urban musical culture. If village culture can seem homogeneous even when it harbors layers of external influence, city culture is by nature heterogeneous. Musical life in Macedonian towns includes remnants of Ottoman music (*čalgija* and *zurla-tapan*); Western classical music; village wedding dance-music, played by clarinet-accordion ensembles and *duvački orkestri*; the music of Rom, Turkish, and Albanian minorities; and Westernized folk ensembles, performing stylized versions of village dance, music, and song for festivals and the media.

Čalgija ensembles

During the Ottoman period, Macedonian towns attracted Turkish, Albanian, Slavic, and Rom Muslims, Jews, and an ethnically heterogeneous Christian population. The urban popular music they shared and patronized was based in Ottoman musical culture and played by an ensemble called *čalgija,* consisting of such widespread Middle Eastern instruments as the *ut* (a short-necked, fretless plucked lute), the *lauta* (a fretted plucked lute), the *kanun* (a trapezoidal plucked zither) and the *daire* (a large frame drum with jingles) and the Western violin, called *ḱemene* after the pear-shaped, three-stringed bowed lute it replaced in comparable Ottoman ensembles in the 1800s (figure 6). Though Turkish amateurs doubtless played these instruments, the outstanding exponents of the instruments were Rom professionals, who played a repertoire of tunes known throughout the Ottoman Empire, sung to texts in Albanian, Greek, Macedonian, Romany, and Turkish. At weddings and circumcisions and in cafes (*kafana*s), they played Ottoman light classical genres (*longa, şarki, peşrev*), urban songs (*turku*), and marches; Rom dances (*čoček, karsilama*); and pieces from local folk tradition with urban melodies, particularly *kasapsko oro* 'butcher's dance' with at least some tunes probably from the Jewish tradition. Musicians interspersed their songs and instrumentals in Turkish rhythmic modes (*usul*s) with highly ornamented *taksim*s (improvisations) in numerous Turkish *makam*s (melodic modes), particularly

FIGURE 6 The *čalgija* ensemble of Radio Skopje. *Front row, from left: ut, kanun,* and *darabuka. Back row:* clarinet and violin. Photo by Blagoje Drnkov.

Radio broadcasts of folk music created a sound with affective, traditional references yet emblematic of a new social consciousness, more Slavic than ethnically mixed, more urban than rural, and more Western than Ottoman.

hijaz, *saba*, and *uşşak*. In the early twentieth century, the ensemble expanded to include—though each town had its own characteristic makeup and style—a clarinet, a *džumbuš* (a long-necked, fretless, banjolike instrument, an inexpensive variant of the *ut*), and by the 1930s an accordion and a *darabuka*, a vase-shaped drum (Džimrevski 1985). As villagers moved into the cities in the interwar period, the repertoire expanded to include village dance tunes and old city songs (*starogradski pesni*), a genre of Turkish urban songs with Macedonian-language texts.

After World War II, Radio Skopje increasingly defined the public sound of Macedonian music. To play folk music, the station hired combinations of Rom and Slav professional musicians, who formed a *čalgija* orchestra. By playing in tempered rather than microtonal tunings, minimizing the heterophonic texture typical of pre-war *čalgija* ensembles and playing mainly a village rather than an urban repertoire, *čalgija* on the radio was effectively reconfigured as a Macedonian, rather than a Rom or Ottoman, and a traditional, rather than an innovative or modern, ensemble (Seeman 1990).

At weddings, circumcisions, and nightclubs in cities and towns, *čalgija* as an ensemble of Turkish instruments has virtually disappeared. Rom musicians (*čalgadžii*) continue the Westernization of instrumentation that began in the eighteenth century, adding trumpet, valve trombone, saxophone, synthesizers, electric guitar, electric bass, and drum sets to create eclectic combinations of instruments. Like urban popular musicians before World War II, they play Albanian, Macedonian, and Rom songs and dances, including village and modern dance tunes (e.g., the lambada) and *starogradski* and popular songs, some of them newly composed folk songs (*novokompanovani narodni pesni*) [see SERBIA], with Greek, Italian, Macedonian, Serbian, and even English lyrics. Though not called *čalgija*, these ensembles preserve the changeability and heterogeneity of the music once exemplified in *čalgija*.

European classical music

Until 1912, composition in other than Ottoman or village styles centered in Orthodox churches and monasteries. Macedonians including Krstan Sandžak of Struga and Georgi Smičkov of Prilep composed church music, and one, Naum Miladinov (1817–1897), wrote a textbook on Byzantine chanting. In the town of Veles around 1830 appeared music teachers, mainly priests trained in monasteries on Mount Athos, Greece, using singing-method books brought by Macedonian merchants who had traveled to central Europe. In the late 1800s, politically motivated choirs and chamber-music groups based on Western and Ottoman urban styles formed alongside groups promoting Macedonian independence, language, and literature. Many of these musicians were students of Atanas Badev (1860–1908), who, born in Prilep, studied in Bulgaria and Russia and became a music teacher in schools in what is now Thessaloniki, Greece, where he taught many in the next generation of Macedonian musicians.

The first orchestras outside schools—including a complete one in a school in Serres (Greece)—were formed in the 1920s and consisted of an eclectic mix of violins, mandolins, guitars, *tamburica*s (long-necked, plucked lutes), flutes, and double basses. With military-style brass bands, they played arrangements of folk songs and popular works by Borodin, Tchaikovsky, and Verdi. Between the world wars, a music school was founded, amateur choral societies were formed in virtually every town, and the military in Skopje sponsored an orchestra led by a Czech conductor. After World II, with extensive support for arts and culture in socialist Yugoslavia, a civilian symphony orchestra and opera company and a university conservatory were founded in the Macedonian Republic. Soloists and composers trained in Croatia, Serbia, and abroad and using folk, neoclassical, aleatoric, and serial techniques have flourished in this environment, but none has yet achieved international fame (Avramovski 1982).

FOLK MUSIC DURING THE YUGOSLAV SOCIALIST PERIOD

From 1945 to 1991, when Macedonia was a republic within socialist Yugoslavia, the government controlled and directed many aspects of cultural, industrial, and agricultural production. Its most important cultural institutions for representation and presentation of village and urban music and dance were Radio Skopje and the recordings its artists produced for Yugoton and RTB (Radio-Television Beograd), and amateur folklore ensembles called KUDs (*kulturno-umetničko društvo* 'cultural-artistic association').

Broadcasts and records defined the sound of new categories of ostensibly traditional Macedonian music, meant to be heard and understood as a symbol of the nation and its ideals and known generally as *narodna muzika* 'folk music'. The radio maintained three orchestras of traditional music: a *čalgija* ensemble; a *mal orkestar* 'little orchestra', of clarinet, accordion, and other manufactured instruments; and a *naroden orkestar* 'folk orchestra', of village instruments that accompanied singers and dancers in a genre called *izvorna muzika* 'music from the source or spring'. Though all the orchestras contained a mixture of Slav and Rom musicians, musically they minimized Rom and Turkish stylistic elements while playing a repertoire of Slavic Macedonian village dance and song tunes and urban *starogradski pesni*. These two moves created a sound with affective, traditional references yet emblematic of a new social consciousness, more Slavic than ethnically mixed, more urban than rural, and more Western than Ottoman. The government viewed these ensembles as progressive in the 1950s, but the need for them to function as symbols effectively prevented further musical development, which occurred at urban nightclubs, weddings, and other occasions not directly controlled by the state's cultural institutions.

The radio's *naroden orkestar* exemplifies the constructed nature of presentations of ostensibly village music, known as *izvorna muzika* in the socialist period. Until this orchestra was formed (in the 1950s), village instruments had not played together. Each had its own functions characteristic of particular ethnic groups: the *gajda* of Slavic Macedonian village dance-music; the *kaval* of Albanian shepherds; the *tambura* of urban-rural interaction with Muslim townspeople and their songs; and the *tapan* of Rom professionals. Mixing Slavic Macedonians villagers (Todor Boškov and later Pece Atanasovski on *gajda*; Mile Kolarov on *kaval*) with Rom professionals on *tambura* and *tapan*, the orchestra created a completely new sound that simultaneously referenced the present and the past and provided a model for village KUDs, some of which created similar orchestras (figure 7). This ensemble also accompanied famous radio singers, such as Vaska Ilieva, Aleksandar Sarievski, and Kiril Mančevski (Dunin, Dimoski, and Visinski 1995). Only rarely was unarranged village music heard on the radio, usually as part of report on a festival or competition.

Village and urban KUDs, often named after important figures in Macedonian

FIGURE 7 The orchestra of folk instruments (*naroden orkestar*) of Radio Skopje, led by Pece Atanasovski, at left, on *gajda.* This version includes three *kavals,* three *tamburas,* and a *tapan,* played by the well-known Rom *zurla* player Muzafer Mahmut, discussed in Rice 1980 and 1982 and heard on CD track 38. Photo by Blagoje Drnkov.

political history, provided recreation and the cultural performance of national identity and loyalty to the state, though Macedonian scholars credit them with reviving many village dances on the verge of extinction. In 1947, an important series of festivals included more than three hundred village groups, after which festivals of village KUDs became popular annual events in Bitola, Skopje, Štip, and the village of Dolneni, near Prilep. The urban KUD Kosta Abraševic appeared in Skopje as early as 1919; one ensemble, Kočo Racin, started in Skopje during World War II. In 1945, some workers' organizations initiated their own ensembles. The airport workers' KUD, Orce Nikolov, was particularly noted for its fine performances of folkloric material from all over Yugoslavia, exercising a responsibility demanded of all KUDs: to perform local and Macedonian material while promoting allegiance to the Yugoslav ideal of brotherhood and ethnic tolerance. By the end of the 1940s, other Skopje KUDs included a university student group, Mirče Acev, and three other ensembles, representing Albanian, Turkish, and Rom minorities.

Tanec, founded in 1949, became a fully professional ensemble with a mandate to represent Macedonia nationally and internationally. Faced with competition at international festivals [see CONTEMPORARY PERFORMANCE CONTEXTS], it soon abandoned its presentation of "pure folklore from the source" in favor of stylized choreographies of dance suites, which in turn provided the standard repertoire for urban KUDs around the country and Macedonian ensembles in Australia, Canada, Germany, and the United States. It featured many of the finest radio instrumentalists and singers.

By the 1970s, Skopje had dozens of KUDs, many smaller towns had two to five, and more than a hundred were scattered in villages, creating a context for many village and urban youths to participate in folklore during the socialist period. Most village KUDs performed local dances in a simpler, though slightly choreographed style than Tanec and some urban KUDs. The recovered and choreographed dances learned in KUDs in turn became part of dance events at weddings and fairs, as young people requested musicians to play them for their amusement. KUDs also provided important patronage to Rom musicians, particularly *zurla* and *tapan* players, paid to accompany village dances on stage, as they were in village squares and church courtyards.

MUSIC OF NATIONAL MINORITIES

For musical life, the Roma constitute the most important local minority, serving as professional musicians to the Slavic majority and other minorities. Musical life within the Rom community includes *zurla* and *tapan*, modern descendants of the *čalgija* ensemble, and songs in Romani [see ROM (GYPSY) MUSIC]. The most popular dance-music, *ček*, exists in 2/4 (3 + 3 + 2) and 9/8 (2 + 2 + 2 + 3), and can be danced in a open circle or as an improvised solo dance with characteristic hip and torso movement. Many Rom vocalists, including Esma Redžepova and Muharem Serbezovski, have emerged as stars. Since 1991, the Rom clarinetist and saxophonist Ferus Mustafov has released recordings abroad.

Turkish music, though little studied, resembles music found in rural areas of Turkey proper, including men's *saz* (long-necked, fretted, plucked lute) playing and the recitation and singing of *maniler* (sing., *mani*), quatrains with an aaba rhyme scheme. Often about love and performed by people of all ages and both sexes, *maniler* are used by women to express otherwise hard-to-express emotions.

POPULAR MUSIC AND RECENT DEVELOPMENTS

During the socialist period, Macedonian popular music was linked more closely to Serbian popular music than to American rock. It consisted of newly composed song styles similar to Macedonian *starogradski pesni* or Serbian popular music performed by ensembles featuring accordion, electric guitar, and bass [see SERBIA]. For most of the socialist period, Macedonian popular music was an amplified version of *narodna muzika*. For local color on a few tunes, the group Tavče Gravče, named for a popular bean dish, added the bagpipes of Pece Atanasovski. Perhaps the most popular rock-influenced group during this period was Leb i Sol (Bread and Salt).

Since independence (in 1991), state support for KUDs has waned, and interest in traditional culture is declining, despite a perceived need to identify those elements of Macedonian culture that distinguish it from its neighbors. Traditional music is being recycled, for example, by jazz musicians, some of whom have added it to their repertoires. One group, Anastasia, which recorded the sound track for the movie *Before the Rain*, employs *kaval, gajda, tambura,* and modern instruments. Another group, Ezgija, has created a fusion sound and recorded with the bagpiper Pece Atanasovski.

The Rom, having become more active in affirming their culture, continue their exploration of new musical possibilities, including rap sung by youths dressed as Los Angeles home boys. Two Rom TV stations broadcast mainly music videos, some with extremely elaborate productions. Religious groups are more visible than during the socialist period, and at holidays Muslim and Christian Orthodox liturgical and ritual music can be seen and heard (Eran Fraenkel, personal communication).

HISTORY OF SCHOLARSHIP

Printed song collections from Macedonian territory first appeared in the 1860s (Miladinov 1861; Verković 1860), many with titles referencing Bulgaria, Turkey, or Greece (Garnett 1885). In the interwar period, collections continued to appear in Serbian (Đorđević 1928; Kuba 1927).

With national recognition after World War II, the Institute for Folklore, founded in Skopje, has published many monographs and *Makedonski Folklor,* a journal with international contributors. In 1955, Macedonian musicologists began recording with tape recorders, and by 1981, the institute's archive held more than sixty thousand recordings of songs. The earliest postwar publications focused on establishing distinctions among Bulgarian, Macedonian, and Serbian styles. Later work has focused on historical questions, including when certain instruments and practices

In comparison to other European countries, many foreign scholars have studied Macedonian music, some contributing song and dance collections and analysis and song-content analysis, and others contributing to themes underemphasized by Macedonian scholars: minorities, especially Roma, and the social and

entered Macedonia; stylistic and ethnographic descriptions of particular regional or village practices; the contents of song texts; and the collection, publication, and classification of repertoires—projects often justified as useful to the KUDs. This purpose has resulted in many printed collections of instrumental music and dance, the latter using verbal description, Labanotation, and a native notation (Firfov and Pajtondžiev 1953).

In comparison to other European countries, many foreign scholars have studied Macedonian music, some contributing song and dance collections and analysis (Dunin 1985; Ellison 1982; Leibman 1992; Traerup 1970, 1981; Ziegler 1979) and song-content analysis (Burkhart 1985, 1987; Peukert 1961, 1978) and others contributing to themes underemphasized by Macedonian scholars: minorities, especially Roma (Dunin 1971, 1973; Rice 1980, 1982; Seeman 1990), and the social and cultural experience of music (Marshall 1977, 1982; Sachs 1975, 1979a, 1979b).

BIBLIOGRAPHY

Aluševski, Ilija. 1980. "Bitolska čalgija." *Razvitok* 18:817–823.

Askari, Mohamed, Rudolf Brandl, and Hans-Jörg Maucksch. 1985. "Das volkstümliche Klarinettenensemble zwischen Orient und Balkan." *Studia Instrumentorum Musicae Popularis* 8:67–85.

Bicevski, Trpko. 1986. *Dvoglasjeto vo SP Madedonija*. Skopje: Institute for Folklore.

———. 1988. *Dvoglasni makedonski narodni pesni*. Skopje: Institute for Folklore.

Brömse, Peter. 1937. *Schalmaien und Sackpfeifen sudslawiens*. Vienna: Rohrer.

Burkhart, Dagmar. 1985. "Der Eliastag 1903 in mazedonischen Volksballaden." *Lares* 51: 479–493.

———. 1987. "Historisches Ereignis und charismatischer Held in mazedonischen Lieder." *Makedonski Folklor* 20(39–40):23–33.

Danforth, Loring. 1995. *The Macedonian Conflict: Ethnic Nationalism in a Transnational World*. Princeton, N.J.: Princeton University Press.

Dimčevski, Đorđi. 1983. *Vie se oro makedonsko: Zbirka na makedonski ora*. Skopje: KUD Goce Delčev.

Đorđević, Vladimir. 1928. *Srpske narodne melodije: Južna Srbija*. Skopje: Skopsko naučno društvo.

Dunin, Elsie Ivancich. 1971. "Gypsy Wedding: Dance and Customs." *Makedonski Folklor* 4(7–8):317–326.

———. 1973. "*Čoček* as a Ritual Dance among Gypsy Women." *Makedonski Folklor* 8(15–16): 193–198.

———. 1985. "Dance Change in Context of the Gypsy St. George's Day, Skopje, Yugoslavia, 1967–1977." In *Papers from the 4th and 5th Annual Meetings of the Gypsy Lore Society, North American Chapter*, ed. Joanne Grumet, 2: 110–120. New York: Gypsy Lore Society, North American Chapter.

Dunin, Elsie Ivanocich, Mihailo Dimoski, and Stanimir Visinski. 1973. *Makedonski narodni plesovi/Macedonian Folk Dances*. Zagreb: Prosvjetni Sabor Hrvatske.

———. 1995. *Orata vo Makedonija/Dances in Macedonia: Scenski del Tanec*. Skopje: Otvoreno opstestvo Makedonija.

Džimrevski, Borivoje. 1985. *Čalgiskata tradicija vo Makedonija*. Skopje: Makedonska Kniga.

Ellison, Judith. 1982. "*Ezgija*: Improvisation in the Repertoires of Two Macedonian Musicians." M.A. thesis, University of Washington.

Firfov, Živko. 1952. "Les caractères métriques dans la musique populaire macédonienne." *Journal of the International Folk Music Council* 4:49–53.

———. 1953, 1959. *Makedonski muzički folklor: Pesni*. 2 vols. Skopje: Kočo Racin (vol. 1), Folkloren Institut na N. R. Makedonija (vol. 2).

———. 1961. "Eden vek muzički život." In *Sto godini Veleška gimnazija*, 169–179. Titov Veles: Opštinski odbor na SSRNM.

Firfov, Živko, and Gančo Pajtondžiev. 1953. *Makedonski narodni ora*. Skopje: Kočo Racin.

Firfov, Živko, and Metodi Simonovski, eds. 1962. *Makedonskite melografi od krajot na XIX vek*. Skopje: Institute for Folklore.

Garnett, Lucy M. J. 1885. *Greek Folk-Songs from the Turkish Provinces of Greece, "I Douli Ellas": Albania, Thessaly (Not Yet Wholly Free), and Macedonia*. Revised and edited by J. S. Stuart Glennie. London: The Athenaeum.

Hadžimanov, Vasil. 1960. "Instruments folklorique en Macédoine–kavalis." *Journal of the International Folk Music Council* 12:21–22.

———. 1963. "The Dvotelnik, a Macedonian Folk Instrument." *Journal of the International Folk Music Council* 15:82–83.

———. 1964. *Soborski narodni pesni*. Skopje: Kočo Racin.

———. 1965. "Les mélodies funèbres du séisme de Skopjé." *Journal of the International Folk Music Council* 17(2):71–77.

———. 1968. *Makedonski narodni pesni (momi tikvešanki)*. Skopje: Makedonska Kniga.

Hadžimanov, Vasil, and Živko Firfov. 1961. "Volksmusikinstrumente und instrumentale Volksmusik Macedonies." *Journal of the International Folk Music Council* 13:77–98.

Hoerburger, Felix. 1954. *Der Tanz mit Trommel*. Regensburg: Bosse.

———. 1967. "Oriental Elements in the Folk Dance and Folk Music of Greek Macedonia."

Journal of the International Folk Music Council 19: 71–75.

International Folk Music Council. 1952. "Programme Notes on the Dances and Songs Performed at the Yugoslav Folk Music Festival." *Journal of the International Folk Music Council* 4: 60–64.

Karovski, Lazlo. 1974. "Macedonian Folk Poetry of Economic Immigration." *Macedonian Review* 4:295–302.

———. 1981. *Klasifikacija na makedonskata narodna pesna.* Skopje: Institute for Folklore.

Katsarova, Raina. 1973. "Balkanski varianti na dve Turski pesni." *Izvestija za Instituta za Muzika* 16:115–133. Sofia, Bulgaria.

Kuba, Ludvik. 1927. *Pučka glazbena umjetnost u Makedoniji.* 2 vols. Zagreb: St. Cecilija.

Leibman, Robert H. 1992. "Dancing Bears and Purple Transformations: The Structure of Dance in the Balkans (Macedonia, Serbia, Bulgaria)." Ph.D. dissertation, University of Pennsylvania.

Linin, Aleksandar. 1978. *Makedonski instrumentalni orski narodni melodii.* Skopje: Makedonska Kniga.

———. 1986. *Narodnite muzični instrumenti vo Makedonija.* Skopje: Makedonska Kniga.

Marshall, Christopher. 1977. "The Aesthetics of Music in Village Macedonia." Ph.D. dissertation, Cornell University.

———. 1982. "Towards a Cross-Cultural Theory of Aesthetics." In *Cross-Cultural Perspectives on Music,* ed. Robert Falck and Timothy Rice, 162–173. Toronto: University of Toronto Press.

Miladinov, Konstantin. 1861. *B'ulgarski narodni pesni.* Zagreb: A. Jakić.

Ortakov, Dragoslav. 1978. "Approaches to the Study of Macedonian Musical History."

International Review of the Aesthetics and Sociology of Music 6(2):307–315.

———. 1982. *Muzičkata umetnost vo Makedonija.* Skopje: Makedonska Revija.

Pajtondjiev, Gančo. 1973. *Makedonski narodni ora.* Skopje: Makedonska Kniga.

Penušliski, Kiril. 1966. "Macedonian Revolutionary Folk Poetry and the National Consciousness of the Macedonian People." *Journal of the Folklore Institute* 3:250–266.

Peukert, Herbert. 1961. *Serbokroatische und makedonische Volkslyrik.* Berlin: Institut für Slawistik.

———. 1978. *Die Makedonische Volkspoesie: Probleme und Praxis des Traditions- und Funktionswandels in der Volksdichtung.* Skopje: Makedonische Akademie der Wissenschaften und Kunste.

Pinto, Vivian. 1955–1956. "Dawn-Courtship in Bulgarian and Macedonian Folk Poetry." *The Slavonic and East European Review* 34:200–219.

Rice, Timothy. 1980. "Macedonian *Sobor*: Anatomy of a Celebration." *Journal of American Folklore* 93:113–128.

———. 1982. "The *Surla* and *Tapan* Tradition in Yugoslav Macedonia." *The Galpin Society Journal* 35:122–137.

Ristovski, Blaže. 1974. *Makedonski revolucionerni narodni pesni.* Skopje: Institut za Folklor, Makedonska Kniga.

Sachs, Nahoma. 1975. "Music and Meaning: Musical Symbolism in a Macedonian Village." Ph.D. dissertation, Indiana University.

———. 1979a. "Chants That Do Not Wound: Concept and Sensation in Koleda." In *Essays in Humanistic Anthropology: Festschrift in Honour of David Bidney,* ed. B. T. Grindal and D. M.

Warren, 253–276. Washington, D.C.: University Press of America.

———. 1979b. "The Facts of Death: An Anthropologist Views Musical Symbolism." *World of Music* 21:36–45.

Seeman, Sonia Tamar. 1990. "Continuity and Change in the Macedonian Genre of Čalgija: Past Perfect and Present Imperfective." M.A. thesis, University of Washington.

Silverman, Carol. 1996. "Music and Marginality: *Roma* (Gypsies) of Bulgaria and Macedonia." In *Returning Culture: Musical Exchanges in Central and Eastern Europe,* ed. Mark Slobin, 231–253. Durham, N.C.: Duke University Press.

Singer, Alice. 1974. "The Metrical Structure of Macedonian Dance." *Ethnomusicology* 18(3): 379–404.

Traerup, Birthe. 1970. *East Macedonian Folk Songs: Contemporary Traditional Material from Malesevo, Pijanec and the Razlog District.* Copenhagen: Akademisk Forlag.

———. 1981. "Mazedonische Bordungesänge." In *Der Bordun in der europäische Volksmusik,* ed. Walter Deutsch, 161–175. Vienna: Schendl.

Vasiljević, Miodrag A. 1953. *Makedonija.* Jugoslavenski muzički folklor, 2. Belgrade: Prosveta.

Verković, Stefan 1860. *Narodne pesme Makedonski bugara.* Belgrade: Praviletstvenom knigopechatnom.

Wunsch, Walter. 1934. *Die Geigentechnik der sudslavischen Guslaren.* Brno: R. M. Rohrer.

Ziegler, Susanne. 1979. *Das Volkslied in Westmazedonien.* Berlin: Harrassowitz.

———. 1982. "The Relation [sic] Text-Melody in Ritual Folksongs of Western Macedonia." *Makedonski Folklor* 15(29–30):159–162.

AUDIOVISUAL RESOURCES

Atanasovik, Pece. N.d. *Macedonian Folk Dances (Reels).* Jugoton LPY 50985. LP disk.

Avramovski, Risto. 1982. *Anthology of Macedonian Music.* Diskos LPD 723–26, 1009–12. 8 LP disks.

Bhattacharya, Deben. 1972. *Songs and Dances from Macedonia.* Argo ZFB 56. LP disk.

Čalgii na RTS. 1982. *Makedonski starogradski pesni.* Jugoton LSY-61633. LP disk.

Dević, Dragoslav. N.d. *Traditional Folk-Music, Macedonia.* RTB 2510081. LP disk.

Liebman, Robert H. N.d. *Traditional Tosk*

(Southern Albanian) Songs and Dances from the Lake Prespa Area. Selo LP-2. LP disk.

Mančevski, Kiril. N.d. *Ajde sonce zajde.* RTB LP 1384. LP disk.

Mustafov, Ferus. 1994. *King Ferus: Macedonian Wedding Soul Cooking.* GlobeStyle Records CDORBD 089. Compact disc.

Ognenovski, Tale. N.d. *Tale Ognenovski, clarinet, svira ora.* Jugoton LPY 61143. LP disk.

Redžepova, Esma. 1980. *Esma Esma.* RTB LP 2110024. LP disk.

Štipski Svadbari. 1980. *Ora i čočeci.* RTB LP 1438. LP disk.

Tanec. N.d. *Tanec igra i pee.* RTB LPV 178. LP disk.

Tavče Gravče. 1985. *Ako imaš srce.* Jugoton LSY 62003. LP disk.

Yugoslav Folk Music. 1968? Lyrichord 7189. LP disk.

Yugoslavian Folk Music from Macedonia. 1976. Olympic 6130. LP disk.

Albanian Music

Jane Sugarman

Overview of Musical Genres and Contexts
Music in Southern Communities
Music in Northern Communities
Music in Institutionalized Settings
Scholarship on Albanian Music

Albanians (Shqiptarë) are the cultural descendants of Indo-European peoples who inhabited the Balkan Peninsula in antiquity. In the late 1990s, more than three million Albanians live in Albania proper (Shqipëria), a 28,748-square-kilometer, largely mountainous country on the western edge of the peninsula. Ruled for most of its history by Roman, Byzantine, Serbian, and Ottoman empires, Albania declared its independence in 1912, only to be partitioned so that today over two million Albanians live outside Albania, in Montenegro, Macedonia, the Serbian province of Kosovo (Albanian, Kosova), and elsewhere in the former Yugoslavia (map 13). Sizable communities of Albanian-speakers and their descendants also live in Greece, Italy, Turkey, Western Europe, North America, and Australia. In Albania, a people's republic, declared in 1946, was superseded by a republic in 1991. Despite the industrialization and urbanization encouraged during the socialist period, Albania remains one of the least-urbanized countries in Europe, with 65 percent of the population living in rural areas as of the late 1980s. This article surveys musical activities within Albania itself and in contiguous areas of the Yugoslav successor-states.

During the nineteenth and early twentieth centuries, Albanians living north of the Shkumbin River were called Gegs; those to the south, Tosks. Today, Albanians are more commonly called north and south Albanians, respectively (see map 13). Each group has its own dialects, but literary Albanian is based primarily on southern speech. In 1945, the population of Albania was roughly 70 percent Muslim (including 20 percent Bektashi, members of a Sufi order), 20 percent Eastern Orthodox Christian, and 10 percent Roman Catholic. In territories of the former Yugoslavia, more than 90 percent of Albanians are Muslim, the rest mostly Roman Catholics. In part because of official discouragement of religious observance in Yugoslavia and its actual prohibition in Albania after 1967, many Albanians no longer retain a strong sense of religious identity. The musical practices of Christians and Muslims in a given region are much the same, but major differences in musical style exist between northern and southern communities. Certain styles of northern music resemble those of Slavs living in Montenegro, southern Serbia, Kosova, and Macedonia. Southern Albanian music has correlates in the music of neighboring Greek, Aromân (speakers of a Latin-derived language), and Slavic communities.

MAP 13 Albanian-populated areas in the central Balkans

OVERVIEW OF MUSICAL GENRES AND CONTEXTS

Before World War II, Albanian folk or national music thrived almost exclusively in the context of family or community occasions. Vocal genres dominated most music making, particularly in rural areas. Song texts provided primary points of reference for moral values, history, and communal identity. Singing accompanied labor and was central to religious and ritual events. Music making and dancing were not merely forms of socializing and entertainment; they also offered creative and aesthetic challenges. Though some genres are no longer performed in community settings, they remain crucial to an assessment of more recent developments.

Most rural communities distinguish between women's songs (*këngë grash*) and men's songs (*këngë burrash*). Women and men traditionally worked and socialized in segregated groups, and developed separate repertoires of songs that address different subjects and are often performed in contrasting styles and settings.

Women's responsibilities have centered around the home, and their songs have been closely connected to family affairs and household activities. Men have concerned themselves with communal welfare, regulating local affairs and defending their homes and settlements from outside attack. Their songs express a broader concern with historical events and political affairs; men have also been the principal instrumentalists. Children too have often had their separate instruments and song repertoires.

Albanian scholars often designate a large group of songs as lyric songs. Women sing lyric songs almost exclusively, but men also sing narrative songs. Lyric song texts address everyday matters and are often associated with specific ritual contexts. In the past, two ritual cycles were critical for a community's survival: seasonal rituals and rituals marking the progression of family members through major stages of life. Many themes and symbols of these cycles overlapped, in that participants intended each type of ritual to assure health, fertility, and continuity.

Seasonal rituals and their music

In the past, when life in rural areas was governed by the agricultural calendar, songs with specific seasonal associations were a prominent element of festivities that occurred during winter or spring, in anticipation of the planting and tending of crops during the summer months.

In southern Albania, carolers went from door to door to wish each household health and prosperity in the coming year. At Christmas, children of both sexes, known as *kolendarë,* participated; for Lazarus' Day (Llazore, the Saturday or Sunday one week before Holy Saturday or Easter), only girls caroled. In each case, the carolers collected gifts such as eggs, walnuts, dried figs, corn, and wheat, which they later shared among themselves. In virtually all Albanian districts, girls were also central participants in springtime holidays, such as the Day of Summer (1 March), Sulltan Nevruz (21 March, from Nawruz, the Persian New Year), the Annunciation (25 March), and St. George's Day (23 April or May 6).

Among Albanians of all religions, St. George's Day (Shëngjergj) was the most elaborate and widely celebrated, since it marked the beginning of the agricultural year. In Muslim communities, the two *bajram*s (Turkish *bayram,* Arabic '*īd*)—the first observed for three days after Ramadan (Ramazan), the second eighty days thereafter—were also celebrated. In early June and late August, some herding communities commemorated the driving of herds to the summer pastures and later their return to the village. During the late spring or early summer of a dry year, children performed a rain-bringing ritual (*dordolec* or *peperona*): usually one child, the *dordolec,* arrayed only in greenery, was paraded from house to house, where he or she was showered with water while the other children sang.

Life-cycle events and their music

The performance of seasonal rituals, officially prohibited in Albania between 1967 and 1991, also declined among most Yugoslav Albanians in that period. Life-cycle observances, however, particularly weddings, are still major events. The climax of a traditional wedding occurs when the bridegroom's party takes the bride from her home and returns with her to the bridegroom's home, where the couple will live. For the period surrounding that moment, professional singers and instrumentalists may be hired, usually by the bridegroom's family, to entertain the invited guests and provide music for dancing. Surrounding the central event, however, are rituals at which songs sung by the groom's and bride's families commemorate their coming of age, introduce the bride to her new household and wifely obligations, and establish relations between the two families (figure 1).

Less common are songs for the birth of a child. In some areas, the pregnant woman, with women and girls of her household, formerly sang in anticipation of a birth. Far more widespread were joyous songs that announced the birth, especially of a son, to nearby households. Lullabies (*ninulla, këngë djepi*) that the mother, a grandmother, a sister, an aunt, or a cousin sings to a newborn boy celebrate the birth of an heir, while those sung to a girl often anticipate her marriage into another household. At circumcision celebrations in Muslim communities, women sing songs that are often variations of wedding songs addressed to the groom.

FIGURE 1 Southern women sing a wedding song to the groom. Lake Prespa District, Macedonia. Photo by Jane Sugarman, 1980.

Singing at social occasions

In addition to ritual contexts, men and women sing at evening gatherings held during weddings and other social occasions. Women's songs focus on love, courtship, and marriage. Where men have gone abroad in search of work, men and women also sing songs of exile (*këngë mërgimi* or *këngë kurbeti*). Men have their own love songs, often more erotic or ecstatic than those sung by women, as well as humorous songs. Some southern communities maintain a tradition in which men drink a shot of *raki,* a type of homemade brandy, before each song during an evening's gathering. As the men become more elated, the evening's final stages are given over to exchanges of rhymed couplets (*bejte,* from Arabic *bayt*). Whether extemporized or delivered in a set form, these are meant to praise the host's hospitality, wish his family well, or tease participants, who must hastily construct a cleverly worded retort.

Most songs that men sing at social gatherings are narratives. These include ballads with themes known throughout the Balkans, such as that of the bride interred in the foundations of a bridge or tower so it will stand. The most famous Albanian narrative songs are the long heroic songs known as *kângë kreshnikësh* (from the Slavic word *krajišnik* 'frontier hero') or *rapsodi* 'rhapsodies', sung by northern epic singers (*rapsodë*). The largest body of such songs narrates events of the 1400s and 1500s, when Muslim and Christian warriors clashed in the northern Bosnian border zone separating the Ottoman Empire from Christian Europe. Closely related to epics once sung by Slavic Muslims in Bosnia and southern Serbia, Albanian epics emphasize fantastic elements reminiscent of fairy tales or classical myths. Singers of past generations extemporized them in performance, drawing on an extensive repertoire of poetic formulas; today, however, singers may perform memorized texts.

Northern and southern men also sing shorter historical songs with more fixed texts. Before formal schooling was available, many rural Albanians acquired their sense of national identity through such songs, which detailed important political events. Among the oldest still sung are those that date from the early 1800s, when many young Albanian men were conscripted to serve in the Ottoman army. These songs are known as songs of the recruits (*këngë nizami*). A larger group of songs deal with resistance to Ottoman rule and the consolidation of the Albanian state, beginning with the founding of the Albanian League in 1878. Northern songs from the early twentieth century detail border skirmishes between the new state and neighbor-

Accomplished younger male singers cultivate energetic styles of singing, whose flamboyant character suits their strong voices and their notions of masculine demeanor. Women tend to sing in a more subdued manner, which highlights their sexual propriety and modesty.

ing Serbia and Montenegro, while southern songs recount guerrilla actions against Greek forces. Similar songs recount Albania's fall to Italy during World War II. Singers continue to create narrative songs detailing contemporary events. In the socialist period, the Albanian government actively encouraged the creation of songs that exalted the Albanian Party of Labor and its chairman, Enver Hoxha.

Singing is not considered appropriate immediately after a family member dies. At such times, the genres performed are not songs (*këngë*) but laments, stylized forms of crying. Laments may be called *me të qarë* 'with crying', *të qarë me zë* 'cried with the voice', and *vaje, vajtim,* or *kuje,* names that derive from sorrowful exclamations like *vaj vaj!* and *kuku!* Family members, usually women, lament, as do lament specialists of either gender who assist at funerals in their district. An unusual feature of women's lamenting is that it was in the past sometimes performed collectively. In some places, a woman soloist was answered by a chorus of other women, who at the end of each line or verse performed a sorrowful exclamation, such as *oi oiii!* and *o lele oi!* In other areas, members of the immediate family alternated verses with a group composed of more distant relatives and neighbors. Men have also lamented for a close family member; among northern highlanders, male lament specialists formerly vocalized an elegy for the dead, known as *gjâmë,* if the deceased was a male.

MUSIC IN SOUTHERN COMMUNITIES
Polyphonic singing

Though a few vocal genres, including lullabies, laments, and songs for seasonal rituals, have been performed monophonically, most southern Albanian singing is polyphonic. This feature is closely connected to the role that singing has played at social gatherings. Usually the host family and their guests gather to sing in groups segregated by gender, and each adult present is expected to participate by leading a song.

Songs are usually unaccompanied and feature two or more solo lines, drawn from pentatonic scales. The soloist who initiates the song is regarded as the singer. Other soloists perform an accompanying function, and all others present provide a choral drone (figure 2). Most songs are sung in duple or triple time or in additive meters, such as 5/8 (2 + 3) and 7/8 (3 + 2 +2). Some men's songs are nonmetric. In certain places, songs with only two lines are performed.

The polyphonic structure of southern singing has its counterpart in dance configurations, particularly where dancing is accompanied primarily by singing. In most such regions, two vocal soloists dance a duet while those droning circle them or stand to the side. In a few areas, the soloists dance first and second in a line while those droning follow behind them, all holding hands.

Tosk and Lab styles compared

Polyphonic styles vary by region and gender. Beniamin Kruta (1980) has identified two main styles of southern polyphony: Tosk and Lab. Tosk polyphony is sung

FIGURE 2 A Tosk women's dance-song for a wedding. Lake Prespa District, Macedonia. Original a major third lower. Transcription by Jane Sugarman.

throughout Toskëri (southeastern Albania), Myzeqe (southwestern Albania), and Çamëri (the border area between southern Albania and Greece), as well as in south-western Macedonia. In this style, two soloists sing vocal lines that interweave over a drone sung on a vowel, such as /a/ or /e/. The beginning of the song is usually sung solo, and subsequent lines proceed in overlapping alternation, with the drone entering last (figure 2). The two solo lines draw roughly upon the same pitches, and in the course of a song they may cross one or more times.

Lab polyphony is found in Labëri, in south-central Albania. In its most common style, two to three soloists sing closely coordinated syllabic lines over a drone sung on a vowel or syllables of the song text (figure 3). Each soloist moves within a specific range of pitches, and in some styles the individual parts may be in different scales or modes. The effect is of stratification in which dense tonal clusters occur on virtually every beat.

Depending upon the locality, singers of Tosk polyphony may refer to the first soloist as singing (*këndon*) or saying (*thotë*) his or her part, or as taking up (*merr*) the song. The second soloist is said to support (*mban*) the song or to cut (*pret*) it, in the sense of interrupting it, since that singer customarily enters after the first. Those singing the drone do a drone (*bëjnë iso*), sustain their voice (*e mbajnë zë*), groan (*rënkojnë*), or boil (*ziejnë*). The most common term for Tosk polyphonic singing is *këngë me iso* 'songs with droning', but singers in certain places also speak of *këngë me të marrje me të prerje* 'songs with taking and cutting', *këngë me të rënkuar* 'songs with groaning', or *këngë me të zier* 'songs with boiling'.

Singers in Lab areas say the first soloist takes up (*merr*) the song, and the second soloist returns (*ia kthen*) it, since that line often circles around the pitches just below the song's tonal center. When a third soloist participates, he or she is said to throw (*hedh*), fill (*mbush*), or cut (*pret*) the song; often this part moves regularly between the drone pitch and another a minor third above it. Those singing the fourth part provide a drone (*iso*).

Accomplished younger male singers cultivate energetic styles of singing, whose flamboyant character suits their strong voices and their notions of masculine demeanor. Women tend to sing in a more subdued manner, which highlights their sexual propriety and modesty. Compared to men's singing, theirs is often more strictly metric, less sharply accented, and less ornamented. As women age, better singers may adopt virtuosic features of the men's repertoire, whereas older men often sing in a more subdued, dignified manner (*shtruar* 'extended, drawn out'). Lab communities

FIGURE 3   A Lab women's wedding song. Gjirokastër District, Albania. Transcription by Mexhit Daiu. After Dheri, Daiu, and Mustaqi 1966b:145.

FIGURE 3   A Lab women's wedding song. Gjirokastër District, Albania. Transcription by Mexhit Daiu. After Dheri, Daiu, and Mustaqi 1966b:145.

distinguish between the repertoires of younger and older generations of each gender, designating songs with terms such as *young men's song* and *elders' songs.*

Singers of ornate men's songs use vocal techniques, often derived from women's solo lamenting, that are intended to imply deep emotion and prompt an emotional response in others. Tosk lamenters fill downward leaps with a portamento and conclude lines of text with ascents of a minor seventh on vowel sounds such as /e-i/ and /o-u/, in which they change into falsetto register. Tosk male singers use similar features in historical songs and songs of exile, as commentary on the tragedy depicted in the song and as marks of the soloist's involvement and elation. Such performances are described as "with crying." Even when features of laments are not incorporated, the phrase "he is crying the song" may be used to praise a particularly emotional performance. In Lab areas, lamenters often render parts of the text using a glottal pulsation—a gesture that has become a standard feature of some Lab singing styles. Falsetto leaps similar to those in lamenting may also occur in Lab women's songs sung for the bride's departure from her home at the climax of a wedding.

Instrumental music

Though singing has dominated villagers' music making, a few men in each community have played locally made instruments, especially herdsmen's flutes (*fyell*), most of which consist of a short (about 20 to 50 centimeters) tube made of wood, reed, bone, metal, or plastic, held obliquely and blown across one end to produce a pentatonic or diatonic scale. In some districts, longer flutes called *kavall* (80 to 90 centimeters), which yield a chromatic scale, have been more common, and duct flutes of similar construction have also been used. Herdsmen in Labëri have also played a type of short, double-bore duct flute (*biculë* or *cylëdyjare*).

Men have played flutes for family gatherings and while out herding. Players often say they have used their flutes to calm the herd or to direct its movement. Generally they play solo, though in some areas a second player may provide a drone. Most of their repertoire consists of expansive, often nonmetric, largely extemporized melodies. Players may give names to their performances, such as "*Kur shkojnë dhëntë për ujë*" ('When the sheep go for water') and "*Bagëtia në kullotë*" ('The herd while grazing'), or they may call them by the Near Eastern terms *avaz* and *kaba,* used also by urban musicians. Related to herding melodies are those that draw on the style of women's vocal laments, which players call *të qarë* 'cried' or *vajtim* 'lament'. Flutists also play local song and dance melodies. Players of the Lab double flute can imitate the top two voices of the local polyphony.

Rural men have also played various types of reed instruments. As their first instrument, boys formerly made a single-reed pipe (*pipezë*) from a piece of cane, carving a reed from one end. Adult men play similar pipes with inserted heteroglot reeds, often performing in pairs in a manner that imitates polyphonic singing. In southeastern districts of Albania, the most popular reed instrument has been the *gajde,* a bagpipe with one cylindrical chanter and one drone pipe, each activated by a single cane reed. Though *gajde* players extemporize melodies, their primary role is to accompany collective singing or dancing. Played as a solo melodic instrument, a *gajde* may be accompanied by a frame drum (*dajre*) or a large, two-headed bass drum (*daulle*). If a player's bag is large enough, he can accompany his own singing.

Urban-based music

For the largest celebrations, rural families hire professional musicians from nearby towns. The ensembles, called *saze* (Turkish 'instruments'), are generally made up of Rom (Gypsy) families. In the early 1800s, the ensemble most likely consisted of a *fyell,* an Ottoman *kemençe* (a small, vertically held bowed lute), a *llautë* (a large, pear-shaped plucked fretted lute), and a *def* (a large frame drum). By 1900, with the increasing popularity of European instruments, the *fyell* had been replaced by one or two clarinets, and the *kemençe* by one or two violins; by 1945, the ensemble had been augmented by one or two accordions (figure 4). Today, the *saze* repertoire is often performed on electric guitar and bass, saxophone, synthesizer, and drum set. Because *saze* travel extensively throughout rural areas and have made recordings since the 1920s, they have transmitted songs and dance melodies from village to village and district to district. Famous leaders of *saze* in recent years have included Laver Bariu and Remzi Lela, both from Përmet. Singers Vaçe Zela, from Vlorë, and Eli Fara, from Korçë, have also recorded songs to *saze* accompaniment.

The older *saze* repertoire consists of songs, dance melodies, and solo instrumental genres, all performed in a polyphonic style closely resembling that of village singing. For women's dancing, *saze* play light (*lehtë*) melodies in a moderate tempo and strict meter. For men's dancing, which often features acrobatic squatting and turning, they play heavy (*rëndë*) melodies in a slower, rubato manner.

The highlights of *saze* performances are evocative, nonmetric improvisations on clarinet, violin, or sometimes *llautë.* Similar to flute melodies, but generally more virtuosic, these are known as *kaba, avaz, vajtim,* or *me të qarë.* Musicians perform these most often for male guests at an event to generate feelings of elation and nostalgia.

Urbanites in past decades also developed their own musical repertoires, known not only in towns, but also in villages where residents had contacts with urban commercial life. In the Ottoman period, men learned to play local versions of Near Eastern chordophones, such as the *ud,* the *bakllama* (Turkish *bağlama*), and the

FIGURE 4 *Saze* playing for dancing at a southern wedding. Bitola, Macedonia. Photo by Eran Fraenkel, 1981.

In the Podgur District, shepherdesses' songs (*kângë të çobaneshave*) have been sung by pairs of girls in a style known as 'with finger on throat', in which each singer vibrates her larynx with her right thumb to alter vocal timbre.

FIGURE 5   A southern Albanian urban song, "*Krehi Leshkat.*" Korçë, Albania. After Osmalli 1958:61–62.

buzuk (Turkish *bozuk*) to accompany pentatonic songs or ones based on the Ottoman system of melodic modes, or *makam*s. After the 1920s, brass bands became popular in some towns, and townspeople created songs modeled after popular tunes from Western Europe, accompanied on guitar, mandolin, and violin. At urban social events, people still sing with relish the urban songs (*kengë qytetare*) of the early twentieth century (figure 5).

MUSIC IN NORTHERN COMMUNITIES

Highland music

Most northern singing is monophonic, but singers sometimes accompany themselves on melodic or rhythmic instruments. There is also a greater emphasis placed on solo performance in northern areas than in the south, particularly of men's genres. Older styles are found primarily in mountainous areas of the north, especially in Malësi, straddling the Montenegro-Albanian border [see MONTENEGRO], and in the Rugovë and Podgur districts, north and west of Pejë (Serbian Peč) in Kosova. People in these districts call themselves *malësorë* 'people of the *malë*', a term that denotes clanlike, patriarchal groups. Their songs have narrow-range melodies with small intervals and nontempered intonation, and use additive meters, such as 12/8 (figure 6). Though men and women have different repertoires, both genders use a loud, focused type of vocal production typical of outdoor singing throughout the central Balkans.

For metric dance songs, women often accompany their singing with one or more large frame drums (*def, daire*). One popular women's dance is a solo form, *kcim*, which emphasizes graceful arm movements, but in some areas line dances are more common. Women have also sung to the accompaniment of a large, round tray (*tepsi*):

FIGURE 6   A young women's wedding song in 12/8 for the "Night of Henna." Podgur District, Kosova. After Munishi 1979: 202–203.

FIGURE 7   Northern girls from the Ulcinj District of Montenegro sing with *tepsi* at the Ohrid Festival, Macedonia. Photo by Eran Fraenkel, 1980.

while one or more women sit beside it and sing into it, another woman places it on a flat surface and with her hand rotates it on its edge; its rotation vibrates the air, affecting the singers' vocal timbre, and its rumbling provides a dronelike accompaniment (figure 7). The player often wears one or more rings that knock against the side of the tray to provide a steady beat. In the Podgur District, shepherdesses' songs (*kângë të çobaneshave*) have been sung by pairs of girls in a style known as *me gisht në fyt* 'with finger on throat', in which each singer vibrates her larynx with her right thumb to alter vocal timbre.

One of the most celebrated men's genres is the "song of the *malësorë*" (*kângë malësorçe*) or the "song of the peak of the arm" (*kângë majekrahi*). One or two men each place a finger in one ear or cup their ear, raise their elbow above eye level, and sing out at full volume. In the past, shepherds or soldiers sang such songs to signal from one mountain to another, but men also sing them at weddings and other festive occasions, even indoors. Narrative songs are most often accompanied by a type of one-stringed fiddle (*lahutë*). The long neck and bowl-shaped body of the *lahutë* are carved from a single piece of wood, to which a skin face is then attached. The playing string and the hairs of the bow are made of horsehair. Players often carve the peg head with elaborate zoomorphic or patriotic designs, highlighting the fantasy and heroism of their songs. The performer, sitting and holding the *lahutë* vertically at a slant while accompanying his singing, is expected through his posture and delivery to convey a forceful and manly affect.

The melodies of songs sung to *lahutë* have just three or four notes, emphasizing stepwise motion. Most lines are sung to the same melodic formula, with a second formula used for the final one or two lines of major sections of the performance. The *lahutë* accompanies with an ornamented version of the melody, providing an introduction and interludes between sections of the story.

Though most older styles of women's singing are monophonic, women in southwestern Kosova and western Macedonia also sing two-voiced polyphony. Against a narrow-ranged melody sung by a soloist, one or more women sing a lower vocal line that sometimes duplicates pitches of the melody and sometimes strikes a pitch a second or a third below it. Men in the same districts in Kosova sing only in unison, but in western Macedonia men have their own polyphonic styles of singing, consisting of a melodic line sung against a drone.

FIGURE 8 *Çifteli*s and a *sharki* on sale in a market in Tetovo, Macedonia. Photo by Eran Fraenkel, 1982.

Instrumental music

Northern herdsmen play various aerophones, the most ubiquitous a short, six-holed, rim-blown flute (*fyell*). Duct flutes of similar size (*bilbil* or *fyelldrejti*) are also common. In western Macedonia, herdsmen play long, eight-holed rim-blown flutes with chromatic fingering, called *kavall*. These instruments, carved from single pieces of wood, are made and played in pairs, in unison or with a melody played against a drone. Also found in Macedonia and Kosova is a double-bore duct flute known as *binjak* 'twin' or *pelqesë*. Villagers have also played single-reed pipes, the most common with two tubes. A popular type is the *zumare*, with two parallel tubes to which an animal horn has been attached to form a bell. Players use circular breathing when playing reed instruments, even, from time to time, on the rim-blown *fyell*. In a few areas, men obtain the same result by attaching a single- or double-tubed pipe to a bag and playing it as a bagpipe (*bishnicë* or *mishnicë*).

Lowland musics

In districts close to large towns, especially the lowland districts of Kosova, Turkish music has influenced Albanian styles, and Ottoman poetry has influenced song texts, especially of men's love songs. Melodies tend to be in additive meters or duple or triple time, and often have a larger range. Some songs are sung to famous Turkish melodies, and others, though not based on a Turkish model, have melodies that resemble common *makam*s. A distinctive feature of singing in these areas is a rhythmic pulsation or vibrato performed on sustained notes.

The most popular stringed instruments among men in lowland areas are fretted, long-necked lutes resembling the Turkish *saz*. Most widespread is the *çifteli* or *çiteli* (Turkish *çift* 'pair' and *tel* 'wire'), with two metal strings and eleven to thirteen frets (figure 8). The lower string provides a drone to the upper string's melody. When these strings are tuned a fourth apart, the scale produced includes neutral second and sixth degrees, so that it resembles the Turkish *makam Hüseyni*. Other tunings produce a scale resembling *makam Hicaz,* or imitate instruments such as the *zumare* and the *fyell*. A larger lute, the *sharki* (Arabic 'eastern'), is popular primarily in Kosova; it may have from three to twelve strings, though most have five or seven, arranged in three courses. The *çifteli* and the *sharki* are steadily becoming instruments of choice in many mountain areas, replacing the *lahutë*.

Men play such instruments to accompany singing and dancing, and for solo improvisations and metric melodies. For weddings and other large family events, particularly in Kosova and western Macedonia, groups of two or more men were once hired to sing and play for men's indoor gatherings. One man would play *çifteli* and another *sharki*, and additional instrumentalists would play a violin, an accordion, and/or a *fyell*. As the men performed, they alternated between longer historical or patriotic songs and shorter songs of love or everyday life, occasionally inserting an instrumental dance tune. In recent years, Hashim Shala and Tahir Drenica, from Kosova, have been among the best-known exponents of this repertoire.

Rom musicians, whose patrons include villagers and urbanites, have also often been hired for family celebrations. Sometimes one or two Rom women are asked to perform at the women's portions of a wedding or circumcision, singing to the accompaniment of *daire* and perhaps performing special dances. To accompany men's activities and for outdoor dancing and processions, families have also hired a group of male musicians to play *surle* (*curle, zurle, cingonë*), a conical-bore double-reed instrument, and *lodër* (also *lodërti, daulle, tupan*), a two-headed bass drum. Such a group includes one to two *lodër* players, plus two or three *surle* players performing in unison, octaves, or with melody and drone, using circular breathing. At evening men's gatherings, musicians have often performed a *nibet* (from Arabic *nawbah*), a sequence of musical genres that includes nonmetric improvisations, song tunes, and instrumental pieces. For dancing, musicians observe a distinction between light, metric women's styles of dancing and heavy, slower, often nonmetric men's styles. Family celebrations have been the major context for such music, but ensembles in the former Yugoslavia have also performed for St. George's Day, the Muslim *bajram*s, and matches by Turkish wrestlers (*pehlivan*s).

Urban-based music

Until the fall of the Ottoman Empire, urban ensembles in northern Albanian areas performed a repertoire closely related to Ottoman urban music. These ensembles were known as *aheng* (Persian *ahenk* 'melody, music') or *saze* in Albania, and *çallgi* (Turkish *çalgı* 'instrument, instrumental music') in the former Yugoslavia. In towns with a large Turkish-speaking population, including Prizren in Kosova and Skopje (Shkup) in Macedonia, such ensembles performed a standard Turkish repertoire, and this music has continued to be performed in both towns for Turkish-speaking audiences. In towns such as Shkodër, Elbasan, and Gjakovë (Serbian Ðakovica), where Albanian-speakers predominated, distinctive styles of Ottoman-influenced Albanian music developed.

In the early 1800s, urban ensembles were made up of male musicians (*aheng-xhinj* or *sazexhinj*), who accompanied their singing on a *kemençe*, a *kavall*, one or more plucked lutes, such as a *saze* 'long-necked lute' or a *llautë* 'short-necked, fretted lute', and a *def.* The group might also include one or more female performers (*çengi*), who sang and danced, accompanying themselves on *def, çapare* 'finger cymbals', or wooden spoons. By the early twentieth century, the *kemençe* had been replaced by the violin (which was at first held vertically on the knee); the *kavall,* by the clarinet. In Kosova and Macedonia, a full ensemble might also include an *ut* 'short-necked, unfretted lute' and a *kanun* 'plucked zither'. In this early period, most performers of the urban repertoire were Roma, but ethnic Albanians have become increasingly prominent in recent decades.

Around World War II, the accordion joined urban ensembles and eventually took over the function of plucked stringed instruments. The typical ensemble thus became clarinet, violin, accordion, and *def* and/or goblet drum (*tarabuka, qypi*), sometimes augmented by *çifteli,* acoustic guitar, string bass, and *xhymbyz* (Turkish *cümbüş*), a large fretted lute with a body like a banjo and tuned like an *ud.* In Gjakovë, *sharki* player Ymer Riza developed an ensemble featuring a *bugari* 'four-stringed long-necked lute', a twelve-stringed, diatonic *sharki*, a *mandoll* 'mandola' (viola-sized mandolin), a violin, an accordion, and a *def*—a fusion of urban and rural instruments. Today, in place of acoustic instruments, many bands feature a synthesizer, an electric guitar, a bass, and a drum set, in addition to a clarinet and/or a saxophone.

Around 1900, the urban repertoire consisted of dance tunes, songs about love and historical events, solo improvisations (*taksim*), and Ottoman instrumental pieces, such as *peşrev*s. Musicians were versed in local variants of the Ottoman *makam*s, of which roughly twelve were used. Since then, many new songs have been created in a style that blends Ottoman and European features. Urban songs often range over more than an octave, and include instrumental interludes performed before each verse or between sections. Though they are now performed diatonically, their melodies often follow the conventions of the Ottoman *makam*s in contour and modulation. In addition to duple time, additive meters such as 9/8, 12/8, and 7/8 are common, as are songs in free rhythm (figure 9). The urban repertoire gained a new popularity in the 1930s and 1940s, when operatic singers, such as Tefta Tashko, began to perform it with piano accompaniment. Since then, numerous singers have

After World War II, the socialist governments of Albania and Yugoslavia instigated policies that affected what types of music were to be performed, and in which settings. The state apparatus promoted new musical genres that came to dominate musical life, eventually subsuming or transforming older genres.

FIGURE 9 The northern Albanian urban historical song "*Ali Pashe Tepelena*", as sung by Luçije Miloti from Shkodër, Albania. After Kruta and Dheri 1968:17–18.

TRACK
39

performed northern songs using bel canto technique. In recent decades, prominent performers have included Bik Ndoja, Luçije Miloti, and Marie Kraja from Shkodër; Fitnete Rexha, Hafsa Zyberi, and Merita Halili from central Albania; and Qamili i Vogël and Mazllum Myezini from Kosova.

MUSIC IN INSTITUTIONALIZED SETTINGS

After World War II, the socialist governments of Albania and Yugoslavia instigated policies that affected what types of music were to be performed, and in which settings. Musicians in rural areas continued to perform older genres, but activities that these genres had once accompanied, including agricultural work and seasonal rituals, were made obsolete by such policies as collectivization of agriculture, settling of nomadic herding families, and, in Albania, prohibition of religious observances.

The state apparatus promoted new musical genres that came to dominate musical life, eventually subsuming or transforming older genres. These policies fostered values consistent with socialism and encouraged new forms of Albanian or Yugoslav identity. Western high culture was promoted so as to place citizens firmly within a European cultural sphere and to democratize the fine arts, and institutions were created to promote research on, and performance of, folk music and dance.

In Albania

In Albania, efforts at establishing new cultural institutions were concentrated in Tiranë, where the Albanian Philharmonia was established in 1949 and the National Theater of the Opera and Ballet in 1953. Semiprofessional orchestras were soon founded in Durrës, Shkodër, Elbasan, and Korçë. These played the standard classics and Albanian composers' new compositions, many of which emphasized nationalist or socialist themes. Most towns had amateur brass bands, plus professional theaters with small orchestras that staged variety shows. Similar amateur organizations were hosted by local Houses of Culture. To foster an interest in Western music and train future musicians, schools instituted a music curriculum that included instruction in Western classical music and Albanian folk music. The most promising students studied in special schools and then at the State Conservatory of Music, housed in the Higher Institute of Arts in Tiranë.

A State Ensemble of Folk Songs and Dances was founded in Tiranë, featuring a chorus and vocal soloists, an instrumental ensemble, and a large corps of dancers. Amateur ensembles were established throughout the country in conjunction with factories, cooperative farms, and town and village Houses of Culture. These ensembles, which staged elaborate choreographies set to folk melodies arranged in Western styles, participated in local and regional festivals. In 1968, a National Festival of Folklore was initiated in the southern city of Gjirokastër, featuring less highly arranged performances of music and dance. This festival, which began to attract foreign visitors, was subsequently held every five years through 1988.

Programming by Radio Tiranë, founded in the 1940s, featured news broadcasts, educational programming, and hours of music, including Western classical music and Albanian performances of "light" music (*muzika e lehtë*) in Western European styles. By far the greatest amount of airtime was reserved for folk music. As electricity reached more settlements, broadcasts on Albanian radio helped break down regional distinctions by disseminating a variety of musical styles throughout the country and into Yugoslavia. A limited recording industry produced commercial discs of radio performances, but these were issued exclusively for sale abroad. Recordings for local use proliferated only with the introduction of cassette players in the 1980s. By 1969, television programs were being broadcast from Tiranë, with programming similar to that for the radio. Feature films often highlighted folk music in the sound track, or included performances by folk ensembles as part of the plot. Through the various media, folk music attained a position of preeminence in Albanian musical life.

Only songs consistent with national or socialist ideals were permitted to be recorded and broadcast; texts were carefully monitored for political content. The men's repertoire of historical songs was the most problematic, and songs representing political factions that had opposed the consolidation of Albania's present borders or the Party of Labor were neither performed nor officially documented. Public performance of popular music from the West was forbidden. The government encouraged the creation of new songs, often set to folk melodies, that specifically addressed aspects of modern socialist life. Songs glorifying the actions of Albania's leader, Enver Hoxha, and the Party of Labor, or aspects of socialist policy, such as collectivization, became known as new folklore (*folklor i ri*), and were prominent in the media and major festivals. Some such songs became popular media hits, not only in Albania, but also in Albanian-speaking areas of Yugoslavia.

The State Ensemble featured an orchestra that combined Albanian rural and urban instruments with others of Western European origin. In its earliest form, the core of the orchestra consisted of six *çifteli,* one *llautë,* and various drums, with a violin, a clarinet, an accordion, and a double bass—a combination that had characterized the older urban repertoires. In arrangements, instruments such as flute and oboe were added to suggest the sound of the rural *fyell* and the *surle.* In later years, the ensemble used Western instruments that could accommodate transpositions and complex arrangements, adding Albanian instruments for local color. Increasingly, singers entered the ensemble already trained in bel canto vocal production. Arrangements also drew on Western techniques, such as tonal harmonies, dynamic shifts, sectional writing, and textural juxtapositions. Choirs and ensembles affiliated with Radio Tiranë, which also arranged performances for full Western orchestra, performed a similar "national" repertoire.

Regional ensembles experimented with other combinations. Instruments such as the *fyell* and the *çifteli* were built in varying sizes and combined in large orchestras, often modified to play melodies in chromatic, tempered scales; ensembles of several like instruments were formed, such as the *kompleks me kavall,* which featured sixteen rim-blown flutes. Such groups then began to accompany vocal genres that had once been unaccompanied. In southern districts, mixed groups of men and women commonly performed polyphonic songs, particularly those with new socialist texts. Women's songs, formerly reserved for family contexts, were now performed in public for large audiences, and female singers adopted a more commanding demeanor and forceful type of delivery to suit these contexts. A greater reliance on Western techniques and instruments, and an emphasis on ensembles combining men's and women's singing with instruments, gradually came to characterize the public performance of folk music in Albania.

In the former Yugoslavia

In Yugoslavia, state sponsorship of Albanian folklore was complicated by the distribution of Albanian communities among three separate republics and by the status of Albanians within the Yugoslav state. Under Yugoslavia's policy of cultural pluralism, Albanians were entitled as a nationality (*narodnost*) to their own schools, newspapers, publishing houses, radio and television programming, and other cultural institutions. The city of Prishtinë, the capital of Kosova, where most Yugoslav Albanians lived, emerged as a center of Albanian cultural and educational life.

In 1964 the folklore ensemble Shota, named after a popular Albanian dance from Kosova, was elevated to the status of a professional ensemble. As with other such ensembles within the country, Shota's performances were required to include

FIGURE 10 A northern Albanian group from Opoje District of Kosova performs at the Ohrid Festival, Macedonia. Photo by Eran Fraenkel, 1980.

suites of dances from all the nations (*narodi*) and nationalities of Yugoslavia, though Shota highlighted songs, instrumental ensemble pieces, and choreographies representing groups within Kosova. In Kosova, Macedonia, and Montenegro, amateur student ensembles performed material much like that developed by Shota, while villages sponsored groups to perform local styles of music and dance that were less highly arranged (figure 10).

Radio-Television Prishtinë broadcast programs aimed at all ethnic groups in Kosova, plus a substantial amount of Western popular music, but it focused on older and newer styles of Albanian music and dance. The most successful performances were then issued by state record companies. Once cassette technology became available, cassettes of Kosova Albanian music proliferated in all Albanian areas. Songs in state-supported contexts were monitored for political content, though less so than in Albania. A song could not endorse an anti-Yugoslav political stance, but it could also not express sentiments that were too enthusiastically pro-Albanian.

Music performed in institutionalized settings in Yugoslavia was more an outgrowth of older styles and repertoires than in Albania. A variety of styles continued to flourish in community settings, which provided a training ground for performers who later made careers in the media or in ensembles. At Radio-Television Prishtinë, the orchestras in most recordings and broadcasts were slightly expanded versions of older types of ensembles. Shota and amateur ensembles used similar, relatively small ensembles, adding *surle* and *lodër* for slower, heavier men's dances.

Since many Albanian men had substantial incomes from working in Western Europe or from small businesses they managed in many parts of Yugoslavia, funds were available for professional musical performances in family-based settings. Such musicians built lucrative careers performing at private celebrations and promoting their recorded performances. Albanians in Yugoslavia enjoyed folk music during the socialist period, because it had a grass-roots character and served as a vehicle for self-affirmation among a sizable yet marginalized group.

The institutionalized forms of folk music and dance fostered in Albania and Yugoslavia came to affect how Albanians saw themselves in the socialist period and how foreign audiences perceived them. The professionalism cultivated through the media and the ensembles helped Albanians view themselves as rooted in national traditions and participating successfully in Western aesthetic models. Women's increas-

Many skilled singers and instrumentalists from Albania and Kosova have emigrated and are now making their careers among expatriate communities in Western Europe and North America. Today, the dominant music in the media and the stores is Western popular music, particularly that of performers from the United States.

ing presence, primarily as singers, but also as instrumentalists, modeled a society that expected women to play a more prominent role in public life. Ironically, for foreign audiences and non-Albanian Yugoslavs, an emphasis on pre–World War II forms of dress and folklore, including demure forms of women's dancing, juxtaposed with assertive, sometimes martial men's dances, risked perpetuating stereotypes of Albanians as a conservative, tribal people, rather than the cosmopolitan urbanites that ensemble members and many of their compatriots were becoming.

The postsocialist period

The fall of socialism has brought about economic hardships, and the dissolution of Yugoslavia has sparked political turmoil in each of its successor-states. Neither set of circumstances supports community music making, which has long served as a symbol of joyfulness and prosperity, and music making in folk styles has decreased markedly throughout Albanian areas of the Balkans. Families in town and countryside who, to host a wedding, once hired a band of musicians and perhaps a large hall, now opt for smaller guest lists, simpler celebrations, and even recorded music.

In Albania, of the many performing groups that once received state support, only the State Ensemble is currently being funded. In Kosova, the rescinding of Albanian autonomy beginning in 1989 brought an end to Albanian-language media broadcasts and state sponsorship of Albanian musical activities, now supported only on a volunteer basis. In the face of such conditions, many skilled singers and instrumentalists from Albania and Kosova have emigrated and are now making their careers among expatriate communities in Western Europe and North America. Today, the dominant music in the media and the stores is Western popular music, particularly that of performers from the United States.

Among the trends counter to this musical decline is a resurgence in Albania of vocal genres associated with the major religions: the Islamic call to prayer (*azan*), Bektashi hymns (*nefes*), and Roman Catholic and Orthodox chants. Also in Albania, non-Albanian communities, such as the Aromân, are forming amateur troupes for the first time. In 1995, such groups appeared in a reconstituted National Folklore Festival in the town of Berat, with Albanian groups from Albania and the Yugoslav successor-states.

The most significant developments are occurring among younger Albanians who have been experimenting with new forms of popular music, producing recordings and videos in small, private recording studios. This is especially the case in Macedonia and Kosova, where more capital is available to local entrepreneurs. Songs may be in a Western rock, techno, hip-hop, or "light" style, or based on Near Eastern genres, such as Turkish *arabesk*. Bands often incorporate the clarinet, the *çifteli*, or other folk instruments into their arrangements, which include updated versions of well-known folk songs. In addition to love lyrics, numerous songs address current economic and political dilemmas facing Albanians.

In Macedonia, recordings of local popular musics are now broadcast by private radio and television stations, and are also sold in stores or open markets throughout the former Yugoslavia, in Albania, and among expatriate communities. Only with greater economic prosperity, however, and a resolution of political tensions will Albanians once again be able to experience a rich and diverse musical life produced by local performers.

SCHOLARSHIP ON ALBANIAN MUSIC

During the 1800s, European scholars, beginning with J. G. von Hahn (1853–1854), studied Albanian language and folklore and published texts of Albanian songs. Inspired by such research, Albanian intellectuals began to publish folk-song texts as an integral component of their nationalist movement. In 1871, Giuseppe Jubany (Zef Jubani) compiled the first collection of songs from Albania proper, published in Trieste, followed in 1878 by Thimi Mitko's collection of northern and southern songs, published in Alexandria, Egypt. With the founding of an independent state, publication of folkloric materials began within Albania itself. Musical notation was included for the first time in two volumes from the 1940s (Dungu 1940; Kujxhija 1943).

Detailed descriptions of rural life and musical contexts, particularly in the northern highlands, appear in early-twentieth-century travelers' accounts (Durham 1985 [1909], 1928; Lane 1923), and in more scholarly studies from the interwar years (Coon 1950; Hasluck 1938, 1954). Research was also conducted then among Albanians in Yugoslavia, largely by non-Albanians. One of the most prolific writers on Albanian epics was the German scholar Alois Schmaus, whose publications span the period 1923–1970. Yuri Arbatsky's dissertation on Albanian drumming in Kosova (Prizren) was published in 1953.

In 1934, the American Milman Parry and his assistant, Albert B. Lord, arrived in Yugoslavia to study epic singing. Though they focused on performances in Serbo-Croatian, most of their informants were bilingual Albanians. In 1937, Lord traveled to northern Albania, where he recorded similar songs performed in Albanian. His classic account of performances in Serbo-Croatian, *The Singer of Tales* (1960), has been supplemented by John Kolsti's study *The Bi-Lingual Singer* (1990), which compares songs from that period sung in Serbo-Croatian and Albanian.

Following World War II, the Albanian government encouraged scholarship on Albanian folklore. In 1957, a team of East Germans participated in a collecting expedition with Albanian scholars. The recordings made at that time became the basis of a national archive, housed first at the State University of Tiranë and eventually transferred to the Institute of Folklore. Folklorists and ethnographers issued research reports in two journals (*Studime Filologjike* and *Etnografia Shqiptare*), and published volumes of song texts, texts with musical notation, and musical analysis. In 1979, both disciplines were combined in the Institute of Folk Culture, which issues the journal *Kultura Popullore*. The archive of the institute contains recordings of more than twenty-seven thousand performances of folk music and other folkloric genres. Similar work has been carried out in Kosova, at the Albanological Institute in Prishtinë, which has published the journal *Gjurmime Albanologjike*. At present, the institute in Albania has only extremely limited funding, and, since the rescinding of autonomy, that in Kosova has operated only on a volunteer basis.

One of the most prolific scholars on Albanian music has been Ramadan Sokoli, whose major publications include a systematic analysis of the structure of folk music (1965), a survey of song texts and their contexts (1966), and, with Pirro Miso, a description of folk instruments and ensembles (1991). Other prominent Albanian scholars have included Beniamin Kruta, Spiro Shituni, and Ferial Daja in Albania and Lorenc Antoni, Rexhep Munishi, and Bahtir Sheholli in Kosova. In the 1950s and 1960s, Erich and Doris Stockmann published several studies of southern Albanian music, most significantly a monograph on Çam singing (Stockmann, Fiedler, and Stockmann 1965), based on materials collected with Sokoli.

Outside the Balkans, expatriate scholars of Albanian descent (Kolsti 1990; Pipa 1978; Skendi 1954, 1980) have produced major studies of epic singing, basing their analyses on printed collections or archival recordings made before the war. The writings and recordings of A. L. Lloyd (1968), one of the few non-Albanian scholars to conduct research in socialist Albania, offer useful introductions to Albanian music making. Other non-Albanians have written on Western classical musical activities in Albania (Emerson 1994), music and dance in former Yugoslav areas (Hoerberger 1962, 1986, 1994), singing and instrumental music of Albanians and Muslim Slavs in Kosova (Traerup 1971, 1974, 1977, 1979), Albanian dance in Kosova (Reineck 1986a, 1986b), and the singing of southern Albanians from Macedonia, including immigrant families now living in North America (Sugarman 1988, 1989, 1997).

BIBLIOGRAPHY

Agolli, Nexhat. 1965. *Valle popullore* (Folk dances). Tiranë: Instituti i Folklorit.

Antoni, Lorenc, ed. 1956–1977. *Folklori muzikuer shqiptar* (Albanian musical folklore). 7 vols. Prishtinë: Milladin Popoviq, Rilindja.

Antoni, Lorenc, and Akil Koci. 1971. "Albanska muzika" (Albanian music). *Muzička Enciklopedija* 1:27–31. Zagreb: Jugoslovenski Leksigrafski Zavod.

Arbatsky, Yuri. 1943. "Proben aus der albanischen Volksmusikkultur." *Südostdeutsche Forschungen* 8:228–255.

———. 1953. *Beating the Tupan in the Central Balkans.* Chicago: Newberry Library.

Askari, Mohamed, Rudolf Brandl, and Hans-Jörg Maucksch. 1985. "Das volkstümliche Klarinetten-Ensemble zwischen Orient und Balkan." *Studia Instrumentorum Musicae Popularis* 8:67–85.

Coon, Carleton S. 1950. *The Mountains of Giants: A Racial and Cultural Study of the North Albanian Mountain Ghegs.* Cambridge: Peabody Museum, Harvard University.

Cordignano, Fulvio. 1943. *La Poesia epica di confine nell'Albania del Nord.* Vol. 1. Venice: Topografia Libreria Emiliana. Vol. 2. Padua: Topografia del Seminario di Padova.

Daja, Ferial, ed. 1982. *Këngë popullore djepi* (Folk lullabies). Tiranë: Instituti i Kulturës Popullore.

———. 1983. *Rapsodi kreshnike* (Heroic rhapsodies). Tiranë: Instituti i Kulturës Popullore.

Dheri, Eftim, Mexhit Daiu, and Qemal Haxhihasani, eds. 1964. *Këngë popullore* (Folk songs). Tiranë: Instituti i Folklorit.

Dheri, Eftim, Mexhit Daiu, and Arsen Mustaqi, eds. 1965. *Këngë popullore dashurie* (Folk love songs). Tiranë: Instituti i Folklorit.

———. 1966a. *Këngë për Partinë* (Songs about the Party). Tiranë: Instituti i Folklorit.

———. 1966b. *250 këngë popullore dasme* (250 folk wedding songs). Tiranë: Instituti i Folklorit.

Dojaka, Abaz. 1979. "Le céremoniel nuptial en Albanie." *Ethnographie Albanaise* 9:117–154.

Dungu, Pjetër, ed. 1940. *Lyra shqiptare* (The Albanian lyre). Novara: Instituto Geografico de Agostini.

Durham, Mary Edith. 1928. *Some Tribal Origins, Laws, and Customs of the Balkans.* London: George Allen & Unwin.

———. 1985 [1909]. *High Albania.* London: Virgo Press.

Emerson, June. 1994. *The Music of Albania.* Ampleforth: Emerson Edition.

Filja, Hysen, ed. 1991. *Këngë popullore të Shqipërisë së Mesme* (Folk songs from central Albania). Tiranë: Instituti i Kulturës Popullore.

Födermayr, Franz, and Werner A. Deutsch. 1977. "Zur Akustik des 'tepsijanje'." In *Neue ethnomusikologische Forschungen: Festschrift Felix Hoerburger zum 60. Geburtstag am 9. Dezember 1976,* ed. Max Peter Baumann, Rudolf Maria Brandl, and Kurt Reinhard, 97–112. Laaber: Laaber-Verlag.

Gjergji, Andromaqi. 1980. *Bibliografi e zgjedhur etnografike, 1944–1979* (Selected ethnographic bibliography, 1944–1979). Tiranë: Instituti i Kulturës Popullore.

Hasluck, Margaret. 1938. "The Gypsies of Albania." *Journal of the Gypsy Lore Society,* series 3, 17(2):49–61, 17(3):18–30, 17(4):110–122.

———. 1954. *The Unwritten Law in Albania.* Edited by J. H. Hutton. Cambridge: Cambridge University Press.

Hoerburger, Felix. 1962. "Erzählliedensingen bei den Albanern des Hans-Gebietes (Metohija)." *Zbornik za Narodni Život i Običaje Južnih Slavena* (Zagreb) 40:193–201.

———. 1986. *Volksmusikforschung: Aufsätze und Vorträge 1953–1984 über Volkstanz und instrumentale Volksmusik.* Laaber: Laaber-Verlag.

———. 1994. *Valle popullore: Tanz und Tanzmusik der Albaner in Kosovo und in Makedonien.* Edited by Thomas Emmerig. New York: Peter Lang.

Instituti i Folklorit. 1961–1962. *Mbledhës të hershëm të folklorit shqiptar (1635–1912)* (Early collectors of Albanian folklore [1635–1912]). 3 vols. Tiranë: Author.

Jakoski, Voislav. 1980. *Baladite i baladni motivi vo makedonskata i vo albanskata narodna pesna* (Ballads and ballad motives in Macedonian and Albanian folk song). Skopje: Institut za Folklor.

Jubany, Giuseppe [Zef Jubani]. 1871. *Raccolta di canti popolari e rapsodie albanesi.* Trieste: n.p.

Koliqi, Ernest. 1937. *Epica popolare albanese.* Padua: Gruppo Universitario Fascista.

Kolsti, John. 1990. *The Bi-Lingual Singer: A Study in Albanian and Serbo-Croatian Oral Epic Traditions.* New York: Garland.

Kongoli, Baki. 1971. "Données sur les temps et la rhythmique dans la musique populaire albanaise." *Makedonski Folklor* (Skopje) 4(7–8):261–273.

Kruta, Beniamin. 1968. "Vështrim rreth këngës popullore polifonike të burrave në krahinën e Myzeqesë" (An examination of men's polyphonic folk songs from the Myzeqë region). *Studime Filologjike* 22(3):161–206.

———. 1972–1974. "Polifonia e Skraparit dhe disa çështje tipologjike të saj" (The polyphony of the Skrapar region and several of its typological traits). *Studime Filologjike* 26(2):209–236, 27(2):131–151.

———. 1974. "Un instrument polyphonique: La culadjyare ou flûte double albanaise et ses parallèles balkaniques." *Makedonski Folklor* 7(13):53–63.

———. 1980. "Vështrim i përgjithshëm i polifonisë shqiptare dhe disa çështje të gjenezës së saj" (General observations on Albanian polyphony and some issues regarding its origins). *Kultura Popullore* 1980(1):45–63. A French version is available as "Aperçus de la polyphonie albanaise," *Culture Populaire Albanaise* 1 (1981).

———. 1989. *Polifonia dyzërëshe e Shqipërisë jugore (Tipologjia)* (Two-voice polyphony of southern Albania [typology]). Tiranë: Instituti i Kulturës Popullore.

Kruta, Beniamin, and Mexhit Daiu, eds. 1969. *Melodi e valle popullore instrumentale* (Instrumental melodies and folk dances). Tiranë: Instituti i Folklorit.

Kruta, Beniamin, and Eftim Dheri, eds. 1968. *Këngë popullore historike* (Historical folk songs). Tiranë: Instituti i Folklorit.

Kujxhija, Gjon Kolë. 1943. *Dasëm shkodrane/Nozze Scutarina* (The Shkodër wedding). Valle Kombëtare/Cori Nazionali Albanese (Albanian national dances), 1. Florence: Il Cenacolo.

Lambertz, Maximilian. 1958. *Die Volksepik der Albaner.* Leipzig: VEB Max Niemeyer.

Lane, Rose Wilder. 1923. *The Peaks of Shala.* New York: Harper & Brothers.

Linin, Aleksandar. 1970. "Šarkija kod albanaca na Kosovu" (The *sharki* among the Albanians of Kosova). *Glasnik Muzeja Kosova/Buletini i Muzeut të Kosovës* 10:355–360.

Lloyd, A. L. 1968. "Albanian Folk Song." *Folk Music Journal* 1:205–222.

Loli, Kosta. 1984. "Kaba me saze" (*Kaba* as played by *saze*). *Kultura Popullore* 1984(2):63–85.

Lord, Albert B. 1960. *The Singer of Tales.* Cambridge: Harvard University Press.

Ministria e Arësimit. 1937–1944. *Visaret e kombit* (Treasures of the nation). 14 vols. Tiranë: Author.

Miso, Pirro. 1990. *Muzikë popullore instrumentale* (Instrumental folk music). Tiranë: Instituti i Kulturës Popullore.

Mitko, Thimi. 1878. *Alvanike melissa (Bëleta Shqiptare)* (The Albanian bee). Alexandria, Egypt: n.p.

Munishi, Rexhep. 1979. *Këndimi i femrave të Podgurit* (Women's singing in Podgur [Kosova]). Prishtinë: Instituti Albanologjik.

———. 1987. *Këngët malësorçe shqiptare* (Songs of Albanian *malësorë*). Prishtinë: Rilindja.

Osmalli, Kostaq, arranger. 1958. *Këngë të vjetra korçare* (Old Korçë songs). Tiranë: Ministria e Arësimit dhe e Kulturës.

Pipa, Arshi. 1978. *Albanian Folk Verse: Structure and Genre.* Albanische Forschungen, 19. Munich: Trofenik.

Pipa, Arshi, and Sami Repishti, eds. 1984. *Studies on Kosova.* Boulder: East European Monographs. Distributed by Columbia University Press, New York.

Pllana, Shefqet. 1968. "Uloga individualnih stvaralaca u razvitku savremenog albanskog narodnog pevanja na Kosovu i Metohiji putem štampe, radija i gramofona" (The role of the individual creator in the development of contemporary Albanian folk singing in Kosova and Metohia by means of the press, the radio, and the gramophone). *Rad XIII kongresa Saveza folklorista Jugoslavije u Dojranu 1966. godina,* 229–237. Skopje: Saveza folklorista Jugoslavije.

———. 1979. "Das albanische Volkslied in Kosovo." *International Review of the Aesthetics and Sociology of Music* 10:215–236.

Reineck, Janet S. 1986a. "The Place of the Dance Event in Social Organization and Social Change Among Albanians in Kosovo, Yugoslavia." *UCLA Journal of Dance Ethnology* 10:27–38.

———. 1986b. "Wedding Dances of Kosovo, Yugoslavia: A Structural and Contextual Analysis." M.A. thesis, University of California at Los Angeles.

Schmaus, Alois. 1971. *Gesammelte slavistische und balkanologische Abhandlungen.* 2 vols. Munich: Trofenik.

Sheholli, Baktir. 1986. "Albanian Vocal and Instrumental Tradition in Kosovo." In *Traditional Music of Ethnic Groups—Minorities,* ed. Jerko Bezić, 205–210. Zagreb: Zavod za Istraživanje Folklora.

Shituni, Spiro. 1982. "Vezhgime etnomuzikore rreth vajtimit lab" (Ethnomusicological observations on Lab laments). *Kultura Popullore* 1982(2):139–151.

———. 1989. *Polifonia labe* (Lab polyphony). Tiranë: Instituti i Kulturës Popullore.

Shituni, Spiro, and Agron Xhagolli, eds. 1986. *Këngë polifonike labe* (Lab polyphonic songs). Tiranë: Instituti i Kulturës Popullore.

Skendi, Stavro. 1954. *Albanian and South Slavic Oral Epic Poetry.* Philadelphia: American Folklore Society.

———. 1980. *Balkan Cultural Studies.* Boulder: East European Monographs. Distributed by Columbia University Press, New York.

Sokoli, Ramadan. 1958. *Les dances populaires et les instruments musicaux du peuple albanais.* Tiranë: Comité Albanais pour les Relations Culturelles avec l'Étranger.

———. 1965. *Folklori muzikor shqiptar (Morfologjija)* (Albanian musical folklore [morphology]). Tiranë: Instituti i Folklorit.

———. 1966. *Chansons lyriques.* Translated by K. Luka. Chansons populaires albanaises, 1. Tiranë: Naim Frashëri.

———. 1971. "Albanian Folk Dances." *East Europe: An International Magazine* 20:41–44.

Sokoli, Ramadan, and Pirro Miso. 1991. *Veglat muzikore të popullit shqiptar* (Musical instruments of the Albanian people). Tiranë: Instituti i Kulturës Popullore.

Stockmann, Doris, and Erich Stockmann. 1964. "Die vokale Bordun-Mehrstimmigkeit in Südalbanien." *Ethnomusicologie III: Les Colloques de Wégimont, V, 1960* (Paris: Les Belles Lettres), 85–135.

Stockmann, Doris, Wilfried Fiedler, and Erich Stockmann. 1965. *Gesänge der Çamen.* Albanische Volksmusik, 1. Berlin: Akademie-Verlag.

Stockmann, Erich. 1960. "Zur Sammlung und Untersuchung albanischer Volksmusik." *Acta Musicologica* 32:102–109.

Sugarman, Jane. 1988. "Making *Muabet*: The Social Basis of Singing Among Prespa Albanian Men." *Selected Reports in Ethnomusicology* 7:1–42.

———. 1989. "The Nightingale and the Partridge: Singing and Gender among Prespa Albanians." *Ethnomusicology* 33:191–215.

———. 1997. *Engendering Song: Singing and Subjectivity at Prespa Albanian Weddings.* Chicago: University of Chicago Press.

Tirtja, Mark. 1979. "Les cultes de l'agriculture et de l'élevage chez le peuple albanais." *Ethnographie Albanaise* 9:155–211.

Traerup, Birthe. 1971. "Rhythm and Metre in Albanian Historical Folk Songs from Kosovo (Drenica) Compared with the Epic Folk Songs of Other Balkan Countries." *Makedonski Folklor* 4(7–8):247–259.

———. 1974. "Albanian Singers in Kosovo: Notes on the Song Repertoire of a Mohammedan Country Wedding in Jugoslavia." *Studia Instrumentorum Musicae Popularis* 3:244–251.

———. 1977. "Wedding musicians in Prizrenska Gora, Jugoslavia." *Musik og Forksning* (Copenhagen) 3:76–94.

———. 1979. "Stimmungen der zweisaitigen Langhalslaute in Kosovo, Jugoslawien." *Studia Instrumentorum Musicae Popularis* 6:98–102.

Uçi, Alfred, et al., eds. 1980. *Probleme të zhvillimit të folklorit bashkëkohor: Simpozium: Festivali Folklorik Kombëtar 1978 dhe problemet aktuale të shkencave etnografiko-folkloristike (28–29 Qershor 1979)* (Problems in the development of contemporary folklore: Symposium: The National Folkloric Festival of 1978 and present-day problems in ethnographic and folkloric scholarship [28–29 June 1979]). Tiranë: Instituti i Kulturës Popullore.

Zojzi, Rrok. 1976. "L'ancienne division régionale ethnographique du peuple albanais." *Ethnographie Albanaise,* special edition: 7–19.

AUDIOVISUAL RESOURCES

Bariu, Laver. 1995. *Songs from the City of Roses.* GlobeStyle CDORBD 091. Compact disc.

Cellier, Marcel. 1995. *L'Albanie mysterieuse.* Disques Pierre Verany PV 750010. Rerelease of *L'Albanie folklorique.* Disques Cellier 010; with some new selections. Compact disc.

Dević, Dragoslav. N.d. *Muzika i tradicija: Pesme i igre naroda Jugoslavije* (Music and tradition: Songs and dances of the Yugoslav peoples). Radio-Televizija Beograd. LPV 190. LP disk.

Dević, Dragoslav, and Bahtir Sheholli. N.d. *Traditional Folk-Music: Songs and Dances from*

Kosovo Performed at the Glogovac Festival of Folk-Lore. Radio-Televizija Beograd 2510073. LP disk.

Encyclopaedia Cinematographica. 1971. Pennsylvania State Audio-Visual Services E01968–E01979. 16-mm films.

Ensemble Vocal de Gjirokastër. 1995. *Albanie: Polyphonies vocales du pays lab.* Inédit/Auvidis W 260065. Compact disc.

Graziani, Jean-Pierre, and Yves Letourneur. N.d. *Folklore instrumental albanais.* Vendémaire. VDE 114. LP disk.

Harding, M., L. McDowell, J. Wozencraft, and S. Shituni. 1990. *There Where the Avalanche Stops: Music from the Gjirokastra Folk Festival, Albania 1988.* Vol. 1. Touch T33.11. Compact disc.

Këngë dhe valle shqiptare (Albanian songs and dances). N.d. Liria Albanian Recording Company CO 2975–2979. 5 LP disks.

Kosova këndon dhe vallëzon (Kosova sings and dances). N.d. Radio-Televizija Beograd LPV 1251. LP disk.

Kruta, Beniamin. 1982. *Albania I: Canti i danze tradizionali: Polifonia vocale e musica strumentale.* Fonitcetra, I Suoni (Italy). Cetra SU 5009. LP disk.

Leibman, Robert Henry. 1974. *Traditional Tosk (Southern Albanian) Songs and Dances from the Lake Prespa Area.* Selo LP-2. LP disk.

Lela, Remzi. 1992. *Famille Lela de Përmet: Polyphonies vocales et instrumentales d'Albanie.* Label Bleu LBLC 2503/Harmonia Mundi HM 83. Compact disc.

Lloyd, A. L. 1966. *Folk Music of Albania.* Topic 12 T 154. LP disk. Reissued on compact disc as Topic TSCD 904.

Lortat-Jacob, Bernard, and Beniamin Kruta. 1988. *Albania: Vocal and Instrumental Polyphony.* Chant du Monde LDX 274 897. Compact disc.

Mauguin, Bernard. 1994. *Islamic Ritual from the Province of Kosovo.* Auvidis/Unesco D 8055. Compact disc.

Rromano Dives. 1996. *Čhaj zibede: Musique rromani d'Albanie.* Al Sur ALCD 172/Média 7 M7 853. Compact disc.

Strictly Albanian. N.d. *Strictly Albanian.* 1001–1003. 3 LP disks.

Tabouris, Petros, comp. N.d. *Albania, Central Balkans, 1920–1940.* Music of the Balkans, 1. Athens: FM Records FM 706. Compact disc.

Tomoaki, Fujii, ed. N.d. *JVC Video Anthology of World Music and Dance.* Vol. 22, Europe 3: Romania/Yugoslavia/Bulgaria/Albania. Victor Company of Japan VTMV-52. Video.

Vaj moj lule (Alas, O flower). N.d. Jugoton LPY–V–853. LP disk.

Vuylsteke, Herman C., and Kaim Murtishi. 1981. *Sous les peupliers de Bilisht. Yougoslavie, 2: Macédoine: Polyphonies tosques.* Ocora 558647 (formerly 558572). LP disk.

———. 1986. *Bessa ou la parole donnée. Yougoslavie, 3: Macédoine: Monodies guègues.* Ocora 558506. LP disk.

Greece

Jane K. Cowan

Mapping the Sounds of Folk Music
Contexts of Folk-Music Performance
Urban Music
History of Music
History of Scholarship

Greece (*Hellas* in Greek) occupies 131,944 square kilometers in the southeastern corner of Europe, one fifth on islands in the Aegean and Ionian seas. Poor in natural resources, the economy is dominated by agriculture, shipping, and tourism. The ancient architecture, philosophy, and politics of Greece have had an unparalleled influence on Europe and the rest of the world. A turbulent history of warring city-states in the pre-Christian era was succeeded by a series of powerful empires: the Roman after 146 B.C., the Byzantine from the sixth century, and the Ottoman from 1453 to 1912, although Greece was an independent kingdom for most of the nineteenth and twentieth centuries. Greece's contentious politics have inspired and censored many songs in urban and rural traditions.

Feature-film images—Anthony Quinn dancing barefoot as Zorba the Greek, Melina Mercouri as the happy hooker dancing with sailors in *Never on Sunday*—often provide non-Greeks with their first encounter of Greek musical life. These characters' penchant for abandoning themselves to song and dance signals their otherness, for films portray Greeks as an emotional people who have retained a spontaneity and naturalness that people in more industrialized societies have lost. Despite romantic stereotypes, such films hint at the importance of music within Greek culture; yet they convey little of the variety of musical sounds, the richness of musical meanings, and the complexity of music making—singing, playing instruments, dancing—as social practices in Greece.

In an overwhelmingly Orthodox nation of 10 million people, Greeks share a legacy of Byzantium in their ecclesiastical music. Secular music, while manifesting the social and cultural variability of the Greek Orthodox world, echoes the modes, melodies, and vocal style of religious hymns. Its variability stems partly from accidents of landscape and history. Before extensive road-building programs after World War II, treacherous, mountainous terrain on the mainland separated regions and often nearby villages. Unpredictable seas isolated Greece's fourteen hundred islands. These barriers enabled dozens of distinct local traditions to thrive in close proximity. Despite the isolation of Greek villages before World War II, Greeks have long been passionate travelers, driven by hunger or curiosity. Shared regional cultures were nurtured at country fairs, where people of neighboring villages or islands exchanged songs, sought spouses, bartered, and bantered. Even before the late 1800s, when massive waves of emigration began, generations of young men had left to travel—as soldiers, seafarers, merchants, traders, and craftsmen—to the rest of Europe, North Africa, and the Central Asian hinterland. Some of the finest stonemasons in Central Europe hailed from remote villages of Epirus and Macedonia, to which they returned every few years to visit wives, beget children, and adorn their houses with Frankish finery. From the 1500s to the early 1900s, an era when Athens was a dusty small town, Greek and Vlach (speakers of a Latinate language related to Romanian) merchants traversed, with oxen, horses, and camels, the paths crisscrossing Macedonia toward the bustling urban centers of Saloniki, Vienna, and Constantinople.

The variety of regional music-making styles shows the traces of specific local histories. Mellifluous *kantadhes,* romantic popular serenades of the Ionian Islands, signal a Venetian colonial presence, while the Macedonian Gypsy ensemble of two shawms (*zournadhes*) and a drum (*daouli*) recalls four centuries of Ottoman rule. Greek musical encounters with East and West reach further back, to a time before the 1400s, when these cultural spheres shared many musical traditions. When Western musical forms and practices began to follow the path leading to the Renaissance (Dragoumis 1975:16), Greek music remained a collective tradition, in which innovation was constant but the formal recognition of individual authorship was downplayed. As a consequence, classifying Greek music as a branch of Near and Middle Eastern music makes musical and historical sense. Ecclesiastical and secular Greek musics have become imbued with tonalities that sound "oriental" to Western ears, though they may also bear witness to more archaic systems, which predate the separation of East and West (Baud-Bovy 1983).

The contemporary array of distinctive folk, classical, popular, and ecclesiastical musics reveals the position of Greece as a geographical and ideological crossroads between Europe and Asia. Orthodox liturgical music, folk songs (*dhimotika*) of the peasantry, and twentieth-century urban popular songs (*rebetika* and *laika*) are clearly, though no longer exclusively, marked by an Eastern musical sensibility. In contrast, Western music, though well known in the islands, was first introduced to the mainland, initially in the form of Italian operas and military bands, in the early years of the struggle for Greek independence (after 1805), by composers and politicians who wanted to Westernize Greek musical tastes (Leotsakos 1980:672–673).

Provoking xenophobic hostility at first, Western music eventually caught on: in late-nineteenth-century Athenian bourgeois society, operettas became popular, and since then, urban Greeks have embraced the harmonies, instrumentation, and dance styles of European popular music. Even *andartika,* songs of the left-wing partisan resistance of the 1940s, borrowed the tunes of Western popular and folk music; one rousing song is set to the American tune "She'll Be Coming 'Round the Mountain."

Classical music, however, remains an elite taste, despite the pride Greeks take in such superstars as Maria Callas and Dimitri Mitropoulos. Avant-garde composers receive little public exposure and less state support, and the talents of some, like Iannis Xenakis and Nikos Mamangakis, have been nurtured abroad. Western music enters Greece primarily as American and European popular music and rock, which young Greeks listen to in the original, influencing an indigenous Greek rock (*elliniko rok*).

MAPPING THE SOUNDS OF FOLK MUSIC

Greek folk music as a whole shares certain general traits: a modal melodic structure; a tendency toward vocal monophony and instrumental heterophony; uneven (Turkish *aksak* 'limping') meters, including 5/8, 7/8, and 9/8, in dance songs; an emphasis on ornamentation; and a common body of poetic images and sung formulas. Within this stylistic unity, distinctive regional musics and local styles within regions have developed. The increase in commercial folk-music recordings and of folklore programs on radio and television has accelerated the movement of songs across regions as folk musicians borrow—or as they say, "steal"—and rework new tunes, as they always have, to expand their repertory. This tendency has diluted the purity of regional and local musics while leading musicians to exaggerate unique regional features. Even with newly borrowed elements and the addition of new instruments (like the now ubiquitous electronic synthesizer), regional musics remain recognizable. In record stores and on city streetcarts, where Gypsy hawkers sell pirated cassettes of commercial recordings, folk music is marketed under regional headings like *Epirotika* 'songs of Epirus' and *Nisiotika* 'island songs'.

On historical and stylistic grounds, folk music can be divided into two major classes: music of the mainland and music of the islands. On the mainland, nearly all of which the Ottoman Empire once controlled, aerophones—*the zourna,* the *karamoutza,* and the *pipiza,* all double-reed shawms; the *gaida,* a single-reed, single-drone bagpipe; the *klarino*; and the brass *korneto*—dominate instrumental ensembles. Meters are usually asymmetric, and rhythms can be complex. Dances often feature upright postures and leaps.

Island musics, by contrast, show the influence of French, Genoese, and especially Venetian colonizers, and of the cosmopolitanism of the Orient. In ensembles, a wide array of chordophones takes center stage. These range from the plaintive violin and shimmering *sandouri* (a trapezoidal dulcimer, struck with wooden beaters) to the Cretan lyra, a bowed fiddle. Melodic lines and the movements of the dances they accompany are supple and lilting. Duple meters predominate, though uneven asymmetric meters—the *karsilamas,* a dance in 9/8, and the *zeibekiko,* a dance in 9/4, both originally from coastal Asia Minor—occur.

The distinction between mainland and island musical styles is also evident in folk-song texts, whose range of themes is extremely wide; however, only on the mainland, in areas that experienced Ottoman domination, does one find heroic songs describing the exploits of the klephts, the bandit-heroes of the resistance against the Turks. Island songs, by contrast, are predominantly erotic, notable for their florid imagery. Structural distinctions are also apparent. Throughout Greece, the most common verse structure is "political verse," a fifteen-syllable verse in iambic meter, comprised of two half lines (hemistichs), the first having eight syllables and the second having seven. The half line is the basic unit from which folk songs are constructed. It is also the unit of the formula (Parry 1930), a group of recurring words, recognizable by conventional syntax, imagery, or sense (Beaton 1980b). Folk songs comprised of political verses are found in mainland and island communities, but the rhyming couplet, unique to islands historically under Frankish control, differs in two ways: it uses rhyme, as virtually no other Greek folk-song genre does, and each verse is a self-contained semantic unit, an epigram, rather than a subordinate (and often semantically incomplete) fragment of a larger song.

Music of the mainland

The mainland comprises the provinces of Epirus, Macedonia, Thrace, Thessaly, Roumeli, and Peloponnisos.

Epirus

Epirus, in the northwest, though one of the country's poorest and most depopulated regions, is musically one of its richest. It is most famous for its *klarino* style, plaintive and unusually slow. The clarinet, with the Albert system of keying, was imported into Greece from Central Europe in the early 1800s, when Ottoman officials and

Polyphonic vocal singing, usually unaccompanied, is found in the Pogoni area of northern Epirus and across the border in Albania. Many songs sung in this style are songs of exile (*ksenitias*), poignant reminders of the loneliness of the emigrant forced by poverty to find work abroad and the despair of those left behind.

FIGURE 1 Excerpt of a three-part polyphonic song from Epirus. The drone (*ison*), on the note d, starts on the last eighth note of the first measure and continues to the end. One part lies mainly above the drone, while the second part lies mainly below the drone. After Baud-Bovy 1983:#57.

local merchants sought for the grand indoor feasts they sponsored a softer, lighter sound than that produced by the *zourna* (Mazaraki 1984 [1959]). In Epirus, the *klarino* is played with a loose embouchure in its lower registers, with descending glissandi and chromaticism, and at cadential points, ascending leaps of a seventh (Chianis 1980:675). Accompanied by violin, *laouto,* and tambourine (*defi*), and in some areas also by a *sandouri* or a struck zither (*tsimbalo*), the *klarino* usually provides the melody in dance-songs. In the characteristic instrumental genre of lament (*miroloyi*), which functions as a table song (*tou trapeziou* or *tis tavlas,* a song sung while sitting around a table with friends and relatives) or a free introductory modal improvisation (*taxim*) preceding rhythmic dance-songs, the *klarino* (or occasionally the violin) plays nonmetrical, weeping melodies (*klapsarika*) over a steady drone, provided by the other instruments.

Rarer and less widely known than the *klarino* is polyphonic vocal singing, usually unaccompanied, in the Pogoni area of northern Epirus, across the border in Albania, and in some Vlach and Slav communities. This musical style, with a pentatonic structure, involves at least three vocal parts: a melodic line, a fixed drone (*ison*) sustaining the tonic, and a *klostis* 'embroiderer', who alternately leads the song and embroiders the melody with a yodeling voice. The interaction of these voices is shown in Samuel Baud-Bovy's transcription of an excerpt of the Epirot song "*Dheropolitissa*," recorded by Domna Samiou and associates (figure 1). Many songs sung in this style are songs of exile (*ksenitias*), poignant reminders of the loneliness of the emigrant forced by poverty to find work abroad and the despair of those left behind.

Macedonia

In Macedonia, one finds a great diversity of musical styles and ensembles, due partly to the region's ethnic diversity during the Ottoman period, when communities of Greeks, Vlachs, Sarakatsani (Greek-speaking shepherds, who moved seasonally

FIGURE 2   A Pontic *kemenje* player strikes up some after-dinner music. The instrument in the background is an accordion. Photo by Jane K. Cowan, 1984.

between highlands and lowlands), Slav Macedonians, Turks, Gypsies, and Sephardic Jews lived in proximity. Their peaceful coexistence, in marked contrast to most of post-Reformation Europe, was largely a consequence of an Ottoman bureaucratic structure that enabled distinctions of language and custom among groups to be mitigated by their common religious identities as Orthodox Christians, Muslims, or Jews.

The Ottomans' renowned tolerance for other "peoples of the book" attracted a hundred thousand Sephardic Jews, expelled from Spain in 1492. From the 1500s to the early 1900s, Saloniki (now Thessaloniki) was a predominantly Jewish city, the cultural and intellectual center of Sephardic Jewry within the empire. Until their near-total annihilation in Nazi death camps in 1941, the Salonican Jewish community, some sixty thousand strong, maintained a tradition of liturgical songs in Hebrew and a female-dominated body of secular and ritual songs in Ladino, the vernacular Judeo-Spanish language.

The rise of nationalism in the late 1800s brought upheaval to Macedonia. Competing groups of nationalists—Serbs, Greeks, Bulgarians, and Slav Macedonians —each claimed Macedonia. The "Macedonian struggles" were followed by the Balkan wars of 1912–1913, out of which Greece doubled its territory and population, acquiring Epirus, Crete, the eastern Aegean islands, and southern Macedonia. Between 1900 and 1920, Greece received small numbers of refugees from Bulgaria, Turkey, and Russia. An unsuccessful invasion of Turkish Asia Minor by the Greek army in 1922 resulted in the Treaty of Lausanne (1923), which dictated a massive exchange of populations between Greece and Turkey, forcing almost half a million Muslims to leave Macedonia for a homeland they had never seen. More than one million Greeks from Asia Minor resettled in vacated properties and new villages. In these refugee communities, music became a powerful symbol of the homeland, and music making forged group identity and social ties.

The Pontii, originally from the southern coast of the Black Sea in Turkey and renowned for their ethnic pride, are accomplished dancers, who maintain an unusually large repertory of dances. Ranging from the delicate *trigona* to the breathtaking war dance *serra* (Kilpatrick 1975), they are accompanied by a single instrument, the Pontic *lyra* or *kemenje*, a bowed lute, with three strings tuned in fourths (figure 2). The *kemenje* player (*kemenjis*) sits in the middle of a circle of dancers, plays in parallel fourths, and often echoes the instrumental melody with tremulous, ornamented singing (figure 3). Because the *kemenje* is difficult to master, competent players are hard to find, and so at celebrations accordions and electric pianos often play at the greater volume most Greeks prefer, with a snare drum removing any ambiguity about the beat. Even Gypsy *zourna* and *daouli* ensembles can play *tik* and *kotsari,* the simple yet exciting dances that indigenous Greek Macedonian customers increasingly request.

Scattered in towns and villages across Macedonia, Greeks from the town of Kosti (in the previously Ottoman region of Eastern Rumelia, now Bulgaria) continue to use their native musical ensemble, consisting of two Thracian *lyras* and a *daouli*. In addition to weddings and festivals, this ensemble is crucial to *anastenaria,* healing rituals, which include dancing, trance, and firewalking, performed yearly on 21 May, the Orthodox feast of Saints Constantine and Helen (Danforth 1989).

The musical legacies of Ottoman pluralism and Balkan nationalism appear in the longer-established communities of Greek Macedonia. The ensemble, consisting of two *zournadhes* and one *daouli*, played by settled and itinerant Gypsies, remains popular in many such villages and towns of Eastern and Central Macedonia (figure 4). This ensemble, often cited in the plural (*daoulia*) to indicate a commanding, percussive presence, was favored by Ottoman and Greek elite families, hence its designation in some localities as Turkish music (Cowan 1990). Its high-status connotations

FIGURE 3 Excerpt from a tune played on a *kemenje* in 9/8 for the dance type *omal.* The harmonies feature fourths, fifths, and seconds. After Baud-Bovy 1983:#51.

A– kri–tas ki on– tes e–la– mnen, A– kri–tas ki on– tes e–la–

mnen e es so me–gan to ne– so–pon, *yiar* es so me–gan to ne– so–pon, *yiar.*

have ensured its survival; Greeks whose peasant ancestors favored the *klarino,* the violin, or even the hurdy-gurdy (*laterna*) for wedding celebrations now consider the *daoulia* essential for them (figure 5). The *gaida,* by contrast, has suffered from its associations as a shepherd's instrument. Once widespread, here and in Thrace, it has gradually been disappearing, except where Macedonian-speaking communities have revived it as a symbol of ethnic identity.

In and around Florina and Edessa and in some Vlach communities, one finds Macedonian brass bands, sometimes called *tzazi,* from *tzaz,* a general term for drums. The ensemble combines a *klarino* and a small drum (*defi*) with one or several brass instruments, like a cornet and a trombone, originally brought to this region in the 1800s by French soldiers serving alongside the Ottoman militia. United by a common meter, these instruments play heterophonically, and sometimes even heterorhythmically. Each player subtly syncopates his part. Only with difficulty do casual listeners find the beat and novice dancers know when to step.

FIGURE 4 A *daoulia* ensemble, consisting of one *daouli* and two *zournadhes,* accompanies a chain dance in Macedonia. Photo by Jane K. Cowan, 1984.

FIGURE 5   The *laterna*. a mechanical hurdy-gurdy, is cranked by its owner, who seeks donations from passersby in the Plaka district of Athens. Photo by Joan Friedberg, 1993.

FIGURE 6   Musicians (*left to right,* a *laouto,* a violin, and a *klarino*) lead a wedding procession in Thrace. Photo by Jane K. Cowan, 1984.

Thrace

Thrace, bordered on the north by Bulgaria and on the east by Turkey, is known for two instrumental traditions. The *gaida* accompanies quick-tempoed dances, like the even-tempoed *zonaradhiko* 'belt dance' in 6/8, and the *baiduska* in 5/8 or 6/8 [see BULGARIA]. In slower, melancholy, nonmetrical table songs, its drone anchors the tune while the melody pipe doubles, and in the instrumental refrain echoes, tight-throated Thracian singing.

The second instrumental tradition of Thrace emphasizes strings but shares a single repertory with the *gaida,* using diatonic and chromatic modes. The *sandouri* and *kanonaki,* struck and plucked zithers, respectively, and the *outi,* a bent-necked, unfretted lute, have nearly disappeared. Ensembles of *klarino,* violin, and *laouto* (or guitar) have replaced them (figure 6).

Thessaly

Nomadic Vlachs and the now mostly settled Karagounidhes ('black-cloak men,' a colloquial expression for a Vlach group whose Latinate language is mixed with Albanian) have left their signature on the music of Thessaly. Their medium- to quick-tempo dance songs are performed by a *klarino* (played in the middle register), a *laouto,* a violin, and sometimes other instruments. In vocal and instrumental performance, the descending melodic slides and anhemitonic pentatonic modes characteristic of Epirus and the more widespread heptatonic (diatonic and chromatic) modes occur.

Roumeli and Peloponnisos

The characteristic ensemble of Roumeli, in central Greece, consists of a *klarino,* a violin, a *laouto,* and sometimes a *sandouri* or a *tsimbalo.* The musical style of this area and the southernmost mainland region (Peloponnisos) differs from that of more northern regions in two ways: the use of tritonic, tetratonic modes and, more commonly, diatonic and chromatic modes and of melismas that replace melodic slides (Chianis 1980:675). Peloponnisos shares a strong vocal tradition with other parts of the mainland, with a large repertory of heroic and ritual songs. In the area called the Mani, professional mourners and close female relatives of the deceased devise elabo-

Nisiotika 'island songs' form a category invented by the Greek record industry. Unlike genres from the mainland, this music has been more accessible to incorporation into the repertories of ensembles playing light popular music (*elafra*) in urban nightclubs.

rate poetic verses (*miroloyi*) to honor the dead, traditionally inciting the deceased's surviving male kin to revenge (Seremetakis 1991).

Music of the islands

Nisiotika 'island songs' form a category invented by the Greek record industry. Recordings sold under this heading draw on an identifiably island sound and lyrics while homogenizing the variations in style and instrumentation on different islands. Unlike genres from the mainland, this music has been more accessible to incorporation into the repertories of ensembles playing light popular music (*elafra*) in urban nightclubs.

Ionian Islands

The Ionian islands, on Greece's western coast along the trade routes between Western Europe and the Levant, enjoy perhaps the most illustrious musical reputation. Before becoming part of Greece in 1864, these islands were the last remaining insular stronghold of Venice, which had ruled much of the Aegean and parts of Peloponnisos since the 1200s. They fell briefly to France in 1797, and to Britain in 1804. Four centuries of Venetian rule heavily influenced cultural life in the islands, whose indigenous aristocracy cultivated Italian tastes. From 1773 on, Italian companies regularly staged operas in Corfu; beginning in the 1840s, amateur philharmonic societies were established throughout the islands, often by composers of the "Ionian School," many of whom had studied in Naples (Leotsakos 1980:672–673). Romantic serenades (*kantadhes*), still popular, are the only Greek folk music that uses Western harmony: men sing in triadic three- and four-part harmonies, accompanying themselves on mandolins and guitars.

Aegean Islands

Two cultures, Venetian and Ottoman, intersect in the musics of the Aegean islands. Venetian-influenced couple dances, like the *ballos,* a form virtually absent on the mainland, are prevalent. Venetian literary forms influenced the fifteenth- to seventeenth-century Cretan literary renaissance and in turn the vernacular oral folk-song tradition, which used the fifteen-syllable political verse developed in the Byzantine period. Rhyming couplets, found throughout the islands, with fifteen-syllable verses and often erotic themes, exemplify this dual parentage. During the late Ottoman period, the musical practices of the cosmopolitan coastal cities of Asia Minor spread to ports throughout the Aegean, where musical cafes arose (Morris 1981). The most typical sort was the *café aman* (probably a corruption of the Turkish *mani khavesi*), renowned for its *amanedhes,* songs in which several singers took turns improvising verses, punctuated by the plaintive exclamation *aman!* 'alas!' to improvised nonmetrical tunes (Holst 1977:20). The incidence of this music increased after 1922, when more than a million Greek Orthodox refugees from Turkish territories resettled on Chios and Mytilene and in Athens, Piraeus, and Macedonia.

FIGURE 7   A man from Kalymnos plays a Dodecanese bagpipe (*tsambouna*) with double melody pipe and no drone. Photo by Jane K. Cowan, 1984.

In the Cycladic Islands (a commercial backwater since medieval times), a tourist boom since the 1960s has taken a toll on traditional music. One may still encounter, however, a wedding or a saint's day (*paniyiri*) when musicians play violin and *laouto*. Syros, the administrative center of the Cyclades, comes alive musically during carnival, though the sonic profusion of *sandouri, gaida, bouzouki,* violin, drums, and *laterna* of the early twentieth century, described in the memoirs of the *rebetis* Markos Vamvakaris (1973), has greatly diminished. On Naxos, young people follow the summer cycle of saints' days as devotedly as religious pilgrims. In the evening, people gather to feast in restaurants that have hired musicians. Each table takes a turn on the dance floor, and members of the audience may honor a male first dancer in a line dance, such as the *syrtos,* by sending up a glass of beer (presented on a tray by a waiter), and a female first dancer by showering her with hard candies. Just to the east, in the northern Sporades, Skyros—for centuries a pirates' lair—has an intriguing genre of unaccompanied table songs called *ikoyeniaka* 'family songs'.

In the Dodecanese, the proximity of the Orient is evident. On Samos, Lesbos, and Chios, ensembles of violin, *laouto, sandouri,* and perhaps *toubeleki* (an hourglass-shaped drum), accompany the *zeibekiko* dance and sometimes the vocal *amanedhes,* whereas in Rhodes and Symi, with perhaps the addition of a *klarino,* they accompany also the *sousta* and *syrtos.* A similar ensemble can be found in the port of Pothia on Kalymnos; however, in shepherd communities of the interior, the *syrtos* is accompanied by a *tsambouna,* a bagpipe with a double chanter and no drone (figure 7). On Karpathos, Halki, and Kasos, the *lyra* and the *laouto* predominate. On Karpathos, the mountain village of Olymbos (home of seafarers and merchants, with a stratified social structure) is renowned for the elaborateness of its summer celebrations (*glendia*), with somber dances and celebrants' ritualized exchange of rhyming couplets (Caraveli 1985). Though tourists relish the spectacle, the celebrations are important locally as occasions that reunite families scattered by emigration, and as the major context for matchmaking between local brides and emigrant husbands.

A musical life of unusual vitality thrives on Crete, where many village singers can sing what seems like an endless stream of couplets from the *Erotokritos,* penned in the 1600s by the Cretan poet Kornaros. They are also adept at improvising new rhyming couplets, known in western and central Crete as *mantinadhes,* and in the east as *kondylies.* They usually sing these couplets to the accompaniment of a *lyra,* which plays the melody, and a *laouto,* which, using one or two chords, provides a rhythmic accompaniment. Gradually quickening and building in intensity, such songs may accompany acrobatic dances (*pidhiktos, pentozali*) [see DANCE IN EUROPE, figure 5, p. 164]. A separate tradition, found in the White Mountains of western Crete, involves unaccompanied table songs (*rizitika*) of fifteen-syllable verses, sung antiphonally by men: a soloist or an ensemble sings a line of verse, which a second ensemble repeats.

CONTEXTS OF FOLK-MUSIC PERFORMANCE
Traditional contexts in rural settings

Singing, playing instruments, and dancing were central activities of communal life in rural communities throughout Greece until the late twentieth century. Mothers soothed babies with lullabies (*nanarismata*), farmers hummed tunes as they walked to their fields, shepherds lazily whittled, then musically mused, on the bevel-edged flute (*floyera*), and in the coolness of late-summer afternoons, adolescents courted through swing songs (*tis kunias*), couplets teasingly exchanged while boys watched girls ride the neighborhood swing. To pass winter evenings, neighbors regularly gathered around someone's hearth, singing, telling stories and jokes, and gossiping.

Elaborate collective rituals and celebrations punctuated the peasant calendar to commemorate crucial moments in individual lives (baptisms, marriages, deaths) and high points of the agricultural and religious year: the twelve days of Christmas, carnival, Easter, and the feasts of the community's patron saint(s)—events that in their most resplendent guise, the *paniyiri,* might include a bazaar, beggars, wrestling matches, and other accouterments of a country fair. These celebrations involved the exchange of gifts, the preparation and consumption of prodigious amounts of food and drink, and the hiring of musicians.

In many places, wedding festivities lasted from Sunday to Sunday, and associated rituals for weeks afterward. Day after day, around the table in the early morning, hours of feasting and dancing led to more pensive, usually nonmetrical singing. Here, surrounded by lighthearted youths, girls, and proud householders, modest elderly folk (excepting women in mourning, who shunned such joyous events as incompatible with their role as public symbols of family grief) rediscovered a forgotten agility as they moved to the first position in the circling dance. Children too stumbled along at its tail, absorbing the rhythms and timbres of local instruments, and the steps and movements of local dances.

Contemporary rural contexts

Making music remains an important collective activity within many rural communities, and in a few is flourishing as never before, but on the whole its traditional forms and contexts have been dramatically attenuated. Since the late 1800s, and particularly since 1945, the transformation of Greece from a predominantly rural society to an urban one (most of the population living in the conurbation of Athens) has had undeniable consequences for music making, as for every other aspect of rural life. With the gradual exodus of young, able-bodied adults and their families seeking better jobs in the cities, countless villages have become "old peoples' homes," with no viable future, save as a holiday destination. As joyful communal events like weddings diminish in frequency, celebratory singing and dancing are superseded by the sounds of women lamenting their loved ones' deaths and the loss of a way of life. Radio and television have altered local patterns of recreation. Rather than spending winter evenings singing and telling stories, each family is more likely to sit at home, in front of a television set, and as children learn songs and dances, not from their elders, but, in supposedly correct versions, from school lessons (a phenomenon imposed on some communities since the mid-1800s, on others much later), a once supple tradition becomes rigid and artificial.

The decline in folksinging has not signaled the end of music making, however, and one can still find coffeehouses where, of an evening, an old man will linger over a glass of ouzo. Closing his eyes, he softly sings highly ornamented, nonmetrical songs, elaborating the klephts' exploits. Though work songs are rare, cassette players ubiquitously blare a stream of folk and popular songs in workplaces from early morning until night, ceasing only during the midday siesta. During an evening out at a tavern, relaxing around a table with friends, many Greeks can recall and sing dozens of old favorites.

Young middle-class Athenians may claim never to have learned how to dance to anything but disco music, but in most rural villages and towns and urban neighborhoods whose residents have strong regional or ethnic affiliations, celebrations such as weddings, baptisms, carnival, Easter, and summer *paniyiria* are still considered incomplete without dancing. Since mass migration to the cities is a late-twentieth-century phenomenon, urbanites usually have a home village to visit for Easter, summer holidays, or a "traditional" village wedding, which nostalgic urban couples increasingly seek. Many village-born musicians, whose tunes villagers consider essential to a proper celebration, have adapted to their customers' migrations by moving to the cities in winter and returning to the countryside in summer. Dancing at festive events remains a highly structured social practice, whose rules vary from one locality to another. In addition to striving for an exuberant high (*kefi*), which comes from copious wine and conviviality, people "perform" gender, class, political, and regional identities, negotiate power relations, and express solidarity or rivalry, with kin, neighbors, and friends (Cowan 1990).

If skill as a dancer, or at least the ability to take command of the dance space, enhances a person's prestige, the status of musicians in Greece is a more complex issue. On the islands and in parts of the mainland, instrumentalists are ordinary farmers, barbers, or shopkeepers, who, having learned to play from a close relative, bring out their instruments when an occasion requires it. They may also sing or merely accompany local men and women who sing, solo or in groups. Accomplished musicians may enjoy fame within their region. On the mainland, many folk musicians from sedentary or itinerant Gypsy families have earned much or even most of their livelihood as musicians for generations, and continue to pass the craft on to their sons.

Throughout Greece, playing instruments is an almost exclusively male activity. Villagers consider women's musical performance in public unseemly. Male musicians' status is ambiguous: though respected for their musicianship and able to earn large sums through the custom of "gifting" from those who request a song, they may receive cavalier treatment, especially if they are Gypsies, as mere "instruments" of the dancer's or singer's pursuit of *kefi* (Cowan 1990:97–133).

In addition to traditional (usually ritual) contexts, other secular events may engage rural communities in making music. Local bands—perhaps an ensemble of schoolmates playing *bouzouki*, guitar, and drums—may play at a youth festival in their own village or a nearby city. Civic associations—soccer clubs, folklore societies, and local branches of national political parties—may hire professional ensembles for an annual dinner dance. At these events, children's folk-dance troupes, organized and taught by the local school or folklore society, frequently perform local, regional, and sometimes Panhellenic dances.

Urban contexts for folk-music performance

As village-based life, within which folk music developed, has changed, much musical activity has been lost. Still, pronouncements of the demise of folk music with modernization are overly gloomy. Certain musical styles and instruments, judged old-fashioned or too difficult, have disappeared, but others are thriving. In the area surrounding Omonia Square in central Athens, one can find cafés where homesick provincials go to drink and dance to nonamplified, old-style folk music, especially *Epirotika*.

With fast-food joints and discos pulsing with rock, Athens remains host to a folk music that lives on in new forms and contexts and with new meanings. This music is performed—sometimes well, often badly, always amplified—in several venues: in regional suburban taverns, where erstwhile villagers and tourists "in the know" go to eat, drink wine, and dance; at periodic social gatherings of regional and island migrants' associations; and, with obvious contrivance but greater concern for an "authentic" sound, in theatrical performances of professional companies, including the Dora Stratou Theater and the Lyceum of Greek Women.

The guises of folk music in commercial recordings testify to its symbolic fluidity in a changing world. Most such recordings are unmemorable renditions of *dhimotika* or *neodhimotika* 'new demotic songs', in which ensembles mix traditional instruments with new ones, such as electric piano and snare drums. At the other extreme, individuals, like the folksinger Domna Samiou (trained at Simon Karras's school),

After 1922, audiences of refugee women and men came to musical cafés to hear Smyrna-style songs— emotional, ornamented pieces, whose lyrics, interlacing Greek, Turkish, and occasionally Judeo-Spanish, proclaimed grief at losing their beloved homeland.

and societies, like the Society for the Dissemination of National Music and the Peloponnesian Folklore Society, have sponsored recordings, usually of high quality, with extensive background information, where authenticity of instrumentation and style is paramount.

Between these extremes, *dhimotika* has emerged as a creative and evolving form. Certain indigenous singers, widely known through commercial recordings, have added memorable voices and unusual interpretations to their local musics. The Pontic singer Chrysanthos's compelling tenor and countertenor moves lithely between steady clarity and intense vibrato while an untraditional high-pitched drum accentuates the relentless rhythms of the *lyra*. The result attracts an audience not confined to his Pontic compatriots. A much-loved singer, *lyra* player, and composer, Nikos Xylouris (whose death, in 1980 at the age of forty-four, sent all of Crete into mourning) was a skilled musician with an expressive voice. From the village of Anoghia, renowned as much for fierce shepherds as for extraordinary *lyra* players, he was the major interpreter of the compositions of Yannis Markopoulos, a fellow Cretan. Both incorporated the harmonies and rhythms of Greek popular music.

Markopoulos is one of several late-twentieth-century Greek composers who have placed traditional Greek folk songs in new acoustic settings. His 1971 recording, *Rizitika*, increased the drama of unaccompanied songs by accompanying them with a small orchestra, which featured the distinctively Cretan *lyra*, *sandouri*, and *floyera*, with a wide range of Greek folk instruments and a few Western classical instruments. The internationally known Vangelis Papathanassiou, in his 1980 album *Odes,* combined synthesizer and folk instruments as haunting accompaniment to the voice of actress Irene Pappas singing *dhimotika*. Ross Daly, an Irish musical polymath based in Crete, is recognized in Greece as a skilled *lyra* player, committed to the Cretan tradition. A proponent of Eastern music, he has brought to his performances an extensive knowledge of Ottoman classical, Turkish, Indian, and Middle Eastern traditions. He and his associates in the ensemble Lavirinthos display a mastery of the timbres, modes, rhythms, and styles of each musical tradition, but create freshness and vitality by recombining them. More accessible to the wider public are the recordings of famous singers who move between Greek folk and urban popular music: *dhimotika* by Yorghos Dalaras and Haris Alexiou and *nisiotika* by Yannis Parios.

URBAN MUSIC

In Greek, the words that distinguish "rural" and "urban" musics are virtual synonyms. *Dhimotika*, usually glossed 'folk songs', literally means 'things associated with the people (as opposed to high culture)'; as a consequence of various ideological and political factors since the late 1700s, the term has come to refer solely to rural society. *Laika*, the general category of urban popular songs, though some Greeks use it in a more restricted sense to denote urban popular music of the postwar era, refers to 'the people' or 'a people' (*laos*). Largely ignored by scholars, urban *laika* are a rich and continuously evolving musical universe; indeed, the *bouzouki*, the instrument outsiders most strongly associate with Greece, is used only in urban musical ensembles.

Rebetika

Rebetika constitute the most distinctive genre within urban music. Sometimes compared to American blues, *rebetika* are songs of the dispossessed, living on the margins of society—songs of love, loss, poverty, jail, and hashish, composed and performed from about 1900 until the early 1950s. Though performing and listening to them were initially confined to members of a small subculture, commercial gramophone records—made in Turkey, Piraeus, New York, and Chicago, as early as 1904, but particularly from the 1920s onward—disseminated them within Greece and to Greek emigrants living abroad.

As a result of associations this had music with the urban underworld and Turkish culture, critics from all sides derided it. The conservative establishment condemned it as immoral, and especially during the regime of Ioannis Metaxas in the late 1930s, systematically harassed musicians and censored recordings that referred to hashish. Left-wing authorities, for their part, considered *rebetika* politically unenlightened, and thought the peculiar mix of defiance and resignation conveyed in *rebetika* lyrics inhibited workers' formation of class consciousness. In the late 1960s, however, *rebetika* began to experience a revival that shows no sign of abating.

The etymology of the term remains obscure (Gauntlett 1982), but *rebetika* are rooted in the traditional singing of the poorer urban classes, who began to migrate to the towns and cities in the 1700s. Though the structures and themes of many *rebetika* show clear links to rural folk traditions (Beaton 1980b:193), this music was shaped by, and came to be the quintessential expression of, a different social world. In the urban centers of the Aegean coast, songs today known as *rebetika* developed within two distinct, if connected, cultural settings: musical cafés, and jails and hashish dens (*teké*).

Musical cafés, humble establishments serving wine and simple food, sprang up in Aegean ports after 1900. One end of the room was usually free for street musicians, many of them Gypsies, to gather and play music for tips (Holst 1977:20–21). After the influx of refugees, including professional musicians, from Asia Minor into Athens and Piraeus after 1922, such cafés typically hosted their own small orchestra (*koumpania*), comprising a *sandouri*, a *laouto*, and an *outi* or a *saz,* a Turkish long-necked plucked lute. A female singer, accompanied by *defi*, spoons (*koutalia*), or *zilia* (metal finger cymbals), often did the belly dance (*tsifte teli*). Audiences of refugee women and men came to hear Smyrna-style songs—emotional, ornamented pieces, whose lyrics, interlacing Greek, Turkish, and occasionally Judeo-Spanish, proclaimed grief at losing their beloved homeland.

Though the music of the cafés had a sophisticated urban pedigree, another stream of *rebetika* developed in underworld haunts. In jails of the mid-1800s to the early 1900s, petty thieves, crooks, and political dissidents developed a unique musical culture. Prisoners carved from bedposts the necks of tiny *baglamadhes* (originally part of the family of Turkish *saze*s) and composed songs of fate, love, and defiance, peppered with jailhouse slang. Out of jail, in the poor neighborhoods of Piraeus, such men gathered in the hashish den, smoking hashish (officially tolerated until 1936) from Turkish hookahs while one of their number quietly strummed a *bouzouki* or a *bağlama* and another stood up to dance an introspective *zeibekiko*. With interpreters like Markos Vamvakaris, the Piraeus style flourished in the 1930s, when it replaced the lavishness of the *koumpanies* with a male vocalist and a spare *bouzouki* accompaniment. Though the *teké* was primarily a male setting, certain "free" women (*derbiderissa*), who made their own living and their own rules, were attached to it. A

1949 song by Vasilis Tsitsanis, paying homage to the *derbiderissa* "who plays men like dice," was popularized by the singer Sotiria Bellou, an unconventional, independent woman.

Laika

After Metaxas (1936–1941), the stigmatized second half of the hyphenated category *laika-rebetika* began to disappear from recording-company catalogs and record jackets, but the music continued to be played and recorded. By the late 1940s, it was becoming respectable. Ensembles grew to include new instrumental combinations: a piano, a guitar, drums, and an accordion joined the *bouzouki* and the *baglamadhes*. Composers increasingly replaced Turkish modes, known in Greece as 'roads' (*dhromi*), with the diatonic major and minor scales of European popular music promulgated by popular dance bands. Eastern sensibilities, which had once permeated *rebetika*, became a conventionalized "orientalism," the new middle-class and nouveau-riche audiences began valuing technical virtuosity more than "soul," and Manolis Hiotis, the most famous *bouzouki* player of the 1950s, added a fourth string and changed the tuning to play faster and produce a more European sound (Holst 1977:59). Dancing in respectable establishments (*bouzoukia*) and their shabbier counterparts (*skiladhika* 'dog's dens', patronized by the working classes) differed greatly from those of cafés and hashish dens. Dancing became an acrobatic, exhibitionist display, complete with ostentatious "gifting" to the musicians, and admiring friends' ritualized smashing of plates at the dancer's feet.

Scholars of *rebetika* identify the early 1950s as the period when this genre ceased to be a creative form. After then, *laika* (understood in its restricted sense as postwar urban music) came into its own. Record companies have continued to produce recordings of *laika*, in its light (*elafrolaika*) and heavy (*varialaika*) styles, with crooning lead singers, accompanied by electrified *bouzouki* and other instruments, performing songs with European harmonies and *rebetika* rhythms [see POPULAR MUSIC IN EUROPE, p. 206, figure 1]. The stuff of Greek musical clichés, a few outstanding singers, among them Marinella, Keti Grey, and Stellios Kazantzides, have transcended the limitations of the genre. Songs of exile, of which Kazantzides remains an unrivaled interpreter, have long appealed to working people, who since World War II have left their villages in search of work in Athens and Thessaloniki, and to the flood of emigrant workers, mostly single men, who found employment in the 1950s and 1960s in the factories of Mannheim and Melbourne. When a group of friends in their forties or older, some of whom may have spent ten, twenty, even thirty years in exile, go out to a tavern, it is these songs, which evoke many memories, that they sing.

Except as old 78-RPM records scoured from the flea markets of Monastiraki, *rebetika* did not survive in the conservative postwar climate. The military junta that seized power in 1967 jailed Elias Petropoulos for publishing his landmark book, *Rebetika Tragoudhia* (1968). Its publication was influential, however: by the early 1970s, many young people were rediscovering in *rebetika* lyrics and subcultures the symbols of resistance to repression. After 1974, when democracy returned, record companies began to reissue old 78s on long-playing disks. The Center for the Study of Rebetic Song, established in Athens during the period of revival, has produced impressive reissues, which, released on the Falirea Brothers label, contain extensive album notes of the songs' social and historical contexts.

After Markos Vamvakaris's *Autobiography* (1973), biographies of major rebetic figures began to be written. Versatile singers, including Yorghos Dalaras and Glykeria, made *rebetika* and Smyrna songs (*smyrneika*) accessible to a wide audience. A spate of nightclubs appealing to aficionados opened in Athens and some provincial cities in the early 1980s, featuring *koumpanies* playing *rebetika* in a meticulously "authentic" style, usually learned from old records. Gradually, the initial focus on reviving old songs and learning to play old instruments was extended to the creation of new compositions in rebetic styles. Stavros Xarhakos' evocative compositions for the 1984 film *Rebetico,* Nikos Mamangakis' melancholy record "Grand Central Station" (*Kendro Dierhomeno*), and the innovative work of groups like Winter Swimmers (Himerini Kolimvites), The Retrograde Company (Opisthodhromiki Kompania), and Aegean Forces (Dhinamis tou Eyeou), exemplify the experimentation accompanying the revival.

New popular forms and fusions

Within urban musics like *rebetika,* an easy circulation of songs in the early years, when musicians felt free to change or add something of their own when they performed, gave way, with the increasing prominence of phonograph records, to a heightened emphasis on individual composers' or singers' ownership of a song.

Some Greek composers and ensembles, drawing on folk and urban musical traditions, have been creating new musical forms since the 1950s. Their music, notable for its appeal to a wide spectrum of Greek society, has attracted the attention of audiences abroad. In the 1950s and 1960s, Manos Hadzidakis, one of the most influential of these composers, developed a style known as New Wave (Neo Kima). An admirer of *rebetika* long before its revival in the 1970s, he often used that tradition's dance rhythms, especially the *hasapikos* (in moderate 4/4), while lightening the melancholy of their melodies. Having a simplicity and a charm that occasionally lapse into sentimentality, his light classical songs, with Nana Mouskouri as their most famous interpreter, retain their popularity with Greeks, at home and abroad.

A second composer of New Wave, Mikis Theodorakis, is internationally famous as much for political activities as for memorable tunes. Film buffs may know him for his music for Cacoyannis' *Zorba the Greek* and Costa-Gavras's *Z,* a thinly disguised account of a left-wing parliamentary candidate's assassination (in 1963), which helped set the stage for the military coup. That the junta made the singing of Theodorakis's songs illegal hints at a phenomenon not limited to him: the widespread use of music in Greece as a forum for political expression. Classically trained, Theodorakis hoped to inspire and express common people's aspirations. His work ranges from elaborate symphonies to unadorned melodies, and his song cycles—musical settings of poetry by George Seferis, Odysseus Elytis, Yannis Ritsos, Pablo Neruda, and others—wed poetry and music as deftly as do Greek folk songs.

The repression of the late 1960s and early 1970s produced other "political" popular composers, including Manos Loizos, Yannis Markopoulos, and Thanos Mikroutsikos, but the most interesting is Dionysis Savvopoulos. Like Theodorakis, he is a controversial cultural figure, but his approach is subversive, rather than heroic. Since his first record (1965), his music has evolved. His guitar-based ballads of the late 1960s, in which antijunta barbs hide in puns and obscure references, range from the frenetic to the lyrical. His later music shows a restless, innovative synthesis of Eastern and Western sounds. Despite a satirical style and an unashamed use of gimmicks (like an extravagant laser show at his major summer concert of 1984), his songs are deeply serious. Many explore the question of what it means to be Greek. Replete with musical references to *dhimotika* and *rebetika,* his song "*Trapezakia Ekso*" ('Little Tables Outdoors', 1983) gently mocks his compatriots' provincial vulgarity while celebrating their patriotism. In his song "*To Kourema*" ('The Haircut', 1989), bossa-nova rhythms and the accordions of French musical cabaret jostle with Byzantine choirs and a plucked *outi,* as he pillories politicians of every hue and all Greeks (see Cowan 1993).

Many Greeks have repudiated the uncritical pro-American stance of postwar administrations and the cultural, political, and economic hegemony it entailed, and, as a consequence, have reexplored their Eastern heritage.

Popular music since the fall of the dictatorship has been the primary cultural site for a renegotiation of Greek identity. Many Greeks have repudiated the uncritical pro-American stance of postwar administrations and the cultural, political, and economic hegemony it entailed, and, as a consequence, have reexplored their Eastern heritage. *Anatolitika,* the Anatolian style of *rebetika* playing, has been particularly popular. In 1989, composer Nikos Ksidakis and songwriter Thodoros Gounis produced an album of compositions entitled *Cairo, Nauplion, Khartoum.* In recordings in the 1980s, a Greek rock group named Fatme, a name evocative of Muslim culture, preceded their jazz-rock compositions with a long, improvised *taxim* in *anatolitika.* Composers of film music, where some of the most imaginative musical syntheses now occur, freely combine seemingly incongruous elements to evoke cultural complexity. Eleni Karaïndrou's theme song for Tonia Marketaki's film *The Price of Love,* set in nineteenth-century Corfu, uses uneven Balkan rhythms with a guitar accompaniment, simultaneously Ionian and New Wave in its nuances.

HISTORY OF MUSIC

An illustrious tradition of musicological and classical scholarship, using the evidence of myths, musico-theoretical texts, poets' and writers' literary works, and visual representations on vases and sculptured reliefs, has revealed the importance the ancient Greeks attached to music. The fragments of ancient musical notations that survive are of late antiquity, mostly post-Christian. Like all systems of notation, they presume a knowledge of the implicit conventions of performance—conventions contemporary interpreters lack. Though we can only guess how ancient music sounded, writers of antiquity described and theorized about other important aspects of *mousikē,* the art of the Muses. They stressed its performative and philosophical unity as "music-poetry-dance," a unity expressed in secular celebrations and ritual drama; the binding quality of rhythm, composed of varying combinations of temporal values, derived from short and long syllables in their language; and the mathematical qualities and ethical—and ethnic, like Doric—connotations of each melodic mode (Winnington-Ingram 1980:750–762).

Without aural evidence, the extent to which the music of antiquity has survived in the music of modern Greece is difficult to assess. Asymmetric meters (like 7/8 and 9/8), common to the melodies of Greek folk dances, with internal patterns of short and long beats, resemble the long-short rhythmic organization of *mousikē.* Ancient Greek music, like most Greek folk music, seems to have been monophonic and melodic, rather than harmonic. Other elements may have survived by a more circuitous route: many scholars believe the Turks reintroduced to Greece during the Ottoman period (1300s to 1800s) certain slightly altered ancient Greek modes, which had disappeared for over a millennium in the Greek-speaking world. The Turks had learned them (as *makamlar* 'Arabic modes') from Arabs, whose ancestors had learned them from the ancient Greeks (Beaton 1980a; Watts 1988:17). If the sounds of music in the ancient world are largely lost, the theories and *vocabulary*—*tónoi, harmoníai,* even *mousikē* itself—survive and, appropriated and reinterpreted, provide a theoretical basis for Western classical music.

Byzantine music

From the sixth century to the mid-fifteenth, the area of present-day Greece was encompassed within the Byzantine Empire, a political structure that developed out of events in A.D. 330, when, over doctrinal and political differences, the Christian world split into Eastern (Orthodox) and Western (Roman Catholic) churches. Ecclesiastical music flourished in Byzantium. Widely scattered monasteries and cities throughout the empire shared a system of modes, but developed a multiplicity of styles of Byzantine chant. These were passed down orally until around 950, when a neumatic notation—graphic signs, roughly indicating melodic motion—was developed as an aid to memory, though learning to chant remained a skill requiring oral instruction, as it still does (Dragoumis 1966; Wellesz 1949).

Because of an association with pagan celebrations, the Orthodox church banned musical instruments from services. Excepting the metallic jingling of a censer and the calling of the faithful to worship with the ringing of bells (or, in some monasteries of Mount Athos, rhythmic hammering on woodblocks), Orthodox music—in Greece, as in all Greek immigrant communities—remains an exclusively vocal tradition. Not surprisingly, Byzantine texts say almost nothing about secular music of their periods. By the eleventh century, visual representations on frescoes show Byzantines with long-necked lutes and pear-shaped bowed lutes (the modern Greek *lyra* belongs to this family of instruments). Brass instruments, introduced by the Roman army, were important in court ceremonies (Beaton 1980a:4). Lively local folk traditions of dance and song doubtlessly coexisted with those of the church and the imperial court, but virtually no knowledge of the former survives.

The Ottoman period

Weakened after several centuries of incursions by crusaders from the West, Seljuk and Ottoman armies from the East, and internal feuds, the Byzantine Empire gradually came under the control of the Ottoman Turks in the 1300s and 1400s. Though Greeks tend to view Ottoman rule as four hundred years of darkness, in the early period the peasantry benefited from enlightened policies of lower taxation and religious tolerance. Under the Ottoman *milyet* system, each religious community—Jews, Muslims, and Orthodox Christians—was permitted to administer its internal affairs and perpetuate its social customs, much as before. The lack of interference by Ottoman officialdom into cultural matters suggests that some continuity of musical practice from the Byzantine to the Ottoman era is likely, but the influence of Ottoman and Arabic traditions in this period is undeniable. Musicians, some of whom were Gypsies who played for Christians and Muslims, introduced to Greek communities many musical instruments from the east and the modes (*makam*s) in which they played tunes. Borrowing was not in one direction: the Ottomans took over the brass instruments of the Byzantine court for their own military bands and reintroduced brass bands into Europe in the 1600s. Many folk traditions coexisted in dynamic relationship with the courtly tradition of Ottoman classical music (itself based on the Arabic classical tradition), whose composers, singers, and instrumentalists hailed from every ethnic community in the empire.

HISTORY OF SCHOLARSHIP

Despite our meager knowledge of folk-musical practices under Ottoman rule, transcriptions of songs began to appear in this period. The first known manuscript to record the text (but not notate the tune) of a "complete" folk song, "The Song of

Armouris," dates from the 1400s. The only other documented folk-song texts before the 1800s are a group of thirteen songs transcribed by a seventeenth-century scribe, with musical notation (Beaton 1980b:82–89).

A fuller picture of Greek folk music emerges in accounts by French and English travelers who visited the Greek-speaking areas of the Ottoman Empire in the eighteenth and early nineteenth centuries. Lured by Oriental exoticism or inspired by romantic views of the uncorrupted life of the "folk," adventurers, antiquarians, amateur ethnographers, diplomats, and wealthy socialites, set off to discover the daily life of rural people.

Many of these travelers were philhellenes who, drawn to Greece by antiquarian interests, dreamed of Greek liberation and the resurrection of Greece's classical glory. The desire to convey what they saw as the continuity of the past into the present sometimes led to fanciful representations: the diligent reader of travelers' texts will see paintings of peasants dancing, not in the village square, but among ruined marble columns, set amid verdant hills (Tsigakou 1981). Prose descriptions of this dancing reveal assumptions about, and use terminology of, ancient Greek dance, but they ignore local nomenclature. Philhellenic sentiments could nonetheless inspire careful scholarship. Starting in 1824, during the establishment of Greek independence, the philhellenes Claude Fauriel (1824, 1825), Theodor Kind (1861 [1827]), and Arnold Passow (1860)—none of whom had set foot on Greek soil—published the earliest collections of Greek folk songs.

From its early manifestations in travel accounts until the 1950s, descriptions of music making focused almost exclusively on singing. Instrumental music was largely ignored as cacophonous: with typical annoyance, the Reverend T. S. Hughes described "a concatenation of discords" produced from "a vile instrument in the likeness of a violin" (1830:269). The approach to singing was also curiously partial: researchers "collected" song texts—that is, they transcribed the words—then interpreted these texts from a literary and philological perspective. Collectors did not notate the melodies, nor did they consider it important to describe the social contexts in which singing occurred. They regarded folk songs as "oral poetry," to be transformed into written texts and classified into genres.

In their approach to folk songs and culture, scholars working with Greek materials were influenced by their contemporaries in Europe. Nikolaos Politis, the founder of the Greek discipline of folklore (*laografía*), adopted the German diffusionist school's concerns to document variants of a song while seeking its original source, the urtext. Collectors systematically—and in their view, justifiably—corrected a folk song they saw as having become corrupted in the process of oral transmission, and they conflated fragments of several performances to obtain a more complete version. Like students of folklore in other new Balkan nation-states, Politis saw folk practices as a manifestation of continuity between the past and the present, evidence of the historical legitimacy of Greece's claims to nationhood. Stressing the archaeological overtones of this argument, he identified folk songs as "monuments of the word" (Politis 1909).

The notion that a folk song is a discrete entity, whose origin is historically identifiable, remains prevalent, but it has recently been challenged. Drawing on the ideas of Milman Parry, Albert B. Lord, and Claude Lévi-Strauss, Roderick Beaton (1980b) has argued that as long as the tradition was an active one, the Greek folk singer did not passively reproduce a memorized, fixed song. Rather, he or she was able to use the tradition's collectively created formulaic conventions and stock poetic images to change or rearrange the song, usually in minor ways, to fit particular circumstances and shifting tastes (see also Sifakis 1988).

This penchant for introducing innovations into performances persists in the singing—in Greek terms, the 'saying'—of laments for the dead (*miroloyia*), almost always performed by women (Alexiou 1974; Auerbach 1989; Caraveli-Chaves 1980; Danforth 1982; Seremetakis 1991). Sung, or sometimes spoken, rhyming couplets are also sometimes improvised. Variously called *mantinadha* (Crete, Dodecanese Islands), *tchiattisma* (Cyprus), *patinadha* (Chios), *pismatiko* (Rhodes), *kotsaki* (Crete), and *amanes* (Asia Minor), this form can be traced to the rhyming poetry introduced by the Franks—French, Genoese, Venetians—on their island colonies in the late 1300s. On Crete, Cyprus, and certain Aegean islands, the performance of couplets to the accompaniment of *lyra* and *laouto* (a long-necked plucked lute) is a highlight of traditional communal feasts. Typically, one celebrant recites a couplet, and then, after a musical refrain by the instrumentalists, a second person offers a couplet that echoes, elaborates on, answers, or challenges the first. Though usually drawn from previous oral renditions or written literature, such as the late-sixteenth- or early-seventeenth-century verse romance *Erotokritos* (by the Cretan poet Kornaros), a successful couplet nearly always must be adapted, by changing a word or a phrase or adding relevant interjections (*tsakismata*), so it says something apt. Couplets can be witty, bawdy, erotic, nostalgic, or insulting, and their exchange is often amiably competitive, a verbal duel.

Inattention to the melodic aspects of song began to be rectified in the 1930s, when Melpo and Octavio Merlier collected onto 78-RPM discs examples of the country's musical riches. Into the project they led other musicologists: the Swiss scholar Samuel Baud-Bovy, who made notations during performances and later produced an important text, *Chansons du Dodecanèse;* and some years later, Markos Dragoumis, a student at Athens Conservatory, who became an eminent musicologist of Western, Byzantine, and Greek folk and popular music and curator of the Melpo Merlier Archives at the Center for Asia Minor Studies (Athens). Melpo Marlier persuaded Dragoumis to enroll in the Society for the Dissemination of National Music, the school run by Simon Karras, and a training ground for middle-class urban Greeks, dedicated to keeping demotic music alive. Believing his students should perform as competently as they could analyze music, Karras insisted they learn to play folk instruments, dance regional folk dances, and sing folk songs and liturgical hymns in the school's choir.

Since then, other researchers, Greek and foreign, have investigated Greek songs. Some, like those associated with the Folklore Archives of the Academy of Athens, collected folk songs on audiotape; the folklorist and renowned ecclesiastical chanter (*psaltis*) Spyros Peristeris (1964) transcribed them into Western notation. From 1972 to 1980, Karras and his colleague, Mary Vouras, undertook an extensive research-and-recording project. Focusing on nonprofessional village singers and instrumentalists recorded throughout Greece, they by 1991 had produced twenty-five long-playing records that represented all of Greece's regional folk music and included four records of religious music. Beginning in the 1970s, scholars began to look at the social contexts of the transmission and performance of songs and funeral laments, at local performance practices, and at indigenous aesthetics (Alexiou 1974; Auerbach 1989; Caraveli 1982, 1985; Danforth 1982; Herzfeld 1981, 1985; Kavadias, Liavas, and Loutzaki 1987).

The bias against the study of instrumental music, noted from early travelers' accounts, no longer obtains, and careful studies of folk instruments and their music have been published, mostly as articles in journals of folklore, and as master's or doctoral theses. Fivos Anoyanakis's lavishly illustrated text *Greek Popular Musical Instruments* (1979 [1965]), produced in Greek- and English-language versions, remains a mine of information about the range of instruments and the variety of playing techniques found in Greece. The social and cultural aspects of instrumental

Despite the similarities of some modern folk dances with pictorial and sculptural representations of certain ancient dances, more recent work has set aside the issue of continuity and focused on what dancing means for Greeks and how they organize it.

practice have not received extensive attention, but one exception is an excellent study of the folk clarinet in Greece (Mazaraki 1984 [1959]).

Finally, dancing has been the object of important scholarly attention, which predominantly documents and classifies the dances found on Greek soil. The criteria of classification vary: they include village or region of origin, the landscape of the place of origin ("mountain dances," "island dances"), structural features of the pattern of steps, and morphological features of the individual body or of the collective body of dancers (Crosfield 1948; Holden and Vouras 1965; Petrides 1980; Singer 1974). Though usually meticulous in their descriptions of contemporary dances, many scholars (including Stratou 1966) have been preoccupied with the continuity of choreographic forms. Despite the similarities of some modern folk dances with pictorial and sculptural representations of certain ancient dances, more recent work (Cowan 1990; Danforth 1979; Loutzaki 1983–1985; Raftis 1985) has set aside the issue of continuity and focused on what dancing means for Greeks and how they organize it.

BIBLIOGRAPHY

Alexiou, Margaret. 1974. *The Ritual Lament in Greek Tradition.* Cambridge: Cambridge University Press.

Anoyanakis, Fivos. 1979 [1965]. *Greek Popular Musical Instruments.* Athens: National Bank of Greece.

Auerbach, Susan. 1989. "From Singing to Lamenting: Women's Musical Role in a Greek Village." In *Women and Music in Cross-Cultural Perspective,* ed. Ellen Koskoff, 25–33. Urbana and Chicago: University of Illinois Press.

Baud-Bovy, Samuel. 1935, 1938. *Chansons du Dodécanèse.* 2 vols. Athens: J. N. Sideris.

———. 1983. *Essai sur la chanson populaire grecque.* Nafplion: Fondation ethnographique du Péloponnèse.

Beaton, Roderick. 1980a. "Modes and Roads: Factors of Change and Continuity in Greek Musical Tradition." *Annual of the British School of Archeology at Athens* 75:1–11.

———. 1980b. *Folk Poetry of Modern Greece.* Cambridge: Cambridge University Press.

Butterworth, Katharine, and Sara Schneider. 1975. *Rebetika: Songs from the Old Greek Underworld.* Athens: Komboloi Press.

Caraveli, Anna. 1982. "The Song Beyond the Song: Aesthetics and Social Interaction in Greek Folksong." *Journal of American Folklore* 95: 129–158.

———. 1985. "The Symbolic Village: Community Born in Performance." *Journal of American Folklore* 99:260–286.

Caraveli-Chaves, Anna. 1980. "Bridge Between Worlds: The Greek Women's Lament as Communicative Event." *Journal of American Folklore* 93:129–157.

Chianis, Sotirios (Sam). 1965. *Folksongs of Mantinea, Greece.* Berkeley: University of California Press.

———. 1980. "Greece, Folk Music." *The New Grove Dictionary of Music and Musicians.* Edited by Stanley Sadie. London: Macmillan.

Cowan, Jane K. 1990. *Dance and the Body Politic in Northern Greece.* Princeton: Princeton University Press.

———. 1993. "Politics, Identity and Popular Music in Contemporary Greece." *Kambos: Cambridge Papers in Modern Greek* 1:1–22.

Crosfield, Domini. 1948. *Dances of Greece.* London: Max Parrish.

Damianakos, Stathis. 1976. *Kinonioloyia tu Rebetiku* (The sociology of *rebetika*). Athens: Hermeias.

Danforth, Loring M. 1979. "The Role of the Dance in the Ritual Therapy of the Anastenaria." *Byzantine and Modern Greek Studies* 5:141–163.

———. 1982. *The Death Rituals of Rural Greece.* Princeton: Princeton University Press.

———. 1989. *Firewalking and Religious Healing: The Anastenaria of Greece and the American Firewalking Movement.* Princeton: Princeton University Press.

Dragoumis, Markos. 1966. "The Survival of Byzantine Chant in the Monophonic Music of the Modern Greek Church." In *Studies in Eastern Chant,* ed. Egon Wellesz and Milos Velimirovic, 1:9–36. London: Oxford University Press.

———. 1975. "The Music of the Rebetes." In *Rebetika: Songs from the Old Greek Underworld,* ed. Katharine Butterworth and Sara Schneider, 16–25. Athens: Komboloi Press.

Fauriel, Claude. 1824, 1825. *Chants populaires de la Grèce moderne,* 2 vols. Paris.

Gauntlett, Stathis. 1982. "Rebetiko Tragoudi as a Generic Term." *Byzantine and Modern Greek Studies* 8:77–102.

Georgiades, Thrasybulos. 1973. *Greek Music, Verse, and Dance,* New York: Da Capo Press.

Henderson, Isobel. 1957. "Ancient Greek Music." In *New Oxford History of Music,* ed. Egon Wellesz, 1:336–403. Oxford: Oxford University Press.

Herzfeld, Michael. 1981. "An Indigenous Theory of Meaning and Its Elicitation in Performative Context." *Semiotica* 34(1–2):113–141.

———. 1982. *Ours Once More: Folklore, Ideology, and the Making of Modern Greece.* Austin: University of Texas Press.

———. 1985. *The Poetics of Manhood: Contest and Identity in a Cretan Mountain Village.* Princeton: Princeton University Press.

Holden, Rickey, and Mary Vouras. 1965. *Greek Folk Dances.* Newark, N.J.: Folkraft Press.

Holst, Gail. 1977. *Road to Rembetika: Music of a Greek Sub-Culture: Songs of Love, Sorrow and Hashish.* Limni and Athens: Denise Harvey and Co.

———. 1980. *Theodorakis: Myth and Politics in Modern Greek Music.* Amsterdam: Adolf M. Hakkert.

Hughes, T. S. 1830. *Travels in Greece and Albania.* Vol. 1. London: Henry Colburn and Richard Bentley.

Kavadias, Giorgios, Lambros Liavas, and Rena Loutzaki. 1987. *Music in the Aegean.* Athens: Greek Ministry of Culture and Ministry of the Aegean.

Kilpatrick, David Bruce. 1975. "Function and Style in Pontic Dance Music." Ph.D. dissertation, University of California at Los Angeles.

Kind, Theodor. 1861 [1827]. *Anthologie neu-griechischer Volkslieder.* Leipzig: Veit.

Leotsakos, George. 1980. "Greece, After 1830." *The New Grove Dictionary of Music and Musicians.* Edited by Stanley Sadie. London: Macmillan.

Loutzaki, Rena. 1983–1985. "O Ghamos os Horeftiko Dhromeno: I Periptosi ton Prosfighon tis Anatolikis Rumelias sto Mikro Monastiri Makedhonias" (The wedding as dance practice: The case of refugees of eastern Rumelia in Mikro Monastiri, Macedonia). *Ethnografika* 4–5.

Mazaraki, Despina. 1984 [1959]. *To Laiko Klarino stin Elladha* (The folk clarinet in Greece). Athens: Kedros.

Merlier, Melpo. 1935. *I Musiki Laografia stin Elladha* (Musical folklore in Greece). Athens: I. N. Sidere.

Morris, Roderick Conway. 1981. "Greek Cafe, with a List of Recordings." *Recorded Sound* 80: 79–117.

Papadhakis, G. 1983. *Laiki Praktiki Organopektes* (Self-taught popular instrumentalists). Athens: Epikairotita.

Parry, Milman. 1930. "Studies in the Epic Technique of Oral Verse-Making." In *Homer and the Homeric Style,* 1:73–147. Harvard Studies in Classical Philology, 41. Cambridge: Harvard University Press.

Passow, Arnold. 1860. *Popularia carmina graeciae recentioris.* Leipzig: Teubner.

Peristeris, Spyridon. 1964. "Chansons poly-phoniques de l'Épire du Nord." *Journal of the International Folk Music Council* 16:51–53.

Petrides, Ted. 1975a. *Folk Dances of the Greeks.* Jericho, N.Y.: Exposition Press.

———. 1975b. "The Dances of the Rebetes." In *Rebetika: Songs from the Old Greek Underworld,* ed. Katharine Butterworth and Sara Schneider, 27–33. Athens: Komboloi Press.

———. 1980. *Greek Dances.* Athens: Lycabettus Press.

Petropoulos, D. 1954. "I piitaridhes stin Kriti ke stin Kipro." *Laografia* 15:374–700.

———. 1958–1959. *Ellinika Dhimotika Tragoudhia* (Greek folk songs). 2 vols. Athens: I. N. Zacharopoulou.

Petropoulos, Elias. 1975. "Rebetika." In *Rebetika: Songs from the Old Greek Underworld,* ed. Katharine Butterworth and Sara Schneider, 11–15. Athens: Komboloi Press.

———. 1979. *Rebetika Tragoudhia* (*Rebetika* songs). Athens: Kedros.

Politis, Nikolaos. 1909. "Laography." *Laografia* 1: 3–18.

———. 1914. *Ekloye apo ta Traghoudhia tou*

Ellinikou Laou (Some songs of the Greek people). Athens: Estia.

Raftis, Alkis. 1985. *O Kosmos tu Elliniku Horu* (The world of Greek dance). Athens: Politipo.

Romaios, K. A . 1973. "Elliniki Hori ke Idhietera o Kalamatianos" (Greek dances, and especially the *kalamatianos*). *Lavirinthos* 1:49–57.

Schorelis, T. 1977–1980. *Rebetiki Antholoyia* (Anthology of *rebetika*). 4 vols. Athens: Plethron.

Seremetakis, C. Nadia. 1991. *The Last Word: Women, Death, and Divination in Inner Mani.* Chicago: University of Chicago Press.

Sifakis, G. 1988. *Yia mia Piitiki tou Ellinikou Dhimotikou Tragoudhiou* (Toward a poetics of the Greek folk song). Iraklion: Panepistemiakis Ekdhosis Kritis.

Singer, Alice. 1974. "The Metrical Structure of Macedonian Dance." *Ethnomusicology* 18(3): 379–404.

Stratou, Dora. 1966. *The Greek Dances.* Athens: Angelos Klissiounis.

Tsigakou, Fani-Maria. 1981. *The Rediscovery of Greece: Travellers and Painters of the Romantic Era.* London: Thames and Hudson.

Vamvakaris, Markos. 1973. *Aftoviografia* (Autobiography). Edited by Angeliki Vellou-Keil. Athens: Papazisis.

Watts, Niki. 1988. *The Greek Folk Songs.* Bristol: Bristol Classical Press.

Wellesz, Egon. 1949. *A History of Byzantine Music and Hymnography.* Oxford: Clarendon Press.

Wellesz, Egon, and Milos Velimirovic, eds. 1966. *Studies in Eastern Chant.* Vol. 1. London: Oxford University Press.

Winnington-Ingram, Reginald Pepys. 1980. "Greece, Ancient." *The New Grove Dictionary of Music and Musicians.* Edited by Stanley Sadie. London: Macmillan.

AUDIOVISUAL RESOURCES

Aidhonidhis, Hronis, Yorgos Dalaras, and Ross Daly. 1990. *T'Aidhonia tis Anatolis: Traghoudhia Thrakis ke Mikras Asias* (The nightingales of the east: Songs of Thrace and Asia Minor). Minos MSM 847–848. 2 LP disks.

Anoyanakis, Fivos, ed. 1975. *Greek Folk Music.* Vol. 1. Peloponnesian Folklore Foundation. Columbia-EMI Greece, MT 3877. LP disk.

Anthony, Alexandra, and Mary Vouras. 1985. *Amarantos, Agrapha, and Aspasia.* 16 mm. Available from 5 Hastings Square, Cambridge, Mass. 02139. Video.

Bakertsis, Argiris, and ensemble. 1985. *Himerini Kolymvites: Apo to parko stin Mirovolo* (Winter swimmers: From the park in Mirovolo). Lyra 3415. LP disk.

Bellou, Sotiria. 1971–1986. *Ta Rebetika tis Sotiria Bellou* (The *rebetika* of Sotira Bellou). Lyra 3224, 3232, 3245, 3248, 3257, 3275, 3290, 3306, 3314, 3526. 10 LP disks.

Center for the Study of Rebetic Song. 1977. *To Rebetiko Tragoudhi* (The rebetic song). Diski CBS AEBE 82290, 82303, 26116, 26117, 26118. 5 LP disks.

Chianis, Sam, ed. 1981. *Epirotika with Periklis Halkias.* Folkways FSS 34024. LP disk.

Cohen, John. 1988. *Pericles in America.* 16 mm. New York: Icarus/First Run films. Video.

Dalaras, Yorghos. 1979. *Rebetika tis Katohis* (Rebetika of the occupation). Minos MSM 391. LP disk.

Daly, Ross. 1987. *Anadhisi* (Emergence). Seirios SMH 87.001-87.002. LP disk.

Dragoumis, Markos. 1976. *Dhimotika Traghoudhia apo tin Sillogi Melpos Merlie* (Folk songs from the Melpo Merlier Collection). Vol. 1. Polydor 2421079. LP disk.

Fakinos, Aris, ed. 1984. *Grèce: Chants Polyphoniques et Musique d'Epire.* Ocora 558631. LP disk.

Fatme. 1982. *Fatme.* EMIAL 9842. LP disk.

Glykeria. 1982. *Smyrneika.* Lyra 3753. LP disk.

Grapsas, Nikos, et al. 1987. *Dhinamis tou Eyeou #2* (Aegean forces). EMI-Columbia 062-1701371. LP disk.

Hadzidakis, Manos. 1965. *To Hamoyelo tis Tzokontas* (Giaconda's smile). EMI-Columbia 14C 062-70243. LP disk.

Hadzidoulis, Kostas, ed. 1975–1976. *Rebetiki Istoria 1925–1955.* Columbia-EMI 2J048–70364, 70365, 70366. 3 LP disks.

Hiotis, Manolis. 1982. *I Megali tou Rebetikou: Manolis Hiotis* (The masters of *rebetika*: Manolis Hiotis). Minos Margo 8244. LP disk.

Karaindhrou, Eleni. 1984. Instrumental Music to Tonia Marketaki's film *I Timi tis Agapis* (The price of love). Minos Matsas and Son, MSM 520. LP disk.

Karas, Simon, and Mary Vouras, eds. 1972–1980.

Songs of Greece. Athens: Society for the Dissemination of National Music. 25 LP disks.

Kazantzidhis, Stellios. 1982. *I Megaliteres Epitihies tou Steliou Kazantzidhis* (Stellios Kazantzidhis' greatest hits). EMIAL 1226. LP disk.

Koch, Mariza. 1977. *14 Tragoudhia* (Fourteen songs). Diski CBS AEBE 82569. LP disk.

Ksidakis, Nikos, and Thodhoris Gounis. 1989. *Cairo, Nauplion, Khartoum.* Lyra 4504. LP disk.

Mamangakis, Nikos, composer, and Yorghos Ioannou, lyricist. 1982. *Kendro Dierhomenon* (Grand Central Station). Lyra 3758. LP disk.

Opisthodromiki Kompania. 1983. *Mia Nihta me tin Opisthodromiki Kompania* (A night with the Retrograde Company). Lyra 3361. LP disk.

Papazoglou, Vangelis. 1982. *Vangelis Papazoglou: To Smyrneiko Tragoudhi stin Elladha meta to 1922* (Vangelis Papazoglou: The song of Smyrna in Greece after 1922). Falirea Brothers ACBA 1132–1133. 2 LP disks.

Pappas, Irene. 1980. *Odes.* Polydor 2473109.

Parios, Yannis. 1982. *Ta Nisiotika* (Island songs). Minos MSM 430–431. LP disk.

Samiou, Domna. 1973. *Domna Samiou: Ehe Yeia, Panayia* (Domna Samiou: Good health to the virgin mother). Commentary in Greek by Markos Dragoumis. Columbia-EMI Greece 14C 064–70115. LP disk.

Savvopoulos, Dionysis. 1983. *Trapezakia Ekso* (Little tables outdoors). Lyra 3360. LP disk.

———. 1989. *To Kourema* (Haircut). Polydor 839728. LP disk.

Shiloah, Amnon, ed. 1978. *Greek-Jewish Musical Traditions.* Folkways FE 4205. LP disk.

Spottswood, Dick, and Jim Palis. 1984. *To Elliniko Laiko Traghoudi stin Ameriki apo 1917 eos 1938* (Greek popular song in America, 1917–1938). Falirea Brothers 22–23. 2 LP disks.

Theodorakis, Mikis. 1986. *Ta Traghoudhia mou 1959-1986* (My songs, 1959–1986). CBS 450186–450187. 2 LP disks.

Tsitsanis, Vassilis. 1984. *Grece. Hommage à Tsitsanis: Bouzouki.* Ocora 558632. LP disk.

Vamvakaris, Markos, and Stratos Payioumtzis. 1981. *Markos Vamvakaris: Stratos Payioumtzis: Zontani Ihografisi stou Vrana* (Markos Vamvakaris: Statos Payioumtzis: Recorded live at Vrana). Falirea Brothers 12. LP disk.

Vouras, Mary, ed. 1975. *Greek Villages.* Sound Image 2. LP disk.

Williams, John, and Maria Farandouri. 1971. *Songs and Guitar Pieces by Theodorakis.* CBS 72947. LP disk.

Xarhakos, Stavros, composer, and Nikos Gatsos, lyricist. 1983. *Rebetiko.* Diski CBS 70245. LP disk.

Xylouris, Nikos. 1971. *Rizitika.* Columbia-EMI Greece 14C 064-70069. 6 LP disks.

Cyprus
Panicos Giorgoudes

Traditional Songs and Dances
The Transmission of Music
History of Scholarship

Cyprus, the chief source of copper in the ancient Mediterranean world (hence its name), is the third-largest island in the Mediterranean, after Sicily and Sardinia. It has an area of 9,251 square kilometers. Since 1960, when Cyprus gained its independence from Britain, it has been a republic, headed by a president elected directly by the people.

The population of Cyprus, approximately 735,000, is composed of two main communities, Greek Cypriots (82 percent) and Turkish Cypriots (18 percent). Communities of Maronites, Armenians, and others—about 2.7 percent of the total—are at their choice counted as part of the Greek Cypriot community.

In July 1974, Turkey invaded Cyprus and occupied 37 percent of its territory, land now inaccessible to Greek Cypriots, some two hundred thousand of whom were forcibly expelled during the invasion. In 1983, the occupation regime in the Turkish-held area declared independence from the Republic of Cyprus, but only Turkey has recognized the secessionist entity. A policy of colonization of the occupied area by Turkey has been matched by massive emigration by Turkish Cypriots, who, because of political instability and dire economic conditions, seek a better life elsewhere.

Cyprus is in every way a contemporary economy. The service sector is growing at the expense of agriculture and industry. The national income is about U.S. $14,000 per capita. The music of Cyprus is connected to the musical traditions of the Greek islands and several other cultural areas of Greek civilization.

TRADITIONAL SONGS AND DANCES

Traditional Cypriot music has a clear relation to some of the eight Byzantine modes (*echoi,* sing. *echos*), which imply not only a set of melodic intervals, but also certain melodic phrases, endings, and important notes. Most songs are in the D mode, known as the first Byzantine mode, *echos* A. The range may be within a seventh, a fifth, or even just a third above the final, with one or two notes below the final. Less common modes include C mode and the E mode, plus a chromatic mode that in its lower tetrachord uses a flat second and a sharp third to produce an augmented second.

A few Cypriot tunes are performed in major and minor scales, which should be

FIGURE 1 A typical
song in D mode
(*echos* A), construct-
ed in the traditional
tune type (*fone*)
called *ishia* 'straight'.
Transcription by
Panicos Giorgoudes.

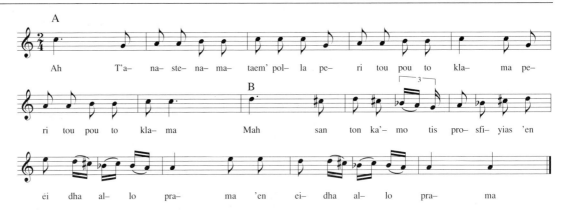

considered foreign cultural elements, imported, modified, and assimilated in Cypriot music. Often played by groups of young people influenced by Western pop music, such tunes are a new phenomenon in Cyprus. These groups usually form when a local song contest or an international festival happens.

Characteristically, singers on Cyprus use traditional tune types (*fones*) as melodic models to create new songs with new texts, particularly in a genre of improvised couplets called *tsiattista*. The most famous tune types of this genre are *ishia* 'straight', *paralimnitiki* 'from Paralimni Village', *avkoritiki* 'from Avkorou Village', and *anamisi* 'one and a half', referring to the one and a half distichs fitted to this melody. *Akritikes* is a famous tune type for *akritika*, songs about the guards of the Byzantine Empire, and *poietarikes* is the tune type for the poems of *poietarides*, professional poet-singers.

Other important tune types are sung during wedding ceremonies and parties, for religious texts, and for traditional swinging-game songs (*sousa*), which often have an erotic or joyful content. Tune types can have AA or AB forms; *ishia*, for example, is in AB form, with A in the D mode and B in the chromatic mode (figure 1). If an instrumental introduction is present, it constitutes a third sectional part, and instrumental music often has an ABC form. Most AA forms are local variants of *ishia*, based on its part A or B. The practice of fitting old or new poetic texts to model tunes also occurs in *laika*, well-known Greek popular songs composed by named composers, especially among the refugees.

In addition to songs created from tune types, many songs (some in AB form) have been imported and assimilated into Cypriot tradition through communication and cultural relations with Greece. These include *kleftika*, heroic songs from mainland Greece; *mikrasiatika*, songs from Asia Minor; and *nisiotika*, songs from the Greek islands. Similarly, Greek dances from all over Greece constitute the main dances of Cyprus, most of them taught in schools, by cultural societies, and in private workshops. These include *tsamiko* and *kalamatiano* from the mainland, *zeibekikos* and *arabies* from Asia Minor, and *sousta* and *syrtos* from the Greek islands [see GREECE].

Dances and instruments

The dances unique to Cyprus, *kartzilamade*s (from *kartzi* 'face to face'), consist of two sequences of five movements, one for men and one for women, who stand face to face. The first through fourth movements are simply numbered (*protos, thefteros, tritos, tetartos*) and performed in the meters 9/8, 7/8, 2/4, and 9/8. The fifth movement (*pemptos*) can be danced in 2/4, 3/4, or 7/9, and usually leads into the line dance (*syrtos*).

For dance music in Cyprus, the typical ensemble (*vkiolarides* 'violinists') consists of a violin playing the melody, a *laouto* (a combination of guitar neck with lute body)

FIGURE 2 Two men dance a *kartzilamades*, accompanied by an ensemble called *vkiolarides* 'violinists'. Photograph from the 1960s supplied to the author by the Levendis Museum, Nicosia.

playing an accompaniment, and a *tampoutsia* (a frame drum) keeping the rhythm (figure 2).

The violin, probably imported to Cyprus in the mid-1800s, seems to have replaced the *lyra,* a bowed, pear-shaped lute still found on some Greek islands. Instruments such as the accordion, the *bouzouki*, and the guitar are usually added to the ensemble today.

To pass time in the fields, shepherds played tune types and other improvised melodies on the *pidkiavli,* a single-reed cylindrical cane instrument in the shape of an *aulos,* an ancient Greek instrument, but few of them remain alive.

THE TRANSMISSION OF MUSIC

Cypriot music used to be transmitted in oral tradition. Most old Cypriots know one or more tune types and sing them with distichs improvised or chosen to respond to a particular occasion. Most music teachers in Cyprus are educated only in Western music, but some of them know the Byzantine music system and traditional music, and act as chanters in the Greek Orthodox Churches or as folk singers. Music education in schools is mainly based on Western classical music, and the piano and orchestral instruments are taught. Few music teachers base their lessons on local music. The traditional way of playing the violin, the *laouto,* and the *pidkiavli* must be learned from relatives within certain well-known families. But young people are not much interested in that.

A new and culturally important environment has been created by refugees driven from their villages and houses during the invasion of 1974. They all live in camps and housing areas in or near the capital (Nicosia), the port at Limasdol, and Larnaca, with its new airport. Though they continue some traditional customs, including music, several new kinds of music can be heard as a result of modern culture and the mass media, which promote international pop hits and contemporary Greek songs (*laika*). Since no record companies have developed locally, Cyprus hosts no countervailing productions. Such new kinds of music are usually published in Athens.

Emigrants from Cyprus living in London, the United States, and Australia continue the musical traditions of Cyprus using new instruments, including synthesizers, electric guitars, and drums, new lyrics relevant to their new lives, and sometimes English words. The 250,000 Cypriots in the United Kingdom sing the old tune types as they change old texts into new ones, describing their feelings of homesickness and desires to return to their homeland. Since most of them are refugees who immigrated to London after the Turkish invasion, many of their songs refer to the struggle for justice in Cyprus in the old tradition of *poietarides*.

HISTORY OF SCHOLARSHIP

Educated laypersons and schoolteachers began the study of Cypriot music as amateurs in the late 1800s, intending to demonstrate a connection between Cypriot and Greek culture. They focused on the texts of the songs, and only in 1910 was the first collection with the music for twenty-one songs and dances published (Apostolides). In 1951, another important collection of Cypriot songs and dances appeared with transcriptions in both European and Byzantine notation (Kallinikos).

After Cyprus gained its independence, Cypriot musicians published several collections, but the discipline of ethnomusicology had not yet been established at any local research institution. Ethnomusicological work started in the late 1980s, the result of efforts by Cypriot students educated in Greece, Europe, and the United States. In May 1997, the University of Cyprus opened. It offers an ethnomusicological research program, which will systematically collect the complete musical-poetic tradition and create an archive to house it.

BIBLIOGRAPHY

Apostolides, Christos. 1910. *Cyprus Songs and Dances.* Limassol: n.p.

Averof, George. 1978. *Kypriakoi laikoi choroi.* Demosievmata Etaireias Kypriakon Spoudon, 5. Nicosia.

Giorgoudes, Panicos. 1990. "Musical Transcriptions: Special Symbols for the Notation of Traditional Greek and Cypriot Music." *ICTM (UK Chapter) Bulletin* 25:16–28.

———. 1991. "Istoria tis erevnas tis Kypriakis mousikopoiitikis paradosis." *Laografiki Kypros* 21:113–119.

———. 1995. "The Basic Structure and Morphology of the Musical Tradition of Cyprus."

In *The Cypriot–French Repertory of the Manuscript Torino J.II.9,* ed. Urs. Günther and Lud. Finscher, 27–32. Musicological Studies and Documents, 45. Neuhausen-Stuttgart: American Institute of Musicology, Hänssler-Verlag.

Ioannides, Kostas D. 1968. "A Short Collection of Cyprus Folksongs." *Kypriakai Spoudai* 32:265–300.

———. 1969, 1970, 1972. "Quasi Liturgical Hymns." *Kypriakai Spoudai* 33:53–123; 34:47–77; 36:197–221.

Kallinikos, Theodoulos. 1951. *Kypriaki laiki mousa.* Nicosia: Etaireia Kypriakon Spoudon.

Michaelides, Solon. 1945, 1956. "Kypriaki (laiki-

demotiki) mousiki." *Kypriaka Grammata* 9:115–126; 21(247–252):105–113.

Papadopoulos, Stelios. 1993. *Paradosiaka Tragoudia kai Horoi tis Kyprou.* Nicosia: Dryma Archiepiskopou Makariou I'.

Tobolis, Sozos. 1966. *Kypriakoi rythmoi kai melodies.* Nicosia: n.p.

———. 1980. *Traditional Cyprian Songs and Dances.* Nicosia: n.p.

Zarmas, Pieris. 1975. *Studien zur Volksmusik Zyperns.* Collection d'Études Musicologiques / Sammlung Musikwissenschaftlicher Abhandlungen, 60. Baden-Baden: Valentin Koerner.

AUDIOVISUAL RESOURCES

Averof, George. 1977. *Cyprus Folk Dances and Songs.* CBS Records 81900. LP disk.

———. 1985. *Cyprus Folk Dances and Songs.* Vol. 2. CBS Records 54694. LP disk.

Cyprus Popular Music. 1989. Peloponnesian Folklore Foundation & Ministry of Culture P.F.F.8–14. 7 LP disks.

Demotike Mousike, Horoi, Tragoudia. 1975. Lykeion ton Ellenidon LCGW 101. LP disk.

Dietrich, Wolf. 1978. *Folk Music of Cyprus: Traditional Songs and Dances of the Greek, Turkish,*

and Maronite Communities. Lyrichord LLST 7329. LP disk.

Kallinikos, Theodoulos. 1933. *Tylliriotissa: Tragoudi tou gamou.* His Master's Voice 400. 78-RPM disks.

———. 1934. *Folklore Music of Cyprus: 10 demotika tragoudia.* EMI Greece. 78-RPM disks.

———. 1973. *Folklore Music of Cyprus.* EMI-Columbia, EMI AL (Lambrooulos Brothers). LP disk.

Music from Thrace, Epirus, Sterea, Peloponnesus,

Dodecanese, and Cyprus. 1975. Peloponnesian Folklore Foundation 2. Compact disc.

Sikkis, Christos. 1987. *Bless This Hour: Folk Songs of Cyprus.* Lyra 3464. LP disk.

———. 1993. *Cyprus, A Paradise on Earth.* Lyra 4708. Compact disc.

———. 1993. *Songs from Cyprus.* Lyra 0108. Compact disc.

———. 1998. *Cyprus.* The Guardians of Hellenism, vol. 12. FM Records.

Glossary

All terms in **bold** are defined elsewhere in the glossary. Page numbers in *italic* indicate pages on which illustrations appear.

a sa seria (also *boghe'e notte*) Songs in slow tempo based on serious themes in Sardinian *a tenore* singing (627)

a să văji A judgment of how well two *strigături* go together in Maramureş, Romania (119)

a tenore A secular polyphonic singing style of Sardinia (627, *628*, 630, 632)

abbaddata A southern Corsican term for a dance around a corpse; see *ballata* (567)

abchodnyja pieśni Belarusan festive "walk-about" songs, sung while villagers make the rounds of their neighbors' homesteads in spring (794)

accordeon (Dutch) An accordion of the Low Countries (530)

accordéon (French) An accordion of the Low Countries (530)

accordéon jurassien The **musette**-tuned accordion of Jura, Switzerland (693)

achangur An Abkhazian four-stringed plucked **lute** (853)

acharpan An Abkhazian whistle flute, made from mountain grass (852)

achetringele A clapper bell of Laupen, Bern, Switzerland (683)

acordeon An accordion of Romania (880)

adaul An Abkhazian double-headed drum (853)

adonai malakh One of the two most common Ashkenazic Jewish **modes** (*shtayger*); see *ahavah rabbah* (253)

Adradžeńnie 'Belarusan Renaissance': a Belarusan movement toward cultural and national assertion, reflected in urban music (800)

adufe A Portuguese square **frame drum** (*577*; *582*); a Spanish **tambourine** (594)

adxoky-pondur A Chechen and Ingush three-stringed bowed **lute** (863, 864)

aeag-ashva Abkhazian harvest songs, performed during traditional feasts; see *arash-vara-ashva* (853)

aerg Abkhazian hunting songs, performed during traditional feasts; see *azhveipshaar-ashva* (853)

afirkhatsar-ashva Abkhazian heroic songs, performed during traditional feasts (853)

agadan iish A Chechen women's lullaby (863)

aguinaldos Spanish Christmas songs (590)

ahavah rabbah One of the two most common Ashkenazic Jewish **modes** (*shtayger*); see *adonai malakh* (253)

aijuma An Abkhazian fourteen-stringed **harp** (853)

ainkjaga An Abkhazian rattle (853)

ajabeba A Spanish transverse flute (594)

akapkap An Abkhazian rattle (853)

akaryna A Belarusan clay ovoid **ocarina**, with eight to ten holes for fingering (796, *797*)

akhima An Abkhazian twenty-four-stringed zither (853)

akritika Cypriot songs about the guards of the Byzantine Empire (1030)

aksak 'Limping': any of numerous asymmetrical, additive, unequal-part meters in Turkish and Eastern European music, also found in some Spanish forms (593, 744, 745, 891, 959, 964, 1008)

alaturka 'In Turkish style': a style of singing used by Sephardic Jewish men in Bosnia-Hercegovina to sing religious songs (968)

alboka A Basque double-pipe aerophone, each pipe having a single reed and a horn at each end, one acting as a bell and the other as a mouthpiece (171, 314, 594)

alborada A Spanish music-and-dance genre of central and eastern Castile-León and Extremadura (596)

Alleluia A proper section of the Mass, derived from a joyous exclamation (Hebrew *hal-lelujah* 'praise Yahweh'), grafted onto a **chant** (106)

allemande A country dance popular in Luxembourg (168, 524)

allspelslåtar The standardized repertoire of Swedish tunes that all fiddlers are expected to know (150)

almschroa An Austrian solo dairymaid's **yodel** (673)

alphorn A usually long wooden trumpet (41, 420, 651, 656, *688*, 689, 690, 696, 697, 872, 875, 878, 915)

alphorn-fa The sharp intonation of the eleventh partial (F in a C scale) as played by Swiss alphorns, a tone also found in traditional Swiss singing (688, 690–91)

alvorada A Portuguese religious festival announced by a civil wind band or a bag-pipe-and-drum ensemble (579)

amanedhes Greek improvised poetry punctu-

ated by the exclamation *aman*! 'alas!' (281, 285, 1014–15)

amarantina See *viola* (582)

amirzakan An Abkhazian accordion (853)

amoureuse A country dance popular in Luxembourg (524)

an dro A Breton line or circle dance performed as part of a three-part suite (559)

añafil A Spanish long, straight trumpet (594)

anamisi 'One and a half': a tune type of the Cypriot *tsiattista* genre; the name refers to the number of distichs fitted to the melody (1030)

anastenaria Macedonian fire-walking healing rituals, performed on 21 May (1011)

anatolitika The Anatolian (Turkish) style of Greek *rebetika* (1022)

andartika Greek patriotic songs of the left-wing partisan resistance of the 1940s (1108)

anglaise 'English' (French): a country dance of the Low Countries (457, 524)

anglas A Swedish contra dance, especially in southern and eastern Sweden (442)

anglois A country dance popular in Friesland (524)

ánimas Spanish songs about the sufferings of souls in purgatory (591)

anninnia Cradle songs, part of the Sardinian *a tenore* repertoire (627)

apandur An Abkhazian three-stringed plucked **lute** (853)

apdziedāšanās Latvian antiphonal, humorous, competitive singing at weddings, with texts largely improvised (502)

apkhertsa An Abkhazian two-stringed bowed **lute** (853)

apocope The loss of a sound or sounds at the end of a word; whispering or omitting the last syllable of a song in northern Poland (703, 711)

arabesk A form of Turkish popular music popular among "guest workers" in Germany and Roma in Kosova (Kosovo) (204, 237, 286, 951, 1002)

arabies A Greek dance of Asia Minor, as performed in Cyprus (1030)

arashvara-ashva Abkhazian harvest songs, performed during traditional feasts; see *aeag-ashva* (853)

archéologie sonore 'Sonorous archaeology' (French): music archaeology (35) *argismo* (also *argia*) A Sardinian spider-poisoning ritual resembling the Italian *tarantismo* (609, 632)

aria In European art music of the **Baroque** and later, an elaborate type of accompanied solo vocal composition, often with a memorable melody; used in **opera** in alternation with recitative (78, 79, 84, 617)

arija A melody to which rhymed couplets are set in Slavonia, Croatia (931)

arinarin A Basque chain dance (314)

arkiestry Orchestras in western Belarus (798)

armailli Herdsmen in Haute-Gruyère, Switzerland, who call their cattle with melodious calls (*ayóber*) (119)

arraial A secular Portuguese celebration beginning immediately after a religious procession, ending in the late evening and including performances of music and dance (579)

arruada A Portuguese religious festival in which a band performs marches in front of each house in a village; also *peditório* and *recolha de andores* (579)

ars musica 'Musical art' (Latin): music theory in the **Middle Ages** (49)

Ars Nova 'New Art' (Latin): In European music history, the period of the early 1300s, when complex polyphonic innovations arose, especially in France (65, 71, 726)

Ars Subtilior 'Subtler Art' (Latin): late-fourteenth-century complex polyphonic music (50, 73)

astalske pesme 'Table songs': café songs in Vojvodina, Serbia (114, 952)

atatsaagara-ashva Abkhazian wedding songs, performed during traditional feasts (853)

Atengenoba A summer ritual celebrated in the mountain districts of eastern Georgia with the sacrifice of sheep and the performance of circle dances (834)

atlarchopa Abkhazian healing songs, performed during traditional feasts (853)

åttondelspolskor A Swedish *polska*, in eighth-note rhythms (435)

aukan'e 'Helloing': a Russian solo lament, sung by women to birds in the forest (760)

aulos An ancient Greek conical double-reed aerophone, typically played in pairs by one player (39, 46, *47*, 1031)

auroras Spanish songs to call people to the rosary (590)

Austropop A term applied since the 1960s to dialect-sung Austrian pop music (674, 676–78)

avaz A Near Eastern term used in Albania and Montenegro to name performances (966, 993)

avkoritiki 'From Avkorou village': a tune type within the Cypriot *tsiattista* genre (1030)

avtorskie pesni 'Authored songs': popular Russian songs distributed by self-published cassette tapes (767, 778)

ayóber Melodious cattle calls, sung by herdsmen in Haute-Gruyère, Switzerland (119)

azar Abkhazian funeral songs, performed during traditional feasts (853)

azhveipshaar-ashva Abkhazian hunting songs, performed during traditional feasts; see *aerg* (853)

ba'al tokeah 'Master of blowing' (Hebrew): a community specialist who plays the **shofar** (259)

badhanim Jewish musical professionals (each a combination of trickster, acrobat, and jester), who often performed at weddings (251, 259)

bagad A Breton *biniou* and *bombarde* band, modeled after Scottish pipe bands (560, 562–63)

bagdaduri A Georgian dance accompanied by Middle Eastern instruments, such as the *zurna*, the *duduki,* and the *doli* (836)

bağlama A plucked **lute** of the Turkish *saz* family, used in Greek *rebetika*; see *bakllama* (993, 1019–20)

baian A Russian version of the Ukrainian accordion (811)

baian A Russian and Belarusan fully chromatic button accordion (771, *798*)

baiduska A Greek Thracian dance in 5/8 or 6/8 time (1013)

baile (Spanish): dance, dancing, ball, **ballet** (596)

Bajram A Muslim calendric feast, celebrated in Macedonia and Albania (975, 988, 997)

bajs A double bass of northwestern Croatia (933)

bakllama Near Eastern long-necked plucked **lute**, played in Albania during the Ottoman period (993)

bal folk Folk-dance nights in the Low Countries (535)

balabaika (Eastern Ukrainian): **balalaika** (816)

balade Romanian **epic ballads** that flourished between the sixteenth and nineteenth centuries; also *cîntece bătrînești*' 'old-time songs' (875)

balalaika A Russian three-stringed **lute** with a triangular sound box, also found in Ukraine (22, 101, 134, 155, 169, 176, 180, 487, 768, 770, 771, 774, *775*, 796, 816–17, 863)

ballad A narrative song in oral tradition, but also transmitted in printed form with the spread of literacy (8, 17, 19, 23, 106, 131, 132, 133, 134–37, 142, 165, 194, 195, 198, 200, 254, 283, 294–95, 296, 297, *327, 328,* 329, 332, 333, 336, 343–47, 353, 365, 367, 369–72, 374, 379, 386, 388, 391, 392, 394, 403–405, 412, 413, 426, 435, 451–53, 458–63, 468–472, 477, 509, 517, 520–21, 523, 541, 542, 545, 547, 551, 559, 576, 578, 589, 592, 596, 601, 605–607, 609, 611, 635, 637, *638,* 646, 663, 664, 672, 674, 695, 709, 740, 742, 760, 792, 795, 798, 800, 806, 821, 875–76, 879–80, 882, 896, 911, 922, 963, 964, 966, 968, 989, 1021)

ballad meter An English poetic meter, composed of eight-syllable lines in four-line stanzas; also long common meter (328)

ballada 'Ballads' (Hungarian): a type of Hungarian folk song (740)

ballade A French fixed verseform, usually consisting of three stanzas with recurrent rhymes, en envoi, and an identical refrain for each part; a musical composition in this form (132)

ballarella A variant of the **saltarello** (609)

ballata A Corsican dance once performed around a corpse; known in southern Corsica as *abbaddata* (566–67)

ballet 'ballad': A broadside in Ireland (386)

ballet A theatrical art form combining conventional movements, costumes, scenery, and music usually to narrate a story or convey a theme (77, 79, 160–61, 287, 369, 444, 460, 472, 781, 800, 882, 921)

ballets de cour Lavish commemorative spectacles hosted by monarchs and aristocrats during the French **Renaissance**, with elaborate scenery, costumes, music, poetry, and dance (160)

balletti (sing. *balletto*) Social dances presented in Italian **Renaissance** courts (160)

balletto polacco A name of the **mazurka** outside Poland (710)

ballos A Venetian-influenced dance of the Aegean Islands, Greece (1014)

ballu A Sardinian line dance; when performed in a circle, it is known as *ballu tundu* (627, 630, *631*)

balon (also *balun*) A dance of the northern Adriatic zone of Croatia 931

bals Breton figure dances (559)

banatske gajde A large three-voiced bagpipe of Vojvodina, Serbia (*945*)

banda A brass band of Ticino, in Italian-speaking Switzerland (695)

banda communale An Italian municipal wind band (617)

banda de música A Spanish municipal wind band (594)

bande A Slovenian band of two to four violins, one or two violas, one or two clarinets, a bass, and a cimbalon; also *goslarije* (917)

bandella A small *banda* of Ticino, in Italian-speaking Switzerland (694, *695*)

bandura A Ukrainian multistringed lute-zither; also *kobza* (101, 815–16, *817*)

bani 'Bass': the lowest part in Georgian three-part singing, the only part traditionally sung by a group (828, *829*, 839)

Bänkelsänger German semiprofessional balladeers (16)

bånsuller Norwegian lullabies (421)

baraban A large two-headed Polish drum (704); a Ukrainian field drum (810, *811*)

baraban z talerkami A Belarusan cylindrical double-headed drum with a brass cymbal attached to the frame (797)

barabanče A Macedonian **snare drum** (977)

barbiton (also *barbitos*) An ancient Greek large **lyre**, used to accompany erotic songs (47)

barcarole A Venetian gondoliers' song, usually in 6/8 or 12/8 time (570, 573)

bard A poet-singer of heroes and their feats; applied in Eastern Europe to any of numerous modern urban singer-songwriters (146,

185, 342, 348–49, 350, 352, 362, 367, 370, 561, 611, 635, 778, 800, 801)

bar mitzvah 'Son of the law' (Hebrew): a Jewish boy who reaches his thirteenth birthday; a celebration, with music, recognizing a boy as a bar mitzvah (143)

Baroque In European music history, the period from about 1600 to about 1750 (65, 69, 76–79, 104, 160, 227, 352, 415, 417, 419, 435, 440, 532, 654, 657, 658, 708, 727, 737)

barva-lur An extant Iron Age animal-horn instrument of Sweden (41)

bas 'Bass': the lowest voice in Slovene three-part singing (913, 942–43)

bas A Ukrainian usually three-stringed bass, about the size and shape of a violoncello (809, 810–12, 818); short for **na bas**, a singing style of the Dinaric Alps and Pannonia (927)

basetla A Belarusan bass fiddle (796)

basiranje 'Bassing': a Serbian singing style in which the lower voice sings in parallel thirds with the melody and forms a perfect fifth at the cadence; also **na ariju** and **na bas** (942)

bassa The lowest voice in Corsican **paghjelle** that implies tonal harmony (569–70)

bassgeige A bass violin in ensembles of Italian southern Tyrol until World War I (615)

basso continuo In European art music of the **Baroque** period, one or more instruments that within an ensemble furnish a partially improvised accompaniment to voices or other instruments; also known simply as continuo (76, 78, 104)

batlejka Belarusan folk puppet theater, having elements of **skamarochi** (minstrel) singing (799)

batonebo A two- and three-part curing song for whooping cough and the measles, sung by women in western Georgia; compare **iavnana** (835)

batta[g]lia German **Baroque** programmatic battle pieces (654)

bayram (Turkish) A Muslim celebration (988)

bayt 'Rhymed couplets' (Arabic); see **bejte** (989)

bazuna A long wooden trumpet of Pomerania, Poland (704)

bećarac 'Bachelor's song': Bosnia-Hercegovinian polyphonic singing in which two voices sing in parallel thirds and cadence on a fifth (964)

bećarci Serbian male youths gathered in cafés to sing and carouse (143, 952)

begii iish Ingush humorous songs (864)

beguine A social dance of Martinique, popular in Italy (619)

bei Polyphonic singing of Tuscany (610)

bejte Rhymed couplets exchanged by Albanian men during social gatherings (989)

bekace A short Polish clarinet (704)

beranče A Macedonian dance in 12/8 time (978)

berceuses French lullabies, usually in 6/8 time

(542)

berda In the Slovene **tamburica** ensemble, a **lute** that plays the bass part (917)

berestiankka A Belarusan horn (*797*)

berikaoba Masqueraders' performances at **kvelieri** in rural Georgia (834, 836)

berimbau A Brazilian musical bow, now used in Swedish folk music (442)

bernerstil 'Bern style' (German): a musical style of Bern, Switzerland, that uses a chromatic accordion and a clarinet to mimic Bernese yodeling (689)

bertsu The improvisation of new verses for an existing Basque tune (311–12, *313*, 315)

bertsulari Basque versifiers who improvise new texts in competitions (311–14)

beshik zhirla 'Cradle song': a Balkar and Karachaevi lullaby (858)

betbut A Maltese whistle (640)

betruf The Swiss "Alpine blessing," having the range of a fifth and important as a national icon (128)

bhangra A popular dance music of Punjabi immigrants in England (207, 232, 236, 240–41)

biarozka A Belarusan dance performed in **žanićba Ciareški** (792)

biasiednyja pieśni Belarusan table songs (793)

bibaw A Welsh **mouth harp**, made of wood or metal, held between the teeth, and struck with the finger, popular until the early 1900s; see **sturmant** (348)

biculë A short, double-bore duct flute played by herdsmen in Labëri, Albania; also **cylëdyjare** (993)

bijambò A Maltese **mouth harp** (640)

bilbil A duct flute played by northern Albanian herdsmen (996)

binbir halka A large **tambourine** played in some Dervish rituals in Bosnia-Hercegovina (967)

biniou A bagpipe of Brittany (France) (545, 559, *560*, 561–64)

biniou bihan 'Little bagpipe' (Breton) (559)

biniou bras In Brittany, the Scottish Highland bagpipes (559)

biniou koz 'Old bagpipe' (Breton): a mouth-blown bagpipe with one drone, pitched an octave above the Scottish Highland bagpipes (559)

binjak 'Twin': a double-bore duct flute, played by Albanians in Macedonia and Kosova; also **pelqesë** (996)

birbyné A Lithuanian single-reed pipe (511)

bisernica High-pitched lutes in the Slovene **tamburica** ensemble (917)

bishnicë An Albanian bagpipe (996)

bîzoi The drone pipe of the Romanian bagpipe (879)

blazeveer A bowed pseudo-bass of the Low Countries (531)

blechbesetzung A Swiss instrumental ensemble of brass instruments (689)

blechmusik 'Brass-band musik' (German) (946)

bleh-muzika (German **blechmusik**): Serbian

rural brass bands; also **bleh-orkestri** (946)

bleh-orkestri (German **blechmusik**): Serbian rural brass bands; also **bleh-muzika** (946)

blokviool A plucked dulcimer of the Low Countries (533)

boben A Slovene drum (916)

bocete 'Laments' in Romanian burial rituals (196, 871)

bodhrán An Irish single-headed goatskin **frame drum**, played with a short stick; also imported into Wales (354, 385, 391)

boerenschots A "Scottish" square dance of the West-Friesland area (524)

boghe'e notte Songs in slow tempo based on serious themes in Sardinian **a tenore** singing; also **a sa seria** (627)

bolgarski rospev 'Bulgarian manner of singing' (Bulgarian): identified in the notation of certain seventeenth- and eighteenth-century manuscripts (904)

bombarde A double-reed shawm of Brittany and the Low Countries (528, 559, *560*, 561–63)

bombardon A dance-band wind instrument of the Low Countries (530)

bombo A Portuguese bass drum (582)

bordi A Maltese contrabass used in small ensembles for ambulatory street music, weddings, parties, and picnics (640, *641*)

borije A Montenegrin folk trumpet, mentioned in literary sources and folk songs (960)

bormliza Improvised or partly improvised Maltese **ghana**, regarded as having originated in North Africa (637)

borona 'Harrow': Russian ritual cacophony, produced as women simultaneously sing calendric songs from all the seasons, to ward off evil spirits (760)

bosanski mekam 'Bosnian *maqam*': a style used by Sephardic Jewish men in Bosnia-Hercegovina to sing religious songs (968)

boselis A stringed instrument from Lithuania with an air- and pea-filled bladder as a bridge (511)

botta u rispota Maltese improvised witty repartee (636)

bourdon A drone played on violin, hurdy-gurdy, and bagpipes to accompany a solo instrumental melody (543)

bouzouki A Greek long-necked, plucked **lute**, the principal instrument of **rebetika** (152, 169, 204, *206*, 354, 366, 385, 656, 1015, 1017, 1019–20, 1031)

bouzoukia Establishments where Greek urban popular music was performed; see **skiladhika** (1020)

božik Macedonian boys' house-to-house caroling Christmas and New Year (973)

bozuk Turkish name of the Albanian **buzuk** (994)

brač A **lute** in the Slovene **tamburica** ensemble that improvises countermelodies (917)

braci A viola that supplies rhythmic-harmonic accompaniment in Romanian and Hungarian music in parts of Transylvania (880)

bragir Melodies of Icelandic **rímur**; see

stemmur (402)

braguesa See *viola* (582)

braguinha Madeiran name of the Portuguese *cavaquinho* (582)

brana A Slovene trapezoidal struck zither; also *cimprekelj, male cimbale, oprekelj,* and *pretl* (916)

branle A French courtly dance popular from the sixteenth to the late nineteenth centuries (523, 546)

Brauchtumslieder German customary songs (664)

brazhotki Belarusan rattles (797)

brindisi An Italian song type preserved in Corsica (570)

briolage French singing to oxen while plowing (128, *540*, 542)

briolées French farmers' cries urging on a team of horses (132)

brnica A Slovene **mouth harp**; also *drumlica* and *drumelca* (917)

brnkač A Slovene noisemaker (made from a piece of wood or bone attached to a string) that produces a whirring sound when spun; also *zingulca* (918)

broadside A songsheet containing **ballad** texts, printed for sale in England between the sixteenth and late nineteenth centuries (137, 142, 296, 328–29, 332, 343, 369, 379, *380*, 386, 435, 452–53, 458, 479, 504, 519, *520*, 522, 549, 561, 606, 611, 664)

broancă A double bass that provides rhythmic-harmonic accompaniment in Romanian and Hungarian music in parts of Transylvania (880)

brungan A Komi zither (774)

b[r]unkula A basset (a small three-stringed bass), played in Resia, Slovenia, to accompany violins; also *ta-velika citira* (918)

bubanj A cylindrical drum played by Vlahs in Serbia and Bosnia-Hercegovina (950, 966)

buben z brazhotkami A Belarusan **tambourine** with jingles (797)

bubon A Ukrainian single-headed **frame drum** played with a small wooden mallet (810–11)

buccina A Romanian trumpet or horn (881)

bucerata A Corsican lament for a violent death; also called *buceru* and *voceru* (567)

buceru A Corsican lament for a violent death; also called *bucerata* and *voceru* (567)

büchel A Swiss small **alphorn** in a coiled shape; see *grada büchel* (687, 688)

bucium A Romanian **alphorn** (872, 875)

bucoliasme Cattle tenders' work songs of French-speaking Switzerland (693)

budeļi Masked, singing Christmas revelers in Kurzeme and western Zemgale, Latvia (502)

bugarija A long-necked **lute** in Croatian and Slovenian *tamburica* ensembles (917, 966)

buhai A Romanian friction drum (870, 877)

buki A Georgian large trumpet popular at court in celebratory contexts and in military contexts (840)

bukkehorn A Norwegian buck horn, with or without holes for fingering (420)

bulerías A Spanish *cante chico* based on a twelve-beat structure (597)

bull roarer In Denmark, an instrument consisting of a hollow reed or a small oblong wooden plate with a hole, tied to the end of a string and swung in circles to produce a whirring sound (455, 655, 682)

burämusig 'Farmer's music': an old term for the Swiss *ländlerkapelle* (689)

burczybas A friction drum used in carnival masquerades in Pomerania, Poland (704)

burłackija pieśni Belarusan nonritual barge-hauler songs (795)

bušen A bark trumpet more than 3 meters long, played by Vlah men of Serbia for St. George's Day festivities; also *rikalo* (950)

busking Performing for money on streets or in subways (336)

buzika A Georgian accordion; also *garmon* (840, 841)

buzuk A Near Eastern long-necked plucked **lute**, played in Albania during the Ottoman period (994)

bygde The indigenous dances of Norway (417, 425, 426, 427, 430)

byliny Russian **epic** songs; see *stariny* (23, 129–30, 201, 754, 763–64, *765*, 768)

byńk A Belarusan dance performed in *žanićba Ciareški* (792)

byz An Udmurt bagpipe (774)

bzhami An Adighian ritual whistle flute (855)

bzhe Adighian women's funeral songs (855)

cabreta A bellows-blown bagpipe of Auvergne, France (545, 547)

cabrette A bagpipe of Limousin and Auvergne, France (560)

cadi A Welsh ritual in which a man wearing women's clothing and wielding a broom, accompanied by dancers in blackface, performs in May to celebrate the coming of spring (343)

café aman Greek musical cafés where *amanedhes* were sung (285, 1014)

café cantante 'Singing café' (Spanish): pubs featuring **flamenco**, especially in Madrid and Seville (*597*, 598, *599*)

café chantant 'Singing café' (French): a nineteenth-century pub in the Low Countries (522)

caixa A Portuguese **snare drum** (582)

čalgadžii Rom musicians in Macedonia (980)

čalgija (also *çalgi*) A Macedonian, Albanian, and Serbian Rom urban professional ensemble (200, 281, 286, 952, 977, *979*–80, 981, 983, 997)

calul (also *caiuți*) 'Hobby horses': a Romanian winter festival with masked dancing in north-central Moldavia and Bucovina (870)

căluş A Romanian healing ritual performed by male dancers to the accompaniment of instrumental music (161, *162, 871*)

căluşari Romanian male dancers who perform a healing ritual (198, 870, *871*, 886)

căluşul 'Little horse': a Romanian young men's ritual dance to create fecundity or to heal or prevent illness, in Oltenia, Muntenia, and parts of Dobruja (870)

calypso A West Indian topical-song genre in duple meter with usually satirical lyrics, typically sung at carnival and popular in Britain (235)

camil An Adighian whistle flute (855)

čampareta Small cymbals of Bosnia-Hercegovina (967)

cana A Portuguese split-cane tube about 60 centimeters long used as a percussion instrument (582)

canção de intervenção 'Song of intervention' (Portuguese): used for political protest (584)

cancioneros Spanish literary anthologies of poetic texts, with or without music, first published in the 1200s (601, 602)

canens "Performing" the verse in Finnish *runonlaulu* (115)

cannacione An Italian countrified version of the medieval *colascione*, derived from Turkish, Arabic, and Greek long-necked **lutes** (615)

canntaireachd The Scottish vocable system for the teaching of the classical piping tradition (*piobaireachd*) (98, 106, *107*, 363)

cantaduras (also *cantadurs*) Historic singing societies from the Romansh-speaking area of Switzerland (692)

cantares ao desafio A Portuguese improvised vocal genre (581)

cantares de ayuda 'Aid-songs': Spanish songs for the gathering of alms (590)

cântaro A Portuguese large clay pot whose opening is hit with a straw or leather fan (582)

cantastorie 'Song-storytellers': Italian itinerant, often blind, professional bards; see *torototéla* (143, 611, 695)

cantautori Italian singer-songwriters of the 1970s and later (619, 698)

cante (Spanish): a song (596, 597, 598)

cante chico 'Small song': any of three types of Spanish **flamenco** singing, with a rhythmic structure less complex than that of the *cante jondo* (597, 599)

cante intermedio 'Intermediate song': any of three types of Spanish **flamenco** singing, a hybrid of *cante jondo* and forms from Spanish folk and popular music styles, especially the **fandango** (597)

cante jondo 'Deep song': any of the three types of Spanish **flamenco** singing, considered the oldest and most serious (134, 591, 593, 596, 597, 598, 599)

canti a pera A type of Italian **lyric song** (606)

canti a vatoccu 'Songs in the manner of a bell clapper': Italian narrow-interval, two-voiced songs (606, *607*, 611)

canti all'altalena Swinging songs of Basilicata, southern Italy (116)

canti alla boara A type of Italian **lyric song** (606)

canti alla longa A type of Italian **lyric song** (606)

canti alla stesa A type of Italian **lyric song** (606)

canti carnascialeschi Italian carnival songs of **Renaissance** Florence (608)

canti di questua Italian begging songs used in seasonal celebrations (608)

canti epico-lirici Italian **ballads**, found mostly in the north (605)

canti lirico-monostrofici Italian **lyric songs**, common south of the Apennines (605, 607)

cantiga 'Song' (Portuguese): a metered **strophic song** (581)

cantimbanchi Italian semiprofessional balladeers (16)

cantiques French religious **ballads** (541, 546, 559)

canto a chiterra A Sardinian guitar-accompanied song (627, *629*)

canto a dispetto 'Song of the despised': an Italian polyphonic form akin to *canti a vatoccu* (610)

canto della passione A central Italian begging song, performed the week before Easter; also *orologio della passione* 'clock of the passion' (608)

cantus Song (**Middle Ages**) (49, 780)

cantus super librum 'Song above a book' (Latin): the improvisation of one or more parts over a **chant** notated in a liturgical book (50)

canu gyda'r tannau 'Singing with the strings': a style of Welsh singing in which the singer improvises the vocal parts to suit the harmonic accompaniment of a **harp** (350)

canu penillion 'Singing verses': a style of Welsh singing in which the singer improvises the vocal parts to suit the harmonic accompaniment of a **harp** (350)

canu'r pwnc 'Singing the text': a form of Welsh folk declamation connected with reciting biblical scriptures at catechismal festivals (345)

canzone Italiana Twentieth-century styles of Italian song (619)

canzoni a ballo Italian **lyric songs** intended for dancing; see *maitinade* and *polesane* (606, 608)

canzune A Sicilian **lyric song** type (606, *612*)

caoine A Irish lament for the dead (128)

caoineadh (also *caoineadh na marbh*) An Irish death lament, anglicized as *keening* (196, 378, *379*, 387, 389)

caper In English **morris dances**, a section in which the instrumentalist is required to play at a slower tempo or at half-speed with note values doubled, while the dancers perform high leaps (329)

capra 'Goat': a Romanian winter festival with masked dancing in Transylvania, Maramureş, Bucovina, Moldavia, and Muntenia (870)

caramusa A Corsican goatskin bagpipe (571)

čardáš A Slovak couple dance with set and improvised steps (721)

carnevale An Italian carnival celebration (608)

carnyx A Celtic horn of the La Tène period, emerging during the first millennium B.C.; it has been defined as an animal-headed trumpet and a war-trumpet (40, 41, 366)

čarojičarske pjesme Songs for masked ritual processions in Bosnia-Hercegovina (963)

carole A French dance tradition that emerged from medieval ring dances and chain dances (132, 546)

čarotki Belarusan reed aerophones (797)

casadh 'The turn': the second of two sections within an Irish dance tune (382)

cascabeles Spanish jingle bells (594)

cascola A Corsican children's game accompanied by verses (571)

cassella A Corsican kettledrum; a large Corsican **frame drum** played with a pair of sticks (572)

castañuelas 'Chestnuts' (Spanish): castanets (594)

častuški Belarusan rhymed poems on humorous themes (796)

catabaucalise Children's nurses' work songs from French-speaking Switzerland; also *nunnie* (693)

caval A Romanian duct flute played by shepherds (875, 878–79)

cavaquinho A small Portuguese guitar with four courses of strings; it diffused to Hawai'i (where it is called *'ukelele*), Brazil, and Indonesia (where it is called *kroncong*) (582)

céilí Irish domestic evening entertainment and visiting where friends and neighbors gather to drink, sing, dance, tell stories, and play (141, 388, 390)

céilí band A large Irish dance band with fiddles, flutes, accordions, **piano**, and drum (388, 390, 391)

ceilidh Scottish evening entertainments, gatherings where people sing, dance, drink, and play music (371)

cembalo An Italian trapezoidal struck zither (609)

ceòl beag 'Little music': Scottish songs, marches, and dance tunes (363)

ceòl mór 'Great music': a theme-and-variation form of Scottish piping that tests a piper's mastery (363)

cerca Corsican dances (571, 572)

cerdd dant 'The craft of the string' (Welsh) (353–56)

cetera A Corsican and Sardinian pear-shaped plucked **lute** with a flat-bottomed sound box (571, *572*, 573, 632)

četrpāru dancis A Latvian dance for four couples (504)

chaba A female Algerian singer of *rai*, a North African music popular in France (*234*)

chabreta A bellows-blown bagpipe of Limousin, France (545)

chalandamarz A celebration in March in Graubünden, Switzerland, with songs that praise the coming spring 685

chang A Persian **harp** (839)

changi A six-stringed **harp** of Svaneti, Georgia (838, *839*, 840)

chanson 'Song' (French): a locally produced popular song (204, 444, 559, 676)

chanson à danser A French term for Breton *kan da gorell* (559)

chanson de bord A French heterophonic responsorial sea chantey (542, 545)

chanson de danse A French **strophic song**, consisting of one or more isosyllabic lines of from six to sixteen syllables; also *chanson en laisse* (540–41, 547)

chansonnier An urban French musical style that uses the accordion; a singer in a style of urban French popular music, especially a cabaret singer (544, 548, 698, 934)

chansons à repouner French heterophonic responsorial dance songs (542)

chansons d'aventure (French): Welsh folk love songs (343)

chansons de geste (French): French and Breton **stichic** heroic songs of the 1100s and earlier (*539*, 540, 561)

chansons de métier French work songs (545)

chansons de travail French work songs (545)

chant In European music, any of various forms of monophonic music employed in Jewish rituals and especially Christian liturgies; see **Gregorian chant** (69–70, 86, 100, 106, 227, 265, 379, 403–404, 447, 600, 650, 652, 737, 779, 881, 885, 943, 960, 967, 968, 980, 1002, 1023)

chapbooks Pocket-sized books printed with texts of **ballads** (137, 365, 368, 369, 387, 549, 755, 907)

charivari A noisy mock serenade to newlyweds (143, 525, 544, 551, 572)

chastushka 'Short ditty': a Russian instrumental-vocal genre in short, single-stanza couplets accompanied by an accordion or a **balalaika** (6, 134, 761, 768, 770, 771, 779)

cheb A male Algerian singer of *rai*, a North African music popular in France (*234*)

cheironomy Hand and finger gestures used in directing music (*100*, 109)

chesslete A winter parade in Solothurn, Switzerland, with homemade noisemakers (684)

chiam' e rispondi 'Call and response': Corsican poetic contests between rival singers (568, 569)

chianuri (also *chuniri*) A Georgian three-stringed bowed **lute**, often played at funerals in Achara and Tusheti (*839*)

chiboni (also *chimoni*) A bagpipe of Achara, Georgia (836, 840)

chifonie A French medieval hurdy-gurdy (545)

chift kavali A pair of *kavals* that play melody-and-drone duets in southwestern Pirin, Bulgaria (*176*, 895–96)

Child ballad Any of a repertoire of popular English, Irish, and Scottish **ballads** with short, usually four-phrase melodies (136, 295, 296, 328–29, 606)

chimoni (also *chiboni*) A bagpipe of Achara, Georgia (840)

chindli jodel Songs of Appenzell, Switzerland, that mainly function as lullabies (691) *chindzembeltti zardjite* 'Songs to accompany the bride': Ossetian best-man's songs (861)

chiphonie A hurdy-gurdy of the Low Countries (532)

chirula A three-holed flute played with a *ttun-ttun* in Basque country and Gascony, France (545)

chishapshina An Adighian two-stringed long-necked plucked **lute** that accompanies **epic** songs and two-part vocal polyphony (855)

chitara 'Guitar' (Romanian) (880)

chitarra battente 'Beaten guitar' (Italian): a central and southern Italian guitar, played with a **plectrum** to accompany singing (611, 615, *616*)

chläuse Carnival characters of Switzerland (140, 683)

chlause A clapper bell of Kaltbrunn, St. Gallen, Switzerland (683)

chlausjage Jingle bells on a harness in Hallwil, Aargau, Switzerland (683)

chlepfe Swiss whip-cracking (687)

chodzony A walking dance in Polish folk music (708)

chona Songs sung during the Georgian ritual of *chonaoba* (834)

chonaoba A Georgian ritual held on Palm Sunday, when maskers go through a village singing a ritual song (*chona*) and begging for food and red eggs, then hold a ritual feast (834)

chonguri Georgian unfretted medium-sized long-necked four-stringed **lute**, played primarily by Samegrelo and Guria women to accompany singing and dancing (*837*, 838, 840–41, 845, 853)

chorale In European music, a hymn of the Lutheran church, usually monophonic in its original (usually sixteenth-century) form, but subsequently employed in polyphonic settings (74, 97, 131, 185, 255, 404, 414, 492, 505, 650, 653, 726)

chorea polonica A name of the **mazurka** outside Poland (710)

chorovod Czech and Slovak line and round dances, particularly by young women (717)

chula A Portuguese couple dance in duple meter (581–82)

chuniri (also *chianuri*) A Svanetian or Georgian two- or three-stringed bowed **lute**, often played at funerals (*839*, 840, 853, 863)

cialambella (also *cialambedda, cialamedda,* and *cialemella*) A Corsican single-reed aerophone with a slightly conical wooden body, a bell, and six holes for fingering; see *cia-ramella* (571, 573)

cialušačka A Belarusan genre that musically depicts the emotions of losing and finding a herd animal (799)

ciaramella An Italian single-reed aerophone played in sets of two or three; see *cialem-bella* (616)

čiftečelli The 4/4 rhythm of Romanian *manea* (278, 279)

çifteli An Albanian fretted long-necked plucked **lute**; also *çiteli* (*996*–97, 1000, 1002)

čift kavali A pair of Macedonian bevel-edged, rim-blown flutes that plays melody and drone (975)

čigāni A type of Latvian masquerader (*budeļi*) meant to evoke the image of Gypsies (Roma) (502)

Ciganski kjuček The 9/8 variant of the Bulgarian Rom *kjuček* (282)

cimbál A Czech and Slovak trapezoidal struck zither (719, *720*)

cimbalom A trapezoidal struck dulcimer, central to Hungarian Gypsy string orchestras (*156, 272,* 273, 274, 275, 511, *738,* 743, 744, 872, 876, 880, 917)

cimbalová muzika An Eastern Moravian and Slovakian dulcimer band with violins, violas, clarinets, a string bass, and a trapezoidal struck zither (*cimbál*) (719, *720,* 723)

cimpoi A Romanian bagpipe (878, *879*)

cimprekelj A Slovene trapezoidal struck zither; also *brana, male cimbale, oprekelj,* and *pretl* (916)

cingonë An Albanian conical-bore double-reed aerophone; also *curle, surle,* and *zurle* (996)

cîntec A Romanian **strophic** song (872, 874)

cîntece bătrîneşti 'Old-time songs': songs performed by professional musicians (*lăutari*) at wedding banquets and other occasions in southern Romania; see *balade* (122, 875)

cîntece ceremoniale 'Ceremonial songs': Romanian burial laments, performed by professional lamenters (196, 871)

cîntece de leagăn Romanian lullabies (869, 873)

cîntece de mahala 'Songs of the neighborhood': urban Romanian Rom songs (277)

cîntece de stea 'Star songs': Romanian children's winter repertoire, with texts inspired by biblical scriptures (277, 869)

cire perdue The technology of lost-wax casting, utilized by ancient Scandinavian and Irish craftsmen to manufacture musical instruments such as the *lur* and the bronze horn (39)

çiteli An Albanian fretted long-necked plucked **lute**; also *çifteli* (285)

cítira A violin of Resia, Slovenia (917)

citra A Slovene zither (*915*, 918)

cittern A guitarlike **Renaissance** stringed instrument with a flat pear-shaped body (200, 331, 366, 422, 571, 572, 601, 658, 686–87)

claca Romanian work parties involving song, instrumental music, and dance (117, 870)

cláirseach An Irish **harp**; see *cruit* (383)

clarine A French cowbell (544)

clarinet-shawm In Denmark, a reed instrument made of pine wood, split and hollowed out, and bound or wedged together (455)

clàrsach A **harp** played by bards in early Scotland and later revived (362, 364, 366, 367)

Classical In European music history, the period from about 1750 to about the death of Beethoven (1827) (79–84, 85, 93, 227, 352, 460, 727–28)

clausula (pl. *clausulae*) 'Close, conclusion, cadence' (Latin): a style of twelfth- and thirteenth-century note-against-note Parisian liturgical polyphony (71)

cliquen A Swiss fife-and-drum band (*685*)

clopote Romanian bells used in New Year's ceremonies and weddings and hung around the necks of cattle and sheep as signal devices; also *zurgālāi* (876)

čobanske pjesme Shepherds' songs of Croatia, Montenegro, and Bosnia-Hercegovina (926, 958, 963)

cobla A Catalonian ensemble that accompanies the *sardana* (593–94)

cobza A Romanian plucked short-necked **lute** (277, 876, 877, 879–80)

čoček A dance of south Serbian and Macedonian Gypsies (201, 282, 951, 979, 983)

colascione A medieval Italian long-necked **lute**; see *cannacione* (615)

colindatori Romanian carolers (869)

colinde Luck visits with singing at New Year's in Romania (131, *132*, 140, 869)

colonne 'The "English" longways dance' (French): a country dance popular in the Low Countries in the eighteenth and nineteenth centuries (524)

comenzi Romanian calls, often integrated into a polyrhythmic texture (872)

compás The complex counterrhythms in **flamenco** (598)

compitu A Corsican lament, especially for the dead; see *lamentu* (566)

complainte The French term for Breton *gwerz* (546, 559)

complainte A song text in French-speaking Switzerland that deals with religious folk themes or political satire (693)

complessi Italian modern soft-rock groups (619)

conca Italian dances preserved in Corsica (571)

concertina A free-reed aerophone with bellows that produces different pitches on a given button, depending on whether air is pushed or pulled through the reeds (4, 170, 197, *329*, 330, 333, 348, 355, 372, 383, 385, 391, 640, 657, 707)

concerto In European art music of the eighteenth century and later, an instrumental composition in which passages for one or more soloists alternate and combine with passages for a larger ensemble (61, 63, 78, 80, 82, 215, 369, 781)

concurso A Spanish competition, especially in **flamenco** (598)

conductus 'Led together' (Latin): a style of twelfth- and thirteenth-century note-against-note Parisian liturgical polyphony (71, 366)

confraternite Sardinian religious brotherhoods, some of which preserve and teach polyphonic singing (627) *congas* Afro-Cuban tall, barrel-shaped or tapered, single-headed drums, now also used in Swedish folk music (442, 656)

consonance In European art music, one of certain musical intervals, including octaves, fifths, and (after the **Middle Ages**) thirds, conventionally regarded as pleasant or sonorous (71, 958, 964)

conterdans (also *contredans* and **contredanse**) A country dance evolved from the minuet in the late eighteenth century in the Low Countries (524)

contră A second violin, which supplies rhythmic-harmonic accompaniment in Romanian and Hungarian music in parts of Transylvania; also *săcunda* (880)

contra dance See **country dance**

contredanse A set or figure dance most popular in France in the late 1700s, an ancestor of the **quadrille** (165, 168, 524, 546, 571, 641)

copla 'Couplet' (Spanish): a poem or song in quatrains of octosyllabic lines, with consonant or assonant rhymes in even-numbered lines (591–92, 594, 595, 598–99, 601); a competitive male pole dance of Spain, involving mock combat (198)

copla de seguidilla A Spanish metric-song form; also *cuarteta* (592)

coraula A dance-song of French-speaking Switzerland in which two choruses sing antiphonally (693)

corn buellin A semicircular Welsh bugle horn (348)

cornamusa Corsican panpipes (572)

cornemuse French bagpipes (559)

cornicyll A Welsh concealed-reed instrument similar to *pibgorn* hornpipes, with a mouthpiece that screwed on and off (348)

cornu A Corsican conch-shell trumpet associated with the struggle for independence; also *cornu marinu* or *culombu* (571)

cornua A Romanian trumpet or horn (881)

corps de ballet A group of dancers, often exclusively female, who dance together as a type of chorus (161)

corridinho A fast virtuosic duple-meter couple dance of Faro, Portugal (582)

cottiljon A Swedish contra dance, especially in southern and eastern Sweden (442)

country dance (also contra dance) Any of various English dances, developed in the 1600s and 1700s and taken to the Continent, in which partners face each other, usually in rows (17, 442, 524, 546, 594)

country dancing English mixed social dancing (331)

courante A dance of Italian origin featuring rapid running steps (168)

cow horn The horn of a cow (478), used as a trumpet, often to give signals (743, 915), sometimes with holes for fingering (41, 455), and fixed with a duct to serve as a horn-flute (527, 571)

crâmignon An open-air *farandole*, danced in and around the town of Liège in the Dutch province of Limburg (522, 535)

crin-crin A French fiddle, played at balls and weddings (544)

criniki A bowed pseudo-bass of the Low Countries (531)

cruit A small, triangular handheld **harp** or **lyre** in Ireland and Scotland; see *cláirseach* (366, 383)

crwth A Welsh rectangular bowed **lyre** with three to six strings, used to accompany bardic declamation as early as the first century B.C. (42, 348, 349)

csárdás The lively 2/4 rhythmic type of Hungarian *nóta*; closed circle dances of Hungarians and Slovaks in Croatia (273, 926, 932, 947)

cuadro The team of dancers, singers, and guitarist in **flamenco** (134, 598)

cuarteta A Spanish metric-song form; also *copla de seguidilla* (592)

cue-system A rubric under which to classify the signal systems used in musical communication: aural, tactile, gestural, and visual (notation) (92, 97–109)

cuisle An Irish pipelike or flutelike instrument (384)

culjke Swinging songs for St. George's Day in Montenegro (958)

culombu A Corsican conch-shell trumpet associated with the struggle for independence; also *cornu* or *cornu marinu* (571)

čumackija piešni Belarusan Chumak nonritual male sociolyrical **epic** poetry and song (795)

cuñeros Spanish cradle songs or lullabies (589)

cununa 'The wreath': a traditional feast at the end of the harvest in Transylvania, Romania (870)

cununia 'The church ceremony': part of the Romanian wedding ritual, accompanied by specific songs or instrumental tunes (871)

cuplé flamenco Spanish sentimental songs from *operismos* (597)

curle An Albanian conical-bore double-reed aerophone; also *cingonë, surle,* and *zurle* (996)

currente A Corsican improvised poem accompanied by a violin, normally played by the singer (568, 573)

cwène A pastoral horn flute of the Low Countries (527)

cykace A Polish **frame drum** with jingles, also a *grajcary* (704)

cylëdyjare A short, double-bore duct flute, played by herdsmen in Labëri, Albania; also *biculë* (993)

cymbały A Belarusan hammered dulcimer (796, 797)

cymbały A Polish trapezoidal struck zither (706)

cynghanedd Welsh verbal embroidery, including alliteration and internal rhyme, used in *plygain* or carols (343)

cyweirdant A Welsh harper's chord, which, in various combinations with a second chord (*tyniad*), made up twenty-four different patterns (349)

czardas A Hungarian dance in duple meter in which dancers start slowly and finish in vivacious whirls; compare *csárdás* (273–74, 721, 747)

czarny kozioł doślubny 'Black he-goat of the wedding': a bagpipe of western Poland, played at weddings (707)

daf An Arabic squarish **frame drum** (838)

daina The basic form of a Latvian folk-song text, a short self-contained quatrain of two nonrhyming couplets (500, 506)

dainas Lithuanian **strophic songs** in long single lines and two-line strophes (131)

daira A Georgian **frame drum** with jingles; see *daf, dā'ira, daphi,* and *tof* (837)

dā'ira An Arabic roundish **frame drum** (838)

dairea A Romanian single-headed **frame drum** (877)

dajre (also *daire*) An Albanian, Macedonian, and Bulgarian single-headed **frame drum** (281, 282, 894, 895, 979, 993, 994, 996)

dajre def An Albanian **frame drum** ensemble consisting of two female frame drummers, who sing and dance (285)

dala-fandir An Ossetian plucked long-necked fretted **lute**, played to accompany solo singing (859)

danaj A duple-meter Moravian couple dance with a hesitation step (717)

dancis 'Dance': Latvian bagpipe dance tunes (504)

danse des pèlerins The pilgrim's sword dance of Marbissoux, province of Brabant, Low Countries (523, 526)

dance des sept sauts 'Dance of the seven leaps' (French): a dance-song of the Low Countries; see *zevensprong* (522)

dans plinn A Breton line or circle dance, performed as part of a three-part suite (559)

danse polonaise 'Polish dance' (French): a name of the **mazurka** outside Poland (710)

danshus A Swedish dancing house, dedicated to preserving dance music and modeled on the Hungarian *táncház* (153)

dánta An Irish lullaby; an Irish religious song performed at Easter (388, 389)

danza A Sardinian virtuosic couple dance (630, 631)

daouli A large, double-headed drum, often played with *zournadhes* by Macedonian Gypsies in Greece (285, 1008, 1011, *1012*)

daoulia Ensembles of two *zournadhes* and one *daouli* in Greek Macedonia (1011, *1012*)

daphdaphi A Georgian large double-headed drum, played with an accordion to accompany dancing; more commonly called *doli* (838)

daphi A Georgian **frame drum** with jingles, played by a female dancer in Kartli, Kakheti, Racha, Samegrelo, and Tusheti; see *daf, dā'ira, daira,* and *tof* (837)

dara A Romanian one-headed **frame drum**, played in Oltenia and Muntenia (877)

darabana A Romanian **snare drum** (877)

darabuka A vase-shaped, single-headed drum, played by Roma in the Balkans (284, 894, 959–60, *979–80*)

darbouka A goblet-shaped Algerian drum, played by immigrants in France (233)

darbuka A Near Eastern vase-shaped drum, played in Swedish folk music (442)

dastgah A Persian musical **mode** (593)

daulbas A double-headed drum of Turkish origin, once played in Montenegro (960)

daulle An Albanian two-headed bass drum; also *lodër, lodërti,* and *tupan* (993, 996)

davluri A Georgian mixed-couple dance with instrumental accompaniment (836)

dawnsio ha' Welsh May-dancing (*140, 343*)

dažynačnya pieśni Belarusan end-of-harvest songs (791)

de bef jagen In the Dutch-speaking areas of the Low Countries, the extinct custom of making noise on instruments and utensils outside the house of newlyweds; see *charivari* (525)

de dragoste 'Of love': a newer type of *doina,* popular in southern Romania (*873*)

dechik-pondur A Chechen and Ingush three-stringed long-necked plucked **lute** (863, 864)

dechovka muzika A Czech and Slovak brass band (719)

def A **frame drum** played in the Balkans (285, 286, 952, 960, 967, 993, 994, 997)

defi A Greek **frame drum** (1010, 1012, 1019)

denkmal 'Monument' (German): used as a term for an authoritatively edited musical score (52)

derbiderissa Greek "free" women who participated in the *rebetika* subculture (1019–20)

deseterac The ten-syllable poetic line of Serbian-Croatian **epic** songs (129, 927, 931, 941)

desgarrada A Portuguese improvised vocal genre (581)

despique A Portuguese improvised vocal genre (581)

deutsche Harmonika See *Handäoline* (657)

dhimotika Greek folk songs (206, 1008, 1017–18, 1021)

dhol (also *dholki*) A Punjabi double-sided membranophone used in *bhangra,* a hybrid genre popular in Britain (236)

dhromi Greek melodic **modes** (1020)

diadizha iish An Ingush women's lullaby (863)

dialekt-rock The Norwegian term for rock performed in the linguistic and musical dialects of specific localities (96, 429, 430)

dideba 'Glory': a Georgian women's circle dance, performed to antiphonal music at the celebration of the Christian saint White George, the central summer ritual (834)

dīdišana The ritual swinging and rocking of a baby by all participants at Latvian christenings in southwestern Kurzeme, accompanied by special songs (502)

dievturīc The Latvian neopagan movement

that occurred between the world wars and developed a special choral style (505)

diple 'Double pipe': Croatian, Montenegrin, Hercegovinan, and Slovene pipes, played with a wooden mouthpiece or as a bagpipe (169, 915, 928, 959–60, 966)

diple s mijehom 'Double pipe with bag': a Croatian bagpipe; also *mješnice* (928)

diple z mehom 'Double pipe with bag': a Slovene bagpipe (915)

diplipito A Georgian set of two or occasionally three to five skin-covered clay pots struck with small sticks, each sounding a unique pitch; see *gosha-nagara* and *nagara* (838)

discantus 'Discant' (Latin): a style of twelfth- and thirteenth-century note-against-note Parisian liturgical polyphony (71)

discant See *discantus* (104, *105,* 134, 610)

dishkant A solo singer who sings an anhemitonic tune with text in the vocal music of the Cossacks in southern Russia; also *golosnik* (757)

diskaner The Breton countersinger of *kan has diskan* who repeats the phrase sung by the *kaner* (559)

dissonance In European art music, one of certain musical intervals, including sevenths, seconds, and tritones, that are conventionally regarded as unpleasant or unharmonious (64, 71, 542, 830, 831, 862, 896)

divisions The figurations of a melody, especially the variations on English dance tunes characteristic of the Northumbrian small-pipes repertoire (331)

diždancis A solemn Latvian couple dance, performed at the beginning of a wedding feast, characteristically involving walking (504)

djeguako An Adighian performer of historical songs (854, 855)

doba A Romanian drum (877, 880)

dodekachordon The modal system developed by the Swiss theorist Glareanus and announced in a book published in 1547 (652)

dodola A summer rain-begging ritual in Serbia (941)

doedelzak (German *dudelsack* 'bagpipe') A bagpipe of the Low Countries; compare *moezel(zak)* (528)

doina A Romanian improvised lyrical song genre; see *hora lunga* (9, 278, 872–73, 875, 878, 879–80, 882)

doli A Georgian large double-headed drum; see *daphdaphi* (836, 838, 840, 842)

dom kultury 'House of culture' (Belarusan): home to regional performance groups (800)

domra A Ukranian folk plucked chordophone (155)

dordolec A rain-begging ritual performed by Albanian children in the late spring or early summer of a dry year; a child dressed in greenery for the ritual; also *peperona* (988)

dosvitky Ukrainian social gatherings for unmarried girls to sew, embroider, sing, and dance (196, 808, 809, 810, 812)

dottagialin iish Chechen and Ingush table songs (864)

draailier (also *lier*) A hurdy-gurdy of the Low Countries (532)

draznilki 'Taunting ditties': a genre of wedding song in Russia (761)

drdra A Slovene noisemaker made from nutshells (919)

dredl (also *dreidl* and *dreidel*) A toy top spun during Hanukkah to sung accompaniment (261)

drîmba A Romanian **mouth harp** (876)

drin drin The French custom of tinkling knives against glasses (546)

drmeš A northwestern Croatian couple dance with shaking (932, 933)

druckvorlage (German): the printer's copy of a score (51)

drumelca A Slovene **mouth harp**; also *drumlica* and *brnica* (917)

drumlica A Slovene **mouth harp**; also *drumelca* and *brnica* (917)

drymba A Ukrainian **mouth harp** (816)

drăgaica A harvest ritual on 24 June in Muntenia, Romania (194, 870)

duadastanon-fandir An Ossetian **harp** having ten to twelve diatonically tuned strings (860)

duan A Scottish narrative song (361)

dube A Romanian double-headed drum, played in Arad, Banat, Bihor, and Hundeora (877)

duda (pl. *dudy*) The common name of the bagpipe in Central and Eastern Europe and the Balkans (707, 719, 743, 797, 813, *932*)

dude A Slovene bagpipe (915)

Dudey A German small shawm with a reed cap (654)

dudka A bagpipe (*duda*) of Hutsul'shchyna, Ukraine (813, 816)

dudka An eastern Slavic aerophone: a Russian duct flute with five or six holes for fingering, also *sopel* or *pizhatka* (770); a Belarusan duct flute (*793, 797*); a small wooden duct flute of Polissia, Ukraine (816)

dudka jazyćkovaia A Belarusan reed horn (*797*)

duduk A Georgian urban reed aerophone (840, 842); a Bulgarian and Macedonian short, end-blown whistle-flute with six holes for fingering (892, 897, 975); a large duct flute of Serbian Vlahs (950); a rim-blown flute played by Montenegrin shepherds (960)

duduki A Middle Eastern fipple flute, used to accompany Georgian *bagdaduri* and *kintouri* (836)

dudurejš A pair of stopped tubes, played by Serbian Vlah women for magical charms and ritual pieces (950)

duende The transcendent emotion often involved in Spanish **flamenco** (598)

duff A North African **frame drum**, the ancestor of the *adufe* (577)

dugački glas 'Long voice': Serbian songs with melismatic sections (942)

duge pjesme 'Long songs': narrative women's **ballads** of Bosnia-Hercegovina (963) *dugi napjevi* 'Long melodies': in Bosnia-Hercegovina, songs having texts subordinate to melodies (964)

dulbas A kettledrum of Bosnia-Hercegovina (967)

dumbuli A Georgian membranophone in medieval court ensembles (838, 840)

dumy Ukrainian **epic** songs (129, 813, *814*, 823)

duru-duru Sardinian infant-dandling songs (631)

duruitoare A Romanian ratchet-type rattle, whirled on a handle for masked dances at New Year's and to scare birds away (876)

dutra A Chechen and Ingush shepherds' whistle flute (863)

duvački orkestri Macedonian brass bands (976, 979)

dűvő A regular rhythm with slurred, offbeat accentuation that often accompanies slow Hungarian dances (745)

dviina fleita A Ukrainian double flute with two pipes leading from one mouthpiece, each pipe with a separate fingering system (816)

dvojanka A Macedonian double duct flute with a melody and drone pipe (975)

dvojice (also *dvojnice*) 'Pair': Croatian and Serbian double duct flutes with three holes in one pipe and four in the other (928, 944, 960, 966)

dyrevisene Norwegian humorous animal songs, often with a moral message (413)

dzeoba A Georgian birth ritual (835)

džez 'Jazz': a drum set used in Albanian *čalgija* ensembles (286)

dzhaz 'Jazz': a Ukrainian drum-cymbal combination (810)

dziavočnik The Belarusan bridal fair the day before the wedding, when girls gather, accompanied by ritual songs; also *na viankach* and *subornaja subota* (793)

dziedāt 'To sing' (Old Latvian): a label for vocal music (499)

dziesmas (also *dziedamās*) Solo Latvian songs with ornamentation, short vocalizations, and refrains (500)

džumbuš A long-necked skin-faced plucked **lute**, originally from the Middle East, but still played in the Balkans (281, 282, 286, 980)

ebani An obsolete Georgian **harp**, mentioned in medieval literary sources (838–39)

echoi The eight Byzantine **modes**, still used in traditional Cypriot music (1029, 1030)

efterklangsviser Danish **ballads**, grouped according to content as spiritual ballads, secular ballads, and historical ballads (451–52)

eglīte A Latvian fir-tree top decorated with colored feathers and hanging bells and jingles, played mostly by women, formerly used to accompany singing of *godu balss* in wedding or winter-solstice rituals (503)

eisteddfod 'Session': a Welsh competitive festival of poetry and singing (147, 185, 342, 349, *352*, 353–56)

elafra Greek light popular music played in urban nightclubs (1014)

elafrolaika Greek "light" *laika* (1020)

Eliaoba A Georgian rain-begging ritual, performed by girls and young women who carry a female figure and sing (834)

élive Weavers' work songs of French-speaking Switzerland (693)

elliniko rok Greek rock music (1008)

entrées 'Entries, entrances' (French): a series of dances in the late-seventeenth-century *opéra-ballet* (161)

enumerative songs In France, songs that are recapitulative, augmenting the strophe progressively (541)

epí trapézios 'At the table': a genre of male singing in Greece (114)

épiaulie Millers' work songs of French-speaking Switzerland; also *hymée* (693)

epic A long narrative poem recounting the feats of a historical or legendary hero and usually sung in formal settings (17, 22, 46, 53, 94, 129–130, *131*, 132, 134–35, 187, 198, 201, 256, 278–79, 307, 399, 400, 413, 452, 469–70, 476, 491, 493, 542, 589, 607, 651, 694, 722, 737, 742, 754, 763–65, 772, 773, 781, 792, 795, 813, 834, 851, 856, 857, 859–61, 863–64, 882, 896, 898, 927, 941, *942*, 957, 959, 963, 965–66, 989)

(e)pinet (also *épinette*) A plucked dulcimer of the Low Countries (533)

épinette des Vosges 'Spinet of the Vosges': a French plucked dulcimer (545, 548)

Epirotika Greek songs from or in the style of Epirus (1009, 1017)

esharsh Chechen and Ingush solo songs with instrumental accompaniment (863)

estradna muzika Bulgarian popular music (903)

estradnaja muzyka 'Staged music' of Belarus, often sung in Russian (801)

estribillo 'Refrain' in the Spanish poetic tradition (591–92)

esz-tam The Hungarian term used onomatopoeically to denote downbeat-offbeat rhythmic patterns in Croatian-Hungarian borderlands (932)

exvoto (Latin *ex voto* 'out of the vow'): a Spanish song of thanks for a miraculous cure or a providential intercession (591)

ezhy 'Everybody': the bass part in Adighian, Balkar, and Karachaevi polyphony (854, 855, 857)

facture French instrument making; see *lutherie* (542)

fado A Portuguese urban genre of song accompanied by one to four guitarists (7, 116, 134, 204, 205, 577, 578, 583–85)

fado canção 'Sung *fado*' (Portuguese) (583–84)

fado castiço 'Authentic *fado*' (Portuguese) (583–84)

falsetas Spanish **flamenco** guitar style that involves plucking the melodic phrases (598)

fam A Mordovinian bagpipe; also *skamóra*, *puzyr'*, and *válonka* (774)

fandango A Basque, Portuguese, and Spanish dance in 6/8 time (198, 314, 582, 583, 589, 594, 595, 597)

fanfares mixtes Instrumental ensembles comprised of brass instruments, from the French-speaking area of Switzerland (689)

farandole A French open chain dance (546, 573)

Fasnacht Carnival festivities in Germany (649, 657, *685*)

fatt 'Fact, true story': a **ballad**, the oldest documented traditional Maltese song form (637, *638*)

feadán An Irish whistle (384)

fedel A Danish stringed instrument of the violin family (454)

félibres Provençal poets and intellectuals dedicated to the revival of their regional dialects (573)

ferrinhos A Portuguese triangle (582)

fest noz 'Night festival': a Breton event featuring songs, dances, and more recently, contests (141, 563)

festa A Maltese and Portuguese religious festival with music (577, 640, 641)

festspiel A German form of folk theater (696)

feuilles volantes 'Flying sheets': French broadsides (549, 561)

Fidel A vielle used to accompany singing in Germany in the **Middle Ages** (651)

fidiog An Ossetian bull or wild goat horn with four or five holes and a mouthpiece, associated with hunting (859)

fiðla An ancient Norwegian **lyre** or **harp**; see *harpa* (423)

fiðla An Icelandic trapezoidal bowed zither (405, *406*, 407)

field drum A side drum (810)

fiesta 'Feast' (Spanish): a holy day, party, or celebration (198, 589, 591, 596)

fifa A single-pitched notched flute, played in Oltenia, Romania, by women who alter its note with yodellike singing (878)

fifra A Maltese fife played with a bass drum for public announcements (640)

fifre (also *fijfel* and *fijfer*) A side-blown flute of the Low Countries (528)

filastrocche Corsican children's songs sung by linking rows of verses, often with nonlexical words (571)

filmi The music of Hindi films, also performed live, popular among Indian immigrants in Britain (240)

firlinfeu Italian panpipes (616)

fisarmonica A Sardinian large, chromatic accordion (627, 630)

fisarmonica a nümar 'Figure-accordion': a diatonic accordion of Italian-speaking Switzerland (694)

fischju A Corsican long, thin, reed flute having three to six holes for fingering; also *pirula* (571)

flamenco A Spanish musical genre generally

associated with *gitanos,* Spanish Gypsies (7, 204, 208, 226, 272, 593, 594, 596–600)

flamenco arabe 'Arab flamenco' (Spanish): the fusion of **flamenco** with Arabic music (599)

flatfele 'Flat violin': a Norwegian name of the standard violin (*vanleg fele*) (415, 418–20, 424, 426)

flatterzunge (Norwegian): flutter tonguing (108)

fleadh A competitive festival of Irish music (392)

flejguta A Maltese shepherd's reed pipe, used in outdoor music (640)

flisak A genre from the Lubelskie region of Poland, often sung by raftsmen (113)

floyera A Greek end-blown, bevel-edged flute played by shepherds (1015, 1018)

fluier A Romanian six-holed duct flute (872, 875, 878–79, 897)

foekepot A friction drum of the Low Countries (526)

fofa A dance found in Brazil and Portugal (583)

fogli volanti 'Flying leaves' (Italian): Italian broadsides (606)

folklig musik The Swedish term for folk music (*gammeldans*) and other forms of popular music since the 1970s (436)

folklore (after German *volkskunde*) Traditional customs, tales, songs, dances, and other art forms (150–52, 326, 551–53, 577–79, 606, 621, 638, 641–42, 647–50, 656, 664, 675, 709, 712, 723, 729–30, 754–55, 758, 771, 773, 774, 782–84, 793, 796, 799–801, 803, 883, 885–86, 907, 934–37, 950, 953, 961, 969–70, 982, 1000, 1002, 1017, 1024–25)

folklorismo 'Folklorism': in Spain, the self-conscious recreation of older folk styles (600)

folkmusik Orally transmitted music of the rural classes in old Swedish peasant society (436)

folknici A Czech and Slovak musical genre that combined music of popular folk singers (*písničkaři*) and rock musicians in the late 1960s (730)

folkparker Outdoor Swedish amusement parks that became important venues for dance music of the modern and old types after 1900 (443)

fones Traditional tune types used by Cypriot singers to create songs with new texts (*1030*)

fonn 'The tune': in Irish dance tunes, the first section, which consists of two four-measure phrases (382)

formes fixes French poetic and song forms of the fourteenth and fifteenth centuries, chiefly the **ballade**, the **rondeau**, and the **virelai** (72)

frajtonarica A Slovene diatonic accordion with buttons (918, 920)

frame drum A shallow single-headed drum often having jingles attached to the frame, usually played by being struck, especially with fingers, knuckles, fists, and knees and sometimes with sticks (169, 194, *195*, 281, 305, 314, 354, 385, 391, 572, *577*, 582, 593, 594, *609, 705*, 707, 810, 837–38, 863, 877, 894, 930, 952, 960, 967, 979, 993, 994, *1031*)

Fränzli music An eighteenth-century Swiss instrumental style (689)

frula A Croatian and Serbian duct flute (897, 928, 931, 944, 947)

fujara A 2-meter-long Slovak duct flute with three holes for fingering, supplemented by a short blowing tube (171, *719*)

fujarka An end-blown, ductless and holeless shepherd's flute of the Carpathian area of Poland (704)

fulyrka A six- or seven-holed duct flute of the Carpathian area of Poland (704)

furiant A triple-meter Bohemian dance with alternating duple and triple accentual patterns (*718*)

fyell An Albanian shepherd's flute (992–93, 996, 1000)

fyelldrejti A duct flute played by northern Albanian herdsmen (996)

gagliarda 'Galliard': a Corsican dance piece (572)

gaida A Thracian bagpipe (285, 1009, 1012–13, 1015)

gaita A bagpipe of northern Spain (560, 593)

gaita A Basque double-reed aerophone of Arabic origin with eight holes for fingering; the variant in Soule is called *txanbela* (314, 315)

gaita-de-foles A Portuguese bagpipe, played especially in the north (583)

gajda A Bulgarian and Macedonian bagpipe (99, *164*, 169, *176*, 282, 283, 892, *893*, 897, 975, *976*, 977, 981, *982*, 983)

gajdaši A player of a Serbian bagpipe (952)

gajde An Albanian and Serbian bagpipe (944, *945*, 947, 950, 952, 993)

gajdy A Czech, Polish, and Slovak bagpipe (707, 719)

galant style A late **Baroque** style that favored regular phrasing, ornamented melodies, and simple harmonies (79, 435)

galdur 'Incantation': a form of Icelandic musical performance (405)

galop A lively couple dance in duple meter (435, 457, 524)

galopp A Swiss regional dance (690)

galoubet A three-holed flute played with a **tambourin** in Provence (545)

gamkivani 'Like the cock's sound': a version of *modzakhili,* the second voice of Georgian three-part singing (828)

gamlestev 'Old stanza' (Norwegian): a poetic form with medieval roots (413)

gammeldans 'Old-time dance-music': music that developed as Swedish urban **folklore** in the 1920s (436, 441)

gammaldansane 'Old dances': dances such as **polkas** and **waltzes**, which went to Norway in the 1800s (419, 420, 427, 431)

gammaldansmusik Scandinavian old-time dance music (671)

gammel vals 'Old-fashioned waltz': a Danish **waltz** (457)

ganga A rural polyphonic vocal genre of Bosnia and Hercegovina (112, 964, *965*)

gangar One of three Norwegian dances characterized by a fairly slow gait in 2/4 or 6/8 meter; see **halling** and **rull** (108, 417)

gara poetica Sardinian poets' sung duels (627, 629)

gardon A Hungarian stringed instrument, roughly the shape and size of a violoncello, played as a percussion instrument by beating the strings with a wooden stick and plucking them with fingers (274, 743, *744*)

garmon A Georgian accordion; also **buzika** (840)

garmon' (also *garmonika* and *garmoshka*) A Russian diatonic button accordion (*771, 774*)

gassenhauer German popular street songs (664)

gastarbeiter 'Guest workers': foreign workers in Germany, of whom a million arrived from Turkey after 1961 (237)

gatački pesni Macedonian short, recitativelike songs (974)

gaval A Chechen and Ingush double-headed drum; see **vota** (863)

gavilēt 'To cheer, exhault, shout, howl' (Old Latvian): a loud, outdoor, solo song, including characteristic cheering or howling formulas (499–500)

gavotte A Breton line or circle dance, performed as part of a three-part suite (559, 594)

gawe A **mouth harp** of the Low Countries (526)

geilwad The Welsh plowboy whose job was to walk backward facing the oxen and sing oxen-songs to keep the oxen calm (344)

geissler Swiss whip-crackers (687)

geitlokkar Norwegian ornamented goat-calls (412)

gema (also *gemanash*) A Chechen and Ingush rattle made of split wood and played during traditional dances (863)

genus durum 'Hard kind' (Latin): the major **mode** as named by Johannes Kepler in 1619 (652)

genus molle 'Soft kind' (Latin): the minor **mode** as named by Johannes Kepler in 1619 (652)

gęśle A Polish bowed stringed instrument found at eleventh- and thirteenth-century archaeological sites (705)

ghana 'Song': a traditional Maltese music form (198, 635–42)

ghana ta' spirtu pront 'Quick-witted song': a Maltese genre of dialogue singing (636–640)

ghannej A singer of **ghana** (639, 640)

ghazal A South Asian vocal genre, performed by immigrants in Britain (232, 240)

ghironda A hurdy-gurdy of Piedmont, Lombardy, and Emilia (615) *gievrie* A South Saami **frame drum**, used by shamans (305)

gigue (also **jig**) A lively English, Scottish, and Irish dance in 6/8 time (168)

Giorgoba The Georgian celebration of Saint George, performed in November with ritual feasts and circle dances (835)

giusto 'Just' (Italian): a term used especially by Hungarian scholars to denote a singing style executed strictly according to a metric framework (739, 741, 742)

gjâmë An elegy for dead males, sung in the northern Albanian highlands by male lament specialists (990)

glagoljaška pjevanje 'Glagolitic singing': a liturgical and paraliturgical form surviving on the northern Dalmatian coast and Kvarner Gulf in Croatia (929)

glamer zither A Swiss board zither, played mainly by women (686)

glas 'Voice' (Slavic): in Bulgarian music, any sung part (115); a system of eight melodic **modes**, used in Russian **chant** until the 1600s (779); a Serbian concept of a melodic type, distinguished by social occasion, musical form, textual content, and ethnic or geographic designation (also *kajda* in some areas) (942, 952)

glas na oj ubava A Serbian song having the refrain *o ubava* (942)

glasoečki pesni Macedonian songs having elaborate melodies; also *vozeni* and *ikoečki pesni* (974)

glee singing An eighteenth-century English form of amateur singing in three or more unaccompanied parts (327)

glendia Greek summer celebrations with singing on some Greek islands (118, 120, 1015)

gnawa A Moroccan musical genre, performed by immigrants in France (232)

gobdas A North Saami kettledrum having a reindeer-skin head (305)

godu balss 'Family celebration tune': a Latvian melodic formula (500, 502, 503)

goebe A friction drum of the Low Countries (526)

goigs Catalan medieval songs that recount the Virgin Mary's seven joys; known in Spanish as *gozos;* compare *gosos* (546, 591)

gol 'Weeping': the textually unfixed, partly sung, partly sobbing expression of grief that followed the Irish *caoineadh na marbh* (379)

gollu A Balkar and Karachaevi circle dance featuring triplets in 2/4 and 4/4 meters (858)

golosnik A soloist who sings a texted anhemitonic tune in Cossack vocal music of southern Russia (also *dishkant*) (757); the second voice in polyphonic vocal music of central and southern Russia (757)

gondolieri 'People who propel gondolas' (Italian): medieval Italian **epic** reciters, who adopted and developed written literature and notated music (53)

Gonjaoba A Georgian rain-begging ritual performed by girls and young women, who carry a female figure and sing (834)

góralski 'Highlanders' dance': a couple dance in the Carpathian area of Poland (708)

gordună A cello that provides rhythmic-harmonic accompaniment in Romanian and Hungarian music in parts of Transylvania (880)

gosha-nagara An Azerbaijani set of skin-covered clay pots; also *diplipito* (838)

goslarije A Slovenian band of two to four violins, one or two violas, one or two clarinets, a bass, and a **cimbalom**; also *bande* (917)

gosos Sardinian religious hymns, part of the Sardinian *a tenore* repertoire; compare *goigs* and *gozos* (627)

Gospin plač 'The Madonna's lament': a song cycle performed by pilgrims during Holy Week in Dalmatia, Croatia (*929*)

gostevye Guests' songs in Udmurt, Mari, Chuvash, and Tatar-Kriashen **folklore** (774)

gozos Spanish medieval songs that recount the Virgin Mary's seven joys; known in Catalan as *goigs*; compare *gosos* (591)

grada büchel A long Swiss straight **alphorn** with a curved bell, carved from a fir-tree trunk and wrapped in birch bark; see *büchel* (687, *688*)

grajcary A Polish **frame drum** with jingles; also a *cykace* (704)

Gregorian chant The chant of the medieval Roman Catholic Church in Western Europe, formalized and promulgated around A.D. 800 and continuing in use (69–70, 86, 106, 227, 403, 447, 600, 650, 652, 737, 881, 885, 960)

grelot A French sheep bell (544)

griot A West African musical specialist, usually a custodian of important historical and cultural knowledge (232)

grotto An open-air tavern of Ticino, a public place for singing in Italian-speaking Switzerland (695)

gruppo folk 'Folk group': any of numerous Sardinian folk-music groups (626)

guci 'Fiddlers': an ensemble of violins and bass of northwestern Croatia; also *gunci* (933)

gudalo A Slovene friction drum made of a clay pot covered by a pig's bladder, with a reed or string inserted through the skin (916)

gudastviri A Georgian bagpipe of Racha and Kartli (840)

gude The Albanian name of the one-stringed bowed fiddle (*gusle*) in Montenegro (959)

gudok (also *guduk*) A Russian three-stringed, pear-shaped, bowed **lute** made of one piece of wood (706, 764, *770*)

gŭdulka A Bulgarian pear-shaped bowed **lute** with three or four metal playing strings and about eight sympathetic strings (*176*, 282, *283*, *893*, 897, 902)

guggemusig Swiss carnival music of Stans, Unterwalden, performed during carnival at Basel (684)

guimbarde (French): a **mouth harp** of the Low Countries (526)

güiro (Spanish): a mainly Caribbean scraped gourd idiophone, used in German folk music after the revival of the 1960s (656)

guitarillo A high-pitched Spanish guitar (594)

guitarra A Corsican guitar (572)

guitarra (also *guitarra Portuguesa*) A Portuguese guitar with a pear-shaped soundboard and six double courses of metal strings (116, 583)

guitarrón A low-pitched Spanish guitar (594)

gukania Yells in the calendric songs of southwestern Russia (758)

gulyaniia Russian outdoor parties (766)

gunci 'Fiddlers': an ensemble of violins and bass of northwestern Croatia; also *guci* (931, 933)

gunggele A cowbell of Muotatal, Switzerland; see *trychle* (685)

gunjci An instrumental ensemble of Istria, Croatia; also *gunci, violine,* and *muzika* (931)

gúnydals 'Mocking songs': Hungarian songs sung in the marketplace (747)

gusla A Macedonian three-stringed, pear-shaped bowed **lute**; also *kemene* (975)

guslari (in Serbian and Croatian also *guslači*) **Epic** singers, derived from the name of the bowed **lute** (*gusle*), with which they accompany their singing (927, *941–42*, 959, 961); blind Macedonian itinerant beggars, who sang and played the *gusla* for money (975)

guslarske junačke pjesme In Montenegro, a *gusle*-accompanied heroic song (959)

gusle A one-stringed bowed **lute** typical of the central Dinaric Mountains of Serbia, Montenegro, and Bosnia-Hercegovina (130, 168, 198, 927, *941*, 945, 957, 959, 961, 963, 966)

gusli A northwestern Russian plucked zither (503, 764, 770, 774)

guslya A Chuvash zither (774)

gwerz Breton **ballads** or narrative songs that recount historical, legendary, or dramatic events; see *complainte* (559)

Gŵyl Fair y Canhwyllau The Welsh festival celebrating the arrival of spring (343)

gŵyl mabsant A boisterous Welsh patron-saint festival, eventually condemned by religious enthusiasts partly because of the use of the **harp** to accompany singing and dancing (353)

haaggeri Swiss whip-crackers of Richterswil, Zurich (683)

habanera A Cuban dance in slow 2/4 time featuring the rhythm of a dotted eighth, a sixteenth, and two eighths, used in Italian popular music (619)

hackbrett A Swiss and northern Italian trapezoidal, struck zither, mainly of Appenzell and the Goms Valley, Upper Valais (615, 686)

haïvky A Ukrainian musical game played by people of all ages and both sexes (808)

hakkebord A trapezoidal struck zither of the Low Countries (532)

halakhah Jewish religious law, which addresses aesthetic and ethical questions concerning music (257) *hałaśeńni* Belarusan laments (793)

hałasnoha śpievu 'Open-air singing' (Belarusan): see *na voli* (793)

halbstarke 'Half-naked' (German): the Austrian youth subculture of the 1960s, with its own popular music (216)

hallgató The slow, rhythmically free type of *nóta* (273)

halling A men's athletic dance of Norway (108, 166, 417)

halsingod A Welsh metrical psalm in the vernacular, born of the religious turbulence in south Wales during the 1600s (349)

halszither A Swiss long-necked lute-zither (686)

hamarreko A Basque dance-song type with five-couplet stanzas (312)

hambo A modernized, nonimprovised version of the Swedish *polska* (443)

Handäoline The later name of the *Mundäoline*, an accordion invented in Berlin in 1821 by F. Buschmann and now known as the **concertina**; also the *deutsche Harmonika* (657)

hanske knap A clapper in the form of a wolf's or bear's head of the Low Countries (525)

hanter dro A Breton line or circle dance, performed as part of a three-part suite (559)

hardingfele A Norwegian modified form of the violin, having four sympathetic strings (*121*, 170, *177*, 415, *416*, 417–20, *421*, 422, 424, 426–27, 429–31)

harmoníai Tunings in ancient Greek musical theory (48, 1023)

harmonica (also *monika*) A small box with free reeds set into slots and sounded by exhaling and inhaling; also **mouth organ** (143, 348, 494, 530, 545, 640, 658, 693)

harmoniebesetzung 'Harmonious composition' (German): a Swiss brass ensemble that incorporates woodwinds (689)

harmoniia A Ukrainian free-reed, button accordion; see *baian* (811, 818)

harmonik A Belarusan accordion (797)

harmonika A Slovenian and Croatian diatonic accordion (918, 931)

harp A chordophone with plucked strings perpendicular to the soundboard; in Ireland, a medieval chordophone known as *cláirseach* and *cruit* (146, 152, 197, 200, 342, 344, 347, 349, 350–55, 364, 366–67, 383–84, 391, 393, 426, 469, 528, 560–61, 601, 615, 618, 651, 656, 658, 672, 743, 838, *839*, 853, 860)

harpa The most frequently mentioned Norwegian instrument in ancient literary sources: either a **lyre** or a **harp** (423)

harppu A Finnish **harp** (479)

harpsichord A Western European keyboard instrument having strings plucked by plectra (traditionally quills), engaged by the action of the keys (55, 75, 78, 82, 101, 200, 366, 367, 422, 654)

harvest home A feast at the close of harvest, often featuring singing (331)

hasapikos A **rebetika** dance rhythm in moderate 4/4 time (1021)

hăulit A **yodel** of the Gorj zone of Oltenia, Romania (873)

haur kantu txapelketa A Basque annual championship of children's singing (314)

hazzanim 'Those serving' (Hebrew): Jewish cantors (253, 263–64, 968)

heilagvisene Norwegian pre-Christian and Christian sacred songs (413)

hemiola The ratio of 3 to 2; musically, the substitution of three beats for two or two beats for three, conventionally notated as the alternation of 3/4 and 6/8 time or 3/2 and 6/4 time (330, 593)

heränneet Finnish Lutheran folk revivalists who embellish their performances of psalms (478)

heterometer The use of more than one metric scheme in a piece of music (521)

heterometric Featuring **heterometer** (127, 475, 521, 541)

hidžaz makam A Turkish **mode** used in singing love songs (*sevdalinka*) of Bosnia-Hercegovina (964)

Highland bagpipe A Scottish bagpipe with a blowpipe, a double-reed chanter, and a single reed in each of three drone pipes (169, *363*, 366, 559)

highlife A popular musical genre that originated in Ghana in the early 1900s and became popular in European "world music" (232, 233)

hiiukannel An Estonian three- or four-stringed bowed **lyre**; see *rootsikannel* (493)

hijaz A Turkish melodic **mode**, used in Macedonia (974, 980)

hirðskáld The oral art of Icelandic court poets (405)

hokh Adighian wishes for prosperity in magical song (855)

hommel A plucked dulcimer of the Low Countries (533)

hora A circle dance of Romania and Israel; see *horo* and *oro* (254, 870, 872, 880)

hora lăutarescă (also *hora tsigăneasca*) A Romanian Rom improvised dance; also *hora tsigănwasca* (277)

hora lunga 'Long song': a name of the Romanian *doina* (128, *129*, 873)

hornpipe A wooden or bone pipe having a single reed and holes for fingering (366, 524, 571); a lively English and Irish dance in 4/4 time, originally accompanied by a hornpipe (168, 330, 331, 382)

horo The generic term for Bulgarian dance, usually an open or closed circle of dancers holding hands; see *hora* and *oro* (891, 897)

horo na pesen A Bulgarian dance accompanied by singing (*892*)

huchage 'Calling': French shepherds' singing over long distances or for herding flocks (540)

huibe A bowed pseudo-bass of the Low Countries (531)

hummel A Swedish plucked dulcimer (439)

humppa A style of Finnish music for dance that mixes jazz, fox-trot, **polka**, *rekilaulu*, and Russian romances (483–86)

hunt supper An English social event, often a context for music and song (331)

hurtkampaniya A Belarusan traditional folk instrumental ensemble; also *kapela, muzyki, skamarochi,* and *viasielnyja muzyki* (798)

hutsul'ka A dance of the Hutsul'shchyna region of Ukraine (812)

hutsul'ka do spivi 'Hutsul'ka for singing': regional melodies played on the *dudka* in market squares and village bazaars (813)

huving Norwegian elaborated shouts; see *laling* (412)

hvësegasse A Danish whirring disk: a button or a round plate of cardboard spun and sounded by rhythmically tightening or slackening a string noose threaded through two holes in the middle of the button or plate (455)

hwyl A declamatory technique used by Welsh preachers in the 1800s and early 1900s to heighten religious fervor (345)

hymée Millers' work songs of French-speaking Switzerland; also *épiaulie* (693)

iablochko 'Beautiful apple' (Russian): a style of Gypsy song (768)

iavnana A two- and three-part curing song for whooping cough and the measles, sung by men in eastern Georgia; compare *batonebo* (835)

iertările 'The forgiveness': part of the Romanian wedding ritual, accompanied by specific songs or instrumental tunes (871)

iet rotaļās A Latvian pastime among youths, including playing games, usually circle dances with singing (503)

igra 'Game' (from the Bulgarian verb *igrae* 'to dance'): a Bulgarian term for games and dances, specifically children's musical games (897, 900)

igranke Spontaneous dance parties in Croatia (926)

igrovoi khorovod A Russian dance game with pantomiming soloists inside a circle of singers (769)

ikoečki pesni Macedonian songs having elaborate melodies; also *glasoečki* and *vozeni* (974)

ikoyeniaka Greek 'family songs,' unaccompanied table songs of Skyros (1015)

il verticale A mechanical **piano** of Italian-speaking Switzerland (694)

ilahije Muslim paraliturgical hymns, also adopted into the religious musical practice of Sephardic Jews in Bosnia-Hercegovina (968–69)

illi Chechen and Ingush historical songs (864)

ilo 'Joy': an alternate name for the Finnish *kantele* (481)

iltamat Finnish public entertainment that concluded with a one-hour dance (483)

îmbrăcatul 'The dressing of the bride': part of the Romanian wedding ritual, accompanied by specific songs or instrumental tunes (871)

Indorock A genre of Dutch rock and roll played by *Indos,* people of mixed Indonesian and European origin (237–38)

infantiles Spanish children's play songs (589)

ingermatura A Corsican children's game accompanied by verses (571)

intermedi Lavish commemorative spectacles hosted by monarchs and aristocrats during the Italian **Renaissance**, with elaborate scenery, costumes, music, poetry, and dance (77, 160)

intonatsiia 'Intonation': a musicological concept developed by Boleslav Yavorsky and Boris Asaf'ev (783)

iron-kandzal-fandir An Ossetian accordion, a woman's instrument (860)

ishia 'Straight': a tune type of the Cypriot *tsiattista* genre (*1030*)

iskelmä A Finnish term for locally produced popular songs (204)

islamei An Adighian fast virtuoso solo dance (856)

iso The Albanian term for a drone (991)

isometer The use of the same metric scheme throughout a piece of music (521)

isometric Featuring **isometer** (71, 127, 414, 476, 521, 539)

ison (Greek): a fixed, wordless drone (904, *1010*)

ispratnica Festivities held in Serbia when a man departs for military service (941)

iÞróttir The essential accomplishments of a well-educated Icelandic gentleman, which included rhyming and harping (405)

itku 'Cry, weep': the term for the lament, one of the oldest Finnish song genres (475, *476,* 480)

ivy leaf Reportedly used in Ireland as an aerophone that vibrated against the upper lip to make a variably high-pitched sound (385)

izglasa 'Out loud': a male vocal genre of Montenegro, characterized by a tense vocal technique; also *izvika* (958)

izvika 'Called out': a male vocal genre of Montenegro, characterized by a tense vocal technique; also *izglasa* (958)

izvorna muzika 'Music of the source or spring': music played on Macedonian radio by a folk orchestra (981)

izvorni 'Original': said of Croatian songs and dances assumed to be ancient, native, and free of foreign influences (935)

jabadao A Breton figure dance (559)

jaleo The encouraging and admiring shouts of the audience in a Spanish **flamenco** performance (598)

Jāņi The Latvian midsummer solstice celebration (*501*)

jaravyja pieśni Belarusan songs sung during the harvest of the spring sowing (792)

jatsi 'Jazz' (Finnish) (483)

jazz balett A Swedish **ballet** accompanied by live jazz; a gymnastic movement for young

people and adults, accompanied by jazz or jazz-derived recordings (443)

jednojke A single-piped duct flute of Bosnia-Hercegovina (966)

jig A lively English, Scottish, and Irish dance in 6/8 time; also **gigue** (166, 168, 330, 331, *381,* 382, 387, 524)

Joaldunak Basque masked carnival characters (314)

joc Closed circle dances of Romanians in the Pannonian zone of Serbia (947)

jocul de pomana 'Alms dance': a dance performed in Banat, Romania, for those who die young (872)

jodel 'Yodel' (German): a Swiss singing technique involving rapid shifting between chest voice and head voice (690)

jodellied Swiss verse songs that incorporate **yodels** as choruses (692)

jodler Austrian **yodels** (671)

joik A Saami vocal genre (96, 117, 143, 299–307, 428–29, 487–88)

jokulatori Czech and Slovak medieval professional musicians and singers (726)

jongleresses Twelfth-century French female traveling musicians who performed for harvest gatherings and the aristocratic elite's amusement (199)

jongleur A medieval French minstrel who sang heroic **chants** (72, 542)

jota An Aragonese couple dance in quick triple time, accompanied by castanets (588, 592, 594, *595,* 596)

jota A Basque chain dance (314)

jouhikko A Finnish bowed **lyre** (479)

juergas Spanish *gitano* jam sessions, one of the earliest contexts for **flamenco** (597–98)

jùjú A Yoruba musical genre, exported from Nigeria and popular in European "world music" (232)

jumpa The Swedish two-step, a local variation of ballroom dancing (443)

junačke pesme 'Heroic songs': Serbo-Croatian **epics**, accompanied by a **lute** (941, 958, 965)

juoi'gat Joik, a Saami genre able to bring about heightened relationships of copresence among ancestors, kinfolk, neighbors, animals, trees, and other features of the landscape or other inanimate objects (117, 447)

juoigan The Fjeld Saami term for joiking (487)

juoigos Saami songs that reference various subjects to master an inhospitable environment (447)

Jurjeǔskija Belarusan St. George's Day (791)

jüüz Swiss natural yodeling of Muotatal; also *jüüzli* (690)

kaba A Near Eastern term sometimes used by Albanian flute players to name performances (993)

kaba gajda A large, low-pitched bagpipe of the Rhodope Mountains of Bulgaria (*896*)

kabardinka An Ossetian couple dance; see *khonga-kaft* (861)

kadeg An Ossetian **epic** song performed by a soloist (*kadeganag*) who provides his own instrumental accompaniment (860)

kadril A Dutch **quadrille** that usually consisted of four or five figures having different tunes in 2/4 or 6/8 time (524)

kadrilj A Swedish **contra** dance, especially in southern and eastern Sweden (442)

kafa An Adighian competitive dance (856)

kafana 'Café': a musical classification used by Vojvodinan Serbs describing where music takes place (952)

kafana A Macedonian café that features the performance of music (979)

kaffeehaus 'Coffeehouse': in nineteenth-century Germany and Austria, a place for listening to popular arrangements of music (51)

kaiga A Mordvinian zither (774)

kajda 'Note': a Serbian concept of a melodic type, distinguished by social occasion, musical form, textual content, and ethnic or geographic designation; also *glas* (942)

kaladki Belarusan carols of the winter song cycle (791, *795*)

kalamatiano A dance of the Greek mainland, important in Cyprus (1030)

kalektyǔnaje halašeǹnie Collective wailing during World War II for Soviet soldiers, partisans, and inhabitants of burned villages (793)

kalektyvy Belarusan amateur rural ensembles (796, 800)

Kalevala The Finno-Karelian **epic**, whose text was sung at all social occasions (*187,* 476, *477,* 480–82, 493)

kalusschellen A clapper bell of canton Glarus, Switzerland (683)

kampfrichter 'Fight judges': Swiss officials who judge **yodels** in competitive festivals (692)

kan da gorell Breton songs for dancing; see *chanson à danser* (559)

kan has diskan Unaccompanied responsorial singing for dance in western Brittany (559)

kandeleh A Karelian plucked zither (493, 503)

kandla A Livonian plucked zither resembling the Finnish *kantele* (493)

kaner A Breton singer of *kan has diskan* who begins each phrase and trades off with the *diskaner* (559)

kângë kreshnikësh 'Long heroic songs': a genre of Albanian narrative songs (989)

kângë majekrahi 'Song of the peak of the arm': performance in which Albanian men place a finger in one ear or cup their ear, raise their elbow above eye level, and sing out at full volume; also *kângë malësorçe* (995)

kângë malësorçe 'Songs of the *malësore*': performance in which Albanian men place a finger in one ear or cup their ear, raise their elbow above eye level, and sing out at full volume; also *kângë majekrahi* (995)

kângë të çobaneshave 'Shepherdesses' songs': songs sung by pairs of Albanian girls (995)

kanklės A Lithuanian plucked zither (170, 503, 511)

kannel An Estonian plucked zither (170, 493, *494, 495,* 503)

kannöl A Votian plucked zither resembling the Finnish ***kantele*** (493)

kanonaki A Greek plucked zither (1013)

kant A Russian three-part singing style with top voices in parallel thirds and an independent third voice (755, 767, *768,* 780)

kanta zaharak 'Old songs': Basque songs that require two voices (121)

kantadhes Greek romantic popular serenades of the Ionian islands (1008, 1014)

kantaduri Croatian singers who sing the extended melismatic lament of ***Gospin plač*** (929)

kantele A Finnish and Karelian plucked zither (170, 475, *479,* 481, *485,* 486, 488, 489, 493, 503, 774)

kantig Breton religious hymns; see ***cantique*** (559)

kantor A Slovakian schoolmaster, responsible for the musical aspect of religious and public city life in churches and schools (727)

kanun An originally Middle Eastern plucked zither, still played in the Balkans (168, 281, 286, *979,* 997); a Georgian urban chordophone played from the 1600s to the 1800s (840)

kanzunetta 'Popular song': a Maltese genre bridging folk and popular music (638, 642)

kapela A Belarusan traditional folk instrumental ensemble; also ***hurtkampaniya, muzyki, skamarochi,*** and ***viasielnyja muzyki*** (798)

kapobalo 'Head of the dance': the dance leader in Croatian dances of the northern Adriatic zone (931)

kappleikar Norwegian fiddle competitions (started in 1888), which have become important manifestations of Norwegian national cultural heritage (150)

karabe Bagpipes played by the Vlahs of Serbia (950)

karadjuzen A long-necked plucked **lute** of northern and central Bosnia (966)

karahody Belarusan spring and summer round dances (792, 794)

karamoutza A Greek double-reed shawm (1009)

karavaj The round wedding bread prepared during Belarusan weddings, accompanied by ritual songs (793)

kargish inar A Balkar and Karachaevi improvisatory antiphonal song competition (858)

karicka An eastern Slovakian women's circle dance having complex heel-stamping patterns (721)

karifu Japanese neumatic notation, set in vertical columns read from left to right (103)

karjapasun An Estonian wooden herding trumpet (494)

Karlovačko pojanje 'Karlovo singing': a type of Serbian liturgical **chant** (943)

Kärntnerlied An Austrian love song of Carinthia, performed by choruses in four-part harmony (674)

kars A Balkar and Karachaevi rattle (857)

karshkuli An Ingush ritual intended to control weather, dedicated to Sela, goddess of thunder and lightning (864)

karsilama A Macedonian Rom dance in 9/8 time (979)

karsilamas A Greek dance in 9/8 time, originally of coastal Asia Minor (1009)

kartinniki 'Picture drawers': a Russian genre in which performers draw pictures suggested by song texts and throw them into the audience (779)

kartsganag Ossetian wooden castanets, played to accompany dancing (860)

kartuli A Georgian mixed-couple dance with instrumental accompaniment (836)

kartzilamades A Cypriot dance, consisting of two sequences of five movements for men and women, who stand face to face (1030, *1031*)

kasapsko oro 'Butcher's dance': in Macedonia (979)

kaside Muslim paraliturgical hymns sung in Bosnia-Hercegovina (969)

katuba A Maltese bass drum, played with a fife for public announcements (640)

kaval A Bulgarian and Macedonian end-blown, rim-blown flute (*164,* 282, 892, *893,* 895–96, 902, 975, 981, *982,* 983)

kavall Eight-holed rim-blown flutes with chromatic fingering, played in pairs by Albanian herdsmen in western Macedonia (992, 996–97, 1000)

kāzu balss 'Wedding tune': a Latvian melodic formula for singing ***apdziedāšanās***; see ***godu balss*** (502)

kcim An Albanian solo women's dance, featuring graceful arm movements (994)

keening A lament for the dead, especially in Ireland (196, 378–79, 761–63)

keenoba Masqueraders' performances at ***kvelieri*** in urban areas of Georgia (836)

kef (also *kefi*) A term used in Greece and the Balkans to label a heightened form of experience created by music and other forms of social experience (118, 143, 1017)

kehillah A term designating different forms of Jewish culture and music (262–63)

kekhat-pondur A Chechen and Ingush accordion, played by women; see ***komuk*** and ***komuz*** (862–63)

kemancha An Georgian urban chordophone, played from the 1600s to the 1800s (840)

kemençe An Albanian pear-shaped bowed **lute**; see ***lyra*** (993, 997)

kemene A Macedonian three-stringed pear-shaped bowed **lute**; also ***gusla***; see ***lyra*** (283, 975, 979)

kemenje A Pontic Greek three-stringed bowed **lute**; see ***lyra*** (*1011*)

kempurvisur Danish heroic songs of the Faroe Islands, sung by line dancers (469–71)

këngë 'Songs' (Albanian) (990)

këngë me të marrje me të prerje 'Songs with taking and cutting' (Albanian): Tosk polyphonic singing; also ***këngë me iso, këngë me të rënkuar,*** and ***këngë me të zier*** (991)

këngë me të rënkuar 'Songs with groaning' (Albanian): Tosk polyphonic singing; also ***këngë me të marrje me të prerje,*** *këngë me iso,* and ***këngë me të zier*** (991)

kerla esharsh Chechen and Ingush new songs for traditional feasts (862)

keserves 'Bitter song': Hungarian lamenting songs with improvised lines (740–41, *742,* 744, 745)

khalkhar Chechen and Ingush dance melodies (863, 864)

khalkharan iish Chechen instrumental music accompanying dances, processions, and horse races (863)

khelimaski djili Vlach Rom duple-meter songs with sung imitations of musical instruments (275)

khelovantmtavari 'Head of the arts': Georgian professional composers who worked in Georgian churches from the eighth to the eleventh centuries (843)

khodiachii A Russian dance in which all participants walk in a circle or in a serpentine movement down a street; also ***khodovoi khorovod*** and ***zmeika*** (769)

khodovoi khorovod 'Walking *khorovod*': A Russian dance in which all participants walk in a circle or in a serpentine movement down a street; also ***kjodiachii*** and ***zmeika*** (769)

khoiisar-fandir An Ossetian two- or three-stringed bowed **lute**, used to accompany **epics**; see ***kisin-fandir*** (859)

khonga-kaft An Ossetian couple dance; see ***kabardinka*** (861)

khöömei Mongolian and Tuvinian throat singing (773)

khorovod Russian collective circle and figure dances; also ***tanok*** and ***krugi*** (769, 770)

khorumi An Acharian and Gurian military dance in 5/4 meter (836)

khromka 'Chromatic': the chromatic Russian accordion (770)

kil-kobuz A Balkar and Karachaevi plucked **lute** (857)

kingir-kobuz A Balkar and Karachaevi **harp** (857)

kingotoner Danish tunes in a hymnbook compiled by Bishop Thomas Kingo (1634–1703); used in the Faroe Islands as the basis for extensive improvisation in informal worship at home (459, 471)

kintouri A Georgian dance accompanied by Middle Eastern instruments such as the ***doli,*** the ***duduki,*** and the ***zurna*** (836)

kiridžijske pjesme Caravan songs, sung by merchants in Bosnia-Hercegovina (963)

kirmaš A Belarusan rural marketplace, often dramatized in government-sponsored staged **folklore** (800)

kisin-fandir An Ossetian two- or three-stringed bowed **lute**, played to accompany **epics**; see ***khoiisar-fandir*** (859, 861)

kitarra biss A Maltese genre of songless guitar

music, performed by an ensemble of lead guitar (*prejjem*) and one or two chord-playing guitars (639–40)

kithara A seven- or eight-stringed plucked **lyre** of ancient Greece, played by professional musicians accompanying choruses (39, 46, 47)

kitka 'Bouquet' (Bulgarian): an arrangement of well-known folk and urban popular songs for bands or a cappella choirs (904)

kjempevisene Norwegian heroic songs (413)

kjuček A Bulgarian Rom instrumental genre in 2/4 or 9/8 time (282, 284)

kjyy A Balkar and Karachaevi women's lyrical song genre (858)

klapa 'Club, group of friends': songs and a singing style in four-part harmony performed by men in urban areas along the Dalmatian coast of Croatia and Montenegro (149, 929, *930*, 936, 959)

klapsarika Greek nonmetrical, weeping melodies (1010)

klarino A Greek clarinet having the Albert system of keying (1009–10, 1012, *1013*, 1015)

klausjagen Swiss whip-crackers of Küssnacht am Rhein, canton Schwyz (683)

klavirka 'Piano accordion' (Slovenian) (918)

kleftika Heroic songs of mainland Greece, imported to Cyprus (1030)

Klenotnice 'The Treasury': a Czechoslovakian program to support traditional folk music activity and collecting (723)

klezmorim Jewish musical professionals, especially instrumentalists (11, 251, 259–*260*)

knari An obsolete Georgian **harp**, mentioned in medieval literary sources (838–39)

knizhnye pesni 'Book songs': suburban Russian songs, drawn from eighteenth- and nineteenth-century literary sources (765–67)

kobza A Belarusan hurdy-gurdy, also *lira* and *rela* (796); a Ukrainian plucked bowl **lute**, also *bandura* (815–16, 818)

kobzari Ukrainian blind peasant minstrels who played the *kobza*; see *lirnyky* (99, 809, 813–16, 820, 821)

koenkelpot A friction drum of the Low Countries (526)

kokles A Latvian plucked zither, carved from a wooden plank and having five to twelve strings (170, 503, *504*, 505)

kolatki Clappers used in annual church ceremonies in Poland; also *terkotki* (704)

koleda The Bulgarian and Serbian winter solstice, Christmas, or New Year's caroling ritual (140, 899, 901, 941)

koledari Bulgarian performers of *koleda* (899)

koledarske pjesme Christmas carols of Montenegro (958)

kolednice Carols sung door-to-door in Slovenia between Christmas and Epiphany (912)

koledniki Slovene carolers who perform from door to door between Christmas and Epiphany (912)

koledovanje Door-to-door caroling in Slovenia between Christmas and Epiphany (912)

kolendarë Albanian children who caroled from door-to-door on Christmas and St. Lazarus' Day (988)

koliada A Russian caroling ritual at Christmas and St. Vasil's Day (758, 760)

koliadky Ukrainian Christmas carols (808, 812)

kolinje Slavonian communal hog-butchering parties, held in the late fall with singing, dancing, and merrymaking; also *svinjokolje* (926)

kolo A Serbo-Croatian circle dance (926, 929, 931–32, 947, 950, 958, 963)

kolo u šest A Serbian circle dance in six steps, also *kolo* (950)

komad s pevanjem 'Dramatic play with singing': a Serbian variant of the Central European singspiel (141, 948)

komuk A Chechen and Ingush accordion, played by women; see *kekhat-pondur* (862, 863)

koncovka A Slovak flute without holes for fingering (719)

kondylies A Greek genre of improvised, rhyming couplets of eastern Crete; known in western and central Crete as *mantinadhes* (1015)

kontra 'Rhythmic-harmonic support': the part played by one musician in a Hungarian folk violin duo (273, 744–45)

kora A West African harp-lute, played by immigrants in France (*239*)

korizne goblice A Slovenian homemade fiddle, made by rubbing two corn stalks together (918)

korneto A Greek brass horn (1009)

kortsili A Georgian wedding in which all songs are polyphonic (835)

kosačke pjesme Grass-cutting songs of Bosnia-Hercegovina (963)

kotsaki A Greek genre of improvised, rhyming couplets of Crete (1025)

kotsari A Pontic Greek dance (1011)

koumpania A Greek ensemble of instrumentalists and vocalists that performed *rebetika* before the 1930s (285, 1019–20)

koutalia Greek spoons, used percussively in *rebetika* (1019)

koza A bagpipe of Podhale, Poland (*707*)

kozak A Ukrainian dance form (812, 821)

kozioł Polish bagpipes (706)

kozioł biały 'White he-goat': a bagpipe of western Poland (707)

krakowiak A popular duple-meter dance in Poland (708–710)

kratki glas 'Short voice': Serbian songs with syllabic text settings (942)

kratki napjevi 'Short melodies': Bosnia-Hercegovinan songs having a melody subordinate to a text and often consisting of one short melodic pattern (964)

kreuzpolka A Swiss regional dance (690)

krez' An Udmurt zither; Urdmurt song; Urdmurt melody (774)

krienser halszither A Swiss long-necked lute-zither resembling a guitar (687)

krimanchuli 'Distorted falsetto, distorted jaw': in three-part singing of western Georgia, the yodeling part (828, *829*)

kriuk 'Hook': the earliest neumatic notation of Russian church music (779)

kroncong The Indonesian name of the *cavaquinho* (583)

krsteno A Macedonian dance in 12/8 time (978)

krugi 'Circles': Russian collective circle and figure dances; also *khorovod* and *tanok* (769)

krusta dancis Latvian dancing and jumping over crossed poles or swords (504)

ksenitias Greek songs of exile (1010)

kücek 'Belly-dance hip movement' (Turkish): the source of *čoček*, a dance of Serbian Gypsies (951)

kudum A small kettledrum, played in some dervish rituals in Bosnia-Hercegovina (967)

kugikly Archaic Russian panpipes; also *kuvikly* (770)

Kühreihen A melismatic Swiss cattle call; also *kuhreigen*; see *ranz des vaches* (17, 128, 683)

kujawiak A Polish folk dance (708, 710)

kukeri Bulgarian masked characters who perform **luck visits** with music before Lent; also *startsi* 1(40, 897, *899*)

kukerski igri The dances of the Bulgarian *kukeri* (897)

kuki A female figure carried during Lazeroba, the Georgian rain-begging ritual (834)

kuku An Albanian lament or stylized form of crying, whose name derives of a sorrowful exclamation (990)

kulning Swedish cattle calls (436)

kulokkar Norwegian ornamented cow calls (*412*)

kulturno-umetnička društva Cultural-artistic ensembles in the former Yugoslavia (959, 968, 981–84)

Kupalle A Belarusan summer-solstice ritual (791)

kupalskie pesni Summer-solstice songs sung in western Russia on Midsummer's Day (760)

kupalskija pieśni A Belarusan summer-song cycle (791)

kuplés Hungarian cabaret songs popularized in the 1930s (746)

kurai A Bashkir and Tatar rim-blown flute (773, 774)

kurnetta A Maltese shawm (640)

kust 'Bush': Belarusan songs for Pentecost, when a girl clothed in greenery is taken around the village (791)

kutok 'Corner': any section of a Ukrainian village that shared a common aesthetic and musical knowledge (807)

kuvikly Archaic Russian panpipes; also *kugikly* (770)

kvæðamaður An Icelandic chanter renowned for special abilities (117, 401)

kvæði (sing. *kvæðir*) The chanting of *rímur* in Iceland (117); lengthy heroic **ballads** of the Faroe Islands, dramatized by singers performing a line dance (*469*–71)

kvelieri The main Georgian ritual complex, the last week of carnival, marking the beginning of the agricultural year (834)

kveða (also *kveðir, kvað,* and *kveðið*) In Iceland, to compose, write poetry, narrate, and **chant** (402)

kveðandi 'Recitation': considered a form of Icelandic musical performance (405)

kviria A Georgian song of Svaneti, connected to the fertility deity (835)

kvirostviri 'Loud-shouting *stviri*: a Georgian metallic military instrument (840)

kvöldvaka 'Evening watch': winter vigils once held in Iceland, when performers (*kvæðamaður*) would recite *rímur* (117, 141, 400–402, 407)

kyoslë A Chuvash zither (774)

kyuchek A solo dance of the Bulgarian Roma (903)

kyuslë A Mari box zither (774)

La condanna della vecchiaccia 'The condemnation of the crone': an Italian mid-Lenten ceremony in Umbria (608)

la grande coquille de Gruyère 'The big shell of Gruyère': a communal dance of French-speaking Gruyère, Switzerland (693)

la marsiliana A Corsican dance imported of France (571, 573)

la tarascona A Corsican dance imported of France (571, 573)

labanorų dūda A Lithuanian bagpipe with a blow pipe, a melody pipe, and a drone pipe (511)

ladkana Monophonic narrow-range wedding melodies of lowland western Ukraine (809)

ladugiju iish 'Melodies for listening': Chechen instrumental music (863)

laduvane A Bulgarian fortune-telling ritual for boys and girls with songs, performed in some areas at New Year's (899, 901)

lahutë A one-stringed fiddle played to accompany Albanian narrative songs (995, 996)

laika Greek popular urban songs (1008, 1018, 1020, 1030, 1031)

lajerkosten A large Slovene hurdy-gurdy on legs (919)

lajna A Slovene hurdy-gurdy (919)

lakodalmas 'Wedding rock' in Hungary (747)

lalim uadindz An Ossetian bagpipe (859)

laling Norwegian elaborated shouts and hollers; see *huving* (412)

Lambeg drums Large, two-headed drums that accompany the keyless fife in Ulster (385)

lamenti di banditi Corsican autobiographical songs of famous bandits (567)

lamentu A Corsican lament, especially for the dead; also *ballata, compitu,* and *voceru* (566–567, 569, 571)

ländler An Austrian waltzlike dance in slow 3/4 time, popular in western Europe (168, 524, 672–74); in Switzerland, the last dance of a common cycle (*räschtli*), often performed fast (690)

ländlerkappelle A Swiss-German instrumental ensemble, consisting of a clarinet, accordions, and a double bass; a corresponding style of dancing and its accompanying music; see *burämusig* (689, 693)

landsgemeinde Swiss open-air parliaments, accompanied by drums in Graubünden and Appenzell Ausserrhoden (686)

landskappleik A fiddlers' festival in Norway (150, *151*)

Landsknechttrommel A medieval German mercenary's drum, revived in the 1920s by German youth groups (656)

langeleik A Norwegian plucked zither (170, 197, 414–15, 417, 422, 430)

langspil An Icelandic bowed zither with two to six strings (*406, 407*)

laoi Fiannaíochta An old Irish genre, known as the Fenian or Ossianic heroic **lay** (379, 388)

laoidh A Scottish lay (narrative song) (361, *362*)

laouto A Greek long-necked plucked **lute** (118, 284, 285, 1010, *1013*, 1015, 1019, 1025, 1030, *1031*)

larchemi 'Cane': a Samegrelian panpipe; see *soinari* and *sastsrapo* (839, 840)

laridé A Breton line or circle dance, performed as part of a three-part suite; see *ridée* (559)

lasowe 'Of the forest': a genre of open-air song of the Zywiecke region of Poland (113)

lassú The slow section of the Hungarian Szék dance cycle, intended for listening (745)

laterna A Greek mechanical music box on legs (1012, *1013*, 1015)

laude (sing. *lauda*) Italian religious **strophic songs**, in Latin or the vernacular (132, 607)

laulaa 'To sing' (Finnish): originally 'to enchant' (480)

laulu 'Song' (Finnish) (475, 480)

launeddas A Sardinian aerophone with three single-reed pipes played by a single player (22, 170, 621, 626–27, *630*–32)

lausavísur 'Loose stanzas': single stanzas or epigrams in Iceland (117, 143, 402, 407–408)

lauta A fretted plucked **lute**, a Middle Eastern instrument, played in *čalgija* ensembles of Macedonia (979)

lăutari Professional Romanian musicians, many of whom are Gypsies (122, 277–78, 873, 877)

lay A simple narrative poem and its music, especially as developed in northern France in the thirteenth century, best known in the works of Marie de France and Guillaume Machaut and preserved in folk repertoires of various peoples (361, *362*, 379, 386, 393, 552, 561)

lazarica House-to-house caroling by young children before Easter in Macedonia (973)

lazarice Serbian girls who sing Lazarus' songs (941)

lazaričke pesme 'Lazarus' songs': songs sung in Serbia, Bosnia-Hercegovina, and Montenegro by girls on St. Lazarus' Saturday to mark the beginning of the agricultural work cycle (941, 958, 963)

Lazaroba A Georgian rain-begging ritual, performed by girls and young women, who carry a female figure and sing the song "Lazare"; see Eliaoba and Gonjaoba (834)

lazarovden 'Lazar's Day': a Bulgarian spring fertility ritual with singing and dancing, performed by women and girls (140, 161, 900)

lehut In Montenegro, the Albanian name of the one-stringed bowed fiddle (959)

lelekanje A Montenegrin men's lament, known in Albanian as *thirrje vaji* (958)

lergøg A version of the Danish vessel flute or clay pipe, also the clay cuckoo (456)

lesavyja piesni Belarusan forest songs (792)

leśna 'Of the forest': a genre of open-air song of the Kurpie region of Poland (113)

leśne 'Forest songs': slow melismatic songs, sung in open woods and fields, of the Kurpie region of Poland (703)

lesno oro 'Easy dance': a common Macedonian dance in 2/4 and 7/8 time; also *pravo oro* (978)

leteuve yered An Adighian song for a child's first independent step (856)

letzim Jewish musical professionals, especially instrumentalists (251, 259)

lev'dd The primary music genre of the Skolts, a Saami people of eastern Finland (486, 487, 488)

lezginka An Ossetian couple dance; see *tim-bil-kaft* (861)

lidovky Czech and Slovak folk music presented in a popular format (730)

Lieder der Bewegung German songs of the [Nazi] movement (664)

Liederschulen German song schools in Berlin, Leipzig, and Swabia (653)

Liederspiele 'Song plays': a folkloric German musical theater with spoken parts alternating with folkloric song (141, 653)

liedertafel A German military male choir (655)

liedmessen German sung **masses** (655)

lier (also *draailier*) A hurdy-gurdy of the Low Countries (532)

ligawka A long wooden trumpet of Mazovia, Poland (704)

līgotnes A Latvian vocal genre connected with *Jāņi*, the midsummer-solstice celebration (501)

lijerica A Croatian three-stringed, pear-shaped bowed **lute** (929)

lile A song of Svaneti, Georgia, connected with the cult of the sun (835)

limena glazba A brass band of Istria, Croatia (931)

lindo A dance of the Dalmatia region of Croatia and Hercegovina (929, 934, 966) *ling* A Chinese small bell (837)

ling dzo A Chinese gong (837)

lini A Georgian pair of copper plates, found in archaeological excavations of the fourth century; also *tsintsila* (837)

lira A Belarusan hurdy-gurdy, also *rela* and *kobza* 796; a Ukrainian hurdy-gurdy (813, *815*)

lira A three-stringed bowed **lute** of the Balkans, especially the central Dinaric Mountains, and of Calabria; see *lirica* and *lyra* (168, 615)

lirica A three-stringed bowed **lute** of Bosnia-Hercegovina; see *lira* (966)

lirnici Ukrainian professional, often blind minstrels (143)

lirnyky Ukrainian blind peasant minstrels who played the *lira;* see *kobzari* (143, 809, 813–16, 820, 821)

liscio Northern Italian songs to accompany rural dances (207)

literátska bratrstva Czech and Slovak literary fraternities of the Hussite era (1400s and 1500s), which formed male choirs (726)

liturgy A rite prescribed for religious worship, often associated with particular types of music (5, 70, 74, 75, 100, 145)

lituus An Etruscan and Roman horn that emerged during the first millennium B.C. (40, 41)

lituus alpinus 'Alpine *lituus*': the Latin name of the Swiss **alphorn** (688)

lityerse Reapers' work songs of French-speaking Switzerland (693)

livret de colportage Small French **chapbook**s of song texts (549)

llautë An Albanian large, pear-shaped fretted plucked **lute** (993, 997, 1000)

llofft-stabal 'Stable loft': the informal entertainment of Welsh farmhands quartered in stables (348, 353)

lnovyja Belarusan songs sung during the flax harvest (792)

löckler Swiss melismatic, nonmetrical solo calls (683)

lockrop Swedish melismatic herding calls (*438*)

lodër (also *lodërti*) An Albanian two-headed bass drum; also *daulle* and *tupan* (996, 1001)

lokarina A Bulgarian clay globular flute with eight finger holes and two thumb holes (892)

loki djili Vlach Rom slow songs (275)

lolling A vocal imitation of the *hardanger* violin in Norway; also *sulling, tralling,* and *tulling* (107, 421)

lolote An Ossetian monophonic women's lullaby (861)

long meter An English quatrain of eight-syllable (or four-stress) lines, of which the second and fourth lines often rhyme (328)

longa An Ottoman light classical genre, played by Rom musicians in Macedonia (979)

lowland bagpipe A bellows-blown bagpipe of the Scottish Lowlands with a chanter and three drones (366)

lubok 'Chapbook': a book of Russian folk songs (755)

luck visit Seasonal rituals in which singers, sometimes masked, visit houses and sing songs of well-wishing in exchange for small gifts (139–40)

luhovyja pieśni Belarusan meadow songs (792)

lulling A Norwegian vocal genre that uses mnemonic syllables for singing fiddle pieces; also *sulling, tralling,* and *tulling* (421)

lumpovanje 'Carousing': drinking, talking, and singing by prosperous young men in Serbian cafés (952)

lundum A Brazilian dance and vocal genre of African origin taken to Portugal (583)

luohti A North Saami **joik** (*301*)

lur An instrument mentioned in ancient Nordic literature (*lúður* in Old Norse), now used to denote long trumpets, especially a Swedish bronze horn (36, 39–41, 146, 420, 422–23, 438, 439, 456, 463)

lute A plucked stringed instrument having a pear-shaped body, a usually fretted fingerboard, and a head with tuning pegs often angled backward from the neck; see **bouzouki**, *lira,* and *tamburica* (51, 75–76, *103*, *104*, 130, *176*, 200, 281, 283, 284, 366, 373, 406, 420, 422, 528, 594, 600, 615, 632, 654, 656, 687, 696, 727, 768, 863, *893*, 917, 926, 945, 959, *961*, 963, 965–66, 979, 981, 983, 993, 997, 1013, 1023, 1025, 1030)

lutherie French instrument making; see *facture* (542)

lydarslåttar Norwegian pieces for listening, played in early evenings, when *sæter* women did their weaving and embroidering (415)

lyóba por la rindja 'Calling-song for the descent': a song sung by herdsmen bringing their cattle down from alpine pastures in Haute-Gruyère, Switzerland (119)

lyra A pear-shaped three-stringed bowed **lute** common in Greece and Crete; see *kemenje* (118, 130, *179*, 929, 1009, 1011, 1015, 1018, 1023, 1025, 1031)

lyre An ancient Greek chordophone having a soundbox made of a tortoiseshell or a shaped wooden frame and covered by ox hide (39, 40, 46, 47, 366, 406, *485*, 601, 839)

lyric songs Songs suitable for singing to the **lyre**: generally nonnarrative songs, often expressing emotions or describing the ritual action they accompany (132–34, 194, 278, 296, 329, 365, 379–80, 452, 492, 581, 605, 606–609, 611, 616, 694, 721, 737, 761, 765–68, 772, 792, 821, 833, 841, 858, 959, 966, 968, 987)

łyžki Belarusan spoons (797)

maa A Chechen and Ingush horn (863)

maclotte 'Sailor's dance': a dance in 2/4 or 6/8 time of Liège and Luxembourg; see *madlot* and *matelotte* (524)

madlot 'Sailor's dance': a dance in 6/8 time of Friesland; see *maclotte* and *matelotte* (524)

madrigal In European art music, any of several types of usually unaccompanied vocal polyphony employed especially in the **Renaissance** and most often set to secular Italian poetry (75–76, 570, 617)

madrigali Italian songs preserved in Corsica, sung in three parts with the leading voice (*secunda*) in the middle (570)

magadis An ancient Greek **harp**, commonly played by women (47)

maggi a serenata Love songs in the Italian *maggio drammatico* (608)

maggio The May ritual (140, 607, 608, 614)

maggio drammatico 'Dramatic May': a drama staged during the Italian *maggio* that treats the life of a saint or a historic hero (608)

magnitizdat' Russian term for cassette tapes (767, 778)

magyar nóta 'Hungarian song': any of numerous songs composed by nineteenth-century Hungarian urban middle-class amateurs, but also known by peasants (738, 745, 747)

mahadjiri-ashva Abkhazian nostalgic migrant songs, performed during traditional feasts (853)

maitinade An Italian song typical of Trent, composed of quatrains or six-line stanzas of eleven-syllable lines, part of the *canzoni a ballo* genre; see *polesane* (606, 607, 614)

maje krahi 'Of the ear': an Albanian men's musical genre of Montenegro (958)

mak'-ye-ups Songs invented by Scottish Lowland Travellers (296)

makam An Ottoman Turkish melodic **mode**, still used in parts of the Balkans and North Caucasia; compare *maqam* and *mugam* (200, 281, 282, 856, 951, 979, 994, 996, 997, 1023)

makkjetta 'Comic sketch': a Maltese genre bridging folk and popular music (638, 642)

makossa A Cameroonian popular urban musical genre, popular in France (238)

mál The Icelandic concept of speech, which in ancient times included forms of musical performance (405)

mal orkestar 'Little orchestra': an ensemble for Macedonian radio, consisting of clarinet, accordion, and other manufactured instruments (981)

malá selká muzika A Czech band consisting of a violin, a clarinet, and a bagpipe (719)

male cimbale A Slovene trapezoidal struck zither; also *brana, cimprekelj, oprekelj,* and *pretl* (916–17)

malhão A Portuguese duple-meter circle dance of the western coast from the north to central Portugal (581)

mane Free-rhythmic improvisation in Macedonian music (281, 282)

manea A highly ornamented dance and musical form of urban Romanian Rom (278)

mani khavesi Turkish cafés where music was performed (1014) *manikarka* A Lithuanian one-stringed cello, used in church (511)

maniler Turkish songs about love of Macedonia (983)

mantinadhes A Greek genre of improvised, rhyming couplets, from Crete and other Greek islands (118–20, 1015, 1025)

maqam Arabic **modes** that influenced some Spanish music; compare *makam* and *mugam* (20, 590, 593, 968)

march A musical composition usually in duple time with a strongly stressed beat suitable for marching (9, 81, 235, 330, 363, 441, 523, 524, 545, 547, 580, 656, 659, 660, 661, 672, 776, 779, 799, 818, 881, 903, 946, 979); an Irish dance in 2/4 time, adopted from abroad (382)

marcia 'March': a Corsican dance (571)

Mari Lwyd 'Gray Mare': a Welsh seasonal festival (140, 342)

Mariamoba The Georgian celebration of the death of Saint Mary, performed in August and centered on the theme of motherhood (835)

marko **band** A Slovenian vocal-instrumental ensemble (920–21)

marranzanu A Sicilian **mouth harp**; see *scacciapensieri* (615)

martellu A Corsican wooden scraper (572)

Martinshorn A German automobile horn, adapted and used in wind bands during the Weimar Republic (1919–1933) (659)

maryna In Great Poland, a bowed instrument played as a percussion instrument by striking its leg against the floor (706, 707)

masa mare 'The grand feast': part of the Romanian wedding ritual, accompanied by specific songs or instrumental tunes (871)

Masleničnyja pieśni A Belarusan spring song cycle performed the day after Ash Wednesday, mainly on swings (791)

maslenitsa Shrovetide songs, sung at carnival in Russia (759, *760*)

masque A short allegorical drama, enacted by masked actors, often with music and dance, especially in the 1500s and 1600s (160)

Mass The liturgy of the Eucharist, especially that of the Roman Catholic Church and other apostolic churches; in European art music, a composition whose text is that of the Ordinary, the invariant portion of the service (75–77, 84, 366)

mastušij rožok A Belarusan horn (*797*)

matelotte 'Sailor's dance': a French dance, introduced into the Low Countries in the late 1700s; see *maclotte* and *madlot* (524)

matenik 'Muddle' (Czech): a couple dance of Central Europe, alternating duple and triple meter (166)

mazanki A small figure-eight-shaped fiddle of western Poland (706)

mazurek 'Mazurka': a Polish folk dance (708)

mazurka A popular nineteenth-century European couple dance in moderate 3/4 or 3/8 time (7, 166, 168, 419, 443, 457, 477, 527, 559, 571, 690, 694, 696, 703, 708, *710*, 711)

me gisht në fyt 'With finger on the throat': an Albanian girls' singing style, in which each singer vibrates her larynx with her right thumb to alter vocal **timbre** (995)

me të qarë 'With crying': an Albanian lament or stylized form of crying (990, 993)

mehterhana Turkish military ensembles, influential in Balkan music (881, 967)

melisma The use of more than one note per syllable of vocal text (70, 98, 106, 328, 345, 350, 381, 404, 414, 436, 438, 487, 519, 570, 581, 589, 591, 593, 598, 604, *612*, 629, 636, 637, 650, 703, 711, 719, 833, 896, 927, 942, 958, 959, 964, 968, 1013)

melodeon A button accordion introduced especially in English and Irish music in the mid-nineteenth century (331, 385)

meraklis A performer of *mantinadhes* in ritual celebrations on some Greek islands (118)

mēslu talka The Latvian ritual of spreading manure on fields, often accompanied by the playing of goat horns (503)

mestvire A Georgian performer of *stviri* (*840*)

metelytsia A Ukrainian dance (812)

mexhelis Albanian men's gatherings; see *muabet* (118)

meyasu Japanese neumatic notation, set in vertical columns read from left to right (103)

Middle Ages In European history, the period from the end of the Western Roman Empire (A.D. 476) to the start of the **Renaissance** (early fifteenth century) (53, 54, 69–73, 127, 265, 366, 378, 383, 443, 470, 481, 518, 533, 540, 560, 600, 617, 647, 650–52, 655, 656, 664, 726, 890, 914, 915–17, 919, 925, 960)

midwinterhoorn A long Dutch traditional trumpet, used for seasonal customs (41, 527)

mikrasiatika Songs of Asia Minor, imported to Cyprus (1030)

Minnesängerharfe A hand **harp** used to accompany singing in Germany in the **Middle Ages** (651)

minuet A graceful, mainly eighteenth-century dance in slow 3/4 time, in which performers bow, point their toes, and move to describe S- or Z-shaped floor-patterns; music for or in the style of such a dance (168, 170, 454, 457, 524, 594)

minuetto 'Minuet': a Corsican dance piece (572)

miroloyia Greek laments for the dead, either instrumental or sung by women (9, 1010, (1014, 1025)

mishnicë An Albanian bagpipe (996)

mišnice A Croatian aerophone with two single-reed pipes (930)

missa 'Mass' (Latin): a Portuguese sung **Mass** in church (579)

mješnice A Croatian bagpipe; also *diple s mijehom* (928)

moda 'Fashion' (Portuguese): a metered unaccompanied polyphonic **strophic song** sung by persons of either sex in any of various contexts (578, 579, 581)

mode In European music, a category of musical compositions defined principally by scale and final note; **Gregorian chant** and **Renaissance** polyphony employed eight modes, a number reduced to two—major and minor—in later, tonal music (69, 258, 327–29, 344, 350, 367, 378, 414, 426, 435, 453, 477, 482, 492, 510, 520, 529, 533–34, 542, 581, 589, 593, 610, 637, 652, 659, 660–61, 671, 703, 719, 721–22, 741, 755, 779, 783, 809, 846, 854, 856, 859, 874, 882, 912, 951, 964, 979, 994, 1007, 1013, 1018, 1020, 1022–23, 1029)

moderna 'Modern': a movement in Slovak music of the 1930s, in which composers utilized folk songs in their compositions (729)

modinha A genre of Portuguese and Brazilian salon art song popular from the mid-1700s to the mid-1800s (583, 619)

modzakhili 'Follower': the high second voice of Georgian three-part singing (828)

moezel(zak) A bagpipe of the Low Countries (528–29)

momačko kolo A showy young men's dance of the Bunjevci minority in Vojvodina, Serbia (953)

mondharp A **mouth harp** of the Low Countries; also *mondtrom* (526)

monferina An Italian dance preserved in Corsica; compare *monferrina* and *monfrina* (571)

monferrina An Italian dance once popular in northeastern Italy and Piedmont; compare *monferina* and *monfrina* (609)

monfrina A dance in 6/8 time of Ticino, Switzerland, originally of Monferrato in the Italian province of Piedmont; compare *monferina* and *monferrina* (696)

monody A monophonic vocal piece; in folksinging performance style, always unaccompanied (520, 523, 607, 794, 882)

morris dance A vigorous central and southern English dance, performed by costumed men wearing bells (*329*, 331, 338, 523)

most 'Bridge': a Bulgarian game similar to "London Bridge Is Falling Down" (900)

motet In European art music, any of several distinct types of polyphonic composition: a variety of sacred or secular medieval work, in which multiple voices simultaneously sing different verbal texts; a sacred work of the **Renaissance** and later, employing several voices that sing a single text not drawn from the Ordinary of the **Mass** (71, 75, 76, 77, 366, 654, 727)

mousikē The Greek term for the arts presided over by the Muses, including music, poetry, and dance (48, 1022–23)

mouth harp A small, U-shaped metal brace with a single vibrating metal tongue, whose overtones are resonated in the buccal cavity; commonly but inexplicably known as Jew's harp (143, 169, *170*, 366, 420, 435, 526, 609, 615, 627, 651, 654, 656, 743, 816)

mouth organ A blown free-reed instrument that produces different pitches on a given key or hole, depending on whether air is pushed or pulled past the reeds; known as the French fiddle in Ireland and the harmonica in the United States (330, 331, 355, 385, 530, 547, 919)

mtiuluri An Eastern Georgian mountain dance (836)

mtskobri A Georgian military ensemble of **bukis** (840)

muabet Albanian men's gatherings; see **mexhelis** (118)

muchafou (also *muchosa*) A bagpipe of the Low Countries (529)

műdal 'Art song': vocal music composed mainly by nineteenth-century Hungarian urban middle-class amateurs (738)

mugam A Middle Eastern modal concept in North Caucasia; compare **makam** and **maqam** (856)

mulatshagos Vlach Rom drinking and singing celebrations (275)

mulatteru A Corsican mule-driver, who sang songs with a long-drawn-out call-like quality (567)

Mundäoline An accordion invented in Berlin by F. Buschmann in 1821, later called the **concertina** (657)

mundharp A Norwegian **mouth harp** (420)

mungiga A Swedish **mouth harp** (439)

murkvamoba-kviriaoba A Svanetian fertility ceremony that retains elements of an ancient phallic cult (834)

musette A French bagpipe (169, 545, 547)

musica lăutarească Urban Rom music of southern Romania (277–78)

musica leggera 'Light music' (Italian): locally produced Italian popular songs (204)

musiikki The Finnish term for music beginning in the early twentieth century (480)

musiikkiopisto A Finnish music college (482)

musique à bouche French mouth music, played on the harmonica (545, 547)

musique de collectage French field recordings (551)

musique ethnographique French traditional music (549, 551)

musique métissée 'Half-caste music' (French): acculturated, pop-folk music (551)

musique résidu 'Residual music' (French): "remnant" music, surviving from earlier times (551)

musique savante 'Learned music' (French): classical music (543)

muška 'Male': distinguishing men's singing styles in genres sung by men and women in Bosnia-Hercegovina (964)

musta-guduchg A Chechen ritual intended to control the weather, dedicated to Sela, the goddess of thunder and lightning (864)

mutettu A poetic form, usually about love, in the Sardinian *a tenore* repertoire; also *mutu* (627)

muwashshah A vocal genre of Muslim Andalucía (265)

muzica orientala A late-twentieth-century genre popular among Romanian Rom (279)

muzika An instrumental ensemble of Istria, Croatia; also **gunci, gunjci,** and **violine** (931)

muzyka (accent on *u*) A Ukrainian term for music (812)

muzyka (accent on *y*) A Ukrainian village term for a trio (812)

muzyki A Belarusan traditional folk instrumental ensemble; also **hurtkampaniya, kapela, skamarochi,** and **viasielnyja muzyki** (798)

na ariju 'On a melody': a Serbian melodic style in which the lower voice sings in parallel thirds with the melody and forms a perfect fifth at the cadence; also **basiranje** and **na bas** (942)

na bas 'On a bass': a singing style of the Dinaric Alps and Pannonian regions of Croatia and Serbia; also **bas, basiranje, bećarac,** and **na ariju** (927, 928, 931–32, 942–43, *944*, 949–50, 952, 953, 964)

na filek Bulgarian songs for games played during Lent (900–901)

na glas A Serbian singing style employing two-part polyphony in which the interval of a second predominates (942, *943*, 944)

na pŭt 'On the road': a Bulgarian term to label songs sung while walking from a village to the fields and back (*897*)

na štrtko Five-part Slovene singing (913)

na trapeza 'At the table': Bulgarian nonmetrical songs, originally sung around a table while eating and drinking (114, 897, 901)

na tretro Slovenian four-part singing (913)

na viankach The Belarusan bridal fair the day before the wedding, when the girls gather accompanied by ritual songs; also **dziavočnik** and **subornaja subota** (793)

na vole 'With freedom, without walls': a Russian style of singing with an open, loud sound (765)

na voli 'Singing freely' (Belarusan): see **halasnoha śpievu** (793)

nacchere A Corsican kettledrum used in the Good Friday procession in Erbalunga, on Cape Corse, also **cassella** and **paghjolu**; a large **frame drum** played with a pair of sticks and used to accompany certain dances like the *tarasco* (*tarascona*) (572)

nachttrichjer A clapper bell of Fiesch, Valais, Switzerland (683)

naduri Four-part harvest songs of Guria and Achara, Georgia (828, *829*, 833)

nagara An Armenian set of skin-covered clay pots; see **diplipito** (838)

nai A Romanian panpipe (277, 872, 878)

naigryt́ 'Dance until you drop' (Russian): instrumental ostinato dance tunes, used to accompany **pliasky** (769)

nana A Georgian ritual lullaby sung a few days after a birth by the mother to protect her infant (835)

nanarismata Greek lullabies (1015)

napevky Czech and Slovak brief melodic and rhythmic fragments, repeated to create a kind of musical mosaic (728)

naprej 'Forward': the middle-range leading voice in Slovene three-part singing (913)

naricanje Slovene laments (911)

naroden orkestar 'Folk orchestra': a Macedonian village instrumental ensemble that plays for Macedonian radio (981, *982*)

narodna muzika 'Folk music, national music, popular music': a broadly generic term in Slavic-speaking Balkan countries (948, 962–63, 981, 983)

narodna orchestra A modern folk orchestra of Serbia (949)

narodna umotvorina 'Folk creation, folklore' (Serbo-Croatian) (953)

narodni muzychny instrumenty Soviet-period Ukrainian folk-musical instruments (816–18)

narodni orkestar The folk orchestra of Bosnia-Hercegovina (968)

narodni orkestri Bulgarian orchestras of folk instruments (892)

narodni pesni 'Folk songs' in Macedonia (974)

narodnjaci Players of newly composed folk music in Serbia (949)

narodno-zabavni ansambli Slovene folk-popular bands (920)

narodnosť 'Nationality, peopleness, national identity': a concept used in the mid-1960s by young Russian composers who turned to Russian folk music for inspiration (782, 1000)

nart Any of several North Caucasian **epic** heroes (851, 859–60, 864)

Nart-Orkurst A Chechen and Ingush **epic** genre (864)

narton simd '*Simd* of Nart': an Ossetian dance in two sections (861)

naturjodel 'Natural yodel' (German): the natural sharpening of the eleventh partial in the overtone series of open tubes (688)

navel (also *nevel*) A biblical instrument cited in various texts written over a period of some seven hundred years, but no specimen exists (36)

nawbah The Arabic source of the Albanian **nibet** (996)

nazm Chechen and Ingush funeral prayers; see **zikr** (864)

neodhimotika Greek new popular versions of folk songs (1017)

népies műdal 'Folklike art song': music composed mainly by nineteenth-century Hungarian urban middle-class amateurs (738)

nestinarstvo A Bulgarian fire-walking ritual, accompanied by **gajda** and **tŭpan** (897)

nevestinsko oro 'Bride's dance': a Macedonian women's dance (978)

nibet In Albania, a sequence of musical genres that includes nonmetric improvisations, song tunes, and instrumental pieces (996)

niggun A textless song genre with vocables that first appeared among Hasidic Jews in

Poland and Ukraine during the 1700s (254, *255*)

ninna-nanna Corsican lullabies sung in a lamentlike mood and style (567)

ninulla Albanian lullabies (988)

nisiotika Songs of the Greek islands (1009, 1014–15, 1018, 1030)

noaidi A Saami shaman who uses **joiks** to induce a trance state in himself (304)

nodas The thematic formulas in a Sardinian ***sonata***; also ***pikkiadas*** (630)

noëls French Christmas carols (542, 546)

nomos aulodikos A solo instrumental piece for the ***aulos*** (46)

nomos kitharodikos A solo instrumental piece for the ***kithara*** (46)

nonstrophic songs Songs in which text and music lack the formal conventions of **strophic songs** (127–31)

noordse balk A plucked dulcimer of the Low Countries (533)

Northumbrian small-pipes A bellows-blown bagpipe of Northern England (*331*)

nóta Hungarian popular art song, disseminated largely by Gypsies (273)

notation Any system of written signs (49–56, 68, 70–71, 90–109)

noviny A Soviet-period genre of new songs celebrating Soviet life (130)

novokomponirane narodne pjesme 'Newly composed folk songs' of Croatia and Bosnia-Hercegovina (934–36, 969, 980)

novokomponovana narodna muzika 'Newly composed folk music' of the former Yugoslavia (279, 948)

nueva canción andaluza 'New Andalusian song': popular music of southern Spain (204, 205)

nuevo flamenco 'New flamenco': a fusion of **flamenco** with other styles of music since the 1960s (226, 599)

nunalca A Slovene children's whistle made of thick reeds (919)

nünichlingler A clapper bell of Ziefen, Baselland, Switzerland (683)

nunnie Children's nurses' work songs of French-speaking Switzerland; also ***catabaucalise*** (693)

nusah An Ashkenazic Jewish form of sung prayer (253)

nüssler Traditional Swiss maskers in winter festivals before carnival (684)

nuta 'Note': a harmonic structure central to the music of Podhale, Poland (705, 707, *708*)

nyckelharpa A Swedish keyed, bowed fiddle (170, 439, *440*)

nystev 'New stanza': a Norwegian musical genre in which each of four lines consists of four stressed syllables, and an end rhyme links the first two and the last two lines; see ***stev*** (134, 413, *414*)

oberek Dance music in the "new style" in central and eastern Poland (122, *704*, 708, 710)

obkrocák A duple-meter Bohemian couple dance (721)

ocarina A usually earthenware duct flute, with an oval body and holes for fingering (176, 528, 616, 743, *797*, 816, 917)

ojkanje 'Singing with *oj*': a Bosnia-Hercegovinan and Croatian vocal technique in which singers perform an emphatic exclamatory section on the syllable *oj* (927, *928*, 963)

okarina An Eastern European and Balkan **ocarina** (816, 915, 917)

olimpiady A Soviet-era Ukrainian musical Olympics, at which ensembles competed in a highly virtuosic style (818)

ommegang A pageant with music of Dendermonde, Oost-Vlaanderen Province, Low Countries (525)

onai An Ossetian women's polyphonic song that accompanied the making of traditional clothing (861)

open-en-toe An accordion of the Low Countries (530)

opera In European art music since the **Baroque**, a compositional genre consisting of a lengthy dramatic text (often in verse) largely or entirely sung with orchestral accompaniment, usually in large theaters with elaborate costumes, staging, and action, including dance (77, 79–84, 95, 97, 160–61, 184, *187*, 188, 199, 205, 215, 219, 235, 274, 368, 369, 370, 444, 601, 604, 617–18, 642–43, 659, 728, 729, 746–47, 759, 780–81, 799, 842, 843, 881, 890, 904–905, 921, 933, 1008)

opéra-ballet A genre introduced in France at the end of the seventeenth century that told dramatic stories in a series of dances (161)

opéra-comique A French operatic genre on light or sentimental subjects, with happy endings and usually until the mid-1800s spoken dialogue (534, 728)

operismo Spanish **flamenco** opera (597–98)

oplakvane Bulgarian lamenting (901)

oprekelj A Slovene trapezoidal struck zither; also ***brana, cimprekelj, male cimbale,*** and ***pretl*** (916)

orchestre champêtre An orchestra featuring an accordion of the French-speaking area of Switzerland (693)

organ A wind instrument equipped with one or more keyboards that control one or more sets of pipes, each possessing a distinctive pitch and **timbre**; used principally in churches for the performance of sacred polyphony (69, *74*, 75, 226, 258, 440, 447, 649, 654, 692, 727)

organetto An Italian small diatonic button accordion (608, 609, *610, 614*)

organum (pl. organa) Liturgical vocal polyphony employed in Western Europe during the central **Middle Ages**, roughly A.D. 900 to 1300 (71, 403, 543)

orgni A Maltese term for the **harmonica**, the **concertina**, the portable harmonium, and the hurdy-gurdy (640)

original appenzeller striichmusig 'Original Appenzell string band': a Swiss band with

two violins, a cello, a dulcimer, and a bowed double bass (690, *691*, 696, 698)

oro A Macedonian, Montenegrin, and Serbian circle dance (947, 958, 978)

orologio della passione An Italian begging song of central Italy performed the week before Easter; also called ***canto della passione*** (608)

orovela Georgian solo male songs of plowing, threshing, and winnowing (828)

orvuolle A South Saami joik (*301*)

oss A hobbyhorse that dances to the accompaniment of melodeons and drums at Padstow in Cornwall, England (331)

ottava rima 'Eighth rhyme' (Italian): a stanza of eight lines rhyming *ababab cc* (607)

outi A Greek bent-necked, unfretted plucked **lute** (285, 1013, 1019, 1021)

ovsenki A refrain of a ***koliada***, sung during winter rituals in Russia (758)

oxen songs Welsh songs that plowboys sing to oxen to keep them calm (344)

oxote Basque choral music with eight male voices singing a cappella (315)

ožragis A Lithuanian goat horn with four or five holes for fingering (511)

ozyn-kyi Tatar long-drawn-out **lyric songs** (773)

päämies The lead singer in Finnish ***runonlaulu*** (114)

pach-pi A Breton figure dance; compare ***passepied*** (559)

pachavalnyja halašeńni Belarusan funeral laments (794)

paghjella A Corsican polyphonic form sung in church with sacred texts and on social occasions with secular texts (542, 566, *569, 570*, 573)

paghjolu A Corsican kettledrum used in the Good Friday procession in Erbalunga, on Cape Corse; a large **frame drum** played with a pair of sticks to accompany certain dances, including the *tarasco* (*tarascona*); also ***cassella*** and ***nacchere*** (572)

pajupill (also ***vilepill***) An Estonian willow flute with duct but without holes for fingering (494)

palavyja pieśni Belarusan field songs (792)

palmas Claps used for rhythmic accompaniment in **flamenco** (597, 598)

palo seco A stick used for rhythmic accompaniment in **flamenco** (597)

palos 'Forms': the three main types of song for **flamenco**: ***cante chico, cante intermedio,*** and ***cante jondo*** (5970)

palos siguiriyas A ***cante jondo*** based on a complex, twelve-beat rhythmic structure; see ***soleá*** (597)

pancharzyna A bagpipe for beginners in western Poland; also ***siersześki*** and *siesieśki* (707)

pandeiro (also *pandeireta*) A Portuguese round **frame drum** with metal jingles (582)

pandero A Basque, Spanish, and Bosnian Sephardic **frame drum** (314, 968) *panduri* A Georgian medium-sized long-necked three-stringed fretted **lute** (*8*, *833*, 838, 840–41, 845, 853, 859)

paniyiri A Greek saint's day celebration (1015, 1016)

paparuda 'Rain-caller': a Romanian rain-begging ritual (194, 278, 870)

paradiddle An onomatopoeic word used by percussionists to designate a quick succession of beats, alternating left- and right-hand strokes typically in the pattern L-R-L-L, R-L-R-R (*108*)

paralimnitiki 'Of Paralimni village': a tune type of the Cypriot *tsiattista* genre (1030)

pardon A Breton annual religious festival (562)

parea In a Greek chain dance, a group of friends who have requested and paid the musicians for the dance (165)

parlando rubato 'Robbed speaking': a singing style with a speechlike, variable beat (134, 275, 380, 520, *540*, 610, 718–19, 721, 740–41, 742)

párosító 'Pairing songs': a type of Hungarian folk song (739)

particello A score showing only the most important voices (51)

pas de deux 'Step for two' (French): in classical **ballet**, a dance for two performers, usually a male and a female (161)

pasbišča pieśni Belarusan pasture songs (792)

passe-pied A lively dance in quick 3/8 or 6/8 time, especially popular in the early 1700s; a country dance popular in Luxembourg; compare **pach-pi** (524)

passu torrau A form of the Sardinian *danza,* based on a six-note rhythmic pattern (631)

pastorale A Basque play accompanied by songs and dances and supposedly descended from late medieval mystery plays dating since the 1500s (314–15)

pastourelles Pastoral songs of French-speaking Switzerland (693)

patinadha A Greek genre of improvised, rhyming couplets of Chios (1025)

pečalbarski pesni 'Songs of workers abroad': songs mourning Macedonian village men who work in cities or abroad (973)

peditório A Portuguese religious festival in which a band performs marches in front of each house in a village; also *arruada* and *recolha de andores* (579, *580*)

pehlivan In Albania, a Turkish-style wrestling match, accompanied by music (997)

pelqesë A double-bore duct flute of Albanians in Macedonia and Kosova; also *binjak* (996)

pemptos The fifth movement of the Cypriot *kartzilamades* dance cycle, performed in 2/4, 3/4, or 7/8 time (1030)

peñas Small Spanish **flamenco** clubs (598)

penna A **plectrum** used with the Corsican *cetera* (572)

pentozali An acrobatic dance of Crete; also *pidhiktos* (1015)

peperona A rain-begging ritual, performed by Albanian children in the late spring or early summer of a dry year; also *dordolec* (988)

peperuda 'Butterfly': a Bulgarian rain-begging ritual, performed as needed during spring and summer droughts (*151*, 161, 900–901)

perepelka A Ukrainian musical game, played only on the day after Easter by girls of a given *kutok* (808)

perkhisa A Georgian suite of line dances in which some dancers may stand on others' shoulders (836)

perkhuli A Georgian circle dance, considered the most archaic Georgian dance 836

pero Slovene leaf whistles (915)

pesenniki Published Russian songbooks (766, 776)

pesennost' 'Songness': a Russian musicological concept developed by Boris Asaf'ev (783)

pesnopojki **Chapbook**s of urban songs published outside Bulgaria during the mid-1800s (903)

peşrev An Ottoman light-classical genre, played by Rom musicians in Macedonia (979, 997)

pevačka društva Serbian singing societies (948)

piano A European keyboard instrument having wire strings that sound when struck by small, felt-covered hammers attached to the keys; popular since the late eighteenth century (82, 83, *85*, 99, 200, 206, 273, 331, 353, 355, 365, 367, 422, 424, 426, 494, 574, 649, 655, 710, 712, 725, 728, 732, 737, 756, 776, 781, 953)

pibau Welsh pipes, a main traditional instrument of medieval and **renaissance** Wales (348)

pibau cod Welsh bagpipes popular, from the 1600s to the early 1800s (348)

pibgorn A Welsh single-reed hornpipe with a cow-horn bell and wood or bone barrels pierced by seven holes for fingering (348, 355–56)

pibroch English for Scottish *piobaireachd* (363, 368, 374)

pichel A local name of the **alphorn** in Uri, Switzerland (688)

picotage In France, the constant alternation of a low note with a melody by a solo instrumentalist to produce a drone effect (*543*)

pidhiktos An acrobatic dance of Crete; also *pentozali* (1015)

pidkiavali A Cypriot single-reed cylindrical cane aerophone, played by shepherds (1031)

piffero An Italian double-reed aerophone, played in sets of two or three (616)

pignatu A Corsican friction drum (572)

pijper(s)fluit A side-blown flute of the Low Countries (528)

pijpzak A bagpipe of the Low Countries (528–29)

pikkiadas Thematic formulas in a Sardinian *sonata;* also *nodas* (630)

Pilipaŭskija pieśni Belarusan ancient **epic** and lyrical songs performed during Advent (792)

pilli A Finnish single-reed pipe (478)

pinna A Maltese guitar pick (639)

piobaireachd The classical Scottish piping tradition; see **pibroch** (98, 106, 363, 367, 368)

píopaî Early Irish bagpipes (384)

pipes An abbreviated term for the Irish bellows-blown *uilleann* **pipes** (383, 384, 385)

pipezë An Albanian single-reed cane pipe (993)

pipiza A Greek double-reed shawm (280, 1009)

pipsac A bagpipe of the Low Countries (529)

pirula A Corsican long, thin, reed flute having three to six holes for fingering; also *fischju* (571, 573)

piščyki Belarusan reed aerophones (797)

pishchik A Russian single-reed aerophone with one or two pipes with a horn bell; also *zhaleika* (770)

pismatiko Improvised rhyming couplets of Rhodes, Greece (1025)

pismice 'Small songs': a song type common in Slavonia; also *pjesmice* (931)

písničkáři Czech and Slovak popular folk singers (730)

pištik A Belarusan reed pipe (*797*)

piszczałka A duct flute with a double pipe of the Carpathian area of Poland (704)

pitos Finger snaps used for rhythmic accompaniment in Spanish **flamenco** (598)

piva A northern Italian and Italian-Swiss bagpipe (616, 694)

pivačka tambura 'Singer's tambura': a long-necked two-stringed plucked **lute** 965–66

pivana A Corsican cow- or goat-horn duct flute with six holes for fingering (572)

pive A double-chanter bagpipe played by the Italian minority in Istria, Croatia (930)

piv-i-røv-hest A Danish vessel flute or clay pipe, also a squeaky-bum horse (456)

piyyutim Nonliturgical sacred Jewish hymns (253–54, 257)

pizhatka A Russian duct flute with five or six holes for fingering; also *dudka* and *sopel* (770)

pizmon A Jewish song genre in which preexisting texts, particularly those for important holidays, are provided with variant musical settings (*255*)

pjesme u kolu Songs sung while dancing the *kolo* in Bosnia-Hercegovina (963)

pjesmice 'Small songs': songs common in Slavonia; also *pismice* (931)

pjevanje uz bešiku 'Singing beside the cradle': in Bosnia-Hercegovina (963)

pkhachich An Adighian rattle, used for dance accompaniment (855)

plastinky A Russian term for phonograph records (777)

plectrum A pick (414, 533, 572, 611, 658, 893)

pliasky Russian solo dances (769)

pliasovoi khorovod A Russian dance with solo dancers inside a circle of singers who step lightly in place (768)

plonarca A two-row diatonic accordion of west Slovenia (918)

plow-whistles A rare category of Irish traditional songs with mostly descending melodies (379)

plugarul 'The plowman': a Romanian festival with music to honor the first farmer to plow his fields; also *pluguşorul* (869, 870)

plygain Welsh carols associated with the winter solstice (343–44, 346, 349–350, *351*)

po-skomorosh'i 'Like a minstrel': a west Russian style of playing the violin (771)

pod draku 'At a fight': a west Russian subgenre of **chastushki**, sung as men engage in fisticuffs (768)

pod iazyk 'Under the tongue': how Russian singers perform instrumental accompaniments in the absence of instruments (768)

podbliudnye pesni 'Fortune-telling songs': Russian songs sung during winter rituals (759, 760)

podkorak 'Lined with the step': a Bosnia-Hercegovinian vocal style in which the rhythm of songs is based on the rhythm of body movement (964)

podruznik A genre of the Lubelskie region of Poland, often played to accompany a wedding procession (113)

podvodka Central Russian polyphonic vocal music, with a lower voice and an improvised descant (757, 773)

poeti a braccio Italian singers of **lyric songs**, such as ***stornelli***, who improvise song texts (611)

poietarides Professional Cypriot poet-singers (1030, 1032)

poietarikes The melodic type for poems of the Cypriot *poietarides* (1030)

poiushchii poet 'Singing poet': a Russian singer-songwriter (776)

pokos 'Haymaking' (Russian): also *senokos* (760)

pol-beat Politically oriented Hungarian music of the 1960s (747)

polanowe 'Of the mountain pastureland': a genre of open-air song of the Beskidy Mountain region of Poland (113)

polesane A type of Italian song for dancing; see *maitinade* (606)

pöliannez A Komi panpipe; also *pölian'ias* (774)

polka A vivacious nineteenth-century European couple dance of Bohemian origin, in 2/4 time (7, 9, 166, 168, 170, 226, 228, 330, 331, 382, 419, 435, 443, 457, 483, 484, 524, 527, 559, 594, 641, 672, 674, 690, 694, 696, 721, 766, 792, 799, 812, 920)

polne 'Of the fields': a genre of open-air song of the Sandomierz region of Poland (113)

polnischer Tanz A name of the **mazurka** outside Poland (710)

polonaise A stately Polish processional dance popular in the 1800s (168, 708, 710)

polonez 'Polonaise': the slowest dance in Polish folk music (708)

polska A Swedish improvisatory dance in 3/4 time (434, 442–43); a Danish dance (454, 457); a Finnish vocal genre based on instrumental dance rhythms (477)

pont-neufs French songs associated with the Pont-Neuf, a marketplace in Paris (548)

popevki Short melodic turns, motifs, and models for traditional Russian melodies (756, 764, 765, 779)

populärmusik The Swedish term for modern urban music (436)

port-a-beul 'Mouth music': Scottish vocal dance music, originally sung when instrumental music was outlawed (363)

portaireacht 'Lilt': singing instrumental Irish dance tunes to nonlexical syllables (380)

posad A Russian surburban zone, also *sloboda*, with its own styles of music (765)

Posaunenchöre German trombone ensembles (657)

posidelki Social gatherings in Russian houses where **lyric songs** are performed (765)

poskočica 'Leaping dance': a dance cycle of the Dalmatia region of Croatia and Montenegro (929, 931, 958)

postranica A Slovene duct flute (915)

potresanje 'Shaking': a singing technique in Bosnia-Hercegovina (963)

powiślak 'Over (or along) the Vistula': a genre of the Lubelskie region of Poland, often sung by groups of women in a bride's home (114)

prapołačnyja pieśni Belarusan weeding songs (792)

pratnja 'Accompanied by instrumentalists': the adjunct to *lumpovanje*, carousing by prosperous young men in Serbian cafés (952)

pravo horo 'Straight dance': the most typical Bulgarian circle dance, in 2/4 time (897)

pravo oro 'Straight dance': a common Macedonian dance, in 2/4 and 7/8 time; also *lesno oro* (978)

prelo Gatherings of women to spin and sew in Croatia, often accompanied by music and dancing (925–26)

pretl A Slovene trapezoidal struck zither; also *brana, cimprekelj, male cimbale,* and *oprekelj* (916)

prichitaniia A Russian lament that resembles **epic** and liturgical narrative singing (761, *763*)

pripevki Bulgarian dancelike songs sung at a *sedyanka* by girls to tease one another about boyfriends (900)

pritrkavanje z zvonovi Slovenian bell ringing on festive occasions (919)

priveghi Romanian wakes, involving humorous games, and, in some areas, masked dancers (872)

procissão In Portugal, a procession that moves solemnly through a village to the rhythm of marches performed by a band: the high point of religious festivities (579)

programmatic music In European art music since the eighteenth century, a composition intended to represent or depict a narrative or a particular thing, person, or other extramusical object (82–83)

protiazhnaia pesnia 'Drawn-out song': a Russian nonmeterical song; also *protiazhniie* (9, 133, 756, 765)

prporuše Rain-invocation ritual songs of Montenegro (958)

przyśpiewka A popular Polish folk song with a two-line text, often containing improvised, malicious remarks (703)

przytrampywane 'Songs with foot-tapping': a local classification of songs performed with dancelike movements in the Kurpie region of northeastern Poland (703)

psalmodikon A Swedish bowed monochord, invented in Denmark in the 1840s and intended to support psalm singing in homes (440)

psal'my Christian songs, the main part of the **kobzari** and **lirnyky** repertoire (813, *814*, 816, 818, 823)

psalterion A **harp** of ancient Greece, commonly played by women (47)

psaltis A Greek ecclesiastical chanter (1025)

pshine An Adighian accordion (855)

psikhere An Adighian ritual melody played on the **bzhami** (855)

pueblos Spanish rural towns (588, 590, 591, 594)

puesia A Corsican song using improvised texts sung to existing tunes (568, 571)

punctus contra punctum 'Note against note' (Latin): the vertical organization of pitches among clerical singers in the **Middle Ages** (50)

Purimspil The Jewish Purim play of the Book of Esther, which recounts a narrative of persecution and freedom (141, 251)

puškaitis A Latvian wooden stick decorated with colored feathers, strips of cloth, and bells, used to accompany singing of **godu balss** in wedding or winter-solstice rituals (503)

pušteno oro A Macedonian dance in 12/8 time (978)

putipù An Italian friction drum (615)

putničke Traveling songs in Croatia and Bosnia-Hercegovina (926, 963)

puzyr' A Mordvinian bagpipe; also *fam, skamóra,* and *válonka* (774)

quadriglia 'Quadrille': a Corsican dance (571)

quadrille A square dance for four couples in a set of five or six figures, mainly in 2/4 and 6/8 time (165, 382, 524, 546, 571, 766, 931)

quadrivium Of the seven medieval liberal arts, those that dealt with arithmetic, astronomy, geometry, and music; compare *trivium* (70, 92)

rabab An Arab fiddle (594)

rabel A Spanish fiddle similar to the Arab *rabab* (589, *590*, 594) *radzilnyja pieśni* Belarusan birth songs, addressed to the parents of the newborn and the midwife (793)

Raffele A German Alpine zither (655)

raffle A Swiss wooden ratchet, a noisemaker; also *rärri* and *rüffle* (685)

ragana A Corsican scraper, a mechanized wooden rasp (572)

raganelle Italian cog rattles (615)

ragas A Lithuanian single-pitched wooden trumpet (511)

ragi Latvian horns or hornpipes, associated with herding (503)

raglja A Slovene children's rattle used at Easter (919)

rai A North African Arabic style of cabaret music, performed also in France (210, 233, *234*–35, 238, 239)

ramoncelle A bowed pseudo-bass of the Low Countries (531)

ramonika A three-row diatonic accordion in Istria, Croatia (931)

ramos Spanish songs for autumn processionals bearing boughs and narrating the lives of saints and Jesus Christ (591)

rancho foclórico A formally organized Portuguese music-and-dance revival group (*577*, 579–583)

rangle A Norwegian rattle, made of large and small iron rings (422)

rantamplan The onomatopoeic imitation of musical instruments in ring dances of the French-speaking area of Switzerland; see *roupioupiou* and *turlututu* (694)

ranz des vaches A Swiss cowherd's song; see *kühreihen* (17)

rappresentazioni Fifteenth- and sixteenth-century Italian songs preserved in the songs of the *maggio* celebration (608)

rapsodi 'Rhapsodies': northern Albanian narrative songs sung by *epic* singers (989)

rärri A Swiss wooden ratchet, a noisemaker; also *raffle* and *rüffle* (685)

räschtli A dance cycle of central Switzerland, consisting of a *schottisch*, a **waltz**, a **polka**, a **mazurka**, and a **ländler** (690)

rasgueado 'Strummed' (Spanish): the characteristic strumming style of **flamenco** guitar playing (598)

raspev Russian long-drawn-out secular songs (779)

raspevshchiki Russian singers of long-drawn-out songs and liturgical music (765)

ražki Belarusan reed aerophones (797)

rebab A Georgian urban chordophone popular from the 1600s to the 1800s (840)

rebetika Greek urban popular music, developed by Greeks expelled from Turkey in the 1920s and popularized internationally in the 1960s (7, 143, 147, 204, *206*, 207, 285, 1008, 1019–21)

recitative In European art music since the **Baroque**, a style of usually accompanied singing whose melodic and rhythmic inflections are intended to resemble those of ordinary speech; used for dialogue in operas and narration in oratorios and cantatas, in alternation with arias (78, 79, 84, 131, 793, 873)

recolha de andores A Portuguese religious festival in which a band performs marches in front of each house in a village; also *arruada* and *peditório* (579)

recomposition The seamless interaction of creativity and presentation (92)

redada Abkhazian wedding songs (853)

redowa A couple dance of the Low Countries (524)

reel A lively Scottish-Highland dance in 4/4 time, characteristic of the British Isles (166, 168, 330, 331, 336, 368, 382, *383*, 391, 524)

reggae A Jamaican musical genre, adopted by the West Indian population in Britain as a source of cultural pride (204, 215, 232, 235–36, 239, 315, 356, 711, 802)

regivärss Ancient Estonian 'runic' melodies; see *runo* (*492*, 493)

reinschrift The conductor's copy of a score for the first performance (51)

reki A Finnish meter with seven feet per line and a variable number of unstressed syllables per foot (477)

rekilaulu A Finnish round-dance song (477–78, 480, 483, 487)

rela A Belarusan hurdy-gurdy; also *kobza* and *lira* (796)

relinchidos 'Whinnies': high-trilling vocal cries in Spanish music (589, 592)

rembetika See *rebetika*

Renaissance In European music history, the period from the early fifteenth century to about 1600 (59, 69, 70, 73–76, 79, 248, 264, 366, 518, 533, 573, 608, 617, 652, 653, 655, 664, 708, 737, 1008)

reque reque A Portuguese wood scraper (582)

requinto A high-pitched Spanish guitar (594)

res facta 'A done thing' (Latin): composition in writing, executed from a score (52)

réveillez French customary begging for eggs and other gifts while singing religious songs at Easter (544, 545)

rhapsodic Extravagantly emotional; in France, said of improvisation using motifs of variable length, rather than measured phrases (541)

ribeba 'Rebab': an Italian regional name of the **mouth harp** (615)

riberbula A Corsican **mouth harp**; also *riebula* and *rivergula* (572)

riddarvisene Norwegian songs about knights (413)

ridée A Breton line or circle dance, performed as part of a three-part suite; see *laridé* (559)

riebula A Corsican **mouth harp**; also *riberbula* and *rivergula* (572)

rigaudon 'Rigadoon': a lively seventeenth- and eighteenth-century dance, still popular in France (547)

rih A curved conical wooden horn of the Hutsul'shchyna and neighboring Carpathian regions of Ukraine, used to accompany *koliadky* (812)

riha A Svanetian ritual Christmas song (835)

rikalo A bark trumpet played by Serbian Vlachs; also *bušen* (198, 950)

rímnaflokkur A cycle of Icelandic rhymed verse, sometimes consisting of thousands of stanzas (401)

rímnakveðskapur An Icelandic genre of music involving repetitions of a short melody (401, 402)

rímur Icelandic **ballads**, sometimes having up to one hundred stanzas (117, 400–404, 407–408)

Rindentrompete A German trumpet made of a bark scroll (*654*)

rindja 'Descent': the annual descent from alpine pastures, when herdsmen of Haute-Gruyère, Switzerland, performed *lyóba* and *tchira* (119)

riondâ A French-speaking Swiss dialect word for singing and dancing (693)

rispetti A type of Italian **lyric song** (606)

rivergula A Corsican **mouth harp**; also *riberbula* and *riebula* (572)

rizitika Unaccompanied table songs of the White Mountains of western Crete (1015)

roženice Double-reed oboes played in Istria, Croatia (930–31)

rockandroll The music of art-punk musicians in Hungary (221)

rog A Bosnia-Hercegovinian animal horn with a single idioglot reed (966)

rog-kaft An Ossetian virtuoso solo dance (861)

rogalj 'Street corners': gatherings of young people in Vojvodina, Serbia, to sing on street corners (952)

rogativa A Spanish prayer song to a local patron saint, asking for the protection of crops from drought and disease (590)

rogovi Slovene horns made of animal horn (915)

roh Belarusan horns made of animal horn, wood, or metal (797)

roitschäggäta Swiss late-winter masking festival in Lötschental, Valais (685)

Rolantskvæði Faroe **epic** songs (*kvæði*) dealing with the exploits of Charlemagne, his uncle, and his daughter (*469*)

rolli Swiss small, closed bells containing little rocks, used on harnesses, worn by women in winter festivals (683)

romance A Spanish and Portuguese **ballad**; also sung by Sephardic Jews in Bosnia-Hercegovina (134, 578, 589, 592 596, 601, 968)

romanceiro A Portuguese **ballad** (136)

romancero A Sephardic Jewish secular narrative **ballad** (254, *256*, 266)

romanse A song genre popular in Croatia between the world wars (934)

Romantic In European music history, a period corresponding roughly to the nineteenth century; its name and certain aesthetic principles derive of the Romantic movement in European art and literature of the later eighteenth and early nineteenth centuries (53, 79–84, 85, 184, 447, 460, 553, 601, 611, 737, 904)

romarias 'Pilgrimages': Portuguese religious pilgrimages with music (577)

romerías 'Pilgrimages': Spanish sacred and secular songs to accompany autumn pilgrimages to local shrines (591)

rommelpot A friction drum of the Low Countries; compare *rumlepotte* (526–27)

rondalla A Spanish guitar-based band that accompanies *rondas* (593, 594)

rondas 'Rounds': in Spain, songs usually sung by groups (590–92, 596)

ronde A French and French-Swiss closed ring dance, sung and danced by the dancers, often in 3/4 time (546–47, 694)

rondeau A French medieval verseform and the music for it (132)

rondes enfantines French children's songs sung in Corsica (571)

roopill An Estonian reed pipe with four to six holes for fingering (494)

rootsikannel An Estonian bowed **lyre** with three or four strings; see *hiiukannel* (493)

Rosh Hashanah Jewish New Year (250, 259)

rospev Russian religious **chants** (779)

rotāšana A Latvian custom between Easter Monday and Whitsunday, when girls gathered on hillsides and sang (501)

roupioupiou The onomatopoeic imitation of musical instruments used in ring dances of the French-speaking area of Switzerland; also *rantamplan* and *turlututu* (694)

rozenhoed 'Hat of roses': a dance in the Dutch-language area of the Low Countries (522)

rozhok A Russian wooden trumpet with five finger holes and one thumb hole (770)

ručhenitsa A Bulgarian solo dance with improvised steps in 7/8 time (897, 901)

rudzu balss A Latvian tune sung in rye fields (500)

ruedas Spanish circle dances (593)

rüffle A Swiss wooden ratchet, a noisemaker; also *raffle* and *rärri* (685)

rull One of three Norwegian dances, characterized by a slow gait in 2/4 or 6/8 time; see *gangar* and *halling* (417)

rumba A ballroom dance of Cuban origin in 2/4 or 4/4 time with emphatic hip movements (204, 205, 233, 234, 619)

rumba catalán A type of Spanish popular music (204, 205)

rumlepotte In Denmark, a friction drum made of a pot sealed with the skin of a pig's bladder and having a goose quill or a piece of reed attached to the middle; compare *rommelpot* (455)

runo An ancient Finnish-Estonian song genre, in which the **Kalevala** was sung (475–77, 480, 482, 487–88, 492)

runonlaulu In Finland, the singing of old poems by a leader and a supporting singer (114)

rusalka 'Mermaid': dramatized in Belarusan

calendrical celebrations at the beginning of summer (*791*)

rusalnyna pieśni 'Water-nymph songs': any of several Belarusan *valačobnyja pieśni* (791)

russkogo 'Of Russians': a style of Gypsy song in Russia (768)

sabii zegakiye An Adighian song to make a child walk (856)

säckpipa A Swedish bagpipe revived in the 1980s (439)

săcunda A second violin, which supplies rhythmic-harmonic accompaniment, played in Romanian and Hungarian music in parts of Transylvania; also *contră* (880)

sadasnje pjesme 'Present-day songs': modern in Gabela, Hercegovina (122)

sæter A Norwegian summer farm for highland pasturing, where the *lur* was traditionally played (412, 415, 420–22)

saga An Icelandic prose narrative, considered a form of musical performance (303–304, 405, 469)

säistäjä The supporting singer in Finnish *runonlaulu*; also *puoltaja* (114)

salamuri A wooden cane flute of eastern Georgia (*833*, 839, 841, 845)

šaljive pjesme Comic or joking songs in Bosnia-Hercegovina (963)

saltarello An Italian **Renaissance** court dance featuring a hop at the start of each measure; preserved in Italy and Corsica as a courting dance, sometimes with gentle, slow movements; also *ballarella, saltarella, savaterelle,* and *stuzzichetto* (571, 572, 608, 609, 614)

sam pa sabie 'Free of restrictions': the Belarusan term for improvisational mastery of instrumental folk tunes (799)

samaia A Georgian women's dance with instrumental accompaniment 836

samica 'By itself': a Croatian plucked **lute** played solo (926, 927)

samizdat 'Self-published' (Russian) (767, 778)

sandouri A Greek trapezoidal struck zither (1009–10, 1013, 1015, 1018, 1019)

sänntumsschölle A Swiss cow bell, worn by male singers in winter festivals (683)

santoer A trapezoidal struck zither of the Low Countries (532)

santouri A Greek trapezoidal struck zither (284)

santur A Georgian urban chordophone of the 1600s to the 1800s (840)

šara 'Ornament, iridescence': small rhythmic shakes that characterize Pannonian dances in Croatia and Serbia (926, 947)

sarabande A stately (originally wild) seventeenth- and eighteenth-century dance in slow (originally fast) triple time with an accent on the second beat (168)

sardana A Catalonian urban-rural circle dance (123, 594)

šargija A long-necked plucked four-to-six-stringed **lute** of northern and central Bosnia (966)

şarki An Ottoman light classical genre, played by Rom musicians in Macedonia (979)

šarkuny Belarusan jingle bells (797)

sarnai A Chuvash bagpipe; also *shapar* (774)

sarronca A northwestern Portuguese friction drum, a clay pot with a narrow opening, covered with a skin that vibrates through the movement of a friction stick (582)

sastrapo 'Urgent': a Gurian panpipe; see *larchemi* and *soinari* (839)

sauelokkar Norwegian ornamented hog-calls (412)

savatarelle A variant of the **saltarello** (609)

saz A fretted, long-necked **lute** of Turkey, imported into the Balkans and Georgia during the Ottoman period and still played by Muslim minorities in some areas (168, 840, 893, 951, 959, 964, 966, *967*, 983, 997, 1019)

sazandari Small Georgian ensembles of Middle Eastern musical instruments (840)

saze An Albanian professional instrumental ensemble, generally of Roma (*993*, 997)

scacciamarzo 'March-chaser': an Italian spring celebration that includes the singing of *canti di questua* (608)

scacciapensieri 'Care-chaser': a northern Italian **mouth harp**; see *marranzanu* (615)

ščadroŭki Belarusan songs sung at the winter solstice and Christmas (791)

scallamanu A Corsican children's game, accompanied by verses (571)

scaloian A Romanian rain-begging ritual, held in spring and summer and involving a mock funeral lament for a doll (870)

scharminkelen Noisemaking on instruments and household utensils in the Dutch Low Countries (525)

Scheitholt The medieval German name of the stringed instrument from which the Slovene drone zither evolved (918)

Scheitholz A German zither revived in the folk revival of the 1960s (656)

schellenschötte 'Bell-shaking': the Swiss technique of ringing bells in regular rhythm to accompany the singing of a *zäuerli* (685)

Schlager Austrian and German popular musical hits (204, 216, 674, 675, 676, 678–79, 934)

schlottere Competitive heelwork in dances of Appenzell, Switzerland; also *bääle* and *solo-doppeliere* (690)

schnelzer Swiss accelerating **yodels** of Appenzell (691)

schnitzelbänke Swiss derisive songs that critique political and social events of the past year (685)

schnulze An Austrian crooning song that recounts feelings of loneliness, farewell, and homesickness (677, 679)

schola Latina 'Latin school': any of several schools founded in Romania during the **Renaissance** (882)

schots (also *schotz*) 'Scottish': a square dance of the Low Countries (524)

schottisch(e) A European couple dance in 2/4 time (7, 166, 168, 435, 443, 457, 484, 524, 527, 559, 571, 690, 694, 696)

Schrammel Nineteenth-century Viennese restaurant music (676)

Schuhplattler A men's presentational dance of Austria and Germany, with elaborate foot and thigh slapping (166)

schuppel A group of Swiss singers in winter festivals (683)

schützenfest A German annual, interregional, civil-militia celebration that uses **tenor drums** in its parades (656)

Schwegel A German fife (654)

schwegepfyfli A Swiss piccololike side-blown flute (687)

Schwirrholz A German **bull roarer** or **thunderstick** (655)

schwyzer zither A Swiss board zither, played mainly by women (686)

schwyzerörgeli A Swiss small, diatonic accordion of Schwyz (689, 696)

schwyzerörgeli quartetten Swiss button accordion quartets (206)

schwyzerpfyf A Swiss soldier's side-blown flute (687)

schwyzerstil A musical style of central Switzerland that incorporates a B-flat clarinet, a *schwyzerörgeli*, a **piano**, and a double bass (689)

sciotiscia 'Schottisch': A Corsican dance (571)

scordatura Any nonstandard tuning of stringed instruments (103, 416, 418, 877)

sean-nós 'Old manner': a style of singing with melodic ornamentation, especially prominent in the Irish-speaking areas of Munster and Connaught (327, 380, 382)

seanchas Old Irish lore (385)

sechseläuten A march performed during Sechseläuten, a Swiss festival, every April (685)

sedlácká 'Peasant dance': a Moravian couple dance with an uneven, offbeat-accented rhythm (122, 721)

sedyanka 'Sitting bee': Bulgarian autumnal social gatherings for spinning or embroidery, accompanied by singing (141, 900–901)

Sega la vecchia 'Saw the witch': an Italian mid-Lenten ceremony with music (608)

seguidilla A southern Spanish couple dance in moderately fast triple time, especially associated with Castile (589, *592*, 594, 595, 596, 601)

seljačko 'Of the village': a narrow-interval singing style of the Croatian Dinaric Alps (927)

seljefloyte A Norwegian duct flute without holes for fingering (416, 420)

semenovna 'Simeon's daughter' (Russian): a style of Gypsy song (768)

semivocale A partial vowel sound, like /n/, as the basis for singing; compare **vocale** (105)

senna 'Quarrel': an Icelandic form of musical performance (405)

senokos 'Haymaking' (Russian): also *pokos* (760)

serpent An English undulating wooden lip-driven low-pitched aerophone with six holes for fingering (330)

serra A Pontic Greek dance (1011)

serragia A Sardinian bowed, one-stringed stick zither with a pig-bladder resonator (627)

sesquiáltera 'Hemiola' (Spanish): alteration between 3/4 and 6/8 times (593)

sevdalinke 'Love songs' of urban Muslim culture in Bosnia-Hercegovina; known as *turčije* or Turkish-like songs before the late 1800s (959, 964–66, 968)

sextondelspolskor A form of Swedish *polska* in sixteenth-note rhythms predominant in southern and eastern Sweden (435)

sezatoarea Romanian social evenings, involving song, music, and dance (870)

shairi Georgian folk-poetry competitions (838)

shapar A Chuvash bagpipe; also *sarnai* (774)

sharki An Albanian large long-necked plucked **lute**, popular in Kosova (996)

sharmanka A Russian street barrel organ (766)

shashmaqam Central Asian melodic **modes** linked to Polish folk music (712)

shedag A Chechen and Ingush double reed with a straight pipe (863)

shiapshe yeredkher Adighian healing songs (855)

shible ydj An Adighian circle dance honoring the god of thunder (855)

shofar A ram's-horn military and religious trumpet of the ancient Hebrews, now blown in synagogues during certain important services (*250*, 259)

shtayger 'Climber' (Yiddish): any of several **modes** of Ashkenazic Jewish music (*253*)

shuvyr A Mari bagpipe (774)

sibizgi A Balkar and Karachevi shepherd's whistle flute (857)

side drum A **snare drum** (364, 523, 527, 528, 810)

sienakosnyja pieśni Belarusan haying songs (792)

sierszeńki A bagpipe for beginners in western Poland; also *siesieńki* or *pancharzyna* (707)

sife A side-blown flute of the Low Countries (528)

Sigmundarkvæði Faroe Island **epic** songs (*kvæði*) that contain a verse of an account of the original settlement of the islands (470)

silväschtertrösche Swiss threshing in rhythmic patterns (684)

silvesterchläuse A clapper bell of Wald, Zurich, Switzerland (683, *684*)

silvesterklüuse Jingle bells on a harness in Oberschau, St. Gallen, Switzerland (683)

simbolo A **frame drum** played by the Italian minority in Istria, Croatia (930)

simd The most popular Ossetian dance (861)

Simchas Torah 'Rejoicing of the Torah': a Jewish autumn religious holiday with processions and ecstatic dances (251)

singing pubs English alehouses or pubs where customers sing for enjoyment (331)

Siomucha Belarusan Pentecost; also *Zialonyja śviatki* (791)

sirató A Hungarian funeral lament (740)

sîrba A Romanian line dance (872, *875*, 880)

sirijna A Balkar and Karachaevi double reed with a flared bell (857)

sirinata a i sposi 'Serenade for the couple': a Corsican *currente* sung at a wedding (568)

sirinato An Italian song type preserved in Corsica; some examples are locally composed and sung to *lamentu* or *puesia* tunes (570)

sirventes French satiric troubadour songs (550)

Sjurdarkvæði Faroe **epic** songs (*kvæði*) dealing with Germanic legends about Sigurd the Dragonslayer (469)

ska Jamaican dance music performed by a small rock-style band and especially popular in Britain (215, 235–36)

skald An ancient Icelandic and Norwegian poet-singer (146, 405, 423)

skamarochi 'Minstrels': a Belarusan traditional folk instrumental ensemble; also *hurtkampaniya, kapela, muzyki*, and *viasielnyja muzyki* (798, 799)

skamóra A Mordvinian bagpipe; also *fam, puzyr'*, and *válonka* (774)

skiladhika 'Dog's dens': working-class establishments where Greek urban popular music was performed; see *bouzoukia* (1020)

skillingtryck Swedish broadside **ballads** (435)

skiparar The leader of line dancing in the Faroe Islands (470)

skomorokhi Russian secular minstrels (122, 770)

Skotse fjoar 'Scottish four': a square dance of Terschelling Island (524)

Skotse trije 'Scottish three': the national dance of Friesland in the late nineteenth century (524)

skripka 'To squeak': a Russian violin made of glued pieces of wood with three strings (770)

skrypka A Belarusan and Ukrainian fiddle or violin (796, 809)

skrzypce A Polish word for violin (706)

skrzypce podwiązane 'Bound-up violin': referring to the Polish practice of binding the neck of factory-made violins to tune them to the bagpipe (706)

skudutis Lithuanian panpipes, played in ensembles of three to seven (511)

skur-orgel A barker's stick, made of building materials and used to accompany the singing of Danish builders as they waited in the workmen's shack for the weather to clear so they could resume work (459)

sláciková muzika An Eastern Moravian and Slovakian string band of two to four stringed instruments (719)

šlageri 'Hits': Croatian songs popularized in operettas and films (934) *slått* A Norwegian *hardingfele* piece (416, 417, *419*, 421, 426, 427, 430)

slava A saint's-day celebration in Macedonia and Serbia, an important occasion for dancing (941, 973)

slavianofily 'Salvophiles': advocates of vernacular Russian traditions (779)

slavonsko kolo Slavonian *kolo*, a circle dance of Slavonia (*932*)

sléttubönd An elaborate Icelandic verse form using palindromic rhymes to deliver coded messages (402, 407)

slide An Irish **jig** in 12/8 time (382)

slip jig An Irish **jig** in 9/8 time (382)

sloboda A Russian surburban zone, also *posad*, with its own styles of music (765)

smørbon A Norwegian butter-making song (412)

smyrneika Greek songs of Smyrna (1020)

snare drum A small cylindrical wooden-shelled two-headed drum with snares stretched over the lower head; compare **tenor drum** (141, 314, 545, 562, 582, 654, *693*, 877, 977, 1017)

sobor A fair with music and dancing in Macedonia (116)

soborski pesni 'Fair songs': urban-influenced Macedonian songs (974)

sofračke pjesme Table songs in Bosnia-Hercegovina (963)

soinari 'The hollow': a Gurian panpipe; see *larchemi* and *sastsrapo* (839, 840)

soitto Improvisation on the Finnish *kantele* (481)

sokačke pesme Street songs sung by young people on street corners in Vojvodina, Serbia (114, 952)

sokak 'Street' or 'lane': a musical classification used by Vojvodina Serbs describing where people sing street songs (952)

sokusarv An Estonian buckhorn trumpet, often with holes for fingering (494)

soldatskie pesni 'Soldiers' song': any of numerous Russian city songs with fanfarelike melodies (767)

soleá A type of Spanish *cante jondo* based on a complex twelve-beat rhythmic structure; see *palos siguiriyas* (597)

solfège The French name of the fixed-*do* system of sol-fa syllables in which vocables signify absolute pitches; sometimes called the **Wilhem method** (106)

solfeggio The Italian name of the fixed-*do* system of sol-fa syllables in which vocables signify absolute pitches; sometimes called the **Wilhem method** (106)

solmization The system of sol-fa syllables that represent interval relationships within the tonal scheme and can be placed at any pitch level (97, 106)

son Breton-language songs; see *chanson* (559)

sonajas de azófar Spanish metal castanets (594)

sonata In European art music since the **Baroque**, a genre of composition for one or several instruments, usually consisting of several distinct sections (movements), each of which may be several minutes to about a quarter hour long (51, *78*, 79, 81, 82, 99, 367, 654)

sonata A Sardinian *launeddas* composition consisting of a series of thematic formulas corresponding to the figures of the dance (630)

sonata form In European art music since the late eighteenth century, a plan (form) employed usually in the first movements of **sonatas**, **concertos**, **symphonies**, and other compositions, incorporating sections called exposition, development, and recapitulation (82, 85)

sonerion A Breton duet of *biniou koz* or *biniou bihan* and *bombarde*; see *sonneurs de couple* (559)

sonettu A Sardinian small diatonic accordion (626, 627, 630, *631*)

söngur An Icelandic song (405)

sonner 'To ring': a playing stroke on Swiss church bells (685)

sonneurs de couple A French term for the Breton *sonerion* (559)

soñu zaharak 'Old melodies': Basque dance tunes with a variable number of bars to each phrase (121)

sopel A Russian duct flute with five or six holes for fingering; also *dudka* and *pizhatka* (770)

sopile Double-reed oboes played in pairs on the island of Krk in the northern Adriatic region of Croatia (930)

sopilka A Ukrainian end-blown flute played especially by boys while pasturing cattle and in other nonritual settings (816, 818)

soukous A blend of Central African and Cuban rumba styles, popular in France (234, 238)

Soul Caking A traditional play at Antrobus in Cheshire, England (331)

sousa Traditional Cypriot swinging-game songs (1030)

sousedská A Bohemian couple round dance in moderate triple meter (717, 721)

sousta A dance of the Greek islands, also important in Cyprus (1015, 1030)

spailpini Irish migrant workers, also called tattie-howkers, important disseminators of song and music in Ireland and between Ireland and Scotland (389)

spasovskaya A local variety of Russian *chastushki*, named after the locality where it is song (768)

spelemann A Norwegian player of a musical instrument (417, 421)

spēlmanis 'Player': the Latvian term for a violinist or a fiddler (504)

spelmanslag A Swedish fiddlers' ensemble (152, *441*)

spelmansstämma A Swedish musical festival (*440*)

spelmansstämmor Informal gatherings of Swedish fiddlers (150)

spelpipa A Swedish duct flute (439)

spielleute German traveling musicians, organized into regional brotherhoods (653)

spilendz-churi 'Copper barrel': Georgian metal percussion, mentioned in medieval literary sources (840)

sprechgesänge German recitative songs (650)

springar A Norwegian couple dance (108, 417, *418*)

spuntini Sardinian weekend picnics, occasions for song dueling (626, 629)

sroteš A couple dance of northwestern Croatia (933)

stabules Latvian wooden flutes with six or seven finger holes or reeds, associated with herding (503)

stadtmusikanten Musicians' guilds in medieval Germany (652)

Stadtpfeifer German professional town musicians who performed music for civic festivities and functions (653)

stalki Belarusan triangles (797)

stanzl A Jewish song genre based on Purim texts and found in rural areas of the former Hapsburg Empire (251)

starchykhy A Ukrainian women's group of vocalists who wandered village roads and performed in regional markets and bazaars (816)

starets A Ukrainian blind traveling singer (*813*)

starina (pl. *stariny*) 'Old song': a Russian folk term for a sung **epic**; also *starinki*; see *byliny* (23, 121, 129, 763)

starinki 'Old tales': a Russian genre known to scholars since the 1830s as *bylina*; also *stariny*; see *byliny* (121, 129–30)

starinshchik A specialized performer of the Russian *stariny* or *starinski*, genres known to scholars since the 1830s as *byliny* (121)

starinske pjesme Ancient songs in Gabela, Hercegovina (Bosnia) (122)

starodávny 'Old-time dance': a dance of eastern Moravia (122)

starogradske p(j)esme Serbian and Croatian old-city songs (934, 936, 948)

starogradski pesni 'Old-city songs': Macedonian urban songs (980, 981, 983)

starosvetská 'Old-world dance': a dance of southeastern Moravia (122)

startsi A Ukrainian group of male vocalists who wandered village roads and performed in regional markets and bazaars (815, 816, 818); an alternate term for Bulgarian *kukeri* (899)

steagul 'The flag': part of the Romanian wedding ritual, accompanied by specific songs or instrumental tunes (871)

Steirisch An Austrian trapezoidal struck zither of Styria (*673*)

stemmur Melodies of Icelandic *rímur*; see *bragir* (402)

step dancing Scottish and Irish virtuosic and competitive solo dancing with elaborate footwork (166, 330, 331, 353)

stev A Norwegian four-line rhymed stanza (134, 412, 413, 426)

stichic Characteristic of songs whose performance repeats a single musical phrase corresponding to a single line of verse (129–31, 539)

Stierische An Austrian multipart dance of Styria; also the name of the button accordion that plays that genre (673)

stili An Ossetian double clarinet with a five-holed melody pipe and a single-holed drone pipe (859)

stilyagi A Russian youth subculture with its own popular music (216)

stock and horn The Scottish name of the hornpipe (366)

stornelli A type of Italian **lyric song** (606, 607, 611)

stradaniia 'Sufferings, cruel romances': a subgenre of *chastushki* and soldiers' songs (765, 768)

strambotti A type of Italian **lyric song** (606)

stranotti (pl.) A type of Italian **lyric song** (606)

stranščice Slovene duct flutes (915)

strigături 'Extemporized verses' shouted during dancing in the Romanian wedding ritual (119, 165, 870, 872)

striichmusig 'Bowed music': a Swiss band consisting of a violin, a dulcimer, a bowed double bass, and a chromatic accordion or a **piano**, in Appenzell and Toggenburg, St. Gallen (690)

string quartet In European art music since the eighteenth century, an ensemble consisting of two violins, one viola, and one violoncello (cello); a composition for such an ensemble, usually in several movements, like a **sonata** (61, 85, 184, 444, 482)

strophic songs Songs in which the same music is repeated for each new stanza (strophe) of music (127, 129, 131, *132*, 135, 540–41, 578, 581, 607, 703, 717, 793, 874, 875, 879, 890)

Stubenmusi Bavarian bar music (656)

sturmant A Welsh **mouth harp**, made of wood or metal, held between the teeth, and struck with a finger, popular until the early 1900s; see *bibaw* (348)

stuzzichetto A variant of the **saltarello** (609)

stviri Georgian wooden aerophones (839)

su concordu A Sardinian three-person chorus that accompanies *gara poetica,* poets' sung duels (627)

subornaja subota The Belarusan bridal fair the day before the wedding, when girls gather, accompanied by ritual songs; also called *dziavočnik* and *na viankach* (793)

sudmalipas 'Mill': the third of four or more sections of the Latvian *četrpāru dancis,* sometimes considered a separate dance (504)

suka 'Bitch': a vertically played bowed fiddle of Poland (705–706)

sulling A Norwegian vocal genre that uses mnemonic syllables for singing fiddle pieces; also *lulling, tralling,* and *tulling* (421)

sunet An Albanian circumcision ceremony with music (*144*)

šupelka A Macedonian shepherds' flute, a short tube open at both ends with six holes for fingering (*975*)

supra Georgian traditional feasts with singing (841)

surdulina An Italian bagpipe (169)

surle An Albanian conical-bore double-reed aerophone; also *cingonë, curle,* and *zurle* (996, 1000–1001)

sutartinė Traditional polyphonic vocal music of southeast Lithuania (*510*, 511)

svadbene pjesme Montenegrin wedding songs (958)

svatba A Bulgarian wedding, which requires specific songs and music for each stage of the festivities (900)

svatovske pjesme Wedding songs in Bosnia-Hercegovina (958, 963)

svilpes Latvian bark or clay whistles, associated with herding (503)

svingbruse In Denmark, an instrument consisting of a hollow tile or a small oblong wooden plate with a hole, tied to the end of a string and swung in circles to produce a whirring sound (455)

svinjokolje Slavonian communal hog-butchering parties, held in late fall with singing, dancing, and merrymaking; also *kolinje* (926)

svirač A Serbian term for a musician (944)

svirale A Serbo-Croatian term for wind instruments, commonly used to denote duct flutes (928, 944, 950)

svirka A Bulgarian short, end-blown, ductless flute with six finger holes and perhaps a thumb hole (892)

svirni Bulgarian nonmetrical instrumental tunes (901)

svrljiške gajde A three-voiced bagpipe of southeast Serbia (945)

symphony In European art music since the **Classical** period, a genre of composition formally resembling a **sonata**, but composed for an orchestra (61, 63, 79, 80, 82, *83*, 101, 149, 152, 184, 186–88, 199, 210, 215, 367, 369, 444, 727, 729, 737, 781, 799, 882, 904–905, 921)

syrinx Ancient Greek panpipes (39, 47)

syrmatika Narrative songs of the Greek island of Karpathos (118)

syrtos A common Greek line dance (1015, 1030)

szopka A Polish Christmas puppet story resembling the Belarusan *batlejka* and the Ukrainian *vertep* (799)

ta-velika citira A basset, a small three-stringed bass, played in Resia, Slovenia, to accompany violins; also *b[r]unkula* (918)

tablak A small version of the Georgian *diplipito* (838)

tablaos Spanish nightclubs where **flamenco** is performed (598, 599)

tabor A small handheld drum that accompanies a pipe or fife, played by the same person in a combination known generally as pipe and tabor and in England as **whittle**

and dub; see *tambourinaire* (142, 330–31, 528, 549)

tabor pipe A duct flute with two finger holes and a thumb hole (528)

tabwrdd A drum known only from early Welsh historical sources (348)

taccule A Corsican wooden scraper (572)

tactus 'Beat' (Latin): the silent waving of the conductor's arm in a downward and upward alternation in medieval Europe to signal the beat (101)

tættir Satirical **ballads** of the Faroe Islands, dealing with topical events and sung by dancers in a line dance (469, 471)

táhle 'Protracted, drawn-out': a term describing eastern Moravian nondance music in **parlando rubato** style (721)

tako'ah The biblical word for trumpet (259)

taksim Nonmetric improvisation in Turkish and Arabic classical music, played also in the Balkans (206, 286, 951, 976, 979, 997)

tala 'Talk, tale': considered a form of Icelandic musical performance (405)

talambas A kettledrum of Bosnia-Hercegovina and Montenegro (960, 967)

talava The principal Rom musical genre in Kosovo, Serbia (286)

talerschwingen A Swiss tradition of rolling a five-franc piece around the inside of an earthenware bowl to produce a sound that accompanies local yodeling (686, 690)

talku balss A Latvian tune sung during communal fieldwork (500)

tałočnyja pieśni Belarusan spring, summer, and autumn team songs, performed by groups gathered to help fellow farmers (792)

talyanka 'Italian accordion': the title of a Russian collection of *chastushka* texts (768)

tamada A Georgian toastmaster who leads the complex structure of toasts with songs at a banquet (841)

ţambal A Romanian trapezoidal struck zither (*277, 872,* 876, 877, 879–80)

tambor A Spanish drum that accompanies flute playing (593)

tamboril A Basque drum, typically played with the right hand while the left hand plays a three-holed flute; see **tabor** and *txistu* (171)

tamboril A drum played in northeast Portugal (583)

tambour A drum (176)

tambourin A snare-drum played with *galoubet* in Provence, France (545)

tambourinaire A French pipe-and-tabor player (549)

tambourine A small drum, especially a **frame drum** with metallic jingles loosely attached to the frame (142, 170, *195*, 280, 331, 512, 517, 594, 609, 615, 639, 640, 654, 656, 797, 798, 967, 1010)

tambura A Middle Eastern fretted long-necked **lute**, imported into the Balkans during the Ottoman period (168, 169, *176*, 198, 283, 743, *893, 894,* 895–96,

902, 927, 932, 945, 953, 959, *963,* 966, 975, 981, *982,* 983)

tamburaši Players of the *tambura* (279, 927, 932, 934, 952)

tamburaški orkestar A *tamburica* orchestra (927, 968)

tamburello An Italian small **frame drum** used in *tarantella* (*609, 610,* 614)

tamburica Related and variously sized long-necked fretted lutes (674, 917, 981); an ensemble of plucked chordophones (*tambure*), also *tamburaški orkestar* (*279,* 674, 927, 931, 933–34, 936, 945–46, 952, *953,* 959, 965, 968)

tamburini Italian **tambourines** (609, 615)

tammorra An Italian **tambourine**; also *tammurro* (609)

tammuriata An Italian couple dance danced to syllabic *strambotti* (609, 614)

tampoutsia A Cypriot **frame drum** used in the *vkiolarides* ensemble (*1031*)

tanbur A Maltese **tambourine** played with a *zavzava* to accompany a *zaqq* (640)

táncdalok 'Dance songs': a general Hungarian designation for pop music (746)

táncház 'Dancehouse': any of numerous revival dance meetings organized by university students in Budapest, Hungary (153, 739, 744, 746)

tango A ballroom dance of Argentine origin in 4/4 time featuring stylized bodily postures (289, 457, 483, 484, 485, 486, 525, 619, 690, 766, 812)

tanok Russian collective circle and figure dances; also *khorovod* and *krugi* (769)

tapan A Balkan cylindrical double-headed drum; also *tŭpan* (201, 280–81, 285, 944, 951, 975–76, *977,* 979, 981, *982,* 983)

taqbil The Maltese art of rhyming, used in *ghana ta' spirtu pront* (636)

taqtuqa Maltese castanets, used in small ensembles for ambulatory street music, weddings, parties, and picnics (640)

tarabuka A goblet-shaped drum, used in Gypsy bands in Serbia (*144,* 951, 997)

tarabuka A Middle Eastern goblet-shaped drum played in the Balkans; also *darabuka* (*144, 176, 281,* 286, 951, 997)

taraf A Romanian instrumental ensemble (277, 278, *872,* 878–79, 880)

taragot A Romanian single-reed keyed wooden aerophone with a conical bore (872, 879)

tarantella An Italian and Corsican dance in vivacious 6/8 time that derives its name from a dance-therapy ritual prescribed to cure a person supposedly bitten by a tarantula (197, 571, 609)

tarantismo The name of the *tarantella* in the area of Apulia (609)

tárogató A Hungarian single-reed keyed wooden aerophone with a conical bore (743)

taures Latvian wooden and birch-bark trumpets with a mouthpiece or a single reed, associated with herding (503)

taxim Greek nonmetrical, instrumental, modal improvisation preceding rhythmic dance-songs (1010, 1022)

tchiattisma Improvised rhyming couplets of Cyprus (1025)

tchira 'Cry': a less melodious version of the *lyóba por la rindja*, a song sung by herdsmen bringing their cattle down from alpine pastures in Haute-Gruyère, Switzerland (119)

të qarë 'Cried': Albanian flute melodies that draw on women's vocal laments; also *vajtim* (993)

të qarë me zë 'Cried with the voice': an Albanian lament or stylized form of crying (990)

techno-lindo Contemporary Croatian popular music that sets traditional Dalmatian dance music on electronic instruments (934)

tegerek-tepsey A Balkar and Karachaevi circle dance in 2/4 and 4/4 time (858)

teicamās dziesmas Latvian songs recited at traditional events and celebrations, such as weddings, lullabies, field labor, and breeding cattle (500)

teké A Greek hashish den, the center of *rebetika* activity (1019)

tekerő A Hungarian hurdy-gurdy (743)

Telemark springar Any of the principal Norwegian dances, with an accented second beat in each measure (417, *418*)

telenn A Breton small Celtic **harp**, revived in the 1950s (560)

telyn A Welsh **harp**; symbolically the most important Welsh musical instrument (347–48)

tenor drum A wooden-shelled snareless drum larger than a **snare drum** (562, 654, 656)

tep A Chechen and Ingush **frame drum**; see *zhirga* (863)

tepežnicw Spanking songs, sung in Slovenia on 28 December to bring fertility (912)

tepsi A large, round copper tray, used by Albanian women to provide a resonator for their singing (994, *995*)

tepsija A copper pan, used by Kosovo Serbs to provide a resonator for their singing (951)

tercets proverbes A Corsican form of *chiam'e rispondi*, in which a traditional proverb sung by one singer had to be answered with a suitable proverb by another singer (568)

terkotki Clappers used in annual church ceremonies in Poland; also *kosatki* (704)

terrimaxka A Maltese barrel organ on wheels with clockwork dancing figures, played for amusement and dancing on Sundays and feasts, often accompanied by a monkey's antics (640)

teško oro 'Heavy dance': a Macedonian men's dance (978)

testamenti An Italian song genre (608)

tetartos The fourth movement of the Cypriot *kartzilamades* dance cycle, performed in 9/8 time (1030)

thefteros The second movement of the Cypriot *kartzilamades* dance cycle, performed in 7/8 time (1030)

thirrje vaji 'Provocation of cry': an Albanian men's lament of Montenegro, known in Serbo-Croatian as *lelekanje* (958)

thunderstick A name of the **bullroarer**; in German, *schwirrholz* (655)

tiba A Swiss term for the **alphorn** in Bundner Oberland (688)

tibia A Romanian trumpet or horn (881)

tibiae pares 'Paired pipes' (Latin): flutes taken as far north as the border settlement of Noviomagus (now Nijmegen, Netherlands) during the first century (39)

tienbasser An accordion of the Low Countries (530)

tiesse di tch'va A hurdy-gurdy of the Low Countries (532)

tietäjä 'Knower, soothsayer': a Finnish singer with above-average knowledge (481)

tiir Italian polyphonic singing style in Primana, Lombardy (610)

ţiituri 'Rhythmic formulas': patterns played on the Romanian *cobza* (880)

tik A Pontic Greek dance (1011)

tilinca (also *tininca*) A northern Romanian end-blown, rim-blown shepherd's flute, lacking a duct and holes for fingering (874, 878)

timbil-kaft An Ossetian couple dance; see *lezginka* (861)

timbre The quality given to a sound by the relative prominence of its overtones (9, 85, 91, 225, 228, 302, 311, 402, 512, 570, 611, 627, 636, 640, 692, 711, 719, 757, 828, 841, 892, 995, 1018)

timbre The French word for a borrowed tune or its title applied to a text (550)

timple A high-pitched Spanish guitar (594)

tin whistle A six-holed whistle flute of England and Ireland (330, 383, *385,* 527)

tintenelle A French sheep bell (544)

tinter 'To ring softly': a playing stroke on Swiss church bells (685)

tiompán An Irish plucked or bowed chordophone, called *timpan* in Old Irish (384)

tiple (also *tiplillo*) A high-pitched Spanish guitar (*594*)

tirade **Epic** tunes of the Lake Onega region of Russia, with stanzas of varying lengths (755, 756, 765)

tis kunias Greek courtship songs, sung while boys swing girls on swings (1015)

tis tavas A Greek table song, sung by men and women sitting at a table with friends and relatives; also *tou trapeziou* (1010)

tjuz tepsey A Balkar and Karachaevi couple dance featuring triplets in 2/4 and 4/4 time (858)

tlŭka Bulgarian autumnal social gatherings for communal work, accompanied by singing (900)

toaca A Romanian wooden plank or metal plate struck with one or two wooden hammers, played in monasteries and by children (876)

toba mare A bass drum played in Romania (877)

toeira A Portuguese term for guitar, usually with five double or triple courses of metal strings, that provides harmonic and rhythmic accompaniment for *fado;* also *amarantina, braguesa,* and *viola* (582)

tof A Hebrew squarish **frame drum** (838)

toggenburger halszither A Swiss long-necked **lute**-zither with a flat body, shaped like half a pear (687)

tolochnye pesni Collective-help songs, sung during the harvest in Russia (760)

tonadilla escénica A late sixteenth-century Spanish short comic **opera** that used folk and popular melodies (601)

tonality In European music, a system of tonal organization characteristic of compositions of the seventeenth through nineteenth centuries (employed in popular and some concert music through the twentieth century), characterized by certain technical features, notably the use of a single key as the basis of each composition; the keys, also tonalities, are understood by reference to a final note and a **mode**, e.g., C major and A minor (79, 187, 237, 275, 330, 425, 453, 505, 518, 523, 534, 581, 606, 609–610, 650, 660–61, 710, 711, 746, 830–32, 1008)

tonnost' 'Toneness': a Russian musicological concept developed by Boris Asaf'ev (783)

tonos A **mode** of ancient Greek music and music theory (48, 1023)

toque 'Touch, beat': Spanish guitar playing (596, 598)

torototela A northeast Italian one-stringed bowed fiddle (615)

torototéla A local term for story-singers of Italian-speaking Switzerland; also *cantastorie* (695)

torra A Corsican children's game, accompanied by verses (571)

torupill An Estonian bagpipe single-reed melody pipe and drone pipes that sound the tonic and the dominant (494, *495*)

torvi A Finnish trumpet made of cow or ox horn or birch or alder bark (478, 479)

tou trapeziou A Greek table song, sung by men and women sitting at a table with friends and relatives; also *tis tavas* (1010)

toubeleki A Greek vase-shaped drum (1015)

touta A Swiss term for the **alphorn** in Anniviers (688)

't patertje A kissing dance of the Dutch-language area of the Low Countries (522)

traccule A Corsican scraper with small wooden slabs, played like castanets (572)

trachten-gruppen 'Folk-costume groups': traditional performers in Germany (154)

tradizioni popolari 'Popular traditions': Italian **folklore** (621)

trallero Florid six-part polyphonic male singing in and around the port of Genoa, Italy (134, 610)

tralling Vocal imitation of the *hardanger* violin in Norway; also *lolling, sulling,* and *tulling* (107–108, 421, 422)

trallning Swedish vocalizations imitating fiddle sounds with onomatopoeic syllables like *tidadi* and *dili-diliadi* (436)

tratto marzo An Italian spring celebration that includes the singing of *canti di questua* (608)

trawantel A sword dance of Westerlo, Antwerp Province, Belgium (523, 526)

trekbuul (also *trekorgel* and *trekzak*) An accordion of the Low Countries (530)

trekkspil A Norwegian accordion (420)

trembita A Silesian long wooden trumpet (704); a Ukrainian long cylindrical wooden trumpet, used to signal danger or villagers' deaths and to perform ceremonial music at funerals (201, 812)

tresche A French dance tradition that emerged of medieval ring and chain dances (546)

treskanje 'Shaking': a Croatian singing style (926)

treskavice A Croatian vocal genre whose name derives from the word *treskanje* (926)

treujenn gaol 'Cabbage stump': a Breton clarinet with four or five keys, often made of boxwood (560)

tribbiera An Italian and Corsican free-metered threshing song, sung in a strained **timbre** by farmers as they drive oxen around a threshing floor (*22, 567, 568*)

triccheballacche A Neapolitan rattle having three or five mallets set in a wooden frame (615)

trideksnis A Latvian wooden stick with hanging bells and jingles, used to accompany singing of *godu balss* in wedding or winter-solstice rituals (503)

trigona A Pontic Greek dance (1011)

trigonon A **harp** of ancient Greece, commonly played by women (47)

trikititxa A Basque ensemble consisting of a diatonic accordion, a drum, and singing (314, 315)

trimitis A Lithuanian wooden trumpet, capable of producing a natural scale through overblowing (511)

triolpolskor A form of Swedish *polska* in triplet rhythms, predominant in western Sweden (435)

triplo A high-pitched Spanish guitar (594)

tritos The third movement of the Cypriot *kartzilamades* dance cycle, performed in 2/4 time (1030)

trivium Of the seven medieval liberal arts, those that dealt with grammar, logic, and rhetoric; compare *quadrivium* (92)

troet An accordion of the Low Countries (530)

Troicskija Belarusan Trinity holiday (791)

troïsta muzyka Ukrainian trio ensembles, a term used by researchers; see *muzyka* (811)

troitskie 'Whitsunday': the seventh Sunday after Easter (760)

trollvisene Ancient indigenous Norwegian songs about the supernatural (413)

tromba A Corsican idioglot clarinet (571)

tromba degli zingari 'Trumpet of the Gypsies': a name of the Italian **mouth harp** (615)

tromp(e) A **mouth harp** of the Low Countries (526)

trønderrock Norwegian rock music; see *dialekt-rock* (96, 430)

trstene orglice Slovene panpipes (915, *916*)

trstenke Slovene reed pipes (915)

truba A trumpet used in Macedonian *čalgija* ensembles (281); a Belarusan shepherds' conical trumpet made of wood wrapped in birch bark or of hammered metal (797); a Ukrainian conical wooden trumpet of Polissia and Volyn' (812); a Serbian trumpet, named in *Zlatna Truba* ('Golden Horn'), a west Serbian festival (946)

trump The Scottish name of the **mouth harp** (366)

trunfa 'Trump': a regional name of the Italian **mouth harp** (615)

trychle A Swiss cowbell of Muotatal; see *gunggele* (685)

trychlen Swiss whip-crackers of Meiringen, Bern; also *übersitz* (683)

tsakismata Verbal interjections in Greek singing (1025)

tsambouna A bagpipe of the Greek islands (118, *1015*)

tsamiko A dance of the Greek mainland, also important in Cyprus (1030)

tsan 'Song': singing by herdsmen in Haute-Gruyère, Switzerland (119)

tschäggätä 'Dappled ones': Swiss masked men in the festival of *roitschäggäta* (685)

tsiattista A Cypriot genre of improvised couplets set to traditional tune types (1030)

tsifte teli A Greek belly dance of Turkish origin (1019)

tsimbalo A Greek trapezoidal struck zither (1010, 1013)

tsintsila A Georgian pair of copper plates, found in archaeological excavations of the fourth century; also *lini* (837)

tsopai An Ossetian circle dance, connected to the cult of thunder and lightning (861)

tsuzam A Chechen and Ingush children's instrument made of a goose feather or a stalk of grass (863)

tsyganochka 'Beautiful Gypsy girl' (Russian): a style of Gypsy song (7680)

tsymbaly A trapezoidal struck zither of Ukraine, Poland, and Belarus (810, *811*–12, 818)

ttiki 'Small lines': a Basque poetic form divided into 7- and 6-syllable hemistichs in the *zortziko* dance-song type (312)

ttunttun A Basque struck zither with six strings struck with a wooden stick (*314, 543, 545*)

tuilage A French singing technique in which two voices alternate, overlapping slightly (542)

tulling Vocal imitation of the *hardanger* violin in Norway; also *lolling, sulling,* and *tralling* (107–108, 421)

tulum A Georgian bagpipe of Meshketi; also called *chimoni* (840)

tumbu The drone pipe of the Sardinian *launeddas* (630)

tunas Portuguese ensembles formed of families of stringed instruments, including different kinds of *cavaquinho*, mandolin, *viola*, and *viola baixo* (582, 583)

tupan An Albanian two-headed bass drum; also *daulle, lodër,* and *lodërti* (164, 996)

tŭpan A Bulgarian cylindrical two-headed drum, played with a thick stick and a thin wand (164, 280, 284, 893–94, 895, 897, 900, 902)

turčije A Turkish song style in Montenegro and Bosnia-Hercegovina, known as *sevdalinke* since the late 1800s (958, 963, 964)

turku Urban songs played by Rom musicians in Macedonia (979)

turlututu The onomatopoeic imitation of musical instruments in ring dances of the French-speaking of Switzerland; see *rantamplan* and *roupioupiou* (694)

turopolski drmeš A couple dance with shaking of Turopolje, Croatia (933)

Turski kjuček The duple meter variant of the Bulgarian Rom *kjuček* (282)

tužbalica A Serbo-Croatian lament, performed by women (941, 958, 963)

tvísöngur 'Two-singing': an Icelandic vocal form and technique of accompanying another voice in parallel fifths (402–403, 407, 423)

twmpath The mound where Welsh musicians traditionally stood to play for dancing (355)

txalaparta A Basque idiophone, consisting of one or more wooden planks beaten by two players to create different rhythmic patterns (171, 314, 315)

txirula A small Basque wooden flute (314, 316)

txistu A Basque three-holed duct flute, typically played by the left hand while the right hand plays a drum (171, 314, 316, 600)

txistulari Basque musicians who accompany dances by fingering a *txistu* with one hand and beating a drum with the other (314, 316)

tympanon A trapezoidal struck zither of the Low Countries (532)

tyniad A Welsh harper's chord, which, in various combinations with a second chord (*cyweirdant*), made up twenty-four different patterns (349)

tzaz A Macedonian and Vlach term for drum (1012)

tzazi A Macedonian brass band with a *klarino* (1012)

u contrastu Corsican improvised poetic dialogue, sung by two lovers or a married couple (568)

u timpanu A Corsican triangle (572)

uadindz An Ossetian ancient whistle flute, sometimes now made of a gun barrel (859)

übersitz Swiss whip-crackers of Meiringen, Bern; also *trychlen* (683)

ud A plucked, short-necked, fretless **lute** originally of the Middle East, still played in the Balkans, and known in Georgia (281, 286, 840, 877, 994)

udj An Adighian collective circle dance, performed in ritual processions (856)

uilleann **pipes** An Irish bellows-blown bagpipe (169, 384, 391, 392, 394)

új stílusú népdal 'The new style folk song': a term used in scholarly writing for nineteenth-century new-song compositions among Hungarian peasants (738)

'ukelele The Hawai'ian name of the Madeiran *braguinha*, a kind of *cavaquinho* (582)

ullagoner An Irish Traveller woman called on to keen or lament at funerals (295)

uniphons Discrete pitches in a scalar system (103, 104, 106)

urările Traditional musical-poetic greetings spoken rhythmically or sung on simple melodies by Romanian children at Christmas and New Year (869)

uravan 'Plain': a singing style in Bosnia-Hercegovina in which the rhythm of songs is based on the rhythm of the words (964)

urlar 'Floor, ground': the term used for the return to the original theme in Scottish *ceòl mór* (363)

urlatori 'Shouters': the generation of Italian singers influenced by American rock and roll and rhythm and blues (619)

urschrift A first full score (51)

ursul 'The bear': a Romanian winter festival with masked dancing, found in north-central Moldavia and Bucovina (870)

urtext 'Original texts': authoritative editions of composers' 'authentic' works (93)

urtyn **dun** A Mongolian long song (772)

uspavanke Croatian lullabies (926)

ustne harmonike (also *ustne orglic*) A Slovene mouth organ (919)

usul A Turkish rhythmic mode, adapted in the Balkans (951, 979)

ut A short-necked, fretless plucked **lute**, a Middle Eastern instrument played in *čalgija* ensembles of Macedonia (979–80, 997)

ut dun Protracted lyrical songs of the Kalmyks of southeastern European Russia (772)

uzliau Throat singing of the Bashkirs of Russia (773)

uzsaukums 'Call, air': slow-tempo versions of Latvian bagpipe tunes (504)

vaj An Albanian lament or stylized form of crying, whose name derives from a sorrowful exclamation (990)

vajdudule House-to-house caroling in Macedonia in case of drought (973)

vajtim 'Cried': Albanian flute melodies that draw on women's vocal laments; also *të qarë* (990, 993)

vakarēšana In Latvia, a gathering of women to do needlework and handicrafts while singing on autumn and winter evenings (502)

vāķēšana A Latvian prefuneral wake, nowadays observed only in Latgale (502)

vāķu rotaļas Latvian games with recited narrow-range melodies, performed beside a corpse the night before its funeral in western Kurzeme (502)

valačobnyja pieśni Belarusan 'wandering' spring songs (791, 793)

vallehorn A traditional horn blown for seasonal customs and related to no-longer-extant ancient horns (41)

válonka A Mordvinian bagpipe; also *fam, puzyr'*, and *skamóra* (774)

valse The French word for the **waltz** (524)

valsu The Corsican word for the **waltz** (571)

vamzdis A Lithuanian wooden flute with few holes for fingering (511)

variaciones 'Variations': the instrumental introduction to a Spanish *jota* (594)

varialaika Greek 'heavy' *laika* (1020)

variété A blend of African and international styles with Western popular instrumentation in the former French colonies of Africa (234)

vasietnija pieśni Belarusan autumn songs (792)

vatoccu 'Bell clapper': a polyphonic singing style of central Italy, with links to medieval discant (134)

vaudeville A French urban popular song of the sixteenth to eighteenth centuries; also *voix-de-ville* (534, 548, 583)

veillée The major context for French recreative singing not associated with meals, rarely practiced in contemporary French culture; compare *viellée* (546)

velike cimbale A Hungarian pedal **cimbalom** played in Slovenia, mostly by Gypsies in Prekmurje and Porabje (917)

velké muzika A Czech large ensemble, consisting of two violins, two clarinets, two bagpipes, and a string bass (719)

vemmalvärss A form of Estonian rhyming folk-song that appeared in the nineteenth century and superseded the runic *regivärss* songs (492)

verbunk A duple-meter Moravian and Slovak recruit's dance in which singing alternates with improvised dance steps (717)

verbunkos A Hungarian military-recruitment dance (162, 273–274, 737, 738, 745)

verşuri Songs based on the literate tradition and composed for burial services in parts of Transylvania, România (872)

vertep The Ukrainian Nativity play (799)

vesnianky Ukrainian spring songs, sung by groups of two or more girls in open or cleared spaces in or near a village (808)

veuze A Breton single-drone bagpipe of southeastern Brittany and northern Vendée, played alone or with an accordion or a fiddle (560)

vevlira A Swedish hurdy-gurdy (439)

viasielnyja halašeńni Belarusan wedding laments (793, 794)

viasielnyja muzyki 'Wedding musicians': Belarusan traditional folk-instrumental ensembles; also *kapela, hurtkampaniya, muzyki,* and *skamarochi* (798) *vièle* The French generic name of a bowed **lute**; also vielle (176, 542, 545, 651)

vielle à roue A hurdy-gurdy in France and the Low Countries (532, 545, 560)

viellée A French evening gathering where people socialized, drank, sang, and danced; compare *veillée* (141)

Vierzeiler A four-line song of Upper Austria (673)

Viggianesi Italian itinerant ensembles from the town of Viggiano that disseminated operatic tunes across Italy, Europe, and Turkey during the nineteenth century (617)

vihuela A high-pitched Spanish guitar (170, 589, 594, 601)

vikivaka kvæði A refrain sung by dancers in Icelandic *vikivakalag* songs (404)

vikivakalag An Icelandic strophic dance-song with refrains performed responsorially by the dancers (404)

vilepill An Estonian willow duct flute without holes for fingering; also *pajupill* 494

villancicos Spanish Christmas carols (589, 592, 596, 601)

villotte A type of Italian **lyric song** (606)

vioara A Romanian name of the violin (877)

viola A Portuguese guitar, usually with five double or triple courses of metal strings, that provides harmonic and rhythmic accompaniment to *fado*; also *amarantina*, *braguesa*, and *toeira* (116, 582, 583)

viola baixo A large bass guitar that plays the bass line in a performance of Portuguese *fado* (116, 582, 583)

viola da gamba In European art music, a fretted most often six-stringed bowed **lute** having a range approximating that of the cello; used during the **Renaissance** and **Baroque** periods for sacred and secular polyphony and revived in the twentieth century (55, 75, 420, 654)

violine An instrumental ensemble of Istria, Croatia; also *gunci, gunjci*, and *muzika* (931)

violon A Breton fiddle (560)

vira One of the oldest Portuguese couple dances, in 6/8 meter and most common in northwest Portugal (581–82)

virágének 'Flower songs': a type of Hungarian **lyric song** (737)

virelai A French medieval verse and song form (132)

virsi In modern Finnish, a Lutheran psalm; also *itku* (480)

viula di orbi 'Blind man's viola': a hurdy-gurdy of Italian-speaking Switzerland (694)

viulinu A Corsican violin (572)

viulu A Finnish violin (479)

viunishnye pesni 'Newlywed songs': songs sung by carolers at newlyweds' houses on the first Sunday after Easter in the Kostroma region near the Volga River in Russia (760)

vkiolarides The typical ensemble for dance-music in Cyprus, consisting of a violin playing the melody, a *laouto* playing accompaniment, and a *tampoutsia* keeping the rhythm (1030, *1031*)

vlačiljske pjesme Wool-combing songs of Bosnia-Hercegovina (963)

vlier A plucked dulcimer of the Low Countries (533)

vlöggelen A chain-dance of Ootmarsum, performed on Easter Sunday and Monday by more than a thousand men, accompanied by religious songs (522)

vocale A full vowel sound, like /a/, as the basis for singing; compare **semivocale** (105)

voceru A Corsican lament for a violent death; also called *buceru, bucerata* (566–67)

voeyesi A Swiss dance-song performed around fountains during the burning of the fields in the French-language areas (693)

voggevise 'Rocking song': a Norwegian work song performed to lull a baby (421)

volksbal Folk-dance nights in the Low Countries (535)

volkshochschulen German public colleges that often offer courses in folk music (659)

volkslied 'Folk song': a term coined in the early 1770s by Johann Gottfried von Herder (17, 551, 646, 662)

volksmusik Folk music, especially popularized forms in German-speaking areas of Central Europe (206, 207, 209, 657, 671, 675)

volkstümlichemusik Austrian commercialized folk music, played by brass- or accordion-based ensembles (671, 675–76)

volksthümliches lied A term for folklike song in German-speaking areas of Central Europe (207, 663)

volochebnye pesni 'Trudging songs': Russian songs sung at Easter when animals are led to summer pasture (760)

volynka A Russian bagpipe (774)

vopli A Russian lament (761)

vorgeige The lead violin in ensembles of Italian southern Tyrol; also *primgeige* (615)

vorzäurer The soloist in the *zäuerle* style of **yodel** of Urnasch, Switzerland (691)

vota A Chechen and Ingush double-headed drum; see *gaval* (863)

vozeni pesni Macedonian songs with elaborate melodies; also *glasoečki* or *ikoečki pesni* (974)

vrličko kolo 'Kolo of Vrlika': a Croatian *kolo* in which the only sounds heard are dancers' footfalls and the bouncing coin jewelry on women's costumes (929)

vučarske pjesme 'Wolf songs': Bosnia-Hercegovinian songs sung after hunting wolves in winter (963)

vuvă A Romanian one-headed **frame drum**, played in Oltenia and Muntenia (877)

wals The Dutch name of the **waltz** (524)

waltz A popular European couple dance in 3/4 time (7, 9, 166, 168, 170, 228, 288, 289, 330, 419, 435, 443, 457, 464, 484, 485, 486, 524, 527, 571, 655, 672, 673, 689, 690, 694, 695, 717, 718, 721, 765, 766, 776, 779, 812, 903)

Wandervogel German outdoor clubs with their own repertoire of folk songs (655–56)

wassailing An English carol-singing custom combining house visits with the performance of specific songs (132, 140, 331, 342–43)

waulking 'Wool shrinking': an occasion in Scotland for singing songs (133, 141, 197, *361*, 373)

werkbegriff The musical product as a finite, conceptual entity (52, 54, 55)

west gallery music English church music between 1750 and 1850 that has survived in oral tradition and involves elaborate fuguing tunes (328, 333, 336)

whittle and dub In England, a term for the combination of a three-holed pipe and a tabor, played by a one-man band (330)

wiegenlieder Christmastime manger songs of Germany in 6/8 or 3/4 time (651)

Wienerlied An Austrian genre from Vienna (673)

wierzchowe 'Of the peaks': a genre of open-air song of the Tatra Highlands, Poland (*113*)

Wilhem method The fixed-*do* system of sol-fa syllables in which vocables signify absolute pitches; see **solfège** and **solfeggio** (106)

wiskanie Women's calls in Poland (702)

wiwat Dance tunes in duple or triple time, popular in Great Poland (708)

Yiftos The Greek word for Roma, synonymous with 'musician' (284)

yodel A singing technique, and in some cases a song genre, involving the rapid alternation of full or chest voice with falsetto or head voice; see *jodel* (14, 19, 127, 128, 142, 194, 412, 607, 651, 671, *672*, 673, 676, 683, 689, 690–92, 696, 828, *829*, 873, 1010)

Yom Kippur The Jewish Day of Atonement (250, 259)

yonika A Bulgarian synthesizer (895)

yule Woolworkers' work songs of French-speaking Switzerland (693)

zabarii iish Chechen humorous songs (864)

zabavna muzika Serbo-Croatian pop or rock songs (204, 934–35, 949)

zaklikatnie viasny Belarusan songs invoking the spring season (791)

žalejka A Belarusan reed pipe (*797*)

zampogna 'Symphony': in Italy and Corsica, any instrument that produces a drone and a melodic line, including bagpipes, hurdy-gurdies, and **mouth harps**; also *zanfoña* and *zumpogna* (36, 169, *171*, 571, *616*)

zanfona A Spanish five-stringed hurdy-gurdy, characteristic of Galicia (589, 594)

žanićba Ciareški A Belarusan calendrical ritual game in which a symbolic mother and father, chosen from older members of a community, pair young unmarried men and women and 'marry' them to each other (792)

zapadniki 'Westernizers': Russian advocates of Western musical models (779) *zapateo* The dancer's footwork in Spanish **flamenco** (598)

zapev The solo introduction to a choral song in Russian polyphonic singing (756)

zapevanje A Serbian lament for the dead (941)

zaqq 'Belly': a Maltese bagpipe, usually accompanied by a **tambourine** and a friction drum (640, 641)

zari Gurian polyphonic funeral songs having structures based on liturgical forms (833)

zarzuela A Spanish court-based musical play with sung choruses and *coplas* alternating with spoken lines (597, 601, 602)

zäuerle (also *zäuerli*) A style of Swiss **yodel** (683, 685, 686, 690)

zavzava A Maltese friction drum played with a **tambourine** to accompany a bagpipe (640)

zbójnicki 'Robbers' dance': a men's dance in the Carpathian area of Poland (708)

zdravice Songs of salutation in Bosnia-Hercegovina (963)

zeibekiko A Greek solo dance in 9/4 time, originally of coastal Asia Minor; the principal dance of *rebetika* (1009, 1015, 1019, 1030)

zelenyj kúsek A Bohemian dance in which duple and triple meters alternate (*718*, 721)

ženska 'Female': used to distinguish women's singing styles in genres sung by men and women in Bosnia-Hercegovina (964)

zerizaykheizh yeredkher Adighian songs of acquittal that try to persuade the community of a singer's innocence of a crime (855)

žetelačke pjesme Bosnia-Hercegovinian harvest songs (963)

žetvarski glas 'Harvest voice': the style in which Serbian harvest songs are sung (942)

zevensprong 'Seven jumps' (Dutch): a jump-dance song of seven steps of the Low Countries; also *danse des sept sauts* (522)

zhaleika A Russian single-reed aerophone with one or two pipes with a horn bell; also *pishchik* (770, 771)

zhil-kobuz A Balkar and Karachaevi bowed **lute** (857)

zhir baschi 'Head of song': the Balkar and Karachaevi term for melody (857)

zhirga A Chechen and Ingush **frame drum**; see *tep* (863)

Zialonyja śviatki Belarusan Pentecost; also *Siomucha* (791)

Ziehharmonika Vernacular German for accordion (657)

zigarella 'Tape': the name of an hour-long Maltese *spirtu pront*, performed at gatherings in bars (639–40)

zikr Chechen and Ingush funeral prayers; see *nazm* (864)

zili Small metal finger-cymbals of Turkish origin, played in the Balkans (960, 967)

zilia Metal finger-cymbals, used in Greek *rebetika* (1019)

ziņģes Latvian popular songs of the 1700s and 1800s (504)

zingulca A Slovene noisemaker, made of a piece of wood or bone attached to a string, which produces a whirring sound when spun; also *brnkač* (919)

złóbcoki A small, rebeclike fiddle of Polish highlanders of the Tatra Mountains (706)

zmeika 'Snake': a Russian dance in which all participants walk in a circle or a serpentine pattern down a street; also *kjodiachii* and *khodovoi khorovod* (769)

znamenny rospev 'Chanting by signs': a Russian notational system for long-drawn-out songs (779)

žniŭnja pieśni Belarusan harvest songs (791)

zonaradhiko A Greek Thracian belt dance in 6/8 meter (1013)

zongora In Romania, the guitar of Maramureş (880)

zortziko 'Made of eights': the most popular Basque dance-song type, in asymmetric rhythm and consisting of eight steps (121, *311*, 312)

zouk A popular music genre of the French Antilles, popular in France (238, 239)

zournadhes (also *zourna*) A pair of conical, double-reed shawms, played by Macedonian Gypsies in Greece (1008–1011, 1012)

zrokha kudi 'Cow's tail': a Georgian small metal military instrument, mentioned in medieval literary sources (840)

zumare An Albanian and Montenegrin single-reed double-pipe aerophone (959–60, 996)

zurgălăi Romanian bells, used in New Year's ceremonies and weddings and hung around the necks of cattle and sheep as signal devices; also *clopote* (876)

zurla (also *zurna*) A Middle Eastern double-reed, conical-bore shawm, imported into the Balkans and Georgia during the Ottoman period; see *zurle* (168, 170, 201, 279, *280*–281, 284, 285, 840, 842, 879, 893, 895, 951, 960, 966, 975–76, *977*, 978–79, *982*, 983)

zurle An Albanian conical-bore double-reed aerophone; also *cingonë, curle,* and *surle;* see *zurla* (996)

zvanočak Belarusan two-clappered hand bells of metal and wood (797)

žvegla Slovene duct flute (915, *916*)

zvon Belarusan bronze clappered bells (797)

zvončari Croatian bell carriers (925)

žvrgolci Bird- or horse-shaped one-to-three-holed clay whistles, played by children in Prekmurje and Lower Carniola, Slovenia (915, 919)

Zwiefache 'Two-Timers': a Bavarian couple dance that shifts between 2/4 and 3/4 time (166, 655)

A Guide to Publications on European Music

Each article in this volume contains an extensive bibliography. This guide contains only a highly selected list of English-language books covering mainly traditional and popular music and associated arts, such as dance, ritual, and sung poetry.

OVERVIEWS

Bohlman, Philip V. 1988. *The Study of Folk Music in the Modern World.* Bloomington: Indiana University Press.

Grout, Donald Jay, and Claude V. Palisca. 1996. *A History of Western Music.* 5th ed. New York: Norton.

Karpeles, Maud. 1956. *Folk Songs of Europe.* London: Novello.

Ling, Jan. 1997. *A History of European Folk Music.* Rochester, N.Y.: University of Rochester Press.

Lund, Cajsa. 1974. *The Sound of Archeology.* Stockholm: Musikmuseet.

Sárosi, Balint. 1978. *Gypsy Music.* Translated by Fred MacNicol. Budapest: Corvina Press.

Wallis, Roger, and Malm, Krister. 1984. *Big Sounds from Small Peoples: The Music Industry in Small Countries.* London: Constable.

West, M. L. 1992. *Ancient Greek Music.* Oxford: Clarendon Press.

Wiora, Walter. 1966. *European Folk Song: Common Forms in Characteristic Modifications.* Translated by Robert Kilben. New York: Leeds Music Corp.

MUSICAL INSTRUMENTS

Andersson, Otto. 1930. *The Bowed-Harp.* London: William Reeves.

Anoyanakis, Fivos. 1979 [1965]. *Greek Popular Musical Instruments.* Athens: National Bank of Greece.

Arbatsky, Yuri. 1953. *Beating the Tupan in the Central Balkans.* Chicago: The Newberry Library.

Baines, Anthony. 1960. *Bagpipes.* Oxford: Oxford University Press.

Bentzon, Andreas F. W. 1969. *The Launeddas: A Sardinian Folk Musical Instrument.* Copenhagen: Akademisk forlag.

Bessaraboff, A. 1941. *Ancient European Musical Instruments.* Cambridge: Harvard University Press.

Bezic, Jerko, et al., eds. 1975. *Traditional Folk Music Instruments of Jugoslavia.* Zagreb: Kolska Knjiga.

Collinson, Francis. 1975. *The Bagpipe: The History of a Musical Instrument.* London: Routledge and Kegan Paul.

Galpin, Francis. 1937. *A Textbook of European Musical Instruments: Their Origin, History, and Character.* London: Williams and Nowgate.

Harrison, Frank L., and Joan Rimmer. 1964. *European Musical Instruments.* London: Norton.

Ling, Jan, et al. 1991. *The Nyckelharpa: Present and Past.* Stockholm: Svea fonogram.

Müller, Mette. 1972. *From Bone Pipe and Cattle Horn to Fiddle and Psaltery.* Stockholm: Musikhistoriska Museum.

Rimmer, Joan. 1977 [1969]. *The Irish Harp.* Cork: The Mercier Press.

COLLECTIONS

Adler, Israel. 1986. *Epic Ballads.* Judeo-Spanish Ballads from Oral Tradition, 2, part 1. Musical transcriptions and studies by Israel J. Katz. Berkeley and Los Angeles: University of California Press.

Bartók, Béla. 1954. *Serbo-Croatian Heroic Songs.* Translated by Albert B. Lord. Cambridge: Harvard University Press.

Bartók, Béla, and Albert B. Lord. 1951. *Serbo-Croatian Folk Songs.* New York: Columbia University Press.

———. 1978. *Yugoslav Folk Music.* Edited by Benjamin Suchoff. Foreword by George Herzog. Albany, N.Y.: State University of New York Press.

Bronson, Bertrand H. 1959–1972. *The Traditional Tunes of the Child Ballads*. Princeton: Princeton University Press.

Chianis, Sotirios (Sam). 1965. *Folksongs of Mantinea, Greece*. Berkeley: University of California Press.

Erdely, Stephen. 1994. *The Music of Four Serbo-Croatian Heroic Songs: A Study*. New York: Garland.

Holmboe, Vagn. 1988. *Danish Street Cries: A Study of Their Musical Structure, and a Complete Edition of Tunes with Words Collected before 1960*. Acta Ethnomusicologica Danica, 5. Copenhagen: Forlaget Kragen.

MacColl, Ewan, and Peggy Seeger. 1977. *Travellers' Songs from England and Scotland*. Knoxville: University of Tennessee Press.

Nielsen, Svend. 1982. *Stability in Musical Improvisation: A Repertoire of Icelandic Epic Songs (Rímur)*. Acta Ethnomusicologica Danica, 3. Copenhagen: Forlaget Kragen.

Slobin, Mark, ed. and trans. 1982. *Old Jewish Folk Music: The Collections and Writings of Moshe Beregovski*. Philadelphia: University of Pennsylvania Press.

Traerup, Birthe. 1970. *East Macedonian Folk Songs: Contemporary Traditonal Material from Malesevo, Pijanec and the Razlog District*. Copenhagen: Akademisk forlag.

Werner, Eric. 1976. *A Voice Still Heard: The Sacred Songs of the Ashkenazic Jews*. University Park: Pennsylvania State University Press.

MUSIC ETHNOGRAPHIES AND SPECIALIZED STUDIES

Bohlman, Philip V. 1989. *"The Land Where Two Streams Flow": Music in the German-Jewish Community of Israel*. Urbana: University of Illinois Press.

Boyes, Georgina. 1994. *The Imagined Village*. Manchester: Manchester University Press.

Cooke, Peter. 1986. *The Fiddle Tradition of the Shetland Isles*. Cambridge: Cambridge University Press.

Cowdery, James. 1990. *The Melodic Tradition of Ireland*. Kent, Ohio: Kent State University Press.

Finnegan, Ruth. 1989. *The Hidden Musicians. Music-Making in an English Town*. Cambridge: Cambridge University Press.

Flam, Gila. 1992. *Singing for Survival: Songs of the Lodz Ghetto, 1940–1945*. Urbana and Chicago: University of Illinois Press.

Goertzen, Chris. *Fiddling for Norway*. Chicago: University of Chicago Press.

Hopkins, Pandora. 1986. *Aural Thinking in Norway: Performance and Communication with the Hardingfele*. New York: Human Sciences Press.

Lortat-Jacob, Bernard. 1994. *Sardinian Chronicles*. Chicago: University of Chicago Press.

Mitchell, Timothy. 1994. *Flamenco Deep Song*. New Haven, Conn.: Yale University Press.

Porter, James, and Herschel Gower. 1995. *Jeannie Robertson: Emergent Singer, Transformative Voice*. Knoxville: University of Tennessee Press.

Rice, Timothy. 1994. *May It Fill Your Soul: Experiencing Bulgarian Music*. Chicago: University of Chicago Press.

Shields, Hugh. 1993. *Narrative Singing in Ireland: Lays, Ballads, Come-All-Yes and Other Lyric Songs*. Dublin: Irish Academic Press.

Starkie, Walter. 1933. *Raggle-Taggle: Adventures with a Fiddle in Hungary and Romania*. London: John Murray.

Sugarman, Jane. 1997. *Engendering Song: Singing and Subjectivity at Prespa Albanian Weddings*. Chicago: University of Chicago Press.

Suojanen, Päivikki. 1984. *Finnish Folk Hymn Singing: Study in Music Anthropology*. Tampere: University of Tampere, Institute for Folk Tradition.

Washabaugh, William. 1996. *Flamenco: Passion, Politics, and Popular Culture*. Oxford and Washington, D.C.: Berg.

COUNTRY SURVEYS

Bartók, Béla. 1931. *Hungarian Folk Music*. London: Oxford University Press.

Breathnach, Breandán. 1977. *Folk Music and Dances of Ireland*. Dublin: Mercier.

Collinson, Francis. 1966. *The Traditional and National Music of Scotland*. London: Routledge and Kegan Paul.

Karpeles, Maud. 1987 [1973]. *An Introduction to English Folk Song*. London: Oxford University Press.

Kodály, Zoltán. 1960. *Folk Music of Hungary*. Translated by Ronald Tempest and Cynthia Jolly. London: Barrie & Rockliff.

Lloyd, A. L. 1967. *Folk Song in England*. London: Lawrence & Wishart.

Purser, John. 1992. *Scotland's Music: A History of the Traditional and Classical Music of Scotland from Earliest Times to the Present Day*. Edinburgh: Mainstream Publishing.

Sárosi, Balint. 1986. *Folk Music: The Hungarian Music Idiom*. Budapest: Corvina.

Sharp, Cecil. 1907. *English Folk-Song: Some Conclusions*. London: Novello, Simpkin.

Warner, Elizabeth, and Evgenii Kustovskii. 1990. *Russian Traditional Folk Song*. Hull, U.K: Hull University Press.

Williams, W. S. Gwynn. 1933. *Welsh National Music and Dance*. London: J. Curwen.

RITUALS AND CUSTOMS

Alexiou, Margaret. 1974. *The Ritual Lament in Greek Tradition.* Cambridge: Cambridge University Press.

Bendix, Regina. 1985. *Progress and Nostalgia: Silvesterklausen in Urnäsch, Switzerland.* Berkeley: University of California Press.

Danforth, Loring. 1989. *Firewalking and Religious Healing: The Anastinaria of Greece and the American Firewalking Movement.* Princeton: Princeton University Press.

Glassie, Henry. 1982. *Passing the Time in Ballymenone: Culture and History of an Ulster Community.* Philadelphia: University of Pennsylvania Press.

Kligman, Gail. 1981. *Căluş: Symbolic Transformation in Romanian Ritual.* Chicago. University of Chicago Press.

———. 1988. *The Wedding of the Dead: Ritual, Poetics and Popular Culture in Transylvania.* Berkeley: University of California Press.

DANCE

Cowan, Jane. 1990. *Dance and the Body Politic in Northern Greece.* Princeton: Princeton University Press.

Flett, J. F., and T. M. Flett. 1985. *Traditional Dancing in Scotland.* London: Routledge and Kegan Paul.

Katsarova, Raina, and Kiril Djenev. 1976. *Bulgarian Folk Dances.* Cambridge, Mass.: Slavica.

Petrides, Ted. 1975. *Folk Dances of the Greeks.* Jericho, N.Y.: Exposition Press.

Popescu-Judetz, Eugenia. 1979. *Sixty Folk Dances*

of Romania. Pittsburgh: Duquesne University Tamburitzans, Institute of Folk Arts.

Sharp, Cecil, and A. P. Oppé. 1924. *The Dance: An Historical Survey of Dancing in Europe.* London: Halton and Truscott Smith.

Torp, Lisbet. 1990. *Chain and Round Dance Patterns: A Method for Structural Analysis and Its Application to European Material.* 3 vols. Copenhagen: University of Copenhagen, Museum Tusculanum Press.

SONG POETRY

Aulestia, Gorka. 1995. *Improvisational Poetry from the Basque Country.* Reno: University of Nevada Press.

Bailey, James, and Tatiana Ivanova. 1998. *Anthology of Russian Oral Epics.* New York: M. E. Sharpe.

Beissinger, Margaret H. 1991. *The Art of the Lautar: The Epic Tradition of Romania.* New York: Garland.

Entwhistle, William J. 1939. *European Balladry.* Oxford: Clarendon Press.

Kolsti, John. 1990. *The Bi-Lingual Singer: A*

Study in Albanian and Serbo-Croatian Oral Epic Traditions. New York: Garland.

Lord, Albert B. 1960. *The Singer of Tales.* Cambridge: Harvard University Press.

———. 1991. *Epic Singers and Oral Tradition.* Ithaca: Cornell University Press.

Vargyas, Lajos. 1983. *Hungarian Ballads and the European Ballad Tradition.* Budapest: Akadémiai Kiadó.

Zguta, Russell. 1978. *Russian Minstrels: A History of the Skomorokhi.* Oxford: Clarendon Press.

POPULAR MUSIC

Butterworth, Katherine, and Sarah Schneider. 1975. *Rebetika: Songs from the Old Greek Underworld.* Athens: Kolomboi.

Cushman, Thomas. 1995. *Notes from Underground: Rock Music Counterculture in Russia.* Albany, N.Y.: State University of New York Press.

Hebdige, Dick. 1979. *Subculture: The Meaning of Style.* London: Methuen.

Holst, Gail. 1977. *Road to Rembetika: Music of a Greek Sub-Culture: Songs of Love, Sorrow and Hashish.* Limni and Athens: Denise Harvey and Co.

———. 1980. *Theodorakis: Myth and Politics in Modern Greek Music.* Amsterdam: Adolf M. Hakkert.

Larkey, Edward. 1993. *Pungent Sounds: Constructing Identity with Popular Music in Austria.* Austrian Culture, 9. New York: Peter Lang.

Mitchell, Tony. 1996. *Popular Music and Local Identity.* London: Leicester University Press.

Oliver, Paul, ed. 1990. *Black Music in Britain:*

Essays on the Afro-Asian Contribution to Popular Music. Milton Keynes: Open University Press.

Prendergast, Mark J. 1987. *Isle of Noises: Rock and Roll's Roots in Ireland.* New York: St. Martin's Press.

Ramet, Sabrina Petra, ed. 1994. *Rocking the State: Rock Music and Politics in Eastern Europe and Russia.* Boulder, Colo.: Westview Press.

Ryback, Timothy. 1990. *Rock Around the Bloc: A History of Rock Music in Eastern Europe and the Soviet Union.* New York: Oxford University Press.

Smith, Gerald. 1984. *Songs to Seven Strings: Russian Guitar Poetry and Soviet "Mass" Song.* Bloomington: Indiana University Press.

Starr, S. Frederic. 1994. *Red and Hot: The Fate of Jazz in the Soviet Union, 1917–1991.* New York: Limelight Editions.

Taylor, Timothy. 1997. *Global Pop: World Music, World Markets.* New York: Routledge.

Troitsky, Artemy. 1987. *Back in the USSR: The True Story of Rock in Russia.* Boston and London: Faber.

A Guide to Recordings of European Traditional Music
Brian Patrick Fox

Each article contains an extensive list of audiovisual resources. A few generally available compact discs are listed here.

COLLECTIONS

Europe. 1994. *Le monde des musiques traditionnelles/ The World of Traditional Music/ Musikkulturen der Welt/El mundo de las músicas tradicionales,* 6. Produced by Christian Poché. Ocora/Radio France C560066. Booklet in French, English, German, Spanish. Compact disc.

Musique à la croisée des cultures/Music at the Crossroads. 1995. Artistic direction by Laurent Aubert. Archives Internationales de Musique Populaire & Disques VDE-GALLO CD 828-29. 75-page booklet in French and English. Two compact discs.

Unblocked: Music of Eastern Europe. 1997. Ellipsis Arts CD 3570. *Eastern Voices, Northern Shores* (CD 3571), *From the Danube through the Carpathians* (CD 3572), *The Balkans* (CD 3573). 72-page booklet. Three compact discs.

World Network. 1991–1997. Recordings made in Germany at concerts, festivals, and studios, and in the field. Edited by Christian Scholze and Jean Trouillet with Jan Reichow of WDR Westdeutscher Rundfunk. Network Medien GmbH, D-6-316 Frankfurt. Distributed by Zweitausendeins Versand, Frankfurt. Notes in German, English, and French. Vol. 2 (1991; Nr. 52.985), Georgia; vol. 4 (1991; Nr. 52.987), Crete; vol. 11 (1992; Nr. 54.038), Portugal; vol. 15 (1993; Nr. 55.832), France; vol. 16 (1993; Nr. 55.833), Ireland; vol. 24 (1994; Nr. 56.982), The Alps; vol. 25 (1994; Nr. 56.983), Spain; vol. 26 (1994; Nr. 56.984), Russia; vol. 31 (1995; Nr. 58.393), Corsica/Sardinia; vol. 32 (1995; Nr. 58.394), Scotland; vol. 41 (1997; Nr. 28.300), Romania. 42 compact discs.

TRANSNATIONAL GROUPS

Atlan, Françoise. *Françoise Atlan: Romances Sefardies: Entre la rose et le jasmin/Sephardic Songs: From the Rose to the Jasmine.* N.d. Musique de monde/Music from the World. Notes and texts in French and English by Sami Sadak. Buda 92574–2. Compact disc.

Basque Country: Traditional and Contemporary Songs. N.d. Ocora/Radio France C 559083. Compact disc.

Chants du pays basque/Songs from the Basque Country. 1993 [1977]. Arion ARN 64223. Notes in French and English by Jean Haritschelhar. Compact disc.

Chants populaires Yiddish/Popular Yiddish Songs. N.d. Musique de monde/Music from the World. Notes and texts in French and English by Sami Sadak. Buda 92595–2. Compact disc.

Klezmer à la Russe: Musiques juives d'Europe orientale. 1996. Recording by Christian Feldgen. Maison des Cultures du Monde W260066. Notes in French and English by Andreas Karpen and Kasbek. Compact disc.

Klezmer Music: A Marriage of Heaven and Earth. 1996. Musical Expeditions. 64-page booklet with essays by Michael Alpert, Frank London, and Andy Statman. Ellipsis Arts 4090. Compact disc.

Máramoros: The Lost Jewish Music of Transylvania—Muzsikás. 1993. Produced by Daniel Hamar and Muzsikás. Notes in English by Muzsikás and Judit Frigyesi. Hannibal Records HNCD 1373. Compact disc.

Musiciens Manouches en Roussillon/Gypsy Manouches from Roussillon: Zaïti. 1992. Recorded by Clément Ziegler. Notes by Pierre Parce, Daniel Elziere, and Hermine Duran. Al Sur ALCD 107. Compact disc.

Rubin & Horowitz: Bessarabian Symphony: Early Jewish Instrumental Music. 1994. Notes in German and English. Wergo Sm 1606–2. Spectrum 281 606–2. Compact disc.

BRITAIN AND IRELAND

Bannal: Waulking Songs. 1996. Produced by Jim Sutherland. Notes and texts in Gaelic and English. Greentrax CDTRAX 099. Compact disc.

Bowen, Robin Hue. 1993. *Telyn Berseiniol fy Ngwlad/The Sweet Harp of My Land.* Notes in Welsh and English. Flying Fish FF 70610. Compact disc.

Ceol Mor, Ceol Beag: Iain MacFadyen. 1996. Producd by Robin Morton. Temple Records COMD2018. Compact disc.

*The Drones and the Chanters: Irish Pipering Volume Two.*1994. Claddagh Records CC61CD. Compact disc.

England. 1998. World Library of Folk and Primitive Music, 1. Recorded by Alan Lomax, Maurice Brown, Douglas Cleverdon, and others between 1939 and 1951. Rounder ROUN 1741. Compact disc.

English Roots Music: The Rough Guide. N.d. The Rough Guide/World Music Network RGNET 1018CD. Compact disc.

From Galway to Dublin: Early Recordings of Traditional Irish Music. 1993. Recorded in Ireland, England, and America between 1921 and 1959. Rounder CD 1087. Compact disc.

The Gentlemen Pipers. 1994. Notes by Ron Kavana. Globestyle CDORBD 084. Compact disc.

Green Linnet Records: The Twentieth Anniversary Collection. 1996. Notes by Myron Bretholz and Wendy Newton. Green Linnet GLCD 106–1–106–2. Compact disc.

Ireland: Irlande. 1997. Traditional Musics of Today/Musiques traditionnelles d'aujourd'hui. Unesco Collection. Recording and notes in English and French by Rionach Ui Ógáin. Auvidis and Unesco D 8271. Compact disc.

Irish Music: The Rough Guide. N.d. The Rough Guide/World Music Network RGNET 1006CD. Compact disc.

McDonagh, John. 994. *An Spailpín Fánach: Traditional Songs from Connemara.* Notes and texts in Irish and English. Cló-Iar-Chonnachta CICD 006. Compact disc.

The Muckle Sangs: Classic Scots Ballads. 1992. Scottish Tradition Series, 5. Produced by the School of Scottish Studies, University of Edinburgh. Greentrax Records CDTRAX 9005. Compact disc.

Music at Matt Molloy's. 1992. Realworld and Caroline CAROL 2324–2. Compact disc.

The Northumbrian Small Pipes. 1996. Produced by Tony Engle. Notes by Colin Ross. Topic Records TSCD 487. Compact disc.

Scotland: Tunes from the Lowlands, Highlands, and Islands. 1995. World Network, 32. Notes by Thomas Daun. World Network WDR 58.394. Compact disc.

Scottish Music: The Rough Guide. N.d. The Rough Guide/World Music Network RGNET 1004CD. Compact disc.

SCANDINAVIA, FINLAND, AND THE BALTIC STATES

Årsringar: Swedish Folk Music 1970–1990. 1990. Notes in Swedish by Per Gudmundson and Ale Möller. 2 compact discs. Musiknätet MNWCD 194–195. Compact disc.

Bjørkum, Per Saemund. *Den våre fela.* 1994. Produced by Hans Fredrik Jacobsen. Notes in Norwegian and English. Heilo HCD 7094. Compact disc.

Buen, Knut. *Knut Buen: As Quick as Fire.* 1996. [Norway: Hardanger fiddle.] Produced by Peter K. Siegel. Henry Street Records HSR 0002. Compact disc.

Ensemble Rasa. *Lettonie: Musiques des rites solaires/Latvia: Music of Solar Rites.* Inédit. 1995. Notes and texts by Valdis Muktupăvels, in French and English. Maison des Cultures du Monde W 260062. Compact disc.

Finlande: Musique traditionnelle/Finland: Traditional Music. 1996. Recorded by Yleisradio (National Radio of Finland) between 1941 and 1995. Notes by Sirkka Halonen. Ocora C600004. Compact disc.

Föregångare. 1993. Folk-music recordings from the Archive of the Swedish National Radio, 1949–1967. Notes by Märta Ramsten in Swedish and English. MNW CD 240–242. 3 compact discs.

JPP: Devil's Polska: New Finnish Folk Fiddling. 1994. Green Linnet GLCE 4012. Compact disc.

JPP: Kaustinen Rhapsody. 1994. Green Linnet GLCD 4019. Compact disc.

Kuulas Hetki. 1993. Sibelius-Akatemian Kansanmusiikin Osaston Äänitteitä, 1. OMCD-46. Compact disc.

Lien, Annbjørg. 1995. *Annbjørg Lien: Felefeber: Norwegian Fiddle Fantasia.* Shanachie 64060. Compact disc.

Lituanie: Le pays des chansons/Lithuania: The Country of Songs. 1997. Recorded by Luetuvos Radijas between 1958 and 1995. Notes by Antanas Fokas in English and Lithuanian. Ocora C 600005. Compact disc.

Lockrop och Vallåtar: Ancient Swedish Pastoral Music. 1996. Musica Sveciae/Folk Music in Sweden, 8. Recorded mainly between 1949 and 1964, with additional contemporary performances. Notes by Anna Ivarsdotter, in Swedish and English. Caprice CAP 21483. Compact disc.

Musica Sveciae: Folk Music in Sweden. 1994–1997. Produced by Anna Frisk. Notes in Swedish, English, and Finnish. Caprice Records CAP 21474–85. 25 compact discs.

Nordisk Sang: Music of Norway. 1991. Produced by Hans Wendl. New Albion Records NA 031. Compact disc.

Suède-Norvège: Musiques des vallées scandinaves. 1993. Notes by Jean-Pierre Yvert in French, English, and German. Distributed by Harmonia Mundi. Ocora C 560008. Compact disc.

The Kalevala Heritage: Archive Recordings of Ancient Finnish Songs. 1995. Compiled from recordings in the Archives of the Finnish Literature Society. Notes in English. Ondine ODE 849–2. Compact disc.

Valimik Eesti Rahvalaule/Anthology of Estonian Folk Songs. 1994. Compiled and annotated by Ingrid Rüütel, Estonian Folklore Archives. Forte FD 0012/2. Compact disc.

Värtinä: Seleniko. 1993. Green Linnet GLCD 4006. Compact disc.

Voix des pays baltes/Baltic Voices: Chants traditionnels de Lattonie, Lituanie, Estonie. 1994. Inédit.

Compiled from recordings in radio archives, 1937–1985. Notes by Mārtiņ Boiko, Daiva Račiunaite-Vičiniene, and Vaike Sarv, in French and English. Maison des Cultures du Monde W 260055. Compact disc.

WESTERN EUROPE

Andalusian Flamenco Song & Dance: Lomas, DeMalaga. N.d. Lyrichord 7388. Compact disc.

Arnaud Maisonneuve: Songs of Lower Brittany. N.d. Ocora C559082. Compact disc.

Ballads, Songs and Dances from Flanders and Wallonia. N.d. Ocora C580061. Compact disc.

Coeur de France: Music from Central France. 1997. Music from Limousin, Berry, Bourbonnais, Cenre, and Auvergne. Notes in English and French. Ethnic/Auvidis B 6848. Compact disc.

Corsica: Traditional Songs and Music. 1990. Music of Man Archives. Recorded by Wolfgang Laade in 1958 and 1973. Jecklin-Disco JD 650-2. Compact disc.

Donnisultana Per Agata: Polyphonies Corses. 1992. Notes by Ghjermana de Zerbi and Ghjacumu Fusina, in Italian, English, and French. Silex Y225019. Compact disc.

Duende: From Traditional Masters to Gypsy Rock. 1994. Ellipsis Arts ELLI CT 3350. 3 compact discs.

Duende: Passion: Voices of Flamenco. 1996. Produced by Angel Romero. Notes by A. Romero. Ellipsis Arts ELLI CD 3351. Compact disc.

El Barullo [and] Maraito: Plazuela. 1995. Flamenco Vivo. Notes in Spanish, English, and French. Auvidis/Ethnic B 6814. Compact disc.

Eriik Marchand and Thierry Robin: Songs of Central Brittany. N.d. Ocora C559084. Compact disc.

Fados de Lisboa 1928–1936. 1992. Fados from Portugal, 1. Notes by Paul Vernon. Heritage HT CD14. Compact disc.

Flamenco: The Rough Guide. N.d. The Rough Guide/World Music Network RGNET 1015CD. Compact disc.

France: Landes de Gascogne: La Cornemuse. 1996. Notes in French by Lothaire, with English and German translations. Ocora Radio France C560051. Compact disc.

Het daghet inden Oosten: It's Dawning in the East, Bagpipes of the Low Countries. 1995. Notes by Bert Lotz, in English. Pan Records PAN 2025CD. Compact disc.

In Dialetto Sardo: Music of Sardinia 1930–1932. 1993. Notes by Paul Vernon. Translation of lyrics by Maria Teresa Orru Babbage. Heritage HT CD 20. Compact disc.

Italia: Donne Della Pianura del Po/Italie: Femmes de ka Plaune du Pô/Italy: Women of the Po Valley. 1997. Notes in English and French. Ethnic B 6846. Compact disc.

Italian Treasury: Folk Music and Song of Italy—A Sampler. 1999. Recordings by Alan Lomax and Diego Carpitella. Rounder ROUN1801. Compact disc.

Italie: Polyohonie Génoise/Italy: Genoese Polyphony. N.d. Musique du monde/Music of the World. Notes by Franck Tenaille in English and French. Buda Records 92514–2. Compact disc.

Melis, Efisio. 1995. *Efisio Melis: Les Launeddas en Sardaigne 1930–1950.* Notes by Roberto Leydi and Pietro Sassu, in Italian, French, and English. Silex Memoire Y225106. Compact disc.

The Music of Portugal: The Rough Guide. N.d. The Rough Guide/World Music Network RGNET 1025CD. Compact disc.

Musical Traditions of Portugal. 1994. Traditional Music of the World, 9. Recorded by Tiago de Oliveira Pinto and Max Peter Baumann in 1988. Notes by Salwa El-Shawan Castelo-Branco, in English and Portuguese. Distributed by KOCH International. Smithsonian Folkways CD SF 40435. Compact disc.

Musique populaire de la Belgique/Volksmuziek uit Belgie/Folk Music from Belgium. 1997. Recorded by Hubert Boone. Notes by Piet Chielens, with English and French translations. Ethnic/Auvidis B6844. 2 compact discs.

Les musiques de Bretagne/The Sounds of Brittany. 1991. Notes by E. Lehtela. Keltia Musique KMCD 19. Compact disc.

Planet Flanders: Music of Allochthones in Flanders/Muziek van Allochtonen in Vlaanderen. 1996. Notes by Al de Boeck. Presented by the Intercultural Centre for Migrants. Distributed by Arhoolie. PAN POCC 1006. Compact disc.

Polyphonies de Sardaigne. 1992. Le Chant du Monde/Musée de l'Homme LDX 274760. Compact disc.

Portugal: Chants et Tamboures de Beira-Baixa/Portugal: Songs and Drums from Beira-Baixa. 1992. Musique du monde/Music from the World. Notes by Murielle Mignon and Manuel Gomes. Buda Records 92542–2. Compact disc.

Portugal: Les voix de l'Alentejo/Voices of Alentejo. 1994. Notes in French and English. Distributed by Auvidis. Ethnic B6796. Compact disc.

Portugal, a Spirit of Fado: Fado Instrumental. 1993. Un Parfum de Fado, 5. Distributed by Auvidis. Playa Sound PS 65705. Compact disc.

Portuguese Traditional Music. N.d. Auvidis 8008. Compact disc.

Quand les Bretons passent à table/Kanomp ouzh taol. 1994. Tradition vivante de Bretagne, 2.

Notes with texts in Breton and French. Dastum DAS 121. Compact disc.

Sacred Music of Corsica: The Chants of Holy Week, Bonifacio. N.d. Ocora C 559086. Compact disc.

Sanacore. *Sanacore—All' aria—Italie: Cants populaire/Italy: Popular songs.* N.d. Musique du monde/Music of the World. Notes by Tania Pividori, in French and English. Texts in Italian, with translation. Buda 92626–2. Compact disc.

Sardaigne: Les maîtres de la musique instrumentale. 1995. Produced by Michel Pagiras. Notes by Roberto Leydi. Al Sur ALCD 157. Compact disc.

Skolvan: Kerzh Ba'n' Dans/Entrez dans la danse/Come to the Dance. 1991. Keltia Musique KMCD 16. Compact disc.

Soñj: Kanticōu E Vro Briez/Musiques sacrées de Bretagne/Sacred Music of Brittany. 1991. Keltia Musique KMCD 17. Compact disc.

Storvvan: Digor'n Abadenn: Ouvrons la ronde/Join in the Round. 1991. Keltia Musique KMCD 24. Compact disc.

Suspiro del Moro: Flamenco and Moorish Roots. 1995. Musique du monde/Music of the World. Notes by Marc Loopoyt, in French, Spanish, and English. Buda Records 92625–2. Compact disc.

Tenores di Bitti: S'amore 'e mama. 1996. A WOMAD Production. RealWorld CAR 2362–2. Compact disc.

Triskell-Servat: L'albatros fou: The Foolish Albatross. 1991. Keltia Musique KMCD 22.

Utrera, Fernando de. 1987. *Cante Flamenco: Fernando et Bernarda de Utrera, Volumes 1–2.* Notes by Antonio Espana, in Spanish with English and French translations. Ocora C558642/43. 2 compact discs.

La vielle en France: Les maîtres de la vielle à roue/Hurdy-Gurdy in France: Hurdy-Gurdy Masters. N.d. Notes in English and French. Recorded between 1930 and 1991. Silex Memoire Y 225109. Compact disc.

Zampogne en Italie: Enregistrements 1969–1989. Produced by André Ricros. Notes by Roberto Leydi, with English translation by Mary Pardoe and French translation by Maria Costa. Silex France Y225111. Compact disc.

Zampogne en Italie/Zampogne Italian Bag-Pipes. N.d. Music of Latium, Molise, Campanie, Basilicate, Calabria, and Sicily. Recorded between 1969 and 1989. Notes in English, French, and Italian. Silex Memoire Y 225111. Compact disc.

CENTRAL EUROPE

Austrian Folk Music—Vols. 1 & 2. N.d. Arhoolie 3003. Compact disc.

Austrian Zither. N.d. Playasound 65067. Compact disc.

Burgenland. 1993 Tondokumente zur Volksmusik in Österreich, 1. 1993. RST Records 915572–2. 2 compact discs.

Czechoslovakia. N.d. Planett 242003. Compact disc.

Fire in the Mountains: Polish Mountain Fiddle Music, Volumes 1 and 2. 1997. Compiled from 78-RPM recordings issued in 1928 and 1929. Yazoo 7012/7013. Compact disc.

Hungary and Romania: Descendants of the Itinerant Gypsies: Melodies of Sorrow and Joy. 1997. Music of the Earth. Recording and notes by Minoru Morita. Produced by Stephen McArthur. Recordings drawn from *Music of the Earth: Fieldworkers' Sound Collections* (Victor Company of Japan [JVC], 1992). Multicultural Media MCM 3010. Compact disc.

Juuzli: Muotatal Jodel. N.d. Chant du Monde 274716. Compact disc.

Moskowitz, Joseph. 1996. *The Art of the Cymbalom: The Music of Joseph Moskowitz 1916–1953.* Recorded in the United States. Rounder CD 1126. Compact disc.

Mountain Songs and Yodeling of the Alps. N.d. Smithsonian Folkways 8807. Compact disc.

Music of the Tatra Mountains: Gienek Wilczek's Bukowina Band. 1996. Nimbus NI 5464. Compact disc.

Musiques Traditionnelles de Hongrie/Hungarian Traditional Music: "Tanchaz." 1993. Distributed by Auvidis. Playa Sound PS 65117. Compact disc.

Pologne: Chansons et danses populaires/Poland: Folk Songs and Dances. 1993. AIMP, 29. Recorded between 1972 and 1992. Notes by Anna Czekanowska. VDE CD 757. Compact disc.

Pologne: Danses. 1992. Texts in French and English. Arion ARN 64188. Compact disc.

Sebö: Hungarian Folk Music. 1993 [1980]. Originally issued by Hungaroton. Rounder CD 5005. Compact disc.

EASTERN EUROPE

Byelorussia. N.d. Auvidis 8005/8805. Compact disc.

Chants des bords de la Mer Noire/Songs from the Shores of the Black Sea: Georgians, Crimean Greeks, Kuban Cossacks. 1994. Produced by Tamara Pavlova and Ekaterina Dorokhova. Le Chant du Monde CDM LDX 274980. Compact disc.

Chants Traditionnels de l'Ukraine/Traditional Songs of the Ukraine. 1993. Notes in French and

English. Distributed by Auvidis. Ethnic/Auvidis B6780. Compact disc.

The Dmitri Pokrovsky Ensemble: The Wild Field. Researched, adapted, and arranged by Dmitri Pokrovsky. A WOMAD production. RealWorld CD RW 17. Compact disc.

Georgia: The Real Polyphony of the Caucausus. 1997. Produced by Stephen McArthur. Music of the Earth. Recording and notes by Minoru

Morita. Recordings drawn from *Music of the Earth: Fieldworkers' Sound Collections* (Victor Company of Japan [JVC], 1992). Multicultural Media MCM 3004. Compact disc.

Géorgie: Polyphonies de Svanétie/Georgia: Polyphony of Svaneti. 1994. Collection CNRS—Musée de l'Homme. Recordings Sylvie Bolle-Zemp. Notes by Sylvie Bolle-Zemp, in French and English. Distributed by Harmonia Mundi France. Le Chant du Monde LDX 274990 Compact disc.

Journey to the USSR. N.d. Chant du Monde 274920–274925. 6 compact discs.

The Music of Eastern Europe: The Rough Guide. N.d. The Rough Guide/World Music Network RGNET 1024CD. Compact disc.

Music of the Tatar People. N.d. Tangent 129. Compact disc.

Musics of the Soviet Union. 1989. Smithsonian Folkways 40002. Compact disc.

Musique traditionnelles d'Ukraine, 1ère partie/ Traditional Music from the Ukraine, 1. 1993. Music of Steppe, Carathians, Western Podolie,

and Boykivshchena. Notes in French, English, and Ukrainian. Silex 225211. Compact disc.

Old Believers: Songs of the Nekrasov Cossacks. 1995. Compiled and annotated by Margarita Mazo, with Olga Velichkina. Notes with texts in English translation. Smithsonian Folkways CD 40462. Compact disc.

Polyphonic Work Songs and Religious Chants. N.d. Ocora C559062. Compact disc.

Rustavi Choir. *Georgian Voices.* 1989. Nonesuch 79224. Compact disc.

The Terem Quartet: Terem. 1992. RealWorld CD RW 23. Compact disc.

Trio of Bandura Players: Ukrainian Folk Songs. 1992. MCA Classics. Distributed by MCA. Art & Electronics AED 10479. Compact disc.

Ukraine. N.d. Auvidis 8206. Compact disc.

Ukrainian Village Music: Historic Recordings 1928–1933. 1994. Produced by Chris Strachwitz. Edited by Dick Spottswood. Arhoolie/Folklyric CD 7030. Reissue. Compact disc.

THE BALKANS

A Harvest, a Shepherd, a Bride: Village Music of Bulgaria: Songs and Dances from the Regions of Pirin-Macedonia (Southwest), Rhodope (South), Thrace (Southeast), and Shope (Midwest) and *In the Shadow of the Mountain: Bulgarian Folk Music: Songs and Dances of Pirin-Macedonia.* 1988 [1970, 1971]. Recorded and produced by Ethel Raim and Martin Koenig in Bulgaria in 1968. Notes by Martin Koenig with Vergilii Atanasov, in English. Elektra/Asylum/Nonesuch Records 9 79195–2. Reissue of Nonesuch H-72034 (1970) and H-72038 (1971). Compact disc.

Balkana: The Music of Bulgaria. 1987. Produced by Joe Boyd and Rumyana Tsintsarka. Hannibal Records HNBL 1335. Compact disc.

Bosnia: Echoes from an Endangered World: Music and Chant of the Bosnian Muslims. 1993. Recorded, compiled, and annotated by Ted Levin and Ankica Petrović. Distributed by Koch International. Smithsonian Folkways CD SF 40407. Compact disc.

Bulgarian All Star Orchestra. 1997. *Dushá: The Soul of Bulgaria.* Produced by Christian Scholze and Jean Trouillet. Network Medien 25.829. 2 compact discs.

Bulgarie: Rhodope-Dobroudja. 1994. Anthologie de la musique Bulgare, 2. Le Chant du Monde CDM LDX 274975. Compact disc.

Chants & Danses Croates/Croatian Folksongs and Danses. 1992. Recordings by Hungarian Radio Broadcasting between 1953 and 1985. Edited by Gábor Eredics. Distributed by Harmonia Mundi. Quintana QUI 903071. Compact disc.

Croatie: Musiques d'autrefois/Croatia: Music of Long Ago. 1997. Recordings by Hrvatski Radio, 1958–1993. Notes by Grozdana Marošević, in Croatian and English. Ocora C 600006. Compact disc.

Ensemble vocal de Gjirokastër. 1995. *Albanie: Polyphonies Vocales du Pays Lab.* Collected by Françoise Gründe. Notes by Pierre Bois, in French, with English translation by Judith Crews. Maison des Cultures du Monde. Compact disc.

Fanfare Paysanne de Zece Prăjini/Žese Prăjini's Peasant Brass Band. N.d. Musique du monde/Music of the World, 2, Roumanie. Notes by Speranţa Rădelescu, in English and French. Buda 92655-2. Compact disc.

Folk Music of Bulgaria. 1994 [1966]. Topic World Series. Collected and edited by A. L. Lloyd. Topic TSCD 905. Compact disc.

Folk Music of Yugoslavia (Croatia, Bosnia-Hercegovina, Serbia, and Macedonia). 1994. Topic World Series. Collected and edited by Wolf Dietrich. Topic TSCD 906. Compact disc.

Gaida Orchestra: Bagpipe Music from the Rhodope Mountains. 1992. JVC World Sounds. JVC VICG 5224. Compact disc.

Greek Traditional Village Music and Dance. 1994. World Music Library, 76. Notes in English. Seven Seas/King Records KICC 5176. Compact disc.

Hungary and Romania: Descendants of the Itinerant Gypsies: Melodies of Sorrow and Joy. 1997. Music of the Earth. Recordings and notes by Minoru Morita. Produced by Stephen McArthur. Recordings drawn from *Music of the Earth: Fieldworkers' Sound Collections* (Victor Company of Japan [JVC], 1992). Multicultural Media MCM 3010. Compact disc.

Jova "Besir" Stojiljkovic & His Brass Orkestar. 1995. *Blow 'Besir' Blow!* Globestyle GSUS038. Compact disc.

Kalesijski Zvuci. 1992. *Bosnian Breakdown: The Unpronounceable Beat of Sarajevo.* Notes by Kim Burton. Globestyle CDORBD 074. Compact disc.

King Ferus Mustafov. *Macedonian Wedding Soul Cooking*. 1995. Globestyle GSUS089. Compact disc.

Krăchno Horo. 1994. *Musiques populaires de Bulgarie*. Produced by André Ricros. Notes by Erik Marchand, in French. Silex Mosaique 225217. Compact disc.

L'orient des Grecs/The Orient of the Greeks. N.d. Rebetika music in the Smyrna style, compiled mainly from historical recordings. Musique du monde/Music of the World. Notes by Philippe Zani, in English and French. Buda 92659–2. Compact disc.

Laver Bariu. 1995. *Laver Bariu: Songs from the City of Roses*. Produced by Ben Mandelson and Kim Burton. Notes by Kim Burton. Globestyle CDORBD 091. Compact disc.

Music From Albania. 1999. Anthology of World Music. Rounder ROUN 5151. Compact disc.

Musique de la Grèce Continentale/Music from Continental Greece. 1995. Produced by Michel Pagiras and Clement Ziegler. Notes in French and lyrics in French, English, and Greek. Al Sur ALCD 138. Compact disc.

Muzar, Virgil. 1996. *Roumanie/Romania: Virgil Muzar: Le maître du violon roumain/ Master of the Romanian Fiddle*. Notes in English and French. Ethnic/Auvidis B6821. Compact disc.

Narodne pjesme i plesovi iz Banije/Folk Sings and Dances from Banija. 1987–1989. Notes with texts by Grozdana Marošević and Svanibor Pettan, in English and Croatian. Jugoton ULP-2050/2286/2464. Compact disc.

Papasov, Ivo. 1989. *Ivo Papasov and His Bulgarian Wedding Band: Orpheus Ascending*. Produced by Joe Boyd and Rumyana Tzintzarska. Hannibal Records HNCD 1346. Compact disc.

Reflections of Romania: Village & Urban Folk Traditions. N.d. Nonesuch 72092. Compact disc.

Rembetica: Historic Urban Folk Songs from Greece. 1992. Produced by Charles Howard and Dick Spottswood. Translations and transcriptions by Charles Howard. Rounder CD 1079. Compact disc.

Roumanie: La vraie tradition de Transylvanie. 1989. Recordings and notes by Herman C. Vuylsteke. Reissue of Ocora 558596. Ocora C 559070. Compact disc.

Serbie: Danses et Melodies Pastorales: Musiques Traditionnelles de la Serbie Orientale/Serbia: Pastoral Danses and Melodies: Traditional Music from Eastern Serbia. 1991. Notes in French and English. Distributed by Auvidis. Ethnic B6759. Compact disc.

Sestri Bisserovi: Pirin Wedding and Ritual Songs. 1995. Choral Series. Notes by Elena Stoin and Lyubimka Bisserova, in English. Pan Records PAN 7005 CD. Compact disc.

Song of the Crooked Dance: Early Bulgarian Traditional Music, 1927–42. 1998. Produced by Lauren Brody. Compiled from 78-RPM recordings. Yazoo 7016. Compact disc.

Songs & Dances of Yugoslavia. N.d. Playasound 65044. Compact disc.

Taraf de Haïdouks. 1998. *Dumbala Dumba*. 1998. Crammed Discs CRAW 21. Compact disc.

Taraf: Romanian Gypsy Music. 1996. Music from villages in the Danube Plain, Muntenia Province. Recorded by Speranţa Rădulescu, Valeriu Rădulescu, and Adrian Hotoiu. Produced by Martha Lorantos and Bob Haddad. Notes by Speranţa Rădulescu. Music of the World CDT-137. Compact disc.

Village Music of Yugoslavia: Songs and Dances from Bosnia-Herzegovina, Croatia and Macedonia. 1995. Explorer Series. Recorded by Martin Koenig in 1968. Notes by Martin Konig. Lyrics in Serbo-Croatian with English translations. Reissue of Nonesuch H-72042 (1971). Nonesuch 9 72042–2. Compact disc.

Wild Sounds from Transylvania, Wallachia, and Moldavia. 1997. Romania, 41. Notes in English, French, and German. World Network WDR 28.300. Compact disc.

A Guide to Films and Videos of European Traditional Music

Brian Patrick Fox

GENERAL

Encyclopaedia Cinematographica, distributed by Pennsylvania State University, has dozens of short, black-and-white films on music from Albania, Austria, Czech Republic, Italy, Germany, Montenegro, Norway, Portugal, Romania, Slovakia, and Spain.

The JVC/Smithsonian Folkways Video Anthology of Music and Dances of Europe. 1996. Footage from Belgium, the Czech Republic, the Faroe Islands, Denmark, England, France, Hungary, Iceland, Ireland, Italy, Romania, Scotland, Spain, and Wales. Directed by Hiroshi Yamamoto. Distributed by Multicultural Media, Barre, Vt. 2 parts. 108 min.

Social Dance Music. 1975. University of Minnesota. 60 min. 16mm.

TRANSNATIONAL GROUPS

At the Crossroads: Jews in Eastern Europe Today. 1990. Oren Rudavsky and Yale Strom. Arthur Cantor Prods., N.Y. 58 min. 16mm.

T'an Bakhtale! (Good Fortune to You!): Roma (Gypsies) in Russia. 1996. Alaina Lemon and Midori Nakamura. Documentary Educational Resources, N.Y. 75 min.

The Last Klezmer. 1995. Yale Strom and Bernard Berkin. New Yorker Films, N.Y. VHS, 84 min.

The Romany Trail: Part II, Gypsy Music into Europe. 1992 [1983]. Jeremy Marre. Shanachie Records, Newton, N.J. 60 min. VHS.

We Have No War Songs. 1994. Abrahami Netz. Filmakers Library, N.Y. 53 min.

BRITAIN AND IRELAND

The Bagpipe. 1970. World Mirror—Realist Productions. University of Illinois. 22 min. 16mm.

Ireland's Whistling Ambassador: Micho Russell of Doolin, Co. Clare. 1993. Bill Ochs. The Pennywhistler's Press. Hinesburg, Vt. 34 min. VHS.

'Oss, 'Oss, Wee 'Oss. N.d. Peter Kennedy, Alan Lomax, and George Pickow. Indiana University. 20 min. 16mm.

Sing of the Border. 1967. British Transport Production. International Film Bureau, Extension Media Center, University of California. 20 min. 16mm.

Song of Seasons. 1978. Canadian Travel Film Library, New York. 27 min. 16mm.

The Story of the Clancy Brothers and Tommy Makem. 1991. David Hammond and Derek Bailey. Shanachie Entertainment, Newton, N.J. 60 min. VHS.

SCANDINAVIA, FINLAND, AND THE BALTIC STATES

Bingsjölåtar i Pekkosgården. 1963. Lars Egler and Bengt Nordwall. Swedish Broadcasting Corporation. 20 min. 16mm.

Jijk (da, när var mannen pa Oulavuoli) (Joik: The art of recall). 1965–1966. Matts Arnberg and Pål-Nils Nilsson. Swedish Broadcasting Corporation, Stockholm, and Pål-Nils Nilsson, Lidingö. 17 min. 16mm

Leticke, Leticke, Korna är hemma (Leticke, Leticke, the cows are home). 1964. Lars Egler and Bengt Nordwall. Swedish Broadcasting Corporation, Stockholm. 24 min. 16mm.

Norwegian Folk Dances. 1962. Jan Wikbor. National Film Board of Norway and Dance Films. 13 min. 16mm.

Taiga Nomads: The School and the Village. 1991. Heimo Lappalainen and Jouko Aaltonen. Fin Image, Helsinki. 50 min. 16mm.

WESTERN EUROPE

Antonio and Rosario. 1961. Janus Films. Pennsylvania State University. 18 min. 16mm.

Danza Flamenco de Hoy. 1991. Pilar Perez de Guzman. Alegrías Productions, N.Y. 60 min. VHS.

Danzas Regionales Españolas. 1966. Encyclopaedia Britannica Educational Corporation. Extension Media Center, University of California. 17 min. 16mm.

Fiesta Gitana! 1994. Rafael Fajardo and Pilar

Perez Guzman. Alegrías Productions, N.Y. 39 min.

Flamenco. N.d. Sueva Films. Brandon Films. 79 min. 16mm.

La Guitarra Española. 1973. Walter H. Berlet. International Film Bureau, Boston University. 10 min. 16mm.

La Jota Aragonesa. 1996. Videos de la Luz, Madrid. 53 min.

Le Carnaval de Binche. 1963. Studio de Balenfer. Gérard Maton, Binche. 49 min. 16mm.

Musica sarda. 1990. Georges Luneau. Centre National de la Recherche Scientifique, Meudon cedex, France. 70 min. VHS.

Of Pipers and Wrens: De Souffle et de Roseau. 1997. Lois Kuter, Michael Bailey, and Gei Zantzinger. Constant Spring Productions, Inc., Devault, Penn., and Dastum, Brittany, France. 58 min.

The Spanish Guitar. 1992. Rafael Fajardo. Alegrías Productions, N.Y 45 min. VHS.

CENTRAL EUROPE

Beruf: Wandermusiker. 1994. Sabine Piechura and Eckhard Schenke. Institut für den Wissenschaftlichen Film, Göttingen, Germany. 46 min.

Kindertänze türkischer Kinder in Deutschland. 1993. Helmut Segler and Andrée Kleindienst. Institut für den Wissenschaftlichen Film, Göttingen, Germany. 20^1/2 min.

Message from Gyimes. 1996. Jeno Hartyandi. Mediawave Foundation, Györ, Hungary. 49 min.

My Blood, Your Blood: The Rock Generation in Today's Poland. N.d. Brighton Video, N.Y. 52 min. VHS.

Village Life and Music in Hungary. 1992. Deben Bhattacharya. Audio-Forum, Guilford, Conn. 27 min.

EASTERN EUROPE

Discovering Russian Folk Music. 1975. BFA Educational Media. 23 min. 16mm.

Soviet Union: Epic Land. 1971. Encyclopaedia Britannica Educational Corporation. Extension Media Center, University of California. 29 min. 16mm.

Soviet Union: Faces of Today. 1972. Encyclopaedia

Britannica Educational Corporation. Extension Media Center, University of California. 29 min. 16mm.

USSR & R: Rock on a Red Horse. N.d. Ken Thurlbek. Tapestry International, N.Y. 88 min. 16mm and VHS.

THE BALKANS

Anastenaria. 1969. Peter Haramis. Extension Media Center, University of California. 17 min. 16mm.

Bryllup i bjergene (Wedding in the mountains). 1966. Erik Elias. Erik Elias Film Production, Copenhagen, Denmark. 45 min. 16mm.

Dances of Macedonia. N.d. Julian Brian, Kenneth Richter and Shirley Richter. Contemporary Films. 10 min. 16mm.

Dancing Songs. 1967. Contemporary Films. 10 min. 16mm.

Fire Dancers. 1974. Fleetwood Films. University of Illinois. 11 min. 16mm.

Jakub. 1992. Jana Sevikova. Documentary Educational Resources, Watertown, Mass. 65 min.

Jugoslav Folk Dances. 1965. Dennis Boxell Films. Extension Media Center, University of California. 55 min. 16mm.

Kalogeros. 1969. Peter Haramis. Extension Media Center, University of California. 12 min. 16mm.

The Mask of the Other Face. 1991. Plamen Sjarov. Plamen Sjarov, Prague, Czech Republic. 18 min. 16mm.

Other Voices, Other Songs: The Greeks. N.d. Sapphire Productions, N.Y. 30 min. VHS.

Piemule. 1992. Jana Sevikova. Documentary Educational Resources, Watertown, Mass. 43 min.

Yugoslav National Folk Ballet. 1965. Dennis Boxell Films. Extension Media Center, University of California. 51 min. 16mm.

Notes on the Audio Examples

1. Jewish instrumental melodies (*niggunim*) (2:08)

   Two melodies, one slow and one fast, from eastern Hungary and Transylvania, performed by Zsigmond Lázár (violin) and Ferenc Kis (folk lute).
   Recorded by Dr. Emil H. Lubej, Institute for Musicology, University of Vienna, 11 June 1999, in Vienna, Austria.

2. Rom (Gypsy) female solo song with tambourine (*dajre*), "*Ajnaja Baktim*" (1:32)

   This song, in Turkish, sung in a bathhouse for female dancing during the Rom wedding cycle of rituals, was performed by Kefajil accompanying herself on a tambourine (*dajre*).
   Recorded by Elsie Ivancich Dunin, 1965.

3. Traveller's song, "The Galloway Hills" (1:44)

   Sung by Jane Turiff, accompanying herself on a harmonium, a reed organ. Her yodeling shows the influence of commercial recordings of country singer Jimmie Rodgers.
   Recorded by James Porter, 1972.

4. Saami joik (0:48)

   A personal joik in the North Saami style, performed by Krister Stoor.
   Recorded by Richard Jones-Bamman, 23 February 1995, in Umea, Sweden.

5. Basque improvised verse (*bertsu*) (1:01)

   Performed by Jon Sarasua at the *Gipuzkoako txapelketa,* a competition of versifiers (*bertsulari*), in Donostia, Spain.
   Recorded by Denis Laborde, 22 December 1991.

6. England: Northumbrian smallpipes, "Jock of Hazeldean" and "Gentle Maiden" (2:39)

   Performed by Colin Ross, each tune has two parts, each played twice. The first is a melody for a ballad associated with Sir Walter Scott; the second, probably Irish.
   Recorded by Burt Feintuch, 20 August 1998, and released on *Northumberland Rant: Traditional Music from the Edge of England,* Smithsonian Folkways 40473. Used by permission.

7. Wales: *penillion* singing with harp (1:27)

   A form combining an improvised vocal melody (with text in Welsh) with a fixed tune, here "The Ash Grove," played on a harp by Robin James-Jones.
   Recorded by James Porter, 1972.

8. Scotland: a Child ballad, "Barbara Allen" (2:26)

The most popular traditional ballad in the English-speaking world.
Sung by Tina Stewart, a Traveller from the village of Fetterangus, Aberdeenshire, and more than eighty years old at the time of the recording.
Recorded by James Porter, 1972.

9. Ireland: old-style (*sean-nós*) song *"Geaftaí Bhaile Buí"* ('At the gates of Yellow Town') (2:20)

A strophic song with relatively long phrases. The text laments in the first person a youthful indiscretion.
Performed by Lillis Ó Laoire, born in the Gaelic-speaking area of Donegal and winner in 1991 and 1994 of the Corn Uí Riada competition for *sean-nós* singing. From *Lillis Ó Laoire: Bláth Gach Géag dá dTig* (CICD 075, 1996). Used with permission of the performer and the publisher, Cló Iar-Chonnachta, Indreashán, County Galway, Ireland.

10. Ireland: jig "All the Ways to Go," on melodeon, followed by lilting (1:18)

Performed by Packy Boner from Arranmore Island, County Donegal.
Recorded by Hugh Shields, 1977.

11. Iceland: song (*rímur*) *"Líkafrón"* (1:18)

Performed by Halldor Einarsson.
Recorded by Theodore Grame and Pandora Hopkins on a freighter bound for Iceland, 1965.

12. Norway: Telemark *springar* 'leaping dance' for Hardanger violin (*hardingfele*) (1:27)

Performed by Finn Vabø in the tradition of Knut Dahle of Tinn, Telemark.
Recorded by Pandora Hopkins in Bergen, 1965.

13. Sweden: *polska* (dance in 3/4 time) *"Di sma undar jårdi dansar"* (1:56)

The tunes are typical of Gotland; the title refers to a Gotland legend about the dance of leprechauns living underground.
Performed polyphonically on two fiddles (*fiol*) by Owe Ronström and Bengt Arwidsson.
Recorded by the group Gunnfjauns Kapell for their compact disc, *Naudljaus,* Selvar Records SJECD 9, 1995. Used courtesy of Owe Ronström, a member of the group.

14. Denmark: sailor's lovesong *"Søde pige, du er så laugt fra mig"* ('Dear girl, I am so far away') (1:03)

Performed by Niels Larson, an 86-year-old bricklayer.
Recorded by Svend Nielsen, 1964.

15. Faroe Islands: ballad (*kvæði*) *"Fípan Fagra"* ('Beautiful Fipan') (1:17)

The ballad, sung by people dancing vigorously, tells of a young, bored shepherdess who surmounts many dangers to reunite with her royal lover in Denmark.
Performed by the Ballad-Dance Society of Hafnar, led by Niels á Velbastað.
From their compact disc, *Alfagurt ljóðar min tunga,* Tutl SHD 16. Used by permission.

16. Latvia: song with moveable drone, "*Steidzies, Dekla, steidzies, Laima*" ('Hurry up, Dekla, hurry up, Laima') (0:52)

    Performed by Alsungas ethnograiskais ansamblis "Suitu sievas" from Alsunga.
    Recorded by the Riga Recording Company, 1978. Used by permission of Valdis Muktupāvels.

17. Low Countries: schottische on plucked zither (*hommel*) (0:51)

    Performed by Leon Maes (b. 1903) from Damme in West Vlaandern Province, Belgium.
    Recorded by Wim Bosmans, 2 July 1980.

18. France: male solo song, "*Mon père a fait faire un étang*" (0:47)

    Performed by François Gloriau, La Garnache, Vendée.
    Recorded by Hugh Shields, 1972.

19. Portugal: choral song (1:47)

    Recorded by two male soloists and choir, the Grupo Coral e Etnográfico da Casa do Povo de Serpa from Sepa, Beja Province.
    Recorded by Salwa El-Shawan Castelo-Branco, 1989.

20. Spain: flamenco *bulerías* for voice and guitar (3:38)

    Performed by Diego del Gastor (guitar), Antonini del Puerto, and Joselero (singers) in Moron de la Frontera.
    Recorded by Robert Garfias, 1968.

21. Italy: ballad in three-part harmony, "*La Rosina la va la rusa*" (1:16)

    This strophic ballad, known to ballad scholars as Nigra 77, "*La bevanda sonnifera*" (fragment), features a lengthy refrain in the middle of each strophe.
    Performed by Iride, Enrica, and Aduana Tagliani from Colleri di Brallo (Pavia), Lombardy.
    Recorded by Luisa Del Giudice, 18 November 1987.

22. Sardinia: *ballu seriu* 'serious dance' "*Beni, dammi sa manu, isfortunatu*" ('Come, give me your hand, unfortunate one') (2:06)

    Performed by the male singing group *tenore Remundu 'e locu* from the village of Bitti, Nuoro Province: Piero Sanna (*boghe*), Tancredi Tucconi (*contra*), Daniele Cossellu (*mesa boghe*), and Mario Pira (*bassu*).
    Recorded by Bernard Lortat-Jacob, 1998.

23. Austria: yodel song "*Apfelbauerndudler*" (2:14)

    Performed by Die Schneeberg Buam: Friedrich Pfeffer, Kurt Lesar, and Otto Dietl.
    Recorded by Dr. Emil H. Lubej, Institute for Musicology, University of Vienna, 10 May 1988.

24. Switzerland: alphorn trio, "*Im Hüenerbachtobel*" (1:41)

    Performed by Ruth, Philipp, and Christian Schneider in three-part harmony.
    From the compact disc *Alphorn pur! Familie Schneider Illnau* (HS 93144), produced by Christian Schneider, 1993. Used by permission.

25. Poland: dance song and music from Podhale (1:16)

A dance sequence *po góralsku* 'in highlander style' at a wedding near Zakopane in the Tatra Mountains.
Performed by a dancer who sings and whistles and a band of five fiddlers and double bass (rather than the more traditional three-string *basy*): Stanisław Styrczula-Maśniak (lead violin), Szymek Karpiel-Bułecka (lead violin), Jurek Niton (second violin), Andrzej Frączysty (second violin), Henryk Krzyptowski-Bochać (second violin), and Tadeusz Styrczula-Maśniak (double bass).
Recorded by Timothy Cooley, 25 February 1995.

26. Hungary: song with violin and struck cello (*gardon*) accompaniment "*Lassú és sebes magyaros*" (1:18)

Performed by János Zerkula (singer and fiddle) and his wife, Regina Fikó (*gardon*, a cello struck with a stick), from Gyimesközëplok in Transylvania (Romania), the song opens with a 10/8 (2 + 2 + 3 + 3) feel.
Recorded by Wayne Kraft, 1995.

27. Russia: song with balalaika "*Skobaria*" ('The man from Pskov') (1:11)

Performed by Konstantin Rybkin (balalaika) and Zinaida Rybkin (singer), both born in 1930, from the village of Slavkovichi, Porchov District.
Recorded by Ulrich Morgenstern, 27 April 1995.

28. Belarus: polyphonic harvest song (0:51)

Performed by women from the village of Kletnaia.
Recorded by Zinaida Mozheiko in the 1970s.

29. Ukraine: *psal'ma* (psalm) with lute-zither (*bandura*) "*Isuse preliubeznyi*" ('Jesus, my great love') (1:34)

Performed by Heorhii Tkachenko at his home in Kyïv.
Recorded by William Noll, 1989.

30. Romania: table song (*cîntec de masa*) for string ensemble (0:47)

Performed by a Gypsy (Rom) ensemble from Maramureş, consisting of violin, guitar, and drum.
Recorded by Ann Briegleb Schuursma, 1969.

31. Bulgaria: wedding dance (*rŭchenitsa*) played on bagpipe (*gajda*) (1:23)

Performed by Georgi Doichev, a former soloist with the Bulgarian National Ensemble of Folk Song and Dance "Filip Kutev."
Recorded by Timothy Rice, 21 June 1993.

32. Slovenia: waltz on bowed and plucked zither (*citre*) (1:03)

Performed by Jože Zajc, who bows the zither with one hand while stopping the melody string and plucking chords with the other.
Recorded by Mira Omerzel-Terlep, 1980.

33. Slovenia: polka, "Dancing on the Green Grass," played by string band (1:00)

Performed by the Cimbalom Band Beltinci, consisting of two violins, cimbalom, and double bass (Miško Baranja, Janči Kociper, Jože Kociper, and Rudi Horvat).
Recorded by Mira Omerzel-Terlep, 1980.

34. Croatia: *klapa* 'club' singing, "*O mili mi je u selu divojka*" ('A village girl is dear to me') (2:10)

   Klapa songs are sung a cappella in four-part harmony.
   Performed by Klapa Šibenik, a semiprofesssional group of seven men from the village of Šibenik.
   Recorded by Mark Forry, 1 August 1993.

35. Serbia: dance (*kolo*) for brass band (1:04)

   This piece has a characteristic section for the accompanying parts minus the melody.
   Performed by the Rom (Gypsy) brass band of Fejat Sejdić from the area of Leskovac, southeastern Serbia, at the thirteenth International Folk Festival (Smotra Folkora) in Zagreb, Croatia.
   Recorded by Mark Forry, July 1993.

36. Montenegro: Muslim Albanian circumcision song, "*Berber bashku*" (1:17)

   The song, in 9/8 (2 + 3 + 2 + 2) time, is addressed joyously to the barber, who traditionally performs the circumcision.
   Performed by male singers from the Malisori minority, accompanied by accordion and frame drum (*dajre*).
   Recorded by Ankica Petrović and Miloš Milošević, 1984.

37. Bosnia: lullaby, "Rest Son, Sleep Son" (1:23)

   This tune resembles an urban love song (*sevdalinka*), and the singer moves from a description of the cradle to a lament for her love life.
   Performed by Emina Zečaj, a well-known Muslim singer of *sevdalinke*.
   Recorded by Ankica Petrović, 1984.

38. Macedonia: Rom (Gypsy) dance (*čoček*) played by two *zurla*s and *tapan* (2:25)

   Performed at a Rom (Gypsy) wedding in the village of Urumleri near Skopje by Muzafer Mahmut and Zulfikar Mahmut on shawms (*zurli*) and Fazli Idriz on bass drum (*tapan*).
   Recorded by Timothy Rice, 6 August 1977.

39. Albanian urban song, "*Na leu dielli n'atë buzmali*" ('The sun rose at the edge of the mountain') (2:24)

   A central Albanian urban song from the late Ottoman era, performed in a style popularized by Radio Tirana during the socialist period.
   Sung by Merita Halili, former soloist with the Albanian State Ensemble of Folk Songs and Dances, accompanied by Raif Hyseni (accordion, synthesizer, arrangements), Gëzim Halili (clarinet), Ardian Ulqinaku (bass), and Kujtim Beka (drumset).
   Recording produced by Raif Heseni, 1994. Used by permission.

40. Cyprus: "*Foni Akathkiotissa*," with violin, lute (*laouto*), and percussion (*tampoutsia*) (1:22)

   Performed by Michalis Terlikkas (singer), Kostas Karpasitis (violin), Yiannakis Souroullas (*laouto*), and Nicos Souroullas (*tampoutsia*), all from the village of Ayios Ioannis of Agros, Limassol District.
   Recorded by the Ethnomusicology Research Program of the University of Cyprus, coordinated by Panicos Giorgoudes, August 1997.

   Digital restoration and mastering by Pantelis Vassilakis, Ethnomusicology and Systematic Musicology Laboratory, UCLA.

Index